1 MONTH OF
FREE
READING

at

www.ForgottenBooks.com

By purchasing this book you are
eligible for one month membership to
ForgottenBooks.com, giving you
unlimited access to our entire
collection of over 1,000,000 titles via
our web site and mobile apps.

To claim your free month visit:

www.forgottenbooks.com/free568290

ISBN 978-0-483-57370-3
PIBN 10568290

Forgotten Books is a registered trademark of FB &c Ltd.
Copyright © 2018 FB &c Ltd.
FB &c Ltd, Dalton House, 60 Windsor Avenue, London, SW19 2RR.
Company number 08720141. Registered in England and Wales.

For support please visit www.forgottenbooks.com

Published every Wednesday at
Ashland, Ohio. All matter for publication must reach the Editor not
later than Friday noon of the preceding week.

George S. Baer, Editor

**The
Brethren
Evangelist**

When ordering your paper changed
give old as well as new address.
Subscriptions discontinued at expiration. To avoid missing any numbers renew two weeks in advance.

R. R. Teeter, Business Manager

OFFICIAL ORGAN OF THE BRETHREN CHURCH

Subscription price, $2.00 per year, payable in advance.
Entered at the Post Office at Ashland, Ohio, as second-class matter.
Acceptance for mailing at special rate of postage provided for in section 1103, Act of October 3, 1917, authorized September 9, 1918.
Address all matter for publication to Geo. S. Baer, Editor of the Brethren Evangelist, and all business communications to R. R. Teeter,
Business Manager, Brethren Publishing Company, Ashland, Ohio. Make all checks payable to the Brethren Publishing Company.

TABLE OF CONTENTS

EDITORIAL

America Failing in the Eyes of the World

Since the world war got fairly, under way the eyes of the world have been turned toward America. At first the warring nations wondered whether or not we would get into the war, then they wondered which side we would take, and when we had gotten in they wondered what our underlying motive was for entering, or in plain terms, what we wanted out of it. When the world had gotten our answer to all these questions, and especially to the last one, it wondered more than ever; it could hardly believe we were so unselfish. After repeatedly declaring ourselves and acting in accordance with our declarations, we finally brought the world actually to believe that we were sincere. The war closed with all eyes looking up to us with admiration and with all nations courting our friendship. We were highly respected and greatly trusted. We were in a position to lead the nations up to a higher standard of international conduct, and we did lead them rightly for a season; so eloquently did we preach our national ideals that the other great nations of the world began to be gripped by them and to aspire toward them. We led in the formation of a program for a great brotherhood of the nations, not perfect by any means, but perhaps as good as could have been accomplished at this time, and far superior to the old policy of "the balance of powers." Thus far we led,—and then we turned aside from our worthy course and began to play politics. Thus far we led with honor, swayed by seemingly worthy motives, and then dismounting from the saddle of leadership and ignoring our opportunities and responsibilities, we became suddenly small and selfish and began to quarrel among ourselves and to become jealous of one another like children at their play. And the world is looking on with wonder and dismay at our petty conduct more than before at our generous spirit. We are falling in the eyes of the world. We are losing our leadership. We are covering ourselves with disgrace, and the sting of it is beginning to be felt.

When the nation takes a backward step it is the church that feels the effects of it first. It is the church and the Christian leaders who first detect the demoralizing effects and suffer more from the reactionary tendencies set going in the lives of individuals in the nation. It is not surprising, therefore that Christian leaders are be-ginning to speak out in very positive terms. When great moral issues are at stake no one has greater right to speak out and to exercise every right influence than the church and her leadership. Among the prominent voices that have been heard on this vital issue is that of Sherwood Eddy, who is close up to John R. Mott as a Christian states-man and has had wonderful success in his evangelistic campaigns in mission lands. The following paragraphs are taken from his article entitled, "America on Trial:"

"Christ stood before Pontius Pilate to be judged; yet in reality Pilate was judging himself. The League of Nations is presented to-day to the American people. Do we realize that not only is the League before us, but America herself is on trial before the bar of humanity? This is not merely a question of the self-interest of America; twenty-six other nations are involved with us, and America alone stands in a position to save the world from disaster.

"I have just returned from a trip around the world since the Armistice, including Japan, China, India, Egypt, Turkey and Europe. I have been lecturing in some fifty cities before business men, clubs, and societies throughout the country and have had an unusual opportunity to observe public opinion.

"In Europe I found a strong revulsion of feeling against the United States. Instead of being, as we were a year ago, the most popular nation, we are becoming the most hated and despised. I have come recently from England and France. A friend of mine in American uniform told me that twice respectable women, recognizing his American uniform, had come up to him, had spit upon him, and said, "That is what we think of America." This kind of a thing is happening more frequently in the other of the two countries than in the one to which I now refer.

"I asked our critics in Europe: "Why do you misunderstand and misjudge America?" In substance, their reply was as follows: "You in America told us that you entered the war not as other nations. You said you wanted no land nor indemnities; you entered from unselfish motives. You proclaimed your ideals to all the world; they were repeated and reiterated in the daily press of Europe and Asia throughout the year that you were fighting. And now you come out of the war not only the richest nation in the world claiming one-third of its entire wealth, not only with all the world in your debt, not only with an enormous merchant marine and much of the world's trade captured successfully while the rest of us were fighting your battles during the first three years of the war, but after proclaiming your ideals to the ends of the earth, you are now threatening to repudiate them, refusing to give the world relief when you alone can do it, seeking apparently to get the world's trade rather than to give the world peace. We ask you: Is America going to stand for world selfishness or world service?' That is the question of Europe today. What is your answer to be?

"As I have gone through the cities of America, I find there is an overwhelming demand among business and professional men that we should settle this matter of the Peace Treaty, and the League of Nations. A large majority are strongly in favor of an early settle-ment for a League of Nations, with mild reservations, omitting the offensive Preamble, but not separating the Peace Treaty from the League. A majority of the business men and nine-tenths of the Christian people of the United States demand such a League. This is the great international question before the world. It has become the paramount moral issue before America.

"'Too long' has this question been treated as a matter of personal prejudice or of party politics. It has been kicked about like a football in the mud from party to party.' The country, is growing heartsick over this delay. If we repudiate our world responsibilities and allow Europe this winter to sink in starvation and revolution, we will place America in the position of being the most detested nation of the world. For America alone can save the situation. Shall we refuse to do it?

"Reader, you and I have been blaming the President and the Senators, but what have you done to avert this disgrace? Have you spoken out? Have you lifted your voice in protest? Can you respect yourself if our country goes down in disgrace and you have not lifted a hand to prevent it? If you agree that this is not a personal or partisan question, but a moral issue and a great world crisis, will you write or telegraph to the senior and Junior Senator of your state, urging that action be taken at once? America is on trial before the bar of humanity, and you and I are Americans.''

And we would add, Christian America is on trial before the bar of God, and you and I are Christian Americans.

EDITORIAL REVIEW

Sister Hillegas reports splendid progress being made at Happy, Kentucky. A revival meeting conducted by Brother Rempel resulted in six confessions. The field is said to be promising and in need of a pastor.

Brother G. W. Chambers, pastor of the Buena Vista ,Virginia, church, writes that the work at that place is on the forward move, that a goodly number have been added to the church recently and that the various departments are doing splendid work.

Brother B. H. Showalter writes of the condition of the Lord's work in the Prosperity congregation near Palestine, West Virginia. He speaks in highly appreciative terms of the service rendered by Brother Barnhart as evangelist.

Brother Mark B. Spacht, pastor of the Williamstown, Ohio, congregation, writes of progress in the work at that place. They are improving and beautifying their house of worship, and are soon to be engaged in an evangelistic campaign with Brother H. H. Wolford as preacher. May God bless them with great success.

Brother Gearhart reports the Home Mission offerings, as well as other offerings. He says the Thanksgiving offering gives promise of being the largest Home offering yet taken, but that some of the churches are just a little slow about reporting. Have you reported? If not, why not?

The first report of White Gift offerings is contained in this issue. Brother Trent is greatly encouraged at the showing thus far. Some of the churches did unusually well. Doubtless there are many pleasant surprises to be reported yet. We dare say that you can delight your secretary-treasurer still further by making your report promptly.

An interesting report comes from College Corner, Indiana. Brother L. A. Myers is delighted with his work thus far with this people. They recently closed an evangelistic meeting in which the pastor was the evangelist and received the loyal support of the entire membership, and especially the choir. A number of confessions resulted.

Brother Bell reports his evangelistic campaign with the Canton Brethren, held in conjunction with the Ohio State conference. Brother Belote is the vigilant and energetic pastor of that flock and he and Brother Bell worked hard during their campaign together. The Canton people do not have all easy going, but by steady and determined efforts they are forging ahead.

Warsaw is heard from again through the pen of their pastor, Brother A. E. Thomas. He has not ben there long, but he has found the people loyal and active. We are not surprised that Brother Thomas is confident of the future, for there are some mighty fine people at Warsaw. They will be launched forth in an evangelistic campaign. Brother Thomas also speaks of the Goshen meeting in which he gave assistance.

The Southern California Conference showing found elsewhere in this issue is one that they may well be proud of. Wouldn't it be fine if not only they but every conference district would make as fine a showing at next general conference. Let's all try. The lateness of this publication is due partly to the crowded condition of the paper for a few weeks and partly to the fact that the reading matter failed to reach us for several months after General Conference.

A good report is given of the work at Bethlehem, Virginia. Brother Chambers is pastor of this church. He and the superintendent keep in close touch with the Sunday school, and doubtless it is largely due to their close contact and suggestions that the classes are so wide-awake to the needs of the church and school. The other auxiliaries too are thoroughly alive.

We are in receipt of a copy of the Pleasant Hill (Ohio) News which tells of the conclusion of "The Most Popular Teacher Contest" conducted in that vicinity by the successful and energetic editor and publisher of that paper, Brother H. C. Marlin. A beautiful gold watch was given to the school teacher who received the most votes within a stated time, and it is interesting to know that Sister Mazie Teeter, who has taught in the village schools there for 21 years received the prize without having solicited a vote.

The live congregation of Lake Odessa, Michigan, has recently experienced a successful revival under the leadership of Brother G. W. Kinzie of New Lebanon, Ohio. According to the pastor's report, it resulted not only in awakening souls to a new sense of their duty to God, but also brought others to realize the value of a man of God in their community, though they themselves do not profess to serve God. It is evidence also that Brother Garrison enjoys the confidence and favor of the community.

Brother Bame reports success for the Brethren church in the simultaneous campaign held in North Manchester. Six churches were holding revivals at the same time, and the Brethren church seems to have been as successful as any of them. Brother McInturff of the Goshen church did the preaching for the Brethren. It would be a difficult field indeed that would not yield to the efforts of a team such as Bame and "Mac." made. And by the grace of God they brought forth results.

Brother Cobb of Dayton is still leading his cohorts forward to victory. The evangelistic campaign, as well as the other "doings" are splendidly reported by our enthusiastic correspondent of that church, Brother W. C. Teeter. The soul-saving campaign was a great success. One happy result of it was the winning of the imported singing evangelist to the Brethren faith. It is hoped the Brethren church may have the opportunity of using him in a large way in the coming days.

Brother Boardman, pastor of the Hudson, Iowa, congregation, has gotten right into the life of the community and made himself a part of it. How much better that the minister should be the leader of the young life of a community than that such leadership should be left to those whose ideals are low and whose motives are mercenary! Much greater fruit will be reaped than that which already is in evidence. An evangelistic campaign conducted by the pastor was successful in spite of the coal shortage.

We are certainly grateful for the loyalty shown the Publishing House, especially as it is manifested in supporting The Evangelist. Long lists of both new subscriptions and renewals are arriving at the business manager's office now, and we are sure still more are coming. We want to extend our hearty welcome to the Third church of Philadelphia and the Masontown church to the Honor Roll. We hope our new subscribers will find The Evangelist a real help and that it shall in time become indispensable to their homes, as it is now in the homes of many of our old subscribers.

We are delighted to see Brother Horner of Goshen coming to us again with an interesting bit of news. Brother Horner truly deserves a word of commendation for the exceptionally neat condition of his manuscript. Our typesetter, Mr. Plank, wishes me to put in a good word in his behalf too, because the manuscript, though written with a pen, is written only on every other line. That makes it easy for him to read. He says if our good friends who use a typewriter would always write double spaced, it would increase both his speed and accuracy.

GENERAL ARTICLES

The Kind of Laymen Our Church Needs.   By Henry V. Wall

(Address delivered at Winona Lake, Indiana, September 2, 1919)

Brother Cassel has spoken of the character of our brotherhood and I shall try to speak along the line of brotherly conduct.

As an introduction to the subject of brotherly conduct, I desire first to say something regarding what constitutes a brother, who is a believer in Christ Jesus, who has really and truly accepted him as his personal Savior and is trusting him in all things.

The true believer has two natures, the old nature and the new nature, the old man and the new man. The Scriptures teach that every regenerate person is the possessor of two natures; one received by natural birth, which is wholly and hopelessly bad; and a new nature, received through the new birth, which is the nature of God himself and therefore wholly good.

The following scriptures will sufficiently manifest what God thinks of the old, or Adamic nature. Psalm 51:5 says, "Behold I was shapen in iniquity, and in sin did my mother conceive me." Jeremiah 17:9 says, "The heart is deceitful above all things, and desperately wicked." Dr. Young's literal rendering of this passage is: "Crooked is the heart above all things, and it is incurable; who doth know it?" Romans 3:10-12 say, "There is none righteous, no, not one, there is none that understandeth, there is none that seeketh after God. They are all gone out of the way, they are together become unprofitable; there is none that doeth good, no, not one." God does not say that none of the unregenerate are refined, or cultured, or able, or sweet tempered, or generous or charitable, or religious but he does say that "none are righteous, none understand God, or seek after him."

It is one of the sorest of faith's trials to accept the divine estimate of human nature; to realize that our genial and moral friends, who, not infrequently, are scrupulous in discharge of every duty, who are filled with sympathy for the woes and aspirations of humanity, and strenuous in the assertion of human rights, are yet utter contemners of God's rights, and touched by the sacrifice of his Son, whose Deity they deny, and whose word they contemptuously reject.

Yes, we undoubtedly have two natures, and sometimes we try in our own strength to corral the old nature, we are almost persuaded that there is a multitude of them . Brethren, it requires more than mortal man to keep under subjection this carnal nature. It required the application of the atoning blood of Jesus Christ to our lives, and the disposition to yield ourselves, wholly up to him, thus giving the Holy Spirit a chance to work in, and through us. The Bible plainly teaches that man cannot of himself, control, even one small member of his body, the tongue. If you think you can, please read the third chapter of James. Many times we have all had a great conflict with this little old tongue of ours, and we have invariably met our Waterloo. God's foreknowledge looked into the future and saw man in his fallen state. His great heart of love was touched and he through the gift of his Son, made the way of escape, whereby man can have his sins covered and the imputed righteousness of God.

Since these introductory remarks we are now ready to say something regarding "Brotherly Conduct."

No Brother Suffers Alone

Therefore there is .the absolute necessity of being exceedingly cautious that we might not in the least bring any offence to our brother.

Paul places a very high value on brotherly relations, and on one occasion we remember he said, "Wherefore if meat make my brother to offend, I will eat no flesh while the world standeth."

What a pleasant condition, would be brought into our church family, if we would be as considerate of our brother's welfare as was the Apostle Paul.

Brethren, do you realize that your brother belongs to the redeemed, bloodwashed body of Christ the same as you do, and that he has rights and privileges in Christ Jesus, as well as yourself? Therefore we as many members constitute the one body of Christ, we should be even more careful not to offend our brother in Christ, than we would to wilfully and maliciously harm or mar the physical body . in which we live. I am quite sure that in God's sight, it would be more preferable for you to mar your own physical body, than it would for you to mar the body of Christ, by offending your brother who constitutes a part of his body, of which he is the head. Brethren, it is really a serious matter when we offend our brother (1 Corinthians 12:26-27).

In reality brotherly conduct belongs entirely to our new nature, and unless the old nature gets in our way, the new nature will treat our brother as he should be treated.

Paul tells us in Romans 12-10 to "Be kindly affectioned one to another with brotherly love; in honor preferring one another.

Romans 14:13 says, "Let us not therefore, judge one another any more; but judge this rather, that no man put a stumbling block or an occasion to fall in his brother's way.

Brethren, do you know what are the three hardest words in all this world for one brother to say to another? But after he does say them, with the meaning that God intended they should have, a great burden will have been lifted from you, and that joy and peace that passeth all understanding will be yours. In order that we might get this God-given peace in a life that is much disturbed because of offending our brother, surely, we as God's children will go to our brother and gladly say these three hard words. What do you suppose these three words are. Here they are. I was wrong.. If you don't think these are hard words to say to a brother whom we have wronged, go try it. I hear some one saying, I never have committed any offence against my brother. That may be possible, but hardly probable, especially if you have been actively engaged in the work of the church.

Also remember this, that the brother who never makes any mistakes while he is tabernacling in this old tenement clay, as a rule he never makes anything else. Brethren, God knew you better than you know yourselves, and he provided an advocate for you even Jesus Christ the righteous who is at God's right hand interceding for those who love, serve and obey him. If you have sinned by offending your brother, go to him and make it right, but above all things go to God in prayer, confess your wrong, and he will abundantly pardon you. Regarding prayer I wish to say this that there are at least two ways that some people use in praying. One way is to p-r-a-y on their knees on Sunday and the other one is, to p-r-e-y on their neighbors on Mon day.

This reminds us of the grocer that had his daily prayer. One morning he said to his clerk, John, have you put dust in the pepper, watered the milk, and sand in the sugar? Yes sir, replied the clerk. Then come on to family prayers. A man may pray on his knees until the end of time, but as long as he p-r-e-y-s on his neighbor he will not reach the ear of God. Christianity is not a cloak for sin; it is a cure for Sin.

Someone said, "Why don't you practice what you preach?" The other one said, "It would be easier for me to practice what I preach than it would for you to preach what you practice."

Galatians 2:20 says, "I am crucified with Christ; nevertheless I live; yet not I, but Christ liveth in me; and the life which I now live in the flesh I live by the faith of the Son of God, who loves me, and gave his life for me.".

This hour and these two addresses are given to the laity, however I desire to say a few words regarding the attitude of the laity toward the actively engaged pastors of our church. In first Corinthians, 9th chapter, 13-14 verses we find these words. "Do you not know that they which minister about holy things live of the things of the temple? And they which wait at the altar are partakers with the altar?" "Even so hath the Lord ordained that they which preach the gospel should live of the Gospel." I am wondering if you know of any church in our brotherhood where the laity is hindering their good pastor from living of the Gospel. God intended that these servants of his should be cared for in a financial way that will permit them to give their very best to him.

If your pastor's salary is so small, that he has to spend part of his time, dodging the grocerymen, or wearing out his lead pencil in figuring out how he can save here and there in order to pay the grocery bill, or any other legitimate bill, you better get the official board of your church together at once, and have an old fashioned prayer meeting, and pray to God to forgive you your trespasses and quit preying on your pastor.

I can't conceive of a more abominable thing in the sight of God, than a thrifty, prosperous laity, (yes, sometimes they are even rich too) of robbing God and his servants in this way. For my part I had rather put on the old black mask, and hide around the dark corner until some old rich tight way came along that had congestion of the pocket book, because of his miserly methods, and hold him up, than I would to sit in the pew of a church where there was one of God's faithful servants underpaid. Brethren of the laity, here are some facts that need our prayerful consideration.

I hear some one saying, we would like to pay our pastor a living salary, but we are not able, the mission board won't help us any more, and I guess we will have to decide to have preaching only once a month. This is just what a lot of worldly church members are looking for. They would then have three Sundays of every month to take their well filled baskets, laden with fried chicken and everything else that goes to make a good picnic dinner, get into an automobile that cost anywhere from the price of the "tin Lizzy" to a Packard limousine, and then drive to the lake or creek and spend the day in fishing and revelry. God have mercy

on you when the day of reckoning and rewards come. To say that we are not able to pay our pastor is equivalent to making God a liar.

For we know that God holds the wealth of the world in his hand, and we are his children, heirs of God and joint heirs with Jesus Christ. Do you mean to say that God will not trust you as one of his stewards with an income sufficient to meet your own needs and have something to give to your pastor's salary? No, no; verily, no. Not if you are really and truly born again.

I believe that God does have a people upon this earth, with whom he can entrust a portion of his great wealth, and if you feel that you as his child are not getting your share, you had better look into life's mirror of the past, and honestly and conscientiously before him upon your bended knees, search the deep things in the secret place of your life and you may find something that will startle you, and that is standing in the way of God blessing you.

I am going to say a few words more regarding our duty toward our pastors. Brethren, I have studied our pastoral situation a great deal, and I am convinced that there are several ways in which our laity can help our pastors to become more efficient in their work. I will only take time to mention one of the many, and that is the one I referred to a few moments ago regarding salaries. Our pastors are not receiving the salaries that permit them to live as they should live. Many of them are struggling hard trying to raise their families, and give them the education that they should receive, and I personally know that as a whole, they are making ten sacrifices to the laity's one. Brethren, these things ought not to be.

In my judgment any pastor whom God has really called to preach his word, and is giving full time to the ministry, should not receive less than $1,500 per year, and many of them should receive much more. Yes, I know that many of us complain, and are not satisfied with our pastors, but really I believe we are getting much more than we have paid for. Laity, I believe if you will give this matter your prayerful consideration and then act as God may direct you, that we will have taken at least one step in the right direction for the betterment of our work. This will encourage the pastors we now have, and will show to God that we are willing to pay our pastors living wages, and then he can call greater men into the ministry to serve us.

I thank God for this privilege of saying these few words to our laity, as I am one of you. May God bless these remarks for our good and his glory.

Long Beach, California.

The Cross the Keynote of Evangelism.   By G. W. Rench

I have been asked to write on the above subject. So here goes. "Like a mighty army moves the church of God." This is what we sing. I wish it were wholly true. If it were, we would not spend so much time disputing the orders of our great Commander.

I like to think of this army as constituted of three divisions: The center is the missionary enterprises; the left wing is pastoral care and teaching; the right wing is evangelism. To the center the orders read, "Go ye into all the world." To the right wing he says, "Preach the gospel to every creature; he that believeth and is baptized shall be saved." To the left wing the command is, "Teaching them to observe all things whatsoever I have commanded you."

But brethren, the noble right wing, upon which so much depends, seems to be hesitating, unsteady, panicky, ready to break and run. Are its leaders at fault, or is it the lack of organization, or both? There is one thing quite apparent to me, and that is EVANGELISM has never received the attention that it should have received. The Evangelistic and Bible Study League is trying to meet that need, and I bless God for its hopes and aims. It has my unqualified support.

But what has the "Cross" to do with evangelism? Why, it has everything to do with it. The finest of steam engines is powerless without steam; and what steam is to the engine the cross is to evangelism. Of course, the cross stands for death—the death of the Son of God. Thi is what makes the cross the world's great magnet. A great preacher recently said, "It took the Father four thousand years to bring his eternal purpose to its conclusion in Christ." It took Christ thirty-three years to execute the plans of the Father, and condense all his work into that last, final command to his army, the right wing of which is to bend every energy in enlisting raw recruits.

The cross is the central fact in Christianity. It is the eternal fountain from whose rivulets the entire well-being of man must be fed. It is not ordinary death on the cross that has opened up that fountain, oh no! but a DEATH WHICH CARRIES WITH IT "RANSOM," (1 Tim. 2:6) and "PROPITIATION FOR OUR SINS". (1 John 2:2). If that ransom—that death of the Son of God—be likened to a comet, then all of your culture and social service tinkering is a part of the tail. Social service important? Why, yes. Soap and water is always important—necessary. But it takes more than clean linen, and brownstone fronts, and flower gardens, and automobiles to keep men out of hell.

"There is a fountain, filled with blood,
Drawn from Immanuel's veins;
And sinners plunged beneath that flood,
Lose all their guilty stains."

"But God commendeth his love toward us, in that, while we were yet sinners, Christ died for us. Much more then, being now justified by his blood, we shall be saved from wrath through him" (Rom. 5:8, 9). Yes, "justified by his blood." This is heaven's answer to a soul struggling to be free from its guilty past. Calvary was foreshadowed in types, in bleeding lambs and tortured beasts. Cain's offering was without blood, and it was rejected by God. From that day until this man has been fighting against his God on the plan to redeem this sin-cursed world. But God's answer has been, "without the shedding of blood there is no remission of sin." Man, self-willed and proud, may cry out in his blindness, "I don't believe it," and with closed eyes walk straight into hell, but his "scientific findings," and "assured results," will not make God a liar, nor pull down his law out of heaven. Oh, no!

The story of the cross conquered the learning and genius of the world in New Testament times, and then human speculation made over the simple story of the cross and clouded the plain path from man to God and from God to man. Scientific investigations have accomplished much whereby mankind have been made happier, but these investigations are powerless to show the necessities there were in the learm of God's thought, his universe or his law which required the sacrifice on the cross. The unknown quantity in the equation is too large. We can afford to leave all that region to be explored by those who delight to spend the time in dreaming. Philosophy can not change the facts, thank God! It is far more important that sinful men should be redeemed than that they should understand the philosophy of redemption. But the cross can never be eliminated, nor its light obscured. It is the known quantity in the equation that can make tangible the light of heaven.

The inexorable law of God had gone forth, "the soul that sinneth, it shall die." Since all have sinned, then how shall there be any escape? Can God be just? Oh, yes. He has provided a way for us to die without the breath leaving the body. He calls that death the DEATH to SIN. "Knowing this, that our old man is crucified with him, that the body of sin might be destroyed, that henceforth we should not serve sin. For he that is dead is freed from sin. Now if we be dead with Christ, we believe that we shall also live with him. ... Likewise reckon ye also yourselves to be dead indeed unto sin, but alive unto God through Jesus Christ our Lord" (Rom. 6:6, 7, 8-11). Why, we are baptized into death. "Therefore we are buried with him by baptism into death" (Rom. 6:4). And to make sure that death is accomplished, and that "ye have obeyed from the heart that form of doctrine which was delivered you," in that last death struggle, the cross is thrust before our vision, and we are to be "planted (buried) in the likeness of his death." There on the cross hung Jesus, bowing his head, and ceasing to breathe (John 19:30). Yes, baptized into death, in the likeness of that death on the cross. "Being then—THEN MADE FREE FROM SIN, ye became the servants of righteousness" (Rom. 6:18). Then made free. Here is the place to shout. Dead, baptized into death, but baptized in the likeness of his death (not burial), this is the divine pattern. "And because ye are sons, God hath sent forth the Spirit of his Son into your hearts crying, Abba, Father" (Gal. 4:6). "In whom also after that ye believed ye were sealed with that Holy Spirit of promise" (Eph. 1: 13). Yes, the cross is the central fact in our remission of sins, and the gift of the Holy Spirit, and the evangelization of the world is by the way of the cross.

South Bend, Indiana.

The Great Objective. By E. A. Rowsey
(Address delivered at Ohio State Conference at Canton)

The Christianization of the world is the great objective facing this generation. Some one in a very apt manner has said, "America has a missionary destiny," meaning that we should recognize all races as the children of God, and not forget the duty of the stronger to serve the weaker. As a church we should study the development of twenty centuries of Christian history and in the light of such knowledge, find our place in the unfolding purpose of God to establish his kingdom in the hearts of men. Since the war, drums throb no longer, and the battle flags are furled. We must establish the parliament of man, and the federation of the world.

The first step in the realizing of our objective is the Americanization and Christianization of America. We must assume a different attitude to the foreigner who is within our gate or refuse him entrance.

My heart was saddened several weeks ago by a scene which I witnessed in the union depot at Columbus. It was just time for the Big Four train to leave the station for Springfield when a bewildered foreigner walked into the station and by the use of a broken English phrase, made known to the ticket agent after some labor of speech that he wanted a ticket in order that he might catch the train that was ready in two minutes to leave the station. As the inexperienced newcomer hurried to the gates in the custom of his homeland, the great crowd of people laughed and made fun of the man who was not experienced in the customs of America.

The man at the gate did not punch his ticket; and an outburst of laughter only added to the poor friendless man's helpless condition. Without information as to the number of track or train, the helpless newcomer to America went out to discover for himself what should have been told him by the representative of Uncle Sam who was paid to impart such information. Can a man remain insensible to such treatment? Will he ever develop into an intelligent American citizen if he is nurtured in such an environment? Therefore I say we must change our attitude to the foreigner who is in our gates or change the hinges on our gates. Thousands of such illustrations could be used to show our attitude toward America's newcomers. As I tried to analyze the case I have just related, I said to myself, How would this crowd of mocking Americans feel in this man's home trying to make their wants known through the medium of the Greek language? If an American should receive such treatment in a foreign port, he would seek to involve the United States in a war with that country for insulting an American citizen.

I would like to spend the remainder of the time on this phase of the subject, but such is not the whole purpose of this address; therefore, I must leave it by saying that we must not forget the objective that constantly looms up before us, namely, that of remolding a plastic, blistered world upon the principles of an undefiled, Christian democracy. The question that is of vital interest to this conference is, How can the Brethren church play the biggest and best part in so worthy an objective? I purpose to mention four facts that in my mind should constitute the great objective Brethrenism during the next century.

I. The making possible a practical democracy by an honest and sincere distribution of interests. In the first place will you ask yourself, What makes a democracy practical? Is it a stipulated form or body of well written sentences? No, such will never make possible a realization of any worth-while objective. Such an attempt would only result in a tragic wreck. As a church we do not stand for formulated creeds as a standard or incentive for service. I am thinking of the spirit that must animate a soul, thus making him willing to go forth and lay down his life for his friends.

Such was the spirit that drove our fathers to the New England shores, that made Socrates willing to drink the hemlock, that gave Stephen the courage to be stoned, that made Paul content to spend his latter days in a bleak, barren, damp, dingy cell in Rome and later welcome the martyr's axe. This same democratic spirit made the immaculate Son of God deem it worthy to suffer the sharp, sting of death on a despised and cursed cross, that we, through his sacrifice might enjoy the same privileges and blessings with his Father, our God.

Such is the ideal of practical democratic service that must penetrate the soul of the Brethren church before we can ever hope for a **proper, sincere, and honest distribution of interests.** If such a spirit or ideal grips the lives of the Brethren church we will understand the electric shock that quickened the step of General Pershing when with uncovered head he uttered in a reverent tone, "Layfayette, we are here."

We will say to the hindering force of progress in our church in the name of justice, and righteousness, we are here to conquer. The two words of the French during the dark hours of the war portray their courage and valor and therefore are immortal as history. First "The will not pass" and second, "They shall not pass," and now we can add the third, "They did not pass." Such must be our attitude toward all the problems we must confront. So much for the spirit of practical democracy. Now if such a spirit is realized how can we distribute properly the interest so sacred to the church and so essential to her welfare.

First: Let us think of college endowment. It is essential. Absolutely, yes. We are rejoicing daily and continually thanking God for the victory of college endowment. May Beachler's name and college endowment never cease to **increase.** Our people are awakening as never before to the need of a properly endowed college. The ear marks of improvement are already visible on the college campus, and with Dr. Jacobs at the helm with his winsome personality and unique ability supported by such a corps of teachers, plus a solid student body, how could things help but go forward? God pity the future of Brethrenism when such a report cannot be given of the college. Yet to focus all of our interest on college endowment would be unwise.

Therefore I would mention in the second place an endowment for church literature. We are in great and urgent need of a church literature. In my humble judgment one of the greatest needs of the Brethren library is a systematic theology. I have had young ministers to confess to me that their early ministry was a failure because they lacked an order of ecclesiastical procedure, and while they were trying to collect themselves in order that they might - swim ashore, they were strangled by confusion, and drowned in the sea of speculation.

Now, despite his modesty for the sake of clarity, I am sure he will pardon the illustration. Take the clear-eyed priest of God, to whom we have looked in this conference as a father worthy of giving council, as you recognize by this description I refer to our honored Dr. Miller. I think instead of teaching in the college he should be writing a systematic theology for the Brethren church. Dr. Miller knows as well as you or myself that he will soon reach the evening of life and God will see fit to transplant his life for the purpose of greater usefulness. And some day the news will be flashed abroad that his sweet spirit has taken its heavenly flight and is now seated in the kingdom of God. If he spends all of his time in oral class room work, he will not leave his rich gold mines of truth immortalized on the pages of history. Should we not through the medium of ink retain his priceless inheritance made possible through over a quarter of a century of ceaseless toil? As valuable as his

counsel is should we not retain the uplifting production of his fertile brain upon pages of immortal literature? I am sure without further discussion (space prevents) you can see the value of a permanent endowment for church literature extension. The proceeds of all books to be added to said endowment.

But should all of our interest be in a permanent literature and college endowment? If so I fear we will have no one to teach or no one to read. So the third distribution of interest should be a National Sunday school and Christian Endeavor Field Secretary. I combine the two for the sake of saving time. As you know I was appointed a field secretary for the northern part of the state of Ohio. As I visit the various societies and observe the organization, or in most cases, the lack of organization, and ask the executive committees to answer a questionaire containing twenty-four questions which I have worked out, I feel like falling on my knees in their presence and praying God to help us so that we may hasten the day when Christian Endeavor can enjoy the benefits of a live wire for field work. During my last tour a young high school boy asked me why Christian Endeavor was so spoken of in the Evangelist. He asked, "Is it really the cow's tail?" And I said "No, Christian Endeavor has no tail." "What do you mean?" was the prompt question of the inquisitive lad. "Well," I said "the other organizations have a tale to tell, but Christian Endeavors story is much like that of Topsy's. The women and girls have a tale to tell. It is this We have a field secretary or secretaries who visit the church and increase interest and promote organization, thus the girls become interested in their girls' organization and lose interest in Christian Endeavor. Now as you know the missionary boards have a field secretary. But the story of Christian Endeavor is in many cases similar to the one you have just related to me." This was his story. "I am interested in Christian Endeavor work. I received a letter asking me to start a society which conscience had asked me to do sometime before. I went to my pastor but he was not interested and from him I received nothing but discouragement. I did not know what to do nor how to do it. So our society is dead." Is that the proper distribution of interest? I would not want the religious aspirations of my brother or sister or child crushed by such a thoughtless distribution of interests. Won't you join us in a prayer for a field secretary?

Our thought thus far has not left the homeland; such is far from honest distribution. So will you consider in the fourth place, our task of helping in the Christianization of the world? Does not the great Interchurch World Movement offer a profitable and fruitful field in which to distribute our interests?

I know some one is saying he is going to butcher denominationalism and slay with heartless criticism the precious doctrine of the Brethren church. But my friends, God forbid; such is far from my intention. This I do not have in mind. Some one else says, Your task is an impossible one. I answer, Is that the way to accomplish a great thing for God? No, such is the attitude of the lazy man or that thoughtless child. I do not expect the victory through man's strength but through man's faith and God's strength. "Attempt great things for God; expect great things of God." Does such a united effort for kingdom extension eliminate denominationalism? It is only a means by which we can, through union and strength save the greatest number of precious dying souls for the heavenly population in the shortest number of years.

Is it valuable for the state of Ohio to be a member of the, the one United States? Does such a union make it impossible for Ohio to revere and protect her state sovereignty? By no means. She feels safer, and increases her own union and at a less expense, because she is a member of the union? Does the size of New York City make it possible for New York to have the greatest preachers in America? Brethren,

(Continued on page 9)

THE BRETHREN PULPIT

Christian Manhood.   By J. I. Hall

Text: Till we all come in the unity of the faith, and of the knowledge of the Son of God, unto a perfect man, unto the measure of the stature of the fullness of Christ: that we henceforth be no more children, tossed to and fro, and carried about by every wind of doctrine, by the sleight of men and cunning craftiness, whereby men lie in wait to deceive; but speaking the truth in love, may grow up into him all things, which is the head, even Christ (Eph. 4:13-15.

There is no other attainment so great as a true Christian character. Every day we should be careful to build our lives with pure, noble, and upright deeds, which will make a beautiful temple honored by God and man. One leak will sink a ship. One flaw will break a chain. So one dishonorable untruthful act or word will leave its impression upon our Christian manhood. Every day we perform our deeds, and one by one the days either grow into noble or ignoble years, and as the years slowly pass, will raise for us either a noble or an ignoble manhood. It is the building that we make with our own hands that must stand and the Word of God that warns us to take heed how we build it; to see to it that we build on the sure foundation, Christ Jesus, for other foundations, can no man lay. We should make sure that we are building a Christian manhood, not simply for the hour in which we are living, but for the hour of revelation, when the whole manhood will be laid before the Great Judge and be seen just as we are.

A healthy child will grow instinctively—the babe, the child, the youth, and the man. But not so with the mere animal. The bird builds her nest now just like she did centuries ago, and in the same way, we see all the mere animal kind living now. But not so with man. He is capable of great development—mentally, morally, and spiritually. In the beginning, man was capable of only one speech, now he can speak many languages. He sees from a higher moral plane than formally. He also becomes more spiritual as he otherwise develops and has a greater conception of God.

The Lord through the different dispensations developed for him a perfect religious system through Jesus Christ, that he may develop and enjoy all his possibilities, and live the life that is possible for him to live.

I. Christian Manhood Is a Growth.

1. He is making progress toward the standard of Christian excellence. But speaking the truth in love may grow up into him in all things, which is the head even Christ from whom the whole body fitly joined together and compacted by that which every joint supplied according to the effectual working in the measure of every part, making increase of the body into the edifying of itself in love (Eph. 4:15-16).

2. We should grow in likeness to him. The human soul is formed for growth. The growth is infinite. The acorn grows into an oak. The babe is capable of developing into a great mental, moral, and spiritual being. He can become a scientist, philosopher, astronomer, etc., but best of all he can grow to the stature of a man in Christ.

3. We can grow in comprehension of him. It is a great privilege that we can comprehend his love and realize that his mercy endureth forever, and desire his truth to be our shield, long for the courts of our Lord, appreciate his long suffering, and have a full realization of him as our personal Savior.

4. A growth that makes the life harmonious. Divine harmonies in accord with his will. Like the harp with a thousand strings and every string in tune. The life of the Christian is in harmony with the Divine will and led by the Spirit of God.

5. His growth is the result of divinely appointed agencies—means of grace. That the blood of Jesus cleanses from all sin and that without the shedding of blood there is no remission. His Word is the sword of the Spirit, God is his father, Christ, his intercessor and the Holy Spirit, his sanctifier. He who lays hold of this triune power will grow into noble Christian manhood.

6. A growth the standard of whose completeness is Christ—the ideal. Jesus is the great ideal for all mankind, and the individual who strives to grow like him will develop a Christian manhood that will give him a great grasp on the real issues of life; and as he grows, his ideals of the greatness of the great ideal grows, and ever keeps him striving and growing into yet a greater manhood.

Let us strive to grow good characters. A good life is a precious thing and should be coveted. Covet the best gifts. They come from God. We may covet the best things that come from God but we dare not covet our friend's possessions.

7. There is no act—however small but what it has its influence upon our manhood. Great actions carry their glory with them as the ruby wears its colors. Whatever may be our condition or calling in life, we should keep in view the whole of our existence. Act—build not merely for the little time allotted for us here in this life, but act for eternity.

II. The Elements of Christian Manhood.

1. Largeness (1) He has enlarged views of the truth. He sees the world as the power of God unto salvation. (2) He himself continues to grow as he is alive—born again. Surely to enjoy the growth that brings us to the largeness of the Christian life, we must be alive—for a dead man does not grow. He is regenerated. He is an heir of God and joint heir with Christ—highest, purest, noblest, and safest. He is making continual advancement till he comes in the unity—the respect in which one grows, the completeness of which is fulness in Christ. (3) He has enlarged views of man's need and the burden of souls is on his heart. He is anxious that Jesus be preached to all the world and lays plans and works for its completion.

2. Dignity. He has that deep inwrought sense of true worth and greatness of his nature, as a renewed man, and of his position as a child of God and joint heir with Christ. He realizes that the lower he stoops in service the higher he rises. Every man should aim to possess the fruits of the spirit, the possession of which develops true Christian character. "He who will not look up must look down." The individual, the community, the nation, tells its standing, its advancement, its worth, its true wealth and glory in the eye of God by its estimation of real Christian manhood or womanhood.

3. Courage and Strength. The spirit-filled man is not afraid of his own shadow but boldly lives and speaks for God. He presses onward and upward, and does with his might what his hands find to do. A gentleman came home one evening very much discouraged and said, "I have lost all, I am a bankrupt. All will be sold." His Christian wife asked, "Will you be sold?" "No," he said. "Will the children be sold?" "No." "Will they sell me?" "No." "Then be of good courage; for you have all that is noblest left—manhood, womanhood, and childhood. You have only lost the result of our skill. Try it over. Profit by past mistakes and failures. Be strong and of good courage. Put the strength of your manhood into your work and finally success will come." The Christian must be of good courage, profit by past mistakes and victory will come in the shape of a fadeless crown of glory.

4. Devotion. Whatever we are most attached to in this life, we are most devoted to.

Thoreau, the celebrated naturalist writer of America, was so devoted to his literary studies and so oblivious to world affairs, that he said, "I wouldn't run around the corner to see the world blow up. I think that I should hear with indifference that the sun drowned himself last night."

A lady applied to her pastor for a district in which she might visit. He said, "I must not ask you to take Blank Alley, it is so wretched and dirty." "All the more needing our help and sympathy," she said, and there she wrought a miracle in cleaning up Blank Alley. So thousands of God's children cut loose all worldly attachments, and go among the heathen with the gospel of Jesus Christ, and from Christian communities.

III. The Out Working of Christian Manhood.

1 Steadfastness. No mere children. No more carried about—borne round and round as in the swiftly whirling eddy of the sea—by every wind of doctrine, but steadfast, unmovable, always abounding in the work of the Lord.

Watch ye, stand fast in the faith, quit ye like men, be strong (1 Cor. 16:13). It pays. It is standing under fire, under trial that tests Christian character. We think of Moses at the Red Sea; Elijah on Mt. Carmel; John the Baptist in Herod's prison; Paul before Felix; Wellington at Waterloo; Washington at Valley Forge; Martin Luther at Worms; John Huss at Constance; and best of all Jesus is the world's greatest example of steadfastness. "For the joy that was set before him, he endured the cross, and despised the shame. Let us therefore be steadfast in the work of the Lord. It brings joy, the grace, the glory.

2. Loyalty. The spirit-filled Christian is absolutely loyal to duty. The spirit-filled pastor is absolutely loyal to the church he serves, from a local and even from a national and whole world sense. The spirit-filled church will be absolutely loyal to the spirit-filled pastor. Pastor and people loyal to the home, community, church, state and nation. Loyal in attending church, Sunday school, etc. Loyal in giving service and in giving of his means as the Lord prospers.

3. Sincerity. Speaking and living the truth in love. Singing and praying and making melody in our hearts. Sincerely working out the great problem of life doing the will of God from pure and noble motives, conscientiously doing our duty toward God and our fellow men.

Our plea therefore for the progress toward Christian manhood is growth in likeness to him, growth in comprehension of him, growth that makes the life harmonious, and growth, the standard of whose completeness is Christ.

It brings for its product, largeness, dignity, courage and strength, devotion steadfastness loyalty and sincerity.

Martinsburg Pennsylvania.

The Great Objective

(Continued from page 7)

let's be honest in our distribution of interest. I would have you retain in the second place,

II. A consciousness of the size of our task Such a realization should bring unity in every church. It should bring first, the co-operation of the Sunday school and the Christian Endeavor and of both the Sunday school and Christian Endeavor to the church proper. Every member should be conscious of the fact that he has a part to play. I love to think of the four men who brought the paralytic to Jesus. They carried him on an ancient bed, which was a blanket, and you can see the four men holding to each corner of the quilt. Suppose one had released his grip! The paralytic would have suffered. So will every church in which there is not perfect co-operation. "To every man his work," which implies that there is a work for every man. In the second place, co-operation issues in loyalty to Christ and the church. Dr. John Timothy Stone of Chicago told a story at Lake Geneva, Wisconsin this summer which illustrates the loyalty of the men to their country's call. He lays on a certain Sunday a number of men were called to report for camp. There were fourteen men who thought they had been called and failed to receive the notice who also appeared to be sent if the call was issued. When the roll was called the names of the fourteen men were not mentioned. One man who could not be present because of sickness left a gap in the line. The man in charge asked one of the fourteen men to volunteer his services in order that the gap might be filled. Instantly the fourteen men were down at the front part of the church every man willing and ready to give his life to his country. Such is a demonstration of patriotism for the country. Do we have such a loyal and patriotism for the kingdom of God?

This question will be answered still better in the third outstanding objective I wish to present.

III. The retaining of a spiritual inheritance, which is national and international in scope.

As a young minister in the Brethren church I have a sacred trust which has been bequeathed to me by those richer in power who have gone before and who must go, soon; in turn I must pass on this inheritance to those who will come after me. The Brethren church has a far greater inheritance than endowments, lands, college and buildings for worship. She has a spiritual entity. This exists in the souls of her choice spirits. This spiritual inheritance must ever be progressive and expanding. As I listened to the report of Brother Kimmel and the address of Brother Shively at Winona this truth was brought forcefully home to me. As Brother Shively traced the development of the church I said surely our present inheritance represents sacrifice and endurance, heroic and unselfish. And if we are to pass on to the next generation a richer inheritance how much more should that spirit of unselfishness appear in our lives? Why speak of an international inheritance? Because I am desirous of an honest distribution of interest. I receive a rich inheritance from the Gribble party in Africa and the Yoder party in South America. They are the children in the great vineyard of God and must be within the scope of my sympathy. If my vision stops at home I am near-sighted and am in need of a pair of God's glasses—the lenses of which are prayer We may have everything I have asked for today and yet fail to realize the great objective; therefore I mention the fourth and last truth I will ask you to consider for me.

IV. The need of deliberation seasoned with reason. I feel that in the past we as a church have been too indifferent to her deep significance of such matters as we are here considering. It is important, therefore, that we should approach the problem now in the spirit of fairness and deliberation rather than in passion. We cannot undo the harm and mischief of the past by rushing blindly to the opposite extreme. We only create new difficulties by pursuing such a course. Popular sentiment is more easily swayed by words than by ideas. When the passions of the multitude are deeply stirred, a catching phrase has more influence with the multitude than the widest reasoning. We have need of all the wisdom and restraint we can summon in order to avoid the danger of religious hysteria. We must be prepared to take all measures with a deliberation born of clear vision and through appreciation of all practical phases of the issue. We must act with that settled purpose becoming to high minded people who, undeterred by difficulties, seek a worthy goal and persist long after the attention of the crowd has been distracted and its passions have cooled. We have in the second place the need of deliberation in the choice of our life work. We may find in twenty years from now that we have defeated the great objective of Brethrenism because we have spent our life on the wrong task. Therefore the greatest objective is the unmistakable realization of God's divine stamp of approval upon our life work.

The saddest picture ever thrown upon the earth's canvas is of the fragments of a mis-spent life. Will you see the saddest picture in the New Testament? It is a judgment scene; as multitudes of blighted souls are turned from the presence of God, they cry for the rocks in the mountains to fall upon them. There is weeping, wailing and gnashing of teeth because in God's mirror they see the reflection of their mis-spent lives. A life work choice that is made deliberately and prayerfully is apt to be an enduring decision, one that will stand the battering day of time and at last safely anchor in the harbor of God.

May we labor that when the rewarding angel comes he will say, "Well done, thou good and faithful servant, come to the heavenly choir."

Sing we of the golden city,
Mentioned in the legions old
Everlasting lights shine o'er it,
Wondrous tales of it are told.
Only righteous men and women
Dwell within its sacred wall;
Wrong is banished from its borders
Justice reigns supreme o'er all.

Then we will have an ideal brotherhood. We will enjoy the parliament of man and the federation of the world —Because

Only righteous men and women
Dwell within its gleaming wall,
Wrong is banished from its borders
Justice reigns supreme o'er all.

Ashland, Ohio.

THE SUNDAY SCHOOL

The Outlook for the Coming Year. By Albert Trent
Address delivered at Pennsylvania Conference, Johnstown

Our estimate of the results in the coming year must be based on what has been accomplished in the past and what we are planning to do at the present time..

It is to be devoutly hoped that we have reached the crest of the wave of war conditions that has somewhat unhinged even the religious interests of the world for the time being and to some extent retarded the advancement of the work of our Sunday schools. This aftermath of an unsettled and apparently unbalanced status in society making its baneful influence felt in all lines of endeavor throughout the world, evidences the need of greater emphasis being given to the teaching of the truths of the Gospel.

The situation of today apparently indicates that the times in some way are out of joint. Seemingly the teaching of the past in our Sunday schools has scarcely yielded the fruitage in the present generation that was expected. May it be that the manner of our teaching the eternal truths of God's word has not been of a character to vitally impress and implant these truths in the hearts of the children to serve as an anchor for the soul in times of trial and great crises like we are passing through.

It is therefore imperative that we learn to present the Bible truths to the children, and all whom we may teach, in such a manner that they will be vitally impressed upon their hearts and become the governing force in their lives: so they may be trained in the great spiritual ideas of love and good will toward all. In a word, that we may teach them to be Christians, realizing that God's word is the only lasting stay for the souls of men and women, and that in the experiences of life God is working out for each a noble destiny.

These are some of the things that face the Brethren schools in the outlook for the coming days. We cannot revolutionize the world, but we can, and we necessarily must, do our share for advancing the Master's cause in the places we occupy, though humble they may be.

The war has taught us some things. It taught us to give without stint when we became clearly impressed with the need of doing so. It taught us that people varying in opinions and capabilities can work cordially together for the attainment of an end. It ought also to have taught us the value of the religion of Christ in the hearts of men and women, and that a victory over military autocracy can be sustained only in a civilization dominated by Christianity. Let us hope therefore that the gloomy haze that has overhung Christian efforts during the recent years is about to be dissipated by the rays of the Son of Righteousness,

bringing cheer and enthusiasm into the outlook for all those who are laboring in the interest of the Kingdom. Let us show in our lives and in our efforts that no phase of war work was more important to us, or can be more important to us, than instilling the principles of the Prince of Peace in the minds and hearts of the children and youths of our Sunday schools.

The following are some of the features in our work that will require careful supervision if we want the year ahead to be successful:

First, and foremost, is the right kind of leadership, wise, enthusiastic and capable of suggesting workable plans. A leadership that can put plans into effect and carry them through to success. Let it consist of those who have a real vision of greater attainments with a determination that will not yield to discouragements nor yet become dictatorial.

Second, and equally important,, a teaching force that is consecrated in Christian living, loyal to the church and the Master. Not teaching, simply, because they are expected to do so, but teaching because they want to be of service in the Kingdom. A force, knowing the Bible and capable of imparting its truths, its doctrines and its precepts, so that those taught can grasp and apply them in practical every day life. In a word, a teaching force that is anxious to make a Christian, a devoted, serving Christian, of every member of the class.

Third, The missionary feature: It is of supreme importance. Let us not fail to give it the place it should hold in our monthly and quarterly programs. Let us see to having missionary propaganda of the strongest type. Have a missionary committee to use at least a part of the opening exercises, occasionally, in giving missionary information, stories and experiences. Some one has said, "Ignorance is the mother of missionary indifference; intelligence is the mother of missionary devotion."

Fourth: A weekly or monthly meeting of all officers and teachers, not simply for entertainment, but to frankly talk face to face over the conditions and vital interests of the school, boosting and strengthening its weak points, and bringing into full and harmonious co-operation all of its forces for greater results.

"I have sometimes wished that I had nothing else to do than to dwell with God in prayer, praise and preaching. Alas! one has to come down from the Mount of Transfiguration and meet the lunatic boy and the quarrelsome scribes at the bottom of the hill."

J. A. Garber
PRESIDENT

G. C. Carpenter
SECRETARY

Our Young People at Work

Daily Suggestions for Christian Endeavor Week, February 1-8, 1920. By Prof. J. A. Garber

Christian Endeavor Day

On Sunday, February 1st, Endeavorers of every land will be privileged to celebrate the thirty-ninth anniversary of Christian Endeavor. We should duly appreciate the privilege of recounting the steps by which the Society has passed thirty-nine milestones, having become a determining factor in the life of more than eighty-five evangelical denominations with a combined membership of more than six millions. Through this birthday celebration the stage may be set for and interest awakened in the activities of the remaining days of the week. The regular topic is "What Does Our Pledge Require?" A special program may be obtained from the United Society at Boston at the rate of $2.00 per hundred. Perhaps the pastor can be induced to preach a sermon on "Young People and the Church." In this event the Endeavorers should attend the evening service in a body, supplying special music and other parts of the service.

Fellowship Day

Monday may be devoted to the cultivation of closer and wider fellowship. Where a local union, city or county, conducts a social, Brethren Endeavorers should join most heartily. If no such meeting is provided, have a society social or banquet. Active and associate members will be invited, but others should be included, honorary now alumni members. A leaflet describing the Alumni Association will be sent on request by the United Society. Then remember the pastor and Sunday school superintendent, asking each to tell how Christian Endeavor has helped them in their work.

Union Day

Many local unions will hold mass meetings on Tuesday evening. At that time vital topics will be discussed, such as, prohibition enforcement, world peace, Interchurch World Movement and the like. The discussion will widen the vision and supply fresh stimulus for enlarged endeavors. Great encouragement will come to all sharing in these rallies.

Church Loyalty Day

The regular Wednesday night service should be made a banner prayer meeting. And, it will be such if the Endeavorers co-operate with the pastor in planning and conducting it. Tell the pastor you will convey his invitation to every family of the church and community. Supply a choir and special music. As a part of general participation have several Endeavorers tell how they have been helped to pray and testify in the Christian Endeavor prayer meeting.

Intermediate Day

Thursday evening may be set apart for the growing number of Intermediates. While the societies are not so numerous, they are increasing in number, and the workers testify to the great importance of this work. A social or banquet for these teen age folks and their parents would help to deepen the interest of both in this method of Christian training. Try it.

Extension Day

The week's activities may culminate in part on Friday evening. If you have been working to double the membership of your society, this night may become the feast of ingathering. Then you may hold an enthusiastic meeting to receive the report of the lookout and special committees, to induct new members—active, associate, alumni—into membership, impressing them with the importance of the Society and giving them the glad hand. If they are still wanting, Junior and Intermediate societies may be organized. If your local work is well organized and developed, have your folks to visit a nearby church to organize its young people into a Christian Endeavor Society.

Junior Day

Make provision for the boys and girls on Saturday afternoon. Invite the parents and give a demonstration of singing, Bible drills, etc. A brief business meeting in which the Juniors make their own reports would impress the parents with the value of the training. A social period with the boys and girls serving would give them an opportunity to make their parents glad.

Decision Day

Sunday, the 8th, should find every society on the crest of the wave of enthusiasm. It promises to be the harvest time, the day of decisions. The general topic is "A Worthwhile Life," and Endeavorers should be led to decide definitely to do those things that help to make life worth-while. Associate members should become Christians, active members comrades of the Quiet Hour, Tenth Legioners, Patriotic Servants and possibly Life Work Recruits. The appeal for full time service will be made through the Ashland College Night program, when societies will receive their offering for the department of Religious Education. Programs with full instruction will be supplied by Superintendent Boardman.

Good News from Altoona

A letter from Mrs. Nora Grosse states that Altoona, Pennsylvania now has three societies: Young People's, Intermediate and Junior. The results are proving that better work can be done than when they had only one society or even two. This seems to be a rather general experience.

The Altoona society has organized a class in Expert Endeavor. The Intermediates desire and expect to share in this work. If they finish the course, as they doubtless will, this society will not lack a trained leadership in the years to come. Other societies will do well to follow this example. Altoona says "Come on! Let's go!"

Mrs. Grosse is Field Worker for Western Pennsylvania, and has arranged to visit some of the societies within the next few weeks. Other societies will profit by arranging for a visit by her. She will help you to prepare for the observance of Christian Endeavor Week. Societies of all the districts should call upon the field workers. They are ready and eager to help you. Make large demands of them if you want to please them.

C. H. Spurgeon once said "If the Supreme Being should say, 'Live forever,' it were a malediction rather than a benediction."

Formerly a drunken Chinaman was a rare spectacle in any Chinese city. Now because the American brewers and distillers, whose business has been made illegal in their own country, Chinese drunkards are becoming familiar sights.

As essential as leather to the shoemaker, or cloth to the tailor, so prayer is to the Christian. It must be the very warp and woof of his character and by means of it he must accomplish his daily service for Christ and his fellowmen. Fenelon used to say, "I spend much time in my closet in order to be prepared for the pulpit, and to be sure that my heart is filled with the Divine Fountain before I am to pour out the streams upon the people." Few men have been better qualified to speak on this subject than the good Fenelon, of whom it was said by one who enjoyed his friendship, "While he watched over his flock with a daily care he prayed in the deep retirement of internal solicitude."—B.

NEWS FROM THE FIELD

GOSHEN, INDIANA

We have failed to measure up to the suggestion of our Edtor in writing up the church news every six weeks short and to the point. We think the suggestion a very good one, and will do our best, at least in the shortness. The only reason we did not write up our splendid evangelistic effort was that we had a promise from Brother Thomas to do that. Come, Brother A. E., where have you been? We surely had a good meeting; the sermons were Scriptural, forceful, and spiritual. The good people stood by the evangelist, just as we always should do for then God blesses his word to the saving of souls. If we remember right, sixty-three came out; about fifty were baptized; a number came by letter and relation. One young man of sterling character, a successful business man of our city came with us. He was born in Aegion Mouria, Greece. He became a member of the Greek Orthodox church when but a youth. He comes to us having received baptism by triune immersion by the Rev. Geo. Choomacos. He is a member of the young men's class of True Blues and he is faithful. We all like "Andy," as we call him. He has a sweet nature and a sweet business. We mention this because of his coming from the Greek church to us. During the absence of our pastor while engaged in a meeting at North Manchester the pulpit was filled by Brother Duker, Brother Vandermell of the Holland Reformed church, also one Sunday by Prof. Wilkinson, superintendent of the city schools, who gave a very practical address on "Practical Education as It Applies to Christian Professors." All did fine and we enjoyed the meeting, but all were glad to see "Brother Mc's." smiling face, when he returned. Our Sunday school superintendent, Brother Milt Wisong is doing his best to get the attendance up to four hundred. The Sunday school gave a cantata on Christmas evening. We took the White Gift offering on the following Sunday.

The Mennonite College Philharmonic society of ninety voices rendered The Messiah at our church on last Tuesday evening; the house was full and to say the least, it was great. Sister Hamman, one of our faithful workers both in Sunday school and church, died at Rochester, Minnesota, after a critical operation. The funeral took place at her home church, Brother McInturff officiating. She was anointed by her pastor and Brother Duker before leaving for the operation. May God bless the bereaved ones.

A merry Christmas and Happy New Year to the Editors and others. M. E. HORNER,
Corresponding Secretary.

REPORT OF EVANGELISTIC LEAGUE

We closed our campaign in Clay City, Indiana, on Monday night, November 3rd and by fast time got into Canton, Ohio, just thirty minutes before we were to appear on the program Tuesday evening.

The Canton meeting was arranged so as to begin at the same time that the Ohio conference was, to be held, so that the evening sessions of the Conference merged into the revival campaign. It seemed like getting back home to be in Ohio and among the brethren whom I had labored with for several years.

The Ohio Conference

The conference was fairly well attended by the northern Ohio churches but less than five delegates from churches in the southern part of the state. The more I study the situation the more I am convinced that states like Ohio and Pennsylvania, covering so much territory would accomplish much more by having two conference districts. California struggled along for years with the same problem in having one conference for the whole state and since the state has been divided into two districts they are doing twice as much work. One

criticism I have to offer, which, in a general, way applies to all conferences, is the failure of those selected to appear on the program to show up or to make provision for their place. This should be reduced to a Christian principle and a moral obligation. The conference was well attended by the Canton members and nearby churches and was generally satisfactory.

Canton Campaign

This city is well known as the home town of President McKinley, in which is erected a fine memorial and tribute to this great man. Brother Belote, the pastor, is an old friend of mine and this was my fourth campaign with him. I held my first revival meeting in the Brethren church with him in Aurelia, Iowa, in 1902. So my association was very pleasant, and I was entertained in a most congenial way in his home while there.

The Canton church is still one of the mission churches of Ohio. Through sacrifice and struggle the faithful here have been building up a work for God and his Christ and soon will be able to take care of the work alone. We have a good class of people here, liberal and faithful to the cause, scattered to the extremes of the city, but on hand nearly every night to give their encouragement and to help the work. Brother Belote's work here has accomplished much; the church expects this year to pay off the remaining debt on the building. The room for the Sunday school is already too small. So many of our churches make this mistake when building—not providing room for Sunday school work.

The campaign was generally, satisfactory, the weather most of the time was good, the crowds fairly good, several found their way to Christ and the Gospel was preached and received. I found three Brethren preachers in the church, whom I trust may soon be found in active work, Brethren Smith, Byers and Eikenberry, all whom are trained, capable and experienced men in the work. Circumstances for a time have compelled them to separate fram active ministerial labor. I shall always remember my. labor in Canton with pleasure and be interested in the future.

Ashland, Ohio

By invitation of President Jacobs, I arranged to stop off at Ashland on my way west to my next meeting and visit the college. I arrived on Wednesday night before Thanksgiving and found many of the students had left for their homes, but enjoyed meeting with those who remained and gave a talk on Wednesday evening to a mixed audience and spoke again on Thursday morning to the Y. W. and Y. M. of the college. I found a good spirit in the school with a good enrollment and from the student body up to the president, all felt full of hope. Everything indicates a bigger and more efficient school in the days to come.

Publishing House

All of you have seen the picture of the publishing house which recently appeared in the Evangelist, which was better described than I can do. Through the kindness of Brother Baer and Slotter I was shown through and am satisfied it was a wise move and a good financial investment. We are securing a good printing equipment and the Publishing Company was never in better position to fill its place in the church.

I am now in Morrill, Kansas, in zero weather, with closed roads and up against the fuel problem, we are going ahead and will continue the meeting unless closed up by officials.
W. S. BELL.

DOINGS AT DAYTON

Being confident that many readers of the Evangelist are glad to know about the work of the First Brethren at Dayton, Ohio, I will briefly offer a few of the interesting features since the report in October. . . . .

Soon after the return of our pastor, Dr. E. M. Cobb, from his campaign in the First church of Philadelphia, Pennsylvania, which was marked with much success, we opened our revival here, November 16th, very auspiciously from the very beginning, with the hope of thoroughly arousing the latent membership and the winning of souls for the Master. Dr. Cobb was the evangelist and preached most excellent revival sermons, as well as some doctrinal and on the ordinances. A great mens banquet was held on Friday evening previous to the opening day with a fine spiritual and inspirational program which set the work going with "pep" and vim. Orion E. Bowman was chairman, and fine addresses were made by home talent. Among the speakers were Rev. Ray G. Upson, Religious Work Director of the Y. M. C. A., Prof. A. A. Maysilles, County Superintendent of Schools, Fred W. Fansher, advertising man, Byron Murr, Lawyer, and Marcus S. Kuns, the pastor and others.

Prof. Arthur Lynn, New York City, known everywhere as "The Golden Tenor," arrived on Sunday morning in time for the opening service. He showed himself worthy of the title, and proved to be a thoroughly consecrated and devoted Christian worker, "not needing to be ashamed." Besides his wonderful solos, he is a great chorus leader of inspirational and spiritual music. He uses the "Great Tabernacle Hymns," published by Myer and Brother, Chicago, a wonderful collection of the best hymns, and almost confined his solos to that book. Brother Lynn is a man of high spiritual conception developed through peculiar hard experiences. He sang on the stage for 12 years and entertained the pleasure loving public, but seeing the emptiness of its bauble, became disgusted with his course and the wasting of his life. He was converted at a little friend's church on the Pacific slope, and decided to give his service henceforth to the Master. He loves the Bible and is scanning its pages at every opportunity, as well as praying, praising and testifying from his marvelous experiences. He greatly endeared himself to the First Brethren church and she is anxious to secure his further service as assistant to the pastor, for which the congregation has issued a unanimous call for them to consider. He became so impressed with Dr. Cobb's messages and the constant scenes during the campaign that on the closing night, December 7th, he was immersed by the pastor with 20 others on the same occasion. And on Monday following he went on his way rejoicing, happy, as a lark, to his next appointment at Lima, Ohio, for two weeks campaign with Rev. R. S. Crosby of the United Brethren church.

On Monday evening the 8th, following the campaign, we observed the communion service and had the largest and best feast ever. The main floor and about half the gallery was occupied, the service lasted two hours.

The visible and immediate results of the revival, were 47 by baptism, 6 yet to be baptized, 5 by relation, 7 by letter, and 2 reconsecrations, making a total of 67. Revival should have continued and we expect to reap its fruits the same as last season when baptisms occurred nearly every Sunday.

At the Wednesday evening prayer, praise and business meeting the congregation authorized the purchase of a Baldwin Grand piano, as well as granted unanimously an evangelist's license to Brother Arthur Lynn, so that he could preach the Word as well as sing the Gospel message. May the Lord greatly bless his ministry is the ardent prayer of the saints at Dayton.

On Thursday night the 11th, the pastor, Dr. Cobb, left for New York City Tabernacle to deliver seven special lectures on the "INCARNATION." During his absence of Sunday, December 14th, the morning service will be featured by a special program on the ''Demobilization of Our Service Flag,'' Vice-moderator Orion E. Bowman, presiding. The Boys will be there, in khaki for the final, we hope! At the evening service, Rev. Dr. Joseph Kyle, D.D., LL.D., of Xenia Theological Seminary, will deliver an address on the optic, ''When We Demobilize the Service Flag of the King of Kings and Lord of Lords.'' Pray for us that the Lord may sustain the membership of the First Brethren at Dayton, by his marvelous grace, is our wish!

    WILLIAM C. TEETER,
    Corresponding Secretary.

DOINGS AT HAPPY, KENTUCKY

It has been quite a long time since the news from Happy have been reported but we are glad to say the work is going along nicely.

Our revival with Brother Rempel, of Krypton, Kentucky, began November 10th, and lasted for ten days. There were six who made a confession and many more whom I believe are under conviction.

We are greatly in need of a regular pastor at this place, also a church. Will the readers of the Evangelist pray that the right man be sent to take up this work?

This is a prosperous field and I believe the Lord has a great work to be done here.

The Sunday school at this place is growing rapidly. We are now getting ready for a Christmas entertainment to be given by the school on Christmas eve.

We have organized a Sunday school at Stacy's Branch about two and a half miles from here and have thirty in attendance.

The new railroad that is being built is just about completed and will soon have a passenger train on the line.

School is progressing very nicely. There are forty-one enrolled and more to come.

We ask the prayers of the Brethren to remember the work and workers here. Wishing you all a Merry Christmas and a Happy New Year.   CHARLOTTE HILLEGAS.

PALESTINE, WEST VIRGINIA

As there has been no report through the Evangelist from the Prosperity congregation for some time, I will try to give a short report of the Lord's work at this place. As one of the smallest and possibly one of the weakest congregations in the brotherhood, we have many discouragements and much opposition. Yet we believe the Master where he says, ''Fear not, little flock, for it is your Father's good pleasure to give you the kingdom.'' And we praise him for the faithful few who always stand firm for the Master and are always ready to help fight the battles for him. We had many pleasant experiences during the month of November. We began our revival meeting the 9th, and closed the 30th, with Brother W. J. Barnhart as the evangelist. Brother Barnhart did us a great service by his evening messages and his morning Bible Studies. We were hindered greatly the last week of the meeting on account of rainy weather. We had no miss three evening services. The immediate results of the meeting were not what we hoped it might be, only one confession. But we are sure it was not the evangelist's fault.

Brother Barnhart certainly did preach the whole gospel with power, and we have reasons to believe that the seed sowed will bring forth fruit, because some people here are like them at Berea where Paul and Silas preached—they are searching the Scriptures to see if those things are so.

We feel sure that the meeting was a success in that it was a great help to the church and the community. We closed with communion service Sunday evening, November 30th and while there were only a few surrounded the Lord's tables we had an enjoyable service. Will just say in regard to Brother

Barnhart that he is a man of great ability and filled with the Spirit and any church desiring evangelistic help will make no mistake in securing his help. Come again, Brother Barnhart. We ask an interest in the prayers of the brotherhood. B. H. SHOWALTER.

LAKE ODESSA, MICHIGAN

We closed our revival meeting at the Campbell Brethren church on November 19th, with five confessions. Brother George W. Kinzie of West Alexandria, Ohio, serving as evangelist and on November 20th, we held our love feast and at that service three more accepted Christ, making a total of eight. They were all young folks but one and we feel that Christ was well pleased with the work, for in Mark 10:14, he said, ''Suffer the little children to come unto me and forbid them not for of such is the kingdom of God.'' There were eighty-four at the table for which we thank God. This shows that Michigan is not altogether dead. Brother Kinzie worked hard but it seemed that the devil and his imps were at work too. And we feel that outside of the conversions, Brother Kinzie did a great deal of good. For the other day an unsaved man came to me and said, ''Do you have a horse?'' I said, ''I do.'' He said, ''I have a half of a load of hay for you,'' and I said, ''All right I will be there;'' and I said, ''I have a cow, too.'' He said, ''A cow! that means a load instead of a half.''

Brother Kinzie, come again. When a man will preach the gospel that will loosen up the unsaved what must it do to those who profess? But that is what the church needs today. We have determined to press the battle harder and try to reach the goal Christ set for us.

Brethren pray for us.
    M. V. GARRISON, Pastor.

NORTH MANCHESTER NEWS

Recently we closed a series of meetings which was one of six simultaneous meetings held in our city. Brother McInturff of Goshen, did the preaching. The total, including all we have received this fall by letter and by relation, gave us an increase of 24 new members of a very fine class, generally. Sometimes we make a ''scoop'' of the children; at other times we get the older. The first class means future strength, the latter mainly, immediate. These people are of the latter class. Brother McInturff did us good work. His evangelism is of a different type than most of the modern preachers, but that does not say it is not good. ''Mac,'' as all soon begin to address him, has a way all his own. He preached some great sermons and did a lot of good mixing among the outsiders. He was entirely true to the Word in his preaching and made a place for himself among us that means an open door to our friendship. I am not sure that the simultaneous idea is a good one for a small town like this. Members, and prospects especially, did too much visiting to get settled to conviction, it seemed. Yet every church that went into the campaign in earnest got a good many new members. All told, perhaps, 125 were added to the churches here during the three weeks.

Communion!

Last night we held our semi-annual communion. The roads were icy and the audience was smaller than we had hoped. Altogether we had 179 at the tables of the Lord. It seems to me that it was the best I ever attended. It is a great joy for a pastor to face practically all of the real force of his church in holy communion with their Lord. It means life, spirit, power. Gradually, this church is coming to its own. A few people everywhere, want the high seats and compel obeisance to them in order to have peace. Too many churches and preachers have to make compromises with the headstrong to succeed as they ought. Under the leadership of our new superintendent, Robert Goshorn, our Sunday

school has grown excellently this fall and money matters are in good shape. We have lost some folks who walk not with the Lord but they have been replaced by a paying, praying class that means strength instead of a load. I am sure that we have been passing through a sifting period in the church generally that means a stronger Brethren church all over this land.

We crave an interest in the prayers of the brotherhood that in the trying days that may be the last of the dispensation, we may be ''watching for the glorious revelation of the saints.''   CHARLES A. BAME.

PLEASANT GROVE, IOWA

We started our year's work out here with a revival, which was hindered from being a succesful meeting by various causes,—corn husking and rain, and the worst of all the church was not in the right spirit to engage in a revival. I am speaking very plain, but God will speak much plainer if I should not declare the gospel that is needful. The Pleasant Grove church needed a revival just for the church. It was like a lot of our churches which think that a preacher should come to them and get a lot of the world saved, but forget that it is expedient for the church members to sit with their faces together instead of their backs before the evangelist comes on the ground. We worked hard the first week to get the church reconciled which we could not do fully in so short a time. Then we looked the last week for lost souls; we received nine in all, seven by baptism, one reclaimed and one by letter. This was as good as could be expected under the conditions. Now if you would like to know a little about Pleasant Grove we have one of as good a Sisters' Society as can be found. And while our Thanksgiving offering was small, as an offering, yet ye have six Home Guards. And do you think this is small? Remember we have not 100 members. I feel that there are churches of more members that can not report as good. We have a fine people here and one of the best attended churches in the township. The cloud is disappearing and light is shining brighter each day, and our heart is made to rejoice in God our Savior who said, ''I will never leave thee nor forsake thee.' We will put in electric lights this month and are going to do our best to increase our subscription for the Evangelist. I and the Evangelist work good together in the field. Watch us.
    HOMER ANDERSON.

P. S.—Don't stop a single subscription. Charge it to the pastor. Pleasant Grove is in for a greater subscription this year. H. A.

BUENA VISTA, VIRGINIA

It has been some time since I have reported our work here at Buena Vista. Let me say we have not been idle, since the last report. We have received about 13 by baptism and several renewals. The Sunday school under the leadership of Sister P. J. Jennings, is moving forward. The mid-week prayer service has been well attended with good interest. The S. S. C. E. is to be praised for their splendid work. This church is in splendid working condition. Pray for us. More later.
    G. W. CHAMBERS.

BETHLEHEM

It has been a real pleasure to serve this church. It can be truthfully said that Bethlehem is a Brethren church. Like many other Brethren churches of the Valley of Virginia, it has had its trials. But through the efficient leadership of Elder E. B. Shaver, it has been able to overcome. The Sunday school with Brother Lee Logan as superintendent has made wonderful progress. In order to get better acquainted with the school we with the superintendent visited each class while in session. This was a really interesting experience. We were made to feel welcome by both the teacher and class. We would like to speak separately of each class but time and space will not permit. On the first Sunday of November '"The Class in the Corner" made its drive and as a result $30.00 were raised which is to be used in building a new Sunday school room. On the first Sunday in December the Bible class made its drive, the result was $48.50 which is to be used in the same way. The Willing Workers' class is helping to pay for having electric lights installed. The Christian Endeavor Society paid for painting the church. The S. S. C. E. will likely help to install a furnace. The brethren and sisters of Bethlehem have a large vision and believe in efficiency and adequate equipment for Sunday school and church work. After serving the church at Buena Vista and Bethlehem for more than two years, we resign and will be open to call after January 1st, 1920. Those wishing to write me can do so by addressing me at Buena Vista, Virginia, Box 122.

G. W. CHAMBERS.

COLLEGE CORNER

The work here is moving along in fine shape. This church has a fine equipment for being located in the country, not even near a rail road. The building is practically new, seated with opera chairs and lighted with Delco lights. They have a Sunday school, Christian Endeavor society, Junior society and Womans' Missionary Society. All these auxiliaries are striving to make their goals.

We commenced our work here with a two weeks' protracted meeting. It started out with good interest and continued to the end. We received the very best of support throughout the entire meeting. The chair platform was occupied every night and the music was all that we could ask. It was at least half of the service. We have some talented young people and of a very high class. This means that the older folks are just as good. When our service closed we baptized and received seven into the church.

We held our Rally Day and promotion exercises, Sunday, November 9th. There was a large number present and the entire forenoon was given to the Sunday school. We expect to be a Front Liner. The general outlook for the year's work is very encouraging. We are enjoying our work with these people to the limit.   L. A. MYERS.

WILLIAMSTOWN, OHIO

As there has been no report from this church for some time, I am sending a brief account of the Lord's work in this part of his kingdom.

Since taking up the work here in September one has been added to the church by baptism.

On Thanksgiving eve, we held services and took an offering for Home Missions. On account of the extremely bad weather there were only about thirty present, but the offering averaged one dollar for the "faithful few," for which we are very thankful.

On Sunday evening, December 7th, we observed the Lord's supper and communion. It seems to me it was, indeed, a "love feast," for surely as we fellowshipped with each other we feasted on that heavenly manna which the Master showers upon those who keep his commandments. There were about sixty that communed, for which, again, we are thankful.

The spirit of the Christ not only rested upon the communicants but also upon the audience. I never beheld more respectful onlookers, and not a few said that they were impressed with our order and manner of observance.

The church here has decided to make extensive improvements—basement, furnace, beautifying the interior—in fact a general remodeling of the building. Plans are well under way and we expect to begin work on the basement in a few days.

On January 5th, Brother Harley H. Wolford of Elkhart begins a three weeks' campaign for the salvation of souls and a general spiritual uplift of the membership here.

We ask for the prayers of the brotherhood

for the success of these meetings and the work in general at thi splace.

We thank our heavenly Father for his part blessings and pray that he may not withhold them in the days to come.

MARK B. SPACHT.

HUDSON, IOWA

Since our last report to the columns of the Evangelist we have been spending the time in getting acquainted with the people and with the field. In the five months we have been in this place we have found much to rejoice over and also much that we are not so glad about. Even in Iowa we find many factors that do not make for the finest type of manhood and womanhood and it would be strange indeed if some of these things were not found in Hudson. We have found however, a mighty fine class of people and we are glad indeed to be able to call many of the folks in this vicinity our friends.

Being just fresh from school when we took charge of this church we found it very hard to settle down calmly and act like a "middle aged brother," so we turned to the local high school as a mighty good avenue thorugh which to let out our surplus energy. The boys needed a "coach" for their basketball team, so we volunteered our services and since that time we have not only been able to keep in the "pink" of condition physically, but we have also been able to claim the boys as our friends. We are not making any prediction regarding this part of our work but I can say that already it has paid big dividends. Along with the job of "coach" came the responsibility of being "Hi—Y" leader, so three fine channels of leadership were opened up to us—viz., spiritual, physical and intellectual. An opportunity like this is worth while.

The evangelistic services closed at Hudson, last Sunday, December 7, after having a short halt on account of the fuel shortage. The meeting was well attended from the start and after counting up the total attendance we found that the attendance for each service averaged 74. This was fine according to the reports of the people who have been members of the church for years and know what to expect in the way of attendance at special meetings. The other churches of the town supported the effort in a due way by attending the services through the week and coming over to our service in a body the last three Sunday nights. The pastor had to be the evangelist in this case and he had the supreme satisfaction of seeing eleven people make the good confession. Nine of the eleven were baptized and became members of our church. The meeting did not only result in public confessions, but also had as a very definite result the encouraging of the membership to renewed efforts for the Christ. Then too, the other people of the town know on just what basis the Brethren church is standing and they have given us a friendly and earnest hearing which bespeaks their continued interest in the days to come. There was nothing "racy" in the meeting nor were the people startled by "sensationalism," but they did hear the message of the Cross with all the comfort and condemnation it conveys to the human heart. We believe God honored his Word.

Our future plans for the beginning of the new year include a Mission Study class, with "Christian Americanization" as the text book, and a Teacher Training class. It will be our earnest endeavor to make our Sunday school count for the greatest possible good in the days to come for we are convinced that if the young life is conserved and trained for God all the other challenges of life will be duly taken care of. The Life Work challenge and the ministry are problems of childhood and the Sunday school is the most potent factor in our hands (as "means" go) to the successful solution of the problems in question.

May God bless his servants and lead them to a fuller, finer service in the new year, 1920.   Sincerely,

EDWIN BOARDMAN, Jr.

WARSAW, INDIANA

This letter comes to the readers of the Evangelist from our new pastorate at Warsaw. We came after being extended a call. We found a loyal band and willingness was written on the faces as we faced them for the first time. The first three months was one of great blessing. The church attendance had grown splendidly and the spirit of the worship is in a high degree of a spiritual nature. So great has been the power of the Spirit manifested that ten people have come to us in the first quarter. The Sunday school is coming back to its own and the other branches of the church showing improvement. We are feeling happy, in being able to shepherd this flock, and we are all confident that the future looks bright. We have never served a more loyal people, nor have preached in a town where we have been greeted by its people more lovingly than here.

During the quarter we were away one month in Goshen-in a revival effort, immediately after state conference. I have been waiting to see the report from the land of Goshen, but so far have heard of none. From the standpoint of the evangelist, we can truly say Goshen has made good. Everybody was on the job. No friction. The pastor, Brother McInturff, who is very popular with his flock, was right with us and we hit the ball together until some of those who had not yet settled the great question surrendered. How many! Official number, 63 in all. A great victory for the Lord and his hosts. Goshen surely did well. It is a great church and one which the Brethren people can be proud of. We hesitate to tell yet we feel we owe it to them to say that we received the largest offering here that we ever received for meetings of this nature. May God bless these dear people, as they go forward with their pastor to victory.

Our pulpit was filled very acceptably here by Brother "Mac," and Dr. Jacobs and Sister Maud Webb, and one service was by a son of the noted English preacher, Dr. Campbell Morgan, who now resides at Winona Lake. Our meetings start here, if the Lord wills, the second Sunday in January and we will be assisted by one of Warsaw's evangelistic singers. We are looking forward to a great victory. But in the midst of these blessings we have not escaped the dark clouds. We have been passing through the deep waters of affliction. My dear father, who was a devoted Christian and a loving parent, passed to his reward December 6, after 68 years of life, which was full of activity and service for the Master. He sleeps today among the hills of Johnstown, Pennsylvania, in beautiful Grandview cemetery, to await the resurrection morning. Heaven is nearer to us today because of his going away and we are living and working to crown Jesus King so that we shall meet him in that home where sorrow and death never come.

May the Lord bless the work everywhere for Jesus' sake.   A. E. THOMAS.

WHITE GIFTS—COMING FINE

The following White Gift offerings have been received already in the order given below:

Berlin, Pa.,	$ 60.00
Fair Haven, Ohio,	26.00
New Enterprise, Pa.,	6.37
La Paz, Ind.,	5.00
Mt. Pleasant, Pa.,	5.00
Denver, Ind.,	6.26
Beaver City, Neb.,	95.15
Dayton, Ohio,	70.00
Columbus, Ohio,	7.60
New Lebanon, Ohio,	22.00
Waynesboro, Pa.,	10.21
Nappanee, Ind.,	190.00
New Paris, Ind.,	33.18
Brighton, Ind.,	12.30
Fairview, Ohio,	20.46
New Enterprise, Ind.,	8.50
Third Brethren, Phila., Pa.,	17.00
Oakville, Ind.,	17.20
Ridgely, Md.,	5.45

Ashland, Ohio,	128.47
Mountain View, Va.,	25.00
Masontown, Pa.,	25.00
Milledgeville, Ill.,	65.00
Elkhart, Ind.,	27.65
College Corner, Ind.,	9.75
Allentown, Pa.,	19.68
Woman's Missionary Society, Allentown, Pa.,	10.00
Maple Grove, Ind.,	11.68
McKee, Pa.,	7.78
	$953.69

To Berlin, Pennsylvania, belongs the honor of sending in the first offering. And to Nappanee, Indiana, that of the largest offering so far. The great number of the above schools have increased their offerings over that of last year, some of them even as high as three hundred percent. Five of the above schools had not paid anything last year. This is, therefore, a most promising start and indicates a splendid offering for our work this year.

Dec. 31, 1919   ALBERT TRENT,
General Secretary-Treasurer.

Showing California Conference in Four Year Program

At the Southern California District Conference held this year a chart was made showing the standing of the congregations on each of the goals of the Four Year Program. This record is not perfect by any means but it shows that the attainment of the goals is not an impossibility in these congregations at least, and that it might lead encouragement to other districts or congregations a cut of the chart was made and is here presented through the Evangelist.

A. V. KIMMELL, District Goal Director.

HOME MISSIONS

General Fund—Receipts for November, 1919	
Brethren Church, Pleasant Hill, O.,...$	27.25
Brethren Church, Ashland, O.,	20.00
Bethel S. S., Berne, Ind.,	15.80
W. M. Society, National,	50.00
Mr. and Mrs. J. A. Perry, Gary, Ind.,	40.00
Mary A. Snyder, Valley Home, Glover Gap, W. Va.,	40.00
Mrs. C. A. Will, Rockwood, Pa.,	5.00
Mrs. R. D. Martin, Pioneer, Ohio,	5.00
Maggie White, Lyndon, Ohio,	2.00
G. C. Brumbaugh, Hill City, Kansas,	5.00
Mrs. H. W. Robertson, Middleton, Va.,	5.00
Fred Horner, Lanark, Ill., H. G.,	5.00
Mr. and Mrs. Guy Pittenger, Wooster, Ohio,	2.00
Arda L. Hedrick, Hallendale, Fla.,	5.00
Laura E. Hedrick, Hallendale, Fla.,	10.00
Geo. W. Hedrick, Hallendale, Fla.,	10.00
B. S. C. Spickerman, Maryville, Mo., (H. G.),	10.00
Martha Armstrong, Atwood, Ind.,	7.50
Gladys Bouch, Bremen, Ind.,	2.00
Scott Richael, Polk, Pa.,	20.00
Sarah J. and Emma Olinger, Meyersdale, Pa., (H. G.),	10.00
Derro Gordo Church, Ills., W. M. Deer, Secretary	17.60
* $4.35 of this was sent to Herman Roscoe for Superannuated Minister's Fund by request of donor.	
Brethren Church, Oakville, Ind.,	60.00
Carrie C. Funderburg, New Carlisle, Ohio, H. G.),	5.00
N. J. and S. E. Paul, Losantville, Ind.,	5.00
E. Oram, Loganport, Ind, (H. G.),	6.00
V. M. S., New Paris, Ind.,	10.00
Brethren Church, New Paris, Ind.,	35.65
W. Gingrich, McAllisterville, Pa.,	25.00
Jackie C. Smith, Bedford, Pa.,	5.00
Mr. and Mrs. Emanual Grice, North Georgetown, Ohio,	2.00
Mr. and Mrs. Whiteleather, North Georgetown, Ohio,	3.00
Brethren Church, Mexico, Ind.,	22.05
Josiah Maus, (H. G.),	5.00
Mable Maus, (H. G.),	5.00
Cora Maus, (H. G.),	5.00
Mexico, Indiana, total,	37.05
Mr. and Mrs. Carl Winterowd, Plymouth, Iowa,	2.00
Samuel Cook and Family, Harrisburg, Ore.,	6.00
Alice Leedy, Fostoria, Ohio,	1.00
Brethren Church, Waterloo, Iowa,	40.00
Austin Miller and Family, Meyersdale, Pa.,	50.00
1st Brethren Church, Phila., Pa.,	5.00
J. H. Sidera, Astoria, Ill.,	2.00
Mrs. Wm. Garwood, South Bend, Ind.,	5.00
Bethel Church, Penn, Mich.,	6.05
Mr. and Mrs. Jacob Swartz, Mt. Clinton, Va.,	2.00
Mrs. Olive Hollewell, Milledgeville, Ill.,	2.00
Young Ladies' Bible Class, Berne, Ind.,	5.00
Mt. Etna Church, Iowa,	5.00
Whitedale Church, Terra Alta, W. Va.,	34.75
Bessie Hook, Lost Creek, Ky., for Brash Valley Church, Pa.,	5.00
Salem Church, Brookville, O.,	31.84
Wilson King and Son, Salem Church, H. G.),	5.00
Salem church total,	36.84
Barbara Musser, Nappanee, Ind., (H. G.),	5.00
Clay City Church, Clay City, Ind.,	41.22
New Troy Church, New Troy, Mich.,	5.75
A Sister of Gretna, Bellefontaine, Ohio,	6.00
Mr. and Mrs. Isaiah Meyers, Fostoria, Ohio,	5.00
D. J. Hetrick, New Bethlehem, Pa.,	5.00
College Corner Church, Wabash, Ind.,	21.25
Fair Haven Church, Fair Haven, O.,	30.00
Mrs. Roy Decker, Augusta, Mich, (H. G.),	2.00
E. F. Miller, Belefontaine, O., (Gretna, Church, (H. G.),	5.00
H. J. Franz, Enid, Oklahoma,	5.00
Total Receipts for November ...$	816.71
Previously reported by former Secretary and myself, $	926.63
Total receipts to December 1, ...$ 1,743.34	

NOTE.—Correction for last month . W. M. S., Dayton, Ohio, should have been National W. M. S. by Mary C. Wenger, Treasurer, Dayton, Ohio.

HOME MISSIONS

Kentucky (Support) Fund. Receipts for November, 1919	
W. M. Society, Mexico, Ind., ...$	15.00
Samuel M. and Lydia A. Baker, Swanton, O.,	10.00
Miss Bell Mast, Spooner, Wis.,	5.00
S. S., Turlock, Cal.,	11.00
Golden Hour Bible Class, Nappanee, Ind.,	5.00
Brethren Church, Krypton, Ky.,	27.50
W. M. S., Elkhart, Ind.,	5.00
Y. P. S. C. E., Canton, Ohio,	5.00
Loyal Women's S S. Class, Canton, O.,	5.00
Dyoll Belote, Canton, O.,	5.00
S. M. M., Portis, Kansas,	20.00
Mrs. Dora Shabe, Austin, O.,	10.00
C. E. Society, Morrill, Kansas, ...	10.00
Mr. and Mrs. Wm. A. Perry, Gary, Ind.,	20.00
Wm. A. Gearhart, Dayton, O.,	25.00
W. M. Society, Milford, Ind.,	25.00
1st Brethren Church, Los Angeles, Cal.,	5.00
O. E. Bowman and wife, Dayton, O.,	30.00
E. W. Longnecker, Dayton, O.,	40.00
Lois Whitehead, Dayton, O.,	5.00
Mrs. R. D. Martin, Pioneer, O.,	10.00
Y. P. S. S. Class, Mexico, Ind.,	5.00
C. E. Society, La Verne, Cal.,	20.00
John M. Humberd, Flora, Ind.,	10.00
Alice and Josie B. Wogoman, Brookville, O.,	10.00
W. Baker and Son, Dayton, O.,	15.00
Jr. and Inter. C. E. Society, Goshen, Ind.,	10.00
S. S., Muncie, Ind.,	5.00
Mrs. D. C. Moomaw, Roanoke,	5.00
Total November Receipts, ...$	373.50
Previously Reported, ...$ 1,163.91	
Total Receipts to December 1, ..$ 1,537.41	

Kentucky Kitchen Shower Fund	
W. M. S., Mexico, Ind., ...$	5.00
Mrs. P. E. Peterson, Bement, Ill.,	2.00
W. M. S., Carleton, Neb.,	5.00
Total November receipts, ...$	12.00
Previously reported, ...$125.05	
Total receipts to December 1, ..$137.05	

Kentucky Electric Light Plant Fund	
C. E. Society, Hagerstown, Md., ...$	18.00
Mr. and Mrs. Carl Winterwood, Plymouth, Iowa,	1.00
N. C. Neilsen and Son, Long Beach, Cal.,	10.00
Mrs. Maria J. Frantz, Enid, Okla.,	5.00
Mr. and Mrs. Orion E. Bowman, Dayton, O.,	10.00
Total November receipts, ...$44.00	
Previously reported, ...$18.00	
Total receipts to December 1, ..$62.00	

Muncie, Indiana, Building Fund	
No receipts in November.	
Previously reported, ...$50.23	
Total receipts to December 1, ..$50.23	

Peru, Indiana, Building Fund	
No receipts in November.	
Previously reported, ...$25.24	
Total receipts to December 1, ..$25.24	
Survey Fund	
No receipts to December 1.	
Tract Fund	
No receipts to December 1	

Summary of Receipts to December 1	
General Fund, ...$	1,743.34
Kentucky Support Fund,	1,537.41
Kentucky Kitchen Shower Fund,	137.05
Kentucky Light Plant Fund,	62.00

Muncie, Ind., Bldg. Fund, ... 50.23
Peru, Ind., Bldg. Fund, ... 25.24
Survey Fund, ...
Tract Fund, ...

Grand total, all Funds, ...$3,555.27

FOREIGN MISSIONS

Receipts During November. General Fund,
South American Fund
Paul R. Humbard, Chicago, Ill., L,
I. M. ....$ 50.00
Cerro Gordo, Church, Cerro Gordo, Ill., 17.40
Mr. Godfrey's Sunday School Class,
Third Brethren church, Philadelphia,
Pa., ... 5.00

Total, ...$72.40
Previously reported, ...$ 22.00

Total Receipts to December 1, ...$94.40
General Fund (African)
St. James S. S., Long Beach, Cal, No.
336, ...$38.17
Mrs. Margaret Kyler, Martinsburg,
Pa., M., ... 5.00

Total receipts to December 1, ...$43.17
Gribble (Personal Fund)
R. F. Hensel, Ohio, Ill., No. 83, M.......$5.00

Total receipts to December 1, ...$5.00
Snyder (Personal Fund)
Mrs. Geo. F. Keim, Dayton, Ohio, No.
7, M., ...$10.00

Total receipts to December 1, ...$10.00
Brethren Missionary Fund
La Verne Cal., Church, by Elsie Rager, $3.50
Mrs. W. O. Mitchell, Newport, Wash., .. .25
G. C. Brumbaugh, Hill City, Kansas, .. .25
Rev. Morton L. Sands, Sergeantsville,
N. J., ... .50

Total receipts to December 1, ...$4.50
Summary
General Fund, South American, ...$ 94.40
General Fund, (African), ... 43.17
Gribble (Personal Fund), ... 5.00
Snyder, (Personal Fund), ... 10.00
Brethren Missionary Fund, ... 4.50

Grand total receipts all funds October
1 to December 1, ...$157.05
Respectfully Submitted,
WM. A. GEARHART,
General Missionary Secretary.

Business Manager's Corner

A WELCOME CHRISTMAS PRESENT

On Christmas Morning we took the mail from the Post Office to the Publishing House to look it over to see if there was anything that needed special attention, and one of the first letters we opened was from the secretary of the pastor of the Third Brethren church of Philadelphia with a list of subscriptions for the Evangelist that covered every family of the active membership of that church. While this was not as large a list as some churches send in, yet it was as complete as any, considering the number of members of the congregation, and it was an increase of several hundred percent over the old list, and we extend to the Third Brethren church of Philadelphia and to its pastor, J. E. Braker, the same welcome to the Evangelist Honor Roll that we do to any of the larger churches. It was a splendid achievement for the Third church.

Then a few days later we received a splendid list of subscribers from the Masontown, Pennsylvania, church that places that church on the Honor Roll. Brother Shively has always been a good agent for the Evangelist and his congregations have been above the average in the number of subscriptions according to the old way of procedure, but still

the new way has increased the list more than two hundred percent.

Brother Shively is a "good sport" and a long-time friend of the Business Manager and helped him to get settled in his first pastorate about twenty-six years ago. Brother Shively is of the honest sort who confessed that when we proposed the plan for getting the paper into all the homes of the congregations several years ago he had little faith in it, but he acknowledges that his opinion was wrong and that the plan will work, and we honor him for his candor, and thank him for his words of commendation that accompanied the list sent us.

Then Berne, Indiana, has again won its place on the Honor Roll by sending in a larger list than it ever did before, and this is the third year for the church at Berne. Here that tireless pastor, W. F. Johnson is in charge and he has a habit of doing the things he sets out to do. We thank Brother Johnson for his confidence in the plan and for his successful manner of helping us to keep the subscription list above the five thousand mark. Then A. L. DeLozier notified us to continue the Allentown list and the corrected list will be sent us shortly. This is also the third year that Allentown has won the place on the Honor Roll. This is another one of our city missions that realizes the importance of keeping all its members in touch with the work of the whole church. Other churches are notifying us that they expect to hold their place on the Roll and still others are notifying us that they expect to win such honors very soon. It is a mighty good thing Brethren, and we would urge you to continue in your good work.

The interruption to our work because of our moving into our new quarters and the delay caused by our not being able to get motors to run our presses, that had been promised us in two or three weeks, in more than three months has made us some late with a few of our Sunday school quarterlies, but most of them have been mailed and ere this reaches our readers they will have been mailed to all who have sent in their orders. We are just as sorry for the delay as any of our schools are, but it was a physical impossibility to do otherwise this time. We hope, however, that no similar delay may occur again and we will do our very best to prevent its repetition.

The Business Manager expects to attend the Interchurch World Movement conference at Atlantic City this week at the very urgent request of the publicity manager of the great campaign. We hope to have something worth while to report to our readers concerning the work of this great conference.

R. R. TEETER, Business Manager.

EVANGELIST HONOR ROLL

The following churches having met the requirements laid down by the Brethren Publishing Company regarding the placing of the Evangelist in the homes of the congregations are entitled to a place on the Evangelist Honor Roll:

Church	Pastor
Akron, Ind., (New Highland),	.... (Vacant)
Allentown, Pa., 3rd Year,	... A. L. DeLozier
Ankenytown, Ohio, 3rd Yr.,	... A. L. Lynn
Ardmore, Indiana,	.... A. T. Wirick
Ashland, Ohio, 3rd Yr.,	.... J. A. Garber
Beaver City, Nebr., 2nd Yr.,	... E. S. Flora
Berlin, Penna.,	.... L. B. Trout
Berne, Indiana, 3rd Year,	.. W. F. Johnson
Bryan, Ohio, 2nd Yr.,	.... G. L. Maus
Buckeye City, O.,	.... Glen Peterson
Burlington, Ind., 2nd Yr.,	... W. T. Lytle
Carleton, Nebr., 2nd Yr.,	.. J. D. Kemper
Cerro Gordo, Ill.,	...... D. A. C. Teeter
Clay City, Indiana, 2nd Yr.,	. S. C. Henderson
College Corner, Ind., 2nd Yr.,	Homer Anderson
Conemaugh, Pa., 2nd Yr.,	...... L. G. Smith
Darwin, Indiana,	.... W. T. Lytle.
Dallas Center, Iowa,	.... R. F. Porte

Denver, Indiana, 2nd Yr.,	...... L. A. Myers
Dutchtown, Indiana,	...... Homer Anderson
Elkhart, Ind., (2nd Yr.),	... H. H. Wolford
Eaton, Ind., (Maple Grove),	.. H. E. Eppley
Eau Claire, Wisconsin,	.... J. A. Baker
Fairhaven, Ohio, 2nd Yr.,	... B. F. Owen
Falls City, Neb., 2nd Yr.,	.. H. F. Stuckman
Fillmore, Calif.,	.... Sylvester Lowman
Flora, Ind., 2nd Yr.,	...... W. E. Thomas
Fostoria, Ohio (2nd Yr.),	...... M. S, White
Fremont, Ohio,	.... H. M. Oberholtzer
Goshen, Indiana,	.... J. A. McInturff
Gratis, Ohio	.... C. E. Beckley
Hagerstown, Maryland	.... A. B. Cover
Hamlin, Kansas, 2nd Yr.,	..... Geo. E. Cone
Huntington, Indiana,	.... J. W. Brower
Johnstown, Pa., 1st Ch., 2nd Yr.	J. F. Watson
Johnstown, Pa., 3rd Ch.,	..... Geo. H. Jones
Lanark, Ill., 2nd Yr.,	..... B. T. Burnworth
La Verne, Calif., 2nd Yr.,	...... T. H. Broad
Leon, Iowa,	.... Geo. T. Ronk
Leon, Iowa, (Crown Chapel), .. Geo. T. Ronk
Leon, Iowa, (Union Chapel), ... G. T. Ronk
Linwood, Maryland, 2nd Yr., .. E. M. Riddle
Long Beach, Cal. (3rd Yr.) ... L. S. Bauman
Loree, Indiana, 2nd Yr., ... C. A. Stewart
Los Angeles, Cal., 1st., 2 Yr., N. W. Jennings
Louisville, O., 2nd Yr., ... E. M. Riddle
Los Angeles, Cal., (Compton Ave)., J. C. Beal
Masontown, Pennsylvania, ... Martin Shively
Meyersdale, Pa., 2nd Yr., .. E. D. Burnworth
Mexico, Indiana, 2nd Yr., ... L. W. Ditch
Milledgeville, Ill., 2nd Yr., .. M. J. Snyder
Morrill, Kansas, 2nd Yr., ... A. E. Whitted
Mt. View, Va., 2nd Yr., ... J. E. Patterson
Muncie, Indiana, 2nd Yr., ... J. L. Kimmel
Nappanee, Ind. (3rd Yr.) ...... E. L. Miller
New Enterprise, Pa., ... Edward Byers
New Lebanon, O., ... G. W. Kinzie
New Paris, Ind., 2nd Yr., ... W. I. Duker
North English, Iowa, ... Homer Anderson
North Liberty, Indiana, ... C. C. Grisso
New Enterprise, Ind., ... P. M. Fisher
Oakville, Indiana, ... W. R. Deeter
Peru, Indiana, ... Geo. C. Carpenter
Philadelphia, Pa (1st Br.) .. Alva J. McClair
Philadelphia, Pa., 3rd church, .. J. E. Braker
Pittsburgh, Pa., ... E. M. Harley
Portis, Kansas, 2nd Yr., ... Roy Brumbaugh
Rittman, Ohio, ... J. Allen Miller
Roann, Indiana (2nd yr.), ... Willis E. Ronk
Roanoke, Indiana .... W. F. Johnson
Sidney, Indiana, 2nd Yr., ... L. A. Myers
Summit Mills, Pa., 2nd Yr., E. D. Burnworth
Telford, Tenn., ... Mary, Pence
Tiosa, Indiana (2nd Yr.) ..... C. C. Grisso
Turlock, California, ... J. Francis Reagan
Washington, O. H., O., 3rd Yr., B. S. Stoffer
Waterloo, Iowa, 2nd Yr., .. H. L. Goughnour
Whittier, Calif., ... A. V. Kimme
White Chapel, Mo., ... G. T. Ronk
Windber, Pennsylvania, ... E. F. Byers
Yellow Creek, Pa., ... Edward Byers
Zion Hill, Ohio, ... A. L. Lynn

VOLUME XLII
NUMBER 2

JANUARY 14
1920

The BRETHREN EVANGELIST

-ONE·IS·YOUR·MASTER·AND·ALL·YE·ARE·BRETHREN-

ONE DEBT WE CAN NEVER PAY

is that which we owe to the Pioneer
Preachers of the Brethren Church

WE MUST ALL FACE UP TO THIS QUESTION:

What will be done to bring material comfort
to the few who remain of those who
first proclaimed and championed

OUR ONLY CREED

THE HOLY BIBLE

?

Give Your Answer on Benevolence Sunday
February 8

Published every Wednesday at Ashland, Ohio. All matter for publication must reach the Editor not later than Friday noon of the preceding week.

George S. Baer, Editor

The
Brethren
Evangelist

When ordering your paper changed give old as well as new address. Subscriptions discontinued at expiration. To avoid missing any numbers renew two weeks in advance.

R. R. Teeter, Business Manager

OFFICIAL ORGAN OF THE BRETHREN CHURCH

Subscription price, $2.00 per year, payable in advance.
Entered at the Post Office at Ashland, Ohio, as second-class matter.
Acceptance for mailing at special rate of postage provided for in section 1103, Act of October 3, 1917, authorized September 9, 1918.
Address all matter for publication to Geo. S. Baer, Editor of the Brethren Evangelist, and all business communications to R. R. Teeter, Business Manager, Brethren Publishing Company, Ashland, Ohio. Make all checks payable to the Brethren Publishing Company.

TABLE OF CONTENTS

EDITORIAL

An Epoch-Making Conference and Its Plans for the Immediate Future

Perhaps the most important religious gathering, unless the Edinburgh Missionary Conference should be excepted, of recent years has just been brought to a close at Atlantic City, New Jersey. It was the very good fortune of a little group of Brethren folk, of which the editor was one, to attend that conference which was in session January 7 to 9 inclusive. It would be impossible for one who had come sensitively in touch with that great gathering to refrain from speaking of that which he had seen and heard. Those of us who rejoice in the inspiration of that conference and feel something of the impact of the great movement that was crystallized there, understand the feelings of the lepers feasting in the deserted Syrian camp outside the gates of Samaria when they said, "We do not well: this day is a day of good tidings, and we hold our peace." This is a day of good tidings for the church.

Immediately you are wondering what was that gathering and why it was so important. It was called the World Survey Conference of the Interchurch World Movement and was composed of more than eighteen hundred representatives and members of practically all the Protestant denominations and religious agencies of the United States. These representatives were come together, to use the words of the chairman, John R. Mott, "In the first place to view the wholeness of the task which confronts our American—you might say our North American—Protestant Christianity as it looks out into the fields of this continent, and as it reaches out beyond the oceans to all parts of the world. In the second place," said Dr. Mott, "we are come together in order that the various bodies represented here may become a formative factor in shaping the final plans of the Interchurch World Movement. And in the third place, we are here to review and to determine the scope and, in a larger sense possibly than some thought possible, the character and the magnitude of the proposed united undertaking."

It was important because of what it proposes to do, because of those promoting it and because of the plans perfected. The Interchurch World Movement has no thought of either directly or indirectly doing away with denominationalism, nor of injuring in any way the future of the small denomination. It is aimed at stirring every church to formulate and prosecute with the greatest possible effectiveness and consecration a challenging program for the hastening of the kingdom of our Lord Jesus Christ, and at the same time to bring all Protestantism to focus their united strength on the accomplishing of the great task before the church. The men who had this conference in charge and who are promoting the Interchurch World Movement are men in whom the religious world has confidence, men who have been used of God in bringing to successful issue great world-involving undertakings. The name of John R. Mott connected with any movement is a guarantee of its worthiness and success. S. Earl Taylor, E. A. Cory, Daniel A. Poling, Robert E. Speer, Fred B. Fisher, names of men at once recognized and trusted everywhere because of their great accomplishments, are leaders in this movement. Many other notable and trusted personages were seen and heard in the conference and will help to give direction to the movement. The name of one of our own leading laymen, Wm. Kolb, Jr., was on one of the leading committees that helped to give shape to certain important plans; and the editor had the happy privilege of representing Dr. J. Allen Miller on the Forward Movement Committee.

This conference was also important because of what it planned in the interest of the kingdom of Christ for the immediate future (not to speak at this time of the more far-reaching plans). It proposed a great concerted plan for all the churches of Christ in America for the first four or five months of the year. The churches are urged to launch a great evangelistic program during January, February and March, bringing it to a climax with an intensive campaign at Easter time. During January special effort is to be made to intensify the spiritual life and re-valuate the spiritual resources of the church; during February special attention is to be given to the teaching of stewardship; during March special effort is to be made to direct young people into life service for Christ and the church, culminating in a great ingathering at Eastertide. Of course, these various phases of Christian teaching and activity cannot be entirely separated, and it is not the intention to attempt it. But it is intended that special emphasis shall be given to these things which are recognizedly a part of evangelism during the months designated. Then following the campaign for souls there will be a great simultaneous financial drive from April 21 to May 2, during which it is proposed that every man, woman and child in the country will be given an opportunity to make a really worth-while gift to the promotion of work of the church of Christ. Following that will be other months of effort at conserving and developing the results of these months of intensive campaigning.

Every church co-operating is supposed to have a great challenging program with which it will go before its people and the people of its fields of labor. It is to be a time when every member of every church is to be urged to press forward in certain vital lines. And at this point the Brethren church has the honor of having taken the lead and pointed the way, for we are on the last lap of our Four Year Program. But like everything else of a pioneer nature, it is soon improved upon. We may be able with profit to center our emphasis on a few vital points and not scatter quite so much, and also perfect our plans for carrying the challenge down to the last man in the last church when our next program is launched at next General Conference time. The more earnestly and faithfully we attempt to complete with credit this last year of our present Program, the better prepared we will be for the program that shall come next.

We shall gain great inspiration and impetus by co-operation with the plans of the Interchurch World Movement. The fact that the whole church of Christ is marching forward together and pressing the battle against the enemy at the most vital points at the same time is going to give great encouragement to the forces of righteousness and discouragement to the forces of evil. A great simultaneous campaign conducted on similar plans with perfect unity of spirit and similarity of effort will result in a great victory for all churches without any church losing its identity, just as the Allies fought in perfect harmony against a common enemy without any nation losing its identity and all won the victory. This co-operative effort will create an atmosphere in which the work of the kingdom can be more easily prosecuted than heretofore. The impact of one single congregation, unless it is able to cover the entire community itself, is too small to create a great pervading religious atmosphere in a given community. Its blows against sin are too feeble. Its influence is too circumscribed. What a mighty force the whole church will be if every community shall endeavor to be at its best and all will work harmoniously together for the one great end—bringing in the kingdom of our Lord and Savior Jesus Christ.

EDITORIAL REVIEW

A word from Brother Oberholtzer states that by this time they are in the midst of a revival meeting led by Brother I. D. Bowman. Good preparation was made for this meeting and doubtless it will tell in success.

A note from Brother Riddle, pastor of Louisville, Ohio, church, states that he is now engaged in a revival meeting there, having begun on January 11. Prayer is requested in behalf of this effort; may God give them great success.

Dr. Jacobs favors our readers with another edition of his ''College News.'' President Jacobs frequently finds himself in pulpits in various parts of the brotherhood. In this way there is being cultivated a mutual acquaintance and friendship. The college is soon to enjoy a treat in the form of a lecture by Dr. Henry S. Cope, the great authority in religious education.

It is a splendid report that comes to us from Milledgeville, Illinois. Brother Snyder and his loyal co-workers are doing a good work there; every department of activity receives its proper emphasis. The spirit of generosity displayed by these people during the Christmas season is deserving of special mention. And in the midst f their giving they did not forget their pastor and family.

In a personal letter to the editor recently, Brother N. W. Jennings said, ''We are now worshipping in the tent while our church difice is going up.'' The good people of the First church of Los ngeles have been struggling with courage and perseverance to overome the difficulties of a building proposition in these times and by he grace of God they are winning out.

Beaver City, Nebraska, is moving along in fine style under the adership of Brother E. S. Flora, according to a report from Sister ohnston, the correspondent. They have recently experienced a very uccessful revival under the preaching of their pastor, and they are ounting up the goals won and making plans for the winning of those ot yet won.

Brother Drushal gives an interesting report of the work at Lost reek. He is still reaping the results of the evangelistic campaign eld by Brother Bowman. Other things that give encouragement are he new light plant, the Christmas activities and offering and the special gift to Brother and Sister Drushal. No one understands quite o well as Brother and Sister Drushal what dividends work among hese needy people pays to those engaging in it.

The Brethren representatives at the Atlantic City conference of he Interchurch World Movement were Brother and Sister Alva J. cClain, Brother Wm. Kolb, Jr., Brother Clarence Kolb, Sister Mae

Smith, Brother R. R. Teeter and the editor. All came away greatly stirred with what they heard and saw, and all were one in the opinion that the hour is at hand when the Brethren church must set before itself a great challenging program and prosecute it with holy zeal, or, to use Brother McClain's expression, it will get ''lost in the shuffle.'' The program we have been working on for nearly three years and a half has helped us greatly, but the time will soon be at hand when must set the standard still higher.

When Brother McClain was in Ashland a few days ago he presented the editor with a neat little hand book prepared by himself. It consists of questions asked on various Biblical themes, the answers to which are given in scriptural language with references attached. It is designed as a guide to Bible instruction and is carefully and compactly arranged.

At Dayton things are doing as usual. ''Over the top'' in regard to home missions would seem to be the right word, judging from the size of the offering. Of course the General Missionary Secretary, Brother Gearhart, would not let his home church lag behind. The Sunday school in particular shows a splendid record of achievement for the year. An unusual feat which that church performed was to call an evangelistic singer into their midst and then turn him into a Brethren preacher before he gets away. That speak much for the convincing way in which the pastor, Brother Cobb, preached Brethren doctrine; it also speaks well for the open-mindedness of the evangelistic singer, Prof. Arthur Lynn. Welcome to you, Brother Lynn!

In a letter to the editor, Brother H. L. Goughnour states that he has resigned the Waterloo, Iowa, pastorate to accept a call to direct the promotion of a federated church movement at Manchester, Iowa. He retains his membership in the Waterloo Brethren church while engaged in this work. He says he is deeply interested in and has the warmest feelings for the Brethren church, but that he believed profoundly in this work and feels very strongly this call. Brother Goughnour is one of the most talented of the young leaders of our church, and during his sixteen years of pastoral work he has served very successfully some of the strongest churches of the brotherhood. We regret that another valuable pastor has been subtracted from our active list, for a time at least, but we pray that God may enable him to accomplish a great work in this new field.

Brother Beachler found some loyal and staunch friends of the college at Williamstown during his canvass there. Brother Mark Spacht, the pastor, is a loyal supporter of every Brethren interest, and the college has not the least place in his affections. It is good to learn that he is planning to spend some time at Ashland in the near future. The Williamstown people have contributed much in the form of life to the Brethren church; aside from contributing four preachers to the Brethren ministry, she has sent a number of students to Ashland College, several of whom entered other types of life's activity aside from the ministry. You can count on such churches doing their part financially, and if this church has not done all that she might have done had she not been burdened with local church repairs, you can count on it that she will give Ashland all the greater lift at some later date. But all will be thankful for the splendid work that Williamstown has done for her own church school at present. She has done well.

TOMBAUGH'S BOOKLET OUT AT LAST. Copies will be mailed at once to those who have ordered them. We have the record of those who paid for them at last conference time. If any one who has paid for a copy fails to get one, please notify us immediately. If you have not ordered a copy, do so at once. Price 20 cents per copy where a dozen or more go to the one address. Single copies by mail, 25 cents postpaid. We had hoped to have this booklet made and ready for mailing before the first of October of last year. But the mechanical department was simply unable to get out the work. All editorial work on it was completed before General Conference. We are sorry for this delay, but the value of the booklet is not dependent upon any particular season and we know when you have your book in your hand, you will say it was worth waiting for. Dr. Tombaugh has put into this little work some of his best thought. You can get nothing better for a popular study of the great fundamental doctrines. Get your order in early for a copy or a dozen copies of ''Some Fundamental Christian Doctrines'' by Dr. J. M. Tombaugh.

FOUR-YEAR PROGRAM PAGE

NOW THEN DO IT.—II Samuel 3:18

Conducted by Charles A. Bame

What's New?

Happy New Year! That's new. It is to be the biggest year in the history of the church, humanly speaking. Nothing so tremendous has ever been dreamed by Christian Statesmen since the Master gave to the world his plan of a world empire. Regardless of the position we may take or what we may think it is, or what it may be the preparation for, it is coming. No, it is here. Already many of our preachers and people are linked up with it and more will be. None can escape dealing with it in some way or another.

Have You Heard of It?

Well, I am sure if you have not, you will. Big things are not easily hid and this one is to be so big that none can miss it unless they miss it awfully. Some of these days, it will come with a "whoop" as they say, and you will be astonished at its pull and push and rush. Already the foreign mission field has been apportioned and mapped—the whole world. Soon, every township and territory of our whole U. S. A. will be. Tremendous contingencies hang upon this INTERCHURCH WORLD MOVEMENT of which I have been speaking. Every church will be tremendously influenced by it, whether they are a part of it or not. How much non-affiliating churches will be affected can not be conjectured. THAT'S THE BIG NEW THING OF THE YEAR.

A Sudden Call

Such will the Master's be when he returns to the earth again. "Two shall be sleeping in a bed; one shall be taken and another left." So, came the call to the officers of all the Boards to assemble with the Committee of Fifteen to consider what should be the action of our people with regard to this movement and its relation to the proposed new program that this Committee was to work out. Brother Garber the secretary of the meeting will make the report of the action taken. I wish to say that the "Committee of Fifteen" in a meeting called after the action of the joint meeting, decided some things that need to be the property of the fraternity at large.

Committee of Fifteen, Look

In order to harmonize more fully with the action of the larger meeting, the Committee of Fifteen enlarged the scope of their inquiry by asking that their study should also comprise, Spiritual Resources; Rench, Wolford and Bame. Religious Education, Garber and assistants. Social Service, The Conference Committee.

What to Do

Study. Work out a program, as a committee. Submit the same to myself not later than March first. Myself to formulate from the matter sumbitted by the various committees a program for the next five years that shall be as staggering as the one with which we shall harmonize. Resubmit it to the committee for final revision and then, submit it to the conference (national) in September.

The Big Day

It is upon us. Big revolutions. Big evolutions. Swift and radical changes. Big gains. Big losses. Big deflections from the things we thought were stable and sure. Big drives. Big surprises. Smallness and bigotry and exclusiveness are past—not passing. We can choose the small things but it will lose us. Unless the Brethren church arouses herself immediately, she may as well "hang her harp on the willows and weep." But she will not. She has as big folks as any church on earth. She will meet the challenge. May

it not be too late that she does it. Nineteen Twenty is the year.

Opportunities—how shall we meet them? Alas!
Opportunities—shall we permit them to pass?
Just idly and carelessly let them glide by,
Not trying to use them, and no reason why? ..
They're coming,
  Ne'er staying;
No moment delaying
  For parley or pay, but passing alway.

Thrice happy the man opportunity meets,
  With courage undaunted that braves no defeats;
Who catches and struggles and wrestles awry;
  Who knows God's rewards all the faithful who try.
Ne'er hiding,
  But chiding
Himself if he loses a moment deciding,
While coming,
  Ne'er staying,
No moment delaying, he hastens to pay
  Their coming a stay.   BAME.

Relief For the Near East. By George S. Baer

Appeals are continually coming to our office in behalf of our brothers and sisters in the Near East, homeless, starving and dying at a sad rate. We have not discharged our responsibility until we have passed the news and the appeals along to our great family of Brethren. The tie of human brotherhood is strong and we believe that those to whom this news comes will respond as unto him who says now as in the days of his flesh, "Inasmuch as ye do it unto one of the least of these my brethren, ye do it unto me.'" Many are giving their lives to this great humanitarian service, and may we at this Christmas season give of our abundance that those who hunger unto death may be fed and life preserved. Men and women of courage and consecration are going in person to minister to the needs of these suffering ones; every follower of him who had compassion on the multitudes will want to help to supply their hands with food and clothing.

Just recently a noble band of American women, who had previously given distinguished service as Red Cross relief workers in France, set sail for the Near East to care for 800,000 homeless refugees. They have gone in response to an urgent cable from Col. William N. Haskell, official representative of the Near East Relief and commissioner for Armenia by authority of the Paris Peace Commission. Col Hoskell says that thousands of women and children are dying daily of starvation and exposure in the Near East and that the relief workers who are on the ground are overwhelmed by the magnitude of the task which confronts them. Many of the men and women who are caring for the destitute women and children in the Near East were formerly engaged in war service and putting into effect the experience gained during the war in ministering to the nations which have suffered such horrible persecution at the hands of the Turkish government.

A recent report from relief workers asserts that 800,000 Armenians will starve if they are not given assistance until next year's harvest and there are more than 120,000 orphans who will require care if they are to be saved from death. Sick and starving refugees who have been wandering for months in the desert are daily being brought to relief centers. Buildings requisitioned as orphanages are filled to overflowing and even by giving the meagerest rations it has been impossible to care for all of those who are in dire need

GENERAL ARTICLES

My Ideal of Christian Womanhood. By Mrs. J. Allen Miller

In the 31st chapter of Proverbs we read of a model matron. We have here a picture of a faithful and kindly wife, mother, and mistress. She performed carefully and properly her dometic duties. When these were completed she gave her time and talent to the performing of duties without the home. Her capable energy might have been repellent without love to soften it. But we know that love ruled for she made a happy home. Godliness must be the source of such a symmetrical character. The fear of the Lord it was which enabled her to keep so even a balance of virtues as to stand forth a perfect pattern to the women of every age and nation. The fear of God had given her a right conception of her duties toward all mankind, and especially of the sacred nature of her relationship as wife and mother. She had an abundant and lasting reward. Her husband's trust in her was complete. Her words of loving counsel and her useful and benevolent life were not lost upon her children, but brought forth filial reverence and noble deeds. And this family blessedness was not a thing that could be hid, but, like a candle of the Lord in a world of moral darkness, it shed its light all around. What an example for **Christian** womanhood!

To Hannah we owe a Samuel. Samuel could hardly have been the mighty power for good in Israel that he was if he had not had the blessing of a godly mother, and early training in the fear of God. Prayers on his behalf ascended to heaven before he drew his first breath; holy plans and purposes were formed concerning him before he saw the light of day. He was consecrated to God before his birth. When pious parents receive their children with calling on God and in his fear, then every child is a Samuel (Heard of God.) What an example for **Christian** mothers does Hannah show us!

If we read the sixteenth chapter of Romans we find Phoebe mentioned as a servant of the church. She was accustomed to noble knight-errantry—to visit, as an angel of goodness, the abodes of poverty, to give bread to the hungry, and good cheer to the sick, to make the widow's heart sing for gladness, to dispel the gloom of earth with the joy of heaven. Many modern women are and more ought to be thus champions of the cause of righteousness. Earth's records do not tell half the tale of the glories of the church's women. The true immortality comes from Christian work and from the possesion of the Christian spirit. There were women at Rome wearing in a single necklace of pearls a fortune of a 100,000. lbs. Their very names have perished

with their follies and vices while Phoebe's name is resplendent for ever in Paul's gospel. "Help those women that labored with me in the gospel, whose names are in the book of life." Phoebe represented ideal Christian womanhood.

Mary of Bethany lost herself in the contemplation of Christ till she forgot all the world, and especially forgot her own self. When she anointed the feet of Jesus with her precious box of ointment she revealed admiration, love, and devotion to her Master. The deeper the religious feeling is in a Christian, the more he fears to weaken it in his effort to express it. Mary was that salt of the earth of which Jesus spoke in the Sermon on the Mount, the savor of Christianity was in her. What then shall she do in order to show Jesus how she holds him for her Master, her sovereign guide, her bread of life, her salvation? Shall she tread in the footsteps of the prophet; shall she celebrate with the psalmist her song of thanks? No. She will not depart from the modest but sacred role which suits womanhood, she knows that the most useful instrumentalities are not always the most brilliant, and that she is none the less appreciated by the Lord because she is less conspicuous. Impatient to testify to Jesus the faith which she has in him she thinks of the precious ointment that she possesses. To give that which is dearest to one is to render the greatest honor. It was in the voluntary and absolute gift of hers to Christ that the rare merit and high value of the anointing of Jesus by Mary consisted. She understood in listening to the Master, in living his life, that Christianity is the religion of love. To give one's self to Christ by a decision of one's own will, to give one's self to him without restriction—this is how Mary understood the preaching of the Master.

Christian womanhood owes everything to Jesus and our greatest service is the least we ought to give.

The fruits of Christian womanhood are legion in service and enrichment to the world. The gift of their lives to the world is hope, comfort, and strength. They give "beauty for ashes, the oil of joy for mourning, and the garment of praise for the spirit of heaviness."

"What we are is God's gift to us; what we make of ourselves is our gift to God."

A fitting prayer for the new year would be the following:

"Make it a passion of my life to be all life, to have in me no death and darkness, and help me to pay unfailteringly the price of life."

Ashland, Ohio.

My Ideal of Christian Manhood. By J. L. Kimmel

Manhood is usually considered the highest conception we can have of a man. Manhood after all means little to him who is no true man. The old saying that a hundred and fifty pounds of avoirdupois does not make a man is only too true. There are many men, so called, in this old world yet there is a woeful lack of true manhood. Man is a three fold being—physical, mental and moral—and to be at his best we are told it is necessary to develop all these, which is no doubt true. Yet a man may be a physical giant and not have manhood. He may be a scholar and yet lack this thing called manhood. Manhood requires character and Christ. True Christian manhood is the highest type of a man.

The moral man is a thousand fold better than the immoral man. Because the immoral man is a continual menace to society and is bent on self destruction. The Christian man is a moral man but he is much more from the fact that he is a follower of Jesus Christ.

Christ's conception of human life was the highest the world has ever known. The code of morals which he taught is far superior to that of any other teacher that the world has ever known. His life was faultless and without guilt and the standard test by him for Christian manhood towers like a mountain peak above anything the world had ever conceived. The ideal Christian manhood is therefore patterned after the ideal man, Jesus Christ our Lord. Any manhood therefore that does not aim at the perfect is not ideal. Too many men are Christians in theory only. They do things of course that are supposed to be essential to Christian manhood, but fall so far short of the ideal that it would be very difficult to decide as to whether they are Christians at all or not. We have become accustomed to saying, He is a big man or He is not a big man, measuring of course by the standard of true manhood. The same could consistently be said of Christian manhood. There are some big Christian men and some that are very small indeed.

Sam Jones used to say that he could put some Christians in a band box, put a two cent stamp on the box and they would go all right by mail. That is a very low estimate of Christian manhood and yet there is entirely too much truth in the saying of the evangelist. But it is not my conception of an ideal Christian manhood; neither is it yours. We are all looking for a man that really is all that he pretends to be, yea, more than he professes to be—a thousand times more. We have the greatest contempt for the mere shell, the empty thing,—that means nothing.

And yet there are so many men who think they can fool the people and pose as great men without manhood. They have gotten it somewhere that men can not discover their true motives, cannot measure them by their true value, cannot weigh them in the balances, so they will never be found wanting. Yet the people laugh at their stupidity and measure them by their true worth, and the whole thing is a very easy proposition. My ideal of Christian manhood is a man who forgets himself and sees the other fellow; a man who is big enough to forget his own interests and to look upon the need of this wretched, miserable old world; a man who is willing to throw himself upon the altar of sacrifice and live and die for the betterment of human society; a man who has the courage of his convictions and will stand by the right as God gives him to see the right; a man who will take the Bible for his guide and the word of God as a weapon of defense; a man who is willing to fight the devil when ever and wherever it is necessary to do so; a man who is willing to exalt righteousness and condemn sin and practice what he preaches; a man who is big enough and broad enough to have Charity for the other fellow, who may sincerely and honestly differ from him; a man who is humble and yet aims at perfection and is continually striving for the higher, the nobler and the better. My ideal is a man who pours out his soul in longing for the spirit of a Bunyan, for the manliness of a Paul and for crowning manhood of Jesus Christ our Lord.

This is my conception of ideal Christian manhood.
Muncie, Indiana.

Love. By N. J. Paul

In the discussion of this subject we want to prove by the Scriptures, that love is the climax of the Christian Religion. When once in possession of true love, we are in position to possess all the Scriptures contain. Love is an attribute of God. According to the Scriptures, God has feelings, affections, toward all mankind. We must derive our conceptions of God from the special revelation which he has given of himself; and this declares his love as strongly as his existence. It is held by some to be inadequate to speak of love as a divine attribute. "God is love". (John 4:8-16). The Scriptures contain no equivalent statement with respect to other qualities of divine nature. Love is the highest characteristic of God, the one attribute in which all others perfectly blend. The love of God is more than kindness or benevolence. The eternal love of God has never been without its object; a fact upon which we receive some light from the Scripture revelation of the threefold personality of God (Matt. 3:17; John 15:9; 17: 23-26).

The Gracious Love of God to Men

Even to sinful men, is most strongly declared in both the Old and the New Testaments (Exod. 34:6; Isa. 63:9; Jer. 31:3; John 3:16; 1st John 4:10). The love of God underlies all that he has done and is doing, although many facts exist which we cannot reconcile with his love on account of our limited understanding. The highest disclosure and most complete proof of divine love is in redemption (Rom. 5:8; 8:32-39; 1 John 4:9, 10).

The Reality and Power of His Love

are properly apprehended only under the influence of the Holy Spirit. "The love of God is shed abroad in our hearts by the Holy Ghost which is given unto us" (Rom. 5:5).

Again love is a Christian virtue. Love is the pre-eminent virtue inculcated and produced by real Christianity. The whole Gospel as well as the law is summed up in love, not in the sense of rendering all other requirements, but in the sense that love is fundamental, and expresses the spirit of all others, and with enlightenments will lead to the observance of all others (Matt. 2:37-39; 5:43-48; Rom. 12:8; John 14:15-21; 15:12-14).

Love, the Highest Motive of Moral Actions

Without this all other motives fall short of furnishing the true stimulus of Christian living. As all sin rests itself in selfishness, so all virtue springs out of love; and yet the love which is presented in the New Testament as the mainspring of holy living is grateful love as distinct from the love that is wholly disinterested. "We love him because he first loved us." are the words which rightly express the whole matter (2 Cor. 5:14; 1 John 4:19; Rom. 12:1-2). Christian love, it is only important to note, is made possible only by divine grace. You see, it is one of the fruits of the Spirit. It is the first fruit which the Spirit bears. And if we bear this first fruit, it will enable us to bear all other fruit which the Lord intended for us to bear (Gal. 5:22; 1 John 3:14). There seems to be at this age, two kinds of love; one kind from the lips only, and the other from the heart. The latter the Scriptures approve; the former is also spoken of but with disapproval and to our shame. It only comes from the lips (see Matt. 15:8). This lip love is in possession of professed Christians, as well as men of the world.

Those who are so fortunate as to possess heart love are the true followers of the Christ. This class will stand the test; this class, will love their enemies. This is where the test begins. Listen to the words of the Master: "Ye have heard that it hath been said, Thou shalt love thy neighbor, and hate thine enemy. But I say unto you, Love your enemies, bless them that curse you, do good to them which despitefully use you, and persecute you; that ye may be the children of your Father which is in heaven:—For if ye love them which love you, what reward have ye? do not even the publicans the same?" Sinners loves sinners; Christian professors should by all means love each other and not forget the more important duty of loving the sinner. "Not every one that sayeth unto me, Lord, Lord, shall enter into the kingdom, but he which doeth the will of my Father which is in heaven." The mission of Christ was not for the saved, but for the lost. The apostles made their missionary journeys, in the interest of lost humanity. What prompted the Father to send the Son to the earth to suffer and to die the shameful death of the cross? What prompted Paul, Peter, James and John and, in fact, all the apostles to forsake all and to endure hardships, persecutions, afflictions, and at last, most of them, to die martyr's deaths? Undoubtedly, it was LOVE. "Love knows no fear." "Let brotherly love continue. If a man say I love God, and hateth his brother, he is a liar; for he that loveth not his brother whom he hath seen, how can he love God whom he hath not seen? He that loveth not, knoweth not God; for God is love. He that dwelleth in love, dwelleth in God, and God in him."

What can adjust all our differences? What can reconcile us, one to the other? What will unite broken family ties? What promotes, (or should promote) the marriage tie? What can unite the Protestant church (and especially the two factions of the Brethren)? Can committees? No, they have been tried. Can elders of both factions meet together and reconcile us, so that we can assist in answering that Prayer of all prayers, made by the Lord in our behalf? Only one solution, and that is LOVE. Love can accomplish more, and do more for the children of men than everything else combined.

It was love that brought the Savior to die for us. He sent the Holy Spirit. The giver will receive no reward for any gift, no matter how large nor how small unless it was through love that he gave it. God rewards only that which is accompanied by love. Without love, nothing is acceptable to God. Realizing then this fact, can we not say with Paul: "Who shall separate us from the love of Christ? Shall tribulation, or distress, or persecution, or famine, or nakedness, or peril, or sword—nay, in all these things we are more than conquerors through him who loved us. For I am persuaded that neither death, nor life, nor angels, nor principalities, nor powers, nor things present, nor things to come, nor height, nor depth, nor any other creature, shall be able to separate us from the love of God, which is in Christ Jesus our Lord." Oh, could we realize this truth, and be prompted by love as Paul was to utter this from the heart. Praise his holy Name.

Love Will Solve the Stewardship Problem

There have been many plans sought by the churches as to how best to raise money to meet their obligations. So far as I know, no device that the church has accepted, has been found to be satisfactory. You have to keep building them up; they are like the electric battery you have for your auto, the more you use them the weaker they get. Why not do away with men's methods, and take God's plan. You pastors preach love, and love supreme to your members, and when you get them full of love, it will work automatically; the more they use it, the more they will have to use.

Here is the Climax

I care not what we give, or what we do, or what we may say, or how much we may work in the interest of the church; if it be not prompted by love, we become as a sounding brass, and tinkling cymbol. If we would even consecrate our bodies to be burned and bestow all our goods to the poor, and yet all this be not prompted by love, what can it profit us. (1 Cor. 13)?

The Bible

It will do good if we shall often read the words of an unknown writer: "This book contains the mind of God, the state of men, the way of salvation, the doom of sinners, and the happiness of believers. Its doctrines are holy, its precepts are binding, its histories are true, and its decisions are immutable. Read it to be wise, believe it to be safe, and practice it to be holy. It contains light to direct you, food to support you, and comfort to cheer you. It is the traveler's map, the pilgrim's staff, the pilot's compass, the soldier's sword, and the Christian's charter. Here paradise is restored, heaven opened, and the gates of hell disclosed. Christ is its grand object, our good its design, and the glory of God its end. It should fill the memory, rule the heart, and guide the feet. Read it slowly, frequently and prayerfully. It is a mine of wealth, a paradise of glory, and a river of pleasure. It is given you in life, will be opened in judgment, and be remembered forever. It involves the highest responsibility, will reward the greatest labor, and will condemn all who trifle with its sacred contents.

Losantville, Indiana.

Miracles of Knowledge. By T. Darley Allen

Hume admitted that "prophecies are real miracles;" and Alexander Keith said, "Each prediction recorded in Scripture being a miracle of knowledge is equal to any miracle of power and could have emanated only from the Deity."

The argument from prophecy is peculiarly impressive because of its simplicity. In regard to the evidence for the miracles of power by which Christianity was established many queries come to the mind of the average investigator. Many instances are on record showing how people have been imposed upon by counterfeit miracles, by Mormonism and various systems of religion; consequently writings dealing with this subject treat to a considerable extent preliminary questions to answer the objections based upon the possibilities when deceit and craft are exercised upon credulous people.

But with prophecy the argument is simple. To foretell the future as the ancient prophets did is plainly beyond human power; and for the argument to appeal with force nothing is necessary beyond establishing the priority of the predictions to the events prophesied. There is nothing that appears wonderful in the utterance of a prediction; as a rule, the same can be said of the event that fulfills it. Only when the two are considered together is evidence furnished that proves the divine inspiration of the prophetic utterance.

That many of the prophecies of the Bible were written before their fulfillment is beyond dispute; indeed, some of them are being accomplished before our eyes. Events occurring at the present time in Palestine afford every reason for believing the long-looked-for restoration of the Jewish people to the land of their fathers, when they shall form an independent state as in the remote past, is very near. Such great numbers of this long-scattered race have expressed a desire to make their home in Palestine that emigration is to be restored because of the impossibility of all being able to be provided for. But of Palestine's soon becoming a land governed by Jews as in ancient times we are assured.

When Frederick the Great asked his chaplain for a brief demonstration of the truth of Christianity he was answered, "The Jews, your majesty."

That the Jewish people have preserved their individuality for more than eighteen centuries of dispersion among all the nations of the earth, as prophecy declared, and are as peculiarly Jewish in features, temperament and other respects as in the days of David and Solomon, is one of the wonders of history.

What could be more wonderful than that many events in the life of Christ was clearly foretold by the Old Testament prophets? And the present condition of Egypt, Edom and other countries, and the ruins of Babylon and other great cities of antiquity are exactly as prophecy declared.

Just as an example of how striking the "subject" of prophecy is, take the prediction that Egypt "shall be the basest of kingdoms," and then consider that as Keith says, "In 1250 the Mamelukes deposed their rulers and usurped the command of Egypt. A mode of government the most singular and surprising that ever existed on earth was established and maintained. Each successive ruler was raised to supreme authority from being a stranger and a slave. No son of the former ruler, no native of Egypt succeeded to the sovereignty; but a chief was chosen from among a new race of imported slaves."

Bishop Newton said that some prophecies are come complete in their description of events than any single written history, that "no one historian hath related so many circumstances and in such exact order of time, as the prophet hath foretold them." We must read several histories to obtain as complete a narrative as prophecy affords.

H. L. Hastings said: "Skeptics know little or nothing of the prophecies; Christians neglect to study them; ministers fail to preach them; critics try to subvert them; but no candid man can read such works as those of Bishop Newton or Alexander Keith, or others, on the prophecies without being convinced that God has at sundry times and in divers manners spoken to the fathers by the prophets."

Cleveland, Ohio.

It is more necessary for us that we should make a discovery of our faults than of our virtues.—C. H. Spurgeon.

THE BRETHREN PULPIT

The Greatest Need of the Church---The Baptism of the Holy Spirit

By R. Paul Miller

TEXT: For John truly baptized with water; but ye shall be baptized with the Holy
Spirit not many days hence. Acts 1:5.

Never before in the history of the Christian church has she been so financially rich and so spiritually poor. Where a few years ago there were thousands raised for missions, today there are millions being raised. The great general cry in Christendom today is that a new era is upon us, a "go ye into all the world and preach the Gospel to every creature" that made the man Jesus the Christ. If we will undertake the big things, and think on them we will have no great world-wide opportunity is facing the church, and that the church must raise prodigious sums of money and men to meet it. But the greatest stress is laid upon the money. The treasurer of a local church told me that when the Centennial movement came into his church its cry was for men, money they got us down in black and white for, they could get along without the others, but they have to have the money." And the enormous sum of one hundred millions was raised with ease. And this same trend is true in nearly every other church I know of. This is heralded by many as the great on-sweep of the church of Christ to victory—a victory bought with money! It looks to me verily like the fulfillment of Revelation 3:14-20 Revised Version. The professing Christian church, rich and great in the world—but with Christ, her Lord, outside of it all.

If the Spirit of God in mercy has taught me anything, the great need of the church today is neither money or men, for either are worthless without God's Holy Spirit permeating both. The great need of the church is the baptism of the Holy Spirit. With a church baptized with the power of the Holy Ghost, these other things would fade into insignificant details in her great onsweep of victory in the power of God.

I believe that the church today is in her decadent spiritual condition because of late years this great truth and blessing has been so little preached and taught. The church is rolling in wealth and starving for spiritual power. They are almost like the poor men that Paul found, "We have not so much as heard whether there be any Holy Ghost" (Acts 19:2)!! I would like to have seen this doctrine among Brother Bell's list of Four Year Program sermons for this year. Perhaps he thought all ministers would use it anyhow. We surely ought to.

The regeneration of the Holy Spirit and the baptism of the Holy Spirit are two entirely different experiences. A man may be regenerated, yet not be baptized with the Holy Spirit. In regeneration, eternal life is imparted to him, but in the baptism of the Holy Spirit, power for service is imparted (Luke 24:49; Acts 1:8). For example, in John 15:3, Jesus pronounces the apostles to be clean or regenerated, and in Acts 1:5, more than a month later he places the baptism of the Holy Spirit some days ahead of them yet. These examples could easily be increased from the Scriptures.

Every true believer has the Holy Spirit in regeneration but not every believer is baptized with the Holy Spirit for service. This is why so many believers have little or no power in Christian service while others seem to be filled; it; some are baptized and others are not. But EVERY BELIEVER MAY HAVE THE BAPTISM OF THE HOLY SPIRIT. It is the normal state of every member of the church of Christ, not the extraordinary or the unusual. Many think that it is only for a favored few, such as preachers, teachers, evangelists, and missionaries, etc. But the Scriptures limit it only to the bounds of the true church. Now, how may every Christian be baptized with the Holy Spirit?

I. We Must Surrender Absolutely to Christ

The great reason why most Christians have so little power is because they have failed to surrender all their sin and sinful habits. The Holy Spirit CANNOT work in a DIVIDED HEART. After the fall of Richmond, in the Civil War, the leaders met to arrange terms of peace. The southern men began to tell what they were willing to surrender and what they would not surrender. After they were through, the northern officers said, "The Government of the north MUST HAVE ALL." As a rule, that's the way Christians do; they begin by telling the Lord what they will and what they WON'T surrender. But GOD DEMANDS AN UNCONDITIONAL SURRENDER IF YOU WILL HAVE POWER. Every sin must be surrendered (Acts 2:38). Repentance does not mean to weep and cry over sin merely, but to RENOUNCE AND FORSAKE IT. To refuse to surrender one sin gives Satan a chance to destroy your whole Christian experience. The law of reserved right, provides that if a man have 1000 acres and sells 999 and reserves one acre in the middle of the plot, he has the right to traverse that 999 acres to get to his own property. So with the majority of Christians; they surrender nearly all yet reserve one little corner for the devil and he drags his dirty claws all over the rest in order to get to his own. The only way out of his clutches is to give every last corner to the Lord. One known sin will lock the lips of praise and testimony as nothing else will. It will stand as a grim specter between the soul and God in prayer. It will take the joy out of every blessing. ALMOST a full surrender is what makes the majority fail. Many say, "The Lord won't care about this little habit or pleasure of mine if it isn't just right." Whether the Lord cares or not, one thing is sure. ONE KNOWN SIN THAT IS NOT PUT AWAY WILL IMPOVERISH YOUR SPIRITUAL LIFE AND POWER AS NOTHING ELSE WILL.

11. The Second Condition is Absolute Trust in the Name of Christ for Cleansing.

"Repent ye and be baptized every one of you, IN THE NAME OF JESUS CHRIST FOR THE REMISSION OF SINS AND YE SHALL RECEIVE THE GIFT OF THE HOLY GHOST." (Acts 2.38).

You don't find those who are trusting in their own goodness, performing miracles of faith. You must realize that of yourself, there is no good thing in you. You must see Jesus on the cross, with your sin upon him, and trust only in the power of his shed blood to cleanse you from all past, present, or future sin.

III. The Third Requirement is Absolute Yielding to the Will of God.

There is a difference between surrendering every sin and yielding to his will. To surrender means to give up the battle and cease striving. To yield to his will means to willingly place yourself in his hands that his will be done in you. We must be self-poured-out that Christ might be poured in. Self-emptying must precede Spirit filling.

All your plans and ambitions must be approved by the Lord. When you lay your plans for the future, what part does God have in them? If you don't submit them to God they will fail in the sight of God regardless of how prosperous they may seem for awhile. When planting ambitions in the hearts of your children, do you first seek the Lord's approval of these ambitions? All plans must be subject to God's approval or rejection. After President Garfield was assassinated, he was taken to a quiet country place. They built a special railroad track from the main line to the house for doctors and nurses, etc. The engineer's began running the line right through a farmer's front yard. He protested. When told that it was for the President, he said, ''O, that's different, why if it's for the President you may run it right through my house.'' Are you willing to give the Lord right of way through all your carefully laid plans for the future? Aren't you a little afraid he would spoil some of them? If you will have spiritual power, you must be willing for him to break up all your plans if need be, that his will for you might be done. Whatsoever ye do, do all to the glory of GOD, and then you shall have power, and he can work a great work through you.

IV. The Last Condition of the Baptism of the Holy Spirit is Faith.

''Received ye the Spirit by the works of the law, or the hearing of faith'' (Gal. v :2) ?

It is not through ''Feelings.'' Thrills and ecstasies are very deceptive. Many think them a sure sign of the Holy Spirit's power. A little fervor and a big imagination fool lots of people. The faith which realizes the baptism of the Holy Spirit, just takes it as its own. ''Believe that ye re- receive them and ye shall have them.'' This faith rests su- pinely upon the promise of God, ''How much more shall the heavenly Father give the Holy Spirit to them that ask him'' (Luke 11 :13).

Surrender every sin and sinful habit absolutely, that you may be a clean vessel, rest entirely in the name of Jesus for your acceptance before God, yield your whole life to him to mould as he sees fit, and finally by faith ask him to baptize you with the Holy Spirit. Meet these condi- tions specifically, and, upon the authority of God's Word I say to you, YE SHALL BE BAPTIZED WITH THE HOLY GHOST AND WITH FIRE. May every member of this church seek it till God shall pour out upon us such a volume of power that we shall literally shake Satan's kingdom. May God bless you all.

Spokane, Washington.

THE SUNDAY SCHOOL

Many Going to the World's Sunday School Convention in Tokyo

Though the first sailing of the fleet of convention steam- ers taking delegates to the World's Sunday School Conven tion in Japan will not take place until next August, 236 have already applied for credentials as delegates. Since there are only about 1,000 reservations that can be obtained on the Pacific Ocean steamers for the delegates, it is impor- tant that all who wish to attend this gathering of Sunday school workers in the Orient should communicate at once with the World's Sunday School Association, 216 Metropol- itan Tower, New York City. The record is kept by states and Pennsylvania is now in the lead with 66 applications. Other states, in their order, are Ohio 18, Illinois 14, Nebras- ka 13, California 11 and Michigan 10. Applications have been received from most of the states and provinces in the United States and Canada. Overseas applicants will greatly increase the number.

Mr. Frank L. Brown, the general secretary of the World's Association, has just returned from London after conference with the British Section of the World's Executive Committee, and the committee representing the Scottish Sunday School Union. He reports that large interest is be- ing shown in the attendance upon the convention on the part of British Sunday school leaders. A number of these leaders, including Dr. F. B. Meyer of London and Mr. T. Vivian Rees, who has headed the Children's Era Movement in Great Britain, are definitely planning to be at Tokyo. Fif- teen inquiries have been received in Wales and in Scotland a number of business men are already forming a delegation for Tokyo. It is possible for the English delegates to travel eastward to Tokyo as well as westward. The eastern trip would include the all steamer journey through the Mediter- ranean and the Indian Ocean, stopping at Egypt, Ceylon, Hongkong and Shanghai, with optional stops at other points en route.

Baron Uchida, a member of the committee promoting the Tokyo Convention, was in London and Glasgow at the time of Mr. Brown's visit and spoke at representative Sun- day school gatherings extending personally, on behalf of the Japanese Committee, its cordial invitation to the British and European delegates. The Baron stated that the Tokyo Committee is preparing to entertain at least half of the dele- gates in the homes in Tokyo. This suggestion was very warmly welcomed by those who heard Baron Uchida.

The British Committee are enthusiastic about the plans for the convention program. They are also interested in the around-the-world plans that are being developed and an- nouncement concerning which is expected shortly.

Had not the Brethren Sunday School Association ought

to be represented at the convention in Tokyo? If we should send a representative who would return with a great vision and enthusiasm such as no leader has yet received, and then travel among our schools and give out what he received, what a world of good it would mean to the Brethren fra- ternity. Have we not been living too much to ourselves? Have we not been too self-sufficient? And have we not been blameworthy in failing to make possible for our lead- ers the very best opportunities for increased efficiency in leadership that the world affords? What we deny to our leaders we deny to ourselves. Think it over, and if the sug- gestion seems feasible to you, write your thoughts through this department.—Editor.

The National Sunday School Association of Japan

There is a National Sunday School Association in Japan which has an affiliated membership of about 160,000. Their annual convention has just been held in Tokyo and was at- tended by delegates from all parts of the Empire. Every ten Sunday schools had one delegate and representatives were present from thirty-three of these local associations. Some subjects that were discussed would be equally helpful for a convention in any country. They were ''Rural Sunday Schools in the United States,'' ''The New Day and Sunday School Education,'' ''The qualifications of the Sunday School Teacher.'' Then special attention was given to the convention of the World's Sunday School Association which will be held in Tokyo, October, 1920. Mr. Horace E. Cole- man, Field Secretary for Japan, who had just returned from the United States, reported the extensive preparations for the convention which are being made in America. The com- ing of this World's Convention is a goal toward which the Sunday School Association in Japan is working. They set five aims as follows:

An increase in the average attendance in every Sunday school of 25 percent by October, 1920.

All Sunday schools to try to organize at least 100 Teach- er Training Departments.

All Sunday schools to strive to bring 1,000 schools up to the standards set for the church school.

All Sunday schools to strive to bring the number of Branch Associations up to 100.

Each Sunday school with an average attendance of 100 between December, 1919 and the end of May, 1920 to be al- lowed to send one delegate to the World's Convention and one additional delegate for an average attendance of 200 or more.

J. A. Garber
PRESIDENT

Our Young People at Work

G. C. Carpenter
SECRETARY

Organization Versus Indifference

Both are to be found in most societies. Their presence would seem to represent a paradoxical condition. Organization is calculated to prevent or destroy indifference.

Is not the explanation to be discovered in the fact that too often societies are organized in name only? This may be due to the manner in which the organization was effected—elect persons to office in hit and miss fashion without careful selection (nomination) or elect them without subsequent notification and installation. In either event the resulting condition is abnormal and should be corrected or disastrous results will follow.

The report from southwestern Virginia shows how one president mobilized his organization to wage war on "indifference" or lack of interest. If more such society-institutes were planned and conducted a revival of interest and effort would ensue in every case. We suggest that others employ this method during Christian Endeavor Week. Let presidents do as President Rowsey did: Decide that something must be done to stimulate interest, then call for counsel other members of the cabinet, including the pastor. Together they may work out a program of Christian Endeavor. They will also be able to find speakers among their own Endeavorers or near-by available helpers.

Then let presidents adopt President Husette's method of letter writing as a means of publicity. There are scores of Endeavorers who would be surprised beyond measure to receive an appealing letter from the president, secretary or any other official of the society. Isn't it a shame—yes, a "burning shame"—that we have failed to communicate through the written page with members of our societies or prospective members? Business enterprises representing thousands of dollars have been promoted in this manner. We must sell Christian Endeavor, and we need not expect folks to become interested through our regular activities when they are unknown beyond the walls of the meeting room. One letter may not get the desired result. Brother Huette, a young business man, understands this, and plans to continue his publicity campaign. Let others do likewise in advertising Christian Endeavor Week.

J. A. GARBER.

Roanoke, Virginia

On November 29 we opened fire on Mr. Lack of Interest who was working against the success of our society and especially playing havoc with our committee work. We opened our work with four simultaneous conferences led by Rev. L. G. Wood, S. M. Coffey, Mrs. L. G. Wood and the writer. Later we had a Workers' Banquet, a meeting with the executive committee and closed with a model Christian Endeavor meeting and a popular Rally with the pastor as speaker.

Buena, Vista, Virginia

On December 31 when we found ourselves at this place the first person we met was Mr. Lack of Interest (who must have come here when we ran him out of Roanoke), who was trying to delay Mr. Organization in his work. After censuring Mr. Lack of Interest and telling of the wonderful work of Mr. Organization in public Sunday and Wednesday evenings and in private when opportunity presented itself we were able to announce a meeting for Mr. Organization. On January 4 we organized a Junior and Young People's society, gave a talk on organization and administration and later met with the executive committee. We leave this work

confident of success because of the workers. Rev. and Mrs. Cook are vitally interested in the work and with Mrs. Cook as superintendent of the Juniors and Roy E. Massie as president of the young people. You may look for victories up this sector of the battle field.

H. H. ROWSEY,
Roanoke, Virginia.

President's Call for Recruits

Dear Friend:

Brother Cobb says, "We always go over the top." Let's show him that we are in the front line trenches and can "go over the top" in our Christian Endeavor work. What part are you going to play in the "Fight for Right?"

How large and how good are you going to help make the society? How much good do you want it to do for your boy or girl, your brother or sister, your Father or mother or your friend or friend's friend?

To "go over the top" in anything means—an increased effort and a combined effort of every one who is directly or indirectly affected by the result to be accomplished.

You may ask, How does all this figure in Christian Endeavor work? Just this: The Christian Endeavor society is the workshop of the church. The Sunday school is the birthplace for Christians but it is the job of the Christian Endeavor societies to help develop and feed the spiritual body of those who are born, also to train them for definite preparatory work.

Your value to the Master is determined by the amount of service you render, and it is imposible for you to render more service than you are trained for. Just ask yourself these questions:

Of how much value am I to the Lord, right now?

How can the Christian Endeavor help me to be of more value to him?

Am I going to give the Christian Endeavor society a chance to help me?

Am I going to help the society help someone else?

If you are not already enrolled in the Christian Endeavor society, either Junior, Intermediate or Senior, ENROLL NOW. Why not? Why not come out on the Lord's side for service?

We who are already enrolled and busy need your encouragement, prayers and your effort combined with ours.

"Come On, Let's Go" is our slogan and that means "Over the Top."

Yours in C. E. love,
EARL HUETTE, President,
Dayton, Ohio.

P. S.—Be in the Christian Endeavor rooms, Sunday evening at 6:29. Start now. Why not?

"Thou shalt not kill" may be broken by anger, hate, malice and the desire for revenge.

Should you be tempted to criticise others for imperfect conduct, first turn the light of Holy Writ on yourself and critically examine your own heart and life, and thus learn if you are able to lead them to a deeper and higher life with our Lord. Otherwise your criticism may prove to be a hindrance to those needing help rather than a blessing.—Wm. H. McLendon.

❖ MISSIONS ❖

KRYPTON, KENTUCKY

As we were looking forward to Christmas, we often wondered what kind of a time we would have here in these mountains. At the same time we could not help thinking back to California and especially to our Long Beach church where we often had spent these days in great blessings, remembering how God had given to this world the most wonderful and unspeakable Gift. But we have found our Savior here also a very present help in time of need. These days were busy days for most of the work was resting on us, but to our joy, Miss Gertrude Ham, who has been teaching here for several years, and who is loved by all the people here, came to spend a few days in Krypton. She was a great help, and also a great blessing to us all at this time.

We had our Christmas exercises on Christmas eve. The church was about filled in spite of bad weather and very bad roads. We felt the presence of the Lord and especially when our offering for the poor and for Brother Rollier, and Marie and Julia, who were especially remembered at that time, went over $30.00.

Our Long Beach church had written to us that they were sending us a piano for our Krypton church, which was to be here for Christmas, and which came Christmas day, early in the morning. Many of these people and children had never seen a piano and it

surely brightened many faces when they saw and heard it. It also helps the looks of the church and will draw the people to come to church, for these people all like music. We can only thank the Lord for a church that prays and also helps to answer their prayers. May the Lord bless each one of those who had part in the gift.

Christmas day in the afternoon, we had another program at Napherd about two miles from Krypton, where we have Sunday school every Sunday afternoon in a private home. The attendance is from 40 to 45, but this afternoon there were about 60 present. We could hardly wait till we tried our new piano, so we had announced a song and praise service for 6 P. M. the last evening that Miss Gertrude was with us. We especially felt the presence of the Lord in this service. When we sang "He Died with a Broken Heart," one of the prominent men of our town, who is not saved but who attends our services regularly could no longer hold his tears back. We believe and pray that the piano will be a great help in our work and in saving souls.

It is a sacrifice to leave home with all its comforts and especially the good schools, as Brother Gearhart says, but the Lord does often manifest himself here in such a wonderful way, that we feel repaid. The people here have been very good to us ever since we have

been here. Our attendance also has been good. The eral influential men who never came to church for years are coming now. Our difficulty was with just two or three individuals, who tried to make the work hard for us, but we see things slowly changing. We hope and pray that the Lord will clear these difficulties away for here is a great work to be done, and especially among the children.

The children are just as bright here as I have seen them. We have two children's meetings a week, Juniors on Sunday evening and the children's prayer meeting on Wednesday evening before the adult prayer meeting. The Lord has answered many prayers in these meetings, and the children are coming to believe in prayer. This morning in our Sunday school class a little girl eleven years old told us yesterday when she was trying to build a fire in the cookstove and it would not burn she stopped and prayed and in a few minutes the stove was red hot.

We have had over forty confessions in the last four months, several of these are true to the Lord and are not ashamed to confess Christ in prayer and testimony. We are so glad when we hear that the people in our churches are praying for this work, for only through prayer and hard work we will be able to accomplish anything for Christ.

MRS. ELIZABETH REMPEL.

NEWS FROM THE FIELD

OHIO CONFERENCE MINUTES
(Continued from previous issue).

Wednesday Evening

The evening session was given over to a Bible lecture by Dr. Miller and the evangelistic sermon by Dr. Bell.

Thursday Morning

The devotions were led by Rev. M. B. Spacht of Williamstown. The early morning hour was composed of a simultaneous meeting of the Women's Missionary Society in the basement of the church and the Men's Conference in the auditorium. The ladies will report the minutes of their meeting. The following program was given in the Men's conference:

A New Day for Brethren Churches, William A. Gearhart. A general discussion of the possibilities of the work of the laymen in the church. The discussion was spirited, instructive and practical. The few minutes remaining between the close of the men's conference and the opening of the joint session was spent in transacting a few items of business.

Discussion of the Standard by which Candidates for Ordination Should be Judged. After some discussion, the conference decided that the standard should be left to the discretion of the Board, but instructed them to take into consideration (1) The life. (2) The academic training; (3) The spiritual qualifications and (4) The faith of the candidate.

Courtesies of the Conference. By vote, the courtesies of the conference were extendd to W. S. Bell, Miss Nora Bracken and others attending from other districts.

Committee on Nominations for Departmental Officers. Mrs. C. W. Abbott, S. G. Worst, and Miss Doris Thorne were named by the chair.

Committee on Resolutions. This committee was composed of E. M. Riddle, R. R. Teeter and D. F. Eikenberry.

The joint session of the conference convened and we were favored by a very helpful address on "A Revival in Every Church," by E. M. Oberholtzer. Another, "Workable Evangelistic Methods" by R. R. Teeter. Both of these addresses will appear in the Evange-

list at an early date and no notes will be given here.

Owing to the fact that several members of the Mission Board of necessity should leave at noon, the report was read by Secretary Miller. The following recommendations were offered and adopted by the conference.

Canton, Ohio, November 15, 1919.

Ohio Mission Board met and was called to order by Brother A. D. Gnagey.

In the absence of Brethren C. E. Beekley and W. C. Teeter the Miami Valley churches were represented by Brother E. M. Cobb.

The time of Dr. Worst having expired as treasurer of the Board; a motion prevailed to recommend to the Conference the name of R. Alger Hazen of Ashland to be elected treasurer of the Board.

It was moved and seconded that the name of E. M. Cobb be presented to the conference as a member of the Board of Evangelists. Motion carried.

The following appropriations for the mission points of the state were made: Columbus, $300.00; Canton, $250.00; Mansfield, $260.00; Rittman, $100.00 and Fremont $100.00.

A motion prevailed that appropriations remain as read with the exception of Fremont and Columbus; the Board reserving the right to withdraw Fremont's appropriation if a joint pastorate could be effected with Fostoria, and to increase the amount to Columbus to $500.00 if deemed advisable.

A motion prevailed requesting Brother Gnagey to go to Fostoria to try and arrange a joint pastorate between said place and Fremont.

On motion the apportionment for the several churches of the state were made as follows to be paid quarterly, beginning October 1st, 1919:

Ashland,	$ 35.00
Ankenytown,	10.50
Bryan,	21.00
Buckeye City,	3.50
Camden,	3.00
Canton,	8.00
Columbus,	3.50
Dayton,	50.00
Fair Haven,	17.50
Fairview,	16.50
Fremont,	6.00
Fostoria,	1.50
Gratis,	25.00
Gretna,	12.00
Homerville,	4.00
Louisville,	18.00
Mansfield,	4.00
Miamisburg,	6.00
Middlebranch,	7.00
New Lebanon,	10.00
North Georgetown,	5.00
North Liberty,	2.00
Pleasant Hill,	12.00
Rittman,	2.00
Salem,	10.00
West Alexandria,	10.00
Williamstown,	12.00
Zion Hill,	10.00
Total,	$325.00

E. F. MILLER, Secretary.

Report of Committee on Special Evangelistic Services, by A. D. Gnagey.

Realizing that the world is calling for the steadying, vitalizing and saving influence of the church today as never before, and that the unparalleled conditions present to the church a challenge and an opportunity for leadership such as she has never before enjoyed, we believe that the churches of Ohio should be urged and encouraged to prosecute their work more vigorously than ever before, especially along the following lines:

We urge that there shall be increased emphasis placed upon evangelism throughout the year from the pupil, in the Sunday school and by means of personal work and various agencies that the church may experience a continued saving of souls, for we remember that the Lord added unto the church daily such as were being saved.

We further urge that rallies for instruction in Bible and church efficiency shall be conducted in the various groups of churches throughout the state and that the Board of

Evangelists shall be authorized to make the proper arrangements.

Realizing the tremendous value of evangelistic endeavors and the vitalizing and uplifting influence of these meetings upon the church and community, we urge that the churches of Ohio make a special effort to employ this God-honored means either under the direction of the pastor or some other man whom the local church wishes to employ; and that the Board of Evangelists co-operate with the pastors and congregations in making provision for an evangelistic campaign in every church; and

We further suggest that the several churches shall loan their pastors for at least one such meeting during the year.

In view of the fact that the investment in childhood and youth is the most profitable investment the church can make; and

In View of the recognized potentiality of childhood and of Christ's attitude toward children; and

Further, in view of the fact that the church has lamentably neglected the cultivation of this most fruitful field; and

Further, believing that the saving of childhood is the most promising evangelism in which the church can engage, and that the strength and power and usefulness of the future church depend upon the preservation and culture of childhood,

Therefore, we urge upon all the churches of the state to give themselves more fully and unreservedly and seriously to the cultivation of this most promising of all fields, especially in the home and in the Sunday school.

As an aid in carrying out these recommendations, we suggest that provision be made for the publication of a series of simple Bible instruction adapted to the use of children, a guide leading to church membership and growth in the spiritual life, and the indoctrination of children in the fundamentals of our faith.

A. D. Gnagey,
George S. Baer,
A. L. Lynn.

On motion the above report was adopted by unanimous vote.

A motion prevailed that the Board of Evangelists be instructed to print the above recommendations in pamphlet form and mail them to the several churches.

A motion duly seconded that the Mission Board comprise a committee to prepare special instructions for the children as suggested in the above report was carried.

Thursday Afternoon. C. E. Session

The entire program of the afternoon was devoted to the Christian Endeavor work. All the addresses were full of vigor and helpful suggestions. They are all in the hands of the editor and will be published in full in the near future so no further reference will be made to them here, except an urgent word to each reader to watch for them and read them. The following program was rendered:

Quiet Hour Talk, by E. M. Riddle. Junior and Intermediate Responsibilities. Miss Nora Bracken.

Making the Program Count. E. G. Mason.

The Great Objective. E. A. Rowsey.

Establishing Young People in the Faith. T. Darley Allen, but read by his daughter.

At this time also, Dr. E. E. Jacobs, President of Ashland College was introduced and spoke for a few moments by way of introduction to his address scheduled for Friday morning.

Business

Action Regarding Evangelistic and Bible Study League. After some discussion, the following motion was carried by the conference,—"That as a conference, we place ourselves on record as in sympathy with the lines of activity, namely, Evangelism, Bible Study and Institutes, proposed by the Evangelistic and Bible Study League."

Report of the Committee on the Call and Ordination of Candidates for the Ministry.

The Call and Ordination of Officers of the

church. In harmony with the provisions of the Manual of Procedure, Chapter I, Section II, Articles 1, 2 and 3, and Section IV, Articles 1 to 5 inclusive, the call and ordination of certain church officers being therein set forth, that part relating to the Elder shall be carefully observed; and further, in accordance with Chapter I, Section II, Article 3, this Conference adopts the following provisions relative to the ordination of an Elder:

I. The Ministerial Examining Board

1. The Ministerial Examining Board shall be composed of three Elders elected by the conference for a term of three years. The Board as now constituted shall be the first board under these provisions, namely, J. Allen Miller, 1920, W. C. Teeter, 1921, and A. D. Gnagey, 1922, and their successors shall be elected in accordance with this provision.

II. Method of Procedure

1. The Ministerial Examining Board shall determine the fitness of a candidate for ordination. Such fitness shall be determined in accordance with the provisions herein set forth and such standards in harmony with these provisions as said Board may adopt for its guidance.

2. The congregation of which the candidate is a member shall in a regular business meeting pass a resolution requesting the ordination of said candidate. This resolution with a request from said congregation for the examination of the candidate shall be forwarded to the Examining Board. The congregation shall be guided by any suggestions the Board may make relative to the candidate or his ordination.

3. The Ministerial Examining Board shall determine the qualifications of the candidate upon the basis set forth in this action of the conference and shall report its findings to the congregation making the recommendation for ordination.

4. If the Ministerial Examining Board finds the candidate qualified for ordination it shall so certify to the congregation and authorize the congregation to arrange for the ordination. Any elders, preferably the pastor and the District Evangelist may perform this ordination.

III. Standards upon which Examination is Based

1. Spiritual Qualifications. The Ministerial Examining Board shall formulate for its own guidance and the guidance of a congregation a statement of the personal and spiritual qualifications essential in a candidate and requisite to ordination. Such standard shall determine:

a. The Candidate's faith in the Christian fundamentals;

b. His Christian character and life;

c. His spiritual attainments and promise; and

d. His personal adaptation for the work of the ministry.

2. Educational Qualifications. The educational qualifications requisite to ordination to the office of Elder shall be:

a. The completion of a standard high school course or its equivalent; or

b. The completion of a course of study in the Seminary equivalent to the English divinity course as now outlined; or

c. The completion of at least two full years' work of the Classical Divinity course of the Seminary as now outlined; or

d. In lieu of the requirements indicated in items, a, b and c of this paragraph the completion of a definite course of reading to be outlined in detail by the Ministerial Examining Board. The requirements indicated in this item (d) shall have reference only to men of high character and personal spiritual attainment, who have the full approval of their home church and who may be so far advanced in age as to make attendance in a school for training impracticable.

e. In determining the candidate's fitness for ordination under this paragraph the Ministerial Examining Board shall exercise wise

discretion and shall have full power to act in each individual instance.

By action of the conference, the Ministerial Examining Board was authorized to have the above rules printed for distribution.

Report of Committee for Nominations of Departmental Officers. "We, the committee on nominations for departmental officers, beg leave to submit the following names, for the Sunday school,—State Secretary, A. L. Lynn; superintendent of the Children's Division, Mrs C. W. Abbott. State Christian Endeavor Officers,—State Secretary, F. C. Vanator; Life Work Superintendent, E. A. Rowsey; Quiet Hour Superintendent. Was left open for the present." Signed, Mrs. C. W. Abbott, Doris Thorne, S. G. Worst. The report was accepted and the persons named elected.

Adjournment.

Friday Morning Business

Committee for Meeting Place of Next Conference. With the permission of the delegates assembled, the moderator, appointed H. M. Oberholtzer, Mrs. Sarah Keim and J. A. Miller to serve on this committee.

Report of Committee on Revision of Statistical Blanks and Credentials.

The report suggesting a more condensed statistical blank and more uniform credential blank was made and the committee was instructed to confer with the National Statistician in order that Ohio's blanks will coincide with those used by the National Statistician. The committee was authorized to prepare and have printed uniform conference credential blanks.

Secretary-treasurer's Report. The secretary-treasurer of the conference submitted the following financial report:

Receipts

Balance on hand from 1917,	$$ 5.34
Received from Credential Com.,	22.00
Total funds available,	$27.34

Expenditures

Printing for Bible St. Rallies,	$ 7.00
Printing programs and ballots,	8.20
Stamps and Stationery,	1.01
Secretary's fee,	10.00
Total expenditures,	$26.21
Balance on hand,	$ 1.13

Owing to the fact that the balance in the treasury is so small and that a goodly amount of printing was ordered for the coming year, the secretary was instructed to collect the delinquent credential fees.

Four Year Program. The following report was read and accepted:

Receipts

Ashland,	$ 2.00
Zion Hill,	2.00
Fostoria,	1.00
Camden,	2.00
Fremont,	2.00
Dayton,	2.00
Louisville,	2.00
Bryan,	2.00
New Lebanon,	2.00
Mansfield,	2.00
Fairview,	1.00
West Alexandria,	1.00
Bear Creek,	1.00
Columbus,	1.00
North Georgetown,	1.00
Fair Haven,	1.00
Ankenytown,	1.00
Total,	$24.00

Expenses

G. L. Maus,	$ 2.25
Printing,	2.50
Stationery and Stamps,	1.08
Total,	5.83
Balance on hand,	$18.17

By vote of the conference the same plan as previously used for collecting the funds for defraying the Four Year Program expenses was adopted.

Report of the Committee on Resolutions. The report was as follows: "Whereas an all wise and ever loving Father has permitted the Brethren churches of Ohio to assemble once again in a state conference with no visible scars of the terrible epidemic through which the church and people passed during the fall and winter of 1918-19, and whereas the Ohio churches have lost few of their number through death, therefore, be it resolved:

First, That we express our deepest gratitude to our Father who has so graciously preserved and cared for us.

Second. That we express our thankfulness for the progress made by our various mission churches of the district and that we especially commend the work accomplished by the Camden Brethren where a church has been organized, a Sunday school maintained, and a church building purchased without aid from our Mission Board.

Third. That as members of the Ohio conference, we express our appreciation of the work done by Dr. E. J. Worst, the retiring treasurer of our Mission Board, who has served the church loyally and faithfully for many years.

Fourth. That we commend the work already done by Brother Beachler among the Ohio churches in the interest of permanent endowment for Ashland College and urge the churches not yet visited to prove their faith by their works, and we further recommend that this conference declare its purpose to give to Dr. Jacobs, President of Ashland College, its united and loyal support.

Fifth. That we hereby express our gratitude and thankfulness to the Canton church and friends for the hospitality of their homes and the splendid provision mode for all human needs while in this conference, also assuring them that our association with them has been both pleasant and helpful.

Signed by the Committee,
E. M. Riddle, R. R. Teeter, D, F. Eikenberry.

Report of Committee on Place of Meeting. The committee recommended the selection of Gratis as first choice and Ashland as second choice.

By motion of the conference the secretary was instructed to affix the conference seal to J. L. Lynn's credential when it is sent in properly signed.

Final Report of the Credential Committee. The credential committee reported the following credentials for ministers presented at this conference: Present,—Dyoll Belote, Alvin Byers, D. F. Eikenberry, Canton; J. A. Garber, R. R. Teeter, Geo. S. Baer, A. D. Gnagey, J. A. Miller, Ashland; Lewis Rang, E. M. Riddle, Louisville; E. M. Cobb, Dayton; E. A. Rowsey, Mansfield; Mark B. Spacht, Williamstown; H. M. Oberholtzer, S. M. Loose, Fremont; G. L. Maus, Bryan. Not present,— Samuel Kiehl, D. L. Minderman, H. C. Funderburg, M. M. Hoover, J. A. Ridenour, W. C. Teeter, Dayton; Jas. S. Cook, T. R. Atkinson, W. R. Deeter, A. C. Hendrickson, T. Darley Allen, C. F. Yoder, A. L. Garber, W. H. Beachler, Ashland; Fred C. Vanator, Homer. Ville, B. F. Owens, Buckeye City. Total 33.

Lay Delegates: Geo. B. Haug, Mrs. M. S. Itskin, Mrs. Wm. Gloss, May Walters, Mrs. J. A. Ginley, Mrs. Frank Smith, Mrs. J. J. Hang, Mrs. B. F. Bowman, Mrs. H. Herbruck, Canton; Louisa Schwab, Mrs G. F. Munk, Mrs. Sophia Keim, Mrs. Henry Eshelman, Mrs. F. E. Clapper, Mrs. E. M. Riddle, Mrs. J. F. Painter, Louisville; Viola Ritchie, Sherman Ritchie, North Georgetown; Mrs. Grace Martin, W. C. Martin, W. E. Martin, E. A. Swihart, Mrs. S. G. Worst, FairhaVen; Mrs. J. A. Miller, D. J. Miller, Mrs. R. R. Teeter, Mrs. E. L. Kilhefner, Mrs. A. D. Gnagey, Ashland; Mary Amstutz, Mrs H. S. Rutt, Zion. Hill; Mrs. Addie Wineland, Bryan; Mrs. N. G. Kimmel, Estella Zimmerman, Gratis; D. S. Workman, Buckeye City; Chas. Baker, Rittman; E. F. Miller, Gretna; Miss Bertha Butts, Miss Doris Thorne, Mansfield; W. A. Gearhart, Dayton; Mrs. M. E. Croft, Mrs. John Barringer, Fremont; Bertha Tombaugh, Williamstown. Total lay delegates 43. Grand total of all delegates, 76.

Election of Conference Officers. George S. Baer was elected moderator, G. L. Maus vice-moderator, and E. G. Mason, secretary-treasurer.

Election of Trustees to Ashland College. The following names were nominated as trustees of Ashland College, W. H. Beachler, F. L, Garber, Orion Bowman.

Election of Church Trustees. G. W. Brumbaugh was re-elected.

Victory Program

This part of the program was devoted to the anticipation of a Victory Year of the Brethren policies in the state of Ohio.

The first address was delivered by Dr. E. E. Jacobs, president of Ashland College on the subject, "Victory Year in the College." Very briefly, this is what he said,—The college has served the church in a very broad way, but it can serve it much more widely. Ashland as well as all schools must enter upon a victory year of expansion so as to meet the demands of the church and times. The future of Ashland College will be crippled, if it does not expand.

The college must meet the conditions laid down by the State Department of Education, the State University and constituency of Ashland.

Ashland College must meet the demands of the church, that of spiritual devotion and intellectual standard. In order to do this the brotherhood must pray for its success.

The endowment campaign not only adds endowment to the college but it places a great many names of interested persons upon the mailing list of the College and thus brings the news of its progress to those who are supporting it."

In the absence of C. E. Beekley, H. M. Oberholtzer, E. M. Riddle, A. L. Lynn, Dyoll Belote, W. A. Gearhart and E. A. Rowsey, and E. G. Mason, briefly discussed "Victory in the Local Church."

The moderator instructed the State Director of the Four Year Program to appoint such aids as he saw fit to promote attendance at General Conference next year.

This conference adjourned after an appeal for increased spirituality and a series of consecrated prayers.

J. A. GARBER, Moderator,
E. G. MASON, Secretary.

SIGNIFICANT MEETING AT ASHLAND

A very significant meeting was held in the College Chapel at Ashland over New Year's Day. It was a two-fold significance: It was the most representative meeting of the church since General Conference, and it dealt with issues that vitally relate to the immediate and even remoter future of the church.

Those sharing in the sessions of the day represented General Conference and the principal Boards thereof. The personnel was as follows: Chas. A. Bame, J. Allen Miller, H. H. Wolford, Miss Mae Smith, Mrs. U. J. Shively, Mrs. W. H. Beachler, A. J. McClain, O. E. Bowman, A. D. Gnagey, E. J. Worst, Wm. Kolb, E. M. Cobb, L. G. Wood, A. C. Hendrickson, E. E. Jacobs, J. L. Kimmel, M J. Snyder, George S. Baer, W. A. Gearhart, G. C. Carpenter, R. R. Teeter and J. A. Garber. R. A. Hazen and Guilford Leslie of Ashland were present, also, during a part of the time.

That all seemed to appreciate the seriousness of the problems confronting them was indicated by the reverent manner with which they approached them. Periods of deep, earnest intercession consumed more time than is ordinarily given to devotions. At the opening Dr. Bame asked the assemblage to join in singing "Come Thou Almighty King." At the request of the chairman Dr. Miller conducted a devotional period, reading from the 4th chapter of Philippians with suggestive comments. The representatives then threw themselves on the Lord in prayer, audible repetitions being voiced by Brethren Cobb, Bame, Kimmel and Miller.

On successive motions the following officers were chosen: Chas. A. Bame, Chairman; J. Allen Miller, Vice Chairman and J. A. Garber, Secretary, On request Dr. Miller recited the steps leading up to the calling and assembling of the meeting. He said a number of the brethren had come in contact with the Interchurch World Movement and felt the need of some authoritative expression from our church. He referred to a letter from Brother McClain, who had attended a meeting at New York, in which he suggested immediate consideration that all might know the position of the Brethren church relative to the Interchurch World Movement. The letter was forwarded to Dr. Bame, Moderator of General Conference, who authorized the call of this meeting.

By general consent consideration was then given to the Interchurch World Movement. Those attending one or more of its meetings expressed their views, and numerous questions were asked by others. The discussion was frank and thorough. That diverse opinions were advanced at times, scarcely needs to be mentioned, but a fine fraternal spirit pervaded the meetings, and every one appeared eager to do that which is best for the church and the Kingdom. Reports from the several district conferences indicated that where they had met recently the Movement had been endorsed or sympathetic consideration given. At a late hour, after the officers and members of the several boards present had considered the question involved in closed session, the conference by an overwhelmingly large vote passed the following resolution:

We, the members of the following boards, namely, Brethren Publishing Company, Board of Trustees of Ashland College, Woman's Missionary Society, General Mission Board, Foreign Mission Board, Board of Benevolences, and Members of Committee of Fifteen (Special Committee on Five Year Program) and Officers of General Conference, assembled in conference, after prayerful and serious consideration of our relations as a church to the Interchurch World Movement, and in view of the fact that the united financial drive will occur prior to the meeting of General Conference, and feeling that Brethren should be afforded an opportunity to designate their gifts for our denominational interests, be it resolved:

First, that it is the sense of this conference that the various boards of the Brethren church prepare and present a program and a budget for one year, and that any board may present its askings to the Interchurch World Movement, deferring the presentation of the budget for the remaining four years until next General Conference; and .

Second, that, pending the action of General Conference, we enter into the spirit and program of the Interchurch World Movement in so far as is consistent with our denominational genius and identity.

On motion the College Board of Trustees was authorized to present the foregoing resolution to and represent the conference in the Interchurch World Movement.

Then, some other matters were presented by Dr. Bame. He announced that the committee previously created by the Committee of Fifteen would continue their studies, reporting their recommendations to him. He stated that three other phases of work had been arranged for as follows:

Spiritual Resources, Bame, Wolford and Rench.

Religious Education, Garber with others interested.

Social Service, Committee, named by General Conference.

Another matter was the announcement of Brother Goughnour's resignation from the Four Year Program Committee. The conference recommended the appointment of Miles J. Snyder as director of goal 16, "Biggest and Best General Conference in 1920."

J. A. GARBER, Secretary.

LOST CREEK, KENTUCKY

Since last reporting for the Evangelist, there have been some remarkable happenings at Lost Creek. We will speak of them in the order of their occurrence.

First, we may say that the after revival effects have been of the best. It seems to me that Brother Bowman, besides giving a powerful appeal to both saint and sinner—for the saint a higher walk in Christian life, and for the sinner a turning to righteousness—does very effective work in building up so, that the pastor only need just keep it going. This is the way it has worked with us.

Our Thanksgiving offering this year, was by far our best yet. It amounted to $22.20. The thing about it that was so satisfying was that so many more gave this year than ever before, and for Lost Creek, considering conditions, we thought it was good. It shows to us that the teaching of these years in the matter of giving is beginning to bear fruit, and that pleases. Some gave way for this offering who never gave for such before.

The next thing to come into our experience here was an electric light plant, and especially the pleasure of the visit of the men who came to install it. They were Wm. A. Gearhart of Dayton, Rev. C. E. Beekly, Gratis, Ohio, Amos and Ira Fudge, Brother Smith, Edward Landis, and Mr. Brubaker from West Alexandria, Ohio. It was a real deluge of pleasure for the workers at Riverside to enjoy the week's stay of these brethren, as they installed the light plant.

If there has ever been any doubt in the minds of any as to the wisdom and need of the light plant, let that doubt be dispelled at once. Riverside will always feel a deep sense of gratitude to the Board for having installed this plant, and especially to Amos Fudge, of West Alexandria, Ohio for his prompt and businesslike way of pushing it along. With Brother Fudge behind it, things did not keep up. And how we wish that you all could see Riverside shine. It means a great deal to the place in many ways.

And lastly, the best Christmas that we have ever passed at Lost Creek is now a matter of history. On Christmas eve one of our neighbors near here and a sister in the church, came in, and said to us, "Santa is coming before Christmas this year," and handed us a package. Upon examining it we found it to contain money to the amount of $25.80, a personal gift to us by the people here. This was Sister Parriett Boling who solicited the money and brought it to us. Later she handed us the names of those who had given, and we find that it includes practically all the people in this community, both children and adults. Sister Boling also had written on paper giving it to us at the same time that she gave the other, the following:

"We know that we have passed from death unto life, because we love the Brethren. He that loveth not his brother abideth in death" (1 John 3:14).

"My little children, let us not love in word, neither in tongue: but in deed and in truth" (1 John 3:18).

"I rejoiced greatly that I found of thy children walking in truth, as we received a commandment from the Father, which we had from the beginning, that we love one another." (2 John 1:45).

"Mercy unto you, and peace and love, be multiplied" (Jude 2).

The above coming after these years of labor with the people here, means so much to us. It seemed to us that the hills never looked so good as they have since receiving this gift of love from those with whom we have labored. It means to us that there is a very real sense of appreciation by the people of what has been done and is being done here. For us it only lays the more firmly, and more largely the foundation on which a strong aggressive church will be built, which will give to the church and our Savior for service both lives and money that wil count in the work of the Kingdom.

Besides this local gift, we have been very kindly and generously remembered by some dear brethren who have sent some gifts. These have all been written personally, and besides that in this way, we want to again say, "Thank you." You have helped to lift the burdens that will enable your servants here to only the better and more effectively carry on the fight against the adversary of our souls, the devil. Pray for us that we may ever be faithful in serving him who gave his all for us.   G. E. DRUSHAL.

MILLEDGEVILLE, ILLINOIS

On our return from General Conference all services of the church were resumed. In fact there was no "summer slump" in our attendance. The Sunday school came through the summer in fine shape.

The first thing of special importance on the program was the October quarterly congregational meeting when the business affairs of the church were attended to. In the election of Sunday school officers W. W. Fike, our able leader of the church choir, was selected as the new superintendent, under whose direction the Sunday school will continue to move forward.

Our Rally Day was held on October 12 with a splendid program and a large attendance and generous offering applying on the pledge for Ashland College permanent endowment.

During the first week of November preparatory services were held each evening looking toward the fall communion service on November 9. These special services were conducted by the pastor for the deepening of spiritual life and the salvation of the unredeemed.

All our churches in the Village united for the week of November 11-16 in a church efficiency and community welfare campaign, conducted by James L. Scofield, a specialist and expert organizer in community work. The activities of the church were quickened and doubtless permanent good resulted from this special effort.

Plans were made in advance for the observance of Home Mission Day on November 23, when our annual Thanksgiving offering was received amounting to $115.00, putting us far "over the top."

As the Christmas season approached the members of our church choir began working on a Scripture oratorio-cantata entitled "Bethlehem." They faithfully continued their work of preparation until the production was given before the public on Sunday evening, December 21. The church auditorium and Sunday school rooms were not sufficiently large to seat the many people who came to attend this musical service, which was generally conceded to have been the best program of similar nature ever given here. At the conclusion of the service a voluntary offering was received for the fund of the starving children of Armenia which amounted to $140.00.

The Christmas services of our Sunday school were held on the evening of December 24. For the fourth successive year "White Gifts for the King" was the service used. The program presented was enjoyed by a large audience, and the offerings given by the different classes totaled $115.00, besides a number of other material gifts. The greatest gift was the gift of a young lady's heart to God and her confession of Christ as her Savior. She was baptized the following Sunday.

One of the surprises on Christmas eve came to the pastor and family when the members of the congregation presented to them a generous supply of flour, groceries, fruit, canned goods, etc., together with several gifts of money. It was the largest donation of material things we have ever received, and our hearts were truly grateful for such an expression of Christmas cheer and good will.

All in all the work of the Kingdom here has been moving along encouragingly. Since our last report in the Evangelist eight new members have been received into the church, five by baptism and three by relation.

MILES J. SNYDER

BEAVER CITY, NEBRASKA

Though a recent report has appeared in these columns of the work at Beaver City, we want to tell you about the meetings we have just held that you too may rejoice with us. Our pastor, E. S. Flora, conducted the services the first two weeks the weather was fine and attendance good, but the last was very rainy and many could not come. Before the break came sixteen souls confessed Jesus the Son of God and accepted him as their Savior. Ten received baptism during the meetings. We do not feel the revival is over, for since closing five more have taken a stand for Christ, making nineteen in all, and six are now waiting baptism, which will be administered next Lord's day. This I believe puts us over the top on goal 4.

The meetings closed with the communion service and a good representation of the membership was present, enough to win goal 2. This makes eleven points on the four year program, however we are not satisfied but are striving to win others and make this a real Victory year, and we feel confident under the splendid leadership of our pastor that we will do it.

I think we are not saying too much when we say we are making a steady growth in all lines of work, especially is this true of our prayer meetings, and right here is where we expect to gain another point, if we have not already.

In a short time we will have another report to make, that of our "White Gift" service, we are planning on a big time at Christmas, but will leave that for some one else to tell.

Let us all pray that much will be accomplished by ALL our churches this year.

LILLA JOHNSTON.

FREMONT, OHIO

We have no flattering report to make of the work at this place, but perhaps a few words from us might help to cheer others on the way. We are pressing the battle as best we can. We have recently lost two of our number by death. Some of our workers have moved away, which has handicapped our work somewhat. Yet we are bravely struggling with our task and looking to God for victory, and we believe that we are making some progress. We have been planning for our revival meetings for some time. For the past month we have held cottage prayer meetings besides our regular prayer meetings, which have been well attended. We expect to begin our revival January 4. Brother I. D. Bowman will lead us in this effort. We are hoping for good results. We desire the prayers of the church for the success of our endeavors, and that we may have a genuine, Spirit-empowered and Spirit-directed revival. May God give us such a revival in every church this year.

H. M. OBERHOLTZER.

DOINGS AT DAYTON

In my report of December 12th, it was incidentally omitted how Dayton First Brethren went "over the top" in her Thanksgiving offering for Missions, which totaled $434.00. Also, that the congregation at their special business meeting had unanimously voted to request the ordination of Brother Arthur Lynn to the eldership after the permission was granted by the State Examining Board which was later secured, and the service was held on the evening of December 22nd in the church. I quote from the Sunday Calendar of December 28th, as follows:

"At the Monday evening service, Dec. 22, Arthur Lynn was ordained by the pastor and Elder W. C. Teeter. Brother Lynn took the examination in a manly and masterful way as he does everything. He certainly feels the responsibility as very few do, but gladly accepted it for him who died for him. Lynn reports a splendid meeting at Lima where many gave their hearts to the Lord for the first time, and where 25 gave their lives specifically to go or stay anywhere the Lord asks them to go. He spends Christmas at home, and after conducting his next three campaigns will then bring his family to Dayton where he will assume his duties as assistant to the pastor and musical director. You might as well get ready to see things move now at the First Brethren church.'

I might also mention that our Sunday school went "over the top" in enrollment on Rally Day, when 716 were present. The record of attendance has exceeded any previous year and the school is growing in numbers and interest under the efficient management and direction of Dr. Cobb, Prof. Brumbaugh and other assistants fully co-operating. During this year the returns show that over $1900.00 has been received through this auxiliary of the church, exceeding all former offerings, and the congregation through all her activities and auxiliaries has raised over $15,000.00, of which $8,000.00 was applied on the church debt.

Doctor Cobb, immediately on taking charge of this church as pastor, followed sternly in the wake of Dr. Bell, his predecessor, to liquidate as rapidly as possible the debt incurred by the building of this modern beautiful church plant, and has proved himself a master in the financial management to cut down the debt. And we trustfully anticipate that another drive next year will cancel the obligation and set us free to do still larger and more efficient work for the Master in this growing, wicked city, though it be the "Gem City" of the Miami Valley.

At the urgent request of over 75 percent of the membership, Dr. Cobb is repeating his wonderful travelogue lectures of the Holy Land during the winter, and has already resumed these studies, and will continue the Bible institute lectures for the season to the profit of all who may take advantage of them. The crowds still come to see and hear. May his grace be sufficient.

WM. C. TEETER,
Corresponding Secretary.

CAMPAIGN NOTES

The report this week comes from the Williamstown church. This congregation does not belong to the class with the larger churches of Ohio, neither does it belong to the smallest. It is about average or medium in numerical strength. But I found here some splendid, loyal people, and my stay among them was very pleasant.

It was from the Williamstown locality that our Brethren H. H. Wolford, Chas. A. Bame, and Alva Spacht came. Brother Mark B. Spacht, a brother of Alva Spacht, is now the pastor of this congregation. My visit to Williamstown gave me my first opportunity to meet Brother Mark Spacht. I found him a very agreeable Christian man, a man worth knowing, and a pastor alive and awake to the interests of his own congregation and the interests of the entire brotherhood. Brother Spacht is yet young among us as a pastor but I have no doubt he will develop into a strong, useful man in our ministry. I was glad to learn of his intention to enter Ashland College for several years' work.

In our canvass here Brother Spacht gave us the benefit of his presence and assistance during our entire stay. The home of Brother Frank Rutledge and wife was our general stopping place, although we were also cared for in the Spacht, Humphrey, and Thomas homes. Needless to say the hospitality in this congregation measured right up to the very best of Ohio hospitality. AND it was Brother Frank Rutledge in this church who furnished the Ford. Thanks many times to Brother Rutledge.

This report, does not show quite the finals from this place. I am able to report at this time $1300. I believe it will go to $1500. On the face of the thing this may not appear quite up to the average for Williamstown. But this word should be said: Necessary improvements in the church building at this place which will cost not less than $1000, had consid-

erable to do in holding back the results for endowment. But I am hoping that at some future time after this congregation has gotten its local improvements out of the way it may still get a little more nearly under its corner of this endowment proposition.

In leaving this field I took my train at Ada, Ohio. This town is the home of what is known as the Ohio Northern University. While in this town I had the time to go out and see the buildings and campus of this institution. Two things impressed me: First that the campus of this college cannot compare in the least possible way with the campus at our college. And the other thing that impressed me was that three of the best buildings of this college were placed there as memorials. This interested me so much that I took the names of these memorial buildings. The one was the John Wesley Hill memorial; another was the S. H. Lehr memorial; and the third was the Dukes memorial. As I turned from these buildings and left for my train I wondered and wondered to myself just why it is that all of the years in our denominational history have elapsed and not one soul among us with money has had such loyalty for our own denomination and college as has led folks in other denominations to do big things for their colleges. No one has thus far arisen among us with a mind and heart to build even a chicken house for Ashland College as a memorial. I wonder again if the people of the Brethren church who have large financial means have never stopped to think how few things have come to our own school to give real encouragement as compared to the many things that come to other schools by way of memorial buildings and large gifts. Our own school just as every school that is getting somewhere must have some large gifts from individuals or else always suffer certain handicaps.

Finals from Gretna put the result there at $2250.

I am now working in the Miami Valley. The mercury is now $135,500.

WM. H. BEACHLER,
Campaign Secretary.

COLLEGE NEWS

School resumed the Tuesday after New Years and is moving off as usual. Six of the resident students attended the great Student Volunteer Convention in Des Moines over the holidays. There were also two alumni in attendance which gave Ashland a very good representation. As might be expected, all came back with a new and high enthusiasm as a result of this experience. One can not come into close contact with the type of men who conduct such meetings without being set on fire in regards to life work and its responsibilities.

We are getting two of the best known Y. M. C. A. men to come to the college to be with us for several addresses, stressing the choice of life work with emphasis upon the claims of the church.

I was at Nappanee and Milford, Indiana, over Sunday, January 4th, preaching at the former place in the morning and at the latter in the evening. Brother Miller has just taken up his work at Nappanee and is just getting acquainted but everything seems to be moving along nicely. It certainly is a fine place and the people are interested and loyal.

Brother Kolb was away from Milford, but the congregation received me cordially. Considering the extremely cold weather, there was a good audience and good interest was manifest. I have very pleasant recollections of both places.

At the morning service at Nappanee, Brother Miller had those who had been at Ashland stand up and all told there were nearly twenty who had at some time been residents here. Hence, I was not wholly among strangers. Moreover, Nappanee promises to send two new

Our Goal: 200,000; We Can and We Must

200	000
190	000
180	000
170	000
160	000
150	000
140	000
130	000
120	000
110	000
100	000
90	000
80	000
70	000
60	000
50	000
40	000
30	000
20	000
10	000

COLLEGE
ENDOWMENT

students to Ashland next year, Miss Price and Becknell.

There has been a call sent out for a meeting of the College Board for January 29 and 30. It is earnestly hoped that there may be a good attendance.

I am to be at Myersdale and Berlin, Pa., over the 18th.

Dr. J. A. Miller spent the holidays mostly at home, meeting with several important committees; Professor J. A. Garber and Professor L. L. Garber likewise. Miss Marie Lichty, Miss Puterbaugh, Miss Wimer, Miss Teeter, and Professor Haun either visited among friends, or spent the time at home.

Miss Pauline Teeter, graduate of last year and now traveling with a musical and dramatic company, spent part of her vacation with her people on the Hill. Among other former students who returned and paid Ashland a visit were Boardman, Ford, Theodore Gnagey, and Glenn King.

I call attention to the college notice to be found elsewhere in this issue. Young people who can do so, should enter for the last semester. Also, those living in Ohio especially should give our summer session serious consideration before planning on going elsewhere for the summer. Our Summer Normal is fully recognized by the state.

We are expecting to have Dr. Henry S. Cope with us here at the College over the fifteenth and sixteenth. Dr. Cope is General Secretary of the National Religious Education Association with offices in Chicago. He is one of the best known men in this field, being the author of several books, and having lectured before many Y. M. C. A. conventions. Ashland College is to be congratulated on being able to secure such an able man and no student should forego the opportunity of hearing him. We are indebted to Professor J. A. Garber for his effort and influence in securing him for the college.

EDWIN E. JACOBS.

THE TIE THAT BINDS

BEAM-ROGERS—Lewis S. Beam and Delta Mae Rogers, both of Roann, were united in marriage by the writer, at the parsonage, November 23, 1919. Both are estimable young people and we wish them many happy wedded years. WILLIS E. RONK.

BEAM-HOFFMAN—George H. Beam who is a member of the Brethren church of Roann, and Ester I. Hoffman, a member of the Christian church, were united in marriage by the writer, on Christmas day, at the parsonage. We unite with their many friends in wishing them happiness. WILLIS E. RONK.

SANFORD-MARSHALL—Howard L. Sanford, of Bristol, Tennessee, and Uneta M. Marshall of Laketon, Indiana, were united in marriage by the writer December 24, 1919. Ceremony at the parsonage.
WILLIS E. RONK.

NYE-LENHART—At the home of the bride, near Milledgeville, Illinois, Russell A. Nye and Beulah Elizabeth Lenhart were united in marriage on December 10, 1919, in the presence of a number of relatives and intimate friends. Both these young people are well known in this community, the bride being a teacher in the Brethren Sunday school and an active worker in the church. The best wishes of their many friends attend them as they start to walk henceforth life's way together. MILES J. SNYDER.

TAYLOR-WOODS—Mr. Elliott Taylor of Kittanning, Pa., and Miss Ruth Woods of the same place were united in marriage at the parsonage of the Third Brethren church of Johnstown, Pa., the pastor performing the ceremony. GEO. H. JONES.

HUTCHISON-BLYLER—Harold M. Hutchison and Alice L. Blyler were united in marriage by the pastor at the parsonage of the Third Church of Johnstown, Pa. The best wishes of a large circle of friends go with these young people. GEO. H. JONES.

BYERS-CARNEY—Brother Roy Byers of Mineral Point, Pa., and Sister Lillian Carney of Johnstown, were united in marriage by the undersigned at the parsonage on Christmas eve. The young people, though not members of the Third church, are old and dear friends of the undersigned, who many years ago was the groom's pastor. It was with the heartiest of good will and best wishes that we performed this ceremony, feeling indeed in our heart that the Lord joined these young people. GEO. H. JONES.

IN THE SHADOW

FLOHR—Jessie Ruth Flohr died November 29, 1919 at her home in Hoover, Indiana, at the age of 25 years and 3 days. She was a member of the Brethren church of Roann and was brought to this her old home, for burial. She leaves her husband, four small children and her parents. WILLIS E. RONK.

ASHTON—Mertha Eltha Ashton departed this life at her home, November 30, 1919, at the age of 39 years, 3 months and 15 days. Mertha was a member of the Brethren church at Roann, was a good Christian girl and loved by all who knew her. She leaves her mother, father, a brother and sister.
WILLIS E. RONK.

SAUERS—Brother Carl Sauers, aged 14 years, after undergoing an operation in one of our local hospitals, passed away on Saturday evening, December 20th. The church extends to the parents its sincere sympathy in their loss and his gain. We had the joy of baptising Brother Carl this past year and feel glad indeed to preach to the sorrowing parents our Blessed Hope in Christ. Funeral services by the pastor the undersigned.
GEO. H. JONES.

COOPER—James W. Cooper, son of Mr. and Mrs. Eli Cooper, was born in hardy county, Virginia, November 3, 1834 and died October 29, 1919, at the age of 84 years, 11 months and 26 days. He came to this county, with his parents at the age of seven years. On December 25, 1864, he was united in marriage with Miss Deborah Kaylor, to which union were born five children, three boys and two girls. Mr. Cooper was a farmer until he retired seven years ago. He with his wife was a faithful member of the Gretna, Ohio, Brethren church. He leaves to mourn his departure his wife, two children, George M. and Claralel Hickman. Funeral services conducted by R. R. Teeter.

PARKER—Thomas B. Parker was born in London, England, October 30, 1827, dying at Aurelia, Iowa, December 11, 1919, being 92 years, 1 month and 12 days old. At the age of fourteen years he emigrated to America with his father's family, living at Savannah, Carroll county, Illinois, and near or in Aurelia until the time of his demise.

He was married in 1855 to Miss Catherine Leonard, with whom he lived until her death in 1913. Since that time he has lived in his home with various members of the family. There were four sons, the youngest of which died in infancy. He officiated as deacon for thirty years in the Brethren church and was one of its most faithful and untiring workers. He was a man of exceptionally strong character and leaves an honorable record that cannot be questioned.

Funeral services were conducted by Rev. G. R. Gilbert, and the remains laid to rest beside those of his wife in Pleasant Hill cemetery. MRS. JESSE McDEID.

TOMBAUGH—Mrs. Emeline Tombaugh was born near Arcadia, Ohio, February 1st, 1853, she died November 3rd, 1919. Sister Tombaugh was from her youth a faithful member of the church. Immediately after marrying Mr. John Tombaugh, who was a deacon in the Eagles' Creek Dunkard church, Sister Tombaugh united with this church. Later she became a charter member of the Williamstown Brethren church. Here she worked loyally and faithfully with the Brethren until she came to California, in 1911. Since then she has been a member of the Turlock Brethren church. She leaves to suffer her loss her six children, Mr. Ira S. Tombaugh, and Mrs. L. A. Buaghman, besides three grandchildren, one great grandchild and a number of friends and relatives. May the Lord comfort all who mourn for her. Funeral services by the pastor. N. V. LEATHERMAN.

GOCHENOUR—On the twenty-eighth day of October, Mrs. Ollie Hyes, daughter of Mr. and Mrs. B. C. Gochenour, formerly of Warsaw, Indiana, died at her father's home here in Spokane. She was 38 years old, having been born at Warsaw, Indiana, May 25, 1881. She leaves a husband, four sisters, and three children, Tom, Nettie and Clyde, and father and mother to mourn her loss. But what is earth's loss is heaven's gain, for she was a most valued and tireless worker for her Lord and Master while among us. It was through her sacrifices and faithful service that our Hollywood Mission Sunday school was begun and established. While on her last sick bed we were holding a revival there and it seemed to be her crowning joy to hear the reports of souls saved there and to know that her humble efforts were bearing fruit for eternity. Her passing has left a void in all the hearts who knew her, not only in Spokane but also in Warsaw, where she became a Brethren many years ago. I'm sure we are all better men and women for having known her. R. PAUL MILLER.

SPECK—Mrs. Anna R. Speck, the wife of Borther J. L. Speck, departed this life at her home in Fremont, Ohio, December 19, 1919, at the age of 63 years, 10 months and 18 days. She was a native of Lancaster, Pa. and came to Ohio with her husband in 1873, locating first in Seneca county and later moving to Sandusky county. For the past eleven years she had resided in Fremont. Although she had no children of her own, she reared to maturity four children who still survive and delight to call her mother. With her husband she united with the Church of the Brethren in Seneca county in 1884. When the church which is now known as the First Brethren church of Fremont was first organized in 1900, she joined with eleven others in the forming of that organization. She filled the office of church secretary from the time of its organization until the illness of recent years interfered. She was active in the work of the Sunday school, the Woman's Missionary Society and all the activities of the church. Her place in the home, in the church and in the community will be greatly missed. Funeral services by her pastor, the writer, assisted by Rev. S. M. Loose.
H. M. OBERHOLTZER.

WOODY—Maxine E. Woody, eldest child and only daughter of Earl and Roxie Woody and only granddaughter of M. W. and Angeline Eikenberry, was born at Russiaville, Indiana, March 25, 1901, and departed this life December 21, 1919, aged eighteen years, eight months and twenty-six days. Funeral services by Rev. Moore of the Friends church at Russiaville, Tuesday, December 23. We cannot say and we will not say that Marine is dead; she is just away.
M. W. EIKENBERRY.

RANDOL—Henry Randol, a member of the Brethren church at Sidney, Indiana, died at the home of his daughter, Mrs. J. W. Sisk, of North Manchester, on December 15, 1919, aged 89 years, 15 days. He was like married, served his country in the Civil war where he was a Corporal, for three years. He leaves two children, several step-children and grandchildren to mourn. CHARLES A. BAME.

STROHL—Wallace Strohl departed this life at the age of 86 years and 12 days. He was a native of Sandusky county, Ohio. He was married twice, but his companions both preceded him in death and he spent the latter portion of his life in the home of his son, Ernest Strohl, in Fremont, Ohio. He united with the Church of the Brethren in early life, and; after a few years of inactivity, he renewed his covenant last February and united with the Brethren church at Fremont. For several months previous to his death he was confined to his room on account of his illness, but he bore his sufferings patiently and hopefully awaited his release. Funeral services by Rev. S. M. Loose and the writer.
H. M. OBERHOLTZER.

The BRETHREN EVANGELIST

NEAR EAST RELIEF
1 Madison Avenue, New York

Published every Wednesday at Ashland, Ohio. All matter for publication must reach the Editor not later than Friday noon of the preceding week.

George S. Baer, Editor

The
Brethren
Evangelist

When ordering your paper changed give old as well as new address. Subscriptions discontinued at expiration. To avoid missing any numbers renew two weeks in advance.

R. R. Teeter, Business Manager

OFFICIAL ORGAN OF THE BRETHREN CHURCH

Subscription price, $2.00 per year, payable in advance.
Entered at the Post Office at Ashland, Ohio, as second-class matter.
Acceptance for mailing at special rate of postage provided for in section 1103, Act of October 3, 1917, authorized September 9, 1918.
Address all matter for publication to Geo. S. Baer, Editor of the Brethren Evangelist, and all business communications to R. R. Teeter, Business Manager, Brethren Publishing Company, Ashland, Ohio. Make all checks payable to the Brethren Publishing Company.

TABLE OF CONTENTS

EDITORIAL

Meeting the Problem of Ministerial Support

Apropos with the support of the pioneer ministry, which the Board of Benevolence is championing and the enlistment of young men for the ministry which is being emphasized at this season by the Christian Endeavorers, the general question of ministerial support is receiving no small consideration. It is a subject that relates more closely to the success of the church than we have been wont to think. It is a subject that has not been much handled because of the modesty of the ministry and the ofttimes thoughtlessness of the laity. The result is that the long-time inadequate salary of the minister has not been much increased in comparison with the increased cost of living. The strain of the situation is beginning to bear fruit in a more than ordinary difficulty to supply the pulpits of our churches. Whatever suggestions are at hand for the remedying of the situation are worthy of a hearing at least, for a remedy we must have if the church is to be adequately manned.

Some one has suggested that the ministers form a union, make their demands and go on a strike until they get them met. This sounds ridiculous, because it is so out of harmony with the spirit of the true minister of the gospel of Jesus Christ. Ministers may form unions for mutual spiritual improvement and the exchange of ideas and methods, but they will never go on a "strike." The men who are burdened with the responsibility of preaching the "good news" will not withhold that message from those who seek it even at the greatest sacrifice. So far as moral right is concerned, they may have as much right to strike as any other class of public servants, but still it is unthinkable that they will do so.

Some have suggested that each minister individually should make demands for an adequate salary and insist upon his church meeting his just demands, that each minister should do his own bargaining with his employer, the church. They say that if the minister would champion his own cause he could remedy the situation and that he himself is to blame for his meager salary. It may be that the minister has been over-modest, but most of them will prefer to continue to suffer injustice because of this fault rather than to run the risk of being accused of having pecuniary motives. Occasional situations may arise wherein a minister may be induced to say, "Give me so much, or I quit," but their infrequency will not remedy the general difficulty. Ministers, as a rule are modest, by the very nature of their calling, and they will not and should not be forced to assume the role of a bargainer with his church.

Some have suggested that the church take the matter in hand and require each congregation to pay its minister an adequate salary, that no parish be supplied with a pastor until there is a guarantee of remuneration that is worthy of the calling. There are certain denominations in which such a scheme is worked, and to some

extent it worked. But it is not feasible in a church of congregational polity. There is no authoritative official to take such initiative, if it were considered advisable, and there is no authoritative body to empower such an official. Conference action is only advisory. And even if such action were taken, whether advisory or mandatory, and if it should prove effective, it is doubtful if it would be the most happy solution to the problem.

Again, others have suggested the plan of enlightening the laity as to the real situation, with the hope and confidence that when they really understand the injustice and hardship under which their servants in Christ have been working, they will apply the remedy. And that seems the most plausible and pleasant of all plans. The church has not done this injustice to the minister because it purposed to do so, but because its attention has never been seriously called to its neglect. The wisest way of dealing with the situation is not by compulsory methods, but by instruction. Bring clearly to the mind of the Christian laymen how meagerly the minister has been supported and how much is required of him in comparison with men in other callings; let them know how unjust the present situation is, and they will not be found wanting in willingness to correct it. Making the facts known will help the situation wonderfully; the people will act if they know. The people cannot be too strongly censured until they know that many ministers are compelled to bury their finest aspirations and waste their talents in a bitter grind for a respectable living. If they are enlightened they will lighten the burden of the minister.

Such statements as the following, published recently by The Christian Herald of New York, in certain daily papers, will go a long way toward enlightening the Christian public on this question of such importance to the church:

"The electricians, plasterers and carpenters who work on the building of our churches are paid from $40 to $50 a week. The average man who preaches from the pulpit is lucky if he receives half that sum.

"1,000,000,000 invested in church property by the Protestant church members of America! And yet the majority of ministers receive less than the minimum sum which sociologists say will support a family decently.

"Surely, as Billy Sunday says, 'Something is radically wrong when a prizefighter in 15 minutes can earn more than a country parson in 15 years.'

"Ministers as a rule do not save. They cannot. Between the ages of 45 and 65, statistics show, many of them supplement their regular work in the ministry by peddling books, writing insurance, or selling real estate in order to earn enough to live on. When old age overtakes them they are too often found in the plight of one minister of 83 who is weaving rugs in order to keep from starving; or another who has been in the ministry for 55 years, and is struggling to support his sick wife with the help of the relief board.

"No class of men has contributed more to this nation's greatness than her ministers.

"By their force of character and their disinterested service, they have set up a spiritual standard for men of all classes; they have given high ideals to our young men and women; they have helped to check lawlessness and give a balance to power.

"In difficult periods of the nation's growth they have thrown their influence on the side of honor and righteousness.

"The country must not sacrifice its ministers. Just as war draws into its ranks the most generous of a nation's youth,—so the ministry, by its very hardships and difficulties, has always attracted men of brilliant attainments and unusual capacity for devotion.

"As a nation we cannot afford to waste these men. The handicap must be taken off the ministers. They must be allowed to use their gifts and their devotion to the fullest, as leaders of progress in the great days that are to come."

EDITORIAL REVIEW

An interesting letter comes from Hallandale, Florida, written by Sister Hedrick. She tells of a golden wedding celebration in honor of Brother and Sister Daniel Crofford. We want to extend our congratulations too.

Brother W. I. Duker, the new pastor of the New Paris, Indiana, church is showing wisdom at the beginning of his first pastorate by more thoroughly organizing the church. His people are loyal in their support of missions, as the report of Sister Frank Roscoe will show.

The work at Los Angeles First church is in splendid condition and Brother Jennings is leading the people steadily forward. They are making progress in their new church building and, as Brother Reed suggests, they are anxiously looking forward to its completion and the larger opportunities it will afford.

Brother Fred Vanator and his "faithful few" of Homerville are getting things turned in the right direction. For a time this little band was discouraged, but things are beginning to look up, due to some extent doubtless to his evangelistic emphasis. The good people were not forgetful of their pastor's material needs.

A note from Brother E. M. Riddle, pastor of the Louisville church, states that the Lord blessed them with five confessions the first week, and that the interest is fine and the spirit good. May God continue to pour out his spirit upon them and turn men's hearts unto him.

Don't fail to take a look at the Christian Endeavor department this week; it's interesting. The biggest Intermediate society in Ohio and its superintendents appear before you there. Brother Boardman has something to say about Ashland College night and C. E. week. Also read Nappanee's plans. Get busy.

We have two reports of the Rittman, Ohio, meeting, one from the evangelist, Brother L. D. Bowman and one from the pastor, Dr. J. Allen Miller. We rejoice with the pastor and evangelist and the good people at Rittman in their success. All Ohio churches will be particularly interested in this report, because Rittman is one of their youngest mission points, and it is promising, too.

One way for the Brethren church to find great leaders and to keep them is to create a great need for them and cause the need to increase with the increasing of their talents. Many an exceptional latent talent has been brought to the surface by the challenge of a great task. No church is worthy of the best until it is willing to make big plans and expect big things.

At Morrill, Kansas, Brother Whitted and Brother Bell were engaged in an evangelistic camping during the month of December, and in spite of difficulties, they were rewarded with good success. The pastor declares that when the conference year closes the Morrill church expects to be among those that will rejoice over having

helped to make this "VICTORY YEAR," and we believe it will, for when the will is coupled with consecrated zeal for a certain noble end, God will supply the strength and direction that will make possible the accomplishment of that end.

In a recent note to the editor when he sent an article for publication, Brother Frank B. Yoder of South Bend, Indiana, stated that he is doing institute work among the farmers of Indiana for the Extension Department of Purdue University. He is also taking a live interest in Sunday school work and is the head of the organization of his home township.

Brother L. A. Myers reports a very successful revival held by the Richer brothers in his church at Sidney, Indiana. Brother Myers is greatly pleased with the work of these evangelists. He is giving his usual careful attention to the direction of the young people of his congregation. Both his churches remembered him very kindly at the Christmas season.

Brother Ashman, pastor of the Sunnyside, Washington, church, tells us that he recently had the able assistance of Brother A. V. Kimmell of Whittier, California, in an evangelistic meeting. They had many difficulties with which to contend but they won the victory. It would have to be a very stiff opposition that would defeat two such capable warriors as Brethren Ashman and Kimmell.

The steady persevering pastor of the Garwin, Iowa, church, reports that his work is in good condition. Brother Ankrum and his co-workers are faithful to every interest of the church, and if the weather hinders them from taking an offering for the general work at the designated time, they will take it at another. We are grateful to Brother Ankrum for taking notice of and complying with our suggestions of some time ago.

Brother C. C. Grisso tells of progress in the churches under his care. He had Brother G. W. Rench of South Bend, with him at North Liberty in a two weeks' campaign which resulted in the conversion of souls and much profit to the members. At Tiosa the pastor's own evangelistic efforts were rewarded with success and when writing the letter he was assisting Brother Kenneth Ronk at Center Chapel in a revival. Brother Grisso is ever at it.

The White Gifts are coming in quite promptly, according to Brother Albert Trent, the Secretary-treasurer of the Sunday School Association. Keep a close watch upon his reports and see if yours is in yet. If you don't find it, perhaps some one has neglected to send it in, or maybe you have not had the opportunity to take your offering yet. Of course if you have been hindered, you will want to take it at the very first opportunity and help along in the good work. Send all White Gift offerings to Brother Trent and not to Brother Gearhart at Dayton.

The Business Manager's Corner tells you how loyally the churches are supporting the Evangelist. One church, the largest in the brotherhood, finds its way into the Honor Roll family of churches, and we wish to say to Dayton, We welcome you and hope you will find the Evangelist as indispensable and many other churches that are continually writing us and we desire to serve you well. We wish to thank the friends who have written us personally about their appreciation of the paper; their words are encouraging and will stimulate us to seek to serve you still better.

REMEMBER: THE ONE DEBT WE AS A CHURCH CAN NEVER PAY IS THE DEBT WE OWE TO OUR PIONEER PREACHERS. When the Benevolence Board asks the brotherhood to contribute to the comfort of these veterans of the cross, they are not asking for charity, but for the discharge of the obligation. than which there is none more binding. He that provides not for those of his own household is worse than an infidel, says the Book we take for our creed, and these fathers of ours are of our own spiritual household. They served the church without hire in the days of its beginnings and what we have and are as an institution we owe to them. With genuine love and deep gratitude may we remember them in the evening of their lives. Not in the spirit of giving alms, but with the feeling that we are simply discharging a divinely imposed responsibility, let us bring our gifts on the second Sunday in February, or the nearest convenient Sunday thereto. Send your offering to Herman E. Roscoe, Goshen, Indiana.

GENERAL ARTICLES

The Church in the Industrial Center. By E. L. Miller

For eleven years after graduation from high school, I was fortunate enough to work in the public works. In that time I had first hand knowledge of several.lines of work, and what is more pertinent at this time, I also met the workers in many trades and callings. In those eleven years I belonged to labor unions and on one occasion came out on strike. This strike was one of the most complete tie-ups in a line of work that has ever taken place, and during that strike we were forced at different times to look into the muzzles of guns held by the militia or constabulary. Now I am no anarchist, bolshevist and neither as I an I. W. W., but I do wish to say that the worker has opinions formed from such contacts that it is difficult for any one to shake. He looks upon the militia and constabulary as the agents of the oppressing capitalist. This is irrespective of your mind in the matter. A peep into the muzzle of a gun held by a none too friendly militiaman might work a change of notions in the minds of you, my dear readers. At least the worker has never had the satisfaction of seeing the muzzle of the gun pointed toward the oppressing employer and that gives him his much criticised but nevertheless firm opinion of the militia.

Now it is not my purpose to say a word against constituted authority, but in order that we may understand the position of the man in the industrial center we must look at these things which have made him the man that he is. To work in the coal mine for a mere pittance and then find all society turned against you when you desire a fair deal does not conduce toward a love of the church which is so often conducted by the very ones who have refused you a living wage while they are living in plenty. There are a few employers of the better type who, like the merchant prince of Philadelphia, do act on Christian principles in dealing with their employees, but to each such one there are dozens, yes scores, of sweat shops and oppressors. It does not matter what you may think concerning the attitude that the worker should assume toward those oppressing him, he will not love the oppressor, and the chances are all against his loving the organizations to which his erstwhile oppressor belongs, among which we find the Christian church. In fact, the church is not making even a dent in the unbelief of the vast number of wage earners in the larger industrial centers.

Not so long ago, perhaps two years, a close friend of mine, a minister in another denomination, while visiting New York stopped to listen-in at one of the many street corner meetings that take place in that busy metropolis. The speaker was dilating upon the rights and wrongs of the industrial system, especially the wrongs, and he was trying to show the way out. Different societies and organizations were named as having some power in bringing about the desired things, but my friend was surprised that at no time was the church mentioned. Finally he could stand it no longer and he cried, "Where does the church come in in your plans?" Imagine his surprise and chagrin when the speaker replied instanter, "It doesn't come in." There you have it bald and fairly before you. And during the last year of the world war a sky pilot who worked among the lumber jacks of the northwest asked a body of them to come hear him preach. They refused point blank. The preacher insisted and they finally consented, but only on condition that they be allowed to choose the text. It was a long shot, but rather than lose them altogether the dominie consented. The shack in which they were to meet was cleaned out and the crowd assembled at the hour appointed. When the time for the sermon came the text was handed the preacher, and can you imagine his feelings as he read that text written in large flaming letters of red on a piece of card-board? The

text read, "To hell with the church." Of course the speaker with ready wit found a way out by quoting on top of it, "But the gates of hell shall not prevail against it." Yet, friend, that did not say that the man in the industrial center has not a different feeling toward the church than do we, the exponents of that institution. It is up to the church to come down out of the clouds a while and meet these fellows where they are. You may invite them until you are blue in the face but they will not come. The Master took the church to the common people, and I am persuaded that it is ours to take the church to many of these or we will not reach them at all. Deporting the Reds may relieve political upheaval, and putting the government control on all industries may result in quieting the unrest in the industrial world, but believe me, all these will not win the unsaved man of industry to the church and the Christ of the church. Anyhow, the man in the industrial center makes quite a distinction between the church and the Christ. With the exception of the ultra-radicals, all the social speakers will use Christ as an example to be followed. They will show his fairness in dealing between rich and poor, with the accompanying befriending of the poor fellow. They will take pains to quote Paul and Christ concerning the reward to the worker and that the idler should not eat. And then they throw the stone at the leisure class and all institutions supported by them. Here is where they make their distinctions between Christ and the church. I have been on strike with them as I said. I have walked the picket line. I have met in their union meetings. I have faced the guns. I have heard their "cusses" as they heaped them upon the sleek employer as he wended his way to church while they were on strike for as much as would guarantee them a living. In short, I think I know how they feel, and it does not do you any good to say they should not feel that way, and then try to square yourself by taking a rap at the fellow who would dare write as I am writing. It is high time that the church is going about preaching the Gospel irrespective of whom it hits and how they like it. A rich sinner is no better than a poor one, and to my way of thinking the striking worker who "cusses" the church is just as good as the oppressor who uses the church to shield his contemptible hypocrisy and lovelessness.

But, say you, cannot the church reach these men and is there no hope? I answer, there is hope and they can be reached. Every man has his point of approach and the worker is a man. He can be reached by sympathetic effort. But I do not believe that he will be reached for God by any other way than the rest of humanity. It is an individual matter. No promise is held out that we shall win any large body by wholesale methods. We must win the confidence of these men by our going to them in sympathy, and by showing them that we are not trying to bamboozle them, as they would call it. Forget some of your starch and dignity long enough to shake an honest, begrimed worker's hand without first drawing on your gloves to protect your lily fingers. Many a man has remarked to me as I worked among them in the centers of industry that the preachers do not usually notice them when they are in their overalls or when their faces are black with the soil of toil. I do not wish to accuse all ministers of this, but I have noticed the same myself during my years of toil in the public works. A dirty hand and a ragged jacket may both be consecrated in the sight of God, even though I do not believe that a man is saved by work or works. Instead of the down-town church quitting business merely because there are no more elite living there, and all that it could do would be to try to interest the working people, they should get the heart of the Master and go to work trying to save the sheep who have no shepherd. Dr. Shelton of Pittsburgh has shown that the down-town church has a mission and he is the talk of the city.' Of course, this church of the industrial center must have people with a vision led by a pastor who has the spirit of the Master in him. The church has lost its hold on the workers because it has felt it necessary to cater to money. It has followed the moves of the monied man rather than stayed among those whom the Lord loved so well, the common people. And now we must show to the worker that we have his soul's interests at heart and that it goes farther than that, that we have his physical, mental and moral and social interests at heart also. "My Father worketh hitherto, and I work," and may God bless the working class of our day. Never will the church fill its mission until there is a more concerted effort at reaching the toilers upon whose backs everything moves. I do not believe that the average toiler has anything against Christianity, he is too intelligent for that. But as I tried to say before, he has a grouch against the constituted order of things, and there is no use of our playing ostrich, and with our heads in the sands of self-satisfaction say, we have builded churches and now it is for all to come to us. We must go to them and make them feel that we have a lively interest in their every activity. The church has failed in part among the working classes, but Christ is still strong with them. So let us obey the Master by lifting him up before them in our lives and churches and not until then will we make an impression upon their hearts. Do not condemn the worker until you have tried to understand him. Give him a hearing and a chance and I fully believe that he will return fruit a thousand fold for any real effort put forth to win him. Not theory but good sound sense backed up by actions which the worker can read easier than your theories, will reach the man who by very nature is a being of action. "Inasmuch as ye have done it to the least of these ye have done it unto me." Pray for the pastors of our city and industrial center churches.

Nappanee, Indiana.

"The Holy Spirit Versus Man as the Interpreter of Our Creed"
By J. F. Garber

One of the chief factors that is instrumental in breaking down the spirituality of the Christian world of today, is the fact that too many people are depending on some man or set of men to interpret the Word of God for them instead of reading it with a prayerful heart and then trusting to the Holy Spirit to guide them into all truth.

The Holy Spirit Promised

We have a definite promise made even before the advent of our Savior into the world, that the Holy Spirit would be poured out upon God's people. In Joel 2:28, 29 we read: "And it shall come to pass afterward that I will pour out my Spirit upon all flesh; and your sons and your daughters shall prophesy. Your old men shall dream dreams, your young men shall see visions: and also upon the servants and upon the handmaids in those days will I pour out my spirit."

Then notice the instructions of Jesus to his disciples just before he ascended up into heaven, to tarry at Jerusalem until they should be endued with power from on high. or in other words, until they should be filled with the Holy Spirit. He made a definite promise to them when he said, "I will pray, the Father and he shall give you another comforter that he may abide with you forever; even the Spirit of truth; whom the world cannot receive because it seeth him not, neither knoweth him: but ye know him; for he dwelleth with you, and shall be in you." He also told them that it was expedient for them that he should go away, for said he, "If I go not away, the Comforter will not come unto you, but if I depart, I will send him unto you." We have in the foregoing Scripture an absolute promise that the Comforter which is the Holy Spirit would be sent into the world.

This promise was gloriously fulfilled on the day of Pentecost when "there came a sound from heaven as of a rushing mighty wind, and it filled all the house where they were sitting." . . . "And they were all filled with the Holy Ghost, and began to speak with other tongues as the Spirit gave them utterance."

Office of the Holy Spirit

But why was the Holy Spirit sent? What was the work assigned to him?

God sent the prophets of old to foretell future events, and to give warning and admonition to his people. John the Baptist was sent to prepare the way of the Lord. And Jesus said of his own mission into the world, "For the Son of man is come to seek and to save that which was lost." He also said, "I am come that they might have life and that they might have it more abundantly." The Holy Spirit was sent from God to mankind to perform a special mission. And we can readily understand what that mission was by reading the following Scriptural references:

"But the Comforter which is the Holy Ghost, whom the Father will send in my name, he shall teach you all things, and bring all things to your remembrance whatsoever I have said unto you" (John 14:26). "Howbeit when he the Spirit of truth is come, he will guide you into all truth: for he shall not speak of himself; but whatsoever he shall hear, that shall he speak: and he will show you things to come" (John 16:13). "And when he is come, he will reprove the world of sin, and of righteousness, and of judgment" (John 16:8). The office of the Holy Spirit then is to guide us into all truth; teach us all things; bring all things to remembrance; show us things to come; and to reprove the world of sin and of righteousness and of judgment.

As the Father has made provisions whereby we may be led into all truth, taught all things, be reproved of sin, of righteousness and of judgment, and even have the future revealed unto us, would we who claim to be true followers of the blessed Master, be acting prudently to reject the Holy Spirit's interpretation of God's Word and accept that of any man or set of men? It appears to me that it would be better for us to adhere more closely to the great plan of salvation as revealed in God's Word. The sending of the Holy Spirit into the world is a part of God's great plan for the salvation of mankind. When we deny his power and reject his official work, we are simply rejecting God's means of grace to us.

If we accept man made creeds, instead of the inspired Word of God as revealed to us by the Holy Spirit, it seems reasonable to me that we will fall under the condemnation which was pronounced upon the Pharisees by our Lord when he said, "But in vain do they worship me, teaching for doctrine the commandments of men."

Dear reader, if we really desire to become the children of God, let us remember that Paul said, "For as many as are led by the Spirit of God they are the sons of God." He also said, "If any man have not the spirit of Christ he is none of his." And we should not forget that our heavenly Father will give the Holy Spirit to them that ask him.

Our creed, the New Testament, contains all of the instruction that is necessary for our salvation, and does not need to be supplemented by any man made creed. It is the perfect law of liberty."

In conclusion let me urge each and every one to drink more freely of that Spirit which shall be in you a well of water springing up into everlasting life.

Weldon, Iowa.

Consistency. By Mrs. O. E. Nicholas

A six weeks' revival has just closed. A splendid interest was shown, there was a large attendance and the church worked as one man.

Great interest was shown in the preaching of God's Word, yet notwithstanding all this the pastor is forced to admit that the primary purpose of the service, the ingathering of souls, has been a failure.

Why do men refuse the call to a better life? Why do men listen to God's truth unmoved and untouched? Why do men say, I am just as good as your Brother A., or Brother B? What is the reason for all this coldness?

Do you ever ask yourself, Do I lack consistency in my everyday walk before men? Are any of my members indulging in the inconsistencies of life on the side?

This is the key, lack of consistency, to the solution of the great problem that confronts every pastor today. The want of consistency on the part of those professing Christianity is what is causing men to lose faith in the church and bring reproach on the gospel. Too many are walking with the church in one hand and the world in the other. I sincerely believe the want of consistency causes more secret uneasiness and more discord than any other failing in man's character.

The inconsistent lives of professing Christians are throwing reproach on the cause of Christianity and making the tongues of enemies to blaspheme. Ah! the wickedness of those professing to be good—of those who set themselves as models of piety and virtue are doing more to hinder the gospel and bring defeat than all the forces of wicked people.

What is the use of preaching to the world against lying, stealing, defrauding your fellowmen, malice and hatred, if the man at my elbow, to whom all look as to an example, lies, steals, hates his neighbor, overreaches in business, speaks unkindly and uncharitably of others and frequents questionable places? What do you gain in the work of saving souls if you refute your own teaching? Which is the more eloquent your words or your acts? We MUST live what we teach and preach. It is the practical everyday living that counts today—consistent living by Christian people.

We are startled by the number of infidels and hardened sinners some men are making. Ingersoll was an avowed infidel caused by the inconsistent life of his father before he was born. The inconsistent lives of men who profess goodness is making more scoffers of religion than the devil himself.

The world's greatest need is more Christlike men and women. The preaching it needs is not only the precept but the practice of pure, heaven-born piety. A cowardly, fashion-loving, covetous, cowardly church will never save men from hell.

But the church of living disciples whose hearts have been cleansed by the atoning blood and whose lives are made beautiful by inward conflict and secret prayer and are made eloquent by noble deeds—these are the men and women that will lead the world to Christ. Their voice is a trumpet, their influence is as salt and their example is a light.

My reader, is your daily walk in life throwing reproach on the gospel of Christ? Is your daily example winning men for the church or is it making men blaspheme Christ's name? Are you causing men to stumble and fall by your inconsistent living?

You cannot live a double life, neither can you serve God and mammon.

Dowagiac, Michigan.

The Church of Jesus Christ, Her Origin, Purpose, Work and End
By H. M. Harley, from his "Brethren Bulletin"

Ephesians 5:25 and 26

"Christ also loved the church, and gave himself for it, that he might sanctify it, having cleansed it by the washing of water with the word, that he might present the church to himself a glorious church, not having spot or wrinkle, or any such thing; but that it should be holy and without blemish."

The church of Jesus Christ is the greatest, grandest and most glorious institution the world has ever known, knows of today, or ever shall know. Jesus Christ himself founded her. He gave to her the inspiration and power, the incentive and the program that is necessary to the perpetuation and the perfecting of the work that he came to do, and did do, until he was called back to the Father. And for a person to accept Jesus Christ as his personal Savior, he will also have to accept his church, for he is the head of the church, which is his body. And however justly some things may be said in criticism about some of her members, the church as an institution is divine, and bears the only saving gospel that the world knows of, or ever has received. She is the body of Christ, and his life in the body, and through it is communicated to its several members.

Now, the life that Jesus gives through the church,—is divine. It is the fountain of perpetual youth, for which men have sought for ages past. And all those who will become a part of her, accept her teaching, and enter into the spirit of her labors, will have a new light imparted to them.

There will be a new hope in their heart, a new ambition in their life, a new warmth in their hand, a new vigor in their feet, a new message on their lips, a new vision of duty and a new knowledge of divine love,—and this is eternal life.

Now then, what is the real purpose and work of the church? The first and foremost work of the church is to evangelize. "Go ye into all the world, and make disciples among all nations, teaching them to observe all things, whatsoever I have commanded them." But before this can be done, there are several things that the church must first do as a groundwork. And the first is to know what Jesus really did say,—why he said it, and what the outcome of either accepting or rejecting his word, would involve. Another duty the church has to perform is to develop Christian character so that there will be those who will be fit vessels through which the Holy Spirit can minister the good things of God and of Christ, to a needy and sin-sick world. She is to instruct, to feed, to call out, and to prepare workers who will enlist in the work of carrying out the world-program that God has ever had in mind for the same.

Then too, it has been given to the church to perpetuate the truths of God so that his good may come to the world. The church has been given several ordinances which help to build up his children in the most holy faith of God, so that they can live lives well pleasing to him, and as well to win others to this same life. And for a person to keep the ordinances as given by Jesus Christ, means that they are going

on record as willing Christians. The Word says, "Show me thy faith without thy works, and I will show you my faith by my works." To observe the ordinances of the church, is to prove our love to him, and also one to another. "Hereby we know that we love the children of God, when we love God, and do his commands."

And say friends, what a difference it would make in this old world, if men would see life from the viewpoint of Jesus Christ, as given to his church! If men would study to understand, rather than to criticize the church, they would join hands in trying to lift fallen men, to have the lost and to bring them back to God. And then too, there would not be so many divisions in the church today, if men would adhere to the "Thus saith the Lord of the Scriptures, rather than to take the say-so of men for it.

And what is to be the end of the church? Some of these times, Jesus Christ shall come for her, and take her out of the world and to himself, but only such part of her as has been faithful to him, to His Word and to the program that he laid down for her. The Bridegroom is coming for his bride, and all who have been true, shall hear the voice, and shall enter in, to enjoy the marriage supper of the Lamb. Will you qualify? God grant that you may.

Pittsburgh, Pennsylvania.

Report of the Great World Survey Conference. By George S. Baer

Last week in the editorial department we gave a cursory report of the great Atlantic City conference, but no one realized more than we, how incomplete it was; it was necessarily so. Some have asked to know more about the Interchurch World Movement and others have expressed a desire to know more about the purpose and significance of the World Survey Conference. And we are conscious that we would not be faithful in our service to our great family of Evangelist readers if, after having had the opportunity of attending a conference of such significance to the whole Christian church, we would not do our best to pass on to them the things we there received. And if our report does not cover any points that our readers want information on, we shall be glad to pass on any information we may have received. In addition to having been an eye and ear witness, we have the benefit of the News Bureau, which enables us to make this report the more complete.

Representatives of forty-two faiths numbering over 1800 men and women gathered in the World Survey Conference of the Interchurch Movement at Atlantic City, January 7, 8, 9 and resolved upon a great common effort to bring nearer the Kingdom of Jesus Christ on earth.

Seldom since the days when the apostles set out from Palestine to carry the Word to all the nations has a meeting displayed such intense spiritual fervor, such wholehearted unselfishness and such unanimous determination to submerge all petty difficulties and do something for our Lord which should go down through the ages.

It was a common remark among the delegates that if only every man on earth could have been present to hear the wonderful presentation of the needs of the world and to catch the divine inspiration, the task of winning all to the altar would soon be done.

Perhaps the most striking decisions of the Conference were the determination to conduct an intensive evangelistic campaign in all the churches from now until Easter time, and the fixing of April 21 to May 2 as the dates of a United Simultaneous Financial Ingathering.

The Conference and later the General Committee of the Movement gave general approval of the proposal for the budget made by the Movement on the basis of the surveys. The budget covers the financial needs of what is considered an adequate Christian program. But each item is to be adjusted with the denomination directly involved. It should also be noted that certain bodies, notably the Methodist Episcopal Church and the Methodist Episcopal Church, South already have raised great amounts through the Centenary and cannot be expected to make another appeal this spring to those who have already pledged themselves for five years.

The total budget is $326,107,837 on a one year basis and $1,320,214,551 on a five year basis. It was recommended that each denomination appeal for the sum needed for one year ahead. On a one year basis, the budget consists of $253,193,400 allotted to boards for regular work; $62,929,05 unallotted for special types of work; and $9,985,232 unallotted—to occupy unoccupied areas.

By types of church activity, on a one year basis, the budget may be divided into: Foreign Division, $104,503,-909; Home Mission Division, $53,773,706; American Education Division, $84,239,050; American Religious Education Division, $2,065,500; American Hospitals and Home Division, $21,368,566; American Ministerial Support and Relief Division, $60,175,326.

The report of the Board of Review said of the expense budget of the Movement, which was presented to the delegates and approved:

"Had the leaders (of the Movement), through lack of vision or fear of present criticism, dared less, and prepared a less adequate foundation, they would have subjected themselves eventually to a far greater censure because of their failure to have constructed a foundation sufficiently broad and strong for the great structure which alone will be in any sense worthy of the united effort of so large an aggregation of the Christian people of the land."

The Movement gained adherents in the course of the Conference, when it was announced that the General Baptists, with 40,000 communicants, have entered into co-operative relationship as a direct result of the surveys of educational institutions in Southern Indiana. Their budget, $1,666,000 for five years, was received too late to be included in the printed budget statements. Another notable event of the Conference was the action of the Administrative Committee of the General Board of Promotion of the Northern Baptist Convention in voting to underwrite its share in Interchurch publicity expense, the largest Baptist publicity appropriation in the history of the denomination was voted.

Dr. John R. Mott opened the Conference with a powerful presentation of the history of the Movement, the unanimity with which the nation's great mission leaders had accepted the plan as providential a year ago and the remarkable victories that already had been won in bringing about Christian co-operation.

"This is the moment of moments for us to find our unity, our spiritual solidarity, without sacrificing our diversity and that which is most distinctive to each of our communions, and which, by the way, is the choicest possession we have," he said.

"The reason why we of each denomination here most value that which is distinctive to us, is not simply because it is ours, but because we honestly believe it is the truth. Without sacrificing our distinctiveness, we want to realize our unity and solidarity as we gather 'round the figure of our Lord with open minds, responsive hearts, and I would say, hair-trigger wills—by that I mean wills that are eager to leap into action when we see a clear path."

Dr. Fred P. Haggard introduced the surveys with the statement that the budget presented included the programs of thirty-four denominations and 147 boards or other denominational agencies. "The denominations co-operating in the Movement enroll 71.06 percent of the total Protestant membership in the United States," he said.

Describing the magnitude of the task of "surveying the world," Dr. Haggard said: "It is not to be wondered at that some shook their heads and said we had undertaken too much."

He quoted the proposal of the Committee of Twenty,

made early in the history of the Movement: "A thorough, united survey of the home and foreign fields of the world for the purpose of securing accurate and complete data as to what ought to be done by the combined churches to meet the needs of the hour, and of at least the next five years."

These surveys were not complete, but they were well enough along to give a cross-section of the results. The preliminary results were placed in the hands of the delegates in fifteen well illustrated pamphlets, giving an unprecedentedly complete picture of Christian duty and opportunity. Dr. Haggard said the surveys when finished would be presented in two large volumes.

Dr. S. Earl Taylor painted a picture of the many little Christian armies at present all assailing the forces of evil, valiantly but without any settled plan and with little co-operation or understanding of the whole task. He showed on the screen the names of the denominations and the denominational agencies at work overlapping each other's fields and thereby failing to make their efforts count for the most for Christ. Both lists were too long to be seen in one picture and, indeed, took several seconds in passing across the curtain. But the last thing in his heart, Dr. Taylor said, was to ridicule denominationalism. He said he was a denominational man and believed in denominationalism. "One of the most precious heritages we have is the prayers we learned at our mothers' knees and the traditions of the churches in which we were brought up," he added. "It is not within the purpose of this movement to lessen denominational loyalty, but to intensify denominational endeavors and increase interdenominational co-operation."

Dr. F. W. Bible opened the foreign surveys with a striking address on China, where he said, at the normal rate of increase as many people as there are now in the United States would be added to the population in the next thirty years. The present number is well in excess of 400,000,000. He foreshadowed a vast, homogeneous Chinese empire, stretching from Siberia across the Asiatic continent and including Malaysia.

"The greatest missionary problem of modern times is to create forces capable of controlling and directing that enormous human mass which ultimately will number between seven and nine hundred millions of people," said Dr. Bible. "America has a peculiar responsibility there. The Chinese government has co-operated with us in the survey, putting in our hands the only copy of the new census at present in the United Sttaes.

"Out of this largest nation on earth, destined in a short time to become a modern, aggressive people, only 312,-000 are communicants of Protestant churches. There is only one evangelical missionary for every 80,000 people and the areas in which there is no missionary agency contains thirty-five to forty million people."

"The Mexican problem is not a question of a revolution to be squelched, but an evolution to be guided," said Dr. S. G. Inman, in describing the opportunities of Latin America. "American mission boards are the only organizations which have developed a practical, comprehensive, inclusive program for solving the problem."

Dr. Inman asked 1,000 new missionaries for Latin America in the next five years and an expenditure of $35,000,000, in addition to what the peoples of the countries benefited would raise.

G. Sherwood Eddy held the audience breathless while he told of the co-operative movement of the native Protestant churches of Southern India, "led by three boys," and described a meeting of 30,000 Christians of the Syrian church in India, a larger gathering than anything of the sort he had ever seen anywhere else in the world.

Dr. Samuel M. Zwemer declared that in dealing with Mohammedanism, Christianity is facing a foe which is bolstered by spiritual forces. He pointed out that the Moslems had a definite and insistent evangelistic program and the number of their converts was increasing at an alarming rate.

"At present there are 2,500,000 of this faith in Europe," he said, "43,000,000 in Africa, 150,000 in South America, 67,000,000,000 in India and mosques are even now being erected in Australia."

Through lack of time only a trifling amount of the interesting and vital material discovered by the foreign surveys could be told. Indeed, that was the case with the whole program—the stress of hundreds of minds working six months with loving care at their task had to be boiled down into ten or even four tense minutes.

Dr. Ralph E. Diffendörfer introduced the home surveys. Dr. Inman, speaking again, said that, "by train and by boat there is liquor sufficient to flood the Woolworth Building; to the twentieth floor being poured into Cuba," and Christian Americans should see every Cuban "has at least as much chance to be decent as to be drunk."

C. L. Fry told of migratory labor in the United States while his audience bent forward to study his unique charts and maps.

"There are in the United States a million and a half men constantly on the move," said Mr. Fry. "This body of men is practically untouched by the church. In the great wheat belts of the middle west alone there are a quarter of a million men following the harvests from Texas into Canada." He also told of the hundreds of thousands leading a wandering life on account of the exigencies of fruit picking, fishing, lumbering and other occupations.

"These are the men of whom the I. W. W. are made," he commented. "And why are they I. W. W.? Because they are subject to the most intolerable living conditions. Because the church has not reached them. We must substitute home life for hobo life."

Dr. Diffendorfer had thrown on the screen colored maps giving a picture of the foreign-born problem in our large cities. To reach these people he suggested an appropriation of $200,000 a year for five years for a press that would touch the five principal nationalities.

Great applause greeted the plea of George Haynes for the education of Christian leadership for the colored race. "Our people are feeling a new consciousness of being 100 percent American," he said. He told of negro denominations voting money to send missionaries to Africa, adding: "They can carry more than money. They can carry this message—that the white race of America has Christianity enough, has democracy enough, to give them a place as men and as Christian brothers."

The home survey presentation was continued on the second day and Dr. James E. Clark described the needs of American education. The importance of this field to the church, he said, was shown by the fact that 90 percent of our ministers come from Christian schools and colleges.

Dr. Walter S. Athearn in outlining the situation of American religious education drew a comparison between the opportunities for religious instruction afforded Protestant, Catholic and Jewish children.

From studies that have been made, he said, it has been shown that Protestant children have only 24 hours a year—30 minutes on Sunday in the Sunday schools—for definite religious training. Catholic children have 84 hours as a minimum and 200 hours of possible opportunity for similar instruction, while Jewish children at the formative age have 85 hours assured and 335 hours of opportunity.

Dr. E. S. Collier showed the work being accomplished in Protestant hospitals of the country. He pointed out that the church is able to do unusually effective work in making good citizens, evangelism, reconstruction and other ways through the hospitals. In one New York hospital, he said, 43 nationalities were treated in one year and in wise ways many conversions were brought about.

Dr. J. B. Hingeley, who has conducted the survey for ministerial relief and support, said that although the necessities of life have advanced 82 percent in cost in the war period, ministerial salaries have increased only 20 percent in twenty years. Fifty-one percent of the preachers of America are receiving less than $1,000 a year, while the income tax returns last year showed that only 1,670 pastors, less than one percent of the whole, received as much as $3000 from all sources.

Dr. Diffendorfer and Dr. Edmund D. S. Brunner told of rural conditions. One map showed three ministers living within seven miles of one another and traveling respectively 85, 90 and 92 miles to preach in three churches located within seven miles of one another and traveling respectively, brought out strikingly the fact that the larger the rural church the greater its proportionate growth (that is, not only the actual numbers, but the numbers in proportion to the size of the congregation). The evils of an absentee ministry were stressed (This is a weakness from which the Brethren church is suffering to a large extent. There has

been too much satisfaction with part time service and an absentee pastor when oftentimes better service might have been afforded if we had realized the need).

Dr. J. Campbell White called attention to the fact that if the church is to carry forward a great program for Christ, she will need 100,000 new paid workers in the next five years. Every church must give attention to the enlistment of its young life into the service of Christ and the church and prepare in the very best way for their training if these great plans are to be carried out. There is not a church but can possibly be discovered. If we can carry the world's great need down to every church, to every home and to every individual heart, the young men and women will be challenged and enlisted in the service of the King of kings and the Lord of lords. "Pray ye therefore the Lord of the harvest that he will thrust forth laborers into his harvest."

Send
WHITE GIFT
OFFERINGS to

THE SUNDAY SCHOOL

ALBERT TRENT
General Secretary-Treasurer
Johnstown, Pennsylvania

Education for Christian Leadership. By President E. E. Jacobs, Ph.D.

Every conscientious and thinking person in America must be impressed with the rather patent fact that this country does stand, and ought by every right to stand, at the forefront in matters of moral leadership among the nations of the earth. If America continues to hold this place, then she certainly will be discharging a very large part of her obligation to the world, for this leadership is of infinitely more worth than leadership in finance or trade. For ideals which revolve around such a leadership, she entered the world war, let us confidently think, and to these ideals let us hope and pray, may she devote the best energies of her future. If America could now step out with a great and glorious program of human betterment which would be at the same time profoundly and thoroughly Christian, then indeed, could every American citizen, who has both intelligence and a conscience, be much more enthusiastic in his patriotism than he can be today.

Now it is perfectly plain, that if life in America is to be increasingly better, it can only come through better men, —men with a keener moral conscience, a clearer vision, a more lively intelligence, and an aroused moral responsibility. To talk of improving the moral life of a people and yet keep the old time dull conscience towards matters of moral obligations, is to talk utter nonsense. The newer wine of Christ's ideals of human blessedness, can not be put into the old wine-skins of low ideals and brutishness. The glorious patch of the new weave of his desire for the future welfare of humanity, can not be safely sewed onto the filthy blood-lust-smeared cloth of iniquitous men! We need a new creation which will take over men soul and body and by all the glorious and etheric process of heaven introduce them into all the mysteries of the New Birth.

Now, how is this to be brought about? How shall we seek to make men over the matchless pattern of the Christ who lived, loved, and died only in behalf of sinful, weak, and unhappy men? Plainly, there must be great souls who are both willing and able to lead the way; men whose souls are flooded and over-flooded with the ideals of Jesus which are rightly coupled with a training for righteousness and clear visioned leadership; men in whose souls the ideals of Jesus never take ebb but which are always at flood tide.

But religious enthusiasms without rational restraint is not wholly trustworthy, it may even be dangerous. If we are to lead men, we must be leaders indeed, for if the blind lead the blind, they will both fall into the ditch. Hence, there is a very great and real need for leadership and that with a vision. Our leaders need both the inspiration that

comes with vision as well as that which comes from educational training. We need leaders who digest, reflect, and who are familiar with facts, stubborn hard facts.

Now, such leadership, the Christian College by its own profession and position is bound to give. It ought to train men for just such leadership. It ought to brush aside the cobwebs of fanaticism and also of unbelief and clear up the mental furniture so that one may discern clearly what is to be done and how to do it. Leadership does not mean being elected superintendent of one's Sunday school particularly, nor a place on a college faculty but it does mean that one is trying to direct moral and religious activities in proper channels. A layman in a community may be ten times the leader his pastor is. A leader is one who has followers.

I see no reason why a church should enter upon the task of making chemists, engineers or even teachers any more than she should seek to make brick masons. But I do see why a church should train men in Christian character and if she is to teach the above noted subjects in her colleges, she must at least have as the excuse for so doing, that she wants to implant Christian character along with the chemistry and what not. Which brings us back to the one fundamental training for Christian leadership, and THAT IS THE SUPREME TASK OF ANY DENOMINATIONAL COLLEGE. Ashland College has absolutely no apology to make, it seems to me, for such a mission and if it could be shown that the College makes here a very large contribution to the educated and trained leadership of the church, it ought to take rank along with any other program of the activity of the church.

Lastly, trained leadership is the demand of the future. America both in her church affairs and in her political matters, needs right now this hour, trained leaders with a vision. Our onward path will be devious enough, but it will be all the more meandering if this sort of leadership is not developed and cared for.

Ashland, Ohio.

ARE THE LUMBER CAMPS NEGLECTED?

In a county of the state of Washington not far from Centralia where I. W. W. recently directed a murderous fire into the Armistice Day parade of ex-service men, the Interchurch Survey shows a population of 45,000, of whom three thousand are church members, with forty-four churches. But in sixty-four logging camps of the county, employing about five thousand men, fifty-six of the camps are entirely without religious instruction and some 500 children are also without the benefits of even a school education.

J. A. Garber
PRESIDENT

Our Young People at Work

G. C. Carpenter
SECRETARY

Intermediate Christian Endeavor

The above picture presents the largest Intermediate Society in the State of Ohio, including all denominations. It is the largest in our church, too. The society is made up of young people of the First church, of Dayton, and every member of it is active in promoting the principles of the organization. Mrs. Charles W. Abbott, their superintendent is aptly fitted for this sort of work as may be easily inferred. The above is a good example of what can really be done where a spirit of willing co-operation prevails.

At the recent state convention held at Canton, Mrs. Abbott was made State Superintendent of the Children's Division of the Brethren Sunday schools of Ohio. This position presents a wider opportunity for Christian service on the part of Mrs. Abbott, as she is eager to help the workers of the Children's Division, (Cradle Roll, Beginners, Primary, and Junior Departments. Correspondence is invited and where arrangements can be made, Mrs. Abbott is willing to visit Ohio schools in person. Her address is 206 Eastern Avenue, Dayton, Ohio.　　　　　　　J. A. GARBER.

First Brethren Intermediate Christian Endeavor Society was organized December 5, 1915. Orion E. Bowman and Mrs. Charles W. Abbott were the first superintendents. Enrollment on the first night was 12 and 53 were present the first month. So we see again that from a small beginning this large society of 1919 to 1920 is the fruit of the labor of those who saw a vision of a great field wherein the teen aged boy and girl might be benefited. Present enrollment is 50. For the first four months 459 were at the I. C. E. prayer meeting, 69 volunteer prayers were offered, 100 Bible verses were learned, 12 chapters in Matthew were studied, beside the regular Christian Endeavor Topic. A

MRS. C. W. ABBOTT
Superintendent

Society of Dayton, Ohio

Christmas program was rendered with the Senior Christian Endeavorers as our guests. Flowers were sent to the sick and magazines numbering 35 were carried to the hospitals. All meetings were opened at 6:29 o'clock. Every leader was present. So far we have met every state standard as required of us. We expect to be a banner society this year. So watch us grow.

Our officers are: President, Hazel Randell; Vice-President, Katherine Roper; Secretary, Alma Baumgardner; Treasurer, Roy Huette; Social Committee, Treva Geohring; Lookout Committee, Charles Wallace. Mrs. C. W. Abbott is superintendent. Mrs. Abbott is better known as Aunt Kate. She has been with us for five years, and records show that she has only missed 7 Sunday evening sessions during that time. Her sterling Christian graces are only manifested best when you come in contact with her through personal work. Boys and girls throughout the city love Aunt Kate. She understands them. She never bosses, but gently leads each in their own way. If Aunt Kate has a hobby it is the teen age boy and girl for Christ and his service. So we go on looking ever forward to the greater blessing which shall be ours if we are faithful to our trust.

FIRST BRETHREN I. C. E.,
　　　　　　　Per Hazel Randall.

Life Recruit Letter

Dear Fellow Endeavorers:

Another year has entered upon its journey and consequently another "Ashland College Night" will soon be here. This year "Ashland College Night" will be observed on Sunday, February 8th, or on Sunday the 29th, and we are most anxious to make it a success in every way. The reason for permitting an alternate date is due to the fact that February is to be "Life Work Month," culminating with National Recruiting Day on the 29th.

Accordingly we are suggesting the use of two programs. The one is based on the regular topic for the 8th. "A Worthwhile Life." The other will be special including, we hope, a life work pageant. Societies should use both to the full extent of their ability.

Appeals looking toward the attainment of the following goals may be made at either or both of the meetings. We are striving for two definite goals—Life Work Recruits and the money to make possible their efficient training at our own college. We ought to have at least twenty new life work recruits and three hundred dollars ($300.00) in offerings for the chair of Religious Education at Ashland College.

Remember that thorough preparation spells success. Begin praying now for these services that God may pour out his fullest blessing on these special efforts; that recruits might be found to carry on the Lord's work; that a real spirit of life giving and money giving might be found among Brethren young people generally. S. D. Gordon has said,

"You can't do anything better than pray until you have prayed." Let us prove the truth of this statement during the days of February.

It may be that your church has no Endeavor Society. If this is the case will you not see to it that the young people of the church are given charge of the evening service on February 8th or 29th, at which time the Life Work challenge can be presented and an offering taken for the support of the chair of Religious Education at Ashland College? The pastor should be asked to preach a special Life Work message, and the young people on that special night might furnish the ushers, the choir, special music and all the program preliminary to the evening sermon. By addressing a letter to Hudson, Iowa in my name I am sure that I could furnish you with some ideas regarding the observance of "Life Work and Ashland College Night"—if you do not have an Endeavor Society. Of course if you have a society in your church the regular program can be carried out. Please let me hear from you if I can be of help.

Yours for service,
EDWIN BOARDMAN, Superintendent,
Hudson, Iowa.

Nappanee Plans for Christian Endeavor Week

On request Miss Cora Culp, Field Worker of Northern Indiana, who was recently re-elected president of her home society, wrote concerning Nappanee's plans for Christian Endeavor Week. On account of evangelistic meetings in the church the celebration will be deferred one week.

On Sunday night we plan to begin with a real consecration meeting. We expect to use the topic—"What does our pledge require?" The program will be conducted by the president.

On Monday night all the Endeavorers will visit some neighboring society. We earnestly hope to attend a society smaller than our own in order that we may help to strengthen and stimulate them along the lines where their need is greatest.

Tuesday night will be fellowship night. Our Social Committee, consisting of sixteen live wire members will conduct the program. To this meeting we expect to invite three other Christian Endeavor Societies of the town. Along with them will be the society of the Christian church at Wakarusa. Last fall eighty of our members visited this place.

Wednesday night is to be Ashland College night. The Ashland College students of Nappanee with the aid of the

pastor, who is one of them, have agreed to "whoop-er up for Ashland." In making our budget up for the year allowance was made for our Ashland College offering. Of course we naturally expect to outstrip the required amount and send that to Ashland also.

"Church Loyalty" will be the theme Thursday evening. This being our regular prayer meeting night the pastor and prayer meeting committee will assume the responsibility of rendering the program.

An excellent program is being prepared by the Intermediates and Juniors for the Friday evening session. This part of the week ought to be one of encouragement, both to the Senior as well as the Junior Endeavor societies.

No meeting Saturday night.

Sunday night will be Decision Night. Coming at the end of a week's effort a climax will be reached in appealing for Life Work Recruits. The need of recruits is pressing and all due encouragement will be given to enlist our required number and more.

In addition to directing these activities Miss Culp continues to visit the societies of the district. She hopes to see all of them in a high state of efficiency by the time of the district convention in March at Nappanee.

J. A. GARBER.

| SEND ALL MONEY FOR General Home, Kentucky and Foreign Missions to | # MISSIONS | WILLIAM A. GEARHART General Missionary Secretary 906 Conover Bldg., Dayton, O. |

NOTICE

"State Missions"

All contributions for state missions should be sent to your state secretary. That is, the apportionment assessed for each church for state work.

"Home And Foreign Missions"

All contributions for home and foreign missions should be sent to the General Missionary Secretary, William A. Gearhart, 906 Conover Building, Dayton, Ohio. If you forget the address, just write Dayton, Ohio, and it will reach me.

"White Gift Offerings"

All contributions for the WHITE GIFT FUND should be sent to the secretary of the National Sunday School Association, Albert Trent, Johnstown, Pennsylvania.

Pastors and superintendents of Sunday Schools should know what the White Gift Offering is for, and see that no pledges made at Winona Lake for the Kentucky work, or

Home Guard pledges, are included in this offering, for the White Gift offering, is not intended primarily for mission purposes, but for the National Sunday School Association which contributes $1000.00 per year to the Kentucky missions, $1000.00 for the Chair of Religious Education at Ashland College, and the balance for the expenses and work of said Association.

We are endeavoring to divide the contributions which are sent either to Brother Trent or myself as nearly as possible in the way which we think you intended it should be done, however if you find that it has not been done as you wanted it, when you see the reports in the Evangelist, you can make it known and correction will be cheerfully made.

Kentucky slides are not engaged far ahead, wish the churches, Christian Endeavor Societies or some organization would ask for them.
WILLIAM A. GEARHART,
General Missionary Secretary,
906 Conover Bldg., Dayton, O.

Isolated But Deeply Interested

Sister Mary Schisler Messenger, of Trout Lake, Washington, writes that she is isolated and that her family is the only Brethren family living at this place, Sunnyside church being their nearest. She states in her letter that they are deeply interested in church work and especially in the Kentucky Mountain missions.

She proves the above statement by sending us a money order for $53.15 for the Kentucky work at Krypton. She conducted a missionary bazaar, and the following are some of the contributors:

Mrs. Ellen Schisler Flickinger, Boardman, Oregon.
Mrs. H. S. Boardman, Boardman, Oregon.
Mr. B. F. Miller, Fredonia, Kansas.
Mrs. Sadia McCune and father, Loraine, Illinois.
Mrs. Lora Cheeney, Portland, Oregon.
Mr. R. T. Caslow, Portland, Oregon.
Mr. John Siders, Astoria, Illinois.
Mrs. Mary Schisler, Astoria, Illinois.

Mrs. LoVa Schisler, Astoria, Illinois.
Mrs. Susan Lehman, Astoria, Illinois.
Mrs. Rebecca Mummert, Astoria, Illinois.
Mrs. Wayne Wherley, Astoria, Illinois.
Mrs. Lola Wherley, Lewistown, Illinois.
Mrs. Chas. Sparts, Basil, Kansas.
Mrs. Millie Messenger, Manhattan, Kansas.
Miss Mary Pence, Limestone, Tenn.
Mrs. O. W. Clemmer, LaVerne, Calif.
Mrs. G. C. Carpenter, Peru, Indiana.
Mrs. W. S. Bagley, Somonank, Illinois.
Sears & Roebuck, Seattle, Washington.
Mrs. E. T. Messenger, Trout Lake, Washington.
Mrs. Mary Messenger, Trout Lake, Washington.

Also a number of Trout Lake friends.

We trust all these dear people will be blessed in their giving, for the Lord has said ''It is more blessed to give than to Receive.''

From The Children:

Miss Marion Watt, age eight, and Zelda MacLennan, age nine, both living in Washington, D. C. have saved their pennies until they have accumulated five dollars each and have sent it to me to be used to cheer the hearts of our missionaries.

I wonder if we can realize what sacrifices these little folks have made in giving their money to the Lord's work. It makes the grown-up folks feel ashamed sometimes, to have the children do such noble work but the Good Book says, "A little child shall lead them" and we trust this example of our little folks will spur us to greater sacrifices in order that the gospel may be proclaimed to the whole world.

Another example of children's support of missionary work: The Primary and Junior department of the Sunday school of the First Brethren church of Los Angeles is supporting Miss Marguerite Gribble, the little mis-

sionary of Africa. She is the daughter of Brother and Sister Gribble.

Let us all, old and young, do our best to spread the glad tidings of salvation to the lost world as soon as possible, for we have been too negligent in the past, many of us, and what will we say to our Master, when we are to give an account of our stewardship.

Easter is not so far away and as this is the time when we make our drive for foreign missions, it is important that we begin to think, pray, and plan for the biggest foreign mission offering that our church has ever lifted.

WILLIAM A. GEARHART.

WHITE GIFTS—COMING SPLENDIDLY

The following White Gift offerings have been received since last report:

Cerro Gordo, Ills.,	$ 13.71
Brush Valley, Pa.,	5.00
Carleton, Neb.,	87.88
Meyersdale, Pa.,	82.00
Gretna, Ohio,	35.34
Listie, Pa.,	5.87
Martinsburg, Pa.,	3.50
Third Bretrren, Johnstown, Pa.,	25.79
Compton Ave., Los Angeles, Cal.,	25.50
Portis, Kans.,	14.20
Uniontown, Pa.,	60.00
Homerville, Ohio,	6.41
Ripon, Cal.,	15.40
La Verne, Cal.,	250.00
Quiet Dell, Pa.,	5.00
Maurertown, Va.,	114.165
Spokane, Wash.,	47.80
Lanark, Ills.,	112.57
Bethel, Ind.,	65.00
Gravelton, Ind.,	5.00
North Georgetown, Ohio,	9.20

Limestone, Tenn.,	30.72
Mexico, Ind.,	65.00
Summit Mills Pa.,	45.10
Peru, Ind.,	12.80
Fairview, Ohio, (Additional)	1.00
Warsaw, Ind.,	29.15
Altoona, Pa.,	31.67
Pittsburgh, Pa.,	62.03
Tiosa, Ind.,	5.00
Leon, Iowa,	8.00

Total,	$1280.29
Previously Reported,	$ 953.69
Grand Total, to date,	$2244.98

This prompt and generous response from our schools for the work of our Association is gratefully appreciated.

You will note that up to this time the La Verne school of California has contributed the largest offering, $250.00.

The fine offering of $47.80 from the mission school in Spokane is certainly worthy of special mention. So far, 14 schools have sent in contributions that had not paid anything to this work last year.

May I call the attention of the schools that have not yet sent in their offering, that all White Gift offerings should be sent to the writer and not to Brother Gearhart. About a dozen schools have forwarded their contributions to the General Missionary Secretary, this adds more work on him as well as additional postage in mailing them to the writer; there is also danger in getting us confused as to what particular account the offering is really intended to be credited, for some are not very explicit on this point.

Jan. 12th, 1920.

ALBERT TRENT,
General Secretary-Treasurer.

NEWS FROM THE FIELD

MORRILL, KANSAS

Having submitted but one or two reports to the readers of the Evangelist since taking up the work here a year ago last fall I suppose many are wondering how everything goes at Morrill. We are still on the job and our efforts have been blessed in the strengthening of the work in many respects. When the reports go in for the closing of the Four Year Program we want to be among the list of churches that can rejoice because we have been instrumental in helping to win ''VICTORY'' for 1920. The reports at the close of the year from the Sunday school, Christian Endeavor, Women's Missionary Society, and Sisterhood of Mary and Martha were most gratifying.

Our plans for a campaign for souls in the fall of 1918 were shattered by that monster that was so frequently seen in our last year reports—influenza, but when the Lord put us on our feet again we immediately began our pleas for such a campaign this winter. We were very fortunate in securing the services of Dr. W. S. Bell for the month of December. Those days of refreshing and real spiritual food for the inner man are now history. This time the fuel situation almost closed our doors but owing to the fact that many of the good men of the church were willing to spend two days in the timber with saws and axes we were allowed to continue. The first two weeks of the meeting the roads were blocked with snow with the thermometer registering below zero, yet we cannot complain for the Lord gave us a great victory. Brother Bell is a man that preaches the whole Gospel in a clear and convincing manner and such preaching is always fruitful. In all twenty-five confessed their faith in the blessed Christ. Of this number all but one have been received into the church, one was received by baptism last summer, making twenty-five additions

since our last report with one awaiting baptism. We rejoice and praise God for this victory. The future looks bright for the Brethren at Morrill. We hope to be able an announce some of our plans for greater advancement in the near future.

At the Christmas season the pastor and family were remembered with a fat purse and many other gifts of real value. These things make the burdens easier and we are truly thankful for them and especially for the spirit that prompted the givers. We ask that the readers continue to remember the work and the workers at Morrill when they talk with God. Let us all strive together to make this the Victory Year for the Brethren church.

A. E. WHITTED.

HOMERVILLE, OHIO

Some time has elapsed since any report has made its appearance in the Evangelist concerning this work. This is not because there has been nothing to report but rather because it has been neglected. First and foremost we are glad to report that since conference time there has been five confessions made, two of those making the stand having been baptised and received into full fellowship, and the other three are awaiting baptism. All of these are young people and it is hoped that before the spring time there will be numerous others to make the same stand as these. We are now conducting a revival on a small scale preaching evangelistic sermons on Saturday and Sunday evenings, with the morning service devoted to instruction. Our prayer is that God may work in the hearts of men and bring them to the feet of Jesus.

At our fall communion the attendance was gratifying, there being about 90 percent of the membership present. On November 18th Dr. Jacobs went with us and preached at the

morning service. This is Dr. Jacobs' home church, his father having been pastor here for many years. He spoke in the interest of the college and the result was apparent when four weeks later Brother Beachler and myself made the canvass for college endowment. I will not make the report of this for Brother Beachler will do that. Suffice to say that we feel proud of the showing that Homerville made, considering the fact that her working membership is thirty-five.

This report would not be complete should we leave out the mention of the splendid manner in which the members came to Ashland in November and loaded up the pastor's cellar with good things to eat. Not only were we glad for the material gifts but also for the spirit of good cheer that came with the twenty-six people who made the trip in autos. It is such experiences as this that makes life just a little more worth living and the bonds of love between pastor and people just a little closer.

Brethren, pray for this little flock that it may be a blessing to that community.

FRED C. VANATOR.

FLORA, INDIANA

After being in charge of the Flora church now for three months naturally we have a few things to say concerning the work here. We had heard a great many good things about Flora before coming here, but now after three months on the field we are forced to say, that half had never been told. We found the work here in fine shape, our predecessors had built wisely and well. We found as fine a class of people as can be found anywhere. They not only believe in the church and her claims but they also believe in living their religion and making it practical in their every day life. We are doing our best to make this a 'real victory year, every goal we have tried to reach so far in the Four Year Program has been reached and we are confident of reaching them all before conference. We have gone "over the top" in every offering so far and expect to go over in all the rest as we come to them. The Evangelist has been put on the budget for the third year and in this way we hope to keep the entire membership in touch with the work of the brotherhood. The attendance at different services of the church has been of the best. The Sunday school under the efficient leadership of Brother Lee Myer and his able corps of workers is making splendid progress. We have one of the finest groups of teachers and officers that I have ever worked with. Recently we have reorganized the Christian Endeavor and expect soon to have a Christian Endeavor Society second to none. The church, Sunday school, Christian Endeavor, Woman's Missionary Society, Sisterhood and every department of the church is doing its work in a very acceptable way. The Flora church in the past has gained quite a reputation for sending out a number of ministers in the work at different places, and she is maintaining that reputation, for just recently Brother Sylvester Whetstone was called and ordained to the ministry and has already taken up the work at Teegarden, Indiana. Brother Whetstone has proved himself in the past a workman that needeth not to be ashamed, and Teegarden is to be congratulated in securing him for their pastor. We bespeak for him a very succesful pastorate.

Just recently we had a "Gospel Team" from the college with us for eight days. It certainly did us good to see a group of young men so earnest, interested and enthusiastic about the work of the kingdom. They certainly made a fine impression on the people here and were a credit to the college. Several young people are looking toward Ashland because of their stay here. Come again boys, we will be glad to have you. The church here being in harmony with the work of the different conferences and trying to follow their advice is sending its pastor to hold a three weeks' meeting at Teegarden the last week in January and the first two in February. We are hoping and praying for a great meeting at that time. Oh yes, we very nearly forgot to mention it. Soon after our coming here the church had a reception for us, I was going to say, the usual reception, but it was not. We never saw anything like it before. Going to the church one evening, as we supposed to an ordinary reception, they put one over on us and it took several trips the next day with a "Henry" to haul everything home. Also at Christmas we were very kindly remembered by old Santa. It is needless for us to say that the future is very bright for Flora, and we believe that the next few years will see great things accomplished for the Lord at Flora. We covet the prayers and good wishes of all God's children everywhere.

W. E. THOMAS.

NEW PARIS, INDIANA.

Since writing you about our dedication service of our church and the ordination service of our pastor, W. J. Duker, we have been having splendid services. The Lord is with us and blessing us in our efforts for Him, and we are looking forward to doing greater service for Him each week.

At our regular quarterly business meeting this week the church adopted a set of rules from which we shall govern our church in all of its activities. This brings about a definite understanding between all members as to just how each office and etc. is cared for. We feel that these rules will be of much good to the church. We then had our church, Sunday School and Woman's Missionary Society treasurer's reports which totaled a balance of $364.14. Probably the best reports ever given at our church.

We then elected our regular church officers and one more deacon. We had one deacon, Brother Smoker who came from the Goshen church, and our selection of another resulted in the call of D. E. Kaser, a good and upright man, well qualified for the requirements of a deacon. Brother McInturff was with us and with the assistance of our pastor, ordained Brother Kaser before the close of this service.

We had a splendid day when we took up our Thanksgiving Home Mission offering which amounted to $444.18. The Woman's ance of 39. And with our little program at Christmas we took our White Gift offering which amounted to $45.65 with an attend-Missionary Society gave $20 included in these two offerings. They are getting along fine with their work.

We are now making arrangements for a revival meeting which we hope to hold in the near future. May we have the interest in your prayers that this meeting may result in many souls won to Jesus.

MRS. FRANK ROSCOE,
Corresponding Secretary.

FIRST BRETHREN CHURCH, LOS ANGELES, CALIFORNIA.

After some delay because of illness we again come to you with some news of the work of the Lord as it has been carried on in our midst. Since our last letter there has been one conversion and one received by letter. Every service has been as evangelistic as possible and the pastor allows no opportunity to pass without an invitation to the people to accept the Savior. There is quite a lot of good material in sight and some of this we hope to reach for the kingdom during the present year. While this is true, yet we must say that Brother Jennings is very conservative and uses no undue influence nor makes any unwise appeals to induce people to unite with the church. Our pastor is meeting with fine success and has the respect and love not only of his parishioners but of outsiders also. The people are pleased with his sermons and one series deserves special mention—a series of sermons delivered on succeeding Sunday mornings on the topic: "The Diety of Christ."

During the year 1919 the membership nobly responded to all the appeals of the pastor not only in giving money for the use of the local church work and for our various benevolences, but also in service in the church. Some instances we now recall as in the case of some members who accepted the responsibility of teaching a class in the Bible School on Sunday morning. And they have been found in their places every session of the school ready to carry on their parts of the work. We may also mention that a spirit of good fellowship prevails and there is perfect harmony among all the membership and among all the ones set forward as leaders in the church and in its auxiliaries.

The standards of the Sunday school are being kept up well. Even in the tent in which we are compelled to worship during the erection of our new church edifice the interest and attendance at all services is being maintained. January 11th we recorded the best attendance in the Bible school we have had for many months—152.

The foundation of our new church is about completed. When it was. determined last year to erect a new building it was thought at first that $15,000 would perhaps be sufficient or nearly so, but as materials went up in price and labor demanded better prices also it was found to be insufficient. When the architect finally had the plans ready for bids, the lowest bid was over $24,000. Since that there has been further advances in prices which will have to be met, so that the writer is informed the total cost will be somewhere between $25,000 and $30,000. All are anxiously watching the progress of the builders and are looking forward to the new opportunities and the new responsibilities the completed structure will bring to us.

During the year 1919 there were forty additions to the church. All the goals of the Four Year Program were reached except one. That is the S. S. C. E. or what is now we believe, "The Woman's Missionary Society." An earnest effort is to be made to reach that goal this year.

Brother and Sister Jennings desire to thank their many friends throughout the brotherhood for their prayers and the warm interest they have manifested in the work here. All the interest that has been shown in any way is deeply appreciated by them. This will save Brother Jennings writing a number of letters to persons who have shown a heartfelt interest in his success here.

As has been our custom, the annual business meeting and election of officers was held on New Year's Day with a splendid supper in the evening between sessions. All the officers of the Bible School were re-elected and a vote of thanks given them for faithful service during the year just closed.

May our Father abundantly bless us during 1920!

Yours in the love of Jesus,
4910 Wadsworth St. A. P. REED.

HOLLINS, VIRGINIA.

I had programmed a two weeks' meeting a Hollins, Virginia six miles from Roanoke, but on account of the good interest at Bittman, Ohio, the brethren would not consent for me to close the meeting in time for me to fulfill my obligation with this church. I had. expected to begin the meeting the 11th of December but I was detained so that I began it almost a week later and I preached only eight days. Brother Patterson, their pastor, began the meeting the 11th, and my brother, J. S. Bowman, preached for them Saturday night and over the first Sunday and I arrived on Tuesday the 18th and closed the meeting the 23rd and arrived home the 24th, the day before Christmas.

I was glad to be home a week as I had only been home four days since the middle of September.

I left home the 3rd of January and I am now at Fremont, Ohio, helping one of the dearest sons I have in the Lord, namely Brother Oberholzer. We started in here with the thermometer four below zero. I have preached here three nights and the congregations have been increasing every night. We will give the report of the meeting here later.

At Hollins we found the work in good condition for a revival. They had the church in a good spiritual condition and had four valuable confessions when I got into the harness. The interest continued to increase. The first night we had a number of confessions so that in one week we had seventeen more, making 21 confessions during the entire meeting.

Had it not been for the holidays we would have continued for several weeks more, but we all agreed that it was best to close the meeting and enter upon a greater campaign next fall if the Lord so wills.

The last night of the meeting several brethren came some 15 or 20 miles to see me and gave a special invitation to come and dedicate their new church in April and hold them a revival.

If I can properly adjust my future engagements I may do so. I found this church at Hollins in a splendid working condition, a small country church built in a wealthy neighborhood, in perfect unity and with one of the best men in the south as their pastor. He preaches twice every Sunday and runs a truck farm of five acres, besides doing some work for his neighbors. This church is near the home of Brother and Sister Ed. Nininger, also near the old Christ Nininger farm. He was a splendid man and a preacher in our church. Several of his children are prominent members of the church.

They have a small country church and the membership is not large, and while they do not. expect a very large ingathering at any one meeting because of the limitations of the field, yet they have already outgrown their house and expect to enlarge it and to equip it for a modern Sunday school and to accomodate a larger audience.

I expect a continual and solid growth until this little church will become one of the strongest in Southern Virginia.

Our dear Brother Wood was there one night and had expected to attend more frequently but on account of sickness was unable to do so.

I was Very glad to meet with my Brother J. S. Bowman, who has been a successful school teacher for more than 20 years and also has been a successful eVangelist and pastor. It seems to me he should give his time wholly to the ministry but he thinks otherwise. He was with me four days in the meeting. Surely there could be done a noble work in the Valey of Virginia and especially in this southern part of the state if one could put a few months of hard work as an evangelist in this field. The same is true of Kentucky. Surely the harVest is ripe but the laborers are few.

Pray for our work here at Fremont. From here I go to Buckeye City, Ohio.

ISAAC D. BOWMAN.

RITTMAN, OHIO

I went from Columbus to Ashland and had a Very enjoyable visit with Brother J. Allen Miller and family and also met other friends there. The next day, Sunday, Brother Miller and I went to Rittman. We opened fire and the crowds began to come almost from the beginning.

The first week I preached prophecy until the house was crowded to the door. We had to get extra chairs, then a number of extra benches, until more than a hundred extra seats were filled and several nights they did not accommodate the people.

When we left the preaching of prophecy and took up more directly eVangelistic sermons there was a temporary lull. But the crowds gradually began to increase till everything was crowded again. Then the bad roads and stormy weather hindered the country people. All in all we had great crowds for our people at Rittman.

Brother Miller nobly stood by the work although he could only be there over Sunday. We were somewhat handicapped because he was not with us and I did not know any of the people.

The field I found to be a Very peculiar one. SeVeral hundred preachers did not do the fair thing there; and hindered the work. But the splendid little bunch of Brethren under the leadership of dear Brother Miller largely bridged over the eVils of the bad preachers before I began the meeting.

There is a great mixture of faiths in the town. The salt works and paper mills haVe brought a great Variety of people to this place. Amish, Swiss, Mennonites, American Mennonites, "Coffee potters," "Come-outers," Catholics, Lutherans, Evangelicals, United Brethren, Presbyterians, Baptists, etc., etc. besides dunkards and Brethren.

I suppose the town has neVer been so stirred up before but there is not a church of any kind that practices immersion in the town. There is a general mixture of religions but only three church buildings in the town—Catholic, United Brethren and Presbyterian.

We had two great difficulties.to overcome in fact three. First, to get such a mixture to attend his church. In this we succeeded above the highest expectations of our little faithful band of workers. Second, to convince them of the doctrines of the Brethren church. Some never heard of trine immersion, feetwashing and the Lord's supper. In this we did not succeed as well as we would haVe liked. But we pounded away on doctrine as best we could and convinced some.

I am Very sure we could haVe done far better along this line had we a place to baptize and at each baptismal service would have driven the doctrine home. We had to take them over 30 miles to Ashland to have them baptized.

Third, as we only worshipped in a hall and there were two denominations that had good churches in the town, this also was a handicap. But in spite of it all we had what I think was a great meeting considering all the difficulties we had to encounter. SeVeral were opposed by parents. Others were written not to join our church and still others were visited as soon as they became under conViction and made to promise to join another church. But in spite of it all we had twenty-six confessions and will receiVe into membership more than half of them. Ten or twelve-were baptized already and one taken in from the Church of the Brethren and others will be baptized. No doubt dear Brother Miller will giVe a more accurate account of the additions.

They have bought a lot and haVe it paid for and will build a church soon. This will greatly relieVe their difficulties and will cause this mission point to become a strong Brethren church. There are a number of the Church of the Brethren who are heartily in sympathy with us. Also some who haVe joined the Presbyterians who required trine immersion. Some of these attended our church and would haVe joined had we had a church. Some of their children joined at this meeting, and once we get a building I believe we will become a strong church in the town. Brother J. Allen Miller, their pastor, is doing splendid work for them and they all loVe him and his careful Bible teaching is leading many of them in the way of all truth. Considering the field and the peculiarities we belieVe this is the best meeting we have held this year in popularizing the whole Gospel in a community.

I am writing this letter on the train bound for Virginia, where I will hold a short meeting up to, and perhaps including the holidays. Then I will go home for a few days and then return to Ohio for another compaign. I want to say in closing this article, we haVe a splendid little band of faithful Brethren here. The expenses of the meeting was considerably oVer $200. They feared the expenses somewhat, but the day the meeting closed Brother Miller said the public offerings has come within fifty dollars of coVering all expenses and he said in the morning serVice all who wanted to help to make that up could do so. And in a few minutes they had $116 promised besides the regular offering both morning and night. So they made all expenses and haVe some left in the treasury. The people fed me well, and I had my home at Brother Holmes, one of the finest places I eVer stopped. We stayed a little more than four weeks and the interest kept deepening to the Very last and while we stayed three days longer than we expected, I belieVe another week would haVe added quite a number more to the church.

ISAAC D. BOWMAN.

SIDNEY, INDIANA; BRETHREN CHURCH

It has been some time since the readers of this paper haVe had any news from Sidney. Nevertheless the work is still going on. It is much more inspiring now than it was last year about this time. SeVeral attempts were made to hold a reViVal, but each time the "flu" stepped in and said no. But it is not so this year. I think we are all glad the "flu" has kept as far in the distance as it has this year and hope it will remain just where it is.

We began our reViVal meeting the 30th of NoVember and continued for three weeks. This led us up to the Sunday before Christmas. We had one of the best meetings Sidney had had. There were 32 came by confession, letter and relation. There will also be a few that will come into the church through the influence of the meeting that did not come directly in the meeting. Twenty-two have already been received. Others are awaiting baptism. We haVe organized a Christian EndeaVor Society and a Junior Society both of which haVe been doing fine. These were organized the last week night of the meeting.

The meetings were held by the Richer eVangelistic party. These people made many friends in Sidney and will not be forgotten soon. They measured up to our expectation in eVery way. The music of the reViVal will mean much to the Sidney church. Brother Harry knows his business as an eVangelistic singer. The three weeks were of real enjoyment although much of the time we had zero weather and many people suffering with colds eVen to the evangelistic party themselves. Working with the Richers is just like working with our own people. They are congenial, reasonable and qualified to bring to a congregation powerful messages, enforced and driven to the heart by the inspiration of the special music of each service. May God bless the Richers in the work of saVing souls.

We closed the meeting with a communion service. It was the largest Sidney has had for several years. We observed Decision Day in the Sunday school during the meeting and the Sunday preceding our reViVal we held Rally and Promotion Day SerVice. It was a fine service and a large attendance was present. Sunday before Rally Day we observed Thanksgiving and took the ThanksgiVing offering. This did not measure up to what we had hoped for, but was good for the number of people present. The day was stormy and but a few people were present. The reViVal interfered with our White Gift offering but that will be received now soon. The work here has a general good outlook for the coming year.

We are now entering upon the new year's activities. But we are still breathing some of the Christmas atmosphere of the old year. Santa was unusually good this year. The College Corner folks remembered us with a general surprise of good things to eat and other tokens of gratitude. When we were ready to leaVe the old Maxwell found it had Very much of a load but even the car was cheerful under the responsibility of deliVering the surprise. We find these people a good-hearted appreciatiVe people. But Santa did not forget us at other places and came in eVery few days before and after Christmas. This all expresses the good will and friendship of those with whom we haVe worked and also those with whom we are now working. May God bless them all in the work of the Kingdom.

L. A. MYERS.

NORTH LIBERTY, INDIANA

We are glad to report the progress of the Lord's work in the Various places where we are laboring. Since the first of October the writer has been diViding his time with another congregation, hence we haVe serVices only on each alternate Lord's Day at North Liberty. I do not feel that we haVe taken a backward step either, but rather forward. I cannot see but that the general interest and attendance at all serVices is equally as good as when we were giVing all our time. EVery auxiliary of the church is working in its particular field. The Sunday school is doing splendidly under the leadership of Brother C. G. Wolf. The Christian EndeaVor is newly organized with Brother Clyde Sheneman as president. Brother Sheneman was with Uncle Sam's forces seVeral years and he knows how to lead Christian EndeaVor workers. The Woman's Missionary society was a banner society last year and will be again, with Mr. C. G. Wolf as president.

We were Very fortunate in haVing our good Brother G. W. Rench with us for two weeks in NoVember. The first week he brought a series of six sermon-lectures on "Our Lord's Return." I only wish that space would permit me to say what I would like to have the readers of the Evangelist know concerning them. I wish it were possible too for him to giVe them in eVery church in the brotherhood, because I know that if there is anything that will awaken our churches; that will cause people to clean up their liVes, and spur them to definite serVice for the Master, it is getting where their lives are gripped by this great truth and absorbed in it. Brother Rench's evangelistic messages were well received; sane, practical, and extremely loyal to the teachings of the Book. During these days of refreshing seven souls were added to the body of believers. It was a great pleasure to labor with Brother Rench who has been a spiritual father to me, for it was during his pastorate at the old home at Mexico that Mrs. Grisso and myself united with the church and it was at his hands that I was ordained to the gospel ministry.

I was privileged to preach in his church three times, and he is doing a great work. My prophecy is, South Bend will soon have to build larger or swarm.

Tiosa, Indiana

Tiosa is still on the map, though difficult to locate. But once found you will have found as loyal a bunch of Brethren as there is in the brotherhood. It was here that I began my ministry sixteen years ago, and was pastor for two years. Here I received my first confessions, baptized my first applicants, preached my first funeral, and performed my first marriage ceremony. So it is a real pleasure to me to come back and preach the gospel to these good people once more. Two weeks of evangelistic effort in December resulted in five persons taking their stand for Christ and the church. These all came the last day of the meeting. We should have continued, but weather conditions being unfavorable we hope to reap later from our sowing. At this writing we are at Center Chapel in the midst of a revival. Here I preached my first sermon, and held several revival meetings in years past. The field is well gleaned, but the Lord is going to give us some souls during these days, we are quite confident. Our young Brother K. R. Ronk is the new pastor, is liked by his people and is aiding us very materially in the campaign. We are having a crowded house at each service. May the blessings of our common Lord be upon us all, and keep us very diligent and faithful in his service until he comes.   C. C. GRISSO.

FROM HALLANDALE, FLORIDA

The Union church of Hallandale was a scene of unusual interest and attraction on Tuesday evening, December 30, when Brother Daniel Crofford and wife, both well known to the older members of our brotherhood, celebrated their golden wedding anniversary. Brother and Sister Crofford came to Hallandale nine years ago from Johnstown, Pennsylvania, leaving there a wide circle of friends and acquaintances, and have added to that another large circle of faithful and true friends.

For fifty years Brother and Sister Crofford have walked side by side, hand in hand, sharing life's joys and sorrows, life's sunshine and shadows, life's prosperities and adversities. His happiness was her happiness. His sorrows and sufferings were here also. In prosperity she enjoys with him his successes. If adversity comes, she stands by him just as faithfully, to share his reverses.

Their home, though commodious, was not large enough for the occasion, for all must enjoy their celebration, so the church was chosen instead. It was tastefully decorated in white and gold crepe paper ribbons with ferns and golden rod.

Promptly at 8:30 P. M., to the strains of the wedding march, the fifty-year bride and groom, preceded by Rev. Carl of the Swedish Lutheran church, and followed by their son Bashor, and daughter Minnie of Pittsburgh, and the bride's sister, Mrs. Myers with her husband, of Johnstown, Pennsylvania, marched up the aisle and passed beneath the arch and marriage bell to the seats prepared for them.

Rev. Carl read a short Scripture lesson from Proverbs, prayed the divine blessing on the happy pair, and then in a short talk paid a beautiful tribute to the lives of usefulness and faithfulness led by Brother and Sister Crofford.

A short musical program of solos and duets both vocal and instrumental, was rendered, and a reading given by Mrs. Barlow, an English lady said to be over eighty years of age. Calm and self-possessed, she recited with all the ease and grace of a young woman, after which Rev. Carl gave a substantial evidence of the respect and esteem in which the twice wedded pair are held, in the presentation of five ten dollar gold pieces from the Ladies' Aid and other friends. Many other useful and valuable gifts had already been received.

Congratulations were then in order, followed by refreshments, and Brother Crofford and wife returned to their home, followed by the good wishes of their friends, and the hope that they may live to enjoy many more happy wedding anniversaries in this life, and a glad reunion over there, where happiness is never marred by sorrow and sunshine never overcast with shadow.

LAURA E. N. HEDRICK.

GARWIN, IOWA

While there have not been any reports recently from here we have not been hibernating, even though the weather has been cold enough. As you will have noticed through Brother Beachler's report, he came on the job here but the weather, cornpicking, mud and some other things interfered, so he decided to come later when there would not be so many things to interfere. I certainly enjoyed my visit with him even though we could not do much toward endowment. You will hear more from here in due time. Our attendance all fall was good, but the weather broke up the roads the day we were to take our Home Mission offering and it became necessary to postpone it. We have taken an offering and will send it when some who were not in attendance have been given a chance to contribute. An offering was taken to apply to the lighting plant in Kentucky. A Christmas program was given that was pronounced by some to be the best given here. Even though there were a number of programs given by different churches we could not have accommodated any other persons without uncomfortable crowding. A community dinner was held in the basement of the church on New Years which was enjoyed by all and was well attended, even though a wedding near kept a number of our folks away who would otherwise have been there. Our attendance this winter has been splendid, especially when the weather permitted. As we are strictly rural we cannot always plan as it is possible in the city churches, and carry out those plans.

The work of the church is in good shape, and we are planning for the summer when we can work to the best advantage.

We would have reported sooner, but as the Editor was getting more material than he could print we thought we would help by not reporting so soon. We appreciate the Editor's advice in regard to making the reports short and more frequent. He could also have applied that advice to sermons to a good advantage. We are glad to read of the progress that is being made throughout the brotherhood, and likewise desire the thoughts of the Brethren in our work here.

FREEMAN ANKRUM.

SUNNYSIDE, WASHINGTON

In our last report, we mentioned our evangelistic campaign. It is now history. Brother A. V. Kimmell of Whittier, California, led us in this effort. His messages were strong, clear, instructive, interesting, uncompromising presentations of Bible truth. As a brother in Christ, he won his way into the hearts of the people at once. As a preacher, he won respect and audience immediately. From the very first service, the church rallied to his leadership. We have never witnessed more favorable interest, attendance, and prospects during the first week of any meeting in which we had a part. Then the mercury began to fall! It was "unusual." For twenty years it had never behaved thus here. It went down until it touched 30. Some of you false optimists who theorize and say, "Blaming the weather is only trying to prove an alibi," ought to get out and buck the rain, mud, wind, and cold a few times and get your feet on the earth again. Well, fuel became scarce and we were asked to close when we were just entering the second week. We refused to do so as long as the dance, theatre, and secret societies continued to meet. But the last 3 nights of the third week we voluntarily closed. Then we held two services on the last Sunday, the only church in town open. The results of the campaign in numbers was 13 confessions, of which 10 have become members. Since the meeting, one aged man has become a member also. Yes, we triumphed in him amid great difficulties.

Our "January the First" meeting was a big success. The largest attendance in its history was secured. The business was ably transacted. Among the numerous items we report two. The church took a firm stand against card playing, dancing, and theatre going. Mrs. Ira Alexander was elected as correspondent to the Evangelist. Hereafter she will report the church news.

C. H. ASHMAN.

RITTMAN, OHIO

One of the latest organized churches of the Ohio conference is that at Rittman, Wayne county. Rittman is a growing town on the Erie railroad numbering perhaps 2000 people. It has two very excellent manufacturing enterprises, namely, The Rittman Boxboard Company and the Salt and Chemical Works. These two concerns furnish splendid employment opportunities. The entire surrounding country is one of the finest Ohio Agricultural districts. I mention this to show the opportunity for the church. Our people have not made a spasmodic effort. All along it has been the quiet and steady work of faithful and determined men and women. I am glad to be able to say that the members of the Brethren church at Rittman belong to the church for conviction's sake. They are as fine a group as can be found anywhere. And I believe constitute the foundation of a strong church in the years to come.

According to pre-arranged plans Brother I. D. Bowman came to conduct an evangelistic meeting. He began on Sunday, November 16th, and continued until December 14th, making four full weeks. The services were held in a hall on the second floor of a business block. Almost from the first the people began to come and many times the hall was filled to the limit. This was especially true of the Sunday services.

The Brethren doctrines were new to very many of the people. But the plain teaching of the Word of God as given by Brother Bowman won the respect of all. It has been said that Rittman is difficult to arouse by the preaching of the Gospel. But Brother Bowman stirred the community. The results of the meeting were fine. The members of the church, and they certainly were faithful in attendance, were aroused to new efforts. The whole community received a spiritual uplift. There were twenty-five who made the great confession. Of this number sixteen have been baptized and one sister was received by relation. Thus the Brethren church is much strengthened. This gives us over fifty members. Each of the other churches in the town received members as the result of our meeting.

Brother Bowman won the esteem of the community. His preaching and teaching of the Word of God has made a strong appeal and we look for the fruit in the days to come. May God bless the dear Brethren who work in the evangelistic field. J. ALLEN MILLER.

Business Manager's Corner

THE AGE OF DELAY

We do not pretend to know whether or not we are nearing the end of the age or of the dispensation, but we do know that we are living in the great "age of delay." Trains are delayed on account of the great white blanket that is covering all the North Central States, and mails are delayed because trains are not running on schedule, and business is delayed because of the failure of the arrival of the mails, and factories are delayed because of their inability to secure material, and material is delayed because of the great unrest in the labor world. Thus altogether the whole world is delayed in its business and even the church seems to be delayed in carrying forward its programs.

It might be well for the entire world to make out a new schedule and then to make a sincere effort to live up to the schedule, for the old schedule has not been an entire success.

The Atlantic City Conference

When we wrote our last notes two weeks ago we announced that it was our intention to attend the Interchurch World Conference at Atlantic City and that after our return we would have something to say about the meeting. At that time it was not thought that any one from Ashland, except the writer, would be able to attend the conference, but it later developed that Brother Baer could also attend, so we have not tried to steal any of his thunder, but will let him exercise his editorial prerogative and speak for himself concerning the great meeting, for it was a great meeting. It was a meeting of the greatest men and leaders of the American churches, as well as a meeting of some of the European religious leaders.

While transacting a little business in one of the stores on the celebrated "board walk" the merchant said to the writer, "I have been in business here for a good many years and have seen a great many conventions in Atlantic City, but I said to one of my clerks this morning, "This is the finest bunch of men I have ever seen going up and down the board walk.'"

One could not help observing the type of men that constituted the body of the convention. They were brainy men, educated men and men of the deepest piety. They had not come to the conference to have a good time, nor to see or to be seen, but they had come on the "King's business," and they were busy about it. One could not sit in the crowded convention hall and sense the atmosphere of the place, and rub elbows and sit jammed together with such men as John D. Rockefeller, Jr. for a half day at a time without knowing that the whole movement is to be taken seriously. And we are in it. It makes no difference whether we want to be in it or not, the movement is so all-comprehensive that there is no escape. All America must feel the impact of the movement, and we are sure that the more heartily we enter into the movement along with the other co-operating churches the more we will get out of it.

The Evangelistic Campaign

We almost forgot that we are only the Business Manager of the Publishing House and had very nearly fallen back into our old editorial habits, but we hope you will forgive us for the slip. Yet we rather like to write things besides business once in awhile. But the business keeps us so busy we scarcely have the time.

Since our last report the largest church in the brotherhood has come in out of the cold and has won a plame on the Evangelist Honor Roll. This time it is Dayton, Ohio, the metropolis of the Miami Valley, the valley of the Business Manager's boyhood, that has won this distinction. Dayton has not yet placed the Evangelist on its annual budget, but its energetic Evangelist representative, Eld. Wm. C. Teeter, a familiar name, that, has by personal solicitation secured enough

subscriptions to win this place for his own beloved congregation, and we are quite sure his pastor, Eld. E. M. Cobb, rejoices over the victory.

Then we have received a number of renewals from churches that have now been on the Honor Roll from one to two years. Prof. E. G. Mason of West Salem writes, "Sure, our church will be on the Honor Roll for the third year, a revised list of names will be sent you shortly." Another brother from the far west writes, "Our church has voted to continue the Evangelist in its budget for the third year. It is the greatest scheme hit upon to date. Keep it up, and don't drop a single name from our list. Thus the First Brethren church of Los Angeles, California remains among the Honor churches of the brotherhood. Then Brother Lowman, pastor of the Fillmore, California Brethren church, not to be outdone by Brother Jennings' church of Los Angeles, writes, "The church has put the Evangelist on the budget for the second year, and I wish every church in the brotherhood could do it that way. I think the church paper is just as necessary for the church as a heating plant is." Thank you, Brother Lowman. If we had about two hundred pastors who would take that view of the matter our troubles would be largely a thing of the past. You see California is to the front this week; but still Indiana must be heard from once again. Brother Henderson of Clay City writes, "The Clay City church has included the Evangelist in its budget, and we expect it to be 100% list we send you for the third year." Let me shout it from the housetop, and if I could get to the highest peak of the Rocky Mountains I would shout it so that every Brethren church in America might hear, "it is the thing to do, so why not do it now." The victory is already ours, but we want to make it a "triumphant victory."

If I have missed any church that has renewed its list within the last two weeks I beg pardon, and will give it mention the next time I write, if my attention is called to the matter.

That Brethren Annual

The first section of the Annual and Conference Report is off the press now and we hope to get it finished shortly. Of course we have been slow, but we have been working our force to the limit for the last five months and it has been impossible to do more. Then too, the last of the copy for the Annual was received only last Saturday, so you see there have been other extenuating circumstances. The price of the Annual will be the same as in former years: single copies postpaid twenty-five cents; in half dozen lots or more at the rate of $2.50 per dozen.
R. R. TEETER,
Business Manager.

EVANGELIST HONOR ROLL

The following churches having met the requirements laid down by the Brethren Publishing Company regarding the placing of the Evangelist in the home of the congregations are entitled to a place on the Evangelist Honor Roll:

Church	Pastor
Akron, Ind., (New Highland),	.... (Vacant)
Allentown, Pa., 3rd Year,	.... A. L. DeLozier
Ankenytown, Ohio, 3rd Yr.,	.... A. L. Lynn
Ardmore, Indiana,	.... A. T. Wirick
Ashland, Ohio, 3rd Yr.,	.... J. A. Garber
Beaver City, Nebr., 2nd Yr.,	.... E. S. Flora
Berlin, Penna.,	.... I. B. Trout
Berne, Indiana, 3rd Year,	.. W. F. Johnson
Bryan, Ohio, 2nd Yr.,	...... G. L. Maus
Buckeye City, O.,	.... Glen Peterson
Burlington, Ind., 2nd Yr.,	.... W. T. Lytle
Carleton, Nebr., 2nd Yr.,	.... W. T. Lytle
Cerro Gordo, Ill.,	...... D. A. C. Teeter
Clay City, Indiana, (3rd Yr.), S. C. Henderson
College Corner, Ind., 2nd Yr., Homer Anderson
Conemaugh, Pa., 2nd Yr.,	.... L. G. Smith
Darwin, Indiana,	.... W. T. Lytle
Dallas Center, Iowa,	.... R. F. Porte
Dayton, Ohio,	.... E. M. Cobb
Denver, Indiana, 2nd Yr.,	...... L. A. Myers
Dutchtown, Indiana,	...... Homer Anderson
Elkhart, Ind., (2nd Yr.),	.. H. H. Wolford
Eaton, Ind., (Maple Grove),	.. H. E. Eppley
Eau Claire, Wisconsin,	.... J. A. Baker
Fair Haven, Ohio (3rd Yr.),	... B. F. Owen
Falls City, Neb., 2nd Yr.,	.. H. F. Stuckman
Fillmore, Calif. (2nd Yr),	. Sylvester Lowman
Flora, Ind., 2nd Yr.,	.... W. E. Thomas
Fostoria, Ohio (2nd Yr.),	.... M. S. White
Fremont, Ohio,	.... H. M. Oberholtzer
Goshen, Indiana,	.... J. A. McInturff
Gretna, Ohio, 3rd Yr.,	.... Edwin Boardman
Gratis, Ohio	.... C. E. Beckley
Hagerstown, Maryland	...... A. B. Cover
Hamlin, Kansas, 2nd Yr.,	.... Geo. E. Cone
Huntington, Indiana,	.... J. W. Brower
Johnstown, Pa., 1st Ch., 2nd Yr. J. F. Watson
Johnstown, Pa., 3rd Ch.,	...... Geo. H. Jones
Lanark, Ill., 2nd Yr.,	.... B. T. Burnworth
La Verne, Calif, 2nd Yr.,	.... T. H. Broad
Leon, Iowa,	.... Geo. T. Ronk
Leon, Iowa, (Crown Chapel),	.. Geo. T. Ronk
Leon, Iowa (Union Chapel),	.... G. T. Ronk
Linwood, Maryland, 2nd Yr.,	.. E. M. Riddle
Long Beach, Cal. (3rd Yr.)	.. L. S. Bauman
Loree, Indiana, 2nd Yr.,	.... C. A. Stewart
Los Angeles, Cal. 1st, (3 Yr), N. W. Jennings
Louisville, O., 2nd Yr.,	...... E. M. Riddle
Los Angeles, Cal., (Compton Ave), J. C. Beal
Masontown, Pennsylvania, .. Martin Shively
Meyersdale, Pa., 2nd Yr., .. E. D. Burnworth
Mexico, Indiana, 2nd Yr., ... L. W. Ditch
Milledgeville, Ill., 2nd Yr., ... M. J. Snyder
Morrill, Kansas, 2nd Yr., ... A. E. Whitted
Mt. View, Va., 2nd Yr., ... J. B. Patterson
Muncie, Indiana, 2nd Yr., ... J. L. Kimmel
Nappanee, Ind. (3rd Yr.) ..... E. L. Miller
New Enterprise, Pa., ... Edward Byers
New Lebanon, O., ... W. R. Deeter
New Paris, Ind., 2nd Yr., ... W. I. Duker
North English, Iowa, ... Homer Anderson
North Liberty, Indiana, ... C. C. Grisso
New Enterprise, Ind., ... P. M. Fisher
Oakville, Indiana, ... W. R. Deeter
Peru, Indiana, ... Geo. C. Carpenter
Philadelphia, Pa (1st Br.) .. Alva J. McClain
Philadelphia, Pa., 3rd church, .. I. E. Braker
Pittsburgh, Pa., ... H. M. Harley
Portis, Kansas, 2nd Yr., ... Roy Brumbaugh
Rittman, Ohio, ... J. Allen Miller
Roann, Indiana (2nd yr.),... Willis E. Ronk
Roanoke, Indiana .... W. F. Johnson
Sidney, Indiana, 2nd Yr., ... L. A. Myers
Summit Mills, Pa., 2nd Yr., E. D. Burnworth
Telford, Tenn., ... Mary. Pence
Tiosa, Indiana (2nd Yr.) .... C. C. Grisso
Turlock, California, ... J. Francis Reagan
Washington, C. H., O., 3rd Yr., B. S. Stoffer
Waterloo, Iowa, 2nd Yr., .. H. L. Goughnour
Whittier, Calif., ... A. V. Kimmel
White Chapel, Mo., ... G. T. Ronk
Windber, Pennsylvania, ... E. F. Byers
Yellow Creek, Pa., ... Edward Byers
Zion Hill, Ohio, ... A. L. Lynn

Volume XLII
Number 4

January 28
1920

The BRETHREN EVANGELIST

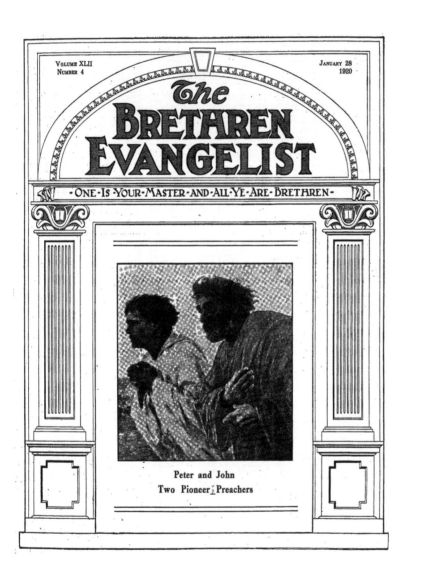

Peter and John
Two Pioneer Preachers

Published every Wednesday at Ashland, Ohio. All matter for publication must reach the Editor not later than Friday noon of the preceding week.

George S. Baer, Editor

The
Brethren
Evangelist

When ordering your paper changed give old as well as new address. Subscriptions discontinued at expiration. To avoid missing any numbers renew two weeks in advance.

R. R. Teeter, Business Manager

OFFICIAL ORGAN OF THE BRETHREN CHURCH

Subscription price, $2.00 per year, payable in advance.
Entered at the Post Office at Ashland, Ohio, as second-class matter.
Acceptance for mailing at special rate of postage provided for in section 1103, Act of October 3, 1917, authorized September 9, 1918.
Address all matter for publication to Geo. S. Baer, Editor of the Brethren Evangelist, and all business communications to R. R. Teeter, Business Manager, Brethren Publishing Company, Ashland, Ohio. Make all checks payable to the Brethren Publishing Company.

TABLE OF CONTENTS

EDITORIAL

The Men Whom the Church Delights to Honor

There are certain men who stand out above the rest in the mind of the church as deserving of honor. They are the men who blazed the way for the Brethren church as a separate and distinct denomination. They are the pioneer ministers of the church, the men who wended their way alone over the mountains, through the woods and across the prairies to preach the simple gospel of Jesus Christ without addition or subtraction and to build up little groups of worshipping saints in every community they might enter. They are the men who fathered the denomination, which stands not for the promotion of a new "ism" or creed, but for the restoration and propagation of the primitive gospel and the practices of the primitive church. They were noble men; God-fearing men, who opposed the requirements and prohibitions of men as much as they loved the laws of God. They were such men as God gives to be the pioneers of a great movement; men in whom certain challenging virtues stand out in bold relief.

These men were men of conviction. They believed strongly in the word of God and its sufficiency for man's salvation and growth in grace. They would allow nothing to be either added or subtracted from the Book of Life. It was their rule of faith and practice, and Christ the Head of the church was their great exemplar. What he taught by precept or example it was theirs to obey. They believed so strongly in this course that they would die rather than give it up.

They were men of courage. They would neither shrink before ridicule nor falter before bitter denunciations or condemnations. When a course was clearly right to them they would undertake it though excommunication would be their reward. Their courage consisted not of reckless daring or a hazarding without fear, but of a firm resoluteness in a just cause. Their sense of duty held them steady in the course they had chosen and would not permit them to turn back. Here conviction and courage went hand in hand. Conviction gave the reason and courage supplied the determination. When once they had taken their stand according to their conviction, they would "stand fast" and would not be moved. They might be persecuted for it, nevertheless they would "stand like a beaten anvil."

They were men in whose lives sacrifice was a large and essential part. Their very calling required it. No one ever pioneered a great cause, especially such as the purification and restoration of primitive Christianity, without experiencing sacrifice in a large way. And these pioneer preachers knew what sacrifice meant. They considered not the goods of this world as things to be prized, which many

might have had in generous portions, in order that they might preach the gospel and turn men from ignorance and sin unto light and salvation. They gave their time freely, not even claiming the hire concerning which the Scriptures says they were worthy, that the kingdom might be preached and the church might be established in needy places. Those who had possessions gave generously for the building of churches, the maintenance of the work and the saving of the church's only and bankrupt school. There were those who parted with their homes in those critical days for the sake of what seemed then to some to be a forlorn hope. I wonder if we know what sacrifice means in these days? Our College Endowment Campaign Secretary has been leading the church in the accomplishment of a great undertaking, the far-reaching effects of which cannot be estimated. But after all, when we consider the fact that no member has yet been found in the brotherhood to give more than $1,500 in spite of the unusual prosperity of our people, one can hardly escape the conclusion that we have simply been doling out our meager sums with the set purpose of avoiding sacrifice. These pioneer Brethren did not seek to avoid sacrifice; they made it cheerfully; it was the measure of their devotion.

They were lovers of freedom. They loved so much "the freedom wherewith Christ hath made us free" that they refused to be "entangled again in any yoke of bondage." To avoid it they would make any sacrifice. When the undivided Israel began to add mandatory decrees to mandatory decrees so that their liberty of conscience was taken away, they parted company with their comrades in Christ. Many friendships were broken, many lives were disappointed, and many futures were clouded because of the rent in the brotherhood brought about by the gospel to deprive men of their religious freedom. The gospel is the fundamental principle of the Brethren church. Recent conversation with some who went through that most unfortunate experience in the history of the Brethren fraternity have elicited this unanimous statement, namely, "The liberty for each individual to read and interpret the New Testament scriptures under the guidance of the Holy Spirit was the issue at stake." They loved the freedom which Christ gave. To have it they were willing to sacrifice all that an otherwise desirable fellowship would mean to them, for they knew that if Christ should make them free, they should be free indeed.

Though they were men of great conviction and courage and though they were strong enough to make any sacrifice and loved freedom passionately, yet they were men of charity and consideration. They had their differences as we today have ours, but they exercised charity one with another. They had not failed to receive instruction from the Apostle Paul who wrote to the Corinthians that however great their devotion and sacrifice might be, it was all for naught if they had not love. That great apostle himself was a strong and unflinching for the right as the rock ribbed hills about him when he wrote, but the granite of his nature was covered with flowers. He was stern in morality, Cromwellian in courage, but Christlke in tenderness and sympathy. The strongest are always the tenderest. And we see in the strongest of these pioneer men of the church a charity maturing with the growing strength of their trying years. Out of their trials they learned forbearance. And those who yet remain of thot noble band seem to possess to a larger degree than those of us who are yet in the strength of our years that love that beareth all things and that never faileth.

These men were not gods, but human beings, with our common weaknesses and possibilities, temptations and aspirations, but in the trials of their faith they found their strength in him whom all the powers of darkness were impotent to overcome. The testings of those pioneer days of the church made them strong and noble and the message of their peerless lives will not pass with the number of their years. Such are the men whom the church delights to honor.

EDITORIAL REVIEW

President Jacobs preached in the U. B. church of Ashland on Sunday, January 25.

Another installment of "College News" is to be found in this issue of the Evangelist. Read it and keep posted.

BENEVOLENCE OFFERING SUNDAY IS FEBRUARY 8, AND THE OFFERING IS TO BE SENT TO HERMAN E. ROSCOE, GOSHEN, INDIANA.

Brother and Sister R. F. Porte of the Dallas Center church entertained quite unexpectedly a large number of their parishioners during the Christmas season.

Brother B. T. Burnworth, of Lanark, Illinois, gives us an interesting account of his "Evangelistic Itineracy" in Pennsylvania. His efforts at both Masontown and Listie were very successful.

Brother I. D. Bowman writes concerning his evangelistic campaign in Columbus with Brother Christiansen and feels well pleased with the results there, in spite of the difficulties.

From La Verne, California, comes a most interesting report written by the church correspondent, Sister H. L. Good. It would be difficult to find a more live missionary, church than this one.

Brother Kinzie speaks of the pleasant relations existing between him and the Clay City, Indiana, church which he recently left and also of the beginning of his work at West Alexandria and New Lebanon, Ohio.

Brother Thomas F. Howell reports his work at Highland, Pennsylvania, and tells of the splendid service rendered by Brother B. F. Owen, as evangelist. Brother Howell states that he has accepted a a call to the pastorate of the church at McLouth, Kansas.

It gives us pleasure to be able to present the first letter from Brother Clarence L. Sickel, who with his wife recently arrived and are now at work in our Argentine mission under the direction of Brother Yoder. We note there was great rejoicing at their arrival.

Very gracefully Brother Paul Miller, pastor of the Spokane church, expresses his appreciation of the encouragement and supoprt received from the brotherhood in the work of establishing the church at that place. Brother Miller states that he is leaving there in the spring.

Brother Beachler reports concerning the Homerville and Salem churches this week in the endowment campaign. Neither are strong churches numerically or financially, but both are loyal to the interests of our only educational institution. Any church that might have the privilege of contributing the president to the college would be expected to be loyal to its interests, and Homerville has certainly proven her loyalty. Her enthusiastic pastor, Brother Fred Vanator,

would hardly be pastor of any church very long without it becoming vitally interested in the college if it had not been before, and he has doubtless lent his influence to make the campaign a success at that place. Salem is shepherded by Brother James Cook, and no one would doubt his loyalty and deep interest in Ashland College. He and his courageous people have done nobly for the college, considering what they have before them locally.

Dr. Tombaugh's booklet on "Some Fundamental Christian Doctrines is being mailed to those who have ordered it. It sells for 20 cents in dozen lots or 25 cents per single copy by mail. Order now. The other booklet on "The Church and Some of Its Fundamental Principles of Work and Worship" by various representative men of the church is not yet ready for mailing.

Brother G. W. Kinzie reports a most stubborn fight in an evangelist campaign at Mulberry Grove, Illinois, which proved to be more of a seed-sowing than of a reaping; but the harvest will come. Besides he dscovered some prospective preachers of whom we hope to hear more later.

Brother Shively makes a most creditable report of his work at Masontown, Pennsylvania. He is backed by a loyal church and they are building steady and strong for the Master in that part of the vineyard. Along with their other giving at Christmas time, these good people did not forget their pastor.

You will be interested in the report of Brother and Sister Teall who recently left Elkhart to assist in the work in Kentucky. As in the case with every one who makes the trip for the first time, they were greatly impressed with their journey and the work they found accomplished at Lost Creek.

In the issue of January 14, the editor made the suggestion that it would be a fine thing if the Brethren Sunday School Association could be represented at the World's Sunday School Convention at Tokyo, Japan, in October, 1920, and asked for comment on the suggestion if any thought it feasible. In reply we received the following telegram: Waterloo, Iowa, Jan. 22, 1920.

"Geo. S. Baer, Editor Brethren Evangelist,
Ashland, Ohio.

"The Brethren church at large should be represented at Tokyo convention next fall. Announce that First Brethren Sunday School of Waterloo, Iowa, will present detailed resolutions next week.

"First Brethren Sunday School."

One of our loyal boosters of The Brethren Evangelist is Brother W. F. Johnson, pastor of the Berne-Roanoke, Indiana, charge. He tells of the progress of the Lord's work in his part of the Vineyard and also lets us know what he thinks of The Evangelist. He considers it a great aid in his work and suggests that if other churches are "handicapped," they should "budget and get the Evangelist." We believe he is exactly right on the method. A church paper is indispensable to every wide-awake congregation, and our experience is that the easiest and surest way of keping The Evangelist in every home, is to put it on the budget of your church just as you put your Sunday school literature on your Sunday school budget. Brother Johnson has done a fine work at Berne in the twelve years of his pastorate there, but he thinks he should give place to some one else and says he is open to a call to some other country pastorate.

Sister Reynolds, our correspondent for the Lathrop, California, church, reports that they are without a pastor at present. She also mentions again the needy condition of Sister Hannah Beer, the widow of Brother J. W. Beer, one of our pioneer preachers who has gone on before. The wives of our pioneer preachers had share and share alike in the trials and sacrifices of the early days and no sister should be allowed to suffer any more than any brother. And when there is a need on the part of these fathers and mothers in Israel it ought to be met immediately by grateful hearts throughout the brotherhood. We would suggest however that inasmuch as we have men elected by General Conference to administer the offerings of the church to such as these that they be used in this case instead of burdening another man who is already heavily loaded with foreign mission interests in additon to his pastoral duties. Brother Herman E. Roscoe, of Goshen, Indiana, is the secretary of the Board of Benevolences and if any one wishes to send a special offering in response to Sister Reynold's appeal, we suggest that it be sent to him and he will see that it is properly administered according to the instructions of the givers.

GENERAL ARTICLES
An Open Letter to Pastors On Life Work Recruiting

Dear Pastors:

Did the great Shepherd were to appear and ask: What is the supreme aim of your ministry, how would we answer the work-searching question? "To seek and save the lost!" Verily, but those words for only a partial answer if we are following the program of the First Minister. Did he not say to those whom he found and saved, "Come ye after me, and I will make you fishers of men?" Seeking, saving and recruiting represent the suggestive trinity of his ministry. Thus he became

A Discoverer of Workers

In doing so Jesus gave full proof of his leadership. A great leader understands that the work does not terminate with him nor his tenure of office. He deeply appreciates the necessity and advantage of discovering, enlisting and training successors. These are frequently associated with him in an apprenticeship. Through such a succession of trained, experienced workers the work is safe-guarded and perpetuated. Is it not incumbent upon pastoral leaders to show a like jealous concern for the well-being of the church and a similar acumen in providing for its continuance and enlargement?

Prospective Recruits Await Competent Guides

Within the church may be found certain gifted young men and women, possessing Christian character, of promising personality and leadership ability, who have not discovered themselves nor the life work for which they are fitted by natural endowments. These splendid persons withhold self-committal, while waiting the counsel of a wise interpreter and the encouragement of an experienced guide. Once the need of and opportunity for unselfish service is made perfectly clear to them they will enter confidently and enthusiastically upon the daring adventure. Who is better fitted, by position and training, to interpret the manifold needs and encourage response thereto than the pastor is the official spokesman for every department of church activity?

A Month of Special Opportunity

He may become the church's recruiting officer during February. It has been marked Stewardship Month, culminating with Life Enlistment Day on the 29th. Every Sunday and mid-week service should carry varied but definite life work appeals. These should be accompanied with prevailing intercessory prayer and followed up with personal conferences. Suggestive literature may be placed in the hands of interested persons. We recommend the following leaflets or booklets:

1. How Can Pastors and Other Leaders Help Young People Find Their Life Work?
2. How to Find Your Life Work.—White.
3. Important Personal Purposes for Young Men and Women.—White.
4. The Path into the Will of God.—Poteat.
5. Stewardship of Family Life.—Poteat.
6. Religion in the Home.—Moore.
7. The Problem of Guidance—Gordon.
8. How to Know the Will of God.—Drummond.
9. The Fulfillment of Life.—Morgan.
10. The Present Task of the Ministry.—Woodrow Wilson.
11. The Claims and Opportunities of the Ministry.—Mott and Others.
12. Life Work Library (Four Fine Little Volumes)—Westminster Press, $2.00.

The other publications may be secured as follows: Numbers 1-3, 1 cent each or $1.00 per hundred; 4-5, 2 cents each, 20 cents per dozen, $1.50 per hundred; 6-9, five cents each, 50 cents per dozen, $2.75 per hundred—all sold by the Interchurch World Movement, 111 Fifth Avenue, New York. Numbers 10-11 may be obtained from the Association Press at 5 and 50 cents per copy, respectively.

We earnestly urge fellow pastors to avail themselves of the opportunity to secure these valuable helps. Presumptuous as it may seem, we would further suggest the wisdom of preaching on these sermon themes:

"The Home, The Seed Plot of Life Work Recruits."
"The Surrendered Life."
"How One May Discover the Will of God for His Life."
"The Claims and Opportunities of the Christian Ministry."
"What Constitutes a Call to Missionary Service."
"Making Every Avocation a Vocation unto God."

Your attention, brethren, is respectfully called to the series of articles appearing in both the Evangelist and Angelus. They will furnish sermonic material. Encourage your young people to read the personal testimonies from recruits. Co-operate with them in the rendition of their program on the 8th and 29th. Command your director of Goal 6, if he can serve you.

Yours Recruiting for Christ,
J. A. GARBER.

The Church's Solemn Tryst
By George S. Baer
Written in honor of our pioneer preachers

They are not many,—those who yet remain
  Of all who stood courageous in the day
When persecution caused stout hearts to wain
  And clash of truth and error caused dismay.

They are not many, yet with tender heart
  We speak their names and count their vict'ries o'er,
And ever till a Voice calls them apart,
  Our love and care shall be their common store.

Their steps are falt'ring; their faces set to sea,
  Yet stand they fast in that for which they fought—
"The freedom wherewith Christ hath made us free—"
  And will not yield that cherished boon for aught.

Soon they'll be gone; their voice of counsel past,
  Yet memory will their noble lives enshrine,
Their loyal sons will hold that freedom fast
  And with their faith cling to the Book divine.

The reformation of the sixteenth century really began a hundred years earlier with the teaching of John Huss, a Bohemian. Today the children of our Bohemian emigrants are taking the highest rank and honors in our public schools in America.

Do you remember James A. Garfield and the incident that happened in New York City just after the assassination of President Lincoln, and a mob started to tear down the office of the New Work World and perhaps precipitate a riot which no man could quell. Garfield rose up before the mob and stood with uplifted hand and said, "God lives and the government at Washington is safe." The mob slunk away. God reigns still and the government of the universe is safe in his hands. So let us quiet our fears.

Ministers in Attendance at the Brethren Convention, Dayton, Ohio, June 7, 8, 1883

Reading from left to right, front row,—A. J. Hixson, H. R. Holsinger, E. S. Miller, Samuel Kiehl. Second Row,—J. P. Martin, George Neff, J. A. Ridenour, R. Z. Replogle, H. S. Jacobs, F. W. Fitzgerald, J. R. Wampler. Third Row—W. L. Spanogle, Edward Mason, J. H. Worst, S. H. Bashor, P. J. Brown, A. A. Cober, T. E. Davis, J. C. Cripe. Back Row,—Wm. Kiefer, J. H. Swihart, W. J. H. Bauman, E. L. Yoder, J. W. Beer, Stephen Hildebrand, D. S. Cripe.

Experiences of the Early Ministry of the Brethren Church.   By J. H. Swihart

(Brother Swihart whose picture appears in the above group is greatly afflicted, yet his interest in the church is still so vital that he has promised a series of articles on the establishment of Brethren churches in Indiana—Editor.)

Having been requested to contribute an article for publication in the Evangelist on the subject as indicated above, I will endeavor to comply in a brief way.

What have been the experiences of other early ministers of the church I can only know as they have been related to me by brethren with whom I had become intimately acquainted. I am alluding to the western brethren, who were denounced by an Annual Meeting committee for no other reason than that they stood firmly to the all sufficiency of the gospel of Christ, as their "'rule of faith and practice." These brethren must be considered as "Early ministers of the Brethren church," for they held in prospect what they realized in fact a few years later—the church fully reconstructed on its original principles. These brethren underwent many trials and faced many difficulties in their efforts and resolutions to obey God rather than man.

Some Personal Experiences

As stated in some former articles, I spent the first years of my ministerial efforts in the west and the work was principally of an Evangelistic character. And in a large thinly populated territory, we had occasion to face many difficulties and privations and experiences. We went from place to place, sometimes on foot; through rain and snow and mud and occasionally had baptism to administer when rain was falling or snow was flying and the water ice cold. I remember baptizing six men and one woman in a rapid running stream when the thermometer indicated 22 below zero. On another occasion when twenty were ready to be baptized no water was available; streams were solidly frozen to the bottom, but providence provided a way for the work to be done on time. The weather began to moderate and snow

melted and furnished water in abundance by next day, running rapidly over the top of the ice in the streams and there in the presence of a thousand or more lookers-on, I stood on top of solid ice and baptized eleven in fresh snow water just formed from the drifts. By that time my hands had become quite numb and I stepped out and went to a fire and a good brother devoid of prejudice and superstition stepped in and baptized the remaining nine. All the converts were wrapped up and taken to the fire, and when the work was finished and all made comfortable we went on our way rejoicing. Such experiences as these would evidently seem real hardships, but standing on the promise of God the yoke is made easy and the burden light.

It is a real pleasure to be and work with brethren who are satisfied with the teaching of Christ and the apostles. But on the other hand, when one comes in contact with chronic grumblers who are never satisfied with anything, he becomes convinced that the Simons and the Ananiases and the coppersmiths are not all dead yet, but are very busy about their Father's business (John 8:44) and although they may appear very friendly to one's face, they may at the same time be forming plots or casting stumbling blocks in the way of others. Should any have doubts about this matter, let them try pioneer work a while.

While yet in the west I had many other experiences of which I cannot now speak in particular. For instance I was sent to district conference thrice as delegate and a participant in the deliberations called "Contest," which finally resulted in a solid union between the two elements—the Western and the Annual Meeting, the latter making the necessary concessions. Then too, responding to a call from Michigan we held a meeting which seemed to give satisfaction to most people except the Adventists who like Daniel's bear raised up on one side and showed fight. They kept up their growling until a year later when I was called back to hold another revival and if need be settle the trouble with the Adventists. On arrival, I was told that three of their elders had come already to attend the meeting, then to have a debate. Although we began the protracted effort, the excitement ran so high in view of the expectation of hearing the discussion that it was considered useless to continue the services, and maybe I got terrified. I accepted the challenge and had an old brother, Elder Lochs, who was a brother-in-law of Henry Kurtz from whom Brother Holsinger learned the printing trade, to be my moderator. The antagonizing party chose Elder Carter of the Adventists and the two chose a third man whose name I can not now recall. Having thus organized, we went into the squabble in earnest. The third evening our opponent proposed an armistice which was accepted, feeling confident that we already had the victory, which also appeared to be the verdict of the Brethren (G. B.) church, the elder included, as well as to many outsiders and the three whom I baptized at the close of the contest. Later I received a letter from a brother who referred to the battle, saying, "I heard every word of it; and I want to tell you that it stirred the greatest excitement that the old Black River church ever witnessed. Many have been baptized and received into the church since." So we thanked the Lord for the power of the Gospel and took courage.

Mulberry, Indiana.

Report of Treasurer of Board of Benevolence. By J. L. Kimmel

There are now twelve beneficiaries on the superannuated list. The following is a brief biographical sketch of these persons:

Mrs. P. J. Brown

was born in Green county, Ohio, November 27th, 1855. Her maiden name was Mary J. Duncan. At the age of 20 years, she was baptized and received into the Beaver Creek congregation of the Church of the Brethren. When the division came she took her stand with the Progressives and united with the Brethren church. She was united in marriage with Elder P. J. Brown of Congress, Ohio, August 7th, 1890. Bishop Brown was one of the leading factors in the Progressive movement and the establishing of the Brethren church. Sister Brown holds her membership in the Fair Haven congregation, close to Congress, Ohio, where she lives.

Mrs. Hannah Elizabeth Beer

was born near Kittanning, Pennsylvania, February 23rd, 1839. Her parents were members of the Episcopal church, and she was christened when an infant. When about 20 years of age, she united with the Church of the Brethren. She married J. W. Beer who became one of the leading preachers and writers of the Dunkard church. He was associated with H. P. Holsinger in publishing the "Progressive Christian" at Berlin, Pennsylvania and was the author of a work entitled, The Passover and Lord's Supper.

Sister Beer's maiden name was Henegan. Her mother died when she was a mere child. She and Brother Beer spent much of their married life in Pennsylvania. On account of the failing health of her husband, they moved to Lathrop, California, where the husband died and Sister Beer was left a widow, and where she still lives.

Elder J. E. Shope

was ordained to the ministry by Stephen Hildebrand and J. B. Wampler.

Brother Shope preached at Jones' Mills, Pennsylvania, for three years; at Mt. Pleasant, Pennsylvania, for four years; at McVeytown, Yellow Creek and at various churches in Bedford, and Somerset counties.

He held the Listie, Pennsylvania, charge for four years. He is now 72 years old and lives at Altoona, Pennsylvania.

Elder Samuel Kiehl

was born in Lancaster county, Pennsylvania, July 23, 1837. He was converted in 1858, while attending school at Otterbein University, Westerville, Ohio, and was received into the German Baptist Brethren church, 1868, by baptism.

He was ordained as a minister in 1882, in Dayton, Ohio, by H. R. Holsinger. He served the Dayton church as pastor for over nine years. Brother Kiehl preached as a supply for many years, and the writer who was his pastor, for three years, can testify to his devotion and to his zeal for the Master's cause. He lives at Dayton, Ohio and is 82 years old.

Elder J. H. Swihart

was born in Hancock county, Ohio, December 15th, 1840. When but a mere boy, his parents moved to Indiana, and settled where the town of Roann is now located. His educational opportunities were poor, but he studied at night and thus improved his time and gained much valuable information.

In 1861 he was united in marriage to Mary Shilliger. The same year they united with the Dunkard church. He was called to the ministry in 1866. In 1872 he was ordained to the eldership, and afterwards spent much time in the evangelistic field and organized twelve churches in Indiana alone.

When the organization of the Brethren church took place in Dayton, Ohio, in 1883, P. J. Brown and J. H. Swihart were appointed National Evangelists to reconstruct churches needing especial care and oversight. Brother Swihart lives at Mulberry, Indiana, and is now 80 years of age, and in failing health.

Elder Christian Forney

was born in Somerset county, Pennsylvania, October 10th, 1838. When he was about twenty years of age, he united with the German Baptist church, in Ogle county, Illinois. September 11th, 1860, he was united in matrimony with Sabina Meyers. He was ordained to the ministry in 1870. He preached about fourteen years before the division of the church took place. Brother Forney was instrumental in organizing Beaver City church, and served as pastor for nine years. He had charge of St. Joseph Mission, for three years, and preached for the Aurelia church for four years. Brother Forney has been a faithful servant of the Master. He lives at Beaver City, Nebraska and is 82 years old.

Elder Samuel W. Wilt

was born July 20th, 1843, was baptized in 1857 by Elder Joseph Shoemaker in Armstrong county, Pennsylvania. In 1843 he was Selected deacon. He was elected to the ministry in 1874, and in 1875 advanced to the second degree. In 1876 he was ordained as elder. Brother Wilt lives at Juniata, Pennsylvania and is 77 years old.

Elder Daniel A. Hopkins

was born in Franklin county, Virginia, January 19th, 1846. He was married to Josephine Booth, October 12th, 1865. They united with the German Baptist church, August 13th, 1866 and soon after moved to Cass county, Indiana. He was a member of the German Baptist church for twenty-three years. August 13th, 1889, he united with the Brethren church and was ordained elder in 1890. By his devotion and able ministry the Brethren churches in Indiana were greatly built up. His consecration and faithful life will be honored and revered for many years to come. He lives at Twelve Mile, Indiana and is 74 years old.

Elder W. J. H. Bauman

was born in Northampton county, Pennsylvania, December 24th, 1837. His father was born in Germany and was educated for the Catholic priesthood, but preferring the medical profession he became a physician. He married Miss

Aurelia Leckington, July. 8th, 1860. He united with the German Baptist church and on April 7th, 1860, he was called to- the ministry. He became a member of the Brethren church at the time of the division, and was the only trans- Missouri delegate at the convention, held at Dayton, Ohio, in 1883. Brother Bauman lives at Long'Beach, California,' and is now 83 years old.

Elder A. J. Hixson

has been one of the prominent ministers in the Brethren church as well as in the German Baptist church. He became identified with the Brethren church at the time of the divi- sion. But on account of not having any data at hand we can not give a complete biographical sketch of his life. He lives at La Verne, California and is 83 years old.

Elder Stephen Hildebrand

was also one of the prominent factors in the Progressive movement. He served the Master faithfully as a minister in the German Baptist church for many years, before the Brethren church was organized. When the Brethren church

was established, Brother Hildebrand became one of its fore- most ministers and supporters. The National Conference of the Brethren church at Winona Lake in 1919, sent greet- ings to this good man on the anniversary of his birthday. He lives at Johnstown, Pennsylvania, and has been an in- valid for some years.

Elder Isaac Ross

lives in Los Angeles, California. He was also a minister for many years, in the German Baptist church, as it was then known. When the Brethren church was organized he cast his lot with the Progressive movement, and largely through his influence the Buckeye City Brethren church was organ- ized, of which he was pastor for many years. He was also pastor of the Brethren church at Middlebranch, Ohio; Wash- ington Court House, Ohio, and Lordsburg, California. Dr. Ross, as he is now familiarly called, deserves the hearty sup- port of his church in his old age, as well as all the brethren and sisters named in this brief sketch.

Muncie, Indiana.

Our Pioneer Ministers and What They Did to Make the Brethren Church What It Is

By Martin Shively

(Brother Shively was Secretary-Treasurer of the Ministerial Association for a number of years and has an intimate knowledge of the older min- isters and we gladly accept his offer to continue the story of the contribution of the pioneer ministers to the Brethren Church.—Editor.)

While it was my privilege to know personally, practic- ally every man who served as a leader in the Brethren church of thirty and more years ago, any mention of pioneer preachers among us calls from the treasures of my memory those whom I knew most intimately. First among these stands the name of our venerable Brother Hixson, because he was the first Brethren preacher whom I learned to know. I was but a boy and a preacher of rare power, living near Parsons, Kansas and not far from my own boyhood home. He was then in middle life, with a splendid family of young folks, who were all in the parental home, except Frank, who was then president of Ashland College. Often did I enjoy the hospitality of that home, and in it I witnessed the first communion service of the re-organized Brethren church. He was a preacher of unusual power, who might have risen to any height in the councils of the mother church, if he had been willing to deny the rights of conscience to determine his course in the trying days of 81-83. Loyal to his con- victions he lived, and still lives, waiting the call to join·his dear ones and his Lord. La Verne, California, is his home while he waits.

On my return to my native state, Indiana, in 1884, I came under the influence of another of the giants of those days. Brother J. H. Swihart was then living at Edna Mills, preaching there at monthly intervals, and at a number of other places, being at the task almost constantly and with great success. So far as my knowledge of preachers reached in those days, he had few equals and no superiors in the presentation of the gospel which he so dearly loved. He was in almost constant demand and did his best to answer every call, serving at a pittance so small, that the wonder is that he survived at all, and has brought with him into his old age a spirit as sweet and uncomplaining as any saint of old. The reader may get some idea of the blessing upon his min- istry, when I say that for a year or even longer, his month- ly appointments at Edna Mills, were always attended with conversions and baptisms. On June 25, 1885, five young men responded to the invitation there and were baptized in Mid- dle Fork at the close of the service. The writer was one of those, and at a meeting held in that congregation during the month of November following, I was ordained to the office of deacon with instruction to preach the gospel. My pastor officiated at this service and three years later he also or- dained me to the eldership at West Independence, Ohio,

where I was then pastor, with Brother Swihart leading in most successful evangelistic service. When I tell you that his ministry has been blessed to the conversion of nearly, if not quite, 5,000 souls, you will know that my estimate of him is not too high. He deserves to spend his remaining days as an honored guest of the Brethren church which he has so faithfully and so successfully served. I have prayed and still continue to pray, that my old age may be as saintly as his. With a frame long weakened by an unconquerable dropsical condition, the inheritance of the Swiharts, he works and waits awaiting for the call from labor to reward. Nothing is too good for such as he. I am of those who do not believe in saving all the flowers for the dead, and I am glad to pay this tribute to my old time friend and pastor while he lives.

Brother Holsinger came into my life in 1884, as I met him at Edna Mills, during his campaign for the liquidation of the debt on the college, I think. I met him frequently thereafter at the various conferences of the church and we became well acquainted, but our intimacy began when he came to Lathrop, California, during my pastorate there, to write the History of the Brethren and. Tunkers. I shall never forget the picture I saw almost every day, as I visited the office in which he worked, Brother Holsinger sitting on one side of his desk, whispering his message to Brother J. W. Beer, who sat on the other side, writing faithfully what he heard. Earlier in life, these two men had worked to- gether in an editorial sanctum, and now, together they wrought out about the last work either was able to give to the world and to the church. Few can realize the difficulty overcome in the preparation of that manuscript. For days at a time the work had to be suspended because the author was completely exhausted. He had done big things before but this was the masterpiece of his great mind. He never recovered from the disappointment incident to the failure in marketing the book as he had expected. A man of deep seriousness and large mental resources was this early leader of the Brethren hosts. Once I saw a side to this man which greatly surprised me. During a district conference held at Turlock, California, when his voice was all but gone, his whispers produced such storms of laughter and applause, that "Mam," as he called his wife, said to him, "Pop, I was ashamed of you." Such witticisms as found expression at his lips that day, as he stood leaning on his cane for sup- port, presented indeed a new side to this big man and deepened the love in which he was held by all. Yes, I knew him well, and as I stood by his grave in the beautiful cemetery at Berlin, Pennsylvania, a few years ago, I thought of what he had struggled and suffered for and what victories have come out of it all. The very things which he so ardently championed and for which he suffered ostracism in the mother church, are a very part of the warp and woof of its life now. If only it might have come without the painful and useless division which has rent the church asunder, how much better it would have been. He was a disappointed old man when his Master called him, but he did not live in vain, even if the victories came some other way than as he had hoped and planned. With a body so enfeebled, it is indeed a great wonder that he accomplished so much.

The space allotted to this paper, forbids that I should go farther in my reminiscences with these servants of God though my heart is full and would fain go on for Bashor, Brown, Kilhefner, Ridenour, Wampler, Nicholson, Knepper, Beer, Leedy and Forney, and still others rise up before me —some having gone home, while a few wait for their call. If the editor will permit, it will be a real pleasure to write of them, as I knew them, at an early date.

But what was it in these men which made its contribution to the present church? First, let us disabuse our minds of any inclination to place them on a plane entirely above their fellows. They were men of like passions as we, and men too, who were not always in agreement upon every question of polity, though there was practically no difference between them on questions of doctrine. They were men of such convictions as made them dare the pains incident to disruption of the associations which had long been a very vital part of their being. And they were men, too, who put their all upon the altar of service to God and to the church, serving for such a pittance that one cannot but wonder how they lived at all. They made their mistakes too, but they were errors of hear and not of heart, for in this they rang true and have left a heritage which above reproach. The church owes much to them for it was their self-effacing service which has made it possible for our splendid body of younger men, who succeed them, to serve as efficiently as they do. Thus, though their tongues are silent, like righteous Abel, being dead, they yet speak. And in the years to come whatever success may crown the efforts of the Brethren church, their own contribution to it, shall not be small.

Masontown, Pennsylvania.

Two Classes. By Samuel Kiehl

(One of the pioneer ministers; his picture is found in the group on page 5)

To be an active member of an orthodox, Christian church is a great privilege for social and spiritual development; but to have the indwelling Spirit of God, received by a living faith in the Lord Jesus Christ as the Son of God and our personal Savior and Lord, is an absolutely indispensable, imperative necessity for entrance into the kingdom of God (John 3:3,'-7).

There may be two classes in any local church; those who have, and those who have not, the Spirit of God dwelling in them. Those in the first class were by nature children of wrath, even as others (Eph. 2:3); but they repented and believed the gospel (Mark 1:15,), were baptized, shall be saved (Mark 16:16), were begotten of God with the word of truth (James 1:18), were born again (John 3:3-8), are children of God (Rom. 8:16), are in the Spirit, (the Spirit of God dwelling in them—Rom. 8:9), are spiritual men and women (Gal. 6:1), are heirs of God (Rom. 8:17), "and joint heirs with Christ; if so be that they suffer with him." Suffering with Christ is the antecedent; being joint heir with him, the consequent; when there is no antecedent there is no consequent.

We are saved by grace (Eph. 2:5); but joint heirship is not received that way according to the "Word" (Rom. 8:1). To him that overcometh will I grant to sit with me on my throne says Jesus (Rev. 3:21). To tell a believer when he receives Christ as his Savior and Lord, that he is now a joint heir with him is not telling him the whole gospel truth as given in Romans 8:17. It is not what a man says he is, or will be, that determines his joint heirship but what he endures and suffers for Christ's sake. For unto you it is given in the behalf of Christ, not only to believe on him but also to suffer for his sake (Phil. 1:29). If we suffer we shall also reign with him (Tim. 2:12). Let us compare our suffering (if we ever had any for Christ's sake), with Paul's (2 Cor. 11:23-27) and others (Heb. 11:36, 37) and then decide, as in the presence of God, what claim we (who have had no such experience and are living in apparent ease and luxury) can have for joint heirship. "God is love; and works all things after the counsel of his own will." Let us honor his word by cheerfully submitting to his will.

The believer who takes God at his word is resigned to his will, and when crossing the "Jordan" confidingly says, Father, into thy hands I commend my spirit (Luke 24:46). Yea ,though I walk through the valley of the shadow of death, I will fear no evil; for thou are with me, thy rod and thy staff they comfort me (Psa. 23:4). I shall be satisfied when I awake with thy likeness Psa. 17:5). In thy presence is fulness of joy (Psa. 16:11).

Those in the second class are said to be in the flesh, are natural men (1 Cor. 2:14), and according to the "Word" their mind is not subject to the law of God, neither indeed can be, consequently they can not please him (Rom. 8:7, 8).

Those spiritual men and women whose mind is controlled by the spirit of God dwelling in them, take great delight in always doing those things that please the Father, as Jesus did (John 8:29). To such he says, I will come again, and receive you unto myself; that where I am, there ye may be also (John 14:3). To those who are in the church and are lovers of pleasure more than lovers of God; having a form of godliness but denying the power thereof (2 Tim. 3: 4, 5) he says, This people draweth nigh unto me with their mouth, and honoreth me with their lips, but their heart is far from me (Matt. 15:8), and because you are lukewarm, and neither cold (dead unto sin) or hot (alive unto God), I will spew you out of my mouth (Rev. 3:16).

Death and the resurrection await both classes. It is written, Many of them that sleep in the dust of the earth shall awake, some to everlasting life and some to shame and everlasting contempt. They that be wise shall shine as the brightness of the firmament; and they that turn many to righteousness as the stars forever and ever (Dan. 12:2, 3).

Dear Reader: To which class do you and I belong? Let us examine ourselves, whether we be in the faith (2 Cor. 13: 5). Not he that commendeth himself is approved, but whom the Lord commendeth (2 Cor. 10:15). And what does the Lord require of us, but to do justly, to love mercy, and to walk humbly with our Lord (Micah 6:8). To walk humbly! Humility is an unknown quantity, and our future abiding place an uncertainty with those (of us) who are not indwelt and led by the Spirit of God.

The Psalmist asks and answers two important questions for our consideration in these words, Lord, who shall abide in thy tabernacle? Who shall dwell in thy holy hill? He that walketh uprightly, and worketh righteousness, and speaketh the truth in his heart (Psa. 15:1, 2). The response of every one in the first class will be, I delight to do thy will, O my God, yea, thy law is within my heart (Psa. 4!:8).

What a power for good the Brethren church will be when every member can joyfully give the above response to the Father. Be it so; we ask in his name.

Dayton, Ohio.

Changes.   By H. B. Lehman

How people will change in their religious customs, as in everything else! This change is especially noticeable in the large branch of the Brethren family. In a certain local paper the name of the church was given followed by the name of the pastor and an announcement something like this: "At the eleven o'clock hour there will be a special program in which a visiting brother, Elder So-and-so will speak an the subject: 'The Church When I Was a Boy.' " I don't know what he said, but since he is a man af about my age, namely, 76, he certainly has seen some changes. About ten or twelve years ago in this same church, a certain elder told in a sermon of the progress that church had made "in his day." He was reported immediately to authority higher up and was made to suffer for it. Now in this same church the same thing is done with everybody's approval.

Now, let us go back to my boyhood days. The German Baptist Brethren church was our church then, but since that time things have greatly changed in both branches of the Brethren. The church said it was wrong to have Sunday schools and we were not allowed to go though there were Sunday schools in our neighborhood. We had no revival meetings and no prayer meetings. These things were considered inventions of the world. Think how it is today. A church is hardly considered up-to-date unless it has a prayer meeting.

About thirty-five years ago, when we lived at Marcus, Iowa, we belonged to the church of that place. There was a charge lodged against me for organizing a prayer meeting. My accusers lost in the local church trial, but they carried the case to the district meeting of Northern Iowa held in Aurelia. In that conference no man defended the prayer meeting except Brother F. D. Arnold and myself. No one else dared to speak in favor of the prayer meeting. One good sister asked the question, If a minister of another church should come to dine with us would it be right to ask him to return thanks for the meal? One zealous brother said, I have done it, but my conscience condemned me. Now, after 40 or 50 years the people of that church past and rejoice in the changes that time has wrought.

Glendale, Arizona.

Send
WHITE GIFT
OFFERINGS to

THE SUNDAY SCHOOL

ALBERT TRENT
General Secretary-Treasurer
Johnstown, Pennsylvania

Correspondence Bible Study in Korea

No less than 1,200 have taken the Correspondence Bible Course in Korea during the past season. This work has centered in Pyengyang and has been under the able direction of Rev. W. L. Swallen, D.D. The students are residents of all parts of Korea. The missionaries itinerate through the remote districts and the Christians became eager for an intensive study of the Word. The Correspondence Course helps to meet their desires. The Men's Bible Institute of Pyengyang gave 99 bright young men six weeks of intensive Bible study during the winter.

The Ancient Samaritan Pentateuch Draped in Mourning

The Samaritan Pentateuch is one of the most ancient manuscripts in existence and is treasured above everything by the remnant of the Samaritan Colony at Shechem in Palestine. When the Samaritans learned of the death of their beloved and very helpful friend, Edward K. Warren of Three Oaks, Michigan, past president of the World's Sunday School Association, they draped their synagogue at Shechem in black and wore mourning for a month. Most impressive of all was the fact that the very ancient Samaritan Pentateuch was also draped in black for the same length of time. Mr. Warren had visited the Samaritans at the time when the World's Sunday School Covention was held in Jerusalem in 1904. Since then he had been their constant friend and had helped the "remnant" on many occasions. A Samaritan Committee had been appointed by the Executive Committee of the World's Sunday School Association and Mr. Warren was the chairman of that committee.

John Wanamaker, World's Sunday School Chairman

Hon. John Wanamaker of Philadelphia has just been elected Chairman of the Executive Committee of the World's Sunday School Association. Mr. Wanamaker succeeds H. J. Heinz, who died in May of last year, at the very time when the Annual Meeting of the Executive Committee was in session. Mr. Wanamaker has been actively engaged in Sunday school work since January 17, 1848. In just a few months he will have 72 years to his credit for continuous Sunday school membership and he is still on duty every Sunday. He is superintendent of the Bethany Presbyterian Sunday school of Philadelphia, which reports an enrollment of 2555. In 1889 he became actively engaged in the Pennsylvania State Sabbath School Association and has been its president since 1894. Not only does this active business man hold these Sunday school offices but he fills them with service. When Mr. Wanamaker was Postmaster-General he continued his activities in the Bethany Sunday school in Philadelphia and made it the rule to return each Sunday from Washington that he might be in his place in the home school on Sunday.

James W. Kinnear, a well known lawyer of Pittsburgh, was elected Vice-Chairman of the American Section of the Executive Committee. Mr. Kinnear was one of the Sunday school tour party that visited Japan in 1913 and he plans, with Mr. Wanamaker, to attend the World's Sunday School Convention in Tokyo next October.

Bible Year--1920

Following a plan adopted in Great Britain, and promoted there by a representative interdenominational committee, of which the Lord Bishop of Durham is president, the New York Bible Society has launched the movement in this country to make the year 1920 Bible Year. The announcement of the plan was made at the Anniversary Service of the Society held on Bible Sunday, December 7th, by Bishop Charles S. Burch, of New York.

Objects: To claim for the Bible a larger place in our individual and national life.

To increase public interest in the Bible as God's revelation to man.

To urge upon all men everywhere the unfailing value of the Bible.

To obtain from individuals in all walks of life testimonials to the significance and influence of the Bible.

To obtain these objects meetings will be occasionally held to claim public attention to the Holy Scriptures.

The culmination of this crusade will be on Bible Sunday, December 5th, 1920, when there will be a great demonstration for the Bible.

"We are but organs mute, till a master touches the keys—
    Verily vessels of earth into which God poureth the wine;
Harps are we, silent harps that have hung on the willow
    trees,
    Dumb till our heartstrings swell and break with a pulse
    divine."

J. A. Garber
PRESIDENT

Our Young People at Work

G. C. Carpenter
SECRETARY

A Promising Week

Christian Endeavor Week—February 1-8—promises much for every department of our work. Its promises, however, can be realized only through careful preparation and sustained effort. Judging from our correspondence some of the societies are planning and working to secure commendable results.

A letter from Brother Carl Grosse, President of the Altoona society, says they are going to do their best to attain every goal on the Four Year Challenge, even though they are trying to attain goals that were set for them in 1916 on the basis of an inflated membership. Other societies may be facing the same difficulty. If so, tackle it with the spirit of those Altoona Endeavorers and the difficulty may vanish.

There should be a determined effort to reach the highest possible mark on each of the ten goals. The first two have to do with the organization of new societies. Let strong societies visit nearby churches having none and help to effect an organization. Every organized society can increase its membership (perhaps double it), win church members, enroll Patriotic Servants, Quiet Hour Comrades, Tenth Legioners, secure additional dollars for missions, enlist Life Work Recruits and graduate Endeavor Experts. Yes, we insist that every society "can," and we decline to accept your denial of the possibility until you have given us an account of your endeavor. It is not enough merely to announce these goals and ask folks in a half-hearted way to lend a hand. They must be solicited earnestly and persistently like the politician solicits votes and the salesman solicits orders. Come on, presidents, officers, committeemen, Endeavorers, all, let's go over the top during Christian Endeavor Week. 　　　　　J. A. GARBER.

Another Life Recruit Message

Once more I desire to state that Ashland College Night may be observed on February 8th or 29th. The latter date is preferable for at least two reasons.

First, the whole of February can then be used as Life Work Month, leading up to the great drive on National Enlistment Day, the 29th. It will be the time of harvesting recruits if good seed sowing is done during the preceding weeks. We wish that pastors and Sunday school superintendents and teachers would become sowers of life work seed. Much material will be found in the articles now appearing in both the Evangelist and Angelus.

Second, the latter date will give more time for the preparation of a life work program. A special Life Work Pageant will be completed and mailed at an early date. It may be used by any group of young people, whether in a rural or city, large or small church. It will prove attractive and effective. Those desiring copies of the same should write Prof. J. A. Garber, Ashland, Ohio.

If, for the above reasons, societies defer the Life Work Appeal and College Offering until the 29th, they may use the 8th very profitably. The regular topic "A Worth While Life" is most suggestive and we have mailed each society an outline porgram, a careful use of which will prepare the way for the subsequent life work appeal and help the society to qualify on other points of the Four Year Challenge. If we can be of further service to you, make known your needs. We are exceedingly anxious to win our specific goals this year: Twenty-five Life Work Recruits and $400 for religious education. "Come on, let's go" is the slogan.

　　　　　EDWIN BOARDMAN, Supt.,
　　　　　　　　Hudson, Iowa.

Just Before Sailing

Dear Friends:

This is my last letter for the present, dear friends, for very soon I shall (D. V.) be on my way to France to carry your greetings and good wishes, and a little of the money of some of you for the reconstruction and upbuilding of Christian Endeavor in war-ravaged Europe. Each week I shall write about what I find, for The Christian Endeavor World, and I shall count on your sustaining prayers in this somewhat difficult journey to the new republics of old Europe.

I leave the work in our central office in good hands,—some new hands, some old hands,—but all of them willing and consecrated hands. The different state unions, too, were never better officered than now; we never had so many seasoned field secretaries, and, from no country in the world, save one, comes any discouraging note concerning our cause.

The goals proposed and accepted at Buffalo are winners, and have already increased the vigor of many societies and unions, though their value and power are just beginning to be felt.

Does any belated person intimate to you that Christian Endeavor "has seen its best days," that it "isn't what it was!" Then tell him he is right,—that it isn't what it was because it is better than it was. If you can do so politely, you might remind him that the trouble is that he isn't up to date in his information.

These are the facts: On the first day of January, 1920, there were more Endeavorers in the world than on any other New Year's day, more Comrades of the Quiet Hour, more Tenth Legioners, more Life Work Recruits, more denominations united in Christian Endeavor, more countries that display the Christian Endeavor banner, more languages into which the pledge is translated.

During the past year two or three of the new republics of Europe have given Christian Endeavor a place, and it has become a greater evangelistic force than ever.

The aggregate attendance at state conventions and union meetings in 1919 has been larger than ever before, and 1920 promises to surpass the old year.

Remind the knockers and the pessimists of these facts, and tell them to pitch in and do their share of the work, and their wails will be turned into songs of rejoicing. Tell them these things, not in a spirit of boasting, but with gratitude to God, and make Christian Endeavor week, 1920, the "best yet," because with new consecration in the strength of our ever-present Lord, we go forward to new victories for Christ and the church.

"Go thy way and I go mine, 　And God keep watch 'tween
　Apart, yet not afar, 　　　　　thee and me,
Only a thin veil hangs be- 　　This is my prayer.
　tween 　　　　　　He looks thy way; he looketh
The pathways where we 　　　　mine,
　are, 　　　　　　And keeps us near."

　　　　"In journeyings oft,"
　　　Your friend,
　　　　　FRANCIS E. CLARK.

Though I have been trained a soldier and have participated in many battles, there never was a time when, in my opinion, some way could not have been found of preventing the drawing of the sword. I look forward to an epoch when a court, recognized by all nations shall settle international difficulties, instead of keeping large standing armies, as they do in Europe.—Ulysses S. Grant.

MONEY FOR
, Kentucky and
Missions to

MISSIONS

WILLIAM A. GEARHART
General Missionary Secretary
906 Conover Bldg., Dayton, O.

What Meaneth this Riverside. By G. C. Carpenter

R is for the **River** Troublesome, so often true to name but which winds and wings through the valley and lends beauty to the choice location of our church and institute

I is for the **Increasing Interest** of Brethren far and near who support our mountain mission work with prayers and money

V is for **Vice** that has been banished from "Bloody Breathitt" through the influence of our mission

E is for **Efficiency** and **Economy** sought in every phase of the work by the mission board and the workers

R is for the good **Roads** which are not but which ought to be as all will readily agree

S is for the **Sunshine** that reaches the valley late and leaves early but which has found a friendly and able assistant in the new electric light plant.

I is for the **Independence** of the rich hills of old Kentucky as they rise around **Riverside** and extend hundreds of miles from state to state.

D is for the **Drushals** who sought the hardest place to work for the Master and who have been hard at it nearly fifteen years

E is for the **Endlessness** of the opportunities to enlarge our mountain mission work in which we are as yet only touching the hem of its garment.

RECRUITS FOR THE HOME MISSIONARY ARMY

G. C. CARPENTER.

Scarcity

Uncle Sam is sending out recruiting officers who are scouring the country for recruits for the nation's army. Uncle Sam is very particular and must have the best. They must be physically fit. Such are very scarce. Should the home mission army set the standard lower? God forbid. Recruits are scarce because so few are willing to serve, although to that end we were created and to that end we were born again. Recruits for the Lord's army must be spiritually fit or willing to become so. The Lord must have clean vessels.

Our U. S. A. army needs recruits, but not as much as does the army of our Lord which is sent by him on a world conquest. Our home mission board is constantly receiving Macedonian calls, from the Kentucky mountain field and from city fields, which they cannot answer favorably because of the lack of men and money, although the lack of men is greater than the lack of money. Find the men and the money will be forthcoming. There are many opportunities for building up strong Brethren churches in needy and unchurched fields. The pressing need is men who will be real leaders, Christlike servants, Christian statesmen in the kingdom of God on earth. This day a pastor and a teacher could be placed in needy fields in Kentucky. Pressing calls for workers are almost unlimited.

How Discover The Recruits.

Pastors and fathers and mothers are the Lord's recruiting officers. Endeavor and Sunday school leaders are also recruiting officers. There are many Christian Endeavorers who should become Christian life-work recruits. Fellow-pastors, let us pray and strive to find some life-work recruits for his army. Parents, are you willing to give your children to the Lord in answer to the Life enlistment call? Young people, are you letting the Lord have his way with your heart? Are you asking, will it pay? The answer is, yes, a thousand times. Just remember that the Lord will not forsake his own. He promises one hundred fold of blessing here and eternal life in the world to come. Trust thou in God.

Two Important Days

Sunday, February eighth is Christian Enlistment Day. Sunday, February twentyninth is Life Enlistment Day in the program of the Interchurch World Movement. May the young people of the Brethren church hear the call of the Kentucky mountaineers and the pressing call of the home field in a thousand places and say, "Here am I, Lord, send me."

PERU, INDIANA.

FROM OUR LATEST SOUTH AMERICAN MISSIONARY

Dear Readers of the Brethren Evangelist:

No doubt we are strangers to most of you but we hope to become better acquainted in the future. Time has passed so rapidly that we hardly realize that we have been here two months and we have been occupied with so many things or you would have heard from us sooner.

Our journey, though long and filled with various experiences was nevertheless a pleasant one. We left home the 23rd of July for New York. But through a delay in the sailing of the boat and a further delay because of the lack of necessary papers we did not leave until the 4th of September. Then a fire on board compelled us to spend two weeks on the Island of St. Lucia in the West Indies which we had not anticipated. The scenery was very beautiful yet it grew old after a couple of days and we were anxious to be on our way. We left there the 23rd of September and after making a few stops we arrived in Buenos Aires the 13th of October. As we had very little trouble in getting our things through the custom house, we were able to leave for Rio Cuarto on the evening of the 16th. A more hearty welcome could not have been given us on our arrival and we feel now that this is indeed a home to us. We found all of our missionaries here to meet us and we enjoy their friendship and fellowship.

Rio Cuarto, Argentina.,
December 23, 1919.

For the present we are busy with the Christmas program and also with the study of the language. We hope to be able to start out with the Gospel Coach by the first of April as the top will then be completed. We believe now that it will take us about three months to make the rounds, that is, if we visit all of the towns that we should. Our work will be to sell Bibles, teach and to get into the homes of the people as much as possible. Right here, may we ask an interest in all your prayers that God might have his way in all that is said and done and that many might be brought into the light.

We recently enjoyed a visit with Brother and Sister Bock at La Carlota. We find the work there as elsewhere growing very slowly for the priest is much in control and the people are very indifferent. The testimony of a clean life counts much and the seed sown will bear fruit. He has a very promising Sunday school started and is doing a good work with them. He has many obstacles against which to work and he needs your prayers.

This is but a short account of our journey as we are writing a more complete one for the Brethren Missionary. Then too, after we are out with the Gospel Coach we will be able to tell you more about the country and the conditions of the people as we find them.

Again we ask an interest in your prayers for the Argentine. We are,

Yours till he comes,
CLARENCE L. SICKEL.

THE TEALLS AT LOST CREEK

To our friends who may be interested in our welfare and also the Kentucky work:

Mrs. Teall and I boarded the train at Elkhart, Indiana, Tuesday, December 30, 1919 at 6:40 A. M. and arrived at Winchester, Kentucky at 6:45 P. M. We rode all day with the exception of fifteen minutes, the time it required to make three changes. This place is located in the blue-grass region where the land sells for $400.00 per acre and the main crop, or one of them at least, is tobacco, which yields $800.00 per acre (but that would be no inducement for me).

At that place we saw lots of colored people, plenty of Fords, but few low necks and narrow skirts. So much for Winchester.

We left this place the following day at 12:50 P. M. for Haddix, a station within two and one-half miles of Lost Creek, arrived at Haddix at 6:30, a town of one dwelling that includes the Post Office. When it was becoming dark the hair fairly stood straight up on our heads, as we often say, for when we would look out of the train in either direction, we at times could only see ten rods distant, and we traveled through such country for 70 long miles. Occasionally, of course, there were open spaces extending as far as forty rods one way and one-half mile the other.

By the way, we met our nurse at Winchester and it was a happy meeting on our part at least, and it gave us new inspiration. She certainly was a great blessing to us, as we were traveling through that terrible looking country.

As Brother Drushal did not get our card that we were coming on that day, there was no one to meet us. But Brother and Sister Pearce went to the station after a box, riding two mules and instead of finding the box, three passengers got off. There we were, five of us besides all our baggage. As Mrs. Teall had not been on an animal since she was a girl it required great courage on our part to undertake the trip. But on considering the work we were engaged in, we placed her upon the back of one of the mules with Brother Pearce on behind. They rode this way until they got to where it was too steep for the mule to carry its burden when Brother Pearce dismounted. I was walking when I wasn't falling down. It was too dark to see the road but I don't believe I could have seen any had

(Continued on page 14)

NEWS FROM THE FIELD

MASONTOWN, PENNSYLVANIA

In a recent report of the happenings in this church, we dwelt almost exclusively upon the very successful revival service which had been conducted by Brother B. T. Burnworth. I am glad to say now, that the interest aroused by the meeting has borne fruit since the close of the meeting, in the confession of three more, making a total of 45 confessions, all but two of whom have been received into the church. The year which has just closed, has been one of exceptional blessing to this congregation, for in addition to the 54 names which have ben written on the roll of members, a splendid spirit of co-operation has been maintained, so that we face the opening of a new year with hope and a deep satisfaction.

The first Sunday of October was observed as Rally and Promotion day with a combined service in the morning, attended by 170 people. There were addresses by Sunday school workers from outside our own number and a program of helpfulness was presented. In the evening of that day we followed a custom which is as old as my term of service here, of having an attorney to deliver the address. The speaker this time was the Hon. Russel Carr, of Uniontown, a prominent lawyer and Christian gentleman, and an officer of one of the leading churches in his city. His theme was, "Jesus Christ, the Hope of the World," and his masterful message was heard by a splendid audience.

Under the leadership of our faithful pianist, another Christmas entertainment was given, which was more than worth while. As usual, it was seen and heard by a capacity house, and all went away helped by the program. How she manages to stage such affairs, is beyond me, and I most devoutly wish that every church could have a leader of her caliber. One of the features not on the written program, was another surprise for the pastor and wife. They were called to the platform and each presented with a $50 check, in the name of their brethren and their friends. Something of this sort has been happening so often during the six years of our service here, that one need hardly be surprised at its recurrence, but this was decidedly the biggest yet, and our hearts were almost too full for utterance. It is needless to say that it made some impression on our purses too, but that was soon adjusted. Such expressions of love and appreciation are very dear to a pastor's heart. Another of the surprises in store for the pastor on that evening was the bestowal upon him of a beautiful watch charm by the Men's Bible class, of which he has been teacher for six years. This men's class is one of the distinct features of this Sunday school, for it is not only the largest in point of enrollment, but also in attendance and in offerings. It is needless to say that the class is very near the pastor's heart, and from this and other expressions, the feeling is not on one side only.

On New Year's eve, a reception was given in honor of the new members received into the church during the past year. The gathering was held at the church and was largely attended by members and their friends. An informal program was rendered in which the history of the local congregation, and of the whole denomination, as well as the doctrinal position of the church, was told to those present. Light refreshments were served at the close, and a most enjoyable and helpful evening was spent thus.

The women and girls of the congregation have organized a Woman's Missionary Society, which promises to take its place among the most active organizations of the brotherhood. One of the local goals is the determination to enroll in its membership every eligible person in the congregation.

The annual business meeting of the congregation was held recently, and was an occasion of much encouragement to us all. All reports were of such character as to make the heart glad for they bore unmistakable evidence of the helping hand of God in all the undertakings of the congregation. Our Sunday school report was another of the kind which it has been showing for several yearst past. With an average attendance for the year of 115, its total offerings amounted to $737.23. The offerings through the regular channels of the church were splendid also. Money is not everything by any means, but like a weather vane, it shows the direction of spiritual interest and when freely contributed, speaks volumes as to human ideals and purposes. At this annual business meeting, the pastor received unanimous call to continue his services for a seventh year at a substantial increase in salary. Thus has the Lord blessed us and we unite in giving him praise.

MARTIN SHIVELY.

DALLAS CENTER NOTES

The Christmas season has passed and another new year has come to us with bright prospects for greater things in the Master's work. The fuel situation prevented us having any Christmas program but we had the Christmas spirit with us just the same. Just after Christmas a knock was heard at the parsonage and upon the invitation to enter a party of 50 friends, laden with good cheer and best wishes for the coming new year. We spent a very pleasant evening together and before departing a material token of friendship and good will was presented to the pastor and his wife. I mention this to state my appreciation of the actual evidence of good will on the part of the people and with the home that some other congregation that thinks the minister is past the sentimental stage of life will awaken to the fact that their minister will feel better and preach better if they will show a sociable and loving spirit in the open and not all the time in secret.

The Brethren at Dallas Center have exceeded previous offerings for Home Missions and for the White Gift. We are encouraged with the greater interest on the part of the congregation in the greater work of the brotherhood. We find that publicity through the Evangelist and other means, of the thought and work of the church creates interest. Our church here is doing her share willingly with the confidence of success in our denominational plans.

We are glad to note the reports of good meetings held and a deeper spiritual life among our people and we trust that the new day into which we have entered in the world's history will find the Brethren everywhere awake and their lamps trimmed and burning brightly.　　　　R. F. PORTE.

LA VERNE, CALIFORNIA

We are rejoicing in the goodness of the Lord to us. To him be all the glory and praise. As is our custom, we held the annual all-day meeting of the church on New Year's Day and then found that the past year has been the most prosperous year in the history of the little church we love.

First of all, the spiritual life seems high. Let us look at the church thermometer—the prayer meeting. Attendance has about doubled—there being 75 percent of the church attendance in the prayer meeting. Then we are becoming more and more of a missionary church. Brother Clarence and Sister Loree Sickel, two of our own young members, now in South America, are proving a great blessing to the church in this line. Brother Allen Pearce and his young wife in Kentucky are claiming our interest, sympathy and prayers. For although Allen did not leave our church directly, it was our pastor who lead him to

know his Savior up in Canada and brought him here for his studies in the Los Angeles Bible Institute and we all know him personally and love him. Another young couple of our Christian Endeavor society have offered themselves for the mission work in the South and expect to go soon, thus making another tie which will bind. The prayer band for the African Mission party is again in operation and to show further missionary interest, about two hundred missionary books have been read, this being under the auspices of the Christian Endeavor.

Our home life is being blessed through a revival of family worship and private devotional life. Then there have also been several cases where faith and anointing have brought about healing and to the effect that others of the community, not known to believe in this doctrine has resorted to it and been blessed.

We have been having two weeks of spiritual feast with Dr. Cook of New York—a man of national fame but one who is not afraid to stand four-square with the old Book. May God continue to use him to strengthen the spiritual lives of many others as he has us. There have been added to the church during the last year twenty-one souls, which speaks well for a small town of four churches.

The financial report of our meeting showed that the church has been forging ahead that way too. The church raised $4,845.00; the Sunday school $555.00; the Christian Endeavor $235.00 and the W. H. M. S. $27.00, making a total of $5,660.00 for the year.

The Sunday school has shown a gradual increase in the last ten years from an average attendance of 56 in 1910 to 136 in 1919—or 150 percent gain. Last year's average attendance was 107. The average collection for 1910 was $1.28, while for 1919 it was $7.36. A beautiful White Gift Christmas program was enjoyed by an enthusiastic and crowded house. The money gift, aside from towels, dolls, and other articles, amounted to $250.00 for the work in Kentucky. The Young People's class raised $80.00 and sent it as a personal gift to Brother Allen and Sister Pearl Pearce. There has been blessed harmony in the Sunday school work and we are going forth in his strength for a still better year for Christ.

The Christian Endeavor has prospered under the leadership of our president, Hilda Broad. We have eighty members striving to live up to the pledge. A class in Expert Endeavor has just been completed. Each committee has been in splendid working condition. The new officers were installed Sunday evening by the president of the Pomona Union and they are anxious to get into their new duties.

The New Year's meeting closed with a most blessed communion service in the evening—about one hundred taking part in it.

MRS. H. L. GOOD.

Pomona, California.

EVANGELISTIC NEWS

After leaving Lost Creek, Kentucky, I went home for about four days and after moving my family from Jersey to Philadelphia, I attended a communion service at the Whole Gospel Mission, and the next day went to Columbus, Ohio, and began a meeting there, November 17, for three weeks. The first week we had good congregations for that Mission, but the second week it rained every day so that when we expected to press our invitations, the unsaved did not come. Only a very few came, each evening. The third week it cleared and we got our congregation back again. We had a good house and interest nearly every night, so at the time we had programmed to close we had a splendid interest.

I had expected to close and rest five days between the Columbus and the Rittman meeting but they insisted upon me preaching while resting. I consented to do so, and we had four more nights of services.

1. I was royally treated by the Columbus Mission. They made up all the finances of the meeting without any trouble. They surely were liberal givers.

2. We had eleven confessions, whether all will be baptized or not I am not sure. There may be one or two who will be opposed by parents.

3. The number of additions was not large but most of them were exceptionally fine people for building a permanent work.

We received some as good as can be found in that part of Columbus and they came with us for doctrinal reasons, and I believe they will stick to the church.

4. I found that the work had greatly suffered from unwise leadership and the community has given it a rather black eye, and many had quit attending.

When Brother Christiansen took the work several years ago about four and five was the average attendance of the prayer meeting, now they have about three times as many. The church is slowly but I think surely gaining the confidence of the community and by the wise guidance of the Mission Board and the pastor, they will gain a solid foothold. The work will not be a rapid growth but a gradual and permanent one, by careful handling.

Brother Christiansen will put the work upon a solid and permanent basis if he can be kept. But the sickness in his family and the high cost of living in a large city is handicapping him financially, but he is gradually gaining the confidence of a good solid class of people that will make the church permanent.

I hope that the state of Ohio will stand nobly by the mission as it will soon become an influential Brethren church.

I feel we have put the work upon a more solid basis than it has been for years and I am hoping to hear that the attendance at Sunday, school and church will continue to improve till in a comparatively short time it may become self supporting.

I would suggest that it be well supported so that the pastor will not be embarrassed in any way and kept from pushing the work to success.

It gives me great pleasure to see one of my spiritual children that I baptized and married and ordained to the ministry having confidence and good of the best people in that part of Columbus, including several of the best teachers of the State University. One of the professors of the university, a clergyman attended several of the services and also spoke in the highest terms of Brother Christiansen.

I feel, during the last year before I began the meeting, took in several good substantial families. So that I feel very sure that if he can be sufficiently supported to live without financial embarrassment that within a few years it will become a self supporting church.

I was well fed and royally entertained in every way while with them.

On the last night of the meeting one of the professors from the university was present and the church gave a free treat of ice cream and cake. So we had a pleasant farewell.

I. D. BOWMAN.

AN APPRECIATION

Expecting to leave Spokane in the spring for a much needed rest before taking up other work, we want to express to the brotherhood and the mission board our deep appreciation of the loyal and steadfast assistance in the establishment of this work of God. Through the long period of struggle when it seemed as though adverse circumstances would crush us, our hearts were constantly made glad by encouraging and strengthening letters with substantial assistance enclosed. And

often are receiving such a message, we would take new courage and strive on. But not least have we prized the assurance that many earnest hearts were holding us up before the throne of God daily, that our faith should not fail.

And now that God has poured out blessing upon blessing upon the work here and brought it to a successful establishment, we want you to know that your prayers, labors and sacrifices have not been in vain. Neither has our gratitude been lacking, and we believe that we have so written to every one that has given to the work.

In the name of our blessed Master, to whom we owe it all, we thank you one and all for your noble support.

R. PAUL MILLER.
W. 402 Montgomery Avenue.

AN EVANGELISTIC ITINERACY

Beginning the evangelism for the winter at home in October we found corn husking and daily rains not very conducive to revival work. After two weeks Brother Beachler came and preached for us a week and also solicited the church for endowment. The result of this experiment, as he called it in his report, was 10 souls saved and $2,000 for the college. This time the Pentecostal 3000 the college got instead of the local work. We closed knowing the end of the revival had not come.

Masontown

Closing our services at home with a communion service with 175 present on Sunday, evening, Brother Beachler left for Waterloo and I went to Masontown, Pennsylvania to assist Brother Shively in a meeting. For three weeks Brother Shively led the singing and I preached. On Sunday afternoons preached at two outside points and on the last Sunday afternoon a splendid communion service was held after which I preached my final sermon. The meeting has been reported. Suffice it to say, that the immediate visible results were 43 additions to the work. We worked hard but it paid well. Never have I been more comfortable than in the Shively home. Never have I enjoyed three weeks of real comradeship more. We had so many things in common concerning us that as we visited we learned to love each other more. I found one secret to Shively's perpetual youth. Sister Shively is a most excellent cook and a very discreet pastor's companion. I have a warm spot in my heart for Masontown. The people received me cordially in their homes, gave me a good hearing at church and a good offering for my services.

Listie

From Masontown I went immediately to Listie. Quite a change to get out of the valley with its gas and coke smoke to the top of the mountain where the air was not only clear but cool. Listie is another church like Masontown in that it has a young pastor. Of course I admit my father is some older than I am but it does not seem to effect him much only in modesty for as I write I now remember that he has not so much as reported the meeting. So here is the literal translation of "He that tooteth not his own horn, the same shall not be tooted." Well the sun shone on Monday when I climbed the mountain and shone again on Monday when I left, the rest of the time the rain just poured straight down. But the people came and in so short a time as a week there were 10 added to the church and a real revival had begun; I hope it has continued. Of course it was a real treat to be home a week. At Listie I found a better church than I expected and also a fine class of people that treated me royally and loyally and gave me a splendid offering for my short stay with them.

We were at Berlin one night, preached to a fine audience and found them loud in their praises of their pastor and planning larger things for the future in the way of a church building. We spent part of one day at Meyersdale, just long enough to help eat a turkey, meet a few people and start for home on an evening train. En route we were at Ashland only long enough to find that the college is going fine and didn't even get to the Publishing House.

On Sunday morning when we stepped into the pulpit we were given a rousing welcome by a loud applause, right out in meetin' on Sunday morning too. During our month at home we have added 11 to the church, had our Christmas services giving $112.50 for a White Gift. I might say that in my absence the church went over the top at Thanksgiving for Home Missions. My pulpit was filled acceptably by Brother Z. T. Livengood and Brother Charles Delp of the Church of the Brethren. At the end of five years here we find we have 380 in Sunday school and 310 members of the church, 139 being added during my pastorate.

B. T. BURNWORTH.
Lanark, Illinois.

HIGHLAND, PENNSYLVANIA

For some time we have been waiting, that we might know just what to write.

On October the 18 Brother Benj. F. Owen of Ashland, Ohio, came to us to assist us in our evangelistic campaign, which proved to be a great success, although the inclement weather was a great drawback. It rained almost every day for the three weeks that Brother Owen was with us. Despite all this the people gave heed to the wonderful messages which the evangelist gave, and several made the good confession and received baptism by the pastor.

The gospel seed sown by Brother Owen, we feel will bring forth fruit in days to come.

The church is taking greater interest in the work of the Kingdom and the people outside were attracted by the timely sermons and Holy Ghost gospel which Owen preached. The meeting closed on Sunday evening after three weeks' effort, all in great spirits and ready for the future. Brother Owen stayed over and on Tuesday evening gave an African lecture which was greatly appreciated, for which he took a freewill offering which amounted to over $50.00. During the three weeks while Brother Owen stayed, there was raised about $100.00. I am sure this speaks for the people as to their gratefulness for the service rendered. Come on, Owen, you are welcome any time.

About the time we were ready to write to the Evangelist, we were surprised by a letter from Brother George T. Ronk, which gave us a call to the church of McLouth, Kansas and the pioneer work of that field. This put us on edge and we were under great perplexity for several days, but after prayer and consideration we put the proposition up to our church and finally, with broken hearts of both pastor and people, we decided it to be the Lord's call and accepted the call to the pastorate of the McLouth church.

It is hard to break loose and leave a people whom one has learned to love and those who have proved their love by their deeds of kindness. We are sure we can never find a people who are more worthy of praise than the people of Highland and vicinity. They are ready to do what they can to advance the cause of Christ.

Since we came here the work has been moving nicely. Several have been added to the church, and the church is in a fine spiritual condition. The church property is out of debt, the building has a new coat of paint, a new Page fence has been erected this spring, also a piano has been installed. All that we can say is to pray God to send a man to lead them on to victory.

As we are leaving this lovable people to go to McLouth, knowing nothing save by recommendation, we ask the prayers of all who are interested in the spread of the gospel and the salvation of souls to remember us with the church to which we go and that there soon shall be many new converts and several new churches in the west through these efforts and sacrifices.

THOS. F. HOWELL.

(Continued from page 11)

it been daylight on account of the rocks and mud.

But thanks be to the Lord, we got here safely and they gave us a cordial welcome. We were sorry to find the matron sick, but she is up again. School is now in session with about forty scholars boarding here, and I can say they are as bright a collection of children as you will find anywhere. But the only way you can appreciate the workers' position is to come and see. And if you knew the sacrifices that some of us are making (when I say some I don't include Mrs. Teall and myself) then you would be thankful that you can stay at home and have the privilege of giving to the work.

Some of our friends may wonder what we are doing here. Well, Mrs. Teall is doing cooking, and I am doing, oh well, just whatever they make me do.

Now I want to say before I close that they are certainly doing a great work here and I believe it is going to continue by the help of God and his children at large.

Yours in the Work,
MR. AND MRS. CHAS. A. TEALL.

LATHROP, CALIFORNIA

Dear Evangelist Readers:

Once again I ask a little space in our beloved paper ot report Lathrop's religious welfare. But first I want to say the Evangelist is surely "a thing of beauty and a joy each week." Lathrop is still on the map—very still just now since our much loved pastor left us for another pastorate. All regretted to see him leave. Since then we have not been able financially and otherwise to secure a pastor. Yet we are bravely holding the fort at this end of the charge. Which consists of Ripon, Colony and Lathrop. We have a very fine Sunday school with a good corps of teachers and a small though lively Christian Endeavor. In my last communication I spoke of Sister H. E. Beer, eighty-one years of age on February 23, 1920, widow of John Jas. W. Beer, one of the founders of the Progressive Brethren church. She lives alone and has no income other than the small and sometimes uncertain sum sent by the Benevolence Board of the church, except what good friends provide as they may think of her necessities. She has been janitor of our church house but is not able for the work longer, as she has rheumatism in her neck and shoulders to a painful degree. Never has she been heard to complain of her lot, though it is widely known that her husband sacrificed a good home for the church in the days of its infancy. And truly by its membership in the Ministerial Association was she provided with means at his death to bury him. He had been incapacitated for active church work for several years before death. The only member of the church seemingly impressed by my former letter to the Evangelist in regard to this matter was Sister H. J. Frantz of Enid, Oklahoma, herself an aged lady of eighty-one years, who sent one dollar to me for Sister Beer and one to start a fund to erect a "modest monument" for Brother Beer. Another incident of the "widow's mite!" If every family in the church would do as much, Sister Beer's care in sickness and health would be assured.

Can there be a concerted movement to do something for her before it's too late? It takes money to buy wood, coal and oil to warm her little home these cold frosty mornings. She would not be allowed to suffer for such things as long as Lathrop has one member living here. Even worldly folks vie with each other in doing for her, remarking the while, "It does not pay to give all you have to churches. When you get old you're forgotten." She is not a mere member of an obscure western church but an honorable member of the first Progressive Brethren church ever organized. Would it not be a fine thing for each member to send even fifty cents each to Brother Louis Bauman, Long Beach, California, he to keep in touch with her needs through her deacons, J. Milo Wolfe and Edward Reynolds of Lathrop? I merely suggest this as a possible solution to a condition that, to say the least, is not creditable to our church. No wonder young men hesitate to enter the ministerial profession when their sacrifices are so soon forgotten. Hoping I may never feel the necessity of mentioning this matter again, I remain,

Your sister for service,
LUDA S. REYNOLDS.

ROANOKE, INDIANA

As we have not seen any report from Roanoke, we feel that a report from there will not be out of order.

We have been serving these good brethren for over one year and must say firstly, that a more loyal people to the pastor would be difficult to find. While the church at Roanoke is not numerically as strong as at Berne yet we have some mighty fine brethren there. We feel sometimes that Roanoke has not had the chance that is due her. We find that there have been many things to hinder the work and it has taken us one year and more to find a way out but thank the God of all Glory that we now see the very brightest year for Roanoke. Now this is human foresight and may we not glory only in the Lord Jesus and yet we are constrained to believe that if the people would only cultivate a forgetful spirit in Christ Jesus, (Paul, says forgetting the things of the past and reaching forward to the great promises of God) we feel quite sure that our churches would be surprised at the end of the year.

Roanoke is handicapped by not holding her young people as residents but it is because there are not many manufacturing plants there, and the people either work in Fort Wayne or Huntington, or move to those towns, or go to some other town for work. So this is one of the reasons why they have been at a disadvantage.

But we also find that in the rural community surrounding that very few of them are believers. So if we can prevail on the rural district we believe there is a great future for Roanoke with the faithful of the city membership. They have lost heavily by death in some of the leaders. Others have moved away so we must depend on the Holy Spirit to send others to replace them. Let us remember that the Christ of God said to his followers that the gates of hell (or hades) shall not prevail against the church (Matt. 16:18). We find that they have some great talent in the young people and may we say that one young brother has promised the pastor that he would send in gleanings from Roanoke from time to time. They have budgeted for the Evangelist with 20 subscriptions and more to follow. So we feel that it will be the means of bringing a great stimulus to the church. We speak from experience here at Berne. This is the third year at Berne and we could not get along without the church paper as a means to a great cause here. If any other church is handicapped and is not budgeting well, just budget and get the Evangelist.

W. F. JOHNSON.

MULBERRY GROVE, ILLINOIS

Immediately after moving my family to West Alexandria, Ohio, it was necessary for me to leave to hold a meeting at Mulberry Grove, Illinois. I have been waiting to see a report of the meeting, but in the absence of a report thus far, this report is given. We began the meeting October 4th and continued for three weeks. This is a very weak church (numerically), located six miles in the country. Besides the most stubborn spirit of indifference I have ever found, there were several rainy spells which, on their typical Illinois mud roads, rendered it impossible for people to come in their machines, hence the attendance was much effected. The meeting closed with communion services the last night with 15 surrounding the Lord's table, but without a single addition to the church. Yet I am very certain that the meeting was far from a failure. The church was greatly strengthened and encouraged, as was partly evidenced by the fact that these good people made us a present of more than $20.00 more than was due me, besides the many expressions of appreciation.

Furthermore, it was my privilege to discover here some mighty promising timber for the ministry of our beloved church. One young man of splendid ability and thorough consecration, Brother Claude Studebaker, will be prepared to accept the pastorate of a church by next September 1. Having taught several terms of school, as well as having a pretty thorough knowledge of the Bible, he possesses splendid ability. His younger brother, John, is also seriously considering entering school to prepare for the work of the ministry. This I believe he will do soon. His zeal is of a very high order.

We had our home with Mrs. Etta Studebaker, the mother of Claude and John, and a splendid home it was. She has had the joy of seeing all her sons and daughters, as well as all her daughters-in-law come into the church. May God abundantly bless these dear people is my prayer.

Lake Odessa, Michigan

The meeting here followed the one at Mulberry Grove almost immediately. This meeting having been reported by the pastor, I shall not report at any great length.

One thing with which I was impressed here was that I did not hear one word of criticism of Brother Garrison by anyone, which speaks for itself as to the confidence of his good people have in him.

It was our privilege to assist Brother Grisso in a meeting here just three weeks ago. We were greatly pleased to find the work in fine shape and the members as loyal and faithful and zealous as before, in spite of the detractions incident to the war. This is just one of the finest churches in the brotherhood, though a decidedly rural church, located six miles from Lake Odessa.

Brother Garrison's home was my home while here, and everything was done by them that could be done for my comfort. Very greatly do I appreciate the many kindnesses shown me by these dear people. May they have a great year together.

GEO. W. KINZIE.

CLAY CITY TO WEST ALEXANDRIA, OHIO

On October first we closed our work as pastor of the Clay City church and left to take charge of the West Alexandria and New Lebanon, Ohio, churches. As we left the Clay City church many happy memories came into our minds which made us rejoice at having had the privilege of working with these dear people for three years, and at the same time brought sadness to our hearts at the thought of severing the ties that had been formed. We shall never forget the many good people here for their faithful co-operation and splendid loyalty to the various interests of the whole church. Few churches will be found in the entire brotherhood which have such a high proportion of live, active and talented people as the Clay City church. I am sure that I covet for them only the best and richest of God's blessings. Under the leadership of Brother S. C. Henderson, my successor, I trust that they may realize great and continual growth.

Concerning the work at West Alexandria and New Lebanon I do not care to speak at any great length as yet for the reason that I have hardly become really acquainted therewith. I had agreed to hold two evangelistic meetings previous to accepting the call of the churches here. These meetings took my time until about November 23. Therefore I have only been on the field here about two months. Then besides this my throat has been giving me a great deal of trouble, thus hindering me from doing pastoral work and becoming acquainted with my new fields. Nevertheless, I wish to speak of the splendid way in which these churches have already responded to the calls of our Mission Boards. West Alexandria while failing to reach the goal for Home Missions at Thanksgiving time, gave almost twice as much this year as last. The New Lebanon church also had an entertainment and White Gift offering at Christmas time. The entertainment was a great success, and the offering amounted to $22.00.

The good people comprising these congregations have also not been unmindful of the physical needs and comforts of their pastor and his family. Different members of the West Alexandria congregation have from time to time contributed various eatables. Then on Tuesday night before New Years Day, when the New Lebanon church held their business meeting, the pastor was directed to one of the Sunday school rooms where, to his complete surprise, he was presented with canned goods, vegetables, meats, lard, flour, etc., amounting to nearly upwards of $25.00 in value. I assure you that these tokens of good will were appreciated most heartily. By the way this donation came near being a birthday present to the pastor. Two days later it would have been such. Prior to this the good people of both congregations united in giving us a "Chicken shower." Beachler, having just been here in the endowment campaign was strongly impressed with the appropriateness of this kind of a "Shower."

We very urgently request the prayers of the entire brotherhood.

GEO. W. KINZIE.

CAMPAIGN NOTES

I am reporting our canvass in two churches this week, viz., Homerville and Salem. I spent Sunday, December 14th, in the Homerville congregation preaching morning and evening. And I suspect that by this time the Homerville Brethren have concluded that I forgot to report them. However, such is not the case. I have simply been deferring the report in order that the non-resident members of this church might have ample time, if they so desired, to contribute their part in making the grand finals for Homerville more nearly what they ought to be. But the time has come when I must report.

Brother Fred Vanator, a young preacher in the college, is serving this church as pastor. Brother Vanator was with us during our canvass among his people. It is only fair to say that his work among this people is highly appreciated, and he has the implicit confidence of all. This congregation is also the home of Dr. E. E. Jacobs, president of the college. It was in this church that Dr. Jacobs enlisted in the service of Christ, and it was for this congregation that his father, Brother Henry Jacobs preached for many years. Homerville is therefore linked up with the college in a unique and vital way.

Though Homerville is a small country congregation with its own struggles and its own problems, I found here very warm, loyal friends both for the college and Dr. Jacobs. The Homerville people have known Dr. Jacobs from his boyhood and they believe in his Christian integrity and his ability to successfully direct the affairs of our school. And what was done for the college by way of endowment was done. Very cheerfully. When I report $500 for Homerville it may not sound very big from a distance; but those who know best the congregation will consent that that result is good.

While in this place I received kind hospitality in the McDaniels, Hummel, and Keyser homes. And to Brother Keyser I am indebted, not for a Ford, but for a good horse. The roads were exceedingly rough at that

time and without that horse we could not have made the canvass.

Salem Church.

Salem church is a small congregation in Miami Valley, but it has some big people in it—not big necessarily from the standpoint of stature but big from the standpoint of faith and courage and loyalty. This is the field in which Brother "Jimmy" Cook is holding forth; and my brief observation of Brother "Jimmy" and his work served to assure me that he is putting into his church the very best that is in him and a whole lot of it.

This was the first church to be visited in Miami Valley. Needless to say there is no place in our brotherhood where I feel as much at home as in Miami Valley, because it was my home and the field of my first work in the ministry. And to labor with Brother Cook among people whom I know so well was a continuous round of pleasure. We had a mighty good time at Salem. I believe Brother Cook will say we did too.

Well this little congregation went $500 for endowment. Now I want to explain that here is a result that ought to make Ohio churches sit up and take notice. Salem is not at all strong numerically, and yet, when there seemed no other way out this little congregation had the grit, and the backbone to tackle a preacher for all time, and they are getting across with it. Besides, the first night I was there I talked endowment so strong that I put the light plant hopelessly out of commission, and so they have the light problem, and other local improvements to meet very soon. But in spite of a stiff local program like that Salem still has $500 to invest in permanent endowment for our college. And I am prepared to pronounce that a very fine result, when all things are considered. Brother Cook has the Salem work humming, and what I saw at Salem served to confirm more deeply two notions I have had in my mind for a long time—first, that God surely does help congregations that try to help themselves. And second, that more than one smaller congregation in our brotherhood would not have died or would not be dying if there were a rebaptism of faith and backbone among us and a renewed determination to tackle big, hard propositions. Some churches die as they sit around waiting for God to rain something down out of heaven into their laps. But Salem refused to die and she refused to sit around and wait. Salem started something. And the outlook for Salem looks good to me.

Miss Josie Wogaman, a member of last year's senior class in the college is a member of this congregation and a strong booster for her Alma Mater. She is a successful teacher in one of the high schools of the Valley. I was entertained in the Wogaman home, also in the Shank and King homes. Besides, Brother Cook took good care of me in his home also, and drove me over his charge in his automobile. I am very much indebted to Brother Cook and his good people for the part they have played in making the mercury move a little higher up.

This brings the mercury now to $136,500. I also have two churches to report for next week—West Alexandria and New Lebanon. I will say that we are getting so close to the $140,000 mark that we can stand on tip toe and look over. Besides, it is interesting to note that the first 13 Ohio churches have gone approximately $21,000. By this time I am measurably sure that Ohio will step up beside Pennsylvania at $40,000.

No doubt by this time many are weary of reading Campaign Notes. But not a soul in the brotherhood is a hundredth part as weary of seeing these notes as I am weary of plugging away at the job. So after all I figure that if I can stand my part of the job the rest of the brotherhood ought to be able to endure the "Notes." The biggest thing about it is the fact that the work we are doing is of a permanent nature. Every thousand dollars reported for permanent en-

---

Our Goal: 200,000; We Can and We Must

200	000
190	000
180	000
170	000
160	000
150	000
140	000
130	000
120	000
110	000
100	000
90	000
80	000
70	000
60	000
50	000
40	000
30	000
20	000
10	000

COLLEGE ENDOWMENT

dowment, invested at 6 per cent will earn $60.00 every year in the long unborn years of the future which will go to maintain our one and only school, which MUST and WILL continually become a larger, stronger, better school. If anybody can give me a plan for speeding this campaign through I am wide open for suggestions. But personally I will say this, that while I have found the people of our brotherhood a fine, loyal people, I have not found them very strong on this "speed stuff." I recommend that we all hold still and steady. A great enterprise in our church is nearing completion and I maintain that we can afford to be patient.

WM. H. BEACHLER,
Campaign Secretary.

COLLEGE NEWS

I was in Berlin, Pa., over Sunday, January 18, and preached morning and evening. I had planned to go over to Myersdale also, but the storm made it impossible. Brother Trout was not at home, being engaged in a series of meetings at Johnstown. However, his church showed me every hospitality and I am under obligations especially to Brother Seibert and family and to Brother Kimmel and family and Mrs. Trout for their very, great kindness to me.

The Loyal Helper's Sunday School Class of the Waterloo congregation recently sent me $3.00 to pay for the framing of one of the pictures I had previously spoken of. The picture is framed and hung. Many thanks. Others please take notice.

Brother Beachler's work has been seriously handicapped by the weather. Still, it is good to have him around the College here occasionally.

Plans are under way for a series of debates with two nearby, colleges, Berea and Bluffton. Dr. L. L. Garber, head of the English Department has this under advisement.

Recent outside chapel speakers have been, Mr. George Hildebrand, president of the Chamber of Commerce, Ashland, Ohio; Dr. H. S. Cope, secretary of the Religious Education Association; and Dr. Young, formerly of the University of Virginia, later of Chicago University, and now of California.

Meeting of the College Board the last of this week.

EDWIN E. JACOBS.

THE TIE THAT BINDS

RICHARDS - LEVIS — Brother Jesse B. Richards and Miss Alice Levis were united in marriage at the home of the bride, Thursday evening, December 18, before a small number of invited guests and friends. The groom is a popular young farmer and the bride was a school teacher. May they be richly blessed as they journey together through life. Ceremony by Freeman Ankrum.

GETTLE-HAYNES — Mr. Ralph Gettle of Green Mountain and Miss Eva Haynes, daughter Brother J. O. Haynes, were united in marriage, Thursday evening, January 1, before a large number of relatives and friends, at the home of the bride. These are popular young people and their many friends wish them the best of life's blessings. Ceremony by Freeman Ankrum.

SMITH-LOVE — On the evening before Thanksgiving, November 26, 1919, Mr. John J. Smith and Miss Myrtle B. Love were united in marriage. The wedding took place at the fine country home of the bride's mother, Mrs. Emma Love, near Somerset, Ohio. Only the members of the immediate families of the contracting parties and a few invited guests were present. The beautiful ring ceremony was used and the service was beautifully appropriate to the whole arrangement of the occasion. At the rendition of the wedding march the two contracting parties with their attendants took their places under an arch of flowers and as the strains of the music died away the writer read the

service. After Congratulations a fine wedding dinner was served. The evening was spent in the social pleasantries of such an occasion. May the blessing of our heaVenly Father rest richly upon these fine young people. J. ALLEN MILLER.

SNOWBERGER-BURNS—Leon Snowberger and Grace Burns were united in holy wedlock at the beautiful home of the groom's grandparents, Mr. and Mrs. John Brumbaugh at Roanoke, Indiana, December 24. After the ceremony a beautiful supper was served. Those present were the groom's parents and grandparents, the bride's parents. Miss Mildred Zant, Misses Alava and Marcell, sisters of the groom and the pastor and his wife. The groom is a member of the Brethren church at Roanoke; the bride is a member of the Christian church. Both are highly esteemed young people of Roanoke. Ceremony by the groom's pastor.
W. F. JOHNSON.

BRATTEN - CORDIER — Friday evening, December 12, was an eventful occasion for two young people at Louisville, Ohio, in F. Bratten and Elsie M. Cordier were united in holy marriage, the ring ceremony being used. Mr. and Mrs. Bratten are both among Louisville's most popular young people and are prominent in church, social and musical circles. May they be richly blessed in the new life. Ceremony by the writer.
E. M. RIDDLE.

PLUNK-YEAGGER — Thomas E. Plunk of Johnstown and Miss Mildred Yeager of Franklin Borough, were united in marriage on the evening of December 24, at Conemaugh Brethren church.
Miss Yeager was one of our faithful young women, was a teacher in the Sunday school and a member of the church choir. May God bless them in their new home. Ceremony by the writer. E. F. BYERS.

FORD-GOOD—Christian S. Ford and Carrie I. Good, both of Conemaugh, were united in marriage on the evening of January 1, at the parsonage of the Conemaugh Brethren church. Mr. Ford and his bride are both active members of the Conemaugh Brethren Church, he being a member of the board of deacons. Mr. Ford has been a member of the Brethren church for 25 years, his wife has also been a life long member of the church. May God richly bless them as they labor together. Ceremony by the writer. E. F. BYERS.

OSWALT-CRUUEA — Harry Oswalt, member of the Brethren church of West Alexandria, Ohio, and only son of Brother and Sister Oliver Oswalt, and Thelma Mildred Cruea were united in marriage by the writer on November 27,1919. Ceremony at the parsonage. May their wedded life be long and happy. GEO. W. KINZIE.

IN THE SHADOW

PRICE—Vergil May Price, the only daughter of Mr. and Mrs. John Price of New Lebanon, Ohio, died December 19, 1919, aged 19 years, 10 months and 11 days. Miss Price died of tuberculosis in a hospital near Cleveland, Ohio. She was a member of the Brethren church, haVing united when but eleven years of age. May the God of all grace sustain and comfort her sorrowing parents and brother. Funeral services by her pastor. GEO. W. KINZIE.

SWIHART—Minnie Luella Bowman was born in Miama County, Indiana July 5, 1877. She departed this life January 17, 1920, at the age of 42 years, 6 months and 3 days. On the second day of April 1895, she was united in marriage to David Swihart, to which union five children were born. Marie ElVira, Lois Alfretta, Orpha Leona, Millard Ugene and Bettie Ann who preceded her mother to the glory land.
Minnie confessed Christ early in life and united with the Brethren church and remained true till death. Although she was a great sufferer, during her last illness, she bore all with patience looking forward with faith to a place in the kingdom of God and departed in peace trusting in her God. She was a faithful wife and mother. Services by L. W. Ditch assisted by C. C. Grisso and the writer. WILLIS E. RONK.

DEFFENBAUGH — George Grant Deffenbaugh was born in Fayette county, Pennsylvania, October 30, 1867. He died at his late home near Wooster, Ohio, January 10, 1920. About thirty years ago the writer baptized him and received him into the Brethren church. On July 28, 1893, he was united in marriage to Miss Anna M. Davidson and since then has lived near Wooster. He leaVes his wife, two sons, two grandsons, five brothers and two sisters and his aged parents, Brother and Sister Conrad Deffenbaugh of the Masontown, PennsylVania church. Brother Deffenbaugh was a good man. His task on earth is done. He has

gone to his reward. For many years he was a great sufferer but he bore his trial patiently. Private services were conducted at the home by the writer. Interment at the beautiful cemetary of Wooster. May God comfort the friends in the hope of a blessed life in heaven. J. ALLEN MILLER.

GRUBB — Brother Henry Grubb of near Mt. Vernon, Ohio, passed away at the ripe old age of more than four score years. Many years ago he united with the Brethren church and remained faithful until death. He liVed a noble and sincere life. He left a memory that the children may cherish with growing love for their father. Though he has passed on, dead as men say, yet he lives. The serVices were conducted by the writer.
J. ALLEN MILLER.

HUMPHREY — Oren E. Humphrey passed away at the Deaconess Hospital, Marshalltown, Iowa, Saturday morning, December 13, following an operation. He was born near Lancester, Missouri, 1891. He was united with the Christian church in Missouri and in the fall of 1918, united with the Carleton Brethren church of which he remained a faithful and consistent member until his death. He leaves to mourn his departure, his widow, daughter Loreta, aged four, and son Edwin, aged 12 months, besides many other relatives and friends. Oren was very popular and an immense crowd gathered to pay their last respects to him. Services were held in the Carleton Brethren church and he was laid away in the nearby cemetery. May the sorrowing widow and friends be comforted in their grief. Services by the pastor. FREEMAN ANKRUM.

OAKS — Allen Elwood Oaks, of West Point near Conemaugh, departed this life on the morning of January 2. Death was due to cancer of the face.
Brother Oakes was a member of the Conemaugh Brethren church, and was a good husband and a loving father, and is worthy of Anthony's compliment to Brutus:
"His life was gentle, and the elements So mixed in him, that Nature might stand up
And say, to all the world, This was a man."
Brother Oaks was called home when in the prime of life, being only 38 years of age. He is surviVed by his widow, Sarah Headrick Oaks, and two children, Leroy and Arlien. May the God of peace, comfort the hearts of those that mourn the loss of husband and father. Services by the undersigned, assisted by G. H. Jones.
E. F. BYERS.

ROLLINS—Charles Ellery Rollins, son of Brother and Sister Ellery Rolling of Conemaugh Pennsylvania, died on January 14, 1920. On account of the illness of Brother Byers, the pastor, the undersigned was called upon for the service. The prayers of a large number of brethren go with the bereaVed parents in their sorrow. Jesus said. Interment in Hendricks cemetery.
G. H. JONES.

KEIM—Jonas M. Keim was born in Holmes County, Ohio, April 21, 1842 and departed this life January 15, 1920. The larger part of his life was spent in and near Louisville, Ohio. August 8, 1862 he enlisted for service in the Civil War at Mapleton, Ohio, in Co. B. 115 Reg. and served 3 years. He was a charter member of the Brethren church at Louisville.
The McKinley Post was present and paid their tribute of respect to their departed comrade. Services in charge of his pastor.
E. M. RIDDLE.

WHERE DO MINISTERS COME FROM?

Do they Just happen?

> *"Trained Christian Leadership is the Supreme Human Need in this Uuprecedented Age of World Upheaval and Adjustment."*

If you had to supply the Brethren Church with ministers and missionaries for the next 25 years, how would you do it?

How many young people has your church sent into definite Christian leadership in the last 15 years?

Published every Wednesday at Ashland, Ohio. All matter for publication must reach the Editor not later than Friday noon of the preceding week.

George S. Baer, Editor

**The
Brethren
Evangelist**

When ordering your paper changed give old as well as new address. Subscriptions discontinued at expiration. To avoid missing any numbers renew two weeks in advance.

R. R. Teeter, Business Manager

OFFICIAL ORGAN OF THE BRETHREN CHURCH

Subscription price, $2.00 per year, payable in advance.
Entered at the Post Office at Ashland, Ohio, as second-class matter.
Acceptance for mailing at special rate of postage provided for in section 1103, Act of October 3, 1917, authorized September 9, 1918.
Address all matter for publication to Geo. S. Baer, Editor of the Brethren Evangelist, and all business communications to R. R. Teeter, Business Manager, Brethren Publishing Company, Ashland, Ohio. Make all checks payable to the Brethren Publishing Company.

TABLE OF CONTENTS

EDITORIAL

A Note of Assurance From A Conservative Guide

Perhaps one of the most widely read among the conservative preacher's magazines is **The Expositor and Current Anecdotes** of which F. M. Barton is editor. We have never heard of Mr. Barton being accused of being too radical in propagating a new movement or of going afield in the theological tone of his magazine. He is everywhere considered safely orthodox and is criticised for being too conservative by some schools. It would be safe to say that more Brethren preachers are readers of this magazine than any other distinctively preacher's magazine published. While Mr. Barton is conservative, theologically speaking, he is awake to and carefully scrutinizes every new move that challenges the attention of the churches and gives his readers the benefit of his interpretation and valuation. We would not expect him to be quiet therefore concerning the Interchurch World Movement. Many of our preachers have already read what he has to say about it, but for the benefit of our great family of lay readers we will give his editorial in the February number of his magazine a place in these columns:

"The Interchurch World Movement has caused considerable misgiving among men who are earnest in promoting the kingdom of heaven on earth. I came to the conference here to question it for the benefit of the 15,000 preachers in The Expositor brotherhood—to report to you—bearing in mind that if it is to succeed that you readers, and the other preachers in America will have to do much of the burdensome work. We all know how heavily we are burdened now. Many of us are worried over inadequate salaries, which are the cause of thousands going into debt for food and clothing. I came to view it as your representative, to weigh it, and to determine for you, whether it was worth the sacrifice it will require from you and your people. The general question in the religious world today is, What do you think of the Interchurch Movement.

"One session of the conference determined one thing for me unmistakably—that is that Jesus Christ is in the Interchurch Movement. What led to that conclusion? For twenty-five years I have been as certain of my own salvation. But I wondered how much he had to hedge or compromise for the Y. M. C. A. during the war. The war has been a severe test to men of high places—even our president, judging from his actions on temperance, seems to have lost his religion under the strain, in Paris, or between there and America.

"But Mott had not been speaking long in the opening address until I was sure he was in close communion with the Captain of our salvation; that his correspondence fixed with heaven, had not been interrupted; and when he said there was no slate, or cut-and-dried program, or an effort to do a big thing merely for the sake of it being big, I believed him. He knows world conditions as no other man. When he said that forces of evil are coming upon us like flood, and that all churches must work together—not unite in one big unwieldy organization—I believed him.

"But when S. Earl Taylor followed him with facts showing results of the multiplicity of our individual activities, clinching the need of co-operation, I began to be sure.

"Dr. P. F. Patton said that China is at a door, looking to America to open it, and that 2,500 missionaries are depending prayerfully on word from the Interchurch Movement, of re-inforcement and support plies.

"Then came Sherwood Eddy, who said that the world war moves masses in India, and that what is practically home rule for India was putting on the leaders responsibilities which they could not discharge without Christian character.

"Then came Dr. S. G. Inman, relating the needs of South America. Our criss-cross occupation by different forces has not touched the fringe of this continent, whose leaders formerly looked up to Europe, but now look to the United States. They are crying to us 'Light, more light.' One class in English increased from 6 to 250 since the war.

"Samuel M. Zwemer, the prime-minister of the Kingdom to the Mohammedan world, told us Mohammedanism united was growing faster than Christianity, and if Christianity fails, that Mohammedanism stands ready to rule the heathen world. Nothing less than the correlated efforts of all the families of churches can stem the black onrushing storm. The powers of evil, anarchy, heathenism, Islamism are acting in concert to destroy the Christian world and a world movement only an interchurch movement can meet these forces. We went into the war not only to save humanity, but with the knowledge that if we did not, the German hordes would do to our America what they did to France and Belgium.

"The Christian churches and forces of America are going into the Interchurch World Movement not only to save others, but in saving others we save our own land for Jesus Christ.

"Therefore the sure knowledge that Christ is in the Interchurch Movements puts me in a different relation to it. It matters not, so much what we think of it, or how we judge it, but it matters a great deal what the Interchurch Movement thinks of our attitude towards it, how the spirit of Christ in it shall judge our co-operation or lack of co-operation.

"The Son of God goes forth to war—a kingly crown to gain—his blood-red banner streams afar. Who follows in his train?"

Illiteracy of American Born Children

That many American-born children are growing up illiterate is n by figures given in the Seventh Annual Report of the Chief le Children's Bureau of the U. S. Department of Labor. These es were collected in connection with the Bureau's administration le Child Labor Act of 1916 which was later declared unconstitul. They cover five states in which the employment of chilwas general.

Of 19,696 children between 14 and 16 years old to whom certiis were issued, more than one-fourth could not write their names ly. Nearly 10 percent had never gone beyond the first grade considerably more than half were in the fourth grade or lower a they left school. Only about three percent were in eighth e and about one in a hundred had reached high school.

These children were native Americans. Of the whole number, 24 were foreign born. The responsibility for their neglect, the rt points out, is not merely a local one. The United States is offering to the states financial assistance and expert advice in iding for the vocational education of children. A similar nationolicy might well be followed in regard to elementary education. "It is generally agreed," says the report, "that . . . . the eduonal opportunities offered the rural child are inferior to those red the children in cities or industrial towns. Illiteracy is everyre higher in the rural than in the urban population. Unless npt attention be given the problem the children of the present >ration will not be assured at least the elementary education ch every citizen in a republic should have. We surely cannot rd to ignore the need of a national guaranty of at least an eletary education for all the children of the country."

Brother Christiansen calls the attention of Ohio pastors to the stor's Interchurch Conference at Columbus, February 16 to 18.

Brother Gearhart gives us quite a detailed report of the receipts both home and foreign missions. He displays great care in his rk which all will appreciate.

A number of the college trustees found time to give us a brief l at the Publishing House. We are always glad to have the Breth. call.

Are you planning to observe Father and Son week in your rch? Think of the opportunities it affords. The time is the third ok in February.

Don't fail to look promptly at the Christian Endeavor departnt this week; it will interest you. It contains some bright Chrisn Endeavor faces and some spicy Christian Endeavor news. Read try word.

Brother Reed, our correspondent at Los Angeles First church ites us that "the new church foundation is now all in and the mework is going up. Brother Jennings is doing fine work and has atly unified the people."

The Business Manager's Report is very encouraging. The Evanlist family is still growing. We welcome Roanoke, Virginia and nter Chapel, Indiana and congratulate their pastors in leading their ople in this accomplishment.

After reading under the Sunday School department concerning a Teacher Training graduates, as reported by the superintendent that department, Prof. J. A. Garber, perhaps your school will be couraged to begin a class, if it has none.

Wherever Brother Homer Anderson goes we know he will be a ral supporter of the Evangelist; he is proving it at his charge in wa. We thank him for his loyalty. He is now in a revival at Milsburg. We pray that God may give him and his people the vicry.

A brief but splendid report comes to us from the Compton Avese church of Los Angeles. A goodly number of new members have en added to the church during the year and the Sunday school has en a large contributing factor. Every department of the work is ported in good condition.

Brother A. D. Gnagey was called to Pittsburgh last week to assist Brother Harley in jubilating over the burning of the note on the First Brethren church. Brother Gnagey reports a most enjoyable trip and states that the church shows every evidence of being in splendid condition. After a long struggle it is now free from debt.

Attention of the ministers is called to the fact that beginning about February 16 there will be held in the various states, conferences to acquaint the ministers with the plans and purposes of the Interchurch World Movement. This is a chance to get first-hand information concerning this great new movement that has come among us.

Brother E. Glenn Mason, the Ohio Benevolence Director, calls the attention of the Ohio churches to the offering that should very soon be in the hands of Brother Herman E. Roscoe, of Goshen, Indiana. That offering is the one which General Conference authorized to be taken for the benefit of the superannuated ministers. Brother Mason wishes that Ohio churches shall make a 100 percent response.

Brother I. D. Bowman calls our attention to an error that escaped the proof reader in his report of the Rittman meeting in Evangelist dated January 21. It should have read "Several preachers" instead of "Several hundred preachers." We are sorry for the mistake and have called the attention of the one who reads the proof to the matter that there may be greater care exercised.

Brother Lowman, of the Fillmore, California, church, writes that his congregation is taking on new life and starting the new year in fine shape after having recovered from a smallpox epidemic during which several Brethren families were afflicted. Brother Lowman announces that he is leaving Fillmore in April and is open to a call to another pastorate or possibly evangelistic work.

The College trustees were in session at Ashland last week and some plans for the further progress of our only educational institution were laid. In due time the brotherhood will doubtless be informed of the larger plans. The church never realized more than now how vitally important Ashland College is to its success and growth and never was interest keener in all that pertains to the welfare of our college.

Brother W. C. Teeter reports that Dayton is making some interesting history under the leadership of Brother E. M. Cobb, and that there has been set before the church for the coming year a challenging program. They have given their pastor a call to continue his services with them for another year and have very kindly granted him a vacation with full pay, so that Brother and Sister Cobb may visit their children on the Coast during the summer.

The work at Limestone, Tennessee, under the shepherding care of Sister Mary Pence, is going forward steadily and surely, and we have no doubt that the future will find, as the pastor suggests, not only a strong church at Limestone, but a number of churches round about. And we are sure those future churches will be loyal to every interest of the Brethren church because every Limestone Brethren home is a reader of The Evangelist.

Brother Cover's report of his work at Hagerstown, Maryland, shows that progress is being realized. A number of new members have been added to the church since last report. The "largest yet" White shirt offering as well as the "largest yet" other offerings show that the pastor's incessant teaching of missions is having its desired result. His good people showed their appreciation of the faithful services of their pastor and his wife by presenting them with a $200 Christmas gift and the teacher training class rewarded their teacher, the pastor, with a gold coin.

Brother Bell writes that the meeting at Morrill, Kansas, was "very satisfactory" in spite of the cold weather and fuel shortage and that the energy of Brother Whitted, the pastor, and his faithful woodmen prevented the necessity of a shut-down. A church that has contributed as many noble leaders to the church as has Morrill, will of course have enough noble men at home to cope with a little difficulty like a fuel shortage. Brother Bell writes from Hamlin where he is engaged in a two weeks' meeting and from there he goes to Pittsburgh in February to assist Brother Harley in a meeting.

GENERAL ARTICLES

Making the Program Count. By Prof. E. G. Mason
(Address delivered at Ohio State Conference, Canton)

How this or that great man or woman achieved his success, is the thing that appeals most strongly to our youth and ambition. If we were accorded the privilege of interviewing any great man, as Thomas A. Edison, Luther Burbank, Henry Ford, John Wanamaker or President Wilson, or any other man of international reputation and of asking him the secret of his success, I am sure that he would answer in much this same way: (1) a vision of the future; (2) a definite program toward making this vision real, and (3) hard and persistent work in working out this program. The policy of such men may well be followed in religious work.

In all work connected with the betterment of a person or a community, a goal to be reached is first of all a necessity. Next, a program must be mapped out carefully planning the work to be done step by step toward the reaching of the goal. Lastly, the doing of the work is a necessity. There are those whose visions are clear and lofty, but these visions are never realized because they are not backed up with the working out of a definite program. These we call dreamers. They are the idealists. They are necessary because they furnish the visions for those who can see none for themselves. But their work would be much more effective if they could follow up their dreams with realization. There are those who are experts at planning a program for others to work out. These are organizers. They are as necessary as the dreamers; but they, too, are most valuable when they back up their organization with hard and consistent work. Sometimes the last class is far the largest. Each of us falls into one class or the other, so there is work for all of us to do. There must be vision, organization and work in every successful Young People's Society. These are fundamental.

The program must be viewed from two angles (1) the weekly program or prayer meeting during the rendition of which the members take an active part. (2) A community program intended for the raising of the standards of the community in which the society is formed.

This leads us to our first consideration, What shall our program count for?

First, it must count for an increased interest in spiritual things on the part of our young people. If our rendition of the weekly program fails to do this our work has lost much that should be done.

In the rush and bustle of a busy world, the quickening of the spiritual life is neglected and it assumes instead, the aspect of a deadening. The past few years have seen the world's history increased by many volumes. Affairs of world wide importance have flashed before our vision with lightning-like rapidity. History is being made so rapidly that most of us can not keep up with it. Local, national and world-wide affairs have occupied our minds so fully that we are apt to crowd interest in spiritual things out of our lives. In no small measure nas it been crowded out of the lives of our young people, and the end is not yet. While America was wrapped body and soul in the problems of the great war, our nerves were screwed up to the highest tension. We were all constantly upon our guard. We served more faithfully; we saved, both food and money, more carefully, and we lived more spiritually. Yes, we lived more spiritually. Men and women who did not ally themselves to any church or religious organization, not only thought upon spiritual things but acted in a spiritual manner and were the better for it. Then the armistice was signed. What then? Just as the farmer or laborer after a hard day's work sits serenely down and rests; or the horse after a hard pull leans back in the harness and rests, so the American people since the tension of the war is over, have settled back and say, "Let us rest awhile, while the world moves on." This resting business is a dangerous business. While closing our eyes a resting, we are apt to let the world slip back again deep than ever into the mire. It is all right if we rest with o eyes open and gather strength for another attack, but if rest and let the load run back it is dangerous. Since t cessation of hostilities, there has been a general relapse our national morals and a rapid return to things not spir ual. It is dangerous for we must preserve the morals of o young people for in them the hope of our future rests. the light of the great good that the Catholic church has do in the late war, it would be far from our purpose to cri cise them, but we will call your attention simply to o practice to illustrate this point. It is a common practice have a great celebration just before the lenten season ushered in as a sort of good-bye to the pleasures of t world and again to have another demonstration and orgy things not rigidly spiritual just as soon as it is over as sort of how-do-you-do to the same worldly pleasures.

It appears that the season of fasting and prayer is mo forced than forceful. If one were really anxious to wors! by fasting and prayer, it would seem that the season shou begin earlier and last longer. I am afraid that much of t spiritual effect of the fast is spoiled by the celebratio We dare not allow the tension of morals to relapse. We, a Christian people, must foster its survival and growth.

Sometimes the morals of people are kept good by pub opinion. We must distinguish between public opinion a religion. Many of us are controlled in our moral progr by a fear of what others may say or think. We are go only because we are afraid of the opinions of others. Pub opinion is not a safe guide. Openly, it is effective, but l hind closed doors it is of no avail. Public opinion, in t past and present, has been a great factor in preserving t public, not the private morals of our young people. Not with religion. With religion, it is not the fear of 'puni ment at the hands of a just God, that guides our mor aright, but the reverence and desire for better and high things. If this reverence and desire can be instilled into t hearts and minds of our young people, we shall make rap strides forward toward the evangelization of the world a the establishing of a brotherhood of man which shall see more wasteful and wicked wars that rob us of our youth a strength.

In the second place, we must develop a social spirit our young people. An interest that will lead them aw from themselves and lend them an interest in affairs outsi of self, a whole-souled and friendly interest in the bett ment of society at large, both national and international well as an interest in the people immediately around the As a cloth is woven from many threads, so our social fab is composed of many individuals. As truly as the thre are, so the cloth will be, just as truly as the individuals a so the society will be. This means that we must be int ested in all classes of people, in the laborer as in the capit ist, in the learner as well as in the teacher, and in the s ner as well as in the righteous. If education is a traini for citizenship, the very fact that we are citizens deman that we must be good citizens. A good citizen is one w by his example and by his acts, raises the general standa of the state. Our public school system is organized so tl its teachings shall ultimately produce a model state. lays its greatest stress upon the development of the intell and leaves the moral development to the church. Primari this belonged to the church, but today it is as much the du of the school as it is of the church. But the church must pace and keep in the front rank. This social interest t be developed early in life when the interest is easily :ured and developed. When the youth once becomes an lt, habits of life are fixed. Thus the interests of the indual are fixed and it becomes a hard matter to interest :m in anything other than that which affects their bread d butter. During youth is the time when questions of :ial importance must be hit hard again and again. The oblems of the missions, the poor and needy and aged, and estions of public concern must be met by careful study d attention. This our youth must learn so that they may rm an important part in our social fabric when they reach e age of accountability.

In the third place, we must develop accuracy and honty. These two factors in character development are the ost needed and the most needed and the most sadly wantg in our national life today. The greatest example of the ck of these factors is found in Germany. So self-satisfied at her thinking and planning were perfect! But how forately (for us) inaccurate in her calculations for world nquest! Germany stands today as the greatest apostle of shonestly before the world. Dishonesty in her dealings ith the world and with her own people. The fate of all ations rests upon the accuracy of their calculations and the onesty of their dealings. The proper place to begin a camaign of teaching to lead toward an accurate and honest ate is during youth. America has long been criticized for ie inaccuracy of her educational results. The Nobel prizes ave gone with but few exceptions to Europeans. The hodes scholars, our most accomplished scholars in America, re criticized by the British professors for their superficial nowledge and inability to apply themselves to difficult roblems for long periods of time. Our public school teachg does not demand and does not secure accuracy. Since ve are all products of our public school system, it follows hat our religious teaching also lacks accuracy. As to honsty, perhaps we are as honest, nationally, as any other ation, yet considering our position as a leader, religiously, ıhysically and financially, we are far from being honest. A young Japanese student before sailing for our shores was onvinced that the average American was a model Christian. This conception was formed from the American missionary who had converted him. He sailed with about $5,000 which vas to cover his educational expenses. He had planned, ifter completing his education to return to his people as a eacher. He sailed upon an American ship manned by Amercans. His faith in the Christianlike character of Americans n general was somewhat shaken while yet on shipboard.

But when he arrived at New York, he listened to the counsels of the first well dressed American he met and gave him his $5,000 for a safe (?) investment. He lost his money but far worse he lost his faith in the honesty of American. He became incredulous and concluded that to pit his wits successfully against Americans, he must meet dishonesty with dishonesty, so his education or the Americanization of this Jap produced a sleek crook instead of a missionary.

In the business and financial world of today, it is hard for a man to be honest. This is all the more reason why honesty must be included in character building. In the business world and religious world, and there are those who believe that these are the only two worlds, and that they are distinctly separate, our standards of honesty differ widely. There can be but one standard and that must be the religious standard. We must project the correct standard of morals into the business world. And this can best be done only through instilling the importance of accuracy and honesty in the minds of our young people. So we must keep these things constantly before them in our weekly programs.

Now, how shall we make the program count? I do not purpose to lay down any set rules, but will only try to make several suggestions as to how it might be done.

First, we can make it count by giving the young people all possible encouragement. We may do this by showing an interest in their meetings by our attendance, applause and financial aid. We may also, profitably give them some of our time in service. But lastly, we may give them great encouragement by living the best possible and the most irreproachable lives as an example for them to follow. Finally we may make the program count by giving our young people the privilege of running their own society. In other words, we make the program count for much by expecting them to do the work and get into the habit of doing it. Our suggestions will go a long ways towards guiding them in the discharge of this leadership, but the fact that they are doing this work themselves independently of the older people, brings about a sense of responsibility and importance needed in their preparation for life.

In conclusion, let me repeat that our programs for the young people's meetings, if they are to count for much in the social framework of the church and of society in general, must result in:

(1) An increased interest in spiritual things.
(2) The development of a healthy social spirit.
(3) The development of an accurate and honest citizenship.

West Salem, Ohio.

Christianity, the Racial Religion. By President E. E. Jacobs, Ph.D.

There is a common notion abroad, that among the religions of the world, some are bad, some rather indifferent, and ıome good; Christianity is listed in this latter class. Or in ıther words, we list many religions as false and Christianity is a true religion.

It is, moreover, suggested that each religion stresses its ıwn peculiar cardinal virtue, viz., annihilation; or devotion, ır respect for the fathers, or fidelity to taboos. Thinking ılong this line, it is said that love is the cardinal virtue of Christianity. It is said too, that the so-called golden rule ıums up Christianity in one sentence and that St. Paul exɔloited it all in his essay on charity.

The geneticist also says that if we had all these gropings ıfter God summed up, we would have the race religion, or ;he totemic religion of mankind, that if we were to leave out ;he ill and keep the good, we would have the perfect human religion. And there is, doubtless, something common to all ;hese feelings after God, something pitiful and yet sublime, ɔomething that will not down.

And yet it seems to me, that there is an error here. For first of all, there is no one virtue which a man may practice ınd make sure that he is a Christian, for a man may, for instance, love his fellow man devotedly, and be only a humanitarian. Or he may love God and yet be only a theist. After one has read the love chapter of St. Paul through and studied the golden rule, one must see that after all the words only partly convey a few facts about a theme that is vastly superior to all that has or can be said about it.

Christianity is new wine that dare not be put into old wineskins. True, but it is more than new wine. It is leaven in the life. Yes, but it is vastly more than leaven. It is as a grain of seed planted in a man's heart. Yes, but it is more than seed. It is life and light. And it is more than life or light or death or powers. It is more than beliefs, more than formularies of faith, or creeds, or ordinances. It can not be bounded by bulls, or conclaves, or conferences, or words or actions of men. It is more than confessions of faith, for a man if left to himself on a waste and dreary desert, could still be a Christian. Yes, if he were once a Christian, he could not be otherwise than a Christian even then. It is more than a set of rules of action for a man might follow every rule and still have his heart far from God. Christianity implies, demands a closer union between the heart of Christ and one's own heart. Christianity is bigger than those who practice it and all the human errors that accompany its expression in the life, is BUT THE HUMAN CONCOMITANT of a thing that is otherwise divine!

Christianity defies description or definition! It is more than the words which attempt to express its meaning. It is bigger than any church. It outreaches the best priesthood and is more than all the books that have been written about it. The best men who have ever lived are after all, only poor expressions of it. Men can not be bought to take it nor, blessed be God, can they be bought to let it go.

Christianity seems to have sounded all the depths of the human heart. It has touched rock bottom. The race is fully satisfied by its findings and there is and can be no other religion which may surpass it. Its plummet leaves no depths below it and its sublimity leaves no space above it, but it is all and in all and may be through us all. Its fire and power and its inner compulsion fills, fulfills and complements the human heart.

It is not one of the religions of earth, then, it is THE religion of humanity. It approves of all that is good in the human heart and bids all that is ill depart; what more could a religion do? Yet we handle it slovenly. We talk all too much about it and practice it all too little. We claim to understand it and yet the Christianity that is practiced by my next door neighbor, who in the weary treadmill of life is faithful and true, is more than I can understand and all the.

wisdom of all the ages can not explain that inner compulsi which urges him on in paths of right.

Christianity, when once it grips the fabric of a ma; or a nation's life, is hard to remove utterly. We talk abc it slipping away, but try to tear it from the heart of Am; ica and what do we have? Could we possibly go back the heathen conception and treatment of childhood? Or the sanctity of the home? Or of marriage and divorce? of womanhood? Or of treatment of those who disagree wi us? Could we ever so lose Christianity that it would nev show itself in our life?

Christianity seems, when viewed from every angle, to in the religion of humanity and has nothing to fear from the ethical culture propaganda in the world. Christ, t blossom and fruition of all that was good in the race, w born in the fullness of time. The whole creation groaned f and up to the time of his birth in the travail of pain.] was at once the divine Son of God and the son of man. him is expressed all the fullness of the glory of God, a glo to which every race and tribe, in some way or other, pere nially strove. And Christ made it possible for the race come back to God, and it need seek no further for its hea may literally bathe in the flood of its highest ideals, idea realised perfectly in Jesus, the Christ of God. Oh, t riches of grace in Christ Jesus!

Ashland, Ohio.

Additional Editorial Report Concerning Interchurch Plans.

Many earnest leaders of the Brethren church, while prosecuting vigorously the plans of our own church for extending the kingdom of Christ, are yet eager to have the benefit of the inspiration and plans and vision of the world's greatest Christian leaders. This, they feel, enables them to do the work God has called us as a church to do more effectively. Furthermore we want to know what is our full shart of responsibility in the task of taking the work for Christ. Keeping in touch with these Interchurch plans helps us.

Pastor's Conferences Between February 16 and March 26

Pastors' conferences will be held in every state in the Union under the auspices of the Field Department of the Interchurch Movement from February 16 to March 26. All the ministers of evangelical churches are invited to "consider the plan of work at home and abroad." Since it is important that every clergyman attend, the traveling expenses of all will be paid through the Movement. Further details will be received directly from the Interchurch Movement officials. Pastors should note the dates and places of their respective conferences and plan to attend. Notice the Interchurch Bulletin also for further information.

The dates of the conferences so far arranged are as follows:

Group A.		Group C.	
Columbus	Feb. 16-18	Wichita	Feb. 16-18
Harrisburg	Feb. 18-20	Lincoln	Feb. 18-20
Hartford	Feb. 23-25	Des Moines	Feb. 23-25
Trenton	Feb. 25-27	Mitchell	Feb. 25-27
Rochester	Mar. 1-3	Minneapolis	Mar. 1- 3
Providence	Mar. 3-5	Fargo	Mar. 3- 5
Boston	Mar. 8-10	Chicago	Mar. 8-10
Bangor	Mar 10-12	**Group D**	
Group B.		Salt Lake City	Feb. 16-18
Kansas City	Feb. 16-18	Reno	Feb. 18-20
Milwaukee	Feb. 18-20	Nampa	Feb. 23-25
Lansing	Feb. 25-27	Helena	Feb. 25-27
Indianapolis	Mar. 1- 3	Douglas	Mar. 1- 3
Parkersburg	Mar. 3- 5	Denver	Mar. 3- 5
Baltimore	Mar. 8-10	Oklahoma City	Mar. 8-10
Wilmington	Mar. 10-12	Little Rock	Mar. 10-12
Group E			
Ft. Worth	Feb. 17-19		
Albuquerque	Feb. 19-20		

Phoenix	Feb. 23-25
Los Angeles	Mar. 25-27
San Francisco	Mar. 1- 3
Portland	Mar. 3- 5
Tacoma	Mar. 8-10
Spokane	Mar. 10-12

Every congregation should see to it that its pastor provided with hotel expenses and is urged to attend the Pa tor's Conference of his state in order that he may be i formed as to this new forward movement of all the Prote; ant churches of North America and bring back whatev benefit is there to be derived. Churches would often increa their pastor's efficiency manifold if they would make it pc sible for them to get away occasionally to conferences at conventions and get inspiration and information concernii new challenges and methods and movements. To these co ferences the pastors will have their traveling expenses pa by the Interchurch World Movement, as stated above, but some cases the hotel expenses will exceed the railroad fai Here is where the local church should give a helping hat to its own pastor; give him enough money to pay his hot bill and tell him you will be glad to have him go and inve tigate this new movement, get a little rest and receive sor fresh inspiration. A hint to the wise is sufficient.

The Evangelistic Campaign

A nation-wide campaign utilizing every church as ; evangelistic center and every Christian as an evangelist, w decided upon at a meeting of denominational leaders at Ne York on January 23. The campaign is to culminate on Ea ter, which is to be known as "Join the Church Sunday Noon-day rallies in the business districts of about 100 citii under the auspices of local churches and in co-operation wi the Laymen's and Field Department of the Interchur World Movement, will be a feature. Similar meetings f women will be conducted under the auspices of women's c ganizations co-operating with the Women's Activities D partment of the Movement. This is a splendid season f evangelism and the fact that every church will be talkii and attempting evangelism will help to create a favorab spirit or atmosphere. Every church should do its whole du in the campaign for souls.

The co-operation of denominational stewardship dire tors in an active campaign for the promotion of the Febr ary Stewardship Educational period, which will reach i

The movement grew out of a conviction which has been spreading rapidly throughout the country that this is the time to start a Christian campaign for the salvation of China. In cities as widely separated as Peking and Canton spontaneous local movements have sprung up, generally calling themselves "The Christianity to Save China Movement." The whole of China is hungering for the gospel of Jesus Christ and it is the only thing that can make China safe for the world.

British and Scandinavian missions were represented at Shanghai as well as American, but after a notable speech of the Chinese secretary of the missionary society of the Episcopal church the conference decided the forward movement in China should be a Chinese movement. It will have a Chinese general secretary, Dr. Cheng Ching-yi, and more than half the directing committee will be Chinese. It is an autonomous movement, although it will co-operate closely with the Interchurch Movement through the Continuation Committee and Dr. E. C. Lobenstine, chairman of the committee, will act as associate secretary of the Chinese Movement.

f Darkness. Mrs. S. C. Kirkpatrick

and with fire and he shall receive power to overcome sin and the devil.

Too many people put too much dependence in John's baptism and not enough in the baptism of Jesus. John said, I indeed baptize you with water unto repentance, but there cometh one after me whose shoes I am not worthy to bear, he shall baptize you with the Holy Ghost and with fire. Anybody can be baptized with water, whether they have forsaken their sins or not, but Jesus will not baptize you with the Holy Ghost until you are willing to give up all sin. Then he will baptize you and cleanse your heart from the Adam's sin, that is, the carnal nature. Some people think we cannot get rid of the carnal nature. But I know from my own experience that we can. For he took all the grouchiness and ill-temper out of me. Praise his holy name!

If every one that has taken the name of Christ would live as the precious Lord taught, how soon we would conquer old Satan! But with so much inconsistency he is not much alarmed. He has gotten the theatres and picture shows and the dance halls to gather in the church members. When one sees the crowds gathered at these places he is made to think that Satan must feel very much encouraged. For he generally is quite sure of the people who are in the habit of entering these places.

Why not every true believer seek the baptism of the Holy Ghost for it is for all who will receive it. The church of Christ could get such power that it would fairly make old Satan tremble if it would seek it. Think what it will mean when we can shout the victory over Satan.

Conemaugh, Pennsylvania.

Prohibition, the long-prayed for event, is now come to pass throughout the land. But the church may not repair to its easy chair and rest and slumber in security. The task is only half finished. The law of the land can be enforced only as the church marshalls and maintains a Christian public sentiment that will require and back up the strict enforcement of all prohibition laws.

Just as the war broke down many families of the world and wrecked many homes, so it is in the greater war of the church of Christ against all the forces of evil many family ALTARS are being broken down and many promising members of the homes being torn away. Before the church can truly win in this warfare she must build up these altars and make less likely the wrecking of lives through the neglect of the home.

THE BRETHREN PULPIT

The Preeminence of Christ's Person.　By Charles H. Ashman

The Scriptures teach that the Godhead is composed of a trinity of Beings. As there are three departments of our government, executive, judicial, and legislative, yet forming the one government, so there are three Persons, but the one Godhead. In the Old Testament, the name for God, Elaohim, is plural. In Genesis 1:26, it is written, "Let us make." In the record of the baptism of Jesus, the attending manifestations clearly imply three Beings. Scofield says, "The Trinity is explicitly taught in the baptismal formula of Matthew 28:19. Yes, the Father is God! The Son is God! The Holy Spirit is God! Yet no one is the other. The Word of God nowhere seeks to explain or prove this but teaches it as a fact of revelation to be accepted by faith.

In the pre-eminence of Christ's Person, we believe him to have been PRE-EXISTENT. He was before his birth in Bethlehem. There never was a time when he was not. His pre-existence really is his eternal existence in the eternity of the past. In Philippians 2:6-8, we are taught that Christ was in the form of God; he was on an equality with God; he took the form of man, being made in the likeness and fashion of humanity. In Hebrews 1:8-12, the pre-existence of Christ is clearly taught. Colossians 1:15-19, with wonderful language, emphatically declares Christ to have been the Creator. In John 17:5, Jesus declared he had glory with the Father before the creation came into existence. In John 16:28, he states that he came from God and would return to God. In John 8:58, he uses this expression, "Before Abraham was, I. AM." Not, "I WAS," but "I AM." He does not cut his existence into pieces, but counts it a unit of continuity. There can be no question in the mind of any honest Bible student, but that the expression in John 1:1, "The Word," denotes Christ. Should there be, a glance at Revelation 19:13-16, will prove that it can apply only to Christ. In that wonderful prophetic forecast of Micah 5:2, the place of the expression of the incarnation of Christ is foretold as Bethlehem, but the Person himself declared to be EVERLASTING. Thus we are brought face to face with the fact that the PERSON of Christ was eternally pre-existent.

The question might be asked, "How then is God the Father of Jesus?" He is not the Father of his Deity! He could not beget what was co-existent and co-equal with himself. The Deity of Christ was never begotten; it was eternal. God through the Holy Spirit, was the Father of the humanity of Christ. The expression, "the only begotten Son," refers to the humanity begotten of God in Virgin Mary. Hebrews 10:5 informs us of all that Christ received in this birth. "A BODY hast thou prepared me." The humanity through which Christ manifested his Deity was the only thing he received in birth. As Deity, he was and is the uncaused, unbegun, self-existent, eternal Being. Any system or person teaching that there ever was a time when Christ did not exist, that his Person was ever created, blasphemes his Person and contradicts the Word of God.

Now, Christ, as the eternal, pre-existent Being was incarnated in a perfect, distinct human nature and body. He became, "God manifest in the flesh." He became God incarnate, Immanuel, "God with us." Only one change was made in his in this incarnation, the change in form or appearance. He was in the form of God. He laid aside that form, appearance, and took upon himself the form of man. His Being, Personality, Person remained the same. As the eternal God, he descended from glory, took of the substance of Mary, the "Seed of Woman," a new, perfect, distinct, divinely created human nature and body, united to it his own uncreated Being and became "Immanuel, God with us." Seven times he is called God in the Scriptures. He is the only GOD-MAN!

In this incarnation, Christ possessed a perfect, distinc sinless human nature. The Deity of Christ could have foun no fellowship with a human nature like that of a carn nature possessed by everyone born of the seed of Adam. Ou nature is never in harmony with the new nature receive when we become children of God. It is conquered by an held in subjugation to it, but is never in harmony with i Paul clearly teaches this in Galatians 5:17 and Romans 7:1 Can you conceive of such a struggle between sinful, carn nature and his Deity going on in Christ! We cannot! The is this difference between the humanity of Christ and ot common humanity,—we are born of the flesh, of the will man, are by nature sinful. We must be born again to b come the sons of God. Christ's humanity was sinless by cr ation. "That HOLY THING which shall be born in th shall be called the Son of God." What was born in Mary Not the Christ, but his body! His nature could not hav been sinless except it had been born of God. "That whi is born of the flesh is flesh" and God has counted all fles sinful before him. But, "Whatsoever is born of God cann sin." The new nature born of God in the new birth nev sins. The sins of the Christian are to be attributed to th old nature still abiding within. The nature of Christ wa sinless because it was born of God. How then was Chri human? He was born "IN THE LIKENESS" of sinful fles! Mary was only used as an instrument to make the incarn tion clear and plain. The body of Christ was not depen ent upon Mary for existence or nature. It received the from the Holy Spirit. The only thing it received from Ma was FORM, APPEARANCE. There is this distinction to b made between the temptations of Christ and ours, when w are tempted we are "drawn away from our own sinful lu (desire), but Christ had no such inward solicitation! E had no fallen Adamic nature! He was perfectly human, b by a NEW CREATION—the second man, the "last Adam (1 Corinthians 15:45). His temptations all came from wit! out! As regards his sinless nature, there is this to be r membered relative to our sins being borne in his body. The were not born in HIS NATURE! In this respect he w holy, undefiled and separate from sinners. His sacrifice wi both exterior and interior,—his body was broken and h soul was offered.

Here then are the things to remember about the Pers of Christ. He was eternal Deity. He was begotten the So of God in his humanity, born of God. His nature as he live upon the earth was sinless and perfect by creation. He die upon the cross, was buried, was resurrected, ascended to th right hand of God where he liveth as God. He will con again as Deity to claim his purchased possession. In all th he is ETERNAL, PERFECT, SINLESS, CHANGELESS!

There rests upon the church of today the solemn oblig again as Deity to claim his purchased possession. nI all th tion to sound forth the Scriptural teachings concerning th Person of Christ. On every hand the false teachings Russelism, Christian Science, and other cults are bein taught with subtle cunningness. In many puplits, the Deit Virgin Birth, Sinless Perfection, Incarnation, and Etern Being of Christ are being denied and scoffed at. The onl way the world will receive or retain a Scriptural conceptio of Christ is for these wonderful facts to be sounded fort without fear, for the unchanging Word is back of then Read Romans 10:8-10.

Sunnyside, Washington.

A great evangelist once said it was his business goin about among the churches "to kick the bushel measure o the lights of church members."

OUR DEVOTIONAL

Quiet Hour Talk--How to Pray. By E. M. Riddle

(Given at Ohio Conference, Canton)

OUR SCRIPTURE

We must be obedient. And whatsoever we ask we receive of him, because we keep his commandments, and do those things that are pleasing in his sight (1 John 3:22).

Our wills must be surrendered to God and this is the confidence that we have in him, that, if we ask anything according to his will, he heareth us (1 John 5:14).

We must pray in the spirit. Praying always with all prayer and supplications in the spirit . . . (Eph. 6:18).

We must pray in the name of Christ. Verily, verily, I say unto you, whatsoever ye shall ask the Father in my name, he will give it you (John 16:23).

We must pray in faith. But let him ask in faith nothing wavering. For he that wavereth is like a wave of the sea driven with the wind and tossed (James 1:6).

We must pray in earnest. I say unto you, Though he will not rise and give him, because he is his friend, yet because of his importunity he will rise and give him as many as he needeth.

And being in agony he prayed more earnestly: and his sweat was as it were great drops of blood falling down to the ground. (Luke 11:8; 22:44).

OUR MEDITATIONS

With these Scriptural passages in mind we surely are ready to consider for a few moments the importance and the need of the Quiet Hour.

The servant of God has need for the Quiet Hour. A few weeks ago, after having made a trip through mud and rain calling upon different individuals, earnestly requesting and urging that they do their whole duty to God and their church, the brother who was with me said, "It surely requires faith and courage to go out and get people to see and do their duty, for after all it is a voluntary service that you ask them to do."

He was right. But where does this faith and courage come from? By observing the Quiet Hour at least fifteen minutes each day in prayer and meditation upon God's Word and thoughts of the Eternal, we can feel that sweet communion with God, who bestows upon the worker true wisdom. He enlightens his servants as to his will and as to pursuing it in the best way. God alone is the source of such faith and courage. The weapons of our warfare must be spiritual, and rightly handling them is true wisdom. In fact, the well-grounded Christian man who is a whole-hearted follower of Christ has learned of him, how to trust, how to obtain strength, patience and humility and courage. A servant who is a stranger to prayer will soon come to grief. But if there is communion with God he can endure; his moral standard will not suffer; nor will dangers and manifold trials do him injury or make him fearful. Jesus knew no fear and he has inspired his disciples with his own courage.

The busy layman needs to take time for prayer. The excuse so often comes, No time to pray. You have 24 hours every day all your own, to be used for yourself or for others from whom you get pay. Isn't there a little time in this 24 hours that is wasted that might be used as the Quiet Hour? Why not get up fifteen minutes earlier when the mind is clear, before any business worries have crept into your life, when there are no disturbances, and begin the day right by using this time for prayer? We take time for everything else, just so we can take time for prayer. If you wait for an opportunity it may never come. We must not wait for time but take time. Do not get the idea that because you are busy is an excuse. It is well known that we go to busy people to get things done and not to idlers. Then covenant with God that you will give him a little unhurried time every day in sweet communion.

There is much seeking for God that is not searching for God with all the heart. There is much praying but too little "prayer." There is a too reckless rushing into prayer and too little patient waiting for the response. Spurgeon said, "Prayer pulls the rope below and the great bell rings above in the ears of God. Some scarcely stir the bell, for they pray so languidly. Others give but an occasional pluck at the rope: but he who wins with heaven is the man who grasps the rope boldly and pulls continuously, with all his might."

OUR PRAYER

Our Father and God, giver of all grace and wisdom, from whom is our strength and joy, we come to thee in the spirit of thanksgiving for all people who know the power and way of prayer. We are also thankful for the great number of Quiet Hour Comrades in the Brethren church and in all churches. Just now we humbly beg that all who read these lines may resolve through the help of the Spirit to give at least fifteen minutes each day to prayer and Bible study. In his precious name. Amen.

Louisville, Ohio.

Christianity in Prophecy. By T. Darley Allen

The wonderful growth of early Christianity cannot be adequately accounted for if the supernatural element in religion be denied. Only by accepting the New Testament estimate of Jesus can we explain how an obscure peasant was able to lift "with his pierced hands empires off their hinges" and turn "the stream of time into new channels."

But were the reasons stated by skeptics to explain the success of the Christian religion in the early centuries adequate to account for the fact, how absurd to deem the world's "great revolution" explainable on natural principles when we consider that the Old Testament prophets described the religion of Christ and declared its extension to the Gentile nations!

The Jewish religion was not a missionary faith, and what could be more wonderful than that the fact should be foreseen and the prophets declare that out of such a religion a faith was to come which should extend everywhere?

The rapid extension of early Christianity was marvelous, to say the least; considered in relation to the prophecies could it have been less miraculous?

The predictions in the Old Testament are admitted by infidels themselves to have been written before the Christian era; and those relating to the rapid extension of a religion to arise among the Jewish people are scattered throughout the writings of the prophets. "All the ends of the earth shall remember and turn unto the Lord—I will give thee for a light to the Gentiles, that thou mayest be my salvation to the ends of the earth—In the place where it was said, Ye are not my people it shall be said, Ye are the sons of the living God—Out of Zion shall go forth the law—The Gentiles shall come to thy light and kings to the brightness of the rising —Nations that knew thee not shall run after thee"—these are a few of the wonderful prophecies in the Jewish scriptures that show that a religion was to arise out of the exclusive Hebrew faith to embrace the Gentile nations.

Cleveland, Ohio.

Thoughtful we ought to be, anxious we must never be. Anxiety does no good, it is futile; more, it does serious harm. We need to be at our best on the threshold of the unknown day: we are not at our best consumed by apprehension.—W. L. Atkinson.

Tennyson says, "For I doubt not through the ages one increasing purpose runs; and the thoughts of men are widened with the process of the suns."

Send
WHITE GIFT
OFFERINGS to

THE SUNDAY SCHOOL

ALBERT TRENT
General Secretary-Treasurer
Johnstown, Pennsylvania

Teacher Training Graduation. By Prof. J. A. Garber

We are pleased to report the graduation of several Teacher Training classes. The report has been delayed for reasons that need not be given here.

Gratis, Ohio

A few years ago, we understand, during the pastorate of Brother George H. Jones, a class or two was graduated in the Gratis school. Another class was immediately organized and later the number was augmented with the members of another class. The combined classes, which had been taught by Brother Holiday, were graduated last August at the close of the Life Work Conference. A splendid program of music and kindred parts was presented under the direction of Superintendent N. G. Kimmel. Pastor C. E. Beekley conducted the devotions, and the writer was privileged to give the address. The class was large as the names below indicate and the presence of a half-dozen ex-service boys added to the impressiveness of the occasion. The names of graduates follow: Orville Ulrich, Pauline Hellar, Mae Smith, Ruth Beekley, Ray Ulrich, Ethel Eby, Ivy Focht, Roy Brubaker, Paul Eikenberry, Lyndow R. Street, Clyde Coleman, Russel Fudge, L. R. Zimmerman, Lowell Ulrich, Ralph Ulrich, Palmer Etter, Carl Smith and Orange Pence. The Gratis school is to be commended upon the graduation of such a large class.

Carleton, Nebraska

More recently a class at Carleton completed a course of study. The teacher was Mrs. W. H. Wearin, who, judging the grades, did excellent teaching. An interested person and helper was Superintendent N. C. Eastabrooks. Both he and Mrs. Wearin have our heartiest congratulations upon the untiring efforts that were put forth in graduating this class. Following are the names of those who completed the course successfully: Alta Rachow, Gladys Miller, Myra Horner, Lulu L. Linsley, Mrs. W. H. Wearin and Jessie Brinegar. Although no report has been given as to their public graduation, we feel confident that those interested received due recognition by the officers of the school and Pastor J. D. Kemper.

Pressing Forward

These classes completed one of the Old Standard courses but each plans to go forward with the New Three Year course. Gratis has already ordered a nice number of copies of the "Educative Process in Religion." Other orders have been received and new classes are being organized. It may not be out of place to suggest that where a school has no training class as yet, it is not too late to organize one. A class in every school is required by point 5 of our Standard of Excellence.

J. A. Garber
PRESIDENT

Our Young People at Work

G. C. Carpenter
SECRETARY

Provide Training for Children and Youth. By Prof. J. A. Garber

Children and youth are not to be forgotten during Christian Endeavor Week. The suggested program made ample provision for both. Superintendents of Junior and Intermediate societies are asked to remember their own. The picture and report of the Nappanee boys and girls emphasize the possibilities of such training. We certainly were glad to learn of their splendid work, and congratulate them most heartily. Last week a similar account was given of the Dayton Intermediate society, and it is now followed with an appeal to others from the Superintendent, Mrs. W. O. Abbott. The other articles are from earnest workers who report their experiences with the children and teen age folks at Winona. Mrs. Wolford superintends a fine Intermediate society at Elkhart and Miss Bracken is our National Junior-Intermediate Superintendent. These workers know the great value of Christian Endeavor training for the young and they are glad to bear these testimonies in the hope of encouraging fellow workers and inducing others to organize Junior and Intermediate societies.

JUNIOR EXPERT ENDEAVOR GRADUATES, NAPPANEE, INDIANA

Report of Junior Endeavor Society. Nappanee, Indiana

The Junior society at Nappanee, Indiana, would like to give an account of itself to the friends among the Evangelist family. During the last six months of 1919 our society made sixty percent on the efficiency chart. We have sixteen subscriptions to the Jr. C. E. World, twenty-two Juniors keeping the Quiet Hour, twenty Tenth Legioners and in November graduated twelve from the Junior Expert course. None of the graduates made a lower grade than eighty-six percent. During the month of August, generally called the summer slump month, our society had an average attendance of eighteen. A few other averages for that month were, sentence prayers, seven; Bibles carried, ten; verses memorized, sixteen; Bible chapters read, sixty-six. Calls on sick with reading to them and carrying flowers, playthings to children and telling stories to children during that one month were twelve. The society also lifted an offering for foreign missions, sent a Christmas box to our home mission field in Kentucky and is supplying a tuberculosis hospital in Arizona with good literature. In May there will be sixteen of this society graduated to the Intermediate society, and you can easily see that the Intermediates are to receive a blessing when they receive these additions. Where is there another society with such a body of prepared Juniors? Maybe this will make glad the heart of Brother Garber, and cause him to feel that Junior work is making good where tried.   MRS. HARRY RICHMOND, Superintendent.

Intermediate Session at Winona

The short Intermediate session at General Conference was held at Westminster chapel. The session was an inspiration to all who attended. Each Intermediate was willing to do his part to make the meeting a success. The coming Senior society in a large measure depends on the Intermediates. It seems to the writer that not enough stress is put upon the Intermediate work. The same time and encouragement that is spent on the Seniors should be given to the Intermediates. This would bring about far greater results for all. The boys and girls are at the age when they are willing to do whatever they are asked to do. This willingness if taken advantage of will train them to do greater work in the Senior society.

The Intermediates are planning great things for their part in the conference next year. Let the program committee take notice.

There were eight different societies represented in the meeting this year, thirty-five or forty being present. Of these twenty-three were from Elkhart. Other societies were urged to send delegations but were hindered from doing so. Next year's plans if carried out will bring many more, especially from nearby societies in Indiana.

The program was carried out by the Intermediates themselves with the help of Professor Garber and three other instructors, Miss Lichty, Miss Puterbaugh and Miss Wimer, from the college. This help was highly appreciated. Get ready for next year.

MRS. H. H. WOLFORD.

Why an Intermediate Society

Throughout the Brethren church wherever there is a Senior Christian Endeavor Society there should be a Junior and Intermediate society. If a man were to build a bridge would he leave out the main support and the center span? Certainly not, and you and I never have seen any construction of that sort, and if we did we know that it was faulty. So why should we as Christian Endeavor people leave the "main span" out of our work? Are not the teen age pupils the very vital spot of our churches? Let us investigate our workshop and see what we are placing our Intermediate aged boys and girls in. Have the corners been cleaned, and fresh air and sunshine let in? Do we give them the very best of our talents, or are we unwilling to be their leader? Let me say that the very best leaders are those who can mould and transform the youthful life. Every one can not be a teen age leader. A leader should first have a clear knowledge of the Gospel of Jesus Christ. There must be an ever-abiding love for the boy and girl. You simply dare not be above them, but be one in their midst. Be a boy or girl while with those of the teen age. Their problems are vital to them, and we ought to be able to understand their difficulties. Our young folks deserve a place in our churches,—the very best room, a good piano, clean chairs and nice new books of their very own. Spend a few dollars to make the teen age pupils feel at home. Let them feel that they are needed; give them work to do. If they should be somewhat noisy, while gathering for a meeting do not quiet them harshly. The man or woman who can smile the best is their leader. The very gates of heaven open to a smile. So give the teen aged boys and girls a smile and in return they will give you back attention, love promptness and quietness. You who are sowers of the seed will see the teen age, budding out spiritually, in so many different ways that you will wonder at the result.

Remember it is easier to teach the teen age scholars the way of the Cross while young than to let them mould their own lives alone. So let us not be weary in well doing. Let us sow, trusting that God will thrust the sickle of love, and the sword of the Spirit into their hearts just at the right time. Every Brethren church needs the teen age society.

What a field there is for the willing workers! When we who live in the city, see our boys and girls going to Sunday afternoon movies, and to the theater in parties at night, then to card parties the rest of the week, there is something wrong.

Is it the church? No.

Is it the Gospel of Jesus Christ? No.

Is it the Individual? Yes. Why! We teach one little short hour on Sunday, then the rest of the week we lay down on the job.

Did you ever hear of the devil shutting up the doors of vice? No. So why should we shut up our churches? Why not make them a place wherein the children love to come? Why build a church so artistically that a child can not be at home within. Some of you older folks will say, They destroy things. Yes, but would it not be better to break a chair, or mar a book now and then than to lose the soul of one boy or girl? Are not their souls worth more than a chair in the kingdom of heaven? Did not the Christ die for them as much as for us who are older? Will we not be responsible to our God, for the lives of our boys and girls, whom we teach should their souls be lost? Oh, men and women, should you feel the spirit of this message, I beg of you to think over the problems of the teen age, then get down on your knees in real earnest prayer asking God to show you the way wherein you can save the soul of a boy or girl. Let us be careful how we handle the lambs of Jesus Christ, awaiting his coming when the day of faithful service is over. May we then hear his glad voice saying, "Come."

MRS. C. W. ABBOTT,
206 Eastern Avenue, Dayton, Ohio.

Our Juniors

At one time our little people were forgotten in conferences. Later their welfare was regarded to the extent that meetings and sessions were held to consider their interests and to train leaders for them. The time is now here when the boys and girls themselves are a part of many conventions and conferences. Provisions are made so that special sessions and meetings are held for them and by them. This is one feature of the Christian Endeavor Conventions of the many states. The Brethren church in her conferences is giving a place to her boys and girls. This was marked at our last General Conference at Winona Lake, As well as our Intermediates, our Juniors found their place.

The Junior Endeavor meeting on Sunday afternoon was such as is worthy of note. A goodly number were present. Nappanee had the largest representation. Our Nappanee superineendent, Mrs. H. B. Richmond, with her enthusiastic wide-awake boys and girls made us feel that the Junior work is truly worth while . A number of other societies were represented, mostly those that are separated from Winona by the least number of miles.

This meeting was very interesting. Our little men and women never tire of the lesson which we had: "The Lost Sheep." The eager and hearty responses from our Endeavor portrayed that in those immature minds there was that vivid picture of the lone lost sheep as it wandered out into the mountains into wild and dangerous places. They heard the shepherd's tender voice calling the lost one. They saw him as he lifted up into his arms the thorn-pierced, bruised and fatigued sheep. Their eager minds did not fail to grasp the deeper meaning of this parable: Jesus Christ, the Good Shepherd, seeking for the lost and sin-sick soul. Mrs. Owen and Joyce Kanauer Saylor assisted in the meeting. They received the lesson picture in song and story.

We hope that our conference in 1920 will find more of our Juniors at Winona Lake, and that we shall have greater opportunities for advancement.

NORA BRACKEN,
Junior and Intermediate Superintendent.

NEWS FROM THE FIELD

COMPTON AVENUE CHURCH, LOS ANGELES

A very successful year at Compton Avenue was closed with a watch meeting New Year's Eve. Thirty seven new members were added to the church during the year. Twenty three of these coming from the Sunday school, shows the great work that may be accomplished through the work of teachers.

The efforts of our Junior, Intermediate and Senior Christian Endeavor societies have been very commendable during the year past.

On New Year's Day was held our annual business meeting, when new officers were elected and plans made for the ensuing year. At noon a bountiful repast was served in our social hall by the men of the church, the change of cooks being much appreciated by the ladies.

We are hoping and praying that the year before us will be one of the most prosperous years at Compton Avenue. May many souls be born into the Kingdom.

K. M. MONROE.

FILLMORE, CALIFORNIA

To the Evangelist Family, Greetings and Best Wishes for 1920:

We wanted to let you know that we are still on the job and working hard. These are busy days and we have been trying to keep up. Our work here is now taking on new life again and we are starting off the new year fine. We have been having some hard experiences with our church work. A couple of months ago smallpox broke out here and three of our families had it. That cast a gloom over our Sunday school and all our church work. But thank the heavenly Father we had no deaths and it is now over for the time. On New Years Day we had our annual business meeting, the best we ever had here. Our members came out, and the election of new officers and planning the work for 1920 were splendidly done. A fine spirit of love and loyalty was manifest all day and evening and we feel that the work is going to take a great move ahead in 1920 if the Lord tarries.

We had 28 additions to the church by baptism during the last year. Not such a large number you say? Well, but we are new here. Hundreds of people in this valley have never heard of triune immersion or the keeping of the Lord's supper and feet washing. They think these are strange things for a church to do.

We had the largest Sunday school last Sunday for weeks and two well attended church services over the first Sunday in the new year.

We are leaving the Fillmore church about April 1, 1920 and if some church in the Central states could use us for awhile we might consider a call. Otherwise I shall go back into the evangelistic field.

SYLVESTER LOWMAN,
Box 261, Fillmore, California.

FIELD REPORT OF EVANGELISTIC LEAGUE

Meeting at Morrill

In December we held a campaign in the Morrill church of which Brother Whitted is pastor. This is one of the oldest churches in Kansas and has contributed largely to the church at large. This is the home church of such men as L. S. Bauman, Charles Yoder, B. T. Burnworth and E. D. Burnworth. This place proves the importance of the smaller churches which are often a more important factor in the work at large than some of the larger congregations.

It was a source of pleasure to labor with the people here who gave the best of support to the meeting. While the first two weeks were the coldest weather of the winter yet the attendance and interest held up until the

last. It seemed as though we would be compelled to close on account of the fuel shortage, but Brother Whitted called together some of his faithful men and with axes went out and secured the fuel to "keep the home fires burning."

The churches and pastors of the town gave the fullest support to the campaign and closed their Sunday evening services during the revival which was a great aid to us. The meeting was very satisfactory and may Morrill be used in the days to come as she has in the past and in the great work of the Master.

Holidays in Washington

Four months had passed since I last saw my wife and children who are in Sunnyside, Washington. After spending ten days in my home I reluctantly left to be gone another five months in the field.

My dates had been arranged to spend January in a campaign at Falls City, Nebraska, but on account of a fuel shortage and quarantine on account of a disease epidemic, the meeting was postponed until May, in the meantime Hamlin who has been without a pastor for some time asked me to give them a short meeting. We are now in Hamlin and working under the handicap of a church without a pastor. We are having good crowds and found a fine class of people and hope to give them some aid and trust that the church will be lined up in aggressive work and secure a pastor. Let us remember that in our zeal for new churches that it is just as important to maintain the ground on which we have already secured a foothold.

Yours in the blessed hope,
W. S. BELL.

HAGERSTOWN, MARYLAND

While we have entered the threshold of another year of grace, we cast a parting glance at the year that is now history. In it, we are conscious of failures and neglected opportunities, yet we desire to take courage anew, profit by those bygone mistakes and push on "for the mark of the prize as it is in Christ Jesus."

Since last reporting, a number have been received into membership; among those three of tender years whom God can use in long service for the interests of his Kingdom; another, the head of a house and of riper years, who may walk the way of intensive service and joy; and five by letter, who strengthen our forces numerically and spiritually.

We had a "White Gift" service at Christmas. However this year, we changed the plan of the service. Instead of presenting the gifts in some novel way, we used a Pageant entitled, "Children of the Christmas Spirit." The children wore costumes representing the different nations which added much to the effect. The closing scene represented the Spirit of Christmas unifying through America all peoples. The "White Gift" offering was made after the play and proved to be the largest yet. At this juncture of the program, our superintendent called upon Rev. Roy Long for an address. He came to the platform, and in a few well-chosen remarks, presented in behalf of the congregation, a purse of $200 to the pastor and his wife. We never desired more to make a speech, but emotion was too deep for expression. But may I add here we thank these dear, good people from the bottom of our hearts. At times our burdens become heavy and we are a bit weary, but such an expression of appreciation, sympathy and love, binds us closer in mutual fellowship in the Lord, and urges us to strive to serve them better. May God bless each one and fit us for higher service.

We were privileged to teach a class in "Christian Americanization." A goodly number of our Endeavorers took advantage of this

opportunity to study the needs and seek to help the foreigner within our gates to become not only American but Christian. The teacher training class passed with very creditable grades the examination of the second book in the First Year's Course. The class very substantially remembered the pastor by presenting him with a gold coin. We praise the Lord for his goodness and pray that he may give Victory Year to the entire brotherhood.

A. B. COVER.

PLEASANT GROVE AND MILLERSBURG UNION MEETINGS

We are in a union meeting at Millersburg, Iowa, which is located two miles east of the Pleasant Grove church. It is a nice inland town with two Protestant churches. The town is too small to support two pastors, and besides the Pleasant Grove church is so close that it weakens the town churches as its membership surrounds the town. The entire field of the Pleasant Grove church takes in a lot of territory. It covers Williamsburg, Parnell, North English and Millersburg. And all the copies of the Brethren Evangelist that come to those towns are for the Pleasant Grove church. The pastor wants all the names of those who are delinquent on their paper sent to him and he will take care of them. Don't forget it. We feel that if we can not do all the goals, we can do this one.

Now let's go back to our revival at Millersburg. We have preached to the most attentive people here that we have met anywhere and things are started. We made our first effort for lost souls last night and one young man heard the call. I preach Jesus Christ and him crucified. I tell you that people want the whole gospel. We are doing business for the Lord. We come to the battle against sin with the cry of David against Goliath, we come in the name of the living God. And God has blessed us. We are writing for the God of heaven and we want people to give God the praise. God works through us and we will receive our blessings at the judgment bar of God. Brethren pray for us.

LIMESTONE, TENNESSEE

Dear Evangelist Readers: We feel as if we were getting on the map down here in the East Tennessee Valley since our Business Manager no longer marks us up "vacant" on the Honor Roll. And we believe that some of these times he will change us from Telford to Limestone which will give us a more exact location on the brotherhood map. We give little concern to the fact that we are an isolated church. One reason for this is we are in close touch with the brotherhood through the Evangelist, and another reason is we are doing what we can to help maintain and broaden out the work of the Brethren church. These things, together with the fact that we believe with you that the Bible is the inspired Word of God do away with any feeling of isolation. We rather look to the future when there will be more and greater Brethren churches in this valley.

Our church work is marked by a slow, steady progress as it has always been. We probably have a stronger organization now than at any previous time. Our machinery is better trained by experience and is running on ball-bearings. It surely means much to a church to have secretaries, treasurers, deacons, superintendent, teachers, and by no means least, janitors that are all on time and on their respective jobs.

Our regular services are Sunday school, prayer meeting; weekly Bible class, monthly missionary society and mission study and church services twice monthly. Our more recent special days since our last report were, Children's Day in August, Thanksgiving, and

Christmas. Offerings were taken on these days in addition to the weekly envelop offering. Our Christmas service consisted of a Cantata of a missionary character. The Sunday school provided a liberal treat for the children. Our White Gift offering was very good. Some expressed themselves as to what they hope to be or do for Jesus during 1920.

New Year's Day the members met at the church for a business session. Before noon there were given reports from the church, Sunday school, W. M. S., Bible Class, and prayer meeting secretaries. These reports were interesting and showed up beyond our expectations. We also went over each goal of the Four Year Program and now we are making every goal we are in a position to make. After lunch which we so much enjoyed, together we took up new business in the way of plans for the year. As we dedicated ourselves and our meeting to God in the beginning we believe the few plans formed were his leading. Some of these plans have already gone into operation and when by the help of God we have carried them out we will so report. One thing we must especially hope to do is win some of these souls to Christ who are not now his. That is our supreme task.

Our Bible class has been very interesting. Having Pauline epistles. At prayer meeting the leaders recently have been selecting passages of Scriptures for our study and meditation. We have started a small Bible Success Band for daily memorizing of Scripture. Our Sunday school superintendent, Dobson Arnold, has also started a band for daily Bible reading.' One of the strongest points of our church life is the fine spirit among the members and the prayer life of the church leaders.

May we have God's leading and power in all our undertakings in our local churches and brotherhood.

MARY PENCE.

OHIO PASTORS, ATTENTION!

The Interchurch World Movement of North America will, during February the 16, 17, 18 hold their Protestant Evangelical Ministerial Conference at Columbus, Ohio. Every minister in Ohio is invited. The fares not EXCEEDING $5.00 will be paid by the Conference. It is requested that the "Clergy Permit" be used. If your "Permit" is not extended please see your ticket agent about extension until March.

Room and breakfast may be had at $1.50 each day per person. I am expecting to hear of some great plans for the future of the Protestant church. Bring your ministerial credentials.

Come, let us get what we can for the benefit of the church of the Lord Jesus Christ.

Fraternally yours in that blessed hope,

S. E. CHRISTIANSEN,
536 W. 3rd Ave. Columbus, Ohio.

BERNE, INDIANA

We believe it has been quite a while since any news has come from Berne. Well, Berne is still on the map. While we have not given any report, we are still busy in the service of the King.

Our Fall communion is in the past. Brother Bell of Spokane, Washington, was with us for a short service in October. He just stopped on his way to Clay City, but he gave us a great message.

Our Sunday school is in fine shape for 1920. They elected Brother Gideon Reisen as superintendent. The outgoing superintendent, Brother M. Baker has conducted the Sunday school in the past year much to the credit of himself and school. The school is, we think, one of the best in the community both in spirit and missions. The offering seldom is

below $10, which is our goal. They remembered the Thanksgiving offering fine, with something over one dollar per member. Likewise the White Gift went beyond our expectations. As the General Secretary, Brother Gearhart, will testify. Our services are attended largely by young people and a great many of them are not Christians in the strict sense, so to speak. So we have great hopes for our coming revival which is to be held by Brother Shively of Masontown, Pa., beginning January 10. But may we say right here that those young people are not of Brethren homes. I do not know of any Brethren homes of this church where the parents are Christians that all the children from nine years up are not Christians also. They have obeyed that portion of scripture where it says "Bring up the child in the way he should go" (that is God's way). And when they come to the years of understanding they will not depart from it.

We are now serving the Berne church for the twelfth year but think it is time for a change, not because we do not like the people (God knows how our hearts are with them), but for the betterment of the cause we love. So if any rural church will be looking after a pastor in the future let us know. We say rural, because all our life work has been in the country, raised a farmer but preach for the glory of God.

We have just attended a week of most blessed service at the Mennonite church at Berne, listening to W. M. Riley of Minneapolis, Minnesota, and C. A. Blanchard of Wheaton, Illinois, on the fundamentals of the Bible. It was surely a glorious meeting to be privileged to attend. And way me just say that Cobb and Bauman gave the church at Bethel as good last winter as can be listened to by any people in the faith. How our churches need more Cobbs, Baumans, Bells, Bowmans and men who dare to stand true.

W. J. JOHNSON.

DOINGS AT DAYTON

The First Brethren church of Dayton Ohio, is making some interesting history at this time under the direction of her efficient pastor, Dr. E. M. Cobb. The annual business meeting was held on the evening of January 7, and proved to be the largest ever held at the church. The general reports as well as all auxiliary and class reports rang with the signal note,—"the largest and best we ever made!" While this was true financially, it was equally stressed of numerical and spiritual growth for the closing year of Nineteen Hundred Nineteen.

The membership is becoming more fully awakened to her opportunity and has a larger outlook from the great program adopted for this new year of 1920. She extended a call to Doctor Cobb to remain with her for another year from September next, as she feels his work should continue under the blessing of God, and granted a furlough to the pastor and his wife during the summer before National Conference, with pay and expenses, so they can visit the children on the Pacific Coast, provided he elects to continue with the First Brethren for another term as indicated.

As the church is growing so rapidly and has nearly 1,100 communicants now she has a vision of a larger plant, and through her representative, Milton J. Beeghly, one of the trustees, had negotiated for the lot next west of the church at a very reasonable price and at the business session in about 15 minutes nearly the full amount was pledged and the ground secured, making a valuable asset to the church. It is fully paid at this writing.

The program outlined by the pastor and endorsed by the church is very intensive until after Anniversary Day in May, but especially till Easter, and has not only Bible study, lecture work, but a special revival booked to begin March 16, as a drive for Eastertide. Following that a series of special meetings to be held at the Bear Creek House, recently acquired by the First Brethren church.

On Sunday, January 11, at the close of the evening service, there was received into our fellowship by baptism from the Christian church, J. E. Eikenberry, wife and daughter, very worthy people we believe. Also at our business meeting there was granted a ten days' leave of absence to the pastor about March 1, to co-operate with Dr. William Evans of Chicago in a Bible conference at some southern city, which sacrifice the church very cheerfully made. A drive is now being made to get on the "Honor Roll" of churches for the Brethren Evangelist. Remember us before him in prayer so that his will may be done through the First Brethren in this city of great need! May the Lord bless his saints everywhere!

WILLIAM C. TEETER,
Corresponding Secretary.

CLEARING THE WAY

Our three weeks' meeting in the South Bend, Indiana, church held during the month of November closed with thirty-two additions. It was held with home forces. There have been several additions since its close. Not quite two years ago the church purchased the adjoining property, giving us a frontage of seventy feet and a depth of one hundred fifty feet, with an alley on the side and the rear. During this time the congregation has paid the interest and $1,500.00 on the principal. On last Sunday, January 11, Evangelist E. C. Miller brought us a great sermon on the theme, "Ye Shall Receive Power." As you read this he is in a great union tabernacle meeting at Alliance, Ohio. At the close of the sermon, two came forward to confess their Savior. Brother Miller then asked the people for $2,000.00 the amount needed to cover our entire indebtedness, and in about twenty-five minutes, he aided us in assembling more than $3,000.00. The surprise subscription was by the choir, made up of about 40 young people, their united subscriptions amounting to $600.00. This means a nice beginning for a larger church-building sometime in the future.

The last Sunday of our special meetings, we had 351 in the Bible school, and if we had room in our building, some schools would have to go some during the next two years, if South Bend did not pass them in the race.

In the evening service, while yet rejoicing in the great victory of the morning, there were three more additions. We expect to be well to the front in the big union tabernacle meeing to be held here soon, with Bob Jones leading the Christian forces.

G. W. RENCH.

REPORT OF RECEIPTS FOR HOME MISSIONS DURING THE MONTH OF DECEMBER, 1919
GENERAL FUND

Mrs. C. E. Mercer, Partridge, Kansas, H. G.,	$ 5.00
Mrs. John A. Myers Williamsburg, Iowa, H. G.	5.00
Interest on monthly balances,	2.13
Brethren Ch., Fillmore, Calif.,	33.50
S. A. Lowman, H. G., $5.00	
Mrs. S. A. Lowman, H. G., 5.00	
Osias Bennett, H. G., 5.00	
Br. Ch., Huntington, Ind.,	32.00
Mrs. Lillie Warren, Silver Lake, Ind.,	3.00
Mr. and Mrs. H. B. Lehman, Glendale, Arizona,	100.00
R. I. Humbard, Chicago, Ill., H. G.,	5.00
Mrs. R. I. Humbard, Chicago, Ill.,	5.00
Miss Mary Elizabeth Humbard, Chicago, Ill., H. G.,	5.00
Paul R. Humbard, Chicago, Ill., H. G.,	5.00
Mr. and Mrs. J. E. Millheisler, Portis, Kansas, H. G.,	15.00
Benj. F. Newcomer, Washing-	

ton, D. C., H. G., ... 8.00
Jacob Thomas, Mt. Etna,
  Iowa, H. G. 5.00
Mt. Etna Brethren Church,.. 10.00
Nettie J. O'Neill, Cone-
  maugh, Pa., ... 10.00
Mrs. Anna E. Grubb, Sacra-
  mento, Calif., ... 2.00
Isaac Rodegeb, Nappanee,,
  Ind., H. G. 5.00
Rev. Ed Miller, Nappanee,
  Ind., H. G. 5.00
Anna M. Beekley, Clarkston,
  Washington, H. G., ... 5.00
Mrs. Anna M. Rorabaugh,
  Conemaugh, Pa., H. G., .. 5.00
E. A. Juillerat and Family,
  Portland, Ind., ... 12.50
Br. Ch., Sergeantsville, N. J., 18.50
1st. Br. Ch., Allentown, Pa.,. 48.20
Rev. and Mrs. A. L. DeLozier, 10.00
Wm. K. Yoder, H. G., ... 5.00
Mrs. Wm. K. Yoder, H. G., .. 5.00
Wm. H. Schaffer, H. G., ... 5.00
Elder E. E. Felmer, H. G., ... 5.00
A S. Kline, H. G., ... 5.00
Arthur B. Turner, H. G., ... 5.00
B. Ch., Fairview, Ohio, ...
Mrs. Armilda Junk, H. G.,.. 5.00
Mrs. Dora Shobe, H. G., ... 5.00
Br. S. S., Ridgely, Md., ... 38.22
Mrs Robert Milholin, Wil-
  liamsburg, Iowa, H. G. .. 5.00
Elva Milholin, H. G., ... 5.00
Raymond B. Milholin, H. G.,. 5.00
Br. Ch., Milledgeville, Ill., ..
Ellen G. Lichty, H. G., ... 5.00
Rev. Miles G. Snyder, H. G., 5.00
Mr. and Mrs. Edward J.
  Meyer, H. G. 5.00
Br. Ch., Beaver City, Nebras-
  ka, ... 85.00
Mrs. Emma Atwood, H. G. .. 5.00
Joseph L. Johnson, H. G. ... 5.00
Rev. E. S. Flora, H. G., ... 5.00
Mrs. Mary Seibert, H. G., .. 5.00
Miss Lilla Johnston, H. G., .. 5.00
Ernest E. Myers, Williams-
  burg, Iowa, H. G., ... 5.00
W. H. Sanger, Millersburg,
  Iowa, H. G. 5.00
Trinity Br. Ch., Seven Foun-
  tains, Va., ... 7.50
Br. Ch., Uniontown, Pa.,.... 20.00
Sunday School and W. M. S.,
  Meyersdale, Pa., ... 41.00
Mr. and Mrs. W. C. Perry,
  Grand Bay, Alabama, ... 2.00
H. S. Myers, Scottdale, Pa.,.
  . H. G., ... 5.00
Aaron Showalter, Adrian,
  Mo., H. G., ... 10.00
Mr. and Mrs. M. F. Mack-
  rall, Conemaugh, Pa., H.
  G., ... 5.00
J. H. Peck, Beatrice, Nebras-
  ka, ... 10.00
S. W. Wine, Afton, Va., ... 3.00
Mrs. P. A. Early, Nappanee,
  Ind., ... 5.00
Matilda C. Antram, New Sa-
  lem, Pa., ... 5.00
Edwin Kent, Wakarusa, Ind.,
  H. G., ... 5.00
Mrs. W. W. Reed, Morgan-
  town, W. Va., ... 1.00
Mrs. E. A. Snowden, Los An-
  geles, Calif., H. G., ... 5.00
1st. Br. Ch., Eau Claire, Wis-
  consin, ... 2.50
Mrs. Sam. Fishtom, Loree,
  Ind., H. G. 5.00
Wesley Miller, Goshen, Ind.,
  H. G., ... 5.00
Mr. and Mrs. A. J. Nurr,
  Bellefontaine, Ohio, H. G., 10.00
Mr and Mrs. C. Rowland,
  Sunnyside, Wash., H. G.,.. 5.00
Alpha S. S. Class, Cone-
  maugh, Pa., H. G., ... 5.00
Mr. and Mrs. Grover Snyder,
  Conemaugh, Pa., H. G., ... 10.00

Mrs. Susan Bezona, Los An-
  geles, Calif. H. G., ... 5.00
Gretna Br. Ch., Bellefontaine,
  Ohio, ... 55.40
Br. Ch., Denver, Ind.,...... 21.55
W. M. S, Denver, Ind., H. G, 5.00
Br. Ch., Louisville, Ohio ... 73.03
Rev. and Mrs. E. M. Riddle,
  H. G., ... 5.00
Viola Knoll, H. G., ... 5.00
Mr. and Mrs. J. F. Painter,
  H. G., ... 5.00
Mrs Sophia Keim, H. G., .. 5.00
Sanford Essig, H. G., ... 5.00
Mr. and Mrs. F. E. Clapper,
  H. G., ... 5.00
Mr. and Mrs. Louis Clapper,.
  H. G., ... 5.00
Mr. and Mrs. John Bricker,
  Rossville, Ind., H. G., ... 10.00
Br. Ch., Limestone, Tenn., .. 10.00
Br. Ch., Columbus, Ohio, ... 8.75
Br. Ch., Nappanee, Ind., ... 50.00
Br. Ch., Martinsburg, Pa.,.. 42.50
Br. Ch., Bryan, Ohio, ... 100.00
Br. Ch., Mt. View, Va., ... 22.25
1st. Br. Ch., Sunnyside,
  Wash., ... 125.00
Mr. and Mrs. Daniel Crofford,
  Hallandale, Florida, ... 10.00
Br. Ch., and S. S. Summit
  Mills, Pa., ... 50.00
M. W. Eikenberry, Kokomo,
  Ind., ... .75
Angeline Eikenberry, Koko-
  mo, Ind., ... .75
J. Warren Eikenberry, Ko-
  komo, Ind., ... .30
Isaac Grubb, Johnstown, O., 10.00
Br. Ch. and S. S., Maurer-
  town, W. Va., ... 100.00
1st Br. Ch., Roanoke, Va., .. 7.40
Gravelton, S. S., Nappanee,
  Ind., ... 10.00
1st Br. Ch., Elkhart, Ind.,.. 90.00
Mrs. Hummel, ... 4.00
Charles Teall, ... 5.00
Mr. and Mrs. C. Rowland,
  Sunnyside, Wash., H. G., .. 5.00
Winifred R. Chandler, Hun-
  tington, Beach, Calif., H.
Br. Ch., Oak Hill, W. Va., .. 53.11
Mrs. A. Gilbert, Farmers-
  ville, Ohio, ... 1.00
Maple Grove Br. Ch., Nor-
  catur, Kansas, ... 23.35
Br. Ch., Morrill, Kansas,.... 132.52
Jno. S. and Lydia E. Wilson,
  Nappanee, Ind., H. G., ... 10.00
Br. Ch., West Alexandria, O,. 16.50
Crown Chapel Br. Ch., Leon,
  Iowa, ... 24.80
Nat. S. M. M., by Mary C.
  Wenger, Treas., Dayton, ·
  Ohio, ... 93.80
Br. Ch., Leon, Iowa, ... 51.45
Br. Ch., Canton, Ohio, ... 58.88
Vina Snyder, H. G., ... 5.00
Rev. Dyoll Belote, H. G., .. 5.00
Mrs. Zilpha Sutton, H. G.,..
Mrs. C. Minnear, Minburn,
  Alta, Canada, H. G., ... 5.00
Br. Ch., Lost Creek, Ky.,.... 25.20
Br. Ch. and S. S., Berne, Ind., 160.00
Frank Johnson, Berne, Ind.,
  H. G., ... 5.00
Prosperity Br. Ch., Palestine,
  W. Va., ... 10.20
Br. Ch., Krypton, Ky., ... 20.00
Campbell Br. Ch., Odessa,
  Mich., ... 107.10
Br. Ch., Hagerstown, Md.,... 112.75
Dr. J. M. Tombaugh, H. G.,. 5.00
Clarence E. Rohrer, H. G., .. 5.00
Mrs. Clarence E. Rohrer, H.
  G., ... 5.00
Mrs. W. G. Barnheisel, H. G., 5.00
Mrs Edith Cunningham, H.

G., ... 5.00
Mrs. B. P. Schindle, H. G.,,. 5.00
Wm. H. Beachley, H. G., .·. 5.00
Friends, ... 5.00 $ 70.00
B. Ch., North Liberty, Ind.,
  J. A. Hostettler, H. G., ... 5.00
C. C. Grisso, H. G., ... 5.00
C. G. Wolf, H. G. 5.00
Polly Hostettler, H .G., ... 5.00
Moses Steele, H. G., ... 5.00
L. L. Kilmer, H. G., ... 5.00
Mrs. L. L. Kilmer, H. G., .. 5.00
Br. Ch., Tiosa, Ind., ... 19.00
Br. Ch., New Enterprise, Pa., 40.00
J. M. Bowman, Harrisonburg,
  Va., H. G., ... 5.00
Mr. and Mrs. D. W. Camp-
  bell, Sandusky, Ohio, ... 1.00
Br. Ch., Roanoke, Va., ... 70.40
Mrs. M. O. Mininger, Roanoke,
  Va., H. G, ... 5.00
Rev. L. G. Wood, H. G., ... 5.00
St Luke Br. Ch., Wood stock,
  Va., ... 5.00
Br. Ch., Washington, D. C., 105.00
Mr. and Mrs. Homer W. Ball,
  Washington, D. C., H. G., . 5.00
Volunteer S. S. Class, Gratis,
  Ohio, ... 1.50
Highland Br. Ch., Marianna,
  Pa., ... 20.00
Br. Ch., La Verne, Cal., ... 102.00
3rd. Br. Ch., Phila., Pa.,.... 35.00
Br. Ch., Dayton, ·Va., ... 21.50
Br. Ch., West Homerville, O., 8.75
Br. Ch., Ankenytown, O.,.. 24.50
Br. Ch., Lathrop, Cal., ... 27.25
Br. Cr., Berlin, Pa., ... 42.00
Br. Ch., Hudson, Iowa, ... 76.21
Union Grove Br. Ch., Eaton,
  Ind., ... 85.00
1st Br. Ch., Dayton, Ohio, .. 414.00
Cliff Askin, H. G., ... 5.00
Mr. and Mrs. Roy Kinzie,
  H. G., ... 5.00
Miss Flora B. Fogarty, H.
  G., ... 5.00
Earl Phillips, H. G., ... 5.00
Mrs. Earl Phillips, H. G., ... 5.00
Rosa D. Longnaker, H. G., .. 5.00
D. W. Keplinger, H. G., ... 5.00
Mr. and Mrs. Jesse O. Garver,
  H. G., ... 5.00
Mr. and Mrs. Freeman Shank,
  H. G., ... 5.00
Dr. E. M. Cobb, H. G., ... 5.00
Aaron Fisher, H. G., ... 5.00
N. A. Teeter, H. G., ... 5.00
John Guthrie, H. G., ... 5.00
A Friend and Brother, H. G., 25.00
Mr. and Mrs. A. D. Grubb,
  H. G., ... 5.00
W. A. Gearhart and Family,
  H. G., ... 5.00
Dr. E. W. Longneker, H. G., 5.00
Blanche E. Hamburger, H. G., 5.00
Miriam Keplinger, H. G., ... 5.00
Dr. J. M. Wine, H. G., ... 5.00
Bertha Wine, H. G., ... 5.00
Susan Wine, H. G., ... 5.00
Orion E. Bowman, H. G., ... 5.00
Della M. Bowman, H. G., ... 5.00
Home Builders S. S. Class,,. 25.00
Mrs. C. W. Abbott, H. G.,.. 5.00
Grace Buck, H. G., ... 5.00   ·
Maude Stoner, H. G., ... 5.00
Mr. and Mrs. Russel Harn,
  H. G., ... 5.00
Mrs. J. C. Ewing, H. G., ... 5.00
A. E. Evans, H G., ... 5.00
Geo. F. Kem, H. G., ... 5.00
Mr. and Mrs. Geo. W. Wood,
  H. G., ... 5.00
Grace Alspaugh, H. G., ... 5.00
Bessie Trubee, H. G., ... 5.00
Br. Ch., Turlock, Cal., ... 120.15
N. V. Leatherman, H. G.,... 5.00
Mrs. Belle Osborne, H. G.,.. 5.00
Mr. and Mrs. C. E. Johnson
  H. G., ... 5.00
Mrs. T. R. Gaddis, H. G., .. 5.00

Ingervel Johnson, H. G., ... 10.00
Mr. and Mrs. Richard Harding, H. G., ... 25.00
Mr. G. W. Powell, H. G., ... 35.00
W. W. Heltman and Family, H. G., ... 5.00
1st. Br. Ch., Fremont, O.,.... 37.45
Mrs. John Baringer, H. G., .. 5.00
J. D. Gilbert, Eaton, Ohio, (Gratis Church), H. G., ...
Br. Ch., Warsaw, Ind., ... 5.00
O. A. Ranauer, H. G., ... 40.00
Friendship S. S. Class, H. G., 5.00
Brighton Br. Ch., Howe, Ind., 19.92
Mrs. Mary M. Young, Bunker Hill, Ind., H. G., ... 5.00
Br. Ch., Ashland, Ohio, ... 98.00
Mr. and Mrs. Geo. S. Baer, H. G., ... 5.00
C. G. Philips and Family, H. G., ... 5.00
H. C. Wertz, H. G., ... 5.00
I. D. Slotter, H. G., ... 5.00
Br. Ch., Charleston, Neb., ...
1st. Br. Ch., Altoona, Pa., .. 41.05
Sylvester Berkeybile, H. G., 25.00
Mrs. W. W. Wertman, H. G., 5.00
Rev. W. C. Benshoff, H. G., .. 5.00
Mrs. W. C. Benshoff, H. G., .. 5.00
Mrs. L. K. Replogle, H. G., .. 5.00
Abram Sollenberger, H. G.,..
Mrs. Irene Sollenberger, H. G., ... 5.00
Mrs. L. Z. Replogle, H. G., .. 5.00
W. M. S., Dayton, Ohio, by Edith Kem, ... 5.00
Vianna Hackett, Hampton, N. J., ... 2.00
Mrs. Edwin C. Hackett, Hampton, N. J., ... 3.00
Br. Ch., Nampa, Idaho, ... 29.00
Mrs. Martha Keller, Washington, D. C., H. G., ... 5.00
Br. Ch., New Lebanon, Ohio, 42.35
John Eck, H. G., ... 5.00
Mrs. George Kinzie, H. G.,.. 5.00
Frank Weaver, H. G., ... 5.00
Mrs. Susie Anderson, H. G., 5.00
Bethlehem Br. Ch., Harrisonburg, Va., ... 25.00
1st. Br. Ch., Fremont, Ohio,.. 2.45
Br. Ch., Cameron, W. Va.,... 10.00
Br. Ch., Hamlin, Kansas, .. 38.25
Minnie Neff, La Fontaine, Ind., H. G., ... 5.00
Miss Edythe O. Fair, Mongo, Ind., ... 1.00
Reimbursement From Foreign Missions, General Fund, ... 52.45
Br. Ch., Meyersdale, Pa., ... 97.00

Total $4,451.60
Previously Reported, ... 1,743.34

Total receipts to Jan. 1st, 1920,.$6,194.94
National S. M. M., by Mary C. Wenger, Treas., Dayton, Ohio, ...$ 50.00
Mrs. L. N. Frame, Long Beach, Cal.,.. 5.00
Harly Roose, Nappanee, Ind., ... 5.00
Mr. and Mrs. Geo. Conrad, North Manchester, Ind., ... 5.00
E. A. Juillerat and Family, Portland, Ind., ... 12.50
Florence Cripe, Goshen, Ind., ... 50.00
Mrs. P. A. Early, Nappanee, Ind., ... 5.00
Br. Ch., Krypton, Ky., ... 23.75
M. W. Eikenberry, Kokomo, Ind., ... 10.50
Mr. and Mrs. D. W. Campbell, Sandusky, Ohio, ... 2.00
Ellis Geidinger, Canton, Ohio, ... 7.00
Br. Ch., Washington, D. C., ... 10.00
Mrs. L. L. Kilmer, North Liberty, Ind., 12.50
Volunteer S. S. Class, Gratis, Ohio, ... 1.50
C. E. Society, Louisville, Ohio, ... 5.00
Mr. and Mrs. P. E. Peterson, Bement, Ill., ... 15.00
Paul N. Brumbaugh, Wash., D. C.,.... 10.00
Jr. C. E. Society, 1st. Br. Ch., Philadelphia, Pa., ... 3.00
Mr. and Mrs. Guy Pittinger, Wooster, Ohio, ... 5.00
Anna E. Grubb, Sacramento, Cal., ... 5.00

W. M. S., New Paris, Br. Ch., ... 11.00
Ella Race, Pittstown, N. J., ... 5.00
Mrs. Lillie Warren, Silver Lake, Ind., 5.00
Br. Ch., Lost Creek, Ky., ... 32.67
Br. S. S. Listie, Pa., ... 5.00
Mrs. W. H. Yagel, Kunkle, Ohio, ... 1.00
1st. Br. Ch., Long Beach, Cal., ... 557.75
Mary Schisler Messenger, Trout Lake, Wash. (Bazaar Collection), ... 53.15
Aaron Showalter, Adrian, Mo., ... 5.00
Br. Ch., Cameron, W. Va., ... 15.00
Mary. A. Snyder, Glover Gap, W. Va., 5.00
Cyrus Snyder, Glover Gap, W. Va., ... 5.00
Mr. and Mrs. W. C. Perry, Grand Bay, Ala., ... 5.00
Lewis Hostetler and Family, Johnstown, Pa., ... 5.50

Total, ... $752.82
Previously Reported, ...,......$1,537.41

Total Receipts to Jan. 1st, 1920, ..$2,291.23

Kentucky, Kitchen Shower Fund
Mrs. G. N. Hammers, Johnstown, Pa., (Collected), ... $ 93.00
Mt. Pleasant Bible Class, ... 6.50
W. M. S. Society, 1st. Br. Ch., Johnstown, Pa., ... 25.00
Gladys Berlin, Goshen, Ind., ... 5.00
Mrs. Geo. N. Hammers, Johnstown, Pa., (Collected), ... 2.50

Total, ... $100.50
Previously Reported, ... 137.05

Total Receipts to Jan. 1st, 1920, ..$237.55

Kentucky Light Plant Fund
Borrowed from General Fund, ... $300.00
Miss S. Elizabeth Gnagey, Oak Park, Ill., ... 10.00
Ira Fudge, Gratis, Ohio, ... 15.00
Mr. and Mrs. Charles Smith, Eaton, Ohio, ... 10.00
Eliza A. Crook, Logansport, Ind.,... 2.00
Miss Ferne Hartzler, Akron, Ohio, .. 5.00
Home Builders Bible Class, Dayton, O., by Mary C. Wenger, ... 25.00
Golden Rule Bible Class, Dayton, O., by Dr. W. D. Long, ...

Total, ... $372.00
Previously Reported, ... 62.00
Total Receipts to Jan. 1st, including $300.00 borrowed, ...$434.00

Summary of Receipts to Jan. 1st, 1920 (Home Missions)
General Fund, ... $6,194.94
Kentucky Support Fund, ... 2,291.23
Kentucky Kitchen Shower Fund, .. 237.55
Kentucky Electric Light Plant Fund, 434.00
Muncie, Indiana, Building Fund, ... 50.23
Peru, Indiana, Building Fund, ... 25.24

Total Receipts to Jan. 1st, 1920, ..$9,233.19

FOREIGN MISSIONS
(December Receipts)

South American General Fund
Br. Ch., Berlin, Pa., ... $ 86.25
Mrs. W. H. Yagel, Kunkle, Ohio, ... 1.00
Br. Ch., Lathrop, Cal., ... 6.50
World Wide Missionary Society, Long Beach, Cal., ... 10.60
Br. S. S., Listie, Pa., ... 10.83
Nettie Brumbaugh, Hill City, Kans.,... 10.00
Br. S. S., Pittsburgh, Pa., ... 157.47

Total, ... $282.05
Previously Reported, ... 94.40
Total Receipts to Jan. 1st, 1920, ..$376.45

African General Fund
343, ... $ 2.00
342, ... 5.00
338, ... 30.00
339, ... 35.00
340, ... 10.00
341, ... 55.00
344, ... 55.00
345, ... 10.00

Total, ... $202.00
Previously Reported, ... 43.17
Total Receipts to Jan. 1st, 1920, ..$245.17

Gribble Personal Fund
88, ... $ 3.00
86, ... 23.00
87, ... 2.00
85, ... 5.00
84, ... 19.50
89, ... 9.75

Total, ... $62.25
Previously Reported, ... 5.00
Total Receipts to Jan. 1st, 1920, ... $67.25

Rollier Personal Fund
36, ... $ 6.00
35, ... 5.00
34, ... 10.00

Total Receipts to Jan. 1, 1920, ...$21.00

Snyder Personal Fund
No Receipts during December, ...$ 0.00
Previously Reported, ... 10.00
Total Receipts to Jan. 1st, 1920, ...$10.00

African Outfit Fund
World Wide Missionary Society, Long Beach, Calif., ... $160.61
Mr. and Mrs. Charles Rush (No Address), ... 31.00
Br. Ch., Flora, Ind., ... 79.80

Total, ... $271.41
Total Receipts to Jan. 1st, 1920, ..$271.41

South American Tract Fund
Br. Ch., La Verne, Cal., ...$125.00

Total Receipts to Jan. 1st, 1920, ..$125.00

Brethren Missionary Fund
No Receipts during December, ...$0.00
Previously Reported, ... 4.50
Total Receipts to Jan. 1st, 1920, ...$4.50

MISCELLANEOUS FUND
Armenian Relief
Mrs. W. H. Yagel, Kunkle, Ohio, ...$ 1.00
World Wide Missionary Society, Long Beach, Cal., ... 5.00
CHINA, for Mrs. Rose Foulke and Children,
1st. Br. Ch., Long Beach, Cal., ...$100.00
India, For S. H. Power
A. W. Mayell, Long Beach, Cal., ...$ 75.00
Clarence Sickel Personal
Young People's S. S. Class, Compton Ave., Los Angeles, Cal., ...$ 5.00

Total, ... $186.00

Previously Reported (None), Total Receipts to Jan. 1st, 1920, ..$186.00
SUMMARY OF RECEIPTS TO JAN. 1, 1920
(Foreign Missions)
General Fund, (South American), ...$ 376.45
African General Fund, ... 245.17
Gribble Personal Fund, ... 67.25
Rollier Personal Fund, ... 21.00
Snyder Personal Fund, ... 10.00
African Outfit Fund, ... 271.41
South American Tract Fund, ... 125.00
Brethren Missionary Fund, ... 4.50
Miscellaneous Fund, ... 186.00

Grand Total Receipts to Jan. 1, 1920, ... $1,306.78
Respectfully Submitted,
WILLIAM A. GEARHART,
General Missionary Secretary,
906 Conover Bldg.,   Dayton, Ohio.

FROM THE OHIO BENEVOLENCE DIRECTOR

Through a slight misunderstanding the appeal to the Ohio churches for Benevolences was not given before.

Sunday, February 8 has been set aside, for this purpose. It is very important that the Ohio churches line up promptly and materially on this proposition. The apportionment is 10 cents a member for each congregation. If Ohio is to hold her place among the Brethren churches of the nation she must meet this goal This is the last year of the Four Year Program and IT MUST BE MET. The day has come when the churches must do some material work and now is that time. Now without any further appeal will not each congregation in the state send its apportionment to Herman Roscoe, Goshen, Indiana. If you do not it will be necessary to write you personally.

E. GLENN MASON.

West Salem, Ohio.

Business Manager's Corner

BUSY DAYS

It was not because we had nothing to report or nothing to say that we had no notes for this column last week, but because we have been having so many things to do and so many things to look after that we scarcely had the time.

Last week the Board of Trustees of the College held its annual two-days' meeting, and as Secretary of the Board we had to give practically all our time for those days to this meeting. It was a most eventful meeting and we trust that the plans proposed for the betterment of the College may be faithfully and successfuly carried out.

How Goes the Battle?

The fight is still on in the campaign for enlarging the subscription list of the Evangelist and we are exceedingly glad to report a most decided forward movement, and to be able to report that not only have fourteen churches, that had already won a place on the Honor Roll, have renewed their lists for another year, but two new churches have been added to the Roll. The new churches are Center Chapel, Indiana, with Kenneth Ronk as pastor, and Roanoke, Virginia, with L. G. Wood as pastor. Brother Ronk is a new man in our ministerial force, but he has gone about his work like a veteran, and though we may be looking at the matter from a somewhat prejudiced standpoint, yet we predict that if Brother Ronk goes about all his pastoral work as effectively as he went about winning a place on the Evangelist Honor Roll for Center Chapel there will be a bright future before him as a pastor. It is the motto, "We will find a way or make one" that counts in the work of a pastor as much as it does in the life of a business man.

We feel extremely grateful to Brother Wood for what he has accomplished for the Evangelist in Roanoke, Virginia. Brother Wood wrote us a year or more ago that he was endeavoring to get his church on the Honor Roll, but that he wanted to be able to claim the honors without any reservations whatever before making any claim at all. We have known Brother Wood personally for a good many years and we know his excessive modesty and knowing this we place the Roanoke church on the Honor Roll before he asks us to. Brother Wood has sent in the required number of subscriptions with the statement, "You need not place the church on the Roll until all the money is sent in." Knowing Brother Wood's systematic methods for many years we have no worry about the balance of the money so we propose to give him and his church immediate credit.

The Renewals

The following churches have renewed their lists: Milledgeville, Ill., third year, Miles J. Snyder, Pastor; Whittier, California, second year, A. V. Kimmel, Pastor; Compton Avenue, Los Angeles, California, second year, J. C. Beal, Pastor; Oakville, Indiana, second year, W. R. Deeter, Pastor; Falls City, Nebraska, third year, H. F. Stuckman, Pastor, Beaver City, Nebraska, E. S. Flora, Pastor; Mt. View, Hollins, Va., third year, J. E. Patterson, Pastor; Limestone, Tenn., second year, Mary Pence, Pastor; Morrill, Kansas, third year, A. E. Whitted, Pastor; Portis, Kansas, third year, Roy Brumbaugh, Pastor; Waterloo, Iowa, third year, W. H. Beachler, Pastor.

We would be delighted to go into detail and say nice things about each one of these churches and their pastors, but you can readily see that would take up too much space for one week, so we will only say "Thank you," to all of you and wish you the same good things that you have wished us in your appreciative letters.

One Thing More

It is one of the besetting sins of a great many preachers to say, "One thing more and I am done," and then keep on for another quarter of an hour, but we will be true to our declaration and say but one thing more this time, but it is an exceedingly important thing. The high cost of living has not been appreciably effected by government investigations and our troubles are far from being ended. Everybody knows how labor costs have advanced during the past year and most of the people know that the cost of paper has almost doubled again in the last six months, with no relief in sight. The other day we placed an order for forty thousand pounds to be delivered in June with no price fixed on it, for no mill in America will make a price on future deliveries. This simply means we will have to advance the price of our Sunday school publications at least; but just how much we have not yet determined. The announcement will be made when our next order blanks are sent out. Last quarter we ordered Westminster supplies for some of our schools, using the same blanks we have been using for a year, and when the invoices came to us we found the prices had been advanced and that we were the losers by the transaction. We sent an order to a New York publisher a short time ago and with the invoice came a slip of paper saying "We have advanced the price of all our publications thirty-three and one-third percent to meet the higher cost of labor." One of the largest printing companies in this section of the country told us a few days ago that they had raised the price thirty percent on everything. So you see it is simply a matter of SELF PRESERVATION with us. We will have to get more for our output or quit putting anything out. We are sorry, but there is no help for it and we ask your co-operation and support in these trying days.

R. R. TEETER,

Business Manager.

EVANGELIST HONOR ROLL

The following churches having met the requirements laid down by the Brethren Publishing Company regarding the placing of the

Evangelist in the homes of the congregations are entitled to a place on the Evangelist Honor Roll:

Church	Pastor
Akron, Ind., (New Highland),	.... (Vacant)
Allentown, Pa., 3rd Year,	... A. L. DeLozier
Ankenytown, Ohio, 3rd Yr.,	... A. L. Lynn
Ardmore, Indiana,	.... A. T. Wirick
Ashland, Ohio, 3rd Yr.,	.... J. A. Garber
Beaver City, Nebr. (3rd Yr.),	... E. S. Flora
Berlin, Pa., (2nd Yr.),	.... I. B. Trout
Berne, Indiana, 3rd Year,	.. W. F. Johnson
Bryan, Ohio, 2nd Yr.,	.... G. L. Maus
Buckeye City, O.,	.... Glen Peterson
Burlington, Ind., 2nd Yr.,	.... W. T. Lytle
Carleton, Nebr., 3rd Yr.,	.... J. D. Kemper
Center Chapel, Ind.,	.... K. R. Ronk
Cerro Gordo, Ill.,	.... D. A. C. Teeter
Clay City, Indiana, (3rd Yr.),	S. C. Henderson
College Corner, Ind., 2nd Yr.,	Homer Anderson
Conemaugh, Pa., (3rd Yr.),	... E. F. Byers
Darwin, Indiana,	.... W. T. Lytle.
Dallas Center, Iowa,	...... R. F. Porte
Dayton, Ohio,	.... E. M. Cobb
Denver, Indiana, 2nd Yr.,	...... L. A. Myers
Dutchtown, Indiana,	...... Homer Anderson
Elkhart, Ind., (2nd Yr.),	... H. H. Wolford
Eaton, Ind., (Maple Grove),	.. H. E. Eppley
Eau Claire, Wisconsin,	...... J. A. Baker
Fair Haven, Ohio (3rd Yr.),	... B. F. Owen
Falls City, Nebr. (3rd Yr.),	. H. F. Stuckman
Fillmore, Calif. (2nd Yr),	. Sylvester Lowman
Flora, Ind., 2nd Yr.,	.... W. E. Thomas
Fostoria, Ohio (2nd Yr.),	... M. S. White
Fremont, Ohio,	.... H. M. Oberholtzer
Goshen, Indiana,	...... J. A. McInturff
Gretna, Ohio, 3rd Yr.,	.... Edwin Boardman
Gratis, Ohio	.... C. E. Beekley
Hagerstown, Maryland	...... A. B. Cover
Hamlin, Kansas, 2nd Yr.,	.... Geo. E. Cone
Huntington, Indiana,	.... J. W. Brower
Johnstown, Pa., 1st Ch., 2nd Yr., J. F. Watson
Johnstown, Pa., 3rd Ch.,	.... Geo. H. Jones
Lanark, Ill., 2nd Yr.,	..... B. T. Burnworth
La Verne, Calif., 2nd Yr.,	.. T. H. Broad
Leon, Iowa,	.... Geo. T. Ronk
Leon, Iowa, (Crown Chapel),	.. Geo. T. Ronk
Leon, Iowa (Union Chapel),	.... G. T. Ronk
Limestone Tenn., 2nd Yr.,	.... Mary Pence
Linwood, Maryland, 2nd Yr.,	.. E. M. Riddle
Long Beach, Cal. (3rd Yr.)	... S. S. Bauman
Loree, Indiana, 2nd Yr.,	..... C. A. Stewart
Los Angeles Cal, Comp. Av. 2d Yr. J. C. Beal
Louisville, O., (3rd Yr.),	..... E. M. Riddle
Los Angeles, Cal., (Compton Ave), J. C. Beal
Masontown, Pennsylvania,	.. Martin Shively
Mayersdale, Pa., 2nd Yr.,	.. E. D. Burnworth
Mexico, Indiana, 2nd Yr.,	.... L. W. Ditch
Milledgeville, Ill., (3rd Yr.),	Miles J. Snyder
Morrill, Kans., (3rd Yr.),	.... A. E. Whitted
Mt. View, Va., (3rd Yr.),	.. J. E. Patterson
Muncie, Indiana, 2nd Yr.,	.. J. L. Kimmel
Nappanee, Ind. (3rd Yr.)	..... E. L. Miller
New Enterprise, Pa.,	.... Edward Byers
New Lebanon, O.,	.... G. W. Kinzie
New Paris, Ind., 2nd Yr.,	.... W. I. Duker
North English, Iowa,	...... Homer Anderson
North Liberty, Indiana,	.... C. C. Grisso
New Enterprise, Ind.,	...... P. M. Fisher
Oakville, Ind., (2d Yr.),	.... W. R. Deeter
Peru, Indiana,	.... Geo. C. Carpenter
Philadelphia, Pa (1st Br.)	.. Alva J. McClain
Philadelphia, Pa., 3rd church, .. J. E. Braker
Pittsburgh, Pa.,	.... H. M. Harley
Portis, Kans., (3rd Yr.),	... Roy Brumbaugh
Bittman, Ohio,	.... J. Allen Miller
Roann, Indiana (2nd yr.),	... Willis E. Ronk
Roanoke, Indiana	.... W. F. Johnson
Roanoke, Va.,	.... L. G. Wood
Sidney, Indiana, 2nd Yr.,	.... L. A. Myers
Summit Mills, Pa., 2nd Yr.,	E. D. Burnworth
Tiosa, Indiana (2nd Yr.)	...... C. C. Grisso
Turlock, California,	.... J. Francis Reagan
Washington, C. H., O., 3rd Yr., B. S. Stoffer
Waterloo, Iowa, (3rd Yr.),	..W. H. Beachler
Whittier, Cal., (3rd Yr.),	.. A. V. Kimmel
White Chapel, Mo.,	.... G. T. Ronk
Windber, Pennsylvania,	...... E. F. Byers
Yellow Creek, Pa.,	.... Edward Byers
Zion Hill, Ohio,	.... A. L. Lynn

Volume XLII
Number 6

February 11
1920

The BRETHREN EVANGELIST

-ONE·IS·YOUR·MASTER·AND·ALL·YE·ARE·BRETHREN-

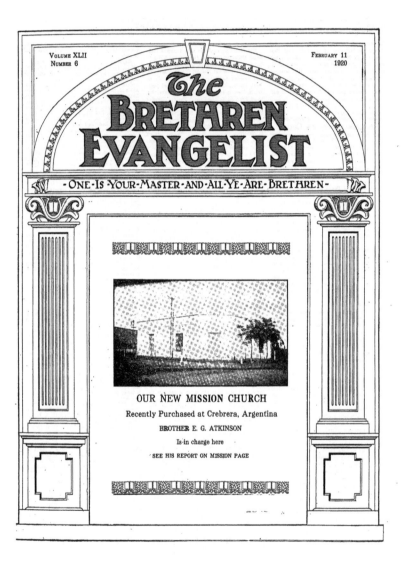

OUR NEW MISSION CHURCH

Recently Purchased at Crebrera, Argentina

BROTHER E. G. ATKINSON

Is in charge here

SEE HIS REPORT ON MISSION PAGE

Published every Wednesday at Ashland, Ohio. All matter for publication must reach the Editor not later than Friday noon of the preceding week.

George S. Baer, Editor

The Brethren Evangelist

When ordering your paper changed give old as well as new address. Subscriptions discontinued at expiration. To avoid missing any numbers renew two weeks in advance.

R. R. Teeter, Business Manager

OFFICIAL ORGAN OF THE BRETHREN CHURCH

Subscription price, $2.00 per year, payable in advance.
Entered at the Post Office at Ashland, Ohio, as second-class matter.
Acceptance for mailing at special rate of postage provided for in section 1103, Act of October 3, 1917, authorized September 9, 1918.
Address all matter for publication to Geo. S. Baer, Editor of the Brethren Evangelist, and all business communications to R. R. Teeter, Business Manager, Brethren Publishing Company, Ashland, Ohio. Make all checks payable to the Brethren Publishing Company.

TABLE OF CONTENTS

EDITORIAL

The Time to Oppose Military Training

Every informed citizen is aware of the imminent possibility of universal military training being made a national requirement by the present congress. The military affairs committees of both the senate and house have had under consideration for some time several bills providing for universal military training. The house committee has not thus far been sufficiently in favor of the principle to be able to report any of them to the house. But by a vote of 9 to 5, the senate military committee on January 26 approved the provisions of a bill drafted by a sub-committee providing for compulsory military training for young men between 18 and 21 years inclusive. It is quite possible that the house committee may soon become united on this or some similar bill. But with that much encouragement, we may now expect a campaign of education in favor of compulsory military training to be launched by those organizations and interests that have favored the policy all along.

It will be remembered that early in December certain army officers appeared before the senate committee urging the passage of universal training legislation. The senators assured them that they favored universal training and urged them to get to work in their home states. "Votes are what count in the final analysis," said one senator, "and if you want this legislation enacted you should build up sentiment for it at home, so that the demand would be felt in Washington. There should be a campaign of education." One of those officers replied that such a campaign would be made as soon as the senate committee should report the bill to the senate for action. So much by way of review to refresh your memory.

Now no one can tell what is likely to be the fate of the proposed universal military training legislation. But one thing is sure, and that is, the final result depends very largely upon what the people say. Most of our congressmen have very keen ears and they are very alert to hear what their constituents say. There are organizations that will talk very loudly in favor of military training. But the churches are opposed to militarizing our land, and the Brethren church in particular is opposed to war and militarism of every sort. Will the churches speak out, so that the men at Washington can hear? And what concerns us more particularly, will the Brethren church speak out strongly? It is this concern that has persuaded us to bring the matter to your attention.

Brother W. M. Lyon, pastor of our church in Washington and our denominational peace representative, has made himself heard on this matter. On January 15, he and some representatives of the Church of the Brethren, the Friends and the Christadelphians were given a hearing by the house committee on military affairs. It is reported that these brethren were received with the utmost courtesy and that for three hours the committee listened, asked questions or debated with these representatives of the churches concerning the questions at issue. This interview will doubtless not be entirely without effect and we are gratified to learn that these brethren discharged their delegated duties so commendably.

But these brethren should be backed up in their objections. Christian people everywhere, who have not forgotten the lesson that Germany taught the world, should speak their opposition to this principle very emphatically. And no church is under greater obligation to express itself at a time like this than is the Brethren church. If we still believe in our gospel-founded peace principles, now is the time to preach them plainly and positively. Now is the time to declare our opposition to any policy that fosters militarism and would tend to make it more likely that our young men should be called upon again in some future crisis to do military service. Now is the opportune time to oppose war, when war is not inevitable, but rather when there is time to prevent it. If we hold our peace now, it will not be to our credit to ask exemption from the bearing of arms if war should again arise. This is our opportunity to demonstrate to the world that we are not a "slacker" church, but that in very truth we are opposed to war, the principle of war and everything that encourages war. If every church of the brotherhood would unanimously draft resolutions opposing universal military training and send them to their respective representatives and senators, such action could not fail to have its effect in determining the vote. These protests, added to the many others that will doubtless come from churches of like faith, will have no small deterring influence upon our congressmen, and at the same time it will keep our consciences clear of any sin on neglect in regard to this matter.

America's Greatest Gift to Near East

One of the many public spirited men enlisted in the campaign of the Near East Relief to aid the hundreds of thousands of people starving or near starvation in Armenia, Syria and Palestine is Bayard Dodge, son of Cleveland H. Dodge, the noted New York philanthropist. He finds, however, from a first hand study of conditions in the Near East that financial aid is not all that is needed for these peoples.

"The greatest gift America can give the Near East," he said in a recent interView, ''is not altogether money, food and clothing. All of these things are vital for the moment but the great gift America can proVide is that of teaching the people again how to live and how to love as Jesus liVed and loVed.

''It is to ingrain again into that population, demoralized by years of war and massacre and spoilation, a true consciousness of character and unselfishness. It is to teach men to live for each other rather than for themselves.

''It is the great achieVement of New England that missionary influences haVe been started throughout the Near East. Thousands of children haVe been given a start in life through the mission schools. The Gospel has been preached throughout the length and breadth of the LeVant, beautiful high schools and colleges haVe been founded and the Bible printed in many languages.

''Through these institutions many leaders haVe been trained for these peoples so long kept under a cruel subjection. High professional training has been given and the graduates haVe been imbued with high ideals to goVern the practice of their professions.''

We should not and will not fail to proVide them with food and clothing and shelter. We must bind up their wounds and heal their diseases even as the Master before us did. And they need these physical benefits in much larger measure than we haVe been supplying. But along with this relief of the body and this proVision of physical needs, we must not fail to proVide them with the higher things of life, the things that perish not. Our Lord was not satisfied with the healing of the body until he had freed the soul of its bondage to sin. And these wretched multitudes, distressed and scattered without a shepherd, Christian America needs not only to feed and clothe but to bring them anew into touch with the loVing character and renewing power and inspiring spirit of Jesus Christ.

EDITORIAL REVIEW

White Gift offerings are still coming in, says Brother Trent. Are yours in?

Brother Kenneth Ronk, the youngest of the '''Ronk preachers'' is pastor of the Center Chapel, Indiana, church and he reports the work in good condition. Brother C. C. Grisso recently assisted him in a Very succesful reviVal meeting.

Brother B. F. Owen recently spent two weeks visiting his home in Montreal, Canada, and is now assisting Brother I. D. Bowman in his eVangelistic campaign at Buckeye City, Ohio, by leading the singing.

Brother L. G. Wood writes concerning the progress of the work at Roanoke, Virginia, and when you read his letter you will agree with him that the work there is ''actually making progress.'' Judging from the ''push'' and the ''pull'' there, it will surely be a ''Victory Year.''

Christian EndeaVorers, don't fail to read the Christian EndeaVor page and then get busy and carry out the plans of Ashland College Night. EVery society should send in an offering this year. ProVe your loyalty by your works.

On the Sunday school page you will find the likeness of the first graduating class in the Three Year teacher training course. Brother L. A. Myers taught the class while he was yet at DenVer. Congratulations to class and teacher.

The Leon, Iowa, field is reported this week by the pastor, Brother G. T. Ronk. The fact that Leon is now independent of the help of the mission board and that they are now paying off their church debt speaks of the progress that has been made. Brother Albert Ronk assisted his brother in a successful eVangelistic meeting at Leon.

A very excellent report comes to us from Brother DeLozier concerning the work at Allentown, Pa. His people remembered their pastor and family in a Very substantial way at Christmas time. Brother DeLozier is doing school work at Lehigh UniVersity along with his pastoral duties and will take his master's degree in June. An increasingly larger number of our young men are giving time to more thorough preparation for the great work of the ministry.

Brother Oberholtzer reports the splendid reviVal meeting recently held in his congregation by Brother Bowman, and he says it was indeed a genuine reviVal. He speaks highly of Brother Bowman's work as an eVangelist and belieVes the church has been giVen a larger place in the city. Brother Bowman also writes concerning the meeting and giVes Brother Oberholtzer much credit for the splendid way in which he backed up the eVangelist.

The Christian Workers Conference held last NoVember in Southern California was not a Church of the Brethren young people's conference as the title of the report might suggest, but a conference of the wide-awake Christian workers of the Sunday schools, Christian Endeavor societies and Women's Missionary Societies of the Southern California churches. Sister Srack shows herself a Very careful secretary.

Brother Gearhart who has recently been on another trip to Kentucky in the interest of our mission work, was delayed in his return by a brief illness. We are glad that it did not proVe to be serious and that he was able to return to his work at Dayton so promptly. He is giving the brotherhood some splendid serVice which no doubt will be more and more appreciated as our people learn more and more about it.

We are pleased to present our readers with a View of our new mission property at Cabrera, Argentina, where Brother Edward Atkinson is in charge. The progress will be much more rapid and substantial now that we haVe permanent quarters. Brother Atkinson is greatly encouraged oVer the prospect and the brotherhood will rejoice with him and support him as well as the other missionaries in that country by their prayers.

It has been some time since we last heard from our little four-year-old missionary who is gradually making her way into the heart of Africa, but we are compensated for the wait by the unusual interest of the letter which we are permitted to publish this week. Our readers will rejoice to learn that the Gribble party is permitted finally to get in touch with the tribes with whom they haVe desired to work and are now learning the dialect. Brother Gribble in a letter to the editor expresses Very generously his appreciation of the brightening up of the EVangelist and especially the first page. We are glad for this encouragement from far away Africa.

After the ''make-up'' of The EVangelist had been arranged we receiVed a special deliVery from Waterloo concerning the suggestion we made regarding representation at the World's Sunday School Convention at Tokyo. We immediately set aside some other material not so urgent and had Mrs. Wisner's proposition inserted. Waterloo is surely wide-awake and the proposition proposed is a most commendable one. We shall be pleased to hear from others in regard to the matter. Mrs. Wisner's reference to Brother Beachler giVes occasion for us to remark that he has accepted a call to the Waterloo pastorate to begin upon the completion of his canVass for College endowment in the late spring or early summer. Since Brother Goughnour's resignation, Brother LiVengood has been supplying the pulpit.

This week Brother Beachler reports for West Alexandria and New Lebanon churches on the endowment campaign. Brother George Kinzie is pastor of both churches and he and Brother Beachler, together with the brethren who supplied the autos, coVered the ground in these pastorates on scheduled time in spite of icy roads. We dare say both pastor and campaign secretary would haVe rejoiced to haVe made the showing double the amount it is, but they pronounce the result that was attained good under the circumstances. We are sure there are many loyal Brethren in these churches and many of them doubtless did their Very best, and if there are those who did not, as is usually the case and as Brother Beachler suggests, we shall pray that they may some day receiVe a vision of their great opportunity and responsibility and make amends for their preVious failure. But we are rejoicing that in these churches we haVe some as loyal and sacrificing members as can be found anywhere and that they are awake to the great need of an endowed college.

GENERAL ARTICLES

Think On Big Things. By J. A. McInturff

(First published in his "Weekly News".)

"Immensity is magnincent medicine," run the words of Mr. Boreham. He is right. That is why your doctor sends you to the hospital or the seaside. We forget the little things in contemplating the greatness of big things. In reading Mrs. Barclay's fiction we hear the physician of one of her characters say to his patient: "Here is your prescription! See a few big things." He then urges her to "go out west and gaze upon Niagara." John Bunyan entered in his notes, "Lord, thought I what ado is here about such little things as these." The tendency of life is to the small things, small pleasures, small troubles, small ideas, small talk. We are like the pebbles on the beach, it is so hard to keep up with the big stones. Put into a can some small beans and two walnuts and shake and the walnuts will stay on top. That is life. John Wesley was weary with that bunch of fellows who buzzed at his feet with little questions. He loved to meet one of his size to talk of the great doctrines of God. We get tired of the plains and long for the mountains. The soul takes its journey and moves among the rugged peaks. Lord Morley tells of one of Mr. Gladstone's letters in which he writes of a visit to Dr. Chalmers. He tells of his impressions in which he saw that Dr. Chalmers would not spend his mind in little things. You may now turn to Gibbon in his Decline and Fall of the Roman Empire and read of the destruction, but after the Huns and Goths did their all, still there remained some of the masterpieces of Roman architecture. Why so? Because of their largeness. The big things were left. Every preacher knows that it is the great subject that holds the field. The preacher of small subjects is doomed. The Canadian Presbyterian relates this farewell to a pastor as he left for a new field; "I am sorry to see you go, I never had but one objection to

you, and that was your sermons were too horizontal." Here is a big truth. A friend was walking in a western desert and looking down said: "This desert is made up of little grains of sand. Little things often make the desert of life. The failure—if there is a failure—of the church is that she has made her God too little. She has made her Christ too small. Men want to live high, and with the big things of life. We have thought on the little things, and we have made the church little in the estimate of the world. Dr. Jowett cries out that, "We must preach more on the big texts of the Bible." The need of the hour is to lay our hands on the big things and do them. It is the small things that often make us fear, but it is the big thing that develops strength and manhood. We read the other day in a Chicago paper that an elephant which destroyed its master was made to plunge in fear when a mouse was produced. In India an elephant carrying a heavy timber, seeing a mole blindly seeking for its underworld, dropped the timber on the driver and killed him. How true to life. We fret and worry over the little things of life and let go of the bigger tasks and drop them. It was the little "gossip" that fell on the Apostle's ear that made him deny his Lord. It was the little "waste" that sent Judas to the gallows. It was the "little complaint" of a few widows that stirred the first church in Jerusalem. It was the "striking" instead of "speaking" that lost the "Promised Land" for Moses. We need a baptism of big things. It was the burning idea of "freedom" that made Moses the great deliverer. It was the money and a great social service program. "But, it was the time for the little things which torment us, and which are after all harmless except as we pay attention to them.

Goshen, Indiana.

Laymen's Conference at Pittsburgh. By Guilford Leslie

In the interest of our beloved brotherhood I will endeavor to tell something about the Laymen's Activities Conference of the Interchurch World Movement, held at Pittsburgh, January 31 to February 2. It was a picked conference of representative laymen of the various denominations, there having been 250 invitations sent out, 221 of which responded, representing 30 states and 28 denominations. Of the number of men invited from the Brethren church the following were present, William Kolb, Jr.; H. F. E. O'Neill; Ira Wilcox and the writer. The chairman of the meeting was Fred B. Smith and the secretary and director of the Laymen's Activities Department was Daniel A. Poling. Other speakers present were, George W. Fowles, Governor Milliken of Maine, Robert E. Speer, George Sherwood Eddy, S. Earl Taylor, Robert W. Babson, Ralph E. Diffendorfer and John D. Rockefeller, Jr.

Among the objects of the meeting were three: to organize bands of laymen to carry the evangelistic note and the ideals of the Movement to their adjacent communities and to assist in creating and promoting a program of lay activities for and within the local church. The chairman declared that this was not a mass meeting, but a board of strategy and that what was planned and done there was to be carried back to the churches.

Speaking of the advantages of co-operation among the churches, Dr. Smith said, "The devil would willingly underwrite the whole Interchurch World Movement, providing the churches would remain aloof and continue to antagonize each other rather than assist each other. Our Lord prayed that we might be one, and the Protestant churches are one in most essentials, then why not co-operate in the things in

which we do agree? Speaking of the Christian's warfare, it was sighted that the Central powers in the great war succeeded by co-operation, and that the Allies' success began only when they co-operated under one leader. We must co-operate under the one great leader, Jesus Christ. Marshall Foch said, "Good divided is easily destroyed by evil united but good united is invincible." When the church goes forward unitedly to the battle it will win, for the gates of hell cannot prevail against it.

It was pointed out that it was time for the ministry to cease trying to save the church and strive to save the world. Dr. Fowles said, "When Jesus was on the cross he saw a bleeding, bewildered, broken bankrupt world. Open now your eyes and see all this which Jesus saw. And may we understand what Jesus knew, that in himself were the resources to heal the bleeding world and a light to guide it in its bewilderment. In him was that which would bind up its broken heart and give riches for its impoverishment. In the broken world Jesus saw the magnitude of the task before the church. May we remove the "blinders" of our denominationalism and see the whole world broken and bankrupt. Do you realize that there are a billion people that know not that God is good and that there may be a real brotherhood? Do you realize that right now during this year there are more people dying than during any year of the war? In Budapest out of 1,000 children 964 are dying.

From Governor Milliken's speech I gathered that we have been exhorted to put religion into business, but said he, we should also put business into religion. He said, We should have business in religion and should have both business and religion in politics. Democracy is organized un-

No one need have any fear that there is any effort or desire to do away with denominations. Nor will the big denominations swallow up the little denominations. The minute anything like that would be attempted, there would be jealousy among the big denominations and the whole Movement would be at an end. The little denomination has a better chance within the Movement than without. I could detect nothing but good motives in the Movement. It is a great desire to forward the work that the church is in the world to do that is at the foundation of this Movement and we as a people ought not to hesitate to do our part in the great program that is being placed before our churches.

Ashland, Ohio.

selfishness; autocracy is organized selfishness. The next war will be in the United States. It is on now, between selfishness and unselfishness. The very life of this nation depends on our interest in the welfare of others. We cannot escape the duty of helping to improve the conditions of this old world and of relieving the sufferings of others. The welfare of a man's soul depends much upon the welfare of the rest of him.

An important work of the conference was in the hands of the Activities committee which brought in some carefully made plans. These were scrutinized by section and adopted, great caution being exercised to maintain the denominations; while co-ordinating all interests that were held in common.

Jesus' Concern for Children An Object Lesson for the Church of Today
By Frank B. Yoder

We are surrounded by a world of matter. In this world is an inviolable law that for every effect there is a cause, and vice versa. Plants grow because they are supplied with plant food and moisture and warmth. We have the conveniences of modern science because men have learned to know certain forces of nature and have made them serve him. Franklin drew the lightning from the clouds and Fulton took steam from the tea kettle and today these two forces are carrying man's messages and bearing his burdens. We have houses in which to live because men have taken material out of which houses are made and have built them.

If our education is broader, more comprehensive today than it was fifty, or one hundred years ago, it is because men have applied their minds to study. If the world is better morally and spiritually today than it has ever been before, it is because men have had a clearer conception of right and wrong and a broader and fuller understanding of the law of love and service as applied to the human family.

Men today engage in business not so much for the pleasure of pursuit but rather for the object to be obtained. The farmer prepares the soil and plants the seed, not so much for the enjoyment he derives from the plowing of the ground or the cultivation of the crop, but for the harvest he hopes to reap. When God made the world he did not do it for mere pleasure, nor out of idle curiosity; he had a purpose, a divine plan. He created the mineral and vegetable kingdoms and the lower forms of animal life and made these subject to the will of man whom he created last. The mineral kingdom is subservient to the vegetable kingdom. The soil is constantly giving itself to the plant. In turn the plant is yielding its life to the animal. And the animal is the servant of man. Man by this same law of the lower giving itself to the higher must give his life to God.

Man is the crowning glory of God's creation. He was made in God's own image and likeness, whatever that may mean. He was made a quickened soul. He was given all the capacities and faculties of the human mind. He has will power, the power to choose and refuse, and the power to reason and think. He can take the simple, the fundamental things of life and build them up one upon the other into the great complex things. He can take the great complex things and analyze them and reduce them to their simple forms. The power to do these things is not possessed by any other creation of God, lower than that of man. Whoever heard of a dumb brute building a suspension bridge, or a New York Sky scraper or of constructing a watch? Such things can be done only by an intelligent brain.

If we may judge by the accomplishments of the past, is it unreasonable to suppose that some day, some time, somewhere, man may have so unfolded the laws of matter and the laws of the spirit that he shall see and know God as he is?

With this conception of life the universe about us ceases to be a playground for man and at once becomes an arena for service.

The world, instead of being a storehouse of wealth and

our fellow-man a tool for unlocking it, that we may add more to our selfish enjoyment, we see it as an opportunity to work together with God in consumating his great plan.

The plan of redemption includes the whole world, none have been left out. It is for every race, for old and young. "Whosoever will may come." But the work of making this plan known to humankind has been given over to you and to me. "How can they know except they be taught and how can they teach except they be sent?" And Christ said before departing this world, "Go ye, therefore, and teach all nations."

We save ourselves by saving others. "He that would save his life shall lose it, but he that loseth his life for my sake, shall find it," Jesus said.

The greatest concern of my life has ever been to know what the will of God is concerning me? What would he have me do? How may I best use the talent he gave me in extending his kingdom here in the world?

Through a study of psychology and from observing men I am convinced that the most effectual work for God and the church must come through work with children.

Jesus likened the Kingdom unto the faith of a child and on numerous occasions he expressed his appreciation for childhood. A most striking example of this is found in the scripture which says, "And taking little children in his arms he blessed them," and again, "Suffer the little children to come unto me and forbid them not."

The wise man of old said, "Train up a child in the way he should go and when he is old he will not depart from it." And again, "As the twig is bent so will be the tree."

We know that by the time we have reached maturity, or anyway, middle life, our ideas and habits are pretty well set. We make but few changes after that. On the other hand, childhood is the formative period of life. The mind is plastic then, susceptible to impressions. In fact, impressions made in that period are never permanently forgotten. They may slip into the subconscious mind temporarily, but during stress, or a crisis they are recalled.

If I may be pardoned for personal reference, I would like to relate an experience of my own when sick with fever and in a delirium. During early childhood my brother, C. F. Yoder, and myself used to compete with each other in committing Bible verses. We sometimes would learn as many as 50 verses a week. As I grew into later life, these verses were apparently forgotten; I could not recall them at all. But when stricken with fever, with the mind and body under a stress these verses came to me and my nurse said it seemed as if I knew the Psalms and Proverbs entirely by heart. Similar experiences have been had by others. Hence, the importance of giving the child the right training.

Did it ever occur to you that we are spending vast sums of money to hire policemen and judges, and guards, to build court houses and jails and penitentiaries and to buy penal farms to re-make the man we made wrongly. Would it not be better to spend at least a part of this money to start the child aright? To give him a good birth, a good home, a good environment, a good schooling, and to place before him high ideals? Then, when this child comes to the years of manhood he will not need to be re-made. Form him rightly and he will not need to be reformed. This business of starting the child in life ostensibly is the work of the church.

Christianity contains the correct standard of morality for the world. Why not take the initiative in putting that standard into pratcice?

In the earlier history of the church, she had no place for her young people. She had no young people's societies, no provision whatever for their social activities. And young people are active, all the laws of life compel them to be so. Why should not the church direct these activities? In one of my meetings this winter I asked the local pastor if he had a young people's society in his church. He replied "No." I asked if there was one in town. He replied "No." I then asked him where the young people were getting their recreation and amusement? He said, "The dance hall and the pool room." He also told me that married men with families were going to the public dance hall, and were dancing with the girls of 15 years to 20 years of age. He also said that trouble had already come to some of the girls from such toleration.

I then asked this pastor his reason for not directing the activities of these young people through the channels of the church?

His answer was most startling. Here is what he said: "If I were to start a movement of that kind in my church, then the other pastor here in town would start a like movement in his church and there would be continual strife between us as to which should have the greatest following." In the meantime this pastor (?), this servant (?) of God, was willing to allow the young people of his congregation to go to hell.

Too many of our pastors are "hide bound." Too many of our churches are dark, dismal, dusty, ill-smelling rooms, where people with long faces congregate, to hear long prayers and uninteresting sermons.

Is it any wonder our young people are seeking entertainment elsewhere? Since young people are active, since they are aggressive, since it is nature's first law for them to be so, it is a physical impossibility to put the cloak of an old man's mind and an old man's habit on a young boy and expect him to wear it. He may wear it for a while, but the time will come when it will be cast aside for a better fit.

I must emphatically refuse to accept the teaching sometimes heard that the natural tendency of man is evil. I believe the natural tendency of the human soul is upward. I believe its intuitive desire is for the good, the true, and the beautiful.

Let us, then, take this life in the very beginning of its earthly career, take it when the mind is plastic. When it is uninfluenced by harmful impressions; take it while it is still in its innocence and purity, and in the home, the church and the school, let us give that child an environment conducive to true manhood and true womanhood.

The child is a builder. He is building the house of character. How well he builds depends almost entirely upon the kind of material we give him. If he gathers his material from the street, the pool room and the dance hall, his building will be constructed of wood, hay and stubble. It will perish with time.

I would not overlook the law of heredity, the advantage of being well born, of having blood from good parentage coursing through our veins.

This has been forcefully demonstrated in the breeding of live stock. Blood tells, and men pay long prices for it. But blood is not all, food and care counts for much even in the scrub.

So in the human family, it is important to be well born. But not to be, is no reason for discouragement. On the other hand, it is a powerful argument for us to make the environment of such a child as nearly perfect as possible. To

one who may be born with inherited weakness let us guard him and protect him with something better.

To whom does this work more properly belong than to the church? Whatever will make a man think a better thought, have a more worthy aspiration, see a nobler ideal should be endorsed by the church.

Why spend all our time trying to uproot the tares sown by the devil?

Let us sow the good seed ourselves. The tares then will have no room to grow.

Can anyone give a valid reason as to why the church should not put on a program of eugenics? Teach the parent as well as the child the laws of life and of health. Teach them how it is that the sins of the parents are visited upon the children unto the third and the fourth generation.

Why should not the church give instruction as to how to grow and care for the body, what food to eat and what kind of clothing to wear? Since one's mental condition depends so much upon his physical condition and the spiritual depends upon both mental and physical, why not have an understanding of the relationships of the three?

In our cities the Y. M. and the Y. W. C. A. organizations are looking after the social welfare of the boy and girl. How about our rural communities? What objection can there be to the country church providing similar amusements for her boys and her girls? Why not have a gymnasium where they may meet in play and exercise, where they can have their shower baths or plunge in the pool, where they can play basket ball or any other game innocent in its nature? Why should not the church own a moving picture machine and give not only the boy and girl but the entire community such views that are at once both interesting and educational? There are many such views to be had. The International Harvester Company, the National Fertilizer Company and the Department of Agriculture, Washington, D. C., have such views which they are glad to loan to anyone desiring to use them. Since about 85 percent of our learning comes to us through the eye, what could be more appropriate than to throw on the screen in our church services some of the gospel songs illustrated, like "Jesus Lover of My Soul," or "Rock of Ages," or "Nearer My God to Thee." While the picture is being shown a single voice, or a duet or quartet of voices could softly sing the words. The effect I am sure would be most impressive.

Picture machines are not prohibitive in price. In fact, the poorer the congregation the more important, do I think it is to have one. For with increased attendance will come increased collections and larger membership.

In the cities there would be no trouble to secure light for operating a machine. An electric lighting plant in the country I am told answers just as well.

Then, there is the Sunday school. Let us teach the child in the language of the child. Let us have the comfortable little chairs, the sand pile, and the charts. Let us make the entire church an attractive place to be. Inside let us have carpets on the floor, clean paper on the walls, suitable pictures hung, curtains at the windows; a library and music room, where the people of the community, especially the young, may gather for reading the best magazines, the best newspapers, the best books, or where they may spend the time in song or instrumental music and social visiting. Let us make the church lawn a thing of beauty with grass, and flowers and shrubbery. And then why not have a kitchen and dining room in the church, where suppers may be served? Men eat, at home, why not have an occasional meal in the church, and enjoy Christian fellowship with each other?

Let us make our church so beautiful, and her services so entertaining and spiritual that men and women, boys and girls would rather go there than anywhere else. When we do this I believe our empty pew question will solve itself. What do you think about it?

South Bend, Indiana.

Christian Humility.   By Mrs. C. E. Nicholas

Humility is that habit of mind in which we do not think more highly of ourselves than we ought—a feeling of inferiority, when compared with others. Humility has been beautifully described as a divine veil which covers our good deeds and hides them from our eyes.

Real humility is the rarest of all virtues—rarest, because it is the hardest to acquire and hardest because it means the getting rid of self, and we all know self is our greatest and persevering enemy.

The conquest of self is the greatest of all conquests and the hardest to win. Many preach humility but very few really practice it. It is easy to look down on others but to look down on ourselves is exceedingly difficult for the average man. It takes courage to look at ourselves as others see us, yet what different lives we would live if we could see ourselves as others see us.

So long as man compares himself with man, he is satisfied but when he enters the Divine Presence he feels his utter worthlessness. When man feels God's love and his infinite mercy the pride of his heart is broken—he becomes humble and penitent. "They that know God are humbled" and "Know thyself and thou canst not be proud." Man must endure afflictions, suffer losses and reverses before his proud heart is humbled.

George Elliott wrote "We can hardly learn humility and tenderness enough except through suffering." Even Franklin said "Through losses and crosses men grow humbler and wiser." Those who suffer most are God's humblest; they have learned by experience that God does give grace to the humble and that his grace is always sufficient.

Humility is the burden of Christ's teaching, yet man is so slow to accept this divine principle.

Of all plants, God has chosen the vine that creeps; of all beasts, the lamb; of all fowls, the dove. Even Christ is referred to as the Lily of the Valley. God appeared to Moses in a bush. Thus you see his great purpose was and has ever been to check the arrogance of men.

Is it not a marvelous fact that God did not select the strong to carry his messages and do his work; he has always chosen the humble that his power might be made manifest.

Moses trembled as he entered the presence of God. David the obscure shepherd boy was the humblest God ever called to a crown. paul who was constantly exposed to humiliations and who continually lamented over his afflictions becomes his greatest apostle. Thus God prepared his chosen for great conflicts and arms them with weakness.

Riches give great power in temporal affairs but poverty gives power in spiritual matters. "Blessed are the poor in spirit for theirs is the kingdom of heaven." He loves to bestow where there is most room. When we are emptied of self then we are filled with the fullness of Christ.

"The bird that soars on highest wing
    Builds on the ground her lowly nest;
And she that doth most sweetly sing
    Sings in the shade when all things rest;
In the lark and the nightingale we see
    "What honor hath humility."

"The saint that wears heaven's brightest crown
    In the deepest adoration bends;
The weight of glory bows him down
    The most when most his soul ascends;
Nearest the throne itself must be
    The footstool of humility."
Dowagiac, Michigan.

One Way of Redeeming "One of the Debts We Can Never Pay"
By Vianna Detwiler

That was a striking appeal on the cover of the Brethren Evangelist for a gift of money for the pioneer preachers of the Brethren church. May the offering of February 8th prove a worthy response to the brave spirit of our early ministers, who dared to stand out for God even though it meant standing alone so far as the church was concerned. Not always is the main body of the church in the right. God's blessings on those pioneer preachers! Is their day altogether gone? Might there be occasion for the same type of ministers today?

Besides the annual offering for the Superannuated Fund, there is another way by which this "unpayable debt" may be lessened. How can I best repay our self-denying preachers of early days? By not refusing to enter the same kind of ministry. A similar condition has developed, the kind that a Holsinger, were he still here or a Swihart were he still active, would not hesitate to undertake.

Here is the situation that is compelling! Ten thousand towns west of the Mississippi are without any regular religious services, was one of the facts again thrust before our eyes as yesterday we listened to the Field Secretary of Religious Education for the Church of the Brethren, Virgil Finnell, Elgin, Illinois. Coming from California, some little stretch before reaching Ashland, he passed through sixteen railroad towns of the same destitution. Elder Sanger one of their district evangelists is also here and together they are exploring the rich mine of opportunity for our God and the whole Bible. Mr. Finnell promises to stop here on his return from the World's Sunday School Convention in Japan and bring his stereopticon report with Japanese coloring. He has had a wide experience as to the feasibility of new fields and he tells me he is going back and ask the mission board for $100,000 to develop their work in this Golden West of unparalleled opportunities. He sees he cannot afford to wait for Annual Conference and assured us that the board would act at once. I inquired "How much money is your church investing among the Mountain Whites?" "Nothing in a special way, helping to support a few preachers in the poorer congregations in Kentucky," he replied.

I have just received the information that no money was appropriated at our last National Conference to develop any new field in this northwest district. The few hundred dollars to be used to reclaim Ashland comes through the self-denial of one of the Long Beach friends. While there are hundreds of towns to be taken, there are six points, two of them large cities, where there is an occasion for us to enter now. Where are the six men of the Holsinger type who dare to step out and occupy even in advance of the mission board? That is not running any more risk than did our early pioneers, because it is only one way in which we can pay the "unpayable debt." Here it is where our foreign mission funds of the future may be generously replenished, for the western people are great givers, once they are organized.

The last three converts baptized New Year's were the result of Dr. Brower's generous services when they were in need of a friend, and now they are the chief helpers in the Win-One Band that meets every Sunday night.
Ashland, Oregon.

"Why do you like the Bible?" was the question asked of a Fiji Islander. "Because it knows me," was the answer.
—Christian Advocate.

I believe that a man should be proud of the city in which he lives; and that he should so live that the city will be proud that he lives in it.—Abraham Lincoln.

THE BRETHREN PULPIT

"Pentecostal Powers." By C. Delbert Whitmer

TEXT: "Ye shall receive power." Acts 1:8.

God works through means in spiritual things as well as in material. The church is his instrument. God will not and cannot violate his laws. Electricity is the best agent known by which to illustrate the workings of the Holy Ghost. Electricity can do almost anything, but only in conformity to law, only by means of conductors, only as its way is prepared. Let the machinery be in order, and see how the electricity flies along the wires, carrying your messages, propelling your cars, furnishing your lights. But let the machinery be out of order, let the wire be cut, and where is your electricity? Even so it is with the Holy Ghost. Let the conditions be complied with, and how he flashes forth power, light and salvation! Let the wire be cut, and even the Holy Ghost cannot overleap the break. The fire from heaven cannot come.

So let us look at this Pentecostal power and see some of its characteristics and conditions. What is it?

First. It is the power of religious earnestness. Half hearted religion is no religion at all. God wants the whole heart or none. Earnestness is working at religion, not playing at it. The disciples knew the power existed. They meant to have it. To get it they would meet the conditions whatever they were. Religious earnestness means ardor, determination, irresistibleness, victory. Without it there can be no Pentecostal power.

Second. Pentecostal power is the power of union. Forty sticks will not make forty separate fires scattered over the prairie. They will all go out. Put them all together and now see what a blaze. Again and again we are told that those one hundred and twenty disciples were all in that upper room—not one hundred and nineteen, but one hundred and twenty. All were there and with one accord. Think how some church members refuse to unite in prayer and will not work with the rest of the church! O how these weaken the strength of the church! Every refusal to co-operate detracts that much from the power and effectiveness of the church. We must be with one accord.

Third. Pentecostal power is the power to witness for Christ. Christianity is a religion that advances by means of testimony; and only so. Where no one speaks for it, it dies. It needs the tongue. The disciples were to be witnesses for Christ. For the first thirty or forty years there were no books written about him. His church grew mightily, but all by means of the witness given by word of mouth. If the first disciples had not talked more about Jesus, than some of his present disciples, his cause would have been dead before the New Testament was written. We are not bold enough to speak on behalf of the Christ who died to save the world.

Fourth. Pentecostal power is the power of God's Word. Have you noticed at Pentecost what a reasoner, what an expositor Peter had become? What gave him such power over men's hearts on that memorable occasion? Read over his address, and you will find that it is founded on quotations from the Old Testament. Peter treated it as the word of God. Have you observed how often we read in Acts, "and the word of God grew and multiplied?" A thought is like a seed—it has life in it and it grows. Did you ever know a church to have Pentecostal power when it did not honor the divine word? They who honor the Word realize a growing grace in their own lives and an increasing power over the lives of others.

Fifth. Pentecostal power is the power of prayer. O how I would like to have heard the prayers in that upper room! Such thanksgiving for the life and death and resur-

rection of Jesus! Such supplications made under the inspiration of the Holy Spirit! Such confessions of sin and unworthiness, and requests for pardon! O, there was prayer, just in the right place, time and manner, just as Jesus had directed! And what an answer it received! Who can explain, analyze or define this power of prayer? Christians, do we want apostolic baptism? Do we want Pentecostal power? Are we willing to pay for it the Pentecostal price of apostolic prayer? They who wait upon the Lord shall renew their strength and go forth empowered by the Holy Ghost.

We have waited six thousand years for steam and electricity; but these forces existed even in Eden, and might have been used had we only known how. We have waited two thousand years for the conversion of the world. The power to bring it about exists. It is the power of the Holy Ghost. It only waits to find human lives through which its power can operate in the world. We can have it in Pentecostal measure if we will comply with the conditions. Then shall the world be speedily brought to Christ. Shall we have it?

South Bend, Indiana.

A New Year Message

The old year has gone with its victories, its joys and its sorrows. We are blessed with life while millions have fallen victims to death and have passed through the door from time into eternity. We are blessed with health while thousands are on beds of affliction. We are blessed with homes while tens of thousands are homeless. All glory be to God for his love and mercy to us, his unworthy servants.

Let us go to our closets often with gladness as if we were going to meet the dearest friend on earth. Let us cast ourselves at his feet and bestow upon him our love until our hearts almost break with a desire to love him more. Let us cast our burdens upon him. Believe, and we will have hope. If we love him and each other all will be well. Let us be more unselfish this year.

Let us take the little foundation stones of our life and place them upon the Chief Corner Stone, and cement them with the precious blood of Jesus until the superstructure, in some measure, answers to the excellence of the foundation —Jesus our Lord.

Let us hunger and thirst after righteousness. May our Lord's rod and staff comfort each of us under all the troubles of life. O! what depths of love and what heights of gospel truth we may enjoy if we but live at his side!

Let each one pray God to fill us with more wisdom, steadfastness, meekness and fortitude. May he enable us to carry the light of the glorious gospel into the hearts of thousands as we represent him here on earth!

Pray for your servant that the light of the mighty Spirit of God may shine upon his pathway and that he may be found walking with God in the beauty of holiness as he goes in and out among you and the people of this part of the city.

With great confidence I give you up to the mercy and keeping power of God, and that all you have and are may be his who bought you with his precious blood.

Let us dig very hard this year in the gospel mines for hidden treasures.

And when he comes, may we be his for all eternity!

Your servant and pastor,
N. W. JENNINGS.

Send
WHITE GIFT
OFFERINGS to

ALBERT TRENT
General Secretary-Treasurer
Johnstown, Pennsylvania

THE SUNDAY SCHOOL

To the Sunday Schools of the Brotherhood

The Brethren church should, by all means have a delegate at the great convention at Tokyo, next October. We can not afford to let a great event like that pass by without some one in attendance.

Sunday schools, like everything else, have undergone a great change since the war and the new problems which naturally have arisen will be discussed and great plans will be made for the future in Sunday school work. We must not get this second handed, but must send some one who is a thorough Sunday school worker and one who can present the plans to us upon his return.

Now naturally two problems will come up: First, who shall go? and second, how can the expenses be met?

Now, this is our proposition: Upon rough figuring, we came to the conclusion that, if every Sunday school would respond with a ten cent per capita offering, as a minimum offering, plenty of money could be raised. The Sunday school at Waterloo stands ready to do her full share in this matter and will forward her share as soon as headquarters can be established.

A splendid time to take this offering would be on Children's Day. The children are taught about Japan in their missionary lessons, and a very opportune time to have the children bring their money to help send some one to Japan would be at that time. I am sure that if it were put to them in that way they would gladly respond. Of course a larger offering than ten cents would be fine, and if any individual saw fit to send in a larger gift, it could not be given to a better cause, at this time.

Secondly, the person as I said before, who should be sent should be a Sunday school worker and one who could come before us and bring to us the great things he will have heard while at Tokyo.

Now, we feel that Brother Beachler is the logical man to send. At first, many people will probably say, "Sure, Waterloo people would want him to go." But, wait a moment! and see if our reasons are not purely unselfish.

Now, we have two very good reasons for thinking, Mr. Beachler should go. First, he is a Sunday school man through and through. Of course he has not been in Sunday school work for the past two years, but nevertheless he is a Sunday school man at heart. He was considered an authority on Sunday school work in Iowa when he was located here. For three years he was state president, and he was sent with a number of international workers on a Sunday school tour at one time. He also was offered the State Secretaryship of the state of Pennsylvania before he came west. So we feel that he is certainly qualified.

The second good reason is, we feel that it would be only fitting that the brotherhood should show its appreciation of the task he has just about completed. Raising an endowment for a college is no mean thing, and we are sure he deserves something big for his tireless efforts for our college.

Before I close, let me again say that Waterloo does not want the Brethren church at large to feel we are selfish in wanting Mr. Beachler to go. For our motive is purely unselfish and we shall be glad to have him go from place to place now and then and report on the great convention.

Now, please, what do the rest of you Sunday schools think of the plan?   Sincerely,

PAULINE LICHTY WISNER, Superintendent.

First Class Completing Three Year Course

The distinguished honor for graduating the first class from the new Three Year course goes to Denver, Indiana. When graduating a class from one of the old First Year courses in 1917, Brother L. A. Myers, the pastor and teacher, and certain other members resolved to be the first to complete the new and more extended course. In line with this resolve they entered immediately upon their studies, pursued them diligently and enjoyed the privilege of graduation on the evening of September 26, 1919.

In the presence of admiring friends an interesting program was presented under the direction of Pastor Myers. After the singing of a song, L. W. Ditch of Mexico voiced the invocation. Appropriate numbers followed by members of the class, the first being the class history by Miss Emma Burkheiser who said in part:

"History deals with what is and has been, poetry with what ought to be and prophecy with what is to be. It has fallen to other members of the class to write the poem and class prophecy. To me has been given the task of reproducing from scanty materials the history of this class.

"This class was organized October 14, 1917, with ten members enrolled. The following officers were elected: President, Mrs. Nora Fouts; Secretary-Treasurer, Miss Emma R. Burkheiser; Teacher, Rev. L. A. Myers. This was the first class in the brotherhood to organize under the new Three Year Teacher Training course. The purpose of organization was to teach and to train its members to be more efficient teachers and leaders in the Sunday school and church. The motto of the class is 'All labor to conquer.' The class had its first lesson on Sunday, October 28, 1917 with Professor J. A. Garber of Ashland, as teacher.

"Since then we have met weekly for our lessons with Brother Myers as teacher. For a time in his absence the

DENVER TEACHER TRAINING GRADUATES AND THEIR TEACHER

members of the class took their turn in teaching, but later feeling that better results could be secured with a regular assistant, Miss Eikenberry was chosen and she filled the position very faithfully. During the two years several enjoyable socials were held. The members of the class are as follows: Ruth Williams, Mrs. Nora Foutz, Rebecca Eikenberry, Emma R. Burkheiser, Charles M. Eikenberry, Mrs. Goldie R. Eikenberry, and Mrs. L. A. Myers."

Other numbers were a pleasing solo by Miss Williams; a witty and entertaining prophecy by Miss Eikenberry and a class poem arranged by Mrs. Eikenberry. The following stanza suggests the spirit of her selection:

"Some classmates to fortune and fame will arise,
    Their lives will be crowned with success,
And none, let us hope, shall fail in the strife,
    And sink into want or distress.
Though rugged the path and steep the ascent,
    And the journey at times sad and slow,
Each day we will strive with energies unbent,
    To achieve life's grand purpose here below."

The writer was privileged to give the class address, speaking on Thwing's definition: "A teacher is one who has time enough, head enough, heart enough, and liberty enough to be a master in the kingdom of life."

We extend heartiest congratulations to the graduates and Brother Myers. He has earned the title of T. T. P.—Teacher Training Pastor. When graduating the first class he graduated another from Tiosa. While conducting the latter at Denver he conducted another at Sidney, which continues to make fine progress under his leadership. Now he is organizing one at College Corner, the last two churches constituting his present pastorate. When one recalls that these are small rural village churches receiving only half-time service, the work is all the more significant.

                          J. A. GARBER.

| J. A. Garber | Our Young People at Work | G. C. Carpenter |
| PRESIDENT | | SECRETARY |

Another Life Recruit Letter

Dear Endeavorers:

February is passing very rapidly. Are you preparing for a big service on the evening of the 29th? The immediate future is pregnant with opportunity for our Endeavorers and we must be found ready to do our part when we are needed.

Familiarize yourself with the missionary situation of our day and you will see how important it is that young men and women be found who will surrender their all to God for life service under his banner. To be a Life Work Recruit does not mean, necessarily that the individual will become a **preacher**. The Lord of glory has great things for mechanics, Y. M. and Y. W. C. A. secretaries, teachers, professional men and women to do, and when we become Life Work Recruits it means that we dedicate ALL our powers to him to be used in his service for ALL our life. This fact however must first be true of the Life Work Recruit, namely, the Recruit must believe God and must have a definite Christian experience of his own. The challenge to life service for Christ is **not** a challenge to the emotions. It is a challenge to the full use of a loving heart, a good keen mind and a prepared life. Stress this fact strongly to your young people.

Then, too, do not be afraid to put the bigness of our task as Brethren young people up to your organization. We will have to learn to see the world through Jesus' eyes and when once we do we will stop frivoling away our life and get down to real achievement. May I not, therefore, plead that you will do your part in helping to win young lives to a life of service for the Christ? The task is a big one but also a blessed one. Will we be found big enough for the task? Don't forget to keep on praying for the outpouring of God's Spirit on our special night—February 29th.

                  Yours in Christ,
                  EDWIN BOARDMAN, JR.
Hudson, Iowa.

Life Work Pageant

The Crusade of Sacrificial Service

As promised in Brother Boardman's announcements and correspondence, we have prepared an interesting and appealing Life Work Pageant. All who have read the copy speak very enthusiastically of the arrangement and its practical worth.

This pageant is simply and briefly arranged. It can easily be used by any society or group of young people in the Sunday school. No special stage fittings are required, not even curtains, two screens will suffice. The cast of characters calls for twelve persons, but none except Sacrificial Spirit has a lengthy part, and this part is not difficult. The other characters represent six ministries: Minister, Teacher, Doctor, Nurse, Industry Expert and Y. M. or Y. W. C. A. Secretary; and five races: Yellow, Brown, Black, Red and White.

Every society and church that fails to use this pageant on February 29th will lose the opportunity of making a winning life work appeal. It can easily be merged with the regular evening service. In this case the minister may conduct a brief, impressive devotional service or even give a short sermon. Then as the climax let the young people present the pageant. Properly advertised it will attract an unusually large audience and its presentation will make lasting, fruitful impressions. Copies have been mailed to some representative of every society. If they are not received, those concerned are requested to write the undersigned. Others desiring copies for use will receive them on request and without cost. Those using them, of course, will, as a matter of appreciation and loyalty, respond to Brother Boardman's appeal for an Ashland College Night offering. He has worked hard to give us this splendid production. Let us co-operate.   J. A. GARBER.

Christian Endeavor at Ashland

No mention concerning the activity of the Ashland Christian Endeavor Society has been made in the pages of the Evangelist for some time. An opportunity now opens the way for a short report. Just recently a faithful member took occasion to voice the fact that the Christian Endeavor was "the shining college organization." During the past few months the society has been unusually active. Although no special work has been attempted other than meeting regularly on Sunday evening, a desire for continued and larger activity has been expressed. As a result, a new mission study class, consisting of all the society members, will be in progress during the next month or so. The plan as worked out by the Missionary Committee for the conduct of same is as follows: The first fifteen minutes of the Christian Endeavor hour will be a period of devotion, in charge of a general leader who will preside over the entire meeting. This part of the service will be made especially impressive. The remaining forty-five minutes will be given over to a systematic study of the book entitled, "World Facts and America's Responsibility." The society has been fortunate in securing Professor J. A. Garber to take charge of this class. By so doing the Christian Endeavor hour can be spent in devotion and study. An orchestra, special music and a lively discussion will be the distinguishing features of the coming meetings. Such a plan is one of great value to any Christian Endeavor society for it brings world missionary problems before young people in a striking manner. We would commend this or any other plan like it to any society that desires to work along this particular line.

              MELVIN A. STUCKEY, President.

Did You Know?

By E. A. Rowsey, Ohio Life Work Superintendent

Ashland College night should be observed during the month of February. In order that the societies may have more time to prepare the pageant, and because of National Life Work Night, it has been suggested, that we observe Ashland College Night the last Sunday in the month.

I What is the purpose of Ashland College Night? It seems to me that there is a three-fold reason for such an observance.

1. To disseminate information about our one and only college. The young people should be informed about the college and its work. Every young person in the Brethren church should have a vital interest in the development of the college. The purpose of observing the night is to impart such information to the young people of the church.

2. To secure "Life Work Recruits," for definite Christian service. I do not mean to secure men for the ministry alone; our need of consecrated Christian doctors, farmers, merchants and lawyers is just as urgent as ministerial recruits. What I mean to make clear is this, When our lay membership is better trained and experience a greater consecration to definite Christian services the. work of the church will experience a growth hitherto unequaled in the history of the church. Why? Because the officials will be better able and more willing to carry forward the work of the church. They will not wait to receive a program outlined in detail by the pastor; they will present to him a program which will cause him to sit up and take notice.

3. To raise three hundred dollars for the Chair of Religious Education at the college. I am surprised that more has not appeared in the columns of the Evangelist about this new department and its support by the Christian Endeavorers of the brotherhood. I fear that some Endeavorer's do not understand what is meant by "The Chair of Religious Education." I am sure that ninety-nine percent of the brotherhood do not appreciate the value of the work given in the department. It was my privilege to take the second course offered in the department and I can say that I have never taken a course in college which did me more good. I am thankful it was my good fortune to take the "phychological principles of Education," under the able direction of Prof. J. A. Garber, a teacher who has immeasurable influence upon the student body of any man on College Hill. The addition of the department and its director, means much to the students of Ashland College.

I have spoken of the department in order that you would be more anxious to contribute to the support of the work. Prof. Garber should have our hearty support because he is an ardent friend of Christian Endeavor. There is no doubt in my mind but that he gives more time to Christian Endeavor work than any other man in the church. His department should not have, "Three hundred dollars," it should have six hundred dollars. But in order to meet even our promise of three hundred and the other expenses that will accrue during the year we must have **five hundred dollars from Ashland College Night**.

II. What My Church is Going to Do?

You will no doubt have received copies of the pageant before you read this article; the question is, how can the pageant accomplish the most good? In our church we are going to give the entire evening program over to Christian Endeavor. The pageant will be given, then a brief appeal for life work decisions will be made. Then a general offering will be taken from the audience the entire amount of which will go to the support of the Chair of Religious Edu-

cation. Mr. President, ask your pastor for such an opportunity in your church.

III. **To the Societies of Ohio.**

As State Life Work Superintendent I have a secret for you. I put it "To the societies of Ohio," so the other states would not read it. Let's work hard to gain all the recruits we can and also the largest offering of any state in the Union. Send the number of Life Work Recruits and the amount of your offering to the writer. Send your Recruit card and your money to Brother Boardman. Let's have our reports in before the other states even decide how much they have given.

Let's Plan and Pay and Pray—Then—
Grow and Go and Glow.
Ashland, Ohio.

Life Work Gems

When the Great Captain commands, soldiers of the Cross are expected to obey.

We must either Pay, Pray, or Go.

The missionary is doing his part. Are you doing yours?

"All that is human must care for all that is human."

Missions:—A supernatural cause resting on a supernatural charter led on by our omnipotent Leader with all his supernatural Power pledged to its support.

"There are one billion non-Christians in the world. There have not been one billion minutes since Christ started his public ministry."—G. Campbell White.

"Surely there can be no joy today that does not know of our inevitable debts, even to those to whom we owe nothing."—Christmas Editorial, Des Moines Register.

"Intercession is the soul of service."

"You can do more than pray **after** you have prayed, but you cannot do more than pray **until** you have prayed."—S. D. Gordon.

"If we would pray "Thy Kingdom come" with intelligent sympathy, we must have knowledge of what the petition implies."

"Love never asks—'How much must I do?' but 'How much can I do?'"

"No one ever fully discovers himself until he identifies himself with universal ends."

"I will place no value upon anything I have or may possess except in relation to the Kingdom of Christ."—Livingstone.

"The world is now an indissoluble unity, and we can no more tolerate the existence of racial slums in that unity than we can afford to allow slums to exist in our great cities."—Bishop Oldham.

"Every man should work in the next ten years as though he were the only man Christ was counting on to carry the Gospel to the world."—G. Campbell White.

"You measure a man by the height of his ideals, the depths of his convictions and the breadth of his interests and sympathies."

"A minister noted for his striking way of putting truth was preaching upon the words that were spoken of paul and his companions: 'These that have turned the world upside down are come hither also.' He said there were three points to his sermon: first, the world was wrong side up; second, it had to be gotten right side up; third, **we're the fellows to do it.**"

"Invest your money in men wherever the need may be."—Gordon.

"Every man who has done something worth while for others has spilled some of his life blood into it."—Gordon.

SEND ALL MONEY FOR
General Home, Kentucky and
Foreign Missions to

MISSIONS

WILLIAM A. GEARHART
General Missionary Secretary
906 Conover Bldg., Dayton, O.

BRIEF MISSIONARY NOTES

I just returned from another trip to our mission points in Kentucky. I did not expect to be sent back so soon after having made the trip to help install the light plant and to study the needs of our work in the mountains.

Some very important business was pressing on the Board for solution, which made it necessary for me to go. Look for a report later in the Evangelist concerning developments for the progress of our mission points.

Krypton has help now, a teacher has been sent from Riverside to assist Brother Rempel's. They certainly did need help, for Brother and Sister Rempel were working very hard to keep the school work going and at the same time doing their house work and pastoral work.

They were very happy when I took a worker to them to help them out. The Lord hears their prayers and they are not easily discouraged when great problems arise for solution, they take them to the Lord in prayer.

The Long Beach church recently sent me over $350.00 to be used at Krypton as follows: $30.00 was designated to start a fund for the purchase of a cow. A piano was to be purchased, and some furniture for the parsonage.

The piano reached Krypton on Christmas morning and it surely was a pleasant surprise for Brother Rempel's, for they needed the instrument very much.

Miss Haddix, our worker at Happy, Kentucky, writes me that they are praying that the Lord will send them a preacher, for the people at Happy are anxious to have the gospel preached, and as I wrote before, it looks to me as if this point was a fertile place for missionary work. Sister Haddix is conducting Sunday school and the work she does is appreciated. The Board is planning to develop some of these points in the mountains. Let every member of the Brethren church pray and give so that the work may progress.

WILLIAM A. GEARHART.

NEWS OF PROGRESS IN SOUTH AMERICA

Cabrera, F. C. C. A., Argentina,
November .11, 1919.

Dear Brethren in Christ:

The new Brethren mission of Cabrera was dedicated on the 26th of October. In keeping with the sublime truth, "Out of the mouth of babes and sucklings thou hast perfected praise," the children were permitted to render an appropriate program which undoubtedly awakened in their hearts the fact that the Culto exists for their development and spiritual welfare. A number of the children of our Sunday school of Deheza participated in the exercises. At the close of the meeting, a social hour was given in the yard. There was a cup of cocoa with cake for every body, and the young people found it convenient to play games.

The property is a corner lot that measures 25x50 meters, and faces one of the principal streets of Cabrera. Our neighbors are a hotel, a drug store, and the railroad station. The building is of brick, and consists of four large rooms. The mission hall is the corner room, and has a seating capacity of 100 or more. Formerly this room was used as a drug store, and has a double door with glass, and a large window. For family use there are three rooms, a closet, a kitchen, and a bath room. The building has been painted, and we are devoting spare time to brushing up around the premises. Friends have given us 75 or more rose bushes. Most of these have been planted to border the playground for the children who come to the mission. The hot winds are cutting down the tenderer flowers. A wall of vines planted along the high woven

wire fence surrounding the premises at the rear would make a good shield. Next spring the small Paraiso trees growing in the yard will be transplanted to the edge of the street, and fruit trees substituted.

Before we moved into our new quarters, our baptized membership was six. Recently three more confessed Christ through this ordinance. While the acquiring of a property was being considered, I wrote Brother L. S. Bauman that a permanent location would yield fifty percent increase in membership within a year. The future is now brighter than was contemplated. Communion services will be observed at an early date. Some of our young converts will be leaving for the harvest fields, to be away for several months, and this means of grace will strengthen and keep them while absent from our midst.

We wish to express our sincere gratitude to the brotherhood for the privilege of enjoying the comforts and opportunity of service that come from this property. We heartily invite all to help in the extension of the Kingdom in this far away land. In your intercessions, remember this mission point, that it may be a blessing to a needy people, and ever be kept true to the Master's wish, "My house is the house of prayer."

Yours fraternally,
EDWARD G. ATKINSON.

FROM OUR FOUR-YEAR OLD MISSIONARY

Nola, French Eq. Africa,
November 8, 1919.

My dear little friends:

I have neglected writing you for a long time. The reason is that mamma has been too busy to write for me. We left Ouesso on September 24th and started for Nola on a little boat called the Ngandu, which was lashed to two other boats, one of them being called the "Stella." That is almost like Aunt Toddy's real name, though we never use it. On Wednesday and Thursday our first days out, everything went beautifully. We enjoyed the pretty river ride and were very happy. We had a very pleasant surprise on Friday for it was then that we met the administrator from Nola, who was on his way down to Ouesso and Brazzaville.

After being out three days without seeing any boat, it was very exciting for us to pull up alongside another little boat very much like our own. The administrator was pleased and surprised to see us, and came on board and had dinner with us. This lasted until very late and we were all very tired when we went to bed. The administrator thought of coming back to Nola with us and would have done so had we been willing to stay at Nola. (Through a mistake a letter of authorization was handed him reading Nola instead of Carnot, so we have had to stay at Nola these six weeks until the mistake can be corrected).

On Saturday we had a very big rain. Our cabin was very leaky and we had to cover ourselves with umbrellas, raincoats etc. We were glad when it cleared off again and we could go up on deck. There were many break downs that day and the next, on the boat. The captain had constantly to be repairing the engine. He himself was ill and so suffered very greatly.

At last, however, we arrived at Nola on Sunday at 9:30 P. M. We could not land that night but stayed on board. Another drenching rain that night made us all uncomfortable, and some of our beds got very wet. The next morning we were all able to land, although some of us were suffering in one way or another. That day we had dinner and supper with the government official at Nola. He gave us two houses to live in, very close together, so that although Marie and Julia have been

in one house and I in another, we have been able to play together every day. We wanted to learn the Baya language here at Nola and so commenced going out to the villages. But we found no Baya villages, only Bakula and Kundu. The first chief that we visited is named Daju. He has eighteen wives and about that many children. Some of his wives are Baya. They live in a large village with the central palace on a high elevation. Daju's wives dress in leaves, except on special occasions, when each drapes herself with a beautiful piece of cloth which is kept in the palace for that purpose. We have been to see them a number of times. They are always kind to us, and usually give us eggs or some other gift on parting. Once when we went Uncle Antoine took his bicycle and we girls took our little wagon. Daju had a ride in the wagon hitched on to the bicycle. The wives thought a circus, and everybody laughed. Sometime we go to other villages near also. One morning when we were returning, Julia and I were in the wagon, and it tipped over, spilling us into a pond of water by the path. I went in first and farthest, but we both got pretty wet and cried about it. So you see we are very human little girls. Daddy rode to the house quickly and got us some nice warm wraps. When we got home, hot baths and drink made us feel all right again.

The first Sunday we were here there was much excitement as another boat came in. I did not bring us any mail, however. We have only received mail once during the six weeks we have been here, and that came sometime later by courier.

Our boys are all Baya boys, and have been teaching us the language, one of them especially. We now have a number of Baya songs The natives love to have us sing them and say the white people are gods because we have learned something of their language in a short a time.

The people here are very strange to us. The women wear a cushion of leaves. Their ornaments are many. Ornaments in their ears, ornaments on their nose, ornaments in their lips ornaments on their ankles, etc. In addition to this, they have their bodies tattooed, and various other things which they think are beautiful but which we think are hideous. We are glad that we know and love Jesus and that we can tell them a little about him. But we do so long to have missionaries come to all these people for they have none.

We had a pleasant surprise on Friday night when the Inspector-General arrived. He came with Monsieur Pineri, the official from Carnot where we are going. They brought the news that the mistake in our papers had been corrected, both by letter and by telegram, so we are going back with Monsieur Pineri on Monday. After we get to Carnot I want to write you another letter and tell you all about our long trip up the river in canoes. I know you will be praying for us and that our heavenly Father's love and care will be with us all the way.

Some of you have been writing letters to me. These my mamma has answered personally for me, but I want to thank you here too, because your letters bring us so much joy.

I forgot to tell you that I was four years old a little more than a week ago. We had a little party, and Marie and Julia and I were very happy. We are celebrating our birth days at different places this year. Aunt Toddy had hers at Brazzaville, Julia had hers at Ouesso, I have had mine at Nola, and I suppose mamma will have hers at Carnot. Mamma says she hopes that very many spiritual birthdays will soon be had in our midst, as people accept our Lord Jesus.

Lovingly,
MARGUERITE

NEWS FROM THE FIELD

ALLENTOWN

Since no news has gone forth since Conference from this place, I now take pen in hand that the Evangelist readers may be posted up to date. Our little church is still on the map. During the pastor's absence at National Conference, a young lady from a new family stepped out for Christ under the preaching of Brother Fennel. Soon after our return another lady, whose little girl we had baptized some months before, came out and now we are praying for the father that the entire family may be together for Christ.

What a wonderful thing it would be to have our families like Joshua's, all for Christ (Joshua 24:15)! If this were accomplished it would strengthen our Allentown church immensely.

Then you see we have had two accessions since last reporting our work.

Our Thanksgiving offering for the National Home work was almost fifty dollars.

Our Christmas entertainment was the best ever—a great success. Our offering through the Sunday school and the Women's Missionary Society on this occasion was over 29 dollars which went to the National Sunday School Association, partly specified for Kentucky. In addition to this we packed a box of "eats," etc., which has gone forward to Kentucky.

A pleasant surprise was in store for the pastor and wife when at the close of the entertainment they were presented with a purse of 40 dollars from the church. We thank the good people of our parish for this kind remembrance.

Several of our people attended the School of Missions "put on" by the Allentown Church Federation a couple months ago. We had hoped to get a mission study class going in the Y. P. S. C. E., but haven't thus far succeeded. However, the week of expert instruction in missions gave a vision to those who were privileged to enjoy it. Our church and auxiliaries seem to have the missionary spirit as evidenced by their willingness to give to that worthy cause from time to time.

Our Y. P. S. C. E. is taking on new life under the leadership of a new corps of officers recently elected. We regret that our Y. P. S .C. E. is not as strong on the "Y" as it should be, i. e., our young people do not take the interest they should. We continue to pray that this condition may change.

Recently Brother Watson was here to "line up" our Sunday school for VICTORY YEAR. Superintendent Turner has already held a meeting of the teachers and officers for the purpose of immediately carrying out the suggestions necessary to make our school a FRONT LINER.

The interest seems to be growing in the Woman's Missionary Society, but it may yet be said that some of our sisters do not have a proper understanding of the purpose and workings of the W. M. S., nor do they appreciate its importance to Brethrenism. Our last communion service was the best attended

yet. Out of 59 members, 51 were seated around the tables.

We are once more holding the prayer meeting in the various homes and are finding them well attended. The First Brethren church of Allentown does not yet believe in the "passing of the prayer meeting." We don't hold our prayer meeting merely to have somewhere to go, but for devotional Bible study and prayer.

For the past three months we have had a building committee, looking forward to a parsonage. Some money is already on hand and we have set the first Sunday in February as a time for giving the committee a little encouragement. According to the "whispers" heard here and there, we are looking for a surprise when the various auxiliaries reveal what they are planning to give, to say nothing of what individuals will give. We hope the furniture of the next pastor for Allentown will not need to go into storage for want of a house as did ours.

Lehigh University

This winter I am taking graduate work at Lehigh University, looking forward to a master's degree in June. For this privilege I am thankful to the Brethren here and trust it may result in advantage to the church rather than to in any way hinder her progress.

Greater Allentown

At a recent banquet tendered the clergy by the new president of the Chamber of Commerce, it was stated that Allentown is to have perhaps a dozen new industries during this year and the population is to be swelled by an increase of 900 new families.

At a banquet of the Church Federation some days later, plans were suggested for the churching of this new district. This has put me to thinking. I wonder how many of the 900 families will be Brethren?

Brethren, if you move to Allentown, or within 30 or 40 miles of here kindly let me know so that we may become acquainted. Indeed I wish that we might have a colonization of Brethren here in Allentown. It would go far toward safeguarding our work in this difficult field.

Yours for VICTORY YEAR, ot only in Allentown, but all over the brotherhood.

A. L. DeLOZIER.

FREMONT, OHIO

On the evening of January 23 we closed our revival meetings at this place. The meetings are considered the most successful ever held in this church. It was a genuine revival in the fullest sense of the word. The deadening influences of the war and post-war conditions have been experienced here, both in the church and out of the church, perhaps as much as anywhere, and the need of a revival was keenly felt by all God's faithful ones. Brother I. D. Bowman came to us January 4 to lead us in our campaign. He began with an earnest appeal for prayer. We have been praying, but we continued to pray all the more fervently. The meetings had been preceded by a number of cottage prayer meetings be-

sides the regular weekly prayer meetings. We advertized the meetings quite thoroughly and Brother Bowman's lectures and sermons soon attracted city-wide attention. Two daily papers each gave us from four to six inches of space in each issue for reports of the meetings and extracts from the sermons, which was a big help. Brother Bowman began with his lectures on prophecy, which seemed to meet a long felt need and a real heart hunger. Brother Bowman at once showed himself to be a master in the interpretation of Bible prophecy. People from the farthest sections of the city came to hear the wonderful messages. Many people of other churches came and hung attentively on every utterance. Many were amazed, for they had never heard God's Word made so clear. What to many people was hitherto only hidden mystery became revealed truth. Every explanation was so clear, every argument so convincing, and every utterance so thoroughly backed up by the Word of God, that no room was left for dispute. No new fangled methods of evangelism were used. Even music and singing did not have as prominent a place as usual in such endeavors. We depended mostly upon prayer and the preaching of the Word, and we are convinced more than ever that the gospel is still "the power of God unto salvation." These meetings clearly demonstrated that it is false that the world needs a new gospel. Some human creeds may be out of date, but the old Book is just as fresh and up-to-date as ever.

We had the largest crowds during these meetings that were ever known in the Brethren church at this place. This gave us increased prestige in the comunity, which will help us much in days to come. There were 34 conversions and renewals in all. A few will go to other churches. 11 have been baptized and received into the Brethren church. Others will be baptized later. The faith and courage of the membership has been greatly strengthened, and new life has already begun to manifest itself. It was the general opinion that the meetings should have continued longer, but Brother Bowman's plans could not well be changed. The prayers of the church go with him as he goes to other fields of labor. He will long be remembered as one of the best evangelists that ever came to this city. Yet to God be the glory forever for he it is that has given us the victory.

H. M. OBERHOLTZER.

ROANOKE, VIRGINIA

The work here is still headed in the right direction and gaining ground and holding what is gained. Our revival held in November was a success. Mrs. Hortense Ropp of this city assisted the pastor in this campaign and her Bible messages were pronounced excellent by all who heard them. Attendance was good throughout the meeting, three were added to the church by baptism and the church generally awakened to an extent that is encouraging to all. The work in all departments is not only alive, but actually making progress.

Eight groups of equal numbers, in charge of leaders are contesting for attendance at all regular services. The Thanksgiving offering was in advance of any before made by this congregation and far "over the top" of the goal. And best of all the congregation has voted to put all of the financial goals over the top this year. The local current expenses are all paid promptly too. We are going on the Honor Roll with the Evangelist also, have already increased the subscription over one hundred percent, and the end is not yet..

The above mentioned attendance campaign will end on the first Sunday in March and this will be Rally Day. Easter Sunday is to be Decision Day, with our communion in the evening. The last Sunday in each month is our continuous service Bible school and worship combined. By this method we hold practically all of the school for the preaching service. At the close of the study period we give a blackboard talk to the children, followed by a short message to all.

This continuous service once per month was recommended by our National Sunday School Board at last conference and I think it is a mighty good thing. I am wondering how many are trying it out this year.

We are endeavoring to keep the banner of VICTORY ever before us in a way that shall call for our BEST.

Several years ago I received a card upon which was printed the following lines:

"Pull! If you can't pull,
Push! If you can't push,
Get out of the way."

No one need to say that now, for the very spirit and circumstances under which we are living is saying it to each one of us in no uncertain way. May we find ourselves in the great task.　　　　L. G. WOOD.

CENTER CHAPEL, INDIANA

We were called to take up the work at this place on the first of last October and since our stay here we have found them to be a very loyal people. All of the branches of the church are progressing as well as could be expected. The Sunday school has kept up the regular attendance during the worst winter weather which to me is very encouraging. On preaching Sundays we have between seventy (70) and eighty (80) while on the odd Sundays in the neighborhood of forty-five (45). The Christian Endeavor is coming along fine but still it is not what I would like to see. The W. M. S. is also active and among other things they have accomplished was the filling of a barrel for Kentucky. Our preaching services are well attended, the building being nearly full in the evening with a good attendance in the morning.

After three months of service we opened our revival meeting with Brother C. C. Grisso in charge. He brought us the message in a way that touched hearts and brought them to yield to the call. On the third evening we had the pleasure of seeing six young people step out for Christ and almost every evening some soul was brought into the Kingdom. The total results for the meeting were twenty-two (22) by confession and letter. Fourteen (14 of this

number were baptized the day after we closed the meeting, while four (4) are to be received into the church by letter and one woman has expressed her desire to go to the Church of the Saints. This leaves us one (1) who is yet to be baptized. Besides these there are several who we believe to be under conviction and we hope to reap more from what has been sown.　　　　KENNETH R. RONK.

EVANGELISTIC NEWS

I just closed the campaign at Fremont last night. The interest became more and more intense until the power of God seemed to overwhelm the congregation. Nearly all who were unsaved made a confession. What few did not were so deeply convicted that they promised to come or renew their covenant in their closets with God.

What helped our meetings so much, Brother Oberholtzer wrote up the meetings every day for two of the daily papers. This seemed to stir more or less the town. Hundreds of inquiries came from those who did not attend at all.

Brother Oberholtzer is a number one pastor and personal worker. His personal life speaks loud and he works hard and unselfishly. The church is unable to pay him what he deserves but I do hope that after this great victory that they may be able to do better. No doubt Brother Oberholtzer will write up the meeting and give you a detailed account. As he is an expert at that I will leave that to him.

This is the greatest victory that the Lord has yet given me, 28 having made confession the last week and three the last night. It seemed a pity to close the meeting but as we had the announcements out for Buckeye City, we closed. The last Sunday night we had 12 confessions, Monday night 7, Wednesday night 4, Thursday night 2 and last night 3. The last night was a desperate night. The worst during the entire campaign but the people came out through the blinding storm and almost filled the house. I am writing this article in a hotel in Mt. Vernon while waiting for a train.

Tomorrow I will begin the campaign in Buckeye City for three weeks, then I go back near Fremont to Fostoria where our Brethren recently bought a church building from the Church of God. I will be there until the middle of March. Brother Oberholtzer will be with me there part of the time during a four weeks' campaign.

Pray for us, especially for the Fostoria work, as that is a comparatively new point for us.　　　　ISAAC D. BOWMAN.

THE LEON FIELD

We have been making steady progress in this field since the passing of the "flu" last fall and can now report that we are still on the highway of progress. Since the first of September we have been independent of the assistance of the district mission board and have a campaign practically concluded for paying off the church debt. Though the statistical reports show no progress since 1916 due to continual losses in this field, still we are getting stronger every year and more able to cope with the local situation.

The great upheaval in real estate values have sent the people of this part of the state scurrying in every direction. The church at Union Chapel which was founded in 1912 has seen the entire community change twice since that time with the exception of a very few families. The wonder is that we have retrieved these losses and kept going at all. The most of these new converts who move away from the church are lost in course of time. It is impossible to follow them up and keep in touch with them.

The county seat work at Leon has profited by these changes, however, and we are continually building stronger. Of late we have begun preaching services twice a Sunday and hope the country churches will consent to afternoon services when the country work opens up again with the break of spring.

While in Decatur county do not believe the church as such has any business footing with social programs, we do believe the church members should be the leaders in all forms of social progress and the Decatur county Brethren are in the van in all such movements in the county. Brethren are leading in the great co-operative farm movement not only in the county but in the state. Brethren are leading in the movement to industrialize this place and give work to keep our young men at home, thus assuring the economic strength of the church.

We have just closed a series of meetings in the county. The meetings in the country churches were almost a failure through bad weather and roads in a thoroughly motorized country. In Leon all joined in a meeting under A. T. Ronk which was greeted with the largest crowds in the history of the church. "A. T." has matured into a powerful evangelist than which there is no stronger in the church. He is spending the winter helping organize our industrial program but expects to give himself henceforth to evangelistic work, within the church as far as its limited field will allow and otherwise in union work. F. G. Coleman is with us this winter also, giving himself to secular work in the interest of his family. This gifted man ought to be in use all the time in Christian work. We have enjoyed the presence of these two brethren and their help but we are conscious of how badly they are needed in the whitening harvest fields.

Let us digress long enough to say that evangelism is becoming an impossibility in the Brethren church due to the high cost of living, of travel, and the niggardly way in which many well-to-do churches reward their evangelists. I know some pastors look at this with a degree of satisfaction because of the resentment they have felt toward the evangelists as an unnecessary institution and the prestige that has temporarily come to him through big meetings. However, I think a careful study of the records will reveal that for the last dozen or more years fully fifty percent of the church increase comes through the labors of a half dozen special evangelists annually. It is useless to talk about big programs of increase without your specially gifted evangelists. Evangelism is a gift of the Holy Ghost like pastoral work and some of the finest and most spiritual pastors in the work cannot draw the net and gather in the fullness of their own increase. They simply do not have the punch and that is all. It does not detract from their gifts at all, without which it would be impossible to run a church. The writer of this article has had some years of experience as an evangelist but is now on a trying and difficult pastoral task; yet in spite of this evangelistic experience he would not think of trying to reap the field without an evangelist annually, when conditions will at all allow. Today it is almost impossible for an evangelist to stay in the field of the Brethren church. The only hope I see is to support the Evangelistic League movement, or something kindred, so the work can be done.

As a result of our series of meetings I will say we have had a splendid and gracious ingathering of souls, which is about as far as good form will allow a report to go.

G. T. RONK.

WHITE GIFT FUND—STILL GROWING

The following White Gift offerings have been received since last report:

Louisville, Ohio,	$ 128.35
Gratis, Ohio,	25.00
Udell, Iowa,	10.00
Roann, Ind.,	38.69
Hamlin, Kansas,	26.50
Conemaugh, Pa.,	150.00
Clay City, Ind.,	17.32
Morrill, Kansas,	55.55
Milford, Ind.,	72.40
South Bend, Ind.,	26.00
Hudson, Iowa,	59.10
Maurertown, Va., (Additional),	4.84
Flora, Ind.,	63.25
Dallas Center, Iowa,	23.83
Muncie, Ind.,	15.00
North Liberty, Ind.,	30.00
Williamstown, Ohio,	12.19
Center Chapel, Ind.,	6.57
Pittsburgh, Pa., (Additional),	5.00
Sunnyside, Wash.,	132.00

Total, ... $ 901.59
Previously reported, ... $2,233.98

Grand total, to date, ... $3,135.57
January 27th, 1920.

ALBERT TRENT,
General Secretary-Treasurer.

CAMPAIGN NOTES

My report this time comes from West Alexandria and New Lebanon. These churches form a circuit which is being served by Brother Geo. W. Kinzie. Brother Kinzie came to this charge from Clay City, Indiana, and he is one of a few of our preachers who was fortunate enough to have to endure me and the endowment proposition the second time. However, Brother Kinzie is a man strong in courage and patience, as well as in loyalty, and he went through this second campaign cheerfully and without complaint. I feel very much indebted to Brother Kinzie for the splendid help he gave me in public and in private and with his "Ford," and I covet for him a rich and fruitful pastorate in his new field. Success on this circuit, as in any field, will come at a cost of hard work and a lot of it, but Kinzie is not afraid

of hard work. I believe good news will come from this part of the brotherhood.

West Alexandria

Beginning January 11th, we preached three nights at this place. Ice and snow hurt out audiences some but we went straight ahead. When I left the result showed a little better than $500 and I believe it will be raised to $600. Under certain conditions this would not be a creditable showing for Alexandria, but after having been on the field I am not inclined to criticize. But my hope is that a day may come under Kinzie's leadership when Alexandria shall want to multiply by two or three what she has done. I shall gratefully remember the Kinzie, Runyan, Hendrickson and Gilbert homes in the West Alexandria congregation. Miss Susie Snyder, a member of this church, is a graduate from Ashland College and a true, loyal friend to her school. I pray that God may use Brother Kinzie to bring good news to Alexandria.

New Lebanon

Immediately following the Alexandria canvass I began the work at New Lebanon. This is one of the younger churches of Miami Valley, having come into existence about the same time the Salem church was born. Although yet young New Lebanon has had a name for doing things. Maybe that is because it is young. Sometimes I am led to feel that churches get too old to do things. They seem to live in the memories of the "good old days," and idly rest on the oars. At all events, I believe there is a general agreement on this, that if "Woe unto them that are at ease in Zion" were taken seriously by every church member everywhere, there would be such a glorious scramble among church folks to get busy as would make the heart of every true pastor rejoice. Pardon me, I forgot I was reporting for New Lebanon.

Well, New Lebanon went a little more than $900 but I could read it in the eye of Frank Weaver and Ora Brumbaugh, and John Eck and others that they will not rest until an even $1000 is rounded out. If those men say so it will be so. This is good for New Lebanon. The Sunday school and Women's organization each did a substantial part in making this showing. We had a fine time with this congregation and even though the roads were icy and dangerous to travel we traveled them just the same—had to because there was nothing else to do. John Eck and Dan Winfield are not men who will back off when there is a little ice on the road. They put the chains on and said, "come on." And so, with either of these men at the wheel, and Kinzie along to help hold things down I felt fairly safe. Thanks to the good Lord and to these good brethren who put their cars at our disposal, we got through all right.

I said $1000 was good for New Lebanon. I should have said that that was good for those who gave. I don't want those who laid down on the job at Lebanon to get any credit for this. That would not be fair, you see. Lebanon, like most churches where I go, have folks who are perfectly willing to have a brass band in the procession provided somebody else pays the band. If that sounds

Our Goal: 200,000; We Can and We Must

200 000
190 000
180 000
170 000
160 000
150 000
140 000
130 000
120 000
110 000
100 000
90 000
80 000
70 000
60 000
50 000
40 000
30 000
20 000
10 000

COLLEGE ENDOWMENT

like a parable I will "splanify" what I mean. I meet folks continually who would not consent for a moment that the Brethren church should be without a college—folks who believe in an educated ministry and who sure do like to hear good sermons, but those same folks consent with amazing ease that other folks shall support and maintain the school. But my own philosophy on this point is this: If a man likes music he ought to be willing to help pay the band.

I shall gratefully remember the Brumbaughs, Weavers, Snyders, Ecks, Motters, and Peters for the kind hospitality extended to me in their homes. This church is the home congregation of Miss Irene Brumbaugh, a former student of Ashland, and a teacher in the New Lebanon schools. I must speak of one gift in the New Lebanon canvass which I consider mentionable. One man in this congregation quit chewing tobacco a year ago. He was a hard chewer, too. So he figured that he saved during the year $36.50 because he quit chewing, and he gave me a check for that amount for endowment. How I wish the "chewers" would all quit ' chewing" and give to college endowment for the next five years what they would save! What a fine memorial building some of our brethren will "chew up" in the next five years! Think of it! I covet all kinds of good things for Kinzer and New Lebanon.

Now the mercury is $458,900.

WM. H. BEACHLER,
Campaign Secretary.

REPORT OF THE CHRISTIAN WORKERS' CONFERENCE OF SOUTHERN CALIFORNIA BRETHREN CHURCHES

By vote of the Southern California District Conference, the Sunday school, Christian Endeavor and Missionary Departments of the various churches held a joint conference at the Whittier church, November 11-13, inclusive, 1919.

Elder J. C. Beal of Los Angeles, F. E. Brower of La Verne and Mrs. Grace P. Srack of Long Beach, were appointed a committee to prepare the program for such conference.

The conference theme was 2 Timothy 2:15. Sunday school motto: "Teach the Word." Christian Endeavor motto: "Efficient Workmen—not to be Ashamed."

Missionary motto: "Information is Inspiration."

The Conference opened Tuesday evening, November 11th, with song and devotional service, led by Elder T. H. Broad of La Verne. This part of the program and also all music throughout the Conference was in the hands of Brother Broad.

Brother Charles Flora of Whittier gave the address of welcome, which was responded to briefly by Brother Brower of La Verne, and Sister Bauman of Long Beach.

Brother Wall of Long Beach gave a stereopticon lecture on Kentucky, which is not only entertaining, but instructive and enlightening to those of us who have never visited that worthy mission field. He explained what has been a query to many, as to the various names for our work at Lost Creek. Now notice: Railway station, "Haddix;" Post Office, "Lost Creek," and the school is at the "Riverside Institute," all at one and the same place, practically.

Evangelist N. W. Jennings, pastor of the First church, Los Angeles, was holding evangelistic meetings in the Whittier church at the time of our conference, but these meetings worked in together beautifully, he giving an evangelistic message as the closing address each evening. Tuesday evening he spoke on "Sin." He said in part: "Sin breaks up our fellowship, one with the other, in the sacred place of the church. Sin does not penetrate into our nature from the outside—it has its spring within. Sin comes to us clothed in light, masked in beauty, radiant with charm. Sin does not reveal the likeness of the devil, but comes to us in the likeness of an angel to deceive. It is an absolute fact, to many many people sin does not appear sin—to many. hell has become heaven, and the devil has become God. Be not deceived—sin is here with its destroying power. Sin is the black cloud through which you cannot see the face of Jesus. Prayer is the wind of heaven that tears asunder the black clouds, and blows them back until the bright and morning Star is seen. Sin pushes the life boat from the shores of eternal life into the black sea of eternal death, where the worm dieth not. It takes the precious blood of Jesus to wash out of the black heart all sin. What this old world needs today is the Mighty Christ—the Christ who stilled the storm on the sea of Galilee, can and will still the storm of today if he is given a chance. The sea of the Nations is swept by the most awful hurricanes, since the nations have been. Oh, if Christ were invited to step on the deck of the ship of this world, peace would come, and peace will not come until he comes."

Wednesday morning. After a short praise and devotional service, the work of organization was taken up. The following officers were elected by acclamation:

Moderator—J. C. Beal.
Vice Moderator—N. W. Jennings.
Secretary and Treasurer—Mrs. Grace P. Srack.
Assistant Secretary and Treasurer—Brother Culp.

Brother A. V. Kimmell gave an inspiring address on the Conference theme: 2 Timothy 2:15, basing his outline on the three points of Study, Approved and Workman. He said in part:

'The publication of our Bibles is largely, at least, in the hands of the Philistines. The circulation is increasing—so also is the price. Many more people are reading the Bible, but there seems to be more "reading" than "real study." Many people plead lack of time for study, but—you take newspapers, and find time to read them; you subscribe for secular periodicals, and take time to read them. Don't make excuses to God. Why are we to study? To show thyself approved, not to the world not even to the church. There are many phases of religious education today, aside from the Bible. Some are good, but many are not. Bear in mind, you are approved unto God—study to this end. Approved as a Workman—study understandingly. God has a definite plan, which is revealed in his Word. You must study his plan to know your business as his workman. You must know how to study 'Rightly divide the word of Truth.' An intelligent workman must know what belongs to the foundation, what to the different stories, and what must form the roof, and how the various parts fit together to make a complete whole, or else he might better never have undertaken the work. God's great plan deals with three classes of people: The Jew, the Gentile and the church of God. Learn God's dealings with and through these three classes, by prayerful study for faithful workmanship.''

Sister Elsie Rager of La Verne (who, by the way, is one of our Missionary experts of Southern California) gave a splendid talk on "How to Secure Missionary Endeavor in all Departments of our church Work." Her outline was about as follows: "Use advertising. It pays in business—it will also pay in missionary work. Good posters and maps should be used in every department. In Sunday school introduce things to interest children in missionary fields; such as handwork. La Verne made a miniature of our South American church for an offering box for South America.

A camouflage ear of corn with plenty of empty space inside the cob, and a slot in one end, was a receptacle for the offering for Kentucky work at one time. A little grass hut, or village of huts, makes Africa more real and interesting. Christian Endeavor societies should have real live missionary committees. Have your honor roll for reading missionary books. Visit missionary enterprises for our foreign population, especially the work amongst the Mexicans. Missionary societies should read, study, give and pray. Study, not only books, but conditions about you, and help wherever you can. We remember 10 percent of what we hear, 50 percent of what we see, 70 percent of what we say and 90 percent of what we do, according to psychological teachings; therefore, 'Let us do.' ''

Sister Rager is very practical, as well as original and creative in her methods, and her talk should be heard at National Conference.

Brother Beal followed with a very practical talk on "The Sunday School Superintendent." He said that a Sunday School Superintendent should be called, set aside, and then trained to superintend. There is no greater work than the Sunday school, and the superintendent is the commander-in-chief. The work of any Sunday school will never be any bigger than the vision of the man at the head. There is a greater demand on the Sunday school superintendent of today than ever before. He must be a man of definite consecration, with the faculty of seeing him, who is invisible. He must be one who can come before his school, buoyant and cheerful. He should use scientific methods and have details of work definitely in hand, always keeping in touch with the best work and help in Sunday school work. Have changes of spice and interest, and don't keep serving up the same old bill of fare. Surprises will keep an air of expectancy, and grip the pupils. Always be on time, or a little ahead of time. Know pupils by their first name, and greet all cheerfully. Put as many as possible to work, Booker T. Washington once said one reason of his success was in never doing anything himself that he could find any one else to do. The Sunday school superintendent should constantly be training workers. A man who has been in office for several years, and has not developed new workers out of his material, has failed.''

The morning and afternoon sessions, each closed with a simultaneous conference of the different departments in separate rooms. These discussions proved helpful and whatever points were thought necessary to bring before the General Conference, were brought up at the opening of the evening session.

The most important topics of discussion in the Christian Endeavor Department was on the line of Sister Clark's paper on "How to Hold the Interest of the Christian Endeavor Society,'' and in her paper she adequately answered all questions of righteous means to hold the interest of our young people. One conclusion was that one wrongly balanced social may throw the young people out of spiritual balance.

Sister Wall of Long Beach spoke of the help she found in drilling the Juniors in Bible verses. A Sunday school query was how to keep children of the Junior and Intermediate Departments of the Sunday school in for the preaching service. Brother Broad advocated having a definite part of the morning service for the children, using the children sometimes for a special song; then a short talk by the pastor to the little folks is very helpful. Make them feel that they are a definite part of the church itself.

The following suggestions for missionary activities were brought out by discussion: Every church should have a Missionary society, whose primary object should be the obtaining and spreading of missionary information, that we may fulfill Christ's command to "Lift up your eyes, and look on the fields," recognizing the understanding of missionary needs as necessary for missionary enterprise.

(To be Continued)

RUARY 18
1920

The BRETHREN EVANGELIST

THIS IS THE HOUR WHEN

The Church Must Find Her Limit

IN A MIGHTY EFFORT TO

Evangelize the World

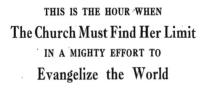

THE CHURCH IS STRONGEST,
HER MEN ARE RICHEST,
HER VISION BROADEST,
THE FIELDS ARE RIPEST,
THE NEEDS ARE GRAVEST,
THE CALLS ARE LOUDEST.

WHO WILL GO FOR US?

....AND...

WHO WILL HELP SEND?

Let the Whole Church Answer in
An Easter Offering On April 4

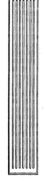

Published every Wednesday at Ashland, Ohio. All matter for publication must reach the Editor not later than Friday noon of the preceding week.

George S. Baer, Editor

The Brethren Evangelist

When ordering your paper changed give old as well as new address. Subscriptions discontinued at expiration. To avoid missing any numbers renew two weeks in advance.

R. R. Teeter, Business Manager

OFFICIAL ORGAN OF THE BRETHREN CHURCH

Subscription price, $2.00 per year, payable in advance.
Entered at the Post Office at Ashland, Ohio, as second-class matter.
Acceptance for mailing at special rate of postage provided for in section 1103, Act of October 3, 1917, authorized September 9, 1918.
Address all matter for publication to Geo. S. Baer, Editor of the Brethren Evangelist, and all business communications to R. R. Teeter, Business Manager, Brethren Publishing Company, Ashland, Ohio. Make all checks payable to the Brethren Publishing Company.

TABLE OF CONTENTS

EDITORIAL

Marshalling the Forces for An Intensive Evangelistic Campaign

(The first of a series of editorials on the above topic, considered apropos to the present season of intensive evangelism and also the aim of many churches of leading up to an ingathering at Easter time)

Evangelism in its root significance is the heart of the gospel and the spirit of evangelism is the pre-eminent characteristic of the church that is faithful to the purpose and genius of that gospel. The gospel of Jesus is "good news;" it is good news to the soul who has wasted his substance in riotous living and good news to the child who is just coming into the possession of his spiritual faculties; it is good news to the individual whose life is wearied and wasted by the cares, troubles and toils of the material world, and good news to the one who is hungering for fellowship with the Infinite. It is good news to everyone who receives it. But it cannot be received until it is made known. And the thing that makes the gospel what it is, is its tendency to move out and on into other lives. The gospel is an evangel, a message to be passed on, a thing of life that is ever reaching out and hastening on to other hearts. It is good news, but it can only maintain its true character by falling upon new ears and finding entrance into new hearts. The church is the messenger of this good news, the body for its incarnation and demonstration and the instrument for its spread into all the world and into all hearts. Evangelism, in its broad sense, then, is the supreme task of the church.

There are various types of evangelism in which the church is called upon to engage. It must save the youth to a life of devotion and service as well as the time-worn prodigal from the horrors of a death in sin. It must save society from its degrading tendencies at the same time it saves the individual from the grip and power of evil. It must save by the daily guidance of spiritual awakenings and instruction in the ways of truth as well as by bringing a mighty array of facts and forces to bear upon the mind to influence to a definite decision of surrender to Jesus Christ as Savior and Lord. But it is the latter type to which we wish to give special attention at this time.

To marshall all the forces of the church in a great intensive campaign for the saving of souls is a problem that is ever before the pastor who takes his task seriously, and especially, is it demanding consideration at this time of unprecedented world need. With the hope of stimulating more serious thought generally along this line and thus increasing the probabilities of success, and not with the presumption of thinking to provide an unfailing and infallible solution to the problem that these and subsequent suggestions are offered.

Certain Pre-requisites

There are certain pre-requisites to a successful marshalling of the church's forces for an evangelistic campaign. First, the marshall, or the pastor, must know the nature and power of the enemy. Whether or not the pastor is also the evangelist would not change the consideration in these present particulars; he is first of all the marshall and must know the field of battle. He must know the sins prevalent in the community, know the dominant hindrances to the cause of Christ, the hindrances that are peculiar to that community. A general is never able to direct his troops wisely until he knows the lay of the enemy's country, and the type of their men, their strength and equipment. How can the general in this spiritual campaign direct wisely his forces against an enemy he knows not, or cope successfully with evils he has not investigated? If an evangelist is imported for the campaign and is without the guidance of a pastor who knows the field, he feels very keenly his handicap. The one who directs the campaign should know as nearly as possible the general characteristics of the unchurched people of the community; he must know their habits, their prejudices, their attitude towards the church and religion and what appeals to them. So far as possible he should know the people individually and collectively, if he would achieve the greatest success.

Second, the marshall must know his own forces thoroughly. He should know their weaknesses and their strong points, in order that he may be able to direct them most effectively. For we have in mind a real campaign, one in which all the available workers are marshalled, coached and directed by a wise, tactful general to carry the gospel into every home and to every individual in the community, whether in shop, factory or on the street. Unless all the church can thus be brought to supplement the pulpit work, it will not be in any worthy sense a campaign, but merely a series of meetings. But to direct the workers wisely, the marshall must know their qualifications. Some will be tactful and some will be awkward in their approach. Some will have self-control in the face of rebuffs and unkind remarks and some will be irritated and likely to retaliate. Some will be persevering and patient while others will be easily discouraged and impatient. Some will possess a deep and genuine passion for souls while others will not have developed a very great concern. Some will have lived very consistently the Christian life before the world while others will have had many discouraging experiences. All these things are important to know, and failure to take them into account may have serious results. The wrong person assigned to a task may work greater harm than if it had been left entirely unattempted.

Third, the marshall must not only know his enemy and his own forces, but he must have the confidence of his people. Without this he shall not be able to lead them into the campaign, direct them in their efforts and inspire them to Victory. This means that he must have proven his worthiness to be their leader by his consecration and unselfishness, his sincerity and dead earnestness, his self-poise and divine direction. He must not be conceited or officious, but must base his leadership upon divine grace and divine authority. He must be nothing more than a Voice from God, willing to decrease that the cause of Christ may increase. He must become partaker of the spirit. of the great Master who took no glory to himself, but said, "I do nothing of myself, but as the Father hath taught me I speak these things. And he that sent me is with me; the Father hath not left me alone: I do always those things that please him." When the marshall of the forces of righteousness shall be able honestly to say these words, he shall have the confidence of his people, and shall be prepared to lead them into the battle.

EDITORIAL REVIEW

The Conference Minutes is now off the press and finding its way to the pastors, as you will observe by the announcement in the Business Manager's Corner. If you don't receive a copy, order at once.

Brother W. C. Benshoff states that Dr. Bame is assisting him in a revival and that the results are good. The meeting is doubtless over now and we will soon hear definitely of the success achieved.

It is not often that we hear from Brother B. H. Flora, but that is our pleasure this week. He is doing some evangelistic work in Indiana and states that he and his wife are to return to Canada the first of April.

The publication in this issue of the sermon by Sister Pence, reminds us of an error that occurred when her last contribution was published last August. We credited it to Miss Mae Minnich instead of Miss Mary Pence. Both have given splendid co-operation, but we are sorry for the error.

The secretary of the Board of Trustees of Ashland College, Dr. Teeter, makes an important announcement in this issue. When the Interchurch financial drive is on Brethren people who may be solicited are urged to designate any gifts they may make to Brethren interests.

Some of our readers have recently sent money to us for the Armenian and Syrian relief, because they did not know the address to which it should be sent. We have forwarded it to "Near East Relief, 1 Madison Avenue, New York" the proper address for such funds.

The Four Year Program page supplied this week by Prof. J. A. Garber deserves the careful attention of every preacher. Co-operation will redound to the benefit of your local church and of the brotherhood. Brother Garber is director of the recruiting goal and is seeking to help the church find more ministers.

We are privileged to have a report this week from Brother Lyon concerning his work at Washington, D. C. They are suffering some from the spread of the "flu" and the leaving of some faithful workers who for a time have been in residence at Washington is being felt by the loyal band, but they are still displaying their customary liberality in the support of the local work.

Economy is a noble attainment; it makes possible ever larger success, wider experiences, deeper enjoyments and higher virtues. Without it many promising lives have the doors of opportunity closed in their faces; even virtue has been supplanted by misery and crime where economy has been neglected. Important as it is, it is often despised, and is daily becoming more and more a stranger in our land.

Gratis, Ohio, does not get into print very often, but they have a good report in this week, and since Sister Andrews made such a good report, we shall welcome another letter from her. The pastor, Brother C. E. Beckley, assisted by Rev. Paul Wright, of Eaton, as song leader, began a revival meeting in December, but sickness caused him to leave the whole task in the hands of Brother Wright. Several confessions resulted from the meeting. The work in this pastorate is going forward harmoniously.

Brother C. A. Stewart, the energetic pastor of the Corinth and Loree churches in Indiana, reports progress at both charges. At the Loree church he was assisted in a successful revival meeting by Brother Wirick, who has frequently given valuable service to this congregation. These people know how to take care of their pastor. He is now comfortably situated in a new parsonage. He was compelled to close a revival meeting at Corinth after a week's duration because of the weather and bad roads.

The editor was very much gratified to receive from Brother W. J. H. Bauman, who is living with his son at Long Beach, California, a letter expressing appreciation of the tributes and honor paid the pioneer ministers in the issue of January 28. Brother Bauman is one of the oldest ministers, both in point of service and in age, but still maintains a vital interest in the welfare of the church. He says he loves the young people and is glad for the superior advantages they enjoy. And I am sure it can be said of practically the younger men of the ministry that they love the fathers of the church and look with pride upon the work they did.

"The Pittsburgh Anniversary" is the subject of a communication from the "Smoky City" over the signature of Miss Isabelle Wilcox. And it was an anniversary long to be remembered, for it was the occasion for the burning of the mortgage on the Pittsburgh church. There are many, in the brotherhood who have had a special interest in this church and rejoice in the progress it has made under the leadership of Brother Harley. Among those who were present and assisted in the celebration were Brother A. D. Gnagey, who was at one time pastor of this church, and Brother Wise who visited many churches of the brotherhood in behalf of this church in the time of its great need.

The Christian Endeavorers are carrying on one of the most important campaigns of the whole year, that of enlistment for life service for the King of kings. Brother Garber, the National Life Work Director in the Four Year Program and Brother Boardman, Christian Endeavor Life Work Superintendent, with the co-operation of others are carrying on an intensive campaign, both in the Angelus and The Evangelist. Where to find sufficient preachers and missionaries is one of the most perplexing problems facing the church. This campaign will help to solve it, if it receives the co-operation that it deserves.

The college endowment mercury is still going up and Pleasant Hill gave it the last boost and a good boost it was. No one can doubt that there are some very loyal Brethren at this place when they read the report of Brother Beachler. Ohio churches as a whole are doing nobly on the endowment proposition and we feel sure that Buckeyes will not be one whit behind the other districts when the finals are all in. And we were particularly pleased when we heard that Pleasant Hill had held up their corner. And it is likely, as Brother Beachler suggests, when some other loyal Brethren have been heard from that the total of Pleasant Hill's gift will be materially increased. Pleasant Hill is not only supporting Ashland College financially, but has some young people who are contemplating coming to Ashland to do school work. We shall welcome them.

The "College News" will doubtless prove of special interest this week, as it is a report of the principal transactions of the Board of Trustees. Dr. Jacobs' report of the attendance of the college and seminary show a good increase over last year. The loss to the college by the leaving of Prof. Hendrickson is being shared by the town people who are interested in the college, as the business men of the town have great confidence in his judgment. It will be noted with interest that Brother Martin Shively has been invited to bring his splendid business ability to do the work which Brother Hendrickson has been performing with such satisfaction. The several financial plans which the college has on foot will be of interest, particularly the one that concerns the Alumni. It is safe to predict that with such a loyal army of students as have passed through the halls of Ashland College the alumni will, under the efficient leadership of Brother A. H. Lichty, will not fail to do something worth while for their Alma Mater, especially since Brother Lichty is in the habit of carrying through to success whatever he lays his hands to.

FOUR-YEAR PROGRAM PAGE
NOW THEN DO IT.—II Samuel 3:18
Conducted by Charles A. Bame

Life Work Recruiting
By the Director of Goal Six

(The following letter was sent out by Brother Garber to every pastor and we are taking the liberty
of running it in the Evangelist for the benefit of all our readers.—Editor)

Dear Fellow Pastor:

February of 1920 presents the ministry with unusual opportunities. This year the month gives us the privilege of preaching on five Sundays, the fifth Sunday occurring thus only once in forty years. Moreover, it has been named "Stewardship Month" with the 22nd set apart for the enrollment of "Tithing Stewards" and the 29th for the enlistment of "Life Stewards."

The latter refers to Life Work Recruits. That is, suitable persons who give themselves definitely to the ministry, missionary service or related work of the church. After taking the necessary training, unless they chance to be prepared, they will become employed workers of the church. Goal 6 of the Four Year Program calls for at least 75 Recruits. Each local church qualifies by enlisting at least one from its membership. Now is the opportune time to make your Victory Drive on this point. Your young people are working under the auspices of Christian Endeavor, and they covet your co-operation. Should your church have no Society, we suggest that you use the Life Work Pageant through your Sunday school.

Another form of recruiting is the forming of "Life Purposes" by those who may be too young and inexperienced to choose finally their life work. Early high school and even eighth grade students may be encouraged on go on record as being willing to follow the leading of God. In this connection we commend the use of the card entitled "Important Personal Purposes for Young People." It was prepared by Dr. J. C. White and may be obtained from him at the Life Work Department of the Interchurch World Movement, Fifth Avenue, New York, at the rate of 1 cent each. Get enough for general use among your young people. Enclose 25c additional and you will receive a fine lot of helps. The titles are given in my open letter in the Evangelist of January 28th. Let me call your attention, too, to related articles in both the Evangelist and Angelus.

Feeling that you appreciate the vital relation between recruiting and a larger Brethren church, let me suggest that we strive to enlist high type, promising young people; to discover such good prospects and land them through personal interviews; to continue to be their interpreter, guide and friend. Let us keep constantly in mind the difficulty and danger of recruiting en masse, also, the uselessness of recruiting unworthy, incompetent, selfish persons or those unwilling to take training. The best are none too good for the leadership of the church and the need is unspeakably great. A class of 30 new recruits should enter Ashland College and Seminary next Fall. Enlist these persons and if they need money for schooling the church must provide it. Please report to me the name and address of all recruits, old and new, early in March.

Yours, praying the Lord of the Harvest,

J. A. GARBER, Ashland, Ohio.

GENERAL ARTICLES

Christian Stewardship. By C. F. Yoder

(Brother Yoder states that this is the first Article he has written aside from reports, since he has been in South America. Our readers will hope he may find time to favor us more frequently. This article was solicited for our booklet, The Church and Kingdom Interest's.—Editor.)

The principle of Christian stewardship is one of the most important teachings of the Bible, but it has been one of the most difficult to learn. The instinct of ownership is so ancient and so firmly established in society as well as the individual that it is hard to replace it by the better idea of stewardship, or the use of property for the general good. Nevertheless the tendency of modern Christianity is to give a wider application to the teachings of Jesus and to promote the social as well as the individual regeneration which they imply.

It is true that this social regeneration is not to be expected in its fullness in this dispensation but in the next, but the church which is being called out in this dispensation must form the social unit which is God's agent in establishing the kingdom of social righteousness in the world, and a proper example of stewardship on the part of the church is necessary to the accomplishment of her mission.

The agencies in the establishment of the principle of stewardship are various. Within the church the Gospel teaching is given more clearly and faithfully than before and without it the socialistic forces are demanding with increasing insistency that wealth be considered a trust for the benefit of all and not a legacy for the benefit of the few.

Before this principle can rule, the world must pass through a period of chaos and trouble and reconstruction as complete as the transformation of a caterpillar into a butterfly. The social structure of the past has been builded on the idea of the dominance of force and this resulted first in slavery and second in industrial oppression and both must pass. The rule of brute force gave way to the rule of mental force and both must give way to the rule of love.

This is the basis and motive power of Christian stewardship. It means far more than the consulting of the Bible as a law book to find out the least amount a Christian must give. It means the joyful administration of everything as the spirit of love directs, and the spirit of love is not limited by ties of blood or race or country. God loved the world. If therefore we know him we shall love as he loves, and our lives with all their interests and activities will be extended to include our neighbors in all the world.

This is not a new principle. Our first parents were told to work in the garden of God, not as owners, but as keepers; and mankind has ever been taught to consider this life, not as a permanent abode but as a pilgrimage. "The earth is the Lord's and the fullness thereof." Thus we read that the Patriarch's "confessed that they were pilgrims and strangers in the earth" (Heb. 11:13) and the law declared "The land shall not be sold forever: for the land is mine; for ye are strangers and sojourners with me" (Lev. 25:23).

The Christian conception of property is not different from this. "The multitude of them that believed were of one heart and one soul: neither said any of them that ought of the things which he possessed was his own" (Acts 4:32). Paul clearly declares "Ye are not your own; for ye are bought, with a price" (1 Cor. 6:19, 20), and the author of Hebrews speaking for all believers says, "We have here no continuing city. but we seek one to come" (Heb. 13:14). Jesus commanded "Lay not up treasures for yourselves upon the earth." In all his teaching he made it clear that God is the owner of everything and believers are stewards to whom he confides only a temporal management and from whom he will exact a strict rendering of accounts. When he said "He that renounceth not all that he hath he cannot by my disciple" he refers to the idea of ownership and not necessarily of administration.

From whence then comes the prevalent idea that every man may use his property as he will? It is an inheritance of paganism and had its origin in the reign of brute force and owes its continuance to a lack of full consecration to Christ on the part of the church. The ownership of everything by the state will not better matters as long as the individuals composing the state are unregenerate and do not recognize that the state as well as individuals must give an account of their stewardship. Not ownership, either individual or collective, but stewardship, both individual and collective, is what the world awaits. The prophets saw the day of its coming and declared "Then shall every man sit under his vine and under his fig tree; and none shall make them afraid" (Micah 4:4). Then shall the world be safe for democracy, but the same prophecy announces a preparatory period of judgment and reconstruction in which all property shall once more be recognized as the Lord's (vs. 13). The new "industrial democracy" shall be a stewardship for nations as well as for individuals (Rev. 21:24).

One of the greatest results of the great war has been the directing of the attention of the world to the fact that nations as well as individuals should be honest and must find their true liberty in renouncing the false liberty of selfish license and accepting the restraint which brotherly love imposes in the consideration of the good of others. "Let no man seek his own, but every man another's wealth" (1 Cor. 10:11). The present economic system and social spirit causes every man to seek another's wealth, but for himself and not for the other. This state of things must end. Its end is predicted as violent but in its place will come the new era of co-operation in which the struggle for life will be at last subordinated to the higher law which Drummond calls "the struggle for the life of others."

Such a change is nothing less than a rebirth of society with all the analogous stages that we experience in conversion as individuals. And as the old man of sin must be crucified that the new man in Christ may live, so the old spirit in society must be destroyed that in its place may come the new in which stewardship shall not be an idle exhortation of a few faithful pastors but the very basis of economic life, accepted and practised by all. Well might the apostles of the new order be referred to as "they that have turned the world upside down" (Acts 17:6). Too long it has been downside up with the underworld in power. Let it be righted that the holy city may come down and fill the earth with the glory of the Lord.

I have said that the church is the social unit which is used in this transformation. In the first enthusiasm of consecration the apostolic church gained heights of power and depths of love which later ages lost. But the glorious example of that church has remained as an inspiration to all ages and faithful witnesses have never failed to exhort the word to follow suit. Why should not we, who proclaim as our plea fidelity to the Gospel, begin to take more seriously

the great doctrine with all its implications and give to the world an example of faithful stewardship. The law of imitation is the great agent of the Spirit in moral transformation. Why should we not with holy enthusiasm enter upon a period of true consecration both of ourselves and of our means? "Like a mighty army moves the church of God"— does it? Where are the millions of volunteers and the billions of money that would furnish the evangelization of the world and put an end to war? Do we "go over the top" with 40 cents or even a dollar a year per member for missions when the state gets a hundred dollars for war? Are parents true to Christ when they hinder their children from going as missionaries only to lose them later in war? Is our country better or more enduring than Christ that we should sacrifice for it so much more than for Christ? No, we have not yet learned what it is to really obey the order to preach the Gospel to all nations and to work for the Lord until he comes.

When once we accept the gospel of stewardship there will be no difficulty with the question of the tithe. The tithe has ever been the proportion demanded by the Lord in recognition of his ownership of all, nor did he ever give to the renter the right to dissipate with the rest. "Ye pay tithes—these ought ye to have done" said Jesus, but the weightier matters of the law—justice, judgment and mercy, are matters of loving stewardship and must not be left undone. The good Samaritan did not count out his tithe money to the innkeeper, much less a partly offering of small coins. He provided for "whatsoever thou hast need of." In Argentina the Roman church has just raised fourteen million pesos to pacify the working class and the working class is spurning the offering. They say that they want justice and not alms. They have lost confidence in those who toss to them an alms with one hand and rob them of their homes with the other. The world will believe the Gospel more readily when it is lived in the beauty of its holiness and the grandeur of its power. Where is the church that will give the example?

And stewardship is gain and not loss for the steward. The windows of heaven are opened upon him and the widow's oil is increased. "He that soweth abundantly shall reap also abundantly," and he that forsaketh father or mother or houses or lands receives a hundred fold. The prodigal son wanted his father's property in his own hands and lost it. The elder brother who left his inheritance in the hands of the father could hear him say "Son, thou art ever with me and all that I have is thine." When we say with Jesus, "All mine is thine" we can also say "All thine is mine." There is no want for those who are joint heirs with Christ. Their Father is rich and their joy is full. Yea "God loveth the cheerful giver." He is preparing the world to be his inheritance and a throne which endureth forever. Not slaves who serve through fear nor servants who give for gain but sons who live and love are the elect of God who shall hear the words "'Well done, good and faithful steward, enter thou into the joy of thy Lord."

Rio Cuarto, Argentina.

THE BIBLE IN CHINA

The president of China, Hsu Shih Chang, has sent the following message to the American Bible Society:

"The instruction concerning all virtue, as contained in the Holy Scriptures of the religion of Jesus, has truly exerted an unlimited influence for good among all Christians in China, and has also raised the standard of all my people along lines of true progress. I earnestly hope that the future benefits derived from the Holy Scriptures will extend to the ends of the earth and transcend the success of the past."

Ye are the light of the world. . . Even so let your light shine before men that they may see your good works and glorify your Father which is in heaven.—Matthew 5:14, 16.

Establishing Young People In the Faith.   By T. Darley Allen

(Address written for Ohio Conference at Canton, but read by Brother Allen's daughter)

De Quincey tells in his Autobiographic Sketches of a beautiful and gifted young woman who was a guest in his boyhood home and who was a zealous opponent of Christianity. His mother dreaded the effect of her arguments upon the servants, and undoubtedly this young woman was a power for harm in that home; for although two clergymen were also guests there at the time, they were unable to counteract her influence, their very inability to answer her arguments no doubt convincing the servants that she was right or men who they supposed to be learned ministers of the church would have been capable of refuting her infidel objections. But it was not because of any weakness in the defences of the Christian faith that the woman carried off the laurels whenever she met opposition but because of the lack of knowledge on the part of the clergymen of the evidences of Christianity.

One of the ministers, De Quincey tells us, was "dreadfully commonplace, dull, dreadfully dull, and by the necessity of his nature incapable of being deadly in earnest, which his splendid antagonist at all times was;" the other clergyman was "holy, visionary, apostolic" and could not be treated disrespectfully, but he lacked the taste and the training for polemic service and could not look upon Christianity as the subject of defence but as a thing only to be interpreted and illumed.

In those days the form of infidelity known as deism was widespread and clergymen who were not familiar with the evidences were not fitted for intellectual and spiritual leadership.

Still less is ignorance of the arguments in support of our religion excusable in the ministry of today. For infidel objections are to be heard everywhere. The newspapers and the magazines and nearly all kinds of literature that come into the hands of young people have much in them to lead inquiring minds to doubt the truths of religion. The way the magazines have been opening their columns to articles on spiritualism from men whose endeavor is to show that the Christian faith is out of date and that a more rational religion is presenting its credentials for consideration, is sufficient to indicate that it is impossible to keep from our young men and women objections which, especially among persons without strong religious convictions, are calculated to sow doubts of the divine nature of our faith.

In the editorial and woman's departments of a great newspaper, the latter being read each day by many thousands of young women, I have found much that openly attacks Christianity, and various special writers to its columns take for granted many of the claims of infidels concerning what most Christians believe are fundamentals. And because infidel arguments are so widely disseminated we are liable to meet them anywhere, in the cars, at the dinner table, or from public speakers on street corners. Most of these objections to Christianity are a mass of misconceptions and due to ignorance, but to many of the people who hear them and are not acquainted with the facts the statements seem convincing.

Some commercial travelers were at dinner in a hotel where a minister of the gospel was a guest. The traveling men had considerable to say on religious subjects and referred to the New Testament as without corroborative testimony from any early secular historian. The minister then asked them if they had examined the history of the times they referred to, and the answer being that their knowledge of the subject was very limited, the preacher told them that it was his business to know the history of early Christianity and he could assure them that the statements they had made were entirely erroneous. He convinced the men that they were unjustified in their criticism and led them without much effort to realize that they had no sensible reasons for rejecting the divine claims of Christianity.

Bradlaugh when a youth was an attendant at Sunday school and once asked his teacher some questions relating to the truth of Christianity. The teacher not being able to answer them laid them before the rector of the church, but this man thought young Bradlaugh should be punished for asking them, which led the youth to conclude they were not only unanswerable but were fatal to the claims of Christianity to divine origin and he became an infidel and in later years the greatest power for the dissemination of anti-Christian ideas of his time in England. Men who know tell us that if Bradlaugh had been treated differently, if the rector had known how to deal intelligently with subjects underlying faith, this man who did so much as an infidel lecturer and writer would in all probability have been saved from unbelief and remained in the Christian fold, a worker of influence for it instead of against it.

Now, the strength of the arguments for Christianity are such that to one who knows the subject not merely superficially, there is nothing to fear from infidelity. I do not mean that all infidel objections can be answered easily. But mean that they can be shown not to be fatal to Christianity. There are objections to the belief of all of us here on astronomical subjects. Some people still hold as important old objections to the idea of the earth's rotundity, but they do not figure largely in the views of us who think we have good reasons for believing the earth is round. Infidels themselves realize that all their objections do not have to be answered in order to prove Christianity true. When Brobinski, the Russian atheist, realized that in the Man of Nazareth God is revealed, he felt that Christianity is true and that objections against a thing proved are of no weight. And the famous Lord Lyttelton, who was convinced of the folly of infidelity through a study of the New Testament account of the conversion of Saul of Tarsus, cared nothing for objections when he realized the incontrovertible character of the positive testimony to Christianity afforded by the acceptance of Christ as divine by the great apostle.

I do not make a plea for an extensive study of the evidences of Christianity by young people. The subject is of such a nature that more than a superficial knowledge of it in some important phases can only be imparted without difficulty by the well-equipped minister. So I think it the duty of ministers to instruct young people sufficiently to keep them from being disturbed when they hear their religion criticised. I think instruction should be given the senior classes of our Sunday schools each Sunday.

Man is incurably religious, as has often been said; and many skeptics have expressed a desire to believe and many have believed when they had their reason satisfied. In one of the editions of McIlvaines' well-known work on the evidences the statement is made that a copy of this book once found its way into an unbelieving neighborhood and as a result all the infidels were changed into believers in the faith of Christ.

C. J. Whitmore, a London (England) preacher, said that out of twenty prominent infidel editors, lecturers and workers he had known in thirty years' experience in the British metropolis sixteen had renounced their unbelief for faith and become workers in the cause of Christ.

Rev. G. L. Griffith, a minister of the Christian denomination, of Troy, Ohio, has said he once preached a series of sermons against infidelity in a Michigan town and at the close of the series a man arose and said that he was president of an infidel club but that he desired to confess as an honest man that "there is not a thread of my coat left and I want to place my feet upon a plank that will stand."

And especially is the young man or woman who has been brought up under church influences desirous of holding on to faith. If the young people of our Sabbath schools are led 'into doubt it is because they have been perplexed by the objections to revealed truth that are to be heard everywhere about them. The desire to believe will hold the young people who have had thrown about them the influences of church and Sabbath school if they have a knowledge of Christian evidences sufficient to show them that on purely intellectual grounds there is reasonable basis for faith.

A writer of a tract who signs himself A. J. P. says, "When the writer was a converted lad in his early teens he was sorely tried with skeptical doubts, so much so that more than once he came within an ace of throwing up all profession of Christianity. But it was the history of the Jews that held him back. This history could only be explained by the power and overruling providence of God."

There can be no question that ninety percent at least of our young men and women are almost entirely without knowledge of the arguments for Christianity. It would be so easy to give instruction in our Sabbath schools that would fortify them to withstand the powers for evil that are so zealous in efforts to undermine Christian faith. And it is because the evidences of Christianity are so strong and there are such interesting ways of showing by argument and illustration that the faith of our fathers is supported by "many infallible proofs" that the fact is easily recognized that there need be no difficulty in imparting to our young people an adequate knowledge of this important subject in these days of doubt and false religious teaching when the very elect are in danger of being led astray and only intelligent Christians, intellectually as well as spiritually strong in the faith, are properly equipped soldiers of the cross.

The Hope of the Church.   By N. J. Paul

In a former article we treated the subject of "The Church;" in this article we want to treat briefly as we can, "What is the Church's Hope or, what should be the hope of the church?" In treating this subject we wish it to be clear that we do not have in mind denominationalism or the different branches of the church. We mean the church which Christ and his apostles instituted. The conversion of the world is not the object of the church's hope. It is quite true this glorious consummation lies in the future, for "the earth shall be filled with the knowledge of the Lord as the waters cover the sea," but the task of bringing this about was not committed to the church. On the contrary, the New Testament descriptions of the last days of the church upon earth preclude the thought. They are depicted in dark colors (2 Tim. 3:1-5; 2 Pet. 3:1-4). The fact is, the history of preaching the Gospel in the world should be enough to show that this cannot be the object set before us, for, while whole nations have been Christianized, not a single community has ever been completely converted. It is a fact the apostles had nothing to say about, the conversion of the world.

While they were busy preaching the Gospel in the world they gave no indication that they expected this work to result at length in the transformation of the world. They were not looking for a change in the world, but for the personal presence of their Lord. Jesus Christ himself was their hope, and his appearing they intensely loved and longed for. The attitude of the New Testament church is represented by the Apostle John in the closing words of the apocalyptic visions of heavenly glory and millennial peace which passed before him. He had seen the new heaven and the new earth wherein dwelleth righteousness, and the holy city, the New Jerusalem, whose light was like a stone most precious. But, at the end of it all the longing of the aged apostle is not for these things to come. Greater than all these glories, dearer than all these dear things, is the Master himself, and the prayer that rises from his heart as he closes his wondrous book is simply, "Come, Lord Jesus." The hope of the church then, is the personal return of her Lord. Let us see how this hope lies upon the pages of the New Testament revelation, and how it influenced the life of the church.

Christ taught his disciples to expect his return. This seems to be the last thought he impressed his disciples with. In the early part of his ministry he seem to have kept his personality in the background; he forbade those whom he healed to tell about him. Then there came a time when he asked the disciples, "Whom do men say that I am?" and led them to think of his divine origin. After that he began to instruct them about his approaching death and resurrection, and his departure which he was about to accomplish at Jerusalem (Luke 9:31). In the last days of his ministry his return to the world largely occupied his thoughts, and he kept it prominently before the minds of his disciples. During his last journey to Jerusalem he foreshadowed his own history in the parable of the nobleman going into a far country to receive a kingdom and return, who left his servants behind with the command, "occupy till I come" (Luke 19: 12, 13).

Oh that we could behold him, as he sat one evening during the last week, on the Mount of Olives, looking down no doubt upon the massive buildings of the temple, the total destruction of which he had just foretold. The disciples gathered about him with the request: "Tell us, when shall these things be? and what shall be the sign of thy coming, and the end of the world" (Matt. 24:3)? It is evident from the form of this question that his coming was no new thought to them. It was occupying their minds already. They knew that he was coming again, and they wished to know how to recognize the approach of that event. In answer to the question, the Lord unfolded a panorama of intervening history, and emphasized the need of watchfulness because the time of his coming would be uncertain. "Watch therefore, for ye know not on what day your Lord cometh. Therefore be ye also ready, for in an hour that ye think not the Son of Man cometh." We should take heed to the Master's teaching on this point. He enforced this teaching with two striking illustrations of the twofold kind of preparation needed on the part of the Christian, the inward preparation the spiritual life set forth in the parable of the virgins, and the outward preparation of diligent service in that of the talents. Then he closed his discourse with a graphic picture of the changed conditions in which he would appear when he came the second time as the Son of Man sitting upon the throne of his glory.

Go with me to the dark hours of the very last night and see how his thoughts were occupied with his return.

In the upper room, when the faithful little band were grouped about him in sorrow for the parting which no doubt all felt was near, he began his farewell words to them with this comforting assurance: "Let not your hearts be troubled. I go to prepare a place for you. And if I go—I will come again." A few hours afterwards he was in the midst of the shameful scene of his trial. Through all the shame of those awful hours, the vision of his return in glory to the world that was rejecting him now shone like a beacon upon his soul; and "for the joy that was set before him, he endured the cross, despising the shame." This one thought should occupy our minds, not what we shall eat; or what we shall put on, or how much we can accumulate in this world, BUT that Christ is coming. Am I ready for his coming? At his ascension the same truth was again brought to the minds of the disciples. As they stood gazing, no doubt in wonder towards the place where the Lord had disappeared from their view, the two angels were sent to remind them of his return. How their hearts must have beat with joy; when their ears heard the message of the angels. "This same Jesus who was taken up from you into heaven shall so come in like manner as ye have seen him go into heaven." This was the thought that sent them back to Jerusalem with

(Continued on page 9)

THE BRETHREN PULPIT

Jesus Yesterday, Today and Forever. By Miss Mary Pence

Text: Jesus Christ the same yesterday, and today, and forever Hebrews 13:8. How like a pearl among pearls is this text among texts. It is a wonderful declarative statement about our Savior. It is a very comforting text for this very age of rapid changing and in its contemplation the heart is calmed. Either change or decay marks nearly every thing with which we have to do so that oftentimes we come near the point of having faith in nothing. But in this beautiful text we are directed to a place of refuge and rest for the soul. When faith finds her resting place all is well within or without. This resting place pointed out is Jesus Christ. We ourselves may change from day to day but "Jesus Christ is the same yesterday, today, and forever."

I Jesus Christ Yesterday.

As early as Genesis 4:4, we read of a blood and bloodless sacrifice. The bloodless offering of Cain, the fruit of his own work, was not accepted which fact proclaims in the infancy of the race that "without the shedding of blood is no remission." And the blood for the remission of sins has always been the blood "of the Lamb slain from the foundation of the world," either the real blood or the blood of some animal which typified the blood of Jesus. The Jews understood the blood they offered to typify the blood of the coming Savior. Nevertheless Jesus then existed and has always existed. "In the beginning was the Word, and the Word was with God, and the Word was God. The same was in the beginning with God. All things were made by him; and without him was not anything made that was made. In him was life; and the life was the light of men. . . That was the true light, which lighteth every man that cometh into the world. He was in the world, and the world was made by him, and the world knew him not. . . And the Word was made flesh and dwelt among us, (and we beheld his glory, the glory as of the only begotten of the Father), full of grace and truth." So says John in the first chapter This was the Messiah to whom the Jews looked forward, the Redeemer promised in Genesis 3:15 as the seed of the woman.

The Gospels of the New Testament is a record of this promised Savior coming to dwell among men. He was manifested in the flesh and in his human body dwelt among men on the earth for about 33 years. Compared with the total area of the earth, he moved in a very limited sphere. He seemed to make no world-wide attempt to restore the divine order of things as they were after "the Spirit of God moved upon the face of the deep" and before Satan destroyed this order in Eden. But wherever he went he bestowed blessings and to a limited extent restored the divine order. He set the temple at rights when after having made a scourge of small cords he drove out the sheep and the oxen and poured out the changers' money and overthrew the tables. And with the voice of authority said, "Take these things hence; make not my Father's house an house of merchandise." He gave life to the dead, health to the sick, bread to the hungry, sight to the blind, hearing to the deaf, speech to the dumb, comfort to the sorrowing, and changed sinners into saints. And not only to one here or there did he impart help and life but the hour struck when on the cross he poured out his blood for all people at all times so that tha whole creation could be redeemed. Now we plead before God the real blood and he is most blessed upon whom God sees the blood of his Son. Thus in the yesterday of history we see Jesus Christ as Savior, "the Lamb slain from the foundation of the world," a risen, living Savior. He was always the Savior.

II Jesus Christ Today.

According to the text Jesus Christ is the same today that he was yesterday, the Savior still. Yesterday he walked upon the earth in humility, a lowly Savior. Today he sits at God's own right hand, an exalted Savior. Romans 8:34 says, "It is Christ that died, yea rather that is risen again, who is even at the right hand of God, who also maketh intercession for us." Hebrews 7:25 says, "He is able to save them to the uttermost that come unto God by him, seeing he ever liveth to make intercession for them." 1 John 2:1, 2 says, "'If any man sin, we have an advocate with the Father, Jesus Christ the righteous.' Christ is entered "into heaven itself now to appear in the presence of God for us." We see from these texts what a great Savior we now have. In him we have forgiveness of sin, we have been saved from the guilt of sin, and now he ceases not to be our daily Savior and pleads our daily cause so that we are being saved from the very dominion of sin. As we tread our daily path we meet with many perplexities. Sorrows, trials, temptations, disease, money matters and what not, these present difficulties which we must meet face to face. We realize our limitations with bitterness. But these things and more seem to melt away before that greatest problem of how to live a life wholly pleasing to God. When we take up God's Word and read such passages as Proverbs 6:16-19, the seven things the Lord hates and as we read passage after passage of the Word, that is sure and steadfast, and the Spirit begins his searchings of the innermost recesses of our being and he compares what we really are and the things we think and the things we do and the things we leave undone, all this he compares to what is God's law and will for his children, then in anguish and humiliation we see how far short we fall of being a glory to him and we cry out, "Who then can be saved?" and "'What shall I do?'" But the promise is that the Spirit shall lead us into all truth and faithful to his office he points us away from ourselves to the fact of the cross, to our Substitute and brings to mind that we have accepted the righteousness of this Savior while he carries away our sin in his own body on the tree. Then the Spirit points upward to where Christ sits at the right hand of God, saying, "If any man sin we have an advocate with the Father, Jesus Christ the righteous" who now appears in the presence of God FOR US! And we receive this message from (eSeecv difirfintatrs—)htnefl nlldo fI'phe' from him: "My grace is sufficient for thee.' It is the sufficient grace alone which gives us daily victory in our Christian life, and frees us from the evils that would otherwise dominate us. "The life that I now live in the flesh I live by the faith of the Son of God who loved me and gave himself for me." O, that Christians would not lose sight of the fact that Christ now appears in heaven for us. We have a faithful High Priest. Glory be to his name!

III Jesus Christ Forever.

Thus far we have dealt with facts concerning Jesus Christ. Now we come to the prophecy of our text, "Jesus Christ forever." If he was Savior yesterday, and if he is Savior today according to our text, and countless other Scriptures, he will be the same Savior tomorrow. In the great untried tomorrow, in the ages yet to come, and the eternity of eternities, he will be the same Jesus, the same Savior. Before the great tribulation period he is to prove himself a great Savior in that he will come with the voice of authority and call for those who love his appearing and catch us out of the world so we will be saved from the tribulation that shall come upon the earth. The dead in Christ will rise with resurrected bodies, and the bodies of the living saints shall be changed from mortal to immortal flesh and all together will be caught up to meet the Lord in the air, "and so shall we ever be with the Lord." Can we comprehend what that meaneth to even be with the Savior, to be in his presence and see him face to face for 1,000 years, all the while knowing that it is as a day with the Lord and that before us lies an eternity of eternities of these days to be with him. It is only by faith in God and his Word that we can comprehend these things.

When we look about us at the little space of earth within our limited vision, and then up into the starry skies with its mysterious untold story we just will have a childish wonder of how our God created the heavens and the earth. And then by faith we turn from the past to the future and we see that "the heavens shall pass away with a great noise, and the elements shall melt with fervent heat, the earth also and the works that are therein shall burn up." And we read on in this third chapter of 2 Peter, "The heavens being on fire shall be dissolved, and the elements shall melt with fer-

vent heat." Nevertheless we, according to his promise look for new heavens and a new earth wherein dwelleth righteousness." And then we wonder if being ever with the Lord does not mean that we shall see the old pass away and be witnesses to the new creation.

It is a fact that a change of existence comes to every man. What a blessed hope is ours in our text. Jesus Christ the same yesterday, today, and forever, a great Savior!" Be diligent that ye may be found of him in peace, without spot, and blameless" when he comes and to be found in him in this life is to be found of him in peace when he comes.

"Change and decay on all around I see,
O, thou who changeth not, abide with me."
Limestone, Tennessee.

The Hope of the Church
(Continued from page 7)

joy, which Luke describes in the closing verses of his Gospel. The apostles taught their converts to wait for the coming of the Lord. Should not this be the first thought to occupy our minds? Is it not HIGH TIME for the pastors, and evangelists to preach and teach their converts of the certainty of the Lord's return, realizing the fact, that our salvation is not complete until the Christ shall come? The conversion of the Thessalonians is described as "turning to God from their idols to serve the living and true God, and to wait for his Son from heaven." The Corinthians "come behind in no gift, waiting for the revelation of our Lord Jesus Christ." To the Galatians Paul writes, "We through the Spirit by faith wait for the hope of righteousness," and to the Philippians, "Our citizenship is in heaven, whence also we wait for a Savior, the Lord Jesus Christ. In the Epistle to the Hebrews the same attitude is disclosed, for there we read, "Christ also, having been once offered to bare the sins of many, shall appear a second time, apart from sin, to them that wait for him, unto salvation." This is where salvation is complete.

After a close study of the Scriptures, it will be discovered that the early church had in mind two views. (1) Their faith was anchored in the past in the facts of the death and resurrection of the Lord, and (2) in the future, in the assured hope of his return. It is evident therefore, that the second coming of the Savior occupied a most important place in the early church, which also the apostles preach, and which the Christians received. The sanctification of all Christians is a preparation for the coming of the Lord. Paul writes to the Thessalonians: "The very God of peace sanctify you wholly, and I pray God your whole spirit and soul and body be preserved blameless unto the coming of our Lord Jesus Christ." John puts the same thing in his own tender way: "And now, little children, abide in him that, when he shall appear, we may have confidence and not be ashamed before him at his coming." Christians should get their encouragement in the same inspiring issue. Paul exhorts Timothy to fidelity, charging him to "keep the commandment, without spot, without reproach, until the appearing of our Lord Jesus Christ." Peter writes to his fellow elders: "Feed the flock of God which is among you, and when the Chief Shepherd shall appear, ye shall receive a crown of glory that fadeth not away." The early church had her suffering and her trial, persecutions and temptations, yet the apostle James does not forget them in their bad hour, but comes to them in their bereavement and says, "Be patient therefore, brethren, until the coming of the Lord. Establish your hearts, for the coming of the Lord is at hand." The life, fellowship, and brotherly love of the Lord's children reaches its holy consummation at the Lord's return. Again, "The Lord make you to increase and abound in love one toward another, and toward all men, even as we also do toward you; to the end he may establish your hearts unblameable in holiness before our God and Father at the

coming of our Lord Jesus Christ with all his saints." Their acts of worship, as for example, their observance of the Lord's supper, washing their feet, giving to them the bread and cup, all have the same end in view. "As oft as ye eat of this bread and drink of this cup, ye do show the Lord's death till he come." Thus, whatever aspect of the church's life and work we consider, we find it to be a stream which moves on towards one glorious future.

The appearing of the Lord Jesus himself fills the whole horizon. Sad, but too true, the church of today is emptied of much of the meaning it had among the early Christians. It has come to be a vague and misty thing—a general habit of expecting things somehow to turn out well. Their hope was no such shallow optimism. It was the light that shone from an expectation of one glad coming event, casting its sacred glow over all their lives. Paul sums up the true Christian attitude in these words: "The grace of God hath appeared, bringing salvation to all men, instructing us, to the intent that, denying ungodliness and worldly lusts, we should live soberly and righteously and godly in this present world; looking for the blessed hope and appearing of the glory of the great God and our Savior Jesus Christ." The word hope was often on the lips of the apostles, "We are saved by hope," "rejoicing in hope;" the epistle to the Hebrews makes frequent use of the word in this way. There was a special reason for this. The Hebrew Christians were a small and despised community, living under the continual influence of that majestic ritual which was still going on in the temple at Jerusalem. The return of Christ was delayed, and there was a strong tendency to slip back into the old ceremonial system. They had need of every encouragement. The writer of the epistle turns their eyes again and again from the shadows of the past to the realities that lay before them. Telling them, their Messiah had indeed come to put away sin by the sacrifice of himself, but he would come a second time, in glory, with a final and complete salvation. This was the hope set before them to which they had fled for refuge (Heb. 6:18). WHEN IS OUR REDEMPTION COMPLETE? The apostles thought of salvation in three different ways: (1) With reference to the past, as a fact already assured at the moment of belief in the Savior. (2) With reference to the present, as a process still going on. (3) With reference to the future, as an act yet to be accomplished. In this last sense Paul uses the word when he says, "Now is our salvation nearer than when we first believed," and Peter also uses the phrase, "kept by the power of God through faith unto a salvation ready to be revealed in the last time," Our Lord refers to the same thing when, after telling the disciples about the signs of his coming, he adds, "When these things begin to come to pass, look up, and lift up your heads, because your redemption draweth nigh." One of the most complete types of the history of redemption is to be found in the ceremonies of the day of atonement.

It was an essential part of the work of the high priest

on that day that he should come forth from within the veil, and laying aside his linen garments, reappear to bless the waiting congregation. Our great High Priest is now within the veil. He has offered the atoning sacrifice on the altar of Calvary, and with the merit of that sacrifice he has gone in to appear in the presence of God for us. But the great day of atonement is not yet closed. When his work within the veil is ended, he shall come forth, arrayed again in his garments of glory and beauty, for the final blessing of his waiting people. As the world was astonished at him when he came the first time, so will it be astonished when he comes a second time, and the prophet's vision breaks upon its view: "Who is this that cometh from Edom, with dyed garments from Bozrah, this that is glorious in his apparel, marching in the greatness of his strength" (Isa. 63:1)? And what will it mean for the redeemed? The happy reunion of all the saints when the dead are raised and the living are changed, for, when the Lord descends from heaven with a shout, "the dead in Christ shall rise first, and we that are alive and remain shall be caught up together with them in the clouds to meet the Lord in the air." This will be a glor-

ious day, a happy time; but only preliminary steps to a higher and holier bliss.

The climax of the redemption will be the manifested union of the church with her Lord in the marriage of the Lamb. For when the Bridegroom shall come to claim his bride, the church, and take her to share his glory and his throne. Then the church that Christ loved and purchased shall be presented to him a glorious church, not having spot or wrinkle. Think what it will mean; after-sharing his humiliation in the midst of a scoffing and unbelieving world, the redeemed, the church, is exalted to his side, and, as the consort of the King of kings and the Lord of lords, stands "all rapture through and through in God's most holy sight.

One more thought, then we close. Do we not know that God will commend us, or condemn us for every word we speak, for every act we do, and every thought we have.

"Therefore, we ought to give the more earnest heed to the things we have heard, lest at any time, we may let them slip.

Losantville, Indiana.

Our Young People at Work

J. A. Garber
PRESIDENT

G. C. Carpenter
SECRETARY

Ashland College Night

For several years the Brethren Christian Endeavor society at Roanoke, Virginia has observed Ashland College Night with great success. In order to extend this blessing to others these Endeavorers started a campaign which culminated in the establishment of the Life Work Department as a permanent department in the Virginia State Union and the election of Brethren Endeavorers as state and district superintendents of the department. One of their unique plans to be used in the society meetings February eighth is given below. (Applicable now to February 29th, National Recruiting Day).

One week or more before the meeting each active member will receive a copy of this notice: "You are hereby summoned to appear before the Exemption Board of the Christian Endeavor Society at 6:30 P. M., Sunday, February 8, 1920 to show cause why you should not be drafted for full time Christian Services. If impossible to appear file exemption papers with the President before Friday. Your name has been registered with the above member and will be selected by Urim and Thummium.

By order————— C. E. Society.

At the meeting, after a special program is rendered the Exemption Board (Missionary Committee) will take its place around a table in the front of the room. The leader, blindfolded, will draw the numbers from a hat, calling upon the members to come forward. After claiming exemption the Board will allow the members to take a seat in the audience or send them into one of the Sunday school rooms to the Spiritual Examiner (Society Life Work Superintendent) who will explain the Recruit's Covenant. Those who sign the covenant will be accepted for full time service and the others rejected. H. H. ROWSEY,
Roanoke, Virginia.

Reports from the National C. E. President

COMMENDATION FROM OTHERS

Our Life Work Pageant, "The Crusade of Sacrificial Service," has been heartily commended by Rev. Frank L. Freet, Quiet Hour Superinttendent of the Ohio Christian Endeavor Union, as will be seen by the following message addressed to Brother J. A. Garber.

"May I thank you for the copy of the Life Work Pageant. Accept my heartiest commendation. It is certainly splendid."

ENROLLING TITHING STEWARDS

Through our Christian Endeavor societies we have been striving to enroll young people as Tithing Stewards. Goal 7 of the Four Year Challenge calls for two thousand by General Conference, 1920. A number of societies seem to have done well in this effort. Some months ago a letter from Brother Thomas Harley of Muncie, Indiana, reported a splendid meeting and stated that thirteen Endeavorers pledged themselves to give one-tenth of their inrease to the Lord. He thought that the number would be increased at an early date. Perhaps other societies cherish a like hope.

Another opportunity to enroll Tithing Stewards will come to our societies on February 22. At this time most of the pastors will preach on Tithing. Advantages should be taken of the impressions made on the young people. A full report of your tithers, old and new, should be sent to Superintendent E. A. Myer, Bringhurst, Indiana.

THE HOPE OF A JUNIOR

Last week those in charge of the Junior and Intermediate sessions at Winona reported their meetings. It was hoped to have messages from some of the boys and girls. Below is one message expressing the hope of having a society for boys and girls in the Brighton, Indiana, church:

Dear Friends:

I am going to write you a few lines about the Christian Endeavor at Winona. On Sunday afternoon, September 7, I attended a fine meeting. Professor J. A. Garber gave us an excellent talk. As yet, we have no society in our church but hope to have a live Junior and Intermediate society as soon as possible.

With the best wishes to all of my fellow Endeavorers.
From a Junior.
KENNETH GOOD, Brighton, Indiana.

Whose Is It? Mine or God's

To whom does it belong—this money I have inherited, this salary I am earning, this house I am building, these sayings I have in the bank? I say my house, my bank account, my property, my salary, my clothes, my books, my education; but is it really mine? Who owns it—this wealth, this power, this influence?

"You do, of course," laughs the world.

"God does," asserts the Bible.

It's queer, isn't it, that after all the centuries of reading the Bible the church has made so little property of a religious question? for the Bible is full of it.

Story· and proverb and poem, legislation. and parable and exhortation—all unite to emphasize God's sole ownership of earth and heaven. Through long centuries of painful training the children of Israel were taught to take the first fruit from the garden, the choicest lamb of the flock, the tenth of all the increase, as a token that they and all theirs belonged alike·to God, the giver and owner of all. The tithe, the free-will offering, the gift at feast day and fast day were only so many reminders of funds held in trust.

The New Testament is not less startling in its emphasis of man's stewardship and God's ownership. Jesus' parable of the talents and his picture of the judgment agree in this, that they weigh the questions of acquisition and expenditure with the issues of life and death.

Whose is it? If it is mine, I may use it to please myself, and it is nobody's business but my own; but if it is God's, I must give an account to the owner for every penny.

Aladdin's lamp never was half so mysterious nor so powerful as these shining bits of nickel and silver and copper that slip through our fingers in an unceasing stream. There are some servants of ours who can speak but one language, but these are the polyglots of the universe. A grain of corn· talks bread, and only bread; a violet breathes of violet; but a nickel will speak whatever you will, facile slave that he is. To one he says beer, to another bread. He turns himself into a trolley ride or puffs himself out in smoke. To the child he whispers ever of goodies; to the student, of books and papers; to the artist, of brush and pencil; to the schoolgirl, of flowers and ribbons. Yet that same little coin may take the wings of the morning and preach the everlasting gospel to the ends of the earth, if you will it so; or it may minister to the whim of some fleeting moment.

Were.they God's—those billion, billion nickels that were drowned in drink last year while his world lay groaning in darkness? Was it God's coin that built those mountains of

candy and volcanoes of smoke and piled those pleasant palaces of pleasure while his world was ignorant and cold and hungry and wicked? Was it God's money that was frittered and fluttered and flaunted and danced and whistled into eternity while his kingdom waited? If it was, shall we not meet his record some day when the books are opened?

Whose is it, anyway, mine or God's? There is not ·a profounder question for Christian men and women to settle. It ought to be settled.—Abridged from the Helping Hand.

What a Tithe Would Do

If every churchman· in the United States gave one-tenth of his income, there would be something over $2,000,000.000 every year for the big enterprise of Christianizing the world, says Harvy Reeves Calkins in World Outlook. Sounds incredible, but we figure it· this way: There are over 40,500,-000 church members in the United States and the per capita income is about $500—multiply and take the tithe of it, and you get a result that is astounding. ·

Sick little children everywhere could have treatment· in hospitals. Eighty percent of · South America's babies would no longer die before they are ʼtwo years old. Fifty million outcasts in India would find new light and new life: Christianity instead of Mohammedanism would win 80,000,-000 in Africa.

In the homeland, every minister's salary could be doubled—some of them need it desperately !—every church could have its own parish house and community center, while as for benevolences—every great board could be increased 1,000 percent, except the boards of education and they could be increased 5,000 percent.

Go on and figure it· out for yourself—the simple matter of giving a tenth of income would mean the beginning of a new world.—Selected ·from The Continent.

THE SUNDAY SCHOOL

That Tokio Proposition. By Wm. H. Beachler

I believe it is fitting that I should be among the first to say a thing or two relative to the proposition which has been submitted by the Waterloo Sunday school through the. superintendent. Mrs. Wisner.

That it is a big, bold suggestion goes without saying. And it is just like the Sunday school forces of the Waterloo church to be doing such things. But I confess that even the thought of such a thing reacts on me very much as the wisdom and wealth and glory of Solomon reacted on the Queen of Sheba—I have no spirit left in·me. To me that is just another way of saying it took my breath. It was my privilege, with some of our brethren, to attend the World's Convention in Washington. D. C. in 1910. And in·1914 I attended the International Convention in Chicago. Each of these were occasions representing rare opportunities. But I confess that the thought of attending a World's Convention in a foreign land takes my breath. To say that that would be the privilege of a life time would be too mild. It would be.more nearly the privilege of about three lifetimes.

Now whatever may be the outcome I want in fairness to myself to say that as far as I am concerned the idea was born absolutely in the minds of the Waterloo people themselves. Never once did I drop the faintest glimmer of a shadow of a suggestion to anybody at Waterloo. or anywhere else for that matter. And I feel a lot better for saying this.

In the next place, even if the way should open. as it looks to me upon first thought I don't see how I could go. The shortest·routes will require from 61 to 65 days. And after a man has been on the "gad" as much as I have for over·two years it would seem about time for him·to settle

down in some corner and stick there for a long . time ʼto come.

In the interest of facts I want moreover to make a correction or two, with apologies to Mrs. Wisner. That I was· ever offered the secretaryship of the Pennsylvania Association is a mistake. I was not. Again,·I was president of the Iowa Association two years instead of three. There is a long established precedent in the Iowa Association that a president can hold the position no more than two consecutive years. If I may, I will say this however, that while I have done considerable Interdenominational Sunday school work, yet I believe I remember with most pleasure the work I have tried to·do in our own denomination. I particularly prize the memory that I happened to be the first president of·the National Brethren Sunday School Association, with Brother A. D. Gnagey as the first secretary. And I also prize the memory of my work as superintendent of the Organized Adult Class Department during which time the number of organized classes registered in our own association went beyond the 200 mark.

I feel sure I will not be misunderstood in these few lines I have written. To be sure I am interested. I certainly agree with Mrs. Wisner that the Brethren church ought to have some representation in this great convention. And I further agree that Brethren Sunday schools can easily provide the way if they are so minded. And beyond that point I say, let God's.will and the will of the majority prevail. If some other man goes he is assured beforehand of my hearty God-speed, and he can even borrow my old black traveling bag if he wants it. I know just how that traveling bag behaves on land for I have seen it put under almost every condition and.circumstance; but I can't say what it might do do when out on the Pacific.

Ashland, Ohio.

NEWS FROM THE FIELD

REPORT OF THE CHRISTIAN WORKERS' CONFERENCE OF SOUTHERN CALIFORNIA BRETHREN CHURCHES

(Continued from last week)

To create interest in missions, have photographs of our missionaries. Use posters. Get people to read missionary stories for "Information is Inspiration." It seemed to be the concensus of opinion that wherever it was possible, it was wise to have a General Missionary Society instead of a Woman's Missionary Society, as the men need the instruction, and would be glad of the opportunity to profit by hearing the programs.

Wednesday afternoon: Miss Leta Hixon of La Verne gave a paper on "The Value of the Expert Class," which was full of good suggestions. This expert class is a class in Christian Endeavor methods, instructing the officers and committees in the duties that devolve upon them, and how to perform them. Each worker needs more knowledge in order to be an efficient workman.

Following this, Sister Lillie Monroe, of the Compton Avenue church of Los Angeles, gave an excellent paper on the "Primary Department." She first stated that the Primary Department includes all children from birth to nine years old, covering the cradle roll and Beginners' Department, emphasizing the following points: "Have competent superintendents, who should keep in close touch with each baby until it is old enough to go into the Beginners' Department. This often results in bringing the mother and, possibly, the whole family, into the church. The Beginners' Department should have good teachers and helpers, who will teach the word of God by story and picture, but always teach the word. Have a goal and work toward it. In the Primary Department, still teach the word.. Often by story and picture, but do not read a story—always tell it, and again whatever you do teach the word. Have prayer and reverence, but avoid long prayers. Avoid, rather than correct, confusion. Rewards are all right, but do not hire the children."

Here Brother Broad asked us to sing the chorus of the Irish Version of "Happy Day," which we did heartily, as follows:

"Happy night, happy night, when Jesus washed my black heart white,
He taught me how to sing and shout, and live for Jesus out and out,
Happy night, happy night, when Jesus washed my black heart white."

Brother Bauman of Long Beach next gave a helpful talk on "The Need and Value of a Missionary Society in each church." He said one might as well speak of the need of money to run a bank. The church is, or, at least, should be, a missionary society itself. Her work is pre-eminently missionary. Christ has committed unto us the work of reconciliation. If the church itself is not missionary, then her missionary society is the most important of all her auxiliaries, even including the prayer meeting. The sole business of the church is to give the gospel to the sons of men, and the program God gave her is found in Matthew 28, 19 and 20, and Acts 15, giving Christ's last command, followed by the direct leading of the Holy Spirit. Different organizations or departments give opportunity to train experts, but all have the same goal—"Go ye, and take the Gospel."

Sisters Kimmel and Jennings gave messages in song at different times during the conference, and Sister Runyan whistled beautifully some of the favorite hymns.

Brother Bauman read a letter from Mr. Ralph Smith of the Bible House of Los Angeles, whose work is to furnish Spanish Bibles, Testaments, Gospels and Tracts for Latin America. This work is conducted strictly on a faith basis. The Los Angeles Bible House is ready to furnish supplies for our Auto Evangelistic Work in South America, and we need $500.00 worth of such supplies. Brother Bauman knew where $250.00 of this money would come from providing the Southern California churches would furnish the other $250.00. It was voted that the conference accept the challenge. On motion of Brother H. V. Wall, it was voted that the Long Beach church pay one-half of this amount ($125.00), and the other four churches of the conference not mission churches pay, the other $125.00. Brother Bauman further stated that the South American Auto work would now require regular Bible and tract fund. Right here, the conference welcomed and extended its courtesies to Brothers Mc-Bride and Kriegbbaum, who just arrived from Dayton, Ohio—in the celebrated "Ocean to Ocean" Bauman Ford.

Wednesday evening we were to have had Mr. Burrows of the Bolivia Indian Mission of South America to speak to us, but owing to an accident on the Pacific Electric Road, he did not arrive, so by urgent request, Brother Bauman gave us a good message from Matthew 5:36, "When He saw the Multitudes, He was Moved with Compassion." He said in part: "Men may have a definite part in foreign missions while staying in the homeland, if that is God's will for them. There is very necessary work of prayer and giving for every one who will have a part. The workers on the firing line must be supported by prayer and money. The pitiful cry from heathen who have heard just a word of a God of Love, pleading for someone to teach them the way of God, was what caused the speaker to "lift up his eyes and look on the fields," and such a look never fails to awaken interest in missionary needs and possibilities. We need to Christianize China, so that in years to come China can send missionaries to the United States. We can take a lesson from China's stand on the tobacco question. When men pray as they should, they will soon learn to pay as they should. The great problem before the missionary advance of the Brethren church is a flesh and blood problem. The Lord of the harvest needs laborers. We must pray out the $1,000.00 necessary to outfit Miss Charlotte Hillegas to Africa.

Brother Jennings followed with an evangelistic sermon on "The Deity of Jesus Christ." This sermon has been published in the Evangelist, so we will not report it, but before beginning his sermon he gave a few suggestions that will be helpful to our Sunday school and Christian Endeavor workmen: Jesus Christ must be the central figure in all Sunday school and Christian Endeavor work. Christ on the cross makes the supreme effort to bring men into oneness with the Father. Sunday school and Christian Endeavor workers should stand together in their work for the one object of teaching the way of salvation.

Thursday morning, at 9:45, Brother Broad opened the meeting with devotional exercises.

At ten o'clock Sister Clark of Long Beach brought a splendid message on "How to Hold the Interest of the Christian Endeavor society." She said the Christian Endeavor society touches the spiritual lives of our boys and girls, but the world is bidding high for young lives, and there are many devices to tempt young feet. Eph. 6:10-18 sets forth the only equipment that makes any life safe from the wiles of the enemy of souls. It is simply folly to even try to hold young people in the church by social life. The greatest problem is not of boys and girls, but of right leaders for them. The leaders of the Christian Endeavor and the superintendents of the Intermediates and Juniors should be spirit-filled leaders—those who will hold up high standards. The young people will not have ideals or visions higher than their leaders have. If the young people are held in the

Christian Endeavor or church by worldly amusements, we have not held them to anything worthy. If we hold them at all, let us hold them to spiritual things. Our part as leaders, is to teach them the word of God, making plain to them the great fundamental truths of the Deity of Jesus Christ, the Blood Atonement, his bodily resurrection, his coming again. These truths, properly presented, will interest and hold young people. One great source of helpfulness is the opportunity of the leader of getting the young people, individually, into his or her home, and getting into the deep channels of the heart life of young Christians. It is possible to have social functions where Jesus Christ has pre-eminence.

The next on the program was a talk by Sister Grace P. Syack of Long Beach on "The School of Missions," but she had no notes, and as she was secretary of the conference, no one reported it, and so—it was breathed into the air, and fell to earth, we know not where—or-what.

Brother Sylvester Lowman spoke on "The Temperance Department at Work." Brother Lowman is certainly awake on this question, and brought out many interesting facts, and some trite and suggestive stories.

The first number on the program Thursday afternoon was a talk by Brother Broad on "Shall we Edit our own Christian Endeavor Topic Cards?" He opened with the query: "Shall we feed our young people on such things as the National Christian Endeavor Topics suggest?" We need topics, the study of which means something in the lives of our young people. Shall we give them negative teaching? How is this for a topic for our boys and girls to study: "The world is being fused into one great Brotherhood." The California Christian Endeavor is known the world over as genuinely out and out for Christ. The best work of the Christian Endeavor societies is done in California. Where else can you find a great Christian Endeavor State Convention, where every worker on the platform is as out and out believer in the pre-millennial return of Jesus Christ? We want topics that bring out the great fundamental doctrines and teachings of the Word, and we want a "Thus Saith the Lord."

Brother Culp of Whittier followed with a paper on "How to Finance God's Work—Give or Raise Money?" He based his remarks on 1 Corinthians 16:2, "Lay aside, as God hath prospered." How little Christendom is giving for the Lord's business—how many know what percent? Listen—it is less than 2 percent. There is altogether too little preaching on tithing. If Israel under the law was asked to pay God one-tenth of their income, surely the church under grace cannot decently do less. Tithing began before the law was given, and it is still advocated in the New Testament. Read Malachal 3:10, and note how God says, "You bring all the tithes in"—and, well you just see what he will do. But remember, if we pledge or vow, we should faithfully keep the vow. God will supply our every need, as he says in his word, but besides that, he will supply his need through us, his children, if we give him the opportunity.

Next Sister Leona V. Kent of Long Beach very beautifully and effectively gave us the story of "Aunt Emiline's Might Box."

On motion the conference voted to hold a Worker's Conference once in three months, taking up the work of but one Department at each conference. The committee for the present conference was asked to arrange for the following conference in about three months, and it was suggested by Brother Bauman that as it would come shortly before Easter, it should be missionary.

On motion it was voted to suggest to individual churches, that as near after the beginning of the year as possible, each church should set aside a day for a Dedicatory Service for newly elected officers and teachers in these departments.

Thursday evening, after the devotional exercises, Sister Runyan beautifully whistled a favorite hymn.

On motion a rising vote of thanks was given the Whittier church for their gracious hospitality and many courtesies extended to all attending the conference.

The moderator announced financial conditions as follows:

Expenses, ...$52.46
Offerings 55.60

leaving a balance in the treasury of $3.14.

Then Harold Cross, Los Angeles County Christian Endeavor President gave an excellent talk on strategic points in Christian Endeavor work. He said in part: "I love the Christian Endeavor because it is a vital part of the church of Jesus Christ. I love it because of its motto, its pledge and its fellowship. I love it because of the Christ it brought into my heart and life. Why are there so many failures in the Christians' life? Just because they are not anchored in Christ, through understanding of his word. The very best things the world has to offer today are far away from Jesus Christ. The Sunday school work is the impression, and the Christian Endeavor work is the expression. The Christian Endeavor should take more vital interest and active part in the evening service of the church. If parents would show as much sensible interest in the Christian life of their children as they do in worldly things, we would have a different crowd of young people. C. E. means living clean, clear cut lives, out and out for Jesus Christ.

Brother Jennings followed with an evangelistic address on "The Red Letter Words of Our Lord" John 1: 1. We did not get an outline of this, but must mention one or two striking points in the address; viz., "What price do you put on your Bible? What if you could never see it again, nor ever be able to get another? God pity those who have time for newspapers, magazines, and, worse yet, novels, but have no time to study the word of God—God's love letters to men and women."

On motion the conference adjourned.
MRS. GRACE F. SRACK,
Secretary.

BANNER BENEVOLENCE OFFERING

New Paris, Indiana, one of the small churches in this conference, with but about fifty active members, lifted an offering for the superannuated ministers amounting to $102.00. This is mighty fine and a good example for some of our larger churches. Let those churches all over the brotherhood who have not yet taken their offering for this worthy cause look at the New Paris example and try to measure up to it. Let us not hew to the line of 10 cents per member. We need and must have more money than that standard will produce, so let the churches forget that part of it and give until it hurts for our aged veterans who surely are finding their lot very uncomfortable in these days of high prices. Good for New Paris! She has set her mark high. If all the rest of us do equally as well, last year's total will shrink into insignificance.

Yours with confidence in our people,
H. E. ROSCOE, Secretary.

COLLEGE NEWS

The Board of College Trustees met two weeks ago with sixteen members present. Some very important matters came up for consideration among which were the following:

The President's Report

Enrollment, in the Seminary, 40; 28 men, 12 women. Last year, 34. In the College, 55; 30 men, 25 women. Last year 48. Total in College and Seminary, 95. Music 71, Total, 166.

Spiritual State. This is very good, but of course not perfect. The religious organiza-

tions are all active and a good interest is being shown. There has been no case of serious discipline so far this year. The self-government at the hall has operated this year so far with unexpectedly favorable results. The spiritual state of no body of people is probably all it should be, but the young people here are uniformly high minded and serious. It is the constant aim to form and found Christian character in the students of the College and no effort has been spared in this direction.

Advertising. Counting in the matter that went out from Professor Hendrickson's office, something over 12,000 pieces of mail have been sent out. Nearly every issue of the Evangelist has had some word from the college and the president has been privileged to preach in fifteen Brethren churches and has attended six conferences in the brotherhood. This does not include many other such engagements outside of the church.

Class Work. This is uniformly good but it must be borne in mind, that, when a student spends his whole afternoon at work in the city as many of our men do in order to support themselves, serious inroads must be made upon what ought otherwise to be study hours. It is a matter of great satisfaction that so many of our young people are thus able to make their way through school, but it is not an unmixed blessing.

Athletics. A reasonable program for the athletic interests of the school was provided for by the addition of a small incidental fee. This was proposed by the students themselves by petition.

The Seminary. No change was made here either in the personnel or in the number of teachers. It was thought best to make no change in this department until the financial campaign, to be noted later, were well under way when the courses will be increased in number and revised. Professor J. A. Garber will be relieved of some or all of his work until he is able to do some work on his own course, a matter that was made impossible by press of work so far. He expects to enter some college this summer for degree work. Within a year his conditions will be removed. It is well to note here, that the professors in the seminary sometimes teach in the college, but the college teachers never do work in the seminary. Also that the board renewed its acquaintance with a minute of some ten years' standing to the effect that no one shall become a member of the faculty with less than a master's degree.

Professor Hendrickson offered his resignation as bursar of the college which was accepted with great reluctance, but business interests call him elsewhere. Brother Martin Shively was invited to take up the work dropped by Professor Hendrickson.

Professor A. C. Hendrickson. An Appreciation. Mr. Andrew C. Hendrickson entered Ashland College some twelve years ago as a preparatory student. He moved here from North Dakota with his family and at once began on his academic work. He took his A. B. from the college in due time and later his M. A. and still later spent a summer in Ohio State University in graduate work. He was, at different times, tutor, bookkeeper, field secretary, professor and business manager of the college. In all these positions he was faithful and efficient. I doubt whether the church at large fully appreciates the splendid work done by Brother Hendrickson. During his financial campaign; Brother Beachler has time and time again expressed his great satisfaction with the way the college office handled its share. Students and faculty alike feel a distinct loss in the removal of Mr. Hendrickson and family from Ashland.

Financial. The proposed financial program is sixfold, as follows:

(1) The Coast Campaign. It is well known that Beachler closes his campaign in the east by early summer after which he will give his time to Waterloo. This leaves the Pacific

coast unsolicited. A committee was appointed to confer with the trustees of the coast in regards to the campaign there. This committee will act in accordance with the best judgments of these trustees.

(2) Campaign in the City and County. This was referred to a committee which will take up the matter very early.

(3) Interchurch World Canvass. A committee has charge of this also.

(4) Budgeting for the College. It was thought that, now since the four year campaign is about over, the Committee of Fifteen which has in charge the proposed campaign for the next five years, should give some consideration to placing the college in this program. It will be recalled that one of the former goals was a permanent endowment for the college. Now that this is in some ways an accomplished fact, it ought to be assigned another goal. A committee was charged with this responsibility, but the Committee of Fifteen might do well to have this in mind as they doubtless already have.

(5) Campaign among Former Students. A committee is being formed to formulate plans to carry out such a campaign. It seems that the former students and friends, who have not been given an opportunity to give to their old college, ought to have such an opportunity offered them. Mr. A. H. Lichty has consented to take the chairmanship of such a committee and plans are under way to carry forward this work with vigor.

(6) Large Givers. There are some who have expressed themselves as willing to make a gift of considerable importance when the time is ripe. That time is now, and this fact ought to be presented to these friends. It ought to be known to all who have Ashland's interests at heart, that now is the time to do what is to be done for Ashland or her future will be exceedingly doubtful. Ashland is standing at the forks of the road. Of this, there can not be the shadow of a doubt.

The church must have it upon her heart for the next ten years as she has not had it within the past ten. These six are the only avenues which are open for money for the school and it was my plan that they should all be pressed with vigor within a year and brought to a culmination and thus see what we can do for Ashland. A short and vigorous campaign is the effective one. I would welcome suggestions and criticism.

(7) Financial Report. Mr. Hendrickson's report showed that the work can be closed this year without deficit. This is wholly desirable.

These are the important points of the work of the board and I am sure that all will agree that they are all important. Other matters of minor place were also discussed which need not be mentioned here. The college asks a continuation of your interest and your prayers.
EDWIN E. JACOBS.

WASHINGTON, D. C.

We have been exceedingly busy, and not having anything special to report, have remained silent for a period longer than usual. At present we are having much interference by reason of the recurrence of the "flu." For several days the health department has reported an average of more than two hundred and fifty new cases daily for our city. This strange malady has not failed to visit several members of our own family. My son's wife has been dangerously ill. In many instances whole families have been stricken at the same time. It is almost impossible to get help, and the hospitals are crowded.

Since our last report six have been added by baptism and three by letter, with two applicants awaiting baptism. An encouraging interest continues. This interest is manifested in part by attendance at the regular services and the Sunday school. The work is supported entirely by voluntary offerings which, I am pleased to say, continues to make a record in liberality, far beyond that of most churches, considering the membership.

Our Sunday school is greatly hampered because we lack rooms for the classes. We still believe that God will supply this great need. Will not others still join us in prayer to that end?

A good brother recently offered to be one of ten thousand to give five dollars toward a new building for our church home in this city. Come ahead; we only need nine thousand nine hundred and ninety-nine more! That's all.

Brother Beachler wonders why the Brethren church has been conspicuous for the absence of large gifts for its object and existence in the world. I think I can answer the query. It is the lack of deep, heart conviction. Let me give a similar illustration. I will refer to my personal experience of years in this city. Why is it that so very many who have come here, representing our membership at large, have failed to report for actual service at headquarters? Scarcely one out of five of those claiming to be members of the Brethren church, either reaching this city, have shown any real interest in the work. I am sorry to have to make this statement. What a record for whole (?) gospel people!

It has been said of certain folks. crossing the Rockies for the Pacific Coast that they left their religion on the east side somewhere. It looks to us sometimes as if the same rule obtains in traveling toward the Atlantic seaboard. The lure of the city, or something else, seems to prove too much of a test for the great majority. It will always be so where there is lacking that real heart and soul conviction and hunger. If I had the time and disposition to write in detail my full experience along this line, doubtless it would be as surprising to most people as it is humiliating to some of us.

I turn now to something brighter. I thank God that we have found some notable exceptions. I must be personal now. For the present I will name those who represent the class that we need in order to do constructive work. First, let me refer to Miss Voda Browsr and Sister Mina, of Ashland, Oregon. We suffered a distinct loss when they had to leave us for their far-away home in the northwest. The same can be truthfully said with reference to our Sister Geneva Strode, (now Mrs. Akens), of Ashland, Ohio. And Miss Lulu Zartman, (now Mrs. Grossman), of Louisville, Ohio, although a member of another church, served faithfully and efficiently while with us, until the matrimonial call snatched her from our midst. And Miss Clara Rogers, the most recent loss we had to meet, who also responded to the hymeneal call and fled to Michigan.

Next? Well, we'll wait and see.

Say, if any of our single sisters have not received a call of that kind, we suggest that you make a break at once for the First Brethren church of Washington, D. C.

But my time is gone and I will give you a rest. I would gladly mention other names and speak of other experiences which possibly might afford food for thought, but for the present must desist. W. M. LYON.

WABASH, INDIANA

Well I have found myself one time more preaching the Gospel in old Indiana. I just closed a two weeks' meeting at New Highland, near Akron. Here I did my first work as pastor 22 years ago. The result of this meeting was three confessions and the promise of another at the time of baptism. The church has an excellent class of middle aged men and women. The mission board should see to it that an experienced preacher is located there.

From here I go to Dutchtown, a country church near Warsaw. This church is also pastorless, which will make it more difficult to hold what is commonly called a successful meeting. Dutchtown was my first work by way of organization.

Mrs. Flora is with me in my meetings. We will be returning to Canada about the first of April. There we have a church federation called Christian Brethren. There are not enough people there of any one denomination to have worship and so all worship together. In view of some of the recent plans for inter-denominational activities we feel that we are quite up-to-date. Sometime ago some Congregational ministers attempted to organize a church of their own denomination, but the Christian Brethren turned them down on the ground that it would "cut too many out." We meet every spring to select a pastor and I have been selected continuously. To show their appreciation, as we were leaving for the winter, the entire congregation gathered in our home and presented us with a purse of money. B. H. FLORA.

GRATIS, OHIO

It has been some time since any report has found its way to the columns of the Evangelist. We may not have a flattering report but we feel it is one worth while. We held our revival in December, commenced with a communion service which was well attended and a splendid spirit as manifested. Our pastor, Rev. C. E. Beekley, did the preaching. Rev. Paul Wight of Eaton led the singing. With two strong men to lead us everything looked very good. But the weather was very unfavorable and the third and last week Rev. Beekley was taken ill. Rev. Wight closed the meeting. Our hearts were made to rejoice to see three young ladies make confession of Christ. Through the good seed that was sown and prayers offered there will be many more to find their way to the foot of the cross. During the meetings the members surprised Brother Beekley with a donation which was very much appreciated. Our Sunday school favored us with a very good entertainment at Christmas time. Songs and illustrated songs were sung. Our Sunday school is moving along very nicely. January first is the day set to hold our annual business meeting. Our good pastor suggested we have an all-day meeting or home-coming. They came from the north, south, east and west. The forenoon was spent socially with a short program, after which dinner was served in the basement. A very good way to reach a man's heart is through his stomach. One o'clock found all ready for business—the King's business.

We use the budget system which we found very satisfactory. A new one was made up for the new year. Harmony prevailed throughout the afternoon. All felt it was a day well spent.

The mercury man was scheduled for here last Sunday. He was here on time; slid in and out; the mercury didn't seem to run right for William so he purchased some sausage and left for Ashland.

We had the pleasure of entertaining Miss M. Mae Smith our Woman's Missionary secretary. This was not only a treat for the women but for the men as well, for she filled the pulpit on Sunday morning and did it very ably. We hope to have her with us again. She left some very good thought and suggestions for the W. M. S. We have surely been blessed in the past year. Death has only claimed two of our members, and every boy that went to serve his country returned without a scratch. May the Father continue to bless us and all our sister churches in the new year, and we will give him all the praise.
SALLIE ANDREWS.

THE PITTSBURG ANNIVERSARY

What joy comes from the realization of things we have striven for years to obtain. For a long time, the members and friends of the church have longed for the day when the mortgage would go up in smoke. Through the noble efforts of our beloved pastor, and the loyal support of friends and members of the church, the debt has been wiped out, and the

mortgage burned. The week ending January 23rd, has been the biggest and happiest week ever experienced in the history of the church. We celebrated our thirtieth anniversary.

Twelve years ago last December our much loved friend and brother, Rev. Henry Wise, started out to reduce the debt on the church. It seemed as though the church doors would have to be closed, and the building sold. But our faithful brother and elder, traveled for more than two years, both summer and winter, soliciting funds to save the Brethren church of Pittsburgh. More than once when sore in body and heart, Brother Wise raised the question in his own mind, whether God really expected it of him or of any other man, to go through the things he experienced on the canvass. But he would ever think of the group of Godly people back in Pittsburgh, who were worthy of his best efforts,—and he would again take heart, and plod on. Perhaps none of us realize how much he has done, and to him we owe a debt of gratitude that can never be repaid.

After his noble efforts, little had been done to reduce the debt until our present pastor, Rev. H. M. Harley came, five years ago. He has worked nobly, and we rejoice with him in the joy of knowing that we worship in a house clear of debt.

The two great events coming together—the 30th Anniversary, and the clearing off of the indebtedness—it was thought fitting that we celebrate with several special services. So on Wednesday evening, January 21st, the first anniversary service consisted of special music, a historical sketch read by one of the charter members, Brother I. C. Wilcox, and a sermon by Brother A. D. Gnagey of Ashland, Ohio. It was a privilege, as well as a pleasure, to listen to one of our former pastors, as he preached a soul-stirring sermon on the subject, "The Supremacy of Christianity." He dealt with the three supreme things, The Supreme Book, The Supreme Being and The Supreme Institution. I'm sure we all went away with a stronger desire to serve Christ and his church, in a larger and a better way.

On Thursday evening, January 22d, a very fine musical and literary program was rendered. The program was made up of vocal and instrumental solos and duets, and readings.

The hearts of all were filled with joy when we gathered together on Friday evening, January 23rd, to celebrate the anniversary proper. After a short opening exercise, Brother Wise made some, very fitting remarks, reminiscent and otherwise. Then letters were read from several former pastors of the church, Brethren Hall, Darling, Koontz and N. W. Jennings. It brought much joy to hear from these friends and to know that they were rejoicing with us. We were very glad to have with us on this occasion, beside Brother Wise, four of the thirteen original organizers of the church, Mr. and Mrs. D. K. Bole, now of Johnstown, and Sisters Nettie and Belle Reynolds. Brother Ira C. Wilcox, with the four original organizers, gave us five of the twenty-seven charter members. Brother Myers, who so faithfully served us several months, was also with us. We heard a few words from each of these, besides others who have done much during more recent years to help bring the church to the place that she enjoys today.

Then came the happy event. Brother Wise held the mortgage, and surrounded by the five charter members, together with Sister Anna Bole, in memory of Brother D. J. Bole, Mother King, our oldest member, put the match to the mortgage. As it went up in flames, every. body sang, "Praise God From Whom all Blessings Flow." And surely, never a happier throng of people sang praises to God, who is the giver of every good and perfect gift. The rest of the evening was spent in social fellowship, and everybody enjoyed themselves immensely, better than 175 being present at this service. A very refreshing plate lunch was served, as the treat of the Men's Bible Class.

We owe much to our pastor. Let us stand by him faithfully, as he labors so ardently in the work of the Master. Most of all, let us keep our eyes on Christ, and strive daily to make our lives and our church more like he would have them.

MISS ISABELLE WILCOX.

CORINTH CHURCH, AT TWELVE MILE, INDIANA

We are still at the same old stand and trying to bring honor and glory to the name of our Lord and Master. Here we have a loyal people. The church is not going by leaps and bounds but is moving along at a steady gait. The situation of the church handicaps us when the weather gets bad. We began our meetings there in December but on account of the weather we were compelled to close after a week's meetings. The roads were almost impassable. There were no accessions to the church and our meetings were postponed indefinitely and prospects are not bright because of the re-appearance of the dreaded "flu" which is raging in that vicinity. We have not been able to accomplish as much as we would have liked to do on this field, but we feel that all was done that could have been done. The community is well churched and we cannot expect great things. Here too it has been a pleasure to work with the church and there is a fine spirit of co-operation on the part of all. Santa Claus did not forget us here. He believes in keeping us warm for he brought us a beautiful comfort and sweater which we prize very highly. We are trying to stress the Four Year Program for we want to have part in the Victory jubilee and are looking forward to the conference at Winona as the biggest and best the church has ever had. We ask the brethren to bear us up to the throne of grace, that we may be able to do a greater work for our Master.

LOREE, INDIANA

In November Brother A. T. Wirick held us a good meeting which was a great help to us in many ways. He gave us some fine sermons which were very instructive and were enjoyed by all. People came from a distance to hear the old time Gospel and good crowds were there to greet the speaker each evening. This was about the fourth meeting that Brother Wirick has held at Loree and he has won a place in the hearts of this people. We feel that the church has been strengthened and all were made to feel their responsibility as a church and their duty towards God and man. There were added to the church some very substantial people, heads of families and young people that will soon be ready to take up the burdens of the church when others will lay them down. Nine came forward in the meetings, but we have baptized eleven and two more are yet to be baptized. Every department of the church is moving along in fine shape. The W. M. S. and Sisterhood girls are reaching all their goals. The Sunday school under the leadership of Brother W. A. Shinn is doing fine work. Two classes of young people are in a contest which will come to a close Sunday, February 15. At present the young men are in the lead. We have a fine class of young folks here which speaks well for the church.

We are now comfortably situated in the new parsonage at Loree, which has been remodeled. These people certainly enjoy to make their pastor as comfortable as possible. They purchased a property last spring, consisting of a house and four acres of ground. So you will know where to find me after the blue birds come and weeds begin to grow. Then after remodeling the house, they, came to Bunker Hill with their wagons and sleds and moved us. Some of the good ladies had cleaned the house and some came and helped us to get things in shape to live. Then one evening about 175 of our friends paid us an unexpected visit which was very much enjoyed and left us two fine leather rockers and

Our Goal: 200,000; We Can and We Must

200	000
190	000
180	000
170	000
160	000
150	000
140	000
130	000
120	000
110	000
100	000
90	000
80	000
70	000
60	000
50	000
40	000
30	000
20	000
10	000

COLLEGE ENDOWMENT

many other things, all of which were very much appreciated.

Our work is not all smooth sailing, we feel some difficulties, but God has blessed our labors together as pastor and people and to him we give all the praise. We set our goal for attendance on Rally Day at three hundred and went over the top with three hundred and one.

C. A. STEWART.

CAMPAIGN NOTES

This time I am prepared to report that the mercury had reached the $140,000 mark. It seems to have been a long, hard pull to reach that place; but I am hoping the $150,000 mark will be reached more quickly and with greater ease. If we could induce our people with large means to talk endowment in terms of $2,500, or $5,000, or $10,000 like folks do in other denominations, it would speed up the old mercury very substantially. But you know it is one thing to say in words that our faith and our practice and our denomination are the nearest right, but it is quite another thing to say it in real dollars. Talk is always cheaper than money. But after all isn't it surprising to see how some people do lay out their money to promote their faith, which, we say, is shot full of error? I was in a small town recently in which, during my stay, three men in an ordinary sized congregation of another denomination laid out $5,000 each for the next five years as their part in the Forward Movement of their respective denomination. We say that denomination is in error in its form of baptism and some other things. Now this is what I have to say on that point. Maybe I don't split hairs and draw fine, sharp lines like some people, but if "error" causes people to open their pocketbooks like that in the promotion of their denominations, then I think the Brethren church could stand a little more "error."

Pleasant Hill was the last field canvassed. Sickness over the state of Ohio is holding me up completely. I had a delightful visit at Pleasant Hill and the results are very gratifying. I have held two meetings in this church during past years and I feel that I have here many close friends. This congregation has been without a pastor for some time and naturally I found the people very hungry for some preaching. Brother Sylvester Lowman will take charge here this spring and his people are anxiously awaiting his arrival.

This is the home congregation of the Business Manager of our Publishing House, Brother R. R. Teeter. It was also a former charge of our Editor, Brother Baer. So our Publishing House awaited with considerable interest the outcome of the Pleasant Hill canvass. It was my privilege to preach to Brother Teeter's mother at each service. Mother Teeter is high in the eighties, but she is of the loyal, faithful kind and bad weather did not keep her at home.

At the time I write this the Pleasant Hill result is $1,775. This however is not final, for there are other members of this congregation who are staunch friends of the college yet to be heard from. If the finals do not exceed by considerable $2,000 I shall be keenly disappointed. This means a fine piece of work for Pleasant Hill and I can truly praise the good people who made this result possible. We had here one $500 gift, also one $200 gift. We also had a very fine line of $100 and $50 gifts. And there was an uncommonly good response in smaller sums. The gifts from school teachers here, and the gift from at least one young man who is now in college were quite sufficient to make folks with their broad acres and fat bank accounts sit up and take notice. At this place as in many, many places, the Sunday school, and the W. M. S. both helped, also one organized class had a nice part in the good work.

As for the hospitality of Pleasant Hill, there is none freer or better. The several Dexter homes, the Long homes, the Staub and Stout and Carey homes will linger long in my memory. Sincerest thanks to all of these good people for their kindness. Brethren Long and Carey were the automobile men at this place. Brother Carey droVe me on one of the most disagreeable days I haVe ridden in this entire campaign. The roads were more icy and dangerous than I eVer saw them before. And sleet on the wind shield made it necessary to haVe the car open all day. As a result my good friend Carey went to bed the next day with grippe. I put up a little harder fight and went to bed seVeral days later, but we both got to bed all right. Well I sure hope Carey is well again. It takes some real nerVe to burn a man's gasoline, wear out his car, take his money, and then top it off with giVing him grippe. I haVe seen some folks in the course of this campaign that I could haVe giVen the grippe with considerable pleasure, but Carey was not in that class. May God richly bless the Pleasant Hill people and may he grant unto them and the man who is soon to come among them a most fruitful sojourn together.

I want to say two things briefly in conclusion: First, I am withholding a report which rounds out the eVen $140,000. And second, in the West Alexandria report the printer or somebody made me say that it was Brother Kinzie's "fortune" to get a second attack of mo. That was a terrible blunder. I meant that it was his "misfortune" and that is different. Since that report was written Alexandria has gone beyond the $600 mark and is still going. Brother Kinzie like many another of our pastors has done some fine followup work since I left. Sometimes I think folks are so glad I am gone that they hand the pastor "thank offerings."

WM. H. BEACHLER.
Campaign Secretary.

IMPORTANT NOTICE

It may not be known to all the brotherhood that at the annual meeting of the Board of Trustees of Ashland College held the last week in January it was decided to haVe the College join in the Interchurch World Movement in its financial driVe in the spring. Saturday we receiVed a telegram from Wm. Kolb, Jr., stating that arrangements had been completed in New York so that any institution in the Brethren church that cares to do so may share in this moVement. Full particulars will appear in the EVangelist next week.

This moVement was entered into partly to conserVe the interests of the different organizations of the Brethren church during the time of this great financial driVe nearing approach. No one is compelled to contribute, but many will do so, and their contributions would be lost to the Brethren church if this precautionary step had not been taken. But wait for Brother Kolb's report next week before you pass decision.

R. R. TEETER, Sec'y. Board of Trustees.

Business Manager's Corner

OUT AT LAST

After an unaVoidable and greatly to be regretted delay the Brethren Annual and Report of the General Conference is off the press and all orders for the same have been filled.

Our plans for getting out this Annual and Conference Minutes were to get them off the press in October or NoVember; but the Good Book says, "Man proposes," but God disposes," and our plans came to naught. When we bought our new building for the Publishing House and began moVing in on the first of October we found that the moVing and the loss of time on account of the inability to secure motors with which to run our presses in the new location would throw us back with our work at least one month.

In fact it was not until last week that the last of our motors bought in September was set up and put into operation, so that for the

---

first time since September we have been able to operate the plant in full force.

We now haVe three cylinder presses and one jobber in operation so that we hope to soon catch up with all our work and then to get a little ahead with it so that no more delays need occur.

We are mailing a few copies of the Annual and Conference Reports to practically all our pastors that haVe eVer sold them for us in the past and we hope they will giVe us their assistance at this time. Last year the Publishing House lost about seVenty-fiVe dollars on the making of the Annual, and it is not done as a money-making project, but simply to serVe the church in the preserVing of Conference Records and Annual Reports that this publication is gotten out each year, so we make bold to ask our pastors and congregations to help make up the cost of the publication of the reports and to buy or sell as many as possible at once. The price for single copies is twenty-fiVe cents, in lots of one half-dozen or more twenty cents each. If we have failed to send a supply to any pastor please let us know and we will forward as many as you want immediately.

Sunday School Literature

We haVe the Sunday school literature for the next quarter well under way and we expect to send out our new order blanks with the new price list Very shortly. We haVe no apology to offer for much of the literature going out late last quarter, we have explained how our moVing the plant made it impossible to do otherwise, but now we expect to be able to fill all orders in good time so that all schools may be able to receiVe their supplies in time to get them into the hands of their pupils before the beginning of next quarter.

We will not say anything about the campaign for EVangelist subscriptions this week, but will saVe that for our next report in the Business Manager's Corner.

R. R. TEETER,
Business Manager.

THE TIE THAT BINDS

RAHN-MOLL—At the home of Mr. and Mrs. OliVer Rahn, their daughter, Ethel, was united in marriage to Mr. Charles H. Moll of Shannon, Illinios. Just the two immediate families were present. After the ceremony promptly at 6 o'clock all sat down to a bounteous wedding supper. The remainder of the eVening was spent in a social maner. Both of the parties are most estimable young people and haVe the best wishes of a host of friends. The bride is a member of the First Brethren church of Lanark. Ceremony by her pastor. B. T. BURNWORTH.

IN THE SHADOW

BURCHAM—Brother Leo Wasley, Burcham passed out of this life January 15, 1920, aged 25 years. At an early age he united with the Baptist church, but after coming to Clay City he formed a very close friendship with Brother G. W. Kinzie, under whose pastorate he united with the First Brethren church at Clay City, Indiana. Brother Leo was of a strong devotional nature; he loved his Bible and the association of Christian people. During the last few months of his life he was stricken by tuberculosis and was depriVed of his customary regular attendance at church services. He leaVes a mother, two sisters and a brother to mourn their loss. The serVices were conducted by the undersigned at the Baptist church near Midland, Indiana.
S. C. HENDERSON.

GOSHORN—Mrs. B. F. Goshorn died at her home in Clay City, after a brief illness with pneumonia, January 16, 1920, aged 57 years, 4 months and 25 days. She was married 15 years ago to Elder B. F. Goshorn, October 1, 1883. To this union were born two sons and three daughters. The two sons preceding her in death several years. She is surviVed by her husband and three daughters also two sisters. At the age of 25 years she united with the Church of the Brethren and has liVed a deVoted Christian life. Since the erection of the Brethren church in Clay City, Mrs. Goshorn and her husband haVe been regular and active attendants. Mrs. Goshorn was a good

---

woman and of an unselfish disposition and will be missed in the large circle of close friends and neighbors. The funeral services were held from the Clay City Brethren church conducted by the undersigned, assisted by Rev. Kelsey of the United Brethren church and Elder John Mitchell of the Church of the Brethren.
S. C. HENDERSON.

CROWL—Daniel Crowl departed this life at North Liberty, Indiana, January 19, 1920, aged 38 years. He was a member of the Brethren church here. He left a companion and 3 small children. Funeral services by the pastor. C. C. GRISSO.

CROWL—Helen Hardman Crowl, wife of Daniel Crowl, deceased, followed her husband to the spirit world after six days. She was a member of the Church of the Brethren until about five years ago she placed her membership with the Brethren at North Liberty. She departed at the age of 35 years, leaving 3 small children. Funeral serVices by the family pastor on January 25.
C. C. GRISSO.

HOFFMAN—Sister Mayme Hoffman, daughter of Brother and Sister Joseph Hoffman of Conemaugh. Sister Hoffman was a patient sufferer for many years and looked forward to the time of her release with unquestioned faith in her Lord. She became a member of the church many years ago and when in health was a regular attendant at the church and Sunday school serVices. She was twenty-three years of age at the time of her demise. Funeral services in the home conducted by the undersigned and Rev. Coleman of the Evangelical church. Interment in Hendrick's cemetery, Janury 24th. The prayers and sympathy of the church are extended to the loved ones in their loss and her gain.

YEAGER—James E. Yeager, son of Brother and Sister Samuel E. Yeager, of Franklin, members of the Conemaugh church, died suddenly January 23rd, 1920, at the parental home. He was buried in Hendrick's cemetery. Funeral serVices by the writer. The sympathy and consolation of the brethren are extended to the young parents in their bereaVement.

P. S. Both of the aboVe funerals were conducted by the undersigned because of the sickness of the pastor, Brother Byers.
G. H. JONES.

MARQUEDANT—Mrs. George Marquedant, of Johnstown, Pa., died January 27th, 1920, at her home. She expired after a long illness which ended in a stroke of paralysis. Sister Marquedant was the daughter of an old Dunkard family, Brother John and Sister Sarah Brown of Jackson township, Cambria county. She was almost 76 years old at the time of her death. Services by the writer. Interment in the Brown Cemetery near Vinco, Pa.
GEO. H. JONES, Pastor.

DREW—Riley B Drew, M. D., died at Eau Claire, Wis., December 28, 1918. Dr. Drew grew to manhood in the Vicinity of Tiosa and his body was brought to the old home for burial. SerVices were held in the Brethren church on December 31, 1919, in charge of the pastor. C. C. GRISSO.

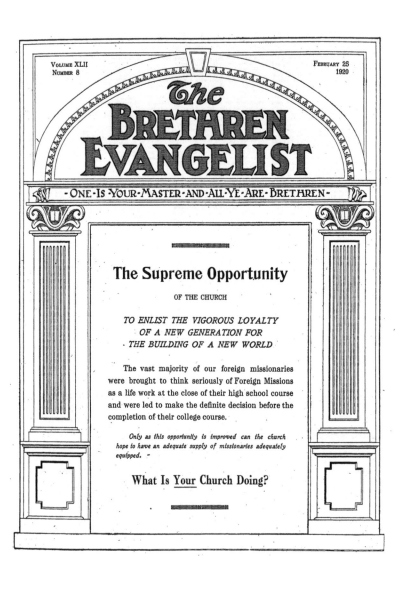

Volume XLII
Number 8

February 25
1920

The BRETHREN EVANGELIST

-ONE-IS-YOUR-MASTER-AND-ALL-YE-ARE-BRETHREN-

The Supreme Opportunity

OF THE CHURCH

*TO ENLIST THE VIGOROUS LOYALTY
OF A NEW GENERATION FOR
· THE BUILDING OF A NEW WORLD*

The vast majority of our foreign missionaries
were brought to think seriously of Foreign Missions
as a life work at the close of their high school course
and were led to make the definite decision before the
completion of their college course.

*Only as this opportunity is improved can the church
hope to have an adequate supply of missionaries adequately
equipped.* -

What Is Your Church Doing?

Published every Wednesday at
Ashland, Ohio. All matter for publication must reach the Editor not
later than Friday noon of the preceding week.

The
Brethren
Evangelist

When ordering your paper changed
give old as well as new address.
Subscriptions discontinued at expiration. To avoid missing any numbers renew two weeks in advance.

George S. Baer, Editor

R. R. Teeter, Business Manager

OFFICIAL ORGAN OF THE BRETHREN CHURCH

Subscription price, $2.00 per year, payable in advance.
Entered at the Post Office at Ashland, Ohio, as second-class matter.
Acceptance for mailing at special rate of postage provided for in section 1103, Act of October 3, 1917, authorized September 9, 1918.
Address all matter for publication to Geo. S. Baer, Editor of the Brethren Evangelist, and all business communications to R. R. Teeter,
Business Manager, Brethren Publishing Company, Ashland, Ohio. Make all checks payable to the Brethren Publishing Company.

TABLE OF CONTENTS

EDITORIAL

Marshalling the Forces for An Intensive Evangelistic Campaign

II CERTAIN PRE-ARRANGEMENTS

(The second of a series of editorials on the above topic, considered apropos to the present season of intensive evangelism and also
the aim of many churches of leading up to an ingathering at Easter
time).

Thorough preparation is the secret on man's part of many a surprising success in evangelism, and on the other hand the lack of
any adequate preparation has resulted in failure to secure the success
that might have been confidently expected. By adequate preparation by no means is meant the effort to work up a revival and bring
about success through man's power and organization with little
dependence upon God. It rather means the endeavor to bring the
whole church and the community as well into such a condition that
will make it possible for the Word of God to have freest course in
the hearts of men. It is no true preparation that does not take into
account man's dependence on God. But it will be found to be a
dead faith that does not realize that God has prescribed certain conditions to be complied with before he will pour out his blessings
in abundant measure. The Lord enjoined thorough preparation on
the part of the apostolic church before it should be baptized with
mighty power for the saving of souls. And we are not warranted in
expecting the blessing of God's power today in such measure as shall
grip and convict many hearts and cause them to cry out, What
must we do to be saved except after honest preparation? Nothing
is more important on man's part than that he be prepared and fit to
receive God's power and to be used of God in the wielding of that
power in the most effective way possible.

In our preparation there are certain pre-arrangements that will
be found worthy of our serious consideration, and to which the marshal must give careful attention before he shall be able to lead his
forces in an evangelistic campaign. First, there must be a mobiliz-
ing of all the forces of the church. All the members must be induced
to leave everything else in a secondary place for the time and give
themselves primarily and supremely to the one great task before
them. If this is to be an intensive campaign, one that will help
to flood the souls of men who have heretofore remained stubbornly
grounded on the sand bars of the world and sweep them by a mighty
effort out into the deep waters of God's love, it will require all the
forces the church can muster. If ever, certainly at this time the
interests of the Kingdom must be placed first by the entire church.
Nothing should be allowed to interfere with their doing everything
in their power to bring success. All social engagements, even those
that are perfectly legitimate at other times, should be dispensed
with during such a season of soul-saving. Community affairs should

be avoided as much as possible. This can often be done by anticipating them and planning accordingly. The work incident to the
daily vocations of the members should be planned so as to afford
the maximum of time for prayer, thought and effort in the interest
of the campaign. Such co-operation cannot be expected of the members unless announcements are made and plans are laid far in advance of the date for the campaign. But if such are done, nearly
always with great unanimity the co-operation of the membership
can be enlisted. Unless this can be secured, unless the campaign
can be made the biggest and most important thing in all the world
at that time, the largest possible success cannot be expected.

Secondly, great care should be given to equipping the forces as
thoroughly as possible before the battle has begun. Great revivals
are not brought about by the efforts of a pastor, or an evangelist
alone, or by the united efforts of the two merely, but by the united
effort and hearty co-operation of pastor, evangelist and the whole
church. Every member counts for success or failure. Therefore all
should be equipped for the campaign. They should be equipped
with a sense of responsibility for the saving of men. They should
be made to feel that they were saved to serve, and that the saving
of men is at once their supreme duty and highest privilege. They
must be made to feel their own unworthiness and need of preparation for such a great work. The soldier without discipline has little
reason to expect victory, and much less right has the Christian to
expect success in his infinitely greater task without preparation. To
feel the need of this preparation is the beginning of equipment.
There must be also a strong faith in God. They must be led surely
to believe that God's Word is true when it says that sin bringeth
forth death, that man can escape from the slavery of sin only by the
power of the resurrected Christ and that God can be depended on to
help, whenever we call upon him, to win men unto himself. They
must be equipped with purity of heart. Whoever would know the
power of God must himself first be clean. We cannot expect God to
bless us with the saving of men when we are compromising with
known sin. They must be equipped with prayer; must have their
quiet hours and spend much time in prayer. The life of the Christian is from above, and when he, like the diver, plunges down into
the ocean of sin in search of lost souls he must keep his connection
unbroken. He cannot live apart from God. There must also be
equipment in the use of the Bible. It must be read for personal
soul culture and studied with a view to presenting it to others,
Christians who love and read their Bibles are the salt of the earth.
No Christians ever became effective as personal workers who did not
love and study their Bibles. The Bible is the sword of the Spirit

and it is important that every Christian should know how to use it skilfully. And with all this preparation there must be also tact. There is no blue-print or set of rules that will solve every problem that may arise in dealing with men. To have tact is simply, to be able to read human nature and to handle each individual according to his own peculiarities. Pray earnestly, oh marshaller of the forces of Christ,—that there may be given to your soldiers insight into life and character, that their sympathies for all men may be quickened and that wisdom from on high may be given to them that they may deal wisely with every man.

Third, when the forces have been gathered and equipped by sermons, prayer meeting talks on personal work and by individual suggestions, the organization of the forces for the battle is the next step in the pre-arrangements. The most effective work can often be done by dividing the forces into groups, as an army. is divided into companies, assigning to each group or class of workers the work for which they are best fitted. Some will be Sunday school teachers and will be able by their instruction to turn the thoughts of their scholars, who are not Christians to Jesus Christ and to press in a wise way his claims on every life. The teachers should be urged as a body to consider the wise use of their opportunities as of vital importance to the success of the campaign. They should prepare their lesson with the idea in mind of winning certain individuals for Christ, enter their classes with a prayer upon their hearts to that end and teach their lessons with that purpose in mind. Other members may be able to witness effectively at opportune times in public meetings or lead in prayer. But to witness effectively does not mean necessarily to be able to speak glibly, but to speak sincerely, briefly, and discreetly out of an up-to-date experience. And to pray with moving effect, in such a way as to touch the hearts of people and to move to decisions, does not mean to use beautiful language necessarily, nor to make long prayers, but to pray briefly, to the point, with absolute sincerity and honesty and with a love that is akin to the compassion of Christ. Some may be counselled to write personal letters to friends seeking to win them to Christ. Here too, brevity and sincerity are cardinal points. Prayer groups may be formed where earnest workers may continue steadfastly in prayer for the conviction of sinners and the empowering of their own lives. There is much need of the upper-rooom meetings in our church life today. Much strength is secured and great results are accomplished by gathering in the Master's name for conference and prayer. Every one should be led to center his thoughts and prayer upon some individual and importune until he has the joy of seeing that soul converted. Nearly every one may be led to feel a divine constraint laid upon him to lead some one to Christ. And there will be no one who cannot find some one whose life touches his own, and whom he ought now try to win. In these and many other ways, the church of Christ may be arranged and organized for the most effective battling for the rescuing of souls from the power of evil. No time or effort should be spared in these preliminaries, for when they are well done the battle is half won.

EDITORIAL REVIEW

Brother G. C. Carpenter's Home Mission News of this week will be of unusual interest. Some things he reports are cause for gratitude and others are cause for more earnest prayer.

The "Devotional" this week is by one of our young Ohio preachers not yet a year old in the ministry but he is going good work and proves himself a good writer.

It is Brother Witter and Prof. Garber who give life to the Christian Endeavor page this week. No department is more interestingly maintained than is this department.

If there is any one who rejoices more than others besides the pastor and resident members over the Pittsburgh success, it is Brother Wise. Read his report of the Pittsburgh Jubilee.

Dr. Bame calls for a "speeding up" of the Four Year Program reports. Brother Bame intended this message for publication last week, but it arrived too late, for which we are sorry. But let every pastor co-operate by reporting now, if you have not already. Every church has received a report card through the District Directors. By this time it should have been in the hands of Director Bame. "Now then do it."

Brother C. W. Yoder, who writes on Church Efficiency is the secretary of the Mid-West conference and a layman who is generally valuable. We hope he will write again. We shall appreciate contributions from more of our talented laymen.

Brother C. C. Grisso reports from the evangelist's point of view the very successful meeting which was recently held at Center Chapel, Indiana. It was not a new field to Brother Grisso as he was at one time pastor of this wide-awake country church. Brother - Kenneth Ronk, the pastor, had everything in readiness for a successful meeting, and the results fully warranted the preparation made.

Brother S. C. Henderson and his faithful co-workers at Clay City, Indiana, are pushing ahead in the various lines of church work. The Brethren Evangelist is now going into every home of the parish. We congratulate Clay City on their achievement and we hope they will find their investment to be abundantly worth while. The pastor was recently surprised by the members supplying him with a young grocery store.

We are glad to hear Brother Belote "tooting his horn," as he expresses it, for he does not toot it any too often and when he does, it gives forth a note of progress. Brother Bell's meeting in the Canton church was successful in spite of the hindrances which that city presents. Brother Belote has been doing some splendid constructive work at that place during the past four years. Now he announces that he is to take charge of the Uniontown church in Pennsylvania, which he served very successfully some years ago.

If there is any class of people we are more anxious to enlist as writers for the Evangelist it is the young people. For if we can train the coming generation to be a generation of writers the Brethren church of the future will be assured of a still more valuable paper than that which is made possible by this generation. Consequently we are always pleased when our college students as well as young people elsewhere, get into print. Miss Raad gives us a very interesting report of the Des Moines Convention. Every one should read t.

President Jacobs' "College News" have a number of things of special interest this week, among which are the recognition Ashland College receives from Harvard University and the other the mention of a farewell reception held in honor of Brother Beachler who is soon to take up his work as pastor at Waterloo. Brother Beachler has performed a great service for Ashland College, whose trustees at their recent meeting conferred upon him the degree of Doctor of Divinity. It is an honor worthily bestowed and in which the brotherhood generally will concur.

Our campaign secretary reports endowment pledges this week from two of our Ohio mission points. It would not be expected that they should come up to the standard set by strongly established churches and there is no reason to be disappointed in the records of these two churches—Mansfield and Rittman. It is fine to see the small and weak churches lifting their portion of the load of the general church along with the large and strong churches. There are some very loyal brethren at these Rittman and Mansfield churches.

Those who have received a number of Dr. Tombaugh's booklets to sell may sell same for 20 cents each and remit the entire amount or sell them for 25 cents and keep the nickel for their trouble and to pay postage. We have made the price just as low as possible in order to encourage a wide sale. Those who have not sent in an order, we suggest that you write for a dozen and turn them over to some Sunday school class to sell. Those having books to sell, kindly remit as soon as possible. Anyone wishing just one copy will receive same for 25 cents postpaid.

Brother Bell's report of the Hamlin, Kansas, campaign brings to our attention one of our small pastorless churches that affords an opportunity for some servant of God to expend their very best energies and resources. There are a number of such throughout the brotherhood and wherever there is any possibility of giving them a life and turning the tide for a renewal of former enthusiasm and activity and the building of a greater church, wisdom would certainly point to the rendering of such help. But these pastorless churches must await an adequate ministry and an adequate ministry awaits among other things an adequate salary.

FOUR-YEAR PROGRAM PAGE
NOW THEN DO IT.—II Samuel 3:18
Conducted by Charles A. Bame

Another Chapter

I should guess that it is about time for another chapter in my writings for the dear people who really try to keep posted on this program. However one can write no better in a case like this than the churches and pastors will allow him to write. I do love to chronicle progress and I am glad that I can do so. I am glad that I can assure you that the church is really making an effort to make this a VICTORY YEAR. I hear about it, and note it in the reports of the correspondents of the churches and I am glad to hear of pastors who are making a fine rush for the final goal at Winona Lake in September. Do you remember the old Gospel hymn,

"What a gathering that will be!"

I do not wish to be sacrilegious, but really, I do feel that we can look forward to this fall and say "What a gathering that will be!" with a good deal of pride and adulation. It will be wonderful that we shall have found out a method of getting us somewhere and to help us to sense, in some small way, at least, our possibilities and our abilities. Had we undertaken any one of the several things our PROGRAM has accomplished, separately, it would have doubtless been as hard to reach the goal as it has been to reach many at the same time.

Reports Are Coming

About the 20th of January, I sent out the cards for the mid-winter report, and I am glad to tell you that they are looking like victory. Of course that is a good look. But we shall be surprised at the number of Gold Star churches we shall have when it is all over. "G" means gained and there are a lot of "G's," I tell you. I have tried hard to fill the small niche the program called for as to this page and this is the first time that I have had a chance to look the cards "in the face" as they came from all the districts. I am finding out a good many things that will make interesting information, too, I dare say.

Only 51 at That

Out of a possible 200, I have but 51 reports and less than half a month till the time has expired. Now, one mail is plenty of time for all the rest to come in, but I do want to say that one week or less is all the time you can hope to claim after this reaches you till you will be marked "tardy." Many of the large churches have not yet reported and no censure is coming for they have still 15 days, but after you see this, you, my fellow-pastor will have to "get a move on," if you do not come under the line, "tardy." I hope that you shall not have forgotten. There will be no further urgings nor appeals. If you do not come across on this with a stamped returnable card to send to me, we shall not expect to get word from you at any rate. You remember the request for the return of these cards was for the First of March. Let them come swiftly and there will be no more trouble. Let's make this look like a Victory Year by the promptitude of our responses. The card says,

"Be Prompt; Be Particular."

But already, we have had more than one mistake. One card is returned without a name or address or name of a church. Who is it from and why did they thus report when it can not be counted? Well, they did not so mean it. They were good on promptness but poor on carefulness. Before I am through with this "call" which I have undertaken myself, I shall have learned some of the trials and tribulations of the District Directors. They have been "good and faithful" bunch of fellows and great credit will be given them at the Jubilee, this fall. If anyone calls them any-

thing but good fellows, they will get into trouble with the General Director.

"For a Time Like This"

How wonderful that we got this Program started just when we did. In a very magnificent way, our church has begun to find itself and to sense its place in the big world of which it is a part. Of course that is not to say that it never did before. But coming out of the "Swaddling clothes" of its youth, she can do bigger and better things. Yet, when we read of the wonderful things that the church is daring to undertake and of the big things we shall have to do in the immediate future not to be lost as the "needle in the haystack," we can see how God in all his goodness was only training us for the day that is coming. By these small doings, he has made us ready for the big demands that the times will put upon us in order to be worthy of our place as a denomination. With our foreign territory already allotted to another denomination and with the home country surveyed as never before and with the terrible frown of a united Protestantism against the forming of new churches in places they may think already overchurched, we shall need more money than ever before and more recruits. If we can not produce them, the husbandman will say, "take away that he seemeth to have." "Beachler's work is about done," says someone; well, if it is, another will need to take it up. We shall not be done with giving to Ashland College as long as we have it. Each new day brings its needs and will as long as time shall last, and if Beachler quits the field of activity, as we hope he may—that of soliciting—it will be because another takes it up or because we have religion or good sense of stewardship enough to go on with the work he so well and nobly carried forward. Just this minute, I threw myself back in my chair and cast a glance up at a motto on my study wall which says,

"The world is not yet made; do your share today."

How true is this of everything with which we have to do! This program, this church of which we are members is not yet made. It is yet in the full bloom of youth, just where it takes money and sacrifice to bring it through college and all the sicknesses of youth. We have really undertaken something in this program and are now conscious of our strength and vitality and so, in every great task before us, we need to prove the world's need of us by what we are willing to do for ourselves.

The Next Effort

It would seem to be a bit early to forecast what the next shall be. But we can not ignore it, seeing we have already a committee working on it. Seriously the brainy men of our church are looking at the next task for our church. But says one, is it not ever the same task? Yes, and no. It is the same task of properly carrying out the last command of our risen Lord. But the Four Year Program has certainly proven that we do not go at the task as well unless we set for ourselves, certain well-defined tasks or goals. The more nearly we can sense the need, the more surely we shall try to do our work. It is a case of life and death. Unless our church shall eagerly and seriously set herself to the task of church extension, we may as well measure our years and size right now. Our church can never become a worth-while one unless we shall begin right now to try to capture strategic places. If the mothers will not consecrate their sons and daughters to this holy cause; if the fathers will not set apart the Lord's share of their income, we shall be still counting our adherents in thousands or less when the Lord comes.

Preachers, missionaries, money—these are the necessary wherewithal that must be next. Not as we have been doing, either. Determined, systematic, consecrated effort must be put forth and he who works out a plan that will set the immense resources of the Brethren church loose on an unsaved world, will be its great benefactor.

The World Needs Brethren

Selfishness of a type never before known—selfishness that profiteers in foodstuffs when babies are starving; in clothes when the poor are shivering; in coal when the world's sick are more numerous than ever—calls for the brother spirit and calls so loud that I trust the Brethren everywhere may hear it as a call from God to go forth with their story of unselfish brotherhood known only when and where the gospel of the Son of God is really lived. The world's need is our opportunity. BAME.

GENERAL ARTICLES

Efficiency In the Church. By C. W. Yoder

The efficiency of a church depends on a number of factors. The old idea that if the members of a church met for worship it was about all that should be required of them is becoming obsolete. Present day Christians should recognize that training and the development of the spiritual life are imperative if the church is to solve the problems and meet the responsibilities that lie before it.

This training should begin early in the life of the child. The writer knows one man who is spending his life on the foreign field, whose mother, before he was born, had dedicated him to the service of the Lord. Some parents magnify the size of the dollar in the presence of their children until it shuts out the view of the whole world. Others magnify the importance of reaching the topmost rung in the ladder of fame, until their children, like the Kaiser, would be willing to drench the world in blood to gratify their ambition. While all too few magnify the life of service as an ideal for their children.

Fortunate is the church which has a consecrated leader, who understands child psychology; who can interpret the great truths of the Bible in story form, for the little tots; who can so mould their expanding lives that membership in the church and service for it comes as the most natural thing in the world. Or, one who can get next to the heart of the boys, who can so present the great characters of the Bible that they shall be heroes for the boys, and who can interpret the Sunday school lesson in terms of the school room, the ball game, or the watermelon patch, so that they may translate the Sunday teaching into their daily lives. It is a principle of psychology that only as good impulses and new ideals are translated into action do they become an asset of value in resisting a future temptation or in raising one to a higher plane.

All the members of the church should be given an opportunity to participate in the activities of the church. A church in which ninety-five percent of the work of the church is performed by five percent of the members is not giving proper attention to the training of its members. One member may be willing to perform a dozen tasks, but the improvement in morale, the increased interest in the work of the church, the development of latent talent, the spirit of co-operation and the ability to do team work that would result from an equitable distribution of tasks is of infinitely more value to the church than any advantage that might come from having a few people do all the work.

The church should serve the community in which it is located. A survey of most any community will reveal a surprisingly large number of families who make no pretense of attending church services, and whose children never hear the name of Jesus except in cursing. Are the white children of America as deserving as the black children of Africa? A large number of these neglected families can be reached if a proper effort is made. A few years ago a union Sunday school was organized in an abandoned country church, and a special effort was made to reach the twenty families were enrolled, the attendance had reached eighty-school. By the end of the second year all but four of these families were enrolled, the attendance had reached eighty-five, with forty-five in the primary department and eighteen members of the school had united with some church. Is it worth while to try to do anything with a bunch of renters?

When the armies of the allies were trained and had learned to co-operate and to co-ordinate their efforts the cause of the Kaiser was doomed. When the members of the churches have been trained for service and have learned to co-operate and to co-ordinate their efforts the power of the church will be irresistible.

Morrill, Kansas.

Brethren and the Interchurch. By Wm. Kolb, Jr.

In general the Interchurch Movement should have the enthusiastic co-operation of all Christian people, because it is an effort to comply in the largest possible way with the Master's great commmission of Matthew 28:19 and 20, and to this end have undertaken a survey of the world's missionary needs, and the enlistment co-operatively of Christians everywhere in an effort to supply these needs.

The backbone is missions, home and foreign, world evangelization, all other activities are supplemental and incidental.

Specifically, selfishly perhaps, the co-operation of Brethren should be accorded because of the opportunity afforded for enlarged usefulness and for arousing ourselves to a realization of our tasks and responsibilities with respect to our church and its various activities and their necessities, and because of the financial advantages. Doubtless there are some among us lukewarm toward the project, due to lack of information or misinformation. I was formerly one of these. The project does not attempt in any way to supplant the denominations or interfere with their activities but to provide a means for their improvement and enlargement.

There is no element of compulsion of any nature connected with the movement and all are wholly free to co-operate or not as may seem best, but arrangements have been effected that will enable all Brethren, either as churches boards or individuals, to help in the work and enjoy the benefits of this year's financial campaign, if they so elect.

At a meeting January 1st, at Ashland, members of the Foreign Missionary Board, Home Missionary Board, College Trustees, Publication Company, Board of Benevolence, Women's Missionary Society, Five Year Program Committee and officers of Conference, it was resolved after careful consideration, to be the sense of the assembly, though not wholly unanimous, that boards desiring to participate should be free to do so and that we enter into the spirit and program of the movement so far as consistent with our denominational genius and identity.

Subsequently at a meeting of the College Trustees January 30th it was decided to co-operate on behalf of the college in the financial drive and to assist in the general under.

writing of the project. Our various other interests not meeting until Conference have taken no official action but in order to make it possible for the church to become a recognized feature, particularly in the financial drive, arrangements have been effected making it possible for Brethren contributors to designate for our various activities, including not only the educational but all other interests. The subscription blanks are not yet ready but they will provide opportunity as above.

The financial campaign plans provide for two groups of contributions; class (a), those specified for a particular object, and class (b), those undesignated. The (a) group fund is to be payable directly to the participating churches as specified. From the (b) group fund, after expenses are paid, a pro rata division is to be made in proportion to the amounts collected from the (a) group. It is apparent that there is every incentive to have the (a) group subscriptions as large as possible. The (b) group fund may possibly provide considerable additional money, depending upon the net results It is confidently expected this will be very considerable.

What do Brethren say to my proposal of the following tentative budget for this year's drive?

$75,000.00 for Education. For necessary addition to plant, buildings and equipment and enlarged faculty. Required if we are going to count ourselves among the colleges.

$40,000.00 for Foreign Missions. For maintenance and extension of our present missionary efforts. We will need to enlarge our vision. It has been too small. Our African effort especially is particularly appealing to the Interchurch. Our South American work also could be made a really large missionary center if we get the vision and act. We are in two strategic fields but we should occupy them.

$40,000.00 for Home Missions, including National and State. It is appalling to realize the unoccupied portions of the United States, vast sections not even churched.

$20,000.00 for Publishing interests for payment of new plant and enlargement of our work here.

$10,000.00 for Women's Societies, Women's Missionary Societies and Sisterhood Societies, for missions, educational projects, etc.

$15,000.00 for Old Folks Home, toward necessary erection and equipment for a home for old people.

Perhaps this would do as a step in the right direction. It is only about the price of a newspaper per day, per member. Our boards can fix up a real budget hereafter, but if all our people will get enthusiastically under a project of this sort there will be a rebirth spiritually and financially in our affairs.

As to the plan of operation, the United Simultaneous Campaign is set to begin Sunday, April 25th, and will end Sunday, May 2nd. This work is to be done through the local churches wherever possible, and solicitors provided where this is not practical. Details here are yet unsettled. It is hoped that the time from now until April 25th will be used for preparations and publicity, and that the campaign shall not be started before April 25th, but shall be united and simultaneous within the dates given. All pastors and others should in the meantime, avail themselves of the opportunities that will come through Interchurch conferences the country over. I believe all drives for money should be delayed until April 25th, to take advantage of the enthusiasm of the campaign and the possible participation in division of undesignated funds.

Should any of our members or churches be not ready as yet to participate fully in the Interchurch Movement, at least our financial campaign could be made in the period April 25th to May 3rd, and the question of more complete co-operation be decided later.

I have through personal conferences and correspondence been keeping in touch with the Interchurch Movement, and have come to be considered a point of contact between them and the Brethren church and expect to report from time to time through the Evangelist, items of interest. We are fully recognized but it remains for us to make the most of our opportunities.

If there are questions in the minds of any that I can clear up I would be glad to receive inquiries. I would be thankful also for expressions of co-operation or criticisms or suggestions, in order that all may have the fullest possible information.

915 Arch St., Philadelphia, Pennsylvania.

THE BRETHREN PULPIT

Mirages of the Great War. By Louis S. Bauman

. TEXT: "They speak a vision of their own heart, and not out of the mouth of the Lord."—Jer. 23:16.

Human nature changeth not. It is the same today as it was when the mighty Demosthenes of Israel cried out: "This is a rebellious people, lying children, children that will not hear the law of the Lord: which say to the seers, See not; and to the prophets, Prophesy not unto us right things, speak unto us smooth things, prophesy deceits" (Isaiah 30:9). The carnal man, forgetting that the Lord hath said, "'Cursed be the man that trusteth in man, and maketh flesh his arm'" (Jer. 17:5), still has a great deal of confidence in his own ability to bring great things and right things to pass. Even when he runs amuck, and sees disaster and death staring him in the face, ostrich-like, he sticks his head into the shifting sands, shuts his eyes against his doom, and remains an optimist to the end. In the carnal heart, pride and vainglory are always present; and the man in whose breast it beats would rather have "smooth things" spoken into his ear, even though those things be "deceits," than to have "right things" spoken against him. How much of this we saw during the recent world-war! Mighty men of renown went over the land, and stood in the pulpits of our churches, telling us what glorious things would come forth out of the agony of the struggle in Europe. They re-

fused to hear the "sure word of prophecy, whereunto ye do well that ye take heed, as unto a light that shineth in a dark place, until the day dawn" (II Pet. 1:19), and prepared to speak "a vision out of their own heart, and not out of the mouth of the Lord." It is now dawning on some, who do not persist in wilful blindness that these good men were victims of mirages; or, as Jehovah Himself put it, "a false vision and divination, and a thing of naught, and the deceit of their heart" (Jer. 14:14).

They spoke their vision of a race of supermen that were to come forth out of this war. But, it was a "vision of their own heart, and not out of the mouth of the Lord." We were told that on the battlefields, amidst carnage and death, men were to at last discover the highest instinct of the soul, —strength, courage, nobility, ungrudging service, infinite tenderness, compassion, generosity, the supremacy of the spirit the purest instances of friendship and death.

"There, near-appearing, the dream that stood far off in times of peace;

Love without bond, love compassing friend and enemy alike;

Unselfish love, a flash of the ideal;

Love of humanity—the Brotherhood of Man!"

We have now waited until those men, those supermen to be, have about all returned to us. Valiant, manly fellows,—yes! For us they faced death, and our gratitude belongs to them in every way it can be shown. But how like the rest of us they still are! In vain we look to discover the supermen to be!

A very popular and patriotic pastor in our own city made a great hit with the carnal man during the war by saying: "When our boys, best men on earth, come home after this war is over, you are going to find them, as a class, infinitely ahead of you in knowledge of the Bible and therefore in the virtues and stamina that count. * * * When he comes back, God bless him and keep him, he may come back with his cards and his tobacco, but he will come back with something he never had before, a practical reading knowledge of the Bible, a positive good that will infinitely outweigh all the negative evils. * * * Worry for yourselves rather, even though you never smoke, for the sorry contrast with him when he comes marching home, Bible-wise." They came marching home with "their cards and their tobacco," all right. The War Department states that ninety-five percent of the A. E. F. men use tobacco, and that its use has greatly increased since the signing of the armistice. The substinence division was still purchasing six months after the war, 425,000,000 of the "little white coffin-nails" monthly, besides 20,000,000 cigars. The "coffin-nails" are in evidence, but we look in vain for that "practical reading knowledge of the Bible." Some one was the victim of a mirage—some one spoke "a vision of his own heart, and not out of the mouth of the Lord." Had this man spoken his vision out of the mouth of the Lord, he would not have claimed for war, what naught but regeneration can do. On all sides now, we see professedly Christian forces making frantic efforts to save our youth from degradation and enslavement by the great god Nicotine, who gave him assistance and condoned his acts during the war. Moreover, some of these very workers stood ready to stigmatize as "Pro-German" those who dared to lift their voices against this great slaver during the war.

They spoke a vision of a world into which the spirit of self-sacrifice would be born as a result of the great war. In vain we look for the reality of their dream. It was "a vision of their own heart, and not out of the mouth of the Lord" who has said, "In the last days perilous times shall come. For men shall be lovers of their own selves" II Tim. 3:1, 2). Probably the world has never seen the selfishness of the human heart made so manifest as now. Some weeks ago, in an address in Kansas City, Governor Allen, of Kansas, said: "The actions of some business interests seem to indicate that they are trying to make up with their greedy profits what they gave out during the war to aid the cause. Human greed in this country during the past six months is unparalleled." One of the greatest problems, if not the greatest problem confronted by our statesmen today is the problem of curbing the profiteers. Scathing and telling are the lines addressed to that human hog we call a profiteer, by a soldier, Major Guy M. Kindersley:

"We died in our millions to serve it, the cause that you told
   us was ours,
We stood waist-deep in the trenches, we battled with hell
   and its powers;
Broken and shattered and helpless, we rotted by land and by
   sea,
For the dream you held before us, the dream of a Freedom
   to be.

"And you? You have gathered your millions; you have
   lined your pockets with pelf,
You have talked of the Rights of Nations, while you worshiped the rights of self;
Your lands are dunged with our lifeblood, your houses are
   built with our bones,
Your temples (and would you could hear them) are filled
   with our children's moans,

"Do you think we shall rise and smite you? Fear not! You
   shall garner your gain.
And we? Will you give us our freedom, just those who have
   not been slain?
No, the tale is the same as ever, and the world will go on as
   before,
Our sons will be fooled and blinded, as our fathers were of
   yore.

"Fooled though we have been by your hirelings—you know
   that we fought for a lie—
We've fathomed a truth that you see not, but one you must
   learn when you die,
That silver and gold and raiment are things of but little
   worth,
For Love is the heir of the ages, and the meek shall inherit
   the earth."

And so, in vain do we look the world over to find the effectual working of the spirit of self-sacrifice that was born of the war. If it can be shown that men have learned to give as they never gave before, it can also be shown that the same men have learned to take as they never took before. Men will still have to turn their eyes to Calvary, rather than to the battlefields of France to learn the meaning of true sacrifice. War breeds hate and not love. War takes but does not give. War is the highwayman of the nations. "War is hell," and nothing good has ever come from it that might not have been attained by nobler methods. God may "make the wrath of man to praise him." He can make the love of man to praise him more.

They spoke to us their vision of a new and better religion that was to come forth from the travail of this war. But, they spoke "the vision of their own heart, and not out of the mouth of the Lord." One of the leading clergymen of the nation made the statement: "Our men and the fighting men of Britain and France are laying the foundation now for the great religion of the future on both sides of the water." One of the most brilliant religious journalists of our day, writing from across the seas, gave us some clue as to what sort of a religion this "religion of the future might be. He wrote: "A really startling radicalism pervades the thinking of the armies, of the chaplains, and of the Y. M. C. A. workers who have been long with the troops. * * * Nobody cares a cootie for 'orthodoxy.' Old usages and old creeds said to have succumbed to the U-boats or some other force, on the way over. All things, from the very existence of a Supreme Being to the right of the church to exist, have had to face the challenge of this new, emancipated, free-thinking warmind." The armistice was signed a year ago, now, and we still are watching for the rise of this "religion of the future" that cares not "a cootie for 'orthodoxy'" which the boys were to have brought back with them. While it is fashioning itself into a tangible thing, some of us will still remain on the job of preaching the old-fashioned "gospel of Christ; for it is the power of God unto salvation to every one that believeth; to the Jew first, and also to the Greek" (Rom. 1:16). We fear that we shall wait in vain for the coming of a substitute of that old-fashioned Gospel able to show forth "the power of God unto salvation." We are beginning to fear that the "religion of the future" so confidently expected to lead man to his golden dream is but a mirage.

They spoke to us their vision of the death of war as the sure result of the great World War. Confidently they told us to give our money to buy cannon and powder and shot to blow the war-god from the face of the earth for all time. The vision was certainly "a vision of their own heart and not out of the mouth of the Lord." More than two-score of wars have been going on ever since the armistice of the great World War was signed at Versailles. Now, one year hence the future never looked more stormy. As this is being written, the United States is about to appeal to Mars as the oily god that can settle her troubles with Mexico. The premiers of Europe are holding once more their secret conferences in groups here and there, forming once more their secret treaties and suspicious alliances, while the poor "League of Nations" hovers between life and death, gasping for breath. The men who make war their business are already figuring hard upon the next war. We are assured that they are preparing cannon that will shoot with deadly accuracy for forty miles; poison gas that will penetrate wool and leather, and one drop of which, falling on the foot will destroy it, and one whiff into the lungs will kill; explosive shells that will dig a hole in which a fair-sized sky-scraper can be buried, and kill every human being for five miles around; submarines that will travel five thousand miles, and throw a shell that will snuff out every life in a great city by asphyxiation; deadly disease germs of cholera and meningitis that will pollute with death great lakes and mighty rivers, etc. And as they plan these things, and call for military training in our public schools to teach our children how to use these implements of death and hell, we are surely made to feel that the prophecies of men who ignored the "sure word of prophecy" have proven to be pipe-dreams indeed. Surely, the day seems yet afar off when "men shall learn war no more."

When will men learn that war, that old-time appeal to brute force, never settles anything; and most of all, it does not settle war. Rather, it begets war. Who does not know that the great World War of 1914 was born of the Franco-Prussian War of 1870? And God alone knows how many terrible struggles of the future, if our Lord shall tarry, are to be born of the great World War of 1914. You may win and shout your victory, but victory does not prove the righteousness of your cause. Aaron Burr was victor over Alexander Hamilton, but it did not prove the righteousness of the cause of Burr. It only proved him a more deadly shot.

A scientist, writing recently, in "The Journal of Heredity," states that man has fought his way upward for millions of years, and that "It is natural then that every human being should have an inborn disposition to war, that once it has been aroused by the appropriate stimuli, the impulse of war is stronger than the desire to live. * * * Militarists have long recognized this fact and made the most of it. The fighting instinct being the strongest that men possess, militarists think that it is utopian to talk of suppressing it. So far as the immediate future is concerned, this is certainly true." We are far from endorsing the statement that "man has fought his way upward for millions of years" and attributing man's "fighting instinct" to that fact; but, we dare say that this scientist understands man's true nature better than many prophets who have prophesied "a vision of their own heart" during the past five years. So long as man's nature remains unchanged by the miracle of Divine grace, just so long he will appeal to the power of the brute within him when he believes himself to be the victim of some wrong, fancied or otherwise. And all your "Leagues of Peace" and enactments of law will fail simply because they fail to change the selfish, self-centered heart of man into a loving and self-forgetful one.

Moreover, one of the outstanding facts of the diplomacy of 1919 is, that is a diplomacy that has ignored the mighty God of nations. In the great "Peace Treaty of Versailles" with its engrafted "League of Nations," not by the slightest breath was any recognition given to the mighty God who happens to have a part of his own for this earth he made. And so long as man plans and refuses to recognize God and his plan, just so long is man's supremest effort foredoomed to failure. There was a mighty world ruler once upon a time, Nebuchadnezzar, by name, whose pride lifted up his heart so high that he was above taking notice whatever of the God of Israel. One day, God's patience was tried to the limit. and Nebuchadnezzar "was driven from the sons of men; * * * and his dwelling was with the wild asses, and they fed him with grass like oxen, * * * till he knew that the most high God ruled in the kingdom of men, and that

he appointeth over it whomsoever he will" (Dan. 5:21). The men who sat at the Peace Council of Versailles seem to have been as forgetful as Nebuchadnezzar. May the grace of God spare them and their nations from the mighty Nebuchadnezzar's fate.

Had the prophets, who, after a "vision of their own heart," told us that the World War would be the death of war,—had they spoken their vision out of the mouth of the Lord," men would know the truth, that man's eternal dream of a day when the war-cry shall no more be heard in the land, when every cannon shall be spiked, and every battle-flag furled; when "the sword shall be beaten into the plow-share and the spear into the pruning hook,"—that dream will only be realized when the Prince of Peace shall come back from the heaven into which he went away, and "shall speak peace unto the nations" (Zech. 9:10). There will never be peace without the coming of the Prince of Peace. Let the effect of that declaration be what it may, the mouth of the omniscient God who sees the end from the beginning hath spoken it. It is not until the "People shall go and say, Come ye, and let us go up to the mountain of the Lord, to the house of the God of Jacob," and "out of Zion shall go forth the law, and the word of the Lord from Jerusalem, and he shall judge among the nations," that "they shall beat their swords into plowshares and their spears into pruning hooks: nation shall not lift up sword against nation, neither shall they learn war any more" (Isa. 2:3, 4). It is not until Jesus Christ shall sit "upon the throne of David, and upon his kingdom, to order it," that it shall be truly said, "Of peace there shall be no end" (Isa. 9:7). Had they spoken of their vision "out of the mouth of the Lord," they would not have placed so much confidence in the flesh (cf. Phils. 3:3), and would have confessed that "Nation shall rise against nation, and kingdom against kingdom: and there shall be famines, and pestilences, and earthquakes, in divers places" (Matt. 24:7), and "great tribulation, such as was not since the beginning of the world to this time, no, nor ever shall be" (Matt. 24:21), up until the very hour that "they shall see the Son of man coming in the clouds of heaven with power and great glory" (Matt. 24:30). Why permit the uncertain desires, born of the pride and vainglory of the flesh, to deceive us and turn us away from "the sure word of prophecy." It is better to prophesy "right things" than "smooth things." It may hurt our human pride, but man's civilization that ignores God's purposes and plans set forth in his eternal word, is doomed to a terrible collapse. God's civilization alone shall endure. And God's civilization shall be built only when man shall have learned that he has been created to work together with God, and always according to the eternal plan of which God alone is Architect. The way to man's peace lies in walking with God, and building in harmony with the eternal purposes of God. When will he learn it?

As a matter of fact, it is not to be expected that the unregenerate man will ever learn it. For, it is written, "The carnal mind is enmity against God: for it is not subject to the law of God, neither indeed can be" (Rom. 8:7). Therefore, for a world that remains unregenerate, we can have no hope. For it, our only expectation is judgment. Beyond that day of judgment lies our hope of a tearless paradise restored. Let us cherish no fool's dream of a paradise in an unregenerate world, born of the efforts of the unregenerate arm of flesh. Let us rather look for the certain fulfillment of "the sure word of prophecy, whereunto ye do well that ye take heed, as unto a light that shineth in a dark place, until the day dawn, and the day star arise in your hearts" (II Peter 1:19).

The "sure word of prophecy" reveals the "vision out of the mouth of the Lord." It reveals a great religious federation, the "great harlot" of Revelation 17, that shall arise and dominate "the beast," who is none other than the Anti-Christ that shall come at the head of the political powers of te world. The hour is coming, and seems even to be upon

(Continued on page 16)

OUR DEVOTIONAL

The Overcoming Life. By Mark B. Spacht

OUR SCRIPTURE

Forwhatsoever is born of God overcometh the world; 'nd this is the victory that overcometh the world, even our aith. Who is he that overcometh the world, but he that believeth that Jesus is the Son of God (1 John 5:4, 5)? Ye are of God, little children, and have overcome them; because greater is he that is in you, 'than he that is in the world. (1 John 4:4). These things I have spoken unto you, that in me ye might have peace. In the world ye shall have tribulation; but be of good cheer; I have overcome the world (John 16:33). Be not overcome of evil, but overcome evil with good (Romans 12:21). And Caleb stilled the people before Moses, and said, Let us go up at once and possess it; for we are well able to overcome it" .(Numbers 13:30. See also Rev. 2:7, 11, 17, 26; Rev. 3:5,12, 21, and 21:7).

OUR MEDITATIONS

When a great battle is being fought we anxiously wait to learn who the victors are. Our lives are the battlegrounds on which the forces of darkness are ever attempting to overcome the forces of light. In the first of the above scriptures we have our starting point in the fight that shall give us the victory over the world. When I speak of the overcoming life, I am speaking to persons who have experienced the saving power of Jesus' blood. I would not, for a moment, think of talking to an unconverted man about overcoming the world. He might just as well throw himself into the rapids at Niagara to block the onward rush of that seething mass of turbulent water, as to try to overcome the "powers of darkness" without Jesus Christ.

How easy it is to bear our burdens and to meet the trials and temptations of the tempter, if we will only let Jesus unreservedly share them with us. I know Paul must have experienced the happiness of the overcoming life when he wrote to the saints at Philippi: "I can do all things through Christ who strengtheneth me." Blessed is he who realizes and has experienced the truth of John's words when he says, "Greater is he that is in you than he that is in the world." Let us ever keep in mind that, no matter what the enemy is that seeks to overpower us, or whence he is, whether he be from within or from without. Jesus is more powerful, and gladly sustains us in our faith and gives us the victory. He is the only one who has conquered this world, and it is through that life that we may be called conquerors.

Adam was tempted by Satan in the Garden of Eden. Jesus was tempted by Satan in the wilderness. The difference between the two is this: the first Adam was overcome by the tempter, the second Adam overcame the tempter. And that is the question that comes ringing into our ears today: Am I overcoming the world, or is the world overcoming me? Think seriously about these questions. Am I more amiable today than I was a year ago? Am I seeking to cultivate a sweeter disposition towards those with whom I labor and associate? Am I offending less as the days go by? Am I less covetous of worldly wealth and honor; more zealous for celestial treasures? Am I more faithful in church services today than I was yesterday? Do I have more of love and fellowship for my fellowman; less of jealousy and hate? In fact, do I let Jesus have his way with me? If we can answer these questions in the affirmative, surely we are overcoming the world; if we can not answer thus, the world is overcoming us.

The church today needs men of the type of Joshua and Caleb. Men who know they are right, and, knowing, will stand for the Christ in face of opposition. Men who will not compromise with evil. Men who are willing to go the second mile for Jesus.

I would like to call your attention yet to the eight promises to the overcomer as found in Revelation. First, "To him that overcometh will I give to eat of the tree of life which is in the midst of the paradise of God." No half-way enjoyment for that person. The promise is that he shall be in the midst of things eternal.

Second. "He that overcometh shall not be hurt of the second death." There is no death for the true disciple. For him the giving up of this life is the beginning of an eternal habitation in heaven.

Third. "To him that overcometh will I give to eat of the hidden manna, and I will give him a white stone, and in the stone a new name written, which no man knoweth save him that receiveth it."

Fourth. "He that overcometh and keepeth my works unto the end, I will give power over the nations; and he shall rule them, etc." I believe God has us in training here, and if we can not overcome, we are not fit to be kings and priests over there. I don't know where the kingdoms are. That isn't of much importance—just so we are ready for service when he calls.

Fifth. "He that overcometh the same shall be clothed in white raiment; and I will not blot out his name out of the book of life, but I will confess his name before my Father and before his angels." He that overcometh shall have friends in heaven. Jesus will be there to proclaim him before God and the angels.

Sixth. "Him that overcometh will I make a pillar in the temple of my God, and he shall go no more out; and I will write upon him the name of my God and the name of the city of my God, which is the New Jerusalem, which cometh down out of heaven from my God; and I will write upon him my new name." How wonderful it is when God calls us his own. I think he looks down smilingly upon us and says: "Those are my soldiers. They are overcoming for me."

Seventh. "To him that overcometh will I grant to sit with me in my throne even as I overcame and am set down with my Father in his throne." What a happy time that will be. Only a short time to overcome, and then all eternity to live with Jesus.

Now the last one, and it indeed shows the fulness of God's love. "He that overcometh shall inherit all things; and I will be his God, and he shall be my son." Oh! but are we not rich? We may not possess much of this world's wealth ,but if we are victors in the overcoming life, we are heirs to all heaven.

OUR PRAYER

Dear Father, we thank thee for thy wondrous love; for the Son of thy love that came to dwell among us and showed us the beauty of the overcoming life. Help us, dear Father, to let him be our close Friend and Guide that we may be able to claim the blessed promises to him that overcometh. In his name. Amen.

Williamstown, Ohio.

Peace is the happy natural state of man; war his corruption, his disgrace.—Thomson.

The capacity to be religious does not guarantee that a man will be Jewish or Christian or Hebrew.—Religious Ed-

MEETING THE ACID TEST

John R. Mott once visited a college in Ceylon where he found a band of students so poor that sixteen of them occupied one room. Near the building was a garden where they spent their spare time cultivating bananas. When he inquired, "What do you do with the money?" they took him to a shore and pointed him to an island off in the sea. "Two years ago," they said, "we sent one of our graduates there. He started a school and it has developed into a church. We are going to send him to another island this year." Their cook laid aside every tenth handful of rice that they might sell it, in order to have Christ preached more widely.

Send
WHITE GIFT
OFFERINGS to

THE SUNDAY SCHOOL

ALBERT TRENT
General Secretary-Treasurer
Johnstown, Pennsylvania

To the Sunday Schools of the Brotherhood. By B. T. Burnworth

In answer to the Waterloo proposal in a recent issue of the Evangelist, that the pastor of the Waterloo church, W. H. Beachler be sent to Tokyo, Japan, to the World Sunday School convention at the expense of all the schools of the brotherhood, ten cents per capita, may I respond thus:

Because of the deep personal regard for Mrs. Wisner who makes the proposal and the intimate friendship of their pastor and the pleasant relation that the writer has with the Waterloo church in general I almost feel that this letter might be interpreted as being personal. But it is not, for the whole brotherhood is at once included and involved. This fact at once eliminates the purely personal aspect. In open forum let me analyze the proposal.

A. "The Brethren church should be represented at Tokyo." This I only could accept under the most auspicious circumstance. If there were not many other things of greater importance to us which are imminent and paramount I might concede the point. But with the life of our very church depending upon the endowment and saving of the college, with a proposal for a new building at Ashland needed badly, and as the president of the Life Recruits reminds us, we must have a fund whereby needy young men and women willing to do the work of the church but in need of training may have it, and if practically every member of the faculty and pastor in the Brethren church did not need a larger salary, and if we could not get this report any other way than going to Tokyo for it, and if it were not a hundred times better for all the Sunday school workers to have their churches and schools send them to a convention where they could all report and benefit rather than send one person such a great distance I might also be willing.

B. "The real reason is that the war has changed things affecting the future of things."

Have we not all been tempted to prophesy that we would have a new world after this war and have we not been keenly disappointed? The United States Senate seems unchanged. The soldiers that were going to return and teach us what real religion is by filling our churches and the important offices, we have found almost universally speaking that they lost what religion they had and they now feel the Lord is under obligation to them and not vice versa. It looks now that the war has added to religious indifference, which may be a Sunday school problem but it won't be solved at Tokyo any quicker than in the United States.

C. How shall the expenses be met? The solution submitted was that every Sunday school should pay ten cents per capita.

Is this the greatest objective our schools can have, to send somebody to a convention on the other side of the globe? Furthermore, there is the remotest possibility that this representative will ever visit your school and you will get a report through the Evangelist, whereas you can get an official report through your state headquarters and still have derived the same benefit and still have your ten cents per capita to send your own pastor who is too poor to attend even a state convention or better yet, send your whole corps of officers of the school to a state or national convention on the same amount that you otherwise would give to have one man go to Tokyo and you and the Brethren church in general will be benefited in the exact proportion to the number of representatives from all the schools sent to some convention, instead of all the schools sending one. There can be no argument advanced that the benefit from a state or national convention visited by several from each school would not be far more beneficial than one report from Tokyo.

Now dear readers, the amount needed for this trip was not mentioned. Do you know that the least estimate yet was $800 (eight hundred dollars) two years ago and that a thousand will not cover it now? Can you think of anything that a thousand dollars could be used for that would be more beneficial to us and others than for a single person to go to this Tokyo convention? As I write, I have two letters before me. One is an appeal from the starving orphans of the "Near East." The other is a receipt for $50 sent them, and the statement that these orphanages are supported by our contributions alone and exactly in proportion as we help, or not, shall these starving children live or die. If my Sunday school takes up a ten cents per capita offering it will be with that fine missionary objective that saves lives now. Dare any man, church, or Sunday school spend a $1,000 to go to Tokyo while children are starving? From our 25,070 Sunday school members ten cents per capita would amount to $2,507.00. Will it pay to spend that much to send a delegate to Tokyo?

Last. Who Shall Go?

Of course, no one is my answer, unless you think that the Japanese can't get along without a representative from the Brethren church of which they have never heard.

So, in reply to the request of my good friends at Waterloo, that the rest of the Sunday schools should tell what they "think," I submit this as being what I think.

Lanark, Illinois.

On to Tokyo. By Mollie Gans Griffin

I was interested in the suggestion that it would be a nice thing if the Brethren church could be represented at the World's Sunday School Convention at Tokyo, Japan. I would like to see our church represented.

It would be a great benefit for us to have some one there. The report he would give and the inspiration and vision he would give to the schools as he would go about among the schools would help us wonderfully. What an inspiration it would be for one of our men to associate with such men as Marion Lawrence, Frank L. Brown, Prof. Athearn and others of like caliber for two months! How it would improve our Sunday school interests in our church and our Sunday school literature to have some one go with that group of expert Sunday school workers and write pen pictures of the trip from start to finish! I believe it would pay us to send some one.

My husband spends all his time in Sunday school work except in mid-summer and we were planning to go to Tokyo. But we are plain farmers and cannot go. It would cost us each $480 from the Pacific coast. Counting the extra clothes and curios we would want to bring back, it would cost us both about $1,500. We would like to see somebody go. At the International Sunday School Convention at Buffalo, we saw at the Pilgrims' Banquet great panoramic views of the trip through Japan. The scenes were great and we were convinced that this convention will be the most noted gathering that has ever come together in the Orient.

Now, I would like to throw a bouquet at Brother Gnagey, who has made our Sunday school literature all these years and nominate him to go.

I will give ten dollars to start a fund to send some one. Brethren, get busy, the berths for Pennsylvania are nearly all gone.

Smithfield, Pennsylvania.

Equanimity, in every condition of life, is a noble attribute.—Cicero.

| J. A. Garber | | G. C. Carpenter |
| PRESIDENT | Our Young People at Work | SECRETARY |

Inspiration for Your Christian Endeavor Work.   By M. A. Witter

One of the most effective ways of awakening our societies to the riches of our Gospel privileges is to lead them in the study of what the Gospel is accomplishing in mission lands. Mission study classes are following some of the most fascinating pages of human history. What can be more thrilling than to watch the effect of the Gospel of Christ as it brings hope and joy and freedom to the sin-fettered lives of gloom and helplessness in unevangelized lands.

Where the number of Christian Endeavorers who could be included in a mission study class is very small it might be a splendid plan for the Christian Endeavor and the Woman's Missionary Society to combine their classes and all together study the wonderful accomplishments and possibilities of medical missions in "A Crusade of Compassion for the Healing of the Nations." In this work Dr. Belle J. Allen brings to the reader the inspiration of her own rich experience as a medical missionary. This book has a stirring appeal for the Endeavorer bringing to his view the thousands who have never known medical aid or Gospel truth. Combined classes of C. E. and W. M. S. members will receive credit for mission study for both the C. E. and the W. M. S.

Where there are enough Christian Endeavor members to form a class of their own it might be well for them to study one of the splendid books on one of the fields where

our own missionaries are at work. If your society has never studied "An African Trail" by Miss Jean Kenyon Mackenzie, they will find a great spiritual uplift if they follow the influence of Christ on darkest Africa as told by this accomplished author who is also an experienced missionary and thorough student of both divine and human nature. "The Lure of Africa" by Patton is equally interesting.

Christian Endeavorers, you can do no greater service for your own society and for the cause of Christ than to interest a group of your fellow-Endeavorers in a mission study class. Right now in the long winter evenings is a splendid time to interest your society. The hours spent in the reading of the work of Christ in mission lands will be filled with rich spiritual treasure for the members of the class. Will you bring this work to the attention of your society at its next meeting?

(Note.—The mission study books, "A Crusade of Compassion" paper, 35c; cloth, 50c; and "An African Trail" paper, 15c; cloth, 25c; may be had from The Central Committee on United Study of Foreign Missions, M. H. Levis, Agent, West Medford, Massachusetts. The Missionary Education Movement, 160 Fifth Avenue, New York, supplies all kinds of helpful literature).

Waynesboro, Pennsylvania.

Christian Endeavor Specials.   By Prof. J. A. Garber

AS OTHERS SEE THE PAGEANT

The writer continues to receive hearty commendations relative to the pageant entitled "The Crusade of Sacrificial Service."

Dr. O. T. Deever, General Secretary of the Young Peoples' Work of the United Brethren in Christ writes the following: "I thank you very much for the pageant. It is very fine. If you will send me three dozen copies I shall be glad to pay for them."

A more lengthy note comes from Rev. James DeForest Murch, the present Superintendent of the Service Department of The Ohio Christian Endeavor Union. He voices his sentiments in this striking manner: "I want to thank you for sending me a copy of your Life Work Pageant, "THE CRUSADE OF SACRIFICIAL SERVICE." It could be used with helpfulness by any Christian Endeavor Society. If it were not for the fact that the forms for the March OHIO ENDEAVORER are closed, I would say something about it in the Service Department, I shall be glad to say a word concerning it in the April issue."

EXPERTIZE YOUR SOCIETY

The Christian Endeavor Expert is not so rare an individual as some of you who belong to societies that have never taken up this work, might think. Only as one becomes an Expert, authorized to sign the significant C. E. E. after his name, and entitled to wear the C double E pin, does he become a real Endeavorer in every sense of the word.

The Expert understands the use of the prayermeeting; he is sure of the interpretation of the pledge; there is no doubt in his mind as to the meaning of the business meeting; he is acquainted with Christian Endeavor history; knows its principles; can tell you its fundamentals; is in tune with its program. He knows the president's job; the place where the lend-a-hand committee best fits in; he knows how to judge a beginner from an active Endeavorer and can tell an associate member from an Alumnus. In fact he is thoroughly conversant with the duties of all the offices and what is expected of the committees.

There is no better month in all the year to begin getting

your society in line, than January. Decide now to qualify on item number six of Ohio's Loyalty Standards. "The efficiency chart in active operation, beginning anew on or after September 1st, 1919." It takes experts to make a good efficiency rating.

Organize a class, order some textbooks, and begin. Give examinations and award the certificates to all who qualify. Give us a chance to explain to you how to do it.

The above from the "Ohio Endeavorer" shows how others regard Expert Endeavor. A class will enable your society to qualify on "Point 10" of our Four Year Challenge. Let us help you.

WESTERN PENNSYLVANIA

Mrs. Carl Grose, the Field Secretary of the Endeavor societies of Pennsylvania sends a most favorable report. She gives an account of her visit to the Third church at Johnstown. One of the first things mentioned is the fact that this society is very active. Mr. M. S. Stutzman, a returned soldier, is the hustling president. While there Mrs. Grose was privileged to meet with the Christian Endeavor cabinet and also shared in a regular meeting. In the cabinet meeting plans were discussed for the future work of the society. Many other things pertaining directly to their new program were also dealt with in a proper manner. Their president seems to have the work well in hand and the future success of the organization is already assured. It might be mentioned in this connection that Brother George Jones is the pastor of this congregation and that the society itself was re-organized two years ago. In the regular meeting Mrs. Grose addressed the society and emphasized definite service as an essential in Christian Endeavor work. An unusual program was rendered. A full house, splendid music and a fine spirit are the three elements that add greatly to the success of this society. The report is closed with the statement that more societies ought to follow the plans of Johnstown third.

I will ever be doing something; that either God when he cometh, or Satan when he tempteth, may find me busied.—Joseph Hall.

SEND ALL MONEY FOR
General Home, Kentucky and
Foreign Missions to

MISSIONS

WILLIAM A. GEARHART
General Missionary Secretary
906 Conover Bldg., Dayton, O.

Home Mission Notes. By G. C. Carpenter

Muncie, Indiana

We have learned indirectly that the Goshen brethren made a very generous financial gift toward the new church building fund. This was accomplished through the personal solicitation by Brother J. L. Kimmel, pastor of the Muncie church. Brother Kimmel holds a large place in the hearts of the Goshen people.

Fort Scott, Kansas

Brother G. T. Ronk is giving time and thought to the work at Fort Scott, as he sees a great opportunity for building up a strong church there. He reports that a regular pastor has not yet been secured and that is their greatest need at present. Brother Ronk states that the place calls for a strong and consecrated man.

Peru, Indiana

With all the hindrances of the past year the Sunday school annual report for 1919 was commendable. The average attendance was 84 and the average offering $8.54. Placing the Evangelist on the Honor Roll was one of the worthwhile victories of the year. The "flu" epidemic here is worse than last year and has cut down church attendance.

Lost Creek, Kentucky

There was quite a change in the corps of workers at Riverside Institute recently. Brother and Sister Pearce resigned and left for Montreal, Canada, where Brother Pearce's father was very sick. Sister Woodmansee is now teaching the school at Krypton. Brother and Sister Teall and Sister Hade returned

to their homes, having resigned also. Our Riverside cabinet seems to be passing through an experience similar to that of President Wilson's cabinet at Washington. Brother Drushal offered his resignation too and the same was accepted by the Directors of the Mission Board but he is continuing the work. He writes that Brother and Sister Claude Akens have arrived and are teaching. Mrs. Akens was formerly Miss Geneva Strode, a niece of Mrs. Drushal. Both Brother and Sister Akens have taught several years at Riverside. The other teachers are Miss Bessie Hooks of Mosgrove, Pa., and John Watts of Lost Creek. Miss Bethke is still assisting in the work. Brother Drushal writes that school is going on with full attendance.

Great Student Volunteer Convention at Des Moines, Iowa: It's Spirit and Personnel
By Miss Clara J. Raad

The most cosmopolitan student conference ever assembled, held its first session Wednesday afternoon, December 31, 1919, when 8,000 delegates swept into the coliseum from 40 nations and nationalities, to open discussion as to the great work of carrying the light of Christianity into the dark corners of the world.

As the "Des Moines Capital" expressed it, "They were just regular young people, those student Volunteers." Yet a most promising alert and keen eyed lot was that big delegation which long before the scheduled meeting time, began to pack the Coliseum from floor to ceiling. And until the meeting opened it seemed that the roof would fairly fly off as with lusty voices the many students gave their college yells.

Seated in section by states, there was some keen rivalry between the different contingents. The Canadian students ripped the air with their college yells. From the right hand side of the balcony came a roar from the Ohio students, and high above, delegates from the Badger state sang, "On Wisconsin," to be almost drowned out on the last note by Minnesota's Ski-U-Mah.

In the front of the house, the big group of foreign students, representing Africa, Arabia, Central America, China, India, Bermuda and Ceylon, Japan and Korea, Europe, Latin and Greek counties of Mexico, Oceania, Persia, Philippines, Siam and Straits Settlements, South America, Turkey, West Indies and other countries, sat quietly, taking no part in the yelling, but smiling with appreciation at the noise and color about them.

Flags of the Allies, and gay bunting concealed the beams and supports of the coliseum. Palms and flags decorated the big platform, upon which sat the missionaries on leave on furlough, and speakers and leaders of prominence at the convention sessions.

As the hour for the meeting approached the roar of college yells grew louder. But sud-

denly as John R. Mott, who presided at every session, stepped out and raised the gavel, the house became quiet. Splendid order was maintained throughout the entire conference. With the exception of twice, there was no applause. The great assemblage maintained a quietness that was intense and attention that showed deep interest. Scarcely a restless head or hand moved throughout the sessions. Noisy enthusiasm had changed to interest, and an intense interest that was superior to every other emotion. The delegates were busy with pencils and notebooks following carefully the words of the speakers.

The happy harmony of personal devotion, moral executive and psychological insight were embodied in the chairman and other leaders.

John R. Mott made the opening address. His deep religious devotion together with his business-like presentation of the purpose of the convention gripped the entire assembly, and won the strong moral support of all.

It was inspiring to listen to such men as Dr. Robert E. Speer, Sherwood Eddy and Dr. William H. Foulkes of New York, who is the leader of the New Era Movement, lay plans for tremendous activities for world evangelization, which they seemed confident would be carried out by allied strategy and the making of a supreme offensive. This was like a triumphant call to every student of every land, to establish such a precedent that the pursuit of education might also become a spiritual adventure.

The Chinese student body, as well as certain individuals whom I had the privilege of being with and hearing at afternoon sessions, were the happy embodiment of searching psychological insight. It was not without irony that they pictured how American civilization has impressed and affected their land and nation through commercial interests and political activities which we know have grossly misrepresented us as a Christian nation. I wish it were in my power to portray to you

some of the fervor and enthusiasm which characterized this keen-eyed world element which is getting its training in our colleges and universities. They are not narrow, but international and so full of ambition and aspiration for their country that even as guests in an American city they made bold to say, and that without fear, "We can not look to Europe or America for the principles of the foundation for our new civilization. The salvation of China must come from within, through God by native Chinese trained in leadership and in Christianity. Europe and America are not what we came expecting to find them. It is true, we owe them much, but in establishing our ideals we must use great precaution. That which is good we should adopt and improve upon. But their civilization is bad at the core. The Christianity which we must strive to establish, must present to the commercial world of China, mental independence, economic independence and interindependence only this will establish co-operation and power. Ah no, The alien is not the only one in this country who needs Americanization.

Mrs. Bennett, President of the Women's Council of the Home Missionary Board, urged that we all work to the end that even in their generation, every missionary to foreign lands may point to Christian America from whence he came, assuring his hearers that their brethren who have gone over there to complete their education, will return with something far more valuable to them than a new language, changed customs and clothes. This means that we must identify our purpose with our principles.

Stevenson gave us a vision of this new world when he described it as a confused and bewildered world. He said, "It is plastic now to a degree that can not be determined. But it is soon to be set and definitely molded." What influence have you in the final formation? (It is essential that the work which might have been done in a century, be done in the hour of the setting sun. Therefore let us lend ourselves to service, not to selfish ends. We as students can not escape in one way or the other, becoming builders in the new world order.

We have all heard a great deal about John R. Mott, but perhaps none of you have heard Mrs. Mott's name mentioned in connection with his great work. It was my invaluable privilege to hear her talk to the foreign girls of the convention. This was a comparatively small assemblage and it was therefore possible to get the full benefit of her lovely personality. Hers was not a studied message, but a heart to heart talk with the girls. In her eyes glowed a deep interest and concern. Her whole being seemed to radiate a wholesome influence which could not be resisted. No mother could be more adored by her children than is Mrs. Mott by the girls who there came under her immediate influence. She was the personification of her own statement, "To live with people is to learn to love them."

Among the other outstanding characters of the convention were Kenneth Saunders, Mr. Nunez and R. T. Sein. Mr. Saunders, for some years a Y. M. C. A. worker in India, reflected in his personality the joy and satisfaction he had found in serving God in the noble calling which he had chosen.

In quoting Mr. Nunez, a Peruvian and student of Dr. White's Bible school, New York,

I see a young man of strong determination and lofty purpose and wish we might catch his spirit. "We in South America appreciate so much what your country is doing for us. We would like to bring all of South America here to see the great work of the Student Volunteers. But we will take our teachings home with us."

Then there was R. T. Sein, a promising young Mexican, so brim full of enthusiasm, fire and fervor that with his red hair and piercing blue eyes he will remain a never-to-be forgotten character. He revealed how the various commercial interests of the United States had invaded his country and exploited the labor, worked its rich mines and agricultural districts and blurred the democratic principles for which the true Christian American stands. Mr. Sein appealed to the delegates to help take Christianity into Mexico as a means of putting the country on a sound economic and religious basis.

Dr. Carl Frier of Stockholm, Dr. Henroit of Switzerland and Dr. Rutgers of Holland were living examples of the spirit of the convention. In their deeply spiritual words there was that underlying moral executive and human understanding which bridged all barriers and made us all one great brotherhood.

Dr. Endicot of Toronto and Dr. H. Cox of New York, are men of great vision and pur-

pose. They spoke in concrete and specific terms, portraying in intimate word pictures the conditions, as they exist, sparing neither our America nor any other nation. They pointed out that no nation should be spared the service it ought to render. We should teach by our example, that success comes by leadership, through service.

It is not necessary here to more than mention the names of J. Campbell White, Dr. James I. Vance, Dr. Mackenzie, Dean Brown of Yale, Bishop McDowell and Dr. Zweamer, that great teacher and missionary of Arabia, to give you a vision of their great personalities. But to sit and listen to their messages and to feel that subtle influence which has swayed so many audiences, is indeed to be privileged. Oh, how the things that are truly great enlarge our visions and give us new vigor. But no less inspiring were the upturned expectant faces in the assembly. Here a black one, there a yellow one, fairly drinking in the messages. Gray haired missionaries looked hopefully out over the great student body as if to say, We know we can depend upon you who are young and vigorous, whose minds are being educated and whose lives are consecrated to the service of God and man, to respond to this new and larger vision and take up our work of sacrificial service.

NEWS FROM THE FIELD

BROTHER WISE ON THE PITTSBURGH JUBILEE

To the congregations and members of the Brethren church, greeting: You doubtless remember that a visit I made to your churches and in your homes, in the interest of the first Brethren church of Pittsburgh, Pa. You also remember I told you if you would raise them a certain amount, we would save the church. Well, the amount was subscribed, and the greater part paid, which greatly encouraged the struggling church, so they went to work fully determined to see the debt paid. I am glad to report to you that with much self-sacrifice and hard work they have reached the goal. With Rev. H. M. Harley, as commander-in-chief, who has been their pastor for the last five years, and has received a unanimous call for the sixth, with a handsome raise in salary, they went over the top with a good surplus for repairs. On the 23rd of January they burned the mortgage, this date being the thirtieth annniversary of the church. There were but four of the thirteen original organizers present. They were, Mr. and Mrs. D. K. Bole, Sister Belle and Nettie Reynolds; they with Brother Ira C. Wilcox made five of the 27 charter members present. So you see the number of the original members but few. Some have moved away and a number have gone to their reward. Their vacant chairs and a remembrance of their social life among us caused a tinge of sorrow to be mingled with our joy on this occasion. And yet if they may know what is passing here, the smoke of that old mortgage and the sound of our jubilation made heaven just a little sweeter for them. I am sure if all of you who helped make this jubilee possible could have been present at the service on the evening of January 21 at which time Brother A. D. Gnagey preached the anniversary sermon and on the 22nd to have heard the addresses and the musical program, both vocal and instrumental and also the readings, then again on the 23 when the jubilee

reached a climax with speeches by all the charter members, the pastor and others and the burning of the mortgage and a banquet, I say if you could have joined in all those festivities, and have looked into the happy faces of the members of the Pittsburgh church, you would have thanked God you had been given a chance to help make that jubilee possible.

I want here, in behalf of the Pittsburgh church, to express heart-felt gratitude for your contributions which you so cheerfully made just for the asking, without any begging. God bless you all most abundantly. And for myself, I say many, many thanks for the service rendered by many of you in directing me around among your people, and to all with whom we visited, for your prayers and sympathy, which we so much needed. God bless all, even any that may not have been in sympathy with our work at that time. And now for the church, it is located in one of our great cities and any of our ministers traveling east or west I think will find a hearty welcome by both pastor and people, if they could arrange with the pastor to stop over any Lord's day and dispense some of the good news they are scattering around. Well, my article is getting too long so I will close.

Your ever grateful brother in Christ.
HENRY WISE,
Parkersburg, W. Va.

FIELD REPORT OF EVANGELISTIC LEAGUE

The Hamlin Meeting

We were limited for time in the Hamlin meeting, being able to give them only two weeks and three days.

This is a small congregation and has been without a pastor for some time. We found here some of God's own faithful and earnest ones. They have a good Sunday school and a fine crowd of young people who can certainly sing the Gospel. The activities of the

church have been kept up even with no pastor.

The attendance was good and more than filled the church on Sunday nights. The meeting gave the church a boost, helped the members and a goodly number accepted Christ and united with the church. The church here must have a pastor and they are a people who will support the right man.

May we not overlook our smaller churches and their need. There is no use of letting some of our churches die for lack of encouragement and help, and talk new fields that will require much money, strong men and years to develop as far along as those we let die by neglect.

Kansas needs preachers. Ft. Scott and other places with church buildings in this state, if neglected much longer will be no more. With money in the district mission treasury and a fruitful field this need should be met.

First Encounter with "Flu"

I came direct from Kansas to Pittsburgh to assist Brother Harley in a meeting. For the first time this year I am up against the "flu" epidemic. While it is of a milder form than last year, yet the memory of its ravages keep people from coming to public gatherings.

So far the services have been poorly attended and while I question the advisability of continuing, Brother Harley and the members have insisted that we continue at least for two weeks. So we will do the best we can under the circumstances.

In his service,
W. S. BELL.

CENTER CHAPEL, INDIANA.

Complying with the plan of State Conference it was the writer's privilege to spend two weeks in an evangelistic effort with the Brethren at Center Chapel near Roann, Indiana. I was pastor of this little flock in the earlier years of my ministry and it was a real pleasure to meet many of my old friends and break the bread of life to them once more. Brother Jacob Flora's was headquarters for us during the meeting and it was like getting back home, for they are real spiritual parents to me, having helped and encouraged me much in the earlier years of my ministry.

We found things in perfect readiness for a revival, so the meeting started by simply throwing out the net. The interest was intense from the very first service. Never did we preach to larger and more deeply interested audiences. Talk about weather stopping a revival? Not here. They came through snow, blocked roads and zero weather to hear the gospel and you would not be surprised to know that God rewards such loyalty. On Monday before leaving for home we led 14 into the baptismal waters and baptized them into Christ. At the same time and place Brother W. E. Ronk baptized two others, a husband and wife who came out in our meeting, but will place their membership at Roann. These with others by reconsecration and statement gave the body of believers a total of 22 additions. Many were men and heads of families and will mean much to the cause in that community.

We made the common mistake of closing too soon. Another week would have added many more. We are hoping that the ungleaned harvest shall not perish but that it shall be gathered in due season. We have been asked to return for another meeting, which, if the Lord tarries and makes it possible, we shall gladly do. I want to say for Center Chapel that it is unlike so many rural churches in these days in that it is a real live church and is actually doing things. It surely is a beacon light and a mighty power for God in that community.

Brother Kenneth Ronk, the youngest of the four Ronk brothers, is the new pastor, is doing his work and his services are highly appreciated. He was with me during the meeting, leading the song service, assisting in personal work and helping in many ways to make the meeting a success. I found him a true and congenial yoke-fellow indeed. I bespeak for him and his church a prosperous future.

As for myself I enjoyed the days immensely. I shall not soon forget the many kindnesses and the many encouraging words from the Brethren. If all our churches were as appreciative of the ministry as Center Chapel there wouldn't be so many going on strikes or dying with frost-bite.

We are indeed sorry that this must be our final meeting for the year. We love the work and it is dearer to us than any other, but other duties call us despite the calls that come to us for evangelistic services. My prayer is that the Lord will graciously bless his church and his ministry in these later days that many souls shall come to him, "whom to know aright is life eternal."   C. C. GRISSO.
North Liberty, Indiana.

CANTON HAPPENINGS

Since it hath been declared in the columns of this publication not long since that "He that tooteth not his own horn, it shall not be tooted," therefore we are going to "toot" a bit. I know that it has been some time since a blast was heard from this region, and because it might be inferred that we are sleeping or just shirking, therefore this report. We have not made any great stir over here in the eastern part of Ohio, but we hope to be considered still alive.

Ever since the first week in November there has been something about the work of the Canton congregation. Beginning on November 4th, the Ohio State Conference met with the congregation here, and the church enjoyed four days of rich spiritual uplift, with the splendid addresses of the conference sessions and the fellowship of the entertaining brethren with their visiting brethren and friends. As previously planned, Brother W. S. Bell was present on the opening night of the conference to begin a three weeks' campaign

for souls, and most ably did he fill the place to which the congregation had called him. Canton is one of the most difficult points at which to conduct an evangelistic campaign that the writer knows of, and yet despite all hindrances there was a total of eighteen people influenced by the services to begin a closer walk with the Savior of souls. Of this number eleven were received into full membership with the church, and others may yet come with us. These days when one is telling us the church has failed and another is saying it is a glorious success, it is difficult to get men to make an out and out surrender, so some are yet undecided. Brother Bell left with the good wishes of the Canton brethren, as well as a very substantial material proof of their appreciation of his services.

It had been hoped to put some sort of a cantata for the Christmas programme of the Bible school, but delay in receiving the samples of the programmes requested for examination made it impossible to attempt anything so elaborate, so a very modest programme was prepared. The affair was quite successful, due in part to the very fine work of the orchestra which has been doing some consistent practicing and made a most creditable showing on the occasion of the Christmas observance.

In the matter of finances Canton is up to her regular standard, meeting all the calls of the various boards with her full quota, and often going over the amount asked for. The report of the financial secretary of this congregation for the year 1919 showed the largest total offering from this congregation of any year in its history, and an increase in gifts in four years of over $1,600. This is especially commendable it seems to me when we say that the increase in membership has not been so great in that time.

The influenza has affected the work slightly again this year, but not so much as last. We have suffered no loss by death from the disease, and have had few dangerous cases. But of course it is having its influence, though we are assured the worst is past for this season.

With the coming of March 31 comes the close of the pastoral year for this congregation. That date will mark the close of a four-year pastorate for us here, and after due consideration we have decided that it will be best for a change. Accordingly, after having served due notice to the folks here we will assume charge of the work at Uniontown, Pennsylvania. Having served these folks for four years in a previous pastorate we feel much like going home, and are looking forward to a pleasant association in the work of the kingdom. We have had four years of real fellowship with the folks here, and we will leave with the most sincere good wishes for a still larger growth and an increasing sphere of influence for good in the city. It is no cinch to take care of the work of the church at this place, but we pray for the Canton brethren that they be led wisely in their choice of a man, and that the new pastor may have given to him a full measure of the grace which is from on high.

DYOLL BELOTE.

CLAY CITY, INDIANA

This new year opens with good prospects and a firm determination on the part of the good people of the Clay City church to make this Victory Year the best yet in their history. The past year has brought added numbers and encouragement so we can enter on 1920 with added momentum. We are expecting to make all or nearly all of the goals set in the Four Year Program by conference time. Our Sunday school is under the able leadership of Brethren Roush and Coan, who are planning for big things through the Sunday school. Some new equipment has been already added which will greatly aid the work. Last year the school made a gain of over 25 percent on the average attendance. Our Christian Endeavor is a live wire and is doing

commendable work. We expect it to be one of the societies in the Southern Indiana district that will meet the "Four Year Challenge." A class in Christian Endeavor Expert has been organized and meets each week following the prayer service. At the business meeting the other week, it was voted to send the Brethren Evangelist to 100 percent of the homes. This makes the third year that Clay City has been on the Honor Roll, and they consider it a good investment. The church also planned to make some needed repairs on the parsonage in the near future.

Several weeks ago Robert Goshorn came home on a vacation and visit with his parents, and filled our pulpit on Sunday morning. This was his first sermon to his home people and it was highly appreciated by all.

Not long after we sent in our last report, we went over to the Wednesday evening service and found an unusually large crowd assembled in the church auditorium. We did not suspect anything extraordinary, as there is generally a large attendance at our prayer meeting here. We had a fine service. Then we were asked to meet with a committee in the Sunday school room. When we opened the door it looked as though a corner of the grocery department of Brother Burger's store had been moved up. After trying to say thank you, all hands helped to transport the store across the street to the parsonage pantry where we have taken it in charge ever since. I think it was all real nice of them. We were also remembered at Christmas time.

If our editor will permit the space we might add, that the churches of the community have recently formed an interchurch committee to look after the social, moral and recreational life of the community. It proposes to make the influences of the church to be felt in the life of the community. In this day of commercialized and pandering amusements our churches must be awake. The New Year was begun with a Community Day; a speaker from Purdue University, a program and a big community "sing" were the features of the day. Everybody pronounced it a great success. I might add that our Brethren gave good account of themselves on the program. A religious chautauqua is being promoted for the summer.

S. C. HENDERSON.

COLLEGE NEWS

I have been working lately over the names which we have here of former students and Alumni with a view to interesting them in the advancement of the college. An organization has been partially effected, called the Ashland College Alumni Forward Movement, of which Mr. A. H. Lichty, class of 1906, is chairman; Professor J. A. Garber, class of 1907, alumni secretary, and Martin Shively, class of 1890 executive secretary. This is the committee referred to in my report of the meeting of the College Board.

The girls of the school have given loyal aid in cataloging these names and addressing the envelopes. We have now, not counting all the special departments for many of the enrollments in these were very young people, in some cases children, 994 names listed. This takes the record back to 1882, although some names are wholly lost.

The copy for the first communication is now in press and ought to reach former students inside of a few days. When Brother Shively arrives on the ground, he will take charge of this matter.

The following letter from the Law School of Harvard University will illustrate the fact that we are receiving merited recognition, not because of our size, but of the quality of work done:

"I am glad to tell you that Mr. Gongwer, a graduate of Ashland College, will be qualified for admission to this school in regular standing upon merely presenting at the time of registration his diploma of graduation. School will open next fall on Monday, September 27th and registration will take place that day or during the preceding week.—Richard Ames, Dean."

Some of the students from the college and Professor J. A. Garber attended the Pastor's Conference called by the Interchurch World Movement at Columbus last week. They met there some of the other Ohio Brethren pastors. They report a very inspirational meeting.

Friday evening of last week, the college held a social in honor of Brother Beachler and family who are soon to move to Waterloo. They have earned a warm spot in our hearts here and will be greatly missed from the "Hill."

On Wednesday evening, a Fathers' and Sons' supper was held in the dining room of the dormitory, which was well attended and helpful.

There are no cases now of influenza among the college people.

I hope you have read my report of the Board meeting in last issue. There were some other matters transacted which are waiting further action, when they will be reported.

CAMPAIGN NOTES

I am reporting for two churches this week—Mansfield and Rittman. I was at Mansfield on January 25th. Brother Rowsey is the pastor of this flock but because of illness on his part at just that time I was deprived of his presence and help in the canvass of his congregation. I always feel myself seriously handicapped when there is not a pastor with me on the field. Mansfield is not as strong numerically as many of the Ohio churches and naturally could not hit the endowment cause as hard as many other churches have hit it. Nevertheless I had a pleasant stay in this congregation, and found not a few people anxious to have some part in the cause. The result was a little more than $300 when I left and it may yet be raised to $500. Brother Harvey Beal's home was my home; and many preachers in times past have found just what I found, viz., that this is a very cordial, homelike place to stop. I feel very much indebted to Brother and Sister Beal for their kind, and genuine hospitality.

Rittman

Rittman is a very nice, busy little town on the Erie railroad, about 30 miles east of Ashland. In this town we have a small but very earnest, faithful congregation. Dr. J. Allen Miller has served this church for a considerable time as pastor; and during the recent months Brother I. D. Bowman held in this congregation a splendid meeting. So I found these people in good spirits notwith-

standing the fact that they have to worship in a hall and keenly feel the need of a church building. I certainly wish the way might open for these good people to have soon the building they so much want.

But in spite of local desires and local plans Rittman was ready to hear my proposition, but Rittman did more than merely hear—when she heard she acted. I meet some folks who are surely fine listeners, but after the talking is all done and it comes time to get right down to definite things and enlist with cash, or a note or a Liberty Bond they are such poor actors. Rittman acted; and when I announce that Rittman gave $500 for endowment let it be clearly understood that that was very fine. Dr. Miller has a perfect right to feel proud of what his congregation has done. And I am sure it must be a real source of satisfaction to Dr. Miller to see this tangible proof of the interest of his people in the institution to which he has given so much of his life. I was in this charge on February 15th, and the Brenneman home was my stopping place. I was also shown rare kindness in the Sheets home, also in the Wertz home in Wadsworth. In addition to these names I shall also remember the Millers, and Pettits, and the Bakers, and the Holmes and the Krafts. Our Rittman people are a true, loyal people, and I covet for them God's richest blessing.

This brings the mercury now to $140,500. Sickness everywhere has greatly hindered me for the last several weeks. But we are hoping for better things in the near future.

WM. H. BEACHLER,
Campaign Secretary.

BRETHREN MINISTERS AT COLUMBUS

In connection with the Interchurch Pastor's Conference at Columbus the Brethren ministers in attendance held a denominational meeting on Wednesday morning. The following persons were present: J. A. Garber, E. M. Riddle, B. F. Owen, H. M. Oberholtzer, A. L. Lynn, C. E. Beekley, G. W. Kinzie, E. A. Rowsey, J. S. Cook. Others attending the general sessions were J. P. Horlacher and S. E. Christiansen.

As one of the denominational representatives named by the late Ohio Conference J. A. Garber was asked to preside. On motion E. M. Riddle was chosen secretary. Prayer was offered by H. M. Oberholtzer. There followed a free and frank discussion of three questions, proposed by the chairman as an outline: 1. What is the Interchurch World Movement as to origin, aims and methods? 2. What should be the attitude of Brethren to the Movement? 3. To what extent does it afford an opportunity to emphasize the goals of our Four Year Program?

Some of the thoughts brought out in the discussion were as follows: Generally the brethren appeared to be favorably impressed with the aim and spirit of the Movement. All were amazed at the bigness of her task and the littleness of the Church's previous programs as revealed through the findings of the several surveys. All were encouraged with the hope of getting these much needed facts

Our Goal: 200,000; We Can and We Must

200	000
190	000
180	000
170	000
160	000
150	000
140	000
130	000
120	000
110	000
100	000
90	000
80	000
70	000
60	000
50	000
40	000
30	000
20	000
10	000

COLLEGE ENDOWMENT

before our people with the use of charts, graphics and pictures, devised and used by the Movement. All felt that we should share in the teaching and emphasis called for in the program schedule, such as, Stewardship in February and Evangelism in March and April. A similar feeling prevailed relative to the coming financial drive, but universal regret was expressed concerning the disadvantages under which we would have to labor. In the absence of any definite goals announced by our Boards, it was decided that pastors and churches might work out a financial schedule on the basis of our Four Year Program with substantial increase. A twenty-five percent increase was suggested for both Home and Foreign Missions and fifty percent to Benevolences. It was thought that education should be included in the budget also.

The sentiment of the hour was crystalized and expressed definitely in the following resolution: Be it resolved that those present register their approval of the Interchurch World Movement and co-operate in their respective churches so far as consistent with their denominational spirit and program. In addition each one expressed his deep gratitude in being able to participate in this great pastor's conference.

E. M. RIDDLE, Secretary.

Our deeds determine us as much as we determine our deeds.—George Eliot.

The love of display which permeates all classes; the ambition to appear "like other people"—that is, like people in a higher social scale or richer than every rank; these are largely the causes why so many are willing to purchase at a low rate the shoddy imitations of what the wealthier classes alone can command.—Professor Flint.

CORRECT ENGLISH

HOW TO USE IT

A MONTHLY MAGAZINE

$2.50 THE YEAR

Send 10 Cents for Sample Copy

.......TO.......

Correct English Publishing Company

EVANSTON, ILLINOIS

The power of God's Word is Great, and a Brother and a Christian can by means of it lift up and console.—Martin Luther.

SOME FUNDAMENTAL CHRISTIAN DOCTRINES

By Dr. J. M. Tombaugh

A 48 page booklet, bound in beautiful golden and brown flexible cover paper.

In this booklet, Dr. Tombaugh deals in a clear, concise and reverent way with the following fundamental Christian doctrines.

God Our Heavenly Father, Christ Our Savior, Our Risen Lord, The Holy Spirit, Man Made in the Image of God, Sin and Its Consequences, The Grace of God, Repentance, Faith, Obience, Prayer, Love.

It will be found a splendid guide to instruction in classes in Christian fundamentals and a valuable handbook in every home. Write today for a copy at 25 cents post paid or a dozen at 20 cents each to one address.

THE BRETHREN PUBLISHING CO.
Ashland, Ohio.

Mirages of the Great War
(Continued from page 8)

us, when the churches of Christendom having forsaken the faith of their fathers and the sure Word of God, will enter into a gigantic and unholy alliance, with the ostensible purpose of conquering the world for Christ and establishing the Kingdom of God on earth. It is plainly revealed within God's Word that the mightiest Wolf that ever came to devour, will come to us clothed in the garments of the Great Shepherd of the sheep. Let not the warning of Christ be in vain; "There if any man shall say unto you, Lo, here is Christ, or there; believe it not. * * * Behold, I have told you before" (Matt. 24:23, 25). The hour of the great Antagonist of our Lord is at hand. And when he first appears, a "harlot" bearing the holy name of Christ will at the first dictate to him, and then be conquered and destroyed by him. (See Rev. 17:16).

The Anti-Christ will be at the head of a great political confederacy, even a "League of Nations" (Rev. 17:12, 13). It is this position of power that will give him the power to overthrow the domineering powers of the great religious confederation of Christendom. As this religious confederation will come to the zenith of its power after the translation of all the true children of God "to meet the Lord in the air" (I Thess. 4:15-17), it will not be surprising at all to find the Pope of Rome at its head. An apostate church could easily drop into the outstretched arms of the papal enchantress.

While this is going in, the children of Israel will be frantically at work rebuilding their desolate country, and gathering their children again into the old homeland, as is often foretold in the Word of God. Little do they realize the sorrows under the reign of the Anti-Christ that will again be their lot. But it will be in that very day, "even the time of Jacob's trouble," that the Lord of hosts will go forth and "break his (the Gentile) yoke from off thy neck," O Israel, and set thy King upon his throne forevermore. (See Jer. 30:1-11). Then shall the vision spoken "out of the mouth of the Lord" become a glorious reality. Then shall "The mountains bring peace unto the people, and * * *He shall save the children of the needy, and shall break in pieces the oppressor" (Ps. 72:3, 4). "With the breath of his lips

shall he slay the wicked. * * * The wolf also shall dwell with the lamb, and the leopard shall lie down with the kid; and the calf and the young lion and the fatling together; and the little child shall lead them. * * * And the lion shall eat straw like the ox. * * * They shall not hurt nor destroy in all my holy mountain: for the earth shall be full of the knowledge of the Lord, as the waters cover the sea" (Isa. 11:4-9). Then, "The desert shall rejoice, and blossom as a rose" (Isa. 45:11), and "There shall be a handful of corn in the earth upon the top of the mountains; the fruit thereof shall shake like Lebanon" (Ps. 72:16). Then, "The inhabitant shall not say, I am sick" (Isa. 33:24),—"Then the eyes of the blind shall be opened, and the ears of the deaf shall be unstopped. Then shall the lame man leap as an hart, and the tongue of the dumb shall sing" (Isa. 35:5, 6). Then "Out of Zion shall go forth the law, and the word of the Lord from Jerusalem. And he shall judge among the nations, and shall rebuke many people: and they shall beat their swords into plowshares and their spears into pruning hooks: nation shall not lift up sword against nation, neither shall they learn war any more" (Isa. 2:3, 4). Then, "There shall be no more thence an infant of days, nor an old man that hath not filled his days. * * * They shall build houses and inhabit them; and they shall plant vineyards, and eat the fruit of them. They shall not build and another inhabit; they shall not plant and another eat" (Isa. 65:20-22). Then, "Of the increase of his government there shall be no end, upon the throne of David, and upon his kingdom to order it, and to establish it with judgment and with justice from henceforth even forever." Dare any man dream that all this glory will be accomplished through the unregenerate arm of the flesh? Of that, we would despair. But, our sure hope is that "The zeal of the Lord of hosts will perform this" (Isa. 9:7). This is the vision "out of the mouth of the Lord." And in that day, "Men shall be blessed in him: all nations shall call him blessed. Blessed be the Lord God of Israel, who only doeth wondrous things. And blessed be his glorious name forever: and let the whole earth be filled with his glory; Amen, and Amen!" (Psalm 72:17-19).

Volume XLII
Number 9

March 3
1920

The
Brethren
Evangelist

-One·Is·Your·Master·And·All·Ye·Are·Brethren-

She who went forth with her own in strength

Now lies buried in the heart of Africa
But her soul goes marching on.
Will you follow with your prayers and funds?

Published every Wednesday at
Ashland, Ohio. All matter for publication must reach the Editor not
later than Friday noon of the preceding week.

George S. Baer, Editor

The
Brethren
Evangelist

When ordering your paper changed
give old as well as new address.
Subscriptions discontinued at expiration. To avoid missing any numbers renew two weeks in advance.

R. R. Teeter, Business Manager

OFFICIAL ORGAN OF THE BRETHREN CHURCH

Subscription price, $2.00 per year, payable in advance.
Entered at the Post Office at Ashland, Ohio, as second-class matter.
Acceptance for mailing at special rate of postage provided for in section 1103, Act of October 3, 1917, authorized September 9, 1918.
Address all matter for publication to Geo. S. Baer, Editor of the Brethren Evangelist, and all business communications to R. R. Teeter,
Business Manager, Brethren Publishing Company, Ashland, Ohio. Make all checks payable to the Brethren Publishing Company.

TABLE OF CONTENTS

EDITORIAL

Marshalling the Forces for An Intensive Evangelistic Campaign

III. CERTAIN CO-OPERATING FORCES

(The third of a series of articles on the above topic, considered apropos to the present season of intensive evangelism and also the aim of many churches to lead up to an ingathering at Easter-time).

Much attention is being given to the preparation for the campaign, but the importance of the issues at stake warrant the most thorough. Great business enterprises are launched only after the most painstaking preparation. Great harvests are reaped only after long periods of plowing, seed-sowing and cultivating. Great movements are set going with sweeping power only after the most careful planning and the most extensive advertising. Is there any undertaking of man that can compare in importance with the great campaign for the winning of men to Jesus Christ? And shall we not make a preparation for such a holy undertaking that is in keeping with its importance? The most successful revival in history required far more time for preparation than was spent in actually preaching. And it may be that more Pentecostal outpourings of the Holy Spirit and ingatherings of souls would occur today if there were more apostolic preparation made for such divine blessings. This matter is so important that it deserved repeated emphasis.

These suggestions, though included in some measure in previous discussions, are nevertheless sufficiently important to receive separate consideration. However their consideration cannot be as extended as they deserve.

It is quite important that the church to engage in an extensive evangelistic effort should have a vision of the bigness of its field, the need and its responsibility. There is little hope for the future of a church that feels that it has reached the limit of its growth. A church will not reach out that has little or no knowledge of the needs of its own field. A church will never be challenged to greater undertakings until it realizes that it is definitely responsible for the meeting of certain urgent needs. A church without a vision is a church without a prospect. And the marshal of a church of that sort will find that all his talk and effort will have little more effect than would his throwing himself against a stone wall, until he can bring them to accept a larger vision.

Of a certain long-established church a new pastor took charge and was planning to conduct a revival meeting. Everybody was expecting a revival to be held, for it was the customary thing; they had always aimed to have one every year. However no one expected much to result from it because the community was gleaned; everybody was a member of some church, so it was thought. No one saw that there could be much done except gather in a few children from the families of the church. The field was very limited and little more

could be expected than that they should hold their own. It would take a stout heart to face a spirit of that kind and launch a campaign with the confidence of victory. But after a survey of the community, made by teams of volunteer workers, had opened the eyes of the leaders of that church to the possibilities before them and had given them a vision of a work larger than they had ever before dreamed of, the pastor was able to lead them into a most successful meeting. Where there is no vision, there people perish.

One reason why a vision is so important is that it is essential to confidence in the successful outcome of a campaign and a general spirit of confidence is so important that to enter into a campaign without it is like trying to back a team with a loaded wagon up hill. If the congregation has little or no confidence in the successful outcome of the meeting they will not give any worthy co-operation. They will not be eager to tell about the meetings; they will not likely put forth any honest effort to win men to Christ; they can not even pray for the undertaking in an effective way, for prayer without faith will rise no higher than the sound of the voice that utters it. Indeed if the lack of confidence is very general, it will be practically impossible to have any real revival. Jesus Christ himself found that he could do no mighty works in a certain town because of their unbelief. And unbelief is as perfect a non-conductor of the almighty power of God in every village and town of America today as it was in old Nazareth.

The church should also be astir with activity, for it is only on Christian people who are active that God can bring his power to operate. There is little chance of a great revival breaking out among a people that is lukewarm, inactive and hard to move. To him that hath life and activity, to him shall be given; but from him that hath not shall be taken away even the little that he hath. The church that is full of life, eager for activity and awaiting for direction can be used of God in a mighty effort for the saving of souls. One thing that discourages a pastor and that stands out as a bold invitation to failure in a concerted evangelistic effort is a people that never get enthusiastic over anything and are never moved to any great degree of activity. Faith is a mighty asset; it laughs at impossibilities and cries, "It shall be done," but the prayer of faith, if it issue not in works, is dead.

There is yet another condition, which if brought about, will co-operate marvelously for success, that is, a favorable community atmosphere, a revival atmosphere, or spirit of expectancy on the part of the community. A successful evangelistic campaign cannot be conducted with the co-operation of the church people alone, there must needs be the co-operation of the community at large. And the more favorable the atmosphere, the greater the spirit of expectancy on the part of the community, the greater the chances of success. It is a great element to success when the community can be made to think and talk about and to look forward with great expectation to the evangelistic campaign. He who does not take into account this factor cannot hope for as great success as might have been attained if he had given it serious attention.

Creating a community revival atmosphere is a matter that has been greatly emphasized by the most successful evangelists, and advertising is the important means by which it is brought about. There are many different ways of advertising. The newspaper is a most important means. A great deal of complimentary advertising will be gladly done by any local paper if the matter is written up in the form of news. Any editor will gladly publish the picture of the evangelist or pastor. And in addition many churches find it profitable to run paid advertising matter. This kind of newspaper advertising has not been appreciated as much as it ought. There are gains to be had from this kind of advertising that cannot be had in any other way. The handbill is a most useful means of carrying your message to the door of every home. For intensive and thorough advertising, there is perhaps nothing more effective, and many a person has been brought to the church and won to Christ by the wise use of the handbill. Small cards that can be carried in the pocket or treasured in the Bible, bearing striking Scripture Verses and tersely written messages, are effective means of securing more studied attention to religious themes and arousing religious interest. The poster is a widely used and important method of enlisting community interests. Some of the most telling advertising of the business world is done by the use of the poster. The placard in the street car is also a popular and highly valued means of advertising. Whole communities and cities have been stirred with a deep interest in religion and revivals have been brought on by its use. In midsummer of 1919, the 1,500 street cars of St. Louis were placarded with Scripture texts. More than a million passengers rode on those cars daily and had opportunity to read a message that called their attention to the value and destiny of the soul. The city was stirred. Passengers and press commented, and even other cities called attention to the campaign. That is what we mean by creating a community revival spirit. In the midst of such widespread serious mindedness, hearts are much more easily brought to conviction and finally to conversion.

Why should not the church make more widespread use of these and many other legitimate means of preparing the soil for the sower and the seed? And if any question be entertained as to the legitimacy and Scripturalness of such means it might be reassuring to remember Paul's "By all means save some" (1 Cor. 9:22); and Christ's "Go out quickly into the streets and lanes" and "compel them to come in, that my house may be filled" (Luke 14:21-23).

EDITORIAL REVIEW

Brother Trent says "White Gifts Continue Coming." Have yours come yet?

Brother I. D. Bowman gives us another detailed report of his evangelistic itinerancy. He is now engaged in a campaign at Fostoria, Ohio.

Brother Ashman states in a personal communication to the editor that he has been struggling with the "flu," and though it has had him down for a while, he is fast recovering. He says the work is prospering there and the future is bright.

Brother C. R. Koontz is leading his good people forward at St. Luke and Liberty, Virginia. Additions have been made to the membership at both places. At the Trinity church a goodly number were received by baptism.

Wouldn't it be a fine thing if every church, whether on the Evangelist Honor Roll or not to present their new converts with a subscription to The Brethren Evangelist? It would help them to become quickly intelligent and loyal members.

Our correspondent from Nappanee is Brother Harry S. Price, who states that they have been led in a successful revival by their pastor, Brother E. L. Miller. Hindrances were met with, but not even the scarlet fever in the pastor's family was allowed to stop operations.

It requires something more than ordinary, forbidding to thwart "Brother Ed's" purposes. The various departments of the Nappanee work seem to be in splendid condition.

We are grateful for the "flashes" that come to us from Brother Bame concerning his brief evangelistic campaign with Brother Benshoff of Altoona. We are also given a hint as to things about to take place at North Manchester.

Hamlin, Kansas, is to be congratulated for keeping their work going and keeping the brotherhood informed about it even though they are without a pastor. They appreciated greatly Brother Bell's evangelistic services. They are in search of a pastor.

Brother Bell is ever putting forth strenuous efforts in the interest of evangelism, but he found about the most strenuous effort of the year at Pittsburgh. But he found also a loyal people and an energetic pastor.

Brother Gearhart says the returns of the Home Mission offering are very satisfactory but that some churches have not yet sent in their offerings. A hint to the wise is sufficient. He also calls attention to the approaching Foreign Mission offering.

The first one to report the sale of the Tombaugh booklets sent out is Miss Doris Stout of Pleasant Hill, Ohio. We congratulate her on the quick sale and prompt remittance. Miss Stout is an ambitious young school teacher and is planning to come to Ashland to attend summer school.

Brother W. I. Duker, the pastor of the New Paris, Indiana, church, writes us that Brother McInturff of Goshen is soon to help him in a revival meeting and he remarks that the Dutch and the Irish ought to make a good team. We are surely agreed and we shall look for a report of a good meeting.

You will be pleased to know that Brother Boardman has led his good people to take their stand upon the Honor Roll of The Evangelist, as announced in the Business Manager's Corner this week. We welcome these new members to our Evangelist family, and we hope they will come to feel, as many others have written us, that they cannot do without the church paper.

That Muncie, Indiana, is awake and doing no one will doubt after reading Brother J. L. Kimmel's letter in The Evangelist this week. Goshen and New Paris expressed their confidence in the Muncie work and its pastor in a most substantial way. If other Indiana churches do as well, a new church building will soon be assured at this promising mission point.

The report from Waynesboro shows the work at that place to have made a good record during last year. Brother Witter tells of a splendid evangelistic meeting held in his church last fall with Brother Benshoff as the evangelist. It would be hard to put together two men who would make a more congenial team than Brethren Witter and Benshoff.

It is a very interesting letter we have from little Marguerite Gribble this week, though it is quite long. But a great many interesting things happen when one is traveling in Africa and we are sure you will be anxious to read it through to the end. We have another letter written just one month later, but arrived only one day later. It is also very interesting and we shall give it to you as soon as possible.

A great revival has recently been held at South Bend, Indiana, by home forces. Brother Rench has been leading those wide awake people forward in a noble manner. They are about to crowd out the sides of their church building and are beginning to talk new church. On a certain day recently they succeeded in raising over $3,000.00 which paid off the debt on their new lot and left a nice sum to apply on the new building. Soon they are to participate in a union revival and we shall hope to hear good news from it.

Louisville, Ohio, is going forward; they are a forward-looking people and they have a forward-looking pastor, and of course they would go forward. We have noticed that they always try to lift a little more than their share of the load of the general church's interests. This is evidenced by Brother Beachler's splendid success there, and also by every special offering that is lifted. They showed their love for their pastor by presenting him with a purse of $48.75 at their annual New Year's meeting.

FOUR-YEAR PROGRAM PAGE
NOW THEN DO IT.—II Samuel 3:18.
Conducted by Charles A. Bame

A New Secretary—An Introduction

Brethren of the fraternity, let me introduce the new secretary of the Four Year Program Committee. He is Pastor Miles J. Snyder, of Milledgeville, Illinois. You have heard of him. A little late for an introduction? Well, perhaps, since it was announced in a single line on the last page of the Evangelist in another report. Well, that was not intended for an introduction, and therefore, this. Snyder seems above all things to be a secretary. His early training and education were both bent that way and whenever he is placed anywhere they need a secretary, it sems a walk away for Snyder.

Why A New Secretary?

Brother H. L. Goughnour whom I lament losing from our Committee in this VICTORY YEAR, having gone into another form of church that took him out of the active workings of our own denomination, resigned from the Committee last fall. I am sorry that he went. He was one of the most tireless and uncomplaining and fraternal of all the men with whom I ever worked. He is a thinker; originally so. He was not stingy with his gray matter; he did not whine for prominence nor take honors to himself that were his due. It was a distinct loss to the Committee to lose him at this time. But that is another story.

In his place at the Conference of Officers on the Boards of the church at Ashland, New Year's Day, the name of Miles J. Snyder was presented and his election to take the place of Goughnour was unanimous. This I wanted you to know for he is the man who will have a good deal of prominence on this page from now on. By his election he becomes the Director of Goal 16 which asks for the largest delegation ever, at the 1920 Conference. That is this year. What all he shall have to say and do; what fine reward he may work out for the church and state and district that really does the best along this line is his to tell and that on this page.

Snyder is O. K.

Snyder is not a new man. He has held places of prominence and has been proven in our church. He, too, is a fine man to work with, for I did it in an evangelistic meeting and that is a good test. He, also, has gray matter that he uses for the glory of the Master. That's one reason he is so often chosen to prominence in the brotherhood. I anticipate good unstinted service and fine results as we pull toward the final goal of the sixteen. Whatever he asks of you, remember he is doing it for the VICTORY YEAR. Victory Year means victory not defeat. Follow the leader and you'll have a time for rejoicing:

The Outlook

Let me tell you that the reports that last week, were reported to be coming slowly are speeding this way in fine shape now. And I will whisper to you also, that the reports look a lot better to me than any other year. If you had a peep at the "G's" that are on the cards that come to me in every mail, now, you would share my optimism. I knew when we got real seriously at this thing, we would make a good showing and this is the year. If you wish to know how seriously one church is taking the program, let me give you some extracts from a pastoral letter that came to my desk only yesterday. Here it is:

....to make our church a VICTORY CHURCH IN THIS VICTORY YEAR.

"If we do this, 25 percent of our membership will have to be present at prayer meeting every week; 75 percent at the communion once a year; all apportionments will have to be met which this year, are as follows: National Home Mis-

sions, 40c (Thanksgiving); State Home Missions, 45c; Superannuated Ministers, 15c; New Winona Auditorium, 17c. Foreign Missions, Easter, 40c; making a total of $1.57 each.

"The Official Board therefore, has decided to classify the membership. If you happen to live away, in order to keep on the active list you should remit by April first, your share of the overhead assessments amounting to $1.57. Also, if you wish, we wish you would include extra $1.50 for one year's subscription to the Brethren Evangelist for your family; and if possible attend the communion of the church set for Easter evening.

If you live here and have not met the above requirements, you will please see the treasurer of the church and do so, and besides, attend regularly as possible all the services of the church not excluding the prayer meeting as the manner of some is. All who do not thus try to help us to keep the church up to the standard required of us by National Conference, will by their very inaction, place themselves on the inactive list to remain there until they make proper restitution and are again listed in the active field.

It is needless to say that we take this action very reluctantly and after more than a year's deliberation as the only possible method of making ours a real church and your Christianity a real thing to you. It is with a prayer that you will at once see the necessity and conform yourself to this action of the Board unanimously taken, that I thus address you for the Board. Money sent me will be receipted by the Treasurer.   Very sincerely yours,
                                           ———— Secretary.

"A Real Church—A Real Christian"

Did you note that statement in the above? Well, that appeals to me. So does the method. What is the use of having a church that is not a real church? Or a Christianity that is not a real gripping, compelling, dynamic thing? If one's religion does not reach down as deep as $1.57 a head; if it does not think enough of its messenger-paper—to make its weekly message worth $1.50, then, I would not give much for the mansion in heaven that the BUILDER is building. If a church meets the requirements of this program, its religion will indeed, be more real. But, after all, how short do some of the Goals fall of a very real church. 25 percent at prayer meeting! 75 percent at communion once a year; $1500.00 to support a half dozen or more old patriarchial preachers who made our denomination possible by a courage that is scarcely matched by the modern preacher! After all, is it a very real thing? With that question, I leave you for this week. May the God of all grace keep us close to him and a real Christianity.   BAME.

WHAT PROHIBITION IS DOING IN PITTSBURGH

The Pittsburgh Chronicle-Telegraph has just given to the public some remarkable figures as to results of prohibition in that city. In the first six months of 1919 there were 7,463 people in the jail, under aggregate sentence of 103,324 days. During the last six months of 1919, while prohibition was in effect, there were only 3,125 jail inhabitants under penalties of 59,139 days.

In the first six months of 1919 (wet) there were 57 murderers in the jail, the second six months (dry) there were 16. There were 55 cases in the jail hospital during the first six months and only 2 during the second six months. There were 10 deaths in the jail during the first six months and none during the second six months.

About 500 of the cells are empty at the present time.

GENERAL ARTICLES

Cause, Work and Purpose of the Organization of Some Early Congregations of Brethren In Indiana

By J. H. Swihart

By request I gave brief sketches of some early work in Indiana some time ago, having in mind to note next the work at Roann. But after further consideration I concluded that to merely sketch the work without giving any particular cause for it could not interest Evangelist readers very much and there the matter rested.

Now that this thing has been stirred up again, I will endeavor to note a few incidents in my experiences that tended to cause this work to take place in Indiana, as elsewhere. As stated in some former articles, I spent the first years of my ministerial effort in the west, mainly in Illinois and Iowa, and the work was chiefly of an evangelistic character. Thus I frequently came in contact with the two elements of the church—the Western and the Annual Meeting. The Western stood firmly on the principles of the Bible alone as a safe guide in all matters of religion. The Annual Meeting element considered the councils of the Annual Meeting to be the safest criterion. This apparently little difference nevertheless gave occasion for more or less unrest and friction. The German Baptists made efforts at various times through their Annual Meeting Committees to get the Western Brethren to adopt their principles and be reconciled to the decisions of the annual councils, but they never got that end fully accomplished.

Being of a progressive turn of mind myself, it was a very easy matter for me to affiliate most readily with the Western element. This I could do without any sacrifice of Gospel principles, or even that of severing my relationship with either, the claim of the one being the same as that of the other—the Bible as their guide. Hence the difference consisted not in words but in works.

Sent to Conference

Owing to the constant carping and grumbling of a few would-be lovers of the "order" causing much disturbance, especially among young converts, the writer was sent to district conference with queries bearing on the points of difference between the two parties and which signified that we ought to obey God rather than man. But to my utter surprise our plain Gospel questions were evaded and ignored, as if Annual Meeting orders must be regarded as paramount authority. Yet those dear old brethren could not be much blamed, forasmuch as it is impossible to serve two masters, and they had become enslaved to the "order" were afraid to face questions that would contradict their order.

This act, although discouraging in its very nature, so enthused the Western Brethren whose liberties had been held in check by the "order" for years, that they resolved to have the matter brought up again at the next conference, at which time there was a National Annual Meeting Committee in attendance. It was said to be on its way to visit some of the Western churches and set them in order. The committee endeavored to curb the influence of the Western

Brethren's action by asking the bearer of the queries to state those points and his convictions about the matter. Here the moderator rose and faced the speaker and paused as if hesitating as to what to say. The speaker said, "Am I out of order?" "Rather," said the moderator, "we are not wanting to debate the questions, we merely want to know what you brought them up for?" The answer was short and sweet. Here one of the Annual Meeting Committee which consisted of three prominent elders respectively from Ohio, Indiana and Illinois, called attention to the minutes of the Annual Meeting which forbade the agitation of the matter for what purpose he brought these questions up. He began to explain by stating his understanding of the Gospel on Then the cry, "TABLE IT, TABLE IT," could be heard all over the house. At this point a Brother Gibson squarely facing the committee and conference said in accents very easy to be understood, "Dont' be too fast about tabling that, you may as well say to the Mississippi flow up stream and to the Rocky Mountains be ye removed as to say dont' agitate it, you have promised us for fourteen years that we should have liberty in these things and we want to know what about it?" Other brethren made similar speeches and all cries of "Table it" availed nothing. By unanimous agreement the matter was laid over to be considered at next conference, a year hence, when it was taken up and discussed in the spirit of brotherly love for one entire day and was settled in so far as the district was concerned, the Annual Meeting element making the necessary concessions.

Now that seemed to be the most astounding and yet the most shocking thing that took place at the close of these deliberations, was the fact that when some of those good pious old brethren were brought to the test of expressing their minds they confessed that they had known better for many years but for peace sake they had refrained from agitating those things but that now they had come to speak plainly in favor of. And the language they used was as plain as could be uttered.

Readers may imagine what effect this confession under such circumstances could have on brethren who stood so long and so faithful in defence of the pure Word of God as against the laws of man. And what confidence they could hereafter have in the integrity of men who would sacrifice plain Gospel truth for the sake of a standing with a legislative body and to keep peace, or maybe, for fear of losing a seat in the "synagogue."

Is it any wonder that local churches were in those early days formed all over the land in order that lovers of the truth might enjoy unrestrained Gospel liberty? Can the reader gather from a few points in this introductory article any just cause for the formation of some early congregational Brethren churches?

Mulberry, Indiana.   (To be continued)

The Interchurch In Columbus. By Prof. J. A. Garber

It was a great pleasure to share in the Pastor's Conference held recently in Columbus under the auspices of the Interchurch World Movement. Despite the extremely cold weather and widespread influenza about 1600 pastors were in attendance.

The Columbus team was composed of Daniel A. Poling, Guy Inmann, Sherwood Eddy, Robert L. Kelly, E. M. Poteat, and other men of prominence. These official and associate leaders presented clearly and definitely the aims, program, and working methods of the Movement.

Thinking in the terms of laymen who are so much exhorted by ministers these speakers sought to convey the maximum of information with a minimum of exhortation. Much of their speeches was devoted to the presentation of stern facts discovered and assembled through the several surveys. These facts were vividly and impressively presented by means of eloquent words, charts, graphics, and stereopticon pictures. Through these media the delegates were astonished with the two-fold staggering fact: The World's need of Christ after more than nineteen hundred years of Christian History and the unspeakable paltriness of the church's little program. To understand and appreciate this astounding truth one must have the demonstration of proof which the Interchurch can surely supply. Even doubting Thomases will become enthusiastic believers once hearing Dr. Inman present Latin America's urgent needs of the gospel, Dr. Eddy tell of the urgency of the situation in the Far East and then behold in statistical mirror the pitiably small gifts given to the extension of the kingdom. At this point one discovers the chief advantage of being connnected with the Movement. No one church, particularly of the smaller bodies, can assemble and present the needs of the world in relation to Christ. What one smaller church could never do, a number of leagued churches have done in an amazingly short time, and all, large and small, may now enjoy the decided advantages growing out of this united effort of securing the much needed intelligence.

The discovered and assembled facts become at once the basis of a united program of education and action. Education—observe—as to world conditions and the church's responsibility therefore, not theology and the Christian relation thereto. Action—mark you—along the lines of Protestant co-operation, and not church union. Those conducting the missionary enterprise, both administrators and missionaries, have been thinking and working with certain recognition of these principles, but the thought and labor of church leaders and members, too often, has been confined to denominational programs and tenets. For Jesus the field was the world, and the servant is not warranted in limiting the boundaries of the parish fixed by his Master. The Promulgation Group of the Interchurch plans to present the needs of the whole world to the whole church. Through 52 Pastor's conferences, 3,000 county conferences and 100,000 community conferences the message will be presented to the last man of the last church—unless the church "walls" itself in and refuses to permit a point of contact. Then denominational leaders and pastors may outline bolder programs and make larger demands. The glorious outcome has been prophetically stated by John R. Mott: "A practical plan of co-operation, entered into intelligently by the leaders of the united and aggressive forces of Protestantism and adhered to loyally without any compromise or sacrificing a single

vital principle, would make possible the easy, world-wide occupation of pure Christianity of all the fields that now concern us. In fact, I see no reason why five years should pass without our having in position in every dominant place the gospel agents and the gospel agencies on both sides of the sea in sufficient strength and working with sufficient precision to bring the victory well within our day." If those luminous words of an accredited Christian statesman are true, is not the church or the individual who stands in the way of this united program of co-operation assmuing fearful responsibilities?

Once the need is understood and the plan adopted, forces sufficient in number and worthy in character, must be mobilized for its successful execution. These are prayer, men and money, and are, respectively, the leading objectives of the Spiritual Resource, Life Work and Stewardship Departments. One can only wish that every Christian would read, "What If Millions Prayed?" You know the answer— A new Pentecost. And he who thinks that prayer is a minor factor in the Interchurch simply does not know the facts. To win the Great War some nations gave one in twenty, while the church has given about one out of two hundred for the ministry and one out of three thousand for the missionary service. As to money, The church has not learned to give. The Protestant churches are said to have given $209,778,535 in 1918 or an average individual offering of 2 cents 7 mills or day. Contrast these figures, if there is enough courage, with the cost of the World War, $450,000,000,000— $7.41 per second since Christ was born. Don't we need a united financial drive? If Protestant Christians can be induced to give a daily offering of 13 cents 7 mills, we can maintain, it is estimated, the work of 1918 with a margin of one billion dollars for advance work. This is the aim of the nation-wide drive scheduled for April 25th to May 3rd. As Dr. Hollingshead suggests, this asking is based not on what the church has given, would, or could give, but upon what the world needs. "This is the most complete change the church world has ever known. All former standards of giving are going to smash."

One cannot seriously consider the world's needs, the proposed program and announced budget without feeling that "It is a crime to be small in these spacious days."

Ashland, Ohio.

Bible Study Essential to Evangelism. By Miss Vianna Detwiler

We are concerned not about the evangelism that is effervescent or evanescent. We are already too familiar with that sort. But the evangelism promoted by Bible study as well as prayer, is the everlasting kind. It follows then, until Bible reading is taken up in a regular way by any group of believers, they have no right to expect God to send them a revival, even though they pray desperately for it. Works make prayer effectual. Without thus giving the Bible its rightful place, you may be making an apparently successful evangelistic effort, but it will be both MADE and a tremendous effort. But conversions will be the natural outcome, when God's order is followed, which recognizes the divine program, making prayer our first responsibility, and placing our effort in purposeful Bible study.

And what is the purpose with which the Bible is to be studied? The same purpose certainly, for which the Bible itself was written. Where could be the advantage in having any other? What is the purpose of the Bible? Not to give us a fine production of great literature, though there is nothing more beautiful to be found anywhere; not to give us a scientific treatise, though there is nothing unscientific in the Book; nor is it written to give us a code of morals, though it is here we find the highest standard of morality; nor is it even a theological treatise, despite the fact we can get our theology nowhere else,—the purpose of the Bible is siemply to show us the "Way of Salvation," to show how

God's love redeems lost man through Jesus Christ. Or if we want the theme expressed in the words of our Lord, by the pen of John, we have it in his third chapter and sixteenth verse. This theme is not developed in a systematic, outstanding way, but so deeply imbedded in the folds of the story of God's dealing with the human race in general, and one nation in particular, that it calls for diligent searching to unfold the divine plan, historically presented instead of theologically.

After we have been listed with the "Whosoevers," have been shown the Way ourselves, then we in turn bring others into the same Way. Since it is the nature of salvation to reproduce itself in bringing others into the Light of life, is it not an alarming indication when we are not being engaged in actual soul-saving? Someone has said "Our salvation stops when we stop saving others." True or not, we want to see to it, that we never run the risk. Our equipment is all provided for us. We have but to apply ourselves to the Word of God, which is the means; and by prayer, apply the power to the unsaved soul, prayer that is undergirded by the Word.

The ultimate purpose then of all true service being winning souls to Jesus Christ, the purpose of Bible study is also that of soul saving, the evangelistic reading of God's Word, —that study which seeks to follow the silver cord of redemption's story, to discover on every page the great theme of the Book—salvation through Christ. It does not call for a critical study, nor yet attention to details. Rather than a mere knowledge of Scripture, we seek to know the mind of God, to learn his way of looking at things (Ps. 105:7).

In this fascinating quest we also gain a knowledge of men's hearts, as the Scriptures unfold the great doctrine of sin, and with it a knowledge of the great heart of God; revealed in his love, forgiveness, saving faith and the keeping power of Jesus Christ. Personal application to the Scriptures, brings the Holy Spirit in the believer into the fullest contact with his own written Word, giving him his own sword to use; this makes it possible for the personal worker to bring the living Word in vital contact with the sinner "dead in trespasses and sin."

But to be fitted for service, we need to know which Scripture to use on every occasion. Many have Bible knowledge, but are not able to handle it. We want to be gathering and cataloguing this knowledge, so we can use it for ourselves, as also for others. In the case of Christ's temptation not only did he use Scripture but used the one particular verse that suited the nature of the temptation. When Satan told him to turn the stone into bread, he didn't then use "Thou shalt worship the Lord thy God," but another quotation from the same book of Deuteronomy, "Thou shalt not live by bread alone." And it was effectual. Knowledge is most powerful when classified or systematized, therefore the use of the note book for our Bible studying. We should give concern "rightly dividing the Word of Truth," else we need to become ashamed (2 Tim. 2:15).

Since the greatest evangelizing force in the world today is the Bible itself, "one of the greatest hindrances to revival work has been the absence of the living Word in the hands of every child of God. It is not enough to have it in the hands of the leader. Every Christian ought to know his Bible and be able to wield it in such a way as to influence souls for Christ. There is very general need of more Bible study.

The Evangelistic and Bible Study League is a long step in the right direction. But better yet if the pastor could form Bible study groups in every section of his parish, months before the time of the revival. With such a course completed, a broad foundation has been laid for the personal workers' class to meet during the revival, for report and prayer.

Given a working knowledge of the Word coupled with regularity of prayer and the revival will break out before the plans are ready for it. It is refreshing to recall an instance of this when there were signs of a revival, and the minister requested they be held back till the first week of the planned meetings, but they would not. The Spirit would not wait. That is the way it works. Do not take my word for it; try it!

In this, the sole business of the Christian though he is but the instrument and the Holy Spirit the chief agent, the Holy Spirit has only so much of the Sword, to handle as he is given him by the storing of the Word in the Christian's mind. He who does not seek to know God's truth can be little used. The Holy Spirit brings to your remembrance only what you have learned.

Do we see then how much the Master places upon us the importance of learning parts of his Book each day? Wilbur Chapman said, when a man is not winning souls for Christ, it is because of sin in his life. Certainly the sin of omission, neglect of properly studying of the Book that inspires and shows us how to win souls ought not to be neglected. The highest efficiency should be sought for this service, for the human soul is a delicate instrument and should not be handled with untrained hands.

Ashland, Oregon.

Christ As a Soul Winner.   By A. T. Moyer

The work of Christ as a soul winner began in the days of John the Baptist, who foretold his coming and finally pointed him out as he was baptizing in the Jordan. His first success in winning souls is due to the quiet influence of his life. As he was walking along the river, John saw Jesus and said to his disciples, "Behold the Lamb of God." They looked upon him and the very appearance of his life caused them to believe in him and to follow him. There was an influence about his life that impressed them with his sincerity and drew them unto himself. That is a fine way to win men today; if we cannot speak to men and convince them of their sins, we can live a life that will attract them.

Jesus won men by displaying the spirit of humility and acting the part of a servant. He was meek and lowly in heart, merciful and long-suffering, benevolent and self-denying. He was heralded broadcast as the one who went about doing good, healing the sick and ministering to the poor and needy. No one was ever turned away, who came to him seeking help. He gave comfort to the weary and distressed, was a refuge to the sin-sick and a wise counsellor to those who sought his wisdom and guidance. His life of helpfulness was one of the secrets of his influence over men.

Jesus was no respecter of persons. He was not partial, but was interested in bringing every one in touch with the higher things. His invitation was to every one to "ask and it shall be given you, seek and ye shall find, knock and it shall be opened unto you" (Matt. 7:7). His invitation was not to the rich alone, but to the rich and poor alike. Had he been a respector of persons, he could have brought to men no true salvation. He was interested in every man's soul. That interest was paramount to him. He was always keen to sense the needs of every weary soul and eager to lead men of every walk of life into life eternal.

Jesus was the great emancipator. He freed men from their narrowness and prejudice, from their spiritual blindness and from their evil habits and love of sinning. He was able to cause men to see their sins and hate them, and stir up in them a love for the good and draw them to himself. He was wise and able to meet every situation. And if men today would have wisdom to meet every problem and to win men to Christ, they should ask knowledge and wisdom of him who giveth to all men liberally and upbraideth not. For if Jesus were here he would be able to meet this busy world of the twentieth century and answer men's questions of doubts and fears. He would understand all the problems of the present day and would be able to solve every difficulty and answer any question, for he is the same yesterday, today and forever, in wisdom as well as being. He will be our wisdom today in winning souls if we ask him and follow his counsel.

Jesus was the great lover of souls and winner of souls. But he was more than a mere winner of souls, for he was the Savior of souls. He was more than mere man, as was proven by his miracles and his death and resurrection. After his resurrection which was witnessed first by Mary Magdalene and later by all the disciples, he was known to be the Son of God and the true Savior of the world. And he is our Savior today and is still winning souls unto himself.

Philadelphia, Pennsylvania.

When ballast is thrown out, the balloon shoots up. Let us throw away everything that hinders the rise of the soul into wisdom and God.—Selected.

The soft answer and the Christ spirit are illustrated in an American missionary who decided for Christ's sake to live the life of an Indian holy man that he might reach the people with the gospel. He went to a village where the plague raged, and began to help the sick. At first the people treated him with harshness. Then one day they told him that they had been testing him. He stood the test and won a whole village.—Selected.

THE BRETHREN PULPIT

The Failing Church.   By M. M. Hoover

TEXT: "And the gates of Hades shall not prevail against it." MATTHEWS 16:18.

I have been told that the church is made up of grafters, and that ministers are in that profession only for what they can get out of it in a material way. It sounds pretty rough, but it surely is partially true. I know it isn't wholly true. I verily believe that there are some ministers, and maybe not such a few, who, are not preaching God's true word truthfully, but are merely tickling the ears of unregenerates, in the church and out, are being lauded for their greatness, their ability to reach the masses, etc., and are being paid substantial salaries for their efforts. Why not remain in such a profession?

Then, again, we are told that the church has broken down because it was not able to avert a great world war. Perhaps it is not to be questioned that a false philosophical and religious teaching in certain portions had much to do wit . bringing on this great world combat. But the true church has not broken down. It has been hindered and the cause of Christian missions has suffered a severe setback on account of the war, yet firm as a rock still stands the church of Jesus Christ, the blood-washed throng, pierced and bleeding, but not defeated. Many are the souls that were ruthlessly slain, whose bodies are strewn here and there, much persecution was endured but the church was not destroyed. On the contrary the result will be like Saul's persecution at Jerusalem. He did not wipe out God's people, as he sought to do, he only scattered them; and by scattering them caused the church to grow more rapidly. While he himself in the midst of what seemed success was halted by temporary blindness. So in this day the church of Jesus Christ stands as surely on that genuine foundation and cannot be wiped out by war, famine or any device of sinful man or the devil himself. Our local churches may fail, and do fail but the true church of God can never fail. With Jesus Christ as the corner stone no storm can overthrow our castle of faith. If you are a member of Christs' true church, you know no defeat: if you are with him, you are secure.

Then some folks seem to get so discouraged that they are just ready to give up. "We're not getting anywhere, might as well quit," they say. Of course the inference is that by pouting around you're getting somewhere. Yes, you're getting under Elijah's juniper tree and Jonah's gourd. and the first and best thing to do is to back out and get on the main line again. We forget about God's seven thousand stiff-kneed anti-Baalites. But suppose you are the only one left. Is God's promise now. of no avail? One with God is a majority. What he says, he surely will perform. Take him at his word; see if he does not make good. I sometimes think God must have more faith in us than many have in him or he couldn't be so merciful in his forbearance. Again I say. if the church has failed it is because we have failed. Our foundation is unmoved, our promises from God never fail. Trust him.

But in my distress over such a poor excuse of a church as we have today, I always look back and study a church that really did things, the Pentecostal church. And about the first thing I note about this church is that they had wisdom enough to listen when God told them to tarry. Some folks are very impatient; they cannot wait. They are doing the work; God has little part in the program. and they expect the glory. I wonder too, if we have noticed what kind of tarrying they did. "These all with one accord continued steadfastly in prayer. with the women and Mary the mother of Jesus and with his brethren." Little wonder the Holy Spirit had such a fine reception when he came. Jesus told them to wait till the Holy Spirit would come, and then they would have power. And there is no question but that the success of this early church was due to the fact that they were all filled with the Holy Spirit. There is much time spent formulating and discussing a doctrine of the Holy Spirit, and little attention given to the infilling or baptism of the Holy Spirit. I cannot find where the promise of the prophetic word quoted by Peter has been recalled: "I will pour out my Spirit upon all flesh." A spirit-filled church is a powerful church. I am told of a church with about nine hundred members, which has a church expense budget of $16,000, and an additional sum of $35,000 for a building fund in one year, and not a pledge is taken, and no record is kept whether its members pay one cent or ten thousand, that's up to them and their Lord. The suggestion at the beginning of the year was that all members tithe for a year. The spirit-filled church knows no problems which cannot be met. They expect great things of the Lord. What a contract in Peter before Christ's death and Peter after Pentecost. I believe that when once the Holy Spirit controls our churches, our great financial problems, as well as our problems of getting workers, and if not too intricate, very likely choir problems, will be easily solved.

Then, further, I like the message of the early church. Folks who like short sermons ought to listen to St. Peter. He must have known when the psychological moment was to stop. But he got results. God is sure to honor his own Word when it is proclaimed faithfully. "This Jesus, whom you slew, and whom God raised up, is the Christ. In him you have remission of sins." And this is our whole message today. A crucified, glorified God will atone for sin, and nothing else will. Holy, sanctified men of God, preach God's word as it is given us in his holy Book. You are not asked to explain; just preach it and let it be self explanatory. A weak-kneed pulpit surely breeds weak-kneed followers.

Then we learn a lesson in real socialism from the Pentecostal church. They had all things in common. I cannot conceive of any body of human beings like you and me having all things in common as the early church had unless they are filled with the Holy Spirit. I am in for that sort of socialism. We seem to be a long way from having this condition in the church to say nothing of the worldly people. The early disciples were missionaries. Did they wait to see if there was a heavy bank deposit to their credit before they went into "Jerusalem and Judea, and Samaria, and the uttermost parts of the world? Out they went, not with fear and trembling but with boldness and power. They could not keep still. God blessed their efforts. The people said, "they turned the world upside down." How can any believer be at ease with his God unless he is telling others of his saving grace?

In conclusion: The early church is proof that God's plans work if he can find people to work with him and for him. He is always on the winning side; are you always on his side? If our local church is failing it is because we are not doing God's will. As has been said in these columns lately, the work of God waits not on money, but on spirit-filled men and women. Lord, send the old time power, the Pentecostal power, and baptize every one of us, preachers and all. Then preachers will have a message to preach: his flock will rally around him and ask for a real job; the treasurer will rest easy and your church will grow.

Dayton, Ohio.

The press of Great Britain comments on the fact that the wets demand the liberties of the people and at the same time hurl temperance speakers from their platforms and otherwise deny the liberty of free speech and action.

OUR DEVOTIONAL

Jesus Our Example.   By Sannie Klepser

OUR SCRIPTURE

For even hereunto were ye called: because Christ also suffered for us, leaving us an example, that ye should follow his steps (1 Peter 2:21). Take my yoke upon you and learn of me; for I am meek and lowly in heart; and ye shall find rest unto your souls (Matt. 11:29). For I have given you an example that, ye should do as I have done unto you (John 13:15). He that saith he abideth in him ought himself also so to walk, even as he walked (1 John 2:6). A new commandment I give unto you, that ye love one another; as I have loved you, that ye also love one another (John 13: 34). Let this mind be in you, which was also in Christ Jesus (Phil. 2:5). Who gave himself for our sins, that he might deliver us from this present evil world, according to the will of God and our Father (Gal. 1:4).

OUR MEDITATION

It was the manner of the apostles upon all occasions, to impress the duty of imitating Christ. God in all ages has raised up persons furnished with rare endowments, assisted by his Spirit, that we may have worthy patterns to imitate.

Many seem to think, "that to go to Jerusalem and tread literally upon the ground that Christ trod, is following the footsteps of Jesus." We are not to follow him in mere form, but if we surrender our lives to him, we will be led by the spirit into paths of duty, and do those things which are pleasing to him, even as Christ said, "I do always- those things that please him;" "I must do the works of him that sent me."

We cannot place ourselves under so great an influence or such a quickening power as the example of Jesus. There is no individidual so great and so easily comprehended as Christ. His life was that of true service, giving life, joy and peace to those who came in touch with him. He lived a prayer life, teaching us many beautiful lessons, as in time of temptation or trials, we should go to him in prayer, and he will help to bear our burdens.

"For what glory is it, if when ye sin and are buffeted for your faults ye shall take it patiently? but if when ye do well, and suffer for it, ye take it patiently, this is acceptable with God" (1 Peter 2:20). Christ here gives us an example of patience, when he was taken for his trial, and to Calvary with all his suffering, scourging and mockery, he made no resistance but "Taken as a lamb to the slaughter, and like a sheep dumb before his shearers." We should bear our sufferings in silence with heroism of patient endurance. It is our duty to show patience toward our fellowmen.

In his suffering, we have an example of love; he manifested his love when he left his Father and came to live on the earth and among the sinful men; also when he was nailed to the cross to suffer and die for our sins, that we might have eternal life. "For love of us he bled; for love of us he died." We learn from his love that he manifested, to help bear the burdens of others, lead them to Christ and obey the command he has given us. "Love your enemies; pray for them which despitefully use you and persecute you" and "Do good to them that hate you; bless them that curse you."

We have an example of his innocent suffering. It was not for any sin that he had committed, for he was without sin, but he suffered for sins of others.

The story of a Bohemian king is an illustration of the help we may find by following the example of the Lord's sufferings. St. Wenceslaus, the Bohemian king, one winter night, went to his devotions in a remote church, barefooted in the snow and ice. His servant, Redevious, who waited upon his master's piety and endeavored to imitate his affections, began to faint through the violence of the snow and cold, till the king commanded him to follow him, and set his feet in the same footsteps which his feet should mark for him. The servant did so, and either fancied a cure or found one, for he followed his prince, helped forward with shame and zeal to his imitation, and by the forming footsteps in the snow. In the same manner does Jesus, for our way is troublesome, full of objection and danger, and apt to be mistaken. He commands us to mark his footsteps, to tread where his feet have stood. He has trodden down much of the difficulty and made the way easier and fit for our feet.

OUR PRAYER

Dear heavenly Father, we thank thee for the gift of thy dear Son, Jesus Christ our Savior! We thank thee for his beautiful life and for the beautiful example for us to follow.

Dear Lord help us to follow more closely in thy blessed footsteps.

We thank thee, that Jesus has taught us so plainly how to live our lives acceptably to thee. Wilt thou give us strength to love our enemies, and to pray for them which persecute and despitefully use us. May we live such lives that will be pleasing to the and an inspiration to thos about us.

In Jesus name we ask it. Amen.

Martinsburg, Pennsylvania.

+++

ARE YOU SAVING ANY MONEY?
By Dr. E. M. Cobb, Dayton, Ohio

Here is a queer situation. In the last five years people have been taught to save as never before—and at the same time others have spent all they have made, and have **NOT ONE THING LAID UP**. That's bad management.

There are all sorts of investments put up to you and so many are not worthy of consideration. Millions are lost in bad corporations and irreputable companies.

If you knew where you could spend 10 percent of your earnings in a **SAFE INVESTMENT** which would bring annual returns much greater than your investment, and at the same time pile up an unearned increment, perfectly adequate with which to secure you a very fine, palatial residence for old age and an endowment fund for your continual use, **WOULD YOU CONSIDER IT**?

We are putting **THE TWIN GOLD MINES** on the market again this year, and offering you preferred stock on a common stock basis. Now listen—dont' turn this down before you read the rest. We've **STRUCK GOLD NOW**. We know it is there. It is no questionable venture any more. We know there is gold there and lots of it. All we need is men and money to develop the mines. These we must have, and have them now. We cannot hold the mines as ours unless we occupy and develop them.

Later you will hear more about our proposition, but let us suggest that you take out a fifty-dollar share if you can; if not, take at least a five dollar share, and get a gold bond certificate. This is the least share that warrants a certificate, but you can take a dollar share in the most common stock, and while it will not secure a certificate, yet it will be a mighty saving that will some day make your heart glad.

WE MUST HAVE YOUR REMITTANCE BY EASTER

+++

Wisdom must be searched for; it must be achieved. We do not drift into heaven any more than we slide uphill. Spiritual improvement means hard work. Are we ready for it?—Selected.

The Daily Chronicle of London says that prohibition in the United States is "perhaps the most wonderful fact in the wonderful times in which we live."

Send
WHITE GIFT
OFFERINGS to

THE SUNDAY SCHOOL

ALBERT TRENT
General Secretary-Treasurer
Johnstown, Pennsylvania

Of Special Interest and Importance to All Sunday Schools in the Brotherhood

This Announcement vitally concerns all Brethren Sunday schools throughout the brotherhood. Elsewhere you will find a reason for the slight advance in the price of our Quarterlies and Lesson Helps. It IS a reason, a real REASON. Read what the Business Manager has to say about it. We would MUCH prefer to publish these Lesson Helps and Papers at the old price, but that would be UTTERLY IMPOSSIBLE, as most of our readers know.

We trust that there may be no falling off in your order by reason of this bit of additional cost in the making. If YOU understood as WE understand you would at once give this matter serious consideration,—it IS serious.

And while we are asking a little more for our output, we are happy in the thought that we are giving something BETTER than ever before, better in quality, which we hope will be appreciated by our customers.

We feel sure that you will agree with us, after you have examined and used our Quarterlies for the second quarter of 1920, that they are the BEST, in the quality of matter and its arrangement, we have ever issued. Special attention is given to the adaptation of the Improved Uniform Lessons to all the grades using them.

Our Motto continues to be, "Better than Ever."

Fraternally,

A. D. Gnagey, Editor Sunday School Literature

PAYING THE PRICE

About fourteen years ago the Business Manager prepared a lecture on the subject, "Paying the Price." He has delivered this lecture before lyceum and chautauqua audiences in one-fourth of the states of the Union, and when he began using it he never expected to live to see the day when the "price of all things" would reach the heights they have now reached.

Had we known of the great changes that were coming in the commercial world at the time we were called into this position four and one-half years ago, we would have been afraid to undertake the task. And even now as we look back over the past and contemplate the changes that have come with the ever increasing cost of all things, we are actually amazed that we have survived the years and we really wonder how it was done.

When we made the first advance in the prices of our publications three years ago we had strong hopes that in a very few years conditions would get back to a normal stage and that these prices could

go back to where they were before the war, but now all hopes for such conditions have fled.

The labor costs have been going up, up, UP constantly and the cost of material has constantly advanced until today, to be really secure we should receive for all publications double the amount we received four years ago. We can get no quotations on prices for paper stock for future delivery at all. Recently we placed an order for forty thousand pounds of paper for our regular publications to be delivered in May, and we have to simply pay the price that prevails at time of delivery, with no idea of what that will be. No paper mill in the country will accept an order on any other terms.

Dire Necessity

NECESSITY compels us to advance the price of our Sunday school publications. If we did not we could not publish them at all. The moment an institution begins sending out its products at a price that is less than the cost that institution is headed for the ROCKS. Practically all price lists we receive from Paper Houses and Publishers are marked, "Prices subject to change without notice." It is the only way they can avoid disaster. We frequently order goods at one price and when the invoice comes another price has been charged us. We have found that most publishers have advanced their prices thirty to thirty-three percent in recent months; but we are going to try to live with an advance of practically sixteen percent. However we cannot survive with this small advance unless our customers stand by us and purchase about the same quantity of supplies that they have been doing. Otherwise we will be left with quantities of goods, that have cost us more than ever, still on our hands.

Just remember that when you are conserving the interests of The Brethren Publishing Company, you are conserving the interests of yourself, for the Company is just as much your property as it is the property of any man living. It is a church institution and must live or die with the church. Please look at it from this viewpoint when you make out your order for Sunday school literature.

We live to serve, and we want to serve you in the best way possible. You can help us in this by promptly filling out your order blank and by including CASH with the order whenever possible. We will do our VERY BEST to serve you promptly,

Very sincerely,

R. R. TEETER, Business Manager.

J. A. Garber
PRESIDENT

Our Young People at Work

G. C. Carpenter
SECRETARY

Church Loyalty

The Special Christian Endeavor Theme for March

By E. P. GATES, General Secretary of the United Society of Christian Endeavor

(Selected from the Christian Endeavor World by Prof. J. A. GARBER. It is an exceptionally fine statement on the subject and deserves a wide reading.)

Church loyalty is the monthly service theme selected by the trustees of the United Society of Christian Endeavor for emphasis during March. Of course, Christian Endeavor stands for loyalty to the church every month of the year, but this March campaign gives opportunity to make perfectly clear that no society is truly Christian Endeavor which is not giving hearty support to its own pastor and church.

Because this is leap year and the extra day falls on Sunday, February 29, it will be well to start the campaign on that day.

The following definite goals are within the reach of every society. They should be presented by the president at the business or executive meeting, and divided among the committees so that every member will feel responsible for the success of the campaign.

1. Church Attendance

a. A Goal of one hundred percent of the Christian Endeavor membership attending every church service during March and the following months.

b. An organized campaign to increase the attendance of those not Endeavorers.

c. A brief season of silent prayer for the pastor and the services of the church, at the close of each Christian Endeavor meeting.

2. Work for the Church

At least one item of service for the church undertaken by each Christian Endeavor committee during the month.

3. Personal Soul-Winning

A definite effort to win young people for Christ. Prayer groups may be formed, whose members will pray each day for certain young people, meeting for prayer together once a week just before the regular Christian Endeavor service. Special work should be done with associate members. Endeavorers who are Sunday school teachers should speak to each scholar individually about accepting Christ. Talk over your plans very fully with your pastor, so that you may do only those things which fit in with his programme.

4. A Sunrise Prayer Meeting on Easter Sunday, April 4

Make this a service of testimony. The regular Christian Endeavor topic may be used, or those present may speak on "Why I am glad I am a Christian." Let your pastor or some older friend of the society close the service with an appeal to accept Christ as a personal Savior. Where there are two or more societies in a community, a union service may be held.

5. Report of Work Done

For the inspiration of other societies, send in a report of work done during the campaign. This report should list the plans used to promote church attendance, the special work undertaken to help the church and pastor, and the general results of the campaign. Letters should be addressed to General Secretary E. P. Gates, 41 Mt. Vernon Street, Boston, Massachusetts. (Brethren societies should also send reports to Prof. Garber for publication in The Evangelist.—Editor.

Ways of Promoting Church Attendance

First of all, of course, every member of the society must be regular in attendance at the church services. Christian Endeavorers cannot urge others to go to church unless they are themselves giving the church the same hearty support. One good plan is to have the Endeavorers enter the church auditorium in a body at the beginning of the service and occupy a special section of front seats.

To promote the attendance of those not Endeavorers, divide the society into teams of two members each, and assign one or more pews to each team. The duty of the teams will be to fill their pews at the morning and evening preaching services.

Try a telephonic campaign. Give to each member of the society the names of ten persons to be called on the telephone Saturday evening and reminded of the services the following day.

Written or printed invitations addressed by name to those staying at local hotels over Sunday will bring many strangers to the church services. Most hotels will be willing to let a representative of the society copy the names from the hotel register for the purpose of addressing such invitations.

Where there are several societies in a community, they may join in an advertisement in the local paper. The announcement should contain an invitation to come to church, followed by the names of the churches and the hours of service.

In one Illinois town the citizens awoke one Sunday morning to find on every doorknob in the village a cardboard hanger announcing the special church services for the day. Members of the Christian Endeavor society had put the hangers in place late the night before. As a result the church was crowded, both morning and evening.

The publicity committee of the society may help in the campaign by seeing that regular notices of the church services are given to the local papers, and by displaying attractive poster and bulletin-board announcements.

The distribution of ticket invitations to special services, a house-to-house canvass conducted by members of the society, and the securing of signatures to cards pledging regular attendance, are all plans that have been used successfully.

Some Plans for Helping Your Church

1. Ask your pastor what he wants done, and then do it.

2. Provide stenographic or clerical service for your pastor. Many members of your society will be glad to give an evening or two a month to addressing envelopes, writing letters, typing sermons, or similar work.

3. Assign a section of the church to each member of the social committee, with instructions that every visitor is to be given a cordial welcome immediately after the service.

4. One Christian Endeavorer, who worked in the public library, collected books and magazine articles desired by her pastor for a special series of sermons.

5. Start a fund for needed equipment for the church or Sunday school, such as Bibles, hymn books, blackboards, a piano, maps, a stereopticon, a communion table etc.

6. One society arranged with members of the church who possessed automobiles to place a car at the disposal of the minister for certain hours each day to be used in making his pastoral calls. Another spaded the pastor's garden, while another assumed responsibility for taking care of his furnace.

7. Devote Sunday afternoons to visits to sick or aged members of the church who are unable to attend the meetings. Conduct song and devotional services, if desired. Send each a lily at Easter. Remember them frequently with books, magazines, flowers and fruit. Secure automobiles to bring them to church on special days.

8. Assume responsibility for the care of the church lawn. Plant flowers. See that the grass is cut. Keep the lawn free from papers and leaves. In one church the Christian Endeavorers did the work of the janitor during his absence because of illness; the boys fired the furnace and shovelled the snow; the girls swept the floor and dusted the chairs.

9. Co-operate with other organizations of the church. Help in a canvass for Sunday school scholars. Entertain the boys' club at a social. Assist Sunday school teachers by following up absentee scholars. Repair the books in the Sunday school library.

10. Maintain a church kindergarten to take care of the children while their parents are in church. Provide flowers for the pulpit. Remember the birthdays of the pastor and other church members.

SEND ALL MONEY FOR
General Home, Kentucky and
Foreign Missions to

MISSIONS

WILLIAM A. GEARHART
General Missionary Secretary
906 Conover Bldg., Dayton, O.

Our Foreign Missionary Appeal.   By J. Allen Miller.

I appreciate most highly the opportunity afforded me by the Editor of the Evangelist to contribute this article. Apart from my daily task in the schoolroom which I count my appointed life-work I cherish no one interest committed to the church more highly than that of Foreign Missions. To be sure every task committed to the church is of supreme worth in its respective sphere. For that very reason no one can say of any work committed to his church by the Lord of the Church this or that is more important. But in the present contribution I shall hold myself to the appeal of the Foreign Field.

The Lord's Command. Here we must always begin. Here is the beginning and the end of the matter. Let us hear his words again. Jesus said: "All authority hath been given unto me in heaven and on earth. Go ye therefore, and make disciples of all the nations, baptizing them into the name of the Father, and of the son, and of the Holy Spirit: teaching them to observe all things whatsoever I commanded you: and lo, I am with you always, even unto the end of the world." When Jesus Christ commands, the true disciple obeys. What he says we should do, we believe we must do. There can be no quibble on the meaning of the words so far as telling us what to do is implied in this Great Commission. The break in our individual life with our Lord comes when we refuse to listen to his commands. The weakness of a church as well as the weakness of the individuals of a church is to be found in the disregard for the Lord's commands. His COMMAND permits of no substitution, alteration or refusal to be obeyed. When He says to HIS Church GO INTO ALL THE WORLD AND MAKE DISCIPLES it remains only for us to go and do what he assigns to us. No one can stress this too strongly or too often. I believe in the whole Gospel for the whole world and I believe our Lord laid it upon us to carry this Gospel to all. As Brethren I covet for us a worthwhile part in World-Evangelization. Jesus Commands. We must obey.

An Unalterable Must. In Mark 13:10 we have what I am fond of calling one of God's unalterable musts. In the 3rd chapter of John we have the "must" relating to the new birth. To enter the kingdom one must be born again. In 2 Cor. 5:10 we have another, the "must" of the manifestation of the believer before the Judgment-Seat of Christ. Mark 13:10 says: "And the Gospel must first be preached unto all the nations." I am perfectly fair with this passage when I insist that the key-word in it is the "MUST" of the original text. No stronger word could be found in all the Greek language to express this idea than the one chosen. Its meaning is perfectly clear and its obligation is inescapable. It is the unalterable "Must" in the plan of God that permits of no cavil or evasion. The Gospel must be preached unto all nations. This makes clear the authority of Christ's command. To be sure it is the GOSPEL that MUST be PREACHED. No more than we can evade duty can we avoid the message. It is the Gospel and no substitute that is to be preached. It is the Gospel that is the power of God unto salvation to those who believe. The Gospel must be preached.

South America. Argentina has become a name that is quite familiar to the greater part of Brethren people. Yet we perhaps know all too little about our particular Mission Field. To put it in a word—Rio Cuarto, Argentina is the center of our missionary endeavors. The Foreign Board has long cherished the hope that we might claim and occupy the territory contiguous to this strategic city, as a center. This would embrace many smaller towns and villages and many rural agricultural communities. Also it would embrace perhaps a million souls. Until the present but few workers have been in this territory except ourselves. Let this be clearly understood: To claim a field and to hold it WE MUST OCCUPY IT. That means that we must have workers on the field in sufficient numbers to give the people the Gospel. It means further that we must have the necessary accompanying missionary enterprises, such as schools, literature, leaders of community interests, to give the very best pos-

sible results to the people to whom we minister. Unfortunately we have been too slow to occupy what I have loved to call our field. ALREADY OUR TERRITORY HAS BEEN ASSIGNED TO OTHERS.

Africa. As for Africa let it be said once for all that the field is large and the task is all but staggering. But even here as in Argentina we must face the actual facts. When once our workers reach their fields and settle themselves to the immediate task before them we shall awake to the fact, if we have not already done so, that SO FEW for so GIGANTIC A TASK can not long be tolerated. And in Africa as in South America we must even NOW look to a large increase of workers and means to carry forward the undertaking. By the grace of God we hope in the name of the Brethren Church to help stem the tide of onsweeping Mohammedanism from the North. But we can not wait too long or else we shall lose our opportunity. Our objective in Africa is in wholly unoccupied territory. We shall doubtless be the first on this field. To be the first is fine. To hold the field because we have won it for Christ will even bring a deeper sense of gratitude and joy. There is a lonely grave at Ikelemba French Equatorial Africa calling to us. See out elsewhere. How can we as a Church fail to hear Sister Rollier's deathless appeal! It is the appeal of the Christ for Africa!

The Pressing Need. In conclusion I wish to say three things in the very strongest possible terms. As you read, pray in deepest sincerity and strongest faith. Only FAITH and PRAYER can avail here and in the matters that immediately press upon us for answer.

The first of these things is the matter of sufficient funds to enable your Board (never forget, WE ARE YOUR BOARD) to formulate and execute an adequate program of Missionary enterprise for the Church we represent. It is the problem of MONEY. One thing more should be said on the matter of Money, and that is, OUR PEOPLE HAVE THE MONEY. May God give us a great offering on Easter for this work. Pray to that end. But what is more also work for that end.

The second matter of supreme importance is trained workers for the fields and the work committed to us. The time is past when untrained workers can be sent out. Men and women who are really highly trained and efficient must be sent. This call goes to all our people and to all our Churches,—LOOK OUT men and women who may immediately give themselves to training for this work. I do not wish to overdraw the picture, the actual conditions that face us in our Foreign Missionary Work. I believe I know the facts and I know the only conclusions that one can draw.

Let me state it plainly and may God give us the faith to accept the challenge. Here is the call to the life of Church to give itself:

Within the next five years we must send enough men and women to these two fields to treble the number. That means that we must send WITHIN FIVE YEARS NO FEWER THAN THIRTY OR THIRTY-FIVE ADDITIONAL WORKERS.

Young men and women, hear me, if you wish to be in this number you must begin now to prepare yourself.

And what is just said is also the call of the Fields to the Church to give her MONEY. We can support fifty Foreign Missionaries.

The third point to which I wish to call attention here is this: The Board as the Servant of the Church can move no more rapidly than the Church makes possible by the gift and offerings of life and money. The Board is anxious to outline a big program. But there must be not only FAITH but the tangible evidence of CO-OPERATION on the part of the whole Brotherhood.

MISSIONARY NOTES

We have been very well pleased with the HOME MISSION offerings thus far and wish to thank every member of our brotherhood who had a part in it. There are some churches that have not sent me their Thanksgiving offerings. We wish that they would do so as soon as possible so we can report that we have reached Goal No. 10. Those who have not paid their "Home Guard" dues should also make a special effort to send it in as soon as is convenient.

Easter is coming and we trust every member from the least to the greatest, will be exceedingly anxious to do their very best to raise the money, necessary to support our missionaries in the foreign field for another year. While we are celebrating his resurrection from the grave, let us remember that he told his disciples to carry the Gospel to the whole world and that he would be with them to the end. Surely every brother and sister will want to have a part in carrying out this great command of our Savior. Now is the time to save your money for that purpose.

Brother Bauman's church in Long Beach, California is surely remembering the Home and Foreign Mission work in a very large way. His members are giving liberally and he tells me he has bright prospects for several splendid recruits to the roll of members who are giving their lives to the work of foreign missions. Many of our young people should be encouraged to prepare for this great work for their Master.

WILLIAM A. GEARHART,
General Missionary Secretary.

NEWS FROM THE FIELD

EVANGELISTIC NEWS

After closing our meeting at a high spiritual tide at Fostoria, Ohio, January 23, we reluctantly left when we should have stayed another week and began a meeting at Buckeye City, Ohio, Sunday, the 25th.

We soon discovered it was not the Lord's

time to have an ingathering here. For the two weeks we were there the ice was so bad that the people could hardly get around. The country people were unable to attend at all. Notwithstanding we had good crowds the first week as the town people almost filled the house. In addition to the ice the "flu"

broke out the first week of the meeting and it soon paralyzed business, shut up the public schools and made it harder and harder for our meeting. In spite of these conditions our people tried to stand by the meetings until half of our people were kept away by sickness. The second week the church members of the town did pretty well against tremendous odds, but the unsaved were scarce at the meeting.

We saw the second week as the "flu" got worse and worse and the ice no better and family after family stricken down, that it was impossible to have a successful meeting. After talking it over with Brother Owen and some of the leading members we decided to close on Friday night of the second week. Brother Owen put the matter to the people as we thought best but not one would vote to close. Then when he asked how many wanted me to stay till Sunday night almost the entire congregation arose to their feet. Hence we closed with a house three-fourths filled in spite of the raging disease. We closed with a good feeling and with two confessions the last night of the meeting. We found here many splendid people but the spiritual tide was low as they have had no regular pastor for some time. We desired to do a good work for them but the Lord ruled otherwise. I feel very sure however that the benefit spiritually was great, and the meeting was surely a good preparation for the future meeting that I promised to hold them when conditions should become more favorable.

They dealt so kindly with me and fair and paid me so well that I could not help but promise them the most suitable date possible for them in the future. I made a date with them and if the Lord wills, I hope to give them a three weeks' meeting, and I believe the Lord will give the increase.

I feel it would not be right for me not to mention the fact that dear Brother Owen, the big hearted Welshman, was with me four nights the first week on his return from Glenford, Ohio and gave us practical service in song and other help in every way possible. He also came back the second week and gave me three nights and was coming back on Monday, and stay until the end of the meeting. This would have been a great help to me, as he lived here for more than a year and has the universal good will of these people.

I was indeed sorry for these good people, but as they knew that the loss to me was greater financially than their loss, they cheerfully made up the finances for two weeks and two days, so that my loss was not more than $25.00 on account of the "flu."

I was all at sea as to what I could do next, so early Monday morning I went to Columbus and there I found Brother Owen. He had gone to Glenford and the "flu" had closed everything there, hence he and I met again at Brother Christiansen's. From Columbus I phoned Brother Oberholtzer, and he said that he had gone over to Fostoria and they decided that it was best to go right on with the meeting and he was getting out the printed matter to begin Sunday, February 15. So I have been resting at Brother Christiansen's and I am certainly pleased with the favorable reports of the Columbus work. They unanimously called Brother Christiansen for another year and agreed to stand by him and help push the work. For this I am glad. They ought to pay him $800 more salary but as they are now giving $100 more than they did last year, they feel it is impossible to do

more. They are certainly standing nobly by their pastor and I am praying that the church here will soon become sufficiently strong to be able to pay their pastor a living salary.

While resting I ran down to Dayton and found our dear Brother Cobb hard at work. He seems to be doing a very, very practical work. I took supper in the basement of the church with the single girls. I was the only boy in the crowd. It was their monthly meeting. After eating a splendid sauerkraut supper, I gave them a short talk and then went up into Brother Cobb's Bible class. I found Brother Cobb has not learned how to do away with the supernatural of the Bible, neither has he become ignorant to deny the second pre-millennial coming of Christ, as many have today who are "wise about that which is written." But he gives the plain literature in teaching of the word, wherever it can be so construed just as Christ, the apostles and prophets taught. He is indeed a splendid Bible teacher.

I went home with dear Brother Teeter and he gave me a place to rest my weary head. We had a splendid talk and I found him thoroughly orthodox and greatly interested in the Lord's work and gives most of his time in church work.

After a splendid night's rest and a good breakfast, he took me to the street car by which I went to see my dear beloved Brother G. W. Kinzie at West Alexandria, Ohio. I spent a day and a night with him and his good family. I have spent many sweet and pleasant hours with him in the past. I have worked with him in at least five revival meetings and I always found him as true as steel. If you have any wirepulling, scheming, underhanded work to do, stay as far away from Kinzie as possible for he will expose you sure, because he hates dishonesty as a true Christian hates the devil.

The twenty-four hour's stay was far too short but duty called me back to Columbus to dear Brother Christiansen's where I am writing this letter and also preparing for a hard four weeks' pull at Fostoria.

Pardon this little admonition. I feel very sure we could double our power as a Brethren church in less than six months if our ministry would become more and more a ministry of prayer and consecration until, we would preach and live the highest possible spiritual life. This I find is THE great need everywhere. Pray for us at Fostoria.

ISAAC D. BOWMAN.

TRAVEL FLASHES AGAIN

It was indeed a flying trip I took to Altoona, to help Brother Benshoff in a short meeting. We planned to put it across as swift as possible but not in the way we had to do it. I was with him just 13 days. We opened with a fine prospect. The response of the people was fine from the start. They said nice things about the preacher and that always makes him better—gives him confidence. But— Oh, when shall we get rid of the "flu" and the smallpox and measles and all the things that hinder progress—oh, yes, including snow two feet deep.

Well, of all the good dinners and suppers, one each every day, and of all the kindnesses,

we can not speak; save to say, that we had a good time in spite of the fact that "flu" came the first night and robbed us of choir people who never got back; then came snow two feet deep, piled high as your head on the sides of the street. We had a good meeting and Benshoff will tell the rest save that Benshoff will not say that he has a good place in the hearts of his people and that he sticks mighty close to his Book and is doing a fine work in a place made big by such pastors as Gnagey and Knepper.

North Manchester is going on in her usual way. We are getting some extensive improvements in the basement of our church, a new piano, a new steel ceiling, new primary rooms. We are planning another campaign, a pre-Easter week and hope to have good things to report by that time. I have the promise of Dr. Fitzwater and will have other help and we want to make it a real Bible Conference revival. More then.

CHARLES A. BAME.

WAYNESBORO

Evangelistic readers have had no report from the Waynesboro work for some time but there are a number of items of interest worth reporting. The splendid meeting conducted for use by Brother W. C. Benshoff has not yet been told in these columns. Brother Benshoff spent three weeks with us in November. His spirit filled messages and genial manner made every service both inspiring and enjoyable. Besides the great spiritual uplift to the membership the meeting resulted in eight additions to the church by baptism. A hearty welcome will be extended to Brother Benshoff at any time he can come again.

The close of 1919 found the financial condition of the church in a gratifying condition. All bills for the year paid, all financial goals met and a nice little balance to start the new year. This is the more gratifying when it is remembered that during the year more than $1,000 of improvements were put into the church. A new furnace has been supplied by the liberality of one of the brethren, another had furnished druggets and gas stoves for the Sunday school rooms in the basement, others had contributed of their labor in making partition for these class rooms, and in giving the walls a coat of plastico, and the W. M. S. had raised the money to purchase a new carpet for the church which very greatly adds to the inviting appearance of our church home. New curtains were placed back of the pulpit and several other improvements were made. During the year a total of $3,117.70 passed through the treasuries of the church and auxiliaries and individual gifts that did not pass through the treasuries would raise the amount contributed for the work during the year to more than $3,500. Of this amount the W. M. S raised $671.46, the Sunday school $310.79 and the C. E. $31.28.

Just now the work of the church is hindered by the great amount of sickness in the community. There was one confession and baptism in January. Commendable progress is being made in the work of the Four Year Program and we hope to report some new goals won in the near future. M. A. WITTER.

NAPPANEE NEWS

We have again closed a successful revival in our church. By a successful revival I do not mean only from the point of additions to the church, but also in the sowing of seed that will bear its fruit in future time. Many who had been somewhat slack in their attendance upon the services of God's house were brought back to their places, and those who were regular were unanimous in their declarations as to blessings received from the good old-fashioned Gospel sermons as preached by "Brother Ed." Surely those sermons will stay with us and help us all to live better lives among the children of men.

We found out that Brother Miller is a plain Gospel preacher, and what is the old world in need of today more than the good old Gospel as we have just had the privilege of hearing from our brother. Indeed they were three weeks of great privilege.

Brother Miller was handicapped in the meetings in that there were seven churches in this town of 2,900 population, all holding meetings at the same time. Then scarlet fever broke out in his own family which necessitated quarantine and this put the brother at a disadvantage, but Brother and Sister Cosper cared for him until the quarantine was lifted and he went on. But to add to the hindrances the "flu" played a return engagement in this locality and we had to close the meetings one week earlier than expected. Among those coming with us were young and old as well as the middle aged. One brother and sisters whose hairs have been whitened by the frosts of many winters will cast an influence that will be felt for good in the community. Two fine young married couples also will add strength to our work. And the others are all of the type that can be looked to for greater things in the church of the future. We were all blessed and made happy to see so many coming to the Lord, and we expect them to help us hold up the banner of the cross until the Master comes again.

Brother and Sister B. H. Flora were visiting with us one week recently and Brother Flora preached for us one Thursday evening. He took as his subject, "The Shadow of the Cross," and it surely brought back memories of days gone by when Brother Flora served as pastor of this charge. We were glad to see them and welcome them back at any time.

Our Sunday school is going along very nicely indeed. Until the "flu" hit us we were averaging about three hundred in attendance, and as soon as we get over the sickness period we feel that three hundred will be left far behind. Christmas services were held and they were well attended. Our White Gift offering as reported by the Mission secretary was a good one, the best we have noticed up to date. Other features too numerous to mention have aided in keeping up the interest, even though we would not use anything that would lower the spiritual tone of our Sunday school.

The W. M. S. is on the job all the time. Their latest stunt was the purchase of a parsonage. This home for the pastor will soon be available, and then no more will the pastor of this church be at the mercy of landlords and their dispossess orders. Surely the ladies are to be congratulated for this piece of good work. It denotes a sort of courage for them to take off such a big bite, but they are of tht kind of stuff that will get away with it. But the men will have their part in it just to show the ladies that they are in for all good things for the Nappanee church.

Our latest special effort here was Christian Endeavor week. We observed it in large measure as the general society heads suggested. But of course we adapted it to our own needs and church with the result that we had a good time together, and Ashland College will benefit somewhat by our efforts. The Juniors and Intermediates need special mention, for they did especially well on the last evening of the week. Altogether we must say that we are moving on and expecting greater things.   HARRY S. PRICE.

ST. LUKE AND LIBERTY, VIRGINIA

It may be of interest to some of the readers of the Evangelist to know that I am still laboring in the beautiful Shenandoah Valley of Virginia. While the work is not going forward by leaps and bounds, yet there is some evidence that the seed is bringing forth some harvest.

Since our last District Conference, which was held in June, seven have been added to the congregation at Liberty, and three at St. Luke. Both of these places are located in a rural section and have their problems to contend with.

Last fall while the weather and roads were ideal for the work of the Lord, a special meeting was held at Trinity, in the beautiful little Fort Valley. It was not strictly an evangelistic meeting, yet evangelism was emphasized, but rather a meeting together of the congregation and pastor for two weeks for the purpose of emphasizing the "Naturalness of Religion." As a visible result of our combined efforts, 16 were added to the church by baptism, and the annual fall communion was the largest that we have had at that place since I have been laboring with them. 93 were seated around the tables of the Lord and all went away feeling that it was good for them to have been there.

However, the days are not all sunny down here. Some of them are dark. The wintry blasts, bad roads, and another siege of grip or influenza have chilled the enthusiasm of summer and fall. Within the past month I have been called to officiate at four funerals, the particulars of which will be reported in another column.   C. R. KOONTZ.

MUNCIE, INDIANA

The First Brethren church of Muncie will enter into a city-wide simultaneous campaign, February 29th, for the salvation of souls.

The Rev. A. E. Thomas of Warsaw, will do the preaching, and Brother Curtis Cruea will lead the singing. The pastor will sit and listen and enjoy the services with the rest of the congregation.

Great preparations are made by all the churches. Prayer meetings are being held twice each week, in every precinct in the city.

We anticipate a successful meeting. We ask the prayers of the brotherhood for victory in this conflict. The church here has deferred the erection of a building until 1921. We believe it will be better for us in many ways.

The pastor has recently solicited funds from the New Paris and Goshen congregations, since we are not able to build of our own accord. We must have the assistance of the churches in Indiana, except those which are helping Peru. I am very happy to say that these churches responded nobly to our appeal, and New Paris gave us three hundred and fifty two ($362.00) dollars and Goshen eleven hundred and twenty-one ($1,121.00) dollars. Goshen I think will make it $1,200.00, as a number have not yet been solicited.

Suffice it to say, that these two churches have the everlasting gratitude of the Muncie people and we know that God will bless them richly for their generosity. If the other churches of Indiana will be as kind to us as these churches have been we will be able to build a church in the city of Muncie ,that will be a credit to us as a denomination, and the debt will not cripple the church for a generation.

We want to second the motion that the Rev. William H. Beachler be sent to the World's Sunday School Convention at Tokyo. The church owes him this honor, and he is undoubtedly the man to go. We might suggest, however, that it will not be necessary for the reverend gentleman to buy any sausage for this trip. All you have to do, William, is to buy a first-class ticket and you will have plenty to eat as you go on your way rejoicing.   J. L. KIMMEL.

HAMLIN, KANSAS

As it is some time since there has been a report in the Evangelist from Hamlin, I will write a few lines to let it be known we are still on the map. We are still without a pastor but are keeping up interest with our Sunday school. We have a splendid corps of teachers devoted to the service of God. We have two classes of young people taking teacher training. Some of our members were privileged to attend the meetings in Morrill while Brother W. S. Bell was there, and when we found Falls City could not hold their meeting on account of the fuel shortage we got busy and arranged to have Brother Bell come to Hamlin for a short meeting. The campaign was started the morning of the eleventh of January, and closed with baptismal services the afternoon of the 29th. Brother Bell was handicapped, there being no pastor, but he ably filled the place of evangelist and pastor and preached with his usual convincing and convicting power. We were fortunate in having good weather and roads and had good crowds most of the time. We were encouraged and helped by the presence and assistance of Brother Whitted and many of his parishioners from Morrill at a number of the services. The immediate results were fifteen baptized and united with the church, three to be baptized later and a spiritual strengthening of the membership. On Saturday following the close of the meetings a ban was put on all public gatherings on account of the influenza. We crave the prayers of the brotherhood for the continuance of God's blessing and that we may soon be able to get a pastor. We are very grateful to Brother Bell for holding these meetings and pray God's blessing on his efforts in the future.

N. P. EGLIN.

LOUISVILLE FIRST BRETHREN

Dear Evangelist Readers:

It may be of interest to all, to hear that Louisville is still in the great Battalion of Life, attempting to serve him whom we love. Many things have been done since our last report that have really been steps of progress in our work.

The Thanksgiving season was observed by a union service consisting of the three Protestant churches. But as usual with such services, it was not largely attended. Our own church made our annual offering at this season to the amount of $73.03.

The next event of note on our schedule was the appearing of Brother Beachler and the Endowment Campaign. Beachler received a cold reception judging from the thermometer but otherwise it was some better. He preached five very powerful messages and we are perfectly persuaded that his messages and presence in the midst of a congregation counts for much aside from the excellent achievement which he is working out. Those who received the greatest blessing from this campaign were those who gave whole-heartedly, as they had been prospered. If Beachler doesn't get a return trip to Louisville sometime it will be because he flatly refuses.

The annual White Gift service was rendered on Tuesday, evening, December 23rd. The attendance was more than could be well cared for. Every class including the Home Department and Cradle Roll had some special part in the program while presenting their White Gifts. The decorations were exceptionally fine. They were white throughout except two beautiful art panels 4x6 feet of the Wise Men and Shepherds, painted by Brother Chester Bratten. The electrical fixtures were furnished by Brother J. F. Painter. The program rendered under the direction of Superintendent Clapper and his committees was, to say the least, very impressive. White Gifts totalled $128.73. The desire is being expressed already that we give a pageant next year.

The afternoon of New Year's Day was the date for the annual business meeting. A definite report was given by the leader of every organization of the church. Also the treasurers gave the financial standing of each, which in every case showed a balance on the interesting side of the ledger. At the close of this meeting a neat little package was presented to the pastor, which when opened revealed $48.75, in love and appreciation for services rendered. We appreciate such kindness.

The first week of January, "The Week of Prayer," was observed with union meetings. Immediately following we began a two weeks' revival. The chief hindrances were snow drifts and icy streets, however the attendance and interest was commendable from the beginning. We called this a revival. Indeed it was such, in every department of our work. The pastor had some very fine support during

this effort and the messenger was never more ably used to preach the Word of Truth and Warning. Twelve were added to the membership and we feel that more will come soon.

The different auxiliaries of the church have united in a mission study class. The text being used, "'A Crusade of Compassion for the Healing of the Nations." Offerings are being received by this mission class and also by the Friendship class of the Sunday school for the Gribble Hospital Fund as suggested in the "Outlook" by Mrs. J. J. Wolfe of North Manchester, Indiana. We hope that the list may grow.

May the blessing of God continue to accompany all efforts put forth in his name.

E. M. RIDDLE, Pastor.

REPORT OF EVANGELISTIC LEAGUE

We concluded our meeting in Pittsburgh, February 15th, after continuing for two weeks in the face of a "flu" epidemic, with many of the members sick and outside people fearful of attending public gatherings. It presented one of the hardest propositions I ever faced in a campaign. Brother Harley and the faithful members stood loyally by us and while the crowds were not large, we had the satisfaction of knowing that the Gospel was declared and the joy of seeing some added to the church.

Brother Harley has done a commendable work in Pittsburgh and is held in high esteem by his people. The church here for many years labored under the burden of a heavy financial obligation and just recently had the joy of canceling all its debts. The church here has a membership of less than 200 and is to be commended for its loyalty and determination to win. They have a very good building and well equipped and with Brother Harley as leader are sure to win new victories.

Johnstown, Pennsylvania

By invitation of the Johnstown church and pastor I spent a few days in the "Flood City" where I served as pastor for nearly six years. It was a real pleasure to meet with these good people and enjoy a few days rest. I preached at both services the Sunday I was in the city to large audiences and received a liberal response to the Evangelistic League. The church here is looking forward to the time of erecting a new house of worship and from what I heard it will be second to none in the denomination. Nearly eleven years have passed since I served here as pastor and during that time many changes have taken place. After spending a few nights with Brother Lyon and his people in Washington City, I began a three weeks' campaign in Philadelphia with Brother Braker.

W. S. BELL.

SPECIAL NOTICE

The next issue of The Brethren Missionary will be one of unusual interest and should find its way into every Brethren home. It will feature the Easter offering for Foreign Missions. If you are not getting it, send 25 cents to the undersigned to pay for a year's subscription today.

J. ALLEN MILLER, Business Manager.

WHITE GIFTS—CONTINUE COMING

Since last report we have received the following "White Gift" offerings:

Falls City, Neb., ...	$ 40.00
Washington, D. C., ...	50.00
Fremont, Ohio, ...	21.01
Campbell, Mich., ...	84.72
Waterloo, Iowa, ...	152.61
Ankneytown, Ohio, ...	16.54
Sergeantsville, N. J., ...	5.00
Philadelphia, First, Pa., ...	150.00
Turlock, Cal., ...	79.63
Johnstown, First, Pa.	180.00
Hagerstown, Md., ...	100.00
Roanoke, Va., ...	12.80
Total, ...	$ 892.31
Previously Reported, ...	$3,135.57
Grand Total, to date, ...:	$4,027.88

February 19, 1920.

ALBERT TRENT,
General Secretary-Treasurer.

THE TIE THAT BINDS

SELLERS-MILLER—Clifford L. Sellers and Faun M. Miller were united in marriage by the writer at the bride's home, February 14. Both are fine Christian people. The groom is a faithful member of the Brethren church here and the bride a faithful member of the Christian church. Their many friends wish them a long and happy voyage over life's sea.

L. A. MYERS.

VANCE-FRANKS—At the home of the undersigned, on Monday morning, February 9, occurred the marriage of Mr. Ralph Vance and Miss Hazel R. Franks. Both these young pople are members of the Uniontown, Pennsylvania, congregation, and well known to the officiating clergyman. The groom has made his home with us here at Canton for some months and has shown himself an industrious, quiet, Christian young man. The bride has for many years made her own way in life, besides acting as parent to two younger sisters, to whom she has faithfully fulfilled her duty. These young people start out in life with the best hopes of their many friends, who unite in wishing them a worthy portion of heaven's choicest blessings. They will reside in Canton for a while at least.

DYOLL BELOTE.

IN THE SHADOW

WEAVER—Mrs. Mary Francis Weaver, the daughter of Mr. and Mrs. George Wogoman, Salem, Ohio, was born February 11th, 1839, and departed this life February 9, 1920. On September 11, 1918 she was united in marriage to Mr. Orion J. Weaver, a faithful member of the Christian church. Eleven years ago Mrs. Weaver united with the First Brethren church at Salem, Ohio, under the preaching of Rev. Martin Shively and since that time has been a very effective and efficient worker in the church. In fact the church feels they have suffered a great loss. The cause of her death was "flu" and pneumonia. She leaves a son of 12 days, a husband, father and mother, three sisters and one brother. Misses Josie and Alice Wogoman, her sisters, were formerly students of Ashland College. The services were held in the Christian church, Trotwood, Ohio, conducted by the writer.

J. S. COOK.

REIGHARD—Gladys, aged one year, daughter of Robert W. and Ethel (Good) Reighard of Conemaugh, passed from this life to be with Jesus, on January 25th. The Master has taken her to himself in that fairer realm beyond, where every bud bursts into bloom and every blossom is filled with fruit. To use the words of a great divine, "Lovely buds these children are, transplanted by death in that larger garden above, where, in pure atmosphere and with heavenly fragrance, they are to blossom through the endless cycles of a glorious eternity."

Funeral services by the writer, assisted by Rev. G. H. Jones of the Third Brethren church of Johnstown.

THOMPSON—Helen Theresa Grumpp, daughter of Albert and Alice Grumpp, was born near Roann, in Miami county, Indiana, September 17, 1897, and departed this life February 8, 1920, at the age of 22 years, 4 months and 21 days. She united with the Brethren church in 1915. On September 3, 1919 she was united in marriage to Lorin Thompson. Helen was a sweet Christian girl loved by all who knew her. Services by the writer. WILLIS E. RONK.

HUFFMAN—Anna Elizabeth Huffman nee Frances was born in Ohio, September 20, 1843, and departed this life at the home of her son Ervin, in Huntington county, Indiana, January 25, 1920, aged 76 years, four months and five days. When quite young she with her parents came to Huntington county, where later she was united in marriage to Jacob Huffman, September 12, 1861. This union was blessed with three sons, two of whom, Ervin and William, survive and live in Huntington county, Indiana. When quite young she united with the Church of the Brethren, and later with the Brethren church of Roanoke, Indiana, to which she was faithful. When her health would permit we always found her at the church services, and by her good works and smiles she being dead yet speaketh. Surely her sons can rise up and call her blessed. She leaves four sisters, two brothers, two sons, seven grandchildren and two great-grandchildren and a multitude of friends to mourn her departure. Funeral services were held at the Roanoke Brethren church, a large assembly of friends and neighbors being present. The sermon was preached by the writer from the texts, John 14.1, 2, 3, and 2 Cor. 5:1. Interment in the beautiful Roanoke cemetery.
W. F. JOHNSON.

SISK—Miles W. Sisk departed this life January 20, 1920, at the age of 75 years, three months and 10 days. He was a resident of this community from early boyhood. His many friends extend their sympathy to the aged companion and other relatives.
L. A. MYERS.

ASKINS—Cleora Coblentz was born in Montgomery county, Ohio, June 21, 1888, and died of pneumonia, at her home in Dayton, February 8th, 1920, aged 30 years, 6 months and 18 days. She ranked high as a mathematician in her profession of teaching and was much loved and respected by her pupils and associates for her life of integrity and uprightness. She was married August 9th, 1912, to Clifford Askins, who, with her parents, three sisters and five brothers, survives to mourn her loss. On March 19th, 1914 she was born into the kingdom of God and has served her Lord as a dear child ever since. She was president of our Women's Bible class for two years and then called to the administration division of her pupils and had taught a class of 31 girls. EVERY ONE OF WHOM SHE LED TO CHRIST. Some record to pattern after. Her pastor was asked to preach her funeral from her most favorite text, Romans 1:16 which has been her life slogan, and when one knows that, it is no wonder that she has accomplished such results.
E. M. COBB.

Business Manager's Corner

THE END IS NOT YET

We have often wondered just when the end would be reached in our campaign for new subscriptions for the Evangelist or when there would be no more churches to win places on the Evangelist Honor Roll. But we have come to feel that the end is still far in the future. Not that we hope to get all the churches to win such honors, for that would be an unheard of thing, but there are yet many churches that should do this thing for themselves and for the church and the Publishing House. Moreover the prospects seem good for a number of other good churches to come in.

Just the other day we received the list from Hudson, Iowa, that places that church on the Honor Roll. Our young friend, Edwin Boardman, is pastor at this place, though we believe we still have a few other friends also at Hudson, even if it has been more than fourteen years since we last visited that church and on October tenth, 1905 baptized Charles Bolt, Verna Waters and Maud Blough. We hope they are still faithful members of that

church. The Hudson subscription list was increased THREE HUNDRED percent, which is a mighty good gain and shows that there is still a good work to be done among many of our churches.

A short time ago we received the renewal of the list from Fremont, Ohio, which places that church on the Honor Roll for the second time. Brother Oberholtzer has been building wisely and well in Fremont and he appreciates the helpfulness of the Brethren Evangelist in his work. One of the first churches to adopt the Budget System for placing the Evangelist into all the homes of the church was Lanark, Illinois, and quite awhile ago this list was renewed for the THIRD year. It works at Lanark and it will work at other places as well. Lanark provides the paper, not for the local membership only, but for non-resident members as well and sends the paper into a number of different states. We should have made this announcement and changed the marking on the Honor Roll long ago, but in some way it was overlooked, and for this neglect we offer our apologies to Brother Burnworth and his church.

Unless the promise of some of the pastors of a number of our best churches fail we will have some more mighty good news to announce in a few weeks. For these prospects we are exceedingly grateful, but we will make no definite announcements until the lists are in. The future looks good to us, and we rejoice.

Sunday School Literature

Last week we mailed to our Sunday schools order blanks for supplies for the next quarter with our revised price list, the announcement of which is made elsewhere in this issue of the Evangelist. Unavoidable circumstances compelled this revision and no one is any more sorry that it was necessary than we are, but you remember the old saying, "What can't be cured must be endured," and this seems to be one of the things that must be endured.

We are doing all we can to get the quarterlies out on time this quarter, and we hope to have them reach all our schools in time to distribute on the last Sunday in the month. But sickness has laid hold upon some of our workers and we are not sure just how we will come out in the end. One of our girls has been off for a week and a half on account of illness, and another girl that heads the "make up" department of the composition room is down with the "grippe" and her mother assures us that she will be compelled to lay off for a week. But we will do the very best we can and it should not be forgotten that "He who does the best his circumstances allow does well, acts nobly, angels could do no more." We are not angels, but we claim to be doing the best our circumstances will allow us to do, so should the unfortunate sickness delay us unduly, we only ask you to exercise Christian patience.

R. R. TEETER,
Business Manager.

EVANGELIST HONOR ROLL

The following churches having met the requirements laid down by the Brethren Publishing Company regarding the placing of the

Evangelist in the homes of the congregations are entitled to a place on the Evangelist Honor Roll:

Church	Pastor
Akron, Ind., (New Highland),	.... (Vacant)
Allentown, Pa., 3rd Year,	.. A. L. DeLozier
Ankenytown, Ohio, 3rd Yr.,	.... A. L. Lynn
Ardmore, Indiana,	.... A. A. Wirick
Ashland, Ohio, 3rd Yr.,	...... J. A. Garber
Beaver City, Nebr. (3rd Yr.),	.. E. S. Flora
Berlin, Pa., (2nd Yr.),	.... I. B. Trout
Berne, Indiana, 3rd Year,	.. W. F. Johnson
Bryan, Ohio, 2nd Yr.,	.... G. L. Maus
Buckeye City, O.,	.... Glen Peterson
Burlington, Ind., 2nd Yr.,	... W. T. Lytle
Carleton, Nebr., 2nd Yr.,	... J. D. Kemper
Center Chapel, Ind.,	.... K. R. Ronk
Cerro Gordo, Ill.,	.... D. A. C. Teeter
Clay City, Indiana, (3rd Yr.),	S. C. Henderson
College Corner, Ind., 2nd Yr.,	Homer Anderson
Conemaugh, Pa., (3rd Yr.),	... E. F. Byers
Darwin, Indiana,	.... W. T. Lytle
Dallas Center, Iowa,	.... R. F. Porte
Dayton, Ohio,	.... E. M. Cobb
Denver, Indiana, 2nd Yr.,	... L. A. Myers
Dutchtown, Indiana,	... Homer Anderson
Elkhart, Ind., (2nd Yr.),	... H. Wolford
Eaton, Ind., (Maple Grove),	.. H. E. Eppley
Eau Claire, Wisconsin,	.... J. A. Baker
Fair Haven, Ohio (3rd Yr.),	.. B. F. Owen
Falls City, Nebr. (3rd Yr.),	H. F. Stuckman
Fillmore, Calif. (2nd Yr.),	Sylvester Lowman
Flora, Ind., 2nd Yr.,	.... W. E. Thomas
Fostoria, Ohio (3rd Yr.),	... M. S. White
Fremont, Ohio (2nd Yr.),	H. M. Oberholtzer
Goshen, Indiana,	.... J. A. McInturff
Gretna, Ohio (3rd Yr.),	... Edwin Boardman
Gratis, Ohio	.... C. E. Beekley
Hagerstown, Maryland	...... A. B. Cover
Huntington, Indiana,	.... J. W. Brower
Hudson, Ia.,	.... Edwin Boardman
Johnstown, Pa., 1st Ch., 2nd Yr.	J. F. Watson
Johnstown, Pa., 3rd Ch.,	... Geo. H. Jones
Lanark, Ill. (3rd Yr.),	.. B. T. Burnworth
La Verne, Calif., 2nd Yr.,	... T. H. Broad
Leon, Iowa,	.... Geo. T. Ronk
Leon, Iowa, (Crown Chapel),	Geo. T. Ronk
Leon, Iowa (Union, Chapel),	.. G. T. Ronk
Limestone Tenn., 2nd Yr.),	... Mary Pence
Linwood, Maryland, 2nd Yr.,	.. E. M. Riddle
Long Beach, Cal. (3rd Yr.),	L. S. Bauman
Loree, Indiana, 2nd Yr.,	... C. A. Stewart
Los Angeles Cal, Comp. Av. 2d Yr.	J. C. Beal
Louisville, O., (3rd Yr.),	.... E. M. Riddle
Masontown, Pennsylvania,	... Martin Shively
Meyersdale, Pa., 2nd Yr.,	.. E. D. Burnworth
Mexico, Ind. (3rd Yr.),	...... J. W. Clark
Milledgeville, Ill., (3rd Yr.),	Miles J. Snyder
Morrill, Kans., (3rd Yr.),	.. A. E. Whitted
Mt. View, Va., (3rd Yr.),	... J. E. Patterson
Muncie, Indiana, 2nd Yr.,	... J. L. Kimmel
Nappanee, Ind. (3rd Yr.)	..... B. L. Miller
New Enterprise, Pa.,	.... Edward Byers
New Lebanon, O.,	.... G. W. Kinzie
New Paris, Ind., 2nd Yr.,	... W. I. Duker
North English, Iowa,	..... Homer Anderson
N. Liberty, Ind. (2nd Yr.),	... C. C. Grisso
New Enterprise, Ind.,	...... P. M. Fisher
Oakville, Ind., (2d Yr.),	... W. R. Deeter
Peru, Indiana,	.... Geo. C. Carpenter
Philadelphia, Pa (1st Br.) ,	Alva J. McClain
Philadelphia, Pa., 3rd church,	J. E. Braker
Pittsburgh, Pa.,	.... H. M. Harley
Portis, Kans., (3rd Yr.),	... Roy Brumbaugh
Rittman, Ohio,	.... J. Allen Miller
Roann, Indiana (2nd yr.),	... Willis E. Ronk
Roanoke, Indiana	.... W. F. Johnson
Roanoke, Va.,	.... L. G. Wood
Sidney, Indiana, 2nd Yr.,	... L. A. Myers
Summit Mills, Pa., 2nd Yr.,	E. D. Burnworth
Tiosa, Indiana (2nd Yr.)	... C. C. Grisso
Turlock, California,	..... J. Francis Reagan
Washington, C. H., O., 3rd Yr.,	B. S. Stoffer
Waterloo, Iowa, (3rd Yr.) ,	..W. H. Beachler
Whittier, Cal., (2nd Yr.),	... A. V. Kimmel
White Chapel, Mo.,	.... G. T. Ronk
Windber, Pennsylvania,	...... E. F. Byers
Yellow Creek, Pa.,	.... Edward Byers
Zion Hill, Ohio,	.... A. L. Lynn

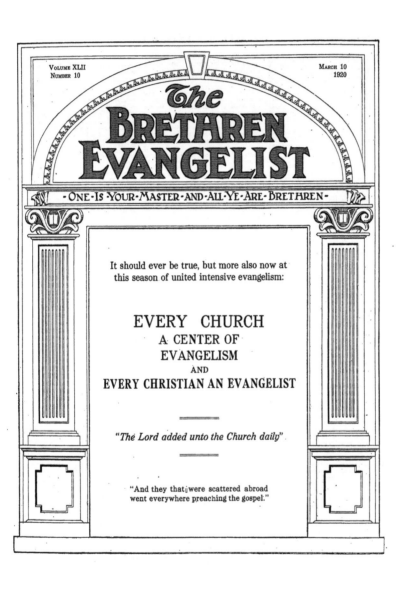

Volume XLII
Number 10

March 10
1920

The Brethren Evangelist

-One-Is-Your-Master-And-All-Ye-Are-Brethren-

It should ever be true, but more also now at this season of united intensive evangelism:

EVERY CHURCH
A CENTER OF
EVANGELISM
AND
EVERY CHRISTIAN AN EVANGELIST

"The Lord added unto the Church daily"

"And they that were scattered abroad went everywhere preaching the gospel."

Published every Wednesday at Ashland, Ohio. All matter for publication must reach the Editor not later than Friday noon of the preceding week.

George S. Baer, Editor

The Brethren Evangelist

When ordering your paper changed give old as well as new address. Subscriptions discontinued at expiration. To avoid missing any numbers renew two weeks in advance.

R. R. Teeter, Business Manager

OFFICIAL ORGAN OF THE BRETHREN CHURCH

Subscription price, $2.00 per year, payable in advance.
Entered at the Post Office at Ashland, Ohio, as second-class matter.
Acceptance for mailing at special rate of postage provided for in section 1103, Act of October 3, 1917, authorized September 9, 1918.
Address all matter for publication to Geo. S. Baer, Editor of the Brethren Evangelist, and all business communications to R. R. Teeter, Business Manager, Brethren Publishing Company, Ashland, Ohio. Make all checks payable to the Brethren Publishing Company.

TABLE OF CONTENTS

EDITORIAL

Marshalling the Forces for An Intensive Evangelistic Campaign

(The fourth of a series of articles on the above topic, considered apropos to the present season of intensive evangelism and also the aim of many churches to lead up to an ingathering at Easter time.)

IV. DIRECTING THE CAMPAIGN

When the field, the workers and the work have all received due consideration with reference to preparation, when no stone has been left unturned that might increase the probabilities of success, we should be at the threshold of a revival with confidence. But when the soldiers of Christ are equipped and in their places and the campaign is begun, the really great task is yet before the marshal, for the successful outcome of the whole undertaking depends very largely upon the wisdom and energy with which he directs it. If he is worthy to direct—if he knows his field and his workers,—he will be found the key man to success. Upon his shoulders falls the great burden of the campaign, and however efficient evangelistic preachers or singers he may summon to his aid, he cannot shift the responsibility. In seeking to discharge this responsibility most faithfully, there are certain suggestions which may be found helpful to consider.

If the pastor has the grasp of the situation, the most permanent good is likely to result if he directs personally the campaign and does not delegate the task to another. Whether the preaching is done by himself or another called for that purpose, no one can direct the forces quite so intelligently as he. We should judge that the situations are rather rare when the pastor should not be the directing power back of the campaign, and the evangelists likely are few who do not prefer to have him discharge that responsibility. This suggestion does not mean that the pastor should always stand in the limelight when he has an evangelist with him. It would be both selfish and unwise for him to seek the center of the stage, or try to eclipse the evangelist. The man who should be the man of the hour and the real drawing card, so far as any human instrument should be made such, is the evangelist. And it is seldom that the pastor does not find it to his advantage to center the attention of the community on an evangelist, who is indeed a man of God and a workman that needeth not to be ashamed, and who knows how to occupy the position of prominence for a season without stealing the hearts of the members. Indeed such an evangelist will leave the place with the pastor stronger with his people than when he came, and more than that his service will redound greatly to the glory of God and the advancement of his kingdom. So the pastor need not seek to be the prominent man; some may even choose to be a part of the congregation at this time. But he should be the first member of it; the leading member of it. He should be the counselling part of everything that takes place. The evangelist's larger general experience should be coupled with and guided by the pastor's larger local experience. In this way, larger and more permanent results are likely to be gained.

If the pastor is to be the real leader of the campaign, he must be found where the leader ought to be,—at the head of his troops. He should not send but lead; should not merely suggest to his people what they may do and urge them to activity, but should set them an example of the most strenuous and effective activity possible. The captain who directs his troops from the rear is not deserving of the greatest success and will not long enjoy the respect of his followers. He who is found in the thick of the fight, who puts every ounce of energy and every moment of time possible into the campaign, who never asks a sacrifice of his members but what he has first set the example of it, will be worthy of and will actually secure the most loyal and active co-operation. He should set a high standard and ask much of his co-workers (for worthy men are not challenged by small tasks), but he should never set a higher standard than he himself is seeking to attain unto, nor ask more than he is both willing and striving to do. Thus he will prove himself worthy to be their leader.

As the campaign progresses the pastor will find it important to keep in personal touch with every worker, for many will need his help in meeting difficulties. Some will want his advice as to how to approach certain individuals. Sometimes personal workers are too abrupt, or patronizing or unsympathetic and they need to be coached in their approach of certain individuals. Some may be baffled in their first attempts and be at a loss to know how to follow up their former efforts. They will welcome his counsel in the matter. It may be the individual whom he sought to influence for Christ should be left alone for a while, or that another should approach him a second time, or that the one who failed should change his tactics and follow up his former efforts. Then again certain of the workers may have come in touch with individuals whom they have been able to interest in their own spiritual welfare, but are not able to answers certain questions or meet certain difficulties and they will desire the help of their pastor. It may be that the pastor himself is the logical man to follow up and clinch the former worker's effort with a visit. Frequently it will be found that earnest personal workers have prepared the soil for the sowing of the seed by the pastor, or evangelist, or other individual who has had special training in handling the Word of Truth. There will be many things to come up about which the workers will wish to counsel their pastor and it will be much to .

his advantage to keep in touch with them frequent personal and group conferences.

In a long drawn-out campaign it is often found very difficult to maintain a spirit of courage and confidence. The spirit of depression and discouragement should be guarded against very carefully. Few things are more fatal to a meeting than just that spirit when it has once settled heavily upon it. It indicates that the people have lost faith, have ceased to work and have settled down in doubtful seat merely to look on and to wonder what the pastor and the evangelist may be able to do. When the members become discouraged, the unconverted people soon sense the situation and cease to be interested.

This danger is often warded off by delaying the invitation until results can reasonably be expected because of the efforts expended and the spirit created. ..ien occasional prayer and conference meetings after the congregation has been dismissed in the evening will send the workers forth with cheerfulness and confidence to another day's work for the salvation of souls and cause them to redouble their efforts. As soon as confessions are made it usually has a wholesome influence on the spirit of the community to have public baptismal service as promptly as possible. It starts the feeling of success both among the members and in the community, and nothing succeeds like success. It is hard to keep courageous in a long siege when results do not readily appear, but often after enduring such testing faithfully fof a season God pours out his blessings in abundant measure, his power is mightily felt and souls are turned unto himself by the score. Let us not be soon weary in well-doing for in due season we shall reap if we faint not.

EDITORIAL REVIEW

Pray for a great ingathering of souls at Easter time.

Prof. J. A. Garber has been ill for several days with something that very much resembles the "flu," but we are glad to report that he is now much improved.

A very encouraging report comes from Brother M. M. Teague concerning the work at Buena Vista, Virginia. The report certainly shows these good people to be alive and growing.

Brother W. H. Miller recently gave the Publishing House a call while visiting in Ashland with his brother, Dean Miller. Brother Miller reported that his work at Oak Hill, Virginia, is progressing nicely.

Another installment of the "College News" is given to our readers this week by President Jacobs. He reports having been recently to Meyersdale to preach. He also was called upon to fill the college pulpit on Sunday, March 7.

Brother J. A. Baker writes from Iowa his appreciation of Brother Swihart's article on Early Ministerial experiences. We wish to add that others have expressed appreciation of this veteran preacher's article also.

Make this Easter the greatest Easter in the history of your church by working and praying for the salvation of souls in your own congregation and by giving of your money to send the saving gospel to the uttermost parts of the earth.

You will want to read over Brother Gearhart's financial report carefully to see if your name is there, and if it is not and has not already appeared, you will want to send in your offering to Home Missions very soon, before it is too late. Do it now.

We received from Brother Bauman a letter written by Brother James Gribble as the door was being opened for them to step out and on towards the field of labor. Now that they are in the borderland, the great passion of their hearts is that they may be kept fit for the Lord's use. To this end they request us to pray.

As we were going to press the sad news came of the death by acute indigestion of Brother I. B. Trout, in Pittsburgh on Friday, March 5, while there on business. The funeral was held on March 9 at Berlin, Pa., where interment was made. Brother Trout was the much loved pastor of the Berlin Brethren church.

The most complete parish year book that has come to our office is the one from the Long Beach church. Among many other things of interest is the following membership summary taken from the pas-

tor's report: "Received into the church,—in 1912, 29; in 1913, 88; in 1914, 57; in 1915, 87; in 1916, 99; in 1917, 79; in 1918, 48; in 1919, 83. Dropped from Roll from 1912-1920,—because of death, 22; letters granted, 57; by dismissal, 29; by excommunication, 12. Present membership, 450. This is a splendid record for an eight years' growth."

Dr. J. Allen Miller calls attention to a most important matter; you have heard much about it before and you will hear much more about it.. It is the important financial call of this season of the year. Foreign missions should bulk large in your thoughts and prayers at this time and should receive generously of your money and your life.

Brother Leatherman has taken charge of the church at Turlock, California. He gives us a report of the work at that place and states that the condition is prosperous. He reports that Brother Reagan, who has taken charge of the Union Rescue Mission of Los Angeles, is at Turlock very ill. Let us pray that he may soon recover.

The Indiana Brethren ministers maintain their record of being among the most aggressive and progressive of the brotherhood. While gathered at the Interchurch State Pastors' Conference at Indianapolis, they took action on the movement and organized for action. They have set a fine example. A group of Ohio ministers gathered at Columbus also expressed themselves in sympathy with the movement.

We are always sorry to lose any of our ministry, but when one of our veteran ministers passes from our midst our sorrow is mingled with a feeling of gratitude for the memory of a long life of service that is left us. It is Brother William Keifer who has been called to his reward, as you will notice by the announcement of Brother Willis Ronk, the secretary-treasurer of the Ministerial Association. We hope to present his picture with an obituary soon.

Rather than see the price of "The Watchman-Examiner," a Baptist church paper, advanced from $2.50 to $3.00, a layman sent in his check for $5,000 to cover the increase on 10,000 subscriptions, in the hope that others would be led to make similar contributions. Gifts to the church paper are something new; but there is a growing sentiment that if the paper is really worth anything to the church it is worthy not only of gifts, but even an endowment.

Still the churches are renewing their subscriptions to The Evangelist. We congratulate them on their wisdom and also their loyalty. We are all one great family working to the interests of each other. You try to get the paper into every home to help your church and to help the Publishing House and we try to make a paper to help every home it enters and also make folks want to buy it for themselves and to sell it to still larger numbers. Let us always seek to co-operate in this splendid manner. See the Business Manager's Corner for the number of renewals.

Wouldn't it be a fine thing for every church to plan its work so as to lead up to an ingathering of souls on Easter Sunday? If you have not had an evangelistic campaign yet this year suppose you arrange to have one just preceding Easter. If you have had one, why not plan another series of evangelistic meetings for passion week? If you cannot secure an evangelist, use your pastor, and if you give him the same co-operation you would expect to give an evangelist, he will hold you a good meeting. If you have planned to have a meeting a little later it will be good preparation for it to stir up some evangelistic fervor at Easter time. At no other time are the hearts of men so tender. There would be great inspiration gained from a situation where every church was engaged in an evangelistic meeting at the same time. Why not?

Our readers will find in this issue some very valuable information assembled and set forth by Brother Orion E. Bowman of Dayton, Ohio. Some of our people are concerned about making provision for certain interests of the church. They will need the official names of the agencies charged with the administration of such interests and will often find it convenient to have at hand or know where they can get in touch with such instruments by which conveyances can be made. Brother Bowman has supplied such information and promises to hold himself ready to answer without charge inquiries for further information. Brother Bowman is thoroughly competent to give trustworthy advice on legal forms as he is one of the leading attorneys of Dayton, and his generosity is the more marked because he is one of the busiest men of his line.

GENERAL ARTICLES

Sleepless Nights Guarantee Spiritual Awakenings.   By Theodore S. Henderson

(Methodist Episcopal Bishop of the Detroit Area, where he has led a remarkable evangelistic awakening, and now manager of the Interchurch United Simultaneous Evangelistic Campaign, sends a message to Brethren people, challenging them as he is challenging every other communion to co-operate in an intensive evangelistic campaign leading to a great ingathering on Easter Sunday.—Editor).

"Give me Scotland, or I die," prayed John Knox.

God did not deny the passionate prayer of this faithful, fearless fervent prophet of God. Scotland surrendered to the mastery of his message. .

Is there anything in us which approaches the spiritual intensity, the passionate fervor of Knox?

Dare we in our agonizing, passionate praying adapt that prayer to our city or town?

Try it.

"Give me Detroit or I die?" Is it true? I tremble before that simple searching test. I am saying it, praying it, meaning it as I write. In the light of Christ's throne, I dare not sham when I say it. ·

· Try it. Speak it aloud. Tell it to your associates without flinching.

PRAY "Give me Scotland, or I die." It will cost you dearly. Intercession is no idle reverie, no pious dreaming, no spiritual recreation. When I read of how David Brainerd prayed I am crushed with the emptiness of my own prayers. When I learned how he prayed, I do not wonder that his Indians were converted. Are my prayers anything like those of David Brainerd? Are yours?

PREACH "Give me Scotland, or I die." You remember with what flaming passion and blood earnestness Rowland Hill preached the Gospel? The people where he preached called him a madman. That is what they said of Paul. That is what they said of Christ. Has anyone said it of you? Unless our mission and message consume us, our people about us will never be kindled with the holy passion of our Lord.

PLEAD "Give me Scotland or I die." All our pleading should not be done in the churches. I wonder if our greatest weakness is not that we fail to follow up our pleading in church with the kind of pleading face to face,

with persons when they are alone, that will reveal to them our heart break for their salvation? Do you remember how Paul did in Acts 20:19-20? As he went from house to house, he went "with many tears." A spiritual revival does not come by organization but by communication. Finney said that the unconverted persons will not become concerned about their own salvation until the converted show their concern about them. Are we manifesting that kind of concern?

There is an incident in the life of John Vassar which tugs at my heart. He was going from house to house distributing tracts and speaking with the people as opportunity offered. An Irish woman heard of the strange little man, and she said, "If he comes to my door he will not be kindly treated." The next day, not knowing of her threat, John Vassar rang the door bell in her house. When she recognized him she slammed the door in his face. Then he sat on the doorstep and sang:

> "But drops of grief can ne'er repay
> The debt of love I owe;
> Here, Lord, I give myself away:
> 'Tis all that I can do."

A few weeks later this woman sought admission to the church. When she was asked how it happened she could only say between sobs: "'Twas those drops of grief. They burned themselves into my heart."

Have we pleaded with our associates with tears? Not forced tears, but with Christlike concern until the people knew we would rather see them accept Christ than to have any reputation or reward they could give us?

Have we followed up the public pleading for Christ, on Sunday, in church, with the personal pleading with one life on Monday? If not, I doubt whether we can say from an honest heart "Give me my city, or I die."

Shall we not with such a passionate, purposeful prayer on our lips and in our hearts, work toward the ideal expressed in the slogan of the Lenten United Simultaneous Evangelistic campaign, that, "Every Christian is an evangelist and every church, a center of evangelism and community service?"

An Offering From Every Member to Take the Gospel to Every Man
By William A. Gearhart, General Missionary Secretary

When great tasks are to be performed, all should be made to understand how very important it is, that there is co-operation and team play, every man doing his best and keeping at it until the task is done. Many of us, who were reared on farms, can remember when we were frequently called together to raise barns or other buildings, how, that when the call was given to "heave to," that every man grabbed hold of the timber and lifted his level best. but if some, perchance, were inclined to be lazy and did not lift their share, it made it doubly hard for the others.

The same principle applies when we do work for the Lord. · Our Foreign Mission Offering is about to be raised, and it will be easily raised if every member will do his very best.

The Foreign Missionary Society is urging every member of the Brethren church to be present on Easter morning in their respective places to worship the Lord and praise him for the hope of eternal life, made possible through his resurrection from the dead, and when the call is given by the building foreman (your pastor) to raise the offering, that every one will touch timber and give a lift. Let not one member shirk his duty, but let every one remember that

just to the extent that each one fails to do his part, it adds to the amount to be raised by others.

Our Master said that "Whosoever will may come and take of the water of life freely." Millions of our brethren and sisters in the flesh are ignorant of the fact that there is a Savior and that through faith in him they too might have eternal life. Many of these millions of unfortunates may never hear of this Savior before they die, and as the prophet Ezekiel stated in the third chapter of his book that it may be that we will be held responsible and will have to answer for this neglect if not taking the good news to them. Please read that chapter. If an eternal life of bliss is worth more than all the world to us, then it behooves those of us who possess it to do our utmost to see that the whole world hears the message of salvation.

How would we feel about it if we were suddenly transported to some heathen land, there to spend the remainder of our days living as the heathen people do, and especially if our hope of eternal life were taken from us? It seems to me we would be of all men most miserable. Why not resolve in our hearts that beginning at once, we will refrain from spending money foolishly for things that we do not really need and lay it aside for the Easter offering. If every member of the Brethren church would do that for even several weeks, it would add thousands of dollars to our offering. Surely there are scores of our brethren and sisters who could give $50.00 and become a Life Member of the Foreign Missionary Society. Hundreds of others who could not possibly give $50.00, but could easily give $5.00 and become a member of the Society, and thousands of others could raise at least $1.00 by Easter. The new Easter bonnets, dresses, ties, shirts etc., which you expect to purchase with the money the Lord desired you to give to save the souls of the unregenerated millions will not bring the blessing to you that your Master has in store for you for he promised a special blessing upon his children who would help to spread the Gospel to those who know it not.

Let us not be selfish with our religion, but let us give it freely to others and we will have more for ourselves.

May the Holy Spirit be allowed to enter our hearts in a fuller sense and fill us with a desire to be faithful stewards for our Master. Let us give as much as possible to carry the glad tidings of salvation through Jesus Christ to our friends in other lands, whom he loves as much as you and me.

Un-christian and Un-businesslike

Editorial in the Philadelphia North American, selected by Dr. E. M. Cobb, Dayton, Ohio

In the last five years the cost of living has soared an unprecedented height. During this period the average wage of workers in eight leading industries has increased from 74 percent to 112 percent, according to statistics compiled by the national industrial conference board.

Meantime, the average salary of Methodist ministers has been increased less than 15 percent—and Methodist ministers, as a whole, are higher paid than those of any other denomination. That is why we choose them as a standard for comparison in once more dealing with a subject far more important than the mass of the people seem to appreciate.

Viewed solely from the standpoint of his moral benefit to the community, the preacher is worthy of sufficient pay to comfortably provide for himself and his family in such manner as his position demands. In many ways that cost money, more is expected of him than of any other worker.

In the first place, he must be well educated. He must keep up his education. This entails constant purchase of books—and books which are not low priced. He and his family must dress acceptably and maintain a standard of living in keeping with the nature of his high calling. It is expected his home shall be adequately furnished and well ordered. A certain amount of entertainment is incumbent on him. He is regarded as a community asset, and as such it is his duty to live the part.

In other words, his congregation says: "We ask you to reflect our best aims and desires; to typify in your person and family and home the outward and visible signs of the inward and spiritual graces of Christianity"—on an average annual salary of $1,111, if he is a Methodist, or of $825 if he be taken as an average preacher in any one of eleven denominations included in a recent questionaire conducted by the Home Herald, of Chicago.

Obviously this is wrong from the ethical standpoint, and virtually impossible from the economic.

Jesus himself, in instructing his apostles in their ministry, said, "The laborer is worthy of his hire." Any reasonable person knows it is unjust to require of an employee more than his compensation will cover. Where this injustice concerns a manual laborer, it is unwarranted. Where it has to do with one whose service is based on a higher plane—one whose direction and guidance are, in theory, accepted as constituting the noblest of efforts—it is inexcusably un-Christian.

"You must lead us in our living," says the community to the clergyman—and pays him less than a living. "You are our standard bearer of morals and spirituality," it says —and gives him a salary which, at its highest average, is less than the wage paid street sweepers in New York. "You are responsible for our progress in conduct and conscience" —and this huge responsibility is "rewarded" with a remuneration which, in some 70 percent of cases, makes it impossible for the clergyman to keep out of debt, though he reduce his living costs to what will cover the irreducible minimum of necessaries.

"You are the caretaker of character, the most valuable of all human possessions"—yet this vital sponsorship is rated on a plane with the caretaking of office buildings. For the average janitor is paid as much as the average preacher.

Stenographers and store clerks average from 25 to 50 percent more than the preacher. Day laborers, whose sole requirements is brawn, do even better. Chorus girls fare twice as well. Yet the preachers never have struck for higher pay, and never will, despite occasional suggestions of such a course.

They, at least, recognize the worth of their calling in something better than dollars and cents. But they can't feed and clothe themselves on this something better. Salvation is free, but butter is 90 cents a pound, eggs 80 cents a dozen, prunes 30 cents a pound, shoes $10 a pair, hand-me-down suits $50 and calico 35 cents a yard!

Congregations are acquainted with these prices. They know, too, that if the preacher is faithful to his long list of duties, he hasn't time to make anything "on the side." Like the doctor, he must hold himself in readiness for calls at any hour. Unlike the doctor, he cannot suggest some one to take his place.

Yet, with a handful of exceptions, congregations have done so little to attest their belief in the Master's dictum that today in every part of the land preachers and their families are forced to go in debt for the bare necessities of life, and forego scores of comforts and pleasures enjoyed by the poorest of their parishioners.

This is the most shameful of all reflections on the present state of religion. For there isn't a church member anywhere who is not pledged to the Golden Rule. It supplies the best of material for those who argue that our Christianity is a veneer. It prompts lovers of fair play to wish the 200,000 clergymen in the United States would strike, and let folk get baptized, married, counseled and buried as best they could until the spirit of Christ is put into the payroll.

So much for the ethical considerations involved. There is an economic side to this matter, however, which few persons have paused to ponder.

The church is a nation-wide organization with business functions which materially affect life at many points. It is a great corporation, with physical property valued at more tan $2,000,000,000. On its proper administration depend many issues as close akin to material as spiritual or moral progress.

For instance, there are millions of persons—among them a large proportion of men and women financially profitable to any community—who would not live in a town or city minus churches. Let some busy manufacturing center try the experiment of ousting all churches, to test this assertion! Will any dare?

Very well. Viewed solely as a corporation, as a business enterprise concerned with the better fitting of people for their daily tasks and their personal and patriotic duties, shouldn't it be managed on somewhat the same basis as any other business organization? Isn't it an economic mistake to expect this $2,000,000,000 corporation, which directly influences the usefulness of 42,000,000 adult Americans and

20,000,000 children to be directed by departmental heads who arent' paid enough to live on?

Would any other business be expected to succeed under similar circumstances? Is there a financier in this city or state who would expect to earn dividends on such a basis?

Why, then, expect Christianity to pay the dividends it might pay, while its temporal administration is based on a condition of managership which approaches mendicancy? Why look for worth-while results from its operation, so long as its salesmen are forced to fight poverty day in and day out?

Incidentally, what would be thought of a manufacturing firm which made its factory ornate with marble counters, stained glass windows and rich furniture, and didn't pay its workers a living wage?

These are pregnant questions which should come home to every church member. They are especially timely at this season, when we approach the season which celebrates the resurrection of the Founder of Christianity. He, of all who have lived, was the most ardent and uncompromising advocate of fair play, justice and altruism. What a reflection, then, that his professed followers should today be dealing out their fullest measure of injustice and injustice and selfishness to his ambassadors!

Church of the Brethren in the Interchurch Movement. By George S. Baer

Many of the members of our large family of Evangelist readers are continually asking for information concerning the Interchurch World Movement and what should be our relation to it. We are always glad to pass on any information we possess or to which we have access. Most of our pastors have gotten in touch with the Movement at the State Pastor's Conferences and have become quite thoroughly informed concerning its purposes, scope and workings. Many have written enthusiastically about it and are informing their people concerning it. One minister expresses himself in this way: "The Interchurch World Movement is every church doing its utmost to take the world for Christ in as short a time as possible and with God's help." Another says: "It is a stir among Protestant Evangelical churches that is destined to challenge our own church with a task that will drive it to prayer and effort in a manner heretofore unknown." Still another says, "It presents us with facts concerning the religious condition of mankind that are challenging, and suggests the best tried methods of meeting the challenge in God's name. But it is up to every church to carry out its own portion of the world task with its own machinery."

This statement strikes at the heart of the Movement. It does not presume to dictate how each co-operating denomination shall do its work, though it suggests methods which may be used or not in so far as they are in accord with the denominational spirit and genius. Accordingly it is of interest to note how other churches are co-operating. Of all other denominations, the most like our own in spirit and practice is the Church of the Brethren. It will therefore be of special interest to our people to know what action they have taken with regard to this Movement. And for the benefit of the thousands of readers who will never see The Interchurch Bulletin we quote the following: "The latest registration (in the Interchurch World Movement) comes from Elgin, Illinois, the headquarters of the Forward Movement of the Church of the Brethren, one of the most important of the smaller denominations of America. Its leaders are arranging active co-operation with the Interchurch World Movement in all its phasis, subject to the action of the general conference of the church, which meets in Missouri in June. However, so splendid has been the response to the appeals already made to the churches in the interests of co-operation with the Interchurch World Movement, that the directors of the Church of the Brethren Forward Movement feel confident they are carrying out the will of the church.

100,000 Strong

That the coming in of the Church of the Brethren to the great campaign, both financial and spiritual, of the Interchurch World Movement, means much to both is indicated by the size and resources of the denomination. The Church of the Brethren numbers more than 100,000 members, with 1,000 churches and 3,000 ministers. Two significant features are that its membership is almost entirely rural, indicating its substantiality, and its support of ten colleges, or a college to every 10,000 members of the church, probably

as high a proportion as any denomination in America can boast.

The budget to which the denomination has set itself in its own Forward Movement and in co-operation with the Interchurch World Movement is $2,670,000 for the next year, or, if it were on the five-year basis of the Interchurch World Movement, it would be $13,350,000. The denomination has set itself at the present time to the work of the one-year drive only, but it is not to be unexpected that if it is successful, the five-year program will be resolved upon and carried out.

Of the budget, $1,000,000 is sought for home and foreign missions, ministerial relief and other benevolences, and $1,670,000 for the colleges. Each of these two major items will be raised in distinct campaigns within the denomination, but the time for the two drives is the same. They will not conflict with the annual conference offering, usually amounting to several hundred thousand dollars. The denomination is strongest in Pennsylvania, Maryland, Virginia, Ohio, Illinois, Indiana, Iowa, Kansas and California.

The entrance of the Church of the Brethren into the Interchurch World Movement means the coming into the co-operative movement of a denomination marked for the keenness of its leaders the high standards of education it has long maintained, and a spirituality among its members that well might be the envy of many of the larger denominations.

They are a conservative people, and as their Forward Movement director said in the Chicago office, they only tie up with a movement or program when they believe it to be expressly in accordance with the Will of God. They see in the Interchurch World Movement the Hand of God working, and believe that through it one of the greatest accomplishments for the coming of the Kingdom of God is going to take place.

The Rev. C. D. Bonsack of New Windsor, Maryland, one of the leaders of the denomination, has been chosen general director of the Forward Movement for the Church of the Brethren. He has taken up headquarters at Elgin, Illinois. The members of the executive committee are the Rev. J. E. Miller, director of the department of young people's work and life resources; the Rev. J. H. B. Williams, department of finance and organization; the Rev. M R. Zeigler, publicity and field work; L. T. Miller, periodicals; the Rev. H. Spencer Minnick, department of Christian and missionary education, and the Rev. Clyde Culp, secretary of the Publishing Board.

Regional Directors

The regional directors are the Rev. P. J. Blough, Johnstown, Pa.; the Rev. J. Walter Englar, New Windsor, Md.; the Rev. A. B. Miller, Bridgewater, Va.; the Rev. C. D. Hylton, Troutville, Va.; the Rev. George A. Snyder, Lima, Ohio; the Rev. D. O. Cottrell, North Manchester, Ind.; the Rev. John Heckman, Polo, Ill.; the Rev. A. P. Blough, Waterloo, Ia.; the Rev. Edgar Rothrock, Holmesville, Neb.; Prof. J. W. Deeter McPherson, Kan.; the Rev. James M. Mohler. Leeton, Mo.; and Prof. I. B. Funderburgh, La Verne, Calif.

"We are on the verge of a new epoch in the spread of the Gospel of Christ," said Mr. Bonsack, "and I believe the next few years will be the greatest in the history of mission-ary and Christian educational effort.. The Church of the Brethren desires its part in the great forward movement of Christianity. Our organization work is going ahead very rapidly, and we will have all preparations in hand for our Forward drive at the time of the general Interchurch World Movement campaign.''

Experience of the Early Ministry of the Brethren Church—An Appreciation

By J. A. Baker

The article written in Evangelist, January 28th by Brother J. H. Swihart pleased me so well that I thought as I was one of the listeners at the debate referred to, I would like, if the Editor would give space, to say a few words as an old friend of Brother Swihart. At the time of the debate I lived at Black River, Michigan, and Elder James Watkins an elder in the Seventh Day Adventist church got so gay we wanted to let him know that we had men that could talk as fast and tell as much truth as he. So he made a challenge to debate in public and we called on Brother Swihart. He came. We made the proper arrangements. The time was set and at it they went. And to tell our honest mind, for the first two nights we were afraid Watkins was getting in the lead for he talked, full time and told his story quite well for an Adventist and our little pop-gun Swihart only said a few words and then sat down.

But on the third night our ''pop-gun'' grew into a mighty big gun and the way he fired into the Adventist camp was not small. All that Watkins could do was to sit with both eyes and mouth open and look and listen. Well, to tell it mildly, I didn't know but the school board might have a job of re-shingling the school house roof! Well this settled Adventism at the old Johnstown school house. Brother Swihart preached some strong sermons while hold-ing meetings in old Black River, Michigan in my boyhood days. Now in his declining years, I wish in this way to re-call some of the happy recollections of years gone by when we could hear the good old Gospel preached with power.

818 Summit St., Eau Claire, Wisconsin.

Returning Apostolic Practice. By N. W. Jennings

Note: The following clipping taken from a Los Angeles paper was sent to us by Brother N. W. Jennings, pastor of the First church of that city. It is interesting in that it shows a tendency on the part of the denominations to re-vert to a practice which Brethren people have long observed. It may be well after all to make James 5:14, 15 seriously. —Editor.

A meeting of about two hundred evangelical ministers and laity yesterday at the Y. M. C. A. Auditorium adopted resolutions which follow. Representatives of practically all the Protestant denominations were present:

''Whereas, we, as a conference of ministers and laymen assembled here, feel that healing is taught in God's Word and that it is possible to utilize those teachings in a very definite and helpful way with scientific facts that are be-coming well known.

''Resolved, That we encourage a study of the subject of healing in all practical and helpful ways and urge all who are interested to make as thorough a study of the sub-ject as possible from a Biblical, psychological, scientific and common sense standpoint, and thus learn how to help and heal themselves and help others.

Urge League of Healing

''Resolved, That we encourage the organization of a Christian League of Healing and Helpful Service, with duly elected officers who shall arrange for meetings in which healing in the churches shall be presented by different speakers and studies on the subject of healing shall be en-couraged, and,

''Resolved, That we also encourage the churches to or-ganize classes and study the subject of healing and learn the definite principles which can be used to help and heal the people and also train persons to help disseminate Bibli-cal, scientific and common sense methods and principles which every one can use to establish health and recover it if lost.''

Return to Apostolic Practice

This action was described afterward by Dr. Henry Stauffer of Park Congregational church, who took part, ''not as a method of combating Christian Science, but of returning to the original practice of the Apostolic church. He said:

''Christ, as was shown at the meeting, exemplified a threefold ministry—preaching, teaching and healing.

''His church in later times became befogged with the-ological discussions and hair-splitting argumentative preach-ing, and healing was forgotten.

''It is to restore this important phase of Christianity that this movement has been commenced.''

Two Questions. By Prof. E. E. Jacobs

In going over the records of the college lately, two questions forced themselves upon my mind.

First, Why have some churches had so many represen-tatives in the seminary and college and why have some had so few or none? Is it because there were no likely young people in the latter churches? Or was it because the pastors did not take sufficient interest to encourage young people to prepare for the work of the church? Or was there some-thing wrong with the spiritual life in those churches? Or was it purely accidental? I could name a few churches which have had representatives here either in the college or seminary ever since I came to the school and they have still other young people in prospect. One thing ought never to be neglected in the local churches—that of inspiring young people to higher education and pointing them to our own church school.

Second, Why are there so few minister's children in the seminary? The other morning in speaking to the members of this department of the college, I found that I was the only one present whose father was a minister. Do our ministers regard their calling in such a light that they do not want their sons and daughters to enter it? We talk much about recruiting the profession but may it be in this case as it was with a bishop in another church? One morning he was urg-ing with much vigor the necessity of parents giving their sons and daughters to the work of the church when his own daughter pressed her way down to the altar rail. He was greatly moved and with choking voice, leaned over and whis-pered to her, ''Why, Frances, I did not mean you.''

WE PREACH—GOD WORKS

Dr. Chapman told this incident: Just to pass away the evening a man came into one of his services in Los Angeles. The power of God seemed at once to take hold of him. He lifted his hand for prayer, and to the consternation of the one who sat with him, he said, ''I am here playing the races and am the owner of five saloons in my home city.'' His conviction seemed to deepen with each service, and at last he boldly stood up and acknowledge his allegiance to his Savior.

CHRIST'S OPPORTUNITY

You may be browbeaten, tormented, excommunicated, driven from your home and friends, lonesome and depressed; but that is Christ's supreme opportunity. He will find you, and in the absence of every other solace, he will be your Comforter, will pour in the wine and oil of his sympathy, and give the supreme revelation of his own wonderful na-ture.—The King's Business.

THE BRETHREN PULPIT

A Prayer Band Letter

February 9th, 1920.

Two letters from our African party reached me at one time, but they were mailed almost a month apart by Brother Gribble. I will not pass the first letter along since most of the items of prayer therein contained have been answered already. The following is a lengthy message, but it is of EXTRAORDINARY IMPORTANCE. Kindly read it over carefully, and then get others to join you in praying it over until you come to have the same burden as have our missionaries, for the pouring out of the Holy Spirit.

A. L. DeLOZIER, Prayer Band Secretary.

Nola, French Equatorial Africa,
November 6, 1919.

Dear members of the Ubangi-Shari Mission Prayer Bands:

After a six weeks' stay at Nola, we will be going on to Carnot. Monday, November 10th, just two months from the time that we left Brazzaville, we are expecting to leave Nola for the last great lap of our journey. How glad we are over it all! To me, the trip from Nola to Carnot the impression is similar to what Joshua must have felt when he was contemplating the crossing of the Jordan right over against Jericho. When at Carnot, we will be in the midst of the great Baya tribe, which is the people that we feel our immediate call to. And by means of the Baya language will be able to converse with the people right over into Ubangi-Shari, possibly nearly as far east as the great military road running from Bangui to Ft. Crampel. Praise God for all of his faithfulness!

Now I will come to the real burden of this letter. While our hearts are full of praise to our God for what he has been doing, they are also heavily burdened for the work to which we have been called. And, not for our work only, but for the sake of the Gospel in the whole of the Eastern French Soudan are our hearts burdened. We feel, from what we have been told by officials at Brazzaville, as well as by officials here at Nola, that our going forth is for the purpose of putting the Gospel we preach to a test among the pagan peoples living in the Eastern French Soudan. As well as I can relate it from my present understanding, this is the situation: Mohammedanism, which is very rapidly spreading all through the country, is not meeting with the approval of the French government. On the other hand, the government realizes that the people need a change; it is not content that they remain as they are. But from what the French government knows about the church and Christianity, for it is the Roman Catholic church with which it has had to deal, it is of the opinion that Christianity also will not help the native to be any better. Officials declare that some of the worst people that they have met in Africa are Roman Catholic missionaries. Their lives are not better than those of any other white people that one meets in the land. And Catholic converts are as shrewd rascals as one can meet anywhere.

But, I am glad to report that the government has a higher opinion of the Brethren party. While at Brazzaville we seem to have passed their inspection successfully. Now, while they are not giving us sufficient permission to make any noise about, we cannot say that we are bound either. At this present time we have all of the permission that we can use to any advantage. The government is going rather slow on opening up the country to missionaries but is anxious to see the Gospel that we preach put to the test. They seem to be satisfied that we are what we profess to be, but they are a bit skeptical as to the power of the Gospel to change the hearts of these natives. They even think that after we have made a trial, we also will give it up as a bad job. And, while they consider the Baya tribe as being one of the most intelligent pagan tribes, they also consider them

one of the most stubborn. You see that now the trial has passed from us to the Gospel that we preach, as far as the government is concerned. Therefore we may well say, the Gospel is challenged in the Eastern French Soudan. Yes, the power of the Gospel is challenged. In this dark land, Christianity is a new thing. None have upheld Jesus Christ in this dark land. In the name of our Lord Jesus Christ, we will accept the challenge, and trust him to vindicate his word and power in the Eastern French Soudan as greatly as he did when the lame beggar was healed at the Beautiful Gate.

Now then for the issue. God has and is helping us greatly in getting the Baya language. We have found and still find great difficulties in getting that language, but some of the party have made such great progress that the Baya people themselves marvel. From what we have heard, our fame has spread quite a distance already into the Baya tribe, and they are all anxious to have us come. But, in order to prove to the world once more that the Gospel of Jesus Christ has not lost its power to change men's lives, we need more than to be able to preach well in the Baya language. It will be found that the natural hearts of the Baya people are as unwilling to be reconciled to God as those of any other people. While they have never been Gospel hardened they will not be "Gospel softened" either. And, no amount of missionary machinery will solve the problem. No, nothing but a mighty working of the HOLY SPIRIT upon the Baya people themselves. Nothing else will do. And, we must not think that anything else will do. While we expect to have schools, medical work, etc., those things will, at their best, only serve as getting us into closer touch with the people and will have no power toward changing their hearts.

Now, realizing that the working of the Holy Spirit alone will bring the needed results, we need to go a step farther. The Holy Spirit will not work among the Baya people except as he goes out through our lives. That is, the lives of the missionaries. We must not only have the gift of the Spirit, which is the heritage of all believers, but we must be actually spirit filled. The Holy Spirit needs to take hold of our lives and absolutely control them. We must be simply swallowed up by him.

I am well aware of the fact that people usually look upon the missionary as being so good and holy that it would seem almost slander for one to pray that they might be swept free from all sin and selfishness, so as to give the Holy Spirit a right of way in their lives. That is a mistaken idea. Along this very line missionaries need your prayers most. We need your prayers that our bodies might be kept strong, but a thousand times more we need them that we may be constantly FILLED WITH THE HOLY SPIRIT, for it is only then that we will fully reveal Christ to these people. Yes, we need your prayers that first of all, there will be a genuine outpouring of the Holy Spirit upon us, and then upon the people unto whom we bring the Gospel. It is almost useless to pray that God would work a mighty work in the hearts of the natives, if the HOLY SPIRIT is not working complete control of the lives of the missionaries.

Therefore, in the interest of the work to which God has called us, and in the interest of the entrance of the Gospel into the whole of the Eastern French Soudan, we earnestly plead with you to pray for a mighty outpouring of the Holy Spirit in the Eastern French Soudan, beginning with the missionaries.

Yours, for the furtherance of the Gospel and for the hastening of his coming.   JAMES S. GRIBBLE.

The above "Prayer Band Letter" from our Brother

Gribble was received during the past week from Brother DeLozier and mailed out to all of the Brethren churches on the Pacific coast, to all of the U. S. M. prayer bands not connected with any Brethren church and to all isolated praying members that I have on my list. If there are any who should have received a copy who did not, or any who would like to be counted as a member of this intercessory band and receive copies of the letters as they come, please send me your name and address and I will be glad to put the same on my roll,—that is, if you are in the Pacific coast division.

I have just been summing up the Sunday school lesson for tomorrow (February 22), preparatory to teaching it, and as I pondered on the fifth verse, which read as follows: "Peter therefore was kept in prison; but prayer was made without ceasing of the church unto God for him." My mind would wander to far off Africa; and I wondered, heart searchingly wondered, if I—yes and the whole church at home—had been faithful. While the Ubangi-Shari band was "therefore kept in prison (1)" did we "pray without ceasing unto God for them!" Could we have shortened that that testing time that will always be thought of by the Brethren church as the Siege of Brazzaville? While that faithful little band was standing by its call, amidst storms, fevers and multiplied testings, shut in by the great iron gates of governmental ruling, yet gently, sweetly, but nevertheless very persistently, knocking, knocking at the fast closed door to Ubangi-Shari; (a door which in all past ages has never swung open to admit the messengers of the gospel of the grace of God) could the Holy Spirit have said of the Brethren church of the United States what he said of that little church at Jerusalem?

Well God has opened the gates of Brazzaville, and the little band so dear to us, has gone on its way rejoicing "as seeing him who is invisible." They have penetrated into the blackest heathendom of the earth, where they have permission to sow the gospel seed amongst a fierce cannibal people know as the BAYA tribe (pronounced Bah-yah). We must continue to pray for the open door into Ubangi-Shari (pronounced U-bahn-ge Sha-re).

God has signally honored us, the band in the field, the Rollier family and dear Sister Mary in particular in that he permitted her to lay down her life on the threshold of this unreached territory, to be the stepping stone for the blessed Gospel of our Lord Jesus Christ. Brother Wm. Haas, who was with our band in the wait at Brazzaville, said "God sowed a laborer that he might reap a harvest of laborers," Who will heed the Master's voice and answer quickly, "Here am I, send me, send me!"

Whether or not we were faithful before, we can by his grace be faithful from now on, and stand in unceasing prayer for those on the front line of battle for the Lord.

We know that the requests in Brother Gribble's letter are in full accord with the will of God, so let us boldly and fearlessly approach the throne and lay hold of God in a very definite way for these things. Then let us pray as persistently and with equal faith that God will hold back the hosts of Islam, keeping the door closed against them, and only open the door to the messengers of the cross of Jesus Christ. The shed blood of the cross of Calvary is just as powerful to redeem the worst savage in Africa as the most enlightened man of any land.

LET US PRAY.

In his service
MRS. GRACE P. SRACK,
118 Locust Ave.   Long Beach, California.

Send
WHITE GIFT
OFFERINGS to

THE SUNDAY SCHOOL

ALBERT TRENT
General Secretary-Treasurer
Johnstown, Pennsylvania

The Adult Division. By L. G. Wood

Before gradation was introduced in the Bible school, there was no Adult Division. The school existed for children only, but if some eccentric grown-ups really cared to go, they could form themselves into a Bible class. Now since practically all schools are graded, it is quite different. This change was brought about chiefly through the Organized Adult Bible Class Movement. The Bible school today is organized and graded.

We have come to see the need of eight departments and three grand divisions. 1. The Elementary division, composed of the Cradle Roll, Beginners, Primary and Juniors. 2. The Secondary division, composed of the Intermediates and Seniors or early and later teen age pupils. 3. The Adult division, comprising all classes whose members are twenty years of age and over. This division has grown so rapidly in the International Association, that it stands today as one of the greatest forces in the religious world. Our own schools report a membership in this division of 6,216.

Ordinarily there should be at least four classes in this division, one for the young men, one for the young women, one for the older men and one for the older women. Every school should have an Adult Division superintendent, who should be a man or a woman of earnest Christian character with a good working knowledge of the Bible and Bible courses of study. The teachers also should not only be "apt to teach" but should be controlled by a love for the BOOK, a love for the WORK and a love for the CLASS. This is the division to which all other divisions naturally look for example, for instance it is sure to be a FORCE or a FARCE in every school. The adult membership of our schools have done excellent work in the last few years by a loyal participation in all of the general work of the church.

The call of the goals of the Four Year Program have been heard and answered in a measure that is encouraging. But the greatest blessings and richest treasures come to those who persevere.

To me the greatest call of the ages is now sounding loudly to the Christian forces of the world, and especially to the Adult Division of the Bible school. How shall we answer this call? 1. By a constant connection with God at the throne of grace. 2. By organizing new classes for efficiency in service. 3. By re-vitalizing classes that are already organized, for power and equipment. 4. By making a practical application of the great lessons are now pursuing.

In the Adult Division of our schools there are 147 unregistered classes reported. These should be organized and registered and receive our denominational seal; this entitles both class and members to the adult class emblem, which is a small red circle with a white center. The significance of which is—"There is no purity of life without sacrifice and no cleansing from sin without the shedding of blood" (Heb. 9:22). The only way to increase our own lives is to live for others. There is no greater opportunity for soul winning than in the adult Bible class. The organized class and personal evangelism should go hand in hand.

The center and climax of the organized class work is Bible teaching. We certainly have at the present a course of lessons that fit into the great movements of the day. A Sunday school teacher was once asked if she ever presented a missionary lesson to her class. She said, "No I am not interested in missions." When asked what she was teaching, she replied, "The Acts." The lesson is obvious. That book of the Bible which give a description of the spread of Christianity in its purity and is at the fountain head and contains the record of the operation of the Holy Spirit in the formation of the infant church, should inspire every student for the greatest effort of all history.

What a great influence the organized adult Bible class can exert on the individual member, on the school, on the church, on the community and on the world! It is a blessed task to teach an adult Bible class, a task fraught with countless possibilities and with results that eternity only can reveal. It is a blessed task to be a member of the class, with a vision of class possibilities and to go out from the class into other fields of service, a stronger, better, more earnest Christian worker.

May God continue to bless the organized adult Bible class and may it be in the future a still more potent force for righteousness than it has been in the past.

We are now ready and anxious to issue our denominational seals to all classes that will organize and register. Seals and registration blanks will be sent free on application. At present you are to secure your certificate of recognition from your International state office, and your d national seal from the writer. We expect to be able soon to issue certificates of recognition direct from our national association. Organize at once and let me hear from you and your good work.

DIVISION SUPERINTENDENT.
1118 Gilmer Ave N. W., Roanoke, Virginia.

| J. A. Garber | Our Young People at Work | G. C. Carpenter. |
| PRESIDENT | | SECRETARY |

Christian Endeavor Specials. By Prof. J. A. Garber

PERSONAL EVANGELISM

In the foregoing number of the Evangelist, mention was made of personal soul-winning in an article entitled, "Church Loyalty" by E. P. Gates. During the month of March various phases of "Church Loyalty" will be emphasized in the Christian Endeavor Work. One of these is Personal Evangelism, a most important factor in the life of any church.

Personal Evangelism is nothing more than a definite effort to win people for Christ. Our program concerns young people and we shall have to put forth our endeavors along the lines of the winning of young people. There are several ways by which this may be done. Prayer meeting groups may be formed, whose members will pray each day for certain young people. The place and time of meeting may be varied. Assembling in the home of an active Christian Endeavorer once per week might be a good plan. Meeting just before the regular Christian Endeavor service, also, ought to be another way by which a soul-winning spirit could be aroused. It might be maintained, in this connection, that no matter where, or under what conditions these meetings may be held, a spirit of prayer ought to be maintained. Prayer is the greatest instrument in personal evangelism and it should dominate the lives of all soul-winners. Discussions centering around questions relating to the conversion of certain individuals might be of great value. Then again, Endeavorers who are Sunday school teachers should speak to each scholar about accepting Christ. The teacher who deals wisely with pupils can easily take advantage of this opportunity and thus do a bit of personal soul-winning. Lest it might be overlooked, special work should be done with the associate members of the Christian Endeavor Society. This can be accomplished effectively in the society itself. Older members may be of great service here because of experience. Moreover, outside individuals should not be passed by. At this point a consultation with your pastor might be of value. It will help in that you may do only those things which fit in his program. By so doing some souls should be won.

ECHOES OF ASHLAND COLLEGE NIGHT

The following is a report from Brother Edwin Boardman, our Life Work Superintendent: We observed Life Work and Ashland College Night last Sunday and we had a fine time. We gave the pageant and its message just seemed to get under the surface of the folks who came to see it. I believe that it was much more effective than a spoken sermon would have been. We advertised the Pageant in the local newspaper and to my surprise we had a fine crowd out on the special evening. Due to the main character failing me the last minute I had to memorize the part and act as the "Sprit." We buttressed the Pageant with two very effective solos at the beginning and the end and this just made it the length of a good service.

I have two churches reported so far and if the other seventy or eighty do as well as the first two we will surely go over the top when the returns are all in. The two who have reported are: Canton, $5.05; Hudson, $16.00. This looks like business to me. It looks as if the churches waited for the later date or I would have had more returns in by now. This week and next will tell the story. Here's hoping that we really have a "victory" year in this objective.

Since receiving Brother Boardman's message a letter came from Brother E. S. Flora of Beaver City enclosing a check for $16.00. This is fine for Beaver City and the response is probably due the presence and work of Brother Flora who is a live Ashland College man.

Other societies should report gifts and names of recruits to Rev. Edwin Boardman of Hudson, Iowa, at the earliest possible date.

| SEND ALL MONEY FOR | MISSIONS | WILLIAM A. GEARHART |
| General Home, Kentucky and Foreign Missions to | | General Missionary Secretary 906 Conover Bldg., Dayton, O. |

A LONG LETTER FROM OUR LITTLE GRIBBLE

Baria, French Eq. Africa, Nov. 15th, 1919.
My dear little friends:

It is about a week since I wrote to you but so much has happened I hardly see how I can get it all into a letter.

On Monday, November 10th, we left Nola. On the Sunday evening before we all had dinner with Mr. Beck, the government official there. It was very strange to hear so much French talked so rapidly. Monsieur Pineri, the administrator at Carnot was there, also Monsieur Bowe, who is in charge of a branch of the large company known as the Forrestaire. We had dinner very late and mamma excused herself and me as soon as possible afterwards, so that might be rested for our trip the next day.

Very early the next morning we were up and preparing for our start. But delays will occur in Africa. We actually started at nine o'clock.

Our boats were baleinieres, small boats made of steel which are used on many rivers of Africa. In one of them was part of our baggage and Aunt Toddy, Daddy, Mamma and I. In the other was Uncle Antoine, Marie and Julia, and some of their baggage. In the little pirogue, or wooden boat which accompanied us was much of our heavy baggage and some of our boys. There were ten paddlers for each boat. We certainly were glad to be starting at last for Bania, after our six weeks' stay at Nola. We ate our lunches on the boat each day. The river was not Very wide and the scenery on both sides was beautiful. The paddlers kept close to the side of the stream as the current was Very rapid, and there were many rapids and whirlpools. The first night at five o'clock we came into a little nook in the trees, where a shelter had been erected under which the boys and men slept that night.

We put up our tents, got supper oVer the camp fire, and soon after eight, we were all snugly in bed. We were tired, the night was cool and morning came all too soon. There were leopards in the bushes around us, but they did not molest us. Mamma told us children to keep Very quiet and especially not to cry, for we do cry when we are tired and hungry and sleepy all at once. But the least thought of the animals quieted, us and as we remembered our heaVenly. Father's loving care our fears were calmed. The' next morning we were up early. Breakfast was oVer and tents down by seven o'clock, and we were off again. · This day was still longer for we were ten hours on the way and it was five o'clock again when we came into our next little camp, where a rest house was awaiting us. In this we put our beds, and were glad we need not put up the tent again. Supper was soon ready and we were all so hungry.

Mamma had a little serVice in Baya with a big crowd of people and one of the oarsmen interpreted in Pandi for those who didn't understand Baya.

The next morning we decided only to cook breakfast on shore and to eat in the canoe. We arose literally at first cock crow, for the rooster slept in the corner of the room, and when he crowed at four o'clock we arose. Mamma thinks he's better than an alarm clock. At 15 minutes of six, we were off again, but it was a long day of 12 hours before we pulled into camp again. Aunt Teddy had a little service with the people that evening. She found the people there understood French better than Baya, so she talked in French. It is a wonderful thing when their people understand for the first time about Jesus, but it was so sad to go from each of these camps and leave them with only one hearing of the gospel story and no prospect of their hearing it again. That night Daddy and Uncle Antoine had to sleep outside. Unfortunately it rained and they got wet, but as there were five beds already in one small room, we didn't know just how to manage. Daddy has a little canVas canopy on · his camp bed, which makes him imagine he is dry when it rains. But Uncle Antoine was on the leaky grass Verandas, and a narrow one at that, so we· were glad when morning came. We got a later start than usual that morning, and at seven o'clock pulled out. Mamma said as we had been eight hours in the canoe the first day, ten hours the next, and twelve hours the next she supposed we would be fourteen hours reaching Bania that day. We were surprised therefore to come into Bania at one P. M., only six hours! We were so glad to get out of the canoes.

I must tell you several things that happened on our journey to Bania that I forgot to mention.

On our second day, I was tired of sitting under the little grass roof which covered the middle of our canoe, and as it was growing cooler, I was sitting outside on Porido's lap. Kobe, another of our boys, was sitting beside me when all of a sudden he commenced saying, "Me si twa, Marguerite, me si, me si." I didn't want to do it for that meant I was to go under the coVering, where I couldn't see the pretty flowers. But the boys pushed me in and I commenced to cry. This made the boys more alarmed than eVer, and they said, "Doknu me, Marguerite." That means literally, "Shut your mouth," and seemed to mamma to be rather unkind. So she said, "Hajugi!" Why? and they responded, "Goh asene'—There is a leopard." Daddy had been reading but he sprang up to look, but too late, for the boys said "Apina," it has gone. Mamma was touched that the little heathen boys had had no thought for themselves, but only for me. The leopard had been in the branches of the tree almost at the side of the canoe. Mamma says we can never know from how many dangers both seen and unseen our heaVenly Father constantly preserves us, not only in Africa, but whereVer a little child may be.

(Continued NeXt Week)

HAPPENINGS IN AFRICA

Dear Brethren in the Lord:

It is with great joy that I am able to write you from a point beyond BrazzaVille. God is faithful, and in his faithfulness would not permit our little party of missionaries to be foreVer retained at BrazzaVille, or any other place short of the part where he has called and is calling them to make the name of Jesus known. The faithfulness of God is our only refuge and we are glad to know that it is a sure one. Inasmuch as he has neVer failed those who have taken him at his word and have obeyed him, he will in no wise desert us howeVer much the adVersary may seem to triumph oVer us. Therefore we are of good courage "though our outward man is decaying, yet our inward man is renewed day by day."

During the years in his serVice some of us have passed through some pretty deep waters with the Lord. We have known what it means to be almost one whole month in a strange land without a cent of money. We haVe known what it means to be without food of any kind for prolonged periods of time and to be sustained by the power of God alone. Yet possibly nothing that we have passed through has been more trying than the long wait at BrazzaVille. God, and God alone could sustain us. And praise his name, he did sustain us. Yet, as one member of the party has well said "The wait at BrazzaVille certainly did take the sap out of one."

After considerable discussion on the subject, on the afternoon of September the 8th, we were giVen the formal information that we were permitted to proceed beyond Brazzaville.

The evening of September the 9th found us all on board the riVer steamer "Djah" which was to convey us as far as Ouesso (Wesso), the first stage of our journey. No more tired set of people eVer started on a journey than we, for we left BrazzaVille almost as hastily as the children of Israel did Egypt. We felt Satanic opposition on every hand. But we knew that the Lord was with us. When the baggage was being taken to the boat on September the 8th, Mary Rollier went down with a severe attack of fever, which threatened to be a prolonged siege. But, in answer to prayer and according to God's faithfulness, she had no feVer the next day. Finally, a bit after 3 o'clock in the morning of September the

10th, the "Djah" began her course up the mighty Congo RiVer from BrazzaVille.

Ar. Dr. Gribble has quite fully written about our journey, I will try not to duplicate what she has already written. HoweVer, I will try to supplement. She has told you of the death of our Sister Rollier. Her death came Very unexpectedly and also as a great blow. Her name was added to the already Very great list of those who have died from the effects of the deadly Congo malaria. Yet she was not the only one of our party who had feVer on the trip. Nearly eVery member of the party suffered from it. There was one day in which she was being carried in a coffin in a smaller boat by the side of the "Djah" and three other members had a rise of temperature. It certainly did look as if Satan would be able to stop the party. But God deliVered and the journey was continued.

The Congo RiVer flows through some very beautiful country and some of which is not so much so. From near its mouth to a point near Bolobo it is bordered by hills, many of which are grass covered. Some places these hills are really mountains, for between Stanley Pool and Matadi the riVer actually breaks through the mountains. (But we have not yet seen in West Africa such lofty mountains as are in East Africa.) But from near Bolobo 'up as far as we journeyed on the Congo, and for a Very long ways up the Sangha RiVer, the country is Very flat and uninViting. At the mouth of the Sangha RiVer the land is just about the height of the water in the river when the riVer is at its highest. As a matter of fact, the water occasionally coVers the surrounding country. A man in the employ of the government told us that at certain times the water of the riVer coVers the floor of his house. When the writer saw the great amount of interior Africa that is not much more than a Veritable swamp, he thought within himself how much better it would have been for the European nations to spend a fraction of the money that the war cost to blast out a bit of the bottom of the Congo RiVer in the Vicinity of BrazzaVille and whereVer there are reefs aboVe that place which would not permit the riVer to deepen its course.

While all of the Lower Sangha is bordered by dense forests, and one does not see a grass covered hilltop until he nears Nola, the riVer banks at many places are quite high. At Ikelemba they are Very high. Also the riVer becomes much narrower. At Ouesso it is about one-sixth of a mile wide, while below there it becomes wider and wider and at most places is possibly a half mile wide. From Ouesso toward Nola the river becomes much narrower and swifter. At one or two places it is only about a hundred yards wide and so swift that it is hard for the riVer steamer to make much headway against the current.

According to all that we have heard, all of the tribes liVing along the Sangha RiVer are cannibals, some of which are Very fierce. Possibly along the same riVer liVe as many large monkeys as can be found anywhere. The forests that border it are the home of the great African gorilla. Just across the riVer from Nola is a high forest coVered hill which is called "Monkey Mountain." We are told that many gorillas are to be found there, and that it is Very dangerous to hunt them as they are considered one of the most dangerous of all animals. At Nola the Sangha RiVer is formed by the junction of two others, the Ekela (which comes from the north at Carnot) and the Kadei.

NeVer have we realized more forcibly that our times are in God's hands. When we reached Ouesso, our going forward seemed to be Very uncertain. The only boat that was there had a number of other passengers aside from us to take up the river, and as, in the eyes of the world, missionaries are the ones least needed in this country, the chances were that we would be left behind while others preceded us. And to make things look worse, the captain declared that he was going to quit. However, he took a liking to us and said that he would do what he could in our favor. (Omnipotence hath servants everywhere). Well, we do not know the whys and wherefores, but this is what happened: After being at Ouesso four days, we boarded the little boat and began our journey to Nola. And, as our little party greatly crowded the capacity of the little outfit, we were the only passengers.

The evening of the second day from Ouesso our boat encountered the other one of the same company which was coming from Nola to Ouesso. On board was the Administrator from Nola who was on his way to Ouesso and Brazzaville. He was rather elderly and had been in the service long enough to be on the retired list and seemed to be sort of a privileged character. In appearance he greatly reminded one of the late Colonel Cody (Buffalo Bill). We have been told that the natives greatly respected him. When first seeing our party he seemed filled with wonderment, but in reading some letters that had been handed him by the captain of our boat, he knew that we were missionaries and seemed very glad to meet us. When he learned that one of the party was a physician, he seemed doubly glad and expressed a desire for us to remain at Nola.

When we reached Nola we found that the place did not appeal to us a bit as far as a place for the beginning of our work is concerned. It is low lying and swampy. Also it is yet within the forest and the tribes living here are not as promising as those farther north. The chief tribe here is the Konde, which, while being pretty large and terribly needy, does not seem to be as promising a one to begin mission work among as the Baya. The Baya tribe is encountered in force just a hundred miles north from here, and sections of the tribe are found much farther south.

Living expenses here at Nola are considerably less than they were for us at Brazzaville. Here we get twenty eggs for a franc and at Brazzaville we never got more than eight and many times not more than six for the same amount. Most other native foods are correspondingly cheap, and we are not in

need of purchasing imported ones. But sleeping sickness is about here and we have a number of mosquitoes also. Now we have a number of Baya boys working for us, some of whom are sons of a chief, and from these we have begun studying the Baya language. ·

We continue to plead with you to remember us earnestly in prayer that we may soon be given an open door for making Jesus Christ known to the Baya people and that we may be so indwelt by the Holy Spirit as to make our work very fruitful. God alone is able for our need. In speaking of our undertaking a friendly official at Brazzaville once re-

marked to our party that attempting to bring "religion" into French territory we have undertaken the hardest thing that we have ever met. But he also said that we trust in and have a Power back of us which will not fail us, and he advised that we forsake not that Power for any other help. And we have no intentions of doing so either, for "Hitherto Jehovah has been our Helper." To him alone be all the praise. JAMES S. GRIBBLE.

Nola, October 4, 1919.

Note: Since writing the above, the party has proceeded one hundred miles further on, and is now located at Carnot.—L. S. B.

THE FOREIGN MISSION OFFERING

The Time.— EASTER SUNDAY, April 4th is the time for the WHOLE BRETHREN CHURCH and all her auxiliary organizations to make an OFFERING as unto the LORD.

The Purpose.—1. This offering is made for the SUPPORT of all our MISSIONARY ENTERPRISES both in ARGENTINA AND AFRICA.

2. The offering is made for the ENLARGEMENT of our present endeavors by sending forth NEW WORKERS into UNOCCUPIED fields.

The Goal.— A Gift of MONEY can never measure our DEBT to GRACE nor dare any earnest Christian ever LIMIT his giving by a suggestion of SO-MUCH-PER member. The "GENEROUS GIFT" (2 Cor. 9:5) falls below or RISES FAR ABOVE the suggested $1.00 per member. "GRACE" measures the gift made to JESUS.

Your Report.— Send all offerings to the General Missionary Secretary of the Brethren Church. Brother WILLIAM A. GEARHART, 906 Conover Building, DAYTON, OHIO.

A Telegram.— Pastors and Churches are invited to send prepaid telegrams or night letters to the Editor of the Brethren Evangelist on Monday, April 5th. Report the success of your EASTER SERVICE both in SOULS won to the Lord and in MONEY given to FOREIGN MISSIONS.

NEWS FROM THE FIELD

WARSAW, INDIANA

Since the last report from this part of God's vineyard we have been going through the blessed state of perpetual revival and the Lord has been adding to the church daily such as should be saved. This report will deal most of all with the result of our great revival meetings which closed recently. They began January 11th and closed February 1st. Our pastor, who was in the evangelistic field prior to coming to us, was the leader of the campaign. He was assisted by a very able party, Dr. and Mrs. F. C. Olds who were engaged to direct the singing and to render special music, and they did their part exceedingly well. Dr. Olds directed a chorus choir of thirty voices, which our pastor says was the best choir he had ever heard in similar meetings held over the country, their singing together, with the special numbers by Mrs. Olds, were very attractive. We also had in the party Prof. Rapp who was engaged to do the playing. His work on the piano was remarkable. He always inspired the audiences to do their utmost to sing and to do their part well. Prof. Rapp was a convert of the Billy Sunday meetings held in Winona Lake last summer. Dr. and Mrs. Olds together with Prof. Rapp are members of the Baptist church, but they did

their work with all heart and soul. Then our pastor did the preaching. Every evening he was greeted with wonderful audiences, and his messages were full of evangelistic fire, deeply spiritual, and doctrinally true to the Blessed Book, which he loves to preach. Another special feature of the meetings was a Junior choir with an average attendance of forty boys and girls at every service. For three weeks the fire burned and the souls of men and women were stirred as East Warsaw has not been stirred for many a day.

Before giving the results, we should like to tell further the far reaching effects of the meetings. The delegations that came were of the noted kind. One night "Ma" Sunday led a delegation from Winona Lake. Her personality and experience in such meetings added strength to the night services and it proved to be one of the best held. Another night the Rev. Percival Morgan, son of the noted London preacher, G. Campbell Morgan, was present together with his brothers, four in all, and all preachers of the Word. So many others came, but these were among the particularly notable.

The results of the meeting, well, they went beyond the expectation of all. We were hindered somewhat with the "flu," but it did

not stop us, at the end the tabulation said that 57 had made some definite stand for the Master, 38 of these have already been received and quite a number more have been baptized but not yet having received the hand of fellowship, while some are awaiting baptism. Since the meetings closed three more have come and the revival spirit is still on. In all, the church will be strengthened by the addition of fifty members and the lives of many others who were Christian in name only received a new power and are doing something for the cause.

Besides this, we rejoice in the great fact that the campaign was a great success financially, over three hundred dollars being raised, and given to the evangelists for their work. The congregation worked a plan by which the pastor was given a neat purse of 100 dollars besides his salary for his part, and the other two were paid as contract called for. This proves that the Brethren church aroused and stirred by the Holy Spirit can if she will take evangelism seriously and pay those who make doing this work a good living wage. Warsaw not by any means the richest congregation, has shown the spirit that wins and God will honor her faith.

Besides the personal check, Brother Thomas

was presented with a beautiful picture of the late Wilbur Chapman, given to him by the sister of the deceased man of God.

Following this great meeting we had a communion, the first one in three years. It was well attended and a deep spirit prevailed. Brother J. A. McInturff of Goshen assisted the pastor.

. The prayer service which is the thermometer of the church is going on with renewed interest, attendance averaging 50. Our pastor is now preaching a series of sermons which is attracting attention and great crowds are coming to us.. This evening we are planning a reception for the new members and trust that they will ever be faithful to their decision which they have made. We are praying for victory in the future. Our pastor is going to assist Brother Kimmel at Muncie for a few weeks and upon his return is planning passion week services of instruction and and evangelism. Busy days are ahead; pray for us.

ALBERT G. HARTMAN.

TURLOCK, CALIFORNIA

The work at Turlock is in good condition, at the present time. Brother Reagan retired from service as pastor here October 1st. He served this church faithfully for one year. Needless to say the church was richly blessed by his ministry, as it was in the fourteen years of service from his predecessor Brother Darling. We took up the work here October 1st. We found many good loyal Brethren here which goes far to make a church stable and successful.

On the evening of October 27th, we were agreeably surprised by a large number of the members calling on us at the parsonage. Each one brought some very practical token of good fellowship. The articles are entirely too numerous to mention in detail; but may be sufficient to say that the warmth of the spirit of the givers was appreciated immensely.

Sunday, November second, the deacons' and deaconesses' organization presented an interesting program of service to the church, which was enthusiastically received by all the members in attendance. The program provides for the care of the sick and the poor who are unable to help themselves. Also to assist any who may be out of employment to find necessary and worthy labor.

Sunday, November 16th, union evangelistic services were opened in a large tabernacle seating nearly three thousand people. John Elward Brown was the evangelist. All who have ever heard Brown know that he is a splendid man, doing a fine work successfully. As a result of these meetings we baptized eight persons whom we received into full fellowship in the Brethren church.

We received our Thanksgiving offering November 30th. The offering amounted to one hundred and twenty dollars and fifteen cents.

On Christmas Eve a splendid program was rendered. The children and young people giving most of the parts. They were trained and prepared exceedingly well by Sister Blewett, Superintendent of the graded work in our Sunday school. A splendid part of the program was when the adults gave their White Gifts which amounted to seventy-nine dollars. After the program the children were each

given a good treat of candy, fruit and nuts. Also the pastor and family were remembered by having handed to them a weighty little box containing fifteen silver dollars. Besides many individual gifts helped in bringing much cheer and happiness of the season to the parsonage.

At the present writing our services have been somewhat handicapped on account of the recurrence of the "flu" epidemic. However we are pleased that the plague is not as severe as it was last year, and that our services are not closed altogether. Several of our people are seriously ill. Our Brother Reagan who has his membership with us here at Turlock is very ill. The church unites in praying for him and the others. Brother Reagan is now superintendent of the Union Rescue Mission of Los Angeles.

The spiritual state of our church enables us to report progress in goal one of the Four Year Program. But with other pastors we can see that this is not sufficient for perfect satisfaction.

We are soon to enter into our Northern California Conference and Bible Institute. A date and program will be submitted to the Evangelist Editor for publication later. We need the Lord's help here in Turlock, and Northern California. Will you pray for this?

N. V. LEATHERMAN.

BUENA VISTA, VIRGINIA

As we peruse the columns of The Evangelist we seldom ever hear from Buena Vista. I think a word would be in order at this time at least.

First, I would like to say that we are not dead but alive to the cause of Christ. Brother G. W. Chambers who served us for two years as a faithful pastor and worker, gave up this work December 31st, 1919. We regret very much to lose him. He was very much appreciated and loved by all. He made many friends in our city. He is worthy of recommendation to any work.

Brother Charles Cooke and his wife came among us the first of January to take charge of this work. They too are alive to the cause of Christ. They have the church at heart. We are anticipating great things for the Master in this year of 1920. Many of those that have been lukewarm and indifferent to the cause have come to the point where they realize their responsibility to God and the church.

Second. We have a fine Sunday school at this place. It is increasing in attendance as well as in interest each week. We have a mid-week prayer meeting with an average attendance of about fifty. We feel uplifted for the interest shown in these meetings.

Brother H. H. Rowsey of Roanoke, the state superintendent of the Christian Endeavor work came down during the holidays and organized a Christian Endeavor union. The good seed was sown. The brethren and sisters took hold of this work with fire and vim. At our last meeting, February 8th, our topic was "A Call to Service or Life Work." Two came out voluntarily and took the Life Work covenant, giving their lives to the Master's service. We solicit the prayers of the brotherhood in behalf of this work. We have material here that can be used in the Mas-

ter's vineyard. The harvest is great and the laborers are few. If our young people can come to a point where they can realize the significance of the great commission as well as the promise as recorded in Matthew 28:18-21, there will be many to volunteer.

M. M. TE...

(HOME MISSIONS)
General Fund

Orin Cause, Apollo, Pa., (H. G.), ...$	5.00
Brethren Ch., Masontown, Pa., ...	50.00
Br. Ch., Roann, Ind., ...	80.00
1st Br. Ch., Los Angeles, Cal., ...	81.24
Br. Ch., Gratis, Ohio, ...	65.00
Ardmore Br. Ch., South Bend, Ind., ...	25.00
Miss Catharine Fields, South Bend, Ind., $5.00 (H. G.), ...	
1st Br. Ch., Long Beach, Cal., ...	130.00
Br. Ch., Dallas Center, Iowa, ...	53.75
Br. Ch., Sidney, Ind., ...	35.85
Br. Ch., N. Georgetown, Ohio, ...	4.85
Will Swinney, Limestone, Tenn., (H. G.), ...	5.00
Interest on Monthly Balances, ...	4.45
Union Chapel, Br. Ch., Leon, Iowa, ..	8.10
Maple Grove Br. Ch., Noreatur, Kans., ..	10.00
Br. Ch., Burlington, Ind., ...	50.00
Br. Ch., Darwin, Ind., ...	15.50
Calvary Br. Ch., Pittstown, N. J., ..	25.00
Br. Ch., Ft. Scott, Kansas, ...	5.00
Br. Ch., N. Manchester, Ind., ...	170.80
Br. Ch., Peru, Ind., ...	46.80
Br. Ch., Ashland, Oregon, ...	8.60
Nat. W. M. S. by Mary C. Wenger, Treasurer, Dayton, Ohio, ...	25.00
Br. Ch., Pittsburgh, Pa., ...	70.00
Br. Ch., Udell, Iowa, ...	35.00
Br. Ch., Falls City, Nebraska, ...	8.00
Br. Ch., Fremont, Ohio, ...	1.00
Loyal Workers S. S. Class Nappanee, Indiana, ...	5.00
Yellow Creek, Br. Ch., Hopewell, Pa.	13.00
Mrs. Harrison Zimmerman, Hopewell, Pa., .$2.50	
Br. Ch., Waterloo, Iowa, 1st Quarter 1920, ...	40.00
Br. Ch., Flora, Ind., ...	85.13
Br. Ch., Ankenytown, Ohio, ...	3.00
Mrs. F. C. Golladay, Mt. Jackson, Va., (H. G.), ...	5.00
D. A. C. Teeter, Cerro Gordo, Ill., (H. G.), ...	5.00
Mrs. Annie Hulse, Flagler, Colorado, (H. G.), ...	5.00
J. L. Kimmel, Muncie, Ind., (H. G.),	5.00
Brother Snyder, Milledgeville, Ill.,..	1.00
B. F. Cloyd, Pittsburgh, Pa., H. G.),	10.00
1st Br. Ch., Lanark, Ill., ...	13.20
Compton Ave. B. Ch., Los Angeles, Calif., ...	94.33
Total, ...	$1,298.10
Previously Reported, ...	6,194.94
Total Receipts to February 1,	**$7,493.04**
Correction—Br. Ch., Cameron, W. Va. should have been, Mrs. E. M. Smith, Cameron, W. Va., H. G., $10.00 for last month.	

KENTUCKY SUPPORT FUND

G. C. Brumbaugh, Hill City, Kans., ..$	5.00
Br. S. S., Camden, Ohio, ...	4.10
Mr. and Mrs. Perl Lowry, Garwin, Iowa, ...	5.00
1st Br. Ch., Los Angeles, Cal., ...	52.88
Br. Ch., Pleasant Hill, Ohio, ...	5.23
Br. Ch., Milledgeville, Milledgeville, Ill., ...	60.00
Roy Kinzie, Dayton, Ohio, ...	5.00
Br. Ch., Lost Creek, Ky., ...	36.12
C. E. Soc. Br. Ch., Allentown, Pa., ..	8.00
Hazel Keiser, Bryan, Ohio, ...	10.00
1st Br. Ch., Roanoke, Va., ...	4.50
1st Br. Ch., Los Angeles, Cal., ...	2.00
Y. P. S. C. E., Ripon Br. Ch., Ripon, Calif., ...	15.00
Br. Ch., Mexico, Ind., ...	25.00
E. A. Juillerat & Family, Portland, Ind., ...	12.50
Nat. S. S. Association by Albert Trent, Treasurer, Johnstown, Pa.,	500.00

Jr. C. E. Soc., Leon, Iowa, ... 5.00
W. M. S. 1st Br. Ch., Flora, Ind., .. 15.00
Samuel Cook & Family, Harrisburg,
  Oregon, ... 5.00
Br. S. S., Oak Hill, W. Va., ... 9.10
Br. Ch., Salem, Ohio, ... 17.35
Nat. S. M. M., by Mary C. Wenger,
  Treasurer, Dayton, Ohio, ... 50.00
Br. Ch., Krypton, Ky., ... 19.25
Nat. S. S. Ass'n. by Albert Trent,
  Treasurer, Johnstown, Pa., ... 500.00
W. M. S., Allentown, Pa., ... 10.00
Br. Ch. & S. S., Canton, Ohio, ... 65.00
Dyoll Belote, Canton, Ohio, $5.00 ...
R. A. Hazen, Ashland, Ohio, ... 5.00
Br. Ch., Falls City, Nebraska, ... 3.00
C. E. Soc. Br. Ch., Columbus, Ohio, 5.00
Primary Dept. Br. S. S., Gratis, O., 5.00
Friends of Strathmore, California, .. 15.00
S. M. M. Br. Ch., Elkhart, Ind., .. 5.00
Lucy Metz, Sibley, Iowa, ... 5.00
Br. Ch., Roanoke, Va., ... 18.00
  Mrs. L. G. Wood, $5.00, ...
  Mrs. W. F. Rippetoe, $5.00, ...
  M. O. Nininger, $5.00, ...
W. M. S., 1st Br. Ch., North Man-
  chester, Ind., ... 7.50
Br. S. S., Leon, Iowa, ... 5.00
J. E. Miller, Milledgeville, Ill., .. 5.00
Fannie Walker, Milledgeville, Ill.,.. 5.00
S. Livengood, Milledgeville, Ill., ... 10.00
B. F. Cloyd, Pittsburgh, Pa., ... 10.00
Highland Br. Ch., Marianna, Pa., .. 25.00
1st Br. Ch., Lanark, Ill., ... 100.00
  Harry Gossard, $5.00 ....
  Frank G. Peters, $5.00, ...
  Alice Garber, $5.00, ...
  Fred Horner, $5.00, ...
N. Eisenbise, $5.00, ...
  J .T. Eckman, $5.00, ... 10.00
C. E. Soc. Br. Ch.; Gratis, Ohio, ... 2.50

Total, ... $1,687.03
Previously Reported, ... 2,291.23

  Total Receipts to February 1, ..$3,978.26
Correction for last month, Br. Ch., W. Va.,
should have been Mrs. E. M. Smith, Cameron,
W. Va., $15.00.

KENTUCKY KITCHEN SHOWER FUND

Mrs. C. L. Sangston, Masontown, Pa., $ 5.00
  Mrs. Martin Shively, ... 1.00
  Mrs. T. B. Shoaf, ... .50
  Mrs. Amanda Griffith, ... .50
  Mrs. W. L. Graham, ... 2.00
  Mrs. G. W. Honaaker, ... 1.00
  Mrs. Harry Berkshire, ... .75
  Mrs. A. B. Kelly, ... .50

Total, ... $ 11.25
Previously Reported, ... 237.55

  Total Receipts to February 1, ..$248.80
KENTUCKY LIGHT PLANT FUND

G. C. Brumbaugh, Hill City, Kansas, $ 5.00
Mrs. H. J. Frantz, Enid, Okla., ... 5.00
Mr. and Mrs. H. B. Lehman, Glen-
  dale, Arizona, ... 50.00
Br. S. S., Long Beach, Cal., ... 28.41
Y. P. S. C. E., Long Beach, Cal., ... 5.00

Total, ... $ 93.41
Previously Reported, ... 434.00

Total Receipts to February 1, ...$527.41
**SUMMARY OF RECEIPTS TO FEBRUARY
1, ALL FUNDS**

General Fund, ... $ 7,493.04
Kentucky Support Fund, ... 3,978.26
Kentucky Kitchen Shower Fund, .. 248.80
Kentucky Light Plant Fund, ... 527.41
Muncie, Indiana Building Fund, .. 50.23
Peru, Indiana Building Fund, ... 25.24
  Total Receipts to Feb. 1, All

Funds, ... $12,322.98
GENERAL FUND (South American)

A Friend, Dayton, Ohio, ...$ 1.00
m Orin Cause, Apollo, Pa., ... 5.00

Br. S. S., (Birthday Offerings), Ma-
  sontown, Pa., ... 12.50
m E. A. Juillerat & Family, Portland,
  Indiana, R. R. No. 7, ... 12.50
m Mrs. Elmer Mock and Daughter,
  Louisville, Ohio, ... 10.00
  Total, ...$ 41.00
Previously Reported, ... 376.45
  Total Receipts to February 1, $ 417.45
    General Fund (African)
No. 346, ...$ 12.50
Previously Reported, ... 245.17

  Total Receipts to February 1, ..$ 257.67
    GRIBBLE PERSONAL FUND
No. 90, ...$ 15.00
No. 91, ... 5.00
No. 92, ... 1.00
No. 93, ... 1.00

  Total, ...$ 22.00
Previously Reported, ... 67.25

  Total Receipts to February 1, .. 89.25
    ROLLIER PERSONAL FUND
No. 37, ...$ 10.00
No. 38, ... 2.00

  Total, ...$ 12.00
Previously Reported, ... 21.00

  Total Receipts to February 1, ..$ 33.00
    SNYDER PERSONAL FUND
No Receipts during January.
Amount Previously Reported, ...$ 10.00

  Total Receipts to February 1, .. 10.00
    BRETHREN MISSIONARY FUND
Mrs. E. P. Kirk, Bellota, Cal., ...$ .25
Previously Reported, ... 4.50

  Total Receipts to February 1, .. $ 4.75
    MISCELLANEOUS FUND
    Armenian Relief
Brethren S. S., Ripon, Calif., ...$ 8.00
Brethren Ch., Krypton, Ky., ... 22.00

  Total, ...$ 30.00
Previously Reported, ...$ 186.00

  Total Receipts to February 1, ..$ 216.00
SUMMARY OF RECEIPTS TO FEB. 1
General Fund, South American, ...$ 417.45
General Fund, African, ... 257.67
Gribble, Personal Fund, ... 89.25
Snyder, Personal Fund, ...$ 33.00
African Outfit Fund, ... 271.41
South American Tract Fund, ... 125.00
Brethren Missionary Fund, ... 4.75
Miscellaneous Fund, ... 216.00

Total·Receipts, All Funds, ...$1,424.53
    WILLIAM A. GEARHART,
      General Missionary Secretary,
906 Conover Building, ... Dayton, Ohio.

COLLEGE NEWS

I was at Meyersdale, Pennsylvania, over the
Sunday of the 31st. I preached at Summit
Mills in the afternoon. At both places there
was a good attendance and a good interest.
These were the sixteenth and seventeenth
churches which I have been enabled to visit
since June. Brother E. D. Burnworth, the
pastor, was not at home but I found everything well arranged. Meyersdale has a beautiful church and the people are earnest and
active. I have very pleasant memories of the
people in whose homes I was entertained, viz.,
Norman Miller and family, including their son
Robert, Mr. and Mrs. Cook, Mr. and Mrs.
Poorbaugh whose son, Jacob is here in college,
and Mrs. Olinger, who was just recovering
from a serious illness. At Summit Mills I
met Brother John A. Miller, one of our older
ordained ministers. It was a pleasure to meet
him after having heard his name so many
times before.

Brother A. C. Hendrickson just returned
from the Pacific Coast where he went on busi-

---

nces. He was asked by the Board of College
Trustees to interview the Trustees of the
Coast in regard to Beachler's financial cam.
paign there. The Trustees expressed their in.
terest in the campaign and their willingness
to co-operate with the college. However, their
plans relative to this campaign are not yet
complete, hence a full report can not be given
at this time.

Meanwhile, the five other remaining finan.
cial programs are getting under way and
there ought to be something to report, one
way or another, soon.

Brother Shively is planning on coming here
to look over the work the first of April, when
he will familiarize himself with the methods
of the former bursar, Mr. A. C. Hendrickson.

Last Sunday at the close of the morning
service in the Chapel, the minister, Professor
J. A. Garber, held a brief consecration service
for the members of the Seminary. All of these
who were present came forward for a brief
prayer of consecration. Of course those who are
habitually absent from this service, missed the
blessing but those who were there have expressed themselves as peculiarly helped by the
service. On these, the future of the church
largely rests, hence the importance of their
complete and full consecration.

Mr. Balch, one of the leading business men
of the city, was present last Thursday morning and addressed us at the Chapel hour. By
having representative business men come to
us, it is hoped that a closer friendship may
be cultivated between the Hill and the City.

Rev. W. H. Miller, pastor of the Oak Hill,
Virginia, congregation, A. B., 1906, is visiting
here for a few days, and conducted Chapel
for us Monday.
      EDWIN E. JACOBS.

OF SPECIAL INTEREST

There have been recently several inquiries
from people who have the welfare of the dif.
ferent organizations of our beloved church at
heart, as to the incorporated name of the sev.
eral incorporations within our church and as
to the proper wording to give a bequest or
devise by will to said incorporations.

I therefore submit the following lists of
incorporations within our church, the object
of each and a sample clause for a will.

1. The National Conference of the Breth-
ren· Church. This·is a corporation organized
under the laws of Ohio not for profit and under the authority of the charter, our church
meets in annual session to lay plans for the
future work of the church.

2. The Missionary Board of the Brethren
Church. This is a corporation organized under
the laws of Illinois not for profit. This Board
has in charge the Home Mission work and
church extension work in the homeland.

3. The Foreign Missionary Society. This
is a corporation not for profit organized under
the laws of Ohio. This Society has in charge
the Foreign Mission work of the church.

4. The Brethren Publishing Company. This
is a corporation for profit organized under the
laws of Ohio. It has charge of the Brethren
publications and is located in Ashland, Ohio.

5. Ashland College, of Ashland, Ohio. This
is a corporation not for profit organized under
the laws of the State of Ohio. It is the one
school of the Brethren church.

6. The Brethren Home of Ohio. This is a
corporation not for profit organized under the
laws of Ohio. It has in charge a fund of over
$10,000.00 with which we hope a Brethren
Home for the old and infirm of our number
can be cared for and also an orphanage for
the children.

7. The Woman's Missionary Society. This
is a corporation organized under the laws of
Ohio and has in charge all the women's work
of the church and also the Sisterhood of Mary
and Martha.

Auxiliary Organizations, not incorporated

8. The National Sunday School Associa-

tion. This is an unincorporated association and has in charge the national Sunday school interests of our church.

9. **The National Christian Endeavor Union.** This is an unincorporated Union and has in charge the Christian Endeavor interests of our church.

10. **The Board of Benevolences of the Brethren Church.** This is an unincorporated Board and has in charge the benevolent work of the church at large.

11. **The National Ministerial Association of the Brethren Church.** An unincorporated Association of our ministers.

12. **The Evangelistic and Bible Study League.** An unincorporated league that promotes Bible study through Institutes, Revivals etc.

Clause in will where a gift in money is given
ITEM.... I give and bequeath unto..........
(Name of Corporation) .... of the Brethren Church the sum of............ ($.....) absolutely to be used by the Trustees of said Corporation in the propagation of the work of said organization as said Board of Trustees may see fit.

Clause in will where real estate is given
ITEM..... I give and devise unto ....
(Name of Corporation)............ of the Brethren Church all of my real estate located in......... or the following described real estate to-wit...... absolutely and in fee simple. It is my will and I so direct that said corporation may sell at public or private sale upon such terms as it may deem just, the aforesaid real estate and use the proceeds therefrom for the propagation of the work of said corporation.

Should there be any one who should desire further information relative to the work of any of the Boards aforesaid, or should any one desire more information about gifts, devises or bequests to any of the above boards, I will cheerfully answer all such inquiries without any charge. Fraternally,
ORION E. BOWMAN,
705 Conover Bldg., Dayton, Ohio.
Attorney for and member of The Missionary Board of the Brethren Church. The Brethren Home of Ohio.

NATIONAL MINISTERIAL ASSOCIATION
To all Members of the Association, greeting: This announcement will notify you of the death of Brother Wm. Keifer. Brother Keifer was one of the pioneers of the church, having affiliated himself with this body at the time of the division. He has been a minister for forty-six years and a member of the Association for ten years. He departed this life February 23, at almost 84 years of age.

This being the fourth death of the year no call will be issued but the claim will be paid out of funds on hand.
Sincerely, your Brother,
WILLIS E. RONK, Secretary-Treasurer.

Business Manager's Corner

THE PSYCHOLOGY OF SALESMANSHIP

Some years ago we listened to a short series of lectures by a noted lecturer on "The Psychology of Salesmanship." He demonstrated quite clearly the advantages that come to a minister of the gospel who has given close study to this question, and since we have come into our present position we have wished many times that every pastor in the Brethren church could have the opportunity to hear such a course of lectures. It would help immensely in furthering the interests of the church and incidentally the interests of the Brethren Publishing Company.

The Brethren Annuals and Conference Reports were mailed to the pastors too late we admit frankly; but we have previously explained why it was impossible to do otherwise this year, so no more of that. But a few days ago one pastor wrote us that it was too late to sell the copies we sent him, and we immediately thought of the psychology of salesmanship. Several other pastors sent us a remittance in full for the entire number of Annuals we sent them in a few days after they were received and one pastor wrote send me another supply at once, and again we thought of the psychology of salesmanship. You know some of us would have a hard time selling cheese to a hungry mouse while others can sell mining and oil stock to hard-headed farmers. It is the psychology of salesmanship.

Dr. J. Allen Miller came into our office last Saturday and took out a number of copies of the Annual and mentioned the fact of their being rather late to sell well, and upon my remarking "that it depends upon trying to sell them," he replied, "You try it," and I said, "I'll do it." I was just getting ready to go to Gretna to preach over Sunday and I put a supply in my grip and took them along. Did I announce from the pulpit, "Now I have here a number of copies of the Report of the last Winona Conference, and although they are out a little late I would be very much pleased to have you come up to the front after the service and get a copy. I see they are marked twenty-five cents, which seems to be a little high high, but I suppose that is as cheap as they can be made by our Publishing House"? Did I? I did—not. Instead I personally handed a copy to the head of every family at the services and said, "Here is a copy of the Brethren Annual and Conference Report, please give me a quarter." And did anybody refuse? They did—not. Now you may call it nerve or what you please, but "we got away with it," and at the evening service one party came and asked for another copy. Yes, I am of the same opinion still. We can sell them, if we want to and we try. We still have about fifty dollars' worth on hand and we would like to have some of our brethren who have not received any as yet to give it a try, and see whether we have spoken truly or not.

The Evangelist Honor Roll
We have no new churches to report for the Honor Roll this week, but during the past week we have received the list of names for the renewal of four of our churches; Namely —Nappanee, Indiana, with E. L. Miller, pastor. This is the third year for Nappanee. Then we received the revised list from Dallas Center, Iowa, R. F. Porte, pastor. This is the second year for Dallas Center and we know it meant real effort on the part of Brother Porte. We want to publicly express our appreciation. Then came the College Corner, Indiana, list for the third year with L. A. Myers, pastor, but in this instance we are sure Brother Myers will gladly share the honors with M. A. Kurtz, the local representative. The fourth list which we greatly appreciate is from the Third Brethren church of Johnstown. We understand this church will be without a pastor April first, as Brother Jones goes to Conemaugh. Here the work of caring for the Evangelist list was taken care of by that faithful worker, Brother H. H. Link.

Sunday School Supplies
Before this reaches our readers we expect to begin mailing Sunday school Quarterlies. Of course they are not all made yet but we want to begin mailing what we have ready as soon as possible.

Sickness among our working force has been greatly handicapping us for nearly three weeks. The forewoman of the make-up department has been ill with the influenza for more than a week now and perhaps will not be able to resume her work for another week. This greatly hinders the work, and with all the quarterlies to finish and The Brethren Missionary to get out just as quickly as possible there will be no respite from hard work for some weeks to come. We only ask our churches and Sunday schools to remember that we are doing our best.
R. R. TEETER, Business Manager.

IN THE SHADOW

BROWN.—Anna Brown the only daughter of Elder P. J. and Mary Duncan Brown was born, September 3, 1891 and departed this life January 16, 1920. She united with the Fair Haven church and was baptized in 1906. She was united in marriage by the writer to Milo W. Holmes June 6, 1918 to which union was born one son, who preceded her to the better land January 12, 1920. Anna was a sweet girl and one to be depended upon in all her tasks. We will miss her in the church, Sunday School and Christian Endeavor society. But our loss is her gain. Our sympathy goes out to her faithful mother and husband and we pray God's richest blessings to rest upon these.
Services conducted at the Fair Haven church by her pastor.
BENJ. F. OWEN.

ORR.—Evelyne Verna Orr, daughter of Perry and Myrtle Orr, was born May 14, 1896 departed this life February 25, 1920, aged 23 years, 9 months and 11 days. She united with the Brethren church and was baptized in 1910 and remained a faithful member until the times of her death. She was united in marriage to H. R. Carnicorn October 4, 1915 and to this union were born three children, two sons and one daughter. She was a kind, loving wife and mother, one who was faithful to all her duties. The whole community loved her and will miss her. Those left to mourn are the husband, three children, father, mother, two sisters, one brother, a number of other relatives and a host of friends.
Services were conducted at the home in Glenford by her pastor.
BENJ. F. OWEN.

NEDROW.—Henry Nedrow was born in Somerset county, Penna., October 4, 1853 and died February 20, 1920, aged 66 years, 4 months and 16 days. In 1883 he united with the Silver Creek Brethren church at Falls City, Nebraska. In 1893 he brought his family to the Colony in Morton county, Kansas, where he became a member of the Maple Grove Brethren church of which he was a faithful member and earnest worker until called to the eternal home. He is survived by his wife and his two children. In the loss of Brother Nedrow the church here lost one of its most zealous workers. His departure will also be a great loss to the community. His home life was thoroughly Christian. Funeral services were held from the house by the writer, assisted by Rev. Earl Flora and Elden C. Forney of Beaver City, Nebraska. J. GILBERT DODDS.

CLARK.—Albert Clark was born in New York, September 15, 1829, died February 18, 1920, aged 90 years, 5 months and 3 days. He was a brother of Walter Clark, who passed away a little over a year ago. He came to Michigan in 1856 and has been a resident of Penn township about 60 years. He was married to Miss Mary Swank, September 16, 1861, who passed beyond February 20, 1907. There was born to this union five children, all of whom have gone before except one son. There are five grandchildren. On March 31, 1909, he was married to Miss Sarah Jane Swank, who survives him. He was an active member of the Brethren church for 50 years and a teacher in the Sundy School, where he will be sadly missed. He has been sick for two years, but his abiding faith and patience have kept him cheerful all this time.
Funeral services by the writer.
J. H. ENGLISH.

SELBY.—Lula Pauline Selby died of pneumonia at her home in Savage, Md. February 8, 1920, aged 18 years, 6 months and 2 days. Funeral services were conducted at St. Luke, Md., by Reva P. W. Wisman and C. R. Koontz. Surviving are her husband, Mr. William R. Selby, of Laurel, Md., her parents and four brothers. She became a member of the St. Luke Brethren church in the fall of 1917.
C. R. KOONTZ.

BARR.—Dorothy Cleo Barr, daughter of G. W. and Nettie M. Barr, departed this life Friday, February 20, 1920 aged 3 years, 2 months and 22 days. The grief-stricken and sick family have the sympathy of the community. Funeral services were held at White Chapel, Detrick, Va., on Sunday afternoon by the writer.
C. R. KOONTZ.

HOLLAR.—Joseph Walter Hollar was born October 27, 1875 and died February 25, 1920. He leaves a wife and four children to mourn their loss. Funeral services were held at his late home and interment at St. Luke cemetery on Wednesday afternoon by the writer.
C. R. KOONTZ.

SHIPE.—Margaret Alice Shipe, 17 month old daughter of Brother and Sister Samuel Shipe, died January 30, and was brought to Trinity on Sunday for burial. Her parents have our sympathy. Funeral services by the writer.
C. R. KOONTZ.

REISS.—Lloyd Kenneth, son of Brother and Sister Henry Reiss was born May 5, 1919 and departed this life February 22, 1920. He leaves a father and mother, four brothers and one sister to mourn his departure.
H. W. ANDERSON.

OUR MISSIONARIES IN SOUTH AMERICA

Reading from left to right: Rev. E. G. Atkinson, wife and two children; Rev. Juan Barrio, wife and child; Mr. Penzotti, South American representative of the American Bible Society; Dr. C. F. Yoder and family; Rev. Clarence Sickel and wife; Rev. W. H. Bock, wife and child.

Read Brother Yoder's Report and Appeal
on the Mission page of this issue.

We ought to put double the number of missionaries and
triple the amount of money in our South American
field at this very hour.

THE FOREIGN BOARD CAN MOVE NO FASTER THAN THE
CHURCH MAKES POSSIBLE BY ITS GIFTS.

Published every Wednesday at Ashland, Ohio. All matter for publication must reach the Editor not later than Friday noon of the preceding week.

George S. Baer, Editor

The
Brethren
Evangelist

When ordering your paper changed give old as well as new address. Subscriptions discontinued at expiration. To avoid missing any numbers renew two weeks in advance.

R. R. Teeter, Business Manager

OFFICIAL ORGAN OF THE BRETHREN CHURCH

Subscription price, $2.00 per year, payable in advance.
Entered at the Post Office at Ashland, Ohio, as second-class matter.
Acceptance for mailing at special rate of postage provided for in section 1103, Act of October 3, 1917, authorized September 9, 1918.
Address all matter for publication to Geo. S. Baer, Editor of the Brethren Evangelist, and all business communications to R. R. Teeter, Business Manager, Brethren Publishing Company, Ashland, Ohio. Make all checks payable to the Brethren Publishing Company.

TABLE OF CONTENTS

EDITORIAL

Marshalling the Forces for An Intensive Evangelistic Campaign

(The last of a series of articles on the above topic, considered apropos the present season of intensive evangelism and also the aim of many churches to lead up to an ingathering at Easter time.)

V. INTERCESSION THE GREATEST AGENCY

More than all efforts and plans in preparation for and in carrying on the campaign, intercessory prayer will be found the greatest agency for the conversion of souls. If the church could but realize this fact, if it could be brought to believe and put to the test the accomplishing power of prayer, how marvelously would the souls of men be turned unto God! Until it can be done, all efforts will fail to bring about the most successful evangelistic campaign possible. All movements for the stirring of souls and turning them to Christ their Savior must be heavenborn. That which gives convicting and convincing power is the Holy Spirit, and that cannot be worked up but must be prayed down.

The whole church or as nearly so as possible should be enlisted in intercession. It is not sufficient that the pastor prays, or that the deacons and a few other leaders pray. The church cannot accomplish its whole task in this manner unless the whole church is enlisted in it. And the power of the church is lessened by every one who subtracts or refuses to add the strength of a petition is increased by every one who earnestly joins in voicing it. Numbers add nothing to the power of God, but God has planned to exercise his saving power through human instrumentality, the greater the number who present themselves before him in earnest prayer as willing instruments in behalf of the unsaved of earth, the greater is the opportunity for the exercise of his power. We shall never know what a wonderful work God might accomplish through his church, until every member shall give himself to earnest prayer for the saving of lost souls.

It is not enough that every member should pray, but that every member should pray earnestly. More than by numbers, the prayers of God's people are strengthened by deep earnestness. How easily we mumble our petitions! How little energy they cost us! How passionless they are! Even many sincere and well-meaning souls pray with as little passion and effort as if it were a matter of little import whether their prayers were answered or not. How seldom do we pray as if the destiny of human souls depended upon the outcome of our prayers. IF we could be made more keenly aware of how much is dependent upon us and how many souls may be saved or lost by the acceptableness of our prayers, perhaps they would not be so feeble and bloodless. When Peter was in prison and the whole church was being tested, no one was without realization of the great issues that were at stake, and so "prayer was made without ceasing of the

church unto God for him." And if we could enter the Gethsemane of passion with Christ, we would understand what it means when it says "being in an agony he prayed more earnestly; and his sweat was as it were great drops of blood falling down to the ground."

But how soon our earnestness of intercession subsides! It is hard to learn the lesson of perseverance in prayer. We look for the fruit so soon, and if it comes not in a day or a week, we cease to pray. We may be sure that it was much more than words that the disciples wanted their Master to teach them about prayer. It was not in the lack of ability to express themselves that they were weak. "It is staying power that tells," and that is what the disciples lacked. Jesus continued whole nights in prayer; not merely one night, but many nights he made his way out to the mountain to pray. And though the people and his own disciples were continually disappointing him, and it would seem that all his prayers would be of no avail, yet he continued steadfastly in prayer. And thus he taught his disciples that they should do. In the parable of the man who came to his friend at midnight to borrow bread, he teaches that it is important that wins the day. In the parable of the judge who dealt out justice to the widow because she kept asking him repeatedly, Our Lord teaches the importance of perseverance in prayer and not the reluctance of God to answer prayer. Be not quick to give up praying, for he who inspired the prayer will also answer it, though the answer be delayed or sent in a different manner than you have directed. The instructions are not merely the "asking" of petition, but the "seeking" and "knocking" of perseverance.

Faith is the thing that gives power to prayer. It connects the inability of our weakness with the all-sufficiency of God's strength. It is that spirit which was found in the Master in such noble proportions when he said, "the words that I speak (and he included also all the things which he did) I speak not of myself, but the Father that dwelleth in me, he doeth the works," the spirit of utter dependence upon God that makes for power. That is the spirit that begets faith and is able to accomplish things for God. It is "the prayer of faith" that saves, both physically and spiritually. "Let him ask in faith, nothing wavering; for he that wavereth is like a wave of the sea driven with the wind and tossed. For let not that man think that he shall receive anything of the Lord." Too often we rise from our prayers fully expecting that the mountains of difficulty shall be still unremoved. Jesus said (and the truth strikes home to us as well as it did to the disciples of his own day), "Because of your unbelief," when asked why they could not cast out the demon from the boy at the foot of the Mount of Transfiguration. "Because of your unbelief?" But how else can we explain our failures in view of such promises as "All things whatsoever ye shall ask in prayer believing, ye shall receive," and "what things soever ye desire when ye pray, believe that ye receive them and ye shall have them?" Indeed faith is the secret for the releasing of the wonderful current of Almighty power by which the dross of men's lives may be burned out and a new life and hope imparted.

Moreover let the heart be clean and the life fully surrendered to God, for until this is done we cannot with grace pray for the salvation of other souls. "If I regard iniquity in my heart the Lord will not hear me." It is when "we abide in him and his words abide in us," when we allow him to have his way with us and we ask "according to his will" that "he heareth us."

Finally let us pray definitely and for particular individuals. Pray for this or that individual by name and enlist others to pray for him also. Scattered, indefinite prayers do not accomplish much. Ask God certain definite individuals and expect to get them.

In these and many other ways you may use this wonderful instrument of intercession for the salvation of souls. How great an instrument it is, and yet how difficult to wield! It entails so much sacrifice to be effective. It means the death of all selfishness and the relinquishing of self-interests. It requires a spirit that refuses not to enter Gethsemane, nor stops short of the cross. But however much it may cost, it is the price of a successful revival and the church must be induced to pay it. The pastor, by word and example, must succeed in leading his forces into true intercession. It is only then that we can fairly lay claim to God's promised blessings, and expect him to open the windows of heaven. It is only then that we shall succeed in casting out the demoniac spirit and in restoring the spiritually dead to life again in Christ's name.

O God and Father of us all, lead us as we seek to lead the forces thou hast placed in our charge, and make us wise, faithful, undershepherds of thy sheep. Help us to have more of thy compassion for the multitudes distressed and scattered as sheep having no shepherd. May thy church be clean and filled with thy spirit, that she may have courage and strength to stand before her enemies. Teach her to pray; help her to intercede for the world, and give her thy hand that she may rise in strength to conquer every foe. Amen.

EDITORIAL REVIEW

Judging from Sister Drushal's report, the people have remembered the work and workers at Lost Creek very kindly during the last few months.

Brother A. P. Reed announces in this issue of the corner-stone laying service of the First Brethren church of Los Angeles. His note arrived too late to serve as an invitation to neighboring Brethren.

We shall be glad to have brief reports of the interest manifested in and the gains resulting from evangelistic efforts preceding and extending up to Easter. A series of passion week services would doubtless result in great good in other lines than evangelism.

Brother Reed tells us that the new church building of the First church of Los Angeles is now under roof and everybody is eager for its completion and expecting that the work will go forward more rapidly than now. New members are continually being added to this church.

After thirty years of service as Salvation Army Commissioner of India, Booth-Tucker has retired at the age of sixty-six. As the result of his labors he leaves 66⅔ social and industrial institutions caring for some 27,000 outcasts from society. There is no greater monument than that constituted by people who will rise up to call their benefactor blessed.

One of the most encouraging reports that Brother Yoder has sent for some time is found in this issue. Among other things reported is the reception of Brother and Sister Francis Edwards and family of seven children into the membership of the Brethren church of South America. The family of talented and experienced missionaries should

prove a most important addition to the work. Brother Yoder calls for the largest Easter offering yet that the work may go forward at that place. The 12,000 dollars he calls for is the minimum; it represents the bare needs. We should give much more, and also give largely for the African work.

Of course those who have given to some mission enterprise lately will be looking over Brother Gearhart's report to see if their names are there and to see who else has responded. If your name is not there and has not yet appeared, suppose you write Brother Gearhart and ask him why. Doubtless he could inform you. He might send you a blank check to be filled out.

Brother Bame gives a stirring message on the Four Year Program page this week. It deserves the careful reading of every member. If we could all have attended the evangelistic Conference which it was his privilege to attend and caught some of the evangelistic fervor with which the great religious leaders of the country are seeking to fire the whole Christian church, it would have been easy to have started almost instantly a great evangelistic campaign that would be felt in the last church of the brotherhood. But though we were not there, yet there should be every possible co-operation given to such efforts and plans as our leaders may devise to bring the church to be gripped anew with evangelistic zeal and to extend its saving influence into all corners which the church is called upon to save.

HOME MADE SQUIBS

A tack points heavenward when it means the most mischief. It has many human imitators.

"Not according to what I try to be when praying, but what I am when not praying, is my prayer dealt with by God!—Andrew Murray.

A life can never become big that persists in being slighted at little things; a magnanimous soul grows only in an atmosphere of love and forbearance.

If men understood how wonderful it is that they were privileged to approach the presence of the great God of heaven and earth and call him Father, no earthly attraction could keep them away.

So many members of the church act as if they were on one long continued furlough. What a mighty army the church could muster if every member realized that he was here for orders!

To start out in life without a purpose is like starting out on the mighty ocean without a destiny; life without a will is like a ship without a rudder; and to be without invincible determination is like running out of coal in mid-ocean.

In the fertile fields of our physical lives our souls may sow what they choose and of that sowing they shall reap in kind; and whether that harvest be much or little depends on how we care for what we have sown.

The King's Business says, "Trust God to send the Word to men who want the truth." And we would add, Permit God to send the Word through you even to the men who do not want but need the truth. There are some who must be evangelized against their will.

"Jesus, I will trust thee, trust thee with my soul;
Guilty, lost and helpless, thou canst make me whole,
There is none in heaven, or on earth like thee:
Thou hast died for sinners—therefore, Lord for me."

Indifferent attendance at the church's services and lukewarm interest in the church's activities will never advance God's kingdom in the world, yet all too frequently such conduct is observed on the part of those who sing lustily, of "A charge to keep I have," and "Send the Light."

It will pay the church to pay its preachers well. No church can prosper and become the power in the community that might become so long as it compels its leader to be the most poorly paid man in the community. A business concern that only half pays its employees is always in ill-repute, and is finally frowned out of existence. Why should we wonder that some churches are no more highly respected than they are?

FOUR-YEAR PROGRAM PAGE
NOW THEN DO IT.—II Samuel 3:18
Conducted by Charles A. Bame

Ninety-five and Still Coming

That, my fellow-pastors, is the tune of the song you are singing right now. Ninety-five of the brethren who report for their churches have come across on time. Some for the first time in the four-year effort and many the best—they have ever made. Some folks who profess to be leaders are very poor followers and so, their reports are not yet here. Of course they may yet arrive before the limit imposed by the delay of my last warning; they may yet reach us before one week after the first of March and be counted; I hope they shall. VICTORY YEAR DEMANDS PROMPTITUDE on the part of preachers as well as givers. I trust we shall not forget.

An Illuminating Trip

For several weeks I have been planning to attend the state conference of pastors at the invitation of the Interchurch World Movement. I was anxious to feel further, my way into the heart of the thing and see what should be my attitude in the face of some opposition among my friends. Then, at eight o'clock on Thursday evening, February 26th, while I was at prayer meeting, came a telegram summoning me to New York to attend a conference on evangelism. This was a further incentive and opportunity and so at eight-fourteen the next morning I was on my way to New York.

Travel Flashes

On this topic, I have written many short observations and so, I shall again use it. On the sleeper, there soon pressed into my acquaintance, two fine looking young men. One a Jew, and the other a Roman Catholic. Neither would have professed religion I presume in some company but both of them were ready to talk about it to one who tries to make it his business everywhere to keep busy in the Master's business. The remarkable thing I wanted to tell was, that one of these, the Hebrew, was on his way to Roumania. Here he had been born sowe twenty years ago. Brought to this country by his parents in his very youth, they had grown rich and he was returning to his native country to start a bank to link up with a chain of banks here. On his person he carried many hundred thousands of Roumanian dollars, in duplicate checks. His stay was to be about the length of a missionary's stay in a foreign country.

The Roman Catholic, a former resident of Kansas City, was on his way to British Guiana, to set up a business for his firm down in South America. On my return from New York to Indianapolis, I fell in with another clean, fine young man and when he had finished his story, I found that he was on his way back to Seattle whence he was to take ship to Hongkong where he was to spend several years setting up a branch of the business of his Seattle firm. Long ago, an old farmer—one of the richest friends of my younger days—had said one morning after I had courted his girl, "Well Charley, business is business" and he slipped on his old overalls and got to slopping his hogs. So, now. Business is going to the corner of the earth and young men are denying themselves the pleasures of home, friends and civilization at the command of business. "The children of this generation"—ah, how well did the Master speak! Are they wiser than we? Are they more busy gripping the opportunities than we? Will business go where Christianity will not, or be busier than the children of the King?

The King's Business

Well, at New York, I was under the roof of one of those great skyscrapers that made it famous and in a room where more big, gripping and compelling programs for the extension of the Master's Kingdom had been planned than anywhere else in the world. And I was there helping to plan one of the most far reaching efforts ever made by United Christendom for an evangelistic and soul-winning campaign. In this room where only what stands for missions and evangelism has been done for a long time—the rooms of the Student Volunteer Movement—were brought together under Bishop Henderson of the Methodist Episcopal church, many of the leaders of the Forward Movements of the churches to see what we might do more, for the gathering of souls into the Kingdom at the Eastertide. Here I met Brother Kolb of Philadelphia who has done everything he can to make possible the entry of the church into this World Movement. Here I also met Brother Kauffman representing the Church of the Brethren who are going into the Movement with all the energy of their wonderful devotion.

Dunkards! No, Dunkers!

In order that you may know what the Church of the Brethren is planning to do, let me give you the "HIGH LIGHTS" as it is stated in the last Interchurch Bulletin. Budget, $2,670,000. $1,000,000, Annual Meeting offering besides. $1,670,000 for education. Ten Regional Directors with a salaried man to be General Director over all. That looks like the King's Business is not to be neglected. $26.70 apiece, in short, is what our nearest brothers are going to try to get for the King's Business, while our own call—God pity us—our call from our General Missionary Secretary that was waiting for me on my return, was $1.00. I hanged my head in shame. Who wants to accept the responsibility for that kind of dullness and lack of vision when the whole Christian world is trying to do wonders?

Indianapolis

From New York I came direct to our state capitol. Here was gathered nearly 1,700 ministers of the state—the first time in the history of Indiana that it could have been possible and the best response that could have been expected. Nine or ten of our own preachers were there and unanimously agreed to get into the game as far and as fast as possible. What else could we do and be loyal to the church—her officers who with a single vote lacking, unanimously voted to enter last January first—how could we when the business is going after business and the leaders of Protestantism are trying to lead us to the spirit of the day in getting big things for the King of kings?

We Are In the Movement

As far as most of the denominations, we are in the movement now. Few of the conferences have met to vote one way or the other on the proposition. Most of them have entered by the same method our own brethren have used—the officers of the Boards and of the conferences. Our action was singularly harmonious and the guarantees are satisfactory to the New York office. It remains for the pastors and churches to get busy and reap. "Lift up your heads and say not there is yet four months to the harvest." The fields are ripening to the harvest—the biggest harvest it is possible to reap in a generation, right now. Let Brethren quit thinking in terms of $1.00 and remember our Brethren whose goal is $26.75. The United Presbyterians voted at Indianapolis or elsewhere to raise this year, $110.00 per member.

The Danger

Some think there is danger in the movement. I have diligently tried to find one. I have failed. When the canvas for funds is made, Brethren will say where it is to go. If it is designated for Missions, Education, Benevolence or Publishing, it will all be due, not to the INTERCHURCH WORLD MOVEMENT but to OUR OWN BOARDS. If it is undesignated—that is, if you do not say where you want it to go,—it will be divided pro rata among the other denominations. Now, the danger is, as I sense it, that our preachers will be asleep and our people uninformed and as they will not escape being solicited, our funds will be misdirected.

Will Our Folks Give?

Of course our folks will give. Can bankers and public people escape? Did we buy Liberty Bonds? We did.. Not because we were especially in favor of war; not because we were investors. We gave because the spirit of giving and sacrifice was abounding. Our people are not the least religious or else we have the poorest appeal for sacrifice. They will give and the way for us to get out of a great movement, all we can, is to fall in line and go after it with as big a vision as others.

How To Figure It Out

Turn to Evangelist, No. 8 under date of February 25, page 5, and you will see the suggested program by Brother Kolb. That estimate is $8.00 per member instead of $26.70. Give on the basis of at least $8.00 per member for your church or much more if you can. Designate what you want it for—any of the five things listed and that you give it for the Brethren church (Progressive) and we shall have one of the biggest funds we ever have had for the spread of Brethrenism. Come on, let's Go.

The Pre-Easter Program

Let Brethren preachers remember that all Protestantism will make a greater drive for members the two weeks before Easter than they have ever done. Get busy for the Lord. Have another campaign if you have had one. Most of this effort will be more silent than usual, but get busy.

Palm Sunday is set for Decision Day in the Sunday school. Do not let it pass without the appeal. Start a "Win One" campaign. Ask your church and Sunday school to get busy and WIN ONE before Easter. Have a Bible conference or something that will bring the members of your church into line with the spirit of the day everywhere so that when the day is done, we shall not be asahmed.

"As For Me and My House"

For myself, the trip has been a revelation and a blessing. I am more determined that my gifts shall be bigger even though for many years I have been giving half by staying in a Brethren pulpit; I am more willing than I have ever been that both of my children shall devote their lives to the world's crying needs for evangelization; I have decided that as for me and my house, we shall this Easter give not on the basis of $1.00 but eight apiece, so that we shall not be ashamed at "His Coming." May the Lord lead us as he is leading the hosts of PROTESTANTISM.

BAME.

Life Work Reports

In an earlier message I requested pastors to report the names of all recruits, old and new, after March 1st. The honor for making the first report goes to Brother H. M. Oberholtzer of Fremont, Ohio. He reports a good Life Work meeting and while there were no definite decisions one young man, whose name was given, is seriously considering the ministry. This church has already supplied two recruits for the ministry both of whom are now in Ashland, namely, Charles Anspach and George Walton.

We trust that this report will inspire other pastors "to do likewise while the impulse is strong." It will add to the value of our records, and will enable us to communicate more intelligently with the recruits, if pastors will observe the following form:

Name .... Address ....
Line of Work .... Date of Decision ....
Age .... Single or Married ....
Education .... Prospects for attending school ......
Any special information ....

Come on with your reports, Brethren, that we may check up your congregation's standing on Goal No. 6.

J. A. GARBER,
Ashland, Ohio.

GENERAL ARTICLES

Taking Our Task Seriously. By W. T. Lytle

The presentation of an article on this subject is in itself an assumption that our task is not being taken seriously. We often speak of taking our tasks seriously, but it is seldom that we really do so. The duties we have set before ourselves will never be accomplished unless we grapple with them with greater concern and more interest than we have usually displayed in the past.

If we have a common task for which we are mutually responsible, we must set ourselves to it with a united front. And if there are problems that confront our church, let us face them squarely and not try to evade them, and at the same time be brotherly and good-spirited about jt. If we have been narrow-visioned, exclusive and backward, let us face the fact and seek to change our ways. If we have not given the co-operation we ought in the plans for advancement and have not tried to work the program we have set before ourselves, let us pray for larger willingness to co-operate and less of the spirit of selfishness and independence.

The time is at hand when we must take our task seriously and center our efforts on certain important things. We cannot all agree on certain matters of detail, but we ought all to agree on the great program of the church. When men debate and differ and selfishly seek to promote their own pet theories and methods, they fall to the rear. We have at times made this mistake greatly to our detriment. While we each insisted on our own prejudices and forgot the great desire of the Master expressed in the great commission, we lost from our rank and file and from our leadership.

First, in taking our task seriously, we must keep in mind the great object for which we are to labor. In John 17:3 we read, "And this is life eternal, that they might know thee, the only true God and Jesus Christ whom thou hast sent." Have we kept our true aim ever before us and so presented it that others might know God and his Son Jesus Christ? Or have we presented geneologies, rehashed Greek philosophies and passing world conditions as fundamental to Christian thinking? If we take our task seriously, we will center our minds on a sin-cursed and blighted people who need the Gospel. There can be no indifference in our hearts when we think seriously of these needy souls, and there will be no discord, no time for discord, as we face the task of meeting this need. Keeping our task ever in mind we cannot be given to petty and trifling schemes of propagating our own ideas which conflict with those of other God-fearing men. "The Whole Wide World for Jesus" cannot be accomplished in our own way, nor must it be undertaken in a way that will bring glory to self, but must be done according to Christ's way, "in his name" and with the co-operation of all his children.

Second, in taking our task seriously we must not be in conflict with those who are seriously trying to solve problems from a scientific standpoint. There may be those who are doing the great work of Christ as earnestly as we but are meeting problems in a different manner than some of us have been accustomed to, but they are perhaps doing it with greater results because they make use of the latest knowledge gathered from th sociological, economic and philosophical fields. Within our own number there may be those who have taken advantage of certain opportunities of learning that others of us have not had. We should not discredit their faithfulness to the Word, nor denounce them as unsafe and heretical because they come at things from a little different angle. They likely have their feet on the Rock, Christ Jesus, the same as we. Let us all with one accord preach the Word and not preach against one another. The less we talk about "Our Creed" and the more we preach and practice the Gospel of Christ, the more rapidly will men be converted unto him who is the Christ. There is not much need for controversy today, but there is great need that men shall hear the Word of God, which is necessary to life. Jesus said, "Man shall not live by bread alone but by every word that proceedeth out of the mouth of God."

Third, in taking our task seriously, we should plan our work carefully and do it systematically. We cannot be serious and be slothful. We need to exercise care to do things systematically and orderly. The church more than any other agent has been slothful in business. It is only recently that we have been putting system and order in our work. We have been careless in the selection of our leaders, and as a result, we have suffered serious set-backs in communities by selecting leaders who have been disgruntled and unfit for their positions. We have been careless in our finances. If we had really taken our task seriously, we should have required or urged every member, both of the ministry and laity to practice the principles of stewardship. Every man ought to be required to give an account of his stewardship to God. Every man, whether doctor, teacher, inventor ,or what not, is handicapped who does not go at his work systematically. And we as a church are handicapped for lack of system.

Fourth, if we are to seek to take our task seriously, we should tarry in the presence of the Father praying that his will may be done in us. Knowing that our task is great and our burden heavy, we should pray not that they should be made lighter but that we should be given grace and strength to meet every requirement. The early church prayed and tarried until they felt the quickening Spirit, to whose presence their own spirits bore witness. Today the great and noble men of God, into whose souls his Spirit has breathed, poured out their souls unto God, ere he filled them with power. And then as they called forth to men in sin, into their ears came the cry, "What shall we do? And they sent back the answer, "Repent and believe."

The kingdom of God, the great struggle of right against wrong, will realize a great impetus in the mighty unselfish movement of the church, the Interchurch World Movement. And we should lay aside our fancied notions abut co-operation and our selfishness, and as true people of God use all the seriousness and wisdom that God imparts. "The field is white unto the harvest" and why sit we idly by and question whether the sickle or the binder is the more valuable. How short-sighted God's people often are! and how foolish they must be in the sight of God in their quibbling over hair-splitting details.

Nay, but we be the true children of God, and by the direction of our energies and the seriousness of our purpose, we are going forward in the performance of the task set before us. We may not all see alike, but we shall all work alike as earnest, serious-minded people of God. "Wherefore seeing we are compassed about with so great a cloud of witnesses, let us lay aside every weight and the sin that doth so easily beset us, and let us run with patience the race that is set before us, looking unto Jesus the author and finisher of our faith."

This is the VICTORY YEAR, and to the victors belong the spoils. Will we possess them? Will we reap the reward of faithful service? These words are in accord with the Scripture. "He that overcometh shall inherit." Let us in his name "overcome" that we may receive the reward that is our due as a church, and that God's vineyard may not be blighted because we have failed. Arouse ye, his saints! Let the dry bones of Israel be quickened with new life for the facing of our task seriously.

Burlington, Indiana.

Delay Is Dangerous in South America.   By Alva J. McClain

"As we have opportunity, let us do good unto all men." Roman Catholicism, the most powerful foe to the truth in South America, is losing its power and influence there because of corruption, superstition and immorality. There is no need to enter into details—they are well known. Everywhere the people are turning away in disgust from the Roman church as it appears in South America.

Several years ago the cry went forth in missionary circles warning us that unless the true faith of our Lord was speedily preached and taught in South America the people would turn to atheism in their reaction against the Roman church. This warning proved to be well-founded. Owing to our criminal procrastination many have already turned to atheism and materialism. Nor is this tendency passed yet.

But there is another danger in South America which is not generally spoken of, a greater danger than atheism, for at its best atheism is never very popular. The Roman church, seeing the writing on the wall, may reform herself outwardly, and thus tighten her grip on those who are ready to leave her fold. By such a course she might even reclaim some already lost and recover lost prestige.

May I remind the readers in these words that the Roman church upon one occasion did this very thing. Prior to that great movement spoken of as the Reformation, people were turning away from her for the same reasons which today appear in South America, namely, corruption and immorality. The Reformers took advantage of the situation to launch a great movement for the truth of God. This movement had an opportunity to sweep the Roman church into obscurity, but unfortunately diminished its effort, and the immoral and corrupt church staged a reformation of its own with lightning speed to counteract the efforts of Protestantism. True, it was only an outward reformation, but it gave Rome a firm grip on those who otherwise would have been lost, and restored her prestige among the people. Her pernicious doctrine remained the same, but she made the outside somewhat cleaner than it had been before, and a moral Rome proved to be a far more dangerous foe than a corrupt Rome.

The Roman church has not lost her cunning. She knows full well that a corrupt and immoral church cannot stand long beside one that is clean. Rome never leads in morals but she can follow with surprising speed when necessary. One of these days there will come a reformation of morals in the Roman church of South America, enforced by the iron hand of its head. When this happens Rome will tighten her grip on thousands of souls who today are held so loosely that the truth of Christ has a wonderful opportunity to win them. And eventually, though now she is in disfavor with progressive governments, Rome will have in South America all the prestige that she at present has in our own country.

NOW IS THE TIME FOR THE BRETHREN CHURCH TO SPEND LIFE AND MONEY IN OUR FIELD OF ARGENTINA.

Ten or twenty years hence our workers there may have to face a Roman church such as we have in America today, an organization which maintains at least an outward respectability. Today the missionary can point to Rome's corruption and immorality in South America as a justification for his presence and work there. Today the striking contrast between the outward life of the missionary and that of the average priest compels recognition, and makes progress far easier than it will be when Rome begins to reform her ways.

If we do not invest our dollars now it will take our tens later to gain for Christ a foothold in South America.

Brother Yoder writes that now the Roman church is losing influence rapidly among the educated people, while our mission is rapidly gaining in favor. The contrast is too glaring. But it will not always be so. Such competition will compel respectability, and the immoral past of a respectable Rome will soon be forgotten. It may seem almost unbelievable, but history has demonstrated its possibility.

Philadelphia, Pennsylvania.

My Impressions of the Interchurch World Movement. By J. A. McInturff

About the biggest thing that has come up lately for consideration by the various denominations is the Interchurch World Movement. I will write my impression of it and will do so in a few words. I have attended all the state meetings. I have talked with our ministers who have been in attendance at the New York and Atlantic City meetings. Also had a conference with some of our ministers who have been in attendance at the meeting of our National Conference officers where there were representatives from some of our National Boards. I have been reading the publications of the Movement from the beginning, and in every way possible I have tried to learn just what it is. At first I entertained considerable fear on certain points, but as I became better informed I lost them. I am still debating some of the things but no one will be able to tell just how the results of this great movement will work out. But I am sure that the only course for the Brethren church is to enter it, and that with all our heart. The Church of the Brethren has gone in and has appointed a denominational general secretary, Rev. C. D. Bonsack. "Our brethren are already in the field; why stand we here idle!" The only objection I have heard is that the movement lacks in spirituality and in clearcut doctrine on the vital subject of the deity of Jesus, and the fundamental doctrines of the New Testament. I do not think this criticism is true. I heard more clear, plain, direct presentation of Jesus' at the Pastor's Conference than I ever heard before in any meeting. Some of our brethren have felt that our distinctive doctrine will suffer. I cannot

see how this can be for the movement does not have any theology as such. It cannot have, for it is simply a movement of the forces of Christ. It would not have progressed this far if it had aimed in propagating a system of theology. If it had any dogmatic theology the Baptist, Brethren, Presbyterian, and Methodist would have discovered it. It will in no way affect us from this point of view. The big thing in it is the fact that it will reveal the church to herself. It will furnish the church the most systematic survey we have ever had. It will give us facts relative to our home and foreign missions. It will also reveal the church to the community in which we are located. I believe that it will lift the financial work of the church to the standard of business. No one can read the World Survey prepared by The Survey Department without being moved by the great mass of information relative to missionary work. It will present the facts, both to the church and community, and if we go on losing ground as we have for years we will do so with our eyes open. However, I think that if some of our brethren are not of the same opinion there should be some effort made to unify our church. If we do not enter the Movement I think we shall lose, but if we enter with a divided church we may also lose. But the truth concerning the Movement will perhaps bring us to the place where we can do the right thing. Fearing no evils from the standpoint of our faith, and believing from my limited knowledge of the great Movement that we shall profit by entering, I say go in with all the force of our church.

Goshen, Indiana.

More About the Twin Gold Mines
By Dr. E. M. Cobb

Since my first installment in the Evangelist concerning the twin gold mines, I have been flooded with mail from various parts of the country, written by men and women of various ages and conditions of life asking for more information concerning the stock in this company, before they make the investment. Since the time is short—Easter being our day set for the final sale of this stock,—I hasten to make specific directions concerning the same.

However, before I make these different prices, allow me to say that a certain scripture comes up before my mind, found in the 19th Psalm. "More to be desired are they than gold, yea, more than fine gold." It really and truly makes me wonder down deep in my heart whether that scripture is applicable to all of us who belong to the Brethren church, and whether or not the real jingle and glitter of gold does not appeal to us more than it should than in the judgments of the Lord; and I wonder, really, when the count is all in, whether all of us who are anxious to make investments in literal gold mines will appreciate the opportunity to invest in one still more real, for the Lord said that the value of a single soul was worth more than all the world including her gold mines.

The Twin Gold Mines are Argentina, South America, and the French Soudan, Central Africa; Brother Yoder and his co-laborers are in charge of the gold mine in Argentina, and Brother Gribble and party are in charge of the gold mine in Central Africa, and any and all who wish to make an investment in either or both of these gold mines should take up further correspondence with Wm. A. Gearhart, Dayton, Ohio, who is the general secretary for both Home and Foreign Mission Boards.

The $50.00 shares in the Twin Gold Mines buys you a life membership in the Foreign Missionary Society, and a $5.00 certificate makes you a Home Member for one year, and the 1.00 certificate gives you a subscription to the Brethren

Missionary. For further information write Secretary Wm. A. Gearhart, 906 Conover Bldg., Dayton, Ohio.

The Wonderful Book. By T. Darley Allen

Rev. Dyson Hague, vicar of the Church of the Epiphany, Toronto, says that an influential citizen of that place, "who has devoted a vast amount of time and attention to the subject, has made the extraordinary computation that through thirty Bible societies and various publishing houses in every land, in over seven hundred living languages of the globe, there are published today probably thirty million copies a year of the Bible."

In this remarkable circulation of the Bible, after so many centuries of infidel effort to destroy it, we have a striking illustration of the law of "the survival of the fittest."

"The man who thinks the Bible is a dead or a dying book," as Dyson Hague well says, "is somewhat out of date." When Voltaire predicted the extinction of Christianity within a century, there were far fewer Bibles in existence than are issued in a few weeks in the present time, and probably the sacred book in the life time of the noted French infidel could have been found in no more than thirty languages. Later on, Thomas Paine declared his work was to bring about the downfall of the Bible.

Well did H. L. Hastings say concerning the old Book: "This book outlives its foes. If you could gather all the books written against it, you could build a pyramid higher than the loftiest spire. Now and then a man goes to work to refute the Bible; and every time it is done it has to be done over again the next day, or the next year. And then, after its enemies have done their worst, some of its professed friends torture and twist and mystify and misrepresent it. Surely it is no fool of a book if it lives through all that. Infidels have been at work nearly eighteen hundred years, firing away at it, and making about as much impression on it as you would shooting boiled peas at Gibralter."

THE BRETHREN PULPIT

The Ministry of Healing.   By H. M. Harley

("Is there any sick among you? Let them call for the elders of the Church; and let them pray over them, anointing them with oil in the Name of the Lord; and the prayer of faith shall save the sick, and the Lord shall raise them up; and if they have committed sins, they shall be forgiven them." JAMES 5:14 and 15.

The people of Pittsburgh and vicinity were greatly stirred a week or two ago, over the coming into our midst of a reputed "Healer," who hailed from England, and who taught and practiced the art of healing by the laying on of hands and prayer, as set forth in the Bible. And why the Christian people of our city should be so stirred up over this man's coming and teaching, is a wonder to the writer,—for he taught no new thing, neither anything that has ever been at least entirely lost sight of by God's people.

There can be no doubt of the fact that the Holy Scriptures represent God as one who heals, and Jesus Christ as the physician of both soul and body. And this power to heal the body did not cease with the departure of Christ, nor even with the apostles. The power was transmitted to the church, and if the apostolic injunctions are to be obeyed, it was intended to be exercised in the church perpetually. And there has been at least a part of the Christian church that has always believed in the ordinance of healing by the laying on of hands and has practiced.

The Brethren church, at the time of her organization as a denomination, adopted as one of the specific tenets of her "Whole Gospel" platform, this doctrine of anointing with oil, and the laying on of hands,—not as a mere preparation for death as some think, but for physical healing as well as for spiritual cleansing, as is implied in the statement of James at the beginning of this sermon. And what is more, every true Brethren minister has both preached and practiced this doctrine with wonderful results. The writer himself has seen many a person who has been given up by physicians, miraculously restored to full health and strength. And this was not only in cases of mental or nervous diseases, but as well in organic troubles and muscular affections. He will go further and say, that he believes that in every case where the conditions were complied with, as they are implied in the promise,—healing was forthcoming.

But note this. No Brethren minister considers himself as "A Healer." This blessed ordinance is not of itself a means of healing. It is merely a symbol of the anointing of the Holy Spirit who does the healing. Jesus himself professed to heal "by the spirit of God" (Matt. 12:28). And the disciples after him prayed, "Grant unto thy servants to speak thy word with all boldness, while thou stretchest forth thy hand to heal" (Acts 4:30). James says that "the prayer of faith shall save (heal is the proper word here, according to the original) the sick." The Gospel minister who performs the anointing is not the healer, but merely the instrument in the hands of him who said,—according to Exodus 15:26, "I am the Lord who healeth thee." To him do we give all the honor and the praise for all he does for us, or through us for the help and blessing of others.

Now just a practical word concerning this doctrine of anointing for healing. We are told that the words "health," "whole," and "holy" all come from the same Greek word, and all refer both to the physical and to the spiritual. Even as sin and sickness are synonomous, so are holy and health, or wholeness. We know that God is interested in our well-being whether of spirit, soul or body. And we have more instances on record at least, where Christ healed physical diseases than where he forgave sins. And surely, there can be no doubt in any sane mind but that God can heal us if he so desires. The Word tells us time and again that he both can and desires to heal as well as to forgive, so that we may be "whole,"—fit creatures of his. And we know further that he does it when he is called upon in faith, and where he

is given the chance to work his power. And this does not necessarily preclude the use of remedies for restoration. The Scriptures nowhere condemn the use of such. The only passage usually so quoted is 2 Chronicles 16:12,—"In his disease, he sought not the Lord, but the physicians." Asa's fault was not in seeking the physicians, but in NOT seeking the Lord. And that's the fault of a large part of Christendom today. They trust only to man's ingenuity and wisdom, and they fail. And then they wonder why God was so cruel as to permit them to suffer, or to take from them their loved ones, when the Lord was not consulted, or even given a chance to work out his good pleasure in the matter. Very many times God does not bestow upon us blessings which we desire above all things else because we seek them in our own way and do not ask him, nor take him into consideration. It may not always be God's will to heal when we ask him, but even then we shall not fail to receive a great blessing. But oftener than we think we might have God's healing grace if we would but ask in faith believing.

While other churches have to a very great extent discarded the divinely given symbol of healing, the anointing of the sick with oil, the Brethren church, and possibly one or two other peoples, have perpetuated it, and are today practicing it most effectively in behalf of those who desire to avail themselves of the same. Why not use it more, and thus prolong life, as well as increase our efficiency as workers with him for the common good. Any Brethren minister is ready at any time to answer the call, and administer this ordinance to all who may desire it, if such are willing to meet God's conditions.

Pittsburgh, Pennsylvania.

Why I Go To Church.   By John Wanamaker

You might just as pertinently inquire, "why do I eat?" or "Why do I sleep?" because I find one just as necessary to my well-being as the other. I could eat well and sleep well, and yet be a very miserable man, without the spiritual uplift that only comes from an attendance upon the divine ordinances.

Then again, it is a great privilege to touch shoulders with the earnest Christian men who are also interested in promoting Christ's kingdom upon earth. For four years, while Postmaster General under the Harrison administration, I traveled nearly 100,000 miles in order to be present each week at my own church.

I have made it the rule of my life to be in my regular place each Lord's Day when in health and in the country, believing that Paul was inspired to write that we should not forsake the assembling of ourselves together for worship. I also believe that the temptations to every man are great, and unless he has more than ordinary groundwork for honesty and faithfulness, he may be caught by the sudden wind of plausible opportunity, and tumble over the precipice, and be ruined.

It is said that a minister once dreamed that he saw rows of beautiful diadems studded with precious jewels. "Is that big one for me?" said he, remembering that there had been many conversions in his church. "No, not for you," said the angel, "that one is for the poor old deaf man, who used to sit by your pulpit stairs and plead with God for souls in the congregation while you preached to them."— From "God's Plan for Soul-Winning."

OUR DEVOTIONAL

"Sharing God's Love." By C. D. Whitmer

OUR SCRIPTURE

Little children, yet a little while I am with you. Ye shall seek me: and as I said unto the Jews, whither I go ye cannot come; so now I say to you. A new commandment I give unto you, that ye love one another; as I have loved you, that ye also love one another. By this shall all men know that ye are my disciples, if ye have love one to another (John 13:33-36). As the Father hath loved me, so have I loved you: continue ye in my live. If ye keep my commandments, ye shall abide in my love: even as I have kept my Father's commandments, and abide in his love. These things have I spoken unto you, that my joy might remain in you, and that you joy might be full. This is my commandment, that ye love one another as I have loved you. Greater love hath no man than this, that a man lay down his life for his friends (John 15:9-14).

OUR MEDITATION

Even as: We begin to understand somewhat of the blessedness of those little words. It is not the command of a law which only convinces of sin and impotence; it is a new command under a new covenant, that is established upon better promises. It is the command of him who asks nothing that he has not provided, and now offers to bestow. It is the assurance that he expects nothing from us that he does not work in us: even as I have loved you, and every moment am pouring out that love upon you through the Holy Spirit. Even so do ye love one another. The measure, the strength, and the work of your love you will find in my love to you, says Jesus.

Even as I have loved you: that gives us the measure of the love wherewith we must love each other. True love knows no measure: it gives itself entirely. It may take into consideration the time and measure of showing it; but love itself is ever whole and undivided. This is the greatest glory of divine love that we have, in the Father and Son, two persons, who in love remain One Being, each losing himself in the other. This is the glory of the love of Jesus, who is the image of God, that he loves us even as the Father loves him. And this is the glory of brotherly love, that it will know of no other law than to love even as God and Christ loves.

He who would be like Christ must unhesitatingly accept this as his rule of life. He knows how difficult, how impossible it often is thus to love brethren, in whom there is so much that is offensive or unamiable. Before going out to meet them in circumstances where his love may be tried, he goes in secret to the Lord, and with his eye fixed on his own sin and unworthiness asks, "How much lowest thou thy Lord!" He goes to the cross and seeks there to fathom the love wherewith the Lord has loved him, and he lays himself on the altar before his Lord,—even as thou hast loved me, so will I love the brethren.

Oh, that Christians would close their ears to all the reasonings of their own hearts, and fix their eyes only on the law which he who loves them has promulgated in his own example, they would realize that there is nothing for them to do but this,—to accept Christ's commands and obey them.

Our love may recognize no other measure than his, because his love is the strength of ours. The love of Christ is no mere idea nor sentiment; it is a real divine life-power. As long as the Christian does not understand this, it cannot exert its full power in him. But when his faith rises to realize that Christ's love is nothing les than the imparting of himself and his love to the beloved, and he becomes rooted in this love as the source whence his life derives its sustenance, then he sees that his Lord simply asks that he should allow his love to flow through him.

From this love of Christ the Christian also learns what the work of his love to the brethren must be. Love teaches the disciple to look upon himself as really called upon to be, in his little circle, just like Jesus, the one who lives solely to love and help others.

Paul prays for the Philippians: "That your love may abound more and more in knowledge, and in all judgment (Phil. 1:9).

The believer who prays that his love may abound in knowledge, and really takes Christ's example as his rule of life, will be taught what a great and glorious work there is for him to do.

The Christian who really takes the Lord's word, "Love one another even as I have loved you," as a command that must be obeyed, carries about a power for blessing the lives of all with whom he comes in contact. Love is the explanation of the whole wonderful life of Christ, and of the wonder of his death; divine love in God's children will still work its mighty wonders.

"Behold what manner of love!" "Behold how he loved!" These words are the superscription over the love of the Father and the Son. They must yet become the key words to the life of every Christian.

As early as the call of Abraham this principle of sharing love was deposited as a living seed in God's Kingdom, that what God is for us, we must be for others. "I will bless thee, and thou shalt be a blessing." If "I have loved you" is the highest manifestation of what God is for us, then, "Even so love yet" must be the first and highest expression of what the child of God must be.

Brethren, Christ Jesus longs for you in order to make you a very fountain of love. The love of heaven would fain take possession of you, in order that, in and through you, it may work its blessed work on earth. **Yield to its rule.** Offer yourself unreservedly to its indwelling. Be not disheartened if you do not attain it at once. Only keep fast hold of the command "Love even as I have loved you." Take time in secret to gaze on that image of love, Jesus Christ. Take time in prayer and meditation to fan the desire for it into a burning flame. Take time to survey all around you, whoever they be, and whatever may happen, with this one thought, "I must love them." Take time to become conscious of your union with your Lord that every fear as to the possibility of thus loving may be met with the word: "Have not I commanded you?" Love as I have loved." Christian, take time in loving communion with Jesus, your example, and you will joyfully fulfill this command, too, to love even as he did."

OUR PRAYER

Lord Jesus who hast loved me so wonderfully and now commandest me to love even as thou hast loved me, behold me at thy feet!

In thy strength, O my Lord, be thou pleased to reveal thy love to me. Shed abroad thy love in my heart through thy Holy Spirit.

Lord, let me understand that I can love, not with my own, but with thy love. Thou livest in me; from thee there streams into me the love with which I can love others. Thou dost only ask of me that I understand and accept thy calling, and that I surrender myself to live as thou didst. Thou wouldst that I look upon my old nature with its selfishness and unloveliness as crucified, and in faith prepare to do as thou commandest. Lord, I do it. In the strength of my Lord, I would live to love even as thou hast loved me. Amen.

217 East Dubail Avenue,   South Bend, Indiana.

Is not Jesus Christ the same yesterday, today and forever? And if he never turned one away who came to him in behalf of a friend or neighbor who was sick, or crippled, or palsied, or possessed with demons, or dead, so he will not can not, turn you away if you, with the same confidence and faith, come to him in behalf of one whose soul is palsied, or possessed with demons, or spiritually dead.—Selected.

Send
WHITE GIFT
OFFERINGS to

THE SUNDAY SCHOOL

ALBERT TRENT
General Secretary-Treasurer
Johnstown, Pennsylvania

Teacher-Training In Japan

At Karuizawa, Japan's famous mountain summer resort, a school is held each summer to give an intensive course in teacher training to Christian workers. Plans are under way for the program of the coming season. Some who will attend the convention of the World's Sunday School Association in Tokyo next October will go to Japan in time to assist at the Karuizawa School. One of these is Prof. H. Augustine Smith of Boston University, who will have charge of the music, pageantry and religious art at the Convention. Frank L. Brown, Joint General Secretary of the World's Association also plans to be present.

Last summer there were 91 enrolled. In addition to a stiff study course there are special features such as two "Goodfellowship" meetings, a reception by the Sunday School committee, and two sunrise prayer meetings. One of these was held on the top of Mt. Atago, and the singing of "Holy, Holy, Holy," was heard by the people in the valley below. When H. E. Coleman Educational Sunday school Secretary for Japan was in this country last year he sought gifts to erect dormitories for the students at Karuizawa. He was present at the Lake Geneva Training School of the International Sunday School Association and the offering on one of the Sundays, which amounted to $25, was given for a scholarship in the Karuizawa Training School in Japan.

Sunday School Work in Brazil

A Sunday school one thousand miles removed from the nearest church or Sunday school is the condition at Manaus, on the Upper Amazon, in Brazil. There are states in Brazil without a missionary and with only one church or Sunday school. The World's Sunday School Association expects to send a field secretary to Brazil in the near future. All Sunday schools there are limited by their inadequate houses, which not only provide no modern Sunday school facilities but do not even house the number of persons who wish to attend. One Baptist Sunday school, whose pastor was president of the North Brazil Sunday School Association, in Torres, a suburb of Pernambuco, has his building completely filled at the opening of the school. The classes are held where they first assemble the teacher rising among the students, one class touching elbows with another. This school has organized a "Home Department," but which in reality is a series of branch Sunday schools. An entirely different set of teachers, some twenty in number, assemble groups of neighbors in their homes at two in the afternoon, and teach over 250 persons—equal to the number in the parent school. The pastor reports these schools as great feeders for the congregation.

Children Reading the Bible in Cairo Streets

Dr. S. M. Zwemer in returning from his office was passing the Bank of Rome in the modern business section of Cairo. He noticed a group of ragged boys including several gamins with newspapers for sale under their arms. They were crouched on the sidewalk and one was reading while the rest listened attentively. Dr. Zwemer stepped up to them to learn what they might be reading. To his surprise it was the Bible. The one boy in the group who knew how to read gathered the others every morning to listen to stories from the book of Genesis. All these lads were Mohammedans. Rev. Stephen Trowbridge, field secretary for Egypt of the World's Sunday School Association, in commenting on the incident said, "There is certainly an open door before us to the hearts of these boys of the streets." All the Sunday school superintendents throughout Egypt have just been written to encourage them to bring in children from the streets to Sunday school.

My Money and the Lord's

(Hugh S. McCord, Tithing Evangelist of the Cumberland Presbyterian Church) Selected by E. A. MYERS

How have I made my money?

Why do I keep my money? For what do I spend my money? The kind of answer I can give to these questions will determine in a measure the sort of Christian I am.

If I am making my money selling intoxicating liquors to my fellow-citizens, there will be no time wasted in determining the sort of a Christian I am.

One-tenth of my income is his, "All the tithe of the land, whether of the seed of the land or of the fruit of the tree is the Lord's." My attitude of mind toward the Lord's money will determine in a measure, the kind of a Christian I am.

If I keep the Lord's tithe and fail to let him have it to be used in furthering the interests of his Kingdom, I am dishonest with my Maker. "Will a man rob God? Yet ye have robbed me. But ye say, wherein have we robbed thee? In tithes and offerings." A robber can not be counted among dependable Christians. When I fail to pay a tithe of my income to help in the Lord's work, I am robbing God of that which is his; I am robbing the people to whom the tithe should go of their rights to the benefits of the gospel; and I am robbing myself of the untold blessings that come into my prove me, now herewith if I will not open you the windows of heaven, and pour you out a blessing that there shall not be enough room to receive it."

"Bring ye all the tithes into the storehouse, that there may be meat in mine house, saith the Lord of hosts, and life when I live in obedience to God's commandments.

Do we believe the Old Book?

If I am saving my money simply for the sake of accumulating wealth, I will in the process of saving become little and mean toward my fellowmen and God. And that spirit will show the sort of Christian I am.

If I am spending my money for myself, and thinking of myself and have no concern about the needy all around me, I can not be owned of him who came, not to be ministered unto but to minister.

But what about the Lord's money?

A Timely Question

Were the whole world good as you, not an atom better,—
Were it just as pure and true,
Just as pure and true as you;
Just as strong in faith and works;
Just as free from crafty quirks;
All extortion, all deceit;
Schemes its neighbors to defeat;
Schemes its neighbors to defraud;
Schemes some culprit to applaud,—
Would this world be better?

If the whole world followed,—followed to the letter,—
Would it be a nobler world;
All deceit and falsehood hurled
From it altogether;
Malice, selfishness and lust,
Banished from beneath the crust,
Covering human hearts from view,
Tell me, if it followed you,
Would the world be better?—Selected.

J. A. Garber
PRESIDENT

Our Young People at Work

G. C. Carpenter
SECRETARY

Echoes of Ashland College Night

Life Work Recruit month for the year 1920 is now a matter of history and at the present writing we are wondering how the Endeavorers of the Brethren church measured up to their opportunity. Last year we fell short of the goals for which we were striving and the defeat was not good for consideration. Only a sweeping victory this year will in any way atone for the failure we had to report in 1919 and unless every society gets busy and sends in the returns immediately we cannot expect to report good news.

The following societies have reported to date (March 9) and their report makes good reading. See if you can add to the list by sending in reports equally as good.

Beaver City, Neb.,	$16.00
Canton, Ohio;	5.05
Altoona, Pa.,	9.00
Clay City, Indiana,	8.60
Dallas Center, Iowa,	6.07
Hudson, Iowa,	16.00
Mansfield, Ohio,	5.23
Meyersdale, Pa.,	15.00
North Liberty, Indiana,	3.00
Total,	$83.95

You will note that these nine societies who have so far re-ported have given an average offering of $9.55 and if the other eighty societies in the brotherhood do as well as these we will have gone way over the top in the matter of helping support the Chair of Religious Education at Ashland College.

But I have something better to report than money given. The Meyersdale report included the names of eleven young people who have made a Life Purpose pledge that no matter what line of work they may follow in the years to come they will so strive to live in that calling as to honor and glorify God. They are not Life Work Recruits in the full sense of the word for all but one of the number are just in the first year of their High school course and do not know as yet what they will do with their life, but the fact that they have formed this Life Purpose at such an early age is fine and is a prophecy of what we may expect in the days to come. That's fine, Meyersdale!

Now let every society send in their reports of Ashland College Night just as soon as they can, for we do not want this matter to "hold fire" for a long time until it becomes monotonous. "Let's go!"

Yours "For Christ and the Church,"
EDWIN BOARDMAN, Jr.,
Life Work Superintendent.

Hudson, Iowa.

The Ever Present Need

At Talas the number of orphans has increased to such an extent that the Near East Relief of 1 Madison Avenue, New York City, has been obliged to open another building for the little Armenians made homeless by the Turkish massacres and deportations. If possible two thousand, six hundred of these children would be placed in private homes, but such homes are non-existent in that part of the Near East today.

Industrial educational institutions are the only practical solution, and for these a large equipment is needed. One or two years of training will prepare the older boys for self support, but for infants and other children, work must continue from five to ten years. The Near East Relief is seeking funds with which to carry on the great and necessary work.

Spring approaches and with it the plowing of the fields and sowing of grain. In Armenia, where the richest farm lands of the Near East are situated, the Near East Relief is preparing to assist the villagers with farm work during the spring and summer; after this, under satisfactory peace conditions the general condition of the country should rapidly improve.

In this, as in all its activities, the work of the Near East Relief is toward 100 percent relief work, whereby the people of Armenia may be made independent economically, the children grow up into trained men and women capable of conducting the welfare of the country, and the country itself, made once more a productive, busy nation.

There are many traps set for the soul—sin, ambition, avarice, and so on.

SEND ALL MONEY FOR
General Home, Kentucky and
Foreign Missions to

MISSIONS

WILLIAM A. GEARHART
General Missionary Secretary
906 Conover Bldg., Dayton, O.

RIO CUARTO, ARGENTINA

We have much to be thankful for in Rio Cuarto. There are new people being interested continually and we frequently find good fruit of the Gospel which we had not known of before.

Work on the auto Bible coach is progressing nicely and we believe that no better work would be done anywhere. It is to be ready for painting by the end of this month.

We are also building a wing to the church to be used for a kindergarten and other classes below and for a home for Brother Sickel's above. It is to be ready for use next month. The money for building all comes from down here and will be repaid by the rent of the rooms.

Of the young lady who is to teach and of other helpers who will probably soon be with us I will write later as arrangements are not yet completed.

We recently enjoyed a visit from Brother Shank of the Mennonite mission in another

province and several members of the Mennonite Mission Board. They came from the States to investigate the work down here. They mean to establish an orphanage and also invest funds as an endowment for the mission. They are doing wisely. We are hoping that after conference Brother Bauman and perhaps some other member of the mission board may be able to visit us here. Our recommendations will be so much better understood after such a visit. We are sure that if some of our good people whom God has blessed with wealth would visit us there would be no further need of appeal for funds for an orphanage or perhaps a colony as well. With thirty percent of the births illegitimate in this country besides the ordinary number and more of orphans without parents living one can imagine the need of homes for children. Such work appeals to the people and if we had a start we could get handsome aid from some of the rich people here. From children of the orphanages will come our best future missionaries.

There is need in most places also for regular day schools for children who cannot go to the public schools because there is no room. Pastors should not be obliged to be tied up with such school but good school teachers could easily support themselves with private schools and would be able to win most of their children to Christ. In some places, as in Carlota, there is a strong demand for a private school in English. Very few English people in this country will consent to send their children to school with the natives because of the corrupting influences of such public schools. There is everywhere also a demand for lessons in English. Such lessons bring nearly a dollar an hour.

We trust that the Easter offering this year may be much larger than ever for the work here just now has prospects of great expansion during the year and there are imperative needs for the support of workers to help in the expansion. The auto Bible coach will be the first in the country. We are looking for great results from it. Do not forget us in our prayers.

Francis Edwards and Family

Since beginning this letter I have received word from Brother Edwards that he and his family have decided to unite with us in the work, and I hasten to communicate the good news to the brotherhood. Brother Edwards is an English preacher with experience in Bible coach work in England but for twenty-two years has been a missionary in this country. He was a Baptist and Mrs. Edwards a Methodist but he came under an interdenominational society which found itself badly in debt during the war and to relieve it he voluntarily became self-supporting. However his work allowed little time for Gospel work and he has longed to give his time fully to missionary work. We have known the family for ten years but only during the past year did they begin to study the doctrines peculiar to the Brethren. The result is their full acceptance of them. Brother Edwards is not only a strong preacher but a man of wide experience and good common sense. Mrs. Edwards is a noted teacher, having been associated with some of the leading teachers of the country. She is an artist and a musician and is the author of a Sunday school song book which is widely used in this country. Their eldest daughter is also a capable teacher and also teaches vocal and instrumental music. There are seven children in all.

Brother Edwards has had offers of fine positions in other churches which he declined because of doctrinal differences. We are hoping that they will be able to move here from the neighboring town where they live in time to open the kindergarten and English school next month. The mother and daughter will take care of this while Brother Edwards will help in the pastoral and Bible coach work. I have been hoping to be able to give up all or nearly all of my work in the college in order to be free for the evangelistic work, but until other arrangements can be made we will try to take care of this increase in our budget, but I am sure that the brotherhood will respond with an Easter offering this year large enough to support these valuable helpers who will be with us. With the purchase of a property in Carlota our total needs for the year in Argentina will be about $12,000.00.

Two of our young men are now out on a colportage tour, supporting themselves by the sale of Bibles. They are meeting with good success and enjoying great blessing. We hope to have a Brethren conference here during Easter week and at that time dedicate the enlarged church and the Bible coach and begin an aggressive campaign.

We believe that this will be a great year for the church both at home and abroad. May the Lord grant it.

C. F. YODER.

Rio Cuarto, Argentina, Feb 4, 1920.

A LONG LETTER FROM OUR LITTLE GRIBBLE

(Continued From Last Week)

On our third day up, we were surprised by the appearance of a canoe downward bound. It was tied up by the side of the river awaiting us. A young white man was standing outside his little "twa," and as we paddled up he at once introduced himself. "I am an Englishman named Brown," he said, traveling for the Carnegie Institute at Washington. I came in by way of Duala, and am studying Variations of the compass and making astronomical observations. I expect to reach Nola today." (One can go down stream very rapidly). "I heard of you," he said, "twelve days north of Carnot, where the news had reached the people that white teachers were coming to them. You have a wonderful field," he said, "for I have traveled in many parts of the world and have never seen another place so needy and so expectant." He said much, much more, which it would take me a long time to write, but we parted quickly, wishing him God-speed, and thanking God for the cheering news he brought.

You little children will be glad to know about our hen. One day at Brazzzaville the big rooster went out and brought in a white hen for his wife. We will never know where he got her, but she was big like himself, although very young. We brought them both up to Nola with us, and there she commenced to lay, and then to set. Her eggs were not yet hatched when we received permission to move. So we brought setting hen, eggs and all along in a basket, and perhaps by the time we get to Carnot, we will have some dear little fluffy white chickens with us.

Mamma says our coming up here has been so wonderful, because God so mightily opened the way before us, and so strangely closed it behind us. The boat by which we left Brazzaville was the last one to come up to Wesso. No more service will be continued between these places by steamboat. Had we not come when we did, we would have had the long overland trip from Bangui or some point on the Ubangi River. The very day we left Nola the company owning the Forrestaire balancieres recalled them all to Uesso. But unconscious of this we had already left Nola, and were plodding laboriously northward in canoes which we were not supposed to have.

After we arrived at Bania, mamma and I climbed the hill to the rest houses on the top. We walked up to the horse and we were about to go in, but a big horse snorted at us, so we just sat down on the veranda and waited until a native thinking we were receiving scant hospitality came and chased him out. As we were coming up the hill we met a superior looking Hansa woman who shook hands with mamma and me in passing. She went on down to the boat and said mamma had told her to bring up our baggage. She proved to be a Mohammedan chief and a "prophetess." (?) She and her people brought up the baggage and charged eighteen francs for it. After we got to the rest house, we were offered a better house some distance on our way toward Bania, so we made the second move that night, although further than the first it cost us less. The Mohammedans are traders and get the best of every bargain.

"We have quite a time arranging for our food when we move. Mamma and I usually go ahead with the "chop boxes" and boys

and soon after exploring, a cook house is found, a fire is built, and by the time the others who have been looking after our many small pieces of baggage, arrive with the loads, supper will be ready, and the famished seven sit down to whatever the Lord may have provided. We have always had money, but sometimes it has been hard to find a market, or a place to buy.

When we arrived at Banya the other night, we had nothing for supper but a few ripe plaintain; no bread baked, nothing ready. But a woman came with what we children call "baby" fish, and Mamma made some pancakes. The next day the chief sent his people with food to sell. Mr. Pineri sent us some mutton, and in the evening some eggs, and we are happy and well fed.

We had the privilege last evening of a call from Mr. Pineri. He was at Nola when we left, but by traveling until late at night managed to make the trip in two days, arriving at Banya on the evening of the same day that we did.

He called on us the following day and we made arrangements about the remainder of our journey to Carnot.

We are to leave on Monday morning the 17th. We must go overland to Ikaya, as the rapids in this part of the river are only to be passed by an empty canoe. We will be five or six days on the river in tiny canoes, and hope to get to Carnot on Saturday night, November 22nd. If Mamma has time she will add a postscript to this at Carnot, before mailing it for me there.

We want to tell you about our salt. It cost us so much to get it here, but it is worth more than money to us now.

Sometimes the people bring us eggs and other food to sell, and will not take money, only salt. It is such good salt, that they have never seen anything like it, and prize it very highly.

The people are strangely ornamented. A woman went by today with her body painted in stripes like a zebra's. In addition to this she had all the ornaments of which I wrote you in my last letter. They call the stones in their lips "talembe." They are smooth and polished, and as beautiful as gems. Ordinary stones are simply "ta."

Mr. Pineri says if we will teach him English, he will teach us Baya. He has been fifteen years in Africa, and speaks Baya like a native. He planted all the large, beautiful trees at Nola and at Banya, as well as those at Carnot, which we have not yet seen.

The natives do not know the name Carnot, but call it Mambeli, after the little river on which it is located.

We are thankful to be so well. There are fewer mosquitoes as we go farther north. We are leaving the rainy season behind us, and that are going into higher altitudes. There are still many tsetse flies and there is much sleeping sickness.

Keep on praying for us, that we may be kept by the Master's power for his use in winning little ones and big ones to him.

Lovingly,　MARGUERITE.

NEWS FROM THE FIELD

FIRST BRETHREN CHURCH
Los Angeles, California

Although we are compelled to worship in a tent during the construction of our new church building, the congregations are keeping up fine. Two Sunday mornings when it rained the Sunday school attendance was cut down quite a good deal. The prayer meetings have been well attended, in fact about as many as they were in the church building before we moved into the tent. This speaks well for the interest the people are taking in all the services.

The roof is now being put on the new building. It is now advanced to a point where its appearance attracts a good deal of attention. It begins to look something like a church and we cannot help but anticipate the interesting and profitable meetings we will hold in it as soon as it is completed.

On Sunday morning, February 15th, two members were received. Brother Harry Toler, who had been working with the Baptist church in a mission on Fifth street, together with his excellent wife, returned to us. We hope to see these two young people entering into the active life of the church.

On the same Sunday we took our offering for the Superannuated Ministers' Fund which amounted to about $25.00, the largest offering yet taken for it at this place. We hope to see this increased in future offerings. Brother Jennings certainly does know how to present such matters to the people and they always respond in a fine way.

A. P. REED.

4910 Wadsworth Street.

INDIANA DENOMINATIONAL MEETING

The ministers of the Brethren church who were in attendance at the Interchurch Pastor's conference at Indianapolis, Indiana met in conference on Wednesday morning, March 2 at the English hotel. After passing a resolution approving of the Interchurch Movement and its program and declaring our hearty approval of the action of the officers of our National Boards in making it possible for our church to co-operate we elected the following State officers: Spiritual Resources, Rev. H. H. Wolford, Elkhart; Life Work, Rev. Charles A. Bame, North Manchester; Stewardship, Rev. Geo. C. Carpenter, Peru; Missionary Education, Rev. Clarence Kolb, Milford. It was agreed to urge all of our ministers to attend the county meetings in order that they may be fully informed concerning the great Interchurch Movement. Rev. Wolford made the denominational report to the conference, in which he assured the conference that our church in this state will co-operate in the largest possible way.

After we had completed the organization the question of holding a Bible conference was taken up. It was agreed to hold one conference at North Manchester, Monday and Tuesday, April 5 and 6, following Easter Sunday.

J. A. McINTURFF, Acting Secretary.

LOST CREEK, KENTUCKY

The following things have been received since our last report: Roll of Sunday School papers from Sarah Phillips, Middlebranch, Ohio; Box clothing, Mrs. H. S. Baughman, North Tonawanda, New York; 48 sash curtains, Gleaners Sunday School Class, Waterloo, Iowa; and 24 curtain rods from the Booster Juniors for the boys' dormitory; box silverware for ourselves, Mr. Berkley, Waterloo, Iowa; box tracts and books, Miss Alice Wimer, Topeka, Kansas; 5 dozen soup plates and 2 platters, Woman's Missionary Society, and $1.50 for wash bowl and pitcher, Mrs. Mary J. Wise, Middlebranch, Ohio; $5.00 for ourselves, Mrs. S. J. Lichty, Waterloo, Iowa; barrel clothing, including stereoscope and pictures for ourselves, Sisterhood, Goshen, Indiana; clothing, Christmas books and toys and comforter for dormitory, W. M. S. and Sisterhood, and Kerr Bros., Bryan, Ohio; box clothing, two pillows, two spreads, quilt for Drushal baby, quilt, silver spoons, pans and cups for ourselves, from friends at Waterloo, Iowa; Christmas package, Mrs. C. W. Landis, Waterloo, Iowa; two comforts, Thanksgiving box, King's Daughters Sunday School class, McKee, Pennsylvania; $3.00 for ourselves, Mrs and Mrs. D. C. Swanger, Tioca, Indiana; box toys, Junior Christian Endeavor, Nappanee, Indiana; two comforts, Mrs. W. S. Bond, Mexico, Indiana; $5.00 each for ourselves, Marion Watt and Zelda McLennon, Washington, D. C.; Christmas box, Miss Mae Minnich, Greencastle, Pennsylvania; year's subscription to Ladies' Home Journal and Country Gentleman, Mrs. Sue E. Cotterman, Farmersville, Ohio! $15.00 for ourselves, Loyal Helpers and Leaders Sunday School classes, Waterloo, Iowa; box Christmas things for ourselves, Sallie Griffith, Sunday School class, Masontown, Pennsylvania; box cards, Altruist Bible Class, Dayton, Ohio; box dormitory supplies, La-Verne, California; barrel clothing, Ella Miller; box children's toys, Opal McKinley, Easton, Indiana; two barrels clothing with toys, Sisterhood Girls, South Bend, Indiana; barrel dormitory supplies, Hagerstown, Maryland; barrel clothing, two comforts for dormitory and some personal effects, Sydney, Indiana; 13 towels for dormitory, Sisterhood Girls, Canton, Ohio; box eatables for dormitory, North Manchester, Indiana; box eatables for dormitory, Maurertown, Virginia; comforter, Welcome Class, Milledgeville, Illinois; 3 calendars, Miss Schrorer, California; box canned goods for dormitory, Church, Allentown, Pennsylvania; $2.00 for ourselves, Alice Ditch, Mexico, Indiana; two comforts for dormitory, King's Daughters Sunday School class, McKee, Pennsylvania; gifts of money for the work, Mrs. Pearl Stuckman, Nappanee, Indiana, $5.00; Geneva Strode, Washington, D. C., $10; Minerva J. Perry, Dodge City, Kansas, $10; Grace L. Buck, Dayton, Ohio, $1; Helen Beyer, Bellefontaine, Ohio, $15; Trinity Congregation, Seven Fountains, Virginia, $6.80; Dr. Milford Brubaker, Troy, Ohio, for work and ourselves, $50.00; Ida Shank, Jenny Lind, California, $25.00. If in the above there has been anything omitted, and there might be,

not intentionally, we will very much appreciate a word from you about it, and it will then later appear in the report.* See last page.

We must not forget to mention the fact that our going to Conference last fall was made possible by the generosity of Brother and Sister Homer Ball and Brother and Sister Munch of Washington, D. C.

This was indeed a treat for the family and greatly appreciated.

We would like to take time to tell how each and everything sent has been so gratefully received. But we have written to all personally, except Sister Ella Miller. Her name but no address was on the barrel. The letter written to Miss Alice Wimer, was returned, so we thank her through these columns for the tracts sent. There were distributed by a committee of Christian Endeavorers.

As on a summer day when things are growing and bearing fruit, oftentimes a dark stormy cloud suddenly approaches, breaks forth, spends itself, then again the skies brighten, so has been the history of Riverside the past few months. Our school opened in January, with a goodly number of enthusiastic students enrolled. That the spiritual life of the students was being developed was evidenced by the prayer meetings held, in the student's rooms and the interest taken in Bible work, and the largest attendance and best offerings at the Sunday services in the history of the work. Of course Satan could not stand all this.

Then to make a long story shirt, misunderstandings crept in. Propositions were made which were accepted by some and rejected by others. Then came resignations, and more or less confusion as a result of all this. Then came the "flu." One by one, or rather two by threes, students and teachers took down. The reception room of the girls' dormitory was turned into a hospital room. Miss Bethke, our faithful worker from California, took upon herself the care of the sick, and did most splendid work as a nurse. Some cases of pneumonia developed, which Miss Bethke so ably nursed back to health, and now we seem to be by it all, with health to go forward in the cause of the Master.

The best part of the whole story is that things are now going fine again. It could not be otherwise; God chastens for a purpose. Could you step in now and see the work of Riverside, you would not see that anything had ever happened outside of the usual. We trust that out of it all may come a better and a bigger Riverside.

MRS. G. E. DRUSHAL.

REPORT OF RECEIPTS FOR MISSIONS DURING FEBRUARY
(Home Missions).
General Fund

True Blue S. S. Class, Warsaw, Ind., $	5.00
Willing Workers' S. S. Class, Dayton, O.,	16.15
First Breth. Ch., Johnstown, Pa., ...	206.00
First Breth. Ch., Waynesboro, Pa., ...	72.00
Bessie Hillinger, (H. G.), ...	5.00
Mr. and Mrs. Jesse E. Koontz, (H. G.),	5.00
Mrs. V. R. Koontz, (H. G.), ...	5.00
Chas. E. Martin & Family, (H. G.),	6.00
M. A. Witter, (H. G.), ...	5.00
Margaret Shearer, (H. G.), ...	5.00
First Br. Ch., South Bend, Ind., ...	50.00
Miss Ethel Ingalright, (H. G.), ..	5.00
Miss Nellie Waddell, (H. G.), ...	5.00
C. S. Jackson, (H. G.), ...	5.00
Willis Sriver, (H. G.), ...	5.00
Mr. & Mrs. J. H. Cunningham, (H. G.),	5.00
Mr. & Mrs. Wm. Meinke, (H. G.),	5.00
Wm. Garwood, (H. G.), ...	5.00
Miss Nellie Garwood, H. G.), ...	5.00

Mr. & Mrs. Clem Garwood, H. G.),.. 5.00
Mr. & Mrs. F. M. Whitmer, (H. G.), 5.00
Nat. W. M. S., by Mary C. Wenger,
　Dayton, O., Treas., ... 25.00
D. Harader, Crescent, Okla., (H. G.), 10.00
Br. Ch., Hagerstown, Md., ... 5.00
Edythe O. Fair, Mongo, Ind., ... 1.00
First Br. Ch., Philadelphia, Pa., ... 52.97
Ellen S. Cassel, Philadelphia, Pa., (H.
　G.), ... 5.00
Junior C. E., Warsaw, Br. Ch., ... 5.00
Orion E. Bowman, Dayton, O., ... 14.00
Third Br. Ch., Johnstown, Pa., ... 12.32
Mrs. George F. Kem, Dayton, O., (H.
　G.), ... 5.00
N. D. Wright, Racket, W. Va., (H.
　G.), ... 5.00
Br. Ch., Whittier, Cal., ... 116.56
W. S. Vickers, Eaton, O., (H. G.), .. 5.00
Willing Workers' S. S. Class, Day-
　ton, O., ... 10.65
Reimbursement, ... 33.75
Br. Ch., Williamstown, O., ... 30.00
Albert M. & Clara Clark, Flora, Ind.,
　(H. G.), ... 5.00

Total, ...$ 685.40
Previously reported, ... 7,493.04

Total Receipts to March 1, ...$8,178.44
Correction for December report: W. M. S.
Hagerstown, Maryland, $26.40 not listed. To-
tal O. K.

KENTUCKY SUPPORT FUND
Montgomery, Ward & Co., Refund,..$ 4.67
First Br. Ch., Waynesboro, Pa., ... 36.00
Laura E. Hedrick, Hallandale, Fla., 5.00
Arda L. Hedrick, Hallandale, Fla., . 5.00
Jr. S. S. Class, Gretna, Ohio, ... 5.00
W. M. S. Soc. 1st Br. Ch., Phila., Pa., 25.00
Br. Ch., Cerro Gordo, Ill., ... 17.50
Br. Ch., Hagerstown, Md., ... 5.00
Chas. Abraham, Uniontown, Pa., ... 5.00
Henry Rhinehart, Flora, Ind., ... 50.00
Br. Ch., Krypton, Ky., ... 15.00
Rev. W. J. Barnhart, Pleasant Hill,
　Ohio, ... 5.00
Br. Ch., Whittier, Cal., ... 25.00
S. M. M., Leon, Iowa, ... 5.00
First Br. S. S., Waterloo, Iowa, ... 40.00
C. L. McShirley, Oakville, Ind., ... 15.00
Mrs. C. T. Metzker, Oakville, Ind.,.. 5.00
Young Peoples' S. S. Class near Leb-
　anon, Ohio, ... 5.00
C. E. Soc., Nappanee, Ind., ... 35.00
Mrs. Barton, Dayton, O., ... 1.00
Dr. Milford Brubaker and Wife,
　Troy, O., ... 50.00
Mrs. Chas. Smith, Eaton, O., ... 5.00
C. E. Soc., Louisville, O., ... 5.00
Albert M. and Clara Clark, Flora,
　Ind., ... 10.00

Total, ...$ 379.17
Previously reported, ...$3,978.26
　Total Receipts to March 1, in-
　cluding $200.00 transferred from

General Fund, ...$4,557.43
KENTUCKY KITCHEN SHOWER FUND
Homer Anderson, North English, Ia. $ 5.00

Total, ...$ 5.00
Previously reported, ...$ 248.80

Total Receipts to March 1, ...$ 253.80
KENTUCKY LIGHT PLANT FUND
Edward and M. O. Nininger, Roan-
　oke, City, Va., ...$ 50.00
Carleton Br. Ch., Garwin, Iowa, ... 13.62
Nat. S. S. Ass'n. by Albert Trent,
　Treasurer, ... 30.00
Br. Ch., Williamstown, O., ... 25.00

Total ....$ 118.62
Previously reported, ... 527.41
　Total Receipts to March 1, in-
　cluding $300.00 transferred from

General Fund, ...$ 646.03

**SUMMARY OF RECEIPTS TO MARCH 1,
HOME MISSIONS**
General Fund, ...$ 8,178.44
Kentucky (Support Fund), ... 4,557.43
Kentucky (Kitchen Shower Fund), 253.80
Kentucky (Light Plant Fund), ... 646.03
Muncie, Ind. (Building Fund), ... 50.23
Peru, Ind. (Building Fund), ... 25.24

Total Receipts to March 1, All
　Funds, ...$13,711.17
GENERAL FUND SOUTH AMERICAN
Br. Ch., Cerro Gordo, Ill., ...$ 17.50
Br. Ch., Hagerstown, Md., ... 6.00
Edythe O. Fair, Mongo, Ind., ... 1.00
Wm. S. Angell, Portis, Kan., (M.), 5.00
Dora E. Hepler, Nappanee, Ind., (M.), 5.00
W. S. Vickeds, Eaton, O., (M.), ... 5.00
A Good Sister, (L. M.), ... 50.00
Frank Clapper, Louisville, O. (M.), 10.00
Isaac Clapper, Louisville, O., (M.), .. 6.00

Total, ...$ 105.50
Previously Reported, ... 417.45

Total Receipts to March 1, ...$ 522.95
GENERAL FUND (AFRICA)
No. 347,- ....$ 10.70
No. 348, ... 16.22
No. 349, M., ... 15.00
No. 350, ... 3.00
No. 351, M., ... 10.00
No. 352, ... 2.50
No. 353, ... 1.00

Total, ...$ 57.42
Previously Reported, ...$257.67

Total to March 1, ...$315.09
GRIBBLE PERSONAL FUND
No. 97, Marguerite, ...$ 2.05
No. 95, Marguerite, ... 9.75
No. 94, M., ... 10.00
No. 96, ... 12.21
No. 98, Marguerite, ... 9.75
No. 99, ... 5.00

Total, ...$ 48.76
Previously Reported, ... 89.25

Total to March 1, ... $138.01
ROLLIER PERSONAL FUND
No. 39, ...$ 8.00
No. 40, (Children), ... 15.55
No. 41, ... 177.95

No. 42, ... 1.20
No. 43, ... 31.20

Total, ...$233.90
Previously Reported, ...$ 33.00

Total to March 1, ...$266.90
**CHARLOTTE HILLEGAS (AFRICAN OUT-
FIT FUND)**
First Br. Ch., Long Beach, Cal., ...$ 1.50
Previously reported, ... 271.41

Total Receipts to March 1, ...$272.91
BRETHREN MISSIONARY FUND
La Verne, Cal., by Elsie Rager, ...$ 1.25
T. J. Gribble, New Cumberland, Pa., .. .20
Mrs. Caleb Gaurn an, by Mrs. T. J.
　Gribble, ... .25
Collected by Mrs. J. A. Myers, Wil-
　liamsburg, Iowa, ... 2.75
Mrs. T. J. Fahrney, Williamsport, Md., .50
Previously reported, ... $ 4.75

Total Receipts to March 1, ... $ 9.70
MISCELLANEOUS FUND
Armenian Relief
Alice Longaker, Phila., Pa., (M.), ..$ 10.00
Homer Anderson, North English, Ia., 1.00
China (Mrs. Rose M. Foulke)
World Wide Miss. Soc. 1st Br. Ch.,
　Long Beach, Calif., ... 19.90
Bolivian Indian Mission
First Br. Ch., Long Beach, Cal., ... 20.00
Rio Cuarto Mission, Communion Set
Mrs. M. P. Holmes White, New
　Smyrna, Florida, ... 20.00
Williamsburg Mission to Jews
World Wide Miss. Soc. 1st Br. Ch.,
　Long Beach, Cal., ... 15.00

Total, ...$ 95.90
Previously Reported, ... $ 216.00

Total Receipts to March 1, ...$ 311.90

The late Professor Henry Sedgwick was describing to a friend a dispute at an academic
council meeting, wherein Bishop Browne of
Bristol had been rather rudely treated. His
friend asked, "And did Browne lose his temper?" Replied Sedgwick, "No, but he kept it
very obviously!"

THE FOREIGN MISSION OFFERING

The Time.— EASTER SUNDAY, April 4th is the time for the WHOLE BRETHREN CHURCH and all her auxiliary organizations to make an OFFERING as unto the LORD.

The Purpose.—1. This offering is made for the SUPPORT of all our MISSIONARY ENTERPRISES both in ARGENTINA AND AFRICA.

2. The offering is made for the ENLARGEMENT of our present endeavors by sending forth NEW WORKERS into UNOCCUPIED fields.

The Goal.— A Gift of MONEY can never measure our DEBT to GRACE nor dare any earnest Christian ever LIMIT his giving by a suggestion of SO-MUCH-PER member. The "GENEROUS GIFT" (2 Cor. 9:5) falls below or RISES FAR ABOVE the suggested $1.00 per member. "GRACE" measures the gift made to JESUS.

Your Report.— Send all offerings to the General Missionary Secretary of the Brethren Church. Brother WILLIAM A. GEARHART, 906 Conover Building, DAYTON, OHIO.

A Telegram.— Pastors and Churches are invited to send prepaid telegrams or night letters to the Editor of the Brethren Evangelist on Monday, April 5th. Report the success of your EASTER SERVICE both in SOULS won to the Lord and in MONEY given to FOREIGN MISSIONS.

SOUTH AMERICAN TRACT FUND
Br. Ch., La Verne, Cal., ...$ 4.00

Total, ... $ 4.00
Previously Reported, ...$125.00
   Total Receipts to March 1, ...$129.00

SNYDER PERSONAL FUND
No Receipts. Previously reported ..$ 10.00

Total Receipts to March 1, ...$ 10.00
SUMMARY OF RECEIPTS TO MARCH 1
Foreign Missions
General Fund (South America) ,...$ 522.95
General Fund (Africa), ... 315.09
Gribble (Personal Fund), ... 138.01
Rollier (Personal Fund), ... 266.90
Charlotte Hillegas (African Outfit
  Fund), ... 272.01
Brethren Missionary Fund, ... 9.70
Miscellaneous Fund, ... 311.90
South American (Tract Fund), ... 129.00
Snyder (Personal Fund), ... 10.00

Total Receipts to March 1, All

Funds, ...$1,976.46
Respectfully submitted,
WILLIAM A. GEARHART,
General Missionary Secretary.

LAYING CORNER-STONE NEW CHURCH
Los Angeles, California
Next Sunday, March 14, will be a great day at First church. Plans have been made for an all day meeting with basket lunch in the big tent. Pastors and members of other Southern California churches are invited to be present and participate in the services in the tent at 2 P. M. and at the corner stone laying across the street at the new church building at 3 P. M.
We are all happy in the anticipation of the completion of our new church this spring.
Yours sincerely,
A. P. REED.

THE TIE THAT BIDNS

NEITHERCOAT-BARCROFT—At the First Brethren church, Louisville, Ohio, 12 M. January 24, Charles A. Neithercoat and Sara F. Barcroft were united in marriage. Mr. Neithercoat is a member of the above named church. Both are estimable young people. The ring ceremony was solemnized by the undersigned. E. M. RIDDLE.

PREAS-MOORE—At our residence in Roanoke, Va., on Saturday, February 14, at 8 P. M. occurred the marriage ceremony of Mr. N. E. Preas and Miss Ora R. Moore, both well known young people of this city. The ceremony was performed by the writer in the presence of a few of their invited friends. They will continue their residence in Roanoke. L. G. WOOD.

LUNDELL-BUCKLAND.—On Saturday evening, January 31, a beautiful church wedding was solemnized in the Turlock Brethren church. Miss Esther Lundell was united in marriage to Mr. Nelson Buckland, Miss Lun-

CORRECT ENGLISH

HOW TO USE IT

A MONTHLY MAGAZINE

$2.50 THE YEAR

Send 10 Cents for Sample Copy

.......TO......

Correct English Publishing
Company
EVANSTON, ILLINOIS

---

dell was a resident of Turlock and Mr. Buckland resides in Modesto, Calif. Both are members of the Turlock Brethren church.
The church was beautifully decorated with palms and flowers. Mrs. Leatherman sang as a solo, "If I But Knew." Miss Alice Bergland rendered the wedding march. There were near a hundred who witnessed the ceremony. The bride and groom retired to the bride's home, followed by the invited guests where a sumptuous reception was enjoyed by all. All unite in wishing these young people a happy and successful married life. Ceremony by the writer.
N. V. LEATHERMAN.

IN THE SHADOW

"GOOD BY PAPA."

These were the last words spoken to me by our dear daughter, Irene, as she departed for Florida two weeks ago. Little did I think nor did any one else that as she started on that long trip to accompany her sister-in-law to see her sick husband, that Irene would be the victim of death instead of the ill husband.
Irene was to me a part of my life for she was the joy and life of the home wherever she went. I baptized her into the Brethren church in her youth at her request. Then when she grew up I performed the marriage ceremony at her request in the Brethren church at Maurertown and now I feel that I should speak a word in this way at her death.
For years I had been hoping to build a Brethren church here at Strasburg where we have a number of members and I had Irene in mind, if no one else could be found, to be the chorister of the church. She was a graduated musician of the Shenandoah Collegiate Institute of Dayton, Virginia, and able to conduct the musical part of the church service. Here at Strasburg she was the soprano singer of the Disciple church when she attended church, as our church is four miles out in the country. Now, since her untimely death I shall abandon the idea of building a church here for I feel that my help which I had depended on has been taken from me.
When we received a telegram that she had developed a mild form of pneumonia, I looked up God's promises to those who would seek him in prayer and faith and I went to my bed chamber and knelt in prayer pleading these promises with tears pouring out to God my heart's desire for her recovery, the God to whom for years I had pointed others as sufficient in any time of trouble and need and who had never before failed me, but all to no purpose. I can not understand, I can not understand the failure. Surely our hearts have been rent as never before. In the past years I have lost two sisters, my father, mother, son-in-law and now my oldest daughter. I can only say, "Good by, dear Irene, good by."
Strasburg, Va.
GEO. A. COPP.

BEER—Elmira Blucher Beer was born in Alleghany county, Maryland, October 11, 1846 and departed this life, January 23, 1920, aged 73 years, 3 months and 12 days. On March 30, in Poweschiek county, Iowa, she was married to J. W. Beer and in April of the same year she, with her husband, moved to Reno county, Kansas, where they have lived, in or near Nickerson ever since except one year in Kingman county. To this union were born eight children, seven of whom are living. They are P. L. Beer of Weatherford, Okla.; A. L. Beer of Pretty Prairie, Okla.; Dr. C. A. Beer, of Enid, Okla; Mrs. L. L. Pate, of Cascades, Montana; Mrs. Catheryne Smalley, of Cayia, Miss; Miss I. A. G. Beer, and Grace Joy Beer. Besides the children there are left to mourn this departure, two sisters, 19 grand children and four great-grand children.
Mrs. Beer was a loyal member of the Brethren church, of which her husband was a pioneer minister. In his absence from home while looking after the work of the church, Mrs. Beer patiently and faithfully discharged the arduous duties and responsibilities of the home, affectionately rearing her children to whom she was so tenderly devoted. Funeral services were conducted in the M. E. church at Nickerson, Kansas, by the pastor of the church.
REV. I. E. McNIEL.

PAINTER—Sister Irene Painter, wife of C. Painter, daughter of Elder Geo. A. Copp, died in Jacksonville, Fla., February 11, 1920, after arriving in above named city only a few days she was taken with pneumonia, following an attack of the "flu." She was a member of the Brethren church and was regarded as an estimable lady. The large attendance at the burial service was an evidence of the respect the general public entertained of her life. Funeral service at Strasburg, Va., by the writer assisted by Rev. J. D. Haymaker.
E. E. SHAVER.

REED.—Mrs. Flora May Reed passed from her earthly home in Stockton, California, to her home in the great beyond, January 7, 1920. She was born at Brownville, Oregon, April 21, 1892. She was aged 27 years, months and 17 days. Sister Reed began the Christian life seven years ago and was very devoted to her Lord. She leaves in her home to mourn her sorely felt loss her husband Harry G. Reed, a son 16 months of age, and a little babe three weeks old. Others who suffer her loss are her father and mother, Mr. and Mrs. Frank G. Smith, two brothers, Ray G. and Harry E. Smith; two sisters, Edna Smith and Mrs. George Watson, besides other numerous relatives and friends whose hearts are saddened because of her departure. May th rich blessings of God rest upon all the sorrowing. Services by the writer.
N. V. LEATHERMAN.

STONEBRUNNER—Sarah M. Stonebrunner died at her home in Sidney, Indiana, Monday, February 24, of bronchial pneumonia. Her going was peaceful while in possession of a living hope. She was a consistent member of the Brethren church at Sidney. Funeral services at the Brethren church at Sidney, Indiana, by the writer.
L. A. MYERS.

OAKS—Arlien, aged one year, daughter of Sarah (Headrick) Oaks, (widow of Allen Elwood Oaks, who died at his home in West Point on January 3) passed from this life to be with Jesus on February 23. Death was due to pneumonia. She has gone hence to find a resting place in the arms of Jesus who said, "Suffer the little ones to come unto me, for of such is the kingdom of heaven."
There remains of this family, the mother and one son, Leroy, aged 13. May the God who raised up Jesus from the dead comfort these troubled hearts. Services by the undersigned.
E. F. BYERS.

HEADRICK.—On February 13th, William Headrick, aged 69 years, 9 months, departed the voyage of this troublous life, to answer the summons of God. Mr. Headrick had been stricken with paralysis about three years ago and twice since that time, the last of which resulted in his death. Brother Headrick, to use the words of Job, came to his grave in full age; like a shock of corn cometh in his season. Brother Headrick was a member of the Conemaugh Brethren church. He is survived by his widow, Isabella (Good) Headrick, three sons and two daughters. May God Comfort the hearts of those that mourns the loss of husband and father. Services by the undersigned.
E. F. BYERS.

Communion Notices

COMMUNION NOTICE
The First Brethren church of Washington, D. C., will hold its semi-annual Love Feast on Thursday evening, April first at seven fifteen P. M. All who love this precious service are cordially invited to attend.
W. M. LYON, Pastor.

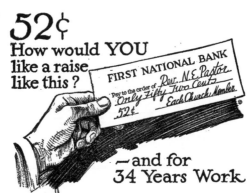

52¢
How would YOU like a raise like this?

—and for 34 Years Work

THAT is the kind of increase in salary the minister has received.

His living expenses have risen just as fast and as far as yours.

But he is paid on the average just 52 cents more *per church member per year* than he was paid 34 years ago.

Is it any wonder that the Minister of God is called "The Forgotten Man?" Forgotten—until we're in trouble. And then we call upon him.

The Minister Never Fails You

The Secretary of the Treasury; the Food Administrator; the Coal Administrator—every officer of the Government with a war message to deliver appealed to the ministers first of all.

And 80% of the ministers receive less income than government economists figure as a minimum for the support of an average family.

When hospitals need money they enlist the support of the ministers —and receive it.

But when sickness visits the minister or the members of his family they must be treated in a charity ward. His pay is less than a day laborer's.

We Pay Him Half the Wages of a Mechanic

Wages have increased 100%; 200%; 300%; in the past twenty years. The average pay of ministers has increased only about 10%.

8 out of every 10 ministers receive less than $20 a week—about half the pay of a mechanic.

And of these pitifully inadequate salaries, how much do *you* contribute? Nothing if you are outside the church; an average of a penny a day if you are a church member.

All of us—inside the Churches and outside—share in the benefits of Christian ministers to the community.

They marry us; bury us; baptize our children; visit us when we are sick. In their hands is the spiritual training of the youth.

We Are All Profiteers at Their Expense

Part of the Interchurch World programme is this—a living wage for every minister of Jesus Christ; an efficient plant, and a chance to do a big man's job.

If you want better preachers, help to pay the preachers better.

It's the best investment for your community—and for your children —that you can ever make.

 THE Evangelical denominations of America have united in a great co-operative work under the name of the Interchurch World Movement. Its object is to encourage church co-operation and discourage duplication; to make the teachings of Jesus Christ the paramount influence in the social, political and economic life of the modern world.

INTERCHURCH WORLD MOVEMENT
of North America

The Evangelical Churches Cooperating in the Service of Jesus Christ
45 WEST 18th STREET, NEW YORK CITY

Volume XLII
Number 12

March 24
1920

The BRETHREN EVANGELIST

-One·Is·Your·Master·and·All·Ye·Are·Brethren-

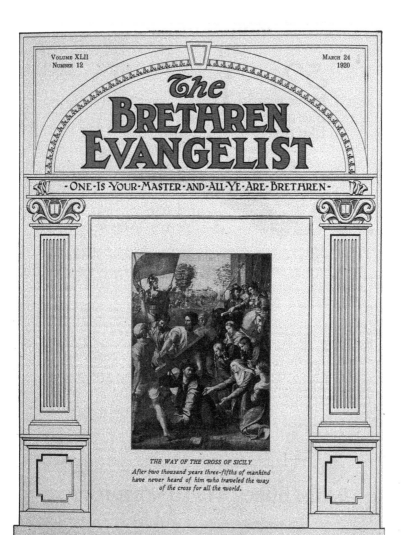

THE WAY OF THE CROSS OF SICILY

*After two thousand years three-fifths of mankind
have never heard of him who traveled the way
of the cross for all the world.*

Published every Wednesday at Ashland, Ohio. All matter for publication must reach the Editor not later than Friday noon of the preceding week.

George S. Baer, Editor

The
Brethren
Evangelist

When ordering your paper changed give old as well as new address. Subscriptions discontinued at expiration. To avoid missing any numbers renew two weeks in advance.

R. R. Teeter, Business Manager

OFFICIAL ORGAN OF THE BRETHREN CHURCH

Subscription price, $2.00 per year, payable in advance.
Entered at the Post Office at Ashland, Ohio, as second-class matter.
Acceptance for mailing at special rate of postage provided for in section 1103, Act of October 3, 1917, authorized September 9, 1918.
Address all matter for publication to Geo. S. Baer, Editor of the Brethren Evangelist, and all business communications to R. R. Teeter, Business Manager, Brethren Publishing Company, Ashland, Ohio. Make all checks payable to the Brethren Publishing Company.

TABLE OF CONTENTS

EDITORIAL

The Two-fold Easter Challenge to the Brethren Church

At this Easter time there is a two-fold challenge to the churches of the brotherhood—the challenge of foreign missions and the challenge of local evangelism. At this season, according to custom, the Foreign Missionary Society is asking for an offering for the support and extension of our missionary work in foreign lands. And at this time also the whole Protestant church is being brought face to face with its responsibility for winning the unconverted souls in the multitude of communities where it is at work to an acknowledgement of the risen Christ as their Savior. This task the Brethren church is facing no less than the other branches of Protestantism. Let us consider these challenges in order.

THE CHALLENGE OF FOREIGN MISSIONS

The day is past when Brethren people need to have presented to them the fact of their responsibility for carrying the gospel to the uttermost parts of the world. We all recognize that as the heart of the commission, and as the most essential requirement of faithful discipleship. We have been holding that before us as one of our distinctive tasks, and we have made considerable progress along this line considering the shortness of the time since we launched our first real foreign missionary project. But our missionary vision has been a matter of growth, and it is not yet as large as it ought to be. We have yet to realize in anything like an adequate way how great is our responsibility for world-wide evangelization. We cannot possibly measure the present duty with the accomplishments of the past and meet the present needs. Such calculation would cause us to fall far behind. It is to be feared that the bigness and urgency of the task at this hour has not dawned upon us as yet. Perhaps this is true of the rank and file of most churches. It certainly is ours. Only the most forward looking leaders of the various communions have any worthy conception of the staggering demands of the present situation. But it is encouraging to see how readily the larger vision is being grasped and the greater demands are being met. And this is the confidence we have in our people,—that when the needs are set before them and the opportunities and responsibilities are made clear, they will move forward and accept the challenge with a courage and a consecration hitherto unequalled.

We are told that at this very season, when we are rejoicing in the knowledge of a resurrected and glorified Christ, there are in South America a million people whom we are as a church responsible for evangelizing. A million people who have never heard the truth about Christ and who look to us for that knowledge! If we carry the responsibility down to the individual, we have for every member of the Brethren church at least forty persons in Argentina to evangelize. Are we taking care of our share? Is the dollar per member we are asked to give likely to pay for the evangelizing of forty people each? But that is only half the story.

We are told that there are a million people in and about our mission station in Africa who are wholly unevangelized and for whom we as a church are responsible. We are told that this is our share of Africa's millions according to our numerical strength. That means forty more unevangelized souls for each member of the Brethren church,—and these are people of the deepest degree of ignorance and superstition. Who had dreamed of such a task? We need not cause embarrassment by asking what we have done to meet this big obligation. It is sufficient to ask what we are willing to do. We have not known the bigness of our responsibility before, but now that the light is come, we have no excuse for our sin.

Our Foreign Board, with much forbearance and patience, is asking for a minimum of one dollar per member, in order that, so far as money goes, they may carry forward in the name of the church the greatest work that God has committed to his people. But how much more they really ought to have they have not dared to tell us. In the provisional budget for our new program, it is calculated that $45,000 dollars annually will be needed during the next five years for foreign missions. But that is scarcely two dollars per member. That is small enough when the need is considered. We have been doing so much less than we were able to do that it is difficult to judge what is the limit of our ability. But the limit of our ability is the least we ought to give.

But money is not all; not even the chief thing in this missionary program. Prayer is needed—prayer that is earnest, definite and persevering. The need is not merely to remember our missionaries in our public worship and group prayer meetings, but in our private devotions as well. We ought to support them daily by our most earnest petitions. We ought to pray not only for our missionaries, but for the Spirit of God to descend upon the hearts of multitudes of unconverted men and women and cause them to seek with sincerity instruction and baptism at the hands of our missionaries. We should pray for our Mission Board that these men may be given vision and wisdom to push the work with the greatest possible speed and thoroughness. And pray for the rank and file of our church to support this work with greater consecration and sacrifice. Prayer has great power with God when it goes forth from earnest, sincere souls; therefore, let us pray at this Eastertide for the tremendous task of foreign missions.

Life also is needed at this time in far greater abundance than it has ever before been given. Young, talented, courageous lives, willing to prepare and willing to go where God may lead them are needed. Money alone will not evangelize the world; it is only the thing that will pay the expenses. Prayer alone is not enough; God works through human agents. The greatest need at this time is life, and that is the hardest thing to give, and the only thing that as a rule requires any real sacrifice. He who gives life, gives all. Many more givers are needed to meet the demands of this hour than we have ever yet dared to ask for, and they must be found in the Brethren church. In proportion as we appreciate the priceless blessing vouchsafed by Easter, will we be willing to make such gifts.

THE CHALLENGE OF EVANGELISM

No season of the year is more appropriate for an ingathering of souls than the Easter season, and it seems that there could scarcely be another time when the prevailing spirit would lend itself better to an evangelistic appeal than this time. It ought to be made to yield the largest possible results in the home fields as well as in the foreign lands. Jesus not only commanded that the gospel be preached to the uttermost parts of the earth, but to the nearer parts as well. He insisted that his followers should begin at Jerusalem. It was the nearest and therefore the most difficult task, which must not be neglected. It was at once a challenge to their faith and courage.

We are challenged to emphasize evangelism in our local churches that others may come to know the joy and consolation and have the hope and assurance which we realize in our own hearts. It seems that no time should enable us to preach with greater fervor and conviction; or with greater faith and courage than the Easter season. The inspiration from this day should give us messages that will burn their way into the hearts of the unregenerate and it should cause us in our conversations to speak with such sincerity and earnestness and love concerning the spiritual welfare of the unsaved that many would be influenced to yield their lives to Jesus Christ, who alone is "the resurrection and the life."

The consciousness that there are men around us out of Christ at this season when our hearts are more tender than usual, made so by the contemplation of the record of the sacred events of passion week, should stir us to new and more earnest efforts for the saving of souls. The crying need of men should touch our hearts and challenge our efforts at this season as at no other. Who could fail to offer to the wounded souls of men the heart-balm of the race at such a time.

At this Eastertide the challenge of the church to apply a message that will prove to be the saving salt of society was never more insistent. All remedial efforts however worthy will be unavailing unless saturated with and supported by the gospel of Christ. As Bishop Henderson says, "There cannot be any permanent world peace without a revival of righteousness through Jesus Christ. There cannot be any lessening of the many evils that are causing unrest until men see themselves as God sees them, and they get into right relationship with God." And if any time, surely this time when the world is becoming so sick of its sinful spree, we should be challenged to do our utmost to proclaim in sermon and conversation the saving power of the resurrected Christ. With the greatest consecration of time, energy and ability possible, let us endeavor to meet this challenge.

The clipping from the Falls City Journal reprinted in this issue bears evidence to the high esteem in which Brother Stuckman is held by his parishioners. It also suggests a thing to our minds that would be fine if copied by many other churches, viz., giving their pastors a vacation, not at his own expense, but with full pay. This is only what the world calls good business, and it is what the church ought to consider good Christianity.

EDITORIAL REVIEW

Dr. Jacobs supplies us with another installment of "College News" which will be found of interest to all friends of the college, and somehow we have a growing feeling that practically the entire brotherhood is becoming a friend to this institution.

Send foreign mission offerings to Wm. A. Gearhart, 906 Conover Building, Dayton, Ohio.

Indiana is to have a Bible conference and it is to be held at North Manchester during the Easter season. Read Brother Bame's announcement in this issue.

Brother Carpenter in his Home Mission Notes calls attention to a number of needs; viz., more workers in Kentucky, a lift on the Winona Auditorium by every church and ten thousand tithers among Brethren people. All these needs deserve your serious attention.

Another letter comes from Africa describing the completion of our missionary party's journey to Carnot. They are now in touch with the tribe with which they feel called to work. The brotherhood will rejoice in their safe arrival at this point, and, it is hoped, will continue to support them with prayer and gifts.

Brother Lyman B. Wilkins, who has been living at Washington, C. H., and engaging in business writes that he has accepted the pastorate of the church at that place. He also states why he could not easily stay out of the pulpit. There are many more scattered throughout the brotherhood who would do well to follow Brother Wilkins' example, by occupying some vacant pulpit.

In Brother Cobb's brief article of last week on the "Twin Gold Mines" he meant to say that five dollars would make one member of the Foreign Missionary Society. His manuscript said "home guarder," but at his request we marked it changed to "member," but the correction was only half made and appeared in print as "home member." But you doubtless understood and "took a Dutchman as he means and not as he said."

It is seldom that a situation occurs such as we have this week. A few weeks ago we wrote to Brother Trout for an article for the missionary number of The Evangelist. He replied that he wrote the article on the same day he received the request,—and our readers will bear witness to the high merits of the article. In a few days after we received word of his death in Pittsburgh. It is a fitting "last word" to his brethren. And we dare say it will challenge us as few things could.

This week we are privileged to publish the promised memorial of Elder William Keifer. He was a noble and faithful soldier of Jesus Christ and for his long service and inspiring life we honor him. It is with a sense of deep regret that we see our veteran ministers leaving us one by one. We have been greatly helped by their counsels in the past and we somehow feel that we still have much need of such san counsel and stalwart defense of Gospel liberty as they displayed. May God comfort his loved ones and bless his memory to our good.

Our readers will be pleased to get another letter from Brother Beachler concerning the endowment campaign progress. And if is good news that comes this week and the church that makes possible this report is the live-wire congregation at Gratis, Ohio. Brother Beekley, the pastor and his loyal people did a fine thing for the college and we are proud of them, especially so because they are helping to vindicate Ohio. When the campaign began in this state it was whispered by doubting Thomases here and there that Ohio would never made a showing comparable to the other districts. But being from Missouri we are "showing them." We are not ashamed of Ohio, nor of such dependable churches as Gratis proves to be. We have a feeling similar to Brother Beachler's, that when Ohio is through with this campaign that she will stand as tall as any of them.

HOME MADE SQUIBS

The faithfulness of every member determines the power of every church.

"EVERY CHRISTIAN AN EVANGELIST AND EVERY CHURCH A CENTER OF EVANGELISM AND COMMUNITY SERVICE" ought to be the slogan of every church at this season of concerted evangelistic effort, and then when it has been tried out for a season, it might be made the challenge for the whole round year.

FOUR-YEAR PROGRAM PAGE
NOW THEN DO IT.—II Samuel 3:18
Conducted by Charles A. Bame

!All In

I guess the reports are about all in. I guess that a good many pastors must be "all in" in another sense, or they had reported. According to my count just about an even hundred answered the last "call" but one. Some of these times they will answer the last and I hope some of them will be a good deal more ready to respond to that or they will be left—where? Just why a pastor will refuse the common courtesy of ordinary correspondence and keep a SELF-ADDRESSED and stamped card that does not belong to him, I can not figure out unless it is a case of pure meanness. Ordinarily, men use another word but I presume the editor would blue pencil that if I'd use it. Of course smallness of action signifies smallness of heart and the man that proves himself small in the testing time need have no hope of big power in the kingdom, no matter how large the church he serves. You can not get a big stream of water through a gimlet hole, no matter how much pressure you put behind it.

The Final Dash

We are now on the last lap of the race. Oh, how I wish I could say that every church is doing the last thing to win and that every one will come in under the line in FRONT LINE STANDING! But if you are greatly in earnest about it, there are a good many things that you can do between now and Conference. For instance, every preacher can use every one of the topics. Most of them have done so, but not all. Every once in a while one asks me what are the topics? Well, had they done as I did, they would have clipped them out and pasted them on a prominent place where they could not miss them. But another fault is that a good many of the preachers are not reading this page as they ought to and thus they miss some of the program. Well,. here are the topics once more:

"The Brethren Church and Her Message," Thanksgiving.

"The Coming Kingdom and Its King," Christmas.

"The Person and Work of the Holy Spirit," February.

"The Message of the Cross, Easter.

Now, there is no use of a preacher missing any of these topics; the Program does not ask that they be used the day designated and I do hope that no preacher will fail the Program and his congregation by not using between now and the first of June, every one of these themes.

Then, there are many churches that can bring their organizations to a higher standard before that time. Look well to the things that your young people can do, to help you to get nearer the goal of Front Line. Start things now, and then keep them going, after.

Then, a good many of the congregations do not have the EVANGELIST in 75 percent of the homes. That can be done and what can be done, must be done and therefore, fellow pastor, if you wish your church people to respond to the appeals of the brotherhood, they must know more than you can tell them in the pulpit at the time of announcements. The Evangelist will do it.

Then, there are the financial goals. Of all times, this is a good year to meet every one of them. And if every congregation will meet each of these goals, and then REPORT THEM, we shall be surprised how much of the yellow will come off at the VICTORY CONFERENCE.

Finally and best of all, there is the increase in membership of 30 percent that your congregation is presumed to make. The INTERCHURCH MOVEMENT is making a tremendous effort to make this the biggest Easter in the history of Protestantism measured by the number that shall confess Christ and join the church. I hope that you, fellow-pastor, are in the game. Since I started writing this, I had a call that said, "Your Easter supplies are here," that is, various cards and leaflets that I want to use in the pre-Easter campaign. Our church is in it. In another column, I hope shall appear a program of what we hope will happen at that time. But this I am saying: you should not miss this opportunity to "get in the game."

Up To Us

That may be slang. But it says in a strong way what I want to say. If all the 30 or more denominations that are aligned with this movement get after the things they have set out to do, where will poor little BRETHRENSIM stand if it is asleep? It will not have a place. Of course I realize that there will be a lot left to evangelize after Easter, but if every church in your town goes after things as I am sure they will, it behooves the Brethren to "go and do likewise," even for self preservation.

Our Plan

My idea is that every congregation should at once get busy with a program as big as any INTERCHURCH plan and see that it goes through at the same time. Carrying out my idea as I put it last week, I am sure that this North Manchester congregation will this week on prayer meeting night vote the biggest program over that has ever been attempted by a Brethren church. If the preliminary meeting of last week is any criterion,- we shall this week vote to raise the biggest budget—so big that at any other time we would have been frightened—and then go after it and thus match what 30 others are doing at the same time.

Make It Yours

Self preservation demands that we at once get busy. We are small enough right now. There is nothing I can see or learn in the world to prevent any congregation in the brotherhood getting into the game right off. And it must be RIGHT OFF. At a time when the Church of the Brethren is voting $2,760,000.00 for missions and education and calling three District Conferences in Indiana to plan for it, when old men who were of the strictest interpretation of the Annual Meeting only a few years ago are as "enthusiastic as boys" for the program that means $27.60 a member above the congregational and district and Annual Meeting expenses, we ought "to begin to commence, to awake and rub eyes" and wonder where we are going to land or float. Not? Here in Indiana, we are going to do it. Every preacher of the ten or so that were in the INTERCHURCH STATE CONFERENCE felt that there was but one thing to do. Get busy. I am glad that hardfisted business men will get into in when they see what is about to happen if we do not.

"Hot or Cold"

The time has come for us to say if we are Laodicean or not. Co-operative Protestantism says "occupy" or "scat." We do no come to you to say that you must move on, but that you must move up. You can not hold this field unless you occupy it. We do not wish to shove you off the map but we do want the Master's will carried out in this generation. We do not wish to be unkind to you, but we must be obedient to our Lord and Master. Get busy or we shall. SO, MY BRETHREN, MAKE THIS THE BIGGEST AND GREATEST EASTER YOU HAVE EVER HAD IN THE MASTER'S BUSINESS, AND THIS YEAR VICTORY YEAR.   BAME.

"The restless millions wait the Light whose dawning makes all things new;
Christ also waits; but men are slow and late.
Have we done what we could? Have I? Have you?"

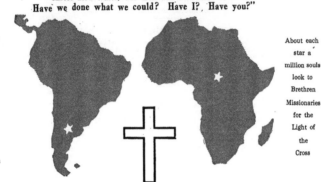

The stars indicate the location of Brethren work in both continents

About each star a million souls look to Brethren Missionaries for the Light of the Cross

The Cross waits to be carried to the farthermost recesses of
these darkened continents. How long must it wait?

GENERAL ARTICLES
The Hour of the Church's Greatest Responsibility

By Elder Isaac Bennett Trout
May 7, 1860 — March 5, 1920

Jesus Christ came into the world to save sinners. In order to do this he gave himself in the supreme sacrifice on Calvary. Upon the rock of his deity and eternity he builded his church, and, having established the work of redemption, he ascended to his Father. However before his ascension he assigned the tremendous task of evangelizing the world to the church, and said to them, "Go ye into all the world, and preach the gospel to every creature." He invested them with the same authority and duty as that given him by his Father, when he said, "As my Father hath sent me, even so send I you." Ever since the Master was here in the flesh till the present hour the church has had a great responsibility, but at no time has the responsibility been greater than in the present hour.

The Great World War involved practically every Christian nation, and put Christianity at a temporary great disadvantage before the world, especially before the non-Christian world. The hour of the church's responsibility is very great in view of the added difficulties thrown in her way by the evils that have grown out of the war. Before the war we were told again and again that the war would bring about the birth of a new and better condition, that the church would come out refined and purified and have greater influence than ever before. Some even ventured to tell us that the Gospel itself needed some improvements and that the war would produce this change. We were further told

that the war would change men's hearts and make them softer and better, more susceptible to the truth and the needs of mankind. The indications are that none of these results have as yet come out of the war, and there is no indication that they will come. The opposite seems to be rather true, that men's hearts are less open for the truth, they are harder to reach, we still have the same church with the same obstacles as before, only intensified. We have the same devil to encounter, the same sins to repent of, the world is practically the same as it was before, only much harder to handle and to win for Christ. The world is hopelessly in debt. Wrath, enmity and bitterness abound that it will take generations to overcome. To swing the world back toward the Christ is the hour of the church's greatest responsibility, for there is no power or organization apart from the church of Jesus Christ that can rescue the nations from the dilemma that they find themselves in.

The Eastern nations find themselves honeycombed with what is called Bolshevism, and our own free America is not without a dangerous admixture of this worst of all forms of infidelity and disbelief. They openly declare themselves as against God, the home, the church, government, and all good morals. In short there is nothing that is moral against which they have not declared themselves. It is very doubtful if the sword can overcome this latest form of infidelity and sin. Indeed it is certain that it can not permanently overcome any form of evil, much less this form. It remains for the church to arise in her strength, put on her beautiful garments and go forth conquering and to conquer in the name of him who bought her with his own blood. "Not by might nor by power, but by my Spirit, saith the Lord." The hour of the church's greatest responsibility demands of her that, she put on the whole armor of God and go forth as a mighty army and overcome the last as well as the least of God's enemies.

Jesus Christ has made no provision for the evangelization of the world and the confusion of the kingdom of Satan other than by and through the efforts of his church. Never have the hosts of sin marshalled themselves with more energy and determination against the church of Christ than in the present hour. This hour, then, is the hour of the church's greatest responsibility. The duty to overcome the combined forces of the enemies of all souls and all ages lies right in our pathway this very hour, and it will demand all the skill, the strength and energy of the church to fulfill the purpose of Christ at such a time as this. Will the church awaken? Will she put on her strength? Will she challenge successfully the onward march of these enemies of God? She will if she realizes what the hour contains. The church has never failed to arouse herself when the critical hour came, and we do not believe that she will slumber now beyond the time of her safety, if indeed, she is slumbering at all.

Then there is the challenge of Mohammedanism in this very hour. Already there is a large commission of Mohammedans on their way from the far East to visit the capitals of the Christian nations for the purpose of securing their consent that the Sultan of Turkey, who is the spiritual head of the Mohammedan religion, may continue to hold the seat of his empire in Europe, in the city of Constantinople, the worst plague spot of the whole earth, religiously speaking. In this critical hour it is the duty of the church to use every lawful means to prevent such a request being granted. How can the church remain quiet when infidels are asking for

a place right by her side and on equal terms with her in the governments of nations? She must speak, and speak for Christ and his church as she has never spoken before in all the ages, for this is the hour of supreme responsibility. This is the hour when he must speak for the generations that are to follow, that they may reap the fruition of her spiritual labors.

The whole continent of Africa lies between darkness and light. Mohammedanism is moving rapidly over the continent from the north, and Christianity is striving to move over the whole continent from the south, where it has gained a foothold. What the result will be, must be decided by the church's action during this hour of greatest responsibility, for it is quite evident that, if Africa is not won for Christ, within the next ten years, that it will likely be lost for many generations to come, and probably for all time till the end of the age. The duties of the hour are supreme. The church must act at once, and act with divine energy and determination. God will give the victory, but we must not stand idle another hour before entering with holy zeal into this great conflict. "Speak to the children of God that they go forward." The victory is ours, if we carry his banner to the front.

As we look out over the world the scene looks dark. Millions of men have been slain in battle, hundreds of cities have been destroyed, countless multitudes of girls and women have been violated, tens of thousands of Armenians are falling before the sword of the Turk and by famine, wicked men are challenging the progress of humanity and of Christianity as probably never before by attempting to overthrow all government and order. Where can suffering humanity look for relief but to the church of Jesus Christ? This is the hour of the church's greatest opportunity. There is no remedy but in Jesus Christ, but Jesus works in and through his church. The world must be helped. The church must do its work of evangelizing. This is her supreme hour.

Berlin, Pennsylvania.

The Challenge of Our South American Field. By Dr. E. M. Cobb

As a member of the Foreign Mission Board it is highly unnecessary for me to say that I am equally interested in our two great foreign mission fields, evidence of which will be seen in Easter Offering literature elsewhere. The Editor of the Evangelist has asked me to speak of the South American Field in particular.

There are a number of reasons why this great mission field should especially appeal to the young men and women of the Brethren church as volunteers and at the same time appeal to the tithers of the Brethren church for sympathy and support. I shall note a few of them.

1. HOTBED OF CATHOLICISM. Since the Brethren church believes in the priesthood of our Lord Jesus Christ, the forgiveness of sin through his blood only, salvation by grace, reward of the righteous, it will at once be patent to the thinking mind that Argentina would furnish virgin soil for a propaganda of this sort; for these poor deluded people have been raised on a double standard of morality, taught intercessory work of the priest and pope, and the reformatory work of purgatory. To say that these poor people haven't the slightest conception of the grace of God, and the righteousness of Jesus Christ, is putting it very mildly. It seems incredible that well educated, wealthy, influential people should be so totally void of a spiritual education; but, we are not advancing a theory, this is a condition that already exists without controversy.

2. PAROCHIAL INSTITUTIONS. One of the potent factors in any country, next in importance to the church, is the school system. The hierarchy in the Southland, sees to it that all children are properly trained in the parochial school. This gives them Catholic instruction from kindergarten to college. When the principles of the catechism and other formalities are drilled into their minds and hearts until

they almost become second nature, it matters little what their teaching be after that—they still remain Catholics.

3. CORRUPT SOCIAL CONDITIONS. With a code of Christian ethics as lax as the one allowed by the Roman clergy in the Southland, nothing remains to be said, except that the Devil sees to it that the carnal mind has plenty of opportunity to push his propaganda. Steam is power, and will propel a boat, but the rudder must guide. Knowledge is also power, but a moral judgment must sit on the throne. Where the moral judgment is patterned after the character of a priest, instead of the righteousness of Jesus Christ, the conscience is not likely to become alarmed even at conditions that we would consider appaling; our missionaries therefore find a very needy field for the exaltation of the righteousness of Jesus Christ.

4. NATURAL RESOURCES AND ATTRACTIONS. This field should especially appeal to those being sent out who fear a radical change of climate and who are adverse to absolutely virgin conditions; for, in the great Southland almost our own climate is duplicated since they are as far south of the Equator as we are north. Roads, railroads, waterways and other means of transportation and facilities for communication are already in operation, and a great deal of the primitive work of civilization has been done, automatically relieving the missionary of much of the initial work usually necessary in the opening of foreign mission work. Years of time, thousands of dollars and hundreds of lives have been saved perhaps to this mission field because civilization has preceded the missionary. On the other hand, however, with this civilization has gone improper and incorrect teaching which naturally, as stated above must be corrected, counteracted, untaught and retaught; so matching assets with liabilities one mission field is as needy, deserving

and profitable as another; but sometimes certain conditions appeal both to missionaries and tithers and it does seem that the wonderful needs of this country should appeal very strongly to the Brethren people.

5. The URGENCY OF THE CALL. With the League of Nations, League of Churches, League of Labor and League of Capital, it is apparent to the student of prophecy that we must hie to the field if we expect to fulfill the last Will and Testament of our Lord. In 2 Corinthians 5:20, Paul very clearly and definitely asserts our ambassadorship, and tells us that God has committed unto us the work of reconciliation. It is our business to represent our King in a foreign land, support the dignity of the fundamentals of the homeland, exalt our Sovereign, execute his orders and stand ready to be called home on a moment's notice, upon the severance of diplomatic relations between our King's country and the foreign shores where we labor. I am made to wonder what our King really thinks as he looks down upon our apathy,

lethargy, negligence, inactivity, carelessness, apostasy and worldliness. What do you suppose he thinks of his subjects who have been especially elected, inaugurated, sanctified and dedicated for a certain ministry plenipotentiary to see these same ambassadors holding back money that belongs to the King, refusing to obey marching orders when the government is subject to disgrace? Do you suppose he really feels that he was justified in paying the price that he did for me and you since he sees how little we appreciate the price he paid for our ransom? We should have the largest offering this Easter for South America in the history of our church. The work has been moving forward with a very normal growth since its incipiency. We are securing some valuable properties, but should have more and have them right away. It goes without saying that we need more consecrated workers. May we have an outpouring of the Holy Spirit that will enlist both for his services at Eastertide.

Dayton, Ohio.

The Threefold Contest for Africa. By A. L. DeLozier

Contest means CALL TO WITNESS, and when a contest is on the witnesses sit around eagerly watching the issue. Such is the nature of an ordinary contest in the form of a game of some kind carried on in the presence of spectators. Some contests are in fun and the outcome counts for no more than a momentary disappointment. Others are for commercial purposes and result in financial gain or loss as the case may be. Still a third class of contests is real serious because the future, the destiny of a nation or a race is involved. Such was the great war. It was a serious contest between autocracy and democracy. There could be only one correct outcome and it happened as it should.

The three-fold contest for Africa is of the serious sort like the great war, only it is far, unspeakably more serious than was that colossal struggle, because this contest for Africa has to do with the eternal destiny of millions of souls, or if the faith of any one is not strong enough for this, it then has to do at least with the physical, mental and spiritual future of those myriads of the sons of Ham.

Just what is the situation in Africa? We have here a continent earnestly coveted by Mohammed, by the god of this world, and one that Jesus Christ would have his children evangelize.

What shall be the issue of this contest? CONTESTOR, I call you to witness. Africa is far off, so was the war, and yet we witnessed it. Let us witness this contest in Africa.

First, let us take the god of this world. What definition shall we give for this contestant? It seems to me that Big Business, National Aspirations, Commercialism, may well represent the god of this world. Accordingly we see the negro on his own native soil put up for auction and three bidders are on hand. The nations of Europe have parceled out Africa among themselves for purely commercial purposes. To this much the African has been obliged to submit and in some respects this being under control of civilized nations is for the best.

But the next step is Big Business going in under the sanction of these nations and claiming Africa as an outlet for trade. Very prominent among these contestants is King Alcohol in all his pomp. The natives are therefore asked to become the devotees of Bacchus and the result is most pitiful as is well known. But another pitiful side to it is that the rum agent is taken for or represents himself as being a Christian and so the poor Africans are asked to do obeisance to King Alcohol; AL: "the" and COHOL: "devil," as some puts it—with the Christian cloak on. Missionaries are constantly testifying to the bad character and influence of government officials, business men and indeed all the representatives of the god of this world in Africa.

Let us "dip into the future" and try to imagine what kind of Africa and African must result under the tutelage of the god of this world. South America is a near picture of

a continent for a few hundred years under the direction of the god of this world with the result that it is still next to a dark continent itself. Is it just to abandon Africa to the god of this world? JUDGE YE!

The second contestant is Mohammed. It would seem that Mohammed is the strongest contestant of all. Mohammedanism sweeps down into Africa like a great irresistible flood. The thing that makes Mohammedanism so strong a contestant, is the fact that every Mohammedan trader is a representative of Mohammed, an exponent of his religion. What is a great flood that sweeps down a valley and overturns a city? It is just so many drops of water each playing its part. Take a single drop and no harm could result, but the drops uniting cause the water to run and to dash irresistably through any obstacle. So a Mohammedan here and there would not count for much, but hundreds of Mohammedans uniting and each doing his part for Mohammed becomes a menace and causes us to sit up and take notice. I tell a solemn truth when I say that Mohammed is rapidly claiming great sections of Africa.

What will Mohammed do for the African? Let us answer the question by asking: "What has Mohammed done for Turkey?" Mohammedanism if anything, leaves the African in a worse state than it finds him. If the future of Africa is to be abandoned to Mohammedanism, our Master way well weep over the situation as he did over Jerusalem.

The third contestant for Africa is Christ. Contestant? Yes, and yet so unselfish and gentle a contestant that we almost refuse to recognize the Christ as such. Now just as it was necessary that democracy win the day over autocracy, not less, yea rather more important is it that Christ be the winning contestant in Africa. This is true because nothing short of Christ will make Africa what it should become. Christ must take Africa because the African is ready to surrender to him.

But above all Africa must be brought to the feet of Jesus because he alone is able to save, and every son of Africa has a soul to save. Now what does this mean? We Christians must "get a move on." We must educate our business men to represent Christ in fact as well as in name. We must PRAY. We must GIVE most liberally. But above all, we must GO in far larger numbers than heretofore. Each one of us owes as much of a debt to Africa and the African as do the Gribbles, Antoine Rollier, Miss Myers, or any other members of the little party now pressing into the interior of the French Congo.

The three-fold contest is not a contest in theory, but one in actual fact. If we Christians mean to act, "NOW is the acceptable time." 1920 is the year of all years to do our utmost.

May God help each one so to do!

Allentown, Pennsylvania.

THE BRETHREN PULPIT

The Whole Church Carrying the Whole Gospel to a Whole World

By Edwin Boardman, Jr.

TEXT: Go ye therefore, and teach all nations, baptizing them in the name of the Father, and the Son, and of the Holy Spirit: teaching them to observe all things whatsoever I have commanded you: and, lo, I am with you alway, even unto the end of the world. AMEN.—MATTHEW 28: 19,20.

The acid test of our Christian faith is to be found in the obedience we give to the commands of our divine Lord. The obedience we give not only to one command, but to all of them will manifest our measure of devotion to Jesus,— "whose we are and whom we serve."

To the Christian church has been committed all the treasures of a divine Master and it is the splendid prerogative of the church to ably execute the last will and testament of the Christ who died to save all men. Into the hands of the church has been laid the only message known among men that has power not only to transform men and nations, but is also able to keep them transformed by the renewing of their minds so that they can clearly come to know what is the good and acceptable and perfect will of God for them.

It was Jesus' dearest wish that this message should be carried to everyone and he gave explicit commands accordingly, in the words, "Ye shall be witnesses unto me both in Jerusalem, and in Judea, and in Samaria and unto the uttermost parts of the earth." Somehow in the busy whirl of things many Christians seem to feel that this command was abrogated when that generation of disciples passed away, or at least, if it was not abrogated it has lost its force and lays no binding obligation upon them. Hence the church has become apathetic and listless—in the large—in striving to obey the Lord of Life.

Let us define some terms for the sake of clarity before we go further, for we do not want to leave any convenient loophole as a means of escape to any who read this message.

1. By the "Whole Church" we mean that "called out" body of believers who have been regenerated by faith in the Christ of Calvary, who have received the blessing of the Christ life, and who have at their command all the omnipotent power of God through Jesus Christ. We believe that every true follower of the New Testament faith is a member of this body.

2. By the "Whole Gospel" we mean the full body of truth regarding himself, his Father, the Holy Spirit, man, and the ethical, social and spiritual truths he laid down for the observance of men and the consequent blessing of their lives.

3. By the "Whole World" we mean every last square foot of land to be found on the globe, where men and women live whom God has made of one blood for to dwell on all the face of the earth. Everyone of these individuals from the lowest, most degraded cannibal of the African jungle to the highest type of educated, spiritually minded white man in America should have an opportunity to hear the "glad tidings of great joy" that so many years ago sounded over Bethlehem's plains and brought peace to troubled souls and surcease from heartache and pain.

There can be no mistaking the fact that when Jesus commanded that his gospel be carried to a lost world that he meant that every Christian should be party to the task. After all what does it mean to be a Christian? When we become Christians we signify in that fact that we are not our own, for we have been bought with a price and hence we have surrendered our will and our life to Jesus Christ. Thus we really have no longer any "say" in what we are to do for we are pledged to the guidance of our Master, whose Spirit dwells within us. The new birth involves this and we are really new people in Christ Jesus. If this truth is absolute will anyone of us dare shirk our responsibility to the last command Jesus left before the clouds of heaven received him out of his disciples' sight?

Permit me to be more specific. What excuse can any one of the twenty-five or thirty thousand Brethren in the United States give to the Master for failing to do their part? What makes us Brethren? Adherence to the teaching of John 13; or because that we have been baptized by trine immersion; or because we take a denflife stand on other certain New Testament passages? Or are we Brethren just because our fathers and mothers were? These reasons are fine but they are not sufficient. Let there be no mistake about this matter in our minds. We are Brethren, not because we observe certain ordinances and because we have a special church history. We are Brethren because we are absolutely pledged as a church to obey the whole gospel of Jesus Christ. Jesus said, "Who is my mother, or my brethren? And he looked round about on them which sat about him and said, "Behold my mother and my brethren! For whosoever shall do the will of God, the same is my brother, and my mother." Hence everyone who is a true Brethren is expected without equivocation or excuse to do his utmost in carrying a whole gospel to a whole world. We must never forget that the Master was not using mere words when he gave voice to the great commission found in Matthew 28:18-20. We cannot be good Brethren if we are not missionary in life and spirit for good Brethren are not "slaves to the letter of formal ordinance" but are—or should be—missionaries of the Spirit and genius of the Gospel.

If we do not believe in missions and missionary enterprise we do not believe in Jesus for his mission was to "seek and to save that which was lost" and he has left us an example that we should follow in his steps. This is no time for trying to excuse ourselves. We are bound to carry the message to lost men for whom the Savior has died that through his death they might have life and have it more abundantly. Not to do this is rank treachery to our Great Captain and to the cause we are aligned with. It makes no difference who we are, or where we are, if we are Christians and if we call ourselves Brethren we must do our part in carrying the whole gospel to a whole world.

The whole gospel is no anaemic or powerless message for we are told that it is the "power of God unto salvation to everyone that believeth." The word for "power" here is the Greek word "dunamis" and it means, "inherent power, power residing in a thing by virtue of its nature." This word is the root for our English words "dynamite," and "dynamo." The Gospel possesses a great, inherent power well able to blast away mountains of sin, unbelief, and false teaching just as dynamite can blast away mountains of earth and stone. The gospel is always able to bring light into the darkness, despair and ignorance of heathenism just as the high power dynamos are able to furnish voltage enough to dispel the gloom of a large city at night time.

If such a powerful factor has been committed to the whole church for propagation, do you not think it is time to get busy and see to it that its power is put to use? The might of the Niagara River amounted to no economic good until engineers harnessed it, and the "Whole Gospel" that we Brethren claim to believe will never do a lost world any good until we concentrate it in enough missionaries and then send these missionaries forth as the high voltage wires who will see that "the power of God" reaches to the last unevangelized portion of the world. It is only as we expose the world to enough of these "live wires" that it will be "shocked" into the faith life.

The world is in desperate straits today. Any Christian reading a description of conditions not only as they exist in heathen lands but also in so-called Christian countries will be shocked at the awfulness of the picture. In the heathen lands we find terrible poverty, maltreatment of children, degradation of womanhood, Paganism, an awful death rate from preventable disease, ignorance and illiteracy, and various other economic and social conditions that beggar description. In so called Christian lands we find unbelief, an awful flood of crime, economic unrest and hardship and a desperate effort to drown our doubts, fears and hardships in a sea of giddy pleasures. Amid all this shame and sin and sorrow Jesus Christ has either been forgotten or he is unknown. The only Personality who can put real values into life, real love into action, real statescraft into national and international policies, adequate power into the nations of the earth, and give men not only salvation but peace also, is absolutely given no opportunity to act. The world does need Jesus and it will never come out of its darkness until it finds him. Every two seconds a heathen soul goes into darkness without the knowledge of the Gospel. Sin demands its awful toll.

Let us face the facts at this time and determine that we are going to do all in our power to change conditions. Let us see to it that not only money but—what is far more necessary—men and women will be furnished to carry the gospel to men in need. Let us really live and act out our prayers. We have no right to pray that the Lord of the harvest will thrust forth laborers unless we are willing to go ourselves or give our sons and daughters to go. As this Easter tide approaches may we not take another look at Calvary and appreciate the fact that the Calvary message is a world message? Let us dedicate ourselves anew to this world task, Brethren, finding new joy in the service of our King. We are one part of the living church that can conscientiously carry a "Whole Gospel to a Whole World." We can do this if we will. Will we?

Hudson, Iowa.

OUR DEVOTIONAL

A Clarion Call to Prayer

This is a time when we are—or at least should be—thinking and praying earnestly as to our obligation to the unevangelized millions of the earth, and especially to those parts of the Lord's harvest field in which he has called us to labor. Now let us have a day of united prayer throughout the entire brotherhood, for very definite praying for our work in South America and French Equatorial Africa.

The little band in Africa, known as the Ubangi-Shari Mission Band, went out from friends and loved ones, the comforts and much of what we deem necessities of life, to enter the most dense heathen darkness of the earth with the light of the gospel of the grace of God; and all they asked us to do, the only pledge they desired was that we stand faithful in prayer for them and their work. In the last "Prayer Band Letter" comes the earnest, heart-stirring plea that we pray earnestly and without ceasing at this time—that they may be fed and clothed? or protected from physical harm? No! not material things, although we must needs stand in prayer for all of these, but they cry to us to continue in effectual, fervent prayer that they may be so emptied of self, and so filled with the Holy Spirit that in every word and deed they shall glorify the Lord Jesus Christ before the natives and French officials, and that there may be a great outpouring of the Spirit of God upon the Baya tribe. Of course we know that this is in the will of God; so if we approach the throne in sincerity, and lay hold of God by faith, he will show forth his power, and prove to the French Government that the gospel of the Lord Jesus Christ is still the "power of God unto salvation."

Then there should be a band of recruits to go forth as reinforcements to that little company. Can we pray them forth at once? They must apply to the Mission Board, be passed upon, outfitted and sent forth, and then it takes some time before they can reach the field. Who will volunteer to step out and fill up the ranks broken by the death of our beloved Sister Rollier? God commands us to pray for laborers.

Our South American work needs more earnest intercession. We must pray for men and money to carry on the work already started, and also to press on and adequately occupy the territory that we believe God would have us cover. If we really pray, God will provide. This call is echoed in his church, that the church be opened and ready, with some faithful intercessor in attendance every hour to carry out the plan for a day of united intercession of all Brethren people throughout the whole United States.

Friday, April 2nd, is the day appointed, from 10 o'clock A. M. to 4 P. M. Let every one who knows how to pray be in attendance as much of the day as possible. Fast if the Holy Spirit so leads. Take a little lunch if you wish to. If you can only be present a part of the day be free in the Spirit to go in when you can and quietly go out when you must; under the guidance of the Spirit any coming and going will in no wise disturb the meeting.

Look to the Holy Spirit for your program of song, scripture and prayer, bearing in mind that the object of the meeting is prayer, and that Satan will divert the time and minds from that as much as he possibly can, so be watchful and persistent to pray.

The following program is suggestive. :

10-11. Singing. Short scripture lesson on prayer. Pray for the Spirit of prayer.

11-12. Song. Scripture promises of answers to prayer. Pray for the work and workers in South America and Africa, for open doors for the gospel and closed doors against the enemy.

12- 1. Lunch hour. Special prayer by groups of "Two or three," for individual missionaries, as the Spirit shall direct.

1- 2. Song. Short scripture lesson on the duty of Christians at home to co-operate with missionaries on the field of faithful prayer. Pray for Africa, for a manifestation of the power of the Holy Spirit in the lives of the missionaries and through them upon the great cannibal Baya tribe, for a band of recruits adequate to the task ahead as God sees it. And pray for all money needed to provide for those on the field, for all necessary building as soon as the Lord would have them to establish a station, and for sufficient funds to thoroughly equip, according to the mind of the Spirit, and send, as many as the Lord shall call out at this time to go forth with the "Good News."

2- 3. Song. Scripture verses showing our grounds for laying hold of God in prayer. Pray for South America, for Spirit filled volunteers to man the field; for money to pay off all mortgages and put up new buildings where necessary, to establish new stations in other centers in our territory, and for plenty of money to equip and send forth all the laborers that the Lord shall call at this time. Shall we not pray also that we may reach out and also carry light to the Indians?

3- 4. Song. Scripture verses setting forth the privilege and power of intercession. Pray that God will put a burden of intercession upon the whole Brethren church for a deepening of her own spiritual life through the work of the cross in individual members, for those fields in which we are laboring, and for an army of intercessory missionaries, those who are willing to be prayer channels through which the Holy Spirit can pray "With groanings that cannot be uttered" for the needs that we cannot know of as well as those that we do not know how to pray for.

May the blessed Holy Spirit lead and control in all of this for the salvation of many precious souls and for the glory of our Lord Jesus Christ. Amen!

Yours in his service for the evangelizing of the world,
A. L. DeLOZIER, Secretary Ubangi-Shari Prayer Bands.
MRS GRACE P. SRACK, Assistant.

THE SUNDAY SCHOOL

Send WHITE GIFT OFFERINGS to

ALBERT TRENT
General Secretary-Treasurer
Johnstown, Pennsylvania

How Will Your School Measure up? By George S. Baer

In a recent letter from the president of the National Sunday School Association, Brother J. F. Watson, Johnstown, Pennsylvania, we discovered printed on the back of his letter the standard of efficiency for Sunday schools and it occurred to us that it would be a service to give it a wider circulation. There are many ambitious schools in the brotherhood and they will want to measure themselves by the standard set. Of course you will want to make every point possible. Determine where you stand now and then decide where you will be at conference time. And go to "Work, work, work."

The Twelve-Point Standard of Excellence for 1919 and 1920 (Briefly stated)

1. RECORDS: Accurately kept and statistics furnished National Secretary-Treasurer.
2. AN ACTIVE CRADLE ROLL DEPARTMENT. For information, write Mrs. H. L. Stroud, Waterloo, Iowa.
3. ORGANIZED. One or more registered Adult classes and one or more registered classes in Young People's Division, all with International Certificates and Brethren Seals, which will be furnished hereafter through the Superintendents of these Divisions. For information, write L. G. Wood, Roanoke, Va., or George H. Jones, Johnstown, Pa.
4. A WORKING HOME DEPARTMENT. For information write Mrs. H. E. Raudenbush, 1231 Firth Street, Philadelphia, Pa.
5. A TEACHER TRAINING CLASS. A class organized or graduated this year, or all graduate teachers. For information, Write J. A. Garber, Ashland, Ohio.
6. A GRADED SCHOOL. With annual promotion day.
6. GRADED INSTRUCTION. The use of regular graded lessons in one or more departments. For information, write J. A. Garber, Ashland, Ohio.
8. MISSIONARY INSTRUCTION QUARTERLY. For information, write C. E. Kolb, Milford, Indiana.
9. DELEGATES TO SOME SUNDAY SCHOOL CONVENTION.
10. TEMPERANCE INSTRUCTION QUARTERLY. For information, write R. R. Haun, Ashland, Ohio.
11. THE USE OF BRETHREN PUBLICATIONS.
12. ANNUAL OFFERING. For National Sunday School Association Work.
13. READING COURSE: "The Sunday School at Work." Secured from Brethren Publishing Company.

Specials for Current Conference Year

CHURCH ATTENDANCE: The last Sunday of each month the members of the school should stay for church services. To promote attendance at church service by Sunday School scholars and attendance at Sunday School by church members. Using a motto:

"All the Church in the Sunday School,
All the Sunday School in the Church,
And everybody in both."

TWELVE HUNDRED additions from the Sunday schools to the church this year. Every school to observe Decision Day and thus help reach this goal.

ASSISTANCE OFFERED: Schools desiring help in any way should use the Officers of the Association. We stand ready to hold Institutes in churches in every district this year. Single churches or groups of churches may secure a worker at the expense of the Association.

THE NATIONAL SUNDAY SCHOOL ASSOCIATION OF THE BRETHREN CHURCH.

Now, having read the "Standard" and noted the various suggestions following, there are some more questions we would like to ask: How many schools are observing "Church Attendance Day?" and what are you doing to make it a success? Do you have children's sermons? Do you let the children sing one of their own songs at this service?

What plans are you making for encouraging conversion and church membership and are you expecting that your Sunday school will win its share of the TWELVE HUNDRED new church members this year?

Again, we wonder how many schools are expecting to take advantage of the offer of the Association to hold an institute in your church. Your day school teachers need institutes; don't your Sunday school teachers need them too? Does not your whole school need one? Write somebody about it.

Attention, Illiokota

To all the Pastors and Sunday school Superintendents of the Illiokota District:

Will you do your best to have a Teacher Training Class in your church during the year and before our District conference this year? I hope many of the schools have them now, and that you will report your progress to me before the conference meets at Lanark. I shall stand ready to assist you in any way I can. Write me about your condition and progress.

Z. T. LIVENGOOD Teacher Training Superintendent.

BILLY SUNDAY ON GOVERNOR EDWARDS

"I regard the action of the New Jersey Legislature on the booze bill as one of the most rebellious, anarchistic, un-American measures ever enacted, and the star that represents New Jersey should be erased from the American flag.

"That infamous business that has left behind it nothing but ragged children and scaffolds, electric chairs and asylums hasn't got a comeback in its system.

"It would turn the calendar back from June to January. It turned a paradise into a desert, but Prohibition turned the desert back into a paradise; and now New Jersey would ruin all.

"No man who is the mouthpiece of that dirty, rotten, vile, hellish, God-forsaken business will ever sleep in the White House as President of these United States. Governor Edwards can no more be elected President than he can cross the ocean on a grindstone drawn by cockroaches. The anti-saloon element in the Republican and Democratic parties accepts the challenge, and we will lick to a frazzle any man that either party nominates who stands for booze."

(From interview in Philadelphia North American).

The gods

Grow angry with your patience; 'tis their care
And must be yours, that guilty men escape not:
As crimes do grow, justice should rouse itself.

—Ben Johnson.

Our Young People at Work

J. A. Garber
PRESIDENT

G. C. Carpenter
SECRETARY

Christian Endeavor and the Church
By J. A. Garber

"For Christ and the Church" has been the chief watchword of Christian Endeavor from the beginning of the society. At first the organization was criticised on the ground that it would rob the church of her young people with all their energy and enthusiasm. The outstanding facts of the history prove just the opposite and give the lie to the ill-grounded criticism of would-be pessimistic or prejudiced prophets. The records show that Christian Endeavor has directed the boundless energies of youth into the channels of the church and related their limitless enthusiasm to the varied activities of the church. Thousands who received their first impulse and elementary training in the Christian Endeavor society have become ministers, missionaries, church officers, Sunday school superintendents and teachers. Ample proof can be had through a little investigation in practically any church, large or small, city or rural. If the reader is a doubting Thomas, let him make a test case of his own or some near-by church where Christian Endeavor has had a fair chance. The Society dies not shrink from examination, nor is it ashamed of its contributions to the church.

But Christian Endeavor does not live in the past, nor rest upon its laurels. True to the spirit of its constituency—young people—it is a forward-looking organization. It is ever seeking to enlarge its capacity. Desiring to serve the church in a larger way, its service themes for March are "Church Attendance," "Church Loyalty" and "Church Support," wanting our Endeavorers to speak for themselves on these themes, we asked three persons for brief messages. Below we print two; one was written by the secretary of the Southern Indiana District and the other by an enthusiastic member of the Louisville, Ohio, society. Both deserve a careful reading by our Endeavorers and all who are interested in young people and the church. We shall be glad to hear from others on these or related subjects, particularly, our young people who have the ability to write.

Young People and Church Loyalty
By Lloyd E. Hang, Louisville, Ohio

Young people should not only pray for a larger vision of Christian Endeavor and for greater opportunity, but what we need to do equally as well, is to secure greater united action on the part of us all, in responding to the vision which we have already seen, and the call we have already heard.

The greatest asset of the church today is young life. Life with high hope, high ideals and a zealous desire to do all it can to promote the work of the Kingdom. The church needs young life, but far greater is the need of the church in young lives. The greatest asset of a life is the "Living Christ," and with Christ in the life, the Master's cause, the work of the church, will always be first. Young people are especially needed in this great work. Many are the things that only young people can do. To be sure there are many duties which must be done by those older, for the reason perhaps, that we simply refuse to do them. It behooves us to seize the opportunities which are ours, and not shirk the responsibilities which would permit the work of Christ and his church to suffer.

Pray for a fuller realization of the fact that his cause is our only challenge, to be accepted by all the spiritual and physical strength that youth can afford. This challenge has been outstanding for centuries past, and now it comes to us. This is OUR DAY. Do you fully realize, just now, that your span of life, no matter how short or how long it may be, is the only time allotted to you here, and whatever work has been mapped out by the Master to be done by you, must be done NOW, or perhaps it will never be done at all.

Should not this fact call forth the best that is in us to a present active endeavor in all lines of the work of the church? True and loyal youth must be counted on not to waver. Loyalty to Christ and his church is the call today. If we believe as we should, that the Brethren church has a definite work committed to it, we must do it whole heartedly as it comes to us, and in so doing we can not be other than denominationally loyal, but I do not mean denominationally narrow. Make the Christian Endeavor pledge the supreme rule of your life and your local church as well as the church at large will never want for your most loyal support.

Young People and Church Attendance
By Mabel Maus, Mexico, Indiana

It is a problem of vital importance in almost every church as to how to keep the young people and interest them in the church service. The reason for this condition, no doubt, is that they do not realize their personal need of building a greater faith through worship. Some are indifferent to their spiritual welfare, while others, who dutifully attend Sunday school or Christian Endeavor or both, think these services very largely meet their spiritual needs. They have the opportunity of receiving instruction and of giving expression to their ideas and it is very commendable that they feel a responsibility and that there are worthwhile gains from these organizations. But these organizations are not ends in themselves. They are not to be separated from the church and are but preparatory training schools for Christian education and enlarged service in the church.

Church attendance should begin in childhood. The child should be taught and trained to remain for worship. This might be a means in later years of overcoming a cause of scarcity of young people at church. Too many leave the church after the Sunday school and Christian Endeavor services. This soon becomes a habit and with it goes the impression that the hour of worship is mainly for older folks and that there is no obligation on the part of young people to attend. This is an error and an idea too prevalent among young people, especially those of the town and city churches. On the contrary, our young people should feel that they have a part to perform which depends upon their reliability, and that their presence and influence is needed.

Perhaps some parents and teachers have been negligent both in precept and example. Christian parents have a great responsibility in not only sending their children but also in going to the Sunday services themselves. When the Sabbath comes it should not be a question of whether or not to go to the services, but an established fact that the family will go unless for some reason justifiable in the sight of God hinders them. Pastors, too, should be interested and sympathetic with the young people in their manifold endeavors and aspirations.

If every young Christian could realize his duty and the influence of his church attendance upon his fellow Endeavorers and also upon non-Christians it would mean much in building up the attendance and in winning souls. The unchurched would be more desirous of what the church has to give if her own people were more faithful and would thus more consistently reveal the Christ whom they serve.

Our Master wants folks who can be counted on and who are loyal in his service. Let us as Christian Endeavorers, everyone during the loyalty campaign and afterwards emulate our Master, who on the Sabbath was found in the place of worship and not amid all the attractions that allure people away from the services of God's house. Hold fast to the much needed command, "Remember the Sabbath day to keep it holy."

willing to help the old school as they find opportunity.

The listing of these names and the securing of the proper present addresses was a very great task, but the faculty members and student gave loyal assistance. These names are now filed alphabetically and the future handling will be easy.

Every friend of the College ought to get some communication from the school at least once a year, but consider this a moment. Beachler has the names of some twenty-five hundred! Former students number twelve hundred. The ministers and board members make at least one hundred more. The total is not far from four thousand. Extra copies of the Purple and Gold, on which we have mailing rates, cost $15 per hundred. So to run off the extras and send them out in sufficient numbers to all, after the type is set, would cost over five hundred dollars—a good part of the pay of one teacher for one year. This does not include the cost of addressing, etc. Hence, those who think that the college does not remember them will need to take these facts into account. And if we used a cheaper publication than the Purple and Gold, the cost would still be comparatively great.

The outlook for the Summer School is very encouraging. Unless all signs fail, we will have at least one hundred teachers in the last six week term.

One of the most successful social functions ever held here and one which was quite new also, was given this past week by the women of the college, including the wives of the faculty. It was a St. Patrick's social, the color scheme being green and white but that was not important. The importance attaches to the fact that there were entertained in the Hall in the afternoon and evening nearly one hundred women of the town. Many of these said that they had always wanted to get better acquainted with the college people but had never had an opportunity and now that a way is open, there will be a closer cooperation than ever before. Others said that they had been students here in the old days, but had not been up for twenty years. Others said that while they had always lived in Ashland, they had never been in the college building, much less the hall. It is hoped to make this an annual affair, when the women of the college will be entertained by the women of the college. I can not stress the importance of this too much. It certainly will have a very desirable influence. Miss Maria Lichty, Miss Puterbaugh, Miss Wimer and Miss Zimmerman, are to be thanked for this innovation.

Professor J. A. Garber is attending the Association of the Teachers of Religious Education in Pittsburgh.

Two intercollegiate debates are scheduled with Berea, under the direction of Dr. L. L. Garber, head of the Department of English. Also one with Bluffton College.

EDWIN E. JACOBS.

CAMPAIGN NOTES

Since the last appearance of "Campaign Notes" the secretary and his family have moved from Ashland, Ohio, back to Waterloo, Iowa. The move was accompanied with the usual amount of "agony" and hard work, but we all landed safely and everything is all right at this end of the line.

Our Goal: 200,000; We Can and We Must

```
200    000
190    000
180    000
170    000
160    000
150    000
140    000
130    000
120    000
110    000
100    000
 90    000
 80    000
 70    000
 60    000
 50    000
 40    000
 30    000
 20    000
 10    000
```

COLLEGE
ENDOWMENT

The report this time has to do with the canvass at Gratis, Ohio. It gives me pleasure to make this report because Gratis went over the top in real fashion. Gratis church is one of the largest, strongest congregations in Ohio, and naturally I went there hoping for big things. I am glad to say I was not disappointed.

Brother C. E. Beekley, a former student and a classmate of the secretary in Ashland College is pastor of this church. His heart beats true for our college and he placed himself and his automobile at my disposal, and without murmur or complaint he put through with me one of the hardest and most disagreeable weeks of the entire campaign. Exceedingly rough roads and cold winds made it a hard week, and needless to say, the automobile tires showed the results of wear and tear more decidedly than did the preacher or the secretary. What we did to those tires was plenty. But the fine results achieved in our canvass made us forget some of the unpleasant things.

Gratis went $4050. That means that Gratis is now first among the Ohio churches thus far canvassed, with Washington C. H. second. I as sorry for Washington C. H., but glad for Gratis. I may say further that if I have looked through the records of the entire campaign correctly (and I believe I have) the result at Gratis places Gratis in fifth place among the churches so far canvassed. Myersdale and Gratis are neck and neck but I think the difference in the two churches, though slight, is in favor of Gratis. I congratulate Gratis and Brother Beekley on this fine record. The only sad thing about the whole affair is that the report would have been still better if every man in the Gratis church had lined up with his brethren and done his part. Not quite all did that.

In this canvass we had three $500 gifts; we also had a $350 gift considered jointly; there were also two $200 gifts; and there was a splendid line of gifts running from $100 on down to lesser amounts. Bith the W. M. S. and the Sunday School had a substantial part in making this result possible, also at least one Sunday School class enlisted in the good cause.

All in all we had a very good time among the Gratis people. I feel very much at home in this congregation. In my early ministry I did some revival work at Gratis. And after their church building burned during the pastorate of Brother Jones, it was my pleasant duty to dedicate their present beautiful structure. The parsonage was my general stopping place and Brother Beekley and his good wife made me feel perfectly at home. But there were so many other cordial invitations into the hospitable homes of this congregation that it was next to impossible to accept all. However, I tried to do my best as I am sure the Andrews, and the Fochts, and the Youngs and the Fudges, and the Smiths, and the Lanes, and the Zimmermans, and the Floras, and the Elkenberrys are ready to testify. Sickness kept not a few of the members away from the services, "Aunt Sallie" Andrew, being among the number. But never mind "Aunt Sallie," some time I will come to Gratis again to raise endowment just so you may have a chance to come to the meetings.

I can't make a more fair proposition than that. I want to thank all of these good people and their pastor and his wife for all of their kindnesses to me, and may God richly bless and keep you all.

In closing, I want to note first that Gratis was the 19th church in Ohio to be canvassed and the Gratis result brings up the grand total of Ohio to date to the even $30,000 mark. Who says it is a disgrace to be born in Ohio? And in the second place I want to register the fact that 19 churches in Ohio going $30,000 means "Good-bye Indiana, halloo Pennsylvania." There is enough work yet to be done in Ohio to make me feel very sure that Ohio is going to go right up along side of and maybe beyond Pennsylvania. If such is the case there sure will be a proud lot of Ohio pastors at the conference this fall.

The mercury now stands at $144,500. Now some of the friends of this campaign will be wondering what about the remainder of Ohio and Maryland and Virginia since I have moved back to Waterloo? Well, these churches will all get a chance in due and proper time. Toward the last of April the work will be resumed again and pushed on to completion. In the meantime let everybody hold steady.

WM. H. BEACHLER,
Campaign Secretary.

PEOPLE OF INDIANA

Pre-Easter week and the two days following, are to be golden opportunity days for us. As chairman of the Ministerium and as a member of the Evangelistic and Bible Study committee of the Indiana conference, I am going to tell you of big plans. First, the plan of the church, for itself. We have engaged Dr. P. B. Fitzwater of Moody Bible Institute to conduct a Bible conference for us beginning March 28 and to last one week. Each afternoon he will speak to the general theme "God's First Days and His Last." Each evening a subject from First Corinthians, at from 7 to 8 p. m. From 8 to 9 the pastor will give an evangelistic appeal. This will be, we think an excellent opportunity for any who wish to sit under the teachings of one of the best teachers we can hope to get in our district. You are invited to come. Nearby churches, we think ought to come in great numbers.

Dr. Frank N. Palmer, Too

Following a resolution of the state conference, we have engaged Dr. Palmer of Winona Lake, for a state conference Bible term commencing Monday evening and lasting till Tuesday evening. This is the tentative program:

Monday Evening
7   Dr. Palmer.
8   Evangelistic Address. A. E. Thomas.

Tuesday Morning
8-9   Stewardship. G. C. Carpenter.
9-10   Dr. Palmer.
10-11   Lecture. Spiritual Resources.

Tuesday Afternoon
1-2   Missionary Education. C. E. Kolb.
2-3   Dr. Palmer.
3-4   Lecture. Life Work. C. A. Bame.

Tuesday Evening
7-8   Dr. Palmer.
8-9   Evangelistic Address. E. L. Miller.

This program was hastily brought together and I am sure will be enlarged some. But this is enough to let you know that we expect a good and helpful time. Every pastor in Indiana must at once get busy and feel that he has a part in making this conference a success as it was by his vote and that of his delegates unanimously taken that it was planned. Dr. Fitzwater could not be held longer and that is the reason Dr. Palmer was asked. Both are top notch men as teachers of the Word. This is Indiana's Bible conference. Will you have a delegation from your church?
CHARLES A. BAME.

PASTOR GIVEN RECOGNITION

The following is a clipping from the Falls City (Nebraska) Journal:

The members of the Brethren church at a business meeting held at the close of the service yesterday unanimously gave their pastor Rev. Stuckman, a vote of confidence, and asked him to stay on indefinitely as their pastor. They also voted to extend to him a two months' leave of absence through July and August. Following this vacation, Rev. Stuckman will begin his seventh year as minister for the local church. He has accepted the leave granted him and will spend the time in a school for pastors conducted by J. Cambell Morgan, and other noted theologians at Winona Lake, Ind. He will also remain over for the national conference of his own church to be held at the same place. The local church feels gratified to know that Rev. Stuckman will remain for another year in view of the fact that his pastorate here has extended far beyond the usual period of time. During his absence this summer a minister will be secured to occupy the pulpit.

IN THE SHADOW

ARNOLD.—Ethel Marian Arnold was born in Lanark, April 2, 1898, and departed March 6, 1920, aged 21 years, 1 month and 2 days. She united with the Brethren church about three years ago. She was faithful to all functions of the church and lived a thoroughly consistent Christian life. Her mother and father survive her. Our loss is her gain. Services conducted by the pastor assisted by Rev. Livengood and J. M. Moore of the Church of the Brethren.

WHIPKEY.—Olive Moore Whipkey, daughter of Mr. and Mrs. John Moore, passed out of this life October 22, 1919, aged 25 years. She was joined in marriage with James F. Whipked September 3, 1907. She leaves to mourn her departure her husband, father and mother and three children, viz.: Orville, Geraldine and Genevieve, also three sisters, viz.: Mrs. Robert Ullom, Mrs. George Ullom and Mrs. Jesse Whipkey, all of Aleppo, Pa. She became a Christian when quite a young girl and has lived a devoted life for her Master. Following the union with the Aleppo Brethren church December 7, 1907. It can be truly said of Mrs. Whipkey that "she went about doing good," was never too busy to visit the sick and lend a helping hand in every way she could. Her going is an irreparable loss to the community as well as the church. Although Mrs. Whipkey has gone to live with her heavenly Father, she will continue to live here in the hearts of her relatives and friends. May we have the pleasure of being with her in heaven that we may hear his joyful voice saying to us as he said to her: "Come ye blessed of my Father, inherit the kingdom prepared for you from the foundation of the world." The funeral services were held from the Aleppo Brethren church, Sunday morning, October 26, 1919, the Rev. H. F. Hilbert officiating and interment was made in the Centennial Cemetery.

BEESON.—Ella May, daughter of Mr. and Mrs. R. W. Beeson, was born March 16, 1884, and departed this life March 3, 1920. In the 18th year of her age, she united with the Brethren church at Roanoke, during the pastoarte of A. E. Whitted. She leaves to mourn her departure a father and mother, two sisters, one of New Haven, Indiana, and one of Detroit, Michigan, and a large number of friends and relatives. Just before departing this life, she asked that the window of her room be opened, as she was to receive a message from glory and shortly the messenger of glory came and bore her soul to the portals of glory. A large number of her friends came from Fort Wayne to pay the last tribute of respect to one who through the associations of life had won their love. Funeral services by the writer from Psalms 17:15. "As for me, I will behold thy face in righteousness; I shall be satisfied, when I awake with thy likeness." The body of her flesh was laid to rest in the beautiful cemetery just outside of the city of Fort Wayne to await the sound of the archangel and the trump of God when the dead in Christ shall rise first.
W. F. JOHNSON.

PATTON.—Robert Delbert, son of Mr. and Mrs. Jason Patton was born near Roanoke, Indiana, July 12, 1919, and departed this life March 6, 1920, after a short illness of the measles and the "flu." His suffering was of short duration, but such is life taken when just a flower ready to burst into full bloom. When leaving the home there were two others of the family hovering between life and death and a fervent prayer went up to the Father of all glory that the relentless hand of the enemy might be stayed from rending asunder the hearts of the parents. Sister Patton has long been a member of the Brethren church at Roanoke. Sermon by the writer from Mark 8:41.
W. F. JOHNSON.

WALKER.—On February 26, 1920, Mary Livengood Walker passed peacefully out of her mortal body into the sunlight of God's eternal day. She was born near Milledgeville, Ill., February 9, 1848. Early in life she became a Christian and was one of the charter members of the local Brethren church when organized in 1884. During all her years she lived an earnest, consistent Christian life, rich in fruit bearing. The memory of her exemplary goodness will long abide in the hearts of all who knew her like the lingering fragrance of a faded flower. Her absence will be sorely missed in the home, the church and the community where she was ever ready and willing to unselfishly perform the gracious ministry of service and helpfulness. Funeral services were conducted in the church by her pastor.
MILES J. SNYDER.

LICHTY.—Lent Lichty, wife of Brother Lewis Lichty, died February 5, 1920, at the age of 34 years, 7 months and 5 days. She was married to Lewis Lichty, January 1, 1908. To this union were born two daughters, Mildred, aged 10 and Margaret, aged 4, who with the husband are left to mourn a devoted wife and mother. Funeral services at the home conducted by her pastor.
A. E. WHITTED.

CARTWRIGHT.—John Ernest, infant son of Louis and Nellie Cartwright, was born September 7, 1919, and as a result of influenza, fell asleep March 3, 1920, being six months and two days old. In Limestone Brethren church March 10, a short funeral service was held by the writer, I Thess. 4:13-18 being the basis of the remarks. Much sympathy goes out to parents and relatives.
MARY PENCE.

STOFFER.—Ethel Marie Stoffer, daughter of Mrs. Elizabeth Stoffer, was born December 31, 1898 and departed this life at the home of her grandparents near North Georgetown, Ohio, February 22, 1920, at the age of 21 years, 3 months and 20 days. Ethel leaves a brother, Paul, a mother and grandparents who will greatly miss her. At the age of eleven years she was stricken with infantile paralysis after which she was entirely helpless. May God comfort the bereaved. Services conducted by the pastor assisted by Rev. F. M. Irvin.
E. M. RIDDLE.

YOST.—Cathrine Yost, oldest daughter of Christian and Elizabeth Yost, was born in Fayette county, Pa., December 4, 1828. She migrated to Ohio with her parents in 1840, first locating at Aukerman Station in Congress township and later at the homestead near Burbank where she resided until death called her home. For a number of years she was the mainstay of a large family, the one upon whom her mother leaned.

She was always a promoter of education and a lover of books. She attended Canaan Academy and Smithville high school, proving by her example the value of education in her home community. As a teacher she was an unusually successful. She taught 16 consecutive terms of school and in 1870 retired from teaching and lived quietly at home caring for the family. This by no means ended her zeal for education. She was a strong supporter of Ashland College and proved this with a substantial gift of $200 for its endowment four weeks before her death. Her literary talents were recognized even late in life. She made several contributions of a religious nature to the "Gospel Messenger" and "Brethren Evangelist." Some were articles on Sunday School work, others letters to the children. As long as she was able she taught a Sunday School class and in her later years became a faithful student and contributor of the home Department.

She loved her church and was a faithful member of Fair Haven, Ohio. She prized above all else her church paper which was read each week thoroughly. A severe illness that caused her great suffering at times, but which she endured with patience and fortitude, ready for her Master's call, came to an end March 11, 1930, when she was called by death to her eternal reward. Especially do we sorrow for her brother David, with whom she lived all her life. Funeral services by the writer at her home near Burbank, Ohio.

BENJ. F. OWEN.

IN MEMORY OF
ELDER WILLIAM KIEFER

Another noble big hearted Christian has been called from the ranks of the Brethren ministry in the person of Elder William Keifer. He was born in Berks county, Pennsylvania, in 1836. When fifteen years old, his parents moved to Ohio. He joined the United Brethren church when he was sixteen years of age, and remained in that denomination until 1861. Then he united with the German Baptist church. He was baptized by Elder Jacob Garver of the Mohican church, of which he remained a member until the division of that body. He was married in 1857 to Sarah Martin, who preceded him to the better land, March 2, 1916.

Brother Keifer was called to the ministry in the German Baptist church November 21, 1874, in the old Mohican church, and remained one of its members until the division, when he espoused the Brethren cause. He preached for the Fair Haven church ever since its organization, in 1882, until February, 1899, when he declined to serve them any longer. The old Mohican church and the Fair Haven Brethren church are in talking distance of each other; thus the above pastor had preached on nearly the same ground, in the same neighborhood, and to many of the same people for nearly twenty-five years without any intermission.

Another product of Brother Keifer's labor is the Zion Hill, Ohio, church. This he organized and became the pastor December 31, 1892. The organization began with only sixteen members and through hard work Uncle William, as he was so well known, brought the work up on a solid foundation so that today the Zion Hill church is a strong unit.

Thus we have some idea of the work rendered by this grand old warrior who began to fail in health some four years ago. He grieved much over the loss of his beloved wife. His eyes began to fail him, until he lost his sight. He could not see; he could not read. Yet with all of this he was most cheerful and praised his God for what he had enabled him to accomplish. He longed for death and waited patiently for the hour, and on Febru-

ary 23, 1920 God called him home. For 84 years he lived in the flesh, but now, after serving his Lord for 66 years, he has gone to wait for his reward. To say that we shall miss him expresses very feebly our feelings at his departure. He will be missed in the Ministerial Association. He will be missed by the Fair Haven and Zion Hill congregation. The writer will miss him. We purpose to hold a memorial for our departed brother at a later date so that all who knew him may pay their last respects. He leaves to mourn, one son, a daughter, twelve grandchildren, four great-grandchildren and a large relationship besides.

Services were held at the Fair Haven church by the writer.

BENJ. F. OWEN.

Business Manager's Corner

Prompt Service

We aim to give as prompt service as it is possible to give without interfering with the regular operation of the plant, but sometimes we are not able to give as prompt service as either our customers or ourselves desire.

It has been our rule to not try to fill any orders that come in on Saturday until the following Monday, but this morning we received three orders from Sunday Schools on the Pacific coast, and that they might receive their supplies in time to distribute them on the last Sunday in the month we passed the orders down the line and in one hour and twenty miutes they were ready for the mails.

Good Business

We are glad that the business of the Publishing Company is keeping up to the standard and even going beyond it. The last two weeks have been the best two weeks for business that the company has ever known. The cash business done was far in excess of anything that had ever been done before in the same period of time. But it is all needed, as the expense of conducting the business of the company was never as great as it is at the present time. But if we all work together everything will come out all right in spite of

high prices and scarcity of materials, etc.

The Evangelist Campaign

Since the last report the following churches have sent in their revised subscription lists for the Evangelist. These are all "repeat orders" and we are indeed thankful that they have found the plan a worthy one. The churches to which we refer as: Falls City, Nebraska, H. F. Stuckman, pastor; Flora, Indiana, W. E. Thomas, pastor; Compton Avenue Los Angeles, Calif., J. C. Beal pastor; Muncie, Indiana, J. L. Kimmell, pastor; Clay City, Indiana, S. C. Henderson, pastor. We have the promise that a few more new churches will win places on the Honor Roll soon and we shall be only too glad to welcome them when they come in with the rest of the churches that have "tasted and found it good."

Honor Roll for the Brethren Annual

We might well start an Honor Roll for enrolling the names of the pastors that dispose of the Annuals and Conference Reports sent them promptly, if we were to do that we would have to enroll our departed brother, Elder I. B. Trout as the first member, as he was the first pastor to send us his check for the full amount a few days after the Reports were mailed. A goodly number of pastors have done likewise, and a number have ordered a second supply of the Reports. This is good. If all the pastors dispose of the small number we sent them there will be no surplus stock on hand this year as the supply we now have is being slowly reduced by the orders that are still coming in. We would ask the pastors to give this matter prompt attention. The special tract prepared for us with the Sunday School lesson in November that dealt with the teaching of John thirteen, was sent only to those pastors and schools that placed and order for it, but to date we think not more than one fourth of them have paid for the tracts. This should not be. Have you paid, brother?

R. R. TEETER,
Business Manager.

THE FOREIGN MISSION OFFERING

The Time.— EASTER SUNDAY, April 4th is the time for the WHOLE BRETHREN CHURCH and all her auxiliary organizations to make an OFFERING as unto the LORD.

The Purpose.— 1. This offering is made for the SUPPORT of all our MISSIONARY ENTERPRISES both in ARGENTINA AND AFRICA.

2. The offering is made for the ENLARGEMENT of our present endeavors by sending forth NEW WORKERS into UNOCCUPIED fields.

The Goal.— A Gift of MONEY can never measure our DEBT to GRACE nor dare any earnest Christian ever LIMIT his giving by a suggestion of SO-MUCH-PER member. The "GENEROUS GIFT" (2 Cor. 9:5) falls below or RISES FAR ABOVE the suggested $1.00 per member. "GRACE" measures the gift made to JESUS.

Your Report.— Send all offerings to the General Missionary Secretary of the Brethren Church. Brother WILLIAM A. GEARHART, 906 Conover Building, DAYTON, OHIO.

A Telegram.— Pastors and Churches are invited to send prepaid telegrams or night letters to the Editor of the Brethren Evangelist on Monday, April 5th. Report the success of your EASTER SERVICE both in SOULS won to the Lord and in MONEY given to FOREIGN MISSIONS.

"HE IS RISEN"

"And ye are witnesses of these things."

Published every Wednesday at Ashland, Ohio. All matter for publication must reach the Editor not later than Friday noon of the preceding week.

George S. Baer, Editor

The
Brethren
Evangelist

When ordering your paper changed give old as well as new address. Subscriptions discontinued at expiration. To avoid missing any numbers renew two weeks in advance.

R. R. Teeter, Business Manager

OFFICIAL ORGAN OF THE BRETHREN CHURCH

Subscription price, $2.00 per year, payable in advance.
Entered at the Post Office at Ashland, Ohio, as second-class matter.
Acceptance for mailing at special rate of postage provided for in section 1103, Act of October 3, 1917, authorized September 9, 1918.
Address all matter for publication to Geo. S. Baer, Editor of the Brethren Evangelist, and all business communications to R. R. Teeter, Business Manager, Brethren Publishing Company, Ashland, Ohio. Make all checks payable to the Brethren Publishing Company.

TABLE OF CONTENTS

EDITORIAL

Some Evidences of the Resurrection Life

The world is quite familiar with the unanswerable proofs of the resurrection of our Lord Jesus Christ, and the human heart cannot be dispossessed of the divinely implanted hope and the Christian assurance of a blessed life after death, but there is always much question as to whether this or that individual is in actual possession of the resurrection life, which is the mark of the Christian. What are the evidences of the resurrection life? That is the thing that claims our attention in tis instance.

The first and perhaps the most convincing evidence of the possession of the resurrection life by one professing to be a Christian, is that he is "dead to sin and alive unto God" (Romans 6:11), according to Paul's admonition. He further admonishes, "Let not sin reign in your mortal bodies," but to "walk in newness of life." No illustration of the ideal could be more perfect and no change could be more complete. The life of the Christian should be as different from the old life of sin as day is different from night. In the high spiritual sense the new life is out of touch with the old; they have no more in common than life has with death, or love has with hate, or white with black. All the old loves, pleasures and ambitions that were unworthy and unwholesome are put away, and life is thrilled with a new love, is charmed with new pleasures and inspired with new ambitions. The change that takes place in the heart of an individual when he is born again is as marked and sudden as the change in climate which one observes in passing from the east of the Cascade mountains in Washington and Oregon to the west. It is said that on the east side the winters are sharp and dry, and the summers are very hot; while on the west the winters are mild and the summers cool and showery. On the east the vegetation is stunted in size and poor in condition, while on the west the sluggish firs and cedars are pictures of vigor and strength. Even the flowers are vastly different in beauty, size and species and the atmospheric conditions are greatly changed. So there is a contrast between the unsaved, unregenerate condition of life and that which is experienced when the Holy Spirit comes into the life and makes all things new. "If any man be in Christ Jesus he is a new creature; old things have passed away; behold, all things have become new." And the newness of that creatureship will be evident; he will reflect as in a mirror the glory of Christ, for Christ will dwell in him. And if Christ be in him, the body will be dead in regards to sin, but the spirit will be alive in regards to righteousness (Rom. 8:10).

Another evidence of the resurrection life is the seeking of the things that are high and holy and heavenly; the things that are from above. Paul admonished the Colossians (3:1, 2), "If ye then be risen

with Christ, seek those things that are above, where Christ sitteth on the right hand of God. Set your affections on things above, not on things on the earth." The resurrection life loves to dwell in a spiritual atmosphere, to think of spiritual things and to seek after spiritual attainments. It loves the Isle of Patmos; it rejoices in the Transfiguration scenes and is at home in the Upper Room. How severely, yet fairly, are the souls of men tested by the intensity of the spiritual atmosphere of places! The man whose religion is merely a nominal affair feels out of place at a prayer meeting where hearts are being directed with much individual searching to "things that are above." He who has not been raised to walk in newness of life with Christ, even though his name be on a church roll, finds it somewhat embarrassing at the communion table where the spiritual atmosphere is so intense that the presence of the Holy Spirit can be distinctly felt. There are those who wear the name of Christ and yet do not enjoy meditating on the beauties of holiness or of dwelling in heavenly places with Jesus Christ, because they do not have the resurrection life. For if they were risen with Christ they would seek the things that are above and would love to dwell in their meditations where Christ sitteth on the right hand of God.

It is evidence of the possession of the resurrection life when we are able to speak of God with sincerity and feeling as, "My Father." God implored backsliding Judah, "Wilt thou not from this time cry unto me, My Father?" (Jer. 3:4). Jesus taught his disciples to pray, "Our Father," and he spoke to them familiarly and frequently of God as "my Father" and "your Father," encouraging them constantly to think of God in that relationship. Paul says to the Roman Christians (8:15, 16), "Ye have received the Spirit of adoption, whereby we cry, Abba, Father. The Spirit itself beareth witness with our spirit that we are the children of God." We can only know God as our Father through Jesus Christ, for he said, "Neither knoweth any. man the Father save the Son, and he to whomsoever the Son willeth to reveal him" (Matt. 11:27). Furthermore we cannot approach God as Father except through the Son, even as he said, "No man cometh unto the Father but by me" (John 14:6). But if we receive the Son, we thereby receive the Father (Matt. 10:40), and, being adopted into the family of God, we shall be his children and he will be "Our Father," and each individual soul will be able to say, "My Father."

It is an evidence of the possession of the resurrection life to have "faith in the operation of God, who hath raised up him (Christ) from the dead" (Col. 2:12). The point that Paul wishes to make is that the resurrection into the new life from the watery grave of baptism is dependent upon faith in the fact that God actually raised up Jesus from the dead. Over and over again do the two greatest preachers of the early Christian church—Peter and Paul—sound forth the declaration that "God raised him from the dead." All the apostles bear witness to this fact, and there is nothing they insist upon more strongly as being true. Upon this point the whole scheme of salvation depends, and the Gospel means nothing if this is not believed. In fact, says Paul, "if Christ be not raised, your faith is vain; ye are yet in your sins." A dead Christ cannot raise us out of our sins to walk in newness of life; we are not surprised, therefore, to find Paul making belief in the resurrection of Christ from the dead by the power of God an evidence of the possession of the resurrection life. Nothing is more essential to Christian faith and nothing is more certainly proven, than that Jesus Christ rose from the dead, according to the Scriptures.

A Campaign for An Adequate Church Program

When thirty denominations can unitedly make a minute survey of the religious conditions and needs of the world and then combine in a United Simultaneous Campaign to raise $336,777,572 with which to meet the needs thus discovered, there is every evidence that the great task of bringing in the kingdom of our Lord Jesus Christ is a live issue in this day and generation. The church is not degenerate; but is rising in the strength and grace of Christ to obey its Lord's commands with greater implicitness and sincerity of spirit than ever before.

Many persons were at first disposed to look upon the Interchurch Movement as a movement to "save the church;" but it is now pretty well understood that the movement is simply thirty or more denominations moving together—co-operating in a mighty effort to take the world for Christ. Some have thought it to be a movement calculated to result in organic church union, or the absorption of the little denominations by the large,—and we at first entertained such fears—but the leaders of the Movement made it clear that they believe that if a church believes it has a reason for a separate and distinct existence, it is highly important that such a church shall continue to preserve and practice these things that give it a separate existence and that wherever a church has a field, it shall work that field with the greatest possible thoroughness. If there should arise to leadership in the movement those who would push for organic union, three-fourths of the co-operating denominations would pull off forthwith; and there is nothing to prevent a church from ceasing to co-operate any time it may choose. Some thought it to be primarily a movement for social service, but we now quite generally understand the facts in the case, that it was first of all a missionary movement and that it has continually given supreme place to prayer, the deepening of the spiritual life and to evangelism. It has no plea except more consecrated attention and effort given to carrying out the will of God, and it leaves to each denomination the task of interpreting the will of God for it. Every church is encouraged to plan and execute its own program on the largest possible scale and, so far as consistent with the denomination's best interests, to carry out its program simultaneously with other co-operating denominations, so as to present to the world a united front and make the efforts of all churches count for the most for the salvation of the world and the glory of God. These two things seem to be the essential desires of the Movement, to stir every church to form an adequate program for the advancement of the Kingdom and to bring about co-operation so far as possible for the sake of greater accomplishment.

In the United Simultaneous Campaign, which takes place between April 25 and May 2, Protestant denominations are proving to the world that denominationalism offers no insurmountable obstacles to unity of action and purpose on the part of evangelical Christianity. This has been demonstrated many times before in union evangelistic campaigns and in union efforts in behalf of temperance and in many other ways, but never on so large and extensive a scale as now. Without the slightest loss to denominational identity these denominations have effected practical co-operation to do a greater thing for the kingdom under God's leading.

In answer to inquiries as to whether certain congregations may co-operate even though General Conference has not acted upon the Movement and though our church as a whole may not participate, we would say that it is possible under our congregational form of government for any congregation to co-operate in the financial campaign or any other part in so far as it may wish to do. We have heard of a district and of certain churches that expect to co-operate. It is their privilege. Neither is there anything to compel a congregation to co-operate, nor to embarrass it if it does not. The utmost Christian freedom is to be exercised with regard to any congregation's or denomination's participation or lack of participation in this Movement.

It is believed that this great united financial drive, regardless of whether or not we are in it, portends a great revival of spiritual interest throughout the world. If this should not be true, the outcome of the campaign, however successful, will be disappointing. It is difficult to see how such a campaign, however successful, will be disappointing. It is difficult to see how such a campaign, which is to be begun with a season of silent prayer, conducted by 5,000,000 workers who pray, among millions of church members who ought to pray if they do not, and many other persons interested in the kingdom of God, can fail to have a spiritual impact that cannot be measured. Surely if this vast army of Christian workers is dependent upon God for strength, wisdom and spirit to accomplish their task aright, as they are admonished to be, there is every reason to hope that we are on the eve of a great spiritual revival. May God grant that it may be so.

EDITORIAL REVIEW

There will be no paper next week.

It would be hard to find a more regular and careful correspondent than Brother Reed who reports for the First church of Los Angeles. In this issue he tells of the experiences attendant upon the laying of the corner stone for their new church.

Brother B. F. Owen reports his work at Fair Haven, Ohio, as moving forward. These people are a loyal group and under the leadership of Brother Owen who is ever ambitious that his people shall not lag behind, they have made a splendid record.

The work of the Sergeantsville-Calvary charge in New Jersey is splendidly reported in this issue by Brother Sands, the faithful and much-loved pastor. That these people appreciate their pastor is shown by their generous treatment of him.

Brother Mark Spacht, pastor of the Williamstown, Ohio, church, reports the revival meeting recently held at that place by Brother H. H. Wolford. Both the pastor and pastor appreciated Brother Wolford's ministrations very much. This was a case where a prophet was not without honor in his own village, for Williamstown is Brother Wolford's home.

Brother Bell speaks of a visit he made at the Washington, D. C., church and of the good work he found Brother Lyon and his co-workers doing. He also reports concerning a very successful revival held in the third church of Philadelphia of which Brother Braker is pastor.

Brother G. T. Ronk gives us a most excellent report of the mission points assigned to his oversight. We shall be glad to give space to similar reports from the other district secretaries any time they may wish to furnish them.

New Paris, Indiana, is rejoicing over "showers of blessings" which they have recently received. Brother MacInturff of Goshen co-operated with the pastor in an evangelistic campaign that was very successful. New Paris is alive to all the interests of the church.

Brother Bauman reports concerning some splendid work done by his rapidly growing and missionary-spirited congregation. This church has set a pace for doing things for the kingdom that few are able to follow, but all doubtless rejoice in their accomplishments.

If you had planned to send a telegram to the editor concerning your foreign offering as requested by Dr. Miller, kindly send a brief post card report instead and it will arrive in time for the next Evangelist to appear April 14.

As we were going to press, a "special" came from Brother Bame stating that "The Indiana Conference scheduled to meet at North Manchester, April 5 and 6 has been postponed on account of conflict with county Interchurch conferences and will meet April 12 and 13 at the same hours. The program will be corrected and we hope to present a still better program. We shall have the slides of the Interchurch on the first evening." A large attendance is desired.

FOUR-YEAR PROGRAM PAGE
NOW THEN DO IT.—II Samuel 3:18
Conducted by Charles A. Bame

Good Friday

According to the usual routine, many of my brethren will get their first glimpse of this page on Good Friday. It might be that some of them do not think of the calendar days of the year as I do, but, raised among the Lutheran people and born half-Lutheran myself, it does have a significance to me. When I write that word as a heading for a meditation, I felt as if I were bowing to my large audience all over the brotherhood and saying, "God bless you," or "How do you do?" Well, I should feel very sorry to take the space of this page if I did not make you feel better by so doing. Good Friday is to remind us of the wonderful sacrifice of the Cross. How much we need to be so reminded of it!

"In the cross of Christ I glory
Towering o'er the wrecks of time.
All the light of Sacred Story
Gathers around its head sublime."

For more than 1,500 years the Roman Catholic church has been calling the church to special remembrance of the event of the day; for a shorter period, some others; but this year, Protestantism as never before, will try to call the world to the meaning of the cross on Good Friday. Whatever the Interchurch World Movement is organized, the business men will be asked to close the shop to repair to a noon-day service at one of the churches of the town or city. Be that as it may, I am trying to call our attention to the need of remembering the Cross. "Without the shedding of blood there is no remission." "The blood of Jesus Christ cleanseth us from all sin." That is the sacrifice he made for us. Shed blood is the price of forgiven sin. The shed blood of the Son of God is the price of our forgiven sins.

"I gave, I gave my life for thee;
What hast thou given for me?"

What? What? That is the question. If thousands of church members should be asked to tell what they had given when they come to the pearly gates before they might enter, they would have to say the "loose change" that I had left after every personal fancy had been satisfied. Do you like the looks of that?

Whose Fault?

Whose fault will it be if the church does not give as it should this year? Who said, "Like Priest, like people?" Well, somebody with a good deal of sense. To be sure the preacher can not compel people to give but he can so well inform them that they can not refrain from giving. The Cross is the most compelling thing in all the universe. If it does not attract, it is because it is not held up. Jesus will draw but not unless he is "lifted up." The sacrifices that are needed the world around will find the offerings—the people and the money,—but not unless it is known by those who can go and give.

Bishop Henderson,

who is at the head of the evangelistic side of the "Interchurch" World Movement has this to say with regard to this Good Friday and Easter:

Good Friday, April 2. Never has there been such a Crucifixion Day since our Lord was crucified as will be witnessed this year. Merchants are requested to close their stores at the noon hour on Good Friday to permit their employees to attend a church service. In multitudes of churches a three hour service will be held to get a new view of the Christ of the cross.

Easter Sunday, April 4, will be the most joyful Easter in the history of Protestantism. It will witness the largest number of new disciples of Christ admitted to the fellowship of the church on one day in the history of Protestantism. Every church in America that believes Christ is a necessary Redeemer as well as a superb example should join in the greatest movement of co-operative evangelism ever undertaken in the name of the Protestant church.

Here are some mighty big assertions. I do not think the bishop is shooting "hot air," as some would say. He is in the New York office where the reports of the big things are coming so fast as to keep them constantly surprised. A bishop ought to be sure he is telling the truth and I believe that he is. The thing that is important to me and you, brother pastor, is to see that while others are going after big things and keeping informed, so ought we. Plan for the biggest Easter in the history of the church where you are the OVERSEER.

Commanding

Writing of the Interchurch Movement, Mr. W. H. Stark, a man of big business said, "This means that I have got to get back into the church. I have been out for years. I don't care a cent about their theological disputes. And the kind of things most of the churches have been doing doesn't interest me in the least. But this is the real thing. You have outlined a plan even for the local church, which means something. If the church is going to put over a proposition of this sort, I have got to get back into it and help."

Are you not glad that the church is thus finding the big men who will bring into it, all the immense strength of their organizing power and purpose and consecrate it to God? Well, if you are, get in the game for big things for the Brethren church this Easter.

Line Up

If your church has decided to go into the Movement as it has a right to do, then go after it with all the power you can get out of yourself and your constituency. If it has decided not to do so, then go after things as big and as compelling as any other church or denominations has dared to try to do. Just so we get past with something like the biggest and best that Christendom has ever heard of or experienced.

Dr. Yoder

Did you read the survey given by Brother Yoder for our work in South America? $12,000 is asked. Doubtless more could be used. But if we need that much there, where will the rest of them come out, if we give but that amount? We must hold the fort or it will be occupied by another. "Occupy till I come," said the Master. That means "Hold the Fort" for I am coming. Do it. Do it for him!

BAME.

The Lesson Taught By Trials

We never have more than we can bear. The present hour we are always able to endure. As our day, so is our strength. If the trials of many years were gathered into one, they would overwhelm us; therefore, in pity to our little strength, God sends first one, then another, then removes both, and lays on a third, heavier, perhaps, than either; but all is so wisely measured to our strength that the bruised reed is never broken. We do not enough look at our trials in this continuous and successive view. Each one is sent to teach us something, and altogether they have a lesson which is beyond the power of any to teach alone.—The Lutheran.

The real hindrance to every reform movement and philanthropic undertaking lies not in the ignorance or viciousness of the people, but in the active and intelligent opposition of those who derive profit from wrong or inhumanity.
—Rauschenbusch.

What Does It Matter to You If at this Easter Time

In South America out of ten leaders one is affiliated with the Catholic church, one is definitely hostile to the church and the other eight are indifferent to all matters of religion?

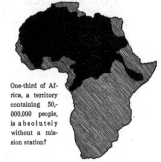

One-third of Africa, a territory containing 50,-000,000 people, is absolutely without a mission station?

(Credit to World Outlook for suggestion and loan of cuts)

GENERAL ARTICLES

Immortality, the Heart-Balm of Mankind. By Miles J. Snyder

The subject of immortality has a perennial interest which abides through all the changing years. More than a decade ago, lecturing at Harvard, a distinguished scientist declared that the interest in immortality was waning and that before many years it would practically cease to concern the minds of serious thinking men. But since that statement was made lectures on the subject have multiplied and books on immortality have come from the press in greater numbers than ever before, showing the utter futility of human prophecy when dealing with great spiritual realities.

Of course, we might as well admit at the outset that immortality cannot be scientifically demonstrated. There is no logically flawless proof of this doctrine which is dearer to us than life itself. Science deals only with sense perceptions and not with spiritual verities. There are many fundamental things which cannot be proved by it, such as the existence of God, the freedom of the will, the survival of the soul. Belief cannot be tested with acid, a thought cannot be weighed in the scales; hope cannot be examined with a microscope.

It is no cause for fear, therefore, to discover that immortality does not depend upon some infallible, scientific demonstration. We accept it by faith, and there is no greater thought or higher hope than this. Long ago Job raised the ever-recurring question, "If a man die shall he live again?" No matter how dulled the consciences and perceptions of men may have become with the opiates of sin and unbelief, sooner or later this question will penetrate their stupor and become a matter of concern. The question of immortality agitates the mind of every man, rich or poor, high or low, wise or ignorant, black or white, male or female, good or bad. It is your question and mine.

Perusing the pages of history we find that the thought of immortality has ever pulled at the heart of humanity. Every ancient Egyptian tomb unearthed shows evidence that this belief was common and unquestioned. The thought of it runs through Greek literature like a strain of music, sometimes melancholy but always there. The literature of the East mentions it, and Roman philosophy is not devoid of intimations of the immortal hope.

Broadly speaking, what have been the answers to the heart-searching question: "If a man die, shall he live again?" Science says he may live again. It has ascertained a continuity of life in nature and admits the probability of the persistence of the soul; but it does not know absolutely. Philosophy takes up the question where science lays it down and answers that man wants to live again, that it is the unceasing hope of the human heart. Philosophy reasons that since nature has provided fish with gills and birds with wings, and air for the lungs and light for the eyes, it is quite probable that man's deepest longing may be satisfied. Conscience answers the question by saying that man ought to live again. There are too many lives unfinished, songs not sung, pictures not painted; too many failures, too many inequalities; too many wrongs unrighted; man simply ought to live again.

It is thoughts like these which make it forever impossible for man to lose interest in the subject of immortality. And besides, loved ones are ever passing away and our thoughts follow them into the unknown with an interest that never ceases, and we instinctively feel that we are related with the eternal. This immortal instinct or yearning is not local nor provincial, but racial and universal. No argument can nullify it and no neglect can stifle it. Faith and hope range beyond earth's sky-line and man is sure there is a life to come.

But, mere persistence of the soul, simply life beyond the grave, is not a boon to be greatly desired. Many dread the prospect and hope for oblivion or annihilation. If only continued existence is all that immortality means, many would not want it as a gift. Even if the life to come promised all this life has given, multitudes would not care to endure it again. There has been too much sorrow, too many heartaches, too much loss, too bitter pain, too relentless a struggle. One of the greatest thinkers a few years ago said, "I believe in immortality, and do not see how anyone can help believing in it. Everything goes to prove it. And I am sorry, for I do not want it; I want rest." This man had been carrying a great burden upon his heart, and he was afraid that immortality would mean the old surroundings in another world. Like him, many would be glad to feel that the evening hour had come, that an endless night would soon be on, and all life's burdens and sorrows be lost in the silence of the grave.

If by immortality we mean simply continued existence, merely life beyond the grave, it calls forth no glad music, no triumphant hope, no carol of springtime, no thrill of a joyous heart. And this is true even of many whose pathway has led through pleasant earthly ways. And then how little must it mean to those whose hearts have been broken, whose spirits have been crushed, whose lives have been bruised under the iron heel of adversity and sore affliction?

But thanks be to God, that is not the meaning of Christian immortality. The thought of an endless life, the assurance of the immortal hope, became the heart-balm of the race only with the coming of Jesus Christ. Without him, the doctrine remains as an instinct in the human heart bereft of joyous anticipation. It is only when we invest immortality with the wealth of its Christian significance that the heart is quickened with joy and beats high with hope. It is only through the transformation of his resurrection life that we pass from pain to power, from darkness into light, from defeat to victory. Not until Christ came did men say "To die is gain," but then immortality became a blessed hope. It was resurrection with glory; it was heaven after earth.

Christian immortality is the heart-balm of the race because of the fact that Christ arose from the dead. By faith he imparts to us that life which bursts tombs and rises triumphant beyond the grave. Dying with him, we too may rise in newness of life. It is the rising into a new glory of life and into a new environment. It is the entrance to peace and the beginning of great blessedness, for "Eye hath not seen, nor ear heard, neither have entered into the heart of man, the things which God hath prepared for them that love him."

The Christian has the assurance of immortality not because it is a proved fact, but because he is a child of God. Our immortal hope is not an inference from philosophy or natural history, but the creation of a religious faith. It is attained by high and holy processes because we shall rise into it through the power of Christ's resurrection life. The Christian's source of comfort and joy and peace is the assurance that the soul of the believer shall pass out of darkness into a great light, out of smallness into largeness, out of sin into righteousness. The entrance into immortality is a time of escape and rich reward; it is the coronation hour when the crown of life is placed on the brow of death.

Immortality is heart-balm because its message is "good news" and "glad tidings." The New Testament portrays immortality as gain, when the sorrows and losses and defeats of time are forgotten in the glory that awaits the triumphant soul. In the Revelation of St. John the Christian is shown as having morning stars in his hand, jewels on his breast, a shout of joy upon his lips, God's name on his forehead, as he walks golden streets stretching between walls of jasper and of pearl. All this is but the author's poetic way of saying that death is gain, enrichment, blessedness.

"O the sweet compensation for heartache and loss,
   In the hope that is given to me;
I shall quickly forget how the road was beset
   When the King in his beauty I see."

And finally, the Christian doctrine of immortality is heart-balm because it promises reunion. It means that severed loves shall be re-united, that broken, golden cords shall be gathered up once more, that angel faces long since lost shall smile again. Jesus tells his disciples that he goes to prepare a place where they may be with him. The Revelation never sings of one man's immortality; it is always the throng of blessed ones who gather about the throne, clothed in white robes, with palms in their hands, singing the new songs of heaven and the joy songs of home.

Immortality then is indeed the blessed hope of the human heart. It does not consist of an argument completed but of a faith begun. It does not rest upon the conclusions of science but upon the plan and purpose and nature of God. What the poets dreamed about, Christ possesses and bestows. What philosophers tried to prove, Jesus simply announces. The one with an unshaken faith in the risen Lord was abiding in him the life eternal. He is not following a mirage but is sustained by a great reality. And a Gospel that can steady the soul with such a belief in the conflict of life is not worthless. A hope that can light up the darkness of the grave is not to be belittled. A Savior who can give victory over death is not to be despised.

This is the Christian's hope. And to those whose lives are scarred with the wounds of battle, who have traveled far and are weary, whose spirits sigh for rest, and whose hearts long for home, this immortal hope is a message from the Infinite descending upon the soul like the strains of heavenly music, filling and thrilling us with the power of the endless life of him who will heal our infirmities, forgive our sins, cleanse us from unrighteousness, and transfigure us into his likeness. It is this blessed hope which leads up the slopes of time to God, and find its fruition at last when its blossoms unfold beside the river of life in the soul's summerland, where the eternal day has dawned and all shadows have passed away, where the wicked cease from troubling and the weary are at rest.

In the light of Christ's resurrection promise all others glow with a borrowed radiance. What music is to the song, what perfume is to the rose, what love is to friendship, that the promise of immortality is to those who are in search of the Father's house. It tells us that some evening the lone shadows of twilight will gather around us and life's sky will glow with the crimson of its last sunset, and the victorious soul will find in death the entrance into life indeed.

Milledgeville, Illinois.

The Heart of the Easter Message. By R. F. Porte

This Easter message is an undying message. The passing years have not robbed Easter of its joy and hope. Who tires of the beautiful fragrant rose, the charm of the gardens of centuries ago? The fragrance of the rose will always be appreciated. Who is not filled with gladness at the thought of the coming springtime with the awakening of nature from her dormant state? Have you ever thought about why we look with joy at the return of spring? It is evidently more than the fact itself. There is an underlying reason why every person feels the melancholy of autumn and the thrill of life in the springtime. Is it not true that Easter bears a message to every Christian all its own? Easter suggests a soul-thrilling message. We want to try to analyze the message of the Easter tide and discover if we can its greatest message. No doubt you will say it is the resurrection of our Lord. That is a most blessed fact yet I want to suggest something that makes Easter even more joyous to every Christian.

Easter does carry with it the story of Jesus' resurrection from the grave. The resurrection was evidently the heart of the apostolic preaching. The sermon of Pentecost is centered around the fact that Jesus of Nazareth triumphed over all his enemies and was raised from the dead giving proof of his right as the Messiah of the Jews and the Savior of the world (See Acts 2:24-37). The use of the triumph of Jesus over his enemies and especially over death which none of the Jewish patriarchs were able to do points Jesus out as the lone man, the very God and Savior of his nation and the world. Peter uses the facts concerning the death and resurrection of Jesus in preaching to Cornelius. The resurrection is the particular evidence of the uniqueness of Jesus. He did good deeds and was a blessing to the needy, but greatest of all he gave his life for many and broke the bands of death (See Acts 10:39-44). St. Paul makes use of the resurrection of Jesus in describing the new life of a convert. In Romans 6:4, we find Paul comparing the death and resurrection of Jesus with Christian baptism, showing that just as Christ Jesus was raised from the dead and glorified so the Christian is to be raised to a new life and new purposes. In Phillipians 2:9, 10, we notice the mention of Jesus' humiliation and death and his wonderful glorification after the resurrection. The resurrection of Jesus was a fact that the Jews could not deny. It was evidence of their failure to destroy Jesus and the power of Jesus to conquer man's unconquerable foe.

Easter is the name we might give to the hope of the Christian world. Easter is a glorious light in the midst of a world of darkness and death. The prospect of the world without the facts connected with Jesus is as black as the human mind could imagine. The Christian prospect on the other hand is as bright as heaven itself. A Christian should not be a pessimist. A cataclysmic view of the world in the light of the facts of the Gospel is out of place in Christian preaching. The Gospel of the resurrection of Jesus brings to all those who believe light and life. We are surrounded by death and decay just as the apostles were and the only message that we can bring is the Easter message of life and light to the one who follows Jesus the Savior of mankind. Perhaps we have failed to use the message of Easter as fully as we should. The apostolic preaching dealt with the more fundamental truths of the gospel while modern preaching has been guilty too often of using merely the complements of the gospel. We never saw a time when we needed to preach the fact of the resurrection more than now, surrounded as we are with evidences of human frailty and weakness. It is the balm that can only heal and save us from the overwhelming tide that sweeps often over homes and communities.

Easter means little to us as a mere historical fact but when we come to believe in its message to our time it means much. Easter is not a time to commemorate an event but a time for deep reflection upon the outstanding mission of our Savior. History may carry a message of warning or give instruction but its value depends upon its translation into the time in which we are living. Easter could not die out in interest for us because we have not passed the point when we do not need the message that Easter brings. As long as the enemy of all flesh is yet unconquered in your life you need the message of Easter to cheer your heart and comfort your spirit. Easter was a test of the immortality of Jesus and I will mention what I consider the text best expressing the heart of the Easter message in the words of Jesus in John 14:19b, "Because I live ye shall live also." That fact cheers my heart more than any other thought about Easter. This word begets hope and confidence to help us break through the darkness that often overshadows our lives. Back in the beginning, God said, "In the day that thou eatest thou shalt surely die." God's warning was against giving death the advantage and then after the disobedience of man God planned the cure for the sting of death. I have quoted the direct statement of Jesus, and the recurrence of this Easter and every succeeding Easter will remind you of Jesus' promise and your privilege in him.

Dallas Center, Iowa.

The Epitaph at Christ's Tomb. By Miss Mary Pence

Many curious epitaphs appear on the tombstones of our cemeteries. The eastern states are especially noted for the unique epitaphs on their tombs. One day in an old cemetery at Hartford, I saw this epitaph:

"Behold, dear friend, as you pass by,
As you are now, so once was I;
As I am now, so you shall be;
Prepare for death and follow me. "

And that was just one of many unique inscriptions, in that one graveyard. Indeed much curious theology is displayed at our tombs.

On the tombstones of most of our cemeteries we see one heading to nearly all: "Here lies," then follow name, date of death, etc. But no tomb is found to bear the inscription that did Christ's. His epitaph was spoken by the angel, recorded in the Word by the Holy Spirit, and is engraven in the hearts of Christ's followers: "He is not here: for he is risen as he said. Come, see the place where the Lord lay." We take flowers and tokens of respect to the graves because "here lies," but there was found no place for the love spices of the women because "He is not here: for he is risen as he said." But on that first Easter morn love was shown a new and better way of expressing itself which was and is, "Go tell." And tell what? "That he is risen from the dead." The central theme of Paul's preaching was, "How that Christ died for our sins according to the scriptures; and that he was buried, and that he rose again the third day according to the scriptures." What are we that we should take anything from that mighty message? And he also tells us of the great cloud of witnesses to the risen Savior many of whom were yet alive when the account was written. Nevertheless some say "That there is no resurrection of the dead." But all the while "some" are so saying, our Savior now exalted at the right hand of God no longer needs the new tomb so lovingly loaned him for "He is not here." He is not seeking a tomb but he has sent forth his Servant the Holy Spirit to seek for him a bride, and he seeks a kingdom. He is to be found at the throne not the tomb. He is not seeking to entomb himself but to enthrone himself in every heart.

If a man die, shall he live again? This question was turned into a declarative statement on that first Easter morn. because "He is not here, for he is risen as he said." There is no question about believers living again when "he is risen," "and become the first fruits of them that slept." "For since by man (Adam) came death, by man (Christ) came also the resurrection of the dead. For as in Adam all die, even so in Christ shall all be made alive. But every man in his own order: Christ the first-fruits; afterwards they that are Christ's AT HIS COMING." To me that is one of the plainest teachings of the New Testament. At his coming they that are Christ's (the true believers) will rise, and in a moment in the twinkling of an eye the living believers will be changed (1 Cor. 15:51-53, and, 1 Thes. 4:13-18).

It is to be noted that the date of our resurrection or our translation is a more definite hour, "movement" than that of our birth or death. No man can testify to the exact time of his birth or death but he can be sure that his resurrection from the dead, or change, as the case may be, is to be when Christ comes "suddenly" with that joyful shout in the air. So the Word says. When the letters are to be chiseled on the tombstone a question often arises as to birth or death, which are far less important than the resurrection, the date of which is certain to be at Christ's coming. Most of our epitaphs, therefore, are unfinished. But the day will come when the finish can be put on: "No longer here:" "Forever with the Lord."

One cannot study the epitaph of Christ's tomb and not fairly overflow with joy at the multitude of beneficient results of the resurrection. They are too numerous to mention them all. In the first place, because of the resurrection we are justified in our belief in Christ. "He was delivered for our iniquities and raised again for our justification." The empty tomb secured for us without question a living Sav-

(Continued on page 11)

THE BRETHREN PULPIT

JOB'S QUESTION. By E. F. Byers

TEXT: "If a man die, shall he live again? All the days of my appointed time will I wait till my change come.—Job 14:14.

As one has said, "The keynote of the world's Easter song is immortality."

In answer to Job's question, "If a man die, shall he live again?" the Easter bells peal forth the blessed assurance, He shall live! The fact is this, man never dies. He simply moves out of one life into another. For instance, I plant a seed in the ground. The seed undergoes many changes, and apparently it dies; but the truth is that it has only undergone a transformation. So we may speak of man as dying; but in truth, his death is but a transformation. The power of death is over the physical body only; the true, or inner man knows no death. Death opens the door to larger possibilities, the investment of superior powers, and to the perfect manhood as revealed in our blessed Lord.

We may deny immortality, but the fact is that the evidences of immortality are a part of our present being. Several days before Columbus saw the coast line of the new continent, he saw birds which he knew must come from the land beyond. So to the thoughtful man there are many indications in this mortal life of the immortality beyond. Perhaps it may be an instinct, but whatever it be; there is something within each one of us that knocks at the door of a larger life. Something that finds itself in a world too small, and a life too short to realize its longings, or to reach the object of its existence. Man is too great for this world. However much a man may develop in this life, he realizes that he has come far short of what he would be. The acquirement of one thing, far from exhausting our capacity or ability to receive more, only enlarges the capacity, and makes us not only able to receive more, but hunger for more. So, in a large sense, we may say that the fact of our immortality indicates a capacity for immortality, and a hunger for it. In fact, in all ages, the thoughtful man has regarded another life necessary for the completion of the present.

Again, there is a strong probability of a future life because in the natural world annihilation is a myth. For example, your house burns down, there is no force destroyed. By a slow process of growth the soil and the rain and sunlight and atmosphere are transformed into the tree which furnishes the building material. Combustion simply releases these forces, and they go to their original condition. There are transformations of energy, but the physical law of the persistency of force prevents destruction. Death is combustion. The body, in death; returns to the earth from which it came, and the soul, released, like a homing pigeon flies back to God.

Then, too, experimental psychologists claim that there is no reason to conclude that the mind dies when the body dies. They say, "The evolution of mind has built up mental aptitudes, and these aptitudes have built up a physical basis for them to rest upon. The rising scale of organic evolution has thus been due to the development of mind. It is the mind that is the man; and mind is spirit, and spirit is immortal, and therefore cannot die.

Again, our affections make the belief of immortality immortal. As has been said, "As long as human love runs like a river to the sea, so long will it shape a shining way upon which men set adrift the ships of their hope to sail into the Ocean of Eternity." As long as the silvery clouds chase each other across the sky, or the stars run their course in the heaven's: the mother lays her babe beneath the sod, and plants a lily upon the lowly mound will believe that sometime, somewhere, she shall clasp it to her breast again. The father who sits the vigil of the night beside his dead; will look up through his tears to catch the beckoning hand that waves him to where his loved one waits.

Again, if there be no life after this, creation is a colossal failure. Better to have been a brute on the hillside than a man, if immortality be a myth! If the Bible doctrine of immortality is a myth, then life is a burlesque, integrity a burden, and conscience a curse!

If it were possible to persuade all men that there is no life after this, personal sacrifice for others would cease and the human family would be hurried to extinction by suicide! Yes, there is a future life, and in the future world virtue will be rewarded, and those who throughout their lives have suffered for the right will be crowned by the Judge of all the earth, who can make no blunders, and "doeth all things well." In that other life there be a correction of the irregularities of the rewards and the punishments of this life.

Then, too, our Master himself, in answer to this question, "If a man die, shall he live again?" comes to us with this blessed promise, "I AM THE RESURRECTION, AND THE LIFE; HE THAT BELIEVETH ON ME, THOUGH HE DIE, YET SHALL HE LIVE: AND WHOSOEVER LIVETH AND BELIEVETH ON ME SHALL NEVER DIE" (John 11:25, 26). Jesus, our Master, is therefore the answer to our questions and doubts concerning immortality. His teaching and resurrection removes the question of a future life from the field of speculation, and places it before us as an eternal reality.

"JESUS! BLESSED JESUS!" as Dr. Maclaren has said, "For us the past should be full of HIM, and memory and faith should cling to his incarnation and his cross. The present should be full of HIM, and our hearts should commune with HIM amidst the toils of earth. The future should be full of HIM, and our hopes should be based on no vague anticipations of a perfectibility of humanity, nor upon any dim dreams of what lie beyond the grave; but upon the CONCRETE FACT THAT JESUS CHRIST HAS RISEN, AND THAT JESUS CHRIST IS GLORIFIED. Our faith should grasp the CHRIST WHO LIVED AND DIED FOR US. Our hearts should cling to the CHRIST WHO IS AGAIN, WHO LIVES AND REIGNS, AND WITH WHOM OUR LIVES ARE HID IN GOD."

Our hopes should crystallize around, and anchor upon, THE CHRIST THAT IS COMING AGAIN, TO PIERCE THE THE DIMNESS OF THE FUTURE AND THE GLOOM OF THE GRAVE. HE WHO IS OUR LIFE, AND WITH WHOM WE SHALL APPEAR IN GLORY.

Conemaugh, Pennsylvania.

California Endorses Interchurch

Church of the Brethren Ministers Back of the Great Kingdom Movement

Brother I. V. Funderburgh, Regional Director for California and Arizona, writing to the office at Elgin, says, concerning the Pastor's Conference for Northern California, held at San Francisco: "A resolution was adopted, urging our people to get behind our Forward Movement, commending the action of the Board, relative to the Interchurch Movement, and heartily endorsing the Interchurch World Movement as a timely one and worthy not only of our interest but our support." Southern California is also behind the Forward Movement and will do her share to reach the standards. Twenty-four of our ministers were present at the Southern California Conference and eleven at the Northern California meeting—not a bad showing.—The Gospel Messenger.

OUR DEVOTIONAL

Our Personal Walk With Jesus
By Miss Alice Livengood
OUR SCRIPTURE

And Enoch walked with God: and he was not; for God took him (Gen. 5:24). And it came to pass that when Moses came down from Mount Sinai with the two tables of testimony in Moses' hand, when he came down from the mount, that Moses wist not that the skin of his face shone while he talked with him. And when Aaron and all the children of Israel saw Moses, behold, the skin of his face shone; and they were afraid to come nigh him (Exod. 34:29, 30). Nevertheless I am continually with thee: thou hast holden me by my right hand. Thou shalt guide me with thy counsel, and afterward receive me to glory (Psalm 73:23, 24). Abide in me, and I in you. As the branch cannot bear fruit of itself, except ye abide in the vine; no more can ye except, ye abide in me (John 15:4). Now when they saw the boldness of Peter and John, and perceived that they were unlearned and ignorant men, they marvelled; and they took knowledge of them, that they had been with Jesus (Acts 4:13).

OUR MEDITATION

Goethe said, "Tell me with whom thou art found, and I will tell thee who thou art." It is true, for we so often hear people say "you can tell what 'so and so' is by his associates." When strangers come into a community they are watched to see whom they will choose for their associates, and they are judged thereby.

The question may come up, How are the wicked to be shown the way, if we cannot associate with them? "It is only when men associate with the wicked with the **desire** and **purpose** of doing them **good**, that they can rely upon the protection of God to preserve them from contamination." We know Jesus ate in the homes of publicans and sinners and good resulted. It is not necessary for us to enter into evil with others in order to win them. We dare not go to them or with them unless Jesus goes with us for he will protect us and open the doors for us.

In the days of long, long ago Enoch walked with God. His family and friends, I am sure, knew by his life that he had holy associations. One day after his years here had been long and, I imagine, while in communion with God, he was not for God took him. His walk had been so perfect that he was greatly rewarded.

In our scripture we find that Moses' face shone because of his association with God while on Sinai. You have seen people whose countenance shone because of their walk and talk with Jesus. They have a source of happiness unknown to the unregenerate heart. They can truly say, "And he walks with me, and he talks with me. And he tells me I am his own, and the joy we share as we tarry there, none other has ever known."

A woman who was left with a family of little ones to support and no means with which to do it except her two hands. She said with her own strength she never could have done it, but each morning as it came, she asked her Lord to be with her and help her that day. Her family grew up into good men and women and she is now able to rest from her hard labor of early years. Yes, he will hold us by "the right hand" and guide by his counsel and is so willing to do it if we will just ask and let him. He will be a very present help in time of need.

Peter and John's boldness and confidence, when before the Sanhedrin, prove the presence of their Lord with them to uphold them. And so he will ever be with those who love him in time of need. Those lawyers had to pause and consider for "they took knowledge that they had been with Jesus." Do our lives show that we are walking with Jesus? Are we abiding in him so thoroughly that we are partak-

ing of and reflecting his spirit? Are we bearing fruit that tells others that we are "his own?" "Every good tree bringeth forth good fruit; but a corrupt tree bringeth forth evil fruit." "By their fruits ye shall know them." The fruit of the spirit is love, joy, peace, longsuffering, gentleness, goodness, faith, meekness and temperance" (Gal. 5: 22 23). We have to walk close to him to bear these fruits and to keep free from the fruits of the flesh.

The last evening Jesus spent with his disciples he said, "Ye are my friends if ye do whatsoever I command you." Now we like to show our regard for our friends by visiting with them and having them in our homes. If we are a friend of his we are glad of every opportunity of going to his house and that includes the midweek and Sunday evening services as well as the Sunday school session. Be glad to "walk and talk with the King."

Someone has said, "It is best to be with those in time, that we hope to be with in eternity." How true! If we do not care to walk with Jesus here, how dare we dream of being in his presence in eternity? Our Sunday school lessons of the last three months show us that companionship with Jesus is the true and safe one. If John had not walked so close to Jesus he would not have had the wonderful vision on Patmos.

OUR PRAYER

Father in heaven, the one and only living God, we thank thee that we live in a land where thy name is known. We are glad that we can have thy Son and our Savior for our daily companion. We pray that day by day we shall crave more of his presence and guidance. When our time here is ended may we be of the innumerable throng that shall worship thee in the heavenly home. Lord, hear and grant our prayer and forgive our sins. We ask in Jesus' name. Amen.

Milledgeville, Illinois.

The Blood of Christ

An old shepherd in England was taken to a London hospital to die. His grandchild would go and read to him. One day she was reading in the first chapter of the First Epistle of John, and came to the words, "And the blood of Jesus Christ his Son cleanseth us from all sin." The old man raised himself up and stopped the little girl, saying with great earnestness:

"Is that there, my dear?"

"Yes, grandpa."

"Then read it to me again—I never heard it before."

She read it again: "The blood of Jesus Christ his Son cleanseth us from all sin."

"You are quite sure that is there?"

"Yes; quite sure, grandpa."

"Then take my hand and lay my finger on the verse, So she took the old blind man's hand and placed his bony finger on the verse, when he said:

"Now read it to me again."

With a soft, sweet voice she read: "And the blood of Jesus Christ his Son cleanseth us from all sin."

"You are quite sure that is there?"

"Yes; quite sure, grandpa."

"Then if anyone should ask how I died, tell them I died in the faith of these words, 'The blood of Jesus Christ his Son cleanseth us from all sin.'"

With that the old man withdrew his hands, his head fell softly on the back of the pillow, and he silently passed into the presence of him whose blood cleanseth from all sin. —Australian Lutheran.

Some years ago a timid Indiana girl made out a prayer list of unsaved friends. At the end of the year only one had accepted Christ, but she kept on praying; and before the second year had ended a great revival had swept over the town and almost every one on her list was saved. But she added new names and has been leading souls to Christ ever since.— Selected.

Send
WHITE GIFT
OFFERINGS to

THE SUNDAY SCHOOL

ALBERT TRENT
General Secretary-Treasurer
Johnstown, Pennsylvania

Sunday School Nuggets from Brazil

More than 125,000 attended the Sunday schools of Brazil on their Rally Day, and this in spite of the fact that the Sunday school enrollment for Brazil is only about 60,000. The special offering for the day amounted to nearly $3,000. The money is to be used for Sunday school work in that country, and especially to pay the local expenses of the Field Secretary for Brazil whom the World's Sunday School Association is urged to send at once.

The State of Sao Paulo held their annual convention in the city of Sao Paulo in November. Popular meetings were held each evening. The seventeen Sunday schools of Sao Paulo participated in the Sunday afternoon mass meeting and by actual count 1,276 persons were present. Many visitors came to the doors, saw the seats all taken and turned away. A very interesting and helpful program was carried out with great enthusiasm; the singing was inspiring. The school were called one by one, arose in a body and sang one or two verses of a hymn, recited a passage of Scripture, or were represented by recitations from little girls especially chosen for the purpose. One item on the program was of very special interest, writes Rev. H. C. Tucker, Field Secretary for Brazil of the World's Sunday School Association, who was present. "Twenty little girls bearing the flags of twenty different nations marched to the platform and formed a semi-circle. When the presiding officer called the name of each country the representative stepped forward and gave the Sunday school statistics for that country. The last who came forward, who not only gave statistics but made a little speech, was Brazil's representative. Just as she was about to begin, the postmaster of the city arose and interrupted the program by saying to the chairman, 'Since Brazil received the Gospel from the people of the United States I propose that the representative bearing the flag of the United States be requested to take her position beside Brazil.' The suggestion was accepted with enthusiasm and the applause was deafening for a time."

"Another item of great interest was the statement of the case of a Sunday school boy in the city, who on two occasions when rally meetings were to be held had been sick: he had looked forward with great expectation to be present at this time, but had the misfortune of being sick again. He was not in condition to walk or travel in the street cars. Five or six chums of his, poor boys who are working for salaries of about $18 per month, agreed to hire a taxi and take this boy to the meeting. When this announcement was made there was a great clapping of hands and calling for these boys to stand up. After insistent calls they finally very modestly arose and thanked the audience. Really the occasion was tense with enthusiasm."

Korea and the World's Sunday School Convention in Japan

The attitude of the Korean Christians with reference to the holding of the Eighth Convention of the World's Sunday School Association in Tokyo next October is clearly indicated in the adoption of certain resolutions at the Korean Annual Conference of the Methodist church. On recommendation of the Sunday school Committee of the Conference the following was adopted unanimously:

"Whereas, the Eighth Convention of the World's Sunday School Association is to be held in Tokyo, in October, 1920, and,

Whereas, we believe that the church in Korea should be represented in any such meeting of the church Universal,

We recommend, that each District, and as far as possible, each Quarterly Conference, endeavor to send representatives to the said Convention."

This represents a much more Christian spirit on the part of the Korean Sunday school workers than that which some reports have attributed to them. Christian Koreans will not hold Christian Japanese to account for any possible injustices of the Japanese Government.

Dr. John F. Goucher, President of Goucher College of Baltimore, represented the World's Sunday School Association, at a meeting of the Patrons' Association in Tokyo, were present at the Bankers' Club in Tokyo where a reception was held. The mayor, Viscount Tajiri, and the Chamber of Commerce joined in extending the formal invitations. Such men as Baron Sakatani, Baron Shibusawa and Horace E. Coleman who is the Sunday school Educational Secretary for Japan were present. The address of Dr. Goucher has been widely printed in the papers of Japan.

Applications for credentials as delegates to this convention in the Far East are being received daily at the office of the World's Sunday School Association, 216 Metropolitan Tower, New York. It is now evident that every reservation that has been made on the Pacific ocean steamers will be taken by those who are eager to attend this Convention.

The Epitaph at Christ's Tomb

(Continued from page 7)

ior who daily imparts life to his followers." He that hath the Son hath the life." There is no death nor darkness about our risen Savior; there is life and light. When he enters he turns dry bones into living, immortal flesh. What a wonderful life-giving Savior! Then in addition to joy, peace, power, daily victory over sin, as believers the empty tomb assures our future state. We have something on which to anchor our hope and it leaves us without a doubt as to whether if a man die, he shall live again.

"I am he that liveth, and was dead, and behold I am alive for evermore." "Because I live, ye shall live also." "He is not here; he is risen as he said." "Go tell" "how that Christ died for our sins according to the scriptures; and that he was buried, and that he rose again the third day according to the scriptures." This is God's wonderful program, brethren; let us follow it.

Limestone, Tennessee.

HAWAII TO CELEBRATE MISSION CENTENNIAL

Hawaii will hold a great Missions Centennial April 11 to 19 next to celebrate the hundreth anniversary of the landing of the missionaries. Hundreds of descendants of the early missionaries will go from many parts of the United States to attend the event, the principal feature of which will be a historical pageant enacted by thousands of the native population and by members of missionary families on the sides of beautiful Manoa Valley, just outside of Honolulu. The pageant is named, "One Hundred Years of Christian Living in Hawaii."

GOVERNMENT BUYS ALL INTERCHURCH COUNTY MAPS

The Office of Farm Management of the Department of Agriculture has just contracted through Charles J. Galpin to buy a copy of each of the 2,968 maps to be produced by the Town and County Division of the Interchurch World Movement, embodying the results of the county surveys. These county maps are concrete expressions of the result of the first thoroughgoing and comprehensive church and community surveys ever attempted on a nationwide scale.

J. A. Garber	Our Young People at Work	G. C. Carpenter
PRESIDENT		SECRETARY

Personal Evangelism

By E. M. Riddle, National Superintendent of Quiet Hour and Evangelism

I offer a brief discussion of this vital subject, knowing that much has been written relative to evangelism, yet knowing that it is being stressed and greatly emphasized in these days as one of the greatest methods of appealing to God's choice creation.

When we take a glance at the New Testament accounts of the work of Jesus, we find that about thirty-four of the people who came to him for healing of the body and soul were brought by others who were personally interested in them. Also we see Jesus himself appealing to individuals, as to the business man (Matt. 9:9) and the woman of Samaria (John 4:7). Next to Jesus, we find the method used by the apostles.

The greatest appeal of Christian effort at this moment is to sign up men and women who will consecrate their lives for definite Christian service. The Interchurch is claiming a need for 100,000 new recruits or more for the next five years. Let us ask the question, How will they be found? My own opinion is that a large percent of this number will be won for the service of God by feeling the call through some personal effort and contact. We Christian people need to come in contact with Jesus. We need to be growing in knowledge; we need that faith such as was revealed by the woman who said, "If I but touch his garment, I shall be whole." Could our Christian lives be guaranteed by affirming that we have had personal dealings with Jesus Christ? If we would be alive to his work and if we are to be his witnesses in the world, it is ours as a privilege to show the need and emphasize the ability that our young people posssess. Too often it is the case that our young people do not realize that their peculiar talent is the very one needed in Christian service.

Personal evangelism has a great effect. The one who serves and the recipient of that service, both receive new vitality. Such service creates confidence, faith and power. personal evangelism has built up some of our weaker churches. They have taken on a new lease of life and have become aggressive forces because the laymen have told the story, have awakened men to the possibilities of their own endeavors and these have bent themselves to the task. Did I say personal work, done by the laymen? Yes. I do not see it anywhere that God particularly branded the preachers to do all the witnessing for him. As I write I recall the noble achievement among about forty groups or teams of laymen who comprised nearly 300 men who lived in a western town. Their journeys in every direction to the extent of one hundred miles, for the one purpose of winning souls resulted in 3,000 actual decisions for our Lord Jesus. You say that sounds like they were soul winners. Why should we not all be? It is only obedience to the command of Christ, his command and his teaching alike summon us to this work. "All authority is given to me in heaven and on earth. Go ye and make disciples." From the calling of the first disciples to the saving of the thief on the cross, our Lord's life was one long record of winning men. Some of the most powerful and effective workers today among the men, who are or have been giving all their time to the work of evangelization and soulwinning, are men who were won by a personal messenger. Dwight L. Moody and John R. Mott were personally called to an enlarging life as a direct result of personal work. Then how great is the obligation resting upon us when we say, where are the men whom we might have won?

The example of every great missionary or Christian leader at home or abroad calls us to this work. William Carry and Dr. Parker in India; Dr. Riefsnyder in China and the early workers in the Philippines and Siam have all taken to the heathen the Word of Life and a touch of healing co-operating all the way. We may think of our own most wor-

thy missionaries in distant lands with the same zeal for souls and power with God, going out with the Gospel of Christ and doing things for the natives that they will not do for each other.

How much must the people of these United States do for each other in order to win for Christ the 2 million boys and girls under twenty-five years of age without religious education, with not even Sunday school advantages? How can we win our States for Jesus Christ except we experience a revival in our own hearts and go out teaching that Jesus is our Savior from sin and also Lord of our very life? This evangelistic spirit is needed in the church; it is needed in the home, to purify and beautify; it is needed in the heart, to quicken and make alive. How much real concern have we for the lost at this Eastertide? "God so loved the world that he gave his only begotten Son." "He that winneth souls is wise." "As the Father hath sent me, even so send I you."

Louisville, Ohio.

Fortifying the Intermediates

The Intermediate society of our First church, Dayton, Ohio, under the superintendency of Mrs. Charles W. Abbott, is employing a program of expression that is calculated to fortify the teen age young people against the evils and temptations of life. These young people are provided with a copy of the little booklet "Bible Truths," consisting of Bible verses topically arranged by Brother Alva J. McClain, and in their meetings they are encouraged to give the Biblical teaching on a given subject in their thought and language. The preparation of these brief talks or papers requires the young people to work over—interpret and assimilate—all the instruction they have received on the topic and the presentation gives the superintendent and pastor an opportunity to observe the progress the young people are making in their thinking. Thus the acquisition of truth may be commended and the acceptance of error discouraged. Truth assimilated by and expressed to one's self becomes the living content of his life and fortifies him against divers temptation. The summary of one of these talks will be found on this page.

The Bible.   By Lois Peirce

The Bible is a book of rare treasures. In it we find the secret of happy living. Through the contents of the Bible we find the Key of Heaven. The Bible contains enough to make us rich for time and eternity. Our Bible is a window in this prison world, through which we may look into eternity.

When you are reading a book, in a dark room and come to a difficult part, you take it to a window to get more light. So take your Bible to Christ and he will give you as much light as you seek. Ask and the promises are yours. We do not want a book that will amuse us, but a book that can save us. The Bible is "God's Chart," for you to steer by, and to keep you from the bottom of the sea, and to show you where the harbor is; so read it with love and devotion.

The Bible, the whole Bible, and nothing but the Bible and Jesus love for me.

Dayton, Ohio.

Faith is not a thing that can stand still; it must grow or die. One conviction must lead on to another, or the fruit will in time be lost. If a man stands by the truth he has, some day, in some form, Christ, who is the Truth, will pour into his heart another and another.—Lawrence.

SEND ALL MONEY FOR
General Home, Kentucky and
Foreign Missions to

MISSIONS

WILLIAM A. GEARHART
General Missionary Secretary
906 Conover Bldg., Dayton, O.

"COME ON! LET'S GO!"

A Final Appeal from the Treasurer of the Foreign Missionary Society

"Come on! Let's Go!" We like that, provided you "go" in the right direction! Many of our dear brethren have a vision for doing something big for Christ—something worth while, and that is right. I think we can all agree that the work of making Christ known where he is unknown is a work worth while. If that isn't the greatest work on earth, then, pray tell, what is? I think that we all have confidence in the men and women at the front. Now then, we have had lots of talk about doing big things—"Come on! Let's go!" How many men among us will prove that we believe in the big forward step by putting across in their churches an Easter offering for Foreign Missions that will be worthy of their professions! Don't you delude yourself into thinking for one moment that the Standard Oil or some other big corporation is going to be drawn into paying our missionary bills. (If they were drawn in, they would raise the price of oil on us again, so what's the use?) Wouldn't it really be unworthy of us to ask this old world that is doomed to judgment to pay our Lord's bills? Ah! be not deceived! The money that will pay our missionaries on the fields lies right in the pockets of THE BRETHREN, and nowhere else! Get that right, and get it NOW. "Come on! Let's go!" "Go" down, "go" deep, "go" cheerfully, into your own pockets and prove your love to him who gave his all to you!

Brother Yoder has written you that it will take $12,000 to care for the South American alone. But Brother Yoder is just about $5,000 low on that. (That is, if the Edwards family is to be taken into our family of missionaries down in Argentina, as he desires.) If we clean up all back bills and pay the full amount on the newly purchased property at La Carlota, which is $3650, then as nearly as we can estimate it and figure safely, it will take about $17,000 to put across our South American program this coming year. Of this, we have in the treasury resources amounting to about $1,500, so let us say that we need at least $15,000 for this work at Easter time. And that means we will not be able to make further expansion this year, which we should do. We are praying that the Lord will raise up some one this Easter time to lift the balance due on the Auto Coach, which is costing $1,500 or $500 more than we at first calculated. We have sent them to date $1,000.

Now, when we remember that Africa also has her claims on us, we can see that $1 per member this year for Foreign Missions is not a bit too high a goal. It ought to be higher. As a matter of fact there are a lot of members in the Brethren church (the shame of it!) who do not propose to give so much as one-third of a cent per day to make Christ known to those who are in darkness! Consequently some of us will have to think of five, ten, a hundred and five hundred times that much. As for the writer's church, $7

per member, from the littlest tot up, is the goal! We don't know whether we are going to get there or not! But—"Come on! Let's go!" The fields are ripe! The harvest waits! The Master is calling! The night is falling! The King is coming! "Come on! Let's go!"

LOUIS S. BAUMAN.

MID-YEAR SURVEY OF MISSION POINTS

G. T. Ronk, Field Secretary,
Central District

Your secretary desires to make this semi-annual report of the home mission work of the central district, and to note progress and some of the problems.

Peru, Indiana

Brother G. C. Carpenter is in charge of this work of the Board. He is president of the Missionary Board of the Brethren church and was drafted to take up this work some years ago. He is making commendable progress. The fine lot on which the wooden tabernacle stands is paid for and they have over $4,000 in cash on hand toward the new building which is fast becoming a necessity. A temporary building like the "Little Brown Church" has a fine appeal for awhile but in time the people expect something more permanent and the time is fast approaching when Peru must have a permanent church building. Brother Carpenter plans on having half the cost of the building in cash and financial arrangements made to handle the floating loan and the permanent debt before he begins building. Peru's greatest obstacle has been the present unrest with the shifting of the population. In five years scarcely a family of the charter members remains and I feel it has been a great piece of work to keep the membership list even, under the circumstances. I spent only a few hours with Brother Carpenter.

Huntington, Indiana

This place like Peru is an ideal city as to size for building Brethren churches numbering from 12,000 to 15,000 in population. I met Brother Brower, the pastor of the church here for a few hours and went over the financial situation and visited through the new church building. Let me say I think it is one of the very best in the brotherhood and in its planning best of all reflects credit on those in charge. I cannot see how it could possibly have been gotten for the price at the time it was built. Certainly it could not be built today for less than $30,000 and cost quite a bit less than half of that. The only thing wrong with the Huntington project whatever has been the lack of an adequate financial plan and proper credit arrangements for handling the building period, which every church must meet when it builds. Being a mission it lacked the local backing to guarantee its own paper and thus was compelled to call upon some of the Indiana churches for endorsement. Now that its surplus property has been sold at the instruction of the mission boards co-operating its debt is reduced to about $8,300, $2,000 of which is pledged. So this magnificent

plant has really less than $7,000 of unprovided debt with resources at present value of not far from $30,000. It appears that arrangements will soon be made for returning the supporting churches their endorsements. Huntington is a great opportunity and I feel sure will yet be a strong church.

Muncie, Indiana

I spent a night here with Brother Kimmel and found everything booming. Brother Kimmel, like Brother Carpenter does not expect to begin building till he has half of the cost on hand and all financial arrangements made for handling the building charges and carrying any permanent debt. The lot seems well enough located and certainly was a bargain at the price paid. The little flock of sixty here are raising $1,700 this year which is about the highest per capita in the whole church. Brother Kimmel is secretary of the Indiana Board and was drafted to take charge of this mission. Now he is returning the favor by going among the churches and asking cash in advance of the actual building to take advantage of the great situation he finds. Money could not be better invested. Muncie is already a city of about 25,000 and the General Motors Corporation are building one of their largest new plants here to employ an army of men. It is estimated this one concern will put the population to near a hundred thousand in the next five years. Our mission has a great field right among the high priced mechanics of two of America's greatest Gear works, the Warner and the Muncie. We are getting in on the ground floor.

Ft. Scott, Kansas

I spent almost a week here visiting among the church members, preaching each night in the new plant, and helping start the financial campaign. We have a fine band of people at this place and though they have been much handicapped by their former location they are now on what three of the city's real estate men informed us is the finest lot in the city. The church for which we paid $3-700 is worth at least $15,000 we were assured by good business men, and the lot is surely worth more than we paid for the plant. The building is fifty years old with the largest and finest bell in the city. It is absolutely sound and is good for another hundred years. Best of all it is in good enough shape for immediate occupancy and can be modernized as the congregation is able. It is a fine specimen of the old spired, arched ceiling church, with main auditorium that will seat four hundred people, a large Sunday school room one-third that size and a suite of living rooms upstairs where former sextons have lived and which can be used for organized class rooms. Our old plant is off in one edge of this city of 12,000, while this plant is two blocks south of the court house, across the street from the Junior High School, on the great paved National Avenue which is a part of the Jefferson Highway from New Orleans to Winnipeg, Canada. It is an interesting fact that our Leon church, lately a mission, is two hundred and seventy miles north, across the street from another high school on the same highway.

When the proper man is secured for pastor I look for Ft. Scott to become one of our greatest fields, with the new plant. Now we are on the inside of our former district and are within reach of the east side of the city which is fully as good a field and where we have a good many people. The new church is almost in the center of our constituency. The old plant is free from debt and when disposed of will leave a very small margin of debt on the new plant. Brethren, let us pray for this field, one of the brightest we possess, as well as for the others.

Other Fields

Des Moines, Iowa is being investigated for the Board by Brother R. F. Porte, pastor of the Dallas Center church, twenty-two miles out. More will be given later.

Decatur, Illinois is a fine city and we believe a great work can be done there. The boards are waiting for the local people to take the initiative as at other places.

Mt. Etna, Iowa, with the county seat of Corning, is a worthwhile field where a group of people are struggling along without a pastor. We are hoping for a more satisfactory solution of this field's problems.

Albia, Iowa, the writer's birthplace is clamoring for something to be done. They are only 22 miles from our pastorless church at Udell and the two working together could form a fine circuit. Albia is another county-seat of about 7,000.

Eau Claire, Wisconsin, is still clamoring for help but they are so far from any other church and so few in number that no way has been seen as yet to help them.

McLouth, Kansas has at last gotten a man on the field in the person of Brother Howell and we hope for good reports. This is the neediest field close in, I know of, being only 45 miles from Kansas City. There is a great rural parish unworked for miles around.

Norton County, Kansas, I have not visited, nor Clay City, Indiana. Everywhere are opportunities. The great cry is for enough of the right kind of men. Throughout this great field, so far as I know, approved methods are being used and results are being won. Let us sacrifice without stint, then pray, then endure and the Lord will vindicate his Word and give the harvest.

NEWS FROM THE FIELD

FIRST BRETHREN CHURCH, LOS ANGELES, CALIFORNIA

Sunday, March 7th, there was one confession of faith at the evening service. Our pastor gives an invitation at every service and we all feel here that it is in perfect harmony with the spirit of the gospel.

The ceremony of laying the corner stone of the new church edifice was held Sunday afternoon, March 14. An all day meeting with basket lunch in the tent had been arranged for, but our plans were very much interfered with. A brisk March wind, one of those "Northers" they are called here, began to come up in the forenoon and by eleven o'clock was blowing quite a gale. The tent was well anchored, but one of the smaller ropes gave way, letting the tent sag sufficiently to strike some upright pieces on the inside, which tore a five foot hole. In a few minutes the tent was torn asunder from cave to top and had to be lowered to the ground to save it from further damage. The morning service was perhaps about one-half through.

The people then either went home or retired across the street to the new church now entirely under roof. The chairs and furniture needed were carried over and lunches were eaten in the new building.

One of the larger Sunday School rooms was made as comfortable as possible by stretching some of the side walls of the tent around it. Here the afternoon service was held, except the short ceremony of laying the stone at the right hand side of the main entrance on the corner of San Pedro and 42nd streets.

The pastors and others were present in the afternoon from the following neighboring congregations: Compton Avenue, Long Beach, Whittier and Fillmore. The following brethren were called upon and gave short addresses suitable to the occasion: N. C. Nielsen, A. V. Kimmell; John C. Beal and L. S. Bauman. Brother Nielsen came from his home in Long Beach every Sunday almost without exception for more than six years to superintend the Sunday School and help to make this work a success in its beginning. Brother Kimmell was pastor of this church for several years. It was fine to have these brethren and friends with us on this occasion and to hear their encouraging messages.

The pastor, Brother Jennings, performed the ceremony of laying the corner stone, which was lifted into place by Brother Kimmell and Brother Bly. Brother L. S. Bauman led in prayer.

The contractor of the new structure was present and said he would have the basement ready for use by Sunday, the 21st, therefore the large tent which was so badly damaged will not be used any longer. It has served our purpose in a splendid way.

The Sunday School attendance is keeping up nicely and all the church services are well attended. We are looking forward anxiously to some good spiritual times during the present year and hoping to see quite a number who will be made willing to come forward and confess the Savior.   A. P. REED.

FAIR HAVEN, OHIO

The work at Fair Haven, Ohio, is steadily moving forward. We are not able to report any large ingatherings at any specific time, but occasionally we receive one or more into the church. The thing that pleases us more than anything else is, we are up as far as any country church is able to go on the Four Year Program. The last feature of the Program realized is the adoption of our budget. This, in the past, was somewhat difficult to realize but it was our only salvation and the church felt the same way in the matter. The amount necessary to meet our expenses for the new year is $900, but we have gone $1,-100 with more people to solicit. Hence it is readily seen what may be accomplished when an effort is put forth. This we consider excellent, but we are not satisfied, we must still strive for larger gains. When we consider the strides we have made in the last three years it makes us glad. We now have the Evangelist going, not to 75 per cent of the members' homes, but to each member's home. We are subscribing our full, and in some instances more, quota to all benevolences. We gave $2300 to Ashland College endowment, with $200 to be added since Beachler was out here, making a total of $2500. Thus Fair Haven is on the map.

This church remembered their pastor in their usual way last December with a substantial Christmas gift and a large donation.

These things are worth much at such a time as the present when everything is so high. The people are pleasant to work with. The writer has preached for them for nearly three years and they have extended the call for another year which will begin June 1. It is our aim to make the coming year a banner year. Pray that the Lord may be gracious to us in this desire and that Fair Haven may uphold its name.   BENJ. F. OWEN.

SERGEANTSVILE-CALVARY CHARGE

We are still doing business for the Lord at the old stand. When we resigned last summer we fully intended to leave for other fields of labor about September fifth, but the churches would not consent to our going. There were some applications for the pastorate but the pastoral committee felt that the writer, being familiar with the field, would give them better service than a new man, so we finally consented to give them another year of service. To show their appreciation they added $200 to the salary. Whether the decision turns out for the best or not it certainly encourages the pastor to know that his people would rather have him than a new man, and that they are willing to make some sacrifice to retain his services.

No great progress has been made since the new church year started, but there have been some things that were encouraging. Because of special meetings in other churches we did not have a revival this fall. (The village is too small to have more than one meeting going on at one time). We did, however, have a very pretty baptismal service in December at which two young girls were buried with Christ in baptism. One of these was Lillian, the youngest daughter of Elder John Porte and sister to brother Robert Porte now at Dallas Centre, Iowa. The other was Vianna Hackett whose name appears in the Evangelist as a contributor to missions and who has always earned her own contribution even when she was a little girl. Lillian joined the Sergeantsville church and Vianna the Calvary church and we are expecting great things from both of them.

January 14 was a great day for the pastor and his good wife. Early in the day a good brother stopped at the parsonage and unloaded several bags of corn and oats. This was followed by others until we had enough feed for horse and chickens to last for several weeks. In the evening though it was exceedingly windy and cold, about 40 people from both churches and community gathered bringing with them enough eats to serve lunch for all present and keep the pastor from going hungry for several days. Among the good things, such as coffee, sugar, canned goods, etc., was ten pounds of real butter. (And butter was 75c a pound, too.) After a pleasant evening spent in love and fellowship the people departing leaving behind a purse of $76.56 to show that they were willing to add a bonus to the increase in salary mentioned above. When we added the value of grain and butter and other food to the $76.56 we found we had nearly $100 in our donation. This was fine indeed and we were made to feel that we had a very real place in the hearts of the community. We appreciate this and hope to continue worthy of the esteem shown by their substantial gifts.

Our work has not been all sunshine and roses, however. There have been problems to solve, difficulties to meet, afflictions to bear. One of the saddest situations the pastor and church have had to meet was the death of Sister May Merrill, our efficient organist and president of our Christian Endeavor society, who died of the "flu." May was one of those splendid Christians who love their Lord, are always in their place and can be depended on to do all they can for the advancement of the Kingdom among men. We shall miss her and her place will be hard to fill but our loss is her gain.

Just now the church here is contemplating some improvements. The order has already been placed for a pipeless furnace and the W. M. S. is talking about a new carpet for the platform and aisles of the church. Some repair work on both church and parsonage will be made which will increase our facilities for greater service for Christ and his church.

The work at Calvary has been moving forward slowly but surely. Stormy weather and snow-blocked roads have hindered our progress a great deal but there were some things that caused us to feel encouraged. The weekly cottage prayer service has kept up well in interest and attendance. The people have a mind to pray and are willing to put something into the meetings s well as take something out and this makes ror an interesting and helpful service. At our recent "All Day Business meeting reports showed that the church was in good condition and prospects were bright for larger activities as soon as weather settled and roads were in condition to induce people to come to service,

Some improvements were made at this point last fall. The people said, "Let there be light and there was light." New 600 candle power mantle kerosene lamps were installed and paid for by the church and W. M. S., thereby greatly increasing our facilities for evening services. Then some work was done on the foundation of the church which will add to stability of structure and if possible we hope in the near future to give it a coat of paint and thus increase the attractiveness of the building in which we preach the old-fashioned gospel of our Lord and Savior Jesus Christ.

Plans are under way for a revival meeting to be held early in May. Brother I. D. Bowman, who had much to do with founding this church, will conduct these services and we are expecting big things of God.

Thus the readers of the Evangelist can see, that while we don't report often, we are trying to advance the cause of Christ among men and bring honor and glory to his name. We pray for God's Israel everywhere.

MORTON L. SANDS.

NEW PARIS, INDIANA

The New Paris church has again experienced a happy time and the cause this time was a two weeks' revival meeting whoch closed last Sunday evening with 11 accessions. We can not express our joy, nor can we thank hte Lord enough for the way he so richly blessed us in this meeting. He has been richly blessing us all along, but this is the best yet. To him we give all the honor, glory and praise.

Rev. McInturff of Goshen held our meeting for us and with our pastor, Rev. Duker, made a fine to work for the Lord: "Bro. Mac" is an able speaker and is well loved by all and from the first night of the meeting, all liked the splendid sermons he brought us, as they appealed to the common sense and good reason of the people, and his every statement was backed by the Word of God.

We certainly appreciate Goshen's goodness in loaning us their pastor for our meeting and we feel quite certain that with the splendid results attained that they will be willing to loan him again when we are ready for our next meeting. We also appreciate the great help they gave us by being present in so many numbers themselves, as this helps so much when the membership is as small as ours. The people from the other churches of our town were present in goodly numbers and helped as though it had been their own meeting. The spirit and co-operation was fine.

Last evening our little congregation attended the Goshen church and shared with them in their prayermeeting, followed by our baptismal services. May the Lord richly bless these new followers of his and may their influence do much toward the upbuilding of his kingdom.

We are now looking forward with keen interest to Easter Sunday, as in the morning we shall take our Foreign Missionary offering and we assure you that we thoroughly enjoy giving to these special offerings of the church and then in the evening we shall have our communion service, and we know that the Lord will bless this big day that we have planned.

May we have the continued interest in your prayers that we may do his will here at New Paris.
MRS. FRANK ROSCOE,
Cor. Sec'y.

WILLIAMSTOWN, OHIO

On Sunday evening, January 25, our evangelistic meetings came to a close. Brother Wolford, of Elkhart Indiana preached earnestly to us for three weeks. His messages were gladly received and reverently listened to by all. They were of the "Whole Gospel" variety for which the world is hungering so much. We could not help but realize

that the Holy Spirit was in our midst and was making his presence felt in our hearts. Although the number that confessed Christ as their Savior was not as large as we had hoped and prayed for yet we believe that much good has been accomplished and that the membership has received added strength to go on with the Lord's work in these times that try and test men's souls. We pray and trust God that much fruit may be garnered from the seed sowing done in these meetings.

Beginning with the first week the weather was against us almost continuously to the close. Roads were blocked with snow and impassable. The use of automobiles was out of the question. After all, we had fair sized crowds, but not near what we would have had had the roads been good.

Three made the great confession. Two young girls were baptized by the pastor on Monday evening following the close of the meeting. They were later taken into the church. If only one soul had been saved for service in the kingdom of Jesus Christ, it would have been worth while. So we feel that we have not toiled in vain.

After the last service of the meeting on Sunday evening, I heard many expressions such as these: "Brother Harley certainly did his best." "He did all he could." "If sinners are not saved they have no one to blame but themselves." After all, what more can we do than our best. Let us keep in mind that duties are ours and that we must labor in the vineyard, but God recordeth the results in heaven.

I know that Brother Wolford has a warm place in our hearts at "Billtown," and our best wishes attend him wherever he may be called to labor in the kingdom of his Lord and ours.   MARK B. SPACHT, Pastor.

FIELD REPORT OF EVANGELISTIC LEAGUE
By W. S. BELL
Washington, D. C.

I met with the church here for three services and was greeted with fine audiences each evening. I was pleased with the work. The church building makes a cozy and homelike appearance, well located being about 10 blocks from the Capitol building and faces Pennsylvania avenue. I found the people of a spiritual type and very receptive of the gospel. I was surprised at the Sunday School and learned that their offerings run between $15 and $20 per Sunday. Brother Lyon has certainly done a good work here and may God's blessing abide on these faithful ones. The work of the league was enthusiastically received and given support.

Philadelphia Pennsylvania

I held this meeting in the Third church of which Brother Braker is the pastor. This is a mission church located in the north part of the city in a locality where the prospects are good for building up a good strong church. The work here with a very small beginning has made a commendable growth, considering that Brother Braker holds a position that takes all his time during the week and can only give Sundays to the work. The Mission Boards should make provision so that Brother Braker could give all his time to the work here. The present building is not large enough to care for the live, growing Sunday School, which in attendance is about 170. A new and larger building is needed badly. The services were well attended and nearly filled the house every night. I found the people willing workers and good helpers. The Lord blessed our efforts and a large number made the good confession and dedicated their lives to Christ. . I enjoyed my trip here and shall expect to hear good news of progress here in the years to come.

My next campaign will be with Brother Snyder at Milledgeville, Illinois, which begins April fourth.

LONG BEACH, CALIFORNIA

These are busy days in the Long Beach church, and even busier days are just ahead of us. We feel we have reason to rejoice because of our offering just forwarded to the Near East Relief. After preaching a sermon on the text, ''She weepth sore in the night, and her tears are on her cheeks,'' (Lam. 1:2); we asked for a freewill offering and over $1400 were cheerfully given. This makes more than $3,000 that has gone forth from this church in the last two years for Armenia. The offering just taken was everybody's offering. We have not heard of more than $100 given by any one individual.

Moreover, though the call for Armenia came closely to Easter, we are not thinking that it is going to lessen our Easter offering a whit. Our goal is $3,000 for foreign missions on Easter Sunday. That is $6.66 per member. We just noticed on the Four Year Program page of the ''Evangelist'' that 40c is the goal for foreign missions. Well, that may be according to the program of the Four Year Program Committee, but some missionaries will be begging for bread before another year rolls about if we do not exceed that pitiful sum per capita. Last year, we received over .80 cents per member. This year we are not thinking of the Brethren church going less than $1 per member on Easter Sunday. We have just read somewhere that ''It is a crime to be small in these spacious days.'' We can say ''Amen,'' to that much, anyway. The Long Beach church has sent out more than $1,900 for foreign missions within the last four months. But what of it? That has just whetted our appetites! Easter is at hand! It is surely ''a crime to be small'' on that day. How will we do it? By everybody, down to the last little tot on the Cradle Roll, doing their ''bit.'' After we have done all we can, what is it beside the unspeakable gift of our God unto us? Nothing! nothing at all!

Moreover, we are planning to begin a revival—''A Bible Conference and Evangelistic Campaign,''—as the coming evangelist wants us to term it. It will be conducted by the well-known evangelist, French Oliver. We are planning for a great campaign of real old-fashioned gospel evangelism. We shall leave results to God. That is his business. It is our business to see that the largest number of men possible in this city shall hear the real gospel of the grace of God. The Lord will add to the church such as should be saved. We are now at work trying to secure the best leader of song we can get. All in all, this campaign should prove to be the

greatest we have ever held in our church here. Pray for us, brethren of like precious faith. Dr. French Oliver will not only conduct our evangelistic campaign, but he promises the officers of our local district conference that he will be with us throughout the ten days' Bible and Church conference that will meet as usual here in our church the last ten days in July.

Another treat before us here in our church comes in the shape of ''The Victorious Life Conference for the Pacific Coast,'' bringing messages from the best expositors of the Word in this country along the line of the deeper things of the spiritual life. The news just came to us over the wire this morning that it was decided to hold this conference here June 20th to 28th. While this is an interdenominational conference, yet, as many of our brethren and sisters in California as possible should try to attend this conference. The times greatly demand conferences of this sort.

Last Sunday, it was our privilege to have with us, Captain Eli Bertalot, of Babbio, Italy, who was the first chaplain called to serve the Protestants in the World War in Italy. He served all through the war and carries three decorations, one of which made him ''A Knight of the Crown of Italy.'' In England, he would be called ''Sir.'' Two members of his church at Babbio serve as governesses of the King of Italy. But he did not come to us with a message concerning the war. He came to Long Beach as a special delegate to the churches of the United States and Canada, from the synod of the Waldensian church in Italy. His message concerning the past history and present status of the only church in the world clinging to the true faith, without having passed through the Reformation, was of intense interest. There are 25,000 members of his faith in the Waldensian valleys'' (really mountain sides) left in Italy. The World War has opened a ''great door and effectual'' for these people to carry the Protestant faith into the Catholic cities of Italy. Doubtless, this is the logical way to evangelize Italy,—assist the the Protestant forces that are now there. We gave him an offering of something over $140 to help the good work along—yes, that we might have some fruit in Italy also.

We almost neglected to mention the fact that it was the privilege of the church here to have with us last month, Dr. I. R. Dean of Toronto, Can', of the ''Tabernacle Church'' of that city. He gave us eight days of Bible lectures on the Book of Romans. These lectures brought us a veritable feast of good things. Dr. Dean proved himself to be one of the richest expositors of the Word we have heard in all our life.

The church here has made a forward step in the employment of Brother Percy Yett, a recent graduate of the Bible Institute of Los Angeles, as assistant to the pastor in the work of the church and Sunday School visitor. He has taken hold of the work like one who has been on the job for years, and his work is already telling on the church and Sunday school attendance. He seems to fit into the work perfectly, for which we are all rejoicing.

One week ago last Sunday night we bap-

tized four. On the preceding Thursday night, we baptized three, of more than ordinary interest, since all three are candidates for the foreign field. One young man, a graduate of the Riverside high school, will enter The Bible Institute in Los Angeles immediately, taking a preparatory course for two years, with the intention of going to the African field. The other two, Brother and Sister Charles Rush, are graduates of The Bible Institute, and are ready for service. They feel that the Lord calls them to the South American field. It may be of further interest to know that Sister Rush is a sister of our beloved sister, Mrs. Mary Rollier, who recently laid down her life for the Master on African soil.

Thus the work here moves along. It moves, but not by the power of that big man—Big Money—Big Machinery Movement known as ''The Interchurch World Movement.'' There has been much said in ''The Evangelist'' in favor of this Movement. For forty or more good and sufficient reasons, the church of which it is my privilege to be pastor, will never give any support either directly or indirectly to this Movement until it can be shown that we are ignorant or misinformed.

Just let me give one reason out of the forty or more. No church of which I am pastor, while I am pastor, will ever form any alliance with any spiritual force or forces that refuses to declare itself or themselves definitely on the great fundamental doctrines of the Deity of Jesus, salvation through his blood by grace and through faith with good works following, the inspiration of the infallible Word of God through the Holy Ghost, the resurrection of the body of Jesus Christ as the earnest of the bodily resurrection of the bodies of all his saints and the personality of the Holy Ghost. The only possible reason for silence on these doctrines that any ''Movement'' can have is that they wish us to ally ourselves in a spiritual work with those who do not believe these doctrines. With such, we can have no fellowship. It is forbidden of the Holy Ghost. II John 8:11. Once again, the program of the Interchurch World Movement is the program of post-millennialism and of Modernism with its ''social gospel'' program. When you get thru trying to ''save society'' with all this cumbersome machinery, you will have little time left for individual soul-winning. As a matter of sheer fact, it is utterly contrary to God's revealed program, as held by men and women of pre-millenial faith. And men and women of pre-millenial faith who are being enticed into it by the holy robes with which it first comes to greet us, need to examine carefully as to the good toward which this movement moves. However, it will never reach its own goal. Why? Because ANY PROGRAM FOR WINNING THIS WORLD FOR CHRIST THAT IS NOT IN HARMONY WITH GOD'S PROGRAM IS DOOMED TO FAILURE. This world will be won for Christ, but it will be done according to God's program, and not man's.

But of these things we expect to speak later. This was not the purpose of this article when we sat down to write. We merely wanted to say here that so far as the Long

Beach church is concerned, we do not expect to give any strength that we may have to the Interchurch World Program either directly or indirectly.

LOUIS S. BAUMAN.

Business Manager's Corner

NEW RECRUITS

No army can long remain efficient without receiving from time to time a goodly number of "new recruits." The "old guard" will, in time, become too old to be efficient unless it is gradually strengthened by the addition of new blood.

The Evangelist Honor Roll has been a mighty factor in the work of the Brethren church for the past three years, and no one can tell just how far-reaching the effect of The Evangelist in thousands of new homes has been in bringing the rank and file of the church to a better support of all departments than ever before. Of course there have been a number of things that have combined together in bringing about these greater results, but we like to believe that the enlarged subscription list of the Evangelist has had no small part in it. But like the "old guard" this Honor Roll must receive new recruits or it will gradually disappear. Now and then we lose a church from the Honor Roll and we just quietly lay them to rest among the "honored dead," and revere their memories for the good they have done and sincerely pray that they may be resurrected at no distant day to again take their places among the churches that have found it impractical to try to get along without having the Evangelist as an assistant pastor to supplement the work their pastor tries to do on Sunday and in his pastoral visitation. The pastor can not call on every family in his parish once a week, but the Evangelist makes its weekly calls and keeps the work of the entire church before the members at all times.

Since our last report we have added two most worthy churches to the Honor Roll. First of all South Bend has come in with flying colors. Not much fuss was made about this campaign, as Brother Rench, the pastor, is not the "fussy" kind; but for a number of months he has had his committees quietly at work and their work counted. A most splendid list was sent us from South Bend and we are confident the new readers of the paper will be delighted with the outcome of their campaign. We certainly welcome South Bend among our number.

We can next report one of the most amazing transformations that has taken place in any church since this campaign was started. It is casting no criticism on any one individual when we say that some of our churches have never realized the helpfulness of the Evangelist and that there has been altogether too little support given to the paper. We have come in contact with a number of that kind. It has not been premeditated lack of support, but simply a lack of inspiration, or something similar, that has kept them from waking up, but when they have wakened up they have done marvelous things. This was true of Mil-

ford, Indiana. We have never had the subscription list from Milford that we thought we ought to have, but it was perhaps our own fault as much as that of any one else. It was perhaps only a lack of system that would reach this field. But, thank the Lord, the "budget system" did the work. Brother Kolb, their pastor, plainly told the official board that their church would not be "in the running" in this victory year of the Four Year Program Campaign, unless they came across with the Evangelist also. While Milford may be a little conservative its members are not "pikers" when it comes to a show down, and they came across gloriously with an increase of NINE HUNDRED per cent in their subscription list. We are just a little afraid the Milford postmaster will suffer from a stroke of apoplexy when this week's Evangelist must be distributed among the good citizens of Milford. Well, we thank you Brother Kolb and all your hosts of loyal Brethren. There are only about three real churches left in Indiana that are not on the Honor Roll and we hope these three will be safely within the fold before the meeting of General Conference. "Indiana unanimous" would be a fine slogan to rally all the churches.

In addition to the two new churches that have been added to our Roll we are pleased to state that we have received the renewal of the list from Bryan, Ohio, and the pastor, Brother Maus, says it was the easiest list to secure he has ever had. His people are all delighted with the paper. This makes the third year for Bryan. The renewal of the list from Huntington, Indiana was also received some time ago, but apparently we failed to make mention of it before. This is the second year for Huntington and Brother Brower is to be commended for the efficient work he has done as pastor of this mission church. Another one of the churches that as won its place on the Honor Roll for the third year is the First Brethren church of Los Angeles, California, W. N. Jennings, pastor. This list was sent in quite awhile ago, but we have not marked the church up until now. We appreciate this list just as much as we do any of the others and it was only an oversight that its credit was not marked up on the Roll long ago.

We have received several more calls for copies of the Brethren Annual from pastors to whom we mailed copies immediately after they were completed. If all the pastors to whom we sent a supply will dispose of the number sent, there will be no "left overs" this year as the supply we now have in the office is just about exhausted. This is as it should be. "Left overs" will destroy the profits in any business.

R. R. TEETER,
Business Manager.

EVANGELIST HONOR ROLL

The following churches having met the requirements laid down by the Brethren Publishing Company regarding the placing of the Evangelist in the homes of the congregations are entitled to a place on the Evangelist Honor Roll:

Church	Pastor
Akron, Ind., (New Highland),	.... (Vacant)

Allentown, Pa., 3rd Year, ... A. L. DeLozier
Ankenytown, Ohio, 3rd Yr., ... A. L. Lyan
Ardmore, Indiana, ... A. T. Wirick
Ashland, Ohio, 3rd Yr., ... C. A. Garber
Beaver City, Nebr. (3rd Yr.), ... E. S. Flora
Berlin, Pa., (2nd Yr.), ... I. B. Trout
Berne, Indiana, 3rd Year, .. W. F. Johnson
Bryan, Ohio, 3rd Yr. .... G. L. Maus
Buckeye City, O., ... Glen Peterson
Burlington, Ind., 2nd Yr., ... W. T. Lytle
Center Chapel, Ind., ... K. R. Ronk
Cerro Gordo, Ill., ... D. A. C. Teeter
Clay City, Indiana, (3rd Yr.), S. C. Henderson
College Corner, Ind, 3rd Yr. ... L. A. Myers
Conemaugh, Pa., (3rd Yr.), ... E. F. Byers
Darwin, Indiana, ... W. T. Lytle.
Dallas Center, Iowa, 2nd Yr. .... R. F. Porte
Dayton, Ohio, ... E. M. Cobb
Denver, Indiana, 2nd Yr., ... L. A. Myers
Dutchtown, Indiana, ... Homer Anderson.
Elkhart, Ind., (2nd Yr.); ... H. H. Wolford
Eaton, Ind., (Maple Grove), .. H. E. Eppley
Eau Claire, Wisconsin, ... J. A. Baker
Fair Haven, Ohio (3rd Yr.), ... B. F. Owen
Falls City, Nebr. (3rd Yr.), ... H. F. Stuckman
Fillmore, Calif. (2nd Yr.), , Sylvester Lowman
Flora, Ind., 3rd Yr. .... S. C. Henderson
Fostoria, Ohio (2nd Yr.), ... M. S. White
Fremont, Ohio (2nd Yr.), H. M. Oberholtzer
Goshen, Indiana, ... J. A. McInturff
Gretna, Ohio, 3rd Yr., ... Edwin Boardman
Gratis, Ohio .... C. E. Beekley
Hagerstown, Maryland .... A. B. Cover
Huntington, Ind., 2nd Yr., ... J. W. Brower
Hudson, Ia., ... Edwin Boardman
Johnstown, Pa., 1st Ch., 3rd Yr. J. F. Watson
Johnstown, Pa., 3rd Ch., ... Geo. H. Jones
Lanark, Ill. (3rd Yr.), .. B. T. Burnworth
La Verne, Calif., 2nd Yr., ... T. H. Broad
Leon, Iowa, ... Geo. T. Ronk
Leon, Iowa, (Crown Chapel), .. Geo. T. Ronk
Leon, Iowa (Union Chapel), .. G. T. Ronk
Limestone Tenn., 2nd Yr., ... Mary Pence
Long Beach, Cal. (3rd Yr.) .... L. S. Bauman
Loree, Indiana. 2nd Yr. ..... C. A. Stewart
Los Angeles, Cal 1st Ch. ... N. W. Jennings
Los Angeles Cal, Comp. Av. 2d Yr. J. C. Beal
Louisville, O., (3rd Yr.), ... A. M. Riddle
Masontown, Pennsylvania,... Martin Shively
Mexico, Ind. (3rd Yr.), ... J. W. Clark
Milford, Indiana .... C. E. Kolb
Milledgeville, Ill., (3rd Yr.), Miles J. Snyder
Morrill, Kans., (3rd Yr.), ... A. E. Whitted
Mt. View, Va., (3rd Yr.), ... J. E. Patterson
Muncie, Indiana, 2nd Yr., ... J. L. Kimmel
Nappanee, Ind. (3rd Yr.) .... E. L. Miller
New Enterprise, Pa., ... Edward Byers
New Lebanon, O., ... G. W. Kinzie
New Paris, Ind., 2nd Yr., ... W. I. Duker
North English, Iowa, ... Homer Anderson
N. Liberty, Ind. (2nd Yr.), .. C. C. Grisso
New Enterprise, Ind., ... P. M. Fisher
Oakville, Ind., (2d Yr.), ... W. R. Deeter
Peru, Indiana, ... Geo. C. Carpenter
Philadelphia, Pa (1st Br.) .. Alva J. McClain
Philadelphia, Pa., 3rd church, .. J. R. Bauker
Pittsburgh, Pa., ... H. M. Harley
Portis, Kans., (3rd Yr.), ... Roy Brumbaugh
Rittman, Ohio, ... J. Allen Miller
Roann, Indiana (2nd Yr.), ... Willis E. Ronk
Roanoke, Indiana .... W. F. Johnson
Roanoke, Va., ... L. G. Wood
South Bend, Indiana, ... G. W. Rench
Sidney, Indiana, 2nd Yr., ... L. A. Myers
Tiosa, Indiana (2nd Yr.) .... C. C. Grisso
Turlock, California, ... J. Francis Reagan
Washington, C. H., O., 3rd Yr., B. S. Stoffer
Waterloo, Iowa, (3rd Yr.), ..W. H. Beachler
Whittier, Cal., (2nd Yr.), ... A. V. Kimmel
White Chapel, Mo., ... G. T. Ronk
Windber, Pennsylvania, ... E. F. Byers
Yellow Creek, Pa., ... Edward Byers
Zion Hill, Ohio, ... A. L. Lynn

Volume XLII
Number. 14

April 14
1920

The BRETHREN EVANGELIST

·ONE·IS·YOUR·MASTER·AND·ALL·YE·ARE·BRETHREN·

PICTURE FURNISHED BY THE UNIONTOWN, PENNSYLVANIA SUNDAY SCHOOL.

THE FAMILY ALTAR

In how many Brethren homes is it found?

What is taking its place?

Published every Wednesday at Ashland, Ohio. All matter for publication must reach the Editor not later than Friday noon of the preceding week.

The Brethren Evangelist

When ordering your paper changed give old as well as new address. Subscriptions discontinued at expiration. To avoid missing any numbers renew two weeks in advance.

George S. Baer, Editor

R. R. Teeter, Business Manager

OFFICIAL ORGAN OF THE BRETHREN CHURCH

Subscription price, $2.00 per year, payable in advance.
Entered at the Post Office at Ashland, Ohio, as second-class matter.
Acceptance for mailing at special rate of postage provided for in section 1103, Act of October 3, 1917, authorized September 9, 1918.
Address all matter for publication to Geo. S. Baer, Editor of the Brethren Evangelist, and all business communications to R. R. Teeter, Business Manager, Brethren Publishing Company, Ashland, Ohio. Make all checks payable to the Brethren Publishing Company.

TABLE OF CONTENTS

EDITORIAL

Some Characteristics of the Home In Which Christ Dwells

The first and most influential institution in the world is the home. Before the state or the church, the home was a vital element in the human race. Its beginning dates from the beginning of man's being on the earth. It is the thing that every man seeks, and without which he is a lone and wandering star. It is the center of life and the determiner of character. The success of every day's labor, the worthiness of every ambition and the brightness and strength of every life is largely what the home makes it. If life has any tender associations, if any pleasing images, if any deep emotions, they are to be found in the home. Here is to be found the law of all hearts and the spell that cannot be broken by time or change. No other single earthly influence is so powerful and so far-reaching; it extends beyond the grave, for it is not broken by death. And nothing is more important than that the home shall be of the highest order. Whether its influence shall be for weal and for woe, whether it is school of Virtue or Vice, whether it turns out saints or villains, depends more largely than on any other one thing on whether or not Christ is an acknowledged and revered member of that household. He alone can make the home what it ought to be. He alone can distill its dross, sanctify its sorrows, refine its pleasures, tender its relations, purify its thoughts, sweeten its spirit and brighten its hope. Only when Christ dwells in the home can it be all that he who ordained it intended that it should be. On such a home it is pleasant to meditate.

The home in which Christ dwells is the home in which prayer is wont to be made. A Christian home is a praying home invariably, for our Lord loves to hold converse with those with whom he dwells. And yet there are homes which claim the name of Christ but never utter a prayer. There are households which pride themselves on their religious pretentions, but they have no family altar and they have no private devotions. Can it be that Christ dwells in such homes? There was a home in which father and daughter had not spoken to each other for years, and yet they dwelt under the same roof. Will Christ dwell an unwelcome guest in a home? Will he remain with those who refuse to pray? No, it is folly to call a home Christian that has no prayer, for there our Lord cannot dwell, nor will his Spirit dominate the lives of those who there abide. And if Christ be not there, what will soften the voice, sweeten the temper, strengthen the patience, brighten the eyes and warm the heart? Certainly prayer is essential to the Christian home.

The home where Christ dwells is a home where much is made of the Bible as a daily guide in the path of righteousness and as a means of cultivating the mind of Christ and strengthening the faith. The Psalmist declares, "Thy word is a lamp unto my feet and a light unto my path," and we too find much need of the light that shines

forth from the enlightening pages of the Bible, that we may be guided aright amidst the winding paths of the home-life and in the various perplexing situations in life's daily toil. Again we hear the aged singer singing, "Thy words have I hid in my heart that I might not sin against thee;" and how sorely do we need the steadying, strengthening influence of God's word in our hearts from day to day. Jesus prayed, "Sanctified them through thy truth," and then declared, "Thy word is truth." What domestic bark can safely sail life's changing sea without the guiding chart which came from God, and who but needs the sanctifying influence of the Truth that makes free, to keep from allowing his own selfishness, personal pride and wilfulness to rock the family boat. If the Bible were read more widely and regularly and devotedly in the so-called Christian homes, husbands and wives would find their lives mingling more in the depths of the truth, and parents and children would be bound more strongly together in "holy, helpful fellowship and mutual reverence and love. Then would the home indeed be a "household of faith" and a place where Christ would love to dwell as he did in the home of Bethany.

The home where Christ delights to dwell is the home where love prevails. God is love and Jesus Christ is the Son of love and surely he who came forth from Love would rejoice to find an atmosphere of love in a home that he might dwell therein. There are many homes where love abides. But love is more unadulterated in some homes than others. In some homes love is like the sun behind an almost total eclipse; it is not permitted to shine out much. There is love there, but it is almost concealed by the shadows cast by family differences. In other homes love is permitted to shine out as brightly as the sun in mid-day, and in every ray of love there are many little expressions of love, just as in every sunbeam there are millions of minute rays of light. Life never seems so sweet as when in a home where love finds continual flow in little acts of kindness, tender words, beaming eyes, sweet laughter and loving confidences. But this love must not be "like the torch-blaze of natural excitement which is easily quenched, but like the serene, chastened light which burns as safely in the dry east wind as in the stillest atmosphere. Let each bear the other's burden the while—let each cultivate the mutual confidence which is a gift capable of increase and development—and soon it will be found that kindliness will spring up on every side." "There is nothing on earth so beautiful as the household on which Christian love forever smiles, and here religion walks a counsellor and a friend. No cloud can darken it, for its twin stars are centered in the soul. No storms can make it tremble, for it has a heavenly support and a heavenly anchor."

God made man to love, and in the fact that man can love he is most like God, for his outstanding characteristic, the one that appeals to man the most is that he is love. The Apostle of Love says beseechingly, "Beloved, let us love one another." And our Lord himself says, "A new commandment I give unto you that ye love one another." And where more than any other place may this love be rightfully expected to be found than in the home. When God gave man a body he must needs give him life, but when he gave him a heart he must give him love. And where hearts are knitted together in the home with love, there Christ makes his abode.

EDITORIAL REVIEW

From Warsaw, Indiana, A. E. Thomas pastor.—"Easter, 1920 will be remembered because we gave the largest offering ever for foreign missions. The amount was $342.00. Praise the Lord, we said, and all the people said, Amen."   "A. E. THOMAS."

Brother B. F. Owen is to preach the baccalaureate sermon for the high school graduating class at Glenford, Ohio, where he is pastor, on April 18, and is to perform a similar service for the high school graduates of Brownsville on May 23.

Your attention is called to "The First Easter Reports," which are most interesting and encouraging. Send Easter offerings to William A. Gearhart, 906 Conover Building, Dayton, Ohio. Doubtless he will be glad to get them as promptly as possible.

Brother William Kolb desires that every one shall read his article on the Interchurch and in view of the fact that a number of pastors have written for information concerning participation in the financial campaign, we call attention to his article.

If you have any public school teachers in your congregation, suggest that they come to Ashland College for a six or a twelve months term of normal this summer. The first term begins May 10. An exceptionally strong faculty has been engaged. Ashland is the most economical place you can find and a beautiful place as well. Write to President Jacobs for information.

Brother Albert Trent reports more White Gift offerings. The persistence with which our churches continue to send in belated offerings when they were hindered from doing so at the proper time shows that there is a genuine desire on the part of nearly all the churches to do their share in the support of the various interests of the church at large. This causes rejoicing to every leader.

Brother Reed who so regularly keeps the brotherhood informed concerning the splendid progress of the First church of Los Angeles writes a complimentary note concerning "The Teacher and Educator," one of our own publications. He says, "I have been using this help almost continuously since it was first published and find it one of the best in the field."

It has been a long time since Brother Braker has personally reported for the growing Third church of Philadelphia, however we have been kept informed of the progress there by some of his able assistants. He is doing a noble work there and has gathered about him a very efficient and faithful group of workers. Brother Bell's ministrations resulted in a great ingathering, which will doubtless mean much for the future of the church.

Brother Horner, our correspondent from the Goshen, Indiana, church, gives a splendid report of the progress of the work at that place. Their pastor, Brother McInturff, recently exchanged pulpits with Brother Wolford of the Elkhart church and the experiment seems to have been greatly enjoyed by the Goshen congregation and we dare say that Brother McInturff was also greatly appreciated by Elkhart.

It certainly took some courage to make an across-the-country trip such as Brother Thomas R. Howell made at the time he made it. But when you put a Brethren preacher and a Ford together they are likely to go anywhere there is a service to render. Brother Howell has taken

charge of the McLouth, Kansas, church, which is composed of about half Brethren and half Church of the Brethren members, and it is pleasing to know how harmoniously they work together. It is a lesson that ought to be learned by the whole Dunker family. Perhaps we are learning it more than we realize.

Brother Clarence Kolb, pastor of the Milford church, has been made director of the financial drive which is to be made in that state at the time of the United Simultaneous Financial Ingathering under the direction of the Interchurch World Movement. He writes that the pastors of that district recently met to organize and make plans for the campaign. It is interesting to note that Indiana led out in the college endowment campaign, and now is leading out in this larger and more inclusive campaign. The "Hoosier" churches usually take pride in carrying to a successful finish whatever they put their hands to.

Quite a number of Dr. Tombaugh's booklets, "Some Fundamental Christian Doctrines," were sent out to those who had ordered them at the Winona Conference, but for most of them we have not yet received remittance. Kindly sell the number you have and remit as promptly as possible. If you were mailed a booklet for which you had not previously paid, please send us 25 cents, the price of a single booklet postpaid. They are 20 cents when bought in quantities. If you have not ordered a copy, you should do so. It is a clear and concise presentation of some Christian fundamentals. It would be a splendid text-book for class study.

Prof. J. A. Garber was called upon to captain a team of workers to present the plans and purposes of the Interchurch World Movement in three county conferences in Ohio last week. In one county Fayette, the richest county in the state, where they held a conference, he was informed by the man who directed the survey that 60 percent of the people are entirely untouched by any direct efforts of the church. At the same time it is said that this county leads all the others in the number of divorces and was second from the standpoint of illiteracy. If the Interchurch Movement does nothing more it will open your eyes to the bigness of the untouched task right around the church doors.

HOME MADE SQUIBS

The man who is continually repenting but never amending is like the foolish man who continually pumps water out of his boat but never stops the leak.

What shall it profit a mother if her daughter become the belle of town and lose her own soul? Or what gaudy fashions and beautiful clothes shall she be able to give in exchange for lost virtue?

What shall it profit a man if he gain the whole world and lose his own boys because he had no time for them? Or what honor, or position, or wealth or service rendered can he give in exchange for his boys when they have once lost their manhood and self-respect?

How shall I be able to live aright amid the anxiety and tribulation of this world? If thou dost once every hour throw thyself by faith beyond all creatures into the abysmal mercy of God, into the sufferings of Christ, and into the fellowship of the intercession, then thou shalt receive power from above to rule over the world, and death and the devil and hell itself.—Jacob Behmen.

MY CREED

"I would be true, for there are those who trust me;
I would be pure, for there are those who care;
I would be strong, for there is much to suffer;
I would be brave, for there is much to dare;
I would be friend of all—the foe, the friendless;
I would be giving and forget the gift;
I would be humble for I know my weakness;
I would look up—and laugh—and love—and lift."

FOUR-YEAR PROGRAM PAGE
NOW THEN DO IT.—II Samuel 3:18
Conducted by Charles A. Bame

Victory Year

After Dr. Bame's words of introduction in a recent number of The Brethren Evangelist, it is fitting that some kind of a response be made by me. In accepting the appointment of director of Goal 16 and secretary-treasurer of the Four Year Program Committee, I am not unmindful of the large task that comes to me. If I had not known something of this before, it would have been very forcibly impressed upon my mind when I recently received by express a large box containing the accumulation of statistical cards covering the past three years and a lot of charts, tables, diagrams, etc., worked out by Brother Goughnour, my very worthy predecessor in this office. If there is anyone in the brotherhood so fortunate and so slow of understanding as to have believed the Secretary of the Four Year Program had a "snap" in a position of "honor," that person would be disillusioned if he looked at the mass of figures and detail work well done which I found in what Dr. Bame terms the "hope chest" recently received.

And so in undertaking to do the work which has been literally thrust upon me I approach it with a high sense of appreciation of the splendid work H. L. Goughnour performed in the first three years of our Program's history, and with the earnest hope that I shall be given the hearty co-operation of every Brethren pastor and congregation in order that this year, which marks the consummation of our efforts in our first great program, may indeed be a Victory Year.

In taking up the work of the director of Goal 16, it will be well to call your attention to the fact that this goal calls for "THE LARGEST AND BEST GENERAL CONFERENCE IN 1920 THAT WE HAVE EVER HAD, WITH 400 DELEGATES PRESENT." Every pastor and congregation ought to begin now to plan for the realization of this goal, bearing in mind that the primary purpose is not merely to have present 400 delegates but the far-reaching results that such attendance will mean in the future activities of the church.

Within the past three weeks it was my privilege to attend two great conferences: the Iowa Pastors' Conference in Des Moines and the Illinois Pastors' Conference in Chicago, under the auspices of the Interchurch World Movement. Similar conferences were held in every state of the Union. What purpose did the Interchurch World Movement have in view in holding these conferences? It was the same purpose for which any conference is held, namely, to put a program "over the top."

The Interchurch World Movement, great and big as it is, would fail utterly to work out its program were it not for its regional, state, and county conferences. Our general conference at Winona is of like value in relation to any program we as a denomination try to put across. We cannot co-ordinate and push forward our work to the best advantage without it. Consequently, every member who has at heart the best interests of the Brethren church should recognize the value and importance of our annual conference,

and lend every influence toward making it the best possible both in point of attendance and spirit of helpfulness.

Let us begin to seriously think about it and formulate our plans and pray for it.

MILES J. SNYDER.

A Good Start

Brother Snyder here makes his bow as the new secretary of the Committee. He makes a good start. His message has a good ring to it and I am sure that it is just what you expected of him. You see he has been keeping in touch with the Page and the Program. I know for I have the evidence right here in my study. He was one of the very first to report and gave one of the best reports, so he has won a right to talk right out in meeting about winning goals.

"Largest and Best"

I am glad that he calls attention to that slogan for our next conference. Now, if it is the best, it will have to be a very good one for during the last few years, we have had some very constructive conferences. Largest, it will surely be. I have not the slightest doubt that Brethrenism will turn out one of the finest delegations that ever graced beloved Winona, and they are fine. But, BEST! Did you notice that in the program? BEST! How can we make it BEST? Well, of course by just making it better than any one we have ever had.

Best is par excellence

If we have the best ever, it will be because we have prayed more than we ever did for a conference. So, we may as well begin right now to pray for it. I do not need to say to my readers that we do not pray enough. We all know it. Until some brother or sister prays like Mueller or Paul or Jesus, and until we see the results, not by what the prayer says but by a superior work for the Lord, I shall feel free to admonish us on the subject of prayer. We must pray for the next conference.

Then too, we must pray for ourselves. Pray that this organism of the body of Christ shall have no disease—no schism. We need to pray that individually, we shall represent the Great Head of the church in the measure of our capacity. "Put off" and "put on" (Col. 3:9-12). If every delegate shall read over and over until next conference that wonderful message and the other of Romans 14 and 15, we shall have a good chance to have the best.

Then third, if we shall have a great conference, we will study well the ambition and aspiration, (to put it into human words) of Jesus our Lord. What I mean is that we shall try to put ourselves into the world dreams of the Christ of God. The angels sang of his world conquest at his Birth. Though born provincially, he talked of world conquest. Never of less than the whole world did he think. Wonderful, that we at last have a generation that is trying to think in his terms. It must be so. Our next conference will be recreant to the Lord she professes to serve and follow, if she does not wisely plan to do her full share in the mighty task of saving the world in this generation.

The King is away but is waiting to return. Let us not be found idle when he arrives to reckon. WILL YOURS BE A VICTORY CHURCH IN THIS VICTORY YEAR? WILL YOU BE A VICTORY SERVANT? HE THAT OVERCOMETH SHALL INHERIT. "LARGEST AND BEST." AMEN!

BAME.

GENERAL ARTICLES

"Restoring the Old Family Altar."   By C. R. Koontz

"And these words, which I command thee this day shall be upon thy heart; and thou shalt teach them diligently unto thy children, and shall talk of them when thou sittest in thy house, and when thou walkest by the way, and when thou liest down and when thou risest up."

In the early Hebrew days the father was the priest, teacher, and lawgiver. He was first to incorporate the will of Jehovah in his own life, and to teach diligently and continually those of his own household. This tradition has been handed down from father to son until the present day when there is to be found practically the same Deuteronomic home among the Jewish people. Among our own people was set up what has been called the "Family Altar." Parents and children would daily gather together and there the father or mother, or both, would read the Word of God and offer prayer. Often during the long winter evenings neighbors would visit each other and during the visit would read and discuss some passage of Scripture. It is true that sometimes there were heated discussions for there was not always agreement over the interpretations of certain passages of Scripture. Be that as it may have been, out of it came an increased desire for the truth, not only among the old folks but also among the young, for at times they had discussions among themselves.

It has been said that "home makes the man." We may want to question this statement in some cases. We may cite such illustrious examples as Lincoln for instance. But it was Lincoln who said, "All that I am, or hope to be, I owe to my mother." Is it not a fact that the other institutions are dependent upon the home for the kind of men and women they produce? School teachers, both public, and Sunday, tell us they can only develop what the home sends. The business world, while in many cases lending a helping hand, has only time to declare what manner of man he is. And the church often can do little more than send Heaven's appeal to his heart.

At present there are grave dangers threatening the American home. These dangers are looming larger than the size of a man's hand. Our homes, many of them, are not the homes of our forefathers. Without stopping to enumerate these dangers, let us stop to consider at least one of the most deep seated of these dangers, namely, "The Decay of the Family Altar."

The father no longer holds the position of instructor of the will of God as did the Hebrew father. Seldom does he talk with his family upon religious topics. Family worship is a custom of the past. The children are growing up without knowledge of the Bible; and are unaccustomed to the hearing of their father's voice in prayer, many not even stopping a moment to give thanks unto God for their daily bread. Go to the "Old Fireside" and ask it what it knows of family worship. The answer returned reads somewhat as follows: Several chairs vacant, not caused by physical but spiritual death; subjects of conversation changed; and the Bible succeeded by papers, novels and other light, trashy literature. To sum it up in a few words, there is a deplorable lack of anything that savors of definite and systematic religious instruction for the young. In short; the old Mosaic injunction has been forgotten.

However, in the minds of some parents, eager to do their full duty, this condition is raising a great problem. They realize that the altar has been abolished, their children are not being instructed and they themselves are not drawing nigh to God as they should. To them the "Old Family Altar" seems inadequate. It would be like putting new wine into old wine skins. If we cannot return to the "Old Family Altar," let us not cease worship, but let us push forward and reconstruct a new altar. Where restoration is impossible, let "Reconstruction" be our motto.

The mere mention of some of the causes of the abolition of the altar may serve to give us a helpful clue toward the setting up of a new one. Hasty marriage coupled with easy divorce has brought the holy estate of matrimony into disrepute. While the woman, under no force of adverse circumstances, has forsaken the home to become an independent wage earner, the man has neglected the home. Necessity often takes him away from home during the working hours of the day, and preference too often the remainder of the time. The mad rush for material possessions and worldly pleasures has caused eventually the loss of many souls.

If the home is to be maintained, the right choice of partners must be insisted upon. The coming generation have a right to be born well. Heredity is a potent factor and should be duly recognized. Our farmers are very careful in the selection of fit stock for the building up of their herds but when it comes to family relationships their care ceases.

The next step is that of atmosphere and environment. From a physical standpoint, our physicians insist upon proper atmosphere. The child that is housed in a poorly ventilated room filled with impurities is liable to contract disease. The child as well as the adult is greatly influenced by their environment. If pure air is so beneficial to the lungs, why would not pure and undefiled religion be beneficial to the home? Having been born well, therefore, the next step is to bring them up in a religious atmosphere. It is no use to try it just on Sunday. or when the preacher pays you a visit, but constancy is the secret of success: The words uttered, All should manifest the Spirit of God.

Another fact that must not be overlooked is that our souls grow in the light of what they receive. The child must receive proper instruction if he is to grow spiritually. And, the adult that ceases to study sooner or later will find to his or her sorrow, that that which he seemeth to have, hath been taken away from them because of disuse. Parents feed, clothe and school their children in the most expensive way, but seldom instruct them in religion. The most potent reason being that they themselves do not know how to speak in no uncertain tone concerning the spiritual realities of God.

Parents, why will you continue to spend your money on your children for that which satisfieth not and withhold from them the religious culture that satisfieth both here and hereafter?

The need is clearly evident, but the question at once arises, how can the "Old Family Altar" be restored in such a busy time as ours? We have as much time as there is, and furthermore, we usually find time to do what we want to do. With the ever increasing demand that is made upon our time, there comes a way of saving time so the two are nearly balanced and it rests with the individual as to what his real desires are. The old form may not be adequate, doubtless will not, but the form is not as important as the spirit of the worship. The important thing is to worship the same God that the Hebrews did and read and teach the same Bible that our forefathers did.

Turn back again to the text and read it. Resolve to give it a fair trial and see if you will not find it the most joyful labor you have ever engaged in. See if it is not the real secret to the truly happy home.

Woodstock, Virginia.

The Christian's work in the world requires much sacrifice, forbearance, courage and hard toil, but it will be found worth all it now costs.

"A silver bell, even when carelessly touched, sends out sweet sounds. A Christian life, to all who meet and touch it, should ring the praise of God sweetly and clearly."

"The Christian Parents' Attitude Toward Some Popular Amusements"

By Mrs. C. E. Nicholas

Sin in the form of pleasure is the hardest of evil to conquer because it is pleasing and agreeable; it is hardest to resist because it appeals to human nature and especially to our youth.

It is right to moderately taste of those pleasures which gratify the innocent sensibilities of our nature and temperately to join in those rational amusements which refresh both the mind and body after exertion, and thereby gain strength for future energies. Sleep is necessary to restore the physical power of our body, so relaxations and amusements are useful in restoring the strength of the mind. The Scripture has said there is a time to dance and a time to sing, but there is a great risk of running to excess in these things and sinking into idleness and frivolity and becoming morally debased.

The love of pleasures and amusements, though many of such are not positively wrong, may come to absorb the whole heart and consume the time, making us insensible to our duties and finally incapable of discharging them—then what may have been a virtue has become a vice.

A Christian's life is a busy life. You can illy afford to spend the time God give for anything other than good. Besides God admits of no compromise with evil.

There may be no wrong in a social game of cards in the home. But should you allow it to consume your time, or stake money on the game, or play for valuables or prizes, then it is wrong; the social game has merged into gambling and gambling should never be tolerated in any home much less a Christian home. Parents should never teach their children crime and should be slow to believe gambling will stop at home any more than raffling will stop in our churches.

To play for favors or trifling expenses is demoralizing and should have no place in our homes.

Honesty should be taught and parents who teach their children it is wrong to steal should teach them it is wrong to win prizes and favors.

Our amusements like our affections should be exercised for themselves and not for profit. When our amusements are captured by our vices it is time to abolish them.

When pleasures and questionable amusements are urged upon you be "purposed in" your "heart that" you "will not defile yourself with them.

Another source of innocent pleasure is dancing—it is a popular amusement and is not wrong so long as each sex dances alone. But man was not satisfied to dance alone, so today the sexes dance in each other's arms with no timidity or thought of the wrong that may be done. So the one time innocent pleasure has assumed the form of one of our greatest social evils. It is doubtful if any one ever engaged in dancing (both sexes) without having an impure thought

suggested. This amusement is the source of many evils. Scores of divorce suits have their beginnings in the dance. Many a pure innocent girl has entered the ball room to return home ruined and disgraced.

Knowing the fascination of the popular dance, why are Christian (?) people so slow to decide against this evil? Instead of consenting to the wrong we should attack it. We are too silent on the subject for our silence oftentimes gives our consent. Christian parents should never consent to any form of pleasure that is associated with evil. Let us put our heels on such amusements as may ruin the purity of our womanhood and endanger our boys.

We are in the midst of the movie craze—it is patronized by all classes of people and because of this fact, its influence is far-reaching. The pictures thrown on the screens are of a sensational character and not a few times excite impure thoughts and are instigators of crime. Many a crime committed by our youthful criminals are traced to the door of the movie. For this reason I am opposed to the movie. We need to exercise care during the formative period of our children; their minds are as clay in the hands of the potter, moulded and shaped at will.

There are pictures of great educational value to the children but these are in the minority because they are unpopular to the movie fan.

The time spent in the movie is just that much time lost. As an institution it is the source of no good; it inspires no one. It is only a source of expense. Thousands of dollars are spent in it that should be put to better use.

There are so many harmless pleasures—pleasures that are not associated with evil,—there are amusements for our children that develop them mentally and physically, morally and spiritually; I see no reason why Christian parents should subject their children to the evil influences of the so-called popular amusements.

Paul says, abstain from all appearance of evil." He also says, "What fellowship hath righteousness with unrighteousness?" We need no proof that God and the wicked can have no fellowship. A man cannot say he has fellowship with God while he loves the world, its pleasures and its follies.

There is no neutral ground in the Christian life. You are either for Christ or against him. You either stand for the evils of today or you are against them. He is with us, who taught the apostles not to be overcome with evil but to overcome evil with good.

Faith gives power in the moral life as well as in the spiritual. I can do all things through him who strengtheneth me. It is our privilege to lay hold of this power that our lives may be living examples for our children. We must be champions of truth and unrelenting enemies of vice.

Dowagiac, Michigan.

Marriage and Divorce Contest.   By John F. Shoemaker

In the city of Muncie, Delaware county, Indiana, for the year 1919, there were 649 marriage licenses granted, and 442 persons asked for divorces. Thus for every three marriage licenses granted, two divorce suits were filed.

This deplorable showing caused the "Muncie Daily Press" to print the following statement: "The Press' wishes to know why this appalling situation exists here. It will give five dollars to the woman telling the best reasons for this condition, and five dollars to the man giving in the best way what he considers the reason and remedy for it. A dollar each will be given to five others whom judges may consider to give the next best five reasons and remedies. The letters to be confined to 150 words and the prizes to be awarded by a committee of five judges. Several hundred

letters were written, the writers representing at least four different counties. Among the contests were lawyers, ministers, newspaper writers, and many others in different walks of life. "The Press says that likely no contest ever attracted so much attention here as this one did. Throughout the entire circulating territory of the "Press" the letters poured in on every mail for days. The judges awarded two five dollar cash prizes as follows:

WINNER OF HIGHEST AWARD OFFERED TO WOMEN
Mrs. Jennie P. Williams of Muncie.

"Marriage and Divorce Editor:

"The divorce evil may be attributed to many things, namely: In the past the sexes have not received unbiased training at the hands of the father and mother; there has been lack of parental co-operation in governing children. The spiritual, moral, and mental development of the child has been neglected. The business woman is especially unprepared, because untrained for the problems of married life. Then, too, there are the war marriages, economic conditions, a desire for things not necessary for comfort, intemperance, gambling, prostitution questionable picture shows. There has been a spiritual relapse on the part of the church, a disrespect for all that is good, pure and holy. We are reaping the harvest of corruption and moral decay, caused by recent municipal conditions. The remedy is equality in married life—not subjection, but a continual walking together in sympathy, respect and forbearance for each other. Our only hope is the home, church and school, brought to a higher plane."

WINNER OF HIGHEST AWARD OFFERED TO MEN

John F. Shoemaker of Eaton

"Marriage and Divorce Editor:

"Five causes for divorce and the remedy. Causes: (1) An improper understanding of the original meaning, intent and purpose of marriage as instituted by God and sanctioned by Christ. (2) Marrying in the 'teen age' and the blinded 'puppy' love stage. (3) Marrying by the 'try-rule,' knowing that the courts will annul unsatisfactory marriages. (4) Marrying for beauty, wealth and popularity alone. (5) Jealousy, caused largely by the too intimate mixing of the married sexes.

Remedy: (1) A perfect understanding of God's idea of marriage. (2) Make the marriageable age twenty for females and twenty-three for males. (3) Make the marriage law too rigid for a trial marriage. (4) Teach young people to marry for real worth. Show them that beauty fades, wealth vanishes and popularity will not meet the high cost of living. (5) Get right with God, be true to the marriage vow, and the divorce courts will have little to do."

The judges in choosing the letter of Mrs. Jennie P. Williams as winner of the first prize for women, and the letter of John F. Shoemaker as winner of the first prize for men, say they were impressed by the fact that they covered the principal reasons as occurred to them as causes of domestic difficulties and also proposed a sane remedy for them. The "Press" says, "As the divorce court is the last resort of the unhappily married, pessimists declare that if two-thirds as many married persons ask freedom from marital bonds as seek marriage, that means that practically nobody is happily married, and that the other third suffer in silence.·

Do you believe that? The Press doesn't, it is frank to say. But the figures are startling and "figures don't lie."

This condition is one that the ministers of every church might well make the subject of more than one sermon. "Anti-congregational form of government, if nothing else, precludes divorce day" in the Muncie pulpits would seem now to be even more important than the "Anti-saloon day" used to be.

Eaton, Indiana.

The Interchurch Movement. By Wm. Kolb, Jr.

I very earnestly solicit special attention to this article. It is imperative that an effort be at once made to inform our people regarding the proposed financial budgets as they relate to our various interests, and to this end I want to enlist the co-operation of all who feel to help in the effort. The Interchurch financial year begins May 1st, the drive for money is to be started April 25th. All our members should be provided with means of designating their gifts for our projects, also for those not distinctively ours, if they wish. While the special drive is to cover the week April 25th to May 2nd, all funds received during the year for budgeted objects are to count in the totals. There will be two classes of funds, the "A" fund which is to include money designated by the givers for specified objects within the churches, and the "B" fund, which will include all undesignated funds. The "A" fund is to be handled within the various communions through their own regular channels. The "B" fund is to be paid direct to the Interchurch treasury and to be available for expenses, and the surplus if any, and it is expected this will be large, is to be divided among the participating churches or agencies in proportion to the amounts they receive within the fiscal year for budgeted objects, division to be made at the end of said fiscal year. Our financial efforts may continue until April 30th, 1921.

It is important to know at once names of pastors and others within the congregations who will help in the effort to inform our membership and friends of the results of the surveys made by the Interchurch, and who will volunteer to see that their churches are taken care of also in the financial solicitation drive. The time is desperately short but the publicity campaign from now on will greatly help. Advise me, please, at once whether or not you will enlist in the above effort. This is vital. I would like to have names of all who will work, including those who have already started. Let us know what you are doing; we want to make an every member canvass as far as possible. It is especially desirable that the facts revealed by the surveys be gotten to the people. They are appealing beyond description and once the people are informed they will be aroused and the result assured.

Subscription blanks for the "A" fund are the subject of further consideration and suggestions would be very useful. How do you say we shall do? The "B" fund subscription blanks will come through the Interchurch Movement. The denominational blanks must be supplied by the various churches.

Our connection with the movement has been the subject of favorable comment and, from some, of unfavorable criticism. There are those who seem to fear that the church has been committed to certain objects or plans that they cannot endorse, respecting this it should be evident, without comment, that nothing of this sort could be done. Our ultra-congregational form of government, if nothing else, precludes it. Nothing is more thoroughly established among us than that the local church is the last resort. Perhaps it would be well to again review our status. At a meeting representative of our various boards and activities, January 1st, after very careful discussion it was the sense of those present, with some exceptions, that while final action should be left until our boards could meet at conference, yet pending this, we enter into the spirit and program of the Movement so far as consistent with our denominational genius and identity, and that Brethren should be given an opportunity to designate that their gifts in the coming Interchurch drive be used in the interest of our denominational projects. Following this at a meeting of our College Board, January 29th, the trustees decided to co-operate in the movement for funds. Arrangements to this end were later made with the Interchurch. As none of our other boards could take official action prior to the time the proposed budget was to be published, all other interests of our church would be unrepresented unless provision could somehow be arranged. In submitting the matter to the Interchurch people they were willing to allow tentative budgets to be subject to the decision of our boards when they should meet. To accomplish this it was necessary to provide underwriting in the amount of 5 percent of budgeted askings. This underwriting has been personally provided, but our various boards are not officially obligated. They have the option of endorsing or rejecting what has been done in their interest. They are in position if they choose, to avail themselves of all the benefits without any risk that they do not care to assume.

(Continued on page 9)

T,HE BRETHREN PULPIT

Spiritualism, or What Is the Secret of the Medium?   By C. H. Ashman

When thou art come into the land which the Lord thy God giveth thee, thou shalt not learn to do after the abominations of those nations. There shall not be found among you any one that maketh his son or his daughter to pass through the fire, or that useth divination, or an observer of times, or an enchanter, or a witch. Or a charmer, or a consulter with familiar spirits, or a wizard, or a necromancer.—DEUTERONOMY 18:9-11; ALSO 12-14.

There are two positions we can take relative to the reputed manifestations of spiritualism. We may declare that they are all a fraud, all expressions of trickery and cunningness of hand. Recently, an eastern broker deposited $1,500 in a bank, offering to give it as a gift to any spiritualistic medium who could produce manifestations which he could not duplicate in sleight of hand. There can be no doubt, but that a large percent of the reputed manifestations of spiritualism is pure fraud. But this will not explain it all to the investigative mind. If we deny all on this basis, we show ourselves to be either ignorant or foolish. The other position we may take is that at least a part of these manifestations are genuine communications with spirits. We do not say the spirits of the dead, but spirits. Science, following the foolish vein that all things can be explained by natural laws, stands baffled by these genuine expressions. It can neither explain, deny, nor understand them. No Bible student dare deny them or he denies the Book itself. It is to the Bible and only to the Bible that we must go for a correct explanation concerning these genuine communications. Such men as Sir Oliver Lodge, having rejected the Bible, fall an easy prey to the deception of spiritualism. Not having real faith in the Bible, they turn to anything having even the appearance of the supernatural in it. Yes, every adherent of spiritualism has rejected real faith in the Bible.

Now, if certain manifestations of spiritualism are genuine, what is the secret of their power? Is it good or evil? We propose to prove from the Bible that spiritualism is the work of Satan through the fallen angels which are always at his command.

There are certain things concerning Satan of which we briefly remind you in this connection. He is a person! A spirit can be a person as much as a human being. A person is one having self consciousness, identification, and direction. Satan has all of these and is a person. Moreover, he is a person of great power. A few incidents in the Word of God prove this conclusively. He worked with great power in the garden of Eden to introduce sin with all its consequences into human experience. In the record of Job's life, the power of Satan stands forth with great force. Satan retvealed the extent of his power and its intensity in the temptation of Christ. We have only to measure the power of the forces of evil about us today to realize Satan's power. Prophecy indicates that this power will be granted terrible expression in the Anti-Christ to be revealed. Yes, Satan is so powerful that it is absolutely necessary to bind him before there can be any millennium! In addition to this, Satan is the head of a kingdom of powerful fallen angels, better known as demons. It is called in the Bible, "the kingdom of darkness." These evil spirits sought to prevent Christ from going to the cross. Colossians 2:14-15 informs us that, "he made a show of them openly, triumphing over them in it." The better rendering is, "he threw them off from him." It is as if a legion of evil spirits leaped upon him, seeking to prevent him from becoming the sacrifice for our sins, but he threw them off! In Ephesians 6:12, we are informed that the people of God today fight against these organized evil spirits. Some day there will be a war in the heavenlies between Satan and his army of demons and Michael and his angels. Then Satan and his kingdom will be cast to the earth. Woe be unto the earth-dwellers in that day! Eventually, Christ will come to bind Satan and destroy his kingdom.

Now there are certain things about these demons we must recall in connection with Spiritualism. They at times possess and use human beings. They possessed the magicians of Pharaoh's court and enabled them to duplicate the first three miracles of Moses. In Acts 16:16-18, they possessed the damsel, giving her the power of divination, the secret of fortune telling. Paul, having the power of discernment of spirits, rebuked the evil spirit and delivered the damsel from its power. We are urged to "try the spirits," because there are evil ones. These demons possessed men in th' days of Christ. They gave unto them supernatural strength, so that men could not hold them or chains bind them. They drove a whole herd of hogs into the sea. Anyone who has attempted to drive hogs can readily realize the power of these demons if they could make a whole herd go straight in one direction. It can easily be seen how that evil spirits could possess modern mediums and use them to perform their purposes. Not only are these spirits able to possess and use human beings, but they are able to communicate with human beings. The first seance meeting was held in the garden of Eden when Satan used the snake, at that time the most beautiful and intelligent of animals, as his medium. Through this seance meeting, all the evil of history has come. Yes, nothing but evil has ever come from any seance meeting. Satan appeared in visible form and talked with Christ. His evil spirits can and do communicate certain information to those whom they use as mediums.

One prominent fact about spirit manifestations is that they are able to impersonate the dead so as to deceive sufficiently to make the living believe they are dead. The impersonated Samuel in the witch of Endor seance. The record will be found in 1 Samuel 28. We make bold to assert that Samuel did not and could not have appeared! An evil spirit impersonated him. The proof of this is seen in these following overlooked facts found in the narrative. The witch alone saw the spirit; Saul did not. He was informed by the witch and believed her report. He "perceived," understood it was Samuel. Why? Because he had seen and knew Samuel? No! Because the witch told him so. Was the spirit of Samuel really present? This spirit came out of the ground at Endor. Samuel was buried at Ramah. If this was Samuel, he must have been doing some tunneling! Samuel himself had condemned witchcraft; would he now become a partner to it? Was he a hypocrite after death? We think not. If this was Samuel, who raised him from the dead? God had ordered all witches slain, stoned to death. Would he then bring forth Samuel at the bid of a witch? God would not thus practise something himself, for which he had pronounced the sentence of death upon others. If God did not bring forth Samuel and this spirit was Samuel, then Satan must have. But, Satan cannot resurrect! Remember, Saul had sought knowledge of God and God had turned a deaf ear to him because he had forsaken God. Saul now turns to Satan through the witch of Endor. An evil spirit impersonated Samuel to receive. But, you say, "how about the message of this spirit?" Most of it was a repetition of past utterances of Samuel with which the evil spirits were familiar. The prediction that the battle would be against Saul on the morrow was very easy for this ambassador of Satan to make, for Satan controlled both armies to fight upon the morrow. The army of Israel had forsaken God as had Saul. This was the reason for their defeat. Satan thus pitted two of his own armies against each other and controlled the issue. Now the result of this consultation was despair and suicide. This result is being repeated today in England. We are informed that with the wave of spiritualism a wave of insanity is also sweeping over the country. Spiritualism today is on the same order as that of the witch of Endor, evil spirits impersonating the spirits of the dead, purposing to lead away from the Bible and true faith.

God's Word is clear and forceful in its denunciation of dabbling in any and all forms of spiritualism. Deuteronomy 18:9-11 speaks like tongues of forked lightning. It forbids the passing of sons and daughters through the fire. This was the worship of Moloch, in which children, slain as sacrifices would be passed through the arms of the image, heated to white heat. You shudder and cry out, "horrible," and so it was, but in the same verse, God condemns all manifestations of spiritualism. He condemns divination, fortune telling, clairvoyance, palmistry. He condemns observers of times, such as lucky stars, lucky and unlucky days, superstitious signs. How about Friday? How about 13? He sternly prohibits consulting an enchanter, witch, wizard, or charmer. He lifts his hand and voice and word against a necromancer, consulter of familiar spirits. Why are these spirits called "familiar?" Because it is their business to know the life of the dead, that they may successfully impersonate them. Spiritualism comes directly under this head. Listen to Isaiah 8:19, the revised version, "on behalf of the living, should they seek unto the dead?" - This is spiritualism and stands condemned!

If you dabble in spiritualism, what will you do with these scriptures? Leviticus 19:31, "Regard not them that have familiar spirits, neither seek after wizards to be defiled of them." Leviticus 20:27,—"A man also or a woman that hath a familiar spirit or that is a wizard shall surely be put to death." 2 Kings 1:6,—"He observed times, and used enchantments, and dealt with familiar spirits and wizards. HE WROUGHT MUCH WICKEDNESS IN THE SIGHT OF THE LORD." These words refer to that wicked king Manasseh. Galatians 5:19 places witchcraft among the works of the flesh. 1 Timothy 4:1, "Now the Spirit speak-

eth expressly that in the latter times some shall depart from the faith, GIVING HEED TO SEDUCING SPIRITS AND DOCTRINES OF DEVILS." Rather fits spiritualism! In Revelations 21:8, the sorcerers are condemned to the lake of fire and brimstone which is the second death. Better be careful or that will be your doom! In Revelations 22:15, it is written, "For WITHOUT are dogs, and SORCERERS, and whoremongers and murderers and idolaters." Spiritualists, sorcerers, how do you like the place and class for eternity? Paul told Simon that he was in the bond of iniquity and must give up his sorcery before lfe could become right with God. So must you give up and keep away from spiritualism if you ever enjoy the experiences of a Christian. In the light of these scriptures, you dare not dabble in these things.

Scripture indicates that the purpose of these evil spirits communicating with the living and impersonating the dead is to deceive and lead away from true faith. "If possible, they will deceive the very elect." Therefore, keep yourselves clean from anything that savors of spiritualism! Keep away from anything that would breed or cultivate a superstitious spirit. Yes, in this class, we put the "Ouija Board." It is a revival of the old heathen "Spirit Machine." Listen to this quotation, "The ancients had a spirit board which had a circular plate on which was skillfully engraved the letters of the alphabet, the pointer falling at regular intervals upon single letters composing verses in answer to questions asked." The description fits the modern "Ouija Board." Beware even of it! It may be introduced first as just simple amusement, testing the power of your thought to direct your hands, but Satan will be quick to see the opening for the entrance of evil spirits into your experience, leading you away from God, his Word, and his church.

Not only keep yourself clean, but lift your voice against this modern menace. Be your brother's keeper as regards it. To keep silent in a time when the magazines of the day are full of the propaganda of spiritualists is to present moral weakness and spiritual cowardice.

Sunnyside, Washington.

The Interchurch Movement

(Continued from page 7)

The proposed budgets as published are as follows:

For Education, ... $75,000
For Foreign Missions, ... 45,000
For Home Missions, ... 45,000
For Publishing Interests, ... 20,000
For Brethren Home, ... 15,000

Of the above $10,000 is suggested as our Women's activities share. That is not separately budgeted because no separate provision had been provided by the Interchurch. The above as explained in revision; any of our boards may decline to benefit or may be considered part of the project. There is no attempt anywhere on the part of the Interchurch to force themselves upon boards or churches, or individuals. Appeals are made and the matter left to individual judgment.

Regarding the amount of the budget proposed for our purposes it is really ridiculously low, being less than three cents per day per member. As to the $75,000 suggested for education, it is doubtless not necessary to explain that the endowment funds that we have been raising are not available for use, only the interest may be expended. It is necessary to provide additional buildings and better equipment and a larger faculty if the school is to continue, and the proposed $75,000 is wanted for these objects. No urging should be necessary respecting our missionary requirements, except to say that they should be put upon a steady income basis. The splendid Easter offerings that we take are fine but spread over the year are extremely small and many give nothing at all. The Publishing Company needs the $20.000 to pay for the new plant and equipment that has been bought and pay-

ment for which must be made. The Brethren Home, on paper for a long time, should be an existing reality.

Some theologians are proving to themselves that the objects of the Interchurch Movement are at variance with Divine plans and some are rejoicing because they see it as a means of preaching the Gospel to all nations, thus hastening the end. Some lament the lack of spirituality and complain that it stops short of essential declarations, etc., etc. In this multitude of counsellors it is hard to know wisdom, but I feel so fiercely busy trying to do the essential thing of going into all the world and preaching the Gospel that I am almost willing to let the theologians arrange their differences and rejoice with Paul, who should be considered a fairly good example in saying, "What then? Only that in every way, whether in pretence or in truth, Christ is proclaimed; and therein I rejoice, yea, and will rejoice." Being willing that Christ shall be preached even of envy.

I am obsessed with the notion that we ought to devote our energies to real things, largely leaving the decisive problems that distress us to our Lord to decide, and in the meantime, using every possible effort to evangelize the world. I certainly would hate to have the Lord at his coming find me disputing about his coming instead of trying to obey his command.

Objection is made that the plans are the program of the social gospelists. I wonder if Jesus himself is really not the best example of the real social Gospel and whether perhaps Cain, the first murderer, is not a fair example of those who cry "Am I my brother's keeper." There comes to my desk only today, the following important resolution adopted by the Interchurch World Movement's executive committee. How does it appeal to you?

"WHEREAS, reports from Europe and the Near East indicate that multiplied thousand of people are under-nourished or starving, and

"WHEREAS, a recognition of the claims of human suffering upon Christendom would not only be in conformity to New Testament standards, but would be an aid rather than otherwise to the Christian purposes of the Interchurch World Movement, therefore,

"BE IT RESOLVED, that the Executive Committee of the Interchurch World Movement recommend to the denominations individually participating that the denominations consider the feasibility of appropriating any over-subscription to their budget, or at least some portion of any over-subscription, to physical relief in Europe and the Near East, these subscriptions to continue to be administered through denominational channels as all other contributions are."

There is boundless opportunity for discussion that will get us nowhere, but I refrain. I am at the moment most interested in practical results. The movement is but a means of helping our church, if we will; with others, to better do our own work in our own way. It is optional with us, I think entirely harmless, does not aim to eliminate any existing church or the activities of any that are useful and helpful, and then should the time ever come when real church union, a thing not now aimed at, should be practical, I am sure we ought all to thoroughly rejoice. It never was intended that things should be as they are, but when that time comes, we are strongly entrenched in being able to offer our own platform, the Word of God, as the only possible platform of union.

As it is hopeless to quickly compose theological differences, I suggest as the basis for present action, that we permit, without question, the various local churches and individuals, as of course we must permit anyhow, to co-operate or not with the movement as they may elect, and in the meantime we could all join in an effort to advance the interests of the Master whom we serve, by better establishing through enlarged resources of men and money, the projects for which we are responsible. Who is on the Lord's side? Let him come on.

Philadelphia, Pennsylvania.

The Church Bells

Written especially for The Evangelist by Mrs. Warren Williams, Gratis, Ohio

(We regret that we were unable to publish the following poem in our Easter number for lack of space, but it is still seasonable and will be appreciated.—Editor.)

As down the cities' busy streets,
The people pass along in throngs,
They hear the church bells pealing out;
They listen to the sacred songs;
Then hurry on where pleasure lurks,
Where vice and sin are seen:
They do not heed the gentle call
Of him, the lowly Nazarene.

To me they tell a story sweet,
Of him, who for the world has died.
I dream of Calv'ry's cross and crown,
The torn hands the bleeding side.
My fancy travels back, far back,
To Judah's plain that holy night,
When by the glitter of a star
The shepherds saw a vision bright.

I see the town of Bethlehem
Beneath a sky so clear and blue.
I see the little crowded inn
And sadly think it still is true—
Naomi's house was full that night;
She turned the Nazarines away.
And so it is with you and me;
We have no room for him today.

Oh, is the old world growing worse,
As we keep greeting Father Time,
Or has the story grown old—
The story of a life sublime?

Can we forget that 'twas for us
That he endured the shame and pain
To bear the cross up Calv'ry's steep?
Oh, has our Savior died in vain?

Above the noisy, sinful world,
Ring out your clear sweet chime
And tell the story old, yet new,
Of Bethlehem at Christmas time.
Ring out and cheer us as we pass
Along life's rugged way.
Until we find a place of rest
With Christ in heaven some time, some day.

Ring on, ring out, o'er hill and plain
At evening when the day is done.
Ring on till all are gathered home,
And all the world for Christ is won.
For on the rock he built his church,
That must forever stand,
Even though the gates of hell prevail
They can not take it from our land.

Then ring, glad bells, of Easter-tide
For this is now the time of year
To celebrate our risen Lord,
And sing glad songs of praise and cheer.
For he who triumphed o'er the grave
Can save a world of sinful men,
And cause the church to reign supreme.
Ring out, sweet bells, ring out again.

Impromptu Flashes.   By W. J. H. Bauman

(Brother Bauman is about the oldest living minister of the church and the church will appreciate and be profited by the counsel which he puts so tersely. Welcome, Brother Bauman.—Editor).

About 35 years ago I began writing "Flashes," either under the heading of "Trans-Missouri" or "Impromptu Flashes." Nearly two years ago I quit. I will not give my reasons, at this time at least, for quitting. Perhaps I did so under a mistaken impression. I have been the recipient of many letters urging me to continue writing them.

Should these requests meet the approbation of the Editor I shall gladly do so, although writing is somewhat difficult for me, on account of nervous affliction. So here goes.

Selfishness contains the rankest and most deadly poison humanity is cursed with. Avoid it, dear reader, as you would avoid the most poisonous viper.

I have made many mistakes in life. Have you?

Jesus tells us to love our enemies—Quite a difficult task, isn't it?

O how thankful we ought to be because God has favored us with the spirit of power: By which we may bring ourselves into subjection.

I love to be loved. Do you? You know Jesus loves us, and wants us to love him.

"I hate the sin with all my heart, but still the sinner love," should mean more to us than mere poetic ryhme.

Men may reach the zenith of worldly wisdom and yet live in utter darkness along lines of spiritual wisdom.

Human life, in itself, is a school in which much may be learned that may not be taught in colleges and universities.

<table>
<tr><td>J. A. Garber
PRESIDENT</td><td>Our Young People at Work</td><td>G. C. Carpenter
SECRETARY</td></tr>
</table>

Christian Endeavor Specials. By Prof. J. A. Garber

"Like a Mighty Army"

Such is the call that is being sounded throughout the state of Ohio. It is a challenge—a call for volunteers. The Christian Endeavorers of our fair state will have a chance to participate in this the "biggest, breeziest, and best," Ohio Christian Endeavor Convention. Every one should have their eyes turned towards Columbus activities to be staged June 22, 23, 24, 25, 1920.

Heretofore conventions of state importance were usually held at a section rather remote to a goodly number of our own societies, but not so this time. Columbus, the central and ideally situated city is extending you the "Come On" invitation. Will you accept it?

It is to be, moreover, a Triangular Convention. Young people, Intermediates and Juniors will have separate conventions, each one filled with attractive, purposeful and uplifting features. Speakers of national and international repute, able and inspiring will conduct the main body of the conference. It is a large "Three in One" affair and promises to give messages of hope, inspiration and fellowship.

It might be a good plan for your society to organize a Columbus Club. Secure the names of delegates that may be able to go and create a "Booster Gang." Now is the very best time to be thinking of some plans by which you can make the conference more effective. Pep meetings, song services and yells will all help to arouse enthusiasm in your own society and then in the convention itself. Names of delegates should be sent in at the earliest possible date. The registration fee for Seniors and Intermediates will be one dollar if in the mail before midnight of May 25, 1920. After that date it will be $1.25. The fee for Juniors will be 25 cents up until May 25 and 35 cents after that date. It will entitle you to the badge, program, official report, entertainment at the regular rate, and the assurance of a good seat at all sessions. Send all registrations to Miss Hazel Worthing, Chairman of the registration committee, 385 East Oakland Avenue, Columbus, Ohio. The slogan is: "ON TO COLUMBUS, 6000 STRONG." Come on Brethren of Ohio. Let's be there.

Our Ideal Christian Endeavor Society

To make our Christian Endeavor the best Christian Endeavor of its size, in the best community of its size, in our state.

To make our society a place where the real spirit of brotherhood prevails and to spread that spirit in the community.

To make our Christian Endeavor furnish a wholesome, happy social center for the community.

To encourage in every possible way, but chiefly by example, the proper Christian conduct in business.

To make our community, a community where people read good things and think high thoughts, and where as fine a type of American citizen is produced as in any place on earth.

To make our Christian Endeavor a place where any one, in any sort of need, can find the Heavenly Friend.

Why Study Missions

In his pamphlet on "Why I Study Missions," J. Lovell Murray gives these four outstanding reasons::

1. The study of missions keeps one in contact with the most momentous issues of the times.

2. The study of missions helps one to be a true internationalist in spirit.

3. The study of missions is profitable for the culture of one's spiritual life.

4. The study of missions equips one to participate in the undertakings of missions.

It is earnestly hoped that the reader of the above will think over these reasons seriously enough to bring about a more general interest in this field of Christian work, first in his own life and then in the lives of others.

From a Junior Society

Mrs. A. O. Horne, superintendent of the Columbus Brethren Junior C. E. Society sends the following report: Ever since Brother A. T. Ronk had charge of the Columbus Brethren Mission, we have had a Junior Christian Endeavor Band. It is a grand and good work and curtails a serious responsibility, especially to the one who superintends. The Juniors have aided greatly in the work of the church and have given to the mission work. Now we have them meet directly after Sunday school in the church basement. We have thirty enrolled ranging in ages from three to fourteen. Also we have memory verses committed, a program arranged and leaders selected on ahead of the time for meeting. In the class session a story is nearly always told. The song service is always helpful in that it creates a spirit of enthusiasm. Prayers are given by the Juniors and they are taught to pray even if only a few words be uttered. Twelve subscriptions to the Christian Endeavor World visit our society. We have also purchased a large map of the Holy Land and anticipate real pleasure in teaching the children the work of the Savior in a more striking way. We bespeak praise for the work of every band and send best wishes to all of our sister societies.

SLIGHT VARIATIONS

I varied the collar I was making but very slightly from the pattern. I cut it exactly like it in the main, but just disregarded a notch here and a slight curve there, but when I had finished it I found that little disregard of a few details had made the piece of cloth I had cut a terrible misfit. There was no way I could alter it that would make it fit snugly and neatly on the garment for which it was intended."

Let us be careful as we set out to model our young lives after the Great Pattern that we follow him in the little things that do not seem to have much significance perhaps. For it is this little bearing with trifling vexations, this little troubling to think of and do a kindness to another, this little touch of sympathy—it is these things in which we follow him that often makes us fit into the place where we can serve abundantly.

Let us be careful not to deviate from our pattern even a little way, lest we make our life a misfit instead of a thing of beauty.—East and West.

We are told that those who go forth weeping bearing precious seed, shall doubtless come again with rejoicing, bearing their sheaves with them (Psalms 126:6). Will those also come rejoicing who have no sheaves to bring?—Selected.

PRINCE OR PAUPER

"A man can pile up a palace of marble and live the life of a pauper within it, or he may be able to build only a hovel and yet live a princely life within its poor walls. The things that can really help or hinder a human soul are, after all, comparatively few."

SEND ALL MONEY FOR
General Home, Kentucky and
Foreign Missions to

MISSIONS

WILLIAM A. GEARHART
General Missionary Secretary
906 Conover Bldg., Dayton, O.

THE FIRST EASTER REPORTS

The first Easter reports are very encouraging, and if they are a fair indication of the response throughout the brotherhood, we are soon to learn of the largest offering for foreign missions that the Brethren church has ever given, and larger than we have ever before dreamed of giving. A number of the churches, complying with the suggestion in the last issue of The Evangelist, sent in postcard notices of their success. One pastor sent a telegram. Every church reporting has gone far over the top. We gladly give space to these "first reports," and hope that they will encourage those who have not yet taken their offerings to do the biggest thing for the evangelization of foreign lands that they have ever done.

First to come was the telegram from Brother H. M. Harley stating that "The foreign missionary offering of the Pittsburgh Brethren church and auxiliaries is $350.00."

Brother R. R. Teeter reported that Gretna, Ohio, gave an offering of $109.10.

From Nappanee, Indiana, E. L. Miller, pastor, comes this post card report: "Nappanee begs leave to report on Easter offering for Foreign Missions. We had about the worst weather of the year over Saturday, and Sunday, with about eight inches of snow and a high wind. Many were not able to get out, but we have the honor and pleasure of reporting an offering of $450.00, and there may be more by the time all is in. That's the best yet for this place and under the worst difficulties. The reason for the good showing is because of the way the Sunday school, the Christian Endeavor and the W. M. S. backed the church in the effort. More than $1.00 per member. Yours hilariously, Brother Ed."

From New Paris, Indiana.—"The Easter offering for foreign missions from New Paris is $350.00, with 41 present. Very truly, "Mrs. Frank Roscoe, Corresponding Sec'y."

From Eaton, Indiana.—"Easter dawned on us here with a very high wind and a pouring rain which continued until noon. In spite of this Maple Grove went $79.00 for foreign missions, and possibly a little more will be added before it is sent in.

"H. E. Eppley."

From Hudson, Iowa, Edwin Boardman, Jr., Pastor.—The Hudson Brethren church went $160.50 for foreign missions. Last year it only gave $35.00. So you will readily see a healthy increase. This offering averages $1.558 per member, including both active and inactive. Edward Boardman, Jr

From Oak Hill, West Virginia, W. H. Miller, pastor.—"Our Easter offering yesterday at Oak Hill was $28.87, or over the mark."
"W. H. Miller."

From Hagerstown, Maryland, A. B. Cover, pastor.—"Our Easter offering not all in, but report $175.00. Accessions to the church, 15."
"Fraternally,
"A. B. Cover."

From Ashland, Ohio, J. A. Garber, pastor.—"Our offering for foreign missions was $265.00. More still to be received. One new member was added to the church during passion week services."
"Andrew Miller, Financial Secretary."

From Dallas Center, Iowa, R. F. Porte, pastor.—"Our Easter service was a real success. Our people did better than $1.00 per member. We have $156.00 to date and more to come. I hope many other churches will have similar reports to make. We are certainly at a crisis in our missionary work. I hope to see the church prove herself."
"Fraternally,
R. F. Porte."

From Salem church, at Clayton, Ohio, J. S. Cook, pastor.—"Just to tell you that our Easter offering was $110.00. One hundred and ten dollars we think very good, with all other expenses, pastor's salary and other things that this little church must meet."
"Best wishes to all."
"J. S. Cook."

From Huntington Mission, Indiana, J. W. Brower, pastor.—"The Huntington congregation went over $50.00 for foreign missions."
"J. W. Brower."

From Bryan, Ohio, G. L. Maus, pastor.—"Bryan went $200.00 for foreign missions.
G. L. MAUS."

From the North Liberty-Tiosa, Indiana, charge, C. C. Grisso, pastor—"Our foreign mission offering from the North Liberty-Tiosa charge was the largest in the history of the two churches. North Liberty gave $100.00 and Tiosa $125.00. We are anxiously awaiting to learn of the measure of the faith of the Brethren as shown by our annual gifts.
"Yours in Christ,
"C. C. Grisso."

From the Rittman, Ohio, mission, Dr. J. Allen Miller pastor.—"Rittman is a small mission point, but it gave an Easter offering for foreign missions amounting to $30.00.
"J. Allen Miller."

From the Zion Hill, Ohio, church, A. L. Lynn, pastor.—We learn that the Zion Hill church gave an Easter offering of $145.00.

From Dayton, Ohio, E. M. Cobb, pastor.—"The drive for the Easter foreign mission offering has yielded very favorable results, and at this writing has reached over $900.00, with the prospects of $1,000.00 or more, thus doubling any former offering for that purpose. In our pre-Easter evangelistic drive, the direct results were seventy s uls added to our number by baptism, letters and relation, and others to be received.
"W. C. Teeter, Corresponding Secretary."

If the offerings continue to come in as these "first reports" show, there is assurance that our Foreign Board shall not only be able to maintain and adequately equip our present mission stations, but also to extend the work into new and waiting fields. But why should we not give ourselves with real seriousness to the greatest task God gave to the church. We have done splendid work in the past, but we are coming to see that we did not do half of what might have been done if we had really been awake to the bigness and urgency of our task. But now the Vision has come and we cannot escape our responsibility. These days are days of "good tidings and we hold our peace. We do not well. Let us hasten to tell to the starving, dying millions across the sea of the Bread of Life whom we have found in such abundance as to satisfy all mankind.—Editor.

NEWS FROM THE FIELD

GOSHEN, INDIANA

Since we last reported the work at Goshen, things have been moving. There is always something to keep us busy. We hardly know what real home life is any more, but it matters not so much just so we are about the Lord's work. On March 14, our pastor and Brother Wolford of Elkhart exchanged pulpits. We do not know what Brother "Mac" did at Elkhart, but if they got a gospel dose on stewardship like we got, they got it good and strong. The brethren at Elkhart must do just as we are doing, wear the shoe if it fits. The dose soaked in at once, for immediately after the sermon the offering was taken for our retired or aged ministers and the result was a little over $200. No doubt some felt a little worked up, but the results followed. Some remarked that that was the strongest sermon on giving that was ever preached in the Brethren church at Goshen. A minister of the gospel should not fear to preach the plain gospel truth, even in his own pulpit. We all need it, preacher as well as laymen. Come again, Brother Wolford. If all professed Christians would tithe their income and lay it by in store on the first day of the weeks as the Book says, the problem of support for the various calls of the church would be solved. Then we would only be returning his own. Then what would happen if we would give to the Lord a part of that he gives us. Our missionaries in Africa and South America, as well as in the homeland could do great service for the Master, and all would feel better. Let us awake to the call of our King. The every member canvass was taken last Sunday by a score of workers the budget has been placed at four thousand four hundred dollars for the Goshen church. Our superintendent has been urging that the attendance at Sunday school be rought up to four hundred. On last Sunday the goal was reached when the attendance was somewhat over that number. In all of our religious work we should keep in mind the spiritual training, and worship should be paramount. Innocent rivalry in our work between classes is all right so long as charity prevails; and it does, between a number of the classes on collections, attendance and chapter readings.

Nearly all the classes are organized and hold their monthly meetings. On next Wednesday night our regular quarterly business meeting will be held. On last Sunday evening, friend Boardman made the good confession, His wife, who is a member is very ill. Let us remember her in our petitions. The mid week services are well attended. On last Wednesday evening the attendance was over one hundred. A traveling man, who happened to be in the city "being a Christian" was on the street seeking a prayer-meeting somewhere, and happened in and volunteered a very interesting experience. The stranger enjoyed the meeting. Come again.

M. E. HORNER,
Cor. Sec.

FIRST BRETHREN CHURCH, LOS ANGELES, CALIF.

A rain storm of such violence, with flooded streets, as to prevent any service at all on Sunday morning, March 21, is the record that will have to be written in our church books for 1920. However there was one baptism at the evening service, a sister who had been brought up under Catholic influences. We are indebted to the Compton Avenue Brethren church for the use of their baptistry for this service.

The contractor is completing the new church as rapidly as circumstances will permit and all future services will now be held in some of the rooms of the partially completed building.

Yours for the honor of the name of Jesus,
A. P. REED.
4910 Wadsworth Street.

THIRD CHURCH, PHILADELPHIA

God graciously poured out his spirit upon the Third church and we are rejoicing in an ingathering of souls as the result of an evangelistic campaign held by Brother Bell, beginning February 29 and closing March 21.

We had prepared for it for several weeks by holding cottage meetings and by much prayer, and when Brother Bell came, with his forceful, spirit-inspired messages, it was but natural (and yet the new birth is ever supernatural) that souls should be born into the kingdom. He preached to crowded houses nightly.

It is an evidence of faithful work on the part of our Sunday school teachers that on a special decision day, March 14, appointed and announced a week in advance, meanwhile the teachers making a personal appeal to each scholar. Brother Bell succeeded in winning 42 boys and girls for Christ. This with about 18 adults, making a total of sixty, will give us, if we succeed in baptizing them all and bringing them into the church, an increase of about 50 per cent in our membership.

With over ten years of hard work here, we rejoice to see this work coming thoroughly established. Our building is now entirely too small for our Sunday school and we are trying to raise money to build a new building. Brethren, we feel that we have as promising a field here as there is anywhere in the brotherhood for a strong church. Our evening congregations almost entirely fill the church. Last Sunday, March 28, we had 179 present in the Sunday school. We expect to take the front line this year.

Our church will, we hope also, according to our proportionate membership, be close behind some of our older sisters in the coming Easter offering. We have also made about 75 per cent of the goals this year on the Four Year Program.

It is some years since I have written a letter to the "Evangelist," having delegated this duty to others. With the care of the Third church and my work with the American Sunday School Union, I am kept very busy.

We hope for the Third church an interest in the intercessions of the brethren everywhere.

J. ELWOOD BRAKER,
848 S. Cecil St., West Philadelphia, Pa.

PROGRAM OF THE NORTHERN CALIFORNIA BRETHREN CONFERENCE AND BIBLE INSTITUTE, TURLOCK, CALIFORNIA
April 18-25, 1920

SUNDAY—EIGHTEENTH
Morning
10:00 Sunday School C. E. Johnson, Supt.
11:00 Opening Services conducted by
N. V. Leatherman
11:30 Sermon .... J. C. Beal
Subject, "Do We Pray?"
Afternoon
2:30 Devotions .... C. E. Doty
2:45 Moderator's Address,
N. V. Leatherman.
3:20 Response .... N. V. Platt
Evening
6:30 Christian Endeavor, Ruth Doty, Leader
7:45 Adult Prayer Meeting,
Geo. W. Powell, Leader
7:3 Praise Service conducted by J. W. Platt
8:00 Sermon .... J. C. Beal
Subject, "Whither—Somewhere but Where?"

MONDAY—NINETEENTH
Morning
9:30 Sectional Conferences:
Layman's Conference. Subject ."The Layman's Position in the Church."
Woman's Conference. Subject, "What Christ Has Done for Woman."
Christian Endeavor Expert Class,
N. V. Leatherman, Teacher
Sunday Bible School Study Hour,
J. W. Platt
Subject, "The Sunday School: Its Nature, and Vital Relation to the Church"
10:30 Devotions .... Mrs. Lois Shank
10:45 Sermon .... J. C. Beal
Subject, "Are You a Tested (G) String or an Untested (D)?"
11:20 Business Session:
Report of Credential Committee.
Reports of Pastors.
Election of Officers.
Afternoon
2:30 Worship in Song, Scripture, Prayer.
2:45 Address .... J. W. Platt
Subject, "The Embodiment of the Holy."
3:15 Address .... A. V. Kimmell
Subject, "Talking with the Dead—Spiritualism."
7:45 Prayer Meeting ... Volunteer Leader
8:00 Worship in Song, Scripture, Prayer.
8:30 Sermon .... J. C. Beal

Subject, "The Question You Must Answer."
TUESDAY—TWENTIETH
Morning
9:30 Sectional Conferences:
Layman's Conference. Subject, "Stewardship and Our Laymen."
Woman's Conference. Subject, "What Women Can Do for Christ."
Christian Endeavor Expert Class,
N. V. Leatherman, Teacher
Sunday Bible School Study Hour,
J. W. Platt
Subject, "The Organization of the Bible School."
10:30 Devotions ...... Mrs. Luda Reynolds
10:45 Address .... A. V. Kimmell
Subject, "Exposition of Matthew 5:
13-16."
11:20 The Evangelistic and Bible Study League the Need and the Objective,
J. C. Beal
Afternoon
2:30 Praise Service ...... C. E. Johnson
2:45 Address .... A. V. Kimmell
Subject, "The Much Neglected Ordinance—Baptism."
3:15 Address .... N. V. Leatherman
Subject, "The Bible Doctrine of Sin"
Evening
7:45 Prayer Meeting ... Volunteer Leader
8:00 Worship in Song, Scripture, Prayer
8:30 Sermon .... J. C. Beal
Subject, "The Question That Causes Anxiety."

WEDNESDAY—TWENTY-FIRST
Missionary Day, Morning
9:30 Sectional Conferences:
Layman's Conference. Subject, "Our Laymen and Missions."
Woman's Conference. Subject, "Our Woman's Missionary Society."
Christian Endeavor Expert Class,
N. V. Leatherman, Teacher
Sunday Bible School Study Hour,
J. W. Platt
Subject, "The Equipment of the Bible School."
10:30 Devotions .... Mrs. Ida Matthews
10:45 Sermon .... A. V. Kimmell
Subject, "Prayer and Missions."
11:20 Address .... N. V. Leatherman
Subject, "Our Home Base."
Afternoon
2:3 Praise Service .... Jacob Shank
2:45 Sermon .... A. V. Kimmell
Subject, "When Prayer Fails"
3:15 Address .... J. W. Platt
Subject, "Our Four Year Program"
Evening
7:45 Prayer Meeting ... Volunteer Leader
8:00 Worship in Song, Scripture, Prayer
8:30 Sermon .... J. C. Beal
Subject, "Why Men Are Lost"
THURSDAY—TWENTY-SECOND
Morning
9:30 Sectional Conferences:
Layman's Conference. Subject, "What Laymen Expect from the Ministry"
Woman's Conference. Subject, "Cumbered with Serving"
Christian Endeavor Expert Class,
N. V. Leatherman, Teacher
Sunday Bible School Study Hour,
J. W. Platt
Subject, "The Pupil in the Bible School"
10:30 Devotions ...... Mrs. Effie Gibson
10:45 Address .... J. C. Beal
Subject, "The Savior or Which?"
11:20 Address .... A. V. Kimmell
Subject, "Self Surrender."
Afternoon
2:30 Praise Service ...... Geo. W. Powell
2:45 Address .... C. E. Johnson
Subject, "The Bible Doctrine of Man in His Relation to the World"
3:15 Address .... A. V. Kimmell
Subject, "The Interchurch Movement and the Brethren."

Evening

7:45 Prayer Meeting ... Volunteer Leader
8:00 Worship in Song, Scripture, Prayer
8:30 Sermon .... J. C. Beal
    Subject, ''How to Be Saved—The
    Newspaper Plan'' (Will It Work?)

FRIDAY—TWENTY-THIRD

Morning

9:30 Sectional Conferences:
    Layman's Conference. Subject, ''What
    the Ministry Expects from Laymen''
    Woman's Conference .Subject, ''Stew-
    ardship and Women''
    Christian Endeavor Expert Class,
        N. V. Leatherman, Teacher
    Sunday Bible School Study Hour,
        J. W. Platt
    Subject, ''The Teacher in the Bible
    School''
10:30 Devotions ... Mrs. N. V. Leatherman
10:45 Sermon .... A. V. Kimmell
    Subject, ''Philemon: A Book Study''
11:20 Business Session:
    Reports of Officers
    Report of Committee on New Business
    Reports of other Committees

Afternoon

2:30 Praise Service .... W. A. Rhyner
2:45 Address .... A. V. Kimmell
    Subject, ''The Communion: a Three Part
    Service''
3:15 Address .... J. W. Platt
    Subject, ''The Message of the Holy
    Spirit''

Evening

7:45 Prayer Meeting ... Volunteer Leader
8:00 Worship in Song, Scripture, Prayer
8:30 Sermon .... J. C. Beal
    Subject, ''How to Be Saved: The
    Bible Way''

SATURDAY—TWENTY-FOURTH

Morning

9:30 Sectional Conferences:
    Christian Endeavor Expert Class,
        N. V. Leatherman, Teacher
    Sunday Bible School Study Hour,
        J. W. Platt
    Subject, ''The Opportunity and the
    Responsibility of the Bible School''
10:30 Devotions .... Miss Mina Coyle
10:45 Address .... J. W. Platt
    Subject, ''The Present Activity of the
    Holy Spirit''
11:20 Sermon .... A. V. Kimmell
    Subject, ''Can a Believer Know He Is
    Saved?''

Afternoon

2:30 Business session:
    Devotions .... Walter S. Reyner
    New Business
    Business Finals

Evening

7:45 Prayer Meeting ... Voluntary Leader
8:00 Worship in Song, Scripture, Prayer
8:30 Sermon .... J. C. Beal
    Subject, ''The World's Present Great-
    est Need''

SUNDAY—TWENTY-FIFTH

Morning

10:30 Sunday School .. C. E. Johnson, Supt.
11:00 Opening Exercises conducted by,
        N. V. Leatherman
11:30 Sermon .... A. V. Kimmell
    Subject, ''The Mastery of Christ''

Afternoon

2:30 Praise Service .... C. I. Shank
2:45 Sermon .... Roger E. Darling
3:15 Sermon .... A. V. Kimmell
    Subject, ''What Is the Business of the
    Church?''

Evening

6:30 Christian Endeavor,
        Miss Vida Elliot, Leader
7:45 Adult Prayer Meeting,
        Volunteer Leader
8:00 Worship in Song, Scripture, Prayer
8:30 Closing Sermon .... J. C. Beal
    Subject, ''Watchman, What of the
    Night?''.
        Benediction.

WHITE GIFT OFFERINGS

The following White Gift contributions have
been received since last report:

North Manchester, Ind. (omitted in
    report of an. 12th), ...$ 148.97
Whittier, Cal., ... 49.51
Falls City, Neb., (additional), ... 4.00
Dayton, Ohio, (additional), ... 30.00
Bryan, Ohio, ... 40.00
Myers Union, Pa., ... 4.00
Claypool, Ind., ... 10.48
Canton, Ohio, ... 65.00

Total, ... $ 351.96
Previously Reported, ... $4,027.74

Grand total, to date, ...$4,379.70

This is an excellent showing for our VIC-
TORY year. There are, however, a few schools
in each district that contributed last year but
have failed so far in sending an offering this
year. We are still hoping to hear from these
schools and a few others who have not been
in the habit of contributing to this work, so
that we may have a 100 percent report to present to Conference this year.
        ALBERT TRENT,
            General Secretary-Treasurer.
Johnstown, March 25, 1920.

McLOUTH, KANSAS

Since our last report our experience has
been great, and unspeakable.

Being called to the work at this place, we
left Marianna, Pennsylvania, on January 31st.

The Ford packed with its burden, the time
came when we must say good-bye to the
Brethren of the Highland congregation. Our
hearts were too heavy to sing ''Blest Be the
Tie that Binds.'' It became a real experience
to us, to separate from those whom we had
learned to love and those who were so faithful to their duty and especially in seeing to
their pastor's welfare. We feel that the man
who accepts the pastorate of the Highland
church, will be a lucky man, and if we ever
find another with whom to work with the characteristics of those we have left behind we
will be fortunate.

Our last day in Pennsylvania was spent in
the home of Brother L. E. Moore, one of God's
tithers who is making a success in life.

Saturday morning the wind was cold and
the roads mostly covered with ice when we
cranked the Ford and made a start for the
West, some 1200 miles away, reaching Washington at one P. M. Then by the way of
Wheeling, West Virginia, we traveled the old
National pike, and arrived at Morristown,
Ohio, about five P. M. and put up for the
night.

Sunday morning we got an early start and
were making good time when bang went a tire.
This replaced, we continued west, when at
length a bolt dropped from the steering gear
and let us down in the road. After two hours
of mechanical labor we were on the way again.

By inquiring we learned that Brother A. F.
Ankrum lived in the vicinity of Graitoo, so
after the use of the telephone we found his
residence on the hill just south of town. We
were received with a warm welcome and
brotherly love. The Ford put in for the night
and the chores all done, we were served with

a most delightful supper. This night with
Brother Ankrum and family, with the comforts of the lovely home will never be forgotten.

All things ready Monday morning, the sun
bright and the sky clear we bade good-bye
and continued west, leaving the National pike
and going by Newark. As we went north we
found snow drifts which checked our drive.
We arrived in Kenton at 7 P. M. and put up
for the night.

Tuesday morning we got started by good
daylight and found more snow and crooked
ruts to contend with. After a hard day with
two breakdowns which caused great delay we
reached Churubusco, Indiana at 10 P. M. By
a little persuasion we found beds and a place
for the faithful Ford.

Wednesday morning at 8 A. M. we made another effort west and north hoping to reach
Niles, Michigan before night. With good luck
we arrived at two P. M. to meet our daughter and her family where we spent five days
While here Elder David Cripe of North South
Bend, called on us to preach for him on Sunday. This we agreed to do and met a fine
crowd of people whom we had learned in days
gone by. It was here in the St. Joe Valley
where we first preached for the Brethren.

On Tuesday, February 10th, the oldest son
and myself started again for the West, leav
ing Mrs. Howell and the two smaller children
in Michigan with daughter. It was a fine cool
morning and we got an early start. We made
the route by South Bend, Plymouth, Logansport, Lafayette, and to Covington, where we
put up for the night, after a drive of 225
miles.

Wednesday morning we were on the road
before eight o'clock. Hoping to make as good
a run as the day before, we found fine roads
from South Bend to within fifteen miles of
the Illinois river when we found mud, which
continued to the Mississippi river at Hannibal, Missouri. After leaving the river region
we had roads equal to summer roads. Saturday night found us in Braymer, Missouri,
within 75 miles of Kansas City.

Sunday morning the cold wind was blowing
but it was clear and bright and we left Braymer, before breakfast, and stopped later to
warm and feed. Talk about the H. C. L.!
You just try it from east to west. The people
haven't any mercy on a preacher. I hardly
think they charge according to salary. It
must be because he is taken as an easy mark.
We met with luck and arrived in Kansas
City a little after noon, and had some difficulty in finding the direction out for McLouth,
which is 40 miles northwest, so we made a
start and arrived in the wonderful little town
at four P. M.

We stopped with Sister J. R. Kimmel, wife
of the deceased Elder J. R. Kimmel. Here we
were refreshed by a fine supper which was
given with great Christian love. After supper the son of Sister Kimmel's brother Claud,
directed us to his home where we were welcomed by his consecrated Christian wife, who
gave us a home and care until further arrangements were made.

On reaching McLouth, we found that the
''flu'' had gotten into several homes and the
quarantine was on,—no school, no church, and

things seemed dead. We hardly, knew what to do with ourselves.

The first thing to consider was a house for the pastor and family, and there was not one in town to rent. Talk about the "blues," we certainly had them.

A suggestion was made for a called meeting of the church on Tuesday night to consider the matter. The results were a committee was appointed to see to getting a house. By this time the "flu" ban was lifted and we had announced a regular business meeting that we might understand and agree for the work of the year. The results of this meeting were efforts to arouse to new life the two mission points in the country, and a revival effort in McLouth beginning April the eleventh, with the pastor as evangelist.

Several houses were suggested for a parsonage and one was agreed upon and purchased, by the church. Here it was our "blues" began to fade.

Mrs. Howell was notified and came to us at once and we are at home again.

On last Friday night we were invited to the church where the Christian Endeavor gave a social in honor of the pastor and family. Here we met about 125 people and enjoyed the evening very much. After refreshments were served, Brother Earl Bowers announced that a gift of appreciation for the pastor and family had been brought which would be presented to our surprise. They had brought many nice and wholesome articles for the home. For this we are truly thankful.

We feel that we have found another church of real Christians.

The remarkable thing is we are serving both the Conservatives and Progressives and I never saw such a spirit of love expressed by any people anywhere.

I only pray that this church will be the means of bringing the church at large into closer fellowship. (One is your Father and all ye are Brethren).

We like Kansas. We find mighty fine people here. There are four churches here; the Methodist, United Brethren, Baptist and Brethren.

Since my last report, I have been so unfortunate as to lose my father. He passed away March the first, at the age of 86 years and 33 days. It seems that my last earthly friend is gone. Yet I have the assurance that he has gone to his reward, which is given the faithful.

We covet an interest in your prayers.
                                    THOS. F. HOWELL.

Communion Notices

The McLouth Brethren church will hold its love feast and communion on April 24th at 8 P. M. We extend an invitation to all who may wish to attend.
                              THOS. F. HOWELL, Pastor.

THE TIE THAT BINDS

STROUP—SUMMERS—At the First Brethren parsonage, Louisville, Ohio, March 1, Wm. B. Summers of North Georgetown, O., and Viola B. Stroup of Homeworth, O., were united in marriage. The ring ceremony was used.
                                      E. M. RIDDLE.

DUFFEY-PRIEST—Mr. Harry Duffey and Miss Mabel Priest were united in marriage at the Brethren parsonage, in Bryan, Ohio, December 9, 1919. The bride is a member of the Brethren church at Bryan. Their many friends wish them the best of life's blessings.

BOISHET—ZIMMERMAN—On the afternoon of February 16, 1920, Mr. G. Boisher and Miss Ethel Zimmerman were united in marriage. The wedding took place in the Brethren parsonage, in the presence of two invited guests. May the blessings of God richly rest upon these young people.
                                         G. L. MAUS.

IN THE SHADOW

BROWN—Nora, daughter of Ephraim and Mary Clemens, was born January 28, 1863. On March 26, 1885, she was united in marriage to Chas. F. Brown. Two daughters were born to this happy union, Bessie, and Addie. She departed this life March 8, 1920 at the age of 57 years, 1 month and 10 days. In 1890 she united with the United Brethren church and on July 16, 1904 she with her husband and family united with the Brethren church of Bryan. Here she was a faithful attendant as long as health would permit. Mrs. Brown was a fine woman, loved by all who knew her. She has gone to her reward. She leaves a husband and two daughters. For a number of years she was an intense sufferer but she bore it all with Christian fortitude, never saying much about it. Services were conducted from the Brethren church by the writer. Interment was in the Fountain Grove Mausoleum of Bryan.
                                         G. L. MAUS.

KEENER—Josiah Keener was born April 4, 1846 and departed this life March 22, 1920, being aged 73 years, 11 months and 18 days. He was born and reared in the state of Ohio, remaining a resident in it throughout his entire lifetime. He was united in marriage to Mary Jacobs on February 1, 1868. To this union were born seven children, all of whom died in infancy. Soon after his marriage, he united with the church. At the time of his death he was a faithful member of the Homerville Brethren church and his kindly face will be missed at all of its services. For the past four years, since the death of his wife, he has made his home with Mr. and Mrs. Emery Kissel, the latter having been reared in the Keener home. Besides Brother and Sister Kissel, there remains to mourn his departure one brother, George Keener, of Kent, Ohio, and one sister, Elizabeth Reed, of West Salem, Ohio, together with a host of other relatives and friends. The funeral service was held at the Kissel home March 26, being conducted by the writer. Interment was made in the beautiful cemetery at Red Haw.
                                    FRED C. VANATOR.

TEMPLE—David Temple was born in Missouri in 1854, and died October 8th, 1919, aged 65 years. He spent the greater part of his life in Kansas, living in Marshall county for a time, then in 1886 moved to Norton county, where in 1887, he united with the Brethren church at Maple Grove and remained a faithful member and constant worker therein up until the last few years of his life, when his failing health no longer permitted him to attend as he would have desired. Hundreds of friends came to pay a tribute of respect to his godly life and splendid Christian friendship on the day of his burial at the Maple Grove cemetery near his old home.

The funeral services were conducted by Rev. C. E. Huff of the Christian church, as the pastor, Brother Dodds, was away at the time.
                                    W. R. DEETER.

WOODRUFF—Emmit E. Woodruff was born near Ada, Ohio and died February 12th, 1920 at his home near Dunkirk, Ohio, aged 26 years, 1 month and 10 days. Funeral services were conducted by the writer in the U. B. church in Dunkirk, assisted by Rev. Sharp. Burial in Dunkirk cemetery. One sister, four brothers and a mother are left to mourn his departure.
                                    W. R. DEETER.

GARRETT—Erminie Veota Garrett was born at Oakville, Indiana, August 2, 1899. She departed this life February 6th, 1920, aged 20 years, 6 months and 4 days. Five brothers, one sister, a father and mother, a host of relatives and kind friends mourn her departure. She united with the Brethren church in 1914 and lived a faithful Christian and member of the church she loved. Her affliction of a few years' duration was born with beautiful patience to the very last. Realizing her going away she called the family all to her side and admonished them to continue to live the good life and bade them good-bye. She was ready to answer her call to the higher life. Funeral conducted by Rev. J. L. Kimmell of Muncie.
                                    W. R. DEETER.

DETRICK—Allie Stevenson Detrick was born December 19, 1853, and departed this life March 28, 1920, aged 66 years, three months and nine days. She was united in marriage to Jonas Detrick, November 15, 1877, and to this union were born three children, Harriet Detrick, Bessie Nichol and Glenna Hutching. Mrs. Detrick united with the Christian church early in life, and in 1885, she with her husband united with the Brethren church of which she was a faithful member until her death. She had her membership in the Gretna, Ohio, church, she was true to her convictions and a staunch believer in her God. She was one of a family of thirteen children, of which only two are living, Mrs. A. M. Lynder of Bellefontaine, Ohio and James Stevenson of Deshler, Ohio. Those left to mourn are her husband, one son, two daughters, and a host of relatives and friends. But our loss is heaven's gain.

ASHLAND COLLEGE SUMMER SCHOOL
ASHLAND, OHIO

NORMAL SCHOOL: A Normal School fully recognized by the State Department of Public Instruction for the Training of Elementary Teachers.

TERMS: Two six weeks terms, the first beginning May 10th, the second June 21st.

FACULTY: A Faculty of experienced and strong College and Public School men.

COURSES: Professional and Academic Courses including,—Education, Psychology, Special and General Methods, School Management, Administration, Law, Play Ground and Games, Busy Work High School and College Subjects, etc.

BRETHREN YOUNG PEOPLE—Why not spend six or twelve weeks at YOUR OWN SCHOOL? The first term will give you an opportunity to attend all the Annual Commencement exercises.

EXPENSES: Tuition for first term $10; for second term $12. Board and Room at moderate cost at Dormitories and in privates homes.
For full particulars address,
                    President Edwin Elmore Jacobs, Ph.D.

Volume XLII
Number 15

April 21
1920

The BRETHREN EVANGELIST

-ONE-IS-YOUR-MASTER-AND-ALL-YE-ARE-BRETHREN-

We have not done all we ought to do until we have done our best.

We have the

MEN, MONEY AND SPIRITUAL RESOURCES

for evangelizing the world in the next five years, if we will draw upon them.

The restless millions at home and abroad await the Light;

And must wait until the church realizes its stewardship.

CHRIST ALSO WAITS

HOW LONG?

Published every Wednesday at
Ashland, Ohio. All matter for publication must reach the Editor not
later than Friday noon of the preceding week.

George S. Baer, Editor

The
Brethren
Evangelist

When ordering your paper changed
give old as well as new address.
Subscriptions discontinued at expiration. To avoid missing any numbers renew two weeks in advance.

R. R. Teeter, Business Manager

OFFICIAL ORGAN OF THE BRETHREN CHURCH

Subscription price, $2.00 per year, payable in advance.
Entered at the Post Office at Ashland, Ohio, as second-class matter.
Acceptance for mailing at special rate of postage provided for in section 1103, Act of October 3, 1917, authorized September 9, 1918.
Address all matter for publication to Geo. S. Baer, Editor of the Brethren Evangelist, and all business communications to R. R. Teeter,
Business Manager, Brethren Publishing Company, Ashland, Ohio. Make all checks payable to the Brethren Publishing Company.

TABLE OF CONTENTS

EDITORIAL

Applying the Budget Idea to the Whole Church

There was a time when our churches raised the money to meet each separate item of expense as the need arose. When coal was needed, a subscription paper was passed and the required amount was raised. When the church needed painting the subscription paper was passed again and this need was met. When new carpet or new church furniture was needed the same method was pursued. When mission money was needed or the pastor's salary was in arrears, an offering was taken or an oyster supper was served and whatever was raised, that was the amount given. There was no effort to foresee all the needs and make plans at the beginning of the year for their being met. But gradually, the inefficiency and frequent embarrassment caused by this means of financing the Kingdom led to a vision of method and efficiency. Churches began to calculate their needs at the beginning of the church year. In other words, they made a budget of the expenses for the year and then took pledges to cover those expenses. It was found that by this method the Lord's treasury was not so often bankrupt, the growth of the Lord's work not so often hindered and the giving of the Lord's money not so grudgingly done, for as pledges were usually made payable weekly or monthly, as suited the individual's circumstances best, there was a continual inflow of funds. While this method has been steadily improved upon, the budget system has long been acknowledged far superior in practice and more Biblical than the old way.

For several years in our church there has been growing the feeling that the budget idea should be applied to the whole church, and little by little we have been endeavoring to make the application. Our Four Year Program has been a most helpful schooling along this line. We calculated how much would be needed for foreign missions each year, for home missions, for the college, and other interests, and then suggested to each church how much per member was expected of them in order to meet the budgeted expenditures. And how much more nobly the several interests have been supported is a matter of common knowledge. Now the budget idea has been applied to The Brethren Evangelist during the last three years and the success that has come to the Publishing Company as a result is a matter of pride. For foreign missions our people are giving several times as much as they were when the Four Year Program began. And for the support of our college there is scarcely a church but has given far more than was calculated per member.

Now the time has come when some of our leaders are suggesting that we take another step forward in the application of the budget idea to the whole church. It is suggested now that we not only calculate how much is needed in each department of the church's work, but that we add the needs of all the departments together into one grand sum and take pledges from the members to cover the entire amount. That is, it is estimated that to enable the college to make the progress that is most essential during the next year, a certain amount of money is needed, for the support and extension of our foreign mission enterprise another definite amount is needed, so also for each of the several interests certain definite amounts are needed. These are all added together, and instead of taking as many different offerings as there are interests we are asked to take one large pledge to cover the entire amount. That amount is to be paid into the local church, weekly or monthly or at other stated intervals as may suit the individual, and the local church will see that the money is sent to the proper boards to be expended in the various fields of activity according as the giver may designate. All money thus given will be handled by our own boards and be expended according to our own plans.

It has been suggested that the entire amount needed in all the departments of our work for the next year, outside of the needs of the local church, will average eight dollars per member. That sounds like a small amount for our churches to give for "others" in a whole year. It is not quite three cents for each working day. But it is perhaps well to begin the plan with a small amount, and small as it may be, it is larger than we have ever yet given, taking the brotherhood as a whole. Therefore those who are leading out in this program, will be greatly pleased to learn of churches pledging even that much. There are some individual congregations that have given more than that amount per member per year for other interests outside their own local needs, but they are few. Yet it is a goal low enough that all churches ought to reach it during the coming year. Our appreciation of the grace of God can be largely determined by the amount we are willing to give for the salvation of others and the building up of his church in other communities. The time is at hand when we ought to heed our Lords' admonition, "Freely ye have received, freely give."

Now it is suggested that during a certain time, April 25 to May 2, when many other churches will be making a similar drive, each church that desires to try out this next step in this budgeting idea shall take pledges from all its members, making an effort to raise an amount equal to eight dollars per member. It is an experiment that is of course wholly optional with the congregations or districts of our church. Doubtless those that do not choose to raise the amount in this way will raise it in another that is suitable to themselves. Every congregation will want to do its full share in the task that the Lord has placed upon our church for the evangelization and Christianization of the world. Those who do not feel themselves ready or willing to co-operate in this plan will not be embarrassed thereby, but those that find themselves so situated or disposed to co-operate will doubtless be greatly benefited by the momentum gathered by the large army of Christians who will be co-operating during those days in the great Simultaneous Financial Drive for the extension of the kingdom of God. Let us make this proposal a subject of prayer and seek earnestly God's will in the matter, seeking not only what to do, but how much to do. The spirit of sacrifice will soon take hold of the individual who gives himself earnestly to prayer. And the kind of gift that has value in God's sight is that which is made in the spirit of sacrifice and prayer.

EDITORIAL REVIEW

Brother B. H. Flora, who did some preaching in Indiana during the winter, holding a revival at Dutchtown, has returned to Canada.

Brother Martin Shively, the new financial secretary of the college, is getting nicely located and may be addressed at 907 Grant Street, Ashland, Ohio.

Our faithful correspondent from the Oak Hill, West Virginia, congregation, reports progress. They have been doing some splendid work in the way of giving offerings for needy and worthy purposes.

Brother Homer Anderson reports a good increase in membership in his parish since we last heard from him. Another thing that is surprisingly fine is the Easter offering of $257.00. Brother Anderson can always be counted on to lead his people to support in a splendid way every Brethren interest.

Brother A. L. Lynn, pastor of Zion Hill, Ohio, church states that the report of their mission offering as it appeared in last week's paper should have been $145.00 above the required forty cents per member'' instead of just $145.00. He says the Ankenytown, his other charge, gave $115.00 for their Easter offering.

We are favored with another report of the rapidly growing work at Dayton. Brother W. C. Teeter, the corresponding secretary, tells of so many interesting things that we hardly dare mention any for fear of slighting others. However we think the splendid revival meeting conducted by Miss Aboud is worthy of special mention. After aiding in the capture of many souls for Christ, she herself was captured for the Brethren cause. It seems to be Dayton's habit.

Brother N. V. Leatherman, pastor at Turlock, California, writes us that "The Northern California Brethren Conference and Bible Institute" will convene at Turlock, April 18 to 25. We are glad to make editorial mention of this fact and to suggest that the churches will doubtless be greatly benefitted by sending a large delegation to the conference. We were notified that a program would arrive in time for publication in this issue, but we regret that it had not reached us when we went to press.

The following request came too late for publication in the church news department:

Public Expression of Gratitude

"I have been instructed to thank the trustees of the Brethren church of Rosedale, through the columns of the Evangelist for the check they sent us, and which was turned into the building fund.

Yours in Christ,   John Leidy Recording Secretary,
                              Conemaugh, Pa.''

Not one dollar of money subscribed by Brethren people for any Brethren cause during the coming financial drive or at any other time goes to the Interchurch World Movement, either directly or indirectly. It all goes through the regular Brethren channels, from your local church to the proper Brethren board which expends it according to their own plans which are always laid before General Conference for approval. Only the money pledged during the financial drive by those who do not care to designate it to any particular church or cause, will go to the Interchurch.

Dr. Jacobs' "College News" are of special interest this week. Our readers will be delighted to learn that the Ashland College debating teams carried off two victories recently. We had the privilege of hearing the one that was held at Ashland and we wish to bear testimony to the unusual forcefulness and thoroughness with which our boys presented their arguments. We are proud of both teams and also proud of the one who coached the boys to victory, Dr. L. L. Garber. The many friends of the college will regret to learn that Miss Marie Lichty, who has proven herself so valuable both in the college and the local church, has decided to leave at the close of the school year. Another announcement made by Dr. Jacobs will bring satisfaction to the friends of the college, it is that Brother H. H. Wol-

ford and Brother A. L. DeLozier have both consented to accept positions on the college faculty. Both are well prepared for this larger service and will add much strength to the faculty.

A most unusual mishap occurred in the postal service last week. The entire Ohio sack of The Brethren Evangelist was lost after it was taken in charge by the Ashland post office and no one has seemed able to discover what became of it. Brother Teeter phoned to a number of the towns where large numbers of Evangelists go and found none had reached their destination. It may be the stray sack will yet be found by the postal authorities. We do not have enough ''extras'' to mail again to all Ohio churches. We can only say we are sorry, and hope that lost mail will be discovered and returned.

Brother Martin Shively, who was elected to fill the place made vacant by the resignation of Brother A. C. Hendrickson as bursar of Ashland College, is now in Ashland and he and his good wife are residing at the "Dorm" until more satisfactory arrangements can be made. The housing situation is a serious problem in Ashland and it may be sometime before they can get settled permanently. In the meantime we are sure they will enjoy the lively atmosphere of student life. Welcome to you, Brother and Sister Shively, into our Ashland circle, and the college and its constituency will welcome your characteristic business efficiency as a worthy successor to that exercised by Brother Hendrickson.

Brother A. V. Kimmell, moderator of the Southern California Conference and secretary of the Executive Committee, makes a statement in this issue concerning the position his district has taken in regard to the Interchurch World Movement. A message came late from Brother Bauman to the same effect but we give place to the official message. No one should criticize them for taking that position, for it is recognized their right. Any district or congregation that conscientiously objects to co-operation undoubtedly has the right to state their position and decline to co-operate. On the other hand there were several districts that voted ''sympathetic co-operation'' at their fall conferences and at least one district has arranged for active co-operation in the United Financial Drive. Brother Clarence Kolb, the Indiana director of the financial drive, writes that he and his fellow pastors are very eager to make the most of this opportunity. A letters from Brother Lytle, the Indiana Four Year Program director speaks with zeal concerning their participation. Pastors of churches, large and small, in almost all the other districts, have written expressing a desire to co-operate and desiring further information concerning the method of participation. The interest that has been manifested in this Movement is wide-spread, and while many are wishing we might have had more time for preparation for our own drive, yet there are high expectations entertained on the part of the leaders as to the good that shall accrue from participation to the extent for which we are prepared. We feel quite sure that there will be a desire on the part of the thoughtful to grant to each congregation and district the right to co-operate without criticism, or not to co-operate as they so elect. If there will be maintained a spirit of charity one toward another and a recognition of mutual rights, in this relation Brother William Kolb, Jr., who is president of the Board of College Trustees and also president of The Brethren Publishing Company and who understands the spirit and purpose of the Interchurch as few of our numbers do, has made arrangements for the co-operation of our people to any extent they may desire. The financial budget that he has suggested is practically that which was worked out at the New Year's meeting of conference officers and board members and officials. It is certainly a challenging program, and to some such program as this or a still higher one all churches will doubtless do their utmost to attain unto, though some may desire to formulate their own method of reaching it. The Evangelist desires to be fair to the many who have expressed themselves as favoring the Movement, and also to those who oppose it and to give privilege for the statement of position. We have had privileges because of our position not accorded to others of investigating the Interchurch Mvement and, as we have previously expressed ourselves, have become convinced that it is a movement of God and that we could lose nothing and could gain much from participation. A goodly number of our several board members and conference officials have made thorough investigation and are enthusiastic about the project. Nevertheless let us grant each other the right to participate or not as each may feel led.

This Oriental sets aside a tithe for his rice and presents a portion to the Lord every Sabbath. Notice the Protestant churches tithe of the grain crop for 1918. Can you imagine how the Kingdom might be advanced during the next (five years) if every Christian should tithe his crops, salary and dividends? Bring ye all the tithe into the store.

PRO RATA SHARE

OF THE

PROTESTANT CHURCHES

IN THE

GRAIN CROP OF 1918

BUSHELS 1,360,339,000	CORN WHEAT OATS BARLEY RYE BUCKWEAT RICE	THE TITHE OF OUR SHARE
VALUE AT FARM $1,742,908,000		BUSHELS 136,033,900 VALUE. AT FARM $174,290,800

Where is your tithe?

GENERAL ARTICLES

Making Evangelism Continuous.   By A. B. Cover

A treatment of the subject of evangelism, in any phase, deals with a profound theme. Jesus himself, was the Great Evangelist and came announcing his program as being evangelistic,—"I came to seek and to save the lost." To make it continuous would be reaching the high-water mark of Christian fruitfulness. Every worker covets such an ideal condition for the church he serves; and in its attempted realization should strive to follow the program of the early church.

After the Master's return to glory ,the disciples returned heavy hearted but obedient to Jerusalem, awaiting a promised power. That power was none other than a baptism of the Holy Spirit. Nothing less than the work accomplished through this self-same Spirit's direction can give us a continuous evangelism. For it is still the Spirit of God that convicts the world with respect of sin, righteousness and judgment, and a conviction of all three is essential to conversion. There is a tendency to belittle, gloss over, and shun the besetting sins of the hour. But in the sight of God, sin is of the devil and separates from God to the same extent as when man first transgressed God's "Thou shalt not." It was loss of the likeness of God, which meant estrangement and banishment. Sin means no less today; it sends the transgressor into the far country to feed among and upon the husks of swine; and amid the applauding throng of worldly-minded multitudes, the awful sense of sin is lost. To make evangelism continuous, the awful consequences of sin must be an ever recurring and vital theme presented by fearless, spirit-filled men and women in no compromising terms. Jesus compromised with no sin, and John in testifying of his Master stated that, he would lay the axe to the root of the tree, purging it. We readily ascertain the process, as Jesus went up and down the land exposing hypocrisy, fathoming secret sins, and calling men and women to repentance. The Church of the First-born must sound the note clearly and positively, that sin is of the world and separates from true blessedness.

The Spirit also convicts the world with respect of righteousness and judgment. It is essential that the positive side of the Christian life be made evident. There is only one standard of conduct, and that is conduct founded upon the foundation which Jesus laid. For every self-denial the positive good must be evident. Thus may we constantly teach both by precept and example that "all things are but loss"in sin, whereas they are gain in righteousnes. It should be evident also that each day is a judgment day in our lives. That we face the issues of eternity today in the building that we construct; not in the future only but in the "Eternal Now." A realization of this truth in the lift of an individual will make life serious, and when serious, the tendency is Christward.

Let us study briefly some of the secrets of success of the early church. In the second chapter of Acts, the last verse, we find these words, "And, the Lord added to them day by day those that were saved," marginal reading, "were, being saved." In this text we have stated an ideal evangelism. The preaching of the Word was continuously bearing fruit. What a rejoicing there must have been in the hearts of those disciples as the continual evidence of the Spirit was made manifest to them! How the heart of preacher, teacher and worker would be made to rejoice by such a harvesting of souls! Some one says, "the outstanding miracle of the world's history is the success of the early church." Humanly speaking, everything was against it. Jesus, its founder, belonged to a despised race. The Jews were held in contempt by the proud and powerful Roman world, under which they were in bondage. Measured by the practical standards of today, Jesus' life was a tragic and pathetic failure. He gathered around himself a handful of obscure, and for the most part unlearned men and women, teaching them for three years by precept and example. The handful was enabled to obey his commands and to realize his prophecy. Into that fierce and strenuous Roman world with all its selfishness, its sensuality, and its materialism, they spread the name and ideals of their Master, until in a few centuries the glittering eagles of Rome surrendered to the Cross of

Christ. The saving power of Jesus was carried into the very household of Caesar, and evangelism reared its head amid the most corrupt worldliness.

In this day of base materialism and cold indifference, can we have a continuous ingathering of souls? What were some of the secrets that made possible the results in the Pentecostal church?

First, their hearts were aglow with a vital message. It was the message of a living Redeemer. Some of those preachers had seen the Master on trial for his life, condemned by lying lips, crucified by heartless soldiers, his body placed in the silent, sealed, guarded tomb! Were their hopes shattered, their plans frustrated, their ideals forever unrealized? The voice of Mary said, "He is risen." The reality of a living Redeemer filled them with a never-dying confidence and a quenchless enthusiasm that was voiced in every message. Peter's voice rang clear and bold, "Him whom ye slew, hanging him on a tree, him God raised up from the dead." That message delivered by men filled with the import of its meaning brought conviction to guilty souls. And when Peter wrote his epistles, he voiced still the fact of a living Redeemer who by his resurrection begat within us a lively hope. The church to be fruitful, must have ministers, teachers, and officers filled with a vital message of a living Redeemer. This is the message that the sin-sick and weary world needs. Faith in gross materialism and worldliness will not long satisfy inquiring souls. The soul will not be transformed by anything less than a personality that is alive, has power over death, and is able to do above all that we are able to think or do. Even so, is Jesus, our great Intercessor. Let our church work abound with this life-giving message.

This message must be known to be realized. The morning of the resurrection of Jesus was an active one. As the news reached the Lord's followers immediately they informed others. People became missionaries. I would, that the same spirit might still prevail in larger measure and I am confident that souls would be born into the Kingdom day by day. In the first great dispensation of Christianity, this seed-sowing was done by the rank and file, the plain men and women of the Jerusalem church. This is God's method for the spread of his Kingdom on the earth. We may be looking for a great revival when in our Sunday schools, there is a field for a continuous revival. That it may be reaped, the teacher, pastor and officers, must witness to the fact of a living Redeemer.

Again, to realize a continuous evangelism, we must be conscious of the power of the spirit, the enduement from on high. Jesus said to his early followers, "Tarry ye in the city of Jerusalem until ye be endued with power." That power must come from on high. Down by the Niagara river is a power-house that sends the electric power over wires in many directions, propelling street cars, giving light to Toronto, furnishes the power for the medicinal touch in the hospital, and may furnish the lightning volt of execution; the secret of its power lies in receiving its power from the great falls, one hundred and sixty-seven feet higher. So must we receive our power of transforming service from on high. As we are engaged in our daily routine work we may constantly drink into our lives that essential power. And as workers in the church, Sunday school and any other organization, one motive should be dominant, seek to save. Such a purpose will be the dynamic for continuous soul saving.

To make evangelism continuous, I would stress last, but not least, the great and urgent need of intercessory prayer. A powerful church, witnessing to the outstanding fact of a living Redeemer, will yield an irresistible power over the powers of darkness. It is the power of prayer that transforms life and projects personality into the vital interests of the Kingdom of God. "The people prayed and the angel of the Lord came, and even the gate of iron trembled vibrant beneath the touch of divine power that shook the very world. We need that prayer today. The modern church does everything else better than it prays. In these times of uncertainty, we have cause in many points seemingly to the end of our resources, and there is nothing left now save prayer; but that will be sufficient," says someone, and there is sufficient evidence to warrant our believing the statement. At any rate, when there were added to the church, "day by day those that were saved," the people, not only the "preacher," prayed. "Behold he prayeth," was written by Paul to allay the fears of Ananias, who knew him as the persecutor. It is the mark of the Godly man or woman, the weapon placed in our hands to build fortifications against evil, and the instrument to call down the saving forces of heaven. Let the church use it in making the redemptive plan operative upon unsaved souls.

To realize the ideal of continuous evangelism, let the theme of our teaching and preaching, be "Jesus Christ and him crucified," which is the power of God unto salvation; the example of our daily lives, the exemplification of the life of the Master, who came to save the last, and let us become in rank and file an intercessory people, that God's spirit working in and through us may daily "convict the world in respect of sin, and of righteousness, and of judgment." Purify us, O God, and may we consecrate ourselves daily to thy eternal purpose of rescue.

Hagerstown, Maryland.

The Brethren Movement. By Wm. Kolb, Jr.

Unprecedented opportunity is at the door of the Brethren church, oblivion awaits inaction. We must choose and wrong choosing is fatal. It is impossible to stand idly still and prosper.

The Interchurch Movement is arousing Christendom to a realization of failures and needs and opportunities as nothing has heretofore done. The Movement, like all human effort, may be, and I think is, faulty in spots, but it is set for the preaching of Christ to the whole world —and deserves earnest co-operation in its efforts to implant Christ in the hearts of men.

The ultra-critical spirit is unfortunate, but then even so loyal and faithful a disciple as John embraced the opportunity of forbidding those who "followed not us." The Master's admonition to him completely covered the case. Something is wrong somewhere when we cannot enjoy the beneficient rays of the sun, because of its spots. It is a sizzling-hot spotted old thing, but the best we have and it gets results. Galatians 5:15 applies, not to our communion only; with stinging force, "But if ye bite and devour one another, take heed that ye be not consumed one of another."

Why not rather verse 14, "For the whole law is fulfilled in one word, even in this, Thou shalt love thy neighbor as thyself."

However, we cannot, do not at least, all see alike, and none are asked either as individuals or churches to consider themselves allied with the Interchurch in violation of the individual conscience, but surely even the conscientious objectors can enlist as supporters of and for enlargement and betterment of established Brethren projects, particularly Ashland College, Foreign Mission, Home, including district, Missions, Publishing interests, Women's Work, and Brethren Home.

The Brethren Financial Drive:

Our College Trustees resolved to co-operate with the Interchurch Financial Drive. For them I speak with authority but for our other activities merely in their interest. They have not officially acted and though not committed may, as previously explained, benefit from the financial drive or not at their option. Churches and individuals and boards, may co-operate as they elect. The time set for the Interchurch financial drive for funds for budgeted objects is April 25th

-May 2nd. It is proposed to start our own campaign at the same time, thus providing our members and friends opportunity to designate their gifts for Brethren activities, or for any projects not definitely ours as they may desire.

The total amount of the Brethren budget suggested to and accepted by the Interchurch Movement is placed at $200,000, divided as follows: $75,000, Ashland College; $45,-000, Foreign Missions; $45,000 Home, including district Missions; $20,000 Publishing Company; $15,000 Brethren Home.

The fiscal year is May 1st to May 1st, amounts received in that period for budgeted objects are to count in final results, not only the amounts subscribed during the period of the Interchurch drive, subscriptions may be made at any time thereafter. Our own campaign will doubtless not be completed within the proposed week, and it is intended to continue our efforts until every member has had opportunity to financially enlist in our movement.

As previously explained money not designated for use by the various churches and co-operating boards is to be paid into the Interchurch Treasury and after expenses are paid, any surplus is to be divided among those co-operating

ONE BILLION DOLLARS
PER YEAR
FOR ADVANCE WORK
WITHIN REACH OF PROTESTANTISM

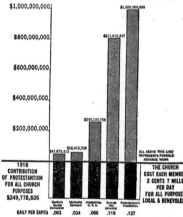

in proportion to the amounts they receive for their budgeted projects during the fiscal year. It is expected this surplus will be quite large and it may be that what we contribute will be materially augmented at the end of the year. All contributions for our own objectives are handled through our own treasury. Note below explanations regarding our several proposed budgets.

$75,000 Ashland College. The endowment funds that we have been collecting are not available for extensive improvement expenditures, now necessary at Ashland. We need a woman's dormitory, at present one building is used for all, for both sexes, as a dormitory. This is not ideal accommo-

dations, aside from being insufficient for our needs. We require also an additional building for library and recitation purposes, and other equipment. It is estimated that $75,000 will be needed for this. We must properly equip our school if it is to continue. Certain state standards, if nothing else, demand it, and it is up to us.

$45,000 Foreign Missions. Our South American and African missions must be vastly extended if we are to be considered as occupying our fields. We are in enviable positions, but we must make adequate provisions. We have but played in the shallows in foreign work. The proposed budget will help to enlarge and better establish our work.

$45,000 Home Missions. Our Home, including district Missions, need money for better development of our established efforts and for launching into unoccupied places of our home field. We have been asleep to the vast opportunity presented for Home Mission work in the United States. Large numbers of men and women are growing up wholly without religious influences of any kind, due largely to wasteful methods and the habit of establishing home missions in easy fields, neglecting the hard places as not worth while.

$20,000 Publishing Company. Our publishing interests are expected to pay their own way. They should really be subsidized and given equipment for better presenting Christian literature to those who need it who may be unable to pay. We are not at the moment asking for this, but we do need $20,000 for payment on account of expenses incurred in the purchase of a new building and installing therein new equipment, required in our work. There is no place to look for this but Brethren contributors.

$15,000 Brethren Home. Who of us is not ashamed of our lack at this point. We all know the need, it should only be necessary to present the project definitely to Brethren people to have this need supplied. It is one of our present and real necessities.

Women's work $10,000. This is not seperately budgeted because no provision under this heading has been made but our women's activities are particularly devoted to education and missions and we guess wrong if they do not go over the $10,000 top.

I trust the time consumed in explanation has not been wasted. It is now time for action. Our appeals have been presented, those who will may help. We want you, if you are a pastor, and you if you are in anyway interested, to help to see that we reach every last member and friend of the Brethren church in the interest of our activities, and too, that we should remember that we do not at all touch many fields that should appeal. We should help as we can in other places of the world. It is heart-sickening to contemplate the vastness of the task and how impotent the approach. I really feel that I owe Brethren everywhere an apology for my part of the responsibility of having suggested such low goals. Our people in general are well-to-do, and to suggest an average contribution, aside from local church work, of three cents per day, is a real reason for apology. Some stewardship! One pair of fairly good shoes per year per member would swamp our treasuries. May the Lord forgive our indifference and inaction, and help us, forgetting for the moment our alliance or non-alliance with the Interchurch Movement, to make this Bretren drive for our necessities in his name and while the driving is good. and now for your subscriptions. not the mighty only but the many, the every-one—prayerfully considering our responsibilities as stewards of the Master, let us put our hands to these tasks and enlist as regular contributors to the work in which we are engaged. making our offerings as unto him, and such as we need not be ashamed to offer him who gave himself for us.

It is proposed to put into the hands of all, subscription blanks, through the pastors or others of our various congregations that will provide for the enlistment of all financially in our different activities. Should any not be so provided. use the blank below for your subscriptions, but it is intended to provide pastors and others with subscription blanks. At the moment the upset transportation facilities may interfere somewhat. In this event pastors should provide themselves suitable blanks. It is not necessary that the subscription be on any specified form; result, not form is wanted.

Subscription blanks are to be supplied from the Publishing Company at Ashland. Write them stating quantity wanted, or let local churches provide their own as convenient. I would like to receive word from all to whom this is sent indicating what to depend upon in the project.

Brethren Movement Subscription Blank

For the purposes below given, I hereby subscribe the amounts stated until May 1st, 1921, and thereafter until changed, payments to be made to my local church, for proper distribution to the purposes designated, with the under-

standing that this subscription is entirely voluntary and shall cease in case of my death, or on due notice.

(Fill in amount and state whether per week, month or year).

(In general, weekly payments are to be preferred).

$........per (week, month or year) For Ashland College.
$........per   "   "   "   For Foreign Missions.
$........per   "   "   "   For Home, including
                                  district Missions.
$........per   "   "   "   For Brethren Pub. Co.
$........per   "   "   "   For Women's Work.
$........per   "   "   "   For Brethren Home.

Name ....

Address ....

Church ....

Agonize   Organize   Vitalize

By Theodore S. Henderson, National Director

United Simultaneous Evangelistic Campaign of the Interchurch World Movement

There will be no revival of religion in America unless these words are kept together. If you drop one of them out of your vocabulary you cannot speak the language of Pentecost. They are all necessary. The minister or church that fails to pronounce every one of these words and to give them their proper place may have a spiritual spasm but no revival of religion.

AGONIZE   AGONIZE   AGONIZE

Revivals are produced by prayer. I have never met a man who could give me a complete explanation of HOW prayer produces a spiritual awakening. The fact is unquestioned. The philosophy of the fact is beyond me. My conviction is that what we need is a demonstration of prayer, not an explanation. We have that demonstration in Christ. How did he pray? "For Jesus during his earthly life offered up prayer and entreaties, crying aloud and weeping" (Heb. 5:7). His supplication had a sob in it. Does God hear the sob in your heart as you cry aloud to him for others? That is what a church official prayed in an after meeting which I conducted; "O God," he cried, "forgive me for my dry eyes. They have never wept one tear over the lost people in my city."

There can be no revival in a church where there is no sob in the supplication of the people. God must know that the sob is genuine. No sham emotion will affect God. No spurious tears will win others. Men will turn in disgust from insincere weeping. The tears that triumph must have the heart-break of God in them. "An agony of distress having come upon him, he prayed all the more with intense earnestness and his sweat became like clots of blood dropping on the ground" (Luke 22:55).

True prayer must bleed before it can bless. To pray for others in cold blood belies our belief in Christ's cross. Prayer that counts is costly. It cost Christ the bloody agony. Dare we kneel with him in the garden and share his agony? If not, there will be no revival. Redemption of others cost God too much to give it to us at a cheap bargain. Ministers of America—ministers of Christ and his cross—do we know the meaning of the "bloody sweat?" Until we do, God will not come in power among our people.

ORGANIZE   ORGANIZE   ORGANIZE

If you agonize and do not organize, your agony will fail of its full purpose. You may agonize over your people who are cold and callous; you may sweat blood over your community which seems as careless about Christ as the soldiers who gambled for his garments. But unless you mobilize your forces for service and sacrifice; unless you organize them by companies and groups for the conquest of the community in the name of Christ no great and permanent revival will come. God does not waste power; he conveys power through properly organized mechanism.

Music is impossible without organization. Music is organized sound. Literature is organized language. Art is organized imagination. Mind is organized thought. Light is organized color. Electricity is organized lightning. Love is organized emotion. Why then despise what God uses so lavishly? Why even think what some one has written me recently: "What we want," says my correspondent, "is not so much organization, as vital Christianity." My reply is that we need both. Jesus Christ organized his officials into the apostolic group. Jesus Christ organized his personal workers and sent them out two by two to win others. Jesus Christ organized his constituency into groups or units of fifty and one hundred in order to reach them with the bread of life. We are to organize as well as agonize.

VITALIZE   VITALIZE   VITALIZE

No machine will run without fuel and fire. No engine will run from New York to Chicago without steam. Your machine may be nothing but cold steel. You must provide both fuel and fire, water and oil, to drive it to its destination. Life must be imparted to that otherwise lifeless mechanism. Your own life must express itself through your organization. Otherwise it is dead. Life must communicate life in your church organization as there is in you. No more, no less. We must breathe the breath of life into every part of our church organism or it will never become a living soul. How did Christ bring life to a lifeless world? "He gave himself," the secret is in those three words. I cannot be done otherwise. My group system will live only as I pour myself into it. My personal work circle will be vital only as I vitalize it by giving myself for it. My Constituency Roll will be a dead list of names unless my blood redeems it and makes it throb with life. Virtue must go out of me before life goes into my people.

I may sob in the night until my heart breaks, and I may agonize until I make the place of prayer ruby red with the bloody sweat; I may organize my people with such efficiency as may make an office expert or a captain of commerce envious of my ability as an organizer but unless I invest every power of mind, heart and will; unless I give myself utterly and with passionate abandon so that my agony of soul and the completeness of my organization become the expression of my truest, deepest, most abiding self, no revival will come. Christ gave himself. He expects me to give myself. Nothing else will satisfy him. Nothing less will raise a dead people into life. "The blood is the life." There never was a bloodless revival. There never will be one while Christ is our Redeemer.

Are we ready for this kind of a revival? Ready to agonize; ready to organize; ready to vitalize? God is ready now to send a revival when you are ready to

AGONIZE, ORGANIZE, VITALIZE

THE BRETHREN PULPIT

The Love Preeminent. By R. Paul Miller

(One of a series of sermons on the book of I Corinthians)

SCRIPTURE: I CORINTHIANS 13.

The Corinthians were great lovers of wisdom and learning and measured a man's worth by his ability and oratory. Being Greeks, they almost worshipped the intellect in its power and attainments. And when the church among them began to receive the gifts of the Holy Spirit they turned their eyes from the source of the gift and began to prize the gift itself as though it were an individual attainment.

So, in the twelfth chapter, Paul shows them that all gifts in the church were from the Holy Spirit, and were given for the edification of the church only, and not for self-exaltation. And then to prevent them from exercising their gifts merely for the sake of the plaudits of men, Paul shows them in this thirteenth chapter that ALL THINGS that they do or say, are worthless if not ministered in love. That LOVE IS THE ONE GIFT PREEMINENT OVER ALL.

Every act of the human heart has a motive behind it. Every word is spoken with a motive: to deceive, gain, hurt, help, hate, love. Some entire lives are lived with but one aim, or motive. Every act of God has one moving impulse behind it—LOVE. As a man grows in Godlikeness, this is the one outstanding characteristic.

But first we would know what love is indicated here. That the Greek word "agape" has here been translated charity instead of love, as is its only proper translation has resulted in much error in thought and practice. As a consequence many have thought that giving alms and kindness to the sick and poor is the sum total of religion, as charity is here exalted above both faith and hope. But this is erroneous, for ' agape'* means love and only that. The apostle here speaks of love in its highest sense, not as an off-shoot of other higher graces, but as the root and fountain of all other virtues the possession of which insures that the life of God has passed into the heart of man. It is not the cheap form of love so prevalent on every hand, which is really more affection and passion than anything else. It is a two-fold love to God and man. It is a love one to another growing out of a fervent and sincere devotion to God. It is taught by Jesus in Matthew 2:36-40, and 1 John 4:20, 21 is John's application of it. "Thou shalt love the Lord thy God with all thy soul, strength and mind and thy neighbor as thyself." When all our dealings and relationships with our brethren are the reflection of our deep, burning love for God, it is indeed "A more excellent way." This love is the death blow to all hard feelings among brethren in Christ. Can we truthfully say of all our dealings with our brethren, "I am doing this because of my love for God?" If there is any real test of genuine Christian faith, it is the doctrine of Christian love, for "By this shall all men know that ye are MY DISCIPLES." "If a man say I LOVE GOD and HATETH HIS BROTHER HE IS A LIAR." "He who loveth God, loveth his brother also" (1 John 4:20). I want these words of Almighty God to carry their fullest power of conviction into every heart in his presence this morning. Let us first judge ourselves that we should not be judged of God. I care not how many great deeds of faith a Christian may do, if he has not a genuine love for every Blood-washed brother, he does not know God. "He that loveth not knoweth not God" (1 John 4:8). So from this we see that this two-fold love to God and man is the one absolute necessity, whether we possess anything else or not, the fountain head of graces out of which all others spring, and without which none others are possible.

Now, we will consider this love from a three-fold point of view.

I. LOVE IS SUPREME IN COMPARISON WITH ALL OTHER GIFTS. VV. 1-3.

1. TONGUES, PROPHECIES, MYSTERIES AND KNOWLEDGE.

Could a man speak all the languages of earth, with all elegancefi beauty and fluency, could he even speak with the transcending power of an angel, and do it without love, it would be empty, useless and futile. Much preaching is of this type today. It is no longer "The trumpet of the Lord with no uncertain sound," but the sounding brass and tinkling cymbal of pulpit essays, by men who "speak of themselves and NOT of the Lord," to tickle the sinful hearts of men and win applause and a better salary. Such a message is not born of a deep love for his fellowmen to help them up to God. Prophecy means to preach or teach, a "forth-teller." This love is the arrow-point that makes the truth preached go to the heart of the hearers. And it is not always the most beautiful lesson or sermon that springs from love, but often the severest censure, the unpleasant warning, is the most profound expression of love. True love warns; it is foolish indulgence that keps silence and permits sin to go unheeded.

2. LOVE IS SUPREME OVER FAITH.

The great works of faith wrought by the Master in stilling the waves, feeding the five thousand, turning water to wine, etc., are not to be compared with the times when he was "moved with compassion" and in love and mercy reached out and touched the poor leper, raised the poor widow's son, heard blind Bartimeus' cry and healed him, raised up the impotent man of Bethesda. These will live on through eternity when the other deeds will have long been forgotten. But on the other hand there are many great deeds of faith done today not done in love. The result is, they are done in vain. (Matthew 7:22 says, "Many shall come to me in that day saying, 'Lord, Lord, have I not prophesied in thy name, and in thy name cast out demons, and in thy name done many wonderful works'? And I shall testify unto them, 'I never knew you.' " Faith without love is vain. In all the great works we are doing and planning today can we treat our deep love for God and man as being at the root of it, or is it not the contagion of desire to do big things? Beware, lest we some day tell him of great works which we did in his name, and of which he will say, "I know nothing of it!" Let us measure our zeal and its source! "The zeal of thine house hath eaten me up."

3. LOVE IS SUPREME OVER SACRIFICE.

Some men seek the favor of God through great gifts. All the liberality in the world is useless if not done in love of the object or purpose of that liberality. Sacrificing with the intent of gaining the favor of God is an insult to him. But when sacrifice springs from devotion to the Savior we love it is eternal. The greatest gift is worthless without love; the smallest gift is priceless with it. IT IS NOT SO MUCH WHAT WE SAY, OR WHAT WE DO, BUT IT IS THE IMPULSE OF THE HEART BACK OF IT!

II. LOVE IS SUPREME IN ITS WORKING. (VV. 4-7).

1. IT IS LONGSUFFERING AND KIND.

How often can you stand for someone to step on your toe and say nothing? This means to suffer injustice, evil, slights, etc., for a long period of time and still BE KIND IN RETURN. To bear deserved punishment or rebuke silently is not longsuffering, but simply, "Taking your medicine." But to bear unjust criticism without resentment is borne of a higher grace than man can bestow, and is the evidence of true love one for another. It is a great heart and a great love that, when under the vicious attacks of smaller hearts, does not feel rancor, but feels that those hearts are really greater than the attitude they assume for the moment.

2. IT IS NOT PUFFED UP, VAUNTETH NOT IT-SELF, SEEKETH NOT HER OWN.

This is what hits most choirs. Because the Lord has gifted someone with a beautiful voice, they think they are peers above all. The sweetest singer I ever heard, was the most humble body to meet. The moment that pride enters into the exercise of any gift it immediately becomes distasteful to both God and man. True love for one another annuls this fault. True love rejoices in another's success. When another begins to absorb our limelight, we cry, "Get off of my chariot." There is room in the world for all great men, and all the good that all can do.

3. LOVE IS NOT EASILY PROVOKED.

How quick we are to get our backs up like a cat on a back fence, when things just don't go to suit us! If some-one happens to say something about the way we do things, how quick we are to retaliate with a burning word of bitter sarcasm. O, temper uncontrolled, how great a fire! How much misery we continually heap upon ourselves and others because of our uncontrolled tempers. There is one sure cure –LOVE. Love and anger cannot live together. Two little boys were playing one Sunday afternoon. Suddenly the sharp words rang out, "You shan't hang it there." "I shall." "I will pull it down." "I won't let you." To pre-vent a tussle they were separated, and were found to be quarrelling over a beautiful card, having the words on it, "God is Love." If contending over the banner of God's love were confined to children, it would not be so bad, but when it comes to those who should have put away childish things, it is shameful and reveals a sad lack of true love.

4. TRUE LOVE REJOICES NOT IN UNRIGHTEOUS-NESS.

The literal rendering of this, is "taketh no account of evil." Do you love to hear of another's misdeeds and then spread it as fast as you can? True love will say nothing if it can say nothing good. That's why a mother has nothing but good to say of a wayward boy or girl. The picture here is of an accountant making entries in his books. Love keeps no books on grudges, offenses, slights, sins of others, etc. Love speaks of others only as it would be spoken of itself. True love will cause your heart to ache because of another's fall. Love has no pleasure in another's sins. Love will pray for the weak and wayward. Too many are like turkey buz-zards,—always looking for some rotten old carcass of scan-dal to pounce on and devour. Remember, the next time you are about to pass on some awful thing another has done, stop and ask yourself if love is prompting you to say it. "If there be any good, if there be any virtue, THINK ON THESE THINGS." Cultivate love and it will grow fast, and your garden of life will soon blossom with beautiful roses of love.

III. LOVE IS SUPREME IN ETERNITY (VV. 8-13).

Love never faileth. All other gifts shall some day pass away, but love goes on forever. Prophecies shall some day be fulfilled. Tongues shall some day cease. Knowledge to-day is limited, and we look as through a glass darkly, but then it will give away to omniscience. What need have we of a candle in the sun's bright days? The three greatest are faith, hope and love. Faith and hove are realized at his coming, but love goes on forever, fuller, freer, grander, un-folding more and more. It is the one perfect gift. They are the deeds done in love that are never forgotten. The words spoken in love never die. Jesus' sacrifice is the theme of heaven's song because it was prompted by undying love. An angel going about through the earth, wanted to take a last-ing souvenir back to heaven. First, he found a beautiful flower and took it. On his way he saw a sweet baby under a shade tree asleep, but with a beautiful smile on its little face. Thinking nothing could be sweeter, he took that too. Farther on he saw a mother crooning over her little child in her arms. "Ah, that mother's love, what can be sweeter? I

must take that too." Then wafting his way to heaven's gates, he stopped to look at his prizes before he entered. But lo, the flower had faded, the baby's smile had turned to a frown, but the mother's love was still true. He cast the others away and took only that perfect love in through the gates. "The greatest of these is love."

Spokane, Washington.

OUR DEVOTIONAL

"The Power of a Sincere Life"
By James S. Cook

OUR SCRIPTURE

Ye are the salt of the earth: but if the salt have lost his savor, wherewith shall it be salted. . . Ye are the light of the world, a city set on a hill cannot be hid (Matt. 5:13, 14). Jesus said . . . I am the light of the world: he that followeth me shall not walk in darkness, but shall have the light of life. (John 8:12). Let your light so shine before men that they may see your good works, and glorify your Father which is in heaven (Matt. 5:16). And behold I send the promise of my Father upon you; but tarry ye. . . until ye be endued with power from on high (Luke 24:49). But ye shall receive power, after that the Holy Ghost is come upon you: and ye shall be witnesses unto me, both in Jeru-salem, and in all Judea, and in Samaria and unto the utter-most part of the earth (Acts 1:8). Be thou an example of the believers, in word, in conversation, in charity, in spirit, in faith, in purity (1 Tim. 4:12). That ye may approve things that are excellent; that ye may be sincere and with-out offense till the day of Christ (Phil. 1:10). Therefore fear the Lord, and serve him in sincerity and in truth (Josh. 24:24).

OUR MEDITATION

The power of a sincere life is a DYNAMIC POWER, most wonderful in it's influence over forces of evil. It is the PEARL OF GREAT PRICE, but too little sought for, though the seeking adds to the worth of the pearl. If sin-cerity could be put off and on as a garment, no doubt, all would add that garment to their wardrobe, as there would be so many occasions for it's use. There is another word akin to the word sincerity, resembling it in appearance, and that word is made up into a loose gown, that can be, if de-sired, worn over other garments, and when used in this way is known as FALSE MODESTY. It is easily seen why the gown of false modesty has become so fashionable it so closely resembles SINCERITY and TRUTH. There are two things to be noted about SINCERITY. It is unchangeable. It is the same yesterday, today and forever. And it is a DY-NAMIC POWER for manipulating the powers of evil for good. It has been the sincere life that has kept the seed alive, that there may be faith on the earth when Jesus comes.

When Jesus said "Ye are the salt of the earth," did he not refer to that life born out of sincerity and truth? "Ye are the salt of the earth, but if the salt have lost his savor, wherewith shall it be salted." It is the opinion of the writ-er that the Lord is greatly in need of salt here on earth, but, be assured, he is not needing it more than we need it. If we are the salt of the earth, have we been sincere? if we are to preach the gospel and shed abroad its influence, have we been sincere? Have we been sincere in our seasoning quali-ties? Have we been sincere in our desire to take the gospel to the ends of the earth? Have we been sincere in the preaching of God's word, "that was once delivered unto the saints? Have we been sincere in all the obligations laid upon us as, children of God and heirs of the kingdom to be, or have we just been playing at the task until we appear to the world as those who have no hope?"

"Ye are the light of the world, a city set on a hill can-not be hid;" as much as to say, sincerity is the light of the world, and sincerity cannot be hid. Sincerity is everywhere and at all times associated with truth and robed with power. Jesus said, Greater thing than these shall ye do, because I go to my Father. And, that greater things might be done, he bid SINCERITY go to the upper room in Jerusalem and there TARRY, WAIT, SEEK, until she should be endued with power from on high, the Holy Spirit. Sincerity obeyed, and came forth groomed in power, to more fully become the salt of the earth.

In speaking of a sincere life what life can be truly sincere, unless that life be subject to the Higher Powers. Therefore the POWER of a SINCERE life is truly a DYNAMIC POWER. This truth is attested by the countless souls that have been won for Christ through the influence of the sincere life. Sincere Peter robed in power, in one day changed the hearts of that skeptical mass of three thousand souls and won them for Christ. Those sincere believers of the early church, had one continual revival, they added members to the church daily, and it was due to the continual sincerity of their lives and their vision of the Christ. It is not to be marvelled at, the remarkable success of the early church, and the power of those disciples over the lives of others, after they had once gotten a vision and had experienced the sincere life. It is however, a hard matter to help men see what we do not see, and experience what we ourselves do not experience. If we are to lift men up, we ourselves must first be lifted up.

The writer has been asked many times, just what Jesus meant when he said, "Greater things than these shall ye do." I have explained it for myself at least from the language of Jesus (in Luke 10:20) where he rebukes the disciples who were rejoicing in a boastful way over the miracles they performed. And Jesus said, Rejoice not over this, but rather rejoice because your names are written in heaven. In other words, it is a greater thing to record names in heaven than to perform some other signs and wonders. It is a greater thing to save souls than to raise men from the dead, calling them back into this old blood-stained, sincursed world. Sincerity never boasts, she never exalts herself, is never puffed up. You have seen her; you have been moved by her mighty influence. She is ever going forth, in that DYNAMIC POWER of a SINCERE LIFE.

OUR PRAYER

O God, thou art omniscient, thou knowest all things, thou knowest our hearts, even better than we know them ourselves, and yet many of us know enough to condemn us. WE know that thou dost despise hypocrisy. We know thou wast grieved once to repentance when thou didst behold this dreadful sin in man. Today; kind Father, we cannot help but wonder what thou art thinking of us in this present age. We see so much, Lord, that is corrupting the earth. But what must thou see!

We thank thee Lord for the light of the world that has come down through the ages, in the lives of those sincere men of the Old Testament, in the lives of the disciples and followers of Jesus in the New Testament, and that one life namely, Jesus Christ, thy Son, Lord help us to be sincere and to live continually a sincere life for the sake of thy Kingdom, and for our own sakes. Amen.

Brookville, Ohio.

California Opposes Interchurch

That is the Brethren church of California opposes taking any part whatever in the Interchurch World Movement.

When the telegram informing the Officers and the Committeemen of California of the meeting to be held at Ashland on New Year's Day, came so late as to make it impossible for any representative from this district to attend, we then called a conference of the pastors and after due deliberation sent a telegram to the meeting informing the gathering that we were unalterably opposed to the church entering the movement. But the committee composed of many of the leaders of the church did vote, with two exceptions, to go as far as the asking Boards desired until National Conference.

When the correct data concerning this move had been secured the Conference officers and the pastors of the Southern California Conference were called in an all day meeting and reviewed the situation from every point of information and as the Executive committee of the District voted again that we would take no part in the Interchurch World Movement. Moreover each pastor was instructed to bring the matter before his congregation and the vote was unanimous in support of the position taken by the District officers and pastors.

A committee was appointed to prepare a statement for the church at large giving the reasons for the stand California has taken and this is now being worked out. The purpose of this article is to say that CALIFORNIA OPPOSES INTERCHURCH.

A. V. KIMMELL, Moderator and Chairman
Executive Committee.

Sunday-school Secretary Sails for Brazil

The Sunday school membership in Brazil has doubled within the past three years and now totals more than 60,000. In Brazil there is a Sunday school organization called the Brazil Sunday School Union, which has been directed by Rev. H. C. Tucker of Rio de Janeiro, who has been able to give only a fraction of his time to this work. The great increase in the Sunday school membership and the consequent enlargement of the work has resulted in frequent entreaties from the Brazil Sunday School Association for a secretary who would devote all of his time to Sunday school upbuilding in this great country. Rev. Herbert S. Harris, of Elmira, New York, will sail on the VASARI in the early part of May, going direct to Rio de Janeiro where he will establish a Sunday school office.

Mr. Harris has resigned as pastor of the Central Presbyterian church of Rochester. He is especially fitted for this work in Brazil, since he is acquainted with both the Spanish and Portuguese languages, Portuguese being the language of Brazil. During the war he was a Y. M. C. A. worker with the Portuguese troops in France and thus acquired greater facility in the use of that language.

Mr. Harris was a missionary at Sancti Spiritus, Cuba, under the Presbyterian Board of Home Missions from 1901 to 1909, and while there was instrumental in organizing the Cuban National Sunday School Association, serving afterward as its first president. In 1911 after attending the International Sunday School Convention in San Francisco, he spent six months in a Sunday school survey tour of South America, inthe interest of the World's Sunday School Association and visited Brazil, Paraguay, Argentina, Chile, Bolivia and Peru. One of the results of this tour was the establishing of a Sunday School Secretaryship for South America in Buenos Aires. Rev. George P. Howard has been the secretary for the whole continent, although his special work has been in Argentina, Chile and Uruguay. Mr. Harris has visited the Brethren mission at Rio Cuarto and is pleased with the success of our work there.

Before sailing in May Mr. Harris will devote his time to the further study of Sunday school subjects, visiting State Sunday school offices and attending some lectures at the Boston University, in connection with their School of Religious education. He will also be present at the meeting of the Executive Committee of the World's Sunday School Association, which will be held in New York, April 27th and 28th. He will be formerly commissioned at that time.

J. A. Garber
PRESIDENT   G. C. Carpenter
SECRETARY.

Our Young People at Work

Junior and Intermediate Possibilities.   By Miss Nora Bracken

(Address delivered at Ohio Conference at Canton)

The possibilities of the Juniors and Intermediates are as great as the world is wide. In all earth's inhabited places we find the child and the youth. The great worth of these young and little people, Longfellow nicely gives us in his poem, "Children":

In your hearts are the birds and the sunshine,
In your thoughts the brooklets flow,
But in mine the wind of autumn
And the first fall of the snow.
Ah! What would the world be to us,
If the children were no more?
We should dread the desert behind us,
Worse than the dark before.

What the leaves are to the forest,
With light and air for food,
Ere their sweet and tender juices
Have been hardened into wood,—
That to the world are children;
...rough them it feels the glow
Of a brighter and sunnier climate
Than reaches the trunks below.

Although Longfellow gives to us these beautiful thoughts concerning the value of the child, can we in our own minds really estimate the possibilities that are hidden in him? Whether he be found in the crowded city street or in the palace, it is hard to determine his worth. Let us go out into the crowded city street some cold winter morning. There in the midst of the busy throng we find the newsboy, a little street urchin with unwashed face, tear-stained eyes, his shoes worn out and his body thinly clad. He possibly sleeps in an old wagon, or in a barrel in an alley. He may not have had any breakfast. His hungry little face and figure show that a great many of his meals are taken from garbage cans. As we look into the face of this child, what do we see in him? The majority of the people pass him by unnoticed, for he is only a street waif; he doesn't amount to anything. What do you see in him? Although his appearance is not attractive, he may be a "diamond in the rough." Some, who were in the same circumstances as he, when given opportunities have grown to be great men.

Jesus saw the value of the child. He called the little children together and blessed them. Can you conceive of Jesus, when he gathered the children together, passing by the poor and unfortunate child and blessing the more fortunate one? Did he make a distinction? If he could have made a distinction do you not think his heart would have been more easily moved to compassion for the unfortunate child? Without distinction between the rich and the poor, we and there are many unpolished gems among the children and the youth. In them lies the future of the church. In them lies the future of the nation. In them lies the future and the wealth of the world.

In order to realize the best that is buried in these our future men and women, it necessitates, on our part, a moulding and fashioning of lives. The potter, who molds beautiful vessels out of clay, is considered very skillful in his occupation, and he is. But friends, it takes more skill than that of the potter, to mould living clay into noble human lives. The child's heart is tender and plastic and easily fashioned but when he becomes a man the shaping is about complete and the early impressions have become hardened as the potter's vessel becomes hardened. Thus, it is very necessary that this work with the young life be wrought with the greatest care. Luke said of Jesus, "And the child grew and

waxed strong in spirit, filled with wisdom and the grace of God was upon him." This should be our ideal for the young lives that are entrusted to our care. They should be so nurtured and trained that the best within them might be developed.

Now where are our boys and girls to get this nurture and training? We usually first think of the home. But we are aware of the fact that in thousands of homes there are boys and girls hungering and starving for this nurture and training. Many parents are unprepared to mold and fashion the little lives that God has given them. We are glad that the church has awakened to the fact that it is necessary to give our boys and girls training in its halls. The church has provided two organizations to meet these needs; the Sunday school and the Christian Endeavor.

We shall now consider the opportunities that the Christian Endeavor society itself affords. The Juniors and Intermediates find here a great place for development. This is one of the best organizations we have to round out the Christian life of our young people. It gives them a great opportunity for service. Our boys and girls want to work. They are very much like grown folks, they must be busy. They want to be busy in the Master's service. They want to serve the Master by serving others. Where is the young Endeavorer who does not like to carry flowers to the sick? Where is the Endeavorer who does not like to carry sunshine into some dark corner? Where is he who does not like to go out and seek for new members? Our boys and girls like to go out to find the little street waif and bring him into the society, and help him in such a way that life, to him, may be more pleasant. These are some of the things they like to do and they are made happier by serving in this capacity. When serving the Master in this way one cannot be discontent or lonely, for as the poet says:

"Seldom can a heart be lonely
If it seek a lonelier still,
Self forgetting, seeking only
Emptier cups to fill."

If all Christians were to do as I have done, would the kingdom of God ever come true?

God greatly prefers that men should keep his laws. He does not desire that any should be sinners, or that they should be punished.—Barnes.

One of the great problems in Porto Rico is that of illiteracy. Though the illiteracy rate has dropped perceptibly since our acquisition of the island in 1899, when four-fifths of the entire population over ten years of age, and 82.1 per cent of the children between ten and fourteen could not read nor write, it was necessary at the time of the census of 1910 to classify two-thirds of the entire population and half of the children between ten and fourteen as illiterate.

Because the road was steep and long
And through the dark and lonely land,
God set upon his lips a song
And put a lantern in his hand.

Through miles on weary miles of night
That stretch relentless in my way
My lantern burns serene and white,
An unexhausted cup of Joy.

—Joyce Kilmer.

NEWS FROM THE FIELD

FROM MULBERRY GROVE, ILLINOIS

I wish to say in connection with the passing of Elder John Cornish, that the Mulberry Grove church is left without an elder. His coming in touch with my father, the late Elder F. Studebaker, was the immediate cause for the organization of the Brethren church at Coffeen, Illinois. My father lived near Coffeen at the time and was isolated from church privileges. Brother Cornish was a member of the Church of the Brethren at the time, but was dissatisfied with their discipline. He got his first knowledge of the Brethren church from my father, and they immediately set about to organize a Brethren church, which was first known as Shoal Creek Brethren church. Later my father moved to Mulberry Grove and the church was transferred to Woburn, Illinois. Still later we built an inexpensive little chapel for worship on my mother's farm, and regular services have been held on it ever since, Brother Cornish doing the preaching without remuneration. But now he has gone to his reward. At one time we had a real active body of young people. But most of them have grown up, married and moved away, leaving us almost deserted. But still we have some faithful members and a congregation that is pretty well taught in Brethren doctrines, so that with a good leader we might be able to build up a strong church. We crave an interest in the prayers of the faithful.

CLAUD STUDEBAᴋER.

DOINGS AT DAYTON

Just a few items of the activities of the First Brethren church, Dayton, Ohio, since our last report, are here given to the readers of the Evangelist. Dr. E. M. Cobb, the pastor, has accepted the earnest and unanimous call to remain with the congregation for another year from September next. The program of specials for the first quarter of the year follows in brief as planned. Through the solicitation of the corresponding secretary of the church the Brethren Evangelist has been placed in enough homes of the church to gain "Honor Roll" recognition.

Instead of Dr. Cobb going south for a ten day convention with Dr. William Evans, the plan was changed and he was directed to go to Rochester, New York, the last of February to assist Mr. Arthur Lught, formerly of Dayton, to start an Interdenominational GOSPEL CENTER Mission, for the confirmation of Evangelical Fundamentals, and he returned highly gratified with the outlook for a successful work in that city. During his absence over Sunday of February 29th, the pulpit was supplied by Miss Emma M. Aboud, a native of the Holy Land, but more recently from New York. Her messages were very well received, and she was invited to assist the pastor in the pre-Easter three-weeks revival campaign.

The Father and Son Banquet given the last of February was a great success when over 200 participated. The good ladies of the church furnished the "eats," very daintily and acceptably. The outside speakers were the Hon. Dayton Clark of Columbus, and Dr. S. N. Salume of Dayton, and the banquet was featured by The Berean Bible Class of young men of whom attorney Orion E. Bowman, is the teacher. Mr. Geo. F. Kem was toastmaster and a very profitable time was enjoyed.

The Coming of the Lynn Family: I quote from the Sunday calendar of March 7th. "Praise the Lord" Rev. Arthur Lynn and wife, Jennie and the son, "Billy" are now among us. They will soon be comfortably located in their home at 1842 West Fifth street. Brother Lynn has come after a successful campaign at Rockford, Ohio, in which 81 souls confessed the Master. The coming of the Lynn family to our church should mean much to us as well as our brotherhood at large. Brother Lynn is an artist of the highest quality, and his splendid leadership in song, together with his consecration and pleasing personality, should be a wonderful asset to us as a church and denomination.

The Mother and Daughter Banquet in the evening of March 9th, was a great occasion. The men of the church had promised to give it, furnish the "eats" and everything, and certainly had a job on their hands, when the ladies sold over 300 plates and taxed the dining room to capacity. But the men proved equal to the situation and would not allow a lady in the kitchen. The waiters looked fine in their white linen togs and turbans, Dr. Cobb being the chief with his scarlet oriental turban. Mr. Arthur Stanye, was chef-in-chief, directing the culinary department. The ladies admitted it was all very accomplished and were pleased with the service accorded them. The ladies were surprised to find a valuable souvenir reminder in a neat white envelope, inscribed Matthew 4:4 and Luke 4:4, bound in linen from the Gospels. Special speakers for the occasion were Miss Emma M. Aboud, and Mrs. Dr. H. E. Palmer, Mrs. Marie Marks, president of the Woman's Missionary Society was toastmistress, and a fine time was enjoyed.

The church calendar of March 14th, has this item: "The Men's Federated Bible Classes of the West Side were the guests of the Ladies' Missionary Society of the First Brethren church last Thursday night, and it is needless to say it was the largest meeting of the kind in the history of that organization. Profuse compliments were afloat as to the service rendered by our ladies, who have an enviable reputation in this city for their great eats.''

The great Easter Drive! All the foregoing has led up to the special revival campaign which began March fourteenth, when Dr. Cobb, the pastor, preached the opening sermons to large and appreciative audiences. On Monday evening following, Miss Emma M. Aboud, before mentioned, gave her first evangelistic message, and thereafter at every service both in the morning and evening during the campaign until its close on Easter evening. The pastor usually gave the invitation, and no undue pressure was brought to force confession of sinners. The sermons were strongly evangelistic, as well as inspirational and doctrinal and very able. They always rang true to the Book. The evangelist appeared frequently in her oriental costume and this was some attraction, but her messages were strong and winning! On Sundays the church was packed to capacity, and as all the churches had simultaneous campaigns on, it was admitted we led in numerical attendance in comparison with all the churches of the city. Rev. Arthur Lynn, our music director and Soloist, was also a great attraction. The direct visible results were seventy souls added to our number, by baptism, letters and relation, and others are to be received.   ..

The spirit of revival continues very pronounced in our midst, and we expect it to bring many more into the fold for the Master. On Monday evening after Easter, the pastor preached a sermon on "Ordinances" for the benefit particularly of the new converts, and in preparation for the spring communion on Tuesday evening following the closing of the campaign. At the close of the service a number were baptized, and among them we were highly gratified to witness the baptism of Miss Aboud, the evangelist, who becomes identified with our denomination.

A representative Communion and Love-Feast service was held on Tuesday evening, and would have been larger but inclemency of the weather prevented many from enjoying the service that would otherwise have been present. Having the Lynns and Miss Aboud with us was an inexpressable pleasure. Miss Aboud has also endeared herself especially to the young women of the congregation, and wields a great influence for good with the younger girls of the church. We are especially pleased to mention that during the campaign Mrs. Jennie Lynn and son "Billy," also were baptized into our communion and added to our fellowship. At the close of the love-feast, the church unanimously and voluntarily authorized the issue of an evangelist's license to Miss Emma M. Aboud.

The drive for the Easter Foreign Missionary Offering has yielded very favorable results, and at this writing has reached over $600.00, with the prospect of $1,000.00 or more, thus doubling any former offering for that purpose. Surely the Lord is blessing the efforts of the pastor, Dr. Cobb, in his fond anticipations for that work.

The drive will now be on for our Anniversary Day in May, when we hope to liquidate our church building debt, and be able to do still better and greater work for the Master in this worldly and wicked city.

May we have the prayers of all the saints to strengthen us in the great work committed to our hands, and we will remember all in Christian fellowship. Praise the Lord.

WM. TEETER,
Corresponding Secretary.

OAK HILL, WEST VIRGINIA

It has been some time since there has been any report of the work here. The Sunday school kept up with good interest through the winter, also the regular preaching appointments. We have had bad roads all through the winter and they are yet too bad for cars to run, which greatly hinders the attendance at church.

Sunday school has been re-organized ready for another year's work.

The collection yesterday, Easter Sunday, amounted to $17.88 and they took $17.88 from the treasury, making $35.76 which will be sent to the Orphan's home in Charleston, West Virginia. After that collection was taken another was taken for a man near Gatewood who is sick. This last one amounted to $9.15.

The collection for Missions will be taken next Sunday. Hope we may have a good year's work.   Pray for us.

MRS ESSIE BOOTHE.

THE MARTINSBURG-McKEE CIRCUIT
Martinsburg, Pennsylvania.

Church work is going along very good. All departments of church work is moving along nicely. Everybody interested and at work. It is a real pleasure to work when all are willing to help.

We are working out the Four Year Program and are having fine results. We are going over the top.

The church here has called the present pastor to continue until November 1, 1921, giving a substantial raise in salary. We feel grateful for this expression of appreciation.

The Woman's Missionary Society has improved the parsonage making home still more pleasant.

McKee, Pennsylvania.

The McKee church is working harmoniously also and going over the top in all lines of church work. At present plans are being made and worked out to improve the church house. Everyone is awake and at work and of course that means success.

This congregation also gave the present pastor a call to continue until November 1, 1921. We greatly appreciate this and with all the energy we can command will continue. We look for good results if the church continues in the future as she has in the past.

Both Martinsburg and McKee have loyally stood by their pastor. It is a real pleasure to work when everybody is concerned and interested in the work.

We trust that this harmony and good will may continue.

May the Brethren church prosper every where.   J. I. HALL.

EATON, INDIANA.
Maple Grove Church

Our work with this congregation began with the second Sunday of last November. The call to the work came much as a surprise as we knew the church had been one of a circuit. We did not come as entire strangers as we had been here to visit them once or twice before.

We arrived on Friday evening prepared to begin the work on the following Sunday which we did. We were not told all that had been prepared for the day. They did tell us it would be an all-day meeting and while we had never enjoyed a meeting of this kind with them we had visions of what would be

taking place soon after the close of the morning service. And it happened just as it always does at one of these meetings when most of the people live on farms—there were "eats" of all kinds and in abundance. Each of the services of the day was well attended and the day was filled with joy and delight.

After getting acquainted in a small way with the work it was decided to hold our revival meeting in January. During the first week neighboring pastors were invited to assist. They responded willingly and gave us good sermons. The pastors of the following churches responded—Eaton M. E.; Eaton Christian; Sheidler M. E.; and Union Grove Church of the Brethren. We are grateful to each of these men for the co-operation and assistance which they gave. The remainder of the preaching was done by the pastor. The meeting continued two weeks and I believe among the worst weather of the entire winter was experienced. With the roads next to impassable and the weather almost too cold to be endured the attendance was above the average. Members and friends should be congratulated for their efforts to attend through such inclement weather. There were no visible results of the meeting.

In keeping with the general program of the church we soon began to look forward to the Easter season. Plans were laid for the receiving of the offering for foreign missions. In addition we decided at a late moment to have meetings each evening during the week preceding Easter. These meetings were well attnded. Brother Kimmel of Muncie, a former pastor, was with us and preached one evening. As a visible result of this effort one was received into fellowship who had been baptized previously and one made confession and will be baptized and received into the church later. Then came Easter morning—one of the most disagreeable I have seen for some time. With the rain pouring in torrents and the wind blowing at a terrific speed the prospects for a big day did not look bright. In the face of this we had a normal attendance in the Sunday school and a very good attendance at the preaching service. Our offering exceeded all hopes. This is the first year this congregation has attempted to support a man full time and on top of this their Easter offering was $81.00. Great joy filled the hearts of all who were present when the amount was announced. It was a great satisfaction and pleasure to see the expressions of delight and joy crowd those of anxiety and wonder from the faces of all. Every one was happy for it was the best ever.

May the efforts of the entire church to carry the gospel to those who have never heard be crowned with victory and great joy.

H. E. EPPLEY, Pastor.

THE EVANGELISTIC AND BIBLE STUDY LEAGUE

The Evangelistic and Bible Study League, composed now of several hundred members, has grown to the extent that it no longer need be considered an experiment. The field worker, W. S. Bell, has been in many churches holding meetings and scores of souls have found a Savior through the old-time preach-

ing of the Gospel. True to the promises of the League at the time of its organization no effort has been made to get into the larger, richer churches, exclusively; but small churches, mission churches and pastorless churches have been sought out and visited in the months that have just passed, and the appreciation shown by these churches is sufficient proof that the organization is meeting an actual need.

Arrangements are now made whereby we add another man to the field force for the spring months and I. D. Bowman will spend some time in his old home state preaching and teaching the old Bible as it is in fact a "Revelation from God."

There are also some Bible Conferences to be held under the direction of the Evangelistic and Bible Study League this spring and summer so for an organization of only a few months' standing it is evident that the demands will exceed the supply unless the membership dollars come in very rapidly.

Nothing much has ever been said about the business end of the League but it is now time to say that the affairs are in the hands of competent men. Men who have vision by faith but also men who have sound business experience and we can assure all members of the organization that the obligations will never be piled up without the money in sight to meet the payments. The only backing the League has is the League itself; therefore the membership fee is a very vital part of the business end of the movement. The fees together with the offerings given by the churches where the workers go, furnish the sole source of revenue. And to report that there is a little money in the treasury above expenses proves it a sound business basis. It will be profitable to some to know that several thousand copies of the little booklet, "The Faith Once for all Delivered to the Saints," in the revised edition written by Brother L. S. Bauman and published by H. V. Wall has been turned over to the League and may be had from the secretary, Brother Wall, at the rate of 7c the hundred, 8c for fifty, 9c for twenty-five or 10c per copy.

In some quarters there seems to be a fear lest the entering into the League by accepting the Preamble and signing the Covenant, will commit the church to a statement of faith. This is caused by a misunderstanding of the purpose of the organization. It is not desired that this movement become a part of the church although the present requirements keep it within the membership of the church, this is in order that it may remain distinctly Brethren. However membership in the Evangelistic and Bible Study League is a matter of individual concern and only as an individual can one become a member. The fact that the movement has been presented to some conferences has been taken up with the sole purpose of spreading information and as a means of getting the confidence of the Brethren in this day of multiplied organizations springing into existence. The League does not want to become the child of any conference. Her constitution is so drawn that only those who accept the Plenary Inspiration and Literal Interpretation of the Scriptures will have any interest in advancing the work but it does bring together hundreds of men and women who are anxious to give the Bread from Heaven to the famishing of earth. The books are always open for membership and any information desired will be given if possible.

A. V. KIMMELL, President.

CANDO, SASKATCHEWAN

We closed a two weeks' meeting at Dutchtown, Indiana, with good interest and the church revived. I am confident they will soon secure a pastor. We have returned to Canada again. I was impressed during my visit among the churches of Indiana with the zeal that many of them are displaying; it is commendable, but I hope they will not be more concerned about "goals" than souls. And in the co-operation with the Interchurch Movement I hope there will not be more seeking of the gold spirit than there is of the Holy Spirit.

I promised my brethren and friends to keep them posted through the columns of The Evangelist concerning my welfare. I think one of the greatest goals of the Brethren church is the budgeting of the Evangelist. It helps wonderfully in keeping the people informed and encouraging the work of the church. Many of the homes I visited I found the people reading the paper. Without a single exception all were anxious to know what Brother Beachler was doing in the college endowment campaign. So the reflex influence of that campaign has become a by-product worthwhile.

B. H. FLORA.

OAKVILLE, INDIANA

Not having reported from this place for some time I now take the liberty to do so. We have come through the winter in fine shape. The prospects of the future are quite promising. The Sunday school attendance is climbing now above the average of last year, which was 83. The offerings are better, running from $5.00 to $20.00 per Sunday. We observe two Sundays a month as "building fund day," which adds to our already growing fund for the new church. Several of the classes have funds started to be used for the same purpose.

The Endeavor is still on top, and has done some efficient work during the winter. We held one social in the Hall which was well attended and a good time was had. Some of the regular meetings have been helpful and inspiring to us.

The Woman's Missionary Society is busy each week, and doing a commendable work for the church. They are indeed a loyal band of supporters. One of the splendid things they did was to purchase a lot for a parsonage, and paid cash for it. The men of the church are now organized and material is on the ground for the new building, so the preacher will have a commodious nest to roost in in the near future, and which he will occupy as soon as graduating from College this year.

Our revival services in March were preceded by two weeks of cottage prayer meetings and the preparations made to co-operate with the other churches in a county-wide simultaneous campaign. We began March 7th

to fire our bombs into the enemy's camp of sin and continued till March 21st. We did our best and the Lord was with us right in the midst of a week's rain, and raging "flu," but we won the victory for God and the church. Six souls made the good confession and were received into the church. We have now added thirty-nine to the list of membership since taking the work in January, 1919. Brother Lester King of the College assisted in the meetings as song leader, and proved himself a helper of many. He brought cheer and comfort to many hearts through song and smile, and especially did the Sunshine Choir receive benefit by the training he gave them.

On Saturday evening the children worked up an agreeable surprise for him in a social hour together and then presented him with a gift in cash which they raised all of their own accord. The church also remembered both singer and preacher with commendable gifts, for which we feel glad, and will endeavor to render our best service in the days to come.

One commendable feature of the church during the past year is that they have maintained and kept up the weekly prayer meetings. This we feel is quite essential, and adds to the success of the work in general.

We are endeavoring to finish out our four years of school work here, and the parting days will soon be here. These days will bring a note of sadness and one of joy, yet as we think back over those four years, the time is short—but well spent, and brings the thought of how swiftly 'tempus fugit'. But we shall go out with a strong desire to be used of God to bring comfort and cheer to weary hearts, and give courage to the weak, and lift up the faltering, in the name of One who has done so much for all. These are days in which some one must lead and stimulate the forces of righteousness to stand firm in the midst of a world of unrest and turmoil. May the good Lord keep us true to do his bidding, in Jesus' name.

W. R. DEETER.

Ashland, Ohio.

PLEASANT GROVE, IOWA

We take the pleasure to report the work of the Lord from this field. We are far behind Long Beach but still proud of the progress here. In six months of our labor, we have baptized seven and reclaimed one in an eleven night revival. We held a two weeks' union meeting in Millersburg, here eleven confessed Christ, with five to come to our church. We have as good a Sunday school as is in the township, with an average of 45. Remember we have no paved streets, nor gravel roads, and we are a rural church. And still we go forward. New faces are adding to our attendance each time of worship. We are defending the Brethren church, and will not support the Interchurch Movement. We need church extension in the First Brethren church, and I am not going to preach that any doctrine is as good as ours. If I do I will throw down the gate and let everybody come into our church with their own baptism. And I do not support dancing, "isms," and card societies. I am in favor of a progressive Brethren movement. And will support that kind of a movement. Let us go to it. What we need is men to go out after souls, and not

after dollars. Let us raise the number of the membership and that will add dollars to our treasury as well. Well Pleasant Grove has one missionary in the Gribble field, Miss Stella Myers. We have one doing mission work in Chicago, Miss Ethel Myers, and one young man in school for the ministry. We gave forty-five dollars to the home mission fund. We gave twenty-three dollars to the Benevolent fund. We put in electric lights at a cost of 250 dollars, they are paid for. We painted the outside of the church, and that is paid for. We have paint to paint the inside. We raised 257 dollars Easter. We have a membership of about 75. And we have the usual amount of dead wood that all churches have. And we are coming. "Come on, lets' go!" As for me and my house we will serve the Lord. And the rest we'll tell next time.

H. W. ANDERSON.

IF IT WAS YOU WHAT WOULD YOU DO?

We have been waiting to hear from the Mission Board as to what the prospects might be for some financial aid in our struggle here in Eau Claire, Wisconsin, for an existence in the Brethren church. We were reading the Evangelist each time hoping to hear and see something said about the future for Eau Claire, if sunshine or gloomy. In a recent Evangelist we read Brother G. T. Ronk in his "Mid-Year Survey of Mission Points." He said Eau Claire was still clamoring for help but we were so far from any other church and so few in number that no way has been seen as yet to help them? I will ask if it were you, what would you do? Does not the Bible tell us that a soul is precious? Well, we have about twenty souls, although somewhat isolated, but all are taking the Evangelist. We are trying to get the members farthest away from Eau Claire to locate here and again I wish to state that we could work with the Presbyterians here in Sunday school and church services, but we would not know what to do when it came to time of communion. A bit of bread and a sip of wine taken in the morning would not satisfy my longing soul. 'If it were you, what would you do?'. Then again at the time of baptism, we would have to stop and wonder. Why not the true way as Jesus taught us in Matthew 28:19, 20. We will stand by the Brethren faith while we live because it is founded on God's Word. And we have faith enough to believe that our dear Lord will some day cause the sun to shine in on us with blessings such as we are continually asking for, a place where we can worship our dear Lord under our own vine and fig tree.

J. A. BAKER.

Eau Claire, Wisconsin,
818 Summit St.

MINISTERIAL EXCHANGE

The Highland Brethren church at Marianna, Pennsylvania is numbered with the pastorless churches, but the people are desirous that the pastorate be filled with an ambitious pastor. They request that any good brother that might be interested please write to, Archie Montgomery, at Marianna, Pennsylvania.

COLLEGE NEWS

The year is fast drawing to a close. Inside of a short time I will be able to announce the Commencement program for the week, Take Notice: Commencement week is from Sunday, May 30 to Thursday, June 3.

Brother and Mrs. Shively are here now and Mr. Shively is hard at work getting the finances in shape for the close of the year.

I have just had word that Brother H. H. Wolford of Elkhart and Brother Arthur De-Lozier of Allentown have both accepted places on the College Faculty for the next year. Brother Wolford was extended a call at the regular meeting of the Board in January but did not desire it to be made public until he had time to consider the matter fully. Brother DeLozier was called by the Prudential Committee, after I had written to several of the other Board members and to several of our ministers, on the resignation of Miss Marie Lichty, who has charge of the department of Modern Language. It is to be hoped that these two men will not find anything to prevent their coming to the College in the fall as we are in need of them both. It is not an easy matter to fill vacancies on the Faculty for several reasons, one of which is the small pay we may give.

This now gives us a very strong teaching staff. The brotherhood is now represented here by Brethren Shively, the two Garbers, Haun, Wolford, DeLozier and Miller. There 'ught to be no doubt in the mind of any a/ to the general stand of the College on all that pertains to Brethrenism.

There have gone out from the College office upwards of three thousand little booklets containing expressions of confidence in and hope for the College. Governor Cox of Ohio has written a very nice note. Also some other very influential persons. If you do not get a copy, which is worth the keeping, let me know and one will be mailed to you. I think it is the strongest bit of advertising that we have ever done. Read and keep the booklet.

Miss Marie Lichty, An Appreciation

Miss Lichty came here as a student six years ago. After the usual four years of work she was graduated as valedictorian of her class. There being a vacancy in the department of Modern Language, she was asked to fill that chair, which she did very acceptable for two years. This past year Miss Lichty has acted as Dean of Women and I am sure that she has set a very high standard for that place. The control of the women of the school has been largely in her hands and few know the load lifted off the shoulders of the President by that arrangement. It is with deep regret that we lose her from that position and from the teaching staff. Her resignation was made necessary by the untimely death of her father. She expects to go home and live with her mother, but she will have an abiding place in the hearts of Ashland College students and faculty.

The Summer School Quarterly, No. 2, is mailed. If interested, write for a copy.

Ashland-Baldwin Wallace Debate

Last Monday evening, there occurred a dual debate between Baldwin-Wallace, an Ohio College, near Cleveland, and Ashland. Question: "Resolved, that the United States Government should control the price of foodstuffs." Ashland won the affirmative here, two to one, and also won the negative at Berea, three to nothing. Naturally, we were pretty well pleased over these two victories. Beside the teams, Messrs. Leckrone, Gongwer and Anspach for the affirmative, and Messrs. Lynn, Horlacher, and Rowsey for the negative, great credit should be given to their coach, Dr. L. L. Garber, of the department of English. If any one has any doubt about our being alive here, and up and at it, consider the above bit of news. Baldwin-Wallace is a member of the Ohio Conference of Colleges.

I am leaving today, for Pittsburgh, where the young people of the church are holding an Ashland College night, which promises well.

Professor J. A. Garber was assigned a place on one of the Interchurch teams which recently held meetings in all the counties of Ohio. He was in Perry, Fayette, and Clinton counties and reports a very profitable time.

Last Wednesday evening, the Philo literary society gave a concert in the College chapel. Miss Pauline Teeter, assisted by her sister, Miss Lucille Teeter, and the Owls, a Philo quartette, rendered the program. Miss Teeter has just returned from an extended concert tour and her work was of a very high order and much appreciated.

The College asks a continuation of your interest and your prayers.

EDWIN E. JACOBS.

Business Manager's Corner

A NUMBER OF THINGS

There are several things to which we wish to call the attention of our readers this week, but first of all we wish to acknowledge the renewal of the Honor Roll subscription lists from Summit Mills congregation, Meyersdale, Pennsylvania, E. D. Burnworth, pastor; and from Sidney, Indiana, L. A. Myers, pastor. This is the third year for each of these churches and it speaks well for the good judgment and appreciation of the members of these congregations. We have no new congregations to add to the Honor Roll this week, but we do not expect to add new churches each week as we are now too nearly the limit of the capacity of the church to do that, but there are yet a few churches that we hope to be able to add to our list from time to time until at least seventy-five percent of our churches are on the Honor Roll.

Breakers Ahead

The publishing business has led a rather precarious existence for the past three years, but about a year ago we thought we could see a small rift in the clouds that hung over the business during the continuance of the World War. However, we were mistaken, as the print paper situation was never in as serious condition as it is at the present time. The Brethren Publishing Company has only enough stock on hand to get out our publications for two more weeks, and with shipping conditions as they are we are not assured that we can get any paper from any source to meet our needs at that time. We bought a car load of paper last January, but we have never had a promise that it would be shipped before May fifth, and we are not sure it will be shipped at that time. We have a promise from the firm from which we secure most of our paper that they will supply us with twenty-five or thirty reams to meet our needs until the car of paper arrives, but a small supply of paper we ordered by telegraph last week could not be shipped because of the embargo on shipping.

Another serious problem that confronts us is the greatly advanced cost of the paper. The car of paper we have coming will cost us nearly double as much as the paper we have been using the past year, and just how we will be able to pay for it with the receipts from our publications at present prices is one of the great unsolved problems.

The Help We Need

One of the most practical things the church can do at this time to help its own Publishing House to a sure financial footing in these days of soaring prices is to help it remove the indebtedness incurred by the purchase of the new business block into which the publishing plant was moved last October. There has not been a day since we have been in our new building but what it has been demonstrated that it was one of the wisest moves the Company ever made. The amount of job work we can now secure is practically limited only by our ability to do the work, but the Company needs the help of the church to make its work an assured success.

At the January meeting of the Board of Trustees of Ashland College it was decided that it would be better for all concerned to have the Publishing Company become the sole owners of the new building rather than to be a joint owner with the college. Arrangements were then made to transfer the holdings of the College to the Publishing Company, but it meant an indebtedness for the Company of the sum of twenty thousand dollars, and this is the amount we are asking the church to contribute to the work of its Publishing Company when the great financial drive in the Interchurch World Movement is made. The contribution of this amount by the church for the payment of the indebtedness on the building will leave the Company with the income from the twenty apartments in the upper stories of the building to be used in the development of a more adequate literature for the Brethren church. This is why we are asking the churches to remember The Brethren Publishing Company when the canvass is made in the Interchurch World Movement. Brother William Kolb, Jr. is right in what he says about the needs of the Publishing House in the appeal he makes this week in another column for co-operation of all the churches and all the members who can conscientiously do it in this great financial drive.

.o may not all view this movement from the same standpoint, but we can certainly recognize the fact that "Where the spirit of the Lord is there is liberty." Let us grant one another the privilege of individual conscience in this matter and we will most certainly discover that the Lord is blessing us in our work.

R. R. TEETER, Business Manager.

How much should I give to make this a better world?

OUR average daily gift for all church causes is
—less than we spend for daily papers
—less than a local telephone call
—less than a third of the day's car fare
—less than 3 cents a day

No wonder that 80% of the ministers of America are paid less than $20 a week. No wonder that the church hospitals turn away thousands of sick people a year. No wonder that China has only one doctor for every 400,000 people. No wonder that every church board and charity society is forever meeting deficits, forever passing the hat.

It isn't because we don't want to help. It's just because no one has ever asked us to think of the work of the church in a systematic businesslike way.

The Interchurch World Movement represents the united program of thirty great denominations. They have surveyed their whole task; they have budgeted their needs: no business could have done it better.

They have united to prevent the possibility of waste and duplication. At least a million dollars will be saved by the fact that thirty individual campaigns are joined in one united effort.

And they ask you who love America to use them as the channel through which a certain definite part of your income can be applied to make this a better world.

Only you can determine what part of your income that should be.

We're passing through the world just once; how much better is the world going to be because you passed through?

The INTERCHURCH World Movement
of North America
45 WEST 18th STREET, NEW YORK CITY

The publication of this advertisement is made possible through the cooperation of thirty denominations

LITTLE ROSEMARY FOULKE

Who, with her mother is Telling the Story of the
Christ to natives in far-away China.

"It Must Be Told"

What are we doing to help?

Published every Wednesday at Ashland, Ohio. All matter for publication must reach the Editor not later than Friday noon of the preceding week.

George S. Baer, Editor

The
Brethren
Evangelist

When ordering your paper changed give old as well as new address. Subscriptions discontinued at expiration. To avoid missing any numbers renew two weeks in advance.

R. R. Teeter, Business Manager

OFFICIAL ORGAN OF THE BRETHREN CHURCH

Subscription price, $2.00 per year, payable in advance.
Entered at the Post Office at Ashland, Ohio, as second-class matter.
Acceptance for mailing at special rate of postage provided for in section 1103, Act of October 3, 1917, authorized September 9, 1918.
Address all matter for publication to Geo. S. Baer, Editor of the Brethren Evangelist, and all business communications to R. R. Teeter, Business Manager, Brethren Publishing Company, Ashland, Ohio. Make all checks payable to the Brethren Publishing Company.

TABLE OF CONTENTS

EDITORIAL

Answers to Some Questions About the Interchurch Movement

In connection with every great movement so much misinformation is passed along for actual fact that it is difficult to know what are the real facts until one goes to the head of things. This is true about the Interchurch World Movement. One prominent New York layman has taken a wise course and written directly to the head of the Movement, Dr. S. Earl Taylor. The clear and definite answers which Dr. Taylor gives to the questions of this layman will be of interest to our readers and possibly help to solve some of the questions with which they have been troubled. We give the letter verbatim:

"I thank you for your letter of the 19th, with its very specific questions. It seems to me that in this letter you have manifested the attitude of a true follower of Christ. In the Good Book the high standard is raised for Christian people that they may presently come to a point where they will think no evil of each other, and where they will in honor prefer one another.

"Instead of adopting this as a rule of conduct, it has seemed to me that in these days of general irritability, quarrelsomeness and seething unrest, Christian people have been especially prone to embrace any opportunity to think all the evil possible of other Christian men and women who are trying to help establish the Kingdom of Christ throughout the world, and they seem to be ready to seize upon and quote any rumor that may be floating around without taking time to investigate the facts, as you are doing. I would therefore most heartily commend your conduct to others.

"May I make the following specific answers to your questions? The first question is, 'Does the Interchurch World Movement deny the divinity of Christ?' The Movement not only does not deny the divinity of Christ, but it is being subjected to great criticism by certain so-called liberal minded men because it confines its work exclusively to the evangelical denominations of the Protestant faith. It stands as solidly upon the evangelical basis as the churches themselves stand, and I have never heard any leader of the Movement even hint at lack of faith in Jesus Christ as Savior and Lord. Indeed, the one and only great purpose of the Movement, so far as I know it, is to extend the Kingdom of Jesus Christ throughout the world. If it were not for this great central purpose I am sure that I should have nothing to do with it, and I do not know of any of my associates who would.

"I note that one minister of Christ has felt called upon to print and circulate a sermon in which he charges that the leaders of the Movement are not men of evangelical faith, and especially mentions Dr. Robert E. Speer and Dr. John R. Mott. How any man who has known these two great Christian leaders as I have known them for twenty-five years could ever get an impression that they are not sound in the faith passes my knowledge.

"Robert E. Speer, above all men that I have ever known, has always exalted the name of Jesus Christ. He is the only man I know who has made it an invariable rule to mention the name of Christ at least once in the course of every public address, no matter what the character of this address may be.

"John R. Mott has stood before students as the greatest advocate of Jesus Christ as Savior and Lord that the students of the world have ever known. Moreover, every address I have heard him deliver since the war began, has emphasized the fact that, while all other foundations have failed, Jesus Christ has remained as the one supreme and central and saving figure now lifted up before the eyes of humanity.

"I challenge any man in the world to produce a sentence with its proper context which would show that any of the men in place of responsible leadership in the Interchurch World Movement have ever uttered a syllable which would give foundation for this unjust and, as I believe, essentially un-Christian and libelous criticism which is being given wide circulation at this time.

"Your second question is: 'Does or does not the Movement believe absolutely in Father, Son and Holy Ghost?' Concerning this question, I must say frankly that while, as I have indicated, the Movement stands squarely upon the evangelical basis of the Christian church; and while, so far as I know, the leaders all believe in the Trinity as taught in the Scriptures, there are doubtless different shades of interpretation in matters of theological interpretation and controversy, and all that I can say is that every leader of the Movement with whom I am acquainted, stands solidly in faith, belief and practice upon the Apostles' Creed as adopted by the evangelical churches.

"Your third question is: 'Why do men like Dr. Reilly refute the movement?' In answer, I would say that I do not know. I observe that one very devout editor of one of the great Christian publications has felt called upon to issue a statement throwing discredit upon the whole Movement on the very eve of the financial ingathering. I notice that other Christian ministers in various parts of the country have felt constrained to do all within their power to block the effort of the leaders of the Christian church to come into co-operative relationship. I hope they have sufficient reason and justification for all this, but I personally feel that any Christian man who for any reason will stand in his place of leadership and oppose a great movement which has as its primary object the lining up of the Christian forces in a great co-operative effort to meet the world's need, is standing in a place which will be very hard to justify in the last great day.

"The Interchurch World Movement may have the wrong leadership and it may have many wrong methods, but all of these are more or less incidental and can easily be changed in the churches. The co-operative principle it stands for is essential to the future of Christianity and to the welfare of the world, and if the churches fail now, may God in his great mercy have pity upon the world.

"Of those who criticize the methods of the Movement, I would simply ask the question which Mr. Alexander asked a distinguished clergyman of England during the days of the Torry-Alexander meetings. This clergyman approached Mr. Alexander and said, 'Do you know, I do not like your method of soul winning.' Mr. Alexander at once replied, 'I thank you' my friend, for coming to me with this statement because we really are not fully satisfied with our method ourselves. Now, please tell me what your method is and how well it has succeeded.' The minister was dumbfounded by the question because it developed that he never had had any conspicuous success in winning men to Jesus Christ.

"To those who say they do not like the method of the Interchurch World Movement, or its plan of organization, or its historic origin, I say that I am not fully satisfied with it myself, but if a great co-operative movement on the part of the Christian churches is needed, and needed in the immediate future, how would those who criticize, launch such a movement, and by what methods would they develop it?

"I think I have quite frankly and fully answered your questions, but if I have not, please write me again.

"With kindest regards, and asking for your prayer and Christian fellowship in this great enterprise, I am

"Cordially yours,
"S. EARL TAYLOR."

EDITORIAL REVIEW

Happiness is the feeling we experience when we are too busy to be miserable.—The Way.

Elsewhere in this issue you will find the announcement of the memorial in honor of the late Rev. William Kiefer, to be held at the Fair Haven church near West Salem, on May 9th. Brother Owen, the pastor will be assisted by Dr. Miller and Brother Hendrickson.

The human race is divided into two classes: those who go ahead and do something, and those who sit still and inquire, "Why wasn't it done the other way?"—Oliver Wendell Holmes.

Brother I. D. Bowman reports a meeting in the "Valley of Virginia" with Brother E. B. Shaver, the father of that section of the Lord's Israel. Brother Bowman found that the field had been kept well gleaned, nevertheless success attended the preaching of the Word.

On April 18th Dr. Miller filled the pulpit of the Ashland Methodist church, and on the 25th Dr. Jacobs preached in that church in the morning and Professor Garber supplied in the evening. The pastor has been sick. Dr. Shively preached at the Fostoria mission. The college preachers are always in demand.

Brother I. D. Bowman reports his meeting at Fostoria, Ohio, mission, where he met with contrary weather and much sickness. Brother Oberholtzer was his helper in the meeting. Though not as great success was realized as Brother Bowman had hoped for, yet a number were added to the membership.

Brother W. T. Lytle maintains his reputation for the regular reporting of his church work. There are some pastors who consider it both a privilege and a duty to keep the brotherhood regularly informed concerning the progress of their part of the Lord's Vineyard. This is commendable. Brother Lytle is ready to exchange revival meetings with some other pastor. Improvements and progress are recorded at both Burlington and Darwin.

You are never to complain of your birth, your training, your employments, your hardships; never to fancy that you could be something if only you had a different lot and sphere assigned you. God understands his own plan, and He knows what you want a great deal better than you do yourself.—Horace Bushnell.

The record of the destruction at Berne, Indiana, caused by the tornado of March 28, will bring sorrow to the hearts of our readers. Seldom is one church called upon to suffer so great a loss and endure so great suffering. Besides the destruction of so many homes, two deaths occurred and many were injured. Our sympathies go out to Brother Johnson and his community of sufferers.

An announcement reached us a few weeks ago of the arrival at the home of Brother and Sister E. L. Miller of Nappanee, Indiana, of a baby girl. She arrived on March 15, and her name is Eleanor Louise. We are always glad to make note of the increase in the number of prospects for ministerial and missionary recruits, and would have made this mention sooner except for the fact that the announcement became misplaced when the editor was moving. Congratulations, to you, Brother and Sister Miller.

In a letter from Brother E. M. Cobb, we learn that Miss Aboud, who recently conducted an evangelistic campaign for the Dayton church and was baptized into the Brethren church at the close of the campaign and licensed as an evangelist, is being booked for revival meetings. Dr. Cobb has her schedule in charge and any one wishing to engage her for a meeting should write Brother Cobb at once. The letter will appear next week, but that this news may reach you the sooner we are making this mention of it.

Brother Wolford reports his work at Elkhart, Indiana, where he has served as pastor for seven years. The church has gone forward under his leadership until what was a half-time pastorate with meager church equipment has become a full-time charge with a splendid church plant. The "Joash Chest" idea was worked with splendid success there recently. Brother Wolford announces that his work there will close at Conference time (when he takes a position on the Ashland College faculty) and that correspondence is welcomed on the part of pastors seeking locations.

An awkward error occurred on page four of last week's issue in connection with the illustration concerning tithing. Instead of saying "This Oriental sets aside a tithe for his rice," it should have read, "This oriental sets aside a tithe of his rice." In this connection we wish to explain that the item concerning the Northern California conference appearing last week was written the previous week before the program came. We then wrote another item and intended that this one should be destroyed, but it was placed in the "Review" last week unawares to the editor.

We recently received word from Dr. J. L. Gillin, who is professor of sociology in the University of Wisconsin, at Madison, stating that he is now on the 17th chapter of his new book on "Poverty and Relief." The book will contain 52 chapters. Dr. Gillin is already recognized as an authority in this line and he is putting in some hard work on this production, and when it is completed we dare say it will be accepted as a standard work. Notwithstanding the fact that he is very busy, he has promised to give the Evangelist readers a production from his vigorous pen in the near future.

We were pleased to receive the following in our mail last week and will share the pleasure with our readers:

"Received Evangelist today. While lying down to take a much needed rest, I took the paper and turned to page 13. How my heart leaped for joy when I read the news "The First Easter Offerings,'' and I said, Praise the Lord.' I felt like going to the phone and calling out 'Praise the Lord, praise the Lord,' for I did so want to tell somebody. Besides the front cover page touched a tender spot in my makeup. I looked at it and studied it, and then looked at it again and again. Many letters written on the 'Family Altar' would not make the impression that picture did. Mary A. Snyder.''

GENERAL ARTICLES

"The Responsibility of the Laymen In the Church's Forward Movement"

By H. F. E. O'Neill

The church, and the Christian life, are like a man on a bicycle, he must keep going or get off. It has been said that there is no neutral ground on a living issue, so, there is no standing still in the life of a Christian or a church, they must either go forward or backward. In our own personal life, we are either better or worse today than we were yesterday. Our great Commander has said, "Grow in grace and in the knowledge of our Lord Jesus Christ," "New born babes need the sincere milk of the word that they may grow thereby." Christ never spoke of **standing** churches but he did speak of growing churches and **dying** churches. You will recall he said of one congregation that was trying to take a neutral position regarding Christian life that "Because they were neither hot nor cold, he would spew them out of his mouth."

When the European nations went into the war of 1914, the American nation took a neutral stand, but after much discussion covering a period of three years, the leaders of our nation decided that as a Christian nation we could not look upon the horrors and atrocities of the "Hun" and continue a neutral position; for the sake of Christ and humanity, we must help settle the struggle of autocracy against democracy. Now that the war is over and our boys have most all returned to their homes, it is very becoming that the church as a Christian body should move together and that move should be forward in a solid phalanx for the promotion of Christ's Kingdom in the hearts and lives of men. There is not one person in a thousand who will resent the presentation of Jesus Christ as their Savior and Lord if he is presented in a sane manner, but to the contrary, you will find men and women whose souls are hungering and thirsting for the message of Christ if WE as Christian people will but present him to them.

There is plenty of room and need for public evangelism and evangelistic meetings and campaigns, and while we need more of this kind of Christian work, it is very evident on every hand that personal evangelism or the method of man to man is more opportune and more needed than ever. Christ did not select the apostles who were to promote his Kingdom from large groups and through large mass meetings, but he selected them from personal contact, and while it behooves the evangelist, and the pastor to win as many people as possible through public meetings, it behooves us as laymen to do the work that God has called us to, for I am convinced that if the world is ever going to be saved it will be through personal evangelism. This thought is not only stressed by clergymen and laymen everywhere as individuals but was stressed very much at the meeting in Pittsburgh of the Interchurch World Movement in their conference sessions in this city, and received the most hearty commendation by that group of men who represented thirty denominations and twenty-eight states of the Union.

The Interchurch World Movement is not trying to correlate all of the Protestant denominations into one church as some have thought, but it is trying to get churches to co-operate in a great united program for Christ, also those churches of like faith to co-ordinate their efforts to do a more progressive Christian work, and in outlying or small communities where there are several churches and all of them dying and none of them enjoying the full time of a pastor to get such communities to combine for union church services and thereby co-ordinate their effort and work and do a definite piece of Christian work and be a real spiritual force in that community.

There are some instances where instead of from two to five preachers traveling from ten to fifty miles once or twice a week to conduct services in the several churches, they could under proper arrangements enjoy the privilege and receive the blessing of having the full time of a regular pastor.

The survey which the Interchurch World Movement has completed in some places and which is in progress in others, is of vital importance and gives to the local churches such a revelation of their community as they had never dreamed of. For instance, an illustration was cited at the conference just referred to above of a borough in Pennsylvania, with a population of about three thousand that had living in its borders at least two hundred Turks. Few were conscious of this condition and many of the churches were sending missionaries to India to convert the Turks and yet nothing is being done in this community for the conversion of these people who live right in their midst.

The Christian church has been criticized many, many times, and rightfully so, not for spending large sums of money in sending our most devoted men and women to foreign lands, for of this there could be no just criticism, but for not spending more time and money in an effort to Christianize the heathen, both American and foreign, in our own communities.

There are comparatively few church members who could intelligently give an answer to the question, "What is the difference between Christianity and Mohammedanism or Confucianism or any other heathen religion? And many professed Christians fail to show any difference between the lives they live and the lives of the persons who make no profession of Christianity.

The church of Jesus Christ must move forward and that right speedily because of the immense responsibility that God has laid upon us in the reputation we hold as a Christian nation and as Christian individuals. We must equip ourselves for a great service. We must remember that if we would be soul winners for him, we must in our inner lives and purpose of soul, "Come out from among them and be a separate people," for thus saith the Lord. This does not mean that we should gather our garments closely around us and refuse to have anything to do with the people of the world, but we must seek to find in them the good spirit which will be our point of contact to win even the vilest to Christ. No better example of the proper kind of spirit to display toward the sinful can be found than in Christ's attitude toward the woman in Simon's house, who was one of the vilest women with whom the Lord came in contact, he was criticized by his own friends for his attitude, but he saw the motive and even found just reason for commending her. It is so much easier for us as professed Christians to find fault with the practices of other people than it is to find the good traits in them. Some of us may not have had seven devils cast out of us, as had Mary Magdalene had, but of how many of us could it be said, like her, that "we loved much." If ye love me, keep my commandments and press forward.

Pittsburgh, Pennsylvania.

Some Good Reasons For Believing In the Interchurch. By Guilford Leslie

As stated in a former article, it was our privilege to attend the great Laymen's Conference of the Interchurch World Movement at Pittsburgh, January 31 to February 1 and 2. At that conference we were brought in close touch with the Interchurch and had set before us very clearly what it aims to do. There we were also led to believe that it was worthy of the support of any Christian. There three things were impressed upon the minds of us laymen about the Movement that made us feel that we ought to get behind it.

(1) It put before us the program of Christ for the world. (2) It was brought out there that the leaders of the Movement were men of faith in Jesus Christ and the church. (3) It was made clear that if the church was to do its work we must all depend much upon God for strength and guidance.

It was stated that the great program of the Interchurch is evangelism. Some one even said that was its whole program—evangelism at home and abroad. Ministers and missionaries were to be trained, money was to be raised, churches were to be built up and every plan was to be carried out in order that the Gospel might be preached to the unconverted at home and in foreign lands and that the needs of men might be met by that Gospel. We were told of the plans to encourage all churches to hold evangelistic campaigns before Easter and urged to co-operate. One of our committees had this statement in its report: "We would urge upon the laymen of America their participation in the evangelistic campaign which comes to a climax Easter Sunday, April 4th, and in the emphasis upon family worship as announced by the Movement." That report further stated, "We have been stirred by the appeal to evangelize the one billion people in foreign lands who have not yet heard the Gospel," also by the religious and social needs of "the vast populations in our own country as presented in the Home Mission Survey."

Realizing how many of the churches have failed to hold the boys of the teen age and older, and not believing it is the will of our Father that any should be lost, it was urged that the churches put forth more earnest effort to save the boys, especially by providing them with men teachers and definite religious and social activities. Our Findings and Message committee said, "In view of the great ignorance among all classes, including many professing Christians, of the teachings of Christ we cannot too strongly urge the necessity of Christian Education. In addition to stressing the work of the Sunday Schools, we believe that the Laymen of the churches should strive to introduce the reading of the Bible in the public schools, or, where that is impossible, to supplement the curricula of the public schools with religious education; that the High School Bible Classes be aided in every way possible, and that Week Day Bible Schools be promoted; that university pastors be placed in every state university, and that the church colleges be given the utmost support."

It was further stated that just as Jesus sought to meet the four-fold needs of men, body, mind, heart and soul, so the church ought to do what it can to lift up the whole of man. Jesus was our example and gave the church its mission. "We believe that the layman identified with the local church should work for the building up of the community life, that they should engage in the ministry of reconciliation between the various classes in society upon the basis of justice and righteousness, that they should become interpreters of life and its possibilities to all the people, and that they should seek to honor God, by declaring the Gospel of Jesus Christ practically applied, is sufficient for all the needs of mankind—spiritual, physical, social and economic." Again, our committee report went on to say, "We believe that the local church should declare itself in sympathy with all those agencies which are seeking to build up the community, in so far as they are in harmony with the spirit and will of Christ?" No one should halt on anything that is in the will of Christ, nor should undertake anything that is not his will.

The faith that the leaders of the Interchurch have in Jesus Christ and his church, as well as all other Christian fundamentals, is such as any one should be able to commend. They have not given a statement of their faith in great detail because they are leading a movement and not a school. Their task is to stir all the churches to do their work with greater zeal and not to engage in theological discussions. For if they should begin to discuss theology they would begin to disagree and would cease working and engage in controversy. But they are men of strong faith in Christ and the church. No one can listen to them speak without being convinced of this fact.

Here is one statement characteristic of many made at the conference: We believe that the church of Jesus Christ is a divine institution, demanding the hearty support of all Christian laymen; that through the Holy Spirit, it is the truest inspirer to the highest service, the best interpreter of the will of God, and the brightest beacon to the oppressed and depressed peoples of the earth. We believe that the outstanding need of our times is the religion of Jesus Christ, the fundamental principles of which are eternal and unchanging.

The leaders insisted that if the churches are to succeed in doing the big work that is before them, they must depend much upon God, and pray and read God's word much. The first thing they had in their program in which they asked the churches to co-operate was the deepening of the spiritual life. The director of evangelism urged that every one should do some real praying for the conversion of souls during the campaign of evangelism. It was urged that we pray for young men to enter the ministry. And when the united financial drive began it was urged that a few minutes be spent in silent prayer just before starting out on the canvass. Frequently in making plans and suggestions, we find them speaking of "the will of God," or "the will of Christ," and other like expressions, indicating their feeling of dependence upon the will of God, and their desire to encourage others to take a like attitude. And doubtless those who seek and depend upon God's will shall find it and be blessed in doing it.

If we shall let that spirit determine our attitude toward the Movement, we shall not go wrong. The question we should have in mind is this: Does this advance movement on the part of the thirty denominations, that has for its object the preaching of the Gospel in all the world, meet with the approval of Jesus Christ, who gave the command to preach?

The wise words uttered by Gamaliel in connection with the activities of the early disciples may be fitting here. "Take heed to yourselves what ye intend to do as touching these men—for if this counsel or this work be of men, it will come to naught; but if it be of God, ye cannot overthrow it; lest haply ye be found even to fight against God."

The Interchurch World Movement Examined.   By Louis S. Bauman

The hour has come! The hour long foreseen by the devout student of the "sure word of prophecy,"—the hour of vast federations and confederations, of collossal amalgamations and alliances, of gigantic leagues and combinations,—has come! The "get together" spirit fills the air. The whole earth seems to be fascinated by it, and ses in it the panacea for all human ills. Labor, capital, nations, religions, are all crying, "Come, let us build, lest we be scattered!" But, so be it! Babylon must again quickly raise her tower heavenward, and again as quickly be humbled in the dust of her pride, before Jerusalem shall return to forever be "the joy of the whole earth."

As for that which the world calls "Christianity," it is becoming famous for its multitudinous "movements,"—movements that for the most part move little or nothing, so far as the world's burden of sin is concerned. Just now, many good poeple are hailing with delight a "Movement" which they believe will bring heaven to earth, and make the "Golden Age" a reality. This particular "Movement is known as "The Interchurch World Movement.". It is heralded as being the mightiest movement in the church in the past four centuries; and, such it may prove to be. But, which way? One thing is certain, no Christian can ignore it. Every church, every pastor, every individual Christian, must take some stand with regard to it. This being true, it is but just and right that we should have as much light on the purposes and plans and possible outcome of this "Movement" as we can secure. It is right that we should examine it in the light of God's Word,—"the more sure word of prophecy, whereunto ye do well that ye take heed, as unto a light that shineth in a dark place, until the day dawn, and the day star arise in your hearts" (2 Peter 1:19).

It is to be expected that thousands upon thousands will "line up" with The Interchurch World Movement, whether it be right or wrong, simply because they are not made of the stuff that can stand against a popular tide. "Better be out of the world than out of the fashion," is still the maxim of the mass. The average man hates to be different, or to appear singular. He likes to "go 'long." It is easier to say "Yes" than "No." It takes a strong man to stand alone against the crowd even for his dearest convictions. When Cain's civilization dazzles the eye, Enochs and Noahs are few and far between. To understand the sort of stuff in the character of old Noah, consider this: "There were giants in the earth in those days, * * * mighty men which were of old, men of renown!" (Gen. 6:4). When Noah went up against those "men of renown," he did a good job in saving his own family. Here we are in the Twentieth Century, worshipping those same old antediluvian idols,—"Men of Renown." Whenever the devil has some damnable doctrine that he wants to pawn off on the human race as God's own truth, he immediately hunts up some "man of renown," and puts him out on the road at a good salary to preach it. When the hour arrived for "giving heed to seducing spirits and doctrines of devils" (1 Tim. 4:1), Satan found his "man of renown" in Sir Oliver Lodge, and made him the Paul of modern Spiritualism.

Even so when this latest "Movement" comes, whether it be of God or of Satan, no matter, we shall find many men falling over themselves to "get in," simply because many "men of renown" are at its head. As we are writing these words, an article comes to our desk in a religious weekly, telling us of a prominent editor of a well-known preacher's magazine who has espoused the cause of this "Movement." His conversion to the "Movement" can best be told in his own words: "I came to the conference (of The Interchurch World Movement) to question it for the benefit of the 15,000 preachers in the ——brotherhood. * * * One session of the conference determined one thing for me unmistakably—that is that Jesus Christ is in the Interchurch Movement. What led to that conclusion? For twenty-five years I have been as certain of John Mott's being a Spirit-filled man as I was

sure of my salvation. * * * And when he said there was no slate, or cut-and-dried program, or an effort to do a big thing merely for the sake of its being big, I believed him * * * When he said * * * that all churches must work together—not unite in one big unwieldy organization—I believed him." In a nut-shell, he decided that "Jesus Christ is in the Interchurch Movement" because John R. Mott is in it. With all due respect to John R. Mott (for whom, by the way, we have a very high regard also), we cannot decide this question that way. Even John R. Mott might be mistaken, and foster a thing that will prove unholy, and that while his motives are right. Yes, even John R. Mott might prove to be human enough" that he himself also is compassed with infirmity" (Heb. 5:2).

The very thing that is going to make this "Movement" exceedingly dangerous, if it be not of God, is the high character of the most of its leading promoters. But wise men will not be carried away by this fact. With the mass, there is too much of this taking things for granted because "men of renown" happen to say so,—too little of spending time in thorough, radical, painstaking investigation. Things being hailed as of a "new order," or belonging to a "new era," or a "new day," are hailed with delight by the crowd which never pauses to examine as to whether in the end those things may not prove impractical or even destructive.

Let us not forget that the present hour is giving to Satan some tremendous advantages. The very atmosphere is surcharged with dissatisfaction. The peoples of earth are like a restless sea, raging, distressed, troubled, tossed, driven. Men want, they know not what. This enables the enemy of our souls to better delude with his deceptive, fine-spun, cleverly-composed and charming anti-scriptural principles and programs. In such a time it is easy to make shallow-minded folks think that "we have outlived the old religion;" or, that "the church has failed." As a matter of fact, men have not outlived what they have never yet lived. It is a thousand times easier to invent a new religion than it is to live up to an old one. As a matter of fact, the real teachings of Jesus Christ have never yet been lived by the majority of the human race. What men are needing is not a new religion nor new schemes of human betterment. What men need is the oldtime Pentecostal power that will enable them to live up to the faith they have for centuries been taught by godly men and women. "A form of godliness," no matter how it may shape itself, will amount to nothing so long as men are "denying the power thereof" (2 Timothy 3:5). It is easier today to get men to open their pocketbooks and pour gold and silver into the coffers of the church, than it is to get men to take to their knees and stay there until "endued with power from on high" (Luke 24:49). But which will avail the more in its working?

Without controversy, there are some things to be said in favor of the professed aims of The Interchurch World Movement. First, of all, it is always a commendable effort that aims to make the church of God realize her tremendous obligation to the heathen world. Shame should sink deeply into the very heart of the church as it contemplates the spectacle of more than two-thirds of the human race without the Gospel after two milleniums of time. Secondly, it is an effort worthy of praise to bring about a better distribution of the forces on our home fields. Thirdly, the effort to make the members of the church of Christ realize that they are stewards of God, and that the vast majority are robbing God of tithes and offerings. Fourthly, there is no more praiseworthy work than to enlist men and women who know the Lord in the ministry of intercession. Fifthly, the tremendous task of making a complete survey of the "field," which is the "world," and furnishing the armies of the Lord with some intelligent idea of the fields to be conquered.—all that is excellent indeed. Sixthly, it is a work of tremendous value to put on a campaign of education and publicity in all the churches of Christ, that shall lift up their eyes unto the fields

that are white unto harvest, at home and abroad. Seventh-
ly, it is commendable to bring about co-operation among all
those who really have a "common cause." The principle of
of co-operation has upon it the seal of God: "How should
one chase a thousand, and two put ten thousand to flight!"
(Deut. 32:30). That figures out that one man co-operating
with a brother, is five times as valuable as when he is "going
it" alone. But we would venture the assertion that these
two men would be five times less valuable in attempting to
co-operate when disagreed as to their "common cause,"
than in each "going it" alone. Unquestionably successful
co-operation demands positive agreement as to "the common
cause."

Now, insofar as The Interchurch World Movement
stands for these seven commendable things, it can but meet
with the approval of all right-minded people. But,—and we
are sorry to have to use that tremendous little word—there
are some other things to be considered. Cheese is good; but
if it is within a trap,—well, then it is the most dangerous
thing about the trap. So before we nibble at the cheese
within The Interchurch World Movement, let us look around
a little farther.

I. The Interchurch World Movement proposes a program
that is contrary to God's program.

In substantiation of any charge we bring against this
"Movement," we shall quote from "The Hand-Book of
The Interchurch World Movement of North America." This
comes form the "Movement" as its authoritative voice,—
"A Source Book of Information for Speakers and Members
of the Organization." In this "handbook," on page 20, its
professed aim is set forth as that of "inspiring and organizing the Christian forces to undertake an adequate world
program." (Black letters used in quoting from this "Handbook" will be ours unless otherwise stated).

Now, let it be remembered that this "Movement" has a
very definite program, or should have, and which it is our
business to understand before we enlist. If this program is
of God, no power can successfully stand against it. If this
program be not of God, it is foredoomed to failure, and effort
in its behalf is worse than wasted. Now, what is this program? Let them state it.

"The Interchurch World Movement seeks to co-ordinate
the forces of Christianity on this continent for their campaign to win the world for Christ." (The Handbook, Pg. 13).

Now that sounds like a glorious program to the support
of which every true child of God ought to rush pell-mell. As
a matter of sheer fact, it is a program that we can fervently
desire and yield our very lives to see carried out! But, what
if it should not be God's program for his church in this age?
To the average person it sounds very much like God's only
program; but, is it? Let us see:

A few years after our Lord returned to glory, the first
council of the church was held in Jerusalem, for the discussion of the vexing question of circumcision. The reception
of the Gentiles into the church brought this question forward. At this council, all the apostles, elders, and other
notables were present. The debate was finished by James,
who arose, and declared without contradiction the program
of God for the church in the present age: "God at the first
did visit the Gentiles, to take out of them a people for his
name. And to this agree the words of the prophets; as it
is written, After this, I will return, and will build against
the tabernacle of David, which is fallen down; and I will
build again the ruins thereof, and I will set it up: that the
residue of men might seek after the Lord, and all the Gentiles, upon whom my name is called, saith the Lord, who
doeth all these things. Known unto God are all his works
from the beginning of the world (ages)" (Acts 15:14-18).

Unquestionably those words set forth the divine program for the Christian church in this age. With Peter's
visit to Cornelius, God began through his church to "visit
the Gentiles to take out of them a people for his name." The
very word, "church," (Gr. ecclesia), the name God himself
gave unto his people in this age, signifies nothing else than

"called out,"—not a converted world, but a people called
out from a world that is doomed unto judgment. The vision
of a world won to Christ in this present age is a mirage, of
which this Interchurch World Movement is one of the hopeless victims. It is the business of the church to evangelize
the nations, and out of them "make disciples," which disciples, called out and separated unto God for his own purchased possession, will be "caught up to meet the Lord in
the air (1 Thess. 4:17) one of these days. "Then shall be
great tribulation, such as was not since the beginning of the
world, no, nor ever shall be" (Matt. 24:21). "After this, I
will return, and will build again the tabernacle of David
which is fallen down." Not until he returns will "the residue of men seek after the Lord, and all the Gentiles," is the
emphatic declaration of the Scripture. Mark you, this world
IS to be won to Christ. For, at the sound of the seventh
trumpet, "The kingdoms of this world are become the kingdoms of our Lord, and of his Christ, and he shall reign forever and ever" (Rev. 11:15). The world will be won for
Christ, but not by the church. It will be won after the translation of the church to the side of Christ, as his bride. It
will be won after he shall restore and sit upon the throne of
his father David, as God has promised him (Luke 1:32, 33).
The Scriptural picture of a converted world is always the
picture of a world with the personal, visible Christ, on
David's throne in old Jerusalem. Look upon it:

"The word that Isaiah the son of Amos saw concerning
Judah and Jerusalem. And it shall come to pass in the last
days, that the mountain of the Lord's house shall be established in the top of the mountains, and shall be exalted
above the hills; and all nations shall flow into it. And many
people shall go and say, Come ye, and let us go up to the
mountain of the Lord, to the house of the God of Jacob; and
he will teach us of his ways, and we will walk in his paths;
for out of Zion shall go forth the law, and the word of the
Lord from Jerusalem. And he shall judge among the nations,
and shall rebuke many people: and they shall beat their
swords into plowshares, and their spears into pruninghooks:
nation shall not lift up sword against nation, neither shall
they learn war any more" (Isa. 2:1-4).

Once again:

"Thus saith the Lord of hosts; It shall yet come to pass,
that there shall come people, and the inhabitants of many
cities: and the inhabitants of one city shall go to another,
saying, Let us go speedily to pray before the Lord, and to
seek the Lord of hosts: I will go also. Yea, many people
and strong nations shall come to seek the Lord of hosts in
Jerusalem, and to pray before the Lord". (Zech. 8:20-2).

Now, if that isn't the picture of a converted world,—
a world won to Christ, then, pray, what is it? If it is the
vision of a world won to Christ, then how was it so won?
Let us read on:

"Thus saith the Lord of hosts; In those days it shall
come to pass that ten men shall take hold out of all the languages of the nations, even shall take hold of the skirt of
him that is a "—Methodist?—no! a Presbyterian?—no! a
Protestant?—no! a Catholic?—no! "shall take hold of the
skirt of The Interchurch World Movement—no!—"shall
take hold of the skirt of him that is a JEW, saying, We will
go with you: for we have heard that God is with you!"
(Zech. 8:23).

No matter whether we Gentiles like the idea or not, the
man called "a Jew" is yet return to his God and do the
work whereunto God called him, leading the world to the
feet of Jesus Christ. Yes, Jonah will return as a miracle
man, and then all Ninevah shall repent. This is God's sure
word of prophecy, and Jesus Christ emphatically declared
that "the Scripture cannot be broken" (John 10:35).

We are told that Jesus, after his resurrection, during
forty days, spoke to his apostles "of the things pertaining
to the kingdom of God" (Acts 1:3). With the clear understanding of the nature of the kingdom they must have had

(Continued on page 10)

THE BRETHREN PULPIT

Your Sins Will Find You Out.   By J. I. Hall

TEXT: Be sure your sins will find you out.—NUMBERS 32:23.

If you will notice the context you will see that Moses was displeased with the Reubenites and Gadites but his displeasure had disappeared on the strength of their solemn assurance. Yet a lurking suspicion of their motives seems to be in his mind, at least he continued to admonish them and concluded by warning them if they failed to redeem their pledge the judgment of God would fall upon them. This emphatic caution by Moses against such an eventuality throws a strong doubt on the honesty of their first intentions, and yet, whether through the opposing attitude or the accusations of Moses, they were brought to a better state of mind, showed that all was right. Moses warned them that if they sinned against the Lord that their sins would surely find them out.

Financially people want to know whether a thing will pay or not. In fact we consider the cost of almost everything but our sinning. If the sinner would count the cost of living in sin he would quit his job and have no trouble in finding one that pays. Yet men go into sin with a relish. If we should search through all literature, both sacred and profane, we could not find one sin committed that paid. No man can escape from his own sin. Every sin you commit will hunt you down and find you and make you pay the penalty. Beware, beware BEWARE.

I want to speak of some of the ways your sins will find you out.

I. In Breaking Human Laws.

A man may be an embezzler, untrue to his neighbor, habitually leave his grocery and other bills unpaid, but at last he loses his credit and the law is enforced against him. I know a man who entered his neighbor's house through the window and stole a large sum of money. No man saw or heard him, but a lurking suspicion and circumstantial evidence caused him to be arrested after a number of years, for his sin and sent to prison. All the money sharks and thugs and conspirators against good government and society will surely be found out and punished. God is displeased with individuals and nations that do wrong and they will finally be brought to justice. It is very important that we be law-abiding citizens, not primarily because we are afraid of punishment, but because it is manly and right.

II. Your sins will find you out in your body.

"Holiness spells health. Sin spells sickness." Violate the laws of health and it will finally shatter both body and mind. The boy who uses cigarettes will never amount to much. This sinful habit blights every prospect, even through his future is very promising. The man who becomes a drunkard unfits himself in mind and body for the great tasks and duties of life, and becomes a weakling and sometimes an imbecile. Quit your cigarettes and your booze and every other sin and live well your place in life.

If we could eliminate all the diseases that come from our transgressions of God's laws, it would be amazing how little sickness would be left. A man may practice secret vices and think no one will know it, but how sadly mistaken he is. It is seen in his blotched face and in his whole makeup, for in his very appearance he will be reckless. Beware, for your sins will surely find you out. Turn from your sinful practices and make your body a fit temple for the Holy Ghost.

III. Our sins will find us out in our character.

Every lie whether spoken or acted poisons the character. Grind a poor man's face and you suffer more in character than he does by the grinding, or suppress a poor man in his wages and you suffer more in your character than he does in his purse. Read an obscene book and you are worse for the reading. One of England's most splendid men was murdered by a young man whose heart became murderous by reading a novel. Listen to an unclean story and you are not quite as good as you were before you listened. Look on obscene pictures and your mind becomes filled with the bestial instead of the true and the beautiful. Witness an indelicate play and the fine sense of propriety is weakened. Turn away from evil or the final outcome will be a besmirched character.

An artist wanted a picture of innocence. He drew the picture of Young Rupert at prayer by the side of his mother who regarded him with tenderness. His hands were clasped together, his blue eyes were turned toward heaven, his cheeks were ruddy, and his face the picture of innocence. The artist hung the picture on the wall, and for years tried to get a model for a picture of guilt to hang beside the innocent Rupert's picture so as to show the contrast. At last when the artist was old, and weary of his search for a model for his picture of guilt, he visited a dungeon and on the damp floor lay a wretched man named Randall, heavily chained. His body was wasted, his cheeks were worn, his eyes hollow, his face showed the anguish, guilt was branded on it as with a hot iron, and the most horrid imprecations came from his blasphemous mouth. The artist drew a picture of guilt from the scene, and bore away the successful effort of his pencil and hung it by Rupert's the innocent. Now who was this young Rupert who kneeled beside his mother and prayed? And who was old Randall? Young Rupert and old Randall were the same. He was led by bad companions into the paths of sin and at last committed a crime that brought him to the dungeon. The face once bright with love, peace and joy was now darkened by guilt and shame. Young man, young lady, take heed lest you, too, may stray away from the paths of virtue and rectitude into the paths of vice. Be careful with whom you associate, or your character too may be darkened by guilt and shame.

IV. Your sins will find you out in your conscience.

Consciousness of sin means agony. Judas could battle off the pleadings of conscience and betray his Master into the hands of his enemies, but the remorse of his conscience made life unbearable. He hanged himself. O, the memory of sin, the remorse of it! Shakespeare says, 'Conscience is a thousand swords and hence, destroyed she becomes the nemesis of the soul.'' Luther said, "I am more afraid of my own heart than that of the pope and all his cardinals." I read of a man who was a murderer, a libertine and a thief. He laughed and joked about his crimes as if they were mere trifles and said he could sleep as soundly and as sweetly as an infant. He was said to be a good soldier, and about the close of the civil war, he killed a Confederate marshal and was executed. Upon the gallows he kicked his hat from the platform and he went off into eternity without a tremor and with an oath of levity upon his dying lips. That man had seared his conscience as with a hot iron by his sinning. "Man with his conscience dethroned is a self-propeller upon a turbulent deep, hurled with the force of his own destruction upon the reefs of an inevitable ruin." "Conscience involves everything." Origin calls it, "The Chamber of Justice," and he who has a good conscience toward God and man will need neither judge nor jury. Coleridge pronounced it, "The Pulse of Reason." Johnson declares it, "The Sentinel of Virtue." Others have styled it, "God's deputy," "God's vice-regent," "God's oracle," in the soul. And so, the heart which heeds and treasures "God's Monitor," as another calls it, needs no further sceptre to sway over his mental and emotional nature. Thousands of people are conscience smitten because they have not dealt fairly with others. Their ill-gotten gain is a sting in their souls. They hear that "pulse". of reason," that "chamber of justice," "God's deputy" crying out against them. Their consciences hunts them down and makes them pay the penalty. O what remorse!

Dear friend, let me beg of you never to fight your conscience. Take care of your conscience and when it tells you to be fair and just with your fellow men, and obey the voice of God—take heed and do and be happy.

V. Your sins will find you out in your children.

The Lord said, I the Lord thy God am a jealous God, visiting the iniquity of the fathers upon the children unto the third and fourth generation of them that hate me (Deut. 5:9). We may not like to think so, but it is true; the Bible reveals the fact. The moderate drinker, may never get drunk but it is overwhelmingly probable that some of his children will be drunkards. We believe many a child has been born handicapped by the sins of the parents. How necessary then it is for parents to lead sober, clean, godly lives for their own sakes and children's sakes. If every act in life is to be impressed upon the character of future generation our lives ought to be filled with good deeds, and with all the strength of our manhood be true and obedient to God's word, which will bring into the life both physically and religiously that which will help unborn millions.

VI. Your sins will find you out in eternity.

Death does not end all. If it were possible for men and women to go through this life sinning and not be found out, their sins would find them out when the great Judge shall come to judge the world. In fact, we shall all appear before the judgment seat of Christ. For it is written, "As I live saith the Lord, every knee shall bow to me, and every tongue shall confess to God. So then every one of us shall give an account of himself to God" (Rom. 14:10-12). The sinner may go on sinning by taking advantage of his friends and never be brought to justice here, and even make an argument that his course of conduct is right, that the pulse. of reason cries out in the depth of his soul and bring agony, yet for the much worshipped dollar he may endure it all, but at the judgment seat of Christ they must give an account of themselves to God.

Men may go through this life despising God and laughing at his word; they may trample under foot the simple teachings of Jesus, and not be arraigned here before a tribunal of justice. No one may ever call them to account for their ungodly conduct. God may permit them to live a long time, but some day they must give an account of themselves to God.

There is a way by which all may be rid of all desire to break human laws, all desire for sins that shatter body and mind and all desire to do the evil which will rob them of their character, their conscience, their strength that will be a foundation laid for future generations and a happy eternity, which will be as sure as the promises of God. That way only way whereby men may be saved. Enter at once and get the experience, the grace, the power, the joy. Do not you are traveling toward eternity on this "way" for it is the No man cometh unto the Father but by me." Be sure that is by Jesus, who said, I am the way, the truth and the life. Wait but do it now.

Martinsburg, Pennsylvania.

OUR DEVOTIONAL

Devotion to Duty. By Albert G. Hartman

OUR SCRIPTURE

What doth it profit, my brethren, though a man say he hath faith, and have not works, can faith save him? If a brother or sister be naked, and destitute of daily food, and one of you say unto them, Depart in peace, be ye warmed and filled; notwithstanding ye give them not those things which are needful to the body, what doth it profit? Even so faith, if it hath not works, is dead, being alone (James 2: 14-17). But let every man prove his own work, and then shall he have rejoicing in himself alone, and not in another. For every man shall bear his own burden (Galatians 6:4-5). And he that overcometh, and keepeth my works unto the end, to him will I give power over the nations (Revelations 2:26). Fear God, and keep his commandments; for this is the whole duty of man. For God shall bring every work into judgment, with every secret thing, whether it be good, or whether it be evil (Ecclesiastes 12:13-14).

OUR MEDITATION

In the above verses of Scripture we are given a keen insight concerning our duties as Christians. It goes without saying, that a Christian should be a righteous person. The Scripture goes farther than that. It contains a definite plea for good works, an unmistakable call for Christian service. What is it that God expects us, as sponsors of the truth, to do? It seems that some people find their places in the Lord's vineyard as soon as their souls are born into the kingdom, while others wander around aimlessly, always looking and never finding.

Our Christian experience will be no less interesting than we make it. It is with church work as it is with things of the world. We get out of it just what we put into it. There is no such thing as defeat to the Christian, except as he allows himself to be defeated by lack of effort on his own part. The chasm of failure is spanned by the bridge of opportunity. We need not fall into the abyss of misfortune, if we keep the faith, and with that faith combine good works. "Whatsoever thy hand findeth to do, do it with thy might." And "Whatsoever ye do, do all to the glory of God."

It is not necessary to lessen our religious activities, as our worldly duties increase in size and number. One good school teacher has said, "My main business in life is to be a Christian and obey the master. I only teach school in order to keep from starving to death." A homely expression, you may think but very true nevertheless. This man does not try to draw a very fine distinction between his religious work and his every day affairs. He takes Christ with him into the school room and into his home. His life reflects it, for he always goes about doing good. He has the true philosophy of life. His ideals are high, and they become the ideals of many others, because his influence is far-reaching. Why should we waste precious moments thinking about our own temporal welfare, when we might better be concerned about our spiritual growth and the welfare of others? God will provide something for you and for me to do every day, some task to perform. Inasmuch as we devote ourselves to these duties, the blessings of life will come. Sweet indeed is the realization that a service has been well performed.

Success is not measured by dollars and cents. The laborer, who earns ten, twelve, or fifteen dollars a week, may be living a successful life, provided he is doing his very best for himself and his fellow men. The business or professional man, likewise, who receives a more liberal compensation for his services, is truly successful only if he is giving his best. to the world. Otherwise he is a parasite and a drain on the community in which he lives. Let us consider well what God has given us to do. May we then be devoted to that service.

Our prayer is that we may all strive to see more plainly just what work we are fitted to do. No task is so large and none so small, but that we should give of our best in return for what God has done for us.

OUR PRAYER

Blessed Father, draw us nearer unto thyself, and show us thy way of righteousness. Give us wisdom and strength to do thy will. May we show a greater devotion to duty than ever before, that our lives may be a greater blessing to those about us. We pray for a broader and clearer vision of what thou would have us do. Dear Lord, we would be more fully consecrated in our service to thee, that our lives

may reflect thy goodness, and our acts radiate thy loving kindness day by day. Forgive our wrong doing; guide us by thy strong hand; and save us at last through Christ our Redeemer. Amen.

Send
WHITE GIFT
OFFERINGS to

THE SUNDAY SCHOOL

ALBERT TRENT
General Secretary-Treasurer
Johnstown, Pennsylvania

The Sunday School Teacher as a Factor In Evangelism. By Thoburn C. Lyon

It might be well to first take a moment to consider in what true Evangelism really consists. It consists in making known the gospel of salvation through Christ, making it known without regard to the number believing: that is the work of the Spirit; and if we have faithfully "made known" this gospel we shall have proved ourselves, in the truest sense, evangelists. "I make known to you the gospel. . . through which . . ye are saved; . . Christ died for our sins according to the Scriptures; . . He was buried . . and hath been raised on the third day according to the Scriptures," that is true evangelism as defined by Paul (1 Cor. 15). .

With this understanding of evangelism, it seems to me that the Sunday school teacher has an unparalleled opportunity; especially is this true in the Junior and Intermediate departments. For this reason, this age is, obviously, an age wherein man, the creature, revels in his self-sufficiency. The Modernists would, for example, have us reject the doctrine of the atonement as insulting to "man's intelligence;" they would emphasize, not what the Creator has done, but what his creature has done; obscuring the deity of Christ by making him but a creature of evolution, simply "at a more advanced stage," and so on. In short, man, always rebellious against God and his plan of redemption, has built around himself a wall of prejudice, otherwise known as broad-mindedness, which is almost impregnable. He says, "I have no need of God." Or, to quote one of the many mural inscriptions in the Library of Congress (a temple in honor of man), "The true Shekinah is Man."

Children to and including the intermediate stage are remarkably free from this prejudice, although each later stage is notably more difficult. Their minds are more receptive and open to conviction, while their impressions and beliefs are still in the formative state. One real point forced home at this period will outweigh a dozen five years later; in fact, a few years later this wall of prejudice may have become so strong that it would be relatively impossible to drive that one point home.

May I repeat, too, that we cannot be too careful in the selection of teachers for these younger classes. The girls will usually fall but little short of worshiping their teacher, copying not only her clothes and mannerisms, but her ideals of life as well, even though they include dancing and other questionable (?) pastimes. The boys, while not so open in their feelings, as a rule consider their teacher as a model of Christian manhood and authority. What a pity, if he has been carried away by the new "social theology," or "higher" criticism! Not only countless opportunities for evangelism lost, but a distinctive force against it.

. . .Too often, on account of the careless attitude of the class, the teacher looks upon his efforts as wasted. Instances might be multiplied, however, where the apparently inattentive scholar has "taken in" everything that was taught. And

even though there be no immediate results, some vivid impression may have been left that, sooner or later, will bear fruit and bring them to that saving knowledge of the grace of God.

However, "success" is not our consideration; from the standpoint of the world there has been no more colossal failure than Christ's own life. Our primary consideration as Sunday school teachers and as Christians, is evangelism— to make HIM known.

And if we do our part prayerfully and carefully, we need not worry about results, for God has said, "My Word shall not return unto me void."

Washington, D. C.

Sunday School Work in Egypt is Increasing

There are two Leaders in Egypt who are co-operating with the missionaries there in developing Sunday school work under the general direction of the World's Sunday School Association. Rev. Stephen Trowbridge, who during the war was "Major" Trowbridge because of his famine relief work, and Sheik Mitry S. Dewairey. Mr. Trowbridge is the Field Secretary for Egypt while Mr. Dewairey assists both on the field and in translating and editing Sunday school literature. Mr. Dewairey has just reported his work at five places which he visited recently. At Cairo he held a convention where over 100 teachers were present. Four schools out of eighteen promised to start teacher training classes. One school is composed entirely of street children. In it there are more than 200 pupils. An Egyptian lady just started another school. She began with three pupils and in three months those three boys had gathered sixty-five by using the picture cards in giving the invitation to attend.

In Alexandria there are now seven Sunday schools. Most of these have teacher training classes. A city secretary has been appointed and he is fostering a spirit of competition among the schools by giving a flag to the school whose monthly attendance is the greatest. More than 600 attended the Rally Day in the Sunday schools of Alexandria.

During the past year Mr. Dewairey has translated the following into Arabic, making a total of approximately 100,-000 words:

Books (1) "The Teacher that Teaches," Wells; (2) "The Boy and the Sunday School," Alexander, and Pamphlets—"Decision Day," "The Secretary and His work," "The Treasurer and the Librarian," "The Sunday School Graded," "The Adult Class Movement." A colporteur is employed who has been very successful in increasing the sale of the more than 25 Sunday school books now printed in Arabic.

The Sunday school workers in Egypt hope to have at least three Egyptian delegates attend the World's Convention in Tokyo next October.

(Continued from page 7)

(else Christ was a very poor teacher!), they asked: "Lord, wilt thou at this time restore the kingdom to Israel?" (Acts 1:6). Christ did not thereupon upbraid them for a lack of understanding, as modern scholars are wont to do, but he rather confirmed their expectations by simply saying: "It is not for you to know the times or the seasons which the Father hath put in his own power" (Acts 1:7). Then he

again stated the work they were to do while the kingdom tarried, and again we have the program for the church from the lips of the Master himself:

"Ye shall receive power, after that the Holy Ghost is come upon you: and ye shall be witnesses unto me both in Jerusalem, and in all Judea, and in Samaria, and unto the uttermost part of the earth" (Acts 1:8). Then, when they shall

Our Young People at Work

Junior and Intermediate Possibilities. By Miss Nora Bracken

(Address delivered at Ohio Conference at Canton. Concluded from last week.)

This organization gives opportunities for expression. Our young Endeavorers like to express their opinion. They like to tell what they have learned about the Bible. They like to read God's word in public and testify for Christ.

Next we might think of leadership. We would have a very weak nation had we no leaders. We would have a weak church had we no leaders. So it behooves us, if we seek to have the best government and organization, to develop leadership in early life. This is what "The Society" is doing for the child and the youth.

One of the greatest things afforded by this organization is that of devotions. There is nothing quite so helpful in a young life as that of Bible study and prayer. John Ruskin once said "All that I have taught of art, everything that I have written, every greatness that there has been in any thought of mine, whatever I have done in life, has been simply due to the fact that when I was a child my mother daily read with me a part of the Bible, and daily made me learn a part of it by heart." There are very few homes wherein the children get Bible training. So it must be gotten in the church. This is very strongly emphasized among the Juniors and Intermediates. You would be surprised, could you hear some of our little Juniors quote their Bible verses and passages of scripture. You would be surprised if you could hear some of them pray.

The Christian Endeavor has proven to be an excellent place for training. What this training means to some is beyond words. Here is where many find the Christ. It is here where some find their way into the pulpit. It is here where some have found their way into the mission field.

There are great opportunities in this field for the Brethren church. The Presbyterians are no doubt the strongest Christian Endeavor advocates among the churches. It was in this denomination where the movement found many of its leaders. The boys and girls in the Brethren church are just as valuable as their Presbyterian brothers and sisters. In comparison with our sister churches, our opportunities are just as great. We have some leaders in our churches who have not yet seen this great need for their young people.

We are praying that they may get a vision and that their young people may have equal opportunities with others.

Again we would say that within these young Endeavorers lie great possibilities. There lie within them innocency and purity; around them lies sin with its snares and pitfalls. Margaret Slattery, in one of her books, has given us a vivid picture of the evils that surround our young people. She first takes us up on a high hill which borders a city. There she shows us a number of beautiful little flowers that are being choked by the deadly nightshade which grows around and above them. The flowers are so entangled in this poison-weed that a person cannot pluck one without coming in contact with the weed. Then she points down into the city and shows us the great number of young lives, as beautiful as the flowers on the hill, that are planted therein. These also are constantly in touch with the deadly nightshade of sin. Many times sin crowds out the good. Again we want to bring back to you Longfellow. He says in his poem, "Maidenhood:"

> Oh, thou child of many prayers!
> Life hath quicksands,—Life hath snares!
> Care and age come unaware!
>
> Childhood in the bough, where slumbered
> Birds and blossoms many numbered;—
> Age, that bough with snows encumbered.
>
> Gather, then, each flower that grows,
> When the young heart overflows, ·
> To embalm that tent of snows.

Friends, life hath quicksands, Life hath snares, and thus it is necessary that our prayers for maidenhood and youth be many. And our care over them should be the best that we can give. What a heavy bough of snow old age must bear when in youth he had no opportunities, no educational advantages and no religious training. Let us help our young people gather flowers to embalm that tent of snows, so that life, to them, may be what God intended it to be.

Ashland College, Ashland, Ohio.

---

have done this work, they had the blessed assurance that, "This same Jesus which is taken up from you into heaven, shall so come in like manner as ye have seen him go into heaven" (Acts 1:11).

"Shall so come?" Yes. For what purpose? "To restore the kingdom again to Israel." Then shall Israel know her "fulness," since God is a covenant-keeping God. They fell,—yes! . But "If the fall of them be the riches of the world, and the diminishing of them the riches of the Gentiles; how much more their fulness" (Rom. 11:12)? Israel will yet know her "fulness," and bring the fulness of the blessing promised through Abraham to all the nations of the world (Gen. 12:3), or God's Word shall fail. And that cannot fail !

Now, at considerable length we have set forth the divine revelation as to the plan and purpose of God for this age. When men shall understand this plan and purpose, they will cease their chatter about "The failure of the church" because of the world that is not won to Christ,—a sadly broken and sin-smitten world as it is. The church was never set to win this world for Christ in this dispensation of grace, therefore she cannot have failed in her mission because it is not yet won for Christ. The church of God shall accomplish that which God sent her to do, even taking out of the world "a people for his name,—be sure of that!

Now, since The Interchurch World Movement has declared for a program that is not God's program for his church, can we be within the will of God and expect his church and expect his blessing if we enter the "Movement" as a church? Verily, God will not change his program to suit the programs of men. As a matter of fact, as we shall later see, the program of The Interchurch World Movement is the "Social Gospel" program of Modernism. We have searched in vain in all its literature for some intimation that its program might recognize the coming of the King to reign again on David's throne, and set the world in order. But never a word have we found. Over and over we have been compelled to ask, "Why say ye never a word about bringing back the King?" Just as sure as the Bible is God's truth, any program that refuses to recognize and work in harmony with the program of the coming King is not of God, no matter who its authors may be. A few months ago some statesmen met at Versailles and laid down a program that contained no recognition of God whatever. As we then prophesied, it is fast coming to naught. The program that fails to give the personal, visible King of kings his rightful place in the "Kingdom" it proposed to build on this earth, is doomed to certain failure.

(To be continued).

Long Beach, California.

SEND ALL MONEY FOR
General Home, Kentucky and
Foreign Missions to

MISSIONS

WILLIAM A. GEARHART
General Missionary Secretary
906 Conover Bldg., Dayton, O.

STATEMENT OF BOARD OF DIRECTORS OF THE MISSIONARY BOARD OF THE BRETHREN CHURCH

Because of the resignation by several workers in the Kentucky field and because of a series of accumulated misunderstandings regarding our mission work in Kentucky, a meeting of the Missionary Board of the Brethren Church was called to meet in the Y. M. C. A. Building at Dayton, Ohio, on April 18th.

This meeting was attended by the following members of the Board: Carpenter, Bowman, Gearhart, Ronk, Fudge, Grisso, Stuckman, Mrs. Wenger and the following members were represented by proxy: Horace Kolb by Wesley Baker; Henry Wall by E. M. Cobb; L. G. Wood by O. E. Bowman; Mrs. G. T. Ronk by E. M. Cobb; J. L. Gillin by C. E. Beekley.

The Riverside field was represented by Brother Drushal and six men from the Riverside community. There were present also Miss Hade, Miss Hillegas and Brother and Sister Rempel or Krypton.

The Board unanimously agreed on the policy printed below for the following year and in addition makes the following statement:

For some years there have been a feeling in some quarters that too large a percentage of our Home Mission funds was being spent in the Kentucky field and too large percent of that was being spent on purely educational work. The policy printed below will show that the Board has cut the total budget for this field in general and of the educational work in particular, as the state of Kentucky is increasingly able to care for the educational needs of the people.

A careful analysis of existing conditions was made by the Board in conference with the representatives from the field and the causes of dissatisfaction were gone into thoroughly and the chief cause of the dissatisfaction was found to be in the financial management. As a remedy the Board decided to appoint a financial secretary and treasurer, who should also be a teacher, thus relieving Brother Drushal of all financial responsibilities and leaving him free to devote his entire time to the church and school work.

With these changes the Board feels that all our interests in the Kentucky field are safeguarded and we can conscientiously urge the continued loyal support of the Kentucky work by the entire brotherhood.

Existing pledges should be met very soon as funds are needed at once.

The conference with representatives sent by Riverside was well worth while as the local people have a far better understanding of the conditions and the purposes of our Missionary Board and also of their own responsibilities and obligations.

Better co-operation means better results.

Statement of Policy

"First: That Brother Drushal be continued as pastor, teacher and superintendent, but that all financial matters such as receipt of tuition and other Institutional funds, all ex-

penditures and the accounting therefore be delegated to a Financial Secretary and Treasurer, who shall likewise be a teacher and shall be provided for by the Board with the approval of the Riverside local committee.

"Second: That no purchase or expenditure be made for the Institute without the approval of the local committee and Financial Secretary.

"Third: That the Riverside church shall provide a committee of three men, who shall have oversight of the local church finances such as raising pastors' salary and other local church, school and farm expenses and shall co-operate with the Financial Secretary.

"Fourth: That it shall be the policy of the Board to engage no other teacher at the Board's expense than the said Superintendent and Financial Secretary and that all work in advance by that supported by the State must be handled by these two workers, unless others are provided by local support.

"Fifth: All donations of food, clothing, etc., from churches or individuals to the Institute shall pass through the hands of the Financial Secretary and shall be checked up and an inventory of same filed.

"Sixth: The Board's administration of the Kentucky Mission field shall be in the hands of a committee known as the "Kentucky Mission Committee" same to consist of three men selected from the Board, one of whom is William A. Gearhart who is to have charge of finances, one Orion E. Bowman one of educational and legal matters and the third Amos Fudge of farm and buildings, and that the dormitory help and care of buildings and grounds be provided by such committee co-operating with the Financial Secretary and local committee."

GEORGE C. CARPENTER,
ORION E. BOWMAN,
GEORGE T. RONK,
Board of Directors.

Attest:
WILLIAM A. GEARHART,
General Secretary.

MISSION NEWS

The "Kentucky Mission Committee" created at the recent meeting of the Home Board in Dayton, has already received an application for the position of Financial Secretary and Treasurer at Riverside Institute. If there are others who desire to serve their Master in such a capacity, and are capable of teaching, will you please write us at once. Further particulars will be found in the "Statement of the Board of Directors" in this issue.

The Committee is also making an appeal for a consecrated, able minister (preferably married) to go to Happy, Kentucky, as soon as possible, for they are asking for this, and state that if our denomination does not send one soon, they will make an effort to interest some other denomination, which no doubt would result in our losing this promising field. Sisters Hillegas and Haddix have been on the field for some time and a splendid work has

been done, but the people at Happy now feel that it is time to place a minister there and they are willing to help to build up a church, for which they already have several splendid workers. Sister Hillegas has been teaching the public school and did what she could for the mission at the same time. She states that it is a very promising field and that the Board would do well to send a minister and his wife to build up the work.

Brother and Sister Rempel, our successors to Brother Cook's at Krypton, brought before the Board some of their problems and went back, feeling that it was well for them to have had the Board's advice, and gave them a renewed courage to continue their efforts to win souls for the Master. They were with us in the Dayton church for the Wednesday evening service, and both gave us very fine talks relative to their work, which were greatly appreciated by all.

The Kentucky slides are now in the General Secretary's office, having recently been shown at several points in the west, and we trust the churches or some auxiliaries of the churches, will make use of them during the summer months. Sufficient funds have not been provided to met the expenses of the installation of the light plant, which Brother Drushal stated is now working fine and was such a great help to them especially for their commencement exercises. Our suggestion is, that wherever these slides are shown, an offering be lifted for the light plant.

We are hoping that all who have made pledges and have not paid same, that an effort be made to do so soon, so that our expenses can be met promptly.

As you give, Brethren and Sisters let us not forget to pray much for all our workers in Kentucky, and not only for them, but also for those in all our mission points both Home and Foreign.

The Foreign Mission Easter offerings are now coming in and we are well pleased thus far. The average per member, when last figured, was over one dollar. We hope it will continue to show over that amount until all the offerings are in. Some of the churches will take several weeks to gather their offerings together, which is all right, just so it will not be put off too long. Brother Duker's church at New Paris, Indiana, was one of the first to send in its offering, and we were wondering what we would do with all the money if all the churches would do as well as this little church did. Their offering was $350.60 and it may be there will be more coming for they had only 41 present when it was lifted. Brother Bauman reports that their first effort to reach their goal of seven dollars per member, resulted in going over the top, and they will have considerable more after all is collected, some having made pledges to pay in thirty days.

Many struggling churches are doing so well that it no doubt will make some of the more prosperous ones feel ashamed, and if they do feel that way, it is not too late to add more to their offerings. The Dayton church is doing that by waiting for some pledges to be paid. We hope to have over $1,000.00 when it is all together, which is more than double the amount ever raised, for which we are grateful, but if we compare ourselves with some other churches that have done much better, proportionately, it makes us feel a little small. A full report of the offerings can not be made for some time on account of the delay in getting it to us.

WILLIAM A. GEARHART,
General Missionary Secretary.

NEWS FROM THE FIELD

FOSTORIA, OHIO

I closed a four weeks' meeting on the 16th day of March at Fostoria, Ohio. In some particulars this was the most peculiar meeting that I have ever held. "Flu" and other sickness kept a number from the meeting from the beginning. Brother Oberholtzer advertised the meeting well and by giving some write-ups occasionally. The first two weeks, in spite of the ice, "flu," etc., we had large and interesting congregations. But as this was a new field, we lectured on prophecy the first two weeks and pressed no invitations. The interest became intense, splendid people became convicted, then zero weather struck us and a great wave of sickness followed that put nearly every person in bed with sickness that was under conviction, and possibly twenty families were stricken that had been attending. This cut our crowds in twain and made the outlook discouraging. We thought of quitting but others thought that we should hold on, hoping against hope that health conditions would become better and that the crowds would again increase. But until the very end but few were able to attend who had been sick.

In spite of all these reverses we had 13 additions to the church the last week. Several of these were prominent members of our denomination. Several had been baptized by triune immersion and were members of other churches. One was reclaimed and several were baptized. Two came the last night when we closed with communion.

Fostoria is a town of about ten thousand people and one of the greatest railroad centers for the size of the town in the United States.

Our people bought a $7,000 or $8,000 church for $2,500. A splendid brick building located at as good a site as any in the city. They made some four or five hundred dollars' worth of improvements and will soon dedicate the church free of debt. One brother alone paid half of what the church cost.

Religion is at a low ebb in the city and Sunday, movies the curse of the town. The churches are selfish and worldly and many of the leading members of the churches need to become converted. We tried hard to push up the spiritual side and proved a great benefit to many of the members of other churches as well as of our own.

The meeting was very unsatisfactory to me in additions to the church for the reasons stated.

The little band of faithful members felt that it was not fair to me nor the church because of the sickness and weather conditions and therefore gave me a unanimous call to come back and hold them a three weeks' meeting next fall which call I accepted. Hence

we hope to fight the battle again when conditions are more favorable.

While there is a small membership of some 35 or 40 they are of such a class spiritually, intellectually and financially which seems to me to be the foundation for a better work than any other church of equal membership.

It would not be right for me not to mention the splendid home that I had at Rev. M. S. White's, right across from the church. All my needs were abundantly supplied. Sister White became very sick while I was there but they just kept me royally all the same. She was yet under the doctor's care when I left.

Then there was Brother Clint Newcomer, who fed me from his bountiful table two meals a day for almost four weeks and he seemed to have just as much to eat when I left as when I arrived. They were indeed very kind to me.

I was indeed very sorry that we had such a poor show but they all took it heroically and invited me to return to fight it all over again. In the middle of March, at midnight, I left Fostoria after a splendid communion service and started for home.

I found all well and happy. After three days' rest, and working hard while resting, I reluctantly pulled myself away from home on a two months' tour in the old Valley of Virginia.

I am now working under the Evangelistic League. We are having splendid meetings which I will report later.

ISAAC D. BOWMAN.

WARSAW, INDIANA

Easter Sunday of 1920 will be a day long remembered in the Brethren church of Warsaw.

First, because it was one of the worst days as far as the weather was concerned that we have seen for many a day, for this time of the year. A blizzard was blowing and the high wind together with the coldness of the atmosphere made one think that a visit from Santa Claus was coming instead of the day which meant so much to all the world, especially to those who have loved,—ones gone over the River to be with Jesus.

Second, it will be remembered because it was the first Easter since my dear father left us. His message of cheer on other similar occasions was missing, and yet through our tears, we could hear the sweet comforting words from the glorious Spirit of our dear Master, "Because I live ye shall live also." Furthermore it was my first Easter in my new parish. This helped to make it a day of pleasant memory, and as well as a sacred one.

Third, it was a day long to be remembered because we went over the top in all the plans which had been laid for the day. We were greeted with a large audience in spite of the

bad day outside and when once in the pulpit we were lost in wonder and admiration of the scenes before. Beautiful fragrant flowers, with their aroma in front of the pulpit silently but surely preaching its message of hope to the waiting congregation. The singing of the chorus choir, "Christ is risen," the pealing forth of the strains of the organ soon brought us to the realization of the glory of the day. The audience attentive and interested brought forth from the messenger the best that was in him. The subject of the message brought was "Easter Meditations." Indeed and in truth our meditations were solemn for we were painfully conscious of the presence of the Spirit.

Again, we will remember the day because we gave the largest offering to foreign missions that we ever gave previously. The amount was 342 dollars. Praise the Lord, we said, and all the people said, Amen. The climax to the morning service was typical of such an outpouring, 26 new members were received by letter and relation and some by baptism. Those that came by letter were from our church at Claypool which has recently disbanded. We made two trips there to see them and got their letters and thereby retained them for the faith which we all love. Two came to us by relation from our church at North Manchester, and four by baptism.

The Easter evening service was given over to the children and they rendered the program of the evening and everybody went home happy and still are speaking praises of the blessings received. May the Lord grant that we shall have many more such spiritual t[....]s, is our prayer.

We are moving thus to victory. The Spirit of God is having the right of way. He is doing the work and we are just the instrument in his hand and doing our best to keep in tune with him.

We are planning another drive soon. Guess what! Well, just wait. Guess awhile and in the meantime pray that we shall be successful in our undertaking for every duty and task before us.

A. E. THOMAS.

FIELD REPORT OF THE EVANGELISTIC LEAGUE

While in Philadelphia we were invited by Brother McClain to present the work of the League and met with a hearty response of the membership. Brother McClain is doing a fine work there and the church is going forward under his leadership. His ability as a Bible teacher has been recognized by the Philadelphia Bible school by placing him on the faculty.

Goshen, Indiana

Enroute to Illinois, I had arranged with Brother McInturff, pastor of the Goshen church to spend a Sunday with him and his people. I had the privilege of speaking to the congregation at both services and presented the League. Many had at the state conference in the fall taken out membership and several more responded the Sunday I was with them. I enjoyed my visit here and the genial hospitality of Brother McInturff and his home.

North Manchester, Indiana

On my way to Dayton I visited Brother Bame and his family and found him and his people in the midst of a Bible Institute, being assisted by Dr. Fitzwater of Moody Bible Institute. They certainly made a good team and I was glad to share one night of the spiritual feast. Dr. Bame is one of the directors of the League and by invitation briefly presented our work.

Dayton, Ohio

I found Dr. Cobb busy on the job and the church a regular bee-hive of activity. Brother Arthur Lynn, one of the sweetest singers of Gospel song I ever listened to, with his family have located in Dayton as assistant to Brother Cobb. They had a revival campaign on with Miss Aboud as evangelist. She is a native of Syria. And preaches the Gospel of Christ effectively. The church was well filled at every service I was present and people were finding the Lord.

We will hear more of Sister Aboud later, and I trust arrangements can be made so we may have all her time. Cobb is making good in Dayton and his motto, "Over the top" is being carried out in letter and spirit.

Announcement

I have arranged to be in the field the coming year for the League. Part of my dates are already taken. I still have a few open. Churches desiring my service should correspond with me early to secure a date. Mail addressed to me in the east will reach me at 28 North Mathison Street, Dayton, Ohio. My western address is Sunnyside, Washington.

The League expects to have other men in the field and we can arrange to furnish the churches with an evangelist. I am now in my eighth consecutive campaign with Brother Snyder at Milledgeville, Illinois, and go from here to Falls City, Nebraska to hold a meeting with Brother Stuckman.

W. S. BELL.

ELKHART, INDIANA

The work here has not been reported for some time but the church is nevertheless actively engaged in the work of the Kingdom. The pastor has been preaching for the church here for seven years. Three years of which was as half time pastor and four years full time. A full report of the seven years' work will be made later.

During the last year a basement under the main auditorium has been excavated and furnished for Sunday school work. The Junior department under their own superintendent with their own opening and closing exercises now occupy the large room of the basement. Besides this classes from the Intermediate department meet for class in the basement. The church has also been repainted and re-papered. The Altruist class of young people also built a choir-loft which cost them about four hundred dollars. All these repairs left the church

with an indebtedness of about five hundred dollars. Plans were laid for raising this money on Easter Sunday, our Foreign Mission offering being provided for in the budget. A "Joash Chest" was prepared to receive the offering. After a brief program by the Sunday school the entire audience marched past the chest and deposited their offering either as individuals or classes. The total amount received was $790.

This is sufficient to clear all indebtedness of the church and meet all obligations outside of the budget.

Every department of the church is in a healthy condition. The church is preparing to make an every member canvass as outlined by the Interchurch World Movement. The presentation of the aims and plans of this greatest of all movements since the Reformation has stirred the church and brought them face to face with the great challenge of the Kingdom of God which calls for immediate and adequate response if we are to meet the needs of the world.

We will close our work here at Conference time. The church here is therefore looking for a pastor and will welcome correspondence from any who are contemplating a change. Write Mr. C. E. Stephany, 1144 Prairie Street, Elkhart, Indiana.   H. H. WOLFORD.

MAURERTOWN, VIRGINIA

I am now in the "Valley of Virginia," the garden spot of the world. Tell Brother Bauman California isn't in it. We surely had a royal time here. I spent two weeks and two days at Maurertown with the seventy-six-year-old boy-pastor and evangelist of this Valley. He seems much younger than he did twenty years ago. Brother E. B. Shaver was old when he was fifty, but now has better health, and while always a good preacher they say he preaches as well as he ever did in his life. He has received several thousand members into the Brethren church, most of them in this valley. I owe to him much for what little success the Lord has given me. He thrust me out into the field when I was a boy.

This church is in a little town four miles north of Woodstock, the county seat of Shenandoah county. This is the home of Brother Shaver and one of the most stable churches in the Valley of Virginia. The field has been well worked. Nearly everybody belongs to some church. We had ideal weather for the meeting and some nights an overflow. Large crowds form beginning to end. As a result of the meeting, Brother Shaver baptized five in the baptistry on Easter Sunday, the closing day of the meeting. There are three others who desire to be baptized in the river a little later. This will make eight additions to the Brethren church.

This was surely about all that could be expected from this well worked field. Many believe, and I think rightly so, that the spiritual benefit of the church was the greatest work of the meeting. They liberally supported me, relieving the League of every dollar for poorer and more needy fields in this valley. And besides liberally supporting me they made up all of the expenses before the Easter offer-

ing was taken and then took an offering for missions of more than $150. So that in a little more than two weeks they paid out about ($300) three hundred dollars. I am also told that they are putting the Evangelist into every home in the church.

I found many here that I had baptized years ago. Among them Dr. Shaver, the most successful doctor in this Valley. He is a radical temperance man, opposing both rum and tobacco.

I had my home with Brother Haun in Woodstock, four miles from the church, but we ran down the Valley pike in his Maxwell nearly every night.

Well it cannot be expressed,—all I will say was that we had old Virginia hospitality at a premium. Haun's is truly a sociable Godly family. Two boys are ministers and the two girls conscientious Christians, the pride of a Godly father and mother's heart.

When the nights were a little cold and I perspired I would ride in Brother Lock's new enclosed Hudson, electrically heated machine. No inconvenience or accommodation was too great for these good people to do for me. I left on Easter Monday for Roanoke, Virginia, and rested one day at my brother's home—J. S. Bowman's. I am now at Boon's Chapel, in the Blue Ridge Mountains holding a short meeting. I will report this meeting later.

ISAAC D. BOWMAN.

Address me, 1942 South 17th St., Philadelphia, Pennsylvania.

BURLINGTON AND DARWIN BRETHREN CHURCHES

We will try and interest the Evangelist readers with a report of our work. We have no excuse to make as the forward movement in many ways speaks for us.

Burlington—The church has called a decorator to do some much needed work on beautifying the interior as well as the outside. The Easter cantata, "In Old Jerusalem," proved to be a fine success in every way and the choir and young folks soon plan to give some other selection which will aid materially to the development of the talent in this community. The church will try to find her place in all the activities to make possible their part in the Victory Year. The church has called us to serve as pastor from October 1, 1920 to October 1, 1921. Also a committee consisting of the three deacons have been appointed to make arrangements with an evangelist to hold a series of meetings following the Indiana State Conference in October. We are planning for a program Woman's Day and for a Great Time with our children on Children's Day.

The Sunday school is moving along with larger and more regular attendance, interested in doing things in a very noticeable way. The Woman's Missionary society is assuming a fine work in beautifying of the church and also planning to do their full measure to meet their goals. In the future when our evangelist comes to us we will expect some great things done for the Lord's work, at Burlington.

Darwin—This church too, has now put in their new light system, and many of the past experiences will be avoided with these better equipments. The folks will enjoy the services better and know that when they come the lights will be on to brighten the gloomy corners. The cantata, "In Old Jerusalem" was given there on the night of April 11, in the absence of the pastor (who was down with something, Dr. said "flu," yet I have my doubts, because, it's out of season). Brother E. A. Myers presided and took up the offering. The church and its various auxiliaries have been handicapped during the winter months, yet we expect some greater results in the future.

The church has called us to serve for the on-coming year and one brother expressed it after the close of the meeting, "As long as we will just keep Lytle." I have not as yet figured this out as a compliment or complaint. I will leave that to the reader. We are also laying plans here for a Woman's Day program and also a Children's Day program which we will be able to report later.

The church here has decided to arrange with some pastor to exchange with the pastor and hold three series of meetings between National and State Conference, in September. Brother Pastor, here is a fine opportunity to do a little working together, if you would like to work with me and allow me to work with you. Write me.

Of course at neither Burlington nor Darwin are wonderful things being done, but with taking all things in consideration our people are loyal, competent, and willing; therefore, we can accomplish if "we faint not."

Pray for us and our work, as we labor together in the Master's service.

We should be in North Manchester attending the Evangelistic Conference, but cannot, and the good Brethren will have to charge our absence up to Mr. "Flu" & Co., whose liabilities far exceed their assets.

W. T. LYTLE.

Burlington, Indiana.

DESTRUCTION AT BERNE, INDIANA

The storm that struck our section here March 28th, surely wrought havoc. The path of the storm here at my place was a mile in width, and left nothing but wreckage in its path. The homes of the Brethren Riffel, Gillispie, Baker, Smitly and Lehman were completely swept away, nothing being left but the foundation. And the miracle is that none of them were killed except at the Riffel home, where the wife and grandfather were killed.

Our own home was partly destroyed, the roof and upper story being entirely destroyed and all the out buildings wrecked beyond repair. The home of W. H. Parr was badly damaged and all out buildings destroyed. The home of W. N. Smitly was wrecked and all out buildings destroyed. His new barn which was just completed is a complete wreck. He had lost a good barn by fire last November. The home of J. F. Sipe was wrecked and all out buildings destroyed. The home of S. S. Egly damaged and out buildings destroyed. The church that is just across the street from Brother Egley was not damaged to any great extent.

The home of Brother Lem. Sipe was completely swept away with all out buildings destroyed. There were nine seriously hurt in the Simeon Riffel home. In the Baker home Dan Baker and his wife suffered broken legs. Archie Smitly was seriously hurt in the Ralph Smitley home, and the entire family suffered considerably. In the Lem Sipe home, he and his wife suffered seriously from falling timbers. In the Baker home a son of six years went out into the darkness and storm and found his baby brother who had been blown some distance in the tornado, and then went nearly a mile to get aid for his parents who were pinned under the debris, each with a broken limb. The homes of Marion Parr and Flora Caffee were badly wrecked and all out buildings destroyed. All these are members of the Berne church.

If we were to tell of some of the freaks that the storm played it would sound unreasonable. My daughter received a letter from a party near Toledo, Ohio, stating they found a post card with her address.

Many families here and in the wake of the storm have not a dish, garment or anything left except what they were wearing at the time of the storm. We were in Pennsylvania at Brush Valley, holding a meeting at the time of the storm and knew nothing of the suffering at home, only on Sunday evening we suffered much, as after retiring for the night our rest spelled as we heard our good wife call out distinctly twice in the night. You may call it mental telepathy or what you please, but it was true just the same.

On Monday morning as soon as we could get a paper we saw the account of the storm which had struck Eastern Indiana near Portland and Geneva, and knowing that these places were near our home, we became quite anxious to learn from home so we left Kittanning, Pennsylvania, on the first train for home and when arriving at Warren, Ohio, a telegram was awaiting us, saying, "Come at once, struck by a tornado, nine of us hurt." So you can imagine our anxiety with this news and at ten P. M. and no train to start us home until five next morning. But you can guess our joy when arriving at Decatur to learn that the telegram had been mis-spelled and instead of nine it should have read "None hurt," a mistake in the receiving.

The storm struck here at six thirty P. M. and moved in a northeasterly direction and for miles both north and south there is nothing but destruction of lives and property. One family southwest of us has five of its members killed. Another had three dead, and others one, two and some one. And yet it seems miraculous that all in those buildings which were completely blown away were not all either killed or crippled. Yet with all the destruction we wonder if those things after all were not for the best. People are getting married to the things of this old world which are perishable at the best, and with all of the calamities of these days, will not people take warning, and flee the wrath to come? For if our Bible be true, and we believe with all our heart it is, these but the forebodings of the great day that is yet to come. See Second Peter three, ten.   W. F. JOHNSON.

CHRISTIAN STEWARDSHIP AND
TITHERS' CORNER

In order to encourage tithing as a plan for financing the Kingdom, and as a means of spiritual development we are giving space to a "Tither's Corner." Much of the material is supplied by "Laymen" whose address is given below. We shall welcome testimonies and brief notes on tithing from our readers. We also would like to hear from churches, Christian Endeavor societies and other organizations as to the number of tithers they have. If you have no tither's band suppose you start one, send to Layman, 143 North Wabash Avenue, Chicago, or Christian Endeavor World, Boston, or Interchurch World Movement, 43 West 18th Street, New York, for tithing pamphlets, and report your progress from time to time. Who will be the first to send a brief testimony or report?—Editor.

Under date of March 16, G. F. Bradford of Sacramento, California, writes:

"I have accepted the position of stewardship and tithing secretary for the Christian Church (Disciples) of northern California, and have been on the job for two months with results beyond my fondest expectations. Have visited eight churches and enrolled an average of eighty tithers to the church. It is surprising how kindly people take to God's plan when they understand it. The majority of these, nearly seven hundred people have been reached at the Sunday morning service for the reason that a very small percentage of the membership of the average church will attend the midweek services.

"My plan is to begin the rally on Wednesday night and close Sunday night. We take pledges at both morning and evening services on Sunday. I also devote a few minutes to the junior and intermediate departments in the Sunday school on Sunday morning, and have found that almost the entire number readily consent to go into partnership with God. I am also urging the teachers to keep the matter before the children with very brief instruction every Sunday morning at the beginning of the lesson study. There is no doubt in my mind but that these children will keep up this system and that it will anchor them to the church in after years through the spiritual development that comes through linking up their lives with God.

"The people of northern California are loyally supporting the work by calling rallies to be held in their churches. I am now dated far in the future. I am being supported by one man who began tithing fifteen years ago when his salary was $60 per month. He is now paying my salary, through his home church, out of a part of his tithe.

"I am going to need thousands of pieces of tithing literature in this work, and wish you would give me prices on large amounts. (They are free to ministers.—Layman.) I secure promises from the ministers to preach on the subject and to order literature from you for follow-up work."

The Methodists of India are having their Centenary in 1920 instead of 1919. They, too, are publishing a "Centenary Bulletin." It is issued in twelve languages in ten different cities. The price is one rupee to those not connected with the Centenary movement. The following is a representative article from the English edition at Lucknow:

"During the year we have made a special effort to enlist our Village Christians as tithers. Letters were sent out from my office to all the members of our Time Legion, numbering about four hundred, urging them to pledge themselves definitely for stewardship. Pledge blanks were sent out to each circuit man and the number of tithers enrolled, aside from our mission workers, is 189. A very large number of these are Village Christians, and we hope to have at least five hundred of these tithers by the end of the year just beginning."

Live Wire Reading Contests

We publish about a dozen different tithing pamphlets by seven or eight different authors. Copy of each will be sent gratis to any leader of a stewardship reading contest upon request. Subsequent orders will be filled, postpaid, at the rate of $1.00 per hundred, or less, for any or all of them.

Address the Layman Company, 143 North Wabash Avenue, Chicago. Please mention The Brethren Evangelist.

The following letter is from Dr. Richard O. Flinn, pastor of the North-avenue Presbyterian church, Atlanta, Georgia. I call especial attention to his methods. They mean education to secure results.

"As a result of several sermons and the distribution of literature and stewardship cards furnished by you, I have received the signature of seventy-three in my church who have accepted the principles of Christian stewardship and have pledged themselves to set aside regularly a portion of their income for Kingdom purposes. Only one of these so far, as the record shows, has been a previous tither.

"I expect after Easter to begin another educational campaign on stewardship, and would like to take advantage of your offer to send more literature. I have already distributed 'How to Tithe and Why,' 'Is the Tithe a Debt?' 'Thanksgiving Ann,' and 'Talks with Money.' I would like you to send me, if you can spare them, about five hundred copies each of 'Reasons for Tithing,' and 'Proportionate Giving,' by Robert E. Speer.

"I wish to express my sincere appreciation of the great work you are doing in the publishing and distribution of this literature, and to assure you of the pleasure it gives me to co-operate with you in every way possible in getting it into the hands of Christians and of trying to persuade them to adopt the tithe as a beginning. In childhood I taught the tithe, but, like yourself, have long ago grown past it in free will offerings."

NIGHT LETTER

Turlock, Cal., April 22-23, 20.''

''Rev. G. S. Baer,

''Ashland, Ohio.

''False impression gone throughout brotherhood because of caption California Endorses Interchurch, Brethren Evangelist, March 31. Northern California Brethren Conference in session unanimously protest against all actions placing our church in wrong light before the world and ask that this appear in next Evangelist.   N. V. Leatherman, Moderator..''

(From what we are able to learn we feel that the news in the above message stating that a false impression has gone forth throughout the Brotherhood will come to most of our readers as a surprise, inasmuch as indications as to the attitude of the California Brethren churches have appeared several times already in this paper. However we give publicity to the telegram.—Editor.)

Memorial services for the late Elder William Kiefer will be held at the Fair Haven church near West Salem, Ohio, on May 9th at 2:30 in the afternoon. The Zion Hill and Ashland friends are especially invited to attend. Dr. J. Allen Miller and Rev. A. C. Hendrickson will be present to assist in the services.
                                BENJ. F. OWEN.

THE TIE THAT BINDS

TEMPLE-SCOTT—Brother Harry Temple and Sister Sarah Elva Scott of Johnstown, Pa., were married by the undersigned, in the absence of the pastor, Brother Watson, in the parsonage of the Somerset Street church. The best wishes of a large circle of friends and brethren go with them in their new life.
                                G. H. JONES.

ECKSTINE-NEWMAN—Mr. J. Leroy Eckstine and Sister Rose Newman of Morrellville, were united in marriage by the pastor, at the home of the bride. After the ceremony a number of relatives and friends enjoyed a splendid wedding feast. The bride is a faithful member of the Morrillville church, to which organization she was aided during the present pastor's administration.
                                G. H. JONES, Pastor.

IN THE SHADOW

SCHWEITZER—William S. Schweitzer was born in Hocking county, Ohio, and when a boy moved to Indiana with his parents. His life was lived near Eaton on the farm. He had the good will of the entire community and was respected by all who knew him. When the Maple Grove Brethren church was organized he became one of its charter members and remained in full fellowship until he was called home. He departed this life March 26, 1920. The length of his earthly abode was sixty-seven years, seven months, and ten days. The heart and the community miss him but we believe our loss to be his gain. Funeral serivces by J. L. Kimmel assisted by the writer.   H. E. EPPLEY.

COX—Harold Cox departed this life at his home near Eaton, Indiana, November 22, 1919, at the age of ten years, one month, and nine days. He had been a member of the Maple Grove Brethren church for two years and seldom has a community been stirred up by the illness and death of a boy as was this one. He had many friends and is missed by all. His parents, two brothers, and a sister remain. We suffer loss but believe it to be outweighed by his gain. Funeral service by the writer assisted by L. Miller of the Church of the Brethren.
                                H. E. EPPLEY.

CORNISH—Elder John Cornish, son of Henry and Susan Cornish, was born in Tionesta, Forest county, Pennsylvania, July 29, 1841, and departed this life March 12, 1920, at his home near Mulberry Grove, Illinois, being 78 years seven months and seventeen days old. At the age of ten years he moved with his parents to Clarion county, Pennsylvania, where they resided till the year 1866, when they came to Bond county, Illinois, where he resided till the time of his death. He was married to Miss Lavina Linamen, August 27, 1862. To this union were born six children, three of whom, with the widow survive. He was converted and united with the Church of the Brethren about fifty years ago, and was ordained to the eldership in the Brethren church about twenty years ago. He lived a faithful and devoted life and was worthy of his calling until he was taken home to his reward. Funeral services by the writer in the Church of the Brethren near his home.
                                CLAUD STUDEBAKER.

MILLER—John S. Miller passed from this life into his future abode on March 8, 1920. He lived to a ripe old age and had been a member of the Church of the Brethren for many years. His wife and one daughter are members of the Brethren church. Funeral services from the Maple Grove Brethren church by Rev. L. Miller of the Church of the Brethren assisted by the writer.
                                H. E. EPPLEY.

RESSLER—Brother George Ressler passed away February 25th, 1920, after a short illness. He died of the influenza. He leaves to mourn their loss a wife and three small children. Interment in the Armagh cemetery. Services by the undersigned.
                                G. H. Jones.

HILDEBRAND—Sister Maggie Hildebrand of Moxham, died at the home of her parents. Brother and Sister Lovinus Hildebrand, after a long illness. She was one of the faithful attendants of the Moxham church and Sunday school. Her presence could always be depended upon and she will indeed be missed. The pastor anointed her shortly before her demise. Interment in Hedricks cemetery.
                                G. H. JONES.

HEIDER—Arthur Heider Jr., the infant son of Arthur and Mary Heider, died suddenly from convulsions. Interment in Grandview cemetery. Services by the writer.
                                G. H. JONES.

Knauer—Brother Dewey Knauer of the Conemaugh church was struck by a train and instantly killed in the Conemaugh railroad yards while returning from his work. Brother Knauer was one of the writer's pastoral family many years ago and his death came as shock to us. His godly father preceded him to the other world some years ago, while driving home from the church services at the Pike church. Both parents have been, with the family, faithful and consistent members of the church for many years.

On account of the illness of the pastor, Brother Watson conducted the funeral services.
                                G. H. JONES.

BORING—Mrs. Nancy Boring, familiarly called "Grandmother Boring," died at her home in Franklin, near Conemaugh. She was a member of the Lutheran church, but the larger number of her children are members of the Conemaugh church. She died after an illness incident to old age. Interment in the Pike Cemetery.
                                G. H. JONES.

Our hearts go out in sympathy to the brethren who have been bereaved of loved ones both by illness and accident. But the Comforter, God's Holy Spirit has been a promised Helper to all who give up loved ones in the Faith. It is with this assurance we send this message to the grieving readers who are one in the common faith.
                                G. H. JONES, Pastor.

KRICHBAUM—Lloyd Dale Krichbaum was born October 6, 1896 at Servia, Indiana, and died March 2, 1920, aged 23 years. In 1915 he graduated from the Warsaw high school. He had been a student at the Winona College and the North Manchester College. When death overtook him, he was a student at the State Normal at Terre Haute, Indiana and just when his graduation was near at this institution, he fell asleep in Jesus.

Lloyd was a devoted member of the Warsaw Brethren church, taking particular interest in the Sunday school. He united with the church during the pastorate of Brother Carpenter and he left evidences that he still retained faith in his Savior.

In the absence of the pastor, the funeral service was in charge of Dr. Breckenridge assisted by a number of other Winona Brethren who knew him so well. May the Lord sustain those who mourn his loss.
                                A. E. THOMAS.

SHOBE—Dora Hagler Shobe, beloved wife of W. R. Shobe, was born February 25, 1865, and departed this life February 7, 1920. She united with the Brethren church at Fairview, Ohio, at an early age and was faithful and loyal to the church, a consistent and exemplary Christian to the last. She was at one time a student at Ashland College and remained always an ardent friend and supporter of the school, giving proof of her interest in the welfare of the Brethren church by liberal donations which she made to it shortly before her death.

Her life of simple, unassuming piety, her tireless devotion to the church and her constancy and steadfastness had so endeared her to friends both in and out of the church, that the congregation has suffered an irreparable loss in her death. Our loss however is her gain, for the church triumphant is more glorious than the church militant—"Mortality is swallowed up"—not in the grave—but—"of life."

The funeral services were conducted by the writer whose good fortune it had been to be her pastor for seventeen years.
                                J. M. TOMBAUGH.

VOLUME XLII
NUMBER 17

MAY 5
1920

The BRETHREN EVANGELIST

·ONE·IS·YOUR·MASTER·AND·ALL·YE·ARE·BRETHREN·

Mother and Her Charge

IN HONOR OF HEAVEN'S SUPREME HUMAN GIFT—MOTHER

Published every Wednesday at
Ashland, Ohio. All matter for publication must reach the Editor not
later than Friday noon of the pre-
ceeding week.

George S. Baer, Editor

The · Brethren Evangelist

When ordering your paper changed
give old as well as new address.
Subscriptions discontinued at expiration. To avoid missing any numbers renew two weeks in advance.

R. R. Teeter, Business Manager

OFFICIAL ORGAN OF THE BRETHREN CHURCH

Subscription price, $2.00 per year, payable in advance.
Entered at the Post Office at Ashland, Ohio, as second-class matter.
Acceptance for mailing at special rate of postage provided for in section 1103, Act of October 3, 1917, authorized September 9, 1918.
Address all matter for publication to Geo. S. Baer, Editor of the Brethren Evangelist, and all business communications to R. R. Teeter,
Business Manager, Brethren Publishing Company, Ashland, Ohio. Make all checks payable to the Brethren Publishing Company.

EDITORIAL

Christian Mothers and the Building of White Lives

"Thou hast a few names in Sardis that have not defiled their garments, they shall walk with me in write, for they are worthy." That is heaven's declaration not only to a church in Asia Minor, but to churches and individuals everywhere that heaven's purity has been maintained. It is a blessing upon the life that has preserved its whiteness in the midst of earth's foulness, and not on the mere innocence of childhood. It praises the pure whiteness of the lily that develops its purity amidst the pollution of its environment and not the whiteness of the fresh-fallen snow whose beauty is soon marred by the smoke and grim of the city. It speaks of positive goodness and not negative innocence. It is the victor's reward in the conflict with evil; the prize which every heart craves; the pass-word to heaven; and the possession that gives the soul the grace to walk and talk with God.

There are many influences that co-operate in making possible the acquisition of this supreme treasure—the white life of character; all have their source and sustenance in the life of character, who alone is the author of all good. But of all the noble instruments of God operating in the formation of white lives, the Christian mother is the most effective and far-reachingly powerful. She gives of her life, her love and her directing influence as none other can. She is heaven's greatest co-worker in moulding men for God and the right. No substitute can take her place and do for the world and the individual what she can do, and not all the contrary influences combined are to be regrotted so much as the absence of this noblest work of God, a wise Christian mother.

If the child is to be well born; if it is to possess a constitution that gives it a consciousness of strength as it grows in years and makes right conduct easy and natural instead of one possessed of all manner of weaknesses which will make the child an easy prey to habits that enslave and incline it to conduct that leads to destruction, the mother must indeed be a hand-maiden of the Lord, a vessel sanctified and meet for the Master's use. No one bequeaths to the child quite so much as she. No one can so surely send the child forth into the world handicapped by inherited weaknesses or fortified by inborn strength. The responsibility of the father is nothing lessened, if the mother's physical relation to the child seems to be more vital; his greater strength divinely given for her protection and provision makes him fully her co-equal in responsibility. But if he fail of his duty (and may God have mercy on the many who have), she is not thereby excused for her failure, and woe be to the race, if she should thus seek to equal man in his shortcomings and share alike in his excuses. The world owes more of its physical strength, keenness of mind, steadiness of nerve and inclination of soul to the Christian motherhood of earth than it has ever dreamed of. If mothers had been generally as derelict as fathers, there would be many more blighted lives than there are today and, many more in their distress would be uttering the reproachful cry of David (and with more truth than he), "Behold, I was born in iniquity, and in sin did my mother conceive me." But thank God for the mothers who have been true and strong, even where fathers have not, for they have thereby made the world stronger and richer in every way than it would otherwise have been. It is not mere sentiment, due to over-wrought emotions, that causes great men to say, as Lincoln has said, "All that I am or hope to be I owe to my angel mother." Such tributes have reference not merely to training, but to physical heritage as well, which inclines the child

Godward. The world may well pause to thank God for, and to do reverence to the Christian mothers who have given to so many sons and daughters the foundation for white lives.

If the child is to be well trained; if its early impressions, its ideals, its habits are to be such as will contribute to its most perfect development and highest attainment in life, it must have a Christian mother. The first impressions are the most abiding; the earliest ideals received are the most powerful in their formative influence; and the habits of childhood are the hardest to throw off. By far the larger part of all that the child ever learns is received during the years when it is under the mother's directing influence almost exclusively. During these years most of its life habits are formed, and the quality of the ideals received at this time will most likely determine the character of the entire life. Nothing is more important than that the child should be rightly instructed and carefully trained during these tender years, if it is to develop the white life that is the fruit of a strong character. No teacher should be so efficiently trained in mind and heart as the mother-teacher and no task is so fraught with responsibility as hers. Sorry is the plight of the children who have mothers who are ill-prepared for their responsibilities and will not take their tasks seriously.

A mother once asked a wise and good man, when she should begin to educate her child, then four years old. He replied, "If you have not begun already, you have lost four years. From the first smile that gleams upon an infant's cheek its education begins." We are continually troubling ourselves about the education of children and youth, and nothing is more important nor deserving of more conscientious study. But the difficulty with most of our systems and efforts is that the education of the child is almost completed when the schools and the churches get hold of him. And that a child makes something of itself, proves itself a credit to the community and makes a worthy contribution of character and service to society is due more to the moulding influence and training of a wise mother than to the instruction of the state or the direction of the church. The character of a community or nation is determined more by the quality of its mothers than by any other one factor. She who has the first training of the child, has the making of the nation for weal or for woe. And for the host of Christian mothers who have helped to give character and training to the millions of noble men and women of America we should never cease to be grateful. Our white garments of character are largely the product of their weaving. And no duty is more binding than that we should give recognition to the great service of motherhood, and do honor to, or show reverence for the memory of, the most influential teacher that ever lived and the greatest human factor in the development of white lives—the Christian mother.

If children are to receive a normal religious development; if they are to grow up in the knowledge of God and in the love of his truth and ways; if they are to be prevented from going off into sin and blighting their lives so that, though they be rescued, they must bear the marks and regrets of sin to their dying day, and instead grow up in the Kingdom as naturally as they grow up in and participate in the affairs of the family, there must be Christian mothers in the homes to begin at the dawn of consciousness to properly impress and gradually to teach them concerning the claims of God and the beauty of the white life. We are wont to contend that the religious faculties are later of development than the other faculties, and there is no desire to disagree with the contention, nevertheless it would seem that parents can not begin too soon to make impressions upon the unfolding mind of character and conduct by which its own spiritual nature may be powerfully influenced and moulded. "A lake is not so responsive to the least breeze that ruffles its surface, as the heart of a child is to the example of piety or impiety at home. If the parents are Christian people ,if they are conscientious, gentle, truthful and godly, the child will take this impression of their lives to be fashioned in spirit like them." Many a soul's history is contained in a poet's acknowledgement of what he owed to his mother, "Looking on her taught me the beautiful," he said,."and I had thoughts of paradise when other men had hardly looked out of doors on nature."

How often we wait too late to begin the making of white lives of character. We wait until the children have developed into young manhood and young womanhood, and have been lured into evil and possibly have become fettered by sinful habits, then we try every conceivable method (sometimes in vain) to win them to Christ. How much wiser if we had guarded them from the evil one and encouraged them to grow up in the purity and strength of the Christian life, which ought to develop naturally as the plant grows and blooms in the sun. If we would only begin earlier, if indeed the mother would begin with the very beginning of her little child's life to think and to plan for its religious development and daily to seek to impress it in ways that will make for purity and holiness in the coming days how vastly different the story of many lives would read! But honor and praise to the multitude of mothers who have realized and sought earnestly to discharge their divine obligation. Thank God for them and the white lives they have thus helped to build. Their works shall abide.

EDITORIAL REVIEW.

IMPORTANT NOTICE

We are compelled to publish The Evangelist this week with only eight pages because our paper stock is exhausted, it is impossible to get more just now and we are printing on borrowed paper. We have had a car load ordered since the first of the year, but the railroads refused to accept paper shipments during the strike disturbances. We are promised a temporary supply by automobile in a few days, but we have not yet received it. We regret having to make this radical change, but every effort possible is being made to prevent having to discontinue publication altogether until railroad conditions make paper shipments possible. We are giving preference to the publication of church news, and believe this plan will meet with the approval of the majority of our readers.

Brother Gearhart requests all churches and individuals to send their Foreign Mission offerings to him as promptly as possible.

The work at Mt. Pleasant, Pennsylvania, is reported by Brother W. A. Crofford, the pastor. This little group of faithful souls is pushing forward; members are being added to the church, the Sunday school is being developed and the house of worship is being improved.

Our readers will be pleased to see the program for commencement week at Ashland College, and we are sure President Jacobs really means it when he invites the friends of the college to attend the exercises of this week.

Brother E. M. Cobb's article concerning Miss Aboud in this issue brings to the attention of the churches seeking an evangelist an opportunity that is well worth considering. Miss Aboud has been meeting with splendid success.

The McLouth, Kansas, church and their new pastor are getting started splendidly together. The people are greatly pleased with their new pastor and his family and Brother Howell is doubtless rejoicing in the co-operation they are giving him. If things keep going as they have started the McLouth congregation will soon be at the beginning of a larger future.

Brother Riddle, pastor of the Louisville congregation writes that the every member canvass being made there in connection with the United Financial Drive of the Interchurch World Movement is showing up nicely. Brother Riddle was survey director for Stark county and is enthusiastic in the Movement.

Sister Maud Webb reports the Indiana Bible and Evangelistic conference recently held at North Manchester. Though the attendance was not large, the effort was doubtless abundantly worth while for those who were there. Similar conferences held in different sections of all our districts would result in much benefit to the churches.

There are a goodly number of the Tombaugh booklets out that have not been paid for. If you received any copies and have not remitted at the rate of 20 cents each in dozen lots, or 25 per single copy, please do so as soon as possible. If you have not received a copy send your order accompanied by 25 cents and you will receive one by return mail. Do it now.

Brother J. F. Watson, pastor of the First church of Johnstown, reports splendid progress in the work at that place. Success attended their revival effort recently conducted by the late Elder I. B. Trout. The pastor has also loaned his services to Brother DeLozier's congregation in a revival effort. The Johnstown church is going forward with their campaign for a new house of worship. They were recently given a splendid lift by Brother J. Leonard Replogle of New York.

Brother Drushal writes that the winter term of Riverside Institute closed in fine shape, and that a number of students made the confession of Christ. The difficulties are to be regretted but the favorable ending is cause for gratitude. The brotherhood will doubtless pray that the Holy Spirit may guide in all the relations of the future and that under the new arrangements the work so nobly carried on thus far may go on to still greater success.

Splendid things are happening at the Warsaw, Indiana, Brethren church under the leadership of Brother A. E. Thomas, as those who read his news letter in last week's issue will witness. Warsaw has gone over the top in practically everything they have undertaken, and we would not be at all surprised to hear of them undertaking the task of getting on the Evangelist Honor Roll soon. If they undertake it, we know they will do it.

Our correspondent from Sunnyside, Washington, reports splendid progress in the Brethren cause there under the leadership of Brother Ashman. Those people certainly did nobly in their Easter offering for foreign missions. We are quite certain that the Interchurch will receive not a cent of this offering, nor any other offering taken for denominational use. We understand that there is no such plan either on the part of the Interchurch or the Foreign Board, and it would not be right to thus divert gifts from their right course if there were such a plan.

Brother Albert Trent, General Secretary-Treasurer of the Brethren National Sunday School Association calls upon the superintendents throughout the brotherhood to fill out the report cards and mail them to him promptly. Surely every one who takes a serious thought about the matter will realize his obligation in this matter. If the local church and Sunday school officials could understand how much time and worry our national officers are put to, and all for naught but the joy of service, they would give more cheerful and prompt co-operation.

The hand may be busy in religion while the heart is hostile in spirit. The hand of Judas was conspicuous on the communion table but his heart was with his Lord's enemies. But Jesus discovers the discrepancy between the hand and the heart. Judas was soon unmasked and before the world he stands as the abhorred representative of hypocrites. The hidden things of darkness will be brought to light.

"A principle is like God's overhanging firmament; its boundaries are horizon lines; but when you go to touch them, and say, 'Here the firmament ends,' they recede before you—things that can never be grasped. Forgiveness is not a thing to be settled by petty rules, and so no petty rule was given. Instead of a rule, God gave us a principle—'not seven times, but seventy times seven.'"—Dr. J. H. Jowett.

GENERAL ARTICLES

Mothers and the Future Leaders of the Church. By President Edwin E. Jacobs, Ph.D

It is needless to say that the future leaders of the church must come from within her ranks. This is particularly true of our own denomination for our ranks are largely recruited from within, so it follows closely upon this fact, that we who are in and interested in the church, must ever be vigilant in our search for material from which leaders may be recruited. I am very happy to write upon this subject for I have come, within recent years, to have some very decided convictions upon it.

I am confident, in the first place, that we as a church have not laid sufficient emphasis in the past upon the selection and training of leaders. I do not recall that we have either had or lived up to, any sort of a definite program in this regard, and yet it is perfectly plain, that our very life depends upon it. It has taken, as a matter of fact, some very stubborn and rather foreboding facts in our own church to bring us to see the tremendous importance of sound, sensible leadership. One of the professed aims of the Interchurch Movement, if not its chief aim, is the selection and development of devout, consecrated leadership. Whether one indorses the program of this movement or not, one must confess that it has seized upon many elements of the crux in several of the weak places of the church programs, certainly so in the campaign for workers.

It is true that the Y. M. C. A. has for some years pressed the claims of life work upon the students in the colleges, but the church has been singularly silent and yet it has been evident for many years past that the major portion of the church leaders must come from the Christian colleges but the churches have failed to formulate any large program in that direction. For one thing, the church colleges have been timid in the not remote past in standing out as denominational schools, fearing discrimination at the hands of the Carnegie and other foundations, but it is becoming increasingly evident that if the church schools are to live, thrive, and be intellectually decent, the churches themselves must back them. A CHURCH WHICH WILL NOT SUPPORT ITS OWN SCHOOL IN THE RIGHT FASHION IS NOT FIT TO HAVE ONE. And by all the present indications, such a church will not long have a college with which she may trifle.

Now evidently, colleges are for training in leadership, and Christian colleges for Christian leadership, but note this fact viz., that it has been pretty definitely determined that about eighty-five percent of all those who enter college have selected their life work before they entered school at all! They come to college, not to find themselves, as some have so fondly believed, but in order to fit themselves for work already chosen. This leads one to conclude that the ages of high school or even before, are the ones in which choices are made. Perhaps one may even be allowed to believe that in not a few cases, choices are made very early in the home and under the influences of the parents. If this is the case, what is the lesson?

Evidently, the lesson to the church is, that bent toward church leadership must be given very early and that is in large part in the hands of the parents, perhaps mostly of the mothers. I verily believe that the mothers of the church could do a very great service right along this line. In the older days, every family was supposed to give at least one child to the church and while we would perhaps not want to re-establish this precedent, yet something of the sort would be helpful.

And the rewards to the mother? Well, I know one college president whose mother could not write her own name yet under her godly and gentle influence her son consecrated his life to the Christian church. What could such a woman have done alone? Her influence for good would certainly have been limited, but in her gifted son, she "being dead, yet speaketh."

Of recent years there has been quite a bit of activity in this direction, viz., of having young people in high school choose their life work. Some have sought to have the teaching profession recruited from the high schools. Lawyers and physicians have spoken again and again to likely young people to enter their professions. Business men have often promised places to those in the high schools who gave promise of making good. How has it been with the church, And what is more, does it not take another kind of solicitation? Would not the mother have the matter more in her own hands anyway? Would not deep consecration on the part of the church mothers coupled with an earnest desire for the good both of her boy and for the Kingdom be determinative in such cases? If ye love houses or lands, or sons, or daughters more than me, etc., is the intent of that familiar passage.

May God lay it upon the hearts of mothers to take seriously the task of helping in the selection of their sons' future, remembering that the rewards are many both in this life and in the one to come. All honor to those mothers who have thus done; but for them, the present would be vastly different. But we need their number magnified, multiplied, and consecrated.

Indeed, if the mothers of a former generation had not in many cases yielded willingly their sons to the cause, our present would be impossible. In the years of the recent past, women have had very small outlet for their energies, for education, the professions and business were closed to them, hence their chief method of influencing the conditions of their times was through their sons. The history of America is full of just such women and it is to be hoped now, that women are entering a larger sphere, that they will by no means forget the tremendous responsibility that is still theirs in rearing sons and daughters fit for special service in the Kingdom of God upon this earth.

If sons were the jewels of the Roman matron in the older day, when life was cheap and loyal Christian manhood rare or impossible, what ought sons to be now? In this age when business and social life take up so much of the mothers' time and energy, is there a danger that they neglect their sons? Is the day passing when the mother has time to sit and read quietly and talk confidentially to her sons? A host of Bible and other illustrations come to mind where the son owed all "he was or hoped to be" to his godly and painstaking mother. As president of the college, I hear ten times to one from the mother rather than from the father in regards to sons here in college. May not that indicate the really great solicitation on the part of the mother, even when the sons are grown and gone from the parental roof-tree?

The college is eager to have the mothers of the church send sons and daughters here from year to year, consecrated, earnest, loyal to right and to the church which we serve, not for our own sakes, but that the church may not have a dearth of leaders, but an increasing supply of leaders of the right stamp. Here, under the grace of God, we may train the intellect and culture the heart, but the major part of all that is fine and high and really essential must be implanted in the home. Christian homes, Christian influences early in life, and Christian mothers,—these three will determine in a very large way, the future leadership of the Brethren church. The college can only work upon the material sent; it can not create it.

Ashland, Ohio.

The Mystery of Mother's Love. By Lloyd E. Hang

It is plainly evident that those things in life about which we understand the least are the most valuable to us. In the material life we may cite electricity; in the spiritual life it is God's love and power; in the child life it is the love of mother. There is something incomprehensible in a mother's love which is not only exemplified in what she is willing to do, but in the sacrifice which she actually and unselfishly makes for those to whom she is devoted. It is impossible to understand such love when there is no condition made, no question asked, and even the dearest thing considered in this world, is given up, which is nothing else than life itself, that those whom she has brought forth may attain greater blessing and opportunity.

It is not possible for us to fathom the depth of LOVE that will cause a mother to cling to her child regardless of what happens, whether in infancy or when manhood or womanhood has been reached. We also see how mother's love impels the most unreserved confidence and trust of the child in its tender years; no harm can come, and nothing evil can happen when mother is near, and whatever mother says and does is nothing else than absolutely just.

It does not matter if the world is friendly and honor and good fortune smiles, or if disgrace has settled on her child and he be spurned and cast off by the world; or even death on the gallows or in the electric chair be the pronounced fate, mother's love can not be quenched. Mother will go along to the very limit, placing complete trust and confidence in her child, and when death comes to those most dear to her, it will only increase her love and devotion.

It seems that the love of a mother's heart is so closely linked up with the divine that it is nothing more or less than a continued invisible thread leading from the great heart of God through the heart of mother and there finding open expression. This it seems to me has been expressed in the fact that God SO LOVED that he gave, and he who was given unselfishly, freely gave up his life that WE might live, for "Greater love hath no man than this, that a man lay down his life for his friends"—Jesus. If then there is no greater love than this, we certainly find it manifested in the life of mother. If we say that we understand and comprehend mother's love, then we could equally as well say that we understand and fully comprehend the love of God, but we know that this is not true, for it can not be understood.

It is true that individuals in common may have affection for one another and exchange kindnesses and good will with the expectation of receiving the same, but this is not true of mother, who without even a thought for herself, sacrifices and completely resigns all she can for the sake of her child. It is this self sacrificing love which is beyond the understanding of man, that will ever keep the memory of mother hallowed.

Louisville, Ohio.

Sermons and Sandwiches. By J. A. McInturff

A few Sundays past we had special sermons, solemn praise, and holy songs. Everything was inspiring, impressive and sublime. Then a day or two passed and we held a social at which a "pot luck" supper was served; sandwiches, meat loaf, baked beans, jello with mixed fruits, and a variety of other foods. All ate as the friendly spirit broke through laughter and chatter. I had taken part in the solemn services of the Sunday before, and had been asked to speak at the supper. I made an effort to collect my thoughts for the evening address, but my thoughts firmly refused to be collected and insisted on propounding this interesting question: What is the relation or connection of the sermons of last Sunday and the sandwiches of tonight? What fellowship has religion and feasting? Why follow the solemn sermons of the Sabbath with such carnival and feasting? I took my Bible and began to search for a clue. I found on one of the very earliest pages of the sacred record this significant statement. It occurred in a crisis in Hebrew history. Here it is: "They saw God, and did eat and drink." "They saw God. There is the principle of the sermon. "And did eat and drink"—there is the principle of the sandwich. Here is revelation and feasting side by side. Here is the secret of all worship and the germ of all feasting. What more could I desire? I read on and found that the two run side by side through all the revelations of the Old Testament. The sermon and sandwich were never far from each other. I found that all the great spiritual elevations of the Old Testament were connected with great feasting. The Feast of Pentecost, the Feast of Tabernacles, the Feast of Passover, the Feast of Trumpets, the Feast of Dedication, and so on. Revelation almost blended with revelry. The record that tells of Israel's redemption from Egypt also gives in graphic detail the eating of the Passover. The angels call at Abraham's tent to deliver a revelation and Abraham rushes to roast a calf and bake cakes. Joseph feasts with his brethren when he desires to reveal the truth. The record that tells how Elijah saw the angel also says that the angel said "Arise and eat." The altar and offering and sacrifice grew out of feasting. The altar was first a table. This was the foundation of all Semitic Covenants. When two parties had eaten together they became participants of a common life, a bond of union is established and they are brothers. Here are the two laws, that of the sermon and sandwich. In the New Testament we meet with the same laws. Jesus performed his first miracle at a wedding feast. Did not Matthew hold a feast directly upon his conversion? Also Simon did the same thing. Look at the feeding of the four and five thousand. Even after the resurrection he feeds them. "They saw a fire of coals, and fish laid thereon and bread." In the very last hours of our Lord's life he desired to eat the Supper with them, and there he gave three of the most sacred services of his ministry. We see in his saying relative to the future world the same relation of these two principles. There we will see God, and also sit down to the Marriage Supper of the Lamb. The law of the sermon brings us into the holiest relations and the law of the supper brings us into relation to all living. This makes us citizens of two worlds, yet we are bound to the most lowly of earth. I look out of my study window and see the birds fly in the air, and it seems that we are strangers, but one alights and eats the crumbs at my door, and we are kin. Visiting this fall in the country we watched a rabbit eating cabbage and we thought how closely we are related. See him eat. So do I. Last Summer I was looking at some fish dart and flash in the shade of a tree. One darted up and devoured a gnat that had fallen into the glassy water. I said they eat and drink, and so do I. The sermon brings me into relation to the spirit world above, but the sandwich brings me down to the bird in the air, the rabbit in the garden or the fish in the lake. But there is another thing, I have always felt that the glory of God was embarrassing, bewildering, dazzling, fearful, repelling, terrifying, paralyzing. I now see different. They saw God and did eat and drink. Not even a bird will eat in a strange cage or a horse in a strange stable. Eating and drinking are evidences of familiarity. We feel at home. Man was made for God and only can be right when he sees him. To see God is to eat and drink, and be at home Peacefully, reverently, restfully, perfectly at home.

Goshen, Indiana.

The Christian church will never know how wonderfully it might realize the blessing of God until it leaves off petty strife and jealousies and every man and group goes to work with all the willingness, consecration and harmony that can be summoned.

NEWS FROM THE FIELD

IMPORTANT NOTICE

Pastors, Church Secretaries or Treasurers, when sending in the contributions for Foreign Missions, should specify the name and address of all persons who gave five dollars, and if more, the amount of each, so proper credit may be entered for every individual as to membership in The Foreign Missionary Society, if they wish to be so recognized. If not so indicated, membership cards cannot be issued to individuals!

WILLIAM A. GEARHART,
General Missionary Secretary.
906 Conover Bldg., Dayton, Ohio.

MOUNT PLEASANT, PENNSYLVANIA
My Dear Editor:

This faithful little organization of the First Brethren church is still on the map and pushing for success, despite the fact that their pastor is obliged to continue road work to make necessary expenses.

Through the efficient head of the Sunday school, that branch of the work is doing nobly, augmented by the Cradle Roll, and Home Departments.

To make our place of worship more inviting, it has been decided to re-paper the class rooms, provide new carpet for the floor of the main auditorium, also dispense with the old gas lights and replace with an up-to-date electric system, as well as to properly paint the entire building.

The attendance is growing at all our services, and to add to our encouragement, two were admitted to the church, by baptism, Sunday, April the 11th.

Yours for the Master,
W. A. CROFFORD, Pastor.
1014 Ash Street, Johnstown, Pa.

FIRST BRETHREN CHURCH, JOHNSTOWN

It has been some time since Johnstown happenings have been reported. It is my purpose to briefly state matters of interest in the work beginning with the New Year. Brother Trout came early in the year and was with us nearly three weeks. The visible results of this effort was that nineteen made confession of Christ as their Savior for the first time. Most of these have been baptized and others will likely come later. Brother Trout gave fine service and his masterly sermons were enjoyed by all who were privileged to hear him. His work was of a high order and resulted in much good to the church.

Brother Bell visited Johnstown on his way east and spent one Sunday with former parishioners. He preached twice for us to large and appreciative audiences. The Evangelistic League and its interests were presented and many became members of the League.

The pastor was given time off to hold a meeting for the Allentown Brethren. We were with Brother DeLozier and his splendid people for nearly three weeks. I surely enjoyed this trip and the fellowship of the pastor and his people. The membership at Allentown is not large but what they have is first class I assure you. DeLozier is a good yoke-fellow. I was glad to get better acquainted with him.

that great good comes from these meetings. He is loved and respected by his people. The results were not large, yet I feel the meeting was not a failure. There were ten who confessed Christ, among these were some Italians. Most of these will unite with the church.

During my absence the Johnstown church closed its financial drive for the new church location and boosted the amount above ten thousand dollars for the year. The church raised about sixteen thousand dollars this year for all phases of work. We just recently received a check for thirty thousand dollars for the building fund. This came from Brother J. Leonard Replogle, son of our beloved Elder R. Z. Replogle, deceased. Of course the church is delighted with this gift for it not only makes possible the erection of a beautiful house of worship but assures us of the steel magnate's interest in our work.

The pastor was delightfully surprised on the evening of his birthday when about a hundred and fifty members came to prayer meeting and brought with them a substantial purse of money as a gift and mark of their good-will. Since this surprise party others have made contributions which brought the amount to an even hundred dollars.

I received a call from the Johnstown church to remain another year, beginning April 1st. An increase of two hundred dollars was also given in salary. I have formally accepted the call and look for the greatest year yet in the progress of the work. We are now looking forward to the coming of Dean Miller and hope to have a great week with him.

J. FREMONT WATSON.

"VICTORY AT SUNNYSIDE"

The Brethren at Sunnyside feel that we have great cause for rejoicing indeed. Under the leadership of Brother Ashman we are going forward. We feel that in him we have a strong leader, one who brings the message in all its forcefulness and blessedness.

The attendance for the past three months has been exceptionally good notwithstanding the fact that we have had our share of sickness, such as "flu," mumps and whooping cough, but the interest in the church has not decreased and we believe with the coming of spring our meetings will be larger than ever. On Easter we had a large attendance both in the morning and evening. The program was especially good, indicating that much thought and time had been given to the preparation of it.

The goal set for the Sunday school was 300, by actual count 347 were present.

Our offering for Missions on this day was $1,075.00. A cantata entitled "Easter Praise" was to have been given in the evening. Owing to sickness it could not be rendered at that time but will be given later. Our pastor brought us a splendid message, however, at the close of which one life was surrendered for missionary work and one public confession made.

A large percentage of our members attend the Thursday night prayer meetings. We feel

and that God blesses us abundantly in this work. At a recent business meeting which was largely attended, we voted to keep apart from the Interchurch World Movement. We have studied it from every possible viewpoint and, although recognizing some good in some things it aims to do, feel that as a whole it is of the world and man and not of God. We feel that as a church we would sell our birthright for a mess of pottage if we sacrificed one principle to co-operate in it. It is unscriptural. It tends toward organic union as its leaders will admit when forced to do so. We are willing to live up with an enlarged program within our own denomination, but will see to it that not one penny of our gifts will go to this Movement, either directly or indirectly. We went far ahead of any church included in the Movement of equal ability with ours, but if the mission board allies itself with this organization not one penny of this thousand dollars will be sent to it. We will send it direct to the mission fields as a personal gift first. A sermon recently preached by our pastor relative to this was sent for publication by the Official Staff of the church, but for some reason has been withheld from publication in the Evangelist. We insist that it be published.

(In this connection we wish kindly to inform our correspondent and the good brethren of the official staff that the mere fact that the publication of an article has been delayed is no proof of its being refused publication. We have articles awaiting publication that have been in our hands longer than the sermon above mentioned. Very few articles except those for special occasions are published immediately upon receipt, inasmuch as we must have a supply in reserve. No one can understand quite so well as the editor, the circumstances that indicate the wisdom regarding the publication and the time of publication of articles. In our effort to be fair and serve the best interests of the whole church we have about 25,000 readers and many correspondents to consider.—Editor).

Wednesday evening after Easter we held our communion. Although not all of our members were present, we had a blessed time together.

The president of the missionary society gave me the following report:

We have had many reasons to be thankful for the increased interest in mission study. The attendance is good, and the prayer service preceding the study has been a great blessing in many of our lives. We have covenanted together to pray each morning at nine o'clock for missions and a world revival, and we believe this has awakened a greater interest in missions, and we have rejoiced to know that over one thousand dollars was given on Easter day for work in Africa and South America.

Our young people are enthusiastic in their work and we believe that much good is being done through their united efforts.

MAY ALEXANDER,
Church Correspondent.

PROGRAM FOR COMMENCEMENT WEEK

·· Sunday, May 30, Baccalaureate Service, Sermon by the President, College Chapel, 2:30.

Monday, May 31, Musical Recital of Advanced Pupils, 8:00 P. M., College Chapel.

Tuesday, June 1, Recognition Service in Chapel, 9:30.

. Tuesday, June 1, Pageant, "The Pilgrims," 8:00 P. M., Campus. ·

Wednesday, June 2, College Banquet, 12:30, Dining Hall.

Wednesday, June 2, Class Address, Dr. Luce, Cleveland, 8:00 P. M., Chapel.

Thursday, June 3, Class Day Exercises, 9:30 A. M., College Chapel.

You are cordially invited to be present at any or all of these events. ·

Class Roster:

.Receiving M. A. degree, Charles Anspach.

Receiving A. B. degree, John H. Gongwer, Darlington Stark, Harvey Becknell, Ruth Lichty, Joseph Gingrich, Elwood Rowsey, (course to be completed by end of summer term, August 1st), Fred Vanator, Ray Mikesell, Nora Bracken, (course to be completed by end of summer term, August 1st), Caryl Miller.

English Divinity,—Helen Vanator, Cora Aksland, W. R. Deeter, Margaret Banghart.

Academy,—Clayton Starn, Beulah Garner, Josephine Clara Raad, George Martin, Helen Gongwer, Howard Leckrone.

Normal,—Ruth Cubbison, Ruth Elliot.

A. B. in Music,—Ada Patterson. ·

· I wish to make two corrections here of errors which appeared in the current number of the Woman's Outlook. First, there · are twenty-three graduates instead of sixteen. The enrollment in the Seminary is 41 instead of 39 and in the College 57 instead of 49.

Friends of the college are invited to attend during Commencement week.

EDWIN E. JACOBS.

INDIANA CONFERENCE ON BIBLE STUDY AND EVANGELISM

The Indiana State Conference for Evangelism and Bible Study was held at North Manchester April 12 and 13. The attendance was small, but all who were there felt that just such conferences are what we need for inspiration and Christian fellowship. · Great oaks grow from little acorns. So we hope that our future conference will be better attended.

We were royally entertained and I think I have never attended a conference where we feasted so sumptuously.

·The first evening the Bible study was conducted by Brother Wolford of Elkhart. His subject was "Prayer." He emphasized the value and power of prayer. He said, Prayer in everything; pray at all times, pray in all places and pray without ceasing. He showed that we dare ask big things of God.

This was followed by a duet. Then Brother Miller of Nappanee delivered a very powerful evangelistic appeal.

·. The Morning Watch was conducted by Brother Whetstone.

Brother Wolford spoke on "Our Spiritual Resources." ··

Brother Harris a converted Jew, lectured on "The Jew and the World War," or "God Moving in the Earth."

Brother W. E. Thomas spoke on "Recruiting the King's Army."

The first address of the afternoon was given by Brother Brower of Huntington, on "Worthy Stewardsip." This was followed by a sermon by Brother A. E. Thomas of Warsaw. Then came a missionary address, "A Map of the World" by Brother Kolb of Milford.

The evening program consisted of a "Bible Study" conducted by Prof. Winger of Manchester College, followed by a stereopticon lecture, "The Whole Wide World," by Brother McInturff of Goshen.

Prayer was given a · prominent place throughout the conference and it was closed with a strong appeal for the consecration of lives to God's service.

MRS. MAUDE WEBB.

KIEFER MEMORIAL SERVICES ·

Memorial services for the late Elder William Kiefer will be held at the Fair Haven church near West Salem, Ohio, on May 9th at 2:30 in the afternoon. The Zion Hill and Ashland friends are especially invited to attend. Dr. J. Allen Miller and Rev. A. C. Hendrickson will be present to assist in the services.

BENJ. F. OWEN.

Communion Notices

The Brethren of Uniontown, Pennsylvania, congregation will observe the ordinances of the Communion Service on Sunday evening, May 9, at 7:30. Neighboring brethren cordially invited to meet with us in this blessed fellowship.

DYOLL BELOTE, Pastor.

·Communion services will be held at the Williamstown church, Sunday evening, May 23. We would appreciate very much the presence of neighboring brethren and sisters at this service. · ·

MARK B. SPACHT, Pastor.

MISS ABOUD.

While lecturing in the New York City Tabernacle some weeks ago, I made a statement concerning my visit to the Holy Land. A Syrian lady, who had been in the audience, came forward and tested me with a few Arabic sentences, and said, "You've been there all right." Subsequent conversations led to doctrinal discussions, and explanations of the observances of ordinances. Finally, she asked me whether my church practised all the ordinances of the original Greek Orthodox church to which she belonged in the Holy Land such as, triune immersion for Christian baptism, feet-washing, the Lord's Supper, Communion, the Holy Kiss, the Anointing with Oil in the name of the Lord, Tithing, etc., etc., and I told her that we did. Then she asked me about the doctrines of the Deity of Jesus, the Personality of the Holy Spirit, the Atonement, the Bodily Resurrection of the Dead, the Coming of the Lord, the punishment of the impenitent, and the reward of the righteous. I told her that I thought a very large majority of our people would endorse every · word she had spoken, but that I was also ashamed to say that it was patent of late that

we also had a few among us who were being led away with divers winds of doctrine, etc., and she said, this was also to be expected in these last days.

She wanted to know where she could find such a church. That she had been hunting such a people for years in this country, and had never identified herself with any people, for the reason she had never found one which went "All the way" in the ordinances of the House of God. I told her to come to Dayton, and I would baptise her after she had seen my people and heard their testimony. She came as soon as she could leave off her evangelistic engagements, for she has been an evangelist for some years in New York and elsewhere. When she came, I happened to be called to Rochester, New York, to open a whole Gospel mission there, and I asked her to preach for me twice here at Dayton, which she did to a packed house, and my people unanimously endorsed her. I asked her to preach for me during my evangelistic campaign which she accordingly did. Brother Lynn led the singing. I sat there and heard her preach for three weeks, and Dr. W. S. Bell heard her for the greater part of a week, and we have been unable to find a flaw in her theology or her presentation of it. She preached at West Alexandria ten days and received over a score of souls. She got seventy-one here, and has a number at Salem already. My church people are going up there tonight to encourage her a little.

At the close of our meeting we had a great love-feast. When she entered the church and saw the house literally filled with white tables surrounded with God's people, she paused and threw up her hands and said "Praise the Lord," and I wish every member of the Brethren church could have heard her testimony after she had washed feet, and was sat at meat. It was the most striking, unique, and convincing because it came from one who lived in the Lord's country and has known of the practices of the early church.

I had baptized her the night before. . Now she had feasted with us. One of the Brethren moved that I give her an evangelistic license, and as quick as a flash it was seconded by several and unanimously adopted. She is now an evangelist of the First Brethren church of Dayton, Ohio. She is booked way into the fall, except a few dates in the summer yet, and as soon as you see this these remaining dates will all be taken. I wish she could speak in every Brethren church in the states. She draws a crowd, holds her crowds, and she tells them something while she has them. To avoid conflicts she has left her booking all with me. You may secure her services by applying to me. I will be glad to send her to you. And may I ask you to observe the following items which we always have to consider:

1. She must have a good private room where she can study and pray.

2. We will be absolutely impartial in the calls; but reserve the right to save you car fare in her traveling if we can do so,

3. She comes to you for the free will offering plus her entertainment and traveling expenses from the last place of meeting.

4. She will begin your meeting on Monday evening and close on Sunday. We treat everybody alike; don't ask selfish privileges.

5. Make your schedule before you apply; do not ask me to extend your time after she is there, for she will be booked a year ahead, and I cannot ask a dozen churches to change their plans for one church who has not had a vision commensurate with their opportunities. Now Brethren churches, here is an opportunity which is seldom accorded to you and the Dayton church offers this evangelist to you with the prayer that you may be strengthened and the name of the Lord magnified. Let me hear from you soon, as I go away for a vacation about the middle of June. And listen, do not wait until you want her to ask for ehr. Good preachers are not idle.

E. M. COBB.

2002 West Third Street, Dayton, Ohio.

LOST CREEK, KENTUCKY

Since our last report, the winter term of school has come to a close. The closing week of this term is a kind of an index to the general health of the work. The temperature this time was almost perfect, for one of the best closing weeks Riverside ever had, was experienced.

The week was featured by two entertainments, this time a commencement, and an especially emphasized prayer meeting service. The high tide of events was reached when at this prayer meeting service, five of the young men made the good confession, and then on the night of our commencement exercises, just a few minutes before the time for the program, Mr. and Mrs. Akens came into our home with another young man, who was wanting to make the confession. His confession was taken, making six for the week. For some years there has never passed a winter term of school without some of our young people making the confession. This year, because of some troubles in the earlier part of the term's work, there were no confessions. Then to see six young men take the stand for the Christ so near the end of the term's work, was pleasing and gratifying indeed.

We had one young woman who completed our course of study, and was given a certificate of graduation for the same. We tried to get one of our elders to give the Commencement address, but did not succeed, and thus called on one of the ministers at Jackson. The Methodist minister responded, a Rev. Vanderpool, and gave us a most excellent address. Odessa Noble was the graduate. The attendance in school held up well to the end, better than usual, the entertainments were enjoyed by large audiences, the order was very good, and the weather ideal. The light plant which had not been operating for a few weeks, got in line for this last week; all this after having passed through some grave difficulties, made this week a very very happy time for those who were holding up the cause of Christ at Riverside.

The matter of the light plant seemed to be a special answer to prayer. For possibly three or four weeks it had not been operating, at least satisfactorily, at all, and some of the time, no service whatever. We needed and wanted this so much. After repairs, writing,

questioning, etc., it did not work. But we never ceased praying that wisdom would be given to make it work. And really, just what we did to make it work we do not know. But on Monday night it gave us the first light for some time, and then by Tuesday night, the night of our first entertainment, it worked perfectly, and has continued so to do since. We praise God for this because we are certain of his hand in the matter.

And now we face the future, which promises well. When trouble assails a place of this kind, or simply a congregation of worshippers, one of the things that can save the day for the place is the unity of the worshipping body, and the scholars. With Riverside, there was the congregation, then also the student body. The saving thing in Riverside experiences this last winter, was the fact that there was no division among the people here. They stood unitedly for what they believed to be right, and doubtless it was that stand which kept things going so well in spite of diverse conditions at times. They still seem so united, and by keeping humble before him who gives power when we are weak, who gives strength when ours fail, who gives wisdom when we cannot see the way, the work which he has so blessed in the past, may go forth to larger things for him and the people. Pray for us.

G. E. DRUSHAL.

McLOUTH, KANSAS

With open hearts our little church welcomed Brother Thomas F. Howell when he and his eldest son arrived February 15, to take up his new pastoral work with us.

By his ever ready and willing spirit he at once proved to us that he was a live wire for the Master.

A week or so after his arrival we were very much pleased to learn that Brother Howell and the pastors of the other three churches, had met and organized a ministerial conference, which means a backbone to our community.

Sister Howell, youngest son and daughter later joined Brother Howell. Surely her true Christian spirit must be a great help to Brother Howell.

Our evangelistic campaign started April 11. Many spirit-inspired messages were brought to us; among them, "Opportunity," in which Brother Howell showed to us that opportunities were never so great as at the present time. If our forefathers had had the opportunities of today, would they not have been wonderfully powerful for God? They drove miles to hear the Gospel. Today opportunity is at our door and we turn a deaf ear. We haven't the time for God but God still strives with us though we will not heed his teachings, for he is a patient God.

The topic, "Adam Where Art Thou?"— Well, we were not lulled to sleep on a flowery bed of ease, for those it did not hit it grazed.

The present generation evades the true teachings of the Gospel, by searching for meanings that may let their souls rest in ease, instead of accepting the old time salvation and religion.

"My church" was not brought to the people as a certain denominational church but as

the church of God. "One is your Master and all ye are brethren." There is too much fighting going on between our churches to Christianize others. We must show that we are at peace one with another and with our God. We all should be striving for the same place and purpose; why not show it by brotherly love to one another?

Other topics were, "What Is a Man?" "Salvation and Religion," "A Man in Hell," "Disobedience." Many other uplifting themes were presented during the two weeks.

Brother Howell shows deep interest in the young folks of our community and has made many friends during his short period he has been here.

We ask the prayers of our Brethren for the work and workers of McLouth.

ESTELLA GROSHING.

VICTORY STATISTICS

The blank report cards for the statistics of the Brethren schools for this VICTORY year of our Four Year Program, ending with the month of March, have been mailed to all superintendents as their names appear on our records for last year. Doubtless a number of schools have changed superintendents during the year and in case any Brethren superintendent has failed to receive the report card he should request one from the writer. We are hopeful that these report cards will receive prompt attention, that all items will be filled out carefully and conscientiously and returned by the 15th of May. Our experience in this line last year was just a bit discouraging. The blanks were mailed in April, and we expected all would be returned by the middle of May. But in this we were sadly disappointed. Not one-half were returned by that time. To over 50 schools the second letter and card were mailed and to quite a number the third; before a response was secured and a few are still holding last year's card. We have faith, however, that in this VICTORY year, every loyal superintendent will realize the importance of forwarding the report at once.

We want a report from every school, large or small, so that a creditable report for National Conference may be given this year. Statistics may not be soul saving, but if carefully given and thoughtfully prepared and presented, they can be made a source of much encouragement in the work. Remember that YOUR church wants to know about YOUR school. So, hustle along that report card, brother superintendent.

ALBERT TRENT,
General Secretary-Treasurer.

AN ANNOUNCEMENT

Easter offerings should be sent to the General Missionary Secretary, 906 Conover Building, Dayton, Ohio, not later than June 1, to be included in the report. If it can not be sent prior to that time, it will be accepted for Foreign Missions, but will not appear in the Easter report. Should any churches or auxiliary organizations, desire to add more to their Easter offerings, they will have ample time to do so.

WILLIAM A. GEARHART,
General Missionary Secretary.

Volume XLII
Number 18

May 12
1920

The BRETHREN EVANGELIST

- ONE · IS · YOUR · MASTER · AND · ALL · YE · ARE · BRETHREN -

IF I THEN YOUR LORD
AND MASTER
have washed your feet,
ye ought also.
to wash one another's
feet.

(JOHN 13: 14)

FOR AS OFTEN AS YE
EAT THIS BREAD AND
DRINK THIS CUP,
ye proclaim
the Lord's death
till he come.

(I CORINTHIANS 11: 26)

Published every Wednesday at Ashland, Ohio. All matter for publication must reach the Editor not later than Friday noon of the preceding week.

George S. Baer, Editor

The
Brethren
Evangelist

When ordering your paper changed give old as well as new address. Subscriptions discontinued at expiration. To avoid missing any numbers renew two weeks in advance.

R. R. Teeter, Business Manager

OFFICIAL ORGAN OF THE BRETHREN CHURCH

Subscription price, $2.00 per year, payable in advance.
Entered at the Post Office at Ashland, Ohio, as second-class matter.
Acceptance for mailing at special rate of postage provided for in section 1103, Act of October 3, 1917, authorized September 9, 1918.
Address all matter for publication to Geo. S. Baer, Editor of the Brethren Evangelist, and all business communications to R. R. Teeter, Business Manager, Brethren Publishing Company, Ashland, Ohio. Make all checks payable to the Brethren Publishing Company.

EDITORIAL

The Duty of Attending the Communion Service

There is perhaps no more important service in the church calendar than the communion service and no time when members of the body of Christ experience a more joyous fellowship and a more vitalizing life that when the emblems of divine communion are brought forth. There should be a looking forward to and a preparation for this event such as no other occasion receives. With joyous anticipation and searching of heart this service should be approached. No other opportunity can compare with that of divine communion and no other function of the church makes the divine presence so real. It is the Bethel of the church, the Holy of Holies in the temple of worship and the tabernacle of Israel to the wandering soul. Here is to be found the fountain of cleansing where the soul may wash and be clean of its accumulated guilt and walk forth in humility and service. Here is to be found the feast for the communion of saints, the pledge of brotherhood, love and equality. Here also are to be found the emblems of the broken body and shed blood of the Savior of the world, emblems which bespeak God's value of the human soul, and of which as we partake we symbolize our sharing of the strength and purity of the life of God. Only extreme necessity should cause a follower of the Lord Jesus Christ to absent himself from such a service. Every concern for the welfare of one's own soul points to the importance of taking advantage of the privileges therein offered. It's benefits are too great to be lightly passed by. And every consideration of one's obligation to other members of the church of Christ lays upon him the necessity of faithfulness to this ordinance of the house of God. No ceremony is more imperative and no privilege more obligating.

Notwithstanding all this, there is a tendency in some quarters to neglect this sacred ordinance and to consider its benefits lightly. There are those who habitually absent themselves from the house of God on this occasion, some with the most frivolous excuses and some with no excuses at all. From the attitude some take towards the communion service, it would seem to be a matter of less importance than a picture show or a ball game. It would be embarrassing to some churches to make a comparison of the number in attendance at the last communion and those crowded in the movie on the preceding Saturday night. It would be unfair to insinuate that this attitude prevails among the majority of church members, yet the number is so large that the Four Year Program committee thought it would be a worthy goal and a commendable attainment if three-fourths of the membership of our churches could be induced to take advantage of this service. It was wise to place a premium upon loyalty of this kind, for nothing speaks more faithfully of the spiritual temper of a congregation than the percentage in attendance at the communion, when conditions are normal. Pastors cannot place their fingers on a more vital spot in their churches' life, and it is with much reason that they are insisting on a re-valuation of and a greater loyalty to this service.

An appeal to the sense of duty may not be the highest appeal, especially when the matter in question is the worship of God. Nevertheless it is likely that most of us live on that plane. And while divine worship ought to be looked upon as a glorious privilege resulting in profoundest joy, and especially ought this to be true of this most sacred service, the love feast, yet for those who will not rise above it, it must rest on the plane of duty. It is, for us all, if

nothing more, a duty to worship God and to endeavor sincerely to engage in the ordinances of his house.

It is a duty we owe to ourselves first of all. Every Christian owes it to his own spiritual attainment to make use of the means of grace which God in his wisdom has provided. No one can be what he ought to be, on the contrary, he will steadily decrease in spiritual strength and quality of life, when he considers lightly and purposely passes by the opportunities of engaging in the ordinances of the holy communion. He who becomes unwilling to yield to the symbol of spiritual cleansing, because of growing pride or indifference to the rite, after having been taught and having once accepted it as the way of truth, will doubtless hear, if he has ears to hear, his Lord saying, more sternly than he spoke to Peter, "If I wash thee not, thou hast no part with me," and gradually upon his spiritual shoulders he will feel the burden of accumulated and unpardoned sins. He who refuses to partake of the common meal because he has somewhat against another member, or because he has so little interest that he will not take the time to attend, will soon discover that he has lost the spirit of brotherhood and will find himself out of joint with his fellows. He who thinks he can neglect the "bread and the cup" with little hurt to himself will sooner or later be awakened to a sadly depleted spiritual life. No one can afford to go in the face of duty, and it is a serious thing to trifle with a duty that concerns the most sacred things of life. No duty is more compelling and exacting than that which a man owes to himself. Every member ought to attend the communion service because it is a duty which he owes to himself; for the sake of spiritual cleansing and the development of the spirit of humility and service, for the sake of cultivating a greater sense of brotherhood and equality, and for the sake of a greater realization of the divine presence.

Furthermore attendance at the communion service is a duty which we owe to our fellow church members. The special form of service which we practice is one of the distinguishing characteristics of the Brethren church. We have agreed together upon the importance of those particular practices and have pledged each other to co-operate in perpetuating them. Whenever a time is set for their observance, it is not only our opportunity, but our duty to be present and to participate, not only to encourage our fellow members but also to lend the weight of our influence to the witness which our church bears to the rightness of such practices. Every unnecessary absence is that much of a discount in the eyes of the disbelieving and of the world as to the necessity and value of these ordinances, and thus the task of those who are faithful is made the harder. He who agrees with a group of Christians to do a certain work, or to bear a certain witness together and then will not do what he can, is as culpable a slacker and as cowardly as he who remains at home and profiteers while his fellow-citizens are fighting his country's battles. Such obligations cannot be lightly passed by.

More binding than all these is the duty we owe to our Lord who gave us the commandment, set us the example and pronounced a blessing upon all who knowing these things should do them. If we profess to take seriously what the Master says in this connection, so much so that it becomes the major excuse for our existence as a separate denomination, and yet we neglect or for other light and frivolous reasons fail to practice these ordinances, shall we not be among those who "say and do not," and shall we be surprised when we hear the Master's words, "Why call ye me Lord, Lord, and do not the things which I say?" Jesus says to us, as to the disciples of his own day, "If ye love me, keeep my commandments."

EDITORIAL REVIEW

The business of life is to be moving Godwards, happy or unhappy. Yet happiness is most likely to come to those who are so moving.—Maltbie D. Babcock.

Touchiness, when it becomes chronic, is a morbid condition of the inward disposition. It is self-love inflamed to the acute point.—Henry Drummond.

"The day will come when the Bible will be read in the public schools just as any other book. There is no good reason why the Bible should not have its rightful place in our school curriculum."—Hon. P. P. Claxton.

Brother L. G. Wood, the Maryland-Virginia district director of the Four Year Program, calls for some "snappy reports" from his goal directors, to which request they will doubtless gladly respond. He is also anxious that the churches in his district shall report promptly as many "G's" (gain)as possible to Brother Bame when he calls for the records.

Brother W. S. Bell reports concerning his evangelistic work. He recently closed a meeting with Brother Miles Snyder at Milledgeville, Illinois. He then visited Brother Burnworth's charge at Lanark, and is now in the midst of a meeting at Falls City, Nebraska, where Brother Stuckman is the faithful shepherd. Brother Bell has been steadily at the evangelistic work ever since last conference time and is beginning to feel the wear of his strenuous efforts.

The editor recently enjoyed a trip to Masontown, Pennsylvania, where he preached to former parishioners over Sunday of May 2. It was evident that Brother Shively, who recently left this pastorate to take charge of the financial end of the college, had enjoyed a large place in the hearts of this people. He not only served this church most efficiently for six years, but performed a valuable ministry to the entire community. This church had not yet decided upon their new pastor, but whoever may go there will find an appreciative and loyal people.

The work at Roanoke, Virginia, is going steadily forward under the leadership of Brother L. G. Wood. They had the "best" Easter communion ever, their Foreign Mission offering amounted to $106.45. Their prayer meeting attendance has recently increased to 50 per cent of the membership, and they are now looking for Brother Beachler's coming that they may have a chance to go over the top on the college endowment campaign. We notice they are also to entertain their district conference.

Word comes from Brother Beachler that the Waterloo church, of which he is pastor, co-operated their greatest year financially. It has also been a year of numerical and spiritual growth, and we are not surprised that this should be true when we note how each department has been working for greater efficiency. The Sunday school has five new Teacher Training graduates, the Woman's Missionary Society has completed a mission study book and the Christian Endeavor Society has graduated nine from the course of Expert Endeavor. Their prayer meeting averages 38; their Foreign Mission offering amounted to $145.50 and they have experienced a successful revival, in the face of most difficult odds, under the leadership of Brother Bame.

"It is a man's job to be a Christian and to recognize that God has first claim on all his talents, strength, time and resources."—George D. Dayton.

Paper Famine Still On.—We are still compelled to publish only half the regular sized paper. We regret this very much, but our paper stock has not yet arrived. We are hoping for and expecting some soon ,and just as soon as it arrives we will restore the Evangelist to its regular size. We know this is a disappointment to our readers, as it is to us, but we hope all will be patient as we are doing all we can to obtain more paper stock. We suggest that you continue to write articles just as you have been and they will be published as soon as we can get to it, especially do we urge our church correspondents to continue their reports regularly, for as we expect to give preference to church news we shall be able to publish your letters about as promptly as usual.

A correspondent recently wrote us inquiring about the proper method of tithing, stating that in his community there were a number of individuals interested in tithing, but were not agreed as to the method. Some thought the tithe should be taken out of their gross receipts or wages; others thought expenses necessary to the business or the earning of the wages should be paid first and then the tithe taken out; and others thought the "living" should be deducted and the remainder tithed. First we should say that any method of tithing is better than none, for it usually results in larger and more regular giving than when a person gives haphazardly and under pressure. But in answer to this brother's question, rather than give our own opinion, we will quote from Dr. C. F. Yoder's book "God's Means of Grace," page 582: "First, all debts and expenses incurred in order to produce an income are to be deducted from the gross receipts. In other words, all money expended for wages, rents, insurance, taxes, advertising, or other necessary expenses, is to be counted as capital invested, not as increase, and therefore not to be tithed. Second, no debt or expenses incurred for other than business purposes are to be deducted from the increase before it is tithed: that is to say, no person in any pursuit, may deduct any sum for home, or living, or personal purposes of whatever sort, from the profits of his industry, until he has deducted the Lord's tenth. He may not feed or clothe himself or his family, pay his house rent, insurance or taxes, educate his children, speculate in property, or otherwise use money which does not belong to him."

We recently received from Brother Lyon, pastor of the Brethren church of Washington, D. C., a newspaper clipping concerning the latest vogue, in the old clothes movement. He states that most of the fads of the world the church cannot follow, but he thinks perhaps this one is right in line with historic Brethren spirit and teaching—simplicity and economy of dress. We should agree with Brother Lyon that it is saner than the overall craze and that it is well for our people to have their attention called to their growing extravagance and extreme pride in dress. It is growing more difficult every year to pick a quarrel with any sect over the "dress question," as it used to be understood, but we are not so sure but that there is needed a little wholesome teaching along the line of economy and modesty of dress. Brethren people are going with the crowd; they are about as extravagant and (the truth must be spoken) immodest as any other class of people. Our women folk are vieing with each other to see who can display the largest number of new hats in a season. Our mothers and grandmothers were quite content with one hat (and often that was a re-trimmed one) a season, and some of them counted only two seasons a year at that. Perhaps actual need had much to do with the getting of new hats in those days, while style dictates today regardless of need. No one has a right to be extravagant in the face of the world's great need, it matters not how much he may possess. Economy is a Christian duty,—not the kind however that seeks to make a gown out of the smallest amount of goods, regardless of the modesty of its appearance. No doubt the men would be willing to pay for a larger amount of goods, and goods heavy enough to make a shadow too, if the women were willing to put it into their gowns, and our ideals would be more nobly Christian. Let the old clothes fad accomplish what it will; economy and modesty of dress is a subject that deserves some really unprejudiced and frank consideration by Christian people today.

GENERAL ARTICLES

Cause, Work and Purpose of the Organization of Some Congregational Brethren Churches in Indiana

By J. H. Swihart

In a former article mention was made of some instances that tended to weaken the confidence of many brethren in the legislative character of the Annual meeting of the German Baptist church, on one hand, and to confirm the belief in the necessity of the organization of congregational churches on the other. But the fact that the article was growing too lengthy I refrained from mentioning other and greater causes for the construction of such congregations. For instance, the wholesale manner of expelling scores of members for trivial, or no lawful reasons, ended in wrecking whole churches sometimes, as in the case of Jasper county, Missouri in 1872, when a church was rent in twain from top to bottom, by representatives of this great ecclesiastical court. Such circumstances would seem very discouraging. But there is a saying, "It is an ill wind that doesn't produce some good." So it was with this and other like circumstances. While it seemed for a time that the whole fraternity would be wrecked from east to west as by a general storm; the final result proved to be a great blessing to the church and to mankind in general. For by this upheaval both parties were stirred to activity and energy, and the good result has been obvious—they have become a great power in the world. The one party now relieved from the busy task of mote hunting (Matthew 7: 3, 4) was then in a better position to preach the Word of God to blood-bought souls for their salvation. The other party now released from the thralldom of ecclesiastical authority was also in a better position to evangelize and secure spiritual homes for the outcast and bewildered sons and daughters of men, who desired to worship God in peace. And so the heralds of the Gospel of grace, accompanied by others who fell in line, went forward to evangelize until, within a very few years local churches were formed almost from shore to shore, Ohio and Indiana not excepted.

Our Return to Indiana

After much has been said in a general way, I must now give attention to some early experiences and personal work after our return to the old state.

In response to an invitation by friends and relations in the year 1878, we made a visit to the old neighborhood at Roann, Indiana, the place where my parents settled from Ohio in an early day, and where I was brought up, spent my boyhood days, was married and with my wife joined the German Baptist (Dunkard) church, but later settled at Bourbon.

While stopping for a few days at Roann, at the request of old friends and brethren, I did a little shot-gun preaching, for I as yet retained my membership with the general body of the church, but on account of conscientious principles, had not communed with the annual meeting brethren for about eight years. Both the congregations in which we lived and had our membership while in the west highly observed, "For I have given you an example that ye should do as I have done to you" (John 13:15). Now, after settling again at Bourbon, protracted meetings were called for, mostly by outside people, for protracted meetings were hardly known among Brethren in those parts. Responding to calls I held many meetings and baptized many converts. This however seemed to stir up a rather ill feeling among the old Brethren.

Once we had a letter from an outside party at Roann, saying, The people would like to have some meetings held down here, but the Dunkards have decided not to let you preach in their house, and have used their influence to have

all the schoolhouses closed. ANSWER AND SET A TIME.

We answered and set a time, stating that the Lord willing and if a place can be found to hold services in, we will preach and will have it very distinctly understood that such as want to attend can do so, and such as don't can stay away. We went at the appointed time, accompanied by an old brother from near Bourbon, where we lived. On our arrival at Roann, we visited with an old man of Campbellite faith, who was taking care of the German Baptist church known as the "Old Fort." After a pleasant little visit with the old man, to my surprise, he asked if I would baptize him. "Certainly, if you believe with all your heart that Jesus Christ is the Son of God," I replied. "I do," said the old man, and immediately we went to the river near by and I baptized him.

Then, by permission, preached in an abandoned church near Roann. After two or three services in this old house which belonged to the Church of God people, some of the German Baptist Brethren ventured out, among them a preacher. After the service he said, "Where have you been keeping yourself?" I said, "We visited some of the old friends, and baptized old father Ivins." "Why," said he, "I didn't know there was meeting" (meaning at the G. B. church). "There isn't," I said. "Well," said he, "who were your witnesses?" "Old Pap Ivins, and old Daddy Whetstone, and God and Christ and all the angels in heaven." "Well, it may do," said he, "but I think it's pretty fast work." "Yes, that is the way Philip worked." He preached the gospel in Samaria and baptized men and women. And the apostles at Jerusalem considered the work of such note that they sent Peter and John down to Samaria to ratify the work by prayer and the laying on of hands, and under the influence of the Spirit of God Philip baptized an Ethiopian officer who had charge of all the treasures of the queen of Ethiopia. As they, Philip and the Eunuch, and maybe one more, were going along the road, and came to a certain water, Philip baptized that Ethiopian, only three human witnesses being present.

On this little visit very little was done other than to scatter some seeds of pure gospel grace. While I had no desire to withdraw from the general body, I felt, after being among energetic brethren for some years, to say, "Awake, thou that sleepest, and arise from the dead and Christ will give thee light." For such a thing as prayer meetings, Sunday schools, Bible readings and protracted meetings were hardly known among Dunkard people in those parts. Not much else than the regular weekly or Semi-monthly meetings scattered around over the territory could be expected, each service being conducted mainly by all the preachers within the congregation, usually from about four to six in number. And then there were the frequent church meetings, designed to keep things in "the order." Such slothfulness as here indicated was evidently responsible for the harvest to be gathered in future days.

(More anon).

Mulberry, Indiana.

CRISIS IN RELIGIOUS EDUCATION

Dr. Athearn recently said, 27,000,000 children in the United States are untouched by religious education. He also suggested that a uniform record of national education, patterned upon the census, be taken from time to time so that more efficient operation of a systematic program of education might be provided.

Returning to Apostolic Practices. By E. E. Roberts

Nothing in the Evangelist has ever given me more pleasure than the selected article by Brother Jennings under the above caption, unless indeed it was the Editor's note on it. My only regret is that I must differ a little with the Editor's note stating that "It is a practice that the Brethren have long observed." Paul said that he was "A Hebrew of the Hebrews;" I can say that I am a "Brethren of the Brethren," being a descendant from the original "Dunkers" and of the one to print the first Bible in America. But my association with the church for forty-five years has shown me that at times they did make attempts to observe it, but when they did it was mostly as the Catholics do, anointing for death, and not for healing, and the few that did anoint for healing did so with the prayer, "If it be Thy will," which is nothing less than a prayer of UNBELIEF.

If Jesus spake the truth, as I believe he did when he told us that he came to show us the Father, i. e., say and do the things that the Father would have said and done, were he present, what did Christ do to show us the Father's will? He healed the sick, cast out devils, raised the dead. Did he ever refuse a healing to any one? The lepers who said, "If thou wilt, thou canst make us clean," did he refuse them? NO, he said, "I will and immediately they were healed." Is there a single suggestion that anywhere or at any time he led them to think that it was not his will to heal them? No, thank God, he did not, but in several cases, he did not wait to have them ask but healed them before they asked, (Matt. 12:15; Luke 8:43; 22:51). And more, he had the disciples do so also, (Acts 3:2), and went so far as to heal all on whom Peter's shadow fell (Acts 5:15).

God declared (Exod. 15:26), "I am the Lord that healeth thee." He had planned to always keep them well, and only ceased to do so when they fell into sin; even then he warned them of the consequences that would follow their sin, all kinds of diseases, even naming consumption as one. He evidently had not changed his plan in Christ's time. Do you

thing he has changed it now? He put in the mouth of Malachai these words, "I am God and change not." Was Paul wrong when he wrote to the Hebrews 13:8, "Jesus Christ the same yesterday, today and forever?" No, Paul must have been right, for in that name Peter healed the crippled man. If Paul was right, that name should have the same power today. That Paul was right, I am convinced by almost daily evidence, supplied by the healing of all kinds of diseases. The best evidence of all is from my own personal experience. Having been pronounced dead by one of four doctors, I was healed by the "prayer of faith" of a dear old, saintly mother. I have lived to bury all the doctors, and feel now that I am good for twenty more years of active service, if the blessed Lord delays his coming. But I hope, expect and believe he will come long before that time. That experience settled it for me; God alone can heal. Praise his name.

Did you ever stop to think what kind of faith it was that justified Abraham? It was FAITH that God would do for his body which was contrary to nature, reason, and human experience. That kind of faith made him the friend of God. And will not God make any other possessor of that kind of faith his friend also? It is no miracle for God to heal us. The miracle is to get men to believe "That all things are possible to him that believeth. May the prayer of that poor father be the prayer of every ministering brother, "Lord I believe, help thou my unbelief."

Thank God that our Brethren are wakening up on this subject. And may they wake up to the necessity of a definite act, i. e., the laying on of hands for the reception of the Holy Spirit. But it is only after the candidates have been fully taught as to what is implied in the act (Acts 8:15) that the laying on of hands and the prayer should take place. Lord, increase our obedience and our faith.

Philadelphia, Pennsylvania.

Man Approved and Blessed of God.

That man may be blessed of God, he must keep God's law. He requires of us a thankful recognition and a reception of his benefits. His love desires that we be faithful followers of his will.

The blessed man in this Psalm is instructed in the negative form, "Thou shalt not." Often man cannot understand the finest things of life except they are put in just this way. A command put in this form cannot be mistaken—it is uncompromising. Naturally man is affirmative—he is practical and energetic.

Therefore we reason, he who is not against us is for us, then it follows that one of the great laws of life is activity and when we refuse to do evil we must be doing good—if we refuse the counsel of the ungodly we must be actively engaged of God.

Man is instructed as to the way in which to direct his life, "His delight is in the law of God."

God never destroys our powers, he does not quench our aspirations, but he does lay his hand on the strength we are misusing and says, "You must use it in another direction and for another purpose."

"Blessed is the man that walketh not in the counsel of the ungodly." So long as man is moving (walking) he has no fixed place or purpose, so that he cannot be changed; he is open to receive any truth that might be presented him,—in other words, he is open to conviction—he may assent to truth and acknowledge the need of a better life. "Nor standeth in the way of sinners." The man who is standing has planted himself in the path of sin—he is hard to move, because he is more firmly set in his position and purpose and we find him hard to convict of truth, yet his position is not so firm that he is lost to conviction.

Psalm 1: 1, 2. By Mrs. C. E. Nicholas

"Nor sitteth in the seat of the scornful." This man is decided—he has gone step by step till he has sat down, thus closing practically all avenues by which his soul may be reached and is not likely to be brought into the saving grace of our Savior.

God blesses the man who does not walk nor stand nor sit in the path of sin, such a man is engaged in doing good. There is nothing abiding in the ungodly, his life has no abiding worth and insecure.

The man who abides in God is safe, while he who puts himself outside the restraints of the divine law, by walking standing and sitting in the way of sinners, forfeits its protection and all its blessings.

He leads us into light—gives us life and peace. Our delight in the law comes from the great flood of light coming into the soul that is actively engaged in the Master's service.

As God unfolds his great plan and his own glorified self to us, our delight increases until we are led to meditate in his law day and night.

Dowagiac, Michigan.

Christ proposed to capture the world by a campaign of personal testimony. Not by controversy, but by conversation. This was to be the sure Kingdom method. Conversation about Christ based on personal knowledge of Christ was to be the particular kind of witness bearing which would produce permanent Kingdom results. It was not mere talk. It was a life transformed by Christ speaking through lips which had been touched by the fire of the Holy Spirit. —Bishop T. S. Henderson.

NEWS FROM THE FIELD

MARYLAND AND VIRGINIA

Each district goal director of the Four Year Program is hereby requested to prepare and boil down a good snappy report of the achievements of your goal in our district during the year. Make it a brief but inspirational report for the "home run" to VICTORY. I am sure we will have a place on the conference program for these reports.

Let every worker in the district be ready to place as many "G's" as possible on Bame's report card when it comes. By all means report promptly.

L. G. WOOD, District Director.

ROANOKE, VIRGINIA

The First Brethren church is moving forward in the work and making commendable progress.

We have nothing sensational to report, in fact we care nothing for sensationalism, but crave constant growth and increase. All departments of the work are in a healthy, growing condition. Attendance at all services is gradually increasing. Our communion service on Easter evening was one of the best ever enjoyed by the congregation. The Easter offering to Foreign Missions was the best ever made by the congregation—$106.45. The congregation has gone "over the top" with all of the financial goals of the program for the year.

The average attendance at the mid-week prayer meeting for several weeks has been 50 percent of the entire membership.

Three precious souls made the good confession last Sunday and yet others are to follow.

We are now looking forward to, and preparing for, two great events, one is the coming of Beachler, perhaps the last part of May. The other our district conference, the second week of June. Here and now I wish to extend a WELCOME GREETING to both and ALL.

Brethren, pray for us. L. G. WOOD.

ALTOONA, PENNSYLVANIA

We have been thinking that perhaps a report from the Brethren in the "Mountain City" might be of interest to the readers of the Evangelist. Our annual business meeting was held Wednesday evening, April 14th. It was to us a great meeting. The attendance was above the average and a keen interest was manifested in every phase of the work of the church. Officers were elected, reports were read and plans were discussed for the future welfare of the church. This was the greatest year of the church financially. There was numerical and spiritual growth. To the Lord be all the glory. With every department of the work well organized, special emphasis is being laid upon the spiritual and intellectual development of the individual. Special classes have been organized in the different departments under competent instructors. In December a class of five graduated in Teacher Training. Since then a still larger class has been organized. The members of the W. M.

S. have just finished the mission study text and a class of nine has just completed the course in Expert Endeavor.

The weather in Pennsylvania on Easter Sunday was no better than in Indiana. But we had a day of spiritual blessing in the service of the Lord. The attendance throughout the day was above the average in spite of the rain. Our offering to Foreign Missions the largest yet—$145.50. This is better than a dollar per member. I have discovered that the best way to increase offerings to missions is by having in your church systematic missionary instruction. And the more we give abroad, the more we have at home.

Dr. Chas. A. Bame of North Manchester, Indiana, was with us in an evangelistic campaign from January 25 to February 6th. Brother Bame has reported this meeting and called your attention to the hindrances. Never, in the experience of the writer in revival work has there been such a combination of sickness and bad weather to hinder as in this meeting. But the Lord was with us and splendid results were realized. Brother Bame proved himself to be capable, consecrated and full of zeal for the Lord's work, and greatly endeared himself to this people and to the writer. As a visible result of the meeting fifteen were added to the church by baptism and six were reclaimed. The meeting was also a means of an awakening among the members as is seen in the increased attendance at all of the services. The average at prayer meeting for the month of April was 48. Since the revival seven have been added to our members by baptism, two by letter and one reclaimed.

The writer was privileged, during the month of November, to work with Brother M. A. Witter and his good people at Waynesboro, Pennsylvania, in an evangelistic effort. This meeting has been reported by the pastor. Brother Witter is a great pastor and, "like priest like people," we have there a great people. In the Waynesboro congregation we have an illustration of what can be accomplished by concentrated missionary endeavor.

We are glad to report that four splendid young people of the Altoona church are this year attending Ashland College. More of our young people are looking forward to the time when they too shall be among the students of Ashland. May the Lord bless his believing children everywhere. Brethren pray for us.

WM. C. BENSHOFF.

YOU MAY HAVE IT, IF YOU WILL

Church folk are too mouse-like. They have cultivated modesty at the expense of greater virtues. All sorts of public evils are tolerated simply because Christians are not as militant as their General Orders require.

So when inclined to grumble about such grave matters as lack of intelligent recognition of religion in the secular press, church members should blame themselves first of all.

Active Christians can just about have anything they want in print, if they are wise and firm in asking for it.

There is not a newspaper in the land that

would not publish a full page every Saturday, devoted exclusively to the churches, if even ten per cent of the professing Christians among its readers were to ask for it.

If you want more and better general news of Christianity in your daily paper, write to the editor and request it. If enough ask, the answer will be quick and sure.

If you would like to read a good sermonic article every week, such as a popular exposition of the Sunday school lesson, write to the editor, and he will get it for you.

If you want a weekly column on Interchurch World Movement activities, why, simply ask for it! The editor will quickly get into touch with the Interchurch Publicity department.

If you want a squarer deal in print for foreign missions, speak up!

If you desire a broad-guage, human interest interpretation of the local religious life of your community, say so to the editor.

News space is apportioned according to the editor's best judgment as to what his readers want. If he hears from the sports followers, and never hears from the church folk, can you blame him for giving a page or two every day to sports, and only a column or two a week to religion?

The text for this homily, is, "Let the redeemed of the Lord say so."

WILLIAM T. ELLIS

FIELD REPORT OF EVANGELISTIC LEAGUE

Milledgeville Campaign

This campaign was one of special pleasure to me as it was formerly the church in which my wife and her parents were members and of which my wife's two brothers who live in Sterling still have their membership. Not only this, but so many of the people who formerly lived here have moved to Sunnyside, Washington, where I knew them while working in that field, that it seemed like being among my relation.

The meeting continued for three weeks and I was given loyal support by the pastor and his faithful people. It was my first opportunity to work with Brother Snyder and found him a good yoke-fellow in the Gospel. The attendance and interest in the afternoon Bible lectures as well as the evening services were satisfactory. We had a good campaign, a pleasant stay and splendid support was given in a financial way to the League.

Lanark

While at Milledgeville, Brethren Burnworth and Livengood came down and made us a visit, and by the invitation of Brother Burnworth I arranged to speak in his church on Monday night following the meeting at Milledgeville. Through mud, rain and snow we were driven over to Lanark, on account of the storm we had a small crowd, but as Brother Burnworth is one of the Directors of the League we left it to him to present the League more fully to his members. It was nearly eighteen years since we were in Lanark and many changes have taken place. Brother Burnworth has done a splendid work in this field, the people under the leadership of their pastor have reared a modernly equipped church second to none in arrangement and equipment. Recently they purchased a fine parsonage and the work here is in splendid condition.

Falls City, Nebraska

Leaving Lanark Monday evening, I arrived in Falls City Tuesday and immediately opened a campaign here. With no rest and my ninth consecutive meeting I feel like Peter when he said, let us go fishing. Brother Stuckman had things in shape for us to begin and we will do our best for the Master and his church.

A tabernacle party are conducting a meeting four blocks from us in the M. E. church and with a carnival show troupe on the borders of the city for the coming week, you can realize we have plenty of competition in a town no larger than this.

W. S. BELL

Communion Notices

The Lanark, Illinois, Brethren church will observe holy communion on Sunday evening, May 16th. Neighboring Brethren are cordially invited.

B. T. BURNWORTH, Pastor.

The Oakville, Indiana church will hold Communion Services, Saturday evening, May 22. Neighboring Brethren invited.

W. R. DEETER, Pastor.

REPORTS OF RECEIPTS FOR MISSIONS DURING MARCH (HOME MISSIONS)

General Fund

Mr. and Mrs. Curtis, Hummel, Nappanee, Ind., (H. G.),...........$	5.00
Breth. Ch., Portis Kans., by R. Brumbaugh, ...	61.00
Thoburn C. Lyon, Washington, D. C.,	5.00
Mr. and Mrs. Henry V. Wall, Long Beach, Calif., (H. G.), ...	10.00
Br. Ch., McKee, Pa., by S. R. Campbell, Sec'y., ...	23.50
Nat'l Woman's Missionary Society, by Mary C. Wenger, Treas., ...	25.00
Interest for Jan. and Feb., ...	13.89
Mrs. Mary N. Huyett, Zanesville, O.,	2.50
Willing Workers S. S. Class, Dayton, Ohio, by Ella Weaver, Treas., ...	12.25
Interest on deposit in Gem City Bldg. and Loan Co., ...	44.64
Mrs. P. N. Auspach, Findlay, O., (H. G.), ...	5.00
Carleton and Garwin, Iowa, Brethren Churches, by Ankrum, ...	39.10
Mrs. W. W. Combs, Lawrenceburg, Tenn., (H. G.), ...	5.00
Total, ...$	251.88
Previously reported, ...	8,178.44
Total Receipts to April 1, ...$	8,430.32

Kentucky (Support Fund)

First Brethren Ch., Long Beach, Cal., by L. S. B., ...$	2.60
Primary Dept. S. S., Nappanee, Ind., by Mrs. Chester Richmond, ...	10.00
Woman's Miss. Society, N. Liberty, Ind., by Mrs. (J. W. Holderman,	25.00
Jr. C. E. Society, Louisville, Ohio, by Mrs J. Frank Painter, ...	5.00
Y. P. S. C. E., Clay City, Ind, by M. Burger, ...	25.00
A loyal member, Brethren Church, Teegarden, Ind., by Whetstone, ..	5.00
Jr. C. E., Nappanee, Ind., by Mrs. H. B. Richmond, Supt., ...	5.00
Woman's Miss. Society, Lanark,	

Ill., by Mrs. Geo. Dimon, ... 10.00
Charles A. Teall, Elkhart, Ind., ... 5.00
Brethren Church, Krypton, Ky., by J. A. Rempel, ... 12.00
Sisterhood Mary and Martha; by Mary C. Wenger, Treasurer, ... 15.64
Brethren Church, Lost Creek, Ky., by Mrs. Drushal, ... 38.80
Mrs. L. S. Stutzman, Cramer, Pa.,.. 5.00
Senior C. E. Society, Warsaw, Ind., by Mrs. C. H. Burnette, ... 15.00

Total, ...$	179.04
Previously reported, ...$	4,557.43
Total receipts to April 1, ...$	4,736.47

Kentucky (Kitchen Shower Fund)

Woman's Miss. Society, Martinsburg, Pa., ...$	5.00
Woman's Miss. Society, Nappanee, Ind., by Mrs. Best, ...'.	5.00
Total, ...$	10.00
Previously reported, ...	253.80
Total receipts to April 1, ...$	263.80

Kentucky (Light Plant Fund)

W. V. Findley, Falls, Pa., ...$	5.00
Brethren Church, Paulina, Iowa, by L. R. Bradfield, ...	10.00
Total, ...$	15.00
Previously reported, ...$	646.03
Total receipts to April 1, ...$	661.03

SUMMARY OF RECEIPTS TO APRIL 1, (HOME MISSIONS)

General Fund, ...$	8,430.32
Kentucky (Support Fund), ...	4,736.47
Kentucky (Kitchen Shower Fund),	263.80
Kentucky (Light Plant Fund), ...	661.03
Peru, Ind., (Building Fund), ...	25.24
Muncie, Ind., (Bldg. Fund) Including Transfer, ...	481.32
Total receipts to April 1, All Funds, $14,598.18	

FOREIGN MISSIONS

General Fund (South America)

Mrs. Nancy Keagy, Orland, Ind., by Horner, ...$	2.00
Frank Clapper, Louisville, Ohio, by L. P. Clapper, (M), ...	5.00
Dr. Ezra and Mrs. Rosa Longenecker, Dayton, Ohio, (M), ...	40.00
Mrs. Mary N. Huyett, Zanesville, O.,	2.50
Mrs. Susan Himes, Indianapolis, Ind., ...	1.00
J. S. C. Spickerman, Maryville, Mo., (M), ...	10.00
Barrie C. Funderburg, New Carlisle, Ohio, (M), ...	5.00
J. J. W. of Milford, Ind., ...	10.00
Maggie White, Lyndon, Ohio, ...	2.00
Elizabeth Gnagey, Oak Park, Illinois, (M), ...	5.00
G. C. Brumbaugh, Hill City, Kans., (Portis Church), (M), ...	5.00
D. J. Hetrick, New Bethlehem, Pa., (M), ...	5.00
Anna F. Miller, McCauley, W. Va., (M), ...	25.00
Mrs. W. W. Combs, Lawrenceburg, Tenn., of Br. Ch., Harrisonburg,	5.00
Brethren Church, Sidney, Indiana, by H. D. Miller, Sec'y, ...	24.87
Mrs. R. D. Martin, Pioneer, Ohio, (M), ...	5.00
Mary E. Storm, Chambersburg, Pa., (M), ...	5.00
Mary E. Chuck, Chambersburg, Pa.,	

(M), ...	5.00
Rosa Johnston, Corning, Iowa, (M),	5.00
Mr. and Mrs. J. D. Millheisler, Eldorado, Kans., (M), ...	16.00
Mr. and Mrs. Eugene Ormsby, Van Buren, Indiana, (M);	5.00
M. W. Eikenberry, Kokomo, Ind., (M), ...	5.00
Angeline Eikenberry, Kokomo, Ind.,	5.00
Mrs. Julia Saunders, Bridgeport, Texas, ...	1.00
Mr. an Mrs. Guy Pittenger, Wooster, Ohio, (M), ...	10.00
Hortense C. Wertz, Crestline, Ohio, (M), ...	25.00
Total, ...$	262.37
Previously reported, ...	522.95
Total receipts to April 1, ...$	785.32

General Fund (Africa)

Number		
354,	....	$ 5.00
355,	....	.50
356, M,	....	10.00
357, M,	....	5.00
358,	....	15.05
359,	....	11.00
360, M,	....	50.00
361,	....	25.00
362,	....	3.00
363, M,	....	5.00
364,	....	24.97
365, (106), M,	....	5.00
366, (107),	....	1.00
367, (108)	....	1.00
368, (109),	....	20.00
	Total,	$181.42
	Previously reported,	315.09
	Total to April 1,	$496.51

Gribble (Personal Fund)

Number		
100,	....	$100.00
101,	....	3.00
102, M,	....	5.00
103, M,	....	5.00
104, Margaret,	....	0.75
105, Dr. Gribble,	....	25.00
	Total,	$147.75
	Previously reported,	$138.01
	Total received to April 1,	$285.76

Rollier (Personal Fund)

Number		
44, M,	....	$ 5.00
45, M,	....	5.15
46, Marie and Julia,	....	2.00
	Total,	$ 12.15
	Previously reported,	266.90
	Total to April 1,	$279.05

Brethren Missionary Fund

Ada Saylor, Los Angeles, Cal., ...$	0.25
Seven Sub'as Breth. Miss (L. S. B.),	1.75
Mrs. J. J. Mange, Kalamazoo, Mich.,	.25
M. W. Eikenberry, Kokomo, Ind., ...	.50
Total, ...$	2.50
Previously reported, ...	9.70
Total receipts to April 1, ...$	12.20

SUMMARY OF RECEIPTS TO APRIL 1, (FOREIGN MISSIONS)

General Fund (South America), ...$	785.32
General Fund (Africa), ...	496.51
Gribble (Personal Fund), ...	285.76
Rollier (Personal Fund), ...	279.05
Brethren Missionary Fund, ...	12.20
South American (Tract Fund), ...	120.00
Snyder (Personal Fund), ...	10.00
Charlotte Hillegas (Af. Outfit Fund),	272.91
Miscellaneous Funds Acct., ...	311.90
Total receipts to April 1, all funds, $2,582.65	

THE TIE THAT BINDS

JORDAN-KLINGAMAN — Miss Helen M. Klingaman of Waterloo and Mr. Herbert Jordan of Cedar Falls were united in marriage on the evening of April 17th, at the bride's home. The wedding was a splendid eVent perfectly arranged and not one of the many relatives and friends present will ever forget it. The bride is the only child of Mr. and Mrs. C. E. Klingaman and the parents and daughter are faithful and actiVe members of the Waterloo congregation. The most hearty good wishes of a host of friends go with these young people as they start out in life together. The ceremony was performed by the undersigned.

WM. H. BEACHLER.

ZIEGLER-MOSER—Vera A. Zeigler, only daughter of Brother and Sister Joseph Zeigler and Lloyd B. Moser, both of Hagerstown, Maryland, NoVember 15, 1919. The bride is a member of the church here. The groom is employed by the W. M. Railroad Company.

A. B. COVER.

MILLS-ARTZ—Mary Eleanor Mills, of St. James, Maryland, and William Henry Artz of Hagerstown, Maryland, February 3, 1920. Both of the contracting parties are members of the church and are esteemed by all who know them. A. B. COVER..

STOLEFHER-HOUSENFLUCK—Marion L. Stolepher of Martinsburg, West Virginia, and William A. Housenfluck of Hagerstown, Maryland, March 24, 1920. The groom is a member of the church here. They will reside in the city. A. B. COVER.

WHITACRE-BEATTY—Wida R. Whitacre of Woodstock, Virginia and Brice Albert Beatty of this city, April 4, 1920. Both are members of the church and will reside in the city. A. B. COVER.

BRADENBURG-RONK—Helen M. Bradenberg of Linwood, Maryland, and Willis E. Ronk of Roann, Indiana, April 7, 1920. The bride is an actiVe member of the Linwood, Maryland, church where her serVices were much appreciated. Brother Ronk is the present successful pastor of the Roann church, also the Secretary-Treasurer of the National Ministerial Association of the church. We rejoice that these liVes are thus united in the Lord's service. They took a short wedding trip to Washington, D. C. After returning a reception was given them at the bride's home. They will be at home at Roann, Indiana, where their many friends will wish them the blessed joys of wedded life.

A. B. COVER.

IN THE SHADOW

JONES—Mrs. Bettie Jones died February 9, 1920, aged 85 years. She had been a consistent member of the Brethren church for years, at Hollins, Virginia. Funeral serVice conducted by Brother L. G. Wood on account of the illness of the pastor.

J. E. PATTERSON.

SINK—James A. Sink died February 7, 1920, aged 30 years. He united with the Brethren church in his youth. He leaves to mourn his departure a brother and sister. Funeral service conducted by Brother L. G. Wood on account of the illness of the pastor.

J. E. PATTERSON.

SINK—Samuel H. Sink died February 15, 1920, aged 64 years. He was one of the most faithful of the Mount View Brethren church. He is survived by his widow asd one daughter. Funeral services in charge of Brother L. G. Wood on account of the illness of the pastor. J. E. PATTERSON.

BRUMFIELD—T. W. Brumfield died March 7, 1920, at the age of 71 years. He had been a great sufferer with cancer on the face for a number of years. He was a consistent member of the Brethren church at Hollins, Virginia. He leaves his widow and one sister. Funeral services by the writer.

J. E. PATTERSON.

COLLINS—Mrs. W. M. Collins, wife of W. M. Collins, died March 9, 1920, at the age of 41 years. She is surViVed by her husband and one daughter. She was a consistent member of the Brethren church. Funeral serVices by the writer. J. E. PATTERSON.

SUMPTION—William B. Sumption departed this life April 14, 1920. For some time he was a resident of Ashland, coming here about twenty years ago. He leaVes to mourn his departure, his widow, three sons, three sisters, and a brother. Funeral services were conducted by the undersigned.

J. A. GARBER.

SAGLE—Mary Dusing Sagle departed this life February 17, 1920. Sister Sagle was sick but a few days; haVing an attack of "flu," which developed into pneumonia. She was a member of the Hagerstown church. She leaVes a husband and a little daughter to mourn her early departure, haVing been but twenty-eight years old. SerVices by the writer, her pastor. A. B.COVER.

SHOOP—Paul F. Shoop died March 13, 1920. Brother Shoop was a sufferer of seVeral years' standing of that dreaded malady tuberculosis. He liVed at Baltimore for seVeral years. He was a member of this church. His body was laid to rest in the city cemetery, the undersigned officiating.

May God who knows and doeth all things well, comfort the bereft. A. B. COVER.

ETHRIDGE—Achsa, the wife of Elmer E. Ethridge, aged 58 years, 10 months and 15 days, passed on from her home here to the eternal home, April 6, 1920. She leaves her husband, two daughters and four sons of the immediate family, and many other relatiVes and friends. She was a member of the Brethren church at Lanark for oVer twenty-six years. Her illness was short; her death peaceful.

Services conducted by B. T. Burnworth, assisted by Z. T. Livengood.

KOONTZ—Sister Sarah E. Koontz passed from this earthly pilgrimage, December 9, 1919. She was a sufferer for some years of nervous affliction, yet she was able to be about her household duties until a short time before her death. She was a mother devoted to her family; she was solicitous to the extent that each one should share her kindly ministrations. It was her pastor's priVilege to Visit with her in her home where she was always kindly receiVed and assured that amidst her busy life, she had time for the things of the eternal. She leaVes to mourn her departure her husband, three daughters, and five sons, one son haVing preceded her to the spirit world. SerVices by Dr. J. M. Tombaugh and the writer. A. B. COVER.

WOODWARD—Elizabeth Woodward was born in Fayette county, PennsylVania, April 23, 1859, and passed to her reward April 13, 1920, in the sixty-first year of her age. Death came at the home of her sister, Mrs. Jennie Vance, of the Uniontown, PennsylVania, congregation. Miss Woodward was a faithful member of the Presbyterian church, but was unable to attend services at her own church and worshipped with the Brethren at Uniontown. Services at the Sandy Hill church, near Uniontown, on April 15, 1920, conducted by the undersigned. DYOLL BELOTE.

McCLELLAND—Blanche Bernetta Miller was born July 15, 1886, a daughter of Elihugh and Nancy Miller, and grew to womanhood in the natiVe state of West Virginia. She was married to Joseph McClelland, NoVember 3, 1908, to which union one child was born. Sister McClelland answered the final summons at the Uniontown hospital on April 14, 1920, death resulting from shock following an operation. 35 years, 8 months and 29 days of earthly pilgrimage had been giVen Sister McClelland to spend with those who loved her, and they mourn deeply at her leaVe taking, but rejoice in her full confidence and hope of immortality. Sister McClelland was a faithful member of the Uniontown Brethren church and leaves beside the husband, one son, father, mother, 3 sisters and 2 brothers, a host of sorrowing friends. Funeral serVices from the family home on April 17, conducted by the undersigned, assisted by Rev. E. S. Hawkins, pastor of the First M. P. church of Uniontown. May God comfort the bereft and give rest to the departed.

DYOLL BELOTE.

SWANK—Mary J. Swank, nee Whisler, was born May 18, 1852, near UnionVille, Iowa, was married to Cyrus Swank April 6, 1871, died May 1, 1920 in Lockwood, Missouri and was buried in Dudenville cemetery. She came to Dawe County, Missouri, in 1902, and to Lockwood in 1909. She had submitted to two operations for that dread disease, cancer, which failed to give relief, and after nearly two years of untold suffering she laid down the burden. She had been a consistent Christian for over 45 years, being a member of the Brethren church. She leaves her husband, 3 sons and one daughter to mourn her departure; also 3 brothers, and 2 sisters. I receiVed a telegram, "Wife is dead. Come." I had known her Godly life, as I had been her pastor when she liVed near Udell, Iowa, as she was called "the good sister." Funeral conducted by Elder H. S. Enslow of the Brethren church.

RAMSYER—George N. Ramsyer was born in Switzerland county, Indiana, June 26, 1837 and departed this life March 28, 1920, aged 82 years, 9 months and 2 days. He was killed instantly by the tornado in the same house in which his daughter met her death. (She however liVed until two o'clock Monday morning). He was united in marriage to Louisa Leslie, to which one daughter, Mrs. Lillis Riffel, was born. His second marriage was to Mariah Latmore, which union was blessed with seVen children, three daughters and four sons, one son having departed this life last April. He leaVes to mourn three sons, three daughters, 21 grandchildren and a number of other near relatiVes and many friends. Father Ramsyer was a member of the Church of the Brethren for many years. He has been living with his daughters since the death of his wife seven years ago. A near relative wrote concerning him:

"Our father dear, thou hast left us and our hearts are bleeding sore,
For our father we loved so tenderly,—we shall never see him more.
Weep not dear friends nor children dear; I am not dead, but sleeping here;
My debt is paid; my grave you see; prepare for death and follow me."

W. F. JOHNSON.

HERRON—Anna S. Holmes Herron was born in Connersville, Oakland county, Michigan, May 9, 1857, where she was united in marriage to John W. Herron, April 14, 1897, and departed this life at her home in Campbell township, Iona county, Michigan, April 15, 1920, at the age of 62 years, 11 months and 6 days. She leaves to mourn her departure her husband, two brothers, three sisters and a host of friends. She united with the Presbyterian church when a girl; later she united with the Campbell Brethren church, of which she remained a faithful member until Jesus came to claim his own. Funeral services by the writer. M. V. GARRISON.

STALEY—On April 14, 1920, at her home near Centerville, Iowa, Mrs. H. C. Staley passed away. Her sickness was of very short duration and the shock to her relatives and friends was Very great. Pneumonia was the immediate cause of her death, though she was suffering from other disease. She leaves to mourn her loss a loVing husband, her aged mother, two sisters, one brother and seven children. Mrs. Staley was known and admired by many people all of whom extend their sympathy to the burieved family. We are sure the brotherhood will extend their sympathy to the family and will note the loss of another sister of the Faith.

GEO. E. CONE.

MOSTOLLER—Katie (Yoder) Mostoller was born April 13, 1862 and died at her home in Listie, Pa., April 10, 1920. She is surVived by her husband, Nathan E. Mostoller, four sisters and a step-son and daughter. Sister Mostoller was a faithful and consistent member of the Listie Brethren church for oVer forty years. During her last illness she suffered much. But through it all she neVer complained, but at all times manifested a true, patient, Christian spirit. Funeral serVices by the writer, in the Listie Brethren church on April 12.

W. S. BAKER.

CATON—In the confines of the Uniontown congregation, Mary Madaline Caton, aged 1 year and 24 days, youngest child of Mr. and Mrs. Robert Caton, passed to be with the Master on April 26. "Of such is the Kingdom of heaVen." SerVices conducted by the writer.

DYOLL BELOTE.

RODABAUGH—Enos Rodabaugh of Kenton, Ohio passed to his eternal reward after dwelling in this life for 77 years, 8 months and three days. He was one of Kenton and Hardin county's pioneer residents and was highly respected by all who knew him. He was a life-long member of the Brethren Church and was a faithful and sincere Christian. He was a man of strong convictions and always advocated high ideals. Five children surVive him. The funeral services were held at the M. E. Church of Kenton and the sermon was delivered by the writer. The pastor of the church, Dr. D. H. Baily, assisted. J. ALLEN MILLELR.

BARTON—Cecil Barton died at the Miami Valley Hospital after a major operation, aged 43 years, one month and 25 days. After being led astray for a time, she was rescued by the Holy Spirit and she cast her lot with the Brethren church and she was happy in the Lord the rest of her days and she had one of the greatest "Passings over" of which I haVe eVer known. Her pastor was summoned to the hospital in the night to see her go across the riVer, but owing to unaVoidable delay he was too late, and no one was there but her son James who became a member of the church during our late reViVal. He was knelt at her bed praying when she said, "What time is it, dear?" He told her and went on praying. She waited a moment or two and he felt her hand slipping out of his and he looked up and she said in a clear audible Voice, "Oh what are all those thousands of people praying for?" And she stepped across. She saw the throng around the throne, and her human Voice was still able to audience to her joy as she was becoming accustomed to the new enVironment. My, what a Victory, and what a glorious close of an earthly life!

E. M. COBB.

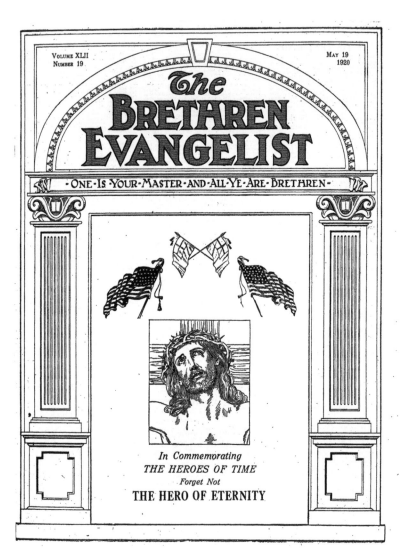

Volume XLII
Number 19

May 19
1920

The BRETHREN EVANGELIST

·ONE·IS·YOUR·MASTER·AND·ALL·YE·ARE·BRETHREN·

In Commemorating
THE HEROES OF TIME
Forget Not
THE HERO OF ETERNITY

Published every Wednesday at
Ashland, Ohio. All matter for publication must reach the Editor not
later than Friday noon of the preceding week.

George S. Baer, Editor

The
Brethren
Evangelist

When ordering your paper changed
give old as well as new address.
Subscriptions discontinued at expiration. To avoid missing any numbers renew two weeks in advance.

R. R. Teeter, Business Manager

OFFICIAL ORGAN OF THE BRETHREN CHURCH

Subscription price, $2.00 per year, payable in advance.
Entered at the Post Office at Ashland, Ohio, as second-class matter.
Acceptance for mailing at special rate of postage provided for in section 1103, Act of October 3, 1917, authorized September 9, 1918.
Address all matter for publication to Geo. S. Baer, Editor of the Brethren Evangelist, and all business communications to R. R. Teeter,
Business Manager, Brethren Publishing Company, Ashland, Ohio. Make all checks payable to the Brethren Publishing Company.

EDITORIAL

Some Challenges to Christian Patriots

As the Memorial season passes by we shall be called upon by churches and patriotic organizations to commemorate the heroic spirit and sacrificial service of the soldiers, both living and dead, who have served their country nobly in times of great need. This no thoughtful Christian will hesitate to do in right and proper ways. We owe more than we can tell to the men who placed their lives on the country's altar during the critical times when the nation was called upon to defend its own integrity, or to serve the peoples of the world. But the worthiness of our commemoration depends upon the sentiments the occasion arouses and the ideals we seek to perpetuate. Whatever heroic deeds we may recount or heroes we may name; whatever issue we may declare to have been at stake and vindicated; however the spirit of gratitude may stir our souls, we will not have made the most of the occasion if we do not ponder and actually face up to the problem of what Christian patriotism requires of us today.

Christian citizens should consider it their task to practice and encourage the acceptance of ideals of peace and aggressively to oppose plans for needless, expensive and competitive armaments that antici- pate, and thus encourage, war and all efforts to establish militarism in our land. The fact that universal military training was defeated by an overwhelming vote in congress does not in itself put an end to all efforts to militarize our nation. It was a great triumph for all lovers of peace, but we must not relax our vigilance under the delu- sion that complete and final victory has come. Two things at least must be kept in mind and ever challenge our sincere efforts. First, we must guard against and seek to forestall by a counter move a possible campaign of education on the part of the militaristic party to prepare the nation for the acceptance of their military schemes at some later period. Second, we must seek to remove every possible occasion or cause for "the president and congress to declare a nation- al emergency," under which emergency all the machinery of universal military training may be brought into operation. This means that more strenuously than ever before, we should seek to bring the whole gospel of Jesus Christ to bear heavily not only upon every individual heart, but upon every relation of life. These things constitute an appeal to every Christian who truly loves his country, but most espe- cially to members of the Brethren fraternity.

The Christian patriots of our land are challenged at this hour to be vigilant and aggressive in the final stages of the conflict against the outlawed liquor traffic. Many and great victories have been won in this field of moral and Christian warfare, but we deceive ourselves, if we think victory is complete and there is only need to enjoy its fruits henceforth. Nothing would serve the interests of the brewers better than that the Christian people of America should relax their vigilance and cease their efforts in the fight against intemperance. The task now is to secure law enforcement and to prevent a liberal- izing government that will seek to make possible the sale of light wines and beer. The liquor interests in certain wet centers, espe- cially in the east, have been working desperately to this very end, but if Christian men possess the right kind of patriotism they will only be, as Editor Best of The Continent says, "wasting their departing strength in kicking against the inevitable."

A most subtle and virulent evil that is growing in our land and that challenges the hand of every Christian patriot is Mormonism. It is subtle because it wins its way among the innocent and unwary as a Christian, evangelical people, without betraying its true char-

acter. The apostles of the Mormon faith are very careful to keep under cover their real character. There are throughout the land many innocent looking chapels over which are inscribed the words, "The Church of Jesus Christ of Latter Day Saints," or some other similarly misleading title, but the mass of the people do not know that they are all paying tithes to the Mormon hierarchy. It is not only subtle, it is virulent. It poisons the minds of its adherents against Chris- tianity, against true Americanism and against the true standards of morality. Notwithstanding the fact that Polygamy has long ago been outlawed by our federal government, it has nevertheless not been stricken out of Mormon teaching or belief, but expediency does not permit its practice. They naturally do not consider it wise to expose to public view their true attitude toward the government, for if it can be judged by the language of some of their vows, it is disloyal. These people are working steadily to get a strangle hold on the gov- ernment, or any public place or position that may be to their hier- archy's advantage. The recent attack of Senator Smoot of Utah on Roger W. Babson, the great statistician and editor of the United States Bulletin, was an effort on the part of this Mormon politician to get a censorship control over this man who is able to deliver facts to the public and to the business interests of the country that are damaging to Mormon strategy.

It is bad enough for any one man to have such a control over Government news; but to think that he is a Mormon! Certainly the Christian churches of America have been asleep to allow such a thing to happen. Christian patriotism requires that we shall awaken to the menace of Mormonism.

The wave of materialism and greed that has caused practically every one who has any chance to take advantage of his fellowmen to become an extortionate profiteer is challenging Christian patriot- ism as few things else are. There has seldom been a time when sel- fishness and greed have been carried to more despicable extremes than right now. Who is responsible for it? Are the profiteers all outside of the church? If they were there could exist no such con- ditions as now prevail. Men who are enrolled on the church books of our land, men who have professed faith in Jesus Christ and pledged allegiance to his principles of love and brotherhood, are driving each man his brother for the last penny. There are many who are still faithful, who maintain their integrity and have regard for the rights and welfare of their fellows, but if their number were recruited by the vast army who have come to worship mammon more than God, their strength would be sufficient to counteract the terrible onrush of the hordes of worldly profiteers.

In these and many other ways, the Christian manhood of our nation is challenged to display a patriotism that is truly Christian. We must have men whom no consideration of the enemy can reach, "men who live above the fog in public duty and in private think- ing." God give us such men.

EDITORIAL REVIEW

Have you paid your apportionment to the Superannuated Minis- ters' Fund? Brother Roscoe says some have not. Do it now!

Maryland and Virginia churches, your conference program is in this issue. Read Brother Wood's notice.

No relief yet from paper famine

Had you forgotten that we were to help build a new Winona Auditorium? Turn to Brother Carpenter's reminder, read it and then act.

Brother I. D. Bowman reports a good meeting on his evangelistic itineracy at Boon's Chapel, Virginia. Brother Bowman is ever faithfully at it.

The aggressive church at Peru, Indiana, experienced a refreshing during Easter week under the gospel preaching of Brother C. A. Stewart, so writes the pastor, Brother Carpenter.

Brother Lowman, who recently resigned the pastorate of the Fillmore, California, church to take charge of the Pleasant Hill, Ohio, church has arrived on his new field, was royally received and is now in the midst of a revival meeting that is proving very successful.

Our readers will be pleased to learn that Brother George E. Cone has taken charge of the work at Ft. Scott, Kansas. They were delightfully received by the membership of that church and the pleasant beginning augurs good success for this promising field. To this end may the brotherhood pray.

You will be pleased to read another installment of "College News" by President Jacobs. Among other things of interest he mentions the fact that the college girls have been winning honors for Ashland College as well as the boys. They did not win their contests, but they beat Baldwin-Wallace and that they failed to win against Bluffton was due rather to the latter's exceptional strength than to our girls' weakness. We are proud of the literary honors of both our college boys and college girls this year. Both have brought honor to Ashland College.

The oldest churches are not always the wisest. This has been demonstrated in Indiana. The Muncie mission invited Brother H. H. Wolford, vice-president of the National Sunday School Association, to conduct a Sunday school institute and they are now wondering why no other church has heretofore taken advantage of such an opportunity. Brother Paul says Brother Wolford is an expert and that their school was greatly benefited. Not only the schools of Indiana, but of every district, have the opportunity of an institute conducted by a Sunday school expert. Has your church had one? or does it not need any such help?

The following "night letter" received from the Dayton church speaks for itself of a success that will be enjoyed by all who read of it.

Dayton, Ohio, May 16-17, 1920.

The Brethren Evangelist, Ashland, Ohio.

The First Brethren church of Dayton, Ohio, enjoyed a wonderful day on their thirty-eighth anniversary. Ex-Governor Brumbaugh of Pennsylvania delivered two wonderful messages and we not only raised the remaining twelve thousand dollars debt on our church, but went over the top. Praise the Lord.   E. M. COBB.

Brother Watson writes an appreciation in this issue of our late Brother I. B. Trout. We wish to add our word of appreciation also. While we have not know him intimately, yet we have come in touch with him on a number of occasions, and was always impressed with his generous spirit and his breadth of vision. We received a copy of the Berlin, Pennsylvania, paper which recorded his death, and we were convinced that he had made a most unusual and lasting impression on the life of that community during his short pastorate there. He was a man of many talents and remarkably efficient in them all. The brotherhood mourns with Sister Trout, for her loss is our loss, though his gain.

GENERAL ARTICLES

The Heroes of War a Challenge to Heroes of Peace.   By H. E. Eppley

Since the cessation of hostilities in Europe the question has often been raised, "What are the results of the war?" It's true heroes may be noted as one. There have been many heroes in each of the fighting armies. A great many of them have been cited and given rewards of honor for their bravery by the warring nations. There are many others who are true heroes in just as real a sense. A young man in Illinois desired to render his country a special service. He went to an auto mechanical school and took a course in that line of work at his personal expense. He then enlisted in this line of service and was sent to a leading university to further prepare for overseas duty. There were five hundred students in the class in which he studied. When the final test had been taken and the grades ascertained his was the highest. Orders were issued to prepare for movement and he had a vision of carrying supplies to the men at the front. However, the commanding officer ordered him to report at headquarters where he was informed he would be retained at the university as an instructor. He remained while his class mates moved on. Was he not a hero? Did it not require the spirit of patriotism and heroism to remain at the school and perform well his assigned duties?

What is a hero? What must a man do to be rated a hero? For the purpose of this article and not as a basis for the awarding of distinguished service medals perhaps we might define a true hero in the war to be, a person who believed in his country; who believed in the cause for which his country was fighting; who accepted whatever responsibility his government imposed; and who used every power at his command, mental and physical, to assist in bringing to pass the desired results. Any person, male or female, meeting this test, in my judgment, should be rated a true hero. Real principles and a genuine spirit are here required,

not mere deeds of bravery much as they should be honored, and on this basis "The Heroes of War" are "A Challenge to Heroes of Peace."

The greatest issues of peace were and are championed by "The Prince of Peace." "Love your enemies, bless them that curse you, do good to them that hate you, and pray for them which despitefully use you, and persecute you." "Take heed that ye do not your alms before men, to be seen of them."

"Heroes of Peace" are challenged by "The Heroes of War" to believe in their country. I am assuming "Heroes of Peace" to be Christians. The true country of all Christians is heaven. The earth is their temporal abode. Peter writes: "To an inheritance incorruptible, and undefiled, and that fadeth not away, reserved IN HEAVEN for you." Paul writes: "For our citizenship (or commonwealth) IS IN HEAVEN; whence also we wait for a Savior, the Lord Jesus Christ." (Revised) "Heroes of Peace" are challenged to believe in their abiding country which is HEAVEN.

They are challenged to believe in the cause for which their country is fighting, namely, the carrying of the gospel of good tidings of salvation to all the world. John the apostle writes: "For God so loved the world, that he gave his only begotten Son, that whosoever believeth in him should not perish, but have everlasting life." When this Son was born, an angel announced to the shepherds, "I bring you good tidings of great joy, which shall be to ALL PEOPLE." And this Son during his earth-ministry said: "I am not come to call the righteous, but sinners to repentance." Have the "Heroes of Peace" accepted the challenge to an unshakable faith in the great cause for which their abiding country is fighting?

They are challenged to accept whatever responsibility their government, the government of heaven, may impose.

The Rulers of this government are the Father and the Son. The Son said: "I can of mine own self do nothing: as I hear, I judge: and my judgment is just; because I seek not mine own will, but the will of the Father which hath sent me." In the garden he prayed: "Not my will, but thine, be done." This shows his willingness to co-operate with the Father. Our responsibility to these Rulers is well expressed by Paul in 1 Corinthians 6:19, 20 (revised): "Know ye not that your body is a temple of the Holy Spirit which is in you; which ye HAVE FROM GOD? and ye ARE NOT YOUR OWN; FOR YE WERE BOUGHT WITH A PRICE: glorify God therefore in your body." Soldiers enlisted in the armies of God are not their own. They are to obey HIS orders, which are to carry the gospel to the uttermost parts of the earth.

Is our Great Commander allowed to exercise complete lordship over our lives?

"Heroes of Peace" are challenged to use every power at their command to assist in winning the victory. As soldiers of the cross we must FIGHT TO WIN. The command from the Commanding Officer is "Go ye therefore and teach all nations." Are the "Heroes of Peace" using their every power to spread the gospel so that with Paul they may say, "I have fought the good fight" and be worthy of the decoration of heaven which is "the crown of righteousness?"

Thus "The True Heroes of War" have issued a challenge to "The Heroes of Peace." Have they accepted the challenge? Do you, reader, accept anew this challenge?

Eaton, Indiana.

A Memorial Address.   By E. M. Riddle

Decoration Day, or as is now termed, Memorial Day, was set apart in the United States for the purpose of commemorating by appropriate exercises the services of fallen soldiers and sailors. In more recent years it has seemed fitting that this commemoration be more than a memorial for dead heroes, that it also be for the living who served in defense of a common cause. The practice originated in the Southern states, and for a number of years was observed by individual parties in northern states. The wide-spread custom owes its origin to an official order made by General Logan in 1868, then Commander of the Grand Army of the Republic. This order contained the following: "The 30th of May, 1868, is designated for the purpose of strewing flowers or otherwise decorating graves of comrades who died in defense of their country during the late rebellion. No definite program has been prescribed, but posts and comrades will in their own way arrange such fitting services and testimonials of respect as circumstances will permit." Such observances are among the beautiful public events of our country and have taken deep hold upon the people.

The incidents and memories of history are next to sacred to the patriotic citizens of today, yet the more recent events of war are more pronounced in their influence upon the average American life. Time and space will not permit the calling of America's roll of honored men, yea, leaders who possessed overmastering virtues that make real manhood. Were we to enumerate America's master men, it would carry us back to the Father of our country in whom was incarnated the American Revolution and republic. Indeed every generation even to the present has had its great men, and they all make a wonderful line, who have given to the world monuments which have not been too much appreciated.

Therefore, we pause for one day in our busy American life to commemorate the personal heroism of those who survive as well as those who fell. We revere the men of the Civil war who fell and sympathetically should be respect the few yet living, since these men fought through all the squalor and wretchedness of war without any clear vision of their country's future. To those heroes of our's we owe debts which can never be paid except in respect, admiration and loving remembrance. We owe to them and to the heroes, both men and women of the recent world war, the demonstration that out of the hideous losses and horrors of war, as out of pestilence, famines, shipwrecks and conflagrations, noble souls can pluck glorious fruits of self-sacrifice and moral sublimity. We reverence the soldier and sailor because in their best we find our better selves and discern in what they did what we tried to do on a less heroic scale.

It is worthy of note that the three great wars in which the United States of America has engaged have been wars of freedom. The Revolutionary war was for the liberty of the colonies. The Civil war was waged for the freedom of manhood and for the principle of the indissolubility of the Union. The war beginning 1914 was fought for the right of small nations to self-government and for the right of every country to the free use of the high seas. Our sons and daughters of America fought for the things which we have

always carried nearest to our hearts,—for democracy, for the right of those who submit to authority to have a voice in their own government, for the rights and liberties of small nations, for a universal dominion of right by such a concert of free peoples as shall bring peace and safety to all nations and make the world at last itself free.

The physical and executive efficiency of our men who were trained in such short duration of time has created wonder in our minds. The mettle and quality of the officers and men we sent over and the spirit of the nation behind them was instrumental in pushing the world conflict irresistibly forward to the final triumph. We were the pupils of other nations for nearly three years, after which we acted with promptness and co-operation giving us now a great pride that we were able to serve the world with unparalleled energy and quick accomplishment. Therefore I am moved to say that the man-at-arms is worthy of our deepest commendation, but there have been others, men and women from every vocation of life, from the administration of affairs at our country's capital to the most menial task performed by men and women of this country. On the part of farmers, miners, builders, railroads, factories, and innumerable others a fine sense of devotion, patriotism and unselfishness was exercised to make our equipment sure of triumph. Millions of gallant eager youths learned how to die fearlessly and gloriously. Millions at home learned how to sacrifice, not only some of the better things of life but the lesser as well. Those who served at home or abroad did it all to teach vandal nations that never more will humanity permit the exploitation of people for militaristic purposes.

We believe the Christian world has laid consecrated hands upon its part of the great task of reconstruction, and we believe it fully realizes the greatness of this movement in the world's history. We fairly hold our breath in high expectancy because of the almost limitless possibilities of good that may be achieved in our day. What kind of peace will the world enjoy? No peace can be a permanent peace unless it be a righteous peace. This is plain from the prophet Isaiah, who wrote, saying, "The work of righteousness shall be peace, and the effect of righteousness, quietness and assurance forever." Christ Jesus our Lord can only create this desire for righteousness. Regardless of language, or color, if an individual yields his life to Jesus of Nazareth, the love of right burns within. In the words of the illustrious Lincoln, "With malice toward none; with charity for all; with firmness in the right, as God gives us to see the right let us strive on to finish the work we are in; to bind up the nation's wounds; to care for him who has borne the heat of the battle, for his widow, and his orphan and to honor all who shall strive for and cherish a just and lasting peace among ourselves and with all nations.

Louisville, Ohio.

Almost every great and useful life was begun by seizing the little and seemingly insignificant opportunities; that is God's true service test to greatness.

The Wells of Salvation. By W. M. Lyon

Text: "Therefore with joy shall ye draw water out of the wells of salvation." Isaiah 12:3.

The prophet delivered a message in the language of the text which still reaches into the future for its ultimate fulfillment. It carries us onward to that time when the Holy One of Israel will have established his reign on the earth. Every time we pray, "Thy Kingdom come," the eye of faith beholds the time of the future fulfillment of Romans eleven, twenty-six. But of that time we shall not speak more at present. It is enough for us to know that God will fulfill his word, "for the gifts and calling of God are without repentance" (Rom. 11:29).

But let us consider some of the things that are suggested by the text with reference to the present. The life of every true believer knows more or less of the meaning of these

Wells of Salvation

Notice in the first place that the text refers to an actual experience. Water is essential to life. In the book of Revelation repeated reference is made to the water of life. Let us turn also to John four, fourteen and listen to the words of the Great Teacher himself as he talks to the woman at the well. Let me just here and now put this personal question to every one who claims to be a child of God. Do you have the experience represented here by the symbol that Jesus used in this sermon by the well side? We talk about the whole Gospel, and surely we can not afford to say less, but let me say that whoever knows by an **actual, personal experience the real meaning** of this inner well of water springing up, will not, and can not be satisfied with anything less than the whole truth! If all the members of the Brethren church really knew the real meaning of this experience, what a wonderful change there would be!

Brethren, we need more of these wells! Yes, we surely do. What if our membership of twenty-five thousand represented that many true gospel wells scattered over the United States, how long do you think it would be until these same channels of living water would bring life to tens of thousands of famishing souls who have never yet tasted of the good word of God? It would settle the question of missions both with regard to funds and laborers, at home and abroad. Yes, and were we as a people once to find our God-appointed place according to his word, we would not be content with **wells**, but we would get so very deep into the great and wonderful things that make up God's plan of human redemption, that we would know something of the meaning of those

Rivers of Living Water

to which Jesus refers in John seven, thirty-eight.

Beloved, shall we not occupy our God-appointed places, and become real channels of blessing? Shall we not pay the price? Do you inquire what that is? There is but one answer:

Unconditional surrender to the will of God, and having once done this, then humbly accept and receive the Holy Spirit!

Dear fellow minister, let us be sure that we measure up to God's standard, and put "first things first." Too many of our people seem to be trusting in the literal observance of the ordinances for salvation, thus having the form of godliness but denying the power. The living water from the word must first flow into and through our lives by the power of the Holy Spirit. Unless this is true, keeping the ordinances, will bring condemnation rather than blessing.

But our text speaks of wells. You notice then that there must be more than one. We have spoken of the well of personal experience. In the next place I wish to speak of

The Well of Prayer

Would to God that more of our people knew more of this wonderful secret. We will make no real advancement as a people until we advance on our knees. We need more knee work. This well of prayer is too often filled with those things which hinder the flow of the water of life. The psalmist said a good while ago that if he regarded iniquity in the heart, that the Lord would not hear him. O, how many wells are choked up today with the rubbish of this world. We can not expect God to answer our prayers if we are covered with the spots of this old world of sin. If we belong to the Lord Jesus Christ, we have cut loose from the world. In fact we have no promise whatever that our prayers will be answered unless we have really separated ourselves from the world.

Beloved, we should see to it that we get the rubbish of worldliness out of these wells.

You remember that Isaac unstopped the wells that Abraham had dug that had been filled up by the Philistines. Here is a great work for us to do. Not only the rubbish of worldliness, but there are other sins, and many of them in these days of awful testing, which have filled up these wells of prayer by the thousands and tens of thousands. Let us imitate the example of Isaac, and see to it that these wells are re-opened.

You ask how this may be done? Listen! Many wells would flow with living water again if only the long hook of repentance were vigorously applied in lifting the rubbish out of the well. What revival fires would spring up all over our land if men and women would only get honest before God and fall on their faces before him in deep repentance. Yes, men and women who profess godliness, but have denied the power, because they have refused to forsake sin. "Be not deceived, God is not mocked." In the next place I would speak of the

Well of the Word

Brethren, our claim is a good one, our slogan, "The Whole Gospel for the Whole World," that is grand, indeed, but many times I feel quite ashamed when I see how far we come this side of its full meaning. It produces a very damaging impression to see a dwarf trying to wear the uniform of a giant! But, let us not fail to apply the remedy. Thank God, we need not be discouraged. God's Word can not fail. It will stand when heaven and earth shall pass away. But it will be of no avail to us if we have not first hidden it in our hearts. We are commanded to be "doers of the Word," but only those who have first "tasted of the good Word of God and the powers of the world to come," can know anything of the real meaning of obedience. And there is no life, no living water, no real well of water springing up, until one has been born again. Yes, we need the baptism of the Holy Spirit before we can know anything worth while in the life of the Christian.

In closing, let me remind you that our text says that we shall obtain this water with joy. This is according to the teaching of the blessed Lord. He prayed that we might have the same joy that he had. Do we have that experience today? If not, we can not lead others to the Christ. If in our hearts we really have that same joy others will find it out. It will manifest itself. If we have really received the Lord Jesus Christ into our hearts, we will without doubt share this joy. In his presence there is fulness of joy. The apostle knew something of its meaning when he spoke of the joy that was "unspeakable and full of glory."

Beloved, let us not be content to live in any other way. In fact, there is no real life without Jesus Christ and with him we possess not only this fulness of joy but all other blessings that make life worth while.

We have the sum total in Psalm sixteen eleven: "Thou wilt show me the path of life: in thy presence is fulness of joy; at thy right hand there are pleasures for evermore."

Washington, D. C.

NEWS FROM THE FIELD

ATTENTION PASTORS

In the rush of present day events in the activities of the Brethren churches not a few of them from all parts of the brotherhood have overlooked or failed to send their offerings for the Superannuated fund. Let all those who have not done so get busy at once on this very important matter as the treasury is badly in need of the funds. Many of our churches have responded splendidly this year in this work and I am sure all of them want to have their part in such a worthy cause. We hope to have an offering from every live church in the brotherhood. Please do not delay.

Yours Sincerely,
H. E. ROSCOE,
Secretary Board of Benevolences.

THE WINONA AUDITORIUM

The new auditorium at Winona Lake is under construction and funds are needed. The new organization of Winona is such that they cannot go into debt, and therefore they have no credit. The material and labor for the new auditorium must be paid for as the work progresses. Hence Winona is asking the Brethren to pay one fourth of her pledge of $2500 at once and the balance in the next few months.

This means that every church in the brotherhood ought to raise her apportionment and send at once to Herman E. Roscoe, Treasurer, Goshen, Indiana. Please do it now.

The Brethren church is under obligations to Winona, having been greatly favored through many years. Accommodations for our conference are furnished at Winona at a very nominal expense. Then our church can enjoy the advantages of the greatest Bible Conference in the world by coming a few days before our church conference.

Will every pastor call on his church or churches at once to care for this appeal. Please do it now.
G. C. CARPENTER,
Member of Auditorium Committee.

COLLEGE NEWS

Three weeks ago I was at Pittsburgh over Sunday and preached for Brother Harley in the morning and spoke to a college rally in the evening. The Pittsburgh church maintains a good interest and everything seem to be in excellent order. The evening service was very inspirational and helpful. College banners, college songs, and college spirit were in evidence. I have very grateful memories of my good hosts.

Last Sunday I was at Louisville, Ohio, preaching for Brother Riddle in the morning and then going to North Georgetown for the evening service. At both places there was a good interest and a good spirit. The Louisville church is one of the strongest and promising in Ohio, it seems to me. At North Georgetown the attendance was good but the membership is not so large. But the building is large and in good repair and it certainly would be too bad to let this work fail. Brother Riddle is doing a good piece of work at both places.

The matter of the local campaign here is slowly shaping up but nothing definite can be announced yet. The campaign among the Alumni is progressing nicely. To date we have received $1,200. Invitations to commencement ought to reach those to whom they are addressed soon.

Since last writing, Ashland met Baldwin-Wallace in a Girls' Literary Contest, in which Ashland won. For Ashland: Essay, Alma Shultz; Short story, Ruth Lichty; Reading, Elizabeth Lentz. We recently lost a contest to Bluffton College.

Dr. Miller left Monday for a week's work in Bible instruction with the Johnstown, Pa., congregation.

The dominating spirit which pervaded the historic Dayton convention in the early eighties, of which my father was a member and who is still living, was an unwillingness to be bound by man-made creeds or the rulings of the Annual Meeting. The ruling of Annual Meeting might have been advisory with them but never mandatory. This was the first factor, if I may rely on what my father has so often repeated to me.

A second feature was the declaration of their unfaltering faith in the Bible as a sufficient rule of action; in essentials unity, in non-essential, liberty, and in all things charity. Each man was free, above and apart from all ecclesiastic authority, to go to the open Book and appropriate its message to his heart.

And the fact that I can thus go and get the spiritual nourishment that my own heart needs, together with the undying belief that thus I am appropriating the whole gospel, has been an unfailing source of joy to me.

These very features ought to be pressed now. That we as a church believe in the essential ordinances, that we have a sound historic basis which we respect, that we cling to the Christianity of Jesus, and that we have no cumbersome hierarchy, intolerant as all hierarchies in time become, ought to make an appeal. There never was a time when the world so needed the simple Christianity of Jesus as today nor was there ever a time when we ought so to insist on, not social salvation alone, but on the individual new birth, as today. If the whole world could be permeated with what I regard as the true Brethren spirit, each heart would be reborn, and "the world through him might be saved."
EDWIN E. JACOBS.

ALUMNI LUNCHEON

One of the delightful functions of Commencement Week is the Junior-Senior Luncheon. At that time, Wednesday at noon, the graduating class will be formally received into the Alumni Association. An entertaining program is being prepared. A delicious meal will be served by the church ladies, the Juniors having secured their services. All members of the alumni and former students may share in this happy event. Reservation, however, should be made in advance. Those

interested may address Miss Elizabeth Lentz, care of Ashland College or the writer.
J. A. GARBER.

FROM CALIFORNIA TO OHIO

Some months ago we had asked to be relieved from the Fillmore work, and on Easter Sunday, April 4th we closed our work with the Fillmore Brethren, after having served for two years as their pastor. In that time we had opened the work under the direction of the Southern California mission board, and from a beginning of two members in the town when we landed there we now have 77 baptized and received into the church. A more loyal bunch of Brethren folks, you will not find anywhere. They are Brethren to the last one, believe in the second personal coming of the Lord and that the Holy Scriptures are the infallible, final and only word of God to man and written by inspired men. And they do not like the new movement, the Inter-church, and in a note by this church they decided unanimously to stay out, believing that it is a post millennial, social gospel plan to get the churches together and establish community centers with all churches united together. Some of that crowd asked the Fillmore Brethren if we would sell our fine new church, worth some $20,000.00, located in the center of town, for that purpose and unite with the other churches; and this preacher said, No.

We had a great final day at Fillmore on Friday night, before leaving on Monday. They called us to one of the member's home, Brother L. F. Robinson and there was a house packed full of our membership and friends and in a social hour showed us a royal good time and at the close of the evening presented us with a purse containing more than $50.00, every dollar of it given out of a heart of love. And then on Sunday, Easter morning our day's work began. And such a day Fillmore Brethren will not soon forget, neither will the preacher. There were several visiting Brethren there from First church of Los Angeles. When the Sunday school report was given it showed the largest Sunday school in our history, 146 present. Then at the preaching service that followed, we asked for the Foreign Missionary offering and without taking any pledges they gave an even $50.00 in cash. Glory. Then came the noon hour and dinner at the church with almost 100 for dinner. Then we had been praying and working to have a soul winning day for that day, so in the evening I addressed the largest crowd since going to Fillmore. When we gave the invitation, six came forward. Five of them were baptized and received into the church that night and the other one later. Then we must say good-bye and that proved the hardest task I ever have been called on to do. There was much weeping and last good-byes, but not for always, for we expect to meet in the clouds some of these days if not sooner. On Monday morning, April 5, we boarded the train for a 3,000 mile trip to Ohio, arriving Saturday, April 10th and on

April 11th met our new folks at Pleasant Hill, Ohio. Here they had planned a fine reception for us and met us at the door with a warm welcome and we began with a Sunday school of 145 present. Then a well-filled house to hear us preach. And again it was a great dinner with cherry pie and home made cakes and all kind of things good. I tell you I believe that Brethren women everywhere know how to cook good dinners. They proved true at Pleasant Hill.

We are now located in Pleasant Hill and at present in a revival. Eleven have already taken a stand for Christ and we trust more will follow before the meetings close. Brethren churches, pray for us, and that the Brethren church may stand true until Jesus comes.

Your servant,
S. LOWMAN.

MARYLAND AND VIRGINIA DISTRICT CONFERENCE

The Maryland and Virginia district conference convenes in the First Brethren church of Roanoke, Virginia, June 8, 9 and 10. We are expecting a large attendance and the best conference ever held in the district. The program will soon appear, and the congregation at Roanoke extends a hearty welcome to all who can attend and assist in making it a real VICTORY conference. Please drop a card to the writer advising of your intention to come and how many may come from your congregation. Our motto is "Increase and Extension." Credentials are in the hands of each congregation; provide your delegates with the same, properly signed.

Come!
L. G. WOOD, Pastor

PROGRAM:

Thirty-third Annual Conference of Brethren Churches of the Maryland-Virginia District to be held at the Brethren Church of Roanoke, Virginia, June 8, 9 and 10, 1920

Conference Motto: "Increase and Extension."
Conference Slogan: "Enlistment and Victory."

Tuesday Afternoon

2:00 Devotions W. H. Miller
2:20 Appointment of Committees on Credentials and Resolutions
2:30 Address of Welcome L. G. Wood
3:00 Response by Delegates.
3:20 Business Session.
    Election of Conference Officers.
    Election of Members of Examining Board to succeed E. B. Shaver.
    Election of Member of Board of Property to succeed J. A. Englar.
4:00 Announcements and Adjournment.

Tuesday Evening

6:30 C. E. Rally Led by H. H. Rowsey
    Statistician's Report of C. E. Work.
7:30 Devotions Quinter Lyon
    Special Music.
8:00 Sermon J. M. Tombaugh
9:00 Announcements.

Wednesday Morning

9:30 Devotions J. W. Leedy
10:00 Victory Drive for Four Year Program
    L. G. Wood
10:30 Discussion of Interchurch World Movement Dr. J. Allen Miller

11:15 Presentation of Sunday School Work
    A. B. Cover, Superintendent
12:00 Adjournment.

Wednesday Afternoon

2:00 Devotions Mrs. Margaret Cook
2:20 Woman's Missionary Society, Led by
    Mrs. A. B. Cover, Dist. Pres.
Mission Board Meeting to be Arranged for.

Wednesday Evening

7:30 Devotions J. E. Patterson
    Special Music.
8:00 Statistical Report and Election of District Departmental Officers.
8:30 Address by Ashland College Representative Dr. J. A. Miller
    Announcements and Adjournment.

Thursday Morning

9:00 Devotions W. M. Lyon
9:20 Reading of Minutes.
9:30 Business Session.
    Statistician's General Report.
    A. B. Cover
    Ministerial Aid Report G. A. Ropp
    Mission Board Report and Election of Officers.
    Conference Invitations and Election of Executive Committee.
10:00 Discussion "Missions" Led by
    H. Harry Haun
11:00 Discussion "Evangelism" by
    J. S. Bowman and H. W. Nowag
    Adjournment.

J. M. TOMBAUGH, C. R. KOONTZ
C. H. ROHRER L. G. WOOD
T. G. LOCKE,
    Executive Committee.

PERU, INDIANA

Brother C. A. Stewart, pastor of the Loree and Corinth churches, was our preacher for the Easter week services and the whole church was pleased with his straightforward and forceful messages. Old-fashioned winter was present for Easter Sunday but the attendance was good and the services were most helpful. A splendid musical program yas given by the children of the Sunday school. Brother Stewart is a good preacher and a successful pastor. Arrangements have been made by which Miss Aboud, a new but successful evangelist in the Brethren church, will come to Peru for a revival campaign beginning October 25. We heard Sister Aboud one evening while in Dayton recently and she is an able speaker and knows the Word of God.

Much sickness among the membership here during the past winter and even now has been hindered the work but all the organizations in the church are active and there is progress.

Our spring "Joash Day" for the church building fund was a success and brought the total in our building fund to the neat sum of $6500.

G. C. CARPENTER.

BOON'S CHAPEL, VIRGINIA

We closed our meeting here the 18th of April with a crowded house. There is a very interesting story connected with this work. It is the outgrowth of the Roanoke church, as I understand it. This is a small union church building but only the Brethren and the Church of the Brethren preach here. Twenty some

years ago Brother D. C. Moomaw did the first preaching here. Soon after that my brother, J. S. Bowman, held a wonderful revival here. He baptized the majority of the old and young people here. While the field has been somewhat neglected our people have had the leading influence in this country ever since.

Following this great revival my brother taught school eight winters here and today he has the universal good will of the people. The influence of several revivals that he held and the eight years teaching has revolutionized the community and has made it one of a high moral standard.

Boon's Chapel is in the Blue Ridge mountains, about 12 miles from Roanoke on the "Pumpkin Vine railroad," one of the twistiest roads in the United States.

These mountain people did well financially for their training in giving, they met about half of the expenses, the balance was paid by the Evangelistic League.

I did more walking here than I have done for many years. Everybody wanted me to come to see them and spend a night with them. I am pretty fat and to walk for two and three miles up the Blue Ridge mountains after preaching would make me puff like a steam engine, but I enjoyed it.

They are indeed a hospitable and conscientious people. I am only sorry I could not have stayed another week.

Brother Enoch Bowman of the Church of the Brethren had a great meeting here last fall, but we baptized 16 of his converts, twice as many as they received. This shows the influence of our people here.

Brother William Beam preaches here once a month and he is liked by this people. He has been sick part of the time and has been scarcely able to fill the pulpit and then he has a very sick daughter in the Richmond, Virginia, Hospital, therefore he could not be with me at all. My brother was with me about a week. We had a real good meeting and the interest became intense at the last but we had to close to begin a meeting the 20th at Garden City, about three miles from Roanoke. We gave them a short two weeks' meeting and had nine confessions. Eight will join our church. Two came out the last night and others were deeply convicted. These with the 16 they received last fall will greatly strengthen this work.

After resting one day I will begin at a new place for our people, in a new church house where I will remain till the 16th day of May.

ISAAC D. BOWMAN.

FORT SCOTT, KANSAS

A few weeks ago we were interested and enthused over the entire brotherhood, by the news which Brother G. T. Ronk had for us regarding the Home Mission work. Among the various places he mentioned was Ft. Scott with its change of location and new advantages. We feel that he has taken a very correct estimate of the situation at Ft. Scott. And we pray that the work may now go forward to the betterment of the people of Ft. Scott and to the glory of God and the upbuilding of his Kingdom here upon earth.

Shortly after his return from the missionary trip, Brother Ronk, as the Mission Board's representative in this field, extended to us a call to take up the work here. After seeing Brother Ronk and personally talking over the situation here, Mrs Cone and I decided to accept the call.

Immediate preparations were made to take up the work here and now we have been here nearly two weeks. So far as we can tell from these days thus far spent here, we believe Ft. Scott will be a place which will soon become, for us, a home. In other words, we think we will readily adapt ourselves to the situation here.

On Thursday, evening of April 29th, we were invited to go to the church with Brother and Sister Otto and when the proper time came we found that a reception for the new pastor and his family had been planned. A short program was rendered after which we were all served with ice cream and cake. We were delighted to be thus received by the church.

There were about 70 present at the reception thus giving us a fair opportunity to meet many of the members of the congregation here.

We hope and pray that God will bless us in our work here together and that the brotherhood at large may be helped by our work.

Brethren, pray for us that we may do the will of him who said, "And all things whatsoever ye shall ask in prayer, believing, ye shall receive" (Matthew 21:22).

GEO E. CONE.

MUNCIE, INDIANA

Brother H. H. Wolford came to our place Monday, May 10, and conducted a Sunday school institute for us, Monday evening, Tuesday forenoon, afternoon and evening, according to the provisions of the National Sunday School Association.

Brother Wolford tells us that Muncie is the first school in the state to call for an institute. That is where our Indiana schools are overlooking a rare opportunity. The Board made no mistake in their choice of a man to conduct institutes in Indiana, for he is both capable and efficient.

Ours is a fine little school, as large possibly as we could well care for in our limited space. We have attained a Front Line standard since 1915, which is encouraging to the superintendent(thanks to my willing workers), but feeling a weakness we called for the institute, which we believe both timely and profitable. To some extent at least we have discovered our weakness and how to overcome it.

Some of our Brethren from Oakville and Maple Grove attended some of the sessions, while Brother Eppley lent his presence and encouragement from first to last. We appreciate these visits of our neighboring Brethren very much. Tonight Brother Wolford will speak at Maple Grove on the theme of "Organization."

The inspiration and enthusiasm created was so evident that Brother Eppley suggested that it would be profitable for the National Sunday School Association to secure some capable person to use their entire time conducting institutes in our church schools, also that our church prepare a uniform system of records for Brethren schools by which we may simplify, yet accurately keep our records, thus supplying a long felt need in many of our schools, and also making it easier for our National Board to get statistics promptly. We heartily endorse both suggestions.

ORA C. PAUL, Superintendent.

WANTED: A Brethren family for the Dormitory of Ashland College; a family which can furnish a matron for the Dormitory and a janitor for the College building.

The College offers free rent, with heat and light and board, besides a substantial salary.

For full information write Ashland College, Ashland, Ohio.

MARTIN SHIVELY, Bursar.

Communion Notices

The spring communion service will be held at the Sydney, Indiana, church on Monday evening, May 24th. Neighboring brethren are invited and members are urged to be present.
L. A. MYERS, Pastor.

The College Corner church, Indiana, will hold their spring communion service on Saturday evening, May 29th. Neighboring Brethren are invited to this service.
L. A. MYERS, Pastor.

First Church, Ashland, Ohio, will observe holy communion on Sunday evening, May 30th. In the afternoon President Jacobs will deliver the baccalaureate sermon. Near-by brethren may find it possible to take advantage of both services, particularly those of Fair Haven, Homerville, Zion Hill, Mansfield, Ankenytown. All are cordially invited.
J. A. GARBER, Minister.

The Brethren church at Gretna, Ohio will hold its semi-annual love feast and communion service on Saturday evening, May twenty-ninth, at eight o'clock. All of like faith are invited to attend.
R. R. TEETER, Pastor.

IN THE SHADOW

BARGER—This notice rightly belongs in two columns: death and marriages. Mrs. Mary C. Barger was united in marriage to John W. Morris in the pastor's study, March 3, 1920. Both were members of the Brethren Church at Spokane for about a year. After a brief and most happy married life one day less than a month, Sister Morris passed on to be with the Lord after a very brief but serious illness, in spite of the continued prayers of the saints at this place. She leaves a husband, and two brothers and two boys whom she had taken to raise, having been denied children of her own. These together with a host of Brethren and friends who learned to love her, mourned her loss. She was a most faithful helper in the Lord's work and a joy to her pastor's heart in the work. Ever seeking opportunities of service instead of shirking, we feel sure that the Lord will say to her, "Well done."
R. PAUL MILLER.

SMITH—Mrs. Elizabeth Smith, wife of Brother S. G. Smith, who preceded his wife to the other world about twenty years ago, died at the home of her son, Brother Jacob Smith, near Vinco, April 9th, 1920, aged 85 years and seven months. She is survived by two sons and three daughters. Grandma Smith, as she was lovingly called by a very wide circle of friends and neighbors, was for many years an active member of the Vinco Brethren church. Her husband while he lived was a deacon in the same church; her son with whom she made her home is now a deacon in the church; her other son Elder E. H. Smith is and has been for many years a minister in the same denomination and is known far and wide for his good work in the church. Her grandson, Brother Garvin Smith, was until recently the pastor of the Conemaugh Brethren church and is now in the Boston University preparing himself for some responsible position in the church. She has another grandson by marriage, Brother Forest Byers, who is the present pastor of the Vinco and the Pike churches. It is not too much to say that Sister Smith in her quiet unassuming way, her optimistic view and words of cheer helped these men in a large way to persevere when thick clouds lowered and storms threatened. Her spirituality was of the highest type, her genial disposition and sunny smile made and held friends for her wherever known. She was faithful in her attendance on the means of grace and was a woman of no ordinary type and will be greatly missed by her friends and neighbors. She died in the triumphs of a living faith and awaits the resurrection of the just. Funeral services by the writer in the Wesley Chapel assisted by Brother George Jones, pastor of the Conemaugh church and by Brother Byers of the Vinco church.
J. L. BOWMAN.

AN APPRECIATION

One of the greatest joys of my ministry has been the acquaintanceship of men who have left their impress upon my life. In a very marked way Brother Trout influenced my life, even though our acquaintanceship was of short duration. I became much interested in him, more especially because he was my successor on the Berlin charge. This brought us close together in many ways and ours was more than mere acquaintanceship, we were friends. During his pastorate we were together many times and I had the opportunity to learn to know him better than most of our ministers did.

Brother Trout was a man gracious in spirit and lovable. He possessed a personality and geniality that drew you to him. A close personal touch brought one to see that he was more than an average man. The pleasure of knowing him was largely due to the many discoveries of qualities far above the average which one was permitted to enjoy.

He was a student of affairs. He possessed a keen insight into the various phases of life which made possible his devoting real service to his fellows. He did no narrow-tread thinking. He was broad minded and never hastily cast aside the convictions of others.

He was a keen student of the Word of God. He possessed strong convictions, yet was not intolerant and bigoted. He was a man of more than average good common sense, sometimes I feel sanctified commonsense, and this was the safety valve of his strong convictions.

As an expositor and preacher of the Word of God, I have heard few his equal. In presenting truth his logic was irresistible. I never heard a man who could handle the Word so that it would pierce the conscience or flay sin as he did. He preached the Word but mightily enforced it with a wealth of human experience. I find myself wishing that his sermon material and sermons be published. If nothing more than the outlines, it would be a creditable and substantial contribution to our literature. It would be of real worth to our ministry.

It was my sad duty to help lay our dear brother to rest. He was buried not far from the grave of Bishop Holsinger at Berlin. A beautiful spot indeed, and overlooking the range of mountains which he seemed to love. I am sure the sympathy of the entire brotherhood goes to Sister Trout and her family. May his grace sustain them until he comes.
J. FREMONT WATSON.

Brethren Evangelist

| VOLUME XLII | NUMBER 20 | MAY 26, 1920 |

And They Twain Shall Be One Flesh

MARK 10 : 8

The surest way of counteracting the marriage and divorce evils is by proper instruction of youths and maidens. Let fathers wisely counsel their sons and mothers give sympathetic guidance to

their daughters and let every effort be made to impart high and holy ideals of heaven's choicest blessing and earth's most sacred institution - the marriage- and there will be little desire to put asunder what God hath joined together.

Published every Wednesday at Ashland, Ohio. All matter for publication must reach the Editor not later than Friday noon of the preceding week.

George S. Baer, Editor

The
Brethren
Evangelist

When ordering your paper changed give old as well as new address. Subscriptions discontinued at expiration. To avoid missing any numbers renew two weeks in advance.

R. R. Teeter, Business Manager

OFFICIAL ORGAN OF THE BRETHREN CHURCH

Subscription price, $2.00 per year, payable in advance.
Entered at the Post Office at Ashland, Ohio, as second-class matter.
Acceptance for mailing at special rate of postage provided for in section 1103, Act of October 3, 1917, authorized September 9, 1918.
Address all matter for publication to Geo. S. Baer, Editor of the Brethren Evangelist, and all business communications to R. R. Teeter, Business Manager, Brethren Publishing Company, Ashland, Ohio. Make all checks payable to the Brethren Publishing Company.

EDITORIAL

The Divorce Problem Again In Public View

Communities are ever and anon being brought face to face with the consequences of their social ills. At such times it is natural as it is customary to seek temporary remedies for the situation. Recently the divorce evil has been brought seriously to the attention of the people of Cleveland by the men whose duty it is to conduct the multitude of divorce proceedings. The judges have become alarmed at the situation and are seeking some way to check the evil. Surely we will grant that the men who occupy our judiciary positions are not alarmists. They are as a rule quite even tempered men and are not too quickly disturbed over a situation. It would seem therefore when they sound an alarm that we should understand that conditions are really alarming and should give earnest heed. We will also grant that these men as a rule are not superficial in their thinking and when they propose a remedy, that proposal is deserving at least of serious consideration. These things the judiciary of Cleveland have done—they have sounded an alarm and have proposed a remedy.

Recognizing the serious condition of the divorce evil, the common pleas judges of Cuyahoga county, Ohio, in which the city of Cleveland is situated, appointed a domestic relations committee, composed of three of their number, to investigate the situation and make recommendations. In short, they recommended a bureau of justice whose duty it shall be to investigate the facts in connection with each divorce case, seek to conciliate the estranged couples where their differences are not too great, and to apprise the judges hearing divorce cases of any previous applications which the persons involved may have made for divorce; it is also recommended that the present state laws which permit the "service by publication" system be amended. Without a dissenting voice the entire common pleas bench approved the recommendations which the domestic relations committee offered. The Cleveland Bar Association, federated churches and civic and women's organizations commended the divorce plan and promised the heartiest co-operation. The three judges who made the investigation were unanimously chosen as a committee to work out details for carrying out their recommendations, and to prepare a list of names of persons available for appointment as members of the bureau of justice. The leader of the Women's Civic Association thinks that "at least two women of mature years and good common sense should be members of the bureau of justice because divorce concerns the home and is essentially a woman's problem." The president of the Federation of Women's Clubs of that city, says, "I favor anything that can be done to remedy divorce conditions." Many other leaders spoke approvingly of this reform movement. It met with universal approbation.

It is encouraging to note all this stir concerning this serious situation. It points to the awakening of men's consciences to an evil that has wrought more harm than has been realized. There has been more or less widespread indifference toward the divorce evil. In certain sections it has been considered as a convenience and in others as a necessary evil against which objections or opposition is futile. There are also certain sections in which very creditable efforts have been put forth to combat it. And the increasing number of places where serious attention is being given to the problem indicates a growing consciousness of the evil involved. And it is only as the public comes to recognize the seriousness of any social evil that any worth-while efforts of reform can be made effective. Many sporadic and local attempts have been made at divorce reform. While good has come

from them, yet the results have been by no means satisfactory, due largely to the fact that efforts applied were too scattered and local to be effective.

There are reasons why satisfactory results have not been realized from efforts to check the divorce evil. As a rule more attention has been given to divorce than to marriage. Very inadequate guards have been placed about the marriage bond, with the result that many ill-advised marriages have been solemnized only to furnish grist for the divorce court mill, almost before the ink on their marriage certificates were dry. Important as it is to have stricter laws and more effective plans for the regulation and prevention of divorce. it is far more important to guard carefully the marriage relation. So long as this sacred relation can be entered without regard to physical fitness on the part of the contracting parties; so long as young people, total strangers to each other, may meet and suddenly in a fit of fancied love secure a marriage license, with no requirement of time for getting acquainted; so long as ministers or justices of the peace continue to solemnize marriages for couples who are strangers to them and require no further evidence of their fitness to be married than a marriage license, perhaps secured by perjury and issued by some indifferent clerk; so long as these and other equally foolish practices are tolerated and even encouraged, just so long will the divorce evil continue persistently unchecked. There is little wisdom in regulating divorce if we do not still more carefully and conscientiously seek to prevent the desecration of the marriage altar.

And this work of prevention must not be left entirely to the state. The church must bear a great responsibility in this matter, a thing which evangelical churches have sadly neglected. We cannot hope that churches as organizations shall speak with authority to members concerning marriage and divorce, but we can hope to cause the teachings of the Word of God concerning marriage and divorce to stand out more vividly in the minds of the people and to be more of a determining factor in such matters. We can hope, and have a right to expect that ministers shall guard more carefully the marriage altar, throw about it more of the spirit of sacredness and solemnity, and insist that those whom they in God's name unite in this holy bond shall be worthy so far as they can possibly determine.

But none of these suggestions go to the bed-rock of the difficulty. Good as they all are, they do not begin at the right place or time. The problems of marriage and divorce will never come anywhere near a solution until through childhood and youth proper instruction is given by parents, Sunday school teachers and pastors concerning the proper relation of the sexes in society and the high and holy meaning of marriage. Perhaps more than to any other one cause, matrimonial difficulties can be traced to the low ideals and perverted notions concerning the most sacred relations of life. Marriage and the marriage vow are ridiculed, caricatured and made the butt of silly jokes on every hand; in the newspaper, in the movies, in the theatre, in social circles, in the home and on the street. It is next to impossible for the average child and youth to get any sane and serious view of the marriage relation, as his growing years and associations force upon him the necessity of making observations concerning this relationship. Even parents by the silly custom of teasing the children about beau-catching and love-making from the time they leave the mother's lap until they approach manhood and womanhood are continually forcing upon the developing minds the idea that marriage is a joke. What wonder that young people pursue the divinely implanted instinct of mating and companion-seeking with frivolous indifference and questionable jesting! What wonder that men and women in increasing numbers look upon the marriage relation as a mere convenience and the marriage bond as of no more consequence than a business agreement! If there is any serious intention of searching out the cause of and applying a remedy to the marriage and divorce evil the beginning must be made with the ideals and impressions of youth. All other remedies are superficial and temporary.

EDITORIAL REVIEW

We are still hoping for more paper.

Brother Carpenter's clipping in this issue points out the vast importance of the vast multitudes of unreached highlanders in Kentucky and elsewhere in the Appalachian range. We have only touched the fringes of the garment of need in our little mission work.

It has been a long time since we have heard from Brother Thomas Allen. He favors us with a report of his visit to the Limestone, Tennessee, church, of which he was formerly pastor, but which is now being so efficiently shepherded by Sister Pence.

We wish to call attention to an error which occurred last week in connection with President Jacobs' "College News." Dr. Jacobs wrote his college news, and also a brief article requested for the "Brethren Day" number of The Evangelist which is to appear next week. The Brethren Day article was accidentally published along with his college news. We regret this very much and hope our readers will take note of this correction.

Our readers will enjoy the report of the very successful evangelistic campaign conducted by Brethren Coleman and A. T. Ronk in a Methodist church. These brethren make a splendid gospel team, and are willing to give Brethren churches the preference in making up their schedule for the coming year.

We have been accustomed for two years or more of reading "College Endowment" news from the pen of Brother Beachler, but this time it is the Waterloo church news. Brother Beachler began the work of his second pastorate at that place with a revival meeting, in which he was ably assisted by Brother Boardman as song leader. As we previously commented, the Waterloo church did a splendid piece of work during the United Financial Drive. We doubtless can expect this church to maintain their excellent Sunday school record, judging from the inspiration they must have received from the convention they recently entertained.

We wish to call attention to Brother Gearhart's notice of the Kentucky Mission Committee's call for an important worker for Riverside Institute. The Willing Workers' Bible Class of Dayton has set a good example for other classes or organizations to follow. Then again the neat little dowry which the Foreign Mission Board recently received from the estate of the late Sister Elsie Showalter ought to be a suggestion to many of our well-to-do brethren. The Publishing Company, for example, could make most excellent use of a little endowment fund, as doubtless also any of the other boards could.

GENERAL ARTICLES

Attendance at Communion Service. By H. M. Oberholtzer

One of the great unsolved problems in many Brethren churches today is, How to get all the members interested in the communion service. It seems strange that this should be a problem at all with regard to such a sacred and important service. It is gratifying, however, that in nearly every congregation there are some who attend regularly every communion service regardless of bad weather or other hindering circumstances; but there is usually quite a large number in every congregation who, for various reasons, seldom attend. Often those who do attend have just as good reason for staying away as those who are absent, but they have the faith and zeal to overcome their hindrances, which might just as easily be overcome by the others, if they would try. There are really very few hindrances sufficient to prevent anyone from attending communion services, if he really wants to attend. Faith and determination will usually overcome hindrances and inconveniences. Sickness, floods, snow-blocked roads, and a few such hindrances may keep some away, but even then they may have the communion service at their home, if they desire. However, it is much more satisfactory to engage in the service with the congregation, if possible. Let conveyance be provided and arrangements made to bring the feeble and the aged to the service, if they can be brought. Let mothers bring their infants, or, if they are not too young, leave them in the care of those who are not members of the church. Let business and social engagements be postponed. Let everyone make every possible effort to attend the service at the church, and then, let the service be taken to those who cannot come to the church. This, I suggest, should be our ideal.

Usually a communion service that immediately follows an evangelistic campaign is well attended. I have seen such services tested by severe storm and cold and yet the attendance was very gratifying, which proves very thoroughly that hindrances can be overcome and that the one thing needed is religious interest.

The attendance of a congregation at communion services is a very good index of its spiritual condition. If any are absent from this sacred service of the church without good reason there is strong evidence that they are not living on as high spiritual plane as they should. It is true that some may attend who are not up very well spiritually and who do not appreciate the significance of the service, but they are not usually as many as those who carelessly and recklessly absent themselves from the service.

The absence of many is doubtless due to a lack of interest and of proper consecration. Live, interested Christians do not fail in such important matters. The love of Christ constrains them so that they find it impossible to remain away from the Lord's table. They delight in the fellowship, they long for the blessing and they rejoice in their obedience. They do not forget their Christian vows, but cheerfully fulfill them. They are fully surrendered to Christ and seek only to please him. All God's commands and the ordinances of his house are a joy to their souls. But without this loving interest and devotion, people become careless and neglectful. They soon come to think more of their carnal desires and their physical ease and comfort than they do of the ordinances of God's house. Nevertheless they wish to be considered members of the church. They seem to have a superstitious idea that without membership in the church they would be lost, and that membership in the church is a guarantee of eternal salvation, regardless of their life or service. Alas! they will learn some day, to their everlasting sorrow, that it is not enough to say, "Lord, Lord," but that we must also "do his commandments." There is positively no hope for the one who uses the church merely as a fire-escape. Christ expects us to "observe all things, whatsoever he commanded us," and the Scripture says "He that offendeth in one point, is guilty of all." And, we must bear in mind that sins of omission are quite as weighty as sins of commission.

Some perhaps are not wilfully negligent, but they are woefully ignorant. They do not understand the meaning nor appreciate the importance of the communion service. Perhaps they have not read their Bibles as they should, or perhaps they have not been properly instructed. These should be carefully and patiently looked after.

Others seem to realize the sacredness of the service, but feeling a deep sense of their own sin they consider themselves unfit and unworthy to participate in the service. They shudder at the thought of possibly eating and drinking condemnation to their own souls. But let me warn such ones that they cannot escape condemnation by wilfully absenting themselves from the communion service. Disobedience and neglect are sins that will not go unpunished. There is no need that anyone who goes to the Lord's table will eat and drink condemnation to his soul. It is not likely that he will do so accidentally or ignorantly. If one goes in faith and in earnest, God will surely accept his service, although he may not fully understand. If this were not true it would be very dangerous for young disciples, whose minds have not yet matured, and who comprehend but little of God's Word, to take any part.

Some do not attend the communion service because they do not wish to fellowship with some whose conduct they question, or whom they consider unworthy of a place at the Lord's table. Paul says, "Let each man examine himself," not others. The guilt of Judas did not in any manner affect the worship of John or either of the other disciples at the supper in Jerusalem when the ordinances were instituted. How then can anyone's sinfulness affect our worship today. Each one must answer for his own sin before God. We gain nothing by staying away from the service because someone else seems unfit to commune. We rather lose. Such experiences are tests of our faith. We should be strong enough not to be disturbed by any such lack of harmony. David said, "Thou wilt keep him in perfect peace, whose mind is staid on thee." Let us have our minds on Christ more than on one another.

Every member of the church should attend the communion service, if at all possible. There is no exception. If one is not right at heart, he should make haste to get right. Repentance is in order at all times. "Today if ye will hear his voice, harden not your hearts." God is merciful and will forgive, if we sincerely repent of our sins. The communion service affords an opportunity for renewing our vows. Christ instituted the ordinances for the very purpose that we should observe them in the churches, and we have no right to ignore them. To do so is to set at naught the holy purposes of God, which is certainly a great offense. Christ plainly commanded the observance of the ordinances, saying, "If I your Lord and Master, have washed your feet, ye ought also to wash one another's feet." And again, "This do in remembrance of me." What he commands it is our duty to obey. Remember that he said, "If a man love me, he will keep my commandments."

Everyone should attend the communion service because of the wonderful and united testimony it gives. Paul says, "Thus ye do show forth the Lord's death till he come." The communion is a most vivid and striking testimony of the atonement of Jesus, and of the disciple's faith in the same. The entire service is rich and replete in divine truth that is symbolized and is thus kept before the church and the world. These are sacred truths that must be kept in mind and lived out in our lives till Jesus comes again. The blessings of the communion service are abundant and of great value to the soul, the consideration of which our space does not here permit.

I fear that many of our ministers and leaders in the churches have failed to properly explain the value and importance of the sacred ordinances and to lay sufficient emphasis upon attendance at communion services. We cannot be too urgent in this regard. The prevailing neglect of the holy ordinances of God's house is doubtless the cause of much of our weakness in Christian character and the lack of power in the church.

I have sometimes thought that it would be well to revive the old time visiting committee, and have each member of the church visited before the communion service, with a view to securing a full attendance of the membership, if possible. If there were difficulties in the way of anyone attending, the committee might assist very much in removing them. Deacons, deaconesses, or other spiritual leaders might serve on such a committee. This would likely add much to the importance of the communion services. Members should be impressed, and many would likely have a better understanding of the meaning and significance of the services.

I have also thought that perhaps our pastors should give more attention to administering the ordinances to those who may not be able to attend the services at the church. The entire service, in its threefold nature, should be observed, if possible. The offer for such service should be made unhesitatingly, and even urgently, that both the minds of those receiving the service and of the rest of the membership may be impressed with its importance. If this is earnestly and persistently done, I believe that people will soon find their places at the communion services whenever it is possible. Too many pastors are guilty of wilful neglect and laziness in this regard. The inconvenience of holding such services is too often allowed to stand in the way. No service for Christ should be considered irksome.

Perhaps I have said but little that is new to anyone. I have only called to mind conditions that are apparent to all, endeavoring to urge the proper consideration and to awaken interest. The present indications are that many of our churches will fail to reach the second goal of our Four Year Program, unless greater interest is in some way aroused in this regard. The standard set is certainly not too high and it will be a disgrace for any church to fall below it. These holy ordinances, with their deep meaning and wonderful impressiveness as they are observed in the Brethren church ought to be more deeply appreciated. If David could say, "My soul longeth, yea, even fainteth for the courts of Jehovah," how much more ought we to long after those courts today with the larger meaning that the services of God's house has for us.

Fremont, Ohio.

The Task of the Temperance Department of the Sunday School

By Prof. R. R. Haun

Four hundred gallons of whiskey per year is to be allowed to each druggist, is the recent statement given out by the federal commissioner governing the handling of spiritous liquors by drug stores and physicians. That is probably enough to make at least five thousand people drunk, which means that each drug store has the right to handle sufficient liquor to make twelve or fifteen people drunk every day in the year.

Alarming as that sounds, there are other conditions relative to the liquor question that are more dangerous than that. Which only serves to show that even though the Federal Prohibition Amendment has been written into the constitution, prohibition is not assured as yet. Indeed prohibition leaders tell us that the situation is now at its most critical stage. And this is due to several causes.

The liquor men have not given up yet. They are very busy on the job. Hostile legislation has united the liquor organizations as they have never been united before. They have been spending money liberally and profusely. They have employed the most able legal talent. With an ever increasing frenzy, they have boasted of their law violation the nation over. By use of the injunction and other legal technicalities, they, in some places, prevented federal officials from enforcing War Prohibition. They have openly organized the "Association Opposed to National Prohibition" which boasts that its purpose is to nullify forever the

18th Amendment. They have organized one movement after another for the same purpose but under high sounding names, in order to catch some unthinking people; the most recent of which is "The American Society for the Perpetuation of Freedom." Among other recent attempts are "The Stability League" and "The Merchants' and Manufacturers' Association." They say they do not want the saloon back. They admit that was a bad thing. They simply want beer, the right to make it and sell it.

The liquor men are making their most desperate efforts through attempted legislation. First by means of referendum. It was hoped by referring the question back to the people, that a reactionary wave sweeping over the country would repeal ratification in enough states. But this method failing, the next move has been to try to have the states define the percent of alcohol in intoxicating liquors. That is to declare that beer having 2.75 percent alcohol by weight or 3.45 by volume is not intoxicating and therefore may be sold. And this has been agitated by them in the states, in the face of the Internal Revenue definition of one-half of one percent as intoxicating drink, which definition has prevailed since 1862 and in spite of the same definition in the Federal Enforcement Code. There are a number of cases now before the Supreme Court involving these questions raised against the validity of the 18th Amendment and the Volstead Enforcement Code. No decisions have been handed out as yet although they are expected at any time. While it is thought that the supreme court will uphold these measures, it must be remembered that here too is another possibility for prohibition to be defeated.

But even if the supreme court does sustain these measures, the fight for prohibition is still not won. The liquor forces will not consider giving up until every possible point of attack has been tried to the limit. Probably the next two moves will be to try and advocate repeal of the Amendment by the same process by which it was written into the constitution, and the more probable method is to elect a Congress that will weaken the Amendment by redefining "intoxicating liquors" to include more alcohol or by failing to provide proper enforcement. And so we must insist that our candidates still declare their policy toward prohibition and again elect only those men, who will stand for its enforcement.

But the thing that the prohibition leaders fear more than the attacks of the liquor interests is the attitude of indifference on the part of the people, who are in sympathy with prohibition,—the prevailing feeling is that the fight for prohibition is won and that they can lay down their arms in peace. One of the very recent issues of "The American Issue" rebukes the people very severely for this attitude.

"Every American Issue reader knows how sure the liquor interests were that national prohibition would never be realized.

"But now the shoe is on the other foot, and there are thousands of drys who are every bit as shortsighted as were the wets.

"With prohibition accomplished, these drys laugh at the thought that the wets will ever come back. They ridicule the warning that the prohibition movement is at its most critical stage. They say there is no danger or need to worry, as prohibition is here to stay, and that nothing will ever come of the clamor from the wet camp.

"Such drys are living in a fool's paradise.

"Prohibition is in danger for the very reason that so many dry men and women are now indifferent and think the dry cause secure by reason that Prohibition is part of the organic law of the land.

"These sleepy drys do not realize that public sentiment must be sustained, that this organized public sentiment must back up public officials, and the enforcement of the law, that the assaults of the wets cannot be successfully repulsed only by organized drys, and that the greatest danger to the dry cause today is the belief of so many drys that the fight is over, the victory won, and there is nothing more to be done.

"These apathetic drys need to take a lesson of the indifferent wets of a few years ago, and then they will understand that eternal vigilance is the price of the recent dry victories."

What then is the task of the Temperance Department of the Sunday school? The task follows very clearly and can be stated in a few sentences. The task is to arouse our people to the folly of thinking that the prohibition fight is over. To show them that the liquor interests have not given up and that they will yet bring about a wave of reaction if we forget that "eternal vigilance is the price of victory." We must arouse public sentiment to enforce the law, or like hundreds of other laws on our statute books, it will amount to nothing.

Ashland, Ohio.

Prayer and Anointing for the Sick. By Samuel Kiehl.

At a certain time Jesus called his twelve disciples together, and gave them power and authority over all devils, and to cure diseases; and sent them to preach the kingdom of God, and to heal the sick 'Luke 9:1, 2). They went out, and preached that men should repent; cast out many devils, and anointed with oil many that were sick, and healed them (Mark 6:12, 13). James gives the anointing service in detail—"Is any sick among you? Let him call for the elders of the church; and let them pray over him, anointing him with oil in the name of the Lord; and the prayer of faith shall save the sick, and the Lord shall raise him up; and if he have committed sins, they shall be forgiven him (Jas. 5:14-16).

Why is it not written that the prayer of the elders shall save the sick? God must have all the glory. Not by might, nor by power, but by my spirit, saith the Lord of hosts (Zech. 4:6). When exigencies exist in which the presence and power of God must be manifested to bring about certain results, Jesus says, It is not ye that speak, but the Spirit of your Father which speaketh in you (Matt. 10:20). Hence, the word spoken by the Spirit of God abiding in the elders, is the prayer of faith that saves the sick.

The three verbs denoting the blessings that follow the anointing are in the future tense; to receive them immediately after the anointing, or at an indefinite time thereafter fulfills the promise. In due time health is restored; and a soul is greatly rejoicing in him whose goodness and mercy endureth forever (Psalms 107:1). But if the sick one does not recover the anointing will not have been in vain. The promise is sure; these blessings will follow; the salvation of his soul, the resurrection of his body, and his appearing with Christ in glory (Col. 3:4). The promise of forgiveness of sins assures his appearing with Christ. Paul had a desire to depart, and to be with Christ (Phil. 1:23). A legitimate desire for a faithful, wayworn soldier of the cross (Psalms 37:4).

From the time that Christ sent out the twelve until the present, laying on of hands (Mark 16:18), prayer for the sick, and anointing with oil in the name of the Lord, by the faithful in Christ Jesus, has been a God-given remedy for the restoration of health, and the enjoyment of a long happy life to multiplied thousands. Since the organization of the First Brethren church in this city its pastors have practised and taught this doctrine with marvelous results. For all these blessings "we thank God and take courage." Wonderful blessings always follow obedience to a "thus saith the Lord." "If ye know these things, happy are ye if ye do them."

Dayton, Ohio.

NEWS FROM THE FIELD

WHO WILL ANSWER THE CALL?

The Kentucky Mission Committee, recently appointed by the Home Mission Board, is anxiously awaiting for some one to answer the call to fill the new position at Riverside Institute, Lost Creek, Kentucky. This position can be filled by any one who has a fair knowledge of keeping accounts and is willing to make the necessary sacrifices which all God's missionaries must make to go to the places he calls them. Of course we expect the party applying for the position, to be able to teach in the school also. Would prefer married man whose wife could help a little with the music. We trust there will be a number of applications for this position within the next week or two, for the time is drawing near to the first of July, the date when it should be filled. Detail of duties will be given to parties making application.

WILLIAM A. GEARHART,
General Missionary Secretary, and Secretary of the Kentucky Committee.

A New Fund

The "WILLING WORKERS'" BIBLE CLASS of the First Brethren church, Dayton, Ohio, has been donating money each month for the support of students at Ashland College who need financial aid. This money is to be for those who are preparing for the mission fields. It is the desire of this faithful class that this fund will grow and be the means of sending many workers into the Lord's Vineyard. The new fund will be known as the "MISSIONARY EDUCATIONAL FUND" and contributors to this fund may designate to whom the money is to be sent, and your General Secretary will be glad to forward it.

Pleasant News

Miss Elsie A. Showalter, Mt. Clinton, Virginia, one of our dear sisters in Christ, who has gone to her heavenly home, left a will directing Jacob S. Swartz to distribute one-half of her estate to missions. As a result of this $1,763.93 has been sent recently for Foreign Missions, and Mr. Swartz states the balance will be given for Home Missions. We wonder why there are not more of our people who are deeply interested in missions, that are willing to make the proper arrangements, before it is too late, to have at least a portion of their estate donated to missions. Our dear brother and attorney Orion E. Bowman, 705 Conover Building, Dayton, Ohio has offered his services free for those desiring to make such arrangements.

P. S.—Counting Long Beach check which will reach me soon, I will have over $20,000 for Foreign Missions since April 1.

WILLIAM A. GEARHART
General Missionary Secretary.

EVANGELISTIC NEWS

On March twentieth Albert T. Ronk, and I arrived in Cedar Rapids, ready to start a meeting the following day in the M. E. Trinity church. Brother Ronk as evangelistic singer, myself as evangelist. For the next three weeks we battled against the powers that be. Pardon me, if I say the meeting was a great success, both spiritually and numerically, I will add to this, financially, the free will offering crowding the thousand mark.

This was the first time I ever had the pleasure of working with our Brother Ronk. I attribute our wonderful victory to the splendid work which he did. Albert sounds a new note in evangelistic singing, wins his way into the hearts of both young and old, insists on a spirit of prayer in the chorus that adds spirituality to the meeting and gives him the calm assurance of victory. Brother Albert had full charge of the opening services and the many readings and expositions which he gave were a great benefit to us all, as were the special services for the kiddies, which he put on.

Some two hundred responded to the invitation which resulted in considerably over a hundred accessions for Trinity church. We felt good over this as we started our meeting five weeks after a big tabernacle meeting had closed.

Brother Ronk and I have decided to work together the coming season. We will book dates for any church or churches for a meeting for the season beginning September twelfth. First come first served. The first date is taken, we go to help Brother Freeman Ankrum September twelfth. This will be my second meeting at Carlton church. No doubt we could fill our year with union meetings but we want to give a large part of our time to our own church, we love the church and want to have at least a small part in helping her win out.

Coveting a large place for the church in the nation's life and a wide field of usefulness for The Evangelist, I am

Your Brother in Christ,
F. G. COLEMAN.

WATERLOO NEWS

One of the older marriage ceremonies asks the contracting parties if they will take each other "for better or for worse, etc.?" Notwithstanding, the record of pastoral repeats has not always been too favorable, yet the Waterloo congregation extended to me a second call to become its pastor, and I accepted the call. I sincerely hope it will be "for better and not for worse" for both the congregation and the pastor. Time alone will prove which it has been.

In the interim between Brother Goughnour's leaving this charge and my resuming the work, Brother Z. T. Livengood of Lanark was in charge of the congregation. Living so far from this field naturally put Brother Livengood to considerable disadvantage, nevertheless the people here counted themselves fortunate that he was available under the circumstances, and they feel highly grateful to him for the faithful service he rendered. Brother Livengood has endeared himself to the Waterloo people, and I am quite sure he will be a welcome guest in their midst at any time in the future.

Immediately following the campaign for endowment in the Gratis congregation which closed February 29th, we came to Waterloo. To say that we were weary and worn out is putting it mildly. On the first Sunday in March we preached our first sermons of our second pastorate here. And we also began at once to settle in our new home. Nor do I find that very restful either. We also began as soon as we landed on the field preparations for our revival meeting. We want the meeting to be in full swing at East time. This gave us very little time for preparation for the meeting and we felt throughout our effort, but we did the best we could under the circumstances.

Brother Edwin Boardman, pastor of our sister church at Hudson had charge of the music in the meeting. Our people were highly pleased not only with his leadership of the chorus choir, but also with his solo work. He was a great help to us, and we are all greatly obliged to Hudson for loaning him to us. The campaign lasted for three weeks and the pastor did the preaching. We had a lot of good weather during that time, and we also had as uniformly good audiences as I think I ever saw in a meeting. I have seen larger audiences to be sure, but taken night after night it was gratifying to see how fine the attendance held up. We observed Decision Day the Sunday school on Easter with quite satisfactory results. And at the close of the meetings we observed our regular spring communion. At this service our people turned out loyally, as they always do. The immediate results of the meetings were sixteen baptized and added to the church. Besides, our people were greatly revived and blessed; and good seed was sown which is bound to bear fruit in God's own time.

Our Easter offering for Foreign Missions was just fairly good—it was $400. While the figure showed an increase over anything the church had done in the past in the way of Easter offering, yet neither pastor nor congregation felt quite satisfied with the result. As consequently we decided that we would not deem the situation in the United Simultaneous Financial Campaign as proposed by the Interchurch World Movement. Parenthetically I want to say that we are not as much afraid of the Interchurch Movement at Waterloo as are some of our good brethren and sisters. To be sure it may be because we are too dense and too ignorant to recognize danger when it crosses our path. But we argued in our own minds, and we still argue, that here was a movement which had created a tremendous momentum; here was a movement which had produced a moment of unprecedented high tide when it was easy for congregations to raise big sums of money for the Kingdom of God, and we said at Waterloo, we dare not let this moment slip by, and we didn't.

After carefully preaching this over to our people, and after carefully praying over it together, and after carefully planning our campaign we launched our little drive on Sunday morning May 2nd, and by the following Wednesday night our results showed $4,600 raised

We understood from the start that not a dollar of what we raised in our own congregation by Brethren folks among Brethren folks would or would go outside of distinctly Brethren channels. Everybody understands that who has taken the trouble to go to the bottom of the matter. Accordingly this money will to to our Brethren interests on the basis proposed by Brother Wm. Kolb—the College so much, Home and Foreign Missions so much, and the Publishing House and Old Folks' Home so much. Let me qualify that statement just a trifle: If either our Home or Foreign Mission Board, or if a single one of the other interests represented feels that this money is in any way contaminated simply because we happened to raise it at the same time 29 other denominations were raising large sums for the promotion of their work, why then we will change our plans and give it all to the College and Publishing House and Old Folks' Home.

Of course we feel good over this: And yet, we are not boasting. Waterloo gave $11,000 to the endowment of Ashland College. And under Goughnour she did a neat piece of work by wiping the slate clean of the remaining indebtedness against the church here which was caused by delinquencies, etc. And besides, this church has always given substantially to all of the interests of the church. And now, in addition to what has been done here in the last several years ,to raise $4,600 purely for benevolences—I repeat, of course we feel good about it. And we believe God has already richly blessed us for doing it. But we are not boasting. We have simply done our duty; and under God we want in the future to do a whole lot more. It has always been Waterloo's policy to render a symmetrical, consistent support to all of our interests. We are not going to get lopsided on any one cause in particular, but we are going to stand back of all of them. We cannot see our denomination strong and stable in the future aside from such a policy in our local congregations.

It was our privilege and pleasure to entertain in our church the Annual Convention of the Blackhawk County Sunday School Association which closed last night. This convention has brought inspiration and a wealth of new ideas to our own teachers and workers. I believe too, that this convention will go down in the Sunday school history of the county inasmuch as it was in the last session definitely decided that this county is to have a paid Secretary or Director of Religious Education giving all of his time to the work. Our county is the first in Iowa to take the step. We believe it is very significant. We are also planning that our school shall be fully represented in our state convention next month. Charles City is the convention city; and one of the unique features of the convention will be that one of the sessions will be held in the world-famous "Little Brown Church" near Nashua, Iowa. The Rotary Club of the convention city will be responsible for transporting the delegates to and from the "Little Brown Church."

Our work in the church is responding very nicely. But we do surely deplore the fact that there has to be a break in the near future occasioned by my going back to take up the last lap of the campaign for endowment. We hope to be at Hagerstown, Maryland, Sunday, June 6th and from there on cover Maryland and Virginia.　　　WM. H. BEACHLER.

SALDEE, KENTUCKY

While on a business trip to Knoxville and Bristol, Tennessee, I stopped at Limestone to visit the dear people with whom I labored in the Lord at the time the Brethren of that place built the nicest little church of that district. We began with about 15 charter members in 1911. Now they have about 60, and the work is doing fine under the leadership of Miss Mary Pence as pastor. Miss Mary is a good worker and she certainly has a fine bunch of helpers to aid her in the work.

I certainly did enjoy my visit with the dear people of Limestone. Mr. and Mrs. B. C. Smith, accompanied by Sister Cartwright and others met me at the station, and I was most pleasantly entertained at the Smith home.

The Washington County Singing Convention was held at our church Saturday, May 1. It was a big day, with nice weather and splendid interest. The Brethren are the leading church about Limestone, and I say they can sing. They are planning for a revival meeting some time this fall. Let us pray that they may go over the top in leading many souls to Christ.

Yours for a greater spread of the gospel and for the advent of our Lord.
　　　　REV. THOS. ALLEN.

Communion Notices

The Campbell Brethren church will hold their semi-annual love feast on June 5th, 1920. Everybody cordially invited. If you wish to come address the pastor. He will arrange to meet you at the train.
　　　M. V. GARRISON, Pastor,
　　　　　Lake Odessa, Michigan.

The First Brethren church, Fifth street, near Tilghman, Allentown, Pa., will observe holy communion Wednesday evening, May 26. All of like faith invited.
　　　A. L. DeLOZIER, Pastor.

An Announcement

The Sunday school and Christian Endeavor convention of the Southern District of Indiana will be held at College Corner, June 16 and 16. The opening session will begin at 8 P. M., Tuesday evening and continue throughout the following day. A worth-while program · has been arranged and pastors and delelgates from each church are urged to be present.
　　　E. A. MYER, President,
　　　Mabel M. Maus, Secretary.

FALLS CITY, NEBRASKA

Following a bad Easter, we had our attention called to the old sign that Moisture on Easter meant seven Sundays of the same brand of weather. Time has proven this true. It worked against us for a few Sundays, and then the people got used to it. Now we go to church rain or shine. The weather forced us to postpone both the taking of our Easter offering and our spring communion, which were planned for Easter Sunday. We were able to carry out our plans later. Our offering this year was a trifle more than five hundred dollars. The communion was not well attended, for we held it during one of the worst rain storms of the season. It proved however a great blessing to those who were present.

Brother Bell came for our revival campaign the last of April, and continued a little less than three weeks. We had perfect weather. Not a rainy night. The people of the church and community stayed by and encouraged in every way possible. Brother Bell brought strong gospel messages, in a way that counted for God and the Kingdom. There were fifty-two confessions. Some excellent young people, as well as older ones who will become strong leaders in the work. The results in the church were beyond our expectations. The church experienced a real awakening. I cannot speak too highly of our brother's work among us. We feel that he was especially sent to us, for certain things that we had been praying for a long time were accomplished.

We are now trying to get our work in shape for the summer. In a few weeks we will leave it in the hands of Brother L. A. Myers of Sidney, Indiana, while we go to Winona Lake for the season. Brother Myers will be privileged to visit his wife's people, and I believe he expects to bring his family along with him. A numbers of years ago he was assistant pastor here, and the people are looking forward with pleasure to his return for a season.
　　　H. F. STUCKMAN.

SALEM, OHIO

Although reports from the Salem church have been somewhat conspicuous by their absence, it does not evidence that things are at a standstill. Quite the contrary.

Since Brother James S. Cook came from Krypton Kentucky, to take up the work here, we have been steadily going forward. We find our pastor, not only a consecrated man of God, but an enthusiastic and tireless worker as well No matter what the odds happen to be, he is busy, visiting and doing personal work.

Many visible results are being realized. We have better church attendance on the part of the members, and those outside the church also. We are having services twice each Sunday, and a mid-week prayer meeting each week. This is the first time in the history of the congregation that we have been able to do so, and we realize it is a vital step in the growth of the church. Besides supporting a pastor for full time we have made a few improvements in the church and are contemplating larger ones. When Brother Beachler visited us during the winter, he talked our lighting system out of service to such an extent that it necessitated a new one. Since then we have installed electric lights inside and out: Come again, Brother Beachler, and we will assure you lighting facilities that you cannot work havoc upon.

We have just closed a two weeks' revival

PAGE 8   THE BRETHREN EVANGELIST

service, our second series since September. Miss About from the Dayton church preached for us. She surely gave us inspirational messages and helped us greatly. God blessed her efforts with an ingathering of eleven souls, besides the sowing of seed that will yet bring forth fruit.

Homes are being touched that are difficult ones, but we feel confident that we shall yet have a greater ingathering. Influence is being gained in the community such that we can expect results.

On Wednesday evening, May 5, we held our communion services.

We are planning special services for Mother's Day, distinctly honoring with flowers, every mother who will be present.

Thus with a capable leader at the head, every department of the church in healthy condition, the Spirit of God directing, we cannot help but press forward and accomplish worthwhile things for the Master.

ALICE E. WOGAMAN.

WHERE IS JERUSALEM?

Note—The following interestion portion of a letter was written by the late Dr. E. O. Guerrant of the Soul Winner's Society and should be read by every member of the Brethren church.—G, C. C.

I certainly think the Gospel should be "preached to every creature in the world" but these, our poor neighbors are in the world, and we should begin at Jerusalem, as he commanded.

Here are more than three millions of our own countrymen, inhabiting a region as vast as the German Empire, who have been left to perish in the fastnesses of their mountain homes. For fifty years I have traveled among them, and may speak with some assurance when I say that I do not know any people who are more deserving of our help, or more anxious to receive it, or more in need of it and grateful for it. There are tens of thousands of them yet without the blessings of education and religion.

In these years our workers have gathered some 40,000 children in our mission schools, instructed by 300 faithful teachers, and built scores of chapels and school houses, and had some ten thousand converts, and yet, there are multiplied thousands of these Highlanders, beyond our farthest missions, which stand like light houses on the shores of a continent of darkness.

They are our own blood, our "kith and kin," and are worthy of our assistance. Most of them are Scotch-Irish, a noble race of people who for generations have been sadly neglected. They are poor, so was Jesus and so are many of the best people. They are not lazy, but work hard to make a living on the mountain sides. Even the little boys and girls, and their mothers, help do the hard work.

Many of them never saw a church or heard a sermon, could not read or write. They are so anxious to learn that they walk miles through snow and cold to attend school. They are very bright and learn fast. I have heard them repeat three Catechisms by heart though they could not read a word. Their teachers read the Bible and Catechisms to them, and they repeat them.

They are so poor many often go barefooted in the winter, and we send them clothing so they can go to school. I never knew any people who were so ambitious to learn; and so grateful for help.

Their houses are generally very poor and cold, and have only one or two rooms. But in spite of it all, they love their homes and the mountains, and cannot be persuaded to leave them.

Few of these children ever saw a doll or a Christmas tree until our missionaries went among them.

We are trying to build them churches and school houses, and to send good men and women to teach them. The Highlanders love them and divide their little store of vegetables and produce with them. Hundreds have learned to love Jesus and some of them are now preaching the Gospel.

ANNOUNCEMENT OF CONVENTION

The Northern Indiana Sunday School and Christian Endeavor Convention will be held at Nappanee, June 8 and 9. Program will appear next week.

MARY LESLIE.

MUNCIE, INDIANA

(This news letter arrived in the midst of the tear-up incident to the editor's moving the first of April, and we regret to say that it was placed away in our desk so securely that it was only discovered this week. We beg the pardon of those concerned for the delay.—Editor.)

The Simultaneous evangelistic campaign of this county and the feast of Gospel truth as preached by Brother A. E. Thomas, of Warsaw, Indiana, is now a matter of history; but the work of the Holy Spirit goes on and the effects of this mountain top experience will last indefinitely in the hearts and lives of the membership of the Brethren here.

Of all that might be said; either in criticism or approval we can find no better words than those of a disinterested attendant— "There is one thing sure, we have heard the Gospel preached!". And "preached" is the correct term. Even, however, with the earnest appeal of this forceful speaker, men were loath to leave the allurements of this world and sin and the material prosperity of the hour and give the cause of their Maker a place of first magnitude in their lives. To be frank on this point we say truthfully, we have never before seen so much indifference in the face of so mighty a message. This is not a note of pessimism, but a fact we must not misconstrue.

However, there were several confessions, and since the close of the meetings, March 19, others have signified their desire to be one of our number. A Catholic home was reached and this we consider a victory of no small import. The final summary of this particular campaign will culminate Easter. The pastor will then give a more detailed and definite report in these pages.

We beg to take this opportunity to express our view on the subject of sending a representative to Japan to attend the World's Sunday School Convention. We have read expressions from several Evangelist contributors and note the points at issue. Some question the person to be sent. Others refer to the financial side.

There is no question but that it would be a fine thing for the Brethren church to be represented at Tokyo. There are perhaps several of our people fitted and worthy, from whom we might choose one for this trip, and there is certainly no question but that such an one would get inspiration and be able to impart more or less to home folks (by much travel after getting home).

In the light of the fact, however, that, to a large extent, every phase of our church activity is handicapped and weakened and halted because of the lack of funds, it might be well to look carefully to the money end of this proposition. We do not know what this expense would be. There have been some hazards on this point in these pages, and neat sums were named.

Suppose, if you please, we held here in our hands a given sum, to be used for God's cause. Now, is it not policy to look about and decide where said amount will do the most good? This long trip to Asia may do this one man (or woman) much good—he may be able to inoculate with his enthusiasm the churches at home, but this would necessarily be limited.

All this pales into insignificance when we read the appeals from our representatives—in South America and Africa, yea from our home desks, in behalf of these fields—when we are confronted with the statement that we must man these fields within five years. Where are the reapers? And what are we doing toward this momentous work?

So, back to the imaginary sum we hold in hand for disposal. Please, we earnestly pray you, can this money be used in a better manner than in a fund to aid worthy, consecrated young people (pledged to go) in a season of preparation at Ashland, unto harvest? In these fields "white already unto harvest?"

FRED V. KINZIE.

IN THE SHADOW

NYSWANER—Mrs. Elizabeth Marble Nyswaner, widow of Brother John Nyswaner, died at her home in Marianna, Washington county, Pa., May 4, aged 85 years, four months and twelve days. She was a member of the Highland Brethren church and was converted at the age of 15, having lived a Christian life for 70 years. She was a noble Christian lady, loved and respected by all who knew her. Funeral services were conducted by
M. C. MYERS.

EHRSTINE—A very sad accident robbed us at Dayton of one of our good loyal Brethren. A speed demon whom it is thought was going at a rate of sixty miles an hour on our principal street ran down his victim by passing a car on the wrong side. The unfortunate man was Brother Willis E. Ehrstine, aged 38 years, 5 months and sixteen days. He has been a very loyal member of the Brethren church since 1909 and was testifying for his Savior within a very few moments of his death. Our large auditorium here was nearly filled with friends and relatives who mourn his loss. He had a brother killed in the world's war two years ago. He leaves a wife, aged father, two brothers and one sister.
E. M. COBB.

MURRAY—Cyrus Murray, the oldest deacon in the Brethren church at Aleppo, Pa., of which he was a member since the age of 23, departed this life in Cameron, W. Va., after a long and creeping illness of creeping paralysis, having reached the age of 76 years, six months and six days. He was loyal to his church and was a faithful attendant until affliction deprived him of the pleasure. He had served his church as treasurer, as Sunday school superintendent, was a faithful teacher and a thoughtful Bible student. Besides his aged and feeble wife, the following children are left to mourn his departure: Mary A. Snyder, Glover Gap, W. Va.; Virginia Snyder, Atwater, Ohio; D. A. Murray, Seattle, Washington; Mrs. E. M. Smith, Cameron, W. Va.; and Myrtle Keefer, a granddaughter, of Cameron, W. Va.. There is also another granddaughter; five grandsons and two great-grandsons. The funeral services were held in his old home church at Aleppo, Pa., Brother W. T. Hilbert, the present pastor, delivering the address, from the text, "And in the garden there was a sepulcher." Besides the relatives, there were many sorrowing friends and neighbors present to pay their last respects to his peaceful-looking form.

VOLUME XLII   NUMBER 21   JUNE 2, 1920

The Brethren Church Characterized, Evaluated and Emphasized--Brief Questionaire Symposium

1. What do you consider has been the historic genius of dominating distinctive characteristics of the Brethren church?

2. What characteristic, practice or plea of the Brethren church has been the source of greatest joy to your life?

3. What should be the chief point or points of emphasis in order to make the Brethren church the greatest agency possible in bringing in the Kingdom of God?

President Edwin E. Jacobs

The dominating spirit which pervaded the historic Dayton convention in the early eighties, of which my father was a member and who is still living, was an unwillingness to be bound by man-made creeds or the rulings of the Annual Meeting. The ruling of Annual Meeting might have been advisory with them but never mandatory. This was the first factor, if I may rely on what my father has so often repeated to me.

A second feature was the declaration of their unfaltering faith in the Bible as a sufficient rule of action; in essentials, unity, in nonessentials, liberty, and in all things charity. Each man was free, above and apart from all ecclesiastic authority, to go to the open Book and appropriate its message to his heart.

And the fact that I can thus go and get the spiritual nourishment that my own heart needs, together with the undying belief that thus I am appropriating the whole gospel, has been an unfailing source of joy to me.

These very features ought to be pressed now. That we as a church believe in the essential ordinances, that we have a sound historic basis which we respect, that we cling to the Christianity of Jesus, and that we have no cumbersome hierarchy, intolerant as all hierarchies in time become, ought to make an appeal. There never was a time when the world so needed the simple Christianity of Jesus as today nor was there ever a time when we ought so to insist on, not social salvation alone, but on the individual new birth, as today. If the whole world could be permeated with what I regard as the true Brethren spirit, each heart would be reborn, and "the world through him might be saved."

Ashland, Ohio.

Miles J. Snyder

1. It was a protest against a growing tendency to substitute "thus sayeth the established church" for thus sayeth the Scriptures." Its outstanding characteristics were loyalty to the clearest meaning of the Word of God and refusal to persecute those who did not agree with its beliefs and practices.

2. Freedom of access to the Bible with only the Holy Spirit as interpreter; and the consciousness that we believe as a church and the things we practice as disciples of Jesus Christ are so well substantiated by the simple teachings of the New Testament.

3. Fearlessly and whole-heartedly proclaim the true message of the old Book to this "crooked and perverse generation" as the only cure for the ills and turmoils of the world, and earnestly try to make our own lives measure up to the profession of our faith. And, in order to conserve and apply in the most effective way for the kingdom our full strength, we need a well-defined program expressive of the best thought and vision of the church, in the prosecution of which we should unitedly and enthusiastically work.

Milledgeville, Illinois.

L. G. Wood

1. The practical recognition of the true foundation of Christian faith. The question of the ages has been, "Who is Jesus Christ?" The historic answer of the Brethren church has been and is, the great confession—Matthew 16:16, "Thou art the Christ the Son of the living God." Every false religion has in some way assailed the PERSON of Christ. Brethrenism always rests its case on the inspired word— 1 Corinthians 3:11: "For other foundation can no man lay than that is laid, which is Jesus Christ."

2. The simplicity and non-sectarian-ism of our whole Bible plea. Brethren teach and practice the "all things" of Christ's commandments. The basis of his beautiful life and the importance of his teaching, is his PERSON. He is Lord of ALL or he isn't Lord at all. This plea won me to Brethrenism, and it is the source of the greatest joy of my life.

3. Ring true to our credal standard, the Bible. Honor the early standard bearers, of our cause, by unflinching loyalty to the historic genius for which many of them suffered the "loss of all things." Their records are written in glory. Never compromise with error. Maintain the "unity of the spirit in the bond of peace." Enlarge our program by a world vision.

Roanoke, Virginia.

A. B. Cover

1. People suddenly plunged into the tossing sea of unrest will most naturally seek stability and anchorage. This is true in all realms, industrial, intellectual, social and religious: Thus the religious chaos following the Reformation found expression, through the counter-reformation, in building upon the Rock of Truth. They wanted the note of authority, and found it fully in the Word of

(Continued on page 3)

Published every Wednesday at
Ashland, Ohio. All matter for publication must reach the Editor not
later than Friday noon of the preceding week.

George S. Baer, Editor

The
Brethren
Evangelist

When ordering your paper changed
give old as well as new address.
Subscriptions discontinued at expiration. To avoid missing any numbers renew two weeks in advance.

R. R. Teeter, Business Manager

OFFICIAL ORGAN OF THE BRETHREN CHURCH

Subscription price, $2.00 per year, payable in advance.
Entered at the Post Office at Ashland, Ohio, as second-class matter.
Acceptance for mailing at special rate of postage provided for in section 1103, Act of October 3, 1917, authorized September 9, 1918.
Address all matter for publication to Geo. S. Baer, Editor of the Brethren Evangelist, and all business communications to R. R. Teeter,
Business Manager, Brethren Publishing Company, Ashland, Ohio. Make all checks payable to the Brethren Publishing Company.

EDITORIAL

The Brethren Church and Its Place In the World Kingdom

Whatever may be our conception of the kingdom of God or the nature of its coming, it is safe to say there is no member of the Brethren church but is concerned about the place his church shall occupy in, and the contribution it shall make to, that coming kingdom. We know of no new discovery that throws light upon the nature of, or the manner of the coming of, the heavenly kingdom; we are satisfied that each individual shall take the same old teachings of Jesus we have always had, and, under the light of the Holy Spirit, interpret those teachings according as his own spiritual grasp makes possible. We desire only to discuss briefly the place and contribution, largely distinctive, of the Brethren church in the great program of making of the kingdoms of this world the kingdom of our Lord and Christ.

It is not in the spirit of denominational conceit and selfishness that we say the Brethren church occupies and will continue to occupy a place of vital importance in the kingdom of God, because 'she has been her mission to espouse fundamental principles of that kingdom. In the first place she has always stood for implicit, humble and loving obedience to the Word of God. We do not claim a monopoly on the spirit of obedience, but if the Brethren church stands for anything that is a distinguishing feature it is a humble and implicit obedience to the most simple commands of our Lord. We do not disclaim that other denominations may espouse very important characteristics of the divine commonwealth, but if there is one thing more important than another it is that of unquestioning obedience, for which the Brethren church has stood in a peculiar way. There is perhaps nothing that more faithfully evidences the quality of character or the worthiness of an individual to enjoy companionship with God and to be a member of his kingdom than the readiness and the loving spirit with which he obeys his Lord's every command. Though the Brethren church be small in numbers, it is great in mission and character and will continue to be so, so long as it exemplifies in a humble and implicit manner this high quality of obedience.

In the second place the Brethren church has stood for equality and brotherhood as few others have. This has been characteristic of our people from the very beginning. When those eight founders of the Brethren fraternity separated themselves from the confusion following the Reformation and dedicated themselves to a policy of implicit obedience to the Word of God, they desired to be known only as ''Brethren.'' And through the years we have been consistently opposed to assigning to any man the position of lord or ruler, insisting that ''one is your Master and all ye are brethren.'' The very nature of some of our most characteristic practices forbids the growth of the spirit of lordship on the part of any of our number, but rather drives home to the heart of every participant the fact of their equality in Christ. We hold that no man is superior to another in church privileges or accessibility to divine grace. Church position represents not mastery but service; not pre-eminence but merely leadership among equals. And before the throne of grace we are all priests unto God. In every way equality and brotherhood are insisted upon in a degree that is unique among the churches.

Christian liberty is also a gospel principle for which Brethren have stood with a consistency and insistency that distinguishes them from other families of God's people. Just as certainly as the throne of grace is free to all, so we have considered the Bible to be a free book which all might approach and interpret each for himself under the direction of the Holy Spirit. That Book, revealed by that Spirit, is considered our sufficient rule of faith and practice. No manmade rules or human decrees have we permitted any one to impose upon us to restrict our liberty of thought and life in Christ Jesus. We have believed that ''as many as are led by the Spirit of God, they are the sons of God'' 'and should rejoice in that freedom. ''For we have not received the spirit of bondage again to fear; but we have received the Spirit of adoption, whereby we cry, Abba, Father.'' The Spirit itself beareth witness with our spirit, that we are the children of God.'' (Rom. 8:14-16). ''Now the Lord is that Spirit: and where the Spirit of the Lord is, there is liberty (2 Cor. 3:17). To every member of the Brethren fraternity this Christian liberty has been a very precious heritage, and to it he has clung with the utmost tenacity even at the cost of great sacrifice. And may we ever ''stand fast in the liberty wherewith Christ hath made us free, and be not entangled again with the yoke of bondage'' (Gal. 5:1).

In addition to these great kingdom characteristics which have characterized the Brethren church in its own inner relations and claims, there is the great passion which characterizes the church in its relation to the unevangelized world. It can be expressed in three brief phrases: The whole gospel to the whole world with the whole heart. Our aim is to take the same complete, unmutilated gospel which we enjoy to those who know it not. We offer no abridged gospel in the form of a man-made creed or catechism; no collection of rules and interpretations, but the simple gospel in its entirety, with both the example and the admonition for complete obedience to all its precepts and commands. We forget not that in the great commission, Jesus enjoined not only the ''going'' and ''discipling,'' but the ''teaching them to observe all things whatsoever I have commanded.'' It is the ''all things,'' the whole gospel without additions or subtractions that we feel it our great responsibility to bear to all the world. That means the gospel of individual regeneration and also the gospel of social betterment; it includes the practice of the means of grace and also the grace to practice the spirit of helpfulness as exemplified by the good Samaritan; it means not only the gospel of personal cleansing through Jesus Christ, but also the gospel of social purity and uprightness made possible only through the prevalence of the spirit of Christ. These with all their implications together with the doctrines and rites make the gospel of Christ so simple and beautiful, so powerful and attractive the Brethren are consciously duty-bound to give to the world.

In our slogan we have idealized our duty to be not only to teach the whole gospel, but to teach it to the whole world. This is the most challenging task with which we could be faced, and it may seem a bit presumptuous for a little band of 25,000 people to undertake or perhaps we had better be wise and generous enough to say 125,000, including the larger branch of Brethren people, but even then it is a most stupendous task. But it is not more stupendous and challenging than the task which Christ presented to the twelve disciples whom he had personally trained. He told them that his gospel must be preached to ''every creature'' and that they should go into ''all the world.'' It is a great task, but it is not greater than the power of him in whose strength we are to work.

But the whole gospel to the whole world will always appear so stupendous as to cause the heart to shrink with fear until we go at it with the whole heart. We have gone at our task only half-heartedly; we have not begun to find the limit of our powers to carry out the great commission. If the Brethren church is to fill the place that God has ordained that it shall fill; if it is to make the contribution that is possible for it to make to the completion of the great kingdom of God, it must not only talk of the "whole gospel" and the "whole world" as objects of its efforts and prayers, but also the "whole heart" being applied to the whole task that God has given the church to accomplish.

EDITORIAL REVIEW

Christian Endeavor and Sunday School programs for Northern and Southern Indiana and the Miami Valley are published in this issue.

Southern Indiana Sunday school and Christian Endeavor workers will find their tenth annual convention program in this issue. They are to convene at College Corner June 15 and 16.

If you know of any teachers contemplating doing school work this summer, urge them to come to Ashland College for the second summer term, beginning June 21.

If taking the whole gospel to the whole world is the task of the whole church, how is it going to be accomplished with so many doing absolutely nothing, and others only a tithe of what they might do towards the task?

Business may demand a man's time and attention; his home and family may rightfully expect their share; friendship may make its demands; and patriotism may claim sacrifice and allegiance; but the land of his heavenly birth should claim his heart in spite of all.

A goodly number of friends were in attendance at the commencement exercises of the college; so many we cannot name them all, but among the ministers and church leaders whom the editor saw were Brethren Carpenter, Beachler, Wolford, Oberholtzer, Eikenberry, Loose, and Prof. Mason. The entire commencement week program was a decided success. We hope to have the pleasure of presenting our readers with a complete report soon.

However rough the exterior of your house of clay may be, you may have a fine finish within; beautiful thoughts will give a beauty to the soul that will delight the eyes of God and the angels.

Our paper stock was completely exhausted and we had to wait for another small shipment by express before we could print and then could print only half a paper. That is the reason you received your Evangelist so late. See the Business Manager's Corner for the prospects.

If life is ever to be successful; if we are ever to enter into the mastery of ourselves; if ever we abandon the disposition to shirk and to dodge life's responsibilities and duties, it will be made possible by the clarifying and enlarging of our soul vision through the indwelling Christ.

Brother I. D. Bowman writes of a new Brethren church at Garden City, Virginia, near Roanoke and of a very successful evangelistic meeting which he conducted there. Brother Bowman says this new church is in a growing community and has a bright future. This meeting was interrupted by a sad occurrence which resulted in the death of Brother Bowman's little grandson. We extend sympathy to our brother.

Brother Kinzie reports some reasons for rejoicing over the work at West Alexandria, important among which are the new members received at that place. The work at his other charge, New Lebanon, is very encouraging and splendid signs of progress are in evidence. Brother Kinzie resigns the former charge to take effect October and gives full time to Lebanon. This is a noteworthy advance for the latter church.

"Canton, Ohio-Uniontown, Pennsylvania" is the subject of Brother Belote's interesting news letter. He and his good wife have recently gone through the experience of separating themselves from their parishioners at Canton where they have done a splendid work during the past four years, and re-attaching themselves to the good people of Uniontown church. The Canton folks gave substantial proof of their high regard for their leaving pastor, and the Uniontown people showed their good pleasure at getting back their worthy leader of former days.

(Continued from page 1)

God. A few pious souls, convinced of such authority, consecrated to an implicit obedience of its plain gospel teachings, launched the Brethren church. The Word of God as the full, final and perfect revelation of God's will to man, as authority; a trusting simple obedience to that authority, as a rule of faith and practice in all life's relationships, and a pure pious life dedicated to God is the apology for the existence of the Brethren church.

II. It has been a source of constant and supreme satisfaction to me in my religious experience that I need make no apology for holding membership in the Brethren church. I find a deep sense of joy in the fact, that amidst an unstable and scoffing world that I may rest my faith upon an unchanging standard, the abiding Word. The means of grace afforded by simple obedience in the ordinances, never fails to strengthen my soul and renew a deeper faith of usefulness in the Master's cause.

III. The slogan, get "Back to Christ." In the world of isms, schisms, unrest and godlessness, Christ is imperative. Christ is the great need of the ages and fully meets every unmet need of the soul. How get back to Christ? By an implicit obedience to him, through his Word, as our personal Savior. "If ye love me, keep my commandments." Individually accept, enthrone, and transmit to others a life, filled and dominated by the indwelling of his Spirit, and we shall contribute our bit to his unshakable, coming Kingdom, and aid our church in fulfilling her mission.

Hagerstown, Maryland.

Charles A. Bame

The dominating, distinctive characteristic of the Brethren church in all her two hundred years of history has been her unreserved and unqualified acceptance of the Bible as God's Word and

as his only message to man. If this has not been its historic genius, then all I have learned of its people from end of the Republic to the next and all I have learned from all her history and literature is false. "Whatsoever he saith unto you, do it," is written on every page of every history.

"Not ours to reason why,"

it is enough that God has spoken. We may think we know why, but if we can not see the reason, "Do it." It is this heroic allegiance to the Bible that has kept in the church, the literal observance of all the primitive practices of the "Apostolic church." Trine immersion, feet-washing, Lord's supper, communion emblems; temperance, anti-war, anti-slavery, anti-secrecy, anti-fashion and withal the liberty of conscience guaranteed by the Christ who set us free, are but the outgrowth of this basic love for the Word of God. To keep true to that history and that profession is the source of my highest joy and my only hope for the greater future of the BRETHREN CHURCH.

H. H. Wolford

The historic genius of the Brethren church, to my mind, is expressed in the declaration of the motto, "The Bible the whole Bible and nothing but the Bible", and also the declaration that "the Gospel of Christ alone is a sufficient rule of faith and practice." This excludes all man made creeds which, through the centuries, have been the cause of contention, and also gives to each individual the freedom of thought and action as the Spirit of God reveals his will and purposes.

Aside from the ordinances which are clearly fundamental to the church as declared at the Warsaw convention of 1892, the plea of the Brethren church which has given me greatest joy is the declaration of the church, "That the only conditions of approved membership in the Kingdom of Christ is obedience to the precepts of the Gospel upon the basis of a good moral character." This gives liberty of conscience aside from fundamentals as stated above. It also renounces all mandatory legislation, creeds and everything that may be construed to holding anything as essential to salvation except the Gospel of Christ (Rom. 1:16.)

The declaration of the principles of the above paragraph and the teaching of the ordinances of the church together with great emphasis upon the world-wide application of the Gospel of Jesus Christ (Matthew 28:19 and 20) is the message that will make the church effective in the extension of the Kingdom of God.

Elkhart, Indiana.

Dean J. Allen Miller

The Historic Genius of the Brethren Church.—1. Worthy of mention as the dominating factor in our church life is the place given the New Testament. This is our only creed. It is God's authoritative and ultimate Word to men. Though a first century book its message is for every century. This message does not grow obsolete, outworn, superfluous. To repeat what I have written elsewhere, "Ours is an unchanging credal standard, perfect and complete in interpretation in every age in the terms of the life and experience of that day."

2. The second factor is just this, that the Christian must live the right life, clean, sincere, consecrated; that he must reproduce in his own life the distinctive characteristics of the Master. This means loyal obedience to God's commands even to their literal observance. This makes for character of a peculiarly fine type. The lesson of the foot-washing and the love-feast, the insistence upon the sacredness of the marriage tie, the separation from the sinful world-spirit of the times,—such elements do make for personal character.

Chief point of Emphasis now.—What can the Brethren church do by way of emphasis in meeting her present obligation to her Lord? Without hesitancy I should say that we need to learn that ours is an obligation that we can not shift upon others. We need to stress the sense of mission, that we are sent of God to do his will. To do our utmost we must feel deeply divine obligation. We must sink minor and individual differences out of sight. We must learn over again the truth which our fathers held so firmly, namely, in essentials unity and in all else charity. We must build a challenging program and consecrate ourselves to its accomplishment. We must have a vision that sees into the future and holds us by its charm to sacrificial living. To save ourselves we must save others. We shall toil only as we see our Lord and own him. In the light of the Cross all else fades away except the word and the will, the love and the glory of the Christ. We need an intensification of the sense of MISSION and consequent RESPONSIBILITY to bring us to fulfill our calling as a people.

Ashland, Ohio.

Prof. J. A. Garber

1. Historically, the Brethren church represents an unmistakable protest. Ordinarily this point is conceded to the Protestant Reformation. But subsequent facts indicate that the very evil which Luther sought to overcome became prevalent in the Lutheran and Reformed churches, which proved to be as intolerant as the Catholic churches had been. Consequently, those who believed in the freedom of conscience in matters relating both to state and church sought relief

from oppressive domination of mind and spirit. Such persons were to be found among the Pietistic Pathfinders in general, and the original eight members of the Brethren faith who were willing to go the full length of separation, after having duly counted the cost.

2. In line with this evident principle of non-coercion this octette of God-fearing, liberty loving persons took the name "Brethren," which would enable them to recognize one another as brothers, equals among equals, and to acknowledge Christ as their Master. Hence the New Testament became at once and forever their sole authority in faith and in practice. Accordingly they yielded to each one entering the brotherhood and acknowledging the Lordship of Christ the liberty to interpret the scriptures in the light of sound reason and under the guidance of the Holy Spirit. It was upon this high ground of religious thinking that the organizers of the Brethren church took their stand in the memorable year of 1883.

3. Obviously enough, the right of private interpretation of the scriptures requires an enlightened people. This requirement was clearly recognized and, the leaders of both historic periods endeavored to provide means of enlightenment, such as schools and printed helps. Few barriers are so difficult to overcome as ignorance and indifference. Spiritual illiteracy works disaster and ruin in both church and state. Righteousness and democracy can be fully realized only through a comprehensive program of Christian education which indoctrinates the people in the word of God and builds up within their life such restraints of character as make for a complete morality, that is, ethical conduct based on the standards of Jesus and exemplified in both private and public relationships.

Ashland, Ohio.

Martin Shively

The thing which gave birth to the Brethren church, and which distinguished it during all its earlier years, was its positive emphasis upon the authenticity and authority of the Bible as being the word of God, and the only safe guide for the soul in its quest for God. It was this slogan, and the ability to drive this truth home to the hearts of men, which won so many converts and which struck terror to the hearts of all who sought to make light of any portion of the word, or to ignore its requirement.

The one greatest thing to me within the bounds of the organization of the church has been the sweet fellowship which has characterized it, whenever it was permitted to do so. It may be partly explained by the comparative smallness of our numbers, but that cannot explain it all. The fact that many had suffered together for the sake of their convictions, and all had denied to themselves the natural desire to be a part of a big thing, united the hearts of the Brethren, until it has often been remarked by those who were not of our number.

While I believe with all my heart, that the gospel of Jesus Christ is as wide in its application, as the needs of men I am profoundly convinced that Peter was absolutely correct when he said, "There is none other name given under heaven or among men by which we must be saved, than by the name of Jesus." That name, with all that is implied in it of supreme loyalty to God and devotion to his purpose, is first of all to be proclaimed as the only hope of man, first singly, and then in the aggregate. In this lies the primary duty of the church, and the hope of its future.

Ashland, Ohio.

"Old Paths and New".   By Fred V. Kinzie

Some years ago we remember of noting in the program of an annual conference of the Brethren church at Winona Lake the above subject, and we believe we even remember who used it; however, this does not matter now. We did not hear the discourse, did not even read the minutes of it, but in some way the four words have stuck in our thought life in a vivid, persistent manner, and many lines of reflection have radiated from the suggestion.

Of course, all this material which we have connected with these words has been directly related to the church and her work.

In every line of activity of the human family there are old paths and new ones, Most of us will agree that to a large extent the new are better than the old.

Industrially, for instance,—here are vast preparations for erect-

ing a business block. The excavation has been made quickly to a depth of more than twelve feet, by the use of a steam shovel, whereas the old method of elbow grease and shovel and wheelbarrow, or later the horse-drawn scoop, would take months or even years to remove such a quantity of earth.

Educationally,—every morning and evening, with the regularity of the clock, there passes the farm house a heated, comfortable, adaptable vehicle containing happy faces, regardless of weather conditions. Many day's school would some little tots miss were it necessary for them to face the elements afoot. Inside the school room we find the best of environments and equipment, and an instructor trained in child psychology, and especially fitted for that particular work. This is all pleasingly significant.

Medically,—yes, we have those who claim modern medicine is not to compare with the old method of ''doctoring.'' A good many cases are ''lost''—perhaps one reason being that great things are attempted and the experimental stages must cost—something—money, time, or lives. On the other hand, many a human being is today enjoying a healthful life who fifty years ago would have succumbed under available medical treatment at that time.

But let us see if there is any new path the human family is following or beginning to travel which might be questionable or subject to condemnation. We might name several, but only one looms up in glaring outline, and causes us to query whether all insanity is in the institution maintained for it. Pen or tongue or vocabulary fail utterly in efforts to express disapproval of modern paths of dress (or undress) in which Dame Fashion leads the millions. Especially womankind—blinded by vanity, until men of even the vilest minds are almost swept from their feet with disgust. Surely there is a better path than this. Where is the correction? One answer and one only—Fathers and Mothers!

The Path of the Christian Church

And so we might proceed in many avenues of endeavor and life. But most important is the lift and activity of the Christian church today. How about her old methods and new methods?

The writer wishes to emphasize in the outset that he readily recognizes to the fullest extent that the methods and activities of the church cannot follow the paths of fifty or one hundred years ago. Conditions have changed; so must our angle of attack change. The greatest and most prominent change is that from rural to urban fields of action. Others might be named.

The duty and the only ultimate goal of the church of Jesus Christ yesterday, today, and forever, till the end of time was and is that of catching men alive (not dead) (Luke 5:10), and the saving of their souls for eternity to the glory of our Lord. Trumbull compares the winning of men for the Cross of Christ to the art of catching fish. Ways of catching vary, depending on conditions, and these conditions have changed in both cases (men as well as fish) in the passing of decades, in that the fishing requires greater skill and tact and judgment. Oh! what a field of thought this opens up, but we pass on.

Now we may easily see that activities and methods may find new paths which are woefully wrong paths. The world—and the church as well—is scrambling for and demanding something new (2 Tim. 4:34). We are not surprised at this attitude in the world; neither dare we frown too heavily upon those in the church who are yet ''babies,'' or who are inactive (''dead'' in reality) but too often there is to be found the third class, and here we are surprised indeed, —those who have spent long, active lives in church work; live-wires, leaders, who are ready to plunge down any abyss or over any gulf for the sake of numbers or fame or money for his own particular congregation, at the cost of quality, spirituality, and that which is really worth while for the cause. This has become true to such an extent that today there exist denominations which formerly practiced many of the teachings the Brethren church holds dear, but now with them they have become only church history.

Some years ago a certain man of the near-infidel type was in conversation with the writer on subjects of the church and Christianity. When he learned the writer's church connections he laughed heartily a demonized laugh and said, ''Oh, that church is no different from any other church, except it is lagging about fifty years behind the others.''

Was He Right?

This slap was not gratefully received at the moment, but it opened our eyes a tiny bit wider than formerly. We began to reflect and query the theoretical phase of his statement. Developments in the meantime have induced us to half way believe he was not altogether mistaken. We put the questions square to you, now, that we put to ourselves then: Is the Brethren church going that road? Will it come to pass, eventually, that we will no longer baptize by trine immersion, or commemorate the communion and Lord's supper and washing of feet, etc.,

Oh, you elders and patriarchs of the church will tap your foreheads at these queries.

But wait a moment! These ordinances will not be dropped all at once. Neither the world nor church act that way. Every change goes by degrees.

It seems that, especially the American people, have gone into a state of mania on the subject of convenience. The advertisements thrust upon us at every turn are full of this term, in connection with household and farm and mill and office equipment. Very well, so long as quality and efficiency are not sacrificed.

Are we letting the matter of convenience overshadow everything else in church activities? Do we go to all manner of ''trouble'' in our homes in preparing to entertain and dine guests, and then, when it comes to preparing for the Lord's supper at his sanctuary, begin to slice and slash customs, scripture, and good sense in order to get the affair over with the least possible effort? and the result,—a mockery. In reality, the greatest convenience would be realized if the ordinance were omitted entirely, and that is exactly what has happened in some denominations. A further result, to get at the point in unmistakable terms, various congregations will be found serving at their Lord's supper observance everything from popcorn balls to blue points on ice. Most assuredly there is no scripture authorizing a specific menu for this meal, but much in the Word will be found which will guide the conscientious thinker aright. The old Jewish passover supper was ordered to be eaten with bitter herbs (Exodus 12:8), and not intended to tickle the palate. At the supper which Jesus instituted there is but the simple mention of the bread and ''sop'' (John 13:18, 26). We do not purpose in the least degree to lay down any specific rule on this point, but do assert that SIMPLICITY, a large amount of good righteous judgment, and not such a leaning toward convenience will make this service more what it should be, and in fact more uniform throughout the churches.

Old and New Paths in Baptism

Our people have always contended our baptism is truly apostolic. Little do we have scripturally describing the character of ceremony in connection with baptismal scenes aside from the simple mode implying immersion by triple action and the presence of the Holy Spirit. It is easy, however, and altogether safe, to read between the lines that it was a SACRED occasion.

From childhood we have witnessed from time to time not a few such scenes; the sanctity of the hour was ever reverenced by young as well as old. However, there came an occasion in later years when the order of services to which we were accustomed has changed and with a marked and undesirable effect. One of the subjects for baptism was a boy in the adolescent age. There had been no hymns sung at the water's edge; no services of any character prior to meeting at the stream. How about the boy? It was early summer. He came out of the water grinning broadly, and yelled: ''Come on, boys, let's go up the river and take a good swim!''

We say, emphatically, without further comment, give us the old baptismal scenes, when much prayer and song, and a certain amount of pre-education on the subject, were used and effectively.

In summary, we declare from the housetops, the path that Jesus trod is the only safe path when it comes to the activities of his church; and in other paths—new paths—we must go, but only to snatch men who are lost, and must fail not to bring them back to the old path,—the righteousness and grace of our Lord and Savior, Christ Jesus.

Muncie, Indiana.

Because the evangelistic appeal has never been heard in many lands and by many peoples, there is a glamour of mind of many preachers which ersts over the ''uttermost part of the earth'' when the plea goes forth to evangelize the world. The glory has departed from ''beginning at Jerusalem.'' The constituency in the city or town or open country which is the parish of an individual minister lacks the imaginative appeal, and all too often lacks in immediate and adequate response. However, the average pastor in the average field will be startled by a faithful and full analysis of his immediate field as an evangelistic opportunity. Facts reveal multitudes out of touch with Christ and with the church. If a constituency roll of responsibility record was carefully made of all the families and folks for whom each local church is spiritually responsible it would quicken to life the dead evangelistic nerve of thousands of pastors in this country.—Bishop Henderson.

NEWS FROM THE FIELD

THE SILENCE BROKEN

While we have been silent for a month or more it has not been because we have had nothing to say, but rather that we have had no paper to spare upon which to print such minor items as the Business Manager's Notes. We thought that so long as the paper famine continued and we were able to make the Evangelist only half size it would be better to let all the space be used for church news and a few of the most helpful contributions. But the Editor insists that we shall lift up the managerial voice once again.

What of the Future?

Many people are wondering about the paper situation for the future, and just how much we will be hindered in our work another year. We are forced to admit that the outlook is not bright. We are not sure we will be able to get out an issue of the Evangelist this week at all, as at this writing there is not a sheet of Evangelist stock in the house, and this is Thursday morning. However, we have the assurance that a little more than one ton of paper was being shipped to us by Express from the Mill at Kalamazoo, Michigan on Tuesday, so we are hoping it will reach us some time today. We also have the promise that a carload will be shipped to us from the same mill on June eleventh, so we are hopeful for the best. We ought to have had one-half the Sunday school quarterlies for the next quarter off the press by now, but we have been unable to get the paper to use in the printing.

Some may think we have been negligent about looking after these matters, but to set any such right in the matter we want to assure you that this paper was bought last January, and we have been fighting ever after the order ever since, but it has been impossible to secure delivery of the order. However as soon as the stock arrives we will get all our presses busy and run them just as many hours per day as we can get feeders to feed them until the quarterlies are completed.

The stock we have ordered is sufficient to run us for ten months, and we are now thinking of placing an order immediately for another supply to be delivered in March, 1921.

The Greatest of These

After all is said our greatest difficulty is not the securing of the stock upon which to issue our publications, but rather to secure sufficient funds to pay for the paper when it is secured. When I tell you that the shipment of paper we have coming will cost us just ONE HUNDRED percent more than the shipment received last July, and that it costs THREE HUNDRED percent more than it did five years ago, you will get some idea of what I mean. It means that twenty tons of paper that cost us three thousand dollars ten months ago will cost us SIX THOUSAND dollars today. Query: Where is that extra three thousand dollars to come from? Will some one who is good in commercial arithmetic please tell us. We are open for advice and information, especially the latter.

The Evangelist Honor Roll

No, the Honor Roll has not died, nor can it be said to be asleep, for while we have said nothing about it for some time the work is still alive and making some progress. Since our last report the following five churches that have already been on the Honor Roll for from one to three years have renewed their lists. Martinsburg, Pennsylvania; Sidney, Darwin and Burlington, Indiana; also Gretna, Ohio. This is the fourth year for the Gretna congregation and the list is larger than ever. Gretna was the first church in the brotherhood to win a place and we predict it will be the LAST one to give it up. The Business Manager has been supplying the Gretna church with preaching for nearly a year. Last summer we visited the congregation one Sunday

to supply them while they were without a pastor, and we have not found a quitting place yet. Brethren Hall, Myers and Lytle are the pastors of the other churches that we report this week. While we have so new churches to report we are able to report that two more churches are working on their lists now and they hope to be able to report that they have won out ere long. This is supposed to be the "Jubilee" year of the church and that should mean that no church that has taken a forward step should turn back. If I were a church myself I would be afraid that the words of the Master who said, "He that putteth his hand to the plow and looketh back is not worthy of the kingdom," might be applied to me. It is the "forward look" that wins out in life and surely we want all our churches to win.

R. R. TEETER, Business Manager.

A NEW BRETHREN CHURCH AT GARDEN CITY, VIRGINIA, WITHIN FOUR MILES OF ROANOKE

We began a revival in the new church here April 20 and continued for nearly four weeks. I was called home for four days on account of my little grandson being lost and then we preached about three weeks and my brother, J. S. Bowman preached one sermon while I was home and Brother Patterson preached four nights also while I was away.

This is a plain but needful wooden building erected at a great sacrifice by a few poor brethren at a cost of $2,000. On the day of dedication we raised nearly $400. They owe yet about $250 which they will pay off $20.00 a month and the pastor, Brother Donohue, agrees to preach for nothing until they get out of debt. This was a mission point and the surrounding Brethren churches helped to build it. Several churches gave about $100 each and then on day of dedication, April 25, we raised nearly $400, leaving the small balance of $250.

Many said these people could never build a church. But the big-hearted liberal Brother Gearhart said, we must build and Donohue and a couple others pitched right in and surprised everybody by getting through as well as they did.

They feel very thankful to the Evangelistic League for helping them in their revival meeting. This was the most needy field I have struck for years. Only two miles to the street cars of Roanoke and yet no school nor church in a community that is growing rapidly. Last year they built a splendid two-roomed brick schoolhouse. The same big hearted Gearhart got the neighbors to bake pies and cakes and erected a large flagpole, put one of the largest flags in the country on it and sent for the school directors. He had 100 children there and all their parents and he said we must have a schoolhouse and they could not resist. Then he said a church is needed worse than a school and we must have that; so persistence, determination and great sacrifice brought a good country church and they are happy. The Baptists, Methodists and a number of Pentecostal people have had the sway but now the Brethren are on top.

We had twenty-one confessions. One joined opposition to contend with but it gradually faded until we had the largest crowds that they have had there in any services for years. And now with the only church in the immediate neighborhood, by careful and persistent work, they will become the leading denomination in the little valley.

We had twenty-one confessions. One joined the Church of the Brethren but his wife and three children joined our church and he says he will support it. Some two or three will join the Baptis church. One was reclaimed, one joined by relation, nine have already

been baptized and I think all the rest will be very soon. Among the number baptized were a prominent man and wife of the Methodist church. They are people of great influence and will be of a great help to this new church. They will now have a membership of between thirty and forty with bright prospects for more. A number from other churches expect to join in the work soon. We have a new church here with a bright future. The interest spread far and near. Many came for miles to the services and I am sure that the spiritual uplift of the community is even of a greater benefit than the number of additions to the church. This meeting cost the league more than any meeting I have held in Virginia, but it was for the most important meeting we have held.

The last Sunday we had four services. Three preaching services in the church and a baptismal service in the First Brethren church in Roanoke. We took the people over in autos and Brother Donahue baptized them in Brother Wood's church.

Near the middle of the meeting, my little three-year-old grandchild, Kenneth Bowman, Junior, wandered away from home. He was as dear to me as my own child. It created the greatest stir for many years in Philadelphia. I went home and hundreds searched but no trace of him. I returned sorrowful to my work. After three weeks he was found dead in the water. I received the sad news after coming to Calvary where I am now engaged in a revival. I went home and attended the funeral. Brother McClain of the Tenth and Dauphin church preached the funeral sermon. I am now back at Calvary, New Jersey, where I am engaged in a two and one half weeks' meeting.

ISAAC D. BOWMAN.

NEW LEBANON

On Monday night after Easter we launched our evangelistic campaign for souls at New Lebanon. We had engaged Brother Arthur Lynn of the First Brethren church of Dayton to have charge of the singing. During the first week of the meeting Brother Lynn could only be with us two nights, being called to Chicago to inspect a new song book which is getting out. But during his absence Brother Cobb and some of his faithful co-workers kindly came to our rescue, furnishing "surprises" for our people. Neither were we permitted to have Brother Lynn for any Sunday services, he having to be at the First church of Dayton. We continued to storm the enemy's camp as best we could for three weeks and three nights. During this time there were several nights when we were without our lights (electric), because of stormy weather and we also had considerable rainy weather. Thus we had some hindrances, yet the Lord gave us great victory, for which we greatly rejoice. The immediate and visible results were 32 confessions, 20 of which were received into the church here by baptism, others came by relation and 3 by letter. Five of those remaining were taken into the Dayton church by baptism. One only has not yet gone further than to make public confession. We had the joy of baptizing five sisters (adults) out of one family. The father mother and two daughters are members of the Church of the Brethren, and this took the remaining members of this family. Twenty-two of those received were adults. Among these were some exceptionally fine young people,—very talented and able, who will be a very great strength to the work.

I can only speak in the highest terms of the excellent services rendered by our dear Brother Lynn. Not only is he one of the very sweetest singers I have ever heard, but he is a man of great consecration and prayer. Any pastor wanting the services of a singer can ot make a mistake in securing the services f Brother Lynn.

The members of the church also were very aithful in the matter of attendance. Indeed he attendance was all that could be expected, onsidering the time of year, etc. On Saturday and Sunday nights the capacity of the uilding was taxed to the utmost. Yet I am ure that these dear people would join with 1e in the words of another, saying, "Not nto us, O Lord, not unto us, but unto thy name give glory!" And again, "The Lord hath done great things for us; whereof we are glad."

The meeting closed with communion services. I am told that this was the largest communion service they have ever had there. There were about 150 who participated in the ordinances.

Previous to the revival there had been 7 additions to the church in the regular church services. Thus there have been 33 added to the church since December 1 of last year.

A Y. P. S. C. E. has been organized and is making splendid progress, considering the handicap of preaching services only every other Sunday evening, etc. However, these good people have received a larger vision of the great possibilities of the church at this place. Hence they have extended a call to their present unworthy servant for full time. Therefore, beginning October 1st, we shall give all our time to the work at this place, provided, of course, that a house be secured in which we can live.

Both these churches (West Alexandria and New Lebanon) have voted unanimously to keep out of the Interchurch World Movement. The endorsement I was represented to have given to this movement at the Pastor's Conference at Columbus, I wish to say, was not quite true to fact. I was not then prepared to commend or condemn the movement, and so stated.

We covet an interest in your prayers and pray that the blessing of the Lord may be upon his people everywhere.

GEO. W. KINZIE.

CANTON, OHIO-UNIONTOWN, PENNSYLVANIA

It has been a good while since any word came to the brotherhood from the church at Canton, Ohio, not because there was nothing to report however. The writer served the good people of the Canton charge for four years, and wants to bear testimony to the continued activity of the various departments of the church. By this it is not meant that all were active and faithful as they might be, for there are always those who feel lightly the obligation to loyalty and sacrifice for the good of the great cause of Christianity. But the constant faithfulness of the few makes up for the indifference of the some, and so the work goes on. When we entered the pastorate of the congregation there we scarcely expected to remain for so long, for the problems of the city church were so many and varied that it was a question to the pastor if he were able to solve them. But when the four years was ended and we knew we had given our word to change, we looked back over the years spent together and with real sincerity of heart could declare that they were pleasant ones. And the good folks at Canton really seemed to care that the preacher was leaving, for they said so, (and they are not given to prevarication), and beside that they announced a meeting of the Executive Board of the Bible school one evening a few weeks before our departure, and by a bit of maneuvering managed to get both the dominie and his helpmeet to go to the Board meeting at the church. And when we stepped into the church it was to find "everyman" and his wife and all the babies assembled, with the superintendent as master of ceremonies. And it was the strangest Board meeting I ever attended. They didn't say a thing about Sunday school matters, but had musical numbers,

by the orchestra, vocal and piano solos and duets, together with readings about preachers and their wives and their troubles, etc. And somewhere toward the last of the programme the master of ceremonies came over where the astounded pastor and wife were sitting and in a very neat little speech presented them with a black bag which was pretty heavy, and which he declared was a visible token of the good will and love of those whom they had served. And $51.00 is quite a substantial and acceptable token in these days of high prices. Well, yes, we said something in response to the presentation speech, but we don't know now what it was, only we know it was very poorly said because we were too moved with feeling to express ourselves very coherently. And then all repaired to the basement where refreshments were served and a social hour was spent. And so the "Board meeting" ended—but will not be soon forgotten by some folks.

We left the Canton church with all departments of the church active, if not so large. When we assumed charge of the work the congregation was carrying a debt of $1,800.00 on the church building. At leaving we have the satisfaction of knowing that the success of the plans is completely assured whereby the debt will be cleared from the property by the time of the next Ohio District Conference, and Canton will be ready to take her place among the independent congregations of the brotherhood. The financial record of the Canton church in four years shows an increase of from 15 percent to 33 1-3 percent in the contributions of the membership to the various departments of the church's activities. And the way the pocketbook responds to the appeals of the church is a kind of index to the spiritual life of the possessor.

We bespeak for Brother Vanator, the new pastor, a most fruitful and pleasant ministry among the brethren at Canton. There is room for plenty of hard work, but the man who isn't afraid of work will certainly see results and find that he has a willing group of followers.

We assumed charge of the work at Uniontown, Pennsylvania on Easter Sunday, and were greeted by excellent crowds at both the morning and evening services. Because of a failure somewhere between myself and the secretary of the Missionary Board the people at Uniontown failed to receive any supplies for the lifting of the Easter offering, and so we had to skirmish around and get some envelopes and work the matter up on short notice. But despite the hindrance the congregation did well on the offering, going well toward the hundred mark (do not have the exact figures). The attendance at the services has been slowly increasing, especially in the Bible school; there having been a gain each Sunday over the preceding until the sixteenth, when none of us were permitted to go to services at all on account of a scarlet fever quarantine in our section of the city. We are hoping this will last but a week or so, both for the good of the work and the health of the people.

Our coming to this work was rather in the nature of a homecoming, for we served this people in a four year pastorate in 1909-1913, and so we were not unfamiliar with the problems and conditions of the field. We found most of those with whom we formerly labored still active beside a goodly addition of substantial folks who have united with the church during the intervening years. And the folks have certainly tried to make it pleasant for the dominie and his helpmeet, since our arrival. On April 15 they held a reception at the parish house, when an excellent programme of music and speeches was rendered and a good social time was enjoyed by all. The congregation have purchased a parsonage, very conveniently located, for the use of the pastor, and here we are very comfortably located, within a block of the church and with a view of the church door from the front of

the parsonage and in a very fine residence district. Already we are feeling very much at home, and we are planning to do some real hard work with the good folks here.

Since arriving on the field we have had three funerals in the first four weeks, conducted all the regular services, preached at an adjoining coke town one Sunday afternoon and conducted the semi-annual communion service on May 9. This in addition to trying to get set up for housekeeping in the new parsonage has kept us pretty busy—and we have visited a goodly percentage of the members also.

We are praying for wisdom and grace to lead these good people into still larger fields of Christian character and attainment, and we crave an interest in the prayers of the brotherhood that we may be kept humble and teachable, so that God may use us to his glory and the extension of his kingdom and the hastening of his coming. DYOLL BELOTE.

THE TENTH ANNUAL CHRISTIAN ENDEAVOR AND SUNDAY SCHOOL CONVENTION OF SOUTHERN INDIANA DISTRICT

at College Corner, Tuesday and Wednesday, June 15 and 16, 1920.

Tuesday Evening, 8 P. M.

Song and Praise
Address of Welcome .... Marie Bowman
Response .... E. A. Myer
.... W. E. Ronk
.... J. W. Clark
Quartette .... College Corner
Address .... W. T. Lytle
Announcements
Song and Benediction

Wednesday, A. M.

8:30 Sunday School Session
Devotional .... Walter Shinn
8:50 Personal qualifications of a Sunday
School Superintendent, Elmer Gunion
9:10 The Nature and Work of the Missionary Superintendent ... L. W. Ditch
9:30 The Temperance Superintendent—His
Place and Work .... J. W. Clark
Song.
10:00 The Value of Adequate Music
L. A. Myers
10:20 Teaching to Win ..... W. E. Thomas
10:40 Getting Pupils to Study the Sunday
School Lessons ...... C. A. Stewart
Violin Solo .... Violet Hoeppner
11:10 Our Educational Task .. C. A. Bame
11:30 Announcements.
Appointment of Committees.

Wednesday P. M.

1:00 Christian Endeavor Session
Music .... Loree. Orchestra
Devotional .... Elmer Ebbinghaus
1:30 Reasons Why Each Church Should
Have a Christian Endeavor Society .
K. R. Ronk
1:50 How to Get the Young People to Sustain a Christian Endeavor,
J. W. Brower
2:10 The Problems of the Program Committee in the Rural Communities,
W. T. Lytle
Song
2:30 How Live Meetings are Conducted,
Nell Wycoff
2:50 Efficiency in Organization,
G. C. Carpenter
Solo .... Edith Brower
3:20 Securing Life Work Recruits,
W. E. Ronk
3:40 Round Table .... E. A. Myer
4:00 Committee Reports
Announcements
Song.

Wednesday Evening

7:45 Praise Service
Installation of New Officers
Special Music .... College Corner

Address .... Dr. C. A. Bame
Closing Song and Benediction.
    E. A. MYER, President,
    MABEL B. MAUS, Secretary.

**THE EIGHTH ANNUAL SUNDAY SCHOOL
AND CHRISTIAN ENDEAVOR CON-
VENTION OF THE BRETHREN
CHURCHES OF NORTHERN
INDIANA**

will be held at Nappanee, June 8th and 9th.

Tuesday Afternoon

2:00 Quiet Hour .... W. I. Duker
2:30 The Teacher and his Message,
                                C. C. Grisso
3:00 Relation of Sunday School to the
      Church .... A. E. Thomas
3:30 Sunday School Round Table,
                                Harry Price
4:00 Social Hour
7:15 Quiet Hour .... W. I. Duker
7:35 Pageant by Nappanee Juniors
7:50 Address by Indiana Christian Endea-
      vor Field Secretary ... E. D. Schmidt

Wednesday Forenoon

6:00 Prayer meeting
9:00 Quiet Hour .... W. I. Duker
9:30 Value of Standards of Efficiency—Ex-
      cellence and Four Year Program to the
      Local Christian Endeavor Societies,
                                C. E. Kolb
9:50 Christian Endeavor Round Table,
                                Glen Carpenter
10:20 Business Session and Reports of So-
      cieties.
11:20 Challenge of the Present World Situa-
      tion to Young Life of the Church,
                                G. W. Rench

Wednesday Afternoon

1:30 Quiet Hour .... W. I. Duker
1:45 Miscellaneous
2:15 Intermediates,
                                Mrs. H. H. Wolford
                                Mrs. Cora Stuckman
      Juniors ...... Mrs. Harry Richmond
      Sunday School ..... H. H. Wolford

**THE MIAMI VALLEY SUNDAY SCHOOL
AND CHRISTIAN ENDEAVOR CON-
FERENCE TO BE HELD AT NEW
LEBANON, OHIO, JUNE 19-20.**

Saturday Forenoon

9:15 Song Service
9:30 Invocation
      Address of Welcome
      Response ..... Miss Alice Wogoman
10:00 Need of a Life Work ..W. C. Teeter
10:30 Meaning of Life Work,
                                Sylvester Lowman

Saturday Afternoon

1:30 Song Service
1:45 —
2:15 Christian Endeavor a Recruiting
      Agency .... J. A. Garber
2:45 Young People in the Church,
                                G. W. Kinzie
3:15 Business Session

Saturday Evening

6:00 Banquet
7:15 Song Service .... Prof. Lynn
7:45 Retrospect .... E. A. Rowsey
8:15 Prospect .... J. S. Cook

Sunday Forenoon

9:00 Prayer Service
9:15 Song Service and Sunday School
10:30 Sermon—The Real Vision of Life
      Work .... C. E. Beekley
11:30 Basket Dinner

Sunday Afternoon

2:00 Song Service
2:30 Conserving Vital Forces of Life,
                                Dr. J. M. Wine
3:00 The Question Box

Sunday Evening

6:30 Model C. E. Meeting
7:15 Song Service
7:30 Pageant
8:30 Young People and the World's Work
                                J. A. GARBER.

Communion Notice

The Homerville Brethren church will observe holy communion Sunday evening, June
13. All of like faith are invited.
                        AUSTIN R. STALEY, Pastor.

Announcements

THE BRETHREN LOYAL AS USUAL

The following is a copy of a letter sent by
our General Conference Temperance Committee chairman to the prohibition leaders of the
several parties. These leaders have pledged
to use such protests and whatever other influence they may be able to wield to bring
the political parties to support the Volstead
enforcement act.—Editor.

The Hon.——
                Washington, D. C.

My dear sir:
    It having been brought to our notice
through the columns of the newspapers that
certain elements in our political life will endeavor to do violence to the Volstead Act
and the national prohibition amendment during the coming campaign, I take this means
of putting the membership of the Brethren
churches in the United States, numbering over
25,000 communicants, on record as having opposed at each annual convention for years, the
sale, manufacture for sale and use of intoxicating liquors for beverage purposes, as well
as candidates for office who approve such
business. Praying that you will use this at
your national convention, and otherwise in
the cause of prohibition, I am
                Very truly yours,
                E. L. MILLER, Nappanee, Indiana.
Chairman Committee on Temperance,
Brethren Church.

The Sunday School and Christian Endeavor
Convention of the Southern District will convene at College Corner Brethren church, June
15th and 16th. This church is out in the
country, about ten miles from a railroad, but
those desiring to come by rail will either notify Brother Ernest Kurtz by letter beforehand or come to Wabash and telephone to him.
In either case arrangements will be made to
meet any such persons. We hope to have a
large attendance with all the Sunday schools

To the Citizens of America

One year of Prohibition has brought more
laughter to children and more smiles to women than any other legislation.
    It has turned almshouses and breweries into
factories, jails into corncribs, and brought
their inmates forward into the great industrial
army.
    It has added untold billions to the nation's
wealth, transferred money from the saloon
tills to savings banks and newly erected
homes.
    The Eighteenth Amendment has increased
farm and city values, quickened industry and
brought to the United States the greatest era
of prosperity ever known.
    The pro-liquor element is doing its utmost
to repeal the Volstead Act.
    It would nullify the Eighteenth Amend-
ment, which would mean the overthrow of
National Prohibition and its attendant prosperity.
    The liquor minority proposes to attain its
ends by capturing the national conventions of
the political parties.
    The dry majority, as demonstrated by rat-
ification in forty-five states, MUST CONTROL
these conventions.
    We ask you to get every state, district and
local organization of whatever kind within
your reach, to ADOPT RESOLUTIONS substantially as follows:
    Be it resolved, that we hereby authorize our

and Christian Endeavor societies represented
and the College Corner folks are making arrangements accordingly.   L. A. MYERS,
                Pastor College Corner Church.

CHRISTIAN ENDEAVOR AT COLUMBUS

All roads are said to lead to Columbus and
they will be much traveled by young people
over June 22-25. They are invited to come
6,000 strong to share in the great triangular
convention, that is senior, intermediate and
junior. Every society is urged to send at
least one delegate. Mr. Chas. M. Alexander
will be the popular song leader. The prominent speakers are Drs. Daniel A. Poling, Ira
Landrith, W. O. Thompson, Chas. F. Wishart.
The departmental conferences will be very
helpful.
                        J. A. GARBER.

A Brethren Secretary

Brethren Endeavorers will find reasons for
particular pride in this convention. At that
time Brother E. A. Rowsey will be introduced as the new Associate Secretary of the
Ohio Union. He just graduated from Ashland
and soon will close his pastorate at Mansfield
to enter upon his new duties with offices in
Columbus. Keenly as we feel our loss of this
energetic pastor, we may rejoice in our ability to give such a promising young man to
the larger cause of Christian Endeavor.

Ohio Conventions

During this month our Ohio people will
have the privilege of sharing the instruction
and inspiration of two great conventions. It
is to be regretted that both meet on the
same days, but the conflict seemed unavoidable. The days to be marked on the calendar are June 22-25.

Sunday School at Hamilton

Hamilton will entertain the Sunday school
workers on the Harvard Plan (lodging and
breakfast free). They will enjoy a three-in-
one convention, consisting of an Association
Officers' Conference on the 22nd, a Daily Vacation Bible School Institute on the afternoons of 22, 23, 24 and the 61st State Convention 23, 24, 25. Speakers of national and
state-wide reputation have been secured. The
head-liners are Professor Wrightsman of Boston, Cope of Chicago and Hutchins of Oberlin. In addition Mr. W. C. Pearce and Prof.
A. M. Loeker will represent the International
Association. Let Brethren schools strive to
send a delegate. Credentials may be obtained
from your county secretary.

names to be used at each and every political
convention to be held in 1920, notifying the
leaders of all parties that we will support such
parties as specifically endorse by platform declaration, the Eighteenth Amendment as interpreted by the Volstead Act, or some measure
equally effective; and nominate candidates
unequivocally committed to its enforcement."
    Immediately wire a copy of your resolutions
to each of the following persons who have
agreed to act as custodians of these resolutions for their respective parties:
    U. S. Senator Arthur Capper, Washington,
D. C. (Republican);
    U. S. Senator Morris Sheppard, Washing-
ton, D. C. (Democrat);
    Congressman Charles H. Randall, Washing-
ton, D. C. (Prohibitionist).
    The crisis is real. Time is short. Republi-
can convention meets June 8. Democratic
convention June 21. Immediate action is necessary.

                ARTHUR DEAN BEVAN
                CLARENCE TRUE WILSON
                E. J. FITHIAN
                IRVING FISHER
                DANIEL A. POLING
                FRANCES E. BEAUCHAMP
                FRANCIS BALDWIN
                J. H. KELLOGG
                MARGARET WINTHINGER
                VIRGIL G. HINSHAW.

Volume XLII
Number 22

June 9
1920

The BRETHREN EVANGELIST

-ONE·IS·YOUR·MASTER·AND·ALL·YE·ARE·BRETHREN-

YOU ARE INVITED

To give one day in 1920 to the children of Serbia

YOUR BIRTHDAY

Just that one day - - - Make it a day of service

While your friends celebrate, you share your gladness
with the world, through a little child in need

"They wander about the country in forlorn, ragged bands, feeding themselves, as the animals do; at night they lie upon the bare ground, or, huddled in the corner of some vacant building, sob themselves to sleep."
—Com. Wm. J. Doherty.

"One out of every seven persons in Serbia is an orphan child."
— Sgt. Ruth Farnam.
"Children's diseases are scourges in Serbia — eighty-five percent of the children need a doctor's care."
—Hon. Homer Folks.

Send birthday offerings to National Birthday Committee of Serbian Child
Welfare Association, 7 West 8th St., New York City.

Published every Wednesday at Ashland, Ohio. All matter for publication must reach the Editor not later than Friday noon of the preceding week.

George S. Baer, Editor

The
Brethren
Evangelist

When ordering your paper changed give old as well as new address. Subscriptions discontinued at expiration. To avoid missing any numbers renew two weeks in advance.

R. R. Teeter, Business Manager

OFFICIAL ORGAN OF THE BRETHREN CHURCH

Subscription price, $2.00 per year, payable in advance.
Entered at the Post Office at Ashland, Ohio, as second-class matter.
Acceptance for mailing at special rate of postage provided for in section 1103, Act of October 3, 1917, authorized September 9, 1918.
Address all matter for publication to Geo. S. Baer, Editor of the Brethren Evangelist, and all business communications to R. R. Teeter, Business Manager, Brethren Publishing Company, Ashland, Ohio. Make all checks payable to the Brethren Publishing Company.

EDITORIAL

Some One Raises An Old Question—"Is the Church Failing?"

Writing under the spell of discouragement, some one asks, "Is not the church failing?" Doubtless every soul who is seriously and zealously concerned about bringing in the kingdom of God has experienced hours of discouragement when he has been disposed to ask the same question. In such times it is very reassuring to lift the eyes from the particular discouraging features with which we have been faced and with one broad sweep take in the whole of God's advancing kingdom. Sometimes our own plans fail and we think the whole church is failing. Sometimes certain ideals fail to be realized and we think the entire foundation of the church has given way. Sometimes in God's long day there come hours when his program for the church seems to be rejected; men leave undone the weightier matters of the law such as love, justice, mercy, and spend their time quibbling over the distance of a Sabbath day's journey, or who is one's neighbor; men are lovers of pleasure more than lovers of God and it seems that the sincere, serious souls are growing fewer every day; men are haters of one another and there is fighting and bloodshed and destruction, at such times we are tempted to think that the power of God is not sufficient and that the world is hastening with all possible speed to perdition. Much of our pessimism is due to the fact that we confine our attention to one or a few discouraging incidents or one small period of time. There is doubtless much desert land yet remaining in the world, but many a waste place has been transformed and made to blossom as the rose. If happily we live in a place or a time of moral and spiritual barrenness, it will save us many a needless gloomy hour if we lift our eyes and look beyond our little desert and contemplate the many fertile fields where the kingdom of God like good seed, is growing and bringing forth abundantly We are too quick to generalize from a few particulars; we thereby do the church much harm and pervert our own judgment. If we are to estimate aright the strength and vitality of the church, its pervading and prevailing power, we must look over the world and across the centuries.

No, the church is not failing; it is not on the verge of failure. The thoughtful student of history cannot but see that the church has been growing more and more triumphant from the first century until now, even though there has been occasional periods of temporary decadence and relaxation. Many and wonderful victories have been won through the all-prevailing name of Jesus. Multitudes of sinners have been reclaimed from the error of their ways, through the instrumentality of the church, and transformed into saints. Womanhood has been exalted; infanticide banished; immorality condemned and the marriage vow sanctified. Slavery has been destroyed; religious freedom guaranteed and the saloon outlawed. Hospitals, asylums and orphanages have been built; libraries and school systems have been established and church houses erected all over the land. Uplifting community centers in the midst of degenerate industrial districts, the reform of penal institutions, regulation of child labor, the establishment of children's courts, these and many other things bear eloquent testimony to the prevailing influence of the church of Christ. And more directly it is inspiring thousands by its noble worship, calling out leaders who give their talents unselfishly to the advancement of the kingdom of Christ and sending its missionaries to the uttermost parts of the earth. It is giving of its money as it has never done before; calling men to more humble and powerful

prayer and more deeply devotional living and sending them forth to more sincere and effective service.

The church is not failing in any of the noble works that have swept within its vision. Not everything that it has undertaken has been, or is being done perfectly, because it is composed of and works through the agency of fallible human beings. Its vision has not always been as broad as it ought to have been, nor has its faith always been as strong as it might have been, because human weakness militates even against a church doing its best. But in spite of its weaknesses and imperfections, it is the world's noblest instrument of uplift and the only means of individual salvation. It has ever gone forward and will never fail. Keep faith in it as you keep faith in God for it is God's church.

A Unique Letter of Appreciation

From the Ecumenical Patriarchate, the highest authority of the Greek Orthodox church, comes this interesting word of appreciation, sent by the Greek Patriarch to those who have so earnestly worked for the destitute peoples of the Near East during their years of suffering:

"Honorable Gentlemen who constitute the American Committee for relief in the Near East.

"We bless your precious Honors praying cordially.

"In accordance to the special decision of the two Higher Administrative Bodies among us, that is, the Holy and Sacred Synod and the National Mixed Council, we beg to express once more to your Esteemed Committee the warmest thanks and the gratitude of our church and Nation for your great and noble help for the relief of the Greeks in Asia Minor and Thrace. Your generous gifts given and continuing to come, out of such a superb philanthropic thought and predilection, on behalf of our brethren in their most difficult circumstances, move us most profoundly.

"May the Lord God reward ten thousand fold all those, who either by their kind care and efforts or by their financial aid contribute to the comfort and strengthening of the poor Christians here who survived the savage and cruel persecution. Invoking blessings from above upon your whole great and glorious country also, we pray that God may grant your Honors the best gifts with many years of health and joy."

There are 11,000 refugees starving in Pergama, Asia Minor one of the "Seven Churches" of Asia mentioned in the book of revelations, now being aided by the Near East Relief. Thousands in the Black Sea region are being cared for in orphanages, hospitals, and relief stations, by this same organization, through which the American people send aid to a stricken people. The need is still great and all gifts sent to the Near East Relief, 1 Madison Avenue, New York, will be applied to this worthy cause. May the Brethren continue their generous gifts and their prayers.

EDITORIAL REVIEW

Sister U. J. Shively announces the date for Summer School of Missions at Winona Lake, beginning June 24 and the Lake Geneva school, beginning August 17.

—The work at North Liberty and Tiosa, Indiana, under the pastoral care of Brother C. C. Grisso is moving forward in fine style. Confessions and baptisms are reported from both places, the communion services were largely attended and the various departments are alive and aggressive.

Brother Freeman Ankrum, pastor of the Garwin, Iowa, congregation gives encouraging news concerning the work at that place. Though the winter months settled hard on this brave people, yet they are bestirring themselves nobly to make up for lost time. They are in a Sunday school contest now that promises much and, though delayed, they gave a splendid foreign mission offering.

Brother Snyder reports the good meeting that Milledgeville enjoyed under the evangelistic leadership of Brother Bell, who was the instrument in God's hands for turning sixteen souls unto their Lord. Aside from the evangelistic success, the generous Easter offering and the largely attended communion bear witness to the good spiritual condition of Milledgeville church under the shepherding care of Brother Snyder.

Brother A. L. DeLozier reports for the Allentown work and it is to be observed that steady progress is being made. He speaks highly of Brother Watsons' help recently given in an evangelistic effort. Brother DeLozier announces his resignation to answer a call to a teaching position on the Ashland College faculty.

President Jacobs favors us with a report of Commencement week exercises. It is gratifying to note the long list of full-fledged college graduates, and among them is one post-graduate student. This is said to be the largest number of degreed students that Ashland College ever turned out any one year. If you want to see your college do that every year, keep continually sending your high school graduates to Ashland for their college course.

Brother Bell reports briefly his evangelistic meeting with Brother Stuckman at Falls City, Nebraska. It resulted very successfully as our readers have already learned through the report of the pastor. We don't doubt that "home looks good" to Brother Bell now after so many months' absence, and we are sure he deserves a much needed rest, which he expects to enter upon at the close of his meeting at La Verne which is his tenth campaign since General Conference.

Progress is again reported from the Beaver City, Nebraska, church by the pastor, Brother E. S. Flora. This progress is evidenced in a number of ways, especially by an increase in membership of 20 percent and their larger gifts to missions and other forms of the Lord's work. These larger gifts are due, according to the pastor to the increase of the tithing band. The pastor and his wife experienced a pleasant and profitable celebration of their first wedding anniversary at the hands of their parishioners.

Our readers were doubtless confused by the typographical error in the first question on front page last week. It took only one wrong letter to take away the clarity of the sentence. F got in the place of B and changed the word or to of. The question should have read, "What do you consider has been the historic genius or dominating distinctive characteristics of the Brethren church?" Get your last week's Evangelist, make the correction and re-read the splendid array of answers.

Brother A. B. Cover, the faithful pastor of Hagerstown, Maryland, church, shares with the Evangelist family the news of the progress in the Lord's work at that place. He and his people co-operated in the Easter season evangelistic campaign and splendid results were realized. The Sunday school is organized for larger work and special attention is being given to training more teachers. It sounds good to learn that the women's organization is concerned about a parsonage for their pastor. If churches realized what an advantage it is to themselves as well as to the pastor to have a parsonage more of them would sacrifice till they get one.

"Campaign Notes" come again like a refreshing shower in the heat of summer. Brother Beachler is at it again. He is now among the churches of the Maryland-Virginia district. But the current report is of the canvass made at Garwin, Iowa, and an excellent report it is. It is evident that Beachler found loyal friends of Ashland College there. We would not expect to find it otherwise with a loyal Ashland College graduate, such as Brother Ankrum is, in charge as pastor. Ashland's graduates have it in their power to make their Alma Mater all she ought to be, and many of them are exercising their influence very effectively. God bless Brother Ankrum and his splendid co-workers. Now all eyes will be turned expectantly to the loyal Virginians and Marylanders.

GENERAL ARTICLES
Made Free Indeed.   By M. A. Witter
(Baccalaureate sermon preached before graduating class of Waynesboro, Pa., High School.)

Text: If ye continue in my word then are ye my disciples indeed; and ye shall know the truth and the truth shall make you free.— John 8:31, 32.

He who builds his life today must build amid the storms of error doubt and discontent. On every hand we are faced by lack of assurance. All is uncertainty, nothing is steadfast and permanent. Old governments are falling and new ones are being born. Great areas lie in doubt not knowing what their government is to be. The good things of yesterday are obsolete today and tomorrow will find today's favorites cast aside for new. Industrial and commercial relations are in a state of ferment and no one is ready to prophesy just what the outcome will be. In religion there are fads and isms innumerable from that of the theosophist with his belief in the transmigration of souls to the Christian Scientist with his denial of the testimony of all of the natural senses. The world is experiencing a deluge of doubt, error, and vague uncertainty.

Above the tumult of these conflicting storms it is refreshing to hear the voice of the Son of God declaring with all authority, "Ye shall know the truth, and the truth shall make you free." We are not doomed to be driven helplessly about by these tempests of anxious foreboding and uncertain conjecture. There is a solid rock upon which we may build our house and it shall not fall though the storms rage and the floods come and the winds beat upon it with demoniacal fury. The sure foundation that will stand the strain is the solid rock of TRUTH. A life built upon error is foredoomed to ruin. A life built upon a series of guesses is destined to certain failure, but

"THE TRUTH SHALL MAKE YOU FREE"

To attempt to build a life without knowing the truth about the world in which we live is as hazardous as the fabled adventure of those who built their camp upon the back of the sleeping sea monster thinking they were on an island until the monster plunged beneath the waves.

To build a life without knowing the truth about eternity is like investing one's whole wealth in a brilliantly lighted palace of ice. It is dazzlingly beautiful but destitute of comfort while it stands and melts away in the first warm day.

To build a life without knowing the truth about eternity is like unwise than to attempt to build a business block in a city without first securing a building permit or without conforming to the ordinances of the city. The laws of city or nation may sometimes be evaded but the laws of God are unerring in their working and evasion is impossible. We are on his territory and if our building is to stand it must be with his persuasion.

To build a life without knowing the truth about self and the purpose of our own being is worse than spending our time blowing bubbles when we might be reigning as kings and queens and meeting the deepest needs of our fellow-men in efficient service.

He who knows the truth is free from the cunning attacks of error, falsehood and deception. He who knows the truth of the love of God is free from all fears of man or devil. He knows that "God is love," and "perfect love casteth out fear."

He who knows the truth about adversity is free from irksome

rebellion against the fiery trials by which his life is purged from its dross, leaving only the purified gold of true worth. He understands that his Master was made perfect through suffering and that "all things work together for good to them that love God."

Those who know the truth about sin do not fall victims to the seductive counterfeits of love, counterfeits of joy and counterfeits of peace.

The truth about service sets free from the drudgery of toil and converts it into a privilege, for across the path of toil is seen the shadow of the Master with saw and plane. Those who know the truth about the Christ, the Son of the living God, are free forever from the questionings, and doubts that make men afraid of his guiding hand. To know his mission from heaven to earth in our behalf, his sinless life of loving service, his willing sacrifice on Calvary for our sins, his resurrection from the dead, his ascension and present position at the Father's right hand our ever-living Intercessor; to know him is to be free from the power of sin, free from the penalty of sin, free from death itself, for to know him is life eternal.

'He is the freeman whom the truth makes free,
And all are slaves beside. There's not a chain
That hellish foes confederate for his harm
Can wind around him, but he casts it off
With as much ease as Samson his green withes."

"YE SHALL KNOW THE TRUTH"

But can the truth be known? Doubt would whisper that it is not possible for finite man to be sure of the truth; that the best we can hope for is a good guess; that in dealing with things of life and spirit, of God and eternity, man is hopelessly beyond his depths and cannot know. But in answer to these whisperings we hear the clear cut statement of the Son of God, "Ye shall know the truth and the truth shal make you free." That promise has been verified by the thousands of his believing children who like Paul have learned to say in truth, "I know whom I have believed."

God has not mocked us by leaving us in a world of a thousand conflicting calls and a labrynth of paths and by-paths without providing a means whereby we may know the truth and find the way to attain the highest possibility of our being.

But let us examine this promise more closely and see to whom it is made and the condition upon which it may be claimed. "If ye continue in my word,"—here is the condition "then are ye my disciples indeed and ye shall know the truth and the truth shall make you free." The promise is to them that continue in his word. "He that willeth to do his will shall know." A knowledge of the truth is conditioned upon willingness to obey the truth. Luther Burbank, the "Plant Wizard," has accomplished the wonders credited to him by the most precise obedience to the laws of plant culture. He has come to know truth in his special field by obedience to truth. Thomas A. Edison has become the master of truth in the field of invention because he has been unwavering in his obedience to truth as rapidly as it was revealed in his special field. This principle applies to truth in every realm. In the great work of building a life spiritual blindness is the penalty of disobedience to known truth. But to the loyal willing soul God himself becomes teacher and opens up great areas of wonderful truth and bids the obedient pupil take possession.

"THEN YE ARE MY DISCIPLES INDEED"

"My disciples," my pupils, what a privilege is here promised. To sit at the feet of the Creator of all and to be his disciples to let him teach us the deep things of life, to hear his voice explaining the mysteries of life, solving life's problems, and directing our journey on the way of everlasting success and victory—this is the privilege of the one who wills to do the will of him whose word is truth.

I visited a factory and saw the workers busily engaged in making the pieces of a complicated machine. I asked a worker to tell me about the piece that he was making and to explain the part it was to play in the finished machine, but he could not tell. He could tell all about the material of which the part was made, he could tell to the thousandth of an inch the size and shape that it must be, but he did not know the part it must play in the finished machine. Thus the inventor took me to another part of the shop and I saw where the parts were assembled and fitted together and he explained to me the place of that part in the finished machine and its work. It is only as we sit at the feet of the great Inventor of all that we can learn the purpose of our lives and the relation of all truth to the life

that we are building and the relation of that life to his great purpose in all.

Any student of history may rehearse to you the facts of history, may tell you of the rise and fall of nations and may trace the shifting races as they have marched to and fro over the battle fields of the world. But it is only the believing and obedient student of God's prophetic word that can discern the invisible but almighty hand of the Lord of Hosts shifting the scenes and lifting up or casting down the nations of the earth according to his eternal and loving purposes for the welfare of his creatures.

Any astronomer may be able to compute the distance to the stars, accurately, to estimate their speed, weigh them and tell you of the elements that enter into their composition; but it is only to the obedient disciples of the Lord that the heavens declare the glory of God.

Any successful business man can give excellent advice as to the careful investment of funds and as to the efficient management of financial interests but unless he has become a learner in the school of our Lord he has not made his investment where neither moth nor rust doth corrupt nor thieves break through and steal.

The sociologist can tell you the conditions in which the people of the world are living. He may tell you more or less accurately of the conditions in which crime thrives and where prosperity and self-respect prevails. His knowledge of the philanthropies of kind hearted men and of others may be cheering; but unless he has been taught by the Spirit of God he has not found either the cure for sin or the recipe for peace, for the only fountain that can cleanse the heart from sin is the fountain of blood shed for sinners and the only abiding peace of the soul that rests in God's forgiving love.

It is only the knowledge of truth as taught by the divine Author of all truth that can make us free. "If the Son shall make you free ye shall be free indeed." Of what use is the knowledge of the achievements of men and nations if we fail to discern the connection between their sin and their ruin or between their loyalty to God and their triumph. What shall it profit us to know every star familiarly by name, if their steadfast obedience to their appointed orbit fails to thrill us with the longing to attune our lives to the will of their Maker and ours. What shall it avail if we achieve the greatest financial success if we have not made sure the inheritance undefiled and that fadeth not away.

Members of the class of 1920, your school days in Waynesboro high school are nearly ended. Four more days and then commencement. Four well spent years have brought you to the well earned goal. I congratulate you. But your school days are not over. Some of you will continue your studies in college. I could wish that for all of you. But wherever your course may lead you, you will be in the great school of life. In that school many have met defeat, discouragement and bondage. They have not continued in his word; they have not known the truth and they are not free but on the way to miserable failure in the final examination of the great judgment. Others, and I pray that these may include every one of you, have met victory and freedom and peace. These have learned truth from the great Master. They are free. They shall not come into the judgment but on the great Commencement Day they shall receive as their diploma the crown of life that fadeth not away.

Waynesboro, Pennsylvania.

Tithing. By N. J. Paul

I feel very much reluctant to discuss this subject. Only by request that we discuss it at all. However we will do the best we can, trusting to the Holy Spirit to assist us. As we understand the scriptures, the Bible gives the church a financial plan, but, to my mind, the church for the last hundred years or more, has practically ignored that plan. Many Bible students acknowledge that the Bible demands that we shall acknowledge our stewardship to God by the payment of the tenth, at least, of our income to the church. Tithe paying can be traced back through all the principal nations of the world—kings and people alike paying the tenth and more to their gods in support of their priests and temples. It is found in Egypt more than 3,000 years B. C., in Babylonia at least 2100 years B. C.; among the earliest people of Europe, including the Pelasgi, the Argives and legendary kings of Rome 1300 B. C., and later "Spartan generals, Roman dictators, lawyers and farmers, Greek shepherds, sailors, merchants, miners, cooks—nay, even dissolute women—thinking it right and religious to offer a tenth to the gods." The Septuagint translation of Genesis 4:7, in reference to Cain's offering, says: "If thou didst rightly offer, but didst not rightly divide, didst thou not sin?" Paul probably had this in mind when, in Hebrews 11:4, he said: "By faith Abel offered unto God a more abundant sacrifice than Cain." The very early Christian writers, such as Tertullian, Clement of Rome, and others claim that Cain failed to bring the full tenth as God had directed, and therefore sinned. Abraham and Jacob recognized this obligation (Gen. 14:20, 28:22); and about 500 years later the law was incorporated in the Bible as we have it in Leviticus 27:30-34. It was obeyed with more or less faithfulness by the Jews to the destruction of their nation, A. D. 70. Malachi charges the people with robbing God when the tithes were withheld (Mal. 3:8-10). About 150 years before Christ a sect of the Pharisees arose, whose main objects were to secure the strict observance of the law of the tithe and ceremonial purity. These Pharisees would not eat with any one who was not a strict tither, but we find this sect invited Christ to eat with some of the chief of them, which goes to show that Christ himself was a tither (Luke 11:37, 14:1). Christ came not to destroy the law, but said, "Whosoever should do and teach it should be called great in the kingdom of heaven" (Matt. 5:15-17). He told his disciples to do what the Pharisees taught because they sat in Moses' seat (Matt. 23:2, 3) and that their righteousness must exceed the righteousness of the Pharisees (Matt. 5:20). He required the rich young ruler to keep the commandments. He did not promulgate anew these laws, including the tithe, but taught and practiced and expanded them, showing that they could be broken in spirit, by thought, word of even look. Paul, in Romans 3:31, says, "Do we then make the law of none effect through faith? Nay, we establish the law." He bases his claim for the Levites, and says, "Even so hath the Lord ordained that they that preach the gospel should live of the gospel," if we acknowledge our relationship to God as stewards of the money we handle, and maintain the public worship of God, not as we will, but as he wills, by complying with the law. Paying tithes is neither typical nor ceremonial and was never repealed. The great heads of the church immediately following the days of the apostles continued to practice tithing and taught it binding upon all Christians. "Our Lord came to expand the law" and taught that, "instead of paying tithes, to divide all of one's goods to the poor, which is not a dissolving of the law, but enlarging it." Tertullian, Ambros, Hilary, Eusebius the great church historian, Chrysotom and Augustine, who says, "Tithes are required as a matter of debt," all bear witness to the importance of paying the tithe. Not a single voice of authority is raised against the tithe among all these great leaders of the church, immediately following the days of the apostles. Tithing was the universal practice of the church for 1,500 years. We shall fail in the battle against the world, the flesh, and the devil and never be able to build up Christlike perfection of character, when we are not willing to give up all, even our life, to secure this end; for our spiritual building is never complete till it is Christlike. "Whoso, therefore, renounceth not all that he hath, he can not be my disciple." This pierces the heart of our selfish nature, and so it should, for the carnal self is enmity against God and the root of all evil. The mind of Christ was flooded with a mighty thought, the thought of the kingdom of God. That thought filled all his moods, his expression, his words, his thoughts. But after his ascension his disciples saw something larger than the kingdom of God—Christ is larger than his kingdom. He said, "I am the way, the truth and the life." He is the way into truth; his is the Life by which we live the truth we know. And so the disciples preached Christ. Christ preached the kingdom of God; they preached him. The two mites of the "poor widow" outweighed the shekels of gold and silver cast by jewelled fingers into the Lord's treasury. The drops make the rivulets, and the rivulets fill the lakes. Nine-tenths of all the money that drives the financial machineries of the church comes from relatively small sums. Where there is one magnificent giver, there are ten thousand humbler stewards. Whose "sacred money" is reckoned by dimes, and not by hundreds or thousands. But listen, the gifts to the Lord are to be weighed rather than counted. God does not look at the amount of the gift, as much as he does at the motive that prompted the gift. Jesus considered the giving of the tenth as a self-evident duty—even beyond any question when he said, "That it ought not be left un-

done" (Matt. 23:23). (The word ought in Matthew 23:23, is a stronger expression of obligation, in the original, than the ought in John 13:14). If one-tenth is commanded, as a just debt we owe the church, and we keep a strict account of our income, and turn over the tenth, then we have only paid that which we owed, and have not given anything, not even two mites.

Paying or giving should be systematic and proportionate. They should be from the first-fruits, and not the dregs. "See first the kingdom of God." The Old Testament gives all the light needed on this matter, and so Paul ordered the churches in Corinth and Galatia (I, Cor. 16:1, 2). to do accordingly, "But you say, "Be led by the Spirit," "We are not under the law, but under grace," Yes, we say, "Be led by the Spirit," but who can believe that the true Spirit leads one to give less than one-tenth so that all shall give in proportion to their ability? The Spirit's leading was very evident in the days of the apostles, and it led men to sell all and lay it at the apostles' feet. No man is led by the Spirit, who is not willing to follow the teaching of Christ, and that would certainly lead to giving more than one-tenth.

Christ lived what he taught. Paul, the apostle of freedom, declares himself to be always under the law to Christ (1 Cor. 9:21). The new covenant is one in which God will put his law in the inward parts and write it on the heart.

Christ's Value of Gifts

When our Lord sat over against the treasury, he saw many that were rich, who cast in much, but it was of their abundance. There was no real sacrifice in their giving. It cost them nothing; their lives were just as full and comfortable as ever. Their abundant gifts did not express any special love or devotion to God. Their giving, like much of ours today, was only part of an easy and traditional religion. The widow cast in her farthing. It was all she had; even her living. It was the expression of her heart's love and devotion. An her self-sacrificing gift called forth the Master's approval and blessing. That Widow's farthings has been shining through the ages with a luster brighter than gold. The world asks how much a man gives; Christ asks how much he keeps. The world looks at the gift; Christ values the gift by the unseen motive behind it. Why ARE YOU NOT A TITHER?

Is it because—
1. You think the tithe system has passed away with the old Mosaic laws?
2. You prefer to fix your standard rather than use God's standard?
3. You think the New Testament does away with the system?
Do you know—
1. That God required one tenth in the Patriarchal dispensation, at least one-fifth in the Mosaic dispensation, and what in the Christian dispensation? Not less surely, but more.
2. That he who fixes on less than one-tenth deliberately excludes all Scriptural instruction and chooses a standard for which no justification can be found in God's Word?
3. That the Old Testament required one-seventh of time and one-tenth of money, and that the New Testament does not require less of either, but rather more? The New Testament does not abolish the law of the Sabbath, neither does it abolish the law of the tithe. He who takes either for his own robs God, his word being witness. Each is a minimum, demanded without reservation. The New Testament did not stress the law of the tithe, because it was accepted as a universal principal and practice and the exhortation is for yet larger giving. We of the Christian dispensation are not justified in falling short of the Old Testament Jew. In the light of the Gospel of the Son of God we are to pay the tithe and then give as God has prospered us.

Losantville, Indiana.

Have you given your life into the direction of God? Do you really believe that you are spirit-led? If you do, let God alone and take what he gives you. What seems bitter in the bud may be sweet in the flower. Rebecca made a great muddle of the life of Jacob by trying to take it out of the hands of God. God had promised, but she was not willing to wait. If you will trust him, God will stand by you.—The Methodist Protestant.

NEWS FROM THE FIELD

MILLEDGEVILLE, ILLINOIS

The work at this place has been moving in the right direction since our last report in the church paper. Both Sunday school and church services were well attended through the winter, and the outlook is good for continued progress and increase.

Our evangelistic campaign this year was held in April, with Brother W. S. Bell as the evangelist. We had favorable weather conditions, and the campaign resulted in much good. The evangelist gave messages designed to build up the church spiritually and to call sinners to repentance; and the writer counts it a privilege and a blessing to have had the opportunity of working with him in this kingdom enterprise. As a result of our meeting sixteen have already been baptized and received into the church, and four more will follow in the good way in the near future.

On May 4th we sent Brother Gearhart our annual offering for foreign missions, amounting to $565.55. This was by far the largest missionary offering this church has ever made, and it is hoped that the blessings which follow such giving will be so apparent that we will be encouraged to exceed this amount next year. The amount given averages more than $2.80 per member. But it should be stated that over two-thirds of this amount was given by one family, a consecrated farmer and wife who tithe their worldly goods. Their worthy example is both a rebuke and an incentive to others who have done so much less.

Our communion services were held on May 9th, and were more largely attended than at any previous time during the writer's pastorate here. In addition to a larger attendance of our own members, over forty of the Brethren from Lanark came over with their pastor and Rev. Livengood. We were delighted to have them with us and share in the blessings of the communion services.

We are now facing the summer months, but shall do all we can to keep the interests of the kingdom moving forward, and believe that with the earnest co-operation of a faithful and loyal people we will go on from victory unto victory in Christ's name.

MILES J. SNYDER.

BEAVER CITY, NEBRASKA, BRETHREN CHURCH

Our correspondent and our brother, Elder Forney have been keeping the brotherhood in touch with the church activities at Beaver City, however, there are some good things better said by the pastor. Nearly a year has passed since we took up the work at this place. We found here a thoroughly well organized work, with good Christian leaders, always ready to do things for the church. During this year there has been no relapse in the work. The Sunday school has been gaining in members and regular attendance. All other auxiliaries of the church are on the forward move. Due to the good work of the people we have added to the membership in the church until the membership shows over a twenty percent increase for the past year. Almost all of these have been admitted by baptism.

Our people are awake in giving to missions and to other worthy causes. Tithing is largely due to the way in which these people respond financially. The number of tithers, which was not small at the beginning of the year, has almost doubled. If it were not for tithing it is hardly probable that these people could have reached the amount of $3,000 or more which they have given in the past year. This does not include the pledges given for the Ashland College endowment. One of the pleasant surprises which recently occurred at this place was in honor of the first wedding anniversary of Mrs. Flora and myself. After the mid-week prayer service, Brother Seibert,

in a fitting manner made it known to pastor and wife that the church wished to present them with a purse of eighty dollars, to commemorate their first wedding anniversary. Our appreciation could not be given in words, but we assured the givers that such a gift was acceptable and highly appreciated.

The outlook for the coming year is good. We ask an interest in your prayers for Beaver City.

E. S. FLORA.

ALLENTOWN

Inasmuch as a few things have happened since our last report, we will once more send in a few lines for the benefit of the Evangelist readers.

Beginning March 15th we had with us Brother Watson who led us in an effort to win souls. We worked together for three weeks during which time our brother brought powerful Gospel messages, every one with a true "ring" as related to the Old Book. One feature of Brother Watson's work with us was illustrated talks in connection with several of the sermons. This method seemed to win in a limited way here, although it would no doubt count for more in easier fields of labor.

Brother Watson had been informed of the peculiarly difficult nature of this field and his three weeks among us served to confirm this fact. But he was willing to tackle a hard field and as a result was not without reward, for nine stepped out for Christ, four of whom were from an Italian family with which we got in touch through our street meetings of last summer.

Due to opposition from the ecclesiastical machinery of our city, we were able to baptize only six of those who confessed.

Watson preached as strong sermons on doctrine as I have heard anywhere, but people of those state churches which persecuted our brethren in Germany two hundred years ago, are not to be easily convinced. No argument seems to suffice. The Allentown church stands straight on the teachings of the Bible. You will therefore know where Watson stands when I tell you that his work here was much appreciated.

Some were afraid that our offering for foreign missions would "fall flat" when we were to ask for more money just after having an evangelist with us. But our offering proved to be $220.00, or over $3.00 per member—our membership at present being sixty-nine. But to put credit where it belongs we must admit that two life memberships in the F. M. S. are included in the offering. Thank God for the Life memberships! May there be more of them! I believe the day is not far distant when Allentown will have more life memberships in the F. M. S. This will be when we have a few more tithers. Already we have a goodly proportion of tithers to our membership.

Our Sunday school shows an increase over a year ago in that our attendance is running several higher than then. Brother Turner is doing his utmost to bring us into the Jubilee Conference as a "Front Liner."

The Y. P. S. C. E. continues about as usual, save that a few socials have been held since the first of the year, and have, we trust, put new "pep" into things. However, many of our young people still do not see their opportunity in the Y. P. S. C. E.

The Women's Missionary Society reports that all the goals are likely to be made and the society become a standard one. A mission study class is now in progress.

Our prayer meetings continue well attended. We have as usual met in the homes of the brethren during the winter, but will now begin to hold church prayer meetings instead.

We had a nice communion service a few

evenings ago. Our average attendance for this year is 79 percent.

Allentown has continued to make the spiritual as well as the financial goals. We will be able to make a good score on practically every point of the Four Year Program.

I have completed the work for a Master's degree at Lehigh University and as a result of having prepared to teach, a call was extended me to teach at Ashland. Although my preparation had in mind teaching in this city, at least for the present; yet after careful consideration, and advising for a month or more, the call has been accepted, and we very reluctantly handed in our resignation here after serving this good people four years.

The resignation takes effect as soon as we can get a suitable house at Ashland.

The Allentown work hasn't made so large a growth in numbers during the past four but in many respects the work has gone forward. The church here is in better condition than it has been for some years. For this I give credit to the faithful members who have come to have a vision, and of course to our Heavenly Father who has heard and answered prayer.

We are very sorry to leave this people and work and, indeed, were it not that we feel that we can serve the church in a larger capacity at Ashland, we should not have considered leaving Allentown.

As stated in my last letter, money has been raised toward securing a parsonage. May 30th has been set as another date for urging the good move.

I do not know who Allentown's next pastor may be, but trust that some one entirely suitable to the field may feel the call and come. Any pastor interested may write to Wm. Schaffer, 626 Washington St., or to Elder E. E. Fehnel, 920 Washington St.

Allentown has a small membership, but the church aims to support a pastor to the full extent of their ability and without outside aid. No church should ask the mission board to help it, if at all able to support a pastor unaided. Tithing will solve the problem for almost any church in the brotherhood. Let's all be more faithful to our stewardship.

I shall have more to say about the work here when we reach Ashland and give our final report.

Pray for the future of the cause at Allentown.

A. L. DeLOZIER, Pastor.

WEST ALEXANDRIA, OHIO

Our reports from West Alexandria and New Lebanon have been held up for some time, awaiting various matters which we hoped to report together herewith.

The work has been very much hindered during the winter by the glare of ice which stayed with us for so long (perhaps six weeks) as well as a recurrence of the "flu" and the prevalence of other diseases. Notwithstanding, we have had at least some reasons for rejoicing. There have been three additions to the church in the regular services, since our last report. Then on March 4th Miss Aboud came to us and continued with us for ten days. During this time there were 9 who made the great confession and were received into the church. There were several more who made private confessions during this meeting who have not been received into the church. In fact a great many of these were already members of other churches of the town, perhaps from 12 to 16 years of age, and seemed not to know why they really had made confession at all. I am inclined to believe that parental influence had been brought to bear upon them. Thus there have been just 12 additions to the church here, in the last six months.

I want to most heartily endorse Miss Aboud

as a speaker. She created a wonderful interest and brought intensely interesting messages from night to night. We were greatly handicapped in that we could not keep her for more than ten days. Her messages were not only most interesting, however, but true to the word of God as well.

The women's organization has been re-organized and become identified with the National organization of the Women's Missionary Society, and the meetings have increased in interest and attendance.

What progress has been made, is being made, however, has been under great difficulties,—so great indeed that I have become convinced of the great difficulty, if not indeed the impossibility, of doing for the church here what ought to be done, and must be done, when not more than one-half of my time can be given to it. Therefore I have tendered my resignation to the church here to take effect October 1. Anyone interested may write to Mrs. Oscar Myers, W. Dayton St., West Alexandria, Ohio.

G. W. KINZIE.

WOMAN'S MISSIONARY SOCIETY, ATTENTION!—CHANGE OF DATE

Through a mistake I just received the official programs for the Summer School of Missions of the Middle West. The date for the opening of the school at Winona Lake has been changed from June 17th to June 24th. The first session will be at 3 o'clock for registration in the Auditorium, and the school will be formally opened at 4 o'clock by Mrs. Vickers, introducing the faculty and missionaries. This school will close at noon July 1st. All women intending to be at Winona please note the change of date.

The Lake Geneva school will convene at Conference Point, Lake Geneva, Wisconsin, August 17th to 24th.

We have a limited supply of programs for each place but to any one interested and planning to attend we shall be pleased to mail a copy. A request to the undersigned on a postal card will bring you a copy.

Mrs. U. J. Shively, Nappanee, Indiana.

NEWS FROM GARVIN

After a long winter in which we had a larger amount of sickness than the preceding one, and with a late spring with impassable roads we have been able to emerge and to plan and accomplish some active work. During the winter all forward work was practically impossible. The bulk of the work here must be done in about eight months of the year.

A workers' conference has been organized for the Sunday school. We meet twice a month at the homes of various members for the discussion of Sunday school problems, the discussion of the lesson and choir practice. Much good has come from these meetings.

We were prevented by the weather and roads from taking our foreign mission offering until a couple of weeks ago. Our offering will average better than a dollar per member, making a total of $195.00. This is the largest mission offering ever raised here. Brother Beachler was rained out in the fall and just recently finished his campaign here for Ashland College. He will have more to report along this line. Garwin realizes the worth of Ashland to the Brethren church and stands ready to support it. We had our spring communion service while he was here and used for the first time our individual communion cups. At the present time we are in the midst of a red and blue contest in the Sunday school which bids fair to crowd us out of all available room. If the start is an indication of the finish with eight weeks to go we will have to hold some classes under as the Sunday school is in good hustling condition. There are a number of added repairs planned for the church and parsonage, which when completed will be well worth while. There is such a spirit of unity and co-

operation here that we cannot but go forward. We are planning for one of the largest campaigns here this fall with Brother Coleman as evangelist and Albert Ronk as choir leader, that has ever been held in the history of this church. The meetings will commence the second Sunday of September and will give us a good season of the year from the standpoint of weather conditions.

We are much interested in the progress of the church at large and desire the interest of the brotherhood in the work at Garwin.

FREEMAN ANKRUM.

COLLEGE NEWS?

Commencement week began Sunday, May 30, with the Baccalaureate service which was Very well attended, the sermon being delivered by the president. On Monday the department of Voice and Piano held their Advanced Pupil Recital in the chapel. It was attended by a packed house. Recognition services at the chapel hour Tuesday was attended by students and friends. Announcements for the coming year were made, the "Annual" was dedicated to Dean Miller and the faculty presented Miss Lichty and Miss Zimmerman with roses as they are both leaving the school this year. There were other interesting features also.

On Tuesday evening a pageant, The Pilgrims, was given on the campus. There was the usual good attendance. Wednesday noon the college banquet was held in the dining room of the Hall. It was the best attended of any, there being over 125 plates served. On Wednesday Dr. Frank W. Luce, superintendent of the Methodist churches of the Cleveland district, gave a very excellent address to the class in the Methodist church. On Thursday morning at the usual hour the class day exercises were held in the chapel. These exercises were of the usual high order. Seniors:

Mr. Charles Anspach, M. A. B.Sc., is employed in an office in the city. He intends to take up further graduate work in the near future.

Harvey Earl Becknell, A. B., becomes County Y. M. C. A. secretary in Harrison county, Ohio.

Nora Pearl Bracken, A. B., is studying in this Summer School.

Joseph Gingrich, A. B., who was married the day following his graduation to Miss Beatrice Smith of near Ashland, becomes pastor of the Masontown church.

J. H. Gongwer, A. B., expects to teach.

Ruth Lichty, A. B., is Visiting with her mother. Her plans for the near future are not fully settled.

Ray Mikesell, A. B., will teach.

Caryl Miller, A. B., will teach also.

Elwood Rowsey, A. B., has a position with the Ohio Christian Endeavor Society.

Darlington Edwin Stark, A. B., expects to enter school for graduate work.

Fred Vanator, A. B., takes charge of our church at Canton, Ohio.

English Divinity Students

Cora Akaland is returning to California.

Ralph Atkinson is in Colorado for the health of a child.

Margaret Banghart expects to enter training for nursing.

Watson Deeter becomes pastor of our church at Oakville, Indiana.

Mrs. Helen Vanator will assist her husband in pastoral work at Canton, Ohio.

Academy graduates go on with their school work.

Faculty

Professors L. L. Garber, Miller and the writer are teaching in the Summer Normal. Professor J. A. Garber expects to give attention to Christian Endeavor and Sunday school work and then enter some summer school for college work. Miss Puterbaugh expects to take Voice training in Chicago. Miss Wimer will spend next summer at her home in Lanark,

Illinois. Professor Haun will do graduate work in Vanderbilt. Miss Luelle Teeter is helping in the Summer Normal. Mr. and Mrs. Landray have returned to their home in Troy, Ohio. Their place has been temporarily filled.

We were glad to welcome many Visitors here during Commencement week. Among those present were Professor Wolford, Dr. Beachler, Brethren Carpenter, Eikenberry, Oberholtzer, Boardman and Professor Glenn Mason. All in all, the spirit was fine and appropriate. It is an entrance at the northeast corner of the college grounds. It consists of a flight of steps at the top of which are two pillars capped by cement flower vases in which are Vines and blooming plants.

When the rush of the closing weeks are over, I shall have more of importance to say.

EDWIN E. JACOBS.

HAGERSTOWN, MARYLAND

As the days glide swiftly by, we pause again with a backward glance for the purpose of finding our bearings. The poet truly sang, "Our todays and yesterdays are the blocks with which we build." So we mark future attainment by past achievement. As we View the months passed since we wrote to the Evangelist family, we are not so certain that we truly shaped and fashioned all the blocks with which we built. A comparison with the infallible standard set by the Great Shepherd of the sheep humbles us and we ask, are we following the crimson trail?

We held a two weeks' meeting preceding Easter. The visible results of the meeting were fifteen accessions to the church. Thirteen of these came from the Sunday school; again demonstrating the fertile field of evangelism in the church. We closed the meeting with our spring communion service. The evening was somewhat inclement, having rained all day yet the Lord's tables were well filled, additional room having been provided. At the morning service, we lifted our offering for Foreign Missions amounting to two hundred dollars.

The Sunday school has recovered from the slump occasioned by the "La Grippe." The attendance is normal and slightly above. This is encouraging in view of the general falling off in Sunday school attendance. The average attendance for the year was considerably above the year preceding. We made a few changes in officers at the beginning of the year, and added some additional ones necessitated by a steady growth. The great and growing need is more trained teachers; our present class in the three years' course have been doing splendid work.

Space forbids mention of the Various other organizations, more than to state they are alive and going good work. The Ladies' Aid Society are live wires and want to see their pastor located in a parsonage.

We are now expecting Beachler, and whatever else happens, we shall have a good time with him in our midst. A. B. COVER.

FIELD REPORT OF THE EVANGELISTIC LEAGUE

By W. S. Bell

Falls City Meeting

This was my first Visit to Falls City and the first opportunity I had to work with Brother Stuckman, who did everything in shape and ready to begin campaign when I arrived. I enjoyed my stay and work with the church, the people were responsive to the preaching and with the pastor gave the very best of support.

The afternoon Bible lectures were fairly well attended and good results followed. It was a great pleasure to get better acquainted with Brother Stuckman and his family, in whose home I stayed. I consider it one of the best meetings I have held during the year. The church responded very liberally to the League.

In California

I am now engaged in my tenth consecutive meeting since last September and the last one for the year, from here I go to be with my family in Sunnyside, Washington, to spend two months in resting up.

I was invited to present the League to the church in Long Beach while here and received a liberal response.

I find the work in Southern California moving forward. Was surprised at the fine structure the First church of Los Angeles has nearly completed; it is a credit to the denomination.

Brother Beal is leaving the Compton Avenue church to take up the work at Fillmore. I am now at La Verne holding a two weeks' meeting with Brother Broad and so far have had good attendance.

The district conference will be held at Long Beach in July and the new church in Los Angeles will be dedicated the last of this month. I regret that I cannot be present at both, but home looks good to me now and expect to land there on the first train after I am through here.

CAMPAIGN NOTES

During the recent lull in the campaign for endowment, the readers of "Campaign Notes" have had opportunity for rest. But once more the wheels have been set in motion and the thermometer is brought forth. This time we are to report for Garwin Iowa. With the canvass at Garwin accomplished the work in the Illiokota district is completed with the exception of Leon.

We went to Garwin last fall in corn picking time with the hope that the canvass would be executed at that time. However, the weather and the roads brought the work to a sudden standstill before the canvass was well begun. Hence we had to return. Brother Freeman Ankrum, a former Ashland College man, continues to shepherd this people. His heart beats true for Dr. Jacobs and the college, consequently I found him ready to enter heart, soul, and Ford into the campaign among his people. We had good roads, good weather, and a royal fine time during our stay among the good folks in this congregation, and Ankrum gave me the most generous help in putting the work across. I was glad to asist on Saturday night in the communion service; and on Sunday, the last day of the campaign we had an all day meeting. I preached, morning, afternoon, and evening to splendid and interested audiences. The ladies of the church furnished a dinner for the occasion which is entitled to a far bigger mention than I shall dare to give it in this report. But I cannot refrain from at least saying that, as one who was there and who knows, it was a one hundred percent dinner. I want also to add that the Sunday school attendance for that Sunday was most gratifying, it being the first Sunday of a contest which gave fine promise of good things for the school.

The results for endowment will go approximately $2,000. Considering the various demands that have been made upon Garwin during the years by way of having to rebuild their church which was burned, also having to provide a parsonage, I consider the result for endowment quite creditable. Our highest gift was $250; we also had two $200 gifts; one gift for $150; also a fine line of $100 gifts and from that on down. By far the greater part of this result was in cash and bonds.

Evangelists and others who have had occasion to sojourn among our people in this congregation will, I am sure, confirm my testimony when I say that the hospitality of the Garwin people is of the most genuine type. I received utmost kindness in the Lowrey,

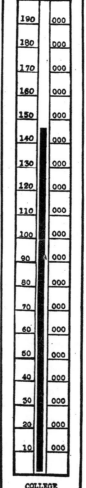

Our Goal: 200,000; We Can and We Must

COLLEGE ENDOWMENT

Hall, Ankrum, Ambler, Dobson, Strong, Richards and Cooper homes. The latchstrings to all of the homes hung out but it was impossible to pull all of those strings. When I was at Garwin last fall the Ronks also opened their home to me. I shall remember with a lot of pleasure my week with Ankrum and his people. Ankrum has a great field before him. And I have no doubt that the meeting to be held for this congregation this fall by Coleman and Ronk will yield large results. May God richly bless Ankrum and his people.

The thermometer ought to indicate now about $146,500. Not having my record at hand as I write this I cannot say definitely, but in the next report I will give exact figures. Am now in the beautiful land of Maryland. The mountains are everywhere so beautiful that if I were poetically inclined I might be tempted to do something rash.

WM. H. BEACHLER,
Campaign Secretary.

Communion Notice

Communion services will be held at the Brethren Church, Fremont, Ohio, Sunday evening, June 20. All members of the congregation are urged to be present. Brethren of neighboring congregations are cordially invited.

H. M. OBERHOLTZER, Pastor.

NORTH LIBERTY, INDIANA

We are always glad to report to the general brotherhood the progress of the Lord's work entrusted to us. On Sunday, May 23rd, it was our privilege to receive six persons into the family of God by Christian baptism. Three of these were very recent confessions, the others were awaiting baptism for some time. Our love-feast was the largest attended for several years. Brother Whetstone was with us at this service and gave us a helpful message. Our Sunday school is booming under the leadership of our good brother, C. G. Wolf. On a very recent Sunday the offering was sufficient to place a hundred new song books in the church. We made selection of Mr. Rhodeheaver's new "Victory Songs."

Our Woman's Missionary Society will be a banner society again this year. They recently gave a splendid Woman's Day program.

We have reasons to rejoice for the continual evidence of interest and growth of the work here. We are pressing the battle as best we can, preaching the old gospel of Jesus Christ without any apology and God is honoring his word.

TIOSA, INDIANA

Saturday, May 29 was the time set for our love-feast at this place. We preached to splendid audiences on two preceding evenings resulting in four confessions. These with three others were added to the body of believers by baptism on Saturday before our love-feast.

Our Sunday school here is above normal the past few months. The attendance and offerings going beyond our expectations. Brother George Riddle is our superintendent and is leading his forces on from victory to victory.

New song books is the order of the day at Tiosa too, and so I am trying to keep my people "singing on the homeward way."

Miss Mae Smith will preach for me at this place on Sunday, June 13, while I am engaged in a united evangelistic effort in the village of La Paz.

These are busy days for us, as we are playing the several parts of farmer, pastor and evangelist. We have just one supreme aim in it all and that is to glorify our Lord and help in our weak way to bring his kingdom to earth. With love to all the brethren, I am

Yours under the Precious Blood,
C. C. GRISSO.

" 'There's no sense of going further---it's the
    end of Cultivation,'
So they said, and I believed it---broke my
    land and sowed my crop---
Built my barns and strung my fences in the
    little border station
Tucked away among the foothills where the
    trails run out and stop.

" Till a voice as bad as Conscience rang inter-
    minable changes
On one everlasting Whisper day and night
    repeated---so:
'Something hidden. Go and find it. Go and
    look behind the Ranges---
Something lost behind the Ranges. Lost and
    waiting for you. Go!' "

TWENTY-SIX MILLION
UNREACHED CHILDREN and YOUTH
CHALLENGE THE QUEST OF THE CHURCH

Published every Wednesday at Ashland, Ohio. All matter for publication must reach the Editor not later than Friday noon of the preceding week.

George S. Baer, Editor

The Brethren Evangelist

When ordering your paper changed give old as well as new address. Subscriptions discontinued at expiration. To avoid missing any numbers renew two weeks in advance.

R. R. Teeter, Business Manager

OFFICIAL ORGAN OF THE BRETHREN CHURCH

Subscription price, $2.00 per year, payable in advance.
Entered at the Post Office at Ashland, Ohio, as second-class matter.
Acceptance for mailing at special rate of postage provided for in section 1103, Act of October 3, 1917, authorized September 9, 1918. Address all matter for publication to Geo. S. Baer, Editor of the Brethren Evangelist, and all business communications to R. R. Teeter, Business Manager, Brethren Publishing Company, Ashland, Ohio. Make all checks payable to the Brethren Publishing Company.

TABLE OF CONTENTS

EDITORIAL

What Is the Church Doing for the Children?

Among the many tasks with which the church of Christ is faced today, perhaps the most neglected, the most difficult and at the same time the most vital is that of claiming the children for Christ and training them for his service. Three observations bear testimony to the fact that the church has been woefully negligent of this important part of her function. First the church's appeal and program in the past has had in mind the adult and not the child. Evangelism, divinely directed as it has been and wonderful as have been the results, has almost lost sight of the child in its effort to rescue the adult. This we say not with the feeling that effort in behalf of the adult ought to have been less, but that concern for the child ought to have been greater. Bible instruction, until comparatively recently, has been adapted almost exclusively to the adult mind. The worship of the church has been planned and conducted with a view to meeting the needs of the individual of mature years, and every place of service, however insignificant, has, until within recent years, been filled by the elders in Israel; there was no place or mission for the young folks except to keep silent and look on.

The second observation follows naturally upon the heels of the first, namely, that there is a discouragingly small proportion of children and young people in the average congregation; in some they are almost totally absent. It seems fair to say that those present represent the chief interest of the pastor and his church; and that the absence of the children is conspicuous because there has been a conspicuous lack of interest in them. Surprise has been experienced at the number of congregations where there actually exists a distinct feeling against children attending church worship lest they by their restlessness disturb the devout thoughts of their elders. But in many congregations where God's youthful worshippers are welcome, their number is painfully small because no one gives any thought to making the worship interesting to them when they do come. Even children will not attend church except by the compulsion of the rod where nothing is done to make it worth their while.

The third observation is in consequence of the other two. The great mass of children and young people are found on the streets, the playgrounds, going on "hikes" or fishing, or are in the community loafing places or in the homes instead of in the house of God at the hour of worship. Even the Sunday school children as soon as they are released rush forth with all the hilarity of a day school dismissal to the streets and to their games, with no thought of the church worship to follow. They go where they are not neglected, where things are made interesting for them, or where they have opportunity to make things interesting for themselves. What multitudes of boys are congregated here and there on the streets, in the baseball parks or in the loafing places, because the church has taken little or no interest in them. If any appreciable portion of the "fifty-eight million unreached people" of our land are ever to be reached for Christ and the church, there must be some intelligent effort put forth to reach the boys and girls. There are twenty-six million children and young people in America under the age of twenty-five who are not even in touch with any Sunday school; these constitute indisputable proof of the church's neglect.

Failure to claim the boy and girl for Christ is not due entirely to negligence, either purposed or unpurposed, but partly to the fact that it is a difficult task. It requires more than ordinary patience, tact and sympathy to capture the hearts of boys, but the difficulty has been enhanced by the fact that too often we have tried to apply the same methods used in working with adults to our efforts with children and youth. So few have any real understanding of the needs and characteristics of the growing years of life, there is little wonder that the church has had such little success at this point. There is a tendency to group all children under one class and apply certain rules to all and when they do not respond we are discouraged. The task is difficult because we do not study childhood, because we do not study the individual child and because we do not use wisdom in making our appeals.

Nevertheless the church has no more important work than that of caring for the religious development of its children, and nothing is more vital to its future. No mistake is more lamentable or more frequently fatal than that of allowing children to grow to maturity without putting forth every possible effort to bring them to a positive and definite acceptance of Jesus Christ as their Savior and Lord. The golden opportunity is usually about the middle of the teen age when the religious appeal is strongest. And if the life is not decided for Christ before it reaches maturity, the chances are strong that it never will. Moreover the perpetuity of the church is at stake along with the future welfare of the child. The church that neglects its children does not put forth faithful and wise efforts to save them for Christ and train them for its service, is jeopardizing its future. He who does not learn to love the church during his formative years and to rejoice in its worship, is not likely to change his attitude in these respects when contrary habits have become fixed. The result will be that the individual will be without the saving influence of the church and the church will be deprived of the strength and support which that life might have brought to it. It is no indifferent matter that the majority of the children are not being brought into vital contact with the Master, that they are almost universally absent from the worship of the church, that they are often not even encouraged to form the habit of church attendance and service; it is grave enough to call the entire church to a replacing of its emphasis.

If the situation is to be remedied a new vision and a more wisely adapted program with reference to three lines of activity seem necessary. First, we must see the need of and work out a more adequate program of religious education. The only religious education that the average Protestant child gets is supplied by the Sunday school. Inadequacy is written over the whole program. The average home has given almost nothing in the way of religious instruction. And in the Sunday school the buildings, equipment, curriculum, administration and teaching force are all failing to measure up to the demands. Aside from these, the time given to instruction concerning the most vital element that enters into life is grossly inadequate. To train the mind the child is given 25 hours a week in the public schools, but to train the Protestant child is given a half hour every week; or about as much time in a whole year is given to religious education as is given to secular education in a week. Over against that the Catholics set aside 200 hours a year and the Jews 335 hours a year for the religious education of their children. The Protestant churches are challenged to provide more adequately in time and equipment for the religious instruction of their children.

A more adequate program of worship must be brought into effect, a program that will meet the needs of the child and youth as well as the adult, if the church of tomorrow, is to possess the children of today. In every program of worship something must be incorporated that is calculated to get the child's mind and heart. It may include a brief sermon that will enable the children to use their eyes and ears, a song that will require the use of their lungs, a favorite seating place, an occasional complimentary mention of their presence, the couching of a thought in simple words for their benefit in the regular sermon, the use of a vivid illustration that will grip their attention and reasonable brevity throughout. If we build and conduct our programs of church worship in such a way that children and young people will enjoy them, we shall likely be rewarded by their presence in greatly increased numbers, and besides the adults will enjoy and attent not less but more.

Then there is needed a more adequate program of training for a service, a program that has the church's young life in mind. Children should be encouraged and given the opportunity of developing in the service of the church. Church leaders are made during the habit forming period, and not after maturity has been reached. More ministers and missionaries are discovered at sixteen than at any other age. Ideals of social relations and habits of helplessness are formed early in life. If the church is to have an adequately trained leadership, and if the church itself is to be trained for service, adequate plans must be made for the religious training of its children.

EDITORIAL REVIEW

On the Christian Endeavor page two Intermediates give evidence of the Bible knowledge they are getting under the instruction of Sister Abbott, the superintendent of the Dayton society.

We invite tithers throughout the brotherhood to send in brief testimonials of appreciation of the plan of tithing their income for the Lord's work, to be published in our "Tithing Stewardship Corner."

We wish to call attention to a letter on our mission page written by one of our little home missionaries, little Edna Rempel. Her interest in the work is unusual for her age. You will appreciate Brother Gearhart's kindness in permitting you to share the letter with him.

We are heartily glad to give our readers a full-sized paper this week, and as our car of paper has arrived you may spurt on normal service from now on. We are still behind due to the fact that we had to wait several days on paper, but instead of dropping a num-

ber we are trying to catch up. We thank you for your patience, and if you will send in your church news we will be able to publish them quite promptly. We are also now able to release articles that we have had in store for sometime, and invite you to write more.

"White Gifts continue coming," says Brother Trent. That is pleasant reading, but it is not pleasant to read that 57 Sunday schools have not sent in their statistical reports yet. Are you guilty? Get busy.

Brother Gearhart requests the payment of Kentucky and Home Guard pledges soon. In another notice he states that Riverside Institute is still looking for a cook and a matron, two separate persons. Who will respond?

"Cobb's Conference Corner" is the title of the first official reminder of the year concerning our coming national conference to meet at Winona Lake, August 30 to September 4. We can assure you that Brother Cobb is planning to stir your minds quite regularly and frequently concerning this matter.

Brother Edwin Boardman writes that Hudson is making progress, and one important evidence of it is the enlarged missionary vision his people are getting and the bigger offerings they are giving. Note what they are doing for their pastor, too; a thirty-five percent increase in salary is fine, and it is what some other churches ought to do for their pastors.

If Ashland College is not given a much more adequate endowment in the near future it will not be because the present administration is not putting forth strenuous efforts. A perusal of President Jacobs's "College News" will convince our readers, if they ever had any doubts, that he is planning and working for a bigger and a better Ashland College, which is essential to a bigger and a better church. Everybody, pitch in and help.

Brother William A. Gearhart, General Missionary Secretary and Brother O. E. Bowman, Secretary of the Home Board, left Dayton on June 19 for a trip among our churches in the west and northwest. They will take the Kentucky slides with them and hope to secure several hundred dollars necessary to meet the balance on the light plant installation expenses at Lost Creek. Brother Gearhart writes that the Easter Foreign offering has reached $27,000.00 and more is still expected.

If we spent more money in building churches, we would have need to spend less in building jails.

"He that winneth souls is wise" is the divine decree of ages ago, then why not heed the enjoining and promising words of the Master, "Follow me and I will make you fishers of men," that we may be truly wise?

Our tasks are no smaller than we make them, and no larger. He who does his work nobly has a noble task, however insignificant it may seem to be; but he who does his work meanly fills a mean position, however high it may be rated.

"My house shall be called the house of prayer," and yet we have made it the house of visiting and hilarity. Too much rowdyism and desecration goes on under the name of sociability in the average Protestant church. May the church people learn the prayer of the Psalmist, "Open thou my lips and my mouth shall show forth thy praise."

"The church is a workshop and not a dormitory," said Alexander Maclaren, and when he said that he put his finger on a tender spot in the life of the church. There has ever been a tendency on the part of many religiously inclined folks to use the church as a sort of a Pullman car whereby they could sleep their way into the kingdom. The Lord supplies no Pullman service this side of the land of death, when all reservations must have been made. Many church members need to hear the Lord say, as he said in parable in the days of his flesh, "Why stand ye here all the day idle," and again "Go work today in my vineyard."

GENERAL ARTICLES
A Vision of Our Task

(Sermon preached by C. H. Ashman, Sunnyside, Washington, and printed at the request of the Official Staff of the Sunnyside Church.)

The first essential of Christian service is to get a vision of the task. Before Nehemiah began rebuilding the walls of Jerusalem, he made a thorough inspection of conditions. He secured a vision of the task. The church of today needs to get a vision of her task. What if all the tremendous power of time, energy, sacrifice, life and money consecrated upon her altars is being misdirected? What if she is missing the goal set before her by her God? What if the church is not actually engaged in the "King's Business?" Jesus said, "Wist ye not that I must be about my Father's business?" What if the church is not about the Father's business? It is of supreme importance that we ascertain the real mission of the church, that we receive a vision of our task.

Is the mission of the church social service? Every day has its fads; fads in politics, business, society and religion. Social service is one of the religious fads of the day. We are hearing much these days about "the inauguration of a new social order." Some speak and write as if they could write out prescriptions which, when filled at certain organizations of an institutional nature, would cure all the ills of society. They emphasize the "reformation of social conditions." From many a pulpit we are hearing about the "social aspect of the gospel" and "the church in her relation to the new social order." Men speak as if society could be saved in sum total form, as a lump. We are instructed concerning, "Christian love regenerating society." This is an absurd impossibility! There is only one power which can regenerate society, the blood of Jesus Christ. There is only one Person who can accomplish this, the Holy Spirit. Yes, and there is not one single hint in the Bible, that this Person and Power will ever regenerate society as such.

No, the mission of the church is not social service. Her call is to the individual, not to society. Her method of winning is "one by one." This appears too slow for the world in this fast moving and fast living age. It appears to be too small a program for a proud haughty church in a proud and haughty world. The individual is being lost sight of today in the group. In the labor world and in business, the individual is absorbed so completely that his identity is almost annihilated. Many a church has caught this spirit from the world and no longer speaks or prays in terms of the individual, but in big terms of society. But the mission of the church is not to usher in any social universal brotherhood of man. This is based entirely upon the natural, carnal, unregenerated man. It is purely a mechanical sentiment which leaves the heart unchanged, wicked, selfish as ever. The church should not waste time and precious energy in that which is only the rubbing of salve upon sores, but which will never touch the source of the disease. Her business is not the reformation of society, but the regeneration of the individuals within society, or rather out of society. This is the only program followed by the Apostles of old and taught by Christ. We believe in every believer doing all the good he can, but if society is ever to be changed, it will be through regenerated individuals going forth to live the regenerated life in society. And the Word clearly indicates that at no time during this present church age will regenerated individuals become so overwhelmingly in the majority that they can rule the world. 2 Timothy 3: 1-5 clearly foretells the contrary.

We are suspicious of the Interchurch World Movement because so much of its program is to be occupied in social service instead of evangelism. In its Church Survey, under the heading, "Church Program," you will find these lines of work outlined: Civic work, such as community improvements, etc. Industrial, such as initiating co-operative movements in credit, marketing, road building, etc. Should the church become a bank, exchange or contractor? Social, recreational, such as play festivals, athletic competitions, etc. Is her business to run a gymnasium or produce entertainments? Educational, such as lectures (there are too many lectures in the church now and not enough sermons), lyceums, chautauquas, etc. Is this her business, or to preach the Gospel? Cultural, such as musical, dramatic, literary entertainments. Is her business to entertain, or to pray? But the crowning link connecting the church with the world in this program is co-operation with organizations, NOT RELIGIOUS, such as boards of trade (legalized gambling), farm bureaus, agricultural college, etc. Is this the task of the church? Shall she link up with irreligious organizations of the world? What about her pilgrim character so often emphasized in the Word? Shall her ministers become walking encyclopedias of social, industrial, commercial affairs? Shall her life and money be thus expended? What does it all point to? It points to the fact that the church is discarding God's plan of personal salvation through personal evangelism and application of the truth of the Gospel for a program worldly in nature, origin, and power. The world is dictating to the church in it all. For ourselves, rather than sell our birthright in the ministry for such a mess of pottage, we will work with our hands for a livelihood. The plea is made by some of the leaders of our church that if we do not ally ourselves with the movement, we will get none of the gifts of money otherwise coming into our treasury. What, has the Brethren church come to the time when, if she must sacrifice principle and convictions and the Word of God for the sake of a few paltry dollars, she will do so? We think not and feel confident that the vast majority of her constituency feels the same way.

Is the mission of the church world betterment? World betterment is based on the assumption of improvement toward perfection of the natural man. It assumes that the natural man can be improved until approved of God and the world. The call is to develop the latent possibilities of the natural powers, to climb to lofty heights through our own attainments, to stand on our own merits, to become SELF MADE MEN! World betterment informs that within our natural, unregenerated self lies the fountain of salvation and personal perfection, we can become our own savior, leader, judge, God; we can lift ourselves by our own boot straps. This is one of the forms of the prevailing tendency of the day, the DEIFICATION OF MAN. In its attempt to get rid of God, the world is seeking to drag God down to the level of man. Mormonism says that God is an exalted man. Christian Science, the religious guinea pig, neither a guinea, nor a pig; neither Christian, nor science, says God is nothing more than mind like man. But the world is not only seeking to get rid of God, but to make every man a god. The devil's lie, "ye shall be as gods," is progressing rapidly these days. Thus the world is deifying man. We are fast developing a state of society that will welcome the anti-Christ, who declares he is God and will demand worship as God (See 1 Thess. 2:3-12).

World betterment is also based on the assumption of proper environment bringing sinlessness and perfection. Its theory is, "if the surroundings, the atmosphere of the life is right, the life will be pure." It says, "close up the saloons, clean up the theatres, reform the dance, solve the slum problems, through eugenics clean up the home and man will become a perfect, happy being.'' But it forgets that often the vilest of earth are to be found in the palace, amid culture. We are in favor of making it as hard to do wrong and as easy to do right as possible, but close every known door of temptation and you have not changed the carnal nature of man one iota. It is still sinful, carnal, and desperately wicked. It will break out in some other place for it cannot be curbed. Close the saloons (we rejoice it is so, yet the heart will turn in amazingly large numbers to tobacco.) The only solution is to close the heart to these things through regeneration. Close the doors and the heart will invent new ones, but close the heart and all the open doors will be in vain.

No, we do not believe that the program of the church is world betterment. Paul taught that there was a dead line between him and the world. He also taught that such a line should be drawn between every child of God and the world. Paul, shall we reach across this dead line of crucifixion and join hands with the world in just polishing the carnal heart? It is foolish to speak of improving the natural, unregenerated man. Can you improve the thorn apple tree by tying figs on its branches? Can you improve sin by whitewashing it? Can you change the sinful heart by putting a dress suit upon it? Can you change the nature of the leopard by painting his spots? Will sin disappear when you polish it with liquid veneer of world betterment? We maintain that although world betterment and social service is the best the unregenerated world can know, that it behooves the church to proclaim that she has a better program, one that will really solve the problem, regeneration of the nature. She should not waste her precious time, life, and money in that which is only a subterfuge, the devil's counterfeit.

Is the mission of the church AMUSEMENT? One would think so to listen to the prevailing programs of modern churches. Concerts, entertainments, fancy fairs, dramatic entertainments, hold sway. The modern church thinks she is called, "to provide recreation for the people." A long distance intervenes between the Puritans and today. They spoke out against such frivolities but the church winks at, excuses, tolerates, accepts, adopts, practices them. God pity the church that must stoop to amuse to win! God pity the church that must stoop to amuse to keep! If I thought for one moment that the few scattering social evenings which you young people of this church spent with each other were responsible for the presence of a single one of you, they would stop this very minute. Yes, you turn out in large numbers, but I am persuaded better things than that of it. It did not seem out of place for you to open your evening of Christian sociability with prayer the other evening. There is a vast difference between an evening of Christian sociability and amusement to win or keep.

No, the mission of the church is not to amuse. Jesus did not say, "Go ye into all the world to provide amusement for the people." God has never given a single gift in the church for such work. For every work ordained of God, he has given a gift to the church. He has given some apostles, prophets, evangelists, pastors, teachers. But never clowns, dancing masters, gymnasium coaches, or entertainers. There is not a single promise of God's blessing upon such work. God has a promise of blessing for every work he has ordained; but never one for amusement. The New Testament standard of attitude between the church and world is "strict separation and uncompromising hostility." Did Jesus ever amuse? Did Paul or any of the apostles. There is a pathetic side to all of this. We have never known a single soul to ever become converted under any amusement provided by the church. True, at the time there is a large attendance. As one newspaper has said, "Movie pictures in the pulpit mean people in the pews." But has it ever meant souls born again? No, but it has meant more than one child of God led into worldliness, indifference, and unspirituality. The devil knows that the distance between the

true church and the world is too great to make in one journey, so he has provided a half way house. "Amusement is the devil's half way house to the world." God pity the church which amuses instead of warning, instructing pleading, entreating.

We maintain that the mission of the church is spiritual in nature. Her task is to gather from among the Gentiles a people for Christ's name. A fair exegesis of Acts 15:13-14 will prove this. There is never a promise that she will ever convert the world to Christ, but that she will gather a people from the world for Christ. In this work, Jesus commanded, not the polishing of the outside through social service or world betterment, but the cleaning up of the inside. Make the inside of the platter and sepulchre clean! Change the nature of the tree if you want the fruit different! Christianity is not something to be rubbed on the outside that soaks in, but the implanting of a new nature within that works out. The business of the church is to clean the inside. With a spiritual message and mission, she is to keep apart from unholy alliances with the world. Christ foretold that the world would hate the true Christian. John informs us that we must not "love the world nor the things in the world." One element of pure religion is to "keep ourselves spotless from the world." Our citizenship is in heaven from whence we look for the glorious appearing of our Lord and Savior. Our treasures are to be laid up in heaven. Our calling is heavenly and also our blessings. Our affections are to be set on things above. Our wisdom is not of this world, but cometh down from above. Our faith is not to stand in the wisdom of men, but "in the power of God." Our hope is for spiritual glories. Our city cometh down from above. Yes, like Israel of old, we must go three days' journey from Egypt, the world, before our worship will be acceptable with God. The message and mission of the church is therefore threefold. First, that of personal salvation, getting people saved from the penalty and guilt of sin. Second, that of personal sanctification, keeping them saved from the dominion and power of sin. Third, that of personal glorification. Call it religious selfishness, if you will; how we wish all were thus selfish then!

When we secure this vision of the task of the church has she been a failure? The world has pronounced her such. Under Constantine, the world wooed the church from her true character and mission into a worldly program which she has more or less been following ever since. Now, because the church has not performed the impossible, cleaning up the world from the outside of the world pronounces her a failure. She is demanding the impossible. But in her real mission, the church is a success. She can sing the song of victory. God's will is being accomplished. Do you suppose God will let puny, insignificant, infinitesimal man to prevent the accomplishment of his purpose? Soon the bride will be complete, then he shall come to call and claim his own. "Even so come, Lord Jesus."

We are suspicious of the Interchurch World Movement because it has so little of the true mission of the church within its program. It boasts that "a united Christendom is invincible." Is it? It cannot do what God never has purposed to be done in this age.

We are fast plunging into the Laodicean state of the church, that state in which the church seks to please the world and the world dictates to thech urch. We have come to the last period of church history when the church is boasting of and trusting in her material power and wealth and forgetting that she is poor and maimed and blind as to spiritual things.

Finally Brethren, since we do not need to spend energy in social service or world betterment, we will concentrate our all upon prayer, upon evangelism, upon Christian experience, upon the divinely ordained program of witnessing to Christ unto the uttermost parts of the earth. We will be a church of great spirituality and missionary zeal.

Sunnyside, Washington.

Why I Am Not In Sympathy With the Interchurch World Movement

By C. E. Kolb

The Brethren church has made some serious mistakes in its history. With your privilege, Mr. Editor, I shall enumerate a few.

1. One of the most serious mistakes of all has been this insane campaign during the last three years to increase the subscription list of the Brethren Evangelist. By this means all the other foolish follies of the church together with the rabid ravings of miscalculating leaders of the church have been propagated. All this has been exceedingly harmful to the church. Not only this but what the future holds for the church in view of the large subscription list no one can forecast. The printing press at Ashland has become very largely a menace to the continuance and stability of the church and should speedily be muffled.

Closely connected with the Evangelist subscription fizzle (about 5500 now) is the effort of the editors of our church Sunday school literature to find sale for their publications. The whole system of publishing any religious literature is all wrong and works against the best interests of the church. Now along comes the Interchurch World Movement, or whatever it is called. I don't know much about it but I understand the editors and publishers are in it and that is enough for me. They are even suggesting that they need more money to carry on their work. Preposterous! The publishers hope to have more and bigger papers and so make it all the harder for the church to exist. Me for the good old days. Time was when we always closed the year with a Publishing Company deficit. That was great; that kept editors and publishers humble. But if we go to work and provide a lot of money for publication interests we will have to increase their salaries and then we will never get rid of them. Then with more money they will employ more workers in their plant and buy more printing presses. That will mean that the Sunday school literature and Brethren Evangelist will get to the users and readers on time and that would be inexcusable in the Brethren church. Woe to the day when Sunday school literature arrives on time. Our people should be kept in ignorance of the church work as long as possible and hindered from using helps to the study of the Bible as much as possible. Editors and publishers are propagandists of the worst type and they should be abolished by our refusing to support them with our money. So I am opposed to the Interchurch World Movement because it proposes to increase the publication interests of the church.

2. Then another very serious mistake of the Brethren church has been the practice of holding special services before Easter for the purpose of getting some "joiners." Now I say this, that one meeting a year is enough for any church and enough to let the sinners of any community know that the church wants to get them; but to have another just before Easter is too much of a good thing. Evangelism is all wrong anyhow. When a man hears the church bells ringing before services, isn't that enough of an invitation? What is the need of holding special meetings for them? Evangelism is too much a passing whim, the result of an over-excited mind to be allowed place in the Brethren church. Now along comes this Interchurch World Movement and the men, who, for all I know, (not knowing them at all) never held, a meeting, at the head of it, suggest that all the churches of the land hold meetings at the same time. the week before Easter. They call it a Simultaneous Campaign of Evangelism. I ask you honestly, Mr. Editor, did you ever hear of anything so foolish and unnecessary? Why, I was figuring on getting some of the members of another church near here into my church, but if all churches have meetings at the same time the members wil likely go to their own services, and—and—they'd miss my good preaching. Now you see that is all wrong. I know some of our preachers have found it just as easy to get members of another church

into theirs as to convert the sinners. They won't have near the chance if all the churches have meetings at the same time. All evangelistic meetings and evangelists are unnecessary and a mighty big expense and I can't see that they have ever done us much good. Consequently I am opposed to the Interchurch World Movement because it proposes to make evangelism and especially simultaneous evangelism one of the great interests of the church.

3. Then another mistake the Brethren church has been making is this business called, Home Missions. The very idea of going into a town and building a Brethren church or doing any kind of religious work. What are we coming to? Then in the cities there are so many foreigners and religion was intended for white people. I contend it is not the business of the church to try to convert a foreigner who comes to this land to Christ. If they want to organize their stiletto gangs, I say let them go to it and we keep our hands off, especially the church should keep away. What if they do teach that Christ was an illegitimate child; what if they are criminals and everything, let them alone. I'd like to ask you what business a peace loving Samaritan had going down to Jericho, when he knew there was a probability of finding some man who had fallen into foul hands? I know that every year a lot of our people move into towns, but instead of our taking the church to them through our Mission Board we ought to let them alone for they should have remained where our churches are. It is too expensive. I don't believe in any kind of missions, much less home missions. I can't see the need of them myself. They tell me, at least, I think that is the idea, that the Interchurch World Movement is in sympathy with home missions. Well. I'm not; and that is another reason I am opposed to the Movement. Spending money to find out that Columbus and Indianapolis are the only two cities of our country with a majority of native born Christians, and to find out that New York has as many Jews as there are people in Philadelphia is all foolishness. I tell you, Mr. Editor, we are fully informed now, and more than for our good; in fact, that is what hurts us. If the Brethren congregations have any surplus money they had better build new churches for themselves rather than helping other congregations. This is a bad mistake the Brethren church has made in being taken up with "home missions" and I am opposed to the Interchurch World Movement because it is trying to interest people in and cause them to pay to home missions and I think our Home Board is just right in being unsympathetic with the Movement. Bravo!

4. And then, Mr. Editor, it does seem to me that we have made the sad mistake of going completely crazy about this so-called "foreign missions." I don't read of any so-called foreign missions in the Bible, the same as I do not read of any Christian Endeavor Union, or International Sunday School Association. And let me say right here, that if the Brethren church gets into any more "interchurch" business like the above mentioned organizations, I can see the finis of our church. It is all of the devil, because,—that is —well, because I believe them to be such. At least if they are not of the devil just now, I think that PERHAPS—and mind you I place great emphasis on that perhaps—they might be later on.

Well, be that as it may, the Brethren church has gotten itself all "het up" over sending the gospel to a land that we never heard about and whose people we don't know. If it hadn't been for the propaganda in the Brethren Missionary and the Evangelist all would have been well. It seems to me if God wanted some black man over in Africa to be saved he would have done it far quicker than the church has been trying to do it. We have heard from time to time that if the Brethren church was not missionary it would have no reason for existence. Now isn't it strange, Mr. Editor, that if that is true that we have only two foreign mission stations in the whole world? I don't believe it pays to send our good, able men down to South America. There is Brother Yoder and Brother Bock, and I don't know the others so well, all able men, and they had far better stayed right here in Indiana where they started from. This Easter offering that takes up so much space in the Evangelist for a month or two before Easter is all wrong and shows that we are all inclined to get excited and be easily swayed by the impulse of the moment. Why, if all goes as predicted we will raise more than $20,000 this year. Terrible waste! I'll tell you, I'm against it.

Now along comes this Interchurch World Movement. And it sure is a "world" movement all right. Just look at the "worldlings" in it. There is Robert E. Speer, John R. Mott, E. Earl Taylor, Sherwood Eddy (he doesn't know anything about foreign missions), Bishop Henderson, Samuel Zwemer, W. E. Doughty, Lyman Pearce and a lot of others. I have no time for these men. They cannot be trusted. Of course I have not been to any of the pastor's conferences or other meetings, but folks say that foreign missions is the very backbone of the Interchurch World Movement. Well, if it is, it is doomed to die and it ought to die. You see we have made the mistake of getting mixed up with foreign missions in our church and if it is wrong in the Brethren church, or, I mean, if it was an error in the Brethren church it will be in this new business. I don't want my church members to have any more missionary appeals than they have had because that would be dangerous to the church. We ought not tell the people that one of the greatest assets of a missionary is his knowledge of medicine. Mission study classes are bad things, because if folks know too much about conditions in foreign lands they will become too sympathetic and so will fly off at a tangent. The first thing you know, if we go into this Interchurch business, we will be giving twice as much for missions as we now are. That would be a disgrace all right, and the greater work of the church would be hindered. It would be a sorry day for the Brethren church if the Foreign Board should come to have more money than it could use. Goodness, we would have to go into other lands and send out more workers and that would be a calamity we would never be able to overcome. The Foreign Board has just about thrown the church on the rocks now by making such strong appeals in the Evangelist. But suppose we would go into this Interchurch business; instead of being asked for $1.00 per member, we would be asked for $2.50. What then? I'll say it is time to call a halt. I think the Foreign Board is doing just the right thing in trying to keep down foreign missionary agitation by being unsympathetic with the movement and I think they will succeed. So I am opposed to the Interchurch World Movement because it advocates and seeks to promote foreign missions.

5. Then there is just one other mistake the Brethren church has been making that I want to write about today. I may write another letter some time soon again, about a lot of other things, but just now the mistake which is causing so much damage is our trying to get young women and young men to enter the ministry and missionary work of the church. I think they call it becoming a Life Work Recruit, or something of that sort. The church does not need any "recruits" for the ministry. I am not bringing up my children to be missionaries or preachers. There is a Student Volunteer Band at Ashland, I am told. Now you see, Mr. Editor, that is all wrong, trying to bring undue pressure upon young people. They ought to go into business and let somebody else do specific church work. The Life Work Department of Christian Endeavor should be discontinued as an unprofitable enterprise and the superintendent made to do penance by having him raised on a platform at National Conference. He is such a "small" man, narrow visioned, and the product of his day. Yes sir! I feel very keenly about

this matter and it sems to me that any preacher who with deliberate purpose try to persuade a man to enter the ministry should be anathema together with all who propound such doctrines of devils.

But the climax of the whole business is just here—that the Interchurch World Movement is organized down to each county of the nation in an effort to get young people for the church service. They say they are after 100,000 in the next five years. That is entirely too visionary. I suppose that would mean a full dozen for the Brethren church. That is more than we need unless we raised all that extra mission money. We ought not to plan to do more than break even year by year in the total number in the ministry. This year we will have a net loss of about five, all of which proves the foolishness of making any appeal for workers. I am opposed to the Interchurch World Movement because of its plan to enlist young people in the ministry and missionary work.

Now Mr. Editor, if the Interchurch World Movement proposes to do the same things that we have been doing in the past, and it does, and if they have been grand mistakes, it would seem unwise to double the mistakes of the past by engaging in this movement. What we ought to do is to get entirely away from all this, develop a scheme of our own and then we know it will be right. I'll write again one of these days.

Milford, Indiana.

Paul's Testimony to Christ's Resurrection
By T. Darley Allen

Dr. James Stalker says that the conversion of Saul of Tarsus "is one of the strong apologetic positions of Christianity." And today, when so much is heard from men and women who are critics of Christianity and the Bible as to the importance of the investigations of Lodge, Doyle and others to find scientific evidence of the life everlasting, it is well to direct attention to the "many infallible proofs" of our Lord's resurrection and especially to the testimony of the great apostle to the Gentiles.

For Paul's evidence is found in writings that are admitted to be genuine by the critics. Greg the rationalist said that Paul's testimony is an extremely strong evidence of the truth of Christianity; and a friend of mine, an agnostic who had given much time to the study of the subject, admitted that he found it far from easy to refute the argument for Christianity afforded by Paul's change from an enemy of the new religion to a convert to and defender of it.

Consider what the conversion of Paul meant. How can we explain why the great apostle, who had for years been zealous in his opposition to the religion of Christ and a persecutor of Christians, should all at once embrace the new faith, sacrificing because of his change in belief all his brilliant prospects, for a life of self-denial and suffering, unless he received overwhelming evidence that in trying to destroy Christianity he was opposing God?

For, it must be remembered that the question of the truth of Christianity was not one of an abstract nature after he had seen the risen Lord. It was not a mere opinion, but a matter of which his senses were the judge.

No satisfactory explanation except that given in the New Testament is possible to explain Paul's change from an enemy of the faith to perhaps the most zealous of all its preachers the world has ever had. And there is certainly good reason for believing that all candid, intelligent investigators will arrive at the conclusion reached by Lord Lyttleton, an eighteenth century skeptic, who was converted to Christianity after investigating the New Testament history of the apostle to the Gentiles, the result of his study being given in his "Conversion of St. Paul," an essay highly praised by the famous Dr. Johnson and one still holding a high place in the literature devoted to the defense of Christianity.

THE BRETHREN PULPIT

The New Day In Evangelism. By J. F. Watson

Text: And Philip ran thither to him and heard him read the prophet Esaias, and said, Understandest thou what thou readest? And he said, How can I, except some man guide me? And I desired Philip that he would come up and sit with him.—ACTS 8; 30, 31.

We see a new day, a new age, a new world. There is firm ground for optimism, for not in a generation has there been such a restless hunger, such a prophetic yearning to know how to bring men to God, how to find and lead the crowd of wandering sheep to the fold.

But in this new day we discover that while the old spirit is all-sufficient, the old methods are insufficient for the herculean task that the Son of God has set for us. There are three or four great characteristics that stand out clear and sure against the background of the evangelism of this new day, which give us hope and courage.

One of them is the new emphasis upon personality. The man is beginning to stand out from the mass. Julia Ward Howe once said to Charles Sumner in Washington, "Come down to my house and meet a personal friend." Sumner's reply was, "I am losing my interest in individuals and becoming interested in the race." Julia Ward Howe wrote in her diary that night, "By the latest accounts God Almighty has not got as far as this." God Almighty never will. And the church is at last coming to see Zaccheus instead of the crowd and to go down to his house for his soul's sake. In every community from which you come—almost every community—there are sections in which it is the ninety and nine that are out instead of the one. But the ninety and nine will be brought back just exactly as the one was brought back—by sending not one after the ninety and nine, but ninety and nine after the ninety and nine. There is a far deeper principle at work when Philip goes out and finds Nathaniel and brings him to Christ than when Peter stands up to preach a sermon that brings three thousand to Christ. The only evangelism that will ever bring this world to God is the evangelism that personalizes itself as evangelism has never done in the past.

Dr. Durbin once said in a great congregation, "No man is ever brought fully and finally to Jesus Christ except through the office of some other man." Dr. Peck being present arose and called his statement in question, saying, "Was not the Ethiopian brought to Christ by reading the Prophet?" And Dr. Durbin replied, "Understandest thou what thou readest? and the eunuch replied, "How can I except some man should guide me?" In that reply Dr. Durbin placed his skillful finger on one of the fundamentals of the coming Kingdom of God.

The sermon that won the three thousand to Christ on the day of Pentecost has dominated our ideals and methods all too long. We have tried to bring in the Kingdom by addition, and the Kingdom will never come except by arithmetical progression.

Another great characteristic of the evangelism of today is the fact that the church is coming to see that its chief business is to save the loss as well as the lost. One of the greatest things that Ruskin ever said, was in a letter to Alfred Tennyson. One day, after he had taken a walk in London and saw the children upon the streets wandering about without a shepherd, he went back and write this to Tennyson: "The more I see the world, the more do I believe that not the sorrow of the world is the wonder of the world, but the loss of world is the wonder of the world. I see by every wayside perfect miracles of possibilities in the lives of the boys and girls going to waste forever without a teacher." The chief business is not to save the lost as we have believed for centuries, but to save the loss, which is immeasurably more difficult and more imperative.

There is just one way to save loss, the incalculable loss which the church has sustained all along, and that is by feeding the lambs instead of hunting the sheep. In God's name brethren, if we cannot do both (we can), let us keep the lambs and let the few sheep stray rather than hunt the few sheep and let the lambs scatter to be found again. We will never accomplish real success until we centralize our work around the conservation of life instead of the reclamation of life. The Brethren church must learn the immeasurable value of the child. Here we can build the church of the future as we want it. If all the energy and devotion and time and service that have been given by the church universal to converting men into the Kingdom of God had been used in keeping the children from being converted out of the Kingdom we would no longer be praying, "Thy Kingdom come." The elder Dr. Tyng was right when, in a public address in Henry Ward Beecher's church, he said: "For years if the choice before me in my work as a pastor has been between one child and two adults, I have always been ready to take the child. It seems to me that the devil would never ask anything more of a minister than to have him feel that his mission was chiefly to the grown-up members of his congregation, while some one else was to look after the children." Then, pointing to the main entrance of the Plymouth Church auditorium, he continued with that peculiar intensity of his, "I can see the devil looking in at that door, and saying to the minister on this platform, Now you just stand there and fire away at the old folks, and I'll go around and steal the little ones."

"'The papal delegate, the official representative of the pope in this country, in addressing a great Roman Catholic gathering in the city of Chicago some years ago, said, 'Whenever there is a decline in faith and in morals it can be restored through the training of the children. From one child rightly reared, a whole generation of Christians can come. What they receive today they will give fifteen years hence,' and then he added, 'The great task of the church of Christ is the training of the young.' We shall never have a generation pervaded by the spirit of Christ and held in the grip of spiritual ideas, motives, and purposes until the church makes a vastly larger investment in the training of the childhood and youth in spiritual things."

I heard a minister say, "Sometime ago my people desired me to look after a certain wayward man about sixty three years old. I camped on the trail of that man for nearly three weeks, until I finally ran him down, brought him to church, got him to the altar, and he was converted to Christ. It was worth all the effort I made." Then he said, "With the time and effort it took me to win that man to Christ I could have won fifteen lads to the Master and saved them from that man's career. Does that not teach us something? Has not the time come for our church to shift its methods? Is it not worth as much to save a lad from becoming a drunkard, as it is to save him after he has become one? Is not formation worth as much to the Kingdom of God as reformation? Is not the business of the church of Christ to minister to lives beginning as well as to lives closing? The thing that I plead for this morning is not that the church do one whit less in behalf of lost men and women who have strayed from God's home. I would that we might do vastly more for those who have strayed from the Father of us all. But the thing that I plead for is that the church be summoned to care for her childhood and youth, to lead them to the church and to Christ. The future of the land is in the hands of that church that makes the largest investment in and the most successful venture with childhood and youth. The next thing that I call to your attention is the matter of your being entitled to know the experience of leading a man to Christ. There are close to four hundred active members in this church that could not do anything this day that would bring them such spiritual vision, such a holy thrill as would come to them by leading a man to Christ. There is no other thing, no other blessing or multiples of blessings that would put the church of Jesus Christ in such a state of grace as that every man and woman in it lead another to Christ. This needed evangelism is going to be very largely propagated, sustained, and extended around the life of laymen and laywomen.

"Pray ye, therefore, the Lord of the harvest that he would send forth laborers into his harvest." **Pray that he may send you!**   Johnstown, Pennsylvania.

OUR DEVOTIONAL

Faith In God's Providence. By O. E. Sibert

OUR SCRIPTURE

"Now faith is assurance of things hoped for, a conviction of things not seen" (Heb. 11:1). "Without faith it is impossible to be well pleasing unto him; for he that cometh to God must believe that he is, and that he is a rewarder of them that seek after him" (Heb. 11:6). "For this is the will of the Father, that every one that beholdeth the Son, and believeth on him, should have eternal life; and I will raise him up at the last day. . . Verily, verily, I say unto you, he that believeth hath eternal life" (John 6:40, 46). "Even so faith, if it have not works, is dead in itself. Yea, a man will say, Thou hast faith; and I have works, show me thy faith apart from thy works, and I wil by my works show thee my faith. Thou believest that God is one; thou doest well; the demons also believe, and shudder. But wilt thou know, O vain man, that faith apart from works is barren" (James 2:17-20)? "Whosoever is begotten of God overcometh the world: and this is the victory that has overcome the world, even our faith. And who is he that overcometh the world, but he that believeth that Jesus is the Son of God" (1 John 5:4-5). "As therefore ye received Christ Jesus the Lord, so walk in him, rooted and builded upon him, and established in your faith, even as ye were taught, abounding in thanksgiving". (Col. 2:6, 7, A. V.).

OUR MEDITATION

It will be well for us as Christians to first make sure of what we mean by faith. Although we as Christians come in contact with the necessity of faith in our early Christian life, many of us have a vague idea of what true faith really is. Let us note again what Paul says: "Faith is the assurance of things hoped for and the conviction of things not seen." That is to say, although we do not see these things which we hope for, we still believe in them and that we shall receive them. It may be belief as a result of a testimony of a friend, or an experience our individual life, or that of an experience observed in the life of another.

Further faith is a necessary element of the Christian life (Heb. 11:6). On our coming to God, faith is one of the first conditions in the plan of salvation: "He that cometh to God must believe that he is and that he is a rewarder of them that seek after him." Yes, even before we were inducted into the fellowship of the Holy Spirit; before we knew Jesus as our Savior, we first believed in him and in his power as the Son of God to save us from our sins. How much more then since we are brought into closer relationship with him, ought we to believe on him and his power among men.

Notice the great reward that is promised to them that believe. He that believed on the Son is to have eternal life according to John 6:40, 46. Yes, God is gracious and is willing to give his followers great rewards but since he is

so kind and loving toward those who met with the requirements, let us not asume that he does not expect something in return. Here is where too many are stopping today. Brethren, are we stopping at this point in our study of the Scripture? If so let us seek with greater diligence. For if we notice the words of James 2:17-20. as quoted above, it will be quite evident to us that faith alone will secure for none of us that eternal life for which we al hope. He who believed in God and does no works has done nothing of which to boast or for which he has any right to expect a reward, for "the demons also believe and shudder." In order that we may see and realize the truth of these statements, let us make a brief review of some of the examples of the Old Testament and of the modern day. Noah believed when the message came from God and proceeded with the work of building of the ark. Moses believed and had faith in the promise of the Lord. It was through this faith that he was able to lead the children out of bondage. It was through faith that the Hebrew children, when thrust into the fiery furnace, were able to pass into the flames unmolested. It was by faith that Daniel was delivered from the lion's den. Christopher Columbus was led through his faith to set sail out into the regions of the unknown sea. But if it had not had work connected with his faith, faith alone would never have accomplished the discovery of the new contentment. Are you connecting works with faith? Or are you like the good brother who believed that he had a plan which would make the Sunday school one of the largest in his community, but he neither did anything to work his plan nor did he tell any one else about it. Of what good was this brother's faith? What did faith in itself do for the school? Was not the faith without the works?

Note that in 1 John 5:4-5, we are told that faith, "is the victory that overcometh the world," and that "he that overcometh the world," is he, "that believeth that Jesus is the Son of God." Often we hear members of the church complaining because some undertaking has not been a success.

Before we go to God with excuses for our failure in carrying out the work of the Master, or for failure in any other phase of life's activities, let us be sure that we have connected with our faith works. Man is the agency which God uses to effect his purpose on earth; so along with our faith we must have a willingness to do whatever God may call upon us to do.

OUR PRAYER

"We praise thee, O God, for Jesus Christ, whose life has revealed to us this faith, and we rejoice that he has become the first born among many brethren. Grant that in us, too, the faith in thy fatherhood may shine through our life, with such persuasive beauty that some who still creep in the dusk in fear may stand erect as free sons of God, and that others who now through unbelief are living as orphans in an empty world may stretch out their hands to the Father of their spirits and find thee near." May we walk in the fredom and joy of faith, that men looking on us may learn to trust and to love thee." Amen.

Ashland, Ohio.

CHRIST'S METHOD DISCARDED

Christ's method of evangelism has been largely discarded in modern times. Christ not only began a campaign of personal evangelism. He trained a small group of disciples; communicated his purpose and passion to them; then he entrusted his program of evangelistic conquest to this group. If that method is followed in America today there can be but one result: a steadily growing Kingdom in strength and size.

If a pastor will secure the evangelistic facts of his parish; then form an inner circle of workers just as our Lord did; communicate to them the passion of his own spiritual program of evangelistic conquest to laymen under pastoral direction, the Jerusalem plan of Christ will prove efficient anywhere.—T. S. Henderson.

Send
WHITE GIFT
OFFERINGS to

THE SUNDAY SCHOOL

ALBERT TRENT
General Secretary-Treasurer
Johnstown, Pennsylvania

The Great World's Sunday School Convention

We are not informed of any delegates from any of the Brethren churches going to the World's Sunday School Convention, but we are sure there are a host of Brethren people who are deeply interested in the convention and would like to go but cannot. It is our purpose therefore to keep our people informed from time to time as thoroughly as our advantages will permit concerning the plans for the trip, the convention itself and the many side-interests connected with this great world gathering. If there are those among our number who are expecting to go to Tokyo, we shall be pleased to have them write us personally about it, so that, if possible, we may make arrangements for some special reports of the trip and the convention. We suggest that every Sunday school and Sunday school worker plan to get in touch with and appropriate as much as possible of the Sunday school vision and momentum which this great gathering will give forth.

HUNDREDS BOOKING FOR THE SUNDAY SCHOOL CONVENTION IN TOKYO

Pennsylvania is still in the lead when it comes to the number of delegates who are going to the Eighth Convention of the World's Sunday School Association which will be held in Tokyo next October. More than 85 have registered from that state and others are asking for information. Ohio stands second with 29 bookings and New York is third with a record of 26. The first sailing will be July 30 on the "Fushimi Maru" from Seattle. That party will visit both North and South China and Manila before the Convention. Four ships carrying delegates will sail in August and the last of the delegates will leave on the "Empress of Russia," September 22, from Vancouver. These and those going on the "Tenyo Maru," September 17, from San Francisco, will arrive in Japan just the day before the Convention begins on October 5th. While some of the outgoing and returning tours have been booked to capacity there are still good reservations to be had on other tours with very interesting itineraries.

Sme who take the Around-the-World tours will stop over in India for four weeks before proceeding to Egypt, Palestine and Europe. At most of these places Sunday school rally meetings will be held. Tens of thousands will have the advantage of hearing the Sunday school specialists who will be among the delegates. More than thirty post-convention meetings will be held in the Far and Near East and the last rally before the delegates separate at Marseilles will be at Jerusalem, where the Fourth World's Convention met in 1904. The great Commission said, "Beginning at Jerusalem," but thisti me it will be from the "uttermost" parts of the earth to Jerusalem. Of course there will be echo meetings in England, Scotland and many in the United States and Canada. Prospective delegates are already making dates to speak upon their return to the home land. All information concerning the Tokyo Convention can be obtained by addressing the World's Sunday School Association, 216 Metropolitan Tower, New York City. Frank L. Brown is the Joint General Secretary.

SUNDAY SCHOOL PLANS IN KOREA

It ought to be suggestive to us to note how Korea is planning for Sunday school advancement and to get the most possible from the World convention to meet so near at hand. The Korean Sunday School Association has requested each of the four major missions working in that country to set apart one of their best equipped missionaries to give special attention to the work of the Sunday school in preparation for and during what will be called "the Sunday school year." This will be in 1921-1922. At present the Christian

workers in Korea are devoting themselves to prayer and evangelism. What this Sunday school year will mean in Korea can be easily visualized by having in mind that the whole church membership in Korea is now in the Sunday school, and that it is possible almost anywhere to gather children even of non-Christian parents in any number.

In order to make the year as effective as possible they have appointed a committee to give particular attention to the preparation of teacher training and inspirational literature. They plan to circulate thousands of copies of this literature and thus educate the whole church as to its responsibility and opportunity. Every part of Korea is to be visited during the year of preparation to explain the whole plan. The existing Bible classes will be centres of widening influence.

Both before and after the World's Sunday School Convention in Tokyo, next October, inspirational meetings will be held in Korea by leading convention speakers. Five post-conventions have already been announced. They will be held at Taiku, Seoul, Pyengyang, Kwangju and Wonsan. At least half of the delegates who go to the Tokyo Convention have chosen an itinerary that will permit them to visit Korea and China.

M. L. Swinehart of Kwangju, Korea, has been appointed by the Interchurch World Movement to give special attention to the delegates, so that in different cities in the Orient full opportunity may be given for visiting mission stations.

Concerning Prayer

"But when ye pray, use not vain repetitions, as the heathen do: for they think that they shall be heard for their much speaking. Be not ye therefore like unto them: for your Father knoweth what things ye have need of, before ye ask him. After this manner therefore, pray ye:

Our Father which art in heaven, hallowed be thy name. Thy kingdom come, thy will be done in earth as it is in heaven. Give us this day our daily bread, and forgive us our debts, as we forgive our debtors. And lead us not into temptation, but deliver us from evil: For thine is the kingdom, and the power and the glory forever. Amen.

For if ye forgive men their trespasses, your heavenly Father will also forgive you: But if ye forgive not men their trespasses, neither will your Father forgive you trespasses" (Matthew 6:7-15).

"If any of you lack wisdom, let him ask of God that giveth to all men liberally, and upbraideth not, and it shall be given him. But let him ask in faith, nothing wavering. For he that wavereth is like a wave of the sea driven with the wind and tossed. For let not that man think that he shall receive anything of the Lord" (James 1:5-7).

"Wherefore let him that thinketh he standeth take heed lest he fall. There hath no temptation taken you but such as is common to man: but God is faithful, who will not suffer you to be tempted above that ye are able but will, with the temptation also make a way to escape that ye may be able to bear it" (1 Corinthians 10:12, 13).

"But the fruit of the spirit is love, joy, peace longsuffering, gentleness, goodness, faith, meekness, temperance: against such there is no law" (Galatians 5:22, 23). "But the wisdom that is from above is first pure, then peaceable, gentle and easy to be entreated, full of mercy and good fruits, without partiality and without hypocrisy" (James 3:17);

Our Young People at Work

Intermediate Bible Studies

Mrs. Chas. W. Abbott, superintendent of the Dayton Intermediate Society, sent us the two Bible talks given by Intermediates of that society. The studies seem to be very profitable.

God.   By Williard Danziesien

There is only one God; one real god, who is "Our Father," in heaven. There are three persons in the true God. The Father, the Son, and the Holy Spirit. No man hath seen God, only the begotten Son, and he has declared him. God's love was so great that he sent his Son to die on the cross of Calvary that we might be saved. God provides us still with what we need. Moses said unto God, behold when I come unto the children of Israel, and shal say unto them, The God of your Father's hath sent me unto you, and they shall say unto me, What is his name? What shall I say unto them? And God said unto Moses, I am that I am; thou shalt say unto the children of Israel, and shall say unto them, The God God said moreover unto Moses, Thus shalt thou say to the children of Israel, The Lord, God of your fathers, the God of Abraham, the God of Isaac, and the God of Jacob hath sent me to you, this is my name forever. And this is my memorial unto all generations. Unto Abraham, Isaac, Jacob, I appeared as, the **"Almighty God"** and was not known as Jehovah to them.

Almighty God means Jehovah, Creator, strength, sus-tainer, power and Supreme Being. Governor of the world. His truths and dominion shall last for ever and ever.

Jesus Christ.   By Myron Kein

Jesus Christ is the only begotten "Son of God." He was conceived by the Holy Spirit and born of a virgin named Mary. Jesus was divine, yet human. At Christ's birth, Augustus Caesar, was Emperor of Rome. Herod, King of Judea, sought to kill the Christ Child, but could not because God warned Joseph, his earthly father to flee with him into a strange country, which he did. God had prepared the world for his coming and yet the Jews did not know him as their Savior and King.

It was the best time in all the history of the world wherein Christ might have become their King. All the world at that time was subject to one government. The world was at peace. The Greek language was spoken everywhere. The Jews had their Bibles and synagogues, yet they did not know their King and thus the Scripture became fulfilled. Jesus Christ was as human as we are. He is our true Savior; he brought with himself wisdom and power for the salvation of the souls of men. He knows our weakness, sorrows and sins. He was sent to preach the truth and to heal the sick. Jesus had enemies when he preached; he also had friends who heard him gladly. And they became his disciples and went about teaching and preaching and thus they have sent the gospel of Jesus Christ unto all parts of the world.

A Modern Epistle to the Church of America

The following letter, beautifully embossed by the monks of Erivan, and expressing the deep gratitude of the Armenian people for the assistance rendered their nation by America, was brought over by the Archbishop Khoren of Arivan, to be presented to the President of the United States.

GEORGE, Servant of Jesus Christ and by the Omniscient WILL of God, Arch-Priest and CATHOLICS OF ALL THE ARMENIANS, Supreme Patriarch of the highest Armenian See of Ararat and of the Apostolic Mother Church at Etchmiadzin the Holy.

To the NOBLE CITIZENS OF THE UNITED STATES OF AMERICA:

AFFECTIONATE GREETINGS AND BLESSINGS from the CATHOLICS OF ALL ARMENIANS and Apostolic Chief of the Holy Church of Armenia.

With placid profound feelings of devotion, we desire, through this hierarchal letter of ours, to place before you and to make known to you the expressions of our deep gratitude for the liberal help which, inspired by a spirit of philanthropy, you have extended to us both by individual personal donations, and through the sustaining assistance and alleviating instrumentality of the Near East Relief Organization. Individually and collectively, combined in one body, as it were, you gave and you brought to us the fruits of your offerings, to the salvation and protection of our flock, during the most bitter days of their suffering.—sufferings which we attribute to the rigours of the War of Liberation, and to the cruelty of our implacable oppressors.

In expressing our thanks for your generosity and for your evangelical commiseration, we, as the recognized head of our spiritual children, comprising the entire Armenian nation, would be glad to view your acts of mercy as tokens of your continued assistance in the future, and that it is your purpose to continue to assist us in our regeneration and complete liberation, in the habiliment of a self-governing nation.

With these things in mind, we appeal to you all; to your devout bishops, our brethren and beloved in our Lord Jesus Christ; to men endowed with political and civil acumen; to those who have been called upon by the Lord in the conduct of public thought; and to every soul in which the spirit of Christian philanthropy glows, come to our defence and to the cause of the freedom of our flock. Come from the pulpits of your churches; from the seats of your council chambers; from the platforms of public associations; from the sanctum of your journals. Raise the mighty voices of your nation and of your sympathetic people, as those of unfailing and unfaltering friends. We need them for the salvation of our flock, tortured in body and soul through centuries of suffering. And our people will forever stand in history as witness that a great nation, prolific of welfare, stretched its helping hand and mighty arm to raise thru up.

The grace of our Lord Jesus Christ, and our thankful blessings be with you all, evermore, Amen."

From the dignified wording of this epistle, one might be again in the ages of the apostles, when the epistles of Paul sent greetings and careful directions to the people of Ephesus, Corinth and ancient Rome. The Christian church in the Near East is suffering prosecutions no less today than in the first centuries, and that oldest Christian nation, Armenia is today sending salutation and appeals for further aid to this strong young country of the west.

Fix your eye on the goal of all spiritual attainment and never take it off.

Power without intelligent direction is a serious menace to the peace and safety of the world.

"Know ye not that ye are the temple of God and that the spirit of God dwelleth in you? If any man defile the temple of God, him shall God destroy; for the temple of God is holy, which temple ye are" (1 Corinthians 3:16, 17).

Impromptu Flashes.   By W. J. H. Bauman

Salvation by grace—unmerited favor—is God's plan of saving mankind from sin. See Ephesians 2:8, 9.

Saving grace is a gift from God, and must be appropriated on our part through faith. See reference above.

Works constitute the life of faith; without works faith is dead (James 2:17, 18).

The simplicity of God's plan of salvation increases OUR responsibility.

The efficacy of our good works in God's great plan of salvation depends altogether on the motive that prompts them. "For with the heart man believeth unto righteousness." Romans 10-10).

Jesus said, "If ye love me keep my commandments" (John 14-15.) Do you love him?

Ancient prophecy, along many lines can never be more literally fulfilled than it is today.

The poetic sentence, "Hate the sin with all your heart, but still the sinner love," is gloriously sublime in poetic love.

Biblical love has grandly assumed a practical character. Its ardency is not founded on mere sensationalism.

If you did not believe any more than you are able of comprehending, how much would you believe?

Are you selfish? If so, get rid of it, for it's the root of all evil (See 1 Tim. 6:10, German version).

In social life, and often in church life, wealth is enthroned; clean character should have the preference .

"Your citizenship is in heaven."

"Ye are not of this world."

Poverty is not piety; but with God is on equality with wealth.

"My kingdom is not of this world; if it were then would my servants fight."

How do the above notations, and many others, justify the church dabbling in politics?

You claim to have faith in Jesus. Have you also faith in his commandments?

Baptism from every correct viewpoint, means a burial. If you can think of something more simple than God's plan of salvation, please inform me.

O how lonesome this life would be for many of us humans, especially us older ones, could we not live in sweet communion with God.

Jesus taught his people to love even their enemies and to do good to those who despitefully used them. Would such love justify them in harming others in any way?

"The Bible, the whole Bible and nothing but the Bible," —that's the way the Brethren creed reads. It is brief in manuscript, but wonderful in meaning, and weighty along the line of responsibility.

Marvelous are thy works, O God.

The greatest wisdom attainable by us humans, comes directly from the triune God of the Bible.

The popular idea of today is that a new day has dawned upon the world. I don't see why it should be regarded as so very new, when we know that the ancient prophets of 3000 years ago, saw it more plainly than we, as yet, do. Astoundingly literally today is ancient prophecy being fulfilled.

Long Beach, California.

SEND ALL MONEY FOR
General Home, Kentucky and
Foreign Missions to

MISSIONS

WILLIAM A. GEARHART
General Missionary Secretary
906 Conover Bldg., Dayton, O.

From a Little Home Missionary

The following letter from little Edna Rempel was forwarded to us by Brother Gearhart. Edna is eleven years old and is taking deep interest in the mission work of Krypton. Our readers, especialy, our little folks, will be glad to learn more about their little home missionary by reading her letter to Brother Gearhart.—Editor.

Krypton, Kentucky, June 1, 1920.

Dear Brother Gearhart:

We are missing those lovely letters from you. Wonder why you don't write any more. Well, we know you are Very busy but we miss your letters just the same. How we would love to hear your knock again some evening. The Lord has certainly answered prayer for our Sunday schools. Mama and myself go to Campbell Creek every Sunday afternoon while papa goes to Chanea. He started a Sunday school there a couple weeks ago. It is a hard field but we pray that the Lord will do what he has done for these other Sunday schools. At Campbell's Creek, we have 43 to 54 every Sunday afternoon. Men, women and children come to Sunday school. They keep the school house locked to keep the Holy Rollers out. So the people who live next to the school house have invited us to hold Sunday school there. Mama has a Bible class and started with the fall of man and is going through the Bible

showing them their lost condition and need of a Savior. It is hard or impossible to get people to help because they don't know the Lord. So we have divided the Sunday school into two classes, and while mama teaches the big class, I tell the children Bible stories. Pray that the Lord will show these dear people the need of their Savior. At Krypton we have had from 76 to 83 present and we expect 100 next Sunday. Our Sunday school offering last Sunday was $2.05. The Sunday before last papa had 17 boys in his class. We are so glad that we have such a good attendance but our prayer is that these may accept Jesus as their personal Savior. It is pretty hard to come home after Sunday school and start Junior right away, but we enjoy it for the Lord's sake. For we have from twenty to twenty-five every Sunday evening. Well, I must close now.

Yours in the Lord's service,
EDNA REMPEL.

Two Evening Calls

By a Mountain Missionary Way Back in the Hills

(Note—The half has not been told by the writer of the following. G. C. Carpenter).

It was at evening that we made the call, in

order to find the whole family at home. On knocking at the door, the response was a call from the farther room, "Come in." As the door was buttoned on the inside, the little six-year-old girl came to open it. We were taken into the farther room and the little girl was sent to the kitchen, the only room, through which we had entered to "get the box." There was not a chair in the home. A part of the broken frame was there of the chair we had given them a few days before. The man of the family sat on the edge of the bunk made up on the floor. The bedstead stood without anything on it, even the slats were gone, and the man remarked that his woman was "too sorry to go get kindling, but had chopped up the bed slats. It was no good for a bed anyway as it dropped them down." (It was an iron bed that a neighbor had discarded, and it sprung in the middle and let the slats fall). I remarked, "I would have push enough to wire it in the middle, so it could not spring and let them down." The "woman" sat on the floor leaning against the side wall. The son was in the other bunk that was made up on the floor. There was a good fire in the stove and absolutely no other article of furniture in the room. The kitchen contained a cook stove, table and a few stove and table dishes.

After seating myself on "the box," and putting my box on the floor, I visited a few minutes, then asked if they wanted some music. With the harp, I, sang a few hymns and read and prayed with them. Then had personal conversation with the man about his soul. His wife claims she is a Christian and a church member, but she can lie, when she thinks it to her personal advantage. The little girl has attended Sunday school a few times.

The second call was at a home nearby, the house built on the side hill, as there is scarcely enough level ground here on which to build houses. One front room with porch, and cellar on the first floor; stairway in porch leads to second floor porch. There are five rooms on the second floor, besides a large porch across the front of the house. On entering,

we found the mother and five children and dog about the fireplace, the mother ''cleaning up'' one of the children. She did a thorough task with her head and hair, rinsing out the soap, then taking the feet. Quite in contrast to the condition of all in the home first mentioned. We scarcely ever see this mother but that she mentions ''cleaning up'' the children and washing. She certainly is clean.

After giving three osteopathic treatments, one for sore throat, goiter and headache, we got out the harp, and all sang some of our Easter and Sunday school songs. The girls have good voices and love to sing. The two boys do not care much about it, and seldom help. The father reads music, when written with the shaped notes.—From the Soul-Winner.

SPECIAL NOTICE

Pledges made at Winona Conference last September for the Kentucky Mission Field should be paid as soon as possible. Also ''Home Guard'' membership dues. We are anxious to secure this money so as to be able to include it in our yearly report.

WILLIAM A. GEARHART,
General Missionary Secretary.

Wanted: A cook and a matron for Riverside Institute, two different persons for two different positions. These positions must be filled by the time the coming school term begins in July. The Kentucky Committee is anxious to have applications from a number of parties. Write to William A. Gearhart. 906 Conover Building, Dayton, Ohio.

NEWS FROM THE FIELD

SPOKANE SUMMARIES

It's been so long since we wrote any church news from Spokane that we're almost ashamed to begin now. We have all the reasons and excuses that anyone ever had for not writing, but we'll take advantage of none of them. We sent in a notice that we would be leaving Spokane in June, but we'll have to take it all back. We aren't going at all. ried to get away, but couldn't make it worth a cent. So we're here for another year and a fine one it's going to be. It has already turned out pretty fair, having had over thirty accessions since the first of the year. Have two or three to baptize now and will baptize again next Sunday night.

The work here is in splendid shape, financially, morally and spiritually, and getting better all the time. Church attendance and interest is fine and the Sunday school stands at the 150 mark. We had an offering of $330 for Foreign Missions on Easter. Our Sunday school is forging ahead under the splendid leadership of our Sister Lillian Bowers. Once a month we have missionary day with a special talk by our missionary superintendent and an offering is taken. Envelopes are distributed to each child the week before for this purpose. The missionary spirit is gripping this people in a splendid way, as they have shown by setting their Foreign Missionary goal next Easter at $1,000! Say, they'll make it too!

All the ministers in this city who believe in the Second Coming of our Lord have joined together in an association to have monthly conferences in the various churches interested. They conferred the responsibility of chairman of this body upon your humble servant. We are glad for this increased opportunity to spread the good news.

Our District Conference of the Northwest will be held at Sunnyside this year from July 28-August 1. We are looking forward to it with great interest and expect a genuine benefit from it. Brother Ashman will have an announcement of it soon. We are planning to have a fleet of Fords and automobiles make the trip of 200 miles up there from Spokane. We are planning a great get-together day

on October 3, when every member of this church within possible reaching distance will be home in the old fellowship for an all day meeting. I believe this is enough for this time, or Brother Baer is likely to get out the scissors on about half of this paper. I guess he thinks I'm rather long-winded anyhow. But every time he asks me for an article it's one of my longest!

Philippians 4:13.

THE BIBLE STILL IN DEMAND

If any one thinks the Bible is becoming an out of date book it will be enlightening to read the following, and then remember that this is only one company of several large ones publishing the Bible on a large scale.

275 miles of Bibles would reach from New York to Boston, on to Lowell and just run over into New Hampshire. And this is the kind of path the American Bible Society could lay with the Scriptures published by it during the past year.

The annual report of the Society just made public, shows that over 3,400,000 volumes were issued during 1919. Of those about 350,000 were Bibles, 550,000 Testaments, and 2,500,000 portions of Scriptures.

Nearly 140 million Scriptures have been issued by the Society during its history of 104 years.

During the World War 6,678,301 Testaments were distributed among the belligerent forces of all nations.

A novel feature of the year is the completion of the great Mandarin Version of the Chinese Bible, which has cost several hundred thousand dollars and took 25 years of work on the part of the translators. This Version makes the Bible accessible to over 400 million people, or one-fourth the population of the world; more people than were ever reached by any one translation in history.

ITINERARY OF MISS ABOUD

To prevent an endless amount of correspondence, to convince some Brethren that this preacher is really dated, to warn negligent officials that they should secure good evangelists a year hence, to allow churches

who really want the services of Miss Aboud, to get in the waiting line as soon as possible, we submit the following:

1920
March 3-13—West Alexandria, Ohio—First Brethren church.
March 15-April 4—Dayton, Ohio—First Brethren church.
April 7-25—Clayton, Ohio—Salem Brethren church.
April 26-May 16—Gratis, Ohio—First Brethren church.
May 17-30—Camden, Ohio—First Brethren church.
May 31-June 13—West Alexandria, Ohio—M. E. church.
June 14-July 4—Berne, Indiana—First Brethren church.
July 5-25—Columbus, Ohio—First Brethren church.
July 26-August 8—Williamstown, Ohio—First Brethren church.
August 9-29—Lanark, Illinois—First Brethren church.
August 30-Sept. 5—Brethren National Conference, Winona Lake, Indiana.
Sept. 6-26—Milford, Indiana—First Brethren church.
Sept 27-Oct. 24—Limestone, Tennessee—First Brethren church.
Oct. 25-Nov. 14—Peru, Indiana—First Brethren church.
Nov. 15-Dec. 12—North Manchester, Indiana —First Brethren church.
Dec. 13-Jan.2, 1921—Berlin, Pa., First Brethren church.
Jan. 10-30—Warsaw, Indiana—First Brethren church.
Jan. 31-Feb. 20—Ft. Scott, Kansas—First Brethren church.
Feb. 21-March 13—McLouth, Kansas—First Brethren church.
March 14-April 3—Milledgeville, Illinois— —First Brethren church.
April 4-April 24—Pleasant Hill, Ohio—First Brethren church.

A number of applications are now in transit and these will be booked in order of their arrival. Too many people in booking for a series of meetings pay more attention to the signs of the moon or the month of the year than they do to the opportunity of getting a strong evangelist and preceding the work of the evangelist by a series of prayer meetings. My address until July 15th will be 6101 Miramonte Blvd., Los Angeles, California.

E. M. COBB.

COLLEGE NEWS

It will be recalled that after the January meeting of the Board of Trustees, I sugested seven features to the financial part of the work here. They were as follows: the financial results of the Interchurch, the campaign on the Pacific Coast, the completion of the campaign in the East, a canvass of the graduates and former students, solicitation among certain large givers, budgeting the College, and the campaign here in the city and county. I want now to state the progress of each up to this point.

1. **The Interchurch.** The financial returns from this source are at present uncertain and inasmuch as this is in the hands for the most part of the president of the Board, I need say nothing further here.

2. **The Coast Campaign.** At present there are no definite plans formulated in this. Whatever is done, must be determined at a later date.

3. **The Campaign in the East.** Dr. Beachler is now in Maryland and from the report already sent in from his first stop, Linwood, it promises well. I have no doubt but that the East will do its full part.

4. **The Canvass Among Former Students** is bringing most gratifying results. Mr. A. H. Lichty is the general chairman of this work and the result so far totals a bit over two thousand dollars and we are just beginning. Shively, J. A. Garber, and the writer here at the college will push this as fast as possible this summer up to Conference time. Just think, what even two thousand dollars will mean to buy books as compared to what we have been having in the past! Surely this looks good.

5. **The friendship of certain men of large** financial means is being cultivated and when the time comes, I believe there will be a good response but at this date nothing definite can be announced.

6. **Budgeting the College.** I have had some rather extended correspondence with different members of the church concerning this and they with no exception think this ought to be done. One fact is absolutely certain, THIS PRESENT FACULTY CAN NOT BE RE-EMPLOYED NEXT YEAR IF OUR RESOURCES ARE NOT MATERIALLY ENLARGED. IT CAN NOT BE DONE. Ne one of the teachers can be accused of having an itching hand, but all have legitimate expenses which must be met. The two new members of the faculty, Brother Wolford and Brother DeLozier are coming at a financial sacrifice and are willing to help lift on the burden, but without further argument, it is evident that the church ought to take as good care of her educational institutions as any other part of her work. Not less for missions, not at all, but more for religious education.

And I write this last sentence with a full knowledge of what I say, for I am perfectly confident that there is not another interest of the church which surpasses in any way the educational interest in importance. It is ardently hoped that at the coming General Conference, steps may be taken in this direction.

7. **The Campaign in the City and County.** I have cultivated this with great care and have been in the closest communication with the men of influence in Ashland for several months. There are several local conditions upon which we must wait and about which nothing can be made public, but I am free to say that the plans are shaping up nicely. I am confident that the city will do a handsome thing for us within the year. The preliminary steps are already taken and as soon as local conditions shape up, the matter will be made public.

A glance over these seven factors in our fihancial success will reveal encouraging progress. I do not believe that any one of the seven will fail when it comes time. If there is such an one, I do not know which one it would be.

The summer sessions are well attended. The first term we had 49 enrolled. Up to this year, the first term never had more than 25. This second term will doubtless total in the neighborhood of 100. This may not seem important to the church, but it is. For, if we are to have a summer session at all, it ought to be a success rather than a drag. And moreover, this is the gateway for many to college work.

I was at Flora, Indiana, three weeks ago and had a very profitable time. Flora has one of the finest church buildings in the brotherhood and the membership seems interested and loyal.

EDWIN E. JACOBS.

HUDSON, IOWA

Hudson has not been heard from for a long time, so I am taking this liberty of writing of some of the happenings uriefly. As we view the work of the immediate past at Hudson we are pleased to note signs of real progress in various departments. The church is beginning to catch the missionary vision and the increased offerings for Home and Foreign Missions bear live testimony to this fact. This is as it should be for when a church fails to see the world through the Master's eyes it is in a deplorable condition. The local services are not as well attended as they should be though the morning services are improving considerably since the roads have become passable. We had fine services on Mother's day and Memorial Day—the latter being a union service of the three churches in the town. The large audience assembled at the cemetery on Sunday morning, May 30, and after the singing of the national anthem and the hymn ''Stand up, Stand up for Jesus'' and a devotional period the audience was ready for the splendid message delivered by the minister of the Baptist church. In this message the preacher referred to the occasion that had brought us together briefly recalling the causes and results of the Civil War. He then portrayed the growing sense of the ideal

of freedom through our 144 years of national life and closed with a splendid appeal to all to stay true to the Christian principles and splendid virtues that played so large a part in the Puritanic spirit of the early settlers. We believe the effect of the message was great.

Hudson got into the Interchurch Financial drive. There were things about the Interchurch we didn't like but we tried to instruct our people aright, held up strenuously the fundamentals of the Christian gospel regardless of what the leaders of the Interchurch believed—for as I recall they did not try to force their beliefs on us at Hudson, and got whatever of good out of the Movement we could. What our future course will be depends on what action our National Conference takes regarding a forward movement program. It appeals to me that the finest and best thing the Brethren church can do at our coming conference will be to put up a program so well balanced and so emphatic in its Christian challenge that misunderstanding will be done away in the striving to achieve the biggest and most lasting results.

The church has called the pastor to serve for the year 1920-21 at a thirty-five percent increase in salary. It feels find to know that you're appreciated.

Fraternally yours,
EDWIN BOARDMAN, JR.

The Tithing Stewardship Corner

A LAYMAN
We Are All Stewards

Whether we are willing to acknowledge it or not, aware of it or not, every one of us is a steward. To escape stewardship is as impossible as to escape death or taxes. Of consequence the word ''stewardship'' needs a defining adjective. Among the Scripture definitions are ''good,'' ''faithful'' and ''unjust.'' Many more, such as ''indolent,'' ''neglectful,'' ''poor,'' ''inefficient,'' ''unprofitable,'' etc. might be added.

The stewardship of every man living needs an adjective to describe it; with many of us several adjectives might be needed. Some of us might be classed as good stewards in the matter if prayer and profession; and—well, call it ''neglectful''—stewards in paying what we owe to God and, consequently, in service to our fellow men. Tithing is the beginning of good stewardship.

May 1, 1920.

My Dear Laymen:

Here is a brief word on the results of Stewardship in the Methodist Church.

First: There is a new attitude toward tithing stewardship. Unfriendliness has given way. Two years ago one or two papers were openly hostile. All our editors are now friendly. Most are now enthusiastic supporters of the stewardship movement.

Second: Misunderstanding has given place to understanding. There is less expression of the fear of legalism and more concern about the blight of covetousness. Much remains to be done in educating tithing stewards already enrolled and the multitude not yet enrolled. But there has already dawned among the rank and file the realization that we are approaching tithing merely as the A B C's of the larger stewardship of all of possessions, time and life.

Third: From the best reports that I can get from the twenty area offices and in conjunction with our central headquarter's files about a quarter of a million Methodists have taken the following covenant:

"In loving loyalty to my Lord and as an acknowledgement of his ownership, I covenant to pay the tithe of my income for the purpose of maintaining and extending the Kingdom of God."

Fourth: In addition, hundreds of thousands of others have increased their giving as an experiment in the matter until such time as faith dares to set apart the tenth.

Fifth: If we can believe the testimony of the leaders of the church, the financial victory of the missionary Centenary was made possible to a large degree by the stewardship campaign. Bishop William Burt says, "The revival of the stewardship obligation gave us our Centenary victory." The testimony of district superintendents is generally that the churches that conscientiously carried out the stewardship educational campaign were the ones that easily reached the Centenary quota.

Sixth: A multitude of transformed churches and individuals attest the value of the tithing stewardship message. The small volume, "Adventures in Tithing," bear witness to this point. As may always be expected, the transformation is not merely financial, but fundamentally a revival of spiritual life.

Seventh: To all appearances the tithing stewardship movement has gained a permanent place in the life of the Methodist Episcopal church. The leadership universally declares that the message of Christian stewardship is essential to the conservation of the five-year Centenary program and to the general reviving of the spiritual life in the churches.

Eighth: A definite educational continuation stewardship program is planned for the future, embracing woman's societies, the Epworth League, Sunday school and the church in general, in co-operation with the stewardship department of the Interchurch World Movement.

Sincerely yours,
RALPH S. CUSHMAN.

A man from Indiana writes: "Last summer at a stewardship meeting a lecturer, in speaking of the misappropriation of the tithe, related the instance of a woman who had charged to her tithing account what she gave to her mother-in-law, and rather derisively criticized her action with the evident approval of the audience. What is your opinion of his attitude?"

I would want to know all the circumstances before venturing to express an opinion, much less criticism. Presumably both were widows, one probably aged and needing help, the other young and willing to help. Which would most please and honor God; helping the mother-in-law or giving the money to the church, in both cases charging the amount to tithing account?

To my mind there can be but one answer. At any rate I would not criticize her action.

Would Comment be Cruelty?

On page 122 of "Money the Acid Test," a text-book on stewardship, after classing tithing as God's "Kindergarten Method" the author says:

"God has taken time to slowly train the race, leading mankind up by almost imperceptible gradations toward the ultimate standard. Growth in the grace of giving seems to have been very like the leading of a little child up a pair of stairs."

On page 122-9 he writes:

"When once the grace of giving is established in the human consciousness the scaffolding of statutes and ordinances is removed."

In the light of the following statistics under the head of "Small Giving," copied from "The Watchman," comment on the above extracts from "Money the Acid Test" would certainly border on cruelty.

"The members of the Northern Baptist church have been giving at the rate of a tithe of 33 cents or 3.3 cents per day for their local expenses and benevolent enterprises.

"The United Brethren church has been giving a tithe of 37 cents or 3 cents and 7 mills per day for local expenses and benevolences.

"The Presbyterian church has ben giving a tithe of an income of 56 cents or 5:6 cents per day for its entire local and general work.

"The Congregationalists are doing a little better. They gave a tithe of 61 cents or 6.1 cents per day for all purposes."

Do we doubt the possibility of living above the level of one's suroundings? Has not the possibility been proved and actualized in all ages of the world's history? Even in pre-Christian times and in pagan lands men have been known to rise above their low surroundings, transformed by the indwelling power of the faith they held. How much more should the faith we hold—the Christian faith—enable us to do this?—D. M. Edwards, in Modern Sermons.

TO THE AMERICAN PEOPLE,

In contrast with our Independence Day, Serbians celebrate the Battle of Kosovo, in which their entire army died fighting in defense of their land against the Turks, June 28th, 1389. They chose death rather than dishonor; and that was but a beginning of five hundred years of almost uninterrupted sorrows, culminating in the tragedy of the recent war, in which all their territory was occupied by the enemy, their land laid waste, their railroads destroyed and one-fourth of the population, including half the tax-payers wiped out by war, famine and disease.

Today in Serbia, there are thousands of helpless children, sick and unprovided for. There are isolated villages of fifteen and twenty thousand people broken in health, reduced to poverty and absolutely without physicians or medicines.

The National Birthday Committee of the Serbian Child Welfare Association, 7 West 8th Street, New York City, appeals to Christian people everywhere for money and clothing for these stricken people. The emergency is most urgent.

On the last Sunday in June clergymen are invited to commemorate in their sermons Serbia's gallant stand for the right and to ask aid for the orphan children. Special literature on the subject will be sent upon request.

Gratefully yours,
STANLEY F. HOWE,
National Chairman.

SEND YOUR OLD CLOTHING

The Near East Relief is asking for our old clothing for the destitute women and children of Armenia. Any substantial clothing will be acceptable, and if it has bright colors, it will suit the natives all the better. They like bright colors to give cheer to their saddened lives. But any kind of substantial clothing and any color will be gladly received. Send to Near East Relief, 1 Madison Avenue, New York, during June and July. From every part of the brotherhood there should come a response to this appeal for an Old Clothes Offering.

THRIFT THAT IS WASTE

Just what is thrift? To place the value of a discarded garment hanging in your closet higher than life? If that is thrift, it is a vice, and not a virtue. That discarded garment will keep some child warm next winter and perhaps save its life. Thousands died last winter because they were almost naked. Decide quickly, for old clothes are being collected this month to be sent to the Near East Relief.

ORPHANS FREEZE

We have peace and we have plenty. We do not appreciate the gift of either unless out of our bounty we give to those who lack. If you cannot afford to adopt one of the 100,000 orphan children in the Near East, by sending a small sum every month to the Near East Relief, you can afford to donate your old clothing to help keep this army of orphans from freezing to death next winter. June is the month for the collection.

WHITE GIFTS CONTIUNE COMING

The following White Gift offerings have been received since last report:

Ardmore, Ind.,	$ 12.43
Goshen, Ind.,	75.00
Windber, Pa.,	4.59
Johnstown, 2nd, Pa.,	5.00
Burlington, Ind.,	20.00
Linwood, Md.,	10.00
Philadelphia, 2nd, Pa.,	5.00
Corinth, Ind.,	10.07
Dutchtown, Ind.,	5.00
Calvary, N. J.,	5.00
Pike, Pa.,	4.11
Vinco, Pa.,	6.00
Mathias, W. Va.,	5.00
Pleasant Valley, Md.,	1.00
Santa Paula, Calif.,	5.00
Los Angeles, Cal.,	52.88
Long Beach, Cal.,	10.00
Liberty, Pa.,	1.00
Total,	$237.08

Some Reports Not Coming

More than two months have elapsed since the Report Blanks were sent to the superintendents of the Brethren schools, and quite a number have been sent the second time, and yet the following number of schools have failed to report to date for each district: California, 6 schools; Maryland-Virginia, 3 schools; Iliokota, 4 schools; Kanemorado, 3 schools; Indiana, 17 schools; Ohio, 8 schools; Pennsylvania, 13 schools; Kentucky (3 schools.

My fellow superintendents, you certainly do not expect me to present a report to National Conference without these 57 schools in the Jubilee Year of the Church!

Will you not get busy at once and return that card?

ALBERT W. TRENT,
General Secretary-Treasurer.

THE TIE THAT BINDS

GINGRICH-SMITH—An interesting college romance culminated in the marriage of Rev. Joseph L. Gingrich and Miss Beatrice Pearl Smith on the evening of June 3, 1920. They were married at the home of the bride's parents, northeast of Ashland in the presence of immediate relatives and friends. The bride graduated from the Normal course several years ago and since has taught school Very successfully. The groom took his A. B. degree in the late commencement when he delivered the Mantle Oration as president of the Senior Class. These promising young people have assumed pastoral care of the Mason-town, Pennsylvania, church. The best wishes of their many friends follow them.
J. A. GARBER.

ROBERSON-WILLIAMS — Bessie Roberson and Hansford Williams of Roanoke, Va., were united in holy wedlock at the home of the bride's parents, May 15, 1920 Ceremony by the writer in the presence of the relatives of the contracting parties.
L. G. WOOD.

KOONTZ-ROCKWELL—At the home of the bride's parents in Waynesboro, Pa., on the morning of March 4, Donald R. Koontz and Hazel M. Rockwell were united in marriage. Both are earnest Christian young people, talented and ready to use their talents nobly. They have the well wishes and the prayers of a large circle of friends for a happy married life. The ceremony which was witnessed by the immediate families of the bride and groom was performed by the writer.
M. A. WITTER.

DILLER-ALMERT—Miss Ella Diller to Frank Gus Almert, May 26, 1920. The bride is a faithful member of the First Brethren church of Peru. May the joys of the best life ever be theirs.
G. C. CARPENTER.

CLAM-GASAWAY—Miss Mildred R. Clam to Ralph Gasaway, May 20, 1920 Both of these young people are workers in the Center Chapel Brethren church. May many blessings attend their way.
G. C. CARPENTER.

IN THE SHADOW

WINEY—Mary H. Mohler Winey, wife of Elder J. G. Winey, was born in Darke county, Ohio. April 19, 1840, and departed this life May 14, 1920, at her home near Lake Odessa, Michigan, at the age of 80 years and 26 days. Immediately after her marriage to J. G Winey, they moved to Union City, Indiana, and later, in 1866 they came to Ionia county, Michigan and settled in the woods and began to clear a home for themselves. In the midst of their toil they did not forget to secure a home at the Lord's right hand, in 1862 Sister Winey was baptized into the German Baptist Brethren church. When the division of the church came she took her place with those who became known as the Brethren church, those who recognize no authority but the Word of God, and to this church she remained faithful until the Master called her home. Her greatest delight was the house of God and her place was seldom vacant. Though she was

faced with the hardships of a pioneer preacher's wife she raised a family of nine children and taught them the way of the Lord. Brother Winey was founder of the Campbell Brethren church and served them as pastor till his health failed him. He preceded his wife to the heavenly home on June 26, 1916. She leaves to mourn her departure nine children, one sister, eleven grandchildren and one great-grandchild, with a host of friends. Funeral services by the writer.
— M. V. GARRISON.

KLEPSER—Frederick M. Klepser died of paralysis May 6th, aged 68 years, 1 month and 21 days. He leaves a wife and four children as well as a large circle of friends to mourn their loss. He was a faithful member of the Brethren church of Martinsburg, Pa. He was a deacon and always willingly and faithfully did his work.

Brother Klepser was a devoted husband and father He lived a life above reproach and was always interested in the cause of his Master. Thus goes out of our midst a loving father, a kind husband, a good citizen and a loyal Christian and he will be greatly missed in the home, church and community. We pray that the Lord may raise up some one to take his place Funeral services were held from his home Monday, May 10th, at 10 o'clock. The services were conducted by the writer, assisted by Rev. W. C. Benshoff of Altoona and Prof. Edward Byers of Morrison Cove College. Interment was made in FairView cemetery.
J. I HALL.

BROWN—John David, infant son of Samuel and Della Brown was born Feb, 18, 1920. and departed this life May 16, aged not quite three months. May the God of all grace and comfort and console them in their sorrow. Services by the writer.
GEO. W. KINZIE.

HENLINE—Christian Henline was born in Saxony, Germany, March 14, 1830 and came to the United States at the age of 27 and settled at Lyons, Iowa. He was united with Miss Frederica Mahnke in marriage Feb 10, 1866. She preceded him in death sixteen years ago. There remain to mourn their loss, William Henline of Garwin, Charles of Luray, Mrs. Emma Knoblech of Toledo and Miss Minnie Henline of Cedar Rapids. Mr. Henline passed away March 27, at the home of his son Charles of Luray. Services were held in the Christian church, Garwin, and burial in the Garwin cemetery. Services by
FREEMAN ANKRUM.

HAYNES—Sarah Olive Haynes was born Sept. 22, 1853 and departed this life at the home of her son at Moulton, Iowa, April 21, 1920. She was united in marriage to Owen Leonard, July 30, 1874 She leaves to mourn her loss, her husband, one son and three daughters, five grandchildren and one great-grandchild. The daughters are Mrs. David Kennedy of Des Moines, Mrs, Fred Wallen of Marshalltown and Mrs. Jessie Hamilton of Kingsbury, Cal. The son is James Leonard of Moulton. She was a member of the Carlton Brethren Church, and had been a long resident in the community before moving away. Services at the Carlton Brethren church by Freeman Ankrum. Interment in Dobson cemetery.

GILLIN—On March 29, 1920, the Hudson church suffered the loss of one of its fine, sweet spirited members when Mrs. Anna Louisa Straley Gillin. was ushered into the Great Beyond. For years Mrs. Gillin had. been a great sufferer and for most of the last few years of her earthly life she was confined to her home, but through all this time of trial she never lost those traits of character which made her life the fine example of Christian fortitude and love that it was. Sister Gillin joined the Brethren church at this place in November, 1890, at the same time as her husband, S. B. Gillin, and daughter, Birdie B. During all her Christian experience our sister was one of those quiet souls whose beliefs are deep and strong and in all the years of her life she wielded a splendid influence for good in the community.

She will be better known to the Brethren at large as the mother of Dr. J. L. Gillin of Madison, Wisconsin, who for years served the church faithfully as a pastor and is now a beloved professor in the big university at Madison. Had Sister Gillin made no other contribution to the church, than she made in the person of her stalwart son her record would have been splendid, but in addition to this contribution, she lived a pure, consecrated life and gave the name Christian a deeper meaning here in Hudson. Her friends and loved ones mourn her departure but they find joy in the thought that the last words of the Apostle Paul to Timothy are so splendidly applicable to her life: "I have fought a good fight, I have finished the course, I have kept the faith. Henceforth there is laid up for me a crown of righteousness which the Lord,' the righteous Judge, will give me in that day and not to me only but unto all them which love his appearing."

Sister Gillin was born near Cedar Rapids, Iowa on December 16, 1850.
EDWIN BOARDMAN, JR., Pastor.

SHOEMAKER—Brother John Shoemaker, one of the oldest members of the Ashland, Ohio, church, departed this life on May 9th. For years he had been deprived of the blessings of sight, but he seemed to have alluring visions of spiritual realities. He gladly received the inevitable summons with unfaltering trust in the Lord. His departure is mourned by a sister, daughter, two sons and many friends. May each be comforted of God.
J. A. GARBER.

CLEMENT—Brother F. M. Clement died May 22, 1920, at the age of 45 years, 3 months and 11 days, death being due to an automobile accident. His car went over an embankment and pinned him under where he remained for seven hours before he was discovered. He only lived a few hours after he was rescued. He was a deacon in the Mount View church, was one of our most loyal members and will be sadly missed. He is survived by his mther, wife, three daughters, one son and a brother. The family have the sympathy of a host of friends in their sorrow. Funeral services by the writer, assisted by Brother L. G. Wood.
J. E. PATTERSON.

Cobb's Conference Corner

Conference is not far away. It is high time that we begin to plan for it. The Brethren church does not seem to place sufficient value upon our Conference. Besides it's spiritual uplift, it has a wonderful influence socially. To get the most possible good from church relationship, we should become personally acquainted with as many as possible in the church; and especially those who have official work to do.

Beside these two strong features, the Conference has educational value, for it is there we learn first-handed about our missions, our educational work, publishing interests, evangelism, Christian Endeavor, Sunday school and the most important thing of all is being emphasized most strongly this year, that of Bible study.

This is our Jubilee year. Let's make it our banner year. Let each church take a special interest in sending large delegations.
E. M. COBB.

Volume XLII
Number 24

JUNE 23
1920

The BRETHREN EVANGELIST

-ONE-IS-YOUR-MASTER-AND-ALL-YE-ARE-BRETHREN-

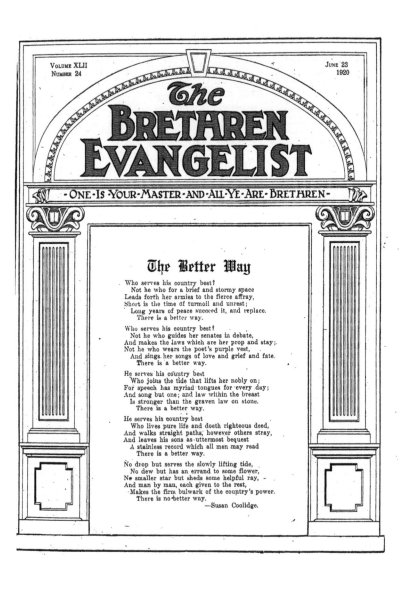

The Better Way

Who serves his country best?
  Not he who for a brief and stormy space
Leads forth her armies to the fierce affray,
Short is the time of turmoil and unrest;
  Long years of peace succeed it, and replace.
    There is a better way.

Who serves his country best?
  Not he who guides her senates in debate,
And makes the laws which are her prop and stay;
Not he who wears the poet's purple vest,
  And sings her songs of love and grief and fate.
    There is a better way.

He serves his country best
  Who joins the tide that lifts her nobly on;
For speech has myriad tongues for every day;
And song but one; and law within the breast
  Is stronger than the graven law on stone.
    There is a better way.

He serves his country best
  Who lives pure life and doeth righteous deed,
And walks straight paths, however others stray,
And leaves his sons as uttermost bequest
  A stainless record which all men may read
    There is a better way.

No drop but serves the slowly lifting tide,
  No dew but has an errand to some flower,
No smaller star but sheds some helpful ray,
And man by man, each given to the rest,
  Makes the firm bulwark of the country's power.
    There is no better way.

—Susan Coolidge.

Published eVery Wednesday at Ashland, Ohio. All matter for publication must reach the Editor not later than Friday noon of the preceding week.

George S. Baer, Editor

The
Brethren
Evangelist

When ordering your paper changed give old as well as new address. Subscriptions discontinued at expiration. To avoid missing any numbers renew two weeks in adVance.

R. R. Teeter, Business Manager

OFFICIAL ORGAN OF THE BRETHREN CHURCH

Subscription price, $2.00 per year, payable in advance.
Entered at the Post Office at Ashland, Ohio, as second-class matter.
Acceptance for mailing at special rate of postage provided for in section 1103, Act of October 3, 1917, authorized September 9, 1918. Address all matter for publication to Geo. S. Baer, Editor of the Brethren Evangelist, and all business communications to R. R. Teeter, Business Manager, Brethren Publishing Company, Ashland, Ohio. Make all checks payable to the Brethren Publishing Company.

TABLE OF CONTENTS

EDITORIAL

The Passion of True Patriotism

The passion of true patriotism is one of the strongest that burns in the human breast and doubtless at this season of the year its flame will receiVe added strength. The heart of eVery true American whether of home or foreign birth cannot help being quickened a pace as he meditates upon the causes that gaVe his country birth, the wealth of its heroic fruitage and the glories of its present high estate. Jacob A. Riis, born in Denmark, yet representing a splendid type of American citizenship, has told us in ''The Making of an American,'' how he discoVered that an American of foreign birth was really made and finished. His words present a picture one will easily remember. He says, ''It was when I went back to see my mother country once more, and, wandering about the country of my childhood's memories, had come to the city of Elsinore. There I fell sick of a feVer and lay many weeks in the house of a friend upon the shore of the beautiful Oeresund. One day when the feVer had left me, they rolled my bed into a room oVerlooking the sea. The sunlight danced upon the waves and the distant mountains of Sweden were blue against the horizon. Ships passed under full sail up and down the great waterway of the nations. But the sunshine and the peaceful day bore no message to me. I lay moodily picking at the coVerlet, sick and discouraged and sore—I hardly knew why myself—until all at once there sailed past, close in shore a ship flying at the top the flag of freedom, blown out on the breeze until eVery star in it shown bright and clear. That moment I knew. Gone were illness, discouragement and gloom! Forgotten weakness and suffering, the cautions of doctor and nurse. I sat up in bed and shouted and laughed and cried in turns. waVing my handkerchief to the flag out there. They thought I had lost my head, but I told them no, thank God! I had found it, and my heart, too, at last. I knew then it was my flag; that my children's home was mine indeed; that I also had become an American in truth. And I thank God, and, like unto the man sick with the palsey, arose from my bed and went home, healed.'' That is a discription of a true patriotic passion.

But patriotism is more than mere sentiment. It may show itself in the carrying of a flag, the cheering of an orator or the singing of a song, but it will do more if it is of the true kind. It will seek to find expression in ways of public welfare.

It will seek to uphold righteous principles. Our worst enemies are not the armies and naVies of foreign countries, but the citizens of our own, who disregard law and repudiate righteous principles. The spirit of coVetousness is abroad; men are in haste to get rich.

The spirit of irreVerence is preVailing; children mature so early and throw out the restraints of their parents. The spirit of carelessness is in the ascendency; men are careless in regard to right and wrong, truth and dishonesty. This is attested by the growing profanity, Sabbath desecration, lust of power, greed, licentiousness, Violence and corruption in public and priVate life.

''Every Christian should stand for righteousness, not only at the polls, but everywhere. Honesty in business is patriotism. So is faithfulness in the family relation. So is faithfulness to the church. A dishonest business man cannot be a good citizen. Neither can an unfaithful husband, or a neglectful son, or a brutal father. A licentious man strikes at national purity, a violent man at national peace and a corrupt man at national honesty. National righteousness is the sum or aVerage of the righteousness of the people. Every bad man lowers the aVerage and eVery good man raises it. He serves his country best and is most patriotic who liVes righteously before God.''

A genuine passion of patriotism will manifest itself in serVice in the hour of ciVic need. There are many who are willing to lay down their liVes for their country when the roar of the battle is heard, but are not willing to serVe in times of peace. They ignore the claims of political life and grow careless of their duties as Voters. Good men Very often refuse to accept positions of public trust in goVernmental affairs, leaVing the waiting places to greedy politicians who make political life a disgrace. It makes the heart sick to see how much there is of graft, corruption and roguery in high places, but the sorry thing of it all is that the men who ought to be the custodians of public Virtues are negligent or unwilling to accept positions of public trust and indifferent as to what sort of men do occupy them. As a result it is often true that the men we elect to make our laws, to eXecute them and to meet out justice are swayed by the money bags of their constituents. The good citizens who stand by and do nothing are responsible; they make such conditions possible by their refusal to soil their righteous fingers with the smut of politics.

But the true passion of patriotism is not selfish nor conceited. While the patriot loVes his own country best, he does not think all the good peõple in the world are within its confines and that all who dwell beyond its borders are barbarians. Neither does he wish for his own country all prosperity and progress, all peace and happiness, all liberty and knowledge to the total disregard of all other nations and peoples. He remembers that ''God hath made of one blood all nations of men for to dwell upon all the face of the earth.'' He knows that the ideal of the brotherhood of man which is the Christian ideal can never be realized by selfish ambition and exclusiveness. In spite of the awful havoc wrought by the late war and the deplorable reaction that has followed in its wake, the ideal of a brotherhood of the nations was brought to the surface and given a tremendous impulse. Underlying President Wilson's message to congress recommending the declaration of a state of war was this conviction of the brotherhood of the nations and the demand that the members of the family of nations shall act in brotherly fashion. Said President Wilson. ''We are at the beginning of an age in which it will be insisted that the same standards of conduct and of responsibility for wrong done shall be observed among nations and their governments that are observed among individual citizens of civilized states.'' Surely when a great country gives forth official expression of such conviction, it means that Christianity is leavening human thought and gradually coming to its own in the ideals of nations. And among these ideals, standing high as a mountain in a plain, is that of brotherhood.

The American people are rising with a desire to embody this ideal, and sorry and disappointed may they well be, when, after having led the civilized world to the verge of accepting this ideal with themselves, the men whom they had trusted as their representatives should turn to playing politics over hair-splitting details of a plan for world peace. May Christian citizens with a passion of true patriotism take cognizance of the lesson we have sought to make clear, namely, that they themselves are responsible for the conduct of selfish-spirited and narrow-visioned men who will not follow the lead of Christian truth. And be assured that this ideal is fundamental and will remain as a rock on which the autocracies of the world will be dashed to pieces.

EDITORIAL REVIEW

You cannot judge a man's generosity by the size of his pocketbook or the quality of his clothes; a thief may wear fine broadcloth and carry a big purse.

The man who is discontented merely finds fault with things as they are. The man who is not contented is cheerfully determined to make things better than they are.—The Youth's Companion.

He who prays for the coming of the kingdom of God, but does nothing to cause the kingdom spirit to prevail in the hearts and conditions of men should hear the Master say ''Ye ask and receive not because ye ask amiss.''

The child who thought he could throw a ball so high that it would never come down was no more foolish than the man who thinks he can violate a moral law and not pay the penalty. The reaction of sin is as certain as the law of gravitation.

If any one is looking for a suggestion as to a place to spend his vacation, he ought to get an idea from this issue of The Evangelist. Brother Snyder re-inforced by Brother Bame, gives the suggestion on the Four Year Program page, which makes its debut after an absence of several weeks, and Brother Cobb reiterates it on page 16. It's a good suggestion.

An interesting report of a most successful circuit trip is given in this issue by Brother S. P. Fogle, of Washington, D. C., who is performing a noble service for some needy churches in Virginia and West Virginia. A goodly number of souls were reported added to the church. He is soon to be on his way to North Dakota for an evangelistic campaign, and asks the prayers of the brotherhood in his behalf.

When a smallpox scare put a stop to all public meetings at North Liberty, Indiana, Brother Grisso takes his hand bag and Bible and gets into an evangelistic campaign at LaPaz, and the Lord gives him seven souls for his hire. Given wide-awake and willing souls to co-operate, God is ever able and willing to cause the seasons of affliction and hindrance in one community to redound to the blessing and victory of another. Brother Grisso's work at North Liberty is in splendid condition.

The Maryland and Virginia district conference which recently met at Roanoke, appears to have been a splendid success both from the standpoint of attendance and program. Brother C. R. Koontz, the assistant secretary proves himself to be a careful secretary, and supplies us with a report for your perusal.

Under the caption, ''From Homerville to Canton,'' Brother Fred Vanator tells of his bidding adieu to his Homerville pastorate and taking charge of the Canton church. Both Brother Vanator and his good wife graduated from Ashland College at the late commencement and begin their ministry together with much promise. Brother Vanator displays a commendable spirit when he speaks so generously of the splendid work done by his predecessor, Brother Belote. He finds himself among a faithful people, and we dare say he will seek to lead them on to greater attainments.

Sister Louis P. Clapper gives a report of a recent Christian Endeavor meeting of the society in the Louisville, Ohio, church. Brother Painter, the wide-awake president was also the leader and demonstrated what faithful preparation will do for a meeting, and such is not the exception for that society. Knowing the Louisville society as we do, we can safely say that it ranks among the leading societies of the brotherhood. We are sure Brother Garber, who conducts the Christian Endeavor page, will be glad to receive reports of interesting meetings from other societies.

We are privileged to treat our readers with a splendid letter from Brother Yoder, of Rio Cuarto, Argentina. It is found on the ''Mission'' page. It reports progress that gives cause for encouragement. It will be noted that Brother Edwards, an experienced missionary recently received into the Brethren church by Brother Yoder, together with his two daughters and Brother Yoder's oldest daughter are coming to the States and expect to be at the coming General Conference. The girls are then coming on to Ashland to school. It will be noted also that Brother Bock and family are soon to return for a year's furlough. With so many returned missionaries in our midst, if our congregations make the proper use of them, the Brethren church ought to be stirred during the coming year to take such advanced steps for the extension of Christ's kingdom as we have never before dared to undertake.

PUT IN A BIT OF COLOR

When you pack a basket of clothing as your donation to the national movement to collect clothing for Armenia, inaugurated by the Near East Relief, don't forget to put in something bright in color.

The story of the Armenian child who found a piece of orange peel in the streets and fastened it in the folds of her waist, is pathetic. She loved bright colors. There was no color in the serviceable gray dress provided for her. Life is full of bright colors for us in this country: so many, we do not dream how despairing and bleak life would be without them. Add woolens, warm and comforting; don't throw aside a garment because it is dull and colorless; add it, and add also a few bright colored hair ribbons your child will be glad to share.

Not Born to Poverty

No honest American may shrug his shoulders and say, when he reads of the suffering of the children of the Near East: ''Oh, well, they are used to it. They were born to privation.'' This is not true. The great majority of these one hundred thousand orphans are the children of parents who were once prosperous, the same as you. The children were sheltered and clothed and fed as indulgently as yours. The Turks killed their fathers, laid their homes in ruin, and drove the mothers to something worse than death. The child whose life you are asked to save was nurtured as tenderly as your own. This is the month to share clothing. The Near East Relief will see it through to the needy ones.

No One Too Humble to Help

There are many ways in which one may help the homeless and orphan children of the Near East. Here is one that should carry an appeal to those whose incomes are small and burdens heavy; clothing, if donated now, will be sent to the Near East at once: Every garment means life for some child. Thousands perished last winter because of the cold. No household is too humble to be denied a share in this. The second way: Five dollars a month, sent to the Near East Relief, 1 Madison avenue, New York, feeds and shelters one child.

FOUR-YEAR PROGRAM PAGE
NOW THEN DO IT.—II Samuel 3:18

Conducted by Charles A. Bame

General Conference In 1920

Those who set the goal, "The General Conference of 1920 the largest and best, with 400 delegates present," had in mind the best interests of our church. The more largely our conferences are attended the more widespread will be the interest created among our people, and the greater will be the inspiration for renewed activity and enlarged vision throughout the brotherhood. To try to reach this goal is a worthy ambition, and the realization of it will be an attainment of far-reaching significance.

Now Is the Time

to plan to attend the 1920 General Conference at Winona Lake. Most people will take some sort of an outing or vacation during the summer, and it is a safe guess that they are thinking about it already. The object of this article is to direct attention to the desirability of planning to go to our conference at Winona. Few people ever get there who do not plan the trip weeks or months in advance.

There is a Reason

why it is very important to begin to plan now. A number of us have to plan ahead in order to have sufficient means to enable us to attend our general conference. By beginning now, many, who otherwise might think it would be impossible for them to incur the expense of such a trip, may be able to save enough between now and the middle of August to make possible an outing at Winona with great pleasure and profit to themselves. Not only by saving, but by earning extra money in various ways, may such a fund be secured. By giving this matter some serious thought now and formulating plans looking toward that end, it will be possible for a number of people to attend our 1920 conference who otherwise would not get there at all.

And There Are Others

who need to give little attention to the financial side of the matter because they have ample means, but their trouble is they have never seriously thought of going to Winona Lake. Perhaps there is some favorite lake or resort where they always spend their vacation. This is a good time to break away from purely selfish pursuits and consider the interest of the church also. And many parents would find it more profitable in every way to take their young people for church conference than to give them an outing at some resort where most of the influences are contaminating, and where, when the vacation is over, nothing of value has been gained and no new ideals and enlarged visions enrich the life. So make a change this year: THINK WINONA. PLAN WINONA. TALK WINONA. GO TO WINONA, AND HAVE A PART IN MAKING OUR NEXT GENERAL CONERENCE THE LARGEST AND BEST.

MILES J. SNYDER.

A Timely Warning

This is a very timely warning sounded by our good Secretary. Brother Snyder is very anxious to make good as our new Secretary. But he cannot do so unless the people of the Brotherhood take seriously his suggestion. The Four Year Program Committee can not make a "Largest and best" conference out of resolutions and words. It must be made out of people who are able and ready to spend time and money or send substitutes.

Why Not a Substitute

If you, my good brother or sister, are unable to spend both the time and money, why not send some one who has the time but not the money? There are a good many such. What a blessing the church would get for herself if she would send some of these good people who work so hard in the organizations at home and never get to see the inside of the great National Conferences!

Begin to Commence

A friend of mine has a way of saying, "It's time to begin to commence to get ready." Well, if you have any such a string of remedies to get, it is time and high time. I happen to know, too, folks who can afford to come to Conference and are not doing so. Just deliberately planning to stay at home! Brethren, it is not fair or right.

Big Things

are bound to confront our conference this year. I pray that it shall be as peaceful as the glorious conference of last year. It can be even though we differ—as we know we shall—if we take with us the spirit of brotherhood. And if we do not take that spirit to the conference we are traitors to our name and ought to give it up.

A Wonderful Auditorium

is under construction and about one month before we arrive at Winona it is to be dedicated by "Billy" Sunday. If there were no other argument, we would need a bigger audience than ever if we make even a small mark in an Auditorium that seats 7500. Brethren people will need to show proper appreciation of the favors Winona shows us in giving this splendid auditorium for our "Largest and Best" Conference.

BAME.

My Confession of Christ
E. M. Cobb, D. D.

I believe in the trinity of God;
I believe that He made the earth and sky;
I believe on the Son who died for me;
And the Parclete, who keeps me ever nigh.

Chorus
Not ashamed of the gospel of my Lord,
With Hallelujah praises I shall sing
Of His Grace, His redemption, and His reign.
Praise the Lord! He is Prophet, Priest and King.

I believe in the virgin birth of Christ;
Let the enemies of God say what they will;
Let Satan hurl the fiery darts of hell;
Praise the Lord, for I do believe it still.

I believe in the cross of Calvary;
His precious blood was shed that I might live;
My crimson stain was washed as white as snow;
He ransomed me; my heart, to Him I give.

I believe that He burst the bars of death;
That He came up triuphant from the grave;
That He conquered the mighty powers of hell;
That we might know His wondrous power to save.

I believe in the coming of the Lord;
That He'll come in His mighty power to reign
With His bride at His side, in glory crowned.
Hallelujah, hallelujah, Amen.

DAYTON, OHIO.

GENERAL ARTICLES

The Value of Literature to Mind and Soul Development

By Prof. Charles Emory Byers

If literature, as Arlo Bates has said, is genuine and typical emotion adequately expressed, then it is a builder of soul. The soul grows rich as it cultivates and develops emotions. Of course to be a great soul it is necessary to grow rich in those great emotions forged in the heat and passion of the smithy of a Shakespeare or Browning. Our own emotions struggling in their infancy or stifling amid the confusion of other things must be shown to us as in a mirror. The poet is that mirror. He reveals us to ourselves. He expresses our thoughts and feelings to us, but does it much better than we could. He is the spokesman, the mouthpiece for the common man.

The human soul does not consist so much of intellect as of heart. Literature has to do with the heart, hence it deals directly with the soul. It hangs beautiful pictures in the galleries of memory and stores up gems of truth for the soul to feed on. These in the normal soul grow brighter and richer with the succeeding years, until age brings the harmony and calm and glory we find in a summer evening sunset.

Literature brings beauty to mind. And beauty is one of the soul's most valuable assets. Browning says: "If you get simple beauty and naught else, you get about the best thing God invents." I take him at his word. I do not aim in this article to get into any theological argument, but wish only to give a bit of philosophy of my own. It may have an abundance of faults and flaws, but I am writing it by invitation and not forcing it on any of the readers of the Evangelist.

The most valuable thing God has given man is art. Art is the wings wherewith we fly to heaven. We have five ways or channels by means of which we get art. They are: painting, sculpture, architecture, music and literature. These five arts collectively are called art. All that man ever dreamed, or wrought or thought are embraced in them. Through these we get beauty of soul provided we employ them to that end. Even nature herself is not man's possession until he converts her into art. Convert joy into art and it becomes a classic. Convert grief into art and it ceases to be grief. This Tennyson has done in "In Memoriam" and death had lost part of its sting. And St. Peter after he had philosophized on the horrors of the grave was touched with this thought when he exclaimed, "O Death, where is thy sting? O Grave, where is thy victory?" Convert the horrors of the battlefield into art and you have turned them into a glory, as many a poet has done, especially Byron on Waterloo. The loathesomeness of prisons and the coldness of the grave is alchemized by the poet's pen. There is a magic, a witchery about it that enthralls.

Physical beauty has served its purpose when it has lasted long enough for the eye of man to behold it and the soul to record. Then it may fade and mix again with the elements, it has its immortality secure. That immortality consists in the part it takes in building soul in the individual who beheld it. An apt illustration of this is Burns' Daisy. If Burns' soul is immortal the daisy is immortal in its humble way, and would have been even if Burns had noted it but never written his beautiful poem.

Physical beauty exists for the purpose of being converted into soul beauty. It exists only long enough for some man of vision and genius to preserve it in amber. Then it may die so far as its physical properties are concerned. It is now the permanent possession of the world. To do this is the mission of art. And to me it is more specifically the mission of literature, the highest of the arts.

I have now stated the ground work of what I have to say. I want to make it plain by illustration and citations from literature.

One man, who lays no claim to literature, says he would rather bequeath to his children the heritage of a taste for good literature than a fortune of one hundred thousand dollars each. He wanted them to travel "in the realms of gold," to build their 'castles in Spain" and to go on the "viewless wings of Poesy."

Browning in Pippa Passes gives the best thought on transforming physical beauty into intellectual beauty of any I have yet found.

"——Last year's sunsets and the great stars
Which had a right to come first and see ebb
The crimson wave that drifts the sun away—
Those crescent moons with notched and burning rims
That strengthened into sharp fire, and there stood,
Impatient of the azure—and that day
In March, a double rainbow stopped the storm—
May's warm slow yellow moonlit nights—
Gone are they, but I have them in my soul."

This is transforming physical beauty into soul beauty. How last year's sunsets, the great stars, the burning rim of the crescent moon and the rainbow in March moulded the soul of this sympathetic observer of God in his works. How the soul can grow great, pure, religious, and climb toward heaven on food like this! Gone are these physical things, but if we follow God's plan for us we have them in our soul, where they are more valuable than anywhere else.

Usually we cannot see the beauty of things until the artist points them out to us. The feeding on the great thoughts of literature as they flow from the minds of inspired men constitutes the value of literature. But literature must not only be read; it must be experienced. It must be felt. The taste for it must be cultivated. We must linger over its lines, we must woo it like we woo and win a beautiful girl. If the girl is worth anything or the literary selection is worth anything we may woo but we cannot win either all at once. It takes time.

Likewise we cannot distill from the sunset, or extract from the rose their spirit without time and reflection. We must take time. Soul growth is slow, and we attain to full stature only by years of diligence. The writers of our great literature are the people who furnish the basis for this. They are spectacles to our blinded eyes and crutches to our limping feet.

The value of literature comes both from perception and apperception. The first poem I ever learned to love was "Little Brown Hands," a stanza of which reads,—

"They drive the cows home from the pasture
Up through the long shady lane
Where the quail whistles loud in the wheatfields
That are yellow with ripening grain."

It was the first one I understood. My eyes were open to it. I lived every word of it. My little hands were indeed brown and I drove the cows home, and I heard the quail whistle. When I read it now as I often do, I cannot do so without tears in my eyes. It is sentiment to me now. I have it framed and hanging on my walls. It brings back a world to me. This is what I mean by experiencing literature.

We are still children, and like the Children of Israel we must have the pillar of fire by night and the cloud by day to guide us. When our Moseses (our great writers and thinkers) stay on Mt. Sinai too long we make and worship golden calves. And with all this teaching in the concrete man got along so slowly learning the principles of God from nature and man, that he was compelled to send Jesus Christ to us to live these principles, so man could see them in the concrete. "O slow of faith to believe all that the prophets have spoken."

These principles of God are the message of the artist. He tries to teach them to us with chisel, with brush and with pen. Let us, then, linger over the message of the artists, especially the great writers, for they enrich the souls of men.

And one of the richest of these mines of truth is the Bible. It is a deep-seated interpretation of the human soul. It shows from Moses to Paul, soul evolution in spite of our efforts to disprove it. It contains the crude conceptions of the world our early ancestors had, as well as the finest philosophy of later scholars. It contains every form of literature extant today,—history, biography, fable, drama, short story, allegory, poetry and the rest. Often do I turn to its pages and watch the stars with its Chaldean sleep out at Bethel and dream with Jacob, watch the dark green cedars of Lebanon, stay with the shepherds as they watched their sheep.

What beauty in the story of David, and what revelry in his psalms! What can be more poetic than, "The heavens declare the glory of God and the firmament showeth his handiwork; day unto day uttereth speech and night into night showeth knowledge."

"The earth is the Lord's and the fullness thereof; the world and they that dwell therein, for he hath founded it upon the seas and established it upon the floods."

Who does not love to dream of this morning of the world when one-half of the world did not intrude itself on the other, and where the tin can did not mark the trail of civilization? Whose imagination is not thrilled by the rivers Pison and Havilah on whose banks was planted the garden of Eden? Who can cease to be charmed by the beautiful story of Ruth? What inspiration is found in the sweep of Isaiah! And what lessons do we find in the master lessons of Job?

The value of the Bible merely as literature is inestimable. The splendid biography of Jesus told in four gospels will be forever an inspiration simply as literature. The strength and force of St. Paul in the 13th chapter of 1 Corinthians has always given me an example of wonderful rhetoric. Many is the time I have read it aloud to myself to hear it trip off my tongue. It is almost a poem.

Then John in Revelation as he writes it alone in Patmos! Any one who reads between the lines can see the rapture in which he writes. Those splendid pictures, those symbols and figures are as magnificent in conception and as artistic in execution as any literature with which I am familiar.

Men have developed into great souls by lingering over the thoughts of the Bible. By imbibing the inspiration, of both human and divine, with which its pages overflow. It shows the ever-widening conception man evolved of God and himself and their relations to each other. The mission of all literature Biblical and other is the building of soul. But with it all we must get "that something far more deeply infused, whose glory is the light of setting suns and the round ocean and the living air and in the mind of man."

"Time wrecks the proudest piles we raise,
    The towers, the domes, the temples fall;
    The fortress tumbles and decays,
    One breath of song outlasts them all."
Huntington, Indiana.

The Motion Picture Menace. By Earl H. Detsch

In the day of Moses Egypt was plagued with myriads of creeping things; despicable, horrid, annoying things. To-day the world is infested and plagued by a huge monster that is entwining its long, green, hateful tendrils about the flowers of the earth. These flowers are the youth of the world. And they are becoming dwarfed. Their leaves are shriveling. Their petals are falling. But alas! they love the monster who is sapping their life. They yearn to be satiated with his venom. They heed not their withering form and declining splendor. What is that to the ecstatic allurement, the rapturous, fascinating charm of this monster—the Motion Picture! Ah! would that some Ulysses would seize a burning coal and bury it into the eye of this abhorrent creature and obliterate its hypnotic gleam! Friends, this is no figment of a prejudiced mind! This is no exaggerated picture of a bigot or fanatic! If so, then all the choicest minds of Canada are fanatical for they have arrayed themselves in armor to regulate the injurious film. Pennsylvania, Ohio, Kansas, and Maryland have also unsheathed their swords against the monster. But if it is but a harmless lamb they have drawn their swords in vain and are sadly deluded. Let us see whether we have in our midst a monster or a lamb.

In the first place the motion picture is a poor, puny, profitless substitute for good book reading. And is not society in general sacrificing the disciplinary, uplifting effects of literary pursuit at the feet of this dumb, uncompensating modern idol? That time which was once spent by the fireside in reading a beneficial book is now employed in a dark, hot, stuffy picture house gazing upon some mushroom production. "Oh, the labor of reading is nerve racking." So speak the movie-goers. "The mental assimilation as the pages are turned over is a process which involves exertion." Oh, dear! the day will come when such people to avoid exertion, will desire their meals injected artificially. "A half-dozen stories can be absorbed," they say, "in the movies in the time which would be required to gather the sense out of one book." Yes, but one book that will cause you to think is of infinitely more value to you than a half dozen pictures that merely play ping-pong with your emotions. The hero passes from one hair-raising adventure to another, defying every sort of villiany within the gamut of human imagination. He is seen in high air, in a sewer without an outlet, in straps on a log while the saw comes nearer and nearer to his shivering form, on a powder keg with a lighted fuse attached, facing a time bomb, with the hands upon the dial pointing to 9:59, with an explosion due at 10, under the torture of serpents, lions, or in the drip, drip, drip of falling water, when lo and behold he escapes it all! It has raised havoc with your emotions. But oh my, what poor culture for the most precious sensibility you have! Preachers do not need to hurl verbal thunderbolts at the dime novel today, The dime novel is a thing of the past. Jesse James and Nick Carter are now beautifully portrayed on the screen, if you please. The alphabet, the school room—all the tedious processes by which a youngster may be made into a reader with a view to bringing him into contact with the literary heritage of the English race, he may put behind him. I would like to see a William Gladstone, or a Henry Ward Beecher raised on a motion picture diet. It would be impossible, for while the picture may allure and fascinate, it has a smouldering effect upon intellectual fire. Allow me to quote the titles of just a few of the pictures that were shown last year: "The Scarlet Road," "The Scarlet Sin," "The Scarlet Woman," "The Flame of Passion," "The Play-things of Passion," "Hell Morgan's Girl," "Hell's Crater," and "Hell" in fifty other verbal combinations, "The Eternal Magdalene," "The Gutter Magdalene," "The Forbidden Fruit," "The Serpent," "Where is My Daughter?" and "Satan's Daughter." And now listen to Ellis Oberholtzer's remarks on these titles. Mr. Oberholtzer is a member of the Pennsylvania State Board of Censorship of Motion Pictures.

"In my experience with human kind I have met very few persons who of their own initiative, except in the regular course of business for the money which comes of it, would write stories and produce pictures appropriate to such titles. Such as do this are, I am assured, subjects for reformation." Behold these modern Ruskins and Emersons whose rotten productions the world is doing obeisance to?

In the second place the motion picture is a colossal deceiver. The blind public bites at the cheese and the trap comes down on its head, but it is too dumb to feel it. When a picture is made to illustrate a very unsavory subject about which people, as a rule, do not freely speak, and that picture is advertised at a great rate, and man, woman, and child are lured to see it, after a payment of a fee, for their everlasting good, then, I say it is time to revolt! Behold them entertaining the people in the theatre and at the same time educating them as to the pitfalls of life! They are like the fakir with a medical museum such as we see in the larger cities. They are like a keeper of a book stall up an alley with a volume about genital processes and sex hygiene. They are seeking the patronage of the curious young. Eugenics or not, such a topic can well be taught only in its own place, and its place is NOT the moving picture theatre. There are churches, and schools and homes for such teaching. When the moving picture man weaves such teachings into a story, and presents it in the form of a picture, and offers it to us for a price, he is nothing but a deceptive speculator. Little does he care what you know about eugenics. But he poses as if he cared. His aim is to swell his income. But his scheme is as transparent as daylight. The energy which has been expended in five years in contriving such stories and in covering them with the garments of respectability for parade in the market place would turn the wheels of a score of honest and useful causes. And yet we patronize the thing!

In the last and most important place the motion picture is in general an immoral machine. Does a serpent's fang eject nectar? Ah, no that is the lily's mission. And enough has already been said to disprove any lily-like assumptions on the part of the motion picture. Did you know that shortly after the signing of the Declaration of Independence our American Congress passed the following resolution: "Whereas true religion and good morals are the only solid foundation of public liberty and happiness; Resolved, that it be and is hereby earnestly recommended to the several States to take the most effectual measures for the discouragement and suppression of theatrical entertainments, horse racing, gaming, and such other diversions as are productive of idleness, dissipation, and a general depravity of principles and manners." Now, were our forefathers fanatics or fools? or do you think their reasons good and wholesome? John Gilbert, the veteran actor, wrote in the North American Review, "I believe the present condition of the drama, both from a moral and artistic point of view, to be a subject for regret. Many of the plays that have been adopted are open to the severest criticism on the ground of immorality." Mr. A. M. Palmer also wrote in the Review that, "the chief themes of the theatre are now, as they ever have been, the passions of men—ambition and covetousness, leading to murder; lust, leading to adultery and to death; anger leading to madness." Now I ask who can help but deem it bad, when its actors, and play writers and critics condemn it as such! Mr. A. C. Dixon after a thorough study of the affair concludes that there is not a theatre in the world which does not pander to depraved tastes in order to make money. Can any intelligent person, any person of refined sensibilities or with a fair knowledge of psychological laws and influences, uphold such an institution? We have not discussed this question from the standpoint of the Christian church. We have interpolated no teachings of Christ nor of Paul upon the subject of amusement in our paper. For this IS a paper and not a sermon. But irrespective of the nature of these words it is plain enough that we have a social and moral obligation to perform. The time has come when we can no longer allow money speculators to play see-saw with the public conscience. They MUST NOT maltreat our moral sensibilities! It is a monster with which we have to contend and not a lamb. It is a gigantic beast, and it challenges VIRILE manhood, and not docile effeminancy! We are to patronize the institution. We are to talk it down. But, you say, I am but a small atom and could do little in influencing this great social mass. Oh, sublime passivity! All David would have needed is a little such doctrine and Goliath would have died triumphantly with his head on. And Patrick Henry with such foppish ideas would have altered his speech to the tune of "Tyranny or no, I'll live!" Listen, a comrade is dying on the battle field. His coat is warm and sticky with blood. His life is ebbing away with every heart pulsation. You are near him. Will you plug the wound and save him? Most certainly you will. Society has a bleeding wound. The Motion Picture is cutting her with poisonous thongs. Will you stand passively by and hear her groan? Or will you do your best to crush her tormentor and heal her wound?

Ashland College, Ashland, Ohio.

Missions and Lace.

(The people of the United States spend $60,000,000 in one year for lace. They gave last year, all Protestant denominations included, $2,000,000 for foreign missions.)

Twenty cents for missions and a dollar bill for lace
Is our index of proportions; shows our zeal to save the race.
Said the Lord to his disciples: "Bring an offering today
For the famine-stricken people who are suffering far
    away."

And his sleek, well-fed disciples, looking up into his face,
Made reply: "We'd like to do it, but we spent so much for
    lace."
Said the Lord: "Seek first my kingdom to establish among
    men;
Teach the dead in sin and evil, they can rise through me
    again."

So they gave their extra pennies and they sent a man of
    grace
To conduct a penny mission—but the dollars went for lace.
Said the Lord: "A tiny army mighty things for God hath
    done:

By William M. Vories

But he calls for tenfold measures that the millions may be
    won."

But they answered: "Lord, have patience: we can't hope
    to win the race.
Leave some work for our descendants; leave us something
    for our lace!"
Said the Lord at last, in sorrow: "Sleep ye on, O faithless
    race;
Take your ease among your rose-patch and your blood-
    bought bolts of lace!"

But his people made remonstrance: "Lord, take not with
    us offense;
We have not forgot thy kingdom—lo, we give thee twenty
    cents!"

Thus twenty cents for missions and a dollar bill for lace
Is our index of proportion; shows our zeal to save the race.

Try this for a recitation in the missionary meeting or
Sunday school.

—The Forward Movement, Church of the Brethren,
Elgin, Ill.

THE BRETHREN PULPIT

"Where Is Your Treasure Stored?"   By A. E. Whitted

(MATTHEW 6: 19-21.)

We are living in a most wonderful time. Yet when we take time to weigh some of the gigantic problems that are confronting us as Christians we are drawn to think of this as a terrible time. Our national as well as our individual life is at stake. We take a good look at ourselves, then we turn back over the pages of the history of the ages past and we behold nation after nation that has risen in splendor only to fall into obscurity. Every time you will find the fall due to a self-centered, self-righteous life. In their selfishness and greed they have forgotten God and have suffered the consequences. As with the nations of the world so it is with the individual life. Self-centered, self-righteous, we fall. Forgetfulness of God and a mind wholly turned to material pursuits bring destruction.

Jesus tells us of two places where our life's treasure may be deposited. In heaven or on the earth. "Lay not up for yourselves treasures on earth." Why not on the earth? Because we cannot be sure of earthly riches. One day we are rich, the next poor. Jesus here names three enemies to these earthly possessions, moth, rust and thieves. The first one is the moth. As time goes on the pleasure found in such wealth is eaten up. Dissatisfied such an one continues in the pursuit of greater possessions until he is not unlike the rich man of old of whom we read in Luke 12:16-20. The verdict being given in verse 21. "So is he that layeth up treasure for himself, and is not rich toward God." The man that is longing for this or that in earthly possessions is allowing his true pleasure to slip, and is wearing out in the effort. What doth it profit?

The next enemy spoken of is rust. How can a man's wealth become rusty or tainted? One has said, "In the getting, in the holding, and in the spending," and we say it is true. "In the sweat of thy face shalt thou eat bread." The wealth we hold must represent certain labor. In the past few years thousands of millionaires have sprung up. Do they represent the true wealth of America? Many of them do not. As I heard one say not long since, "The true wealth is found in those who have been so busy serving that no time was left for collecting, while in those who hold vast material wealth, the art of serving was swallowed up in the art of collecting."

But our wealth may become tainted in the holding. Bread becomes moldy and grows stale if not used. So it is with our silver and gold. Is the miser happy? Easily answered, No. Wealth is somewhat like knowledge. It cannot be a source of pleasure to the one that possesses it nor helpful to others about him unless it is lent. We must send it on to the other fellow to keep it bright and shining.

The spending is also to be considered. We remember the story of Cleopatra, how she dissolved her precious pearls in a goblet and drank the contents. The American people seem to be following very closely upon her heels. If there is anything wanted we will have it without even considering the price. It seems to whet our extravagant minds, if the price tag reads high. Think of our recklessness along this line when thousands are hungry and in want, while millions more are ignorant of the blessed story of the gospel. Yet extravagance is not the worst result of earthly possessions. It perhaps leads to that place where we will disregard that which is noblest in life. The loss of character is to be feared. The golden earrings of the daughters of Israel were not so bad, but out of them came the golden calf which caused Israel to forget the true God. What happened in Israel? The calf was ground into dust and scattered upon the water from which they must drink. So men who bow to ill-gotten riches—who devote their entire time to the getting of money and material things will sooner or later come to drink of the cup of misery that such living brings.

The last enemy named is the thief. There are numerous kinds of thieves, but the one I want to speak of in particular is DEATH. He is no respecter of persons. He has no pity. He visits every mansion, every hovel. No matter what our holdings when this enemy comes to us, all is gone. We brought nothing into this world, and with nothing we must leave it. I cannot say what another is worth unless that one would let me into his affairs, but I can tell how much he will be worth when death comes, so far as dollars and cents are concerned. So cometh the warning of Jesus, "Lay not up for yourselves treasures upon the earth, where moth and rust doth corrupt, and where thieves break through and steal." Surely man does not expect to live on in this same state forever. If not there is but one alternative, and that is found in the continuation of the Master's thought in this same connection. "But lay up for yourselves treasures in heaven where neither moth nor rust doth corrupt and where thieves do not break through and steal." I hear you say, Can we lay up riches in heaven? You surely can. In connection with this thought let me lead you to Luke 16:9, "And I say unto you, make to yourselves friends of the mammon of unrighteousness; that when ye fail they may receive you into everlasting habitations." Money spent in doing good returns a hundred fold. And after all our treasure does not consist of silver and gold alone. There is truth, nobility of character and the art of being useful. These things time cannot erase, no enemy can take away.

We have heard men say that because a man had lost all his material wealth he was ruined. Money cannot make real men, neither can the loss of money ruin a man. If he keeps his good name and noble upright character he yet holds in his possession all that will one day count. That we might come to see the value of righteous living as well as the value of dollars and dimes. Shall we heed what the Master says? The clinching argument is found in the 21st verse: "For where your treasure is there will your heart be also." Home is where the heart is. If you make your home on the earth, you must some day leave it behind. If you plan your home in heaven you will one day go to possess it. The riches and grace found in God's blessed Son are the real wealth and glory of man. Let us earnestly strive to attain them.

"Riches of earth I may not have,
    God may prevent;
Heavenly honors are my own,
    I am content."

Morrill, Kansas.

A Lost Art

(Brother H. M. Harley's counsel to his parishioners)

A very beautiful custom our fathers used to observe, was to enter the House of God reverently, and bow the head for a moment of silent prayer, after having reached their seats. We wish such a habit were general today. Aside from the blessing derived from prayer, what an excellent preparation such a habit is for the services which follow. It puts the heart and mind of the worshiper into a fit frame for the service. And perhaps one reason why we fail to get more good from the service is just this lack of fervent preparation.

Pray for the preacher. He comes to you with a message from God's word, and he needs to be strengthened and sustained through the prayers of those who worship. Pray that he may be filled with, and led by the Spirit of the living God. (Continued on page 11)

OUR DEVOTIONAL

"Making Jesus Real" By Nettie J. O' Neill

OUR SCRIPTURE

For God so loved me (us), that he gave his only begotten Son, that if I (we) believe in him I (we) should not perish, but have everlasting life (John 3:16). For I have given you an example, that ye should do as I have done to you. (John 13:15). A new commandment I give unto you, That ye love one another; as I have loved you, that ye also love one another (John 13:34). That they all may be one; as thou Father, art in me, and I in thee, that they also may be one in us; that the world may believe that thou hast sent me (John 17:21. For the Son of man is come to save that which was lost (Matt. 18:11). And when the Lord saw her, he had compassion on her, and said unto her, Weep not (Luke 7:13). For we have not a high priest which cannot be touched with the feeling of our infirmities; but was in all points tempted like as we are, yet without sin (Heb. 4:15). Let every one of us please his neighbor for his good to edification (Romans 15:2). For even Christ pleased not himself: but, it is written. The reproaches of them that reproached thee fell on me (Heb. 15:3). But as he which hath called you is holy, so be ye holy in all manner of conversations (1st Peter 1:15). I will declare thy name unto my brethren; in the midst of the congregation will I praise thee (Psa. 22:22). The woman then left her waterpot, and went her way into the city, and saith to the men. Come, see a man, which told me all things that ever I did: is not this the Christ? They went out of the city, and came unto him (John 4:28-30).

OUR MEDITATION

If we would have our friends and neighbors know that Jesus is real and that he is the loving, helpful, all-powerful Savior and Friend that we would like them to know, he must first be a real, living, vital personality in our own lives. This result can only be obtained by our first seeking, finding and following him closely in every thought and act of our lives.

In thinking of this fact, I am often impressed with the unreality in the minds of most people, both so-called Christian and Non-Christian, of Jesus as a living, ever-present personality to whom they could and should go with any burden or difficulty, but those who do know him as a real personality, it is mostly under these circumstances; that we should go to this same Jesus with our joys and pleasures and tell him how glad we are for the blessings he is constantly bestowing upon us and how pleased we are to have been born in a Christian land, in Christian homes, with Christian friends around us.

If we would make it a habit in our lives to tell him of our pleasant experiences as well as to go to him for comfort in times of trouble most of us would be surprised to know how much more real he would be to us.

If we would make Jesus real to others, we must put more of ourselves and our effort into the cause he represents, for after all, those people get most out of life and Christianity who put most of themselves into it. This fact was plainly demonstrated by the statement of the President of a South American republic who recently asked a question of a citizen of the United States, "What is the difference between your country and mine?" When the American said to him, "What do you think is the difference?" After serious consideration, he said, "The difference is this, Our country was settled by the Spaniards who came to South America for all they could get out of it of gold and other thing of material value. The United States was settled by the Pilgrim Fathers who came for religious freedom. They came for what they could put into it and our settlers came for what they could get out of it."

The best way to make Jesus real in the lives of others is to have a contagious case of Christianity and then all with whom we come in contact will be infected with this contagion and Jesus will then be a real factor in their lives.

OUR PRAYER

Our Father in heaven, we thank thee for the privilege of being children of thine and for Jesus Christ, thy Son, our Savior and Lord. We thank thee for making him so real in our lives through the power of the Holy Spirit.

We thank thee that through the Spirit and the Word we can make Jesus real to those about us.

May we have the infilling of thy Holy Spirit that we may have the out-flowing into the lives of those about us.

We ask these favors with the forgiveness of our sins, in the name of our real, personal Savior, Jesus Christ.

Amen.

Conemaugh, Pennsylvania.

The Argument for Christianity
By T. Darley Allen

Some men who have long been infidels, have been persuaded to give the evidences of Christianity a careful examination, and as a result have become believers in the Bible. This shows that the arguments for our religion are exceedingly strong.

Chalmers the famous Scottish divine, was an unbeliever in his early years but became a Christian through the study of writings in defense of Christianity, his careful reading of Butler's Analogy of Religion convincing him that more could be advanced in support of religion than he had supposed and the reading of this book leading him to the study of other works that resulted in his conviction that infidelity could not stand in the light of a thorough examination.

Guizot, the historian, was convinced of the truth of Christianity through study necessary in the preparation of notes for an edition of a great historical work.

John Marshall was changed from a skeptic to a believer by study of the prophicies of Scripture.

Many Christians think that infidels, as a rule, are well acquainted with the Bible, but men who have met many unbelievers and listened to their reasonings assert that the average skeptic is extremely ignorant both of Scripture and of the evidences of Christianity.

Rev. A. T. Pierson, the well-known divine, said that he never met an infidel who knew much about the Bible, but once talked with one who claimed to be a student of the book and well acquainted with its contents. But within ten minutes, said Dr. Pierson, this man proved by his conversation that he was far from being familiar with the Bible history, for "he did not know the difference between Job and Lot, and thought it was Job that lived in Sodom and dwelt with his two daughters in the cave.

H. L. Hastings said that he once met an infidel who requested him to present some strong evidence of the truth of Christianity. Mr. Hastings furnished the man with a copy of a well-known book on prophecy and later learned that the volume had destroyed his infidelity and that he had united with a Christian church.

Dr. Howard A. Kelly, a professor in John Hopkins University, was a skeptic for years, but his study has brought him to accept Christianity as divine. "Perhaps," he says, "one of my strongest reasons for believing the Bible is that it reveals to me as no other book in the world could do, that which appeals to me as a physician, a diagnosis of my spiritual condition. It shows me clearly what I am by nature—one lost in sin and alienated from the life that is in God. I find in it a consistent and wonderful revelation, from Genesis to Revelation, of the character of God."

Cleveland, Ohio.

Send
WHITE GIFT
OFFERINGS to

THE SUNDAY SCHOOL

ALBERT TRENT
General Secretary-Treasurer
Johnstown, Pennsylvania

The Sunday School as a Missionary Training School.   By Viola Knoll

We note with gratitude to God that all over the brotherhood the offerings for Foreign Missions are much larger this year than they have been heretofore. This seems to be the result of getting people to realize the great missionary needs of the world, the responsibilities of Christians and the great blessings that come to those who offer freely their prayers, time and money. But we can and must do better.

At two seasons of the year, Thanksgiving and Easter, the special attention of our people is called to the subject of missions. At these times the conditions existing in the mission fields are reviewed, and strong appeals made showing the needs and possibilities for the future. Throughout the year letters and reports from the various fields come to us through our church papers, and mission study classes are organized to acquaint people with conditions in other countries and to show them what has been and is being done now. Prayer bands, with limited prayer and support for an object, are also organized in some places.

All this is good, very good, but it is not sufficient. If we want to accomplish great things for God in the mission field it is with the children that we must work. The church must begin to train its workers when they are young, when their minds are plastic and impressionable, for later the task is more difficult and the results not as thorough. Definite missionary instruction in the period of youth will indeed fall upon good ground and bring forth fruit abundantly.

The elementary department of the Sunday school seems to be the ideal place to begin missionary training. It is the desire of each teacher there to teach "Jesus" to the children, to have them love him and want to grow to be like him. Besides teaching them the Bible stories, what better way have we than telling them stories of the missionaries? For they teach and heal, lift up the oppressed and downtrodden and continually go "about doing good" in the name of Jesus. At times children are inclined to think that Jesus lived on this earth a long time ago and that things were entirely different from what they are at present. But missionaries are living now, doing these things in the world about us.

Again children of the early adolescent age are hero-worshippers, each chooses some one like whom he wants and tries to be. Is it not well then that their minds be filled with stories of missionaries? But you say that children want something exciting, with plenty of adventure in it. That is true, but what could be more exciting and adventuresome than many of the experiences through which the missionaries of all foreign fields have gone? What will make the children more appreciative of the blessings they enjoy because the blessed story of the Christ is known here than to know about the wretched lives of the boys and girls of other lands? And what will make them more unselfish than to teach them to pray for and give to missions? Those who receive such instructions are anxious to do what they can.

But how can this be done? A part of each Sunday school service should be devoted to missionary teaching so that the process may be a continuous one. In the first place the children should become thoroughly familiar with our own missionaries and mission fields. Pictures of the missionaries may be posted on the wall where the children can learn to know them by name. Pictures of buildings and groups of natives will add interest. Maps may be used for the older children to get an idea of the location of the fields but the names will be sufficient for the younger ones. The superintendent of our school used a "world globe" to show where our missionaries are working. She also had a large outline map of Africa made on which she traced the route taken by the Gribble party, marking the places where they stopped.

Besides having our children thoroughly acquainted with the efforts of our church they should know something of other fields. They are very much interested in the children of all other lands. They want to know how they dress, what kind of homes they live in, what they do at school, (if there are such), how they eat, sleep, what they play and above all what their ideas about God are. Then we can tell them how the lives of these children are transformed by the power of the Christ and how anxious they are to learn of him and pass the glad tidings to others.

Along with these stories we must not neglect to bring in continually the teachings and example of Christ on this subject. And while the Sunday school is primarily a place for impressions, we must give the children a chance to express themselves. They can do this through prayers, giving of money, making of scrap books and giving of their own things when boxes are sent.

So, realizing the importance of the missionary teaching of Christ and that the future work depends on the children of today, let us renew our efforts with them and consecrate our lives to his service until he comes again!

Louisville, Ohio.

Plans for the Accommodation of the Convention

The Japan Educational Secretary of the World's Association sends word concerning the activities in Japan in preparation for the coming of the thousand or more delegates from all parts of the world. The Convention building is to be erected on the Plaza in front of the Tokyo Railway Station. A restaurant seating 1000 will be attached to the Convention Hall. These buildings are near the Y. M. C. A. where the great Sunday school exhibit will be set up. The hearty enthusiasm on the part of the missionaries and native Christians is manifested in all the preparatory work of the General Committee.

Music An Interesting Feature

Mr. Coleman has just returned from a trip to Korea where he found that the Koreans wanted the number of delegates which have been assigned for that country increased from 100 natives to 200, and 50 missionaries are planning to be present. One of the very interesting features of the convention will be the pageantry, music and religious art under the direction of Professor H. Augustine Smith of Boston University. Professor and Mrs. Smith will sail in August and at once take up the matter of drilling the chorus, choir and pageantry groups. Some of the pageants will be introduced in the post-convention meetings that are to be held in strategic centers of the Orient, such as Peking, Nanking, Shanghai, Hong Kong, Canton and Manila. Korea has asked for no less than five post-convention meetings and has indicated the places for them, namely, Seoul, Pyengyang, Fusan, Taiku, Kwangu and Wonsan or Hamheung. The delegates going on this trip to Tokyo, including tours in other parts of the Orient, will receive an educational value that is worth far more than the money expended.

"It has been said that there are three kinds of people in our churches today; the row-boat people, who always need to be pushed and pulled and urged along; the sail-boat people, who go only when there is a favorable wind, and the steam-boat people, who go along bravely and steadily, what ever the wind or weather. In which class are you?

J. A. Garber
PRESIDENT

Our Young People at Work

G. C. Carpenter
SECRETARY

Variety Wards Off Summer Slump

Monotony tends towards staleness. Variety adds freshness. Young people are keen to detect both the stale and fresh; the former they shun, the latter they seek.

Some days ago Brother J. F. Painter wrote saying the Louisville, Ohio, society was planning something new for a coming meeting. With the letter was enclosed a blank telegram for a return message. It was sent immediately. The report below tells the whole story.

Other societies will find it possible to ward off the dreaded summer slump by introducing something new. Let the prayer meeting committee meet with the leaders and together plan some novel programs. Merely to meet in another room will have a good effect. Try several outdoor meetings, say a vesper service on the lawn of some church home. "Breezy Echoes" would make a good topic for one meeting. Should you be so unfortunate as to have no delegates at the state convention, secure reports by mail and have them given by persons representing themselves as delegates.   J. A. GARBER.

Louisville Leads the Way
By Mrs. Louis P. Clapper

A novel way of conducting a Christian Endeavor program was used by the Louisville Endeavorers Sunday evening, June 13th, when the topic was "Common Mistakes in Daily Living."

J. F. Painter, the leader of the meeting, planned the program and about two weeks in advance sent blank telegrams to quite a number of former members and out-of-town friends of our society with the request that they send a short message on one particular phase of the topic. At the Sunday morning preaching service, just before Brother Riddle was ready to deliver his sermon a messenger boy brought to him a telegram announcing the evening meeting. Then in the evening the program began right on time (which gives any meeting a good start) and to the click of a telegraph instrument. Mr. Painter operated the instrument and his son, Josef, a Junior Christian Endeavorer, sat at a small table nearby to perform the duties of a messenger boy. Each one taking part in the meeting was given a number, so that instead of the program being called in the usual manner, it was when the telegraph instrument clicked our number that we responded. Besides the telegrams which were read there were talks by several members of the local society, the pastor's talk, a talk by a county Christian Endeavor officer, song service and devotionals and a selection by the Clapper-Bratten male quartette.

It is just such variety in conducting Christian Endeavor prayer meetings that keeps them interesting and we as a society have found that the results more than repay for the time and effort spent in planning for such meetings. We hope Christian Endeavorers will find this method profitable and we would be glad to know of methods others are using.
Louisville, Ohio.

Letters from Our Little Home Missionaries

The following are letters from the little Rempel sisters of Krypton, Kentucky to Mr. Gearhart, our General Missionary Secretary:

We all wish you could come and visit us. How are you folks? We are just fine. Verna is not very strong yet. Brother Gearhart, we would just love to peep in that shed and see those little milk goats. When you come down the next time you may bring us one if you have one to spare. Our attendance was better today than it has been for a long time. I visited a little stranger girl today and we had a fine time together. First we sang and played on the organ and then we went into a little room where no one could disturb us. Next we read the Bible and then knelt down and prayed. Miss Bethke gave Verna and myself each a promise box. I took that over to this little girl's house. We had a great time together. Well I think it is about time for Junior.   Yours in Jesus,
EDNA REMPEL.

Dear Brother Gearhart:

I want to thank you very much for praying for me when I was sick. The Lord certainly has answered your prayer. My how I would love to peep in that goat shed of yours. Papa had to sell my little lamb and its mamma. Brother Gearhart, the next time you come down here bring your wife and children. Mamma will roast a fat goose for you. We made some garden and hope to have a lot of green things when you come. It is nearly time for Junior. I must close.
VERNA REMPEL.

A New Christian Endeavor Society

The Conemaugh Brethren church has very recently established a new Christian Endeavor Society. Brother E. F. Byers was until recently pastor of this church and is largely responsible for this piece of work. Brother Byers was once a very active Christian Endeavorer and gave his life to the work of Christian ministry as an immediate result. The officers elected stand as follows:

President, ... Miss Ruth Constable
Vice President, ... Miss Alice Stutzman
Secretary, ... Miss Winoma Sigg
Assistant Secretary, ... Mrs. Clara Miller
Treasurer .... Miss Lilian Smith
Organist, ... Margaret Rorabaugh
Assistants, ... Miss Stella Stifler and Miss Mildred Boring

It is earnestly hoped that this society will progress rapidly. Under the supervision of Rev. Byers, or of the new pastor, Rev. G. H. Jones, naught else but a growing society could be expected. Who will follow in "Conemaugh's Train!"

A LOST ART
(Continued from page 5)

Pray for yourself. It is no easy matter to banish all foreign thoughts which fill the mind as you enter the House of Prayer. Pray that God may put your soul into proper condition for worship.

Pray for the other worshipers. God only knows the needs of those who assemble with you. Some need comfort and strength. Some need warning. Some need to be turned from evil paths. There are burdened souls present, and there are some who need conversion. Pray that the various needs may be met.

Pray for the stranger. Every Lord's day there are strangers with us. Pray that they may be helped by the service, and that they may feel at home in God's House.

Pray for the absent ones. Some are absent because of circumstances over which they have no control. Others are absent because of a lack of interest. Whatever the reason for their absence, they should be remembered in the prayers of those who come to worship.

Significance of the Oil In Anointing the Sick
By Samuel Kiehl

As the wine in the communion service symbolizes the presence and cleansing power of the blood of Christ, so the oil in the anointing service symbolizes the presence and healing power of the Holy Ghost, the spirit of God. "By my spirit, saith the Lord of hosts (Zech. 4:6).

SEND ALL MONEY FOR
General Home, Kentucky and
Foreign Missions to

MISSIONS

WILLIAM A. GEARHART
General Missionary Secretary
906 Conover Bldg., Dayton, O.

Rio Cuarto, Argentina. By C. F. Yoder

For several months we have been so busy trying to finish up the enlargement of the church and the building of the auto-coach that we have neglected writing for the Evangelist. Now we hope to write more regularly. The dedication of the church took place on the sixth anniversary of the dedication of the first building and was followed by a week of special meetings in which Mr. Penzotti, superintendent of the American Bible Society, helped. He also participated in the love-feast which we celebrated at that time. At the close of the meetings we baptized three candidates in our new baptistry two of them being daughters of Brother Edwards and both are to go with him to the States to be in school for a few years. Our oldest daughter is to go also and hopes to be at the coming Conference at Winona Lake and then at Ashland.

We are hoping that Brother Edwards with his twenty-two years' experience in this country will be of great help to the mission cause through his presence at the Conference and by a tour among the churches, and that he will return to the work here inspired to new enthusiasm by his contact with our people in the homeland. We have other candidates for baptism and also for missionary work of whom we may write more later.

We dedicated the Bible coach which is named "El Auto Evangelico" on Easter Sunday and began to use it for meetings in Rio Cuarto, but our first trip to others towns of the district began May 6. Brother Sickel with Mrs. Yoder and our boy Robert, went as far as Carlota. On the way we visited la Gilda where there is one family interested, and then Las Acequias where, in the country, we have a Sunday school in the home of Brother Gaychet. We had twenty-five at the meeting there, all eager for the meeting. This family bought a nice tablecloth which they keep for use only when we have meetings in their home. A daughter teaches the Sunday school and is doing splendidly. We visited the homes of the neighborhood and then hurried on to Carlota in order to have meetings there before the leaving of Brother and Sister Bock.

The authorities were good to us and gave permission for meetings in the plaza and to go about with the auto without paying the tax which is generally collected from vehicles.

We had an English meeting in the morning. Carlota has been fortunate in having a group of English speaking people who have helped considerably in the work. Generally the English are no help whatever to the missions. I might say Americans also, but there are as yet so few of them that they are hardly worth counting. The country needs colonists of the Puritan type to build up Christian homes and communities. The temperament of the Latin race is very different from that of the Anglo-Saxon and lacks the element of stability so necessary in Christian work.

The Spanish meetings at Carlota were also well attended from first to last although there are some special difficulties in this town. It is very much scattered and there is little police protection. In fact many suspect the police of being in partnership with the thieves so that people fear to leave their houses alone at night. The priest at this place is one of the most notorious rascals in the country and although he is losing his influence is still feared by many. Recently however he got a little of what he deserves when a man in a neighboring town came home and caught him with his wife and at the point of his revolver made him sign a check for twenty thousand pesos (about $8600.00) to hush the matter. Brother and Sister Bock are well spoken of in Carlota and we deeply regret the circumstances which call them away from the work there. We are already overburdened here but we will try to take care of the work in Carlota by going there the first Sunday in each month until better arrangements can be made. While we have no members there yet, there is a nice little group of Sunday school children which deserve our care and there are people interested who in time should be fully converted.

After a week in Carlota we went on to Los Cisnes, about twelve miles nearer to Rio Cuarto. Here we held a meeting at the railway station at which there were about 130 present out of a total population of only about 500. While here we were entertained in the home of Mr. Debanne, the leading business man of the town. He has a large family, well educated and refined and all trying to follow the Gospel. We are hoping to have a Sunday school here with one of the daughters for teacher. There is a great demand for a day school here as there is none worthy of the name and there are many bright children from Swiss families. One young man and his wife here brought their baby to consecrate it and although they were brought up Catholics, promised to accept and follow the Gospel. We have arranged to preach here each time that we go to Carlota.

The next town on our way back was Alejandro, a town of about 4000 but with many signs of growth. We found a few families at once who are in sympathy with the Gospel from having heard it elsewhere. I was obliged to leave the coach here in order to return for my classes which come on Wednesday and Thursday. Mrs. Yoder had returned before but Brother Edwards came to join Brother Sickel and arranged to speak in the fine hall of the Italian Society. There were about seventy out and cheered heartily at the close of the sermon. Here as elsewhere Brother Sickel helped much by his stirring solos. He is also a model driver for the auto and a good helper all around. Sister Sickel came to Carlota also while we were there and remained to help Sister Bock prepare for their long journey.

We find that the auto behaves beautifully with the load it carries and the people every-where come out to see the auto that looks more like a street car. We can stop most anywhere and have people to talk to from morning till night and those who have heard of the Gospel before at once make themselves known. We distributed thousands of good tracts and portions of the scriptures and are quite enthusiastic over the work. We sleep better in the coach than in a house and have it conveniently arranged for cooking as well. On the way from one town to another we can take all the quails, pheasants, rabbits we want, and sometimes armadillas and ducks. The roads are very sandy in places and when it rains are full of ponds but the auto goes everywhere so far. We are now finishing up some details which we left till having some experience on the way so as to know better how to have everything, and next week hope to go down the line the other way and spend a week or ten days at Cabrera and Deheza with Brother Atkinson.

We have just received the Evangelist with the first reports of the Easter offering and are delighted to see the advance over other years. But our expenses have doubled also and in order to extend the work we must go on to larger giving as well as larger efforts. May God bless the dear friends who have made it possible to have the auto. We pray that there may be enough for a second machine by another year. The field is large enough for a number of them and ripe enough too.

THE SIZE OF A BABY'S BACK

The remnants of flannel and woolen goods you find in an old scrap bag are so small you think there is no use for them.

Did you ever notice how small is a baby's back? Babies in the Near East perished of the cold last winter because they hadn't a piece of cloth to cover them. Add the largest and smallest of pieces of cloth to your bundle to the clothing you sent to Near East Relief Headquarters in June; a use will be found for the tiniest scrap.

PHOTOGRAPHS DON'T TELL IT

It is unfortunate that photographs coming from the Near East, the Tragedy Spot of the World, cannot be passed around, from hand to hand, till every one in the United States has seen them. It is only by seeing pictures of children, clad in one thin cotton garment, standing in the snow, waiting to be served a piece of bread, or a bowl of soup, that the majority may realize the suffering in that section. To prevent a repetition of what was told last winter in the digging of thousands of graves for those who perished of the cold, the people are called upon to contribute to the collection of clothing now on under the Near East Relief. The movement is nation-wide, and the clothes will be baled and sent to the Near East as rapidly as collected. It is up to you; will you save a child's life or feast the moth?

NEWS FROM THE FIELD

FROM HOMERVILLE TO CANTON

Homerville

From time to time we have reported this work through the columns of the Evangelist, but it has been some little time since any report has been forthcoming. During the past winter and spring we have not been handicapped by either sickness or bad roads as we were last year. Consequently the attendance at both Sunday school and the church services steadily advanced and the interest increased. We have reason to feel proud of our faithful though widely scattered band of workers. Though under many difficulties they are doing their bit and it was with great hesitation and with a mighty heavy feeling in our bosom on the morning of April 18th, that we told them that it would be necessary for us to leave them. Other fields were calling and as we were nearing the end of our school year and the completion of our course, it did not come to them as a sudden decision. This is the really hard part of a pastor's work—the severing of bonds of love thus formed. But while we leave them as pastor, we know that we do not lose them as friends. Moreover we did not feel quite so badly about it as we know we were leaving them in the hands of another whom they will love just as well, if not better, than the one who is leaving them. On the second day of May Brother Austin Staley went in among them to lead them on, and knowing him as we do, we do not fear for the future. May God bless you, brethren of the "Homer" church, and may you follow in the way as directed by your chosen leader.

Canton

On April 11th, at the request of the Canton church we made an acquaintance trip to that place. To say that we were well pleased at the reception we received would indeed be putting it mildly. To make a long story short, they gave us a call and we accepted it and at this writing we are all torn up and only waiting for the truck to take us to our future home among these good people. We have been waiting for Brother Belote, the former pastor, to report the work of the Canton church and at last he has made such a report. But the trouble with his report is that he did not "blow his horn" hard enough. Listen, Brethren, truly it is a mighty fine piece of work that he has done for the church. When we took charge and made a rapid survey of the work we found that things were in fine running order with all the gears well oiled up and plenty of "gas" in the tank for the journey this year. Before Brother Belote was content to relinquish his work to another he had led the flock to several victories. Primary among these victories was the paying off of the church debt, the last payment being made April 15th. Then not content with this he had so enthused the people that when the smoke of battle had cleared away for the Easter Mission offering it found Canton with over $1.00 per member, for with a membership of 159 Canton gave nearly $170.00. Thanks,

Brother Belote, for the inspiration your work gives to the one who follows you.

But it did not all happen before Brother Belote gave up the field. A few things have happened since he left. For example, on Mother's day the Sisterhood had charge of the devotional service of the morning hour and with a little extra effort on the part of the workers of the Sunday school in conjunction with these fine young ladies we had a great service. When the final count was taken for the Sunday school report the total was 164. This was a great jump from the previous Sunday which was only 110. But that is not the best part of it. We have had the joy of seeing the attendance hold up and instead of just a little over the 100 mark we are now averaging about 140. Brother J. J. Hang, our live superintendent and Sister Guiley, who is in charge of the children, together with a great number of fine workers are making the school mean something. Of the other departments we have not been able to learn very much but know that they are going forward. But the best event since we have been with them was the semi-annual communion service. This was the largest communion service that has been held in the Canton church, I am informed. Over 100 taking part in the blessed service. For this we are more thankful than for anything else, for it shows that above all else the spiritual status of the church is high. A church is just as big as its spiritual life allows it to grow. Brethren, blend your prayers with ours for a sustaining of this relation to God and to one another. We hope from time to time to report progress, not of the flighty kind, but a steady, onward, forward movement that means victory in the end. FRED C. VANATOR.

A VIRGINIA CIRCUIT

It has been some time since I have given a report of the neglected and almost helpless places of our needy little Brethren neighborhood, and while we have not tried or could not make a glowing show for a report for the Four Year Program report, we are trying to make a program that will speak from the fair pages of the eternal records. We find Jesus taking those that no one else would have and we have some little bands longing for the Gospel to be fulfilled, where it says the Gospel shall be preached even unto the poor. Unfortunately for our Ashton, Virginia church, my childhood home and where the night whippoorwill's warble is still to be heard, is still without a pastor. The main workers and the faithful are gone, but the Spirit of God still works with the faithful few. Last fall they appealed to me to come again, and I went to them for one week and over two Sundays. I baptized two good young people and received two fathers and one son by relation, which will be a help to us financially as well as spiritually. Brother Dan Bozzel was one, and he is now a Bible class teacher. Since then we have returned as often as possible. On June 12 we went back and held four ser-

vices. Our subject on Sunday night was "The Prodigal's Return," and three clean young men and three young ladies came forward, asking baptism. Monday morning was baptism and in the evening was the confirmation service, when a young mother with a babe in her arms came.

I asked how many would raise their hands to say they would pray for a harvest of souls to be gathered on my call trip for a three weeks' meeting in North Dakota. All hands were eagerly raised. But they said, Please come back to us once before you go in July. I go to Piney Hill on the east side of the Blue Ridge mountains, but I make very little fuss about it. For three years now we have gone there and have eighteen members. I preach out by the wayside. They are glad to see me come, and often they send me parcel post boxes of eats. Often at these times our eyes are filled with tears and our lips are made to say God bless the little far-away flock. I think I can tell God in tenderness that they try to do their best.

We are thankful for the twenty dollars that the mission board gives for the Hammer mission of West Virginia. There are twenty odd members there 150 miles from their shepherd. We try to go there four times each year, and add a few of such as will be saved. But oh, the loss of our leader there, Brother Bud Hammer! He will be missed by us all for some time to come.

We have added five to our Reliance Mount Zion church since our last report. Is there any brother who will offer himself to help me this fall in this work on the same financial basis that I am on? Bear ye one another's burdens and so fulfill the law (love) of Christ.
S. P. FOGLE,
22 Third St., S. E., Washington, D. C.

P. S.—Our dear Brother Balen VanHook who wrote us last fall to come this July says they have heard not one real gospel sermon in eight years. Brethren, pray that on this voyage souls may be gathered. _ S. P. F.

LA PAZ, INDIANA

On Tuesday evening, June 1st, we began an evangelistic effort in the village of La Paz, twelve miles distant from North Liberty, and continued for twelve days. La Paz is a village of 276 souls, 73 of which hold membership in some church there or elsewhere. Twenty-six are members of the Brethren church and these with some others maintain a union Sunday school in a union church.

It was in the union church that the meeting was held. Our audiences were not all that we had hoped for but there were many who heard the word gladly, and the Lord gave us seven souls for our labors, all of which are adults and four are heads of families. No doubt all will become members of the Brethren church. During the meeting we baptized two, preached a funeral and anointed a sick sister.

This is a splendid field for the Brethren, there being about a hundred members of the church in the town and nearby communities, but they are unorganized and without a pastor. Here is an opportunity for our state evangelists to investigate and help them get started again and take the community for Christ.

A smallpox scare in North Liberty, putting a ban on all public services for two weeks, made it possible for me to hold the above meeting. Sunday, June 20, we began our open air meetings here at home for the third season. They are a great success in every way. At our last appointment we also added two splendid people, a husband and wife, coming from the Church of the Brethren. Our work was never better prepared to go forward here than it is now. The Lord is blessing us abundantly in these days. He has given us more than a score of souls in the last month in our several fields, but we have been busy, because the time is short, the Lord is at hand, let us help to prepare this old world to receive him.

I think I should state in closing that we are standing aloof from the Interchurch World Movement. In the light of God's word it appears to me as a huge joke.

Yours under the Precious Blood,

C. C. GRISSO.

MINUTES OF THE 33RD ANNUAL CONFERENCE OF MARYLAND AND VIRGINIA DISTRICT

The 33rd Annual Conference of Maryland and Virginia District met at Roanoke, Virginia, June 8-10, 1920.

In the absence of the moderator, Dr. J. M. Tombaugh, the vice-moderator, L. G. Wood called the conference to order. In the absence of W. H. Miller, the devotions were conducted by Amzi Weimer, who read for our edification and instruction Romans 12:1-12 and invoked God's blessing and guidance upon the conference.

In the absence of the secretary, A. B. Cover, was elected secretary pro tem. and the following committees were appointed: Credential—L. G. Wood, A. B. Duncan and Miss Mary Pence; Resolutions—J. S. Bowman, J. M. Bowman and W. H. Stem.

Next on the program was the Address of Welcome, by L. G. Wood, pastor of the Roanoke church. Brother Wood extended to the delegates and friends of the conference a most cordial welcome and expressed a wish that we might all be profited by coming together and that the cause of Christ might be advanced.

The following delegates responded: A. B. Duncan, E. B. Shaver, J. W. Leedy, Miss Mary Pence, J. M. Bowman, Mrs. P. J. Jennings, and A. B. Cover.

The courtesies of the conference were then extended to Rev. J. F. Watson of Johnstown, Pa., who also responded to the Address of Welcome.

After the singing of "On Higher Ground," the Credential committee made its initial report. The report was accepted and committee continued. The following business was then transacted:

J. E. Patterson, A. B. Duncan and Mary Pence appointed tellers.

First ballot resulted in election of A. B. Cover moderator.

L. G. Wood was then elected vice-moderator.

Upon second ballot for secretary Mary Pence was elected, and C. R. Koontz was declared assistant secretary by acclamation.

J. S. Bowman was elected treasurer.

C. R. Koontz was elected statistician.

A. B. Cover was elected a member of the examining board to succeed E. B. Shaver.

G. A. Copp was elected a member of board of property to succeed self.

After the making of several announcements the benediction was pronounced by A. B. Duncan and the afternoon session closed.

Tuesday Evening

The first on the program was a Christian Endeavor Rally led by H. H. Rowsey. Many helpful suggestions were given out at this time and the report showed that progress has been made in the district. This session was closed by the usual Mizpah benediction.

Conference again assembled at 7:50 P. M. and after the singing of a hymn, C. R. Koontz conducted the devotional service, reading for a lesson 2 Timothy 2.

At this time we were favored with special music by the choir, which prepared us for the annual conference sermon which was delivered by J. M. Tombaugh in hi sown forceful way. His subject was "The Preacher and His Message." In brief he said as follows: The highest station in life to which a man can be called is to preach the Gospel, to be an ambassador for the King. It is of divine appointment in perfecting the plan of salvation. In all ages God has blessed the public proclamation of his own truth, and the pulpit has been the chief human agency by which the world has been led to Christ. From the human standpoint preaching has not always been successful. In some cases failure may be the fault of the preacher, and in some it is the fault of those in the pews. His theme is the everlasting Gospel, and he has no right to convert his pulpit into a lecture platform. Furthermore, his "Emancipation Proclamation" is world wide,—to every nation, a kindred tongue, and people.

After the rendition of a beautiful anthem by the choir, and the making of some important announcements, Dr. Tombaugh pronounced the benediction.

Wednesday Morning

The devotional service was conducted by Brother J. W. Leedy, who read a few verses from the 14th chapter of John and invoked God's blessing upon the day's work before us.

First on the program was the "Victory Drive for the Four Year Program" by L. G. Wood. After urging every member to make a full report when Brother Bame calls for it in July, he asked each goal director to give a brief report of his or her goal or goals. The directors reported progress in the work and in the case of Foreign Missions we have gone over the top. While progress has been made there is yet more to do.

Next on the program was a brief discussion of the Interchurch World Movement. It was expected that Dr. J. A. Miller would lead this discussion but unfortunately he could not be with us. In his absence A. B. Cover opened the discussion, after which various questions were asked and answered but the discussion closed without any definite action being taken in relation to the Movement.

"The presentation of the Sunday school work," by A. B. Cover, district superintendent was next on the program. His subject was twofold: "The New Ideal for the Sunday School and the Teacher Come From God." He said in part, that the most fundamental problem of America today is religious education. For the solution of this problem we must know the principles of the Master Teacher. The agency through which it can be best solved in the Sunday school. To do this there is need of a new realization of the effectiveness of the Sunday school; a new conception of the Sunday school as a Bible school; a new realization of the importance of the Sunday school as the chief agency of religious instruction in the nation today. In all the teaching realm, Jesus is the Model Teacher. Therefore, let us study again his life and teaching. Preparation for his work was full of meditation, study, prayer, communion with the Father; he was courageous, free from prejudice, and placed confidence in men. The characteristics of his teaching are intensity, brevity, nearness to nature. He appealed to the will; used induction, and question; he taught with effect and power because he and the truth he taught were one.

Credential committee reported 20 ministers and 33 lay delegates present.

Benediction pronounced by Brother Chambers.

Wednesday Afternoon

The service was opened by the singing of "Brighten the Corner Where You Are," after which Brother J. E. Patterson conducted the devotional services, reading for a lesson 1 Corinthians 13.

Credential committee reported 24 ministers and 47 lay delegates present.

Statistician's report of Sunday school work was read and accepted. It showed that 16 schools reported a total of 84 officers, 1487 pupils, 101 teachers and total membership of 2043. Offerings $3206.98. Two Front Line schools and two Teacher Training classes.

After a beautiful duet by the Misses Pence the following were elected:

J. E. Patterson, District Superintendent of Sunday schools to succeed A. B. Cover.

C. C. Haun, district secretary of the Sunday schools.

G. Harry Haun, president of the district Christian Endeavor work.

Miss Edna Bovey, secretary of the district Christian Endeavor work.

Brother J. F. Watson of Johnstown, Pa., brought a very helpful and vital message in behalf of the Sunday school work. He said in part that the statistics represent the real facts of the case; they are the life and energy of our work. They are the scales in which we are weighed. Are we found wanting? The day of modern evangelism is passing, what shall be done to supplement it? Revitalize our Sunday schools. We had better 1000 times burn out our energy in the saving of a whole life in the Sunday school than to save the remains of a wasted life in a revival.

The service was closed with an inspiring solo by Miss Arnold, and benediction by J. F. Watson.

Wednesday Evening

The forepart of the evening was given over to the women's work. The devotional service was conducted by Sister Cover and Sister Pence. Little Miss Eleanor Plunket brought us a twentieth century parable, after which the choir favored us with special music.

Miss Hillegas of Pennsylvania brought us a message based on the first chapter of Romans and emphasized the fact that the heathen were greatly in need of Christ. Miss Hillegas expects to go to Africa in the near future and asked that we pray for her as well as the other workers in the field.

After a very impressive solo by Miss Arnold, five of the sisters presented in native costume the needs of their home lands. Miss Pence closed this part of the program with an appeal based on "Go Ye! Pray Ye! Give Ye!"

The congregation sang one verse of "If Jesus Goes With Me," after which Prof. R. R. Haun gave a brief report of the work at Ashland College. He said in part, that there were 25 graduates, mostly long course men; that the college had passed through a very successful year financially; and that best of all there had been a fine spirit of harmony prevalent throughout the year.

Last but not least, was a message by Rev. J. F. Watson. His subject was the Stewardship of Life. The following lessons were drawn from Peter's call to feed his Master's sheep: Peter must be sifted from Simon. The same questions come to us today. Do we love Christ enough to give of self; to give of substance; to give of time. May the Master shift us and raise us from our dead selves.

Special music by the choir.

Annual conference offering amounting to $14.15 was lifted.

The following recommendation was made by the Mission Board: The Mission Board of the Maryland and Virginia District Conference recommends to Conference the repeal of Article 7, Section 1 of the Constitution and that the following amendment be adopted instead: That the Mission Board of this District shall consist of two laymen and three ministers holding certified credentials.

Motion was made and seconded that recommendation be adopted. After a few remarks the question was called for and the vote was 31 to 1 in favor of the amendment.

The following were elected by acclamation: E. B. Shaver, G. Harry Haun, A. B. Cover, J. S. Bowman, and C. C. Haun.

Benediction by Brother E. B. Shaver.

(To be continued next week)

SOCIOLOGIST REPORTS FAVORABLY ON EFFECTS OF NATIONAL PROHIBITION DENIES EXODUS OF FOREIGNERS TO AVOID DROUGHT

A carefully balanced report by a practical sociologist on the effects of national prohibition, showing numerous favorable results and some yet in question, has been submitted by Dr. W. E. McLennan, Director of Welcome Hall, a large social center at Buffalo.

Dr. McLennan undertook this study some months ago at the instance of the Commis-

Our Goal: 200,000; We Can and We Must

200	000
190	000
180	000
170	000
160	000
150	000
140	000
130	000
120	000
110	000
100	000
90	000
80	000
70	000
60	000
50	000
40	000
30	000
20	000
10	000

COLLEGE ENDOWMENT

sion on the Church and Social Service of the Federal Council of the Churches of Christ in America. He was told to get the facts, no matter where they might lead. In order that the survey of the situation might be thoroughly representative the cities of New York, Philadelphia, Washington, Harrisburg, Columbus, Chicago, and Detroit were visited and consultation was had with social workers, police officials, business men and others in daily contact with all classes of people.

Unsettled Questions

"Some questions," says Dr. McLennan, "I have not been able to clear up, even to my own satisfaction. One of these, has to do with the influence of prohibition on what we call the general prosperity. We know, for instance, that the banks in workingmen's districts have lately received extraordinarily large deposits. Bankers themselves are inclined to believe this condition is principally due to prohibition. They may be right, but it is clear that no amount of prohibition can of itself provide workingmen with funds for deposit, if there is not steady employment at good wages. On the other hand, the possession of money easily earned is not in itself a guarantee against the lure of drink. It may be said, indeed, that as a rule the larger the wage of the drinking man the more he will spend for his favorite beverage.

Another question that cannot be settled at present is the relation between prohibition and accidents. It is perfectly clear that accidents due to drink have been reduced since prohibition went into effect. But as to industrial accidents we must wait until we know not only the number of accidents but also the number of employees in the different industries, the hazards in the different employments and the physical and mental condition of employees when injuries occur.

(To be continued)

CAMPAIGN NOTES

The campaign in the Maryland-Virginia district opened at Linwood. It was the original plan to open at Hagerstown, but Brother Cover's attendance at the Maryland-Virginia conference caused me to change to Linwood for the first church to be canvassed in the east. Nor have I any particular regrets that circumstances led us to this decision; for the Linwood result is such as to set a very good pace for the churches of the entire Maryland-Virginia district.

Linwood does not represent very great numerical strength. Moreover, since Brother Biddle has closed his work there Linwood has had no regular pastor. And even though the pulpit has been ably supplied in this interim by Brethren J. M. Tombaugh and Roy Long, nevertheless the Linwood work has suffered in the absence of a pastor. And I have learned in the course of the present campaign that my work is always harder when there is no pastor on the field.

I did not go to Linwood an utter stranger, having been there at two different times before. Hence my work among the Linwood people was pleasant because it was a process of renewing acquaintances. It is needless to say that Ashland College has some warm friends and supporters at this place. And the presence of Dr. Jacobs at the Maryland-Virginia conference at Linwood a year ago only served to intensify and deepen the interest of Linwood in Ashland. I preached each night

I was at Linwood to appreciative audiences and my work was a pleasure throughout.

Linwood went $1,000. In view of what I have already said I consider this very good. And I am glad to report that the first church visited in this district has to its credit a $500 man. I hope many other churches here in the east may share in this distinction. We also had one gift for $150, and the next were for one hundreds and on down. I was received with royal welcome in all of the Linwood homes; and am especially indebted for entertainment to the Inglars, and Drachs, and Measlers, and Buckeys. The home of Brother John A. Inglar was my general stopping place, but I also spent considerable time in the home of Brother J. C. Buckey at New Windsor. Thanks to all of these good folks. Brother Earl Detsch a student at Ashland who is spending his summer vacation in his home at Philadelphia will care for this congregation this summer.

While at New Windsor I visited the Blue Ridge College located at this place. This is a Church of the Brethren school. And as I looked over the beautiful grounds with their splendid buildings already erected, and also a fine dormitory building in course of construction, quite a number of thoughts went chasing through my mind and the one that I shall mention now was this: "Surely some people in the Church of the Brethren have learned to give big, substantial gifts to their colleges, else I could not have seen such buildings at Blue Ridge as I was looking upon." And the only comment I have to suggest is that we as a denomination cannot yet flatter ourselves that we have learned to think in big terms and big figures when it comes to giving to our only educational institution. Even though we are measurably sure to round out $200,000 for permanent endowment in this campaign, when it is all done I shall still have to feel that we have only "nibbled." Maybe we shall reach up to better and bigger things some time. Let us all hope so.

Our result now is approximately $148,000. My next report will put us beyond the $150,-000 mark and that will be a grand and glorious feeling.

WM. H. BEACHLER,
Campaign Secretary.

Business Manager's Corner

ACCEPTING THE INEVITABLE

The heading of these notes may appear to be somewhat high-sounding from a business standpoint, but there is nothing else to be done, so why not face the music and call things by their right names? For some time it has been known by all the readers of the Evangelist that the paper famine had at last reached The Brethren Publishing Company and that for some time the Evangelist was made only half size. We might find comfort in the fact that a number of other papers, both religious and secular, had to do the same thing, but that would not help matters. However we may congratulate ourselves that we now have enough paper stored in our

stock room to get out all our publications for the next ten months.

BUT here is the problem; this paper cost us exactly TWICE as much as the same amount of paper cost last July. The question is, Who is going to pay the bill? It is quite evident that it will be an impossible task for the Publishing Company to pay this bill from an income no larger than its income has been during the year drawing to a close, and yet this has been the BIGGEST year by far that the Publishing House has ever known.

The inevitable conclusion can be nothing else than that the church at large, or the users of Sunday school literature and the readers of our church papers will have to PAY THE BILL. Every quarterly that is sent out to our Sunday schools this quarter is being sent out at a financial loss, and every number of the Evangelist that is sent out printed on this new supply of paper is sent out at a loss. Something will have to be done to meet this situation and it will have to be done QUICKLY. It will not do to wait until the Board meets at Winona Lake the last day of August, for by that time the order blanks for Sunday school supplies will have been sent out to all our schools.

This Quarter's Literature

We are sorry that we are somewhat late in getting out our Sunday school supplies this quarter, but no one who has any reasoning faculties at all will find fault or complain about it when they understand that we simply had to wait for the arrival of paper upon which to print the quarterlies. As stated in a former article this paper was bought last January and should have been here long ago. Then some of the cover paper for the quarterlies was on the road just eight weeks in making a one hundred and fifty mile trip to Ashland. It arrived only this forenoon. We have been running our publishing plant to its capacity with the number of workers we have been able to secure, working nights as well as days for a good deal of the time, and on Wednesday, June 23rd we began mailing our first quarterlies, and we are mailing them every day just as rapidly as we can get them off the presses. We hope to get them to practically all of our schools in time for use on the first Sunday in the quarter, though they may not have them in time to distribute the last Sunday in the previous quarter.

The Evangelist Honor Roll

We have almost lost track of the Honor Roll during the past few weeks as we have been so busy with other things, but one church at least has renewed its list since our last report, and that is the Maple Grove church, Eaton, Indiana, with H. E. Eppley pastor. We have also received the preliminary list from another church that is going after a place on the Honor Roll. We hope it may succeed.

Cutting Off Subscriptions

Ever since the campaign started to increase the Evangelist subscription list we have been extremely liberal with delinquent subscriptions to the Evangelist, and it has paid in the long run. We have lost some money by doing as we have done, but we believe we have made infinitely more, and many readers have

written us how much they have appreciated the extension of time we have given them. BUT NOW WE MUST CHANGE our system. We can no longer afford to send the paper after the subscription has expired and take our chances on its renewal. The paper COSTS too much. We will be compelled to cut off subscriptions as they expire. We will give two more weeks' extension of time and then we must CHOP the unpaid subscriptions off. It is a movement for self-preservation.

LOOK AT YOUR LABEL

Let me explain the marking on your label once more and you can then know whether your subscription has expired or not. We publish FIFTY copies of the paper each year and they are numbered from Number One to Number Fifty. If the label on your paper says 50-19 it means that your subscription expired with the last number in December. If your label says 4-20 it means your subscription expires with Number Four of the present year. If it says 24-20 it means your subscription expires with this week's number of the Evangelist. So EVERY subscriber whose label is numbered before 25-20 is now a DELINQUENT subscriber, and it is time to get busy to save yourself and to save us the trouble connected with taking names off our mailing list and then in a week or two putting them back on again. Pastors, your help is needed in this matter. Please explain it from the pulpit and help your members to understand. They will appreciate it I know, and I am sure we will appreciate it very highly as well.

R. R. TEETER,
Business Manager.

MINISTERIAL EXCHANGE

The Brethren church at West Alexandria, Ohio, is looking for a pastor. Any one interested may write to Mrs. Oscar Myers, West Dayton Street, West Alexandria, Ohio.

Cobb's Conference Corner

VACATIONS

Nowadays, nearly everyone has a vacation, sometime during the summer. Why cannot the Brethren people arrange far enough ahead for their vacations that they might enjoy the Conference? It will do the person good, make a bigger Conference, and increase the interest in the home church upon the delegates' return. Of course it will not be possible for everyone to get away, but if arranged for in time, a great many more can be in attendance than are usually there.

It will speak well for the spiritual interests of our church if more of our members take their vacation at Conference, than to go off on some fishing trip, or to some pleasure-resort. When once Conference begins to grow numerically, it will easily justify a stronger program, and the stronger the program, the deeper the interest. So let us work hard, for a great Conference this year.

E. M. COBB.

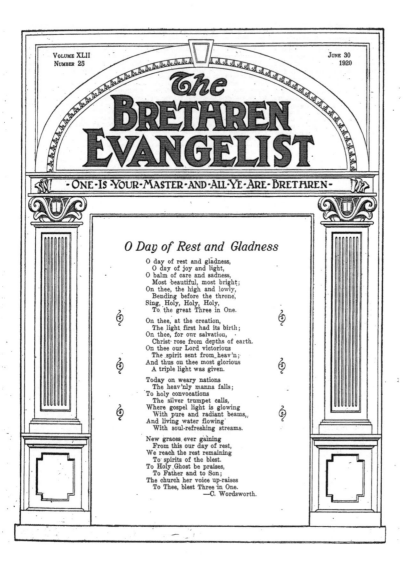

Volume XLII
Number 25

June 30
1920

The BRETHREN EVANGELIST

-ONE·IS·YOUR·MASTER·AND·ALL·YE·ARE·BRETHREN-

O Day of Rest and Gladness

O day of rest and gladness,
 O day of joy and light,
O balm of care and sadness,
 Most beautiful, most bright;
On thee, the high and lowly,
 Bending before the throne,
Sing, Holy, Holy, Holy,
 To the great Three in One.

On thee, at the creation,
 The light first had its birth;
On thee, for our salvation,
 Christ rose from depths of earth.
On thee our Lord victorious
 The spirit sent from heav'n;
And thus on thee most glorious
 A triple light was given.

Today on weary nations
 The heav'nly manna falls;
To holy convocations
 The silver trumpet calls,
Where gospel light is glowing
 With pure and radiant beams,,
And living water flowing
 With soul-refreshing streams.

New graces ever gaining
 From this our day of rest,
We reach the rest remaining
 To spirits of the blest.
To Holy Ghost be praises,
 To Father and to Son;
The church her voice up-raises
 To Thee, blest Three in One.
 —C. Wordsworth.

Published every Wednesday at Ashland, Ohio. All matter for publication must reach the Editor not later than Friday noon of the preceding week.

George S. Baer, Editor

The
Brethren
Evangelist

When ordering your paper changed give old as well as new address. Subscriptions discontinued at expiration. To avoid missing any numbers renew two weeks in advance.

R. R. Teeter, Business Manager

OFFICIAL ORGAN OF THE BRETHREN CHURCH

Subscription price, $2.00 per year, payable in advance.
Entered at the Post Office at Ashland, Ohio, as second-class matter.
Acceptance for mailing at special rate of postage provided for in section 1103, Act of October 3, 1917, authorized September 9, 1918.
Address all matter for publication to Geo. S. Baer, Editor of the Brethren Evangelist, and all business communications to R. R. Teeter, Business Manager, Brethren Publishing Company, Ashland, Ohio. Make all checks payable to the Brethren Publishing Company.

TABLE OF CONTENTS

EDITORIAL

The Need of a Revival of Sabbath Observance

There is scarcely another moral law more flagrantly violated than that which requires the observance of the Lord's day. By Christians and non-Christians, by corporations and individuals, for business and for pleasure, of necessity and by choice, Sabbath observance is being broken down, and the day set apart for rest and worship is becoming more and more a day of ordinary business and pleasure seeking. During the war under the "camouflage" of patriotism the most serious Sabbath desecration was tolerated and even encouraged. And during these days when the post-war reaction in morals is being felt in so many lines, many and effective arguments are being used for its continuance. Commercial interests for selfish ends are seeking to legalize the operation of non-essential industries on Sunday. Advocates of professional and amateur baseball are persistently urging legislation for Sunday baseball. The motion picture trust companies are determined to legalize their business in all parts of the land. Nearly four million laborers are at work every Sunday, half or more of whom should be released. There are 150,000 caddies on the golf links on Sunday in season, tempted away from Sunday school by men (many of them church members), who for selfish Sunday pleasures are robbing the boys of moral and religious opportunity and training. Sunday automobiling for pleasure, sports and similar activities are keeping hundreds of thousands of church members away from public worship on Sunday and furnishing an astonishingly bad example for the young people of our day.

All over the country efforts are being made to break down the bars that guard the Sabbath as a separate and sacred day. The battle is being waged ceaselessly in the New England states and the situation has been described as a "perilous and dancing balance." In New York some adverse bills were defeated and some were passed. In the southern states the struggle has been vigorous, but in general the adverse bills have been defeated and the courts have sustained the existing laws. In Pennsylvania and Indiana the friends of the Sabbath have been victorious. The District of Columbia, the home of our national capitol, and the states of California and Oregon have no Sunday laws. "In the Rocky Mountain states the Sabbath laws are few and feeble and the people are satisfied with what they have," says F. M. Barton. "Once the Sabbath is gone, irreligion will follow, which may lead to atheism and anarchism." History is replete with object lessons which drive home the importance of safeguarding the Sabbath. "It is perfectly natural, therefore," says the supreme court of Pennsylvania, "that Christian people should have laws to protect

their day of rest from desecration. Regarding it as a day necessarily and divinely set apart from worldly enjoyment, and for the enjoyment of spiritual privileges, it is simply absurd to suppose that they would leave it without legislative protection from the disorderly and immoral. The sentiment that sustains it should be expressed through those who are elected to represent the will of their constituents."

With the present tendency steadily increasing there is certainly a need of a revival in the matter of the proper observance of the Sabbath. And the church must take the lead if such a revival is ever to come. Early in the summer before the abnormal hot weather rage toward Sabbath desecration has set in, every Christian should take his stand resolutely and every church wield every proper influence against the common and flagrant misuses of God's holy day, sanctified to man's highest use. It is a matter that is vital to the highest spiritual development of every Christian and the most abundant life of every church. A man cannot treat God's day lightly without experiencing a corresponding disregard for God's Book, God's name and everything connected with God. And a church cannot encourage or look askance on the wrong use of the Sabbath without cheapening itself in the estimation of the world and causing the worship of its divine Lord to be looked upon as a matter of indifference. The church owes it as a duty to its own life, the spiritual welfare of its members and to the best interests of every moral and material good to seek to bring about a renewed concern for the observance of the Lord's-Day. God told Jeremiah to stand in the gates of Jerusalem through which kings and people pass to and fro, and there renew the covenant in hallowing the Sabbath, urging each and all to neither bring in nor bear out any burdens on that day, nor do any work, so that the people might truly prosper and the city remain forever. This is the duty with which the leaders of the church are faced today.

We must call for a revival of Sabbath observance for the sake of physical rest. The primary purpose for the institution of a Sabbath was that man might have a day of rest from his labor. It is a physical necessity. Any one who has been interested enough to observe has noticed how those who persistently take no Sunday's rest suffer a fatigue and a weariness that finally puts them behind in the race of life. The law of one day's rest in seven is written as certainly in our physical and mental constitutions as in the Decalogue. A man is duty bound to conserve his vitality and to conserve his physical strength, for these are his best assets. By numberless tests from the days of the French Revolution, when the tenth day was substituted for the seventh, down to the days of the World War when England threw restrictions on working hours to the winds, but for the sake of efficiency was compelled to restore them, it has been demonstrated that a man can work efficiently and continuously only six days out of seven.

We need a revival in Sabbath observance in the interest of mental improvement. This is especially true of those whose work day by day does not bring them in touch with the world's accumulation of learning and ideals. And even for those whose pursuits bring them in touch with these things, the day should afford opportunity to fields of learning not of a professional nature and thus broaden the sympathies and enlarge the vision. The study of the highest themes and the social discussion of them in the Bible school and in prayer meetings, gives the ordinary person more mental training in the course of his life than all his school days give. Far too few have any appreciation of the beauty and divinity in nature, or any acquaintance with the world's noble writers, or understanding of God's leading of the nations or the great reform movements and heroes of history, or even the holy Word of God. These and a hundred other things might be the subject of profitable meditation and study on the Sabbath and would result in the enrichment of the mind and the inspiration of the heart.

There is need of a proper Sabbath keeping revival for the sake of spiritual nurture and training. The soul must be trained to enjoy spiritual realities in this life, if it is to rejoice in those things in the life that is to come. Our preparation for immortality must be made during the days of mortality. And in the rush of life's every day duties there is not found sufficient time for the development of the soul; there is a need of the still hours of the Sabbath when the soul may tarry and grow accustomed to the holy atmosphere of divine communion. That does not mean that we should or can be expected to sit all day with the Bible on our knees, wrapt in meditation and prayer, for it is quite contrary to our nature to sustain a state of mind and heart so continuously. But it means we must have time to "practice the presence of God"—time to hear God speak and to speak to him. It does mean that we must take time for soul-refreshment, for the replenishing of our spiritual vigor. The soul wearies and becomes exhausted under the strain and stress of daily trials and vexations, just as the body becomes tired and worn. It must have time to come to the inexhaustible fountain of spiritual power and be renewed with strength in the inner man.

The Sabbath is also a day of spiritual service, and for this purpose it should be reclaimed. The Lord of the Sabbath said, "It is lawful to do good on the Sabbath days." Every day should be a day of service, but they are not. Our days are so filled with selfish service and self-seeking, that we are inclined to become fixed in selfishness, while the needy and weak suffer without help. We need the Lord's Day in which we find time to give ourselves in a special way to Christian service. It is not enough to spend the day in mystic contemplation on things divine; we must give ourselves to divine service. This is a day on which we should demonstrate the practical side of our religion, or prove our faith by our works, a thing which the Apostle James prized so highly. "Pure religion and undefiled," he says, "before God and the Father is this, to visit the fatherless and the widows in their affliction, and to keep oneself unspotted from the world." So, we shall improve the day, not only by saying "Lord, Lord," but by "doing the things" which the Lord says.

EDITORIAL REVIEW

We are sharing with our readers a word of appreciation coming from Brother Thomas Gibson, Wasco, California.

The summer slump divides the "annuals" from the "perennials" among Christians, just as the autumn frosts do with plant life.

If your soul is dark and gloomy, let the sunshine of God's love fill your heart and all will be cheerful and bright.

Brother Cobb again directs your attention to the importance of preparing to attend conference. See his "Cobb's Conference Corner" on page 16.

You cannot be heard of God with loud, empty words, nor seen of him with a proud, haughty demeanor.

If the world is to be saved for Christ there are thousands of idle people in the churches who must go out and get to work.

So long as our nation spends more money in building "men of war" than the Christian people of America spend in encouraging the building of men of God we can expect that the spirit of war shall be dominant.

On the Christian Endeavor page you will find a report of the Ohio Christian Endeavor convention, recently held at Columbus. It was written by Prof. J. A. Garber, who is now doing school work at Northwestern University at Evanston, Illinois.

"You cannot 'catch up' in life, as you can at school; you are marked on your daily average." "Complimentary tickets are never given out to the great theater of success. Success is not a bequest; it is a conquest. For the dead one it is an inquest."—Exchange.

The employer, whether corporation or individual, who takes a part of his employee's Sunday's rest for gain by compelling him to work on that day is a thief, as surely as is the man who breaks into a house and takes his neighbor's goods. And the crime is no less blameworthy when the employer is a church corporation.

The first itemized report of the Easter offering is to be found in this issue. Nearly every church has increased its offering over last year and some have done exceptionally well. It is the largest mission offering ever given by our people but it is no larger than the needs demand. From this splendid victory we will take courage and press forward.

"The Annual Brethren Bible Conference" of Southern California will be held at Long Beach, July 16-25, 1920. Brother Kimmel states that they are expecting to make this the best conference yet. That ought to be the ambition of every district concerning each successive conference. We hope it can be truly said of our coming General Conference when it is past.

"Travel Flashes Again" writes Brother Bame and reports two evangelistic campaigns recently held by himself, one at Huntington, Indiana and the other at Oak Hill, West Virginia. Both campaigns resulted in victory for the Lord's work. Brother Bame speaks highly of the present condition and future prospects of the Huntington mission, which has gone forward under the leadership of Brother Brower. At Oak Hill, Brother Bame and his able assistant, Mrs. Bame, were received with much appreciation, not only by Brethren people, but by members of other churches as well.

We came near thinking our little friend, Marguerite Gribble had forgotten us, but not so; she sends us another interesting letter which is published in this Evangelist. Our little friends throughout the brotherhood will be interested especially in the fact that little Marguerite was baptized, as were also Marie and Julia Rollier. It is surprising to know how early in life the Lord can speak to the souls of children who are given careful religious instruction from their first conscious moments and are permitted to grow up in the attitude of prayer. It is in accordance with the word of Jesus who said, "Suffer the children to come."

A SAD ACCIDENT

On Friday, June 25, Prof. Edward Byers was killed near Martinsburg, Pennsylvania, a fast train having struck the automobile in which he was riding. Brother Byers was owner and president of Morrison Cove College and at the same time was pastor of two Pennsylvania churches. It will be remembered that he was for years a teacher in Ashland College, and also for a time professor in Defiance College at Defiance, Ohio. Thus in the midst of a most useful life another most useful servant is taken from time into eternity. Further obituary notice later.

GENERAL ARTICLES

When Is a Boy Too Old to Go to Church? By Bruce Barton

(Through the courtesy of "The American Boy" we are permitted to pass on to our family of readers this excellent article in which Mr. Barton answers the above interesting question together with such questions as, "Why is your mother respected and honored?" "Where did America's ideals of liberty come from?" "What is the biggest, most powerful business in the world?" It is a stirring, manly article and we trust our readers will make the best possible use of it. After you have read it, pass it on to some one, especially to some friend among the boys.—Editor).

I have a friend of nineteen who quit going to church last year; and when I asked him why he had quit, he answered that a church was doubtless a good thing in its way —a nice place for women and children to meet on Sunday mornings, but no real place for a man, or a boy who was almost a man.

After he left me I got to wondering about what he had said. Is a church merely a place for women and children to go and sit and be preached to, or at? What is the church anyway? And at what age is a boy too old to take any more interest in it?

All of us have the very human habit of judging the big things of the world from a few small facts. We pick up the telephone receiver, and because central does not answer in a jiffy, we say: "The telephone system is all gone to pieces." We ship a parcel to Chicago by express, and if it happens to be delayed twenty-four hours we think that the express companies are terribly inefficient. We see a little unpainted church, with a preacher who is struggling to support his family on starvation wages, and we think that the church is losing out all along the line.

But if we could see the thousands of miles of wire, the great army of trained employes, and the huge central stations that are the telephone system, we would never make a telephone call without feeling a sense of mystery and awe. Think of the miracle of it—to be able to sit in your own home, and without lifting your voice, have it carried across waters and mountains for hundreds of miles. If we stopped to remember that it took weeks to carry the news of Cornwallis' surrender from Yorktown to New York, we would marvel at the better appreciation of the marvelous feat that the express company performs when it carries our parcels from Chicago to New York not in weeks, or in days, but in hours.

In the same way we would get a very different picture of the church if we could see its world-wide sweep. We would gain a new respect for the unpainted buildings at the country crossroads, for it is not an isolated unit, alone and unrelated.

It is really a branch office of the greatest business in the world. That business—which is the church—has more paid employes than the greatest corporation; it has headquarters in every country; its total budget amounts to hundreds of millions of dollars. It supports hospitals in every great city; it cares for thousands of babies in orphans' homes; it is curing sick people in India and China with its doctors; and teaching the boys and girls of Turkey and Hindustan in its schools. Don't despise the little white church, then, because it is having a hard time.

Remember, first of all, that it is just one part of a great big whole—the local headquarters of a business that is bigger and finer and more inspiring than the business of the biggest trust or corporation that America has ever known.

To run a business of that size is a job for men—big, red-blooded men; women can help wonderfully, but they cannot do it alone.

But suppose we go a little farther back. Every institution has a right to be judged not by what folks say about it, but by what it really stands for, by the things that it has done. Suppose we judge the church on that basis; and in making our judgment we'll omit every argument that is in any way theoretical. We'll limit ourselves to matters that affect you and me, as young Americans, living in the year 1920.

Who is the most important member of your household? Who is the one whom all the other members of the family delight to honor? Who is the one to whom your father pays greatest respect? Who has influenced your life the most? Your mother, of course. It is our pride, as Americans, that we honor our mothers above everyone else on earth. Perhaps it never occurred to you that honor to mothers is comparatively new thing in the world. But that is the fact. When Jesus of Nazareth started his preaching women were hardly better than slaves. It was an unheard of thing which he did—he made them his companions. Of the people closest to him, whose names we know, more than half were women. He gave mothers a wholly new place in the world and his church, in all the ages, has been the champion of women and of motherhood.

There are plenty of places under the sun where men still treat women as slaves. In the New Hebrides, for instance, it was the custom, when a man died, for his wife to be strangled to death and buried with him. That custom would still prevail in the New Hebrides, probably, if it had not been for a Christian missionary named John G. Paton who was sent out by the church. He carried reverence for women to those savage islands, just as Christian missionaries have carried it into every land. Wherever the influences of Christianity spreads, the lives of mothers are made brighter and happier. And any boy who is not too old to feel a love for his own mother, is not too old to support an institution that is making life more worth while for mothers all over the world.

Some day you will fall in love with a wonderful girl and have a home of your own, and some boys and girls that will call you "Dad." When that time comes you would be willing to die rather than have any harm come to those babies of yours. But do you know what used to happen to babies in the olden days? Men did not value them highly; often they were regarded as a nuisance. Sometimes they were sacrificed to the heathen gods; in Egypt for instance the great iron statue of Moloch was heated white hot, and mothers threw their screaming infants into its flaming arms. In Greece babies were left out on the mountains to die; in China they were drowned. The world had a very poor opinion of babies until Jesus of Nazareth came.

He said: "Suffer the little children to come unto me and forbid them not; for of such is the kingdom of Heaven." It is to him that we owe our reverence for babyhood. His gospel, wherever it has been carried, has changed the thought of men about children. And any boy who some day expects to have boys and girls of his own, ought to stand up for the church; for the church has been forever, and forever will be, the best friend that boys and girls have.

You hope to go to college perhaps. And who was it that started our colleges? The state? No; the state universities are all of them comparatively young. The first colleges were started by ministers of the church. Harvard was founded by John Harvard, a Christian minister. William and Mary, the second college, was founded by a Christian minister. Yale was founded by a group of Christian ministers. Amherst, Williams, Dartmouth and scores of others were started by church people and supported for many

many years by contributions from the churches. Today there are said to be about 450,000 students in colleges, universities, and academies in this country. And more than half of them are in institutions supported by the churches. So any boy who expects to go to college ought to be glad to go to church; for if it had not been for the churches we should have had no colleges.

You may be sick some day, seriously sick; you may have to go to a hospital and that hospital may perhaps save your life. The chances are it will be a hospital that was made possible by the churches and still depends upon them for most of its support. There are thousands of boys and girls in the land whose parents died in their youth. Things would have gone very hard for them had it not been for the children's homes that the churches built and maintain.

Indeed you can hardly mention a single institution of society which exists for the common good that does not have its roots in the church. And you know enough about trees to understand how short a time a tree can live after you have severed the roots.

We celebrate this month the Fourth of July, the birthday of our nation. Have you ever stopped to think who it was that gave us the ideals of liberty that have made America? Those ideals came across the ocean in a little boat named the **Mayflower**. In the cabin of that boat the first constitution was drawn up by a Christian minister and the members of his congregation. The government they established for the state was modeled after the government they had established for their church. They chose, their governors in the same way that they had chosen their preachers—each state choosing its own governor without the consent of kings or emperors as each congregation had chosen its own pastor. The very institutions which we are proud to call American are institutions that were developed and tested first by Christian people in the organization and government of the Christian church.

And the men who have made America great—did they think when them came to manhood that they were too old to go to church? Washington drove to church with his family every Sunday morning.

Daniel Webster was in church the Sunday before he died. His was the greatest brain that America has produced; scientists studied and weighed it after, his death because it was so great; and it was a Christian brain.

Abraham Lincoln almost never missed Sunday morning worship. "God bless the churches," he exclaimed, "and blessed be God who, in this our hour of trial, giveth us churches." Nicolay and Hay, his biographers, say that in all the crises through which he was called to pass the churches were always at his back, ready and eager to respond to his call for support.

And Theodore Roosevelt declared: "I think it is the duty of every man to go to church. Frequently I have to listen to sermons that bore me. But the church has contributed so enormously to civilization, its service to society is so great, that irrespective of all other considerations I feel I ought to support it and to attend whenever I can."

Let us put away this idea that the Church is merely a place for women and children to go. It is not a place; it is an influence, greater and more powerful than any other in the world. An influence that has made motherhood mean what it means to you and me; an influence that has given childhood a place of reverence in the thoughts of men; an influence that has created our colleges, and our social service institutions, and inspired the men whose names we honor most. Washington did not outgrow it; Lincoln never was too old to worship under its roof; Webster and McKinley and Roosevelt, and all the men whose names we remember on the nation's birthday, were glad to do honor to its name and service.

Surely no boy of your age or mine need be ashamed to follow in the footsteps of men like these!

The Christian and Politics. By Mrs. C. E. Nicholas

Never in the history of our nation have we needed the influence of real Christian men so much as today.

We need men of high moral principles—men of Christian character—men who are ready to sacrifice everything except **truth** and **justice**—men who have the interests of the people they are serving at heart—men who cannot be bribed to sell his country for Judas' thirty pieces of silver.

The love of money and the sin of greed is scaring the conscience of men that they are no longer touched by the cries of the suffering poor.

Every day the rights and liberties for which Washington and Lincoln fought are being sacrificed to political bosses and money hoarders.

We are pained to acknowledge we have men who are daily betraying the confidence of millions because of selfish aggrandizments. Just how long the Christian people of our land are going to be satisfied with existing conditions is a question. Just how long the Christian people are going to allow the morals and lives of our people jeopardized and the progress of the Christian religion retarded, is more than can be foretold. One of our great politicians recently made the following statement, "Not more than half of the American people belong to churches yet they are receiving benefits of Christian ideals in this country.

We must look to Christianity to bring labor and capital together, all other plans and efforts have failed. Christianity, if applied, will solve the profiteering problem. Are we going to take the challenge and measure up to our opportunity and accomplish the work others cannot do and calm restless humanity? It would seem to me this is our opportunity to prove to the world that Truth properly applied will rule the political world as well as the spiritual.

The spirit of the Golden Rule needs reviving. The BIG I and **Little you** has taken its place and rules everywhere.

We must have men with clean hands, to meet the demands of today, Christian men who are absolutely free from political taint. We must have men whom the interests of Wall Street cannot control, men who under pressure will be able to keep an eye single to the interests of the people they represent.

Do you say impossible? That they are not to be found? Have faith! There are no impossibilities for those who both **work and pray.**

We pray for our rulers but if our prayers are answered we will have to **work** as well as **pray.** God never answers prayers without corresponding works.

There are prayers that are never answered because they are not linked with **works** as well as faith. The absence of **work** spells defeat.

Not so many years ago one lone Kansas woman started a crusade against saloons with her hatchet. She did not depend on prayer alone but works brought the results desired in the end. While we did not approve of her radical methods yet great reforms have started in just that way. Her frantic efforts to rid the country of the curse of whiskey, awoke the people, the crusade spread from state to state and finally became a national question—not a political question but a great moral issue which thousands were supporting. Today our nation is rid of the saloons and barrels of whiskey have been hauled to the dump. The victory has been won but we must still fight to hold our ground. Shall we retreat? The forces of the wets are working day and night to undermine our victory and to make the enforcement of National prohibition ineffective. We will find it harder to hold what we have already won, than it was to win the victory at first.

Temperance won because there was strength in union —people put aside political objections and religious differences, united their efforts,, worked with just one object in view—that of putting down one of the greatest evils of our fair country.

If the affairs vital to the morality of our nation are to be rescued from the hands of "money changers" and political bosses, it will be because the Christian people unite. their efforts to break their power, and seek to bring the people generally to recognize the Golden Rule as the higher authority.

The opportunity is golden. Will we grasp it? If we are saved from national disgrace, if we are to experience great moral reforms, if the power of God's Truth is to be felt throughout the nation, it will be because her christian people have lived it and worked for it as well as prayed for it.

Reforms are slow; men naturally cling to their old ways of thinking and living and are not easily turned to new thought and practices. It takes a great force to arouse people out of their stupor yet it can and must be done.

Everything of value must come by strife and struggle.

Dowagiac, Michigan.

"Heads I Win, Tails You Lose."   By N. J. Paul

In the discussion of this topic, first I want you to get the thought before us that in any business, or occupation that we may choose, or engage in, there is a chance to lose, as well as to win. I want to bring to your mind a story of two Irishmen who had newly landed in New York City. Both secured jobs, but at different places. One Sunday morning Pat was walking about the city taking in the sights, when he met his old friend Mike. After a hearty hand shake and a good morning, Pat suggested that they flip a half dollar to which Mike agreed, at the same time slipping two bits into Pat's hand. "Now, Mike," says Pat, "heads I win, tails you lose." "Alright, Pat, flip the coin." The coin was flipped; up came tails. Pat set his foot on it, and said, "I win." "Hold on there," says Mike, "I chose tails." "Sure," says Pat, "did I not tell you, heads I win, tails you lose?" While we meditate on the story of the two Irishmen, we are introduced to a great lesson in the study of God's word. We win heaven step by step. After we claim faith in God the Father and the Lord Jesus Christ his Son, the first step is baptism, and that by trine immersion, by the forward action. Here we meet many times with opposition. Some tell us one dip is all that is required. Others tell us pouring is sufficient. Others say, Just sprinkle a few drops water on us and we are satisfied. While still others say, No water at all for me, give me the baptism of the Holy Spirit, and that will suffice. To all of those requesting these different modes of baptism I will say, If you can be saved and reach heaven by them, I am satisfied. If one dip will answer for one, and sprinkling will answer for another, and pouring will satisfy another, and another is satisfied with none at all, and all will reach heaven, surely I can get there by taking the three dips and we will not fall out about this baptism at all. "Heads I win, Tails you lose." Under the old law the priest always washed, or cleansed themselves with water before entering into the holy part of the temple to prepare themselves to wait upon the people, or to offer sacrifice.

Next, in the New Testament, Jesus teaches foot washing. He not only taught it, but gave the example. Yet you say no need of that, it was only an old Jewish custom, and was nailed to the cross. No trouble between you and me on this command, if you can get to heaven without doing it, surely I can by obeying it; on top again, "heads I win, tails you lose."

Again. In the Old Testament the Jews were required to observe the passover once a year, in order that they might not forget their deliverance from bondage out of Egypt. In the New, we have it given to us in the form of the Lord's supper. What for? To carry our minds forward to the great supper in the evening of this world, when Christ himself will serve us. How queer, you say, scarcely any church observes a meal in that way; the bread and cup is the Lord's supper. There is no need at all of a full meal before the bread and cup. All right, if you can get to heaven by never eating the Lord's supper, I surely can get there by eating it. "Heads I win, Tails you lose."

Under the Old Law the blood was to be applied, and wherever the death angel found the blood he passed over; but where he found no blood, a death was the result. In the New, it says, "likewise after supper, he took the cup after he blessed it, etc." "Except ye eat of my body, and drink of my blood, ye have no life in you." "Just another one of the old customs," you say. You see nothing in it? Very well, we will have no falling out about this command, if you can reach glory by not obeying it, surely I can by obeying it. Once more, "Heads I win, Tails you lose."

Under the old law they were required to give a tenth. Under the new, we are admonished by the Apostle Paul; who says, "Upon the first day of the week let every one of you (not a part of you) lay by him in store. as God hath prospered him, that there be no gathering when I come." This is just as great a command as the Book contains. I don't find any other one more needful than this one. Here we strike the cord that seems to reach the heart. Your head drops; the mind at once begins to fix the excuse to get you by. Here are some of them: "I am in debt; I have a large family; I am only a renter; the H. C. L. is so high, I can hardly make both ends meet; let the preacher do as Paul did, labor with his own hands for his support; what little I could give would not amount to much anyway, I think the church can get along without my help." Listen, remember the poor women with her two mites. If you can get to heaven be too glad to meet you there. We will have no trouble between us in the matter of giving to the church: If I assist the church, surely I can get there too. Once more I score, "Heads I win, Tails you lose."

We as a church, believe in the anointing service. In fact, the Apostle James says, "Is any sick among you? Let him call for the elders of the church; and let them pray over him, anointing him with oil in the name of the Lord; and the prayer of the faith shall save the sick, and the Lord shall raise him up; and if he have committed sins they shall be forgiven him." See what a wonderful promise to those obeying this command. There are none greater connected with any that we have a chance of obeying. It comes to us on the sick bed when we most feel our need. I have assisted in this solemn service, and can witness to the times when God raised the patient, and restored him to health. No, we are not Christian Scientists because we believe in, and practice what God's word teaches. It is the same old question you come back with, "If that is a command, why don't all the Christian churches teach, and practice it?" And then you retort, "For my part, I think medical skill can do all that can be done, and when medical skill fails, there is nothing more to do. I haven't anything for such a practice. All right, we will not fall out about it; if you can get to heaven not observing this great command, I can get there by observing it. You see it is, "Heads I win, Tails you lose."

You are invited to join the church, and to assist us any way you can, to herald the gospel to all the world: You say, "There are too many unfaithful members in the church; I know men who are not connected with any church, who could set some professed Christians good examples. As for me, I can do as much good out of the church as I could in it." Jesus says, "Let the wheat and the tares grow together." "He that is not for me, is against me." If you can get to heaven out of the church, I hope I can by being in it. It is the same old story, "Heads I win, Tails you lose." So it is all the way through life. I prefer to take God at his word, and take nothing away from it and add nothing to it. If you can-get to heaven by adding substitutes, surely I can get there by obeying the whole Word of God. So to the last, let us have no trouble among ourselves. By obeying the teaching of the Master, we have everything to gain and nothing to lose. The way is plain and there is no risk to run. "Heads I win, and Tails you lose."

Losantville, Indiana.

The Verdict.   By Martin R. Goshorn

(The following poem was recently sent us, with the accompanying explanatory note, by Brother Robert R. Goshorn. His father, Brother Martin Goshorn, is one of our educated farmers who occasionally serves the church with his pen. We hope that by this time Brother Goshorn is completely recovered from his accident.—Editor.) -

"Today I got hold of a poem which my father had just written. Father was badly injured in an accident a few weeks ago and has been confined to his bed ever since. This poem was written under those conditions."

She stood before the Mighty Judge,
Dejected, spurned, forlorn;
No friend she knew to plead her cause;
The crowd was there to scorn.

Accusers bold, on every hand,—
She must be stoned they cried;
The law demands the penalty,
It cannot be denied.

Poor trembling soul, bowed low with shame;
Her grief she could not hide,
And then unknown by sinful men,
A friend bowed near her side.

We know not what passed through his mind,
But this we think is true;
He thought of human weaknesses,
And all he came to do.

He thought of those self-righteous men,
Who always sought a flaw,
To crush some weaker being
Neath the punishment of law.

He thought how bright the world would be,
If love should reign instead.
A man would lift, and love, and help,
And spite and hate were dead.

So calmly to the mob he spoke,
In accents firm and clear,
Go! Throw the stone you sinless man,
If any such is here.

Did any dare to do the deed,
In scorn they sought to do?
No! conscience' darts pierced hard their hearts,
They all were sinners too.

Again the Master bowing low,
Wrote calmly in the sand;
We wish we knew the precious thoughts,
That moved his loving hand.

No doubt he thought of leaving heaven,
Where real perfection reigns,
To live upon this sin-cursed earth,
And drive away it's pains.

Perhaps he thought how men had failed,
And fallen o'er and o'er,
Then to the sinful woman said,
Just go and sin no more.

The curtain fell, the scene was closed,
The verdict all can read,
No sentence marred her future life,
She now was free indeed.

A Mighty Judge with power supreme,
Had sat in court that day,
The whole world heard the verdict,
The law was changed for aye.

The law of Moses ages old,
Had served it's time and place,
A fuller meaning now was taught—
Man should be saved by grace.

A friend had come to aid the weak,
New light and life to give;
He'd lift the fallen from the mire,
And teach them how to live.

.   .   .   .

Age after age has come and gone,
His star still brighter growing,
Age after age has felt the stream,
Of gentle mercy flowing.

.   .   .   .

The tempter still our weakness sees,
And oft we fall and stumble,
But mercy watches all the way,
And bows to lift the humble.

Thanks! Thanks! to him our Mighty Judge,
Enthroned forevermore.
While sinful men would cast the stone,
He says, Go sin no more.

Clay City, Indiana.

Music.   By Mary Louise Switzer

Originally music was a general name for any art over which the muses presided but now we use it to specifically refer to that art which concerns sounds and their combinations.

So far as we know and as far back as our records go, all people who lived long ago even before the time of Christ showed a love for music. Even savages attempted to sing or make some musical sounds. Music is a part of us a part of our nature by which we express thoughts that cannot be expressed through words, gestures, or writing thoughts, which cannot be expressed through the art of painting of sculpture, etc. There are probably but few people in the world so morose as to find no pleasure either in the exercise or the receipt of music and only these few will regard it as an undesirable or useless factor in our human life.

Music has been described as the purest, the noblest and the most universal of all arts and though the most abstract of all arts, it is the only one that can be learned and understood in early childhood. A child sings and learns to sing almost as soon as he learns to talk. Songs fills a space between infancy and the time that a child learns to read and write. Music cannot debase a child's mind for even though the melody is simple, it possesses something which lifts the mind above the ordinary things. Music should have an educational value; should be taught at home and at school, and should not be considered in the light of a fashionable accomplishment rather than as an indispensable part of an education.

Music has played an important part in education. The Greeks looked upon it as having power to mold the nature of man because their music included poetry and dancing

(Continued on page 11)

THE BRETHREN PULPIT

A Glimpse At the Social Religion of Paul

By J. L. Gillin, Professor Sociology, the University of Wisconsin

"I say the truth in Christ, I lie not, my conscience bearing witness with me in the Holy Spirit, that I have great sorrow and unceasing pain in my heart, for I could wish (Marg. "pray") that I myself were anathema from Christ for my brethren's sake, my kinsmen according to the flesh." Rom. 9:1-3.

The profoundness of the religious genius and the depth of his religious experience has been recognized by every student of the Christian religion. No one either in the Apostolic Age or since has equalled him in the variety of his religious interests, the breadth of his spiritual horizon, the mystic feeling of his religious life and the thoroughness with which he thought through the various complex problems which his religious experience thrust upon his attention. He knew as few of his day the theology of the Jews. He was steeped in their history. He had a profound belief in the central place which they had held in the economy of God for the revelation of himself to all men. Theirs were the promises, and theirs the heroes of the faith. Yet, the puzzling thing was that they were rejecting the Messiah foretold by their prophets, and revealed to them by the most wonderful life which men had ever known, and who had revealed himself in a special manner to Paul, when he called him to his service.

Paul has been looked upon by some as the teacher of individual salvation. The eleventh chapter of his Epistle to the Romans pictures in a most realistic fashion the struggle through which he went in his own experience between his sense of his sin and his desire for delivery from the consciousness of sin. The eighth chapter reveals his sense of freedom and joy at the release which his own experience with Christ brought to him. It is a shout of liberation and triumph. Over and over again he exhorts his disciples to conform their individual lives to the life of Christ. Occasionally he expresses his desire to be with Christ.

Yet, how often we lose sight of his unselfish devotion to others. How clearly we see that he is more interested in the salvation of others than even in his own, if we but take a comprehensive view of his writings. His whole life was one solemn dedication to the service of others without regard to his own welfare. Evidently, if we take his activities into serious consideration we can see clearly that his motive for his abundant labors was not inspired primarily by his "Woe is me if I preach not the Gospel," in the sense of fear for his own salvation in the next world, but rather by the attitude expressed in our text. Even his desire to depart and be with Christ he subordinates to his desire to be of service to the Philippians. (Phil. 1:23.)

In the passage of our text, however, Paul's social passion in his religious life comes to clearest expression. As he contemplates the condition of the Jews his "kinsmen according to the flesh," his sense of social unity and his passionate longing for them as a community leads him to the finest expression of the social Gospel which ever fell from the lips of any man aside from the savior himself. So desirous is he for the salvation of the Jews that he could wish himself anathema from Christ, if that would win them to him in whom Paul himself found freedom from the consciousness of sin, joy in life, a new source of power in labor, the capacity to suffer anything with joy, and the hope of heaven—in short, all that Paul means by "salvation."

One cannot measure the depth of Paul's self-abnegation and the profoundly social character of his religious passion, unless he remembers what Christ had meant to Paul. Picture to yourself a highly gifted man, brought up in the strictest sect of the Jewish religion, steeped in the traditions and literature of the Race, conscious from his earliest years of the proud claim of that Race that they were the chosen people of God, and sharing in all the rich treasures of spiritual exaltation and profound religious experience; imagine him drinking in with thirsty soul from early boyhood the sweet waters from the Prophets' and Psalmists' wells of religious literature. Remember also that with the growth of his knowledge of spiritual realities there came that sense of his own personal relation to Christ that enabled him to realize in his own life the nobility of character and that sense of unity with God which his own sensitive soul demanded and which the Old Testament literature had quickened. Add to that the detail that as a native of a Greek city he had lived in the atmosphere of Neo-Platonism, which emphasized the contrast between the flesh and spirit, and which placed in the flesh the seat of all the ills to which humanity is heir and which prevented the realization of the ideals of life inculcated by a highly ethical religion. Imagine also the struggle between his desires to be a "perfect man" ethically and socially and his own "fleshly" desires, so vividly pictured in the seventh chapter of his Epistle to the Romans. Remember further that it was Christ who appeared to him on the road to Damascus who resolved these personal difficulties of Paul, that through that experience with the risen and exalted Jesus of Nazareth, whom he was persecuting in the persons of his disciples, Paul had found freedom from his struggle to attain unto righteousness and a sense of that perfection of character which he sought. Furthermore, do not forget that it was that same Christ who had given him the power to "labor more abundantly than they all" and who yet conceived himself to be the least of the apostles, that it was the satisfaction which he found in his experience with Christ that enabled him to gladly "count as dung" all the emoluments, all the honors which had come to him in the Jews' religion. Then, with all these things in mind, one can see something of the scope of these words of the text in which Paul finds himself willing to be anathema from that Christ, that he might win to Christ the Jews—these Jews who had persecuted him from city to city, who had corrupted his disciples and who had made his life one long agony.

What shall one say of the contrast between the unselfish, social passion of Paul, willing to be damned from from Christ, that he may win his persecutors, and those short-sighted selfish Christians who think first and last of their own salvation and let the devil take the hindmost? And what think ye of the appeals to men to be saved, when salvation means only saving their own skins? Brethren, too often our appeals to people to "get religion," or "to come to Christ," or "to join the church" is a selfish appeal to them to consider their own selfish interests rather than an appeal to the heroic in them, to lose their lives for a great cause.

What a different conception of the nature of salvation had Paul in the words of the text! He was willing to be accursed from Christ in order that the Jews might be saved. Nothing more unselfish, and in that sense social in its attitude and concern, could be imagined. He was following his Master in that attitude. I wonder if Jesus did not have something of a sense of alienation from God the Father, when on the cross he cried out that word, which has puzzled expositors ever since, "My God, My God, why hast thou forsaken me?" To Paul Jesus stood in the place of God. Hence, nothing darker and blacker in prospect could be imagined by him than alienation from the Christ who had meant so much to him. Yet, even from him he was willig to be anathema, if by that means he might win the Jews the riches of life which he had found in Christ.

The unselfish, the emphasis upon the social rather than the individual's selfish advantage, the consideration of the welfare of the individual in the group, or church, the emphatic statement that "no man liveth to himself and no man dieth to himself," marks the whole ministry of St. Paul as it did of Jesus himself. The greediness for numbers characteristic of some of our militant Christians—or shall I say ecclesiastics?—today, with the resort to appeals a fear for their own personal safety here or hereafter was not so characteristic of Paul or Jesus. They were concerned with the Kingdom of God; the individual was of importance only as he was a part of that Kingdom and as he became a member of it. And—mark you!—becoming a member of the Kingdom was not a matter of joining a church or other ecclesiastical organization, but of partaking of the spirit of it. "But if any man hath not the Spirit of Christ, he is none of his." (Rom. 8:9.) That spirit was a self-sacrificing spirit, the willingness to lose one's life, yea, as Paul puts it, the willingness to be anathema from Christ that others may know what salvation means by actual experience.

Madison, Wisconsin.

OUR DEVOTIONAL

The Consecration of All to Christ
By W. W. Wertman

OUR SCRIPTURE

"I beseech you therefore, brethren, by the mercies of God, that ye present your bodies a living sacrifice unto God, which is your reasonable service. And be not conformed to this world, but be ye transformed by the renewing of your minds, that ye may prove what is that good and acceptable and perfect will of God. For I say through the grace given unto me, to every man that is among you not to think more highly of himself than he ought to think; but to think soberly, according as God hath dealt to every man the measure of faith. For as we have many members in one body, and all members have not the same office; so we being many are one body in Christ, and every one members one of another. Having then gifts differing, according to the grace given unto us, whether prophecy, let us prophecy according to the preparation of faith; or ministry, let us wait on our ministry; or he that teacheth, on his teaching; or he that exhorteth, on his exhortation; he that giveth, let him do it with simplicity; he that ruleth, with diligence; he that showeth mercy with cheerfulness."

OUR MEDITATION

The word consecration and its meaning has a value far beyond the value usually placed upon it. The consecration of all literally brings us to the point where we are giving our all to the Master. And how few of us do consecrate our lives, time, and worldly goods and all to his work. In 1 Chronicles 29:5 we read: "The gold for things of gold, and the silver for things of silver, and for all manner of work to be made by the hands of artificers. And who then is willing to consecrate his service this day unto the Lord?" In these days of unrest in the church, and in civil life the scripture just quoted has a far deeper impression for us if we read the latter part first. There are many folks who have done this, and God has richly blessed them and prospered them in all their trials and temptations.

Our missionaries in the foreign fields are examples of the consecration of all to Christ. They have been borne up by the hope and promise of life eternal, which is promised all of us if we only obey the call. The dedication of one's life to Christ and his works, is called to the writer's attention by a note, in the report from the convention held by

The Methodist Congregation at Harrisburg. A young and promising minister, being offered a larger pastorate, and of course, a larger salary, "Resolutely set his force to the duty and call, going to a smaller congregation, and necessarily less salary," He has consecrated his life, and all, to the Americanization and Christianization of the foreign population of this locality.

In the consecration of one's life to the Master's work, we meet obstacles placed by the world, "being called fanatics and shunned by worldly people; but then we must remember that, the blessed Lord Jesus, also was shunned, and hated by the world. I Peter 2:9 tells us if we are God's children, we are a peculiar people. The aftermath of the world war has left many seared and bleeding hearts. Mothers and Fathers who have lost sons, in the struggle have lost the love of Christ, and have gotten farther and farther away from Jesus. Spiritualism has taken hold in America, to such an extent, that we Christian people should all consecrate our lives and prayerfully preach and teach the "Faith of our Fathers," and there is need that the Brethren church, the whole Gospel church, shall consecrate itself to its task and that down to every member we shall present our bodies as a living sacrifice, wholly acceptable to God, which is our reasonable service.

We must, if we are going to live up to our teaching, prayerfully give our lives to some definite Christian service. We are not delinquent in our business, and we must realize that everything comes from our God, and every thing returns to Him so we should be faithful in our spiritual service. If we cannot give our time to missionary work, we can at least give our dollars, for he has commanded, "Go ye and teach the gospel to all nations," then shall the end come. And we shall be heirs and joint-heirs with Christ, if in our hearts we have his love and have been faithful in our service.

The training and consecration of our children's lives to service for our Master is indeed one which we, as a people have been slowly drifting away from. How many of the homes in our land has fallen away from family worship, and in thanks to God for our material needs? The home should be headed by Christian parents, and at least try to consecrate our lives and the lives of our children to some definite work for Christ. In the hurry and bustle of our life we are becoming thoughtless, and the awaking will be to late.

Our Father, we earnestly pray for the awakening of our brethren to greater obedience to the inspired teaching of thy word as did the apostles, "We need to feel Christ's presence more closely and the one and only way for this is through the earnest and consecrated prayers of the ministry and laity. Our prayer is that through our missionaries and field workers, also through the personal efforts of us Christian laity, that the whole gospel of Jesus Christ may be taught so strongly that the world at large will see the light. Through the consecration of all Christian people this can, and must be accomplished; or we have failed in the sight of our Lord and Master. Let us pray, Brethren, for strength, is our earnest plea.

OUR PRAYER

Our Father, who art in heaven, we pray that we may be more fully consecrated to our tasks and to thee. We have often sought our own work and our own way when thou didst seek to lead us into larger spiritual experiences and work. Forgive us for our willfulness and our lack of consecration, and help us to see our duty of giving our all to thee, withholding nothing. May we as a church consecrate ourselves to our tasks as we have never done before and seek to carry the whole Gospel to the whole world even as thou didst command us. Strengthen us in our purpose to this end. In the name of Jesus, our Lord and Master, we pray. Amen.

Altoona, Pennsylvania.

Send
WHITE GIFT
OFFERINGS to

THE SUNDAY SCHOOL

ALBERT TRENT
General Secretary-Treasurer
Johnstown, Pennsylvania

Is Any One Going to Tokyo?

It seems out of the question for the Brethren church to send a delegate to the World's Sunday School Convention at Toyko, Japan, but it is possible that some member of the church is planning to go on his or her own initiative. If such there is, as we hope, we should like to hear from them. If any one finds it possible to go, it will be abundantly worth all it will cost, if the trip is made with eyes, ears and heart open. It is the opportunity of a lifetime, and will be worth more than a year's schooling in any college in the country. However the great mass of us cannot go, but we can get much of the inspiring convention spirit and information if we seize upon every bit of news that comes within reach. Why not appoint a World Convention Committee, whose duty it will be to gather news concerning the Tokyo Convention or interesting events connected with the trip and report to the Sunday school. Let us make the most of this convention even though we cannot go.

THE TOKYO SUNDAY SCHOOL CONVENTION BUILDING

The Convention Hall that will house the main meetings of the Eighth World's Sunday School Convention, which will convene in Tokyo next October, will be erected on the great plaza in front of the Tokyo railroad station. Plans have been drawn and the work will begin soon. The building will be in barracks style and will seat at least 3,500. Even more than that amount of space will be needed, for in addition to the 1,000 delegates who will go from America many will come from other countries. Korea has asked for the privilege of sending 250. Of these 200 will be members of the native Korean church and the other 50 will be missionaries. Then there are thousands in Japan who would like to gain admission. The delegates from Japan will be in proportion to the number of schools in a given district and the size of the school.

Five hundred can be accomodated on the large platform. This will furnish places for the chorus choirs and especially for the pageants which are to be both instructive and attractive features at the evening sessions. A dining hall will be one of the sections of this large edifice and will seat 1,000 at a time. Many delegates will be entertained in Japanese and missionaries' homes over night and for breakfast, but provision in restaurants will be made for the other two meals. Some will be cared for in the Imperial Hotel and in the Tokyo Railroad Station Hotel, opposite which the Convention hall will be erected. Baron Okura will entertain 50 or more in his home.

Around the World With Sunday School Delegates

Two ships will leave Japan after the World's Sunday School Convention has concluded, with delegates who will return by way of China, Singapore, Colombo, and Port Said to Marseilles. There the conducted tour will end and railroad tickets to a Channel port and Trans-Atlantic steamship tickets will be provided. If possible, detours through India will be arranged for at additional cost. It is likely that special sightseeing can also be planned for Egypt and Palestine. Special information on the subject can be obtained by addressing World's Sunday School Association, 216 Metropolitan Tower, New York City. The ships to be used for these Around-The-World tours are the "Kitano Maru" and the "Kamo Maru" of the Nippon Yusen Kaisha line. The first tour, without the detour in India or Palestine, will arrive at Marseilles December 14 and the second on January 11, 1921.

An Additional World's Sunday School Tour Party

So many World's Sunday School Convention delegates have desired to take Tour 15, sailing by the Empress of Asia on August 26, that no more reservations can be obtained for that particular trip. To meet the demand for just such an itinerary another tour has been provided which will go to Manila and South China before the Convention begins. The new tour is No. 23 and the sailing will be on the Korea Maru, of the Toyo Kisen Kaisha line from San Francisco, leaving August 21 and stopping at Honolulu en route. After visiting Manila for two days and spending 8 days in Hong Kong and Canton the delegates will journey to Shanghai and thence to Tokyo via Nagasaki. They will arrive in Tokyo on the second day of the Convention but the program for the remaining days will be abundantly rich and satisfying.

Reservations are being made daily on the ten steamers that will carry the delegates to the Convention. The sailings are from July 30 to September 23. Three ships are for the exclusive use of those going to the Toyko Convention. All are popular Pacific ocean steamers—"Monteagle," "Siberia Maru" and "Suwa Maru." On some of the steamers, where not more than 50 or 75 reservations could be obtained, all berths have now been taken, but good accommodations can be had on other tours. Some of the trips provide for touring in Japan only, while others include in their itineraries Korea, China or the Philippines. The privilege of Christian companionship during the entire tour is one of the very attractive features that is assured to every delegate.

Sunday School Delegates Seeing Mission Stations

Those who go to the World's Convention in Tokyo next October will have unusual opportunities of coming into close contact with the work at many of the mission stations. The itineraries are planned with this in view. Receptions are being planned by the missionaries and members of the native churches. Tokyo, of course, will extend a gracious welcome, as will Yokohama. Special courtesies are contemplated in such places as Osaka and Kobe, where there are large Christian educational institutions.

The Interchurch World Movement has placed the matter of directing the deputations of tourists in the care of M. L. Swinehart of Kwangju, Korea. He is now in Tokyo making advance arrangements in cooperation with Horace E. Coleman, World's Association Secretary for Japan. Korea has requested that at least five post convention meetings shall be held in that country at such centres as Taiku, Seoul, Pyengyang, Kwangju and Wonsan or Hamheung. Similar meetings will be held in China, Philippine Islands, and by the Around-the-World tourists at Singapore, Colombo, India, Cairo and Jerusalem.

Groups of business men, educators and Sunday school specialists will visit just as many parts of Japan and elsewhere as may be possible. Women, specially qualified for that work, will hold meetings for the girls and women of these countries. The personnel of the delegates who have registered thus far indicates that there will be an abundance of speakers who can do these types of work. World leaders are among those already chosen by the Program Committee for Convention speakers. A number of State Sunday school secretaries will lead the delegations from their respective states.

World Wide Representation at the Tokyo Convention

Applications for delegates credentials to the World's Sunday School Convention are being received from the very ends of the earth. It will be truly a world's convention which will meet in Tokyo next October. In addition to the hundreds who will go from the United States and Canada there will be representatives from different countries in South America and from the Continent of Europe. All sections of the British Isles will send delegates. Then they will come from Australia, India, Java and Africa. All parts of the Orient will send many delegates, both from among the missionaries and from the native churches.

J. A. Garber
PRESIDENT

G. C. Carpenter
SECRETARY

Our Young People at Work

Christian Endeavor In Columbus.   By Prof. J. A. Garber

(We are indebted to Prof. J. A. Garber for this splendid report of the Ohio State Christian Endeavor convention which met in Columbus, June 22 and 23. As he sat in the convention hall, in the midst of the inspiration of song and address, he wrote this report as it comes forth to you. We hope you will catch something of the convention spirit and your enthusiasm for Christian Endeavor stirred as you peruse this message.—Editor.)

Memorial Hall is rapidly filling with young people possessed of shining faces and happy hearts. Amid the deafening din of enthusiastic delegation songs and yells, Chas M. Alexander mounts a chair on the high platform. His magnetic personality and musical voice are sufficient to transform confusing choruses into heavenly harmonies. "Higher Ground," the opening selection, strikes the dominate note. The chorus song follows. It was written by the pianist, Mr. Voke. Here are the impressive words, replete with evangelistic faith and fervor:

"Jesus is mighty to save,
Jesus is mighty to save;
Tell the glad story wherever you go,
Jesus is mighty to save."

Representing the City of Columbus, M. Naylor, the acting mayor ,said: Youth is the most active force in the land. When girded by Christ youth becomes a most potent factor in civic as well as church life. Speaking for the churches Dr. Maurer, pastor of the First Congregational church, testified that his early Christian training was received in a Christian Endeavor society in a small church that was not sympathetic toward the young people's organization, but from it have come three congregational ministers within the last ten years. If you young people will tie yourselves to a blazing ideal for which you are willing to die, Ohio will become the kind of a state we want her to be.

In his keynote address President Sine described youth as possessed with the spirit of the conqueror. Youth is full of daring, and knows not the meaning of failure. Impressed with the conquering spirit of Christian youth men will be impelled to exclaim

"Oh Gallilean, thou. hast conquered."

After a prolonged ovation, Daniel A. Poling said, This demonstration of youthful vigor and Christian potentialities calls for the continuing program of Christian Endeavor. It prepares for intelligent service, and enables young people to apply the strength of their life to the tasks at hand. Pledged for service to Christ, they serve not haphazardly, but under his direction. With enthusiastic, passionate eagerness they help to quicken the pace of the church. Youth, unspoiled, free of cynicism and conservation, is to change this world under God and bring in the fulness of Christian possibilities. The great objective of the service of Christian youth is to give Christ preeminence.

In the Quiet Hour message of Wednesday morning Miss Elinor Millar spoke conserning the meaning and blessing of prayer. She pointed out the danger of deifying youth, saying that youth unrestrained by Christ is dangerous. Through prayer the lawlessness of youth may be overcome. Praying youth may push the needed spirituality into these busy, rushing, compromising days. Such praying voices our conscious dependence on God and represents an outlay of spiritual energy. Prayer is not overcoming God's reluctance but taking hold of his willingness. You, Christian young people, should know how willing he is to save others through your prayer and service.

The character of the young.people will be determined by what they do between seven and eleven in the evening. Those pregnant words formed a text for General Secretary Gates to discuss the social program of young life. In many communities there is no place for them to go, except to the bad. It will do little good to lecture them in a prudential way. To tell them not to go to certain places, nor to indulge in questionable amusements, will prove ineffective. Instead of discussing doubtful matters, use the same energy in planning and promoting a social program that will attract and minsiter unto the perfectly natural needs of the young people. Have socials for fun and fellowship, recreation and entertainments, and not to raise money.

At the Wednesday evening session Dr. Chas. F. Wishart, president of Wooster College, elected to speak of "Those on the Reserve Line." Most of us are on the reserve line, not because of option, but reason. If these are reasons for our being here, we have duties to perform. As to relation there are about two on the reserve line to one at the front. In some instances the proportion is much larger. If detained, responsibility for world-wide vision and service rests with the reserves. It is their business to get the supplies to the front. The reward of him that remaineth by the stuff is the same as that of the one who goeth forth to battle. Then we sang:

"Hast Thou, O Lord, a work to do?
The field is white, the laborers few.
My heart now longs and yearns to go,
To reap thy harvest here below."

Music

(Continued from page 7)

and thus was connected with certain fixed aspects of life. They used it for patriotic purposes, for religious services and for expressions of love. Luther praised music because of its moral significance and advocated its use in early training. Spencer taught that it developed the speech and aroused feelings in others. He said it affords a pure and high type of pleasure. It is a relief from toil and fatigue. It serves as a framework, dignifies the commencement exercises, aids in the entertainment of friends, lends emotional power to the worship of God.

Is not this proof enough that this art should be cultivated and taught in all communities and to all peoples? Wonderful as the victrola and piano-player are they will not and cannot replace the pleasure that one obtains from actual playing and singing. There is no self satisfaction which comes from playing these instruments; the feelings of your own soul cannot be uttered by these devices

It remains to the people of today to determine the future of this art, and if this generation can understand a little at least, of what music really means and how it has come to be what it is, perhaps it will encourage the composers and they will be able to make it an honored and enriched art. Surely that which the spirit of man has labored with for centuries cannot be a mere plaything, for by the use of this art, a man's life may be widened and deepened and even inspired.

Wabash, Indiana.

Education and money in a sense are much alike. Either one may be instrumental, when properly used, of a great blessing, and an equally great curse when improperly used.

The stubborn man is blood-kin to a mule. To balk is no sign of character.—The Methodist Protestant.

SEND ALL MONEY FOR
General Home, Kentucky and
Foreign Missions to

MISSIONS

WILLIAM A. GEARHART
General Missionary Secretary
906 Conover Bldg., Dayton, O.

Another Letter from the Heart of Africa

Carnot, French Equatorial Africa,
Feb. 25th, 1920.

My Dear little friends:

This is daddy's birthday and I think I will celebrate by writing you a letter, especially as I have been very negligent and haven't written you a single word in 1920.

First of all I will tell you that people are still trying in vain to get that leopard. Traps have been set for it, guns have been shot at it, so far in vain. But God has kept it from attacking any of us. And now that I have set your mind at rest on that question, I will go back to the beginning of the year and try to tell you all that has happened since.

On January we all had dinner with Monsieur Pinelli the government official here. We certainly do enjoy those lovely dinners, and Mousieur Pinelli was so kind to us children. Each of us received a new dress as a New Year's gift. They are pretty bright-colored cloth such as the natives wear here. We haven't had the dresses made up yet, but some day all three little girls will appear in gala attire.

Soon after the beginning of the New Year we commenced our prayer meetings on the veranda of the upper house belonging to the Company. We were at that time living in their lower house, a few steps removed. Mama called that veranda the "upper veranda," and the older people had precious seasons of prayer there. Sometimes we children ,too, would attend the prayer meeting, and at other times we would creep away and have a little prayer meeting all by ourselves. At this time Monsieur Romeuf was away and the house was unused. About January 25th Monsieur Dufont arrived from France, and that same evening Monsieur Romeuf returned. Soon after this two other gentlemen connected with the Company arrived. We had to discontinue the use of the veranda but after that we met for prayer in Aunt Toddy's room.

On the last Sunday in January we had a love feast. We children sat at a little table by ourselves and did not take part in the breaking of bread, and the footwashing. We all felt so sorry because we had not been baptized that we could not take part in the other ordinances, as baptism comes first. From that day I commenced to want to be baptized. I asked mama if I might be, and she said, "Yes," but didn't say when. So I asked daddy and he looked rather perplexed and said "Ye-es," rather hesitatingly. So I said, "Mama can I be baptized tomorrow?" and she said, "Perhaps." So when I woke up the next morning, I said, "Mama, is this tomorrow?" and she said, "No, dear, it is today." I was puzzled, but I said, "Well, mama, why can't I be baptized today. I do love and trust Jesus." I heard mama talking with daddy about it and they said they hardly knew what to do as I am so very young. On January 28th I was taken ill with fever, and was anointed again and healed. Just as soon as I was taken sick, I said, "Mama, can I be baptized when I get well?" and without a moment's hesitation mama answered "Yes." The next day I had to stay in bed, although I had no fever, but on January 30th at four o'clock in the afternoon when the water in the Mambeli River is the warmest we all went down to its shores. Uncle Antoine took me first of all because he was afraid I would be frightened if I saw the older children baptized first, and I would have been too. But Jesus helped, as he always does when we trust and obey. Mama says she wonders what church I will belong to in America. Marie and Julia know their church home is at Long Beach, but I do not know whether mine is at Falls City, where I belong to Miss Cleaver's Cradle Roll, or at Dayton, where mama belongs, or at Philadelphia where daddy has his membership.

On February 1, Marie had another attack of fever. She had one in January, and was not strong yet from it when the second one came. On February 3rd we thought she was going to be with Jesus, but in answer to prayer God gave her back to us once more. She was no sooner out of danger than mama was taken down, the first illness, except influenza since we came to Africa. But God healed her wonderfully, and she was up as soon as Marie. On February 9th mama, Marie and Julia were all in bed, but Julia had only a slight rise of temperature, and all were up again on the next day.

It was so nice to help take care of mama when she was sick. I was the doctor and Julia was the Red Cross nurse, and we would go together to make our professional calls. We certainly were glad when our patient made so prompt a recovery, and glad that mama can recommend us so highly.

On February 10th we moved again. You see the Company needed the house we were living in, and as there was no other house for us, we had a camp cleaned and moved into our tents. We put up two of the tents first, and Aunt Toddy and daddy and mamma and I moved. Uncle Antoine and Marie and Julia came up a week later. On the Sunday after we came up, I went down to have dinner with Marie and Julia, and while I was there I was taken ill. Daddy went down and carried me up to camp in his arms. I was put to bed, and anointed, because Jesus always blesses obedience. At two o'clock the next morning my fever was all gone.

On the 19th, Marie was taken with fever again, and now after seven days of illness she is in bed still. It is a hard, hard test for us all, but we believe Jesus will heal her as surely, though not as quickly as he did me.

We were so glad that the Lord is giving us a house to live in here. It is almost completed now, and we are so happy, as the rains are beginning. Aunt Toddy and Marie moved in the unfinished house today, as it is so much better for Marie to be under a roof than in the tent alone.

I am so happy in Jesus and when I trust him he gives me victory, but, oh, Satan tempts me so, and I so often yield to temptation and grieve the heart of Jesus and of all my loved ones. I know you will pray for us children that we may be true soldiers of the Cross, and worthy missionaries of his Word in this dark land.

Yours lovingly,
MARGUERITE.

A LINE OF ORPHANS

Those who have seen the bread line in a large city say it is a sight they can never forget. How, then, could they look upon a bread line—not of men and women, the majority of whom have squandered their lives and opportunities,—but a line composed of orphan children. They may claim they have never seen such a line, and hope they will be spared the sight. But if their consciences are on the job, they are seeing such a line at this moment. Children, those who are fortunate enough to be clothed, wearing a collection of vermin-infested tatters and rags; the majority half naked, no difference what the weather, and all hungry. Some half starved. This is a familiar Bread Line in the Near East. You can remove a child from that line by adopting one. Five dollars a month sent to the Near East Relief, 1 Madison Avenue, New York, feeds a child. Clothing sent to your nearest Near East Relief Headquarters will be forwarded.

IF STOCKINGS HURT YOUR FEET

There are mothers in America who do not let their children wear a stocking that has been darned, claiming that the darned spots hurt the tender little feet. Not a bad idea if the mother remembers at the same time that the tender feet of thousands of children in the Near East have been blistered, frozen and burst with chilblains because of lack of shoes or stockings. It's a good place to send all discarded stockings; as well as warm clothing. The Near East Relief is collecting clothing this month—a receiving station is open in your locality.

DIRTY RAGS HAVE NO WARMTH

What does "the return of the children" mean to you? Excitement, anticipation ,preparation, joy, laughter? This is what "the return of the children" means in another part of the world: From the desert to which, nearly four years ago, they were driven by the Turks to perish, come the children of Armenia—those that are left of them. In groups of twos and threes they come, thin and hungry, clad only in dirty rags. With them sometimes are their mothers; more often they come alone—their fathers having been butchered, their mothers carried into slavery to die of abuse. They are coming back to shelter and food and clothing if you do your part in sending the clothes you can spare to your nearest Near East Headquarters.

NEWS FROM THE FIELD

MINUTES OF THE 33RD ANNUAL CONFERENCE OF MARYLAND AND VIRGINIA DISTRICT

Thursday Morning

The service was opened by the song "If Jesus Goes With Me," after which Brother C. C. Haun conducted the devotional service.

The next on the program was a brief business session.

Owing to a mistake in the nominations for the Mission Board, Brother C. C. Haun tendered his resignation so as to put another layman on the Board. His resignation was accepted and Brother Samuel Hounshell was elected in his stead.

Minutes of previous sessions were read and adopted.

G. A. Copp, treasurer of the Ministerial Aid, read his report. The report was accepted and Brother Copp re-elected for the ensuing year.

J. E. Patterson tendered his resignation as superintendent of district Sunday school work. Resignation accepted and Dr. J. M. Tombaugh elected in his stead.

A financial budget was created for the district Christian Endeavor work.

Dr. J. M. Tombaugh tendered the Conference an invitation to meet at Hagerstown next year. Invitation was accepted.

The following constitute the Executive Committee for the coming year: A. B. Cover, J. M. Tombaugh, J. S. Bowman, Mary Pence, C. R. Koontz.

Credential committee made final report, which showed a total of 22 ministers and 50 lay delegates present. Report was accepted and committee discharged.

The next was a discussion of "Missions" by G. Harry Haun. In his absence Brother C. C. Haun gave a vision of the opportunity that lies before us in regard to a Bible conference. The challenge is before us.

Brother A. B. Cover made final statistician's report. His report was accepted and in brief is as follows: Total membership 2211; Gain 214; Loss 67; Valuation of churches, $81,050; Parsonages $3,500; Salaries $7,595.70; District Missions $211.50; Home Missions $711.02; Foreign Missions $1,038.17; Benevolences $1,172.08.

The Resolution committee tendered the following resolutions which were accepted:

Resolved, that we offer thanks to God, our heavenly Father, who in his divine providence hath permitted us to meet in this conference as co-workers with him in the work pertaining to his kingdom.

That, we thank the local church as a body and as individuals together with their friends for their splendid entertainment and genuine hospitality as manifested in their homes and at the church during this conference.

That, we sincerely thank the Melrose Baptist church for the use of the basement of their parsonage for the purpose of serving meals.

That, we offer our sincere gratitude to the choir and volunteers for the excellent and inspiring music rendered during the sessions, and to all the officers of this conference and others that have contributed in any way to the enjoyment and spiritual uplift of this body.

That, we extend special thanks to Brother J. F. Watson, Johnstown, Pa., General Superintendent of our National Sunday school work, for his presence, and stirring messages of instruction and encouragement which he brought us.

Be it further resolved that, it is the sense of this body that we feel the need of its deepening of the spiritual life in the church and that we as individuals and as a body urge the use of all means to that end.

J. S. BOWMAN,
J. M. BOWMAN,
Wm. H. STEM.

Treasurer's report read and accepted.

Motion made and passed that $10.00 be sent to J. F. Watson to defray his expenses in coming to our conference.

Brother J. S. Bowman next discussed in a very plain and practical way the subject, "Evangelism." He said in part, that the Gospel should be preached to the whole world; that a great deal had been done toward this end, but that there was a great deal yet to be done. Narrowing his subject to our own district he said that much of the work had been of the "Hop, Skip and Jump" kind. Real evangelism has for its purpose the saving of souls and establishment of churches. Hence, the importance of the following: Location of Mission; Permanency of Mission; and Character of Evangelist. There is a great need of that abiding zeal produced by the indwelling of the Holy Spirit that causes God's children to produce much fruit.

At the close of this address Brother Wood made some announcements relative to dinner and trains leaving Roanoke, and a motion for adjournment was passed.

Dr. J. M. Tombaugh invoked God's parting blessing and benediction upon the conference and the 33rd Annual Conference of the Brethren Churches of Maryland and Virginia district adjourned.

A. B. COVER, Moderator.
C. R. KOONTZ, Assistant Sec.

Report of the Easter Missionary Offering

By churches and districts, from March 1 to June 1, 1920. The report by items and of memberships will appear in the July Brethren Missionary Magazine.

Pennsylvania District:	S. A. or Gen'l Fund	African Fund	Other Funds	All Funds Totals
Johnstown Brethren Church,	$ 360.00	$	$	$ 360.00
Philadelphia Brethren (3rd),	71.50	54.50		126.00
Uniontown Brethren church,	99.75		.25	100.00
Waynesboro Brethren church,	189.84	54.50		230.34
Allentown Brethren church,	163.63	58.62	.75	223.00
Conemaugh Brethren church,	119.85			119.85
Altoona Brethren church,	117.75	27.75		145.50
Highland Brethren church,	45.00			45.00
Pike Brethren church (Conemaugh),	31.00			31.00
Vinco Brethren church (Conemaugh),	27.40			27.40
Sugar Grove Brethren church,	7.00			7.00
Yellow Creek Brethren (Hopewell),	13.00			13.00
Jones Mill Brethren (Pleasant),	6.00			6.00
Listie Brethren church,	27.88			27.88
Summit Mills Brethren & S. S.,	100.00	100.00		200.00
Aleppo Brethren church,	25.74			25.74
Johnstown Brethren church (2nd.),	5.00	15.00		20.00
New Enterprise Brethren S. S.,	31.00			31.00
Masontown Brethren church,	36.67	18.33		55.00
Martinsburg Brethren church,	67.28	28.50		95.78
Martinsburg Rose Circle S. S. Class,	5.00			5.00
Johnstown Brethren church (3rd.),	38.70			38.70
Berlin Brethren church,	148.07			148.07
Liberty Brethren church (Saxton),	6.20			6.20
McKee Brethren church,	24.00	24.00		48.00
Pennsylvania District, All funds, Total				$2,135.46
N. B. Add Myersdale Brethren to Pa.	100.00			100.00
Grand Total				$2,235.46
Maryland and Virginia District:				
Bethel Brethren church (Harrisonburg),	$ 50.25	$ 56.65		$ 106.90
Terra Alta Brethren church, W. Va.,	64.00			64.00
Roanoke Brethren church,	37.85	68.65	.15	106.65
Mt. View Brethren (Hollins) Va.,	33.18	84.55		117.73
Liberty Brethren church, Quicksburg, Va.,	14.38			14.38

Trinity Breth. church Scorie F'ns, Va., ...	16.93			16.93
Maurertown Brethren church, Va., ...	164.69			164.69
Woodstock, Va. Brethren church, ...	9.03			9.03
Hammer Br. church (Franklin, W. Va.), ...	9.20			9.20
Mount Zion Brethren church, ...	1.70			1.70
Arkton, Va., Brethren church, ...	2.00			2.00
Round Hill Brethren (Strasburg, Va.), ...	20.00	31.00		51.00
Oak Hill, W. Va., Brethren church, ...	16.87			16.87
Salem, Mission (Oak Hill Brethren), ...	25.00			25.00
Sugar Grove S. S. (Cameron, W. Va.), ...			28.53	28.53
Buena Vista, Va., Brethren church, ...	10.17			10.17
Dayton, Va., Brethren church, ...	32.38	32.38		64.76
Palestine, W. Va., Brethren church, ...	19.00	20.00		39.00
Hagerstown, Md., Brethren church, ...	200.00			200.00
Ridgeley, Md., Brethren church, ...	38.56			38.56
St. James Brethren church, Lydia, Md., ...	5.00	78.02		83.02
Happy Mission, Ky., (Hillegas), ...	5.00			5.00
Krypton, Ky., Brethren church, ...	65.00			65.00
Lost Creek, Ky., Brethren church, ...	38.23	7.68		45.91
Limestone, Tenn., Brethren church, ...	25.26	25.27		50.53
Sergeantsville, (N. J.), Brethren church, ...	30.00			30.00
Washington, D. C., Brethren church, ...	358.95	111.00	19.00	488.95
Maryland, Virginia and Washington, D. C., District, Totals				$1,855.51
Ohio District:				
Ashland Brethren church, ...	$ 235.00	$	$ .25	$ 235.25
Canton Brethren church, ...	161.19	5.00		166.19
Columbus Brethren church, ...	25.35	11.90		37.25
Dayton, First Brethren church, ...	425.05	273.00	223.23	921.28
Fremont Brethren church, ...	59.71	41.30	5.00	106.01
Fostoria Brethren church, ...	5.00			5.00
Gratis Brethren church, ...	34.45			34.45
Gretna Brethren church, ...	50.37	60.63		111.00
Fairview Brethren Ch., (Washington C. H.),	66.30			66.30
Louisville Brethren church, ...	139.87	54.75		194.62
West Homer Brethren church, (Homersville),	10.50	1.00		11.50
West Alexandria Brethren church, ...	46.75			46.75
New Lebanon Brethren church, ...	54.00	12.50		66.50
Miamisburg Brethren church, ...	36.00			36.00
Pleasant Hill Brethren church, ...	27.50			27.50
Salem Brethren Church (Clayton), ...	54.00	54.00		110.00
Ankenytown Brethren church, ...		115.00		115.00
Bryan Brethren church, ...	136.15	63.85		200.00
Camden Brethren church, ...	5.61			5.61
Fairhaven Brethren church, ...	75.00			75.00
North Georgetown Brethren church, ...	16.27			16.27
Effie Kennedy, Pioneer Brethren, ...	1.00			1.00
Frank Clapper, Louisville Brethren, ...	5.00			5.00
Ohio District, All Funds Total, ...				$2,593.48
Kanemorado District:				
Beaver City, Neb., Br. church, ...	$ 84.50	$ 139.50	$ 20.50	$ 244.50
Carleton, Nebraska, Brethren church, ...	137.78			137.78
Nampa, Idaho, Brethren church, ...	55.00			55.00
Hamlin, Kansas, Brethren church, ...	40.00			40.00
Morrill, Kansas, Brethren church, ...	140.25	119.50	40.25	300.00
Ft. Scott, Kansas, Brethren church, ...	5.00			5.00
Nickerson, Kansas, Brethren church, ...	250.00	329.00		579.00
McLouth, Kansas, Brethren church, ...	15.18			15.18
Maple Grove, Kansas, Brethren church, ...	54.90			54.90
Portis, Kansas, Brethren church, ...	80.51	26.25		106.76
Kanemorado District, All Funds, Total, ...				$1,538.12
Indiana District:				
Maple Grove, Brethren church, (Eaton), ...	$ 76.61	$	$	$ 76.61
Tiosa, Ind., Brethren church, ...	50.00	50.00		100.00
Burlington Brethren church, ...	10.00			10.00
Warsaw Brethren church, ...	337.08	5.00		342.08
North Liberty Brethren church, ...	50.00	50.00		100.00
Denver Brethren church, ...	83.00			83.00
Mexico Brethren church, ...	83.00	3.00		86.00
New Paris Brethren church, ...	355.60			355.60
Roann Brethren church, ...	193.41	22.50		215.91
North Manchester Brethren church, ...	18.00	247.93		265.93

OAK HILL, WEST VIRGINIA

On Tuesday night, June 1st, Brother Bame began an evangelistic campaign at the church in Oak Hill, and continued until Monday night, June 14. To say that we enjoyed his excellent sermons, to say that he and his good wife entertained us with their sweet singing, to say that they won the hearts of all whom they met, but lamely expresses our feelings of Brother and Sister Bame.

The attendance was good from the first, considering we had some very rainy weather the first week which kept some of us from attending, especially those living very far out of town. But the last week the church was filled and people came who could not find seats. We have never had the hearty co-operation of the other churches as in this meeting. The Baptist pastor, Brother Fitzgerald, was a regular attendant and the Methodist pastor was with us almost every night. On the last night of the meeting the Baptist pastor, the pastor of the M. E. church and the pastor of the M. E. church South all stood up and expressed their appreciation of the excellent service Brother Bame had given to their own churches as well as the good others had received. While there was no great ingathering of souls we think it was a wonderful meeting. All the churches speak only praise of Brother and Sister Bame.

We believe there has been a great good accomplished. At no previous time has there been such good feeling existing for our people in Oak Hill. We are praying that the time will not be long until Brother Bame can come back and finish his campaign as the time he could give us now was entirely too short. Twelve made confession. Four were baptized last Sunday in the Baptist baptistry, thanks to Brother Fitzgerald and his church for their kindness. We feel that the harvest of Brother Bame's labors will yet be gathered.

The people showed in more ways than one, their appreciation of the services. When the collections were taken, we had no especial soliciting to do but just announced that a collection would be taken, the results were $211.00 for Brother Bame. Then the last night of the meeting a collection was taken for Sister Bame which amounted to a few cents less than $20.00.

May the Lord richly bless them wherever they go. We ask an interest in your prayers.
MRS. ESSIE BOOTHE.

THE ANNUAL BRETHREN BIBLE CONFERENCE, LONG BEACH, CALIFORNIA, JULY 16-25, 1920

First Brethren Church—Fifth and Cherry

Why a Bible Conference?

The tremendous situations of the day demand that those of like precious faith, stand steadfast, unmovable, always abounding in the work of the Lord.

Ten days of Devotion, Prayer, Fellowship, Song, Bible Study, Sermon and Lecture under the presence and power of the Holy Spirit will give us a vision that will inspire through the years.

The Speakers,

French E. Oliver, E. M. Cobb, J. Wesley Platt and N. V. Leatherman.

Our Own Pastors: T. H. Broad, L. S. Bauman, J. C. Beal, N. W. Jennings and A. V. Kimmel.

The Singing

T. H. Broad will direct the congregational singing, assisted by the choir. Special numbers will be furnished by the different congregations.

Entertainment

Rooms will be furnished by the Long Beach members and their friends. If the homes available should be taken, visitors will be directed to places where reasonable prices maintain.

Privileges of cooking and eating in the church basement will be as at previous conferences subject to the rules adopted for the good of all. Convenient conveyance to and from the business part of the city.

Tents for camping can be pitched at Belmont Pier.

NOW FOR THE BEST CONFERENCE YET. PROGRAMS WILL BE READY IN A SHORT TIME.

Address, A. V. KIMMELL, WHITTIER, CALIFORNIA.

TRAVEL FLASHES AGAIN

Huntington, Indiana

By the good graces of my church I was allowed to go to Huntington, Indiana, during the month of May to assist our mission there, in a revival campaign. The opening week, it was our good fortune to have with us, Jacob Moses Harris and his wife; himself a converted Jew and his wife a Gentile. His lectures were the best along the lines of prophecy and the Jew, I have ever heard. Mrs. Harris is a splendid help and gave afternoon "Victorious Life" lectures. Before the week had ended, we had filled the house to capacity several times and had a splendid start was made toward the final results of the meeting. Of course there was some reaction when, at the end of the week, they left us to carry on the work alone, but we came out victorious at the end. It was a hard battle and a pretty fight that near a dozen girls gave us. They came to almost every service for the weeks of the meeting and at the last Sunday night, were still fighting against God. But we had faithful workers and on the Monday evening when we met for the Communion, the last one of "the bunch" had been baptized and partook of the sacred emblems. This is not an easy field but one of great promise. Brother Brower has brought them through to where he sees the end of their debt—by the help of the Indiana churches—and the sooner he translates that vision to these churches, the better it will be. A number of fine people were added to the roster of the church that will help to change the history of Brethrenism in Huntington, among them several heads of families. Former differences among members will not longer hinder the work here, I predict, because the new members together with others that had been gathered can and will help to guide the bark away from troubled waters. One of the great results of

(Continued on page 16, 1st column

Bethel Brethren church,	210.00	90.00	300.00
Milford Brethren church,	148.00	10.00	158.00
South Bend Brethren church,	164.17		164.17
Nappanee Brethren church,	294.19	109.59	403.78
Cambria Brethren church (Rossville),	10.00		10.00
Loree Brethren church,	107.79		107.79
Elkhart Brethren church,		100.00	100.00
Flora Brethren church,	174.25	5.00	179.25
Corinth Brethren church,	33.18		33.18
Center Chapel Brethren church,	32.00		32.00
Poplar Grove Brethren church,	2.00		2.00
Sidney Brethren church,	30.88	24.87	55.25
Muncie Brethren church,	31.75		31.75
College Corner Brethren (Wabash),	37.20		37.20
Teegarden Brethren church,	5.10		5.10
Peru Brethren church,	15.00		15.00
Loree Brethren S. S., Special,	15.30		15.30
Huntington First Brethren church,	14.00	36.00	50.00
Brighton Brethren church,	25.00	5.00	30.00
Indiana District, All Funds, Total,			$3,364.90

Michigan District:

Campbell Brethren church, Lake Odessa,	$147.50	$	$ 99.26	246.76
New Troy Brethren S. S.,	4.00			4.00
Glendora Brethren S. S.,	3.00			3.00
Bethel Brethren church, Cassopolis,	16.00			16.00
Michigan District, All Funds, Total,				$ 269.76

Illiokota District:

Carlton Brethren church, Garwin, Iowa,	$95.05	$100.00	$	$ 195.05
First Brethren church, S. S., Waterloo, Iowa,	400.00			400.00
Brethren church, Mt. Etna, Iowa,	13.05			13.05
Brethren church, Udell, Iowa,	99.58			99.58
Brethren church, Hudson, Iowa,	160.50			160.50
Brethren church, Dallas Center, Iowa,	122.58	52.50		175.08
Brethren church, Leon, Iowa,	138.97			138.97
Pleasant Grove Brethren Ch. Williamsburg, Ia.	8.62	270.00		278.62
Breth. Ch., Milledgeville, Illinois,	350.00	215.55		565.55
Cerro Gordo, Ill., Brethren church,	35.35	10.00		45.35
Woburn Brethren church, Mulberry Grove, Ill.,	20.00			20.00
Total of unclassified gifts in this district, viz., Sundry individuals,	143.00		7.00	150.00
Illiokota District, All Funds Total,				$2,241.75

Southern California District:

Long Beach, 1st Brethren church,	$1,806.53	$1,005.82	$1,025.47	$3,837.82
Los Angeles First Brethren church,	75.10	154.20	.25	229.55
Whittier Brethren church,	243.25	260.75		504.00
La Verne Brethren church,	145.40	188.50	107.00	440.90
Fillmore Brethren church,	24.00	25.25	.75	50.00
Unclassified individual gifts,	8.00	20.00	5.50	33.50
Interest,	8.52			8.52
Southern California, All Funds, Total,				$5,104.29

Northern California and Pacific Coast District

Turlock, Calif., Brethren church,	$ 193.67	$ 169.95	$ 10.00	$ 373.62
Ripon, Calif., Brethren S. S.,	30.95			30.95
Lathrop, Calif., Brethren church,	45.00	65.05		110.05
Manteca Brethren church, Ashland, Oregon,	6.00			6.00
Sunnyside, Wash., Brethren church,	603.00	527.50	9.50	1,140.00
Northern Calif. and Pacific Coast District, All Funds, Total,				$1,660.62

Elsie Showalter,	$1,763.93			
Unclassified gifts of,	659.49	$90.00		$3,013.42

These latter will also appear in the Brethren Missionary of the July issue, as well as classified churches, etc.

Falls City, Nebraska, of over $400 and other reports too late for entry will appear in later regular report!

Grand total of All Funds noted to June 1st,	$23,796.80
And Miscellaneous receipts,	88.97
Total Showing,	$23,885.77

Respectfully submitted,   WILLIAM A GEARHART,
General Missionary Secretary.

the first sermon was to bring together those who had differed and one of the most cheering things at the close was to see them all at the Lord's table. Rather unthoughtedly, I ventured the prophecy that in five years, North Manchester that is now helping Huntington might be helped of them.

Oak Hill, West Virginia

After a flying visit to my home charge, lasting two weeks, I went to Oak Hill, West Virginia, at the invitation of Wm. H. Miller and the church there, for a two weeks' vacation campaign. In some ways, it was the most remarkable meeting I have held for 18 years. From the very first, the church was filled to capacity and more, and also to the last. This is the home of the Duncans. One of the finest sights that ever greeted my eyes was one where the octogenarian father, Elder A. B. Duncan, was on the platform and his four sons singing in a male quartet. It was enough to fill an aged father's heart with pride thus to see the good results of his training and more, still to see it following to the grand children, as one of his granddaughters was at the organ and one grandson is not adverse to entering the ministry.

I had been in the south some, but had never been in a mining community like this. Wonderful wealth is here. Vein upon vein of the finest furnace coal underlies all this land. More people are hidden among the cliffs and the woods of these mountains than the uninitiated could imagine.

From the first, people of the other-denominations came as if it were their own meeting, and never let up till the last farewell was said. A M. E. preacher told me that he never missed a service that it was possible for him to attend. The Baptist preacher did as well, I think. Much good was done that will not be named in the report of the meeting. The time was too short and the people moved too slow to get the results we had hoped for. But it will doubtless result in a union meeting later in the year when I expect that the "Word that does not return void," will reveal what is its power.

Pleasant memories will cling to some of the splendid meetings and people and times we had here. The wonderful southern hospitality shone in all its glory and we hope—really hope—to return again when we can do more good and have more time for it.

Back Home

Well, you know how you feel when you get back, back home where they take so much for granted. Where the commendations do not come; where the service rendered is a matter-of-fact; where they do not need to fear they will miss something if they do not hear every sermon; where people do not try so hard to please and commend and compliment; where they do not insist so much on a visit; where they do not evaluate on the same basis —well, we are back home. It is nice to be at home and here we expect to spend the rest of the summer quite close. With Winona Lake but twenty miles away and a new Ford; with plenty of lakes nearer, with friends coming and with our trips here and there, we shall hold the fort as best we can. We have been drifting too much here—just going along

keeping pace but we have decided to "contest" some and we have finished the basement in fine style and we shall tell you in the future what shall be in North Manchester after we have "done it."

CHARLES A. BAME.

AN APPRECIATIVE VOICE

In the midst of the difficult and sometimes trying task of making a church paper that will please and serve the best interests of the largest possible number of the multitudes of varying tastes throughout the brotherhood, our task is occasionally lightened by receiving a word of appreciation. We wish to say in this public way that we are very grateful for these kind and encouraging words. Most frequently perhaps do these words come from our isolated friends. And that our friends in the churches may understand the loyal and warm feelings of our isolated readers we are sharing this expression coming from Wasco, California. In connection with his renewal to The Evangelist, Brother Thomas Gibson says,

"As we have been isolated from the church of our choice for twenty-five years, The Brethren Evangelist is a welcome visitor in our home, as it sets forth the fundamental doctrines of the Bible and is loyal to the truth. We are continually grieved to see how professing Christians are persisting in "going onward and abiding not in the teachings of Christ." When the word emphatically declares "such have not the Father." It was because the Jews did not know the Father that they persecuted the disciples (John 16: 3.) Christ is not being acknowledged as the Son of God by those who reject the ordinances of the church. "He that rejecteth me, rejecteth him that sent me." "Believest thou that I am in the Father and the Father in me?" "No man can come unto me except the Father draw him." "He hath my word and keepeth it, he it is that loveth me." It is not

possible for any one to know the Father and not know the Son also (John 8:19), as they are one and Jesus "dwelleth in the bosom of the Father." Let us honor the Father by honoring the Son and keeping his word. Jesus said, "If any man serve me, him will my Father honor" (John 12:26). He that doeth the will of the Father shall eventually enter heaven (Matt. 7:21). Unto God our Father be glory forever. Amen. (Phil.4:20)."

O health! health! the blessing of the rich and the riches of the poor! Who can buy thee at too dear a rate, since there is no enjoying the world without thee.—Ben Jonson.

Of the professions it may be said, that soldiers are becoming too popular, parsons too lazy, physicians too mercenary, and lawyers too powerful.—Colton.

A Ghost City in Armenia

We have read and heard much of the destroyed cities and villages in Belgium and France. We are not so familiar with the ghost cities and villages of the Near East; cities and villages into and out of which there have swept hordes of Turks, leaving desolation and death in their wake. Such a city is Aintab, once a propterous city of 43,000 inhabitants on the caravan road from Aleppo to Constantinople; now a collection of roofless houses, with the few Syrians and Greeks left alive living in the ruins of their homes; with the voices of children not the voices of laughter, but the voices of pitiful wails. The Near East Relief is exerting every effort to bring back life to this Ghost City; it is supplying money and materials for reconstruction; it is housing and feeding and nursing the babies; it is bringing a hope of happiness to these afflicted people, a work in which every American helps. June is the month for a nationwide collection of clothing. Bring your bundle.

Cobb's Conference Corner

Delegates

The pastor of each church, should have sufficient interest in General Conference, to see that each department of his church is properly represented by delegate at Conference. Let the Sunday school, Christian Endavor, Women's Missionary Society, and the church proper, select delegates at an early date, that they may plan ahead, for Conference, and let these delegates be such as will properly represent the department by which they are sent. It may be that not all departments are financially able to pay all expenses of delegates, but at least they should be encouraged sufficiently, that they will be present at the Conference sessions, participate in the work, and secure material for reports, to bring to the people who sent them. Too many delegates fail to appreciate the responsiblity entrusted to their care. It has been my observation that even some pastors spend more hours at the lakeside, than they do in Conference session. Let us remember "First, the Kingdom."

E. M. COBB.

S. 59465

Brethren Evangelist

Ashland Theological Library
Ashland, Ohio

VOLUME XLII	NUMBERS 26 & 27	JULY 7, & 14, 1920

THE NEW FIRST BRETHREN CHURCH
OF LOS ANGELES, CALIFORNIA
DEDICATED JUNE 20, 1920
(SEE PAGE 12 FOR DESCRIPTION)

Published every Wednesday at
Ashland, Ohio. All matter for publication must reach the Editor not
later than Friday noon of the preceding week.

George S. Baer, Editor

The
Brethren
Evangelist

When ordering your paper changed
give old as well as new address.
Subscriptions discontinued at expiration. To avoid missing any numbers renew two weeks in advance.

R. R. Teeter, Business Manager

OFFICIAL ORGAN OF THE BRETHREN CHURCH

Subscription price, $2.00 per year, payable in advance.
Entered at the Post Office at Ashland, Ohio, as second-class matter.
Acceptance for mailing at special rate of postage provided for in section 1103, Act of October 3, 1917, authorized September 9, 1918.
Address all matter for publication to Geo. S. Baer, Editor of the Brethren Evangelist, and all business communications to R. R. Teeter,
Business Manager, Brethren Publishing Company, Ashland, Ohio. Make all checks payable to the Brethren Publishing Company.

TABLE OF CONTENTS

EDITORIAL

The Growing Popularity of the Prize Fight and New York's Experience

Every age has its moral issues. Christian patriots must be continually alert to guard against the rise and enthronement of some outstanding evil. Now that the liquor traffic has been outlawed and capital is no longer able to exploit the cravings of men for intoxicants, there is a widespread movement on foot to exploit men's fighting and gambling desires. In March, 1920, at Albany, New York, it was announced that an attempt would be made in every state to secure a law licensing prize fights. Since then Kentucky, New York and Massachusetts have passed such a law. In the latter state the law which was enacted June 4, 1920, was suspended by referendum petition. In Montana, by referendum in the spring of 1919, the county prize fight bill, which gave fifty per cent of the door receipts to support a State Home for Needy Soldiers, was defeated.

Not only must the citizens of Massachusetts be awake to their responsibility and wield every possible influence against the threatening curse, but in every state watchfulness must be exercised and agitation must be carried on to stir the unwary to a realization of the danger of being overtaken by a prize fight and gambling monopoly.

If such a law as is hanging in the balance in Massachusetts becomes operative in that state and then spreads throughout the nation, it will cause an increase in crime by increasing gambling, robberies, gangsters, thugs, quarrels and many acts of violence. It will increase taxes because the increase in crime will necessitate more police, courts and prisons. The five per cent of the receipts of the admission fees will no more pay the expenses of legalizing prize fights than have the saloon license fees paid the state for the crime, poverty and disease caused by the liquor traffic. The fact is, the whole agitation is simply an effort on the part of greedy fight promoters to restore a brutal and demoralizing game for the sake of the great profits they may reap.

As a warning to the citizens of other states—for this scheme to revive prize fighting will surely come up in many of the state legislatures next winter, and every candidate for state legislator or governor should be tested on this issue—a few paragraphs from the history of New York's experience with prize fights may be given:

From 1896 prize fights were legalized in New York State by the Horton law. In 1900 Governor Roosevelt, in a message to the legislature, recommended the Horton law be repealed. Personally he liked boxing, and later lost an eye in that sport. As Police Commissioner he had tried in vain to regulate prize fights in New York City under this Horton law. In his message asking repeal he said:

"Boxing is a fine sport, but this affords no justification of prize fighting, any more than the fact that a cross country run or a ride on a wheel is healthy, justifies such a demoralizing exhibition as a six day's race. When any sport is carried on primarily for money—that is, as a business, it is in danger of losing much that is valuable, and of acquiring some exceedingly undesirable characteristics. In the case of prize-fighting, not only do all the objections which apply to the abuse of other professional sports apply in aggravated form, but in addition the exhibition has a very demoralizing and brutalizing effect. There is no need to argue these points. They are expressly admitted in the Horton law itself. Moreover, the evils are greatly aggravated by the fact that THE FIGHT IS FOR A MONEY PRIZE, and is the occasion for unlimited gambling and betting."

The Horton law was repealed and the law recommended by Governor Roosevelt was enacted and remained in force till 1911, when the Frawley law permitting prize-fight exhibitions with admission fees was enacted.

In 1907 Governor Hughes vetoed a bill which permitted sparring exhibitions in certain associations provided the contests should not continue more than fifteen minutes. He wrote:

"In my judgment this is a step in the wrong direction. The bill is not necessary to support a wholesome interest in boxing as a sport. There is no reason why amateur associations should not encourage it, and why lovers of the sport should not engage in it under suitable conditions. This they can do without charging an admission fee for exhibition."

Governor Whitman on February 1, and May 7, 1917, in messages to the New York legislature urged the discontinuance of the Frawley "State Athletic Commission" by which those interested in it financially believed or pretended to believe boxing could be regulated or controlled so as not to offend public decency. The experience of six years demonstrated that it could not be done. On May 7, 1917, Governor Whitman asking for the repeal of the Frawley law wrote:

"It has again become a public disgrace to the greatest state of the Union, and early this year I urged the legislature to repeal the statute and protect the good name of the state.

"There seems to be an inclination on the part of some members of the legislature to shirk their responsibility upon this question, and to protect and keep in existence a statute which is the cause of this disgrace and serves only to satisfy the greed of a few who exploit prize fighting, and prize-fighters for the money return, which is by no means small. It is urged that it is a manly sport and men of only good red blood can indulge therein. There is an abundance of opportunity now for men of good red blood who are anxious to fight to gratify their desire in a good cause.

"It was after the most mature and deliberate consideration on my part that on February 1, 1917, I urged the legislature in a special message to repeal the State Athletic Commission Law. One of the evil effects of the statute was brought home to us recently. Here, in the capital city of the state, a disgraceful and brutalizing contest was held when a young man in the prime of life was allowed to enter a contest and receive a blow which killed him. Even the people, who were present sat calmly by and the remainder of the program for the evening was carried out. This boy was done to death under the rules, and none of the regulations adopted in the interest of this so-called manly sport was violated.

"I urge the legislature to take up this subject and to repeal the Frawley Law. Every honest and right thinking person in this state, familiar with conditions, must, I believe, demand this repeal."

The Frawley law was repealed in 1917. In 1920 the New York legislature again legalized prize fighting under pressure of international commercial interests that are seeking to legalize the brutal sport that has long been outlawed in every state. They are going at it quietly, but keeping persistently at it. They have succeeded in New York and Kentucky and if they can influence the popular vote in their favor they will win in Massachusetts. Encouraged by this measure of success the campaign for the restoration of the prize fight will be carried on with great determination and power. There are fortunes to be made in the game and the promoters will not surrender their hopes of gain without a fierce battle.

The time has come when Christian men and women everywhere must be awakened to the fact that they are being faced with a gigantic organized evil that is seeking to entrench itself in our pleasure-loving American life. It is scarcely another sport that is so demoralizing and brutalizing. It awakens the average nature to such an extent that for the time the spectators show themselves more beastly than human-like, and the far-reaching evil effect cannot be estimated.

That such fights really have a degrading influence is recognized not merely by preachers and church leaders, but also by men who know them intimately is evidenced by some words written by an experienced sport writer. For twenty five years he had been a chronicler of pugilistic happenings and on the occasion of the Williard-Moran fight in Madison Square Garden in New York City, in 1916, he wrote, "There were thousands of howling blood-thirsty, fight-lovers in the Garden waiting to see one man knocked unconscious by another. Many a mind was made more brutal, and some may have been turned toward crime and toward murder itself by that shameful exhibition on Saturday night. What could do more to inflame and make criminal the mind of a weak lad than just such a disgraceful spectacle, when one huge brute with a blow of his fist brought blood pouring from the eye of another man?"

When one thinks of the brutalizing influence of such sport, of the persistent and energetic effort to legalize it and of the growing popularity of fistic encounters, even where prize fights are not tolerated, one is convinced that it is time to raise the voice with all possible influence against. It is time that the church shall seek to create public sentiment against it and that every Christian citizen shall do what he can to oppose it.

EDITORIAL REVIEW

Brother C. E. Kolb, who is spending a few weeks at Winona Lake, Indiana, supplies some desired information for those who are looking forward to attending the coming General Conference.

Members of the Pennsylvania conference should not fail to read Brother Witter's notice to pastors and delegates. Pennsylvania means business in the matter of getting statistical reports.

Brother G. C. Carpenter writes in the church news department this week, giving some admonitions against worldliness and indifference, and at the same time reporting progress for the "Little Brown Church" of Peru.

Mrs. Bessie Clingaman of Denver, Indiana, is rightly concerned about reporting the activities of her church in the Evangelist. It pays the church to keep checked up on its own interests in this manner

and it is of much interest to the many readers of the paper. The work is going nicely under the leadership of Brother Wirick.

Mrs. Margaret E. Dill of Ashland, Oregon, writes a highly complimentary note concerning Sister Vianna Detwiler and her work, and no doubt the expressions of appreciation by the people there are entirely merited. There are rewards more than gold for those who prayerfully, energetically and humbly give themselves to making Christ known and building up his kingdom.

Brother Carpenter supplies us with another interesting selection dealing with a missionary's experience in Kentucky. We should say that such an experience would only "test the nerves of some of us dignified parsons," but it would greatly test the staying qualities of our average audience to be faced with four preachers, all of whom were to exhaust their vocabularies and test the strength of their voices.

You will notice by President Jacob's "College News" that the Summer School is proving a splendid success, and if the pastors and other church leaders respond to Dr. Jacob's suggestion in his open letter the regular school year will be even a greater success. Send your young people to your own church school for their education, and when they return to you, they will have higher ideals and be more thoroughly Brethren than when they left home.

One of the most interesting news letters we have received for sometime is the report of the dedication of the First Brethren church of Los Angeles, made by Brother Reed, our faithful and efficient correspondent at that place. The new church house is a beautiful and splendidly arranged structure and will afford opportunity for greater efficiency and space for larger expansion in Sunday school and all the other departments of church work. The Brethren of Los Angeles are to be congratulated for the sacrifice, perseverance and good judgement displayed in bringing about this remarkable accomplishment. Such a beautiful and substantial structure could not be built in these times without sacrifice and perseverance which are fed by a great faith.

As our readers well know, the Publishing Company got behind in printing its publications when compelled to wait for the arrival of paper stock. When the paper came in and we were able to restore The Evangelist to full size, we were a week behind. We did not wish to drop an issue and promised to catch up, but so far we have been unable to do so and have been advised to combine two numbers in one issue, which we have decided to do. We are sorry that circumstances have cooperated to make this necessary, but we do not wish to continue dating papers a week behind, and so this issue bears two dates and numbers, thus making our numbering unbroken.

Brother Beachler is meeting with a splendid response in the Maryland-Virginia district in his effort to still further increase the college endowment fund. Everywhere he finds noble people on whose faces is written loyalty, and it is these who bring joy to the secretary's heart and make possible the splendid reports which make us more and more confident of the future of Ashland College. Linwood did splendidly and gave us reason to be proud of her. Now Hagerstown comes across with a worthy gift to prove the genuineness of its gratitude for the service Ashland College has done in training its present minister and his wife, as well as other ministers who have served it in the past. All eyes are on the Maryland-Virginia district to see what it will do for Ashland, and if we can judge the final result by the first returns, it will be worthy to be compared with what the other districts have done.

Seldom is the church and the kingdom interests called upon to suffer such a sad and vital loss as now in the death of our beloved brother, Professor Edward E. Byers, a memorial of whom is written in this issue by Dean J. Allen Miller. Seldom has so young a life accomplished so great a work in the face of such difficulties as Brother Byers has done. He was always modest and unassuming; but those who knew him well loved him, and the better he was known the more he was loved. He was thoroughly unselfish and counted no sacrifice too great that he might be of service to some one. It was this quality of self-forgetful service coupled with his genuineness that won for him such a large place in the community where he accomplished his last work. He will be greatly missed not only by his wife, parents, brothers and sisters, but by all who had the privilege of calling him friend. May God's gracious Spirit comfort all who mourn.

GENERAL ARTICLES

The Child Garden of the Church

By A. D. Gnagey, Editor of the Sunday School Publications

(A General Conference address buried in the Conference Minutes, but deserving of a wider reading. Few are so well qualified to speak of the importance of a permanent church literature as Brother Gnagey, and few understand so well as he the particular phase of its importance dealt with in this article—the inspiration and direction of young lives through the printed page.—EDITOR.)

In a small corner of a church in New York City, not widely known outside of a specially interested circle, is a little room which in every way is worthy of the name given it by a visitor twenty years ago. In itself the room has no particular attractions, but the early visitor soon forgets the architecture in studying the pictures on the wall. They are neither expensive nor numerous, but well chosen in their relation to the lessons taught, and hung low enough for the smallest child to see. However, before the picture study is finished, a beautiful woman, modestly attired, her face shining like an angel's, enters the room, and no prophet is needed to predict spiritual growth and development under such embodied sunshine. The class numbers more than one hundred, and is divided into sections of ten or less. Promptly at the appointed hour all doors are closed and late-comers are obliged to remain in an outer room until after the opening exercises, which begin with the greeting. "Good morning, children," to which comes a hearty response, and the teacher's work begins. The unseen motto written on this teacher's heart, and controlling her work with teachers, mothers and children, is: NOTHING IS UNRELATED. From beginning to end the pictures, music, lessons, are all related in some way. The greatness of the work is found in its simplicity. Christ is brought to those tender plants not as one afar off, but as a dear Friend, a glorified Savior, who is always nearby to love and help little children·

An interested lady, a true child of God, came half way across the continent to spend thirty minutes in that room, to which she gave the significant name, THE CHILD GARDEN OF THE CHURCH, and the teacher as the true Child Gardener, consecrated to God and humanity, who studies her human plants in every detail. Both room and teacher are worthily named.

If, while telling this story, there has arisen in your minds the question, what all this has to do with an address on the publishing interests of the church, I shall not censure you. As briefly as possible I shall endeavor to show you that it is by no means unrelated to the thought which is to occupy our minds for the hour.

In view of the fact that the work to which the church has called me, in a very large measure, touches childhood and youth and young life, I feel justified in the use of this story as my introduction. Further, I trust there may be no objection on the part of the Company and the members of the Executive Committee who prepared the program to my making the burden of this address the church's opportunity and its resources in its youth, emphasizing the importance, not only of conserving its energies, its enthusiasm, its heroism, its faith, but of giving proper direction to this group of qualities which have in them spiritual possibilities unmeasured and unparalleled for spiritual conquests and achievements.

If only I could say something that would bring the church to a realization of the tremendous resources God has placed at her command in her youth, and for the training and direction of which he will hold us responsible, then would the church give herself more enthusiastically and with greater determination to the development and utilization of these resources, going forth again to her world tasks with the new assurance of the ultimate triumph of the kingdom of God on earth. The church that does not in every legitimate way cultivate this virgin soil and conserve its productiveness, making the largest possible investment in

her youth, fails in her supreme task and as a consequence will be without adequate leadership for her future,—if she has any.

Here then lies our FIRST duty, first in consciousness, first in importance, first in order of procedure,—it is the CULTIVATION OF THE CHILD GARDEN OF THE CHURCH. Why is the church so slow to accept this responsibility? The future of the church absolutely hinges on the cultivation and conservation of her youthful soil with all its tremendous potentialities,—youth as yet untrammeled in mind and heart, unspoiled by world association, with a soul that aspires, thirsts for the living springs, hungers for God, impulses within his being to feel, to do and to know. Youth is restless; to it passivity is an intolerable burden and quietness is oppression. To be going, to be moving, to be doing, that is the characteristic of youth's ceaseless impulse. What shall the church do with it? Are the barriers to the kingdom's coming which keep so many without the door to be reproduced in the church's youth? Is there no way to save its back from the burden of the ages? Youth today is challenging the church to a larger faith with its mighty prophetic appeal to expect great things from God; to attempt great things for God. Youth is not satisfied with anything less than that. Will the church accept the challenge and make the investment? Hear me, friends, you, men and women, not much longer for this world, you, fathers and mothers, you, of younger years, I say it deliberately, but with absolute knowledge of the facts, and as a warning, youth offers itself with all the eternal possibility of its being to the cause, the kingdom that will first come, satisfy his mind and soul hunger, answer his yearnings and claim him for its own. Will the church be wise and claim her own? If not, I despair of our future·

Furthermore, if the church in her earlier history had given herself more enthusiastically and persistently to the cultivation of the youthful soil with its marvelous possibilities, or to change from the figurative to the literal, if the church had invested her talent in the creation of a permanent literature, her youth would not have sought elsewhere for mind and soul food, and we would not have suffered this awful leakage, which in some localities has well nigh depopulated our ranks,—we would have been saved that drifting away from the moorings of the old faith, the faith of our fathers, which many of us deplore.

I am minded to quote here, with your permission, some very striking statements from the loquacious Frank Crane.

OUR FIRST DUTY

"The first duty of a people is to take care of the children. What are you doing to train fitly the human beings under twenty-one?'

"Beside that question all other questions of politics and economics are almost piffle. Run the tariff up, or run the tariff down, have a gold or silver basis of currency, build your Panama Canal or let it fill up, construct three dreadnaughts a year or send all the battleships to the scrap heap, it all makes little difference in the end; we can adjust ourselves to anything—these are questions that hit upon the ridge-pole of national prosperity. But the care of the children, that is a question that sits at the hearthstone of the nation's existence.

"The United States of America has done more toward education than any other nation in history, yet all we have done is pitifully little. Socialists, Progressives, Republicans, Democrats, stand to one side! For there is but one

Great Issue in the twentieth century. It is for every child to have the privilege of being equipped for life."

John R. Morris uttered a great truth when he said: "There is always time to do the things which ought to be done, and surely there is nothing which imposes stronger obligations than our duty to the child.

I have never yet been able to understand why the church has been so slow, and is so slow now, to recognize and appropriate the truth long since recognized and appropriated in the world of politics, business and amusement, namely, that if we would enlist the men and women in our cause we must claim them in their youth. There is a strikingly significant incident recorded in the Acts of the Apostles, the healing of the cripple at the gate of the temple called Beautiful. The attendant circumstances are communicated to us by St. Luke, who, being a physician, significantly dwells upon the mature age of the man as something which rendered a natural cure impossible,— ABOVE FORTY YEARS OLD. Why above forty? Do we realize that defects, moral and spiritual, as well as physical, so stereotype themselves in middle life, that few people ever change for the better past the age of forty? Character and conduct tend to fixity. The limitation which a man has placed upon his effort in the direction of righteousness becomes a yoke, and in most cases will be borne to the end rather than lifted and replaced with something better. The incident at the gate Beautiful is a pathetic parable of human life,—a marvelous achievement because the man changed was "above forty years old."

Let us disabuse our minds of the delusion that time automatically exerts an uplifting influence upon human character. It requires a mighty effort, a stupendous reinforcement of the will, an avalanche of divine grace, to enable the average man of middle life, rooted and grounded in the kind of life he has followed, whose relation to righteousness has been a dream rather than an actual experience, to do and to become what he has always expected to do and become "above forty years old." If this sounds too much like preaching, let me remind you of the unparalleled opportunity of early years—how great! The desirability of establishing youth promptly and firmly in the ways of Christian living and Christian doctrine. Shall not the church with intense earnestness and with renewed vigor set itself to the task of saving its youth before the sands of life are running low, and as far as possible place it beyond the defiling touch of cruel, outward circumstances?

That is why I plead for a literature that shall be worthy of our Christianity and commensurate with the claims that we make for ourselves as a church. Such a literature would go a long ways toward furnishing food for the empty yet hungry mind of the child, so woefully lacking in our pulpit ministrations and too often in the homes of our youth. "REMEMBER" began the preacher in the pulpit forcefully. A tiny girl in a pew caught the one word. Snuggling up to her mother, she lifted her clear, seeing eyes, and whispered, "Tell me something to remember." A childish thought, did you say? No, but a child-thought. That cry voiced the hunger of a little empty mind. The baby wanted something to think about, to ponder through the long service, to remember when she, too, went out of the temple of worship. You and I may smile at the words—they seem so foolish. For OUR memories are burdened to the breaking point; OUR minds are so crowded with diverse knowledge that we often feel overwhelmed and unable to retain what we read and hear and experience. But the wee girl in the story had only put words to the cry of childhood; "Tell me something to remember." This mind hunger insists on being satisfied. If we do not put something there to be pondered, other sources of information will. The little brain is not going to stay empty because of our sins of omission. That is the need and here again lies our duty and our opportunity. Put clean, beautiful thoughts into it and the low, the trivial, the sensual will be crowded out. Put something in that young mind that will be but the gateway into a

whole garden of beauty and food for the soul. So when the child-like appeal comes, "Tell me something to remember," be sure you have something worth putting into the empty brain. Can you think of a better way to meet the cry of childhood than with the simple story of classic literature, a literature adapted to the child-mind? The church is not lacking in talent for the creation of such a literature; my relations with the publishing interests covering a period of twenty years have given me ample opportunity to discover such talent, and, I say it modestly, I KNOW WHERE IT IS. It only needs to be called forth and directed. Think of how barren the church is in anything like juvenile literature. It is little less than criminal negligence—our failure to provide wholesome mind food for the childhood which God has committed to us, and for whose development and utilization he will hold us to strict accountability. I appeal to you in the name of the Christ who redeemed you, does this cry of childhood, this challenge of Almighty God move you? The thought staggers me, when I think of how trivial, how meager are our efforts to put into the empty mind of the child the food for which it hungers and thirsts and aspires. Are we guiltless?

All that I have said has been but preparatory to what, in a few brief words I want to emphasize and press home upon the conscience of the fathers and mothers and the educators and all others who may hear me tonight who are responsible for the MORAL training and education of the children, who, under the providence of God, have been committed to our care and keeping. Within the domains of Uncle Sam there is an army of more than thirty million that come within the circle designated as young life. The alarming thing about it is that this very night there are 20,000,000 children and youth under twenty years of age absolutely without any ministrations in the name of Christ. Ladies and gentlemen, fathers and brethren, think on that amazing fact for a moment, a fact fraught with awful possibilities. An army of 20 million godless children and youth growing up around us into a yet more godless manhood! And the church persists in the awful spectacle of spending its energies and its time in an effort to save a meager portion of grown-ups, saving the LOST, we call it, but men and women, what are we doing to save the LOSS? Shall the church go on forever hunting lost sheep, doing comparatively nothing to keep the lambs from going astray? Is it good policy—is it good sense? In less than ten years the twenty million youth under twenty will have grown into an army of so many godless men and women, in a land of churches and Bibles and Sunday schools. I submit to you the proposition whether the supreme duty of the church at this very hour is not that of SAVING THE CHILDREN from growing up into an army of anarchists?

I make my appeal to you, men and women, for the loyal and unstinted support of your publishing interests, one of God's agencies for the promotion and the spread of the gospel principles of righteousness. And to the men and women in the church who have peculiar talent. Use it for the glory of God. You think of Paul, the chosen of God because of his intellectual, moral and spiritual furnishings, going from city to city preaching Christ and him crucified with marvelous persuasive power,—the church's greatest preacher, but Paul did not immortalize his name as a preacher; as such his name might have easily passed from the memory of men within his own generation. Paul immortalized his name because he was numbered with the League of the Golden Pen; he put his feelings, and thoughts, and experiences into an epistolary literature which is mightier today, eighteen hundred years since his lips have been sealed and silent, part of a literature of an unending eternity. I would rather have written the love chapter (1 Cor. 13) than have built the Panama Canal: I would rather be the author of John 14 than of Milton's Paradise Lost. The man who wrote the 23rd psalm has been singing its sweetness and comfort into human hearts for 3,000 years. Think of how bare and poor the world would be if bereft of the four Gospels, the letters of Paul, John and Peter, and all that great body of literature that clusters about these masterpieces! The power of Christianity impact upon human thought and feeling is evident in the abiding influence and power of the literature that it created.

THE BLOSSOMING

Dear Master of the Garden, unto thee
  I bring these blossoms, tended by my care;
I pray thee to receive them tenderly,
  And find them fair

These many days have I with longing eyes
  Waited and watched for seed long sown to
    spring,

Eager to see (oh, heart grown strangely wise!)
  Its blossoming.
So graciously and softly fell the dew
  Of blessed promise on the precious seed,
As if the Lord of Harvests saw and knew
  Its daily need.

Until, at last, in radiant life and light,
  To fragrant bud and bloom I saw it spring;
I pray thee, guard from hurtfulness of blight
  Its blossoming.

Dear Master of the Garden, unto thee
  I bring these sweet child-flowers with a
    prayer;
Lord Christ, wilt thou receive them tenderly,
  And find them fair.

How Laymen Can Strengthen the Ministry---By Encouraging Them
By Albert Trent

(Address Before Laymen's Division of General Conference. Publication Requested by the Laymen)

The infuence and power that the Brethren church may exert in the world depends to a great extent on the strength of her ministry. Our church's growth and advancement rests in a great measure with the potency that emanates from her pulpits.

The attitude of the lay membership toward the ministry is a significant factor in determining the standards to be maintained, and the measure of her success numerically and spiritually.

A creditable, efficient and adequate ministry cannot be developed under an indifferential purpose of Christian work demands on the part of the layman a live, sympathetic interest and co-operation in the plans of the pastor and a warm appreciation of his efforts in the advancement of the kingdom.

Criticism of the ministry, so common in our newspapers, conversation and every day gossip, is doing the interests of the church a vast amount of harm and nullifying her efforts. It is not difficult to find instances where the pastor has lost his place of leadership in the moral and spiritual realm of his church and community, without any faults of his own, but it is altogether due to thoughtless remarks and petty faultfinding regarding his efforts among the membership of the congregation. Anybody seems to feel that he has the liberty of taking a "fling" at the preacher. Some one has recently said, "All kinds of missiles, save gold nuggets, are thrown at the minister. We know he is not, perfect, neither are we, my brother laymen; he has his faults and so have you and I; he sometimes fails, and so do we. Let us remember, however, that he is, nevertheless, the "anointed of the Lord," the chosen vessel of the church to bear the golden treasure of salvation to a sin stricken world. The pastor should therefore be accorded the place of honor he deserves, and the dignity of his work and position should command the respect and esteem of his entire membership.

The pastor is sometimes discouraged because the members of the official board of his church lack vision and faith, failing to measure up to the important affairs of the kingdom, thus crippling his plans and leadership instead of responding with a liberality and a generosity that they would show in secular interests. Forcing him to folow a narrow, close-fisted policy in the work that blasts his ambition, leads to falure and is responsible for some able congregations failing to bear their share of the burden for kingdom extension.

Let us come to the practical duty of the layman to his own pastor. How can I encourage my own pastor?

The apostle Paul, in his own matchless words answers the question: "We beseech you brethren, to know them that labor among you, and are over you in the Lord, and admonish you, and to esteem them exceeding highly in love for their work's sake."

Do we as laymen measure up to that standard? Do you know your pastor? What do you know about his life, his thoughts, his purposes, his ambitions—the place where he really lives? Do you know the things he is mostly interested in? The matters that give him the greatest anxiety? His difficulties, his burdens, his greatest care? Pauls says "Know them."

Once we are in possession of the knowledge regarding our pastor that Paul had in mind our opinion of him may change our judgment of his actions may be more considerate and we doubtless will take a greater interest in his work. I feel sure we will be more ready to speak a word of encouragement to the pastor.

"Esteem them exceedingly high in love for their work's sake." Oh! the high standard of honor and dignity to which Paul elevates the pastor in his calling! And we have sat in the "amen corner" criticising mentally, if not openly, his manner, his delivery, his bearing, his language and eagerly listening for any slip of tongue that might be considered as stepping outside the lines of orthodoxy.

Brethren, the Bible accords the pastor too high and sacred a position to permit this general indiscriminate criticism that is so common among church members. With a higher appreciation of the surpassing sacredness of his calling there will be less tendency for fault-finding and a greater inclination to give him encouragement. Vacate your seat in the Knockers' Fraternity and organize a Boosters' Club for the preacher and get every layman to join it.

Our pastors are not spineless creatures, fearing to stand alone or unable to bear their burdens. Not so, their spinal columns have more rigidity than those of half the laymen that are continually croaking about them. He needs your encouragement because in addition to his own burdens he is called to bear the burdens of the many in an almost inconceivable variety of ways and often exceeding grevious, of which the average layman knows nothing. He needs your help, your sympathy, your love.

Cultivate a real listening attitude during the sermon, nothing encourages a speaker more than a good listener. Introduce him to your business friends and others not members of your church, he will appreciate that Express your appreciation when he has said or done a good thing.

May I yet bring to you the words that were addressed to a congregation more than fifty years ago at an installation of a pastor, that are as pertinent now as then and most fitting to the subject in hand: "I suggest that you pray for your minister daily; guard his reputation carefully; hear him preach weekly; listen to the word wakefuly; treasure it up joyfully; practice it faithfully; labor with him sympathetically both individually and collectively; attend the prayer and conference meeting constantly; support the Sunday School heartily; pay him promptly; give him a bit of meat and a ball of butter occasionally; call on him frequently, but tarry briefly; greet him cordially, but not rudely; and may the God of all grace bless you abundantly."

If this recipe for treatment of the pastor by the laymen were applied in all of our churches; we would not have a poor preacher or an unsuccessful church in the brotherhood, and the work of the church would advance by leaps and bounds under such cordial Christian co-operation between laymen and pastors.
.Johnstown, Pennsylvania.

An Open Letter. By President Edwin E. Jacobs

To Ministers, Sunday School Superintendents and Teachers and to Leaders of the Church Generally:

The next semester of Ashland College will open September 14th. This is the second Tuesday after the close of our National Conference. Quite naturally, the college is anxious to have a good enrollment. The purpose of this article is to urge upon the above designated and others the importance of directing the attention of the young people within their circle of influence to the college.

Attendance. It is highly important that the young people of the church take their membership so seriously that they will be willing to enter her college and prepare for some definite Christian work. This past year saw two of our most promising young men enter fields of Christian service, in highly important places, the Christian Endeavor and the Y. M. C. A. The graduating class of two years ago furnished the Y. W. C. A. with a recruit. Along with these are many young people who entered other useful fields. This year's class now has a young man who has refused $2000 a year in the public schools. There never was a day like this, when young men and women of training were in such demand. The college could fill a score of places right now, if we had the young people. And as I write these words I am waiting the visit of a superintendent of a town school seeking college graduates but I can only refuse him as we have none to offer. I urge this not only because salaries are good, but because the college trained man or woman is in a position as never before to be of real service to the world. But we are here at the college, especially interested in recruiting the ministry. There ought to be twenty-five young men who will enter this fall, not to go into other fields of Christian work, but into THE MINISTRY IN THE BRETHREN CHURCH. Pastors, make this a loud and clear call to the young of your congregations.

More workers are needed in South America, the Mission Board tells us Ashland covets the opportunity to train these. More are needed also in Africa. The college is anxious to train these. Brethren pulpits are vacant. The college is waiting and anxious to fill these pulpits. The public schools need trained and Christian teachers. We are equal to the task of assisting in the supply of this need. But above all, perhaps, the world needs sound Christian leadership, not only in the pulpit, the schools and in the church but in the several communities. Under the blessing of God and with Christian professors, Ashland is able to do her bit here. There needs to be a revival of primitive self-sacrificing Christianity—a following of the simple Gospel of Jesus in the family, in the church, and in society generally. I have every reason to believe that Ashland College trains to supply this need also.

Now, pastors and others, the college can do all the above as indicated upon ONE CONDITION ONLY, and that is, that young people come to us in sufficient numbers to make it possible. May there not be a drive, say during the latter part of July and the early part of August, for students for Ashland?

Dean Miller, Professor J. A. Garber, Dr. Beachler, and myself have covered much of the church as representatives for the college, but we can not visit every congregation. Hence, the matter of attendance must be left in part to others who are interested.

It does seem to me that with all the demands the world is making for trained men and women, with all the demand within our own church, and with the very urgent demand for Christian leadership everywhere, not only Ashland but all Christian colleges should anticipate and realize a large enrollment of high minded, serious young men and women in September.
Ashland, Ohio.

Paul Runs the Gauntlet of Persecution

When you think your Christian way is hard and you seem to be the victim of more than ordinary persecution, it will help you to think of Paul and the gauntlet of persecutions he was compelled to run. Have you yet suffered as he said he did?

"In stripes above measure, in prisons more frequent, in deaths oft, of the Jews five times received I forty stripes, save one, thrice was I beaten with rods, once was I stoned, thrice I suffered shipwreck, a night and a day have I been in the deep. In journeyings often, in perils of waters, in perils of robbers, in perils of mine own countrymen, in perils by the heathen, in perils in the city, in perils in the wilderness, in perils in the sea, in perils among false brethren. In weariness and painfulness, in watchings often, in hunger and thirst, in fastings often, in cold and nakedness."

And yet in self-forgetfulness he was able to say, "Above all taking the shield of faith, wherewith ye shall be able to quench all the fiery days of the wicked." A man who could give counsel like that must himself have lived the shielded life. And what the shield of faith did for a man like Paul, it will do for you and me today.—B

If I Could Pluck a Rose

If I could pluck a rose in June and keep it all the year
Fragrant and fair and full of grace, just as it meets me here;
If I could wear it on my breast, could feel its subtle spell.
Which roses have the power to cast o'er those who love them well;
If I could steep my soul in bliss, ne'er feel one pang of pain,
Ne'er struggle, suffer, toil, or weep, to what would I attain?
Would other days be just as sweet if I could always keep
Unwithered roses in my hand, could neither sigh nor weep?
Ah, if the pain of loss for aye my soul had been denied,
Should I with life be more atune? Should I be satisfied?
—Selected

Service

Hon. Henry W. Watterson, the great Kentucky journalist, said of George D. Printice, "He did more for others and less for himself than any other man of his day." It was largely through his unselfish influence that the state of Kentucky was saved from secession at the time when the action of a single state meant so much to the nation.

"The corn of wheat "falls" and "dies," yet its best does not die, but transcends the earthly. Thus blooms the flower of immortality."

Those who bring sunshine into the lives of others can not keep it from themselves.—Barrie.

THE BRETHREN PULPIT

Meditation At Eventide.   By B. T. Burnworth

A Sermon Preached at a Funeral Service

Text: And Isaac went out into the fields at eventide to meditate—Gen. 24: 63.

My text has to do with a family scene in the home life of the patriarch Abraham. When he was old and well stricken in years and the Lord had blessed him, he became solicitously anxious about his son Isaac, that he should follow in his steps and live the life of his father that he might be the inheritor of the same divine promises and blessings. He calls his servant "Eliezer of Damascus" and bids him go to Nahor of Mesopotamia and seek a wife for his son, not an ungodly and idolatrous woman, for said he, "this would bring down my gray hairs in sorrow to the grave."

In Eliezer's absence and at his return we find Isaac in meditation in the field at eventide·

The Evening of Our Common Day

Meditation well becomes any of us. This is a bleeding, agonizing and bewildered world. Never before has there been such confusion. The masses rush to their tasks and when the day with its rumbling, roaring factory and loom is augmented by the shriek of locomotive and the grinding at the curb by traffic, then night finally comes, and, who is it that should not desire and who does not need the quiet of the eventide? How refreshing to walk as did Isaac into the fields and meditate! The poet was right when he said, "The world is too much with us early and late." It is a mistake that our evenings are all taken. The quiet evening of the day is used partly to finish up the day's business and partly in foolish amusement, until our home life is completely wrecked and no time is found for meditation. As Abraham feared such a status would send him to his grave, it is surely sending us prematurely to ours. The world is impoverishing herself by the improper use of the eventide.

There are just two times in the day practically adapted to meditation. First in the early morn—before the world is astir. The second is when the shop and factory have closed and the sun calmly sinks to rest casting its last brilliant ray upon the bosom of the lake, and when not a leaf is stirring. When this calm is mirrored in the soul and the shades of evening are falling and the dew is beginning to distill that is time for meditation. Our fathers in the gloaming sat about the fireplace with no other light kindled, engaged in family conversation or in holy meditation. Later a tallow dip was lighted and a book was read aloud by some member of the family and then as a mighty climax the Book of all books was gotten down from the mantle shelf and a venerable and patriarchal father read perhaps where the Master said to his tired disciples, "Come ye yourselves apart and rest awhile." The day was closed in prayerful meditation. From such homes heroes and giants have come and stalwart men of high and noble endeavor with deep and unalterable conviction·

Now I infer by finding in the context both father and son in meditation; that it was a fixed habit with them, and a practice we might well imitate. There must be a season when the muscles can relax, the mind unbend the knitted brow and iron out its wrinkles, smooth out the furrows of the cheek and forget the weariness of the day, for the repose and tranquility of meditation at eventide. And as the lengthening shades confess the shortening day, that time so peace-prevailing, so soul-quieting, it were even a sin to rush into this holy time of day where angels fear to tread with our unrestful programs, so often entirely void of meditation. The time to leave business anxieties behind is when the sun retires, then walk forth in the quiet fields or sit down in pensive mood, free from all the things that confuse modern society and agitate the human breast, this is

the time to gather strength to shield us from life's animosities on the morrow.

II The Divine Objective of Meditation.

In this historic and biblical scene we find Abraham and Isaac in meditation upon the home life—Isaac in the contemplation of the establishment of a home, and Abraham hoping that his companion for that home will encourage his instruction to his son and their home be like his, truly righteous. When I ponder the home life I can not but be solicitous about the future. The meditative hour at eventide now is a lost art, and is given over to social diversion, not always of the wisest nature. Among the many suggestions here, this one must not be overlooked, "No civilization has ever risen higher than its hearth stone." Our men are on the level of our homes, our towns on the level with our men, our states on the level of our towns and the nation on the level of the state—all revert back to the home. There is no more sobering or serious meditation than this. No wonder Isaac meditates as to who shall be his home maker. The word's greatest asset has been the mothers. God bless the true mothers in Israel who have recognized the dignity of their high calling and the opportunity of being home builders. No one so influences life, forms character, or helps to shape destiny as our mothers. They by kindly word and prayerful solicitation for the future seek to build well our lives and we should be constrained by their beautiful lives and counsel· There is nothing more natural, more beneficient or more important than the desire and the establishment of the home life, and it is a divine objective that we should meditate with Isaac on this great Theme, for our earthly homes should be types of the heavenly home.

III The Evening of Life.

Meditation at eventide is highly symbolical of the evening of life. When the burden and heat of the day is past, with gratitude we look back and remember when the sun shown in its strength at noontide. Life was at its highest pitch; vigor and strength were in fullest exercise. But the sun's settings bespeak the declining years; they are emblems of the close of this life's brief and little day. But when I see a life in its complete fruition, mellowing to the harvest like the full corn in the ear, like the cap sheaf of harvest, and an Abraham only waiting until Isaac can perpetuate his godly home, I exclaim, "Let me die the death of the righteous and let my last end be like this." Let us then in meditation join the Psalmist and say, "So teach us to number my days that we may apply our hearts unto wisdom." Let us find time amid ouh labors, strain and rush to listen to the still small voice that our strength may be renewed from day to day and we become more confident in the ways of holiness and heaven. Let us improve the calm of the day that at the eventide of life we shall be able to look back upon a life well spent and that our sun may sink in glory. The soul now exultant in the very sunbeams of strength, bouyant with a thousand hopes may soon retire beyond the western "golden gates." It is well to note here that Abraham knew his life was exemplary and his home commendable. Remember it was Jacob, that mighty wrestler, who obtained his blessing in the calm of night; that Jesus knew Nathaniel under the fig tree and he drew near to the disciples on the way to Emmaus when they were in deepest meditation.

A final meditation then upon this solemn occasion is that the sun sinks to rise again; even so shall we rise again in the glorious sunshine of the eternal presence of our Redeemer. May we all meditate upon this hope that cheers our saddened hearts today. May these stalwart sons and daughters never forget the Godly example of this mother.

Let us all prepare for the eventide which is drawing near, nearer perhaps than we think, that our sun may sink in glory and rise in the splendor of a new and perfect day.

Then fresh from converse with your Lord return
And work till daylight softens into even,
The brief hours are not lost in which ye learn
More of your Master and his rest in heaven.

Lanark, Illinois.

OUR DEVOTIONAL

The Cleansing Blood of Christ

By Rhetta O'Rourke

OUR SCRIPTURE

Hebrews 9:11-14; 10:19, 22, 24.

But Christ being come an high priest of good things to come by a greater and more perfect tabernacle, not made with hands, that is to say, not of this creation, nor yet through the blood of goats and calves, but through his own blood, entered in once for all into the holy place, having obtained eternal redemption. For if the blood of goats and bulls, and the ashes of a heifer sprinkling them that have been defiled, sanctify unto the cleanness of the flesh; how much more shall the blood of Christ, who through the eternal spirit offered himself without blemish unto God, cleanse your conscience from dead works to serve the living God. Having therefore, brethren, boldness to enter into the holy place by the blood of Jesus, let us draw near with a true heart in fulness of faith having our hearts sprinkled from an evil conscience, and let us consider one another to provoke unto good works.

OUR MEDITATION

There is no sorrow like the sorrow of a great and sincere repentance. There comes a loathing of sin, a hating of self together with the burden of an unclean conscience that scourges the soul and drives it to the cross of Christ for cleansing and relief.

"Come unto me all ye that labor and are heavy laden and I will give you rest. Take my yoke upon you and learn of me, for I am meek and lowly of heart and you shall find rest unto your souls." The blood of Christ is the blood of peace. How quickly the penitent realizes this when kneeling at the cross; the Saviour lifts the burden and gives us the yoke of meekness that takes the sting out of the trials and disappointments of our daily lives. He has made our peace with God through his cross and given us the mind of the Spirit which is the mind of peace, peace with God and peace with our fellowmen, and all the former warfare —the struggle between right and wrong, between the desire to be free from the burden and the love of sin for the pleasure it gives—has given place to a calm and quiet desire to do God's will and his alone, trusting him for grace to conquer.

The blood of Christ is the blood of cleansing. It washes away our sins and God remembers them no more against us. If the blood of goats and bulls.... sanctifies .... how much more shall the blood of Christ..:....cleanse your conscience from dead works to serve the living God." Repentance leads to confession and upon the fullness of that confession depends the whiteness of the soul. The burden of dead works is not laid down until the sins are confessed in their entirety. The only way to get them under the blood is to lay them bare before God in a deep contrition that has but one aim—pardon. Then our conscience is cleansed, not that we may sit idly by in the sunshine of God's favor, but that we may serve, that like as the Saviour offered his body as a sacrifice for many, so we bring our bodies to God as living sacrifices, keeping them holy that they may be acceptable in his sight, having our souls not conformed to

this world but transformed into the spiritual image of the world to come by the taking away of the mind of sin and the giving of the mind of holiness.

To serve God means not only to do good but to be good. Leaving the dead works that were such a heavy burden to carry and pressing on to the mark of the prize of our high calling. And we are called to be heirs of God, which means that we are heirs of His righteousness, of His kindliness, of His spirit of forgiveness of his right to show mercy to the penitent. It is not His fault if we fail to lay hold of our inheritance, that we forget that the blood of Christ has cleansed us, not for our own selfish comfort and relief, but to fit us to serve and to press on, through service, toward our high calling—godliness.

The blood of Christ is the blood of hope . The Lamb slain from the foundation of the world is the hope of the world and upon him and his servants are the eyes of the world fixed. The challenge of the world to the church today is a challenge to individuals. Does the blood of Christ avail for salvation? The answer is in our daily lives. The church has not failed. The Bible has not changed. It is you and I who have failed, and failed because we have not taken possession of our inheritance. In the eyes of the world we are either stars of hope or rocks of offence and the virtue of the atonement is judged by the quality of our service. To do good and to be good should be our aim. It is here that faith and works unite and of that holy union is born the purifying hope that bridges the chasm between this world of endeavor and the promised land of fulfillment.

OUR PRAYER

Our Father, we thank thee for Calvary, its fulfillment and its promise. We thank thee for the power manifested in our own souls, for a change of mind and purpose and for peace of conscience that enables us to serve thee with an open heart. We pray for humility and patience, for knowledge and understanding. Grant unto the wandering the Spirit of conviction that their sins may become burdensome to them and drive them to the cross for peace and pardon. Give us the Spirit of hope that spurs to holy living and binds to useful service. Grant us day by day our daily portion of thy grace that we may endure unto the end, and with the light of eventide bring us home rejoicing, not empty handed, but with bundles of golden sheaves, to keep the Harvest Home, in Jesus name. Amen.

Mattawan, Michigan.

What Can You Do For Your Church?

Attend her Lord's Day and mid-week services regularly.

Take some part in every service.

Pray and work for the success of the church.

Invite strangers to her services.

Greet the stranger that may be in our midst.

Give to the support of the church as liberally as God has dealt with you.

Visit the sick and infirm, the needy,—the careless and indifferent, and any who may be interested.

Be ready to serve wherever and whenever needed, or are asked to do so.

If you will do this, our's will be a live, warm, serving, spiritual church, used of God for great good, and to the saving of many souls.

Enjoying Religion

"And at midnight Paul and Silas prayed, and sang praises unto God; and the prisoners heard them." (Acts 16:25.)

A preacher, approaching his new appointment, asked a boy, "Do the people at Billbrook enjoy religion?" "Them that has it does," was the reply.

Send
WHITE GIFT
OFFERINGS to

THE SUNDAY SCHOOL.

ALBERT TRENT
General Secretary-Treasurer
Johnstown, Pennsylvania

An Array of Items for Your Convention Committee

Have you appointed a Convention Report Committee? If not, we suggest that you do so at an early date. Select some person or persons, who can take a bit of news and present it in a brief but interesting way. It would not be wise to encourage long reports. No matter how much information they have to give, the report should be brief and spicy. From two to five minutes at a time is enough to give to the convention news. If it can be given a local coloring, it will be all the more interesting. This will be a splendid opportunity to revive an interest in Sunday school methods and plans. Give your Sunday school a fresh interest in its own work and a new vision of its possibilities by making this world convention a matter of vital and practical concern to your own school.

Christian Japanese Awaiting Sunday School Delegates

"The Sunday School" a publication by the National Sunday School Association of Japan, dated May 25th, has just reached the office of the World's Sunday School Association in New York. The English page tells of the extensive preparations on the part of the Japanese who are looking for the arrival of their Christian brethren from overseas. The ninth Conference of the Federation of the Japanese Churches passed the following resolution: "The Church Federation expresses its hearty approval of the World's Sunday School Convention to be held in Tokyo next October and prays God's blessing upon it and also expresses the desire to help as much as they can to make it a great success." Receptions are being planned not only in Tokyo at the residence of Marquis Okuma and in the Imperial Gardens, but in Yokohama, Kyoto, Osaka and Kobe. Japan as a whole will have intimate knowledge of the work and worth of the Sunday school. Two groups are now touring West and North Japan to promote Sunday school work and to create added interest in the coming convention. Mr. Horace E. Coleman, Educational Secretary for Japan, has just returned from a trip as far as Sapporo in Hokkaido, and reports that interest is keen even that far north.

Sunday School Tourists Enroute to Tokyo

The conducted tours for delegates to the Tokoyo Sunday School Convention in October will officially begin at the point of embarkation on the Pacific Coast. Many are already planning to travel in groups for the trans-continental portion of the journey. Special cars will be used and special trains provided if the travel warrants it. Since travel is so heavy during the summer some have already been wise enough to make their pullman and hotel reservations for this country.

Each steamer-group will have a leader who will act as special host. Lectures will be arranged which will be given to those who are not too indisposed to attend! These lectures will give valuable information concerning the countries to be visited. There will be missionaries on each steamer and these will also be invited to address the traveling delegates. Some of these missionaries can be visited when in Japan, Korea, China or the Philippine Islands. Life-long friendships will be established and a vital point of contact between the field of the church at home and that of the church abroad.

A great chorus will lead the convention singing in Tokyo. Those of the delegates who have ability as singers will have opportunity of rehearsing the anthems and choruses while on the ships, as a song leader will be appointed for each of the ten groups traveling on that many Pacific Ocean steamers. The music at the convention will be under the direction of Prof. H. Augustine Smith of Boston University. Mrs. Smith will assist Prof. Smith, as she does so helpfully, at the musical services in this country. The Smiths will sail on the "Fushimi Maru" July 30, and will spend the two months in Japan before the Convention in completing the preparation of the music and pageantry of the program.

Sunday School Business Men in the Orient

A large number of leading business men of America are booking for the Tokyo Convention. Many of these men have expressed the desire to be of service in connection with the Tokyo Convention and the other Conventions following Tokyo. It is planned to have these men introduced to Chambers of Commerce in Japan, China and other parts of the Orient by similar bodies in the United States and Canada. This will give opportunity for a Christian message from these men to business bodies throughout the Orient. Hon. John Wanamaker has been deeply interested in this plan and both native leaders and missionaries in these fields believe that this plan of reaching the civic and business leadership of the Orient will be unusual and very fruitful.

It is also planned that leading educators, who shall be delegates, will meet with groups of educators in these countries to tell the value of religious education in the production of character. It is at this point that the need is greatest in the Orient and in every land, and here is eager inquiry on the part of native educators for some effective plan of producing character.

Through these and similar approaches, it is expected that the Convention delegates will do some of their best work and the plan is attracting the interest and attendance of those who are looking upon the Convention as an opportunity of special service at this critical time.

Sunday School Books: From One to a Thousand

The exhibit of Sunday school books and material used by up-to-date Sunday school workers wil be a feature of the Tokyo Convention. Under the direction of Allan Sutherland of Philadelphia, Chairman of the Exhibit Committee, assisted by Miss Alice B. Hamlin, the best in books, maps, charts, pictures, etc. has been assembled and are now on their way to Japan. One thousand books in twenty boxes, were sent in May. Other boxes left in June. Many Sunday schools have sent special demonstrations of their hand work, while photographs of large organized classes have been sought. Any Sunday school that has a photograph of a class or of any special activities in connection with the work of the Sunday school is requested to forward the same by mail to Horace E. Coleman, care Y. M. C. A., 3 Sanchome, Mitoshiro-cho, Kanda-Nu, Tokyo. Mr. Coleman is educational secretary for Japan of the World's Sunday School Association. Following the Convention in Tokyo this exhibit will remain intact in that city. Efforts are being made to raise a fund for the erection of a permanent Sunday school building in Tokyo. This edifice, in addition to meeting many needs would become the home of the exhibit.

The China Sunday School Union, with headquarters at Shanghai, has asked permission to print a special edition of each book written by Miss Margaret Slattery and which has been translated into Chinese. Both Miss Slattery and her publisher granted this request. These books will have an extensive circulation among the thousands of teachers in China and special interest attaches to the fact that Miss Slattery will sail on July 29th, on the "Empress of Russia" that she may take part in the Tokyo Convention. First she will attend some of the late summer conferences in China. Following the Convention Miss Slattery will be one of the Sunday school specialists who will make the return tour through Korea, China, Singapore, India, Egypt and Palestine.

J. A. Garber
PRESIDENT

Our Young People at Work

G. C. Carpenter
SECRETARY

The Miami Valley Life Work Conference.

held at New Lebanon, Ohio, June 19 and 20 was considered by those in attendance as the best ever held in the Miami Valley. The Conference was opened Saturday morning, by song service and prayer followed by an excellent address of welcome by Miss Brumbaugh of New Lebanon and a splendid response by Miss Wogaman of the Salem church.

Our missionary secretary, W. A. Gearhart, told us of the great needs in our mission fields and made a strong appeal for recruits in all lines of mission work. He said, if we knew that one soul was required yet to complete the bride of Christ, no effort would be spared to save that soul, yet how few of us realize that this could be possible. Rev. Sylvester Lowman, in speaking on The Meaning of Life Work, said, It meant much to surrender self to this work but emphasized the great reward that awaits the true and faithful servant. Rev. G. W. Kinzie spoke along the line of the "Church as a Recruiting Agency" and told of the great task ahead of the church to hold its young people in active Christian service

A large number of young people enjoyed the banquet Saturday evening which was followed by a spirited evening session in the conference

"Retrospect" was Rev. E. A. Rowsey's subject; he told us that out of the mistakes and failures in the past should come the dawn of a new day and reminded us that the sacrifice of our soldier boys leads us to think of him who gave all that we might have more abundant life.

Rev. James Cook spoke on the subject, "Prospect" and helped us to look into the future for better things and urged us to be prepared for their coming. He said that many Christians were like the old rain barrel in their living, in as much as they became so loose and careless that when God did send his showers of blessings, they were not prepared to retain them.

Union Sunday school services were held Sunday morning under the leadership of Superintendent F. J. Weaver followed by preaching services in charge of Rev. Beekley, of Gratis, who spoke very forcefully on the conversion of Paul as recorded in Acts 26. Dr. J. M. Wine of Dayton spoke Sunday afternoon on Conserving the Vital Forces of Life· His talk was timely and to the point, coming as it came from a practicing physician and one who knew whereof he spoke, some of the main points of his address were, "If you waste the vital forces of life when young, you will not have them when they are needed in old age," "How long could we live if we did not violate laws of nature?" "God conserves the vital forces of nature for his children."

Prof. J. A. Garber followed Dr. Wine in a short address and presented the new seven point five year Christian Endeavor Program, which apparently was well received. He spoke on the future state of affairs both religious and political and said if we secure the future we must take care of our youth.

The Model Christian Endeavor meeting was led by Rev. Stoyer and Rev. E. A. Rowsey. This meeting was very inspiring and was much appreciated by all

The Pageant written by Brethren Garber and Boardman for National Enlistment Day was presented by the Dayton society, followed by the closing plea for life work recruits by Prof. Garber. He said in making his plea that the day of narrow and selfish living is past and that we must now think in world terms in planning our future, and that the experience of the past should be a lesson for the future· In relating his experience in selecting a life work

Prof. Garber spoke of the plans of his parents which were very different from those which he felt duty bound to follow, but through kindly consideration they were led to see his call as it came from God. His plea was to be true to father and mother as far as possible but above all to be true to the voice of God.

While there were no visible results as the outcome of this Conference, yet we know that the Holy Spirit was at work and left the people with a deeper and keener sense of their duty toward their fellowmen and above all to their God and for these blessings we "Praise the Lord."

(Note.—either through oversight or undue modesty, the writer failed to sign the above splendidly written report, and as the editor is not informed and knows of no one in town who does know, we are unable to give credit to the writer.—Editor.)

Maryland-Virginia Christian Endeavor

Previous to the recent Maryland-Virginia Conference there had been no effective Christian Endeavor organization in the district. At the conference cash and pledges were received for the financing of the work and the folowing enthusiastic Endeavorers were elected to ffice:

Mr. G. Harry Haun, President, Woodstock, Va.

Miss Edna M. Bovey, Secretary-Treasurer, 119 King St., Hagerstown, Md·

H. H. Rowsey.

Copy of Letter Asking for Statistics

Dear Co-Worker.

Enclosed you will find statistical blanks for the annual report from your society. The report should be filled out at the earliest possible moment and sent promptly to the undersigned district worker, who will summarize the reports for the district and report the totals to the national officers.

Thus your society will be asked for only one report in our denominational work, and it is most important. In making it up, follow the duplicate of last year. If it has been misplaced make out the best report within your power. Failure here will rob your society of its deserved standing in national and district conference.

Every report will help us to indicate our standing in the finals of the Four Year Challenge. Moreover, it will aid us materially in preparing our new Five Year Program. A tentative draft has already been prepared under the title, "Our Seven Point Program," which correlates nicely with the newer programs announced in the enclosed literature from the United Society. More about all this at Winona. Be sure to send as many delegates as possible.

J. A. Garber, National President.

(Signed) ...., District ....

....

A Scotch preacher told of a Scotchman who did not like the Sermon on the Mount: "there was too much morality in it."

EDUCATION AND CHARACTER

Horace Mann, the great educator, would not allow a person of poor character to graduate from Antioch College, of which he was president, howeVer fine a scholar the person might be. Mr. Mann held that an educated rascal was just so much the worse rascal, and he would not help to inflict such a peril upon the community.

SEND ALL MONEY FOR
General Home, Kentucky and
Foreign Missions to

MISSIONS

WILLIAM A. GEARHART
General Missionary Secretary
906 Conover Bldg., Dayton, O.

A Saturday Night Meeting In the Kentucky Mountains

By a Presbyterian Missionary

Note.—Some experiences in meetings like the one described below might test the nerves of some of us dignified parsons, but a few meetings of that kind might do us good too. —G. C. Carpenter.

One Saturday night I heard there was to be a typical mountain meeting where I was staying, and as I had no meeting on Saturday, I decided to go and see for myself how they preached.

When I arrived the house was filled with men, women, children and dogs in about equal proportions. There were four preachers on the platform, and I learned that they all were to preach. But I was in for it, and as I do not often get the opportunity of hearing a sermon I thought to make up somewhat for lost time.

After three of them had preached, I was approached and told that as they had heard I was a preacher, my turn would come next. I arose in my place and told them that as they had heard three sermons and one more was to come, I thought they might excuse me. But I told them that in the cities where I had lived I would not have heard so much Scripture quoted in six months in the pulpit. The only books in most houses, where there were any at all, were the Bible and the almanac, so that perforce they read the Bible when they read at all. But alas! mainly for the purpose of argument in supporting some dogma learned from some one as ignorant as themselves.

I noticed one curious thing—that a bucket of water was placed on a chain in front of the pulpit ,and there was a constant stream of children passing back and forth for a drink. I found later, however, that it was placed there so it could be watched to keep the dogs out of it! Along the middle of the meeting the babies got to crying and the dogs to fighting at the same time and raised quite a hubbub. The tall mountaineer who was preaching raised his voice and said,

"Now friends, don't you think that noise is worrying me; when I tell you that I am the oldest of a family of twenty-nine you will know I am used to noise!"

The beloved Dr. Guerrant has gone, but the work moves on under the auspices of our Southern Presbyterian church. And when I see the growth and progress in fifteen years, my soul exclaims, "What hath God wrought! and happy are they who have a part in this unique work of God, which combines both home and foreign missions."

Canyon Falls, Kentucky.

The First Chinese Bible

It was a missionary named Morrison who made a first attempt to translate the Bible into Chinese. An Englishman he was, but history tells that he started out from Boston in one of the years shortly after the Civil War—started out from Boston with the backing and approval of the American Missionary Societies then in existence.

The record of his voyage around the Cape of Good Hope sounds more like a story of adventure than a missionary journey. His boat was beset with storm and shipwreck; he suffered from lack of water and insufficient food.

Half a century ago China was a vastly different country—on the surface—than the China of today. It was openly hostile to strangers. And so it happened that Morrison, at the end of his pilgrimage, found nothing confronting him but a blank wall.

Morrison begged for admission to the land, and then, when that admission was denied him, he looked about for some "next best" location in which to do his work. And he found it on the island of Macal, just off Hong Kong.

It is not hard to picture his progress once he got started. Though he never really own his way into China, he made the best sort of a translation that could have been made. For he used as his medium the Mandarin colloquial language, which according to present day authorities, is a near approach to the original language of the Scriptures. Of the many dialects (there are eighteen) of China this was the most suitable. And so it is that the first effort has been used as a foundation for all other translations.—Margaret E. Sangster, in The Christian Herald.

NEWS FROM THE FIELD

DEDICATORY SERVICES OF THE FIRST BRETHREN CHURCH
Los Angeles, California

We are now congratulating ourselves on the successful consumation of our plans for a new church building for this congregation. The new edifice stands on the location used for the old building at the corner of Forty-second and San Pedro streets. It is a structure of the English Gothic style, finished in white stucco plaster. At the southeast corner of the building stands a stately and substantial tower, the ground floor of which serves as the main entrance Vestibule. This tower with its buttresses running high up in the walls and its curved windows carries out the general architectural treatment in a particularly fine way.

The main Vestibule leads directly into the auditorium which has a seating capacity of approximately 350 persons. The rostrum is placed across the corner opposite the main entrance and is semi-circular in form. The baptistry is to the rear of this and set back in a nook with well selected plush curtains to cover the opening when the baptistry is not in use. A beautiful river scene has been

painted on the wall of the baptistry, the work of one of our church members. Sister Hazel Shively, without charge.

N. W. JENNINGS
Pastor the new First Church of
Los Angeles, Calif.

One of the most attractive features of the interior design in the main auditorium is the ceiling and walls. The intersection of the ceiling and the walls is covered and a border of wood carried around the square of ceiling. An interval of five feet was left and another placed around. This one is of beautifully decorated plaster staff with circular plaster medallions at the four sides, out of which project the indirect lighting fixtures.

The woodwork throughout the entire building is Douglas fir, oak stained and varnished which gives it a beautiful gloss and shows the slash grain of the wood. The roof and ceiling over the main auditorium is held up by three heavy and strongly constructed wooden trusses.

To the right of the rostrum the east wall is framed by a rolling partition which opens up the main Sunday school room into the main auditorium. This room has a capacity of 185 persons, which added to the capacity of the main audience room, makes a total seating capacity of 535. There are eight class rooms in the main Sunday school room—three on the first floor and five on a balgony which extends around three sides of the room.

To the north and across a four-foot hall is located one of the departmental rooms (20x32). There are three of these rooms extending along the north side of the building each with folding doors, making it possible to turn them into one big room. The street vestibule to these rooms is on the San Pedro street side, and also serves as a second vestibule to the main auditorium. A basement extends the full width of the church on the east side, and is about twenty-five feet wide one section to be used as a kitchen.

Good lavatories have been placed on the first floor, off the hallway. There is a small room. The auditorium has been so constructed will be used for a class room and prayer room. The auditorium has ben so construdto'l that a balcony may be put in at any time in the future.

The windows of the main audience room are made up of small panes of stained glass leaded together. The different colors are so blended as to cast a soft light over the entire room, which will greatly add to the comfort of those who attend the services.

The heating system is one of the most effective used in present-day construction. Gas radiators are to be used, and their satisfaction has been assured by past records.

This new church building is the result of the united, consecrated and self-sacrificing efforts of brethren and sisters who have dreamed and prayed for a larger and better equipped house in which to worship God. We look upon it as a monument to the prayer of faith, and we dedicate it to the glory of the Father, Son and Holy Spirit.

The following pastors have served this church since its organization in 1905: M. M. Eshelman, J. R. Keller, A. V. Kimmel, W. C. Benshoff, F. J. Reagan, and N. W. Jennings, the present pastor.

After several years in evangelistic service, Brother Jennings came to Los Angeles January 1st, 1919, to take the pastorate of this church. The membership at that time was about 120 and the church edifice was too small and was poorly equipped. There was a debt of about $2,000. This was quickly paid out after the pastor had made an appeal, and the building of a new church was taken up. It was thought about, talked about, and prayed about until it all crystallized into the appointment of committees and the raising of funds.

An architect was engaged, and the actual work of removing the old building and constructing the new one was begun about November 1st last. The congregation was compelled to worship in a large tent during the erection of the new church.

During a little more than a year approximately $20,000 has been given toward our new church home the total cost of which is something more than $30,000. The building committee consisted of the following brethren: I. A. Miller, chairman; Jos. Shively, Morris Leffer, H. W. Hedrick, Arthur Sherer, Carl Coverdale.

Sunday, June 20th, the new church was formally dedicated to the worship of God.

The services were planned to continue throughout the day beginning with the Sunday school at 9:45. Brother Jennings preached the morning sermon. Subject: "The Church of the Living God and Her Mission."

At noon there was a free dinner served in the basement consisting, among other good things, of stewed chicken and noodles with pie and watermelon for dessert. About 300 persons were fed during the day.

At the afternoon services. Visiting ministers and others were given an opportunity to make brief addresses. The sermon was preached by A. V. Kimmel of Whittier. His subject was "Giving the Word a Place in Your Life." L. S. Bauman of Long Beach made an appeal for funds and about $3400 was subscribed toward the building fund. Brother Bauman made the dedicatory prayer and also preached the evening sermon. There were quite a number of Visiting members from neighboring churches, the Long Beach brethren especially showing their interest by their presence and by generous gifts.

Several came forward at the morning service and took their stand for Jesus. Others came out at the evening service, making a total of eleven. Ten of these received baptism in the new baptistry at the close of the evening service. The services were continued each evening during the week, closing with a well attended and deeply spiritual communion service on Friday evening. One soul made the good confession at the Wednesday night meeting.

During the week some canvassing was done in the interest of the Sunday school About 25 or 30 new scholars were promised for the school and many of those residing in the neighborhood spoke very highly of the new building and promised their cooperation.

Brother Earl Hedrick called the Sunday school cabinet together recently and laid before them for discussion the re-organization of the school on account of the added room and better accommodations afforded by the new building. It was decided to increase the number of separate departments and to provide for some new equipment very much needed for efficient work.

Our congregation, in all of its departments, faces a great responsibility, and our pastor is wisely urging us all to be very humble and prayerful and to look to the true source of strength.

May our Father richly bless his work here as we go forward to face the tasks that await us.

A. P. REED.

ASHLAND, OREGON

Last January, a little lady came to Ashland, Oregon unknown. This June, she was the inspiration of one of the most delightful social gatherings of neighbors from every part of the city at a noon picnic dinner in the beautiful bungalow building in Lithia Park at which over a hundred were seated at the first table. The table was decorated with roses and on one center side was a flower decked chair, decked by young girls who adore the little lady and in which

she, as honor guest, was seated. The dinner was a loving tribute from the neighborhood Bible classes to Miss Detwiller who past six months has conducted the Six Months' Course of Synthetic Studies in the Old Testament as outlined by Dr. Gray of Moody's where Miss Detwiller formerly studied for a short time. Miss Detwiller is recently from Dr. White's Teachers Training School of New York. An opportunity was offered her to come to Ashland which is a town of six thousand or over and she made the Venture. The result has been most wonderful. Over a hundred have given regular attendance at the neighborhood classes and many others have followed the Bible readings who could not attend. Miss Detwiller considers the attendance remarkable for so small a town and is enthusiastic over Ashland's appreciation of the Neighborhood Bible classes, however the Ashland folks feel that the personality behind the teacher had much to do with the remarkable response as the classes are made up of girls and boys and older folk.

MRS. MARGARET E. DILL.

PERU, INDIANA SOLILOQUY AND NEWS

The world is gaining momentum in worldliness in this city about as fast as anywhere else. The automobile will send many souls to hell. Blessed is the automobile that goes to church regularly. Better walk on crutches to heaven than ride on cushion tires to death. The movies are enjoying full Sunday liberty here, to the enrichment of the owner's pocketbook and the cursing of the youth of the community.

The devil is not to blame, for he is scoring a big victory while the church is suffering a terrible defeat. It is the people whom the demon of the pit has asphyxiated with the gas of worldliness who are to blame.

The profiteer prospers on, unmolested by Uncle Sam or anyone else. Government inspectors drop in and make a few pretensions but never a prosecution, and before the dust of the inspector's visit has settled the profiteer shillingly marks his merchandise up another fifty or one hundred percent and advertises a "July Sale—Regardless of Cost." Not how much should I get but how much can I get determines the sale price, and the gullible public who according to Barnum like to be humbugged swallow his bait, hook and all and go on their way rejoicing. The fact is that many people have the high-price fever and refuse to buy merchandise that happens to bear a reasonable price mark.

The religious indifference of the majority of the members of all the churches is appalling. What meaneth this apostasy? Is this the hour of low tide and will high tide come again or are we in the last days as many would have us believe? Is the Brethren church faithful to her mission as given by Jesus Christ the Head of the church? What part of the members of the Brethren church are guilty of lowering their moral and spiritual standards for the sake of passing profit? How many members of the Brethren church were once on fire with religious zeal but are now lukewarm if not down to zero when tested by the Old-time-religion,

Holy-Ghost, Hallelujah, Amen thermometer. Most ministers would die from the sudden shock before restoratives could be secured if the church deacons would chorus an amen to some good point in the sermon.

Awake, O Zion! Rescue the perishing, care for the dying! The harvest is white and good grain is being lost. Awake O church of the Living God! Apply the Gospel of Jesus Christ to the affairs among men. Live the Christ life and thus show the Savior to a dying world. Seek first the Kingdom of God and his righteousness and reverse not God's plan for his world.

I started out to write some church news but soliloquized with the accompanying result. Three have been added to the church since our last report, one by letter and two by, baptism. The Christian Endeavor society has a hot weather contest on for six weeks with an expert endeavor class thrown in for good measure. The Sunday school averaged seventy-seven in attendance during the past three months. Mrs. Charles Abbott of Dayton, Ohio, spent a week in Peru recently, having been given a week early date for the Winona school of Missions and having learned of tre same on her arrival here. During the wek Sister Abbott gave several very helpful talks, endearing herself to the young people of the church. All who heard her expressed their appreciation. She was with the Brethren church at Loree on Sunday morning and her message was appreciated by Brother Stewart's congregation. This visit occasioned by a mistake worked out for good. Thanks to Sister Abbott for her kindly service.

We are expecting a larger representation than usual at the Winona Conference. Those who go once, want to go again. The blessing is double to those who attend and to the local church during the whole year.

Your for Victory,

G. C. CARPENTER.

DENVER, INDIANA

As nothing has been reported from this place for a long time I take the liberty of making a brief report myself. Although we have been quiet we are not on the dead list yet awhile. Our Sunday school is moving along nicely with a fair attendance but could be better. By hard and faithful work we are keeping up to the standard for which we are glad. Through the faithful work of an excellent program committee the Juniors and Primary members of the school rendered a fine Children's Day program on Sunday evening, June 20th.

Our W. M. S. have struggled hard trying to make the goals for this year. Miss Mae Smith gave us a call two weeks ago and gave us a very helpful talk which we appreciated very much. At our next meeting we reelect officers for another year's work which we hope will b a more successful one than the past one has been. Although we have had very few accessions to the church the past year every part of the work is moving along smoothly with Rev. A. T. Wirick as our leader. We didn't seem to accomplish much through the revival last winter as the "flu" scare was abroad causing us to have

a slim crowd most of the time. Brother Wirick did the preaching and gave us some fine sermons, and Brother Harley Zumbaugh of Tiosa, Indiana, had charge of the singing which he very ably conducted. (I might add here that anyone wishing a singer would do well to get Brother Zumbaugh.) Although only two united with the church a much better spirit existed throughout the church as a whole so we don't feel our effort was a failure entirely.

If this doesn't find the waste basket you may hear from Denver again. We ask a united interest in your prayers.

MRS. BESSIE CLINGAMAN,

Denver, Indiana.

CONCERNING CONFERENCE ACCOMMODATIONS

— Winona Lake, Ind., July 5th, 1920.

Rev. G. S. Baer,

Ashland, Ohio.

Dear Brother:

I have been living at the park for several weeks and feel that some word should appear in the Evangelist concerning accommodations here. At the present time all the cottages are rented until the close of the Bible Conference. After that during our conference it will be possible for families to rent cottages if they desire. Notice should be given of such plans in advance so that the gas, light and water need not be turned on again. A great many of the boarding and rooming houses have all their rooms engaged for the Bible Conference. Those of our conference desiring to attend the Bible Conference from Aug. 20 to 29 should make reservations at once. Last year all beds in the park were occupied during the Bible Conference and many, were sent to Warsaw.

During our conference the usual rooming houses will be open together with the Inn. The rates at the Inn, during our conference will be $1.00 per day, per person, European plan. Meals will be served Coffee House style, dinner and supper without desert 45 cents each; breakfast regular A La Carte service. Rooms by the week will be $5.25 each two in a room.

It will be possible for some families to secure rooms with light-housekeping accommodations during our Conference. Mr. V. M. Hatfield, Winona Lake, Ind. should be written to concerning cottages; The Pauley Hotel Company, Winona Lake, Ind. for reservations at the Inn and the Hotel. The Hotel will be open if occasion demands. I shall be glad to answer any inquiries concerning cottages, rooms or rates.

Hoping for a large conference and with best wishes for your work, I am,

Very truly yours,

C. E. KOLB.

COLLEGE NEWS

Summer Sessions

The first term of six weeks, the enrollment was 49. This term the enrollment is 80. This does not include either pupils of the model school or any of the teachers. Total 129.

Churches Visited

I have been able within the year to visit

the following churches, preaching in many of them both morning and evening: Ohio— Ashland, Fair Haven, Homer, Mansfield, Dayton, New Lebanon, Gratis, Canton, North Georgetown, Louisville. Indiana— Milford, Nappanee, Warsaw, Goshen, Flora. Pennsylvania — Masontown, Myersdale. Johnstown, Summit Mills, Berlin, Pittsburg, Cerro Gordo. Maryland—Linwood. Total 23. To this should be added the following churches: Presbyterian, Baptist, Reformed, United Brethren, Church of the Brethren, Evangelical. Church of God, Methodist (8). I count a duty and a privilege to bring the the college to the attention of our own congregations and at every one of the above places, I have ben exceedingly well received. My last place was Masontown. One of this year's graduates, Brother Gingrich is to serve this congregation. The church is much interested in the prospects and I am confident that Mr. and Mrs. Gingrich will render them a good service.

Dr. Shively, has been able to secure Brother and Sister Pettit of the Rittman, Ohio, congregation to take up the work of the dormitory. Mr. Pettit will have general care of the property and Mrs. Pettit will superintend the work of the dining hall. Miss Amy Puterbaugh, teacher of Voice, will be Dean of Women. Girls wishing to be assigned rooms should communicate either with her or the writer. Men will write to Prof. Haun or to myself. I also call attention to the college advertisement soon to appear in The Evangelist. Pastors, will you kindly read it over and then be reminded to urge upon your young people the desirability of coming here this fall? Local prospects are good. Let the church respond.

EDWIN E. JACOBS.

CAMPAIGN NOTES

From Linwood we came to Hagerstown Having held a meeting in this church some years ago when Brother Tombaugh was still pastor I knew many of the Hagerstown people. Brother A. B. Cover is now the shepherd of this congregation. And he and Mrs. Cover both being graduates of Ashland College, I found them eager and willing to do the utmost to put the canvass across in the most successful manner. And Brother Tombaugh being a life long friend and supporter of the school, shared with the Covers a desire to see Hagerstown go over the top for college endowment. But it would be very unfair not to add that very many others of the Hagers town folks felt the importance of the movement and wanted their home congregation to do its very best.

It should probably be said at this point in this report that unfortunately for both Hagerstown and the college the purchase o a pasonage property and the campaign fo endowment came at practically the same time So in view of the local plans at Hagerstown the results there for endowmen were quite good. And needless to say, some men in the Hagerstown church who have been blessed with a generous portio of the things of this world had done eve the widow's mite for the college the result would have been still better.

Brother Cover gave me every possible assistance and when the results were reckoned up we found that he had gone almost $2200. Our top notch gift from an individual here was $250. But the Hagerstown Sunday school enlisted at a fine, substantial figure —$500. That puts the Hagerstown school right up very near the top among the Sunday schools of the brotherhood in their gifts to endowment. The other organizations including the W. M. S., the Ladies' Aid, and the S. M. M. also did nobly. So it is needless to say, Ashland has many strong backers at Hagerstown.

The home of Brother and Sister Tombaugh was our general stopping place and it was a pleasure indeed to be in this home. We were also treated most royally in the Cover, Rohrer, Schindle and Barnheisel homes. To all these kind folks I feel greatly indebted. I am also particularly indebted to Brethren Brown and Beachley for the service they gave us with their automobiles. Brother Beachley is superintendent of the Hagerstown Sunday school and he has just reason to feel proud of his school for the fine showing it made in the canvass.

It was also my privilege to visit in the home of Brother and Sister Roy Long during my stay here. Brother Long was a student at Ashland while I was there and we had many a good time together. And after a long period of separation it was a real pleasure to me to visit in his home and meet his family.

I shall not soon forget the splendid co-operation of Brother and Sister Cover, nor the many good people who make up his congregation. I covet for this field God's rich favor and blessing.

This now brings the mercury up to $150,-000. It has taken a long time of working and waiting to reach this point. But I don't believe the fault has all been mine. If I had had my way we would have been away beyond that long ago. But it is after all up to the folks who hold the pocket books to say how fast the mercury shall rise. If I had been blessed with the money some of our people have I would have hit this thing so hard that I would have made the thermometer look like the "Old Faithful" geyser in Yellowstone Park. But thank the Lord, we have reached the $150,000 mark. Next will be the report from St. James.

WM. H. BEACHLER,
Campaign Secretary.

Pennsylvania Churches Take Notice

At the last district conference the following action was taken and is now in full force:

"That after this year (1919) the conference seal be withheld from credentials of ministerial delegates failing to furnish Statistical Reports and that lay credentials be refused from churches failing to make Statistical reports."

Blanks have been mailed to all churches. If you have not received them write at once for blanks to the statistician. Reports should all be in my hands before July 20.

M. A. Witter, Statistician. Pennsylvania District.

Our Goal: 200,000; We Can and We Must

COLLEGE ENDOWMENT

THE TIE THAT BINDS

BAKER-HELVIE—Near Huntington Indiana, at the home of the bride's parents, Mr. Walter L. Baker, and Miss Rosa B. Helvie, March 23, 1920.   CHARLES A. BAME.

BROWN-WRIGHT—At the home of Rev. I. B. Wright, father of the bride, in the presence of immediate friends and relations, Mr. Dwight L. Brown of Chicago and Miss Lois Wright, of our church. May 29, 1920.
CHARLES A. BAME.

MUELLER-LANDIS—At the home of Sam'l Landis, father of the bride, June 16th, 1920, Mr. Daniel E. Mueller and Miss Ruth Landis.
CHARLES A. BAME.

OLINGER-ULERY—At the home of the bride's parents, Mr. Geo. Ulery, on June 19th, Mr. Devon Olinger and Miss Lois Ulery, both members of our church.
CHARLES A. BAME.

BRANSTRATER-FOSTER—Mr. John Branstrater of Mishawaka, Indiana and Miss Ruth Foster of Tiosa, Indiana, were united in marriage at the Brethren parsonage in North Liberty, Indiana, June 13, 1920. The undersigned, the bride's pastor, performing the ceremony. Mrs. Branstrater is a member of the Brethren church at Tiosa, and a successful teacher in the public schools of Fulton county. May the blessings of God be upon this union.

C. CLARENCE GRISSO.

FORD-WOGAMAN—Mr. Wilbur H. Ford and Miss Josie Wogaman were united in marriage, May 1, 1920 at the home of the writer, Clayton, Ohio. Both Mr. Ford and Miss Wogaman were students of Ashland College where they first met. Miss Wogaman was a faithful worker in the Salem church at Clayton and has for some time been employed as a teacher in one of the high schools near her home. Following their marriage they went at once to assume their duties at a County Home near Toledo, Ohio, where Mr. Ford is rendering a faithful service as manager. They have the good wishes of their many friends for a long and happy life.
J. S. COOK.

Thus we are called to give away to other cities, three or four of our best choir girls. Two of them to South Bend, one to Chicago. All are prominent and promising young people who will grace any community.
C. A. B.

IN THE SHADOW

HARTZEL—Leonard Hartzel was born near Elberton, Ohio, August 20, 1839, and departed this life May 30, 1920, at the age of 80 years, 7 months and 10 days.

About twenty-five years ago he, with his companion, united with the Bear Creek Brethren church, of which he continued to be a faithful member until his death.

He leaves to mourn their loss his wife, five children, 25 grand children and 6 great-grandchildren. May they be sustained in this hour of their sorrow by a loving heavenly Father. Services from the Bear Creek church by the writer.
GEO. W. KINZIE.

PURCELL—Mary Gertrude Purcell, daughter of John Calvin and Almeda Winterringar was born at Millwood, Knox county, Ohio, October 5, 1866, departed this life May 31, 1920, aged 54 years, 7 months and 2 days. She was united in marriage to C. B. Purcell, and to this union were born three daughters, Grace, Helen, Lucile. She united with the Brethren church under the ministry of Dr. J. Allen Miller and remained a faithful member of the same until the time of death. Those left to mourn are her father, mother, two brothers, a husband, three daughters, a number of other relatives and many friends.

Services conducted at the Buckeye City church by the writer.
BENJ. F. OWEN.

BY THE GRACE OF GOD —CHRISTIAN GENTLEMAN
Minister of the Gospel, Teacher of Youth.

On March the 8th, 1877 there came into life on earth a little child. The birthplace was Woodbury, Pennsylvania and the parents were Brother and Sister Martin Byers, now of Ashland, Ohio. The child was their first born, our esteemed brother in Christ, Dr. Edward E. Byers. The child grew to manhood and into usefulness and service. He acquired a splendid training for his life's work, though not without a struggle. Then at the very threshold of a career that promised much to the church of his choice, to the cause of education and to himself and his friends—suddenly, instantly, his life was snuffed out in a fatal accident. On Friday evening, June 25, 1920, while riding in an automobile with a fellow teacher and a friend, in crossing the railroad near Martinsburg. Pennsylvania, a passenger train struck their machine and ended his career. At the time of his death he was aged 43 years, 3 months and 24 days. His "Sun went down at noonday."

Brother Byers came to Ashland, Ohio and entered the college, in 1803. He completed the A. B. course here. He earned the A. M. at Defiance College. Elon College, South Carolina, honored him with the degree of Litt. D. He studied and taught at Ashland College 9 years. During this time he also served the Zion Hill Church as pastor for several years. He taught at Defiance College for five years during which time he was Dean of Men. While at Defiance he preached for our Bryan Brethren for two years. Since 1917 he has been the President, as he was the founder, of Morrison Cove College located at Martinsburg, Pennsylvania. During the three years of work here he with his faithful wife directed the building up of a splendid educational plant. The work he did here alone is sufficient monument to any man if we may judge by the impression made upon a community.

Brother Edward E. Byers united with the Brethren Church at Martinsburg when about twenty years of age. He was baptized by Dr. W. L. Spanogle. He soon heard the call of his Master to a life of service and surrendered himself. Immediately he set to the task of better preparation for the work of the ministry. Later he was ordained to the eldership. He was ready wherever and whenever opportunity presented itself to preach the Gospel. Thus while teaching in the school he founded he served the circuit of churches in Morrison's Cove as pastor and spiritual leader.

In June 1909 he was united in marriage with Miss Rose Summers of Canton, Ohio. Together they planned their work for Christ

DR. EDWARD E. BYERS

and humanity. Together they toiled to fulfill their mission. Upon Sister Byers falls the shadow of a supreme loss. Only love and devotion to a high cause can break through the cloud and bid her complete life's tasks.

Funeral services were held at the place of his residence. The following paragraphs are taken from the Altoona, Pa., Times-Tribune:

If the loss felt in any community may be be measured by the number of people attending the obsequies of one lately departed, then Morrison's Cove is mourning its greatest personal and community loss in the death of the late Professor Edward E. Byers. Attended by a concourse of 4,000 people conveyed to the Morrison's Cove college by a cortege of more than 500 automobiles, by Pennsy train and pedestrians from the town

and community, the funeral of the deceased educator was held yesterday afternoon.

Long before the hour for the services—2 o'clock—people began arriving and when the opening moment came with close friends and relatives within and the majority of friends, neighbors and sympathizers standing in front of the college building, which had been the home of Professor Byers for three years prior to the unfortunate accident which had snuffed out his life like a candle, the Rev. J. I. Hall, pastor of the Martinsburg Brethren church, took charge as master of ceremonies.

Rev. Hall opened with prayer and a short eulogy on the deceased, with whom he had been very closely affiliated in church and school work for a number of years, then one by one twelve other ministers and one layman spoke words of eulogy for the dead, drew lessons from his life for the good of those who remain and words of comfort for the bereft.

The body was brought to Canton, Ohio, for the final service. Here the aged parents, brothers who could not attend the service at Martinsburg, sisters and friends, assembled. A brief but impressive service was held. The following brethren ministers were present and spoke. Dr. E. E. Jacobs, A. C. Hendrickson, Eli Hoover, Earl Riddle, Fred Vanator, the writer and Elder Walter Keller of the Church of the Brethren. At Martinsburg, Brother W. C. Benshoff took part in the service.

Of the fine personal characteristics, the humble spirit, the clean and pure heart, the sincerity of life, the loftiness of purpose, the supreme desire to serve his master in the best possible manner—of these one might write much as exemplified in his life.

His was not a life so long as that of some but it was crowded full of worth and usefulness. The writer felt that he could sum up his message to the friends in three short but meaningful sentences: Edward Byers was a thoroughly sincere, high-minded Christian Gentleman; Edward Byers lived to serve his day and generation with his best endeavor utterly forgetful of the sacrifice and cost to himself; Edward Byers is not dead—he can not die for his life was hid with Christ in God, he lives with his Lord.

May the Grace of the Lord Jesus, the love of our heavenly Father and comfort of the blessed Holy Spirit sustain Sister Byers, the aged father and mother, the brothers and the friends.

J. ALLEN MILLER.

Cobb's Conference Corner

Music

Music will be strongly featured at our Conference this year. Good music is a wonderful asset to a successful conference. We have secured this year as inspirational song leader, Prof. Arthur Lynn, who is known on two continents, as "The Golden Tenor of Glasgow," He is a personal friend of Homer Rhodeheaver, William J. Kirkpatrick, Geo. Myer, Charles Gabriel and has been featured in some of the largest Evangelistic Campaigns in the U. S. A., by the most noted song leaders of our day.

We are fortunate indeed to secure such talent. It is his purpose to visit a number of churches in Northern Indiana, during August, and spend a night or two at each church, drilling chorus' out of which he expects to build a grand chorus at Conference. Any churches desiring a night or two might confer with me, and I will try and arrange. Address me 2002 W. 3rd St., Dayton, Ohio.

E. M. COBB.

Thine Is the Kingdom

A PRAYER

By Dwight E. Marvin

Almighty God, thou rulest over all thy creation. Thy kingdom is an everlasting kingdom and thy dominion endureth forever.

Thou rulest over all this world. Make it a new paradise. Restore sinful man to a life in thee. Cause thy law to be the law of nations and thy service the glory of all people, through Jesus Christ our Lord.

Thou rulest over this land. Make it a holy land. Set up thy throne here. Purify and strengthen our national life and deepen our spiritual power and influence, through Jesus Christ our Lord.

Thou rulest over us. Make us thy true children. Come thou and abide in us and constrain us to do thy will, through Jesus Christ our Lord.

Thine, O God, is the kingdom forever. Amen.

Published every Wednesday at Ashland, Ohio. All matter for publication must reach the Editor not later than Friday noon of the preceding week.

George S. Baer, Editor

The
Brethren
Evangelist

When ordering your paper changed give old as well as new address. Subscriptions discontinued at expiration. To avoid missing any numbers renew two weeks in advance.

R. R. Teeter, Business Manager

OFFICIAL ORGAN OF THE BRETHREN CHURCH

Subscription price, $2.00 per year, payable in advance.
Entered at the Post Office at Ashland, Ohio, as second-class matter.
Acceptance for mailing at special rate of postage provided for in section 1103, Act of October 3, 1917, authorized September 9, 1918.
Address all matter for publication to Geo. S. Baer, Editor of the Brethren Evangelist, and all business communications to R. R. Teeter, Business Manager, Brethren Publishing Company, Ashland, Ohio. Make all checks payable to the Brethren Publishing Company.

TABLE OF CONTENTS

EDITORIAL

The Way Into the Kingdom

Sometimes we find certain Bible truths set forth so simply, beautifully and effectively, that any attempt to explain or emphasize only detracts from their effect. In such cases it is well just to let the Bible speak and give its own message in its own way. Concerning some of the most vital teachings of the Word, this is true. Multitudes of hearts are asking today as in the days of the apostles, "What must I do to be saved?" "What is the way into the kingdom of Christ?" Let the Bible speak for itself.

1. FAITH

"Moreover brethren, I declare unto you the Gospel which I preached unto you, which also ye have received, and wherein ye stand; By which also ye are saved, if ye keep in memory what I preached unto you, unless ye have believed in vain. For I delivered unto you first of all that which I also received, how that Christ died for our sins according to the scriptures; and that he was buried, and that he rose again the third day according to the scriptures" (1 Corinthians 15;1-4).

"Be it known unto you all, and to all the people of Israel, that by the name of Jesus Christ of Nazareth, whom ye crucified, whom God raised from the dead, even by him doth this man stand here before you whole. Neither is there salvation in any other: for there is none other name under heaven given among men, whereby we must be saved" (Acts 4:10, 12).

"He that believeth and is baptized shall be saved; but he that believeth not shall be damned" (Mark 16:16).

"Ye see then how that by works a man is justified, and not by faith only" (James 2:24).

"But showed first unto them of Damascus and at Jerusalem, and throughout all the coasts of Judea, and then to the Gentiles, that they should repent and turn to God, and do works meet for repentance" Acts 26:20). "Then Peter said unto them: Repent and be baptized every one of you in the name of Jesus Christ for the remission of sins, and ye shall receive the gift of the Holy Ghost" (Acts 2:38).
"And the times of this ignorance God winked at; but now commandeth all men everywhere to repent" (Acts 17:30).

2. REPENTANCE

"Now the works of the flesh are manifest, which are these: Adultery, fornication, uncleanness, lasciviousness, idolatry, witchcraft, hatred, variance, emulations, wrath, strife, seditions, heresies, envyings, murders, drunkenness, revellings and such like: of the which I tell you before as I have also told you in times past, that they which do such things shall not inherit the kingdom of God" (Galatians 5:19-21).

3. CONFESSION

"That if thou shalt confess with thy mouth the Lord Jesus, and shall believe in thine heart that God hath raised him from the dead, thou shalt be saved. For with the heart man believeth unto righteousness; and with the mouth confession is made unto salvation" (Romans 10:9, 10).

"Whosoever therefore shall confess me before men, him will I also confess before my Father which is in heaven. But whosoever shall deny me before men, him will I also deny before my Father which is in heaven" (Matthew 10:32, 33).

4. BAPTISM

"And Jesus came and spake unto them saying, 'All power is given unto me in heaven and in earth. Go ye therefore and teach all nations, baptizing them in the name of the Father and of the Son, and of the Holy Ghost.'" Matthew 28:18, 19). "Then Peter said unto them, 'Repent and be baptized every one of you in the name of Jesus Christ for the remission of sins, and ye shall receive the gift of the Holy Ghost'" Acts 2:38). "And now why tarriest thou? Arise and be baptized, and wash away thy sins, calling on the name of the Lord" (Acts 22:16). "He that believeth and is baptized shall be saved; but he that believeth not shall be damned" (Mark 16:16).

"Know ye not that so many of us as were baptized into Jesus Christ were baptized into his death." (Romans 6:3). "Buried with him in baptism, wherein also ye are risen with him through the faith of the operation of God, who hath raised him from the dead" (Colossians 2:12). "For he that is dead is freed from sin" (Romans 6:7) "Therefore if any man be in Christ, he is a new creature: old things are passed away; behold, all things are become new; (II Corinthians 5:17). "There is therefore now no condemnation to them which are in Christ Jesus, who walk not after the flesh, but after the spirit" (Romans 8:1).

The Greatest Story Ever Told.   By A. D. Gnagey

In the early part of the year, while returning home from New ark, Ohio, my attention was attracted by an apparently unassuming passenger who was reading with seemingly deep interest what afterwards learned was a huge advertisement covering the entire back page of the Cincinnati Inquirer. Stepping across the aisle and begging the passenger's pardon, I inquired what it was that so in terested him in a newspaper advertisement. He was a Christian gentleman on his way home to Defiance, and answered very politely.

The headlines of the advertisement had caught and held his eye, "THE GREATEST STORY EVER TOLD." It was a wonderful message he was reading, a message which the Editor has kindly consented to publish and which appears on another page of this issue of The Evangelist. We discussed in a very friendly way, the religious problems of the day, and both agreed that it was a hopeful sign that a secular paper should give an entire page to an announcement of the simple story of Jesus which has come "down to us through ages," accompanied by an illustration of the Christ in the person of a shephard.

I asked my fellow-passenger if he would permit me to clip the advertisement, explaining to him at the same time that I could make good use of it. Very graciously he handed me the entire paper.

After my return home I read it to the family and told them that sometime I shall offer it to our good editor for publication. It appears on another page, though in smaller type, yet large enough to give the reader a very fair idea (lacking the picture) of what it was like in its original setting.

Probably it will not appeal to the reader as it did to me personally, but it made an impression upon my mind that time itself will not easily efface. It is my prayer that the message may find its way into the hearts of our worthy editor's readers and enlarge their thoughts of the Kingdom.

EDITORIAL REVIEW

GENERAL CONFERENCE AT WINONA LAKE, INDIANA, AUGUST 30 to SEPTEMBER 5.

Brother Herman E. Roscoe reports the status of the churches and districts on the Benevolent Fund. Some churches have contributed nothing and some not their full quota.

The church's obligation is every member's obligation. This applies to the Winona Auditorium Fund as well as to any other obligation which the church at large has assumed.

The Brethren of the First Church of Los Angeles are pressing forward and making the most of their enlarged opportunities in their new church building. Brother Reed continues to keep us informed.

It will pay every pastor and church secretary to read Brother Dyoll Belote's letter in this issue. Our faithful conference secretary is seeing to it that every congregation gets its full quota of credentials in good time. If you have not gotten yours write him.

The Evangelist Honor Roll is not a dead issue, because it is still growing. The latest "joiners" are North Manchester, Indiana and Maple Grove, Kansas. We give these churches a warm welcome and congratulate them on the fine spirit of loyalty thus displayed.

La Verne, California, church, shepherded by Brother Thomas Broad, is looking up and onward. They recently enjoyed a two weeks' meeting under the evangelistic preaching of Brother Bell. This church appreciates its pastor and lets him know it in very substantial ways.

Brother Drushal writes enthusiastically concerning the conference he was recently privileged to attend at the Moody church in Chicago. He speaks also of some of the difficulties they have been encountering in their work at Lost Creek, as well as the progress and prospects. The school term now beginning promises to be the best.

"The Last Call," says Dr. Bame on the Four Year Program page, and he urgently requests every church to make prompt and accurate report of what has or has not been accomplished of the goals we set before ourselves nearly four years ago. Your church may not be to blame for not "gaining" all the goals, but it will be blamed if it is not reported.

It is not our custom, as it would be manifestly impossible, to make editorial mention of all obituaries, but in view of the fact that the publication of the obituary of Brother S. J. Giffin, who was Brother H. F. E. O'Neill's co-worker in Y. M. C. A. work and for many years was a faithful deacon in the Brethren church, has been

so long delayed, it is due the friends to state that the original obituary sent to the editor by the officiating minister, Brother H. M. Harley never reached its destination. The one herein published over the name of Brother O'Neill is the first we have received.

We can see how Sister Detwiler's faithful teaching of the Word and consecrated personal work are having their effect on the people of Ashland, Oregon. Sister Detwiler is very modest in her reports, but the spontaneous report recently published from Mrs. Margaret Dill and the present report forwarded by Miss Detwiler help us to understand what splendid fruit her work is bearing.

Brother Ira D. Slotter, who for so many years has had charge of the mechanical department of the Publishing House, writes concerning the work of the Ashland Brethren church. Brother Slotter is the faithful secretary of the Sunday school. The work is going forward under the efficient pastoral care of Professor J. A. Garber, and all are looking forward to the time when we will have a church house in Ashland and will no longer be compelled to worship in the college chapel. Brother Garber, as we have before announced, is taking work in Northwestern University at Evanston, Illinois, and if any churches in the vicinity of Chicago have need of a pulpit supply during the vacation of their pastor, write him either at Ashland or at the above address.

Brother Gearhart is visiting the churches in behalf of the Kentucky Light Fund and showing the Kentucky slides. During his absence from his office Brother W. C. Teeter is taking care of the important business, and it was from his hands that we received the recent Easter offering report, recently published. Brother Gearhart takes occasion in his letter to speak in behalf of some who took exception to a certain article published in Evangelist number 23. We do not feel it our duty either to defend or pass judgement on the article in question in this public way, but it is perhaps due the author to state, as some have failed to understand, that it was written in a vein of sarcasm, the writer meant just the opposite of what he said. It is perhaps only fair to say that we have received words of depreciation concerning both of the articles published in that issue on the Interchurch World Movement. One writer gave his reasons for opposing it and the other gave his reasons, in a sarcastic way for favoring it. In view of the fact that the Interchurch Movement has recently ceased to exist on its former elaborately organized basis and is no longer an issue, and also that further articles pro and con can accomplish no good but may tend to be further divisive, we have decided to exclude further discussions of the merits and demerits of the Interchurch Movement. We believe the large majority of our readers will sustain us in this decision. We have yet in our hands unpublished articles dealing with both sides of the question, but we are hopeful that their authors will be kindly considerate and not feel that they have been discriminated against. We do this in the interest of the largest good in which we are all concerned.

Brother Beachler is finding cause for encouragement among the Maryland-Virginia churches. That district is proving itself loyal to the college in a very substantial way. When we realize how far removed they are from the college and yet see how liberally they are giving (most of them), we are made to realize that the Evangelist has been preaching college endowment very effectively and has proven an able assistant to Brother Beachler. Brother Beachler's "Notes" and President Jacob's "News" have been carrying the needs of the college to every nook and corner of the brotherhood where the Evangelist has been placed in the homes of the members. And we must continue to work together in this way, for with the growth of our college every department of our church will be benefitted, and with the growth of the Evangelist and other publications of the church all other interests are benefitted and with the growth of missions the Evangelist becomes the more essential as a medium for diseminatnig missionary news. Thus all departments of the church go forward together. And every department should be vitally concerned about the success of this particular campaign, the adequate endowment of our college, for it lies at the base of our denominational growth. We therefore rejoice with you, Brother Beachler, in your success and we congratulate the many churches that have given on their wisely placed interests. And we congratulate the St. James and the Washington, D. C. churches on their splendid contributions to this most worthy cause.

FOUR-YEAR PROGRAM PAGE
NOW THEN DO IT.—II Samuel 3:18
Conducted by Charles A. Bame

The Last Call

The call has gone forth. The Four Year Program has almost reached the 'finis.'' I am not sure that I shall have another message to this column. The final record is to be made to OUR NEW SECRETARY. Your reports are called to be at MILLEDGEVILLE, ILLINOIS by AUGUST FIRST, 1920. If every pastor has not received his card by the time this message appears in print, he will still have time to ask me for another and get it in on time.

Be Prompt and Particular

We cannot afford to do less. The encouragement or discouragement of a generation will go with this report. VICTORY CHURCHES will not forget it in either of the four winning classes. If they have a framed reminder of their VICTORY you will be reminded of it often by the absence of one.

How Brethrenism Responded

Is best shown by these figures; read them and study them: Last year out of a possible 2814 points, we know we gained only 772. We know we have progressed on 225 and lost 417. But if the 1400 unreported points had been reported and the same ratio as the 1414 points maintained, we should have had 1980 gained and progressing and only 817 lost. By these figures, we know what we have gained, only in part. We know full well that our churches over the land gained many more points than we had reported; but we can not count them until they are reported. We do not know how many to count in big strong churches that we know make goals even though they do not tell it unto the churches, as the Apostle of Patmos was to do.

This Is The Year

And this year is VICTORY YEAR. A whole evening is to be given to a JUBILEE. What a jubilee it would be if the 1400 unreported points of last year were reported and the same ratio maintained!

Progress. Remember that PROGRESS is loss or LOST, this year. You may mark your cards as usual, but the Secretary will mark all progress points lost, as, for the sake of this program they are lost. For the larger cause we have had at heart all these years, progress is away ahead of LOST. We are glad if you can report progress which will mean that you are still working at it; but we are sorry if you have not had all progress made over into GAINED.

Do It Now.

Maybe you can make progress into gained yet, before it is too late. Look closely over your assessments and see if you have cleaned up on all of them. Check up on the Goals that call for percents and see if you have not made them. Do not miss reporting all the gain you have made.

Look Out For 16

Not 16 to 1, but you might need to look out still for what William Jennings Bryan might do before November 4. But get your BOOSTER COMMITTEE to work so that Goal 16 may be counted before it is won. That is one chicken we shall have to count before, but if you will get to work right away and keep right on working, you will win that one. But look out! But here the muse is getting me and we shall see whaet he has to tell:

The Last Call

Pastors! Pastors! Hear the summons
Heralding the finis call.
Now it comes with echoes ringing
For great faithfulness from all.
If you hear the tocsin sound,
Ring the brotherhood around,

Think how you the changes, too,
Rang on those who worked with you.

Workers! Workers! Soon rewarded
For your striving, you will be;
At Winona, banners waving,
We shall sing of Victory.
If your duty you have done,
Your own viet'ry will be won.
Quickly your report, return.
For that Victory, we yearn.

Brothers! Brothers! Turn your purses,
Up-side-down for once in life
If it has a scanty portion,
Talk it over with your wife.
Churches only reach the goal
If we all, with heart and soul
Make this Anno Domini
One of greatest VICTORY.

Pastors! Brothers! Sisters! Workers!
Time is short to August First.
And without our being twisters,
Let us do our best, not worst.
When we reach Winona, fair,
Victory in all the air.
"Best and Largest" it will be
With a hard-earned VICTORY.

Teaching to Win.   By W. E. Thomas

I am afraid that a good many times Sunday school teachers go into the presence of their classes without a definite purpose in view or a heaven-born determination to win. Of course the ultimate purpose of every teacher should be to win the scholar for Christ, but there are certain things which we believe are essential before that victory is reached. The teacher that is not sufficiently interested in his or her class so as to be burdened with their soul's welfare is not worthy to be a teacher. First of all if you are teaching to win you must have the confidence of your class. How can any one expect to win souls for Jesus Christ if your scholars do not believe in you as a servant of Jesus Christ. The question of the church, How can I, except some man should guide me (Acts 8:31), is the question that the scholar is asking of the teacher. The teacher must know the way. The old saying, Do not as I do, but do as I say, will not work in the teaching of the Word. You must be a living testimony of the saving power of the cross. There is one thought that I just want to touch in passing, you must be able to adjust yourself to the class you are teaching. In other words, if you are teaching boys you must be a boy, or girls you must be a girl. Again if you are teaching to win you must have an adequate knowledge of what you are trying to teach. Too long have we tolerated teachers who went before their classes with this excuse, I have been so busy this week that I haven't had time to study the lesson. The teacher who is able to present the lesson in a fascinating, inspiring way that will cause the scholar to go out and seek to bring others into the class is the teacher that has spent time in preparation and prayer and has an adequate knowledge of the Word. My last thought is this, if you are teaching to win you must seek to bring the pupil to the place where he will decide for Christ. I do not need to add that if you have failed to win the scholar for Jesus you have failed in teaching to win.

Flora, Indiana.

The Greatest Story Ever Told

From Out of the Ages a Message Has Come That Never Held a Clearer Call To Us All Than It Does Today

Thousands of years have come and gone since a Babe was born in Galilee.

Thousands of years!

And because this Babe was born, Wise Men came from afar to worship at the shrine of his manger-cradle.

But a little while—and he whose cradle had been a manger was called away, even in the very bloom of the most glorious manhood.

Yet the message that He left behind was never to perish!

Wise Men of to-day still worship His message, His memory and His name—even as did those other Wise Men of ages gone.

For that message was as clear as it was direct —as powerful as it was good. Interpreted, it involved Character in terms of Love and Service.

As never before—men of to-day are turning back to that simple message which has come down to us from out of the ages, because it is as practical as it is beautiful.

And what is practical is what we want.

It is practical to want peace and content-ment—and the power to find these was left to us by Jesus of Nazareth.

The story of the Babe who was born in a manger is the Greatest Story Ever Told!

Down to us through the ages has come the Church of God.

The church is not an end unto itself. The function of the church is but to bring to pass our Eternal Destiny expressed in a universal realiza-tion of the Fatherhood of God and the Brotherhood of man.

How well the church performs this mission depends upon the people in the church—upon that and nothing more.

Fundamentally, there is nothing wrong with the church—there is not, and there never has been.

If there be strong men and women in the church, her power for good is just in proportion— it can be no greater and no less.

It is a gratifying fact that the future of the church never looked brighter than it does to-day. There is a trend of strong men and women toward the church—a recognition that organized religion with a program is indispensable to the nation and the world.

Men and women are at last beginning to see that it is not a question as to whether we need the churches or not. That is not an open question.

Frankly, it reduces itself to this: Whether we shall strengthen and maintain the churches to our own lasting good—or neglect them to our con-fusion.

GENERAL ARTICLES

"The Church Compared to a Vine" By C. D. Whitmer

"Return, we beseech thee, O God of hosts; look down from heaven, and behold, and visit this vine." Psalms 80:14.

The ancient church which the Lord brought out of Egypt, is here compared to a vine. Christ, the Great Teach-er, used a like figure when he said: "I am the vine and ye are the branches." Let us consider some of the ways that the church may be compared to a vine.

1st The Root of the Vine.

The root of the vine is Christ. Now you know the root of a vine is not beautiful in appearance, but is an unsight-ly object. If you were to see the root, and nothing but the root, you would never dream that it was of any value. So when men saw Christ, they said: "There is no form, nor comeliness in him that we should desire him." When he is spoken of as a stone, he is said to be, "a stone disallowed of the builders," but this rejected stone has "become the head of the corner—" "the chief corner stone."

He was the root, but to men he appeared to be worth-

less, "a root out of dry ground." But this frail root, this root of David has sent forth a vine whose branches are filling the whole earth, and the nations are eating of the fruit with gladness and joy.

2nd The Weakness of the Vine

It is a clinging plant; it cannot stand alone; it cannot support itself. Consequently it throws out tendrils, and clings to some object for support. Well, Christians are weak; the church is weak. Nearly all the figures used to describe the church represent it as weak. For example, is the world compared to a harvest field and the disciples to "reapers?" Then the harvest is great and the laborers are few; is the church compared to a "flock?" it is a little flock to whom the Father will give the kingdom; is the church compared to a "bride," then she is represented as "coming up from the wilderness leaning upon the arm of her beloved." And here it is compared to a vine, that must have a rack, a trellis, or a frame to cling to for support. It is when the church feels this weakness that she is strong. Israel was safer when dwelling in tents amid desert sand and war-like tribe, feeling her weakness, and trusting in God, than when dwelling in fenced cities, trusting in her own might and the strength of her walls and towers.

3rd The Vine Though a Frail Plant, Grows Rapidly

How weak a plant Christianity appeared to be at the first, but how rapidly it grew. Peter planted it among the Gentiles when he preached to Cornelius, Philip, the Evangelist, carried it to Samaria; next it took root in the Syrian Antioch. Paul planted this precious vine all along the shores of the Mediterranean and in the towns and cities of Asia Minor. Long before his death it had taken root in the palaces of the Caesars. The Ethiopian eunuch carried a little slip of this vine into Africa, and there it took deep root and flourished for ages, yea, and about the same time it began to grow in the island of Great Britian where it has continued to flourish and bear fruit even to this day. And what more shall we say? For the time would fail us to tell how this vine has spread in the present age.

4th It is the Fruit of the Vine that Makes it of Value

It is for this and this alone, that men cultivate it. Some plants are valued for their roots, some for their bark, and others for their wood, but the vine is chiefly valued for its fruit. Christ says to his church, to his people, "In this is your Father glorified that ye bear much fruit." And again he says, "My Father is the husbandman," and every branch that beareth fruit, he purgeth it that it may bear more fruit.

5th The Vine Requires Pruning

Fruitless branches must be cut off. Christ says of such, "Men gather them and burn them." Or is it true that men and women may even be members of a church, prominent professors of religion, and yet be burned as worthless branches.

You will notice that this is actually necessary; the vine must be pruned if it is to be fruitful. So, too, the church must exercise gospel discipline; the worthless and barren must be cut off. But bear in mind that this pruning in the church must be done with great skill and prudence. A man with a sharp knife might soon spoil and ruin a splendid vine. And how much wisdom is needed in dealing with fruitless professors! A vine dresser might easily cut off branches that ought to be spared; or again, if he used the knife in an improper season, the vine may bleed to death. Alas, how many churches have been ruined by injudicious dealing with the members!

6th The Vine Grows on, and Beautiffies and Adorns Rocky and Unsightly Places

Such places as the sides of old buildings, the rocky and barren sides of hills and mountains are thus adorned. Vineyards were the beauty of Palestine. That land is almost a desert today. Its hillsides are rocky and bare; the terraces have been broken down. Where the vines once flourished, desolation now reigns. So, too, this vine beautifies and adorns the earth. Wherever it has been planted and carefully cultivated, there is spiritual beauty, and wherever it has been allowed to die, there desolation and ruin reign. How must the thoughtful traveler feel depressed as he surveys the barren and desolate appearance of Palestine, and remembers that where nothing stands today but naked rocks, vineyards once flourished. As he examines the face of the country, he sees the remains of the terraces that once supported the soil that nourished the vines. And the ruins of aqueducts that once furnished the water to irrigate them in the time of drouth.

And what must be the feelings of the thoughtful Christian who visits those lands where the Gospel once flourished, but where it was allowed to die, and where pagan darkness now reigns! Such a land for instance, as Asia Minor or Italy, and the greater part of Europe. There he can survey the ruins of the Seven Churches of Asia, there he will find the ruins of church edifices, the remains of baptistries, the relics of primitive Christianity—but about them a moral Sahara Desert.

7th The Vine Can be Propagated in Two Ways

(1) From the Seed and (2) from cuttings or branches. So, too, the Gospel churches are propagated, and Christianity extended in two ways,—by the seed of the kingdom, which is the Word of God; and by branches of the vine, that is, by believers themselves.

There are various ways in which the good seed may be sown by tracts, Bibles, etc. To propagate the vine by cuttings seems a severe way, but it is one that God has often used. When the storms of persecutions fell on the first church in Jerusalem, "They that were scattered abroad went everywhere preaching the word," and so the vine spread and took root in new places.

SOUTH BEND, INDIANA.

Character Building In Adolescence.   By H. E. Becknell

(An essay read during the late commencement exercises upon Mr. Becknell's graduation from Ashland College. He kindly granted the editor permission to publish his essay in The Evangelist; it was also published in the Purple and Gold, the college paper. Mr. Becknell is soon to leave as a Y. M. C. A. missionary to the Hawaiian Islands. —Editor.)

This is the age of child-worship. Never before in the history of man has such emphasis been placed upon the value of the child as at the present time. The place of youth in a nation's life indicates the future outlook for that nation. I use the term child-worship indiscriminately. We hear so much about the ancestor-worship of China and we have but to look at her standing in the progress of civilization to understand that such a reverence for age and decay can only beget stagnation and retrogression for her national life. Now that Christianity and the western civilization has penetrated China's wall of superstition and ignorance she too is casting away the shackles of her ancestor-worship and is turning to the training and educating of youth. The most hopeful sign for America's future is the attention she is now giving to her children. We have just recently been celebrating "Children's Week." A week set apart for the observance of the conditions and the possible improvements of childhood in our country. To the most casual observer the importance of the high value of a vigorous and well trained youth to our national life must be apparant.

It is with this realization of the importance of the training of our youth that I invite your attention to that particular period of human life commonly known as Adolescence. Generally youth begins from thirteen to fifteen years in boys and from eleven to fifteen in girls. It is a time of change, of new birth, for the higher and more completely human traits are now born. The qualities of soul and body that now emerge are far newer. Nature at this period arms youth for conflict with all the resources at her command—speed, power of shoulder, biceps, back, leg, jaw—strengthens and enlarges skull, thorax, makes man aggressive and prepares woman's frame for maternity. This is the period of plasticity, both mentally and physically. In no other period of life is the individual so receptive to the influences either for good or for ill as now. Now is the time when youth is ready to take upon itself the culture accumulated through ages of civilization. The habits formed during adolesence remain with the individual throughout life. Certainly it is highly important that youth shall be wisely guided through this storm and stress period and that only those qualities of manhood and womanhood which are high and noble shall be encouraged in their development.

Character might be in a sense defined as a plexus of motor habits, Dr. G. Stanley Hall says: "Habits determine the deeper strata of belief; thought is repressed action; and deeds, not words, are the language of complete men. The motor areas are closely related and largely identical with the psychic, and the entire muscle culture develops brain-centers as nothing else demonstrably does. Muscles are the vehicle of habituation, imitation, obedience, character, and even of manners and customs." Let us apply this information to the problems of youth. Adolescence is fraught with momentous changes of motor functions. These changes in a large part determine character. Youth at this period is intensely physical. At the beginning of adolescence a boy or girl is facing the critical character-building years of life. During this time of rapid growth and motor change good habits may be acquired and the bad ones already formed can be rooted out. Formation here saves the necessity of reformation later. A boy will develop, very generally, along lines chosen carefully for him by others, or in a haphazard way according to his own instincts and interests. In which of these two ways he will develop is a matter for careful concern. And what I have to say here concerning the development of the boy is equally as true for the girl.

It has not been until recently that educators and social workers have recognized the importance of this phase of youth. They consider it now almost a divinely bestowed gift to be able to take an adolescent boy or girl and so train and direct his or her interests and possibilities so as to realize the highest possible type of manhood. It is like the potter taking a shapeless although plastic pliable lump of clay and fashioning therefrom a beautiful vase. Youth is capable of being moulded into any form of character during these plastic years. It is for us who are leaders and who have caught the vision of the greater life to furnish the mould and to point the way. It was Mr. Roosevelt who said: "In the long run it is character that counts." This great American understood the problems of youth. He understood the needs of our nation. He saw that the future of our country depends, not upon our great wealth, nor upon our unlimited natural resources, nor upon our commercial position, but rather upon the ideals inculcated in the minds of the youth of our land. Character is the lasting, worthwhile reward for living. Adolescence is the time for setting the moulds. Character-building is the real adventure in life.

Nappanee, Indiana.

"Gogetter"

By J. A. McInturff, in his "Weekly News"

It was John A. Dickson of Chicago who according to the editor of the Evening American, coined this word, and gave the definition: "A gogetter is a man who goes and gets it." The editor then tells us that there are three kinds of "gogetters." First, the one who goes and gets. Second, the one who goes but fails to get. Third, the one who neither goes nor gets. Here is food for thought. The third class is represented by the "goods-box-carver" at the country store, the well dressed city street "parader" who has time to always "butt" into a business conversation, the girl who has no higher ideal of a lady than to spend her time on the streets looking at "low-browed" men, the son of a "a rich" man living off the gift of the dead, the fellow who has no interest in life but to eke out an existence, the "beast" who has no interest in humanity. Here is the most good-for-nothing class of people They are the fathers of the "red-men," the parents of the Bolshevik. No interest in self, except to live off others. This class of people "sometimes" get religion and enter churches. They want to live in the church just as they do in the community. They want the church to keep them from sin, take care of the children, cover up their sins, stop gossip about their life, and in a general way hold them up as "Christian people."

But let us consider the second class, those who go but

fail to get. In this class we have those who only "pretend," those who act out the character as a "stage-player." Also those who start on the run and stop before they get there. They either lose interest or become exhausted. Or perhaps, someone "laughs" at their walk, or they see another just before them who appears in the way. We have them in the church, but not a large number. Then, we have some who feel that they should reach the goal in a short time. Time is the Father of all success. Things obtained in a moment leave us in the same way. This class is the to-be-helped, they should be the object of "pity" and 'sympathy."

The first class—the one who goes and gets is the honorable man He is the man we look to as an example. But remember that this man is the product of a long "going" before he "gets." The great Hebrew Moses spent 80 years getting ready to free his people. The Great Man-God spent 30 years preparing to preach for only three years. The great missionary of the N. T., the Apostle Paul, was a "gogetter" and he went after the world and he "got" it for the church. He spent three years in Arabia before he preached to the world. Take as an example some of the great men of science. Darwin wanted to know how the soil of the earth was made so he covered a certain amount of ground with chalk, then waited and measured how much soil the earth worm would throw up above the chalk. It took him 30 years, but he got it. Prof. Michelson of the University of Chicago who is the winner of the Nobel prize for physics wanted to know how "rigid" the earth was so he planted a long pipe in the ground, and as you know that the tide rises in a glass of water or a small pond or even in a dewdrop, only it does not rise so much as on the ocean he measured the pull of the moon on the earth in his pipe, allowing for the times that the moon was off to one side. He figured how much the moon pulled the earth out of shape, and he was able to tell how rigid the earth is. He learned that the earth would not be more solid if it was cold steel But this took time. So let us in our "religious experience" remember that it takes time to do great things. To be a real "gogetter" we must first "go" and "keep" going, and after a long time we will "get." In India where one of the apostles went after the "suffering" of the early church we have an unwritten saying of Jesus which was taught by him, and it is carved in the cold stone of an ancient city's wall: "Jesus on whom be peace, has said 'The world is merely a bridge; ye are to pass over it, and not to build your dwellings upon it.' " Real life is a "going" and after we go far enough we will receive the reward. We "get" the "dwelling" after we "pass over."

Goshen, Indiana.

The Fourfold Gift

A physician has said that every human being needs the blessing of God through the fourfold gift of work, play, love and worship.

Work of some useful sort there must be, if life is to be sane and worth the living. To keep tense nerves from snapping and toil from becoming drudgery the rest of recreation must be found in some form. It is love that supplies the motive for endeavor. No one seeking only his own good ever reaches his highest success or finds satisfaction in achievement. And the life that does not link its efforts, its affections and its pleasures with God Himself is missing the meaning and the crown of existence. The swelling tide of thankfulness when days are sweet, the uplifted look for guidance when problems bewilder, the swift cry for help in time of danger, and the belief that all our treasures are safe in a Hand more strong and tender than our own, belong of right to every soul.—Exchange.

"If our love were but more simple,
    We should take Him at His word;
And our lives would be all sunshine
    In the sweetness of our Lord."

THE BRETHREN PULPIT

The Present Need of and the Challenge to the Christian College

(Baccalaureate sermon, Ashland College, May 29, 1920 by President Edwin E. Jacobs, Ph., D.)

TEₓT: But ye are a chosen generation, a royal priesthood, a peculiar people that ye should show forth the praise of him who hath called you out of darkness into his marvelous light.—I Peter 2: 9.

These words were, of course, addressed to an earlier people than we are today and they bore at the time a deeply religious significance yet in the light of present day conditions, they could as well be addressed to the members of a Christian college. For, young people, who live in the atmosphere of a modern Christian college, who imbibe from day to day from all that is best of the world's ideals and thought, who enter so largely into the rich inheritance of all time, who enjoy all the advantages of a society to which they as yet have made but small contribution, certainly are a peculiar people, a chosen generation. They by all the gifts and graces of society ought to constitute a regal priesthood dedicated to holding high the best in our present day civilization.

Now the institutionalization of a people's ideals is the best measure of their civilization. That is, the making certain both by legal enactment and by force of public sentiment, their ideas of what is of most worth, constitutes their best achievement. Greece institutionalized her ideals of physical beauty in her games. Rome did likewise with her legal ideals. The Hebrews are remembered today because of their religion. These elements together with others are the priceless inheritance of these decayed nations. And while we stand in awe before the earthworks of ancient Egypt or the Mound Builders of America, the imposing element is not their size, for they are insignificant when compared with even the humblest mountain, but it is the fact that they represent some ideal of these all but forgotten people, that they were conceived by the human mind and brought to perfection by the human hand.

So the evolution of the ideal, the quest eternal of that which is just above us and all around us and which is just within our reach by standing on tiptoe, that which we may get only when we are in our second breath—this has been the lure of the world's true elite. And now if it could be shown that the Christian college contributed in any large way to the realization of this idealism, if it is a lantern over the road, then the college would need no other excuse for its existence. This occasion offers time for the discussion of but a few of these ideals, viz., America's ideals in culture, education and religion, and I may be allowed to weave all these together as I go along.

Now in the establishing of a nation's ideals, education and religion have always played the major role. Neither religion nor education is directly concerned with material greatness but it must be regarded as the technique necessary to ends far greater than itself. Quantitative production belongs to business, not to education. So many dollars invested, so many dollars returned, is a matter for Dunn or Bradstreet, not for college boards or faculties! Quality of production is the true measure of the usefulness of both the school and the church. Hence, the institutions and ideals of a civilization must always be the concern of the school and the church. Commerce may wish to leave a nation's ideals as it found them but religion and education can not so do. It is their business to energize, enthuse, emotionalize, and reconstruct the individual and to develop whatever of idealism is possible.

Now the question at once arises, What is the need this hour in America in regards to her idealism? Is it as high as it ought to be? Does she need more of greed or more of grace? More of wealth or more of welfare? More politics or better policies? More of commerce or more of conscience? Now that the war is over, does America need to be buttressed by the best ideals of her men and women? Does she need to revive that race idealism with which she entered the war, when, as Lord Churchill said, she presented the grandest spectacle in all history when she flung her wealth and blood into the struggles for world-wide ideals of Democracy?

1. Well, out of this conflict we were told that America would emerge shorn of her greed, chastened of her lust for power, that the spiritual would superceed the material, that the worship of money would no longer replace the worship of God.

2. We were also assured too, that this war was one to end war.

3. And we were to emerge with a newer Christianity, sometimes called the dough-boy religion. Man was to live by deed, not by creed, to live by works, not by words. The cup of cold water given in the name of a disciple was to be the test of religion and service was to spell salvation.

4. Moreover, America was to lead the world in her culture and in education. Now, out of the war we did get some good things, beyond any question. Whether we got the above as set down, might well be questioned, but we did get a fine sense of cooperation, of sacrifice, of the extension of the function of the government. We got something of a world consciousness, certain mechanical improvements, and certain other and intangible values. Also certain educational changes.

But we also got an outrageous increase in the use of the cigarette, which may, at some time, become a national peril, for aught I know. We got government by injunction and interference. We got a limitation of freedom of speech, high and in many cases extortionate prices, certain Bolshevism, strikes, the killing of many of our best physical men, and the unsteadiness of business and of labor generally. But our idealism, what of it? Is not the rather fine idealism which we hugged to our hearts in '17 passing? Are we not a bit disappointed over the results of the struggle? Are not at this very moment the politicians of the country playing football with what promised to be the finest achievement of the race?—an opportunity for lasting peace? And the two great political parties are both right now blind and halt and dumb and lame in their idealism! But ye? Well ye are a chosen people, a royal priesthood set apart to life's best and noblest idealism.

Now if I am right in my analysis of the situation, if we are suffering from an after-war depression in our idealism, what is the cure? First of all, we ought to lament no failure but by all the etheric processes of the new birth, get genuine Christian idealism to be again the goal of our endeavors. What a charge!—for men to live from day to day careless of all that Christ taught, defying the powers of righteousness, laughing to scorn the golden rule, sneering at, "faith, hope, charity, but the greatest of these is charity," praying with lips of brass, "our Father who art in heaven, thy kingdom come, thy will be done on earth as it is in heaven," but not believing in it, and then bemoan a world war of unprecedented horror and blood! What else could be expected? Building not upon Christian ideals, but upon the ideals of Hegel and Nietasche, magnifying, not the spiritual, but the material; relying, not upon justice, but upon force; trusting, not in brother man but in twenty-five mile guns; putting trust not in diplomacy, but in secret treaties, what could the world not expect in nineteen fifteen? And what may we not expect again, say, in nineteen thirty?

The challenge now is to try, really try, Christian culture—the Christianity of Jesus. Stop babbling about its failure, but give it a trial. Pay less attention to deporting "Reds," but deport "red" ideals! Fear not Bolshevism, but make Bolshevism impossible in America, the America of Washington, Jefferson and Lincoln! Support Christian schools and colleges. Make both schools and teachers, churches and preachers, not beggars and paupers, but give them the means of power. Let us set our faces as flint against self-seeking, time-serving politicians. Put men of vision at the head of affairs. Turn the dishonest, the incompetent, and the ignoramus out of doors and no longer make "democracy the cult of the incompetent," either in government or in the church, or in the school.

It is not too late to catch up the tattered ends in America and go forward. Idealism is not dead, but must it take another world war to arouse a sentiment such as this? Must it take a world war to arouse a sentiment such as this?

I have a rendezvous with death
At midnight in some flaming town
When spring trips north again this year
And I to my pledged word am true,—
I shall not fail that rendezvous.

This sentiment, that of a young American who laid his life a willing sacrifice upon the altar of his devotion, is worth more to the world than millions made in high prices of steel or in extortionate prices for sugar! But, of what value would they not be, if they could have been the ideal of all the long and happy and lasting days of peace? I think one could be hopeful of America if such ideals could be translated into ideals of peace.

Did not the poet speak, not only for the heroes of this late war, but for those also of every war and of every time, and of all of those good and true who have labored and passed on, when he said

"Take up your quarrel with the foe;
To you with failing hands we throw
The torch. Be yours to hold it high,
If ye break faith with those who die,
We shall not sleep though poppies grow
In Flanders field."

Not to break faith with all those choice souls who have lived and labored, and loved and passed on before, from the days of Jesus until now—that is the challenge, that is the need. Men and women, clear of vision, strong of purpose, trained in intellect, and chasten of soul, alone can make this happy ideal an accomplished fact.

Ashland, Ohio.

Faithfulness, the Crowning Characteristic

(The following was taken from a daily paper of Johnstown, Pennsylvania)

"The Crowning Characteristic, Faithfulness or Loyalty," was the theme of the baccalaureate sermon delivered at the Conemaugh Brethren church last evening to the 12 girl graduates of the Conemaugh High school by the Rev. George H. Jones, pastor the church. The Rev. Mr. Jones took his text from Isaiah 11:5: "And faithfulness (loyalty) shall be the girdle of his loins."

He said in part:

Through Toil and Drudgery.

"In a land where no royal monarch sits enthroned and confers titles of nobility, there must be some way in which the citizens of that land can have conferred upon them recognition for nobility of character—natures made noble by self-conquest. An aristocracy established superior to that of birth. (We must distinguish between enobling a name and enobling a nature.) One is conferred as a royal gift, the other patiently acquired through toil and drudgery.

"Natures manifest themselves by characteristics. Characteristics are the expression of the natures which come to us through heredity or self-conquest or through both. The hereditary traits we have found to be largely physical, those of self-development; spiritual, expressing themselves in social and religious observances. The latter are the product of environment and self-expression.

"The text is a prophecy concerning the coming deliverer. It is a message primarily referring to Jesus. It reveals the prominent characteristics of the deliverer when he should come, faithfulness or loyalty. The prophet speaks of it as a girdle, compassing about, binding, encircling, or belting him. The loins were a symbol of strength to the Hebrew mind. The imagery called into his consciousness readiness for struggle. It is thus referred to in the message of the prophet. 'Symbolizing strength in labor and loyalty shall be the symbol of his strength?' This does no outrage to the prophet's meaning.

Importance of Loyalty

"Prof. Royce of Harvard university published a book some years ago. It was a powerful plea emphasizing the supreme importance of loyalty to every human soul. He contends that loyalty is one of the most essential traits of the most noble human characters. He says further, 'that it is impossible to sustain any of our most cherished virtues without it, whether to a man, an institution or a principle. With-

out it the individual becomes unreliable, undependable, vacillating, weak and worthless for any undertaking.

"It is the foundation for the future, whether of church school, home, political liberties, or social industrial relationships. It is a task beyond human effort to inculcate it in any life after youth has passed. It must be instilled in childhood and youth.

"Nobility of character emerges from loyalty to ideals. Better not be at all, than not be noble," writes Tennyson. "My road," said Canning, "must be through character to power. I will try no other course, and I am sanguine enough to believe that this course, though perhaps not the quickest, is surest." Shakespeare wrote: "First to thine ownself be true, and it must follow, as the day the night, thou canst not then be false to any man.'"

Await Loyal Leadership.

"O! Youth! the time for foundations! The time for great loyalties! The time for life's challenges! Great movements are only possible through great loyalties. Today we wait some great loyal soul's leadership. Without such the turmoil and unrest will irresistably lead to chaos. Great objects that challenge our loyalties are made to loom larger each succeeding generation. The power to do this is the secret of America's greatness. Lack of vision in this respect makes the youth of any land helpless and only too often worthless.

"The compulsion of an overpowering objective is the challenge of the day.

"The growing menace to the home life of the land, called divorce, would fade and disappear, if there were larger numbers of young people loyal to the home.

"Here parental wisdom and firmness are the safeguard that control youth and point out the danger of excessive recreation of a doubtful nature and lead or guide into sensible garb and expenditure.

"The homes of the nation are its last bulwarks against evils of any kind; relaxing here opens the way to the end that the most powerful nations of antiquity reached. Extravagance, youthful folly, disobedience, sowing of wild oats and a myriad of lesser excesses all point to the same end.

Loyalty to The Church

"Piety, a term so often used scornfully, yet is essential to our highest natures, here gets its birth and impetus.

"Here absence and carelessness or indifference give rise to all kinds of moral and ethical disturbances.

"To the observant student of history, there has been no notable advance in Christian civilization unless preceded by a revival of Christian faith and piety.

"The great uplifting and levelling power of the public schools is one of the phenomena of American social life. Here social intercourse makes the nation a real melting pot. Here are fused the colder blooded northern immigrants with the hot-blooded southern types.

"Here common studies are making likeminded the rising generation of new Americans.

"Here Jew and Gentile form friendships that no ancestral bias nor animosity can undermine.

"Here teacher and custom are slowly building into the future citizens a respect for a distinctive American institution that prolongs the life and increases the happiness of our people—the American Sabbath.

"Here in this great mass of youth appeals are made and again for hospitals, homes, welfare organizations, sanitary precautions, and hygienic rules that promise greater things yet to come.

"Toleration too, for the religious beliefs of the other home is unconsciously developed.

Loyalty to Political Liberties.

"The chief objections to our political life have come almost entirely from those who have been born and trained under another form of government. Acquaintance, thorough and broad, with our political principles, has made loyal citizens out of all who have learned, guided by a right spirit.

"The perpetuation of all that is best in our political life can only be assured, when those who make what changes are necessary, have proven to be loyal citizens. The elimination of what is proven bad can only be safely entrusted to those who are in hearty accord with our best thought and interests.

Loyalty to Our Social and Industrial Relationships

"It is the lack of such loyalty that makes the present orgy possible. The lack of contact in a social way with manual laborers, and seeking of recreation abroad, has severed almost every tie but that of business interests with capitalist and laborer.

"Customs which benefit and with which there is no contact will receive less attention as the citizen absents himself from them. The growing abuses in our industrial life must be corrected but only by the loyal and religious thinkers. For back of all loyalty is the spirit of the Man of Galilee.

"This Deliverer, eagerly anticipated by Isaiah, has the secret of all real progress and stands ready to reveal it to every disciple. The secret is the possession of the same characteristics that he had. First and fundamental in importance was that of the text: 'And faithfulness shall be the girdle of his loins.'

"Youth is the time to engrave characteristics on the soul. Divine revelation points out the crown of life to the seeker after royal qualities. The destiny of the soul is determined by the characteristics acquired in the present world. 'Be thou faithful, loyal, until death and I will give thee a crown of life.'"

J. A. Garber
PRESIDENT

Our Young People at Work

G. C. Carpenter
SECRETARY

To the Christian Endeavorers of America

A Fortieth Anniversary Crusade, from September 1, 1920, to February 2, 1921, has just been approved by the Board of Trustees of the United Society of Christian Endeavor. The affirmative vote is probably the largest ever cast for a Christian Endeavor campaign. The five goals of the Crusade are as follows:

1. 600,000 vacant seats filled at Sunday and mid-week services.
2. 600,000 new Christian Endeavors.
3. 600,000 young people enrolled for systematic Bible study, study of Church History, Stewardship, Missions, Personal Evangelism, Social and Expert Endeavor.
4. At least 600,000 young people urged to accept Christ and unite with the church.
5. One week of solicitation of funds from individuals for the adequate financing of Christian Endeavor at home and abroad. (The exact date of this campaign and the amount to be sought will be determined at a meeting of the trustees and field secretaries to be held in Boston July 21 and 22, 1920.)

Ten Thousand Christian Endeavor Societies Must Enlist For This Great Crusade Before July 15, 1920

We ask your society to do these three things now:
1. Endorse the Crusade by vote of the society or Executive Committee.
2. Appoint a Captain and five assistants to organize and direct the Crusade for your society.
3. Send in your enlistment to Executive Secretary, Carroll M. Wright, on the attached blank.

A Manual of Information, giving full suggestions for reaching every objective of the Crusade, will be sent free as soon as the enrollment of your society is received. Everything is ready for a great campaign that will strengthen your society and church and help win and train the young people of the world for Christ.

See that your society is one of the first to respond. Send in your enlistment blank today.

Yours in His Service,
E. P. GATES,
General Secretary.

United Society of Christian Endeavor
Mt. Vernon and Joy Streets, Boston, Mass.

YOU CAN COUNT ON US

Our Society Will Do Its Best in The Fortieth Anniversary Crusade

We have appointed ....

Whose address is ....
to serve as Captain for our society.

Name of society ....

Location ....

Name, official position and address of person sending in this enlistment ....

....

....

Please fill out this blank at once and send to Carroll M. Wright, Executive Secretary, Mt. Vernon and Joy Streets, Boston, Mass.

"Help Our Church"

The New-Old Slogan of Christian Endeavor.—Illinois Leads in a New Campaign

A New Folder That Will Help Your Society

By Rev. Francis E. Clark

President of the Unitey Society of Christian Endeavor and of the World's Christian Endeavor Union

"HELP OUR CHURCH"

The first Christian Endeavor society was organized to

help the Willston Church, and because it "helped our church" the plan has been adopted by more than a hundred thousand other churches in all parts of the world; and most of them have called their "help-our-church" societies by the Christian Endeavor name.

But it has remained for the Illinois union to suggest a special campaign with "Help Our Church" for the slogan. The suggestion of these wide-awake leaders is that two months be set apart for increased emphasis upon definite support by Christian Endeavorers of their own churches and their own denominations.

Of course, in a sense this should be a campaign that knows no end, but to call special attention to these important features this idea of spending two months in a special campaign, with "Help Our Church" as a war cry, is an admirable one. It emphasizes the most fundamental of all Christian Endeavor principles, loyalty to church and denomination, and calls attention anew to the things for which Christian Endeavor has been striving from the beginning.

The campaign calls for emphasis on four lines of society activity: church-attendance, denominational study, Sunday school evangelism, and increased financial support of denominational missions.

The plan and standards are as follows:

1. Church Attendance.

a. Evening Service. 100 per cent of the society membership at each Sunday evening service for the two months. Society sitting in a body.

Systematic effort to bring outsiders to Sunday evening service by personal invitations. Each member to speak, write, or phone an invitation to at least one person a week. Lookout committee responsible.

b. Midweek Prayer Service. Organized campaign for attendance and participation.

Society prayer meeting committee to be responsible

for notifying members in advance as to topic and urging their participation.

2. Denominational Education.

a. A series of short talks at the society prayer meetings on the different boards of the denomination. President responsible.

b. Correspondence with denominational secretaries to find out what is expected of the society—results to be reported to the society. Secretary responsible.

c. A mission-study class, with particular emphasis on denominational work. Missionary committee.

3. Sunday School Evangelism.

Each teacher to speak individually at least once to each member of his class urging the acceptance of Jesus Christ as a personal Saviour.

4. Increased Financial Support of Denomination.

a. Enrollment of members in Tenth Legion.

b. Presentation of needs of denominational missionary work by the pastor or a denominational leader.

c. An "every-member canvass" for missions.

Missionary committee, treasurer, and finance committee responsible.

Here is a splendid method for making effective Sections 26 and 27 of the Efficiency Chart.

The executive committee of the board of trustees of the United Society of Christian Endeavor unanimously indorsed the plan, and recommended that it be pushed by every union and adopted by every society.

A simple method for introducing the plan would be for each union to secure a supply of these leaflets (which will be furnished by the United Society for $1.00 a hundred, postpaid), and send the leaflet, with a letter heartily commending the plan and signed by three or more representative pastors, to every pastor and society represented in the union.

SEND ALL MONEY FOR
General Home, Kentucky and
Foreign Missions to

MISSIONS

WILLIAM A. GEARHART
General Missionary Secretary
906 Conover Bldg., Dayton, O.

LOST CREEK, KENTUCKY

Since our last report of the work, different things have come into our lives. The Lord has especially this spring and summer opened the way for us to attend different conferences, the greatest of which was the one at Chicago, The Victorious Life Conference, held in the Moody Tabernacle Church. For some years now, or recent years, (This conference was only organized in 1915, an interdenominational conference on the Fundamentals of the Bible) it has ben our desire to attend this conference. This year, the last of May, the way very unexpectedly opened, as we did not know that we could go until a couple hours before we started, and we had the glorious privilege of spending one week under the greatest spiritual uplift that it has ever been our privilege to enjoy. I was very hospitably entertained in the home of Brother Russell Humberd, who with his good wife were very kind to us.

This conference was great, and the Holy Spirit was present in a remarkable way, because Christ was exalted, the whole Bible was accepted as the inspired word of God, more attention was given to prayer and the spiritual life than to the machinery of it, and as a result of this, the spiritual uplift was very marked.

There were two marked surprises to us in this week's Conference. The first was, to

see in what kind of a building the great Moody Church worships, and the second to see and know something of what that church, not a denomination, is doing for the Master.

This church is located in the heart of Chicago, near Lincoln Park, about as fashionable as any place in the city. we should believe. But the building, inside and out, is very, very plain, no plush covered pews, yea no pews at all for seats. Only benches made from scantlings and planks. No polished, or carpeted floor, but a floor of shavings, and other things about it in keeping with this simplicity. And should you criticize them for worshipping in such a place, as a Kansas City man did when shown the place by its pastor, Mr. Rader? If so, listen to what this Church is doing. "Be ye doers of the Word and not hearers only deceiving your own selves."

This church, besides supporting two pastors, and other local expenses, which are heavy, the last year raised $42,000, with which, seventy two missionaries were supported on the Foreign Field, and this coming year they have pledged $61,000 for the same work. One woman's class or organization, of about eighty members, many of whom work for their living, raised $6,000 last year, and this coming year have pledged $8,00 for the same. One woman of this class, who washes

for her living. gave $200 of this money, and others somewhat accordingly.

The climax of the Conference came on Thursday night, when it closed or merged into the Missionary Rally of the church. The sermon was preached by Mr. Rader, and at its conclusion, when the invitation was given for volunteers among the young men for the Foreign Field, eighty one young men stepped out for this service. To see these young men take this stand, was indeed a sight never to be forgotten. Surely any church or people with the Bible and missionary vision which these people have will have life, and have it these people have will have life, and "have it more abundantly."

Our work here has been holding up fine, though we have been hampered some by contagious diseases, which are now about over. We have ben having a hard fight with the "moonshiners." With the closing of the open saloons, came the opportunity of the Mountaineers to make the stuff, and he took advantage of it. The lure of the dollar was too strong for them, and to our surprise, some of the people living right near Riverside engaged in its making. They received $40 per gallon for the stuff, and of course that was a temptation to some. When we learned of it, we fought them, with the sword of the Spirit. At first we went into the woods helping to try to locate the stills,

Then we repeatedly preached against it. Then later we went to the "Shiners" and had personal talks with them: It now looks as if they are going to quit, and if they do, that will mean a big forward step for us. Our county officials like it so well themselves that we are helpless in getting help through them. But the National Prohibition Enforcement organization is giving help, and that counts.

Our three Sunday schools are now booming. The one on the Big Branch seems to be taking on such a new life not heretofore evident. Then one of our Christian Endeavor workers, a young woman, has opened a Sunday school up on Lost Creek, right near the heart of the citadel of the "shiners." She is having good attendance and is roing fine work there.

Our Sunday school gave a 4th of July program, on Saturday the 3rd. There were two or three hundred people here, and we had a fine time. A program by the Sunday school, then two addresses by local men, then athletic contests, dinner. etc. We were very happily surprised to see our nearest "moonshiners" present, one of whom said, "This is the first time I ever spent a day like this with good people, and I did enjoy it." This looks very good too, for the future.

School opens the 19th of this month. The attendance now promises well, in fact it now looks as if we would be overcrowded, especially in the grades. To see the situation as it actually is now, and to know it, does not lead one to believe that our work at Riverside in the grades is yet over, or that there is not the need any more. A young man who attended here last year, and boarded at the dormitory, but at the close of school in March, went to Georgia. writes that he will be back for this next year, and is bringing a Georgian with him.

Our revival will begin the last Sunday in this month, led by Evangelist I. D. Bowman.

May. we ask that you pray for us, that the church members here may be strengthened, and sinners won from the darkness of sin into the marvelous light of the glory of God?

G. E. DRUSHAL.

A LETTER FROM OUR MISSIONARY SECRETARY

Here I am in the land of flowers, fruits, delightful climate, splendid opportunities and best of all, faithful and happy brethren and sisters of the Brethren churches.

I have been royally entertained wherever I have been. Thus far I have visited the following churches: Whittier, Long Beach, First Church in Los Angeles, La Verne, Lathrop. Manteca and Turlock. Showed the Kentucky slides in nearly all of these churches. Opportunity was given to these dear people to contribute to the Kentucky Light Plant Fund, and without urging in the least, these churches have given liberal donations. We still lack several hundred dollars in having sufficient to meet the entire expense of the installation of the plant.

Maybe there are some of our dear brethren and sisters over the brotherhood who did not read the appeals we had in the Evangelist some time ago for donations, will be glad to have the privilege to help pay for the plant.

I am now in the home of our dear Brother Leatherman, pastor of the Turlock church. Brother and Sister Leatherman are doing a great work for the Master and he will surely continue to bless them in their labors. Brethren Kimmel, Wall, Bauman, Shively, Milo Wolfe, Platt and others have been so good to me, and have entertained me so royally that I feel very much at home out here in California. In many respects. this country makes us think of the Garden of Eden, where Adam and Eve enjoyed the many beautiful things of God's creation.

I will leave here this P. M. for Sunnyside where the lecture will be given Sunday the

11th and at Spokane on the 13th. Expect to visit the Waterloo church and perhaps several others in that vicinity.

It is a great blessing to me to meet our people face to face and I am sure it will make my work as General Missionary. Secretary more pleasant and profitable in the future. I hope to visit most of our churches in our brotherhood as time and opportunity presents itself. I have started with the western churches because this is the best time for me to be away from my work for several weks. Rev. W. C. Teeter is looking after the most important matters in my absence.

The brethren out here on the coast are very much disturbed over the article written by our Brother Clarence E. Kolb, which was published in Evangelist number 23 on the subject, "Why I am Opposed to the Interchurch World Movement." They feel that if it is sarcasm (and most of them are inclined to think it is) it misrepresents this facts, and would lead those who read it to infer that all those who are opposed to the Interchurch World Movement, are not deeply interested in Home and Foreign Missions, Publishing House, Evangelism, etc. They would like to call the brotherhood's attention to the Easter offering reports in the Brethren Missionary and the Evangelist, which will appear soon, to indicate their interest in missionary activities, and other reports printed from time to time which show their interest in other lines of activity, which have to do with the progress of our denomination. If the article was not intended to be sarcasm, they think it should never have ben printed for the reason that it opposes the best interests of our beloved brotherhood. We trust every member of our brotherhood will strive to exercise charity in all things. Will write later concerning my visit to the other churches.

Fraternally,

WILLIAM A. GEARHART,
General Missionary Secretary.

NEWS FROM THE FIELD

ASHLAND, OHIO

Commendable progress is being made by the First Brethren congregation, worshiping in the College chapel, under the helpful leadership of J. A. Garber as pastor. The membership has ben increased materially during the year. Among the recent additions were Brother Martin Shively and wife whom we welcome into our midst. As the result of a canvass for funds with which to erect a church building $9,488.17 has been subscribed, $4,415.17 of which is already paid. The church lot was purchased sometime ago. The Sunday school is fortunate in having Geo. S. Baer as superintendent. He is quite successful in overcoming the usual "Summer slump" by inaugurating June 13 an eight weeks' contest between classes. Based upon enrollment it is possible for each scholar to make five points every Sunday as follows: Two points for attendance, one point each for on time, lesson studied, Bible read daily. In addition a class can gain 25

points for each new scholar enrolled. At the close of the contest August 1 a recognition service will be held for the class securing the largest percentage.

The Woman's Missionary Society. is an important factor in this congregation. The weekly prayer meeting and Christian Endeavor are also maintained.

We are hopeful that the Ashland City church will continually extend her influence for good.

IBA D. SLOTTER.

LA VERNE, CALIFORNIA

Some time ago we had Brother Bell with us for a two weeks meeting and we had a very blessed time, got well acquainted with Bell. and the verdict on every hand was "He rings true to the Bible."

Ten souls came out, and have since been baptized and received into the church,then the church was most wonderfully blessed for while the messages were saturated with

evangelism there seemed to be a point of contact in which the Christians were blest.

We shall be glad to have Brother Bell with us again at the first opportunity. and for a more extended period.

It may interest you to know that the pastor at this place was driven to build a home for himself, and that when it was finished the members gave us a house-warming, after a short program the family were called into a room in which a paper rose had been hung and from which six strings were hanging, each member was to take a string and shake the rose, then see which one had shaken the most petals down, we pulled all right, but there fluttered out a shower of one dollar bills—one hundred and eleven in all.

At the quarterly business meeting the church concluded to put up with their pastor for another year, and raised his salary.

At this writing Eld. A. J. Hixson (who is eighty-six years of age) is very weak, it seems to be a general break down of his system, but he has a most blessed hope of seeing "The King in his beauty," and is earnestly longing for that time.

We are praying that the National Conference may be led by the Holy Spirit, and that great things will be planned for the future of our church.

Yours in the Blessed Hope,
THOS. H. BROAD.

WINONA TABERNACLE FUND

Herewith find report of those churches having paid their apportionment to the Winona Tabernacle building fund.

Muncie, Indiana,	$ 11.56
Mexico, Indiana,	17.00
Corinth, Indiana,	7.16
Ardmore, So. Bend, Indiana,	8.50
Denver, Indiana,	21.25
Roann, Indiana,	9.00
Goshen, Indiana,	85.00
Loree, Indiana,	34.00
Nappanee, Indiana,	72.25
Wabash, Indiana,	15.47
Pioneer, Ohio,	4.00
Uniontown, Penna.	13.00
Berne, Indiana,	25.50
Geo. Barnhart,	1.00
Total	$324.69

I presume that a misunderstanding exists among the churches of most states for as you see Indiana has most of the representation. Our total apportionment to the new Tabernacle as a Church whole is $2500.00. May we not have a response from the churches' at once as the Tabernacle is almost finished and the money is badly needed. We have pledged to pay now let us do it. Make all checks payable to Herman E. Roscoe, Goshen, Indiana. The apportionment is 17 cents per member from each and every congregation.

Yours Truly,
H. E. ROSCOE, Treas.

BENEVOLENCE REPORT

I beg to submit for publication all funds received to date for the Superannuated fund of the Brethren Church in conference districts as follows:

Indiana

Goshen,	$201.50
New Paris, W. M. S.	10.00
New Paris, Church,	92.00
College Corners,	8.75
Muncie,	12.00
Teegarden,	3.50
Roann,	5.00
Tiosa,	15.00
North Liberty,	21.60
Mexico.	14.00
South Bend,	50.00
Flora,	26.30
Burlington,	14.61
South Bend (Ardmore)	12.00
Clay City,	11.96
Dadwin,	10.00
Nappanee,	50.00
Roann, (Center Chapel)	6.00
Loree,	32.00
Total	$596.22

Tennessee

Limestone, (Vernon Chapel)	11.00
Total	$ 11.00

Kanemorado

Portis,	5.00
J. S. C. Spikerman (Marysville, Mo.)	4.00
Morrill (Kansas)	20.13
Beaver City (Nebraska)	37.00
Total	$ 66,13

Pennsylvania

Uniontown,	20.50
Allentown,	20.00
Martinsburg,	14.71
Altoona,	21.74
Vandergrift,	7.00
Masontown,	20.00
McKee,	15.00
Johnstown,	20.00
Meyersdale,	50.00
Highland Church (Mariana)	12.75
Philadelphia S. School,	32.06
Philadelphia Church,	19.29
Berlin,	37.22
Waynesboro,	29.05
Listie,	7.91
Johnstown 3rd Church,	18.00
Total	$353.14

Ohio

Bryan,	20.00
Bellefontaine,	22.00
Louisville,	17.81
Canton,	30.23
West Alexandria,	6.35
New Lebanon,	14.03
Ashland,	45.00
Ankenytown,	12.80
Clayton,	11.70
Fremont,	22.64
Middlebranch,	10.50
Fairview Church, W. Samel,	7.50
Fostoria,	7.25
Smithville (Zion Hill)	5.00
Total	$232.81

Maryland-Virginia

Pleasant Grove (Williamsburg)	28.73
Roanoke.	14.50
Washington, D. C.,	30.00
Hagerstown,	45.00
Hollins (Mt. View Church,)	10.00
Total,	$128.23

California-Oregon

Turlock,	22.85
Los Angeles 1st Church,	25.10
Pomona,	30.92
Sunnyside, Wash.,	45.45
Long Beach,	50.00
Lathrop,	7.80
Torlock S. School,	10.00
Total,	$192.12

Illikota

Hudson, Iowa Church,	16.13
Cerro Gordo, Ill,	13.05
Pleasant Grove W. M. S.,	6.25
Waterloo,	50.00
Leon Union Chapel,	2.00
Leon Crown Chapel,	2.36
Total,	$ 89.79

Michigan

Campbell Church,	48.75
Total,	$ 48.75

Have also received contributions from individuals from various parts of the Brotherhood amounting to $64.50. These amounts as given above total about eighteen hundred dollars and I believe we can make our total at least two thousand dollars by conference time. Let those churches that are still on the delinquent list made a special effort to send their money as soon as possible in order that we may make a full report at Winona.

Sincerely yours,
HERMAN E. ROSCOE.
Secretary Benevolence Board.

FROM ASHLAND, OREGON

"Editor Brethren Evangelist:

While we have no great report to make here in Ashland, still under the leadership of Miss Detwiler, we are reaching the people of Ashland by Bible study classes. She has five regular classes during the week held in homes in different sections of the city, and the people are all very much interested in their studies. The lessons began with Genesis and are going right through the Old Testament.

"On Sunday evenings, the Young People's Win-One-Band meets, and already three of them have confessed Christ.

"The adverse conditions here are doubtless known, and we realize it is only through entire faith in the Lord, that we can go forward at all, for everything depends upon our willingness to let God work out his plans through us.

"At this time it would be a very material help to have Brethren locate in Ashland, which is a desirable home city, with delightful surroundings. To our eastern friends we would like to advise that there are wonderful possibilities on this coast for Christian work, as well as good opportunities for making a livelihood."

(Left Unsigned).

Miss Voda Brower was appointed church correspondent in the winter, and the above was her first effort, written a few months ago, since which time the hospital has been her lot and death her close pursuant. But God gave the victory, despite the repeated operations, and there is one more young life which promises fair for future service. Her letter was left in my care, but I was voluntarily with her in the hospital at first, then of necessity for a few days more. But Psalms 103:3 is still as true as ever. This much to explain why correspondence had to be pushed aside for the time.

The weekly Bible classes had to be kept up till the course closed in June, when the work had progressed far enough for the Evangelistic and Bible Study League to come in and hold their promised meeting. They did not respond, and now the Summer is full of Chautauqua, followed by a Summer Bible School. This latter may help to lay the foundation still broader for the initial open meeting for the Brethren in the fall, before cold weather comes, as the Brethren own no building in this town.

Should I not have another opportunity to write this summer, I want to say a word in behalf of the Ashland people. Personally I have never had better treatment by the Brethren anywhere, often just as good, as one would expect, but never has the Lord given me such a large place in the hearts of the Christian people of the town as here. They have shown such a splendid response to the Word of God, taught to them as it was written, as far as we have gone through the Old Testament. How much greater are the opportunities for the Brethren here in the west than any other place.

VIANNA DETWILER.

FIRST BRETHREN CHURCH
Los Angeles, California

We are now enjoying the comforts and conveniences of our new church building and every one seems to be encouraged to do his or her best.

Although it is now vacation time, the attendance at the Sunday school has taken an upward leap from what it was a year ago, and we hope that as soon as the summer time is past there will be renewed interest and increased attendance at all the sessions.

Since the dedication services there have been three confessions and all three received baptism at the close of the service Sunday night, July, 4th.

The Christian Endeavor societies spent the holiday of the 5th of July at Hermosa Beach. Many of the holidays are thus spent by our people getting together at some picnic place where all can be together and have a social time.

Our pastor is having things pretty much his own way at home now since Sister Jennings is on a visit to her people in Virginia, but we suspect he appreciates the invitations to the homes of the members, especially if it includes the meal time, and will be very, very glad indeed to welcome her home at the end of her vacation and to hear the sound of her voice calling him to the dining room.

The weekly prayer meeting is being well attended while the pastor is leading us in a study of the subject of The Kingdom in the gospel of Matthew.

A. P. REED.

4910 Wadsworth St.

THE CREDENTIALS ARE COMING

The season has arrived for the annual flight of credential blanks from the office of the secretary of the National Conference, and the migration has already taken place—that is it will have taken place by the time this appears in print.

The following points should be remembered concerning the use of the credential blanks, viz.

1. The blanks have been sent to the pastors except in a few cases where the church is without a pastor, or where the secretary is not sure as to whom they have as pastor now but does know some good member who will attend to the matter.

2. Any pastor who has formed the habit of taking a vacation about this time should either arrange with some member to take care of his mail or else send me word as to whom to mail the blanks.

3. If not enough blanks were mailed to meet the rights of any congregation more

can be secured by addressing the one whose name appears at the bottom of this article.

4. Delegates and alternates should be elected early and then get your credentials signed up in good time so you do not have to run about just before you want to leave for Winona to get one of the necessary signatures. AND REMEMBER THAT—

5. Your credential is supposed to have the signatures of all the officers asked for, unless you do not have them.

6. PLEASE, please, please fill in the space showing the number of the membership of your congregation, and then the secretary can more easily determine how many blanks you will be entitled to when he mails the blanks next year.

7. And read carefully the printing appearing in red ink across the face of your credential, so you will not be embarrassed when you approach the credential committee with your papers.

There are a few congregations who do not have pastors, or concerning whom I have no information as to names of members to whom I can mail blanks. Such will have to address me for blanks. Kindly tell me how many members you have when you write. And do not wait too long before writing, for it were better that you have too many credential blanks than not to have any at all. And they are to be had for the asking.

Yours for a GREAT conference,

DYOLL BELOTE, Secretary.

61 Highland Ave.
Uniontown Pennsylvania.

CAMPAIGN NOTES

After the canvass at Hagerstown I came to the St. James congregation. Brother Walter Nowsg is pastor at this place and inasmuch as he came from the Moxham charge to St. James he had a second period of tribulation with me. However, he took it all good naturedly and without complaint. What is commonly called the St. James congregation represents a membership of over 500 members, covering a very large area and maintaining four different preaching places. Consequently I found that Brother Norwag is serving one of the largest fields and most difficult to cover of any of our fields that I have seen. He placed his Ford at my disposal and helped me put across three of the busiest days I have had in the entire campaign. He sure did drive like "Jehu," or more so, not just for the fun of it, but because we had it to do. But thanks to the good Lord and Nowag's skill with a Ford, we got through safely; however, there were moments when it seemed to me we were certainly "flirting with the angels."

Considering the size of this congregation the result for endowment was not near what it should have been. However, we did our best. Rain the first two nights I was there hurt the work some. But the biggest drawback at St. James was the same as I have found in a number of other places—the people are not taking the Evangelist hence the great majority knew little or nothing about the campaign. And when I find people unacquainted with the campaign and not interested I always count that I have very little

foundation upon which to build. We went $800 at St. James.

I feel very much indebted to Brother and Sister Nowag for their extreme kindness to me. It was a real pleasure to be in their home again. And I am also grateful to Brother Harvey Poffenberger and his good wife for the excellent home they gave me. Nor can I refrain from mentioning the kindness of Brother Clarence Roher of Hagerstown, who, with Sister Roher, and Brother and Sister Tombaugh come out to St. James the last night of the canvass and took me back with them to Hagerstown. It has become evident to me long ago in this campaign that I shall never in this world be able to repay the many good people of our church who have rendered help and kindnesses to me. But I trust God shall richly reward them all.

Washington, D. C.

On June 29th, I began work at Washington and remained there until the following Wednesday night. I preached at each service to large, appreciative audiences. The result for endowment was very good considering that our Washington people do not represent great wealth. We raised $800 in the canvass. Here and I must testify, that I have at no place seen the people enlist more freely and cheerfully than at Washington. This is undoubtedly due for the most part to the fact they have been carefully schooled for years by Brother Lyon in the very important matter of Christian stewardship and giving. When a pastor has dared to faithfully and patiently teach his people Christian giving it never fails to tell its own story. But on the other hand when the pastor himself is stingy and when he is scared to death to have his congregation give something to an outside cause for fear he may lose fifty cents on his salary, that always tells its own little story too. It tells the story of a "little" pastor. Well, anyhow the Washington people know how to give cheerfully and liberally. There are many tithers in this congregation.

I found a live Sunday school here under the leadership of Brother Dooley. On the Sunday I was there, and the preceding Sunday, this school raised a cash gift of $10 for endowment and it was done so quietly that I didn't know anything was going on. I did not hear a single "groan" and nobody said "ouch." But it became very clear to me later when Brother Lyon told me that during the last year the offerings in the Sunday school went $1200, just lacking seven dollars. They don't have "penny" collections in the Washington Sunday school. A penny is ashamed to show its face around anywhere during the Sunday school hour. And the Sunday school also gave a note for $50.00 more, and I don't believe there will be much trouble getting that note paid either. The W. M. S. also took a part in the good work.

It was a real joy to be associated with Brother Lyon and his family in his home. I shall not soon forget the time we spent together. And I am also very thankful to Brother and Sister Harrison for the rest and kindnesses I received in their quiet hospitable home. I greatly enjoyed my stay in a national capital. May God richly bless the Washington work.

I think St. James and Washington now put the mercury at $151,000. But at the time I am writing this the Maryland and Virginia canvass is almost completed; and I know some mighty good things but I am not going to tell them now. But if anybody thinks Maryland and Virginia are asleep they, have quite a different thought coming to them.

WM. BEACHLER,
Campaign Secretary.

MINISTERIAL EXCHANGE

CERRO GORDO WANTS PASTOR

We would like to correspond with some one who would be free to take up the pastorate of this church October 1st or soon after. Address

MARY WISE,
Cerro Gordo, Ill.

The Tithing Stewardship Corner

Under date of March 31, the Rev. L. M. Delaney, pastor of the Rivermont avenue Presbyterian church, Lynchburg, Virginia, writes:

"The splendid supply of tithing literature came in due time and has been used to the best advantage. Our stewardship campaign closed Sunday with an enrollment of over one hundred percent in pledges for the ensuing year. The best thing is that we now have forty-five tithers signed up and others have decided to become tithers. We expect to continue our efforts along this line throughout the year. We are having a real revival of stewardship and religion, which are always inseparable. Your literature has factored greatly in bringing about our blessing and spiritual awakening."

Education in tithing does not differ from all other education.

This letter from Toledo, Ohio, contains merited enthusiasm:

"Some time ago you sent me a supply of tithing literature for the Maumee Presbyterian church, a church which has been aided by the Home Mission Board for thirty years, and which previously has raised $700 annually for the minister's salary. The literature you sent was read by church officials and one of four pamphlets was mailed to each member of the church preceding the financial canvass. The canvass was a decided success. The canvass produced $2,300, which has enabled them to call a minister of ability at a salary of $1,800 per year and manse. I feel very sure that your tithing literature had much to do with the present hopeful condition of the church.

"T. L. RYNDER."

THE TIE THAT BINDS

BELLES-DESIPIO—George Belles and Fannie DeSipio were united in marriage June 12th at Allentown, Pa. Both are members of the Allentown church and have the prayers and good wishes of a multitude of friends. A. L. DeLOZIER, Pastor.

Our Goal: 200,000; We Can and We Must

COLLEGE ENDOWMENT

IN THE SHADOW

OVERHOLSER—Geo. Overholser died June 14, 1920, aged 78 years, 2 months, 15 days. Father of eight children. Member of First Brethren church, North Manchester. Funeral by the writer. CHARLES A. BAME.

WESTON—Evelyn Jeanne, two-days' old daughter of Charles and Thelma Weston of North Manchester Brethren church. Funeral by the pastor. CHARLES A. BAME.

RIPPETOE—Susan C. Bond was born in Virginia, September 17th, 1853. She was married to W. F. Rippetoe, June 13th, 1879. To this union were born five daughters. The husband preceded her by 24 years, since which time two daughters were also called home. She leaves three daughters and a very large circle of friends to mourn their loss. She departed this life June 14th, 1920, in Roanoke, Virginia. Sister Rippetoe had been a member of the Brethren church for many years, and a member of the Roanoke congregation since its beginning. For many years she had made her home with Mrs. W. H. Sanders of Roanoke. She was well known and loved by all who knew her. Her sincere Christian life and devotion to her church were above question. A very choice soul has been called home at the age of 66 years, 9 months and 27 days. Funeral service was conducted by the writer, who was her pastor nearly five years. The body was laid to rest by the side of her husband and daughters, at Port Republic, Virginia. L. G. WOOD.

Brawner—Death is sure and life uncertain. Most true do we find the words of the Master: "Watch and pray, for ye know not the hour when your Lord doth come." While seemingly in good health, Samuel J. Brawner answered the call. Come. home. He died suddenly and was found by members of his family in his kitchen about one hour after his death. He was born in Washington county, Iowa, Oct. 18, 1849, and departed this life June 22, 1920, being 70 years, 8 months and 4 days old, a few months over the allotted time, three score years and ten. He was a faithful member of the Brethren church for forty-five years. He leaves one sister, eight children and a host of friends to mourn his departure. N. W. ANDERSON.

Evalson—Sarah A. Freas was born in Jefferson county, Pennsylvania, Feb. 20, 1844. She united with the Brethren church at Milledgville, Ill. in her girlhood. She was married to Charles Gibbons in October, 1868. He died soon after their marriage. Shortly after his death, she was ordained to the ministry. She served as pastor at Chicago, Illinois, Crown Chapel in Decatur county, Iowa, Fortis, Kansas and St Joseph, Missouri. She was married to J. W. Evalson on September 8, 1915. She passed away June 14, 1920. She leaves her husband, a stepson, Martin W. Evalson, two step-daughters, Helen and Alice Evalson of this city, a brother, F. W. Freas, of Pawhuska, Okla., three sisters, Mrs. H. W. Tasker, of Caney, Kansas, Mrs. Frank Sheedy and Mrs. Edward Harper, of Independence, Kansas, and an unnumbered host of friends. Funeral services were conducted from the home in St. Joseph, Missouri, Sunday, June 20, by the writer. A. E. WHITTED.

Giffin—Samuel J. Giffin, Senior Deacon of the Pittsburg Brethren Church, died of pneumonia, Tuesday, Feb. 17th, 1920, after an illness of about a week.

Brother Giffin was seventy-one years old and had been a member of the Brethren church ever since its organization. Until twenty years ago, he had been a member of the Johnstown Brethren church, when he came to Pittsburg and united with the church here.

Up to the time of his death, he had been employed in the Railroad Y. M. C. A. in Pittsburg.

He leaves to mourn him his widow Salina L. Giffin, now living at Saltsburg, one brother and one sister.

Services were held at his late residence Oakland Ave., Pittsburg, Pa., Thursday evening, Feb. 19th, by the pastor, Rev. H. M. Harley. Interment was made in Saltsburg the following day.

H. F. E. O'NEILL.

Baringer—John Baringer, born near Marion, Ohio, Feb. 17, 1841, departed this life at his home in Fremont, Ohio, June 16, 1920, at the age of 79 years, 3 months and 29 days. Although his health had not been good for some time, his condition did not seem to be alarming. He seemed to be as well as usual when he retired in the evening, but was found dead in bed in the morning, by his wife, which was a severe shock to her.

Brother Baringer was converted early in life and united with the United Brethren church and later transferred to the Methodist church. He was very fond of the Bible, which he had read through many times. He served thirteen months in the Civil War, receiving a disability discharge prior to, the close of the war.

Interment took place at Marion, Ohio. Funeral services were conducted by the writer, assisted by Rev. S. M. Loose and Rev. Caldwell, pastor of the Trinity Evangelical church in Marion.

The bereaved relatives, and especially the widow and the step-son, E. W. Baringer, who by their faithfulness have endeared themselves to the church, have the earnest sympathy of the Fremont Brethren and their pastor. May the Lord comfort and sustain them.

H. M. OBERHOLZER.

Business Manager's Corner

The Home Stretch

We are nearing the end of the Four-Year Program period; the three quarter pole has been passed and as we come down the home stretch the wire is in sight. The question is, How many winners will pass under the wire? So far as the Brethren Evangelist goal is concerned it has ben reached by a goodly number of our churches. Some have been resting from their labors for some time, having passed the goal so long ago and so often that it has become a habit with them, while others have found a new sensation in experiencing the victory for the first time, and still others have passed under the wire so recently that they hardly realize that the race has been won, and yet there are others now coming down the home stretch that may win only by a "nose," but if they win even by that so all margin it will be a victory nevertheless and they will receive due recognition for it.

The Honor Roll of the Evangelist has not been published for some time, but we are glad that the addition of two new churches to the Roll last week gives us the opportunity to bring the Roll out to view once more.

The churches that have won these honors are the North Manchester, Indiana church with Dr. Charles A. Bame, pastor, and the Maple Grove church at Norcatur, Kansas with J. G. Dodds, pastor. No small degree of credit for the achievement at North Manchester is due Frank L. Kohr, a business man who put business methods to work for Christ and the Church and won out in the effort. The Maple Grove church is only a small church on the western prairies, but we are sure Brother Dodds rejoices as much over victory in Kansas as Brother Bame does in Indiana. We extend our best wishes to both.

Since our last report the Fairview church at Washington C. H., Ohio has renewed its budget list for the Evangelist, making this the fourth year for that congregation. The good people at Fairview have become established 'budgeteers" so far as the Evangelist is concerned and we predict it would take a four-horse team or a 'Ford" to pull them back into the old rut that has been followed by so many churches. Brother L. B. Wilkins is again serving this church as pastor. The Zion Hill, Ohio church has also renewed its budget, making the second year for this church, with A. L. Lynn, pastor

A number of other churches have notified us that they will renew their budget lists soon, while still others are striving to reach the goal for the first time. We sin-

cerely pray that they may be successful before the meeting of our Winona Conference.

A Friend in Need

One of our most modest western pastors has manifested a most heroic spirit in a recent communication. In ordering a small supply of extra quarterlies for the Sunday school he enclosed TEN cents EACH and said: "This is more than the price I know, but it is what all the schools ought to pay until that expensive shipment of paper is paid for." He then added: "I also have a ten dollar bill I will contribute toward a fund for the purpose of meeting that extra cost of paper, if the churches will take that method of meeting this extra burden." We are glad this brother has it in his heart to stand by the institutions of the church no matter what the stress of the times may be. Other Brethren have written words of encouragement also, and we feel sure the church will in some way come to the help of the Publishing Company so that all the literature of the church may be sustained.

As we view the matter now we can do nothing less than to slightly increase the price of our Sunday school quarterlies for the next quarter and then to withdraw the special rates made to churches who win places on the Evangelist Honor Roll, immediately after conference. The business has gone fine the past year but no business established as ours has been and continued for the purpose it has been can meet a ONE HUNDRED PER CENT increase in the cost of paper and other printing material. But we shall have more to say about this in our annual report at our Winona Conference.

R. R. TEETER, Business Manager.

P. S. In checking up our books preparatory to our annual report we find entirely too many unpaid accounts for a concern with no more working capital than the Publishing Company has to carry. Statements are being mailed to all who are indebted to the Company and we trust they may find some way to meet these accounts before July thirty-first, the day we are to close our books for the year's business.

Among those who are indebted to the Publishing Company we find twenty pastors who have not yet paid for the Conference Reports and Brethren Annuals sent to their churches last winter. The total of their accounts is only forty three dollars; but if there was any profit at all in the publishing of these reports it is all tied up in these unpaid accounts. Please pay up brethren, and if you have any unsold copies on your hands return them and we will give you credit for them. We need a few more to keep in our files than we have left at the present time.

EVANGELIST HONOR ROLL

The following churches having met the requirements laid down by the Brethren Publishing Company regarding the placing of the Evangelist in the homes of the congregations are entitled to a place on the Evangelist Honor Roll:

Church	Pastor
Akron, Ind., (New Highland),	.... (Vacant)
Allentown, Pa., 3rd Year,	... A. L. DeLozier

Ankenytown, Ohio, 3rd Yr.,	.... A. L. Lynn
Ardmore, Indiana,	.... A. T. Wirick
Ashland, Ohio, 3rd Yr.,	.... A. Garber
Beaver City, Nebr. (3rd Yr.),	... E. S. Flora
Berlin, Pa., (2nd Yr.),	.... I. B. Trout
Berne, Indiana, 3rd Year,	.. W. F. Johnson
Bryan, Ohio, 3rd Yr.	.... G. L. Maus
Buckeye City, O.,	.... Glen Peterson
Burlington, Ind. (3rd Yr.)	.... W. T. Lytle
Center Chapel, Ind.,	.... K. R. Ronk
Cerro Gordo, Ill.,	.... D. A. C. Teeter
Clay City, Indiana, (3rd Yr.), S. C. Henderson
College Corner, Ind, 3rd Yr.	.... L. A. Myers
Conemaugh, Pa., (3rd Yr.),	... E. F. Byers
Darwin, Indiana, (2nd Yr.),	... W. T. Lytle
Dallas Center, Iowa, 2nd Yr.	... R. F. Porte
Dayton, Ohio,	.... E. M. Cobb
Denver, Indiana, 2nd Yr.,	..... L. A. Myers
Dutchtown, Indiana,	...... Homer Anderson
Elkhart, Ind., (2nd Yr.),	... H. H. Wolford
Eaton, Ind. (Maple Grove, 2nd Yr.)	....
....	H. E. Eppley
Eau Claire, Wisconsin,	...... J. A. Baker
Fair Haven, Ohio (3rd Yr.),	... B. F. Owen
Falls City, Nebr. (3rd Yr.), .	H. F. Stuckman
Fillmore, Calif. (2nd Yr), . Sylvester Lowman
Flora, Ind., 3rd Yr.	.... S. C. Henderson
Fostoria, Ohio (2nd Yr.),	..... M. S, White
Fremont, Ohio (2nd Yr.), H. M. Oberholtzer
Goshen, Indiana,	........., J. A. McInturff
Gretna, Ohio, (4th Yr.)	...... R. R. Teeter
Gratis, Ohio	.... C. E. Beekley
Hagerstown, Maryland	.... A. B. Cover
Huntington, Ind., 2nd Yr,	... J. W. Brower
Hudson, Ia.,	.... Edwin Boardman
Johnstown, Pa., 1st Ch., 2nd Yr. J. F. Watson
Johnstown, Pa., 3rd Ch.,	...... Geo. H. Jones
Lanark, Ill. (3rd Yr.),	... B. T. Burnworth
La Verne, Calif., 2nd Yr.,	... H. L. Broad
Limestone Tenn., 2nd Yr.),	... Mary Pence
Long Beach, Cal. (3rd Yr.)	... L. S. Bauman
Loree, Indiana, 2nd Yr.,	... C. A. Stewart
Los Angeles, Cal 1st Ch. ... N. W. Jennings
Los Angeles Cal, Comp. Av. 2d Yr. J. C. Beal
Louisville, O., (3rd Yr.),	..... E. M. Riddle
Martinsburg, Pa. (2nd Yr.)	..... J. I. Hall
Masontown, Pennsylvania, ... Martin Shively
Mexico, Ind. (3rd Yr.),	...... W. C. Clark
Milford, Indiana	.... C. E. Kolb
Milledgeville, Ill., (3rd Yr.) Miles J. Snyder
Morrill, Kans., (3rd Yr.),	... A. E. Whitted
Mt. View, Va., (3rd Yr.),	... J. E. Patterson
Muncie, Indiana, 2nd Yr.,	... J. L. Kimmel
Nappanee, Ind. (3rd Yr.)	..... E. L. Miller
New Enterprise, Pa.,	.... Edward Byers
New Lebanon, O.,	.... G. W. Kinzie
New Paris, Ind., 2nd Yr.,	... W. I. Duker
North English, Iowa,	.... Homer Anderson
North Manchester, Ind,, ... Charles A Bame
N. Liberty, Ind. (2nd Yr.), ... C. C. Grisso
New Enterprise, Ind.,	.... F. M. Fisher
Norcatur, Kansas	.... J. G. Dodds
Oakville, Ind., (2d Yr.),	..... W. R. Deeter
Peru, Indiana,	.... Geo. C. Carpenter
Philadelphia, Pa (1st Br.) .. Alva J. McClain
Pittsburgh, Pa., 3rd church, .. J. E. Braker
Portis, Kans., (3rd Yr.), ... Roy Brumbaugh
Rittman, Ohio,	.... J. Allen Miller
Roann, Indiana (2nd yr.), ... Willis E. Ronk
Roanoke, Indiana	.... W. F. Johnson
Roanoke, Va.,	.... L. G. Wood
South Bend, Indiana	.... G. W. Bench
Sidney, Indiana, (3rd Yr.)	... L. A. Myers
Tioga, Indiana (2nd Yr.)	... C. C. Grisso
Turlock, California,	... J. Francis Reagan
Washington C. H., O. (4th Yr.) L. B. Wilkins
Waterloo, Iowa, (3rd Yr.), .. W. H. Beachler
Whittier, Cal., (2nd Yr.), ... A. V. Kimmel
White Chapel, Mo.,	.... G. T. Ronk
Windber, Pennsylvania,	...... E. F. Byers
Yellow Creek, Pa.,	.... Edward Byers
Zion Hill, Ohio, (2nd Yr.)	..... A. L. Lynn

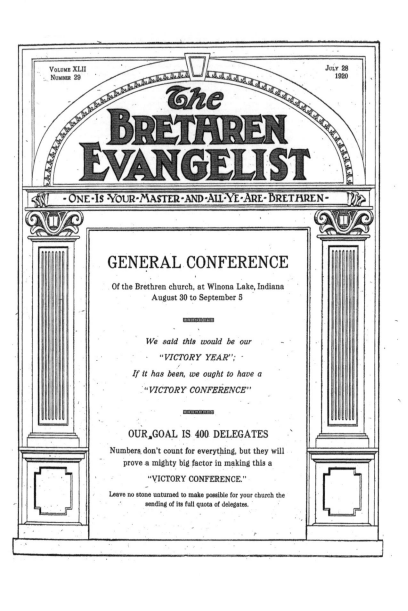

Volume XLII
Number 29

July 28
1920

The BRETHREN EVANGELIST

-ONE·IS·YOUR·MASTER·AND·ALL·YE·ARE·BRETHREN-

GENERAL CONFERENCE

Of the Brethren church, at Winona Lake, Indiana
August 30 to September 5

We said this would be our

"VICTORY YEAR";

If it has been, we ought to have a

"VICTORY CONFERENCE"

OUR GOAL IS 400 DELEGATES

Numbers don't count for everything, but they will
prove a mighty big factor in making this a

"VICTORY CONFERENCE."

Leave no stone unturned to make possible for your church the
sending of its full quota of delegates.

Published every Wednesday at Ashland, Ohio. All matter for publication must reach the Editor not later than Friday noon of the preceding week.

The Brethren Evangelist

When ordering your paper changed give old as well as new address. Subscriptions discontinued at expiration. To avoid missing any numbers renew two weeks in advance.

George S. Baer, Editor

R. R. Teeter, Business Manager

OFFICIAL ORGAN OF THE BRETHREN CHURCH

Subscription price, $2.00 per year, payable in advance.
Entered at the Post Office at Ashland, Ohio, as second-class matter.
Acceptance for mailing at special rate of postage provided for in section 1103, Act of October 3, 1917, authorized September 9, 1918.
Address all matter for publication to Geo. S. Baer, Editor of the Brethren Evangelist, and all business communications to R. R. Teeter, Business Manager, Brethren Publishing Company, Ashland, Ohio. Make all checks payable to the Brethren Publishing Company.

TABLE OF CONTENTS

EDITORIAL

The Prevalent Lack of Self-poise

To maintain one's poise—mentally, morally and religiously—is perhaps one of the most difficult tasks with which we are faced. There was a time when to maintain physical poise was a real problem for a large number of American people, but with the banishment of the saloon men are able to walk upright and alone with greater ease. But it is equally possible for men to become mentally intoxicated as it is physically, and there is equally as great a tendency in that direction. Men are impressed with a certain fact, or statement, or imagination and there is a tendency to hold that matter in mind and to continue to think along that line, unless something is permitted to dislodge it and to start another train of thought, until the mind is fairly overbalanced in that particular. For example, a man is impressed with the power the mind has over the body. He sees that certain individuals are acutally made ill by having induced into their minds a fear and a dread of a certain disease, or by the mere imagination that they are in ill-health. Tho suggestion that they are ill tends to induce a corresponding feeling and unless a counter suggestion is brought into play the individual is likely to become really ill. He sees also that suggestions of health and good cheer have a remarkably wholesome effect on the body and he observes that certain individuals in ill-health are actually restored to normal health by having induced into their minds wholesome attitudes and uplifting thoughts. The more he dwells upon the matter of mind-influence over the body the more he sees in it and the more widely he applies the principle, until he comes to think that all disease is due to the wrong sort of mental attitudes and suggestions, and that every physical malady will yield to the proper mental suggestions if they are maintained with sufficient concentration and persistency. And if he keeps on thinking in that direction he may come finally to the conclusion that diseases are not physical realities at all, and that the cure of all disease lies in merely eradicating it from the mind, which is the only reality. And so thought goes on in its fanciful flight in the line of the one idea, excluding all other legitimate and equalizing ideas, until it has become an abnormal, monstrous thing and mental poise is lost.

One of the greatest intellectual needs of our day is mental poise. One mind becomes possessed with the idea that the whole of truth lies in one particular direction of thinking, or that one line of investigation is the secret to all truth. One has emphasized the scientific side of life so much that he insists that everything must be explained from a scientific point of view, and that which cannot be thus explained is given no place in his life. Another has ignored science and is averse to scientific explanations and prefers to hold to signs and tokens and explanations that have no basis in scientific fact. Some minds are prejudiced against higher education, colleges and universities, thinking that such are opposed to the values of faith and inspiration, and that it redounds to their credit to speak slightingly of such centers of higher learning and to declare themselves free from their influences. On the other hand there are those who imagine that there is nothing of intellectual value that can be discovered outside the walls of a great university. In either case it betrays a lack of intellectual poise; it indicates a mind that is decidedly partial or out of balance and finds it impossible to give due credit to truth and intellectual values that do not appear in molds of their own fashioning nor are presented by persons of their own liking. Therein is to be found the secret of the Jews' rejection of Jesus. He did not appear in the form and manner they had anticipated, and they were determined in their own minds that the Messiah could not appear in any other manner and therefore Jesus could not be the true Messiah, nor could they accept his teachings as truth.

One of the most frequent and at the same time saddest occurrences is to find men losing their moral poise. This is lost in much the same way that intellectual poise is lost. One indulges in conduct that is wrong, or cherishes unworthy desires in his heart, or speaks words that are unbecoming. He perhaps relishes the taste of sin somewhat even though his conscience lashes him for it. He repeats the indulgence, once, twice, and then many times. At the same time he seeks to justify himself in it. More and more with each indulgence and each excuse, he loses the power to distinguish accurately between the right and the wrong. Men often go into a new community, get confused as to directions and call south east and north west. So do men become morally confused and call good evil and evil good.

Not only is a man who has thus lost his moral poise in a sad plight personally, but he is perhaps the most dangerous kind of person in the community. The man who indulges in conduct that he and everybody else knows is sinful is not going to deceive anybody with it, and not many people are induced into sinning by observing the glaring, undeceptive, and publicly discountenanced kind of sin. But the man who engages in conduct that is merely questionable, conduct that has evil results and yet has a semblance of respect, conduct after the commission of which a man may stand up and with a fair show of sincerity maintain his innocence—such a man, who believes or pretends to believe that the evil he is doing is not evil, but perfectly legitimate and good conduct, is the treacherous man of any community. Who will say how many young and innocent lives are induced to indulge in many of our modern demoralizing amusements because some one who has lost his moral poise has maintained he saw no harm in them! How many young girls have cheapened their self-respect just a little by gowning themselves in styles that required a compromise of modesty, because the devotees of fashions have declared they were perfectly proper! How many young men have been led to sacrifice their high native sense of honesty by underhanded business and political tricks done by men who profess innocence of any ulterior motives and who stand high in the popular estimation! How much wrong-doing will be placed to the charge of the man who has lost his moral poise!

The lack of religious poise is scarcely less common than the lack of moral poise, and it is the cause of more controversy. Certain individuals are inclined to be introspective, and by nature take delight in spending much time in deep spiritual meditation. To them the all absorbing theme is their personal relation to Jesus Christ their Savior and their standing before the throne of God. Persistence in thinking almost exclusively along this line causes them finally to forget their social relationships and their duty to others. They spend so much time in adoring in their mystic way the great God and Father of our Lord Jesus Christ, which is indeed the first duty of man, that they forget the second commandment, "love thy neighbor," they lose sight of the individual's and the church's obligation to "others," which is "society," and any mention of this duty is as a discordant note in their songs of praise. They have lost their religious poise. There are others who are by nature very practical and estimate religion more in terms of service than of devotion. Many such do not spend much time in cultivating the power of keenly sensing the Divine presence; they seldom become deeply absorbed in meditation; their disposition is to activity. They are more concerned about the fight against some social evil than the attendance at the prayer meeting. And as they continue to think and act along the line of social service, often so busy that they neglect to give proper attention to their contact with God and the culture of their spiritual lives, they come to the place where they fail to appreciate the importance of spending much time in communion with God and spiritual meditation as they ought. Then again there are those who take special interest in the multitude of details connected with religious worship and practices, and often they persist in giving their attention to these with such concentration that other and more vital interests are crowded out and they must share the rebuke of Christ to the Pharisees, "for ye tithe mint and anise and cummon, and have left undone the weightier matters of the law, justice and mercy and faith; but these ye ought to have done, and not to have left the other undone." In these and many other ways is the tendency manifested to over-emphasize certain elements of religious truth which we especially favor and to under-emphasize or to neglect other elements that do not appeal to us so forcibly or which we have not grown to understand. How often we prove ourselves lacking in that fine religious balance, that perfect poise which Jesus manifested on all occasions! And yet however one-sided our views may be, and to whatever views we may have given ourselves, we are all inclined to bring support to our views by accusing our Lord of sharing our personal prejudices along those lines; in other words we say, This is what Jesus believed and taught. Is there any one who has a right to say in the spirit of absolute certainty that he is in full possession of the thought and teachings of Jesus on any particular subject, or that what he believes and teaches is fully and purposely sanctioned by the teachings of Jesus on the subject? We are all more or less lacking in ability to grasp the whole of a particular truth, or to give every phase its due emphasis.

EDITORIAL REVIEW

Brother G. C. Carpenter supplies us with another selected article for the Mission page. It relates some interesting experiences which should help us to appreciate more the need of aggressive endeavor among the mountain people.

Brother Joseph Gingrich, who recently took charge at Masontown, Pennsylvania, makes his first report of his first pastorate. Brother Gingrich was one of the very promising graduates of Ashland College this year, his wife also having graduated from the same school, and they are being royally welcomed by the Masontown

people and loyally accepted as their leaders. That fine "shower" that was given the bride and groom was characteristic of Masontown hospitality. Their former pastors will testify that not only at the beginning of a pastorate, but all through and to the very end do they look well to the provision of their pastor.

Brother H. W. Anderson reports his work at Pleasant Grove, Illinois and besides pushing his local work enthusiastically he is, as ever, loyal to all the interests of the church, including the Publishing. If all the members of the Brethren church were as willing as he to furnish full proof of their loyalty to the Publishing Company would soon have a neat sum as an endowment.

You will find the General Conference program in this issue. Read it carefully and decide that you will be there to enjoy the good things that are in store. Every interest of the church calls for the largest possible attention and support. People will support them, we believe, if they only understand their needs. Here is where the needs of these various interests and their vital importance to the church will be set forth. Among the most important elements of a successful church conference two things at least must be included, namely, a large and representative attendance of the churches and a thorough, hopeful and positive discussion of the essential needs of the church as represented by the various authorized interests. There will also be some special inspirational addresses which will be worth your going to hear. Dean J. Allen Miller, whose ability as an expository preacher and a teacher of the great doctrines of the Bible is so highly appreciated by the brotherhood, will be one of the special speakers. Dr. William Evans of Wheaton College, Illinois, will be the other. Brother Arthur Lynn of Dayton will have charge of the song service, and from that we may expect great inspiration.

An Unusual Complaint

One good brother while renewing his subscription to the Evangelist took occasion to write the Business Manager that he did not believe in the stand The Evangelist took on prohibition. His complaint is so distinctly a voice from the past that even he will not fail to recognize a point of interest in noting the progress we have gained by comparing the ideal he expresses with the ideal that has become universally popular in America today. Among other things he says, "John the Baptist came neither eating bread nor drinking wine. The Son of Man came eating and drinking and the Pharisees called him a gluttonous man and a winebibber. But wisdom is justified of her children. He made wine at the feast of Cana in Galilee and told the servants to draw out and bear to the feast. The Samaritan had oil and wine on his person. Saint Paul in Colossians the second chapter says, Let no man judge you in meat, or in drink, or in respect of a feast day, or a new moon or a sabbath; which are a shadow of the things to come; but the body is of Christ. Are we contending earnestly for the faith once delivered unto the Saints. . . I teach temperance instead of prohibition. For Jesus taught the way . . . and if we follow him we will make no mistake all the way, and not follow Wayne B. Wheeler or Bryan." These words sound like queer argument in favor of temperance in drinking, but it is the kind that used to be common. Temperate drinking has been given a long try-out, but it has only heaped upon itself the reproaches and accusations of the awakened consciences of every age. Both the uncontrollableness of the human appetite and the injury of alcohol to the human system in any measure is so universally understood, that we believe the publication of such arguments as our brother has written in favor of moderate drinking will only strengthen the determination of the great mass of Christian men and women to see that our national prohibition policy is both maintained and enforced.

We thank our brother for affording us this opportunity of presenting to our readers an argument for temperate drinking which in itself will serve as a warning to our people that they be not found thoughtlessly aiding the interests of the liquor traffic which is trying desperately to gain a new lease on life. And we pray that our brother may seriously reconsider his attitude toward the drink question and come to the conclusion that practically our entire brotherhood and also our nation have arrived at; namely, that the only safe and truly Christian kind of temperance is total abstinence and prohibition, remembering that the judgements pronounced upon those who defile "the temple of the living God" or "putteth a stumbling block in a brother's way" are too serious to be trifled with.

FOUR-YEAR PROGRAM PAGE

NOW THEN DO IT.—II Samuel 3:18

Conducted by Charles A. Bame

Here is the Measuring Stick

Last week Dr. Bame issued his "Last Call" for reports on the Four Year Program. Previous to that the report cards had been sent out to the various congregations through the district directors. Every district director, as well as the national director, is anxious for a quick and complete response and is willing to do every thing in his power to get it. As Ohio director, I have sensed a need which I will supply, not only for the benefit of the Ohio churches, but the churches of the entire brotherhood as well. From one church (a church that has not had a regular pastor) comes the word that no one has a copy of the Program and no one is able to make a report on it without it. I immediately mailed a copy to a member of that congregation. But in view of the possibility of there being other churches experiencing a similar need, the entire Four Year Program is herewith presented to all our readers. For the Ohio district our slogan is "A prompt 100 per cent report." Every church has received that message and we are entertaining high hopes that every church will cooperate to make it a reality. No report is worse than a poor report. "Now then do it," now.

　　　　　　　　　　GEORGE S. BAER,
　　　　　　　　　　　Ohio Director.

FOUR-YEAR PROGRAM OF BRETHREN CHURCHES, 1916-1920

The Denomination's Goals	District Goals	Congregational Goals
	How they may be attained	*How they may be attained*
1. A Quickening of the Spiritual Life of Every Member of the Church.	1. Ten per cent Increase in Attendance or 25 per cent of Members at Prayer Meetings.	1. Ten per cent Increase in Attendance or 25 per cent of Members at Prayer Meeting.
2. A Deepening of the Spiritual Life of Every Member of the Church.	2. Seventy-five per cent of Members present at Communion Services during year.	2. Seventy-five per cent of Members present at Communion Service during year.
3. The Zealous Heralding of our Distinctive Plea, Principles and Practices.	3. Ministers using seventy-five per cent of Four-Year Program Subjects.	3. Ministers using ninety per cent of Four Year Program Subjects.
4. A Membership of 30,000 by General Conference, 1920.	4. An Increase of 30 per cent over the membership in 1916.	4. An Increase of thirty per cent over the Membership in 1916.
5. The Founding or Re-establishment of 10 Congregations.	5. An Increase of five per cent or at least one Congregation over the number of Active Congregations in 1916.	5. Payment in full of District Missionary Apportionment.
6. Seventy-five New Recruits for the Ministry and Missionary Service.	6. An Increase of 25 per cent over the number of Ministers and Missionaries, or such Candidates, in 1916.	6. The Gaining of at least one Recruit to the Ministry or Missionary Service of the Church.
7. Eighty per cent of the Congregations using the Budget System of Finance.	7. Eighty per cent of the Congregations using the Budget System of Finance.	7. The Use of the Budget System of Finance.
8. Ashland College Endowed with $100,000.	8. The Contribution of the District's percentage of $100,000 to Ashland College.	8. The Contribution of the Congregation's Percentage of $100,000 to Ashland College.
9. The Brethren Evangelist in seventy-five per cent of Homes.	9. The Brethren Evangelist in seventy-five per cent of Homes.	9. The Brethren Evangelist in seventy-five per cent of Homes.
10. Annual Offering of $15,000 to Home Mission Board.	10. The Contribution of the District's percentage of $15,000 to the Home Mission Board.	10. The Contribution of the Congregation's percentage of $15,000 to the Home Mission Board.
11. Annual Offering of $10,000 to Foreign Mission Board.	11. The Contribution of the District's percentage of $10,000 to the Foreign Mission Board.	11. The Contribution of the Congregation's percentage of $10,000 to the Foreign Mission Board.
12. Annual Offering of $2,500 to Board of Benevolences.	12. The Contribution of the District's percentage of $2,500 to the Board of Benevolences.	12. The Contribution of the Congregation's percentage of $2,500 to the Board of Benevolences.
13. Seventy-five per cent of the Sunday Schools reaching Standard of National Sunday School Association.	13. Seventy-five per cent of the Sunday Schools reaching Standard of National Sunday School Association.	13. A Sunday school reaching the Standard of the National Sunday School Association.
14. Seventy-five per cent of Women's Organizations reaching Standard of National S. S. C. E.	14. Seventy-five per cent of Women's organizations reaching Standard of National S. S. C. E.	14. A Women's Organization reaching the Standard of the National S. S. C. E.
15. Seventy-five per cent of C. E. Societies reaching Standard of National C. E. Union.	15. Seventy-five per cent of C. E. Societies reaching Standard of National C. E. Union.	15. A C. E. Society or Societies reaching the Standard of the National C. E.
16. The General Conference of 1920 the Largest and Best to that Date, with 400 delegates present.	16. An Increase of fifty per cent over number of Delegates present at General Conference of 1916.	16. An Increase of fifty per cent over the number present in 1916, or a full Quota, at General Conference, 1920. If not represented in 1916, at least one Delegate.

NOTE: Reaching the 16 Goals gives the Denomination, District or congregation Front Line Standing; or a Gold Star. Reaching 14 Goals gives Banner Standing; or a Blue Star. Reaching 12 Goals gives Star Standing; or a Red Star.

GENERAL ARTICLES

How to Secure a Trained and Active Laity. By Roy A. Patterson

In these days of apparent apostacy and lethargy on the part of our church people, one of the greatest tasks of the church and her ministry is to secure men and women who will really allow themselves to become very much engrossed with the affairs of the church, and if we will actually make a canvas of the situation in our own congregations, it will be found that the "Old Guard" is very much in evidence and that a very small percentage of our people care to assume any responsibility in God's work. Too many of us are "hearers" rather than "doers" of the Word."

The hope of our church does not lie in the hands of the present generation to such a marked degree as our ideals have been largely formed, as well as our characters and our years for training, especially the older ones, have nearly past, but it is to the coming generation, the boys and girls, that we must turn for a trained and active laity as well as ministry.

To state that youth is the time of development and action is superfluous as no one will dispute the fact that as soon as children come to the age where they observe and understand things about them, ideas and thoughts are being formed and impressions made that will never fade. Young hands will find something to do, for where life and health exist, action can always be expected. Young tongues will speak, speak of the things they know and inquire of the things they know not.

These are some of the attributes of young life that must be jealously guarded. Into the hands of parents and teachers is placed the responsibility of training these boys and girls who will soon become men and women to glorify Christ or bring shame and reproach on those who trained them. Regardless of whether we care to assume it or not, the responsibility is there and may our prayers be, that we shall be found worthy of such trust.

The life of a child can be compared very favorably to a lump of clay in the hands of a potter, easily shaped and designed into a masterpiece or cast aside as unfit for any use. This is the office that I should choose for the Sunday school to perform, the shaping and designing of young lives for Christ's service and may we never be found guilty of teaching, either by example or precept, lessons that would mar this masterpiece and render it unfit for service.

Let our guide be Christ and him only in the performance of such a sacred privilege as the teaching and training of boys and girls.

If we would train a generation for action in our churches, care must be taken in the selection of those who would teach. It would be far better if we had but one teacher, whom we knew to be thoroughly grounded in the faith and who believed the Bible from lid to cover and who practiced such beliefs, to teach in our Sunday schools rather than twenty-five who had very few well grounded beliefs and who failed to live what they did know to be right.

It is sad to know that in many of our homes, Jesus Christ and his salvation is briefly hinted at if mentioned at all, after we have exhausted ourselves in talking about our work, the movies, the dance, our card parties and other worldly pleasures that only damn our souls, while our children sit by taking it all in and then, how we wonder when one of these precious ones go astray.

It is strange to say that some of these worldly affairs have crept into our Sunday schools and that the one hour we give to the study of his Word each week is often spoiled in the discussion of things that have no bearing on our lesson.

Parents and teachers, permit me to say that if you would expect your boys and girls to grow up active in the church, you must give them the proper food for such growth. Cereals are good for a man who earns a livelihood through brain power but the man who makes a living by the use of his hands must have more substantial food. The movies, dances and card parties are alright for those who have no regard for their own souls or the souls of others but to those who would do Christ's will, must be given food from on high that they may never perish. No opportunity should be passed by either by parent or teacher, to impress upon the young mind, the proper way of living toward his fellowmen and his God. The home and the Sunday school are the only agencies to whom we dare look for this desired training.

When this life has been shaped, as the vessel, in the hands of the potter has been formed, it is ready to be filled and used, and may it not be filled with unworthy things but with the Holy Spirit to be a "Living Epistle written in our hearts, known and read of all men."

Dayton, Ohio.

Tolerance. By Theodore Parker Gnagey

Virtue is one of the first and highest requirements of character. It is the stimulus which makes nobility of the soul, and a noble soul is the heighth of great character. Even honor, says Emerson, "is always ancient virtue." So that virtue, then, or all of the true virtues, such as goodness, kindness, honor, truthfulness, chivalry, bravery, are the elements of real character. Thus a man who possesses these elements we may well pronounce a virtuous man. Of what a noble pedigree does this make him!

Now virtue is ancient. It is as ancient as humans are. As far back as the records of history go, men possessed and revered virtue. The ancient Egyptians and Babylonians had it. The Greeks, in a world of transcendent art and culture, had it. The Romans, amid a degrading and a corrupt society, were not without virtuous men.

But virtue alone has come to be a word of common meaning. It is only since the advent of Christ that the word has become expanded. Now it is Christian Virtue. Yet, after all, the expansion is not so much in the tacking on of the adjective Christian, for the real virtues, such as those above mentioned, were Christian elements always, before

the days of Christ and since, because they are elements of the ethics which Christ taught. Jesus did not bring virtue to the world. He simply emphasized the exercise and the veneration of virtue. But still, there is a way in which virtue has been expanded since the coming of Christ. It is in the addition of a few other virtues which heretofore were not recognized as such. One of the greatest of these is TOLERANCE.

Tolerance, then, I should call one of the most supreme Christian virtues or graces. It is that magnanimity of the mind which duely respects the thought of other men. It does not smack of weakness but of strength. It is not a giving way of opinion or possession, but the fine sense of mental humility which understands, and understanding is aware that the opinion is changeable, the possession less valuable. It is only the most obstinate mind that does not admit of the possibility of being mistaken. That is a true case of actual narrow-mindedness. It is proper and fitting for all of us to have a firm and steadfast belief, opinion, or idea, but it is a tyrannical abuse of tolerance to condemn another man if he does not believe, or hold the same opinions, or have the same ideas that we have. Christ emphasized the exercise of tolerance. Do you recall that occasion, recorded in the gospel of St. Luke, in which James and John said, "Lord, wilt thou that we command fire to come down from heaven, and consume them, even as Elias did?" But he turned, and rebuked them, and said, "Ye know not what manner of spirit ye are of. For the Son of man is not come to destroy men's lives, but to save them." Ah, is not that the expression of a tolerant spirit? And do you remember when Christ talked with the Samaritan woman at the well? Was not that tolerance, too?

Yes, for a long time this old world has been full of intolerance. History itself is a checkerboard of intolerant acts—a record always marred by despots and tyrants. Before the days of Jesus this hardly could have been called a sin against the virtue of tolerance, however; for not until Jesus stamped tolerance a virtue was it recognized as such. But the greatest and most outrageous sin of which men are guilty is their insistent abuse of tolerance since Christ has a better way. Even in christendom history has been checkered by intolerance. That is why noble men have been hung or burned as martyrs. That is why the man who discovered the telescope, and first saw heaven, was paid with a dungeon. That is why he who invented the microscope, and first saw earth, died of starvation, driven from his home. Yes, that is why Christ himself was forced to the cross.

But my chief purpose here is to point out the extreme need of more tolerance in this modern age. It may be a matter of wonder to some why this need is more insistent now than at any time. But only those who do not belong to the modern age in spirit can possibly wonder at this. For this century, this decade, is an epoch of progressivism in thought. The time was when men accepted authority without investigating the evidence. They adhered to established customs for customs' sake, and they believed in iron-bound doctrines for doctrines' sake. There was no science at all that we now could call science, and theology was as mysterious as astrology. But science dawned. It came as an awakening in thought just as the Renaissance was an awakening in art. But science, at its birth, did not flourish like the culture of the Renaissance. In the first place, it was not born all at once, and in the second place, it was not universally accepted. The seeds of science were born with men like Sir Isaac Newton and Galileo. Then out of it grew a new philosophy the sponsors of which were men like Francis Bacon and Descarte. Slowly but surely all of the elements of nature and of the mind were measured,

tabulated, and systematized as indisputable facts. Out of hypothesis grew theory, and out of theory grew law. Many an hypothesis was untrue, and many a theory failed to work. But men kept on investigating, and these first results, while perhaps unstable in themselves, served as stepping-stones—as beginning places, as it were—for higher structures and more perfect conclusions, until the operation of natural laws became positively known and even variation was measured.

Now the world today is in that indomitable state of advancement which is the result of scientific investigation. But it is yet much more so than was the world of yesterday. Of all that we know about electricity, who can say what is yet to be learned? Who can say that sociologists will not make an exact science out of sociology? Who knows but that the theory of relative motion will teach us vastly more than Newton ever dreamed? Theology itself is now a contestant for the ranks of the emperical sciences.

Yes, modern men have the heritage of a greater knowledge than the ancients had. But by virtue of this greater knowledge they have greater doubts. And let me say here that doubt is not, as it has been falsely stamped, "a traitor." Good, progressive doubt is the path which leads to truth. Only the doubters ever struck the heart of truth. Those who never doubted grew stagnant. Galileo doubted the doctrines of the theologians of the Middle Ages. Yes, he was thrown into prison for it; but today we know that he was right; they wrong. They were not tolerant! And where is our need of tolerance. Men today are doubting those things which long have been taken for granted; but men today are discovering the facts of existence and the truths about life. This is a scientific age which should not have the scorn of men, but their support. Only those who "live blindly" are afraid of science. Science has never hurt religion. It always has benefited it. It is inevitable that God should seem vaster with every extension of human knowledge.

So let us be tolerant! If we belong to the old school and cannot see God and Christianity in enlightenment as well as darkness, let us not put a shadow in the path of enlightenment. If we prefer to nourish our thought on prophecy rather than discovery, let us be prophets if we can, but not raise a hand against the discoverers. In short, if we can not believe as others, let us believe as we will, but let us be Christian-spirited enough to be tolerant and to let others have that same liberty of belief.

Ashland, Ohio.

Coordinating Church Work. By L. G. Wood

These are days of extravagance, notwithstanding the high cost of living; this extravagance is not only in habits and conduct, but also in belief and teaching. It seems to me that a campaign of Conservation, Consecration and Consentration by all Christian forces is the only safe remedy for the present need.

This may be called the day of "drives," for it is a drive for this and a drive for that. Governments seem to set the pace and now nearly all institutions have caught the spirit. Such campaigns are all right if rightly used for a worthy object. But it is very easy for one to become lost in a drive, so as to lose sight of the goal for which they are driving. That means disaster and defeat. The church of Jesus Christ must keep herself "in the clear," yet she must LIVE and ACT in the atmosphere of the present. The progressive spirit of the age should quicken the spiritual pulse of every member of Christ's body.

Spiritual energy and influence should be increased, conserved and concentrated. The organization of the local congregation is five-fold, this is in order to the grading of both the work and the workers. These departments may be called auxiliaries, for they represent all of the churches activities and are equally dependent upon the church and

responsible to the church. Each of these departments occupy a unique place, distinct in its program and method, yet coordinate with all others in aim and purpose. We represent the church by a circle, and around this circle we place five circles representing its life and work, and named as follows:

FIRST

The Bible School. This institution stands for three great principles of action, evangelism, education, equipment, for it is "The teaching service of the church, to win souls to Christ and train them in Christian service."

SECOND

The Christian Endeavor Society. It has for its principles of action, expression, enlistment and expansion. The Bible school and the Christian Endeavor Society are most beautifully linked together by their missionary departments.

THIRD

The Women's Missionary Society. Its great and noble task may be classed under three words, enlighten, enthuse, energize, and is related to the Bible school by an educational program.

FOURTH

The Church Prayer Meeting. The great purpose of the prayer meeting may also be expressed in three words, engage, enthrone, endue, relating its self to the Woman's Missionary Society, by their devotional program.

FIFTH

The Official Board. It also has three principles of action, plan, purpose, provide, relating itself to the prayer meeting, by means of the spiritual thermometer, also related to the Christian Endeavor Society, by the executive committee.

Thus we have five cooperating, coordinating agencies, representing fifteen distinct, but harmonious principles of action and with no over-lapping. These five agencies are joined by a cord that represents the fundamentals of church life.

As a denomination we are making splendid progress in coordinating our general work. At last conference the election of a General Missionary Secretary, also the election of a committee of fifteen, to coordinate and concentrate the sixteen goals of the Four Year Program into about five goals.

It is just as necessary that the congregation coordinate its work, that there be no lost time, energy or motion, neither over-lapping in these great and opportune days. This arrangement is based upon 1 Corinthians 12:12-31.

Methods are many
Principles are few
Methods may vary
Principles never do.

Roanoke, Virginia.

Every Wheel In Place. By G. C. Carpenter

This is a necessity. Illustrations are numerous. Any piece of machinery must be efficiently organized that efficient service may be rendered. Any wheel in that machinery must itself be efficiently organized, and be properly "connected up." One spoke gone or one cog broken and the wheel is weakened. Who has not had some experience with a disorganized automobile? A watch disorganized is useless. The human body is one of the best examples. One member afflicted affects the efficiency of the whole body.

While in an auto hospital the other day the telephone rang and somebody said, "Come and pull me in." In a few minutes I heard an old man saying, "The old thing kicked and kicked until I was scared and gave up trying to start her." And soon the auto doctor said, "Your timer is loose." That meant only a few turns with the wrench to remedy it, but the slight disorganization destroyed the efficiency of the whole machine, and failure to do the work of a Ford was the result.

The school and the home and the church furnish timely illustrations. Each represents a family, having definite tasks for the individual members to perform, and failure on the part of any individual spells failure more or less for the whole unit.

We are told that when Campbell Morgan went to Westminster church, London, the attendance was small at the services. Before long the church was crowded. "Do not give me credit," said the minister, "give it to the twenty deaconesses that have gone from house to house, from heart to heart, pleading the cause of Christ." It was the personal touch plan worked out through an efficient organization.

With much profit can we apply this principle to the Sunday school and the Christian Endeavor Society. Each is a family wherein the individual members have specific duties. Standards of efficiency, carefully tested and proven, are furnished for both organizations. The Endeavor efficiency chart outlines a plan that assures success and "Expert Endeavor" tell all about it, even to the smallest details.

Sometimes people tire of looking after the Sunday school and Endeavor machinery and soon they are standing as still as a neglected Ford. Eternal vigilance is the price of success, whatever the organization may be.

Harding and Cox are in a race for the White House and each will have the most efficient organization possible to help win the goal next November. Surely none will question the necessity of efficient organization that a certain end may be obtained.

Then how can this be secured in Sunday school and Endeavor? Real Convictions concerning the necessity must be held by the pastor and the officers and they must be everlastingly on the job in rain and shine, hot and cold, early and late, but always on time. They must keep the machinery running smoothly. Oil is sometimes necessary

and pincers and wrench are sometimes essential. The standards need to be studied. The advice of experts must be sought. The directions must be followed, although there must be individual study and analysis of the individual case. Many an organization fails because some part of that organization stopped working or failed to cooperate with the other parts of the whole.

A teacher said to Willie: "Don't you know that punctuation means you must pause?" Willie answered, "Course I do. An auto driver punctuated his tire in front of our house the other day and he paused a half hour." There are too many punctuations in our church organizations. There are punctuated officers, and committees and lay members and we have heard of some punctuated preachers. The punctuations must be fixed and the pauses removed if success in the highest degree is to crown our efforts in the work of the church. No punctuated praying but every member living the prayer life! No punctuated giving but every member giving systematic support according to the directions furnished by God himself in his Book of Directions! No punctuated serving but every member rendering efficient service, whichever way the wind blows! No punctuated consecration but every member abiding in Christ every day! Let the members of our church organization meet these conditions and victory will be certain!

Peru, Indiana.

Unfilled Promises

A young woman and her Sunday school teacher were strolling arm-in-arm through an orchard in full bloom. In every direction stretched dazzling vistas of pink and white, making the orchard a veritable fairyland. The young woman exclaimed in ecstasy. "Yes, it is wonderful," remarked her more mature companion, "but to me there is a touch of sadness in the thought that so many blossoms will bear no fruit."

How many lives in the early spring of their careers give promise of usefulness, and then bear no fruit! Evil habits, insidious temptations, sinful allurements do their fruit-destroying work. Every pathway of human experience is sown thick with the white petals of blossoms that have failed to fulfill their earlier promises. Youth needs constantly to be on its guard against the enemies that lie in wait.—Forward.

THE GREAT REVIVALISTS

All the great revivalists of the church have had the passion for souls at the root of their work. John Smith, the mighty Wesleyan preacher, used to say, "I am a brokenhearted man; not for myself but on account of others: God has given me such a sight of the value of precious souls that I cannot live if souls are not saved. Oh, give me souls, or else I die."

THE BRETHREN PULPIT

"After 2000 Years." By T. C. Lyon

"TEXT: Ye say that He is your God, yet ye have not known Him."—John 8:54,55.

SCRIPTURE LESSON: The Parable of the Unjust Judge.—Luke 18:1-8.

A prominent Baptist minister, in objecting to the Interchurch World Movement not long ago, among other reasons gave this, that the movement "held out the hope that the world was growing better, while the Son of God declares that it will grow worse and become as it was in the days of Noah." A certain editor, in reviewing the article, takes great delight in ridicule. He says, "If that was the best that Divine Omnipotence had to offer, the world in general, fortunately, did not know it. Imagine going out to convert a heathen with this beginning: 'Join my church; we guarantee that the world is growing worse.'"

In reality, that beginning would make one of the best of arguments: "Join my church and escape the doom of a sinful world." The newspaper man, however, does not see that, and the fact remains that, on account of man's sinful heart, that was the best that Divine Omnipotence had to offer; and it is equally true that the world in general does not know about it. In fact, although nearly 2000 years have passed since the time of Christ, the world in general, and even some of his professed followers, knows but little of the truths which Christ actually taught. "Ye say that he is your God, and ye have not known him."

I am reminded of the old lady who made so many pies; but of all the pies she made there were just two kinds; mince pies and other pies. Wishing to distinguish between them as they lay on the shelf, she labelled them. The mince pies she marked "T. M." meaning "'Tis mince." The others she marked "T. M." meaning "'Tain't mince." It seems to me that there is about as little difference between the great body of men and nations marked Christian and un-Christian as there was in those labels.

In looking back through our Bibles, however, we find that Christ's simplest words and teachings were misunderstood even at the time they were given out, and by his closest friends. It must, indeed, have been discouraging. Let me give a few instances of this. In the 21st chapter of John, we find Peter asking Christ concerning John, "Lord, and what will this man do?" Jesus answered, "If I wish him to remain till I come, what is it to you? Follow me." This saying, therefore, went forth among the brethren, that that disciple should not die; yet Jesus did not say to him that he should not die, but, "If I wish him to remain till I come, what is it to you?" And so have his simplest words been perverted from the beginning.

In Luke, 9th chapter, we have a still more painful example (vs. 51-56). Let us try, for a moment, to visualize the scene: here it was nearing the end of Christ's ministry; one of his chief burdens had been to teach love and forgiveness to enemies, and here were two of his best-loved disciples, asking permission to destroy some unbelievers with fire, for what was, comparatively, but a petty insult.

Perhaps it would seem to you that his disciples must have been very dull, not to have understood him better, but for them there was some excuse: to them all this was new. Before the time of Christ such doctrines were practically unknown, and it was little wonder that some of it seemed strange to those simple folk. But for us there is no such excuse. These doctrines were given to the world nearly 2000 years ago, and nearly all of us have had them in our homes, in book form, all our lives. And yet I doubt if the real doctrines of the Christ are better undertsood by us today than by those first disciples so long ago.

There are a number of reasons for this. In the first

place, the doctrines of Christ are not pleasing to the natural man. They offend his (or her) dignity and self-respect. Christ taught that his followers should be humble, dress and live simply and without show, love their enemies, suffer rather than cause suffering, give up your cloak and coat rather than go to law to defend the coat, the sacredness of marriage and the evil of divorce, in short that his followers should be in the world but not of the world; not in its politics and reform movements, not in its wars and strifes, but in the world as teachers and preachers of the crucified Christ and the need of regeneration. Doesn't that sound popular? As some of those early disciples said, "This is a hard saying and who can hear it?" We find this illustration in the 11th of Matthew, verses 16-19; they didn't want to believe John—his teachings made them uncomfortable—so they rejected them because he didn't eat and drink; and they rejected Christ because he did! Oh consistency! After all, men believe what is MOST PLEASING to them and disturbs them least: that is why the doctrine that there is no hell is so popular.

Another reason is that much of our "knowledge" of the Bible is based on tradition rather than of the Bible itself. For instance, let me ask what is your idea of a cherub. See if I can describe it: a cherub is a cute, chubby little child, generally represented with wings; some people think of it as a beautiful young woman, and a few as a finely proportioned young man, but most commonly as a little child. Ezekiel, however, gives us a very different picture; he says it is part ox, part eagle, part lion, and part man! Some youngster! If you would read just a few references to the cherubim in the Bible you would soon see that the other idea is preposterous. Where did we get it? Some of the earlier painters, being better artists than Bible sutdents, so conceived them, and they have been perpetuated in that way. It isn't found in the Bible.

Another source of error is that many people believe every word in the Bible, but I don't. You didn't know I was an agnostic, did you? Well, I' not. Maybe you'll quote that "every scripture is inspired of God, etc.," but the better translation of that is, "Every scripture inspired of God is profitable," and so on. The Bible is a record not only of the words of God and his saints, but also of the words of the devil and his followers. A difficult case in court was won on the strength of a Bible quotation. When it was read the judge could scarcely believe it was in the Bible, but the reference was given, and his clerk looked it up and read it. Afterward the judge, still unconvinced, looked it up for himself, and found that the passage quoted was the direct advice of the devil in tempting some saint! It is well to examine into the authorship and context of a quotation before we accept it as truth.

I just mentioned context, and that brings me to the Mizpah. A beautiful little prayer as we use it, and I would not for anything say a word against its use. Let us continue to use it with the same meaning we have always attached to it heretofore, though that is not its true meaning as found in the Bible. Let us go back, just for a minute, and recall some of the events that surround it. You will remember how Jacob had matched his wits against Uncle Laban for so many years, and had at last been victorious and fled, taking with him a great deal of property that Laban might well have claimed, and, worst of all, Laban's stone gods: that was unforgivable. Laban's pursuit of Jacob was no loving affair, but an armed pursuit with murder in the heart.

Finally he overtook Jacob on the edge of his own land, but Jacob deceived him again and matters were patched up. However, Laban was still suspicious; a boundary was established between them and Laban called on Jacob's God to watch as a sentry between them and keep them apart lest they fight with one another. Our use of this as a prayer name from a misunderstanding as to its original meaning, but as we use it it is a beautiful sentiment and well worth preservation as such, though it is not the thought expressed in the Bible.

Let me give one more reason, found in the last verse of a little poem I came across not long ago.

> "When religion goes a begging
> And the Bible is forgot,
> And the preacher preaches nothing
> Only scientific rot;
> There the faithful old believers
> They are getting mighty few
> When (science) rules the pulpit
> And the devil rules the pew."

'Scientific rot'—I thought that was pretty good! About half our people, and even more of our ministers (though they usually deny it if you put it up to them), have laid the Bible aside and are spending their time studying philosophy, sociology, psychology and the other "ologys," trying to find the panacea that will reform man. But God says, 'The heart of man is sinful and desperately (that word means hopelessly) wicked above all things." Man needs regeneration, for a reformed sinner is still a lost sinner. To put your faith in reformation is to put the cart before the horse; hitch up to regeneration, and reformation will follow along naturally and without any fuss. But men get so wrapped up in their sociology and this business of reforming people, that they can't get loose and get back to the faith that was once for all delivered to the saints.

Makes me think of the man with the wooden leg who stayed too long at a souse party. On the way home his wooden leg stuck in a knot-hole in the board walk, but he was too far gone to know the difference and kept right on going, round and round, all night. Oh, let's get that old wooden head—I mean leg—out of the knot hole of human wisdom (which is "foolishness with God") and get back to the Bible itself as the one source of knowledge of God and his truth.

Oh, the things that are taught in the name of science! Not long ago I saw a "pointed paragraph" reading, "Some time a lot of loose cogs are rattling behind that high brow." Listen: I was talking to a young fellow the other day who claimed he didn't believe in Christian Science, but before he got through he proved conclusively, to his own satisfaction, at least, that neither the pencil in his hand nor the table before him was real. "I'd like to know," he said, 'what the soul is, or where it is. Every doctor knows you have a soul, or something that leaves you at death, but they don't know what it is, nor where. A runner puts his soul in his feet, when I use this pencil, I put my soul in my fingers, and so on. But I don't believe any doctor really knows; I don't believe they ever will. Do you?" "No," I said, "I don't believe they ever will either." In Luke 24: 45 we find this: "Then he opened their minds that they might understand the Scriptures." And if we would understand these things, it is to him that we, too, must go, and not to the stuff that God calls foolishness.

All these reasons for this condition of misunderstanding might be briefly summed up under one or the other of two headings:

1. Lack of a vital and life-giving interest individually.
2. Absorption in the "wisdom of this world."

Let us just briefly now consider a few of the most vital things that are so commonly misunderstood:

First, does "redeemed" mean to be saved? We have the old song "Since I have been redeemed, etc." Right here let me give out a warning against some of our hymns. A great many of the hymns that have the prettiest tunes and so become the most popular are hymns that are exactly contrary to the teachings of the Bible. This is the one consolation to be found in the fact that most people sing their hymns without taking the slightest thought as to what they are singing. If you don't believe they do, just listen some time. In the meaning of the scriptures, to be redeemed does not necessarily mean to be saved. The word itself means to buy again. In other words, we once were God's, but left him for bondage under the devil. He bought us back again with the great price of his only begotten Son: that constitutes redemption. We are not saved until we take advantage of the freedom he offers us. The worst sinner in the world is a redeemed man—the price has been paid—but he is not a saved man.

Second, should a Christian tithe? You often hear the point made that tithing was only meant for the Jew "under the law," and does not apply to us "under grace." But suppose you were legally bound to support some person at a distance, one you had never known. Then, later, it so happened that you moved nearer to this person and learned to know and love him. Do you think for a minute you would want to give any less than you did before? I recently heard a very good story about tithing. It is said that a certain Chinese mandarin was walking along a country road when he was accosted by a beggar. The mandarin had ten pieces of Gold strung on a string, as the Chinese carry their money, and he answered the beggar by taking off one gold piece and telling him to buy himself something to eat with it. Then he gave him another, telling him to buy himself some clothes; another for education, and so on until he had given him nine of the ten pieces; the tenth only he reserved for himself. But the beggar, still dissatisfied, followed him at a distance, and when the mandarin lay down beneath a tree to rest, as soon as he fell asleep, the beggar crept up and stole away the tenth piece. A pretty low down trick, wasn't it? And yet, are we not worse than this "heathen Chinese" if we steal the tenth from God after he has so graciously given us the other nine?

By the way, if you really want to find out what Christ taught, just talk to some Jew about it. I've tried it, and I know. Let me read just here part of a statement by a Jewish rabbi on this subject: "For the purpose of learning to what extent the teachings of Jesus have been followed, let us hastily review them. He prohibits wrath and anger, persecution and punishment. He teaches non-resistance, bids man when smitten on one cheek to turn also the other, when robbed of his cloak to give also his coat; rather than get into strife or go to law. In opposing resistance, and punishment he opposes the courts. He prohibits the oath." (And doesn't that include even the oath we little government clerks have to take?) "He bids men love their enemies, to bless those who curse them, to do good to those who do them evil. In these teachings there is no room for ruler or subject, for army or police, for courts or prison. Hatred is to be conquered by love, wrong by forgiveness, curse by blessing. The hand of man is never to be raised against a fellowman no matter how grievous the offense. But go where we may in Christendom, and as far back as we choose . . . we see everywhere oppression and injustice and class distinction, notwithstanding that the dominant religion of these lands is Christian, and the dominant clergy is Christian, and the deity most worshipped is Christ, he who taught peace and love and equality. It illbecomes the Christian to denounce and persecute the Jew for not accepting Jesus, seeing that he himself has not yet accepted him."

Is it any wonder that a Jew should thus accuse Christians? I think not. You will find that all the things mentioned here are in strict accord with the teachings of Christ.

(To Be Continued Next Week)

Send
WHITE GIFT
OFFERINGS to

THE SUNDAY SCHOOL

ALBERT TRENT
General Secretary-Treasurer
Johnstown, Pennsylvania

The Sunday School An Asset and a Liability.   By Mrs. O. W. Lewis

The Sunday school has rightly been called The Kindergarten of the Church, for here it is, that many children hear for the first time the blessed words of truth, here it is that many have caught the vision of the great work of the church, and have dedicated their lives to the work of the Master. Here also many have found the joy of service —a service that calls for the giving of self unreservedly, that Christ might be enthroned in the minds of the girls and boys of today who will be our men and women of to- morrow.

It is the planting of the seeds of truth in the minds of youth that brings forth rich harvest in the minds of men. Some one has said, "Give me the youth and I will give you a new earth." Think how vastly different would be the condition of the people in Europe, if the youth of Germany had been trained as carefully and earnestly in the way of Christian living as they were in the ways of militarism. "Train up the child in the way he should go and when he is old he will not depart therefrom," says the Good Book. Think of the wonderful opportunity of the Sunday school as it stands, a dispensary of the things of God and eternal life. Think of the God-given commission of the teachers as they stand between Christ and the child. Does it see Christ in us? Has some one seen Christ in you today? Christian, look to your heart I pray. The little things you have done or said—did they accord with the things you prayed? Have your thoughts been pure and your words been kind? Have you thought to have the Savior's mind? The world with a criticizing view has watched; but did it see Christ in you?

The Sunday school as an asset has much to offer but as a liability has it no debt to pay?

The world is looking to the church as never before and if it ever had a message to the world it has now. The world needs true witnesses. Christ was crucified because he had to proclaim truth alone. Let the church rise to meet the challenge of the hour and recognize that this is indeed her day. Let her fill her place. Let her claim her right to lead out in this great world-saving enterprise.

It did not take America long to see her place in the great world war. They recognized their opportunity and filled their ranks, marching forward with a determination to win and they won. In unity there is strength. Now the same loyal spirit manifested in the great war and the same loyal support must be in evidence in the work of the kingdom. To carry the message of love to our home people as well as our world neighbor will require a united effort, a tremendous effort on the part of all those who profess to know and follow the Lord Jesus Christ. The Sunday school is the recruiting station to which we are looking for the material with which to fill in the ranks of Christian warfare. Are we supplying the demand? If not, why not? The Red Cross has taught us to minister to the needs of our soldiers. May the cross of Christ enable us to meet that greater need—"the need of the soul." Our response will be the measure of our love for the Christ, whose command comes ringing down the ages to us, "I have given you an example that ye should do as I have done."

Falls City, Nebraska.

World Sunday School News

It is interesting to all Sunday school workers to know what a big movement they are connected with. It is a world movement and is world-wide in its influence. When we tussle with the problems of our own little school or revel in our local success, we are apt to think that we have the whole story of Sunday school success or failure. It is therefore wholesome for us occasionally to be reminded of the great world reach of the Sunday school movement and to get a broader vision of its possibilities and achievements. With this in mind it is our intention to give occasional bits of Sunday school news from various parts of the world.

Sunday School Dividends in Egypt

Candy gifts produce half dollar returns in Egypt, writes Rev. Stephen Trowbridge, Sunday school secretary representing the World's Sunday School Association at Cairo. This story follows: "In many schools a special effort is being made to reach the children of the streets. A pastor in a rural parish tells how he used to fill his pocket with pieces of sugar. He gave to every street child a piece of sugar if he would follow him to Sunday school Most of these gamins were Moslems. At first the congregation was not pleased to find the church full of these dirty, mischievous children. At the end of the year, however, some of these very urchins came to the pastor with half dollar pieces. 'We have been working in the cotton fields,' they said, 'and these are our tithes.'" Most important of all they had the boys too.

There has been an increase in the Sunday school membership in Egypt since the report was prepared for the Zurich Convention in 1913. There are now 294 Sunday schools with 894 officers and teachers, 22,236 pupils making a total enrollment of 23,130. While the increase in population has been 9% the increase in Sunday school membership has been 26% and 51% in the number of officers and teachers. There are 10 teacher-training classes in Egypt.

Sunday Schools in Asia Minor

Many Moslem boys are studying the Bible in connection with Sunday schools connected with institutions. At St. Paul's College, Tarsus, 85 Moslem boys were members of the Sunday school before the war. These boys were constantly committing to memory portions of the Psalms and Gospels. Many were Christians in heart and called themselves "Turkish Protestants." Since the war they have professed Christ openly.

Need of Sunday School Leaders

The Director of Sunday schools at St. Paul's college, Kevork P. Damlamian, in an interview at the office of the World's Sunday School Association, Metropolitan Tower, New York, stated that there is no greater need in Asia Minor today than the upbuilding of the Sunday school. Many adult Christian leaders have been killed. The leadership of the immediate future depends upon the young men who must be obtained from the Sunday schools of today. Request has just come from Constantinople that a Sunday school field secretary be sent there at once. Then there are insistent calls that another worker be located at Adana. Many new Sunday schools have been organized recently. These are often among the refugees and the soldiers. The Blakesley graded lessons have been translated into both Armenian and Turkish and printed in the local weekly paper at Adana. There is great need for teacher-training courses in both Turkish and Armenian and these will be prepared as soon as a secretary can be assigned to these fields. This man will be a well-known Sunday school leader. He may be a State Secretary or one of the officers of the World's Association.

How many a life has been kept pure and sweet by the living realization of that one truth, "Thou, God, seest me?"
—Farrar.

J. A. Garber
PRESIDENT

Our Young People at Work

G. C. Carpenter
SECRETARY

A Christian Endeavor Tool-Chest
By Albert A. Rand, in the Christian Endeavor World

"We had a great present given our society the other day," said the Carpenter.

"Is that so? What was it?"

"A tool-chest."

"A tool-chest? Why, I don't see anything very great about that. What do you do with it? Are you planning to build an addition on to the church, or somethin'?"

"Oh, no we use it in our society work; and you ought to see how things have improved since we started using those tools."

"How many tools are there, and what are they like?"

"Well, first there's the hammer."

"Oh, yes," I interrupted. "I've heard about hammers before. They use them for knocking. I don't see—"

"Now you just hold on a minute. You're going ahead too fast. They do use some hammers for knocking, but not ours. It is to be used for driving things in with. We use it to drive home the worth-while points of the topic; we use it to drive the fact into the heads of the members that they ought to attend the meetings more regularly and be more active. We use it for driving live facts about what the local, county and state unions are striving for. Yes, sir, our hammer is used only in building and constructive work."

"That's good, of course. What are some of your other tools?"

"The saw. It was made by the firm of B. Brief and Company; and we use it to cut off long arguments in the business meeting with. When the meeting gets to rambling along without any point except turning out talk, we bring around the saw, and start using it. We don't use it nearly as much as we did at first; for nobody likes to see it coming, and so we make what we have to say short and to the point.

"There are still plenty of places left where it comes in handy, though, like the cutting short of refusals and saying, 'Let somebody else do it.'

"Then there's the plane. At first we had to use it quite often in smoothing out difficulties about the work, or hurt feelings and jealousies. Some members wouldn't come, because some other member had or hadn't said something to them; and we used to have it pretty hard getting things fixed up until we got the tool-chest and found this plane of charity in it. It's proving to be one of the best tools in the set."

"I'm beginning to see the value of your chest now. But what are some of the other tools?"

"It would take too long to tell about them all, as the set is very complete, but I will mention a few more. You might be interested in the bit and auger."

"Yes; how are they used?"

"We use them for boring into things and finding weak places. You see we used to have considerable difficulty in telling what was best for the society, and whether it was wise to attempt certain things or not. Several times we would adopt a plan that looked first-rate from the outside, and we would go ahead with it enthusiastically. Then, when we started working it out, we would find that it wasn't sound.

"Now, if we have anything of the kind, we take our auger of prayerful consideration, and just bore down through that plan. If we find it to be sound clear through, we go ahead with it. Of course we don't move ahead quite as fast as we did before, but we don't have any rubbish to clear away either. Then I want to tell you about our rule."

"What rule is that?"

"The rule that we measure ourselves by. We measure the length of our absences from prayer meeting with it, as well as the length of the pauses between testimonies, and the number of minutes lost by not beginning the meeting on time. Our rule is, of course, of standard length.

"Then we use the chisel and wedge in opening ways of doing things that people tell us can't be done. These two tools are known as the wedge of prayer and the chisel of faith.

"But there's one thing more I must not forget, and that is our spirit-level. It is a wonderful help to us in telling whether we're standing exactly level or are tilting away from the perpendicular and leaning too much toward things that do not belong to Christian Endeavor. With its aid we can detect the slightest deviation in any of our members, and can correct it. This is really the most valuable tool in the whole set, and is known as the pledge."

"Well, I admitted as he concluded, "I never realized before how valuable a tool-chest could be in keeping a society in good trim."

Bradford, Mass.

The High-School Crisis
A Serious Situation in the Public Schools of the United States

The United States Bureau of Education has been making investigations with alarming results. It has proved that next fall our high schools will face the most serious shortage of teachers in the history of the nation.

Mr. A. O. Neal, who conducted the inquiry, had before him the problem of more than 7,000 high schools that wrote him of their needs. These schools now have a force of 65,857 teachers, a considerable army; and they will need, as the superintendents estimate, 17,275 new teachers in September. This large number will be needed to provide for the usual increase in the enrollment of pupils, and to take the places of the high school teachers that are leaving for other work, lured by the high salaries everywhere prevalent—except, to be sure, in such brainy occupations as teaching.

But of course the 7,000 schools from which Mr. Neal heard are only a part of the high schools in the country. Believing that they represent the general condition of the schools, Mr. Neal estimates that in the fall 25,978 new teachers will be required to fill up the high school ranks.

Now that is a tremendous number of teachers. Are they in sight? They certainly are not.

The Bureau of Education has corresponded with all the colleges and universities of the country, and has asked how many persons they would graduate this year and how many of these graduates expect to teach in the high schools. The Bureau received 323 replies. The graduates of these 323 institutions number 10,680 men and 9,327 women (almost an equal number, it will be noted); and of the twenty thousand only 1,630 men and 4,742 women are looking forward to high school positions.

Supposing that this proportion will continue in the institutions that did not reply, the Bureau figures that 10,620 of this year's graduates may be counted on to fill the yawning gap in the high school teaching force.

The difference between 10,620 and 25,978 is 15,358. How are these 15,358 teachers to be obtained?

If they are not found, many high school classes will be sadly overcrowded, many others cannot be taught, at all, perhaps many high schools must be suspended.

Such a condition is sure to bring back many old teachers to the desks from which they have been driven to make way for younger teachers. It is sure also to put in charge of the young folks large numbers of teachers who are far below the best educational standards. Twice as many high school teachers as there are in all New England must be found; more high school teachers than there are in the great states of New York and Pennsylvania. Many "poor sticks" must be picked up, or the school fires will go out altogether.

The emergency calls imperatively for the raising of teachers' salaries everywhere, and for a decided improvement in the lot of the educator. After the children remain untaught for a while, or taught by incompetents, we shall bitterly regret our parsimonious and short-sighted policy. Incomparably the most important product of our nation is its children. To allow the factories, the mercantile establishments, the banks, and the lawyers' offices to attract all our bright young folks, and starve the teaching profession, is the quickest and surest way to national degeneration.

SEND ALL MONEY FOR
General Home, Kentucky and
Foreign Missions to

MISSIONS

WILLIAM A. GEARHART
General Missionary Secretary
906 Conover Bldg., Dayton, O.

Interesting Experiences Among the Mountaineers

(Note: In many districts in the mountains conditions similar to those described in this article still prevail and such conditions existed in the communities where our Brethren missions are located. This personal experience of a mountain missionary emphasizes the pressing need of spreading the knowledge of our risen Lord among the mountains.—G. C. Carpenter).

By a Mountain Worker

On the morning of Good Friday, I arose at four a. m. to take the morning train, as one of my preaching appointments is usually filled on Friday. After travelling about twenty-five miles we came to a landslide which prevented further progress. The engineer of the train predicted that the workers would not be able to get the track cleared before evening, so I decided to walk the other fifteen miles to my appointment.

It was a beautiful day, coming just after a period of heavy rains. The sunshine was very refreshing and intensified my thought of how the sunshine of God's love warms the soul, and how great an expression of that love was manifested when Jesus died for me.

After travelling about five miles the sky became overcast and soon the rain began to descend. Taking shelter in the depot of the nearest settlement, I spent the time in contemplation of the darkness of the cross. Soon I heard a train whistle and to my welcome surprise the train which I had left back yonder in the mountains came puffing into sight. I climbed aboard and resumed my journey, arriving at my destination about eleven, a. m., hungry (for I had nothing to so far), but happy. After breakfast I walked another two miles to visit some shut-ins, to bring them a message of comfort at the Eastertime. When I returned it was time for supper.

Services had not been held for the past three weeks at this point, due to the unsettled condition of the workers. "Moonshine" whiskey had been very much in evidence of late, and it was not safe to try services during this period of unrest. However, I was rejoicing that we were to resume our worship on this Good-Friday, and I prayed that it might be a Good Friday indeed to many who had never taken Jesus as their own personal Savior.

Just before the time of meeting I was advised that it might not be best to hold, per-

vices that night; for I was told that it was suspected there was a still in the immediate neighborhood and the Deputy Sheriffs were going out to try to locate it that night. After praying the matter over, I decided to hold a service just the same. We went to the school house, the place of meeting, and had one of the best meetings that it has been my privilege to hold at this point. The attendance was fine and the attention good; and hungry souls drank in the story of the Cross. As I knelt in my evening prayer I thanked God for the privilege that had been mine in His service that day. But the day was not over and little did I dream of the events that were to follow before I laid my head upon my pillow.

While preparing to retire I heard a boy's voice crying out on the night air, so I stepped out to see what was wanted. There sat a boy of about 12 years, astride a mule, and in excited tones he said, "There's been some shootin' up thar," indicating with his thumb the direction of the creek, "and they need help." My host and I started out in the direction given. On our way we aroused a Deputy Sheriff in the camp and then we proceded up the creek towards the head of the stream.

It was a beautiful moonlight night so we were able to make good progress over the uneven ground of the creek bed. After walking about half a mile we saw someone coming through the tres. At this apparition came staggering into view we saw a man carrying two gallon jars of Moonshine; and with his shirt front dyed crimson with his life's blood, he looked ghastly in the moonlight. He was one of the Deputy Sheriffs, and said that he and a companion had started out to try and locate the still. On the way they had come across two men on muleback, loaded with Moonshine. As the two Deputies approached them they immediately commenced to shoot. He said his partner had been badly shot and the two "bootleggers" were also badly wounded, he being the only one that was in a condition to go for help. This he had done, and then after the boy had started out, he had returned in order to get the Moonshine that he was carrying. As I was unarmed it was decided that I had better go with this wounded man to the nearest house (for he was pretty weak by this time) and do what I could for him, and also telephone for the sheriff and doctor.

We entered into the home of the boy who had first gone for help, and for the benefit of those who have never seen what once was a typical mountain home, such as still exist in large numbers, I shall describe this one. The room into which we entered had but one small window which was about two feet square. The only light we had came form the open fireplace. The walls were papered with old newspapers, and the rough boards of the floor would afford poor protection against the wind if the cracks were not filled with dirt which was the accumulation of years. Although this room was only about ten by twelve feet, two full sized beds were crowded into it and upon our arrival, about six children and a number of grown people were in these beds. The mother, father, and one of the older girls were up awaiting our coming. There was another room in the house and the children were soon hustled into this.

After heating some water, we stripped the wounded man and found that he had been shot through the right side. When he was as comfortable as we could make him, I went back down to the settlement and telephoned for the Sheriff and doctor. Returning to the house I found that by this time quite a crowd of men had gathered. My host and his companion had returned saying they had found the other Deputy, who was wounded in three places, and they needed more help to bring him in. Taking a sheet with them as an improvised stretcher, they soon brought him in. He was in a sad condition, having been shot through the left forearm, the left leg above the knee, and through the right lung. No attempt was made up to this time to go out after the renegades, as it was too dangerous, for if they were in a condition to shoot they would have the advantage of anyone coming upon them.

About one a. m. the Sheriff and two doctors arrived and a posse was formed to go out after the other two wounded men; and as the men had taken a little courage from the moonshine while waiting for the Sheriff, it looked like bad business before we were through. I remained with the doctors, and gave what assistance I could. After the men had been made as comfortable as possible, under the circumstances, the doctors left for the house farther up the creek; for we had received word that one of the "bootleggers" had crawled to this house and was there, very badly wounded.

After the doctors had left I turned to those who had remained to look after the wounded and said, "Friends. I do not know how you feel at a time like this, or whether you ever think of the Life that is to come; or not; but I believe in a God who hears and answers prayers. A God who shed His blood that we might receive pardon for sin; and not only this but He died and rose again that we might receive comfort and strength to sustain us in a time of need, and He is the only one who can help us at a time like this." So we knelt and took our case to the Great Physician, and I hope that the tears that were shed by hardened men were truly from repentant hearts.

Then I thought that I might be of service to the other poor fellow in the house up the creek where the doctors had gone, so I inquired how to get there, and they told me. Following the directions as best I could I made my way up the mountain, but soon came to the realization that I had lost my way so retraced my steps. Upon returning to the house the woman implored me not to go again, but I thought it best. She gave more explicit directions, and again I started off and soon came upon an old logging trail, and

believing that to be the road, followed that. For the next half hour I passed over the roughest stretch of country I think I have ever traveled. Through mud and water, over logs and through underbrush, I was often disappointed for everything that looked like a house turned out to be rocks in the shadows. Once again I realized that I was lost, and as I was in the neighborhood of the shooting and also liable to run into a still, and as my actions there in the moonlight might not appear as those of a man who was seeking the benefit of his fellow men, I decided to turn back. This I did feeling that my purpose had been defeated. Upon my return I found the dirt road going over the mountain—a fairly good dirt road, the last thing I expected to find in that country.

It was then almost three, and as I had to catch the train at six-thirty I went to bed, it having been over twenty-four hours since I arose from my bed the day before.

At the train—the next morning I met my companions of the night before, taking the badly wounded sheriff to the hospital. I learned that both moonshiners had been found, the last one having fallen exhausted from loss of blood as he was attempting to

go through the gap at the other side of the range of mountains.

As we view these things in the light of the Cross, how much we have to thank our Heavenly Father that Jesus shed His blood for our redemption and for all the fullness of joy that we have in a life of service for Him. The thought comes of our responsibility for these conditions in the mountains, for the people have been slow in going to these parts to tell them the Old Love Story. Today there are hundreds of homes in which the name of Jesus has never been heard except in blasphemy, and it is safe to say that never in the history of that home was voice ever raised in prayer to God before. What are you going to do about it? There is one thing you can do, pray for us, for we need your prayers so much.

Upon my return home I had services on Easter Sunday morning and evening, and as our prayers were going up to the Father thanking Him for the blessings of the day, a woman shot her husband through the right shoulder, their home being on the hillside, and in plain view from the church door. This, too, was the result of a drunken brawl.

NEWS FROM THE FIELD

PLEASANT GROVE, IOWA

With God as our Father and the leadership of Jesus before us, we push forward, and on our forward march, sing, "Savior more than life to me. Lead us gently, gently as we go, Trusting thee, we cannot stray. We can never, never lose our way." The last Sunday in June our church house was too small for the people all to get seated. We have the best cooperation in helping to interest the people in our community. Our program was a success, and reported the best they ever had. Do you know why many churches are dying? It is because people will not take time to train their children in religious exercises. I was told once by a good sister that she never saw any spiritual good from a harvest meeting or a children's day exercises. The only reason that we can not see any spiritual good is due to the fact that we do not want to take time to prepare for the occasion. The trouble is in the church. It is running a race with the world—wanting something for nothing. If we want the child to be a religious worker we must train that child to sing and speak from the platform of our churches and this takes time and patience. And the church that has no time to teach their children this important lesson will die.

It is a pleasure to work with a church, when the church works with you, dear pastors. I do not know whether the Pleasant Grove people really know what was best for them, but they gave their pastor a unanimous call for another year. And we have decided to stay with these good people for another year. We preach the Gospel and are working for the interest of the first Brethren church. And if providence does not fail, we will be represented at General Conference with all the delegates that the law allows us. We are proud that we are Brethren. Some people are a little timid about telling that they are a Brethren. Well, if I were afraid to tell it, I would not belong to such a church. I love the very meaning of Brethren. We go to conference, preachers and laity, as Brethren. And if the world stands until the Brethren church is as old as the Methodist church is or the Presbyterian; we will be stronger in numbers than they, considering our short life. And we have cast a line of Brethrenism from the Atlantic to the Pacific, and from the Dominion of Canada to the Gulf of Mexico and even to South America and the middle of Africa. God is helping us to great things and the gates of hell shall not prevail against us, as long as we follow the Leader, Jesus Christ. But do we consider the strain on our little Jerusalem! What do I mean when I say "Jerusalem?" I mean Ashland, the Jerusalem of the Brethren church. Look at the job she has on her hands, to supply her readers with the news of the field, the needs of the Sunday school, the needs of preachers and to urge the carrying of the Gospel to the four winds of the earth, with our Publishing House in a losing proposition! What shall we do? The time to use some home mission money is here. Brother Teeter, surely there is money enough to pay for a car load of paper. If there isn't, we can soon raise it by a call through the Evangelist. I have ten dollars to start it. This is my way to do it. I would not give a cent for a Brethren that would not stand by the institutions of our church.

H. W. ANDERSON.

MASONTOWN, PENNSYLVANIA

Perhaps many have wondered whether the "Masontown Brethren" are on the map or still living. If the readers could have been here for the last month that question would not occupy any place in their minds any longer. Brother Shively answered the call to succeed Mr. Hendrickson as Bursar of Ashland College. As former pastor he left the place in splendid condition. We came to Masontown June the tenth, and considering the long absence of a pastor the work is moving along nicely.

The first evening we spent in Masontown one good brother succeeded in diverting our attention from the parsonage by taking us on a little touring exhibition. Upon our return we were ushered into the parsonage and out on the lawn where a great donation was awaiting us. To say the least, the entire affair was a complete surprise for the pastor and his companion. The members were all filled with enthusiasm and seemed to be running over with joy and happiness. Brother and Sister Belote came all the way from Uniontown to witness our surprise and the state of satisfaction expressed by all. Yet he claimed that he knew nothing whatever concerning the event. Among the many things that were so generously and so bountifully given were eats of all kinds, bedding, dishes, towels and apparatus for washing. They kindly remarked that the tub and washboard were for the pastor but later on I noticed a rolling pin—thanks to providence, it is a glass one. After an enjoyable evening, during which time refreshments were served, one by one they all dispersed feeling that they had achieved their goal, their ideal was realized. Every one reported having had a very pleasant time. We all felt we were well acquainted already. These dear people at Masontown will always occupy a preeminent place in our memory and were we not to express our deepest and most heartfelt gratitude we would be ingrates indeed.

Our work at this place is going nicely. The Methodist people and we have united in union services during the summer months. Last evening the children of the Brethren church rendered an excellent program. There is splendid material among the young folk and we expect that you shall hear from them later.

We are anticipating a very interesting and pleasant work with the Masontown Brethren in the days to come. Brethren, pray for us, for we covet your support.

Fraternally yours,
JOS. L. GINGRICH.

Program of the Thirty-Second General Conference of the Brethren Church Winona Lake, Indiana August 13 to September 5, 1920

Moderator .... Dr. Chas. A. Bame
Vice Moderator, ... Elder J. A. Garber
Secretary, ... Elder Dyoll Belote
Assistant Sec. .... Elder Miles J. Snyder
Treasurer .... Norman G. Kimmel
Sec. Ex. Com. .... Dr. E. M. Cobb
Slogan—Stand Fast in the Faith.
Platform—The Bible, the Whole Bible and Nothing But the Bible.
Text—Forever, O Lord, Thy Word Is Settled in Heaven (Psalm 119-89).
Theme—Go Ye Therefore and Teach all Nations.

Conference Speakers

Dr. WILLIAM EVANS, ... Wheaton, Ill.
DR. J. ALLEN MILLER, ... Ashland, Ohio

Music Director

ARTHUR LYNN, ... Dayton, Ohio

Ministerial Program

Wednesday—
Devotions—G. L. Maus.
Annual Report of Secretary-Treasurer.
Annual Election of Officers.
Thursday—
Devotions—L. A. Myers.
The Minister as a Leader—H. H. Wolford.
Business.
Friday—
Devotions—Edwin Boardman.
Church Problems (Query Box).
Discussion led by Martin Shively.
Report of Committees.
Saturday—
Devotions—E. B. Shaver.
Memorial Services.
Unfinished Business.

Christian Endeavor Program

Tuesday—
Young People and the Church—
Arthur Lynn
Culturing Their Spiritual Life—
E. M. Riddle
Wednesday—
Young People and the Kingdom—
M. A. Witter

Training Them to Use Their Money Aright— E. A. Myer.
Thursday—
Young People and the State—
A. E. Whitted
Keping C. E. Prominent—Earle Huette.
Friday—
Young People and Their Education—
Dr. E. E. Jacobs
Enlisting Them for Service—
Edwin Boardman
Saturday—
Young People and Christian Endeavor—
F. C. Vanator
On the Lookout and the Outlook—
E. A. Rowsey
Sunday—
Junior Endeavor—Nora Bracken.
Intermediate Endeavor—Mrs. H. H. Wolford.

Laymen's Program

Wednesday—
How Can the Layman Assist the Pastor?
—Henry V. Wall.
Open Discussion led by Chair.
Thursday—
The Laymen's Place in the Church Services—Herman Roscoe.
Open Discussion led by Chair.
Friday—
The Laymen's Responsibility in Prayer Meeting.
Open Discussion led by Chair.
Saturday—
What Can We Do to Encourage Our Very Best Young Men to Enter the Ministry?
—Arthur Lynn.
Open Discussion led by Chair.

Sunday School Program

Tuesday—
Frankly Facing the Facts—J. A. Garber.
The Place of the Bible in the Life of the Child—W. H. Beachler.
Wednesday—
The Church's Educational Program—
J. A. Garber.
Religious Education in the Home—
W. H. Beachler.
Thursday—
A Statistical Mirror—Albert Trent.
Forward March! A Call to Advance!—
J. Fremont Watson.
Recognition Service—Albert Trent.
Friday—
Officer and Teacher Training—W. I. Duker.
Curriculum—H. H. Wolford.
Saturday—
Adolescent Problems—Miles J. Snyder.
Children's Division Activities — Pauline Wismer.

Home Mission Program

Tuesday—
The Highest Efficiency in Brethren Home Missions—G. T. Ronk.
The Home Mission Call and Accomplishment West of the Rockies—A. V. Kimmel
The General Secretary's Message—
Wm. A. Gearhart.
Wednesday—
The Home Mission Call From the Cumberlands—Orion E. Bowman.
The Outlook—G. E. Drushal and J. A. Rempel (10 min. each).
Stewardship—W. H. Beachler.

Foreign Mission Program

Thursday—
Pray for Our Ambassadors—A. L. DeLozier
The South American Field—Edwards.
Friday—
Missionary Motives That Are Biblical—
A. J. McClain
The African Field—L. S. Bauman.

Educational Program

Saturday—
The Function of the Small College—
Miles J. Snyder
Facing Up to the Situation in the College world—Dr. E. E. Jacobs.
Sunday—
The Present, an Opportune Time for the Emphasis of Religious Education—
J. A. Garber.
The Present Challenge to the Christian College—Dr. E. E. Jacobs.

The Publication Program

Wednesday—
Business Manager's Report—
Dr. R. R. Teeter.
A Representative Church Literature—
Dr. A. D. Gnagey.
Thursday—
Editorial Address—Geo. S. Baer.
The Need Most Important and Most Neglected.—Dr. A. D. Gnagey.

Evangelistic and Bible Study League

Report of Officers—Henry V. Wall and J. C. Beal.
Reports of Field Workers—Dr. W. S. Bell and I. D. Bowman.
Wednesday—
Preparation for Revival by Pastor and People—Dr. Chas. A. Bame.
Round Table Discussion.
Thursday—
The Evangelist, His Message and Methods—By B. T. Burnworth.
Round Table Discussion.
Friday—
Bible Study in Evangelistic and Regular Services—By L. S. Bauman.
Round Table Discussion.
Saturday—
The League, Its Objective—George Ronk.
Round Table Discussion.

SOCIOLOGIST REPORTS FAVORABLY ON EFFECTS OF NATIONAL PROHIBITION DENIES EXODUS OF FOREIGNERS TO AVOID DROUGHT

(Continued from June 23)

"No reliable data could be secured bearing directly upon the effect of prohibition on community life, especially among the poor though, as the superintendent of the Philadelphia Society for Organizing Charity said 'We know what way the wind is blowing. The men who used to spend their money in the saloon are now inclined to give it, or at least a portion of it to their families. It is true that there is still drinking and in some instances there appears to be a tendency to increased gambling.

Emigration

"But if there are some mooted questions that cannot now be definitely answered, there are others that have been cleared up. One of these is the persistent charge that the recent emigration from America has been due to prohibition. In an interview with the official at Washington who has most to do with the issuance of passports to aliens I was told there had not been discovered a single in tance of prohibition being named as a reason for wanting to leave America. The reasons given are to visit relatives, to look for property to bring back relatives to America, spend last days in the place of birth and so on. These 'reasons' were confirmed to me by two educated Italians who had spent much time visiting among their countrymen and there, either when they were contemplating leaving the country or when on the high seas. It may be added that there is a report that steamship agents are using the prohibition argument to induce aliens to leave. The best answer, however, to the charge that prohibition is the cause of recent emigration is in the 'Report of the Commissioner of Immigration for 1919, which shows that the total emigration for the last year was only 123,522, which is 44.73 percent less than the average migration since 1908, in which the total number leaving our shores was 395,075.''

Drug Habit

"There appears to be a general impression that prohibition has caused an increase in the drug habit. Dr. George H. Simmons, editor of the Journal of the American Medical Association does not think so. Moreover he has just published an editorial in his journal showing that the restriction of the use of alcohol in Germany during the war was followed by a diminution of the use of harmful drugs.' In an interview with Dr. Arthur Dean Bevan, former president of the American Medical Association, he dictated and afterward signed the following statement: '' It is possible that in this transition period a few people cut off from the use of alcohol have resorted to drugs as a substitute, but if this is true it is simply a temporary matter and due to this transition from the free use of alcohol to prohibition and the number of these cases is very small compared the number that were made drug addicts the free use of alcohol in the past.''

LABOR

Dr. McLennan reports Frank Morrison, Secretary of the American Federation of Labor stating that the wide spread opposition of union labor men to prohibition, due largely to their sympathy for brewery and distillery workers who supposedly would be thrown out of employment, has largely disappeared since has been found that these men have rapidly been absorbed into other lines of work at in most cases are more remunerative than the old.

Police Records

The most tangible evidences of the effects of prohibition are found in the police and court records of our cities. These show a decrease in the number of ostensible criminals confined or on trial running from 30 to 90 percent, Columbus and Harrisburg showing improved conditions approximating the latter figure.

Hospitals

''Returns from seven hospitals under the department of Public Welfare of New York city substantially agree with the statement Dr. G. Kremer of Sea View Hospital, west New Brighton, 'that the intoxicated raging house and hospital rounder type is w the exception, while he was formerly the le. In the psychopathic pavilion a marked crease in the number of admissions for alcoholism is noted . There is a wonderful ange for the better in the appearance and aduct of many employees who formerly ank to excess.'

''Dr. J. C. Deane, chief resident physician the Philadelphia General Hospital, reported on April 14 that the alcoholic ward of s hospital was then running with from 15 20 inmates. Formerly the number was out 300.

''Dr. Karl Meyer of the great Cook County Hospital, Chicago, said: 'We practically have no alcoholic patients any more. The typical hospital bum seems to have disappeared.' ''

Even the Brewers are Happy

Rescue Missions are finding so few of the old time ''down and outers'' to deal with that they are having to recast their methods of work. Practically all the liquor ''cures'' are closing their doors. Public sentiment seems constantly growing stronger for prohibition. Even the Secretary of the United States Brewers' Association, Hugh F. Fox, with whom Dr. McLennan spent an hour, says that he does not want the saloon to come back, and that his clients will be satisfied with the manufacture of non-intoxicating beer to be sold under respectable conditions to respectable people.

Prohibition in Other Lands

Word from Sudan

''As to the situation here, I do not see how it could be much worse. Nothing at all that I have heard of is being done to better conditions.

''The sale of whisky to the Sudanese is prohibited by the government, as this country is under British control, but there is a great deal of illegal selling. Those who do this, do it at a great risk and charge exhorbitant prices, and then sell only a very low grade of badly adulterated whisky. You can imagine the result to the native. I was asked what his religion was. He said: 'I have the religion of the Englishman; I drink whisky and say no prayers.' The Greeks do much of this unlawful business and as their shops are to be found everywhere, it must be a wide-spread business.

''The natives drink 'marisa;' used by men, women and children. It is perhaps a greater menace to these people than whisky. This drink is made of dura or native corn and is brewed much as beer is made. However, it has a higher percentage of alcohol, and doctors say it is more intoxicating. I was told by a Sudanese woman that rarely do you find a Sudanese girl that has not been raised on 'marisa.' They are put on this diet as babies and get little besides for years. This woman has a small school for girls and she told me that practically all of the little girls who came to her were 'marisa' users.

''A mother would only laugh when a child became so drunk that it reeled around. I have visited some of the 'marisa' shops, which are to be distinguished by the small white flag which floats above them and is the sign of government approval of the traffic, and they are loathsome places. However they are popular resorts for all classes. The native village is usually very quiet in the day time but resounds with the singing and revelry of its inhabitants at night, of which the 'marisa' shop is the center.

''It is amazing the quantities they are able to consume of this drink. A Syrian doctor, who has practiced here for eighteen years and knows conditions pretty well, told me that one person could drink gallons in a day. It is not hard to imagine the effect on the people

as a race. They are very thin and poor, unable to withstand disease, and are a ready prey to tuberculosis, pneumonia, influenza, and the like.''

—From a letter from Miss Aulora McIntyre, American Mission, Khartum North, Sudan, Africa.

What One University President Has Observed of the Effects of Prohibition

''Having resided for fifteen years in a great whisky and beer manufacturing center, and witnessed the effect of the liquor business on other industries and the evils of the saloon control of most public concerns, I am convinced that the only way to eliminate the saloon is to prohibit the manufacture and sale of all alcoholic liquors, I am ,therefore, opposed to any modification of the law which would permit the manufacture or distribution of beer and wine, and thus bring back the saloon, as it would certainly do, with all of its political, as well as physical and moral evils.

''Since the saloons have been eliminated here, conditions are improving rapidly. There is less crime, as shown by the police, the court, and the workhouse reports, and much better health as shown by the hospital records. The people are, for the most part, adapting themselves to prohibition with excellent spirit. The only complaints are from the old habitual drinkers and those commercially interested in the liquor industry. Business is better, more money is going into the savings banks and into the homes, and the women and children are happier.''

—Charles Wm. DABNEY, President Cincinnati University (Just resigned), Cincinnati, Ohio.

The Tithing Stewardship Corner

Practically every interest of the Brethren church is in need of more liberal financial support than is possible under the present plan and proportion of giving. This is true particularly of the College and the Publishing House. The publications of the Brethren are not what they might be made if the means were supplied whereby improvements could be made possible. There are many commendable methods to which we might resort make possible the larger need financial support, but any method that is temporary is not adequate. It is likely that we shall find that our people will only give adequately continuously when they shall be induced to make it the practice of their lives to give a tenth of their income to the Lord's work. More and more tithing is being encouraged by the various denominations as the most satisfactory and just method of financing the Kingdom. Brethren churches that have tried the plan are rejoicing in the success it has brought. For the encouragement of others the tithing experiences of individuals and churches are welcomed.

A Remarkable Record

In the January 3 Christian Observer,

LouisVille, Ky., apears, in the church news department, the following account:

"The first Sunday in January was the seVenth anniVersary of the pastorate of the Rev. E. D. Brownlee in Sanford. The church bulletin for the day called attention to the remarkable growth. A fine church plant has been erected, which is worth at least $50,-000. A work among young people has been inaugurated which has been quite successful. Its Senior Christian EndeaVor for several years held the highest efficiency record eVer made by a Christian EndeaVor Society. It has an enthusiastic Junior Christian Endeavor Society. The Sunday school has been developed into a gold seal school. An unusually large number of mature men haVe been received into the church on profession of faith. The year 1919 has been the best in the history of the church."

Immediately following the aboVe was printed an article by the pastor:

"The Sanford Presbyterian church has been deeply stirred by the tithing movement. Ninety-two members enrolled as tithers in one day. The pastor and eVery elder and deacon enrolled themselves before speaking to anybody else. It has stirred the religious circles of the town; especially so because of the prominence of many of the tithers. Among some of them are chairman of the board of county commissioners, the mayor of the city, the president of the board of trade, the editor of the daily paper, president of one bank and Vice-president of another, Various directors in the three banks of the city, and a number of prominent merchants, capitalists, and Vegetable growers. It is expected that more will enroll themselVes as a result of this movement."

Before publishing the aboVe, I decided to write the pastor for a brief account of his methods in obtaining the remarkable results above described. The following is his reply:

"Sanford, Fla., February 12, 1920.
"Dear Layman:

"I thank you for your letter in reference to the tithing campaign in our church. The following were the preparatory steps:

"1. A general educational campaign through the use of the tithing literature from the Layman Company. This literature was distributed pretty regularly for a year.

"2. About a month before Commitment Sunday, the prayer band of the church united in prayer for the success of the tithers' campaign.

"3. A strong personal letter from the chairman of the board of deacons was sent to eVery member of the church, laying the privilege and responsibility of tithing upon their hearts. A pamphlet on tithing was enclosed in this letter.

"4. The campaign was next taken up by the officers of the church, and the pastor and eVery officer enrolled themselves as tithers.

"5. The matter was then presented to the congregation by a sermon by the pastor, followed by a number of short, snappy talks given by men not accustomed to speak in public but prominent in the business affairs

---

of the community. These men were new tithers.

"Sincerely,
"E. Darnall Brownlee."

When we look into the long aVenue of the future and see the good there is for each of us to do, we realize, after all, what a beautiful thing it is to work and to live, and be happy.—Robert Louis SteVenson.

MINISTERIAL EXCHANGE

The Elkhart, Indiana, church is seeking a pastor due to the resignation of Brother H. H. Wolford to accept a position on the Ashland College faculty. Any one wishing to correspond with the church should write to C. E. Stephey, 1144 Prairie St., Elkhart, Indiana.

The pastor of the SergeantsVille, New Jersey, charge is leaVing this pastorate September 1. Any pastor contemplating making a change may correspond with the following committee:

Willis C. Myers,
Joseph D. Wilson,
M. H. Wilson.

Brother C. D. Whitmer writes that he will be open to a call to a pastorate for full time serVice following General Conference. He may be addressed at 217 East Dubail AVenue, South Bend, Indiana.

THE TIE THAT BINDS

WYCOFF-WENTZ—On June 30, 1920, at the home of the writer in Peru, Indiana, Miss Nellie Wycoff and Earl R. Wentz of Portland, Indiana, were united in marriage. Miss Wycoff is a faithful member of the Center Chapel Brethren church and has also been

---

prominent in the Woman's Missionary ciety in the national organization. groom is a highly respected business m We join their many friends in wishing th the best that life offers.
G. C. CARPENTER.

BRUBAKER-FUDGE — On Wednesd June 30th, 1920, at 8 o'clock, A. M., a dou ring wedding ceremony took place at t Gratis Brethren church. Mr. Roy M. Br baker and Miss Dorothy Lucile Fudge w united in marriage in the presence of i mediate friends and relatiVes.

These promising young people have well wishes and prayers of a large host friends for a happy married life. Both members of the Brethren Church and earn Christian workers. Ceremony by their p tor.
C. E. BEEKLEY.

IN THE SHADOW

RICKMAN—Warneda Christine, and M Nadine, infant twins of Brother and Sis W. E. Rickman, died at their home in R noke, Va., July 8th, 1920, at the tender a of two months and twenty days. Fune service was conducted by the writer at cadia, Va., and the bodies were laid to n near the old home. They were members our Cradle Roll and as buds of prom were carefully gathered for the heave flower garden.
L. G. WOOD.

TURNER—John W. Turner, aged 18 ye departed this life in New York, being a me ber of the U. S. Army. The body shipped to his parents in Roanoke, Va., t funeral was conducted from a little chu in the old home neighborhood, in Bedf county, Va., where the body was laid to r conducted by the writer on June 26, 1920
L. G. WOOD.

NIEBEL—Jeremiah Niebel was born J 4, 1838, and departed this life June 3, 19 lacking but five hours of being eighty-t years old. He united with the Breth church of Miamisburg, Ohio, in 1873, serv as a trustee till his death, and was the fi of its charter members to pass beyond. 1855, he was married to Henrietta Spelln who was called home ten years ago. F children were born, three of whom died infancy. SurViving him are his son Cha with whom he made his home recently, daughter Clara, who faithfully cared for father to the last. Services conducted in home at Miamisburg by the writer, assis by Rev. Sweat of the M. E. church.

"Thou shalt come to thy grave in a full a Like as a shock of grain cometh in its s son."
M. M. HOOVER.

Thou Shalt Love the Lord Thy God
... And Thy Neighbor as Thyself.

But he . . . said unto Jesus, And who is my neighbor?
Jesus made answer and said:

A CERTAIN man was going down from Jerusalem to Jericho; and he fell among robbers, which both stripped him and beat him, and departed, leaving him half dead. And by chance a certain priest was going down that way: and when he saw him he passed by on the other side. And in like manner a Levite also, when he came to the  place, and saw him, passed by on the other side. But a certain Samaritan, as he journeyed, came where he was: and when he saw him, he was moved with compassion, and came to him, and bound up his wounds, pouring in oil and wine; and he set him on his own beast, and brought him to an inn, and took care of him. . . . Which of these three, thinkest thou, proved neighbor to him that fell among robbers?

And Jesus said unto him, Go, and do thou likewise.

Published every Wednesday at Ashland, Ohio. All matter for publication must reach the Editor not later than Friday noon of the preceding week.

George S. Baer, Editor

The
Brethren
Evangelist

When ordering your paper changed give old as well as new address. Subscriptions discontinued at expiration. To avoid missing any numbers renew two weeks in advance.

R. R. Teeter, Business Manager

OFFICIAL ORGAN OF THE BRETHREN CHURCH

Subscription price, $2.00 per year, payable in advance.
Entered at the Post Office at Ashland, Ohio, as second-class matter.
Acceptance for mailing at special rate of postage provided for in section 1103, Act of October 3, 1917, authorized September 9, 1918.
Address all matter for publication to Geo. S. Baer, Editor of the Brethren Evangelist, and all business communications to R. R. Teeter, Business Manager, Brethren Publishing Company, Ashland, Ohio. Make all checks payable to the Brethren Publishing Company.

TABLE OF CONTENTS

EDITORIAL

The Fine Art of Neighboring

"Neighboring" is suggestive of "others," of unselfishness and of helpfulness. It suggests activity very noble and most essential to the right relations of men one to another, and yet very difficult oftentimes to accomplish. It is necessary to the making of life happy both on the part of the neighbor and the neighborhood. It is required by the teachings of our Lord and by high moral necessity (Of such kind are all of Christ's teachings). It is a pressing demand, ever present with us, and yet never was there a time when it was more needed than now, when suffering and distress are everywhere present and many are laboring under handicaps too great for their strength.

Neighboring is never a great task, beyond our means or power. It is simply the doing of the little acts of kindness that are more sorely needed and more highly prized than the bestowing of great riches. It is not embarrassing another by unnecessary charity, nor pauperizing the improvident by making it unnecessary for him to struggle for his own provision. It is not doing the things which the enactments of civil government require, but things that are voluntary and show the spirit of friendliness and good will. The laws of the state do not require one farmer to exchange work with another in the busy harvesting and threshing season; or loan the use of a horse for some urgent work when a neighbor's horse has sickened and died; they do not require the hoeing of a garden of a poor widow who has been weakened by her struggle for a livelihood, nor the loaning of a loaf of bread to a neighbor in a time of pressing need, nor the loan of a book or magazine, nor the giving of time to a friendly chat or some words of good cheer and encouragement to a soul in the grip of loneliness and discouragement. These and a thousand other things, small but so necessary, are not demanded by any legal requirements, but how much of joy and value they add to life! And who cannot recall when he has felt himself greatly in need of just such little acts of kindness and neighborliness.

Some one has said, "Is there one among us all who cannot remember days—hard, disheartening days—when a neighbor's loving act or presence came like a benediction, filling our hearts or moving us to tears as he who had 'fallen among thieves' must have been moved when the good Samaritan bent over him? Our 'thieves,' perhaps, were not of the kind that run away on two feet, but rather of the deadlier sort; discouragement, mayhap, or loneliness, or failure, or sorrow, or disgrace, or want. Yet our help came to us as it came to him of old, through a great-hearted 'neighbor;' a neighbor who chanced to be driving by, and who did not 'pass by on the other side.'"

We have all known such hours, and have had such neighbors. We have known how great a blessing came into our lives because of them—because of the lovingkindness they showered upon us. Is there anything more binding upon us than the passing on to some one else—lonely, disheartened or defeated—whatever act of kindness our ability makes possible and their need requires? Too often we live isolated and selfishly in the midst of many who need the kindness of a good Samaritan neighbor. Too often we "pass by on the other side" to avoid being brought face to face with needs we are unwilling to supply. We do not wish to be embarrassed by refusal to perform the neighborly act that is needed, and so we seek to escape meeting it.

Not only individuals but churches fail to play the part of a true neighbor very often. Some churches are indifferent to the needs of the community. They go along in their ruts of religious worship never branching out into other lines of interest and activity, never seeking to do anything to break down the barriers of mutual disinterestedness that so often exists between the world and the church. Other churches are proud, selfish and exclusive; those who worship there do not wish to be disturbed by the cries of need being brought to their ears; they do not wish to be inconvenienced by going out of their way to help the wretched community; and they do not wish to be humiliated by having objects of distress and need presented to their door. None but the truly elite can worship in their magnificent courts of praise, and it would be a disgrace to their exalted dignity to take their religion either in the form of worship or practical helpfulness to the community. Still other churches, because of their self-righteousness and feeling of exceeding superiority, hold themselves aloof from the community and refuse to perform some most important kinds of service. The true church must indeed come apart from the world and touch not that which is unclean, but it must at the same time make itself a vital part of all life and conduct and be the saving salt of every worthy function and institution of man. And more than that, it must keep in mind the fact that it is necessary not merely to "preach the gospel" to those who will come to the house of God to hear it, but to go out into the community and "become all things to all men" in order to win them, even as Jesus not only preached the gospel to the poor, but healed the sick, cleansed the lepers, cast out devils, comforted the sorrowing, and ministered to all the needs of humanity. He himself is the one who enjoined neighborly conduct; will he not require it of his "body" and "bride?"

The nation, too, that would be worthy of wearing the name of Christ should show itself a neighbor to other nations—weak or strong, civilized or savage, near or far. The day when a nation may be selfish and exclusive, disregardful of the needs and distresses of other nations and yet maintain its self-respect is fast passing. It has been a long hard process, and we have not yet completed the travail of it, whereby we are being freed from the selfish isolation of the past and permitted to rise, into that nobler and truer freedom of service and the recognition of mutual relationships and obligations among the nations. We are coming to realize that there is a responsibility resting upon us as a nation to neighbor other nations and peoples, especially those that are weak and defenceless.

To illustrate, let us have brought to our minds the fact that there exists in America a great body of people deeply sympathetic with Armenia, anxious that America shall not fail in its duty toward her. So far as food and clothing and temporary rehabilitation go, the Near East Relief accomplishes their desire. But they feel that America has duties toward Armenia that the Near East Relief cannot carry out because they involve government and political action, not necessarily the assumption of an American mandate, but very certainly the assuring that the Armenians shall not be slaughtered and that the new state shall have safety and the best chance possible for success.

But to play the part of a good neighbor is not so easy; that is, it is not so easy to become willing to do the neighborly act. We are naturally selfish and averse to seeking the interests of others. Neighborliness is not an inheritance, or a talent bestowed upon us; it is an acquirement, a quality that must be developed. Neighboring then is an art; something that requires much training to be able to do with skill and naturalness that gives effectiveness. There are a few who seem to be artists by nature, so there are some to whom it comes natural to be a good neighbor. They take delight in it; their unselfishness is evident. But for the most of us it comes hard, and requires much practice. With definite purpose, wise planning, persistent determination we must seek to play the part of a neighbor. Even then we shall often find ourselves discouraged by repeated failures. It will require more than all the perseverance that human will can master; it will require the spirit and power of the infinite God to perfect in us the fine art of neighboring.

EDITORIAL REVIEW

When a Christian with holy purpose and a heart filled with love goes on a quest for souls, all the power of heaven is at his command.

If you are acquainted with happiness, introduce him to your neighbor.—Brooks.

The men and women who are lifting the world upward and onward are those who encourage more than criticise.—Harrison.

The reason why some folks do not enjoy life is because they put so little into it.

Brother Shively finds the busy life of financial secretary of the college is made more strenuous by frequent calls to conduct funerals, a number of which he reports in this issue.

Brother W. I. Duker writes us personally, while sending in his article published in this issue, that the work of the New Paris church, of which he is pastor is "going very nicely."

How strong is the power of a lofty fellowship! Jesus knew it was one of the mightiest forces that girds and upholds a life, and so he said to his disciples, "Abide in me."

Statistical reports in? Well, they must be in for Ohio churches or you will be shown up. Brother E. G. Mason, Ohio conference secretary and statistician, writes that three churches have reported thus far. He promises to send in names of others reporting next week. If your name doesn't appear it is a bad sign. Get busy!

A card from Brother George Kinzie, pastor at New Lebanon, Ohio, mentions the "arrival of a new preacher" in their home, a few weeks ago, "thus necessitating a great deal of 'theological' training." Congratulations to Brother and Sister Kinzie. This is one important way of recruiting the ministry.

When we consider the great price that the Father placed upon the life of man, that he was willing to give his own Son to win him unto himself, we should regard man of more value than we are wont to do. Man is not a worthless worm, but a potential son of God. This should give to every life great meaning and value.

We can never be made to realize how far-reaching is the influence we are wielding every day; but we should so walk, every hour and minute, that no one shall be led astray by us. We must have no "off times," for during such times we may wield a bad influence that will require eternity to tell the story.

There are many, trying and disheartening experiences in life; scarcely is there one who can evade them. But by the grace of God they can all be made more bearable than we think, and out of them all we can come, stronger, nobler and more sympathetic. Diamonds must be ground before they sparkle and lives must be tried and proven e'er they glow with beauty.

Mexico, Indiana, is heard from over the signature of Brother Loren T. Black. He reports the work in good condition under the leadership of Brother J. W. Clark and that at a recent business meeting, the church extended him a call to serve as pastor for another year. Brother Black takes occasion to state that they "are loyally behind our church college." That shows both wisdom and gratitude.

In the stress and need of war men realized their common brotherhood to a degree heretofore unknown, but it was only temporary in as much as it was based upon mutual need and not upon love. This is the opportune time for the Christian church to press upon the world its need of a brotherhood based upon love and a common fellowship in Jesus Christ.

If you had to make out and arrange a report of this year and of the entire four years of our "Program" you would understand why Brother Miles Snyder is in earnest about your reporting immediately as to what your church has done or has not done. When you stop to think how much time and nerve-energy these Four Year Program directors are spending in order to get pastors and church leaders to do what is their plain duty to do, and that they are getting nothing out of it except the joy of service and a few "knocks," we wonder that they are willing to do it. Let us all come across with our report right now, if we have not already.

Brother Wm. H. Beachler and Brother Claude R. Koontz had a great time together in the latter's parish, soliciting for college endowment. Brother Koontz being an Ashland College graduate was thoroughly interested in making the campaign a success in his parish and Brother Beachler says it was a success. They had to travel a great many miles to cover the territory, but they were royally received wherever they went. Besides Brother Koontz's pastorate, the churches of St. Luke, Fort and Liberty, the church at Mathias, West Virginia, was canvassed, and here some warm friends of the college were found. We cannot but comment again on the splendid loyalty displayed by the churches of the Maryland-Virginia district. Their response is fine considering the opportunity these churches in general have had of coming in touch with men from the college. It may be that this district will surprise the brotherhood before the canvass is completed.

"Home Again," says Brother William A. Gearhart, and he says he has returned from his visit among churches on the Pacific Coast and other western districts full of "vim and pep" ready for work. Perhaps he means to suggest by that expression that you need not delay sending in your mission offerings thinking he may need a rest after his strenuous trip, but that he is fully able to take care of all monies that may be sent in. In other words, it is likely he would be delighted to have every church and individual pay all pledges and apportionments before conference time. That a goodly number of churches and individuals are getting squared up in this line is evidenced by the splendid financial report made in this issue.

Brother E. L. Miller has a custom which is worthy of being copied by all pastors of the brotherhood; he reports his church work to the brotherhood every quarter. The pastors who report their church work frequently find that it results in much benefit to their own people. It not only increases their interest in the church paper but makes them feel that they count for something and thus are encouraged to do better service. A word of encouragement or commendation is worth ten of reproof and criticism and complaining, and is far more valuable than keeping silent. Brother Miller has a number of good things to report about his people and the work being done there.

FOUR-YEAR PROGRAM PAGE

NOW THEN DO IT.—II Samuel 3:18

Conducted by Charles A. Bame

"HO, HEAVE!"

Most people, at some time or other, have seen a number of sturdy laborers working on a job which required united and honest effort. Again and again the call, "Ho, heave," was heard and each time every man responded and joined his strength and ability with the concerted action of all, with the result that difficulties and obstacles were overcome and the task was accomplished with right good will.

THE SECRET

of success in any good enterprise which is undertaken by a group of individuals is loyalty and whole-hearted co-operation. Our General Conference is such an enterprise; it concerns the entire brotherhood. The interests of all are involved in what General Conference does or does not do. It is an enterprise which cannot be rightly carried through by only a few individuals; but to accomplish the best work there must be loyal and widespread co-operation throughout the brotherhood. This necessitates the interest and active enlistment of every pastor and congregation.

OUR GOAL

for the coming General Conference is "the largest and best conference in the history of the church, with at least 400 delegates present." It is a goal which can be reached, but to do so will require the help and co-operation of all pastors and congregations. It would be a great thing to have every congregation in the brotherhood represented by one or more delegates at Winona. Not only would we reach our goal then, but every church would receive the benefits which result from having delegates attend General Conference and bring back inspiring reports to help advance the work through the coming year.

NOW IS THE TIME

to definitely plan for that effective co-operation on the part of each and every church which will culminate in the largest and best conference we have ever had. Churches far from Winona should do what they can, while those located nearer Winona ought to have their full quota of delegates present. To reach Goal 16 in our Four Year Program requires each congregation to have an increase of fifty percent over the number of delegates present at the General Conference of 1916, or, if not represented in 1916, to have at least one delegate present in 1920.

THE CALL

"Ho, heave!" comes down the line. Let us all respond and throw our interest and loyalty into the task that is before us, and by one big united push put the General Conference of 1920 on the map as by far the largest and best we have ever had. IT OUGHT TO BE DONE; IT CAN BE DONE; IT WILL BE DONE IF ALL PASTORS AND CONGREGATIONS UNITEDLY WORK TOWARD THAT END.   MILES J. SNYDER.

NORTH MANCHESTER CHURCH'S SLOGAN

"Every Member of the Church at Winona Once," is the slogan of the Brethren church of North Manchester. We shall be sure to send every delegate possible to send so that we shall not be lagging on that score, either. But if this Conference is to be "Largest" the Indiana churches will have to do a full portion. We are thus trying to set a good example for our sister Indiana churches.

Your Turn, Officials. A good many times I have called for a large attendance at Winona. Our Secretary is doing

well along that line, also. But it is right now, time for the officiary of the churches to get busy. Pastors, it is "up to you" to try to put your churches on the map, this year as to Conference attendance. If you are indifferent your constituency may be also, and all our Jubilee come to naught. Get in the game. Heave, ho!

BAME.

Go To College. President E. E. Jacobs

I want to stress in about three short articles the advisibility of young people entering college this coming fall. First of all, what kind of a college shall the young person choose?

1. Choose the smaller Christian college. Unless there are very urgent reasons why this type of college can not offer the work demanded, it is best to choose a colleg with a limited enrollment and which is manned by men of Christian culture and character. The reasons for this are manifold, but the most essential reason of course is, that under such an environment the development of Christian character is more certain. There are those who seem to feel that to come to Ashland is quite a sacrifice on their part because Ashland is small. The contrary is quite true: it is QUITE A SACRIFICE in many cases, at least, to go to a large and godless state school. They are good for graduate work but are not always the best for under-gradute work.

A teacher in a large state university said in my hearing this past fall that out of one hundred students to whom he put the question, "Why did you choose this school?" over ninety replied, That they might be near a certain well known football star. Now, this university has one of the best known presidents in America, an enrollment of some six thousand, an equipment second to none, a library of unusual merit, yet these did not seem to draw, as the teacher referred to, himself commented. If this represents the seriousness of any large number of college men, no wonder they would not want to choose a school where football is not the whole thing, as President Wilson said, when the president of Princeton University, and the college the "sideshow," but where football is only incidental and secondary.

It is estimated that over eighty percent of all the ministers of the Protestant denominations came from the small college. Moreover, the graduates of Ashland are accorded the same recognition as the graduates of larger schools, and in some cases are given the preference. So far as the teaching profession is concerned, they have never been discriminated against but have been sought out. It was wholly refreshing this summer to have superintendents from large city schools come here for teachers and to hear them express themselves, without exception, as wanting just such men and women as we turn out. Young man and woman, in nine cases out of ten you would be making no sacrifice at all to choose a small, well-equipped, well-manned, Christian college in which to do the major part of your undergraduate work.

Ashland, Ohio.

THE GREATEST THING

When Dr. Lyman Beecher was on his dying bed, a brother minister said to him, "Dr. Beecher, you know a great deal; tell us what is the greatest of all things in Christian ministry."

"It is not theology," he replied, "and it is not controversy. It is to save souls."

GENERAL ARTICLES

A Vision of Western Possibilities.   By Earl S. Flora

Greeley said, "'Young man, go West." These who did go west were of a certain type of manhood. Only those' who were strong and broad in vision could endure, for there were many hardships to encounter in this new country. Undaunted in faith these men and women came to this country which was either a wilderness or a desert, and took out their homestead rights. In the timbered regions houses were made of logs; while on the prairie, dugouts or sod houses served as shelter. Through privation and prosperity these pioneers have lived to see the fruition of their hopes, and to see this region blossom as a rose. With the coming of man the wilderness and barren land has become a fruitful garden. The timber and buffalo grass has given over to the vast grain fields.

A half century is a short time in reckoning the time of states or nations, but the west of which I write has barely reached the half-century mark. There are still living about us these sturdy, broad-visioned pioneers, who have lived to see civilization over-rule the wilderness of the west. These were the victims of the fever to "Go west and grow up with the country."

This country did grow. No other country in the world, perhaps, has been so quick to do away with old methods and adopt the new. The west today is modern in thought quicker method by the use of the header, which in turn is and deed. The very latest type of machinery in city or on farm, crowds to the junk heap that which is in the least out of date. The reaper and binder, which held dominion in the grain fields has surrendered it's place to the much now being called upon to give way to the combination harvester and thresher. There are no sacred traditions handed down from generation to generation which stays a change. In this way the west is unhampered in growth, which brings prosperity.

The question which is of concern to the Brethren church is, Has the church kept pace with the growth of this country? This can be answered by "yes" and "no," in a manner of comment. The same progressive spirit prevalent in other activities of western life is found carried into the western church work. The church, with her auxiliaries, is on the lookout for something new, by the way . . . ." or equipment, which will enable her to do a more . . . . work unhampered by a staid past, the churches are growing with the country. But, the brotherhood has not kept pace with the growth, by expansion in this growing country. There are thousands of places in this area which bid as fair for development as the well worked places and which are wholy untouched by the Brethren. Unlike so many eastern places, these are under-churched. We have but a few mission points in the whole of the Middle West district which could be considered as babes, nourished by the mother churches. This is not because they soon become full-grown, but because of our failure to seize this opportunity of expansion by the method of multiplication. Of course they are not calling for us from these places, but, nevertheless the places are there with souls ready to be woven into the fabric of our brotherhood. Their need should be considered as the call. Their open mindedness should be an appeal to us to take to them the God-given truths as we find them in his Word, unthwarted by the thoughts and works of man. The trend of thought among these people will favor an acceptance of God's Word on nothing short of par.

When lifting up your eyes, and looking on the fields that are white already unto harvest, why not take a far look to this changing, fast-growing, but underchurched district of the Middle West? Other churches are endeavoring to care for this district. One church now has two hundred and forty ministers in the state of Nebraska, actively engaged in the church work, while the Brethren have but three. The state of Kansas has but few more Brethren ministers, engaged in the work than does Nebraska. Soon this will be a changed and worked-over country, developed and nourished by other denominations, so now is when "Time is golden," to send forth the reapers to help care for this bountiful harvest. "The harvest indeed in plenteous, but the laborers are few. Pray ye therefore the Lord of the harvest, that he send forth laborers unto his harvets."

Beaver City, Nebraska.

What Is Your Life?   By W. I. Duker

"To be or not to be," is a question of the stage, propounded by a half-crazed character in a plot. The question of the real man on the stage of life is "Being, how shall I make the most of life?"

The question of LIFE and what it is, has been the source of much discussion and thought in times past, and still we find it taking toll of our time with interest in no wise abated. We can more easily grasp the meaning of life if we can see it by illustration rather than by definition. So let us take a view of life that will not be taken as a basis for a theological discussion, but merely as an illustration of an otherwise difficult subject. May we see a picture. We see a large central plain surrounded by a dark, impenetrable forest. In the center of this plain we see a large fire, illuminating and making bright the entire plain. As we look again we see the figure of a man who seems to be caring for the fire. But as we look again, to our surprise, we see the fire or rather the illumination to come from the very presence of this man, rather than from a fire which he may have kindled. I look again, and I see this man, who now has taken on the appearance of some wonderful being, as he moves about, here and there, to cast his great loving eyes out toward the dark and gloomy forest, as though the darkness there seen, disturbed the beauty of the plain. Now I see him pick up a burning faggot from the great fire and with one sad look of renunciation turn his face to the forest, and soon I see a little gleam in the otherwise dark wood. Soon the presence of this wonderful personage, now blessing the forest with his love for light, is shown by innumerable lights, here and there, until the old gloomy wood shines as the plain. He now returns to the great central plain in which He is the illumination and which was rather darkened by his absence, but now as I see him again glance toward the forest the brightness that is the result of the innumerable little lights that he had kindled, causes his face to shine with a resplendent glory, displacing the evident sorrow that had been there before his journey to the forest that had known no light. So, kind friends, we see the "Life" of the world to be a "spark" of the great heavenly fire brought to a world of darkness through the love of the Father of light. When the many sparks of the great light of God will have made the forest to shine as the plain, then and not until then, will the plan of eternal redemption be completed.

Now, again, by definition we shall try to see what we may mean by the term life. First life is a gift. We have not been solicited in reference to our willingness to receive this wonderful gift, because in the very absence of the gift there would have been no appreciation of its value. With many today that lack of proper appreciation still prevails because of a reluctance or ignorance in the proper use of said gift. A good old mother living in Scotland, whose only son had gone to America many years before, upon being asked by interested neighbors relative to his financial care of his mother, said, "Sandy is a good son and writes me many kind and interesting letters and soon hopes to have me with him in the 'New World.'" "But," said the neighbors, "doesn't he send you any money?" With just a bit of perplexity written upon her kind old face, she said, "No, he doesn't, but each letter contains a small blue paper with the picture of some man upon it." "I suppose," said the mother, "that this may be the picture of the man for whom my boy is working." Upon investigation it was found that in each letter through all these years, "Sandy" had been sending his mother, a substantial check in the thought that she would understand how easily it could be turned into the "coin of the realm." How well this story of the old mother may be made to apply to those whose lives are filled with God's uncashed checks.

Then again we see life as a preparation. Of all sad men, he is the one most to be pitied, who lives from one day to the next, not as a preparation but just as an existence. Today, tomorrow—and then again tomorrow! Of all the days of my childhood that stand out with remarkable distinctness are those days in which we were preparing to go somewhere, or planning for some event in our home. All other days of mere existence are forgotten in the most important days of preparation .So may our life, today, be seen and experienced as a period of intense joy, if we regard it in the light of a preparation.

While traveling across the continent toward the "Rockies," we were amused to watch the porter of our car in his intense desire to be of use to us. As he would anticipate some wish that we ourselves hardly realized as a desire, we were amazed at his power of appreciation and willingness to turn his appreciation into service. But when we saw him busy with the "lamps" of the coach, lighting them in the middle of the afternoon, we nudged each other as we silently enjoyed his evident over-anxiety to please. We shall never forget how we sat there in broad daylight, as he turned on the lights with haste and evident care, while we smiled in derision and wondered why more in the coach did not smile with us. Suddenly, without the slightest warning, we found ourselves in our first tunnel. The lights that a moment ago had lost their glow in the greater light of the day now shone forth as the sole illumination of the car. The smile of derision now changed to a look of wonder and acknowledgment of superior judgment. Now, for the first time, we realized that our guide had gone that way before,

and knew the way. In after years the lesson has returned with added application. Now we see the value of caring for our "lights" while the sun is still high in the heavens and no tunnels are in evidence. Also the thought of having with us one that has gone the way before and knows all of the turns and twists in the way brings a feeling of security and pleasure that could be attained in no other manner.

And again "Life" is seen as a conflict. Now, as never before, we find that there are no "flowery beds of ease." We find that "flowery beds" do not beget ease. The only ease that is lasting is that ease found in conflict. Every fiber of our being calls out for a struggle. God has made us fighters, not for evil but for good.

Too often, however, we misinterpret the kind of conflict into which we have been called. With what should our conflict be? Should it be with one another? Many today feel quite justified if they can find themselves busily engaged in some form of controversy with those with whom they work, a controversy having to do with matters that should be molded into a factor of progress rather than one of retarding influence.

The giant vessel that crosses the great ocean in an incredible time is, to me, a good example of a life conflict. The one desire is progress. The conflict is with the waves that tend to retard progress. As the old boat steams' valiantly on we see that which would impede progress is thrown high before her as she meets it and is instantly cast aside and forgotten as she presses on to encounter new difficulties As each giant wave is overcome she forges ahead to meet another. Never does she turn about in her wake to re-enter into a struggle with waves that lies behind her. May we, as we love our God given conflicts, find them only as they lie in our path of progress, a path that appears as we face our goal. That type of conflict to be avoided, and in which we should take no pleasure is to be found without stint in the struggles of ungodly men about us. The type equally undesirable is the type commonly known as "worry." Surely in no wise the type recognized as, "Life's conflict."

"Why do we worry about the nest?
  We only stay for a day,
Or a month, or a year, at the Lord's behest,
  In this habitat of clay.
  Why do we worry about the road,
  With its hill or deep ravine?
A dismal path or a heavy load
  We are helped by hands unseen."

New Paris, Indiana.

The Pastor—His Life. By Mrs. C. E. Nicholas

The Christian ministry is the greatest trust ever committed to man. No other calling or vocation can equal it. The solemn call comes from God through his church. It takes men from their chosen fields of life work and consecrates their lives to the saving of souls, entrusting to them destinies of men and women, making them ambassadors of Christ and ministers to all classes of people in health and sickness, sorrow and death.

Good brethren, you are God's highest representatives of the Kingdom of Grace among men and nothing less than the noblest imitation of the Divine Pattern will make you a worthy servant. We look to you as our example of God's daily saving power from sin. The Christian ministry is a most wonderful work, and leads every other profession for high attainments and far-reaching results. It is a calling of greatest activity and touches every phase of human life. Need we be reminded in view of the responsibilities, the possible results and great work to be accomplished, that the gospel demands purity of character, high spiritual attainments, unquestioned consecration, the losing sight of self on the very threshold of entrance into the sacred office? No serious minded minister but realizes that. To be

a Christian means to be an imitator and follower of Christ. Our ministers lead us in our imitation and following of Christ. How nearly we are like him depends largely upon the efforts they are making to follow his example.

There should be no occasion of doubt as to their identity—"A living epistle, known and read by all men." It is for many a sad commentary on the power of the religion of Jesus Christ when a Christian minister turns aside from the straight course, betrays the sacred trust placed upon him and brings reproach upon the cause of Christ. In reality it does not indicate a weakness of Christ's power, but a failure to make use of the strength he affords. Yet his cause is reproached just the same. Instances may be recalled when men who have ranked high in this noble calling have yielded to temptation in an unguarded moment and have brought disgrace upon themselves and cast a shadow over the church. But why do men fall with so much of grace at hand? Why do any of us fall? Our hearts will tell us the answer to much of self and not enough of Christ. We grow self-confident, depend on our own strength, yield to the infirmities of human nature and do not give to God the praise that belongs to him, and consequently fall.

For the pastor more than any one else it is needful that he keep himself in the back-ground, giving God all the praise. It is hard to keep down expressions of human praise but many a prominent man has been caught and ruined by his own folly. Human nature needs encouragement but encouragement is one thing and human praise is quite another and need not be coveted by a true servant of God. The greatest thing that any consecrated life can rejoice in when he leaves the world, is to be able to say, "I have done my work to the best of my ability; I will leave the praise to God; I will give God all the glory."

There must be less of self within and more of the Holy Spirit to make a servant of God effective. That Spirit alone will enable one to make that complete consecration that puts self out of sight and exalts Christ and the Truth. The greatest desire of the true servant is to make his life tell for God that the world may know his life, his work is from above. The one great question of a minister's life is "How much of that Spirit will I be able to get into my life that I may be a true ambassador of heaven?"

A pastor of all men, must be a true man. There can be no justifiable excuse given for a minister of any other kind. Every characteristic belonging to true manhood must be a factor in the make-up of his character. He must be a man of his word. He must be conscious that every word preached must be lived to make it active and practical. God gives no man permission to live one life and preach another.

It is a fact that if the spiritual inward man is vivid, the outer becomes effective. I have met ministers who made me feel their daily lives were lived with God; every truth they uttered, even though not eloquent, burned into the hearts of their people. I have also come in contact with those whose very entrance into the pulpit sent a chill through the audience and killed the spirituality of the

service. The one kind possessed the Spirit and lived the true life while the other possessed the spirit of the world and lived a worldly life outside the pulpit. Heavenward and worldward are opposite to each other, a life in either course is eternally fatal to one in the other. It is folly for one to suppose he can live differently from your message and hold the confidence of his people. We do not look for pure sparkling water from an impure source.

A pastor must be truthful—any attempt at concealment or misrepresentation is productive of no good. His life at this point must be above question. He must be free from any entangling alliances. Money obligations must be held sacred. No explanation will clear up the neglect on his part. The tables will be turned against him, his work will be crippled and his influence gone. He may be forgiven but even the tears of Esau did not bring back his birth-right or his father's dying blessing.

It is to be regretted when it is necessary for the world to insert the conjunction "but" into a pastor's life and thereby spoil what might have been a model life. I like to regard a pastor as a really good shepherd, faithfully leading his flock into "green pastures" and by the "still waters."

The lowly life of Jesus teaches his servants "All glory is thine" I am only a very humble instrument in thine hands.

May all ministers let their prayers, their preaching, their dealings, their walk, their all, combine to impress their people with the intense consciousness of a pure life within. They have no right to be other than faithful, representatives of Jesus Christ, bearing about in their every walk in life marks of our Divine Master. And then may all disciples of Jesus be faithful and true as they expect their leaders to be.

Dowagiac, Michigan.

"After 2000 Years." By T. C. Lyon

(Continued from last week)

Take the doctrine of non-resistance; if you are one who does not believe in this doctrine, let me ask you for a minute to put aside all your previous ideas on the subject and listen to a few verses from the 5 th of Matthew: "Ye heard that it was said, 'An eye for an eye and a tooth for a tooth,' but I say to you, resist not the evil (man); but whosoever smites you on your right cheek, turn to him the other also; give to him asking you, and from him who wishes to borrow of you, turn not away. Ye heard that it was said, 'You shall love your neighbor and hate your enemy;' but I say to you, love your enemies; and pray for those who persecute you, that ye may be sons of your Father who is in heaven; because he causeth his sun to rise on evil (men) and on good; and sendeth rain on the righteous and on the unrighteous, (all except the Germans.)" That's the way some people would have read that during the war. "For if ye love those who love you, what reward have ye? Do not even the tax-collectors the same? And if ye salute your brethren only, what more than other do ye? Do not even the Gentiles the same? Ye, therefore, shall be perfect, as your heavenly Father is perfect." Honestly, now, is there more than one thing you can make out of that?

And this matter of going to court about your disputes. In the same chapter we find several verses which should effectually settle that question: "But I say to you, Resist not the evil (man); but whosoever smites you on the right cheek, turn to him the other also; and to him who is desirous that you should be sued at the law, and to take your coat, grant him your cloak also; and whosoever shall impress you to go one mile, go with him two." I would refer you, then, to the parable of the unjust judge in the 18th of Luke, which was read awhile ago. This parable has always been interpreted as teaching importunity in prayer, but I think it means something infinitely more than that. Its lesson is not so much persistency in prayer as to show

the court to which we should present our petitions. The woman appealed to an unjust judge, and it was a long hard struggle before she got what she desired. "Hear what the unjust judge saith." Asmuch as to say, "Isn't that a hard way to get an answer? Here is a better way. Appeal to my Father, for will he not avenge his own elect which cry day and night unto him? I tell you that he will avenge them speedily. No long waits there. But it is "a hard saying, and who can hear it?"

Then is it the Christian's duty to mix up in matters of Government and reform movements? I think not. "Oh, but if Christ were on earth today he would do anything he could to make life more worth living for the masses." But would he? That depends on how you mean it. You will probably begin by telling me that conditions are different now, but are they? Dr. Jefferson says, "In Christ's day the people wanted him to do everything. That was their conception of the Messiah. The air was filled with questions, political, social, economical, ecclesiastical, but he refused to touch them, so eager was he to say just one more word about God. Evils lifted their hoary heads on every side—slavery, Roman tyranny, the social evil, false customs, economic tragedies—but he never lifted a hand to strike them. So narrow was he, so blind was he. No age ever had more problems than his. But to him there was only one fundamental problem, and that was the problem of sin. The intellectual people of his day had no use for him. Men of acumen and large mental grasp smiled at the poor peasant telling people little stories about God. Men of patriotic fervor, alive to the needs of the day, sneered at him because he did not fall in with their plans and adopt their panaceas. To all practical men who believed in grappling with problems and suggesting solutions, he was a visionary, so much talking about God."

(Concluded on page 10)

THE BRETHREN PULPIT

The Church's Commission.   By I. D. Bowman

TEXT: MATT. 28:19, 20; MARK 16:15, 16.

In a word the church's commission is to do all with its power to have its membership:

1. **Saved.** That means a new creation, regeneration.
2. **Spirit-filled.** This means to receive the gift of the Holy Ghost after regeneration.
3. **Spiritually developed,** by receiving more and more of the living, active Word of God in their life. The church has power over self, sin, and the world in proportion to the amount of the Word of God received. If you take a man and cut off his head and his feet you need not wonder that there is no life in him. So the Word must be received as a whole.

When a young man in Virginia I had the largest fishing net in our community, and by putting bait upon it I caught many fish. If I had taken my knife and cut off both sides, then ripped out the center, taken away the bait, I could have fished all day and not caught a fish. So with the Gospel net. Cut off the Creation story in Genesis, cut off Revelations at the other end, rip out Ecclesiastes, Isaiah, Daniel and Hebrews in the middle, take away the blood of Christ, the bait: then wonder why the church has no power.

The church's commission is to give a WHOLE gospel, backed up by a **consecrated** Christian life; to a WHOLE world.

I. Notice more in detail the commission of the church.

1. Preach the Gospel as a witness, "And this Gospel of the kingdom shall be preached in all the world for a witness unto all nations, then shall the end come.) (Matt. 24:14). Acts 1:8 gives us the program, "But ye shall receive power after that the Holy Ghost is come upon you: and ye shall be witnesses unto me both in Jerusalem, and in all Judea and Samaria, and unto the uttermost parts of the earth. In Acts 15:14-17 we have further instructions that help to make the commission of the church clear. "Simeon hath declared how God at the first did visit the Gentiles, to take out of them a people for his name. And to this agree the words of the prophets; as it is written, after this I will return, and will again build the tabernacle of David, which is fallen down; and I will build again the ruins there of, and I will set it up: That the residue of men might seek after the Lord, who doeth all these things."

Here we have (a) the commission of the church in this gospel age—Gather out the church from all nations. (b) Then the second coming of Christ; followed by (c) the conversion of Israel; and lastly (d) the conversion of the nations, some of whom came out of and some through the terrible judgments after the church is taken, when Christ comes for his bride.

This world, including all nations and kingdoms, is doomed to destruction except the church, and the tribulation saints saved immediately after the second advent. "In the days of these kings shall the God of heaven set up a kingdom. . . . It shall break in pieces and consume all these kingdoms and it shall stand forever. " "I saw. . . one like the Son of man come with the clouds of heaven. . . and judgment was given to the saints of the most high and the time came that the saints possessed the kingdom. And the kingdom and dominion and the greatness of the kingdom under the whole heaven shall be given to the people of the saints of the most high whose kingdom is an everlasting kingdom, and all dominions shall serve and obey him." See Dan. 2:44; 7:13, 13, 2, 27 and II Pet. 3.

2. Preach the Word. Need not spend much time to **prove** the Word to be true. Preach it with authority and it will prove itself. If you let a lion out of a cage you need not prove that he is not a mouse. The lion will do that. So with

the Word. The Word is declared to be "as silver purified seven times," "the law of the Lord is perfect.". "All scripture is given by inspiration of God and is profitable for doctrine. . . that the man of God may be perfect." Paul declares that if he or an angel from heaven should preach any other gospel let him be accursed. It also declares that Jesus will come in "flaming fire taking vengeance" on all who do not obey the gospel. In the Revelations we are forbidden to add to or take from. Hence we are forbidden to add to or take from his Word.

Rightly Divide It. Preach the first principles **first**; all of the: (a) repentance (b) faith, (c) baptism, (d) laying on of hands, (e) resurrection and (f) eternal condemnation. See Heb. 6:1-3. The writer of the Hebrews says, "This will we do."

Today we need a modern John the Baptist to go through the formal church and the world and cry "Repent." The church today needs to surrender **completely** its will to God's will. We need not only to accept the apostolic baptism which is triune immersion; but **heart** obedience is essential, believe with all thy heart and **then** be baptized. Baptism belongs to repentance; no one has properly repented who knowingly rejects water baptism.

We should teach, and the members of the church should accept, the **gift** of the Holy Ghost by faith through the laying on of hands. This gift of the Holy Ghost is a distinctly New Testament gift; not for salvation but after regeneration. Many are confused here. Brethren, I laid hands on a thousand people who never received the Holy Ghost by my teaching; some no doubt received him, but I had not received him myself. I was regenerated, honest and sincere in purpose, but hardly knew there was any Holy Ghost. I was acquainted with his **name**, but not with **him**. When we believe that he is nothing but an "influence" or an "it," I fear we do not so much as know there is any Holy Spirit. No people ought to understand this any better than the Brethren church. I fear many of our teachers need to be taught again this first principle of the gospel of Christ. I want to repeat it for the sake of emphasis, that the laying on of hands, out of the water after baptism, is the form of doctrine obeyed when we are to receive the Holy Ghost **after** salvation. Conviction is the work of the Holy Ghost, regeneration is also the work of the Holy Ghost; there is also the penetration power of the Holy Ghost that fills one sufficiently for him to **know** the Holy Ghost; all this is only the preparation for the person of the Holy Ghost to come into that convicted, converted and strengthened one, as a distinct and separate gift and blessing. I believe that it is not only possible to be saved, but one may have the **gifts** of the Spirit, and yet not have the **Pentecostal Gift** of the Holy Ghost. I want to make this plain, **first** by noticing this dispensationally. 1. From Adam to Moses we have a world without a Bible. Conscience and nature and handing instructions from father to son, their only teachers. Abel, Enoch, Job, Abraham, Isaac and Jacob, and others were saved. They looked prospectively for and to Christ. For these twenty-five hundred years all mankind could have been saved through the teachings of conscience and nature. See Rom. 1:20; 2:12-16; 5:13-18. II. From Moses to Pentecost. In addition to nature and conscience and mere salvation, we have the addition of the written law and visible sign of the invisible presence of God—cloudy pillar by day and the fiery pillar by night. Here we have salvation plus the presence of God, and with this presence a new name of God. "I appeared unto Abraham, unto Isaac and unto Jacob by the name of God Almighty, but by my name of Jehovah was I not known unto them.'' (Exodus 6:3. In this dispensation of law we have conscience and nature and a written revelation the spiritual blessings—God constantly with them in addition to mere salvation. III. Now in the gospel dispensation we have, conscience and nature, as we had for twenty-five hundred years, from Adam to Moses; plus law of Moses from Moses to Pentecost, fifteen hundred years; plus the gospel from Pentecost to the second coming of Christ. The spiritual blessings, salvation by faith in Christ—Adam to Moses,—plus Christ with them,—Moses to Pentecost,—plus Christ in you,—Pentecost to the second coming.

God does not repent of blessings but adds to. The indwelling Christ, the gift of the Holy Ghost, the more abundant life, New Testament sanctification; it may be designated by any or all of the above names. There is an impregnable wall at Pentecost, back of which none can go to find this blessing.

I believe there are four classes in the visible church: 1. Unsaved. 2. Saved, but in experience living back of Pentecost and even back of Moses. 3. Others saved, plus God with them, but not in them. Living experimentally on this side of Moses but back of Pentecost. 4. Thank God all of us have the privilege of living in the New Testament dispensation experimentally. Salvation plus God with you plus God in you. ''Ye know him; for he dwelleth with you (they were yet under the law experimentally until Pentecost) and shall be in you.' (After Pentecost). ''The mystery which hath been hid from ages and from generations, but now is made manifest to his saints. . . which is Christ in you the hope of glory. Col. 1:26, 27. Here is a mystery hidden for 4,000 years. "Christ in you." See-also Eph. 3:14-20; 1 Cor. 2:7, 9; II Cor. 6:14-17:1; 1 Thess. 5:22-24.

It is stated forty times in the New Testament that the human body is the temple (Naos—only of holies in which God dwells) of the Holy Spirit. God dwelt in the burning bush, but not in Moses; he came down into Mt. Sinai but not in Israel; in the Tabernacle and Temple of Solomon, but never until after Pentecost was the human body the temple of the Holy Ghost,—Jesus only excepted.

The mass of God's people, like the Ephesian brethren, believed, we are baptized and saved, but they had not yet received the indwelling Christ. Read carefully Ephesians 3: 14-20. Yet every one should receive the gift of the Holy Ghost by faith immediately after baptism when they receive the laying on of hands we receive salvation when baptized and the gift of the Holy Ghost when hands are laid on.

3. Then we should go on unto perfection. Aim at Perfection. Don't be afraid. Christ should be our aim and he is absolutely perfect-.I would rather aim at perfection and miss it than at imperfection and attain it.

4. Then after salvation and the reception of the Holy Ghost, by prayer and earnest endeavor we will receive a passion for souls. God will give one and all a ''Can't help it movement.''

5. Among the ''all things'' (Matt. 28:19) Christ and the apostles place special emphasis upon the second, personal, visible coming of Christ. He made this—

(a) An Imminent Event. Because of the purifying effect of faith in the Lord's coming, he made it an imminent vent. More than twenty-five years ago A. J. Gordon, of Boston, wanted to give his two daughters an impressive lesson of the meaning of this word. He said, ''I am going to a two weeks' Missionary convention and I want you to meet me at the train when I return. I will be home Monday, Tuesday, Wednesday or Thursday. Monday they put on their new dresses and at seven A. M. were at the depot. They looked for him, they were watching. ready to meet him. They were not much disappointed because he did not come. They did the same by going to the train five or six times each day until Thursday evening at seven P. M., the last train from New York, when as he stepped off the train

he met the happiest girls in Boston. So for almost two thousand years we were to have on the wedding garment, looking, watching and being ready for his coming. The disciples as well as us he taught us to look for, love, and pray for the Lord's return. Knowing the purifying effect of this doctrine, he made it an imminent event; wanting us to live day by day ready for his coming. It puts iron into the blood and fire into the nerves. Only to those who ''look for him'' will he appear without sin, only to those who ''love his appearing'' will he give a ''crown of life.'' We are to hasten his coming, pray for it, ''the bride says, Come.'' Tell others so that ''whosoever heareth may come,'' until from church to church, town to town, country to country the bride will say Come, then the Lord will hear that prayer and arise from his father's throne and say, ''behold I come and my reward is with me.''

(b) It is not only an imminent event, but a little while before he comes, the near, but not the exact, time of his coming shall be known. At ''the time appointed the end shall be;'' the vision of his coming was sealed up and closed until ''the time of the end'' then the wise shall understand, but none of the wicked shall: Jesus says that we shall know as surely the near time, but not the exact, as we know that summer is near when we see the leaves upon the trees. He tells us to lift our hearts and rejoice when we see these things begin to come to pass and that we shall know that it is nigh, even at the doors.

So many false doctrines advocate and abuse this precious doctrine and have set dates, etc., of his coming and have been disappointed and this causes many to be prejudiced against it. Every good thing is counterfeited. This doctrine of the second, personal, visible coming of Christ was taught of Jesus, and the apostles and universally believed by the early church.

In these terrible days, when the last apostasy is developing, and nearing its climax, the whole church is slumbering and sleeping and nothing will awake it but the midnight cry. Thank God, all over this world there are a faithful few among all the churches and on all the mission fields who are crying ''Behold the bridegroom cometh, go ye out to meet him.'' Thank God many. are rubbing their eyes, arising and trimming their lamps. This cry is all that will awaken the church, and half of those awake, half of the few that are looking for him, half of those separated from the world and are trimming their lamps, will not be ready for want of oil to enter into the marriage.

O Brethren, let us awake, watch and pray, exhort and admonish one another more and more as we see the day approaching. Let us not neglect the house of God. Make first things first.

In conclusion, let us as pastors.be sure that we are saved, spirit-filled, going on unto perfection by earnest prayer and study of the Word, with a passion .for the church, and the salvation of souls. Then move heaven and earth in our endeavor to give a Whole Bible to a Whole world. Paul, without any steamboats, railroads or modern means of conveyance, gave the gospel to every creature under heaven in one generation. Let us see the same vision.

Philadelphia, Pennsylvania.

HITTING THE MARK

By ''hitting the mark'' in its relation to preaching we have reference to so presenting Gospel truth as to make it applicable to the needs of the hearers. It is opposed to clubbing, which seldom hits the mark and at most hardly leaves more than a scar.

Much preaching is aimless and can accomplish but little. We should have the truth well in hand and so far as possible know the tradition of the hearer and then present the word so that it can be understood.

The effect of hitting the mark will depend upon the will of the hearer and the power that is behind the message.—A. I. Yoder, in the Gospel Herald.

"After 2000 Years

(Continued from page 7)

But you object, "What would happen if all good people stayed out of Government and politics?" But they wouldn't. Governments, "the powers that be," are ordained of God, and for a specific purpose; the Christian, however, has a very different purpose. We haven't time to go into it in detail just now, but you will find this distinction very closely defined in the 12th and 13th chapters of Romans, the 12th applying to the Christian church, the 13th to the state. I will just give a few parallel references from the two chapters for the sake of comparison:

Romans 12— Church

So we, being many, are one body in Christ.

Duties—Ministering, teaching, exhorting, giving, shewing mercy. (No politics in this).

Abhor that which is evil.

Continuing instant in prayer.

Avenge not yourselves. Vengeance is mine; I will repay, saith the Lord.

Overcome evil with Good.

Romans 13—State

There is no power but of God; the powers that are ordained of God.

Duties—mete out judgement, bear the sword, terrorize evil works, execute wrath on evil doers.

Execute wrath upon him that doeth evil.

Attending continually upon this very thing (destruction of evil by force).

He (governments) is a revenger.

Execute wrath upon him that doeth evil.

There you have the two, each instituted for a different purpose, and dominated by different laws; the 12th chapter would wreck the state, the 13th would ruin the church. Let the state, as a penalty, feed its enemies, let it give a cloak also for every stolen coat, let it go twain for every mile it is asked to yield in matters of principles and justice; let it bless and ardently pray for its lynchers and riotous anarchists; the result? I guess it needs no answer.

The very phraseology of the two chapters is different and strikingly significant. In the "church" chapter, Paul uses the first person throughout, showing that he considered himself a part of this; but in the "state" chapter, it is always the third person—he never places himself in that group. Does it mean anything to you?

To sum up, the powers that be, the governments, are ordained of God for a purpose—to keep law and order, by force is necessary. But the Christian is not to take part in all this. His work is not to kill, but to keep alive; not to wound, but to heal. Ootherwise, we shall have to include with the "Good Samaritan," as men who did the Christlike thing, those also who wounded the poor fellow, stripped him of his raiment, and left him, half dead, along the road-side.

Divine healing is a doctrine that is beginning to come into some prominence again. The meetings recently held in this city have opened a great many eyes to that. I saw an interesting editorial the other day on that subject. It says: "Mr. Hickson believes that he cures the sick. There is no doubt that he gathers them together and gives them a chance to infect each other. He said, 'Christ gave to his church the wonderful power of healing, and that healing has ceased because faith died.' Since the days of miraculous healing men have learned to think and to cure themselves."

At any rate, you can see where the editor's faith is.

Old John Brown, colored messenger at the office, gave me this story recently. It's about "Ole Caesar." Ole Caesar was one of those old darkies that for years attended church and took up a great deal of time at every meeting telling how ready he was for death and how he would like to go home. Finally it got on the nerves of some of the younger ones, so one night about three o'clock Ole Caesar heard a knock on the door. He was too scared to answer, but when the knock was repeated, finally he said, "Who dar?" "De angel ob death, come to take pore ole Caesar home." "Uh-uh-uh, Ole Caesar don' lib yere no mo'. Caesar done mobe las' week." We've all heard people talk that way; I think mostly it's because nearly all of us think of death as being something far off, until it rears its ugly head right before us, and many of us would be like Ole Caesar and find we were not quite so anxious to go as we had thought. The best way to be prepared for death is to be prepared to live. But there is something that is to most of us, perhaps, more imminent than death, and that is the second advent of our Lord. Within the last few weeks one of the last remaining signs to be fulfilled has been accomplished in the formal return of Palestine to the Jew, under the protectorate of Great Britain. This was done at the recent conference at San Remo. It simply can't be far away if God's words are true. "Watch, therefore, for ye know not on what day your Lord cometh."

A little quotation yet from "Sartor Resartus," and I am finished. It is a picture of life in a city which he shows us; "Upwards of five-hundred-thousand two-legged animals without feathers lie around us, in horizontal positions; their heads all in night caps, and full of the foolishest dreams. Riot cries aloud, and staggers and swaggers in his rank dens of shame; and the Mother, with streaming hair, kneels over her pallid, dying infant, whose cracked lips only her tears now moisten.—All these heaped and huddled together, with nothing but a little carpentry and masonry between them—crammed in, like salted fish in their barrel—or weltering, shall I say, like an Egyptian pitcher of tamed vipers, each struggling to get its head above the others; such work goes on under that smoke-counterpane!—But I mein Werther, sit above it all; I am alone with the stars."

It is just so that the Christian, surrounded though he be with the strife and confusion of this world, yet sits above it all and is alone with God. Let me refer again to Luke 24:45, "Then he opened their mind, that they might understand the Scriptures." Let us all pray for him to open our minds, that we too might undestand his scriptures aright.

Washington, D. C.

Moslems as Gospel Propagators

Dr. Alexander, a mission worker in Egypt, gives a most encouraging report about the missionary zeal of converted Mohammedans and some, even, not yet in church fellowship. As they happen to meet, they are eager to discuss Bible topics, and they can readily point out the superiority of the Blessed Book over the wholly inferior Koran, the sacred book of Islam. On the trains in Egypt, in places of business, in the shops, in the khans, Moslems are frequently seen with a copy of the New Testament, which they read to their fellows. As a rule, all educated Moslems have a copy of the Bible in their libraries. Many of them have committed to memory portions of the Gospels and of the Psalms. They are free to admit that Mohammedanism has nothing so exalted as the sublime teachings of the "Sermon on the mount."—The Gospel Messenger.

A Marked Transformation

When Henry Howard began work among the Terro Indians of Brazil, six years ago, he found them to be drunken, lazy, brutal, illiterate, immoral and diseased. They were without God and without hope. During his years of strenuous effort, in the uplift of these people, he was opposed by Romanism, by drink-selling traders, who imposed upon the natives on every occasion, and by other unscrupulous exploiters. When Mr. Howard left on his furlough, recently, he could point to one hundred earnest converts. eight native preachers, and a day school of 580 pupils. The drunkards of bygone days are now sober; immoral men are now clean-minded and God-fearing; profligate youths are now staunch defenders of Gospel principles. The wonderful change is a demonstration of God's wondrous grace.—The Gospel Messenger.

| J. A. Garber | Our Young People at Work | G. C. Carpenter |
| PRESIDENT | | SECRETARY |

ASHLAND CHRISTIAN ENDEAVOR AND A SPECIAL MEETING
By Mrs. George Stanley Baer

As the reports from the various Christian Endeavor societies are of interest to us we thought that perhaps a report from our society might be appreciated by others. The conditions in our society are a little different from others owing to the fact that our membership changes with the coming and going of the student body which makes it necessary for us to elect a new corps of officers for the summer months. During the school year we have so many young and qualified people that most of the work is carried on by them, but when they are gone our own (older) young people are called into service.

Our work for the season is progressing nicely under the splendid leadership of R. A. Hazen, president, and his qualified assistants, namely, Verne Stoffer, vice president, Harriet Abrams, secretary, C. A. Anspach, treasurer, Fern Hendrickson, pianist.

The Fourth of July meeting was worthy of special mention. The chapel was neatly decorated in flags, including the Christian flag. After the singing of patriotic songs and a solo "The Red, White and Blue" by Miss Myrtle King, and offering of prayer, the leader Brother Guilford Leslie, unfurled a large American flag which he held while making the following remarks:

"Our duty to our country is varied and of very great importance and demands our best individual effort at all times and on all occasions. With the greatest good to the greatest number in mind with the cause of Jesus Christ uppermost and foremost. Our country includes our state, our town, or homes. Our country is the product not only of great men who have made it what it is but also of the innumerable number of little men who have made it what it is. We may not be among the great but we have our duties, our influences, our responsibilities. This flag is the emblem not of a mere sentiment, but of a noble history."

The leader then passed the flag to Dr. L. L. Garber, who gave a most excellent talk on "The Making of Our Flag." He spoke—not of the sewing together of the stars and stripes, but of the ideals that entered into the making of what the flag stands for. He said the making of our flag began back in England with the Magna Charta; that it was given beautiful form by the founders of our country; and that it had been continually perfected and made more beautiful through our national history. Dr. Garber then passed the flag on to the audience for general participation, each in in turn being to pass the flag and giving his or her part

that had been previously assigned. It proved to be a very enthusiastic and helpful meeting, closing with song and prayer.

May every Christian Endeavorer do his best in the great work of the Master is our prayer.

Ashland, Ohio.

Statistical Special.   Prof. J. A. Garber

Statistical blanks with certain printed helps for Christian Endeavor have been distributed through various district workers. The names of the persons concerned with their addresses follow:

Md. & Va., G. Harry Haun, Woodstock, Va.
Pennsylvania, Miss Nora Bracken, Ashland, Ohio.
Ohio, F. C. Vanator, Canton.
Southern Indiana, Miss Mabel Maus, Mexico.
Northern Indiana, Miss Cora Culp, Nappanee.
Illiokota, Edwin Boardman, Hudson, Iowa.
Middle West, Miss Jennie Bailey, Carleton, Nebr.
Southern California, A. V. Kimmel, Whittier (Or his appointee).
Northern California, N. V. Leatherman, Turlock.
Northwest, C. H. Ashman, Sunnyside, Washington, (Or his appointee).

The Plan

These persons will distribute and collect the blanks in their respective districts. They will also tabulate and summarize the statistics, keeping a copy for the district conference and forwarding the duplicate to the undersigned for the benefit of the National Union. Corresponding secretaries and presidents of local societies are expected to co-operate with these district workers with a view of making our reports as complete and accurate as possible. If any society failed to receive the blank, let some officer communicate with the district officer at once. In many instances this can be done by telephone. Or better still, make out a report following the outline of the duplicate of last year and mail it without further delay. This matter is of the greatest and most urgent importance. We want to make a good showing on our Four Year Challenge. Moreover, the report of this year will help to form the basis of our new Five Year Program. Our present Four Year Challenge overreached because of imperfections in the 1915 report. With the help of all this mistake can be avoided in our next concerted effort. Come on, society officers and district workers!

A Thousand Dollar Church With $75,000 Worth of Autos.   By P. E. Burroughs

"There are seventy-five automobiles on these grounds." The speaker was a farmer; the scene was a home-coming at a country church. "What are these automobiles worth?" After a moment's thought, the farmer replied, "On an average, they are worth $1,000 each."

"What is your church building worth?" It was a small, one-room frame building, erected many years ago. "When we put it up," the farmer said, "it cost us $1,000."

This bit of incident is typical; it is worthy of careful study as reflecting pretty accurately the present situation in regard to country church buildings. Seventy-five thousand dollars in automobiles had come to church that day. The average cost of the automobiles in which a farmer's family rode to church was the same as the building in which the whole community worshiped God.

Buildings for country churches are not keeping pace with the buildings for country schools. The United States Bureau of Education and the several States have been co-operating in a persistent effort to secure better-designed

school buildings. Similar intelligent and co-operative help in behalf of country churches would bear similar wonderful fruitage.

The new style building is neat, usually striking, churchly. It would attract favorable attention in the suburbs of the city, in the village, or in the country.

As to strength, the old-style building has a bad reputation in withstanding storms. It has long been among the first to go down or to go over when wind comes. After the famous Galveston storm, literally scores of churches had been crushed in or blown over. This new-style building is clearly strong to resist wind. It could not be blown over; it could hardly be crushed in.

The old-style building offers no suitable provision for the teaching of the Bible. The writer has during the past winter tried to teach a class of intermediate boys in an open space with many similar classes. He is prepared to say that it cannot be done—at least, that it ought not to be undertaken.

The new-type building offers ample provisions for classes and departments. The building is excellent both for teaching and preaching.

As regards general conveniences, the one-room building offers no suitable meeting place. In the new-style building, if the women wish to bring and serve dinner for the all-day meeting, if the Young People's Society wishes to meet in two sections, if it is desirable to hold two or more small meetings at the same time, if the evangelist wishes to hold

an inquiry meeting, if—but it is needless to go further; the new building will meet practically all the demands which may be made upon it.

Since the new-style building offers so many and such marked advantages over the old style, we would naturally suppose that the new-style building will involve a correspondingly greater cost. This is not true. The new-type building can be erected for less money than the one-room building which offers the same floor space.—In Home Lands.

NEWS FROM THE FIELD

MEXICO, INDIANA

When you think of Mexico, you likely think of Mexicans with all their law-breaking, cruel, and murderous raids. Terror reigns supreme because relations between men on the basis of true brotherly love have been broken (or have never been formed) and because men have willfully severed themselves from the Power from on high. The inevitable has occurred in 'Old Mexico.

But I am not going to tell you any more about Mexican history for you already know considerable about that, but rather briefly to tell you some news about a little church in the Hoosier state. We are not so strong numerically. Oftimes strength comes from numbers not necessarily so with the church. Our strength comes from the Master. Rev. J. W. Clark is our faithful shepherd and he is diligently caring for his flock. As a result the church as well as its auxiliaries, the Sunday school, Christian Endeavor and Women's Missionary Society are doing creditable work. At a recent business meeting we showed our appreciation for his good work by calling him to serve us for another year. Brother J. L. Kraning is our Sunday school superintendent, and with his willing workers he has increased the standard of attendance as well as interest at least twenty per cent. We are teaching graded lessons to five classes. The results are very gratifying and surely justify their use. Never before has the church been so dependent on the Sunday school. It must needs train the young folk for service in the church. If the Sunday school trains them, then the Christian Endeavor Society is surely needed to give them a fuller and more thorough development for church activities. Our Christian Endeavor officers are working but I am sure we are all falling short of what our Lord expects of us. The Woman's Missionary Society consists of the loyal sisters of the church. We have learned to depend on them in a time of need.

Our people are trying to meet as many goals as possible in our church, especially the Sunday school, Christian Endeavor, and Woman's Missionary Society. The Sunday school is caring for one Armenian orphan this year.

The church as well as its auxiliaries is invariably represented at their respective conventions and conferences. We find that it pays in more ways than one. The best ideas are the ones that the other fellow has, so if we wish to profit by them we must

find them out—that is what conventions are for.

Last but not least we are loyally behind our church college. We are deeply interested in its achievements. Christian training pays and for this reason we are endeavoring to fit all our young people for some kind of Christian work. The logical place for this is at our dearly beloved Ashland College.

LOREN T. BLACK.

PASTORS, ATTENTION!

Dr. Charles A. Bame has already emphasized the importance of all pastors getting their Four Year Program reports to the secretary by August 1st, 1920. Now August 1st is past, and many churches have not yet been reported. It is just such carelessness or indifference on the part of certain pastors which tends to make this work a burden instead of a delight. Why will pastors absolutely ignore a matter of this kind? It will not be easier to fill out a report card in August than it was in July, and it will take as much time, and nothing whatever is gained by such negligence. On the other hand it is a disregard of a request kindly made by our General Director and shows a lack of consideration for those who have the large share of this work to do.

The work of tabulating and classifying and ascertaining percentages requires time and effort, and it is asking a very small thing of each pastor to get his card in to the secretary at a specified time. This expiration date cannot be extended indefinitely. There must be seals and certificates printed and gotten ready before General Conference; and it is altogether out of the question, and beyond reason, to hold up these reports until conference time and then expect recognition based on a report received at that time. Reports coming in then must be disregarded; they will be too late. The pastor who delays very much longer sending in his report will have to do his own explaining to his congregation for failure to receive recognition at the JUBILEE service.

The thing for those who have not yet reported to do is to get busy at once and send in report cards without further delay. Please do not neglect this any longer, but send your cards to the undersigned at the earliest possible moment. If there is any pastor who did not receive a blank report card from his state or district Goal Director so advise the secretary at once.

This is the LAST CALL through the columns of the Evangelist. The cause of any

poor showing in the final windup at General Conference will rest wholly upon those who fail to respond promptly with the necessary reports.

MILES J. SNYDER,

Secretary.

Milledgville, Illinois.

WAKE UP! OHIO PASTORS!

Your statistical reports must be in in order that Ohio, the home of Ashland College, shall hold up her part in the conclusion of the Four Year Program. Here is a list of the Ohio churches reporting in the order of their receipt. Don't let your church be the last. Bryan, Pleasant Hill, Fair Haven. Will report again next week.   E. G. MASON, Secretary and Statistician of the Ohio Conference.

HOME AGAIN

I am back again full of vim and pep for the work. It is about time to get matters in shape for Conference. I certainly had a very pleasant and profitable journey, visiting the people of our beloved brotherhood, giving the Kentucky stereopticon lecture in quite a number of the churches and incidentally taking in the wonderful sights.

I was royally entertained everywhere by our dear people, so much so, that I felt at home wherever I found a Brethren church.

After leaving the California churches, visited Sunnyside, Spokane, Waterloo, Milledgville and Lanark churches, lectured in each one and visited in the home of many of the Brethren.

At the close of the Kentucky lecture, the peoples attention was called to the ''Light Plant Fund'' and without pressing the matter in the least, liberal offerings were given to help this worthy cause.

We also received several additional prospective missionaries names, who are now, or will soon be, ready for the mission field. Praise the Lord, for brethren and sisters who are willing to give their lives to this.

Then on July 14, Masontown had calle again, because the grim messenger had once more taken from earth the soul of another of those who had long served their Lord there. This time it was Sister Elizabeth Haught who was called, and at the age of 72 years, 6 months and 26 days, she had exchanged the infirmities of old age for the eternal youth of a spirit made free from the entanglements of flesh. Since her early life, she had been a member of the Mastontown church, and in her quiet practical way, given constant expression to those qualities of most important work in all the world.

I tried to encourage the churches to send a splendid delegation to our National Conference this year, for which we should all be praying and planning that it might indeed be a great spiritual feast for the entire brotherhood. Sincerely and fraternally yours,

WILLIAM A. GEARHART,

NAPPANEE, INDIANA

The time for my quarterly report through the Evangelist being about here I will try to deliver. Since our last report we have been moving along in the right direction. We held our Easter offering as one of the first events of the quarter. In spite of the day being the most inclement of all the year we went about one dollar per member, which says that some did valiant work while others were not quite doing their best. Absence from the Easter services due to any cause whatsoever should not make us feel that we are not obligated to assist in carrying the Gospel to the needy. After Easter comes the spring time and what is known as spring fever. Well, some developed the disease and have not recovered, the summer "slumpitis" having developed from the original trouble. But we thank God for the faithful who do not go by fits and starts, more fits than starts, and it is on that body that the work moves. So we have had occasion to rejoice over what may be called good attendance so far through the summer. On Memorial Day we preached the sermon to the veterans of all wars, there being some thirty-five of the boys who fought in the late war present in a body. Our Children's Day services were pleasing as were the Mother's Day and Woman's Day services. The communion service held during June permitted us to make the communion service goal on the Four Year Program. We had three communion services during the year and the folks seem to think that we ought to have no less any year. I feel the same way about it myself. Our evening church attendance is a revelation to me, for in the cities where I have served hitherto the larger crowd was in evidence in the morning but here it is in the evening that the most folks get to church. Nappanee with a population of about 2700 and eleven churches is quite a church-going town. Then our Sunday school is keeping right at it and so far during the summer we have been able to maintain an attendance averaging 250, which is not so bad considering all the Sunday schools in this town and all the automobiles also. Vacation time does work against the best attendance, but we hope that our folks are attending services elsewhere when on vacation, just like those vacationing in our midst do NOT attend while here, but keep others away because they are COMPANY. The little girl was correct when she bid God good-bye as she and her folks were about to leave for their vacation, for, as she said it, they were going to Atlantic City. It makes little difference where they are going, God does not seem to go along on their vacations.

The W. M. S. and the three C. E. societies are alive and doing excellent work. If all the people were as earnest as some what a

church ours and every other church would be! I must not forget the Sunday school and church picnic which we held on the 4th of July. It was a very enjoyable affair and as some said the best ever held by this Sunday school and church. Good clean games and plenty of fun of all kinds kept everybody interested from beginning to end and all went home happy even though some were sore, in the muscles not in the heads. Our financial work also deserves a word. The members have stood by the work like never before in this way. All our obligations for the year for outside affairs have been paid and we will meet all the local obligations without any trouble. The officers made report that last quarter's financial effort was the best of which they have any record. So here too we are alive and going strong. The people are standing back of us nicely and making us feel more at home every day, and with a goodly praying body, which we know we have by the attendance at prayer meeting, we are certain that Christ will be magnified and his church built up here. It is our aim to have the largest representation at conference this year that Nappanee has ever had. Will we all try to do that? Let's go. We pray for the brotherhood and ask an interest in the prayers of all.

E. L. MILLER.

A TOLL OF DEATH AMONG THE BRETHREN

When in response to the call given me by the Board of Trustees of the College, I landed in Ashland, on April 9, to assume the duties of bursar, I supposed that mine would be a quiet life, so far as calls for ministerial service would be concerned. At an early date I want to tell you what I have found, and what my impressions are, of the college and its outlook, but for the present, I owe it to some of my dear friends and to the whole church as well, to speak of some special services in which I have been called to participate, on account of the ravages of death in our ranks.

On May, I was called to the Middlebranch church to officiate at the funeral of Sister Sabilla Brumbaugh, who had for years been an active and faithful member of the band of Brethren who worship there. In the presence of a very large concourse of her Brethren and friends, the last solemn service was held, with many and unmistakable indications of her high standing in both church and community. She had been called home on her 50th birthday, to meet her Savior and many dear ones who had gone before.

On May 1, I was called into what had once been the bounds of the Farmersville church, to lay away all that was mortal of one of God's noblemen. In my early ministry, it had been my good fortune to work with Brother Joshua Gilbert, who lived near Farmersville, Ohio, and to be his pastor for almost four years. He was my senior by a good many years, but an attachment sprang up between us, which held until his death, at the ripe age of 84 years, 7 months, and 22 days. I had no more faithful friend among men, nor God a more faithful servant. From early manhood until his death, he had lived and wrought in this one community, and

when he left it for the better one, the manner in which his neighbors from near and far came to the funeral service left no doubt as to his high standing among them. His good wife and sons, as well as all the others who loved him, are comforted with the thought that he was ready, and nothing more comforting can be said of any one when death rends asunder the ties of earth.

My next call was back to the congregation which I had served for six years as pastor, Masontown, from which I had come but a few weeks before. There on May 27th, we committed to the earth the mortal remains of Sister Amy Provins, who had lived to the ripe age of 74 years, 7 months and 11 days. She was a member of the Sterling family, one of the oldest and best known and most highly respected families of southwestern Pennsylvania. Until recently, or comparatively so, there had been no break in the family outside of the father and mother, but an invasion of its ranks was begun in the death of Ephriam, a bit more than a year ago, and then his good wife, Emma, last December, and now Amy, next oldest, and all who remain have had their warning. She was a deaconess, having been ordained by the writer. She was a good woman too, and not afraid to go. Her children and others who knew and loved her, mourn her going, but Christian faith offers foundation for a hope which brings comfort.

A week later, I was called back to Masontown again, to bring the consolations of gospel truth to the family of Sister Susan Marshall, who at the age of 75 years and 11 months, had gone to be with her Lord and the loved ones who had found an abiding place in him. She had been greatly afflicted for a number of years, a victim of paralysis, and I could only rejoice that she was thus finally relieved of her physical handicap.

On June 6th, the congregation at Gratis, Ohio, was called upon to say "farewell" to one who had been among its most faithful and efficient workers, in the days gone by. Sister Naomi Stover, wife of Brother John C. Stover, was the victim of death's shaft, and if the great crowd of folks who gathered at the family homestead, could be taken as an indication of her standing in the hearts of men, then there was no room for doubt as to the place she held. And we who had known her for so many years, knew that love had drawn her friends to thus join in paying a last sad tribute of respect to one whose sterling qualities of character had won and held their love. For years she had been a member of the church there, and one upon whom I could always depend during the term of my pastorate, more than a quarter of a century ago. When she knew the end was approaching, she requested that I should say the last words over her form, but spiritual attitude is shown in the fact that two ministers of the Church of the Brethren, a minister of the Old Order church, and three ministers of the Brethren church, sat together in the service, and each was sure he had lost for a while, one of his best and most helpful friends. She was a daughter of Dr. George Henkle, and died at the age of 55 years and 5 months.

character which are the product of association with Christ.

July 24 found me at Clayton, Ohio, to conduct the funeral of Sister Grace Bucklew, wife of Walter Bucklew, one of my first associates in the effort to build up a congregation at Salem. For years, I had been the family pastor, and it was my privilege to hear the confession of the good woman whom death had now claimed, and to lead her into baptismal waters. She was a good woman, a devoted wife, and noble mother, and an all round Christian, which facts went far toward comforting the hearts of the great congregation of her friends and brethren, as they assembled to join in this last service, held in her honor. I was here too, at the request of the dead, and in her going, another of my dear friends has gone to join the company, beyond, which grows apace, and which, with my Savior, will make loneliness in heaven an impossibility for me.

MARTIN SHIVELY.

Ashland, Ohio.

REPORT OF RECEIPTS FOR MISSIONS DURING APRIL (HOME MISSIONS)

General Fund—

Mrs. Roy Decker, Augusta, Mich., H. G.	$ 3.00
G. A. Hoover, Thornville, O.,	3.00
Dr. J. L. Gillin, Madison, Wis., H. G.	10.00
Mrs. U. J. Shively, Nappanee, Ind., H, G.,	5.00
Mrs. Sarah Teague, Roann, Ind. H. G.	5.00
Mrs. Anna E. Ruble, Blackwell, Okla., H. G.	5.00
Nat'l Women's Missionary Society, Mrs. Wenger, Tr.,	25.00
Brethren Ch., Masontown, Pa., per Graham, Treas.,	25.00
Martin Shively, Masontown, Pa., H. G.	5.00
Fairhaven Br. Ch., (Zion Hill) W. Salem, O.,	1.00
Nettie J. O'Neil S. S. Class, Conemaugh, Pa.,	5.00
(From Mrs. Kate Yost, Burbank, O.) Geo. Barnhart (Corinth Ch.) Twelve Mile, Ind.,	2.00
J. H. Siders, Astoria, Ill.,	2.50
Brethren Church, Cerro Gordo, Ill.,	29.65
Dr. and Mrs. J. W. Tibbls, Des Moines, Ia.,	10.00
Total	136.16
Previously reported	8430.32

Total receipts to May 1st, ... $8566.47

Report For May (Home Missions)

General Fund

Amos Fudge, West Alexandria, O., H. G.,	5.00
Mr. and Mrs. G. C. Brumbaugh, Hill City, Kans.,	16.00
Nell M. Zetty, Phoenix, Ariz.,	4.00
A. J. Hixson, LaVerne, Calif.,	10.00
Mr. and Mrs. Chas. H. Keplinger, Sturgis, Mich.,	5.00
Brethren Church, Goshen, Ind., Trimmer, Treas.,	200.00
Brethren S. S., Loree, Ind., (Birthday Off.)	13.08
Brethren Ch., Long Beach, Calif.,	

(L. S. B.)	15.00
Martha Armstrong, Atwood, Ind., Int., Mar. 6. 24, Apr. 5. 68, May 3. 34	7.00
	15.26
Total	290.34
Previously reported,	8566.47

Total receipts to June 1st, ... $8856.81

Report For June (Home Missions)

General Fund

Nat'l W. M. S., by Mary C. Wenger, Treas.,	25.00
1st Brethren Ch., Waterloo, Ia., 2nd quarter, 1920,	40.00
Trustees of Br. Ch., Nickerson, Kans. (Proc. of Sale),	200.00
I'll Try S. S. Class, Warsaw, Ind.,	5.00
Brethren Ch., Falls City, Nebr.,	100.00
Maude Wingard, South Bend · Ind., H. G.,	5.00
Total	375.00
Previously reported	8856.81

Total receipts to July 1st, ... $9231.81

(HOME MISSIONS)

Kentucky Support Fund

(From April 1st to July 1st

G. A. Hoover, Thornville, O.,	2.00
Trustees Rosedale Br. Ch., Johnstown, Pa. (Church Sold)	150.00
Mr. and Mrs. Lemuel Kilmer, No. Liberty, Ind.,	12.00
S. M. M. Gretna Church, Bellfontaine, O.,	5.00
Brethren Ch., Masontown, Pa.,	25.00
Geo. Barnhart, (Corinth Ch.) Twelve Mile, Ind.,	1.00
Brethren Church, Krypton, Ky.	17.50
Volunteer S. S. Class, No. Manchester, Ind.,	5.00
Mrs. T. J. West, North Liberty, Ind.,	5.00
Geo. F. Kem., Dayton, O.,	10.00
Brethren Church, Lost Creek, Ky.	9.47
Mrs. Anna E. Robinson, Long Beach, Calif.,	100.00
C. E. Society, Sergeantsville, N. J.	14.00
W. M. S. Gretna Ch., Bellfontaine, Ohio,	10.00
Mrs. Wm. H. Cox, Gaston, Ind.,	5.00
W. M. S. North Manchester, Ind.	7.50
Brethren Ch., Lost Creek, Ky.,	13.36
Brethren Church, Oak Hill, W. Va.,	12.00
C. E. Society, Nappanee, Ind.,	30.00
Lydia Ann Baker, Swanton, O.,	5.00
Brethren Ch., Krypton, Ky.,	72.50
Kendall Br. Ch., Lake Odessa, Mich.,	5.00
Ever Faithful Class, Roann, Ind.,	10.00
C. E. Society, Denver, Ind.,	5.00
W. M. S. Darwin, Ind-Darwin· Br. Ch.,	5.00
Brethren Church, Long Beach, Calif.,	24.00
Edwin Boardman, Jr., Hudson, Ia.	25.00
Brethren Church, Lost Creek, Ky.,	12.24
Y. P. S. C. E., Mexico, Ind.,	10.00
Mrs. Clara M. Hartle, Hagerstown, Md.,	4.00
C. E. Society, Dallas Center, Ia.,	15.00
Brethren Church, Krypton, Ky. (Rempel)	13.00
Total,	640.07

Previously reported to Apr. 1st	4736.4?
Total receipts to July, 1st,	$5376.5?

Kentucky Light Plant Fund

(From April 1st to July 1st)

Brethren Church, Beaver City, Nebr.,	10.0?
Gratis, Ohio Brethren Ch., per Amos Fudge,	20.0?
Brethren Church, Salem, O.,	9.0?
Total,	39.0?
Previously reported to Apr. 1st,	661.0?

Total receipts to July 1st, ... $ 700.0?

Respectfully submitted,

WILLIAM A. GEARHART,

General Missionary Secretary

General Foreign Missions Report for June

1920

	Gen'l Fund	African Fun?
Brethren Church, Clay City, Ind.,	68.20	
Mr. & Mrs. Jas. W. Hunt, 1st Br., Johnstown, Pa.,	20.00	
Lost Creek, Ky., No. 445,		11.00
Br. Ch., Lost Creek, Ky., AB	12.33	
Br. Ch., Falls City, Nebr.,	402.25	
1m·Austin Miller, Meyersdale, Pa.	50.00	
Sunbeam S. S. Class, Johnstown, Pa., No. 123		12.00
Chapparrel Br. Ch. Jenny Lind, Cal	50.00	
Chaparrel Br. Ch., Jenny Lind, Cal. (446)		40.00
Chaparrel Br. Ch., for Hillegas Outf.	10.00	
Brethren Ch., Rittman, Ohio,	80.00	
Junior S. S., Los Angeles No. 124		9.75
Round Hill Ch. Strasburg, Va.,	10.00	
Zion Chapel, Leon, Ia.,	9.00	
Crown Chapel, Leon, Ia.,	.19.00	
Zion Hill Br. Ch., Smithville, O., (447)		151.00
Totals,		
Grand total		.904.53

Note—Detail report of Foreign Missio[n] contributions will appear in the July nu[m]ber of the Brethren Missionary, which h[as] been delayed somewhat on account of [a] trip among our churches in the West.

CAMPAIGN NOTES

On June 23rd, I began work in the circu[it] which is being served by Brother Claude Koontz. This field comprises three churche[s] viz., St. Luke's, the Fort, and Liberty, a[nd] is another of the hardest circuits to cover have seen. Pastors of circuits in Maryland and Virginia have many miles of rough roads to travel in the discharge of their duties, But when they arrive at their points they have splendid, appreciative audiences to whom to preach. I can testify that the most uniformly good audiences I have had in this entire campaign, I had in my seven weeks in Maryland and Virginia. And during part of that time people came out of the harvest fields for midweek services.

Brother Koontz, being an Ashland student, was anxious to do his utmost to make the canvass a success among his people. By the time we had covered his own circuit, and had also returned from our trip to Mathias, West Virginia, the speedometer showed that Koontz and I had travelled together over 225 miles. It was a noble piece of service Brother Koontz rendered Ashland college and me. I might add that a liberal part of that 225 miles was over some of the real mountain roads of Virginia and West Virginia. Not all of my readers will understand what this implies. (It means more than merely pretty scenery.)

Well the Koontz circuit went $834. Of this amount, $125 goes to the credit of St. Luke's; $133 to the Fort; and $576 to Liberty. The great majority of folks in these churches were not situated to give big gifts, but what they did give they gave cheerfully. While at St. Lukes I was well cared for in the hospitable home of Elder P. W. Wisman. Brother Wisman has given many years of preaching to the churches about Woodstock, Virginia, and he has been all through the years a staunch supporter of our school. Nor has he grown weary in well-doing as was evidenced by his substantial gift in the present campaign. Thanks to the Wismans for their kindness to me.

I shall remember the Fort particularly for the great number of fine young people I saw there. I am sincerely, hoping that some of these young people may make their way to Ashland College. Every home in that beautiful little valley seemed wide open to us but we only got as far as the homes of the Barrs, and Bakers, and Coverstones, and Smiths. It would have been a real pleasure to have remained longer among this splendid people.

At Liberty we struck a neat little surprise. Two $200 gifts represent the secret of the surprise. This is a small congregation and it has its full share of discouragements; and $576 was a fine showing for this place. I preached here just one night: In the light of results I regretted that I had not planned to give more time at Liberty. But a smallpox scare and busy harvesting seemed to make some atonement. I shall remember with much pleasure the homes of Samuel Houndshell and Sister Golliday. Our welcome into those homes was genuine and complete.

Needless to say, Brother Koontz is doing a fine work in this field, and he enjoys the confidence and respect of his people. For him and the people he serves I covet God's abounding favor and blessing.

MATHIAS, WEST VIRGINIA

Mathias is a little town snugly hid away in the mountains and surrounded by some

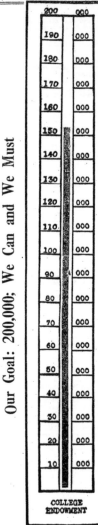

Our Goal: 200,000; We Can and We Must

COLLEGE ENDOWMENT

of the most beautiful scenery of West Virginia. None of the crowded highways of life touch this village; but what it may lose by that it more than makes up in other ways. Our church is in the town and it is at once a very neat, attractive building both inside and out. This is a comparatively young movement, being only little more than a decade since it was launched. Here lives Elder Samuel Mathais who was the leading spirit in the starting of the Mathais work. The movement from the beginning has been self supporting, and it has been characterized by very gratifying growth. Brother Arthur Snyder is the pastor now serving this congregation. Brother Snyder is a busy business man but he takes the time to preach at, at least, two different points. I counted it a privilege to make the acquaintance of these two brethren, Mathais and Snyder. It was here I also met for the first time Dr. Moyer, a most kind and faithful doctor. And I certainly hope to meet all these men again. Brother Koontz and I can both testify that the Snyders and the Moyers are royal in their hospitality.

The needs of Ashland College have perhaps not been brought to the attention of this congregation as much as to some other congregations; consequently I regarded our visit to this place as much a process of getting acquainted as anything. And while $275 may not look so big at this time, yet I am sure that among this people the college has some true friends; and what has been done in our recent visit I consider only a gentle suggestion of the larger things that will be done later. I shall remember with much pleasure my visit to Mathias.

The mercury now stands at $152,000. The next report will come from Maurertown.

WM. H. BEACHLER,
Campaign Secretary.

THE TIE THAT BINDS

SMITH—McCUL—Rev. L. Garvin Smith and Miss McCul, daughter of Hon. and Mrs. James McCul of Stockholm, N. J., were united in marriage on April 5, 1920, by Rev. Dr. W. J. Thompson, of the Drew Theological Seminary faculty. Mrs. Smith is a graduate of the Hamburg, N. J. high school and the Montclair State Normal school. She is at present teaching in the Montclair schools. She is also an accomplished musician. Mr. Smith graduated from the DePauw university with the degree of A. B. in the class of 1911, after which he did a year's graduate work in the Divinity School of the University of Chicago, and in the Ohio State university. He received the B. D. degree from Drew Theological Seminary in 1916, and in 1917 received the B. D. degree from the Union Theological Seminary of New York City and the M. A. degree from Columbia university in the same year. He is now finishing the work for the doctorate of philosophy at the Boston University School of Theology, and at the same time is preaching for the Mayflower Congregational church of Kingston, near Boston. Mr. Smith comes from a long line of preachers, both his father and grandfather having been preachers before him. He recently concluded a pastorate at Conemaugh, Pa., his boyhood home. He began preaching when but sixteen years old, assisting his father, and for twenty years has averaged two sermons a week. He has also had experience in teaching school.

Both Mr. and Mrs. Smith have a host of friends who wish them much happiness and success as they go through life together.

WHITEHEAD-STEPHEY—Boyd A. Whitehead and Katherine A. Stephey at the home of the bride's parents, Mr. and Mrs. C. E. Stephey, 1144 Prairie St., Elkhart. Mrs. Whitehead is a member of the Brethren church. They will reside at Goshen. May God richly bless them with long and happy life.

H. H. WOLFORD.

SMITH-HOKE—Ray H. Smith and Miss Goldie Hoke at the First Brethren church at the close of the morning service, Sunday, June 20. Both are members of the Brethren church and teachers in the Sunday school. May God richly bless them with a long and happy life.

H. H. WOLFORD.

IN THE SHADOW

Singer—James McElroy Singer, son of John and Jane (Rodgers) Singer, was born in Edenburg, Cambria County, on August 12th, 1838. He answered the summons of God and passed from this life at the Memorial Hospital, Johnstown, Pa., an June 30th, 1920. Age 81 years, 10 months and 18 days. Death was due to infection following two operations.

Mr. Singer was a veteran of the Civil War having served in Company C, Nineteenth Infantry during the entire conflict between the North and South. And was one of the oldest and most honored citizens of Cambria county. In his death the community lost a man whose life was spent in usefulness towards both church and state. He was a member of the Brethren Church for nearly forty years, and for many years was an active member of the official board of the Vinco Church.

Mr. Singer was a man who found his inspiration at his fireside, and approached the ideal in his domestic life. He and his faithful wife, Matilda (Sell) Singer, who was both helpmate and companion, inhabited as tennants in common that sacred spot called home, and needed no court to define their relative rights and duties. The invisible walls which shut in the home, and shut out all else, had their foundations upon earth and their battlements in the skies. No force could break them down, no poisoned arrows could cross their top, at the gate thereof, love and confidence stood ever upon guard. We may say of him as Anthony has said of Brutus,

"His life was gentle, and the elements
So mixed in him, that Nature might stand
Up and say to all the world,
This was a man.'"

There survives, his widow mentioned above, 7 children, 20 grandchildren and 5 greatgrandchildren. May the God of peace comfort the hearts of those that mourn the loss of a husband and father.

Services at the Singer home in Vinco, by the undersigned, assisted by Rev. J. F. Watson of Somerset St., Johnstown.

E. F. BYERS.

Tyre and Prophecy.　By T. Darley Allen

The prophecies of the Bible concerning Tyre are among the most interesting of all the illustrations the sacred book presents of the reality of the miraculous in the present generation. Fulfilled prophecies have been termed "miracles of knowledge," and in the present-day condition of the once great city of Tyre we have a number of such miracles, which are as clear an evidence of the supernatural as are afforded by miracles of power. To describe with accuracy, as the Scriptures do, events many centuries in the future is possible only through divine power. The raising of the dead is due to omnipotence; to look down the age and describe events of which no visible sign exists is due to omniscience. God alone is omnipotent and omniscient.

The ancient city of Tyre in Phoenicia was long the emporium of the world. Among its numerous colonies was Carthage, the rival of Rome.

Isaiah and Ezekiel predicted the fall of Tyre when at the height of its power. And although there were two Tyres, the more ancient one being on the continent and the other on an island, the latter inhabited by the same people and perhaps occupying in part the same ground as the older city, the prophecies of Scripture have reference to both.

Passing by the predictions relating to the more ancient Tyre, such as those concerning the capture of the city by the Chaldeans and occurrences relating thereto, we come to the prophecies referring to the more modern city that are being fulfilled today.

In Ezekiel 26:14 we read: "I will make thee like the top of a rock; thou shalt be a place to spread nets upon," and these and similar words by the same prophet find in Tyre's present condition their exact fulfillment.

Tyre, at the beginning of the Christian era, was a city of some importance. The Saracens came into possession of it in the seventh century; and five hundred years later it fell into the hands of the Crusaders, it then being a great commercial city.

Travelers tell us that its condition for more than a century could have no better description than the words of prophecy afford. Early in the nineteenth century Maundrell said of Tyre: "You find here no similitude to that glory for which it was so renowed in ancient times. You see nothing here but mere babel of broken walls, pillars, vaults, etc. Its present inhabitants are only a few poor wretches, harboring themselves in the vaults, and subsisting chiefly upon fishing, and who seem to be preserved in this place by divine providence as a visible argument how God hath fulfilled his Word concerning Tyre."

Volney, the infidel said: "The whole village of Tyre contains only fifty or sixty poor families who live obscurely on the produce of their little ground and a tribing fishery."

To Bruce, a noted traveler, Tyre was a "rock whereupon fishers dry their nets."

Cleveland, Ohio.

The Most Important Conference Yet

AUGUST 30—SEPTEMBER 5

GENERAL CONFERENCE - 1920

The
Closing
of the
Old
Program
with
Honor

The
Beginning
of the
New
Challenge
with
Faith

Published every Wednesday at
Ashland, Ohio. All matter for publication must reach the Editor not
later than Friday noon of the preceding week.

The
Brethren
Evangelist

When ordering your paper changed
give old as well as new address.
Subscriptions discontinued at expiration. To avoid missing any numbers renew two weeks in advance.

George S. Baer, Editor

R. R. Teeter, Business Manager

OFFICIAL ORGAN OF THE BRETHREN CHURCH

Subscription price, $2.00 per year, payable in advance.
Entered at the Post Office at Ashland, Ohio, as second-class matter.
Acceptance for mailing at special rate of postage provided for in section 1103, Act of October 3, 1917, authorized September 9, 1918.
Address all matter for publication to Geo. S. Baer, Editor of the Brethren Evangelist, and all business communications to R. R. Teeter,
Business Manager, Brethren Publishing Company, Ashland, Ohio. Make all checks payable to the Brethren Publishing Company.

TABLE OF CONTENTS

EDITORIAL

An Appreciation of the Four Year Program

In keeping with the prevailing custom of writing appreciations of worthy men and things when they are gone, we are moved to give expression to some sentiments along this line at the time when our Four Year Program has all but completed its existence. It sometimes appears to be a sort of a stupid, ungracious custom,—this thing of writing appreciations when some one or some thing is passing out, —stupid and ungracious, because it indicates a sudden awakening to the appreciation of something of worth when it is gone. But that is our common human failing. Whoever saw a really great man? They are all dead. Great men are not recognized while they are alive and among us. We are too close up to them, It is seldom that we ever really appreciate the worthy things of life until they are slipping from our fingers. And since we are naturally so slow in arriving at the values of things present, it is perhaps better that we express our appreciation of them when they are passing than not at all. It would be most unfortunate never to speak our gratitude for the good things of life, and so it is better to pay our debts late than never.

Is this case it is only a "Program" that is passing, and no person, with sorrowing friends out of deference to whose feelings we must say gracious words. It is only a thing, and there is no one to be offended if we hold our peace. But it represents values the appreciation of which if we have failed to arrive at during these four years of mutual exhortation and endeavor we are beyond all hope of a future. It points out ideals the importance of which, if we have failed to understand after all that has been said and done to bear them to the heart, we must surely be spiritually blind beyond hope of recovery. It sets forth challenges to special endeavor along spiritual lines which if we have failed to accept and to seek to accomplish, we certainly are lacking in that virility and courage, that faith and consecration that would make us worthy of being counted a part of the great church of Christ. And so failure of appreciation of this "Program" that has been challenging us during these four years would reflect a discredit upon us that we would not care to bear. And out of the fulness of the heart's appreciation the mouth and pen cannot but speak.

Our Four Year Program has been a great program. It has been great not because it outlined anything particularly new to be done, nor because it was perfectly planned. It has been great because of what it has done. It has challenged and thereby drawn out spiritual energy and activity that would otherwise have remained latent. Sometimes very worthy and capable people are inclined to drift along with the current, venturing little and accomplishing little, until a challenge is thrown out to them that stirs and energizes their whole being. Then life becomes full of interest and ambition, and time and talent are jealously guarded and spent to some purpose. As with men so with churches, the thing that is needed to transform many an inert, indifferent and doless congregation into an active, wide-awake and aggressive force is to have a taunting challenge thrust before them. Many of our churches were going along in a quiescent sort of way, realizing only half the life and power they might have possessed, until they were awakened by the challenge of the Four Year Program. And though many of our congregations, for one reason or another,—many of them legitimate reasons too, may not have been able to reach all the goals, yet the good derived by all who have rallied enthusiastically to the "Program's" appeal is such as should cause the entire brotherhood to praise the service it has wrought.

The Program has not only stirred us and aroused us from our lethargy, but has brought to our attention the fact that we can do bigger things and be bigger than we ever imagined before. In other words, it has set us to dreaming dreams and seeing visions. Surely after being tutored by the Four Year Program for these years no one shall be able to say of us, "Their people perish for want of vision." We have been awakened to the fact that there are possibilities which we may realize and bigger things which we may undertake that had not occurred to us before. We have learned to look out of a disappointing present into a brighter future. Therein lies the hope of our church. There is no future to them who can see no vision.

We have been giving definite direction to our spiritual energies by this Program; that has been possibly its greatest contribution. Too often in our admonitions to the young we have said, "Be good," instead of saying, "Be good for something." Abstract admonitions are next to useless. We must make them concrete and specific if they are to be real factors in influencing character and conduct. So it is in the work of organized Christianity—the church,—instead of saying, "Be efficient," our Program has said "Do certain things and cultivate a certain spirit that will count for efficiency." It has pointed out certain specific things to be done, which if done sincerely will redound greatly to the strengthening and upbuilding of our denominational life.

This Program has also made us aware of the fact that our church can accomplish far more than we have been able to do if we but focus our thoughts and unite our efforts on certain definite things. It made us realize that if we are to work together as a denomination and not merely as a number of entirely separate and independent congregations, we must have certain things in common which we seek to accomplish, and which shall characterize our endeavors. For example, we have been made to realize that if we are to have a denominational existence, all congregations must unite in supporting a certain definite school. Now there are many good Christian colleges besides Ashland College and many worthy theological training schools, besides Ashland Seminary, but Ashland College and Ashland Seminary are the only institutions founded with the distinct purpose of forwarding the interests of the Brethren church. And every Brethren congregation that has caught the spirit of the Four Year Program has come to see how important it is that they shall give their money and their sons and daughters to the one educational institution which stands for the promotion of our denominational interests. If we scatter our support among many different schools, none of which have any concern for the success of the Brethren church, we will get nowhere as a denomination. The same concerted action is needed in behalf of the only publishing house of the Brethren church, and of every other denominational interest. This does not mean denominational selfishness, intolerance and conceit, but merely denominational loyalty, against which no churchman, with fairness, can say aught. Our Program has in very definite words sought to focus our attention on certain interests very essential to our denominational existence, and to encourage united effort and hearty co-operation along those particular lines.

These considerations, and others that might be mentioned, bear testimony to the great service that has been wrought by the Four Year Program, that passes into history with the coming General Conference. It has been no magic instrument that would work marvels without our effort; it was profitable only as we gave ourselves earnestly, definitely and with consecration to the accomplishment of the things it pointed out. It has been a noble leader, a worthy guide and has brought us forward a pace, and in our "Jubilee" we shall crown it with gratitude. But what of the future? If we shall only hold a "jubilee" and not plan largely for the future, we shall have failed to learn the lesson that these years of effort sought to impress upon us. And we cannot crystal the old Program over into the future. It was good when we made it ,not only stirring our own churches to noble endeavors, but furnishing the inspiration to other denominations for the making of programs. But now we must plan anew. The old program will not do, and to fail to set before ourselves a new program would be fatal. This conference will have failed in the greatest thing before it, if it does not outline under the direction of God, with utmost wisdom, consecration and unanimity, a program that will challenge our highest faith and most strenuous effort, and enable us as a denomination to meet the needs of the world in the largest possible way. But having done that it must make plans whereby the challenge of such a program shall be carried down to the last member in the last church, if we are to profit by our previous mistakes.

EDITORIAL REVIEW

The Virginia Christian Endeavor field worker is not a mere figurehead, but is active in extending the influence of Christian Endeavor as will be noted by his letter on the Christian Endeavor page.

We wish to call attention to our correction in the "News from the Field" department on page 13, of an error that occurred last week in Brother Shively's article "A Toll of Death among the Brethren."

You will notice in the Business Manager's Corner that another new church has been added to the Evangelist Honor Roll. It is Harrisonburg, Virginia, and we wish to extend a most hearty welcome to these new members to The Evangelist Family.

The corresponding secretary of the Hudson, Iowa, church, Sister Gutknecht, writes that they are "always busy" and their "workers are increasing." An every friend of Brother Boardman this church has experienced an "increased interest along many lines." A prayer meeting which was recently started is resulting in much good.

We suggest that pastors call attention from their pulpits to the conference articles in this issue, and in case every home is not getting the Evangelist ,that extra copies be sent for to hand out to create enthusiasm for conference. Those in positions of responsibility should do everything possible to make conference attendance a success.

Just as we were about to go to press the news reached us of the death of Mrs. David Augustine, wife of Elder David Augustine, of South Bend, Indiana. Her death was due to apoplexy and occurred

on August 5th. Sister Augustine was widely known and a host of friends will be made to sorrow at this news. The Evangelist bespeaks the sympathy and prayers of the brotherhood in behalf of Brother Augustine and other sorrowing relatives.

Brother C. C. Grisso, who is leaving North Liberty at the coming conference time, states that the work is in good condition and that the people are ready to follow on to greater victory whoever may be their next leader. He reports additional members received into the Lapaz church. The North Liberty church expects to have a large delegation at conference at Winona.

The secretary of the Board of Benevolences, Brother H. E. Roscoe, of Goshen, Indiana, compliments Brother O'Neill's Bible class and the Pittsburgh church, of which Brother Harley is pastor, for their most excellent offering to the Superannuated Minister's Fund. That is a cause often neglected by many of our churches.

Brother I. D. Bowman's evangelistic effort at Calvary, New Jersey, was attended with handicaps. Bad weather and bad roads are hard things to contend with. He speaks most highly of Brother Sands and his work. At Ankneytown, Ohio, his evangelistic meeting was more successful, and the handicaps were not so great. Yet he was denied the help of Ankneytown's efficient pastor, Brother A. L. Lynn, on account of school work during most of his campaign.

STATISTICAL REPORTS IN? Yes, I know we said the same thing last week, but we are co-operating with Brother Mason in his desperate effort to get the Ohio conference statistical reports in before General Conference time. Only four more churches have reported since last week. If you were the statistician, how would you like such lack of co-operation? A little application of the Golden Rule would help much in this case. Brother Mason's address is West Salem, Ohio.

The Clay City, Indiana, church under the leadership of Brother S. C. Henderson, is aggressive and progressing. The pastor claims it will be a banner church according to the Four Year Program schedule. The Sunday school is wide awake and growing and the Christian Endeavor has recently graduated a class in Expert Endeavor. The parsonage has been repaired and improved, and is now in fine shape. They are looking forward to an evangelistic campaign under the leadership of Brother A. E. Thomas in October.

Brother Alva McClain, pastor of the First Brethren church of Philadelphia, writes an interesting letter concerning the progress of the work there. He and his wife are the proud inhabitants of a fine new parsonage. Churches without a parsonage would do well to follow the example of the Philadelphia Brethren. This people's generosity is further evidenced by the splendid foreign mission offering they made. Not only financial but numerical growth is registered. Brother McClain recently accepted the church's unanimous call to remain as its pastor for another year. Notice also that this church is not forgetting to give proper attention to its pastor's salary in these days of constantly increasing "high cost of living." And they are coming to General Conference twenty delegates strong.

One thing that is sometimes discouraging to the ambitious is that when they have done exceedingly well, there is always some one comes along and does a little better.' That has been the history of the endowment campaign all along, and the Maryland-Virginia district is no exception. The Hagerstown church had given the largest offering until Maurertown gave a larger one. And we half believe Brother Beachler enjoys seeing one church outstrip another in giving to this worthy cause, though he says he is "sorry." The fact is, every friend of the college is rejoicing in these splendid gifts to the endowment fund. It is not half large enough yet, but if the awakening to the needs of the college that has been realized during the last three years, continues another three years, we will be in better shape to begin to talk about an adequate endowment. For when the second hundred thousand dollars is raised, we ought to have a third hundred thousand piled right on top of the second. We congratulate Maurertown for their realization of the need of Ashland College. There is a reason, or we had better say, There are reasons, and Brother Beachler has told them. Whenever a church is as vitally connected with a college as this church is (having had students in the school and having a member on the faculty), you can expect it will show its friendship in very practical ways.

GENERAL ARTICLES

Why Every Congregation Should Be Represented at General Conference By One Or More Delegates

By William H. Beachler

I am writing on this subject by request. The privilege was granted me to change the wording of the subject if I so desired, but I had no inclination to do so. I consider the subject just right as it stands. It implies that, regardless of size or geographical location (at least in our own country) every congregation should have representation in our General Conferences, and, allowing for conditions which might occasionally arise in a congregation making it impossible, the subject represents my conviction greatly.

It is a fact greatly to be deplored that we have congregations which, in their entire history, have not been represented in a single one of our General Conferences. If each and every such congregation in our brotherhood were to have one or more delegates in the coming General Conference it would swell by considerably the grand total of delegates and it would mean far more in a number of ways than I can indicate in this short article.

But why should every congregation be represented at General Conference by one or more delegates? I assign three reasons—there are doubtless more.

First, for the sake of what a congregation owes itself and the community in which it is. I maintain that a Brethren congregation is under obligation to represent the brotherhood of which it is a part in a consistent, intelligent manner. Now I am not going to say that a congregation cannot do this in a way if it has never been represented in our General Conferences, but I will say that any congregation is giving itself very decided advantages that keeps in touch with the thought of the church as it finds expression in those conferences. I have observed congregations which never fail from year to year to have their delegates in our General Conferences. Then, too, I have observed congregations which have never been represented. And with no thought at all of being unfair or unkind I must insist that there is a radical difference to be noted; and the difference is in the favor of the churches that go to General Conference. I contend that while a Brethren church may be a good Brethren church having never had representation in a General Conference, yet that same church will be a better Brethren church, more effective in its respective community, and more clearly and correctly representing the ideals and thought of the general brotherhood of which it is a part, if it does keep in touch with our General Conferences. I am very certain that no congregation can habitually ignore our General Conferences, content to live and move in a world all by itself and not sustain great loss. Every congregation should be represented in every General Conference because of what it owes itself and the community in which it works.

Second, each congregation should be represented in our General Conferences because of what it owes the brotherhood. The moment a band of people organize themselves into a Brethren congregatoin, being by their own consent a part of the general Brethren fraternity, that moment they assume obligation to the general brotherhood. And any congregation is doing a substantial part in discharging that obligation when it has its delegates in our General Conferences who are willing to share their respective part of the responsibility for the conferences, and also willing to lend their voice and their assistance in the framing and shaping of the policies which are to govern our various general interests. To say the very least it is not fair for any congregation to habitually sit back and allow other congregations to carry the whole burden of responsibility for the promotion of the general movement of which it claims to be a part. I maintain that this is a place where each one should bear his own burden. For all too long a time, a comparatively few people from a comparatively few congregations have been bearing the burden of our General Conferences in their relation to the general interests of the church. The moment has come when more people and more congregations must assume their legitimate responsibility to the denomination. Nor is it putting it a whit too strongly to say that it is imperative that the General Conference habit must become more general among our people in all of the districts and congregations of our entire brotherhood. Hence, every congregation should be represented in our General Conferences in order that they may discharge the obligation they sustain to the general brotherhood. A congregation failing at this point suffers as a result in loss of individuality. As with an individual so with an organization; failure to assume our responsibilities and to live up to and exercise the rights and privileges which belong to us stifles and kills individuality. Strong effective churches have individuality. I need say no more at this point.

Third and last, every congregation should be represented at our General Conferences for the sake of the inspiration and enlarged vision which is to be had there and which is not nearly so likely to be found at our State Conferences or by reading the Brethren Evangelist. I am not disparaging our State Conferences or the Brethren Evangelist, not at all. But I am insisting that there are some good things to be had at our General Conferences for every congregation, but somebody must be sent to get them and bring them home, else they are lost as far as the congregations are concerned. I mean good things for the Sunday school; for the W. M. S.; for Y. P. S. C. E.; for the Sisterhood girls, etc., etc. And besides, a whole lot of fire and inspiration. Think what our congregations have missed that have never had a representative in a single General Conference! Think what our ministers have missed too who have never had the privilege of being in a single General Conference! No congregation can afford year after year to allow all these good things to go by unheeded. And what is more, I believe God holds congregations as well as individuals responsible for the opportunities brought to us which we disregard and ignore. And so I say, by all means every congregation should send a delegate or delegates to General Conference for the sake of the good things they will bring back home for the local congregation. It has been proven time after time that the best possible investment a congregation can make is to send some of its people to General Conference. Very often the first thing that happens in a local congregation when delegates get back from General Conference is a resurrection. God give us a lot of resurrections!

Now then, whatever I have said thus far, I do want to try hard in this closing paragraph to say something practical—something that will get us somewhere, and it is this: I know literally scores of people in the Brethren church who have an abundance of the things of this world, and who never spent a red cent in their lives to go to a General Conference. Over against that I know scores of other loyal folks, among them a lot of poor preachers, who have, in the last twenty years actually spent hundreds of dollars to attend our conferences. Now you folks who never spent anything going to conference, let me give you this bit of valuable suggestion: you get busy right away quick and pick up some poor preacher (maybe your own pastor), or some other faithful young man or woman in your congregation and YOU literally send him or her to the coming conference, with all expenses "prepaid." If you can't think of the "poor preacher" or the worthy young person write me and I will give you some names. If you, my brother, my sister, will dare to do this magnanimous thing it will prove to you the genuineness of your Brethren loyalty, and at the same time it will enhance your own respect for yourself at least fifty percent. I dare somebody to do just this sensible, practical thing.

Yours for a record breaker attendance at the coming conference.

Waterloo, Iowa.

The Spirit That Should Characterize a Brethren Conference. By J. I. Hall

We are now looking forward toward the convening of the Brethren National Conference. We hope and pray for the best conference in the history of the Brethren church. There is no reason why we should expect anything less than the best. But if it is the best it will be because we make it so. Certain things must be observed heartily to make it the best.

(1) Go to conference repeating our slogan, "Stand fast in the faith." Stand four square on the Brethren platform—"The Bible, the whole Bible and nothing but the Bible. To stand anywhere else in a Brethren conference will make trouble. But don't be theological hair splitters. Contend earnestly for the faith once delivered to the saints. Pray for the guidance of the Holy Spirit.

(2) The spirit of harmony. Pray for it. Talk for it. Sing for it. Work for it. Let the coming conference be like a harp with a thousand strings and each string in tune with the others. If we should go there in the spirit of debate—walking around with a chip on our shoulder, daring any one to take a crack at it, we will undoubtedly have a stormy conference.

(3) Go for business and inspiration. The King's business must be attended to. Do not want everything to go your way, because you are not the King. Advise and be advised. Thus we will get inspiration and wisdom to do business for our Master that will count for much good, for in the multitude of counsellors there is safety.

(4) Do not pout if you are not given an office. Everybody at conference cannot have an office. Maybe you have been tried before and failed through incompetence or at least, you failed. Do not be jealous because someone holds an office a long time, but wish him well, and thank the Lord that he has proved himself competent and that we have men, and women too, in the Brethren church that can do things.

(5) If you have any personal schemes or an old dull axe to grind, leave your personal schemes at home, bury them, and take your axe to the shop and grind it,—and be sure you pay the boy that turns the grindstone. Go to conference in the spirit that St. Paul taught the Romans (Romans 12:10), "Be kindly affectioned one toward another with brotherly love in honor preferring one another."

In an art show at the Royal Arcade, Mr. Turner took down one of his great conceptions to make room for a picture made by an unknown artist. Christ's servants should be ruled by a like spirit. Go to conference with the spirit that prefers another.

(6) Be willing to make some concessions. Take it for a fact that other people know a few things at least and that it is well to respect an honest Christian gentleman's opinion now and then. Do not go there riding a hobby. The hobby rider never dismounts, hence never makes any concessions.

(7) If you are not given a place on the conference program do not get your back up about it, and stay away, thinking you are not needed nor wanted there; or if you go do not go with a grievance because you have not an opportunity to tell the wonderful message that you have prepared for the occasion. Maybe you have been on the program before and made a fizzle of it, or may be you delivered a wonderful message, especially in your own estimation. Just be reasonable and charitable, too. The program committee cannot put everybody on the program. Therefore do not feel slighted or belittled. Go praying that everybody on the program may be present and acquit themselves nobly.

(8) Go there for recreation. Yes, but be sure that you go rowing or swimming, or hiking or lounging or resting, or sleeping when the conference is not in session, for your Master's orders are that you be present to help boost the most important work that is given men and women to do. Remember that the King's business after all is the most important. If we have the spirit of our Master we will do with enthusiasm the work of the conference. Then we will be conscious of being absolutely loyal to the Master and his work.

(9) If you get angry or disgruntled, indignant or insulted at something that is said on the conference floor, do not lose your head and get hasty or you will say something you may regret. An insult is like mud, it will brush off better when it is dry. Just wait awhile until you cool off, and then the trouble can be easily mended. Most likely no insult will be thought of.

(10) And lastly, but not the least, use brotherly love. Go in the spirit of love. Be patient, long suffering, gentle. Use brotherly kindness. Be charitable. Obey the Golden Rule. Do not use your brother in such a way that you know if he used you so, you would be like Charles Spurgeon said, "You would get your monkey up." We believe if the above rules were observed the conference would be all that the most sanguine could expect. Let us pray and try.

Martinsburg, Pennsylvania.

Why the Laymen Should Attend Our General Conference. By H. F. E. O'Neill

First. The General Conference should be a cosmopolitan body and to make and keep it so there should be a large attendance of laymen in order to get their interest and attention and to give the benefit of their suggestions and advice as well as their moral and financial support. The ministers are not willing to conduct all the business of a National Conference and this is right, for with all respect to our ministers, most of them were educated and trained in a profession and many of them have had no experience in the business world. "The King's business requireth (accuracy as well as haste."

Second. The local church should be represented by the largest possible number of laymen so that she may have her proper share in the Conference and get the best possible return from it, as no one person either clergy or lay, can give a report of the National Conference that will interest and enthuse a congregation, and when the local congregation gets enthusiastic reports from the National Conference, the result will be reactionary for good.

Third. That the spiritual life of both the General Conference and the laity might be the very best possible there should be a larger attendance of laymen at the conference. Those who go to the conference filled to overflowing with the spirit of Christ will be able to put inspiration into those assembled and those laymen who are not so spiritually minded will do well to be put in touch with the spiritual dynamo at the conference and will come back more efficient members of the local church.

Fourth. There should also be a larger attendance of laymen at the conference so that they may know and appreciate the work that is being done throughout the country, for the more who attend the General Conference the more interested and enthusiastic workers there will be in the local congrgations. This is one of the many rules that works both ways. The most interested members of the congregations will attend the conference and those who attend the conference will be the most interested and helpful members of the local church.

Fifth. There should be a larger attendance of the laity at the General Conference as a matter of vacation. The trite saying, "All work and no play makes Jack a dull boy" was no more true when it was said than it is now, and after having taken a vacation for a good many years, I can speak from experience when I say that those members of our church who have not made the General Conference their summer vacation have missed a great blessing in their own lives as well as being a blessing to others. Many good people have had the sad experience of coming back from a seashore and other public summer resort, having their spiritual if not their physical health lessened, (if not ruined), where experience has proven that people who spend their vacation attending a church conference at a beautiful place like Winona Lake, both spiritual and physical health is really re-created.

Sixth. A larger attendance of laymen at the General Conference would not only increase the spiritual life of the individual but it would tend to strengthen the erection and maintenance of family altars in the homes of our church.

Pittsburgh, Pennsylvania.

How to Make the Coming Conference Count for the Most for the Future of the Brethren Church

By George H. Jones

Somewhere between Chicago and New York on a train coming from the Democratic National Convention of 1896, the following conversation took place. Two delegates were comfortably disposing of themselves for the long journey home. They began discussing the results of the meeting. One, after comfortably lighting a cigar, remarked with a sigh of contentment, "Well, I saw everything worth seeing in Chicago." The other answered with an earnestness in strange contrast with that of his companion, "I heard one of the most marvellous speeches a man ever listened to, and I met one of the most brilliant men America has produced. His very tones carried conviction. Both men while in Chicago, found the very things they had been most interested in.

Just behind the two delegates, sat two officers of the convention. One remarked enthusiastically, "With such a leader capable of such a speech, and a platform such as we adopted, I honestly believe it will be possible to carry even Pennsylvania for the Democratic party." "Pshaw!" said the other gloomily, "I could have carried New York, had I been nominated." The convention meant different things to these different men, but in their comments, the motives and condition of their minds were plainly apparent.

Conventions and conferences are alike epoch making only as the delegates and leaders alike are dominated by unselfish devotion to a high ideal. Selfishness and indifference both narrow the spirit of a conference.

The Indifferent Delegate

Fortunately the delegate who is not interested is rare. He comes because he would have been lonesome back home, had he remained there when the more interested members of the family planned on attending. He looks bored, he feels bored, and he seldom gets anything of real value out of the conference. His tribe is increased by the delegate who plans for only one day at conference. The rest of the time he spends in auto rides, in visits to neighboring cities and points of interest. He does not know who are on the program or when it begins or ends. He just knows, "It starts Monday and ends Monday—or Sunday, is it?"

Then there is the fellow who came just "to have a good time." "What's the use of listening to dry old speeches? We'll boat all day, or fish, or visit. I can read that 'stuff' in the Annual." The indifferent delegate is almost as valuable to the local congregation which sent him as to the Conference body.

The Inspired Delegate

By way of contrast there is the inspired delegate. He realizes the value of a conference. Back home there is a department of the church work in need of repairs. It isn't functioning right. It is crippling the related departments. In fact it seriously threatens the progress of the whole congregation. Because of its inefficiency it is causing hard feelings upon the part of the officials concerned. Matters are serious. So he comes to get the benefit of another's experience. He wants, too, the "hill-top" view. He wishes to get off at a distance, above the feelings and the local viewpoint, and see from a higher standpoint. He generally succeeds. He comes with a local longing, he leaves with a mountain-top vision. He has enthusiasm, too. To him church leaders from "California" are a source of inspiration. His feelings are infectious. The leaders absorb the contagion. He brings his vessel empty. It goes away filled. He likes to tell you what a fine crowd of people he holds his membership with. His pastor is as good as any in the brotherhood.

Then too he thinks Brethrenism has a future. His work is not paralyzed by unbelief. He can see the need of doctrines like ours. Spring and fall communion and love feast are a real need to him. The inspired delegate is an inspiration.

The Self-Seeking Official

The officials loom large in the value of a conference to a church. What an embarrassment, yea more, what a detriment, are some of the tribe. We need grace to bear with them. The officer who plans to put himself in the prominent place, who looks for a possible call to a wealthy church pulpit, or one of large membership, who has a network of wires running in all directions, like a spider's web, himself at the center and the terminals located where possible a fine berth might be secured. Such a one remarked to the chairman of the executive committee, "I think my position entitles me to more prominence on the program than you have given me." (He was already programmed more than any other man on it).

> "Wud some power the giftie gi'e us,
> To see oursel's as ithers see us."

The heartaches such a condition of mind brings upon some of our conference officers is lamentable. It has its "souring" effect. Sometimes we have felt that our conferences would be a hundred times more effective if we could only unload all of these who are self-seeking leaders. Such a fever of hurt vanity we have tried to cure! Truly the Great Physician has been needed badly at some conferences. There have been self-seeking delegates returned disappointed from church conferences as well as from political conventions. Let us pray that such a spirit might be banished from our 1920 Conference.

The Loyal Official

What a big soul is a business-like, consecrated conference official. May his tribe increase. How we have voted for and sung the praises of a man big enough to be a real executive. How gladly have we mounted into the realm of certainty and faith, when our loyalty has been worth while. Big, loyal-hearted, unselfish leaders help to make a conference worth while.

Three things make a conference count for the best. The foregoing message has had just three in mind. First, a big vision is needed. Second, a big motive is equally as necessary. And lastly, these two combined make an inspired delegate and a loyal official. Have these two and this Conference will count for the most in future years.

Conemaugh, Pennsylvania.

The Coming Conference a Time for Visualizing Our Task. By E. L. Miller

"Your old men shall dream dreams, your young men shall see visions." It is quite preacher-like to set a text at the beginning of an article. but it is not our intention to preach. As we look at the attainments we are in a measure dreaming, and it is well that we have some grounds for good dreams; whether our effort has given us such ground it is ours to see and say. The older ones are to dream, perhaps of things enjoyed in the past and with a flavor of happier things beyond. But it is the part of the live, vigorous young persons to see visions, visions of bigger and better things that their vitality may bring to pass. Surely none present at the closing sermon of last conference can forget the tremendous stress laid upon those fateful words spoken by God to Moses. Dr. Morgan laid upon us the necessity of GOING FORWARD. I do not like to emphasize the word of direction alone but also the word of action. And it says GOING. Now we must not be satisfied with what we have gained ,but we must be going to better things in the field of promise, which, as it was with the Children of Israel, is still ahead. We will have a jubilee over what has been done by the faithful during the past four years, but to me that is only an earnest of what we ought to do the next four years. Each year better than its predecessor ought to be our aim. We ran well, that is, some did, and those doing it know what blessing the Four Year Program was to them. Perhaps the goals were high, but it is low aim that is crime. No church making a decent effort at attaining the goals set but received some good from it. And the ones making a majority of the goals are the ones loudest in their demands for something definite at which they may aim the coming years. And as one committee lays down its work for another to pick it up and push forward, may we not bespeak a more earnest effort in attainment than was made the past four years? It is well for us to look backward and count the gains made, but no true business man would do that without also looking ahead and planning for greater prosperity during the period known as the future. I am reminded of the colored man who was made the victim of a practical joke. A mammoth "ghost' pursued and fear lent such speed to the colored gentleman's heels that he outdistanced the "ghost," even though it did make him extend himself. Then while resting on a stump the "ghost" pulled up behind him and touching him on the shoulder said, "That was a dandy run we had, wasn't it?" The darky answered, "Yas sir, but it ain't nuthin' lak we're goin' to have." So we have made a good run, at least some have, and it is the hope of the writer that it is nothing like the one we are going to make. The mistakes of the committee and program of the past four years can be corrected, or at least guarded against, and no reason exists thaat would excuse us from doing better work the next four years than we have the past four. We are only getting our eyes opened to the fields of endeavor that are open before us, the vision of service is just unfolding, and shall we refuse to enter into the "joys of the Lord" which are the rewards for well-rendered service?

Now since the coming conference is the time and place where the ends will be picked up and where we will have made known to us just how well we did, or poorly for that matter, during the past four years, it will be by the same token be the place where we can get the vision and inspiration for the task that is ahead. No one would deny that we are living in a time when the church is being put to the test, but Jesus said that his church would prevail, and if we are part of that real church of Christ we will lay plans to prevail. We have pulled up stream somewhat, but we must not rest on our oars or the stream will carry us back even farther than the starting point. Tell the Brethren that they Go Forward. And the coming conference will show us the way. Let's go!

Nappanee, Indiana.

Understanding Our Children

Heavenly Father, we pray that thou wilt show us how to enter into the lives of our children and learn their thoughts and feelings. The years have blunted our memories. We are not able to clearly recall the impressions of our own childhood, how can we understand the quest of our little ones for knowledge? Give us, we beseech thee, a new vision of the past. Renew our youth, deepen our sympathies and guide us that we may more fully take possession of their hearts and teach them thy way.

Keep us from unwisely repressing their impulses and inquiries, from misdirecting them through impatience and self-indulgence, so that we weaken their confidence and cause them to go astray.

Enable us through thy spirit to show them by word and example the paths of truth and righteousness, through Christ Jesus. Amen.

A Campaign of Iniquity

Much indignation has been aroused by the pernicious activity of the British-American Tobacco Company, in seeking to win the people of China for the cigarette habit by every possible expedient. Already more than $5,000,000 has been spent in the distribution of samples, and the promoters are hoping to reap a most copious harvest from the sowing thus made. For several months, a package of cigarettes was wrapped in every parcel of dry goods, sold at the stores to the Chinese women. As a result, the cigarette habit is being fastened on the unsuspecting people of China, upon whom, hitherto, opium had a strangle-hold, which could only be dislodged by the most stringent governmental edicts. How can so-called Christian nations allow this cigarette propaganda?—The Gospel Messenger.

Proposed Union of Mennonites and Amish

There has been a strong pressure among both Mennonites and Amish, that the two bodies—so similar in religious sentiment and general practice—enter upon negotiations that will eventually bring about a close organic union. A conference to that end was recently held at Milford, Nebr., which gathering is described by the editor of the "Gospel Herald" (Mennonite) as a more harmonious meeting than any he ever attended. He frankly says: "As the two wings of the church have been one in fact for a number of years, it is fitting that the last remnants of the 'middle wall or partition' be wiped away." This promising effort of our Mennonite and Amish friends well deserves to meet with success. Incidentally it might suggest a course of action by which other denominational units, closely affiliated in general religious belief, might join their forces in a united and constructive campaign for righteousness.—The Gospel Messenger.

THE BRETHREN PULPIT

The Call of the Master.   By George W. Kinzie

(Sermon preached at New Lebanon, Ohio, June 27, 1920)

TEXT: The Master is come, and calleth for thee."—JOHN 11:28.

Jesus has just come from Jerusalem to visit again the place of his baptism. While here he received a message from Mary and Martha telling of the sickness of their brother Lazarus. Now there seems to have been no home in all that country where Jesus so loved to be as in the home of Mary and Martha and Lazarus. He greatly loved them,. and was much loved by them. And no doubt his heart was much touched by the sorrow which he knew was about to come to these he so greatly loved. There was none to whom he would go in greater haste, none whom he would more readily shield from grief and sorrow than these. But he was in the midst of a great revival, and some three or four days' journey from them, and many souls were believing on him. Furthermore, he knew this very incident would give him greater opportunity to reach men. And so he waits two days before starting to go to them. As soon as Martha heard that Jesus was coming, she hastened to meet him, and to lament the loss of her brother. Jesus comforts and consoles her in her sorrow, then she stole away to call Mary her sister, in the words of my text: "The Master is come, and calleth for thee." And I am sure the Master has called, or is calling every one of us here today. Will we arise and heed his call?

Let us remember that it is the **Master** who calls. It is not our Sunday school teacher, nor the superintendent; it is not the president of the Christian Endeavor Society, nor is it even the pastor who calls—but the MASTER. He may use any one or several of these human agents, yet it is he who calls. We might ignore the call of these if it were merely their call—without any serious consequences; not so the Master's call. He is the **Master**; we are his servants (slaves). He has bought us with his own blood, and his we are, and all that we are and have, for, "Ye are not your own, for ye are bought with a price" (1. Cor. 6:16). And "To whom ye yield yourselves servants to obey, his servants (bondservants) ye are to whom ye obey; whether of sin unto death, or of obedience unto righteousness" (Rom. 6:16). And the Master has the absolute right to command as he will, and true servants have no recourse but to obey. Yet, though slaves, and to be in such complete subjection, it is wholly voluntary and enjoyable to the true child of God; for his delight is to do the will of God.

The call of the Master is a persistent call—"He calleth for thee." Those of us who have responded to his call can testify to the persistency of that call—first of all to give him our hearts, and then to definite service. How that call still sounded in our ears, though we sought to evade it ever so long! It is also a personal call for he calleth for thee. No one else in all the world can answer that call for you. What will your answer be? Will you answer as did some in the days of his flesh, when one would follow him without counting the cost; or another who would follow but he would first attend to temporal matters; or yet a third, who would give his homefolks first consideration? Or will you answer his call as did Peter and Andrew, and James and John, who immediately, upon being called, forsook their all, and followed him? Are we saying, "Yes, I will follow thee, BUT?" What excuse are you making for denying him your whole service?

His call is a call first of all to salvation. But once we are saved he calls us to service. We are saved to serve. He has saved us that through us he may reach and save others. In this call there are no exemptions, and to refuse is to rebel. And if salvation means anything, it means that we are no longer rebels against God. It means that our former enmity

against God has been removed. It is also, it may be, a call to great sacrifice. It may be that in heeding this call of the Master, we may have to give up our homes and loved ones perhaps even to be shunned and rejected by relatives and friends. Was not the Master also "despised and rejected" for our sakes? It may be that heeding the Master's call would mean to go among strangers, of strange speech and habits, and to endure hardships and loneliness. We are told to "endure hardships (hardness) as good soldiers of Jesus Christ." Do soldiers have "soft times?" And let us not forget that "If we suffer with him, we may be also glorified together." Furthermore, the Master has also suffered hardships and loneliness for our sakes, when, after his baptism he was led of the Spirit into the wilderness to be tempted of the devil. For forty long days he fasted and prayed, and in the loneliness of the desert fought against and overcame the temptations of Satan, that he might succor them that are tempted. But, blessed be God, at the end of that terrible struggle, and at least partly compensating it, "Angels came and ministered unto him." And so they will minister also unto us, should his call lead us through paths of trial, if we are but true.

The Master's call is a challenge to your heroism. It means to deny and renounce and spurn the ways, fashions methods and pleasures of the world and of self; to follow him despite ridicule, peril or other consequences. Not always an easy thing! Indeed it is extremely hard on the flesh. It is easy to rest on one's oars and to dream and drift with the current, to go the way the crowd goes, but this also means separation from Christ. And to the real Christian truly

"How tedious and tasteless the hours
  When Jesus no longer I see!
Sweet prospects, sweet birds and sweet flowers,
  Have all lost their sweetness to me.
The midsummer sun shines but dim,
  The fields strive in vain to look gay;
But when I am happy in him
  December's as pleasant as May."

His call is a challenge to your devotion. How much do you really love him who first loved you? He says, "If ye love me keep my commandments," and "If a man love me he will keep my words." Regardless of the loudness of one's profession, obedience, prompt and unquestioning, is the sure proof of love.

Again, the Master's call is a call to closest fellowship as well as to the greatest and grandest of achievements. It is only in obedience to his "Go ye," that we may expect to realize the "Lo, I am with you alway." And what greater work can there possibly be than to be instrumental in enthroning Jesus Christ in even a single heart and life? Turning souls from the power of Satan to God?

But what constitutes a call? Is not the realization of the need a sufficient call to any one who is able to supply the need? That people are starving is the only call we need to share our crust of bread, to say nothing of our super abundance. Only a criminal would deliberately withhold the healing agency from a dying people. Perishing souls going out into a Christless, endless eternity, are beckoning and calling to you and me, and this should be a sufficient call to a child of God. We have the light; they sit in darkness. We have the bread of life; they are perishing. Can we sit idly and carelessly by while their cry mingles with the call of the Master for us to arise and give them from our abundance? The Master's "Go ye into all the world is as applicable to you and me as it was to the apostles. Shall we rebel, and refuse to obey? There are various fields from which urgent calls are coming for volunteers to fill up the depleted ranks of the workers in those fields. They call evangelists, pastors, Bible teachers, medical missionaries, to the ministry, mission fields, Sunday school work, etc., as nurses, evangelistic singers, pianists, personal workers, etc. Has God been calling you to some special work of this sort? Then do not refuse. It is quite certain, however, that it is hardly according to the will of God that all should be pastors, etc. But it is just as certain that God would have every Christian to be a soul-winner—this to be the chief business of life. No doubt he would have many like William Carey, who said, when asked what his business was, "My business is winning souls. I cobble shoes to pay my expenses." Perhaps he would have you farm, or work in the store or office or factory to pay expenses, but, if you are a Christian, he would have you "By all means save some."

Suppose some one were to offer me a thousand dollars for every soul that I might earnestly try to lead to Christ, would I endeavor to lead any more souls to him than I am endeavoring to do now? Is it possible that I would attempt to do for money, even at the risk of blunders or ridicule, what I hesitate or shrink from doing now in obedience to God's command? Is my love of money stronger than my love of God or of souls? How feeble then my love of God! Perhaps this explains why I am not a soul-winner.

"Suppose I were to see a blind man unknowingly approach the brink of a high precipice, and that I were to sit by without concern or any effort to warn or save him from certain death, would I not be as guilty of his death in God's sight as though I had murdered him outright? The death of a body, which might have been (but was not) prevented, is a terrible thing, but how about the preventable death of a human soul—perchance of many souls—for which God may hold me responsible? If my murder of another body by neglect is an unspeakable crime, what shall be said of my murder by neglect of another's soul?

"Suppose I were to be asked how many persons I had persistently tried to win to Christ during the past month, or even during the past year, what would my answer be? How many have I spoken to? How many have I on my prayer list now? If I am not interested enough in the salvation of others even to have a daily prayer list, is it any wonder that I am not a soul-winner?

"If I speak with the tongues of all the dialects and languages of men and of angels, but fail to win men, I am become as the cry of a beggar in the streets of famine. And if I have the gift of making money, and know all about politics, business, science and war, and if I have great influence and many acquaintances, yea though I have great power of adaptation so that I can move with equal ease among the most cultured and refined or the most degraded and needy, but win not men, I am not living. And if I spend all my life and means in famine relief, giving physical life to multitudes, and give my body to be buried in the end, and win not men, it profiteth me nothing.

"To win men one must suffer long and be kind. To win men one must not envy. He who vaunteth himself, who is puffed up, who behaveth himself unseemly, who seeks his own, who is provoked, who taketh account of evil, who rejoices in unrighteousness and not in the truth, such an one winneth men for the evil one and his reign of death.

"He who would win men must bear all things, believe all things, hope all things, endure all things. He who wins a man to a life with God, wins that which never faileth; but whether there be prophecies of winning men, they shall be done away either in achievement of it or in failure. Whether there be tongues, they shall continue only as they win men.

An Ode to the Divine Logos

BY WILBUR FISK TILLETT

In the beginning was the Word, and the Word was God; and the Word was made flesh and dwelt among us, full of grace and truth; and we beheld his glory. In him was life, and his life was the light of men. (St. John.)

God hath in these last days spoken unto us by his Son. (Author of Hebrews.)

Words are thought bearers, love bearers and will bearers from man to man. (Plato.)

I

The Thought Bearer

O Word of God incarnate,
    Thought bearer to mankind,
Who, clothed in flesh, dost translate
    To men 'th' omniscient mind,
God's thought to earth thou bringest
    That men in thee may see
What God is like, and, seeing,
    Think God's thoughts after thee.

II

The Love Bearer

O Word of God incarnate,
    Love bearer from on high,
Men's hearts are all insatiate
    Till thou dost satisfy;
God's love to earth thou bringest
    In living deeds that prove
That they see God the Father
    Who see thy life of love.

III

The Will Bearer

O Word of God incarnate,
    Bearer of will divine,
Who didst our free wills create
    That we might make them thine,
God's will to earth thou bringest
    That all who would obey
May learn from thee their duty
    And see in thee the way.

IV

The Life Bearer

O Word of God incarnate,
    Life bearer sent to men,
Who at thy fountain satiate
    Their thirst ne'er thirst again;
God's life to earth thou bringest,
    And, though the thorn-path trod
Led thee to death on Calv'ry,
    Thou wast the Son of God.

V

The Light Bearer

O Word of God incarnate,
    O Light of Truth divine,
So bright thy light is, so great,
    To all men it doth shine;
God's light to earth thou bringest
    To drive sin's night away,
And, through thy life so radiant,
    Earth's darkness turns to day.

VI

The Word Complete

O Word of God incarnate,
    O Mind of God made plain,
O Heart no man need placate
    God's gracious will to gain;
O Light of Life eternal,
    In thee God and man meet;
When God through thee hath spoken,
    Thou art God's Word Complete!
        —Vanderbilt University.

Whether there be knowledge it shall be done away. For we know in part and we prophesy in part; but when all men are won that which was in part shall be done away, for the perfect day shall have come.

"And now abideth at the disposal of each one of us here today a body, a mind and a spirit, but the greatest fruitage of each and all is the winning of men."

Shall we not therefore, here and now, determine that by his grace we will give ourselves from this day forward to the definite business of saving the lost, that we will have a daily prayer list and do what we can under the guidance of the Holy Spirit to help accomplish the supreme work for which our Lord and Master came into the world, and the work to which he calls every follower of his? May God help us so to do.

New Lebanon, Ohio.

Send
WHITE GIFT
OFFERINGS to

ALBERT TRENT
General Secretary-Treasurer
Johnstown, Pennsylvania

THE SUNDAY SCHOOL

Of Interest to Sunday School Workers

Every wide-awake and up-to-date Sunday school worker is interested in what promises to be the greatest Sunday school event in years. If we cannot attend personally the World's Sunday School Convention to be held at Tokyo, Japan, we will be interested in reading about arrangements for the trip and the convention. He who does not permit this convention to be the occasion for a new awakening in Sunday school interest and an enlarged vision of its mission and possibilities will miss a wonderful opportunity.

Increasing Interest in the Tokyo Sunday School Convention

By telegrams, letters and in person, applications for reservations are being made at the office of the World's Sunday School Association, 216 Metropolitan Tower, New York, by those who are eager to go to the Tokyo Convention. Special interest is shown in the Around the World tours. Plans have been completed for a detour of four weeks in India. The visits to the mission stations of the different denominations will be experiences never to be forgotten. Inspirational and educational meetings will be conducted at each stopping place. Berths can still be had on most of the tours. Immediate application for reservations is of great importance. Each registered delegate, in talking over the plans for the trip, makes others want to go. The first steamer sails July 30th and the last one September 23rd. Those who take a later tour can see Japan, Korea and China after the Convention concludes on October 14th.

Each of the ten outward bound tour parties will hold meetings in the Orient and it is interesting to note the combined talent in each group. Trained workers and speakers of marked ability will be ready to conduct profitable Sunday school gatherings whenever the opportunity offers. Leaders in the different centres abroad are now arranging locally for the coming of the Sunday school pilgrims.

A number of the delegates have already announced that they will write books on their experiences while in the Orient. One writer will have his photographer along that suitable illustrations may be obtained. Many others will become personal correspondents for various papers in the home land. The World's Association will mail its "World Wide Sunday School News" for November from Tokyo at the conclusion of the convention. It will be a brief report of the great meetings in Japan and mailed to about 600 papers in many parts of the world. Arrangements are being made with the Associated Press to flash Convention news daily around the world.

About a Noted Sunday School Worker.

We could as well consider ourselves informed American citizens and worthy of our opportunities and yet not know the name of the president of the United States as to think to be considered up-to-date in Sunday school matters and not know something about the great Sunday school leaders of America and of the world. Frank L. Brown is one of the outstanding figures in the Sunday school world and few are more widely known.

Frank L. Brown of the World's Sunday School Association has just received the honorary degree of Doctor of Laws from Albany College, Oregon. The conferring of this degree is a special recognition of the all important place that the Sunday school holds in the work of the Christian church. President Williams in announcing the degree said, "Albany College conferred the degree of Doctor of Laws on Frank L. Brown in recognition of his statesmanship in affairs of the Kingdom of God and his leadership in International Friendship between the United States and Japan."

Dr. Brown is Joint General Secretary of the World's Sunday School Association. In the interest of Sunday school work he has been to the Orient three times, has traveled around the world on Sunday school missions both by way of India and through Russia. He was the leader of the Sunday school party that visited South America in 1915. On one of his trips to Japan he was instrumental in organizing the National Sunday School Association of Japan. He also organized the Korean and Philippine Island Sunday School Associations.

On July 29th Dr. Brown will sail on the "Empress of Russia" from Vancouver to prepare for and participate in the Eighth Convention of the World's Association, which will convene in Tokyo October 5th. While in Japan preceding the Convention, he will complete the plans for the one and two day conventions which will be conducted by the Sunday school delegates in at least thirty cities of the Far and Near East. In November Dr. Brown will, with forty others, sail from Shanghai, China, on another Around the World tour solely in the interest of Sunday school work. The party will spend a month in India, holding meetings in many cities and then continue to Egypt, Palestine and Europe.

The Foes of Our Own Household

The most perfect machinery of government will not keep us as a nation from destruction if there is not within us a soul. No abounding material prosperity shall avail us if our spiritual senses atrophy. The foes of our own household shall surely prevail against us unless there be in our people an inner life which finds its outward expression in a morality not very widely different from that preached by the seers and prophets of Judea when the grandeur that was Greece and the glory that was Rome still lay in the future.
—Theodore Roosevelt.

There is something finer than to go right against inclination; and that is to have an inclination to do right. There is something nobler than reluctant obedience; and that is joyful obedience. The rank of virtue is not measured by its disagreeableness, but by its sweetness to the heart that loves it. The real test of character is joy. For what you rejoice in, that you love. And what you love, that you are like.—Henry Van Dyke.

"If every man in the United States would read one chapter of the Bible each day, most of the nation's troubles would disappear."—Woodrow Wilson.

J. A. Garber
PRESIDENT

Our Young People at Work

G. C. Carpenter
SECRETARY

Vacation Hints for Endeavorers. By Albert A. Rand

For such Endeavorers as are still looking ahead to vacation or are perhaps now enjoying it the following timely hints are offered in the hope that they may help some doubtful one to decide concerning what is the proper way to conduct himself in this situation.

First, a few suggestions as to packing may not be amiss. One of the most puzzling questions confronting the vacationist is the one of "To take or not to take." As it is impossible to take everything, it is obvious that something must be left at home. The purpose of these suggestions is to help solve that problem of what should be left behind.

In the first place, you should carefully remove your Christian Endeavor pin from the lapel of your coat or from the front of your dress before packing said garments away. This simple action may save you from much embarrassment later on, especially when called upon by some thoughtless creature to divulge before all those gay butterflies at the resort where you are staying just what those letters mean. Of course you don't want those people to suspect that you are a Christian Endeavorer; it might hurt your standing with them. And, furthermore, the pin would look out of place at some of those gatherings at which you wish to be present. There are times when it is rather awkward to be reminded that one is an Endeavorer.

Another thing to be left at home is your Bible. Of course, after all your clothes are packed there won't be much room left, and it would be the height of folly to waste that space by putting a Bible in it. Then think how embarrassing it might be if some of your friends or acquaintances should happen to catch you reading it.

The chances are that you won't need the Bible anyway, for it won't be possible to take the fifteen minutes a day for reading it, since one's time is always so limited when on vacation. A vacation should include a rest from religion too.

You might manage, however, to squeeze in a copy of the "Afflictions of Ann" or the "Peregrinations of Pearline." These books will take up only about twice the room that your Testament would take, and they are so uplifting for vacation reading.

Possibly these hints are sufficient to guide in the packing. After you reach your destination remember to forget all about everything that you said you wouldn't forget to remember before you left. If there's a little church in the neighborhood that is keeping open during the summer months, don't go near it. Some one you know might see you going in. Never mind if they do need a piano player badly or some one to lead the singing, and you're the one who can do it; don't let them find out about it. Remember you're on vacation.

If you happen to hear of a Christian Endeavor society that is struggling along and sadly in need of a little encouragement, you are not under any obligation to give it to them. Your pledge is on vacation, too. They ought to know better than to try and run their meetings during the hot weather; so don't encourage them by going near them.

In all your conversation and meeting with others be careful to let no word slip that will give you away. If you are in a company where they are making sport of the things that Christian Endeavor stands for, make no attempt to defend the society. You might hurt somebody's feelings. It is terribly bad form to speak about religion to any one while you're on vacation. It isn't done. So just laugh with them, and let them see that you appreciate their humor.

By all means don't be so rash as to waste any time while you're away in thinking about plans for making your society more efficient when you get back to it in the fall. What

if you did say that you were going to return brimful of plans for your committee? The chances are that the others won't worry themselves over anything like that; so why should you? There'll be time enough to think about what should be done after the time has arrived to start doing it.

There may be other suggestions that would be of value in helping you enjoy a good time, but at present we do not recall them. Should there arise any situation that is not covered by the above instructions, it can be met by observing the following rule: Conduct yourself in such a manner at all times that on your return home you will be able to say:

"Oh, I've had a wonderful vacation. Not a single person suspected that I was a Christian Endeavorer."—Christian Endeavor World.

The greatest of all pleasures is to give pleasure to one we love.—de Bonfflers.

Where Friendship Deepens

By Emily Beatrice Gnagey, in St. Andrew's Cross

"The best education," some one has said, "that any soul can have is not an incrustation, not a commandment, but a friend." Is there any life more ideally conducive to education than that of camping?

There is first the deeper friendship with one's fellows. Removed from the artificial things that fetter our spirits, freed from the routine of shop and school and factory, we enter into a fellowship otherwise unknown. One's part in the machinery of life and in the toil of the world is forgotten; and we think of each other rather than of our calling; we see each other's lives rather than merely our stations in life. Men who have campaigned together and men who have pioneered in common know the meaning of the rugged friendship that is not conditioned by the material circumstances of life and which may be cultivated when we are thrown back upon ourselves in camp.

There is also to be gained a deeper friendship with nature. The glory of dawn and sunset, the pageantry of the heavens, the majesty of the wooded hills and the peace of the fields are the familiar possession of those who pitch their tents against a bulwark of sheltering trees whose tops touch the sky. They are strangers to the earth who have never slept close to its benign breast, who have never found companionship in the winds that sweep across spaces laden with star-dust and pregnant with messages of other worlds. "The wind bloweth where it listeth"—our Lord's own words—and thou hearest the sound thereof, but canst not tell whence it cometh, and whither it goeth."

And what of those who have never followed a vagrant stream or plunged into the cooling depths of a quiet river? who have never felt the redemptive tang of rain in the face, nor yielded to the enchantment of a bird's call and the marvel of its flight? nor dwelt in the consciousness of wild companions, the unoffending neighbors of the forest and the night? who have never been awed by fireflies at dusk nor charmed by the melody in a thicket of reeds? nor spent interminable afternoons watching the slanting shadows and the clouds and the sun and things that pass? Nature's secrets are for him who "holds communion with her visible forms."

Earth's beauties symbolize spiritual beauties; they are expressions of the Author and Maker of all things. Deeper acquaintance with the natural world draws one closer to the unseen world. The least of the lovely things one delights in out-of-doors to the most sublime manifestation of the Eternal foreshadows a higher world where we shall know unbroken friendship with the Lord of all life. "No chaffinch but implies the cherubim"—where there is nothing to deface or destroy the world as God made it, we may recognize the presence of the angels that encamp around those who fear him.

Garden City, Virginia

Sunday, July 25, we opened a Christian Endeavor Campaign in the new Garden City church recently dedicated by Dr. Bowman. We went into details concerning the origin, principle and practice of Christian Endeavor; organized a Young People's society and assisted the executive committee in planning the work. We hope to have a model Christian Endeavor prayer meeting Wednesday evening and close our campaign with a one or two day Christian Endeavor Institute. We hope to be assisted in the institute by Roanoke and Hollins' Endeavorers.

Besides an enthusiastic pastor, the Rev. George Donahue, the following officers will direct the activities of this new society: President, Bud Guthrie; Vice president, Ernest Gearhart; Secretary, Miss Viola Stanley; Corresponding Secretary, W. H. Stanley, and Treasurer Miss Essie Gearhart.

We have calls for Christian Endeavor Institutes in the valley which we hope to reach before General Conference.

H. A. ROWSEY, Virginia Feld Worker.

NEWS FROM THE FIELD

THE BRETHREN CHURCH OF PHILADELPHIA

A pastor remarked the other day that he was in a field where "Christian work" was very difficult, to which we answered that his field of labor was not an exception but rather the rule. A Gospel which proceeds upon the assumption that "there is no difference, for all have sinned;" which condemns the best man utterly before it saves him, has never been exactly a popular proposition with a world which considers itself quite respectable. Nor is it likely to become more acceptable in these days of growing self-sufficiency and pride of accomplishment. But in spite of this the Word of God is powerful, and God proves himself faithful as we are faithful to his Word. Our own field here is not the easiest, and our accomplishments during the past year and one-half do not satisfy us, nevertheless, the Brethren church of this place feels that some real substantial progress can be reported in various phases of the work.

The coming General Conference will close the second year of our pastorate in Philadelphia, and we have come to love this body of believers for their zealous desire to know and make known the Word of God, and their faithful support in whatever has been attempted. If there have been exceptions in these respects, they are not worthy of mention.

Our relation with this church began with the "flu" epidemic (which more than one pastor will not soon forget) and consequently work did not really begin until January, 1919. One of the first matters attended to was a revision of the roll by which the membership was reduced to about 195. By confession, letter and affiliation about 36 have been received into the church. By death and letter about 10 have been lost. From this it will be seen that we are started in the right direction.

It also gives us pleasure to report that the First church now has a parsonage of which any church in the city could be proud. It is ideally located second door from the church, the house next door having been purchased by the sexton for a permanent home. Both properties have been appraised so as to have an entrance to the church from the rear. The parsonage is a seven room house with laundry room and bath. When it was purchased about April first, 1920, its interior was in almost unspeakable condition. A building committee from the church looked it over and laid plans for a complete remodeling. Walls were ripped out and old plumbing done away. About $1,200 was spent in remodeling. Besides this, the men of the Brethren church donated at least $1,200 in labor, much of it being done at night. We had our own electricians, furnace-man, plumbers, carpenters and painters. The only professionals we needed to hire were for the plastering and paper-hanging. Two months were required to do all the work and the finished result is a beautiful home with every modern convenience. The plumbing is the last word in such things, the woodwork is all in white enamel, the doors are mahogany, the walls are papered in light colors throughout, the electrical fixtures are in silver to match the other light colors and the floors were given a hard-wood finish with a coat of "bar-top" varnish on finish (This is one of the advantages of prohibition. "Bar-top" varnish on a parsonage floor is almost like "beating swords into ploughshares!) The house now compares very favorably with houses farther out which have been selling for eight to ten thousand dollars. When the work was all completed and the pastor moved in a reception and housewarming was held to give every member an opportunity to inspect the new parsonage. Everyone was delighted with the remodeling plans of the committee and the manner with which the work was executed. It was also a distinct relief to all concerned that the problem of housing the preacher was settled for all time. In case the present incumbent should be "fired," the next pastor may rest assured that he will have a place to live without passing through the horrors of "househunting." (During the month of June there were over 3,000 couples married in Philadelphia and 14 new houses begun!)

Too much cannot be said in commendation of the fine spirit shown by the men who labored at the work, and also by the whole church which promptly provided for the financial needs. All expenses were paid and a sufficient payment made on the property to cut the carrying charges down to about half what the house would rent for at present prices. This makes very cheap rent for the pastor.

The parsonage problem is very real in most congregations. The method we have taken would no doubt solve it in most places. There is scarcely a church in the brotherhood which does not have men who would be glad to lend a hand in work and money in a co-operative effort such as has made possible our splendid parsonage here.

At the last business meeting of the church the writer accepted a unanimous call to continue as pastor for the coming year. The salary has been substantially raised twice within the past year, each time at the suggestion of the church. God has marvelously blessed this body of believers with the spirit of giving. At Easter the offering for Foreign Missions was about $700, over twice as much as last year, which had been the largest offering ever made here. This was well over $3 per member. No great appeal was made. We asked everybody to pray, organizations, Sunday-school classes and individuals, and the result justified the method. When Brother Bell was here the Evangelistic and Bible Study League was merely mentioned. The result was 50 memberships. It is a growing conviction with us that where the Word of God is taught and the Lord Jesus exalted, "Money drives" are not only unnecessary but harmful.

Among the accessions to the church this year we have one young man who has answered the call of God to the ministry. He is at present attending the Philadelphia School of the Bible, and at the conclusion of his course expects to take up Seminary work. This gives our church three young men actively engaged in preparation for the ministry. In addition to these we have another young man who has signified his intention of beginning such preparation when his high school work is finished.

On the roll of the church we have now two missionaries both of whom are in Africa. Brother Gribble is the first and needs no introduction. The other is Brother Carl Urban who at one time was a member of the Long Beach church when we were there. In fact we were in the same Bible class. Brother Urban originally offered himself for Africa under our Board when the Gribbles went out but was refused a passport because his name looked a little "German." Being determined to go to Africa he volunteered under the African Inland Mission which works in the Belgian Congo, where strange to say, German names are not so hated as in the French Territory. He left New York about the first of the year and at last report by letter he was on the Nile past Khartoum. Before leaving he requested the Philadelphia church to carry his name as a member since the African Inland Mission is an Interdenominational mission. It is a faith Mission like our own African work. Brother and Sister Gribble were with it before beginning work under the Brethren society. Let all those interested pray for Brother Urban. He is really a Brethren missionary.

In January of this year the writer was invited to become a member of the faculty of the Philadelphia School of the Bible, of which Dr. C. I. Schofield is the president. The invitation was accepted with some hesitancy on account of the great pressure of work in connection with the church, and health which is not the best. However, by giving up Monday as a "Pastor's rest day" we have been able to carry the extra work, and have found it very pleasant to teach God's Word in an atmosphere of such deep spirituality and devotion to the Lord Jesus. The work there has also been a real help to our church, bringing it to the notice of many strangers.

We are praying for a great conference this fall and expect to have a delegation from this church large enough to hold a conference of our own. If nothing happens we will have around 20 and perhaps more. It costs $40 for a ticket but we are saving our money and regard it as in the nature of a vacation as suggested by Brethren Bame, Cobb and Snyder. We want to do our share in making this conference the biggest in history.

The church has kindly granted the pastor six weeks vacation this year with which to relieve "that tired feeling." During our absence, Dr. Smith, a former classmate in Seminary and member of the faculty of the Philadelphia School of the Bible, will act as pastor of the church.

Concerning the Interchurch Movement, "we have many things to say" but will merely state that the church here did not co-operate with the Movement, and, has passed resolutions, without a dissenting vote, stating why we could not as Christians co-operate, and requesting all the interests of the church to sever whatever connections they may have with the Movement.

ALVA J. McCLAIN,
2255 North Tenth, Philadelphia, Pa.

A CORRECTION

In Brother Martin Shively's article, "A Toll of Death Among the Brethren," that appeared in this department last week.

A handful of slugs (every slug represents a line) that belonged in Brother Shively's article was inadvertently placed in Brother William A. Gearhart's article, entitled, "Home Again." It was the paragraph reporting the death of Sister Elizabeth Haught of Masontown and was as follows:

Then on July 14, Masontown had called again, because the grim messenger had once

more taken from earth the soul of another of those who had long served their Lord there. This time it was Sister Elizabeth Haught who was called, and at the age of 72 years, 6 months and 26 days, she had exchanged the infirmities of old age for the eternal youth of a spirit made free from the entanglements of flesh. Since her early life, she had been a member of the Masontown church, and in her quiet practical way, given constant expression to those qualities of character which are the product of association with Christ.

We are very sorry for this error and hope all who noticed it will also notice this correction.

NORTH LIBERTY, INDIANA

A few Sundays ago it was our privilege to baptize four persons, two husbands and their wives, in the beautiful lake near Lakeville, Indiana, in the presence of about four hundred persons. These good people will place their membership with the LaPaz Brethren. The field about LaPaz is indeed promising and if some one who has some authority would give them some attention, I believe a strong work could be built up there, with the splendid start that they have. They are anxious to go forth, but they must have some one to lead them.

We are closing our work at North Liberty with the conference year. This is a splendid church and whoever our successor will be will find a good people with whom to labor and conditions in every way conducive to continual progress.

As for ourselves we are not certain where we shall labor the coming year. We only know that we shall be busy somewhere in the Lord's work.

We are expecting that our church shall have a large delegation at General Conference. May nothing interfere with our having the best Conference ever.

Yours in the Blessed Hope,
C. C. GRISSO.

CONCERNING BENEVOLENCES

In the summing up of experiences of a year's work, one finds many new things which are very valuable not only for their present worth but serve in a special manner for the future. During the year just drawing to a close in the work of Benevolences one or two churches and Sunday school classes have distinguished themselves in a manner worthy of special mention; not that they wish or ought to be advertised for the mere sake of publicity, but because such special work was done cheerfully and no thought of praise, it is right to mention such as an example with the admonition to others "go thou and do likewise."

I speak particularly of Brother H. F. E. O'Neill's class of men in the church at Pittsburgh, Pennsylvania. A class of fellows numbering not more than twenty but surely hustlers all of them, set their goal for One Hundred dollars and made it One Hundred Twenty-five dollars for the Superannuated fund. That surely is mighty fine. Congratulations and thanks, Brother O'Neill and your

faithful bunch of hustlers. A mighty good work and a good example for some of our large Bible classes of the brotherhood for another year. I know Brother O'Neill is too modest and too good a Christian worker to take the credit for such a fine piece of work, but I am sure that it was his splendid enthusiasm and effort that made it possible for the work to be done.

The church at Pittsburgh has not been slow in past years along the line of giving for last year only one church in this district gave more for the superannuated work. The Sunday school is wide awake and contributed nicely this year so that Pittsburgh's total offering for this fund this year amounts to $228.62—very fine for what has been considered a mission point, and unless some church comes to the fore between now and conference time with a larger amount Pittsburgh will take the banner for this year, and I am sure such faithful work deserves high praise. God can and will bless them in their efforts.

Sincerely yours,
H. E. ROSCOE,
Secretary Brethren Board of Benevolences.

CLAY CITY, INDIANA

Several weeks have passed by since Clay City was last heard from through the Brethren Evangelist. We may have kept still but we have not been still. Although several of our good workers and regular attendants have been detained away from services the greater part of the summer on account of illness or caring for those who were ill, we are glad to report that the church work has made progress. Now as most all are able to be at their posts again, we are looking forward with hope of greater things still before us.

The other day when we mailed the card reporting the Four Year Program from this place, we were glad to see what great progress this church as one of our new churches has made. It is going to take a stand among the banner churches this year. We do not take the credit for it ourselves, but the people here are open to all good works.

The Sunday school has been gaining in enrollment and average attendance. On the second Sunday evening in June a fine Children's Day program was rendered to an overflowing house, and again on the evening of the Fourth of July our school assisted in a large open air community Sunday school program. Our Christian Endeavor still continues to go forward. It recently graduated a class of six in Expert Endeavor and thus gaining all the points in the Standard of Excellence.

One addition has been added to the church by letter since our last report. At our Love Feast in the latter part of June we were glad to have Brother W. T. Lyttle of Burlington with us to assist in the service. We are now planning for our series of meetings in October. We are expecting to have Brother A. E. Thomas of Warsaw, Indiana, with us as the evangelist. We are hoping for an ingathering through the grace of God and his laborers with us.

Three years ago, the Brethren here wisely purchased a property for a parsonage. It was well that they did as houses have become scarcer and rents higher in Clay City until it would be impossible for them to have a pastor now if it were not for the parsonage. But the building was in need of repairing, so last spring the church decided to make the repairs and improvements at once. An addition was made to make it larger and more convenient. The entire building was re-shingled and re-painted. Now they have a nice well arranged home for their pastors for sometime to come. They are now planning walks about the church property. This will be a great help to our work as they have long felt the need.

Last Sunday (August 1) the church held a Harvest Home. It was the anniversary of the organization of the church. Everyone enjoyed the day. A number of our isolated members were present with us.

Several are expecting to attend conference from this church. S. C. HENDERSON.

STATISTICAL REPORTS RECEIVED

The list to date of statistical reports received from Ohio churches is as follows: Bryan, Pleasant Hill, Fair Haven, Louisville, North Georgetown, Rittman and Zion Hill. Please hurry up, the days of grace will soon be past. It will take no longer to do it now than it will to do it later, so do it now. If any one failed to receive a statistical blank, write me at once.

E. G. MASON, Secretary and Statistician of the Ohio State Conference.
West Salem, Ohio.

EVANGELISTIC REPORT
Calvary, New Jersey

Our meeting at Calvary was not all what we expected or would have liked for it to be.

1. They had expected that corn planting would be over but it was four weeks later than usual on account of the unusual wet weather.

2 Most of the people come a distance and travel in autos; but the roads most of them were either impassable or almost impassible so that many of the people could not attend regularly at all.

3. It rained about one week of the three and the roads were very bad for two weeks so that we only had one favorable week of good roads.

4. Being behind four weeks in corn planting they worked from daylight till dark to get their corn in and were still planting when I closed the meeting. They aimed to have the meeting after corn planting but they missed their aim.

5. We were all very sorry for those conditions and we hoped against hope that the conditions would be more favorable but they remained bad to the very end.

6. Then it is a very hard field at best. Some of our good evangelists held meetings here in good weather with but few additions, and some had none.

7. They insisted upon me to stay, so I pounded away, some nights entirely rained out, sometimes almost rained out and a few times we had the largest crowds that they had had for years.

8. They said the spiritual uplift of the

members was the greatest that they have had for many years and they paid me splendidly for the meeting.

I regretted to take the money when conditions were the most unfavorable of any meeting that I have ever held. But they realized that it cost me as much to live when it rained and the roads were muddy as when they were good, and therefore they liberally and freely did above my expectation. I promised the Lord that if it was his will I surely would go back some time when the conditions were such that we could have additions to the church.

Brother Sands, their pastor for five years, stood nobly by this work. He is universally loved and I honestly believe that he is one of the best men in our church to be so little known by our brotherhood. By what they told me here he is by far a stronger preacher than I had supposed; and then he is spiritual, unselfish and every inch a man.

There is considerable material to work upon in the community but it was impossible to get them to the church regularly because of the conditions that I have stated.

Two Sunday mornings I preached at Sergeantsville to an attentive congregation. The last Sunday I was there they gave me a liberal freewill offering.

The field is a peculiar one. Sergeantsville and Calvary should each have a pastor but they are unable financially for the support. The churches are seven miles apart and in the winter time it is very hard for a man to preach at both places.

Ankneytown, Ohio

After resting at home two days I left home for Ankneytown, Ohio, where we opened up fire, June 12. We found here wet weather, bad roads and busy times, somewhat similar to Calvary, New Jersey, but not so bad.

Here we had a great meeting in spite of the bad conditions, but I feel that we would have had twice as many confessions had we had normal conditions.

Thirty years ago I had one of the greatest meetings that ever been held here. And I found many of the best members of the church were those who were baptized then.

We had here about a score of confessions, all but one united with the church. Brother Lynn the pastor promised me that he would give a detailed report of this meeting, hence I will not say very much about it. Brother Lynn was busy in school work part of the time and also preached at his other church so that he could not be with me much of the time. He was with me the last week and was a great help to the meeting. He and his good wife are universally loved and he is bringing this church forward and if he remains pastor long there will be a great and strong church there.

I was treated royally and well supported financially and we closed the meeting with a splendid communion service, July 5 and I took the train the same night for home.

After spending four days with my family duty called me to turn my back to wife many loved ones in the city and travel days and a night to Old Kentucky.

We are having a splendid meeting here

Krypton, but we will report it after we close here. In a few days we will close here and then go to Lost Creek where we had such a splendid time last year. From there we go to Virginia for 10 days under the Evangelistic League, then home one day after a seven weeks' absence, then to National Conference.
ISAAC D. BOWMAN.

HUDSON, IOWA

Hudson Brethren church has not been silent because we are not working. The workers in a church are always busy, and our force is increasing. It has been one year since our pastor, Brother Boardman came to Hudson, and since that time there has been an increased interest along many lines. All departments of the church are working earnestly and trying to advance. Our pastor recently started a mid-week prayermeeting and Bible study that is intensely interesting. From the mid-week prayer service should come the spiritual force of the church and no one can attend this service without receiving inspiration and strength to go on with the work for Christ and the church.

During these hot summer months the three churches of our town are holding union services on Sunday evening in the park. These services are well attended and enjoyed by all. We have good lively singing and fine sermons.

Co-operation and faith in God can bring about such great things for the Master and we are praying for such results in the coming year with Brother Boardman as our pastor.
MRS. GUTKNECHT,
Corresponding Secretary.

CAMPAIGN NOTES

On Sunday, July 4th, I began work in the Maurertown congregation and preached five times, always to good audiences. Dr. E. B. Shaver has served this congregation faithfully and well for a number of years as pastor. I may say this organization, like the St. James congregation for example, has one central organization with several outlying preaching points. Elder Geo. A. Copp, who is a member at Maurertown, preaches regularly for our people at Round Hill. This church is the home congregation of Prof. Haun now on the faculty at Ashland, as it is also the place of worship of his parents, Brother and Sister Harry Haun. It is also the home of former students of the college including Brother Winnett Shaver who is a booster one hundred percent strong for the college and the Brethren church. Needless to say I had a splendid time during the Maurertown canvass.

Brother Shaver was ready with his characteristic snap and rush to put the campaign across in his congregation in real fashion, nor was he disappointed. Maurertown went almost $2,300, which entitles her to first place among the Maryland and Virginia churches. I am sorry, Brother Cover, but Maurertown did it and we have to give it to her. In the course of this canvass we are brought to light '00 gifts and that always helps a whole rand totals for a congre- be. I am glad for our $500 friend and brother at Linwood that he now has company. And I would simply hint that he shall just hold steady because we have more company for him. The Sunday school under the leadership of Brother Glenn Locke also took a substantial part—$200. Brother Locke may justly feel proud of his Sunday school. The W. M. S. and the Y. P. S. C. E. also took a part Ashland College has many warm friends among the Maurertown people and I shall not soon forget the fine co-operation given me by Brother Shaver, nor the kind hospitality I enjoyed in his home, and the Locke home, also the Haun and the Hockman homes. Neither shall I forget the splendid automobile service rendered me by Brethren Winnett, Shaver, Locke, and Hockman. Thanks again to you, brethren. And may God richly bless you in your work for the Master.

This now places the mercury about $154,000. The next report will be of the canvass of our churches around Harrisonburg, Virginia.

WM. H. BEACHLER,
Campaign Secretary.

MINISTERIAL EXCHANGE

Dr. Charles A. Bame announces that he has resigned the pastorate of the North Manchester, Indiana, church and will give himself to evangelistic work at least until Christmas. Address him at North Manchester, Indiana, for dates for evangelistic meetings.

The church at North Liberty, Indiana wishes to secure a pastor for half time the following year. Any minister desiring to consider this field communicate with the church secretary.

Yours in Christ,
CLYDE H. SHENEMAN, Sec.
North Liberty, Indiana.

THE TIE THAT BINDS

GISH-SHANER—Minnie Gish and Charles August Shaner, both of Roanoke, Virginia, were joined in holy matrimony on July 1st, 1920, at my residence. Ceremony by the writer.
L. G. WOOD.

GOSHORN-GILLASPE—On July 31, 1920, at the Brethren parsonage at Clay City, Indiana, occurred the marriage of Brother Robert R. Goshorn and Miss Evalyn Gillaspe of Terre Haute, Indiana. The groom is the eldest son of Brother and Sister M. R. Goshorn, near Clay City, Indiana. He has attended the Indiana State Normal at Terre Haute and North Manchester College. He was a member of the A. E. F. during the World War, and is at present holding an important position with a large manufacturing concern at Brazil, Indiana. The bride is an accomplished young lady. She has been employed as a designer in a large furniture plant at Terre Haute. We wish them years of happiness and blessings.
S. C. HENDERSON.

IN THE SHADOW

DIEL—Mrs. Blanche M. Diel, daughter of Elder B. F. and Ida Goshorn, was born at Coal City, Indiana, June 20, 1887 and departed this life at Clay City, Indiana, June 26, 1920. She was an active member in the First Church of the Brethren at Detroit, Michigan, being one of the charter members of the organization. She leaves a father and two sisters to mourn her departure. The funeral services were held from the First Brethren church at Clay City by the pastor, S. C. Henderson,

(center thermometer graphic)

Our Goal: 200,000; We Can and We Must

200	000
190	000
180	000
170	000
160	000
150	000
140	000
130	000
120	000
110	000
100	000
90	000
80	000
70	000
60	000
50	000
40	000
30	000
20	000
10	000

COLLEGE
ENDOWMENT

derson, assisted by Elder Mitchell of the Church of the Brethren and Rev. Kelsey of the United Brethren church.

HARDIN—Mr. Charles Hardin departed this life at his home near Clay City, Indiana, July 10, 1920, being at the time of his death 49 years, 1 month and 26 days old. He leaves a wife, two daughters, a son and an aged blind father. Funeral service was held at the First Brethren church, Clay City, Indiana, conducted by the pastor.
S. C. HENDERSON

MILLER—Albert Miller died at Clay City, Indiana, May 20, 1920, aged 66 years. Funeral from the home of his brother. He leaves a brother and two sisters. The service was conducted by the undersigned.
S. C. HENDERSON

KLINE—Sister Dora A., wife of Brother Milton Kline, of the Middle Branch Brethren church, died July 31, 1920, aged 41 years and 11 months. In the presence of a great congregation, her mortal remains, as well as those of her little babe, were laid to rest August 3rd, to await the resurrection call. Her husband, a daughter and a son are bereft in her death.
MARTIN SHIVELY.

THOMPSON — Catharine J. Thompson, daughter of John and Nancy F. Johnson, was born August 3rd, 1836, died July 7th, 1920, aged 83 years, 11 months and 4 days. She was married to Abner Briggs October 19th, 1858. To them were born eight children, two of whom, Freddie W., and Charles, died in infancy. John S., died November 31st, 1902, at the age of 38 years; the remaining five are Oscar L., Almer E., Werter C., Stella J. Parrett and Dora F. Swope. At the time of her death nine grandchildren and one great-grandchild survive.

In 1889 Mrs. Briggs was married to John Thompson now deceased. Her entire life was spent in Fayette county with the exception of a few years with her daughter in Columbus. Her birthplace being at the old Johnston homestead near New Holland.

In her early life she became affiliated with the Brethren church at Fairview, Ohio, to which she remained steadfast until her death.
L. B. WILKINS.

FIVECOATS — Gladis Irene Fivecoats passed to her reward July 4th, 1920, aged 10 years, 11 months, 27 days. She was a member of the Brethren church at Denver, Indiana. Funeral at the Church of the Brethren, Mexico, Indiana, by the writer.
L. A. MYERS.

STONEBURNER—Mrs. Jessie Stoneburner departed this life July 24th, 1920, after a short illness at the age of 27 years, 9 months and 2 days. She leaves four small children and a husband to bear the burden of their great loss. She was a member of the Brethren church at Sidney, Indiana, where funeral services were held by the writer.
L. A. MYERS.

ARTHUR — Elsie Lenora, twelve-year-old daughter of Mr. and Mrs. G. W. Arthur, of Roanoke, Virginia, departed this life at her home on July 26th, 1920. Funeral service was conducted by the writer. Burial was made in the Red Hill neighborhood a few miles out of Roanoke.
L. G. WOOD.

DETRICK—Jonas Michael, was born at Gretna, Logan county, Ohio, may eleventh, 1847, and died at the home of his daughter, Mrs. R. S. Hutchings, at Lockington, July 21, 1920, at the age of seventy-three years, one month and twenty days. On November 15, 1877 he was united in marriage with Miss Allie Stevenson, who preceded him in death just fourteen weeks. To this union were born three children who survive him.

Brother Detrick was a Christian from his youth up, and for many years was one of the honored members of the Gretna Brethren church, serving in the capacity of deacon.

The funeral service was conducted by the writer in the Baptist church at DeGraff, Ohio, in the presence of an exceedingly large concourse of people who gathered to pay their last respects to an honored neighbor and friend.
R. R. TEETER.

Business Manager's Corner

ONE BY ONE

One by one the churches are winning places on the Evangelist Honor Roll. Though the time is exceedingly short until the Four Year Program must be brought to a close there is still time for a few churches to win this distinction before it does close. The latest church to win this honor is the Bethlehem Brethren church near Harrisonburg, Virginia.

We really do not know who the pastor of this church is, but the list of names was sent in by the church secretary, H. A. Logan. Brother Logan stated that they had just closed a successful evangelistic meeting, led by J. A. McInturff of Goshen, Indiana, and that through his efforts the church had decided to put the Brethren Evangelist in the home of every active member of the congregation.

Brother McInturff knows something of the value of the weekly visits of the Evangelist to a congregation as his home church receipes more than two hundred copies each week.

We wish to thank Brother McInturff, and Brother Logan, and the Bethlehem pastor, if they have one, and any one else that helped in any way to make it possible for this church to win this place on the Honor Roll.

Since our last report we have received the renewal of the list of subscriptions from the Roann, Indiana, congregation. This is the third year for this congregation with W. E. Ronk as present pastor, and Monroe Jones as the Evangelist Agent. Thank you, Brethren, you have done a good work and it is greatly appreciated.

There is plenty of room yet for other churches to find a place among their more distinguished sister churches and we hope these last days may be fruitful days.

The Gretna, Ohio, church was the FIRST church to win this distinction and it has held its place throughout the entire four years. We wonder now what church will be the LAST one to win this honor. Of course there will not be as great honor go to the last church as to the first one to win in the campaign, but yet there will be a distinction that is unique come to the church that CLOSES the campaign. Will this distinction go to Bethlehem? or will it go to one of the Indiana or Pennsylvania churches that is still striving to reach the goal before the meeting of our Winona Conference?

In our last report we stated that we were in receipt of a letter from a pastor in the middle west who said he was ready to contribute the sum of ten dollars toward a fund to cover the excessive cost of the print paper we had recently received. The other day we received another letter from this Brother in which he said, "saying is not doing, so here is my ten dollars to help pay for that paper." The letter and the gift of money came from Homer Anderson, Williamsburg, Iowa. It is just like Brother Anderson to pull a stunt like that. We have had no more loyal booster for the Evangelist during the entire campaign than he has been. We certainly appreciate Brother Anderson's generosity. Then a few days later we received a letter from a good sister from Rockwood, Pennsylvania renewing her subscription to the Evangelist with an additional dollar to apply on the "big" paper bill. Thank you Sister Will. You have the right spirit, and every little bit makes just a little bit more. Five thousand more Sister Wills would get us over this financial handicap.

"Be not weary in well-doing, for in due season ye shall reap, if ye faint not."

R. R. TEETER,
Business Manager.

EVANGELIST HONOR ROLL

The following churches having met the requirements laid down by the Brethren Publishing Company regarding the placing of the Evangelist in the homes of the congregations are entitled to a place on the Evangelist Honor Roll:

Church	Pastor
Akron, Ind., (New Highland),	.... (Vacant)
Allentown,.Pa., 3rd Year,	... A. L. DeLozier
Ankenytown, Ohio, 3rd Yr.,	.... A. L. Lynn
Ardmore, Indiana,	.... A. T. Wirick
Ashland, Ohio, 3rd Yr.,	.... ʹ. A. Garber
Beaver City, Nebr. (3rd Yr.),	... E. S. Flora
Berlin, Pa., (2nd Yr.),	.... I. B. Trout
Berne, Indiana, 3rd Year,	.. W. F. Johnson
Bryan, Ohio, 3rd Yr.	.... G. L. Maus
Buckeye City, O.,	.... Glen Peterson
Burlington, Ind. (3rd Yr.)	..... W. T. Lytle
Center Chapel, Ind.,	.... K. R. Ronk
Cerro Gordo, Ill.,	.... D. A. C. Teeter
Clay City, Indiana, (3rd Yr.),	S. C. Henderson
College Corner, Ind, 3rd Yr.	.... L. A. Myers
Conemaugh, Pa., (3rd Yr.),	.... E. F. Byers
Darwin, Indiana, (2nd Yr.)	... W. T. Lytle
Dallas Center, Iowa, 2nd Yr.	.... R. F. Porte
Dayton, Ohio,	.... E. M. Cobb
Denver, Indiana, 2nd Yr.,	...... L. A. Myers
Dutchtown, Indiana;	...... Homer Anderson
Elkhart, Ind., (2nd Yr.),	... H. H. Wolford
Eaton, Ind. (Maple Grove, 2nd Yr.)	......
	.... H. E. Eppley
Eau Claire, Wisconsin,	.... J. A. Baker
Fair Haven, Ohio (3rd Yr.),	... B. F. Owen
Falls City, Nebr. (3rd Yr.),,,	. H. F. Stuckman
Fillmore, Calif. (2nd Yr),	. Sylvester Lowman
Flora, Ind., 3rd Yr.,	...... S. C. Henderson
Fostoria, Ohio (2nd Yr.),	...... M. S. White
Fremont, Ohio (2nd Yr.),	H. M. Oberholtzer
Goshen, Indiana,	.... J. A. McInturff
Gretna, Ohio, (4th Yr.)	...... R. R. Teeter
Gratis, Ohio	.... C. E. Beekley
Hagerstown, Maryland	.... A. B. Cover

Harrisonburg, Va. (Bethlehem)

Huntington, Ind., 2nd Yr,	... J. W. Brower
Hudson, Ia.,	.... Edwin Boardman
Johnstown, Pa., 1st Ch, 2nd Yr.	J. F. Watson
Johnstown, Pa., 3rd Ch.,	...... Geo. H. Jones
Lanark, Ill. (3rd. Yr.),	.. B. T. Burnworth
La Verne, Calif., 2nd Yr.,	...... T. H. Broad
Limestone Tenn., 2nd Yr.),	... Mary Pence
Long Beach, Cal. (3rd Yr.)	... L. S. Bauman
Loree, Indiana, 2nd Yr.,	...... C. A. Stewart
Los Angeles, Cal 1st Ch.	... N. W. Jennings
Los Angeles Cal, Comp. Av. 2d Yr.	J. C. Beal
Louisville, O., (3rd Yr.),	...... E. M. Riddle
Martinsburg, Pa. (2nd Yr.)	...... J. I. Hall
Masontown, Pennsylvania,	... Martin Shively
Mexico, Ind. (3rd Yr.),	.... J. W. Clark
Milford, Indiana	.... C. E. Kolb
Milledgeville, Ill., (3rd Yr.),	Miles J. Snyder
Morrill, Kans., (3rd Yr.),	... A. E. Whitted
Mt. View, Va., (3rd Yr.),	... J. E. Patterson
Muncie, Indiana, 2nd Yr.,	... J. L. Kimmel
Nappanee, Ind. (3rd Yr.)	... E. L. Miller
New Enterprise, Pa.,	.... Edward Byers
New Lebanon, O.,	.... G. W. Kinzie
New Paris, Ind., 2nd Yr.,	... W. I. Duker
North English, Iowa,	...... Homer Anderson
North Manchester, Ind,	... Charles A Bame
N. Liberty, Ind. (2nd Yr.),	... C. C. Grisso
New Enterprise, Ind.,	.... P. M. Fisher
Norcatur, Kansas	.... J. G. Dodds
Oakville, Ind., (2d Yr.),	..... W. R. Deeter
Peru, Indiana,	.... Geo. C. Carpenter
Philadelphia, Pa (1st Br.)	. Alva J. McClain
Philadelphia, Pa., 3rd church,	.. J. E. Braker
Portis, Kans., (3rd Yr.),	... Roy Brumbaugh
Rittman, Ohio,	.... J. Allen Miller
Roann, Indiana, (3rd yr.)	...... W. E. Ronk
Roanoke, Indiana	.... W. F. Johnson
Roanoke, Va.,	.... L. G. Wood
South Bend, Indiana	.... G. W. Rench
Sidney, Indiana, (3rd Yr.)	... L. A. Myers
Tiosa, Indiana (2nd Yr.)	...... C. C. Grisso
Turlock, California,	... J. Francis Reagan
Washington C. H., O. (4th Yr.)	L. B. Wilkins
Waterloo, Iowa, (3rd Yr.),	..W. H. Beachler
Whittier, Cal., (2nd Yr.),	... A. V. Kimmel
White Chapel, Mo.,	.... G. T. Ronk
Windber, Pennsylvania,	...... E. F. Byers
Yellow Creek, Pa.,	.... Edward Byers
Zion Hill, Ohio, (2nd Yr.)	...... A. L. Lynn

The Brethren Evangelist

The Living Teacher

The living teacher is an artist. He paints for every one he teaches, a masterpiece, and brings him face to face with it. Whether it be a boy with the world all new before him, or a girl filled with the joy of living, a man or woman who has tried life and found it hard--as he looks at the picture of himself there is a new light in his eyes and a new look on his face, "Am I that?--Can I be that?" And perchance the teacher who stands by to answer "Yes" may hear him say, "I will be that", and see him go with courage and confidence into this world.

—Margaret Slattery

Published every Wednesday at Ashland, Ohio. All matter for publication must reach the Editor not later than Friday noon of the preceding week.

George S. Baer, Editor

The
Brethren
Evangelist

When ordering your paper changed give old as well as new address. Subscriptions discontinued at expiration. To avoid missing any numbers renew two weeks in advance.

R. R. Teeter, Business Manager

OFFICIAL ORGAN OF THE BRETHREN CHURCH

Subscription price, $2.00 per year, payable in advance.
Entered at the Post Office at Ashland, Ohio, as second-class matter.
Acceptance for mailing at special rate of postage provided for in section 1103, Act of October 3, 1917, authorized September - 9, 1918.
Address all matter for publication to Geo. S. Baer, Editor of the Brethren Evangelist, and all business communications to R. R. Teeter, Business Manager, Brethren Publishing Company, Ashland, Ohio. Make all checks payable to the Brethren Publishing Company.

TABLE OF CONTENTS

EDITORIAL
Getting Enthusiastic About General Conference

The success of a thing depends largely upon the stir that is made about it. When enthusiasm runs high things are going to take place; when the spirit of apathy on the other hand prevails little or nothing can be expected. It is as true about General Conference as anything else in the world. When one gets concerned about Conference; when one gets anxious or worked up about it, he is going to do something about it; he will sacrifice or put himself to much trouble that he may do something for it. And when such concern is not only felt by one or a few, but by many all over the brotherhood, much is going to be done to make Conference a success, and that is practically its sufficient guarantee..

Some folks are very much averse to getting enthusiastic over anything. Some do not like it because they do not have the material to make enthusiasm of; they do not have the energy and it does require that. A dead man cannot become enthusiastic, neither can men half dead. And some do not like to get enthusiastic until they know what it may cost them. It does usually cost folks something to get enthusiastic over a thing, for enthusiasm that is worthy of the name will lead to action. Therefore the man who lets go of things of value grudgingly is not going to get enthusiastic until he knows where it is going to lead him. There are those also who are averse to getting enthusiastic over religious matters. It seems just a little beneath their dignity. They are still possessed with the old idea that matters pertaining to religion are not quite worthy of a strong man's best efforts. Religion, they think, is a sort of an emotional affair, more suited to women and children than to strong men. They will get enthusiastic over their fraternal orders and put themselves to the most extreme inconvenience for them when occasion demands. They will get enthusiastic over political matters and with hot words and energetic fists they will debate the political issues in the barber shops and on the street corners until they have made very successful fools of themselves because of their lack of self control. But religious matters are different. They are not the kind of folks to get enthusiastic over such things. It does not become them. And of course it would be out of the question to expect to stir up enthusiasm among such people over a church conference.

There are others who do not get enthusiastic about Conference because they are not informed. They seldom.read the church paper; they have never heard any one say much about Conference, and they have never attended one. So it does not mean much to them. Where such lack of enthusiasm exists there is chance of overcoming it if there are those who are interested in doing so. It is possible to get copies of The Evangelist containing articles on Conference and put them in the hands of the uninformed and by some tactful suggestion

get them to read about it. It is possible for the pastor to speak frequently and optimistically about Conference, telling of what it has meant to him and to others, how churches and individuals have gotten vision and new life there, what it has meant to come in touch with certain missionaries and other men of deep spirituality, and of soul-stirring addresses, inspiring music and forward-looking plans for the church,—it is possible for the pastor to so speak of these and many other encouraging features that even the most indifferent will come to have a desire to learn more of these things and to consider whether or not it is worth their while to attend. It is possible to have pre-conference meetings calculated to create interest in and stir up enthusiasm for Conference. It is possible for those who have been in attendance at Conference and know its value to visit certain individuals who because of their situation and position ought to go but are indifferent and in a tactful way subject them to an evening's exposure of their own enthusiasm in behalf of Conference. It is possible for the pastor to pick out certain promising young or middle-aged people of his congregation, kindle within them a seal for Conference and encourage the church or some auxiliary to send such individuals as delegates. It is possible for those who have the.money to go but not the time to select some worthy individual and.say, "You go in my stead and bring home the best report of the Conference you can and I will pay your expenses. You give the time and I will give the money, and we will do it in the interest of our church and a successful conference." In these and many other ways it is possible to overcome the indifference due to ignorance or inexperience and cause a zealous and wholesome enthusiasm in its stead.

Then there are those who having been regular attendants at Conference have at times felt little enthusiasm for it because there have been contentions when discussions were not tempered with brotherly love and motives prompting certain actions seemed not to be inspired by the Holy Spirit. It is certainly to be regretted when men gather in conference to conduct the business of the King and are careless of Christian proprieties and manifest a lack of the Christian spirit. However, the more wholesome enthusiasm there has been created for conferences and for the things for which they were convened in times past, the less of irritation and the lack of consideration there was present. And so the features that have been discouraging in the past can be obviated in a very large measure if effort is centered on the creation of enthusiasm for the real purposes of conference and the benefits that may rightfully be expected to be derived from it. Contention does not .thrive in an atmosphere of genuine Christian enthusiasm, and such atmosphere is largely determined before Conference convenes. If one could know the counsel that is being given to prospective delegates, the ideals that are being set forth and the spirit that is being encouraged in all the churches throughout the brotherhood, he could predict very certainly what kind of a conference we will have. There is little real excuse for being indifferent towards Conference because of what has taken place at different times in the past, for by encouraging enthusiasm for a conference characterized by Christian forbearance and mutual consideration we can make it the kind that will give pleasure to think back to.

So much depends on the kind of enthusiasm we create or whether we get up any enthusiasm at all or not! Every church leader of whatever station ought to be concerned about doing what he or she can to predispose the representation to a wide-awake interest in the vital things of the Kingdom and to harmoniously plan for more aggressive measures for taking the world for Christ. It is the business of the Son of God we are called to transact, and it is in view of the fact that we are workers together with God in the great task of reconciling the world unto himself that we are called to plan ways and means whereby we may make our talents count for the most as a church; surely that is enough to warrant the most fervid and deeply seated enthusiasm. It is not a matter of passing worth that calls us together, but the interests of the church of Christ and the eternal destiny of human souls that demands our attention. About such things we can well afford to be enthusiastic.

EDITORIAL REVIEW

The hope of the church lies in its children, and the church that is without children is without a future.

"Beautifiers" do not add any real beauty to a lady, nor do precious jewels give value to life, yet how many indifferent lives consider themselves respectable behind the mask of such false values.

The moth is attracted by the flame, but the flame has no mercy on the moth; so also the human soul is enamored by the glare and glitter of sin, but sin when it is conceived bringeth forth death and hath no compassion on the sinner.

It is when men seek to slip out of touch with and out of sight of their great Friend, Jesus Christ that they find the Christian life hard. Our Lord had in mind human necessity when he said, "I am with you alway."

Brother Kenneth Ronk reports his work at New Enterprise and Center Chapel, Indiana, and though he sees the clouds as well as the sunshine, yet the progress he reports is worth while. He is closing his pastorate of these churches the first of October.

Under the "Ministerial Exchange" head the North Liberty, Indiana, church makes inquiry for a new pastor. Two churches and one minister made use of this department last week. The Evangelist is anxious to be of service to both churches and pastors in this manner, and offers free use of this department to the brotherhood.

A good sister from Van Hook, North Dakota, reports a very successful meeting recently held in that vicinity by Brother S. P. Fogle of Washington, D. C. More than a score of souls were converted and a new church organized. Brother Fogle very wisely introduces them to The Brethren Evangelist and we hope they will soon subscribe and become permanent members of The Evangelist Family.

The work at Sidney and College Corner, under the pastoral care of Brother L. A. Myers, is making splendid progress, according to the pastor's report in this issue. The various departments are doing good and the young people especially are being well cared for. The pastor is to continue in this charge next year and the churches have increased his salary.

The Washington, D. C., church continues its ingathering of souls, and Brother W. M. Lyon, the faithful pastor, states that besides the seven recently baptized, several others have confessed Christ. They are looking forward to a Bible institute led by Brother L. S. Bauman. Brother Lyon states that the Sunday school has outgrown the size of the church and that a new and adequate buiding is needed badly.

Every little child is at once a gift and a trust—given of God and entrusted to the parents, to the church and to society to be molded into strength and holiness of character, to be developed in clearness and balance of mind and to be trained in efficiency and unselfishness of service.

From Milledgeville, Illinois, comes a splendid report from the pen of the pastor, Brother Miles J. Snyder. New members have been added to the church since the last report and the Sunday school, instead of experiencing a summer slump, is outstripping previous records. The church is continuing its pastor for another year at nearly a thirty percent increase in salary.

Brother L. G. Wood closes a very successful pastorate at Roanoke, Virginia, the first of September and immediately after Conference takes charge of the Third church of Johnstown. The visible fruits of his ministry at Roanoke are such as may rightly give him joy. He announces the coming of two young people from that church to Ashland College this fall. Brother Oberholtzer is to take charge of Roanoke.

You will not fail to read what Brother Gearhart says about the success attending the efforts of Brother Bowman who is engaged in evangelistic work in our Kentucky missions, but before you get that far, you will have read what he says about Home Guard pledges. Are you a Home Guard? No, its not a military organization, but a host of men and women who have enough interest in the cause of missions in the homeland to stand guard to the amount of at least $5.00. Now, are you a Home Guarder? If you have pledged, it's time to pay up. If you have not joined, do it now, by sending $5.00 to Brother Gearhart.

Marguerite Gribble through her amanuensis, Dr. Florence Gribble, sends us another most interesting letter from the heart of Africa. Many friends that had become uneasy concerning their safety will feel a relief to know that in spite of sickness and danger they have been preserved and were at the writing of this letter all well. They have been hindered in their work but the prayers of God's people in the homeland united with those of the missionaries will help to bring about the freedom that is needed. May every missionary heart pray for their health and safety as well as for their spiritual keeping.

The good work for college endowment continues among the Virginia churches. Brother Beachler's report this week comes from the Bethlehem, Mt. Olive and Dayton churches and it shows a splendid interest in the welfare of the college on the part of the Brethren in that section. Go where you will, north, south, east or west, and it will be found that those who are awake to the demands of the times for a Christian leadership and the absolute necessity of a Christian college to supply our church with a trained ministry, are ready and willing to give what they can to endow Ashland College. The good people in these churches have proven that they have a vital interest in our only church school. In this section are homes that have contributed much to the welfare of the Brethren church and they are endeavoring to lift their load in this most worthy cause.

Have you noticed how many of the churches this year are increasing the salary of their pastor? It is an indication of a better day for the church when it begins to see both the unwisdom and the sin of keeping its pastors on a starvation wage. It brings discredit to the church in the eyes of the world to underpay its pastor; the pastor finds it impossible to give himself heartily to his work when he must worry about his "living," his doctor bill and the education, to say nothing of a bit "for a rainy day"; and talented young men are not attracted to the ministry very strongly when they know tradesmen in the congregation are getting twice the salary that their pastor is getting, and when professional men, who have spent similar time and money in getting their training, are getting two, three and four times as much salary. Pastors have not done much complaining; they are not possessed of the mercenary spirit of the age, but are still dominated by the spirit of sacrifice. Nevertheless the church has no moral right to deny them a living wage simply because they would endure the injustice rather than complain. And the churches are recognizing this fact, and on every hand they are coming forward with splendid increases in salary. The church that refuses to do this will not long be able to command the talent that it desires. This statement is as much in the interest of the churches as the pastors.

GENERAL ARTICLES

Why Every Pastor Ought to Attend National Conference. By George H. Jones

1. Because he needs the uplift, always possible there.

2. Because he can do better work, if he backs off and sees his work from a distance.

3. Because he does not know it all. Conference is a splendid place to learn things.

4. Because he can help the other fellow who lacks his experience.

5. Because he can only become likeminded through personal intercourse. "Association begets assimilation."

6. Because his vision lengthens and broadens with a widening circle of friendship.

7. Because his knowledge of the need of a particular field is made more definite by acquaintance with the leaders in that field.

8. Because the devotional life gets out of the rut and is refreshed by a change of diet.

9. Because he isn't a specialist in every field, the specialist from some one field might be of unusual benefit to him.

10. Because church business methods can be improved, Sunday schools made more efficient, prayer meetings more interesting, woman's work in the church more vital, Y. P. S. C. E. revived, all these and many more living reasons why a pastor ought to attend National Conference.

But if the pastor is indifferent and is simply satisfied to be the preacher, this list of reasons won't appeal to him, he is already dead and only needs burial, a ceremony some of the churches are already engaged in.

"Anything will do for an excuse when one does not want to do a thing."

However sickness will be a sufficient reason, when a man has planned on going and is prevented by sickness.

Or, financial reasons are sufficient, if the church is too penurious to make a free-will offering, when the preacher overlooked the matter in his contract.

The benefits are so evident that all denominations, where it is at all possible, make the matter of attending conference compulsory with every pastor.

SURE, WE EXPECT TO SEE YOU AT CONFERENCE.

Conemaugh, Pennsylvania.

He Is Just the Same To-day. By J. M. Tombaugh

(See Hebrews 13:8.)

The story which the biographers of Jesus tell in the Gospels is the sweetest, the most marvelous ever written. The picture which they present of Christ, of his teaching, of his character, his goodness, gentleness and sympathy, is so human and so lovable that we all feel that we have missed something infinitely precious in not being permitted to know him in the flesh, and to feel the elevating and purifying influence of his presence. We feel that the world of unhappy men and women suffered an incalculable loss when he departed out of this world unto the Father.

If only he could have remained here! If such a life, so helpful, so full of inspiration and yielding so much of comfort to weak, discouraged people—if such a life only could have continued! We all alike yearn for the intimate fellowship with the Lord which it was the good fortune of the early disciples to enjoy.

If we had lived when Jesus was on earth would it not have been a comfort—when we were discouraged and sad or weak or tempted or burdened with a consciousness of guilt—would it not have been a comfort then to go to him for his forgiveness and love? When we study his character in the New Testament, when we admire him and love him as he was when he was on earth, we think how easy it would be, how delightful a task, to follow and serve forever such a dear Friend and Savior. When we feel that he is farther off from us now than he was from those with whom he was physically present then, it is eivdent that our hearts need fresh realization of the truth that "He is just the same To-day."

There is change everywhere else but there is no change in him. You have not lived very long in the world but you have lived long enough to witness very many changes. Social customs are different from what they were when you were a child. Manners and habits have changed. The views of the people concerning many things are different and you are conscious of many changes in yourself. The old neighborhood where you were brought up is not at all like it was fifty years ago. If you were to go back there today you would doubtless feel very sad at many of the changes the years have brought about. Perhaps you would go again to the little country school house where you began to climb the rough path of knowledge and as you sat again on the old bench where you used to sit as a boy, and in memory call over the names again—the roll the teacher used to call every morning at the opening of school—the names of the boys and girls who were your classmates and playmates long ago, what a sense of loneliness will come over you when you remember that so few are left. Your seatmate and particular chum moved to the west years ago, you wouldn't know him now. Your little sister has been sleeping under the sod for many a year, the teacher is dead and the friends of your childhood are all scattered and gone.

If you would go back on a Sunday to the old church you would find just as many changes there. Here is where you went to Sunday school. Here long years ago you were converted and gave your heart to God. Down at the creek yonder you were baptized and you joined the church and you started heavenward with a new light in your eyes and a new joy in your heart. How the blessed memory of it all comes back again after all the years. Here, on the front pew, you sat one day broken hearted when they preached your mother's funeral sermon. It is a sacred place to you, this old church, and it will always be, but still it is very much altered. You used to know everybody at church, now it is a congregation of strangers. The old deacons are gone; your father is not in the pew where he used to sit every Sunday morning, and a different preacher occupies the pulpit now.

And if you should re-visit your old home you would find that time had wrought great changes here too; it would hardly seem like the same place. The circle which used to gather round the fireside at the time of evening prayer is broken and it can never be united again on earth. Physical changes too have taken place; the old house is almost a ruin; the orchard is gone; the barn where you and the other children used to play on rainy days is no more; only the rich store of golden memories of those far-off happy days is left to you. The old friends are gone, some are dead and the others scattered far and wide .

Yes, we have all lived long enough to realize that time brings many changes, but it is a comfort to know that the best friend of all never changes; "He is the same yesterday, today and forever."

When Jesus was on earth, his heart was a rich mine of

love. He loved as tenderly, as faithfully, as patiently as a mother loves her child. He loved those who were undeserving of his love. He loves blind, rebellious, sinners so well that he wept when he thought of the awful fate their sin would surely bring upon them; he loved them so well that he endured poverty and pain and reproach and even death, to save them. When we read the life of Jesus we have no trouble in believing that he loved man then. He is just the same today.

When he was on earth he was ready to sympathize with all forms of suffering and distress. Blind people, crippled people, poor people, people who were sick, or whose friends had died or who had any kind of trouble found ready sympathy and help yhen Jesus was here. He is just the same today. Jesus was very tender and compassionate and ready to forgive every penitent who came to him even though he

had been guilty of very grave sins. Remember how tender he was to that sinful but penitent woman who knelt at his feet—"Neither do I condemn her." If you, dear reader, are not a Christian, if you are not forgiven, would you not gladly go to Jesus and receive full pardon if you thought he would receive you as he used to receive penitent men and women long ago? He is just the same today.

As the helper of his people he is still the same. The disciples had so learned to love him and to lean upon him that they were troubled when he announced that he was about to go away, but he explained that it was expedient for them that he should go that he might send the Holy Spirit who would abide with his people always. Now Jesus stands in heaven as our Advocate, but he is still our Elder Brother and our loving friend, he is just the same today.

Hagerstown, Maryland.

The Light of the World. By T. Darley Allen

The transformation of Fiji, Korea and Uganda since the coming of the missionaries affords as striking an evidence of divine power as does the apostle history.

The history of modern missions contains chapter after chapter showing that God blesses the work of those whose aim is the evangelization of the heathen. The critic of missions is the critic of the only means that has been shown to be capable of bringing the blessings of civilization to the most degraded races of humanity.

A visitor to the Hawaiian Islands said to Kamehameha V, then king: "Really, now, don't you think that things are in a worse condition than before the advent of the missionaries?" "I want you to judge," was the reply. "Since you have come into my presence you have broken the ancient law of tabu in three ways. You walked into my presence instead of crawling, you crossed my shadow, you are even now sitting before me. In the old days any one of these things would have cost you your life."

F. A. McKenzie, an English journalist, connected with the London Mail, has said: "A stranger stopped me one day. 'I cannot understand,' said he, 'why you, a newspaper man, should advocate missionary work, It is not your business. Why do you meddle with it?' 'I do so because I am a Christian imperialist,' I replied. 'The white man's civilization is the best the world has ever seen, and the white man's

civilization is rooted in Christianity. I know that every missionary is an active campaigner, not merely for a new theology, but also for a new life based on the foundation stone of our civilization, the cross. I want the white man's ideas to triumph, not for the glory of the whites, but for the betterment of woman-life and child-life throughout the world.'"

The "Light of Asia" has been shining in India for ages, but the only hope for that sin-cursed land is in Christianity, which already has done wonders to better the condition of the population of that country and in bringing them some of the blessings of civilization.

As late as the year 1870 a sign was to be seen in China on the bank of a body of water telling the public that girls were not to be drowned there. Directly and indirectly China has been greatly blessed by the work of missionaries. And while the number of converts to the religion of Christ in China are few compared to the vast population of that land, yet they are not inconsiderable and will repay all the effort spent to carry the gospel there. And everywhere is the evidence increasing to give us assurance that only in Christ is there hope for the world and that the glorious time is nearing when the kingdoms of this wolrd will become the kingdoms of our Lord and of his Christ.

Cleveland, Ohio.

Putting on Strength. By Mrs. C. E. Nicholas

"Awake, awake, put on thy strength, O Zion."

There are two commands embodied in one, "Awake, awake" and "Put on thy strength."

The voice that would awaken us is divine, it is a powerful voice and is full of reassurance to him who listens to it. The voice that cries "awake, awake," is the voice of Zion's God.

There are periods of energy and languor in the church. Every live worker desires a steady growth. An uninterrupted growth is best even though it be slow, yet if such has not been the case, then if the ending of winter and the coming of spring will supply the dry branches with new life and vitality, the resumption of retarded growth is next best and the only alternative to withering away.

God requires his church to be faithful, therefore wakeful. Sleep indicates weakness. Sampson was shorn of his strength while asleep. Whole armies have been taken by the enemy because one man fell asleep at his post.

Churches have declined because her individual members fell asleep, thus becoming weak and inactive.

There is nothing so fatal to the growth of an individual as inactivity. To grow we must exercise. The enemy is watching the church that is inactive, he is alert and knows the strength and knows just where and when to deal the death-blow. "Awake," there is a work for Zion to accom-

plish, there are borders to be strengthened,—there are battles to be fought and victories which Zion alone can win.

The second part of the command, "Put on thy strength," implies there is a strength that has not yet been put on.

Primarily, the strength of a community lies in the individuals of that community; so the strength of the church of God is in the separate members. There is strength in all life—Zion has the fullness and richness of eternal life. The church has power in truth—she has intercession before God which is a source of power and strength.

God says, "Put on thy strength"—be ye clothed with strength as with a garment. Put on faith, love and obedience; wrap around you the garment of righteousness; gird thyself with truth. Let your light shine before men that others may see your good works.

Strong winds are heard, strong sunshine is felt and a strong life asserts itself.

The church of God can only rest and be joyful as she puts on strength. To receive the blessings of God we must be awake.

God calls his church and individual Christians into a life of activity. We must face our duties with a stout heart and do with our might what our hands find to do.

Never in the history of the church was there so much

to be done and so few to work. We need men who are clothed with strength and power and who are bent on victory.

The mighty voice of God is calling, "Awake, put on thy strength for world evangelization." God endows us with strength and expects us to use it. The same voice in powerful tones is calling Zion to raise her hand against military training. We have strength, will we use it? If we fail to use it in fighting this system and continuing to fight it nothing remains for us finally but to live under its galling yoke.

Awake, today, put on strength that all peace measures and gospel plans may be placed in the ascendency. To sleep now means, DEFEAT.

Defeat is oft the discipline we need
To save us from the wrong, or teaching heed
To errors which would else more dearly cost;
A lesson learned is ne'er a battle lost.
Whene'er the cause is right, be not afraid;
Defeat is then but victory delayed—
And e'en the greatest victories of the world
Are often won when battle-flags are furled.

Go To College (II). By President Edwin E. Jacobs

In my last article I suggested that the young person who intends to go to college, should select a Christian school with a limited enrollment. In this article I want to stress the spirit which should actuate the entering student.

A recent educator made the statement that the first element in the securing of an education is the desire to secure one. That is to say, that the four years spent in college will be well nigh fruitless unless one comes with a very serious purpose. There are in every college every year, those who come only to loaf, yet college is the most expensive place to loaf in all the world. The young person some way graduated from high school. He pays his railroad fare and sets out for college. He lands, enrolls, buys the books, and gets all ready, and then forgets to study or to give himself to the seriousness of college life. If one wants to spend time this way, the place to do it is on a soap box before the little country store at home. Companionship there is of like kind, the cost is small, and the general atmosphere is right. But not so at college.

Let me invite you into the waiting fields. Are they ripe for your harvesting? They are. First, there is the whole domain of literature with the best of old earth's thoughts. There is science, thinking God's thoughts after him. There is history with its brilliant deeds. There is sociology, anthropology and philosophy and religion, such a domain as to challenge the studious mind to enter and win dominion. These fields are calling. The harvest awaits. The text books clamor for readers. The whole of college life is a blaze of brilliant glory,—and yet our student sleeps!

He irks under the restrain of study. The picture shows allure, the pool rooms attract, the easy-going life appeals. And so one may come to college and grovel in the mud, or one may lift up one's head and have visions as real as ever came to man!

Ashland College is anxious to serve high minded young people and so invites such to come. No matter what the occupation may be in later years, life will be fuller, richer, and more worth while if the soul is chastened, the mind enlarged, and the powers increased by four years of serious study. The first semester opens Tuesday, September 14th. Plan to enter.

The Main Motive in Tithing. By Mrs. Fred C. Vanator

The first question that came into the mind of Paul when he received the true vision of the Lord Jesus Christ was,

"Lord, what wilt thou have me to do?" Has not this been the experience of each of you when you received the vision? I am sure not one of us started the Christian life with the express intention of doing nothing to show the change which had come into our lives. This question which St. Paul asks although intuitively felt by each of us has not always been audibly expressed. This perhaps, is the reason we have been so reluctant in telling to the babe in Christ the blessing of this service. If this message could be indelibly impressed upon the mind of each Christian, the difficulties of the church would be at an end. "O yes," you say, "money is all the church is after and with that they could accomplish their goals." I say this is not the solution, for tithing must go farther than the systematic division of money. We could make no advance in any line, although we had millions in our treasuries, if there were not men who gave their time and strength to the cause. You cannot pay your tenth and say, "Now I have done my duty to the Lord and I will do as I please with the rest." The one who gives in this manner has entirely missed the spirit of this service.

At this point I am reminded of an instance which came to my attention some years ago. A lady of very comfortable circumstances said to me, "The tithe is not a fair division. I give a tenth, but I do not sacrifice to do so. Now there is Mrs. Blank who makes but three dollars a week washing dishes at the hotel and she gives thirty cents of that to the church." (You notice that she said "to the church" and not "to the Lord." This is the spirit in which so many of us give). Now I knew this to be true but I am sure not one member of the financial committee of that church would have deprived that poor working woman of the blessing and joy which she receives by paying this debt. It is easy to see the difficulty in the case of the wealthy member. She was giving systematically and seemingly automatically, not according as she was able, nor with the deep joy and spirit of giving. She was giving the minimum rate when she belonged in the maximum class. This same lady referred to this service as "giving the tithe." In the light of this you can readily see that she was missing the spirit of tithing; for this service is only the payment of the usury for that which has been entrusted to us for our comfort, pleasure and gain. Not until this debt has been met can we say "We are giving."

It might not be amiss to say here that tithing is not a plan for raising church finances, but rather the plan by which to order our lives; to teach us to put first things first. When do we lay aside the tithe? The last day of the week, after all other bills have been met? Not at all. On the first day of the week when we can pay out of the first fruits of our abundance. It is wonderful to witness the change in the lives of those who have received the blessing after placing Christ first in their lives. I think this is never made so real to the individual as when he places Christ first in his financial budget. After this is done he feels that he is an honest man and can look the Lord squarely in the eye and not feel that he is a defaulter.

No one knows the joy of giving like the man who has paid the tithe and then makes a gift out of the remaining nine-tenths for some worthy cause.

I have tried to make clear that the financial side of tithing is not the side on which to lay the stress, but rather, it is the spiritual side. It is the beginning of an orderly, consecrated life. Keeping in mind the scripture that has been so much stressed by the Woman's Missionary Society this year, "Seek ye first the Kingdom," how can we put the Kingdom first in our lives and not in our bank account? You say you have no income and that your husband does not believe in this method, therefore you cannot tithe. You have the most valuable thing on earth—TIME. Will you tithe your time and strength for the Lord?

If you want a sure cure for selfishness just take a six months' treatment of tithing. A man cannot put God first in his expense account and at the same time have self first in his heart. No other service so broadens a person's view as that of paying God the first tenth of your abundance. The common plea is, "Study missions and then you will give." The converse is much more true. Get a man to give for missions and he will study the subject in order to know what good his gifts are accomplishing. It has been said that it is much easier to lead a man from tithing into church membership, than it is to lead him from church membership into tithing. Be that as it may, it cannot be denied that conse-crating portion of your income to God does deepen and broaden your spiritual life.

The one who is not a tither gives to a worthy cause, when it is presented to him, as he feels he can spare. But the tither sees the Lord's money accumulating in his treasury and he seeks out the cause which he deems the most worthy and gives out of the Lord's abundance for its support. Never does the individual feel his partnership with the Lord as he does when he pays a debt of this kind from the Lord's share of the profits. Our place as servants of God and co-workers with Christ is kept increasingly before us by this thought of responsibility. It is not a mere acknowledgement by word of mouth, but a real, concrete expression of our lives by means of which we are linked a little closer to the life of the One, "whose we are and whom we serve."

Canton, Ohio.

The House by the Side of the Road

Let me live in a house by the side of the road,
Where the race of men go by—
The men who are good and the men who are bad,
As good and as bad as I,
I would not sit in the scorner's seat,
Or hurl the cynic's ban—
Let me live in the house by the side of the road
And be a friend to man.

I see from my house by the side of the road,
By the side of the highway of life,
The men who press with the ardor of hope,
The men who faint with strife;
But I turn not away from their smiles nor their tears—
Both parts of an infinite plan—
Let me live in a house by the side of the road
And be a friend to man.

Let me live in my house by the side of the road,
Where the race of men go by—
They are good, they are bad, they are weak, they are strong,
Wise, foolish—so am I.
Then why should I sit in the scorner's seat
Or hurl the cynic's ban?
Let me live in my house by the side of the road,
And be a friend to man.

Admirers of Sam Walter Foss' poem, "The House by the

Side of the Road," are many. The story of his writing it is known to few. He was an enthusiastic traveler, and on one of his trips through New England he came, at the top of a long hill, to a little unpainted house set almost in the road, so near it was. Near one side was a queerly constructed signpost finger, pointing to a well-worn path and a sign, "Come in and have a cool drink." Following the path, he found in the side of the bank some distance from the house a spring of ice cold water into which a barrel had been sunk, and above which hung an old-fashioned gourd dipper. And on a bench near by—a wonder—was a basket of fragrant apples, with another sign, "Help Yourself."

Scenting a story, he went back to the house, where he found a childless old couple in straightened circumstances, with the rocky farm as their only source of livelihood. But it was rich in the delicious spring water and an abundance of fruit, so the sign was placed guiding to the water, and from the time of the ripening of the first purple plum to the harvesting of the last red apple, a basket of whatever fruit might be in season was placed near, that anyone passing might rest upon the long hill and refresh himself.

The old gentleman explained that they were too poor to give money, so took this way to add their mite to the world's well-doing.

The beautiful thought and its real helpfulness so impressed Foss that he immortalized with his pen the spirit of the ideal home.—Selected.

A Friendly Admonition. By Samuel Kiehl

Any democrat, republican, or prohibitionist, who takes a greater interest in his party and its belongings than he does in Jesus Christ and his teachings, is the enemy of God according to the "word" (Jas. 4:4, last clause). Ye cannot serve God and mammon, says Jesus (Mat. 6:24; Luke 16:13). The lust of the flesh; the lust of the eyes, the pride of life, and "self-determination," are not of the Father, but are of the world. And the world passeth away, and the lust thereof! but he that doeth the will of God (not his own will) abideth forever (1 John 2:16, 17).

If we take David's advice in Psalm 15, and obey, we shall be "unmovable, always abounding in the work of the Lord." The Psalmist asks two important questions. "Lord, who shall abide in thy tabernacle? Who shall dwell in thy holy hill?" and gives the following answer in eleven statements: (1) "He that walketh uprightly, (2) and worketh righteousness; (3) and speaketh the truth in his heart. (4) He that backbiteth not with his own tongue, (5) nor doeth evil to his neighbor, (6) nor taketh up a reproach against his neighbor. (7) In whose eyes a vile person is condemned; (8) but he honoreth them that fear the Lord. (9) He that sweareth to his own hurt, and changeth not. (10) He that putteth not out his money to usury, (11) nor taketh reward against the innocent." "He that doeth these (eleven) things shall never be moved;" whatever his political aspirations along the lines of right may be, for the good of the people, and the glory of God.

Dayton, Ohio.

A pastor longed for a genuine and thorough work of grace among his people. He sent for a neighboring minister, who had recently enjoyed a marked visitation from the Lord, which resulted in large accession from the world to the church. The brother came. A fair audience greeted him. He preached with plainness, force and earnestness upon the duty of removing the stumbling blocks out of the way of the Lord's coming. A deep impression was made. One present, a man of fervent piety, and who delighted in the displays of divine power, at once remarked, "We are going to have a revival of religion among us." He was quick to see that the key-note had been sounded, and that the people were thoughtful. Nor was he mistaken. Night after night the meetings grew in interest, and numerous conversions followed, so that the occasion became memorable in the history of the church.—Selected.

THE BRETHREN PULPIT

"Our Creed."   By H. M. Harley

TEXT: "Teaching them to observe all things, whatsoever I have commanded you."—Matthew 28: 20.

We are told in God's Word that we are "to be able to give a reason for the faith within us." And if this is true of the individual, how much more ought it be true of the church or denomination. If the Brethren church, or any other body of God's people have no distinct message to offer to the world, than that offered by some other people, then there is no excuse for her existence. We believe that the Brethren church has such a plea.

The only creed ever accepted by our people has been, and is the New Testament Word of God. We believe that the "Thus saith the Lord" of the Scriptures is· adequate ·and sufficient as a rule for the faith and practice of God's people in the world, and that the primary business of the church is to teach men to observe all things, whatsoever Jesus has commanded. In· fact, he assures us that as we · go about doing this, he will accompany us in our efforts, and for him to be with us means that we shall enjoy his aid and blessing.

Now, there are several principles which characterize our stand as a church. And the first and fundamental one is that Jesus Christ is the supreme and final authority in matters pertaining to faith and doctrine, as well as of church polity and government. Men are coming more and more to recognize and acknowledge the fact which the Brethren church has advocated for more than two hundred years,— that the authority of Jesus Christ, as expressed in his life and teaching, is the only religious authority that will stand the test. The authority of the church must be subservient to, and in perfect harmony with the spirit and will of him who organized, and has ever since energized .the church for the work to which she has been called.

The second principle that has ever dominated the Brethren church, is that the ordinances which Jesus instituted for, and gave to the church, are essential to the proper development of the spiritual life of his followers. The purpose of an ordinance is to. visualize and vitalize the truth in question, and. to make it real to those for whom it was intended, and at the same time to perpetuate the truth, as first given. If· then, the teachings of Jesus are as vital and as essential

today as they were when first uttered by the Great Teacher himself, why should not the ordinances of the church · be needed as well, in order to make the truth more real and vital. And if the ordinances as instituted are of any value, why not adhere to them as first given, and as understood and interpreted, and practiced by the early disciples who received them first-handed? The disciples of the first century of the Christian Era ought surely to have been able· to grasp the mind of the Master, and we believe they were led · of the Spirit of God in their interpretation, as well as in the enforcement of the several ordinances as given to the church. And at least all Bible students and readers of church history know how they understood and practiced the teachings as recorded in Matthew 28:19-20, John 13, 1 Corinthians 11, James 5:13-16, together· with other important scriptures that might be mentioned.

If the truths symbolized in these several ordinances were necessary to the life of the church in that day, why not even more so today, with our complex life, and our increasing obligations and temptations. God's Word is eternal and unchanging, because the truths contained therein are needed in every age, to meet the needs of the children in that age. And only as we take those truths to ourselves, and apply them to our lives in the way he thinks best, can we hope for the greatest possible good.

Men differ as to certain passages of Scripture, and this difference has resulted in the divisions among God's people. Why not take Christ's Word at its face value, and if there is any uncertainty as to their meaning, compare it with other like utterances. Then see how those who were with him, understood them, and be guided accordingly. And you can't go far wrong. Remember ,the Word says, "He that willeth to do, shall know of the doctrine." Others may be content to accept man-made rules and ordinances, but as for me and my church, we will strive both to do and teach "All things," —whatsoever he has given to us,—nothing less and nothing · more.—The Brethren Bulletin, published by the.Pittsburgh· Brethren church.

The Union of Faith and Works.   By Roy Brumbaugh

Time and again have the words been quoted, "Without faith it is impossible to please God." I sometimes think we put too much stress on a passive faith. The apostle might just as well have said, for it is plainly taught throughout the Scripture, Without works it is impossible to please God. "Faith without works is dead." We are to hear the voice of God that says Do this and live.

To be sure we are not saved by our works. If we could be saved by our works the sacrifice and death of the Son of God were useless. .We might as well talk about sailing to England in a wooden shoe or lifting ourselves with our bootstraps as to talk about earning our salvation. Salvation is the.free gift of God. But we are asked to keep this gift by being faithful and passing the good news on to others. We are to work out our salvation with fear and trembling. Labor broad as the earth had its summit in heaven. God worked six·days and rested on the seventh. But do not think that God is still resting. The Builder of the mansions in the sky said, "My father worketh hitherto and I work." Jesus was always busy. He was often weary and footsore. But he delighted to work the works of him that sent him while it was day. He knew the night was coming when no man could work. The long night of death will soon overtake us and we will wait in silence until our work in review passes

before us. What a joy unspeakable it must be when men hear the summons to know that life's·work is well done. Perhaps the work allotted to us is waiting on us, how much longer it will wait I do not know. But this I know for a surety, "The night cometh wherein no man can work" and nobody else can do the work God has assigned us to do.

Whether our life is an eternal failure or an eternal success depends entirely upon our union and co-operation with, and our faith in the Son of God. We can be assured whatever we have done or failed to do when we are through it is done for all eternity.· We are not so·foolish as to think of living life over again, and yet how many folks live that ought to live life over again. It is true we shall pass through this world but once. Each day we live brings us one day nearer eternity. I once saw a cartoon picturing a man who had fallen in the mire standing with outstretched hands towards a passerby who was making towards him to help him out. Below the picture were words similar to these: "I shall pass through this world but once. The good that I should do· let me not defer or neglect it, for I shall not pass this way again." Then you have heard of the boy that was given a candle and sent to the basement to do a certain amount of work. He lit the candle, looked at the work and said, I will play awhile. He came back and saw that the candle was half gone and said, I still have time and went to play. When he came back at last the candle was flickering and the work was not done. We have been playing too long and have left the work Jesus has asked us to do go undone. We dare not say there is time enough yet. Or "time enough" may sometime hiss and shame us. Dust to dust is the eternal decree and earthly frames will soon be dusty. There is just time enough from the cradle to the tomb to fit us for that eternal habitation. Life will soon be done. The wind will soon pass over us and we will be gone for all flesh is grass. Let us be working for the glory of God while the candle of life still burns.

It is true Jesus said, "Only believe," time and again, and that Paul said, "Believe on the Lord Jesus Christ and thou shalt be saved." But they put so much in that "believe." They meant a belief that would lead a man to repent and to a new life, that would lead them through the baptismal grave and to a life of service for the Master, for so they taught and preached. A lack of faith does nothing worth while for the world. It curses and damns and ruins it. But the men who have moved this world onward and upward, and Godward and Christward and heavenward, have been men with a real and abiding faith in God. Without faith there is no true repentance, no regeneration, no baptism with a meaning, no pearly gates to swing ajar, no seeing and enjoying the fellowship of the city of God, no heaven, no hope of immortality, no promise of life beyond the grave, no dependence upon God. For without faith it is impossible to please God. We might do all that we are able to do, yet it will not be accepted but be a rejected sacrifice if it is done without faith. Men may pile up their works until they reach the sky, but without faith they are rejected. "The just shall live by faith." True faith is leaning on Christ. It will not save me to know Jesus is a Savior, I must trust him if he is to be my Savior. His atonement is only a sufficient safeguard from the wrath to come, as you make the atonement your trust and your refuge. Faith is walking down the fire-escape; it is buckling on the life preserver; it is stepping into the life boat. Faith is walking life's highway with your hand in Christ's. Faith is stepping across the Jordan with Jesus.

No one in the sacred record ever pleased God without faith. Think of the men in Hebrews eleven. Faith was their stepping-stone to success and the approval of God. Faith is necessary because works cannot save. The key to heaven is at the girdle of Christ; he has the keys of hades and death; he it is that openeth and none shutteth, and shutteth and none openeth. You cannot work your way to Jesus without faith in his atoning blood. This is the key. Then you say works are useless. No, let us see. We work and labor for our rewards. The rewards of God are for doing something, for being faithful, for feeding the flock, for loving his appearing. But salvation or eternal life is a free gift through Jesus Christ our Lord.

We need to have faith but we need to get busy as well. "Not every one that sayeth unto me, Lord, Lord, shall be saved but he that doeth the will of my Father in heaven." "Whosoever heareth these sayings of mine and doeth them not, I will show you unto whom he is like." He is like a man that built his house on the sand and when the crises of life came it revealed his folly. "As the Father hath sent me even so send I you." "Occupy till I come." Paul says, "We ought to give the more earnest heed to the things we have heard lest at any time we let them slip." We have left too many things slip—family worship, prayer meeting service, money for missions. Jesus said, Say not there are four months till harvest; the fields are white and the gleaners are few. Too many folks have something big they are going to do by and by. They want to cut ice in the summen and shock wheat in the winter. Jesus said to his disciples, Let us go to work. Today is the day we ought to pitch in and get busy. Stand no longer idle, harvest day is here, thrust in the sickle and reap. Jesus said, "He that reapeth receiv-

eth wages and gathereth fruit unto life eternal. Pay day is coming. Jesus always pays liberally all whom he calls. At the end of all sowing and reaping comes a completed harvest. The last wagon will be loaded, the last word spoken, the last prayer offered and the last hymn sung. The last day for worshipping the Lord with your gifts will one day come. What will the harvest be?

Let me say ere I close, we are not saved by our works, we are saved to work. We are saved to serve. And we need faith, for without faith we cannot please God and he will not accept our service. "Not by works done in righteousness alone" but by the life we now live, being lived by the faith of the Son of God. No, we are not saved by works but to work. The disciples were to pass on the good news of salvation and to serve others. We have the same mission and the same message to take to the world. And the test of our faithfulness is whether or not we love Jesus. "If ye love me ye will keep my commandments."

It pays to have a vision of service and yield ourselves to the doing of the will of God. It was a vision of the ripened harvest that sent men across the sea to glean for their Master. It sent Moffat and Livingstone to make bright a dark continent. It led Judson to decline the finest home parish that he might be the apostle of Burmah. It made Paton and Chalmers a blessing to the South Seas. It made Burns and Morrison the seed of the Kingdom in China. It made Verbeck the creative force of the new Japan. It sent the Gribbles and their party, to the blackest, daarkest, vice-molested and disease-infected spot on the globe—the heart of old darkened Africa. It has sent the Yoders and Boeks to the heart of Roman superstition and degradation and damnation in Argentina. And God only knows the price they pay. But it will pay. God always pays his workers. One soul is worth more in his sight than the whole world. And after all the world's captains with guns and drums are silent, and when every gun fired for selfish purposes yielding destruction, havoc and damnation is spiked, these men shall shine forth as the real benefactors of mankind. Simply because they had faith in God and gave themselves to the doing of his will. May the Lord increase our faith and our willingness to do his will. Let us plant the anchor of faith by the work we undertake so that what we do, we may do to the glory of God.

Portis, Kansas.

Feminine Attire

That New Orleans priest certainly aroused the natives who interrupted a wedding the other day because the bride-elect was not wearing enough clothes. He declared he was so shocked by what he saw that "he ordered the lights turned out until the girl could clothe herself properly." The editor's traveling companion on the train read this aloud, and made the characteristic comment: "Fools rush in where angels fear to tread'; but even at that I admire the priest for his nerve; no Protestant minister I know would dare to hold up a wedding for such a reason, and yet goodness knows the way some girls undress in public these days is an outrage on decency." Possibly if other priests follow this example, or if more institutions challenge the decrees of fashion as Hood College has done in its recent announcement imposing restrictions on decollete attire, there will be a chance to halt what appeared to be an inexorable process of elimination. It requires no little courage on the part of a mere man—perhaps some of the ladies would prefer the word presumption—to lay down the law on such a question. We venture merely to suggest that if the present modes of attire are not quite decent, it is because the parents of America have permitted and encouraged it. It is only when a pagan spirit is in the ascendancy that restrictions are necessary in such a matter as decency of attire.—Selected.

Send
WHITE GIFT
OFFERINGS to

THE SUNDAY SCHOOL

ALBERT TRENT
General Secretary-Treasurer
Johnstown, Pennsylvania

World's Sunday School Day Service

For use in Sunday Schools throughout the world as a service of worship preceding the lesson, or as a merger service with the church on Sunday, October 10, 1920 during the progress of the Eighth World's Sunday School Convention at Tokyo, Japan, October 5th to 14th.

(Prepared by Professor H. Augustine Smith, of Boston University.)

(It is to be hoped that our schools very generally may plan to use this very suggestive service.—Editor).

GOD-CREATOR   CHRIST-REDEEMER!

1. God, the Creator and Supreme Giver

INSTRUMENTAL PRELUDE

HYMN (All Standing)—
"The Spacious Firmament On High."

LEADER—
In the beginning God created the heavens and the earth. (The first words which Joseph Neesima read from the Bible and which led him from Japan to America, from Buddhism to Christianity, and eventually to the founding of Doshisha University).

ASSEMBLY—
And he made of one every nation of men to dwell on all the face of the earth, having determined their appointed seasons and the bounds of their habitation.

ASSEMBLY (Doxology)—
All people that on earth do dwell,
Sing to the Lord with cheerful voice;
Him serve with fear, his praise forth tell,
Come ye before him and rejoice.
(The first hymn sung on Commodore Perry's boat in Yeddo Bay, July, 1853, at the opening up of Japan to the world).

LEADER—
"Japan's progress and development are largely due to the influence of missionaries exerted in the right directions when Japan was first studying the outer world." (The words of Prince Ito, former Premier of Japan).

ASSEMBLY—
The God that made the world, himself giveth to all life, and breath, and all things;

LEADER—
Every good gift and every perfect gift is from above, coming down from the Father of lights.

ASSEMBLY—Hymn ("Italian Hymn")
Thou, whose almighty Word
Chaos and darkness heard,
And took their flight;
Hear us, we humbly pray,
And, where the gospel's day
Sheds not its glorious ray,
Let there be light.

LEADER—
There shall be One that ruleth over men righteously, That ruler in the fear of God, He shall be as the light of the morning, when the sun riseth, A morning without clouds.

ASSEMBLY—
His name shall endure forever; His name shall endure as long as the sun: And men shall be blessed in him; all nations shall call him happy.

LEADER—
Blessed be the Lord God, the God of Israel, Who only doeth wondrous things.

ASSEMBLY—
And blessed be his glorious name forever; and let the whole earth be filled with his glory.

ASSEMBLY (Doxology; Seated)—
Soon may the last glad song arise
Through all the millions of the skies,
That song of triumph which records
That all the earth is now the Lord's.

2. Emmanuel, Prince of Peace

LEADER—
For unto us a child is born, unto us a son is given; and the government shall be upon his shoulder;

ASSEMBLY—
And his name shall be called Wonderful, Counsellor, Mighty God, Everlasting Father, Prince of Peace.

LEADER—
And he shall judge between the nations, and arbitrate for many peoples.

ASSEMBLY—
And they shall beat their swords into plowshares, and their spears into pruning-hooks;

ASSEMBLY—
Nation shall not lift up sword against nation, neither shall they learn war any more.

ASSEMBLY—
In his days shall the righteous flourish, and abundance of peace till the moon be no more.

LEADER—
He shall have dominion also from sea to sea, and from the River unto the ends of the eadth. Yea, all kings shall fall down before him; all nations shall serve him.

ASSEMBLY—
The kingdom of the world is become the kingdom of our Lord, and of his Christ, and he shall reign forever and ever! KING OF KINGS, and LORD OF LORDS.

ASSEMBLY (Hymn, "Antioch"; Standing)—
Joy to the world! the Lord is come:
Let earth receive her King;
Let every heart prepare him room,
And heaven and nature sing.

He rules the world with truth and grace,
And makes the nations prove
The glories of his righteousness
And wonders of his love.

3. The Cry of the World for a Savior

LEADER—
We are the voices of the wandering wind,
Which moan for rest, and rest can never find.
Lo, as the wind is, so is mortal life,
A moan, a sigh, a sob, a storm, a strife.
So many woes we see in many lands,
So many streaming eyes and wringing hands.
("The Light of Asia," Matthew Arnold.)

Lo, in the darkness I wander,
Where is the light?

Nothing know I, but I wonder ·
Is there no light?
Lord, in thy vastness I wander,
Where is the way?
How may I reach thee, I wonder—
Is there no way?—(Hindoo Song).

The doors of the world are heavy and tall,
But the cry of a child can pierce them all.
(A cry of a child in anguish sore;)
And though it sounds from a land apart,
'Tis at our threshold and at our heart.
(A child is crying beyond our door).
—(Theodosia Garrison).

LEADER—
The 80,000,000 people of Central Africa are still pagan.
60,000,000 or 80,000,00 boys and girls of school age in
China are growing up with limited educational advantages. More than 99 percent of the college students in
South America profess no belief in God. Seven out of
every ten Chinese babies die. Ninety-five percent of the
women of India may be classed as illiterates. One-half
of the world's 600,000,000 boys and girls under fifteen
cannot read or write in any language, are ignorant of
Jesus Christ, never have had a Christian home.

PRAYER (All uniting)—
"Almighty Father, we are made in thy likeness to do
thy work. Thou hast shown us what we can do in making this world a part of thy kingdom. May we carry
the glad tidings of thy love everywhere, that every child
may see thee, and find thee, and every nation become
that happy nation whose God is Lord. Amen."

4. The Missionary Christ and His Ambassadors

LEADER (Standing)—
The Spirit of the Lord is upon me, because he anointed
me to preach good tidings to the poor: He hath sent me
to proclaim release to the captives, and recovering of
sight to the blind, to set at liberty them that are bruised,
to proclaim the acceptable year of the Lord.

ASSEMBLY (Hymn, "Webb")—
Hail to the Lord's Anointed,
Great David's greater Son!
Hail, in the time appointed,
His reign on earth begun!
He comes to break oppression,
To set the captive free,
To take away transgression,
And rule in equity.

LEADER—
Go ye therefore, and make disciples of all the nations,
teaching them to observe all things whatsoever I commanded you: and lo, I am with you always, even unto
the end of the world.

LEADER—
And they that are wise shall shine as the brightness of
the firmament;

ASSEMBLY—
And they that turn many to righteousness as the stars
forever and ever.

LEADER (Prayer of the Viceroy of Manchuria)—
O spirit of Dr. Jackson, we pray you intercede for the
twenty million people of Manchuria, and ask the Lord
of Heaven to take away this pestilence. "He died for
us," said the Chinese of Arthur Jackson.

ASSEMBLY—
Forth to the fight he fared,
High things and great he dared;
He thought of all men but himself—
Himself he never spared.
He greatly loved,
He greatly lived,
And died right mightily.
("In Memoriam of David Livingstone," John Oxenham.)

ASSEMBLY—
For God so loved the world, that he gave his only begotten Son, that whosoever believeth on him should not
perish, but have eternal life.
The Son of man came not to be ministered unto, but to
minister, and to give his life a ransom for many.
As the Father hath sent me, even so send I you.
Greater love hath no man than this, that a man lay down
his life for his friends.

PRAYER HYMN ("Elmhurst"; Sung softly as a solo or
quartet)—
Send thou, O Lord, to every place
Swift messengers before thy face,
The heralds of thy wondrous grace,
Where thou, thyself, wilt come.

Send me whose eyes have seen the King,
Men in whose ears his sweet words ring;
Send such thy lost ones home to bring;
Send them where thou wilt come.

5. The Coronation of Christ

LEADER (Standing)—
In Christ there is no East or West,
In him no South or North;
But one great fellowship of love
Throughout the whole wide earth.
(John Oxenham).

ASSEMBLY Hymn ("Coronation")—
Let every kindred, every tribe,
On this terrestrial ball,
To him all majesty ascribe,
And crown him Lord of All.

Lord's Prayer and Benediction—
"O thou strong Father of all nations, draw all thy great
family together with an increasing sense of our common
blood and destiny, that peace may come on earth at last,
and thy sun may shed its light rejoicing on a holy
brotherhood of peoples. Amen."

The Value of Adequate Sunday School Music.   By L. A. Myers

(Address given at Southern Indiana Sunday School and Christian Endeavor Convention at College Corner.)

God gave man a musical nature and also the ability to
respond to the impression of music. Music is one of the
means by which men give expression to the various emotions
of their own being. Thus it has been a very important factor in all religious services. It is a natural way for the human soul to give vent to the feelings of praise, honor and
adoration for a superior being. It has always had an important place in the entire history of man's religion. Its nature
and kind always partook of the nature of the service, thus
it was adapted to the service of which it was a very important part. These facts are also true of the modern religious

service. They are lifeless and cold without the inspiring
force of song. The very nature of the soul is to praise God
through hymns.
The Sunday school is not only the Bible school but also
the school of worship. We seek to know God and his will
and endeavor to worship him in the same service. Thus in
securing Sunday school music the fact of worship should not
be forgotten. The songs should be selected that have a worshipful nature. They should be songs that touch the heart
and not the feet. A large number of our modern Sunday
school songs have too much of the ragtime, the hop-skip-and

jump movement to them to inspire the heart and prepare it for a real worshipful hour. The utmost care should be taken in selecting the songs that inspire and are worshipful. There is no better way to open up any subject of the Bible than through a song service that bears on that subject. But too often it is true that the proper interest and care is not given to the selection of the Sunday school songs. We fail to have the songs of worship because it becomes a hit and miss matter of selection, convenience being preferable to care and interest in preparing for the service. When we have such songs as "All Hail the Power of Jesus Name," or "Holy, Holy, Holy," to open our Sunday school service we start it out with a reverence and feeling toward God that is worthy of him and inspiring to us. When we sing "All Hail the Power of Jesus Name," the imagination is set in action and the singer gets the image of all people giving special regard to the name of Jesus; the angels prostrating themselves at his feet and all the precious jewels brought to him and crowned Lord of lords and King of kings. There are many other worshipful songs that should have the preference, especially for opening the service. The average school sings the song the superintendent first sees when he opens the song book to select the song. We need to learn that our song service in the Sunday school is not mere custom or filling of space, but is a vital part in the life of the entire service. When the school is opened and the subject presented through the sentiment of soul stirring, worshipful songs the teacher and the pupil are both prepared to enter into the discussion of the subject with interest and a feeling of reverence as soon as the lesson period begins.

The music of the Sunday school should be adapted to the subject for consideration for that particular hour. A careful program should be prepared beforehand and songs selected that bear upon the lesson; the subject should be sung as well as taught. Too many schools are woefully wanting in this particular phase of Bible work. There is too much of a tendency to merely get by with the Sunday school and satisfy the feeling of duty that we should have some kind of a Sunday school. Frequently the Sunday school superintendent will come late or if on time wait for the organist. When they are both on the job they hurriedly meet and find a song to sing because it is past time to begin. It is not a matter of adapting the song to the subject but a matter of convenience. The lesson subject receives no attention whatever. If the song book opens at "Asleep in Jesus Blessed sleep, from which none ever wakes to weep; a calm and undisturbed repose; unbroken by the least of foes," this is the song that is sung. It serves as a lullaby to place the school in sweet repose while the lesson is being taught in some poor weak way. One can readily see the effect of singing a song with that sentiment, to the subject of Israel's Conquest of Canaan or some other subject of kindred nature. Music selected in such a thoughtless way loses its entire value to the teaching period. We need to see that the music of the Sunday school has more to do with the making of a valuable hour to all than just filling space. The entire song service should be in harmony with the thought of the hour. This helps to secure concentration of thought and feeling.

Then, too, the music of the Sunday school should be adapted to the grades of the school. Songs should be used that would apply to the various stages of life as found in the Bible school. Hardly any one song will apply to all ages as we have them in the Sunday school. Each different grade represents a different temperament, varying, ambitions and activities. The adult songs do not apply to the children. The sentiment is not expressed in child thought and language. The adult should have adult music; the children children's music.

This would suggest an elementary department for the children of the school. Here they can meet and sing the songs that are adapted to child nature. This would enable the music of the entire school to be adapted to the various stages of life. We have been mistaken in that we have tried to give the child the adult head and hear. In many of our schools we meet and sing the adult songs while the children spend the time in waiting for the teaching period, the only part that is really theirs. The overworked, discouraged adult that feels a long, long rest is the one thing he desires above all other things wishes to sing "On Jordan's Stormy Banks I stand and cast a wishful eye; To Canaan's fair and happy land, where my possessions lie." This is soothing to his soul, but what are the children doing? They are not tired nor overworked. Neither are they thinking of a happy land of rest. They have not had enough of this one, yet to satisfy their natures. Thus the song has but little for them, except to make them restless and weary. The child nature is full of activity and movement. The child loves and desires to be loved. The child desires recognition as well as the adult. Then while the adult is singing the song that applies to his or her place in life have the child sing the ones that appeal to his nature, for example, "Jesus wants me for a Sunbeam" the idea of doing something is expressed, also something that appeals to the child. Or, "Jesus loves little ones like me." The fact that even Jesus loves the child appeals to the children and they take delight in singing such songs, because they apply to them. It is much different from the state of waiting and watching and being tired out and weary of life. If such intelligent attention is given to the children, by the time they are sixteen or seventeen they will feel like they have something in the Sunday school and also in the church.

Then to have adequate Sunday school music it is necessary to give more time and attention in adapting the music to the grades of the Sunday school, and to the lesson subject, not forgetting the value of worship to the Sunday school pupil. When we have more adequate music for the Sunday school we will accomplish more in teaching and training and will have more real worship in the Sunday school hour.

Sydney, Indiana.

SEND ALL MONEY FOR
General Home, Kentucky and
Foreign Missions to

MISSIONS

WILLIAM A. GEARHART
General Missionary Secretary
906 Conover Bldg., Dayton, O.

News From the Heart of Africa

Carnot, French Equatorial Africa,
March 26, 1920.

My dear little friends:

Another month has quickly passed since I wrote you last. Daddy's birthday came and went but we did not celebrate because at that time Marie was so sick, and our hearts were all burdened with prayer for her. God wonderfully answered prayer, and Marie recovered. On the following Sunday she was able to be up, and although weak we all rejoiced in her recovery.

About this time also another event occurred which caused us all great rejoicing. The leopard got in the big bamboo trap which had been made for it a long time before by Mr. Pinelli. The shooting of the guns, the howls of the wounded leopard, and the running of the natives awakened us all, and Daddy and Uncle Antoine went to the trap to see the animal. It was not so large as the East African leopards but it was hideous indeed. The next day its skin and head were prepared for preservation, and we children all went to see them.

The next Monday Marie made a cake for Daddy, because he didn't have a birthday celebration. Would you like to know how she made it? Of a queer African grain called sesame, of native chocolate, eggs, native honey, flour, sugar, and soda. Every one pronounced Marie's first cake a great success, and so the month of March commenced in joy, none of us knowing of the afflictions which were so soon to befall us.

For since then Daddy, Marie, Julia, Uncle Antoine and Aunt Toddy have all had illnesses. Sometimes three have been in bed with fever at once, and those who were up were hardly well enough to take care of the sick. Mama says the place seemed like a little hospital. Marie and Daddy were sickest of all. Daddy had two attacks of fever, four days apart. The first time he was sick three days and the second time six. During the four days that he was up, Uncle Antone had his attack, and Daddy nursed him. He was very sick for a time, but soon recovered During those days we would take the hot-water bottles, still warm, from the beds of the convalescents to put them in with those who were just in the throes of a severe attack. Daddy was put to bed the second time with a temperature of more than 103 degrees. We had been having prayer meeting that morning and Daddy had been lying down during the service, but no one realized how ill he was until after the meeting, when Mama took his temperature. Aunt Toddy's and Julia's sicknesses were fortunately very slight, and they soon recovered. Marie had a severe, but shorter attack of fever than usual with her, and then there came a glad day—now more than a week ago—when everybody was up, and beginning to get strong again. The rains have commenced, and with them we hope, a time of better health.

We children have swings up in the house in which we spend many happy hours.

I am beginning to learn to read and enjoy it very much, although I enjoy still more looking at the pictures in the little primer.

We haven't had any mail at all from home since before I wrote you my last letter. The Afrique's going down may account for some of it, but we are all so hungry for news.

Bananas are getting more plentiful and mangoes will soon be ripe. Sweet potatoes are scarcer than ever now, so we are glad for the fruit. We have fried bananas for breakfast, baked bananas for dinner, and banana pudding for supper. We don't eat them raw very much, as they do not agree with us when we have so much malaria to fight. We, do not have very many eggs now, but we appreciate every one that comes. Monsieur Du Mont gave us children some chickens. Mine was a rooster, and we ate him. Marie and Julia each have little hens which we hope will lay us some eggs. Aunt Toddy's chickens that were babies when we came here, four months ago, are big now, so we have quite a flock.

Monsieur Du Mont loaned us a little monkey for a few hours one day and we did enjoy playing with it so much. They are very cute, but we have to watch them because they will sometimes slyly bite us.

You ought to see Monsieur Du Mont when he goes out riding. He has a chair which is harnessed between two horses. When the horses behave nicely both in front and behind the chair, all is well, but when they stand on their hind legs and do other naughty things, it is a circus. But Monsieur Du Mont is not afraid of them and always controls them.

We thank God for our home, and for all his care. We are awaiting his wonderful deliverance from these days of hindrance. We know you still pray for us and will never grow weary of doing so.

May our Heavenly Father keep you true to him and give you blessing and light every day. We are happy in him.

Lovingly yours,
MARGUERITE GRIBBLE.

April 17th. Almost another month has gone by, Daddy has continued ill, but now is up again. Marie, too, has had another severe illness. A big event occurred April 13th when we received mail for the first time in over two months. There was so much of it belated Christmas mail, and there were so many packages and so many good things to read, that we were extremely happy. It seemed like another Christmas. We are all well today as we write. We are hoping for the mighty working of our God to be soon manifest in our midst.

May his blessing be with you,
MARGUERITE.

NEWS FROM THE FIELD

WASHINGTON, D. C.

Some of our good friends have been inquiring why we have been silent so long. Well, as we continue in the work of the Master and the years multiply, we find that our cares and responsibilities also increase. We have simply been too busy to write.

Since our last report seven others have been baptized, several have confessed Christ recently and will probably follow the sacred rite before this letter appears in print.

Our congregations have been good until the last few weeks. Vacation season takes a heavier toll each succeeding year. Doubtless this is largely due to the spread of the "Motor" fever. We read of a time long ago when blessings were changed to curses. History is a great repeater. The "Motor" car can be used so that great blessings may result, but surely the facts prove today that they have become an awful curse. But few seem to use them to the glory of God.

At present we are looking forward with deep interest to our Bible Institute, when, (D. V.) we expect to have Brother L. S. Bauman with us. We are confidently expecting a rich spiritual feast. We earnestly request a personal remembrance before the throne of grace.

The Institute begins on September eighth, to continue ten days, perhaps longer.

Mention has been made before this of our need of a more modern and suitable building. Our Sunday school work is greatly hindered on this account. We are thankful, indeed, for what we have but we could accomplish much more if we had a building adapted to our needs. Let all who really know the secret of prayer, pray very definitely in regard to this matter. God is able. He can touch hearts and fill them with a desire to open pocket books.

For years we have had an impression that eventually God would lay it upon some heart to supply this need. We are still holding on to that belief. How many will join us definitely in our intercession in this matter? His all-searching eye can easily find the person who will come forth and erect a "memorial" building in this great city. Pray that his will may be worked out and that we may be found in the center of it!

W. M. LYON.

A FEW CHURCH NOTES
New Enterprise, Indiana

After so long a time we shall try to send in a short report of the work at this place.

With the odds against us we managed to pull through the winter with colors flying. With the help of a small handful of good loyal people we opened the church doors every Sunday thus far during the year. Many times we were greeted with only from twelve to fifteen faces and at other times we were compelled to dispense with our evening services on account of sickness, bad weather and the like. We were unable to hold our revival service, as the "flu" came around on the date set.

The fair weather of spring and summer has brought encouragement for us as we see new faces coming nearly every week and we can also see a new interest in the work.

Center Chapel, Indiana

We are still pounding away here amid the encouragements and discouragements and there are times when the discouragements are at the top. Our attendance is staying at about the same level and at times we feel that the church as a whole is taking a new interest. and again it seems to center in just a few.

The church has not advanced as we had hoped she would after the success we had in our revival. In spite of the fact that we received a goodly number into the church at that time I consider the meeting a failure in so far that the church herself was not revived. In fact some of those who took the most important part in that meeting seems to have lost all interest in the welfare of the church and some who came out at that time have scarcely darkened her doors since. But

"Behind the dark clouds
Is the sun still shining."

We know there are many here that are stronger spiritually than they were a year ago. To them our revival was a blessing and has inspired them to serve the Christ better than ever before. It is upon the shoulders of these that the burden of the future of this church rests and we feel assured that they will keep the banner floating high.

We are leaving the work at both Center

Chapel and New Enterprise the first of October and we hope the new man whoever he may be, will be able to bring out the hidden possibilities that lie within these two churches.

KENNETH R. RONK,

Winona Lake, Indiana.

MANNING SCHOOL HOUSE AND VICINITY,

North Dakota

In past years we had a large Sunday school and services, but we have been without a pastor for three years and our Sunday school was given up. We all became scattered and were as sheep without a Shepherd. In July Rev. S. P. Fogle of Washington, D. C., came into our midst and preached the true gospel as we had heard it in our childhood (nothing added and nothing taken away). With earnest and devoted love for God and his holy Word and for all mankind, he preached repentance unto salvation and baptism. God has given us a refreshing shower of his love. We all have renewed our covenant to God and are more fully determined to carry forth the good work in this beautiful spot of God's moral vineyard.

The spirit of God came with wonderful power to convict and to save. Those who came through idle curiosity remained to pray.

The meetings continued three weeks, closed last Tuesday night by confirming those who united with the church by baptism.

The number of conversions were 21 and by triune immersion in the River Knife. A large and reverential audience was in attendance and the ceremony was very impressive.

One middle-aged man hearing of the meeting came 22 miles, declared his belief, accepted salvation and was baptized.

On Wednesday night a church and Sunday school was organized which will hold weekly meetings in the future.

It was the expressed desire of many that Rev. Fogle will endeavor to be with us again next year. His exemplary life, his loving kindness, his words of wisdom, his Christlike charity for all has endeared him to all the people in this community.

Asking an interest in the prayers of God's people that this little band of true worshipers may ever be faithful, we will close, by giving God all the praise and glory for this manifold blessing which we have received at his bountiful hand.

Yours in Christ,

ONE OF THE CONGREGATION.

SIDNEY AND COLLEGE CORNER

Some time has elapsed since we gave the readers of the Evangelist any news concerning the work at College Corner and Sidney.

The auxiliaries of the church at Sidney are active. The Christian Endeavor elected officers at their last regular meeting in June. The members are not so active through the hot summer weather as they plan to be later in the year. The Christian Endeavor has been doing good work in view of the fact that they have been organized only a few months. The Senior Christian Endeavor and Juniors had a joint patriotic meeting on Sunday, July 4th, their service occupied the regular time of the Christian Endeavor meeting and church service. The Juniors have part in the morning service each Sunday morning.

The W. M. S., Sunday school and Sisterhood have all reached their goals that were required by the various standards. This manifests the interest and work of each one during the past year. The Sunday school gave an excellent Children's Day program one Sunday evening in June.

The Sunday school committee deserved much credit for their untiring persistency in training the children. The W. M. S. recently met and elected officers for the coming year.

Since our last report six have been baptized and received into the church. This makes a total of 28 since December. There are others yet to be baptized. At the last business meeting the church voted to make some improvements in the basement of the church and install a new baptistry with modern conveniences. The church also extended a call to the present pastor for another year with an increase in salary. This is our fourth year with this church.

The auxiliaries of the College Corner church have also been doing good work. They have not been as successful in reaching goals as Sidney, but they have made the effort. The W. M. S. made their standard. The last one was to organize the girls into a Sisterhood. This will be a good thing for the girls. The Christian Endeavor has its devotional meeting each Sunday, one Sunday in the morning after Sunday school, the next Sunday in the evening before church. Much credit is due Sister John Knee who is chairman of the program committee. The young people take part in the services freely. The Junior Christian Endeavorers and the Seniors held a joint patriotic service on Sunday evening of May the thirtieth. The service was well attended and a good offering given to the societies. The Sunday school had a children's service on Children's Day that was largely attended. It was appreciated by all who were present. It was through the earnest efforts of the committee that made the program worthy of the comments it received.

The church services are all well attended. We have had no real summer slump here as yet. Our attendance has been above normal. Sidney and this church kindly granted the pastor a four weeks' vacation through August In September we will hold our evangelistic services. Other plans for the coming year are being made. The church also extends a call to the present pastor for another year. The call included a voluntary increase in salary. This with many other similar deeds express the appreciation of the people.

At present we are making our home in Preston, Nebraska, and serving the Falls City Brethren as substitute pastor for Brother Stuckman who is taking his vacation. It gives us pleasure to work with these people and renew the old ties of friendship which were made more than ten years ago. The Falls City Brethren are an appreciative people and manifest it through their very favorable comments of Brother and Sister Stuckman. Brother Stuckman has been pastor here six or seven years. The life and activity of the church is evidence of the pastor's wise leadership, and his good pastoral care.

May God bless Brother and Sister Stuckman in their work.

L. A. Myers.

MILLEDGEVILLE, ILLINOIS

As a general thing the summer months are not very prolific in "church news." However, we are glad to see the work here moving along so encouragingly. The Sunday school has continued normal all along; and accurate record show that the church attendance through the past quarter has averaged more than in any corresponding quarter during my entire pastorate here. These results were produced by no special effort or sensational method, except an earnest effort to preach the plain Gospel from week to week. Since our last report through the columns of the Evangelist four new members have been added to the church four by baptism and one by letter.

On June 18, our annual Sunday school picnic was held at Point Rock Park near Mt. Carroll, Illinois. It was our good fortune to have an ideal day, and consequently we had a large attendance. A memorable twelve-inning base ball game was played by the "farmers" and "professionals," which, with the enjoyment of other forms of recreation, afforded all a pleasant day's outing.

Our regular business meeting was held on July 7, and was well attended as all congregational business meetings ought to be. The church extended the present pastor a call for another year, beginning October first, and also voted a raise of nearly thirty percent in his monetary remuneration for the coming year. This action on the part of the congregation is characteristic of these good people; and since our work has been mutually pleasant and not without marks of gain for the Kingdom of our Lord, the present pastoral relations will be continued.

We had the pleasure of having with us on July 25 Brother Wm. A. Gearhart, our General Missionary Secretary, who addressed the Sunday school and congregation at the morning service.

The work of preparation for General Conference is now the matter of chief concern. With Conference time yet a few weeks away, it now appears that we will have a very good representation at Winona—more than our full quota of delegates—and it is earnestly hoped that present plans may be fulfilled and the the coming Conference will indeed be the largest and best in our history.

MILES J. SNYDER.

ROANOKE, VIRGINIA

Some things have been happening here since our last that are worthy at least a brief mention.

The congregation here is well pleased with the success of our district conference held here in June. The success was due to the good attendance from the various churches of the district. Our only regret is that we could not do a better part in entertainment. Our people appreciated Brother Beachler's great messages, and his personal work during his brief stay among us, and we are hoping for additionals in the more substantial expressions of appreciation—College Endowment—before he reports his work here.

Sister Pence of Limestone, Tennessee, and Brother Lynn of Ashland, Ohio, have been with us and added inspiration to the work by their splendid messages.

Have received one into the church by letter, and have several on our "prospective" list for whom we are working and praying.

We will close our work here the first of September and expect to go immediately after conference to our new field, which will be the Third church of Johnstown, Pennsylvania. We are certainly pleased to have our dear Brother H. M. Oberholtzer succeed us in the Roanoke work. We are doing, and will continue to do all we can to make his work here both pleasant and profitable. I consider my experiences here profitable and never have I been more conscious of the Lord's leadership than in my work here. Have received 82 into the church, some of these have been called to their reward, a few have moved to other parts but we are thankful that the greater number of these are still here in the faithful service of the King. Two of these, H. H. Rowsey and Essie Albridge, will enter Ashland in September. These young people will be greatly missed from the local work, but we rejoice in their consecration and preparation for full time service for Christ and the church.

Our Christian Endeavor work will be reported soon. We have found many precious souls with which to work and fellowship in this field. There is lots of hard work to be done here, but the prospect is better and brighter than ever before, and with the efficient leadership of the in-coming pastor and the loyal co-operation of the membership, the future is bright with light.

May we "love the brotherhood,"—"fear God." Pray for us.

L. G. WOOD.

CAMPAIGN NOTES

We have three churches near Harrisonburg, Virginia, viz., Bethlehem, Mt. Olive and Dayton. None of these churches at the present time have pastors. The preaching that is being done now at Bethlehem and Mt. Olive is being done for the most part by Brother E. B. Shaver.

Bethlehem

I canvassed Bethlehem first. This is a country congregation located in a beautiful country. The church building is a neat, attractive building. I preached three times at this place to splendid, appreciative audiences. And I found among this people a fine interest in the college. I was especially glad for the enlistment made for endowment by the Sunday school, also the noble part taken by the organized classes. The W. M. S. also took a part. We had several $100 gifts at this place. And we had a grand total of $1,525 to Bethlehem's credit. However, it was through one of the pleasant surprises in Virginia that I am able to report such a figure for the Bethlehem church. This was the home church of the late Sister Elsie Showalter the bulk of whose estate has been left to the various interests of

Our Goal: 200,000; We Can and We Must

COLLEGE
ENDOWMENT

the Brethren church to be administered according to the discretion of her brother-in-law, Brother Jacob Swartz. And Brother Swartz I think acted very wisely when he decided to place at least $1,000 to the permanent endowment fund. And it was this action that put Bethlehem up to the point where she went.

I very much enjoyed the work in this congregation. I shall remember always the Swartz folks, also the Logans, the Dowells, the Showalters, the Bowmans, and many others of this congregation. This is the home of Brother J. M. Bowman; and the treatment rendered me by himself and his good wife was such as to send the pilgrim on his way refreshed and rejoicing.

Mt. Olive

This is another country congregation, and like any other congregation I have ever known—it needs a pastor and it needs him badly. Oftimes a congregation misses the opportunity of its lifetime during some interim that it has no pastor. I found an exceptionally fine lot of young people here and they need good pastoral care and leadership. I preached four times at this place, and it was a busy time but I had good audiences; I worked hard here for the cause of the college and we had a fairly good result. I got a little over $500 here in four gifts; and the total result was $725. I received the best of care in the Rogers and VanLear homes. And I am particularly indebted to Brother VanLear for the excellent service he gave me with his Ford. It was a real pleasure to be in the many homes into which my work took me here at this church, but especially do I feel indebted to the folks whom I have mentioned. I am hoping to meet them all again.

Dayton

This is the home of Prof. J. A. Garber. It was my privilege to visit his aged mother in her home. I found in this lady one whose heart beats true to the church with her various interests. I only preached one night in this church, but my audience was very appreciative. This congregation has had its discouragements and what the future holds in store for the work here is hard to say. The result for endowment was $175. I am glad I went to this place. The people who invested in endowment did so cheerfully. It was here I met for the first time Brother Rash. I also made the acquaintance of Brother John W. Thompson. This man's loyalty to the school assumed a practical form and I shall remember him in a pleasant way.

Finally

This puts the mercury now at $154,500. The last report from the Maryland and Virginia trip will come from Roanoke.

WM. H. BEACHLER,
Campaign Secretary

EVANGELISTIC NEWS FROM NORTH DAKOTA

Some of you dear readers may wonder the result of my trip to northwestern North Dakota which I mentioned in my last letter to the Evangelist, June 23.

As I stated, the call came from our dear Brother J. W. Bolen Van Hook to come by

July 10th, but circumstances at home were such we could not get there to begin till Sunday, July 18. A well filled house was waiting the stranger at the door. Many said they had heard but one Gospel sermon since they lived there. I introduced myself by saying, "This is what I had heard of, this desire to hear the Gospel, and I am come, knowing nothing but the Gospel of our Lord which is the power of God unto salvation." The first subject was Man's Fall and His Punishment. Through disobedience he caused the tree of Life to be cut away which resulted in sin and death. This was followed the next evening by the subject: Sin; What is It—the Extent and Evil Thereof. In each argument we brought forth, we ended with its first and last meaning, disobedience. Gently weaving in our Lord's Commandments one by one, we pressed harder and stronger the fact that our salvation was not wrought by the doings of the flesh—its thoughts and deeds, but by obedience to and a living faith in our Lord's teachings. We gave them 22 sermons in all, simple, plain Gospel sermons, and by request one sermon on "Baptism; its Purpose and Origin," and praise God for victory to a people who never heard it that way in North Dakota before.

We organized a church with 20 members on the roll. Sister James A. Graham is our church secretary. Brethren J. W. Bolen and Arthur La Brant were chosen as deacons and officers. By continued, urgent requests we have promised to go back the middle of next June for one month's meeting. They will go on in Sunday school work till cold weather. Sister Herbert J. Hoffman, who was once a school teacher in Pennsylvania and other states, asked me for our church paper's address. I think she wanted to write something about the meeting. I'll stop as I want her to have the privilege of giving the results. I want to say yet that our secretary, Sister Gra-

ham is a fine organist and music leader and her husband is a good tenor singer.

Dear ones of North Dakota: I want to thank you for your loyal kindness to me and let us all pray and ask others to pray that your number may be multiplied by at least three next summer. I promise to pray daily for you till we meet next time. I am paying for the church paper for a little while for you as a surprise gift and a sample. Hope you may renew the subscription very soon.

There were some whose address I did not know. Please read and pass your papers on to them. Let's have every member taking the church paper.

S. P. FOGLE.

IMPORTANT NOTICE

We are pleased to report that we have a fine response to the call for clearing the last National Conference Kentucky pledges which comes in very nicely since we need all of that fund to fully prosecute that worthy work in the Home Mission field. However, in looking over the list of Home Guard memberships we find a marked shortage of responses, which we believe has only occurred through a little oversight or neglect on the part of our loyal Christian supporters of that division of our worthy missionary enterprise. May we suggest that at least most of those who have not yet renewed, might send their contribution for active continuance before the next Conference convenes and make a better showing in that division of our work.

We are glad for the recent information from the Kentucky Field resulting in the salvation of souls. Elder I. D. Bowman was with the brethren at Krypton, and the evangelistic effort resulted in 27 confessions, and already 19 of that number baptized. The church did well in raising over $100.00 to defray expenses of the campaign. Elder Rempel,

makes a fine report for the July work in that field.

Elder Drushal also sent us a recent report of the work just begun at Lost Creek, by Elder I. D. Bowman and already 6 have been baptized, with a bright outlook for a large ingathering of souls there, and says the Institute is opening with good attendance at the school for this season of the calendar year.

WILLIAM A. GEARHART,
General Missionary Secretary.
906 Conover Bldg., Dayton, Ohio.

MINISTERIAL EXCHANGE

The First Brethren church of North Manchester, Indiana, is in search of a pastor. Any who are interested in filling this place are invited to correspond with the Secretary.

Yours very truly,
HOMER G. BAKER, Secretary.
North Manchester, Indiana.

Where boasting ends, there dignity begins. Young.

"In the reaction from formal methods of evangelism there is danger of permitting this important function of the church to go by default. Whether or not one day is observed as "Decision Day," some plan is necessary, to make certain that no child of the parish shall be permitted to pass through the periods favorable to religious awakening without an opportunity to make and affirm his decision to become a loyal follower of Jesus Christ. No less important than the decision itself is the instruction which should follow and which should make clear to the young Christian in plain terms of everyday speech the meaning of the new life and the new responsibilities which it involves."—E. P. St. John.

Two New Faculty Members

Harley H. Wolford, A. B., A. M., who becomes professor of History in Ashland College, is a man of strong native ability as student and speaker, has splendid training and is loyal to the Brethren faith.

Arthur L. DeLozier, A. B., A. M. becomes prpfessor of Modern Languages, and by his remarkable linguistic gifts, his careful training and Brethren loyalty adds much strength to the faculty.

Published every Wednesday at Ashland, Ohio. All matter for publication must reach the Editor not later than Friday noon of the preceding week.

George S. Baer, Editor

The
Brethren
Evangelist

When ordering your paper changed give old as well as new address. Subscriptions discontinued at expiration. To avoid missing any numbers renew two weeks in advance.

R. R. Teeter, Business Manager

OFFICIAL ORGAN OF THE BRETHREN CHURCH

Subscription price, $2.00 per year, payable in advance.
Entered at the Post Office at Ashland, Ohio, as second-class matter.
Acceptance for mailing at special rate of postage provided for in section 1103, Act of October 3, 1917, authorized September 9, 1918.
Address all matter for publication to Geo. S. Baer, Editor of the Brethren Evangelist, and all business communications to R. R. Teeter, Business Manager, Brethren Publishing Company, Ashland, Ohio. Make all checks payable to the Brethren Publishing Company.

TABLE OF CONTENTS

EDITORIAL

Our Ashland College Faculty

The Evangelist takes pleasure in presenting to its readers just previous to the opening of the school year the members of the Ashland College Faculty and some statements concerning them. If there is one department of our church's program that has received a more general awakening of interest on the part of the brotherhood than any other in the last three or four years it is the educational. Ashland College has grown in favor with our people by leaps and bounds, because they have had its needs presented to them and they have invested to help meet those needs. And where our investments are there will our thoughts and concerns be also. And undoubtedly our readers will be interested in knowing "Who's Who" in the college faculty.

Many indications of a brighter outlook for Ashland College have been observed recently, but none are more propitious nor give greater cause for rejoicing than the strength of the present faculty. We like to see the college endowment fund mount up higher and higher; and it must continue its climb. We have high hopes,—and we shall rejoice in their realization—of seeing new buildings and added equipment on "College Hill" in the not far distant future. It is encouraging to see new students flock to Ashland College in ever larger numbers. But the keenest pleasure of all comes with a realization that the faculty of our college is worthy, so far as quality is concerned, to be compared with that of any other reputable denominational college. A strong faculty will involve larger expenditure and thus necessitate still larger endowment; it will draw more and better students and students and faculty will demand better equipment and more buildings. And so, our college faculty, which has been steadily growing in strength and was never stronger than now, is one of the surest indications of the larger future of our college. A glance at the personnel of the faculty will help us to appreciate this element of strength.

President Edwin Elmore Jacobs, M.Sc., Ph.D., who did his undergraduate work in the College of Wooster, took his master's degree in the University of Chicago, did graduate work in Harvard University and took his doctorate of philosophy in Clark University, has not only a highly trained scientific mind, but is a man of high spiritual attainment and is loyal to the Word of God. Moreover he is well equipped for the management of our college by his thorough understanding of college standards and requirements, the confidence he enjoys of our people throughout the brotherhood and his democratic spirit which makes him loved and respected by the student body.

Dean J. Allen Miller, A.M., D.D., who got his education in Hillsdale College, Hiram College, Ashland College and the University of Chicago, is without a peer in the brotherhood as an expositor and teacher of the Word and is scarcely equalled for intimate knowledge of the Scriptures, its original languages and times. While his special field is theology, yet his education is remarkably well rounded, and he is able to teach mathematics or science when occasion demands. After his twenty-five years of continuous teaching of the Word, is still a constant student, and at the same time keeps in vital touch with the needs and experiences of the pastorate, and so is abundantly equipped for his position of Dean of the Seminary.

Professor Levi Lucius Garber, A.M., Litt.D., was educated at Ashland College, Ohio State University and the University of Chicago, and is a most thorough student of the English language and literature. For years he has been at the head of the English Department, and every student who has gone through Ashland College has reason to be grateful to Dr. Garber for the way in which he has imparted clarity and skill in the use of the English language and enlarged the appreciation of literature.

Clara Worst Miller, A.M., Litt.B., gained her education in large part side by side with her husband, Dean Miller, in Ashland College, Hiram College and the University of Chicago. She has an understanding of the Latin language, which she teaches, such as few teachers have, and she knows how to impart her knowledge to others, former students will testify.

John Adam Garber, Professor of Religious Education, is a graduate of Ashland College and of Bonebrake Seminary. His mastery of his subject is recognized not merely by Ashland College students, but by his fellow members of the Religious Education Association and also by our brotherhood in general, for he is Educational Superintendent of our National Sunday School Association and is in constant demand for Sunday School conventions, institutes, and Christian Endeavor rallies. He is doing special work in Northwestern University. He is pastor of the Ashland Brethren church.

Ray R. Haun, A.B., A.M. is a graduate of the University of Virginia and of Vanderbilt University, and so is well qualified and able teacher of his subjects, Chemistry and Physics. He is a young man of marked ability as a student, is still pursuing studies along this line and work done with him is fully recognized by the best schools.

Harley H. Wolford, A.B., A.M., who is an alumnus of Ashland College and the University of Chicago, has been a successful pastor for a number of years, has done evangelistic work and work in religious education, he now being vice-president of the National Sunday School Association of the Brethren church. He was elected to the faculty to teach History by the Board of Trustees at their meeting last spring.

and will be in charge of that department at the opening of this school year.

Arthur L. DeLozier, A.B., A.M., a graduate of Ashland College and Lehigh University, has also been a successful pastor, is vitally interested in foreign missions and is a member of the Foreign Board of the Brethren church. He, too, was recently elected a member of the faculty and is well qualified both by native ability and training to teach the subjects assigned to him, Modern Languages. He will be at his post at the opening of this school year.

Lucille Teeter, A.B. is a graduate of Ashland College and has done work in Ohio State University. She is a young lady of splendid capabilities, has taught in high school and is now Instructor in the Academy.

Amy Genevieve Puterbaugh, Teacher of Voice and Dean of Women, has an exceptional voice and is well versed in and fully able to teach all that pertains to her department. She has done work in Lake Forest Summer School, two years in Chicago Musical School and is studying with Gustaf Molmquist, and Sybil Sammis McDermid. She also has charge of the Ashland church choir.

Lucy Cowan Wimer, B.Mus. M.Mus., is a graduate of Francis Shimer School of Music, Cox Conservatory and is now doing work with Maurice Aronson in the Chicago Musical College. She is Teacher of Piano and her natural musical ability and splendid training make her fully worthy of having charge of that department.

Mrs. Edna Gamertzfelder is Supervisor of the Model School and a teacher of years of experience and excellent training.

Walter Leckrone has charge of the Physical Education of Men and will endeavor to see that the men students keep in physical trim for their studies. There will also be selected a director of Physical Education of Women, but as yet her name has not been announced.

Of vital concern to every lover of Ashland College are two other men, one of whom, for three years has been going in and out among the churches gathering endowment for this institution which is perhaps the key to the future of the Brethren church. To him, William H. Beachler, D.D., belongs large credit for making possible the strengthening of our faculty, and as an expression of the college's appreciation of his splendid service, the Board of Trustees conferred upon him the honorary degree of Doctor of Divinity. The other man referred to has recently come into vital connection with the college, but his love for the college, his enthusiasm and boundless energy have already established his value to the future welfare of our only church school. He has taken up the work which was formerly so efficiently done by Prof. A. C. Hendrickson, and is also doing work in the field in the interest of the college. His name is Martin Shively, D.D. and his duties are briefly comprehended under the term Bursar and Field Secretary.

This is our present college faculty, a group of men and women whose professional ability cannot be doubted, and whose religious convictions and consecration to the church constitute an even greater asset. They are worthy teachers of our young people and deserve our prayers and support.

EDITORIAL REVIEW

You will not want to miss Brother Carpenter's interesting "Mountain Mission News" on the "Mission" page.

Every church should do its very best to send its full quota of delegates to General Conference. Don't forget the date, August 30th to September 5. "Whosoever will, may come."

Sister G. C. Powell, corresponding secretary of the Harrisonburg, Virginia, congregation, reports that Brother J. A. McInturff recently assisted them in an evangelistic meeting that was quite successful.

Brother E. H. Smith reports successful evangelistic work which he recently did among the Brethren near Holidaysburg, Pennsylvania. He is continuing his services with them until a pastor can be secured.

Brother Earl Detach, another Ashland student, who has spent his summer doing pastoral work with the Linwood, Maryland, congregation, reports in this issue. He has found a loyal people at that place.

Brother G. E. Drushal writes that the benefits of the evangelistic campaign recently conducted there by Brother I. D. Bowman did not consist merely in the addition of new members and the reconsecration of others, but also in the good effect the meetings had upon the "moonshiners." Brother Drushal is evidently teaching these people concerning the grace of giving as well as other Gospel virtues. The school at that place is progressing nicely.

Sister Frances Nielsen writes some news items from the Long Beach, California, church and states that their pastor, Brother Bauman, is on the program of the Northwest district conference held at Sunnyside, Washington.

A few brief items from Peru, Indiana, shows that work is progressing there under the leadership of Brother G. C. Carpenter. The pastor and his wife have recently moved into the church's "log cabin parsonage."

It is fine to note the enthusiasm of our student pastors and the way they throw themselves into their work. Brother Pfleiderer who has spent his vacation in the Armstrong county, Pennsylvania, circuit, writes concerning his experiences.

Running through the whole life is the unceasing effort to break up old and wrongly formed habits; how much time might be saved and how many regrets might be avoided if we but took more care to form only right habits!

Brother W. I. Duker may well be proud of the church of which he is pastor, New Paris, Indiana. It would be hard to find a church that exceeds this little congregation in loyalty to every Brethren interest and in the joy it seems to find in giving. By their noble gift to their pastor recently they gave evidence of their appreciation of the splendid leadership of their pastor.

Do not fail to read the splendid list of testimonies to tithing under the "Tithing and Stewardship" department. The editor will be glad to receive others for publication in this department. If you have a tithing band in your church, ask each one to write his or her own testimony to the benefit and importance of tithing and mail them to us. Do it now; it will be an important kind of missionary work. It matters not if you say what some one else has said; say it for yourself and breathe a prayer that it may carry its blessing to some heart.

The Dayton, Ohio, church writes through its secretary, Brother Wombold, that they would like attention called to the distinction between the names E. M. Cobb and C. E. Kolb, inasmuch as there has been a tendency to confuse the names. Brother E. M. Cobb is pastor of the Dayton church and Brother C. E. Kolb is pastor of the Milford, Indiana, church. However these brethren, living in different towns, can hardly experience the difficulties in being distinguished the one from the other as do the editor and another man living in Ashland. The other man's name is George Bear and the editor's George Baer.

Brother Beachler found in Brother L. G. Wood, pastor of the Roanoke, Virginia, church a loyal supporter of Ashland College, when he made his canvass there for college endowment. It is not a surprise to any one who knows Brother Wood, however, for he is openly and enthusiastically loyal to all the interests of the Brethren church. And "like pastor, like people," so the Roanoke church was ready and willing to do what it could in this noble cause. The Mountain View congregation of which Brother J. E. Patterson is pastor, also lifted its corner on the endowment proposition and did it in the spirit of genuine Brethren loyalty. Then in the Garden City congregation, a courageous group of people who have built themselves a church home without outside assistance, he found a number who had also laid the matter of college endowment upon their hearts and a nice gift was realized. And when Brother Beachler was just saying the Virginia result is all reported for the present, along came another $100 gift from an isolated member of the Dayton congregation, so that he had to mail us a "Post Script" which we attached to his main report. We will not be surprised if other gifts will yet come in to necessitate another report. In fact, Brother Beachler leaves a lurking suspicion in our minds that Brethren loyalty has not yet fully expressed itself in Virginia. But with what has been done we can truly say that the Maryland-Virginia district has done as well. She has proven her loyalty in gifts of money, is sending her sons and daughters to Ashland College in ever larger numbers.

Ashland College—Our Own Church School

Main College Building and Dormitory

Introductory

President Edwin E. Jacobs, Ph. D.

I am under deep obligation to the Editor of the Evangelist for this opportunity of presenting the members of the Faculty of Ashland College to the readers of this paper. They are all, without exception, members of the Brethren church and are Christian men and women of deep spirituality and devotion. The church has a spiritual wealth here of which it might justly boast. It is the earnest prayer of the president that the church together with these Godly men and women may strive earnestly to promote both education and Brethrenism so that the Kingdom of God may be extended upon the earth.

Outstanding Impressions of Ashland

By Martin Shively, D. D.
The New Bursar and Field Secretary

The substantial stateliness of the buildings on the college campus cannot fail to impress him who first sees them with the thought, that in the mind of those by whom they were conceived, the estimates placed upon their purpose, were indeed of a high order. Like the imperishable value of the kind of culture it was intended here to develop, they were erected not for a short period of service, but for the generation then to be served, and for those which were to come. The lack of ornamentation suggests the thought, that in the mind of the builders, as in the mind of him for whom they wrought, service, the kind which is spelled with a capital, was to be the objective aimed at. The beauty, therefore, of the College, and all that is included in the name, is not that of a showy ornamentation, but that of a quiet stateliness, which reflects the whole spirit which permeates the place. The splendid trees which line the drive and walks, invite the weary passer by to find rest and comfort beneath their shade, accenting the primary purpose of the institution to give anchorage, mental and spiritual, to the soul, buffeted by its wavering thought.

The spiritual atmosphere which permeates Ashland College cannot fail to make a lasting impression upon him who spends any length of time amidst its activities. During every morning of the school year, all who are associated here are called to spend a half hour or more, together in a devotional period. Here, led by President Jacobs, or other members of the faculty, or others who are from time to time invited to do so, the Word is read and its message amplified and applied, in some of the most appealing messages which I have ever heard. No one can question the supremely high place which God's Word holds here, who knows the college with any degree of intimacy. Every student who enters our halls is required to spend at least one hour each week in definite Bible study, under the direction of consecrated and thoroughly trained teachers. In addition to this, both Y. M. C. A. and Y. W. C. A. have weekly meetings of an hour each, where students and teachers join in such definitely religious service, as the organizations suggest. The mid-week prayer meetings, the Christian Endeavor societies and Volunteer Bands, furnish outlet for every spiritual longing and are inviting avenues to that spiritual culture, without which all else is comparatively worthless. The soul, and all associated with it, both as to time and eternity, is the chief concern of Ashland College. The observing visitor cannot fail to reach this conclusion, if his stay is of sufficient length to enable him to catch the spirit which is uppermost here.

Another thing which cannot fail to impress the newcomer to Ashland, is the persistent activity which characterizes it. From early morning until after night fall the halls are vibrant with the effort which goes on within them. The hours are not limited to eight nor even ten, for I know I am well within the truth when I say that from the president on through the entire membership of the faculty, the hours spent in class room or study, will easily average at least twelve per day. And that is not limited to a few months per year either, for not a single member of the faculty has thus far had any vacation this year, nor will there be one, for most of them at least. The summer school for teachers is holding some of them to their tasks and others are in school, preparing for more efficient work, when they return to their class rooms. After years of experience outside these halls, I say without hesitation, this is one of the busiest places which I have ever seen. The dawdling, ease seeking student, gets no comfort here either in precept or example. Such are among the outstanding impressions which the college makes upon one who has come recently again under its influence.

Ashland, Ohio.

The Need of Advance In Our Educational Work

By J. Fremont Watson, Member of Committee on Education

A short time ago one of the New York dailies, one friendly to the church, said editorially: "What is the matter with the preachers? Have they lost their fire, their inspiration, their grip on the people? They seem to be busily engaged in confessing that they have.——It is proper to say, however, that the searching of hearts now going on among the shepherds of the flock is entirely timely."

No thoughtful and well-informed person will deny the increasing difficulty of attracting the masses to the churches or of bringing them into hearty co-operation with the program of Christianity. The reasons for this difficulty are manifold. The changed conditions of our civilization; the insane lust for money getting; the negative influence of the press itself; the rage for pleasure; the possible failure of the church to adjust itself quickly and safely to these modern conditions, and numerous other reasons may well be studied earnestly.

Careful reflection convinces me that no single cause is so potent as the negative attitude of our whole system of public education to the religious element in education and life. As a nation we are constantly saying to successive generations of youth, "The three 'R's' the fundamentals of a liberal education, are of vital importance. But religion is optional. As a nation we have no concern about it. The churches are supped to be concerned about it, but if they fail to reach the problem, let the subject take care of itself.
Education, wherever one gets it, is the chief formative force in a man's development. To omit religion from the training of our youth is to insert the germ which will result in the lingering death of the church, and will lead to national deterioration. George Washington told the new nation, in his "Farewell Address," "Of all the dispositious and habits which lead to political prosperity, religion and morality are indispensable supports. Let us with caution indulge the supposition that morality can be maintained without religion. Whatever may be conceded to the influence of refined education on minds of peculiar structure, reason and experience both forbid us to expect that national morality can prevail in exclusion of religious principle."

It is not a question of maintaining a school or schools as a denominational propaganda. It is the larger question of finding a way to let the breath of God breathe through the bones of a life withered and dry without that vital breath. It is a question of the preservation of national purity on an eternally safe basis. I make bold to say, that no greater question can engage the minds of our people at this time. It is of supreme importance, and we are not at this moment alive to its deepest significance. What is the use of sending millions of money every year to foreign lands to Christianize alien people, if we cannot make the program of Christianity effective in the noblest nation of them all?

The state starts its educational policy from the doctrine of duty, growing out of the child's right to an education; the church starts hers from the Christian impulse of love of God and of men. The church believes that duty can never be fully met while there is indifference to the underlying forces that develop men and perpetuate civilization. To the church spiritual ideals are supreme. The denominational college is and will remain her great fort where the freedom of religion will be maintained with the same courage as in the state institutions the freedom of science will be defended. The church college must never falter on its insistence on these moral and spiritual essentials. I would have the church college to be less and leass a denominational propaganda, and more and more the defender of Christian ideals and the champion of the vitally religious element in all education.

The church college should lay less and less stress on religiosity, cant, and Churchianity, and more stress on the great Christian fundamentals. I want the church college never to surrender on the incontrovertible principle that we can get ultimate and final truth if we leave out the moral and spiritual elements in the culture of men. We must consistently place the perfected education by the side of the education imperfect because of the lack of the religious element, until the world realizes the lack and supplies it.

To serve her purpose the church college must be well equipped and endowed. They cannot do their great work if their libraries are composed of antiquated books and their laboratories ridiculously defective. Their equipment must be the best. The skilled workman demands the best tools. The man who works beneath his ideals soon degenerates. Great teachers cannot get along with inferior equipment. Their faculties must be composed of noble men of proved and accurate scholarship, reverent toward God and devoted to their fellow-men. We need Ashland College for the sake of an efficient leadership in the church. Look at the men who are leaders today. Take the man who are filling our pulpits. Take the men who are making our church literature. Who are the outstanding men in all the various church activities? Almost without exception they are graduates of Ashland College.

For her positions of greatest responsibility, when leadership of the highest type is required, the Brethren church is almost wholly dependent upon the men who have been trained in her own schools. Is there any prospect that it will be otherwise in the future? I see no sign of it. I believe that our very existence as a denomination depends on Ashland College. The vision of the Brethren church for her must be large, for the future of the church depends on what we see for Ashland College. Ashland College is the lens through whihc we must look at our future. We must not forget that the future of Ashland College depends upon the church and the future of the church upon Ashland College. It means denominational suicide to fail to meet her every need. The wheels of our denominational progress will move slow or fast in proportion as we meet these needs. Brethren, the best has not been reached. We could not be good Brethren and believe that. The best is none too good for Ashland College and the Brethren church. And since we desire that both help extend Christ's kingdom, the best is the least we should do for him who did so much for us.

Johnstown, Pennsylvania.

Educating Our Workers

By J. Allen Miller, D.D., Dean of Seminary

The education of the leaders and workers of the church is the most insistent because the most indispensable and essential task that faces our people today. This has been so for thirty years of our history. Space forbids recalling the critical and tragic facts that attest this statement. And therefore once again, though at the risk of censure for repetition, the present writer insists that the Brethren Church has no obligation quite so great as that of training workers for the present and the future.

And the church must do this for herself. No other organization will do it. No other organization can do it. The Brethren church must train her own ministers, religious teachers and church workers. We can not look to other denominations to do this for us. Equally certain is the fact that our own teachers must be trained under our own auspices. Our own teachers in our own school must do this work for us. No others can do this. What others recognize as well established in fact, it would be worse than folly for us to quibble ever or dispute.

Once again I beg the privilege to say to the readers of the Evangelist that the most insistent, persistent and inescapable obligation that rests upon the Brethren church is the ADEQUATE EQUIPMENT OF ASHLAND COLLEGE.

We as a people have never taken this matter of Christian education seriously. We have thrown the burden of all that has been accomplished upon too few men. The load has been a heavy one, all but unbearable. Yet under the grace of God blessing has attended the effort. The whole church must NOW RALLY TO THE STANDARD SET AND MAKE ITS REALIZATION POSSIBLE.

Three indisputable facts stand out in great definiteness and boldness as we ask the question, Do we really need a Brethren college?

The first of these facts is that our BRETHREN YOUNG PEOPLE WILL GO TO COLLEGE. They go to the schools of other denominations or they go to state institutions. In either instance observation shows that for the most part they are lost to the Brethren church. It is not narrow bigotry to insist that our OWN YOUNG PEOPLE belong to us. We must hold them to the faith that we hold. Every reason that holds us true to Brethren faith and practice must hold them. There is no escaping this conviction or this conclusion unless we are set of conscienceless time-servers. THE BRETHREN CHURCH OWES IT TO HER YOUNG PEOPLE TO OFFER THEM THE BEST EDUCATION POSSIBLE UNDER THE HIGHEST CHRISTIAN IDEAL. This ideal we are praying may be realized in Ashland College.

The second fact is, as already indicated, that as a church we must have a thoroughly equipped and efficient leadership. This means an educated leadership. It is a mere shifting of responsibility and a blind refusal to see the facts of past experiences that fail to take cognizance of our immediate and urgent obligation to supply this leadership. ASHLAND COLLEGE is the only institution in the church which has set this high purpose for itself.

The third fact is that now more than ever before do we need the CHRISTIAN elements of an education emphasized. Ashland College is a Christian college. Faith in the Word of God, respect for the church and her institutions, the deepening and strengthening of the Christian life, the beauty of the Christ-like life,—these are some of the things that receive constant stress.

In view of these facts ASHLAND college appeals to the brotherhood for the sons and daughters of the church. They will be educated. They must be educated. The church has a claim upon the life of her young people. Let ASHLAND COLLEGE help stress that claim. Let the College help these young people to find themselves. Let the College train them for life and life's service.

Ashland, Ohio.

Department of Religious Education

By Prof. J. A. Garber
Head of Department

While the religious element has always been dominant in the education provided in Ashland College the organization of a department of religion dates back only to the autumn of 1915. Prior to that courses in Bible and religious education were offered chiefly for seminary students. In line with the growing demand on the part of patrons, the increasing need on the part of students and the deepening convictions among college administrators generally, President Furry and Dean Miller urged upon the Board of Trustees the establishment of a particular department through whose ministry the message and meaning of the Bible and religion would be presented to the entire student body. The Board appeared willing but funds were wanting. Fortunately the National Sunday School Association and the National Christian Endeavor Union came forward with the assurance of the needed wherewithal.

The writer was invited to Ashland to take charge of this new department and to cultivate a virgin field. The following courses were organized: For the Academy-Normal group, "Life of Christ," "Life and Letters of Paul," "Heroes of Israel," "Hebrew Prophets;" for college Freshmen and Sophomores, "New Testament History," "Old Testament History"; for Juniors and Seniors, "Social Institutions of the Bible," "The Bible as Literature." (The last two have been taught by Dean Miller). The first course in the "Principles of Religious Education" was elected by twelve persons who generously provided about two hundred dollars with which a splendid room was renovated and equipped. These courses have been continued with the addition of others in "Child Study," "Religious Pedagogy," "The Psychology of the Christian Life," "Teacher Training" and "Expert Endeavor."

From this curriculum the aims of the department may be inferred, correctly or incorrectly. The reader with preconceived notions may infer that the aim is to train and equip religious educators. That is the aim when certain courses are elected by prospective ministers and religious teachers. Through this particular group a direct and immediate contribution is made to the religious educational strength and efficiency of the church. But the vocational is transcended by the life aim. The chief concern is to educate all in and for religious living. Unto this end the student is guided and inspired by the acquisition of knowledge of the Bible and the fundamentals of religion. Information, however, is encouraged as a means to motivation. While these materials of religious knowledge are presented and pursued after approved educational methods the studies are not merely academic. They seek to introduce the student to interpret life in the terms of religion, to cultivate religious attitudes, to commit himself to religious ideals. Thus religion becomes a vital element, positive factor, controlling force in his life. A real religious experience during four years of college residence becomes the pledge and prophecy of a supremely effective reality in the life which the graduate will live amid varying social relationships.

Ashland, Ohio.

Romance Languages

By Prof. A. L. DeLozier, M. A.
Department of Modern Languages

By the Romance or Romanic languages we mean all those tongues that are derived from Latin, including Portuguese, Roumanian and a few others. But ordinarily only three languages are emphasized in the Romance group: Italian, French and Spanish.

However the statement may sound, I am convinced that until quite recently we Americans have been entirely too provincial in spite of the large country in which we live. We have been a one language people. Even our business men have been guilty of saying, "If Spanish-Americans want to deal with us, they'll have to 'come across with good old United States' (i. e.,) English." One manufacturer went so far as to send a car load of catalogues to South America, but they were all printed in English. We are now coming to see things differently. We must be more cosmopolitan in our thinking and even in our speaking.

"Quit langue a, a Rome va," say the French, i. e., He who has the speech may go anywhere. I will modify this to, He who has French and Spanish may go anywhere, especially if he has English also. A queen once said, "A man with only one language is like a bird with only one wing." No doubt she referred to Europe, but this is coming to be true in America as well.

Why should we study Roman languages?

1. There is a cultural value. The Romance are the most beautiful languages in the world. Other languages have their strong points, but the Italian, French and Spanish hold first place as to actual beauty, musicalness, euphony. The literature, especially of the French, is extensive and worthwhile.

2. Present commercial relations strongly indicate a

ed of French for the Eastern and of Spanish for the West-
n Hemisphere.

3. For Brethren interests there is a pressing need now
r Italian, French and Spanish.

a. Of Italian for every city pastor and Y. M. C. A.
orker, that he may be able to reach many a family now
touched by the gospel.

b. Of French for our African work in the French Con-

c. Of Spanish for our South American work, but also
r reaching the Mexicans and Cubans who are now to be
und in large numbers in most of our cities.

A final word as to our purpose this year at Ashland.
e shall attetmpt to impart both a literary and conversa-
onal knowledge of these beautiful languages. We hope no
udent may leave the class room next summer without being
ble to help himself considerably in one of these Latin
ngues.

Ashland, Ohio.

The Contributions of the English Department

By Prof. L. L. Garber, Litt. D.

Head of Department

The contributions of the English Department to a satis-
actory education and to the work of a college are so many,
o diverse, and so fundamental that it is difficult to state
hem clearly or interestingly in brief space. Emerson some-
here says, "The Anglo-Saxons are the hands of the world:
hey turn the wheels of the world, do its work, keep things
oving." In a somewhat similar way, the department of
iglish is the hands of education.

First, the English department trains in that convention-
l correctness of speech which everywhere distinguishes the
uccessful intelligent man from the unlettered failure and
nakes possible that happy exchange of desires and ideas
hich lies at the basis of a well-ordered life.

Second, English furnishes the tools and trains in the
orms of systematic and effective thinking. We cannot
hink without words. We cannot think effectively without
roper sentence forms. We cannot think convincingly with-
ut proper devices and methods of procedure. Such tools,
uch devices, such methods and procedure our English de-
artment now emphasizes.

Third, English trains in expressional power; the quality
hat makes great speakers and writers. It is this quality
hat compels attention, that "gets across," that stirs the mul-
itude, that bequeaths to posterity an imperishable bequest
n the form of great literature.

Literature as a phase of the English work is in itself of
ast importance to all who would prepare themselves for the
est and happpiest life. President Harper has said, "Next
o the study of the Bible, the study of Literature is most im-
ortant." In fact in creating and moulding noble senti-
aents and in developing high and moving ideals, it is akin
o religion itself, not to mention its many other important
ontributions to the education most worthwhile and most
eeded in the present day.

In sanity of aim, in wise adaptation of means to ends,
n concentration upon the most worthful and useful things
f education and life, the English department of the Col-
ege, it is believed, ranks with the best.

The Voice. By Amy Genevieve Puterbaugh

Department of Voice

Voice is one of the branches of fine arts which relates to
he agreeable combinations and successions of sounds, and
mbraces melody and harmony. Its history is older than
hat of civilization, extending back to the remote ages and
ntedating the deluge.

Voice is the sound produced by the vocal organs of man
and nearly all higher vertebrate animals.

Vocal sound is made only when the vocal cords are less
than one-tenth of an inch apart, and the different tones of
the voice depend upon the width of the opening and the tension of the cord. When the cords are short, tight, and
closely in contact, the higher tones of the voice are produced, while the opposite conditions cause the lower tones.
Loudness depends on the strength of the expiratory current and quality depends chiefly on the physical structure
of the cords. All tones are the cadences which emotion gives
to thought.

The female voice has a higher pitch than that of the
male, this being due to the circumstance that the cords of
the latter are longer.

At about the age of fourteen years the larynx of boys
enlarges and the cords grow proportionately longer and
coarser; hence the voice becomes about an octave lower and
is said to change or break. The voice changes with old age,
this being due to the muscles that move the cords losing
their elasticity. Soprano, tenor, and baritone voices depend
respectively on the length of the cords, but all voices are
modified to some extent by the form of the throat, mouth,
teeth and lips.

"God sent his singers upon earth
With songs of gladness and of mirth,
That they might touch the hearts of men,
And bring them back to Heaven again.
—Longfellow.

Music, the Language of Emotion

By Lucy Cowan Wimer, Mus. M.

Department of Piano

Music is regarded as the direct language of the emotions. Musical sounds are fascinating as the refined physical
medium on the very borderland of spirit, which, when directly excited, deal with and control the springs of this mysterious inner life of feeling. Music has its morals, its rights
and its wrongs, its high and its low, like any other art.

"Emotion colors all life, inspires all words, nerves all
for action." What would life be without it? What is the
grandest thought without it? The noblest passages in the
Bible are living and inspiring thoughts when read aloud
with impassioned religious eloquence. Music creates the
atmosphere in which thoughts are born, it deals with the
mystic states in which thoughts are steeped and colored.

A great awakening is taking place all over the United
States. Publishers are publishing more of the better music.
The public is beginning to take greater interest in the best
music writers and showing a hunger for information and
guidance. Books on "How to understand music" find a
vastly increasing audience. People are being thoroughly
trained to comprehend the classics and by having a knowledge of classical literature will find a life-time's pleasure
in listening to concerts and coming in contact with great
things which has an enormous developing influence on every
human being. "Music, the Civilizer, the Recreator, the
Soother and Purifier of the emotions" shall continue to be
the great language of the emotions and trainer of morals.

Stubbornness we deprecate,
But firmness we condone.
The former is our neighbor's trait,
The latter is our own.
—Boston Transcript.

When one is right about a thing, he can afford to keep his temper under control; if he's wrong, then he can't afford to lose it.—Selected.

THE BRETHREN PULPIT

The Vital Power of Spiritual Want.　By S. C. Henderson

TEXT: "Blessed are they which do hunger and thirst after righteousness for they shall be filled."—MATT. 5: 6.

Startling as it may seem to us, there is a vital power in man's wants. We generally feel that our wants make us miserable beings. Want dries up the currents of the soul and stifles life's ambitions. The child wants a toy and feels unhappy because he is denied the desire of possessing his want. The girl wants a new gown and feels anything but blessed because her purse is too meager to exchange for its purchase. "In the haunts of wretchedness and need, on shadowed thresholds dark with fear" we find anything else but power and happiness. Want is cartooned as a gaunt grim, grey wolf at the cottage door.

Yet in spite of all these dire facts and experiences, want contains a striking paradox. Some one has recently said that "a paradox was a truth standing on its head." It is a truth contained in an apparent contradiction. Our wants have a power potency. The old adage had it, "Man gets what he wants." Some few who have suffered life's defeats will deny this. Yet in our wants there is a creative force developed that spells all kinds of human progress.

Several years ago, a big New England cotton mill wishing to get nearer the source of supply moved to Georgia. All conditions argued for the change. There was better water-power, cheaper labor, less freight rates, so the new mills were erected and a shanty town sprang up over night. Thousands of negroes flocked in. A little dingy company store was erected to furnish the colored employees with the necessities of life. The mills started up in full tilt and ran until the first pay day. The next morning when the whistle blew, there were not enough laborers on hand to man a single line of machinery. The negroes would not work as long as they had a cent in their pockets. Scolding, threatening, bribes, cut-wages, advances, were all resorted to but to no avail. The situation was becoming serious. It looked as if the mills would have to move back to New England where the people felt poorer and would work. But about this time, the young son of one of the mill owners presented himself for employment. He was just fresh from college. The foreman was at a loss to know where to place him, because he distrusted his ability. But finally he was placed in charge of the little dingy company store. The young fellow knew a thing or two about commercial psychology that the foreman never dreamed of. His ideas were at first ridiculed as whims but because he was the mill owner's son he was allowed to go on with what was ridiculed at the office as "a freak notion." But he went to work. The sides of the little dingy store were cut out and big plate glass windows were set in. Then the curtains were drawn. A mystery was being planned within. On pay day there came the big opening, and the window was an enchanted fairy land to the colored people. There were big red plush albums, large family Bibles with gilt edges, phonographs, and all sorts of colors in clothing for both men and women. As the mill-workers compared their pay checks with the articles in the display window, they turned and started off to the mills with a determination to possess some of the coveted luxuries that had hitherto been unknown to them. The mills did not have to move because the wants of the laborers had been enhanced. Because they wanted, they worked.

It was John Quincy Adams who once said, "Give me some of the luxuries of life and I will get along without the necessities." A social settlement worker had long been trying to help a poverty stricken family. The mother in particular, was discouraged and without ambition. The visitor talked about diet, sanitation and efficiency without success. Finally one day, with a woman's insight she said to herself, "That woman loves blue. She has not had a new dress for a

long time. I will give her one because she needs it more than advice." The dress was presented and from that day the family's fortunes began to improve.

Extravagance is a vice, but there is a field that lays between the bare necessities of life and extravagance in which mankind finds the comforts and enjoyments of living. The cry of the laborer is not a living wage but a livable wage. As the standards of life are increased human wants are likewise increased. In many cases the luxuries of one age become necessities in the next. The average home today have comforts that kings and nobles did not or could not have a century ago. What our grandfathers classed as comfortable luxuries would seem crude and awkward to us if we could be transported back to their times.

Faber said, "The ill of all ills is the lack of desire." Not long ago a man died in a poor-house in an eastern state having spent his life of seventy years within its walls. We wonder why the man at some period of his life did not make an effort to get out of the institution and live for himself. Very likely he didn't want to. Perhaps he argued this way: Here I live without worry. The H. C. of L. doesn't bother me. Those outside are constantly worried and fettered by about making ends meet. Here I have no worries or wants. Social workers know the peril of the poor is to drift into pauperism. It is the state where they do not care to rise out of their condition. It is poverty plus the sense of want that is ever making the poor boy to become famous. His wants are the stimulators to his ambitions.

After Count Bismark had retired to private life by the overbearing egotism of his nephew, the young Kaiser William, a deputation of citizens came to pay their respects to their aged chancellor. In reply to one of the speakers that hinted that his past achievements could be to him a great element of satisfaction, he responded, "No one is ever satisfied, and it would be a misfortune for one to be; all striving would be at an end and we would be like the South Sea Islanders who have nothing to do but to lie under the palm trees and eat the dates that fall in their mouths." It has been truly stated, that necessity is the mother of invention. So wants are the parent of progress. Howe felt the want of the housewife when he made the first sewing machine. McCormick sensed the need of the farmers when he invented the reaper. The same was true of the line of great inventors: Awkwright, Whittney, Bell, Morse, Stephenson and Edison in their creative geniuses they sensed the needs that lifted loads of toil and drudgery. The successful merchant is the one that not only senses his customer's wants but also creates them. The teacher and the preacher likewise are not mere reservoirs of intellectual and spiritual knowledge, but one of their important tasks is to create a hunger and a thirst for these things.

It is the sense of spiritual want that moves the soul. When Jesus said, "Blessed are they which do hunger and thirst after righteousness for they shall be filled," he uttered a great spiritual fact. When he spake those words, he was looking over the multitudes of people as they flanked the mount's side. He knew that in that great out-of-doors meeting there were hungry and thirsty hearts. He knew that they had left their flocks and nets, shops and homes, farms and vineyards to hear the words of divine grace which he spake. With his great loving insight he looked down into their hearts and lives. Too true, there were those that were seared and stained by sin. Yet there were those who were looking and hoping for something better. He knew how the mass of his countrymen were oppressed by the iron hand of a despotic government. He too knew that their souls were kept in darkness and ignorance by the spiritual leaders, the Pharisees, who wrangled over minute points of theology and the law and gave no inspiration or enlightenment. As those longings were for the right and righteousness, he made the promise that they should be met.

Did not you ever note the strong desire expressed in the text, Blessed are they which do HUNGER and THIRST after RIGHTEOUSNESS, for they shall be satisfied. No stronger terms could be used for the cravings of soul than to say it hungers and thirsts. Hunger is the most primitive, universal and imperilous of our physical wants. Nay, but thirst is even more so. The famished Esau, bartered away his chieftianship of the patriarchial clan of Abraham to appease his hunger. Hunger makes wild beasts brave human habitations. Hunger makes men and women desperate beings. Thirst produces insanity and raving maniacs. An ancient king bartered away his kingdom to his enemy for a drink of water for himself and army.

In every normal soul there are longings that must be filled, if it lives the full and complete life. It was the Psalmist who sings, "As the hart panteth after the water-brooks so my soul panteth after thee O God." It was not a draught from the river Lethe that made them forget all their troubles that these poor thirsty souls craved, but rather the Water of Life that refreshed their weary hearts. It was not ambrosia, the fabled food of the gods, but the bread of life which was sustenance to the soul. It has been estimated that from six to twelve million American children are the victims of malnutrition. They are not getting enough food or not enough of the right sort to sustain the physical needs. This is a startling fact in this land of plenty, but just as startling is it that millions are suffering from spiritual malnutrition. 27,000,000 normally protestant children are without religious instruction and 16,000,000 more with barely thirty minutes per week and then often at the hands of very incompetent teachers. Others undernourish by feeding on unnourishing things. Food chemists tell us that it is not at all in the quantity of food, but a diversified quality is needed to make up a perfect diet. Men cannot live by bread alone. High wages, good prices, pleasure, music, art, literature, automobiles, etc. are good and in a certain degree helpful, BUT THE SOUL FAMISHES IF NOT FED ON THE VITALS OF SPIRITUAL THINGS.

These common people that pressed Jesus daily and heard him gladly are to be contrasted by another class in his day, WHO DID NOT WANT. Some of the Savior's severest words are directed against this class. He utters, "Woe be unto you who are full." These people had no sense of wanting anything. They were contented. Their goal of self-righteousness had been reached. Their heaven was already won. The Christ ever finds a more cordial welcome across the threshold of the cottage of the toiler than in the mansion of the rich. The salvation of the beggar Lazarus was that he wanted. The rich man lost his soul because he had no wants, for he fared sumptuously every day. The Pharisee and the Sadducee felt no need of what Christ had; they did not want. They and their nation were lost because they fell into the malady of not wanting.

It is the sense of want and the desire to possess righteousness, that leads a soul to Christ. When the early missionaries encountered, they found that few of the Patrician class and officials heard their messages. Not many wise, rich or noble became followers of the WAY; they thought they heard this Rome say "I am rich and want for nothing." They could not move her as they did the Rome of the poor freedmen and slaves. The prodigal son did not awaken in his prodigality until penury, rags and famine had reduced him to want, and out of his wants he came to himself. In this day of reconstruction and social-unrest men are battling with their wants, but they have not come to themselves. They need to want Christ and his kingdom. The old human race has been playing the prodigal and it needs to get back to God. Men and women need just now to see the value of spiritual want. Our famine is as acute as Armenia's, but

only in another direction, and the sad thing is, we fail to know our want.

The desireless heart is a desert heart. You may till it, and seed it, but it yields no harvest. You plant trees on the western parched plains and their leaves wither and they give you no shade. So it is with a "not-wanting" heart. Too many like the men of Gadara, they love swine more than the presence of the Lord. They want what they want, but they do not want Christ.

But "Blessed are they which do hunger and thirst after righteousness for they shall be filled." Our spiritual wants can be filled, and satisfied. Eugene Ware found an answer in the poor widow washerwoman's song:

"Human hopes and human creeds,
Have their roots in human needs."

That is the pragmatic test of Christianity. Christ meets all the soul's needs. The other religions do not. To the woman at the wellside the Lord said, The Water that I shall give will slake all thirst and shall become like a flowing fountain bubbing up into everlasting life.

Our spiritual wants become dynamics of power by which we rise upwards to God. The heart that is void of want languishes, but blessed are those that want the deep things of Christ for they shall be satisfied.

Clay City, Indiana.

Church Loyalty During Summer Months

By M. E. Horner

In offering a few thoughts on the above subject there is but one standard to measure up to. That is the standard given by "The Book" and all through the pages of that sacred volume we are told of our duty to God and man. Our duty to God is first: He who has created and given us all good things which we enjoy in this life and points us to the greater and far more sublime in the life to come deserves our most faithful service. That is the test of our love and worthiness to be his disciple. And besides it has been said and proven true by so many faithful witnesses that real, true comfort, joy and happiness comes through loving service to our Lord and King. If this be true why excuse ourselves from the hour of joy and worship during the summer months.

There are fears in this present time that "the love that binds," is too easily severed by so many who absent themselves from the hour of worship, for pleasure at the lakes and groves. We all enjoy the beautiful shade, the balmy cool breeze about the waters. They are the creation of God and were pronounced "good." But too often we use them in a wrong way and their proper use is desecrated. They were never intended to lead us from God.

We are living in a day when family ties are frequently renewed by an annual meeting called a "reunion." The family reunions certainly are commendable but they should not work against our meeting with God. They should be held other than on the Lord's Day, not because it would be wrong to have a meeting of the kind on that day, but because it takes worshipers from their Christian duty. Just recently we attended a reunion when at the close a non-worshiper stood up and suggested the next reunion be held on Sunday so all would have time to attend. Then came the time as it often does, for those to speak who believe the worship of God of more value than even a family reunion: A number contended for a day when it would not interfere with the church service and in this case we won. We must show our colors and be loyal to God: Let us remember that it has been said that "neither heights nor depth, nor any other creature shall be able to separate us from the love of God, which is in Christ Jesus our Lord (Romans 8:39).

Goshen, Indiana.

Send
WHITE GIFT
OFFERINGS to

THE SUNDAY SCHOOL

ALBERT TRENT
General Secretary-Treasurer
Johnstown, Pennsylvania

Tithing—As a Recognition of God's Ownership and An Acknowledgement of Our Stewardship
By Mrs. Ira D. Slotter

Every beast of the forest is mine, and the cattle upon a thousand hills.

I know all the fowls of the mountains; and the wild beasts of the field are mine.

The silver is mine and the gold is mine, saith the Lord of hosts.

And again we read, The earth is the Lord's.

In the light of these facts, can we claim anything as our own? God owns the property, land, money and income which we call our own. It is God's world. This point many church members do not and will not recognize, much less acknowledge. Here the tithing system is vital. The teaching is that at least the tithe in a special sense belongs to God. We do not ask a person to tithe to pay the preacher, or the church debt, or build a new church, but we ask him to pay to God what already belongs to him. If a Christian will recognize God's ownership of the tithe, he will recognize God's ownership of all. He renders unto God the things which belong to God.

This disposition on the part of man to give material things to God is a creation or gift of the Spirit, hence Paul calls it a grace and his exhortation is, "See that ye abound in this grace also," that is, the grace of giving.

The church has been waiting for a hundred years to be taught a spiritual motive for giving. The time has come for the church to launch a systematic campaign, teaching the high motives and purposes of systematic stewardship; these purposes and motives to become life principles among Christian people, financially expressed by religiously giving at least the tithe to the work of the Lord.

Christian stewardship is a present day movement whose practical message is that the money test is the acid test of genuine devotion to the Kingdom of God. It's easy enough to exclaim, "All that I have is the Lord's," but the honesty of such words is proven only by laying down some definite and first proportion of income.

Dr. Henry Clay Trumbull puts it this way: "The Christian stewardship applies to the nine-tenths, the one-tenth not being given to us, to use as we may see fit. That is the Lord's from the beginning. The tithe is indeed the basket in which the Lord sends us the nine-tenths which he commits to our keeping. If we do not hand that right back to him we steal his basket. Could anything be meaner than that? Yet many men and women, members of Christian churches, have been storing up these stolen baskets for years, thus robbing God."

A modern Christian statesman put a great truth in a nutshell when he wrote: "The money that belongs by every right to God, but is kept back from him by his people, is probably the greatest hindrance to vital spirituality that there is in the world today."

The tithe is a debt of honor, a sacred and supreme obligation that rests upon every Christian believer. Trust God. The Christian, though he may be pinched by poverty, should remember that God will make nine cents go farther than ten and nine dollars go farther than ten dollars, when the tithe is faithfully paid. Only those disbelieve who have never trusted God enough to try it. Willing obedience in tithing will bring prosperity, financial and spiritual, and withal an overflowing joy and gladness of heart and mind, wholly unknown to all but the obedient.

"Honor the Lord with thy substance."

"He that honoreth me, him will I honor, saith the Lord."
Ashland, Ohio.

World's Sunday School Day, October 10th. By George S. Baer

In last week's issue we published a program prepared for use by the Sunday schools of the World on the Sunday when the World's Sunday School Association will be in session at Tokyo. It is an attractive responsive service, the work of Prof. H. Augustine Smith of Boston University and will doubtless commend itself to Sunday school leaders all over the brotherhood. It will be used by hundreds of delegates as an opening service at Tokyo on that Sunday and it will aid in bringing about a great feeling of world harmony and oneness to know that in all Sunday schools the world over the name of Christ is praised in the same forms of speech and on the same day. A limited number of copies of this program may be had by addressing the World's Sunday School Association, 216 Metropolitan Tower, New York.

THE SUNDAY SCHOOL CONVENTION IN JAPAN

Delegates are now on their way to the World's Sunday School Convention which will convene in Tokyo, Japan, October 5th. The first of ten tour parties sailed from Seattle on the "Fushimi Maru" July 30. They will be touring in Japan, Korea and China, returning to Tokyo just before the opening day of the Convention. Three other groups will sail on August 21, going from both Seattle and San Francisco. The last August tour party will be larger than the others and will sail on the "Empress of Asia" from Vancouver on the 26th. The "Asia" delegates will be joined at Shanghai by the "Fushimi" party on September 10th and together they will sail to Manila where a Sunday school Convention will be held. Sunday school workers in the Philippines are preparing to give this company of delegates an enthusiastic reception. On two different steamers these Convention pilgrims will proceed to South China where two or more conventions will be conducted at Hong Kong and Canton. Each of the outgoing and returning tour parties will hold similar conventions before and after the great Convention in Tokyo. Four steamers bearing convention delegates will sail from a Pacific port in September.

Tour Captains for Sunday School Pilgrims

Each tour party that goes to the Sunday School Convention in Tokyo will be captained by a special representative of the World's Sunday School Association. Those who have accepted this interesting work are: A. L. Moore, Pontiac, Michigan, on the "Fushimi"; Rev. E. F. Evemeyer, Easton, Pa., on the "Korea"; A. T. Arnold, Columbus, Ohio, on the "Asia"; W. J. Frank, Akron, Ohio, on the "Katori"; D. W. Sims, Raleigh, N. C., on the "Colombia"; George W. Penniman, Pittsburgh, Pa., on the "Monteagle"; W. G. Landes, Philadelphia, Pa., on the "Siberia"; Rev. Joseph Clark, D. D., Albany, N. Y., on the "Tenyo Maru;" Rev. W. E. Chalmers, D.D., Philadelphia, Pa., on the "Empress of Russia."

These men will begin their work by registering the delegates and supplying them with one of the Convention badges. On the "Monteagle" and the "Siberia Maru" each passenger will be wearing the Sunday school insignia since these boats are exclusively for those going to the Tokyo Convention. The captains of each vessel will be presented with a badge and thus made an honorary delegate.

The badge is decidedly picturesque. Mount Fujiyama is depicted with the sun rising over its snow-capped summit. In the lake at the base an island with a pine tree is shown.

and a boat is also seen. An open Bible is represented in the immediate foreground with the text indicated thereon: "I am the light of the world," John 9:5. A tori is placed around the general design. On the cross piece of the tori is the word "Tokyo" and on two sides are "W. S. S. A." and "1920." "I am the light of the world" is the Convention motto. This inscription appears on the credential and will also be placed on the large design which will be constructed in Tokyo and placed above the platform in the Convention hall.

Brazil will be well represented at the Convention. Rev. Alvaros dos Reis and a number of other representative Brazilians will leave Rio de Janeiro on August 17 for Tokyo via New York. Word has been received from Australia that a tour party is also being formed there. Two Egyptians will sail this month from Port Said that they may participate in the Convention and its program. All information concerning the Convention and the various tours can be obtained by addressing the World's Sunday School Association, 216 Metropolitan Tower, New York.

| J. A. Garber PRESIDENT | Our Young People at Work | G. C. Carpenter SECRETARY |

Some Games That We Like for Young People's Recreation

1. One-Finger Polo

We usually meet in the basement of the public library. The ceiling is low, but otherwise it is a fine room. A small, hard-rubber ball was put on the middle of the floor. The goals were two tables pushed against the wall at either end. It does not matter how many boys play. They choose even sides. In front of each table was a goal keeper. One boy from each side was chosen for a bucker. The buckers faced each other over the ball. The whistle blew, and each bucker tapped the floor with one finger, and then they tried for the ball with one finger only. A player was disqualified if he used more than one finger for a polo stick. If the ball was knocked behind the table without going between the front legs, the ball had to be brought to center and bucked over again. A "half" was five minutes. Sometimes we played "one-hand polo," when either hand, the whole hand, could be used in place of one finger.

2. Harness-Ring Shuffleboard

We bought six harness-rings and six curtain-rings, all made of wood. We set two polished tables end to end. Two feet from each end of this shuffleboard we drew a chalk-line all the way across. There were two boys on a side. Each partner had three rings of the same set. No. 1 slid, then an opponent, No. 3; then No. 2 slid, then an opponent, No. 4, until all six rings were slid. The idea was to knock your opponent's rings off the table, and place yourself in the best position beyond the chalk line. Touching the line counted one to go over it, two; and to go over the end, without falling off, three. Twenty-five was the game. Iron rings in place of wooden ones can be used if they don't scratch the table. Plain kitchen tables do very well if sand is sprinkled on them.

3. Waste-Basket Ball

We tied a waste-basket to a table-leg with a boy's belt. Then we took turns trying to throw a large, inflated rubber ball, about a foot in diameter, into the basket.

4. Comic Obstacle Race

Four boys ran in a heat. The course was like this: Over a table, under a table, over two hurdles made of brooms laid across chairs, over two chairs put back to back, under six brooms tied into a wigwam. Every racer had to carry a shoe in one hand and a broom in the other. The soft side of the broom was up. Sometimes we made the race harder by adding two tables. One table had to be vaulted. In getting across the other one it was a foul for the racer to touch his feet to the top of this table.

5. Jousting

This, of course, is done in various styles. We put ordinary old mattresses on the floor, as we had no gymnasium mats. A rope was tied from one table to another. Two boys were the horses. They got down on all fours on each side of the rope; but facing each other. Two smaller boys were

the riders, the knights. They took brooms for lances. The soft ends were the points. It got exciting when the knights tried to push each other off their horses with the brooms. It was against the rules to use hands or feet in unhorsing an adversary. And the horses were not allowed to help their riders.

6. Live Hurdles Outdoors

It took a lot of boys to work this wonderful outdoor race. Four boys knelt on the grass. They faced the same way, on all fours, and were close against one another. About ten feet further on there were four more boys, who acted as hurdles; and then another four—as many fours as we had boys to spare. At the whistle the first four boys stood up, ran, and jumped over all the other line of live hurdles, until they reached the end, when they quickly knelt down at the proper interval. Then the next further set stood up, and hurdled over the other sets. The race stopped after each set had run about six times. There was no winning team, but the game was great sport, and won big applause at our school field-day.—Christian Endeavor World.

West Park, N. Y.

TEST YOUR BIG SENTIMENT

About "love for humanity" by what you are doing to lead individuals to Jesus Christ.

Does the power of Christ in me reach others through me?

"It takes a philosopher to whistle and weep at the same time."

People who say they do not amount to anything, they cannot do anything, they have no talent, they do not know anything—never speak the truth.—Jefferson.

A holy man will have eyes to see holiness in others. Holiness is never hypercritical. Some men who claim a large degree of holiness, toward human weakness are merciless. The Son of God did not bring a railing accusation against the sinner. He was pitiful and full of compassion.—Reformed Church Messenger.

UNLIMITED BACKING

God never gives a command without giving with it the power to obey. A Scotch lord gave his old servant, Donald, a little farm. He said, "Donald, I am going to give you that little farm that you may work it for yourself and spend the rest of your days on your own property." Donald replied, "It is nae gude to gie me the farm; I have nae capital to stock it." His lordship looked at him and said, "I think I can manage to stock it also." "Oh, well," he said, "if it's you and me for it, I think we can manage it!"

SEND ALL MONEY FOR
General Home, Kentucky and
Foreign Missions to

MISSIONS

WILLIAM A. GEARHART
General Missionary Secretary
906 Conover Bldg., Dayton, O.

Mountain Mission News. By G. C. Carpenter

Evangelist Bowman

Splendid revival campaigns have been conducted at Krypton and Lost Creek by Brother L. D. Bowman. All will be interested in the final reports.

First Bible at Eighty

Miss Andrews, a mountain missionary told of Mr. John Black, who received his first Bible in the winter, and who, past eighty, may be seen almost any day sitting on his little porch painfully spelling his way through the New Testament, in which he has now read through Acts. It was before she told this that she said Mr. Black was changing and softening, and then we afterwards found out why.

Health Instruction Needed

Another mountain mission worker writes: "The mission work goes on slowly. At both of our stations we have been having mumps, chicken pox, measles, whooping cough and scarlet fever. The diseased children seem to be allowed to go wherever they like, and the

well ones are quarantined (by their parents). Nearly all the children at both stations have whooping cough. It looks like none will escape. The attendance at all services is cut down, of course."

Community Service

The editor of the "Soul-Winner" writes as follows of the work a consecrated woman is doing in a new and needy center.

"It is real community service that she is doing, though it is hard to get from her many of the details. Her cottage is nearing completion, and is now ready for the roof, and of course must be gotten under cover before fall. This cottage she hopes to make a real community center, with its garden in which she grows new vegetables never before heard of in the mountains, trying in this way to persuade the people to vary their diet and improve their health. Her pure bred chickens, and a good cow to serve as an incentive for them to improve their live stock. Through her sewing and cooking classes she is broad-

ening the interests of the women and children."

Dr. J. W. Tyler's Testimony

This appeal coming from the leader in the mountain mission work of another denomination ought to appeal to every loyal Brethren and insure his loyal support of the mission work of the Brethren church. Dr. Tyler says:

"Transformations are rapidly taking place in the Southern mountains and now is the time of all times in their whole history to be diligent and prayerfully earnest in hearing these 'cries from Macedon.' We believe that the next twelve months are beckoning us to a more rapid and fundamental realization of our dreams in these sections and that our church is given the supreme invitation of Providence just now to take the very leading part in causing the waste places of the mountains to "blossom as the rose." God grant that in the threefold way—by prayer, by activities, and by giving of our means—you and I may fill to the fullest the days, as one by one they stretch out into the beckoning months."

TITHING AND STEWARDSHIP DEPARTMENT

Some Tithing Testimonies By Tithers

Mrs. Ira D. Slotter, Ashland, Ohio:

"I have long believed in tithing and have long practiced it. Ever since the establishment of our home we have recognized the tithe as being sacred unto the Lord. The Lord's treasury receives its portion regularly, and this practice has brought into our lives one of our greatest blessings. The spiritual benefit received from tithing is the greatest good of all.

Mrs. Fred C. Vanator, Canton, Ohio:

"As my testimony, I want to tell the tithing experience of a church of which I was a member. It was a small church and had been struggling for years with finances. A new pastor took charge of that church and began to teach tithing. The people thought they ought to have a new church building so as to give room and encouragement for the growth of the Sunday school. The new pastor said nothing about a new church for a long time, but kept on teaching tithing and enrolling a tithing band. Finally the band reached an enrollment of 55. Every year the offerings to foreign missions and home missions increased as the number of tithers increased, the church grew and the spirituality was deepened. At last the time came when they were ready to build the new church. The pastor put the proposition up to the people and they were ready to undertake it. The new church was built and paid for in a remarkably short time when the members had learned how to give. The Lord kept his promise with that church when it fulfilled the conditions."

Mrs. George Stanley Baer, Ashland, Ohio:

"In the beginning tithing appealed to me from the standpoint of obedience and the hope of realizing the great promise of the open windows of heaven. I was not disappointed for in a few years my salary was doubled and the pleasure of giving "tithes and offerings" was beyond expression. And who can know the far-reaching results of the gifts? Now obedience has lost itself in the beauty of worship and in the pleasure and value of putting God first in all things. Of all other considerations this seems to me to be most important.

"While the giving of at least the tithe by all Christians would solve the financial difficulties of the church it is by no means the greatest thing that it would accomplish. If God's plan had embodied only closest observance. It will do that; but the paramount object of tithing is to build character. The foundation of all character building worthy of the name is a deeply implanted sense of dependence upon and responsibility to God. The motive of giving should be spiritual. Tithing puts God, not self, first in thought and life. It is obedience to Christ's command 'Seek first the Kingdom of God.'"

Mrs. H. C. Wertz, Crestline, Ohio:

"I tithe and I could not do any other way. Since I tithe I have dollars to give instead of nickles and dimes. And I think every member of the Brethren church ought to tithe if they believe in the sayings of Jesus: 'Give and it shall be given unto you.' I think if Christians would tithe the world would soon be converted."

Mrs. I. M. Murray, West Salem, Ohio:

"In the first place we believe tithing is God's plan and therefore take pleasure in following it.

"In the second place, we believe it is only giving back to God that part of our income which belongs to him. We do not believe we have any more right to use for ourselves the money that belongs to the Lord than we would your money if we held it in trust."

Mrs E. L. Kilhefner, Ashland, Ohio:

"I am truly grateful that for a number of years we have been giving as the Lord has prospered us. The tithing system is wonderful to me as it brings so many blessings in so many ways. Some might think it a sacrifice at first, but it soon becomes a very great privilege. Just to be able to supply a need, both in the church and wherever a real need is seen among the sick and poor, is a very great joy to me. I do believe most emphatically that God does prosper, and in a material way too, those who honor him."

Mrs. G. C. Carpenter, Peru, Indiana:

"Permit me to quote a great truth recently uttered by Dr. Ralph S. Cushman: 'The first requisite for a successful stewardship is a RIGHT MOTIVE. The acknowledgement of the ownership of ALL THINGS BY GOD by the setting aside of a definite proportion of the income is not, first of all, a matter of raising money to pay the church's debts or to solve its financial troubles. The acknowledgment is SPIRITUAL and is THE TEST OF CONSECRATION which SYSTEMATICALLY AND PROPORTIONATELY PLACES MONEY UPON THE ALTAR.'

"It is first a question of consecration. If

the heart gets right a faithful stewardship will follow. After years of tithing which has always been a pleasure I am glad to give my testimony in its favor and to assure my friends that it pays in every way to be honest with God. And in order to do that we need to adopt the divine plan and form the holy habit of giving systematically and proportionately of our resources and first of all to give ourselves in full consecration.

"Horace Bushnell said: 'One more revival, only one, is needed, the consecration of the money power to God. When that revival comes, the Kingdom of God WILL COME IN A DAY.'"

NEWS FROM THE FIELD

NEW PARIS, INDIANA

As we are just closing the conference year in our work with the good people of New Paris, we feel that a brief report of the year's activities will be of general interest. We take keen pleasure in giving this report for we have had an unusual year.

The active members of the church are working in perfect harmony, and all efforts that associate themselves with the greater work of the church, as indicated by General Conference, have been cared for with that degree of enthusiasm and support that characterize our larger churches (larger in membership.)

We do not deem it wise to give a review of definite items, for this can easily be found in the Conference Reports. But to those interested directly in our work, we take pleasure in being able to say that if the work would go any better we would be compelled to turn our services over into a jubilee.

Possibly a few definite examples will serve to illuminate. After caring for all our "goal" obligations, and in many instances going so far beyond as to lose sight of the "goal," the membership began to look about for new "goals" to conquer. About this time the pastor was compelled to undergo an operation that placed him in the hospital for a time and we were obliged to forego our church service for a period of three weeks. During our convalescence, a representative of the membership, with his good wife, called upon us, and in the name of the membership of the New Paris church presented us with a generous supply of vegetables and fruit; and, will wonders never cease! a purse of ($225.00) two hundred and twenty-five dollars. There! the secret is out. Does anyone wonder why the New Paris church is prospering when a spirit so magnanimous and unselfish is extant?

W. I. DUKER.

LONG BEACH ITEMS

The local district Conference, held as usual in our church, the last ten days in July, afforded unusual opportunities of spiritual uplift. It was a privilege to have with us again Dr. French E. Oliver; also Brother Cobb of Dayton, Ohio. The Conference secretary will give a complete report of these sessions.

Immediately following the Conference Brother Bauman left for Washington where he is to give a series of addresses on prophecy, at the Northwest District Conference held in Sunnyside; and afterwards at Spokane. He will leave Washington to attend the National Conference at Winona; from there he goes to Washington, D. C., for a two weeks' Bible conference, before returning to Long Beach the last of September.

During Brother Bauman's absence, the assistant of the pastor, Brother Percy Yett, will

have charge of the work. Part of the time the pulpit will be occupied by our own boys who have been attending Xenia Seminary. Also Brother Rush, who with his wife, hopes to start for Africa, before long. Mrs. Rush is a sister of Mrs. Rollier, who gave her life for that field.

This past week our annual Sunday school gathering was held at Bixby Park, located about a block from the ocean. This year we enjoyed a family basket picnic with about three hundred in attendance. Brother Yett skillfully directed the sports, after which many jolly groups went to the beach for a dip in the surf.

A great many of our workers are away on vacations at present. From this number we are expecting to have a representation of at least twelve at the National Conference. Last week Sister Rush and Sister Srack left for the east enroute to National Conference. They will stop at different churches in the brotherhood, showing a new set of stereopticon slides from our missionaries in Africa.

MRS. FRANCES NIELSEN.

ARMSTRONG COUNTY FIELD

As soon as college closed we hastened to our home in Indiana and after having spent a week there we moved on to old Pennsylvania. When we arrived on the field and saw the place in which we were to spend our vacation we never have had the privilege of being in the eastern hills before. Arriving in Kittanning in the dead of night, due to the high water at that time, we didn't see anything of the place until the next morning. On looking out of the window the following morning I saw that the town was wedged in between two hills. With little difficulty we found the home of Brother J. Herbert John, who is the superintendent of the West Kittanning Sunday school. Brother John and his fine wife sure know how to make a person feel at home. I have been in their home during my stay here and I have come to regard it as my home. Brother John is an old A. C. man and as a result we have spent many happy hours in living over student life on the hill. We have one young man who is counting on going to Ashland this fall and several others who may go.

Brush Valley

This place has been well named as it is all grown up with brush especially around the church. I will never forget the impression that part of the country made upon me at first sight. I thought that must have been the last place God created and that he had to hurry to get done as it was getting dark Saturday night. He must not have had time

to arrange the forest anyway. I thought that we had some crooked roads out in Indiana, but they are all straight. When I started for this place they told me to get on the Pittsburgh and Shamut Railroad, a coal road, then to get off at Dickey, taking the left road and going around a bend I would find a watering trough by the road, then a schoolhouse; I thought that would be easily done. Well, I got off and started up the road as they told me but the one bend that was to bring me to the watering trough proved to be about half a dozen. It was a long old tramp but we finally arrived at Sister Hooks' in time for dinner. They were not expecting me and as a result they had two preachers for that week. Brother Smith Meyers of Scottdale was there too. I spent my first week out there and visited the members. Tramp, tramp, tramp, was all that I got done. I found the people down among the hills and was surprised to see that it was so thickly settled. The people gave us a hearty welcome every place we went and we didn't need to go hungry either.

I found a Front Line Sunday school and a growing one too. Brother C. L. Hooks, the superintendent, is sure some worker and deserves praise for placing the school where it is. He has an efficient corps of workers and he is busy training others. His Teacher Training class took their last examination last Sunday, (August 15) and now they are going to take an advanced course. The people out there are some stickers when they once take hold. All that began this course finished and that is something that cannot be said of very many classes. We have organized a Christian Endeavor at this place and it is remarkable how the young people take a hold and get behind the movement. The second Sunday we took up a collection for the Kentucky work and the young people raised $3.02. We have about twenty-seven that have signed pledges but in a short time this number will be greatly increased. The prospects are for a good and flourishing society at this place. There had been no regular services here since Brother Smith left, but it only took a little while for all to get back at work again. I never saw a place where people attend church as they do out here. The church is filled and often there are more on the outside listening through the windows than the number who have managed to get on the inside. People go for miles and never think a thing about it. The church building that we now have isn't large enough to hold the crowds and besides it is old and inadequate for Sunday school purposes. We are counting on starting our new church building in the spring and that will be a big boom for the church. They are raising money now and the indications are that the largest part will be paid into the treasury before the building is started.

Beginning on August 9 we began a week's meeting, holding our communion on Friday evening and then continuing the meeting over Sunday. The weather man was against us all week. It rained every day and the roads were almost impassable but yet the people came. It doesn't make any difference how hard it rains you can expect some out to church. Although the results were not what they should have been we had a fine meeting. Four made the great confession and on Friday afternoon we baptized three and the other is going to be baptized in the near future. Sunday evening a part of the West Kittanning choir came out to help with the music but due to rain only one-third got there. We thank the Lord for the success he gave us even if the weather was against ut.

On the Sundays that I preach at Brush Valley I have been going down to the Meyers school house and preaching. Here they have a fine Union Sunday school and a splendid troop of workers. Friday evening, August 13 after the communion services the people came around and presented their pastor with a purse for his birthday present. It wasn't empty, either. The good people had placed about thirty dollars in it. It was a surprise to us but we appreciated the way they remembered our birthday.

West Kittanning

At first sight the work here looked very discouraging but after a rather close investigation we found that it wasn't as bad as we first anticipated. We have about fifty members but they are scattered all over this part of the state of Pennsylvania. In fact we only have about twelve members in West Kittanning and about that many in Kittanning and Wick City but the distance, river and the hill makes it impossible for them to attend regularly. We have several dozen down at Cudagon but unless you have an auto it is too far to go. The Sunday school at this place is a Union affair and is not even manned by Brethren people. We have a Brethren superintendent and the teacher of the adult class is a Brethren man. I find that all the Christian people are ready and willing to fall in line and work to make things go. The people are loyal and have given exceptionally good support. We have a Sunday school that averages about eighty-five and the high water mark is one hundred sixty-five. We are planning to go beyond this before long. An effort is going to be made to get a 100 per cent attendance plus on the day of our Teachers' Training graduation exercises. Some day this possibly can be made a Brethren school but at present it is advisable to let it remain Union.

The church had never been completely organized up to the last preaching service when we re-organized the work. The members seem to be taking a new interest in the work. We are going to ordain two deacons and one deaconess after the services on August 22. The finances of the church are in better condition than they ever have been before. The prospects for a Brethren church are good if things are worked right. It is going to take some hard work and time but I believe that it can

be made self supporting inside of the next five years. If we can get a strong Brethren evangelist upon the field and then concentrate our efforts for the next few years things will come our way. We have a fine building and when it is finished it will house us for years but right now we are sadly in need of the basement for Sunday school purposes. I know if we set ourselves at the task the West Kittanning work can be well established.

FLORIZEL PFLEIDERER.

LINWOOD REPORT

The church of Linwood has held no conspicuous place in the "report" columns of our church paper of late. This privilege has been denied her by reason of the fact that for several years the church has been without a permanent pastor. The writer has served the church at Linwood throughout the summer months, and now at the expiration of his temporary term thinks it not presumptuous to write a few words in behalf of the Brethren of Linwood.

Even as the picturesque village itself might well be the pride of Maryland, so might the Brethren church in that town be Linwood's boast. The church building is modern. I have found few country churches that can compete with it from the standpoint of a building. At the end of the town, upon a slight elevation where one may stand and see the purple summits of the Blue Ridge Mountains, 'surrounded by the exquisite scenery that characterizes the Golden-rod State, stands our Brethren church. Her high, eminent bell-tower may be seen for miles around. And when the tones of the high-hung bell reverberate across the hills, we are glad to say that with few exceptions the entire community responds to the call.

The structure of the church is of stone and brick. It is electrically equipped throughout, even to an electric reading lamp on the pulpit. The pews are of oak and highly polished, and the platform furniture is heavy and richly carved. On either side of the auditorium proper is a Sunday school room, and beneath is a spacious basement. This beautiful little church (it may be noteworthy) was built through the generosity of a dozen members some fifteen years ago, and if is a church that ten dozen charitable members might be proud of. I am reminded of several country churches that have come under my observation that were well nigh ready to totter and fall for the want of repairs or rebuilding, while on the outside stood a score or more automobiles! Oh shame! To let the place you worship God in decay while the thing you have your pleasure in glitters and glares with attention and care!

The people that worship in the Linwood church are just as splendid, every whit, as the church structure itself. Socially, they are hospitable (in the Southern sense), exceptionally kind, and the sort of people that when you enter their abodes you may hang your hat up, and feel "at home." And if I am allowed to use the church paper as a medium of expressing my gratitude I wish to thank the following folk for their almost inimitable kindness and entertainment while among them: Brethren and Sisters Drach, Essler, Koontz,

Dahoff, L. Messler, W. Messler, Englar, and Stem.

Now, spiritually as well as socially the Linwood church is to be lauded. The fires of religious zeal burned low without a leader, but it did not take much to rekindle them. The attendance in general has been doubled during the summer, and the smouldering Christian Endeavor Society is now aflame again. "But," said a member last Sabbath, contemplating the fact that the old regime of a "preacher every other Sunday," will soon have to be resumed, "but—we will soon be back in our old slump again." Oh, I would that Linwood had a permanent pastor! How natural it is for a church to fall into a "slump" when there is no leader among them to spend time in "the personal-touch work," to create and maintain spiritual enthusiasm, to "preach the Word," and to "be INSTANT in season and out of season; reprove, rebuke, exhort with all longsuffering and DOCTRINE." How natural! It is a thing to be profoundly regretted that our staggering churches are without help BECAUSE they are without pastors. If there were no other reason in all the world for a prosperous church to give HEAVILY to the "College Endowment Campaign," the cause of pastorless churches should be sufficient For a strong college spells strong leaders,— and many; and many strong leaders spells many strong churches. Does it not?

Without further deviation,—here's a pleasant retrospection of the summer at Linwood and a hopeful prayer for her immediate future.

EARL H. DETSCH.

Philadelphia, Pa.

CAMPAIGN NOTES

The last report from Maryland and Virginia district for the present comes from Roanoke, Mountain View, and Garden City. There are a few points in this district to be visited at some later time.

Roanoke

This being the last group of churches visited in the Maryland and Virginia campaign naturally I landed at Roanoke very much worn out. But Brother L. G. Wood did all in his power to make my work light. Though deprived in his early life of attending school at Ashland, Brother Wood is nevertheless one of the most ardent supporters in the brotherhood of our college. And viewing with keen interest the campaign for endowment from the very beginning, Brother Wood had for many months faithfully reminded his people of the challenge that would come to them in the interest of our only school. Hence I found the Roanoke people thoroughly conversant with the campaign. I also found here a splendid lot of young people, two of whom will enter college this fall at Ashland. This, I am sure, is due in very large part to the influence of the pastor on the lives of these two young people.

I am able to report for Roanoke at this time a little more than $1,800 for endowment. However, I consider myself fully warranted in saying that when the final word is spoken by Roanoke, whether it be in the immediate future, or the more remote future, the college and the brotherhood will have occasion for rejoicing. We had one gift here that belongs in the $1,000 class—it was a little more than that. We also had a $200 gift; and from that on down to smaller gifts. But when I speak thus I do not forget that very often what may seem to be a small gift, may, from the standpoint of sacrifice be a very large gift indeed. The Sunday school, the Y. P. S. C. E., and the W. M. S. each had a part in the Roanoke result. I shall remember with much pleasure the various homes in this congregation wherein I was shown the rarest of hospitality; And especially shall I remember gratefully Brother and Sister Wood for their kindness to me in many ways, among which was the "Ford way."

Mountain View

The Mountain View congregation is mostly rural and it worships in a beautiful little church property out several miles from Roanoke amid some of the fine mountain scenery of Virginia. I was at this place for a Sunday afternoon service. But I want to say that though this was not a regular time for their service and though the notice was very short, and notwithstanding rain, I preached to a fine audience; and in that audience there were not a few young people too. Brother J. E. Patterson is serving this people as pastor. I was very glad for the privilege of making his acquaintance. He operates successfully a truck farm during the week and preaches on Sundays. And I found him interested in Ashland College and anxious that both himself and his people should have a part in the campaign for endowment. It is never hard to do business under such conditions. The result at this church was a little better than $550, which was every good. We had here one $200 gift, also several $100 gifts. And the Sunday school also helped. I am glad to have met Brother Patterson and his people, and I am sure I wish them God's abundant blessing upon their labors for him.

Garden City

Garden City is another rural congregation out in another direction from Roanoke. Brother Wood took me out to preach in this congregation on Monday night, and while Monday night is not always the most favorable night for preaching, yet I had a good audience at this place too. Brother G. D. Dunahoo is the pastor of this congregation. He too operates a truck farm for his livelihood, and preaches on Sunday. This congregation is yet young and struggling. It has had to build for itself a place for worship and now the debt is almost paid off on the building. And I can say for Brother Dunahoo that while in stature he belongs in the "Zacchaeus" class, yet, he was not "up in a tree" on the matter of college endowment. He was very sure that he wanted himself and his people to have an opportunity to give to endowment. And he was one of the men, who, so to speak, came down the road to meet me to talk endowment with me. Oh, how rare and sweet is the memory of such folks! I met Brother Dunahoo at his market stand on a Roanoke street. And while he sold cabbage, and beets, and beans, and huckleberries, I fixed up the note; and while he signed the note I took charge of the market trade and I didn't cut prices either. Well,

COLLEGE ENDOWMENT

| |
| 200 000 |
| 190 000 |
| 180 000 |
| 170 000 |
| 160 000 |
| 150 000 |
| 140 000 |
| 130 000 |
| 120 000 |
| 110 000 |
| 100 000 |
| 90 000 |
| 80 000 |
| 70 000 |
| 60 000 |
| 50 000 |
| 40 000 |
| 30 000 |
| 20 000 |
| 10 000 |

Our Goal: 200,000; We Can and We Must

we had a good time anyhow, didn't we, Brother Dunahoo? And this little congregation went $135 for endowment. The Sunday school at this place also had a part.

This brings Maryland and Virginia up to $13,000. We wanted it to be at least $15,000 or even more. Among the number who helped to create this result are many who did their downright, level best. Then there are some that just "nibbled." And sad to say, there are some that were willing to lose out entirely and not even attempt to stretch a tug. Of course quite a few who belong in that class know exactly what I think of that type of "Brethren loyalty," because I told them frankly. And I may say here that since a very early period in the endowment campaign, peoples' loud assertions of Brethren loyalty have been mere cheap, empty words with me, when, in the next minute those same people would "excuse themselves out" or "hard luck story" themselves out from giving a single dollar to our one and only institution that stands for the express purpose of raising up men who, in the future will perpetuate and preach the doctrines of the Brethren church. To resume, I still hope and pray that the slackers in Maryland and Virginia and also the "nibblers" may yet repent and "bring forth fruit meet for repentance." But I want to register this testimony that I greatly enjoyed my canvass in this district and shall always remember the many noble people I met in the various churches where I visited. May God richly bless and lead forward the great district comprising Maryland and Virginia. The mercury is now $159,000.

WM. H. BEACHLER,
Campaign Secretary.

P. S. Since making my report for the churches around Harrisonburg a hundred dollar gift has been received from an isolated member of the Dayton, Virginia, congregation. This puts Dayton $276 for the present.

W. H. B.

FOREIGN MISSIONARY BOARD MEETINGS

The Board of the Foreign Missionary Society will meet for the transaction of business during the week of Conference at Winona Lake, the first session being at one o'clock, on Monday, August 30th at the Inn.

J. ALLEN MILLER, President.

LOST CREEK, KENTUCKY

On July 31st, Elder I. D. Bowman came to us from Krypton, for a series of meetings of two weeks' duration. For about five weeks we had been preaching sermons preparatory to this revival effort. At our Wednesday night prayer meeting, i e., the one just preceding the opening of the revival effort, five confessed the Christ, and the next day were buried in baptism. This all made a good setting for revival meeting.

Brother Bowman came on Saturday, and the meetings began in earnest. There were some handicaps,—the dark nights, the high humidity making the most sultry weather we think we ever experienced, and the rains, which never let up during the second week of the meetings. But nothing daunted our brother in his work; he labored most earnestly, and efficiently. His sermons were wonderful revelations of the Word. And when the Word is preached in its entirety and fullness, with nothing out out, but God justly honored by such preaching, there are bound to be results. "My word shall not return unto me void." Indeed fortunate is the congregation that has the whole Bible preached as Brother Bowman preached it. The visible results were twelve confessions and baptisms. This with the five just preceding it, made a total of seventeen for the period.

But another important result was the strengthening of the membership. This was seen in different ways, but especially was it so with some of the moonshiners. Some such, who had not been coming to services, came to these services and we believe that they were much helped. We shall try hard to conserve this result, and in the future we believe that it will b a big help in the work. Really, the persons above referred to, had dropped out of service, i. e., out of the church service for the service of John Barleycorn. We are highly pleased to see them show evidences of dropping his service now.

Our revival closed on Sunday evening with a baptismal service, followed by the communion service. The severe rain storm doubtless kept a number away from these services, as it came just before the time of meeting. But as it was, there were about thirty-five around the tables, and among these some new faces. We had a happy, blessed time in the Lord, and all felt strengthened.

Another evidence of the growing spiritual power here was the offering Sunday. This was $55.40. It was much the best single offering we have ever had here, and came with less coaxing than heretofore. When we remember that Riverside has no work of any kind about it, save a little farming, that it is located in a really non-profit-producing community, and that the old folks have control of what money there is here, we felt very good over it. We thought it good. We believe the time is not very far away, when conditions will wonderfully change in this valley about Riverside, i. e., conditions financially.

The school is progressing quite well, considering the lack of help. The school rooms are now overcrowded. It is very lamentable that we cannot at all properly take care of all who want to come to Riverside. We are told by some that we have reached the time when the grade work ought to be dropped, and the church cease supporting it. Outside of the workers, we now have twenty-two boarders at the dormitories. All of these are doing grade work but one. Were we to drop the grade work now, we could not have much use for some of the things that money has been spent for. Then all the other mission points similar to Riverside, ARE DOING THE GRADE WORK. And only a few days ago, Brother Bowman and I rode by a place where eight or ten wagons were loading up building material for a dormitory about 20 miles from us, and they there, instead of dropping out the grade work, are even making greater preparations for continuing it. It is very plain to us now that if we are going to let the conditions be the guide, the evidence is all for the grade work yet. If there are any "doubt-

ing Thomases," we would like to have you investigate the matter and learn the conditions not theoretically but experimentally. We now have a bunch of three children here, all from the same family, but father and mother dead. These children are all in the grade work. From Krypton there are now eight children in school, all in the grade work. The mother of three of these left $5 here for these children to put into the offerings Sundays. Brother and Sister Rempel now have their oldest child in school here, in the grade work.

Thus through the grade work, we get much the largest number of pupils, both boarders and otherwise. These give their offerings here, when in school, and better than all, come under Brethren influence. If we did no grade work, these all would go to the schools where they give it, and thus we would lose them very largely for Brethrenism. The public schools are yet, and will be for some time to come, in such a condition that parents will not send to them. This is hard for some to see, as it is in the United States. but such it is.

Pray for us, that we may only be led by him who never leads wrongly, and that in no way may we get or go ahead of his leading in all things. Lord help us, that we may not be deceived, and that we may not lag too far behind his leading.

             G. E. DRUSHAL.

HOLIDAYSBURG, PENNSYLVANIA

According to a promise I made to some of my people I will give a report of a meeting I recently held on the field recently made pastorless owing to the recent death of our highly esteemed Brother Edward Byers. Prior to the sad accident resulting in his death, I promised to give him some assistance in his work, owing to his school work he was necessitated to neglect a portion of his church work, especially on the farthest portion of the field. I agreed to hold a short meeting at what is known as the "Bunker Hill" and "Liberty" churches providing my physical condition would permit. They had not had a communion for three years. Well, we went, and met the enemy with a straggling, almost disorganized army, but at the bugle call we were surprised to see how they did rally and meet the enemy, neither asking or giving "quarter." For two weeks we did our best, then had one week's rest and went to work for another siege. In our three weeks' effort we baptized thirteen and received them into the fellowship with the church.

Quite a few others were worked over, or "renewed" as some say, yet I never felt like reporting "prodigals" as additions.

The communion was well attended, we had the pleasure of having Brother Arthur DeLozier and wife with us at most of our meetings and Brother DeLozier preached a couple of splendid sermons during their stay, as they were visiting Sister DeLozier's parents who are members of the Bunker Hill congregation. Brother Himes, her father, is the only deacon in both churches.

I feel justified in saying that the additions the church received at this meeting are all from the ranks of the Sunday school and ranging in age from 35 years down to 10 and means a great deal more to the church at that

place than can be described by tongue or pen.

I presented a plan for their future consideration and assured success, and if the plan goes through the church at large will rise up and take notice. I will try and supply them with preaching until they can secure a pastor. I would advice any young man who wants to work to glorify God and save men, desiring a field with unlimited resources as to a pro-life field, to apply here. As to finances I would say they had no promise as to monies when we began and none in sight, however at the end of three weeks, they gave me $75 and a nice substantial amount over to place in the treasury for future needs. I can't say like our dear Brother Bowman that I took the money reluctantly. I took mine mightily gladly. I earned it and the "labor is worthy his hire" and the church was ahead.

I think paying helps a congregation the same as a curry-comb helps a poor horse—it helps to stretch the hide and assists in the fattening process. And as they grow larger in giving, more will be given them, pressed down and running over.

Yours looking for the Kingdom,

       E. H. SMITH, R. R. No. 1.

PERU, INDIANA

A class in Expert Endeavor is just finishing the course. A hot weather contest in the Endeavor society proved a real help during the summer.

Two members were received into the church by baptism on Sunday, August 15.

We are planning on the "Largest Yet" delegation to Conference.

The Sunday school has made a good summer record. Loyal teachers is the secret of winning out in Sunday school work. Our corps of teachers deserve much praise.

The pastor and his wife are moving soon into the "log cabin" parsonage. The house which is weatherboarded will make a cozy home when some improvements are completed. The church has rented the house but the scarcity of houses and the sale of the house in which the pastor was living brought about the decision of the pastor and his wife to begin life over again in a "little log cabin" on the Wabash. The location is ideal and will be a fine spot for a new parsonage at some future time. "The Little Brown Church" and the "Log Cabin Parsonage" make a fitting combination. Call on us and find an old fashioned welcome.

       GEO. C. CARPENTER.

BETHLEHEM, BRETHREN CHURCH
Near Harrisonburg, Virginia

We have been silent for some time but not our hearts and hands. We have been unusually busy during the last few weeks. Brother J. A. McInturff of Goshen, Indiana, came here July 18 and began a meeting which closed in two weeks with 17 confessions, 13 being received into the Brethren church. Two came by relation and two are yet to be baptized. Brother McInturff preached powerful sermons. Every line of church work is going fine. Several from here expect to attend General Conference. Pray for us.

       MRS. G. C. POWELL,
       Corresponding Secretary.

Volume XLII
Number 34

September 1
1920

The BRETHREN EVANGELIST

-ONE·IS·YOUR·MASTER·AND·ALL·YE·ARE·BRETHREN-

SOME BRETHREN PUBLICATIONS
FOR BRETHREN PEOPLE

Are these coming into your home?

NO PAPER NEXT WEEK

Published every Wednesday at Ashland, Ohio. All matter for publication must reach the Editor not later than Friday noon of the preceding week.

George S. Baer, Editor

The
Brethren
Evangelist

When ordering your paper changed give old as well as new address. Subscriptions discontinued at expiration. To avoid missing any numbers renew two weeks in advance.

R. R. Teeter, Business Manager

OFFICIAL ORGAN OF THE BRETHREN CHURCH

Subscription price, $2.00 per year, payable in advance.
Entered at the Post Office at Ashland, Ohio, as second-class matter.
Acceptance for mailing at special rate of postage provided for in section 1103, Act of October 3, 1917, authorized September 9, 1918.
Address all matter for publication to Geo. S. Baer, Editor of the Brethren Evangelist, and all business communications to R. R. Teeter, Business Manager, Brethren Publishing Company, Ashland, Ohio. Make all checks payable to the Brethren Publishing Company.

TABLE OF CONTENTS

EDITORIAL

Should the Small Denomination Make Its Own Literature?

Should the small denomination, such as our own, make its own literature? There are so many large and well-equipped publishing houses, with large funds and great writers at their command, that can put out religious literature of every imaginable kind to suit every possible occasion at the very lowest cost; is it advisable for small denominations to build their own publishing houses and make their own medium of communication, or paper, and it must make its own. denominations, and save the money that would be required to make our own literature and use it in missions and the building of new churches? It costs as much to make a Brethren Sunday school quarterly as it does to make a Baptist, or a Presbyterian, or a Methodist quarterly, and yet there is only one chance to sell a Brethren quarterly to fifty chances to sell a quarterly made by the Northern Baptist church, or to fifty-five of the Presbyterian, or to a hundred and fifty of the Methodist Episcopal. A fair estimation is that for every Brethren quarterly made and sold, there are at least a hundred and fifty Methodist Episcopal quarterlies made and sold. About the same ratio obtains with regard to other forms of Sunday school and church literature. When it comes to permanent church literature, the contrast is even more discouraging from our standpoint. When we compare wealth, facilities, constituency and consequent demand for religious literature, we are so insignificantly small, we are made to wonder if we can ever make a worth-while church literature, or whether indeed it is advisable for us to try it.

But we do not wonder long until we have forced home upon us the answer,—We must make our own literature if we would live; it is necessary to our denominational existence. No church can live without its own church literature, for it is by that means that it indoctrinates and denominationalizes its people more than in any other way. It is just as essential that a church shall have its own publishing house as that it shall have its own educational institutions or its own missionary agencies and enterprises. A church must have its own medium of communication, or paper, and it must make its own. It must have its own Sunday school helps in order to give to its own children and young people as they grow up its own approach and method of interpretation of the Bible. It must create its own books and pamphlets for the defence of its distinctive practices and doctrines. No other church will do that for us. Our denominational existence depends on our having our own church literature; and if we are to have it, we must make it. And if we are to make it, we must have our own publishing house, supply our own equipment and use our own men. It would have been much cheaper to have bought our religious literature of some large and well-equipped house than to

have gone to the expense of buying our own building, machinery and labor required to make it ourselves, but we could not buy a literature that would carry our distinctive message. And because we believe we have such a message and have a desire to preserve its character and to spread it abroad, we must pay the cost of making our own literature.

This cost involves three requirements, three different manifestations of loyalty—buying and using our own literature, doing what we can with the pen to make our own literature and helping to supply our church with the necessary equipment and funds with which to make it.

If we are to make our own church literature, our own church people must use it. We cannot expect to sell it to another denomination. Our patrons must be those of Brethren faith. When we cease to sell our output to Brethren people, our Publishing Company will go bankrupt. No such danger seems to threaten us, however. The support we have received is a matter of much gratification to all concerned. Taking our brotherhood as a whole, there is perhaps less cause for complaint now than there has ever been regarding buying from other publishing houses supplies that ought to be bought from our own. This is doubtless due to two things: (1) the increasing loyalty of our people and (2) the growing quality of our own publications. Nevertheless, in view of the extensive advertising and insistent bids of non-denominational publishing houses for the patronage of Christians of every faith, we must not fail to remind ourselves occasionally of the importance of loyalty to our own denomination in this particular. No non-denominational supplies, whatever be their character, are as good for Brethren people as similar supplies that can be secured from our own Publishing House. And the more loyally Brethren people support Brethren publications, the higher will be the quality of those publications. Brethren support at this point is absolutely essential to the maintenance of a worth-while church literature.

Another requisite to the building up of a Brethren literature is the training and practice in writing on the part of our own people. Not only must we publish our own literature, but we must write it as well. We cannot ask others to do that for us, and they could not if we should wish them to do so. We have not given the attention that we ought to the service of the pen. Our young people have grown unable to write, not because they were incapable of doing so, but mainly because no one has seriously brought before them the importance of such service, nor held up to them the opportunity. It is a form of service that God has wonderfully blessed; it has had an untold influence in world advancement and the growth of the Kingdom. The men whose messages have lived to bless the world, are the men who, with all their other accomplishments, learned how to write. The churches that have the best denominational literature are the churches that have given most attention to the encouragement of writers. We need preachers who can speak well, but we need also preachers who are able to write. By developing their writing abilities they become the better preachers. We need laymen trained to do the work of the church and that are able to grapple with the many problems of life, but we also need laymen who can and will write for the enlightenment of others concerning life's problems and Christian activity. If we are to have a periodical literature of increasing value, and if we are to have a permanent literature that is worthy of our denomination and that will meet our needs, we must discover many among us who shall be willing to pay the cost of learning to write by careful training and patient toil.

Our third great need, and one that is indispensible to the making of a worthy denominational literature, is financial backing. We can scarcely make the official organ of our church on the subscription price alone. It is doubtful if there is any church paper published that is a money making proposition; in fact it is hard to find one that pays for itself. No fortune is to be made in the selling of Sunday school literature when separate supplies are made for the various departments and classes, according to the requirements of modern Sunday school methods, especially with a constituency so small as our own. The making of books is inadvisable from a money standpoint when the only market we can hope to have for them is within the confines of the Brethren church. And so it can be easily seen how necessary it is that the Brethren Publishing House shall be supplied with funds outside its regular sources of income, if it is to be able to make for Brethren people a denominational literature that will meet their needs. The day has come when we ought to begin talking Endowment for a Brethren Literature. Money could scarcely be given to a more worthy cause than the publishing of a literature calculated to bring to the hearts and minds of men and women at home and abroad the "whole gospel" of our Lord and Savior, Jesus Christ. And few needs are more vital to the life and growth of the Brethren church than the making of an adequate denominational literature.

Should we make our own denominational literature?
We ought!
Can we do it?
We can, if we will!
"We can have it, if we want it; if we want it hard enough."

EDITORIAL REVIEW

Brother W. B. Sell of Fredonia, Kansas, reports a number of accessions to the Brethren faith.

We call your attention to a "review" in this issue written by Brother T. Darley Allen of a pamphlet entitled "The Ethics of Dancing."

The Indiana District Conference program is to be found in this issue of the Evangelist, sent us by the secretary, Brother C. C. Grisso. The Conference is to be held at Flora, Indiana, October 4 to 7.

A successful evangelistic campaign was conducted in the church at Columbus, by Miss Emma Aboud, as reported by the pastor, Brother S. E. Christiansen.

If you are not now getting all our periodical publications, take a glance at the picture on front page, see what ones you have not and get them coming to your home.

It is of little worth for one to say he honors Christ and then stand before him eclipsing his glory, causing all eyes to be turned upon him instead of his Lord.

There is no path that leads to "yesterday," so it behooves men to take time to live this day aright, that there may be no need of wishing it might be lived over again.

The last light of lingering day is God's smile before night falls. It seems to say, "I am with you through all the darkness, and will bring to you a new dawn."—The Methodist Protestant.

If your church is not on the Honor Roll, we invite you to write us for some sample copies of this issue, place them in the hands of those who are not subscribers of The Evangelist and get their subscriptions.

However much American Christians have given to the relief of the distressed millions in war-devastated and famine-stricken lands, they have not finally discharged their obligation so long as there are people who are starving and homeless while we revel in plenty and even luxury.

He who would win men from their indifference and sin, must be more concerned about his possession of Christ than his profession of Christ. Nothing will be more quickly resented by the man of exemplary life than the effort of a nominal but inconsistent Christian to lead him to Christ.

From the "land of Goshen," Indiana, comes a report over the signature of Brother M. E. Horner, the corresponding secretary of the Goshen church. The pastor, Brother McInturff, has been enjoying a vacation, but the work has not been allowed to lag during his absence, as you will see by reading this letter.

Brother E. M. Riddle's report shows that Louisville is a "church with a future" and that the people there have gotten a vision of a "Greater Brethren Church." And who could doubt its realization with such a happy combination of efficient leadership, a loyal church and a growing town?

Jesus' promise to be with us alway was made on the assumption that we would be on the go into all the world. The professing Christian who idles his time and is not busy about his Father's business, need not complain if he fails to sense the presence of his Lord. He could hardly be with the idler, for he said, "My Father worketh hitherto and I work."

The kind of Christians the church is sadly in need of is the kinds that keep everlastingly at it. There are brilliants that glare for a moment and then disappear like a skyrocket. But no worth-while piece of work was ever accomplished by the light of "fireworks." Give me rather the steady light of the humble lamp and I will keep the gospel light in the window of the church the whole night through.

We are told that character is vitally affected by associations and therefore we should not be indifferent as to who our friends are. That is true. But how often have we lowered the ideals and weakened the lives of those with whom we have associated. Let us consider the influence we have been wielding when we are about to shun the association of others.

Another message comes from our missionary party in Africa and our readers will rejoice to know that notwithstanding frequent illness on the part of various members of the party, they have been steadily blessed with a return of health and that conditions seem to be improving. They are doing some splendid work in the way of translating the Bible and other missionary helps into the several languages of the people with whom they are to work.

Brother N. J. Paul, a contractor and builder, living at Loaantville, Indiana, and who occasionally writes articles for The Evangelist, says, "It certainly affords me great pleasure to write you my appreciation of our church paper. I enjoy writing for it as well as reading it. As I understand, the paper has about 5,000 or more circulation (About 5,500 at present.—Editor), and of these 5,000 papers going into Christian homes I wonder how many are passed out ta non-professing Christians. It seems to me that we ought to use our good paper for missionary work, for getting hold of those who never come to the house of God. There ought to be some means devised in our churches whereby the Evangelist could be used to carry the glad tidings to those around us. Suppose, when we get through reading it, we pass it on. This is only a suggestion, but I think it would prove a good one if it were practiced. I may have more to say along this line later on." This is a splendid suggestion, and shows a fine, intelligent loyalty. If every reader of The Evangelist were as thoughtful and as much concerned both about the success of our church paper and the winning of souls to Christ as this brother, what might be done for the Kingdom's interests?

GENERAL ARTICLES

The Need of An Adequate Publishing House, for A Growing Denomination

By Martin Shively, D. D.

So long as all the members of a denomination are confined to a single group, or are so situated.as to permit them to get together frequently, nothing further than the spoken word is necessary to insure enlightenment and co-operation. In proportion as they are widely separated from each other, some mediums of communications between them becomes absolutely essential to this end. When no such medium exists, they are bound to drift apart in matters of faith, and their achievements be multiplied for want of united action. Since any group of sufficient numbers to warrant the name of "denomination," is too large to be efficiently served by a herald with his personal message, only one other means of communication offers itself, and this is the printed page. And in this our day of incomparable activity, and competition, not a single printed page will suffice. There must be many, they must be diversified, they must be constructively clean, and appealing. It is needless to say, following this, that even the mechanical side of an institution which is to supply this need, will, or ought to be adequately large, in proportion to the number of the people whom it is to serve. Its equipment must be such as will enable it to send out not only the

regular periodicals, but books, and tracts of every kind, essential to the highest service it may be capable of rendering to its constituency. Such a plant will require not only equipment, but men,—men in sufficient numbers, but also men of ability, and of consecration, both to furnish and arrange the material, and to keep the equipment in operation.

Such a plant as has been indicated in the foregoing, can be created and maintained only by the use of ample funds. Such funds must come from the people who are served, or from others who desire to join in rendering the service. Here is offered a field for the perpetual activity of money contributed as endowment. Taking "The Gish Fund" in The Church of the Brethren, as example, one readily sees its possibilities for good. Books are furnished to her ministry at such low cost that there is no reason for not possessing them. The intellectual horizon is advanced, and efficiency increased, and he that contributes to such an end, like righteous Abel, though being dead, yet speaks, and speaking, ministers to man's real well being, and glorifies his Lord.

Ashland, Ohio.

The Brethren Evangelist As An Aid To Every Church Interest

By Prof. A. L. DeLozier

By way of introduction, let me say that no enterprise can be successfully promoted today without some official organ in the form of a magazine or paper. Labor unions have their papers and the industries have theirs. All the ISMS that are making inroads upon the church have their papers. We have Journeyman Barber, Bethlehem Steel, Bremen Derrick, Christian Science Monitor, Zion's Watch Tower, etc.

Then all the denominations have their papers and the Interchurch World Movement had its official organ, The Bulletin, which was sent free of charge to pastors and other workers, preceding the great drive. The boys in the trenches and even those in prison camps had their papers or magazines.

Let me use one illustration of a paper which I have read somewhat, The Christian Advocate of the Methodist church. We all know the Methodist church has been going forward. I was a constant reader of the Advocate during the Centenary drive and I am sure that this paper was the greatest possible asset to that move. I also know that it is an incalculable aid to all the interests of the Methodist church.

But I am thinking now about The Brethren Evangelist as an aid to every interest of the Brethren church. In one sentence I can state a fact which will prove the efficacy of our own paper in this respect. This is the fact: For years back our church records show that the church which is of most value to the brotherhood at large and to its own community, is the one in which the most copies of the Brethren Evangelist go each week.

Let me briefly specify a few of the interests of our beloved church.

1. EDUCATIONAL INTERESTS: This has to do with the College, of course. Without a college no church can hope to fulfill her mission in the world today. Brethren people are coming to see this and are responding nobly. But Beachler himself will tell you that he gets most money where the Evangelist is most read. He has even said that it would have paid the college to put the Evangelist in some homes

free of charge six months before his canvass for endowment.

One more thing under educational, namely, sons and daughters are most likely to come to Ashland College from homes where the Evangelist is a regular caller. Some of our folks who don't take the Evangelist, forget that we have a college and send their children elsewhere to school. More Brethren boys and girls are attending Ashland today than ever before. Why? Because the Evangelist is going into more homes.

2. PUBLICATION INTERESTS: The Evangelist is itself one of the publication interests, but if people read it they will and do take our own Sunday school literature and they will also order needed books through our own publishing house. Our publishing house is growing. There have been years when this could hardly have been said. Why is it growing now? Because the Evangelist is going into more homes than it used to.

3. MISSIONARY INTERESTS: We never had such missionary offerings as we have been getting the last couple years. The future of our church is beginning to look hopeful as it relates itself to the first part of the Great Commission. We have a splendid little missionary magazine called THE BRETHREN MISSIONARY. We have a new and efficient secretary in the person of Brother Gearhart. But overtopping all these agencies, is the propaganda of the Brethren Evangelist in behalf of missions and the fact of its wider circulation by being placed on the budget system.

4. MINISTERIAL INTERESTS: It may sound funny for me to say a word about ministerial interests. We preachers have not yet decided to strike, but we have stronger reasons for doing so than the many who are constantly doing it. The war brought high salaries for our parishioners, while quite a few of us had to economize just a little more to meet the higher prices. But cheer up, brother pastor! Do you want to raise your salary? Get the Evangelist into all your homes and it will increase rather than decrease your salary. Your people may read of some other brothers' salary being raised. Yours may then be raised. You may miss it

if your people don't get to read about this. But the Evangelist will boost a lot of other preacher interests besides salary.

5. LAY INTERESTS: Yes, the laymen have interests that need consideration. We preachers do not need to run everything. The laymen are going to have a larger voice and a larger place in the church of tomorrow. The Brethren Evangelist is prepared to take care of these interests and will be an aid to them as well as to any others.

In conclusion, if I have omitted any interests of the church, I humbly beg your pardon, and will wager that the Brethren Evangelist will prove an aid to those interests as well.

Ashland, Ohio.

Pastoral Calling. By J. L. Kimmel

(Read before the Muncie, Indiana, Ministerial Association)

In compliance with the request of the committee I have written on this subject. It seems however superfluous from the fact that this subject has been discussed before this body, not so long since. Again all ministers are so very familiar with this topic by experience and otherwise, that it makes it more difficult to say anything of much interest. In the third place I suppose it would be conceded by all ministers that pastoral calling is a part of their work and consequently there is not much room for argument here. Nevertheless Pastoral Calling is a subject of vital importance and must be emphasized again and again, "lest we forget, lest we forget."

I realize that there are two sides to this question, and that even the faithful pastor is confronted with many difficulties when it comes to discharging his duties along this line. Furthermore it must not be forgotten that some of the greatest preachers the world has ever had, have done little or no pastoral calling.

When Alexander Maclaren contracted with his church at Manchester, England, for his charge he had it specified that he was to do no pastoral calling. He held his charge for forty long years and became famous as one of the greatest expounders of the Word the world has ever known.

Dr. Russel H. Conwell of Philadelphia, who has built up one of the largest Baptist churches in the United States and who also has held his charge for forty years has done perhaps very little pastoral calling. The same no doubt could be said of many other preachers who have climbed the ladder of fame, in their profession. A great temptation comes therefore to the young minister, who has entered this sacred calling, he is faced with the problem of how to make his life count for the most.

Should he devote his time to study and become a great thinker, a great leader of men, an orator who could sway the thousands and lead them in the paths of righteousness? Or should he spend his time among his people and thus help them to bear their burdens and share their sorrows?

Indeed the pastor might take even a different course. There is a possibility of his spending about all his time among his parishioners, talking to them about the every day affairs of life, telling them about their splendid traits of character, their fine homes, and especially, about their bright and pretty children, and intimating that they are really the foremost people in the whole church, and that he would be willing to eat chicken with them any day as that was all he had to do. Hundreds and thousands of the laity have this conception of the ministry. They say the minister works two hours on Sunday and then has nothing to do all the week, and yet never calls at our home. The men in the shops, with this idea in mind, are inclined to look on the pastor as a mere parasite, who is hanging onto society for a living and who is a kind of a necessary nuisance. This unfortunate misunderstanding has done much to prejudice the non-Christian world against the minister of the gospel of Christ.

These people do not realize that the man who would be a power for good, in the ministry must be a devout student. First, he must be a careful and constant student of the Bible, the book of books, a book that is a library in itself, a book so simple that the wayfaring man though a fool can not err therein, and yet so profound that it has challenged the most gigantic intellects of all the ages. No sage has ever been so wise, that he has been able to fathom its depth, no one so

learned that he could unravel its mysteries. A book that solves all the problems of this world and opens up the gateways to the world beyond.

Secondly, he must be a student of literature. He should know everything that takes place in the world today and about everything that has taken place since the world began. He must read the daily papers, and the leading magazines, and all the books that are worth reading. He must be a student of philosophy, psychology, sociology, and economics. He must be able to preach two sermons each Sunday, that will keep his auditors wide awake, while the sermon lasts. He must attend all the social functions, serve on the most important boards and committees, lead the prayer meeting, officiate at the weddings, visit the sick, comfort the brokenhearted, and bury the dead. He must hold himself in readiness to deliver an address, on any subject he might be called upon, without any previous notice and acquit himself nobly on every occasion.

Then again there are ministers who have a thousand, perhaps two thousand members in their congregation. How could they call on all these people once or twice each year and thus multiply their work a thousand-fold? Should not a minister also call on the people who live in his parish but are not Christians? Common sense would suggest that the Christian people should come in touch with those, who are not Christians, and lead them in the paths of righteousness and it is generally conceded, that no one is so well qualified for this task as the pastor. All these and many more demands are made of him. When we consider the minister of the gospel from this viewpoint it becomes apparent at once that it is almost an utter impossibility for him to do much pastoral calling.

There is, however, brethren, another side to this proposition and I shall now proceed to give the other side to the best of my ability.

The pastor is a clergyman or minister having Spiritual charge of a church and congregation, says "Webster." The word pastor seems to be derived from the word pasture, to feed—hence a shepherd—originally one who had charge of flocks and herds. Jesus said, "I am the good shepherd; the good shepherd giveth his life for the sheep. But he that is a hireling, and not the shepherd, whose own the sheep are not, seeth and fleeth and the wolf catcheth them and scattereth the sheep. The hireling fleeth because he is a hireling and careth not for the sheep. I am the good shepherd and know my sheep and am known of mine, and I lay down my life for the sheep."

These marvelous words of the Master have, no doubt in them a scathing rebuke to many so-called pastors, who do not comply with the example and precepts of the Great Teacher. It is said the oriental shepherd knows all his sheep by name and when he calls them they immediately follow him. How about the pastor of our day? Does he know his people and can he call them by name or would he not know them if he met them on the street at noonday?

I know what an effort it requires on the part of the faithful minister to do much pastoral calling. Having had considerable experience, I appreciate this fact very keenly. Nevertheless I contend very earnestly that pastoral calling is an important part of the Christian ministry and should not, yea must not, be neglected by the faithful pastor. In this regard I think the Master could truthfully say again, "And they all with one consent began to make excuse." We all mean to do better than we do. But there are so many things to take our time and attention that we defer these things, putting them off from day to day and from week to week and from year to year, until procrastination becomes a fundamental principle with us and a part of our very natures.

A traveling man was approaching the depot heavily loaded with his baggage. He heard the train whistle and for fear that he might miss it, started to run. Just as he reached the station platform the train passed by with the rapidity of sixty miles an hour. The disappointed man turned to a colored policeman and said, "Doesn't that train stop here?" "No sir," was the reply, "it doesn't even hesitate." With all the obstacles that loom up before us, with all the difficulties that confront us, we must not procrastinate, we must not even hesitate. If we do, we lose the battle and suffer everlasting defeat.

Some pastors are better fitted, by nature, to come in contact with all classes of people, than others, but what we lack in temperament God will supply with grace, if we ask him, who giveth liberally unto all men. A certain pastor said he was prevailed on by his congregation to call on a certain family, who was not identified with any church. He took the unpleasant and arduous duty upon himself and when he reached their home-and had rung the doorbell he wished in his heart they were not home. If pastoral calling seems to us an unpleasant task we must cultivate until what was once an unpleasant duty becomes a joy and a delight.

It is true that sometimes the pastor does not get the most welcome reception. A certain priest called on a family that was a member of his parish. He rang the doorbell and the children came to the door and the priest stepped in. "Mother is not at home, she has gone down town," the priest was told. The priest happened to look into another room where there was a screen and noticed below the screen two feet. "And so your mother has gone down town," said the priest. "Yes, sir, she has gone down town." "Well, you tell your mother," said the priest, "That when she goes to town next time she shall take her feet with her. While this illustration brings forth an unpleasant phase of the subject, yet it is also true that when a minister uses tact mixed with grace ninety-nine percent of the people will treat him with the greatest cordiality and respect. May we not forget that the great Apostle to the Gentiles said, "I have become all things to men that I might save some." We must not overlook the individual if we would follow the meek and lowly Nazarene. When an angry mob had taken up stones to stone him the great Teacher stopped by the wayside to correct a false doctrine and open the eyes of the man who was born blind. To an individual, he preached the doctrine of regeneration and to a woman of ill-repute the great doctrine of the inward work of grace.

Philip left a great and successful revival and went out into the lonely desert to preach to a single individual. The name of this convert is given as well as his official position. While on the day of Pentecost we have not the least intimation of the name or station in life of one person of all the three thousand converts.

Following close on the work of the preacher is the work of the pastor, the shepherd of the flock. How many good men are today drawing back from this task and saying, "If I am to give the time necessary to make strong sermons I cannot find time to also do pastoral work. Yes, gentlemen, we can, and we must. No man can do brain work all the time. I know many fine fellows, who, under the delusion that they are getting needed knowledge, read themselves into insensibility and when they begin to write, their productions has no spring, no gripping power. If there were no other reasons a man must do systematic and extended pastoral work to be able to declare the worth of God with heart-binding power. Let it be said again, It is the man behind the message that sends it to the human heart.

I quote from "Building a Working Church" by Samuel Charles Black, D.D.:

A preacher must know the heartaches and throbs of humanity by meeting his people in the intimate intercourse of their own homes before he can speak a language they understand. Few men ever know the value of personal contact, as did the lamented Maltbie Babcock. In conversation, by letter, by telephone, or message, he kept in personal touch with his people. They loved him like a father and hung upon his words as a maiden, upon the words of her betrothed.

Furthermore, pastoral work is absolutely necessary if a man desires to win new members in any large numbers. It is while in the homes of his people that he learns of members of those families still unsaved or of new residents, who may be reached. Seventy-five percent of the members won by a pastor, who is building up his congregation at the rate of two hundred a year, are discovered while making pastoral calls. Two or three afternoons a week will work marvels and every man needs that much time out of his study to keep him from going to seed or becoming a mere spinner of impracticable theories. "You are the first minister that has called at our home in eleven years," said a lady to me since I have come to Muncie. Such testimony is no honor to the Christian ministry.

O Master, let us walk with thee
In lowly paths of service free.
Tell me thy secret, help me bear
The strain of toil, the fret of care.
Help me the slow of heart to move,
By some clear winning word of love.
Teach me the wayward feet to stay,
And guide them in the homeward way.
Teach me thy patience, still with thee,
In closer dearer company.

In work that keeps faith sweet and strong
In trust that triumphs over wrong,
In hope that sends a shining ray
Far down the future broadening way,
In peace that only thou canst give;
With thee, O Master, let me live."
Muncie, Indiana.

The Pastor----His Work.   By Mrs. C. E. Nicholas

The Christian ministry has long been regarded as a life of sacrifice yet is it not the kind of sacrifice that brings to the faithful servant God's choicest blessings?

The world scarcely appreciates the consecrated efforts of a faithful man of God, yet it is slow to acknowledge it could move on just as well without these sacrifices in behalf of humanity.

The pastor's field and mission is world-wide and it leads you from the lowest hovel of sin and vice to the most refined of society. In all walks and conditions of life and everywhere his services are needed. And there is never a time

when his work is completed. It is an endless chain making its revolutions with no stop.

The working machinery of the church must be kept in repair and running smoothly. There is always a certain amount of community work he is expected to do. He must serve on committees, because his opinion is valued. He must make visits and do errands which no one can do quite so well as the pastor.

If there are dissensions among the people, he must smoothe the ruffled feathers and solve the many knotty problems that the serenity of the church may not be jarred and the work retarded.

He visits the sin-sick soul and holds to him a light to light his pathway. He visits the sick and dying and gives them hope for the future. In short, he is continually in demand and his life is not his own.

He is expected to sacrifice all personal inclinations and go when and where he is called.

He must be able to suit himself to all conditions. Failure to do this means a failure to his work.

The personal work a pastor is able to do during the six days of the week does more to build up his church and increase his influence in the community than all the eloquence and persuasiveness he may be able to display in the pulpit. It is personal contact that tells on the lives around us.

He must be friendly to all people—the poor as well as the rich, the sinner as well as the saint. He cannot be a respecter of persons. The Master was not—and he must seek to be his true representative. Christ came to seek and to save the lost and the servant should be as his master.

The pastor's message to his people must be chosen with reference to the needs of his congregation. He must master his chosen theme and himself. Too often a minister chooses a subject beyond his ability. In other words, the subject is bigger than the man. Before he presents his work to the public he should become its master. To do this means study, preparation, consecration and prayer. He must make the truths of God to be felt—it is within his power to make his people feel and know for a certainty, by his life and message, that he is an ambassador from the very court of heaven.

His life must be aflame with divine love ere he will be able to lift others into a holier communion with their Savior. The power of God's word depends on the spirit that stands behind that Word. He may preach the Word, yet preach it so coldly and unfeelingly that men cannot receive it. It is said in Siberia milk is sometimes delivered in chunks to the customers. It is a lamentable fact that the milk of the Word is sometimes delivered in the same way.

Preach! Yes, but his sermons must be thawed before they can be assimilated.

We need men who will proclaim old truths with new energy—not bundling them in a mass of drapery. A good preacher preaches from the heart to the heart and uses such plainness of speech that while offending none, at the same time makes the truth plain.

A preacher's success cannot be measured by the crowded churches or by the "yeas" and "amens." Elijah thought so, but when he discovered his mistake he suffered disappointment and was heart-broken. Success lies in altered lives, in obedient and humbled hearts. Most people know enough but want to be made to feel and to do. This is the preacher's work.

Power in the pulpit is not measured by eloquence and gesture but by the thrusts made at sin, by demonstrations of the Holy Ghost and by the personality visible in the message. Flowers and rhetoric have their place, but the pure, plain, simple truths of the Bible give more joy, comfort, peace, and rest than all the oratory the world has ever known.

God's plan is for man to perform his part and to do it with all available means, Therefore the workman of God must work, toil, pray, trust and meditate.

He needs fire from above and must put himself in readiness to receive it that he may impart it to others through his messages.

If he is to meet with success today he must be an instrument under the control of the Holy Spirit, as the prophets and apostles were. The inspired men of the Bible wrote and spoke as they were moved by the Holy Spirit.

Just as God used the preachers of the Bible so he wants to use the preachers of today. Just as he endowed his prophets of old with the Holy Fire from above, so he will endow men today if they will adjust themselves to his plan and put themselves in readiness to receive the unction from on high.

Dowagiac, Michigan.

Only One Soul; Who Shall That One Be?   By Samuel Kiehl

Just before his ascension Jesus gave to his disciples the following commission, promise, and warning, according to Mark 16:15, 16 (R. V.): "Go ye into all the world and preach the gospel to every creature. He that believeth and is baptized shall be saved; but he that believeth not shall be condemned." John 3:18 says, "He that believeth on him is not condemned; but he that believeth not is condemned already, because he hath not believed in the name of the only begotten Son of God." Paul says, "Those who know not God, and who obey not the gospel of our Lord Jesus Christ shall be punished with everlasting destruction from the presence of the Lord, and from the glory of his power" (2 Thes, 1:8, 9). Three classes; those who shall be saved, those who are condemned already, and those who shall be punished. To which class do you and I belong? Take notice! "It is appointed unto men once to die, but after this the judgment" (Heb. 9:27). "Then every one of us shall give account of himself to God" (Rom. 14:12). Shall we then hear, "Well done thou good and faithful servant, enter thou into the joy of thy Lord" (Mark 25:21), or, "I never knew you, depart from me" (Matt. 7:23).

Dear reader, you may be called any moment, from time to eternity. Amos 4:12 says, "Prepare to meet thy God." Jesus says, "No man cometh unto the Father but by me" (John 14:6). "Christ Jesus came into the world to save sinners" (1 Tim. 1:15). "He gave himself a ransom for all" (1 Tim. 2:6). He died for your sins according to the scriptures (1 Cor. 15:3). He was delivered for your offences, and was raised again for your justification (Rom. 4:25). His own self have your sins in his own body on the tree, that you, being dead to sins, should live unto righteousness (1 Peter 2:24). He loved you, and gave himself for you (Gal.

2:20), and is now saying to you, Come unto me (Matt. 11: 28-31). Do not resist his gracious invitation. They that resist shall receive to themselves damnation (Rom. 13:2). "Flee from the wrath to come." There is danger in delay.

If you have not yet received Christ as your personal Savior and Lord do not neglect the present opportunity. Open now the door of your heart, and let the Savior in. He will sup with you, and you with him (Rev. 3:20). What a joyful experience you will then have, sitting together, as it were, in heavenly places in Christ Jesus (Eph. 2:6). "He that hath the Son hath life; he that hath not the Son of God hath not life" (1 Jon 5:12). That is final. Eternal life, or eternal death—which shall it be? Will you now joyfully receive this loving Savior, who died for you, that you might live? God give you grace to do so, today. Now is the accepted time; now is the day of salvation (2 Cor. 6:2). No promise for tomorrow.

Should the preceding quotations from "the Word of God" be instrumental in bringing one soul to Christ, there will be "joy in the presence of the angels of God," over that one soul (Luke 15:10). YOU CAN BE THAT ONE, NOW (Jno. 6:37 last clause). Be it so. We ask in his name.

Dayton, Ohio.

GOOD CITIZENS

One writer has said, "Liberty consists and depends upon respecting your neighbor's right every bit as fairly and squarely as your own." That is the idea being carried forward by the Junior Red Cross, which is teaching that service for others and respecting the rights of others is the badge of good citizenship, and a Junior is, first of all, a good citizen.

THE BRETHREN PULPIT

The Church and The Labor Problem.   By H. M. Harley

TEXT: "Study to be quiet, and to do your own business, and to work with your own hands, that ye may walk honestly toward them that are without, and that ye may have lack of nothing."—I Thess. 4: 11, 12.

This is a subject that should. interest everyone, because the problem of labor effects very materially every man, woman and child. And we all recognize the fact that the labor problem is one of the gravest problems that is staring us in the face today. The present feeling between capital and labor, is contributing as much, if not more to the present unrest and high prices of all that goes to make up life, than anything else.

None can get away from the fact that there are two sides to this labor problem; yes, indeed three,—the side of the employer, the side of the employee, and the side of the gneral public, which side is too often forgotten. And if only we could get all parties concerned to get together and talk things over unselfishly and with a view to arriving at a course of action for the greatest good of all concerned, things wuold not be in the present state of chaos. The church says to all sides, "Come, let us reason together, and see whether we cannot find a line of procedure that will be fair to all, and result in the largest possible prosperity for all involved."

Labor, or work, is a great bessing to humanity, even though there are some people who cannot see it that way. It is not only the way to health and wealth, but to happiness and usefulness. An idle person is a sorrow to himself and to his neighbors. He is a parasite, living at the expense of other folks, and not contributing to his own or other's welfare. He expects a living from the world, but gives nothing to the world. The Word says, "If a man will not work, neither shall he eat." And that man is to be pitied as well as shunned, who has nothing to do. He is like a barnacle on a ship, or like a floating derelict at sea—useless to himself and dangerous to others. Work is positively necessary to keep body, soul and mind alive. Parasites always degenerate, and in time die out altogether, according to natural law. To live means to be active. When God created the human being, he made the body with an idea of work. A plow or a locomotive is not more evidently built for work than is the human frame, the human machine. Hands, feet, eyes, brain, heart,—all are fitted and ready for action, and each lives only as it works. A human being not at work is like a great machine, wonderfully constructed, but standing idle, useless and in time worthless. To this end were we born, and for this cause came we into the world, that we might work, and in that way help to further the world's good. If we fail to do this, we fail in the very end of our being, that which is stamped on our constitution, and built into our very bones and blood.

Let me repeat then, that work is one of the greatest blessings that God has conceived for man. We are happiest when we are using the powers of body, mind and soul for the accomplishment of God's will in the world. And earth's greatest and best have always recognized this fact. At the close of his autobiography Admiral Dewey writes a characteristic paragraph. It reads like this, "A most gratifying feature of the rank of Admiral of the Navy which Congress has given me, was that I was to remain in the active service of the navy for life. While I lived, there would be work for me to do." You know, there are people in the world who look forward to the time when they can retire and live a life of rest and ease, as they say. They think that when duty is all done, then their pleasures will have begun. But they are mistaken. and Dewey was right. Work means health and pleasure and long life. I verily believe that if Roosevelt had remained in the active service of the government, he would

have had at least a good chance of living today and for some time to come. But his was a forced retirement, and this brought great grief to his heart and shortened his days.

Work then, is the natural thing for man, and the very best thing for him, so far as his own physical and mental makeup is concerned. It is also true of the physical universe. You and I live in an unfinished world. We find it with forests unbroken, its fields unplowed, its mines undeveloped, and all of its forces untamed. Man must sink his axe into the forest, but first he must invent and make the axe. He must plow the fields, but first he must invent and make the plow. He must raise his own food, weave his own clothing and build his own house, or else he will go hungry, and naked, and perish. This planet on which we live, was handed over to man in a raw state, and man had to clean it up and develop it into its present condition. And this work must go on unceasingly, and on an ever increasing scale as time goes on. The battle for bread ever has been, and is today a tremendous factor in human history. It has made and unmade men and nations, and even civilizations. If we did not do this work, the world would remain or relapse into a dense wilderness.

The Word of God is very plain on this line, and says that while labor is honorable, laziness is dishonorable and destructive. And we find too that the godliest men of whom Scripture speaks, each had his occupation. Abraham, David, Peter, John, Paul, Luke, even Jesus,—all worked with their hands, as well as with their minds and hearts. In fact, Christ dignified and made sacred the work of the hands. And at one time we hear him saying, "I am among you as one who serveth." Under the seal of a well-known college are the words, "Learn and Labor." And this is a most fitting expression of our ideal for a country as ours. Some people have a great desire to learn, but they consider it beneath their dignity to labor. We should all learn in order that we may labor. Otherwise our learning will be in vain.

Now, so far as the problems of labor are concerned, as far back in history as the time of Jacob and Laban, conditions of industry have caused sharp differences and bitter feelings between employer and employee. True, the situation has changed in many ways, but the problem has only taken on a different angle. There is really no difference, and it certainly has become no easier or better. It seems as though no generation has ever faced labor difficulties so great, and so complex, and so uncalled for and unreasonable, as those which are with us today.

It seems as though the idea of "get-rich-quick," and with the very least amount of work possible, has taken hold, not of a class, but of the great majority of people, whether employer or employee. They all want a whole lot of returns for a small investment of time or money—profiteers, whether among the capitalists or the laborers, or the merchants.

What so many people want today, is not an honest or worthy piece of work, so much as a good income. It's the wdekly pay envelope or the return on their investment that interests them, rather than the work that they are doing. And while we dare not, and do not want to ignore the wage aspect of work, yet it is a fact that a truly worthy worker in any line whatsoever, is first of all interested in his output. And that's the trouble with the world right now,—over-consumption and under-production. There is right now a trade in Pittsbtrgh that pays just four times what it did five years ago, and by common agreement, men of that trade are going to do less than half the work they did for the old wage. Every one who consumes should also produce, and in pro.

portion as he consumes or receives. But the fact of the matter is that conditions are no better now than they were during the war, no, not nearly so good. And if anything, they are becoming worse, industrially at least. We cannot expect a lowering of the cost of living, so long as this battle between the higher wages on the part of the employee, and the inflated returns of the profiteer is allowed to continue. But what can be done? Something must be done, or life will become unbearable, and it may take the direct interposition of God Almighty to stop, and adjust things. Indeed some of us are looking for that very thing.

I know that there have been many plans and schemes suggested, which were supposed to settle all of these various differences and grievances. Many have tried, and thus far have failed. Men have looked to most everything but the real thing or place for a remedy that will be effective, if properly applied. The Gospel of Jesus Christ has an application for and concerning modern industry, that cannot be gainsaid. Jesus, when he came into this world, not only dignified labor, but he elevated the standards of the laboring man. And wherever these principles have been accepted and followed, they have been responsible for the greatest advances and benefits for all concerned.

The real problem of labor is not merely one of economics, or if wages or returns financially. It involves the question of human rights and human duties of and for all classes, a matter on which the church of Jesus Christ seeks to give light and help. In the past, the church and labor especially, have been most greviously misunderstanding each other. The laboring man says that the church is the rich man's club. This is a false charge, for there is a far greater percentaeg of laborers or employees in the church than employers,—at least ten to one. And then remember, too, that Jesus Christ, her founder and leader, was a laborer in the true sense of the term.

And listen, what the church offers to men today is positively the only solution to the problem as we have it. Religion is not something that concerns only the church and the Lord's Day. It concerns everything that is connected with every-day life. If a man is a Christian on Sunday, he will be one on Monday and on every other day of the week. If he is a Christian in his church-life, he will be one in his home life, his social life, and as well in his business life. He will work he will work honestly, fairly, and will always strive to give value for value received. In other words, he will at the very least, do as he would be done by.

It's the business of the church to persuade men of all classes, to learn to know God, to obey his teachings, and to learn to love and trust each other, and to give to all men the same chance in life that they desire for themselves. And in proportion as that end is accomplished, will hatred, and differences and problems disappear; fair-play to all will become the dominating spirit, and the working man and the employer will become brethren; and each will rejoice in the other's prosperity, and each will labor to the other's interests. Then, and not until then, in spite of whatever else men may say or do, dare we hope for anything better than what we are contending with today?

And while we are talking about work, and the need of doing a real day's work, and of doing it fairly and for the interests of all concerned, let us not forget that we as Christians especially, owe a work to the One who makes every good possible, and that only as we fulfill that obligation will we really be happy and successful as Christian men and women.

When Dr. Winfred Grenfell was a medical student in London, he yielded himself to D. L. Moody's invitation to follow Christ. The Christian world knows what took place in his life. The young man gave himself, first to the mission among the deep-sea fishermen, and later found his field on the bleak coasts of Labrador. Fourteen years after his conversion, Dr. Grenfell called on Moody in Boston. The Missionary said, "I realize my debt to him, and I want to say. 'Thank you.'" Moody listened to what he had to say, and then, treating religion as the religion of the Lord should be treated, he said, "Good, but what have you been doing since you were converted?" "Doing," said Grenfell, "Well I've been living and working among fishermen from the Bay of Biscay to the coast of Labrador, instead of staying in London, and merely plying my profession." "And do you regret it?" asked Moody. "Regret it! No sir, I should say not," was the reply.

Friends, the only regret will be for the person who once met Jesus in the way, and yet must hang his head in shame when he comes face to face with the question, as all will have to, sooner or later, "What have you done or what are you doing now? Merely making a living? or making a life?" Have you been working merely for time or for eternity? That's the church's message. So live, and so love and so labor, that at the end of time there will be no regrets, but men that men may say, O "There's a person who labored willingly and cheerfully, one who always played the game fair, and ever gave value for value received." That's the church's message, and only as men will heed it, dare we hope for that condition that all desire, and God most of all.

"God worketh, let me work too.
God doeth, let me do.
Busy for God my work I ply,
Till I rest in the life of Eternity."

Pittsburgh, Pennsylavnia.

The Supremacy of Jesus
By T. Darley Allen

Jesus Christ alone of all the teachers of the world was conscious of perfection. Other men gave to humanity wonderful moral codes, but Christ was not only the author of the grandest of all systems of ethics, but lived in exact conformity with his teachings. He practiced exactly what he preached.

And Jesus, besides being the one perfect pattern of virtue, is the highest incentive to others to be righteous. The heathen moralists well knew the weakness of human nature and how difficult it was even for themselves to approach near to what they desired to be morally. They recognized their many defects.

Paley says that the faultlessness of Christ is "more peculiar than we are apt to imagine. Some stain pollutes the morals or the morality of almost every other teacher and of every other lawgiver. Zeno the Stoic and Diogenes the cynic fell into the foulest impurities, of which Socrates himself was more than suspected."

Christ was not only sinless but, as has been well said, "faith in him is declared to be a means of imparting to human nature a moral and spiritual strength of which it was previously destitute," and through all the centuries since his advent men and women have sought strength from him and been able to resist temptation and live holy lives although formerly the greatest of sinners.

James Martineau said that Jesus can be called "the Regenerator of the human race," and that "the world has changed" because of him.

"Many great men," says J. W. Jenks, "have deeply affected the history of the world. Jesus has changed the fundamental nature of society."

Harry Earl Montgomery says: "If we compare the teachings of Christ with those of the world's greatest leaders in philosophy, eloquence and song, as to their regenerative effects on the lives of mankind, we will be compelled to admit that Christ 'spake as never man spake.'"

Well may we say with Browning, "I tell thee the acknowledgment of God in Christ, accepted by thy reason, solves for thee all problems in the world and out of it."

Cleveland, Ohio.

Send
WHITE GIFT
OFFERINGS to

THE SUNDAY SCHOOL

ALBERT TRENT
General Secretary-Treasurer
Johnstown, Pennsylvania

Lessons on Teaching from the Great Teacher.   By Prof. E. G. Mason

The present plan for child development is three-fold, mental or intellectual, moral or spiritual and phsical. Yet in our public schools greatest emphasis is placed upon mental development with an ever increasing emphasis upon physical development. Educators are learning each year the importance of physical education in conjunction with mental.. They must find out in the future that moral education in Christian teaching must be included. We are very sorry to say that the education of the morals is left to some other organization and that organization must reach out and touch all classes of people. Although our school courses are lengthening and becoming more complex year by year and more attention is being paid to play and play grounds as a means of developing the bodies of children, there is sadly lacking the same progress in moral and spiritual teaching. The organization that comes the nearest to filling this great need, today, is the Sunday school.

There are no state laws compelling the attendance of our young people in the Sunday school. It is all a matter of choice. In order that the worldly lure of automobile trips, fishing, Sunday baseball games, moving picture shows, and the like shall be successfully overshadowed the Sunday school must be made exceedingly attractive. It has a great task before it if the young people outside of Christian homes are to be brought into and held by the Sunday school. Our only hope for the success of the project is the steadfast faith in God that right shall conquer in the end.

No organization is stronger than the individuals that compose it. So the most essential part of the Sunday school is the teacher. We may all learn much of teaching from the Great Teacher, our Lord and Master, Jesus Christ. These thoughts are as old as time, yet we see them used by so few, that another telling shall do no harm but rather renew them in our minds.

The methods that Jesus employed were most effective for they founded a faith that has stood the test for nearly 2,000 years and its growth has been marvelous supplanting in the minds of thinking men the earlier faiths. His methods were direct, simple and earnest. Now if we combine in our teaching these three things, the whole world shall flock to our doors, as the whole world is even now beginning to bow at Jesus' feet.

(a) Directness is sticking to the lesson and driving home each truth and thought with such force that lasting impressions shall be left on the minds of the Sunday school students. Directness also means making modern- applications of the lesson teaching. Jesus was always direct. He used nothing more than was absolutely necessary to make his meaning clear. He went directly at the heart of his lesson and did far more,—he left much room for thought— upon what he had said.

(b) His simplicity is marked. His language and parables were spoken in the simplest form in order that all people might understand. He chose as objects for his parables, those things which the people were most familiar with. This in itself a very valuable lesson. How easy it would be to hold the attention of our Sunday school pupils, if we could so simply and clearly state the great lessons of the Bible!

(c) Lastly, Jesus was in earnest. Anyone who would suffer the physical tortures and mental anguish that Jesus suffered for the sake of teaching the people of this world the greatest lesson of sacrifice in all history, must be in earnest. What could not a Sunday school teacher do with the earnestness of Jesus? He felt the burden of sin in this world; He felt the necessity of showing men why they should turn from the paths of sin and his heart bled for the eternal punishment that all the sinful should suffer. When we feel this, then we can attract and hold all those who may fall within our influence. These in brief are the greatest lessons we may learn from the Great Teacher. We may not all be able to teach either directly or simply yet we may all inspire others by our enthusiasm and earnestness for the safety of the souls of our young people.

West Salem, Ohio.

The Power in the Book

By T. Darley Allen

D. L. Moody declared the Bible to be inspired because it inspired him. The great argument for the divine inspiration of the book is that it leads to God and to a life of righteousness.

Clayton Sedgewick Cooper tells of a Hindu student of the Bible who at the beginning of the second year of his study of the book was asked what impression he had gained from his reading, and replied, "The influence I have gained is not one of thought merely; it has changed my life and my life work."

"I know all that argument can say against my faith," said the Archbishop of York some years ago. "In moments when I can escape the distraction of daily life and the pressure of the senses, I am still conscious of a yearning which is at once satisfied and sure of its rightness—an instinct of divine fellowship. I still know that there is no power on earth that can so lay hold of my last self and satisfy and stimulate it as the thought of One who long ago spoke the words of eternal life and died for love of me, his brother. That is the evidence of my faith; it is enough."

Says a writer concerning the Bible: "It tells me about righteousness and faith and immortality. It has been the guide and the teacher and the comforter of multitudes of people in every age and country. All men find there what they most need. There alone can they find the satisfaction of their deepest wants."

Cleveland, Ohio.

Christian Endeavor's Soliloquy on the Closing of the "Four Year Challenge"

By George S. Baer

I stand now at the ending of four years
    And backward look, and forward strain my eyes;
Upon the blotted record fall my tears,
    While brushing them aside, a glad surprise
Breaks like a new day on my anxious face:
    Though unattained—the goals I held in view—
The Master didst supply me daily grace
    And, as I struggled, gave me strength anew.

Not all attained,—though strove in full accord.
    They've borne with me; and now has come the day
Of reckoning and meting out reward.
    If crowned or no, I've stood not by the way.
And now, in Christ my trust through all the days,
    I pause not from a nobler work to rest,
But, heart sincere, with instant prayer and praise,
    Prepare to make the coming years the best.

J. A. Garber
PRESIDENT

Our Young People at Work

G. C. Carpenter
SECRETARY

Dr. Clark's Birthday Celebration

(Note—You may not have received the following letter through the mails, as many other Endeavorers did not, but we know you would be interested in learning of Dr. Clark's birthday and the nature of its celebration, and so we are sending it to you in this way.)

August 14, 1920.

Dear Friend:

Dr. Clark expects that the attached letter will be sent out early in the fall, but there is a special reason for sending it to you now.

Sunday, September 12, is Dr. Clark's Birthday, and we want to delight him at a surprise party on the day before by presenting him with a book containing the greetings of at least two thousand of his friends and admirers from all parts of America, and by assuring him that a large part of the amount for which he asks has been raised.

You have marvelled at the physical sacrifices he has been willing to make in order to carry the message of Christian Endeavor. You feel, I am sure, that it is not fair that in addition to leading our movement, Dr. Clark should be required to raise single-handed the seventy-five thousand dollars necessary to make this work possible.

May we have your greeting and contribution in time for this birthday celebration? I am enclosing a greeting card. The upper half is for your name and address. The blank space is for a special message if you wish to write one. The attached stub gives a place to indicate the amount of your pledge or contribution. These greeting cards (without the stubs) will be attractively bound in a leather volume and presented to Dr. Clark. If you can send full or part payment with your pledge this will be appreciated, as we would like to show to Dr. Clark as much of the actual money as possible. But if this is not convenient, your pledge will be equally acceptable. (Though you did not get the greeting card referred to, you might send a greeting and an offering anyway, if you care to do so.)

As the sheets must go to the bindery on Monday, September sixth, I shall be very grateful if I may hear from you before that date.
Sincerely,
E. P. GATES, General Secretary.

A Christian Endeavor Partnership

August 14, 1920.

Dear Friend:

A friend of mine, in sending a generous sum for the Christian Endeavor cause, tells me he would like to be my partner in advancing Christian Endeavor throughout the world. He says: "You can visit other countries and tell us of their needs, while I am a stay-at-home partner to furnish some of the funds for the enterprise."

A Partnership Proposition: Dividends Assured

Will you, too, not become a partner in this work? I know you must be interested in the cause, or you would not be a reader of the Christian Endeavor Department of the Brethren Evangelist, and as such you must be acquainted with the needs of Christian Endeavor and its vast possibilities for good.

The constantly growing success of Christian Endeavor makes it impossible for us at the central office to finance it in all lands without the aid of those like you who are interested and well informed.

I have recently returned from Central and Eastern Europe, and found that in many of these countries the distress is terrible, the need of Christian work appalling, and, happily, that Christian Endeavorers are doing far more than their full share of physical relief work and genuine Christian service.

For instance, most of the Endeavorers in Budapest, Hungary, have been killed, captured, deported, or have died of actual starvation during the war, or the more dreadful days of revolution and communism that followed. Yet, in spite of all this, the 131 Endeavorers who are left in the city carry on nine weekly evangelistic meetings in two great hospitals, have especially helpful work for blind soldiers and other blind people, for juvenile delinquents, for fallen women, and even for would-be suicides. Has such a record ever been surpassed?

The Endeavorers of Finland, who have suffered almost as much, out of their deep poverty and distress, and with a little help from America, have sent two field secretaries to Esthonia and Latvia to help evangelize these new republics, and their visit has been attended by a wonderful revival.

In China our secretaries have denied themselves even

the necessities of life, that the small amount of $2,500 sent to them for all purposes might be used in extending Christian Endeavor throughout that great republic.

In Japan and India more money is imperatively needed if Christian Endeavor is to hold its own, to say nothing of expanding its numbers and its work five-fold, as it easily might do, if the necessary funds were at our disposal.

The same is true of Mexico and South America and Africa.

Many a church in America would be saved from spiritual decline or extinction if a live society could be started among its young people. Our own American fields were never so white for the harvest, if we only had laborers to send into them. Indeed, the laborers are waiting, but we have not the means to send them.

These are our resources in opportunities and in willing workers. We lack only sufficient working capital to realize enormously greater spiritual dividends.

We have a partnership account in which everyone who gives will be listed, and will be a sharer in the dividends. Your dividends will be fully 100 percent., perhaps 1,0000 percent., on money invested, in souls saved, young Christians trained for service, churches built up, and many good causes enlarged and strengthened by our societies.

The Governor of Colorado, who is noted for his wise and extensive material investments, when sending one thousand dollars to the State Christian Endeavor Union, at its last convention, declared it was the best investment he had made that year.

If you will make an investment of at least $10.00 in world-wide Christian Endeavor, a quarterly bulletin will be sent, telling of some of the spiritual dividends your money is earning. You will also be elected, if you desire, a member of the United Society, with voting powers, and a certificate of membership will be sent you.

Smaller sums than $10.00 will be gratefully received, and larger investments in this partnership are earnestly solicited from those who can afford them.

Hoping and praying that we may count you our partner in prayers and gifts for the great work Christian Endeavor has to do throughout the world, I am

Faithfully and sincerely yours,
FRANCIS E. CLARKE.

SEND ALL MONEY FOR
General Home, Kentucky and
Foreign Missions to

MISSIONS

WILLIAM A. GEARHART
General Missionary Secretary
906 Conover Bldg., Dayton, O.

Another Letter From Africa

Carnot, French Equatorial, Africa.
May 16th, 1920.

My dear little friends:

It has been a month or more since I wrote you last. Daddy has been well and is getting strong like his old self again. But Marie and Julia have both been ill again. Julia was Very ill for a few days, but God has restored all to health again.

We are all busy. Marie and Julia and I play, and the older girls study when they are well enough. I am making a very small beginning too. Mama and Aunt Toddy have both had light attacks of fever, and were both in bed at once, so we had rather a hard time for a few days. But we girlies like to help with the nursing and can do many little things in sickness. Julia especially likes to nurse and mama says she is a great comfort when others are ill.

The Lord has been so gracious in supplying all our needs. We sent checks to Brazzaville in February. They came back three months later as money orders. But we haven't got them cashed yet, as Monsieur Du Mont who has been away, just returned last night. This is Sunday, but tomorrow we hope to get the money orders cashed. We didn't think last July when the last checks were cashed at Brazzaville how long it would be before we would be able to cash any more, almost a year!

The Lord has done many wonderful things for us. The government built a house and refused to take pay for it. Many, many times mama has been able to buy eggs and other necessary food with salt. The boys have been willing to take their pay in salt or sometimes in old clothes. The government officials, the Hausas, the native clerk of the Company, etc., have all been moved of the Lord to send us food. Pork, chickens, eggs, fish, rice, sweet potatoes, have come in from time to time as donations. Aunt Toddy sold her young rooster to help pay the milk bill. We still have the big old "bafambwa" (rooster) much admired by all the natives! Just when we needed the eggs most the hens commenced to lay. The stores of oatmeal, flour and sugar which Uncle Antoine brought out with him are not yet used up, and so our expenses have been very light. We found a few francs in a trunk which we had forgotten. It was wonderful the way God seemed to multiply the money we had left when we came to Carnot. Mama says God knows how to multiply our blessings as well as to add them to us. There were only a few days that we were actually without money, and only once that mama had to turn away the beef from the door because we didn't have money to pay for it. That very afternoon some porters came and wanted to buy salt. Daddy sold 36 francs' worth, and we felt it was a special working of the Lord for never before nor since have we been able to sell salt for money. Those 36 francs aren't all spent yet, and tomorrow we shall have more! How good God is!

Our yard is barren except for mango trees which are simply laden with delicious fruit, and cost us nothing. We eat them raw, cook them as sauce, use them green in soups, (when they taste like carrots) and make pies and puddings of them. I must simply stop counting our blessings for there are so many—too many to number! I just happened to think perhaps you don't know what mangoes are! They are more like a peach in form and structure than any other fruit of which you know. But they are much larger. When one eats them, one slices off the rosy "cheeks" makes criss-cross marks across the yellow pulp with a knife, and eats with a spoon out of the saucer-like rind. There still remains the stone to be eaten, which is a rather difficult and "mussay" process. There are no "freestone" mangoes. All of them not only cling to the stone but there are long fibers passing from the stone through the surrounding pulp. But the flavor is so excellent that we always like the stone best of all. There is a common question in East Africa: "When is the best time to eat a mango, before your bath or after it?" The answer is, "In it."

Just as I write this, little Julia is taken ill with a temperature of 101 degrees. In the midst of life here in Africa we are surrounded with sickness and suffering. But we always look to the dear Lord for his deliverance, and he is so wonderfully gracious to us, Aunt Toddy is nursing Julia, and we all trust she will soon be well.

We children just came back from Sunday school, just three of us with Aunt Toddy for the teacher. You would laugh if you saw the funny little place where we have it. Just a little grass hut used on week days for a study. Here Daddy typewrites, or mama translates the Bible into Baya or Sango, or Aunt Toddy teaches us in school. Although so small and so uninviting, there is usually some one in it, for it is quiet, and one can accomplish so much more away from Africa's confusion.

We also have a boy's house in our little camp, used in rainy weather as a cook house. There is another little shelter for a cook house also, so little by little our camp is growing. And will no doubt continue to do so.

Our present house is full and when the dear expected missionaries, including Aunt Mae, arrive, we will have to build another if we are still at the Carnot camp. Mama says she hopes we will be able to commence work on our station then, and they will not be detained as we have been.

We talk daily about Miss Hillegas who is coming and the others who are thinking of coming, and ask Jesus to keep them safely through all the dangers of the way.

We are doing language work of some kind all of us, little and big. We little folks think the language is so easy and wonder why the big folks must work so hard on it.

How happy we are that our Heavenly Father knows the end of all these years of waiting and prayer. (Just here mama jumped up to kill a centipede just crawling toward one of my sandals).

It is afternoon now and already Julia is better. It seems that this attack of fever will be a slight one. Mama says it is another of God's many deliverances. How we shall praise him now and through eternity! We have been six months at Carnot now. We were three times that long at Brazzaville. But our times are in his hands.

Mama says she is so glad for Brother Mc-Clain's catechism. Already it is translated into Baya, and arranged in French. Next week the Sango translation will, we hope, be finished. We find Sango difficult now as we use it much less than Baya and French. We are so glad for the Sango songs arranged at Brazzaville, for there are quite a number who enjoy them here.

The English-Baya dictionary is finished (the first edition). Aunt Toddy is typing the gospel of Mark. The next big works will be the Baya song book and the Baya-English dictionary, and, oh, so much. But mama says we must learn not to plan in Africa, only to plod. Mama says she is so glad that in these days when we are shut away from the people we have so much that we can do for him.

We are looking forward to that glad day when the Word of the Lord shall have free course and be glorified with us, even as it is with you. Even in these dark days when your missionaries are bound, we rejoice that the Word of God is not bound, and that every word which has been and is being preached shall redound to his glory and honor.

Yours Very lovingly,
MARGUERITE EDNA GRIBBLE.

A Missionary Hen

She was not a comely hen. Her legs were very short, her body rather long and slim, and her head of no special kind at all—just a common barnyard pullet of last summer's late hatch, a dusty Dominique. But she was the delight of our small hero, who himself was not Very large, considering his ten happy years.

Because she was a late chick, he had been allowed to adopt her; and never was hen more loved, more petted, or responsive more fully to a child's affection.

This bright Sabbath morning in early April the boy stood gloating over fifteen brown eggs in a small chip basket which he had Very carefully lifted from the high shelf in the pantry.

There was no question about it, Pet was broody. Tomorrow probably he would bring fresh straw from the stack and, having dusted it well with sulphur, he would make a new nest and place therein these golden prospects and soon—not Very soon either, but in three weeks—he'd see.

The minister had delivered a searching address, a powerful appeal for missions. So interesting was it that the child had not noticed how long it was; and as he slipped stiffly down from the high bench and stood on his feet, he almost tumbled over, for his sitting so long in one position had stopped the circulation of the blood and his feet had "gone to sleep."

Walking homeward along the side of the road, he was so quiet and absorbed in his thoughts that his mother spoke to him twice before he heard her.

"Mother," the childish voice was eager; "mother, I'd like to give something to take the story of Jesus to the heathen, but I haven't anything; and if father gives me money, it wouldn't be my gift, would it?"

"Have you nothing, dear, that you could give?"

The small head was working hard. "Yes, mother; I have Pet. O. I know!"

It was considerable sacrifice; but once having engaged to do this thing, he stuck closely to his bargain.

The young hen took kindly to the new nest and the fifteen brown eggs. She sat so faithfully that her small owner was wont to drag her from the new duties to feed her. But one attempt was sufficient; for from one evidence of the effectiveness of Pet's beak.

There were fifteen of the hatch, a most remarkable result, and only one casualty in the rearing. One adventuresome one stepped

into the water trough and before assistance came was past help. But the fourteen thrived. Not even gapes attacked them; and when August arrived, they were so near the size of their mother that it was hard to distinguish between them.

The White Sulphur Springs wagon, which regularly visited the farm, carried away the flock; and though the price received was only fifty cents each, it was for that time and day a fair one.

The seven dollars, after the history was told, looked rather large to the preacher, and he asked the child if he meant to give it all.

NEWS FROM THE FIELD

INDIANA DISTRICT CONFERENCE
Flora, Indiana, October 4, 1920
Monday Evening, October 4

7:30 Service of Song and Prayer led by
C. A. Stewart
8:00 Welcome by pastor, W. E. Thomas.
8:15 Annual Conference Sermon,
Dr. G. W. Rench
Assignments, announcements, Benediction.

Tuesday A. M.

8:30-9:30 Simultaneous Conferences—
Ministerium, Woman's Missionary Society. (Note—W. M. S. program will appear separately in Evangelist).
Ministerium.
8:30 Devotions.
8:45 Election of officers and other business.
9:00 The President's Message, C. A. Bame.
9:30 Devotional, J. W. Brower
9:45 Brief Addresses by Delegates.
Theme: The Challenge of the Hour, or What I Would Like to see this Conference Do.
10:15 The Conference Moderator's Message,
J. A. McInturff
10:45 Pastor's Annual Reports; Business.

Tuesday P. M.

Sunday School and Y. P. S. C. E. Session, Sylvester Whetstone Presiding.
1:15 Quiet Hour, W. R. Deeter
1:30 The Superintendent's Message,
S. M. Whetstone
2:00 Reports of District Conventions:
(a) Northern, President of District
(b) Southern, President of District
2:30 Our Young People, G. C. Carpenter.
2:50 Special Music
3:00 Address, B. L. Miller
3:30 S. S. and Y. P. S. C. E. Business Session
4:00 Adjournment.
7:00 Service of Song and Prayer,
J. W. Clark
7:30 Our College, Dr. E. E. Jacobs
8:00 Special Music
8:10 Sermon, C. C. Grisso
Benediction.

Wednesday A. M.

8:30-9:30 Ministerium and W. M. S. Conferences
8:30 Business

9:00 Address—The Place of Theology in Brethren Conferences and Pulpits,
A. T. Wirick
9:30 Public Session of W. M. S.,
Mrs. Elmer Burkey, Presiding.
10:30 Address—Pastoral Evangelism,
W. E. Ronk
11:00 Business Session.
11:50 Adjournment.

Wednesday P. M.
Our Mission Interests

1:30 Quiet Hour, H. E. Eppley
1:45 Address—"Our attitude toward the Open Doors of our District,"
Dr. G. W. Rench.
2:15 Mission Pastors Reports
3:00 Report of Members of Mission Board
Election of Members of Board.
Business
Adjournment.
7:00 Praise and Prayer, C. A. Stewart
7:20 Brethrenism—Past, Present, Future,
C. E. Kolb
7:40 Special Music
8:00 Evangelistic Sermon,
Evangelist A. T. Wirick

Thursday A. M.

8:30-9:30 Simultaneous Conferences.
Ministerium
8:30 Devotional
8:45 Business
9:00 Address—"How Shall we Get More Successful Evangelism in Our District?" W. T. Lytle
9:30 Quiet Hour, L. A. Myers
9:45 The Five Year Forward Movement as National or State Director Applied to Our District,
10:15 General Discussion of Forward Movement Program
10:45 Final Conference Business Session.
12:00 Good-bye.
Notes—The church at Flora is planning for large delegations and will spare no means to entertain in a great way.
Let every church send their full quota of delegates.
Persons whose names appear on the program finding it impossible to be present will do us a favor by notifying us at an early date. C. C. GRISSO, Secretary,
North Liberty, Indiana.

THE OUT OF SEASON

There is no doubt that every city pastor will agree that the months of July is one of the most difficult of the year for a revival service. However we had one in Columbus, Ohio, and a good one at that. We further say that we never had such big crowds at any revival service in Columbus. If the weather had been nice the house would not have held the attendance at several services. The people of the community and the church speak very highly of Miss Emma M. Aboud not alone as an evangelist but as a deeply consecrated woman and a tactful, earnest, devoted servant of God, always ready for personal work. I must say even more than ready, for she doesn't wait for opportunities but tries by all means to make them. You Brethren who have not yet had this opportunity of having her, get in line to get Miss Aboud for next year. The work done in our service did not show so great in numbers, but the influence of the Brethren church is greater; the church is better known in the city than ever before. People came from the other end of Columbus to hear and see one from the land where Jesus walked and talked. During the three weeks' campaign there were twelve that made confession. Two of these were reclaimed, five were baptized, and there were five young girls whose parents forbid them to unite with our church. Two of these last girls mentioned were Catholics or of Catholic parentage and when the parents found out that these had made a confession in a Protestant church they worked it otherwise, and now their children are not allowed to play with our children. The follow-up work is now laid on the pastor and the members, and the future will show our earnestness in this respect. The field in Columbus is great and a wonderful opportunity for the Brethren church. In my judgment every effort should be put forth, not by one but by all, to erect a strong work, based upon the whole doctrine of the Lord Jesus Christ, with an active life for Christ to prove the doctrine, in truth and in deed. We found the truth in love and deeds to be the main object in Miss Aboud's heart. May God richly bless her in the endeavors to win souls for the Master and his Kingdom. I am safe to say we could not have had a better evangelist for this place, she has the spirit for indoor and out-door work and the main-issue in her life is a Redeeming Savior for a Lost World.

Since the service we have had a good chance to talk with some that came to the revival services and have the promise of others to yield their lives to the Lord's will. One has been received by letter. Many of the churches in this city have no services during the months of July and August, others have but one service each Sunday. We continue two services although the congregation is small beside what it is in the winter. As a whole the attendance has been larger this year than the other two years. Our choir has proven a great help in attendance.

S. E. CHRISTIANSEN,

536 W. 3rd Avenue.

ANY BRETHREN IN COLORADO?

Brother A. J. Ramey of Manassas, Virginia, states that he is going to locate in Colorado and desires to know the names of any Brethren living in that state. He requests any members living in that state to write him at the above address.

LOUISVILLE, OHIO

We delight in reading church reports from every part of the Brethren Vineyard and trust that there are those who may be wanting to read a brief message from this place.

Louisville as a town is now in the making. We are thinking that it will soon be a wide-awake business place. The erection of two large steel mills, with one now in operation has brought and is still bringing new people to our town. Every attempt is being made to locate the newcomers and interest them in the work of the church. These corporations are under the direction of estimable men, who are selecting their employees. Hence a remarkably fine class of people are coming here for mill work.

As a church, with a splendid organization, we are glad to report that some very fine families are showing a great interest in our church work. Our Sunday school is making a strong appeal to the strangers and many have already become members of that body. Some of these have been teachers and leaders of societies in their home churches. The word that sounds encouraging to our ears is, "we have come here to stay."

A wide-awake Sunday school having a good orchestra, a consecrated corps of teachers and officers; a Women's Missionary Society that has recently captured fifteen new members; a Sisterhood and two good Endeavor societies; all directed and used for his sake, by the Spirit of God ought to make some wholesome environment for a rapidly growing town.

Summer conditions have not affected church attendance with us. In fact Sunday school and church attendance during the past six months has been much better than for the same months last year.

Our latest event was the annual picnic of the Brethren Sunday Schools of Louisville and Canton at Nimishilo Park, on the afternoon of August 11. The children were kept busy by races and contests. A ball game be-

tween the single and married men furnished excitement for the older folks. A picnic supper was served in the open pavilion.

We expect to be represented at Conference by a full quota of delegates.

We have every reason to be optimistic about the work here. We urge continually the responsibility of each for a greater Brethren church.

We covet your prayers for the sake of the Kingdom.

E. M. RIDDLE, Pastor.

FREDONIA, KANSAS

I baptized five applicants, Sunday, August 15. They all live near Middleton, about 16 miles north of Fredonia. Others seem near the kingdom and prospects are very favorable for an organization. One of the new members came from the Quaker faith. Pray for me and the Lord's Cause.

W. B. SELL,

Box 804, Fredonia, Kansas.

FROM GOSHEN, INDIANA

We have put off writing longer than we really expected to, not because we did not have any news, because there is always something doing at Goshen. Brother McInturff our pastor, and family are enjoying their vacation at present. More than a month ago they motored to Virginia to see the old home friends. We sure thought he would write a bit of news for the Evangelist while absent. We expect him home Tuesday, then he will tell us all about his trip and why he did not write for the Evangelist.

The work at Goshen was not called off during the pastor's absence, all departments at work, "save the Senior Endeavor." The pulpit has been filled by Brother W. I. Duker, Sister Maud Webb, and Brother J. A. Garber. All did well. Brother Garber seems to enjoy preaching to the Goshen people and we sure all enjoy his good sermons. He preaches for us this evening.

Brother Duker submitted to an operation at the Goshen Hospital, and is doing fine so far. The operation took place two weeks ago tomorrow. While on his bed a meeting of the deacons and others was held and Brother Duker took the confession of Mr. Culp, eighty-three years old. It is blessed to see the aged come to Christ.

Our Sunday School Superintendent announced the annual Sunday school picnic for Thursday the 12th of August. Usually these picnics are largely attended and all plan on having a good time. This is right for a good time for Christians means a Christlike time, doing just what we would do if he were here in person. The Sunday school is holding up fine in attendance, not getting far from the three hundred mark. Conference time will soon be here. Some of the Goshen folks expect to attend. Some usually plan to spend their summer's vacation at Winona at that time hoping to get something good and we usually get what we look for, so it is said. Sometime during the early fall, Brother Bell will conduct the evangelistic campaign for the Goshen church. We ask for the prayers of all.

M. E. HORNER,

Corresponding Secretary.

THE ETHICS OF DANCING
A Review

A pamphlet on "The Ethics of Dancing," by Rev. R. Lee Kirkland, D.D., of Flemington, New Jersey, and published by him, is an able and interesting treatment of its subject. First, he discusses the holy dances, those participated in by David and the holy men and women of old, then deals with the pagan dance, such as was indulged in by Aaron in the absence of Moses, where "the people were naked unto their shame." He follows this type of dancing down the ages to the present, showing its influence over the homes, even the church, and through all eternity. Colleges and schools that encourage dancing receive their share of criticism from Dr. Kirkland. A most excellent treatment of the subject is this 12-cent booklet, and church people would do well to read it for their own enlightenment and pleasure, then hand to some person who is unable to see any harm in the dance.

It is invaluable to ministers as it is filled with suggestions to aid them in preparing sermons on the subject of dancing, and is highly deserving of the widest possible circulation.

T. DARLEY ALLEN.

15th International Congress Against Alcoholism

Under Auspices State Department, U. S. A.

Washington, D. C., Sept. 21-26

(Special Correspondence)

Washington, D. C., August 19, 1920—For the first time in America, and the first time ever outside of continental Europt, the great International Congress Against Alcoholism will convene in this city at the beautiful building of the Pan American Union under the auspices of the Department of State, from Tuesday noon September 21 to Sunday evening September 26, 1920.

Practically every country with which the United States maintains diplomatic relations will be represented by an official delegation. There will be delegates from up under the Arctic circle from Iceland and Finland and Russia. Scandinavia, the land of the midnight sun, will be represented in force. The new republics of Poland and Czecho-Slovakia will answer to their names for the first time. The democratic kingdom of the Serbs, Croats and Slovenes will answer "Here" when "Jugo-Slavia" is called. The Antipodes will be present, and all of the countries of Central and South and North America. England and France, China and Japan, will be there likewise, while Italy in addition to its formal delegation is sending a commercial representative with an exhibit of unfermented wines to show what can be done with a great native industry if ever there is an 18th Amendment to the Italian Constitution.

The Congress is a governmental body, and is strictly scientific in character. It is in effect an open forum for the free discussion of alcoholism as a disease, and is without prejudice for or against any particular method of dealing with the problem. Because of its scientific and governmental character, the Congress passes no resolutions nor does it commit to a definite policy the official delegates attending it. Its purpose is to meet every two years, listen to the reports of those who are studying scientifically the various phases of alcoholism and leading the fight against it, analyze and discuss their conclusions, and exchange among the delegations world-wide information on this great international topic.

Distinguished scientists, prominent educators, well-known physicians, and men and women who are taking an active part in the public life of two hemispheres, will either read papers or lead the general discussions which follow the papers. They will be present as guests of the United States Government, who is official host to the Congress. Aproximately half the program will be given over to the United States, as is the customary courtesy of the Congress to the country which has issued the official invitation. The program, which will be announced soon by the State Department, is divided into three sections, scientific, economic and industrial, and social and historical. A particularly searching examination will probably be made by the Congress into the method and results of Constitutional regulation of alcohol in this country.

This will be the fifteenth session of the Congress since its foundation in 1880, and the first session in almost a decade due to the upheaval of the World War. The last previous Congress met at Milan, Italy, in 1913, and it was at this session that the invitation of the United States was formally accepted. The date was fixed originally for the autumn of 1915, and the American Executive Committee appointed at that time by the State Department to have charge of the details of the Congress has been continued in office by the Secretary of State to direct the meeting which now will take place in September. The Committee consists of: Edwin C. Dinwiddie, of Washington, D C., chairman; Charles Scanlon LL. D., of Pittsburg, Pa., 1st vice-chairman; Rufus W Miller D. D., of Philadelphia, Pa., 2nd vice chairman; Earnest H. Cherrington, of Westerville, Ohio, secretary; Very Rev. Peter J O'Callaghan C. S. P., treasurer; Mrs. Don P Blaine, of Washington, D. C.; and Bishop James Cannon Jr., of Richmond, Va. Mrs. Ella A. Yost, of Morgantown, West Virginia, is Director of Women's Activities, Miss Laura R. Church of Washington, D. C., is Assistant Treasurer, and Thomas Quinn Beesley of Washington, D. C., is Assistant to the Committee. The offices and headquarters of the Committee are at 756-759 Munsey Bldg., Washington, D. C.

THE PASTOR'S NEED OF RECREATION

A great many years ago there was a test of endurance in one of the English factories. A set of men worked the seven days of the week; a corresponding set of men worked six days and rested the seventh. At the end of a given time there was an examination of results. It was found that the men who worked six days and rested the seventh had produced more work, had rendered more satisfactory service, and were in better physical condition than those who had taken no rest. No test

has been made in the matter of vacation or no vacation, but we feel safe in assuming that we would get like results. The pastor, above all others, is an outstanding example. He works seven days a week: he is hard at it from morning till night, except Sunday, which, by all odds, is his easiest day—if he has an easy one. And when the oppressive summer heat comes he needs a few weeks' rest to steady his nerves, invigorate his bodily powers, and give his mind a chance to spring back to its former bent. And as the year revolves it will be found that he renders more service and more efficient service, than if he had plodded on in the same old round of duties; while, as a purely physical effect, his dial will turn back many a degree because of the spell of rest. The congregation that does not give its pastor a month's vacation is not only forgetful of his wants but negligent of its own interests.—The Lutheran.

RAMONA, KANSAS

Dear Editor: I wish to announce through The Evangelist that I will be free after the first of October to do some evangelistic work for those desiring my services. If there are weak churches that are not financially able to pay for such services, do not hesitate to correspond with me, as my desire is not to make money but to build up Christ's church and spread this glorious Gospel of Jesus Christ and see souls saved. Address

F. E. BUTTON, Ramona, Kansas.
Box 96.

When the Mists Have Rolled Away
By George Kinzie.

I may not know the reason why
The dark clouds gather in the sky;
Why grief so great should come to me,
While others seem to go so free;
But blest be God, I'll know some day,
When the mists have rolled away.

O my heart is almost breaking,
And my brow so weary, aching;
Yet I know he's not forsaking;
For so near He seems to stay;
Ever telling me "Be faithful,
Till the mists have rolled away."

Tho' my sorrow 'most o'erwhelms me,
And I feel my grief compels me
To rebel, and say Him, "nay;".
Still His love divine impels me;
"Follow on," His spirit tells me,
"Till the mists have rolled away."

When the mists have rolled away,
His dear face I then shall see,
And again my loved ones meet.
There no sorrow e'er shall be;
It will be just one glad day,
When the mists have rolled away.

When that glad eternal day
Sheds its glories on our way,
How we'll shout, with joy untold!
As we tread the streets of gold;
Matchless love we'll then unfold,.
When the mists have rolled away.
New Lebanon, Ohio.

"A penny for your thoughts," we sometimes say; but thoughts, good thoughts, are golden. Would you be ashamed to have your father or mother, or your Sunday school teacher, know what you are thinking about just now? Only good, pure thoughts will make you fit company for yourself. Here is one of the great verses, this beatitude: "Blessed are the pure in heart: for they shall see God."

The Tithing Stewardship Corner

What Is Stewardship?
By Mrs. Sarah Keim

Mr. Reeves Calkins, in his book on Stewardship, gives in the first place a few illustrations as to what stewardship is not. We will give at least one. When the will of the late Richard T. Crane, of Chicago, was probated, it was found that, under its terms and by verbal instructions to his two sons, certain public charities were to receive more than a million dollars for endowment, and another million was to provide pensions and disability benefits for employees of the Crane Company. This was generous and praiseworthy. But the question forms itself into words: Was the Crane will an act of stewardship? And we must conclude it was not. We might give many more illustrations like this one but let this suffice.

Stewardship is not merely giving, for the steward is not administering zor himself but for another. Stewardship is the recognition that God is the owner of all economic Value, and, therefore, that private property can be no other than a sacred trust. The earth is the Lord's and the fullness thereof. The cattle upon a thousand hills are mine, the gold and the silver are mine, and ye are not your own but ye have been bought with a price, therefore glorify God both in material gifts and spiritual talents.

Stewardship is the Christian's attitude toward his possessions that causes him to recognize God as owner and himself a trustee. But it is very much more than that. Stewardship is the Christian's law of living. The stewardship of privilege, of opportunity, of mental and spiritual gifts, of experience, of education is acknowledged. We remember the parable of the Talents, given by the Master. Stewardship is under one compulsion and only one, but this is absolute. "It is required in stewards that a man be found faithful." It is the loyalty of friendship. It implies vital partnership with God. "Let that Word measure the quality of a man's fidelity'.
Ashland, Ohio.

Business Manager's Corner

A SUMMARY AND A FORECAST

The annual report of the business of The Brethren Publishing Company appears on this page and while it does not seem proper that the Business Manager should make any complimentary remarks about his own work, we only want to say we are not ashamed to present the report as it is and we are willing to leave it to our readers to determine whether or not the work has been creditably done.

By far the largest volume of business ever done in any one year by the Company has been done the past year. But volume of business does not mean much unless it has been a profitable business. It is not with the publishing business as the old Jewish clothier explained about his great "below-cost" sale of clothing, "that while losing on the sale of a single suit of clothing he came out ahead because he sold so many of them...

In the publishing business every sheet of paper used must be paid for at the market price and every hour of labor of each employe requires the outlay of a definite sum equal to the market price of labor, and unless more money is received for the finished product than the cost of material, the cost of labor, the cost of wear of machinery, the rental value of the building occupied and at least six per cent interest on the amount of money invested, there is no profit no matter what the volume of business has been.

Thus while the report for the year shows a very decided net gain for the year it is only just to say that this gain is principally the result of a wise real estate investment and not the result of the printing end of the business. The cost of material and the cost of labor the past year has been too great when compared to the prices we have received for the completed product to net any profit that has been worthwhile, and the outlook for the future is less promising than the results of the past year have been.

Sunday School Supplies

We have received revised price lists from several other publishers of Sunday school litterature and they have increased their prices considerably, and we have been compelled to follow suit, not because they have done so, but because it is impossible to make a literature for anything less.

We sent out order blanks to our schools last week and we trust that they will all understand the necessity for the change, and that they will also understand that if they attempt to avoid meeting their share of the increased cost of production by reducing the amount of supplies ordered they will effect a direct loss to the Publishing Company, because the same number of quarterlies will be made that was made last quarter, and if there remains unsold any large number of quarterlies printed on the expensive paper that has to be used for the year it will mean just that much direct loss. So please remember that the Publishing Company is your company and that its losses are your losses and its gains are your gains.

The Evangelist Subscription Campaign

The four year campaign is over and it has been a worthy one. Only the final report of the campaign managers will determine what departments of the church have been most successful in their efforts to reach their goals. We can only say for The Evangelist that it went nearly one thousand subscriptions beyond anything we hoped for when the campaign was begun. But this campaign for The Brethren Evangelist is exactly like a

Sunday school contest, it counts for but little unless the momentum gained can be made into a permanent driving or impelling power.

The Budget System has worked admirably for four years and we hope it can be continued indefinitely by our churches, but it will have to be done on a different basis. This system has been giving the paper to perhaps three-fourths of our subscribers at the same price that was paid in 1915, and since then the cost of paper stock has increased nearly THREE HUNDRED percent. Our local daily paper and the Cleveland daily that comes to our home have increased their subscription price fifty percent, and something must be done for The Evangelist, but this is one of the problems that will have to be dealt with at our Winona Conference and we can make no prophecies here:

We are still printing nearly 5,500 copies of The Evangelist each week and we would regret very much to see the list cut down to any large extent.

In order to give every church an opportunity to win a place on the Honor Roll before

the close of the campaign we have been extremely lenient, even to the point of carelessness in continuing subscriptions after they have expired and now a rough estimate would place 1,000 subscriptions on the delinquent list. Immediately after conference we will go after this matter and those who fail to renew will be discontinued, but we still hope they will all renew.

Since our last report, two churches have been continued on the Honor Roll, New Enterprise and the Akron, Indiana, congregations. We believe this is the second year for New Enterprise and the FIFTH year for Akron. Even before we began our Four Year Campaign Brother A. E. Dickerhoff of Akron sent in a list of subscriptions with the statement, "this includes every family belonging to our church," and they have never lost their place.

After our Board meeting at Winona we will be able to make definite announcements for the future.

R. R. TEETER,
Business Manager.

FINANCIAL REPORT
Of
THE BRETHREN PUBLISHING COMPANY
For the Year
August 1, 1919 to August 1, 1920

R. R. Teeter, Business Manager

Year's Business	
Cash and Credit	
Cash Balance Aug. 1, 1919	$ 1,868.94
Evangelist Subscriptions	7,595.92
S. S. Publications	9,345.20
Commission Goods	1,144.45
Job Work	9,530.91
Engravings	171.35
Paper Stock	20.66
Rents	1,381.36
Loans	2,800.00
Miscellaneous	4,578.90
Total	$38,456.50
Cash on hand Aug 1, 1919	$ 1,868.94
Received during year	32,446.35
Total	$34,315.29

RESOURCES	
Cash in Bank	$ 2,471.49
Printing Outfit	6,700.00
Composing Outfit	5,700.00
Paper Stock	5,414.00
Furniture and Fixtures	400.00
Accounts Receivable	2,101.53
Buildings and Grounds	32,000.00
Total	$54,787.52

Year's Expenses	
For Labor	$10,850.68
Composition	2,340.93
Postage	578.63
Commission Goods	862.27
Engravings	249.72
Transportation and Dray	531.81
Paper Stock	3,616.58
Insurance	182.59
Interest	939.67
Light, Power & Fuel	750.96
Miscellaneous	10,939.92
Total	$31,843.80
Cash on hand Aug. 1, 1920	$ 2,471.49
Total	$34,315.29

LIABILITIES	
Accounts Payable	$ 5,921.77
Book and Tract Fund	500.00
Bills Payable	24,525.00
	$30,946.77
Total Resources	$54,787.52
Total Liabilities	30,946.77
Net Resources	$23,840.75
Resources Aug. 1, 1919	11,170.06
Year's Net Gain	$12,670.69

Ashland, Ohio, August 20, 1920:

We have this day audited the above report of the business of The Brethren Publishing Company, and find it correct according to the books of the Company. Signed,

J. ALLEN MILLER,
MARTIN SHIVELY,
Auditing Committee.

The BRETHREN EVANGELIST

Impressions and Reports
of the
JUBILEE CONFERENCE
AT WINONA LAKE, INDIANA

The Launching of the
BRETHREN BICENTENARY
MOVEMENT

Comparative Figures
of the
FOUR YEAR PROGRAM

It will pay you to preserve
this issue of The Evangelist

Published every Wednesday at Ashland, Ohio. All matter for publication must reach the Editor not later than Friday noon of the preceding week.

George S. Baer, Editor

The
Brethren
Evangelist

When ordering your paper changed give old as well as new address. Subscriptions discontinued at expiration. To avoid missing any numbers renew two weeks in advance.

R. R. Teeter, Business Manager

OFFICIAL ORGAN OF THE BRETHREN CHURCH

Subscription price, $2.00 per year, payable in advance.
Entered at the Post Office at Ashland, Ohio, as second-class matter.
Acceptance for mailing at special rate of postage provided for in section 1103, Act of October 3, 1917, authorized September 9, 1918.
Address all matter for publication to Geo. S. Baer, Editor of the Brethren Evangelist, and all business communications to R. R. Teeter, Business Manager, Brethren Publishing Company, Ashland, Ohio. Make all checks payable to the Brethren Publishing Company.

TABLE OF CONTENTS

EDITORIAL

The Forward Look of the Jubilee Conference

We have been there—more than four hundred of us, besides departmental delegates—and now we are home again thinking it all over. The thirty-second General Conference is now a matter of history, but the inspiration received, the visions experienced and the plans laid are not in the category of mere historical facts; they are present possessions in the hearts and minds of practically every serious-minded delegate who was there. No one in a receptive frame of mind could have spent a week at Winona Lake attending the various sessions of our Jubilee Conference and returned home the same as he went. Those who participated sincerely in those high spiritual experiences could not but have had their souls greatly uplifted and their strength renewed. The Spirit of God was manifestly present, and, in a very large measure, must have had its way in the direction and messages of the Conference, and also in the plans and problems that had to be worked out there. And, as is always the case where the Spirit is permitted to speak and where there is a willingness to hear and to heed its wisdom, the delegates purposed in their hearts that they would ''go forward.'' This prevailing attitude is the thing that sent us to our homes with brighter hopes, stronger faith and greater zeal as regards our common task. This is the thing that makes us desire to speak of the things we have seen and heard. This is the thing that is likely to be the dominant note in the report of most of the delegates to their home churches. And if everything else should be forgotten, this is the thing that should remain with us and be held up before us throughout the coming year—the vision and plan of a larger future for the Brethren church. For if this forward look becomes the permanent possession of every member of our fraternity, it is certain under God to be realized.

In every department of our church's interests this forward look was evident. There was rejoicing over the accomplishments of the past, but we had scarcely taken inventory of our credits in store until we began to consider what greater things we might and ought to do. The one department in which perhaps the greatest revival of interest and increased support has been experienced is the educational work of the church centering in Ashland College. Here the Four Year Program goal has been far outreached. From all over the brotherhood endowment money has been coming in through the strenuous campaign of Brother Beachler until we are made to hang our heads at the smallness of our faith of four years ago. But rejoice as we may over the success of the endowment campaign, we are very conscious of the fact that we have made only a small beginning at meeting the urgent needs of Ashland College. This fact has been continually set before

the brotherhood by President Jacobs and other leaders of the college, and was also brought to the attention of the conference. Plans were laid whereby our educational institution should share continually in proper proportion in the church's gifts to the Lord's work from year to year. And there is a growing conviction that its proper proportion is larger than that of any other interest just at present in view of its strategic position in the work and growth of the church—it bears the responsibility of discovering and training the workers of the church for all its various fields. That Ashland College must be adequately endowed if the church is to do her proper work is coming to be the conviction of every informed member of the Brethren church, and we are looking forward not to $200,000, but to $500,000 and then to a million. This high ambition will not be fully realized during the next three years of our Bicentenary Movement. But the decidedly forward look taken by this conference indicates that the brotherhood will not long be satisfied with doing this task in mincing bits.

At our Jubilee Conference we had much reason to rejoice in the great advance in missionary giving and activity. At the beginning of our Four Year Program we were giving only a little more than four thousand dollars for foreign missions, while last year more than twenty-six thousand were contributed for that purpose. Our gifts for home missions increased thirty-three and one-third percent. These facts were gratifying, but the delegates were not content with rejoicing. They set still higher goals and planned how we as a church might demonstrate still more worthily the seriousness of our purpose to carry out the commission of our Lord.

The impetus given to our publication interests by the Four Year Program has caused a remarkable growth along all lines, but especially in the number of subscriptions to The Brethren Evangelist. The various publications have been increasing in efficiency and the Publishing Company has grown in a remarkable way. But it is coming to be realized that if our Publishing House is to serve the brotherhood in the largest way it must be supported and endowed by the gifts of the people. We are also coming to see how the various publications can be still further improved and made to serve the brotherhood in a larger way. In these and many other ways there is indicated a growing outlook and the fact that our late conference took cognizance of these things is cause for encouragement.

The work of the Board of Benevolences showed a remarkable progress during the Four Year Program, so that it is able to pay the aged ministers or aged widows of ministers a larger sum than ever before, but still more worthy work along this line is being planned. The leaders of this work are looking forward to the time when our benevolences in behalf of those who need and deserve the help of the brotherhood shall be to our credit, and not to our embarrassment, as has been the case in the past. Hearty co-operation with this board's plans for the Bicentenary Movement will make possible the realization of this worthy aim.

In still other ways it might be pointed out how our Jubilee Conference gave expression to the sentiment that has been steadily crystalizing among our people that the hour has come when we should press the battle with all possible vigor in every department of our church's interest. We are awakening to the fact that we can no longer afford to dally with the most important matter in all the world—that of advancing the interests of the kingdom of Christ. This conference revealed a noble work done during the recent four year drive, a work comparable to that of another people, but it also showed without a doubt that our people are not satisfied to date over the accomplishments of the past (they are not worthy to be mentioned compared with what must needs be done), but have their eyes fixed upon the challenge of the future. And it was a great conference, not because of its record attendance, but because of what it did to enable the church to meet that challenge.

EDITORIAL REVIEW

Be careful of the man who mistrusts everybody, for rarely will that man trust himself.—Selected.

Moderators of district conferences should not fail to heed Brother O'Neill's "Special Notice" concerning the election of representatives for the Superannuated Ministers' Fund.

Brother Enoch Fetters writes that his wife, Mrs. Grace P. Fetters, has been removed from the hospital in Battle Creek, Michigan, to her home and is very critically ill. He asks that the brotherhood make united prayer on Sunday, October 3 for her recovery.

Brother S. P. Fogle reports concerning his evangelistic labors in Allegheny county, Virginia, which resulted in a goodly number of confessions though some difficulty was experienced in the matter of deciding church relationships.

Another Brethren missionary died in the heart of Africa— Myrtle Mae Snyder of Dayton, Ohio. Word to this effect reached Dr. J. Allen Miller, president of the Foreign Missionary Society, on the afternoon of September 13. Fuller notice and particulars will appear later.

The Brethren Sunday school at Garwin, Iowa, kept interest very much alive during the summer by a "Red and Blue" contest. Brother Ankrum, the pastor, states that it is likely that they will either have to "stop growing or soon enlarge." It is encouraging to learn of places where the Lords' work was kept going at full force during the season when there were the greatest temptations to lag.

Brother Belote brings to the attention of the churches of the various districts a very urgent matter; it is the payment of our denominational pledge to the Winona Tabernacle Fund. Read his letter in this issue and let every congregation do its part immediately. We wish to urge this matter upon the Ohio churches in a special way. We hope every church will have paid its apportionment of 16 cents per member before our state conference meets.

Our correspondent from the Compton Avenue Brethren church of Los Angeles reports that they lost their pastor, that the district mission board called him to use his splendid talents to develop the difficult field at Fillmore. Brother Beal is one of our strongest pastors and preachers, and we can understand how they would miss him. But they have secured a splendid young man in the person of Brother Victor Leatherman to take his place. Brother Leatherman has been out of school only a few years, but he is rapidly developing into a strong and efficient leader.

Brother E. G. Mason, our new General Conference secretary, gives a brief report of the business proceedings in order that the brotherhood may know promptly concerning the things that were done at Winona. The complete report is promised to be forthcoming in November. Brother Dyoll Belote who served the Conference so efficiently in this capacity for eleven years demanded a release, and with a vote of thanks for his faithful services the Conference acceded to his demand. But in the person of Prof. E. G. Mason, a worthy successor has been found.

The work is going forward in a splendid way in the new First church of Los Angeles. The spirit of evangelism continues to run high, and conversions are of frequent occurrence at the regular services under the stirring evangelistic sermons of the pastor, Brother N. W. Jennings. We notice that the church paid its pastors' expenses to General Conference, which was a fine thing to do, and was as Brother Reed suggests, an expression of their appreciation of his splendid services. It ought to be the custom of every church to pay their pastors' expenses to the conferences. Either that or pay him enough larger salary so that he may pay his own way without financial embarrassment. The paying of conference expenses is a delightful custom on the part of many churches.

Brother I. D. Bowman was quite successful, as has been learned by previous reports, in his evangelistic campaign at Krypton. It proved to be a "revival" as well as an evangelistic campaign, according to Brother Bowman's report. He found many difficulties with which to contend. It would probably be a revelation to many of our pastors to be called upon to work among these people for a few weeks. The vices which Brother Bowman mentions as being prevalent at Krypton are such as have been reported by our workers there and at Lost Creek from the beginning. But the gospel has been steadily proving to be the power of God unto salvation for the people and conditions there. However we must expect that old habits and customs will not all be suddenly done away, but will cling to individuals and communities to vex us. It takes time to regenerate a whole community. But if we plant the good seed of the Word and faithfully care for it, God will give the increase in good time—his time.

Every loyal Brethren who can possibly do so, ought to heed the appeal of the business manager for a contribution to help meet the emergency in which our church paper finds itself. You will understand what is meant when you read the Business Managers' Corner of this week. There ought to be a great many "one dollar bills," "fives" and "tens" and even higher finding their way into the office at an early date. This ought to be considered as much a part of the Lord's work as meeting a deficit on some missionary's salary or helping to erect a chapel in which the Gospel was to be preached. We have said repeatedly that the publishing of a church paper is not a money-making proposition. A church paper's mission is publishing the Gospel and we ought to support it the same as we do any other missionary or evangelistic agency. This is an opportunity to do more than simply pay for the good you get personally from the Evangelist. Make the matter a subject of prayer and let the Lord direct you in making your gift.

This is the time for state and district conferences, that is the time to prepare for them and plan to attend. The efficiency of each district work depends very largely on the loyalty with which the various churches support the conferences of their respective districts. This year more than usual demands a large attendance at our various district conferences in order that the districts may get all their congregations started on the new Bicentenary Movement at the outset. Note the dates and places of the district conferences whose programs are found in this issue of The Evangelist:

Pennsylvania at Pittsburgh, October 4 to 7.
Illiokota at Lanark, Illinois, October 6 to 8.
Middle West at Fort Scott, Kansas, October 12 to 14.

And the Women's Missionary Conference Program to be held in connection with the Indiana conference at Flora, October 4 to 7.

The Ohio conference will be held at Ashland, Ohio, during the last week in October, the definite date and program will appear promptly.

THE OLD

FOUR-YEAR PROGRAM PAGE

NOW THEN DO IT.—II Samuel 3:18

NOW BECOMES

THE BRETHREN BICENTENARY MOVEMENT PAGE

1723 · - · · · · 1923

The old Four Year Program was brought to a close with the late General Conference and a new three-year program, known as The Brethren Bicentenary Movement, has taken its place. The new program and the organization to put it into effect are as follows:

EXECUTIVE COMMITTEE

G. W. RENCH, Spiritual Life   WM. A. GEARHART, Missions and Extension

EDWIN E. JACOBS, Education   R. R. TEETER, Publication Interests

MILES J. SNYDER, Stewardship   H. F. E. O'NEILL, Benevolences

W. S. BELL, Evangelism

CHARLES A. BAME, Chairman and Executive Secretary

MILES J. SNYDER, Secretary–Treasurer

SPIRITUAL LIFE

1. The family altar maintained by habits of daily prayer and Bible reading in every Brethren home.
2. Faithfulness in all the services of the church.
3. Continued zeal in heralding doctrinal truth in pulpit and Bible conferences.

EDUCATION

I. College and Seminary

1. Our educational institutions increasingly endowed and supported on a proportionate basis with other general interests.
2. A growing student body from Brethren homes to receive worthy education under positive Christian guidance and influence.
3. Sufficient scholarship funds to encourage and enable young people dedicating their lives for definite Christian service to take the needed training.
4. Particular emphasis given these objectives on Educational Day, the first Sunday in June.

II. Religious Education

1. The home made the initial center of Christian education.
2. Active co-operation with related community agencies in the promotion of universal religious education.
3. The local church organized and equipped for religious education under the direction of a competent Board, maintaining regular training courses and an annual school of missions.

STEWARDSHIP

I. Of Life

1. A standing, urgent life stewardship appeal before every church with a view of securing (a) at least one recruit for full time employed service, and (b) definitely enlisted trained voluntary workers. A call to service is a call to necessary preparation.

II. Of Possessions

1. An effective educational campaign on stewardship conducted throughout the year, with one-tenth the minimum basis of giving; including (a) the observance of the last Sunday in October as Stewardship Day with appropriate sermons preached, and (b) timely articles in the Brethren Evangelist supplemented by the distribution of stewardship literature.
2. The budget system of finance with the every-member canvass in each operating church.

EVANGELISM

1. An evangelistic meeting in every church of the brotherhood annually.
2. The work of evangelism to be carried on through local official boards, district evangelistic committees, or the Evangelistic and Bible Study League.

MISSIONS AND EXTENSION

1. The full consecration of life and possessions to the task of missionary endeavor.
2. A systematic campaign of missionary education in every church.
3. A vigorous program of conversation and extension to fortify weak places and to claim new opportunities.
4. Friendliness to a working agreement with the Church of the Brethren for the saving of all Brethren people to the faith.

PUBLICATION INTERESTS

1. An adequately equipped publishing house to meet the growing need for Brethren literature.
2. A proportionate share of the budget funds devoted to the publication interests.

BENEVOLENCES

1. The fullest possible provision for the care and maintenance of the aged ministry and missionaries of the church.
2. An active effort properly to finance by gifts and bequests the Brethren Home of Ohio.

COMPARATIVE FIGURES

Following the Activities of The Four-Year Program---1916 - 1920

NUMERICAL SUMMARY OF GOAL REPORTS

Heavy figures show summary for the year 1919-1920 and accompanying light figures indicate corresponding standing for the year 1917-1918

The number of congregations reporting in 1920 show the following results:

GOALS	ABRIDGED REQUIREMENTS	CONGREGATIONS			
		Gained	Progress	Lost	No Rep.
1 Quickening of Spiritual Life; 10 percent Increase in Prayer Meetings		58—32	16—29	56—59	60—80
2 Deepening of Spiritual Life; 75 percent of Members Attending Communion Service		81—60	16—23	33—37	60—80
3 Heralding of Brethren Plea; 90 percent of given subjects used		88—99	20— 8	22—13	60—80
4 Membership of 30,000, by 1920; 30 per cent increase over 1916		53—27	21—32	56—61	60—80
5 Founding of 10 New Congregations; Payment District Missionary Apportionment		104—91	9—17	17—12	60—80
6 75 Ministerial and Missionary Recruits; Gaining at least one Recruit		56—39	—19	74—62	60—80
7 80 percent Congregations using Budget System; Using Budget System of Finance		79—70	14—27	37—23	60—80
8 Ashland College Endowed with $200,000; Reaching Congregation percentage		105—	2—	23—	60—
9 Brethren Evangelist in at least 75 percent of Brethren Homes		80—46	11—30	39—44	60—80
10 Annual Offering of $15,000 Home Missions; Contributing Congregation's percentage		86—72	15—22	29—26	60—80
11 Annual Offering of $10,000 Foreign Missions; Contributing Congregations' percentage		94—78	12—21	24—21	60—80
12 Annual Offering of $2,500 for Benevolences; Contributing Congregation's percentage		79—64	12—25	39—31	60—80
13 75 per ct. of Sunday Schools reaching Standard of National S. S. Association		38—41	38—31	54—48	60—80
14 75 per ct. of Women's Organizations reaching Standard of National W. M. S.		54—33	26—33	50—54	60—80
15 75 per ct. C. E. Societies reaching National Standard of C. E. Union		22—17	34—23	74—80	60—80
16 The 1920 General Conference Largest and Best; 50 per ct. Increase over 1916, Full Quota		109—	7—	14—	80—

NUMERICAL SUMMARY OF DISTRICT REPORTS

Heavy figures show summary of points for the year 1919-1920 and the accompanying light figures indicate corresponding standing for the year 1917-1918

DISTRICT	Number	NUMBER OF GOALS			
	(of Churches Considered)	Gained	Progress	Lost	No Report
Illiokota	15	122— 96	23— 39	95— 75	— 28
Indiana	38	327—160	54— 93	147—139	80— 140
Maryland-Virginia	35	89— 63	58— 17	93— 88	320— 322
Michigan	4	18	4—	26—	16— 70
Middle West	12	91— 65	15— 8	54— 39	32— 84
Northern California	5	28— 28	9— 41	11— 15	32— 14
Northwest	3	10—	3—	3—	32—
Ohio	33	187—153	40— 53	93—116	206—196
Pennsylvania	39	230—161	37— 71	117— 90	240—336
Southern California	6	80— 42	13— 18	3— 10	
Entire Church	190	1182—788	256—340	642—572	960—1190

From M. J. Snyder's printed report to General Conference

ECHOES OF GENERAL CONFERENCE

Some Impressions of the Jubilee Conference

By H. E. Eppley

What impressions did the Jubilee Conference make upon my mind? They were many and varied in nature. I shall note only a few.

I. Accomplishments

To anyone who has been a regular attendant at Winona and who was on the grounds for the first session on Monday evening this fact must have been noticeable. The goal was 400 delegates, and how they came! Even those not connected with us were heard to say, "You are having lots of people here this year," and we did have. The goal is an accomplished fact. (For some comparative figures on the Sunday school, see the report on another page.)

The next evidence of accomplishments was in the reports made. Every phase of the work had some victory to report. How we shrank from the financial goals of the Four

Year Program when they were announced, thinking they were impossible! And today, how ashamed we should feel of the fears we entertained then!

It is true we failed in one or two of the goals but a close inspection of these will even reveal progress made and sure foundations for future efforts laid. How could any one listen to the reports made during conference and witness the 45 churches receiving their certificates of recognition for victories won and not feel that something had been accomplished.

II. The Value of a Program

The value of a program is evident. When the program was launched its goals seemed beyond the possibility of attainment. Sighs—almost groans—were heard and but few people believed many of the goals would be reached. BUT THEY HAVE BEEN. Why? Because there was a definite program, a race to run, a finishing line to cross, a vision of a victory to be won.

III. Willingness to Work

This was impressed upon the observer at every turn. At no conference were men called upon to work harder and sacrifice more. There were nights when almost no rest was enjoyed and days when the getting of meals was almost impossible. Not a complaint was heard on this account. There was a willingness to work, and if all the laity practiced the same willingness to work in the home church, what could not be accomplished in the next three years!

IV. A Christian Spirit

There were problems—hard and perplexing—to be solved. Yet in the attempts to solve them charity prevailed. This is as it should be. May it please God ever to keep us in this spirit and may the next Jubilee conference be even greater than this one.

Eaton, Indiana.

My Impressions of the 1920 Conference
By Edwin Boardman, Jr.

The National oCnference of 1920 was a real "jubilee" conference. In the first place, we topped all previous records in the matter of delegates in attendance, especially remarkable being the number of laymen present. When the laymen of the church really become interested in her growth and progress we are going to see things happen that will be startling in their results. Another fact of the attendance which impressed me greatly was the fine large group of young people who were there to add their interest and enthusiasm to the assembly. More and more our conference season is becoming a time for the reunion of classmates and friends and this bespeaks for the years to come a continually growing interest in the conference itself.

A second outstanding fact to me is the seriousness with which the church at large is taking its world task. Running throughout the whole conference this year was the fine thread of missions, which in the final summary of the conference bulked especially large. Among the manifestations of this missionary consciousness which is developing I might mention the following: 1. The more earnest heed given to the Life Work Recruits of the church and some plans that are being developed to continually increase their number and value to the church. 2. The number of men and women who, this year, offered themselves as volunteers for the foreign mission work of the church. As long as the Lord can find volunteers for this work in the Brethren church he will see to it that that branch of "his body on the earth" does not suffer. 3. The increasing willingness of the whole church to give large sums of money for the propagation of the gospel of God. During the year ending with this conference the church gave for Home and Foreign Missions the fine total of $50,116.03. The money raised in the various offerings of the conference made plain that this spirit of giving is growing among us. May it increase is our prayer. 4. The increasing program of the church for continued progress in all departments is another very fine manifestation of the missionary spirit. During the next three years the Bicentenary Program is to occupy all the effort of the church and if we can but reach up to the standards set we have the conviction that our church will step into the front rank as a missionary church. God grant that it may be so.

The third fine impression of this last conference that I received was the especially large place given to the Word of God in the program. With Dr. Evans holding us vitally interested for an hour each morning on some fundamental teachings of the Book, and Dr. Miller carrying us into the depths of the teaching regarding the person and work of the Holy Spirit during an afternoon hour, especial prominence was given to the place and power of the Word of God in our life. I am sure that every delegate who attended the last conference went back to his or her home with deeper convictions of truth and a finer more wholesome love for the Word

of God than they ever had before. I am frank to say that such was my experience.

In conclusion I would pray that those of us who were privileged to enjoy the Conference of 1920 will see to it that the message of that fine assembly is adequately interpreted to our home churches.

Hudson, Iowa.

Echoes from the Conference
By A. E. Thomas

While the inspiration of the conference is still within me, I will, at the request of the Editor, write my impressions of the doings.

We were rather worn and tired as we entered upon the work of the week as we had been through similar conferences and Bible work all summer. However, we can say without the slightest hesitation that we have just closed the greatest conference of the Brethren church that we have ever attended. I say, "greatest," for it really was, if results count for anything. Everything was done for the glory of God and the advancement of the church and the work of the Lord. It was a greatest in the point of attendance, over 400 delegates were there from all parts of the country. And what a happy crowd they were! Preachers and laity alike! We have been impressed with the great tasks that have been accomplished.

To us it was not only the greatest conference but the happiest. We were happy to look into the faces of our brethren in the ministry with whom from time to time we have been associated. Whatever else the readers may think of the preachers of the Brethren church, it is the profound conviction of the writer that no church can boast of a cleaner set of men. And they are men who have zeal for the truth, and love for the Word of God and the salvation of men. Indeed, amongst us there is a unity that is sacred, and to mingle together was indeed a pleasure. Then the laity was well represented. Old friends were met and the scenes of other days were brought vividly before us. Old friendships are more appreciated as the years go by.

Second, it was greatest in the things accomplished. Think of the tasks of the past four years and note the results as given to us. Indeed who of us could not rejoice in them! Our mission offerings were greater than ever. Our churches reported more signs of progress and life. A deeper spirit and a greater faith prevailed as we beheld the goals brought to a successful end.

Third, it was the greatest ever as to program. The Moderator, W. H. Beachler never for a moment lost his smile. He kept the conference always in a happy vein. The Bible lectures of Dr. Evans and Dr. Miller were of high order. Dr. Evans, strengthened still more our faith in the great fundamentals of Christian doctrine. The music throughout under the direction of Prof. Lynn was inspiring. Then the Jubilee service was one long to be remembered! The Conference closed with an address by Miss Aboud, and at midnight the great delegations, tired yet happy, began to pour out for home and fireside.

The future—well, it is before us. What will be doing? Well, you will hear more later. However, it calls forth still greater effort. Watch for the announcement of another great drive. In the meantime, pray, and let us keep humble before the Lord.

Warsaw, Indiana.

Vivid Impressions of the Jubilee Conference
By George H. Jones

With ideal weather and a crowd full of enthusiasm, there was only one outcome—inspiration soared to the heights.

California gold was in abundance. So many wore her

colors that it looked like California's meeting. They came a long journey too. They were indeed Pacific brethren.

The Four Year Program was great when it was really worked at, but in too many cases it was only a placard now and then, and a prod from the Directors. In such cases it "pestered" a church, but it was meant to awaken where there was life to "wake up."

Doctrinal discussions can be practically applied. A short season under Dr. Evans, a prince of expositors and you would certainly have agreed.

Apropos Bible Exposition, those of us who have been refreshed by Dr. Miller, a teacher of teachers, rejoiced to have the opportunity again. The Dean is perennially inspiring.

A new voice filled the auditorium. "Filled" is correct. It was both clear and pleasant. Compass and tone were fine. Prof. Lynn was capable and a revelation. A new and genial personality has been added to our ranks. We shall be disappointed if the great mass of our people do not get to know and enjoy the splendid talent of our brother. He is a master of music and voice. May the Lord bless his labors.

"The old are gold; the new, silver," quoted the observer. Transmuting silver into gold is a miracle of friendship, when association ripens our affection.

We missed many old friends. We hope their absence is only temporary. Possibly another year will find them with us bringing new cheer and fresh vigor.

From 1920 to 1923. Christmas to Christmas. Three golden years of achievement. What we can do if we WILL. Bi-Centenary, big with possibilities. Brother Bame will tell us how to "go to it."

"We found ourselves," avers Bame, "now we'll do something." He seems to think we can, through a Bi-Centenary movement. Contrary to the objection to the word "Movement," the capable Secretary thinks that movement means movement, while program might mean contemplation. We agree with him.

"Committee of Twenty-Five" sounds like a big committee, but if it gets accomplished what Brother Bell has in mind, it will do a big thing.

Bridging over a valley is a difficult engineering feat, but human differences are not such mountains as they look, especialy if they "be brethren" to begin with. Love and good-will are splendid abutments.

The Philadelphia crowd was there with banners. This is more than a figurative expression. Blue and white were the colors. California's were black and gold. Geographically the extremes met. And they set a fine example. Such interest from east and west ought to stir our loyalty. They came a long distance.

The program was very largely carried out as planned. Almost without exception, the speakers came with well prepared messages and were thoroughly appreciated. We heard many commendations and wish to pass the kindly expressions on to the faithful workers.

The arrangement of the program was quite different from what we have been accustomed to, but it had many features worth continuing. Some we felt were innovations that were not so much needed as others, but we can heartily commend many of the changes.

It was a well balanced program. Particularly was the selection of Dr. Evans' felicitious. The vote for his presence another year was proof of the hold he got on our affections.

Blocking off the program with time, place and person was fine, if only we might have had the subject matter and the hour of delivery more conveniently placed. But so much was praiseworthy that we found little to criticize.

Such a crowd! It looked as if we had become interested. The auditorium was well filled again and again. The cottages were straightened for accommodations for the crowd. It was common for groups to go hunting everywhither for rooms. This was the first conference such a condition prevailed. And such a spirit of hearty good fellowship, it was worth going far to enjoy.

We had a typical illustration in the great new auditorium one morning. The ministers were occupying the rostrum, almost a hundred of them. The good sisters were having a meeting in the rear of the auditorium. Both groups were singing, when by that subconscious feeling both sensed what the other was singing, and, strange coincidence, both were singing, "He Included Me." In the rare experience that followed, it was a glorious sensation to feel that as far apart as we were, and as diverse as our discussions were, unconcious to ourselves the hymn was a real expression of our innermost feelings. There are mountain-top experiences that linger in the memory longer than others. This one will in the minds of all that took part. It thrilled us.

The rain on Sunday prevented the record attendance for Sunday school and church such as we had planned. But we had a record attendance and offering after all. Sunday school offering of $825.13 and $150.47 at the church service were splendid. The attendance almost reached the 1,400 mark. It was great.

The ladies, both the Sisterhood and the W. M. S., surely gave encouraging reports. What a pity the men cannot match them with similar organizations among the other sex.

New and promising methods of work are in process of launching with field secretaries employed for more or less of their time. Bi-Centenary and Sunday school boards are pioneering in the effort. Both deserve our prayers and hearty co-operation.

If each Conference lays the foundation for the success of the next, we shall have a hummer next year. Time fails to mention half of the many good things we heard and to name the many splendid men and women who quietly contributed their share of inspiration and appreciation to the sum total. It can best be summed up, "A Great Conference," made so by a great spirit of fellowship and love, in the Lord Jesus Christ.

Conemaugh, Pennsylvania.

THE LAST CALL

At the General Conference at Winona Lake, all Goal Directors holding bills of expense against the old Four Year Program Committee were asked to turn them in to the Secretary-Treasurer for payment in order that all matters pertaining to that work might be closed. None were turned in. This last call is now made to give everyone an opportunity to close up such accounts. The Treasurer of the Four Year Program Committee was instructed by the late General Conference to turn any remaining balance over to the Brethren Bicentenary Movement, and this will be done at an early date. Should anyone desire payment of legitimate expenses incurred in the Four Year Program work, such bills must be sent to the Treasurer at once.

MILES J. SNYDER, Secretary-Treasurer.,
Milledgeville, Illinois.

How Can the Layman Assist the Pastor?

Address by Henry V. Wall, at the Brethren General Conference, Winona Lake, Indiana, September 2, 1920

The layman can assist the pastor first, last, and all the time by prayer. Paul knew this to be true, and in Second Corinthians 1:11 he says, "Ye also helping together by prayer for us, that for the gift bestowed upon us by the means of many persons, thanks may be given by many on our behalf." One of the rules of my life is to pray daily for my pastor. The surrendered layman's life in meditation and prayer before Almighty God, under the direction, power and influence of the Holy Spirit, will see the pastor as God would have him see him, and then only, is he capable and competent to render unto his pastor the assistance that is most needed. Doubtless many a pastor would have rendered good service in your church, had you given unto him this kind of support, rather than criticizing him because he does not do everything just to please you. Remember that your pastor was not called for the purpose of preaching just to please you, but he was called of God to preach the Gospel. Many times the layman's life is not in harmony with the teachings of our Master, and then it is that makes the very best destructive critic.

Brother Laymen, I urge you to pray daily for your pastor, not because he alone needs your prayers, but your own life needs it. Remember that **prayer changes things**, not alone in your pastor's life, but in your own life also.

John 15:7 says, "If ye abide in me and my words abide in you, ye shall ask what ye will and it shall be done unto you."

1st John 3:22 says, "And whatsoever we ask we receive of him because we keep his commandments and do those things that are pleasing in his sight."

Prayer is the great key that unlocks many a closed door. Through prayer the unsurmountable obstacle can be removed. Through prayer the old Philippian jail doors were opened and Paul and Silas walked out free men.

James 5:17, 18 says, "Elias was a man subject to like passions as we are, and he prayed earnestly that it might not rain; and it rained not upon the earth by the space of three years and six months. And he prayed again, and the heaven gave rain, and the earth brought forth her fruit."

Brother layman, you can not be the power of good in this life that God intended you should be, except you spend a part of each day in prayer.

Second: The layman can assist the pastor by temporal support. Read 1st Corinthians 9:7-8. The 14th verse of the above mentoned chapter says, "Even so hath the Lord ordained that they which preach the gospel should live of the gospel." My brother, do you know any pastor that is preaching the gospel, and his salary is so small that he is compelled to work outside his profession to support himself? If you do, surely there is a fault among us somewhere. Brother layman, don't be a party to employing a pastor for his full time, that you don't pay at least fifteen hundred dollars per year. Many of our pastors should receive much more. Why not encourage our pastors by paying them good salaries. Then we could expect them to give us their very best. If your pastor's temporal needs are not properly cared for, you cannot expect the good gospel sermons and shepherding care that you should have.

Why are you not willing to pay liberally for the things pertaining to your eternal destiny? Meditate, soberly and prayerfully, on matters of such great importance. Show me a member of your congregation that is stingy and not willing to carry his or her part of the expense, and invariably this person's spiritual life is dwarfed, and readily recognized by all other members as being so. If you really love Jesus Christ, and the church, which is his body, you will support whole-heartedly, things which you love. Therefore, examine yourself by God's Word, and see whether you are put-

ting most of your life and money into things temporal, or those that are eternal.

Third: The layman can assist his pastor by kindly and **direct criticism.** This is one of the tender spots in all our lives, and is likewise true of our pastors. It is one that is often neglected because of this very fact, and if criticism is made it is not made to the pastor himself, or if made to the pastor, it is not made in the proper manner, and with the spirit of love. I have often heard people say, "That was a fine sermon, if the pastor had not said———" so, and so. It would be very much better to say such things to your pastor; if said in the spirit of constructive criticism, and in a manner that he would know you were trying to help rather than hinder him.

Unless you are on the best terms with your pastor, and he has high regard for what you say, you had better leave the kindly criticism to others, as he might misunderstand you. Of course, if you have prayed over the matter, and the Spirit leads you to kindly criticism of your pastor, you need not fear, as God is abundantly able to take care of the situation.

Don't criticize your pastor unless your heart is overflowing with love for the cause of Christ, and you are certain that such criticism is without any selfish motives on your part.

Fourth: The layman can assist the pastor by **praise when deserved.** My brother, I would advise you to use praise quite liberally, yes, much more liberally than criticism. There are very few pastors, if any, but what are sadly neglected by the laity on **deserved praise.** If your pastor preaches a good sermon and says many things that are helpful to you, don't hesitate to tell him. He will then know that his earnest efforts are appreciated by you, and it will help the honest, conscientious pastor, to preach a better sermon the next time.

Nearly every congregation has some old "wind-jammers" that will sleep soundly until the sermon is over, and often they are first to praise the pastor for his great message. This is not the kind of praise that he appreciates most. The praise that comes from the wide-awake, consecrated, active Christian, is the kind that will help your pastor, and I urge all of this class of laymen to be free with their praise, and encourage their pastor in every possible manner. Don't forget that it will take a lot of praise from the laity to off-set the accusations which are brought against our pastors by the Old Serpent, the Devil. Let us have more flowers for the living and less for the dead.

Fifth: The layman can assist the pastor by **personal work in winning men for Christ.** The early church for the first four centuries of its history, without regular places of worship, without wealth, without social prestige, without governmental toleration, spread like a mighty conflagration. Every member was a firebrand in its irresistible onward sweep. Why? Because every Christian was a witness for Christ. Every member, even the least, felt under obligation to advance the cause of Christ, and there was a genuine joy in his service. Personal evangelism was the fundamental secret of growth and achievement. After Christianity became the religion of the Roman world, more and more such personal witnessing fell into disuse, and preaching came to fill a larger program of the church. There are those today who, while not in the least discounting the value of preaching, deny that the church's full duty is fulfilled by supplying it. We know that personal witnessing for Christ by laymen whose lives are dedicated to him, is not only a duty, but a necessity. Such witnessing is necessary for the layman himself. There is no self-salvation. The pathway to spiritual victory is through the valley of self-renouncement.

Let me repeat again that progress in spiritual things is

possible only through self-renouncement. The Gospel is "Good News," but news is not news unless it is published. Its goodness and sweetness must be heralded by the laymen as well as the pastor. We cannot keep our spiritual blessing. The only way to enjoy them is to give them away. Spiritual life grows by self-renouncement. Like the bread cast on the waters, it returns with enlarged harvest, having blessed him who received, but much more him who gave. The joy of personal salvation is great, but the joy of leading others to Christ is greater. To this, every personal worker will agree. There is no passion comparable to the passion for souls. It is God-like. It makes a man not only more a man to be animated by such a passion; it makes him more than a man—it makes him Christ-like. One of the needs of the church today is for laymen with a passion for souls.

I hope we laymen will soon comprehend the strategic importance of our own personal efforts at evangelization. We have been engrossed in our business and our professional life. We have been glad to support the church, and attend its services. But we have not considered that our responsibility for the church could not cease with these things. We are now almost ready to say with a certain devout layman of a former generation, when asked what his business was, he said: "My business is serving the Lord, but I cobble shoes for a living." We will have to put first things first, all of us, before the spiritual baptism for which we so earnestly pray shall descend upon us in quickened power. We must not only be Christians, but we must work at our job. We cannot delegate our responsibility for the salvation of our brothers to anyone else. We cannot hire the minister to do it for us, nor the professional evangelist. We must do it ourselves, or it will not be done. Nothing so exalts little folks into big ones; nothing so transforms weakness into towering strength; nothing so magnifies babes into giants and heroes, as joyful willingness to do the will of the Master, and to do it in the Master's own way. God has always blessed the evangelistic efforts of the laymen with startling results. In the acts of the Apostles, after the rich Pentecostal outpouring of the Holy Spirit, only three of the original twelve are mentioned, but seven simple-hearted laymen became world famous. It was given to a layman to be the first to yield up his most priceless possession, his very life, for the Master's sake.

The missionary journeys were planned and executed largely by laymen.

Brother laymen, let us double our diligence and get busy in the soul-saving business, and assist our pastors in his, as well as every other way possible.

Long Beach, California.

OUR DEVOTIONAL

Living In Communion With Christ
By J. Gilbert Dodds

OUR SCRIPTURE

"If we love one another, God dwelleth in us, and his love is perfected in us: hereby we know that we abide in him and he in us, because he hath given us of his Spirit. And we have beheld and bear witness that the Father hath sent the Son to be the Savior of the world. Whosoever shall confess that Jesus is the Son of God, God abideth in him, and he in God. And we know and have believed the love which God hath inus. God is love; and he that abideth in love abideth in God, and God abideth inhim." "I am the vine, ye are the branches: He that abideth in me and I in him, the same beareth much fruit: for apart from me ye can do nothing. . . . If ye abide in me and my words abide in you, ask whatsoever ye will and it shall be done unto you. Herein is my Father glorified, that ye bear much fruit; and so shall ye be my disciples."

OUR MEDITATION

The word "communion," as defined by the Standard Dictionary, means "sympathetic intercourse," "religious fellowship." But the meaning of our subject is not half implied by the definition of this one word. One may have sympathetic intercourse with another, yet, because human conditions and viewpoints are subject to sudden changes, an hour later the intercourse becomes grossly unsympathetic. Two persons of the same religious faith, work, purposes, and ideals may have perfect religious fellowship one with the other. But one meets a religious experience, not met by the other, his faith and purpose reverts to other work, consequently their religious fellowship ceases.

The key to our subject is the word Living. It is more possible to have living communion with an unchangeable Person than one who is changeable. Two changeable human beings cannot live in communion, one with the other, except they be joined by an unchangeable influence.

Living in communion with Christ implies more than plans and talk, it signifies activity, love, faith, hope, brotherly kindness, passion for souls. It means to develop our lives according to the pattern which is Christ. It means doing our work according to the will of the Father even as Christ did.

The vine sends its roots into the ground to collect life-giving food from the soil. In turn the vine gives this food to its branches. The leaves on the branches breathe through their many pores life-giving elements from the atmosphere. The sap that touches every tiniest fibril of vine and branches feeds them with the food collected through rootlets and leaves. So long as the food-filled sap enters the branch, the branch shall live; but the day that the branch no longer allows the sap to enter, it shall die. To live requires co-operative living with the source of life.

Thus it is to live in communion with Christ. The Christian must mould into his character the attributes of Christ's character. Note these attributes: Reverence for his heavenly Father; obedience to God's will, so forcibly taught us by his Gethsemane experience; love for all people, even his enemies,—he died for them, saying on the cross, "Father, forgive them;" patience; kindness; honor for his Father's house; and his habit of being ever busy teaching God's living message. His character was the revelation of God's character. The great passion of his life was the passion for souls.

Even as the vine with its life-giving sap nourishes the branch, so does Christ, through the Holy Spirit, which he promised, nourish them who strive to live in communion with him.

Even as the branch, through its leaves, absorbs from the atmosphere the food required by the vine, so does he who lives in communion with Christ, and sharing Christ's life, he also shares his passion. "Go . . . and disciple all nations, teaching them to observe all things whatsoever I have commanded you." As Christ's great passion was for the salvation of souls, even so is that the passion of Christians.

Worry, trials, temptations, discouragements and troubles assail all people. But he who lives in communion with Christ will remember Psalm 50:15, "Call upon me in the day of trouble: I will deliver thee, and thou shalt glorify me." Again, 1 Corinthians 10:13, "God is faithful, who will not suffer you to be tempted above that ye are able." The Bible contains thousands of promises to those who will to live in communion with Christ.

The great need of the church today is not machinery, it is not organization; it is not finance. It is an unction from on high; a closer and more vital union unto Christ. Machinery is good; organization is good; finance is good. All these are needful. But except they be God-filled they are worthless and become a stumbling block to the advancement of God's purpose in this world.

Let us meditate upon what the vine has given to us: life, love, forgiveness, redemption, Bible, Sabbath, Christian associations, churches, and numberless opportunities for Christian work. What have we as branches given in return? Father, help us to be unlike the friends invited to the feast, who one and all began to give excuse. Our life is the testimony of its faithful communion with Christ. "Remember the Sabbath to keep it holy." "But to do good, and to communicate, forget not: for with such sacrifice God is well pleased" (Heb. 13:16). "The fruit of the spirit is love, joy, peace, longsuffering, gentleness, goodness, faith, meekness, temperance. And they that are Christ's have crucified the flesh with the affections and lusts thereof. If we live in th Spirit let us also walk in the Spirit" (Gal. 5:22-25).

OUR PRAYER

Our Father, we pray that our lives may be used in th service for the fulfillment of thy purpose. May we so liv in home life, church life, prayer life, Bible study life, an social life that thy holy name may be honored, and that thin only begotten Son may be lifted high to draw all men unt him. In Christ's name we pray. Amen.

Norcatur, Kansas.

Send
WHITE GIFT
OFFERINGS to

ALBERT TRENT
General Secretary-Treasurer
Johnstown, Pennsylvania

THE SUNDAY SCHOOL

The Jubilee Conference Sunday School

A great many Sunday school scholars could not be at Winona to be in the great Sunday school session. You will want to know something about that session.

It was held in the new tabernacle and some of the outstanding features were as follows:

Attendance and Offering

The attendance was the largest ever assembled in a Sunday school session at our conference and the offering the largest ever taken. Comparative figures for the last six years follow:

Year	Attendance	Offering
1915	1,009	$222.76
1916	1,025	245.35
1917	1,056	400.63
1918	856	401.00
1919	945	530.94
1920	1,394	825.13

All classes whose offering amounted to one dollar o more per capita were to receive special mention. Followin is the list:

10	H. M. Harley,	$1.19
20	E. L. Miller,	1.07
24	Geo. Ronk,	1.05
9	Martin Shively,	1.05
11	James Cook,	1.01
21	R. Paul Miller,	1.00

Class number 24 gave the largest offering amounting t $76.16.

H. E. EPPLEY, Conference Sunday School Sec'y.

J. A. Garber
PRESIDENT

G. C. Carpenter
SECRETARY

Our Young People at Work

Christian Endeavor In General Conference. By Prof. J. A. Garber

Among those who constituted the personnel of our latest and largest General Conference there was a conspicuously large number of young people. Strangers visiting our conferences are often heard to remark: "Yours seems to be a church of young people." Without disparaging in the least the excellent older people, the comment is true, and it should become the occasion for deep gratitude with both old and young.

At the outing by Indian Mound several spoke of the large number of boys and girls of high school age. This happy event was prepared for by Florizel P. Pfleiderer, cheer leader of the College, and Miss Alice Wogaman, a former student, and their associates. So great was the response to the invitation that the "eats" were found to be insufficient. However, the resourceful young hosts and hostesses kept the road hot with machines going back and forth to Warsaw until sufficient provisions were secured to satisfy the appetite of all. Every one appeared to enjoy greatly the social fellowship, college songs and yells and greetings by President Jacobs.

The addresses announced in the printed program proved to be carefully prepared, and were effectively delivered. The early morning hour seem to affect the attendance at the opening of the session, but for the most part the attendance was good. A keen interest prevailed throughout the sessions. Since the messages of the speakers will appear in these columns it is unnecessary for us to attempt a digest at this writing. In a special meeting at four o'clock on Sunday our new program was read, studied and adopted by persons representing societies from all but two conference districts. The adoption of the program was followed with challenging messages from the newly elected national officers. If the Endeavorers present caught the spirit of their leaders an will help to enthuse the folks at home who were denied a inspiration of conference, the new program will usher in period of prosperity and be carried through to a successfu completion.

BICENTENARY PROGRAM FOR BRETHREN ENDEAVORERS

I Membership

1. Active membership increased annually by 10 percent ne gain.
2. Associate membership increased annually by 5 percen net gain.

II Meetings

1. At least forty-two weekly meetings during each year.
2. Regular bi-monthly committee meetings and semi-annua business meetings.
3. Several social gatherings each year to promote whole some fellowship.

III Devotion

1. The value of private Bible study and prayer faithfull stressed.
2. The enrollment of Comrades of the Quiet Hour.
3. Individual participation in society and church praye meetings urged.

IV Education

1. A yearly class in Expert Endeavor or similar study.
2. Co-operation with the annual school of missions.
3. Participation in the training classes of the church school
4. Helping to provide and use the library of religious edu cation.

V Denomination

1. Two particularly prepared programs on Brethrenism.
2. Regular attendance at Sunday and mid-week services encouraged.
3. Representation at church and interdenominational conventions.
4. Statistical reports carefully prepared and promptly returned.

VI Stewardship

1. The enrollment of stewards who will give of substance on the basis of the tithe.
2. The adoption of a society budget which shall encourage systematic giving.
3. Liberal contributions to missions and Ashland College.
4. The recruiting of life stewards who will enlist for full time service.

VII Service

1. Some definite service for the local church.
2. Some community service that makes for civic betterment.
3. Service relating to the training of Juniors and Intermediates.
4. Special leagues of service for prayer, evangelism and good citizenship.

Changes in the National Organization

The Committee on Nominations consisting , of Edwin Boardman, Alice Wogoman and Alva Evans recommmended several changes in the national cabinet when presenting their list of nominees.

Miss Frieda Price was nominated to take the place of Miss Nora Bracken who was elected superintendent of the Children's Division of Sunday school work. Miss Price has been a successful superintendent of Junior work in her home church and has specialized in children's work. She is willing and eager to serve Junior and Intermediate superintendents and societies.

For sometime there has been a desire for a full time field worker, but various conditions seem to make the selection of such a worker impracticable for the present. Last year partial provision was made in the appointment of voluntary district workers, most of whom rendered commendable service. When one of our own number became Associate Secretary of the Ohio Union regret was expressed that we were not ready to command his services. He, however, has agreed to give us as much time as his numerous duties will permit. consequently the committee nominated E. A. Rowsey for the office of General Secretary, nominating G. C. Carpenter for the position of Missionary Superintetndent. This change is not as new as the report might indicate. Ever since the writer came into his present position Brother Carpenter has been specializing on the missionary phase of our work, being until last year wholly responsible for the Kentucky Funds. This

charge enables him to continue this particular line of endeavor, and certainly no one of our number is better prepared to keep before our young people the missionary message and program of the church. Being in constant touch with the latest and best methods in Christian Endeavor, Brother Rowsey will keep us informed and enthused as to policies, programs and methods. Moreover his work will take him into every county of Ohio where he can counsel the leaders of each of our Ohio societies. In addition he will be able to respond to calls from Indiana and Pennsylvania, and plans to attend both of the coming conferences. Heavy demands upon him will increase his love for Brethren Endeavor and Endeavorers.

A new department was added. It is entitled Publicity, and the superintendent is Earl Huette who gave a most suggestive address on "Keeping Christian Endeavor Prominent." We have known Brother Huette for several years now, having received him into the church and observed his development. He plans to tell you how to advertise and sell Christian Endeavor. Watch both the Evangelist and Angelus for his suggestions.

The National Cabinet 1920-21

President, J. A. Garber, Ashland, Ohio.
Vice Presidents, The District Presidents.
General Secretary, E. A. Rowsey, Columbus, Ohio.

Departmental Superintendents

Junior-Intermediate, Miss Frieda Price, Nappanee, Indiana.
Quiet Hour, E. M. Riddle, Louisville, Ohio.
Missionary, G. C. Carpenter, Peru, Indiana.
Tenth Legion, E. A. Myer, Bringhurst, Indiana.
Good Citizenship, A. E. Whitted, Morrill, Kansas.
Life Work, Edwin Boardman, Hudson, Iowa.
Publicity, Earl Huette, Dayton, Ohio.

Fortieth Anniversary Crusade

Some weeks ago we announced the goals of the Fortieth Anniversary Crusade, which extends from September 1, 1920 to February 2, 1921. Since it dovetails nicely with our Bicentenary Program we are reprinting the five goals. Let Brethren Endeavorers share in their full attainment.

1. 600,000 vacant seats filled at Sunday and mid-week services.
2. 600,000 new Christian Endeavorers.
3. 600,000 young people enrolled for systematic Bible study, study of Church History, Stewardship, Missions, Personal Evangelism, Social Service, and "Expert Endeavor."
4. At least 600,000 young people urged to accept Christ and unite with the church.
5. A systematic canvass of individuals for contributions for the adequate financing of Christian Endeavor at home and abroad.

The New Testament a Sufficient Present Day Creed.   By S. M. Loose

The word creed as used in this connection means a system of Christian faith. We hold the New Testament to be a sufficient system for all ages. Paul tells us the Gospel is the power of God unto salvation to every one that believeth; to the Jew and also to the Greek. The New Testament is sufficient creed for every one who has true faith in the Gospel. It was given to be everybody's creed and is all any one needs. It opens the way to the sinner to become reconciled to God. It teaches that we are all sinners and must repent and be converted; that we must confess our sins and be baptized and then grow in grace; that we must both believe and obey the whole Gospel. We need nothing more than what we find in the Gospel, no different creed. The Gospel gives us a plain outline of how to live and walk and deal with one another; how to be laborers together with the Lord. I don't see that we can get a better creed or system, and so, I say, stay by it.

The duties of the ministers are plainly lined out. They are to preach and teach and bring all unto Christ that they possibly can. They are to teach men to observe all things whatsoever Christ has commanded. The duties of deacons and their wives are clearly set forth, telling them what to do and how to live. Every need is met. I do not see that anything is lacking in this perfect law of liberty. It is a perfect system and cannot be improved on in any way. I do not think either men or angels can give us a better and creed than the New Testament. It will abide forever. Other creeds will not. Heaven and earth may pass away, but the Word Christ has given will not pass away. Man must fix up a system to please the carnal mind; he may make the way broader and easier, but it will not stand neither will it be safe. The narrow way is the only safe way.
Fremont, Ohio.

NEWS FROM THE FIELD

AN EXPLANATION AND A REPORT

At the National Conference of the Brethren church in 1919 a resolution was adopted pledging the Brethren church as a whole to raise the sum of $2,500.00 as a denominational contribution toward the erection of a new tabernacle at Winona Lake, Indiana. A special committee was appointed by the conference to make equitable appropriation of the $2,500.00 among the various districts, with the understanding that the various districts would take care of the raising of the money and forward it to the committee of the conference chosen for receiving such funds. The commitee appointed to apportion the amount among the districts performed its work and reported to the conference of 1919, but by some slip somewhere the report was missed by most of the districts and consequently went by default, only a very few scattering churches over the brotherhood lifting the offering and forwarding it to the committee.

At the conference of 1920, Dr. Sol C. Dickey, general secretary of the Winona Assembly and Bible Conference, appeared before the delegates and asked that the denomination make good its pledge—and that it do so at the earliest moment possible—as the said Winona Assembly was then facing debts to the amount of $24,000.00 which debts had been contracted on the supposition that we, along with a lot of other people, acted in good faith when we made our pledge to contribute $2,500.00 toward the tabernacle.

As a result of the appeal the undersigned was appointed as temporary third member of the committee on Winona Tabernacle to secure as much of the money as possible. As a result of the conference and the activities of the moderators of the various district conferences present the following report can be given. If there is any error I shall appreciate it as a personal favor if those who see such will call my attention to the same. This report covers only the moneys collected at the conference and shows the amounts due from the various districts—where there is a balence due:

Dist.	Apportioned	Per Capita	Pd.	Balance
Penna.	$350.00	.12	$ 93.00	$257.00
Ohio	600.00	.16	272.96	327.04
Indiana	900.00	.17	85.00	815.00
Illiokota	250.00		184.00	66.00
Mid-West	100.00	10	82.50	17.50
Md.-Va.	150.00		150.00	—.—
S. Cal.	100.00		115.00	—.—
N. Cal.	25.00			25.00
N. W. Dist.	25.00			25.00
Michigan	25.00		25.00	—.—

After collecting all of the above the committee was still short about $1,000.00. This they were authorized to borrow from some one of the standing Boards of the conference with the understanding that the various congregations should get busy at once and raise their quota and forward it to the proper parties. If this is done promptly the Board will not have to be out of the use of its funds for very long!

The loan of $1,000.00 was made by the Foreign Mission Board through L. S. Bauman. That there may be less cause for mistake I am giving below the sums received by me to be applied on this fund from the various districts, the church and amount being indicated in each instance.

District:

Penna. Pittsburgh, $25.00 Philadelphia, $50.00; D. Belote, $5.00.

Ohio. Dayton, $176.96; Ashland $32.00; Gretna, $15.00; Salem $10.00; Fair Haven, $12.00; Williamstown, $16.00; M. Shively, $10.00; Mansfield by DeLozier, $1.00.

Indiana. Roann, $34.00; South Bend, $51.00. Illiokota. Maple Grove, $3.00; Cerro Gordo, $20.00; Lanark, $35.00; Udell, $10.00; Milledgeville, $36.00; Leon, $10.00; Pleasant Grove, $20.00; Waterloo, $50.00.

Middle-West. Ft. Scott, Kan., $5.00; Morrill, Kan., $20.00; Hamlin, Kansas, $12.50; Falls City, Nebraska, $30.00; Beaver City, Nebraska, $15.00.

Md.-Va. Limestone, Tennessee, $5.00; St. James, $20.00; Jacob Swartz, by balance from estate of Elsie Showalter, $125.00.

S. Cal. Check from L. S. Bauman—for Wall—for total, $115.00.

Michigan. Check for district's apportionment—Garrison, $25.00.

Now there had been between four and five hundred dollars already sent in toward this fund, and this does not appear here nor do the congregations which contributed that sum get mention here—and neither is this intended to be in the way of a reminder to such, but only for those churches which have not made contribution to this cause. Upon such latter it is urged that you immediately get busy and do your share. If you do not know what your quota should be write your district moderator and he will tell you.

And in order that there may be no misunderstanding as to whom this report is to be made I will give below the name and address of the men in each district—in which there is still some balance—to whom all inquiries are to be sent:

Penna.: H. M. Harley, 5002 Dearborn St., E. E. Pittsburgh, Pa.

Ohio: George S. Baer, Ashland, Ohio.

Indiana: J. A. McInturff, Goshen, Indiana.

Illiokota: R. F. Porte, Dallas Center, Iowa.

Middle West: A. E. Whitted, Morrill, Kansas.

N. California: J. W. Platt, Manteca, Cal.

N. W. District: C. H Ashman, Sunnyside, Wash.

Finally: In case of any question as to the amount you are supposed to raise, write your district moderator as indicated above, or to me. When you have taken your offering send it to Mr. Herman Roscoe, Goshen, Indiana, indicating the name of the congregation, the district to which your congregation belongs and the purpose for which it is intended—and remember our note has been given to the Foreign Mission Board for sixty days only, so PLEASE GET BUSY AT THIS AT ONCE. Fraternally,

DYOLL BELOTE,
61 Highland Ave., Uniontown, Penna.

Look back often to the Reformation, that fiery furnace in which the makers of our modern world walked in unharmed, because protected by the presence of the Son of man. Do not stop at the Reformation. Take in with the sweep of your eye the thousand years that preceded Luther, in which God moved in mysterious ways in the work of subjugating barbaric Europe to a gentler temper. Let your glance take in all the epochs of the Christian era, back to the days of the apostles.—Jefferson.

COMPTON AVENUE BRETHREN CHURCH
Los Angeles, California

About April first Brother Beal, our pastor, handed in his resignation to take effect July first. To say we were shocked and disappointed is putting it very mildly. At first we thought we just would not and could not accept the resignation. But after praying over the matter the church accepted the resignation, because we felt the Lord was leading that way. If there was ever a church and pastor in harmony it was the Compton Avenue church and pastor. But the Lord's will must be done.

Brother Beal accepted a call from the Southern California Mission Board to the work at Fillmore.

The last week Brother Beal was with us the church gave him and his family a farewell reception at which a fair representation of the membership was present.

Since July first we have been without a regular pastor. But the work has been going on just the same.

Two of our own boys, Brother J. C. Caldwell and Brother John Lienhard, have been doing most of the preaching. On Sunday Brother E.-M. Cobb of Dayton, preached for us. At the close of the evening service a man expressed his desire to be baptized. So arrangements were made to baptize him at prayer meeting on Wednesday night.

Last Sunday Brother T. H. Broad of La Verne, California, preached for us while Brother John Lienhard preached at La Verne.

We have called Brother N. V. Leatherman of Turlock, California. He expects, the Lord willing, to begin his services with us the first Sunday in October (October 3rd.)

We are planning to have our Rally Day and Annual Home Coming Day on that date. A program is being planned already for an all day service. The program starts with the regular Sunday school session, then the program by the children. Everybody brings their lunch. The tables are spread in the Sunday school room. Well, you know the rest. Then in the afternoon we have another service at which the visiting Brethren do the speaking. Usually are great days for the Brethren.

Saturday, August 14th, we had our annual

Sunday school picnic, which proved, as usual, a great success. We went to Exposition Park in four truck loads—one hundred and sixty of us—with sixteen gallons of ice cream and well filled baskets. A program and a lot of prizes were features of the day. All expressed themselves as having a good time. And they are already asking when the next picnic will be.

Thursday evening, August 26, we will hold our regular love feast. Brother Broad will be with us, to help conduct this service.

We are all looking forward to October 3rd to the coming of our new pastor. We ask an interest in your prayers that we may be faithful till he comes.

Yours in the blessed hope,
A. E. NEHER.

FIRST BRETHREN CHURCH
Los Angeles, California

Notwithstanding a large number of our people have been taking their summer vacations, the attendance at both Sunday school and church has been remarkably good. A number of strange faces are seen in the congregation almost every Sunday.

The high prices asked for real estate and high rents are making it somewhat difficult for some of our members to find homes within easy reach of the church.

There have been some more responses to the earnest evangelistic appeals of our pastor and Sunday evening, August 8th, a young sister was led into the baptismal waters, and we hope there will be seen the evidences of a spiritual resurrection. At the close of the evening service, August 15th she received the laying on of hands and was ushered into our fold. The same days at the close of the morning service two of our intermediate boys stepped to the front and gave their hands to the pastor signifying their choice of Jesus as their life-long and eternal friend. One of these boys received baptism at the close of the service the same evening. These are the first fruits of the new and separate Intermediate Department of our Sunday school with their own room and their own opening exercises.

At the last regular quarterly business meeting Brother Jennings was called unanimously to serve us for another year beginning October 1st. It was also decided to raise enough money by subscription outside the regular budget to pay his way to the National Conference at Winona Lake, Indiana, and return. We all felt that such a journey and such a privilege was due him and we wished to show our appreciation of his faithful work among us. We were also not without the mildly selfish feeling that we would receive some slight benefit in an indirect way by his presence at our National Conference. We hope he'll be able to return inspired with new zeal and knowledge and with great visions of things to be accomplished. On the return trip he will no doubt have the pleasure of the company of Mrs. Jennings, who has been visiting relatives in Virginia during the summer. And we'll surely be glad to welcome them back home again to the "City of the Angels."
ALBERT P. REED.
4910 Wadsworth Street.

KRYPTON, KENTUCKY

I began a meeting here July tenth and closed July thirtieth. I found this a very peculiar field. The first ten days there seemed but little hope that we would have a successful meeting. Brother and Sister Remple have a hard pull here. I by accident was permitted the pleasure of spending a night with them nearly a year ago and I almost wept when I saw the state of things there. The morals of Krypton are very low. It is a mining town and gambling, drinking, moonshine whiskey, and swearing seem almost universal among the men. I heard more swearing in this little town the three weeks I was there than anywhere I have ever been. Nearly all the little boys and men swear. Outside of Brother and Sister Remple and their two little children there were only about two members that would pray or testify in public. These only lately began. I believe there was a man that prayed when he attended, but he would also swear, play cards, drink and gamble, so I was told by a number of the best people there. He only came one night. I found a large part of the membership a hindrance instead of a help in the meeting. The spiritual tide was slowly rising before I came upon the scene. A very influential man, the superintendent of one of the mines and a child were baptized before I arrived. This created an interest and almost a sensation. Then the "holy rollers," as they are called there, had a meeting in full swing before I began and took quite a number of people that would have attended our meeting had it not been for the excitement. The "holy rollers" would dance, go off in swoons, speak in tongues and roll on the floor, and many went for the fun they saw in it and some were infatuated with them.

We pounded away the best we could and walked over the mountains and made 100 calls with Brother and Sister Remple. This gradually produced fruit. Then I preached New Testament Sanctification and showed how the holiness among the people there was full of "holes." I made ten charges against this counterfeit. About the middle of the three weeks the tide rose rapidly. First, about six or more of the church members that said they had never been converted repented and accepted Christ. From this moment on the tide rapidly arose. The mine superintendent's wife was baptized, also her single sister and the superintendent's brother-in-law. Then other prominent persons joined. They were the best people in the community, so that the interest became the best of any meeting I have held this year. It was the highest at the very last. About a score were baptized and a half a dozen members of the church became converted so that there were about twenty-seven made confession during the last two weeks of the meeting. I should have stayed another week but I could not do so because of other pressing engagements.

The volunteer offerings netted 100 dollars, about twice as much as I expected, and a hearty invitation to return again very soon.

One gambler shot and killed another gambler in broad daylight in the center of the town; both were drunk. Two others were

killed in the community, I was told, one above Krypton, near another mine and one below Krypton.

They had a communion, and I was told that it was more than four times as large as any ever held there before.

This field is indeed a hard one and Brother and Sister Remple need the united prayers of the brotherhood in their behalf.

They are wonderfully devoted people; nothing is too much for them to do. Mrs. Remple walks miles and miles every week over those mountains, nurses the babies, prays with the people and teaches the Bible, and they tend three Sunday schools every Sunday. It is wonderful how they are wearing themselves into the hearts and minds of these shy people. It will take great wisdom, much prayer and a lot of hard work to build up a spiritual church there. But it surely is coming forward and the secret of their success is the living of a high spiritual life and the teaching of a pure and high gospel. This they surely are doing. If any of you people think that the Kentucky field is an easy one, go and try it. I thought southern Philadelphia was hard but it doesn't compare with Kentucky. I have studied the people by being in their homes for eight weeks at Riverside and Krypton and also being raised within a few miles of the Mountain Whites in Virginia. I think I almost perfectly understand the field. It is white for the harvest, but O, the prayer and work and wisdom it takes to build permanently! A social gospel is a failure and there by all who have tried it of all denominations. You must preach salvation by the blood, repentance, the second coming of Christ and hold up a high spiritual life and live it out before them. They see through insincerity, and a superficial religion easier than most places. They are shrewd in their primitive way and see through insincerity like through a glass window.

If we would have pressed finances a little more we could have made up all, but on account of the very hard beginning little was done along that line until near the close.

The Sunday school has more than doubled within the last year at Krypton and if the brotherhood would send them second hand clothing it would be doubled again. A judicious disposition of clothing would do wonders there. At Lost Creek we have a different story to tell, but also a good one, but I will tell it in another letter.

I think it's only fair to say that it is expensive to live at Krypton and much good food is hard to get there. Hence the mission workers should be well supported, because as the missionaries in foreign lands they have enough troubles without having to scratch around to get something to eat and wear.
ISAAC D. BOWMAN,
1942 South 17th St., Philadelphia, Pa.

GARWIN, IOWA

As we have not reported from here recently, we will give a digest of the work at the present time.

Our Red and Blue contest came to a close the last Sunday in July. As predicted we were crowded out of available room for the conduct of the classes. The indications were and are, that we must either stop growing or soon enlarge; we have no intention of the former. Our attendance for the Sunday school and church service has been good with a splendid interest. Even during the month of August when many are away on vacations the attendance has been good. The Sunday school under the efficient superintendency of Brother Oscar Rank has been moving forward very favorably.

We are continuing to labor among these people. The outlook at present is for a very favorable and progressive year. While much has been accomplished here in the past few years, there is much yet to be done. We have been granted a vacation during the month of October and will spend this among friends and relatives in Ohio and Virginia. This will be after our meeting, conducted by Brother Coleman and Albert Ronk, will have come to a close. Our next report will be when the meetings have come to an end. May we have the interest of the brotherhood in the work of the Kingdom. FREEMAN ANKRUM.

A BRIEF REPORT OF THE NATIONAL CONFERENCE
By B. G. Mason

Inasmuch as the great body of the Brethren people did not attend the conference they did their part in other ways toward making this conference a great conference, it is due them that a brief report be published as early as possible. Considerable work and about two month's time will be required before the completed minutes can be published. Meanwhile this brief report of the business transactions will put the brotherhood in touch with the work done.

A better week, as to weather conditions could not have been chosen. The conference was both inspirational and instructive. All who attended felt overpaid for their effort. From the standpoint of attendance, the goal set four years ago was passed, a total of 417 delegates being in attendance. This did not include the delegates from the auxiliary organizations of the church. The general sessions were attended daily by from 500 to 600 people.

The new officers chosen were,— Moderator, W. H. Beachler; Vice-moderator, A. V. Kimmell; Secretary, E. G. Mason; Assistant Secretary, E. M. Riddle; Treasurer, H. F. E. O'Neill

The district delegates to National Conference were elected as follows,—Pennsylvania, Dyoll Belote and W. C. Benshoff; Ohio, E. M. Cobb and Martin Shively; Indiana, J. L. Kimmel and A. T. Wirick; Illiokota, M. J. Snyder; Middle West, Marie Lichty; Michigan, M. V. Garrison; Maryland-Virginia, A. B. Cover and H. M. Oberholtzer; Southern California, L. S. Bauman; Northern California, J. Wesley Platt; The Northwest, C. H. Ashman.

By motion, the district conferences were requested to hereafter elect members for the Executive Committee of the General Conference.

A rule providing for the creation of a Committee on Committees was made and J. F. Watson, B. T. Burnworth and A. V. Kimmell

were elected to constitute that committee.

The following standing committees were named by this committee and elected by the conference:

Committee on Christian Endeavor Organization,—Edward Boardman, Miss Wogaman, Miss Pence.

Committee on Conference Membership,—C. E. Kolb, C. C. Grisso, W. E. Thomas, Perry Horlacker, James Cook

Committee on Peace,—C. A. Bame, J. F. Watson, L. S. Bauman.

Committee on Interchurch Co-operation,— J Allen Miller, Martin Shively, J. A. McInturff.

Brethren representatives on Board Winona Assembly,—A. E. Thomas, H. E. Roscoe.

Committee on Resolutions,—O. E. Bowman, L. E. Srack, W. C. Benshoff.

Committee on Brethren Home,—O. E. Bowman, H. F. E. O'Neill, J. Allen Miller, H. V. Wall, J. L. Kimmell.

Committee on National Sunday School Organization,—M. J. Snyder, A. L. DeLozier, A. E. Whitted.

Committee on Finance,—H. E. Eppley, F. C. Vanator, W. T. Lytle.

Committee on Education,—L. L. Garber, J. C. Beal, B. T. Burnworth.

Committee on Rules and Regulations,—Dyoll Belote, G. W. Rench, E. L. Miller.

Committee on Temperance,—E. M. Riddle, Sylvester Lowman, Earl Flora

Committee on Social Service,—H. H. Wolford, G. S. Baer, E. D. Burnworth.

The various reports of these committees were given but neither space nor time will allow their publication at this time; they will appear later with the full report of the Minutes

The following Boards made detailed reports of their finances and accomplishments for the year together with their recommendations,—Benevolence Board, Publication Board, Board of Trustees of Brethren Home, Committee of Fifteen, Foreign Mission Board, Home Mission Board.

Owing to the fact that not all the churches had sent in their statistical reports, the National Statisician was not able to make a complete report. Since this is Jubilee year and the completion of the Four Year Program, H. H. Wolford, the statistician, was authorized to publish his report when completed instead of giving at the conference incomplete as it was. H. E. Eppley was elected to succeed H. H. Wolford as Statistician.

The detailed reports of these Boards will be printed in the Conference Minutes so will not be given here, but there are importants parts of these reports which we will mention here, as they are of immediate concern to the church at large.

First,—The Foreign Mission Board confirmed the appointment of the following persons to the Foreign Mission Field, to be sent as soon as the opportunity presents itself,— Edwin Boardman, for South America, Brother and Sister Rush and Miss Charlotte Hillegas for Africa. Brother and Sister L. E. Srack were candidates but not confirmed on account of their age and condition of health. These devout people must be given special praise for

volunteering for the foreign field and the conference so recognized it.

Second,—The Committee of Fifteen recommended that this conference adopt a new program to be concluded at the conference of 1923. This movement to be called the Brethren Bicentenary Movement, inasmuch as 1923 marks the two hundredth anniversary of the birth of the Brethren church in America. Since most of the goals set by the Four Year Program were passed, the financial budget of the church was set at half a million dollars to be raised during these three years and proportionately divided among the various boards.

A general secretary was named in the person of C. A. Bame, to devote his full time to the promotion of this Movement. This Movement means the completion of greater work and a greater forward movement of the church and should be boosted by each member from this moment on.

Very many other important and interesting items of business were transacted but this report will serve to acquaint the people in general with the action of the conference.

FROM ALLEGHENY COUNTY VIRGINIA

Stopping on my way home from the North Dakota meeting to see my sick brother at Charter Oak, Iowa, the Spirit of the Lord called me in a letter from our dear Brother J. S. Bowman of Roanoke, Virginia, to hold two meetings in his mission field in Alleghaney county, Virginia, which I agreed to do on my homeward trip. We began here at Arritts, Sunday, August 22 and closed on September 2. The Lord blessed our efforts with 27 confessions and renewals. Two mothers came from the Baptist church, while three of the converts of Baptist parentage will unite with the Baptist church. All the rest would have united with our church had it not been for some very uncharitable work done by a preacher of another denomination. He has caused great harm among the converts by his unwise efforts. It may result in eight converts going to the Methodist Episcopal church. Brother Bowman could not be with us in our meeting, but we are glad to say that we had the presence of Brother F. M. Arritt who is the local preacher at this place. He is a good preacher. We had his help in the excellent love feast held on the last night. All enjoyed the thoughts on loyalty he so forcibly delivered. Nearly all his old and substantial helpers have moved to other parts, but he is well liked and those who remain and the new workers are rallying about him. And he will prove a worthy shepherd for them. This is my third visit to these dear people, and I can say they are nobly holding together. Sister F. M. Arritt and Sister David Bowyer are the leaders in the Sisters' Society and the Sunday school. Brother David Arritt, whose subscription to the Evangelist I am sending in, has been in ill health for several years, but is getting better. Brethren, pray for him that he may be able soon to take up his work again. During the meeting I made my home there, and they surely made me feel at home by their loving kindness.   S. P. FOGLE.

SPECIAL NOTICE

It is the desire of the National Board of Benevolences that each state or district elect representative for the Superannuated Minister's Fund, and who will also promote the interests of the Brethren Home. As soon as the district representative is elected, I would greatly appreciate it if name and address of said representative is sent to H. F. E. O'Neill, . R. R. Y. M. C. A., 43 Street, Pittsburgh, Pennsylvania.   H. F. E. O'Neill.

The Illiokota District Conference of Brethren Churches

At the First Brethren Church, Lanark, Illinois, October 6, 7, 8, 1920

Wednesday Evening

7:30- 9:00 Opening Session.
    7:30 Songs of Praise and Prayer.
    7:45 Lanark's Welcome,
         B. T. Burnworth
      Response by Delegates.
    8:00 Special Music.
    8:20 Conference Sermon,
        Moderator R. F. Porte
    8:45 Announcements and Assignments

Thursday Morning

8:45-10:00 Simultaneous Conferences.
       a. Woman's Missionary Society.
        Program arranged by and for Women only.
       b. Ministerium.
    8:45 Devotions.
    9:00 Laymen Encouraging Recruits for the Ministry,
         B. F. Puterbaugh
    9:20 Problems Facing the Choice of the Ministry,
        Edwin Boardman, Jr.
    9:40 Discussion and Business.
10:00-11:45 Conference Session for District Problems.
   10:00 Devotional Service.
   10:10 Enrollment of Delegates.
   10:20 Moderator's Message,
        R. F. Porte
   10:35 Report of Mission Board,
      Secretary B. T. Burnworth
      Treasurer's Report,
        B. F. Puterbaugh
   10:50 How Advance Cause of Missions in District, G. T. Ronk
   11:15 Discussion and Business.

Thursday Afternoon

1:30- 2:00 Bible Study, Homer Anderson
    2:00 Challenge of The Brethren Bicentenary Movement,
        Miles J. Snyder
- 2:25 Discussion of the Bicentenary Program.
    3:00 Open Conference Program of Woman's Missionary Society

Thursday Evening

7:30- 9:00 Session for Worship and Inspiration.
    7:30 Song and Praise.
    7:40 Preparation by Pastor and People for a Revival,
        Z. T. Livengood

   8:05 Announcements and Special Music.
   8:15 Sermon, W. H. Beachler
   8:5 Benediction.

Friday Morning

8:30- 9:30 Ministerium Meeting.
   8:40 Devotions.
   8:30 Devotions.
   8:40 Problems of the Modern Pastor, and How Solved,
        D. A. C. Teeter
   9:05 Discussion and Business.
9:30-11:45 Sunday School Session
   9:30 The Primary Department, Importance and Methods,
        Mrs. H. E. Stroud
   9:45 Preparing Young People for Church Leadership,
        Freeman Ankrum
  10:00 Teacher Training and How to Promote It, Miss Alice Garber
  10:15 How to Teach Missions in the Sunday School,
        Mrs. G. T. Ronk
  10:30 Present Status of Temperance Instruction,
        Mrs. Robert Truman
  10:45 Administration Work in the Sunday School, Mrs. Frank Wisner
  11:00 Music.
  11:10 The Sunday School, the Right Arm of the Church,
        W. H. Beachler
  11:30 Business.

Friday Afternoon

1:30- 3:00 Session for Denominational Interests.
3:00- 4:00 Business Session and Election of Conference Officers.

Friday Evening

7:30- 9:00 Worship and Inspiration.
    7:30 Praise and Thanksgiving.
    7:45 Christian Endeavor, Why and How? Edwin Boardman, Jr.
- 8:10 Special Music.
    8:20 Sermon,
       Evangelist F. G. Coleman
    8:55 Closing of Conference.

Middle West Conference Program Fort Scott, Kansas, October 12, 13, 14, 1920

Tuesday Evening, October 12

7:30 Devotions, J. G. Dodds
8:00 Sermon, E. S. Flora
    Appointment of Credential Committee.

Wednesday Morning October 13

9:00 Devotions, J. S. C. Spickerman
9:15 Address of Welcome, E. E. Otto.
9:25 Response by delegates.
9:30 Report of Credential Committee.
9:40 Moderator's Address.
10:00 Organization.
10:30 Home Missions.

Wednesday Afternoon

2:00 Devotions, Marie Lichty.
2:15 Stewardship of Life, Roy Brumbaugh
3:00 Women's Missionary Society Session.
4:00 Adjournment.
7:30 Devotions, T. F. Howell

   7:45 Problems and Progress in Home Missions, G. T. Ronk
   8:15 Religious Education,
      Ashland College Representative

Thursday Morning, October 14

9:00 Devotions, J. D. Kemper
9:15 Unfinished Business.
9:30 The Bicentenary Program,
        H. F. Stuckman
10:00 The Stewardship of Possessions,
        T. F. Howell
10:15 The Laymen's Responsibility in the Prayer Meeting, D. E. Wagner
10:30 Open Discussion led by the Moderator
11:15 The Sunday School Curriculum,
      Ashland College Representative
12:00 Adjournment.
       C. W. YODER, Secretary.

Pennsylvania District Conference, Pittsburgh, Pa., October 4th to 7th, 1920

Monday Evening at 8

Music and devotions, led by E. E. Roberts.
Address of Welcome, H. F. E. O'Neill.
Response, by Mr Darr of Johnstown.
Music, announcements and offering.
Moderator's Address, H. M. Harley.
Assignment of delegates.
Closing song and benediction.
A time for social fellowship.

Tuesday Morning, 9:15 A. M.

45 minutes of devotion, led by M. A. Witter.
Music.
Conference Business.
11:30 A. M., Memorial Service,—
For Brother I. B. Trout, J. F. Watson.
For Brother Edw Byers, J. L. Hall

Tuesday Afternoon, 1:30 P M.

Sunday School Session. In charge of the State Sunday School President.
Music and Devotions.
Addresses by Sunday School Specialists,—
"Our Sunday School goals for 1920-21,"
        J. F. Watson
"Teacher Training," Wm. C. Benshoff
"Our Present Status, Albert Trent.
ALSO,—A State Sunday School Specialist,
Sunday School Business.

Tuesday Evening, 7:45

15 minutes of music and devotion, led by
        Mr. M. C. Myers
Address on "Our Publishing Interests,"—
        R. R. Teeter
Music, Announcements and offering.
Sermon, by Dyoll Belote
Closing song and benediction.

Wednesday Morning, 9:15

45 minutes of devotion, by E. E. Fehnel
Conference Business.
Missions, Albert Trent
Benevolence, H. F. E. O'Neill

Wednesday Afternoon, 1:30

Christian Endeavor Session, in charge of Miss Eleanor Wilcox, State C. E. President.
Devotions, led by the President
"Our Juniors," by Miss Marguerite Rau.
"Our Young People," Alva McClain
ALSO, A State Christian Endeavor Specialist.
Christian Endeavor Business.

3:30 P. M., W. M. S. Session, in charge of Miss Mae Minnich

Wednesday Evening, 7:45

Music and Devotions, led by H. C. Cassel.
"Our Bicentenary Movement."
"The Spiritual," M. A. Witter
"Evangelism," L. G. Wood
'Religious Education," J. F. Watson
'Benevolence," H. F. E. O'Neill
"Missions," Alva McClain
"Education," E. D. Burnworth
Music, Announcements, Offering and Benediction.

9:30 P. M., A trip to the Old Fort Pitt, where the Pittsburgh Christian Endeavor will entertain the delegates to a marshmallow toast.

Thursday Morning, 9:15

15 minutes of devotion, led by Osmer Tress-Conference business and organization.
A Round Table on "Church Organization," led by Horace Kolb.

Thursday Afternoon, 1:30

15 minutes of devotion, led my Osmer Treasler
Address, "The Message of The Brethren Church for Our Day," E. D. Burnworth
2:30 o'clock, An automobile tour of the city, with stops at a few of the leading places of interest.

Thursday Evening, 7:45

Music and Devotions, led by J. I. Hall
Address, "Our College,"—by
　　　　　　　A College Representative
Music, announcements and offering.
Sermon, Alva McClain.
Closing words and song, and benediction.
The Pittsburgh Brethren church is hoping that every church will send her full quota of delegates, and she will do all in her power to make their stay both pleasant and profitable.
The above program is the result of much study and prayer, and is intended to help our churches to find themselves in the light of the new Bicentenary Program which has just been studied out for, and presented to us at the recent National Conference.

Program of Woman's Missionary Society of the Brethren Church.

Indiana District Conference
Flora, Indiana, October 4
to 7, 1920. Conference
Slogan, "Serve to
Save"

Tuesday, 8:30—9:30 A. M.

Song Service and Devotions, Mrs. J. J. Wolff
Business, 　　Appointing of Committees
"Serve to Save," 　　　　Mrs. Berkey
Reports, 　　President and Treasurer
　　　　and Patroness of S. M. M.
Report from Summer School of Missions,
　　　　　　　　　Mrs. Shively
Announcements and closing hymn.

Wednesday, 8:30—9:30 A. M.

Song Service and Devotions, Mrs. J. E. Ham
Business, 　　　Election of Officers
Goals 1920-1923, 　　Miss Mae Smith
Goals 1920-1921, 　　　　　President
Problem Hour, 　　　　　Delegates
Closing hymn and prayer.

Wednesday, 8:30—9:30—Public Session

Song and prayer, 　　　　Mrs. Shively
Installation of Officers, 　　J. L. Kimmel
Address, 　　　　　　C. A. Bame
Benediction.
Note.—Time for Mission Study class will be announced later.

MRS ELMER BERKEY, President,
　　　　　　Goshen, Indiana.

THE TIE THAT BINDS

KYLE-TEETER.—On Wednesday evening, August 18, 1920, at the home of the acting pastor, Samuel J. Kyle and Miss Laura B. Teeter were united in marriage. The bride is a member of the Third Brethren church of Johnstown, Pa.
　　　　　　　　W. S. BAKER.

GLASS-HUSTON.—On Wednesday evening, August 25, 1920, at the home of the bride's parents, Brother and Sister J. C. Huston, of Johnstown, Pa., their daughter, Louise M. was united in marriage with Homer H. Glass, of Altoona, Pa. The bride is a member of the Listie, Pa., Brethren church. Ceremony by the writer.
　　　　　　　　W. S. BAKER.

SMITH - WEITZELL — Mr. Raymond B. Smith and Miss ElVira Weitzell were united in marriage at the home of the bride near the Carlton Brethren church, Wednesday afternoon, July 7. There was a small number of invited guests and relatives present. These young people will make their home on a farm in the community. May their life together be enriched by many blessings. Ceremony by 　　FREEMAN ANKRUM.

IN THE SHADOW

BRACKEN.—Mildred Geraldine Bracken, the two-year-old daughter of Brother and Sister William Bracken, passed out of this life into the life everlasting, on August 19, 1920. May God bless and comfort the bereaved ones. Funeral services from the home in Johnstown, Pa., by the writer.
　　　　　　　　W. S. BAKER.

STAHL.—At his residence near Jones Mills, Pa., July 22, 1920, Amos Stahl died at the ageof 48 years, 7 months and 14 days. He is survived by his wife and twelve children, all of them in the church. Brother Stahl was a faithful and highly esteemed member of the Jones Mills Brethren church. His high standing in the community brought a very large number of people to his funeral. Among the number were even ministers representing four denominations. Services were conducted by the writer.
　　　　　　　　H. S. MYERS.

RICHARDSON.—Following a comparatively short illness, John Lincoln Richardson, aged 56 years, 8 months and 27 days, peacefully passed beyond earth's shadows on July 19, 1920, to greet the dawning of eternity. He united with the MilledgeVille Brethren church in 1884 under the pastorate of S. H. Bashor. A devoted wife and an only widowed daughter are left to mourn his absence, and also many friends who knew him as a good citizen, a congenial neighbor and a real friend in time of need. May the Father's grace comfort and sustain the bereaved in this time of sorrow. Funeral services in the home conducted by the writer and assisted by Rev. Z. T. LiVengood, Lanark, Ill.
　　　　　　　　MILES. J. SNYDER.

Business Manager's Corner

AN URGENT APPEAL

Among the many perplexing questions which came before the meeting of the Brethren Publishing Company at the General Conference at Winona Lake was that of meeting the tremendous increased cost of paper-stock without increasing the subscription price of the Brethren Evangelist. While this has been a serious problem for a little more than three years it has never been quite as serious as it is at the present time.

While the cost of paper is practically four times as great as it was five years ago, yet by the Budget System or the Honor Roll System about two-thirds of the subscribers of the Evangelist get their paper for the same price that was charged five years ago.

It is absolutely impossible to publish the paper at this price without suffering loss. The Publishing Company is facing an actual deficit of two or three thousand dollars during the coming year unless relief is secured in some manner.

The question of increasing the price of the Evangelist to two dollars and a half for single subscriptions and to two dollars for the Honor Roll churches was considered seriously. But it was agreed that this radical advance should not be made providing some other way could be found that would enable the Company to meet this added cost of paper. It was felt that the Evangelist is as many Brethren homes as possible is vital to the growth of the church and its institutions and the Board of Directors was reluctant to take any steps that would have a tendency to reduce the number of subscriptions.

A Remedy .

One brother stated that he would rather contribute fifty dollars himself toward a fund to meet this emergency than to have the subscription price advanced, and another brother remarked "that will mean a ten dollar bill out of my pocket also." So this is the conclusion arrived at: A general appeal shall be made to the entire Brotherhood for contributions sufficient to meet the impending deficit. This will mean that between TWO THOUSAND and THREE THOUSAND dollars must be contributed voluntarily by members of the Brethren church who love their church enough to make a personal sacrifice for it. If this appeal does not receive a ready response the price of the paper will have to be increased fifty cents on January first.

The need is urgent and what is to be done must be done NOW. We will endeavor to keep this appeal before our readers for a period of six weeks and we pray that within that period of time the emergency may be fully met.

We hope to be able to use this column weekly to record the contributions that are made from week to week, and we trust the splendid example set by our good brother, Homer Anderson, who gave the first ten dollars for this cause as well as a number of others who have already contributed smaller sums will move a large number of our readers to follow this example.

With the great Bicentenary Movement just entered into by the church and which is to continue for three years, it would be almost suicidal to allow any appreciable slump in the Evangelist subscription list.

We hope to enlist the large majority of our pastors in this work for we know that without the co-operation of the pastors no work touching the general brotherhood can be successfully carried on.

Who will be the first one to answer this appeal with a substantial contribution?
　　　　　　　　R. R. TEETER,
　　　　　　　　Business Manager.

Volume XLII
Number 36

September 22
1920

The BRETHREN EVANGELIST

-ONE·IS·YOUR·MASTER·AND·ALL·YE·ARE·BRETHREN-

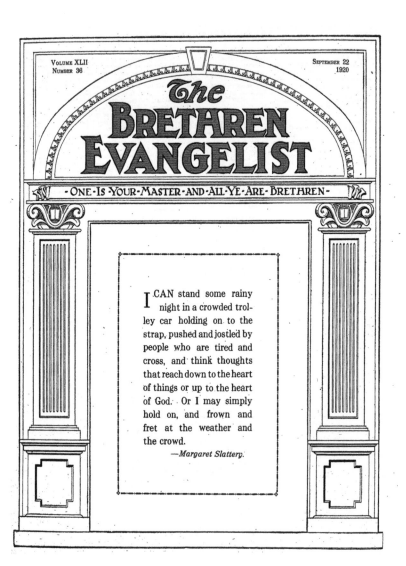

I CAN stand some rainy night in a crowded trolley car holding on to the strap, pushed and jostled by people who are tired and cross, and think thoughts that reach down to the heart of things or up to the heart of God. Or I may simply hold on, and frown and fret at the weather and the crowd.

—*Margaret Slattery.*

Published every Wednesday at Ashland, Ohio. All matter for publication must reach the Editor not later than Friday noon of the preceding week.

George S. Baer, Editor

The
Brethren
Evangelist

When ordering your paper changed give old as well as new address. Subscriptions discontinued at expiration. To avoid missing any numbers renew two weeks in advance.

R. R. Teeter, Business Manager

OFFICIAL ORGAN OF THE BRETHREN CHURCH

Subscription price, $2.00 per year, payable in advance.
Entered at the Post Office at Ashland, Ohio, as second-class matter.
Acceptance for mailing at special rate of postage provided for in section 1103, Act of October 3, 1917, authorized September 9, 1918.
Address all matter for publication to Geo. S. Baer, Editor of the Brethren Evangelist, and all business communications to R. R. Teeter, Business Manager, Brethren Publishing Company, Ashland, Ohio. Make all checks payable to the Brethren Publishing Company.

TABLE OF CONTENTS

EDITORIAL

The Movement Begins With the Right Emphasis

The first point of emphasis in our Bicentenary Movement is the "Spiritual Life." Beginning here indicates its wisdom, for no movement worthy of the effort of the church can be launched without seeking first of all to deepen and vitalize the spiritual life of its membership. This was the beginning point of the old Four Year Program and to the extent that the spiritual note was sounded in all the various congregations and spiritual vigor was induced in the lives of the members success was attained. But the Bicentenary Movement profits by an omission in the spiritual emphasis of the old program; it makes the family altar the starting point in the campaign to quicken and intensify the spirituality of our people. That is the proper place to begin, for we have already discovered that it is impossible to take men very far into the spiritual experiences of God's house until they have become accustomed to spirituality in their homes. And so it occurs to us that the Movement begins with the right emphasis.

There is a great need of emphasizing religion in the household, both because of its great importance and its widespread unpopularity. That the family altar has become very unpopular and almost extinct is very evident to those who are at all observant. Religious leaders of every phase of interest and of every denominational affiliation are concerned about the disappearance of this evidence and expression of home religion. How few are the homes in the average congregation where family worship is the rule we have no statistics to tell us. Perhaps few pastors really know the exact condition of affairs in their own parishes, and if they did they would be too much humiliated to make it known. But go where you will, you seldom find a home that has time to call the members of the household together for morning or evening prayer and the reading of God's word. People are too busy; too much is crowded into the day to give time for family prayer. One member of the family must hasten to work in the morning before the rest are up and ready for prayer and another returns home too late at night. Worship has been literally crowded out of our homes by the multitude of earthly cares entering in.

Besides the family interests are too varied to enable the members to concentrate in such a matter as worship. And the failure of the family to take a few moments together in prayer is largely to blame for the growing lack of the spirit of family unity and oneness of interests. There is something to be little or nothing that the entire family has in common, nothing in which all are interested, nothing to bind them together except a place to eat and sleep. This is one of the most lamentable changes that is taking place in the modern home—the lack of a feeling of unity and the wide separateness of interests. Such a spirit can hardly grow up where the various members of a home have grown accustomed to the uniting influence of the Bible readings, the meditations and the prayers of the family altar.

Nothing is more important for us as a church to face than this situation, and no effort more worthy than that which is calculated to remedy it. If we are to have a genuine revival of religion with more than temporary results and if we are to press the task of extending the Kingdom with any promise of worth-while success, it behooves us to begin with vitalizing and intensifying of the religious life of the home.

Nothing can take the place of the home in making religion popular and effective. We may encourage our young people to pray and discuss religious themes in Christian Endeavor meetings, and it will be helpful to them. But if the spirit cultivated there is not a part of the home life, it will be hard for them to make it real and apply it to their daily problems. It will seem more like an enjoyable sensation which they must go to church to experience and not a part of life. Children may go to Sunday school and perchance gain a fair knowledge of the Bible and receive something of the spirit of devotion that is there imparted and their lives will be ennobled thereby. But if the Bible is a strange or sealed book in the home and its precepts are not applied to the home relations, it will be a long and tedious task with all their Sunday school instruction to learn how to make the application and the chances are against them ever coming to look upon religion as a really vital part of life. Men and women may be induced in one way or another to attend church worship, and children may be compelled to go, and while they may be benefited to some extent by their presence there, yet if the practice and spirit of worship is omitted from the home life, religion is likely to be looked upon as a Sunday affair, something that may be put off with one's Sunday clothes.

Many ways and means have been devised to aid in the cultivation of the spiritual life and in promoting the spirit and practice of worship and we have no desire to minimize the importance of anything that has been used as a means of grace, but nothing is so fundamental to the building of strong, stalwart, useful Christian characters as a religion cultivated in the home and made as familiar, as customary and as essential as the daily meals and the nightly sleep. Until the value of family religion is re-estimated and given a higher rating, all our public efforts at the promotion of religious zeal and the development of Christian lives will be greatly discounted. Until the church insists on the erection and maintenance of family altars with equal persistence as it does on the practice of church ordinances, all the church's ritual will be more or less formal and powerless. Until we recognize the fact that the spiritual weakness resulting from the deplorable lack of family religion can be made good not by substituting religious organizations and institutions but by the re-building of the family altars, will we as a church have the power to prosecute our high commission divinely given with the effectiveness and rapidity which the urgency demands. In view of this let us rejoice that our new Bicentenary Movement has begun with the first emphasis on home religion.

An Amusement Test for Christians

It is not uncommon in this amusement loving age (and doubtless every age has had its amusement craze) to hear Christians ask some religious leader whether or not they can engage in this or that amusement. The very fact that one is caused to hesitate and ask the question ought to make one suspicious as to the rightfulness of the thing about which he inquires. But when people are concerned about doing the light of that which is permissible instead of living safely within the bounds of right, they are very much concerned about having a definite line of demarkation between the right and wrong. They are continually asking for rules and decisions whereby they may be guided. They do not wish to accept the responsibility of judging for themselves. If only some one would be conscience for them! Or, if they could have given them some rule that would cover every case and relieve them of the necessity of deciding! But no such rule can be given. No man can answer for another's conscience. Nor will one decision, if properly made apply to every case. But there is a principle enunciated by the late Dr. J. Wilbur Chapman, which would seem to be a safe principle to follow in making our decisions concerning questionable amusements.

Being asked, concerning certain amusements which his inquirer hoped might be considered permissible, he said, "It is a very difficult thing for one to make a rule for another to live by. The rule which governs my life is this: Anything that dims my vision of Christ, or takes away my taste for Bible study, or cramps me in my prayer life, or makes Christian work difficult, is wrong for me and I must, as a Christian, turn away from it."

That is very good counsel and would solve many a Christian's problems concerning amusements, as well as many other interests of life. We owe it to our Lord as well as to our fellow Christians to "keep fit" all the time. We ought to live at the maximum and not at the minimum of spiritual power and efficiency. The athlete contending in the games, the soldier fighting the battles of his country and the physician diagnosing the disease of his patient, all owe it to those who put trust in them to keep at the height of physical strength and mental alertness. And just so no less than the highest spiritual fitness is to be expected of every Christian. This cannot be maintained if we indulge in things that are knowingly weakening, simply because the flesh desires them. We dare not ask the question whether a thing is permissible or not, for God may permit things he does not sanction, even as he permitted Balaam to curse Israel, but did not sanction it. Anything that lessens our spiritual efficiency, however much we desire it, we cannot afford to engage in it.

"How far that little candle throws its beams!
So shines a good deed in a naughty world."

It seems that the hardest tenet of the Christian faith for man to believe is that God is everywhere, for man invariably and continually acts as if there were places where God is not. We are ever saying, "God is a God of the hills and not of the valley."

EDITORIAL REVIEW

A very carefully written report of the Southern California conference, with lists of the many addresses and sermons is found in this issue of The Evangelist.

Prof. H. H. Wolford is to represent the College and the National Sunday School Association at the Pennsylvania state conference to be held at Pittsburgh, October 4 to 7.

Brother Austin Staley, one of our student preachers, spent his vacation with the Brethren at Udell, Iowa, where he was formerly pastor. He had a very enjoyable and successful vacation. He is now preaching at Homerville, Ohio, along with his school work.

On the Bicentenary page last week under the sub-head "Missions and Extension" in item 8 occurred a typographical error. Instead of the word "conversation" which appeared substitute the word "conservation," the word intended, and it will read, "A vigorous program of conservation and extension to fortify weak places and to claim new opportunities."

From Oriskany, Virginia, comes a report of the meeting recently held by Brother I. D. Bowman and reported by his brother, J. S. Bowman, who teaches school and makes occasional trips of "more than fifty miles" to minister to the spiritual needs of the little group of Brethren at Oriskany.

Brother Reed reports the maintenance of a fine interest in the work of the First church of Los Angeles with conversions frequently taking place in their regular services. Brother Jennings is doubtless now on the job again after his visit in the east and attendance at General Conference.

Brother E. M. Cobb calls it "A Real Vacation" that his people of Dayton gave him; it was six weeks long in time and covered several thousand miles, but it was not spent in idleness. He made himself generally helpful among the churches of Southern California, and particularly at the Southern California conference held at Long Beach.

The Lanark, Illinois, church is always alive and doing things under the energetic leadership of Brother B. T. Burnworth. They recently held an evangelistic campaign with Miss Aboud as the preacher. A number of souls were born into the Kingdom and Brother Z. T. Livengood, our faithful correspondent, pronounces the meeting a success.

A correction in the Illiokota conference program that failed to reach us before the paper went to press last week is as follows: On Friday forenoon Mrs. Robert Truman is scheduled to speak on "The Present Status of Temperance Instruction." The name of A. T. Ronk is substituted for that of Mrs. Truman. We are informed that on Friday afternoon at the session entitled "Denominational Interests" Prof. J. A. Garber will represent the College and also the National Sunday School Association.

Our readers will appreciate the letter of Brother Edward Atkinson to the Foreign Board in this issue. Among other observations that might be made these two give cause for encouragement: First the sense of permanency and confidence that the people are coming to feel regarding our mission at Cabrera due largely to the purchase and well-keeping of our mission property will give our missionaries increased influence and their message increased power. Second, the wonderful transforming influence of the true Word of God upon hearts who read it with anxious and sincere purpose is beginning to manifest itself before the eyes of our workers there.

Dr. Bame, who was given the task of directing us in our Bicentenary Movement, supplies us with his opening message in this issue. The page that was formerly devoted to the Four Year Program will now be be dedicated to the promotion of the new three-year-program, and Brother Bame will supply us with the material, either from his own pen or from the pens of those whom he may invite to write. We have no way of knowing what he may have to tell us during the year, but we feel sure it will be of vital interest to every congregation and individual and the page should be read carefully.

Among some of the churches there seems to be some indifference manifested towards the appeal made in behalf of the Winona Tabernacle fund. This could hardly exist if our members were generally informed concerning the matter. The various denominations using the Winona grounds for conference purposes are uniting in the building of a new and larger tabernacle. Our General Conference last year pledged our denomination to pay the small sum of $2,500 and then apportioned the amount among the districts and churches. This year we were privileged to use that new tabernacle, though it is not fully completed. We could not begin to build one like it, if we had to depend on our own funds for the entire amount; but it is there for us to use every year. We said we would pay the amount within the year, but the year is gone and the amount is still unpaid by the churches. Conference made provision for the payment of the amount promptly, as reported last week by Brother Belote. But the churches must promptly pay back the amount that was borrowed from the Foreign Board on a short time loan. The church that fails to pay its apportionment of this pledge at the earliest possible moment can hardly rebuke the member who fails to pay his grocery bill. This is a legitimate obligation on every congregation, and we cannot but believe every one will make good when it is understood.

THE BRETHREN BICENTENARY MOVEMENT PAGE

1723 · · · · · · 1923

Dr. Charles A. Bame, Editor

"Ring Out the Old; Ring In the New"

This is the topic for the times. For that is just what has already happened. To the many friends and readers of this page, let us say that we are glad to have had a chance to do it. You notice the new heading to this page? Well, that tells the story of what has happened. The old was the Four Year Program; the new is the Bicentenary Movement. In this article I wish to tell you a good many secrets; how the old went out and how the new came in. We were at Winona. It was Jubilee night. On the program were the best singers and the best speakers of the conference. A year

before, one of the finest men in Winona Lake had said of our Committee, "That is a mighty fine, keen bunch of fellows." Well, I think he said it right. That is what they were and are. Both of these Programs represented the good thought of many of the brethren without whom our church could not well get on. You will be happy to know that we came out big on most of the Goals of the Program. Jubilee night told us that three of the churches of the brotherhood had come out ahead on all of them. All hats off to a church that can reach such a standard. Here they are:

Front Line Churches: Won 16 Goals

ASHLAND, OHIO   FLORA, INDIANA   FALLS CITY, NEBRASKA

I feel that it would have been a good thing to have gotten a special banner for these churches. But it is honor enough I guess, that they may always, by their certificates, tell the other Brethren churches that they were one of three in nearly 200. But if some of the churches did not make every goal, it is some achievement for a program to have so many winning all goals but two out of fourteen. Hats off to the Banner churches:

But still, if all the churches could not climb that high on the scale of fame, let it be known that a greater number still reached 12 goals and hence we can again take off our hats to the Star churches because they are in the majority; you want to see their names, too? Well, here they are

BANNER (Won 14 Goals)

Altoona, Pa.
Canton, Ohio
Dayton, Ohio
Goshen, Ind.
Lanark, Ill.
Beaver City, Neb.
Clay City, Ind.
Elkhart, Ind.
Hagerstown, Md.
Louisville, Ohio
Martinsburg, Pa.
Meyersdale, Pa.
Morrill, Kans.
Muncie, Ind.
Johnstown, Pa., (First)
Los Angeles, Calif., (First)
Nappanee, Ind.
North Manchester, Ind.
Roanoke, Va.
Whittier, Calif.

STAR (Won 12 Goals)

Bellefontaine, Ohio (Gretna)
Eaton, Ind., (Maple Grove)
Allentown, Pa.
Bryan, Ohio
Fremont, Ohio
Huntington, Ind.
La Verne, Calif.
Limestone, Tenn.
Long Beach, Calif.
Masontown, Pa.
McKee, Pa.
Milledgeville, Ill.
New Paris, Ind.
North Liberty, Ind.
Philadelphia, Pa., First
Philadelphia, Pa., Third
Portis, Kansas.
Sidney, Indiana.
West Salem, O., (Fair Haven)
Summit Mills, Pa.
Waynesboro, Pa.
Sterling, O., (Zion Hill)

Anyway you look at the work of the Program just finished, you are happy over the progress made. Progress, when other churches were making the poorest show of a century. Progress when the great denominations were fighting hard for progress and withal, lost. To win at such a time and

under such conditions ought to encourage the most faint-hearted and discouraged. To win when the world was war-torn and literally ransacked for funds and men to carry on the work of destruction, is an achievement that has not found sufficient appreciation and laudation, as I see it. Just take a look:

	1916 Report	1920 Report
Amount of Permanent Endowment for Ashland College	$37,000	$185,000
Money Contributed to Home Mission Board	10,013	15,000
Easter Offering for Foreign Missions	4,262	26,414
Amount of Contributions to the Board of Benevolences	779	2,263
Number of Women's Organizations Reported	88	94
Number reaching the National Standard of the W. M. S.	22	54
Number of Subscribers to the Brethren Evangelist	2,500	5,350
Congregations receiving Evangelist in 75 per-ct. of homes	1	80
Number of Churches using Budget System of Finance	30	79
Number of Recruits gained in Four Years		75
Number of Congregations Founded or Re-established		6
	1917-1918	1919-1920
Congregations on the Four Year Program Honor Roll	22	45

Of course, made without experience and hastily as was the Four Year Program, some goals were too high and some too low. The new program which you had a chance to study last week, will profit by that experience. About that, I

wish to say more next week. But for now, turn back to your last week's Evangelist and see what it contemplated and get busy.

BAME.

GENERAL ARTICLES

Symposium: What Is a Successful Rally Day?

I. BY G. W. BRUMBAUGH

Rally Day is a great reunion day for the Sunday school. It should be a home-coming day for all the members of the Sunday school family. The most suitable time for such a day is in the early fall soon after the opening of the public schools when all the children, young people and others have returned from their vacations. Since the Sunday school is a department of the church suited to all ages, from the youngest baby on the Cradle Roll to the oldest member of the Home Department, a successful Rally Day should take into account in its plans and purposes every member from every home in the entire community. The new school year opens for increased activities of school work in class and community. Our aim is set before us; every pupil and teacher in place, new families visited and interested, and indifferent parents brought in touch with the Sunday school and church. A search should be made for children and others not connected with any school.

A successful Rally Day will depend much upon the preparation that has been made previous to the day in the way of advertising and general publicity given to it by all who are interested in the growth of the school. There should be first of all, a strong committee appointed whose duty it is to get every worker and teacher in every department of the school in co-operation with them to look after all absentees and delinquent members of the school. This committee should have general charge in the planning of the program for the day. There are three ways to give invitations and all can be used to advantage for the same occasion.

(1) Send specially prepared printed or written invitations from the school or classes in each department.

(2) Personal calls to invite, made by teachers and friends.

(3) Interesting notices and write-ups in the local papers where such is practicable.

There should also be a committee on decorations who should make the church or school just as attractive as possible with harvest fruits, sheaves, autumn foliage and flowers. The surroundings should be made as home-like as possible.

On the Rally Day a spirit of optimism and good cheer should pervade the entire school with any special features which the committee on program and preparation may see fit to plan and carry out for the day. Above all else there should be the very best teaching of the regular lessons in all the classes in each of the departments of the entire school. A combined Sunday school and church service is a splendid thing for Rally Day. The pastor, superintendent, and some prominent Sunday school worker, outside of the local school may have a vital part on the program. Good music should be provided in which the children and young people should all have a prominent part. The plans and purposes of the year should be set forth and every one who is interested in the success of the school each Sunday throughout the year following should become a booster for the school.

The program of the day should inspire, encourage and interest every one in the school to such an extent that each will desire to be regular in attendance throughout the year. Also the great aim of the Sunday school to win souls to Christ and to build up real, strong, Christian character should be strongly emphasized by teachers and officers in a practical way that will bring results at every opportunity.

If some of the simple suggestions which have been made can be carried out in each of our schools in the brotherhood, and every worker is inspired with a desire to become more efficient in his work for the Master, the cause of religious education will have received such an impetus as will be felt throughout the entire year.

Dayton, Ohio.

II. HARRY E. PRICE

To answer this question in brief I would say, A successful Rally Day would be to have laid definite plans, set reasonably high goals for attendance, offering, etc., and on Rally Day to have "GONE OVER THE TOP" in every department of the Sunday school in reaching these goals. This would be a successful Rally Day but in order to discuss a question of this kind in a way to make it beneficial to others I will try and give some plans that would bring about a successful Rally Day in any school if properly carried out.

The superintendent has gathered his officers and teachers about him for the last camp fire of the year; he has been pondering over plans that would bring the best results and make it the biggest Rally Day in the history of the school and that it would mark the beginning of a year of large accomplishments,—if he could only communicate his vision to his officers and teachers so that the flame of enthusiasm could be kindled in every department.

Some of the teachers and officers are very conservative and it takes them so long to see new possibilities or to recognize the value of a new plan or method. Every year much time and precious energy is wasted in trying to create interest in various projects for the good of the school but here is the place and now is the time to build the fire of enthusiasm for a successful Rally Day.

Our Sunday schools are so well organized that we can distribute the responsibility for each department and outline some plan whereby each department superintendent can carry out his or her plans to a successful end. Let us begin with the Cradle Roll and we will ask the superintendent

of this department to see that every member of the Cradle Roll has a written invitation to Sunday school on Rally Day, October 10. Have the invitation on a neat postal card, also see as many mothers of the babies as possible and give them a special invitation to bring the babies. Then go to the Beginners' superintendent and have her ask the teachers of the classes to make a list of the scholars who have not been regular and try to see them personally and give them an invitation to Sunday school several Sundays before Rally Day and then send written invitations to all the pupils in the department the week preceding the Sunday of October 10, using some attractive card. Now your Junior superintendent is waiting for the plans to be used in this lively department for indeed it is the BEE HIVE of the Sunday school and a large part of the enthusiasm of the school is always alive in this department and they are always willing to do even more than their part to make the Sunday school wht it should be.

Now I ask the Junior superintendent to give each teacher in this department these plans to begin the first Sunday in September. Starting with a contest for attendance and offering leading up to and including Rally Day and giving to the Junior class for having the most teachers in regular attendance and the largest offering per member each Sunday a nice banner to be hung up in the class room. The competition will soon raise the proper enthusiasm to carry this department successfully over Rally Sunday, making a special effort the week before Rally Day.

For the Intermediate, Senior and Adult Departments,

I would work through the organized classses, as each class in these departments is organized. I ask each teacher to take the responsibility for his or her class along with the president and secretary of the class, secure a list of the membership enrolled, take out the names of those not attending regularly and divide them among a committee in the class and have each one urged to personally invite them to come to Sunday school during the month of September and then on the week previous to Rally Day have a solicitation of every member of the class by the committee.

The Home Department superintendent should also be asked to send invitations to every member of this department. Ask them to co-operate with the school in having the largest attendance on this day ever; urge them in the invitation to bring every person in the home, young and old, provided health permits, and to be present at 9:30 sharp.

After these plans are laid before the Cabinet a few things of general importance must be discussed:

First, our school aim is 500 for a school of 250 average attendance. By making your aim, high, your plans large, you will get big results.

Second, every member of the Cabinet willing to forget themselves and do everything in their power to boost toward the objective.

Third, appoint your committee as follows:

Program Committee; Reception Committee, including transportation, seating and nursery; Advertising Committee; Decorating Committee.

Fourth, use a motto for the school, "EVERYBODY WORKING!"

I believe if these suggestions are carefully and prayerfully carried out a most successful Rally Day is assured.

Nappanee, Indiana.

III. BY IRL F. BRATTEN

A Sunday school Rally Day Service, which is attended by nearly twice the average turnout, and which consists of an entertaining program, interspersed with live singing, does not in itself constitute a successful Rally Day, in my opinion.

Candidly, I grow weary of hearing the term, "Sunday school" sarcastically referred to by outsiders, as a place where they "Sing from page so-and-so, while the brother takes up the offering"—as though that were to be inferred as being the extent of Sunday school work! It is appalling how few there are who realize the importance of the Sunday school, an organization which in my opinion will be very largely responsible for the social as well as religious ideals upheld by our citizens of the coming generation. I do not wish to speak discouragingly, but merely want to suggest to my readers the necessity of impressing upon the minds of our people the importance of Sunday school work. Only this is fully realized, every Sunday will be Rally Day. In order to accomplish this, I would offer the following plan of procedure, as a suggestion:

First, arrange for a "Rally Cabinet Meeting," in which different members will be asked to report on the aims of the Sunday school, the necessity of maintaining the Sunday school, a history of the Sunday school generally, and its accomplishments in the past, the present condition of our school, and problems we are now facing, our future possibilities and responsibilities, etc. After thoroughly discussing the various problems, follow up by formulating a definite plan of action, to cover a period of, say, the remainder of the year.

We are now ready to prepare our Rally Day meeting. For this service I would suggest that the lesson study be dispensed with, and a number of three-minute talks be given, presenting to the school the matters discussed in the Rally Cabinet Meeting; and then, of course making a strong appeal to each individual to do his part in the carrying out of the plan presented by the cabinet. Everyone should be strongly impressed with the fact that this day shall mark a New Beginning, and not an end in itself.

At this point the real effort should begin. Where good music was rendered on Rally Day, better music should be planned for the following Sunday; and where the program has been well planned for Rally Day, the program for the following Sunday should be prepared and executed with more zeal than the preceding Sunday, and so on until everyone gets in the habit of doing his BEST EVERY SUNDAY. With this plan under way, and each teacher preparing each week, (through earnest prayer and study), something really worth while to the pupil, I believe the school would make remarkable progress.

In conclusion, I would say, in answer to the question "What is a Successful Rally Day?" that it is a day which marks the beginning of a new era well planned, and not a "one-day soap-bubble."

Louisville, Ohio.

Coordinating Religion and Education. By Miles J. Snyder

Address at the late General Conference, Winona Lake, Indiana

In times past there have been those who regarded religion and education as things separate and apart. More than once the question has been asked: What has education to do with religion? Down through the centuries gone by, people have wondered whether religion had anything in common with education, and whether each had need of the other.

Before trying to point out what relation should be recognized between religion and education, or what relative rank each should occupy, it is not irrelevant to remind you that the outstanding leaders in the history of the world's religious life have been educated men. Moses graduated form the best schools in the world under the most brilliant minds of his day. Elisha went to school to Elijah until his master passed away. Of Jesus it was said, "Never man spake as this man," and even his enemies recognized that he "taught as one having authority." Paul was a student in the Greek schools of Tarsus, and also a pupil of the greatest teachers of the Jews. The twelve apostles had the finest course of instruction with which human beings were ever favored—three years under the tutelage of the world's Master Teacher. The illustrious Fathers of the primitive Christian church were men educated in schools fostered by the early church. From the history of our own church we find that Alexander Mack was a well educated man, that Christopher Saur was a university graduate, and sent his own son to the best schools of the day. And in the more recent centuries the pages of church and missionary history are resplendent with the names and deeds of men and women who drank deep at the fountain of learning, only to go forth and serve the Christ in the beauty of holiness animated by religious zeal.

In fact, one must be blind to the history of the past if he cannot see that true religion and Christian education are closely related and vitally important, and that each has been and can be of great service to the other. Christian religion stands for man's highest welfare; it regards the sacredness of the body, the powers of the mind, and the spirerate only, but also the greatest scholars and philosophers. It meant to carry the Gospel to the greatest civilization the itual possibilities of the soul. It is unlimited in the scope of its influence upon human life; but it needs the help of education to realize and exert its transforming power. In other words, education is necessary as a means or handmaid to open up the world's storehouse to the eye of the soul, to measure things at their proper value, to discover and to throne high ideals, and to formulate a program of life that will appeal to the best and worthiest in an individual.

A close and vital relation then exists between religion and education, and each enhances the meaning and value of the other. Religion without education becomes superstitious and inefficient, while education without the spirit and truths of religion wholly misses the mark and may even become dangerous. In religion we have that which is regenerates the heart and governs the will and purifies the springs of conduct; while true education means the orderly development of body, mind and soul. The two working together constitute a creative force in society for the building up of a desirable and permanent civilization.

That an intelligent co-ordination of religion and education is important, is evident when we look about us in the world today. Rumblings and threatenings are in every corner, and industrial and social unrest and uncertainty are everywhere. Governments that seemed stable yesterday are tottering today and will go down tomorrow. Age-old loyalties are gone; and without loyalty lawlessness lifts up its head.

More and more clearly it appears that the solution of the present world problems, the one cure for the world's ills, is the kingdom of God through Christian enlightenment; or, in other words, a proper co-ordinating of religion and education. This alone can produce and maintain a desirable civilization. It is only as the Christian forces of today succeed in educating the manhood and womanhood of tomorrow in the principles of the Gospel of Jesus Christ that a permanent civilization will be assured.

Every child born into the world comes with latent possibilities, with capacities for many things either good or bad, and Christian education is the thing which determines what they shall be. If we want clean, strong men and virtuous women, if we want a world of peace and order, if we want bonds of happiness and brotherhood, we must put the right truths and ideals into our educational policies in the home and church and school.

But, unfortunately, right here is the crux of the whole situation. The great question which faces us is: How shall this be done? Multitudes of homes are delinquent in this respect, most churches are neglectful, and the public schools and universities do nothing to help the matter. There is but one agency left, and that is the denominational school. The Christian college stands before us as the one glorious hope in our day. We must have religion and we must have education, and the Christian college will give us both together.

While we frequently hear it said that "man is incurably religious," many are persuaded that in multitudes of cases the "cure" is almost complete and religion is gone. Man is not as "incurably religious" as he is often represented to be. The fact in the matter is, religion depends upon education. Religion is not a finished product inherited from nowhere, but a growing thing developed in the life that now is. Whether an infant will grow up in the Protestant faith, or the Catholic faith, or the Mohammedan faith, or in the Hottentot faith, will depend altogether upon its education and training. Christianity is not a thing of inheritance so much as of education. No argument is necessary to prove that our moral and religious beliefs and customs and ideals come to us through the social order that transmits through a process of education its inheritance to the younger generation.

Furthermore, not only does the whole fabric of religion depend upon education, but its kind and quality likewise depend upon it. Those who have had the most meager religious instruction and who know the least about the Bible and its revelation of God and the Christ, have the crudest religious ideas and ideals. While the greater one's knowledge of the Bible is and the truer one's conceptions of God

are, the deeper and purer and nobler will the religious life be.

But, not only should religion and education be properly co-ordinated in our individual lives. The importance of this is the greater when we think of the church. As a denomination we have distinctive doctrines. We believe they are altogether Scriptural; we think the world needs them; and we feel they must be propagated because they are good and true and essential. The question naturally arises: How can we best preserve and propagate these doctrines and ideals? The logical answer is: There is only one way, and that is by education. Our children will not get the doctrines of our church merely by heredity; nor will they find them out in business or politics or in other schools. If the Brethren church wants to maintain her doctrines, and desires her sons and daughters to know them and love them and practice and promote them, there is only one way to secure the desired results and that is through a process of education.

Any one who thinks at all knows that the people who are young today will make up the church tomorrow. It naturally follows that if the church tomorrow is to have growth and power and influence, the youth of today must get vision and consecration and preparation and loyalty now. And the possession of these elements depends upon proper education. This should begin in the home and continue in the church and Sunday school and Christian Endeavor; but, let it not be forgotten, that the Christian college is pre-eminently fitted to train the body, mind and soul in orderly development and to inculcate and nurture the great spiritual truths which make for Christian manhood and womanhood.

Of course, I am not referring primarily to the ministry. If there is going to be a future Brethren church there must be more than ministers who have consecration and devotion and loyalty. Young men and women who become educated for business, for the professions, for the farm and the home, need to be made loyal to the church and her cause through the moulding influence of our own Christian college. We cannot send young people from Brethren homes to educational institutions which are strangers with strange doctrines, and then expect them to come back with increased loyalty and devotion to the church we love. In the training and development of the laity, as well as of the ministry, religion and doctrine must be properly co-ordinated with education.

Furthermore, the importance of Christian education is seen when we remember how the welfare of the future depends upon Christian leadership. The outstanding need in the church today and the outstanding need in the world is one and the same, i. e., leadership. In the present and in the future, as in the past, God must have leaders to guide the masses in the way of life and truth and righteousness. We still need prophets and preachers and statesmen and teachers and evangelists and missionaries; and all these to do their most efficient work must be trained and fitted and prepared through the process of education. A larger Brethren church waits upon a larger and better trained leadership, which must of necessity come through the Christian college. And it is of no particular advantage to a church to have Christian leadership and not use it. Men and women of unspotted Christian character who are trained and qualified for leadership should be used in the most effective ways. That denomination is circumscribing its own possibilities and putting rocks in the pathway of its own progress which fails to give large place in its councils to those who are capable of wise leadership.

The task assigned to the followers of Christ was a stupendous one, "Go ye into all the world." "Preach the Gospel to every creature." "Teach all nations." This Great Commission did not include the humble and the illiterate world had known, even unto the uttermost parts of the earth. It is a mistake to think that the multitudes of the world yet untouched for Christ are all ignorant and easy to

(Continued on page 10)

THE BRETHREN PULPIT

"Securing the Needed Laborers."   By A. B. Cover

In the program of Jesus, this was considered a stupendous task. Jesus said, "Pray ye the Lord of the harvest to send forth laborers into his harvest" (Matt. 9:37, 38). Jesus himself made it a matter of intercession. Until the church feels this burden of responsibility, fields will be lost to the Lord of harvest. I fear that we are too engrossed with the fading things of life too deeply to even consider the importance of the above injunction, and our beloved church is losing, daily, fields ripe unto the harvest.

A closer study of the Word, reveals to us that the word send has a stronger meaning than our English implies; the word in the original means "to cast out, to drive out"—"thrusting forth laborers." If this matter of securing the needed laborers were made a matter of intercession, then undoubtedly the church would be aroused to do the "thrusting." God help us to place this matter where Jesus placed it.

World conditions today demand efficient laborers. I am a reader of the "Independent" and I have perused it with much satisfaction and at the same time concern, because the standard of the work is constantly advancing; hence laborers of efficiency are demanded. In the Biblical phrase, "the harvest is indeed plenteous," ripe. Harvest is reaping from previous sowing. The Gospel of grace has been sown long and widely by the prophets of the Old Testament. They stood upon the mountain heights of inspired vision, beckoning their generation to more righteous living and pointing to the coming of the world's Savior. Then followed John, the Baptist, a man sent of God, to prepare the way for the coming of the Son of Man; he cried "Repent ye, for the kingdom of heaven is at hand." Then came the long-looked-for Messiah, inaugurating a new dispensation built and founded upon the Old, but placed in "new wineskins." The burden of his message was "repent ye, for the kingdom of heaven is at hand." He vitalized the decadent religion and made it a dynamic that shook the powers of the world. He went forth as the Savior, as "the sower to sow." His will directed that his disciples, and every follower since then, should carry this same Gospel unto the ends of the earth. We need willing laborers to carry forth the provisions of the Master's will.

We may, with some profit, compare world conditions then when our Savior lived and world conditions today. There was then a universal world power. Rome's flag was recognized as the swaying symbol in the then Roman world; her state language was the rich Greek in which was written the New Testament Scriptures; and there were laborers who were endued with the Holy Spirit to carry this Gospel even unto the very household of Caesar. Today we must recognize a world power, authoritative. It seems to me significant that our own glorious United States, "the melting pot of the world," is playing so large a part in world statesmanship. We have a rich, flexible language, in which were drafted the principles of world-peace; a language already translated into many dialects to make known Jesus. Our educational institutions are already the tutors of the cream of the Orient, and soon may be of the Near East; and lastly a world democracy is conducive to the reaping of the world's spiritual harvest.

Today then, conditions seem "ripe" and to the church has come to her supreme opportunity. We are living in a new world, politically, economically, socially and religiously; old systems, old institutions and nations have been weighed in the balances and passed into oblivion. The new world is plastic, "ripe" unto harvest. What is the crying need of Mexico, India, China, Japan? You will agree with me, it is nothing less than the Gospel of Jesus Christ.

We may ask, what about the Near East? What does a decadent regime need most? Diplomats say, Republican form of Government; steel magnates, greater instruments of destruction, but the church must say with no uncertain voice, the religion of Jesus Christ.

And for this work, I think the opportunity will open. Recently we were told of the number of American boys who had returned with English and French wives. This means that we will come into contact with Europe in social relationships. These new families will visit back and forth with a widening acquaintance and relationship. Will the religious forces of America grasp this opportunity to instill into the lives of this people and engraft upon the shores of Europe the ideal life of the Master? Thus the opportunity has presented itself to reap for the kingdom of Jesus. Can we secure the needed laborers? How can we secure them?

The first fundamental, in my way of thinking, is vision. Pray the Lord of the harvest to give young men and women a vision of the world's need. I have already stated that we are living in a day of unprecedented opportunity for service for the Master. The alert will ask seriously, "how shall I invest my life?" Life is a trust loaned us by the Lord of life; what shall we do with it? The vision of Isaiah is essential first of all. In his book, we are told, "In the year that King Uzziah died, I saw the Lord high and lifted up." We notice in connection with the vision of the Lord high and lifted up, a temporal affair is associated,—"in the year that King Uzziah died." That king was not a contributing factor to the highest development of Israel's religious life and his death brought about a political condition that was conducive to such development; just as world political conditions may be utilized for the Kingdom's advancement. So today we need a leadership with a vision of the "Lord high and lifted up." A leadership not given to spending itself in little quibblings, but alive to the larger opportunities; a leadership that will give the world a dynamic unrealized since the days of Pentecostal glory.

Secondly, we need laborers who will say with Isaiah, "Woe is me for I am undone, I am a man of unclean lips." The great task and the stupendous responsibility should send us humbly consecrated, dependent to authority that is divine. A band of workers removed from professionalism, clean, pure, high-minded, consecrated to the service of Jesus Christ. Laborers who are qualified for the tasks that present world conditions demand.

Let us, for a moment, look into the field, "ripe unto the harvest," from our own denominational view-point. I thank God for the lives that have been laid, willingly, sacrificingly upon the church's altar; those who labor in South America, Africa, Kentucky, and all others. But to expand these fields, we must have still others, and others. Jesus made the field the world; true Brethrenism dares make it no less; this means both home and foreign. We have observed with keen delight the slow, but steady growth of our church since affiliated with her; but where are the laborers to "thrust forth" into greater endeavors of demanding fields?

How shall we secure the needed laborers is the still unanswered issue. We have endeavored to point out some of the qualifications of the needed laborers, but that we may secure and equip these laborers, the church must play a very conspicuous part.

The laborers need vision and consecration, but what they need more, they must be trained. Among the qualifications that Paul names, in writing to Timothy, is "apt to teach." The great function of the church is teaching, and if the church would have teachers she must train them. The church must establish and maintain an institution of learning adequate to the present day and coming day's demands. I am gratified for the splendid work that has been done and is being done for Ashland College in the way of permanent endowment. We may rejoice with a sense of just pride for such men as Beachler, Jacobs, Miller, Furry, Gillin and all others who have made possible our present Ashland College, and will make possible a greater Ashland College, by the consecration of intellect, life or substance. The task is not completed; we must have still better equipment as a growing church demands a more efficient corps of laborers.

Again, the church can help secure the needed laborers by taking a bit of thought on the pecuniary side. We, as most all denominations, are conscious of a dearth of needed laborers; we are not ignorant of the plea for laborers coming through the Evangelist and otherwise. But dear Brethren and sisters, do we assume any of the responsibility for such a state of affairs? There is a dearth of ministers in a measure because the salary paid is so pitiably small that many of gifted talent seeks other fields of labor where there is promise of at least keeping body and soul together. I believe it to be entirely beneath the dignity of any laborer in the Lord's vineyard to be considered an object of charity. Paul writes that "the laborer is worthy of his hire."

I make no apology whatever for the above statement and I believe that if the church generally would submit to a baptism of pocket books for religious purposes one cause for a dearth of laborers would be removed. The minister with a family of children to educate finds himself in a deplorable plight. He must choose between marring the educational advantages of his children, and thus their lives in the world, or quit the ministry and find other more lucrative employment that he may educate his children.

But, beloved, I would not be misunderstood; I do not put this uppermost; I am only making what I believe to be a just plea that our laborers shall be regarded as "worthy of their hire;" that they may be able to live.

To secure the needed laborers we would appeal to a higher and nobler sentiment, viz., the vision of the ideal life of service.

Let me again state that the demands of the day are for more adequate laborers. In this tremendous task come discouragements and burdens at times almost too grievous to be borne; the financial side offers no panacea for this. But as we turn to God's Word and seek the promise of reward, the answer echoes back, **IDEAL MAN.** In Genesis 1:26 God says, "Let us make man in our image and after our likeness; and let him have dominion, etc." Man created in the image and after the likeness of God, is to rule over God's creation. What a high and holy place God has given a man! We ask, what has man done with this God-given trust? You know. Man sinned. In the wake of sin, as history records, are rioting, bloodshed, wars and worldliness.

I look to the future where the wave of time must yet pass, and I ask, "What of man and his God-given trust? The book of Hebrews answers: "What is man, that thou art mindful of him, or the son of man that thou visitest him? Thou madest him a little lower than the angels; Thou crownedst him with glory and honor, and didst set him over the works of thy hands; thou didst put all things in subjection under his feet * * * * But now we see not yet all things subjected to him. But we behold him who hath been made a little lower than the angels, even Jesus." Jesus is the ideal man, the Savior who died, who arose triumphantly, who reigns supremely at the right hand of God. I behold him amid the universe; the winds and the waves obeyed his "peace, be still," the water was turned into wine instantly at his touch; and the fevered patient arose at his touch; and the grave gave up its dead at his bidding. In him we see ideal man, the laborer rewarded. Let the church pray with the Master, "send forth laborers into the harvest." Amen.

OUR DEVOTIONAL

All Things Through Christ Who Strengtheneth Me

By Miss Alice Livengood

OUR SCRIPTURE

I can do all things through Christ which strengtheneth me (Phil. 4.13). And he said unto me, My grace is sufficient for thee: for my strength is made perfect in weakness. Most gladly therefore will I rather glory in my infirmities, that the power of Christ may rest upon me (2 Cor. 12:9). There hath no temptation taken you but such as is common to man: but God is faithful who will not suffer you to be tempted above that ye are able; but will with the temptation also make a way to escape, that ye may be able to bear it (1 Cor. 10:13). God is our refuge and strength, a very present help in trouble (Psalm 46:1).

OUR MEDIATION

So long as time is, so long will there be tasks hard to do, duties unpleasant to perform and temptations to overcome, and just so long will there need to be a source of strength from which to draw to do these things. Jesus the Christ is that source.

Paul tells us this in the first verse of our scripture and he knew because he had tested and found it not wanting. But for every test in his life and he had tests a plenty in afflictions and all kinds of persecutions—he went to the Fountain-head and drew the strength to meet and conquer the enemy. The Lord knoweth how to deliver the godly out of temptation (2nd Peter 2:9).

If Paul, the valiant soldier of the cross, found it needful to rely on Christ, the more do we need to rely on that same strength. The world today has so many pitfalls and also needs so much help that daily must that strength from above be sought. So very often we are asked to do something or say a word and we feel utterly unable to do them but if they are things that are for the upbuilding of the kingdom and for the glory of the Christ he will give us power if we ask him. Then too, we need to ask for strength to keep from doing a wrong deed or saying a harmful word. It requires strength for that too.

Again suffering, almost unbearable, and sore disappointments come to us but someone has truthfully said, "Under the shadow of earthly disappointment, all unconscious to ourselves, our Divine Redeemer is walking by our side." Jesus said to Paul, "my grace is sufficient for thee." Of course it is for did not he, while on earth, suffer all that we suffer and so is able to intercede for us and pity us? "God had one Son on earth without sin, but never one without suffering." Blessed is the man whose strength is in thee (Ps. 84:5).

Such a comfort it is to know that we are not tempted above that we are able to bear and that with the temptation a way is made to escape. But we must not walk open eyed into it and say, "Lord help me out;" neither must we rail against God when loved ones are taken. He expects us to take heed where we go and what we do and say.

"To attempt to resist temptation, to abandon our bad habits, and to control our dominant passions in our own unaided strength, is like attempting to check by a spider's thread the progress of a ship borne along before wind and tide." Another has said, "To be like Christ in this world, we must, more or less, be the subjects of temptations. But he instantly and successfully resisted temptation, so that though tempted, he was "without sin." We also to carry out the Christian character, must resist to complete victory, all the temptations with which we may be assailed.

Our missionaries, especially the foreign ones, surely do their work "through Christ which strengtheneth" them else.

how could they endure separation from home ties and the privations they meet in their work. Not only that but often persecutions and illness come pouring upon them. Through it all they live in that abiding faith that is the "cure all" for all troubles.

The story of Mary Slessor's life and work in Africa is thrilling. Granted that hers was an unusual work, but never for a moment do we doubt but it was all accomplished through Christ's strength in her. A frail woman could never possibly do it otherwise. And no glory for herself did she claim. "All for Christ" seemed her motto, for certainly such was her life.

I am sure when any Christian fails it is because he is living by self and not by the strength of Christ. It is well to remember Paul's advice, "wherefore let him that thinketh he standeth take heed lest he fall" (1 Cor. 10:12). Tryon Edwards warns us thus: "Do all you can to stand, and then

fear lest you may fall, and by the grace of God you are safe." So after all it is only close acquaintance with and leaning on the strength of Christ that we are enabled to do the things that are pleasing and resisting the things that are not pleasing in his sight.

OUR PRAYER

Loving Father, we are glad that thou hast provided a source of strength by which we can do all things that are for the glory of thy name, whether in suffering or rejoicing or in definite work for thee. Thou knowest our needs better than we can tell them, so we ask thee to give us and do for us as thou seest best. Lord, help us to always trust thee and lean on thee and when our work here is done receive us in heaven with all the redeemed. These favors are asked in the Saviour's name. Amen.

Milledgeville, Illinois.

Send
WHITE GIFT
OFFERINGS to

THE SUNDAY SCHOOL

ALBERT TRENT
General Secretary-Treasurer
Johnstown, Pennsylvania

Making Our Contest Ideals Permanent.   By Guilford Leslie

(Explanatory Note: For eight weeks during the late summer the Ashland Brethren Sunday school was engaged in a lively contest over the attainment of certain points agreed upon. Each class was pitted against every other class, and the class winning the largest proportionate number of points won the contest, at the end of which a recognition service was held in honor of the winning class and also of the good all had gained. The ideals set before the classes during the contest were, faithful attendance, promptness, daily Bible reading, studied lessons and new scholars.—At this recognition service the accompanying address by Brother Leslie was given.—Editor).

Early in the history of man we have records of contests. The eternal contest between good and evil is ever present. Elijah "pulled off" the notable contest between the only true God and the gods of the heathen. Paul compared the Christian life to a race. Ideals of supremacy in one line or another are the goals of many lives. Habits, good or bad become a permanent part of our character, and are determined by the things we strive for. Habits of negligence or indifference, following the line of least resistance surely lead to a weakened and vacillating character. Punctual and regular attendance to any known duty tends to fortitude and strength of character. To be punctual; to be on time; to begin on time requires determination. A determined soul will do more with a rusty monkey-wrench than a loafer will accomplish with a machine shop. Lots of fellows have the right aim in life but are short of ammunition.

A determined mind is the ammunition necessary to carry the goal. If a man says I will, something may be done. If a woman says I will, something has GOT TO BE DONE. It is the determination there that counts. Men need more of it. How we all long and love to attain, and rightly too. But the pursuit, the strong striving and the straining against odds is what gives permanent strength and courage and enables us finally to overcome and reach our goal.

It is right that we have set the aims before us, and we should keep them before us and seek with determination to reach them. Let us ever aim high. Some one has said, "It won't be any harder on your gun to knock the tail feathers from an eagle than to splinter a barn door."

A contest in right living is a method of adopting the injunction of Paul, "Provoke one another unto good works." Covet fitness rather than place, always mindful that God cares more for quality than position.

Some of our classes have attained a high standard of efficiency, much to their credit. We honor them; honor is due them. It is hoped the contest will continue and all will determine to reach a higher scale, that habits of faithful attendance and punctuality, daily devotions and Bible study may become the perpetual achievement of every member of our Sunday school.

Ashland, Ohio.

Coordinating Religion and Education

(Continued from page 7)

handle. Some of the keenest intellects have not yet been enlisted under the blood-stained banner of Jesus Christ. In his missionary journeys Paul met some of the most learned men of his day; and it was his education and intellectual training pitted against theirs that saved the day for him and for the cause which he championed. And no less today, in going where the Great Commission sends us, in order to successfully meet the opposition that is sure to be encountered we need all of education's contribution to the religious life. In these days of materialism, skepticism and sin, we need facts and figures and wisdom and intellectual skill, as well as the Spirit's power, to meet the opposition and confound destructive criticism and all the satanic brood of erroneous teachings and "isms' and "ologies."

This then is no time to neglect or minimize the part education must play in the full-orbed religious life. There is no other way to build up and maintain a Christian civilization save by education; and the higher that civilization is to be,

the more education is needed, just as the higher the standards of the church the greater must be the efforts to maintain those standards.

Concluding then, let us remember that in the Christian college we have that which combines and creates and makes possible the two things absolutely essential to this old world's greatest good, namely, Christian character educated and Christian leadership. This being true, it would be suicidal for any church to let her denominational college fail or be unnecessarily handicapped. If the doors of religious schools were closed in one generation, it is altogether probable that doors of churches would be closed in the next. We want neither religion without education nor education without religion, but the two combined and co-ordinated in one Christlike life. And the Christian college that steadfastly works toward that end is an institution in our life and activity which merits and should have the united and wholehearted support in the entire church for which it exists,—a support finding expression in the giving of students, money, prayer, sacrifice.

Milledgeville, Illinois.

J. A. Garber
PRESIDENT

Our Young People at Work

G. C. Carpenter
SECRETARY

Tom's Talks. From the Christian Endeavor World

With Christian Endeavorers of All Kinds. — On Christian Endeavor Topics of All Sorts
Just When and as the Notion Takes Him

A Methods Man

If I were president of a Christian Endeavor union—which I am not, nor likely to be—I should pick out the best-informed and brightest Endeavorer of the bunch (best-informed Christian Endeavorly, I mean) and get the executive committee to appoint him the Method man of the union. It would be his business to advise every officer or committee chairman in the union how best to carry on his work. To that end he would hold workers' conferences all over the union and in the separate societies, and he would talk and write incessantly. I, Tom, am a sort of Methods Man at large—at least, I am at large at present.

By the way, one of the duties of the union Methods Man would be to get every society to appoint a little Methods Man of its own.

An Inquisitive Keystoner

An Endeavorer in the Keystone State rises to ask Tom a few questions. They are good questions, and Tom is glad to answer them. As follows:

First, this inquisitive Keystoner asks how a before-the-Christian-Endeavor prayer meeting is conducted. The pre-prayer meeting, some call it.

Well, all the members of the prayer meeting committee are present, with the leader of the meeting; sometimes others. It should be understood that any member of the society may come that wishes. The president, for instance, will often drop in, and the pastor.

The meeting will be held in some little room just before the regular prayer meeting. It will be held for five minutes, no longer. All will kneel, and the entire company, one after the other, in the order in which they sit, will pray for the meeting that is to come, for the leader, for all that take part, for the society and the pastor and he church. Very short prayers, seldom more than a sentence each. That is all there is about it,—and that is a lot.

Should the prayer meeting committee conduct this meeting? asks my Pennsylvania friend. Yes.

What are the chief duties of the prayer meeting committee? she goes on to ask. Get leaders for the prayer meetings. Help the leaders plan the meetings. Prod the music committee to get up interesting music. Prod the social committee to make everybody feel at home. Prod the flower committee to have pretty and appropriate decorations. Prod the missionary and citizenship committees to take care of their meetings. Get the pastor to occupy the closing five minutes. Introduce fresh prayer meeting plans (find them in every week's prayer meeting page of this paper). Get the members of the society to take part better and ever better in the meetings. And by the time you have done these things, you will see a heap of other things to do.

Finally, Miss Keystoner inquires which I consider the more important, the work of the prayer meeting committee or that of the lookout committee. The work of the first—when I am on it. The work of the second, when I am on it.

Ask me some more, Pennsylvania.

The Devil and the Cross

An outline of a very interesting meeting held by the First Friends Christian Endeavor society of San Diego, California, has been sent me by Julien A. Welles. The meetings of this society are held in the church auditorium, and a cord was strung along the ends of the back pews, thus forcing the society up front, while the very first pew was reserved for the late comers. Good scheme. Among the novel fea-

tures of this particular programme was a whistling duet by two young men. Questions typewritten on separate slips of paper were placed in a convenient place, with the placard, "Take one." A large board was set in the front of the room bearing a graphic representation of the devil, vividly painted in red and black. Above the picture, in blue were the words, "Our wrestling is against the spiritual hosts of wickedness in heavenly places—Eph. 6:12." At the left, in purple, were the words, "Resist the devil and he will flee from you.—Jas. 4:7." A sheet of paper was prepared, bearing a large red cross and the following words in green, "For the word of the cross . . . unto us who are saved . . . is the power of God.—1 Cor. 1:18." This sheet was placed behind the board, upside down, facing backward, and was fastened to strings running around the board at each side, so that it might be pulled up in front of the board an inch at a time, seeming to rise from the bottom of the board and cover the picture of the devil with the picture of the cross. As each person gave his testimony the leader pulled the paper bearing the cross a little higher; after each prayer also it was lifted one space. After the cross had climbed about half-way up the board the leader added interest by swinging into place from behind the board another head for the devil exactly covering the first one, with an expression changed from one of wicked glee to one of angry disappointment. The cross came fully into place with the last testimony, and then it was found that the crown on the devil's head had a slit cut through the paper at its lower edge into which the top of the cross entered, so that the devil was completely covered up and the crown was on the cross. This plan brought about an almost one-hundred-per-cent participation, people praying and giving testimony that had never done so before in public; and all were resolved to make the victory over the devil continuous in their lives.

An All-Around Lookout

What would you think, brother lookout chairman, if a sailor, sent up to the lookout, should confine his attention to only one point of the horizon. You should want to tell him to come off the perch, wouldn't you?

Well, what do you think of a lookout committee that confines its attention to only one point in the Christian Endeavor horizon, say the point of new members, or the point of attendance? The lookout committee is to look out for the betterment of the society in all points. Wherever the society is weak, the lookout committee is to strengthen it. Is it disorderly in the meetings? Look out! Is it forming disagreeable and harmful cliques? Look out! Is it unsocial to strangers? Look out! Is it neglectful of the prayer life? Look out! Is it disloyal to the church and pastor? Look out! Sweep around the entire horizon. A submarine may pop up from any direction.

"Record of Christian Work" says that when a Kavirondo convert in Africa confesses Christ he promises six things: "To learn of Christ and serve him, to pray every day in public and private, to give up all that is contrary to God's Word, to agree to monogamy, to contribute to Christian expenses, and to teach relatives."

The Fourth Presbyterian church of Chicago carries an unusual note on the church calendar. After doxology, creed, invocation and hymn comes "organ interlude," together with the page and reference of "Scripture suggested for silent reading." It is thought that this silent reading is more effective than the later reading from the desk.

SEND ALL MONEY FOR
General Home, Kentucky and
Foreign Missions to

MISSIONS

WILLIAM A. GEARHART
General Missionary Secretary
906 Conover Bldg., Dayton, O.

A Letter to the Foreign Board

Provincia de Cordoba
Cabrera, F. C. C. A., Argentina,
July 23, 1920.

To the Members of the Board of the Brethren Foreign Missionary Society, Dr. J. Allen Miller, President, Ashland, Ohio.

It is a pleasure to render a report for the past year covering the progress made at Cabrera and at Deheza, two of our mission points in the Argentine Republic.

In the first place, I wish to express my gratitude to the entire brotherhood, whose money and prayers have made the work possible. I also acknowledge that God has dealt graciously with us in providing our physical and spiritual needs, in keeping us from serious sickness, and in giving us a spirit of cheerfulness to lighten the tasks incident to our work as missionaries.

At Cabrera, the new property if of much advantage. It is winning for us the confidence of the people, that we mean to establish a permanent and helpful work in their midst, for the sake of making known the Gospel of Jesus Christ. Since establishing ourselves in our new home, the attendance has increased, especially so at the Sunday evening service. During the year, five people have made public confession of faith in Christ through baptism. We now number thirteen, but two have moved to other points. Two communion services were celebrated, and it was a blessed privilege to see that all our ordinances as a church were willingly obeyed by nearly all who participated, although some were affiliated with other denominations.

The mission property is now in rather good shape, and presents a neat appearance before the public. The building has been painted (white-washed) inside and outside, the yard thoroughly cleaned, and numerous rose bushes planted. A playground has been leveled for the children (which would also serve as a tennis court), and a corral made for the horse that my brother-in-law is lending us. The small shade trees that grew in the yard now line the walk at the side and at the front of the lot. I find that there would be ample room on the premises for twenty-four fruit trees and a grapevine arbor. The planting will be done as soon as I have a few extra dollars.

The enclosed photograph was taken of our "culto" on July 4th. Five or six of the group are from Deheza. We are not always so numerous, yet all present sympathize with us, and attend services at one time or another. I had planned on sending you other pictures, but the photographer failed us, as is evidenced by the one that I am enclosing. I wish that you would send me the booklet of instructions that usually accompanies the Auto-Graflex camera. There are many views obtainable at Cabrera and also at Deheza which would present the need of the Gospel before the church in a very appealing manner. I have a camera, and am now taking a few pictures, but these pictures would be too small,

I am thinking, for use in making lantern slides.

Regarding our needs at Cabrera, I must say that a day school is badly needed. The children of our Sunday school attend either the public or private schools, and they are catechized against Protestantism, and are also frequently driven to the Catholic church, to practice for picnic programs, etc. At our last Field Council meeting, it was recommended "That a school be organized at Cabrera, the instruction to include Bible study," but I do not know where there is a capable teacher for the work whose influence would tell for Christ.

The mission at Deheza promises a rich harvest, but there were difficulties encountered in the seed sowing. Two Plymouth Brethren taught against feet-washing as a Christian rite. This caused a little hesitancy on the part of a few of our congregation, but the people have now read St. John, chapter thirteen, and the sentiment is now in our favor. The Plymouth Brethren have permanently withdrawn from the field. Some time ago, I wrote Brother L. S. Bauman on this matter, and I am enclosing you a copy of my letter. While no one has been baptized, yet the people are thinking Godward. One lady, on hearing the teachings of Christ, persuaded her husband to abandon his work as saloon keeper. To enjoy the privileges of Christian fellowship, she has gone to Rosario to live near her father, who was converted several years ago. The property in Deheza is for sale, and as no suitable offer has been received, the husband shifts the blame on the presence of the Bible in his home, which our "almost persuaded" is reading. Then, there is a man, regular in attendance, who has an interest in a wine shop. His business is becoming an abomination in his eyes, and he is wondering how he could make a living in an honorable way. Recently he bought a New Testament that is sold by a Catholic Publishing Society, and is carefully comparing it with our New Testament. He tells his friends that the greatest difference between the two Testaments is that the footnotes of the Catholic Testament are exceedingly numerous, and man-made. Our Sunday school numbers about twenty-five. The children can sing remarkably well. One of my brothers-in-law has been teaching them. Two preaching services are held each month. Our sulky gives us an opportunity to visit during the week. For the hall, we are paying only $12.00 a month, not $35.00, as indicated in our budget. I now have on hand enough money for another year (in case the bank finally honors the check received some time ago).

At our last Council Meeting, no budget was made. However, as Brother Yoder has written me that I could make you an estimate, I might say that, at Cabrera, $72.00 will be needed for lighting, and $50.00 for Sunday school literature, to be used at both points. I am wondering just what could be done

with the balopticons sent us. As yet one has not been put into use at Cabrera. My understanding is that there are no slides available.

I trust that you have read these brief notes, feeling that we are all one in the Master's service. On to victory!

'Finally, brethren, pray for us, that the Word of the Lord may have free course, and be glorified, even as it is with you.''

Yours in the blessed hope of his second coming,

EDWARD G. ATKINSON.

(Note.—Through the kind permission of the Foreign Board, we are privileged to publish for the benefit of our large family of readers this splendid letter of Brother Atkinson.—Editor).

TESTIMONIES TO THE SCRIPTURES

The first and almost the only book deserving of universal attention is the Bible. The Bible is the book of all others to be read at all ages and in all conditions of human life; not to be read once or twice through and then laid aside, but to be read in small portions of one or two chapters every day, and never to be intermitted except by some overruling necessity. I speak as a man of the world to men of the world, and I say to you, "Search the Scriptures." I have for many years made it a practice to read through the Bible once a year. It is an invaluable and inexhaustible mine of knowledge and virtue.—John Quincy Adams.

It is astonishing how much a man may know of the Bible by learning a text a day and how much he may know experimentally by watching the events of the day and interpreting them in the light of the text. If you cannot retain by memory a whole passage, never mind that; take a short text and be looking out for a commentary upon it. I do not mean Matthew Henry, or Scott, or Gill —I mean your own daily experience. Be looking out to see how the Lord translates that text to you by his own providence, and you will frequently see a striking relation between the verse that was given in the morning and the trials of the mercies that are given you during the day.—C. H. Spurgeon.

From the time that, at my mother's feet or on my father's knee, I first learned to lisp verses from the sacred writings, they have been my daily study and vigilant contemplation. If there be anything in my style or thoughts to be commended, the credit is due to my kind parents in installing into my mind an early love of the Scriptures.—Daniel Webster.

Ten thousand different kind of animals eat ten thousand different kinds of food. But they all drink water. That is nature's way. It is a source of much pleasure to note that man is coming back to nature and is taking to drinking water.

NEWS FROM THE FIELD

FIRST BRETHREN CHURCH

Los Angeles, California

During the absence of our pastor at the National Conference, the preaching has been done by one of our own number, Brother Harry Toler, which was very acceptable. The attendance and interest was kept up in a fine way; and the Sunday school attendance increased from Sunday to Sunday.

At the close of the morning service, August 28th, two of our Intermediate boys from the Sunday school who had decided for Christ stepped forward when the invitation was given thus signifying publicly their intended allegiance to the Master. Last Sunday, September 5th, one of these boys received the ordinance of baptism and will be a member of the church. Another boy from the Sunday school also came forward at the invitation which is always given at the close of every service.

Next Sunday we expect our pastor, Brother Jennings and also his good wife with us again. And it will be a real pleasure to see them both in their accustomed places zealously engaged in the work of the kingdom.

A. P. REED.

4910 Wadsworth Street.

UDELL, IOWA

Some time has elapsed since the readers of the Evangelist have been given any news concerning the work at Udell. These people have been without a pastor for some time yet they have kept up a good Sunday school.

We spent our summer vacation with these good people and it was one we will not soon forget. At each service we were greeted by a large audience. The last Sunday we were permitted to spend with them we united with three other churches of the community and enjoyed an old-fashioned basket meeeting! I feel that it was a day well spent. It helped the churches to see that they would be more efficient in bettering the conditions of the community if they would put forth a more united effort. In the evening we went to the church for another union meeting. As we left the building that night we could not help but feel that, not only the Brethren people, but the people of the entire community, appreciated the effort we had been making for the advancement of the Kingdom among them, and our bank account had grown far beyond our expectations. Altogether we received a purse of about three hundred dollars.

As we returned to Ashland we were permitted to bring with us another young man who is preparing for the ministry. This gives the Udell church a credit of three preachers at home and one in the foreign fields, which we feel is something worth being proud of. This church is seeking a pastor. We are sure that the man who takes up the work with this church will find them a splendid people to work with and he will also find that the opportunity is great for the advancement of the Lord's work in this community. We pray that God's work may continue to "Go forward" in this field and that he may send them a good leader.

AUSTIN R. STALEY.

A REAL VACATION

After two years of close application to the work here, my church very kindly gave us a much needed vacation. And this church knows how to do that. It was not a week's "lay off," but a real vacation of six weeks. Long enough that a man could shake off routine of the pastoral work. This is only a small part of the game too. My church set themselves to the task of keeping the wheels running while we were gone. Some of the oldest members in this church say that the summer attendance was the best in the history of the church. (I think I will go away again; especially if Brother Lynn stays and sings and preaches to hold the crowds). Our deacons and laymen as well as the auxiliary organizations deserve credit for invaluable help. Happy may be the pastor who has a band of members who have the best interests of the church at heart.

We went to California and while there we visited every church in the state except Fillmore and we had our plans laid to go there, but they were foiled. We held a week's Bible Conference at Turlock in the heat of the summer with respectable crowds and remarkable interest. Brother Leatherman has done a good work there, but has been there but a year. We went to Manteca, but Brother Platt's were at Fresno attending the State Christian Endeavor convention and we missed them. At Lathrop the Brethren informed us that they are going to remodel and enlarge and equip their house of worship.

In Southern California we visited Brother Broad at La Verne, and note an addition to their work since we left home. We were privileged to preach at Kimmell's church at Whittier, and twice at Compton Avenue, where we once served regularly. At Long Beach we attended the State Conference and assisted in a small way much to our enjoyment. The Brethren in California are making things go in many ways. At the First Church in Los Angeles, we were at the dedicatory services of the new church building which is a magnificent structure, and one of the most conveniently arranged churches in the brotherhood. Brother Jennings has done a great work there sure as you live. The old debt is wiped out, the new church paid for except a small mortgage, and the membership in harmony and unity as far as we can see and we think we know them pretty well.

We had the very great pleasure while there to conduct the secretary of the Home Mission Board and the General Missionary secretary, over 300 miles of asphalt boulevard through the oranges and flowers, and since that they will hold still and let us tell them anything we want to about California. We found several towns where there ought to be Brethren churches and it may be some day that there could be assembled a lot of Brethren families from all over the brotherhood and establish a new church in a new field where real missionary work might be done. There is lots of room in California.

E. M. COBB,

Dayton, Ohio.

ORISKANY, VIRGINIA

The last ten days of August were a spiritual feast for the small but faithful band at Oriskany. This congregation, never large, has suffered much of late years by members moving to other parts of the country. Our church has held no revival for several years, and the outlook was not promising. Our brother in the flesh, Elder Isaac D. Bowman, did the preaching and good crowds greeted us from the beginning in spite of some rain and an exceedingly busy season. Several prophetic discourses and one distinctly doctrinal were given eager attention by people that were not familiar with this kind of teaching. A fruitful revival had been held a few months ago by the Methodist church in the same village and the easier reaping had been done, nevertheless three were added by baptism, one reclaimed, and one other made the good confession. The meeting was too short for so well worked a field as evidenced by the two confessions on the last night. We thank the Lord for the precious sheaves reaped but feel that probably the greater success was in the seed sowing. We pray that the way may be opened for our brother to return to this field again when not so definitely limited as to time. We feel to ask a special interest in your prayers for this needy field as we are laboring under some severe handicaps as we live more than fifty miles away and cannot minister to this church oftener than once per month in the summer and less frequently in the winter.

J. S. BOWMAN.

FROM LANARK, ILLINOIS

Sister Aboud came to Lanark on Monday evening, August 9th. She was scheduled for the evening service, but because of a train being taken off which arrives here at 12:45 P. M. she came too late for the sermon. Our pastor took her place on Monday evening. The meetings continued until Sunday evening, August 29th. On this Sunday three young men, one boy and a mother and her daughter were baptized. One young man remains to be baptized, and one to unite by relation. So far six have united with the church as a result of the meetings, with at least two more to follow. The first week of the meetings the weather was very warm, the second week the weather was fine, but the Carroll County Old Settlers' Association had their annual meeting day here at Lanark. The last week of the meeting Carrol county had their annual Fair for four days. All these attractions greatly detracted from the attendance. Sister Aboud is not ashamed nor afraid to preach the whole gospel as she understands it.

Upon the whole the meetings were very well attended. On the second Sunday evening the entire seating capacity of the church was filled, with a number of chairs in the aisles.

One peculiar thing about this meeting was the conversion of four young men and one boy. This meeting has given us a hold upon two new families, and in the judgment of your correspondent was a success.

Sister Aboud is a Bible student and is very well acquainted with it and loves it and her Savior, with a tenacity that would cause her to suffer a great deal before she would renounce it. I imagine she would die for him if necessary.   Z. T. LIVENGOOD,
                    Corresponding Secretary.

DR. BAME AT OPENING SERVICE OF NORTH MANCHESTER COLLEGE

A clipping was recently sent to the editorial office from the North Manchester, Indiana, daily paper, containing a write-up of the opening of the school year of the North Manchester College. C. E. Jackson, the writer, says in part:

"Although considerably handicapped by the extensive improvements in progress at the present time, Manchester College opened Wednesday morning for the fall term with an enrollment totaling 357 students, the largest representation in the history of the school. Work on the spacious new building which will join Chapel hall with College hall is being pushed to the limit in order that adequate accommodations may be in readiness for the many more students who are expected at the opening of the winter term."

The editor wishes to remark that the splendid growth of this college is due to the support which the Church of the Brethren people are giving it, both in terms of students and funds. When will the Brethren people awaken to the necessity of giving in large amounts so that new and much needed buildings and equipment may be added to our our church school, Ashland College? Our brethren who once were called "Conservative" can teach us who were called "Progressive" a lesson in progress along this line.

The clipping continues:

"The opening chapel service was held in the gymnasium Wednesday and a special program was arranged for the occasion. Rev. T. E. George, D.D., pastor of the Church of the Brethren of this city conducted the devotional services. The principal address was delivered by Rev. C. A. Bame of the First Brethren church.

"Fears for America".

"In the message of the morning Rev. Bame impressed the fact that it was a belief that America was in a perilous condition and that the Red Flag of the Bolshevik was swiftly sweeping toward this country and that it was high time that something be done. He also pointed out that the young people training in religious schools were the salvation of the country and impressed them with the fact that unless they could give America something better than she already had they had better stick to the fundamentals upon which she was founded."

NOTICE TO PENNSYLVANIA CHURCHES

This is the last call for Statistical Reports from the churches of Pennsylvania. According to a ruling of last Conference only churches furnishing Statistical Reports are entitled to representation in Conference. Send your reports at once to the District Statistician.   M. A. WITTER,
                    Waynesboro, Pa.

MINISTERIAL AND CHURCH EXCHANGE

Brother C. E. Kolb writes that he will be open to engagements for evangelistic work, either as a song leader or as preacher. Address him at Winona Lake, Indiana.

The American Churches and Armenia

The assertion is being made throughout our country that America is indifferent as to what becomes of Armenia. This cannot be true. The statement probably arises in the fact that President Wilson's suggestion that we take a mandate for Armenia was declined by the Senate, and the further fact that the platforms of the two leading political parties look with disfavor upon the President's proposition, because there is no present prospect for the taking of a mandate for Armenia by America. We cannot say, truthfully that America is indifferent as to the fate of Armenia. The reports received at the office of the Near East Relief in New York furnish abundant evidence to the contrary. Last year, for instance, the people of America contributed over $15,000,000 toward the succoring of Armenia through the Near East Relief. That is a generous amount. And this year a similar amount will be forthcoming if the current receipts are a reliable basis of estimate. In addition to this contribution in money there have been large contributions of clothing and of other necessary and acceptable items. And better than either has been the contribution of personal service on the part of a large number of American men and women who have gone to Armenia and are giving themselves in fine devotion to the ministr of humanity.

Armenia — persecuted and plundered— makes a special appeal to the Christian churches of the world. Sir Philip Ginns, the well-known war correspondent, speaks of Armenia as "the bridgehead of Christianity for many centuries." And it has been just that, and it is because Armenia has bravely borne witness to the Christian faith in the midst of hostile surroundings that the Turks are determined to efface that people once and for all. It is obnoxious to the Turk to have a flourishing Christian community in the heart of his country. He will go to any lengths of perfidy and cruelty to root it out. He is not disturbed about the recognition given to the Armenian Republic by Europe and America. A Turkish official is reported to have said: "We do not mind if the western powers proclaim a free Armenia. We will make it a desert without people. It will

be free for us." The Armenian knows what the program of the Turk is, and that gives point to the remark of an Armenian in Aleppo: "It is to America that Armenia cries for help now, before there is a tragedy more terrible than any in the past"; and to this other word that comes from an Armenian woman in Asia Minor: "Unless America acts quickly my people will be slaughtered in greater numbers for their danger is greater now than ever before."

The governing bodies of many American churches have expressed their sympathy for Armenia, and have urged their people to do their utmost for the immediate relief of these stricken people. One result of these endorsements and exhortations is the constant flow of the golden stream into the treasury of the Near East Relief. And because of this the organization has been able to continue and to expand its gracious ministry, to Armenia. It is of interest to review some statistical items based upon the report of Col. Haskell, United States Commissioner to the Near East, covering the month of March, 1920; during the month 20,779 children were housed, clothed, fed, given medical treatment and taught in 81 orphanages under the administration of the Near East Relief, and 43 hospitals and 58 clinics and ambulatories cared for a daily average of 5,589 cases and 3,037 clinical cases. In addition to that good work the 60 soup kitchens scattered throughout Armenia fed 55,039 little children; and 561,970 homeless refugees were saved from starvation.

That is a fine piece of humanitarian service, and America has a right to glory in it, for if America had not done it the present existence of thousands of Armenians—men, women and children—would be doubtful. But the feeding of starving people, worth as it is, does not meet all the requirements of the case. A starving person needs food day after day and the process needs to be carried on. It is better to establish Armenia upon a basis that will ensure independence and self-support within a reasonable period. To do this requires the moral support of a strong and worth nation—such as America is. If we cannot take over a mandate for Armenia politically, we can at least buttress that bruised and battered nation and demand that it have a fair and square chance for self-existence. A liberty-loving people, such as we are, ought not to stand by and see, without protest or offer of assistance, another group of people of like passion and purpose slowly, crushed to death by its cruel and inveterate enemy.

What can the Christian people of America do? The can continue to express sympathy for Armenia and keep on contributing their money through the Near East Relief. That is certainly something. But it is not enough. The situation in Armenia is critical. There is no other nation but America that can meet the demands of the hour. And there is no other force in America than the churches that can stir up the nation to do its full duty toward its sister republic in Asia Minor in this hour of its peril when it is marked for slaughter by its ancient and implacable foe.

THE POWER OF QUIETNESS

A score of years ago a friend placed in my hand a little book which became one of the turning points of my life. It was an old mediaeval message, and it had but one thought, that God was waiting in the depth of my being to talk with me if I would only get still enough to hear him.

I thought that this would be a very easy matter, so I began to get still. But I had no sooner commenced than a perfect pandemonium of voices reached my ears, a thousand clamoring notes from without and within, until I could hear nothing but their noise and din. Some of them were my own cares, some of them my own prayers. Others were the suggestions of the tempter and the voices of the world's turmoil. Never before did there seem so many things to be done, to be said, to be thought; and in every direction I was pulled and pushed and greeted with noisy acclamations and unspeakable unrest. It seemed necessary for me to listen to some of them, but God said, "Be still, and know that I am God." Then came the conflict of thoughts for the morrow, and its duties and cares; but God said, "Be still."

And I listened and slowly learned to obey, and shut my eyes to every sound; I found that after a while, when the other voices ceased, or I ceased to hear them, there was still a small voice in the depth of my spirit. As I listened, it became to me the power of prayer, and the voice of wisdom, and the call of duty, and I did not need to think so hard, or trust so hard, for that still small voice of the Holy Spirit in my heart was God's answer to all my questions.—A. B. Simpson.

As a white dove looks fairer against a thunder cloud, so Christ's peace is brightest in adversity.—H. B. Stowe.

EARNING A LIVING

"Why do you peg away at your college work, Marcia, when you might be having so many good times?" asked a girl of her classmate. "I should think that a girl with your prospects would be satisfied with barely getting through. It isn't as if you'd have to earn your living, like the rest of us."

"I don't see so much difference," replied Marcia with her friendly smile. "It seems to me that everyone ought to earn a living—in one way, if not in another. I know it doesn't look how as though I'd ever have to earn money. But I want to live a really rich full life. And is it any more than fair and honest that I should earn the right to do so, should give something in return for all I get—something besides dollars and cents, which are supplied to me by someone else, and so are not essentially mine at all? That is why I am working as faithfully as I can now. No one can earn a living without being properly equipped for doing so, and so I feel that I must make the most of this opportunity for getting ready. I shan't accomplish anything to boast of, even then. I'm not clever, like you and some of the other girls. But I can always do my best."

If only every girl had discovered the truth that Marcia expressed, and would loyally put it into practice! The life that is all taking and no giving is small and mean. It is, in truth, not very different from a pauper's life. Some of you who read this have no necessity to earn your bread by paid labor. It may even be that you have no right to do so. But there is no one who is not under obligation to make some return in service—and the best service of which she is capable—for the good things that she enjoys.—Selected.

Brethren Bible Conference, Long Beach, California
July 16-25, 1920

Officers

Moderator—A. V. Kimmell, Whittier.
Vice-Moderator—J. C. Beal, Fillmore.
Secretary—Hazel Shively, Los Angeles.
Assistant Secretary—A. E. Neher, Los Angeles.
Treasurer—H. V. Wall, Long Beach.

Speakers

French E. Oliver, D. D., noted author, lecturer, preacher and evangelist. Dr. Oliver, who is at present connected with the Bible Institute of Los Angeles, is a man of superior education and wide experience. He is one of the foremost figures in the religious world today, having been engaged in active Christian work for more than twenty-four years.

Dr. E. M. Cobb, Dayton, Ohio, well known Bible teacher and preacher. Dr. Cobb is so well and favorably known in the Brethren church little needs to be said about him. His clear and forceful delivery combined with his pleasing personality make him a man of great power and influence.

L. S. Bauman, Long Beach, expositor pastor. He is always in demand as a speaker or Bible teacher at conferences and conventions and absolutely second to none in any line of Christian work.

Royal J. Dye, M. D., Secretary, Foreign Missionary Society. More than ten years of service in the African Mission field, a man who knows the conditions there and the great need of workers. A wonderfully interesting and inspiring speaker.

N. W. Jennings, Los Angeles, pastor and evangelist. A forceful and convincing speaker.

J. C. Beal, pastor of Fillmore church, a very sincere and conscientious preacher.

T. H. Broad, pastor of La Verne church. "A mighty man of prayer." He impresses all with his earnestness and sincerity.

N. V. Leatherman, Turlock, California. A most welcome addition to the Brethren ministry of California. A speaker of power and conviction.

J. Wesley Platt, Manteca, California. The church at Manteca is certainly to be congratulated on having such enthusiastic and earnest leaders as Brother and Sister Platt.

A. V. Kimmell, Whittier, California. Following a resolution adopted by the conference: "Whereas our Brother Kimmell who has served our conference district as moderator for the last four consecutive years so faithfully we have resolved as a conference to express our appreciation of his untiring efforts in making the conference such as we are now engaged in, possible. Brother Kimmell has labored hard under difficult circumstances in keeping the tenor of our conference well balanced and orderly. He has lead us to depend upon the Lord's leadership throughout. It is needless to say that we regret very much that his office expires with the concluding of this conference. May the Lord bless him."

Singers

T. H. Broad, director of conference singing.
Mr. and Mrs. Wm. Wheatley, Los Angeles.
Byron Burdett, San Dimas, an experienced Christian Endeavor worker and song leader.
Hazel Shively, Los Angeles.
Clarence Shively, Los Angeles.
Bert Hendy, Hollywood.
Ada Visiek, Long Beach.
Lelia Neher, Los Angeles.

Esther Sargeat, Los Angeles.
Miss Campbell, Long Beach.
J. W. Platt, Manteca.
Miss Elliott, Manteca.
Mr. and Mrs. Gnagey, Whittier.
Mrs. Hooper, Los Angeles.
Dora Zimmerman, Turlock.
Mr. Poole, La Verne.
La Verne Ladies' Quartette.
Mrs. Seymore   Mrs. Bath
Mrs. Pager   Mrs. Swank

Long Beach Ladies' Quartette:
Mrs. Grace Srack   Mrs. L. S. Bauman
Mrs. Thomas Lovejoy   Mrs. Campbell

Pianists

Johanna Nielsen, Long Beach.
Mrs. Frances Nielsen, Long Beach.
Ivy Bauman, Long Beach.
Vera Hessler, Long Beach.
Lelia Neher, Los Angeles.
Leslie Keller, Los Angeles.
Mrs. Metcalf, Whittier.

The Addresses

Friday (July 16)

10:40 Address: "Facts or Fancy," E. M. Cobb. Based on six facts—(1) The Bible is the word of God; (2) Jesus is the Son of God; (3) All men have sinned; (4) Jesus died for all men; 5(1) Jesus arose from the dead; (6) Jesus is coming again.

8:00 Address: "African Missions," Dr. Royal J. Dye. In the northern part of Africa there are 40 million Mohammedans. In the south 10 million nominal Christians. Between are 80 million pagans. Who will win this great continent?"

Saturday:

8:00 Sermon: "The Mirage of Ono," E. M. Cobb. Interchurch World Movement likened to a mirage.

Sunday:

11:00 Sermon: "Elijah in Training." L. S. Bauman. "The heights to which Elijah attained are not inaccessible to us because 'Elijah was a man of like passions with us.' He rested on the promise of God."

3:00 Address: "The Psychology of Sound Doctrine," French Oliver. "The psychology of sound doctrine sends a man who would be used most to his knees. A man of sound doctrine can get victory."

8:00 Sermon: "The Doctrine of God," E. M. Cobb. "The instincts of animals the reasoning power of man, the system of the human body and of the universe shows us that there is a God."

Monday:

8:00 Sermon: "The Doctrine of Christ," E. M. Cobb. "He has all power on earth over disease, death and nature, in heaven over thrones, angels and the judgment and in hell over demons, evil angels and Satan."

3:00: Sermon: "Elijah in Prayer," L. S. Bauman. "Elijah's prayer was definite, expectant and persevering. Man does his most effective praying when he is driven by an urgent need."

8:00 Address: "The Psychology of Prayer," French E. Oliver. "The devil degenerates a man by these steps: imagination, thought, desire, action, habit, character, destiny. The keynote of Christianity is prayer."

Tuesday:

10:00 Address: "The Doctrine of the Holy Spirit," E. M. Cobb. "The personality of the Holy Spirit is often questioned because we make the mistake of speaking of him as 'it.'"

11:00 Sermon: "Fellowship with God," N. V. Leatherman. "We have fellowship with God if we like to do what he wants us to do."

2:00 Sermon: "Elijah in Conflict," L. S. Bauman. "When a man can live peacefully with the Lord's enemies, there is something the matter with him. We need Christians out and out for God. There is too much false sympathy with the devil and his agents."

3:00 Address: "The Psychology of Faith," French E. Oliver. "Without faith it is impossible to be pleasing to God. The psychology of faith is best manifested in men who are looking about for some new manifestations of the love of God."

8:00 Sermon: "The Doctrine of Man," E. M. Cobb. "There is nothing in nature to compare with man. He is a triune being having body, soul and spirit. Human nature is the same now as at the time of man's creation.".

Wednesday:

10:00 Sermon: "The Doctrine of Satan," E. M. Cobb. "The ridicule we have placed on the devil has given the idea that he is not a real being. The devil's power is subtle, strong and ever present. But his power is made of no avail if we stand in the shadow of the cross."

11:00 Address: "The Holy Spirit—His Work," J. C. Beal. "We should take great comfort in the fact that two divine persons are praying for us. The Holy Spirit leads men into lives of activity that will please God."

2:00 Address: "The Test of Discipleship," French E. Oliver. "Christ never called a lazy or an idle man. The greatest thing a Christian can do, is soul winning. There is nothing so much in the way of the progress of the church as the hypocrisy of its members."

3:00 Sermon: "The Old Rugged Cross," N. W. Jennings. "The hope of the world is in the dynamic power of the cross of calvary. God forbid that I should glory save in the cross."

8:00 Sermon: "Elijah in Despair," L. S. Bauman. "Sometimes we lose in spiritual power because we do not take more care of our bodies. Elijah was lonely—the Value of Christian fellowship cannot be overestimated."

Thursday:

2:00 Address: "The Impotence of Influence," French E. Oliver. "If you operate the church on the basis of a political campaign or a lodge, it loses its power. Power with God is vital, influence with men, incidental."

3:00 Sermon: "Elijah in Restoration," L. S. Bauman. "The love of God sometimes follows us even when we have wandered away from him. God can provide food for the soul as well as the body."

8:00 Sermon: "The Doctrine of Angels," E. M. Cobb. "Angels are the servants, ministers, slaves of God. Don't worship angels; worship God."

Friday:

10:00 Sermon: "Prayer," N. W. Jennings.

"Prayer is the highest privilege we have. We should pray the prayer of faith."

11:00 Sermon: By J. Wesley Platt. "The church is trying to compete with the world and is losing. The church has in no wise received a blessing in coming down from its high standard to cater to the world."

2:00 Sermon: "Fellowship in Him," T. H. Broad. "Fellowship with Christ will make the things of the world unsatisfactory. We fall down as Christians because we haven't gone in deep enough in the beginning."

3:00 Address: "Gethsemane to Calvary," French E. Oliver. "In saying 'My God, why hast thou forsaken me?' Christ uttered the wail of the lost. He represented you and me."

8:00 Sermon: "Elijah in Translation," L. S. Bauman. "The translation of Elijah is neither the first nor the last translation. The next great translation will be that of the saints. If the Bible doesn't teach the translation of the saints, it doesn't teach anything."

Saturday:

8:00 Address: "The Curse of Modernists," French E. Oliver. "It is not so much what ministers of today say, but what they leave unsaid that does the most harm. Their teachings are so nearly like the real factor that they deceive and blind the people."

Sunday:

11:00 Sermon: "Elisha, Elijah's Successor," L. S. Bauman. "Elisha made the mistake of putting earthly things first. When you start to work for God burn the bridges behind you."

3:00 Address: "A Towel Glorified," French E. Oliver. "Think of the Creator coming down in the form of a man and humbling himself by taking a towel and girding himself and washing the feet of some Galilean peasants. If you are honest enough to live up to the light that you have, God will give you more light."

8:00 Address: "The King's Ferry," French E. Oliver. "The only way to get passage on the King's ferry is by the grace of God. You must be a member of the King's household. There are a lot more sad people in the world today than glad ones. Sin is at the bottom of the tears and broken hearts."

Business

Friday (July 16)

10:00 Special prayer for Brother and Sister Reagan.
Roll call of churches:
Long Beach, 3 elders, 18 delegates.
Whittier, 1 elder, 7 delegates.
La Verne, 2 elders, 6 delegates.
Los Angeles, First Church, 2 elders, 6 delegates.
Los Angeles, Compton Ave., 6 delegates.
Fillmore, 1 elder, 4 delegates.
Credential committee appointed:
N. C. Nielsen, Long Beach.
Mrs. Leffler, Los Angeles.
Leonard Robinson, Fillmore.
Committee on committees appointed:
T. H. Broad, La Verne.
C. S. Kreitor, Whittier.
Rose Runyon, Los Angeles.
Courtesies of Conference extended to E. M. Cobb, Dayton, Ohio; David Churn, Kansas; Greetings from W. J. H. Bauman, Long Beach, who has to his credit nearly 62 years of membership and more than 60 years of public ministry.

2:30 Election of officers for coming year:
Moderator—J. C. Beal, Fillmore.

Vice-Moderator—N. W. Jennings, Los Angeles.
Secretary—A. H. Kent, Long Beach.
Assistant Secretary—Clarence Shively Los Angeles
Treasurer—H. V. Wall, Long Beach.
E. V. Hand, Whittier, re-elected member of Mission Board.
N. C. Nielsen, Long Beach, was elected member at large of the Mission Board.
L. S. Bauman, Long Beach, elected member of Executive committee of National Conference.
Committee of 12 appointed to consider and bring in resolutions relative to: (1) Publishing interests; (2) Ashland College; (3) Interchurch World Movement:
T. H. Broad, T. J. Steves, N. W. Jennings, Ray Runyon, L. S. Bauman, H. V. Wall, J. C. Beal, C. H. Flory, A. V. Kimmell, Harry Hooper, A. E. Neher, N. C. Nielsen.
Final report on four year program by District Director, A. V. Kimmell.
Report of N. C. Nielsen, President of District Mission Board.
Present officers of this conference were constituted a committee with authority to select 2 persons, to represent this district as members at large at the coming National conference. Adjourned.

Saturday (July 24)

2:30 Courtesies of conference extended to N. V. Leatherman and J. W. Platt, Visiting ministers.
Statistical Report for district by T. H. Broad:

Value of church property, ...	$ 154,000
Total funds raised, ...	42,070.99
Pastors' salaries, ...	10,770.61
Paid for Evangelistic meetings, ...	788.31
Current expenses and improvements,	24,279.01
State or District Missions, ...	1,075.02
National Home Missions, ...	1,090.88
Foreign Missions, ...	4,534.95
Miscellaneous Benevolences, ...	1,266.51
Churches owned, ...	6
Parsonages owned, ...	1
Membership, ...	1,148.00
Deacons, ...	20
Deaconesses, ...	19
Elders, ...	20
Revivals held, ...	7
Accessions at revivals, ...	119
Accessions at regular services, ...	74
By letter, ...	16
By relation, ...	1
Baptized, ...	191
Lost, ...	65
Net gain, ...	150

Motion that this district pay, toward Winona auditorium fund on basis of ten cents per member carried.
Motion that a special offering be taken Saturday, July 24, to go toward payment of Auditorium fund, said offering not to reduce payment on basis of ten cents per member carried.
Reading of report of Committee of Twelve concerning (1) Publishing interests; (2) Ashland College; (3) Interchurch World Movement.
Motion that conference concur with, accept and adopt resolutions drawn up by Committee of Twelve carried unanimously.
Motion that A. V. Kimmell be named as chairman of Southern California delegation at coming National conference, carried.
Motion that Secretary of this conference notify the Board of Trustees of Ashland College that this district wishes to elect their representative on the College Board of Trustees, carried.
Reading of Report of Conference Treasurer, H. V. Wall. Total expenditures, $345.00.
Motion that Home Mission apportionments for coming year be same as last year, carried. Adjourned.
A. V. Kimmell, Moderator,
Vivian Yett, Acting Secretary,
Long Beach, California.

ELDER STEPHEN HILDEBRAND

Oldest Living Brethren Minister, at the age of 91 years

Rejoices in Song and Praise with friends who gather in
his home

(SEE PAGE 13)

Published every Wednesday at
Ashland, Ohio. All matter for publication must reach the Editor not
later than Friday noon of the pre-
ceeding week.

George S. Baer, Editor

The
Brethren
Evangelist

When ordering your paper changed
give old as well as new address.
Subscriptions discontinued at expiration. To avoid missing any numbers renew two weeks in advance.

R. R. Teeter, Business Manager

OFFICIAL ORGAN OF THE BRETHREN CHURCH

Subscription price, $2.00 per year, payable in advance.
Entered at the Post Office at Ashland, Ohio, as second-class matter.
Acceptance for mailing at special rate of postage provided for in section 1103, Act of October 3, 1917, authorized September 9, 1918.
Address all matter for publication to Geo. S. Baer, Editor of the Brethren Evangelist, and all business communications to R. R. Teeter,
Business Manager, Brethren Publishing Company, Ashland, Ohio. Make all checks payable to the Brethren Publishing Company.

TABLE OF CONTENTS

EDITORIAL

The Great Labor Turn-Over Among the Profession

Denominational church government has both its advantages and its disadvantages. We are jealous of our congregational independence; it is a very precious possession in Brethren denominational life, and we would sacrifice much rather than give it up. But it is not an entirely unmixed blessing in some of its outworkings. It sometimes develops into congregational selfishness and inconsiderateness for a co-operating congregation. This is especially noticeable in the matter of securing pastors. In our extreme congregational government there is quite frequently detected in this connection a weakness that deserves our attention with a view to its correction.

Every congregation is practically a law unto itself in the matter of securing and dismissing its pastor. Here is a weakness and a source of evil, the unsatisfactory results of which are growing more exaggerated with the increased scarcity of ministers. A congregation may go anywhere at any time, without the knowledge or consent of any other congregation or individual and seek its pastor. Every congregation feels it a duty of getting the very best minister possible, and if perchance it has its heart set on the pastor of another congregation, and if it is not too conscientious about breaking one of the Ten Commandments, it makes him an offer and tries to allure him away. Or if it has no one definitely in mind, it may write to a half dozen or more different pastors and ask them if they will "consider a call." There are unfortunate consequences due to such methods which are coming to prevail among a goodly number of our churches.

There are at least three parties to whom injury is often done as a result of some of our unwise, if not unscrupulous, ways of securing pastors. First, the church whose pastor is suddenly taken is often injured greatly. Very likely that church is just discovering itself under its present leadership; it is just becoming awakened to the possibilities of its field and its future is redolent with hope. It is coming to have every confidence in its leader and is willing to follow him in sacrifice and service to ends heretofore unknown. The church is united, harmonious and every one seems anxious to pull his load. A great work is about to be undertaken and there is every reason to expect success. Just then some congregation comes pastor hunting and snatches away the leader of this expectant band. Disappointment takes the place of hope, plans are interrupted and visions of greater things to come are delayed of realization. It means the spending of months going through the "get acquainted" stage again, and possibly, the months may number into years before any really intelligent and aggressive piece of work can be done. While this readjustment is going on, it may be that the day of supreme opportunity for that church is passing, and its whole future may be blighted or the future possibilities greatly lessened

because an inconsiderate sister congregation lured away its pastor when it could least afford to lose him. More than we think, perhaps are the distressingly short pastorates due to this custom, and more often than we have been wont to recognize has the future of some promising work been cut short by a sudden and unwarranted change in pastors.

The church which gets the pastor often finds it has done itself an injury by the method it employs. Perhaps it finds its new pastor unfitted for the place. He was doing a great work in his former pastorate and they thought he would duplicate his record in their church but conditions are different and he doesn't seem to meet their expectations. Perhaps they selected him because of some spectacular thing which he was supposed to have done, and which was no true indication of his ability as a pastor. It is likely that they failed to make any thorough investigation as to his ability to meet the needs of their field; they could not make inquiry of those whom he was serving, for they would meet vigorous objections to their making overtures to their pastor, if it was not opportune for him to leave. At any rate it often occurs that the church that steals away a pastor from another congregation finds that it has not chosen wisely, and there is a dissatisfied congregation and a dissatisfied pastor soon to make another change.

Moreover the questionableness of the method they pursued may have reacted against them. It can hardly be denied that they were prompted by selfish motives when they sought to take a good pastor from another congregation that needed him badly and with whom he was doing a good work. Heaven's choicest blessings can hardly be upon a people that are actuated by such motives. And the lives of the members can hardly fail to be affected by the quality of such motives. The reaction will come. It may come in a failure to send any personal responsibility for the success of the work, or in an unwillingness to sacrifice for the good of the cause, or in a headiness and selfishness that will make harmony and co-operation impossible. In some way the reaction will come, so that in the long run, the church that seeks to take away another church's pastor, without high, Christian consideration of the other church's needs, merely because it wants the best preacher and has the money to pay the price is not likely to win out.

The preacher is also done an injury. He may have been satisfied before another congregation tried to pry him loose, or suggested their interest in him, but now he is somewhat undecided whether he should remain where he is or whether he should seek a more profitable field. It as taken away his feeling of permanency with regard to his relations with his present field, and there is the danger that it shall grow upon him with the result that he shall take less seriously his present task, prosecute it with less vision and aggressiveness and of maintaining the attitude of being about to close up his work. Even if he should not allow the matter to affect him so radically, he is almost certain to have suggested to him the question whether the present field offers sufficient opportunity for the exercise of his talents and the accomplishment of a worthy work, a thing which may take away the joy, he has heretofore found in his present field.

The "Reformed Church Messenger" has written in this strain and says editorially, "One of our popular young pastors has written a suggestive complaint to this office which is typical of some other convictions expressed to us by other pastors within recent months. This man says he was happy in his work until a few weks ago; but within the last few weeks he has had four or five offers to consider other places, and he suggests something of the method and the temptation held out to him which has added to his restiveness, and has also made him feel the inadequacy of our entire method of placing ministers." There has been something of the same feeling experienced by our own ministers. Occasionally we hear complaints on the part of pastors against churches which when in need of a pastor have the habit of writing to as many pastors as they think might meet their requirements, asking them if they would consider a call. They are not satisfied with settling on the man they want and going after him; they must disturb a half dozen or more. The pastors object to having their feelings of contentment broken in upon in wholesale fashion, and when there is little chance or desire of serious and definite consideration of them individually as pastors. They do not appreciate being grouped together and having a committee pick out the one that may happen to make the best appeal, or having their fate decided by the drawing of their names from a hat by a person blind-folded. The pastor likes to feel that the call to a certain pastorate is a call of God to him definitely, and that wisdom and great seriousness has been exercised by those through whom the call has been extended. Such a call no pastor can afford to take lightly. But a pastor can hardly consider an inquiry or call with such seriousness when he feels it is prompted by selfishness and inconsideration of others, or as a result of a desire of some church to flirt with as many different preachers as possible or drive the best "bargain" possible before selecting their pastor.

We do not advocate the Methodist system of the appointment of pastors by superintendents who have studied the fields and the ministers; our jealous regard for our congregational independence would doubtless make us unreceptive of such a system. We do think however that a little exposing of weaknesses that have crept into our congregational operations will help to correct the defects. Our plea is for the exercising of greater care, wisdom and unselfish consideration in the selecting of our pastors. This will go a long way towards overcoming the wasteful habit of too frequent pastoral changes, and will give encouragement to pastors to consider the call of a church in very truth the call of God to a field of service.

EDITORIAL REVIEW

Brother Teeter reports "progress" in his Business Manager's Corner, but he is anxious to have more progress along the line of gifts to help meet the heavy payments for print paper. Read his "Corner."

Manteca, California, church just organized, is enthusiastic over the prospects of a new church building and also of growth spiritually and numerically. Under the efficient leadership of Brother J. W. Platt, the pastor, they will doubtless go forward to victory.

Brother B. T. Burnworth outlines an interesting and full program for several weeks to come. When we look for an explanation for the remarkable growth of the Lanark church, we find no small portion of it in the tireless energy of its pastor.

Anything that adds to the comfort and good cheer of our pioneer ministers is of interest to the brotherhood. Brother A. O. Dannenbaum of Johnstown writes concerning a recognition service in honor of our aged brother, Elder Stephen Hildebrand. And we are glad to honor this veteran by presenting his picture on first page.

Our correspondent from the Bethlehem church (Virginia) reports encouragement and progress. The good condition of the church and its auxiliaries speaks well for the faithfulness of the membership at this place, in view of the fact that they are without a pastor.

Our readers will be pleased to learn through Marguerite Gribble's letter that there is hope of the health of our missionaries becoming better and that a little group of "cottages" is springing up there. They report some splendid work done in the way of translations of scripture and other missionary helps.

The Ashland Church and the College authorities unite in extending an invitation to all Ohio churches to send large delegations to Ashland to attend the Ohio State Conference, October 25 to 27. The program is to be found in this issue. "A Full Quota From Every Church" is our slogan.

Doubtless few really appreciated the courage and noble work of our departed Sister Myrtle Mae Snyder. After reading Brother Cobb's article in this issue all will appreciate more what she was and did. Sincere sympathy to her loved ones, and may her heroic example inspire others to be willing to make the supreme sacrifice.

The first installment of "College News" since the opening of the new school year is found in this issue. Dr. Jacobs points to certain encouragements connected with the opening of school, and also points out the urgent necessity of new buildings and equipment. The school is the brotherhood's and the brotherhood must meet its needs.

It sometimes seems almost as great a loss to lose by death the mothers of our ministers as our ministers themselves. All who knew Brother G. C. Carpenter's mother loved her and she was known to all the students and Brethren at Ashland, when she lived here while Brother Glenn Carpenter was here in school. She and Brother Cook's mother and the editor's mother were three widowed mothers here together and they became fast friends. Mother Baer and Mother Carpenter are now in the glory world and who shall say they are not rejoicing again together. We extend sincere sympathy to Brethren George, Ira and Glenn Carpenter, and as well to the other children.

HOME-MADE SQUIBS

It is no task at all to be generous with that which costs us nothing; to give liberally and cheerfully of that which comes by hard struggle or costs greatly is the thing that tries us.

No man is little except he who wants to be. Neither race barriers, nor poverty, nor pain, can defeat and keep down that life that is determined to be large.

If we would only stop to consider the fact that worldliness disqualifies an individual for spiritual greatness, we would not wonder why there are so many small and discredited Christians in our churches.

How human it is and yet how unchristian, to rebel against God because he fails to interfere in our behalf. We forget the hundred joys we have received and let the one unavailing sorrow unfit us for service and life.

Christianity is not something superimposed on life, not something that may be put off or on at will, but it is a new and distinct type of life, a higher quality of life infused into our own which transforms us until we are no longer our former selves.

This country which we love and of which we are justly proud in so many ways, has lately furnished a most striking example of the Levite of Bible story. Stricken Armenia has called to us for relief from the robbers and Christian persecutors, but America, "the land of the free and the home of the brave," has passed by on the other side, and left Armenia in her misery.

THE BRETHREN BICENTENARY MOVEMENT PAGE

1723 · · · · · · 1923

Dr. Charles A. Bame, Editor

Evangelism

The "Go" and "push" of our Bicentenary Program is up to the evangelistic drive of the church. If we are to have a larger membership, bigger churches and more churches, it must be through the agency of evangelism.

Concentration on Evangelism

The past few years we have been flooded with money drives, methods and booster campaigns, will it not be wisdom to study the methods of Jesus and his program for the church, take time to "tarry" before God and be infused with the Holy Spirit and go forth with holy enthusiasm to make Christ known, the only hope and Savior of a lost world?

The Need of the Hour

The world was never so reckless and daring as today, a tidal wave of money thirst and pleasure seeking, has all but swallowed us up. The nominal church is asleep, listless and indifferent to her mission. If the church is to be awakened and sin halted, it will be through intensive and extensive Gospel evangelism.

The Gospel Outflow

Evangelism is and always has been the outflow of Christian zeal and fervor. It is the "Go ye" of the great Commission of Christ to the church; the medium through which the Holy Spirit makes the Christ message known.

The Bicentenary Slogan

Is "An annual evangelistic campaign in every church of the brotherhood." Let there be no excuses or postponements. A church can have a revival anytime it is ready to get down on its knees before God, and go out and win men for Christ. Let there be no slackers. There is something wrong with a church that cannot have an annual meeting for special soul winning. God's time is "NOW." The question is, are we ready?

Evangelists

This year we will have in the field more men than ever before in our history. The Evangelistic and Bible Study League will have Brethren Bowman, Ashman and myself. The Gospel team, of Brethren Coleman and Ronk and also Miss Aboud will give all their time to evangelistic work. Brethren Bauman, Burnworth, Thomas and others will give part of their time. Brother Bame the secretary of the Bicentenary program will be out for six months. Arthur Lynn of Dayton will give as much time as he can spare to the work. This is certainly encouraging.

Some Plans

As program director of Evangelism, I desire to do all I can to further this work. With a congregational form of church government, the preference and choice of the individual church has to be considered and dealt with; in the light of this we suggest the following:

I. That every conference District appoint an Evangelistic Board of three members, who will assist in the supervision of evangelism in their respective district, to co-operate with churches and evangelists in carrying out our program.

II. The Evangelistic and Bible Study League, which is a national organization, will co-operate and work with the local churches and districts.

III. Evangelists in the general work like Ronk, Coleman and Miss Aboud should be corresponded with personally in making arrangements.

Finally

Has your church arranged for a meeting this year? If not get busy and make your plans now. May we make this the biggest year for evangelism in our history. We can, if we will. Let us say WE WILL.

W. S. BELL, Director of Evangelism.

Evangelism Ahead

This stirring appeal from the Director of Evangelism is at the right time and of the right ring. It is "Evangelism Ahead" both as to getting in the first appeal of the directors, and "Ahead" because it is the thing the churches should be looking after in, quick order. But this is not all appeal. Director Bell offers good, practical suggestions for immediate use and the church that gets going right off, will succeed. It would seem that a small body as our church is mighty fortunate to have so many good folks in the field of evangelism as he names. Besides, there are many pastors who will be glad to have the opportunity to do a bit of it themselves. Indeed, we have many who are wonderfully gifted for just such work as helping the churches to get done, this will of the Master. Of course, we know how sure we may be that Jesus wants it done. If he has nothing else, he has that; when the church has carried out all of his will, the last corner of the earth will be evangelized and then he will return in glory with his holy angels. Since I was a member of a committee on evangelism last winter, I know where the failure comes about. It is not the preachers; most of them seemed anxious to go and do. But many of them have to hold their own meetings or have none and some do not get the proper encouragement from the pews. This idea that because the place is small or because it has been well worked, little need be done, no attempt need be made this year, is all apart from the way of the Man of Galilee. "In every church" this year, does not mean part of them. This is a new program and thus a new opportunity. Our goals are more general but we hope to make them thus, more practical. I am in for more evangelism, not because I need more dates, but because the churches need to be dated. Not because evangelists need more to do (perhaps they do) but because more churches than ever need to be evangelized. Every district and each church has a part to do in this drive for lost souls and we all do well to read Dr. Bell's article as well as our Bibles until we get the spirit of the conference that asked for "a revival in every church in the brotherhood."   BAME.

AN OBJECT LESSON

A few weeks ago a "Near East banquet" was held in New York and seventeen hundred persons were in attendance. The tables were bare save for the white cloth, and when the banquet was served all that each one received was a piece of coarse bread, made of oatmeal and barley flour, and a small bowl of very weak barley soup.

This, they were told, was all that the people of the Near East had been living on once a day. The object lesson made a deep impression. The banquet will be long remembered. The speeches found the people ready to har and heed the appeals that were made.—The Christian Work.

GENERAL ARTICLES

Joys of the Winona Bible and Brethren Conference. By N. W. Jennings

It was a real joy to pass through the gates into the park which is a very sacred spot, where one is always greeted by a spiritual atmosphere and caught up in such a spirit that he cannot help but feel at home.

It was a joy to attend a part of the great Bible conference and be at the feet of great thinkers who themselves sit at the feet of Jesus, the great Teacher, and who live under the deepening shadows of the cross of Calvary. It was a joy to dip our bucket deep into their well. It was a joy to think of his promise that if we drink of the living water "wells should spring up within us, and rivers would flow from us."

It was a joy to enter into the spirit of our own conference which followed the Bible conference, to listen to the moderator's address which had a true ring, to listen to the singer and the choir which added much to the conference, to be at the early prayer meeting which paved the way for the leadership of the Holy Spirit during each day.

It was a joy to be at the feet of Dr. Miller and hear the blessed and beautiful doctrine of the Holy Spirit and to hear Dr. Evans on the doctrine concerning the eternal Son of God. The work of these two men meant so much to the conference! They both ought to have been paid well for their work, for no little time was required in getting together the material which they gave out to the people.

It was a joy to be at the Jubilee service which had to do with our Four Year Program, to note the victory; and yet there was plenty of room for all kinds of improvement. Machinery is not all, in fact, it is useless unless oiled and manipulated by the Holy Spirit.

It was a joy to be at the College rally. It was like old times. It was a joy to see the intense earnestness of our president, Dr. Jacobs, and the enthusiasm of the present student body. To meet some of the dear young men whom God gave us in the ministry, who are now in Ashland College preparing for the work of the ministry, this brings double joy into the life of a minister of the Gospel of the Son of God.

It was a joy to meet hundreds of good friends which we had met throughout the brotherhood. It was a joy to be with McInturff and his people at Goshen and to break the bread of life to them once more, and to share their fellowship.

It was a joy to see how nice and cheerful so many of our Brethren in the ministry were who had no place on the program, who held no office and who sought none. But many such men whom we see plodding on in their ways are traveling with visions in their souls, perhaps nobody knows it but themselves and God. In my humble judgment, such men are the true representatives of the church and her King Jesus. So loud rings that verse, "Seekest thou honor unto thyself? Seek it not." Saul may hide but God will bring him to the front when he wants him. A Goliath may rush into battle and never get to strike a blow.

Brother Wm. H. Beachler was made moderator of the conference by the vote of the people and he served well, as it was no new place to him. Brother A. V. Kimmell, Vice-moderator, was also at home in the work. Others served in a noble way whose names we cannot mention for the lack of space.

It was a joy to see our conference come to a close with the dove of peace in our camp and with white wings outstretched, and to see the rainbow of love bend over the camp. May we all be kept by his almighty power until we meet again there, and if not back there, then over there where all is love and peace.

It was a joy to meet our dear consecrated flock at home, who were anxiously awaiting our coming. After the first morning message one young man came into the church.

Brother Harry Toler did the preaching while we were gone and did good work. We expect to launch our revival soon, and we do ask the prayers of all God's children.

Los Angeles, California.

"Brotherhood and Some of Its Implications." By Prof. I. R. Senseman

The ramifications of such a subject are so many and varied that under it one might discuss all phases of Christian conduct or relationship. The brotherhood of man is necessarily just as broad as the Fatherhood of God, and so our relationship with God involves directly and indirectly all our relationsips with our brethren. However, there is just one problem, seemingly a fundamental one among the many implied in the term brotherhood, that the writer wishes to stress. It is this: Do we in all respects really and sincerely desire to be brethren? Or, have we in our human relations, been playing house keeping with strangers; and thus living in a superficial fashion not very well united by common interests, easily torn asunder when the testing time comes? We do not mean to imply that the difficulties of real brotherhood are not severe; severe enough, probably, in spite of our deepest desires to tear us asunder, but there are reasons for seriously doubting whether many Christian communities, states, nations, denominations and other groups have risen to a level where they sincerely desire to throw off their cherished little distinctions, their pride and pique and enter into full brotherhood with all others.

As "brothers" to the weak, insane, criminal, and so forth, we seem to have made comparatively good progress. In the case of the treatment of criminals, we had really become so refined in our feelings that we have been compelled to react in some ways, remembering that the criminal was not the only "brother," and that the offended community as well as the offender must be considered. Our scientific study of insanity and the consequent charitable regard for and treatment of the insane has become notable. Likewise our concern for the poverty-stricken and otherwise unfortunate is quite keen and solicitous, and all things considered we do very well by them. But are these really our brethren in the full sense, and capable of brotherly reciprocation, or are they only potential brothers, who through misfortune or sin have fallen to the condition of wards? And have such imposed upon us the severest test of Christian brotherhood? We believe they do not.

There is a subtle characteristic in human nature, a kind of personal pride, or feeling of self-importance that is satisfied by helping the weak or unfortunate. And so, however humble in spirit the giver may be, it is very apt to be even in a selfish sense, more blessed to give than to receive. So may we add the thought that "to give and take" is more blessed still. "To give and take" implies equality, toleration, co-operation, and sympathetic understanding, and appears to even higher spiritual characteristics than those that lead us to help the unfortunate.

We are thinking, at this point, especially of peoples, nations, communities, denominations, etc., for although in God's sight there is only one kind of soul, the personal, individual soul, the stress of human affairs has compelled us to think of society as a whole, somewhat to the neglect of individuals. We think of America, for example, as having set a new standard in the treatment of subject peoples. Our treatment of Hawaii and Porto Rico, though not perfect to be sure, is an advance over old methods. Yet, we cannot believe this to be the final test of America's ability to practice brotherhood. The real test is probably now upon us, and involves not our attitude toward our wards, but toward our equals. Can we unite with Great Britain, France, Germany, and other Christian nations, and with them "give and take" in the accomplishment of things all Christianity holds dear, and higher than any national self interest? Or shall we, in self-righteousness, stand apart as more democratic than Germany, purer than France, and more intelligent than Russia? We believe this burden is not only upon America, of course, but that it rests equally heavy upon all Christian nations to meet such a test now.

Applying the same thought to the church, it does not seem to us that the severest test of brotherhood in the church comes in the problem of foreign missions, and the Christianizing of backward peoples, but that it comes now in the challenge for all denominations to unite in this and other works, thus practicing and proving brotherhood as well as preaching it. Of course, there are difficulties in the way, but what are difficulties for, but to overcome? The doctrines and teachings of each denomination espoused and developed by spiritual cultivation are not to be easily forced aside. But need the things that are vital be done any violence by such a union of efforts? Isn't there in Christian humanity by this time, enough of toleration and sympathetic understanding that individual and small group distinctions can be preserved and yet not stressed and accented in a manner or in a spirit that will result in the injury of others and the undoing of united effort? Can we not maintain our cherished distinctions (and they are doubtless inevitable and

serve a worthy purpose) and yet show ourselves magnanimous enough to unite on the high plans of our common aims for the sake of a wider brotherhood? This would prove a severer test than any other of the highest and most genuine spirit of brotherhood, and yet the strength that would accrue to us and the good that would be accomplished would more than pay us for the effort.

Unless there shall develop a willingness on the part of individuals, organizations and nations to minimize differences and magnify and unite on agreements that are essential how shall the righteous and constructive forces be able to meet the demands of the world today? We must all grant each to the other the right of personal opinion, but at the same time we must not be unwilling to unite on some process or method by which we may arrive at the fulfillment of the promised day when there shall be peace on earth and righteousness shall prevail. Mere criticism will not satisfy in matters of such moment. And apparently we haven't much longer to hesitate in doing something constructive to ward off a worse world crisis than the one we have just gone through. The crisis is a challenge, not only to nations and denominations, but to individuals to cultivate a real desire for brotherhood, not as superior elder brothers but as equal brothers, willing to tolerate differences and to co-operate in true "give and take" spirit. My nation, my church, my community, my club, my self need now if ever to show their greatness by their willingness to sacrifice the emphasis of their cherished distinctions for the sake of our common cause, our common principles and our common safety.

Chicago, Illinois.

Stewardship.　Wm. H. Beachler, D. D.

I consider that stewardship has been up until comparatively recently one of the greatly neglected doctrines of the Bible. And as a consequence of that neglect grave harm and loss has come to the church and the cause of Christ, and individual Christians have forfeited from their lives and experience immeasurable power and joy and growth.

True, this doctrine is not popular with all professing followers of our Lord—not even in the Brethren church however, because an individual happens not to like this doctrine is not proof positive that there is something wrong with the doctrine. My own personal notion inclines to the belief that it is proof that there is something wrong with the individual. And certainly because a man or woman may not like this doctrine will not lead God to disapprove of the doctrine; rather it may lead to God's disapproval of the man or woman. And therefore if any man has a quarrel with the doctrine of stewardship his quarrel is, in reality, with God. For God himself is the author of the doctrine and it has a large place in the Bible.

What does the doctrine of Christian stewardship imply? I believe the average Christian's idea of stewardship is like the average Christian's idea of temperance—only partly correct and altogether too limited. When the average Christian thinks of temperance he thinks of abstinence from intoxicating liquors, whereas temperance has to do with far more than merely a man's attitude toward liquors. Likewise when the average Christian thinks of stewardship it calls to his mind the thought of money and earthly possessions. To be sure, Christian stewardship has to do with money and earthly possessions, but it has to do with some other things far more fundamental and vital than money and things perishable.

This is my own understanding of the doctrine of stewardship: It is the Christian's acknowledgement that he is not his own. His life, his time, his power, his influence, his wealth, his all are not his own, but belong to God. For me no other text in the entire New Testament strikes at the quick of the matter as does 1 Corinthians 19, 20: "And ye are not your own, for ye are bought with a price." When

this great fundamental fact dawns with the light of noonday upon the mind and heart of a Christian many problems in his life find easy solution, including the problem of the use of his money. As further confirmation of my own idea of Stewardship I quote from one of the strongest writers of the present day on the subject. "In the first place, we must keep in mind one fundamental fact,—Stewardship is the Christian law of life. It does not refer primarily to property and money, though it certainly includes these. Paul writes, 'Stewards of the mysteries of God.' The whole of life is a stewardship. This is the teaching of Jesus Christ."

The texts in both the Old and New Testaments emphasizing God's ownership of all things and the fact of man's stewardship are almost countless. I can only hope to call attention to a few of the most striking ones:

Psalms 50:10—"For the world is mine and the fulness thereof."

Ezekiel 18:4—"All souls are mine; as the soul of the father, so also the soul of the son is mine; the soul that sinneth it shall die."

Leviticus 25-38—"And the land shall not be sold in perpetuity; for the land is mine; for ye are strangers and sojourners with me."

Habbakuk 2:8—"The silver is mine and the gold is mine saith the Lord."

1 Peter 4:10—"As every man hath received the gift, even so minister the same one to another, as good stewards of the manifold grace of God."

1 Corinthians 4:11—"Let a man so account of us, as of the ministers of Christ, and stewards of the mysteries of God. Moreover it is required in stewards that a man be found faithful."

1 Timothy 6:7—"For we brought nothing into this world, and it is certain we can carry nothing out of it."

I may say again that these are merely suggestive of the many texts and passages in the Bible which bear on the subject of God's ownership of all things, and man's stewardship. Nor can I pass without mention of David's striking recognition of all this. As the spokesman of his people, who had just made a marvelous offering for the house of the Lord, he said, "Of thine own have we given thee."

In the remaining time I will say this: As I view the church today—the Brethren church, if you please,—her needs and her problems, it is my firm belief that our slogan should be no less than this, Back to the doctrine of Christian Stewardship This slogan should never be long absent from the lips of our ministry and the teaching force of our Sunday schools. For old and young alike should be faithfully and unceasingly taught the doctrine of Christian Stewardship. I am going to assign the following reason for my conviction on this point:

First, it is thoroughly Scriptural, and that is the best reason of all. No doctrine of the Bible should be neglected or slighted; certainly not this one.

Second, I believe that a full acknowledgment on the part of Christian people of their stewardship to God would give back to the church its power. We cannot fail to see the significance of the fact that in the days of the church's greatest power and spiritual life it was said of the believers, "Neither said any one of them that aught of the things he possessed was his own." There is certainly a most vital relation between our spiritual life and growth and the quality of our stewardship. As a rule poor stewards are very puny, sickly Christians. No wonder a lot of these poor stewards have to go to a milder climate for the winter, they are so delicate. I believe the philosophy is sound in the familiar lines:

"To give is to live, to deny is to die."
"He is dead whose hand is not opened wide
   To help the need of sister or brother;
He doubles the length of his life-long ride
   Who gives his fortunate place to another;
Not one, but a thousand lives are his
Who carries the world in his sympathies.
To deny is to die."

Moreover, a full acknowledgment on the part of our people of their stewardship would go far toward solving our problem of an adequate force of workers. I argue it this way, If Christian parents recognized that even their children are not their own, they certainly would not exercise quite as much liberty and authority in pointing out to their children what they shall do in life. And on the other hand if young Christians acknowledged their stewardship they would choose their life work only after long consultation with their Lord and Master. Oh for more Elis who will speak the right word to the young Samuels! Oh for ever increasing numbers of young men and women who, as they stand face to face with life, shall be willing to say, "Speak, Lord, for thy servant heareth!" Is it not indeed apparent that when once parents recognize that their children are not their own, and likewise when once our young people recognize that their lives are not their own, I say, is it not apparent that then many of the worldly considerations which are robbing Christ and the church of ministers and missionaries will have been robbed of their attractive power?

Yet again we have here the solution, I believe our only solution, to the financial problem. Where there is a general acknowledgment among God's people of their stewardship there can be no financial problem. Stewardship does to the financial problem what the sun does to snow—it puts it out of business. Most people like to spend their money; I like to keep mine. True stewards don't talk like that. I want my money while I live. After I am dead it will have a long time to do good. Nor do true stewards talk like that. True stewards don't go west or south where it is nice and warm for the winter leaving God and his cause to shiver around the North pole. True stewards never consent to ride in a Packard or a Cadillac and make God and his cause ride in a Ford or walk. No, no, that is not true stewardship. True stewardship recognizes its partnership with God

and it leads men and women to give until they feel it and they give cheerfully. When some Christians give to the Lord they kiss the money good-bye, and then they sing, "When we asunder part, it gives us inward pain." Whereas true stewardship deadens the nerve that runs to the pocketbook, and giving to the Lord becomes a painless, joyous operation. A true steward is never afraid he will give too much to the Lord; but rather he is afraid he might fall below the level of true faithfulness.

Back to the doctrine of Christian stewardship,—let this be our slogan! And let us fervently pray God to give the Brethren church a glorious baptism of the spirit that lies at the very heart of this great doctrine!

It has been well said, "Happy is the man who is thrice the master of his money,—in getting it, in saving it and in using it." Livingstone said, "I will place no value on anything I have except in relation to the Kingdom of Christ." That, beloved, is true stewardship talk. The prayer of some great soul was this, "Give me a hand to get and a heart to give." And that, beloved, is a true steward's prayer.

I close by giving you the following which appears on a tract on Christian Stewardship, put out by one of our Waterloo citizens:

DO YOU KNOW THAT

Christian Stewardship succeeds even when consecration seems to fail?

Christian Stewardship is true consecration in working clothes?

Christian Stewardship is "Cashing-up" on what has been consecrated?

Christian Stewardship is the only true test of actual consecration?

Christian Stewardship is in full accord with all scripture readings?

Christian Stewardship begins with giving a tithe of our increase to God?

Christian Stewardship goes beyond by additional free-will offering?

Christian Stewardship does not increase the burden of giving in any case?

Christian Stewardship brings back the joy experienced at conversion?

Christian Stewardship is recommended by everyone who has tested it?

Waterloo, Iowa.

SINS OF OMISSION

Matt. 25:45. "Inasmuch as ye did it not." Life's omissions must be taken into account; not merely what one does, but what one neglects or avoids doing reveals character. Nor is one always conscious of the opportunities missed. Perhaps we have not deliberately passed "by on the other side"—quite as often we step over, without seeing and without knowing, the duty that lies in our path. Our Lord has much to say about the sins of omission. The buried treasure that remained uninvested, the slighted invitation, the neglected beggar, the foolish virgins without oil, the guest without a wedding garment, the barren fig-tree—each of these tells the story of what was not done that ought to have been done. The only safe rule is to travel the second mile, when one mile only is the standard requirement. "What do ye more than others?" My soul, be on thy guard, lest it be said of thee, "Ye did it not!"—Selected.

So, at the last analysis, is is the ideal value that determines life. What we think of the world determines what we do in the world. We may fail or our success may be long deferred; but at last the ideal conception of the world and our relation to it enters into and determines all that we do.—Ozora Davis, in Modern Sermons.

THE BRETHREN PULPIT

Soul-winning---The Church's Supreme Business. By A. E. Thomas

TEXT: "As the Father hath sent me, so send I you."—JOHN 20:21.

These are the words of Jesus. In a nutshell we have the real, supreme mission of the church, the real object which we as preachers have before us.

Let me present two questions: First, What is the mission of the church? Second, How can this mission be realized?

First, "What is the mission of the church?" Jesus said, "As the Father hath sent me, so send I you." May we make answer to this question by first saying what the mission of the church is not. 1. The church is not a political institution. I do not mean to say that the church should not be foremost in the making for better governments. Everything that affects humanity she should be interested in. Her work is varied, and I haven't much use for a religion that does not affect conditions here and now. The church long since has been criticized because of her indifference to the conditions that are against the teaching of practical Christianity. So, while I believe this with all my heart, this is not the mission of the church. 2. It is not educational. Education is intended as a means to an end. As a part of the great object for which the church stands education is valuable. We are, perhaps, altogether too lax on this question. Today we see around us a great need for religious education, and it has its place in the work of the church. We, brethren, are to be promoters of knowledge and not to parade ignorance, which has always been a foe to the progress of truth. 3. It is not institutional. Some have the idea that the main object of the church is to feed the hungry, etc. I do not belittle this work. It must be done and done by the church in some measure I feel sure.

It is not primarily the mission of the church to edify the saints. The church, in the conception of many, is a sort of sheep pasture, a place where the saints must be fed. I again do not decry this, I have too much respect for those preachers who love to teach the Word to the saints. That is an important and necessary ministry. This is a duty of the pastor and he has discharged it in a commendable way. It is not because he has not fed the people that they are not interested but because they have had too much food. They think that they must be fed, and they become terrible peevish if they are not fed. Brother, if you think that your preacher ought to give you spiritual food all the time, just go home or go in your room alone with God, and ask him to help you digest and put into blood that which he has given you.

Now, what then is the supreme mission of the church? Listen to the text again, "As the Father hath sent me, so send I you." What is, then our mission, supreme, above all else? I answer, for what did Christ enter the world and leave it on a cross? Let him answer, "For the Son of man is come to seek and to save that which was lost." "For God sent not his Son into the world to condemn the world, but that the world through him might be saved."

The salvation of sinners, soul-winning is our supreme business, brethren. Jesus Christ came with one great object in view, the salvation of the lost. What object above all others have we, brethren, when we stand before our people? Salvation, that is our business. We are to become all things to all men that by all means we might save some. Everybody having their name on church records, this is the mission you have to perform—to save some. Are we doing it, brethren? There needs to be a more determined effort made if we are fully to realize our great and wonderful mission. There is no greater object on earth than this. The greatest business on earth is our business. Solomon said "He that winneth souls is wise."

Soul-winning, then, being the supreme business of the church makes it necessary that the preacher be first and foremost a soul-winner. I do not believe that the work of the pastor is separate from that of the evangelist or the teacher. Anyone working in spirit and in truth for the Master has the one great object in view. The pastor often feels the fire burning in his soul.

We have, I fear, brought evangelism into serious complication by trying to say that it is the work only of the evangelist. We have necessarily not given it the rightful place. It should be given the best, and the best possible preparation should be made for this important work; the ripest mind and the widest culture is needed in the work of soul-saving. The greater the intellectual equipment, the greater will be the success, providing the spiritual life is equally strong. However, the church must save men or be untrue to her mission. Brother pastor, ours is a noble task. A big undertaking, SAVE Men, that is IT.

Now as to method. We may not all have the same method. Jesus never was the same in the manner in which he preached. However every act of his life, whether at a wedding, a dinner, or a feast, his great purpose was "to save that which was lost."

The faithful pastor Sunday after Sunday working constantly amid discouragement is doing all he can to save men. The teacher in her Sunday school class works hard. If true, she does it to save her scholars. Different methods, but the same end in view. Paul said exactly how it was with him when he declared "I am willing to become all things to all men, that by all means I might save some." I take it these words mean that the methods he used were of little avail —to save was the great idea. To put his idea in modern language Paul would say, "To the outsider I became an outsider; to the scientific I became scientific; to the musical I became musical. I fear that too often we have become accustomed to certain methods, when any method will do, since to save some is the end in view. Go out after them. How far? As far as they have strayed. Brethren, let me ask you, what will we say in the last great day if we have sought to amuse and entertain those whose souls have been committed to our care?

Second, "How is the church to become a soul-winning institution, and so fulfill its mission? 1. We must realize that there is something to save men from. We very much need to show the importance of what we are saved from. There is surely a great need of preaching against the terribleness of sin. Sin is not preached upon as it once was. When we realize what sin is and the consequence of it, we will surely become soul winners. During the Great War we were talking about the deadly power of the German submarine; we were working overtime as a nation to find something to master it. SIN is worse than the submarine—worse than anything. I remember we contemplated taking a trip east about the time Infantile Paralysis was at its worst in New York City, and what precautions we took. But what are these things compared to sin?

Note that "sin lieth at the door," sin croucheth at the door is a later translation; sin waiting, ever ready to devour you. Sin separates from all that is best in life. Sin separates the husband from the wife, homes are blasted, mothers' hearts are broken, everywhere we see records of broken vows. What is it that causes this? SIN! Brethren, sin must be preached as the great enemy of man. I fear sin is not enough preached against. To many sin is not real, it is but a delusion of the mortal mind. But sin crucified the Son of God. It is not something to be trifled with.

Beloved, when we see the seriousness of sin we will then become great soul-winners. When we realize that sin will keep our loved ones out of heaven, when we see that it will mean separation from each other forever, then it is that we will be willing to save some.

These are days of separation. During the holocaust I saw partings that were heart-rending. Mothers said good-bye to their sons, children to their fathers. But sin will cause eternal separation. Think, mother, of that baby of yours lost because of sin this day. We are in sin. We can not say we have never sinned, for we have. SIN! SIN! Now the mission of the church is to show the world its true condition, that we are sinners and must be saved from such. That will keep us busy, no need of other things—plenty to do in this great task. What a mission is this!

1. We must realize that we have something to save men with, something that needs no human addition. We have the cure, and we are to show the world the disease and the cure, which is salvation through the blood. When I see a poor sinner, tears in his eyes, misery written in his face, I am glad that I can point him to the Lamb of God that taketh away the sin of the world." Jesus said, "If I be lifted up, will draw all men unto me." Lift Christ up, brother, and the world will find a remedy for its ills.

No doubt men see Christ with different eyes. He appears as he did to the two men on the way to Emmaus, in different forms. Yet I am here to say that we must all see him as our Savior or die in our sins. We must see the blood as the atonement for sin, or be forever lost. I care not in what form you preach him, only present him as Savior. We may all see the same object and not be impressed alike. To some Jesus is a great teacher. To others he is the friend of the down trodden. To still others he is the Savior of a broken fragment of humanity. The conception of Jesus may vary with the individual, but we must see him as OUR Savior. No man can be saved only by the great fact that Jesus died for our sins. Today we can say to a world torn and bleeding through sin, "For unto you is born in the city of David, a Savior." A SAVIOR! That is it—LOOK AND LIVE.

Warsaw, Indiana.

Do We Know Our Bibles. By T. Darley Allen

Rev. T. T. Shields, a well known minister of Toronto, was once present where a group of men were discussing the published memoirs of a noted detective. "He was a very religious man," said one. Another disputed the statement, saying, "not in his job with the things he'd have to do."

"Why not?" asked a lawyer. "The Bible says, 'Do evil that good may come.'" A warm discussion followed and the crowd grew. Mr. Shields who had been sitting silently while the others were speaking, then arose and asked the lawyer to finish the quotation from Scripture, for instead of meaning what it seemed to teach from its partial quotation —that is, that the Bible commended doing harm that good might result—the passage (Romans 3:8) explicitly says that the statement was slanderously reported to the Christians: "And not rather (as we be slanderously reported, and as some affirm that we say), Let us do evil that good may come, whose damnation is just."

The Bible is often misquoted not only by men who are not professing Christians but by church members of long standing and even by ministers and professors in theological seminaries. Some years ago the head of a great institution of learning, one of the best known divines in a great church, was corrected through the press for an error in scriptural quotation made upon the public platform during a famous debate.

For many centuries the Bible was almost a lost book, and the result was the dark ages. Martin Luther, when twenty years of age, found a copy of the Bible at the library at the university at which he was a student, and although he had been brought up in a Christian home, this was the first time he had seen the Book of God.

Today Bibles are in almost every home, yet to vast multitudes it is as much a sealed book as in the far-off past when printing had not brought the Book within the reach of all and made it the most common book everywhere, not only the "best seller" every year but constantly circulating in greater numbers than all the leading "best sellers" in fiction combined.

Of 150 freshmen entering a great college in a certain year, an examination of their knowledge of the Bible revealed that 79 knew nothing of the fall of Jericho, 37 had no knowledge of Cain's murder of his brother; 40 were ignorant of the history of Daniel, 102 knew nothing of Gideon and 107 nothing of Timothy.

In a recent issue of the Saturday Evening Post, George F. Parker says in his article on "Grover Cleveland's Career in Buffalo" that this distinguished man was fond of the home. "The Bible reading which he began early as a child," says Mr. Parker, "had grown into a habit wherever he was, and was kept up during the whole of his life. He followed the habits of boyhood days in reading it before going to bed. He never read it critically—that is, from the point of view of a doubter—but always with the utmost faith in the page before him. He had the perfect confidence of the Christian of the time and of his surroundings. He always insisted that the Bible itself was good enough for him."

Theodore Roosevelt and all our great men in political life have been deeply appreciative of the Book of books, and President Wilson has given testimony to his high regard for its divine teachings in some of his notable statements.

The man who is trying to make something of his life is doing himself an injustice if he fails to study the Bible, for from its pages he will absorb that which will enable him to think clearly and develop his intellectual powers.

But the greatest plea for Bible study is not that it is a great power from the intellectual point of view, but because we require its help in our spiritual development. The Christian cannot be strong spiritually who fails to read from it daily. Theodore L. Cuyler said: "A vital need of the hour is more Bible—more knowledge of the Book of books, and more study of the Word of words. If a sea captain is worthless who is ignorant of his charts, a Christian is ill-equipped who is ignorant of God's Word. It is the soul's 'corn.' The more thoroughly it is ground and baked and eaten and digested, the more you will grow thereby. It is the 'sword of the Spirit.' The more it is scoured the brighter it shineth; the more it is wielded the safer you are against the adversary. God's Book is every man's book."

He who searches the Scriptures, as every Christian is commanded to do, is the strong, spiritual believer. When we read of God's children who lived in the far-off past when Bibles were few, and think how little they cared for dangers in their eagerness to read or hear read the Words of life, going long distances often before they could find a copy of the then rare and expensive Book, how thankful we should be that it is now the most easily obtained of all books and that we have access at all times to the Words able to make us wise unto salvation.

Cleveland, Ohio.

We need not predict the future—we can determine it if we educate the whole of every child for the whole of life.

The children of today are the church of tomorrow. How much do we hold and train them for the church? The Church School.

Send
WHITE GIFT
OFFERINGS to

THE SUNDAY SCHOOL

ALBERT TRENT
General Secretary-Treasurer
Johnstown, Pennsylvania

The Monthly Worker's Council. By Prof. J. A. Garber

[The following program for the Worker's Council was worked out and presented by Brother Garber at the recent Ohio State Sunday School Convention and was subsequently published in "The Ohio Sunday School Worker." We are glad for the privilege of presenting this careful study to our readers with the hope that they will profit by the suggestions.—EDITOR]

This outline statement represents the speaker's analytical study of the subject and does not include his apt illustrations.

The assigned subject seems to have been thoughtfully worded. The words employed suggest certain points worthy of observation and emphasis.

Time. In some schools council meetings are held annually; others semi-annually; others quarterly; but in the well organized school councilors meet monthly for consultation and deliberation. To meet less frequently is to deprive the council of sufficient time. To meet more frequently is to incur the displeasure of the members who feel the burden of numerous meetings.

Personnel. All the workers are included, viz., the minister, educational director, superintendents, principals, teachers, secretaries, treasurers, leaders of music, librarians, ushers. Class presidents may attend on invitation. In the case of the large school with many officers the list may appear to be too inclusive. If one fears an unwieldy mass among so many, the apparent disadvantage will be offset with the opportunity to foster unified thinking among the larger group. With a wise general in charge the difficulty vanishes.

Council. The Council, therefore consists of selected workers who meet monthly to take counsel one with the other, which will issue in deliberate purpose and represent the collective judgment of the assembly. Jointly these regularly assembled councilors consider the "Stop, Look and Listen" signals which have come within the scope of their vision during the month. Unitedly they assume the role of specialists, diagnosing conditions prevailing in their charge and prescribing both correctve, preventative and promotive formulas.

Program. A carefully prepared program will give relish and reach, pull and push, direction and decision. Without some guiding agenda, to be closely followed as the order of the day, the meeting may degenerate into inane talking and fruitless discussion, the participants departing while floundering in the mire of discouragement or sinking in the slough of despond. Business should be reduced to a minimum through assignment to the several committees to whom will be given discretionary power to dispose of routine items, reporting to the council only matters of major importance. Certain points of school administration may be committed to the departmental conferences which follow the general session. In addition to a business provision should be made for a brief devotional period which will deepen religious purposes and the study of some timely topic which will strengthen educational ideals. Certain outstanding characteristics are:

1. Vital yet visioned (forward-looking).

2. Comprehensive and continuous.
3. Proportion and progress.
4. Variable yet seasonable.

Sample. Illustrative of these points, observe the following suggestive program for ten months of the year, omitting the vacation months. Note the monthly theme and sub-topics in each instance.

September—**R**ecovering and **R**ebuilding.
1. Rallying our Forces.
2. Working Policies and Standards.
October—**R**eligious Education of Childhood and Youth.
1. Their Religious Educational Needs.
2. The Ministry of the Home.
3. The Function and Aims of the Church School.
(Have one open meeting for parents, too).
November—Cultivating Worshipful Attitudes.
1. Worship; Its Meaning and Cultivation.
2. Thanksgiving and Thanksliving.
December—Developing Stewardship Ideals.
1. Giving of Self, Substance and Service.
2. How Christ May be Born Anew in Each of Us.
January—Measuring Ourselves and Our Work.
1. Good Tests for Officers and Teachers.
2. Our work Measured by Approved Standards.
February—Creating Missionary Enthusiasm.
1. The Church School and Missions.
2. How Create the Missionary Spirit.
March—Preparing for Evangelistic Ingathering.
1. A Study of Spiritual Awakening and Conversion.
2. Bringing Our Scholars to Christ.
April—Indoctrinating and Training Churchmen.
1. Needed Lessons in Christian Evidence.
2. The Work and Workers of the Church.
May—Evaluating Special Days and Programs.
1. Their Purpose and Educational Worth.
2. Children's Day, Fourth of July, Temperance Sunday.
June—Making Ready for Vacation Months.
1. Opportunities for Self and Professional Developments.
2. Providing Substitute Workers.

Advantages. Few of us can imagine all the advantages accruing from such a carefully prepared and faithfully observed program. Negatively, it will keep the school out of unseemly ruts, prevent working at cross-purposes and minimize individualism. Positively, it will add freshness, make the cherished ideal of leaders commomn property of the group and foster team work. It will promote unity and continuity, harmony and efficiency. It will free the school of a legion of pedagogical blunders and enable it to enter the promised land of achievement.

Ashland, Ohio.

J. A. Garber
PRESIDENT

Our Young People at Work

G. C. Carpenter
SECRETARY

Our Publicity Superintendent and Department

As suggested two weeks ago the addresses given in our conferences at Winona will appear periodically in these columns. The one given in this issue appears so timely we are giving it first place. It evoked such appreciation and con-

fidence among the delegates as to make them feel that we should use the advertising ability of Brother Huette in promoting our work.

Consequently he was chosen Publicity Superintendent

and will supply material for both the Evangelist and Angelus. Endeavorers reading both publications are asked to give careful consideration to his suggestions. His messages, particularly this one, should be preserved as property of the eecutive committee. The fruitful suggestions presented in the accompanying paper can be used throughout the year.

Special use may be made of them in launching our Bicentenary Program and in attaining our share of the goals set forth in The Fortieth Anniversary Crusade, both of which were given weel before last. The Master's business requires active attention and persistent promotion.

J. A. GARBER.

Keeping Christian Endeavor Prominent
By Earl Huette, National Publicity Superintendent

On the evening of February 2, 1881, in the parsonage of Dr. Francis E. Clark, then pastor of the Williston Congregational church, was originated the idea of Christian Endeavor. Dr. Clark called together, in a social meeting, the young people and their parents, for the purpose of finding a way to get his young people into definite and active Christian work. This movement was suggested and immediately sensing its great value, these people together with their pastor got busy and organized themselves into a society under the name of "Christain Endeavor."

Naturally, every young person in the church boosted for this new movement and soon it began to grow until today the Society of Christian Endeavor has over 4,000,000 members and about 80,000 societies. This tremendous growth can mean only one thing. That is "There has been a continuous campaign of advertising in behalf of this great work during its forty years of existence."

Certainly, there has never been a cause more worthy of the advertising which it receives, and I am sure that no "advertising manager" ever had a proposition to present to the public in which he could have more confidence than the fellow who boosts Christian Endeavor. We can have absolute confidence that if the policies of Christian Endeavor are carried out that the results obtained will be very favorable.

Confidence is the keynote of success in the career of any advertising man, and it is confidence in Christian Endeavor that will make us the best kind of Christian Endeavor boosters.

Study Christian Endeavor, Pray for Christian Endeavor, Work for Christian Endeavor, then it will be a successful Christian Endeavor.

Besides having confidence in a proposition, it is also very important to know the "Whys and Wherefores," so that they may be readily given when necessary.

In our discussion, I shall assume that all of us know the "Whys and Wherefores," but are just anxious to learn of new ways of doing the work. So, in order to give you the most I can in the short time which we have together, I shall condense every item as much as possible.

The first and one really important thing is, "Select one fact and then drive it home."

Let us tell the world that "C. E." means Christian Endeavor and that Christian Endeavor stands for Christian Training and Christian Service."

During my study of this topic, I found it logical to divide our prospects into two groups:—Christian and non-Christian. Also, to distinguish three places where we shall exert our efforts.

(1) In the local church.
(2) In denominational and inter-denominational work.
(3) In the community.

In dealing with those who are already Christians, we must arouse and keep an interest, then train them, and finally put them to work.

But in our work among non-Christians, we must first prove to them that the Bible is the Word of God, and that it is he whom we serve and whose name we magnify.

After we have brought this before them and they see that we do as well as say, then we can use the same kind of advertising as we do for the fellow who is already a Christian. However, we have yet to show them the wonderful satisfaction that comes to them who work for him and

prove to them the titanic power which belongs to him.

Now that we have the real foundation for our efforts in "Keeping Christian Endeavor Prominent," let us suggest "WAYS AND MEANS" for the first item in our study, viz., Keeping Christian Endeavor prominent in the local church.

1 Prayer is the secret of success in this work as well as in any other work of the church.

2. Enlist the support of the parents.

(a) Some member of the Lookout Committee shall make a personal call and explain the benefits which John or Mary would receive by being a Christian Endeavor member.

(b) Send them Christian Endeavor literature, choosing such literature as will give them direct information concerning the work of the C. E.

(c) Get their permission to hold a business meeting or a cabinet meeting in their home. This will awaken a desire to have their child belong to your society.

3. Enlist the Pastor, if he is not already doing his bit.

(a) Typewrite, if possible, all of your announcements which you may hand him.

(b) Prove to him, by the things that your society does, that the church could not, positively could not, get along without a Christian Endeavor society. How to do this is a sub-question:

1. At your next annual business meeting of the church, when the office of secretary is mentioned, produce an experienced secretary.

2. Appoint some member to handle and file all magazine or newspaper clippings, so that they will be in good shape to use in research work. Every member should be wide awake and keep his eyes open for good articles to hand in. Different members offer their service to him to help in his research work.

3. Offer to address envelopes, write letters, fold circulars, make calls or do errands as he shall direct.

4. See that the church lawn is kept in good condition.

5. Make the society so useful to him that he would be lost without his Endeavorers.

4. Chairman or some other member of Lookout Committee be at the door at every church service, inviting folks to attend your meetings.

5. Make every member of your Sunday school a booster for Christian Endeavor.

(a) Place a "booster" in every class.

(b) Make sure that every Christian Endeavor member is a member of Sunday school.

(c) Organize a class of substitute teachers who study the lesson together, once a week. Let them be prepared to take a class at a moment's notice.

(d) Unless there is already a Teacher Training class, organize one. If there is one already, do your level best to bring in recruits for it.

(e) Help in the campaign for Sunday school scholars. A larger Sunday school means greater chance to enlarge in C. E. work.

(f) Prayer meeting committee to arrange to take charge of the opening devotions once in a while. The Citizenship committee to be responsible for something different in connection with the regular temperance lesson.

(g) Establish the habit of "Decision Day" in your Sunday school for Christian Endeavor membership.

Some one has said, "When you have money, you have friends." I suggest that, "If you want friends, do something for them." Make a friend of your Sunday school superintendent.

6. Place short "squibs" in your church calendar.

7. Have a separate and distinct bulletin board.

Use of suggestive cartoons, poetry and other novelty is very good to impress upon the mind the importance of your meetings. Do not try to be funny; remember Christ was very prominent but never funny.

8. Variation in your programs.

(a) Get "52 varieties of C. E. meetings" from the publishers.

(b) Create a friendly rivalry between classes, suggesting largest class attendance and the best program, not entertainment.

9. Have good live socials, picnics and other wholesome and entertaining gatherings.

10. Pre-prayer service. This will give inspiration to the leader and all others who attend. The Holy Spirit will surely lead your meetings.

11. Locate a Mission Point. Appoint a Mission Superintendent from your Christian Endeavor society. Then help him in his work.

Second, keeping C. E. prominent in denominational and inter-denominational work.

1. Ask for a special place on the program at your conventions. (Thanks to our Convention Committee, we have that place.)

2. Boost county, state and national Christian Endeavor conventions.

3. C. E. Talks in church papers, giving facts not fancies, about Christian Endeavor.

4. Exchange of letters, helps, challenges, pictures of C. E. groups and any other live suggestions. Let several societies get into this.

5. Visit back and forth between societies. Some Sunday evening, just literally pick up your society and go to some other. Both societies will thus receive an inspiration and each society will have gained something from the other which is helpful in their own work.

6. Send out "couples" every Sunday evening to other societies. Let them report on the next Sunday. They will receive many good pointers which may be used in your own society successfully, also, they may be able to give to the other society something beneficial to their society.

7. Choose some one who will be responsible for bringing in news and helps that will be helpful in building up the society. Some outsider may have an idea that is good, but would hesitate to come into the meeting and express his opinion. Thus you will make a job for every Endeavorer and at the same time gain publicity by getting suggestions from the one who is not an Endeavorer.

8. If your church paper has something unusually good send a copy of it to several other societies.

As a denomination, let us keep awake to the possibilities which lie in having a good live Christian Endeavor society in every Brethren church, for therein lies the where-withall of the future church.

BOOST THE OTHER FELLOW AND HE WILL BOOST YOU.

(To be continued).

Dayton, Ohio.

SEND ALL MONEY FOR
General Home, Kentucky and
Foreign Missions to

MISSIONS

WILLIAM A. GEARHART
General Missionary Secretary
906 Conover Bldg., Dayton, O.

Another Letter From Africa

Carnot, via Brazzaville, French E. Africa.
June 22, 1920.

My dear little friends: It certainly is time for me to write you again. The weeks go by as rapidly here in Africa as they do with you, although more monotonously.

We are hoping that the worst of our sickness is over now, for we have had so much of illness since coming to Carnot. Aunt Toddy and Marie and Julia and I were all ill at once for nine days in June. Once in a while one of us would have normal temperature for a day and try to get up but the fever would simply come back again, and we would crawl in between our blankets with hot water bottles again. But there came a glad Sunday, the thirteenth of June, when we got up to stay up. Oh, how happy we were that day and have been in the nine days since that we have all been well!

Little houses are going up all over our place now. We are almost beginning to think of it as a station, for as it was all jungle when we came here it requires constant and heavy work to make it livable.

The place is triangular. On one side of it is the road, on the other side a race track, sometimes used by M. DuMont and M. Pinelli in exercising their horses. But it is so little used that daddy says it will soon be a good place to get grass for thatching. On the third side is a narrow path which separates the plot from the government post and the embryo park beside it.

In this little triangle, the largest house is the one put up some time ago for us by the government officials. Toward the point of of the triangle is a little grass house for our boys. Just in front and near the corner of the house are two small cookhouses. At the right, and near a much frequented path is the little house, occupied at different times of the day by different persons. Below this toward the government post, is a little house occupied by Uncle Antoine's boy, Basaba, and his wife. Basaba is the only married boy on the place. Between this and the study another house is going up for the workmen.

All around are the gardens. A pine-apple patch, the mango trees, etc., we trust will furnish fruit in the various seasons as long as we are here. Already we have had a few tomatoes, other vegetables, etc., from the gardens, and the rains promise much more, to follow during the season.

In order to do all this work, it is necessary to have boys and men, who work for small wages, under oversight of the missionary. So you see we are as busy here as a beehive, busy as any other mission station although we do not yet have the name of being one.

School goes on every day when we children are well. Aunt Toddy is the teacher.

The medical work is growing bigger ever since we came to this place. Mamma or Aunt Toddy have a dispensary every morning at eight o'clock. There is no open door yet for

the native school but there is a wide open door for the medical work. Aunt Toddy does the dressings and the dental work and mamma does the prescribing. At least mamma thinks that is the best way to divide our work at this place. Aunt Toddy has commenced the dental work by pulling a tooth for M. Pinelli for which he was so grateful that he made her a valuable present of carved ivory. When Aunt Mae comes up we will have another medical worker and when Miss Hillegas comes to teach how happy and busy we will all be! The officials won't let us have a native school yet but we are hoping that we may before long for we love the little black children and want to see them come to Jesus and learn to read the Bible.

Brother McClain's catechism is ready in three languages for them now French and Baya and Sango. The gospel of Mark is translated, the English-Baya vocabulary and about thirty Baya songs. Every day we are trying to do more for Jesus. Mamma says some day all hindrances will be removed, and we will be as free and happy as they are on any other mission station in all Africa.

We can't do so very much in the evenings yet for we burn a native resin for light which is very "flickery." Lately, we have made some little lamps and have commenced burning "sundu" (sesame) oil in them. Mamma thinks they are very much like the lamps which the virgins of the parable had.

Mamma says the apartments of the homes of our great grandfathers were no doubt elegant as compared to those of a pioneer missionary's temporary shack.

We cannot scrub, for our floors are already dirt. The best we can do is to throw water on them to keep the dust down, and partially cover them with native mats.

We cannot wash our windows, for they are just airspaces between the upright bamboo poles which form the walls of our house. We do sweep, but it is done not with a broom, but with the branch of a tree, or a bundle of twigs, or grass.

We cook over an open fire on the ground, and our kitchen is a thatched roof without walls.

We have a kitchen table, but it is a slab board placed across two stumps. We eat with knives and forks and use dishes yet, although so far removed from civilization. But our dishes are enamel or aluminum for Africa is so far removed from "China."

We have cocoa, but we prepare it ourselves from the bean, and it is not fine and valuable like yours.

We have potatoes, but they are sweet. Seldom in all these years have we tasted a good "Irish potato." One of papa's cousins wrote that he would trade his whole civilized dinner for some of our sweet potatoes. We would gladly make the trade, but perhaps he wouldn't want to do it more than once.

We have peanuts here but we are seldom allowed to eat them as mamma says they "cause congestion of the liver and predispose us to fever." We have chickens but we don't enjoy them very much, for their portable house is too tiny for nests and they come in the house to lay. Daddy is going to make a bigger chicken house, but until he can finish it, the "mamma" hen and all her half-grown chicks sleep in Aunt Toddy's tent. You see our life, although full of blessing is a little different from yours. But the chickens lay fresh eggs and the "bos-

sies" at the Hansa's give fresh milk, oh, so sweet! When our white sugar failed, we found we could buy brown at the "Compagnie Magazine" here, no dearer than at Brazzaville.

Sometimes we can buy rice and we children are, oh, so fond of it. So you may come and spend a day with us whenever you like, and I am sure when you go home you will have many things to tell your little playmates that mamma and I forget to mention.

We know you are praying that we may grow to be Jesus' true little missionaries here, and that we will honor and glorify our Father in heaven. We will soon meet our dear Lord Jesus in the air. In answer to your prayers, may there be with us, his messengers, many, many black boys and girls to be among his own precious jewels.

We all send our love to you all. I am glad to be

One of your little missionaries,
MARGUERITE EDNA GRIBBLE.

NEWS FROM THE FIELD

THE OLDEST BRETHREN MINISTER

A service of prayer and praise to cheer the heart of our aged Brother Stephen Hildebrand was recently held at the home of his daughter, Mrs. Lemon Philippi, of 412 Thomas Avenue, Johnstown, Pennsylvania, where Brother Hildebrand is making his home. Elder Hildebrand is perhaps the oldest living minister of the Brethren church. He was born in Jackson Township, Cambria county, 91 years ago. He has been a minister during the last 56 years, and an elder since 1883. He lived for many years in east Taylor township where he gave the church a long and faithful service.

Elder Hildebrand, though in the last decade of his century, is in full possession of his mental powers. He eats and sleeps well; enjoys visitors and can tell many interesting and amusing incidents from his long life. He is confined to his bed and has been for nine years, his right side being paralyzed. The most remarkable and outstanding feature about this aged veteran was the evidence that his faith is growing stronger with his years. He loves to talk on spiritual themes and is looking forward willingly to meet the future with a feeling of security in the faith he has in Jesus Christ.

At this service some old time hymns were sung. And having charge of the service, it fell to my lot to make a short talk, which was on the subject, "Life and the Fruits Thereof." To me, a young man, it was a great privilege and a blessing to be there, and to see this patriarch of the faith. It was an inspiration and mark and impression on my mind that I shall not soon forget. Another veteran minister was present at this recognition service; it was dear Brother Benjamin Goughnour, who is assistant pastor of the Somerset Street church and a protege of Brother Hildebrand. He recounted some interesting experiences of the early days and told of the great blessings of God on the life and work of our aged Elder Hildebrand.

It was good for his friends to be there and enjoy the inspiration of this veteran of the cross, and we believe he was inspired and cheered by our service. It was a good thing to show consideration for these aged ministers and give them recognition while they are yet among us.

A. O. DANNENBAUM.

MANTECA, CALIFORNIA

Sunday, September 19, 1920, was a day long to be remembered by the Brethren of Manteca. After the Sunday school hour in the morning, and all were again assembled in the main room, the regular preaching service was opened by singing several fine old hymns, such as "Pentecostal Power" and "Work, for the night is Coming." A number of prayers were offered by brethren in the audience and these were followed by one of the best sermons it has been our privilege to listen to in many months, and we have heard quite a few in that time.

The lesson was taken from the latter part of Acts two, beginning about the 37th verse; and also the 4th chapter of Ephesians, giving particular notice to the 110th verse. The blessed Holy Spirit was manifest in the speaker and in the hearts of the hearers.

There were about 60 people present, a very good number we think for having held services in the city less than 2 months. Considering also the long flight of stairs to climb. We are holding our meetings in the Odd Fellows' Hall, but we expect soon to have definite plans to start a church house of our own, the Lord willing.

Immediately after the sermon we all had the joy of extending the right hand of fellowship to Mr. Cecil Johnson and wife and Mr. Frank Larson, they having been baptized the evening before. On Wednesday evening next, Mrs. Frank Larson will receive baptism, also Mr. Rube Elliott and possibly 8 more adults and one girl.

Those who intended to stay for the after-

noon meeting brought box lunches, and so we all repaired to the dining hall for a season.

Following the lunch the meting was called to order by Brother Platt, and the organization of a Brethren church in Manteca was begun. Throughout the entire afternoon the Spirit led and as soon as the organization was completed, Brother Platt was unanimously called to serve us as pastor.

So we had cause to rejoice and praise God with baptisms the night before, the blessed association of dear Brethren all day, a much loved pastor with us, and more baptisms to take place during the coming week!

The day was far spent when we adjourned, yet a number returned for Christian Endeavor at seven o'clock. Brother Platt preached again at 7:45 from the 12th chapter of First Corinthians. So our day of joy and profit came to a close.

There were 19 charter members, but on account of sickness a number were unable to be present. We expect to have about double that number within a week or two.

MRS. SUSIE G. REYNER.

BETHLEHEM CHURCH
Near Harrisonburg, Virginia

Our work here is doing nicely and growing in interest. This is very encouraging to us, especially in view of the fact that we have no pastor at present. Elder E. B. Shaver has promised either to fill the pulpit or send some one to do so until we can secure a regular pastor.

Our Sunday school has reached the one hundred mark and over. Promotion day is near at hand, and there will be eighteen to promote from the various classes. Our Christian Endeavor of which Brother J. M. Bowman is president, meets every Sunday night, and the interest is good. The Junior Christian Endeavor meets at nine in the morning. This hour makes us country folks hurry to get there in time, over the rocks and hills, but we feel that it pays. We are teaching the young children to lead these meetings and it does us good to see the progress they are making. The Women's Missionary Society has its regular monthly meetings, which are well attended. We have twenty-five on our Sunday school cradle roll, and when any of the children have a birthday we send them a token of remembrance. Every member of our little congregation has the privilege of reading The Brethren Evangelist, which we appreciate very much. We give the credit for making this possible to Brother McInturff of Goshen, Indiana. He was here and held us a good meeting this summer. He worked hard when he was here and got the Evangelist in every home. No wonder he did not have time to write for the paper when he was here. He visited Virginia to take a vacation, but he worked for us while he was here.

We need the prayers of all God's children.
MRS. G. C. DOWELL, Correspondent.

COLLEGE NEWS

The College opened Tuesday, September 14, with a good enrollment. There are 17 out of a Freshman class of 41 who are graduates of last year's class of Ashland high school. This is encouraging, for it indicates a deepening interest on the part of the local young people in the College. The entering class, it will be noted, is very materially increased over former years.

These young people can only be kept and satisfied if we go forward with our building plan here. This is absolutely imperative. The total enrollment will be announced later.

Professor Wolford and Professor DeLozier have taken up their work and are making good records. I am confident that they will fit into the work here in a fine way. It is a matter of deep satisfaction to the president that all of the College teachers with but slight exception have done considerable graduate work. It is a pleasure to note that Professor R. B. Haun, of the department of Chemistry and Physics, took his M. A. at Vanderbilt this summer.

Convocation Sunday. This past Sunday, September 26, was Convocation day at Ashland College. The sermon was delivered by Dr. E. M. Cobb of the Dayton church. This was the first time we have tried the dignify the occasion by full academic costume and also by having an outside speaker. The occasion furnished opportunity for two things. First, it gave us an opportunity to look us over and get better acquainted with the College. In the second place, it gave opportunity to dignify religious services in connection with the school. Dr. Cobb's sermon was splendid and generally appreciated and approved.
EDWIN E. JACOBS.

TO THE CHURCHES OF OHIO

At a recent meeting of the official Board of the First Brethren church, Ashland, Ohio, the following official invitation was authorized and ordered published in the Brethren Evangelist:

The First Brethren church cordially invites the ministers and laymen representing the Brethren churches of Ohio to meet at Ashland for the Conference of 1920.

The College and Seminary heartily concur in this invitation. Parents of Ohio homes, and those of nearby districts, with children in school at Ashland may find this an especially opportune time to visit the College.

A large attendance for the coming conference is definitely desired and eagerly expected. "Ashland's welcome light is shining still."

For the church: J. A. Garber, Minister,
　　　　　　　　J. L. Hamilton, Secretary.
For the College and Seminary:
　　　　　　Edwin E. Jacobs, President,
　　　　　　J. Allen Miller, Dean.

CALENDAR OF THE FIRST BRETHREN CHURCH
Of Lanark, Illinois.

For isolated members, friends and all who worship with us.

September 26. End of six and beginning of seven years' pastorate.

Sermon subject: "A Resume of Six Years."
Fine men's chorus in the evening.

October 3. Promotion and Rally Day in Sunday school.

Harvest Home in the church service.

Every member canvass in the afternoon.

Communion services at Milledgeville in the evening.

October 6, 7, 8. District Conference at Lanark.

October 10. Home Coming of all members of the church.

Communion services at 7:30 P. M.

Following this date the pastor will conduct revivals in Burlington, Indiana, and Louisville, Ohio.

November 14. The pastor will return and begin a series of sermons on "The Parables of the Kingdom."
　　　B. T. BURNWORTH, Pastor.

Myrtle Mae Snyder
Brethren Missionary to Africa

Myrtle Mae Snyder, daughter of the late John William Snyder and Elizabeth (Finfrock) Snyder, was born on December 5th, 1882, in Shelby county, Ohio, and died of malarial fever, at her post, on her chosen field of labor, at Incongo Sankaru, Congo Belge, Equatorial Africa, on August 28th, 1920, aged 37 years, 8 months and 23 days.

She was the second of nine children, eight of whom remain to mourn her loss. She was left an orphan at a tender age. When about fifteen years of age, while with a relative in Indiana, she accepted Christ under the ministry of Elder E. M. Cobb, who happens to be her pastor at the time of her death. She was baptized by Elder Cobb in Eel river at North Manchester about 23 years ago, into the Church of the Brethren.

Later on, she changed her church relation to the Brethren church, and about 1905 she went to Philadelphia, and entered the International Training School for Nurses, graduating with honors in 1908. While in that city she was under the efficient pastorate of Elder L. S. Bauman, who, upon hearing the sad news of her death, writes her pastor: "The sad news of Sister Snyder's death has just reached me. My heart is sore indeed. To me, this loss is terrible. For a long time, I was her pastor in Philadelphia, and knowing her as I did, I realize that we have sustained a great loss to our work in Africa, but the Lord knoweth best."

Dr. J. Allen Miller, president of the Foreign Mission Board, of which Elder Bauman, and her pastor are also members, writes upon hearing of her passing on: "I am in receipt of your communication announcing the death of Miss Myrtle Snyder. I was deeply moved as were all the Brethren to whom I have transmitted the intelligence. This seems a great and irreparable loss, but we have long since learned that God's ways are not our ways. He does 'move in a mysterious way his wonders to perform.' Please communicate to the relatives of Sister Snyder, the deepest sympathy of all here at Ashland, and especially the members of the Foreign Missionary Board."

In a very beautiful letter to her sister's pastor, Mrs. Minnie Edith Green, of Lima, Ohio, says: "The last letter received from her was written in June, and received in August. In it she told, as usual, of her great love for her work and that she was beginning to see the fruits of her labors in her chosen field. How glad she was to be there at her post doing his will. How greatly the good Lord was blessing their efforts, and, oh, how she did urge the rest of us children to enlist our services in behalf of the unenlightened African. Her whole life was filled with kindly deeds. She always speaks so eloquently of her Savior's guidance."

Miss Snyder, according to the physicians of Dayton, was a very efficient nurse, and evidently had before her a very promising career, but in 1917, she bade adieu to all that was near and dear to her in the home land, and turned her face toward the darkest spot on the face of the earth—the Congo Basin. After a brief wait at Brazzaville, rather than suffer an extended delay, caused by the closed doors of the French Soudan, she chose rather to go to the Belgian Congo where she has ever since the day of her arrival been ministering to the physical, mental and spiritual needs of her dark-skinned brothers and sisters, whom she said over and over she loved.

Mae was a member of the Sisterhood of Mary and Martha here and the girls have received many, many letters from her since there on the field, and never once has she said she wanted to come home, but always asks for more to come and help in the great work. The Willing Workers' Bible Class, who has a silver star in the Mission Service flag for each of our missionaries and mission students, have now replaced her silver star with a gold one, since she has gone to receive her reward for her faithful and cheerful stewardship while in the body.

If we could but lift the curtains of distance and behold her fifty or more little colored boys, tenderly pulling tufts of grass, and laying them on a rudely made mound which holds all that's mortal of the only real mother they ever had, perhaps we could more easily make the sacrifice we are called upon to make. If her pastor could have the honor to chisel a single epitaph upon her stone, it would be her favorite scripture, II Corinthians 6:10.   E. M. COBB.

A MEMORIAL TO A SAINTED MOTHER

Mrs. Mary Carpenter was born in Germany, May 7, 1851 and came to America at two years of age, living most of her life near South Bend, Indiana. She was married, May 14, 1872, to Chauncey C. Carpenter, who preceded her in death in 1900. Six children were born, two dying early in life. Those living are George C., Peru, Indiana; Mrs. Edith Huston, Cincinnati, Ohio; Ira V. and A. Glenn, both of South Bend, Indiana. There remain also two brothers, many other relatives and a very large circle of friends, for to know her was to respect and love her.

Mrs. Carpenter with her husband became a member of the Fairview Brethren church early in the organization of that church and for the past three years has been a faithful member of the Brethren church at Ardmore, near South Bend.

After failing health for the past six months her death came quietly and peacefully in the early morning of September 8, 1920, at the age of 69 years, 4 months and 1 day.

Her love of her Savior and her faith in his wonderful salvation grew stronger and more and more steadfast as the days and years passed. The testimony of her children is that God never gave to children a more loving and faithful Christian mother.

"Mother! That precious name,
For evermore the same,

Earth's sweetest word!
Though ages past have flown
No sound has ever known
Like that dear name alone,
Or ever heard.

"From childhood's earliest day
She guarded all our way
With tenderest care.
She shared our every woe,
Each cherished hope did know,
Heard every whisper low
Of childish prayer.

"Our mother's God, to thee
In deep humility
We lift our prayer.
She loved us and served us
Through every trial and test,
And may she ever rest
Safe in thy care!"

The funeral service was held at the family home near South Bend, on September 10. A most appropriate and heartfelt message was delivered by Rev. G. W. Rench and our sainted mother was laid to rest, thought she still lives and shall live for evermore.
                         GEORGE C. CARPENTER.

The Annual Conference of the Brethren Churches of Ohio

Entertained by the First Brethren Church of Ashland, Worshipping in the College Chapel October 25-27, 1920

OCTOBER 25, MONDAY NIGHT—SPIRITUAL LIFE

7:30 Prayer and Praise, A. R. Staley
7:45 Ashland's Fraternal Greetings,
          The Conference Response
8:00 Appointment of Committees and Announcements
          Special Music.
8:10 Religion in the Home, G. L. Maus
8:35 The Church Culturing the Spiritual Life,
                              Prof. A. L. DeLozier

OCTOBER 26, TUESDAY MORNING

8:15 Prayer and Praise, S. E. Christiansen
8:30 Reports: The Brethren Home
          Ministerial Examining Board
          State Statistician
          Secretary and Treasurer of the Mission Board
9:30 Bible Study (College Chapel Hour), A. D. Gnagey, D.D.
10:05 Moderator's Address
10:40 The Bicentenary Movement, Dr. Charles A. Bame
11:10 Ohio's Participation and Realization, Dr. R. R. Teeter
11:40 General Discussion of the Movement

TUESDAY AFTERNOON—SUNDAY SCHOOL SESSION

1:30 Prayer and Praise, J. P. Horlacher
1:45 Present Emphases in Religious Education,
                              Prof. J. A. Garber
2:10 Our Sunday School Objectives, Prof. H. H. Wolford
2:25 Special Music
2:40 Possibilities of the Young People's Division,
                              Prof. B. R. Haun
3:05 The Sunday School Gleaning the Community,
                              A. L. Lynn
3:30-4:30 Simultaneous Sessions:
          Board Meetings
          Women's Missionary Society Meeting
          Song Service and Devotions
          Reports: President Mrs. E. F. Miller
          District Patroness of S. M. M., Mrs. G. L. Maus
          Secretary-Treasurer, Mrs. E. M. Riddle
          Presentation of Year's Work
          New Program, Miss Mae Smith

TUESDAY EVENING—MISSIONS AND EVANGELISM

7:30 Prayer and Praise, M. L. Sands
7:45 The Missionary Challenge of the Bicentenary Movement,
                              Dean J. Allen Miller, D. D.
8:15 Special Music
8:20 Advance Steps in Evangelism, Dr. Charles A. Bame

OCTOBER 27, WEDNESDAY MORNING

8:15 Prayer and Praise, S. M. Loose
8:30 Unfinished Business and Election of Officers
9:30 Bible Study (College Chapel Hour), George W. Kinzie
10:10 Business Continued
10:40 Mission Board President's Message, A. D. Gnagey, D.D.
11:10 Ohio Missionary Opportunities and How to Meet Them,
                              Sylvester Lowman
11:40 General Discussion of Missionary Opportunities

WEDNESDAY AFTERNOON—CHRISTIAN ENDEAVOR SESSION

1:15 Prayer and praise, M. B. Spacht
1:25 New or Unfinished Business
1:45 Principle Points in Our Bicentenary Program,
                              Fred C. Vanator
2:10 Christian Endeavor's Contribution to the Local Church,
                              E. M. Riddle
2:35 Special Music
2:40 Christian Endeavor Inspiring Missions, J. S. Cook
3:05 Marks of Endeavorers for Our Day, Dr. L. L. Garber
3:30-4:30 Simultaneous Sessions:
          Special Men's Meeting
          The Demand for a Masculine Christianity,
                              Martin Shively, D.D.
          Men and Missions, Wm. A. Gearhart
          Women's Missionary Society Meeting
          Song Service and Devotions
          Business, Election of Officers
          What Shall Ohio Do? Mrs. E. M. Riddle
          Problem Hour, Miss Mae Smith

WEDNESDAY EVENING—EDUCATION AND STEWARDSHIP

7:30 Prayer and Praise, B. F. Owen
7:45 Education and Kingdom Progress,
                              President E. E. Jacobs, Ph.D.
8:15 Special Music
8:20 The Call for Reapers, Dr. E. M. Cobb

Communion Notices

Communion services will be held in the Bethlehem Brethren church near Harrisonburg, Virginia, on Saturday night, October 2 at 7 P. M. All Christians are cordially invited. MRS. G. C. DOWELL, Correspondent.

The Garden City Brethren church near Roanoke, Virginia, will hold communion services on October 16, at 7:30 P. M. Brethren of like faith are invited to attend.

G. D. DONAHUE, Pastor.

The Lord willing, on Thursday evening, October 14, love feast services will be held at the First Brethren church, 12th and Pennsylvania Avenue, S. E., Washington, D. C., beginning at 7:30. The usual invitation is hereby cordially extended.

W. M. LYON, Pastor.

MINISTERIAL EXCHANGE

The Brethren church of Altoona, Pennsylvania, will be without a pastor after October 1st, and we will be glad to hear from any one who may be available and cares to consider the place. Kindly address

S. E. KING, Church Clerk,
Altoona, Pennsylvania.

Business Manager's Corner

REPORTING PROGRESS

Frequently when but little has been accomplished along a definite line a report of progress is all that can be made. In this case it is of the greatest importance that we are able to report progress, because that is the one thing we wish to be making at all times.

Two weeks ago we made our first appeal in this column for the help from the brotherhood that the Publishing Company must have, if the price of the Brethren Evangelist is not to be increased. At the time of this writing we have had but two responses to the appeal. Dr. E. J. Worst, Ashland, Ohio, was the first to mail us a check for ten dollars, and Brother H. J. Schrock, Goshen, Indiana, was the second to respond with a gift of five dollars. Brother Worst is a dyed-in-the-wool Brethren and to his mind no publications on earth can take the place of Brethren publications for Brethren people. And Brother Schrock wrote, "We will pay, first and then pray." We are glad to have the prayers of the whole brotherhood, but Brother Schrock has the right idea and he knows that prayers will not pay paper bills. With about fifteen dollars reported previous to our recent appeal we have received thirty dollars to apply on the "excess paper bill," but it will require ONE HUNDRED times this amount to make up the difference in the cost. Last week we paid one note of $1,000.00 on the paper bill and on October sixteenth we have another note for the same amount to meet and thirty days later another of the same amount and still thirty days after that we have a $2,000.00 note to meet finish paying for this one shipment of paper. It is impossible to secure that

amount of money through the regular channels of business and at the same time meet our weekly pay roll of nearly $300.00, so unless the interested Brethren come to our rescue before that time we shall practically be driven to the wall. But we are not anticipating such a contingency as we expect the friends of the work to come to our rescue. But what is done should be done quickly. Our churches and Sunday schools owe thousands of dollars to the Publishing Company which should be paid immediately as the Company never has been in a position to carry such accounts any length of time. We think we will have to do like a great many other business concerns do, charge six per cent interest on all accounts more than thirty days old. We have to pay interest on our delayed payments, so why should not those who owe us do likewise?

The Honor Roll

We are glad to be able to publish the Evangelist Honor Roll once again. This time it is the Brethren mission in Columbus that has won this distinction, and we congratulate Brother Christiansen on his perseverance that has resulted in success. We are also glad to be able to say that since our last report the churches at Loree, Indiana; Fremont, Ohio; and Rittman, Ohio have renewed their lists. This is the second year for Rittman and the third year for both Loree and Fremont. We congratulate them on their perseverance and faithful work.

Books and Tracts

For several years we have been calling the attention of the church to the fact that there is a great dearth of Brethren books and tracts. None have been written or published for several years. No funds have been forthcoming to finance such work. But at last a Book and Tract Fund has been established with a substantial gift from Kansas. Most of the members of the Nickerson, Kansas, Brethren church having died or moved away the remaining few, realizing the impracticability of trying to continue the organization, under the leadership of Elder Jacob W. Beer decided to sell their church property, and from the funds received from this sale $500.00 was sent to the Publishing Company to be used as a circulating book and tract fund, with the understanding that from the sale of tracts, etc., the fund be replaced as it is used and that additional funds be solicited so that in time it may grow into sufficient proportions to enable the Publishing House to do something really worth while. in putting out a Brethren literature. We are certainly thankful to Brother Beer and the few remaining Nickerson members of the church who have made this liberal initial gift.

But the thing we need most at this time is sufficient money to meet our paper bills as they fall due, and we are anxious to know whether the Brethren really mean business and are going to give the help that must be had to save the day. How many more will follow the example of Brethren Anderson, Worst, Schrock and others with liberal gifts for this worthy and needy cause?

R. R. TEETER,
Business Manager.

Volume XLII
Number 38

October 6
1920

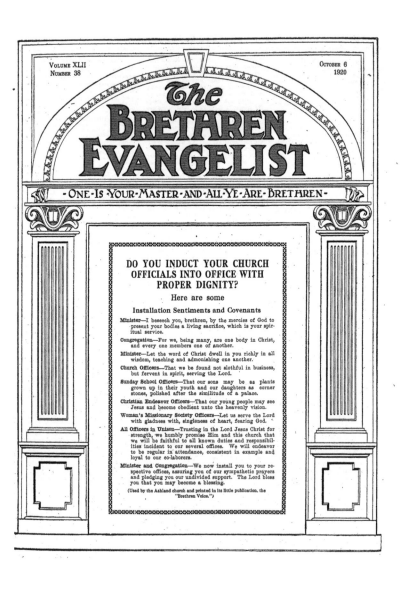

The BRETHREN EVANGELIST

-ONE·IS·YOUR·MASTER·AND·ALL·YE·ARE·BRETHREN-

DO YOU INDUCT YOUR CHURCH OFFICIALS INTO OFFICE WITH PROPER DIGNITY?

Here are some

Installation Sentiments and Covenants

Minister—I beseech you, brethren, by the mercies of God to present your bodies a living sacrifice, which is your spiritual service.

Congregation—For we, being many, are one body in Christ, and every one members one of another.

Minister—Let the word of Christ dwell in you richly in all wisdom, teaching and admonishing one another.

Church Officers—That we be found not slothful in business, but fervent in spirit, serving the Lord.

Sunday School Officers—That our sons may be as plants grown up in their youth and our daughters as corner stones, polished after the similitude of a palace.

Christian Endeavor Officers—That our young people may see Jesus and become obedient unto the heavenly vision.

Woman's Missionary Society Officers—Let us serve the Lord with gladness with, singleness of heart, fearing God.

All Officers in Unison—Trusting in the Lord Jesus Christ for strength, we humbly promise Him and this church that we will be faithful to all known duties and responsibilities incident to our several offices. We will endeavor to be regular in attendance, consistent in example and loyal to our co-laborers.

Minister and Congregation—We now install you to your respective offices, assuring you of our sympathetic prayers and pledging you our undivided support. The Lord bless you that you may become a blessing.

(Used by the Ashland church and printed in its little publication, the "Brethren Voice.")

Published every Wednesday at Ashland, Ohio. All matter for publication must reach the Editor not later than Friday noon of the preceding week.

George S. Baer, Editor

When ordering your paper changed give old as well as new address. Subscriptions discontinued at expiration. To avoid missing any numbers renew two weeks in advance.

R. R. Teeter, Business Manager

The Brethren Evangelist

ASSOCIATE EDITORS: J. Fremont Watson, Louis S. Bauman, A. B. Cover, Alva J. McClain, B. T. Burnworth.

OFFICIAL ORGAN OF THE BRETHREN CHURCH

Subscription price, $2.00 per year, payable in advance.
Entered at the Post Office at Ashland, Ohio, as second-class matter.
Acceptance for mailing at special rate of postage provided for in section 1103, Act of October 3, 1917, authorized September 9, 1918. Address all matter for publication to Geo. S. Baer, Editor of the Brethren Evangelist, and all business communications to R. R. Teeter, Business Manager, Brethren Publishing Company, Ashland, Ohio. Make all checks payable to the Brethren Publishing Company.

TABLE OF CONTENTS

EDITORIAL

The Great Labor Turn-Over---The Pastor's Responsibility

Last week we pointed out a weakness that sometimes is noticed among churches of the congregational type in regards to the manner of securing ministers. We pointed out the fact that greater care should be exercised that with greater wisdom and more unselfish consideration the churches might select their ministers. So long as we cling to our present method, or as some would term it, lack of method, of placing our preachers, it is inevitable that churches will at times correspond with men to ascertain if they may be open to a call. This, in itself, when it is done with proper consideration, is not to be descried. It was pointed out that the lack of consideration of the other church's rights, the opportuneness of a change and the wholesale method of the inquiries, as is the practice of some churches, are the source of much harm, and also that churches that look upon a change in pastors as a matter of such little moment and light consideration are in no small degree responsible for the regrettably short pastorates.

However there is another side to the consideration and while last week we dealt with certain phases of the church's responsibility and this week we wish to give consideration to the pastor's responsibility and point out some advantages of a long pastorate.

Whenever one congregation succeeds in taking another congregation's pastor at a time when a change can ill afford to be made, there is a pastor who must be held equally responsible with the church that made the advance. A pastor cannot be stolen away against his will, and when he receives a letter of inquiry from another pastorate, he is responsible for giving it consideration if he knows, or believes his work in his present field is not about completed. Sometimes one meets with a church that is so penurious with its pastor that the only way it can be brought to pay its pastor a living wage is to be faced with the situation of having its pastor about to leave for another pastorate that offers more justice along this line. However this is not the principal cause, nor is it often the excuse for the frequent labor turn-over in the ministry. By far the larger number of Christian ministers are more concerned about the good they may do than the salary they receive.

One great cause for the frequent changes, so far as the pastors themselves are concerned, is the spirit of discouragement that often overtakes them in the midst of the almost universal difficulty with which Christian work is done. It is doubtful if there is any field that offers worth-while opportunities, where the work of Kingdom building comes easy. But pastors sometimes, when they occupy isolated fields, or fail to fellowship occasionally with fellow-ministers, or measure success too much in terms of results that are "visible," become discouraged, think they are accomplishing little or nothing and look for more fruitful fields. When one's heart becomes discouraged his hands become weak and his efforts ineffective until he is inspired with new courage for his field or betakes himself to a new field.

Another thing that gives cause for frequent changes in pastorates is the failure on the part of the pastor to recognize adequately the needs and conditions of his field and to adapt himself to them. A pastor may have principles that are very dear to his heart, and may have worked out methods that seem ideally perfect for the accomplishment of certain ends, and yet what has seemed perfect in theory may need to be revised greatly in practice, and what has worked in one pastorate may not be at all suitable for another. The ability to adapt oneself and one's methods to one's field is a great accomplishment. Paul had learned the secret of successful pastoral work when he declared that he became "all things to all men that he might win some."

Sometimes pastors are induced to change fields before they have finished their work because certain pastorates seem to offer greater opportunities for distinguishing themselves, and with less difficult problems. It is a most natural ambition, that of desiring to distinguish oneself; and doubtless the ministry would not claim to be immune to it. Yet it cannot be denied that it is selfish; and however natural a thing may be, if it is selfish, if it is not Christ-inspired, it should not be encouraged. Nor should one yield to the impulse of running from difficult tasks. A task may be ever so hard, but if it is God's work for me, I cannot succeed so well, nor perform such worthy service, nor find such joy in labor anywhere else. Besides, if one would distinguish himself for Christ's sake, there is no way so full of promise as that of accepting any task, even the most difficult, to which the Holy Spirit may lead and being able to say with Paul, "I can do all things through Christ who strengtheneth me."

And there are some ministers who seem to owe their frequent changes of pastorates to a spirit of "wanderlust." They seem to have gotten the habit of staying only a short time at a place; they seem to enjoy the frequent changes. The new pastorate has a sort of a fascination for them. There are pastorates like that,—churches that have the habit of changing pastors every two or three years because they like the novelty connected with it. It is needless to say that neither such a church nor such a pastor ever accomplish anything very permanent or worth while.

There are many advantages that accrue to the pastor from long service in one field. First, there is the more thorough knowledge of the field that is made possible to him. For a pastor to know his field means more than to know the names and places of abode of all his members; it means so much more that the average pastor has scarcely gotten acquainted with his field until he is planning to go to another. Every pastor understands what an advantage it is to know his people (not merely their names), to know every non-Christian as well as every member of other churches in the community, to know all the school children, every business man, every organization of the community and to understand and be able to take an intelligent attitude toward every community interest and problem. It is a great privilege, that the man of a short pastorate does not know, that comes to him who remains long enough in a community to become identified with it and to be accepted as its leader. One of the most unfortunate things about the short pastorate is that at the time when the pastor is becoming able to render efficient service to the church and the community he is preparing to leave.

The pastor who remains on the field for a long service enjoys the confidence of the people as the man of short pastorate cannot. It takes a man who is genuine, one who has wearing qualities, to remain in the same field until all his ways have become familiar to all the people and he has gone in and out of all the homes, giving comfort in death, cementing the marriage bond and consecrating the children, and all the while become more honored and loved. But the man who thus remains until he is commonly accepted as the high priest of the community can render a service that others cannot. He who has thus won the confidence of the people can "reprove, rebuke and exhort," with a candor and an influence that is not possible to the new or short-time pastor.

The man who remains by his pastorate as though he were a "permanent fixture" can plan more wisely and build more permanently than the shifting pastor. Too often our plans are for immediate results and we work for immediate results. We give attention to those things that can be done quickly and with little preparation, and yet will make a "show." If we are going to be in a place for only a short time we are likely to plan to do something that will produce results while we are on the field. We must leave some visible signs of our having been there. Short pastorates ever tend to emphasize showy and temporary results. Far-reaching plans for the future of the church or the community receive very little attention; the results are too slow. And more than that, the man who has recently come to the community is not able to plan with statesmanlike view, nor to build with permanency, his vision and knowledge are too limited. Neither in nature nor in Christian work does God crown with oaklike strength and permanency a structure that springs up over night. And one of the greatest weaknesses of the short pastorate is the tendency to temporary, quick results. Let the ministers co-operate with the churches in an effort to extend the length of our pastorates for the sake of greater strength and permanency, and the greater glory to God and the greater gratitude of the future church will be our reward.

THE NEW EDITORIAL COMMITTEE

An "Editorial Committee" whom the editor might consult in regard to the policy and various problems that arise in connection with the management of The Evangelist is not a new thing. For years the editor has had the benefit of the counsel of such a committee. Nor is it a new thing for a committee of such men to co-operate with the editor in the writing of editorials, but for the last two years the editor has not had the benefit of such help. The work placed upon the editor's shoulders two years ago when he entered office has been recognized as too heavy, but until at the last Conference no relief seemed to be in sight. He not only edited the Evangelist and did his own correspondence in connection with the work, requiring fully a day each week, and without any office assistance whatever, a thing required of the editor of no other denominational paper so far as we have been able to learn, but also attempted to give a fourth of his time to assisting Editor A. D. Gnagey on the Sunday school literature. But that arrangement was the best that could be made at the time. Now additional help has been added to the Sunday School Editorial Staff so that the editor of The Evangelist is relieved in that line, and in addition he has been given an Editorial Committee whose members shall act as associate editors. This new staff is composed of five members, as representative of the thought of the church as it

was possible to make. Each associate is to write five editorials during the year for the Editorial page, and the editor will write the remainder. We enter upon our new arrangement with the month of October and next week the first editorial by a member of this staff will appear. The names of these associate editors are J. Freemont Watson, Louis S. Bauman, A. B. Cover, Alva J. McClain and B. T. Burnworth, and they will appear permanently at the top of page two. We believe there are possibilities of great improvement in this arrangement and we covet the continued co-operation of the brotherhood to the end that this shall be the best year in the history of our beloved paper.

EDITORIAL REVIEW

Brother Fogle is still on the "go" in the name of Christ and success is attending his evangelistic endeavors.

Prof. DeLozier who has charge of the department of Modern Languages in Ashland College, writes his final report of the work at Allentown, which he recently left to answer the call of Ashland College.

Brother Lyon reports a very successful meeting under the leadership of Brother Bauman, who recently gave a series of Bible lectures in the Washington, D. C., church, closing with an evangelistic service which resulted in a number of conversions.

Brother I. D. Bowman, who has done some evangelistic work in Kentucky at both Lost Creek and at Krypton, declares his conviction as to the great importance of educational work in the uplift of the backward peoples among the southern mountains. His investigations confirm convictions that a number of us have held for years.

Brother Bame's "Travel Flashes" appear again and our readers will rejoice to learn of his success as he goes about preaching the Gospel, in connection with his other work of directing the Bicentenary Movement. The reports of all our evangelists are read with deep interest by our entire Evangelist Family.

We wish to suggest to our readers that they give consideration to the public letter of Brother Melvin A. Stuckey, the Circulation Manager of the college paper, The Purple and Gold. Send in your subscriptions, singly or in clubs, the paper is abundantly worth your reading.

Allentown, Pennsylvania, reports its work over the signature of Brother E. E. Fehnel. The work was in splendid shape when Brother DeLozier left and the people are keeping together in fine style under Brother Fehnel's leadership. But this arrangement is only temporary. They are looking for a pastor.

The following communion notice was received too late for publication under the proper head on page 16, and so we give it space in this department:

The Homerville, Ohio, Brethren church will observe communion services on Sunday evening, October 17, at 7:30 P. M. All of like faith are cordially invited.   AUSTIN R. STALEY, Pastor.

The Business Manager is able to make a splendid report this week of gifts received to be applied on the paper bill. It is hoped they will continue to pour in from individuals and churches. If the churches generally will set aside a Publication Offering Day, as suggested, it will result in a much larger offering than would otherwise be possible.

Brother Frances Edwards, an experienced missionary, who some time ago cast his lot with our South American workers, affords us a rare treat by relating some of the experiences of a missionary trip in the Bible auto. With this sort of work made possible by our Bible auto, we imagine that the seed thus sown will demand the opening up of permanent mission stations in the next few years in larger numbers than we have in the past.

It is not often that Brother A. L. Lynn gets into print with a report of his work, but he is busy all the time, and we are pleased to get a word from him concerning the progress of his work at Zion Hill and Ankenytown. The Zion Hill church is a country congregation whose members have drifted mainly into two village centers where two congregations have been organized to take the place of the old country congregation. Brother Lynn reports that these two new churches are starting off with bright prospects.

THE BRETHREN BICENTENARY MOVEMENT PAGE

1723 - - - - - - 1923

Dr. Charles A. Bame, Editor

Stewardship.   By Miles J. Snyder, Stewardship Director

One of the great subjects included in The Brethren Bicentenary Movement is "Stewardship." This embraces two phases, namely, the stewardship of life and the stewardship of possessions. By way of emphasis let me quote the stewardship goals as they appear in the Bicentenary program:

1. Of Life

A standing, urgent life stewardship appeal before every church with a view of securing (a) at least one recruit for full time employed service, and (b) definitely enlisted voluntary workers. A call to service is a call to necessary preparation.

2. Of Possessions

1. An effective educational campaign on stewardship conducted throughout the year, with one-tenth as the minimum basis of giving; including (a) the observance of the last Sunday in October as Stewardship Day with appropriate sermons preached, and (b) timely articles in the Brethren Evangelist supplemented by the distribution of stewardship literature.

2. The budget system of finance with the every-member canvass in each operating church.

My object in calling attention to this particular part of our program just now is that suitable preparation may be made for the observance of Stewardship Day on the last Sunday of October. That date is not far away, and no pastor should permit it to get by without stressing the subject of stewardship in the most effective way. This cannot be done on the spur of the moment, but it should be wisely planned for and made the subject of much thought and prayer.

The attainment of the stewardship goal requires the making of a strong appeal for recruits for the ministry and missionary service, as well as for enlistment in various lines of religious work. There is a stewardship of life. We are not our own. Life is not a probation which ends in reward or punishment in another world; but it is power to be used. It embraces the stewardship of time, strength, opportunity and ability.

Furthermore, the attainment of this goal means an educational campaign on the stewardship of possessions. The last Sunday in October should be used to inaugurate and give impetus to such a campaign. The theme is one upon which every minister should be able to preach with conviction and power. Principles of Christian stewardship which, among others, should be emphasized are: 1. God is owner of all things. 2. Every man is a steward and must give account for all that is entrusted to him. 3. God's ownership and man's stewardship ought to be acknowledged. 4. This acknowledgment requires as part of its expression, the setting apart for the extension of the Kingdom of God such proportion of income as is recognized by the individual to be the will of God. 5. The separated portion ought to be administered wisely for the interests of the Kingdom of God, and the remainder recognized as not less a sacred trust.

One of the best ways of educating people along any line is through the distribution of good literature. Fortunately, there are now available a lot of splendid tracts and booklets on every phase of stewardship. Every pastor is urged to supplement his sermon on stewardship on the last Sunday in October by distributing appropriate literature. There are different ways by which funds must be secured to purchase

such literature, but no doubt in most cases the pastor himself will have to buy it. But it is an investment which will bring large returns and yield much interest through the coming years. There is little or no stewardship literature worth having which can be had for nothing. But The Layman Company, 143 N. Wabash Avenue, Chicago Illinois, will furnish to pastors who wish to educate their people in tithing a very good line of pamphlets in quantities at one-half the published price. Every pastor should get their package of eighteen or more pamphlets free.

In order that all interested may know where good stewardship literature may be secured, until better arrangements may be made by our own church to supply the same, I give the following names and addresses, together with a few of their publications and prices per hundred. Single copies are two and three cents. In most cases samples may be had free.

The Layman Company, 143 N. Wabash Ave., Chicago, Ill.
"How to Tithe and Why" $1.00 per hundred.
"What We Owe and How to Pay It," $1.00 per hundred.
"Proportionate Giving," $1.00 per hundred.
(These may be had at one-half price if name of denomination is given).

The Hubbard Press, Box 636, Auburn N. Y.
"Money the Acid Test," A text book, 60c paper.
"How Much Owest Thou?" $1.50 per hundred.

Interchurch World Movement, 4 West 18th St. New York.
"Scriptural Stewardship," $2.00 per hundred
"The New Emphasis," $2.00 per hundred.
"Thine Only Son," $1.50 per hundred.
"The New Christian," 25c in paper; 50c in cloth.
"Why I am Glad I am a Minister,"
What Constitutes a Missionary Call,"—Speer.
"How to Find Your Life Work."—White.
Stewardship of Family Life.—Poteat.
"How Pastors and Other Leaders Can Help Young People to Find their Life Work.—White.

Bible Institute Colportage Association, 826 N. LaSalle St., Chicago, Ill.
"What Mean These Constant Calls for Money?" 40c per hundred.
Milledgeville, Illinois.

HELPFUL THOUGHTS

Four things a Christian should especially labor after, viz.: To be humble and thankful, watchful and cheerful.—John Mason.

I'll bind myself to that which once being right, will not be less right, when I shrink from it.—Kingsley.

You are waiting to do some great thing; you are waiting to pull down some great evil. Perform the small things that are unseen, and they will bring other things for you to perform.—John Bright.

Whoever is satisfied with what he does has reached his culminating point—he will progress no more. Man's destiny is not to be dissatisfied, but forever unsatisfied.—F. W. Robertson.

The Mohammedan is an isolated man; he regards himself as superior to all other human beings; he looks down upon every people; he is therefore, unfit for service to any man, and especially for the governing of other people.

GENERAL ARTICLES

Brethren Ideals Which the World Needs Today. By S. B. Grisso

In this hurriedly written article I want to preface it by a few plain truths as they occur to me.

1. No organization has the right to exist which is not the messenger of some truth not advocated by another.

2. The Brethren church has certain "Ideals" and such "Ideals the World Needs Today."

3. She can not, and does not, perform her mission in the world if she fails to bring these ideals to the world.

The Brethren Church Is Idealistic

From the earliest existence she has been idealistic. In fact, it was this spirit that brought her where she now stands. She was born idealistic. It was this idealistic, visionary spirit that was fostered in the hearts of a few faithful men and women which made them realize that there was a mission to be performed that up to the time of her organization was not yet performed by those with similar doctrinal views. The Brethren church is not the Kingdom of God on earth, but she is a part of it. The "Field is the world," said the Master. The Brethren church has a part of this field to cultivate. If she fails, she must give an account before God in the last day.

In missionary zeal she is becoming more and more idealistic. She is distinctly missionary in spirit. She realizes more and more that no church can be a part of the Kingdom of God that is not missionary in spirit. The great commission confronts every organization at her very beginning. "Go ye therefore and make disciples of all nations," is the imperative command that is laid at the threshold of every religious organization. Mt. Olivet's echo is still heard and must continue to be heard until every land has heard the message of the risen Christ. It remains yet to be fully demonstrated what God can do when he finds a people who are willing to work with him in the accomplishment of his ends —the salvation of the world to the uttermost. That the Brethren church is not pushing her share of the work as fast as she can is evident. Not so much that there are not workers who are willing to go, but for the lack of more adequate support. There are at least two columns in the Brethren Evangelist that are especially interesting to me, and those are Ashland College and the Missionary news. God in no instance has ever laid a burden on his people too heavy for them to bear, nor has he ever failed to provide the means wherewith to carry it out.

Never in the world's history has there been a more opportune time to enter the field and possess the land. Never was there a time when the world needed Christ more than now; and never was there a time when the world was more willing to receive the gospel than now.

The Brethren church is idealistic in an educational line. Here, I must say, she has not as yet grasped her whole vision as she should. However, the church is realizing more and more the necessity of educational training in all the various realms of life. We are living in an age entirely different from that of our forefathers. The young man or woman without an education finds himself or herself handicapped at every turn of the road. The time was when a man with a common school education could be a competent merchant or school teacher, or minister. This was due simply because the average man or woman had not yet possessed the higher vision of the world's possibilities. But that day is past. The engineer who can tunnel the Allegheny Mountains, cross the Rockies and can tell the cost, is the man that is in demand. Likewise the man who can take a piece of steel in his hand and tell whether it is fit for a machine or not is the man who finds ready employment. It is the man that knows, that the world wants. The time was when if a man could turn a good smooth furrow he was a good farmer, but not so now, the man who can analyze his soil and tell what it is best adapted for is the successful farmer. Booker T. Washington once said, "The colored graduates of Tuskegee have raised 250 bushels of sweet potatoes on an acre of ground in the same location where an uneducated colored man raised less than fifty. Bishop Vincent, a man of authority and wide experience, said "If my son were to be a blacksmith I would want him to have a college education." Dr. Orson Warden, editor of Success Magazine, said, "Will an education pay? We might as well ask, Will it pay a rose bud to unfold its petals and fling out its fragrance and beauty to gladden the world." The highest services one can render to his God, to himself, and to his fellowman is to make the most out of the talents God has given him; to develop them not narrowly, not in a one-sided way, but systematically as a trust from God. It is one's first duty, not to make money, but to make the best possible man out of himself, as God gives him grace to do.

I think it next to a crime, if not a crime, for parents in this day to send their children away from home to do for themselves without an education, if it is at all possible to give it, them, for uneducated, their children will find themselves handicapped in every undertaking in life. An education is the richest heritage one may possess. Bank accounts may go into an embezzler's pocket, buildings into smoke, but an education remains as a resource to draw upon when everything else fails.

A Whole Gospel to a Whole World

This was the challenge our Savior threw down, when standing on Mt. Olivet, and with outstretched hands blessed his disciples. How his heart must have yearned for them at this critical moment,—blessing them, he said, "All authority is given to me both in heaven and earth. Go ye therefore and make disciples of all the nations" and then, as a safeguard to their future reward, added, "Teaching them to observe all things whatsoever I have commanded you." Less than this the Brethren church dare not teach. Have we this vision? Are we idealistic in this matter? The world needs it now. Shall it be given?

Hannibal, Missouri.

The Church Securing Its Future. By Ray A. Emmert

The events of the next generation are largely shaped by the education of the children of today. As a nation or a church educates its children, so shall it reap.

In 1885, the State of Iowa passed a law requiring all teachers in the public schools "to give and all scholars to receive instruction in physiology and hygiene, which study in every division of the subject shall include the effects upon the human system of alcoholic stimulants, narcotics and poisonous substances."

It has taken just a generation for education under this law and similar laws of other states to secure national prohibition.

Bismarck by carrying out a policy of "blood and iron" united the smaller provinces of Germany into a strong nation. This policy of "blood and iron" was taught in the schools and universities of Germany. In 1914 Germany started out to conquer Europe.

Practically the only way to secure the welfare of our country is to properly educate and train the children of the present.

Not so very long ago scientists began to find new truths and to disapprove things that had long been accepted as true. Scholars developed an openness of mind and an attitude of doubting. This spirit of investigation and questioning was carried into many theological schools and into many of our church schools. The same spirit has been carried into many pulpits. The congregations have adopted the attitude of questioning religious matters but have failed to apply themselves sufficiently to secure answers to the many questions which arise in their minds. Often they doubt like Thomas, but unlike him, fail to get in reassuring touch with the Master.

Note the result of this kind of teaching and preaching as reflected in empty church pews that should be occupied by the present generation. Let us analyze for a moment the present situation in regards to the religious education of the children of your community:

1st. Are there many children attending your Sunday school whose parents are not associated with the church?

2d. How many of the pupils in your Sunday school could pass a written examination upon the Bible, if such an examination were as thorough as their public school examinations?

3d. How many of the pupils in your Sunday school are more ignorant of the Bible than of Shakespeare's works?

4th. How many of the school children are not attending Sunday school?

If your community is like the average community, your answers to the above questions will compel you to act; especially is this true when one realizes the great importance of present religious training to the period beginning thirty years from now.

If the church is to make its future secure, it must see that every child's education shall include a thorough religious education. If this be a Christian nation or if we believe that every child's education should include a religious education, why not have a definite program along that line for the United States? For example, would it not be desirable to have the Bible studied in connection with our public schools?

Of course, I know there are many who will object to this, but let me remind you that in the United States not so very long ago, there were many who objected to having free public schools supported by taxation, that there was bitter opposition to equal suffrage and to prohibition; and I call your attention to the fact that the existence of opposition to teaching the Bible in the public schools is not an argument against the desirability of doing so.

It is reported that in New York they are dismissing school for a fraction of a day each week and requiring that the children attend during that time some religious school, selected by the child or his parents. I regard this as a step in the right direction.

The Sunday schools are making and have made great progress in giving the children a religious education and the results of their work will grow and be more and more apparent as generation after generation is trained. It is the thousands of children who are not regular attendants at Sunday school who constitute a menace to the security of the future of the church.

The direction we must go to make secure for the church her future, is toward universal religious education of the children. The road we must travel is not mapped out, but the necessity for making the effort is commanding.

Des Moines, Iowa.

The Influence of Good Cheer On Christian Work.   By Ner Guy Stoner

Every one hates a grouch. A grouch is a person who is never satisfied with anything, no matter how good the movement might be, or how much good could be derived from it. His main satisfaction in living is to be contrary to every one that he is in contact with. His whole influence and his whole life must be a negative impulse to any good that is brought before him.

The opposite of such a person just described is a person whose living is characterized by good cheer—one whose pleasant countenance is always a reflection for good. I am beginning to realize each day that the greatest asset to a Christian life is good cheer.

We are living in an age when the business world demands men of the good cheer type to carry on its business; especially must salesmen be men who are cheerful. It is necessary that the men who are to go before the public and meet all kinds of people successfully shall possess a cheerful spirit. If this type of men are the ones who carry on the business of today, why should not such a spirit be required in the church? Surely the business of the church is just as important, if not more so than any other business in the world. The one class of people whom we so often neglect are the foreigners. If we would only give these people a bit of good cheer their education would certainly be aided instead of hindered. We too often give them a "short answer" rather than give them a word of cheer. By so doing we create a hatred in their hearts and surely if this cannot be neutralized in some way we can not expect to fulfil the great Commission.

There is another element in our great nation which we too often neglect, frown down and speak roughly to rather than give a little of good cheer. That element is the negro. We call the negro a problem. He is so primarily because we have been unkind to him, have ever discouraged and never appreciated him. In the most common matters it will pay us to treat them with consideration, that we may cheer them in their struggle. The following homely incident impressed this fact upon my mind, especially with reference to the more ignorant type. During the war it was my privilege to spend my army career in one of our Southern states. On one Sunday morning several other boys and myself were taken home from church to be entertained by a family for dinner. They employed a negro "mammy" whose duty it was to cook and wait on the tables. For our last course we had pie and after each one was served by the hostess a few pieces remained on the plate. The hostess insisted strongly that we eat all of it, as the old "mammy" would think the pie not good as we had not eaten all of it and would feel badly about it. This, of course, seemed somewhat strange to us boys and we made way with the pie. Then in a rather incidental way our hostess remarked that if we as a people want to Christianize the negroes, especially the lower classes, we must constantly show them that we appreciate all that they do, as that is the surest method of gaining their confidence and subsequently winning them.

The people on the outside of the church are constantly looking for mistakes whereby they can have some grounds to excuse themselves for not being Christians and joining the church. If they see by our actions that we are not giving encouragement and showing good cheer through all our walks in the Christian life, how can we expect them to see what a pleasant thing it is to serve Christ and be a member of his church?

The sick room is another place where good cheer will play a great part in Christianity. Good cheer will have more effect on a sick person than medicine in some cases. I am beginning to realize more and more each day that psychology plays a great role in the healing of the sick. If such is the case why can't we show good cheer to sick people, especially to the non-church people? On the other hand a Christian person who is sick can have a wonderful part in Christianizing others by always showing good cheer. Surely non-Christians would notice this and the influence from it could hardly help but be for good.

Let us as a Christian people strive to constantly show good cheer to every one that we meet. No matter how small it might seem, the influence may be more far-reaching, than we think. Let us all set high ideals and standards of living so that by so doing we may be cheerful. Such a life might be instrumental in molding another "Billy" Sunday or Dwight L. Moody.

Louisville, Ohio.

Unremedial Mistakes. By C. E. Nicholas

Esau and Jacob are two most conspicuous characters in Bible history, widely different in their character. Esau, a hunter, belonged to the open air and was a lover of wild sports, while Jacob, a shepherd living at home, cared only for quiet pursuits and was a schemer and sharp dealer—a real Jew.

Esau had no sense of spiritual things, yet was nobler in character than Jacob, more generous and more forgetful of self. But with all the cunning, the scheming and craftiness of Jacob, he possessed the divine aspirations that Esau lacked and by a long stern discipline God educated him for himself. The one was a man of cruel fate, the other of destiny. The one had a pathetic, tender love for his old blind father, the other was submissive to the wishes of his mother. Esau came to the end of life as he began, while Jacob, developed by God's chastening, became the Prince of God.

In Esau's character we find ourselves. He was not a repulsive character but a lovable man, naturally free and unreserved and his life was open alike to friend and foe.

From the beginning he suffered because of hereditary influences; he was "sinned against from birth." Thus many a soul begins life under adverse circumstances. Many a father and mother shape the career of their child for ill from the beginning.

The evil influences of home enter into the "makeup" of many a boy and contribute to the direction of his life in ways that cause regret and failure. There are many who are taught by precept and example, like Esau, from infancy to hold lightly things sacred in life.

With no hallowed influences of home, with no guardian angel, no mother love, with no heavenly music from within the home, it is not strange that Esau's life was open to evil influences and his baser passions. Neither is it strange that your boy or mine should desecrate the sacred things of life under such circumstances.

Not unlike many today, Esau was concerned only with the present and the good things of life, and in a moment of physical exhaustion he sold his birthright for a mess of pottage. This rash act cost him the right to the priesthood, the promise of the inheritance of the Holy Land and the promise that of his blood the Christ should be born. In a moment of weakness and folly, we part with the honor and truth with which God crowns every life, for a "mess of porridge," and like Esau we seek the lost birthright and the blessing "with tears." In one rash moment we open the avenues of our life to the consequences of sin. While the mistakes were not such that cost Esau heaven, yet the issues growing out of them were such as could never be changed. Thus with one heedless act of our lives we bring unalterable and lamentable results. A man squanders his fortune, afterward grieves over his recklessness and wishes he had been more careful, but he cannot retrieve his loss "even with tears." A man by dissipation loses his health and when lying on his bed of pain wonders why he disobeyed the simple laws of nature and longs for recovery. But it comes not.

It is far easier to harden your heart than soften it. A man may be sorry over his sin yet finds it very hard, and in many instances impossible to repent of his sins, "even with tears." We may repent of our sins but we cannot hope that every effect of the sin shall be erased. A cut in the hand may heal but the scar always remains. I believe God intends us to feel the full force of our sins even when his great mercy frees us, God forgives but the consequences are beyond our recall. We cannot erase bitter memories and blot out the effect of bad habits. "Whatsoever a man soweth that shall he reap." Souls are selling their birthrights and even bartering their interest in heaven for the follies of the world.

There is such a thing as repenting too late. Repentance brought neither the birthright nor the blessing back to Esau. They were lost and lost forever.

We may repent of our sins but the issues growing out of our mistakes are unremedial,—a thing done is done forever. Esau's cry was intensely bitter but the results remained unchanged. "He found no place for repentance though he sought it carefully with tears."

How many parents are neglecting the proper home instruction of their children concerning life's habits, to say nothing of their neglect of their spiritual welfare. How many are uninterested in the society of their boys and girls and are concerned only that they be troubled as little as possible with them! How many parents give little or no attention to the reading matter their boys and girls become interested in. They do not supply them with good literature nor guard them from the unwholesome kind, with which they are often being unconsciously moulded for life.

Parents are thoughtful enough about the temporal and immediate needs of their children, but sadly neglect the soultraining. An unremedial mistake which brings so much sorrow to the parents as well as the children in after years.

How often we have heard a father say, "Let the boy sow his wild oats." Never was there a more fatal mistake and more ruinous in its results.

Many a son and daughter's life have been filled with bitter memories and pangs of regret because they "sowed wild oats." Like David of old they implore their God, "Remember not against me the sins of my youth."

The arrow striking deepest in the human heart now and hereafter is and will be "lost opportunities"—What I might have been—what I might have done.

Dowagiac, Michigan.

The momentary circumstance was too strong for him: he failed to look beyond the shadowy scope of time, and, living once for all in eternity, to find the perfect future in the present.—Hawthorne.

WHAT AMERICA MEANT TO ONE FOREIGNER

The following illuminating dialogue took place between a student and a Polish native a few years ago in a village in Poland where many of the workmen had been in America:

"How do you like America?"

"I hate your country."

"Hate it? And why?"

"All they want of us in America is our muscle. I hate it."

"Ours is a great country. We have the finest school system in the world."

"That may be. I was never in one of your schools."

"My country, too, is a land of religion, of churches."

"I was never in a church in America."

"Why not?"

"No one asked me to go. I was there six years."

"Well, what do you think of American homes?"

"I was never in an American home. I slept in a bunkhouse, ate at an eating house, and worked all the time. I went to America a strong man; I came back broken in health. All your country wants of us is our muscle. I hate it."—"Expositor."

THE BRETHREN PULPIT

The Ministry of Healing. By H. M. Harley

TEXT: "Is there any sick among you? Let them call for the elders of the church; and let them pray over them, anointing them with oil in the Name of the Lord; and the prayer of faith shall save the sick; and the Lord shall raise them up; and if they have committed sins, they shall be forgiven them."—JAMES 5:14 AND 15.

The people of Pittsburgh and vicinity were greatly stirred a week or two ago, over the coming into our midst of a reputed healer, who hailed from England, and who taught and practised the art of healing by the laying on of hands and prayer, as set forth in the Bible. And why the Christian people of our city should be so stirred up over this man's coming and teaching, is a wonder to the writer,—for he taught no new thing, neither anything that has ever been at least entirely lost sight of by God's people.

There can be no doubt of the fact, but that the Holy Scriptures represent God as one who heals, and Jesus Christ as the Physician of both the body and the soul. And this power to heal did not stop with Christ, or even with the apostles, but was given to the church as well. And at least a part of the Christian church has always believed in the ordinance of healing by the laying on of hands.

The Brethren church, at the time of her organization as a denomination, adopted as one of the specific tenets of her "Whole Gospel" platform this doctrine of anointing with oil and the laying on of hands,—not as a mere preparation for death as some think, but for physical healing as well as for spiritual cleansing, as is implied in the statement of James at the beginning of this sermon. And what is more, every true Brethren minister has both preached and practiced this doctrine with wonderful results. The writer himself has seen many a person who has been given up by physicians, miraculously restored to full health and strength. And this was not only in cases of mental or nervous diseases, but as well in organic troubles and muscular affections. He will go further and say, that he believes that in every case where the conditions were complied with, as they are implied in the promise,—healing was forthcoming.

But note this. No Brethren ministers considers himself as "A Healer." This blessed ordinance is not of itself a means of healing. It is merely a symbol of the anointing of the Holy Spirit who does the healing. Jesus himself professed to heal "by the spirit of God" (Matt. 12:28). And the disciples after him prayed, "Grant unto thy servants to speak thy word with all boldness, while thou stretchest forth thy hand to heal" (Acts 4:30). James says that "the prayer of faith shall save (heal is the proper word here, according to the original), the sick." The Gospel minister who

performs the anointing is not the healer, but merely the instrument in the hands of him who said, according to Exodus 15:26, "I am the Lord who healeth thee." To him do we give all the honor and the praise for all he does for us, or through us for the help and blessing of others.

Now just a practical word concerning this doctrine of anointing for healing. We are told that the words "health," "whole," and "holy" all come from the same Greek word, and all refer both to the physical and to the spiritual. Even as sin and sickness are synonomous, so are holy and health, or wholeness. We know that God is interested in our well-being whether of spirit, soul or body. And we have more instances on record at least, where Christ healed physical disease than where he forgave sin. And surely, there can be no doubt in any sane mind but that God can heal us if he so desires. The Word tells us time and again that he both can and desires to heal as well as to forgive, so that we may be "whole,"—fit creatures of him. And we know further that he does it when he is called upon in faith, and where he is given the chance to work his power. And this does not necessarily preclude the use of remedies for restoration. The Scriptures nowhere condemn the use of such. The only passage usually so quoted is 2 Chronicles 16:12, "In his disease, he sought not the Lord, but the physicians," Asa's fault was not in seeking the physicians, but in NOT seeking the Lord. And that's the fault of a large part of Christendom today. They trust only to man's ingenuity and wisdom, and they fail. And when they wonder why God was so cruel as to permit them to suffer, or to take from them their loved ones, when the Lord wasn't consulted, or even given a chance.

While the other churches have to a very great extent discarded the divinely given symbol of healing, the anointing of the sick with oil—the Brethren church, and possibly one or two other peoples, have perpetuated it, and are today practicing it most effectually in behalf of those who desire to avail themselves of the same. Why not use it more, and thus prolong life, as well as increase our efficiency as workers with him for the common good. Any Brethren minister is ready at any time to answer the call, and administer this ordinance to all who may desire it, if such are willing to meet God's conditions.—The Brethren Bulletin, Pittsburgh, Pennsylvania.

OUR DEVOTIONAL

Living Sincerely. By Joseph Gingrich

OUR SCRIPTURE

Ye hypocrites, well did Esaias prophesy of you saying, This people draw nigh unto me with their mouth, and honoreth me with their lips, but their heart is far from me. But in vain they do worship me, teaching for doctrines the commandments of men (Matt. 15:7-9). But all their works they do to be seen of men: they make broad their phylacteries, and enlarge the borders of their garments, and love the uppermost rooms at feasts, and the chief seats in the synagogues, And greetings in the markets, and to be called of men, Rabbi, Rabbi. But be not ye called Rabbi: for one is your Master, even Christ; and all ye are brethren (Matt.

23:5-10). Therefore when thou doest thine alms, do not sound a trumpet before thee, as the hypocrites do in the synagogues and in the streets, that they may have glory of men. Verily I say unto you, They have their reward. But when thou doest alms, let not thy right hand know what thy left hand doeth: that thine alms may be in secret: and thy Father which seeth in secret shall reward thee openly. And when thou prayest thou shalt not be as the hypocrites are: for they love to pray standing in the synagogues and in the corners of the streets, that they may be seen of men. Verily they have their reward. But thou, when thou prayest, enter into thy closet, and when thou hast shut thy door, pray to thy Father which is in secret; and thy Father which seeth in secret shall reward thee openly (Matt. 6:2-6).

OUR MEDITATION

These are a few noted passages from only one writer bearing on this subject. If we care to read the other three Gospels, we will find them replete with the same or similar passages.

Sincerity denotes truth and uprightness, an agreement of the heart with the tongue. Sincerity is opposed to double-mindedness. Deceit and insincerity denotes a condition where the sentiments of the heart are contrary to the lips. No one cares to associate intimately and confidentially with a person who is not sincere and misrepresents things. No one is more detested and abhorred than a hypocrite and it is no wonder that Jesus, being what he was, was compelled frequently to frown upon and often rebuke the Pharisees who were often hypocritical in their lives.

The word sincere is derived from two Latin words, sine—without and cera—wax; hence without wax; originally it meant pure honey without wax. Anything without wax is pure and genuine. When a person buys anything sincere he gets his money's worth. Not long ago a gentleman purchased a pearl and, after examining it thoroughly, discovered that the top was pure pearl but, alas! a large portion of it was filled with wax. That is what I mean by not being sincere. In studying humanity as a whole one notices that there are a good many people just like this little pearl; they look so good, talk so good and many times act so good, when in church or in the presence of the preacher or sacred place or circumstance. Under other circumstances they seemingly depreciate in value. They are not pure and solid,—sincere if you please. Jesus could not tolerate the outward manifestations of the Pharisees who always wanted to appear so holy while inwardly were, as he said, "Full of dead men's bones." You and I could not sanction such actions either and we too rebuke those poor Pharisees who, by the way, were apparently the best people of their day, at least they had been. What the Puritans were to the earliest settlers of America, the Pharisees had been to the people of their day. But gradually they became formal and insincere. The Pharisees are dead and it is very easy to condemn them now. Turn the telescope the other way and take a look at ourselves once in a while. It will cost a searching struggle for some of us to give up our own contentment with the approval of man, who "looketh on the outward appearance" and seek inwardly to be such that we will have the approval of God who, "looketh on the heart." Jesus never did and never will appreciate or be satisfied with mere lip service or perfunctory and formal worship. Not long ago the writer had an opportunity to attend a very large funeral of a citizen of a certain town. Three-fourths of the service consisted of pure formality, which, I venture, was not comprehended by three-fourths of the people. "They that are of the Spirit must worship in the spirit." There is not much spirit in such service. Jesus further states that "This people honoreth me with their lips but their hearts are far from me. Howbeit in vain do they worship me, teaching for doctrines the commandments of men" (Mark 7:6, 7). To illustrate, in our Sunday school class last Sunday morning, we men entered into a rather lively discussion on a teaching of Scripture, viz., "There shall be infants in hell a span long." After discussing at length I asked them to show me where that was found. They failed to point out the particular verse and finally admitted that they had heard some preacher state that it was a teaching in their creed. I kindly remarked that what I cannot find, in my Bible, the only creed, is no teaching for me and will cause me no anxiety. Too many people are satisfied by simply listening to the preaching of the doctrines or precepts of men. Sincere men will read and teach the Bible only.

Addressing the Pharisees again, Jesus said, "But all their works they do to be seen of men." This passage portrays the hypocrisy that Jesus so much abhorred. Does it not consist in caring little for the real goodness and usefulness of life, so long as an admirable, or at least respectable appearance can be maintained? How modern this sin is! Some one has written, "He stands having his loins girt about with his religiosity and having on the breastplate of respectability. His feet are shod with ostentatious philanthropy, his head is encased in the helmet of spread-eagle patriotism. Holding in his left hand the buckler of worldly success and in his right the sword of 'influence', he is able to withstand in the evil day, and having done, all to stand." Compare this picture with the original portrait in Ephesians 6:10ff. Be not deceived, God is not mocked; while we may continue to live respectably for a short time on this earth, it will not always last. The heart of man is deceitful; so therefore, let us keep it with all diligence for out of it come the issues of life. How easy it is for one to fall when he thinks he is strong. It is little wonder that the Psalmist cried out in the prayer, "Create in me a clean heart, O God; and renew a right spirit within me."

Sincerity was the great characteristic of our blessed Lord and Savior while he spent that period of great moral struggle in the wilderness. He could not be bribed. He would not compromise. He was the unchangeable, immovable, steadfast Servant in the service of his Father. He was not only sincere himself but taught sincerity to his followers and enemies. The person who is most honored and respected; the person who will live longest in the hearts and memories of their fellowmen; the Christian who loves and serves best and whom God can bless, is the follower of God who is thoroughly sincere in word and deed. Many a man becomes a hard rock covered with a soft moss of words, and we never learn how hard the rock is until we slip on the moss and fall. Such men break up the mutual relationship of trust, on which all worthy human life depends; they are the arch traitors against the race. Have you grown lax about insincere and deceptive speech? or do you hate a lie as the Master did, so that your friends know that they can depend absolutely upon what you say? "I'd rather be a violet and be a little blue than be a big man and be untrue." May God help us all to be more sincere in all our relations with God and our fellowmen.

OUR PRAYER

Our heavenly Father, may the sincerity of thy truth fall upon us and the genuine purity of thy great Spirit enter our hearts and prevail upon us to be sincere in every part of our being. Keep us from becoming formal and shallow and hypocritical and may our lives ever conform to our speech and our heart's deepest desires. There is so much of superficiality and insincerity in us all. Take it from us and forgive wherein we have thus been untrue to thee. May we do always those things that are pleasing to the Father; not as eyeservants or men-pleasers, but because we love thee and are at one with thee in purpose and spirit.

Masontown, Pennsylvania.

CONSIDERATION FOR OTHERS

"Look. . . every man also on the things of others."—Phil. 2:4.

The sweetest joys and the truest successes are the outgrowth of self-forgetting, self-effacing kindness to others. Joseph owed his promotion largely to such kindly consideration. One morning, seeing the countenance of two of his fellow-prisoners full of sadness, he inquired: "Wherefore look ye so sadly today?" Two years later one of these men remembered the kindness of Joseph, and spoke the word which exalted him to the second place in the land. It is safe to affirm that no act of unselfish kindness is ever lost. It may not exalt us to places of honor and power; it may not bedeck us with chains of gold; but it will live in the hearts of those to whom it was shown, and at the last great assize the Judge of all will say: "Inasmuch as ye have done it unto one of the least of these my brethren, ye have done it unto me."—J. R. Miller.

Send
WHITE GIFT
OFFERINGS to

THE SUNDAY SCHOOL

ALBERT TRENT
General Secretary-Treasurer
Johnstown, Pennsylvania

The Challenge of Adolescence.   By R. F. Porte

The challenge of adolescence is a call to develop unused possibilities. Our progress materially has come because venturous and brave men and women were willing to develop the virgin resources of a new country, and return the products to a needy world. We look with wonder at the rich farms of the Mississippi valley, but perhaps few can appreciate the daring it required to reduce the wild to its present productive state. It is the people who saw years ago who today look over the broad fields of a fertile country such as we have in our middle states. It is the time of adolescence that tries our patience and requires boldness to conquer. Many people see nothing but swamps and sink holes and the bad, and consequently avoid doing anything for this virgin territory for a spiritual harvest. Just as some of our best farms have been reclaimed from the most dismal wilderness, so we may reclaim some of the best souls from this dismal swamp of adolescent badness. The challenge of adolescence comes to the individual who wants to make the world rich by giving it spiritual souls reclaimed from waste and idleness. · It will require a brave spiritual person who will exercise good management and do hard work to get the results we seek.

The adolescent period is the period of transition and unrest. The child is passing from childhood into the period of manhood and womanhood. Have you ever noticed how easy it is to lead and suggest to a newcomer into the community? He will give attention to you if you approach him in the right way because he has no preconceived conclusions about the new country, and he respects the one who has lived there and knows. Let the individual settle down without the help and fellowship of the old residents and the chances are few to really direct and mould his methods of doing things. He has solved his own problems in his own way and is very slow to surrender his personal solution to his problems and thus seems incapable. So it is with the child passing from childhood at twelve years of age into the adolescent period. He enters into it uncertainly and open to advice and suggestion. He will be influenced by somebody's ideas and here is one challenge to the Christian people of the community. Young people can be lost to the Brethren church at this period if they are not made to know for a surety that the doctrines of the church are right. If they must hear only the ridicule of the unbelievers, you must break down that prejudice, a thing well nigh impossible. The uncertainty of adolescence is the field to get rich in. We will make more real Brethren by indoctrinating the Sunday school and Christian Endeavor than in preaching whole series to the adults. The best and most loyal young people in our church are Brethren because some good, loyal member of the church got in when the field was virgin and tilled the soil and drained the bogs. If we want to make our own church bigger and richer spiritually, I believe that this is the place to do our work. Why spend time trying to undo what others did wrong when we can enter an uncultivated field and own our own farm. There is no prejudice on the part of the adolescent as to who moulds his life in this uncertain period. He can become a Christian just as well as remain in spiritual idleness, and of course better so for all, and it is our duty and privilege to enrich the church with this virgin material.

The next challenge is that of pent up energy seeking escape. The adolescent has it and he will use it. It is quite immaterial to the adolescent who gets the benefit just so he gets the relief from the energy expended. The ambition to do things is what we need in our churches. The older folks have had their day; why harness their years of requirement with work in the church when the energy of youth is waiting to be used? The challenge is for directing this energy upon the wheels of power that will turn the wheels of the church. Civilization has taught men to harness the dynamic forces of nature and do greater things than were ever possible before, and the church must harness the youthful energy in our midst to the creative spiritual duties. We need ministers, missionaries and church workers and we fail to get them in sufficiently large numbers to supply the need because the youth is not made acquainted with the good to be done in this line of work. We are hindered by the idea that energy must be turned into a dollar to be worth anything. We ought to know that gold is worth its weight in the bar as well as in the gold eagle. The energies of youth are more valuable in the form of some spiritual service than if turned into the cold material of the earth. If we hope to turn the world's attention from the spiritual things to the spiritual we must change the idea of the value of these energies, stored away for the glory of God and the blessing of humanity.

There is another great challenge of the adolescent, and that is the love of the ideal. The child's transition toward manhood and womanhood makes him select some one as his pattern. This is a more or less hit-and-miss selection, unless some consecrated soul is wise enough to become a friend to the young man or woman. The individual who loves the youth becomes the companion and also the ideal. The Master of the Boy Scouts and director of the Camp Fire Girls have a wonderful field in which to mould the ideals and hopes of the youth of the community. It is just as much our business to make good the ideal. The church must awaken to the possibilities of being the ideal of youth. Jesus, the bridegroom of the church, is the ideal and perfect man, and the church must likewise not be ashamed to become ideal and attractive by presenting the high claim of the Christ, who died to save us. This does not, and must not, mean any lowering of the standards, but appealing to the ambitious youth to achieve.

The challenge of youth is a challenge to the church for religious education. The child holds much which will characterize the youth, the youth holds the possibilities of the future men and women, all proceed in logical progression. Childhood is the time of action and adolescence the time of forming character out of these activities. We believe in training men and women for commercial and professional life. We believe that a person ought to have a high school education in order to get the most out of life and we have our compulsory graded schools. If this be true and the child must be fitted for better living here in this life, why not the spiritual life? The adolescent demands of us proper spiritual training. The church must train the youth to meet the religious needs of the life before him. If knowledge will keep a person right and make him a successful and useful citizen, why not educate him to be a Christian? Ignorance is an invitation to ruin. The adequate church school can not help but meet these challenges of youth and help the youth find his place. The day is past when intelligent people believe a boy or girl should sow wild oats. This condition is a direct evidence of the lack of proper leadership. Every Christian college man and woman should have at least one course in religious education, necessarily to be a candidate for church office but to help them be what they should be as Christian citizens. If the youth can not look to the adult as a pattern right and make him a hard fight to maintain decency. Educated bookkeepers and lawyers are needed, but people educated in religion and morals are needed worse. The modern youth demands a director of religious education in every community. He may be the pastor or any prepared Christian worker, who shall lead the adolescent in his activities. The challenge of adolescence means to me the saving of the church of the future.

J. A. Garber
PRESIDENT

Our Young People at Work

G. C. Carpenter
SECRETARY

Ho! Patriotic Endeavorers!

Did you realize that Good Citizenship Day was so nearly upon us? Did you really have any thought of the day? Does your Endeavor Society observe the day? Well I might just keep on asking questions but perhaps if I don't "keep on keeping on" in this instance you will try and answer those that I have asked. Now be honest, will you? The first one is—Do you realize that Good Citizenship Day is so nearly upon us? I cannot imagine how you will answer but I do know that regardless of your answer, IT IS UPON US! When? The third Sunday in October. October 17. Now isn't that soon?

The next question—Did you really have any thought of the day? Well, I can about guess your answer here, if you are a genuine Endeavorer—a true American. Let me guess. Here you are, "Sure, I've thought a whole lot about that day. Why yes, it comes just before the great election in November. It means we are out with an effort for better voting and better living in general. We are out to arouse inter-

est in folks concerning the vital problems of our day." Why sure I guessed your thought. That is what I had hoped for, since you elected me as your Good Citizenship Superintendent. Now that third and last question, the one I quit "keeping on" with. Does your Endeavor Society observe the day? Well, I trust it does and that you will make it a meeting of great importance. Work it up. Advertise IT. Talk about IT and for IT. Make your religion and your life count for true righteousness.

I have asked for a few articles to be run in our church paper on themes vital to this particular department. Watch the paper and do not fail to read and digest each article. And as we close this little announcement,—it will make your Good Citizenship Superintendent feel better if you report what a rousing time you had on the evening of October 17. Will you observe the DAY and REPORT IT?

A. E. WHITTED, Good Citizenship Superintendent.
Morrill, Kansas.

Keeping Christian Endeavor Prominent.   By Earl Huette

(Continued from last week).

THIRD—KEEPING C. E. PROMINENT IN THE COMMUNITY

In dealing with the public at large in these days, we must consider the fact, that whenever we make a statement, the other fellow is there to receive it and weigh the veracity of it, therefore it behooves us to be very careful what we say in our publicity work.

It is for us to know that our Christian Endeavor Society is doing what it is intended to do, before we make any statement that may be just a "little high colored." Let us be careful about the stress which we place upon our announcement that there will be Something "Special" tonight, or that this social has received more hard work than any which has been held recently, therefore, we assure you of a good time.

The other fellow may know the truth of the matter.

Getting closer to our subject now let us suggest the following:

1. **Community Service.**

(a) Co-operate in evangelistic campaigns.

(b) Co-operate in taking community census, then turn the information needed over to the proper church authorities.

(c) Keep the children off the streets by establishing or maintaining a children's playground. Supervision of the right sort is needed greatly in these places.

(d) Conduct a "story-telling" hour for the children, every week.

(e) Introduce community athletics. (For information address the Association, 1 Madison Avenue, New York, N. Y.)

(f) Hold regular services in the jail, poor farm, hospital and other public institutions. See that the inmates are provided with well printed Bibles.

(g) Help the Rescue Mission in her work of bringing lost souls to the feet of Jesus.

(h) Promote the growing of flowers and vegetables on the vacant lots that are now being left to grow up in weeds. Give the flowers to the sick or sell the vegetables and give the proceeds to Missions.

2. **Place C. E. Literature in the Racks Provided in Most Public Buildings.** Especially in hotel boxes. Written

invitations to attend your meetings will often get into the hands of just the fellow who needs Christ. Always be sure to give the name of the church. Time of your meetings and the way to reach your church.

3. **Newspaper Advertising.**

Here is one that we could talk about for an hour but we will pass it up with just a few remarks.

(a) Don't try to put anything "across" the editor.

(b) Don't try to get Free Space. Pay for it.

(c) Don't give him C. E. poetry or a plate reading "Be at Christian Endeavor tonight."

(d) Don't try to be funny. Most newspapers carry a column for "Mutt and Jeff," or "Bringing up Father," or some other such column.

Mr. Dana, of the New York Sun said, "When a dog bites a man, that is not news, but when a man bites a dog, that's news."

In our newspaper advertising let us use this motto and standard—"Do Something Startling, Then Tell About it."

4. **Street Car Advertising** is suggestive of great possibilities.

5. **Do not allow the movies and Theatres to monopolize all of the electric lights.** Put plenty of light around the church, remembering that it is "the light places that offer refuge while it is the dark places that offer seclusion." Prove to the world that the church is a place of refuge.

6. **Close up the poolrooms, Sunday movies and the dance halls.** Also provide proper censorship for the movies that are operated daily.

Let us urge that people do not attend the "movies" so frequently if for no other reason than for their "eye's" sake and the overtaxation of the mind in trying to keep pace with the film as shown on the screen.

The scenes flash past so quickly that the eye is fed faster than the mind can digest the movements, thus, the mind loses the faculty to absorb.

7. **Put Christian Endeavor Literature on the Public News stands for sale.** As it is, when we want any Christian Endeavor literature it is necessary to write to the publisher then wait a week or two before we can get it. More than that, there are literally thousands of people who go into the news and magazine stores that do not have the slightest idea what kind of literature they want. Let us put some attractive and good literature there and ready for them to buy.

Right here in this connection I want to say "that there is plenty of room for improvement in the kind of magazne covers and literature which litters almost every newsstand. Why not make an effort to regulate this by establishing a 'Magazine Censor' movement?"

It is my humble opinion that if the Christian Endeavorers of the United States would get behind their publishers, that the publishers in turn, would put Christian Endeavor literature where it belongs.

I want to go on record here and now as saying "that Christian Endeavor literature has as good a right to be sold on the public news stands of our country as has the literature of Christian Science and the other 'isms' with which the minds of so many thousands of people are becoming polluted?"

Cannot we Endeavorers who are now assembled in this convention make some kind of a start, that will clean up some of this hearsayic doctrine that is at present so rampant? Is it impossible to get an amendment to our national laws that will compel every religious sect to come out in the open and make public their dogmatic belief?

Come on! Endeavorers, the organization is big enough now to do a real man-sized job, and it is high time now that if the work is to become really and truly prominent, that

we get busy and do something that is worth while.

Let us make these opportunities for doing the will of Christ become a reality instead of a phantom.

8. **Adopt a Slogan that means something** to be used in all of your C. E. literature, on your advertising, in your letters and wherever it is possible and practical.

Here is one for you, "Bring back the family altar."

Surely there is nothing which can be more desired and nothing from which so much good would be derived in the way of bringing about more earnest Christian activity as would the family altar in every Christian home.

Show me a good home without the family altar, then establish the altar in that home and in a month's time I will show you a better home than you showed to me.

Christian Endeavorers of the Brethren churches of the world:

Let us not forget that we have the opportunity of helping to make one hundred percent of the additions to the church better informed in the Word of God, and of helping them to be better trained workers in the cause of our Lord and Savior, Jesus Christ.

Let us not slack in our efforts to make Christian Endeavor stand out prominent among the organizations of the world that are listed as those that DO THINGS!

Dayton, Ohio.

SEND ALL MONEY FOR
General Home, Kentucky and
Foreign Missions to

MISSIONS

WILLIAM A. GEARHART
General Missionary Secretary
906 Conover Bldg., Dayton, O.

"El Auto Evangelico"

On July the 29th, Brother Sickel and I started out for a trip with the Coach: "there's muckle adae when cadgers ride." Our store of provisions, cold meat, eggs, tea, etc., has been replenished by the good wives. The tanks are full of gas and water, the bed clothing is neatly packed away in the cupboards, a good supply of Bibles, Testaments, portions, tracts, etc., are on board, so off we go. Passing through the outskirts of the city to avoid the uneven cobblestones, we cross the bridge of the Rio Cuarto River and head for the north.

Only a mile or two out of town and we are up to our necks in sand—not exactly but up to the axle; the little Ford pants hard but struggles on bravely, and soon we have passed the heavy piece of the road. Our first customer keeps a small "boliche" (drink shop) where two roads cross. We enter and offer him some gospel literature; he is not over keen on study; asks us to have a drink, but we are both dry men. He can read a little, and surrounded by a curious assortment of bottles, sprawling over a dirty counter with his wife peering over his shoulder, curious to see what the evangelical book contains, we leave him to his perusal of the Gospel and pray that the seed of God's word may find an entrance into this dark indifferent heart.

No rain has fallen since March so you can imagine what Brother Sickel and I look like, covered with dust as we journey on towards Coronel Baigorria, the next railroad station on the line from Rio Cuarto to Cordoba. Occasionally we meet somebody, pass a solitary farm house, see someone working in the fields and to all the message is given, either in leaflet or portion form. "Cast thy bread upon the waters" . . . "He that goeth forth". . .

are promises which encourage us as we journey on. But the unerring clock within tells us that it must be dinner time; so we halt by the road side. Opening up our small dresser, lowering a small folding table, and seating ourselves on the opposite side we have just room to eat comfortably inside the coach, and enjoy our dinner of cold roast mutton, eggs, tea, etc., and are soon on our way again.

Entering the village of Coronel Baigorria we manage to sell two Bibles, find a ready reception for free literature, chat with an Italian who once lived in North America and who is very anxious to air his little English —very little—and then head again for Gigena to the north. Sixteen o'clock (four o'clock) and we have reached our journey's end for one day, having covered about thirty miles. A short run did you say? Yes, according to the North American speedometer, but come and see our roads and you'll understand. At Gigena we are immediately surrounded by a crowd of curious onlookers. "What is it?" we hear them ask. A van carrying goods and wares for sale like Turks use? A mode of advertising cigarettes No. 43? No, a coach for the distribution of Gospel literature. But what is the Gospel anyway? We have heard of numerous saints, but never of the Santa Biblia. Here again we find the same mixture of nationalities, Italian predominating and here again the same ignorance of the Gospel, indifference and open rebellion against God. So far as the Devil's territory has never been disputed and he is the god of this age.

In reply to our question, "Where can we hold a conference tonight?" the owner of the largest hotel came forward and offered a

room free. Immediately we turned the side windows of the coach around (painted black on one side in order to use as a blackboard) and having written a notice in chalk inviting the people to attend at twenty-one o'clock (nine o'clock) we drove through the town distributing tracts and successfully advertised the conference. But to our disappointment, when we entered the hotel at night prepared to preach the Gospel, we found the room so full of half drunken men all armed with revolvers and knives, that we decided it would be best to distribute a fresh assortment of tracts and wait for some more convenient place to preach in.

Leaving next morning we journey on to Elena and Berotarran and in both places were well received, selling some books and distributing a large quantity of tracts. At La Dormida I asked permission to visit the public school and made a gift of "Porciones Escogidas" to each child. At first the head mistress Catholic objected, but after using persuasive powers she finally consented and also received a New Testament for herself. About sundown we arrived at a friend's farm where Senor Stoller gave us a hearty welcome. During the night it rained hard—an untold blessing for the country but obliging us to stay with our friends until Sunday morning. Although the roads were still heavy we set out good and early for Almafuerte crossing over the foothills, but did not arrive until fifteen o'clock (three o'clock.) I had lived and worked near this little town some years ago, as administrator of an Estancia. On arriving we found that two priests were holding special services. The auto was soon surrounded by a bunch of children seeking for literature; but alas I had forgotten the priests who very soon came upon the scene and destroyed all the papers they could get hold of. However this act of persecution made no small stir in the town and many of the people who already knew me came to apologize for such an act of fanaticism. Many of the children who had lost their books returned for more promising faithfully not to let the priests destroy them. At Almafuerte we visited many families, spoke personally to the people, and distributed a large number of tracts.

Leaving on Tuesday morning we traveled over to Cabrera to visit our Mission and Brother Atkinson there. It was already late when we arrived but received a royal welcome, and arranged to stay for some days and hold special meetings. The seven meetings were well attended and at the close of one meeting several professed to accept Christ as their personal Savior. The work in Cabrera and Deheza is very encouraging. The Mission has a nice property in Cabrera and Brother Atkinson and his wife are doing a good work. They have been able to get in touch with a large number of families. The two Sunday schools are well attended as also the different weekly meetings. Our Brother and Sister need to be upheld in prayer, so that whilst isolated much more than we are in Rio Cuarto they may have grace to continue bravely in the work. One of the most hopeful signs in the work at Cabrera is the actual opposition of the local priest, who, feeling the effects of our brother's preaching, has started to write against the Mission. A day school is very much needed in Cabrera, also seats for the Mission Hall, the ones in use have no backs.

After eleven days out we returned to Rio Cuarto on Monday, praising God for his blessing on our efforts to spread the gospel.

FRANCIS EDWARDS.

NEWS FROM THE FIELD

ANKENYTOWN, OHIO

Some time has elapsed since a report issued from this part of God's great vineyard. Be it known, however, that Ankenytown is not dead, neither can it be catalogued as in a moribund condition. This church like many another church has been subjected to the painful experience of seeing many of her young people depart to the urban centers. Despite this reduction of her forces Ankenytown is making a pretty good showing. The work of the Sunday school is going forward under the efficient leadership of Mrs. Edna Guthrie and her faithful teachers. The church's services are fairly well attended. Dr. I. D. Bowman came to us for three weeks in June and preached the old time gospel in a masterly way. Despite the many handicaps Brother Bowman held a splendid meeting. As a result nineteen were added to the church. The majority of these were young people whose life will mean much to the church. Brother Bowman is a flaming evangel of the truth and as such I recommend him to those who are looking for a nevangelist.

A. L. LYNN.

ZION HILL, OHIO

Many interesting events have transpired in this congregation during our sojourn with these splendid people. We have had the high privilege of receiving forty into the church and the sad experience of preaching the funeral of dear friends such as John Moines, Walter Winter, Mrs. Beal, Miss Curie and two sweet little infants. May the God of grace comfort the bereaved ones. There has also come to the writer the pleasure of uniting several young people in holy wedlock. The most recent the writer failed to report. Mr. Dave Boss and Miss Beulah Amstutz, both inestimable young people and loyal members of the Zion Hill congregation. May the blessings of God attend this young couple through life.

The Zion Hill brethren are doing things. Forward seems to be the dominant note of this people. When the brethren saw that progress depended upon and necessitated a change of location many reluctantly, and yet decisively abandoned the old Zion Hill church and now possess new fields. Yes, fields. They now occupy two fields instead of one. They bought a splendid little church from the Mennonites in Sterling, and are renting a church in Smithville. It was a wise move. We save the old field and make possible the conquest of new ones. We are having interesting crowds in our new locations and the outlook is mighty encouraging. We held an all day meeting at Smithville in August. This was a Wayne county get-together meeting. Despite the unfavorable weather we had a splendid time. Dr. Miller and Dr. Shively were with us and gave to us inspiring sermons. Thanks to the sisters who prepared for us such an excellent dinner. We think the signs point to the erection of a new church at Smithville in the not far distant future.

Brethren, we solicit an abiding interest in your prayers that we may tactfully and courageously possess the fields for our Master as they open unto us.   A. L. LYNN.

LOST CREEK, KENTUCKY

After some delay I will write an article concerning the Lost Creek work as I found it. Brother Drushal has already written concerning the meeting there.

I have received inquiries from the south and west concerning the Kentucky work since I was there. I want to make an honest confession that I had a very wrong conception concerning the Kentucky work. I find in traveling over the brotherhood that almost the entire brotherhood has the same mistaken conception that I had.

First, after carefully and prayerfully studying the field, after being there eight weeks and talking to prominent men from the various states, who are in the mining business and other pursuits, after talking with the most prominent missionary pastors and prominent men and women of the different churches, as well as talking to the natives who are prominent members and other citizens of note, as well as politicians, I believe I can speak with authority concerning the "mountain whites" of Kentucky and their needs. I went there feeling as I believe a large majority of the brotherhood feels, that we should send more missionaries to preach the Gospel and less school teachers to teach the children. I have taken special pains to investigate this subject to the bottom, because I found I was either wrong or every person that I have talked to that knew the field was wrong. I am now thoroughly convinced that neither I nor the brotherhood know the facts concerning this field.

I feel positively sure that a consecrated, sacrificing teacher and preacher can do ten times the good that a consecrated preacher alone can do. Every mission school in this part of Kentucky proves my statement. The Presbyterians have learned this well and are enlarging all their schools, and every person with whom I have talked says the school at Lost Creek has helped to revolutionize the place more than anything else.

I had a talk with a prominent, wide-awake Baptist, a splendid man, who has two brothers who hold prominent political positions in the state. He told me voluntarily that the influence of our Kentucky mission was greater than any other in all that part of Kentucky.

A prominent spiritual Presbyterian mission worker told me the same. Every family for miles around told me the same. Even the "moonshiners" all admit the same, although they say, "We would vote for Drushal to stay but we do not want him to know where our stills are, for he would close them and put us in jail."

In the second place, the great reasons why we are all deceived concerning this matter, are the following: (1) That the public schools here are unlike those we know. Many teachers are very poor. Some drink and gamble and swear. (2) The hope of Kentucky is in the training of the child. (3) Both the school authorities and the parents are willing for a consecrated school teacher to teach all the Bible that he wants to teach; many send their little children from six years up to mission schools because of the moral and religious training they get. Many of these little tots are in boarding schools away from home because the parents want them to have the intellectual, moral and religious training that they cannot get in their poorly managed public schools. Parents just plead and weep, when Drushal says our school is over-crowded and we cannot take any more. AND ABOUT ALL BECOME CONVERTED TO THE BRETHREN FAITH AS SOON AS THEY ARE OLD ENOUGH. You find them for many miles around Lost Creek these young people come and go through school, and while there become soundly converted. They go home, get married and establish Christian homes, and every one that I have found believes and advocates the Brethren doctrine. This school does ten times as much to spread Christianity and Brethrenism than Drushal could do by simply preaching the Gospel without this school.

For the above reasons, the need of Kentucky being so different from the needs of our brotherhood elsewhere, there is danger of the entire brotherhood failing to appreciate the needs of this field and therefore of cramping the work.

Third. I am thoroughly convinced that the Kentucky school must be enlarged and several additional consecrated teachers put there or it will gradually go down and we will lose out. The Lord's work either goes forward or backward. The apex is reached in going forward there, as they now have one-third more pupils than they can properly provide for. Therefore it cannot go forward without more room and teachers. Hence unless this provision is made it will begin to go back. It seems therefore imperative that this great need should be provided for at once.

Fourth. I want to say that I went there last year with misgivings. I had been told some things that were not favorable. To my utter surprise I never found in any church in the brotherhood such a love for the Bible, such quoting of the Word from six-year-old children up, such testimonies and prayers. I wept with joy when I saw the good that was being done. I only judge the tree by its fruit. I was in the home of Brother Drushal five weeks, I went from home to home with him and he read the Word and prayed in every home. And as far as I was able to learn, and I made special inquiry, I did not find a family that did not have confidence in him and his work. And it seems to me that nothing but the Holy Ghost could have made it possible for him to have gotten such a hold upon these suspicious people, who are exceptionally wise in reading character.

I saw the pupils sitting under trees, on the swinging bridge, on the grass, reading their Bibles, and then scores of them quoting verse and some chapters in the church service. I never saw anything like it anywhere before.

Lastly. I sometimes think that Drushal is too modest to teach them to give as liberally as they should. Although they are improving along this line. But like in old Virginia, many have been taught all their lives that it is a sin to pay a preacher, therefore the poorest and most ignorant do the preaching. Brother Drushal no doubt has not the time but I feel with his influence, if he could be released from teaching and preaching a couple of months and would go out in that community, he could obtain much money for an endowment or a fund for the immediate expenses of the school.

If the macadamized road that has been surveyed through there is built it will, result in the mines being worked and lumber camps being established that will make money much more plentiful than now.

I feel that Brother Drushal needs our special prayers. He has a church to look after, a dormitory to vex his righteous soul, a constantly increasing school to look after, besides his own family and the families of scores of others.

We had a splendid meeting, with large crowds, and those received in the church during the preparation for the revival and during the revival I think were seventeen. This was excellent for a field that has been so well worked. A number of the "moonshiners" were deeply convicted and some of them are of more than ordinary intelligence, and I believe will quit their business and come to the church.

One man was shot and killed while I was there on the day of the primary election. But he lived some miles away, as also did the desperado that killed him. The murderer will likely be cleared as they usually are there.

ISAAC D. BOWMAN,
Buckeye City, Ohio.

EVANGELISTIC TRAVELS

Our last report was made at the close of our meeting at Arritts, Virginia, September 2. Then I went on into the old home neighborhood of our dear Brother J. S. Bowman, where he taught school and labored in the Gospel for several years. His amiable life and faithful preaching of Brethren doctrine resulted in the planting of seed which grew into eight or ten Brethren families. Among these dear ones I found some of the richest treasures of Christian love and influence.

When I arrived in this section on September 3, our dear Brother George Simmons met me at the little station called Clift, Virginia. His home was my home during the entire fourteen days of the meeting, and I cannot find words to express my thanks and gratitude for all the kindness and hospitality shown me during all my stay with these dear people. We went home with Brother Rexford Humphries one night. He had a truck-padded with straw and brought twenty-one with him to church. He belongs to the Christian church, but we baptized his wife and four of his brothers and sisters. When we came here we did not know personally one family, but we leave with many friends, and have promised to return in the near future. The glorious results of the meeting were 31 confessions, eighteen of which were baptized at one time. One was baptized by the M. E. pastor. It was not convenient for some to be baptized at this time; these Brother Arritt will baptize later. We rested a couple of days and then held a love feast on Sunday evening, September 27 in the Mount Union church, with 32 around the tables. This was the first service of this kind ever witnessed in this community, but it was enjoyed by all.

Our dear Brother Fred M. Arritt came over to our meetings as often as he could, as did also some of our new converts at Arritts. This was encouraging to us, and also had a good influence on the people at this place. Brother Arritt will preach for our people in the M. E. church at eleven in the morning of

each fourth Sunday and at three in the afternoon of the same Sunday at Mt. Union. We are loath to leave these dear people, but duty requires us to take the parting hand.

The offerings exceeded by far the amount we expected. And our dear Brother and Sister Simmons, with whom we made our home while here, with the help of their uncle, James Wolf, and two other families, converts of the meeting, all living in sight of each other, kept me on my knees one afternoon, packing two good-sized boxes with peaches, apples, quinces, grapes, pears, cucumbers, and a lot of beans to send to my home in Washington, D. C. I can never forget the sweet influence of these dear people and their generosity, nor the ties of Christian friendship that were made here. But how do we know that we have passed from death unto life unless we love the brethren?

I am enclosing cash for The Evangelist for one year to be sent to the following enclosed addresses. I repeat, God bless these dear ones till we meet again.

I am on my way home after an absence of 74 days, including a week spent with my sick brother in Iowa. The full visible results were 83 who confessed Christ at three different meetings. Besides one husband and three daughters, whose husband and the father, who could not read, refused to allow them to be baptized by triune immersion. They had been baptized by single immersion, but were not satisfied. We will still pray God's blessing on them that they may work out their souls' salvation in fear and trembling. This is September 23, and I am on my way home. I will spend one night there and then will go on to Reliance (Mt. Zion church), Virginia, which is my regular work. And before you read this letter, we will hold a love feast there on Sunday evening of the 26th.

S. P. FOGLE.

TRAVEL FLASHES AGAIN

If my plans carry as now made, my friends will have the privilege or the burden of my "flashes" again. I am right now enroute to Oak Hill, West Virginia, to my first fall engagement in evangelism. It was here that I spent two weeks this summer in one of the most spirited meetings that I have held for twenty years and it was that, I presume, that prompted a call from four of the five churches of the town to return to help them in a union effort this fall. Here, Wm. H. Miller is pastor of the Brethren church which is a good working church and here are more people supported to the square mile by the natural resources of the country than any place I think I ever was. But "travel flashes" are not always so flashy and, so here is a pause. A wreck ahead is holding us back and with reservations on the night train in jeopardy, it is not easy to wait. But how many wrecks we meet and how many are still ahead! It is to stop the wrecking of the human life of the world that we leave our lovely folks at home and start to wave the red banner of the Lord's Kingdom to the careless and restless world that we go to save. How many trials I have had in getting ready, too! Two singers agreed to go and agreed twice each, and here I am many miles on my way and do not know what the leading of the Lord is. It is all darkness but he has a way. If he wants me to have a singer, one will be there and his will is what we hope to have done. Last summer I had the best singer ever with me, but she is a mother and had to stay by the stuff and the youngsters. It was quite a denial for her and for me but that seems clearly her duty. By the way, our home is at North Manchester. We have one of those houses that are more the renter's than our own, this winter at Plymouth I'd hate to be a big householder in Indiana; the laws seem all to be made for the other fellow; it may be right but it keeps us out of a house we thought was ours, perhaps nearly a year—all because we trusted a "good fellow." If you wish to write me, address me at North Manchester so that the lady will get it first. She is a good censor, and if you do not talk right, she will blue pencil it, to be sure. I hope this shall be the greatest year for the Brethren church in her history.

CHARLES A. BAME.

WASHINGTON, D. C.

Our Bible Institute, conducted by Brother L. S. Bauman, of Long Beach, California, came to its close on last Sunday night. We began this series of Bible lectures with high expectations. We can truly say that we were not disappointed in the least. Eternity alone will reveal the great good accomplished during those ten days.

God is surely using Brother Bauman in a wonderful way. Thank God for men who still believe the old book! In these days of tremendous peril, they never fail to draw a crowd. If you don't believe we had the crowd, inquire of Brother Bauman. On the last night he gave an evangelistic sermon. At its close seven came forward and made the good confession.

Our hearts were encouraged, too, during the meeting, because of the presence of Brother and Sister Wall and son, of Long Beach, California, and Brother and Sister Stutz of Dayton, Ohio.

In closing we repeat our request for all who really know the secret of prayer, to ask our Heavenly Father to supply us with the building we so greatly need. W. M. LYON.

ALLENTOWN TO ASHLAND

After spending four of our best years at Allentown, we at last found it necessary to say good-bye, to those whom we had learned to love, and move west in order to answer a call to another line of service for our beloved church.

It will be unnecessary for me to say much here about the Allentown work since Evangelist readers are likely familiar with it through past reports.

But I remember the time when Allentown was not taken seriously as a pastorate among my brethren in the ministry. I want to bear this testimony after serving said church four years: I don't know of any other place I would rather go than just to Allentown, if I were again seeking a pastorate. I never left a place and people that I was so reluctant to leave as Allentown.

Had we obeyed our feelings we should doubtless have remained in the Pennsylvania Dutch city, but sentiment must be put aside at times and cold realities be faced if we want to take seriously our future as a church. The work at Allentown is hard. I know of no harder field in the brotherhood. But the folks are responsive. There are some tithers and I believe there will be more ere long.

With less than seventy-five members Allentown pays the pastor's salary without aid from the Mission Board. They do not keep their money all at home to do so either. You need only to consult financial reports to learn what our brethren there have done.

Very few churches beat us in foreign missionary offerings, Ashland College endowment, contributions to Board of Benevolences, etc. We made a splendid score on the Four Year Program as those who attended know.

During our sojourn in the "Grundnis Shdedle," progress was made along various lines in the church, but the additions were not so many. Yet when we measure even accessions with results attained in many other congregations during the past four years, we need not feel ashamed, for we added to our number during that time thirty-three souls—thirty by baptism and three by relation.

As a parting word for Allentown, I will say that my prayers continue for that work and to the end that the Lord may definitely lead in sending to them the very man they should have as pastor.

Our Elder E. E. Fehnel, whom I learned to know as a consecrated servant of the Lord, is serving the Allentown congregation until a pastor may be located. Aufwiedersehen, Allentown.

On the Way

We spent nearly a month visiting along the way in Pennsylvania. Most of the time was spent in Bedford county. I had the pleasure of assisting Brother E. H. Smith in a special meeting at Bunker Hill, one of the Bedford county circuit.

The untimely death of Prof. Ed. Byers left these churches without a pastor. I am glad to know that Brother Smith is arranging to serve two of them. The present scarcity of preachers necessitates a larger use of our older brethren in the ministry. But above all, we must get more young men into the service. Churches must encourage young men to take up the work of the ministry. New Enterprise and Yellow Creek are pressing a young school teacher into service and there is likelihood that he will reach Ashland for further preparation by another year. More of our churches must do this sort of thing.

Mansfield

Leaving Pennsylvania behind once more, we came on to Mansfield, Ohio. We took charge of the work there August first. I cannot say much about the Mansfield work until we get better acquainted. Suffice it to say at least that the field is very difficult like Allentown. Mansfield needs better organization and she must take her work more seriously. By the help of God we hope to see victory here!

Rally Day has been set for October 10th and already gives promise of being a real success. We ask your prayers in behalf of the work at Mansfield.

Ashland

Then we came on to Ashland and once more caught a glimpse of the Alma Mater where I am now teaching.

Owing to scarcity of houses we were obliged to room temporarily in the dormitory, but we are now at last located at No. 923 Grant Street.

Thus my story ends, except to say that I keenly feel the need of the prayers of all those who are interested in the future of Ashland College that I may prove a real asset as a newly added member of the faculty.

A. L. DELOZIER.

THE IMPROVED COLLEGE PUBLICATION

Ashland Ohio, Sept. 28, 1920.

Friends of Ashland College:

The Brethren church and Ashland College are entering upon a new day. At no time has there been such a general enthusiasm among the young people of the Brethren church. This enthusiasm is expressing itself in the enlargement and better organization of the various activities of the church and the College.

In harmony with this enlarged enthusiasm and better organization, the Purple and Gold, our College paper, will be circulated throughout the whole brotherhood. You no doubt will be interested to know that the Staff and Management have been completely re-organized. The thing that commands the greatest attention, perhaps, will be the "up-to-dateness" of the magazine. It will contain the best literary productions Ashland is able to produce. Illustrations and cartoons will be intermingled with the jokes and news in the most attractive manner. The latest happenings of the Alumni Association will be penned by J. A. Garber, its secretary. Every page will be of interest to you. As an Endowment Subscriber you will find that every issue will really be an interesting report on your investment.

In view of these facts, we are asking for the co-operation of all the churches. Several of our churches have already organized P. & G. Clubs. The regular subscription price is one dollar per year but in clubs of ten or more, the eight issues can be secured for seventy-five cents. The first issue will be ready for distribution about the fifteenth of October. A response in regard to this matter will be appreciated.

Thanking you for any favors and anticipating a better future for Ashland College and the church, we remain,

Cordially yours,
MELVIN A. STUCKEY,
Circulation Manager.

ALLENTOWN, PENNSYLVANIA

At our regular quarterly business meeting in April, Brother DeLozier, our pastor, handed in his resignation, to take effect as soon as advisable, which later developed to be July 5th, 1920. While to be sure, the church as a whole was shocked, and yet to at least some it was not unexpected. The church however feels gratified that the pastor, Brother De-

Lozier could leave under such favorable circumstances, and that there was perfect harmony between church and pastor. But all of
us will come to that place in life, when we
must submit our will unto his will, for the
Lord's will must be done.

After receiving a call from Ashland College, which Brother DeLozier seriously considered he finally accepted that call. What is our
loss will be the gain for the church at large.
And the church at Allentown always stands
for the progress and advancement, of the
whole church, it finally accepted, the pastor's
resignation with deep regret.

Since the church was without a pastor, it
extended a call to the elder of the church, to
take the work until a regular pastor could be
secured, to which call he consented. The work
here is coming on nicely since we took charge,
three souls have made the good confession,
two of whom have been baptized and united
with the church.

Just a word in regards to a mistaken idea
concerning the work at Allentown, Pennsylvania.

It is noted as a hard field by some of the
strongest men of the church, but it is not a
hard field, due to the fact of the church itself. There is a good spirit manifested as
you can judge by the average attendance at
our midweek prayer meeting, an average of
more than 30 percent present, even during vacation season. Our financial standing is excellent, as you can readily see by the report
of our Easter offering, and we are nearing
the $1,000.00 mark towards a parsonage. So
the reason why this is said to be a hard field
are rumors from without, and lack of information and other causes.

Since Brother DeLozier left here, we enjoyed the pleasure of having a son of this
congregation, now pastor at Pittsburg, Pennsylvania, Brother Harley, spent his vacation
with us, and he preached powerful sermons
for us, ringing true to the good old Book.
Come again, Brother Harley.

The delegates that attended the National
Conference from this place came back with a
splendid report which was received by the
church with much pleasure. Our Sunday
school superintendent, Brother Turner, has
the work at heart. On Temperance Sunday,
he planned a special program, such as singing,
recitations, and asked the pastor to give a
short address upon the subject which was concluded by a demonstration of the white of an
egg, and alcohol. The white of the egg represented the brain and we showed the effect
that alcohol would have upon it. The superintendent also gave some helpful remarks.

On Sunday, September the 26th, our school
observed Promotion Day, thus keeping our
school in front line.

The church here is anxious to correspond
with anyone who is open to a call.

Address all communications to Wm. H.
Schaffer, 626 Washington St., or to E. E.
Fehnel, 920 Washington St., Allentown, Pa.

MARYLAND-VIRGINIA CHURCHES,
NOTICE

If you have not yet sent in your money for
the Tabernacle Fund (as per notice), please

hold same until further instructed. Your
moderator complied with instructions at Conference and was not aware of payment made
until reading notice in The Evangelist.

A. B. COVER, Moderator.

Communion Notices

Communion services will be held at the
Maurertown, Virginia, Brethren church on
October 17th at six o'clock in the evening.
We extend an invitation to all who may be
interested.   E. B. SHAVER.

Business Manager's Corner

HELP IS COMING

In our last report we stated that thirty dollars had been contributed toward the fund to
help the Publishing Company meet its excessive charge for paper stock without increasing
the subscription price of The Brethren Evangelist. We are glad to be able to report contributions from the following faithful members of the church since our previous report.
Mrs. J. W. Weidenhammer, $1.00; W. W.
Meyer, $5.00; R. R. Boone, $5.00; J. L. Hudson, $5.00; J. S. C. Spickerman, $5.00; Mrs. H.
M. Cook, $10.00; Mr. and Mrs. Israel Penrod,
$10.00 and H. B. Lehman, $25.00—total $96.00.

We greatly appreciate these gifts and desire to say "thank you" to each one of the
givers from the least to the greatest. We
wish to call attention to Brother Lehman's
gift, not because it is the largest we have received to date, but because Brother Lehman
is a frequent contributor to the needs of the
Publishing Company, and because he reports
that it is possible for him, an old brother past
his three score years and ten, who makes his
livelihood by raising chickens, to make such
gifts because he sets apart a "tithe" of his
income for the Lord's work. A few thousand
such members of the Brethren church would
assure the financial success of all the institutions of the church. May the Lord bless all
such and increase their number.

A Publishing Company Offering Day

Since the new Bicentenary Movement of
the church includes in its scope an adequate
financial support of The Brethren Publishing
Company, and since the Board of Directors
has authorized this present appeal for assistance to meet the present emergency before
the real program can be gotten under way,
and since members of the church have asked
why we do not have the churches take up a
special offering for the fund, we are going to
give every church such an opportunity.

We will designate Sunday, October thirty-
first, as PUBLICATION DAY and will ask
all our pastors to make it a subject of prayer
for that day and to take up an offering for
the cause for which we have been making
appeals for the past few weeks. The smallest
amount any one church should be content to
contribute on that day should be TWELVE
CENTS per member. This seems the only
way possible to meet this emergency and we
trust every church in the entire brotherhood
may be led to feel and to assume its portion

of the responsibility. Churches that have
services only twice a month should lift the
offering either the preceding Sunday or the
Sunday following the thirty-first.

Amounts already contributed by individuals will be credited to the churches they
represent.

This is no small matter for the Publishing
Company, but rather a matter of life and
death; but we are confident it will mean continued life if our loyal pastors will rally to
the call and add this one more burden to their
already heavy loads and give their people an
opportunity to follow where the Lord will
lead them. We CAN and we MUST meet
this emergency.   R. R. TEETER,

Business Manager.

THE TIE THAT BINDS

KILPATRICK-SEIBERT.—A wedding was
solemnized by the writer Sunday evening,
September 12 at the home of brother and
sister G. B. Seibert when their daughter
Fern, became the wife of William H. Kilpatrick, Jr., of Beatrice, Nebraska. The bride
is a member of the Beaver City Brethren
church and has been a zealous worker in
church activities. The groom, who is a member of the Beatrice Christian church is a
young man of good Christian character. Both
Mr. and Mrs. Kilpatrick have the best wishes of the church   E. S. FLORA.

IN THE SHADOW

VERNON.—James Delbert, son of Mr. and
Mrs. Wesley Vernon, aged one year and three
months. The funeral services were conducted
by the writer at Masontown.

JOS. L. GINGRICH.

ROTHARMEL.—Within the confines of the
Uniontown, Pennsylvania, congregation, Mrs.
S. B. Rotharmel, aged 78 years, 4 months and
22 days. Death occurred on July 23, 1920,
after a lingering illness consequent to a paralytic stroke. Sister Rotharmel was descended from Brethren ancestry and had been a
life-long member of the fraternity, making
the transfer of membership to the Brethren
church on July 13, 1920, at her own request.
Funeral services at the home on July 25, in
the presence of a large concourse of friends
and relatives. Services by the writer, assisted
by Rev. Dr. W. Scott Bowman, pastor of the
Second Presbyterian church of this city.
Music by a quartette from the First Brethren
church, and the body was laid to rest in the
beautiful Church Hill Cemetery at McClel-
landtown, Pennsylvania.

DYOLL BELOTE.

MARTINDALE.—Following a long illness,
Sarah Deeter Cable Martindale, aged 74
years and 22 days, departed this life to be
with the redeemed. Sister Martindale early
in life united with the Church of the Brethren and when the Brethren church was organized in Pleasant Hill, she became a charter member, continuing faithful to her church
until her death. The funeral services were
conducted in the home church with her pastor in charge, using as his text John 14:1:
"Let not your heart be troubled." He was
assisted by Elder Isaac Frantz, a lifelong
friend of the family.   S. LOWMAN.

PLEW.—Pearl Marie Tenney was born in
Kosciusko county, Indiana, February 5, 1884,
and died September 8, 1920, at the age of 36
years, 7 months and three days. She was
united in marriage to John W. Plew, April
16, 1904, to which union was born one son,
Lester, who with the husband, survives.
Pearl united with the Brethren church at
Dutchtown at the age of 14 years. She was
always a true and loyal member and always
ready and willing to "do what her hand
found to do." She will be greatly missed by
her church and the community in which she
lived. She expressed her faith in her Lord by
being anointed by Rev. A. E. Thomas, while
she was yet a patient at the Lutheran hospital at Fort Wayne, Indiana, where she was
a great sufferer for five long weeks. Her last
wish was to return home and pass away
among her relatives was granted. Funeral
services were conducted from the Dutchtown
Brethren church, Saturday, September 11, by
Rev. A. E. Thomas.

MRS. H. L. MAUZY, Warsaw, Indiana.

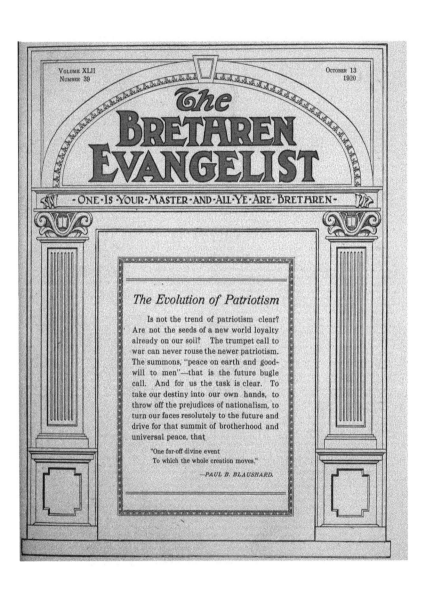

Volume XLII
Number 39

October 13
1920

The Brethren Evangelist

· One · Is · Your · Master · and · All · Ye · Are · Brethren ·

The Evolution of Patriotism

Is not the trend of patriotism clear? Are not the seeds of a new world loyalty already on our soil? The trumpet call to war can never rouse the newer patriotism. The summons, "peace on earth and good-will to men"—that is the future bugle call. And for us the task is clear. To take our destiny into our own hands, to throw off the prejudices of nationalism, to turn our faces resolutely to the future and drive for that summit of brotherhood and universal peace, that

"One far-off divine event
To which the whole creation moves."

—*PAUL B. BLAUSHARD.*

Published every Wednesday at Ashland, Ohio. All matter for publication must reach the Editor not later than Friday noon of the preceding week.

George S. Baer, Editor

The
Brethren
Evangelist

When ordering your paper changed give old as well as new address. Subscriptions discontinued at expiration. To avoid missing any numbers renew two weeks in advance.

R. R. Teeter, Business Manager

ASSOCIATE EDITORS: J. Fremont Watson, Louis S. Bauman, A. B. Coven, Alva J. McClain, B. T. Burnworth.

OFFICIAL ORGAN OF THE BRETHREN CHURCH

Subscription price, $2.00 per year, payable in advance.

Entered at the Post Office at Ashland, Ohio, as second-class matter.

Acceptance for mailing at special rate of postage provided for in section 1103, Act of October 3, 1917, authorized September 9, 1918. Address all matter for publication to Geo. S. Baer, Editor of the Brethren Evangelist, and all business communications to R. R. Teeter, Business Manager, Brethren Publishing Company, Ashland, Ohio. Make all checks payable to the Brethren Publishing Company.

TABLE OF CONTENTS

EDITORIAL

Ministry for the Times

In the discussion of our theme—the kind of a preacher our age demands—two questions naturally suggest themselves: What are some of the outstanding features of the age in which we live? How may the message of the pulpit be so shaped as to effectively meet present-day conditions? To answer these two questions, even though the answer be brief and cursory, may enable us to reach, the conclusion our subject proposes.

What are some of the dominant features of our present age? Analyzing our present century—the most marvelous and progressive the world has ever known—one cannot fail to note, among others, four special features:

In the first place, ours is an age of earnest, intense, unsatisfied search after truth—not so much an age of doubt, as "an age of struggle against doubt in the interest of a finer faith and a nobler spirituality."

In the second place, our age is, in a remarkable degree, an age of social unrest, reconstruction, and reform. Men are studying and emphasizing today as never before sociology, social psychology, social ethics, and social politics. There are visible today—in field and factory, in mill and mine, in store and shop—great social problems which call for solution.

In the third place, our age is an age of unparalleled intellectual advancement and opportunity, an age of public schools, public libraries, of widely diffused intelligence.

In the fourth place, our age is an age of marvelous enterprise and activity—of progress and improvement everywhere and in all directions—in material conditions, in social relations, in philanthropic endeavor, in educational movements, in moral elevation, in Christian attainment and growth.

We come back, then, to the question: What kind of preaching is demanded by our time? Our age, possessed of a fourfold character, demands and must have, a ministry marked by a fourfold aim and power: a truth-seeking age, a minister faithful to him who is the Way, the Truth, and the Life; a socially restless age, a ministry expounding and emphasizing the practical application of Christian principles to all human relations; an intelligent, cultivated age, a ministry abreast of the times and possessed of a culture worthy of its high position; an active, aggressive age, a ministry alive, alert, aflame with enthusiasm for God and man. Give the church a ministry like this and it cannot fail to bring rich and radiant trophies to the mediatorial grace of our Lord Jesus Christ.

Nothing can satisfy this truth-seeking age of ours but a ministry of strong evangelical convictions and of fearless evangelical proclamation. A ministry true always and everywhere, with a Pauline fidelity to the faith once for all delivered to the saints. Dr. Theodore Cuyler said, that the secret of power of such giants of the pulpit as Guthrie and Hamilton, Spurgeon and Parker, Beecher and Brooks, was "their adamantine faith" in essential Christian truth. "If asked to state the great specific of human sin and sorrow," said William Ewart Gladstone, "I should say this: The old, old story of the greatest, noblest, richest gift of God to man, the gift of Jesus Christ as friend, and brother, sovereign and Savior. Give mankind this," continued the Grand Old Man, "and you give it all."

There is Paul—in a sense he knew nothing but the gospel. Whether in the great center of religious truth—Jerusalem—or in the extreme limits of his missionary field among the heathen; whether in the synagogue of the Jew or the school house of the Greek; whether in the barbarous Lystra or elegant Athens or cultivated Corinth—everywhere his theme was the glorious evangel of Jesus and his redemptive love. Not simply Christ the perfect man, nor Christ the transcendent teacher, nor Christ the majestic miracle worker, but Christ mighty to save through the irresistable power of a sacrificial death. One thing covers the whole range of his being—thoughts, words, acts and that is Jesus and him crucified. This great, ennobling truth, of God in Christ reconciling the world unto himself through the blood of a transcendent, an all-sufficient, an unrepeatable atonement for human redemption—Jesus Christ and him crucified. This, I say, was the keynote of Paul's preaching, and its power too.

Much of the preaching of our day, is pitched to a lower key. "It deals much with the life of Christ, in its tender human sympathies—the Christ whose face was sculptured benevolence, whose hand was friendship's symbol, whose eye was liquid sympathy for all human burdens and woes; much with the works of Christ as the pattern and inspiration of helpful doing; much with the words of Christ as a divine philosophy, with heights to which no human imagination has ascended, depths which no human plummet has fathomed, and breadths which no human mind has compassed." Now, these are well enough, in their places, but they are not fundamental. The cross is Christianity's hope as well as Christianity's center. This is the theme for our day that hungers after truth.

Secondly, The pulpit must proclaim with vigor and earnestness the office Christianity takes to man in all his human relations and conditions. We need a ministry that makes men see that no man can lead an unrelated life; that absolute independence is an impossible relation; that to live for others is not a gratuity, but a duty and a debt.

Once again, our intelligent, cultivated age demands a ministry of ripe scholarship and broad intellectual culture; a ministry, as far as possible "with the scholar's taste, the poet's touch, and the prophet's torch." The day certainly is gone by when the minister can give his people anything and satisfy them. No efficiency outside of the pulpit will make amends for deficiency in the pulpit. It is true that the Spirit of God is the power that sends the arrow of truth on its all-conquering way; but it is also true that man is the bow through which the arrow is driven, and the better the human adaptation the finer the divine execution. It is a strong saying of Brierley: "Every religious teacher from Paul down who has cut deeply into his age has been an intellectual athlete as well as a spiritual man." And in our day, as never before, in the world's long history, the pulpit needs scholarly men, learned men, great-brained men, and great-souled men —men with minds developed, organized, trained by communion with higher forms of thought—men able to stand up and out before this proud, progressive age and declare with marked, effective force that with all its learning our world has not outgrown the mighty Master of the ages.

It must be confessed that in many instances the Christian Ministry of our day lacks flaming enthusiasm, dynamic energy. Some one has recommended to our preachers Hosea Bigelow's definition of eloquence: "Thoughts that burn in phrases such as stick." An American writer has described preaching as gathering material in the study and setting fire to it in the pulpit. He tells us that while a man may preach out of the head like Edwards, or out of the cultivated imagination like Fenelon, or out of his human nature like Brooks, in each case the truth of God must fill and thrill him if he would move men. Kingsley's sentiment is fine—"Would that I were an Apollo for his sake!"
J. FREMONT WATSON

EDITORIAL REVIEW

Brother Bryan Stoffer has accepted a call to the pastorate of the Elkhart, Indiana, church, which he will serve in connection with his school work at the University of Chicago.

Sister Elizabeth Haddix makes an appeal for help in meeting an obligation incident to the closing of the mission at Happy, Kentucky. See her letter in the "News from the Field" department.

Brother Lowman, pastor of Pleasant Hill, Ohio, church reports the work in good condition and increasing. Brother James Cook recently assisted him in an evangelistic campaign with good results.

Brother W. C. Teeter reports that the Dayton church has discovered two more preachers for the Brethren ministry. We hope the Brethren church will prove to be a real home to them and that they will prove to be a real contribution to our ministerial force. Welcome, Brethren Ronk and Eikenberry!

Begin now to look forward to and to plan for the General Home Mission offering to be taken at Thanksgiving time, either the Sunday preceding or the one following that festal day. The needs are greater and the offering should be greater than ever before. Plan and pray that the church may do its best.

According to Brother H. E. Roscoe's report of the Winona Tabernacle Fund, there are a number of congregations that have not come across with their apportionments to that cause. This ought, rather must be gotten out of the way in the very near future or somebody will be embarrassed by not being able to meet an obligation in which all the churches have agreed to co-operate. Do it now.

Brother G. E. Drushal has the matter of advancement at Lost Creek, Kentucky heavily upon his heart and he is seeking to place it upon the hearts of the brotherhood. It was he and his faithful co-worker, Mrs. Drushal, who first had the Kentucky field upon their hearts and place it upon many Brethren hearts. We dare say his zeal at this time will not be in vain, even as it was not then.

If the "love of Christ constrain us we will go anywhere even to the ends of the earth, or do anything even to the laying down of our lives for Christ's sake. But if we do not feel that constraint no irrefutable arguments, no unquestioned divine command, no sweeping wave of spiritual enthusiasm will carry us very far, nor exact from us any very great sacrifice.

It was a banner Sunday school rally held in the First church of Johnstown. Both the offering and attendance indicate that the school is back of the church in an effort to get a new church building. We shall be pleased to have reports of other successful Rally Day services. Your school may not be so big; but if you had success, tell the rest about it for their inspiration.

"Whether prophesy, let us prophecy according to the proportion of our faith," says Paul. How advisedly he writes! Faith differs greatly in different men and in the same men at different times. One reason for the success of some men and the failure of other men under equal circumstances is the difference in faith. The same man may have failed under circumstances which at a later time resulted in success, because his faith had grown. It is inevitable that the success of our work is always in proportion to our faith.

We have previously received a report of the evangelistic campaign held at Garwin, Iowa, written by one of the members, but this week the pastor, Brother Freeman Ankrum gives his version of it. But the pastor's letter has something decidedly new; he gives us a glimpse of the vision he has of the possibilities of his church's future. When every pastor gets a vision of that sort concerning the future of his parish, there will be greater growth: Where there is no vision, there people perish.

Brother J. C. Beal tells in this issue concerning the growth of the Compton Avenue, Los Angeles church during his pastorate and of the loyalty and promise of the faithful little band he found at Fillmore where he has taken charge of the work at the request of the district mission board. Few churches can excel the splendid record made at Compton Avenue under the consecrated leadership of Brother Beal and we can expect great things under his leadership at the Fillmore charge.

OHIO CONFERENCE AT ASHLAND, OCTOBER 25-27. Every Ohio church should keep this in mind and not fail to send a full quota of delegates instructed to remain throughout the entire conference. Parents who have children in college at Ashland will find this a fine opportunity to visit them and get acquainted with the school. And those who have no friends in school here will enjoy a visit to Ashland, the seat of the College and the Publishing House. The Ashland church is anxious for a large attendance and is making arrangements for your entertainment in a royal way.

The Business Manager's Corner has something of interest this week. Contributions for the paper bill are coming in and the size of these gifts is becoming larger. And another encouraging feature is that the churches are taking up the matter, and when this is done quite generally, as we believe it will, the fund will grow not "slowly", but by leaps and bounds. We are very thankful for all these expressions of co-operation and vital interest, whether large or small.

Brother A. V. Kimmell, vice-moderator of the General Conference, was called home, to Whittier, California, it will be remembered, before the close of the evening program on account of the serious sickness of their little child. In a communication just received from Brother Kimmell concerning a manuscript for publication, he stated that the little one died the day he reached home. We bespeak the sympathy of the brotherhood in behalf of Brother Kimmell and family in their sorrow

---

Brother P. H. Beaver, another veteran minister, died October 5, Tuesday morning. "He went to bed in his usual manner and went to sleep peacefully," his son, E. B. Beaver, states, "and in the morning we found he had gone home quietly and peacefully in the Lord." Thus one by one the aged veterans of the cross are answering the final roll call. We miss their counsel and encouragement as they pass from us, but they have earned their reward. May God bless and comfort those who most keenly feel the loss of this stalwart Christian soldier.

THE BRETHREN BICENTENARY MOVEMENT PAGE

1723 · · · · · · 1923

Dr. Charles A. Bame, Editor

The Story of the Making of Our New Program—The Brethren Bicentenary Movement

Back of every great movement in the world's history there has been a story of human interest. Inasmuch as the new Brethren Bicentenary Movement promises to be a thing of far-reaching significance in the history of our church, a brief story of the movement will not be without interest. As temporary secretary at the beginning, and later Secretary-Treasurer of the movement, it seems fitting that I should record some of the salient facts pertaining to it.

In the deliberations of the Four Year Program Committee at the general conference in 1919, the idea originated to ask the conference to appoint a committee on church extension whose duty it should be to formulate a "follow-up program" for use after the termination of the Four Year Program, same to be presented at the 1920 general conference.

In response to conference action, the committee on committees reported what was to be known as the Committee of Fifteen, and the following members were duly elected on said committee: Chas. A. Bame, W. H. Beachler, J. A. Garber, J. Allen Miller, O. E. Bowman, Horace Kolb, Miles J. Snyder, Norman Statler, H. V. Wall, G. T. Ronk, G. W. Rench, H. H. Wolford, A. V. Kimmel, W. S. Bell, and L. G. Wood.

Before the 1919 conference closed this committee met and formed a temporary organization and prayerfully considered the work delegated to it. It was thought wise to try to build a new program upon only several great outstanding church activities instead of having many goals. Accordingly, sub-committees were designated and assigned specific work for the following year. The chairmen of these sub-committees met at Ashland, Ohio, on January 1, 1920, and together considered the work done and also planned for the future.

Realizing something of the importance of the work in hand, the Committee of Fifteen was called to Winona Lake, Indiana, two days prior to the meeting of our late general conference, and began the work of formulating the new program. Reports were received from the several sub-committees, and then as conference came on there followed session after session of the committee, when the various suggestions were gone over and every phase of the work carefully considered. In that part of the work there are a number of things which cannot be incorporated in any "story" of it. Only those who have worked on similar committees will appreciate anything of the thought and prayer and effort that have gone into the making of this program.

But at last, by the grace of God, the work was done, and The Brethren Bicentenary Movement was presented to the general conference on Saturday, September 4, 1920, where it was enthusiastically and unanimously accepted, without a single change, as the program of the church for the next three years.

The program with the Executive Committee and its organization has already been published in the Brethren Evangelist. It presents a big undertaking. It challenges the Brethren church to the greatest effort she has ever put forth. Its goals can be attained only with the abiding help of God, whose we are and whom we seek to serve.

From the very beginning, Dr. Charles A. Bame was one of the leaders in the formation of this new program, and has been untiring in his efforts for the largest success of the Brethren church. It was altogether fitting and proper, therefore, that the promotion of the Bicentenary Movement be entrusted to him as Executive Secretary. The church was fortunate in securing his services in this capacity. Let us one and all uphold him in prayer and actively support his efforts by the most effective co-operation in every possible way.

MILES J. SNYDER.

More of the Story

I am glad that Secretary Snyder has written so much of the story; but there is a lot to it, as he hints, that is not written. The part I was anxious to add is, that it represents a great lot of study. Fifteen men of the church had it more or less in their hearts for the entire year. As it is presented to you, it is not as any one had planned. It represents the growth and devolopment of a great idea and as I now behold the work, it is a marvel of the completeness of the next work of the denomination. If the various organizations and secretaries will take seriously the work entrusted to them, the next jubilee will be something to go to and be a part of. Bicentenary! 200 years ago, in 1823, was started a small insignificant church on American soil. Its growth has been steady and sure, if slow. All these years, it has exercised its influence and who knows that until 1923, the Lord shall have made very clear that we have been preserved to the world for just such a time as this. It is my candid conviction that each succeeding day and year shall reveal more clearly the purpose the Lord has for the Brethren faith. It is to get ready for that day that we are planning this wonderful program. And, if Brethren generally, will try to attain the ideals therein set forth we shall be ready in three years for the greatest work the Brethren church will ever have the opportunity of doing.

This Movement as no other we have ever had, plans for the consecration of life and property of our membership as well as the fitting to the field of workers thus found, so that we shall not go on in haphazard nor unplanned method, with the work of spreading the gospel of the "Bible, the whole Bible and nothing but the BIBLE." In all these three years, this must ring out with fuller and stronger note than ever. If we do not live for the fullest possible adherence to and devotion for the truth as it is in Christ and as it has been preached for all of the 200 years of Brethren history, then movements like this need not be encouraged nor organized.

But the church has already put on this Movement, through its Conference, its most hearty approval. The silent raising of more than $1,000.00 on one evening of the Conference shows unmistakably the enthusiasm of the conference. Now, do not forget, Brethren, that you at home ought to come across with some "dough," also. If you will speed up and send your gift to the BICENTENARY FUND, M. J. Snyder, Secretary-Treasurer, Milledgeville, Illinois, you can do a bit of encouraging also. Two sisters at Conference gave $100.00 each; what will you give? BAME.

GENERAL ARTICLES

Enlisting Young People for Service.   By Edwin Boardman, Jr.

Jesus still wants his people to meet him at Calvary. We are to meet him there not merely to have our emotions stirred; nor to hide behind the skirts of a tragedy that means for us eternal salvation; but he wants us to meet him at Calvary to die with him. Calvary must spell for us not only salvation through the death of the Son of God, but also death to self and selfish ambition. Many centuries ago the Apostle Paul voiced the truth in those immortal words: "The love of Christ constraineth us in that we thus judge that if one died for all, then were all dead; and that he died for all, that which live should not henceforth live unto themselves but unto him who died for them and rose again." Centuries later another consecrated man breathed the truth, for as Raymond Lull was being martyred for the love of Christ his Mohammedan butchers heard coming from his dying lips the words, "He that loves not, lives not; and he that lives by the Life can never die."

There can be no Christian life without Calvary in it; and there can be no joyous Christian experience without the bitter-sweet experience of dying with Jesus. To die with Christ is really to live, for once that death to self comes we will reach that state where we will be willing to do his will. This will bring us to know his teachings and Jesus himself said, "My words they are spirit and they are life." The Master always thought of the Christian life in the superlative degree. Life to him meant obedience to the Father's will for he said, "I do always those things that please the Father." Hence obedience was the keynote of life to the Master and it is not strange that he passed the truth on and makes obedience the organ of spiritual knowledge for us. "If ye love me ye will keep my commandments," is the Master's pointed way of showing us the path of life's supremest enjoyment.

We therefore make bold to state the two truths to the young life assembled here today, that if you would know what life really means you will have to "set the cross up in the heart," and you will thereafter implicitly obey the One who has called you into the true life.

Each Christian in this presence today is face to face with the authoritative "Go ye" of the Master of men and it behooves each of us to earnestly heed the command. To young people especially is the command a pointed one. We have a life to give as a living sacrifice and if we are Christians in heart and purpose there are very few excuses we can offer for neglecting to carry the truth to the uttermost parts of the world.

There are three important human factors that enter the question of young people giving their life in service for God, and, sad to relate, the three have all too often acted in a negative way toward the matter.

The first of these factors is the attitude taken by Christian ministers and Christian workers. All too many times those who should be fired by a holy zeal for world saving are negative in their attitude and instead of filling young life with an enthusiastic desire to do big things they have chilled them into indifference by counseling against Christian service as a life calling. Their argument is generally the material argument of poor pay and when a young man finds a servant of God seeing only the gold side of the call of Jesus he comes to believe that the God side is but a poor and secondary matter. I am not foolish enough to fail to recognize the necessity of material returns in Christian life service, but I do most earnestly contend that the man who advises a young man against Christian life service solely on monetary grounds is a traitor to the cause he has espoused and will some day have to pay the price of his shame. Ministers of Jesus Christ, we must be blazing firebrands for God in this matter, letting the fire of the Holy Spirit so permeate our life and thought and words that when young people seek us for counsel regarding life service for the King they will have been so advised that they will leave us with heart and face aglow to go out and give their all for their Christ. One of the sweetest memories of my own life is the counsel I received from a godly pastor when my decision was still to be made. He was an idealist and by his ability to forget the material and exalt the spiritual conception of Christian life service he led me to know the glory of such labor. May we as ministers and Christian servants encourage young life to the noblest kind of activity for Christ.

Then, too, parents play an important part in this matter. There was a time when parents counted it all joy to see their sons and daughters enter the ministry and mission service. In fact it was a habit with them to dedicate their children to God's service from birth and endeavor through their young life to help them to see the wonderful privilege and power of a Christian life work. That's the reason we had such characters as Moses, Samuel and John the Baptist in the old days. They could not be other than they were because the fact had been thoroughly impressed on them that they were servants of the Most High and they had also the glorious power of a godly parentage behind them. Today the story is different. Parents have forgotten their godly prerogatives, seemingly, and instead of dedicating their children to God's service and advising by precept and example the necessity of answering God's call they positively fight such a thought. Even ministers have been heard to say, "Well, I'll never advise my boy to be a minister." Our whole attitude as parents is that of pushing the responsibility onto someone else. We're perfectly willing to talk to young people about a life service for God providing the young people are the children of someone else. With a shrug of the shoulders and a deprecating smile we say, "Oh, you know how it is. I don't want my boy to be a poor preacher, and I don't want my daughter to be in some God-forsaken land as a missionary. I want them to have the comforts of life; to be famous; to have them near me." In this manner we turn sons and daughters into a hundred other channels of activity, give them a poor conception of Christian service, and then sit piously in church on Sunday and complacently watch the heathen go into Christless graves. Shame on us!—fathers and mothers—that such is all too often our attitude to the claims of Christ on our children. Is it any wonder young folks are turning a deaf ear to the pleading Christ? May the Holy Spirit melt our hard gold-seeking hearts, and so destroy our idols that we will be able to see the "Lord sitting on the throne high and lifted up, with his train filling the temple."

The third human factor in this matter of life enlistment for God is the individual himself. To most young men the Christian ministry is a "soft job," something effeminate and consequently no place for a strong red-blooded man to exercise his powers. To him it's a case of making a series of short calls on parishioners, of looking perpetually pious, of chaining up all the vibrant vital qualities in one's personality and becoming by middle life a dried up specimen of manhood that has lost its power and point because of living in perpetual fear of cantankerous deacons or sarcastic, fault-finding church members. If such a picture were the true story it would be bad indeed, but I want to register a strong protest against any such conception of the Christian ministry or general Christian work. Christian service demands the most vibrant vital quality of life possible and the man of God should be strong, healthy, vigorous and happy in his work for he is handling the things that make for life and joy and prosperity. It is true that discouragements come; that temptations to ease and real downright laziness are very present, but these deterrent factors are everywhere. The youth must see the big work, the big opportunity that the ministry and mission field present before they condemn them as soft, effeminate callings. Jesus calls us to a hard life, a high life, a happy life, and it were better a thousand times to be a poor preacher with the knowledge of a good task well done than to be a material worlding, successful in making money, but absolutely crippled in making a life.

So much for the human factors in enlistment for life service. There is the Divine side to the question. The great wish of God's heart, yes let me say—the burning desire of his heart—is that men might be saved. Being God he cannot complacently stand by while his dark skinned children of the Orient and the South go down into Christless, hopeless eternities. So strongly did he feel about the matter that he gave the world the best he had so that salvation, hope, joy might come to the race. Hence we read that in the fulness of time Jesus came. Jesus carried on the great thought of God and he with compassionate heart and tear-filled eyes looked out on the world of men beholding them as "sheep having no shepherd." With intense yearning he cried from the depths of his soul, "The Son of man is come to seek and

to save that which was lost." His heart was big enough to embrace all men and the craving of his life was that those who love him should "feed his sheep;" that no servant of his should fail to carry the "Bread of Life" to those who are hungry. Though confined to the limits of Palestine the Master's vision took in the mystic palaces and shrines of China, the storied beauty of India; the cold forbidding regions of the north and the fabulously rich lands to the south. Being creator of all things, he was definitely, absolutely committed to the welfare of all. Hence his world challenge.

Now that the Master is at the right hand of the throne of God, the Holy Spirit is here telling of God and his dear Son, leading men to believe, urging Christians to carry the news everywhere that "a fountain has been opened in the house of David for sin and uncleanness." We have been looking for some miraculous challenge to life service, and just because the Spirit is here urging, pleading in the "still small voice" we turn a deaf ear to the call. Thus the three personalities in the Godhead are calling positively and clearly to us to carry the gospel everywhere and to do this we must enlist in the service of the King.

(To Be Continued)

A Few Thoughts on John 15; Matthew 15 and 20:8. By N. J. Paul

1. Our Relationship to Christ. "I am the true vine, ye are the branches"—a vital connection. Each branch is a partaker of the vine's life,—"partakers of the divine nature."

2. Entire Dependence. "The branch can not bear fruit of itself; no more can ye. Fruit-bearing is the Christian's chief business, and this demands abiding in Christ. (See Philipp. 1:11, 27-29; Rom. 5:1-5; 8:4-6; Gal. 4:6).

3. Co-operation. "Without me ye can do nothing." Christ must have a chance to work in us, both to will and to do Philipp. 2:13; 2 Cor. 13:5; Col. 1:12, 13.

4. Great Possibilities. "Ask what ye will, and it shall be done." The key to unlimited power is here placed within reach of all. See 2 Cor. 5:17; Gal. 6:7, 8.

II. Our Relationship to One Another,—(Col. 3:12-17).

1. Oneness of life. There are many branches, but one vine; many believers, but one Head—Christ; many creeds, but one Gospel. All are born (or should be born) of the same Spirit, and members of the same family. See Psa. 119:63; Amos 3:3; Mark 10:42-45.

2. Oneness of love. "Love one another as I have loved you." The words of the Master. How do we, as professed Christians understand this Scripture? Not all, but sorry to say, a great many of us, seem to understand it to mean to keep strife up among one another; to tattle, and carry news to one annther, and last of all to become jealous of one another. Listen, "love one to another" is the universal mark of discipleship. See 1 John 3:14; 4:21.

3. Oneness of Friendship. "I have called you friends." "Whosoever shall do the will of my Father, the same is my brother, sister, and mother."

4. Oneness of Work. "Bring forth fruit." Unity of life and privilege leads to unity of service.

5. Our Relationship to the World. Verses 19-27.

6. Separation. "Ye are not of the world." Called by his grace, cleansed by his blood, we are made meet for his fellowship by the indwelling of his Spirit.

7. Opposition. "Because ye are not of the world, therefore the world hateth you." As sons and daughters of God, the world knows us not; we are but strangers and foreigners.

8. Witness-bearing. "Ye shall bear witness, because ye have been with me." In the midst of a dark, sin-stricken world, Christians should, and do shine (Philipp. 2:15).

III. Reasons Why We Should Be At Work (Matt. 20:1-7).

(a) Because God is our Master. He is the "Householder." We are the servants.

(b) Because we are able to work. Our hands, our heads and our hearts may do noble service for God and man.

(c) Because we are called to work. The Divine call comes to men in all ages. The same call that came to Peter was addressed to others, long years before. Every soul is expected to respond.

(d) Why are we not at work? "No man hath hired us" —a satisfactory excuse in the case of the laborers of the parable. They were willing, and wanting to work; but were not called until almost the last hour. A similar condition prevails in the church today. Many noble young men who have united with the church, have heard the call, but the church fails to see their talents and unmindful of the service they might accomplish let them remain unnoticed and idle. The young men (or ladies as the case may be) have perhaps sought other fields where they could be employed. The church should always find work for all its members, and advance them to new fields of labor, as they prove worthy and opportunities offer.

IV. Willing to take our place (Matt. 15).

"A woman," a Greek, a Gentile, a mother in trouble. "O Lord, thou Son of David, etc." Her prayer was short, humble, persevering, full of faith, both right and wrong. It was conceived in a wrong name. Therefore, "He answered her not a word." "Send her away," they said. How quick the Jews gave command to the Master. Jesus never sent any one away (John 6:37). If he could not bless a true seeker where he found him, he led him to where he could bless him. "Lord, help me!" Compare this with the prayer in verse 22 and note the change. "Not meet"—proper, fitting. "Truth, Lord,"—is not meet to bring the children down to a level with the dogs; nor is it fitting to bring the dogs up on a level with the children. "Yet the dogs eat of the crumbs." I am but a dog, Lord, bringing for a dog's portion —the crumbs, just the crumbs,—a cure for my afflicted daugter, which is but a crumb compared with what thou hast done for the children (the Jews) yet of the same loaf. This poor woman, full of grief, full of sorrow for her afflicted daughter, had faith in Christ. Though she was considered as a dog, she simply took her place, and only begged for the part which belonged to her. Listen, "O woman, great is thy faith: be it unto thee as thou wilt." Take what thou comest for, and use it as thou wilt.

This woman was blessed because she was willing to take her rightful place. Great faith will endure the misery of silent suspense, and yet get comfort out of reubke. All people get, just what they work for.

Losantville, Indiana.

New Citizens and the Ballot.   By Bryan S. Stoffer

The time of the year is approaching when those who have the right of franchise will have an opportunity to exercise that right. Millions, who have not had this opportunity heretofore, will have it this November. Upon their votes will depend the type of men who will guide the destinies of municipalities, states and nation, during the next few years. Some will loyally respond to their duty as new-born citizens; others will neglect and thereby lose their privilege.

In this article the remarks will be confined to those who during the last four years have reached the legal age of citizenship. Theirs is not only an opportunity, it is also a responsibility. These young men and women must prove that they are worthy citizens of a great nation. It is a right; it is a duty, but it is more than either of the former; it is a privilege to feel that one is a part of this commonwealth. Her problems are our problems and we must accept her responsibilities just as eagerly and enthusiastically as we glory in her achievements.

This year is one of especial importance because of the great issues involved. Some of them are too great to be bound up with what we usually term politics. Those of us who are of legal age should cast our ballot and that ballot should be intelligently considered. The years of the war ushered in a great spirit of idealism. Since that time it has declined, but it is not dead. It has helped us win victories, such as prohibition which dare not be lost. Every man who is seeking a seat in our National Congress ought to be compelled to announce his position with regard to the Volstead Act. We, as Christian men and women, dare not allow our great moral victory to slip from our grasp. We must also try to eliminate the hatred which some are breathing against nations and governments both home and foreign. The spirit of "Good Will," between men and nations who differ, is one of the crying needs of our time.

The limit of this article will not permit a more detailed analysis of the problems facing us. It is to be hoped that all citizens of legal age will inform themselves and exercise the privilege which is theirs as an integral part of this nation.

456 Goshen Ave., Elkhart, Indiana.

Pulpit Preparation.   By T. Darley Allen

In the Brethren Evangelist of September 1 is an interesting article on "Pastoral Calling," it being a paper read by J. L. Kimmel before the Muncie (Indiana) Ministerial Association.

It is not the purpose of the present article to refer to the statements of Mr. Kimmel concerning pastoral work, but to what he says about the necessity of a minister's being capable of preaching "two sermons each Sunday that will keep his auditors wide awake."

Not only must the minister of the gospel be able to help his people spiritually but he should be an intellectual leader.

Indeed, he cannot be a spiritual leader unless he is intellectually well equipped also. In this intellectual age he must be capable of dealing with the great questions, especially those underlying faith, that engage the attention of thinking people.

Bishop Waldorf of the Methodist church once referred to a minister who declared that no one had the right to relate his experience in prayer meeting without careful preparation and that he had no reason to expect people to give their time to anything less than his very best.

The late D. L. Moody said, "A man cannot be giving out all the time. He wants to receive something. What the Christian people of this day need is more time to study the Word of God. I know of wrecks of Christian evangelists and ministers all over the land because they did not get time to study. A man who does not get at least two hours a day for study will soon run out of ammunition. I do not believe any Christian work is worth a snap of the fingers that is not based on study. Experience is a good thing, but a little of it goes a long way. The man who is continually talking about his experience has a harp of only one string, and continual thrumming of it becomes tiresome."

The person who does little or no study but is satisfied with telling of his experience will not have a worth-while experience long. For his spiritual development he must study. To neglect to do so means that he is likely to lose interest in spiritual things and perhaps become a backslider.

Many years ago an article in a religious paper quoted a deacon as saying of two candidates for a certain pastorate: "The first one did well for about three trips; after that his sermons lost interest and instruction, and the congregation fell off, so he quit. . . The truth is, he did not study. The second minister came; he was a good speaker, he had a large congregation. But he preached Mr. T's sermon on 'The Beautiful Name' verbatim and represented it as his own. This lost him his influence, and of course that tells the rest."

The following illustrates the methods of sermon preparation followed by Dr. Frank W. Luce, district superintendent of the Methodist Episcopal church, Cleveland, and one of the leading preachers of the denomination. Says Dr. Luce, "Having chosen my text and subject and evolved the general plan of the discourse, having made copious notes of various points, my library—so far as books bear on any of the themes suggested—is gone over by indexes and paragraph readings, careful note being made of thoughts suggested, facts gleaned, incidents and other illustrative matter discovered. . . Usually a few hours each week are spent in the public libraries in consultation of periodical literature and such authors as are not in my private library. The mass of noted material is then one over and logically arranged . . . This arranged and selected material is then worked into a pencil sketch of some two thousand words, carefully looked over, re-arranged, interlined, erased and rewritten in some of its sentences. Usually three forenoons of about four hours each have been diligently and systematically spent when the 'pencil sketch' is completed. Some sermons cost me many times that length of time. . . For me there is no substitute for patient, diligent, prayerful toil."

"In Life's Small Things Be Resolute and Great"

Every action, down even to the drawing of a line, or utterance of a syllable, is capable of a peculiar dignity in the manner of it, which we sometimes express by saying, it is truly done (as a line, or tone, is true), so also it is capable of dignity still higher in the motive of it. For there is no action so slight, nor so mean, but it may be done to a great purpose, and ennobled therefore; nor is any purpose so great but that slight actions may help it, and may be so done as to help it much, most specially that chief of all purposes, the pleasing of God.—John Ruskin.

What would I have you do? I'll tell you, kinsman;
Learn to be wise, and practice how to thrive,
That would I have you do; and not to spend
Your coin on every bauble that you fancy,
Or every foolish brain that humors you.—Ben Johnson

THE BRETHREN PULPIT

Taking the Community for Christ.   By E. L. Miller

TEXT: For God hath not given us the spirit of fear; but of power, and of love and of a sound mind. Be not thou therefore ashamed of the testimony of our Lord, nor of me the prisoner: but be thou partaker of the afflictions of the gospel according to the power of God.—II Timothy 1: 7, 8.

Thou therefore endure hardness as a good soldier of Jesus Christ.—II Timothy 2: 3.

Since no instance of a community having been taken for God in toto has ever come to our notice, we must speak in the subjunctive. All that we can do is work suppositionarily. That is, if we are to take the community for God, what must we have and what must we do? It was Christ himself who said that if he were lifted up, he would draw all men unto himself. Now since so many are away from him, there must be need of putting him before the people as he is. In order to make good in community or individual soul-winning, we must have—

1. Indomitable Courage.

The largeness of the task dare not appall us. We must get the drop on the enemy and this can be done only by showing courage and alertness. Those were the two elements evidenced by Pat, as when he came into camp driving a score of the enemy ahead of him at the point of his bayonet his captain commended him, but said, "Pat, how did you do it?" Pat very soberly replied, "Shure and oi surrounded thim." He did, that is, his courage and alertness surrounded them and so must it be with us. We must put our ten thousand to flight. Verily the wicked fleeth when no man pursueth, but he maketh better time when God's warrior getteth after him.

Then the orders of our commander must be followed even to our extreme sacrifice. When a young naval officer approached Senator Sumner at the outbreak of the Civil War and said, "Senator, I am a South Carolinian by birth and rearing. My ship has been ordered to southern waters. What shall I do?" Sumner said, "Read your commission." "But," expostulated the young officer, "suppose we are ordered to fire on Charleston?" "Read your commission," replied Sumner. "But suppose I am ordered to point the guns toward father's plantation?" "Read your commission," thundered Sumner. So with us, we should read our commission and take it to heart seriously.

In short, each soldier of Christ needs the revised version of the three G's in his makeup, Gumption, Grit and Git. Live lay members and not dopey, drowsy lay members are needed in the church before we can make an appreciable dent in the parish for God.

Then too, the preacher must desist from his namby-pamby, rock-me-to-sleep-mother sort of preaching. The devil is a relentless, no-quarter-granting foe and we must mercilessly, unrestrictedly shell, storm and torpedo his positions for God.

The true servant of God, and earnest soul winner, will have no time for creedal fusses or denominational scraps. We must not equivocate nor dare we compromise, for not only he that hesitates but also he that compromises is lost. But the spectacle of Christian fisticuffs will help no soul toward God.

Nor yet must we make faint-hearted approach of the sins of the world through the Word. It isn't a matter of "you must desist from your sin in a measure, or you may be condemned, as it were, and then perhaps you may be punished, after a fashion;" but it must be, "if you don't quit your meanness and sinning you are condemned and where God is you can not come."

For the cause's sake, don't ride any hobbies, but don't neglect preaching some notable but disliked truth for fear of being called a hobbyist.

Proclaim the whole counsel of God, don't preach human sufficiency and gloss over the various mistakes of the preached-tog. A young minister after preaching his initial sermon to an ultra-fashionable congregation was called into the vestry room and kindly told not to speak again in opposition to the liquor traffic, secretism, narcotics, gambling, etc., as he had done that morning. So inclusive was the inhibition that in sheer desperation the young clergyman asked, "Well, against what may I preach?" The reply was, "Give it to the Jews, there isn't a one in our congregation." Such churches ought to be pastorless, and the pastor who would yield to such persuasion ought to be churchless.

Further, have courage enough to proclaim the essential doctrines without any fear of being called narrow.

In short, be a good soldier of Jesus Christ, casting aside every unnecessary weight, and you will be able to make at least a dent in the breastworks of the enemy.

Again, I might say that in order to make any appreciable effect upon the community for God we must not only be possessed of indomitable courage but

2. We must preach Christ and him crucified.

These are days of woeful neglect along this line. As an old Scotchman put it in a Lancaster county, Pennsylvania, church after he had listened to a series of sermons on popular subjects, ending with three on the life, works and death of Garfield; he was asked how he enjoyed it and his reply was, "Weel, my mon, in days gone by one mought at any time hear a sermon in this kirk on Jesus Christ and him crucified, but noo it is Garfield and him assassinated." The criticism was well taken and very timely. Let us take heed.

We must gospelize the social body, and not prate so much about socializing the gospel. Preach the old Book and leave profane hands off its sacred content. The book has always done the work wherever and whenever preached. So don't try to edit, revise, deny or argue the Word, just preach it.

Fearlessly, forcefully, but kindly, face both community and individual sins, and fight both to the finish. No quitters need apply in God's army.

As already intimated, the preacher must cut all strings that influential members in sin may have tied about him, and then "go to it."

Don't tolerate balkers, shirkers, jerkers, stingers or babblers in high church places. Particularly must the gossip be quieted. With their tongues put out like a weather vane, they buzz around and hit at all four points of the compass with little or no difficulty, but with awful results. If you can't preach their funerals, at least preach them quiet or out of the church.

And hold Christ forth as a Man, and not as a pink-tea weakling. Imagine him spending his time as engineer-in-chief to some Ladies' Aid Society or bean supper. It takes the presentation of him as a man—a real man—to properly appeal to men and women. I can tolerate a tom-boy girl, but a sissy boy or man nauseates me. So don't preach my Christ as one afraid of his task. Read Matthew 23 for a type of fearlessness, and that person was the Christ we should preach.

We must get the church on a platform of clean living, wholly sanctified and consecrated in order to move any in the community for God.

We are aware that Roger Williams maintaining that the

nearest way to a man's heart was through his stomach. Yet I am persuaded that a little more stress on the spiritual and a little less on the physical—oyster suppers, bean feeds, turkey spreads, grab-bag bazaars and the like—would lead more men and women to God. And how preaching the tithe would improve upon the above-mentioned questionable methods of money raising.

But ere I close I must emphasize the "greatest of them all." No Christian work will be effectively accomplished without prayer and more prayer. Besides, we must remove all restrictions to good, prevailing, intercessory prayer. Some are hindered by one thing, others by another. With an illustration from my own family circle, I close. My oldest daughter, a girl not quite five at the time of the incident about to be related, was collecting pennies for the last Easter offering. She had some twenty or thirty and was pleased all to pieces about it. On the Sunday preceding Easter when she got home from the evening services she was busy counting her pennies for the poor boys and girls who have no Sunday schools. As she counted and arranged them in rows and circles on the table her mother said to me, "Papa,' you ought to have heard Margaret lead in prayer this afternoon at the Junior C. E." Mind you not quite five and leading in extemporaneous public prayer. Then the mother said, "Margaret, pray for daddy now." No answer. Again, "Pray for daddy now, won't you Margaret?" Can you imagine the looks that passed between the two parents when the money counting tot replied, "Please don't bother me now, I have too much money to pray."

Nappanee, Indiana.

OUR DEVOTIONAL

The Christian's Daily Provision
Wilma E. Garber
OUR SCRIPTURE

The Lord is my shepherd; I shall not want (Psalms 23:1). Happy is he that hath the God of Jacob for his help, whose hope is in the Lord his God (Psalms 146:5). Blessed be the Lord, who daily loadeth us with benefits, even the God of our salvation (Psalms 68:19). Your Father knoweth what things ye have need of, before ye ask him (Matthew 6:8b). My God shall supply all your needs according to his riches in glory by Christ Jesus (Philippians 4:19). The young lions do lack, and suffer hunger; but they that seek the Lord shall not want any good thing (Psalms 34:10) Thou makest the outgoings of the morning and evening to rejoice (Psalms 65:3, b). Thou visitest the earth and waterest it: thou greatly enrichest it with the river of God, which is full of water: thou preparest them corn, when thou hast so provided for it (Psalms 65:9). Every good gift and every perfect gift is from above and cometh down from the Father of lights, with whom is no variableness neither shadow of turning (James 1:17). The Lord openeth the eyes of the blind: the Lord raiseth them that are bowed down; the Lord loveth the righteous (Psalms 146:8). And the peace of God, which passeth all understanding, shall keep your hearts and minds through Christ Jesus (Philippians 4:7). For the Lord God is a sun and shield: the Lord will give grace and glory: no good thing will he withhold from them that walk uprightly (Psalms 84:11). The Lord lifteth up the meek (Psalms 147:6). He keepeth the paths of judgment, and preserveth the way of his saints (Proverbs 2:8). By grace are ye saved through faith; and that not of yourselves: it is the gift of God (Ephesians 2:8). The Lord will give strength unto his people; the Lord will bless his people with peace (Psalms 29:11). Let us therefore come boldly unto the throne of grace, that we may obtain mercy, and find grace to help in time of need (Hebrews 4:16). The Lord shall reign forever, even thy God, O Zion, unto all generations. Praise ye the Lord (Psalms 146:10).

OUR MEDITATION

Our God is continuously providing us unworthy beings of this universe with necessities of life. He is ever on the lookout for the needs of our body and soul. If God should forget to watch over us we would immediately perish. He provides us with comforts regardless of whether we are Christians or not.

Among the many things that he provides are food for the nourishment and strengthening of our bodies. He gives us water to refresh us and fresh air, which is one of the richest and most abundant of blessings, to sustain life. Along with these gifts we receive many blessings which add to the beauty and happiness of this universe. Flowers which most everyone enjoys at some stage of their growth; birds are supplied us by our Father, adding a touch of sweetness to our sorrows or disappointments. He gives us the animals to break the silence of the woodland or dispell the loneliness of the prairie and to supply us with physical food. In order that this world may be more beautiful and pleasant, he has painted the charming roof above us a magnificent blue at times adding to this a cluster of golden or swarthy clouds edged with gold or silver; at other times lighting the heavens with a brilliant radiance from the sun; at still other times our roof is a sea of darkness dotted like so many diamonds with twinkling stars made still more wonderful by the moonlight. At our side he has placed a range of mountains or perhaps a city of huge rocks of various hues or maybe beyond is a rolling prairie decked with trees and perhaps drained by a sparkling wandering river supplied with fish for use as food; the banks of this river often hemmed in by a wall of massive trees or bending bushes.

On the surface of this wonderful universe we are permitted to wander and seek happiness and along with us many persons of whom we may make companions and with whom we may share our happiness.

Do I hear someone say that he has given the sinner all of these? True, he has, and we Christians are glad that he has, but he has given his children more. He has given them an appreciation of the beautiful, a love, a spirit of mercy and sympathy for the useful which no sinner can ever understand. He helps us to understand what these all mean to us.

God has given us his holy inspired Book in which we may read daily and each time gain new thought, new desires, new aspirations, a knowledge of the world, our beginning, our end and best of all, our God.

He has given us the privilege of coming to him in prayer daily, hourly. He talks with us daily and provides us with instructions for doing his work.

He gives us strength to carry out his instructions through communion with him.

He daily leads his people by a still small voice which is heard by no one except the one to whom it is directed.

He gives us heavenly and earthly wisdom.

He gives a happiness in serving others which is felt by no one in the same true sense as the Christian.

God provides daily a contentedness and satisfaction to his people which one who is not his child can never enjoy.

He gives us the privilege of organizing his people into working groups as churches, etc., and devoting our energies to his needy people.

Best of all he gives us his love and guidance. He permits us humble, sinful, unworthy creatures to love, praise and adore him and calls us his children. We have been sinful and unworthy. But because of his great love he has lifted us up and made provision for our every physical and spiritual need. And he wants us to love and serve him in return.

OUR PRAYER

Dear all-wise, all-powerful, merciful Father, we come to thee in our weak, unworthy condition as humble servants of thine, seeking thy love, thy guidance and the in-dwelling of thy Holy Spirit. We would put our hand in thine and ask thee to lead us into righteous paths lest we dash our feet against a stone of sin and stumble and fall. We are very weak; thou art strong. Strengthen us; help us to do thy will. Father we thank thee for the daily gifts thou art showering down upon us. We thank thee for the beautiful things thou hast given us. We thank thee for the useful gifts. We thank thee for the Holy gifts; for thy Book and a desire to read it, for thy church and people, for a Christian

land and the privilege of coming to thee in prayer. We would ask thee to continue to bless thy people; Father, wilt thou especially bless thy servants who are at work in foreign lands. Do not withhold from them the strength which they so much need. Guide and bless us all and at last take us to the heavenly home above, for Jesus Sake. Amen.

Weldon, Iowa.

Send
WHITE GIFT
OFFERINGS to

THE SUNDAY SCHOOL

ALBERT TRENT
General Secretary-Treasurer
Johnstown, Pennsylvania

Children's Division Activities.　By Mrs. Pauline Lichty-Wismer

"Children's Division Activities" is, indeed, a big subject, in fact, too big for treatment in a single paper. The activities of each department in the division, namely, Beginner, Primary and Junior, could profitably be treated at length separately. However, we shall try to sum up a few activities that have actually been tried and have proven successful and may be used in any department.

A fine scheme for getting pupils to Sunday school on time, is to arrange a so-called "pre-lesson period." This, in other words, is for the superintendent to provide some work, which the children will like to do, and which is to be done entirely before ten o'clock or before Sunday school opens. This may consist of making scrap books, nature books, coloring pictures, collecting post cards, arranging them and pasting them together, etc.

Most of these things the children make can be used, if the superintendent is careful to supervise the work. The scrap books can be sent to children's wards in hospitals, or to sick children, whom the children know or to orphans' homes. Likewise the nature books. The post cards can be sent to mission points for the less fortunate children there. In fact, it is surprising the interest that children take in doing these things, especially if the superintendent will have announced the previous Sunday that the children shall bring pictures next Sunday for making scrap books. And if the work is done neatly the books will be sent to "some definite place" when completed.

The little nature books which consist of pressed flowers, leaves, pictures of animals, birds, butterflies and the like, and the scrap books may be taken to a printing office to be stitched and cut. Ofttimes if the object of these books is explained to the printer, he will be more than willing to do the work free of charge.

Some classes, especially Junior boys, will enjoy making monthly calendars and posters for their rooms. Some classes, use paste and the boys might enjoy making little wooden spatulas for spreading the paste. Boys will also enjoy making little make-believe paste board volumes representing the books of the Bible. This will help them to learn the names of the books, and also some of the boys could make a small imitation bookcase to hold these little volumes. These later could be used in the classes where commmitting of and the location of the books of the Bible are a part of the memory work. However, the thought must be in the child's mind all the while he is working, that what he is doing is needed and not that he is coming early, merely to play and have a good time. For this reason if for no other, the one in charge should plan definitely for using the things the children make. The question of pre-Sunday school discipline will be almost entirely solved if some such method as this is used.

The outside activities of our Sunday school children are ofttimes sadly neglected. We do not hold as many social gatherings for the children as we might. In fact, I think once a month is none too often for these parties. Now, in planning for these parties, try to make them instructive as well as entertaining. Also try to impress upon the minds of the children that to have a good time does not depend so

much on what some one else does for them as on what they can do for some one else. Keeping this in mind, the children can be asked to bring something for charitable institutions or for needy families. Some time it might be soup for the day nursery, some time crackers for the grandmas in the Old People's Home, or if no such institution is at hand, for some old ladies that the children know, or jelly or fruit for children in the hospital, etc. If there are no charitable institutions near your school to give these contributions to, perhaps there are poor families or "shut ins" in your community to whom the things could be sent.

In February the children could make Valentines for crippled children or they might even send them to the children of our missions. Easter time, they could color eggs, or make pretty little gifts from egg shells. The children could be taught that these parties are not just for something to eat. Refreshments could consist of candies, cake or cookies furnished by mothers, whose children had birthdays during the month.

Realizing how children love stories, and the benefit to be derived from them, try to have a story for each party. These can be obtained from "The Children's Hour" by Carolyn S. Bailey and Clara M. Lewis.

Each month naturally suggests the nature that the parties could be, i. e., October, Hallowe'en; November, Thanksgiving, etc.

Activities for third and fourth year Junior girls might consist of dressing dolls, piecing quilts, hemming dish and hand towels, etc., for hospitals or the church kitchen and the like. They could meet one evening each week or each fortnight, or even each month and get many things done. They might even form into a club, for we know that at this age, girls have a natural tendency for "cliques," clubs and the like. This might be the very way for teachers to get a firm hold onto these girls. It can certainly, with a little thought and preparation, be made attractive enough that they would rather come to these meetings than spend the evening at the "Movies."

Then Junior boys of this age are the most serious persons about the things in which they are interested. They are apt to be trifling in relation to matters with which they feel no vital concern. The teachers of older Junior boys are apt to make the mistake of trying to catch or win them by trifling games or amusements. Also they ofttime make the mistake of attempting to make the boy take seriously matters which he has not recognized as vitally related to his well being. Rev. Harnish says, "Boys are not interested in the history of Josiah's reign, or even in the eighth commandment, but let a boy's suit case be disturbed at camp, or a box of cookies be "crooked,' 'the detective work that follows is worthy of a high-grade police department. "The wise teacher will take occasion to impress on the boys' mind, in connection with this that boys ought not to steal apples from his neighbor's tree, etc."

Boys have much of the traditional "rough house" spirit. They sometimes are disposed to turn the Sunday school service to ridicule and some try to make a farce of every lesson. Now—how can we get this boy? Here is one way.

not give them parlor games, or soon they will turn the room into a baseball field, using anything available for balls, bats and bases. Anyway, this will not reach the serious side of the boy, and that is what we must not lose sight of. Try this plan, simple of course: Find an available room somewhere and fit it up as a work room. Let the boys make things that may be used. They can make toys, bird houses and the like. These can be sent to hospitals, sick children, poor children, etc. A boy likes nothing better than hammer, saw, nails, and a can of paint. The boys could also be encouraged to bring articles from home to be repaired or even make simple things for their own homes. The spirit of this room, supervised of course, will soon be reflected in the church school.

There are many so-called activities. If only the children's Division workers could catch the vision of the tremendous opportunities open to them for getting hold of the children. And after all, all these things are nothing more than another way to worm our way into the hearts of the children and save them for Jesus, our Lord.

Let us not forget the social natures of the children, for if the church neglects this side, you know as well as I, who will not let this side of their natures lag, and it will not be long until the bright lights of "the great White Way" will lure them their way and we shall have lost our big opportunity.

Waterloo, Iowa.

| J. A. Garber | Our Young People at Work | G. C. Carpenter |
| PRESIDENT | | SECRETARY |

"Young People and the State"

By A. E. Whitted, Morrill, Kansas, National Citizenship Superintendent

We are all proud of the fact that we are American citizens. That we are Americans means that we are protected by the best form of government ever framed by man. Our forefathers planned for this day. They not only planned but they carried their plans out in their lives even though doing so brought hardship, toil, sacrifice,—sacrifice even unto death for many of them. Because of these sufferings and sacrifices they were able to hand down to their posterity the protection and liberty you and I enjoy in this day.

They laid the burden of this republic on the shoulders of the men of this hour without fear for they had so shaped and moulded the life of their young that they felt no uneasiness concerning the piloting of the old ship of state. I am wondering whether such nobility of character, such true Christian patriotism is being fostered in our young men and women of today. If this spirit is fostered and kept alive we have a labor to perform in their midst. If the state is made secure through the decades to come this work must be accomplished.

The great work to this end is education. It takes men of mental ability,—full rounded men—to shape the state. It is said that education is the bulwark of any nation. It surely is the pre-requisite of a free government such as we are under in these beautiful states. Kaisers and Kings might be able to rule a people that are ignorant but presidents could not. In this free government we, the people, are compelled to stop and think things out. Matters of vital importance cannot be left with one man. Each has his part of the problem to solve.

O, what a great future faces the young man and woman of the church of the living God! How they are called upon in this day of so much unseen, unthought of evil, to prepare, to fit themselves for the biggest and best service that they can render to their country and their God! Democracy—what a big word! A democratic government is a big government. We believe democracy has come to stay. Dare we believe less? It has been tried and proven to be the best. Under its banners the hand that is hard with toil can hold high the scepter, and the brow once wet with perspiration for its daily bread may one day wear a crown. So all ought to be trained to be kings in a peculiar sense.

What is the great need in our land today? One great and imperative need is a better knowledge and better understanding of public affairs. Too often those who have no conception of righteous government, no fitness for leadership, no sense of true citizenship are placed in positions of trust. Here is where the monsters of inside peril of which we have heard much in the past week are eating their way into our life. When true citizens once learn of the true facts they rise, in righteous indignation to drive them from our midst.

We are facing problems of no little bearing. Great and overwhelming is our task. Tomorrow thees young men and women must arise to make and enforce laws that will solve these problems. These laws, if the state remains secure, must be just and indiscriminate. And even greater questions than these will arise to test the metal of men. These questions our young people will be called upon to answer. Will they be equal to their great task?

The moral life of the land is in the hands of its people. So it will always be. The moral life will soon be dependent on the young man and woman of today. God alone is their Superior. He alone is their sufficiency. We must lead them to know this, that they may be able to control themselves and become powerful to influence others! A stream cannot rise above its source. Water does not flow up hill; it flows down and out to meet the quiet power of the waiting sea. The moral life of a nation cannot be expected to be raised up by some unseen, unnatural force above the moral life of its citizens. Of what does our nation, or any other nation consist, anyway? Of these wonderful institutions of these great commercial systems, the magnificent laws? No, but rather the nation consists of folks, plain folks, men and women for whom and by whom these very things exist. The structure for our future state then will depend very largely upon the material raised up in our young life. Yes, and as water will not rise above its source, neither will a building excel the material of which it is built.

Can you not see the importance of fitting the young for places of leadership. Leaders—Christian leaders — are needed. The need grows as the nation advances, for men and women of ability. No victory was ever won without a commanding personality. How can we finish the task which I have said is so great without seeing to it that the young are so trained as to be strongly stamped with outstanding personalities. Great battles were never won by the spear and sword. All great battles which have changed the course of civilization have been fought upon the fields of men's thought, by the help of a righteous, divine God. We must train our youth to be thinking men and women, an education gives one the power of independent thought and teaches us to weigh matters, to find the main, primary issue involved. It develops self-control, self-confidence and a distinct and separate personality. Every one of these are very essential to the one who expects to carry his part of the burden of guiding the destiny of men. We are afraid of these terms. Because of this we truthfully say, "Pioneers have always been scarce." Only a few are willing to blaze the new trail, to rise to become commanding in their personality.

What part has education played in the building of the nation? I think if you will consider the matter for a few moments I can show you that it has had a large part throughout the growth up to this present day. The author of the Declaration of Independence was a college man; out of the sixty who signed it, 40 were college trained; two of the three men who led to the assembling of the constitutional convention were college men, and the three who contributed most to its adoption by the different states were college men. So the great issues arising in days before us must be met by men who are trained.

Yet there is more needed than the mere training of the mind; the heart must be touched and kindled with the wisdom of God. The young men and women of a democracy must be educated as men and women of principle. They must be trained in their moral life. We can have a moral state only as we have moral men and women. We boast of a Christian nation. If its citizens are Christian, only thus can we have a Christian nation. The ideals of a free government cannot rise above the Christian ideals of its people. The ideals of this same people cannot, will not, rise above their own thoughts. It therefore becomes the duty as well as the privilege of every young man and woman to make his and her thought life the very best, the highest, the noblest that he can. To do this he not only needs head-training but he needs heart-training as well. He needs to drink at the fountains of living water. He needs to sit with the Master Teacher. He needs to apply to his own life the thought of the song writer when he said:

Take time to be holy,
Speak oft with thy Lord,
Spend much time in secret,
Believe in his Word.

We've been trained too much to selfishness, and so long as our ideals rise only high enough to meet the demands of selfish interest we cannot become fitted to handle aright the affairs of a righteous government. As one has said, "We need men educated to be citizens and citizens educated to be men. Men—citizens, who know their rights and dare to maintain them. Men who know the rights of others and dare to grant them." How near like the principles of Jesus. How like the golden rule, How we need men of this type in today. Today as never before are earnest whole-souled, consecrated men and women needed.

Let me close by quoting from a little pamphlet, read recently, "The air is pregnant with great news; great news of glories yet to be, when we have answered to the age, when we have awakened to the light! Let us train men and women who will be able to answer to their age. Strong men and true great men and good, brave men and wise in simple faith; men warm with love and rich with hope; men with high aims and lowly hearts. The supreme test of every Christian citizen of our land is: Are you fitted to grapple with the questions of your day? These are many and serious. Lord help us to so teach and mould the lives of our young people that they will be able to intelligently answer.

Policy or Principles? By Dyoll Belote

Topic for October 17: "Principles in Politics." Luke 22:24-27.

[The following is a portion of the Christian Endeavor lesson helps written for the Angelus, but arrived too late for the issue intended and were given to us by Brother Gnagey for publication in The Evangelist. It is a very timely topic and should be made much of.—EDITOR]

Make up your mind that you are going to have a program a bit different from the one last Sunday evening, if in but one point,—but let that point be one that is helpful. This suggestive outline may be used, but is not to be followed slavishly.

Open with silent—or sentence-prayers, the LEADER to close the period.

Repeat the motto—the whole society standing.

Song.
Reading of the Lesson.
The leaders own thoughts on the topic.
Song.
Announcements.
Committee reports—Information, etc.
Special numbers—Music, recitation.
3 minute address "Politicians or Statesmen?"
3 minute address "Women and Politics"—by a woman.
General participation, including the use of the illustrations, quotations and questions.
Song.
Pastor's five minutes.
Benediction.

Thought Provokers

Do we need more laws or better enforcement?

What should be our attitude toward our officials?

What is our first duty as to our government?

Is it a Christian duty to vote?

Should Christian men run for political office?

Does "principle" or "policy" rule in politics?

What connection is there between our voting and our praying?

Gladstone said "We must make it as easy as possible to do right, and as hard as possible to do wrong." What has politics to do with this?

How has the Civil Service law helped to clean up politics?

The Bible and the State

" * * * Then saith he unto them, Render therefore unto Caesar the things which are Caesar's; and unto God the things which are Gods" Matt. 22:21. The conclusion is inevitable from this Verse, that a man's political duties are duties, and are not to be ignored. Read Matthew 17:24-27 and 1 Peter 2:13-16.

The True Citizen

He does not vote for bad men, and then plead that he did not know they were bad. He takes time to investigate the characters of candidates.

He loves his country, but he will not sully his loyalty to God to gain an earthly, material advantage, no matter how great the inducement nor how great the risk of refusal.

He believes that it is better to live for his country now, setting an example of Christian fortitude and forbearance, than to wait until he can die in some dazzling blaze of publicity —which may never come.

The true citizen pays all taxes justly assessed against him without attempt at evasion.

Such a citizen takes an active interest in public affairs and in the history and welfare of the country.

On election day he is found at the polls, voting for and exerting a positive influence for righteous men and measures.

Next to the affections of the heart and the labor of the hands which such a man feels due to Christ's kingdom comes his allegiance to his country.

Tell It Again

"A weapon that comes down as still—
As snowflakes fall upon the sod,
But executes freeman's will,
As lightning does the will of God;
And from it force, nor doors nor locks
Can shield you—'tis the ballot box."
—J. Pierpont.

Doubtless in every city and county the good citizens are in the majority, but too frequently they make the fatal mistake of dividing on political questions—and too frequently wrong wins as a result.

That patriotism is purest that disregards opportunities for personal honor, and falters not when called to do the difficult duty, though it must be done in obscurity, far from the blaze of public approval. Patriotism burns brightest in the unselfish heart.—Herald and Presbyter.

It is easy to get up sentiment for reform measures and the cleaning up of existing evils, but it is quite another thing to find enough who believe in the need strongly enough to give time and labor for its accomplishment. If you do not love and serve the part of your country that you can see—your neighborhood and your town—how can you love and serve the part of your country that you cannot see?—Amos R. Wells.

No one is likely to live for one's country if one is ignorant concerning its history—ignorant of its heroes and heroines, of its present perils and its great possibilities. The first step toward becoming a worth-while American is to learn about America.—Amos R. Wells.

Our country calls not for the life of ease, but for the life of strenuous endeavor. Let us, therefore, boldly face the life of strife, resolute to do our duty well and manfully; resolute to uphold righteousness by deed and by word; resolute to be both honest and brave, to serve high ideals, yet to use practical methods.—Theodore Roosevelt.

A patriotism that inspires us to give all to our native land and die for it ought to teach us to live those same lives in the service that will best help our native land.—Rev. Albert Bryant.

The world is in need—as it has always been—of men; men for every walk of life, and nowhere are real men more needed than in politics. The country wants men who will stand four-square for the best interests of the people for whom they have been chosen to make laws. And there is no place that should be able to furnish more of that soft than the church.

The boy who is going to be a statesman must be brave, and he must be afraid of nothing in the world except doing wrong.

Be strong!

We are not here to play, to dream, to drift.
We have hard work to do, and loads to lift.
Shun not the struggle—face it; 'tis God's gift.

Be strong!

Say not the days are evil. Who's to blame?
And fold the hands and acquiesce—oh, shame!
Stand up, speak out, and bravely, in God's name.

Be strong!

It matters not how deep intrenched the wrong,
How hard the battle goes, the day how long.
Faint not—fight on! Tomorrow comes the song.

—Maltbie D. Babcock,

First of all it is the duty of every young man and woman to be a Christian and to live the Christian life. And it is his or her next duty to be an American and live the true patriotic American life. And such people should not be content to leave the government of the country in the hands of unscrupulous politicians, but consider it their duty to work and live that this country may be constantly becoming a finer, greater, truer exponent of freedom and justice for all.

If the government is not what it should be, it is the duty of ourselves and the many other Christian people in this land to make our government ideal,—and not to leave it to the domination of unscrupulous and dishonest men.

Breathes there a man with soul so dead
Who never to himself hath said:
"This is my own, my native land!"
Whose heart hath ne'er within him burned
As home his footsteps he has turned,
From wandering on a foreign strand!
If such there breathe, go mark him well.
For him no minstrel raptures swell,
High though his titles, proud his name,
Boundless his wealth as wish can claim;
Despite those titles, power and pelf;
The wretch concentered all in self,
Living shall forfeit fair renown,
And doubly dying, shall go down
To the vile dust from whence he sprung,
Unwept, unhonored, and unsung.

—Sir Walter Scott.

In the enjoyment of liberty's prizes men are tempted to shrink liberty's pain. For the great rights which this western world possesses under the law may be maintained only at the cost of watchfulness and service. The peril of self-government is the indifference of the majority to the obligations of citizenship.

A Motto

"If laws are to win obedience they must first win the consciences of men."

Daily Readings

Principle of justice .... Mal. 2:4-7
Principle of freedom .... Gal. 5:1-14
Principle of service .... Mark 10:35-45
Principle of honesty .... Isa. 5:22-25
Principle of integrity .... Ezek. 18:5-9
Principle of reform .... John 2:13-22
Topic—Christian Principles in Politics.
Luke 22:24-27.

Additional Material

If we are going to be of real service as citizens of our great land we must be impartial, we must treat the foreigner as we should like to be treated if we were to go to his land to live. We must so conduct ourselves toward him that the words of the following verse may be duplicated everywhere.

"American"

Just today we chanced to meet
Down upon the busy street,
And I wondered whence he came,
What was once his nation's name.
So I asked him, "Tell me true,
Are you Pole or Russian Jew,
English, Irish, German, Prussian,
Belgian, Spanish, Swiss, Moravian
Dutch, or Greek or Scandinavian?"
Then he gave me his reply,
As he raised his head up high:
"What I was is naught to me
In this land of liberty;
In my soul, as man to man,
I am just American."

If ever in the history of the world it was true it is now doubly so that we need the sentiment of these lines projected into reality in our own and all lands:

"God give us men! A time like this demands
Clear minds, pure hearts, true faith and ready hands.
Men who possess opinions and a will;
Men whom the desire for office cannot kill;
Men whom the spoils of office cannot buy;

Men who have honor, men who will not lie;
Tall men; sun crowned, who live above the fog,
In public duty and in private thinking;
Men who can stand before a demagogue
And denounce his treacherous flatteries without winking.
For which base tricksters, with their worn-out creeds,
Their large professions and their little deeds,
Wrangle in selfish strife. Lo! Freedom weeps,
Wrong rules the land, and waiting Justice sleeps."

These two poems could well be used, being spoken by two boys who might come before the society at the same time and both remain standing until the recitations have been given.

The Politician

Carven in leathern mask or brazen face,
Were I time's sculptor, I would set this man.
Retreating from the truth, his hawk eyes scan
The platforms of all public thought for place.
There wriggling with insinuating grace,
He takes poor hope and effort by the hand,
And flatters with half-truths and accents bland,
Till even zeal and earnest love grow base.
Knowing no right save power's grim right of way,
No nobleness save life's ignoble praise,
No future save this sordid day to day,
He is the curse of these material days.
This worshiper of Dagon and his flies.
His monument the people's true acclaim,

The Statesman

Born with a love for truth and liberty,
And earnest for the public right, he stands
Like solitary pine in wasted lands.
Or some paladin of old legends, he
Would live that other souls like his be free;
Not caring for self nor pelf nor pandering power,
He thunders incessant, earnest hour by hour,
Till some old despot shackles cease to be.
Not his the gaudy title nor the place
Where hungry fingers clutch his country's gold;
But where the trodden crouch in evil case
His cause is theirs to lighten or to hold.
Juggling with mighty wrongs and mightier lies,
And title high, a love more great than fame.

W. Wilfred Campbell

NEWS FROM THE FIELD

A CALL FOR HELP

Dear Evangelist Readers:

I suppose almost every reader of the Evangelist knew about our mission we established at Happy in 1919 but was closed when a year old. When the mission was closed there was a debt to be paid and I began to work to pay this off, but before it was all paid I unfortunately took a severe case of bronchitis and then—tuberculosis, (of which I suffered a few years ago, and have been unable to do any work since in July and I have been asking the Lord to help settle this matter, for it must be paid. The answer has been coming, "Ask the Brethren to help," and I wonder if there are some who would like to help in this. No matter how small, a gift surely would be appreciated and would mean lots.

I do not feel that this matter is personal, although I was in charge of our mission and did the best I could on a meager salary and praise the Lord, his work is far greater than

any salary. The debt is about thirty-five dollars.

I was glad to hear such good reports from our conference and to hear it was so well attended.

I hope you brethren will remember me in your prayers.

May the Lord bestow his richest blessings upon our brotherhood and inspire each of us for greater service for our Lord and Master, is my prayer. Romans 8:28.

ELIZABETH HADDIX,
Lost Creek, Kentucky.

COMPTON AVENUE, FILLMORE, CALIF.

After more than three years of fellowship with the Compton Avenue Brethren church as pastor I left that field July first to take up the work at Fillmore which is under the direction of the Mission Board of Southern California.

To tender my resignation to these good people was one of the most difficult things

I have been asked to do since I have been in active church work. The perfect harmony between pastor and people made the work a real joy but the call of the Mission Board was considered the call of God and the writer felt constrained to forego the pleasure of working with these people that the Lord might have his way in the matter.

The time spent in this place were days of real fellowship. Compton Avenue can boast of as good people as are to be found anywhere in the brotherhood, men and women who are loyal to the Lord Jesus and his work. These people stood by the pastor in prayer and effort and the work accomplished was due in a large measure to the spirit of prayer that pervaded every department of the work. Never have I been in a place where such a large percentage of both old and young knew how to pray. I shall always remember with much pleasure the days spent with these people.

During the time the writer was with this church he had the pleasure of receiving into the membership a number of people who have proven themselves a real help in the church work—people who have added real power to the spiritual life. That the spiritual condition of the membership is fine is evidenced by the fact that although they have been without a regular pastor for nearly three months the work has gone on unhindered. Such a thing could not have been possible had there not been the finest spirit of co-operation and if the people had not been spirit led.

It was with a great deal of pleasure that the writer witnessed the growth of the foreign mission spirit. The offering for the foreign work the first year of the pastorate was $65.00. The second year it was about the same amount. At that time the people considered they were doing well in giving. By constantly stressing the duty of stewardship and keeping the demands of the unsaved and unevangelized before them the spirit of giving grew and one year ago the offering was $180.00 and on last Easter the offering was more than $466.00, an average of nearly $4.00 per active member. This amount was raised without in any way taking away the support of the local work. When the work as pastor closed every bill was paid and besides more than $600.00 was in the treasury to care for the work under the leadership of the new pastor. Not only were the current expenses met but the indebtedness on the church property was all provided for and practically all paid. The new pastor will find no old bills to meet with an empty treasury staring him in the face. Again I want to say that these things were made possible by the leadership of the Spirit and the co-operation of the membership.

I love these good people and wish them the richest of God's blessings and I know he will lead them out into still greater service for him. I bespeak for Brother Leatherman who will take up this work with the beginning of October, the same loyal co-operation in prayer and effort that was given me. If this could be done only success can be theirs.

I have been in the Fillmore charge since July first, and am just getting really acquainted with the work. I have found a most loyal membership, a membership which is worthy of praise. Although but young and forced to be without a regular pastor form Easter until the writer took charge of the work, they kept up the services in a remarkable way. The midweek service was led by the members and was largely attended. In fact, they had a larger percentage of the membership present under these circumstances than some old established churches have with a resident pastor. Since coming here the midweek services have been attended by from thirty-five to fifty people. When it is known that the active membership does not number more than around 60 I think this is a record that can not be excelled by any congregation in the brotherhood. These people love the Old Book and are anxious to learn its truths. A short Bible study is held in connection with the midweek service.

When I tell you ours is the only prayer meeting of any consequence in the little city of Fillmore you will appreciate what this means. There are two other churches with several times as many members as we have in our church and yet the spirit of prayer is almost entirely lacking. One of the pastors recently told me that the prayer meeting in his church had dwindled to almost nothing. We are to have Dr. French Oliver with us in a union meeting in December and it is to be hoped that some people who seem to be sleeping may be aroused to duty.

The work is gradually taking on life. The offerings are better than ever before, the crowds are increasing and I am sure with the deepening of prayer life and with the spirit of co-operation which is manifest on the part of the membership this work must grow. These are good people but this work needs the prayers of our people.

The church here at Fillmore has shown the pastor and his family every kindness and I want to thank them in this public way.

I would not close this report without a word of appreciation of the work done by Brother Lowman. Brother Lowman was called by the Board to inaugurate this new work. Upon him fell the responsibility of building a church in a new field and of moulding into an active membership those who were almost wholly new to Christian work. That he did good work is evidenced by the beautiful little church building erected to the honor of God and by the band of loyal members he gathered into the ranks. Brother Lowman is universally loved not only by the membership but by many outside of our own ranks. Much of the faithfulness and loyalty displayed by these people are with him in his work at Pleasant Hill, Ohio.

We are planning our Rally Day and Home Coming Day on October 3. We are setting as our goal an attendance of 150 in the Sunday school and are planning to have every member of the church present, also the friends of the work. From the spirit manifested we are going to reach our goal. Pray for the success of the work.   J. C. BEAL.

FIRST BRETHREN, JOHNSTOWN

Splendid Sunday School Rally

The Sunday school of the First Brethren church, Somerset street, held its annual rally day exercises Sunday, September 26. The school normally has an enrollment of 450, with an average attendance of about one-half that number during the summer months and from 300 to 350 during the balance of the year. It is customary, after the vacation season is over, to make a special effort to get every student back to the school on this particular day and attempt to get every one in line for this winter's work, which usually marks the best season of the year in Sunday school and church endeavor. Several months ago it was announced that special effort should be made to increase the offering on this day which is usually applied to some particular branch of the work. This year, as was the case last year, the offering is to be applied to the building fund for the new church edifice

to be erected at the corner of Dilbert and Napoleon streets.

Following is the result of Sunday's achievements from the different departments of the school, with the names of the teachers and the class offering:

Beginners' Department, taught by Mrs. George Hunter, Mrs. J. F. Watson, and Mrs. W. S. Fritz, $31.10; Primary Department, taught by Marion Trent, Mrs. S. S. Foust and Grace Goughnour, $58.32; Junior Department, taught by Lottie Hellman, Mrs. George Hammers, Mrs. Berwyn Evans, Mrs. Oscar Brant, Frank Goughnour and Mrs. Charles Ott, $113.06; Intermediate Department, taught by Mary Snook, Verna Fyock, Effie Goughnour, Harry Statler and Donald Statler, $123.30; Senior Department, taught by S. A. Snook and Miss Gertrude Lake, $140.86; Adult Department, taught by L. B. Furry, Harry Wissinger, Norman Statler and H. W. Darr, $2,034; officers, $26; Woman's Missionary Society, $100; Sisterhood Girls, $50; Mrs. Edward Smith's Circle of ladies, $40; total, $2,715.43.

The attendance for the day was 454, four more than the total enrollment of the school. In addition to the enrollment of 450, the school has a Cradle Roll and a Home Department, each having about 150 members.

There is nothing but praise and kindly feeling toward the corps of officers, headed by Superintendent Albert Trent, who has served in that capacity for more than 37 years, for their efficient methods of leading the people to success in reaching their goals set before them.

At a special business meeting of the congregation last Wednesday evening the plans for the new edifice were presented with more than usual interest being manifested by the laity of the church. With a full determination to forge steadily ahead to the final completion of a new church, every member of the congregation is lending every effort possible under the general leadership of J. Freemont Watson, pastor of the congregation.—The Daily Tribune (Johnstown).

LOST CREEK, KENTUCKY

Though you have not heard from Lost Creek for some time, yet there has been an abundance of life here. Riverside has been very much alive. This has been the time of "Funeral Meetings," which usually cut down the attendance at our services. But this year these meetings have not bothered us so much, though there have been many of them. One of the things that continually surprise us here is how Riverside holds up under the "handicaps," or circumstances that have been imposed on the work. Under such conditions, one would think that the attendance at all services and the school would wane. But, as it was last winter, so it is now, the attendance keeps up fine, though the rumblings of discontent can be heard. There may come improvements or Riverside's great opportunity will pass.

Often we hear of things that show that so many of our people do not understand Riverside. Riverside is strictly a religious work, but its work involves so much more than just straight church work, that it cannot become self-supporting like a church only. We have the church work, and that, buttressing that work very emphatically, is the school work. There has been a kind of county fair established at Jackson, our county seat, by the county agricultural agent. It has been going two years. This year Riverside competed for the awards on the school day. A man of influence whom I have known all these years, told me that Riverside's school showing outranked that of any other school there, and we took some of the awards for community singing, etc.

Our scholars outranked, both in age and development those from the other mission schools about us. This was clear. And we are bringing this to you, dear reader, that you, too, may know something of what you have in Riverside; that you may know that Riverside has the morale; that you may know that Riverside ranks high in the development and age of its pupils; that Riverside stands very high in the thought and estimation of many people in eastern Kentucky; that Riverside honors the Bible as the fully inspired Word of God, and the cross with its blood propitiation, above everything else; and that finally Riverside has everything in a local sense that should go to make its work successful. But there are things that cannot yet be supplied locally, sufficient funds and workers. These must yet come from the brotherhood. Here are our imperative needs now:

1. A good woman for cook. As it is now, Miss Bethke cannot do the work of two women and be where two women ought to be. The result of this is that we are losing out in both food and dormitory clothing. Anywhere else, a boarding house with from thirty to sixty boarders, a man would be necessary to have around, but here it goes any way, with girls, boys or whoever can be gotten, and now one woman to be where two ought to be. Is there not some man and woman who will respond to this need? These young people are especially need quite close supervision if things are to go right at all.

2. A music and domestic science teacher. We have the apparatus and pupils who want to take it. And who can question the need of music in religious work? Who will answer this opportunity?

3. Then after the holidays there will be serious need of two teachers, one for the first five grades, and one for the work above the grades. Who will respond?

4. Finally there is great need of a, shall I say, respectable dining room. The kitchen, store room for food, and dining room, are in sorry plight. There is need of a new building for these things. To some here last winter, this was promised, for anyone seeing the place can quickly see the need. But to date, we see no move for the building so much needed. The need has increased since last winter. The dormitory is now about full of pupils, something that we do not usually have at this time of the year. For the above needs we are having special prayer services, looking to the Lord to have them met. Will you, dear reader, join with us in praying for the same?

But we are told that the Brethren church is too small in numbers, and that it cannot keep up a place like Riverside. Of course, if this is actually true, THEN IT SEEMS TO US THAT THERE HAS BEEN SOME VERY, VERY FOOLISH WORK DONE IN SPENDING WHAT HAS BEEN EXPENDED THUS FAR. IF RIVERSIDE IS A MISTAKE FOR THE BRETHREN CHURCH, WHY CONTINUE IT ANOTHER MINUTE? WHY HAS IT TAKEN FIFTEEN YEARS TO DISCOVER THE MISTAKE? WHY DO THE OTHER DENOMINATIONS KEEP ON MAKING SUCH MISTAKES, and mark you, increasing their plants and work, instead of cutting them down. But if Riverside is a mistake, then by the same logic that proves it such, we can prove our other mission work MISTAKES ALSO. But, thank God, Riverside has not been a mistake in his sight, else he would not have planted it, and fed it and led it to its present status. God does not make mistakes. Men do.

Eastern Kentucky is now approaching a period of great financial development. This is evident on every hand. Self-supporting churches will grow up here in this field, that is, the coal mining center, just as they have in other coal fields. But a place like Riverside is different. Its work differs or rather, is many times larger and includes so much more than simply straight church work. Nowhere else, either on this field, or other home fields, or foreign fields, are similar places self-supporting. If that is not true, we shall be very glad to have our error pointed out, and we will then make the correction in our next article in the Evangelist. Then why expect something from Riverside than other places do?

We also feel like saying this, that Riverside has cost the church but little, considering the work it has done, and its field. We know of one place with about the same attendance as ours, but eleven teachers, while Riverside has never had more than six or seven, and usually four. Circulars on our desk from another mission school, The Pine Settlement School, which states that they spent $26,000 last year, and will need this year $30,000. This place was started about seven years ago. Riverside's expenditures from September 1, 1918, to September 1, 1919, were $2,905.51, this alone being received from the brotherhood at large. This is a fair average for the years past. You can see that Riverside's expenditures have been very meager compared with others, and the work it has done.

Comparisons like the above could be continued. If there are "Doubting Thomases" in this matter, we would be very, very much pleased to have the different places in the field investigated, and the figures published. The fact is that Riverside in the past has kept well within the realm of expenditures for such a place, and those who know what has been done here, ask us "how it can be done with that amount?"

Yes, the evidence is indisputable that this work is of the Lord and his planting. It has attained unto a growth that ought to please. Why should we, his servants, let this plant languish because of improper support? We have been so often told that missions is not a problem of money but of workers for the field. But here is the Lord's plant, a truly missionary one, that is now languishing, because it is not given the financial support that would make its work go as it might. The plant, the soil, the souls, but there is little rain. How, long, oh Lord, how long! Pray for us that we may so humble and so submit ourselves to his will that he may the better use us for his glory. G. E. DRUSHAL.

DOINGS AT DAYTON

The Dayton church has two more preachers. These men were preachers in another church, or rather churches, but felt that they were somewhat hampered and handicapped in the matter of preaching a full gospel. They have been attending church here for some time and finally united with the church. They both have been using their ministry for the benefit of the church and so the official board asked the church for their ordination, which was granted by the examining committee, and consequently, the pastor, and his assistant, Brother Lynn, ordained to the full ministry, Brethren Jesse Eikenberry and Clifford G. Ronk. Brother Eikenberry is already stationed at Camden and has baptized eight, and will soon begin a revival there. Brother Ronk goes to West Alexandria next Sunday to preach with the hope that he may help these brethren until such time as they may be able to secure a pastor on fall time.

WILLIAM C. TEETER,
Corresponding Secretary.

GARWIN, IOWA

A two and a half week's meeting under the direction of Brother Coleman as preacher and Brother A. T. Ronk as singer came to a close Sunday, the 26th of September. Brother Coleman was called to another field during the second week and left Brother Ronk to do the preaching and lead the singing too, which he did in a very able manner. Brother Ronk was here four years ago and held a meeting for us, so he was not a stranger to us. He had a large chorus choir, which fairly made the church ring with their singing. The entire meeting was so much enjoyed that we were sorry when it was brought to a close. During the meeting they met many difficulties in the way of success. There were many people who made excuses. The weather, however, was fine most of the time. During the short time of the meeting there were thirteen made the good confession and were baptized. There were a number under conviction and would have made the start if the meetings had continued longer. The attendance was good; a number of times the church was hardly able to accommodate the crowds. We held our communion services on Monday evening, when a goodly number were present to take part in the sacred ordinances. We trust the Lord will lead Brother Coleman and Brother Ronk back to the Garwin church in the future. They have our earnest prayers for a successful meeting at the place where they are now laboring and throughout the coming year. MRS. BELLE DOBSON.

PLEASANT HILL, OHIO

Yes we are still here and the Pleasant Hill church is still alive. We have not written the Evangelist lately, but we have been busy. Our church work kept up fairly well during the summer months. This field is well churched, but still there are many people who do not belong to any church, and there are many more that just belong to some church and are spiritually dead, becoming driftwood to the church, holding others back. But that is to be expected in these days of apostasy when the leaven of Satan is working to corrupt the whole world and is getting things ready for the Man of Sin of Second Thessalonians 2:3, but watch and pray.

Our Sunday school work is growing. The attendance is good and increasing all the time. We have a contest on now, the Lincoln Highway Auto Race, which is creating a good deal of interest and enthusiasm. Our Christian Endeavor is fine, with good meetings and from 30 to 35 almost every Sunday night.

The last two weeks of August Brother Cook of Salem came to us for a meeting and brought to us the Gospel in a plain, straightforward way. There were good crowds, considering the time of year, and as a result four were added to the church. Praise his name for those willing to accept Christ. Pray for us.

S. LOWMAN.

WINONA TABERNACLE FUND

Herewith find list of churches in the entire brotherhood who have paid their apportionments to the Winona Tabernacle Fund:

Indiana District

Muncie,	$11.56
Mexico,	17.00
Corinth,	7.16
Ardmore, So. Bend,	8.50
Denver,	21.25
Roann,	9.00
Goshen,	85.00
Loree,	34.00
Nappanee,	72.25
Wabash,	15.47
Berne,	25.50
North Manchester,	72.59
North Liberty,	25.50
Tiosa,	20.10
Peru,	20.00
Elkhart,	35.00
Center Chapel,	12.00
Roann (at Conference),	34.00
South Bend,	51.00

Illiokota

Cerro, Gordo,	$20.00
Lanark,	35.00
Udell,	10.00
Milledgeville,	36.00
Pleasant Grove,	20.00
M. Grove,	3.00
Waterloo,	50.00
Leon,	10.00

Ohio District

Pioneer,	$ 4.00
Louisville,	30.00
Bryan,	35.00
Dayton,	176.96
Ashland,	32.00
Gretna,	15.00
Fair Haven,	12.00
Williamstown,	16.00
Mansfield,	1.00
Salem,	10.00
Martin Shively Indv.	10.00
New Lebanon,	30.00

Pennsylvania

Pittsburgh,	$25.00
Philadelphia,	50.00
Uniontown,	13.00
Dyol Belote Indv.	5.00

Middle West District

Ft. Scott, Kan.	$ 5.00
Morrill, Kan.,	20.00
Hamlin, Kan.	12.50
Falls City, Neb.,	30.00
Beaver City, Neb.,	15.00

Maryland-Virginia District

Limestone, Tenn.,	$ 5.00
St. James,	20.00
J. Swartz gave personal for Bal.,	125.00

California-Oregon

Long Beach, Calif.,	$115.00
Los Angeles, Compton Ave.,	15.30
Michigan,	25.00

M. V. Garrison gave personal check for the Michigan total.

Most of these subscriptions from the above districts with the exception of the Indiana churches we received at National Conference this year and were made by individual delegates who gave their personal checks to cover their respective amounts; this of course will be paid to them by their district. Brother L. S. Bauman, as treasurer of the Foreign Missionary Society, loaned the committee $1,-000.00 or the balance due on the Tabernacle pledge in order that our obligation might be made good. This money must be refunded before November 1st, 1920. Those churches in the Pennsylvania, Ohio and Indiana districts and elsewhere who have not paid their apportionment will confer a great favor on the church and this special committee by sending to the undersigned at once their checks to cover their respective amounts.

Fraternally yours,
H. E. ROSCOE, Goshen, Indiana,
Treasurer Winona Tabernacle Fund.

RAILROAD "Y" CONFERENCE

We take pleasure in advising our readers that the Fifteenth International Conference of Railroad Young Men's Christian Associations of North America will take place in Richmond, Virginia, November 18-21, 1920.

These conferences are usually held at intervals of three years, but a considerably longer interval has elapsed this time because of the war intervening.

These meetings are attended by from 1,000 to 1,200 railroad men representing every section in the country and every department of the railroad service.—The Editor.

TO THE OHIO CHURCHES

Attention has been called to the fact that the Ohio conference will be held at Ashland, the program has been published, as has also the invitation of the Ashland church and college, and letters urging attendance have gone out to all pastors, yet we want to take this, another opportunity of urging the matter upon all members of Ohio conference district. We believe that Ohio conferences ought to be made the big event of the year for all Ohio churches. It can be, if pastors and people will make it so. And the extent to which it is made the big event will determine the success of our state work. And the success of the local church work will be found to depend in no small way upon the inspiration received from and the co-operation given to state conference. Let every congregation plan to send its full quota of delegates to Ashland and instruct them to stay until the conference is closed in order that they may participate in all the business, get all the inspiration possible and do their part toward making the last session as good as the first. Don't forget the date, October 25 to 27.

Yours for the biggest and best conference ever, GEO. S. BAER, Moderator.

Communion Notices

The Brethren church at Fairhaven, Ohio, will observe the Lord's Supper and the Communion service on Sunday evening, October 24th. All Brethren are invited to attend and enjoy this service with us.

B. F. OWEN, Pastor.

The First church of Canton will hold its semi-annual communion and love feast on Sunday evening, October 24th at 6:30 o'clock. All brethren of like faith are invited to this service. FRED C. VANATOR, Pastor.

Business Manager's Corner

THE FUND IS GROWING—SLOWLY

We will have just a few words to say this week, but they are important words. Since last week we have received the following contributions for the Evangelist paper bill: Mrs. Eugene Ormsby, $1.00; G. C. Brumbaugh, $5.00; John Wisler, $5.00; L. L. Kilmer, $10.00; A. Brethren Family, $20.00; Mr. and Mrs. J. E. Miller, $20.00; Richard Henning, $25.00; Previously reported, $96.00. Total $182.00. In addition to the above we have been informed by the pastor that the Fairview church, Washington, C. H., Ohio has voted to send $50.00 for the fund and Brother A. B. Cover writes that the Hagerstown, Md., church has voted to contribute $25.00 to the fund, provided a sufficient amount is contributed by the other churches to insure against the increasing of the price of the Evangelist. Both of these churches are Honor Roll churches, and Brother Cover writes that they realize the real value of the church paper to the local work of the church since they have had it in the homes of all the active membership of the church. Of course we will get that twenty-five from Hagerstown. We are bound to meet this paper bill without increasing the subscription price of the Evangelist. If all the churches will remember to observe PUBLICATION DAY on October thirty-first, and make a proportionate offering it will be done "hilariously," as Brother "Ed" says.

We are sending a personal letter and appeal to all the pastors this week, and we trust they will all heed the call and make good use of a most splendid opportunity to do good along a line that has never been put squarely before our Brethren churches.

If any pastor fails to receive one of these letters it will be because of an oversight or a wrong address. If you do not get the letter, just be good natured about it and take up the special offering any way and show that you are determined to do your full duty even though you may have been overlooked in the matter of a personal appeal.

R. R. TEETER,
Business Manager.

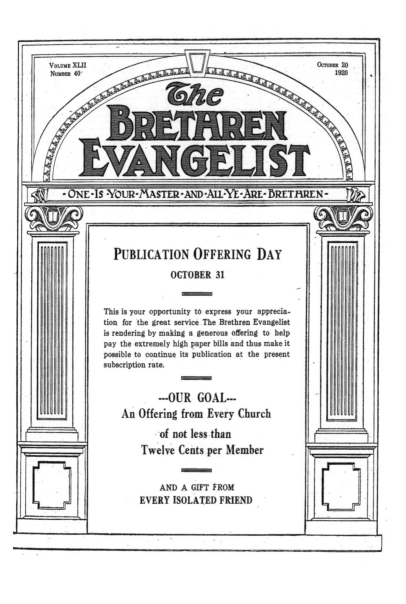

Volume XLII
Number 40

October 20
1920

The BRETHREN EVANGELIST

- One - Is - Your - Master - And - All - Ye - Are - Brethren -

PUBLICATION OFFERING DAY

OCTOBER 31

This is your opportunity to express your appreciation for the great service The Brethren Evangelist is rendering by making a generous offering to help pay the extremely high paper bills and thus make it possible to continue its publication at the present subscription rate.

---OUR GOAL---

An Offering from Every Church

of not less than

Twelve Cents per Member

AND A GIFT FROM
EVERY ISOLATED FRIEND

Published every Wednesday at Ashland, Ohio. All matter for publication must reach the Editor not later than Friday noon of the preceding week.

George S. Baer, Editor

The
Brethren
Evangelist

When ordering your paper changed give old as well as new address. Subscriptions discontinued at expiration. To avoid missing any numbers renew two weeks in advance.

R. R. Teeter, Business Manager

ASSOCIATE EDITORS: J. Fremont Watson, Louis S. Bauman, A. B. Cover, Alva J. McClain, B. T. Burnworth.

OFFICIAL ORGAN OF THE BRETHREN CHURCH

Subscription price, $2.00 per year, payable in advance.
Entered at the Post Office at Ashland, Ohio, as second-class matter.
Acceptance for mailing at special rate of postage provided for in section 1103, Act of October 3, 1917, authorized September 9, 1918.
Address all matter for publication to Geo. S. Baer, Editor of the Brethren Evangelist, and all business communications to R. R. Teeter, Business Manager, Brethren Publishing Company, Ashland, Ohio. Make all checks payable to the Brethren Publishing Company.

TABLE OF CONTENTS

EDITORIAL

Christian Idealism and Political Responsibility

The time is at hand when every loyal citizen must face the responsibility of casting his influence for or against certain great and vital issues by means of the ballot box and otherwise. To what extent will the Christian carry the idealism of his religion into the discharge of his responsibility to the state? There have been those who have decried idealism in politics as impracticable, but such are usually the type of men who have little or no sympathy with Christian idealism. To be sure it will be found impracticable in him who is committed to unworthy aims and methods. The high ideals and righteous methods that are inspired by the spirit of Christ cannot be made to contribute toward the accomplishment of questionable ends. A good tree will produce good fruit. But when the purposes are undoubted in their worthiness and there is a desire for methods that are above reproach, Christian ideals and principles will be found most practicable.

Then again there are others—very religious and good-intentioned people—who because their citizenship is in heaven, feel themselves justified in disowning any political responsibility whatsoever. If we do count ourselves mere "strangers and pilgrims in a foreign land," even yet we are obliged to "render unto Caesar the things that are Caesar's", which in this case would be the discharge of our political responsibility. Moreover we are commanded to pray "Thy kingdom come, thy will be done on earth as it is done in heaven." How can we consistently pray that expressed wish of the Master without doing what we can to make it a reality? We may fairly question whether he who prays "Thy kingdom come," but does nothing as a member of the earthly kingdom (or commonwealth) of which God has made him a part to bring in the reign of righteousness, will be found worthy of a place in that kingdom when it does come in its fulness. We are warranted in fearing that he who petitions "thy will be done on earth," but does not seize the opportunities to cause God's will to be done in organized society, will be met at last with the rebuke, "Why call ye me Lord, Lord, and do not the things which I say?" It is to be doubted whether he who is not a good citizen of our earthly commonwealth will make a good citizen of heaven's Kingdom.

But by far the large majority of those who have taken upon themselves the name of Christ will acknowledge their political responsibility, and most of that number will also agree that Christian idealism is both practicable and desirable in the affairs of state. To them we must look as the saviors of our country and of the world in this time of stress and instability. On their attitude much depends, and it is to them that appeal must be made.

There are some who, in spite of their acknowledged responsibility for the promotion of good government and the triumph of right principles, will assume an attitude of indifference toward the opportunities that face them. All that they might say or do will count for little. Their vote is an insignificant affair, and no issue will be lost or won by it. Their business is too important, their work is too pressing and their time is too valuable to go to the polls, or to give themselves to a study of the issues or to exercise themselves for the right. It matters little to them what sort of men or policies prevail, so long as they personally are not affected by the outcome. They are not moved by the privileges of their citizenship nor stirred by its responsibilities. It makes little difference under what kind of a government they live; whether they are privileged to have a part in determining the affairs of the state or whether all things are determined for them; whether public servants are faithful to trust or whether corruption prevails. They go blindly, indifferently on, while the devil, undisturbed, entrenches himself in the places of power and influence and delights himself in wide-spread ruin. It seems hardly imaginable that such indifference should exist among those who are accounted as members of Christ's body, but such is the case. And it is because of such as these that the church has often been compelled to blush with shame because of failure to cope with outstanding evils that have publicly challenged their power.

There are others who, recognizing their political opportunities and responsibilities, take part enthusiastically in such affairs, but always in the spirit of party prejudice. Politics is always a partisan affair with them. An issue is good or bad according as it is being promoted or opposed by the party of which they are members. They see everything through their party's glasses and permit their party bosses to focus the lenses. Whatever kind of candidates or issues are thrust upon them, it becomes their immediate duty to unearth or create arguments for their justification. They are party "regulars" and are a delight to the eyes of scheming politicians. They neither vote nor think independently, but with becoming submission, they do all according to party expediency. They are not necessarily dishonest to conscience; for many, conscience is held in abeyance, or not permitted to pass judgment until they receive the party dictum and justification. To be independent of party counsel would be a grievous fault, and would cause party leaders distressing uncertainty. Recently a high aspirant complained about the spirit of independence becoming so prevalent and the tendency to break away from party lines and landmarks. Doubtless the feeling of uncertainty and suspense on the part of self-seeking politicians when independent voters are in considerable number is very displeasing and distressing, especially when they have little of real merit on which to base their appeals. And the large numbers who have been unwilling to incur the displeasure of party leaders by voting independently, even when conscience and right principles demanded it, is a sad revelation of the failure of professing Christian voters to carry the idealism of their religion into their politics. Far too many cast aside or compromise their Christian ideals when dealing with political issues.

But it is a delight to know that there are others who hold their political privileges as sacred trusts, to be discharged as conscientiously as they would pay an honest debt or lead a prayer meeting. To them the right use of the ballot is a matter of religion; they can not therefore be indifferent to its obligations. The stand they shall take regarding issues and candidates is a matter of conscience and right; they cannot therefore be swayed by party prejudice. They seek first not the success of a particular party but the triumph of righteous principles. They submit to the dictation not of party bosses, but to the Spirit of truth. They give their allegiance not to partisan selfishness, but to Christian patriotism, not to political expediency but to principles of Christian service. They may wear a party name but they are not slaves to the party. They are the high-minded, independent Christian voters, whose numbers are rapidly increasing and whose influence if steadfastly directed by lofty Christian ideals, are destined to be the saving salt of our national life. These are they who in very truth are co-operating to make the world safe for democracy and democracy safe for the world, by leading first America and then the world to put trust not in armies and navies, but in those spiritual forces resident only in the church of Jesus Christ.

EDITORIAL REVIEW

Ohio Conference at Ashland, October 25 to 27 and Every Church Represented by Its Full Quota of Delegates.

Brother Shively makes an appeal to the children of the Sunday school. On the Sunday school page he says there is ''Wanted—a Hen.'' Read it.

Brethren Coleman and A. T. Ronk recently closed a successful evangelistic campaign at Garwin, Iowa. The meeting closed with a well attended communion service.

''America first'' is as selfish and unworthy of our own country as ''Germany over all'' was of our former foe, and if followed to its logical conclusion will lead to the same ending.

As we were going to press announcement arrived concerning communion services to be held at Oakville, Indiana, church, on Saturday evening, October 30, at 7 o'clock. The usual invitation is extended.

Brother Vanator, pastor of our church at Canton, Ohio, reports splendid progress and displays a fine spirit of optimism concerning the work there. There cannot but be a bright future for the church whose pastor and people are thus unitedly confident and aggressive.

Indiana is first with its conferenced report and we wish to comment Brother Grisso, the secretary, for his excellent report. We feel certain that the Evangelist family will find it quite readable. The report reveals that the Indiana churches are very wide awake and are blessed with an aggressive leadership.

Brother L. G. Wood, always faithful in keeping the brotherhood informed concerning the progress of the Lord's work in his part of the vineyard, writes concerning his new field. Those who know Brother Wood's record for faithful service agree that we are warranted in predicting that the Third church of Johnstown will go forward under his consecrated and efficient leadership.

The paper fund is growing, as will be noticed by a glance at the Business Manager's Corner this week. Some splendid gifts are coming in,—all are splendid, in fact,—but some are of good size. We are convinced that the welfare of The Evangelist is on the hearts

of a great many of our readers. And as the present emergency is brought to the attention of more and more of our readers we believe they will respond in ever larger numbers to make possible the meeting of our paper bills without raising the price of The Evangelist. Let churches and individuals make their gifts as promptly and as liberally as possible.

President Jacobs, in his ''College News,'' sounds the note of hope that in the not far distant future College Hill will begin to take on some new signs of improvements—a new building. It will cause rejoicing in the hearts of all former students and friends of Ashland College when that day arrives. It will cause us all to take still more seriously the task of adequately equipping and endowing our own church school.

Pastors are requested by the Stewardship Director of the Bicentenary Movement, Brother Miles J. Snyder, to preach on the subject of Stewardship on October 31. This subject is very vital to the welfare and progress of the church of Christ and the sooner Brethren people are brought to a realization of the fact that the proper acknowledgment of our stewardship is as binding upon us as is feetwashing or baptism, the sooner will the Brethren church enter into the larger future that awaits it.

Every Christian voter in Ohio should not fail to vote for House Bill 620, which provides for the enforcement of state wide prohibition. We have put a prohibition clause in our state constitution, but the ''wets'' called for a referendum on it, thus delaying its enforcement until ratified by the people. The people should see to it that its enforcement is no longer delayed and that the State of Ohio cooperates with the national government in making the destruction of the liquor traffic complete. That bill is designated as House Bill No. 620. Vote ''Yes'' on it.

The General Home Mission offering to be taken at Thanksgiving time, either on the Sunday preceding or the Sunday following that day, should be the largest yet given in the history of the church. Now is the time to prosecute the cause of Christ in the homeland as never before. The present mission points must be built up and new fields ought to be opened. The Kingdom of God waits on human co-operation. The Master is ready to lead us into the possession of the long-promised land if we but have the faith and courage to ''go over and possess it.'' We have not yet begun to do home mission work in a serious way. Let us launch out into the deep and not remain longer in the shallows and see if he will not give us success beyond our fondest anticipations.

Our readers will not fail to appreciate the article on ''The Importance of Missions'' on the mission page, and in connection with the publication of this article which was sent in at the request of members of the Conemaugh Sunday school, we wish to say that we welcome the sending in of such articles unsolicited. If some one prepares a good paper for some local meeting and you think it merits a wider hearing, the editor will be pleased to have you submit it to him. We want to make the Evangelist more and more a medium of expression on the part of the brotherhood of those things that are helpful and constructive and inspiring. It has been our constant effort during the last two years to encourage those who can write for the inspiration of others to use their talents, and it has resulted in the greater value and wider appreciation of our beloved paper. We will be grateful for your co-operation in this matter to further enhance the value and service of The Evangelist.

Look up! not down! It is the upward look that takes in the ''certain flight'' of the birds, the giant strength of the oak and the purity of the blue empyrean. It is the upward look that enables one to see the silver that lines the clouds though the sun is shut out from the sky, that catches a gleam of the star of hope when courage is almost gone, or that floods the soul with a sense of delight at the infinite majesty of God and pauses it to exclaim in a burst of enthusiasm, ''The heavens declare the glory of God and the firmament showeth his handiwork.'' The downward look sees nothing but mud and dust, and the creeping, crawling, forbidding things of life. It is the upward view that enables one to walk in heavenly places with Christ Jesus.

GENERAL ARTICLES

The Home Mission Call and Accomplishment West of the Rockies

An address delivered at General Conference by A. V. Kimmell.

In order to make myself clearer I will transpose the subject and take up the last phrase first.

I. WEST OF THE ROCKIES

There are six states which properly lie west of the Rockies and unless you have been through them or have made careful calculation as to their size you will not be able to comprehend the vast territory about which I am to speak even though I spend considerable time in trying to make it clear to you.

It is in the West that water appears to run uphill. It is in the West that a mountain fifty miles away seems to be a little walk before breakfast, so just let your imagination run as I try to tell you that Washington, Oregon, Idaho, Nevada, California and Arizona cover an area of about 625,000 square miles. You do not get it yet? Well little wonder, let me put it in this way: Take a trip through the United States just east of the Mississippi river, running north and south, now count in Wisconsin, Michigan, Illinois, Indiana, Ohio, Pennsylvania, Virginia, Kentucky, Tennessee, Mississippi, Alabama, Georgia and Florida; THIRTEEN STATES IN ALL AND NO SMALL STATES EITHER; and you still have room for three states the size of little Rhode Island before you equal the extent of territory west of the Rockies.

That you will not be mistaken as to the physical aspect of this country I will remind you that there is another majestic range running the whole length of the section—The Coast Range—thus we have high mountains with perpetual snow, deserts hot and dry, and broad sweeping valleys with the most productive soil on earth.

The marvelous growth of the West Coast cities from Seattle to San Diego a distance of over 1,500 miles, will cause the nineteen twenty census enumerations to report a population of several million, perhaps as high as five or six million people in this territory.

Scattered throughout this great expanse and among these millions of people are some two thousand Brethren.

II. THEIR ACCOMPLISHMENT

There are three centers of Brethren activity in the West, almost five hundred miles apart, giving to each of the districts a territory six times as large as the state of Indiana. We note them in the order of their organization as follows:

1. **Northern California.** Their accomplishment dates from before the division in the years gone by. Lathrop was the center of Brethren activity in the early days and has never lost her identity. A number of preaching points have been opened, but many of them have not been maintained so that in all this district regular services are held only at Lathrop, Turlock, Manteca, and occasional services at Ripon, East Colony and Jenny Lind. This great district has been shepherded by two pastors, one of which is leaving and until a successor is secured some 200,000 square miles of Brethren territory will be under the care of one pastor. I ask it with deep sincerity—let us remember Northern California in her needs.

2. **Southern California.** The extent in square miles in this district is less than that of the others, yet within eight miles of our LaVerne church lies the western line of a county —a single county as large as this state, Indiana—so do not shorten your vision as we review the accomplishment in this section.

Fifteen years ago there was one lone Brethren church in all Southern California with a membership of seventy-five scattered in every direction. Today there are six active growing congregations with a total membership of 1,148. There are six splendid church buildings four of them prac-

tically new. The total property valuation is given at $154,000.00. The total of all money raised during the last church year is given at $42,070.99 which does not include the last Foreign Mision offering, the largest yet given by any district.

If I speak with feeling and even a degree of pride concerning the accomplishment of this section it is because I have been privileged to live in Southern California during the time covered by this report and have been in a position to know the facts whereof I speak. Through the mail, by personal interview and in a general way we are asked to give the secret of the success we have had and in reply I can only say that there is no secret.

I would not forget the splendid men and women who have helped in all the years, the best laymen in any field, nor would I take one single mark of credit from the noble pastors who have done more than their share, but the whole success of the effort is because the foundation upon which the work has been built is "Jesus Christ, himself being the chief corner stone." In thus building upon this Rock especial emphasis has been placed upon the following:

(1) THE BIBLE IS THE VERY WORD AND REVELATION OF GOD; INERRANT, INFALLIBLE, GOD-BREATHED. A favorite passage of scripture in the churches is 2 Timothy 3:16-17, "All scripture is given by inspiration of God, and is profitable for doctrine, for reproof, for correction, for instruction in righteousness: that the man of God may be perfect, thoroughly furnished unto all good works." And where there may be any question on this point the whole force of Peter's testimony is urged as he claims to be an eye witness in the second Epistle 1:20-21, "Knowing this first, that no prophecy of the scripture is of any private interpretation. For the prophecy came not in old time by the will of man: but holy men of God spake as they were moved by the Holy Ghost." Hence little time is spent in interpreting the scriptures but much time is used in urging men and women to accept by faith him whom the scriptures hold most dear.

(2) JESUS CHRIST IS DEITY—GOD MANIFEST IN THE FLESH. The evidence of this is incontrovertible.

First, by the Virgin Birth. "Fear not Mary for thou hast found favor with God. And, behold, thou shalt conceive in the womb, and bring forth a son, and shalt call his name JESUS. He shall be great, and shall be called the Son of the Highest: and the Lord God shall give unto him the throne of his father David: and he shall reign over the house of Jacob forever; and of his kingdom there shall be no end." Second, by the Substitutionary Atonement in his Death. Hebrews 2:9, "But we see Jesus, who was made a little lower than the angels for the suffering of death, crowned with glory and honor; that he by the grace of God should taste death for every man." Also Romans 5:8, "But God commendeth his love toward us, in that, while we were yet sinners Christ died for us." Third, by the Physical Resurrection of Jesus Christ a proof of our own bodily resurrection. 2 Corinthians 4:15, "Knowing that he which raised up the Lord Jesus shall raise up us also by Jesus, and shall present us with you." Fourth, by the Second, Visible, Personal and Pre-millennial Coming of Christ. Acts 1:11, "This same Jesus which is taken up from you into heaven shall so come in like manner as ye have seen him go into heaven." John 14:2-4, "In my Father's house are many mansions: if it were not so, I would have told you. I go to prepare a place for you. And if I go and prepare a place for you, I will come again, and receive you unto myself; that where I am ye may be also."

I am not making this fourth point to bring you to my way of thinking but to state emphatically that this teaching of the "Blessed Hope" has occupied a large place in the succesful growth in this district.

3. THE GREAT NORTHWEST

For a number of years the only center for Brethren of the Northwest was at Sunnyside, Washington. Their most progressive and successful growth dates from the time they withdrew from the hindering influences of the Federated church. Their progress continues and we point to this church as being the next largest on the Pacific Coast full of life and spiritual power. They rest upon the same sure foundation to which reference has just been made.

Spokane of this district is so new to our memory that we need only to recall the early Bible classes, the struggle for the building, the final victory and success all in true western spirit, building on the same sure foundation.

Ashland, Oregon, is also of this group. Here there are a few loyal Brethren, whose hearts have been stirred anew through the holding of Bible classes. How the Lord may lead to satisfy the longing of their lives remains to be worked out.

III. The HOME MISSION CALL.

In spite of reports and surveys to the contrary I am compelled to say that there are but few if any permanent, populous centers without regular religious worship. The idea that there are large towns and cities calling for churches is all wrong. There are a number of church mission boards continually looking for places to open new fields that will grow into self supporting churches in a reasonable time.

The Brethren Mission Board in Southern California has spent much time and money looking up such fields and other denominations are doing the same thing.

However you must not forget that we are dealing with the marvelous West where houses are actually built in a day. Towns spring up over night. Mining camps, lumber camps, pleasure camps spring up before time to think twice and often disappear as quickly. It is here that a real problem in home missions sends up a call. A traveling preacher, a church on wheels or a gospel coach almost entirely supported by churches, individuals or mission boards are some ways in which the call can be answered.

At present the greatest need is more work among the Indians. It is a shame that a civilized nation calling itself Christian will permit, abet or encourage the heathen superstition of their fore-fathers. When I say encourage I use the word advisedly. The ancient superstition the snake dances, the medicine man, the pow-wow are kept up even today. The sun-god is worshiped. The rain-god receives his adoration and instead of sending missionaries and teachers to tell the simple gospel story, trainloads of American citizens, traveling tourists and moving picture makers are actually paying with their money these poor helpless people of the red race to continue in their heathen worship. And some of you people who visit the movies and are entertained by these ungodly forms of worship will be contributing your full share to keeping these human souls in darkness. Will they stand before us in judgment and say, "No man cared for my soul?"

Whittier, California.

Pray for Our Ambassadors.   By A. L. DeLozier

Synopsis of General Conference Address

I should like to suggest that this subject read: "Pray for Our Substitutes." For as a matter of fact the missionaries are not our ambassadors. They are God's ambassadors, but they are our substitutes.

Tennyson wrote:

More things are wrought by prayer
Than this world dreams of. Wherefore, let thy voice
Rise like a fountain for me night and day.
For what are men better than sheep and goats
That nourish a blind life within the brain,
If, knowing God, they lift not hands of prayer
Both for themselves and those who call them friend?
For so the whole round world is every way
Bound by gold chains about the feet of God.

At this critical time we are liable to lose sight of the potency of prayer. We need to remember as John R. Mott wrote a decade ago in his Decisive Hour of Christian Missions that:

"Every marked advance in the missionary enterprise has been preceded by prayer."

Either this statement is true or it isn't true. If true, it is fraught with great meaning.

Did you ever know that God rules the world and his church through the prayers of his people? God's work is dependent upon you and me.

To what purpose do we live? In heaven Christ lives to pray.

It is wonderful and beyond our thinking, but God actually commits the fulfilment of his desires to our keeping. No matter what you and I may choose to think about it, intercession is an essential element in God's redeeming purpose. We will not realize how solemn is our responsibility until we come to see the place of intercession for the Kingdom of God.

And so in spite of our materialistic way of looking at things we must admit that our Lord makes it a condition of the setting up of the Kingdom that we "Pray to the Father."

I was in the wonderful and complete harmony between the Father and the Son that the great redemption was accomplished. It will be only through a similar harmony of ourselves with God that the great commision will be carried out.

Who are our ambassadors or our substitutes? I am thinking of Yoders, Atkinsons, Sickles, Edwards, Barrios and all the other in South America, and I may add of Books at home on furlough.

But I come related in a peculiar way to the African work. I am acting as Prayer Secretary for that work. As you know it is on the faith basis that our workers have gone into Africa. They have undertaken a herculean task. We should not criticize them either. Because they have undertaken a thing which in terms of our faith looks rash, we have no excuse for criticizing. Rather should we examine ourselves and see if our faith isn't too small. At least let us pray before we criticize.

Never once in all the records do we read that Jesus turned to man for help. Always and everywhere he went to his father to be shown what to do and what to say. This seems to be the spirit of our workers in Africa. They look to God to make good his promises. They don't look to man. Said Buddha, "The greatest prayer is patience." If our little African party is able to pray this greatest prayer through their waiting under every adverse circumstance, why can't we pray it here at home while comfortably situated?

Now the title of this address is PRAY for our Ambassadors. I know that you are busy. We are all busy. But some one says:

"The Christian will find his parenthesis for prayer even in the busiest hours of life." So I am going to ask you to find this parenthesis. It is not absolutely necessary to go down on your knees to render this service. Assume the attitude in which you are in the habit of thinking. If you think best on your feet, then stand up. If you think in your chair, then sit down. Get into the place where your mind is free from any thought that can hinder, and then talk to the Master about our ambassadors, or rather his.

As John R. Mott says: "Prayer is the putting forth of vital energy. It is the highest effort of which the human spirit is capable."

But you and I are called upon thus to contribute vital energy and high effort as well as are our missionaries.

They crave our prayers. Shall we disappoint them? A certain missionary once said: "Unprayed for, I feel like a diver deep down in the sea, but without any air or like a fireman up in a blazing building without any water in his hose."

May God help us to be true stewards in prayer.

Ashland, Ohio.

Preparation by Pastor and People for a Revival. By Z. T. Livengood

In the presentation of this subject, three propositions come to my mind, first, the need of a revival; second, the pastor's part in a revival; and thirdly, the people's part in a revival. Then we begin by asking the questions, Are conditions such that we need a revival, and What is a revival?

There is a constant wear upon every living moving thing. Our bodies are constantly wearing out and need renewing and reviving. Of necessity there is a consuming of energy, and this used up energy must be supplied. Isaiah says, They that wait upon the Lord shall renew their strength." (Isa. 40:3). We ought to be supremely grateful for this fact, that the Lord will renew our strength, when we wait upon him. This same divine fact runs through all living things, even through business enterprises, and it also is true about the church of the Living God.

Christ's command to the church was, "Go and make disciples of all the world," of "every creature." The early Apostolic church was in a continual revival. So ought the church be today. Does the church and the world need a revival today? Pessimists of today are ready to say that the world is alarmingly full of sin and greatly needs a thorough cleansing, if civilization is to remain. Really, the dishonesty and crime and robbery and gambling and stealing and social evils and national sins are appalling. I need not particularize; every day the newspapers are replete with them.

Who is to do this work of saving men, the lost men and women? The church is the instrument God uses to do it. The pastor and the church members are to do this work of keeping themselves alive and bringing the dead in sin unto life.

The pastor is a prominent factor in any successful revival. He must believe in revivals. He must have a passion for lost souls. He must love his church. He must be a good Bible student, a teacher of the Bible, and a God-fearing man. The nearer he lives the Christ-life the more effective he will be. Above all, he must be divinely guided.

The people must also believe in the revival. They too must be good Bible students, and have a like passion for lost souls, and godly living. The pastor and people must fully co-operate in Bible study and continual prayer before a revival is begun, and when pastor and people are led by the Holy Spirit, the church will receive new life and the dead in sin will seek the true and living Light. And as they continue thus in fidelity and prayer many will find him who is the true Light of the world. When pastor and people work together with God in a revival no power on earth can defeat them.

If your church is spiritually dead, a genuine revival will bring it to life. If she is a quarreling church, it will make them co-operative. If they are divided, it will unite them. If they are cold and indifferent, it will make them hot and zealous. If they are lazy it will make them active. If they are covetous, it will make them liberal. If your church is not growing, have a revival. But do not forget to fully prepare for this revival, and seek divine guidance in the entire work.

Lanark, Illinois.

Enlisting Young People for Service. By Edwin Boardman, Jr.

(Continued from last week)

Now, young people, let me talk very earnestly with you about your own individual life enlistment. Are you satisfied to be a mediocre servant of God or do you really love him enough to go the limit in his service? Is the spirit of St. Mihiel and the Argonne dead already? There young men bled and died willingly for the propagation and perpetuation of an ideal of liberty. Counting their lives, their careers, their hopes for the future, as nothing they dashed into the jaws of death with a cheer on their lips and a song in their hearts because they had learned the glory of serving a great cause. Young women behind the lines served in hospital and dressing station and "Y" hut until they were completely exhausted, because they felt this was their part in the fight for international honesty and good faith. Am I to believe that the young people of today are any less noble or heroic than the young people of 1918? Will men and women dare more for their country than they will for their God? Do the "Stars and Stripes" of America bring out more of the true spirit of sacrificial service than do the "stars and stripes" of the Christ of God? We read in the Word, "And they that turn many to righteousness shall shine as the stars forever and ever." In another place the Word says "By his stripes we are healed." Do stars and stripes like these make no challenge to us? Must our country's history read like a record of triumph while the history of Christian achievement reads like an obituary, and all because young men and women absolutely refuse to heed the challenge of Christ in their life?

Young people, the call of a vital need comes to us to-day. The world is dying. Notwithstanding our automobiles, our inventions, our luxurious mode of living, our increasing intellectualism, the world is dying. It does not have Christ Jesus; does not know him, and without him all the mere paltry gains we make are but so much tinsel and gold lace trying to cover up a putrefying corpse. One billion souls are dying without Christ in this generation. Every two seconds that I have been speaking to you a heathen soul has gone out into the outer darkness without the Light of the World to lead him. The fetich doctor has been plying his nefarious business in the meantime and some helpless little tots have been literally sacrificed to the Molochs of Ignorance and Superstition. The foul spirit of Mohammedanism has pushed some Arabian trader just a bit further into Africa and a few more converts have been enlisted in the shame of Islam. The disciples of Mormon have visited just a few hundred more homes in the meantime preaching their false doctrines and wrapping the slimy coils of their cult around a few more Americans. The worshippers of Brahma and the three hundred million idol gods of India have also climbed down into the filthy, unspeakable depths of the dirty Ganges hoping to wash away not the filth of their bodies, but the filth of their souls. At the same time thousands of heavy-eyed and a million times heavier hearted, little temple girls have been carried a bit further into the shame of being wedded to the gods; and multiplied millions of poor little Hindoo widows have felt a bit heavier the awful yoke of life that is virtually a living death. Oh, had I but the power of a supernatural magician so that I could paint clearly scene after scene of what is going on right now, while I am talking in the various places where Jesus is unknown, and—let me whisper it sorrowfully—the shame that abounds in places where people have had a chance to know Christ.

Beloved, I call to you today to reverently, honestly hear and heed Christ's call to you right now. He needs you to help carry the news of salvation to those who grope blindly in the darkness. You dare not excuse yourself. Preachers are needed and whether you think you can preach or not the big thing for you to do is to give God the chance he wants. If you are slow of speech, as was Moses, and **God wants to use you**, he'll make arrangement for you to have a good mouthpiece before he sends you into the hard place. We must remember that God not only uses preachers by precept, but he uses much more, preachers by example. If you cannot preach by word of mouth therefore it may be that the Master will speak through you by the skilled hand, the trained voice, or in a multitude of other ways. "What is that in thine hand?" was God's question to Moses of old and many, many times since then the Almighty has put his rod of power not in our mouths, but in our hands and we must of necessity use it. There is no need therefore for anyone of us to sit back and say, "There is nothing that I can do." There is something for us to do and the splendid prerogative that we have is to "become all things to all men, if by any means we might save some."

There is not only the call of a vital need, but also the call of a supreme helpfulness that is ours. The troubles of the world have as their basis a spiritual foundation; that is, many of the misunderstandings, economic injustices, political crimes, and international scandals are at heart spiritual, not material. If men would learn to see each other truly there would be no unfair practices indulged. The real things of life are the unseen, but men have gone so far astray in their judgment that they are ready to fight at the drop of the hat for a bit of gold or a strip of land or a few oil wells —something with material value,—while ideals that are lofty and ennobling are relegated to the scrap heap.

The servant of God has an opportunity to change this crude and false conception of values by bringing to bear on the hearts of men and nations all the wonderful dynamic of Jesus Christ—a power sufficient in itself to change the course not only of individuals, but of whole worlds. It was said of the men of old who were filled with this same power of God, "These that have turned the world upside down are now come hither also." There was no military organization behind these men, no power of material wealth, no striking intellectualism—only the power of the Holy Spirit in their hearts and the glory of the cross in their lives, and yet these men were accounted world-changers. We have access to that same power; we have the same prerogatives as had they and the responsibility devolves upon us to discharge our trust. The Apostle Paul tells us in II Corinthians 4:18, "For the things which are seen are temporal, but the things which are not seen are eternal." It is our privilege to emphasize the eternal values and place the beauty and wealth of the unseen things before men. I can say, without fear of successful contradiction, that all the really worthwhile things of life are those that transcend human reason and wisdom. No one can adequately tell us about life itself. We know its manifestations, but we do not know its essence. The same thing is true of love—a quality magnificent because we cannot fathom it. And what shall we say about our God, who while he is a consuming fire is also Spirit and Love and Father?

Ah, young people, we do possess those eternal verities as servants of the Most High that place us in the position of being supremely useful to the world. It is our privilege to help men to think right and to do right and the use of any power that produces such results is not only significant from a spiritual standpoint, but is infinitely valuable to the world at large from an economic, material basis. Such a power has eternal weight and worth and we, as young men and women, should count it all joy to enter into a service

that makes us pre-eminently useful to our fellowmen.

But enough has been said. Apart from all the material worth of Christian service, apart from all the reasonableness of such service, apart from all the need of the world for the Christ message, we must get this angle to the situation, viz., it is our bounden duty to obey Jesus Christ in all things and he commands us to go into all the world and preach the gospel. Dare we refuse to heed his call? Dare we sit by while the people whom Jesus would save go to eternal ruin? Will we seek our own material comfort and well being while the cry comes insistently from the outer darkness, "Come over and help us?" Men and women—young people—God calls, and while vast continents lie shrouded in darkness the burden rests upon us to carry to them the Light of Life so that the glory of that great prophecy in Isaiah might speedily shine out." The wilderness and the solitary place shall be glad for them, and the desert shall rejoice and blossom as the rose." Amen.
Hudson, Iowa.

Impromptu Flashes. By W. J. H. Bauman

His satanic majesty is at the head of a mighty host. The Bible informs us that devils are very numerous.

Among all the acquaintanceships you may form in life, get acquainted with God and your self. Say to Satan "get thee behind me."

The wonderful harmony in the realm of nature is **conclusive** proof of just such a God as is represented in the Bible.

How a person with acute mental powers can deny the existence of a God like our Bible's God, is a mystery to me.

Were New Testament Christianity to control the world's character, there would be no dishonor of any kind; locksmiths would have to close their shops; tattling tongues would be paralyzed; divorce courts would be discontinued; and bloody wars would be unknown.

To the writer of these "flashes" there seems nothing more simple than God's plan of salvation, so far as human attitude is concerned. A short poetic sentence expresses it all—"Trust and obey."

Human weakness can be overcome by Christian hopefulness.

Both Old and New Testament prophecies are so rapidly and clearly being fulfilled in our day, that all doubt as to the veracity of the old Book should vanish.

Every moment in human history is graced with a vision of our Bible's God.

From the standpoint of honor Christians of today are covered from head to feet with responsibilities.

That detestable old tattler is engaged in the meanest and most detestable business to be found in human ranks.

Christlike humility is superior to mere intellectuality.

The old proverb, "Where ignorance is bliss, 'tis folly to be wise," is about as true as it is poetic.

Dear reader, you and I have infirmities which we keep hidden from each other, and justifiably; let us be glad that God is sympathetic and loves to forgive.

I know from personal experience that it is a **tremendous** task to be kind to those who harshly treat us. But hark, from Calvary's cross comes the cry, "Father forgive them, for they know not what they do." Let's join in.
Long Beach, California.

THE BOOK OF TRUTH

We search the world for truth; we cull
The good, the pure, the beautiful,
From graven stone and written scroll,
From all old flower-fields of the soul;
And, weary seekers of the best,
We come back laden from our quest
To find that all the sages said
Is in the Book our mothers read.—Whittier.

THE BRETHREN PULPIT

One Master, Many Brethren.   By J. A. Garber

TEXT: One is your master and all ye are brethren. Matthew 23:8.

In these challenging words Christ makes an exclusive claim for himself and proclaims an all-inclusive fellowship for his followers. How strangely the bold declaration must have sounded to the men selfishly appropriating for themselves places of leadership and wholly disregarding the principles of brotherhood! How strangely the fearless proclamation would sound to the men of today assuming similar attitudes were it not for the cumulative verification of more than nineteen centuries!

One is your master. "Master" is the striking and significant title which the disciples applied to Jesus and with which he wanted them to address him. In the Gospels he is spoken of as King but nowhere does he ask the disciples to employ that appellation with reference to himself. With marked frequency the Evangelists speak of him as "The Son of Man" and "the Son of God" but he does not urge the usage of either when speaking of him. He does authorize the use of "Master." One is your master; "If I your Lord and Master have washed your feet you also should wash one another's feet;" "Why call me Lord and Master and do not the things I command you?"

The pregnant idea of a supreme master had not gotten inside the brain of Jesus' contemporaries. Infatuated with the possession of high-sounding titles the scribes and Pharisees had a mania for the term Rabbi like some modern self-opinionated teachers have for the degree of Doctor. It never occurred to them, like others today, that position is not to be sought for the name but for the service one can render. With characteristic discrimination Jesus distinguishes sharply between the office and the men who occupy it. Had they been true to their trust they would have been worthy of due honor, but they were false men who say and do not. Through a series of "woes" they are characterized as blind guides! impious, irreligious scribes! You are very exacting about keeping clean the outside of the cup but inside you are filled with self-indulgence and self-seeking. Having severely indicted these false teachers with a full length portrait of them Jesus exhorts his disciples not to be called Rabbi. Be ye not like the scribes, but unlike them in every particular. One is your master.

Although the mastery of Christ is being more largely recognized many persons speak of him as master without comprehending the meaning of the term. Certain people who have never acknowledged him as Savior refer to him thoughtlessly and even profanely as the "Master." Others impelled by a full measure of religious enthusiasm glibly talk of their "Master" but subsequent conduct indicates that their gushing words were outbursts of cant and insincerity. It is very doubtful if any one of us has yielded his life fully and completely to him who would have us call him Master. Reviewing the work of the past year has Christ or self been the master? Are we ministers sure that we served the churches by the counsel and under the direction of the Overseer? Or must we with the blush of shame confess: Master we have toiled all the year fruitlessly because we did not let down the net at thy bidding, our plans were not brought reverently under thy control? Have you laymen

attended and supported the church with the chief desire to please the Master? Did any of your appointments relative to mid week engagements or Sunday auto trip occasion disappointment in his heart? As Sunday school teachers and Christian Endeavor workers, can we truthfully say that we have worked for the pleasure of him whom we fondly call Master? Tested by the plans we have for this conference and the coming year, are we really planning to do what we believe is his will? Are we not men and women under authority?

Like the Centurion we are men and women under authority, and no one needs to expect exemption. Not a single person can plead ignorance, for the Teacher has come. It is superfluous to ask: Master, where dwellest thou? His wonderful teachings have become general possessions, even though we may not be possessed generally by them. Moreover our Schoolmaster has set a copy for us to reproduce, "I do always the things that please him," said Jesus. While the Revised Version gives the word Teacher in the text, the primary meaning is Guide or Leader. Here we hav no mere peripatetic meeting with groups of truth seekers, disseminating knowledge, but the incarnation of truth wrought out in ideal conduct. Here we find satisfaction for one of the inmost yearning and highest aspirations of the soul. Napoleon and Frederick the Great may satisfy the heartless militarist. Gladstone and Lincoln may satisfy the coming statesman; Shakespeare and Ruskin may satisfy the literary critic; Luther and Wesley may satisfy the religious devotee, but Christians will be satisfied with none other than the example of the sinless one, who though he was rich, yet for our sakes he became poor, that we through his poverty might become rich, and who went about doing good.

To all this fine idealism our hearts yield ready, willing and unwavering assent. Yet we experience certain practical difficulties. It is relatively easier to submit to Christ the Savior than Christ the Ruler. The one aspect of his mission suggests the idea of the similitude of children we take refuge in love represented by mother but we shun the sterner discipline suggested by the presence of father. Enamored with the loveliness of the Lover we are prone to overlook the masterliness of the Master. Viewed through a contracted perspective we see a single pose of his balanced character and deprive ourselves of the moral fibre resulting from the contemplation of the dual picture. The sovereign consciousness of being under the control of spiritual firmness, not laxness, begets character. Mastery produces stability. He that has no masters will never become a master. As the stars are kept in their courses through strictest submission to the king of heavenly bodies so the Christian will be steadied in the paths of eternal righteousness through fullest obedience to the righteous One. Unlike the early disciples we sometimes try the pleasanter way of following him and keeping our nets. To make the attempt is to enter into a practical repudiation of our Master like those mentioned by Jude, who denied their only Master and Lord. We will not become the best vessels for the Master's use until he is homed in the throne-room of the heart. Why sing "Crown him Lord of all" when he is not crowned Lord at all? Why call me Lord and Master and do not the things I command ye?

Conspicuous among those commands is the brotherhood commission. All ye are brethren. In relation to Christ we may be disciples, friends and servants; but in relation to one another we are brethren. Others may call us Christians out of irony or sincerity; but he has named us "Brethren." Judging their utterances, which, doubtless, reflect his teachings, his immediate followers were profoundly impressed with the appropriateness of "Brethren" for a church name. Peter, who made the great confession and preached the initial sermon, assumes that church members are brothers when he admonishes the Christians of the Dispersion to "Love the Brotherhood." John, the beloved disciple, says, "We know that we have passed from death unto life because we love the brethren." Paul, the unmatched interpreter of Christ in a later day, writing the church in Thessalonica, says, "Concerning the love of the brethren, ye have no need that one write unto you, for ye yourselves are taught of God to love one another; for indeed you do it toward all the brethren which are in Macedonia. But we exhort you, brethren, that ye abound more and more."

One cannot peruse those inspired deliverances proclaimed by the pathfinders of Christianity, without being persuaded that they regarded it their perennial duty to build the dissimilar elements of society entering the folds of the church into an indissoluble brotherhood. And, a like obligation rests upon those who take pardonable pride in their apostolic practices. Clear thinking at this point will save us from foolish blunders and help us to determine the points of emphasis. When the church is criticised and discounted people are tempted to magnify unduly some Christian association or Salvation Army, failing to recognize these as adjuncts; when the church's sphere of usefulness seems circumscribed and limited ministers are lured into some forum where they can lecture on social reform or they are enticed into the field of evangelism, forgetting that moral problems are best solved by educating groups of persons in the fine art of living together and that men must not only be evangelized but builded together in a brotherhood. The crowning and far-reaching ministry is the ministry which cultivates a fellowship of persons whose sympathies intertwine, whose purposes interlace, whose lives blend. Where neglect weakens one, domination disrupts ten churches. No man nor coterie of men dare think of himself or themselves as being the church. In thinking so both forget that the faith was delivered to the saints, which certainly would include all of the Lord's followers. Furthermore, those who essay to lord it over others forget that one is your Master. Contention about positions of leadership among his followers now is as deeply grievous to him as strife among the first disciples was when he sought to institute the Lord's supper. It cannot proceed with hearts estranged. To rebuke them, to purge their hearts of selfishness, to show them the royal pathway to greatness, he girds himself with a towel, pours waters in a basin and washes their feet. In the self-same hour he said "A new commandment I give unto you, that ye love one another, even as I loved you. By this shall all men know that ye are my disciples, if ye have love one to another." Were he in our midst tonight, and he is; should he discern the secret thoughts of our minds, and he does; could he know our plans for this conference, and he can; he would deliver no other key-note message. Mark its implications: Love knows no jealousy; love is never selfish, never irritated, never resentful; love is never glad when others go wrong; love is gladdened by goodness, always slow to expose, always eager to believe the best, always hopeful, patient; love never disappears. If we love one another differences arising in our quest of the truth cannot harm us. If we are poor in love for the brethren they will wreck our gospel boat on the rock of ecclesiastical controversy. But if we know not our brothers whom we see, how can we profess to love him whom we have not seen?

While the love of the brotherhood begins with the household of faith it does not end there. The Christian idea of brotherhood is unique in that it transcends all boundaries, racial and national, social and religious. It apparently did not occur to Moses when he sought to mediate the struggle between his Hebrew brethren that the Egyptian whom he had slain was also his brother. A Roman would be provoked to fiercest indignation when seeing a fellow countryman mistreated but he could witness the slaughter of other people as a bit of pastime. The Stoics taught that men should be considered brothers but the Greek despised the Syrian. Christ's novel conception of brotherhood escaped the narrowness which hampered the national idea and the helplessness which rendered impracticable the worthy teachings of Stoicism. He threw down the dividing prejudices of nationality and taught universal love without distinction of race or rank. According to his precept and example all men, from the slave to the master, from the lowest to the highest, from the poorest to the richest, were children of one Father, and should feel and act toward each other as brethren. Studying his teaching and beholding his conduct men began to understand that in Christ, and for his Father whom he revealed, there was neither Jew nor Greek, barbarian nor Scythian, bond nor free. Adjusting ourselves to new world conditions which are changing the boundaries of nations and liberating enslaved peoples we must earn that in Christ there is neither American or Britain; Belgian nor French, Slav nor Teuton: Formulating our Americanization and Christianization program we must purge our vocabularies and enlarge our sympathies.

He shall see the travail of his soul. He is the desire of all nations. His grand ideal of equality will be realized. Our man-made differences and prejudices may delay but cannot defeat the brotherhood program. It synchronizes with the times and coincides with the tendencies of the age both in church, society and state. Within the brief span of our denominational life almost a score of men's brotherhoods have been organized, many of them bearing the name of the church or its revered founder. Churches having the episcopal form of government have modified it so as to place the conduct of the church on a more brotherly basis. Churches adhering to the congregational principle are discovering the mistake of being democratic in government and autocratic in spirit. Personnel not polity becomes the determining factor. Time fails us to number the legion of lodges, fraternities and unions which carry the brotherhood label. Most of these are organized on the principle of exclusion rather than inclusion. Unless the applicant can meet a physical, social or industrial test he must stand alone in an unbrotherly world. If he is fortunate enough to be admitted into membership he must rigidly conform to every rule even though conformity thereto outrages his conscience or imposes upon him an intolerable hardship. That with which sympathetic souls gropingly seek the church must supply and may, if she will maintain a brotherly atmosphere that will light the flame of brotherhood in human hearts to kindle the altars of daily life. Even patriotism is taking on the brighter hue. Men can no longer content themselves with the thought that they are citizens of a county, state or nation. Modern invention has brought the ends of the earth together and made us world citizens. Increased contracts necessitate enlarged sympathies. The neighborhood created by the nineteenth century must be converted into the brotherhood of the twentieth century. Unbrotherly attitudes on the part of nations precipitate wars. The preventative is the toxin of brotherliness. Once injected in the citizenry of the world strong nations will regard the rights of the weaker as being sacred, and each will enjoy the opportunity of working out its own destinies without let or hurt. The League of Nations represents a most significant step in that direction. But the sisterhood of nations is conditioned by the brotherhood of man, and it waits for the brotherhood of Christians

When men accept the Fatherhood of God and the Mastery of Christ. Only under the influence of their majestic authority and the unifying force of their supreme love can fraternity grow to be a ruling passion capable of mastering human selfishness. When men distrust systems of personal interest, discard quack remedies for social ills and discriminate between the genuine and spurious the golden days by prophet bards foretold will surely dawn. When men begin to brother the foreigner into a Christian citizen, the drunkard into a Christian man, the employer and employee into workingmen like unto the Carpenter of Nazareth we will have reached the

> "One far-off divine event,
> To which the whole creation moves."

When men know themselves children of God through fidel-

ity to the Elder Brother they will not be found wanting in brotherliness to any one of the human family. Above nations humanity and above all national anthems we must hear the international anthem

> All hail the power of Jesus' name
> Let angels prostrate fall
> Bring forth the royal diadem
> And crown him Lord of all.

Send
WHITE GIFT
OFFERINGS to

THE SUNDAY SCHOOL

ALBERT TRENT
General Secretary-Treasurer
Johnstown, Pennsylvania

Sunday School Progress In South America

Soiled Linen

A steam laundry in the suburb of Bahia Blanca, Brazil, is the meeting place for a growing Sunday school. Rev. George P. Howard, Sunday School Secretary for South America representing the World's Sunday School Association, states that this school was the first one begun in that community. He writes, "This Sunday school meets in a steam laundry, surrounded by machinery, boilers, etc. I thought this was the most novel place for a Sunday school. The youngsters file in through a door labelled "soiled linen" when they come to Sunday school. These children are gathered up from the tenement district and they look like "soiled linen" when they come to Sunday school. But just wait. Come back a year from now and you will notice that a moral and spiritual cleaning up has been going on in that laundry on Sunday mornings, and that inward change will register in an outward cleaning up. Little bare feet will begin to don shoes and stockings, little dresses and caps will be washed and ironed on Saturday so as to be in readiness for Sunday morning, and in this way that whole neighborhood will be changed.

Five years ago Bahia Blanca placed a Sunday school in Villa Mitre, a suburb of the toughest. The crowd of children that gathered there was the filthiest I had ever seen. But you ought to see the crowd of fine young people they have now! They are the same youngsters, but the leaven of the Gospel has been at work: they all work better, they go to school longer, they save more, use more soap, and ten days ago a local bank advanced them a loan of $6,000 to purchase one of the finest properties in that neighborhood for church and Sunday school purposes. That Sunday school has become a powerful plant for the formation of the finest type of Christian citizenship. When I was in Bahia Blanca recently I had a long talk with a fine young man belonging to

this Sunday school who is thinking seriously of going into the ministry. Our own missionaries in Argentina are witnessing similar transformations as a result of their Sunday schools. We have not realized what a wonderfully uplifting and regenerating agency in the hands of God the Sunday school is.

Wanted---A Hen

When Brother Beachler visited the churches of the brotherhood, his principal appeal for the college was to the older folks, though not a few of the boys and girls gave also for permanent endowment. But this appeal is one particularly to the boys and girls in the Sunday schools, or out of them if it has not been possible for them to attend.

In spite of our effort to save in every way possible, there is still a good deal of waste at the dormitory, when so many are being fed every day. We have determined to convert this waste into something with profit, and here is the plan. We have built a splendid poultry house, capable of housing at least 200 chickens and I think the boys and girls will want to supply them. We are expecting you all at Ashland College some day, and the help you give now, will pave the way for fresh eggs and fried chicken, when you do come. I know you all want to help stock this poultry plant, and so I am giving you the opportunity to do so. Intermediates, Juniors and Primary classes, can each send a chicken, or better still, send money to buy one, for I can buy it here. I will report every week the names of classes or persons who contribute to the fund. You are already too late to be first, for since I told of our plans at the Indiana conference, Brother C. A. Stewart has sent me $2.00, and Brother Bennett of Ashland has added another to it, so the fund is really started. Come, who is next?

MARTIN SHIVELY, Ashland College, Ashland, O.

J. A. Garber
PRESIDENT

Our Young People at Work

G. C. Carpenter
SECRETARY

A Welcome Letter

At Winona we requested the delegates of the Christian Endeavor conference to send us the names and addresses of new officers whenever elections were held in the societies. Below we print the first response to that request. The writer will be surprised with its publication, but we publish it as a reminder to all who may read these lines. Such letters are welcomed because they supply information that enables us to keep an up-to-date directory or mailing list. This we most earnestly desire that we may communicate from time to time with our societies. Another commendable feature about this particular letter is the concern of the writer for the education of the young people. We hope she will continue to direct their attention to Ashland. Here is

a fruitful suggestion for others associated with young people's work in local churches.

J. A. GARBER.

Meyersdale, Pa., October 1, 1920.
Dear Brother Garber:

Just had our business meeting and elected our officers. I will send you the names of our new President and Secretary: President, Cedric Miller, Meyersdale, Pa.; Secretary, Lynnette Morgan, Meyersdale, Pa.

I trust you can visit our Christian Endeavor some day for we have quite a number of boys and girls who are soon through school. I would like to see them in Ashland College.

Sincerely,   VESTA N. HOOVER.

On the Lookout and the Outlook

An address delivered at General Conference by E. A. Rowsey, Associate Secretary, Ohio Christian Endeavor Union.

When I first began to think upon this subject, I wondered just what the difference was between the "lookout" and the "outlook." At first I could not see that there was any particular difference. Later I saw a world of difference.

I was at the New York State Christian Endeavor Convention at Rochester, New York, and one beautiful afternoon, State President Collins and wife took Dr. Ira Landrith, Dr. Poling and myself out on a sight-seeing trip. We left the hustle of the crowded streets of Rochester, and soon we were sailing across that glass-like road which leads to Lake Ontario.

While sailing over hill and plain we were busy discussing the reasons for the recent death of the Interchurch World Movement. As our conversation became more and more intense, we became less and less conscious of the beautiful paradise through which we were passing. We had lost sight for the moment of God's handiwork and our eyes riveted upon the dusty sides of the traveling car. All at once, Mrs. Collins cried, "Oh, look!" and as our eyes were lifted they were caught by a marvelous picture. Just to our right was a most exquisite flower garden blossoming in indescribable splendor, and just back of the flowers a background of nature-clipped shrubbery which gave a symmetrical design to the divinely painted reality.

While dazed at such a natural splendor the car climbed to the top of the summit, then the human eye was checked only by its own makeup, for before us the most beautiful picture yet—the howling Ontario was dancing and leaping, falling and filling, and when human sight could see no further, the sky of dark velvet blue seemed to come down and kiss the angry water to sleep.

It was beyond description for beauty; it tugged at the beautiful and powerful in man. I whispered to myself "I see the distinction between 'Lookout' and 'Outlook.'

The outlook was here, but I had to take my eyes from the dusty car and direct correctly the human gaze before I had the Lookout.

The Outlook is before us, but the saddest picture of the century is the refusal of the so-called Christian faces to Look out.

1. The Outlook

The outlook was never darker; nor was it ever brighter. We stand at the cross-roads awaiting the marching orders of a convalescent age. We have camped in the valley of drouth and at present are building molds into which the liquid world will be poured. The size of our molds will determine the volume of our progress.

The religious forces are in quest of a reasonable solution to the world's problems insofar as religious education is concerned.

Dr. Mott says, "We are called upon to deal with an entirely new world. This is a shaken world—one that is still vibrating. What we called foundations yesterday we have discovered were shifting sand. The pillars of our so-called civilization to which we point with so much pride and confidence have one by one crumbled into dust at our feet; until at least we are to appreciate the words of the Belgians in their darkest hour, taken from their oldest book, "Sufficient is thy arm alone, and our defense is sure."

II. The Lookout

We see the outlook as it is created by the special whole. We see the lookout through the peculiar idiosyncracies of individuality. There are at least four pre-requisites to a reasonable "lookout."

1. A Look Backwards.

The past plus the present equals the future.

I wish to make myself very clear when I say we dare not do our work as we did yesterday, and hope to achieve desired victory; neither dare we hope to ignore the lessons of the past, and steer clear of similar pitfalls in the future.

When we look backwards over the avenue of Christian Endeavor's progress, our minds fall upon Dr. Clark's first society, which was organized in Williston Church, Portland, Maine, February 2, 1881. In October of the same year, we see the birth of the second society organized by Charles Perry Mills in North Congregational church of Newburyport Massachusetts. The first conference June 2, 1882, was represented by six societies. It was during these days that the grain of wheat had been dropped into the ground to die, that in the beginning of the nineties it might come forth with abundant life force.

Christian Endeavor swept over the United States, and soon the Macedonian call was given from the Canadian forces and Christian Endeavor accepted the opportunity to warm the cooler hearts of our beloved friends. The spark of friendship has multiplied until just a few months ago through the United Society, it was posible for Canada to have an "All-Canadian" Secretary. This, to me, is the vindication of a great faith.

Christian Endeavor ploughed her way into the snows of the Arctic Circle and planted her joy smile on the cheeks of the inhabitants of Alaska.

Then to Mexico, the Canal Zone, South America, Asia, India, Burma, China, Korea, Turkey, Persia, Great Britain, France, Switzerland, Spain, Italy, Germany, Scandinavia, Finland, Russia, Poland, Hungary, the Balkan States, Africa, Australia, the Islands of the Sea, the Marshall and Caroline Islands, Samoa, the Loyalty Islands, the Ellice Islands, the Islands of the Atlantic, Formosa, and Madagascar, and the Philippines.

I saw a few days ago the pictures taken by Dr. Clark on his recent trip to the war-ridden countries of Europe. I also heard from his own lips a great testimony as to the power of Christian Endeavor. Dr. Clark distributed thousands of dollars among the disheartened, down-trodden, flocks of humanity, who before his arrival would have welcomed the hand of death, and who after his arrival were strengthened to the point that it was possible for them to regain their stolen strength.

Christian Endeavor gave soup, meat, bread and clothing to the orphans of a nation that had been crucified upon the bloody cross, for humanity's perpetuation.

In Finland, where at one season they have twenty-three hours night and one hour of light, and another season they have twenty three hours of light and one of night, I saw helpless, homeless children helped by the loving gift of America's loyal Christian Endeavor to an unfortunate friend. Surely such a dynamic demonstration should encourage us to a greater and more loyal and willing service "for Christ and the church."

2. A Look In.

"TRY IT"

Say, What's the use of taking stock
In all these things we hear?
Why rip the lining out of Jones,
And make Smith look so queer?
You cannot always tell, my boy,
Perhaps 'tis all a lie—
Just step around behind some tree
And watch YOURSELF go by.

In business as in pleasure,
And in the social life,
It doesn't play to speculate
Or let your thoughts run rife
But try to see the best in those
Who in your pathway lie—
Just slip around behind some tree
And watch YOURSELF go by.

When we are just ready to stick the poison fang of criticism into the progress of our work, if we would halt and look in, I am sure silence would reign in our souls. We can never hope to achieve until we look into our own lives, until we look upon and estimate the destructive tendencies of our bias and personal belief. Too often we break partnership with ourselves. The "Inward Look" will prevent the presentation of such a sad commentary upon our own fail-

ures. It is easy to criticize the work of another but suppose you were the other fellow, could he criticize your work? Or would it be above human criticism? From the way some people judge the efforts of another, you would think that their achievements would by far transcend Divine criticism.

SEND ALL MONEY FOR
General Home, Kentucky and
Foreign Missions to

MISSIONS

WILLIAM A. GEARHART
General Missionary Secretary
906 Conover Bldg., Dayton, O.

The Importance of Missions. By Mrs. George C. Wyke

A paper read at a missionary rally of the Conemaugh, Pennsylvania, Sunday School

When we hear the subject of missions discussed the most of us do not give the matter very serious thought. Oftentimes we dismiss it from our minds entirely, or else pass the responsibility on to some one else. We seldom take the cause to heart and feel that the task is our own. In this we fail to prove true to one of the most vital principles of Christianity, that is, concern and thought for others. When one gets the true spirit of Christ in their hearts they immediately want some one else to know and experience that great blessing for themselves.

If we are to be true to Christ, we must be interested in missions. When he said to his disciples, "Go ye into all the world and preach the gospel to every creature," he had in mind not merely the disciples of his own day, but all those who should become followers of him. He meant you and me, and every professing Christian of our day. There are some of us who may not be able to "go," but we should help others to "go." We should see to it that those self-sacrificing ones who do go, are supplied with the means with which to carry on their work effectively.

Sometimes we hear people say, "I believe in home missions but not in foreign missions." Some of those people are sincere and some are merely making excuse. Those who are sincere are ignorant concerning that the field of Christianity is the world, and that with God there is neither "home" nor "foreign" missions. But it seems that the larger part of such people are merely making a flimsy excuse, when they make such a statement. They claim to be interested in home missions when approached by foreign missions, but the chances are, if we were to investigate, that we should find them doing little or nothing along the line of home missions.

After all, why should we hesitate to give either to home or foreign missions, when that which we are asked to give is the Lord's? Why should we withhold from God that which belongs to him? It will do us no good. We may labor and save, and use all our energies in trying to accumulate riches in this life, but what can we do with them at the last? "There is no pocket in a shroud" is an old saying but very true. When we hear the last call, we must leave our monies and houses and lands and go alone across the dark river, taking none of our possessions with us. We shall find that it will be worth while to give all we can and do all we can to evangelize those who have not the gospel. When

we reach the other shore, if there is one soul there who has had the gospel preached to him through our instrumentality, we shall find it worth infinitely more to us than all the wealth of this world. And then there is the possibility of seeking and hoarding the things of this world until we shall not be able to save our own souls, even as by fire. "What shall it profit a man though he gain the whole world and lose his own soul" has always seemed to me to point to a terrible tragedy, but it will have no terror for him who gives gladly and cheerfully of his abundance for the Lord's work.

Missions involves a sacrifice, when we engage in it as we ought. Whether we go into the foreign field or use our talent in the home field, or merely give for the support of missions, it will mean a sacrifice if we really put our hearts into the work. But when we remember that the Son of God became poor for our sakes and had not where to lay his head, and that he made the supreme sacrifice for us on Calvary, we consider it a privilege to do all that lies in our power for him. When we realize how much he loved us, it stirs a love in our hearts for him and we want to show our love in ways that count. If we understood the love that Jesus sought and longed for we would appreciate more his words when he said, "Simon Peter, lovest thou me more than these?" Peter said, "Lord, thou knowest that I love thee." Jesus replied, "Feed my sheep." Three times he repeated the question and the command that he might impress on him the importance of showing his love in practical ways. Right here is the great test: if we loved the Master as we intended that we should, we would pour out our all on the altar for his service. Then there would be no need of societies to forward the interests of missions, and no need of making appeals through our church paper, for every soul would be doing his utmost to give the gospel to those who have it not.

If we could learn to prize not so much the treasures of earth, and more the treasures of heaven, we would not withhold that which we ought to give and do for missions. In our human frailty we lose sight of the fact that the only abiding and safe treasures are those that are laid up in heaven. "Moth and rust doth not corrupt, nor thieves break through and steal" what we lay up there. One of the most important ways of laying up treasures in heaven is to do all we can toward sending

or taking the gospel to those who have never heard the name of Jesus.

To be alive unto God and to be a live church we must have the missionary spirit in deed and in truth, and do all we can to preach the gospel unto the uttermost parts of the earth. We must heed the Master's command or we cannot have his life.

Conemaugh, Pennsylvania.

Bibles for the Immigrants
New York Bible Society Makes Large Distribution

While thousands of immigrants are crowding through Ellis Island in these days, they are not being overlooked by the New York Bible Society. Hundreds of Bibles are distributed every day in many languages, so that it is possible for each immigrant to obtain a copy in his mother tongue. The Society giving this friendly welcome to the immigrants is the oldest Society rendering service to the immigrants. For nearly eighty-seven years the representatives of this Society have without interruption been meeting the incoming strangers and presenting copies of the Bible to those who wished to accept the Book. In the olden days the workers met the immigrants as they came from the ships at Castle Garden.

The present representative of the Society, Mr. Charles Carol has been at Ellis Island for nearly ten years and has distributed more copies of the Bible in that time than have been printed of almost any other book. With the number of immigrants increasing to over seventy thousand per month the demand for Bibles is very great. Mr. Carol speaks thirteen languages and rarely makes a mistake in offering the right book to an immigrant, for he has learned to know the different nationalities by sight. In one week recently he distributed the Scriptures in more than thirty languages. These Scriptures are presented as a free gift to the immigrants and they make a fine expression of America's welcome to the strangers.

This work is maintained by those who love the Bible and our country. The office of the Society is at 675 Madison Avenue, the Treasurer, James H. Schmelzel and General Secretary—Dr. George William Carter.

What the powder is to the ball; what the dynamo is to the wire; what the electricity is to the black carbon—just that the home mission work is to the salvation of the world.

NEWS FROM THE FIELD

GARWIN, IOWA

. Our meeting closed recently which was started immediately after General Conference by Brethren Coleman and Ronk. We were met with rain at the start and had just commenced to going good when through a misunderstanding and confusion of dates it was necessary for Brother Coleman to leave and start the meeting at McLouth, Kansas. We regretted very much having him leave but in view of the situation considered this the best for all concerned. Brother Ronk then took the burden of finishing the meetings upon his shoulders and worked hard. The final result when we had run a total of two weeks and three days was sixteen. Thirteen of whom have been baptized and received into the church. A mistake was made in not planning at the start for a longer meeting, as there were a number prevented from attending until the last week. This field is so large that anything under a four weeks' meeting will not be full justice to either evangelist or people. While some aims were not realized, in view of the conditions, the meeting was a success. Coleman and Ronk are a very versatile team and should meet with success during their campaign together. Brother Coleman is a power in the pulpit, and delivers his messages with telling effect. Brother Ronk handles the music to good advantage.

Our work here does not make much progress during the winter owing to the weather and bad roads, but must make its gains during the summer.

The interest and attendance is good. There are a number of improvements planned that will make the parsonage at least a warm place in which to live, and improvements also along other lines. There is room here for much growth and sometime not far in the future this church can be a leading church in the brotherhood. With an active membership now of two hundred and ten, a possible membership of four or five hundred in the next decade is not an idle dream. We have taken sixty into the church membership during the past three years, and there is still opportunity for that many more additions in the next three years.

Our prayer is that God may use Coleman and Ronk mightily for his kingdom. May we also at Garwin have an interest in your prayers.

FREEMAN ANKRUM.

INDIANA CONFERENCE REPORT

The thirty-third conference of Brethren churches of the state of Indiana met in the First Brethren church at Flora, Indiana, October 4-7, 1920. The weather was ideal, the attendance good, and these with the inspiration and entertainment that the great church at Flora gave, tended to make one of the largest and best conferences ever held in the district.

All conference sessions were presided over by Vice-moderator J. A. McInturff, who in his fair and impartial way kept things running smoothly throughout. In his annual message he very heartily commended the work of the ministry, the splendid efforts of the laity as well as the work of the several auxiliaries of the church. He called attention to the fact that out of 47 churches receiving recognition by General Conference, eleven of them were in Indiana. Six recommendations were offered which with a few alterations were approved by the conference.

The sermons of the conference were brought by Brethren G. W. Rench, A. T. Wirick and C. C. Grisso. The sermons were all well-prepared, clear and forceful, ringing true to the Book, and each speaker held the large audiences to the last sentence. Addresses were given by the following brethren, W. E. Thomas, Sylvester Whetstone, G. C. Carpenter, E. L. Miller, W. S. Bell Martin Shively, Willis E. Ronk, A. E. Thomas, W. R. Deeter, H. E. Eppley, A. T. Wirick, W. T. Lytle and G. W. Rench. The addresses were timely, dealing with various phases of the work of the church. Some of these addresses will be printed in full in the Evangelist.

One of the most touching scenes of the conference was when Brother W. F. Johnson led our aged veteran of the cross, J. H. Swihart to the front and spoke very feelingly to the conference concerning his labors for the church in the years gone by. Brother Swihart addressed the conference briefly after which the district showed its appreciation in a small way by presenting to him a purse of one hundred and ten dollars.

Missions

The reports of various mission pastors and members of the mission board showed that the work was in a splendid condition in every way. The budget as presented by the Board for the coming year is as follows: For Huntington, $960; Muncie, $600; Peru, $420; Clay City, $100; Teegarden, $75; and for pastorless churches, $250. This budget calls for a 45 cent per capita apportionment according to 1920 statistical report, and that all funds be paid quarterly.

Committees and Officers

The conference officers and various committees for the year are as follows: Conference Secretary and Treasurer, C. C. Grisso; Member of the Mission Board, C. A. Stewart; State Evangelists, G. W. Rench, J. A. McInturff and J. L. Kimmel; Ministerial Examining Board, G. C. Carpenter, G. W. Rench and J. L. Kimmel; Conference Trustees, J. W. Brower and Henry Rhinehart; District Director of Benevolences, H. E. Roscoe; District of "Our Bicentenary," W. E. Thomas; Director Old Folks and Orphans' Home, G. E. Eaton; College trustee, J. W. Brower; District Delegates to General Conference, George Barnhart, Henry Rhinehart, Albert Hostetler, A. J. Wineland, Walter V. Pearson; Members of Executive Committee of General Conference, J. A. McInturff and G. W. Rench. Sunday School Officers: State Superintend-

ent, S. M. Whetstone; Children's Division, Miss Naomi Wilson; Young People's Division, Grace Ebbinghous; Adult Division, Mrs. J. E. Ham; Administrative Division, Wm. Widmoyer; Educational Division, W. I. Duker. Conference Executive Committee: J. A. McInturff, Moderator; A. T. Wirick, Vice-Moderator; and C. C. Grisso, Secretary.

Some Advance Steps

(1) A resolution from the Ministerium was presented and approved by conference as follows: That the Indiana Conference indorse the movement to build up a religious center at Shipshewana Lake, Indiana, and we urge our Indiana churches to contribute toward the material for a tabernacle, and that this conference appoint a committee of three to solicit the necessary funds and that said committee consist of J. A. McInturff, E. L. Miller and A. E. Thomas.

(2) A motion was heartily approved by conference urging each church to lend its pastor for a revival somewhere in the state within the year.

(3) That some time during the year, at the Evangelistic and Bible Study League Conference that the distinctive doctrines of the church be treated in a series of addresses. It was arranged that this conference be held at Warsaw some time next spring.

The conference for 1921 will meet with the Brethren church at Oakville, the first full week in October. The minutes of the W. M. S. conferences, the ministerium and certain features of the work of the Sunday schools of the district will be reported separately through the columns of the Evangelist by those having the work in charge. The resolutions offered and approved are as follows:

Resolutions

Inasmuch as it has pleased our heavenly Father to again permit us to assemble in his name, and in this the thirty-third Annual Conference of the Brethren churches of Indiana, we deem it proper first of all to than him for his kind Providence and gracious care over us since last we met. And further, that we especially praise him for the sweet spiritual fellowship so manifest among us all.

So be it resolved:

1. That we extend to the Flora Brethren church our hearty appreciation for the kindly welcome received, and the generous hospitality rendered while among them.

2. That, we extend our most grateful appreciation to the program committee for their efficient forethought in placing before us a program which is far-reaching in effect, and especially for the splendid way and manner in which it has been carried out.

3. That we are in hearty accord with the proposition of Mr. Ash of Shipsawanna Lake, Indiana, in offering to the Brethren churches of Indiana a location for a tabernacle in which to hold Summer Camp meetings, and Bible Conferences. In having a central place of meeting we shall be able to create within us a desire for deeper spiritual fellowship in

the Lord, thus forming a basis for a more extensive growth in our district.

4. That, both ministers and laymen seek to keep the vision of a larger working church constantly before them, that many souls may be brought into the fold of the Lord Jesus Christ in the coming year.

5. That, we especially recognize the place the Woman's Missionary Society has come to hold in our church. Their splendid co-operation in all departments of the church is worthy of our acceptation, and is a powerful asset whose influence shall not wane in the ages to come.

W. R. DEETER,

W. E. RONK,

W. T. LYTLE.

C. C. GRISSO,

Conference Secretary.

FIRST BRETHREN CHURCH

Los Angeles, California

After an absence of nearly a month Brother Jennings was greeted with an interested audience on Sunday, September 12. All of us were glad to welcome home again both the pastor and his wife. Sister Jennings was accompanied home by her parents, Brother and Sister Allen of Virginia.

That same day we had the pleasure of receiving by letter Brother Percy Hawk formerly of the Brethren church of Fremont, Ohio. If he is a fair sample of the kind of folks in the church there, we know they have some good, dependable people, such as one likes to meet.

At the last meeting of the Sunday school cabinet, September 21st plans were made to secure some much needed equipment for the new departments that have recently been organized. Our school is still growing in numbers. On Sunday, September 19 another lad from the Sunday school was baptized and a brother who had formerly been baptized was received into the church by the laying on of hands.

The following Sunday, September 26, another boy from the Sunday school received baptism, and Sister Gates of Oak Hill, West Virginia, was received by letter. Also Sister Hade from our Mission in the mountains of Kentucky worshiped with us that day for the first time.

Sunday, October 3rd was our Rally Day and we had the church well filled for the program given at the regular preaching hour. The pupils acquitted themselves well, showing that the teachers had been teaching them the true principles of Christian living. Quite a number received promotions to advanced departments and it was both a pleasure to give the certificates and to see the appreciation of girls and boys on receiving them. We had the highest record of attendance yet attained —183. At the close three of the lads of the school, already mentioned as having been baptized, were received into the fold by the laying on of hands.

That afternoon it was the pleasure of a number of our people to attend the "Home Coming" and reception to the new pastor, Brother Leatherman, at the Compton Avenue

Brethren church. Some were also present from Long Beach and Whittier. The program consisted of music, testimonies and addresses by visiting ministers and a response by the new pastor, Brother Leatherman. He is one of our Ashland College boys and is no longer so very new in our state, having already served 2 or 3 years the churches in Central California. We are glad to welcome him to our district and shall pray for his success as a minister of the Word of God in this difficult field. As a rule our Ashland College boys have given a good account of themselves. Brother Jennings remarked on the excellent showing made at our late National Conference at Winona Lake by Ashland College men when more than (200) two hundred of our ministers occupied the platform. I think we all brace up just a little more when we know that a good deal is expected of us. Ashland College is certainly a great unifying force among us. The fellowship of school boys is not easily thrown off but its power to hold together is experienced by every one who has been in attendance for any length of time sufficient to form associations and permanent friendships.

A. P. REED.

4910 Wadsworth St.

CANTON, OHIO

It has been some time since any report has been made of the Canton work but nevertheless it has not been because there has been nothing to report. To begin with we are glad to report that the Sunday school has successfully resisted any attempt of "Old Hot Weather" to make inroads into the attendance record. In fact there has not been any occasion to even think about a summer slump. Instead there has been a gradual increase in the attendance and with the exception of one Sunday when it stormed so hard that it was impossible for those living at a distance to come, the attendance has never been lower than 110. Then too we have been having fine attendance at the regular church services and an increased interest in the work of Christian Endeavor.

On the morning of September 19 a most impressive consecration service was held in behalf of Miss Marie Snyder, who accepted the call to the secretaryship of the national work of the Sisterhood of Mary and Martha. The writer was assisted in this service by Elders Alvin Byers and D. F. Eikenberry. At this time Miss Snyder signified her desire to enroll as a recruit in the Life Work Department. This had a real significance to us in that as the first Life Work Recruit of the old Four Year Program, we have the honor of presenting to the Bicentenary Movement the first Life Work Recruit of this new movement. May God bless this new official and inspire her to do great things for the work. She has a live Sisterhood to help her work out her plans and they are already beginning to take up suggestive plans with the view of testing out the work.

But the half is not yet told. On Sunday, October 3rd, we reached new heights for both school and church. It was Rally Day and Promotion Day in the Sunday school and Mortgage Burning and Jubilee in the church

services. Our goals were 100% of the Enrollment of the school present and a special offering over and above the regular offerings of the day of $300.00. This looked large to us at the beginning but the more we studied the situation and the more we prayed the more confident we became. We were not disappointed. Note the result. Present at Sunday school 185, this being 20 more than we have ever had in attendance before. Special offering, made for immediate needs, coal, insurance, needed repairs, etc., $401.00, $101.00 more than we asked, and the beauty of it all was that it came without any begging. We could scarcely keep track of the amounts as they came in. After this amount was given, how joyfully we watched the flames as they quietly consumed the paper that had once been called a mortgage. Standing around the tray upon which the mortgage burned were the old war horses to whom belonged the glory of planning and helping carry out the plans which relieved the church of debt: P. M. Snyder, George Hang, M. S. Itikin, J. J. Hang and L. D. Ellis. With what fervor we sang "Praise God from whom all blessings flow" and joined in hearty "Amens" as P. M. Snyder offered God thanks for the joy of the hour. Our only regret was that Brother Belote, under whose ministrations this work was done could not be present to enjoy the scene with us. After the mortgage had been consumed we enjoyed a short musical program and an address, after which we departed to our homes, feeling that the morning was well spent in the Master's service. In the evening we had a wide-awake Endeavor meeting under the leadership of J. J. Hang. We had announced Dr. Jacobs as the speaker of the evening, but owing to a conflicting engagement he sent as his substitute Prof. R. R. Haun of the College. While we were sorry not to have Dr. Jacobs with us, yet in a great measure was the regret lessened as we listened to Prof. Haun who brought us an excellent message upon the subject, "Why I believe in God." Taking it all in all we feel that we are just beginning to do things and that the future promises great things for the Canton church under the leadership of God in whose name we are all working.

FRED C. VANATOR, Pastor.

OHIO CONFERENCE DELEGATES

We cannot emphasize too strongly that every church send its full quota of delegates to our Ohio state conference to meet at Ashland, October 25 to 27. The success of each congregation's work as well as the success of our conference and state work depends upon it. Each church is entitled to one delegate for every twenty-five members or fraction above fifteen. And each auxiliary organization, such as the Sunday school, Christian Endeavor, Woman's Missionary Society and Sisterhood, is entitled to one delegate. The delegates from these auxiliary organizations use the same credential blank as the church delegates and all are members of the conference. The church is assessed twenty-five cents for each delegate allowed whether the delegates are actually sent or not. This is found necessary to take care of the expenses of the conference, and enables every church to bear its proper share. Every church should send with its delegates a check for the amount of its delegate fees, made out to E. G. Mason, Secretary-Treasurer of the conference. A word from Brother Mason just informs us that he sent out National Conference credentials, when he discovered at a late date that the supply of state conference credentials was exhausted. The dollar credential fee, mentioned on the National Conference credential should not be given any consideration, for the state fee is twenty-five cents, and is to be paid by the church whether the delegate comes or not. The credentials for the auxiliary organizations are to be exactly like those of the church with the exception of the name of the organization instead of the church. If the National Conference credential is used the "Ohio Conference" should be written on the face of the credential. In case no credential blanks arrive, the church may write its own credentials, but be sure they are properly signed by the pastor and church clerk or secretary of the organization sending the delegate. The name of the organization represented should be written on the blank.

By the way, if your church has not paid its Winona Tabernacle Fund apportionment, and also its state mission apportionment, we suggest that these items be taken care of before conference. "Let all things be done decently and in order.

Now, for the "biggest and best conference ever" with a full quota from every church, I am faithfully yours,
            GEORGE S. BAER, Moderator.

FIELD REPORT OF EVANGELISTIC LEAGUE
By W. S. Bell
After spending two months with my family in Washington, I am once again in the field.
Sunnyside Conference
We had a very profitable Bible Conference in Sunnyside, Washington which was well attended by the people of the district. There are only two organized churches in this district, Sunnyside and Spokane, but they are live ones. Brother L. S. Bauman gave valuable assistance, with Brethren Ashman, Paul Miller and myself, who completed the speakers on the program.
Winona Lake, Indiana
We were glad to be present at this largest and most enthusiastic National Conference ever held by our denomination. Progress and onward was the spirit that dominated the plans and program. While there were problems to be met, they were met, and the future of Brethrenism looks promising.
Cerro Gordo, Illinois
My first campaign was held in the church at Cerro Gordo where Brother D. A. C. Teeter is pastor. This church is somewhat isolated from other churches of our denomination. I found here a willing people and enjoyed my work with them and the pastor. I found here a willing people and enjoyed my work with them and the pastor. I found Brother Teeter a mighty fine fellow to work with. We had good crowds, fine weather, and a good meeting with satisfactory results.

Indiana Conference
I was glad to be able to be present for part of this Conference. Indiana has the best district conference I ever attended—in attendance, in enthusiasm and in doing things. I hope the step taken to have a state Bible conference annually will mature.
Pennsylvania Conference
This conference was held in Pittsburgh and we enjoyed meeting old friends and renewing past acquaintances. We were only able to be present the last day, but found a fine spirit and a good conference.
I am at Uniontown, Pennsylvania with Brother Belote in a meeting. It is the fifth meeting I have held for Brother Belote and it is a pleasure to work with him. We have appreciated the courtesies of the different conferences attended and the support given the work of the League.

COLLEGE NEWS
Faculty Reception
On Friday, October 1, the Annual Faculty Reception was held in the library of the college. The weather was bad but the attendance was very gratifying. The entire building was opened and lighted and the occasion was in the nature of open house.

The big thing, however, was an address by Mr. J. L. Clark of this city, a local trustee and a former student, in which he gave public assurance that Ashland would go over the top in the proposed local financial campaign, contemplated for the early spring. Plans are now forming in regards to advertising, cuts, and notices in the Cleveland and Columbus papers, so that when the time comes, we will move right off. If things go right, the Board at its next meeting, will have the unusual pleasure of planning for a building within the year.
Enrollment
While I have not been able to consult all the departments, yet it is evident that the enrollment is up to or likely past the usual number, over 150.

I wish hereby to acknowledge the receipt of a barrel of fruit for the Dormitory from the W. M. S. of Lanark, Illinois. Also two comforts from Fairview, Ohio, W. M. S. For both gifts the College is grateful.

Professor Wolford attended the Pennsylvania Conference, Dr. Shively the Indiana and Professor J. A. Garber the two western conferences. They were all pleased with the reception accorded their messages from the College.

Dr. Miller recently gave a series of Bible addresses before a Union Bible conference of the churches of Peru, Indiana. So pleased were they with them that they expressed a desire to have him appear on the Winona Bible Conference program next year.

Professor Hahn of the department of Physics and Chemistry, recently spoke to the Sunday school at Louisville, Ohio and filled the pulpit for Brother Vanator in the evening at Canton. Please note that he is professor of Physics and Chemistry.
            EDWIN E. JACOBS.

JOHNSTOWN, PENNSYLVANIA
Third Church
It occurs to me that a brief report from my new field of labor might be of interest to the Evangelist family. It is never an easy task to sever the relation of pastor and people, and there were experiences which formed special attachments between the Roanoke church and ourselves during our five-year sojourn among them.

Then again the "Magic City" of the Blue Ridge mountains was attractive and very homelike to us. But many years ago we decided that "Where he leads we will follow."

We were also pleased, and highly gratified with the fact that the church at Roanoke was expecting their new pastor, Brother Obochetzer, within three days after we left, and knowing him to be a man of deep and consecrated efficiency it lightened the burden of leaving.

We started from Brother Edward Nininger's on Thursday morning in the For i and reached Johnstown Saturday evening and took lots of time to see the sights along the road. We furnished the gas, oil and water and the Ford did the rest.

We found the work here in good condition, which speaks very highly of our predecessors, Brothers Jones and Baker and others. It also reveals interest on the part of the membership and a fine spirit of co-operation between pastor and people. The Sunday school, Woman's Missionary Society, Sisterhood of Mary and Martha and Young People's Society of Christian Endeavor are not only intact, but well officered and going forward.

I find my people awake to the great interests of the brotherhood and with a purpose of launching into our Bicentenary Movement. This congregation is also making some large plans, for the necessary equipment and extension of their home base.

We enjoyed the splendid fellowship of the recent state conference in Pittsburgh; and feel very fortunate in being able to attend a conference so soon after coming to the state.

We are pleased with our work and people, and hope to be of service to our King. We are also glad to be in the old "Keystone" state. When we hear mentioned (as we often do), Berlin, Meyersdale, Somerset and Conemaugh, it brings to our minds the names of many of the old defenders of the faith, whose memories we cherish.

I heartily agree with what Brother Bame calls the "meaning" of our Bicentenary Movement. We must ring clear to the principles that distinguish us as BRETHREN. Many of the old Standard Bearers "suffered the loss of all things," to hand these principles down to us. The success of this Movement in 1923 will be measured by the spirit of devotion and sacrifice that has gripped our people for BRETHRENISM.

We should look upon the past with reverence, "other men labored and we are entered into their labors" and their records are written in glory. We should face the present with diligence and the future with hopefulness and determination.

Remember us at the throne of grace.
            L. G. WOOD.

Business Manager's Corner

ANXIOUSLY WAITING

Many of our readers are anxiously awaiting the reports from the churches after the special offering has been made on Brethren Publishing Company day, October thirty-first. We trust all churches will report promptly, as we desire to publish the reports and the amounts they contribute just as promptly as possible.

Of course we will not publish the names of the churches that possibly may fail to make an offering to this most worthy cause, but by the simple process of elimination it will be an easy matter for our readers to learn what ones fail in this by noting carefully the list of churches, as they will be published, that have made the offering.

We have heard from a number of pastors since sending out our personal letters, and they have promised to do the best they can for the cause.

We are glad to be able to report a number of splendid gifts since our last week's report was made. These gifts have been as follows: Mrs. H. B. McEntyre and father, $12.50; Eld. L. G. Wood, $3.00; J. A. Baker, $5.00; Fair-View Brethren church, $50.00; A Friend, $2.00; Edward and Mrs. M. O. Ninninger, $50.00.

Previously reported, $182.00. Total $304.50.

R. R. TEETER,
Business Manager.

Communion Notices

The Brethren church of Berlin, Pennsylvania, will observe Holy Communion Sunday evening, October 24th. Brethren of like faith are invited to enjoy this service with us.

W. C. BENSHOFF, Pastor.

The Listie, Pennsylvania church will observe Holy Communion on Sunday evening, October 31. Neighboring Brethren are invited.

W. S. BAKER, Pastor.

The Gretna Brethren church will observe the Lord's Supper and the Holy Communion on Saturday evening, October thirtieth. Not only the local membership, but all of like faith who may be able to attend are cordially invited to do so.

R. R. TEETER, Pastor.

IN THE SHADOW

WHITELEATHER.—June Vinetta Whiteleather was born June 16, 1920. May heaven's blessing be upon the father, mother and two little brothers. Services at Sebring, O., by the undersigned.

E. M. RIDDLE.

HALL.—Ira Hall, at the age of 93 years and 5 months, died suddenly at the home of his daughter near Louisville. He was a member of the Methodist church. Services by the writer.

E. M. RIDDLE.

WHITELEATHER.—Vinetta M. Kerr White-leather of Damascus, Ohio, departed from this life September 22, 1920, at the age of 59 years and 5 months. She was a faithful, consistent Christian woman throughout her life.

The deceased was a member of the North Georgetown Brethren church. May God's comforting spirit be with those who mourn.

E. M. RIDDLE.

KAGEY.—Jacob Kagey of Louisville, Ohio, passed to his eternal home October 2, 1920, at the age of 77 years, 11 months and 20 days. He lived a beautiful Christian life and was a trustee of the First Brethren church. He was widely known, having served his community in a public capacity for a number of years. May the God of love and compassion comfort his widow and sons. Services in charge of the undersigned assisted by Rev. F. W. Hoffman.

E. M. RIDDLE.

MILLER.—Mary Elizabeth Miller, daughter of Andrew and Rebecca Cunningham, was born in Ross County, O., October 5, 1849, and departed this life at her home in Washington township, Miami county, Indiana, October 3, 1920, aged 70 years, 11 months and 28 days. At the age of four years she with her parents came to Indiana and lived the remainder of her life in Washington township. In the year of 1875 on March 25, she was united in marriage to Joseph Miller, to which union were born six children, one dying in infancy; two daughters, Ida F. and Sadie departing this life at an early age, and Charles of Peru, Edward D. and Clarence of Washington township, and one foster daughter, Mrs. Elba Runyon now at home.

About 34 years ago Mrs. Miller united with the First Brethren church at Loree, Indiana, and has been a faithful member of the church. Christ and his cause were always upon her heart and his kindness and love were made manifest in her life. The religion of Jesus Christ was not a cloak for her that she put on or laid aside at her will, but was a part of her life, and like her Master was always living for others. Day by day she displayed that unselfish spirit that dominated the life of her Lord, and God will only know how much better the world has been made because she has lived in it. Although she has left us for a season and we bid her adieu, her influence still lives as the fragrance of the faded flower.

Besides the bereaved companion she leaves to mourn their loss, three sons, one foster daughter and a brother, Jacob Cunningham, one sister, Mrs. Ella Fox, of Washington township and eight grand children and a host of relatives and friends.

Mrs. Miller has been poorly for some time but the last two weeks was confined to her bed.

Funeral services were held at the residence conducted by Rev. W. T. Little and Rev. C. A. Stewart, pastor.

SRACK.—La Vosier Ellsworth Srack was born at Hopkinton, Iowa, on January 20, 1867. He departed to be with Christ on September 26, 1920, at the age of 53 years, 8 months and 6 days. His parents moved to Nebraska when he was seven years of age and he grew to manhood on a farm near Cedar Rapids, Nebraska. He was converted at the age of 17 years, in the Methodist church, and to the day of his death lived a conscientious Christian life. While in the mercantile business in Fremont, Nebraska, he was married to Grace Helene Powers, on May 10, 1890. In July, 1891, Mr. and Mrs. Srack came to California, which state has ever since been their home. They came to Long Beach to reside on January 1, 1912. They both united with the First Brethren church in Long Beach in August, 1913, the month following the organization of the church and were therefore practically charter members, having been identified practically from the beginning with the work of the church. Both of them have been among the foremost factors in making the First Brethren church of Long Beach what it is today. Their influence in both the spiritual and temporal affairs of the church has always been great. Brother Srack has been identified almost from the beginning of the church in an official capacity, serving most of the time both as deacon and as trustee. While always following a useful and busy life in the affairs of men, his work in the church was made the business of his life. He loved his church dearly. It was only at the National Conference of the Brethren church less than a month ago, that he presented his application to go to Africa as a missionary and to a part of Africa that has been known as "the graveyard of missionaries." Thus he offered to make the supreme sacrifice, if necessary, that the message of his Lord might be told. Its place on earth will be a hard one to fill. We look "through a glass darkly," but know that God knoweth best.

As he survived by the wife, a sister, and a number of more distant relatives. His father, mother, one sister and only brother, several years ago preceded him into the life beyond.

Funeral services were conducted by the undersigned, his pastor. A large congregation of people testified to the esteem in which he was held in Long Beach.

LOUIS S. BAUMAN.

PASSING OF THE DRUNKS

The Washington (D. C.) Herald recently printed the following story:

"The appalling scarcity of drunks in Washington has resulted in there being about one inebriate to every forty of pre-prohibition days, a canvass of institutions for inebriates showed last night.

"Belated hard-working husbands who in the damp past used to tack into the welcome doors of sheltering benevolent establishments and request assistance in repelling the truculent attacks of pursuing cerise rabbits, have almost disappeared with the advent of prohibition.

"We don't have anywhere near as many men under the influence of liquor as we used to,' said H. W. Kline, superintendent of the Gospel Mission, recently. 'Where we used to have 40 or 50 drunks we now have one. Prohibition has entirely changed the character of our work.

"'Most of the men here now are hardworking, poverty-stricken employees. We try to set them on their feet by crediting them with a few weeks' board and after that, for the most part, they make good. Several of them have bank accounts.

"'When Washington was wet,' said N. N. Smiler, the resident physician at the Emergency Hospital, 'we had several cases of inebriety every day. The number dropped off considerably when prohibition came to Washington, but we still sent the ambulance out frequently while Baltimore was supplying the drinks.

"'But now that national prohibition has come,' he said, 'it's seldom that we see a man paralyzed by drink.'

"'At Casualty Hospital the resident doctor said a number of drunks had fallen off from 'a great many every day to three or four a month.'"

THE REAL REASON

He was a splendid type of a man in a northern church, and at the close of an altar call for Christian stewards he said to me, "You noticed that I did not go forward to the altar on your call for tithers?"

"Yes, and could not help wondering why."

"Well, you see, I do not like altar services, and I was sure that some who went there were not in dead earnest, and I give that much anyway."

My reply was brief as the diagnosis of a doctor who has been called to his 9999th case of measles, "Brother, isn't the real reason why you hang back the unbelief in the daily care of God? You haven't the nerve to trust God with your first tithe in faith that he will see you through on the other nine-tenths." His reply was honest, "I guess you hit about right."

Thousands of men would enroll today if they could screw up their practical faith in God to the point where they could trust him in this daily partnership.—Wm. H. Phelps.

"O Lord and Master of us all,
Whate'er our name or sign,
We own Thy sway, we hear Thy call;
We test our lives by Thine."

Volume XLII
Number 41

October 27
1920

The
BRETHREN
EVANGELIST

· ONE · IS · YOUR · MASTER · AND · ALL · YE · ARE · BRETHREN ·

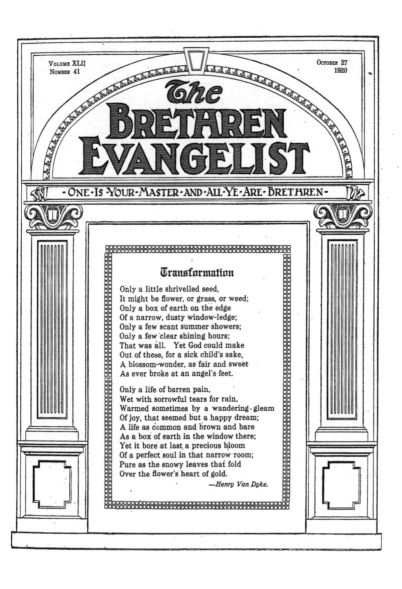

Transformation

Only a little shrivelled seed,
It might be flower, or grass, or weed;
Only a box of earth on the edge
Of a narrow, dusty window-ledge;
Only a few scant summer showers;
Only a few clear shining hours;
That was all. Yet God could make
Out of these, for a sick child's sake,
A blossom-wonder, as fair and sweet
As ever broke at an angel's feet.

Only a life of barren pain,
Wet with sorrowful tears for rain,
Warmed sometimes by a wandering gleam
Of joy, that seemed but a happy dream;
A life as common and brown and bare
As a box of earth in the window there;
Yet it bore at last a precious bloom
Of a perfect soul in that narrow room;
Pure as the snowy leaves that fold
Over the flower's heart of gold.
                            —Henry Van Dyke.

Published every Wednesday at Ashland, Ohio. All matter for publication must reach the Editor not later than Friday noon of the preceding week.

The
Brethren
Evangelist

George S. Baer, Editor

When ordering your paper changed give old as well as new address. Subscriptions discontinued at expiration. To avoid missing any numbers renew two weeks in advance.

R. R. Teeter, Business Manager

ASSOCIATE EDITORS: J. Fremont Watson, Louis S. Bauman, A. B. Cover, Alva J. McClain, B. T. Burnworth.

OFFICIAL ORGAN OF THE BRETHREN CHURCH

Subscription price, $2.00 per year, payable in advance.
Entered at the Post Office at Ashland, Ohio, as second-class matter.
Acceptance for mailing at special rate of postage provided for in section 1103, Act of October 3, 1917, authorized September 9, 1918.
Address all matter for publication to Geo. S. Baer, Editor of the Brethren Evangelist, and all business communications to R. R. Teeter, Business Manager, Brethren Publishing Company, Ashland, Ohio. Make all checks payable to the Brethren Publishing Company.

TABLE OF CONTENTS

EDITORIAL

Growing Sentiment for the Bible in Public Education

There is a growing sentiment in favor of using the Bible in public education that bids fair to assume the proportions of a nationwide movement. And notwithstanding the special interest of ministers in this wholesome tendency, they are not the fathers of it. It is being brought about by educationists, who are coming to realize that the school's function is to educate the heart as well as the mind. Moral education and character building are coming to be recognized in a very definite way as a part of the school. teacher's responsibility. This is encouraging in view of the mistaken conception so prevalent in the past that the public school's business was restricted to the training of the mind, and that the Bible had no rightful place in the school room.

There are those who hold that there is a very definite relation between crime and the lack of religious instruction in the schools. Walter L. Hervey, Ph.D., says, "It is even alleged that the steady increase of crime in the United States during the past fifty years—from there being one criminal in each 3,000 of the population to one in 300—is due to the deliberate omission of direct religious instruction from the curriculum of the American public schools during the same period."

Mr. Edward E. Van Cleve, under the direction of Prof. W. C. Bagley of the University of Illinois, made an extensive study a few years ago of the relation of religious instruction to crime. He says, "The strong and clear indication of these facts is that the best results in moral outcome are secured by making religious instruction a part of the daily training for every child in home and school. The gradual casting out of the Bible and religious instruction from our public schools has been practically simultaneous with the increase of crime to which we have already referred."

Many testimonies might be quoted showing the deepening and widespread conviction that religious instruction, not mere Bible reading, is essential to well-rounded and wholesome education and character building on the part of students, and that where such is lacking for any considerable time, there is a noticeable increase in crime.

As a result of this and other things that contribute toward a revelation of our present folly, the sentiment in favor of religious instruction in our schools is increasing. President Robert W. Kelly of Earlham College, has said, "We are in the midst of a nationwide revival of interest in promoting Bible study for pupils in our schools, and students in our colleges and universities."

P. P. Claxton, United States Commissioner of Education said,

"The day will come when the Bible will be read in the public schools just as any other book. There is no good reason why the Bible should not have its rightful place in our school curriculum."

From Prof. Clyde W. Votaw of the University of Chicago, we have these words: "What the children in the public schools need, and what the Bible if reasonably used, can help them to get, is an understanding of life from a simple, practical standpoint. To train boys and girls in the right way to live, to teach them the right things to live for—this is the goal of public school education. We should find a way to use the Bible in the schools solely for this purpose. Religion as an ideal of life, therefore, is at the foundation of our public school aim and work."

Prof. George Albert Coe, one of the world's greatest present-day scholars in the field of Religious Education, has made this statement, significant of the trend of modern thought: "The psychology of the day finds that religion is as deeply rooted in human nature as any of the higher instincts or impulses that distinguish men from lower orders of life. . . Frobel's whole plan of education revolved around the thought that God is a present reality within us and within Nature about us, and that the end of education is to make us conscious of his presence. . . Religious education is not a part of general education, it is general education. It is the whole of which our so-called secular education is only a part or a phase."

In an address by Dr. A. P. Peabody of Harvard University, there is found this paragraph which is reassuring both as to the faith of modern scholarship in the Bible and also as to its place in public school instruction:

"We are asked to exclude from our schools the Bible, and, by parity of reasoning, all instruction drawn from the Bible. What is this, in the first place, but garbling and truncating history? There are important, momentous portions of the world's history of which the Bible is the only manual. The Jewish people have exercised an influence upon mankind far exceeding that of all other ancient nations, and outside of the Bible how scanty and fragmentary is all that can be known or taught concerning this people! Shall our children be forbidden to learn that Christianity in its own universally acknowledged manual? Jesus Christ, whatever be His actual character—whether he be or not, as I believe him to be, all that his biographers claim for him—is so far the most influential personage that has ever appeared in the history of the world. To exclude his life and character from the narrative of human existence for the last nineteen centuries is an immeasurably more gross, foolish, and stupid mutilation of history than it would be to omit the names of Washington, Franklin, and Adams from American history. Shall not our children be permitted to learn what he was from the only authentic record of his person, words, and works?''

President W. H. P. Faunce, of Brown University, sees in the present state of affairs a lamentable situation. He says, ''The State has handed over religion to the church, and the church has handed education over to the State. Who then, is henceforth responsible for religious education? The State says, 'It is not me;' and the church saith, 'It is not me.' Hence we have in America millions of children growing up without any religious training whatever—a situation which would have seemed inconceivable to ancient Athens, or medieval Florence, a situation such as no pagan nation ever tolerated.''

President Wm. Douglas Mackinzie of Hartford Theological Seminary, a man whose vital interest in foreign missions is widely known, declares religious education absolutely essential to the safety of the state which is responsible for its encouragement. ''For in the modern world no less than in the ancient, public morality, which is the very life of the state, is closely bound up with religious ideals and motives. And if the state formally separates itself from the inculcation of those ideals and the awakening of those motives, it is in danger of seeing generations arise whose very education makes them not only the slaves of individual impulse, but more powerful in wrong-doing.''

There is a general conviction that the type of religious education which the state could supply would not be wholly satisfactory or sufficient; its work must be supplemented by the church. Neither is it expected that the state could give direction to the distinctively spiritual impulses; the church must bear this responsibility, and must not neglect it if the religious education which it is desired that the state should supply is to become a vital and determining factor in life. To this point President W. A. Mills of Hanover College has written the following significant statement: ''My own judgment after twenty-five years of public school supervision and some years of college experience is that 'incidental' teaching of morals has proven a failure. It is possible to teach a body of moral principle, with pertinent application and exemplification, which will be of great value to the pupil in setting up for him a standard of conduct and at least opening his mind to moral issues. But it is also my judgment that no moral instruction will be of greatest value until it finds its sanction in a definite religious faith, and is motivised by a consciousness of personal relationship to God. I am aware of the administrative problem this involves, yet to this we must return, or get deeper into the mire.''

EDITORIAL REVIEW

Brother C. W. Abbott of Dayton announces his readiness to answer calls to direct evangelistic singing. See his notice in this issue.

Publication Offering Day on October 31. While making your offering of money to help pay our bills, make an offering of prayer for God's blessing upon us that we may serve the brotherhood more efficiently.

The report of the W. M. S. sessions at the Indiana conference show that the women of that state are not letting their work lag. They have the same aggressive spirit that characterizes the entire district.

Home Missions is now called to your attention by the General Missionary Secretary, Brother Gearhart. Read his message on the Bicentenary Page. Make it a matter of prayer from now until the offering is lifted, that not only you but others also may make just the offering that God's cause needs.

Stewardship Day, October 31. It is the time when your pastor will likely call to your attention in whatever way the Lord may lead him the fact of your stewardship and God's ownership. You doubtless have already recognized that fact, but have neglected to acknowledge it. This is the time to make public recognition of the fact and decide from henceforth to pay the tithe as the minimum expression of your stewardship.

Brother Bame recently closed a very successful union evangelistic campaign at Oak Hill, West Virginia. He gives us a few ''flashes'' of his trip, to which our readers will be interested in giving attention.

Our readers are always anxious for news from our foreign mission stations and especially to learn of the progress in our South American field. Brother Yoder writes an encouraging letter. The growth has been commendable and outlook is bright. It is a pleasure to learn of Sister Yoder's improved health. Yet she still needs the special prayers of the brotherhood for her complete recovery.

The Illiokota conference minutes, written by the careful pen of Brother Miles J. Snyder, are in this issue. It proved to be a very successful conference under the direction of a wide-awake group of leaders. One thing we notice in the way of new steps taken was the appointment of a Board of Religious Education to take the place of the district boards of Sunday school and Christian Endeavor departmental superintendents.

Brother E. E. Roberts writes an interesting letter concerning his trip and experiences in connection with the Pennsylvania State conference. We are impressed with two things about Brother Roberts as they are revealed in his letter; first, his strong, implicit faith in God's providential care and second, his youthful spirit that enables him to enjoy the fun and frolics of the young folks, though he is counted among our ''veteran ministers.''

EDITORIAL SQUIBS

Until a man has learned to praise God at his work bench, he will not be able to render worthy praise by any ritual in God's house.

Blessed is the man who sendeth in his news early in the week, who writeth upon one side only of his paper, useth double space on the typewriter, maketh his lines far apart when he writeth with the pen, observeth paragraphs, and readeth over and correcteth his manuscipt before he submits it. His name shall be praised and his memory cherished.

The Herald of Gospel Liberty quotes Dr. E. A. Watkins as saying, ''The peril of the Christian life is in our willingness to trust God with our souls, but unwilling to allow him to have anything to do with the management of our property.'' But if we really recognized the Christian principle of stewardship, we would not be willing to speak of ''our property,'' it would all belong to him who created both it and us, and we would be his stewards.

The individual Christian who has no appointed time for prayer, will soon find that he has no time for prayer.

The local church that gives up its mid-week meetings for prayer and intercession soon becomes a church spiritually prayerless and powerless.

The time to think about it and plan for it is now. There has been a deepening longing on the part of thousands for a revival of the old-time Watch Night meetings, ''to watch and pray'' the old year out and the new year in; yea more than this, unitedly to pray new life and new power into the church. In the old revival days of a half century ago almost every evangelical church throughout the length and breadth of this land had its annual Watch Night meeting —not for entertainment, not to listen to addresses or to hear reports of ''progress,'' but primarily for prayer and praise, for confession and supplication,—and in hundreds of cases revival fires were kindled that swept churches and communities and brought not only local blessing but general uplift. In these days of moral laxity, of loose social customs, of industrial turmoil, of broken down family altars, might it not be helpful to have a revival of this old custom? Think it over.

THE BRETHREN BICENTENARY MOVEMENT PAGE

1723 · · · · · · 1923

Dr. Charles A. Bame, Editor

Home Missions

For a number of years the Brethren church has found Thanksgiving Day a very appropriate time to secure the funds necessary for the promotion of her Home Mission work. We feel it should be left to each individual church to decide as to the advisability of making this offering on the Sunday before or the Sunday after Thanksgiving Day. The important thing is, to be sure that it is not neglected.

In order that the brotherhood may know where the money will be spent and the amount necessary to success-fully carry forward the plans for this Conference year, we give you the following information:

Financial Help Has Been Voted To

Kittanning, Pennsylvania.	Peru, Indiana.
Third Brethren, Philadelphia, Pennsylvania.	Huntington, Indiana.
Whole Gospel Mission, Philadelphia, Pennsylvania.	Fort Scott, Kansas.
Columbus, Ohio.	Norcatur, Kansas.
Canton, Ohio.	McLouth, Kansas.
Salem, Ohio.	Spokane, Washington.
Camden, Ohio.	Limestone, Tennessee.
Clay City, Indiana.	Krypton, Kentucky.
Muncie, Indiana.	Lost Creek, Kentucky.

Note—Spokane has already become self-supporting and several others soon will be.

The Budget

For our mission points in the Kentucky Mountains, ... $ 5,210.00
For all other points, including General Secretary's Salary, ...:........................... .... 10,336.67

Grand Total, ... $15,546.67

The Goal

ONE DOLLAR per member is the amount set by the Board and approved by Conference as the goal to be attained, which amount, if reached, will provide for the needs indicated above, and will give us a little surplus money to answer other worthy calls. WILL We Do It, BRETHREN? Come on, and let us go over the top. The goal last year of FORTY CENTS per member to be raised at Thanksgiving time, did not include the Kentucky work. It was decided this year to include in the goal to be attained, the balance necessary for our Kentucky Missions, which was not provided for by pledges at our Annual Conference. Hence the increase in the goal. It will be easy to raise, if we will WILL to do it.

Extension and Fraternal Relations

As Director of Missions and Extension, which includes Fraternal Relations, I am exceedingly anxious to secure suggestions from all points in the Brotherhood as to the prospective points for missionary endeavor, and I want to urge all organized Bible classes and auxiliary organizations to plan some definite mission study and to do practical missionary work. We have already begun to do this in Dayton and the result is that ere long we expect to have several new churches in and near Dayton. Let us be prepared to give financial aid to the many new mission points which we are confident will be started if we get in earnest. ONE DOLLAR PER.   WILLIAM A. GEARHART,
Director of Missions and Extensions.

How to Organize for the New Movement

It may be a bit late for the instruction that I intend to give to the churches as to the new Movement of the Brethren churches; if it is, then we ought to with all the more vigor proceed to the organization. It is my plan that each church of the brotherhood should organize itself so that each of the functions of the Movement shall have a local representative. That is, each church ought to have seven secretaries whose duty should be to look specifically to the department of the work intrusted to them. Too many times, all the work of the departments of church work are left to the pastor. How many times the church treasurer has to run to the pastor to find out where to send the "collection" when, if he were Secretary of Missions in his church he could tell the pastor where to "get off at," or tell him a lot of things that he ought to know about the organizations of various mission enerprises inside and outside of the denomination.

As an instance in point, I conjecture that Secretary Snyder of the Stewardship Department of the Movement recently gave a lot of pastors and others, information as to where to get literature on he subject of Stewardship for Stewardship Day which comes the last Sunday of this month and for which all pastors and workers are supposed to be getting a good ready. We are hoping that each church of the brotherhood will appoint, as soon as possible—say on Stewardship Day,—a Stewardship Secretary whose duty it shall be to keep the church awake to the duty that must be tremendously stressed for the next three years, and then on "till the Lord comes." Keeping the subject ever before the congregation and reminding the preacher if he does not often preach about this topic; enrolling members on the Tithing Scroll which this Movement hopes soon to furnish every church, or on the Life Recruits Roll of Honor, which we hope to have hanging in each church and one at the headquarters of the movement, where we hope to "match dollars with men," or, in other words, to make the dollars ready for the man who is ready to go. It is the plan of the organizers of this Movement—and they do it at the behest of the Conference—that it shall not be lop-sided; that as soon as we find folks who are ready to prepare for the ministry or missionary work, that we shall also get the money to help them to prepare; as fast as we find an institution of the church lagging, it shall be known by the brotherhood and helped at the earliest possible time. But we can not thus co-ordinate the work of the church without the help of the entire denomination. Each state or district as fast as they meet in conference will appoint an Executive Secretary through whom the district work will focus. It is expected that several will be appointed before this date. Others will, as fast as the conferences meet. They may appoint more than one, as they see fit, but for the purpose of the Movement, this man will be wholly responsible.

The Local Church

But for the work of the Movement, the local church will need a seven-fold organization if it accomplishes all that is to be done, if it is to get rightly into this Movement. In each church, at the earliest possible time, there should be appointed the following secretaries:

SPIRITUAL LIFE, EDUCATION, EVANGELISM, MISSION, PUBLICATION, STEWARDSHIP, and BENEVOLENCE.

Of course, it is plain that these secretaries should be appointed several weeks before the special day for which they are to help the pastor to make ready. Indeed, they ought to be appointed right now. The General Committee might get a good many suggestions from them as to organization as they go along. If a Stewardship Secretary had been appointed in each church as soon as Conference was over, and if that person had been busy getting live literature and a live program and if the General Committee had ready, the scrolls that they hope soon to have, we should get good results from October 31st. But it is not possible to have all this on the spur of the moment, and so, we shall have to do the best we can for this year. Indeed, this Movement will go to such proportions, we think as a renewer of church activities, that we shall be very happy for the effort when it is over.

Now, Therefore,

Pastors, get busy with this much of the organization. The helps that we hope to furnish you as soon as we have the time to get them, will come along; but the work of Stewardship needs to be done at once.

Now, Now!

Now is the accepted time! Delay is dangerous! If one special day is thrust aside and put off, it will disarrange the whole year, as you know it has done before now. It is of enough importance that you could well hold a separate council meeting for this purpose. We evangelists get so used to saying "Now is the time and today is the day" that you may know why I urge this as the most important single duty you have for the present.

The good Lord wrote most of the Bible to the professing believers. That "Now" means as much to the church worker as to the unsaved. If it is not done right away, who knows if it will get done at all? Remember it is the duty of every church to get this Movement on its way and do it quick! Almost a whole year was lost by most of the churches on the Four Year Program because we did not know rightly how to go about it. Into the new Movement, we hope to write the experience of that one, and so, we offer, as the first duty, this organization, the seven-fold local organization.

Excuses

We pray that you will not "begin to make excuse." I have heard so many times, "Well, our church is so small" or "These people do not take much stock in such things," that I know where a lot of the trouble is. It is with the supposed leaders. Yet, we are here offering the leaders an opportunity to get help from folks in their number and thus to shift some of the heavy responsibility they have been needlessly carrying. There is no church so small that it can not function along the lines of this Movement. Indeed, there is no reason why most every nucleus of the several districts should not find many reasons to co-operate along every line of this work. If we cannot accomplish this in this Movement, we are getting ready for the toboggan.

I do not anticipate needless delay. I know I am repeating, but I'll repeat any number of times if I can get action on this work. We ought to enroll 5,000 tithers in the brotherhood on October 31st and out of active congregations, 25 Recruits. But it is your duty, Brother Pastor! Do the best you can. Prepare your sermon and make your appeal. Do your duty and be blest.   BAME.

GENERAL ARTICLES

Counterfeit Premillenialism

Selected by Noah A. Teeter from the Sunday School Times

(We are pleased to give place to this article selected by Brother Teeter, for it encourages the right spirit. Regardless of one's views concerning the coming of Christ, "By this shall all men know that ye are my disciples if ye have **love one to another**," and we should "abide in him; that, when he shall appear, we may have confidence, and **not be ashamed** before him" at his coming."—Editor.)

There is an outstanding fact concerning the truth of our Lord's coming upon which there is perfect agreement among all Christians, whatever may be their view as to the relation of Christ's coming to the "millennium." All agree that the period in which peace and righteousness will prevail universally in the world has not yet come, and that the Lord Jesus has not yet returned in the sense in which the New Testament speaks of his coming. That is, we are now living in premillennial days.

And yet is it not true that many Christians who contend earnestly for this or that view regarding the coming of Christ have somehow forgotten the bearing of this important fact on the discussion? Is there not such a thing as being a "true premillenarian" in the sense that our attitude toward these premillennial days in which we are living is the right attitude?

A Christian worker whose sweet spirit toward other Christians who may differ from him, and who is noted for his desire to avoid harsh judgments, recently remarked to a friend: "You did not know me in my tigerish days. I imbibed the critical spirit when I was led into the truth about Christ's coming, and found myself tearing to pieces many other Christians who did not see truth as I saw it."

This Christian worker had his life revolutionized through a discovery of the Bible truth concerning the Lord's coming. But Satan insidiously passed on some counterfeit at the same time, and this worker got not only the illumination of the Holy Spirit but a strong slant toward another spirit, even the spirit of "the accuser of the brethren."

Satan hates God's truth. If he cannot prevent a Christian from getting a clear conception of what God's truth is he will be eager to sow some of his own tares in the midst of the true wheat, to use this figure in a somewhat different application from that originally intended. Nothing will so greatly choke the truth, and indeed often render it worse than useless so far as winsomeness is concerned, as to hold God's truth in a contentious, critical attitude.

A Christian business man who is standing for the fundamentals of God's Word in a blessed way recently read to a group of friends a letter from an earnest Christian worker expressing his grave question as to the gain of emphasizing the truths concerning Christ's coming. He told of Christians he had come in touch with who contended zealously for what they considered the Scripture teaching regarding the premillennial coming of Christ, who were trouble makers in their church, and discounted the service of Christians who did not hold their views, and in general had a decidedly unloving and critical attitude. A member of this little group who had had wide experience in Christian work in different parts of the country, and who himself is eagerly looking for the coming of the Lord, remarked: "I know just what he is talking about, for I have come in touch with just such 'premillenarians,' and they do more harm to the truth than those who are outspokenly against the premillennial teaching."

May not this fairly be called "counterfeit premillennialism?" The intellectual conception of these Christians may be very clear, and in some cases may be entirely in accord with the Word of God. How then can it be called "counterfeit?" Because the Word of God can never unfold its true meaning except as the truth is held in the Spirit. Truth is always personal. The central fact in all the teaching concerning the coming of Christ and the results of that coming is, not this system of doctrine or that, but the Lord Jesus himself. One who is truly looking for the coming of the Lord, and who understands the full meaning of this event for a sin-torn world will have the Lord Jesus in his personal presence as the center and secret of all his knowledge of the truth.

One of the most widely known Christian leaders of our day was led into the truth concerning Christ's coming through a missionary statesman who did not give him any counterfeit along with it. In the tender love of Christ he received it and it broadened his sympathy and love for his fellow Christians and for the lost world. This Christian leader's honored father for many years had studied his Bible with the viewpoint that Christ would not come until the close of the "millennium," or the period of universal righteousness and peace. The father and son one day were discussing the question, and the father said: "I cannot see this thing as you see it. But I want to say to you that if you are right and I am wrong, and Jesus Christ should come today, there is nothing that could happen which would fill me with such joy. I love him so, and I long to see him face to face."

It was the missionary statesman who was used to lead this brother into the truth who told the incident, and he remarked: "This Christian father, an earnest postmillenarian, is more truly looking for the coming of the Lord than many ardent premillenarians whom I know."

True premillennialism includes a right conception of these premillennial days in which we are living. Are we ready for his coming? Are we living as in his personal presence? Are we contending for the truth with the recogniton that the truth is just Jesus himself?

That the truth of the Lord's Coming, like all living truths of the Word, results in just this way is evidenced by the statement made again and again and never contradicted, that a large proportion of the missionaries and evangelists who today are most notably used in soul-winning, both on the foreign mission fields and at home, are looking for the return of the Lord Jesus to usher in the Kingdom age. This is ever the fruit of true pre-millennialism, for it exalts not a doctrine, but a Person, the One who is coming, and who has commissioned us to preach his Name in these premillennial days of grace.

We shall lose nothing, nor weaken the truth, by strengthening the bond of Christian love with those who may not see things just as we see them. If we have the truth, one of the evidences men have a right to expect is that the fruit of the truth shall be in all love and gentleness in the manifesting of the Spirit of him who is the Truth.

There is a startling contrast between two men in their attitude toward the coming of the Lord, and toward this "present age." The name of one of these men is Paul; the name of the other, Demas. Paul writes in the last chapter of his second letter to Timothy concerning himself and also "all them that have loved his appearing." Then follows this word: "Give diligence to come shortly unto me: for Demas forsook me, having loved this present age." Here is the clear choice between two attitudes, two contrasting views of life that cannot be reconciled: love of this present age, or love of his appearing to usher in a new age.

There is a man living in one of the great Eastern cities of the United States whose life has been completely revolutionized by the Lord speaking to him through that text, "Those that love his appearing." It could not be said at all that he loved this present world, for he did not. But he dreaded "his appearing." It meant to him only "the end of the world," with an angry God appearing in judgment, and men and women in terror calling on the rocks and mountains to fall on them and hide them from his frowning face. But one evening he heard a Christian layman weave the text about love of Christ's appearing into an address. He had never known the glorious side of the "appearing." He had never heard it preached about. He wrote to the speaker, secured "Jesus is Coming," Blackstone's wonderful book, discovered more fully the hopefulness and glory of Christ's appearing, led many others into the truth, and now, in addition to his daily calling, is conducting a Bible school on which God is setting his seal of approval.

Do we love his appearing? The answer is found in the way we are living in this present age, these premillennial days. That passage in Timothy gives a clear indication of what it means to love his appearing. The veteran warrior, near the end of his conflict, gives a solemn charge to young Timothy, charging him by Christ's appearing and his kingdom to fulfil his ministry and live blamelessly. Then he appeals to his own record: "I have fought the good fight; I have finished the course, I have kept the faith: henceforth there is laid up for me the crown of righteousness, which the Lord, the righteous judge, shall give me at that day; and not to me only, but also to all them that have loved his appearing."

Here is a clear link between the faithfulness of such a ministry as Paul's, and the love of his appearing. Those who love his appearing will suffer hardships as good soldiers, and will not love this present age. Let us not lightly regard the meaning of that profound word of the love of his appearing when we remember its connection with the life ministry of such a one as Paul.

Are we loving his appearing?

Dayton, Ohio, October 6, 1920.

Rev. George Baer,
Editor, The Evangelist,
Ashland, Ohio.

Dear Brother: I am enclosing herewith copy of an editorial which appeared in the Sunday School Times of August 28th, entitled "Counterfeit Premillennialism."

When I read this editorial my mental comment was, "Well, that certainly hits me pretty hard," for I had had my 'Tigerish attacks' as well as the editor of the Times.

How well we all know that there are some of our Ministerial Brethren in our denomination who even now are similarly afflicted, and by the way, this class is not wholly confined to the Pacific Coast, for I am very sorry to state that this intolerant spirit is very frequently encountered both in ministers and laymen in our State of Ohio, both inside and out of our denomination and by both "Pre" and "Post."

Personally I am and have always been a dyed-in-the-wool Premillennialist, but I can see no good reason NOW why I should "set at nought my brother for whom Christ died" because he does not see this truth just as I see it.

So in view of the fact that I was sure the above editorial might prove helpful to others as well as it has to me, I wrote the Sunday School Times for permission to have it reproduced in the Evangelist, and under date of October 1st they replied as follows:

"We are very glad to give our cordial permission to reprint the editorial from the Sunday School times entitled "Counterfeit Premillennialism" in your own denominational paper. You will, of course kindly give credit to the Sunday School Times for the article. We are glad to know that you approve us heartily of it and that you feel that it will be helpful."

I most sincerely trust that you will be able to find space for this article in a very early issue of the Evangelist.

Fraternally yours,
NOAH A. TEETER.

Adequate Pay for Teachers. By P. P. Claxton

(An abridgement of an address read before the National Education Association and forwarded to the Evangelist for publication. We have had much to say in these columns concerning the ministry, its rewards and remunerations, but little has been said concerning the profession of teaching, which ranks close up to the ministry in loftiness, abiding worth and the unmeasured values with which it deals. There are many Brethren young people not possessing the peculiar talent required for the ministry, but who ought to be encouraged to give themselves to the noble work of teaching. These words by Mr. Claxton offer encouragement both concerning the loftiness of the profession and the prospect of adequate remuneration. Moreover, this paper should be of interest to the ministers inasmuch as it might well be applied almost in its entirety to this noblest calling. The growing appreciation of work having to do with spiritual values is encouraging.—Editor).

Teachers worthy of places in the schools in which American children are prepared for life, for making a living, for the duties and responsibilities of democratic citizenship, and for eternal destiny can never be fully paid in money. Men and women worthy of this highest of all callings will not think first of pay in money or in any other form. For teachers, as for all other workers, Ruskin's saying holds: "If they think first of pay and only second of work, they are servants of him who is the lord of pay, the most unerect fiend that fell. If they think first of the work and its results and only second of their pay, however important that may be, then they are servants of him who is the Lord of work. Then they belong to the great guild of workers and builders and sevairs of the world together with him for whom to do the will of him that sent him and finish his work was both meat and drink."

Workers Paid Largely in Kind

It has ever been and probably must always be that workers of whatever sort received the largest part of their pay in kind, as millers take toll of the grist they grind. Those that work with material things that have easily measured cash values receive their pay chiefly in money or in things whose values are most easily measured in money. Other rewards will be less in proportion and in importance. Those who work largely for other than the material results that can be measured by money must continue to be content to receive a large part of their pay in the consciousness of work well done for a worthy cause, and in participation, by faith at least, in the results, both near and far away in time and in space.

The Teacher's Spiritual Rewards

Teachers who do their work well and who, either in fact or by faith, see the world made better as a result; individuals made healthier, wiser, happier; sin and suffering made less; the common wealth made more; social purity and civic righteousness increased; public laws made more just; patriotism broadened and purified; state and nation made stronger and safer against attack from without and decay from within; and the world lifted on to a higher plane and into a brighter sunshine and a purer atmosphere, are possessed of wealth unseen and for most unseeable.

All true teachers will think on these things and many of the best will be attracted to and held in the profession by them. It will be all the worse for the profession and the world when it is not.

But this should not be made an excuse for putting public or private education on a charity basis, nor for paying teachers the miserably low wages they are now paid. It should not be made an excuse for paying such wages as will not permit school boards and superintendents to fix reasonable minimum standards of qualifications for teachers because young men and women who expect to teach can not afford to incur the expenses necessary to prepare themselves to meet the requirements of such standards. It should not be made an excuse for failing to increase the pay of teachers, as the pay in other professions is increased, in recognition of proved merit and in proportion to increasing ability gained through experience, continued study, and constant devotion to duty.

Improved Salaries Benefit the Schools and the Nation

Not for the sake of the teachers primarily, but that the schools may be made fully efficient; that children may be well taught; that the material wealth of sate and nation may be increased so that we may have the means of paying our debts, building our highways, caring for our unfortunates, and meeting other public expenses and at the same time have enough for all the people to live in comfort; that our democracy may be preserved, purified, and made more effective; that scientific discovery, useful invention, and artistic expression may be promoted; that we may act well our part in the commonwealth of the world, we must pay such salaries as will bring into the schools as teachers men and women of the best native ability, men and women strong and well organized physically, mentally, and spiritually; men and women of the finest culture and the most thorough and comprehensive education, academic and professional, and so adjust their salaries as to enable them to hold all those who show themselves most capable and best fitted for the work. In this most important of all our enterprises we can not afford to pay less.

Many Able Men Have Taught

Our traditional policy of paying to young and inexperienced men and women with little or no question as to their professional preparation salaries as large as we pay to those who have had many years of successful experience had at least one merit. It brought into the schools large numbers of young men and women of unusual native ability and of strong character and sometimes such men and women having also good scholarship and fine culture, willing and eager to do the best they could while saving from their comparatively good wages enough to start them in business or home making, or to enable them to prepare themselves for those professions for which adequate preparation is required and demanded. Many of the ablest men and women in all walks of life have been school teachers. A good-sized ex-teachers' association could be formed of members of any recent Congress of the United States. We have just nominated two ex-teachers as candidates for the Presidency. Unfortunately, however, most of these have remained as teachers in the schools only till they had begun to gain some little comprehension of their task and some little skill in executing it. But despite their lack of preparation and experience it was good for boys and girls to come in contact with them. From this contact many gained inspiration and purpose.

Other Occupations Pay Better

The time has come now when men and women of unusual native ability and strength of character can make more money in any of hundreds of occupations than they can in teaching. A few of them will teach while waiting to find themselves, or to make money for a start in business, or for paying for preparation for other work. They will accept employment which is at the same time more attractive and more remunerative. From now on schools will be taught (1) by unprepared and inexperienced young men and women of mediocre ability and less, while waiting for the maturity which is required for employment in the minor and more common occupations; (2) by the left overs of such men and women who have failed to find more attractive and remunerative employment elsewhere, but have not wholly failed as teachers; or (3) by men and women of better native ability, stronger character, more thorough education, and the professional preparation which will enable them to succeed to such an extent that they may be induced by the payment of adequate wages to continue to serve their country in a high and valuable way as teachers.

This is the real crisis in education.

We have come to the parting of the ways. Which shall we accept? Makeshift teachers of the first two classes we may continue to get in sufficient number by paying salaries relatively as large as those paid in 1914. To have the same relative value and purchasing power as salaries paid in 1913-14, the present salaries and salaries for some years to come must be approximately twice as large as they were then.

We Must Have Strong Teachers

For teachers of the third class—and we should be satisfied with no other—we must pay salaries larger relatively than we have paid at any time in the past, and must adopt a policy which will give such recognition to teachers of unusual ability as will hold them in the service of the schools against the temptation of better pay elsewhere. Temporary increase in pay of teachers will not be sufficient. There must be such guaranty of good wages in the years to come as will induce young men and women of such native ability and character as good teachers can be made of to accept teaching as a profession and take the time and spend the money necessary to prepare themselves for it. The demand for professional preparation and continued service, coupled with adequate pay, can only result in supplying the schools with teachers of small caliber, unfit to become the inspirers and guides and educators of those who are to make up the citizenry of the great democratic Republic, solve the problems, and do the work of the new era. Such teachers are not fit seed corn for the new harvest to which we should and do look forward.

The Money Can Be Raised

Can we pay such salaries? At an average wage of $2,000, it will take a billion and a half dollars to pay 750,-000 teachers. Increase this by 50 percent—a liberal amount—to pay for administration, supervision, buildings, equipment, and supplies, and we have a total of two and a quarter billions—a quarter of a billion short of Spaulding's two and a half billions and only 140,000,000 more than the amount the Department of Labor reports that we paid last year for tobacco in its various forms. Our part in the World War, in which we fought for freedom and democracy, cost us not less than fifty billions of dollars all told. At 5 percent the annual interest on this amount is two and a half billion dollars. Without education there can be neither freedom nor democracy. Unless we educate all the people in such way as to enable them to possess these in fullest measure we shall have spent our money for naught and the men who sleep in France and Belgium shall have died in vain.

Missions and Tithing.   By M. Florence Wineland

And all the tithes of the land, whether of the seed of the land or of the fruit of the tree is the Lord's, it is holy unto the Lord, it is the Lord's, hence it cannot be given to the Lord by a special vow. No man can give away what belongs to another or give God what he has already.

The dedication of the tithe in various forms, as an acknowledgment of dependence upon and reverence to God, is one of the most common practices of antiquity. The Romans, Greeks, and Phoenicians as well as the Hebrews adhered strictly to this custom.

A very practical question emerges just here, as to the continuation of the law of the tithe. Although we hear nothing of the tithe in the first Christian centuries, it was again established in the fourth century as the law of the church. This system passed from the Romans into the Reformed churches, but met with severe criticism because of the development of a system of voluntary giving.

In attempting to settle this question in the light of the New Testament teaching, the fundamental teaching, as given by the Apostle Paul in his instruction that on the first day of the week everyone should lay by him in store as God hath prospered him, is that a certain fixed sum belongs to God, and should be set apart for his work.

The moral element of the law of the tithe is still in force, it forbids the Christian to leave, as so often, the amount he will give for the Lord's work to impulse.

If any ask how much should the proportion be, one might say that by fair inference the tenth might safely be taken as an average minimum of giving, counting rich and poor together.

It sounds impressive to say that the Protestant churches of the United States and Canada give twenty million dollars a year to foreign missions, but if you will do a little figuring you will find that this means less than two cents per member per Sunday, considerably less than a postage stamp a week from the Christian people of America, in order to win the world to Christ.

It makes a big story in a missionary magazine to tell about a city church taking up a ten thousand dollar collection for a mission board but when you learn that there are ten millionaires sitting at the ends of the pews in that church, how do the figures look then? Can anybody, even in his most enthusiastic frame of mind, regard the situation complacently when not more than one-fifth of our church members, according to the best authorities, give any appreciable amount for world evangelism. Read what the Apostle Paul says on the subject in Second Corinthians 8th and 9th chapters, then look at the matter through the eyes of Christ sitting over against the treasury and consider what would be his comments were he to watch the offerings in the well-to-do churches of today.

Perhaps rich men are not approached with missionary projects that are large enough, by either pastor or mission board; this was the experience of a member of a prominent mission board. He relates the following:

A western business man, after having attended a convention, manifested great astonishment at the intellectual ability and fine personality of the men and women engaged in missionary work, he ventured to ask one man the amount of his salary and was told it was $500. He decided that if a man of such calibre is willing to go to China and work for $500 a year, he ought to make it possible for such a man to go. He expressed this desire to a member of the mission board who called and the following conversation ensued; "Well, have you got that missionary for me who will go out to China?" "Yes, I have a man in mind, but before mentioning his name I want to explain some of the business details involved." "Well, I told you I would contribute $500 a year and you can count upon me to keep this going as long as I live." Then the secretary followed with explanations which meant added expenses as follows, support of wife, $500; children, 10 percent of salary; outfit and traveling expenses, $1,200; house $4,000. "All right," said the financier, "I want to do this thing in the proper way. I set out to support a missionary without any extra cost to the board. I did not realize all these expenses, but I have the money and I am going to do it. I want you to select the missionary as soon as possible, and let him come and spend a week at my house. If we are going to be partners in this enterprise, we ought to know each other. Now who is the man?"

The man was named, the plan was consummated by a letter in which all the business details were put in writing, pledging himself to continue this support for thirty years, and the secretary of the mission board left the office with a pledge of double the original $500 and extra charges totaling not less than $5,350.

It is not the wealthy only who can help. Sherwood Eddy says, I know of one poor girl who has worked as a stenographer for years in a big city. She offered to go to the foreign field and was rejected on account of her health. Since then she has been saving and sending her money supporting native workers at $30 each a year. As a result there is a community in North India where there more than a thousand souls that have been brought to Christ, solely through native workers supported by this one frail girl. A thousand who have passed from darkness into his marvelous light because one girl cared. How many are in the light because of what you have done? How will you answer the money test of Christian Stewardship?

Martinsburg, Pennsylvania.

Some Important Testimonies.   By T. Darley Allen

Life is not safe and property is not worth very much where the Gospel is not preached; and even infidels are far from desirous of living in communities that have no houses of Christian worship.

A few years ago the statement was made in Leslie's Weekly that a soap manufacturer of Zanesville, Ohio, said in his will that while not a professing Christian he so respected the work done by the church that he bequeathed $1,000 to every house of worship in Zanesville, regardless of denomination.

A minister and an agnostic met in a railway train and entered into conversation. The latter saying that he never attended a place of worship, the minister asked him his opinion of the value of the work done by the church. The agnostic admitted the church to be a power for good. He was then asked if it would be a calamity if the church were allowed to go down. He replied with emphasis that it certainly would. Then the minister asked him if he did his duty as a citizen in failing to help along the work of such an institution. He replied, "No, I don't, and next Sunday I am going to church." He surprised his wife when he reached home by telling her that he was going with her to church. He kept his word and became a stalwart supporter of the institution.

In one of H. L. Hastings' pamphlets reference is made to an infidel who preferred to have his boy attend Sunday school rather than play about the wharves. Mr. Hastings also told of a dissipated lawyer who had a Sunday school established in a godless settlement in Wisconsin as a shrewd business operation. Said this lawyer, as quoted in Mr. Hastings' tract: "I organized the first Sunday school in the county. A few of us Americans came here early. We wanted to get in decent, industrious settlers and keep the rowdies out. So I said, 'A Sunday school will draw the folks we want. It will be the best and cheapest way to blow for the settlement.' They all agreed to it. There wasn't a soul of us that pretended to have a grain of piety. So they pitched upon me to carry out the plan. I did it, sending to Mr. Rice of the Sunday School Union for a library, and ran the school all summer. It did the blowing for us splendidly. Several Christian families came in, and as they had a better stock of piety, I handed the Sunday school over to them. It was a grand thing for us. We secured a good, moral settlement. In fact, sir, it got to be so pious that I couldn't live there myself."

An employer claiming in Rhode Island, although an infidel, said he always preferred Christian workmen to men of his own way of thinking because he had found out that they did more satisfactory work than unbelievers, the latter as a rule not being dependable.

It has been well said that if men desire prosperity, "they must have a society based upon the principles laid down in the Word of God. This is the honest thought of honest and intelligent men in general. Skeptics and scoffers like to live in a Christian community. Real estate is not worth much in Sodom or Gomorrah; and much as infidels hate the Bible they do not hate it enough to go to live where its influence is unknown."

Cleveland, Ohio.

The Spirit of Sacrifice a Necessary Factor for a Greater Brethren Church
By A. P. Reed

This is but another way of saying that the members composing the great body of the Brethren church must be full of the Holy Spirit. They must be predominated by the Spirit of God, which is the spirit of sacrifice.

We are using the word sacrifice here in the sense of giving up something for that which is better. Truly, the Christian not only sacrifices for that which is better, but seeks the very best, even the grace of God, which bringeth salvation through Jesus Christ our Lord.

Perhaps a better way to express what we want here would be to use the term "self-sacrifice," for it is often easier for us to give something else, as money, or goods, or mere words, than it is to give ourselves.

I shall never forget a passage in one of the school readers in use when I was a boy, "there is no excellence without great labor." We have seen this demonstrated again and again; and we may apply that idea to the present topic and say, there is no excellence to be attained in the Brethren church without great labor or much self-sacrifice. And we cannot have the spirit of a thing without the thing itself. The spirit of sacrifice is the unseen force which expresses itself in service and shows openly before the world that itself does really exist. The secret prayer is heard by him who sees in secret and "He shall reward thee openly."

But how shall this condition be attained? It must first be desired. And then the wish will be father to the deeds of sacrifice necessary. But as a basis for all this, before the desire, there must be understood and properly estimated by each individual, the worth and value of the Brethren church.

This result will be attained no doubt by the high standard of Christian character of those who constitute the body of Christ, which is the church. Good is contagious as well as evil. Like fire, it will "catch" in whatever or whoever it may come in contact with. That is the philosophy of the crowd, or of the revival, or of the "movement" and that (at least in a large measure) is the philosophy of the new "Bicentenary" or Three Year Program.

With sincere prayer accompanied by the Holy Spirit, these conditions are intensified and there is a continuous growth and advancement toward a "Greater Brethren church."

Los Angeles, California.

Send
WHITE GIFT
OFFERINGS to

THE SUNDAY SCHOOL

ALBERT TRENT
General Secretary-Treasurer
Johnstown, Pennsylvania

What We Owe the Children of the Elementary Division.   By Nora Bracken

We owe the children of the Elementary department the best that we have. Yea, perhaps we owe them more than we have to give. I fear that often-times we do not have enough to give the precious, hungering children.

We often speak of the debt we owe Christ, the one who suffered and died that we might have life and have it more abundantly. We owe him a great debt that we cannot pay, and the nearest we can come to paying it is by surrendering our lives completely to him and giving him our time and talents.

So, likewise, are we indebted to the children. The debt is probably greater than we can pay. To many people it means a surrendered life of service.

The child comes into this world a weak, helpless being, waiting to be molded and fashioned by men and women. Now when we think of this hackneyed expression, "As the twig is bent the tree inclines," we are reminded that the child is the foundation of the man. And we find that the most important period for development is in the elementary department.

Now in thinking of what we owe the children we shall first think of the teacher. We owe the children a teacher, a living teacher. What do we mean by the teacher? What title is more honorable than that of "teacher?" Teachers are oftentimes more highly honored than men and women of other high callings. The word "teacher" carries a great significance with it. To the child, the teacher is often the best and greatest person in the world. What is the living teacher? Is there such a thing as a dead teacher? We have teachers who are dead and do not know it. What do you think of a teacher who arises at a late hour on Sunday morning, looks over the lesson for about fifteen minutes and then goes off to Sunday school to teach her class? She comes home from Sunday school, lays away her work and does not look at it until the next Sunday. She has no books on child life, or none pertaining to the child world in her library. She tries not to secure these from other sources. She takes no time to read. She takes no time to study the child in his world. This teacher may have at some time or another taken the work that we call "Teacher Training" and other courses of study, but her books are closed and laid away. She considers this essential, and no longer does she grow. Such we call a dead teacher. When water has no inlet, no outlet, it becomes stagnant. So, too, do teachers become stagnant when they have no source from which to get the fresh, sparkling water. We have no use for this kind of teacher; we want living teachers. We want those who are real, genuine and Christ-like.

Christ was the great teacher, a living teacher. He was a real teacher because he had something to give. He had something to give that he felt would make the world better and make the people happier. He was so glad to teach that he crossed and recrossed the Sea of Galilee. He walked miles in order to give the Word to those who were hungering and thirsting. He met his enemies in the Synagogue. He taught individuals who came to him privately.

Jesus taught because he wanted to teach. No one urged him to do it. He saw the great need and he said, "I must teach." So with the living teacher today. She teaches because she sees the need, she wants to teach, she has something to give.

The living teacher implies a growth, a change. The man or woman who refuses to change mind and thoughts is not growing. A great change is continually taking place in the outside world. Times change and seasons change. Man changes in his way of living. Think of the great change that has taken place since the time of Christ. See how dif-

ferently we must teach today than did our forefathers. If one would be a growing teacher then she must change in many ways, and she must come in close touch with Christ the great Teacher.

The wide-awake teacher will share love with her children, and show interest in them. A few years ago I visited in the home of a girl friend. This girl had a little sister. I loved the little sister, Elizabeth. I spent as much time with her as with the remainder of the family. So one day when Elizabeth and I were out walking, she looked up in my face and said, "Miss Bracken, do you know what I thought before you came?"

"No, Elizabeth," I said, "What did you think?"

Her answer was, "I thought you were a big, tall girl. I thought you had yellow hair and blue eyes, and I didn't think you'd go out walking with me. I thought you'd spend all your time with Ruth."

"Then you were disappinted in me, were you not, Elizabeth?"

In child-like simplicity she looked up into my eyes and said, "Yes, but I like you better just as you are."

If you love the children, if you are interested in them, if you give them of your time and talents, they like you better just like you are.

The living teacher is beautiful. That is, she lives a beautiful life. Did you ever have one of your little children put their arms around your neck and say, "Teacher, I think you are pretty," and down in your own heart, probably because of some physical defect, you knew you were homely? The child did see something beautiful in you. He saw beneath physical beauty, he saw the heart of love that you had for him. He saw that beauty of Christ dwelling in you.

We owe the children the beautiful. What do we mean by owing the children the beautiful? We mean that we owe them everything that is beautiful, everything that tends to beautify a life.

"In early ages man was content if his house was dry, his coat warm and his tools sharp. In far-off times Pericles had his palace, Athens the temple, but the common people dwelt in mud huts, beauty was found only in cathedrals and palaces."

Now the time has come when beauty is scattered everywhere. This is an era for the beautiful. No longer is man content to live in mud houses, clumsy tools are no longer found, garments must be neat and have harmonious lines. No longer is the worshiper satisfied with harsh hymns, but his songs must be melodious and have a beautiful sentiment.

The children that come from the ordinary homes of today come from homes that are well furnished. Homes are decked and adorned with things which appeal to human needs. And the Sunday school rooms should not fall short of this, yea, in some ways they should be better furnished. They should be light and roomy. They should be well furnished with comfortable chairs, tables, sand-tables and instruments. The walls should be adorned with pictures, such as will be elevating to the child. Each picture has a silent story to tell. And when the child once grasps the story, then it springs up and grows within him. Flowers brighten the room, and they, too, speak in a wordless language. We may not know the value of the plant in the Sunday school room.

Beside the living teacher and the beautiful, we owe the children the best seed we have to sow. The child is the soil, and in him we plant the seed. The harvest will depend on how we sow and what we sow. Much of the seed that is sown depends upon the teacher. The living teacher will sow good seed.

To every teacher there is given a number of packages of seeds and among these the best package contains a book, the Word that was left with us in order that we might be guided aright. This Book contains many stories and truths. Within it lie the stories of man and his creation, his fall, his struggle to live and learn. We can follow man as he progresses in life. We see God's guidance. We see God choose the Israelites. We see him lead them into Egypt, through the wilderness and back into the land of Canaan. Sometimes we find them prosperous and other times—when they are disobedient—they are failures and God punishes them. We hear the sweet songs and prayers of David and other Psalmists. In this Book we become acquainted with the Manger, the Christ-child, the boyhood and manhood of Jesus. We see the Garden, the cross on Calvary, the tomb, the resurrection, the ascension, the home above, the church organized here on earth. All this is in this one package, and yet more. What truths shall we sow in the heart of the

child? There the little beginner sits on his tiny chair, there is the bright-eyed Primary child waiting for a story of truth, there is the Junior child bubbling over with enthusiasm. Can the teacher give the same truth to all these children? She must be careful in the selection of the seed, for what she would sow in the Junior would probably not take root in the Beginner.

We owe the children the seed of truth, the seed of life and the seed of light. We must teach them to love God, teach his loving care and tender protection, and his love for them. We must teach them to love Jesus, father and mother, brothers and sisters. We must teach them to give. We must give them the best we have.

"An angel paused in his onward flight.
With a seed of love and truth and light.
And cried, "Oh where shall this seed be sown
That it yield most fruit when fully grown?"
The Savior heard and said, as he smiled,
'Plant it for me in the heart of a child.' "

| J. A. Garber
PRESIDENT | Our Young People at Work | E. A. Rowsey
SECRETARY |

Why Christian Endeavor Should Be Interested in Citizenship
By Ellwood A. Rowsey, Associate General Secretary of the Ohio Christian Endeavor Union

A nation's best assets are its loyal, true-hearted, Christ-spirited people. A nation is poor or rich just as its men and women believe in equality and justice, truth and righteousness, love and service.

Christian Endeavor has always stood for the highest type of citizenship, and is one of the greatest organizations of the church in its advocacy for the thing that is clean, pure, wholesome and uplifting. Christian Endeavor is too big to remain within the four walls of any church. Its plan is to reach out into every section of every community and teach life and lift it to the highest possible standard of efficiency.

She is training mothers of men to be model citizens. We should form classes in our Citizenship Department for the study of the problems in our community.

The following is a suggestive study:
1 The Public School System
2 The Public Charities
3 The Prisons
4 The Courts
5 The State Legislature
6 The Sabbath
7 The Social Evil

The age in which we are living demands the highest type of Christian citizenship. Every effort that is put forth for the betterment of a community or an individual should receive the hearty support of every member of the Citizenship Department, and any influence that seeks to destroy the moral life of a community or individual should receive the censure of every good citizen.

We, as a Christian organization, should feel that we have a part in helping to make our community what it should be morally. The question might be asked, "How can we promote good citizenship?" Good citizenship not only can be promoted by educational means, but a chief essential for ultimate success in social requirements is that we train up citizens that the people be taught to understand better the nature of social institutions, that they may realize that not all but a large part of our social evils come not from wickedness, or hard-heartedness, or injustice; but merely from mal-adjustment of social relations.

They should realize also that these evils can be overcome at times by merely slight changes in methods of social work if only students of society can be found to suggest wise changes in methods. But most important of all is the edu-

cation of the people to that flexibility of temperament and culture that will enable them readily to adapt themselves to new conditions; that judicial habit of thought, that fostering of personal responsibility, which will enable them to see truth, when unwelcome.

Some Definite Plans
In the Evangelical Endeavorer of September first is an article by Mr. Stanley Vandersall, of Boston, Massachusetts, entitled "Citizenship Suggestions for Young People." With his permission, I quote the following as suggestive plans to carry out for the young people of Ohio:

"First: Every Christian Endeavor Society could well serve as a training class in civic duties. A series of special meetings may be arranged in which details of local government may be discussed, even to the extent of having a mayor, or the chief of police, or other officials to come for the purpose of making addresses; or a mock Town Meeting; or a meeting of the City Council will create pleasure and instruction. There can be a discussion of improvments needed for the community, together with plans for securing them. Public Institutions may be made the subject of investigation and report.

"Second: Do direct citizenship work in behalf of foreigners who need the principles of American Government. In many sections a class in the study of the Constitution of the United States or the principles of our political institutions, etc., will be a distinct Christian service.

"Third: The Citizenship Committee can and should be alert to the actions of local, state and national lawmakers. Legislation detrimental to health or life or to morals or to religion should be promptly opposed. Bills to break down the Lord's Day or to legalize prize-fighting, or to foster gambling, etc., call forth immediate action by Christian Endeavorers. Many effective means are available. Signatures may be secured to petitions, telegrams and special delivery letters may be sent, and public sentiment aroused.

"We should be as quick to commend as to criticize. The zealous Citizenship Committee called to this special task through meetings, bulletin notices, posters, announcements, petitions, etc., can keep the whole sentiment of the church and community awake to pressing needs and plans for betterment. Let no Christian feel that this is a small and inconsequential task."

The Liquor Fight
To touch so vast a subject—and only touch it—is diffi-

cult. Let us not think for a moment that the liquor fight is a closed issue, and that there is no more need of agitation. If there was ever a time when we needed to be aroused to the real situation it is NOW. Great moral issues are at stake. Civilization must entirely destroy the liquor traffic, or be destroyed by it.

Shall We Proceed or Recede?

We dare not turn backward. "Forward" is the watchword of the age. Mr. McAdoo says, "To restore breweries to political power means the re-establishing of the debasing and immoral liquor traffic and the nullification of the prohibition amendment." He further says, "Even if the saloon were not reopened, light wines and beer would be sold at every soda fountain, at every lunch counter and in every restaurant and hotel. If we turn loose upon the country light wines and beer, we have destroyed the prohibition amendment and brought back upon humanity a cross greater than war itself."

The light wine and beer clause will be the great issue in Congress. Prohibition has stood the test for the past year, and thus far it has done for us what it promised. People are happier, more prosperous, and are succeeding far better in life than ever before. Shall we turn backward? Shall we permit the saloon to come back and trample under foot the highest type of American citizenship? No, Never! We will never be satisfied until we have worldwide prohibition.

The Coming Election

Every good, loyal citizen in the state of Ohio who believes in law enforcement should vote "Yes" on this question. The good people of Ohio should give the proposal a majority so big that there can be no doubt where the state stands on law enforcement.

House Bill No. 620

Last winter the Ohio Legislature enacted a law to enforce the state-wide Prohibition Amendment. This bill is known as "House Bill No. 620." The brewery interests have petitioned for a state-wide vote on this law, and the referendum will be held at the November election this year. If you will notice the unofficial ballot carefully, you will see that the law enforcement proposal is the only referendum on the ballot this year.

Six Reasons for Voting "Yes"

1 Its brief.
2 Provides that one half the fines go to village trying case.
3. Gives lower courts power to hear Still and Bootlegging cases and thus saves Federal Courts from being Police Courts.
4 Makes putting of wood alcohol in beverages murder if death results.
5 Protects the home (if only a room) from unrestricted search and seizure.
6 Protects children; defines intoxicating liquor for Ohio; would be effective even if Congress should change the Volstead Act.

(To be continued next week).

SEND ALL MONEY FOR
General Home, Kentucky and
Foreign Missions to

MISSIONS

WILLIAM A. GEARHART
General Missionary Secretary
906 Conover Bldg., Dayton, O.

Our Work In Argentina. By C. F. Yoder

There is a saying, "Blessed is the nation that has no history," which means that such a nation has no record of wars, which according to the mistaken standards of the past, have made up most of the pages of history. If Evangelist readers have not had frequent reports from Argentina during the past year it is because the work has been going smoothly and keeps us all so busy that we have neglected to write.

The first half of the year we had the extra work of enlarging the church property and building the Bible coach and now we have the work of the coach and several new points to care for. First, we have Carlota, which though a hard field in some ways, is too promising to abandon. I have been going there once a month and thus far have been able to keep the Sunday school together. The last time we had 28 present. A brother-in-law of Brother Atkinson went with me and we canvassed a part of the town from house to house and found several new families interested.

Then we have begun meetings in Los Cisnes, ten miles from Carlota. A believer from there takes me over from Carlota in his auto on Sunday afternoons after Sunday school and another in the evening in a vacant bakery. The street meetings draw from 150 to 200 people, which is about half the population here. There is no church of any kind, but the school teacher is an agent of the priest. On my last visit I spent half a day teaching her and she went immediately after to Carlota to see the priest. I do not know what may result.

In Deheza we were obliged to give up the room we had been using but Brother Atkinson found a much better place on the main street at a little higher price, and the work is going forward better than ever. This is another town where there is no priest to do the devil's work.

In Cabrera we have also improved the property by putting in a well, improving the benches of the hall and planting the lot with trees and flowers. Brother Atkinson is using one of the new balopticans with good results.

Then we have begun work in a new town a little over a hundred miles south of Rio Cuarto, called Huinca Benanco.

Brother Edwards has gone there with his family and will write later all about the work. The town has about 5,000 inhabitants and is growing rapidly as it is the center of a rich agricultural region on the edge of the pampa. There is no church or priest but a number of evangelical believers and a general desire for a mission. Brother Edwards writes: "We had two good Sunday schools yesterday with about ninety in all, a funeral of an English child in the afternoon and a splendid meeting at night, about sixty present, all our room would hold. Mrs. Edwards has begun womens' meetings in another part of town." There are other good towns around this place which are also unoccupied and this should form a good center for propagating the work.

As Brother Sickel will not be able to go out with the auto coach for a few weeks we will push the work here all we can until that time. We now have street meetings Sunday afternoons and have begun cottage meetings on Wednesday evenings and also a Sunday morning meeting for members. A number of our members have moved away but there are new applicants for baptism and we have reason to feel encouraged.

The Salvation Army has opened a work here and have meetings in the plaza on Sunday afternoons. In a town of 33,000 there is room for them, and we hope to co-operate some with them.

We are eager to hear the report of the Conference which we trust has been the largest and best in the history of the church. Mrs. Yoder has not been well for several months, but is slowly improving. Our two girls are away in school. May we have the prayers of all at home.

The Call for a Cook

Sister Huldah Ewert of the Dayton Brethren church, a consecrated, conscientious Christian lady, has answered the call to go to our Lost Creek, Kentucky, Mission and cook for the dormitory students and the mission workers. How happy we are that this call has been accepted, for we have been praying and seeking for the right party to do this work for some time. She will leave on Tuesday, October 26th, for the field. Let us pray for her that she may be a great factor in this mission station.

WILLIAM A GEARHART,
Secretary of the Kentucky Committee.

NEWS FROM THE FIELD

Minutes of the Illiokota District Conference Held at Lanark, Illinois, October 6-8, 1920

Wednesday Evening

The pastor of the conference church, B. T. Burnworth, presided at the opening session of the Illiokota District Conference at Lanark, Illinois, on Wednesday evening, October 6, 1920.

"To the Work" and "True-hearted, Whole-hearted," were sung. A portion of the fourth chapter of Matthew's gospel was read as the Scripture lesson, and prayer was offered by Miles J. Snyder, invoking God's guidance and blessing upon the conference.

A men's chorus choir gave a special number after which B. T. Burnworth gave an address of welcome to the visiting delegates. Responses were made by R. F. Porte, Miles J. Snyder, Elizabeth Hildebrand, and Mrs. Emmert.

Following the singing of a duet, the opening conference sermon was delivered by Moderator R. F. Porte, whose theme was "Jesus' Method of Advancing the Kingdom of God." He emphasized God's purpose for the redemption of the human race, and portrayed his plan as the only plan and showed that our conformity and obedience thereto was the secret of peace and joy and power. He urged the importance of evangelism, doctrinal preaching, and religious education.

Thursday Forenoon

On Thursday morning simultaneous conferences were held by the Ministerium and the Woman's Missionary Society.

After brief devotional and business sessions, both groups assembled in the church auditorium to listen to addresses by B. F. Puterbaugh and Edwin Boardman, Jr. The former spoke on the subject, "Laymen Encouraging Recruits for the Ministry." He presented the dire need of ministers confronting the church, and showed how Sunday school superintendents, Bible classes, and religious homes may and should be vital and effective factors in securing recruits for the ministry.

The theme of the latter speaker was "Problems Facing the Choice of the Ministry." His splendid address centered around three points: problems relating to the preparation and delivery of sermons; problems of occupational limitation and environment; and problems arising from low monetary returns.

By motion of conference it was requested that Edwin Boardman's address be published in the Brethren Evangelist.

At the beginning of the conference session for district problems, "Nearer Still Nearer" was sung, and prayer was offered by Z. T. Livengood.

The Moderator appointed a credential committee consisting of Z. T. Livengood, Freeman Ankrum and B. F. Puterbaugh, and the delegates present were enrolled.

The Moderator's annual message was given by R. F. Porte. He pointed out the great need of pressing forward in our district, to fortify weak places and enter new inviting and strategic fields now open; and made an appeal for continued loyalty and devotion to the Word of God as sufficient to meet all needs.

Report of the district Mission Board was given by Secretary B. T. Burnworth, who told of the plans the Board had under consideration for the coming year.

The Treasurer's report was given by B. F. Puterbaugh showing a balance on hand of $775.10.

By motion the reports of the Secretary and Treasurer were accepted. A period of discussion and business followed. Decatur, Illinois, Eau Claire, Wisconsin, and Des Moines, Iowa, were considered as prospective places where aggressive work may be done the coming year.

The credential committee reported in attendance thirty-four lay and seven ministerial delegates. The report was accepted and the committee continued.

By motion B. F. Puterbaugh and Miles J. Snyder were elected members of the district Mission Board for a term of three years.

"He Included Me" was sung, and a benediction brought the morning session to a close.

The first of the good meals provided by the Lanark Brethren for the visiting delegates was then served in the basement of the conference church.

Thursday Afternoon

In beginning the Thursday afternoon session, the audience joined heartily in singing "The Touch of His Hand on Mine." W. H. Beachler read the Scripture lesson and offered the opening prayer.

The first address of the session was given by Miles J. Snyder on the subject, "The Challenge of the Brethren Bicentenary Movement." A period for discussion followed in which a number participated speaking on various phases of the new program.

The open conference session of the Woman's Missionary Society followed. "I Have a Friend, You Ought to Know Him," was sung and Psalm I was read by Miss Alice Livengood, who had charge of the devotions. "Presentation of This Year's Motto—'Serve to Save'" was the subject of Mrs. B. T. Burnworth. She reviewed the slogans of the past and showed their practical importance as ideals and moulding factors in Christian Endeavor.

Mrs. W. H. Beachler gave an illuminating presentation of "Our Goals;" after which she conducted an interesting and suggestive period on "The Problem Hour."

Election of officers resulted as follows for the coming year: President, Mrs. B. T. Burnworth, Lanark, Illinois; Vice President, Mrs. R. F. Porte, Dallas Center, Iowa; Secretary-Treasurer, Miss Elizabeth Hildebrand, Waterloo, Iowa. Mrs. W. H. Beachler will represent Illiokota district at the Summer School of Missions next year.

The session was closed with benediction.

Thursday Evening

The evening session opened with a spirited song service in which a large audience united in singing "Silently the Shades of Evening" and "O That will be Glory for Me." The devotional service was conducted by Edwin Boardman, Jr., following which everybody joined in singing the great chorus song, "All Hail Immanuel."

The first address of the evening was on the subject, "Preparation by Pastor and People for a Revival." Z. T. Livengood very ably discussed this theme, strikingly showing that the church which is not evangelistic in spirit and life is on the road to deterioration and death; and that the work of saving souls is the greatest task in which the church may be engaged, meriting the most careful preparation on the part of pastor and people in the way of prayer and Christian activity.

"Sing Praises" was sung by the Lanark choir as a special musical number, after which the sermon of the evening was delivered by W. H. Beachler, who spoke on the theme "The Christian, God's Fellow-Worker." He showed how the Christian sustains a vital relationship to God and has a share in promoting and executing his plan in every generation. The Christian is not his own, but God's possession, whose privilege and honor is not to work for God but with him.

"To the Work" was sung and a benediction closed the session.

Friday Forenoon

The audience united in singing "Mighty Army of the Young" at the opening of the Friday morning session. Devotions were conducted by G. T. Ronk, who read from the twelfth chapter of Hebrews and led in prayer.

This was the Sunday school session of the conference.

The first address was given by Freeman Ankrum whose theme was "Preparing Young People for Church Leadership." He showed how the leadership of tomorrow depends upon the training of today, and emphasized the vital importance of finding interested young people of ability and preparing and encouraging them for Christian work.

"Teacher Training and How to Promote It" was the subject of the next number on the program. In the absence of the person who was to present this theme, the subject was opened for general discussion; and an interesting and helpful period followed with talks by Moore, Ronk, Puterbaugh, Snyder, Burnworth, Livengood and Garber.

Mrs. G. T. Ronk discussed "How to Teach Missions in the Sunday School." She pointed out the importance of teaching missions to young people through class instruction, special missionary exercises and programs, the reading of leaflets, and books, and practical lessons in Scriptural prayer and giving.

A splendid paper on "Administration Work in the Sunday Schools" was read by Mrs. Frank Wisner. She clearly set forth the imperative need of wise administrative work, both in the school as a whole and in the several departments, in order to secure the most desirable and profitable results.

The closing address of the session was given by W. H. Beachler on the theme "The Sunday School the Right Arm of the Church." His address centered around three main points: The Sunday school's relation to the church as a factor in religious education, in evangelism, and in character building. And despite all the Sunday school has done, as confronting it in the way of a challenge, he enumerated the problems of enlistment, of holding, of attendance, and of efficiency.

The session adjourned with benediction by R. F. Porte.

Friday Afternoon

"Holy, Holy, Holy," was sung as an opening hymn, after which R. F. Porte offered prayer.

Prof. J. A. Garber, of Ashland, Ohio, representing denominational interests, was introduced by the Moderator and spoke enthusiastically in turn upon the Publication interests, Ashland College, and the National Sunday School Association. The very close attention and unmistakable interest of the audience, clearly indicated the high appreciation of the people in having Prof. Garber attend the conference and bring the encouraging reports from our leading denominational auxiliaries.

Conference Business Session

The organization of the district Mission Board resulted in the election of the following officers: President, W. H. Beachler, Waterloo, Iowa; Secretary, B. T. Burnworth, Lanark, Illinois; Treasurer, B. F. Puterbaugh, Waterloo, Iowa.

The Mission Board recommended to conference that its officers be appointed as a committee with power to act to visit Des Moines, Iowa, and go over the situation there with a view of establishing a Brethren church in that place.

Furthermore, the Mission Board recommended that forty cents per member shall be the basis for the apportionment of district missions for the coming year.

By motion both these recommendations were adopted by conference.

By motion Miles J. Snyder was elected a member of the General Conference Executive committee to represent Illiokota district next year.

By motion W. H. Beachler was elected Illiokota District Secretary for the Brethren Bicentenary Movement, and given discretionary power either to represent the seven departments of the Bicentenary program himself or to appoint assistants.

By motion the Conference Moderator and Secretary were authorized to appoint delegates at large to represent Illiokota at the next General Conference.

By motion S. P. Hoover and Samuel Livengood were named as Illiokota nominees for Ashland College trustees.

The Moderator was instructed to appoint a committee of three to bring in nominations for a Board of Religious Education to supersede the district boards of Sunday school and Christian Endeavor departmental superintendents. The committee appointed consisted of J. A. Garber, Z. T. Livengood, and Edwin Boardman, Jr.

The final report of the credential committee showed an attendance of 37 lay delegates and 9 ministerial delegates, making a total of 46. The lay delegates were from the following churches: Lanark, Illinois 10; Milledgeville, Illinois, 9; Dallas Center, Iowa, 2; Hudson, Iowa, 3; Leon, Iowa, 1; Waterloo, Iowa, 12.

The committee appointed to bring in nominations for the district Board of Religious Education reported as follows: B. T. Burnworth, Chairman, Edwin Boardman, Jr., and Elizabeth Hildebrand. On motion properly sustained this report was adopted and the parties elected.

By vote of conference, the selection of the place for the holding of next year's conference was left in the hands of the Executive Committee.

The election of conference officers took place at this time, with the following result: Moderator, Edwin Boardman, Jr., Hudson, Iowa; Vice Moderator, Freeman Ankrum, Garwin, Iowa; Secretary, R. F. Porte, Dallas Center, Iowa; Treasurer, Mrs. B. F. Puterbaugh.

By motion G. T. Ronk was re-elected a member of the Ministerial Examining Board for a term of three years.

The benediction closing the afternoon session was pronounced by Freeman Ankrum.

Friday Evening

The evening session opened with Edwin Boardman, Jr., the newly elected Moderator, presiding. "Faith is the Victory" was sung and devotions were conducted by R. F. Porte. After the audience united in singing "Love Lifted Me," Prof. J. A. Garber spoke on the subject, "Christian Endeavor and Its Program." He stressed the importance of proper guidance in the growing life and its best preparation for effective Christian service; and showed the contribution young people have made and what they can do in the advancement of the church and the kingdom.

"Rouse Ye Soldiers" was sung by the audience and an offering was received.

In the absence of the one who was to preach the closing sermon, a missionary lecture was given by Miles J. Snyder entitled, "Seven Wonders of the Modern Missionary World," which was beautifully illustrated with a number of stereopticon slides.

The closing number on the conference program was a stirring appeal for Life Work Recruits by Edwin Boardman, Jr.

"To the Harvest Field" was sung and B. T. Burnworth offered the closing prayer and benediction.

MILES J. SNYDER, Secretary.

BRIEF REPORT OF W. M. S. SESSIONS OF THE INDIANA STATE CONFERENCE AT FLORA, OCTOBER 4-7, 1920

All sessions were presided over by Mrs. Elmer Berkey, the District president. The devotional periods were all instructive and uplifting spiritually. The motto for the year "Serve to Save" was forcibly emphasized by our National President, Mrs. U. J. Shively, as the ideal of all of our endeavors and toward which each one must strive earnestly throughout the coming year.

The president's report for the year showed commendable growth and interest in the work and increased mission study.

Mrs. Shively gave a stirring report from the Summer School of Missions, telling of the wonderful inspiration she received from hearing the discussions and talks by returned missionaries. She also conducted mission study classes each day, benefiting those who expect to teach the classes in their respective societies.

The address of the public session was delivered by Rev. A. E. Thomas upon the subject, "Can a Woman Make Good?" He pointed out the fact that women have made good in the spiritual, national and home life of all ages.

An offering amounting to $13.45 was given for the purpose of purchasing knives and forks for the dormitory at Lost Creek, Kentucky.

Mrs. Wolfe the district patroness of the S. M. M. reported growth in the work during the year. She imparted plans for each sisterhood to make and send necessary articles for the comfort and brightening of the home life of the girls in the Kentucky Mission.

The following officers were elected for the coming year: President, Mrs. Elmer Berkey, Goshen; Vice President, Mrs. J. J. Wolfe, North Manchester; Secretary-treasurer, Mabel M. Maus.

Per M. M. M. Secretary.

TRAVEL FLASHES

I wonder if it will happen this winter, that all the travel flashes will be written on the train. I am speeding along at a fine rate along the "Beautiful Ohio." It has a good name; it is a beautiful name and is as distinctive in its individuality as anything God ever made. It is really unlike any other river I ever saw. There is just one trip I should more enjoy than this one on the C. & O. and that would be one in a boat. But I presume it will be a long time before I shall feel that I have time to go that slow!

Beauty, Beauty!

How gorgeous is nature as we look across from the Kentucky side! The hills of Ohio draped in the autumn shades, some of them low, some of them high but all painted by the Master hand of Providence is unequalled by all that man can do and as wide as the world in its sweep. How can anyone help but offer thanks to Almighty God for this artist touch to all nature this fall.

Chestnuts

Not the kind that we "kid" about but real ones. For the first time in my life, I got them right off the tree and so many that— well I hate to tell it—I did not know they would make one sick. But it did not take me long to recover and ready to eat some more. West Virginia has a lot of chestnuts of various kinds.

Oak Hill

Oak Hill, it seems to me, ought to be Chestnut Hill, for the only grove in the town is a Chestnut grove. It is from Oak Hill that

I am returning from my first evangelistic effort.

Here after a two weeks' engagement when we reached the most of the available prospects of the Brethren church, last June, we were invited to return for a union campaign to be held in the Baptist—the largest church in town. All the churches co-operated in a splendid manner and only once did any jar occur and that was immediately avoided. From the very first, the meeting house was too small. At the first audience, an overflow was turned away and that was the style in all but a few of the meetings. More beautiful weather the Lord never gave any place. As I remember there was rain but one night of the four weeks. The money raised for the campaign reached near the thousand dollar mark and the good inestimable.

Distractions

Oak Hill surely passed through tribulations during this time. It is a mining community, and many poor fellows who toil in the dark for your warmth and light, are maimed and wounded and the hospital is full all the time. This cheapens life. So, it is not at all strange that one of the leading business men of the town was stabbed to death after church one night. Political discussion is rife and it is a wonder that we got much good done; but the people were with me in all my fight against the common evils of the day, the entire audience standing against cards, dance and theaters. All the men standing for the pure life. Perhaps there were one hundred conversions from sin who will definitely line up with the churches of the town of whom the Brethren will get a just share. May it be a great year for EVANGELISM.

CHARLES A. BAME.

FROM ALLENTOWN TO PITTSBURGH

Some weeks before the state conference, Brother Harley, the able, and beloved pastor of the Pittsburgh church wrote me insisting on wife and me coming to the conference in their church. I promised to do so, providing God gave my dear wife the necessary strength, and provided the way for us. Then I would accept it as evidence that it was according to his will for us to go. A very marked improvement in wife's health soon became very apparent, then came Brother Shaffer's letter insisting that we come to Allentown and go with them. That was just like him—while he is big in physique, he is bigger in heart. We felt that God had provided both, and accepted them as evidence that it would be pleasing to him to have us go, and so we went and had the most enjoyable time of our lives, one we can never forget.

Now just a few words about the conference. First, it was I believe one of the largest and best ever held in Pennsylvania. Too much praise cannot be given to Brother Harley and the church for the way they did it. They certainly went the limit. As you will doubtless have an account of the conference from the secretary I will not attempt a description of it, leaving it to him, but of some novel features I wish to speak. On Wednesday evening, at 9:30 after the evening services, the

Christian Endeavor society, gave a reception on the site of old Fort Pitt, now a playground, but I assure you that it was no play to get there as it required both wind and muscle, for it is about two hundred feet above the city. Arriving there, we were treated to sandwiches and frankfurters, or as they call them in the west "weiners." They had built a big, raging fire, and provided several armsfull of straight "suckers" or shoots from trees, some four to six feet long, then more frankfurters which were placed on the suckers and toasted in the fire. This done, then a supply of marshmallows, which were also toasted in the fire, after which the Ashland boys and girls let loose some college yells. And they were some yells, believe me. After some Ashland songs, then we sought our beds.

Thursday afternoon, they provided autos for 94 to tour the city. Beginning at the H. J. Heinz Company plant, which was a wonderful sight, we saw the preparation of the world-famous 57 varities. Then an illustrated lecture showing their different depots in the different countries throughout the world, as well as the sources of supply in distant lands. Then they set us down to a banquet in which we tasted in a seven course feast the quality of their products so well known all over the world. Hardly necessary to say that it was enjoyed by all. They had planned to take us to many other points of interest, but so much time was consumed at the Heinz Company that we had only time to run through the section occupied by the rich, and then to the park. The Pittsburgh church certainly deserved the gratitude of those attending the conference. But come to the city of "Brotherly Love" next year. While we can not hope to equal such strides, we will do our best.

Another matter I wish to speak of, is the delightful trip over the mountains in Brother Shaffer's car. Leaving Allentown at 9 A. M. we ran to Everett, I feel by God's appointment; for we thought we were in Bedford, where we had purposed to stop. We secured excellent accommodations at very reasonable rates. Asking about churches, we were told that there was the Baptist, Methodist, Dunker,—that will do, I said and, being directed we went to the Dunker church and were warmly welcomed and invited to speak for them, which Brother Fehnel and I did.

Starting out at 8 A. M. we arrived in Pittsburgh at 4 P. M.

I should like to speak of the trip over the seven mountains but language fails me. Paul had some things that even he could not describe, and these are beyond me. Returning we stopped over night at McConnellsburg, arriving in Allentown at 4 P. M. We preached (or tried to) for them on Sunday and felt all very much at home there, having known about all of them, since we gave a part of our time to them a few years ago. Just a word for the dear ones there. Were it possible for me to leave this city, I know of no church that I would rather go to than it. Brother Fehnel is ably filling the pulpit until they can secure a pastor, with his business it is too much for him to do, continually. After spending several delightful days

visiting among them we turned our faces homeward, arriving safely.

Now a few words for the glory of God. Wife and I definitely committed our way unto "Our Father" trusting him for health, strength, and protection from all harm, or accidents. Then the whole party started from their knees as well, having committed ourselves to Father's care each morning, and each night thanked him for the blessings of the day. Results: While we saw autos in the gutter and upset, yet we traveled the 600 miles without a puncture, or trouble of any kind, save that a fan belt wore out and caused us about 15 minutes delay. To God be all the glory. Oh, that we would all learn to love him better and trust him more.

E. E. ROBERTS.

ANNOUNCEMENT

Charles W. Abbott, of the Dayton, Ohio church, wishes to announce that he is prepared to do evangelistic singing and take full charge of music for revival meetings.

He has had wide experience in this line and can prove himself valuable to any meeting.

Also, he is an Expert Christian Endeavor worker and organizes and lectures to young people. Address

CHARLES W. ABBOTT,
206 Pleasant St.   Dayton, Ohio.

ENDORSEMENT

I take pleasure in endorsing Charles W. Abbott, of the Dayton church, as evangelistic singer, as he was one of my standbys in the Dayton church.

While he may not be the polished solo singer that some others are, he is a spirit-filled man and is a truly "Gospel singer" and no church would make a mistake in engaging him.

W. S. BELL.

The Tithing Stewardship Corner

By Layman

In the "Record of Christian Work," Northfield, Massachusetts, under the head "Flooding the Storehouses with the Tithes," appears the following:

"The great outpouring of subscriptions for the Southern Baptist five-year fund is, we imagine, one of the greatest occurrences in the history of large scale giving. The $75,000,-000 asked for was over-subscribed on the first day of the week of offerings. There were a few large gifts, but the mass of the millions was given by the masses of the people. Country churches remote from the railroads and holding services only once a month have given with a generosity which has astonished the leaders of the denomination."

The Southern Baptists were three or four years in advance of their Northern brethren on the subject of teaching and preaching tithing. The above account is a perfectly natural result.

Can a country church do things Here is one that does: The East Jordan United Brethren church, in northern Illinois, is located in a farming community with no village for miles around. The Rev. B. Lee Towsley is the pastor. His membership is wide awake and the Sunday school as good for its size as can be found in any city church. In addition to a full benevolence budget, this church regularly supports two missionaries, one in the home and one in the foreign field, and some individual members are in other ways doing large things for the progress of the gospel. The striking thing about it is the ease with which all this work is done. When renewing the home and foreign missionary support a few weeks ago, no special effort was made. The subject was presented, after which the pastor offered a fervent prayer, and slips of paper were quietly passed through the congregation. The sum for the day amounted to nearly $1,130.

Where is the secret of the East Jordan church? One at least is that for about a quarter of a century one man with consecration and vision has been superintendent of the Sunday school. He himself has all this time practiced and earnestly advocated the paying of the tithe to God. The result is the people of the whole community have grown up from childhood with their lives permeated thoroughly with the tithe principle. This tithing community is a prosperous community, both in spiritual and temporal things.

In the February 11 number of the Christian Observer under the head of "Editorial Notes" appears the following:

"A revival of the study of the scriptural teachings of Christian stewardship is sweeping over the entire church. The final solution of all church problems, including the evangelization of the world, waits for a new emphasis on God's ownership and man's stewardship. 'The Presbyterian Progressive Program' is urging that classes be organized in every church for the study of stewardship, and the text-book suggested is 'The New Christian,' by Ralph S. Cushman. The Presbyterian committee of publication has sent a complimentary copy of this book to every pastor in our Assembly."

So nigh is grandeur to our dust
So near is God to man,
When duty whispers low, thou must,
The youth replies, I can.
—Ralph Waldo Emerson.

Business Manager's Corner

THE LAST CALL

This is our last opportunity to call upon the churches and the pastors of the brotherhood to rally to the need of the Publishing Company on Sunday, October thirty-first. In fact, there likely will be some of our readers that will not see this appeal until after Sunday. But it is not absolutely necessary that the offering be taken on that day. Any day soon will answer the purpose, just so we receive the funds in time to keep our notes at the bank from going to protest.

Since our call for the offering on the day set went out our attention has been called to the fact that October thirty-first is the day set to be observed as Stewardship Day by our Bicentenary Committee. We happen to be a member of this committee, but we can not recall having been in the meeting of the committee when that day was set, and we wish to explain that no conflict was intended when the Publishing Company Day, was set. Both notices went out in the same number of the Evangelist. We would not have set that day had we been informed concerning the plans of the committee on Stewardship. But there need be no conflict, as it will certainly be a manifestation of the responsibility of stewardship to make a financial offering on the day set for the relief of the embarrassed condition of our Publishing Interests.

We are expecting large things and we pray that our expectations may be realized. No institution or department of the church has made any progress in the last twenty years without the constant and loyal support of the Brethren Publishing Company, and it is only an act of justice that the churches at this time come to the assistance of their servant that has served them so faithfully for so many years.

Let every church make a gift, and make it accordingly as the Lord has prospered it. With such gifts we will be perfectly satisfied. With the announcement of the special offering to be made by the churches the individual offerings became less, but we are glad to record the following since last week: Dyoll Belote, $10.00; Beulah Hartle, $2.00; H. F. E. O'Neill, $5.00; Mary A. Snyder, $1.00; Ellen G. Lichty, $3.00; Geo. A. Smith, $1.00. Previously reported; $304.50; total, $326.50.

Evangelist Honor Roll

The Evangelist Honor Roll is not yet dead, nor does it seem to be dying. Since our last report we have been glad to add to the Honor Roll the Mansfield, Ohio church, A. L. DeLozier, pastor, with an increase of subscriptions of more than TWO THOUSAND per cent. Is there any one left who says there is no more room for the Evangelist family of readers to grow? If so, please stand up and let us have a look at you. Then the New Paris, Indiana church, W. I. Duker, pastor, has renewed its list for the third year, and the Goshen, Indiana church, J. A. McInturff, pastor, has come along with its renewal of TWO HUNDRED FIFTEEN subscriptions, and Tiosa, Indiana ,Sylvester Whetstone pastor, has sent in its first installment of renewals for the third year.

At the present time we have more than fifty of our leading churches that have tried the "Evangelist in every home" plan for from two to four years and it seems good to them. The wonder is that any church will now try to get along in the "old fashioned way." We will continue the Honor Roll system so long as the results justify the means, and so long as there is a single church not on the Roll there will be room for one more and a warm welcome will be awaiting any that still feel inclined to come in with the leading churches of the brotherhood.

R. R. TEETER,
Business Manager.

THE BRETHREN EVANGELIST

HOW THEY SPENT THEIR MONEY

Selfishness.

I kept all my wealth—and I mourn all my loss,
For gold in a skeleton hand turns to dross;
Love, friendship and gratitude might I have bought,
But I kept all my wealth 'till it moulded to naught.

Pleasure.

I spent all my gold, I danced and I sang,
The palace I built with hilarity rang,
Plays, revels and frolics from even to dawn
But I lie here with nothing—I spent it—it's gone!

Avarice

I loaned my good money, at grasping per cent—
'Twas I who got all that you kept and you spent;
While I counted my millions, death plundered me bare,
And this grave that I sleep in belongs to my heir.

Charity.

It was little I had, but I gave all my store
To those who had less, or who needed it more;
And I came with death laughing, for here at the grave
In riches unmeasured I found what I gave.

Robert J. Burdette.

‡ - ‡ - ‡

What Will You Do for Home Missions?

AT THANKSGIVING TIME?

Published every Wednesday at Ashland, Ohio. All matter for publication must reach the Editor not later than Friday noon of the preceding week.

Che Brethren Evangelist

When ordering your paper changed give old as well as new address. Subscriptions discontinued at expiration. To avoid missing any numbers renew two weeks in advance.

George S. Baer, Editor

R. R. Teeter, Business Manager

ASSOCIATE EDITORS: J. Fremont Watson, Louis S. Bauman, A. B. Cover, Alva J. McClain, B. T. Burnworth.

OFFICIAL ORGAN OF THE BRETHREN CHURCH

Subscription price, $2.00 per year, payable in advance.
Entered at the Post Office at Ashland, Ohio, as second-class matter.
Acceptance for mailing at special rate of postage provided for in section 1103, Act of October 3, 1917, authorized September 9, 1918.
Address all matter for publication to Geo. S. Baer, Editor of the Brethren Evangelist, and all business communications to R. R. Teeter, Business Manager, Brethren Publishing Company, Ashland, Ohio. Make all checks payable to the Brethren Publishing Company.

TABLE OF CONTENTS

EDITORIAL

Some Essentials to the Success of Our Bicentenary Movement

More than any other one thing, so far as human plans and methods are concerned, the thoughts of the brotherhood are upon the Bicentenary Movement. It is right that it should be so. It represents the aim we have set before ourselves as a denomination. It is natural that our aim should stand out big in our minds. Besides this new program represents the united wisdom of the foremost leaders of the brotherhood, and it is worthy of the first place in the thought-life of our people. It is a great program because it holds up ideals that are vital, and it is a challenging program because those ideals are beyond anything we as a church have set before ourselves.

It has been designated a "Movement," but it is not yet that; it is only a program. It is hoped that it will soon result in a movement however, and that the life and activity of every church will steadily increase through these three years, so that we may be able finally to speak truly and with pride of our Bicentenary Movement. But there are certain things essential to the success of our new program,—so essential, in fact, that little can be accomplished until they are taken properly into account.

In the first place it is important that we get started promptly and properly. A great deal depends on getting started right and without delay. A successful evangelist wrote us recently, as he was just beginning a campaign that promised great success, and used this significant phrase, "We got off on the good foot." That ought to be our experience in this three year campaign, if we are to accomplish what we hope. We must not repeat our mistake at the launching of the Four Year Program. The entire first year was gone before we got started on it. The fault did not lay with the churches then, however, but it will now if they lose time in getting in to this program. The plans have been well laid, and the instructions and suggestions have gone out to every church. Dr. Bame and his co-workers are sending out messages almost every week to the readers of The Evangelist. It is important that every church organize immediately according to his suggestions and do its best to accomplish every proposed undertaking at the proper time. Delay always puts one to a disadvantage, and in this case it may cause a church to fail in something that is important to be done. This program challenges our best efforts practically the year round; there are no off seasons when one can make up for lost time. It is important that we get started promptly and keep going at "full capacity."

In the second place it is important that there be ready and loyal co-operation on the part of all the ministers and church leaders with the plans and suggestions of those who have been chosen to direct the Movement. The brotherhood will likely be disposed to hold these directors responsible for the success or failure of the undertaking. But it is very evident that they cannot lead the Movement to success without the hearty co-operation of the local church leaders. Too often in any general movement of this sort there is a tendency on the part of local leaders to stand back and look on. Some even hold themselves aloof and resent any suggestions as to plans and methods for increasing the efficiency of the local and general work of the church. Some ignore all appeals for statistical and other reports and seem to regard with indifference the most earnest pleas for united effort along a particular line. Such was occasionally found to be the case during our Four Year Program effort. But surely we have learned much as to the value of united-efforts and the necessity of co-operation in such efforts. We have learned something of the importance of co-operation to the success of our Home Mission, Foreign Mission, College, Publishing and Benevolent interests; we have come to realize that if the Brethren church would do anything worth while along any of these lines, it is important that every pastor of every church shall get back of the movement with all his influence and power. And in this new Movement no one should stand apart and speculate as to what it may accomplish, but every one should identify himself with it, give it his most enthusiastic co-operation and do everything in his power to bring about the largest measure of success that glory may redound to the name of Christ.

Not only should every church with its leaders co-operate with the Movement, but every member of every church should be in it. The same measure of loyalty that is desired by the national leaders from the local leaders should also be exemplified by every Brethren member towards their congregational leaders. Unless the message and task of our Bicentenary Movement can be carried down to the last member of the last church and there receive intelligent response and loyal support, it cannot result in the great good that is hoped from it. The success of the Movement will be determined by the unanimity of the response given it by the members of every congregation and by what it is able to accomplish for every member and for the souls yet unborn into the Kingdom. Our slogan, at least our aim and ambition with regard to this Movement should be every member of every church in it for all there is in it.

That suggests and leads to the consideration of another essential factor in the success of our Bicentenary Movement, namely, that we shall take seriously the challenge that is thereby thrown out to the churches and to Brethren people everywhere. The program we have set before ourselves is not merely the winning of certain goals and the receiving of honors; it is carrying out the will of God for his church; it is the challenge of the task which he has assigned to us who are members of his body; it is the privilege of working together with God for the realization of that coming Kingdom, for which the Master taught us to pray. It is an organized movement that proposes by co-operation and wise direction of effort to make the church more effective in accomplishing its divinely given task. It is designed to encourage the church to prosecute its mission with greater enthusiasm, aggressiveness and consecration than heretofore. All organizations and plans are to be counted as mere machinery, important as means to the accomplishment of the church's task, but not regarded as ends in themselves. The great aim is the high commission of the Church of Jesus Christ, and this deserves to be taken seriously by every congregation and individual that presumes to wear the name Brethren and professes to be a member of that great body of believers of which Christ is the Head.

There is no time for aloofness and indifference, but for co-operation and vital interest. It is no time for dallying and half-heartedness, but for prompt and enthusiastic endeavor. It is no time for the people to be at ease in Zion, or for unwarranted insistence upon one's favorite methods or theories; it is rather a time for complete consecration to our common task and for a whole-hearted entrance into a fellowship with the Master's passion for the saving of a lost world, where the souls of men are distressed and scattered as sheep having no shepherd.

During the late terrible war when the Germans were pressing farther and farther into French territory and devastating all they possessed, a most gifted and eloquent professor was lecturing in a certain French university where there was a group of students,—quite young—who had not yet gone to the front. One day he closed his books and declared he would not stand before them again until his country was free. He left their midst to join the army and face the enemy as a common soldier. Whatever gifts he had, he put aside; he sacrificed them for the sake of the cause so dear to his heart. So Paul, impressed by the needs of men and the greatness of the mission committed to him, said, "I determined not to know anything among you save Jesus Christ, and him crucified." It is consecration of that sort that our task and our times demand of every one who would prove himself true to the name of his adoption—Christian—and prove himself a worthy member of the blessed fraternity, called Brethren.

EDITORIAL REVIEW

Brother Wm. H. Miller states that he has accepted a position as teacher in the high school at Oak Hill, West Virginia, and is serving the church only half time until some one else can be secured.

Brother C. C. Grisso reports that he has closed his work at North Liberty and Tiosa, Indiana, and taken up the work at La Paz. He is now engaged in one of a series of evangelistic campaigns for which he is scheduled.

Sister F. G. Peters, our correspondent of the Lanark, Illinois, church, writes enthusiastically concerning the progress of the Kingdom's interests at that place under the able leadership of Brother B. T. Burnworth.

Another letter comes to us from little Marguerite Gribble, written by her mother, Dr. Gribble, while little Marguerite lies ill. The faith expressed in God's healing power impresses us; the description of the celebration of the French "Fourth" of July interests us; and the hopes of the arrival of a party, one of whom God has already taken home saddens us. But there is one short sentence which we imagine tells more than any other part of the letter. It speaks of the work as being "very quiet, very tedious, and very monotonous."

We wonder if this does not reveal to us the severest trial this little group must undergo? May we not pray with them that God may open up the way for them?

A very successful evangelistic campaign was held by Brother Bell at Cerro Gordo, Illinois, immediately following Conference. Besides the good number of confessions which resulted, the entire church and its auxiliaries seem to have been stirred to new life. The report is made by Sister Helena Bogue.

One only needs to read the report from La Verne, California to be convinced of the fact that the people of that church are thoroughly alive and awake to the various interests of the Lord's work and the many opportunities of service. If every congregation were as active as this one the church would go forward more rapidly than it does.

Brother Boardman is leading the Hudson church forward in a splendid manner and is encouraging them to adapt a very all-inclusive type of loyalty. The College and the Publishing House is placed on their annual budget for their rightful portion of benevolences. This is the proper thing to do and we congratulate Brother Boardman for his thoughtfulness.

Brother Gearhart was in our office a few days ago and said in view of the fact that the special Home Mission number of The Evangelist to be published November 17, would not reach all parts of the brotherhood before Sunday, November 21, that he would suggest, where convenient, that the offering be lifted on the last Sunday in the month.

The McLouth, Kansas, people have experienced a great spiritual refreshing under the leadership of Brethren Coleman and A. T. Ronk. It was a union meeting and the fact that these men were selected by others than the Brethren pastor is a compliment to these brethren. We dare say that Brother Howell had no small part in inaugurating this evangelistic movement and in awakening the community spiritually.

Brother Bame "flashes" more news concerning his evangelistic travels. His last trip brought him through Ashland where the Ohio conference was in session and which had the benefit of several addresses from him. While here aside from his address to the students at chapel hour, he presented the the Bicentenary Movement in the morning and spoke with his characteristic effectiveness on evangelism in the evening of the same day. The conference greatly enjoyed his presence and service.

The Elkhart, Indiana, people appreciated the worth of their pastor, Brother H. H. Wolford, who served them with such aggressive leadership for seven and one-half years, but when the College called him to a position of greater service they were willing to submit to what seemed to be God's leading and now God has supplied them with another splendid leader in the person of Brother Bryan Stoffer whom we predict will prove to be a worthy successor to Brother Wolford.

Are you planning and praying concerning your share in the General Home Mission offering that is to be taken at Thanksgiving time? Your church will doubtless lift the offering either the Sunday preceding or the Sunday following Thanksgiving day. Remember the goal—$1.00 per member—and take into account the fact that some will not be able or willing to make an offering of $1.00, and if we are to reach an average of $1.00 per member it will be necessary for some to give much more.

In our editorial note preceding the letter of Brother Yoder to Brother Gearhart on mission page, we suggested the writing of letters by churches and individuals to our missionaries in South America, and also to those in Africa. We wish here to urge the matter upon the attention of our people generally. If you write immediately to Africa, your letter will likely be late for Christmas, but better late than never. But if you get a letter off to our missionaries in South America by the middle of November it will likely reach them by Christmas. Send each one a Christmas letter, but send your gifts of money to the Foreign Missionary Society.

THE BRETHREN BICENTENARY MOVEMENT PAGE

1723 - - - - - - 1923

Dr. Charles A. Bame, Editor

How Do You Feel About It?

I am asking this question in all seriousness. I'd like to have a few letters from friends and foes of the Movement as to how they feel towards the Movement and the work so far attempted. You know that there is nothing much more terrible than silence. I may go on saying things on this page for a year and never have any way of knowing if I am hitting the mark. If you were hunting and shooting all day and never picking off any game, how would you feel? You want to know if you are getting the game. So do I! Yes, I know all the conferences, to this time, have passed resolutions of some kind and appointed officers but there are a lot of people who think, and yet do not get a look in at the conferences.

What Do I?

Well, I guess you know that I feel that this Movement is both important and necessary; if it is needed, I can say with equal candor, it is compulsory. If you do not sense the importance of it, let me pass on the words that will go on the charts you will get to adorn your church walls. I put them down some time ago and was astonished how we had taxed the English language to describe the Movement. Here they are: FAMILY ALTARS, DOCTRINE, CHURCH ATTENDANCE; STUDENTS, BIBLE STUDY, ENDOWMENT; RECRUITS, TITHERS', BUDGET; ANNUAL EVANGELISTIC CAMPAIGN; SUPPORT, LOYALTY, EXPANSION; MISSIONS, CONSERVATION, FRATERNITY; MINISTERS, MISSIONARIES, BRETHREN HOME. What an array of great words and they are all needed to describe the Movement! If an attempt to put all these words into reality and meaning in 23,000 lives is not worth while, then what is? If it is, then let us do it and do it with all our might. That is what we need to do.

Again

Besides, we have our part to do. What a few men did in the generation past, we are enjoying. Many of us had a small part in it—very small. What shall we leave as our mark for the next generation to laud and commemorate? What would we do better than to just endow and equip and renew and revive as this Movement plans, the whole church? It is our task, under God. The times demand that we shall not enter on an extensive building campaign among the churches. We shall do with what we have hoping that soon, there will be a better time for that kind of sacrifice when it will count for more than it can, now. So, this is extensive and intensive.

Besides

Then there is another angle. It is the appeal to make worthwhile the sacrifice of those who made them for us. Your fathers and grandfathers and further back, the founders of the church made their contribution for the sake of conscience. It will go far to naught unless we match that sacrifice with another. We shall all need to go back to the beginning and live over the life of he founders, in order to properly sense the meaning of this program. Go back to Germany, Holland and even to the early settlements of this country and see, once more, what they did to give us a Brethren church with "The Bible and Nothing but the Bible" slogan, and then say, "Who will pass this on if we do not?" Somebody must or it will be lost. "Who will go for us," they cry from their graves. Who will make lasting our devotion to the truth? Who? Who?

The Crux of It

And, so, here is the crux of the thing. Unless we can write into this generation of Brethren, the feelings and the sacrifice of the founders of it, we shall fail. Brethrenism is still small; insufficient for the world task, it must intensify and grow at the same time and all calls for what made it in the beginning, devotion to the truth. We can not grow by the same methods as made us. Emigration is too criss-cross, now. Our planning must be definite and our giving commensurate. While young men and women offer themselves for service, Brethren of means must offer the money or we shall fail as in too many cases we have failed in times past.

Recruits Plus Dollars

For instance: Suppose that last Sunday, there were 25 young people all over this land of ours that offered themselves for definite service for the church either as minister or missionary. Suppose, too—for most of them come from homes of poverty,—that all but five of them are too poor to go to make the preparation for their chosen work. Suppose, too, that we just delay the possibility of their doing the things we have preached to them while we preached that the members of the church tithe. How shall we encourage them? When will they get ready to do the thing they set out to do? PERHAPS NEVER. IT HAS TOO OFTEN HAPPENED THAT THEY COULD NOT GO because they could not prepare.

That's How I Feel

Will you tell me how you feel? May I not expect a word from you about it all? Have you done all you feel you ought and shall wish you had when you stand before the Great Judge? Tell me; and if you have not, will you not yet make the amends you can while it is yet day with you?

Chisel in hand, stood a sculptor boy,
　With his marble block before him;
And his face lit up with a smile of joy
　As an angel dream passed o'er him.
He carved that dream on the yielding stone
　With many a sharp incision
In heaven's own light the sculptor shone
　He had caught an angel vision.

Sculptors of life are we as we stand
　With our lives uncarved before us
Waiting the hour when, at God's command
　Our life dream passes o'er us
Let us carve it then, on the yielding stone
　With many a sharp incision
Its heavenly beauty shall be our own
　Our lives that angel vision.

　　　　　　　　　　　　　　BAME.

Programs for Every Church

(From the Secretary-Treasurer of the Movement).

As soon as the work could be done after General Conference, a lot of leaflets were prepared giving the new Brethren Bicentenary Movement program in convenient form. These are attractively printed in two colors for general distribution, especially to all pastors, officers, Sunday school superintendents, teachers, and workers. Supplies of these programs were sent to the different state and district conferences which have already met, with the hope of getting them carried into every congregation. The churches of Ohio will be supplied at their state conference. In districts where conferences will not be held until next year, a number of these handy programs have been mailed direct to the pastors for distribution in the various congregations. If your pastor has not yet distributed these in his congregation, ask him about it.

An effort has been made to get these programs into every church in the brotherhood, in order that all leaders and workers may become thoroughly familiar with it and be able to intelligently and effectively help to promote its every activity. If there are churches which were not represented by delegates in state and district conferences already held, or, for any other reason are not yet supplied, the writer will be glad to mail programs to all such upon receipt of request either from pastors, members of congregations, or state and district secretaries.

Every member of the Brethren church ought to know what the program of the Bicentenary Movement is in order that he or she can rightly pray and work for its largest success. A supply of programs is available, and, as stated, they will be gladly furnished upon request to the undersigned.

MILES J. SNYDER, Milledgeville, Illinois.

Our New Program

(From the Director of Spiritual Life)

In the Bicentenary Movement, it is planned to touch the spiritual life of the membership. One of the objectives set is "Continued zeal in heralding doctrinal truth in pulpit and Bible conferences." Perhaps a good beginning would be to use the following subjects in a series of sermons. If this first application is thought too drastic in its entirety, select what you can use.

The New Testament Church and Its Creed.
The New Testament Church and Its Terms of Admission.
The New Testament Church and Its Organization.
The New Testament Church and Its Form of Baptism.
The New Testament Church and Its Form of Communion.

The New Testament Church and the Holy Spirit.
The New Testament Church and Its Standard of Prayer-life.
The New Testament Church and Its Missionary Supervision.

It is planned to have a list of subjects every three months. A few published reports from congregations selected at random will reveal how generally the subjects are being used.

In the meantime let every pastor get ready to report on how many of his homes have some form of daily prayer.
G. W. RENCH.

Evangelistic Flashes

(From the Director of Evangelism)

Harvest season is here. A number of our evangelists are in the field. Some of the churches have already had their meetings, most of them that have not, have made arrangements. How about your church? Do not let the year roll around without an Evangelistic Campaign.

Important to Churches

Here are the names and addresses of men who have offered their services for one or more meetings:

C. C. Grisso, North Liberty, Indiana.
C. A. Stewart, Loree, Indiana.
C. E. Kolb, Winona Lake, Indiana.
H. E. Eppley, Eaton, Indiana.
W. R. Deeter, Oakville, Indiana.

Brethren Coleman and Ronk, also Miss Aboud are giving full time this year and if their dates are not all taken, are open for more work.

If there are any other men that desire to give some of their time to holding one or more meetings, address me, 61 Highland Avenue, Uniontown, Pennsylvania, until October 30th.
W. S. BELL.

GENERAL ARTICLES

Prayer and the Anointing with Oil for the Sick.   By Alva J. McClain

God is indeed interested in the souls of his people but his interest does not by any means end there. He is also interested in their bodies. He has saved the soul of the believer, and the promise is that he will also save the body at the coming of Christ. In the case of sin God has made gracious provision for the restoration of the soul. Likewise, in the case of sickness he has made gracious provision for the restoration of the body.

James 5:14-15 lays down very explicit direction for the believer to follow in the case of sickness,—"Is any among you sick? Let him call for the elders of the church; and let them pray over him, anointing him with oil in the name of the Lord; and the prayer of faith shall save him that is sick, and the Lord shall raise him up; and if he have committed sins, it shall be forgiven him" (R. V.)

I. HOW SOME HANDLE THIS PASSAGE

1. The Roman Catholic church makes it teach a sacrament which they call Extreme Unction. When a member of that church is expected to die, the priest anoints with consecrated oil upon the supposition that by this act the dying sinner is cleansed from the last stains of sin. In short the Roman church uses the rite taught in this passage for the purpose of getting men ready for death! But the most superficial reading of James 5, shows that the rite was intended to be used for the very opposite purpose! It was to be used in the restoration of health and strength.

2. Most Protestants simply ignore the passage. The

most fitting answer to this attitude is that no passage of God's Word is to be ignored.

3. Another class admit that the early church was accustomed to anoint the sick with oil but say that this was in the days when the miraculous gift of healing was yet present in the church. They argue that since this gift has ceased, it is also proper to drop the anointing service which was used in connection with its exercise. To this it may be answered that even if it be true that the miraculous gift of healing is no longer present in the church, still we are absolutely certain that God heals today in answer to prayer. And James states that the anointing is to accompany prayer for the sick, not the exercise of a miraculous gift of healing. The same argument that would do away with anointing would also do away with prayer for the sick.

4. Still another small class of Christians claim that the book of James was not written to the church of this present age. They say this is plain from the address which reads, "To the twelve tribes which are scattered abroad." But such an argument proves too much. According to such argument Hebrews is not for the church, neither the epistles of Peter. The proof that James was writing to believers of this age may be found in 2:1, where the recipients of the letter are addressed as "My brethren," who "hold the faith of our Lord Jesus Christ, the Lord of glory." This is the faith of the church. Besides it is true that all believers are accustomed to apply certain passages from this book to

themselves (cp. 1:12, 17, 18; 5:8). If these belong to the church, why not 5:14?

5. Our own position is that this passage of Scripture is given to us who "hold the faith of the Lord Jesus Christ, the Lord of glory," and therefore should be obeyed literally.

II. SEVERAL OBSERVATIONS ON THE PASSAGE

1. The primary and fundamental thing set forth in James 5:14 is prayer for the sick, not the anointing with oil. The anointing is secondary. The elders are to "pray over the sick, anointing him." They are not directed to "anoint the sick, praying for him." It is to be feared that some have exalted the "anointing" above the "prayer." We have chosen to speak of this service as "The anointing of the sick with oil" when we should have named it "Prayer and Anointing with Oil for the Sick." The result of placing the emphasis upon the "anointing" instead of upon the "prayer" has led some to imagine that the "anointing" saves, whereas the passage plainly declares that "the prayer of faith shall save the sick." And the Spirit of God is careful to guard even this statement from misconception by going on to say that it is "the Lord" who raises up the sick. There is no actual efficacy in prayer. The efficacy comes from the "Lord" to whom prayer is addressed. Though it is proper for us to say that prayer accomplishes things, we must bear in mind that it is after all not prayer, but God who "changes things." Some modern theories of prayer have stumbled sadly at this point, making it almost wholly subjective.

2. The first step in the anointing service is to be taken by the one who is sick, not by the elders of the church. "Is any among you sick? Let him call for the elders." The elders are not to take the initiative for a very good reason. God does not want preachers running around anointing indiscriminately people who may not believe the Word of God. Certainly the pastor of a church should teach his people what to do in case of sickness, but when sickness comes the one sick must take the first step in calling for the elders. If a sick believer calls on the elders of the church for prayer and anointing with oil in the name of the Lord, it is evidence that such a one has faith in the promises of God. And such faith is always the essential prerequisite for healing.

3. The calling for the elders of the church in the case of sickness is not something left to our own judgment and discretion. It is a definite command. How much better it would be for all concerned, if Christians obeyed this command. Sometimes it happens that a member of the church falls sick and the pastor for some reason fails to hear of it. In the meantime the sick member is wondering why he doesn't call and unfortunately is sometimes terribly offended because he didn't call. In a church where the pastor has taught his people what to do in case of sickness, they have no one but themselves to blame if they do not receive attention. "Let him call for the elders of the church." I believe this is a wise provision. I would a thousand times rather visit the sick and pray for them when I am called for that purpose than to go when I am not called for. Sad to say, some professing Christians don't like to be bothered, and some don't like to be prayed for unless they are about to die. When a Christian sends word for me to come and pray for his healing, I know that I am really wanted, and also that there is in that person faith that God heals in answer to prayer. The pastor must be ready day or night to answer a call for prayer, but in all ordinary cases the sick must do the calling. It is a command.

4. Nor should the calling for the elders be left as a last desperate resort. It should be the first resort if we would honor God. Too often the believer tries every doctor, all available remedies, and then when all human hope has been given up the elders are called for. This is not only dishonoring to God, but it relegates the "anointing to a place which is little higher than the "Extreme Unction" of the Roman church. I am sorry to say that in some places where this service is observed, it has come to mean little more than this. To say that a certain person has been

"anointed" is the same as saying that all hope for recovery has been abandoned and death is expected.

5. The "calling for the elders" in the case of sickness does not at all preclude the calling of a doctor. Some have taught otherwise. But they forget that God heals in his own way. All healing is of God, and it has been shown abundantly that God does use the skill of physicians and surgeons in healing. No one has ever yet produced one solitary passage of Scripture which forbids the calling of a doctor in the case of sickness, or the use of ordinary remedies. On the contrary God has blessed in a marvelous way godly physicians who have gone to the foreign fields as medical missionaries. By ministering to the body they have gained thousands of opportunities to minister to the soul. This idea that we cannot be trusting God if we call in a physician is mere foolishness. It is true that "my God shall supply all your need according to his riches in glory by Christ Jesus." We believe it absolutely. We have put it to the test. But we do not therefore sit down and do nothing, expecting God to put bread into our mouths. Likewise it is true that God "healeth all our diseases." But to refuse to use such means as we have in combatting disease is not faith but presumption. It savors of the ancient suggestion, "Cast thyself down, for it is written, he shall give his angels charge concerning thee." The answer is, "Again it is written, thou shalt not tempt the Lord thy God." Neither foolhardiness nor laziness is encouraged by the Word of God.

6. If our churches expect and desire their members to follow literally the directions of James 5:14-15, then we must make it possible for them to do so. How can the members of a church call for the elders of the church when that church has only one elder? In the Apostolic age every local church had a plurality of elders (Acts 14:23). I hope I shall not be misunderstood on this point. The office of these elders is purely local. They need not be preachers or pastors, but rather spiritually minded laymen who know the Word of God and believe in prayer, who will stand ready to assist the pastor in just such matters as the one under discussion.

7. We should note also that this anointing service is in no case for unbelievers. "Is any sick among you?" plainly limits it to believers. This shows that the anointing with oil is not connected with the miraculous gift of healing, for the gift of healing was exercised in the case of all who came for healing (Acts 5:16). The anointing service is no more for the unbeliever than is baptism or the communion.

III. THE PROMISE ATTACHED TO JAMES 5:14-15

This promise is unconditional. There are no strings attached. "The prayer of faith shall save him that is sick." But some one may say, "Why then are not all healed who are prayed for in connection with the "anointing?" It is a legitimate question and the answer is that not every prayer is "the prayer of faith."

What is the "prayer of faith" in this instance? May I make three statements before attempting a definition? (1) Prayer must be according to the will of God or it cannot be answered. "If we ask anything according to his will he heareth us" (1 John 5:14). (2) Faith is assurance of things hoped for" (Heb. 11:1 R. V.). (3) Faith is the gift of God (Eph. 2:8). Combining these three statements we may define "the prayer of faith" as "prayer for the sick accompanied by a God-given assurance that it is the will of God to heal the one prayed for."

Now the results prove conclusively that not all prayer for the sick is the "prayer of faith." "The prayer of faith shall save him that is sick," but not all prayed for are healed. Therefore it is evident that we do not always pray "the prayer of faith."

Is it our fault if we do not pray the "prayer of faith?" It may be, but not necessarily. We do know that it is not always the will of God to heal the Christian (See Heb. 12:5-11). That the "chastening" spoken of in this passage refers to "bodily sickness" primarily may be seen by comparing 1 Corinthians 11:29-32 where the same word is used to explain what it was that caused the "weak and sickly" condition of some Corinthian believers. Also the death of a few. It is also worthy of notice that Hebrews 12:5, "despise not thou the chastening of the Lord," is taken bodily from Job 5:17 where the context plainly shows the reference is to Job's physical condition. Again, Paul is a concrete illustration that it is not always the will of God to heal entirely one of his children. Paul was given "a thorn in the flesh" and when he besought the Lord thrice to remove it, was told that he must endure it, as God's "grace was sufficient" to sustain him. Whatever the precise nature of "thorn" was, only the most desperate exegesis can make it mean anything else than physical infirmity. In fact Paul so speaks of it in Galatians 4:13. Nothing is more certain from the Word of God and also from the experience of God's choicest saints than it is sometimes the will of God for them to "suffer" for a reason.

Now it is certain that, if it was not the will of God to heal one of his children, he would not give any one the confident "assurance" that he would heal in that case. And if God withholds such assurance it would be impossible to pray "the prayer of faith." I fully realize some will argue that it is always the will of God to heal, and therefore we are always responsible to pray the "prayer of faith." But as shown above such a position cannot be sustained from the Scriptures. The fact that believers die reveals the fallacy of that argument.

Do we always know certainly whether or not we are praying "the prayer of faith"? Some affirm that they do, but I doubt it. I do know that there are times when we have an overwhelming conviction that God is going to answer our prayer for the sick. But I know also that at other times such a conviction is not present, and yet our prayer is answered just as faithfully. Human feelings cannot determine such things infallibly. If we were always empty "vessels" our convictions might always be trusted to register accurately the will of God. But who is there that claims to be always such a vessel?

Should we pray for the sick, anointing them with oil, when we do not have the absolute assurance that it is the will of God to heal the one prayed for? YES. The command is, "let the elders pray over him, anointing him with

oil." We are responsible to obey. The result is in the hands of God. It is worthy of note here that God does not command us to pray "the prayer of faith." He knows that sometimes it would be impossible. We are to pray for the sick. Our prayer may be the prayer of faith, or it may not be. The result will determine that.

In every case we should follow the example of our Lord Jesus Christ, who, when he prayed for deliverance in Gethsemane, said, "Nevertheless Father, not my will but thine be done." This is the highest reach of faith. Mortal man can ascend no higher than to say with Job, "Though he slay me, yet will I trust him." If we pray this way, we shall always be praying in faith, though our prayer may not always be "the prayer of faith" spoken of by James.

IV. SIN AND SICKNESS

James 5:14-15 makes gracious provision for the forgiveness of sin in connection with the healing of the body. This presupposes what other Scriptures plainly teach—that sickness may be the chastening of our Father on account of some sin to which we are clinging. If such be the case there is need for confession and forgiveness. But mark the "IF" "IF he have committed sins." Not all sickness is chastening for sin (John 9:2-3). Also compare the case of Job whom God designates a "perfect" man in his sight. By the form of his statement, James repudiates the doctrine that sickness is invariably the evidence of unconfessed sin.

V. THE SYMBOLISM OF THE ANOINTING

Anointing with oil sets forth a great truth of the Scriptures. Oil is a type or symbol of the Holy Spirit. Now it is a remarkable fact that of the three Persons in the Godhead, the Holy Spirit is the one whose blessed work it is to "give life to these mortal bodies" (Rom. 8:11).

I believe that it is highly important that members of the church should take advantage of the provision God has made for the healing of their diseases and infirmities. Definite prayer for the sick, with anointing, has been neglected too long. The unfortunate result is that false cults and "isms" have been given an opportunity to make their appeal on the ground of healing the body. Eddyism can make no converts from the church in which the "whole counsel of God" is faithfully taught.

Philadelphia, Pennsylvania.

First Thanksgiving Offering for Home Missions.   By G. C. Carpenter

The coming Thanksgiving offering for Home Missions will be the first in our Bicentenary Three Year Movement and will be an indicator concerning the faith of the church in this new program. The best days of the church are at hand if opportunity is grasped. The biggest things in the history of the church can be done in these three years if every member in the whole brotherhood will rally to the Lord's call and say, Here am I, Lord, you can count on me. The time has come for

Moving Mountains

Our General Missionary Secretary has outlined the work of the Home Mission Board, giving the budget and the list of places being helped. The board is the created servant of the church and is doing conscientious service in building up the home base to the end that the Brethren church may help in a large way to give a whole Gospel to a whole world. He has given you the goal set by Conference, namely, one dollar per member for every church. This is to cover all the home mission activities. Each church will include in the dollar per member apportionment the amount paid to the support of Kentucky missions outside of the White Gift offerings, only a minor portion of which goes to Kentucky missions. The goal is not too high if the Brethren church wants to obey a whole Gospel and do big things for the Lord. The goal is not too high if the pastors will lead their churches up the hill to its attainment. The goal is too high for church members who want to continue robbing the Lord and play

Penny-purse

It is a hopeful sign that the Brethren church is paying to the Lord more and more of what he says is his own and is to be returned to him as rental by his stewards. Nothing will so increase the spiritual power of the church and provide life-work recruits so quickly as the consecration of the material wealth in the hands of the members of the church. It is a source of joy that the Brethren church is getting more and more disgusted with the missionary penny-purse, and is becoming less and less afraid of the

Dollar-Purse

Special recognition will be given by our secretary through the Evangelist and at next General Conference to the churches reaching the dollar-per-member goal by the end of the year. The best way is to reach it at Thanksgiving time and then rejoice over the victory the rest of the year. Give liberally and cheerfully and your board will do its best to use the funds to bring the largest and best results. The board welcomes also any information or suggestions that will increase the efficiency of the mission work.

Peru, Indiana.

The events of life are a sacred text on which the mind may ponder and comment. How can we fail to follow with attention and respect the chain of circumstances which has accomplished a thought of God?—Madame Swetchine.

OUR CONFERENCE PLATFORM

How Can the Laymen Help the Pastor in the Church Service? H. F. E. O'Neill

May I say in the beginning, that I was thinking mostly in terms of men helping the pastor, but what I shall have to say of men is equally true of the women in most cases.

I am sorry Brother Roscoe could not be here to present this subject but in his absence and on short notice, I will do the best I can. I have consulted a number of pastors and laymen as well as my own experience in the matter and the following are the suggested ways that the laymen and women can help the pastor in the church service:—

Be Regular in Your Attendance

If we went to work as irregularly as we go to church, most of us would not have our positions very long, and if the Lord dealt with us as we FREQUENTLY deal with him, especially in our church attendance, most of us would not be here to tell the story, for it would be so long between "drinks", (if he had to be guided by the number of times or regularity with which we attended church) that he would frequently forget that we existed. I believe the Lord's business requires regularity as well as haste.

Be On Time

When you plan a trip, you arrive at the station on time to get your train, and you give yourself sufficient time to buy a ticket and make whatever other arrangements are necessary. If you find your time is getting short, you will speed up your car or drive the horse a little faster or run two or three blocks in order to be in time for your train. Why not apply the same principles to the attendance at the church service. If you want to know how the preacher feels to have the congregation coming straggling in throughout the whole service (and some of them are late so many times that the preacher can tell what time it is without looking at the clock) you should have the experience of being allowed to sit in church from five minutes to one-half hour and wait on the preacher or the choir. Then you will have some idea of how the preacher feels to have you late.

Keep Awake

Those of you who have had any experience in public speaking know that it is hard enough to speak to a large attentive audience and it is still harder to speak to empty pews and it is hard in the superlative degree to speak to an audience that is asleep. To admit to this, of course, is a reflection on the speaker and I would not expect you to make this admission regarding your own experience, but it is amusing to say the least (as most preachers will acknowledge) to have some person who has slept comfortably through most of the service come up at the close of it and tell you how good your sermon was and how much he enjoyed it.

Be Attentive and Receptive

There is more to church attendance than simply keeping awake during the sermon. Most ministers have studied psychology enough and have enough experience in public speaking to know when their audience is simply hearing and a the same time their minds are at a picnic, or an auto mobile ride, or in their office, or making a new dress, or cooking dinner or whether they are really attentive and receptive to the truths the preacher is presenting. This is also determined by the result in the lives of the parishioners. Most preachers can emphatically quote with considerable feeling "Be ye not hearers only but doers of the word."

Pray While He Preaches

While it is not possible to successfully have your mind centered on the things suggested in the paragraph above and listen attentively to the sermon at the same time, it is possible to be in the spirit of prayer and to hold up his arms by prayer like holy men of old did while Moses was talking to God. Pray first that his message may deepen your own conversion and spiritual life and that it may quicken other Christian men and women in the audience, and that it may lead to the conviction of and conversion from sin of those who have not accepted him as their Savior.

Respect for God, His House and His Word

Your attitude of respect for holy things while in God's house will have a decided influence over non-Christians and especially young people. It is not a place for public conversations and gossip but a place for reverence and prayer. "My house shall be called a house of prayer."

By our very posture and position and the nodding of the head or an occasional amen or an assent to what he is saying in some manner that will be recognized by him and will be an inspiration to him.

Conduct Occasional Services

Either as an individual or as groups, such as Sunday schools, Christian Endeavor, Women's Missionary Society, Sunday school classes, etc. Both the preacher and the public will enjoy these innovations in a regular program.

Spend part of your week days visiting and inviting strangers and non-church going people to the service. Be one of a committee to welcome them when they come and to invite them back.

Act as Invitation, Welcome and Reception Committee

Make helpful suggestions of changes from the old routine, and of new things, a service which most preachers will gladly welcome.

Be Spirit Filled and Not a Fault Finder

To be filled with the spirit means that we shall not only strive to attain to the highest realm ourselves but out of our own lives shall flow rivers of living water that shall touch the lives of those with whom we come in contact and we will not be near so apt to find fault with what the preacher says and how he says it, the tone of his voice, his manner of delivery, or how he and the congregation are dressed and other faults that we are so prone to find.

This does not mean that we should not be constructive critics. If we have a suggestion to make, though it may eliminate a present practice or custom of the minister, if what we suggest is better, and if we suggest it in the right spirit, it will be gladly received by a majority of the preachers.

ACTING and Securing others to Act as Ushers

It is very embarrassing to go into a strange church and have to wander around like a blind dog in high oats to find a seat. You are all aware that the regular attendants at church have regular places to sit and naturally they feel most at home in those pews. Strangers are just as naturally at sea to know where to sit, for they recognize that regular attendants have regular pews. And may I suggest that you should find a stranger in your pew, even if you don't feel happy about it, don't be discourteous and unChristian enough to show your feelings by your scowling looks at the stranger who happens to be in your pew.

Volunteer Your Service if You Can Sing or Play an instrument or both.

Do not think because you cannot sing like Caruso or cannot play like Mendelssohn that you cannot be of any help in the church service. One of the first qualifications of a good musician is willingness, and no person is much of a success without it.

Be Ready and Willing to Serve in Any Capacity that the Pastor May Suggest

Last, But Not Least, Have a Passion for Souls

Do personal work. You will recall that Jesus did not get the disciples by public addresses but he selected them by individual work. If you want fruit that lasts longest and keeps best, you select what has been hand picked. The same principle is true of Christian work. While evangelistic services and appeals to large crowds are necessary, the results should not be left entirely to this method, but we as Christian people, should prepare ourselves by prayer, study and practice for this the most remunerative work for both here and hereafter that we can do. It will be a great consolation when we reach the other shore to meet those whom we have personally led to accept Jesus Christ as their Savior. On the other hand, it will be an equally great embarrassment to be in the position which is expressed by the poet in that song:

"Must I go, and empty handed,
    Thus my dear Redeemer meet,
Not one soul with which to greet him,
    Lay no trophy at his feet?"

Pittsburgh, Pennsylvania.

OUR DEVOTIONAL

Our New Life in Christ
By Mrs. Rhetta O'Rourke

If ye then be risen with Christ, seek those things which are above, where Christ sitteth on the right hand of God. Set your affection on things above, not on things on the earth. For ye are dead and your life is hid with Christ in God. For when ye were servants of sinf ye were free from righteousness, what fruit had ye them in those things whereof ye are now ashamed? For the end of those things is death. But now being made free from sin and become servants of God, ye have your fruit unto holiness and the end everlasting life. For the wages of sin is death but the gift of God is eternal life through Jesus Christ our Lord.

OUR MEDITATION

Our life in Christ is a NEW life with new thoughts and new aims and a new standard of values. We learn to value the things of this world in proportion to their relation to the things of the next world. Everything with which we come in contact is divided into two classes, the transient and the eternal, and its value determined accordingly. Thus gradually our mind is changed, things that were of first importance in the old life fade into the background and become mere casualties, while many things that once seemed of little import become necessary to our existence. Thus we pass from death to life, while we are yet in the flesh, letting go the things of this world, the transients, and clinging to the things above that are eternal.

Having this new view of life the people round about us appeal to us no longer merely as associates who have characteristics which we like or dislike, but as souls that may be saved or lost,—souls upon whom our daily lives must and will have an influence.

As humiliation and its attendant regrets is often mistaken for repentance, so the change of mind is sometimes confused with the change of heart of which it is but the beginning. A change of heart is a change of mind became habitual, that has reached the root and core of the soul life and grounded it in righteousness. It is a kind of spiritual instinct that unerringly guides the thoughts and words and actions and keeps them under divine control. Many believers never reach this state. Too many are content with knowing how to do right, without actually doing it. Having a knowledge of truth but never coming to the point of spiritual understanding. Spiritual understanding is a knowledge of the blessedness of obedience gained from actual experience.

Our life in Christ is a free life. "Ye shall know the truth and the truth shall make you free." Free from what? From sin and death. But the truth alone can not make us free, the very fact that truth exists does not free us. We must come to a knowledge of the truth before we can be free. Jesus said, "I am the truth," so to know the truth means to know the Lord and we know him when we are walking with him down the blazed trail of obedience, sacrifice and kindly deeds. We can be free from sin. Jesus said so. We can not be free from temptation, but we can be free from the desire to yield to temptation, and we can be "more than conquerors through him that loved us."

Our life in Christ is eternal. "If a man die shall he live again?" questioned Job. And centuries after the Man of Galilee flung back the reply, "Whosoever liveth and believeth in me shall never die." But it is not enough to believe in him, we must live in him also; then our life is eternal, because he is eternal. Jesus brought to this world a new concept of both death and life. What to Job was death became through Jesus not death, but life, not the end, but the beginning, not a valley to tread in fear but a hilltop to gain with rejoicing.

But our life is not in Christ unless it is new. Vows and promises do not change us unless step by step and day by day we keep gaining in righteousness and losing in worldliness. If our lives are no different from those around us who do not confess Christ as their Savior, then they are not new; we are living the same old lives; we have not changed. It is only through pure and holy living that we get in touch with the Eternal. We have not put on Christ until we have put on his righteousness and laid aside our own worldliness.

OUR PRAYER

Our Father in heaven, we thank thee for the comfort and peace of the new life. We thank thee that we are no longer bound by the opinions and customs of the world but are free to serve thee and to grow into a knowledge and understanding of thy mysteries. Help us to hold fast to the ground we have gained and to win the reward at last. May we not falter but press on to the mark of the prize of our high calling, which is perfect righteousness. In Jesus name Amen.

Mattawan, Michigan.

ECONOMIC BENEFITS OF PROHIBITION

A dispatch from New London, Connecticut states that in the five counties of the second congressional district of that state they were going to close four of the county jails and utilize the other one for the entire district.

Dr. W. C. McLennan, special invesigator for the Federal Council of Churches, states that the decrease in the number of inmates in the houses of correction, jails, etc., in New York City under the first year of prohibition, amounted to 39.73%.

Comparing the number of inmates in the Chicago, Illinois, house of correction, for the first three months of 1919 with the first three months of 1920, a decrease of 41.68% is shown.

In the state of Connecticut, approximately twenty-eight million dollars is the amount of increase in the savings bank deposit during the first year under prohibition. The increase was from $387,646,445 to $415,584,817.

The city of Miami, Florida, which has been under prohibition regime for ten years, shows an increase in population during that period of 441%. Property value has gone from $2,000,000 up to $39,000,000 in that period and bank deposits have increased form $1,500,000 to $14,500,000.

Moving picture theatre managers in Baltimore say that patronage has increased 50% since the dry law went into effect.

Send
WHITE GIFT
OFFERINGS to

THE SUNDAY SCHOOL

H. H. WOLFORD
General Secretary-Treasurer
Johnstown, Pennsylvania

The Adult Division.   L. G. Wood, Superintendent Adult Division

As we arrange for greater and more aggressive work in the launching of our Bicentenary Movement, we naturally emphasized religious education. And religious education naturally looks to the church school as its parent and promoter. "Religious Education" is being stressed, in all church conferences and conventions as never before. May we not hope that it is being seriously emphasized also in all Adult departments of our church schools, for it is here the responsibility largely rests. Conferences may plan, conventions and programs may enlist and enthuse, but the work must be done largely by the adults of our local schools. We now have a national board of Religious Education, also district boards and it is urged that each congregation elect its board and in the main, the organized adult classes will furnish these boards. Therefore this most worthy movement is depending upon the local congregation for its final success and achievements.

The primary aim of the Adult Bible class is to study the Bible. This is the first essential. The name "Adult Bible Class" is a misnomer if the class does not put Bible study first. The Bible is the great text book on Religious Education, therefore this division should be admirably fitted for this very important work. The natural result of Bible study is Christian service and personal evangelism, and these will make any class a success in the highest and deepest sense of the word. The following statement from the Teacher and Educator is to the point here—"Out of the swift and mighty tides of progress in religious development of the past century, the Sunday school emerges as the central institution of the churches for the education of the millions in the first truths of the Bible." This program is a challenge to our best preparation and greatest endeavor, let us meet it with determination.

We do not need to transform our organization, either of classes or departments, but strengthen all weak points and extend the registration to the 128 classes that are still reported "Unregistered" and of course bring in some new ones.

Organized Adult classes in a school does not constitute an Adult Department, any more than babies in the homes constitute a Cradle Roll. Each school should have an Adult Division superintendent. This is necessary in order to federate class activities, and unify class aims. Four classes can undertake a larger program than one, yet each class can work out its own ideals.

Above all things keep the organization in touch with the Spiritual Dynamo, by prayer and the study of the Word.

Take time for personal devotions and let the Holy Spirit, with the camera of truth, take a "time exposure" not merely a "snapshot" of your life resources. The Educational program of our great Movement is certainly an appeal worth while; let us move forward and possess the goal. The Adult Division of each school should maintain at least one Bible Training class.

The writer is anxious to be of any assistance possible in a forward march. Denominational seals are waiting to be sent to classes that will organize according to the International Standard. I also keep a supply of International Application blanks. Let me hear of your good work and of your problems, if you have any. I will be glad to hear from district Division superintendents for co-operation and service.

Johnstown, Pennsylvania.

That College Hen

Only a week ago, I told you about an opportunity to help stock up the new poultry house at the college dormitory. The response has been splendid, as I knew it would be. The more I know of the folks in the Brethren church and Sunday schools, the more I am convinced that they are always ready to help in any worthy cause, if that cause is presented to them. Here are the givers to date:

C. A. Stewart, Loree, Ind., ...$ 2.00
Ed. E. Bennett, Ashland, Ohio, ... 1.00
Nettie O'Neill's class at Conemaugh, Pa., ... 5.00
Sunday school, Tiosa, Ind., ... 11.75
Junior and Primary clases at Brighton, Indr., sent by
    Mrs. Sam C. Good, ... 2.00
Ellen Lichty, Milledgeville, Ill., ... 1.00
Rev. L. R. Wilkins, Washington C. H., Ohio, ... 1.25
Carrie McCoy, Washington C. H., Ohio, ... 1.00
Robert Himiller, Washington C. H., Ohio, ... 1.00
Adult Class at Fairview church, ... 10.00
"Rosebuds," Hagerstown, Md., Mrs. C. L. Rohrer,
    teacher, ... 2.00
Mrs. Long, Rittman, Ohio, ... 1.00
Mrs. A. J. Miller, Rittman, Ohio, ... 1.00
Florence Burkholder, Rittman, Ohio, ... 1.00

This makes a total of $41.00 to date, so you see that ten of yours will not be lonesome. Come on, who is next?

Send your gifts to   MARTIN SHIVELY,
                    Ashland College, Ashland, Ohio

J. A. Garber
PRESIDENT

Our Young People at Work

E. A. Rowsey
SECRETARY

Advertising Christian Endeavor

By Earl Huette, Publicity Department

‡-‡-‡

YOUNG PEOPLE!

U. R. introduced to

The MOST Up-todate, LIVE and HELPFUL organization in the church, which will TRAIN young people for
SERVICE FOR THE KING.

C. E.

That is the topic which will be discussed in this column. Get the one next week).

Pennsylvania State Christian Endeavor Work

The State business meeting was held Thursday, October 7th at the State Convention held at Pittsburgh, Pa. The following officers were elected:

President, Eleanor Wilcox, 5145 Dearborn St., Pittsburgh.

Vice President, Mr. Carl Grosse, 2512 Eighth Ave, Altoona.

Sec'y. and Treas., Agnes Simpson, 4094 Howley Ave, Pittsburgh, Pa.

Eastern Field Secretary, Mr. E. E. Fehnel, 920 Washington Street, Allentown, Pa.

Western Field Secretary, Mrs. Carl Grosse, 2512 Eighth Avenue, Altoona, Pa.

At the same session it was voted to set aside fifteen.

minutes, preferably 7:15 to 7:30 P. M. at the Christian Endeavor meetings held on November 14th, for special prayer. The prayers to be first, for the state work; second, for the field secretaries, that they may be consecrated and given God's blessing; third, that the churches which haven't any Christian Endeavor may be led to desire one, and may open

their hearts and their homes to the Christian Endeavor and its interests.

It is suggested that each society appoint the leader now for that meeting and have him, or her, correspond immediately with the state president or secretary.

Yours in Christian Endeavor,
M. ELEANOR WILCOX, President,

Why Christian Endeavor Should Be Interested In Citizenship

By Ellwood A. Rowsey, Associate General Secretary of the Ohio Christian Endeavor Union

(Continued from last week).

Why Citizenship Day?

In 1907, the largest number of immigrants in the history of our country registered their appearance on the shores of America, the number being 1,285,349.

During the year ending July 1, 1920, there came 800,000 friends from afar.

Since July 1, 1920, an average of over 3,000 immigrants are landing daily at our ports, and the year July, 1920 to July, 1921, according to present earmarks, promises to smash all previous records.

About 10 percent of all our population, or 10,145,014 people, live in our three biggest cities.

Sixty-eight of our biggest cities contain over 25 percent of our entire country's population.

Over 53 percent of our population is in communities of 2,500 or over; that is, we are no longer an agricultural, food-producing nation.

The larger percent of American newcomers go into our cities, mines and mills where they are destined to remain, ignorant and un-American.

America's goal today should be more food and fewer strikes, more Americanism in the same amount of Americans; and more of Christ in professing Christians. This means we must distribute our friends over the endless stretches of God's great out-of-doors and present to them the highest ideals of a cross-fertilized race that professes to follow the idealism of a Christ-painted program. This is a vital challenge to America as she bows in worship on Citizenship Day.

Citizen-Shipped

One of the bloody questions that gnashes with flesh-crazed teeth at the cage of American mixups is: "Should we allow the Bolshevists, the Red and the Rogue to ravish their thriving ideals in the gilded garret of American civilization, or should we with Germanic selfishness cork with heartless seals our ears to the bootless cries of a besmirched unfortunate, ignorant and superstitious group of home- and fortune seekers?"

No question in the catalog of entanglements is more difficult to answer and a brief "Yes" or "No" will not add credit to our already negligent ledger.

We dare not profess to nurture a Christian conscience and kick to the scrap heap one good intention that rests beneath the fringes of a sun-freckled or weather-beaten frock, neither dare we overlook the immortal endlessness of the anarchist's soul. Which road leads to a conclusion? We can not hope to even approach a conclusion until we brand most emphatically the good-intentioned foreigner who because of fate is dumped in the cargo with the green-eyed gobblers whose motto is "Self plus selfishness equals success."

The only escape from the catechism seems to be by the establishing of rigid yet attainable means as a minimum measurement, not with the intention of citizens-shipped out of America; not with a hope of citizen-dumped-into America. We must forever cease to manipulate our laws in order that we may have from foreign shores a constant stream of livestock to be butchered by corporations and trusts. As fodder is fed into our silos, so humanity is fed into our factories; and we have not had time to educate them before they were smitten by the icy hand of death.

Our need is not more men; our need is more man.

In the name of a liberty-named republic, may the chariot of time hasten the birth of a new day when America's influx will be a credit to the Stars and Stripes that pronounce liberty, loyalty and life, as she whispers across the dwellings of God's blessed creation.

One Day in Seven

With all our whisperings and murmurings under our breath about "how much we know the theatres in our town are breaking the Sunday closing laws," we are guilty of contributing to the condition ourselves.

Suppose, if you did not on October 17, that on some later date you have a Citizenship Day in Christian Endeavor and that in your meeting you take a census by ballot to find out how many of your members are guilty. By means of a marked "yes" or "no" ballot folded up and dropped, unsigned, by each member into a box, no one need feel embarrassed in being truthful.

Put the question squarely, "Those who even occasionally attend Sunday baseball, Sunday movies, Sunday theatres, or spend much of their time each Sunday motoring during the hours of church services."

If you live in a community where they have NONE, then perhaps the test will reveal nothing unusual, but our observations lead us to believe that the average society will find its percentage of those who will answer "yes" among its members.

But then your work has only begun. Start right at home. To help change conditions you MAY NOT get farther for a beginning place. Look this thing squarely in the eye. Don't you begin to make excuses. If you hedge, nothing is to be gained by following this suggestion.

If you have an average society, drag out your wall pledge from where it has been so long, quietly reposing on the south side of barrels of ashes in the church basement, carefully hidden by the cobwebs that have accumulated during the musty days of summer while your society was on its "vacation."

Talk about circulating petitions! Negative measures won't get you anywhere and you will defeat your own efforts in harping all the time on the "don't" side.

Why not spend a little time in earnest thought preparing a comprehensive "do" program for "Sunday" for your young people. Acquaint folks with what kind of reading, what kind of physical and mental exercise, what social enjoyment one may participate in, what activity one may share, and still be able to say, "This has been a wonderful Lord's Day."

Why not try this for a few weeks, and then some Sunday night let six persons occupy 18 minutes talking, three minutes each, on some such subject as "The Happiest Lord's Day I have Ever Spent."

Any right-minded person will not try to deny the fact that our theaters are swamped these days with trashy stuff that does more in one performance to tear down all that years of ideal home life has built up in thousands of young men and young women, but let's have MORE emphasis on keeping the Christian Endeavor Pledge.

Columbus, Ohio.

SEND ALL MONEY FOR
General Home, Kentucky and
Foreign Missions to

WILLIAM A. GEARHART
General Missionary Secretary
906 Conover Bldg., Dayton, O.

MISSIONS

Another Letter From Africa

Carnot, French Equatorial Africa,
August 9, 1920.

My dear little friends:

It has been seven long weeks since I wrote you. For six weeks of that time we were without any mail. Now two mails have come in only a week apart, and we have been very busy answering our many letters.

Marie and Julia who have had so many serious illnesses have been very well since we wrote you last. But I have had three illnesses, from each of which Jesus is raising me up. Mama is sitting now by my bed writing for me as I am lying ill. In the latter part of June mama and I were very happy to have every one so well. We spent most of our afternoons down in mama's little study. Mama studied, wrote, or translated, and I played with paper dollies, etc. In the mornings we were busy with all our other work, for I help mama whenever I can, and there are many little things that I am learning to do for her.

Very little of interest to you is happening. For our work is very quiet, very tedious and very monotonous in many ways.

We had a very quiet "Fourth." It was Saturday. We are the only Americans here, and no one else was thinking of the American holiday, but all were looking forward to the French holiday the 14th of July, in memory of the falling of the French prisons, the Bastile.

That day came quickly. We all put on our best clothes for it is not often that we have a chance to wear them. All of us at some time during the day went down and called on Mr. Pinerri, the government official here. Mr. Du-Mont was away, and we had only one place, therefore, to call.

Many parades and processions passed during the day. Native chiefs came in from long distances, curiously and wonderfully dressed. Some were riding horses, some were carried in chairs or litters. Each was surrounded by an immense retinue and accompanied by bands with various musical instruments.

Everything was so godless and there was so much foolish pomp and display, that mama says she thought over and over again of Nero and other foolish kings in history, who like these chiefs were wicked and godless. The government official gave away large amounts of money, to the chiefs and their retainers, a custom which is observed here on New Years' Day as well.

In the evening everybody put on all the "la," (cloth), that they possessed and went to the dances. Mama and daddy and I came by one of these dances on our way home from the officials'. Everybody looked so hideous and were making such faces, and twisting their bodies in such odd shapes, that I was afraid and clung to daddy with all my might. Mama said I need not fear for the very wickedest man in all Baya land, loves every true

missionary, and so far from hurting us would protect our lives in every possible way. Mama says it is only themselves they injure in their wicked dances.

The days since the fourteenth have been very much the same as those before, except that Mama and Aunt Toddy are free to go out now, and they had not been out for four and one-half months before. So I have more walks and more pleasure. But mama finds the people are bound by fear even more than they were in January and February. Whenever mama and I go out to preach, we find that the devil is there, too. Mama says she can feel his tremendous power, as he beats the words back into her mouth, or through some of his agents causes her audiences to be scattered. Mama has come home from an afternoon of such preaching so exhausted that she could hardly move, and yet in her heart has been a tremendous joy and a profound peace, and the deep assurance that it will not be long until throughout all this land the Son of God will destroy the works of the devil.

But mama still spends most of her afternoons in the study, for language work is a joy which Satan does not control, and many a boy or girl or older person comes there quietly to hear the wondrous story of the Cross.

Today is Aunt Toddy's birthday, but as I am ill it is a very quiet one. Truly when one member suffers here all the members suffer with it."

We are rejoicing in the presence of the Lord, and in his promises. We are glad to know of the party so soon coming to Africa. We know that God can bring Brother and Sister Srack, Brother and Sister Rush, Sister Hillegas and all the others in his own good time.

We are trusting him to bring them through all the opposition of the way safe to the point, to which he is calling them.

We are praying for them every step of the way, and we know that God is faithful.

We thank you for your letters. All of them we answer personally, but we know that sometimes letters are lost, and some of you who have not received personal letters sent to you may see this.

Just this afternoon the mail is closing. We hope the many letters which it carries will go safely to all you dear ones in the homeland, and that messages of peace and encouragement may be yours, even as your messages have brought such joy and happiness to us.

Lovingly,
MARGUERITE.

A Personal Letter

(Brother Wm. A. Gearhart very kindly shares with the brotherhood this personal letter to himself from Brother Yoder. It contains some things that Brother Yoder's recent open letter to the churches did not, especially the reference to Sister Yoder's health. Notice also the reference about the letter from friends in the homeland. Suppose your church sends a Christmas letter to our missionaries both in South America and Africa.—Editor).

Dear Brother Gearhart:

Rio Cuarto, September 6, 1920.

Your letter of May 27 arrived several weeks ago and should have been answered sooner, but there has been an unusual amount of work for me on account of the sickness of Mrs. Yoder. She has been ill for several months but is now better and is able to be up again, but cannot see to read or write. The trouble began with a cold which caused inflammation of the kidneys. She will have to be on a diet of milk and fruit for many months yet.

We thank you very much for your kind letter. It helps us a lot to get such letters, but there are very few who think to write them. We have been thinking of you and the members of the Mission Board very much these days when the Conference is in session. We would like very much to be present also. We hope to hear within a month of all the great events of the Conference.

Here our work goes forward slowly but steadily. Brother Edwards and family have gone to Huinca Renanco, a town about a hun-

dred miles south of us where there is a splendid opening for a mission and are opening a work there. We are getting a new addition to our working forces in the person of the father-in-law of Brother Atkinson and his family. He is a Swiss nobleman who married out of his caste. His wife is a fine woman and his two sons are good preachers and good singers.

They have an auto coach somewhat like ours in which they have been doing evangelistic work from town to town. They are now headed this way and should be here in a week or so and then we will plan our campaign with them.

The Salvation Army has opened a work in Rio Cuarto so that we have company. In a town of 33,000 there is room for both of us. We also have street meetings after Sunday school every Sunday that I am here. I go to Carlota the last Sunday of each month, or rather on Saturday, as there are no Sunday trains, and preach also in the streets in Los Cisnes, a town ten miles from Carlota. I am thus keeping up the work which Brother Bock had in Carlota.

We feel proud of the brethren at home who have contributed so generously this year and have made it possible for us to go forward in our work. May God bless you all.

We will be glad to hear from you again at any time.

With kind regards from all,
Your brother,
C. F. YODER.

NEWS FROM THE FIELD

MCLOUTH, KANSAS

To the Brethren scattered abroad, may the grace of our Lord Jesus Christ be with you, and bless you and your efforts in the great forward movement for the Kingdom.

It has been some time since we have attempted to tell you of our work and the blessings of God upon our church and town.

Many events of interest have transpired since we came here. Sin was abroad, running rampant, worldliness on every hand, church members cold and indifferent, without the proper concern for souls of men and the Kingdom of God.

As we had prayed to God before leaving the hills of Pennsylvania, to use us to his glory in the salvation of the lost in the west, we set out to help in the answer of our prayers. To do this I must say it takes a great deal of grace and grit. When the old devil stands out in public with the imps of hell, to induce if possible the very elect of God, using the open dance pavillion, crap shooting, betting on ball games, and many other sins, which are looked on as only social affairs, it means something to go against them.

In the face of it all we feel that prayers have been answered and God has visited his people.

Early in the season the three pastors of our town put their heads and hearts together and got busy. The dance pavillion is gone and other sins are more on the quiet.

The great question came to us, What must we do, that we might work the works of God?

This suggestion sprang up before us, Let's organize and hold a union meeting. Some came to us and said, It has been tried before and failed insomuch that the preachers fell out and became unfriendly. This brought us to no halt whatever. We kept working and praying, and insisting on our churches lining up. Then we began to correspond with many evangelists in regard to leading the meeting.

With the many answers received written on letterheads spread on the table before us, looking into their faces and catching their spirits, the choice was first made by the U. B. minister, with which the Baptist minister heartily agreed. That choice was in the person of Brother F. G. Coleman, as evangelist and Brother A. T. Ronk as singer, and what could a Brethren preacher do but agree to this? The date for the meeting was set for September 19, at which time these brothers were engaged in a meeting at Garwin, Iowa. Nevertheless, the good people of Garwin gave way and Coleman came to us on time, leaving Ronk to fight the battle at Garwin, after one week he joined us in our effort. I must take time here and thank the Brethren of Garwin for their loyal love to God's Kingdom, and we pray his richest blessing on them. The people of McLouth feel that their pastors made no mistake in calling the Coleman-Ronk party to come to us.

Considering Coleman's short experience in the work he is a great preacher. When we say this it is with consideration, and we mean

every word. We say he is a Gospel preacher and stays by the word of God. We must say the messages were convincing and convincing.

We cannot say anything that would express our heart's gratitude for Brother Ronk, a man of God, filled with the Holy Spirit, and music, which is a great power for calling the lost to Jesus Christ.

We feel that we should congratulate Flora for the wise selection in "Coley and Ronk" and we know that if the church will get behind the throne with their prayers that the works of God will be witnessed among them.

During the four weeks of the meetings we had fine crowds, estimated from three hundred to one thousand people. The most blessed thing is that 74 walked down the "sawdust trail" and took a stand for Jesus Christ. Yet it was sad indeed to close and see such great numbers under conviction, such was never before seen in this little city.

On Sunday, the last day of the meeting, we held a union Sunday school. Coleman preached, after which a great dinner was spread. Nearly seven hundred partook and were satisfied. Ronk gave us a mighty message in the afternoon which will be long remembered. Coleman gave his farewell address in the evening and said good-bye and was off to see his dear family.

There is one other thing we would not fail to make mention of. The good people showed their appreciation of the great work of Brother Coleman in a freewill offering which amounted to $990.79. We also paid Brother Ronk $150.00 for three weeks. We paid all expenses of which the total was about $1,400. The remarkable thing is the greatest amount given by any one was $25.00. Of this we do not boast, but we are thankful to know that the people here touched from the heart to the pocketbook.

The good work is going on with a full house at our union prayer meetings and a good number at the business and men's prayer meeting.

The Brethren church has been revived and has taken greater interest in the work. We baptized three Sunday night and some others approved for baptism.

As we come to a close, we must give God the glory for what has been done in our midst and pray his blessings upon the church at large and Coleman and Ronk with Flora. Pray for us.

THOMAS F. HOWELL.

TRAVEL FLASHES

Yes, my friends, I am traveling again. This time enroute to Ashland, Ohio, where I hope to look over the Mecca of Ohio Brethren. There I hope to get smart and "go through" college; get sharp and go over the Publications plant and later, tell you if you ought to send the money to the folks that ask you for it; attend the Ohio conference and tell them how they do it in Indiana; and incidentally tell them that they must get busy if they would measure up to some of the states on the Bicentenary program.

Back to West Virginia

Then, after a day, I start back to within eight miles of Oak Hill, in another union meeting with six churches—all there are in the town—co-operating. I like these people and this section and they seem to like me, and so, "we work together." Brother Sam Duncan of the Oak Hill Brethren church is to be my song leader, as he was in my last. He is a splendid man who has lived so well and so good that they instinctively turn to him in all that section for a music leader. So, while the meeting will this time have no co-operating Brethren church, we shall have a Brethren team. We also have promised to preach the whole gospel and no one has ever accused us of not doing so.

Nice to be at Home

It was really nice to be at home though the short week we were there flew by so fast that we did not get near all done that we had hoped. Some of it will wait and some will have to be finished by the lady and her two helpers. While there, I had the pleasure of hearing and meeting for the first time, Brother Hilbert of Aleppo, Pennsylvania, who was with the North Manchester Brethren church for that Sunday. It was much of a surprise to both him and myself. I am praying that the Lord will raise up the right leader very soon for the church at home, however small may be my part in choosing him. Our big churches need active leaders for the work of the next three years.

The Bicentenary program will not do itself and no church shall dare to do less than its share if we get where we hope to get in the next three years. I hear that some of the churches have not taken the announcement of Brother Teeter seriously and have made no effort to raise an offering and that means that they will get the price of their Evangelist raised. Too bad!

At Ashland

I have been there. I saw the Publishing House. If you had been on the Publication Board as I was for several years when we were so low that we had to RENT a poor substitute for a linotype and now had the privilege of seeing two operators working on real linotypes and could see other gains in proportion, you would not censure nor criticize. I am sure the men are doing the best they can and angels can do no more. Let's stand by the guns and—after the election—no difference whom we elect. we shall have good times!!!

At Chapel

At chapel, I saw the student body and had the privilege of addressing them seriously on the task we shall soon pass on to them. They have the tools; we had to buy them. They have the churches; we had to build them. They have the opportunities; we had to find them. So, I told them we expect them to do the things we had hoped to do. It is a fine group of youngsters and we have a first-class faculty now, and as soon as we give them the needed equipment, we shall be what a college has to be to go right and serve rightly our boys and girls, a "Standard School." It can not be done too quickly and Brethren, let's do it.

The Conference

The Ohio Conference will do advanced things for Ohio. I am watching closely the reports of the district conferences to see what they attempt for the Movement. You do the same. We have machinery enough to carry it all out and I feel that we shall soon "possess the land" as we ought. We had some splendid sessions the day I was with the Ohio Conference and when I made the appeal to the delegates to "start the revival in Ohio Brethren churches" they stood like a solid phalanx. God bless the Brethren everywhere to insure the progress that his program and ours demand.   CHARLES A. BAME.

PASTORAL AND EVANGELISTIC SKETCHES

North Liberty, Indiana

We closed our pastoral relations with the above church on October 1. Here at North Liberty we have one of our best churches in Indiana. They are intensely loyal to the faith and are actually doing things for the Master. Our labors among them with but a few exceptions were both pleasant and profitable. In our three years of service here, though the field had been well gleaned previous to our coming, we were permitted to add about 35 persons to the body of believers. They have a very good Sunday school under the leadership of C. G. Wolf; a banner W. M. S. with Mrs. C. G. Wolf as their president, and a splendid Y. P. S. C. E. with our esteemed Brother, Clyde Sheneman leading the forces. It is my conviction that the work is in every way prepared to go forward and do great things for the Master. This church received recognition at the late General Conference as a star church. We very reluctantly gave up the work, having received a call for the fourth year with a substantial increase in our salary, but because of certain local conditions over which we had no control, we deemed it best to turn it over to another. Our good friend and brother, A. T. Wirick has been chosen as our successor, is already on the field, and is pressing the battle. We have learned to love these good people and will remain among them for the present where my family can have the advantages of a Brethren church while I am in the field.

Tiosa, Indiana

The past year we gave a part of our time to the work at Tiosa. I was pastor here when I was a mere lad, and have many here whom I count among my dearest friends. We much appreciated the help of the young people here, especially our good brother, Harley Zumbaugh, who was our very faithful and efficient song-leader. And this reminds me to say that any pastor needing a good song-leader for a meeting would do well to write him. Then Brother George Riddle, a teacher in the schools at Rochester, kept the Sunday school machinery running smoothly. The Tiosa church has a great field, and when they once get the vision and apply more and more the principles of Christian stewardship, they no doubt yill yet have a great future. They met all the financial goals as set by

General Conference, going far beyond any previous record for home and foreign missions. Our good brother, S. M. Whetstone has accepted a call from this church. May the Lord bless him graciously as he labors among them.

La Paz, Indiana

Near the village of La Paz is located the old County Line church where many a victory has been won for the cause of the Brethren in years gone by. But reverses have come and for three years they have had only a few months of pastoral care which was very acceptably given them about a year ago by Brother J. W. Clark. Since then they have done practically nothing. Last spring a union effort in La Paz by the writer resulted in several additions to the Brethren. In fact this meeting awakened the entire community to the extent that the Brethren at County Line were no longer content to stand by and see the work go to the rocks, and after a careful canvass for funds it was found that their fondest hopes had been realized and sufficient funds had been obtained to push the work forward the coming year. I have arranged to give them both pastoral and evangelistic service. The work is starting nicely with splendid crowds and good interest. Brother C. D. Whitmer preached for them on Sunday October 17. Our revival effort will begin there soon. Now brethren of Indiana, as secretary of the district, I think I am in a position to say, that there are at least six other places in Indiana that are going to pieces in the same way. What is going to be our answer to the great Head of the church for our indifference and our indisposition to help them?

Terra Alta, West Virginia

After the great Conference at Flora, where we met so many of our friends and good brethren and where we found so much fruit of our own labors of other years, we moved on into West Virginia. Terra Alta is rightly named, it is indeed a "high terrace," being almost 3,000 feet above sea level. Here nestled among the mountains, is a little flock of God's own people. If there is a finer, cleaner, or more loyal bunch of Brethren anywhere it has not been my privilege to meet them. Indeed, I was much impressed with the personnel of the people generally. There are in this little congregation, I think, fourteen school teachers, several college graduates and three ordained elders. This is the home of Elder C. E. Glenn a great preacher for the Brethren in his day. I think it was he who stood up in that memorable convention at Ashland, Ohio, in 1883 and moved that the name "Brethren" be retained. Brother Glenn still preaches some and his services are appreciated in the local church.

Brother V. W. Flora, one of our own spiritual sons, is pastor here. They speak in the very highest terms of his services and he is universally liked. They say he preaches splendid sermons. Sorry he could not be with me in the meeting. He is teaching school and could only be in the meetings over Sundays.

When we commenced we were informed that there was no available material. Indeed it looked that way to us for awhile. But after the first week, the interest became intense. The crowds came and the Lord rewarded us

with thirteen precious souls. Twelve by baptism and one by relation from the Church of the Brethren. The converts are in the main men and women and are such that will mean much to the little flock here.

A communion service at the close of the meeting was conducted by the writer and Brother Flora with 57 at the tables and the church has a total membership of 53. If there is any church that has been able to go ahead of that record for attendance at communion service it has done well, I am sure. The evangelist has had his home with our aged veteran of the cross, J. M. Freeland and "Aunt" Mary. God bless them; it was a "home" indeed for this weary preacher. I shall never forget their many kindnesses. Our only regret is that we didn't arrange in the beginning to stay longer. But we had planned for a week at Accident, Maryland, and thus we called a halt here in the very midst of the fight. They gave us a unanimous call for a second meeting. May the Lord open the way. We have a number of meetings ahead. We solicit your prayers, brethren, that we may preach none other than the old fashioned gospel of the Son of God.   C. C. GRISSO.

HUDSON, IOWA

The church in this place is planning to meet the increased demands of the Bicentenary Movement and at the last business meeting took steps to incorporate in the budget both the College and the Publishing House, putting them on a basis with Home and Foreign Missions, the College on the average of 35 cents per member and the Publishing House 25 cents per member. This is merely a little start in the right direction, for we hope to do better than this later.

The church is in a fairly sound condition with the membership increasingly finding their place in the work of the church. The response to our efforts to organize a prayer meeting have not been as good as we had hoped, but when it is remembered that for years the people have never felt the need of such a service, their lethargy is not to be marveled at. The church services are being well attended in the morning but in this region people seem to have an antipathy for the dark and as a consequence our evening audiences are small. We are steadily preaching the realities in Christ Jesus and are striving consistently to lead the Brethren into the larger and fuller experiences of the Christian life.

Three delegates besides the pastor "Forded" it to the district conference at Lanark, Illinois, and since the pastor was the "driver" we have the conviction that at least three members of the church know how to pray, for there were times in the journey when prayer was mighty necessary, due to several "close calls." We all made the trip safely, however, and enjoyed the conference immensely. Illiokota is in line for big things and we are confident that our record in the Bicentenary will be good.

Hudson is still moving and though we have not yet attained the speed of a "Super six" we can report that we have no engine trouble for we're "hitting on every cylinder."

EDWIN BOARDMAN, JR.

LANARK, ILLINOIS

Quite a number of important and interesting events have transpired in the First Brethren church at this place during the last few weeks, mention of which was made in an outline of special days by our pastor, B. T. Burnworth, in a previous number of the Evangelist.

Sunday, September 26th, marked the closing of the sixth years and the beginning of the seventh year of Brother Burnworth's pastorate with us. The morning service address was given by the pastor on the subject, "A Resume for Six Years." In the brief survey of his work with us in the past six years, he called attention to the real progress made in the various departments of church work. First, by the Sunday school having greatly increased its enrollment and regular attendance; second, by the increased interest and membership of the Women's Missionary Society, and lastly, the splendid results having been accomplished in a spiritual way by the addition of many new members to the church and also in a material way, with regard to our financial progress which enabled us to remodel and enlarge our church building so as to meet the growing needs of the Sunday school and church. In addition to this, the church was also able to purchase a parsonage so that the pastor and his family now have a permanent home for their future work with us. In his closing remarks he made a splendid appeal to all to stay true to the Christian principles and splendid virtues that had played so large a part in the success of his six years' work with us.

Beginning with October, our newly elected Sunday school officers began another year's work. October 3rd, we had Rally Day and Promotion Day services in the Sunday school and Harvest Home service during the worship hour and communion service at Milledgeville in the evening. We are pleased to be able to report a successful Rally Day service. We had a splendid program and an attendance of 317 and an offering of $16.23. The church in general is rallying in a very commendable way and seems to be thoroughly alive to all the needs of the work in Sunday school and its activities. The attendance and interest is being kept up in a fine way with the result that the Sunday school steadily grows. Rev. Z. T. Livengood is our superintendent and with him to lead us we expect to keep right on growing.

The Harvest Home service which immediately followed the Sunday school session was also well attended. The decorations were many and beautiful, giving us ample proof of how wonderfully God does bless his people. The pastor's sermon was in keeping with the service, placing special emphasis upon the truth that as Christian men and women we ought to show greater appreciation to our God for his wonderful gifts by giving greater service to him. In the evening, quite a number attended communion service at Milledgeville.

Next came the District Conference. The Illiokota District Conference this year was held at this place October 6, 7, 8. A very important program had been planned for and which afforded unusual opportunity for spiritual uplift and the planning of our future program for construction work. There was a goodly attendance of delegates from all parts of the district. The weather and roads being favorable, many of them came across the country in their autos.

The Sunday following conference, we had Home Coming Day for all isolated members, friends and all who worship with us. The pastor gave a very impressive sermon on the subject of "Home," discussing it in a threefold manner. First, with regard to our earthly home; second, the home of the soul, and third, our heavenly home. In the afternoon, a young man was received into the church by baptism.

About the most important of all the events was the communion service which was held in the evening following the Home Coming service of the morning. This, I believe, was the largest service of its kind ever held in the Lanark church. We are more thankful for this than anything else, for it shows that above all else the spiritual status of the church is high, for after all, a church is just as big as its spiritual life allows it to grow.

On the following Monday, October 11th, Brother Burnworth left for Burlington, Indiana, where he will conduct a series of revival meetings. From there he goes to Louisville, Ohio. He expects to be gone until the middle of November. Rev. Z. T. Livengood will occupy the pulpit on Sunday mornings during his absence. Following this date, on November 14th, the pastor will return and begin a series of sermons on "The Parables of the Kingdom." MRS. F. G. PETERS,
Corresponding Secretary.

LA VERNE, CALIFORNIA

We are still advocates of the spirit of thanksgiving here. Almighty God is justly showering blessings upon us.

We have just closed a three days' prophetic conference led by four Doctors of Divinity, well known in Southern California for their faithfulness to the Word of God. These men were secured through the Bible Institute of Los Angeles. The themes showed us the believers' security in Christ, discussed the problems and apostasies of the present day and pointed us to the blessed hope of his coming, for his saints. Many people heard these truths for the first time and were blessed by them. In the evening meetings the church was hardly able to accommodate the crowds. We are all looking forward to the time when we shall have another such conference.

Our Sunday school is flourishing. At our Rally Day exercises, 184 were present as compared to 168 last year and we saw then our great need for more room. A large class was graduated from the primary department and all the other classes were adjusted, a new one of high school age being formed.

The prayer meetings continue good both in spirit and numbers.

Christian Endeavor is still active. The meetings are well attended and very beneficial. Once every month we go to our valley hospital to sing. A few weeks ago eight auto loads of us went into Los Angeles to the County Hospital to hold a service in the chapel and take gifts of fruits, jams, scrapbooks, clothing and infants' wear to the inmates. We also had a praise meeting in the open court in front of the tubercular ward. We are now planning for a "concentionette" to be held in Pomona.

The Women's Missionary Society is doing much practical good at their all day meetings. Three quilts, 43 infants' garments, 10 infants' blankets, and 27 other garments have ben made in the last quarter. The Women's Bible Class at their regular class meetings have also made rugs and quilts to be given to the needy.

Our pastor, Brother Broad, is still as busy as ever keeping up his sermons and always going on his missions of love and mercy. In an accident, which wrecked his old car, while on his way to Whittier to take charge of the funeral services of Brother Kimmell's little one, he and four women of the church were all more or less injured, but God spared them miraculously. All of them are quite well over it now, and Brother Broad has another machine to use to God's glory.
MRS. HARRY L. GOOD.
Pomona, California.

OAK HILL, WEST VIRGINIA

September closed a year of service with the church here. There are three preaching points on this circuit, and services here held occasionally at a fourth point. The results of the year's work are: Four additions by baptism.

Beginning October 1st, I am giving only half time services here. Having accepted a place to teach in our high school, my time is limited and I am serving as pastor only until such time as a pastor may be secured. So here is an open door for some pastor who wishes a field in a district where good opportunities are a healthy climate and room for work.

Praying great success for the year to all of our churches, I am,
Fraternally,
WM. H. MILLER.

CERRO GORDO, ILLINOIS

On coming home from Conference, Brother Bell began a three weeks' revival meeting, September 12.

We had a good attendance at all meetings, but never the interest put forth in church work as in any other thing that might be on at the same time.

Such sermons as Brother Bell gave us we ought to have had more people than our church could hold each night. We did have to get chairs and then on Sunday night turned some away.

Nineteen made the good confession. Fourteen were baptized; two having been baptized and two went into another church; one remains to be baptized yet.

On Monday evening following the baptismal and consecration services our communion service was held with an attendance of 90 members.

Brother Bell stayed with us for these services which we certainly enjoyed as we, learned to love him very much as he worked among us.

One thing fine in our meeting was that all the confessions but three were young people from our Sunday school, and it surely makes all those that have worked among these young people feel happy to see them step out and take their stand for Christ.

While we know there are still many who are out in the world and we are praying for, we feel that our meeting was a great success. The auxiliaries of the church are all doing good work. In July we started our prayer meetings again and having fair attendance. Brother Teeter is giving 30 minutes before prayer service to the Bible study part of "Teacher Training," which I think will help us all to know how to study our Bibles as well as encourage us to study them more. On last Sunday evening we organized a Christian Endeavor society which we hope will be a great help for encouraging our young people for further work of the church.

A young man and wife and two little boys have moved here from the Mulberry church. We surely welcome them into our midst and want to make them feel at home among us, as they are much interested in the work of the church.

On the last Sunday of our meeting, Brother Teeter accepted our call to stay with us another year, for which we are truly glad as we hated very much to think of him and Sister Teeter leaving us at this time.

Brother Bell has our prayers in the great work which he is laboring in, that he may be the means of bringing many lost souls into the kingdom.

Pray for us that we may be more faithful and willing in all we are called to do.

MRS. HELENA BOGUE,
Corresponding Secretary.

Communion Notices

The First Brethren church of Elkhart will observe its semi-annual communion service, Friday evening, November 5th at 8 P. M. All of like mind are cordially invited to worship with us.

B. S. STOFFER, Pastor.

The Brethren church at Williamstown, Ohio, will observe Holy Communion, Sunday evening, November 7th. Brethren of like faith are invited to enjoy this service with us.

AUSTIN R. STALEY, Pastor.

MINISTERIAL EXCHANGE

As I wish to get into the Master's harvest field again to work, I wish to notify the readers of the Evangelist, especially the isolated members, that anywhere I can serve, I will come at any time. With the united efforts and prayers of God's children we will endeavor to save souls from death to the glory of God. I was pastor of the church at Altoona, Kansas, for seven years, and then had

to leave and travel around for eighteen months on account of the health of my son. Last August he passed to his eternal reward. At present I am located at the address below and wish to get into active service again for the Master.

F. E. BUTTON, Ramona, Kansas.
Box 96.

ELKHART, INDIANA

I will write a few lines to let the readers of the Evangelist know that we are still moving forward. Many were the regrets expressed, and in strong terms, when Brother Wolford was called to the College. The church was moving forward and every department was in excellent condition. He gave us seven and a half years of his services. All were very sorry to have him go, but God's will must lead. We trusted and depended upon this leading.

We have secured the services of Brother Bryan Stoffer, who is yet in the University of Chicago. And many expressions of "We won't get another preacher like Wolford" have changed to "Well, we certainly got another good preacher." He has taken hold of the work in earnest and we are looking forward to greater things. We hope that we can continue to report progress from Elkhart.

A formal reception was held for our new pastor on Monday evening, October 18. The following report of it appeared in the "Elkhart Truth":

Reception for New Pastor

Rev. Bryan Stoffer, the new pastor of the First Brethren church on Goshen avenue, was tendered a reception last evening by about 150 members of his congregation. Following the formal preliminary proceedings, in the church auditorium, during which Peter Pontius welcomed the new pastor, to which the latter responded with a few appropriate words, the members retired to the church basement, where a bounteous supper was served, cafeteria style, by the ladies of the church. Rev. C. B. Croxall of St. Paul's Methodist church, representing the Elkhart Ministerial association, also extended a welcome to Mr. Stoffer, after the assembly had returned to the auditorium, and an interesting program was given. It consisted of a piano duet by Fern Baugher and Pauline Cripe, a violin duet by Dorothy McManus and Mary Harden and a saxophone solo by Lee Willis, whose piano accompaniment was played by Guy Hall; several selections by the Golden Rule quartet—Fred Taska, H. L. Carr, D. D. Stutsman and R. H. Smolinske—and a repetition of the tableau, "Sewing for the Heathens," by the Sisterhood girls, coached by Mrs. W. D. Hall. Mr. Stoffer came here six weeks ago from Alliance, Ohio, to succeed Rev. H. H. Wolford, who resigned to take a professorship in the denominational school at Ashland, Ohio.

PETER PONTIUS.

Business Manager's Corner

FIRST FRUITS

Several weeks ago we asked the question, "What church will be the first to report the offering taken on Publication Day?"

As we go to press we are glad to report from two churches, and as we announced previously, any amount contributed by the individual before the offering was taken will be

included in the amount credited to the congregation making the offering.

The first offering comes from one among the smallest congregations in Ohio, the Gretna church, and amounts to $53.00; nearly one dollar per member for the congregation. The second offering received is $35.00 from the Ashland congregation. If one hundred of our churches will do as well as Ashland and Gretna we will be able to pass through the present crisis in splendid shape.

We hope to have a larger report to make next week.

R. R. TEETER,
Business Manager.

The Tithing Stewardship Corner

Last week we gave a portion of the methods of Dr. and Mrs. A. T. Robinson in securing tithers. Following is a continuation. I cannot too strongly endorse Mr. Robinson's method of treating the relations between tithing and stewardship.

"Our work has certain characteristics. (1) In the first place, we stick to tithing and let stewardship alone. In my judgment we should distinguish more sharply between these two than we usually do., Stewardship is a New Testament, word, a divine word, a fine word, and we cannot get along without it. It presents a goal, an ideal. Hold it up and the life will certainly gravitate toward it, for the life swings to the look always.

"But stewardship in practice is the goal of our teaching, the last consummate flower of religious experience. Why expect the goal in one day by ordinary means? It is essentially a New Testament doctrine taught by men and to men filled with the Holy Ghost, and to folks whose ancestors have tithed for over a thousand years.

"God is the God of things as they are. He never started in on a campaign of stewardship, asking that they hold all they had as in trust for him. God met them on the level on which they lived and asked for one-tenth as their recognition of his over-lordship and sovereign rights in the case.

"Tithing is the first step toward the goal of stewardship. Better take the first step first and one step at a time. That is God's method. Tithing is the alphabet of stewardship. We do not start a child in on Kant's 'Critique' when learning to read, but at the alphabet. In music we start them in at the staff and scales, not at one of Beethoven's sonatas. Tithing is a short cut to stewardship, and if you want stewardship, get your people to tithe, for the peculiar thing about this divine method is that people no sooner begin to tithe than they want to do more and are now ready for the second lesson in stewardship. For tithing is stewardship so far as it goes. It is the practical, the very real acknowledgment that another owns the plantation. After that the way is easy. The undeveloped soul can understand the tithe for it is essentially a reasonable proposition. For this reason you can both teach it and expect people to come across with it."

Volume XLII
Number 43

November 10
1920

The BRETHREN EVANGELIST

-ONE-IS-YOUR-MASTER-AND-ALL-YE-ARE-BRETHREN-

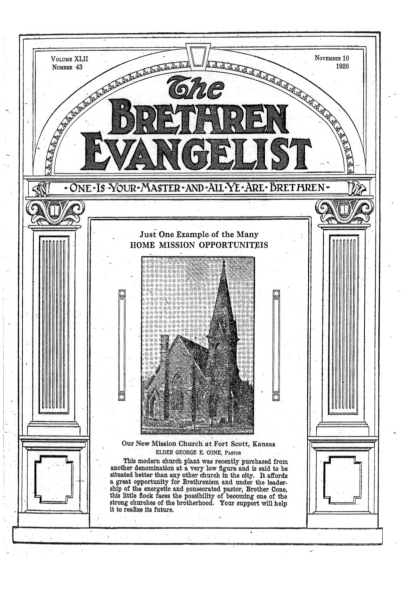

Just One Example of the Many
HOME MISSION OPPORTUNITEIS

Our New Mission Church at Fort Scott, Kansas

ELDER GEORGE E. CONE, Pastor

This modern church plant was recently purchased from another denomination at a very low figure and is said to be situated better than any other church in the city. It affords a great opportunity for Brethrenism and under the leadership of the energetic and consecrated pastor, Brother Cone, this little flock faces the possibility of becoming one of the strong churches of the brotherhood. Your support will help it to realize its future.

Published every W·-'nesday at Ashland, Ohio. All matter for publication must reach the Editor not later than Friday noon of the preceding week.

George S. Baer, Editor

The
Brethren
Evangelist

When ordering your paper changed give old as well as new address. Subscriptions discontinued at expiration. To avoid missing any numbers renew two weeks in advance.

R. R. Teeter, Business Manager

ASSOCIATE EDITORS: J. Fremont Watson, Louis S. Bauman, A. B. Cover, Alva J. McClain, B. T. Burnworth.

OFFICIAL ORGAN OF THE BRETHREN CHURCH

Subscription price, $2.00 per year, payable in advance.
Entered at the Post Office at Ashland, Ohio, as second-class matter.
Acceptance for mailing at special rate of postage provided for in section 1103, Act of October 3, 1917, authorized September 9, 1918.
Address all matter for publication to Geo. S. Baer, Editor of the Brethren Evangelist, and all business communications to R. R. Teeter, Business Manager, Brethren Publishing Company, Ashland, Ohio. Make all checks payable to the Brethren Publishing Company.

TABLE OF CONTENTS

EDITORIAL

HOLD FAST

When we realize the imperative of the words, "Hold Fast," it arouses the sense of imminent danger. These words were addressed to Christians at various times and in divers circumstances. Today they come to us with a peculiar force. We are living in times when the injunction is of the utmost importance. Like the "few names in Sardis," who had not defiled their garments, amidst corruption, the Lord rejoices for the evidence of a living faith. When the Lord comes will he find faith upon the earth? That we may not find ourselves drifting with the tide of materialism and agnostic indifference may the words of Paul addressed to Timothy be applied in daily conduct.

Keep that good thing, the good deposit. The great essential to guard is life, the new life in Christ Jesus. "I am come that ye might have life and have it more abundantly," was the purpose of the incarnation. That life has value above everything else. What will a man give in exchange for his life? Sad commentary on the present day drift, that the things sought are not the things from above but rather the things that are of the earth earthy. In this earthly life are things of infinite value when made to serve the higher purpose and aim of life. Intellect is not to be discredited. Make it serve the purpose of losing live to save it, which utilizes the best in the lower or earthly life.

Environment may be made to present an opportunity of serving the higher aim of life, even though it may be adverse, as the remnant throughout the Scriptures attests. Hold fast the life, the good deposit, the life portrayed in the Gospels.

Keep the good things which God has given to struggling humanity. These good things are not to be kept in a napkin carefully secluded, but used that they may multiply. Each one has been given the ability to propagate the faith. No man liveth to himself. Christians are the torch-bearers of good news. If given a sack of grain, we choose to lay it by and refuse to plant it, there will be no increase; on the other hand if the wheat is sown there will be more wheat; the blessing multiplies forty, sixty, a hundred fold. Thus the good deposit is kept, by using it. Hold fast the faith. Let the light of Christian loyalty blaze the way through a crooked and perverse generation. Grow daily in knowledge that we be workmen unashamed.

How shall we keep or hold fast in these days of testing? There is an unfailing source, all sufficient. God, our Father. Keep the covenant with him. How lightly are those sacred promises made before God and man ofttimes regarded. The fervor of faith dwindles ere the words of confession and acceptance have died upon the lips. Business demands occupy the whole of the day and social engagements take the leisure time of night, and there remains no time for God. Hold fast in the midst of it all and help others by living true.

Hold fast by permitting the Holy Spirit entrance into your life. He unfolds all our powers. He energizes all our activities. He gives to the hand steadiness, to the eye spiritual outlook and uplook, to the tongue the power of witnessing concerning eternal verities. In our lives he unifies the powers of mind, body and soul. In the church, he unifies the aim and purpose of the Master so that the "Gates of Hell" cannot prevail against her even in the days of indifference and materialism.

Like as the Spirit spoke to the church at Sardis, "Thou hast a name that thou livest, and are dead," so does he speak today. Worldliness must be eliminated, garments kept undefiled, if she, the church, shall walk with him "in white'—worthily. May these words burn into our hearts and may we be able to hold fast the faith that we may be worthy. —ALBERT B. COVER.

Getting Ready for the Banner Offering

Of course it has occurred to you that you must "get ready" to make an offering. You must if you expect to make a success of it. A real up-to-date missionary offering, one that measures well up to the needs of the hour, does not come without preparation. This fact we must all take into account in looking forward to our Home Mission offering at the Thanksgiving season.

We must have a great offering this year. We cannot open missions and build churches in this day on penny collections. Our Home Board has asked for one dollar per member. That will come easy with proper preparation, but hard without it. That is to say, people must be enlightened, stirred and moved to give adequately. They must be enlightened by a vision of the needs, stirred by some one who is enthusiastic about the needs and moved by the Holy Spirit to give to meet those needs. Unless that sort of preparation is made the chances are that we will get only a collection of the left-overs of our selfish spendings.

In some churches, perhaps, the preparation is going on continually. There is instruction concerning our missionary needs and obligations throughout the year. Both our home fields and our foreign are being made to unfold before the eyes of congregations, Sunday schools, Christian Endeavor Societies and Women's Missionary Societies. In many ways,—by public address, stereopticon, the printed page and by study classes, missionary intelligence is being passed out to the members of many of our churches. They are stirred and made to feel concerned about the situation by the enthusiasm of aggressive, awakened, and Spirit-led leaders. And the Holy Spirit moves their hearts to give themselves or their substance or both to meet these needs which have steadily grown in their minds to be the most important in all the world. To such people it is only necessary to offer an opportunity of giving to such a cause and a missionary offering that seems impossible to the indifferent and uninformed is the result.

If a church has not had the benefit of systematic missionary instruction and encouragement in giving (and there are places where it is very difficult to maintain these), yet it is possible to launch a campaign of intensive preparation that will bring about great results. Nearly all our churches can be brought quickly to respond in a very generous way to a great and plainly divine call. They only need to have a truly worthy cause put up to them in a wise, enthusiastic and convincing manner to win their loyal support. If the great task and responsibility of home missions and church extension is placed repeatedly before Brethren people and the value and urgency of such work is emphasized they will not fail to measure up to that which is expected of them. But if nothing is said or done about this most important matter until the day on which the offering is to be received the congregation is not to be blamed if it does not make a worthy offering. The big reason why the church has not done better in the past in giving for the preaching of the gospel and the building of churches in new communities is because the task and the challenge has not been properly presented to its membership. We have faith that the church will readily respond to what is expected of it when it is properly acquainted by its task. Advertise, agitate and challenge and pray.

EDITORIAL REVIEW

In this issue Brother Henry V. Wall gives a report of the election of officers in the Evangelistic and Bible Study League.

Home Mission Sunday, either November 21 or 28. Let us make it the largest offering ever given for the extension of Christ's kingdom in the homeland.

Brother Drushal writes an interesting letter from Lost Creek, giving a very significant experience which occurred recently in their chapel services. He also speaks of the importance of maintaining the grade school work.

Brother I. D. Bowman reports concerning his meeting in the Oriskany church, Virginia, where he sees a bright future for our church if it could have the proper care. He also speaks of a week of Bible instruction at Berne, Indiana.

Brother Bryan Stoffer gives his version of the reception which was reported by Brother Pontius last week, and also speaks of the loyalty of the Elkhart people and of the splendid condition in which he found the pastorate. These people are already finding that they have again been fortunate in the selection of a pastor.

Our good-spirited reporter from the Goshen church, Brother M. E. Horner, tells of some of the accomplishments of that wide-awake and still growing congregation, under the leadership of a wide-awake pastor. We are sure our readers would have enjoyed it if Brother Horner had gone more into detail concerning the big program which the Goshen church set before itself, seeking to stimulate spiritual growth as well as financial. Perhaps he is reserving some of that for

another good report. We are in receipt of one of Brother McInturff's church bulletins which sets forth the challenging program in detail. We hope to give it to you later as it will be suggestive to others.

There is a movement launched by the American Bible Society to celebrate November 28 as Mayflower Universal Bible Sunday as a part of the Pilgrim Tercentenary Celebration. We wish to endorse the movement and suggest that it is a fitting way to celebrate the coming of the Pilgrims to America.

Brother Homer Anderson shares with the brotherhood his joy over the "showers of blessings" which the Lord has bestowed on the Pleasant Grove church. The Lord sent them a helper in the person of Miss Nell H. Malen, who was wonderfully used together with the pastor for the conversion of souls and the reconsecration of life.

If any one has had a doubt as to the value of Rally Day in the Sunday school when accompanied with the right kind of preparation, Brother J. C. Beal's report from the Fillmore, California, will go a long ways toward dispelling it. We dare say that this efficient school which is being built up under Brother Beal's leadership will prove an important factor in building up a greater Brethren church in that city. The people recently showed their appreciation of their pastor in a very practical way.

At Limestone, Tennessee, the Brethren seem to be thoroughly alive, wide-awake and aggressive. And we would not expect to find them otherwise under the efficient leadership of Sister Mary Pence, who is proving to be an excellent spiritual housekeeper. They have recently enjoyed a splendid revival under the leadership of Sister Aboud.

The Evangelist family will be glad to learn that Sister Detwiler has been greatly improved in health. "It is fine in fact," so she states in a communication to the office. Her many friends who have written to her will find a reply to their letters in this week's Evangelist. Her address for the winter is 1242 West 42nd Street, Los Angeles, California.

Don't fail to turn to the Business Manager's Corner and see that some of our churches and individuals are responding in a splendid manner to the Publishing Company's financial call. Many others will yet respond, and we believe in sufficient numbers and generously enough to make it possible for us to keep The Evangelist subscription where it is.

One of the "high spots" in our church news this week is Terra Alta, West Virginia. This congregation is not only "high" terrestially speaking, but is in a high spiritual state. They have recently enjoyed a spiritual feast under the evangelistic leadership of Brother C. C. Grisso who reports the meeting last week. Brother Vern Flora, who took the work for the summer expecting to return to Ashland to continue his school work in the fall, proved himself so worthy a leader that the people would not let him go and his report indicates that he has the work very well organized and in high spirits. And with such a talented and loyal membership at his back we shall expect to hear of further progress in the future.

There is something wrong spiritually with the man who professes to love and follow his Lord and Master and yet will not take his place at the communion table, habitually absents himself from the prayer meeting, has not the courage nor the desire to lead his own family in worship and never allows his voice to be heard in prayer. He needs a more vital touch with the Master, and a clearer vision of his own sinfulness and of divine grace.

The Red Cross did a noble work during the war, but its work did not cease with the close of the conflict. It still has a great mission in helping the unfortunate, making strong the weak and teaching the gospel of clean living and well being. You will have an opportunity to help along in this noble work by joining the Red Cross during Roll Call weeks, November 11 to 25. And if you have been a member you will likely want to renew your membership.

THE BRETHREN BICENTENARY MOVEMENT PAGE

1723 - - - - - - 1923

Dr. Charles A. Bame, Editor

A Real Thanksgiving

Save the Cities

The time has come for us rightly to express our Thanksgiving this 1920, A. D. It has been a wonderful year. From whatever standpoint we look, we are compelled to say it is a great year. While no other country has had so few disturbances as ours and none among the civilized peoples of the earth have had so much of their natural resources left undisturbed as we, the question of questions, to all who have the salvation of our country at heart is, "How shall we save our cities?"

The Drift

The drift of population as you know is to the city. More farmers left their farms this year than during the war. Thousands of families are waiting outside of every large city of our country for entrance while all students of the times and of social conditions know well, that too many are there right now. Commercial clubs are busy evoking plans by which their city can receive this population and thus augment their own number. But is the church in a very real sense trying to keep pace with this drift?

How Church Members Act

The trouble with so many church members is that they do not take with them to their new places of citizenship, their religion,—at least not their church letters. They cease not to drift as they go and so drift from membership altogether, or to some church in which they can not enlist all their energy and ardency and so, Christianity, and especially the small church, has lost by their migration. But if the churches are to maintain their place in American life they do not dare to thus lose out. If the peoples from the country are to forget or forsake their religion when they migrate, and if the major population of the cities are to be unChristian, America is on the road of all other nations; she is loomed to oblivion and she will go as sure as the God of heaven has spoken.

How to Keep Pace

The answer is simple. Raise churches and missions everywhere members move. That is good Dunker missionary policy. It is responsible for about all the growth our peoples made until 1880 and much of it since that time. Than this method, I can conceive none better. If we have one good family indoctrinated into what Brethrenism really is, then, around that glad family if we should build a mission and then a church, we could soon have churches in most of the cities of the land. But there is one of our weak places. We do not pretend to follow up in places where we have more than one such family. Why?

Why? Why?

The reason is simple. We have thought more of our money and worldly things than we have of our brothers and sisters in the faith. We have made no systematic effort to raise churches for these who isolate themselves from their church. The task has been rather too large for our faith and we have made some few mistakes along that line that forever are hashed forth when another is made, and consequently discouragement and inaction has been too often the result. But,

The Bicentenary

This Movement has coupled up all the agencies of the church so as to co-ordinate them. This Movement designs to unify and utilize as never before the actions of all our organizations and thus results that could never have been possible before are to be reached. Last week, Brother Gear-

hart gave an outline of all that the General Missionary Committee hopes to do this year and says they ought to have ONE DOLLAR per member this year for that work. To back to number 41 Evangelist and read again what the Board intends to do. It is a small program, you say? We then do not give less than it calls for. This is perhaps more than a church of our size ought to do to save the citi of America. Sodom, Gomorrah, Nineveh, Tyre, Sidon, Capernaum, what a host of cities have been lost to earth because they had not or heeded not. The gospel of God and his Christ! Let us not think that cities with far greater opportunity can be saved by any other means.

Election-Day

I am writing this on election day. Thousands of my fellow-citizens are traveling many miles and much money being spent for the right of franchise. All right. But never be fooled into the hope that the Millennium will be ushered in by either political party that seeks your vote. Nothing but the gospel of our Lord Jesus will ever redeem them and we do not do justice to the founders of our church if we do not sacrifice for it. One of the candidates made a lot quoting the "Peace on earth" of the angels but do not believe that that can ever come to pass until it is accomplished through the will of HIM of whom the angels sang.

"The Lord is Not Willing"

that any should perish. Are you? Well, we can tell, my brethren, after Thanksgiving, when the accounts are made up. We shall prove it by whether we give at least one dollar per member for this work. One is measly small for many. One hundred would be more like it for many of us. Not only the cities of the U. S. A. but the whole world is HIS goal. But for this Thanksgiving our goal is ONE DOLLAR PER MEMBER.

National Service

I feel that this is quite specifically a National service. When we preach the Gospel, we help to save the nation. I wish every one might be an evangelist just for a single meeting. I wish you might have the happy feeling that comes to him who has preached the Gospel for three or four weeks to the same people. At the close of my last meeting there came to me a millionaire and said, "My life will be different from now on." I had not spared to preach from James 5 either. Nor had I slighted the parable (?) of the rich man in hell. His son was a convert; his wife definitely aligned with him in his church. The policeman said similar things without uniting with any church. By-products of the meeting, perhaps, but who can deny that it will tell in the purifying of the city in which the meeing was held?

Your Dollars Count

Thus when you preach the Gospel in the city they count in the saving of the city and thus in the saving of our country. As goes the city so, goes the country from now on in America. Now, therefore, give DOLLARS, many DOLLARS, MIGHTY DOLLARS, SAVING DOLLARS, CONSECRATED DOLLARS, SURRENDERED DOLLARS, BUT SURELY, DOLLARS. "Give as the Lord has prospered thee" and know thyself a man. Get the feeling of duty manfully and well done. Realize what it is and how it feels to have done your full share. Give with the memory of the sacrifice made by those whose BICENTENARY we have already begun to celebrate. Above all, give, remembering the Jesus gave all and said, "Follow me and I will make you to become fishers of men." To him be the glory.

BAME.

GENERAL ARTICLES

Attractive Power of Christ. By H. C. Funderberg

(And Jesus came and spake unto them saying, All power is given unto me in heaven and earth (Matt. 28:18).

Jesus in commissioning his disciples to go forth in the iverse to execute the work he had assigned unto him, ould have them understand that he was fully authorized delegate them. And to make his power more attractive, pledges his presence with them always (Matt. 28:20), t for a limited time, but till the end of the world. They ust have been assuring to the disciples.

When Jesus and his disciples took their Galilean voyge, the **Master** you will remember fell asleep and a storm rose on the lake, so terrific was it that their boats were lled with water and their lives were in jeopardy. Their aith had become exhausted and they realized their extrem.y. But man's extremity makes possible God's opportunity. nd they began to be conscious of the fact that the one allowerful was on board, so they awoke him, saying, "Master, aster, we perish." Jesus responded to their call (A friend need, is a friend indeed), arose and rebuked the wind and aves, and they obeyed him (Luke 8:22-25). This demonstration of his wonderful power so impressed them and cenered their attention on him that they began to consider him s never before and to say, "What sort of a man is this that e commands he winds and waves and they obey?

Jesus had drawn the fishermen to himself as they were o draw others—not by craft or force, but by the river of is living Word and the spirit of love. Their loyalty was ree and spontaneous. The calm greatness of the character of Christ shines out in such an unpretending beginning as is manifested in our Lord's dealings with the humble fishermen. It is the germ and center of a movement which is to revolutionize the world.

Insignificant as it might seem, it is only so when judged by a human standpoint, the men touched with the love of heavenly truth, and eager to win others to embrace it, were powerful living spiritual forces, destined by a law of nature to repeat themselves in even wider circles through successive generations.

If blooming flowers are placed in a window, though the window is closed and the blinds drawn yet the bees discover the presence of the flowers. You will see them beating against the window-pane in a vain effort to reach them. This illustrates how the soul is drawn to Christ and also how the Christian filled with Christ's spirit has a power over

other lives. I do not mean by this illustration, that when we are the possessors of the Christ (or in life) that we should close our hearts, as the window is closed. Rather our lives should be as David said concerning his cup: "My cup is full and running over" (Ps. 23:5). That generous outgoing kind is the attractive kind. Jesus said, "And I, if I be lifted up will draw all men unto me" (John 12:32). And he desires to be lifted up in us. If all professing Christians would live as they should, our lives would be so saturated with the attractive power of Christ that each would be as a magnet drawing men to Christ. Someone has said, "All great souls attract smaller souls." Strength is an irresistible magnet to weakness. Every good impulse in a sinner's heart, however weak it may be, is drawn out by that soul's admiration and love for strong-hearted Christians and for Christ himself.

Jesus went about in all Galilee teaching and preaching the gospel of Christ, and everywhere that attractive power was felt. When he spake he did it as one having authority and this attracted the people. It was unusual to hear such words as these. "No man can come to me except the Father (which hath sent me) draw him" (John 6:44). The commanding authority of the Master is in evidence when he called Peter and Andrew, James and John, and also when he finds Philip, and again when he finds Matthew sitting at the seat of custom. The obedience of these disciples to the call of their Lord as well as Master's power to heal the sick, made him the center of attraction. The people thronged about him on all sides. On one occasion he taught the multitude from a boat. On another occasion they let the sick down through the house top before him. No obstacle was too great to hinder people from being drawn to him. Jesus told the people on one occasion that they thronged him for his loaves and fishes. But whatever the purpose, they sought him on every hand and always Jesus' mission was two-fold —preaching and healing. As Jesus would heal the body, so he is able to heal the soul. Sin is the source of all disease and we are taught that the blood of Jesus Christ cleanseth us from all sins—not part but all. He makes a complete job of it. A thing is attractive on account of what it is able to accomplish. I wish I had space to enlarge on this, but will pass it by.

May we all make our lives attractive by the good we may do to mankind and to Christ.

New Carlisle, Ohio.

Can We Stand the Test? By N. J. Paul

If we have never thought of this subject before, is it not time we were thinking about it? In all of the late models of machinery before the parts are assembled, they are all pested out. Why? To see if all parts are perfect. Again, after all parts are assembled and the machine is complete, it is taken through another test before it goes upon the market. So will our works as we journey through life, be brought to light; they will be tested. Our minds, our thoughts, and our acts should be that of kindness toward our friends and neighbors; and also toward the brethren. "For if you love not your brother whom you have seen, how can you love God whom you have not seen?" In doing these acts of kindness as we journey through life, we are creating or making the parts, so that when they are assembled we may be able to stand the test. "Every man's work shall be made manifest: for the day shall declare it because it shall be revealed (or tested) by fire; and the fire shall try (or test) every man's work of what sort it is.

In all kinds of business men take an inventory at least

once a year. Brother, sister, did you ever take up the Book of all books, and compare your daily life, with its teaching? The teaching of God's Holy Word will catch men in all walks of life. We may think we are in the true service of the Master, and yet, when we come face to face with his Word, it makes our blood run cold to think how far short we come from what is expected of us. Here is a text we will have to face, and one that will test us sorely: "Lay not up for yourselves treasures upon earth, where moth and rust doth corrupt, and where thieves break through and steal; but lay up for yourselves treasures in heaven, where neither moth nor rust doth corrupt, and where thieves do not break through nor steal." Oh, what a clincher he puts here! "For where your treasure is, there will your heart be also." How many of us, as professed followers of Christ can stand the test of this one text? How few have left all, that they might win Christ? "But I say unto you. resist not evil: but whosoever shall smite thee on thy right cheek, turn to him the other also. Give to him that asketh of thee, and from him that would borrow of thee turn not thou away. Ye have heard that it hath been said, Thou shalt love thy neighbor, and hate thine enemy. But I say unto you, love your enemies, bless them that curse you, do good to them that hate you, and pray for them which despitefully use you, and persecute you; that ye might be the children of your Father which is in heaven'' Can we stand the test?

You will notice with me in the parable of the talents, that we are all servants; some profitable and some unprofitable; some goats and some sheep. ''And he shall set the sheep on his right hand, but the goats on the left.'' What are we? Let us ask the question, and make it personal. What am I? a sheep, or a goat? I am one or the other in the light of God's Word. ''Then shall the King say unto them on his right hand, Come, ye blessed of my Father, for I was an hungered and ye gave me meat: I was thirsty, and ye gave me drink: I was a stranger, and ye took me in: naked, and ye clothed me: I was sick and in prison, and ye came unto me. Then shall the righteous answer him saying, Lord, when saw we thee an hungered, and fed thee? or thirsty, and gave thee drink?—sick and in prison, and came unto thee?. . . Inasmuch as ye have done it unto one of the least of these my brethren, ye have done it unto me.'' Can our works stand the test?

Paul says, ''Let love be without dissimulation. Abhor that which is evil; cleave to that which is good. . . Distributing to the necessity of the saints; . . . Recompense to no man evil for evil; . . . But rather give place to wrath: for it is written, vengeance is mine; I will repay, saith the Lord. . . Therefore, if thine enemy hunger, feed him: if he thirst, give him to drink: for in so doing thou shalt heap coals of fire on his head. Be not overcome of evil, but overcome evil with good.'' Quite different from the way we treat our enemies, is it not? Can we stand the test?

''Think it not strange when we suffer persecution, yea, and all that will live godly in Christ Jesus shall suffer persecution.'' ''Set your affection on things above, not on things on the earth, . . As we have therefore opportunity, let us do good to all men, especially unto them who are of the household of faith.'' ''Judge not, that ye be not judged. For with what judgment ye judge, ye shall be judged.'' ''Judge not!'' We judge and condemn, and thereby violate the Word. Evil thinking always precedes evil speaking; the love we ought to have for one another thinketh no evil. Paul, having in mind the teaching of Christ, said: ''Bear ye one another's burdens and so fulfill the love of Christ.'' How often we fail in living out these teachings! Another passage we want to call our attention to, lest we forget, is ''Brethren, if a man be overtaken in a fault, ye which are spiritual,

restore such a one in the spirit of meekness; considering thyself, lest thou also be tempted.'' This was Paul's plan of dealing with a brother who had been overtaken in a fault. What is our plan? Here are some of the plans we take: First, we run to the pastor, if we don't happen to see any one before we see the pastor, tell him all we know, and possibly add some to it; second, tattle it to some one else, third, keep on and on until we can see no one else to tattle to. Paul says of such Christians, ''They are wells without water, whose mouths must be stopped, they profess that they know God; but in works they deny him, being abominable, and disobedient, and unto every good work reprobate.'' Is it any wonder the Bible lies on the center table until it gets dusty? These texts we must face in the judgment. Can we stand the test?

So many of us try to see how little of God's word we can observe, and then think we can stand the test. ''Put on the whole armor of God.'' What for? ''That ye may be able to stand against the wiles of the devil! Again, we must have on the whole armor, so we can withstand in the evil day. We must have our loins girded about with truth and and have on the breastplate of righteousness; and our feet shod with the preparation of the gospel of peace; having on the shield of faith, in order to be able to quench all the fiery darts of the wicked, and the helmet of salvation, and the sword of the Spirit, which is the word of God. ''And besides this, giving all diligence ,add to your faith virtue; and to virtue knowledge; and to knowledge temperance; and to temperance patience; and to patience godliness; and to godliness brotherly kindness; and to brotherly kindness charity. For if these things be in you, and abound, they make you that ye shall neither be barren nor unfruitful in the knowledge of our Lord Jesus Christ. But he that lacketh these things is blind, and cannot see afar off, and hath forgotten that he was purged from his old sins.''

We are passing this way only once, how careful then should we guard our thoughts, our words, our actions and above all our temper. Whenever temper is in control, sin abounds. When our Savior looked over the doomed city, he was made to cry out, ''O, Jerusalem, Jerusalem, thou that killeth the prophets, and stonest them which are sent unto thee, how often would I have gathered thy children together, even as a hen gathereth her chickens under her wings, and ye would not.'' He would gladly have saved them, had they only given him a chance. May God help us to a closer study of his Word, may we search the Word daily, for the acid of sin is striving to burn its way into hearts of pure gold. CAN WE STAND THE TEST?

Losantville, Indiana.

Ths Man Jesus. By J. A. McInturff

About 1924 years ago this man was born at a small town called Bethlehem in the ancient land of Palestine of a Jewish woman. This woman was a virgin engaged (at the time of conception) to be married to a man by the name of Joseph. Mary, the mother, and the men who followed this wonderful man on earth, believed that his birth was unnatural, and that he was born by the power of Almighty God, born of a virgin. This is the plain teaching of the New Testament., Early in life he showed signs of extraordinary personality and intelligence. At about the age of thirty he appeared at a meeting held by one John the Baptist who was preaching a new spirituality of the Law and the Prophets. He requested baptism and began to preach and for three years he taught his ideas of religion. After his death his disciples were inspired to write a record of his life and teachings, and upon the New Testament was builded the churches of Christendom. About all we know of this historical man is found in the Gospels written by his followers. But this will be enough for our purpose.

First, this man felt conscious that he was unlike other men in that he was THE Son of God. He claimed to be the

Son of God and the Savior of men. He believed that he was to live a certain life and die a certain death and teach certain things for men to believe and do in order to be what he believed he was. He laid down his program upon two things. First, himself. Second, his teaching. This was one program, not two, but there was in it two things, not one. He demanded certain beliefs about himself and then about the things he taught. To believe in what he taught and to practice it is worthless unless we believe in him. Christianity is built upon him, not his teaching. But to believe in him is to believe in his teachings. The Brethren church has been building upon his teaching and forgetting the Christ. This is true of all churches. Belief is in him, not his teaching; but the doing relates to his teaching. Let us believe in him and do his teaching. He demanded belief in himself as the Savior of men. He told his disciples that all life, even eternal, depended upon him. ''I am the resurrection and the life?'' Who? I. Not what I teach, but what I am. Salvation, hope of eternal life, comes from our belief in him, not from our doing his teaching. Our doing his teaching will result from our faith in him and our sense of future security in that faith. The test of his claim to be God is proven in the history of his life. He possessed the power to suspend natural law, to create, and by abundant proof demonstrated that he possessed divine power. He was unlike other men in that his friends and enemies say he lived a sinless life. Take his claim to be God, his demonstration of divine power and the historical sinless life and you have the positive proof of his claim. Now, let us take the suggestion. Think of Christ, study him make him real, and believe in him. To believe less than his claim is to lose your Christ. His teaching will appeal to you with force after you have

really consecrated all your faith in him. May the Brethren church think on Christ. O, thou great Son of God, reveal thyself to us. O, mighty Christ, mighty God, hear us when we pray to know thee. It is hard for us to feel the responsibility of doing thy bidding when we do not know who thou art. But if you are the Son of God to us, we would not disobey one word that fell from thy lips. On this we stand or fall. A Christless church although they keep all commands will fall, but a church with Christ, the Son of God, will do all the commands and all the powers of evil will not crumble her walls.

Goshen, Indiana.

Constructive Labor. By G. T. Ronk

One of the most comforting assurances in the Word of God is that we are laborers together with him. Being made in God's image we partake of the divine nature and have the satisfaction of achievement, of looking on what our minds have purposed, our spirits have enforced and our hands have wrought. No words can paint the human happiness that comes through the mere satisfaction of the desire to do and to accomplish.

But in the specific labor of the Lord which Jesus came incarnate to inaugurate, that work which has to do with the regeneration of the spirit of man, we have the added joy of divine partnership and of direct spiritual illumination for the combined task of ourselves and our Great Elder Brother. All our labor in this service should be doubly fruitful and blessed if we never lose sight of the partnership of it and the divine wisdom which guarantees its success.

That great partnership labor heads up in mission and

church extension work as the progressive and constructive end of a divine program. I cannot but feel that in the pioneering end of his service the great Head is especially busy and especially concerned. His last great commission was a pioneering charge for the church as though he were reminding us of the dangerous inertia of mere content, fixed habit and vested custom.

The annual Thanksgiving tide call for church extension offering thus goes out to all like a trumpet blast, calling to constructive labor, the blazing of new trails, the launching of new hopes, the scanning of a new horizon and the capitalizing of a new zeal. It is for all, reminding us that the unorganized, the unclaimed, the unredeemed, the unpossessed, the unplanned and the unprogrammed are heavy on the heart of the great Founder of our faith; and that if we are to be laborers together with him we must partake of his travail of spirit and enter with him on the untrodden way.

Leon, Iowa.

The Sinless Christ. By T. Darley Allen

Our Lord makes a universal appeal because all men recognize in him a complete character. As Alexander Henderson says: "He blends love with holiness, grief with joy, tenderness with severity, gentleness with courage. He can stand alone and yet mingle with men in the social life. He can be a mystic and yet be practical. Like the picture of the face whose eyes are looking straight at you from whatever angle you view it, so Jesus seems to be looking right at us from whatever angle of life we view him. In him is completeness of character."

We realize that Jesus is man always at his best. Never does he do anything that shows an undesirable attribute in his character, and we all would feel as did the celebrated literary man who, speaking for the company he was in when one of their number asked what they would do if Jesus appeared among them, said, they would fall on their knees.

Men feel their unworthiness in contemplating the wonderful life of Jesus. Other men who have been great moral teachers of humanity have recognized their imperfections. But in Jesus was no sin, and of this he was conscious.

Horace Bushnell well said that the character of Jesus "forbids his possible classification with men," and Philip Schaff maintained the perfection of Christ is proof of his divinity.

It cannot reasonably be claimed that the sinlessness of Christ is merely literary, that the evangelists invented that side of their Master's character, for to admit this would be to assume that the writers of the gospels performed the miracle of literature.

Henry Van Dyke says: "Jesus is such a person as men could not have imagined if they would, and would not have imagined if they could. He is neither Greek myth nor Hebrew legend. The artist capable of fashioning him did not exist, nor could he have found the materials. A non-existant Christianity did not spring out of the air and create a

Christ. A real Christ appeared in the world and created Christianity."

The only reasonable view is that the evangelists were merely biographers describing a life that actually was before their eyes.

Rousseau, in "Emilius," showed that he felt the force of the argument that the fiction of such a character as Christ is more inconceivable than the reality.

Bishop Hogue says: "The boldest writer of fiction in the world would never dare, were he able to do so, to make the leading character of one of his works flawless, sinless, perfect, since it would be so overdrawn so absolutely disconformable to facts, and so universally shocking to society as to result on a verdict that the writer was a fool, a knave or a madman. Yet in the case of Jesus we have one in the form of man who was flawless, sinless, perfect, and the world has been studying his character for well nigh two millenniums and in each succeeding age has placed a higher estimate upon it and has paid it increasing reverence." And, again says Bishop Hogue, "if we were to reject the miracles of Jesus we should still have the miracle of Christ himself."

Cleveland, Ohio.

SENTIMENT IN FRANCE

Miss Anna Gordon, National President of the Woman's Christian Temperance Union has just returned form a five months' trip in Europe in the interest of prohibition. She reports a strong movement and a growing sentiment in France for prohibition of distilled liquors. This movement is led by prominent women of the country, and is destined to make a considerable impression within the next few years. The French people are watching with interest the effects of prohibition in America. Miss Gordon also told of a strong dry movement in Scotland which will culminate in local elections in the near future.

THE BRETHREN PULPIT

Christ's Church.   By J. F. Koontz

TEXT: Upon this rock I will build my church; and the gates of hell shall not prevail against it. MATTHEW 16:18

God planned many things for the best good of mankind. These plans existed originally in the divine mind of God, beginning with eternity. For example, the ark built by Noah. God lifted to his eye the telescope of time and looked down through the ages and saw that the time would come when the world would become so wicked that it would be necessary to destroy it with a flood of waters. All who would not obey him would be buried in a watery grave. But to save all the obedient and a pair of each kind of living creatures an ark was necessary. There was need of a vessel which would float on the bosom of the waters until the waters would subside. God gave Noah full directions how to build the ark (See Genesis 6:14-22). Solomon's temple was also an example of the wise planning of God. It was a place where the Ark of the Covenant, the tables of the Law, etc., could be kept and also a place where his chosen people could meet to worship. The plan of salvation also emanated from the divine mind of God. This involved many things, one of which was the erection of Christ's church. The materials of which this is composed are the souls of men, all Christian people of every clime, age, and race. God being both the designer and the architect of this marvelous structure, ordained his Son, Jesus Christ, master builder and master mechanic and sent him into the world to do his part of the work and also to direct the work of this marvelous and stupendous undertaking.

Let us notice the Builder. (I will build). This was an extraordinary undertaking. It required more than human skill, human intellect, and human sacrifice to succeed in this tremendous work. There was no fault in the plan and in the execution of it, it required a leader, who was without fault. Christ was the one personage who would measure up to the requirements. Pilate confessed to the chief priests and to the people, "I find no fault in this man" (Luke 23:4).

In the survey of this subject we at once see in a very great measure, what Christ had to face. A wicked and rebellious world was before him. A world groping in darkness. Sin seemed to be predominant. On the very verge of his undertaking, he came to his own, and his own received him not (John 1:11). Then according to the Divine plan he went entirely among strangers (The Gentiles). He there began his arduous task assigned to him by the originator of the plan. I can say without the fear of successful contradiction that he is gloriously succeeding. I am aware that this success is not conceded to him by many in this enlightened age.

His advent into the world to carry out his Father's plan, was a fulfillment of prophecy. "And speak unto him, saying, thus speaketh the Lord of hosts, saying, behold the man whose name is the BRANCH: and he shall grow up out of his place, and he shall build the temple, (church) of the Lord. Even he shall build the temple, (church) of the Lord: and he shall bear the glory, and shall sit and rule upon his throne: and he shall be a priest upon his throne: and the counsel of peace shall be between them both" (Zech. 6:12-13).

It was 712 years before Christ, that Isaiah told how the Lord God planned the foundation of this wonderful edifice. "Therefore saith the Lord God, behold, I lay in Zion for a foundation a stone, a tried stone, a precious corner stone, a sure foundation: he that believeth shall not make haste (Isa. 28:16; 1 Cor. 3:11. and Eph. 2:20). Christ not only is made the master builder, but he acts the part as the chief corner stone in the foundation of this edifice (See Isa. 28:16 and Eph. 2:20-22). Christ becomes the chief angle of this structure, the connecting medium, connecting the church militant and the church triumphant. The foundation on which the church is built is the apostles and prophets, Christ himself being the chief corner stone (Eph. 2:20). A corner stone in a stone wall is the most carefully laid stone in a wall. It ties the two walls together, hence a connecting medium. A corner stone means something more than a mere stone in a wall. The Lord places this special emphasis on Christ, as the corner stone.

The master builder conducts the preparation of the material to be used in the erection of this edifice. In the obtaining of his material he approaches the human quarry. He with heaven's blasting powers proceeds to secure his material. The material is in its crude state. "Know ye not that the unrighteous shall not inherit the kingdom of God? Be not deceived: neither fornicators, nor idolaters, nor adulterers, nor effeminate, nor abusers of themselves, with mankind. Nor thieves, nor revilers, nor extortioners, shall inherit the kingdom of God. And such were some of you: but ye are washed, but ye are sanctified, but ye are justified in the name of the Lord Jesus, and by the Spirit of our God (1 Cor. 6:9-11). In the preparation of the material, a marked change is brought about. Let us illustrate. A man takes a stone in its crude state just from the stone quarry and places it on the stonecutter's bench. Here time is spent with mallet and chisel until it is shaped into the design of the designer and polished to perfect beauty and it is completed as a tombstone. Comparing the finished product with the raw material you readily see the marked change. So is all material used in the erection of Christ's church, notwithstanding the condition of this material in its crude state. When Christ touches blasphemers they undergo this radical change, and their blasphemies are changed to praise. When Christ touches cannibals, a class who are enemies to mankind, they learn whom they once hated, to love with a fervent love. When Christ touches the Hottentots, a race so low down that the are hardly recognized as belonging to the human family they are so wonderfully changed that they become members of the family and fold of God.

It is Christ's work to provide himself with helpers or laborers who shall assist him in this all important work. Christ while walking by the sea of Galilee, saw two brethren, Peter and Andrew, his brother, he saith unto them, Follow me, and I will make you fishers of men. (Matthew 4:19). I glean the thought from the above statement that God saves man by man. Man cannot by his Christian deportment, Christian life, Christian zeal, and Christian energy, save his fellowmen, but he can bring others in such proximity to Christ that he can save them. Let us illustrate. The photographer agrees to make one dozen photographs for a certain stipulated amount, a thing which he cannot do. All he can do is to adjust the card board to the negative, and the sunlight paints or transfers the picture from the negative to the card board. Just so men can adjust the crude material to the Power that can cleanse and in this way God saves man by man, which is according to the divine plan.

This makes man a heaven sent messenger to man. If this statement is not according to the divine plan of God, then I ask, Why did God send Elijah to Mt. Carmel? Why did he not send an angel? Why did God send Daniel to interpret the hand writing on the wall? Why did he not send an angel? In many other instances he set men through whom he could accomplish some divine work. Why did God send Joseph as an interpreter of dreams? Why did he not send angels to do such work?

It is Christ's business to complete the erection. And that he will do in his own good time. I can safely say, "That he knows no defeat." He has, and always will be victorious in all he undertakes to do for the welfare of mankind. True, he encounters many hindrances. The opposition of the devil. Many professed Christians have cold feet. Many have cramped knees, they cannot get down to pray. Many have a zeal, but not of God. I like to compare the growth of the church to the mighty oak of the forest, which grows and continues to grow until it towers its head above its surrounding neighbors and crowns itself king of the for-

est. Likewise, the church will grow until it towers its head, high above all other organization and crowns itself queen of the world. The completing work will be when Christ comes again into the world and gathers its own unto himself and sets up his eternal kingdom where he will rule his people throughout all eternity, girding himself and serving his redeemed.

I am glad to think of the safety of the church: "The gates of hell shall not prevail against it." In the sight of Christ, the church is very precious. It is the bride, the lamb's wife and very precious indeed (Luke 21:5-18).

Washington, D. C.

FROM OUR CONFERENCE PLATFORMS

Education In Its Relation to the Progress of Christianity

An address delivered at the late Ohio State Conference by President E. E. Jacobs, Ph. D.

I can not overestimate the importance of Christian education, for in those two words, education and Christianity, are wrapped up about all that is worth while in the world. I want to define, as best I can, what I mean by Christian education. I mean the putting of all learning under the spirit and genius of Jesus. I mean that the life shall be frankly Christian. I think the world has had about enough of those nations which would exalt the intellect at the expense of the heart, where survival power was the touchstone of all existence and progress, where the struggle for existence and the survival of the fittest was the shibboleth of the would-be powerful, and where God, heaven, love, and sympathy for the weak were laughed out of court.

Christian education is something more than a method of teaching geometry and chemistry. It relates to one's philosophy of life, to one's outlook on life, how one relates one's self to the great problems,—social, industrial, education, moral—of life. It is one's rapport with life.

Now, Christianity as lived and exemplified by Jesus was a very simple matter. Nothing could be simpler than his law of love, the golden rule and his going about doing good. But there are also problems and mysteries. There is the doctrine of the Deity of Jesus, his resurrection, the indwelling of the Holy Spirit, his miracles, providence, the after life, etc. These are some of the points of attack. The power of a good life has never been the point of attack, but these and others present what is often regarded as vulnerable points. Hence, there must be no mental wabbling about the Lordship of Jesus, about his sonship, personal responsibility, a reckoning in the after-life, about God in history, or about salvation through grace.

Now there are some tendencies in modern education that need curbing. I want to stress three. 1. There is in some cases, a tendency to slur over, underestimate, and minimize religion as a potent agency for good. There are those who can see no real good in religion. This thought was headed up some years ago by Spencer, Huxley, Comte and by Lester F. Ward in this country and by Ernest Haeckel, now abroad. There are those who look upon religion as something which may even be tolerated but certainly not to be engaged in heartily. But these are profoundly mistaken. I want to insist that the fine idealism of religion which has impelled and driven onward, with a perfectly wonderful power from the days of the cave-man on up to now, is the most precious heritage of the race. Without this almost cosmic force in human life, history would be unthinkable.

2. There is, moreover, a tendency in some parts to explain away religion—your theosophist doctrine. This flattens out religion and makes not for grace of heart, but for sharpness of the intellect. I confess I am a bit alarmed today over the tendency to erase the miracle of grace from

Christianity. Sin still stands out as the tragedy of the universe and all the intellect in all the world, apart from grace, can not win man back to God. Therefore, I want to stress an education that needs make no apology for a belief in Christ and his church, or for a religion that is something more than highly emotionalized intellect. God knows we have about enough of that sort of religion as it is and Ashland need not contribute more!

Take those who would teach the Bible just as they would any other subject, say history. The children of Israel were to encompass Jericho and the walls were to fall, not through the miraculous power of God but by the sympathetic vibrations of the ram's horns. Very well, then so could you and I do likewise, and then where is your miracle? Or, Jesus was not really dead but the cool moist earth revived him. Well, so also with you and me, but then where is the doctrine of the resurrection, of which Paul made so much and which caused him to say that if Jesus be not raised, then is our preaching vain? Or again, Jesus was only the son of God in that he sustained unique relations with him. He differed not in kind, they would say, but in degree from us. So then are we all sons of God, redeemed and saved. Then where is your doctrine of redemption? Christian education ought to step right in here and make these great fundamental doctrines secure and not allow them to be subverted as suggested above.

What then, is the task of a Christian college? (1) Face facts. Meet hard problems. Ye shall know the truth and the truth shall set you free. (2) After facing these stubborn facts, uphold Christianity.

(3) Do not attempt to force the living, fiery ferment of the Gospel into molds of a bygone age. Christianity is a thing alive in our hands. It will not be taken by force. It will not be compressed within confines. It must work, expand, and work the miracle of the ages—convert men.

And in the last place, (4) There is a tendency to entrap education in the meshes of materialism and intellectual joyriding. If education is not idealistic, then it is not education at all. Ideals still rule or ruin a nation.

Make firm, O God, the peace our dead have won,
    For Folly shakes her tinseled head
And points us back to darkness and to hell,
    Cackling, "Beware of Visions," while our dead
Still cry, "It was for visions that we fell."

I dare to believe and venture to say, that education need not be antagonistic to religion, but it may be made the very vehicle of Christianity. And a problem right now in our church is, that she make her educational institutions, not liabilities, but assets to her progress. Support her school and publications so that they may in turn support her. Educate her ministry so that it may in turn educate her. Infect her learning with the spirit of Jesus so that it may in turn infect her. Let all life and learning be put and kept in sweet accord with the spirit and genius of Jesus.

I therefore pray, that the young people of our own faith and of America may take their lives so seriously that they will make full preparation for living. And I pledge myself and the dear men and women of my faculty again to put our ideals of learning increasingly under the spirit of our risen and living and glorified Lord.

Ashland, Ohio.

Send
WHITE GIFT
OFFERINGS to

THE SUNDAY SCHOOL

H. H. WOLFORD
General Secretary-Treasurer
Ashland, Ohio

Our Present Status.   By Albert Trent

In bringing to you a brief message on the present status of the Brethren Sunday schools of the Pennsylvania district, permit me to digress for a few moments from the subject in hand, to bring to your attention in a reminiscent way, the beginning of these gatherings in the interest of Sunday school work.

The Brethren people have always been strong advocates of religious education for their children and young people. It is a well known fact that the followers of Alexander Mack, Tunkers or Brethren, conducted a Sunday school in Germantown, Pennsylvania, years before Robert Raikes opened his school on the Sabbath day for street urchins in England.

In later years the Brethren of Western Pennsylvania became so interested in the the work for the sake of their children, that they felt the imperative need of getting together to discuss methods, develop plans and to give inspiration to a movement for better organization and improvement in the teaching of the Word in our Sunday schools. The Annual Meeting of that day had frowned upon movements of this kind, and those who were loyal to its dictations directly opposed all such attempts.

Nevertheless, a call was issued to the Brethren churches of Western Pennsylvania for a Sunday School Convention to be held in Berlin in the fall of 1879, just 41 years ago. This convention was held in the German Baptist Meeting House on the outskirts of the town of Berlin. My recollection is that the sessions continued over two days. It was largely attended, and so successful, enthusiastic and conducive of good to the work, that before adjourning it was unanimously voted to make the convention an annual affair, and arrangements were effected for the next meeting in the fall of the following year, 1880, at the same place.

At that time the Pennsylvania State Sabbath School Association was only in its teens, in fact but eighteen years old. The third year it was held in Salisbury, then Johnstown, then back to Berlin, to Conemaugh, to Masontown, then to Berlin for the fourth time, to Meyersdale, and then to Johnstown for the second time, in 1886; when it was merged with the First Brethren Conference held in the Pennsylvania District that year. It has continued covering a part of the sessions of our conferences up to the present time. The records therefore show this to be the 40th Annual Convention of the Brethren schools of the Keystone State.

Just twenty-one years ago, in 1899, we met in Pittsburgh, and that Conference was scheduler as the Eleventh Annual Conference of the Brethren Churches and Twentieth Annual Convention of the Brethren Sunday Schools of Pennsylvania. This became too cumbersome a title and was changed to the Brethren Conference, covering the sessions of the churches and the schools as it ought.

My object in calling your attention to these facts is to impress you with the truth that the record of the Sunday school work of he Brethren of our state is not a mean one, but most commendable, and reflects great credit on the leaders of the church of thirty and forty years ago who devoted so much time and energy in the interest of religious educa-

tion of the young people of the church. These facts should prove an inspiration to us today to emulate the splendid efforts of the men and women of the past years and maintain the standard they have given us, and by our devotion bring our schools to the highest possible attainment.

This brings me to the subject properly assigned to me; Our Present Status from the earliest movement of our people in this work a growing interest has always been maintained, as evidenced by the reports given year by year, showing a regular increase in enrollment, a more complete organization for work and training of teachers, as well as the adoption and application of the modern methods in the management of the local school. However, about the second year of the great war this advancement received a rather discouraging check in the features of enrollment, attendance and general interest in the work of the schools. Since then our schools have experienced a downward trend as our reports show with the other schools in general throughout the state. Even the State Association shows a loss of 250,000 during this period in enrollment.

Our losses, however, are not so great that they might be regarded as a source of discouragement to the workers, and when compared with the losses of the past few years of some of the large denominations there is much for which we may feel encouraged and abundant reasons for gratitude to the Master for the success that has been ours. The small losses in some of the features of the work are offset by gains in the others. The report for this year in comparison with last year shows a loss of but 77 in enrollment, or less than two percent. The loss on total membership of our schools is 144, also less than two percent. The most serious loss we have had during the year is that of 15 percent on the adult enrollment. We have made however some very encouraging gains: on regular offerings our gain has been over $12,000, or 170 percent; on missionary offerings, 7 percent; on Teacher Training students, about 8 percent and on additions to the church from the Sunday school, almost 100 percent over last year.

The facts of the present status of the Brethren schools of Pennsylvania is such that it should afford us to stimulus to overcome the slight losses of the past year and re-assure u that by a reasonable effort on the part of all we can come to next year's Conference showing a gain on every feature of our work.

Johnstown, Pennsylvania.

"Yea, my King,"
I began—"thou dost well in rejecting mere comforts that
   spring
From the mere mortal life held in common by man and by
   brute:
In our flesh grows the branch of this life, in our soul it bears
   fruit.
Leave the flesh to the fate it was fit for! the spirit be thine!
By the spirit, when age shall o'ercome thee, thou shalt still
   enjoy
More, indeed, than at first, when, unconscious, the life of a
   boy."—Browning, in Saul.

J. A. Garber
PRESIDENT

E. A. Rowsey
SECRETARY

Our Young People at Work

On the Lookout and Outlook

By A. E. Rowsey, Associate General Secretary of the Ohio Christian Endeavor Union

(Continued from issue of October 20).

3. A Look up.

Prof. Amos R. Wells says, "The outward look cannot be true until the upward look is strong."

Back of every successful Christian Endeavor organization there is a strong prayer life. Prayer alone will not build a Christian Endeavor Society, but human power, apart from prayer cannot build a society for permanent growth. Are your habits of prayer good enough to be recommended to anyone in your society? or to any society in the foreign countries which were mentioned in the earlier part of this address? If not, our "up-look" is not strong enough for your own uplift. It is easy to look out and look in after we have looked up. The up-look produces a clear outlook. Let us look up to him as the Author and Finisher of our plans.

Our Morning Prayer

"Take my life and let it be
Consecrated, Lord, to thee."
"To thee, thou bleeding Lamb
In all things one,
All that I have and am,
And all that I know
All that I have is now no longer mine
And I a mnot mine own; Lord, I am thine."

Our Evening Prayer

"Far, far away like bells at evening pealing
The voice of Jesus sounds o'er land and sea,
And laden souls, by thousands meekly stealing,
Kind Shepherd, turn their weary steps to thee."

During Our Temptation Hours

Breathe through the pulses of desire
His coolness and his Balm"
Calm me, my God, and keep me calm,
While those hot breezes blow;
Be like the night dew's cooling balm
Upon earth's fevered brow."

These expressions are the outgrowth of the upward look. The poetic future is revealed through the power of Christ to calm the panting heart and purpose it to know and do his will.

4. A Look Forward.

"Life is real, life is earnest:
And the grave is not its goal;
'Dust thou art, to dust returnest'
Was not spoken of the soul."

"We are living, we are dwelling
In a grand and awful time,
In an age on ages telling
To be living is sublime."

We have reviewed the past; we have considered the enduring elements of the present; now logically we must face the future. We are challenged with a stupendous task—that of remolding a program of religious education and changing our points of emphasis. We must lay more stress on formation and less stress upon reformation.

Our forward-looking program is to save the developing youth and use wasted energy of past years in reconstructing in these days of reconstruction. "Trusting in the Lord, Jesus Christ, for strength," we must undertake the biggest

Advertising Christian Endeavor

By Earl Huette, Publicity Department

‡‡‡

YOUNG PEOPLE!

U R THE SUBJECT

C. E. means Christian Endeavor.

Christian Endeavor stands for Christian Training and also Christian Service.

Mother, Father, PASTOR, Young People.

This column will carry interesting FACTS about Christian Endeavor every week.

(Save every item).

---

task we have ever tackled; we must attempt great things for God. We must expect great things of God. We have not given enough of ourselves over to God. We have not asked God for enough of himself for us, for our strengthening.

We are passing through a crisis in a transitional development. If we could become more conscious that we can never pass this way again, our service would be more intense, and our sacrifice more cheerfully made.

I Shall Not Pass Again This Way

The bread that bringeth strength I want to give
The water pure that bids the thirsty live,
I want to help the fainting, day by day,
I'm sure I shall not pass again this way.

I want to give the oil of joy for tears,
The faith to conquer crowding doubts and fears,
Beauty for ashes may I give away,
I'm sure I shall not pass again this way.

I want to give good measure running o'er,
And into angry hearts I want to pour
The answer soft that turneth wrath away,
I'm sure I shall not pass again this way.

I want to give to others hope and faith.
I want to do all that the Master saith.
I want to do aright from day to day,
I'm sure I shall not pass again this way.

As we look forward we must have:

1 Faith in God—we dare not break faith with God.
2 We dare not break friendship with man.
3 We dare not break partnership with ourselves.

Our is a challenge unto life. If we are willing to so consecrate and discipline our own lives, the future has in store for us blessings which far surpass our wildest expectations. We must frankly face the outlook and with the eye of an eagle we must look out; we must not only look, we must SEE; we must not only see, we must acknowledge what we have seen; and there must be interest, love, fellowship, friendship and fidelity in our acknowledgment.

SEND ALL MONEY FOR
General Home, Kentucky and
Foreign Missions to

MISSIONS

WILLIAM A. GEARHART
General Missionary Secretary
906 Conover Bldg., Dayton, O.

How One Pastor Is Advertising the Home Mission Offering

(If you have not yet put the matter squarely up to every member of your church, here is a suggestion.—EDITOR.)

Our Thanksgiving Offering

(By E. M. Cobb in Dayton Church Weekly Bulletin).

In just one month, we are to have our feast of ingathering. We used to call it our "Harvest meeting." The Lord used to have his people to bring him their first sheaf of the field, the first fruits of the orchard, and the first of the herd and the flocks, and do not forget the first of the family, too. Oh we get off easy now. We have been shaving off a little here and there, until about all there is to a Thanksgiving, is for the President to copy off the proclamation he had in the papers last year, and we all go to some of our friends in the country and see how much turkey we can surround and defeat the undertaker by paying a little surcharge tax to the doctor. We all have a good time, but how much do we think of the other fellow?

Now this time we are sure going to have a good time. We are counting on a great program and a great offering. One number on the program will be well worth the entire evening. We dare not tell you yet what it is,

but maybe we can next week or the week after. But we want to give you this notice a month ahead that you may not have any other date made for that evening, for you really do not want to miss this event.

Now about the offering. That will be for Home Missions. That means all of our missions in the U. S. A. and not any of our foreign missions. The Home Board asks us this year for a dollar a member. We nearly did that the last time and it will be easy this time if we think ahead a little. Begin now to save up. Some of the little ones, and some of the careless ones who do not really know that there is a Thanksgiving service, or that they owe a debt, to the unsaved, or that there is a reward for the saving of a soul, such as these will not give a dollar. But there are those who have been so wondrously saved, and some who have ben so wonderfully blessed this year that they can not contain their souls if they do not give the Lord some real tangible token of their appreciation of their blessings. There will be many a twenty, ten and five go in out of pure gratitude.

The Gospel Mandatory

(This clipping from the Christian Herald selected by Brother Gearhart carries a message that is especially timely. The mandatory character of the Gospel has a bearing upon home missions as well as foreign. We have no more right to be indifferent to the irreligious and unchurched conditions in our own land than we have to non-Christian conditions in foreign lands. The responsibility is upon us and we must face it.—Editor).

Matt. 28:19. "Go ye therefore and preach the Gospel to all nations." There are people who say, "One religion is as good as another, so long as you live up to it." The Mohammedans live up to their religion, and behold the result. "By their fruits ye shall know them."

We profess to be a Christian nation; and as such we have been asked to assume a mandatory over certain peoples who have suffered at the hands of the Moslem. However, the far stretch of the Seven Seas or the terms of our Constitution may forbid, we are, nevertheless, not absolved from responsibility in these premises. By the teaching of our Lord as to the universal brotherhood, we are under bonds "to do good and to communicate as we have opportunity unto all men." And we have an unmistakable "mandatory" from his own lips: "Go, evangelize!" Our propaganda is to be carried on not with any dripping Yemen blade but with the "sword of the Spirit which is the Word of God."

The responsibility rests upon us not only as a Christian republic but as individual followers of Christ. For nations are only as the units that constitute them. Let us therefore bring our lives up to the summit of our light.

We have a God who says not "These to hell, and I care not!" but "As I live, saith the Lord, I have no pleasure in the death of the wicked but that all should turn unto me and live!"

Our symbol of conquest is the Cross, on which self-sacrifice was made the crowning virtue of life and character. By all the privileges of the Gospel, let us so live that men—even those dwelling afar off—shall see our good works and glorify God.   D. J. B.

Lost Creek, Kentucky

One of the most impressive things it has ever been my privilege to witness here, or anywhere, in a religious way, occurred one recent Friday morning at our chapel exercises. It has become not an uncommon thing to hear some of our grade pupils repeat from memory, a chapter from the Bible. This they have quite frequently done, both at regular and chapel services, and it was always impressive. But the following was so much more so. The teacher who had the chapel exercise to give this morning, asked her High School class to arise and give the Scripture lesson. This class of young men and women, from sixteen to twenty years old, thirteen in number, arose and repeated from memory in unison, the third chapter of Second Timothy. To hear young men and women of their age, quote Scripture like that, as a class, WAS SOMETHING VERY, VERY IMPRESSIVE INDEED. Then when we remember that the Lord has said, "That my word shall not return to me void," what or who can measure the force and power for righteousness set

going by such work, and remember that this they did while they were doing their regular school work; YEA IT IS THEIR SCHOOL WORK, THE MOST IMPORTANT PART THEY GET AT RIVERSIDE.

Now, anyone who knows the work here knows that the grade work is the feeder for this higher work. BRETHREN, DO YOU WANT TO CUT THIS OFF? IS IT ACTUALLY TRUE, AS WE ARE TOLD, THAT YOU DO NOT WANT TO SUPPORT THE GRADE WORK ANY LONGER AT RIVERSIDE? In our judgment the testing time is not very far away, when as far as we can humanly see there is no provision made for this very, very IMPORTANT PART OF RIVERSIDE'S WORK, THE GRADE WORK.

The Presbyterians of late have been holding a Conference on the Mountain Work, at Jackson, Kentucky, the county seat of Breathitt county. Below I quote from two speakers at this conference, both of whom have labored many years in the mountains, and one of which is a native of the hills—the first one quoted. These quotations are self-explanatory.

"A great many things are said about the mountaineers of Kentucky, the back yards of these eight states, and so many different views are expressed that I find myself puzzled as to what you, or we, really know of the mountains. A man rides around on the railroad, stops over night at the hotels, talks to some of the mountain men who lounge around, goes back home and writes a book about the mountains. YOU CANNOT KNOW ABOUT THE MOUNTAINS IN ANY SUCH FASHION. We cannot know a people just by meeting them for a few weeks or a few months.— When anybody speaks about how easy it is to manage a mule, I known right then that he has never managed a mule. I think I know something of the mountains. Talk to Guerrant, Scott, and others, who are giving their lives to the work, and find out how much sin and ignorance is blocking the way. Sin is blighting every cove in the mountains. It is no easy task in which we are engaged; it is a momentous task; yea, a hopeless task, did we not remember that God would give the victory."

From the other speaker we quote: "When we speak of a mountaineer, I am not thinking of people in Jackson, or Knoxville, or Ashville, or any of the large cities and towns of the mountains, because they are like any of the cities of the southern states, but of those people back in the coves, about two millions of them. Now in speaking of the mountain people, I believe that if I stay in the work a few years more, I shall reach the stars where I cannot make a speech at all. The shorter time we are in the work, the better speech we can make. The problems become so complex that it becomes more and more impossible to make a speech.

"Speaking of the schools, in 1870, the Synod of Kentucky, started the work in the mountains. The evangelists started out and organized churches here and there, and to-day you can find the deserted buildings. It seems that we do not appreciate, as a church this mountain problem, we do not back it up, and then it dies out. The 'Soul Winners' came to this conclusion, after the organization of these churches, that the way to do is to place a school beside the church, and that is now the policy of every place I know of, and of every denomination. They make a very effective weapon toward the reaching of the mountain boy and girl. Now, I do not say that the church could not succeed without the school, but I do not know of a single instance where a church without a school, has succeeded. Someone has said that the Apostle Paul did not fool with a school. Conditions were different. We have to train our leaders. We have no educated people to work with. Dr. Erdman was talking of a very pious Episcopalian who thought that the Episcopal church was the only church. Someone asked him if one could be saved another way. He said, 'Well, there might be some other way, but I do not think any gentleman ought to take advantage of it.' There might be some other way of developing the mountain church, but I do not know of it."

G. E. DRUSHAL.

NEWS FROM THE FIELD

LIMESTONE, TENNESSEE

Since our last church report many things have taken place of a constructive nature. We can praise God that little has happened of a destructive nature. There may be some members who cheat themselves of great blessings by contributing very little of themselves to the church life but we can point to no kickers. There is a feeling of fellowship among the members.

In the spring our church building was given some new coats of white paint on the outside, wall-finish for inside wall, varnish for woodwork and pews, and oil for the floor. Some of the young men are doing some grading about the grounds and some other work about the building is being done. All this makes our place of worship a more attractive place.

Our regular services have been very well attended and much interest shown. Our weekly Bible Class deserves special mention.

In May the Washington County Singing Convention met in our church. Several churches and Sunday schools were represented so we entertained many strangers on that day. We had some good singing and the spirit of the day was so fine that it was a day long to be remembered. At this same period Brother Thomas Allen of Kentucky, who was the first pastor of this church was here visiting his daughter. While here he conducted two services for us. Brother Allen has a warm place in the hearts of the people here. Later in the summer we had a combined service for the children and young people.

In July we held our communion and had with us Brother Wood of Roanoke, who preached four excellent sermons for us. Brother Wood proved a good friend to this church while he was in this district. In August, Prof. J. M. Bowman of Harrisonburg, Virginia, spent a week among us taking part in all our services and gave us some splendid talks on tithing. If every layman loved Christ and the church as does Brother Bowman there would be no complaint of lack of interest nor any empty treasuries. None but an isolated church can know how much all these visiting brethren were appreciated.

The last event of the church was the evangelistic meetings from September 29th to October 24th conducted by Sister Emma Aboud. These meetings were of unusual interest to both church and community. During these meetings the Lord blessed us with unusually fair weather after a prolonged wet season. There was no rain during the entire time. For a busy farming season the people came to church in a wonderful way. Several times the seating capacity was overtaxed. Some became offended at the preaching of the Word but in the main the community was greatly blessed because many heard the Word gladly and were more noble than some because they searched the Scriptures to see if these things be so. The church was gratified with the way Sister Aboud stood for the whole Bible. The church was edified. Many members received blessings through fastings and prayer and some through the anointing service so we were built up in body, mind and soul. There were twelve confessions, eleven of whom have been baptized and added to the church. Ten of this number came from the Sunday school. We praise God for giving us these eleven souls two of whom are yet children, one middle aged lady, and eight fine grown up young people whose bright faces are an inspiration to the church to continue to teach the Word of God that countless others may follow Jesus. The meeting closed with many under conviction. We have reason to believe much seed sowing was done for a future crop. We have much praise for our dear Sister Aboud who is such a tireless worker for Christ. Her example of faith surely would edify the most indifferent church.

We give the Lord the praise for all the mercy drops and showers of blessings bestowed upon us during the past year. The Lord has blessed us hitherto. And so in faith the church goes forth anew to sowing and reaping.

MARY PENCE.

FILLMORE, CALIFORNIA

Sunday, October 3, was a great day in our history. This was the day selected for Rally Day and Home Coming Day. The goals for the day were more than reached. The number set for attendance in the Sunday school was 150 and the total offering for the day was to be at least $100.00. The membership rallied to the support of the undertaking and when the record was completed we had "gone over the top" in a real way. The attendance in Sunday school was 188 and the total offering for the day was but a few cents short of $260.00. When it is recalled that Fillmore is but a new work and that three months ago the Sunday school attendance was less than 60, you can realize the way the Lord blessed our efforts. When the news reached one of the friends of the work, he said, "How did they do it?" The result was accomplished by a liberal use of printers' ink, by the most excellent co-operation on the part of the membership, and by definite prayer. God makes success possible when there is a willingness on the part of the people. Nothing was taken lightly and there was no cessation on the part of the workers until the job was completed. Possibly the most effective part of the printed matter was a promise to be present on Rally Day. This was used by the workers as they solicited attendance and by the middle of the week before Rally Day 135 people had signed these promises. On Wednesday evening at prayer meeting the pastor was able to announce to the people that we were to have more than the 150 which had been set as the goal. This added to the enthusiasm of the workers and they continued the work with increased zeal. On Saturday a postal card was sent out by the pastor to each of those who had signed the blank, thanking them for their promise to attend and assuring them it would be a very great personal disappointment to him if they were not present. This clinched the matter and practically 100 percent of those who had signed the blanks were on hand. The success was a great encouragement to our people and we are now reaping the results of our efforts. We are having the largest attendance in the Sunday school in our history and it is the determination of the workers that there shall be an increase in attendance shown each Sunday over the previous Sunday and we shall not be content until many of those who are not now in Sunday school shall be reached.

The work of the Young People's class in the Sunday school is worthy of notice. When the present teacher took charge of the class the attendance was two or three. At present the class has an attendance of from 18 to 20. This result has been accomplished within a month. The class is now definitely organized and every prospect points to an attendance much in advance of the present number within a comparatively short time. The Bible class has taken on new life. This class was but recently organized and definite plans for more aggressive work have been made. With these two classes setting the pace we shall soon see the attendance in the Sunday school largely increased.

The prayer meeting continues to be well attended. The interest in the study of the Bible in connection with the mid-week service is marked. These people have a simple faith in the Old Book, they love it and are anxious to learn God's will for their lives.

We are now in the midst of preparation for

the County Christian Endeavor Convention which is to hold its sessions in our church. The convention is to be held November 12, 13, 14. On December 5 we are to enter a union meeting led by Dr. French Oliver. All the churches of Fillmore are to share in this special effort. The present plans are that this union meeting is to be held in our church. The First Brethren church has been selected because of its location and because it will seat a larger crowd than any other church in the place. These things bring our work into prominence which will mean much to our work in the future.

We have at present three Christian Endeavor societies. For some time past our church has had the distinction of having the largest Christian Endeavor society in Ventura county. We now have three societies each nearly as large as the old society before these new organizations. Some weeks ago an Intermediate Society was organized which is doing excellent work. Two weeks ago a Junior society was organized which promises much. On last Sunday evening the attendance at the Junior society neared the 20 mark.

The work here has been much opposed from the very start but I feel sure the Lord has set his seal on the undertaking and the work is bound to succeed. The workers are seeing that glory may come to the Father and that Jesus may have his way in the hearts of many people.

On last Friday evening after the organization of the Bible Class the members of the class sprung a real surprise on the pastor and his wife. People began bringing packages and bundles of all sizes and placed them on the table in the church basement. The list included flour, spuds, sugar, bacon, coffee, tea, apples, canned goods, and even oil for the automobile. This was such a surprise that the pastor could only say, "Thank you." The pastor appreciates this great kindness not alone because of the real worth of the gift but more because of the spirit that made this gift possible. The spirit that maintains can mean nothing but definite success in the Lord's work.

Pray for the work here. The field is a difficult one but he can bring success.

J. C. BEAL,
Fillmore, California, Box .61.

TERRA ALTA, WEST VIRGINIA

Greetings from the midst of "Those West Virginia Hills." It would be a self-centered church indeed which could feel content and at the same time keep itself ostracised to the extent that the church at large could not know of its activities or perhaps its existence. Yes, we are down in the hills of West Virginia. We are an active little congregation, with a personnel which is, as far as Terra Alta is concerned, "The salt of the earth." Within the gates of the Terra Alta congregation, there are more school teachers, I suspect, than in any one congregation of its size in the entire brotherhood, for one-fourth of the membership is made up of school teachers. The remainder is made up of carpenters, retired ministers (there being only three) and farmers, merchants, mechanics, in fact the

city is very well represented in the Brethren church. We are located in one of the most healthful parts of the United States. Due to this fact hundreds of people every summer come here to breathe in the pure mountain air and drink in the beautiful natural scenery. These various assets are encouraging and certainly help us to visualize a bigger and better work at Terra Alta. Now you know about the place, I want to tell you about the activities.

When the writer came to this part of the country four months ago he was confronted with several almost impossible tasks but along with the difficulties he found a band of people willing to co-operate with the pastor in surmounting these difficulties. The Senior C. E., although it has not reached the realms of perfection is not at all discouraging. The Junior C. E. is the pride of the church. The average Sunday school attendance has stayed very close to one hundred percent. And a thing unknown is, for the Sunday school to remain for the church service. The finance of the church is in better condition than heretofore due in part to the creating of the budget system of finance. Sister Mae Smith, the general secretary of the W. M. S. was with us recently and organized the sisters of the church into what we hope will be an effective auxiliary of the church. So much for the mechanism of the church.

The spiritual life of the congregation, the dynamic of the mechanism, like the high physical elevation of Terra Alta, is at a high point. For this encouraging aspect we are indebted in part to Brother C. C. Grisso who was with us for a two weeks' meeting which resulted in thirteen additions to the church and a noticeable revival among the people in general.

So, Brethren, we are on the map. Don't be surprised if you hear from us again soon, and support us, as every church should support every other, by prayer.   V. U. FLORA.

ELKHART, INDIANA

At our late General Conference I was asked to consider the pastorate at this place. After a conference with their former pastor, Brother H. H. Wolford, and the Pastoral Committee arrangements were made for a visit to Elkhart.

On the 17th of September I returned from a pleasant visit with my home folks and with friends at Ashland to Elkhart and had the privilege of preaching to these loyal Brethren people.

As a result of this visit we have decided to labor together as pastor and people for the coming year.

The people of Elkhart are loyal. Their former pastor will testify that they gave him a whole-hearted support. I always like to hear a pastor speak well of his former congregation. It signifies that the spirit of Christ has been the dominating factor in their labors together. On the other hand it is just as significant if the members of a congregation speak well of their former pastor. Just here, I will say that not only the people of the Brethren church but those of the city speak

well of Brother Wolford. They extend to him their best wishes in his new field of labor.

The church here at Elkhart is in good condition. The various departments all seem to be full of life and vigor.

The people of the church and community have demonstrated their interest and loyalty by the way they have welcomed their new pastor. He usually leaves his pastorate for his university work each Monday afternoon, but on October 18th he was asked to remain, for what reason he only dimly perceived. On Sunday morning at the close of Sunday school he was suddenly asked to speak to the Beginners and Juniors in the Basement upon the subject, "Oh! Just Anything." After the reception I realized that the superintendent hadn't even had time to think of a subject. The reception was certainly an enjoyable occasion. The speeches of welcome by Peter Pontius and response by the pastor were followed by a bounteous dinner, served cafeteria style. An excellent program was then rendered in the auditorium. Rev. Croxall brought a welcome from the ministerial association: piano duet, Fern Baugher and Pauline Cripe; violin duet, Dorothy McManus and Mary Harden; saxophone solo by Lee Willis, accompanied at piano by Guy Hall; selections by the "Golden Rule Quartet," and a playlet, "Sewing for the Heathens" by the Sisterhood Girls. Everyone enjoyed this splendid social evening together and especially the pastor. The large number present assured him of an increasing interest. May the bonds of friendship and fellowship grow deeper between pastor and people. B. S. STOFFER.

REPORT OF LEAGUE ELECTION

As a result of the recent election the following persons were elected as officers of the Evangelistic and Bible Study League:

A. V. Kimmell, President.
J. Allen Miller, 1st Vice President.
Martin Shively, 2nd Vice President.
Ben T. Burnworth, 3rd Vice President.
N. H. Nielsen, Treasurer.
Henry V. Wall, Secretary.

Directors

For Three Years

Geo. W. Rench, Chas. A. Bame, W. S. Bell, E. M. Cobb, L. S. Bauman.

For Two Years

Ed. Miller, Geo. T. Ronk, A. J. McClain, Chas. H. Ashman, A. E. Thomas.

For One Year

Horace Kolb, W. C. Benshoff, H. M. Harley, J. F. Watson, Chas. H. Flory.

The work of the League for the coming year looks very encouraging W. S. Bell and I. D. Bowman are devoting all their time to Evangelism and Bible Study.

We are praying that God will bless this work and make it possible to have at least ten consecrated men in the field all the time, preaching and teaching God's word.

When this is accomplished, our membership will increase at least twenty-five hundred each year. I am sure this is a very conservative statement. Brethren, will you help to accomplish this in the name of him who died on

Calvary for you? If you will, first of all, pray for the success of this great work. Second, give liberally of the money that God has entrusted to your care.

Send all money to
HENRY V. WALL, Secretary,
1330 East Third Street, Long Beach, Calif.

AN OPEN LETTER

To the Friends among the readers of these columns:

Since resting is still the order of my program, I may be allowed this short-cut in my correspondence to respond to the hundreds of letters of encouragement and inquiry since my illness during the summer. I appreciate every thought and gift. But to answer each separately, would be to defeat the purpose of my temporary withdrawal from church activities. Let me assure you that your prayers have not been in vain, for my health has been restored, though not yet my strength, which seems to depend upon my continuing yet longer to wait upon the Lord." They that wait upon the Lord shall renew their strength." In the several attempts to resume work, the lack of strength was the reminder that I had not yet learned to appreciate the place that resting holds in the Victorious life. "Come ye apart and rest awhile," calls for obedience as promptly as "Go ye." Twice within the last few years the call came to rest, and an unusual invitation for a vacation, with the provision for every need, but I felt I could not, so long as the goal set for the number of new churches, in the Four Year's program had not been reached. I saw the unparalleled opportunity in the scores of cities and towns of the Northwest different from the East, and where a six months' course in Bible study, would lay the foundation for a new congregation, if the Mission Board could see that far fo direct their new ministers and means thus. But being so far east, they could not, and my spirit was broken. I gave up but not till they forced me to go to the hospital. Crushed, and only with my lips could I repeat my favorite, "All things work together for good." Now I see it was the best day's work done for me, for I learned a new lesson in yielding. It is when we surrender that which is good, that cuts the deepest, and for the first time in seventeen years or more, I gave up to the entreaties of friends to take drugs as a medicine. With it went everything else, even my undue ambition for the enlarging of the borders of the Brethren church.

Not as formerly, the healing was delayed after the anointing service, and three thousand miles away mother was wiring Dr. Brower to put me under medical treatment. No small task for the Doctor and Sister Brower. They argued that their tithe, together with the assistance of other friends, would meet all hospital bills and that it would still be the Lord's healing. Never have I had better treatment from any Brethren than those in that unique town of Ashland, Oregon. May I say further for Dr. Brower, while he is a medical doctor, is always ready to minister in the anointing service, and he stood between the hospital doctor and his threatened operation for appendicitis. And the dropsy,

caused by poor heart action, yielded quickly, after I had given up. So the friends who were concerned as to the outcome of the operation, I am happy to inform them, that I was spared the knife, and am now in my former realm again of trusting God only for health.

I have failed to bear testimony for the wonderful healing from inflammatory rheumatism, the first year I came into the Brethren church, when the Philadelphia church prayed for my recovery and their pastor, I. D. Bowman, administered the anointing service. The doctors had stopped coming, because of the feeble heart action, which was beyond their help. Surely our Lord is worthy of more praise than we give him.

For the winter, my brother's address will be mine, Los Angeles, California.
VIANNA DETWILER,
1242 W. 42nd St.

REPORT OF THE EVANGELISTIC LEAGUE WORK

Oriskany, Virginia

This report of this work should have been made sooner but I have been in one continuous strain for the last two months till now I have a breathing spell for a few days.

My brother, J. S. Bowman has given a brief report of this work some time ago.

The meeting here was too short but I had to close at miss National Conference. As it was I missed a day and a half.

This work is being revived. They only have preaching every four weeks and then my brother has missed about three months a year on account of his school work.

I have heard good reports of the after-effects of this little meeting. We closed with a full house and an intense interest with two confessions the last night and several others during the short meeting. We had ten days' services.

This church is in the Allegheny Mountains some 30 miles, perhaps, from Roanoke City, Virginia.

This is one of the churches built largely by the efforts of my brother, J. S. Bowman and a remarkably intelligent and up-to-date community. Some of the best judges and educators of Virginia have come from this mountain settlement.

If this church could have the attention it should have there could be built a creditable work here for the Brethren. They are very anxious for me to come back and finish the well began work but whether I will be able to do so or not I cannot tell now. I believe this is a hopeful field for our people and it is not very far from where Brother Fogle held a very successful meeting that has recently been reported in the Evangelist. There could be built a chain of good churches here by persistent effort.

Berne, Indiana

I stopped here and gave a week of Bible teaching and prophetic lectures. This is the fifth time I have given lectures here on the Prophecies and they seem to be well pleased. I was royally entertained and all expenses were borne so that this meeting has cost the

League nothing. They gave $34 on the League Cards, besides a liberal offering. These are surely noble and loyal people. I have held two other successful meetings that I will re port soon.   ISAAC D. BOWMAN,
1942 S. 17th St. Philadelphia, Pennsylvania.

PLEASANT GROVE, IOWA

I suppose that you would like to hear from us once again as we have been silent for a while. Well, there are a few things that have happened in the last three weeks. We have been cleaning house at Pleasant Grove. And our way was not the Lord's way this time. On our return home from General Conference the church was hungry for a revival. On the spur of the moment we decided to secure an evangelist. A message sent to Brother I. D. Bowman which brought the answer, No. Then we sent another to G. T. Ronk, and got the same answer. Once more we called to A. E. Thomas with the answer, No. Then the call came to Anderson to hold his own revival. A request of the pastor that the church give him a choir leader was consented to. The long distance call was sent to Miss Nell H. Malen with the answer, "I'll be there." God answered our prayers. And what a blessing to find such a person as Sister Malen ready to go without even a promise of a cent. Now, if we had more ministers and churchworkers who would be ready to trust the Lord for results, perhaps some of our dead churches would be brought to life. Miss Malen came on the job, and we began to clean house. The old devil began to tremble. Miss Malen is more than a singer. She can preach as well as she can sing. And she is on the job every hour. She took us off our feet the first song we sang, and we were not singing "He lifted me," either. And then she said, "Singing is one part of a revival. But prayer is the power of God unto salvation; we must pray." Well, when, and where? Well, "Charity begins at home," so does prayer. In the morning at 8 o'clock and four mornings out of the week there will be prayer. She did not ask any questions about whether we wanted it or not, whose home is opened tomorrow at 8 o'clock with two doors opened for prayer? She did not give us a chance to say, I can't." "There will be prayer meeting tomorrow morning at Alva Pope's," she said. Now "can't" is the substitute word for I don't want to. There were 8 persons there. Then the next morning there were 13. And the net morning, 18. Oh, what we can do when we want to! The next morning 28 were there, and God was there every morning. The Holy Spirit touched our hearts. There's no task too great for Miss Malen. Then Sunday afternoon she talked to the women while I talked to the men. On Tuesday we listened to Miss Malen talking on the full surrendered life, and when the call was made 14 came. Then, lo, we turned to the Gentiles. We closed our meeting with twenty-nine accepting Christ. With 12 baptized, 12 reclaimed, and 5 yet to be baptized. We have also other helpers who are sharing honors. Sister Ethel Myers was a worker among the children, and then Sister Hillegas was with us and will stay here until she sails for Africa to join those over there of our number. Brother Garden of Leon, Iowa, was with us one night. We closed the revival with the Lord's supper, with 65 around the Lord's table.

Brother Boardman of Hudson was then called to help organize a Christian Endeavor Society. Our Young Peoples' Class has outgrown their seating capacity and moved to the basement. As the C. E. is not fully organized, we will report it next time. Miss Malen is one of the best all-around evangelistic workers we have ever met and we can recommend her to anyone wishing a song leader and personal worker. Write to Miss Ethel Myers or to the writer if in need of a helper. Miss Ethel Myers' address is, Williamsburg, Iowa, Route 2.   H. M. ANDERSON, Box 126, North English, Iowa.

GOSHEN, INDIANA

Today all over this nation in which we live men and women are casting their ballots for the leaders of our government and no doubt too many are governed by political favor rather than a God fearing leader, which we so much need at this present time. According to past history all nations who forgot GOD sooner or later were obliged to step down and out, therefore, we had better heed this warning, "Blessed is the nation whose God is the Lord."

On next Lord's day, Brother Bell of Sunnyside, Washington, comes to Goshen to conduct a campaign for lost souls. We ask all who are interested in the lost to pray for the effort being put forth that many who are in darkness might see the light and decide to walk therein. From the first time we were permitted to hear Brother Bell we were impressed by his real devotion to the cause, and we are persuaded that God is wonderfully using him to the saving of souls.

Last Wednesday evening after prayer meeting, Mrs. D. Miller and daughter were baptized and received into the church, also yesterday two more were baptized. It surely should cheer us all to see them come into the fold, and should inspire us to live more devoted lives.

Several years ago the Goshen church purchased a beautiful home for a parsonage just across the street from the church, and if I remember right the good women of the church had paid the only payment that had been made. At least, there was a debt of around two thousand dollars so it was decided "as suggested by the pastor" to put on a special program by all the auxiliaries of the church to make a supreme effort to raise the debt. To some of us it looked like a big task to raise it all at one time, and we confess our faith was a little weak, but all pulled and pushed and it had to come. Brother McInturff says "it will all come before we let go." The goal set was to raise twenty-five hundred dollars on October 31. Now I imagine I can hear Brother Teeter, the Business Manager say, "That was our day, so that belongs to the Publishing Company." If you get it, Brother Teeter, Brother McClain will be obliged to move as he wants to live in a house free of debt. You might get him to put

on another big program for he says, Goshen can do anything she undertakes. The Sunday school raised more than thirteen hundred dollars. The Sisterhood offering was one hundred and fifty. The W. M. S. one hundred dollars. The C. E. offering sixty-one. A neat tithing box was made by Brother Ira Stutzman. It had been requested that the members tithe their income the last two weeks of October and on Sunday, October 31, put it in the box. The amount deposited was five hundred dollars. Pardon me for saying this was fine while it lasted, but it did not begin soon enough and quit too soon. Where in the Book do we read that God's people tithed for a short time, then quit? There are a number of regular tithers in the Goshen church and I hope the time may come soon, too, that we may return to the ancient method of raising means for the Lord's work and cease depending upon socials, feasts and the like for the support of the Lord's Kingdom. I am told that Brother Kimmell tithed and preached tithing while in Goshen. A number of the Sisterhood Girls are tithers as a result of Brother Kimmell's effort. I must say in the late program the Sisterhood in their offering according to numbers did the best of any and did it first. No doubt there were many in the church who did not observe the tithing for two weeks but one can soon see what it would mean for the Lord's work at two hundred and fifty dollars per week, for the Goshen church. Do we really love God who owns us and all we have, when he only asks for the small sum of the tenth and fe refuse him even that? What will the answer be? Some say We are not required under grace to give the tenth or tithe,. The Book says, Lay by in store on the first day of the week as the Lord has prospered us (do we do it?) Dare we think he will require less of us than he did of the Israelites?

Brother, sister, we had better ask God to forgive us if we have robbed him, and from now on claim the promise "One hundred fold in this life and in the world to come life eternal.'

M. E. HORNER, Corresponding Sec'y.

Business Manager's Corner

REPORTS COMING SLOWLY

We do not mind if the reports from the offering taken on Publication Day come in slowly, just so they come in surely.

Last week we mentioned but two churches that had reported at that time but we should have also mentioned a few individual members who had sent in their contributions. The first is $2.00 from Forrest E. Reed. We do not know Brother Reed personally, but more than thirty years ago his father and the Business Manager played football together in the same High School. Other personal gifts are as follows: F. E. Button, $2.00; Mr. and Mrs. E. M. Riddle, $5.00; Mrs. E. C. Mercer, $3.00; J. H. Peck, $1.00; Member Brethren church, Michigan, $2.00; Austin Miller and Family, $15.00. The following offerings have been received from churches, Martinsburg, Pa., $8.40; New Enterprise, Pa., $6.08; Bryan, Ohio,

$36.10; Sidney, Ind., $10.00; Miamisburg, Ohio, $4.50; Fort Scott, Kansas, $7.80.

Other churches have reported that their offering was postponed one week on account of bad weather, and others that they were waiting until a little more would come in from scattered members before making their reports. We trust the pastors and churches have taken this matter seriously, for we firmly believe the Publishing Company was never brought face to face with as critical a situation as it is at the present time, and the churches simply MUST rally to its support to save the day.   R. R. TEETER, Business Manager.

Communion Notices

The Conemaugh church will hold its fall communion on Sunday evening, November 14th, at 7:00 P. M. The brethren of the surrounding community are cordially invited to attend.

G. H. JONES, Pastor.

The Tithing Stewardship Corner

Tithing Egg Money

The following is a letter from Indiana: "Have you any publications explaining what to tithe and how? Example: I have a dozen hens; I raise and use my own feed and do my own work. The hens lay, say one dozen eggs, which I sell for sixty cents and put aside six cents for my tithe. The next week I have to buy my feed. It costs me $1.00. They lay a dozen eggs and I sell them for sixty cents but have some feed left. What would be the solution for the tithe? This and similar questions come to me from those wanting to tithe. I have my solution, of course, but there are some examples that are not so simple. Can you help me out?"

I send him copies of "How to Tithe and Why" and the tithing account book and write him in substance as follows: "In addition to keeping your tithe money separate, use the account book I send you, and your problem will solve itself. Feed is business expense. Deduct the cost of feed from the total income and tithe the reminder."

H. E. Beckler, stewardship secretary of the Texas Christian Missionary Society, under date of February 3, writes: "I have just returned from a trip through Oklahoma into Kansas and at two places in Arkansas. Signed up 100 preachers and 300 laymen in seventeen days. Had calls for 45,000 pamphlets on the trip. Am getting some of them out here. Have secured 2,004 tithers in the past four and a half months."—A Layman.

Never fancy you could be something if only you had a different lot and sphere assigned you. The very things that you most depreciate, as fatal limitations or obstructions, are probably what you most want. What you call hindrances, obstacles, discouragements, are probably God's opportunities.—Horace Bushnell.

Volume XLII
Number 44

November 17
1920

The BRETHREN EVANGELIST

- ONE·IS·YOUR·MASTER·AND·ALL·YE·ARE·BRETHREN -

A Song of Thanksgiving

THE PAYMENT OF OUR VOW FOR HOME MISSIONS WILL
PROVE THE GENUINENESS OF OUR THANKSGIVING

*"Offer unto God thanksgiving; and pay thy
vows unto the most High."* Psalm 50:14.

Published every Wednesday at Ashland, Ohio. All matter for publication must reach the Editor not later than Friday noon of the preceding week.

George S. Baer, Editor

The Brethren Evangelist

When ordering your paper changed give old as well as new address. Subscriptions discontinued at expiration. To avoid missing any numbers renew two weeks in advance.

R. R. Teeter, Business Manager

ASSOCIATE EDITORS: J. Fremont Watson, Louis S. Baumat, A. B. Cover, Alva J. McClain, B. T. Burnworth.

OFFICIAL ORGAN OF THE BRETHREN CHURCH

Subscription price, $2.00 per year, payable in advance.
Entered at the Post Office at Ashland, Ohio, as second-class matter.
Acceptance for mailing at special rate of postage provided for in section 1103, Act of October 3, 1917, authorized September 9, 1918.
Address all matter for publication to Geo. S. Baer, Editor of the Brethren Evangelist, and all business communications to R. R. Teeter, Business Manager, Brethren Publishing Company, Ashland, Ohio. Make all checks payable to the Brethren Publishing Company.

TABLE OF CONTENTS

EDITORIAL

Our Pilgrim Forefathers—Their Evaluation of the Bible and Ours

This season is pregnant with noble thoughts. One cannot be thoughtful at Thanksgiving time without a flood of ennobling sentiments coming into the mind. Important among these are the sturdiness, courage and faith of the Pilgrims, their love for the Bible and the vitality and expressiveness of their religion. There is perhaps no other special day in the year, save Christmas and Easter, that presents a more inspiring scene than that of the pioneers of Christian liberty kneeling on the shores of a new continent at the close of their first harvest to thank God for the blessings he had bestowed upon them. This Thanksgiving season is more suggestive than usual, because it is just three hundred years since those strong-hearted men and women landed on Plymouth Rock with their Bibles.

That they came with their Bibles is the significant fact. That explains all they were and did. Dr. W. H. P. Faunce, president of Brown University, says, "Their whole story can never be understood unless we realize that their fundamental impulse was from the spirit of the Scriptures. They believed themselves to be as they were,—followers of the apostles and prophets. Their ideas of government as well as religion, their conception of social life, of national destiny, of individual achievement—all came out of the Old Testament and the New." They had few books, but the Bible was their library for guidance in all matters both public and private. It served these Pilgrims not only as a guide in their perilous journey from the Old World to the New, but in every action of their daily lives. They were profoundly religious and in all their affairs they were actuated by the highest motives. There are few parallels in history where the Bible was given so large a place in the life and thought of a people.

These Pilgrim forefathers have a message of vital importance for us. They would point out to us the necessity of a revaluation of the Bible as a guide book for all matters of conduct, as well as religious belief. Their example has endured through three centuries largely because of their adherence to the precepts which they gained from the Book. If we would understand them and appreciate the sacrifices which they made and the dangers which they fearlessly faced we must turn again with new reverence and faith to the literature from which their faith and energy were derived. And if we would celebrate in a fitting manner the tercentenary of the Landing of the Pilgrims, nothing would be more in keeping with the spirit that animated those sturdy Christian pioneers than to emphasize their virile faith in the Scriptures as the rule by which their lives were governed and nothing could be more important than the direction of the public's attention to that great Book which has remained intact through centuries of criticism and has wielded an unmeasured influence in the midst of the turmoil of worldly affairs.

We are not giving the Bible a large enough place in our lives, as individuals or as a nation. And if there seems to be a careless giving way to the spirit of the world; if there seems to be a growing prevalence of disregard as to the importance of Christianity and its high idealism, the cause is likely to be found in our wide-spread neglect of the Bible. Nothing is more essential to our continued strength and influence as a people than a firm underpinning with the word of God. Testimonies of many worthy witnesses might be cited, but we mention only a few. Samuel R. McKelvie, governor of Nebraska, says, "I have long felt that the Christian religion is the cornerstone of American citizenship; and when the people of our nation disregard this fact, we shall be upon the brink of decay. Hence the necessity for the ideals and teachings of the Bible." It is reassuring to find men in high station bearing witness to the importance of God's word in public life. It gives hope that the swelling tide of disinterestedness is about to recede. Governor A. E. Roberts of Tennessee says "If the people of this republic should for one day forget or abandon the teachings of the Bible, our institution would tumble about our heads in a heap of ruins." Josephus Daniels, Secretary of the Navy, speaking of the faith of the Pilgrims in the Scriptures as a rule for the governing of their lives, declares that, "Today we need a return to the simple faith in the Bible as the unerring guide of human action. The foundations of our republic were laid on faith in the Word, and all these blessings are to be perpetuated by a return and a consecration to the old Book." President Sills of Bowdoin College, Maine, says, "The neglect of the Bible, not only by the younger generation, but by so large a part of our population is one of the saddest characteristics of modern life; and to remind Americans that to the Pilgrims the Bible contributed sturdiness, courage and faith will be of great service."

Truly the Christian Bible and the religion of Jesus Christ therein set forth have done more for the advancement of civilization and the adjustment of men's relations with one another as well as men's relations with God than anything else in the world. And surely there never was a time when the study of the Bible and the adaptation of its message to human needs and relations was more essential to the welfare of the whole world than now. It must prove to be the cure of the world's ills or there is no cure. That great Christian statistician, Roger Babson, says, "Our industrial problems will never be worked out through legislation; the only solution of our social, political and industrial affairs lies in the truths presented in the Bible. Only as these truths become more and more known and recognized will the nation make any permanent progress.

These statements are both challenging and reassuring. It is reassuring to have this testimony borne to the fact that we have within our hands the certain cure for this sin-sick world. And it is challenging to be brought face to face with the fact that the gospel of Christ is unknown and unapplied to the great mass of human hearts and relations. These warnings and testimonies coming from men who stand upon the watch-towers of our national life ought to stir our souls. Every professed follower of our Lord Jesus Christ should seek to make the Word increasingly vital to his life and never go forth ungirded with its keen edge by which he may be able to quench all the fiery darts of the evil one. And the lamentable ignorance concerning the Bible, the surpassing indifference to its importance and the unrestrained and unabashed disobedience to its most primary teachings ought to challenge every one who has the interest of the Kingdom and the welfare of human life at heart to do his utmost to bring about an attitude of greater concern and appreciation for and response to this Book of books.

EDITORIAL REVIEW

Don't forget the Home Mission apportionment—one dollar per member—and if you are an isolated member, you will still want to do your share and the church counts on you.

Apropos of our Home Mission number, we present three Kentucky reports on the Mission page this week; one from Brother Gearhart, one from Brother Rempel and one from Sister Drushal.

If any one has ever had any doubts as to Terra Alta's being on the map, these doubts must be dispelled. Since Brother Grisso's splendid meeting there a few weeks ago, they are still rejoicing in the enthusiasm then created. Brother S. K. Whitehair writes his appreciation of the meeting this week.

Dr. Bell reports his evangelistic travels, and particularly his meeting with Brother Belote at Uniontown, Pa. This, he states, was his fifth campaign with Brother Belote, and we think it speaks well for the congeniality of both these brethren, to have worked together successfully in so many campaigns.

Brother H. W. Anderson recently reported a very successful revival conducted in his church at Pleasant Grove, Iowa, and now he writes that the enthusiasm of his people is still keeping up to a high point. It looks as though he were getting his people very thoroughly organized for a country congregation.

Brother S. C. Henderson, pastor of the Clay City, Indiana, congregation, reports a splendid evangelistic campaign in his charge. "The Welsh Evangelist," Brother Thomas of Warsaw, did the preaching in the enthusiastic manner of which he is capable, and Brother H. E. Eppley of Eaton led the song service. Brother Henderson bears witness to the fact that these brethren made a winning team.

The reports of Publication Day Offering are beginning to come in nicely. And we believe this is only the beginning of a surprisingly big offering. Many churches which did not find it convenient to take the offering on October 31, will take it later, for we are confident that we can count on their loyalty. See the Business Manager's Corner, for the report.

GENERAL HOME MISSION OFFERING ON EITHER NOVEMBER 21 OR 28. Send your offering to William A. Gearhart, 906 American Building, Dayton, Ohio. You have been accustomed to address him at Conover Building, but from now on write American Building instead. Brother Gearhart has not changed his office; the building has changed ownership and the name has been changed in the transaction.

If there are still those who think it is a matter of indifference whether the college is adequately endowed and equipped or not, President Jacobs' "College News" should help to dispel that attitude. Dr. Jacobs is possessed with a great passion in behalf of your school and mine, and in the interest of the young people of the Brethren church and our future ministry, but his hands are tied until the brotherhood comes forward in much greater strength than it has up till now.

This week we present the first installment of the Pennsylvania conference minutes, from the careful pen of Brother Witter, the conference secretary. The number of years in which Brother Witter has served in that capacity shows what the Pennsylvania conference thinks of his efficiency. A reading of the minutes will reveal to you what a successful conference this district had and also what a royal host the Pittsburgh church proved to be.

Our correspondent from the Zion Hill, Ohio, congregation, Sister D. L. King, tells of a successful evangelistic campaign recently held among that people by their pastor, Brother A. L. Lynn. Brother Lynn is a student in the graduating class of the College this year, but he has long since proven himself as a pastor and evangelist, and we are not surprised that his people at Sterling and Smithville want to keep him.

We are privileged to present to our Evangelist family a picture of "The Little Brown Church" of Peru, Indiana. You will find it on Mission page. We inadvertently omitted the pastor's name from the statement on that page. Brother G. C. Carpenter is pastor and has been from the beginning of the organization. We have presented this church this week and the Fort Scott church last week because they are typical of our home mission needs, and also because neither of them were presented in this connection last year.

In this Thanksgiving-Home Mission number of The Evangelist we are privileged to publish several beautiful cuts supplied by the Home Missionary Society. Occasionally our readers speak of their appreciation of pictures that appear in the paper and express a desire to see more of them. The Publishing Company, itself is not in shape to spend very much on cuts, but if any of our friends are concerned about this matter enough to send us from three to five dollars to apply on cuts, it will please us greatly and we will see that the money is spent for that purpose. But be sure to state definitely that it is to buy cuts or it would likely be applied on the paper bill.

As we were going to press we received from Brother G. W. Rench of South Bend, Indiana, a newspaper clipping informing us of the fact that the Brethren church located on South Michigan street was destroyed by fire at 11:30 Friday night, November 12th. When the firemen responded to the general alarm they found the brick edifice a mass of flames and it was several hours before the fire was under control. The fire started, according to the firemen, from an overheated flue. A series of meetings was in progress and it is said that a too hot a fire was left in the furnace at the close of the evening service. This church had been considering the enlarging of their structure to take care of the increase in the congregation. We bespeak the sympathy and prayers of the brotherhood in behalf of these Brethren in their great misfortune.

The leaders of our Bicentenary are placing special emphasis on evangelism at this season of the year, and it is not likely that they will slacken their emphasis on this matter during the winter. It is to be hoped that they will not, but rather press the campaign with increasing vigor. There is little doubt but that we can count on them to do that. But if the evangelistic fires are to be kindled all over the brotherhood, and if they are to burn in every church with the intensity and wide-reach that will bring about a really great harvest, there must be many others besides the directors and evangelists getting themselves concerned about this matter. The task and burden of evangelism must be carried down to every member of every church. What is the membership ready to do to bring about a great ingathering of souls? Are the laity ready to share with the ministry the responsibility of preparing the way for another Pentecost? It was prayer and concord and self-surrender that brought about the first mighty awakening of souls. Are we ready to accept the responsibility?

THE BRETHREN BICENTENARY MOVEMENT PAGE

1723 - - - - - 1923

Dr. Charles A. Bame, Editor

Evangelism on the Map

This is to tell you that Evangelism which some weeks ago was "To the Front" is still there. We are planning on keeping you awake on this topic while it is yet day. The day for evangelism soon passes and we wish to keep it to the front so well that no pastor nor board can forget his duty. I am more sure each day I live that the pastors are anxious to help their fellows in evangelism. I am just as sure, or a bit more so, that the people are more ready to support evangelism than they are to back up the pastor. Why then shall we not have "A revival in every church, annually." We have here a live director, too, as you will see when you read these lines. That bodes well for the New Movement of which it is a part. Bell is ready and has already become a good focus for this work. Get busy for the spread of the kingdom by Evangelism. If you need help, write Bell, or send a wireless to Bame and we shall see what we shall see.—Bame.

Evangelistic Firing Line

The evangelistic drive is on in the church and already great victories are being reported. The following churches have had good meetings, with hundreds won for Christ, with churches strengthened and the faith of believers deepened.

CHURCH	PASTOR	EVANGELIST
Oak Hill (Union meeting)	Miller	Bame
Clay City	Henderson	Thomas and Eppley
Philadelphia, 3rd Church	Braker	Bowman
Cerro Gordo	Teeter	Bell
Camden	Eikenberry	Eikenberry and Cobb
Garwin	Ankrum	Coleman and Ronk
Uniontown	Belote	Bell
Sunnyside (Union)	Ashman	Bulgin
Los Angeles, First Church	Jennings	Bauman

Several churches are now engaged in meetings and from all indications this will be the greatest year of evangelism in the history of our denomination.

Some Things Consider

As a church remember the GOAL of the Bicentenary Program—"A revival annually in every church in the brotherhood. Have you arranged this meeting in your church? If not, get busy.

I find so many of our pastors and churches think they must have their meeting at a certain time in the year or not at all. This cannot be done for we have not men enough to cover the denomination in three or four months. Select your man and choose the time that you can have meeting regardless of the season. We can cover the denominational needs in this way, but if you are going to insist it must be at a certain date or not at all, you may be without a meeting.

Additional Workers Volunteer

Alvin Byers of Canton, Ohio, is open for a few meetings and Brother Lloyd King offers his services for December as an evangelistic singer. We are off with a good start with a fine line up for the winter months. Keep the fire burning.

W. S. BELL, Director of Evangelism.

STOP! LOOK! READ! DO!

W H A T ?—Offering for Home Missions.

W H E N ?—Sunday before or Sunday after Thanksgiving Day.

W H Y ?—To obey our Lord in the command to scatter the Gospel seed.

G O A L ?—ONE DOLLAR per member.

WILL WE DO IT?—We should.

WILLIAM A. GEARHART,
General Missionary Secretary.

Fourteen Points on Killing a Church

1. Don't come.
2. If you do come, come late.
3. When you come, come with a grouch.
4. At every service ask yourself, "What do I get out of this?"
5. Never accept office. It is better to stay outside and criticize.
6. Visit other churches about half of the time to show your pastor that you are not tied down to him. There is nothing like independence.
7. Let the pastor earn his money; let him do all the work.
8. Sit pretty well back and never sing. If you have to sing, sing out of tune and behind everybody else.
9. Never pay in advance, especially for religion. Wait until you get your money's worth, and then wait a bit longer.
10. Never encourage the preacher; if you like a sermon, keep mum about it. Many a preacher has been ruined by flattery. Don't let his blood be on your head.
11. It is good to tell your pastor's failings to strangers that may happen in; they might be a long time finding them out.
12. Of course you can't be expected to get new members for the church with such a pastor as he is.
13. If your church happens to be harmonious, call it apathy or indifference or lack of zeal, or anything under the sun except what it is.
14. If there happen to be a few zealous workers in the church, make a tremendous protest against the church's being run by a clique.

—From The Christian Work.

The First Thanksgiving

Was inspired by a spirit of genuine gratitude to God for his sure protection and loving provision and therefore it was a real thanksgiving. If the Pilgrims had cause for gratitude, we have much more. Will our Thanksgiving be real? The answer will be found in our Home Mission Offering.

GENERAL ARTICLES

A Blessed Privilege.   By A. B. Cover

A blessed privilege comes to every member of the Brethren church at the Thanksgiving season, in the Home Mission Offering. We lay aside the cares and duties of routine life for a day and gratefully acknowledge God as the Giver of all gifts. This devotional spirit is expressive of true Americanism, and dates from the first Thanksgiving Day in our land, when the Pilgrims humbly knelt upon the bleak New England shore, thanking God for blessings received. We can perpetuate that spirit, and the greater program of Jesus with it, by planning with our gifts, to extend God's Kingdom.

It seems to me that if we want to do our part in the great program of church extension, now is the time. May God give to all Brethren the vision of the privilege of consecrated service. How simple is the message, "Go!" It is not said that you must change your occupation, but give as the Lord has prospered you, and help some one whom God has called and who is willing to "Go," to make that sacrifice. You will be blessed.

I am thinking of the unoccupied territory in our own land where the Gospel is not preached, and where people grope in darkness, while the church has been negligent. May the vision of lost souls become a burden upon our hearts, and then may God be made to rejoice, in that we as his professed followers are willing to render unto him consecrated gifts for the salvation of unregenerated souls.

I am appealing to the Brethren of the Maryland-Virginia district to "go over the top" in this Home Mission offering. Our showing in Foreign Missions last year was a credit to us; may this offering be likewise the largest and most creditable that we have yet given. Remember that in the budget of $1.00 per member is included the Kentucky work. Now let all members and all organizations of the district rally around the standard for the largest Home Mission offering yet.

Hagerstown, Maryland.

Come Over and Help Us.   By Horace Kolb

Always the cry for help is heard, but at this Thanksgiving time in particular the voice comes clear and loud from all over the land.

It is our Lord speaking to his children requiring an offering of the goods he has intrusted to us as his stewards. His test of our thankfulness is our giving, and the way we do it. Far better to let our gifts without words speak, than to presume we can please him by our words alone, while we withhold the gift. He requires that both shall be given together, and he will not accept either without the other. We can not go acceptably to a Thanksgiving service in the church and leave our pocket books at home.

Our Board is the channel through which we are enabled to properly and orderly do the Home Missionary work. It is making the regular appeal for money. It has carefully and under direction of the Spirit, considered the various fields and made necessary appropriation. Their work having now been completed it is the duty, I should say high privilege, of each loyal member of the Brethren church to back up the Board by doing all he can to make this year's offering the largest in our history. Will you help to bring this result to pass?

The call comes not to a portion of the churches and the membership, but to all. No one should falter. The dollar per member goal set by the Board and approved by Conference, should be met very easily and even this should not be the measure, but let all first give themselves to the Lord, and all give as the Lord has prospered them, and then the dollar mark will be superceded by a much larger amount, with the result that the Home work will be greatly strengthened and built up, and as a logical consequence, the church will be in a position to extend the work in foreign lands.

Philadelphia, Pennsylvania.

The Great Northwest and Missions. By W. S. Bell

By the request of the Missionary Secretary of our church I am writing a brief review of our work in this section.

In the early development of the Yakima Valley in Washington, some of our Brethren located here and shared an active part in the development of this fertile and wonderful country, among whom were S. J. Harrison, Chris Rowland, H. M. Lichty, W. S. McClain and others. Our people kept their church identity and united in a Church Federation with five other denominations. Brethren Harrison, Early and McClain filled the pulpit in sharing with the ministers of the other denominations in the Federation. This arrangement was followed until I was called as pastor for full time in the fall of 1909.

Independent Denominational Work

When I took over the work as pastor we had something like seventy members. The first two years of my pastorate we continued in the Federation, which only consisted of two other denominations, the others in the Federation having started an independent work of their own.

At the close of the second year we began an independent work of our own, buying the Federated church, which we remodeled and installed a pipe organ. Brother Bauman held us a wonderful meeting in which we had over 100 accessions and our numbers grew very rapidly. Later on through the kindness of Brethren Harrison, Rowland and Lichty three lots and a large building adjoining the church were deeded to us, upon which was built a modern parsonage. We have here a fine church property well equipped and one of the best churches in the denomination with a membership of about 350.

The Work in Spokane

This work was first opened by myself. I received a letter from Brother Sam Lichty of Falls City in which he enclosed a communication from the Mellingers of Spokane and with whom I got in communication and made arrangements to investigate the field. Upon arriving in Spokane I found three Brethren families, Goughenours, Browers and Graybills. I spent several days with them, holding meetings in different homes. In these services Brother Mellinger and his wife and Mrs. Mellinger's sister and Mrs. Robinson confessed Christ and were baptized in the Spokane river and

were the first converts to our work. After organizing into a little band for prayer services and Sunday school, Sister Detwiler came to their aid and did a great work and prepared the way for a tent meeting which was conducted by Brother Bauman, which gave great encouragement in securing several additions. Shortly after this meeting Brother Paul Miller, the present pastor, was secured and under his leadership and the loyal support of the members, a beautiful brick church has been erected and the membership increased until now they must have about 135 members. This is a very promising field and under proper care is bound to make a good strong church.

Why This Review?

I have briefly sketched the history of these two points for information and to show what can be done in this district BY WHAT HAS BEEN DONE—an irrefutable argument.

We have scattered in this district outside of the churches named some seventy members of the Brethren church. There are two groups, one at Ashland, Oregon, where we should have a good congregation and would have, if it had not been for mismanagement and incapable leadership. There is another group in Nampa, Idaho, where they have a small organization which Brother Neher is caring for. We have members in Seattle, Portland and other smaller places. Two years ago this district was organized, which includes Oregon, Washington, Idaho and a part of Montana.

A Land of Opportunity

I have traveled quite extensively the last few years and I know of no part of the United States that offers the opportunity for homeseekers and makers as this great undeveloped country, because of this there is bound to be a great exodus of homeseekers from the overcrowded East. Some of our own people will be coming this way and in my judgment the Northwest offers a fertile field for church extension. This country is bound to attract people of thrift that make a work permanent and not of the shifting class. In time we should have churches in Portland and Seattle and the only thing that is holding us back, is finances and leadership. May we take courage from what has been done and enlarge our gifts and efforts to make more of the same kind of work possible.

Sunnyside, Washington.

Working Together. By Mrs. G. T. Ronk

The only way a church can accomplish its purposes is for all to work together. Do you remember the old cartoon picturing the average church? The pastor is seen hauling a wagon full of his church members up a steep hill. They are going slowly for the load is heavy and the road is rough. The pastor is bent almost double, while streams of perspiration are pouring from his furrowed brow.

A more cheering picture shows the pastor again pulling the wagon but the members are behind pushing and getting it safely out of the ruts and through the mud holes, while all are smiling because of their achievement. They are working together.

Now the only way the Brethren church can reach the goal of one dollar per member for our Home Mission offering is for ALL to work together; the pastor, the leaders of the various organizations, and the general body of the church.

In this work the women can do a great deal for the days are past when women can truthfully say that they have no influence over their families or neighbors. Women have as much if not more influence than men if they will but use it. Just recently a hospital project was to be voted upon in our county. A few days before election it was discovered that violent opposition had developed which if not combated would cause defeat of the measure. So women were sent out to canvass the districts and explain why the project

should be voted for. After the elections returns were in, it was found that the measure carried by a goodly majority and largely through the efforts of the women. Surely Christian women will do no less, rather more, for the advancement of the Kingdom and the saving of souls than for the saving of the body. And in doing our share let us talk, let us agitate, let us give, let us pray that our goal may be reached.

By all working together, men, women, children, pastor, leaders, laymen and women, success shall be ours.

Leon, Iowa.

And thus it is that the Christian life, because it is a splendid venture, is also a bracing exploration and a magnificent discovery—

"And what to those who find? Ah, this,
  Nor tongue nor pen can show."

It is life's greatest "find," compared with which everything else is as nothing, for it is "the Pearl of Great Price."—Dr. J. H. Jowett.

In this world we are subject to alternate exaltation and humiliation, prosperity and persecution, light and darkness; but in the hereafter we shall be unchangeably rich in everlasting munificence. "It doth not yet appear what we shall be; it would overwhelm us to know it all now. We could not endure the brightness of the possessions of the sons of God.—E. W. Caswell.

Thanksgiving. By Mrs. C. E. Nicholas

"In everything give thanks," says Paul, "for this is the will of God in Christ Jesus concerning you."

To give thanks in everything means not only a silent submission on our part but it also implies a constant trustful acceptance of everything God sees fit to send into our lives.

There are periods in every life when to give thanks is easy. There are days of sunshine when the pulse of life beats strong, when to live means joy and hope—when all nature seems to sing a song of thanksgiving to the Maker.

But there are times when the days are sad and gloomy, when clouds obscure the sun, when disappointments come, when the dearest hope of life is crushed to earth, when days of broken health come,—it is then we feel God has forsaken us, and we are not inclined to give thanks, but are apt to grieve and murmur against Providence. But Paul, says, "Give thanks in everything."

Man is a very ungrateful creature, he alone is capable of giving praise yet he seems to feel it is beneath his dignity to acknowledge his Benefactor. There is also a repugnance in his nature to own itself dependent.

We accept the daily comforts and necessities God gives us as small and common, yet these same blessings cost Christ's blood as purchase money.

There are blessings man regards as evils. We owe God our thanks for even these blessings.

Our afflictions are many and varied. God does not allow them to come into your life and mine without a cause and purpose. A true child of God will not only be content but rejoice in all his troubles.

God gives strength for every affliction. He does not try us above that we are able to endure—a submissive child will feel and believe that "All things work together for good."

You feel your particular trial is just a little harder than that of any other. You complain because God has allowed this affliction to come into your life, yet it is evident that just such a chastening is needed to teach you meekness and submission.

It is your duty and mine to bear every trial, every affliction and every disappointment with thankfulness by praying God's will be done in us, that the afflictions may become subjects of praise also.

The life that is completely given to God and has come up out of much tribulation, purified and sanctified, knows what it means to say, "I am happy, O Lord, for each lesson thou hast taught me." It takes a complete resignation to look to heaven and say, "Thy will be done," yet this is just what every child of God must do.

Our Father requires his children to love him with all their heart, soul, and strength and they who do this will not thank God for one thing and murmur at another but will be thankful for all things that our Father is pleased to give them.

No Christian can have the true life without the love of God which causes joy, and no one can have that life-giving faith in him, without being thankful at all times and for all things.

No one can be thankful without being humble and we cannot be humble without being conscious of our need of God's refining power.

We delight to give to those who show themselves thankful; so also the Lord loves to bestow his mercy and blessings where he may have the most praise. "Whoso offereth praise glorifies me."

May God's people learn to thank him for all things at all times,—not only for daily blessings being constantly received from his hand, but also and above all for his Fatherly chastisements.

Dowagiac, Michigan.

Essentials of Denominational Progress. By Miss E. Marie Lichty

Jesus Christ is the very first essential of denominational progress. Whatever other essentials there may be, they are empty of lasting value, even though realized in the height of efficiency, if Jesus Christ stands not at the head and is not the Leader under whom we take our orders to progress.

With the real presence of the Christ and a sincere realization of his love, there is little need for further essentials but we feel the editor desired that we specify what we feel a denomination must have within its organized body to help insure this progress.

There must be harmony. And harmony is bred only of unified purpose. The one demand for attainment is tolerance. Some one in a recent edition of a religious weekly has said that the need of the denominations of today is not half so much of unity as it is of genuine co-operation. And we feel that tolerance is and must continue to be linked with co-operation.

Further, a growing denomination must have a dynamic program. Today that means a program which takes special cognizance and plans to meet the spiritual needs of the laity as well as of the ministry; a program which is alive to publication interests with support to the denominational press which in turn makes that agency vital and necessary; a program which includes an increasing educational program, an endowment not only of money but of students from the de-denominational homes. And we are pleased to note that leaders in our denomination have been at work on such a program. When the times comes to launch it, we dare not fail the challenge which it presents. It must be a program which discounts non-essentials and centers on fundamentals.

Another essential seems to us to be a sense of responsibility felt on the part of the laity regarding their real share in either making or unmaking the progress in the denomination, and an appreciation of the drastic need of their loyalty to the cause of Christ and the church.

To grow and to meet growing needs a denomination ought to have comparative councils with other denominations. Inasmuch as the same needs are ofttimes being felt by the different evangelical denominations, we believe that through conferences plans for strengthening through co-operation can be evolved. An instance of the result of this is noted in the benefits received by our National Woman's Work in their participation in the Interdenominational Summer School of Missions held annually at Winona Lake.

And this leads us to the suggestion that a denomination should not progress by growth alone in its own borders but also by growth gained through the co-operation with other Christian bodies. The Interchurch Movement has been retarded, and in fact discontinued but some other means will arise whereby the Protestant churches can co-operate on the World Program for which they are all working.

In summary, may we say, that with Christ as the first and most powerful of all essentials, the real demand follows for the denomination that would progress to exert a real dynamic stewardship.

Falls City, Nebraska.

LIQUOR LIMIT IN SWEDEN

Prohibition of all drinks having an alcoholic content exceeding 2.8 percent is recommended in a report of a government committee appointed in 1911 to consider the liquor question. In addition the committee proposes that absolute prohibition be submitted to a vote of the people and made effective if three-fifths of the electorate favor it.

THE BRETHREN PULPIT

A Thanksgiving Sermon.　By Miles J. Snyder

Text: Oh that men would praise the Lord for his loving-kindness, and for his wonderful works to the children of men. And let them offer the sacrifices of thanksgiving, and declare his works with singing.—Psalms 107:21:22.

At the call of those in authority in state and nation, and at the bidding of our own grateful hearts, we meet once more in public assembly to give thanks to our heavenly Father for all his mercies, temporal and spiritual, individual and national. It is well for the whole nation to cease its feverish activities and pause in adoration before the Giver of every good and perfect gift.

Through these age-old Psalms there sounds forth a grand chorus of thanksgiving and praise whose echoes were caught by our Pilgrim forefathers in this new world, and their lusty voices gave fresh impetus to the Psalmist's reverent refrain. The little company of Pilgrims at Plymouth thanked the Captain of their salvation for their safe arrival in the western world. And farther south the Godly William Penn lost no time in establishing an altar of religion in the colony of Quakers, and heart-felt thanks were offered to the Lord for all his gracious goodness. On November 19, 1621, Governor William Bradford issued the first public thanksgiving proclamation in the new world, since which time the custom has been followed by those in authority until it has come to be commemorated annually as a memorial of thanksgiving.

There are different ways of observing this day. Sometimes it is used as an opportunity for mourning over national sins and failures. Of course, as patriotic citizens of a beloved country, we cannot be blind to the fact that ofttimes politics are corrupt, that profiteers are criminals, that strikes are a peril, that graft is rampant, that the multitudes are pleasure-mad, that our domestic life is decadent with a greater annual number of divorces than any other country in Christendom, that large sections of our social life are as godless as ancient Babylon, and many other dark clouds equally as foreboding. But there are three hundred and sixty-four other days in which to bewail our national sins and imperfections, so none of that for me on this Thanksgiving Day!

Others observe the day as one of feasting and gluttony, and think no farther than the dinner table. The day suggests to them only an elaborate menu, and is remembered only because of what has been eaten. The physical satiety which follows a bounteous dinner is considered a suitable response to the Thanksgiving proclamation. While physical enjoyments are not to be despised, this day has lost its true significance when it does not add to physical pleasure a spiritual joy.

Still others go farther than the physical satisfaction and find intellectual revelry in recounting the material treasures of the past year. They ponder the tables which the statisticians supply, and glory over the size of our crops, the volume of our business, the value of our manufactures, and the incalculable wealth of gold and silver amassed in our banks. But, when such is the extent or chief end of our thinking, the day becomes a curse instead of a blessing to us. Too often people meditate on our broad expanse of acres and whirling machinery and expanding markets, until God is banished from their thoughts. The prophet Hosea, speaking for the Lord, uttered no sadder sentence than this: "They were filled, and their heart was exalted, therefore have they forgotten me."

The Roman empire in its day built the largest number of triumphal arches, but the sad commentary upon that nation are these words of Paul, "Knowing God, they glorified him not as God, NEITHER GAVE THANKS." That marked the climax of the nation's degradation. Overflowing prosperity tends to coarsen the heart, and superabundant riches puffs up. It is when men are gloating over their bursting barns and laying plans to build new ones, that the fires of devotion die down and they forget God and "neither give thanks." Thanksgiving Day is poorly spent in measuring crops and reveling in the marvelous resources of our land, if the heart is not moved to exclaim:

"O praise the Lord;
　Give thanks unto him, for he is good.
　Bless the Lord, O my soul,
　And all that is within me
　Bless his holy name."

Therefore, let us make this a real day of rejoicing as we think of the unalloyed blessings which have come to us both as individuals and as a nation: "Oh that men would praise the Lord for his lovingkindness, and for his wonderful works to the children of men. And let them offer the sacrifices of thanksgiving, and declare his works with singing."

Only a little knowledge of America's history is enough to enable us to see God's guiding hand in the crisis of every one of the great periods through which our country has come: the period of discovery, of colonization, of political liberty, of expansion, of the struggle for union, and in the Great War. He is blind who can look upon our country's broad plains, its majestic rivers, its rugged mountains, its vast forests, its government established in the interests of all the people, its institutions of home and church and school and hospital and asylum, and not clearly see that God's most gracious providence is our inheritance.

And, more important still, we dare not forget our spiritual inheritance; but remember the star that glided out of the east and stood over the Bethlehem manger, and then witness the ministry of the Savior, and gaze upon the Cross, and into the empty tomb. Then behold the glory of the resurrection, and recall the gifts of apostles and saints and martyrs whose lives enriched our spiritual legacy and shed abroad the light in which we walk.

And then, in our personal lives, who has not cause for great rejoicing when recalling the gifts and innumerable blessings of the Lord? Hours and days have come freighted with good things both temporal and spiritual. Of course, there has been a wide range of experiences resulting in different causes for individual thanksgiving. In the lives of some there has been sunshine almost without a cloud, while in the experience of others gleams of light have shot through the mists of sorrow. Some have enjoyed abundant prosperity, while others have struggled through the valley of adversity. But, coming through the varied experiences of life, multitudes have been conscious of God's sustaining grace which, through joy or pain, brought the soul into closer fellowship with him.

As our minds revert back over the year, we know that God's blessings without number have come into our lives new every morning and fresh every evening. Three hundred and sixty-five days in the year we have sat at the Lord's table and been fed of his bounty. Three hundred and sixty-five nights we have had comfortable beds for rest while watched over by One who "neither slumbers nor sleeps." He has kept us in health and strength and given us grace for all our needs. He has made possible cherished friendships which enrich and uplift us. He unites the loving ties of comradeship as with others we climb the glowing hills of victory. He calls us to tasks that claim our time and strength: and by means of which we are enabled to provide for our own and also glorify him.

"Ten thousand thousand unnamed gifts
　Our daily thanks employ;
Nor is the least a grateful heart
　　That tastes these gifts with joy."

And we all ought to thank God for the place we call home,

"Where love supreme holds gentle sway,
To bless anew returning day,—
. That spot is home."

Above all other places, it. is in the home, sanctified by prayer and God's Word, that

"We come to read our daily chart;
Here, for our duties, strength and grace obtain;
Here find direction for our faltering feet,
And peace to keep us in life's stress and strain."

And then, finally, we need to remember that all which has been mentioned or hinted at is only the beginning of God's goodness to us. He looked upon us in a world of sin and hopelessness and "so loved the world that he gave his only begotten Son, that whosoever believeth on him should not perish, but have eternal. life." And history is but a corridor down through which the Christ has walked carrying the burdens of men, healing their wounded lives and saving their souls.

All the argosies of wealth and banks of diamonds and mines of gold and the glories that glow in the heavens are not to be compared with the riches of grace that are ours in Christ Jesus. Let us praise him then, not one day. in the year, but every day "for his lovingkindness and his wonderful works to the children of men." For it is to the glory and praise of Jesus Christ that he provides in our lives for all that is lacking, that he makes up not only for our failure, but for the failure of others, for he is a very present help in time of trouble and of need.

Milledgeville, Illinois.

FROM OUR CONFERENCE PLATFORMS

Stewardship of Life. By Roy Brumbaugh

An address delivered at the late Middle West Conference

The Psalmist said, "My son, give me thine heart and let thine eyes observe my ways." Jesus said, "Follow me and I will make you fishers of men," and again," "As the Father hath sent me even so send I you." Again we are to, even as Christ said concerning himself, work the works of him that sent us while it is day for the night cometh when no man can work.

We are to study to show ourselves approved unto God, workmen that need not be ashamed, rightly dividing the word of truth. We are to present our bodies as living sacrifices which is our reasonable service. "And he hath showed thee, O man what is good, and what doth the Lord require of thee, but to do justly, and to love mercy and to walk humbly before thy God."

God has made us, or better, we are men in the making under God. He is lengthening out the threads of life day by day, for in him we live and move and have our being, and he has a right to our service and he demands it. But how reluctant we are to give it, or to give it without restriction. Too often we seek to hold back something here or there. Too many folks say, I will pay but will not pray, at least by action they say that. Some say, I will read my paper and send my children to church and Sunday school. I will give dollars for missions and to the college but will not send my boys or girls to be preachers or missionaries. This is the way we do. Have we awakened to the fact that we are stewards of our lives, yes, we are stewards of the manifold grace of God.

Paul says we are to give the more earnest heed to the things we have heard lest at any time we should let them slip. The Revised Version reads, Lest haply we drift from them. We are doing too much drifting. We are going with the tide and the crowd. We have let too many things slip. Men have drifted into isms and unbelief and further from the truth eternal. Men's foundations are being shaken and faith seems to crumble. Men have been torn loose from their moorings and are drifting from God to do as they please. We need to call a halt and be reminded that we are stewards of our lives and. through faith need to link our lives with Christ's. We have failed to give heed. We profess and do not possess. There has been enough good preaching to have saved the United States long ago, but it is not saved yet because men have not heeded and we have not recognized that sovereign claim of God upon our lives.

We seek everything else first but the Kingdom. It is so easy to drift with the current and so hard to stem the tide. We drift from attending church and prayer meeting. We put the Bible on the parlor table and leave it there while we read catalogues because they have pictures in them and concern us more. Of too many folks it can truthfully be said as it was said of Samson of old, The Lord is departed and they know it not. Too many are steeped in gain and greed and commercialism, they have been trying to keep up with the world in going the pace and have lost their peace and power. Salvation is not nearer than when we first believed because we have left too many thing slip and have left our first love. The devil has worked the shell game on many folks who have their name on the church roster. The devil promised them something and when they shut their hand on it, it was gone. It was only a conjuror's trick. We are stewards of our lives and ought to fall in line and follow the Captain of our salvation who leads the way. and who is our guide. We ought to be on the firing line for King Jesus. As we face the future we need a guide. We know not what the morrow holds in store; it is all new and unseen to us. Its waters may be chilly and its frosts bite and sting. And as we face the future we need him who has come on before, and he who comes again to walk by our side, and to guide us in the way of peace and safety and service.

We ought to say from the depths of our heart and mean it:

There is surely somewhere a lowly place,
In earth's harvest field so wide—
Where I may labor through life's short day
For Jesus the crucified.
So trusting my all to thy tender care,
And knowing thou lovest me,
I will do thy will with a heart sincere,
I will be what you want me to be.
I'll go where you want me to go, dear Lord,
Over mountain or plain or sea,
I'll say what you want me to say, dear Lord,
I'll be what you want me to be.

John spake of a church that had a name to live by but was dead. A church is composed of individuals. We ought to hear and heed the voice that says do this and live. "Whatsoever thy hand findeth to do, do with thy might for there is no device or work in the grave to which thou art going." We are to work the works of him that sent us while it is day, for the night cometh. We have a divine call and sending to this service, "as the Father hath sent me even so send I you." But how few are working on the job.

(Continued on page 10)

Send
WHITE GIFT
OFFERINGS to

THE SUNDAY SCHOOL

H. H. WOLFORD
General Secretary-Treasurer
Ashland, Ohio

Thanksgiving Message to Our Sunday School Children

GOD CARES FOR HIS OWN

God provides for all his creatures. The little squirrels that live in the woods eat nuts that grow on God's trees and are supplied by his tender care. They do not lay by in store great quantities of nuts, enough to last them many years, as some people do, but depend on God's provision every year. They have no thought of distrusting God's willingness and power to supply their every need. By their very nature they depend on the God who made them to give them food and shelter. And how happy and contented they are with their day's supply.

People are not always willing to trust God for the things they need. They lay by great stores of food, clothing and money, and, still unsatisfied, they keep on getting and laying by more wealth. With all their wealth they are not happy nor contented, for happiness and contentment are not to be gained by great possessions.

The Bible does not teach us that the getting of wealth is a sin, but it does say that it is wrong to love money, to hoard it and to be selfish with it. After all, everything in the world belongs to God; the money, clothing, food and houses and lands. And we have no right to keep getting and holding in a selfish way as if all were our very own. What we have no more belongs to us than the trees and the nuts belong to the squirrels. All is a gift from our heavenly Father. It ought to make us happy then to think that God has been so good to us in supplying us with the many things which we enjoy. We ought to love such a great and good God and be very grateful for what he has done for us and is doing for us every day.

If we do love him, and if we are truly grateful, we will want him to know it and, will prove it by what we do and say. We will sing songs of praise and thanksgiving unto him and we will be telling of God's goodness to others. There are many who are too far away for us to tell them about God's love and kindness, but we can send messengers to them. Out of the many good things which God has given to us we may give at this Thanksgiving season gifts to help send the "Good News" of God and his Son Jesus Christ to others in our land, who have not learned to rejoice in the love of God. Every Sunday school scholar who knows Jesus and is thankful for the goodness of our loving heavenly Father, will want to have a part in the great Home Mission offering that is soon to be made. Jesus said, "Freely ye have received, freely give."

That College Hen

The chicken fund has not grown so very much since my last report, but has grown some, and that encourages me to tell you about it and to ask that you help make it grow more. When Brother A. E. Whitted, away out at Morrill, Kansas, read the first appeal, his little daughter Dorothy, eight years of age, said to her papa: "I want to send my pet blue pullet." And he did, and her pet traveled four days, but came through all right, the first hen in the new house. Others sent the first money, but to Dorothy Whitted, goes the credit of having supplied the first live chicken, and the fact that she did that, makes me feel that perhaps others would like to do that too. Let the boys and girls of the Sunday schools put their hens together in a coop, and send them to us. We will appreciate it just as much as if they sent us the cash to buy them here.

The fund at present, is as follows:

Previously reported, ...$41.00
Charles Baker, ... 1.00
Winners Class, Gretna, Ohio, ... 1.50
W. D. Humke, N. Manchester, Ind., ... 4.75
Ruby Seibert, Beaver City, Neb., ... 2.00
June Hartzler, Sterling, Ohio, ... 1.00

 Total to date, ...$51.25
There is plenty of chance for the rest of you.
MARTIN SHIVELY, - Ashland College, Ashland, Ohio.

The Stewardship of Life

(Continued from page 9)

Must I go empty handed, thus my dear Redeemer meet?
Not one day of service for him, lay no trophies at his feet?
O the years of sinning wasted, could I but recall them now,
I would give them to my Savior, To his will I would gladly bow.

Must I go and empty handed? Must I meet my Saviour so?
Not one soul with which to greet him? Must I empty handed go?
Yes you must go. And whether you are empty handed or not depends upon what you have done with your life.

Jesus said, "We must work while it is called today for the night cometh. Jesus had a conception of time. He knew his work in the flesh would not end. And the work allotted to him he was determined to do and did do. If we want to work after the example of Christ it is easy to find the work for the fields are still white. Here again we have stewardship: "I," or "we," must work—note they are personal pronouns. We dare not substitute someone else. Then Jesus said, "Must work." Yes, "must work;" we use it in business and on the farm and elsewhere but when it comes it comes to the Lord's work, we think there is no compulsion about it. So many things are allowed to interfere. If everything goes just right; if supper is ready just on time and there is no place else to go, then perhaps we will be at church. We feel no responsibility or obligation in religious matters. Work? Yes we work, but not for the Master. All are looking for work except work for Jesus. All are looking for a job and big wages except in the Kingdom of God.

It is said that Sam Jones went to a southern city to hold a meeting where George Stuart was pastor. As he entered church they were singing "One more day's work for Jesus, one less of life for me." Sam arose and said, "Stop singing that hymn, you have not worked a day for Jesus, else there would not be all these empty pews." He said he would like to meet the following morning in the basement of the church all who would volunteer to work a day for Jesus. It is said the next morning about thirty gathered bringing their dinner to work a day for Jesus. They had a word of prayer and then Sam Jones sent them out, not for a moment for business, or pleasure or social chats, but to talk Jesus. They came for dinner and he sent them again with the same instructions, and at night as Sam walked up the front steps of the church, he saw them coming bringing the lost to the church and to Jesus. They assembled in the church and sang the song they tried to sing the night before, "One more day's work for Jesus, one less of life for me." And it is said here, Sam Jones held his greatest meeting because thirty folks recognized the claim of God upon their lives and that they indeed and in truth were stewards of their lives.

I said, Let me walk in the fields; He said, No, walk in the town,

I said, There are no flowers there, He said No flowers, but a crown.

I said, But the skies are black; there is nothing but noise and din,

And he wept as he sent me back, There is more, he said, there is sin.

I said, But the air is thick, and fogs are veiling the sun.

He answered, Yet souls are sick, and souls in the dark undone.

I said, I shall miss the light, and friends will miss me, they say.

He answered, Choose tonight, If I am to miss you or they.

I pleaded for time to be given, He said, Is it hard to decide?

It will not seem hard in heaven to have followed the steps of your guide.

I cast one look at the field, then set my face to the town,

He said, My child do you yield? Will you leave the flowers for the crown?

The Lord, he had a job for me,
  But I had so much to do;
I told him, you get somebody else,
  Or wait until I get through.

I don't know how the Lord came out,
  But he seemed to get along.
But I felt kind of sneaking like
  'Cause I knowed I had done him wrong.

One day I needed the Lord myself,
  And I needed him right away.
He never answered me at all,
  But still I could hear him say,

Way down in my accusing heart,
  I've got too much to do.
You better get somebody else,
  Or wait till I get through.

Now, when the Lord, he has a job,
  I never tries to shirk,
I drops whatever I'se got on hand
  To do the good Lord's work.

My own affairs can run along,
  Or wait till I get through.
For I've learned nobody else can do
  What God has marked out for you.
    Portis, Kansas.

Then into his hand went mine, and into my heart came he, And I walk in the light Divine the path I had feared to see.

Here is an admonition to use our life aright for the night cometh. Eventide with its closing shadows is swiftly approaching. Night is coming for all of us. But for some the morning cometh. "Weeping may endure for a night but joy cometh in the morning." For gambler, dancer, farmer, mechanic, banker, carpenter, business man, night is coming. Will our work be done? Will Jesus be honored by the lives we have lived? Will we have so lived our lives as to have blest others and to have left the world better?

Jesus said in the parable of the Good Samaritan as he spake of him who had mercy, Go thou and do likewise. We are to be a friend to the friendless, feed the hungry, clothe the poor, minister to those in prison, and visit the sick. In short, be a blessing. Jesus spent his life in being a blessing to other. This is our business here, and our business beyond the stars will be to be a blessing. In all other occupations some fail, this is one thing we all can succeed at if we will. We ought to work harder at it. The most lucrative professions of life are crowded. But the best in all this world and the only thing that has the stamp of eternity upon it has been overlooked. We need to recognize the claim of God upon our lives, and follow his guidance that we may be a blessing.

Let me say ere I close, we are attempting too much work today by proxy. We will give but not work. What do you suppose the Lord thinks of us? We will hire a preacher and spend all of our time at business, getting the world's goods. This shows what men put first in their lives. We try to excuse ourselves on the ground that we attend church and pray. Yes, but we usually attend church at night or on Sunday when we cannot work. Yes, we pay but only our spare cash and give that grudgingly, singing "God be with you till we meet again." We do not stop any plows or factories or places of business for the Kingdom of God. I say again, it shows which we have made the most valuable in our lives. Jesus left all and gave his all for us; the disciples followed in his steps; and now we are asked to take up the work where it was laid down and carry it on. God helps us to realize and recognize the claim of God upon our lives, for we are not our own, for we were bought with a price—Christ's sacrifice. Let us resolve to give unto him the rightful place in our lives, yielding unto him our service.

PRESIDENT WILSON'S THANKSGIVING PROCLAMATION

"The season approaches when it behooves us to turn from the distractions and pre-occupations of our daily life, that we may contemplate the mercies which have been vouchsafed to us, and render heartfelt and unfeigned thanks unto God for his manifold goodness.

"This is an old observance of the American people, deeply imbedded in our thought and habit. The burdens and stresses of life have their own insistence.

Cause for Thanksgiving

"We have abundant cause for Thanksgiving. The lesions of the war are rapidly healing; the great army of freemen which America sent to the defense of liberty, returning to the grateful embrace of the nation, has resumed the useful pursuits of peace, as simply and as promptly as it rushed to arms in obedience to the country's call. The equal justice of our laws has received steady vindication in the support of a law-abiding people against various and sinister attacks which reflected only the baser agitations of war, now happily passing.

"In plenty, security and peace, our virtuous and self-reliant people face the future, its duties and its opportunities. May we have vision to discern our duties; the strength, both of hand and resolve, to discharge them; and the soundness of heart to realize that the truest opportunities are those of service.

Should Give Thanks

"In a spirit then, of devotion and stewardship we should give thanks in our hearts, and dedicate ourselves to the service of God's merciful and loving purposes to his children.

"Wherefore, I, Woodrow Wilson, president of the United States of America, do hereby designate Thursday, the twenty-fifth day of November next, as a day of thanksgiving and prayer and I call upon my countrymen to cease from their ordinary tasks and avocations upon that day, giving it up to the remembrance of God and his blessings, and their dutiful and grateful acknowledgement."

SEND ALL MONEY FOR
General Home, Kentucky and
Foreign Missions to

MISSIONS

WILLIAM A. GEARHART
General Missionary Secretary
906 Conover Bldg., Dayton, O.

Kentucky News

Brother Arch G. Bradenbergh and wife together with Brother Thomas, all from Defiance, Kentucky, have recently organized a Sunday school at a point called Acup, and they are asking for our prayers that souls may be saved through their efforts to bring the true Gospel seed to their dear friends in the Mountain regions.

I had the privilege of lodging overnight with the Brandenbergh and Thomas families on one of my trips to the Kentucky field. I found them to be very hospitable and kind. They are eager to work for their Lord and Master. We predict that with the proper support from the Brotherhood with our prayers ,they will build up a splendid Bible school and some day we may have a Brethren church at Acup.—Praise the Lord for these dear people.
WILLIAM A GEARHART.

Krypton, Kentucky

Some time has elapsed since we gave the readers of the Evangelist any news concerning the work at Krypton.

When looking upon God's goodness in the past, our hearts get full of praises to him, but according to his promises good things are ahead. We do praise God for the many blessing he has bestowed upon us in the work here at Krypton. And for the opportunities he has given us, to go into the mountains preaching the Gospel, telling the great story to people who are ready and eager to listen.

We love, and enjoy the work among these dear people, have never found hospitality as we have found it in the homes here in the mountains. They are ready and willing to share the last they have with their friends.

The LORD has answered prayers in a wonderful way for this place.

Satan has tried hard from outside and inside the church to destroy this work, but we thank the Lord for the victory. Satan always fools himself.

Our prayers are that the Lord may send us a good teacher. Good schools are what we need more than anything else, because the children are the future and they are just as bright and capable as any other children. These people, after accepting Jesus Christ as their Savior, make just as good Christians as at any other place.

About fourteen children from Krypton are at Riverside Institute, which has a reputation as being among the best schools in the mountains. That community would not be what it is now if it would not be for the school. And we would see a great change at Krypton if we had a good school.

Pray that the Lord may have his own way here at Krypton, that souls might be saved and that we might be flexible instruments in his hand. Our success depends greatly upon your prayers.

J. A. REMPEL.

"The Little Brown Church" at Peru, Indiana

This is one of our very interesting and promising mission points. This temporary house has served a splendid purpose, but it must soon be replaced with a new and substantial church building. This is only one of the many urgent needs you should remember when making your Home Mission Offering.

Lost Creek, Kentucky

We again have a good report to bring of how our brotherhood is helping our mountain work.

We have received clothing from the following W. M. S., Lanark, Ill.; Church at Center Chapel, Ind,; Mr. M. E. Smith,: Mexico, Ind. All of this was quickly disposed of at our "sales."

A comfort for the "Dorm" came from the Ever Faithful Sunday school Class, . Lanark, Ill.; Fifteen towels from Sisterhood of the Third church of Johnstown, Pa. Two pillowslips and one towel from M. E. Anderson, Mexico, Ind.; Six sets of knives and forks for "Dorm" from State W. M. S., of Indiana.

If you would visit . our dormitories, . you would see how all of these things were greatly needed.

Another important need which had been met by Mr. and Mrs. McConnell of Denver, Colorado, was the two different shipments of Testaments, Gospels, tracts, and eleven of the Moody Colportage books for our . school library. We have realized for some time that a serious lack in our school and among our young people was that of good reading material. Hence we were pleased also to receive a box of good books from Miamisburg, Ohio.

Some have remembered the work with gifts of money, leaving the workers decide what was most needed. Those who have helped in this way are Mr. and Mrs. C. A. McConnell, Denver, Colorado, $10.00; Mrs. W. V. Wilmer, $5.00; Miss Alice Wimer, $10.00 to be sent to Krypton; Mrs. Homer Ball, New Jersey, $30.00; Mrs. James Stuckman, Nappanee, Indiana, $5.00. With these offerings, a book case has been purchased for the school library, and the rest used to meet the dormitory expenses.

In the spring a nice lot of bulbs were sent by Mrs. S. E. Cotterman, Farmersville, Ohio. After planting some about the place we gave the rest to our neighbors, who were delighted with them.

A personal gift from dear old Sister Swonger at Conference was greatly appreciated.

Mrs. Dora Rose of . Nappanee, Indiana, did not forget our temporal needs and mailed a box of good beans for our personal use.

I feel that I must also acknowledge our debt of gratitude to the two sisters who helped bear my personal expenses while at Winona Lake. I refer to Sister Elizabeth Rodabaugh, and Sister Dora Rose of Nappanee, Indiana.· God will not forget their labor of love.

Every one at Riverside was pleased over the gift of the Dayton church. This gift was Miss Ewert, a cook for the dormitory. She was accompanied by Mrs. Wenger, who helped install her in her new and important position.

One need that has not been met is a nurse. It is impossible for Miss Bethke, our matron, to be a matron and nurse too. We have had two quite serious .cases of illness this year. The many minor ailments have to be neglected.

This will .perhaps be my last report before the beginning of the new school year, but we are hoping that before another report is sent in we can tell you that not only has a nurse arrived on the field, but that we have also a music and domestic science teacher, and that the grade work is being continued for the next term, as it should be with the necessary helpers.

Having a little fellow six years old with a sister and a crippled brother a few years older were brought to us. It is so hard to care for the little ones, but harder to turn them away.

MRS. G. E. DRUSHAL.

The Lord's Day

This is the beautiful way to think of the Lord's Day. It is the shadow of Christ on the hot highway of time. We pause in it as in a shelter from the heat, and are refreshed. In proportion as we carry the spirit of it into all days do they also become . Lord's days, and yield us the same refreshment and peace as the Sabbath day.—Robert E. Speer.

NEWS FROM THE FIELD

ZION HILL, OHIO

The Zion Hill congregation purchased a church at Sterling, Ohio, last spring. This is the first building in our history which we can really call our own. Heretofore we always worshiped in a Union church.

We also rented a church at Smithville and hold services alternately at these two places. We think we have made a wise move as our attendance at both Sterling and Smithville has been better than it had been when we held services at only one place. We held our first revival at Sterling beginning Monday evening, October 11 and closing Sunday evening, October 24. It was a very busy time for the farmers but most of them considered the Master's work first and most important and the crowd continued to grow larger at each meeting. Even nature smiled down upon us, for we were certainly blessed with the most ideal weather. There was not one bad evening. Brother A. L. Lynn, our regular pastor, conducted this revival. We can only speak of him in words of highest praise. The immediate results of the meeting were eleven confessions, nine were received into the church by baptism, and one by relation. The church as a whole was very much revived and strengthened. At our last Sunday's service the Sabbath school volunteered to give Brother Lynn their offering which amounted to $17.22. The church also gave their morning and evening offering. The entire voluntary offering amounted to over $113.00. At our closing service on Sunday evening, the house was packed long before the hour for services to begin and many were turned away because of lack of room. Many remarked that at no religious gathering in this town did they see the house filled at such an early hour.

We might tell you many more good things about Brother Lynn but we hesitate to do so, fearing some other congregation might get interested in him and take him from us. We desire to keep him as long as we can for we believe there is much good yet to be accomplished during his stay with us.

MRS. D. L. KING,
Corresponding Secretary.

PLEASANT GROVE, IOWA

The midweek prayer meeting has been well attended. We have a good start to make the goals for 1928. We have a full program each Sunday now. Sunday school at 10 A. M., preaching at 11 A. M., Christian Endeavor at 7 P. M. and preaching again at 8 P. M. and the midweek prayer meeting on each Thursday night. We expect to start our teachers' training class also. The first night of prayer meeting we had 30 people there. Some of these came seven miles. And this week we had 28. Now we are in the midst of corn husking. See what we can do when we have a mind to work and pray. The church is dying because we do not pray. Jesus the only begotten Son of God prayed. Why do we not pray? Oh, say folks, do you know that the church of God must pray for lost souls? If we would stop

our everlastingly calling each other pro-Germans and German sympathizers and look at our own sins, and do more praying, the church house would not be empty every Sunday morning. Jesus said we should pray for each other, and to judge ourselves and not our brethren. Now the day of judgment will tell it all; it will show how you and I stand before God. The sin of evil speaking is increasing. I find it spreading all over the entire church. People surmise something and then they gossip about it. And even if some one has done wrong the slander keeps him from repentance. If you saw a person drowning, would you try to save him, or would you stand on the bank and say, "You fool! You had no business to fall into the water?". The latter is just what some folks do to sinners. Instead of praying for them and helping them to believe in Christ, they drive them away from the church by this everlasting gossip. If you can not pray for them, do not do anything else. We should try to save the lost by prayer.

H. W. ANDERSON.

COLLEGE NEWS

The work of the College goes steadily forward with a few new enrollments from time to time. We have this year a very fine body of young people. The Seminary is not as full as one could wish for but it is hoped that when we go forward with our new building program it will have a generally stimulating effect on the attendance. This week marks the mid-semester examinations.

Recently I attended a gathering of the college presidents of the state and talked with many of them about our plans for enlargement and gained some very valuable suggestions. But it makes one's heart sick to see other colleges planning campaigns for one or more million dollars when we have a hard time to reach several hundred thousand. The College right now ought to have $200,000 in order to step right out and take the place due by right merits. One hundred thousand ought to be used for building a new building and for repairing those we have and the other hundred ought to go towards permanent endowment. Every cent put here into the college stays, is not lost, and becomes an increasingly large asset to the church. We talk as a church about expansion when we forget that the very first step in that expansion is the proper preparation of young men for that expansion. There is no hope for expansion unless we have men keen of intellect, trained of mind, and consecrated in heart for the work of life. We might as well face it again, the college must have at least $200,000 more money within the next five years, or,—well, I cannot say what! This ought not to be a gloomy statement, or one that suggests defeat. It ought to challenge our church to its fulfillment. It may not be wholly possible, but it would be a very good tonic for the church to face the challenge. I am very hopeful that the Bicentenary will see this accomplished.

Let me add a list here of colleges and what the towns mentioned gave them, to say nothing of the churches which controlled them. In many cases the city did not contribute half of the general sum raised. That will suggest the very large amounts raised for these schools. All are Ohio colleges but one.

College "A" recently raised $53,563 in Canton (not located there).

College "B" raised $61,555 in Marietta.
College "C" $75,000 and over in Wooster.
College "D" $100,000 in Defiance.
College "E" $90,000 in Wilmington.
College "F" $250,000 in Stark county.
College "G" $200,000 and over in Clark county.
College "H" $200,000 in Allentown, Pa.

This suggests what Ashland has to compete with right here in Ohio. Educational Day for our people comes in latter May, I believe, and by that time, I hope the church will see the seriousness of the situation and respond heartily.

Some one asks, will the College never be satisfied? The answer is, Not so long as we are behind in the race. So that question ought to be settled once and for all.

The College asks a continuation in your interests and in your prayers.

EDWIN E. JACOBS.

FIELD REPORT OF EVANGELISTIC AND BIBLE STUDY LEAGUE

Uniontown Meeting

I was specially interested in the work here as I was one of a committee, including Brethren Wampler and Myers, who first visited this field and recommended it to the State Mission Board as a field to operate in.

This was my first meeting with Brother Belote and a more congenial pastor I never labored with. I enjoyed the hospitality of his home and his congenial fellowship. It was under his leadership that the work here was developed and the church building erected. He was recently recalled to serve his second pastorate, which speaks of the esteem of the church for him.

The church here had had its struggles, difficulties and problems, but there is no question as to its future success with a whole Gospel and a consecrated people.

The attendance at the services was ordinary, but made up of faithful supporters. It was a good meeting and while it was not large in number of converts, yet several were added to the church.

Masontown

With Brother Belote, I had the pleasure of visiting the Masontown church by invitation of Brother Gingrich, the new pastor, who succeeded Brother Shively. I was glad to meet Brother Gingrich as he is one of our new pastors, serving his first congregation, having graduated from Ashland College last spring. While it was on Saturday night when we had no service in Uniontown, yet we had the privilege of speaking in the church to many of its members and presented the work of the

League, to which several gave support. Brother Gingrich is now in the midst of a revival which he is conducting himself.

Johnstown, Pa.

By invitation of Brother Watson and the congregation, I arranged to stop over to preach three nights and to assist in their communion service. It was a privilege to be with the people whom I served for six years as pastor. We had large audiences and a fine communion service that was well attended.

Keep your eye on Johnstown for the days to come, they have a great program ahead of them. When their new building is erected it will be the finest and best in the brotherhood. I went over the blue prints and saw the picture of it as it will look when completed.

I enjoyed the hospitality and fellowship of Brother Watson and had the privilege of dining in his home with Brethren Jones and Wood. Their revival will be conducted by Brother Ashman in January.

Now at Goshen

I began a campaign with Brother McInturff in Goshen, Indiana, Sunday, November 7th. This is my second meeting here and we hope for a good time in the Lord.

W. S. BELL.

CLAY CITY, INDIANA

On the eleventh of October, we opened an evangelistic campaign with Brother A. E. Thomas of Warsaw, Indiana, as our evangelist. The Monday following Brother H. E. Eppley came over from Eaton, Indiana, to lead the singing. They made a good team. Eppley put life and inspiration into the service of song, and it is almost needless to say that Thomas put his best characteristic "pep" and enthusiasm into every sermon. But mind you, this is only a bit of seasoning to his unique expositions of the Word that brought home a telling message. The meetings continued three weeks, and in spite of the many political meetings, lecture course dates, Hallowe'en parties and a spell of bad weather during the closing week, the meeting was a success. A pastor of another church said to me since the meetings closed, "The meetings at your church have left a deep impression on the community." The visible results were fourteen. Ten by baptism and two by relation have united with the church. Among those who answered the call and have been baptized is one of the leading physicians of the community, whose influence will mean much to the cause and the church in the community.

The revival closed with an all day meeting at the church and our brethren kindly consented to remain over for the communion service on Monday evening.

S. C. HENDERSON.

TERRA ALTA, WEST VIRGINIA

It has not been long since a report has appeared concerning the Whitedale congregation. Our splendid revival has already been reported; but I want to speak my appreciation of it.

The services of Evangelists C. C. Grisso of North Liberty, Indiana, who was secured by our pastor, V. U. Flora, have had a wide spreading influence over this section. Brother

Grisso began his evangelistic campaign here October 9th and continued for two weeks. Good interest was noticeable from the very beginning. The sermons were masterful, especially the sermons from the following named themes, "The Unpardonable Sin;" "What Then Shall I Do With Jesus?" "The Conversion of a Moral Man;" "Why Men Are Lost;" "The Lost Christ and Christian Baptism." This last was one of the greatest sermons we have ever heard on that subject. It was a masterpiece. If any of the brethren had any doubts as to baptism by immersion, those doubts were removed through the hearing of this discourse. The church has been strengthened.

But the sermons were not all that was good and inspiring about the meetings. For in addition to all this, Brother Grisso's leading in the singing, and his solo work was inspiring and appreciated by every one.

Brother Grisso's untiring efforts shall not be forgotten. The meetings closed Saturday evening, October 23rd, with a communion and love feast, in which fifty-seven members participated. At the close of this meeting, a unanimous call of the church for Brother Grisso's return for an evangelistic campaign next year, was made, which shows appreciation of good services rendered. And we mean to go forward with renewed energy, under the splendid leadership of our pastor, feeling stronger as a congregation than ever before.

S. K. WHITEHAIR.

Terra Alta, Virginia.

MINUTES OF THE THIRTY-SECOND CONFERENCE OF THE BRETHREN CHURCHES OF PENNSYLVANIA, PITTSBURGH, PA. OCTOBER 4, 5, 6, and 7, 1920

The opening session of the thirty-second conference of the Brethren churches of Pennsylvania was called to order by the Moderator, H. M. Harley, the pastor of the entertaining church, at 8 P. M., Monday, October 4, 1920, in the Pittsburgh Brethren church.

The hymn "Day Is Dying In the West" was sung with spirit and Elder E. E. Roberts of Philadelphia was introduced and conducted the devotional exercises reading the 84th Psalm and leading in fervent prayer for the blessing of God upon the work of this conference. He pleaded for a deep realization of the importance of the work of the church, citing Nehemiah as an example of zealous devotion.

"Leaning on the Everlasting Arms" was sung earnestly.

Brother H. F. E. O'Neill on behalf of the Pittsburgh church extended a hearty welcome to the delegates. His address follows:

Address of Welcome

Delegates to the State Conference of the Brethren church of Pennsylvania:

Following the language of General Pershing on his arrival at the shores of Lafayette in France, may I say Brethren and sisters you are here to attend the thirty-second annual conference of our church and we, the people of Pittsburgh, are here to welcome you. In doing so, I want to express the appreciation of Brother Harley, the pastor, and the people of the Pittsburgh church in having you here as our guests.

We hope you will not find this but rather make this the greatest and best conference we have ever had. In welcoming you, may I suggest that the best way to do this is first to be here at every session and be on time.

Secondly Listen attentively to every address and if possible, participate in, and profit by every discussion. Third: Contribute something of your thought and substance to whatever is for the Kingdom of Christ and the life of men. Fourth: Reconsecrate and re-dedicate your all exclusively and unreservedly to the service of Christ in whatever way and place he may call you. Fifth: Be as generous as God would have you be but don't be so generous that you give someone else all the work to do. Do your own share and thereby glorify your Heavenly Father, for no one else can do the work God has planned for you, and if you do not do it, it will go undone.

May I set the goal and slogan and sound the keynote for this Conference? Goal—The largest and best conference ever held in Pennsylvania and every member stay throughout the Conference to the closing session, Thursday evening and every delegate at every session on time. Slogan—Every delegate at this Conference shall be fully consecrated to the service of Jesus Christ in winning men and women to know and accept him as their Lord and Savior, whom to know aright is life eternal, and we shall all go back to our local congregations filled to overflowing with the spirit of God as evangelists for him. Keynote—Complete surrender and consecration, to him and Christlike service to every man in the community in which we live.

In my closing word of welcome, with the Pittsburgh church extending to you a most hearty welcome, we do not follow the custom of giving you the key to the city, but we leave the doors of our homes wide open for you to come and go at your pleasure. We hope your stay will be both pleasant and profitable to you and us and pray that you will be a blessing to us both in the Conference and in our homes.

The response to the address of welcome was brought by Elder J. F. Watson of Johnstown. After a few pleasantries regarding the ability of the delegates to do ample justice to the splendid hospitality of the Pittsburgh church he called attention to the tremendous tasks before the church and the problems to be solved. He emphasized the truth that while many solutions may be offered for our problems the preaching of the plain Gospel of Christ is the solution of all problems.

The choir rendered "Great God of Nations" to the enjoyment of all. An offering was taken amounting to $15.59. Elder W. C. Benshoff of Berlin returned thanks for the offering.

Elder Walter C. Warstler of the Church of the Brethren, Pittsburgh, brought a word of hearty greeting from his church, expressing a most cordial spirit of fellowship and a desire to see the Church of the Brethren and the Brethren church united in one great body. The twenty members of the Church of the Brethren present were asked to stand and the conference greeted them heartily. "The King's Business" was sung and Brother Warstler offered fervent prayer for the guidance of the Holy Spirit in the work of this conference.

The Vice-Moderator, W. C. Benshoff, took the chair and called for the Moderator's address by Moderator H. M. Harley. This inspiring address will be published in full in the Evangelist.

The hearty singing of "It's Just Like Jesus" and benediction by Elder W. C. Benshoff closed this session.

Tuesday, 9 A. M.

The forty-five minute devotional period was conducted by Elder M. A. Witter. Elder W. C. Benshoff led the singing of two spirited hymns after which prayer was offered by one delegate after another until fifteen minutes had passed in earnestly petitioning God for his guidance and for his power in doing his work. "Love Lifted Me" was sung. Ephesians 1:3-14 read with comment and the devotions closed with brief prayer.

The Moderator named as a Credential Committee, Elder Geo. H. Jones, Andrew Bell, and

D. K. Bole. Credentials were collected and while the committee was preparing its report some discussion was had as to the custom of conference in receiving ministers into this conference district.

The courtesies of conference were extended to Elder B. T. Showalter, Palestine, West Virginia.

The Credential Committee reported 38 Lay credentials and 25 Ministerial credentials approved. They also reported the receipt of $45.50 in conference fees. The report was accepted and committee continued.

The Moderator appointed as a Committee on Resolutions Elders J. F. Watson, W. C. Benshoff, and E. E. Roberts.

The courtesies of conference were extended to Elder J. L. Gingrich of Masontown, Pa., it being understood that certificate of ministerial standing in this district be issued when approved evidence of ministerial standing in Ohio district be furnished the Ministerial Examining Board.

The Johnstown delegates were granted the privileges of the conference pending the arrival of their credentials which were delayed.

At this time conference passed a memorial session in honor of the two noble men of God who had been called by death from fruitful Gospel ministry in this district. "Wonderful Words of Life" was sung.

The memory of our beloved brother, Elder I. B. Trout, was honored in the address of Elder J. F. Watson, who spoke with deep feeling, paying a beautiful tribute to the life of this highly accomplished and noble spirited man of God and tower of strength in the Christian ministry.

A touching tribute to the memory of our dear brother, Elder Edward Byers, was paid by Elder J. I. Hall who spoke of the unusual accomplishments of this faithful gospel minister and educator who met his death in the train-auto accident near his home last June.

Tuesday, 1:30 P. M.

SUNDAY SCHOOL SESSION—

President Albert Trent of the District Sunday School Association presided at this session. "The King's Business" and "My Jesus, I Love Thee" were sung with enthusiasm, Brother Benshoff leading the singing.

Elder W. S. Baker led the devotions, reading 2 Timothy 2:1-26 and offering prayer.

The Vice-President, W. C. Benshoff, took the chair and called for the address of President Albert Trent on "Our Present Status." This address will appear in full in the Evangelist.

Elder J. F. Watson, President of the National Sunday School Association of the Brethren church addressed conference on the subject, "Our Sunday School Goals for 1920-1921." His address gave a clear explanation of the goals of the new standard and kindled a flame of inspiration to their attainment.

"The Importance of Teacher Training" was the subject of a helpful address by Elder W. C. Benshoff.

"The Sunday School's Greatest Need" was the subject discussed by Elder George H. Jones. Each of these addresses have been requested for publication in the Evangelist.

The election of District Sunday school officers was the next item of business.

A motion prevailed that instead of the corps of officers that we now have we elect a President who shall also be Director of Religious Education for the district and who with three other members shall constitute the District Board of Religious Education.

A motion having carried that a nominating committee be appointed to bring in nominations for these offices the moderator appointed Elders J. F. Watson, Dyoll Belote, and George H. Jones as that committee.

"Higher Ground" was sung, announcements were made and the Nominating Committee brought in its report which was accepted, the following District Sunday school officers being elected:

Albert Trent, District Sunday School President and Director of Religious Education.

Alva J. McClain, L. G. Wood, and Joseph L. Gingrich, members of the District Board of Religious Education. (Note.—At a later session on motion by Alva J. McClain the name of Horace Kolb was substituted for that of A. J. McClain as a member of the District Board of Religious Education).

"Love Lifted Me" was sung and Elder E. E. Roberts pronounced the benediction.

Thursday Evening Session, 7:45 P. M.

The spirited song service was led by Brother Sheldon Smouse of Altoona. "If Your Heart Keeps Right," "Awake, Awake," and "Saved, Saved" were sung. The devotions were conducted by Elder M. C. Myers who read Colossians 1:1-29 with comment and offered prayer.

A solo, "Hold Thou My Hand" was beautifully sung by Mrs. Wm. Smith.

Dr. R. R. Teeter, Business Manager of the Brethren Publication Board was introduced and spoke on the subject "Our Publication Interests." He stressed the importance of the religious press drawing parallels from the political world to show the power of the printed page in any propaganda. He plead for an enthusiastic and loyal support of all of our publication interests.

A quartet, Mr. Rishel, Miss Amelia Dewall, and Mr. and Mrs. Wm. Smith sang "No One Can Help But Jesus" and an offering of $18.43 was taken.

Elder Alva J. McClain brought the closing message of the day in his inspiring Gospel sermon based on 2 Timothy 4:6-8. We expect to see this sermon in the Evangelist.

Wednesday Morning Session, 9:15 A. M.

The 45 minute devotional period was led by Elder E. E. Fehnel. The song service was led by Brother S. Smouse. "Jesus Included Me," "Just When I Need Him Most" were sung. About 15 responded in earnest prayer after which Elder Fehnel read Colossians 3:1-4, 12-16 and brought a helpful message based on Colossians 3:3. "Wonderful Words of Life" were sung.

The first item of business was the report of the Credential Committee, showing 42 lay delegates and 27 ministerial delegates, a total of 69 approved. The committee was continued.

A motion prevailed that the courtesies of the conference be extended to all Visiting Brethren representing the general interests of the church.

A motion prevailed that this conference pay the bill of $34.45 for the traveling expenses of Elder L. G. Smith in attending the meeting of the Board of Trustees of Ashland College, also that the expenses of Brother Wm. Kolb in attending that meeting be paid.

A motion prevailed that hereafter this conference pay the expenses of Ashland College Trustees in attending Board Meetings until such time as the College can provide for that expense.

Brethren Albert Trent and S. A. Snook were re-elected to membership in the District Mission Board. Term expires 1923.

Elder A. J. McClain was elected a member of the Ministerial Examining Board. Term expires 1923.

Elder Henry Wise was elected member of the Board of Appeals. Term expires 1923.

Elders Dyoll Belote and W. C. Benshoff were elected members of the Executive Committee of the General Conference for the year 1921-1922.

Brother H. F. E. O'Neill was elected District representative of the Board of Benevolences.

At this time Dr. M. E. Poland, Educational Director of the No-Tobacco Army was introduced and addressed conference on the tobacco problem and the work of the No-Tobacco Army.

"Love Lifted Me" was sung.

Secretary Albert Trent of the District Mission Board made the following report for the Board. The report was accepted.

To the Moderator and Members of The Brethren Conference of Pennsylvania District:

Brethren:

Your Mission Board respectfully submits the following report of its work for the year ending October 6, 1920.

Throughout the past year, the conditions have been such in the Pennsylvania District that we were practically unable to do any aggressive work for lack of pastoral and evangelistic service at the points where help of this nature was so greatly needed. The dearth of ministers in the Brethren church is so great at present that we cannot secure pastoral care in one place without depriving some other church of its pastor.

We have therefore had to confine our efforts toward taking care of the missions in hand without attempting any new work. Some of the points were taken care of in a temporary or substitute manner where we ought to have had pastors regularly located in order to be successful.

In Armstrong County, where the services of a regular pastor are sorely needed, Brother M. C. Meyers of the Pittsburgh church and others gave Kittanning services every two weeks for the greater part of the year. And Brush Valley was taken care of in a similar way by Brother H. S. Myers of Scottdale for a part of the year.

During the college vacation season, Brother Florizel Pfeiderer, a young theological student of Ashland, spent his vacation on this field and accomplished efficient work among the people and in organizing the young people for service. He also added a number to the church by baptism during his short stay.

Calvary, New Jersey, continues in about the same condition as in previous years, an evangelistic meeting was held for them by Brother I. D. Bowman with some additions. But here we are also without a pastor at present.

Johnstown, Third church, where your board and the National Board have promised assistance in enlarging their building which is entirely too small for their present needs, has continued its splendid growth throughout the year notwithstanding the handicap due to crowded condition. Dr. Bell gave them an evangelistic meeting which resulted in the addition of 55 souls to the church.

Bedford County Circuit lost its pastor through the lamentable death of Prof. Byers and has been without regular services for a time. New Enterprise and Yellow Creek are under one pastorate, served by Brother Fyock. Bunker Hill and Liberty are being taken care of temporarily by Brother H. E. Smith.

Jones Mills, since Brother Clifford has left the pastorate, is now under the ministry of Brother H. S. Myers and receiving no support from your board.

Terra Alta and Pleasant Valley had no regular services during the year until the college vacation period, when the services of Brother V. U. Flora, another Ashland student, took up the work. His services have been so efficient that they have persuaded him to take up teaching in the public schools in that section and serve them as pastor.

The responses from the churches on the Apportionment have been most commendable during the past year. In fact more funds were received this year than in any single previous year.

Our difficulty is not the lack of funds for the work but the men to serve as pastor or evangelist. We have tried to secure preachers from various sections of the brotherhood, but have been unsuccessful so far.

Our field is indeed ripe for the harvest but the laborers are too few.

The following contributions on the apportionment were received during the year:

Contributions Received During Conference
Year Ending October 6th, 1920

Aleppo,	$ ....
Allentown,	29.00
Altoona,	70.30

Berlin,	113.00
Brush Valley,	30.00
Bunker Hill,	4.00
Calvary,	22.00
Conemaugh,	100.00
Highland,	
Johnstown, First,	258.00
Johnstown, Second,	26.00
Johnstown, Third,	76.00
Jones Mills,	25.00
Kittanning,	
Liberty,	17.00
Listie,	25.50
Martinsburg,	40.00
Martinsburg, Ever Faithful Class,.	4.00
Masontown,	100.00
Maple Grove,	19.00
McAllisterville,	5.00
McKees,	36.50
Meyersdale,	186.00
Mt. Pleasant,	20.50
New Enterprise,	31.74
Philadelphia, First,	93.00
Philadelphia, Second,	
Philadelphia, Third,	27.00
Pike,	55.00
Pittsburgh,	90.00
Pleasant Valley, Md.,	
Quiet Dell,	
Salisbury,	
Sergeantsville,	29.00
Summit Mills,	65.00
Sugar Grove,	
Terra Alta, W. Va.,	68.00
Uniontown,	
Vandergrift,	
Vinco,	27.00
Waynesboro,	85.00
Windber,	25.00
Yellow Creek,	20.00
Interest on Savings Account,	35.80
Sale of Bethlehem church,	50.00
Mrs. Jessie M. Friedline,	50.00
Rosedale church,	150.00

Total,	$2,113.34

Expenditures for Conference Year Ending
October 6th, 1920

Armstrong County, Missions,	$ 194.28
Bedford County,	175.20
Third Brethren, Johnstown,	161.00
Windber Church,	66.00
Jones Mills Church,	30.00
Bethlehem, Interest on Mortgage,	60.00
Calvary Church,	50.00
Traveling Expenses,	7.89
Printing and Postage,	21.43

Total Expenditures,	$ 765.80
Balance on hand, October 9, 1919,	$1,928.09
Received during year,	2,113.34

Grand total,	$4,041.43
Expenditures during year,	765.80

Balance on hand, October 9, 1920,	$3,275.63

ALBERT TRENT, Secretary.

SUNDAY SCHOOL EQUIPMENT IN SOUTH AMERICAN CHURCHES

MonteVideo, Uruguay, is setting a great example for every community in the United States as well as in other countries in the matter of recognition of the essential place which the Sunday school holds in the life and growth of every church. "No plan for a new church in my district will receive my approval," said a District Superintendent, "unless proper provision is made to house the Sunday school." This sensible statement was reported by Rev. George P. Howard, Sunday School Secretary for South America. Mr. Howard offered a real Methodist "Amen" when he heard the Superintendent express his decision. Brethren leaders too are coming to appreciate this point, but too often in the past those who had charge of the erection of new church buildings had no vision of Sunday school needs.

Mr. Howard tells also of our work in Rosario, Argentina. "I was in Rosario a few Sundays ago. In our Central church one Sunday school with 80 members which I founded four years ago has grown to two Sunday schools, one meeting in the morning with 140 members and the other in the afternoon with 270. The MonteVideo Central Sunday school is spending this year $10,000 for additional class rooms. This school has a teachers' institute weekly that contributes richly to the efficiency of the teaching staff. A rather novel idea is also being carried out: one class of young men is being led by a missionary in a course of studies leading up to a theological course in our local Seminary. MonteVideo church is hoping to turn out some preachers for this field." How do our Sunday schools compare with this one in growth and accomplishments?

Dr. John Clifford says, "God is always preparing the world's kings. True rulers are never absent. They do not sit on thrones. They are with us in our families, or looking after our sheep, or keeping our books, despised by their elder brothers, and unrecognized-by all; but when the clock of time strikes they take their place and do their work."

God tests young men with opportunities; their worthiness is evidenced by the readiness with which they seize them and the willingness with which they pay the price for success."

—W. H. Burleigh.

Business Manager's Corner

GROWING BRIGHTER

The prospects of our being able to meet the notes, given in settlement for the last car load of paper we received, as they come due are growing brighter as the days go by. Today we must pay a $1,000.00 note at the bank and in thirty days we must meet another note for $2,000.00.

With the assistance given us by the churches that have reported their offerings taken on Publication Day we are able to meet today's obligation, and we trust the churches that have not yet reported, together with those that have not yet taken their offering, will swell this offering to an amount that, added to what we may receive through our regular business, will enable us to meet our December obligations as well. The need is still great, and no church should let this opportunity to come to the help of one of the oldest and most useful institutions of the church pass by without improving it. If October 31st did not suit your church for this special offering, any other day will do just as well. We are not a bit choicy about the matter. The one thing we want is results.

One thing we are glad to report this week is the help that came to us from good old Nappanee, in the renewal of their entire list of ONE HUNDRED FIVE Evangelist subscriptions with a check for the full amount accompanying the order even though their subscriptions do not expire for two months yet.

We do not know how orthodox our theology was considered the years we served as pastor of these people, but we do know that we taught them sound financial doctrine, as we always tried to teach all the churches that we served in a similar capacity, and we are convinced that this is just about as essential to the welfare of a church as theological views are, though we would not minimize the importance of straight theological thinking for a moment. This makes the fourth year for the Nappanee church on the Honor Roll, so the plan still WORKS. You have heard that expression before, but we want to remind you of the fact that our best and most successful churches find it the best way to handle the matter of church literature.

We are also glad to report the following offerings from churches, Sunday schools and individuals for the paper fund: North Liberty, Indiana, $20.50; Hagerstown Brethren church, $25.00; Mrs. J. M. Morgan, $1.50; Mr. and Mrs. Albert Landry, $5.00; Waterloo Brethren church, $60.00; Meyersdale Sunday school, $30.00; Allentown church, $17.65; Beaver City church, $15.00; Milledgeville church, $48.77; Columbus church, $6.00; Pittsburgh church and Sunday school, $57.95; Maurertown Sunday school, $11.00; Washington, D. C., Sunday school, $15.00; Lucy Metz, $1.00; Mrs. H. J. Frantz, $1.00; Salem Brethren church, $12.00; New Paris, Sunday school, $11.11; Calvary, New Jersey, church, $5.00; Louisville Brethren church, $10.32; Fort Scott additional to last week's report, $2.00; Flora Brethren church, $13.16, and in addition to this several subscribers of the Evangelist have voluntarily raised their subscription price as they have renewed to $2.50. All these things help and are surely appreciated. But there are many, many churches that should yet be heard from to make this a general offering.

R. R. TEETER,
Business Manager.

Communion Notices

The Brethren of Roanoke, Virginia, will hold their love feast and communion service, Sunday evening, November 28. All members of the church are urged to attend. Brethren of neighboring churches are cordially invited.

H. M. OBERHOLTZER.

The First Brethren church of Fremont will hold their Fall Communion service on Sunday evening, November 21. All neighboring Brethren are cordially invited to share the blessings of this service with us.

M. L. SANDS.

Communion service will be held at Milford, Indiana, Sunday evening, 8:00 o'clock, November 21st. All who believe that Jesus is Christ are welcomed to enjoy the service of sacrament with us.

EARL H. DETSCH.

The Brethren church at Masontown, Pennsylvania, will observe Holy Communion on Sunday evening, November 21. All of like faith are invited to share these blessings with us.

JOSEPH L. GINGRICH, Pastor.

VOLUME XLII
NUMBER 45

NOVEMBER 24
1920

The BRETHREN EVANGELIST

- ONE·IS·YOUR·MASTER·AND·ALL·YE·ARE·BRETHREN -

THE TIME OF
SPIRITUAL HARVEST

Is Here and Before Us Is

THE CHALLENGE OF RIPENING GRAIN

Thrust forth thy sickle. Dost thou not care if the harvest be lost? Thousands are going down to spiritual death every day. Dost thou not care? Lift up thine eyes and behold how great is the harvest, and that it is all around thee. Scarcely one Christian in a hundred seems to care or offer a single prayer for the salvation of those for whom God gave everything he possessed— his only begotten Son, his Holy Spirit, his Word, his love, his all.

How Shall We Answer If at the Judgment
An Accusing Voice Should Say,

"No Body Cared for My Soul?"

Published every Wednesday at Ashland, Ohio. All matter for publication must reach the Editor not later than Friday noon of the preceding week.

George S. Baer, Editor

The Brethren Evangelist

When ordering your paper changed give old as well as new address. Subscriptions discontinued at expiration. To avoid missing any numbers renew two weeks in advance.

R. R. Teeter, Business Manager

ASSOCIATE EDITORS: J. Fremont Watson, Louis S. Bauman, A. B. Cover, Alva J. McClain, B. T. Burnworth.

OFFICIAL ORGAN OF THE BRETHREN CHURCH

Subscription price, $2.00 per year, payable in advance.
Entered at the Post Office at Ashland, Ohio, as second-class matter.
Acceptance for mailing at special rate of postage provided for in section 1103, Act of October 3, 1917, authorized September 9, 1918.
Address all matter for publication to Geo. S. Baer, Editor of the Brethren Evangelist, and all business communications to R. R. Teeter, Business Manager, Brethren Publishing Company, Ashland, Ohio. Make all checks payable to the Brethren Publishing Company.

TABLE OF CONTENTS

EDITORIAL

The One Safe School of Theology

It has been said upon more than one occasion by men who ought to know that the "safe" theological schools of the country may be counted upon the fingers of one hand. There is undoubtedly much of truth in the statement. Be that as it may, there is in our own mind a growing conviction that after all there is but one school where we may safely study the Scriptures and formulate our theological views—and that school is the one located at the foot of the Cross! Only the truth can prevail here! False theories wither up and die! The Cross is the only place where questions of theology can be settled. No answer is to be accepted that cannot endure the blazing light of the Cross.

Are the Scriptures the Very Word of God?

Come to the Cross! The Lord has been hanging there for several hours. Prophecy after prophecy has been fulfilled. He is about ready to "give up his spirit." "Knowing that all things are now finished," he says, "I thirst!" Why does he say it? He was thirsty, answers some one. Ah, but that will not exhaust the purpose. He said it "that the Scripture might be accomplished!" Back in the 69th Psalm there was a prophecy that read, "In my thirst they gave me vinegar to drink!" The Son of God refused to die until that last prophecy of his sufferings was fulfilled to the letter? Those men who teach that prophecy is not prediction, that we must not expect it to be fulfilled literally, did not learn their doctrine of inspiration at the Cross.

Does the World Love God?

To this some have answered, Yes, humanity loves God and is seeking him. The cross brands this answer as a lie! Man is not seeking God! God is seeking man! And as the proof that humanity does not love God, when God came into the world in the person of Christ to seek and to save, humanity seized and nailed him to the Cross. Surely, a strange way to manifest love.

Nor can this greatest of all crimes be charged to any one section or party of the human race. It was a representative mob which crucified the Lord of glory. Pilate's superscription is a striking symbol of this fact. It was written in three languages—Hebrew, representing religion; Greek, representing learning; Latin, representing power. Man's religion, man's wisdom, man's power—behold their work—the Christ of God upon the Cross!

For the past few years we have heard it said with tiresome iteration and reiteration that the crimes of humanity are not committed by "the people," but by their rulers. Dr. Frank Crane has written, "The People are as wholesome as the sunshine, or the wide sea, or

the mountains. They are more deeply moral than any saint or church. They are utterly incorruptible. . . The People are the true Supreme Court. The People's eventual word is as the Day of Judgment. The Voice of the people at last is the Voice of God."

Over against these "great swelling words" let us put the Word of God in Luke 23:13-23, "The chief priests . . . rulers . . . people . . . all together . . . shouted, saying, Crucify, Crucify him! . . . And their voices prevailed." Could any movement be more purely democratic? It is worthy of note that out of all this crowd there was only one individual who made a serious attempt to prevent the crucifixion. That man was a king, the despised Pilate!

Does God Love The World?

"God commendeth his own love toward us, in that while we were sinners, Christ died for us." Such is the answer of the Cross.

"O Love divine, what hast Thou done?
The incarnate God hath died for me,
The Father's co-eternal Son,
Bore all my sins upon the tree!"

But the Cross was no mere exhibition of God's Love. It was not something given us merely to look at and grow sentimental over. It was Love in action, providing a way by which every sinner might escape the wrath of God and be saved forever. The Cross was not given merely to inform us that God loved us in order that we might have an incentive to pull ourselves out of the mire of sin. It was the Power that reached down into the mire and plucked us out and set us with our faces toward God. And the Cross will appear the more glorious when we remember that it was not a moral necessity on the part of God. If, when man fell into sin, God had left him to his doom, no man could ever have questioned his righteousness. The Cross was pure Love, unmixed grace. Let us never forget it.

What is the True Estimate of Sin?

There is an easy-going doctrine, a convenient philosophy which has attained quite a large place in our modern world. Namely, sin is not, in the eyes of God, such a reprehensible thing as we have always supposed. Eddyism denies its existence altogether. Spiritualism tells us that sin will be somehow out out of our souls when we "go west." Theosophy promises deliverance from it after a few million years of reincarnations. Modern theology assures us that sin is not a criminal act committed by a responsible agent and deserving of eternal punishment, but rather an abnormal condition in the individual caused by the "shape of his head" or the "block in which he lives," something to be dealt with by surgeons and social service experts.

The Cross of Christ gives us the true estimate of sin, God's estimate of sin. He hates it! And his hatred is so inexorable that when the only-begotten Son took upon himself our sins, though he himself was without sin, the judgment of divine wrath fell upon him. Not even the Son of God could be spared when Jehovah raised his holy arm against sin. The Cross is the measure of God's hatred against sin, and no man can know its awful intensity and fullness until he has stood by the Cross and beheld the suffering of the Son of God.

What is the Precise Nature of the Atonement?

Come to the Cross and hear the cry of its Victim, "My God, my God, why hast thou forsaken me?" Yet some have dared to say that Christ died not in our stead. That he did not bear the penalty for our sin. That he was not standing in the place where sinners deserved to stand. Men have set forth various theories of the death of Christ. They have said that he died merely as a martyr. That he died merely to show God's love for men. But if Christ did not die as our substitute, if he was not punished for our sin, then why did God forsake him on the Cross? WHY? The martyr theory cannot answer. The love theory cannot answer. The men who have advanced such theories did not stand at the Cross when they originated them. If a man wishes to form correct views on the Atonement, let him take his stand at the foot of the Cross, let him listen to the cry, "My God, my God, why hast thou forsaken me?" His theories will die while the sound beats upon his ears. After men have stood there, they come away beating their breasts and crying, "Bearing shame and scoffing rude, In my place condemned he stood; Sealed my pardon with his Blood, Hallelujah! what a Savior!

No man can explain his cry apart from the fact that he bore the sins of sinners, that he was "made sin" on our behalf. It is not the habit of God to "forsake" good men in the hour of death! When Stephen fell under the cruel shower of stones he was looking into heaven and beholding "the glory of God and Jesus." It is only when men stand "afar off" that they can theorize on the atonement, failing to see the divine substitute for sinners.

How Can God Be Just and Forgive Sinners?

The answer is to be found in the Cross. The justice of God in forgiving sinners was vindicated by the Cross. The Cross proclaimed God to be "holy and just." Every unsatisfied demand of broken law in past ages was satisfied in the Cross. This is the great sweeping argument of Romans 3, "God hath set" forth "Christ" to be a propitiation . . . to declare his righteousness for the passing over of sins done aforetime in the forbearance of God; to declare, I say, his righteousness, that he might be JUST and the JUSTIFIER of him that believeth on Jesus."

Forgiveness through the Cross does not violate justice and make void the law. It establishes the law and exalts justice. And it is for this very reason that God can forgive NO man apart from the Cross of Christ, and that he can forgive ANY man who comes to the Cross.

Christianity is not a sickly sentimentalism like Eddyism and Unitarianism and the New Theology which forgives the sinner, and says of his sin, "It is nothing." NO! True Christianity does forgive the sinner, Thank God for that. But it does something besides. It bids the forgiven sinner look upon the Cross and there behold the glittering "sword" of a just God "smiting" the Lamb of God as he stands in the sinner's place. It is just this that makes the Cross, where it is truly preached, the mightiest moral force in all the universe. Where the Cross goes sin dies and righteousness becomes the ruling passion of men. The Cross makes forgiveness safe. Forgiving sinners without the Cross would wreck the universe.

Will There Be a Day of Judgment Upon Sinners?

The logic of the Cross is pitiless on this point. When the holy, sinless, undefiled Son of God took upon himself the burden of our sin and carried it to the Cross, he was not spared. The judgment of God fell upon him with eternal force. In the face of the Cross, dare any man who rejects the offer of the Son of God and elects to bear the burden of his own sin—dare such a man hope to escape the judgment of a just God?

When a man rejects the Cross of Christ as the place of pardon, the Cross becomes to that man the guarantee of his final judgment and doom.

Let every unbeliever who scoffs at the idea of eternal judgment contemplate the Cross. Let him behold the unutterable sufferings of the Son of God. Let him weigh carefully the terrible import of his cry, "My God, my God, why hast thou forsaken me?" Let him ponder well the divine explanation of that awful scene, "Christ died for our sins." And finally, let him tremble at the warning,, "If we sin wilfully after we have received a knowledge of the truth, there remaineth no more sacrifice for sins, but a certain fearful expectation of judgment." But above all, let him remember the gracious promise, "He that believeth . . . hath everlasting life, and shall not come into judgment."   A. J. McClain.

EDITORIAL REVIEW

Brother C. C. Grisso reports a brief but successful meeting held by himself at Accident, Maryland, where seven souls accepted Christ as their Savior.

Brother O. E. Bowman, the Secretary-Treasurer of the Home Mission Board, has a splendid letter on Mission page which every one will want to read. It deals with our Kentucky work.

Brother I. D. Bowman had a very successful revival meeting at Buckeye City, Ohio, in spite of the fact that the church is without a pastor and has been for some time.

Brother W. B. Sell reports briefly concerning his evangelistic meeting recently held at Row Valley, near Fredonia, Kansas. The result of a score of converts was most splendid.

A report from Brother A. B. Cover shows that the Hagerstown church is still pressing forward toward greater efficiency in the Lord's work, especially in their Sunday school. A splendid communion service is reported.

Pleasant Hill, Ohio, has experienced a real revival of interest along all lines under the enthusiastic leadership of Brother Lowman. The Sunday school and prayer meetings are especially noteworthy examples of this greater awakening.

Brother E. H. Smith makes a brief report of a brief evangelistic meeting, but the results are not brief. These nearly a dozen souls should be a great encouragement to the Brethren at Hollidaysburg.

Brother Belote has something to say in this issue concerning the Winona Tabernacle Fund, which some of the Brethren have not allowed to trouble them. He also makes some suggestions which are worth considering.

Brother McInturff raises the question as to how long it has been since he wrote a news letter to the Evangelist readers, but since he writes us quite a nice letter at this time we will not "give him away." He has had a good correspondent in the person of Brother Horner, so we have been kept informed. But we appreciate this word concerning the splendid program which the Goshen church has put across.

Now that you have made a banner offering for General Home Missions, it is not too early to look forward to the White Gift offering which, according to our custom, will be taken at Christmas time. This is the time when the Sunday schools furnish proof of the missionary inspiration and information they have received during the year.

Brother Gearhart passes on to our readers the sad information that also came to the editor recently, concerning the death of the little son of Brother and Sister George Cone, who have charge of the Fort Scott, Kansas, mission church. It seems that the fatal result came more from the fumes and smoke which the little one inhaled than from the burns which it received. Brother Cone is suffering greatly from burns which he received while endeavoring to rescue his child. In behalf of The Evangelist and its many readers, we extend the most sincere Christian sympathy to Brother and Sister Cone in their deep sorrow.

That our people are proud of the heroes of our faith is evidenced by the kindness shown to Brother J. H. Swihart by the members of the Indiana state conference. Brother Swihart writes concerning his great appreciation of the experience. We are of the conviction that we cannot do too much for nor be too thoughtful of these courageous veterans of our fraternity.

GENERAL ARTICLES

Some Congregational Essentials to Successful Evangelism.   By George E. Cone

To my mind the very first essential is that the body of the membership have a very real sense of what constitutes the work of the church. It is a very evident fact that too many of our people have an extremely narrow view of the mission and work of the church. It is not for me to analyze the situation to find the cause for this. Nor is it for me to lay the blame. To be sure there is a deep lying reason or reasons to be found. Each one will make his own analysis and place the blame. To me, it would be very interesting to have these analyses and the conclusions you come to. I am here pointing out the fact that people do not, in the main, appreciate the great responsibility resting upon the church. So long as we have a contracted selfish view of her work we need not expect "Successful Evangelism." To be specific here I refer to the attitude of so many which is best expressed by the proverbial "me and my wife and my son John and his wife, we four and no more." In other words, it seems to be far from general for our people to see the great multitude of unsaved people and our obligation to them. This obligation Christ himself laid upon us. It is the obligation to take the gospel message to all nations and to the people near at hand. I repeat then, that to my mind the first congregational essential to successful evangelism is that we get a clear and compelling vision of the many lost souls to be found everywhere and all around us and that we are commissioned to be instruments in God's hands for their salvation. It is necessary that every member, and not alone the pastor and a few of the faithful workers shall get this vision. We must have a wide-spread evangelistic spirit in the congregation if we are to succeed in evangelism.

Once we have gained the proper vision of the lost world and our own part of the task of bringing it to the saving knowledge of God we will then be ready for the next step. We will then see the utter folly of attempting the task in the strength of mere organization and administration. We will see that to undertake the task without God as advisor and partner is to invite disastrous defeat. It will be easily apparent that without the guidance and power which God alone can give we can but expect failure. Realizing this we will at once make use of the provision for gaining that vital touch

with God. We will pray, definitely, earnestly and compellingly. We will intercede as has never seemed possible to us before. Life will be laid in God's hands. He will give it back to us to use mightily for him and the extension of his work in the world. The accomplishing of great things, for him, will be put definitely into our hands. Why? Because he will know that we are working, not for self, not for any glory save as it glorifies his name. Because the life has been so given that he can use to the utmost.

Following these two essential steps comes another, namely, it is necessary that the congregation be a harmonious working unit. How can we expect God to add souls to us by his saving grace if we will not let him exert his power to the extent that we will be in Christian unison? Can we expect him to use an organization for his glory when it is divided within itself? Was there division among the Apostles on the day of Pentecost? Could God have worked so mightily among and through them if there had been? Would the Spirit have been their helper if they had been split into petty factions? I say emphatically, "No," to all these. And it is essential that we be in unity and in the bond of Christian love and fellowship within before we expect God to add to our numbers. In all things there must be prayer in the congregation. Organization and administration must be in the spirit of prayer and by the guidance of the Holy Spirit. Successful evangelism can not come into a divided, quarrelling congregation. Then let us get together and work together for his glory, minimizing our differences and in his Spirit keeping faith one with another.

I have named, what seem to me, three of the essentials to successful evangelism in the local church. The congregation will find other things. Each congregation will find some peculiar difficulties but if we are a unit on the great outstanding essentials, other things will find their rightful places. God must be given the pre-eminence all the way through but we must not forget that he works through human beings in carrying out his work among men. God and man as well as man and man must work together if the salvation of the peoples of the world is ever to be realized.

Ft. Scott, Kansas.

The Dress Question.   By Martin R. Goshorn

This subject is one that is generally considered unpopular to discuss as it touches almost every class of worldly people. It touches the vain and gaudy dresser because his heart is in his dress and being so near the surface it is easily hurt. It touches the person who desires to make a show in the world and because of his inability to hold a high position in society on better grounds, tries to hide his shortcomings behind a garb which he supposes will give him the standing which he craves. He who seeks the reward of the world usually finds it. But its promised beauties and satisfaction vanish like the rainbow and in the end when it is all too late the victim awakens to the knowledge of the fact that it was only a mocker, and his being deceived thereby is a sure evidence of his lack of wisdom.

To the true Christian the dress question is a minor one as regards his individual feelings. He lives in a different atmosphere to that of those who worship the world with its changing fashions and follies. The Christian really lives in a different world because he has been transformed by the renewing of his mind and no longer conforms to the world of fashion and pride. The things he once loved he has forgotten or hates, for in Christ he has become a new creature.

The dress craze is one of the great worries of the world today. It is common to both sexes. With it comes a spirit

of rivalry perhaps not surpassed by any other desire of men. This rivalry is greatest of course among the people of the world, but it exists among professed Christians to an astonishing degree and is evidence that the "ego" in them has not yet been crucified. They are usually a class of church members who are seeking peace where there is no peace, because they have not accepted the peace of the Master. They seek the abundant life but have not yet passed from death to life and become participants in that abundant life which Christ came to give.

When we speak of the worries and hardships endured by fashion loving people we refer to such as are endured by mothers who are eking out their lives in slavery to a proud spirit that tells them that dress is the one thing that is necessary to make the lives of her children a success, and to keep them in a position of high standing in the social world. Poor mother! Of course she loves her children, but her dream of dress, show and social standing has in it more of the coloring of Satan and his desire to despoil her child than it has of the Christ who came to give the abundant life, which takes no thought of raiment. Too many of our boys and girls grow up too much like the Feathertop of Nathaniel Hawthorne and are almost as worthless.

When we speak of the worries and the hardships induced by the fashion loving people we refer to such as are endured by many young husbands who because of their love for their frivolous, extravagant, fashionable wives have resorted to dishonest and dishonorable means of getting money to maintain their wives in their luxuries and who are now serving time in our penitentiaries because of being convicted of gambling, embezzling, or stealing the funds of their employers.

Church people should not be so much bothered about the dress question. However, go to some of the prisoners mentioned above and you will find that frequently the wives for which they stole the money in order that they might be dressed in the highest fashions, were women that stood high in the churches, but who had become crazed after fashion. Be honest, is it not true that you have seen some of the frivolous and extreme fashions in the choir of the churches? And have you not heard over and over the statement, "We would like to go to church and take our children to Sunday school, but we just simply can't dress well enough to go?" Would it be sacrilegious to say that there is something wrong with the church on the dress question? And would it be wrong to suggest that it might be possible Satan is blinding our eyes to these conditions to such an extent that we have become blind to the truth and that we are being led by him more than by the spirit of the lowly One of Nazareth?

There are some people who are so spiritual and devoted to their Master that they really have little thought about their clothing. They dress themselves neatly and modestly and care more for the inner man than they do for the outer raiment. To such the fashions in dress have no fascination. They are the class of people that after all almost everyone admires. They are a stumbling block to no one. As a result they have less of worry and more of peace.

So far we have only discussed such dress and fashions as are regarded in a general way as being suitable to cultivated and refined society. Other fashions in dress we leave to your own minds to discuss. Are they moral or are they immoral? Where does the one begin and the other leave off? And if there is no evil purpose in one what is the purpose of the other? How much of it can receive the "Well done thou good and faithful servant?" It is Christian to think on, and to cause others to think on, those things which are good, true, honest, just, pure, lovely, and of good report.

For ages the church has been trying to fight the evils of the dress question. Our mother church, as many others, tried to combat the fashionable dress of the world by enforcing uniformity in order to bring about nonconcormity among its members. Truly they were sincere and in a way successful. For the world looked upon them as a church of modest dress. Yet uniformity required much anxiety and thought to maintain it. Christ taught us not to be anxious about our raiment. We believe he meant that we should not bother our minds about our dress. Then it seems that Satan takes the opposite stand and tries to get the whole world anxious about the fashions of the world. Shall we follow Satan or Christ?

Christ taught us to seek first the Kingdom. Being subjects of the King, being sons of the Father, being heirs and joint heirs with the Son, who would care for the fashions of the world? Or who in such a state would worry about the dress of the worldly except to pray, "Father, forgive them for they know not what they do?"

If we are a "Whole Gospel People," we have come out out from among the world in the matter of the evils in dress as well as the evils in all other things. We should be a separate people. The world seeks the fashions and follows them at any cost. Should not Christians be entirely heedless concerning them and think more of the things pertaining to the welfare of the soul, clothing the body in such raiment as is convenient, modest, unassuming and Christlike and thus avoid all entangling alliances with the world?

Clay City, Indiana.

On the Duty of Man and the Attainment of Happiness.   Theodore Parker Gnagey

The world of ideals is not the insignificant world it is often thought to be. It is the world in which the greatest highlights in all history have lived, from the most practical of business men to the most brilliant of educators to the most incorporeal of idealists.

I think of ideals in terms of the totality of life and in the individual relation. "One adopts a life purpose and pursues it with a belief in its effectuality. For every individual, his life is all his power and riches, and is not to be spent save for the greatest good that he can reasonably pursue." This implies the fact of individual importance—self-development for personal achievement; and it is interlinked with the fact of ultimate importance—self-cultivation for the purpose of service to humanity. The former involves the idea of what people generally call "practical," the latter "idealistic."

In modern college circles, where the value of ideals should be more profoundly realized, there seems to be a confusion of these two elements of life. The practical and the idealistic are too often thought to be opposing entities, entirely unrelated, while the truth of the matter is they are inseparable in terms of the most efficient success.

Self-development for personal acheivement embodies for many, more than anything else, the unaltruistic idea of utility. Great numbers of college and university students find themselves in their respective institutions with the sole idea of developing their proficiency for the purpose of becoming able to bring to themselves the largest possible income with the least possible exertion. There is no harm in desiring such a state until that state becomes in itself a utility working for a utility. When once it has developed into that, the very ethics of a man's relation to his own self becomes corrupted and it often leads him to be parasitic in his relations with society. When a man works solely for the purpose of increasing his personal comfort and riches he has lost his hold on that high morality of duty and has slipped out of the realm of truest happiness, for that happiness is not to be found in the satisfaction of material wants but only in the path where conscience is unconstrained by higher dictates because it is free and in harmony with them.

Personal welfare, then, is the immediate desire which motivates the pursuit of self-development. Than this there is nothing more natural in human nature; yet, as I have suggested above, care must be taken that it does not become an end in itself. Although it concerns the individual, his personality and his individuality, it is not, if righteously continued, the purpose of existence. Man's own self is a big world. In him the sun of his own fate rises and sets. But he is only one world in a vast universe. That universe is humanity, and to humanity he owes not only his existence as a member of the race, but his circle of influence for the betterment of mankind. Inasmuch as he is an inevitable organ of humanity, just insofar must his ultimate purpose in life be service to humanity. A wheel is a piece of junk detached from the machine of which it is a part. To be of any individual value it must work in harmony with the mechanical whole. So it is true with the individual man. If the powers of his mind are cultivated and used only to satisfy his mind's own desires he is a worthless being. His ultimate purpose in life must be to serve the mind of humanity. And it is much more stringent in man that he serve the rest of his kind than that a wheel work in connection with the machine to which it belongs, because a man is an intellectual and a moral being, a machine only a mechanism. While a machine has only a material end to satisfy, a man has an ethical and spiritual end to fulfill. His life is not only a span of time through which he must exist, but he has the power of reproducing his kind so that his race will sustain; he has not only a personal duty to perform, but owes a portion of his gift to the society which gives him room to move, and all to be done in the spirit of him who was the Supreme Servant of men.

I think there is a supreme desire in man himself and in humanity which it is the purpose of all endeavor to satisfy. That is happiness. Man seeks personal happiness, and the highest state of the race is a happy humanity. There may be no such thing in the world as a final state of happiness which is full of contentment and free from dissatisfaction; it is a good thing there is not, else there would be an end to the value of life itself. That involves a new situation: happiness is a scale reaching toward an ideal mental and spiritual state. The attainment of happiness is to be found in the ascension of that scale.

To have happiness, then, one must ever climb upward. That implies constant work. The college student who is preparing himself for a definite purpose must be obsessed with the thought that his trained ability is to be directed not only toward the betterment of his personal welfare, but to serve humanity in the highest sense. Self-cultivation directed toward the goal of service as the Master served is the ideal state. When one adopts a life purpose, he has taken a serious step and has realized the value of life; and when life is spent for the greatest good, the Kingdom will be advanced, mankind will be benefitted and happiness will be the personal reward. Gold and pearls are only riches; happiness is the only real or enduring or intangible wealth a man can possess. To know that you are doing good and to desire continually with the highest motive to do good is to live a happy life. The possessions of the heart are far greater than anything the hand can touch.

Denison University, Granville, Ohio.

Ashland College from a Canadian's Standpoint. By B. F. Owen

Many have wondered and some have asked me, What is my attitude toward Ashland College? This question has weight because I happen to be one of a number that came to Ashland College from Montreal, Canada, some of whom were not loyal to the institution that opened its door to them. I left Montreal on a Saturday morning and arrived in Ashland on Monday night at 10:30 in the January of 1912. The college sent a student to meet me and he ushered me into an old time hack which took us to the dormitory. This was quite a new life for me and the thing that made it more strange was, that every room I passed going to the room reserved for me had the door openwide enough for the eyes of the occupants to peep out and see what this new Canadian looked like. I arrived at my room and being tired and the hour being late I retired until next morning when I received my first impression of college life.

I found that Ashland College stood for Christian ideals. Before I left Montreal, Canada, I was pressed hard by some to go either to The Moody Bible Institute or The Los Angeles Bible Institute for my training, for it was said that Ashland College was not a Christian school. I told the parties, one of whom had been in Ashland College, that if a man wanted to be a Brethren minister he should go to a Brethren school and I for one was going to Ashland and stick to the school of the church. I believe in The Moody Bible Institute and have sent money to both institutions, but my contention still is, and I say it in all sincerity, that if an individual feels called to preach in the Brethren church and is able to afford an education he should get the training at Ashland College. Further, all Brethren ministers, whether they have received training at Ashland or not, should encourage future students, especially for the ministry, to enter Ashland College. It is a Christian school, and I say this after studying the situation for eight years, having somewhat of a prejudiced mind to begin with. It does stand for Christian ideals. Its students are of a high type. These conclusions come through first hand observation and not heresay.

I found that Ashland College was moulding the students in harmony with these Christian ideals. A college is usually no place of reform. At least that was always my impression. But from my observation I have come to the conclusion that no individual can pass through Ashland College without his being better for having been there. Let us look at some of the few facts that are open at any time for inspection. The students of the dormitory never eat a meal without giving thanks. Then there is the regular daily chapel service conducted especially for the uplift of the individual life and character. This is entirely devotional. The best of hymns are used, followed by a discourse from some vital Bible truth applied to every day life and the service is concluded with a heart searching prayer. In fact, these discourses are the same as would be used at conference, in a pastorate or any place where they could be applied. The professors of Ash-

land College are not one thing at home and another abroad. Then there is the Bible study hour when once each week each and every student is required—there is no choice about it—to study God's Word. That means no one escapes, no matter what his course, they are no respecters of persons. This is constructive work and not destructive. Again, each Sunday there is the Sunday school, church service, Christian Endeavor of the local church in charge of the pastor, Rev. J. A. Garber, who leads the student body with the members of the Ashland church into the deeper things of God and life. Will these instances suffice? I know I am right. Students who have come to Ashland College not knowing Christ may find him through these influences. Dr. Miller when pastor at Ashland received them into the church. Rev. J. A. Garber, the present pastor, has and is receiving them into the church. Time will not permit me to tell of the work of the Y. M. C. A., Y. W. C. A., the Student Volunteer Mission Band, etc. I think enough has been said to show that Ashland College believes in moulding Christian ideals into the lives of her students.

I found that the professors of Ashland College lived up to these ideals and are thorough Christian gentlemen. I have never seen a professor of Ashland College under the influence of liquor. I have never known of one that used tobacco, neither have I heard one use profane language. These habits I have witnessed in professors of other institutions. In fact I picked up a drunken professor in Montreal one day when he would otherwise have frozen to death. It was said that he was a clever man. I have listened to sermons preached by the professors of Ashland College and they all stand for the highest and best ideals of the church. For instance, Dr. Jacobs, the president of our College, preached for me at Fair Haven this summer. I did not tell him what he should preach but left that to his judgment. His discourse was a strong appeal for the Brethren to return to that simple life that has long characterized the Brethren church. He urged all to intensify their faith in Christ and live for him each day. He denounced amusements, especially the dance hall. He said that America and its people could not be great until she upheld the Christ and the church that the Pilgrim fathers, believed in. I believe in standing for the right and defending right with all my might. I for one wish to say that Ashland College has as good a class of professors as you will find anywhere. A class that I believe are conscientiously working all the time to live out the ideals of Christian stewardship so that they may render the best possible service to those that come to be instructed by them from time to time.

This is a simple endeavor to show my appreciation for the school that has given to me a training that I could not have secured elsewhere. No one asked me to write an article of this type. I took it upon myself to do so. I am ready to defend any statement involved in this article, for I believe and mean every word. I am glad I came to Ashland College. I will always remember what she has done for me. I will boost her cause wherever an opportunity arises and defend her till the last. I have already subscribed to her endowment and expect to do more. I was glad for an opportunity as student pastor to help Brother Beachler in raising endowment at Fair Haven, Ohio. Finally I hope that we may one and all place Ashland College on our prayer list, praying that God may guide her in the channnels that will enable her best to provide for and to prepare those who enter her walls, for the task of the church, society and the world.

Ashland, Ohio.

Christian Baptism.   By E. E. Roberts
I. What Is It ?

(From a tract published by the author and sent us for the benefit of Evangelist readers.—Editor).

After all the strife and contention upon the subject of baptism, the face remains that no scholar of any note would risk his scholarship by contending that the   Greek word **baptizo**, in its primary meaning, means anything else than "to dip," "plunge," "immerse." Briefly stated, we contend—

(1) **Baptizo**, in classical Greek, means "to dip, plunge, immerse."

(2) That it has the same meaning in Biblical Greek.

(3) That **baptizo**, or forms of the word, is in every other place translated "dip."

(4) That words meaning "sprinkle, "pour," "wash," "purify," etc. are never used for baptism.

(5) That when **baptizo** is translated into any language other than English, it is always translated "to dip" or "immerse."

(6) The prepositions used to indicate immersion being everywhere **in** or **into**, not **on** or **upon**.

All of these propositions we stand able and ready to prove to anyone, and do not do so here for the reason that we only desire to briefly state the subject.

Our next, or (7) **The testimony of Ancient Baptistries**, prove that **immersion** was the practice of the early church. We can only quote one of the many: Mr. Cote, in his "Archaeology of Baptism," p. 324, says: "In company with Drs. Fish and Harvey we visited the ruins of St. John Cathedral, at Tyre, but recently discovered and said to be the most beautiful one in Phoenicea. Professor Epp pointed out the old baptistry to his visitors, remarking: "They baptized people here;" and to prove it he went down the steps at one end, and lowering himself by kneeling and projecting his head and shoulders forward, and below the level of the top, said: "This is the way they baptized them."

Dr. Harvey says, speaking of the same scene, "The baptistry is of white marble, has three steps leading down one end by which the candidate descended, and kneeling, according to the ancient usage, bowed his head **forward** and **under** the water."

(8) **The pictures on the walls of buildings and other places**, indicate that baptism was by immersion. One must suffice: St. Callistrus has a picture reproduced in "Smith's Christian Antiquities," p. 168. It is of a youth standing undressed in the water, with the baptizer's hand on his head, —which would be entirely unnecessary was he to be sprinkled or poured, as is proven by the practices of today.

(9) Every practice, other than triune immersion, can be traced to their origin, as we will show later; but triune immersion can be traced to the Apostles. The earliest being "The Teachings of the Apostles," certainly written in the first one hundred years, and some placing it as early as A. D. 65 or 70, which would be before the Gospel of Matthhw, and which is quoted by Ignatius, who with Polycarp, were students of St. John, in his epistle to Philadelphia. It quotes the Commission, Matthew 28:18-20, as authority for triune immersion.

Impromptu Flashes.   By W. J. H. Bauman

Loving God in reality, means love of service in his vineyard.

Christian love is of an exceedingly practical nature. Read the 14th and 15th chapters of John's gospel.

If you feel hateful toward anyone, even though it be a cruel enemy, turn to Matthew 6th chapter and read from the 38th verse to the end of chapter.

Human feelings are often exceedingly deceptive.

Our highest aims in life should be founed on Christian lives.

If you are a Christian simply to get to heaven, or to keep out of hell you are too selfish. We ought to be Christians because it is **right**.

If intellectual knowledge were piety ours would be the most pious age in human history.

True love for God means love for his service. Jesus said, "If ye love me keep my commandments." Any other motive would prove a failure.

Good works are not the cause on our part, in the plan of salvation but the fruit.

The writer of these "flashes" has more than once in his day enjoyed great kindness from infidel neighbors. Did that kindness they rendered save them?

"Words fitly spoken are like apples of gold in pictures of silver" is surely, a fine and important proverb.

Yes, Sir, condensation in speech often means avoidance of confusion to the listener. In fact, I believe it would often lessen the number of sleepers during church services.

Perhaps we are not as careful as we ought to be along the line of self-esteem.

If weighed in the scales of ignorance the most cultured of us humans, along mental lines would weigh quite heavy. Knowledge scales would convince us that A. D., 1920 does not know it all.

The entire realm of nature confronts us with proof of just such a God as we have revealed so plainly in the Bible.

If you want to tickle the devil just be stingy, you know "coyetousness is the root of all evil."

His satanic majesty is quite a hanger on. If he can't win us on one line he'll try another, and so on, **ad infinitum**.

If we would use the tenacity Satan uses in his efforts to ensnare us, only in an opposite direction, God would help us and we would come out winners every time.

Long Beach, California.

THE END OF THE PATH

"Not long ago," said a minister, "I was visiting a friend in the country. On the second morning I started for a walk, taking my host's little boy with me. We chose an inviting path through the pastures, fringed with clover blossoms and buttercups; but the lad held back. 'Why don't you want to come along this path?' I asked. 'That path was made by the pigs,' he replied, 'and before you get very far you'll get into the awfullest patch of mire and weeds you ever saw.' " It is well for us all when bent upon some pleasure to ask, where does this pleasure lead to?—Selected.

FROM OUR CONFERENCE PLATFORMS

Moderator's Address at Pennsylvania State Conference. By H. M. Harley

Through the kindly providence of a loving God and Father, we, the Brethren churches of the Pennsylvania District are again privileged to assemble in this, the 32nd Annual Conference of our district. And we are here for three definite purposes. First, to unite our hearts and our voices in praise and gratitude to a loving heavenly Father for the way he has blest and prospered and used us hitherto,—because we are coming to realize more and more the fact, that without his help and direction, we could certainly not have made the advances which we have made during the trying days of the past few years. And I want you to note that we as a church did advance, when other larger, better organized and better financed organizations than ours were not even able to hold their own. In the second place, we are here to review the work of the past, and to get a proper estimate of our present status ,as a part of his great corps of workers in the interest of the common good, as well as for the advancement of his Kingdom in the world. Or in other words, we just want to glance backward for a moment, in order that we may secure the proper forward look, or outlook upon the work of the coming year or years. And in the third place, we are here to deliberate and plan for the future growth and advancement of our church, not only so far as our own district is concerned, but having in mind the needs and the opportunities of our entire brotherhood, and even the needs of the world, for they are indeed many and grievous. And in order to do all of this properly, we will certainly need first to get the up-look, before we dare hope to have the proper outlook upon our field and our work.

But before we take up any of the actual work of the church, whether such as pertains to our district, alone, or that of co-operating with National Conference, let me remind you of the fact that our conference district has lost five able workers since last we met together in conference session, —two by death and three going to other and larger fields of labor. Brethren I. B. Trout and Edward Byers, both exceptional men in their line, and wonderful assets to our church, men whom God has been using mightily for good, were stricken down suddenly and tragically in the very midst of their labors. And while the church militant is the poorer because of their decease, the church triumphant is made the richer by their coming. And fellow-workers, instead of losing valuable time over the question of "Why they were taken in the manner and at the time that they were," let us then rather busy ourselves to fill the gap made in our ministerial ranks, by praying the Lord of the harvest, that he thrust forth other laborers into the harvest, and at the same time, that we who are in the ranks may be both more willing and more able to carry on the work which they were compelled to lay down. May the inspiration of their lives spur us on to larger and more unselfish endeavors, working while it is called today, for the night will come, when we too shall no more be able to carry on his work.

Then, too, our district has lost three able men during the past year in the persons of Brother Martin Shively, "the Bishop of the Pennsylvania district;" Brother Arthur DeLozier, "the linguist!" and Brother "Ed." Miller, "the Cyclone from the east,"—all three of whom have been called to larger fields of labor. Brother Shively is now Bursar and Business Manager of Ashland College, and Brother DeLozier is Teacher of Modern Languages in the same institution. While we shall miss the faces, voices and co-operation of these two brethren from the ministry of our state, yet we are glad that we could give them to this larger and more important work of our only and much-loved institution of learning, "Old A. C." And we should feel honored that Pennsylvania had men of sufficient calibre, and who were willing to sacrifice for this larger good. Then too, we shall

all miss "Brother Ed," whose genial smile, strong personality and very aggressive spirit, were ever manifest in our conferences. We certainly wish all of these brethren Godspeed in their new fields of labor, and trust that their every effort for good may be abundantly blest of God.

And while we regret these losses, we also rejoice that we have at least in part made up for them, by the coming into our midst of three brethren from other parts within recent months. Our dear and faithful Brother Belote has come back home again to the "Old Keystone State" after an absence of several years, having no doubt known a good thing when he saw it. And the thing that speaks especially well for him is that he was able to come back to the charge he left when he assumed the duties of Business Manager of our Publishing Company. Then too, we have Brother Joseph L. Gingrich, a recent graduate of Ashland College, coming to take the place left vacant by Brother Shively's going. Brother Gingrich brings to our district the enthusiasm and inspiration acquired while in college, and we feel certain that he too shall prove to be an asset to our work. Then there is still another addition to our ranks in the person of Brother L. G. Wood, who has just come to us from Old Virginia. Brother Wood needs no introduction to any of our ministers, for he has been at the forefront of every aggressive piece of work that has been proposed by and for our people. And we know that when the laity of our district come to know Brother Wood, they will all come to love him, as we of the ministry do. We certainly welcome these three brethren into our state, with the hope that we may all be of mutual help to each other.

Our work as a district has certainly been blest and used of God during the past year, due at least in part to the Four Year Program as mapped out for us by our leaders, and as carried out by both the pastors and laity of the several churches. And while we have not done nearly all that might and should have been done, yet we are encouraged to go on to larger and better things. The Four Year Program is a matter of history, but its fruits are still with us; and will continue to be so increasingly, we trust, for years to come. As retiring moderator, Brother Bame said a few weeks ago at National Conference, The next few years will see even greater results from the efforts of the past four years, than we have yet realized.

And, to conserve both the efforts and the fruits of the past, and as well to make still greater advances along all lines, the leaders of our fraternity have very carefully mapped out a new program of effort, which is to be known as The Bicentenary Movement, extending over a period of three years, from Christmas of 1920 to Christmas of 1923, at the culmination of which time we will be celebrating the 200th anniversary of the organization of Brethrenism on American soil. And it is very fitting that this event should be celebrated with the completion of our three years of special effort for advance along all lines, for the extension of his work in the world. Christmas day of the year 1923 ought to have a triple significance to the members of the Brethern church, and we are hoping and praying that every member of our church will enter into the true spirit of this Bicentenary Movement, so that they will be able the better to celebrate and to enjoy the event when it comes around, and still better, that they may have this larger share in bringing God's good to men, both at home and abroad.

This program is to include every phase of church work, and will have something for all to do. It will be explained at a later session of this conference—the Wednesday evening session being given over entirely to it—at which time we want every member and friend, whether of the conference or of the church to be present, to give careful and prayerful heed to, and immediately get into the spirit of this program, with the determination that by the help of God, we shall make these next three years the most fruitful for good in our entire history as a district and as a church.

Coming then to the more practical part of my message, I want to say first of all, that one of the greatest needs of the Brethren church today is a real revival of genuine Bible study and of prayer. Wherever you find, either a minister or a church, that is saturated with the blessed truths of The Book, you will find one who is alive with the spirit of God, and awake to the needs of the times. And when these two come together—our need with his Spirit,—needs will vanish, our wants shall ever be supplied, and great good will be accomplished. But best of all, souls will be saved. And that after all should be the final aim of all of our endeavors, —to bring the unsaved to the saving knowledge of their Lord as their own personal Redeemer.

And right in line with this, let me say that the mid-week prayer service needs more emphasis, and better thought and study on the part of our pastors, as well as a larger and more loyal support on the part of the laity. Instead of this service having outgrown our day, it is more needed than almost any other service, for where the midweek service is made a service of real prayer, praise and Bible study, it will become a source of spiritual strength and power to every member and part of our church. Oh, that we might get our people to search the Scriptures, that they would come to see their own needs, and both God's ability and willingness to supply them, that they might find out his wish and will concerning them, and then plan and work in perfect harmony with his Divine purposes. While we need a carefully studied and planned program for coming years, and while we will increasingly need both men and money to effectively carry out this program, we need first and foremost of all, the spirit of the Living God possessing our minds and hearts and lives, to the end that we are ever open to know and do his whole will. And when the mind of Christ and the spirit of God is ours, our plans will be both wise and far-reaching, and all that will be needed to bring those plans to a successful issue, will very readily be forthcoming.

"Oh! for the Spirit of Christ we plead,
Pure and unselfish in word and deed.
Humble and lowly; fearless and holy,
The Spirit of Christ we plead."

The Sunday or Bible school should have a large part in instructing our people, both young and old, in the ways and the will of God, and this end of the work of the church should be made so efficient and far-reaching that it will not only touch those who come to its regular sessions, with the Book, but it should in some way reach out and bring under its teaching and influence, every home and every life in the community, whether Christian or not. And until it does this, it is not 100 percent efficient, neither is it measuring up to its opportunities. Special emphasis should be given to Teacher Training, and to the Home Department, together with the giving of our best thought, study and prayer to every other department of the work. Today spells opportunity to the wide-awake Bible school, and where folks are on the job, tomorrow will see them far in advance of anything they have yet attained.

Another great need of our day in all lines of activity, whether political, social or religious, is leadership—men and women who have given themselves over to a very careful and detailed study of the work they are especially interested in and particularly fitted for, and who are both able and willing to give to and do their best by, and as well who are capable to draw the best out of others for, the good of the cause in question. Never has either the church or the world lacked leaders as right now. And unless something is done to raise up and prepare such leaders, both the world and the church will not only fail to advance as they should, but even will they not be able to hold the ground already gained by past prayer and effort. The church has within herself an organization intended for just this very thing—of raising up, instructing in, and preparing for leadership along all lines of church activity. And it is none other than the Young People's Society of Christian Endeavor, the organization which has already done so much good for our churches, and which is very much needed today, to meet the present crisis in our ranks as workers with God for the bringing of his good to men throughout the whole world. Too much of prayer, time and effort cannot be given to this branch of our work at this time, and the pastor who fails to link himself up with his young people through Christian Endeavor, is both limiting his own usefulness, and as well is robbing the church of future leaders, and consequently of future advancement. If the real purpose of Christian Endeavor is put to the front, and stressed in our local churches, many of the problems now confronting us as pastors, will be conspicuous by their absence. Let us make a careful study of Christian Endeavor, its intent, method and opportunity, and then let's give it our best self, and we know that we will not only save our young people for the church, but we will make of them efficient workers in the church and community for the common good, as well as for the advancement of his Kingdom among men.

And what we say for Christian Endeavor can and should also be said for the Women's Missionary Society, and for the Sisterhood of Mary and Martha. Each of these auxiliaries aid the individual to a better, larger and more useful life, and as well very materially aid the church, whether locally or at large, both to become more efficient and also to branch out into new and larger fields of activity. They all deserve our most loyal support, and are worthy of our largest possible co-operation. And the fact of the matter is that without them, we will fall far short of attaining to the goal set for us in our Bicenenary Movement program.

Now, along with the suggestions already offered, for a more constructive and effective work, there is still another thing that needs our attention, and that is the matter of church extension. One of the few points that we failed in during the last four years, was the organizing and building of new churches throughout our brotherhood. It was not that the opportunities or the means were not at hand, but other reasons existed which hindered our progress along this line of work. Why not for the next three years, put special effort and emphasis each year upon some one new and opportune field within our district, or better yet, upon some weak church already established, but struggling for an existence, and strive to make it both self-supporting and aggressive, and then find a pastor who will give his best efforts to and for that church? We surely ought in this manner, to put at least one weak church upon her feet each year, while at the same time we would keep our eyes open for new fields.

Then too, we should insist on a revival in every church in the state during this year, however strong or weak the church may be. Let the local church give all the aid possible, and where she is pastorless, or too weak either numerically or financially to hire an evangelist, the District Mission Board can come to her aid, while the larger and stronger churches can give the loan of their pastors for at least one such meeting. What this district needs along Home Mission lines is some definite object to work for. And surely, there ought to be some opportunities for the preaching of the "Whole Gospel Message" in this, the state that gave birth to Brethrenism in America. Let us keep our ears to the ground, our eyes upon the fields that are white unto the harvest, and our hearts lifted up to him who has promised to bless our efforts and to give us souls for our hire, let us not become weary in well doing.

May God forgive us where we have failed or come short in the past, and may we determine that in his name and by his help we shall go forward in every good work, conquering and to conquer, And whatever he will do for us, or through us for the good of others, to him shall we give all the glory.

Pittsburgh, Pennsylvania.

Send
WHITE GIFT
OFFERINGS to

THE SUNDAY SCHOOL

H. H. WOLFORD
General Secretary-Treasurer
Ashland, Ohio

World Convention By One Who Was There

(For sometime we have been endeavoring to get for our readers a report of the World's Sunday School Convention by one who was there. A few days ago we received the following report prepared by Mr. Arthur T. Arnold, General Secretary of the Ohio Sunday School Association. Mr. Arnold was secretary of the World's Convention. It gives us pleasure to pass on to our readers this splendid report.—Editor.)

The Eighth World's Sunday School Convention held at Tokyo, Japan, from October Fifth to Fourteenth in its outstanding features was the greatest event of its kind in history.

Before its close the 1814 accredited delegates from five continents and seventeen countries of the World saw this great gathering assume an international significance of first magnitude, assuring that it would go down in history as a potent influence for universal brotherhood and world peace among the nations.

The Patrons Association

In preparing for this Convention the National Sunday School Association of Japan, of which Hon. E. Ebara, M. P., is chairman had the active support of "The Patrons' Association" which included great leaders of high rank as well as many of Japan's distinguished business and professional men. Viscount Shibusawa and Baron Sakatani were the leading spirits in this big enterprise.

This great Christian enterprise also had the moral and financial support if His Majesty the Emperor of Japan who contributed Yen 50,000 ($25,000).

The Convention Building

The first design of the great Convention Hall was made by a missionary architect, Mr. W. M. Vories, and, was developed and executed by Mr. Furuhashi, a Christian architect of Tokyo. The building had every modern convenience, providing for offices, accommodations for the chorus and a dining hall seating 400. It was located near Tokyo's Central Railroad Station at a cost of yen 180,000 ($90,000).

Building Burns

Three hours before the first session of the Convention, due to an unavoidable accident, the building was entirely destroyed by fire in less than thirty minutes, without the loss of life, though the building at the time was swarming with people including a great chorus of 500 voices.

Statuary Spared

A beautiful piece of statuary designed by one of Japan's leading sculptors entitled "Christ Blessing the Children of the World" was spared and still stands before the ashes of the consumed building as a reminder of the munificence of the Japanese people and the earnest of the extension of his Kingdom through the cultivation of "the seed ground for the future."

Imperial Theatre Opened

Premier Hara of the Empire expressed his willingness for the Halls of the Imperial Diet to be used for the Convention.

The strong men of the nation rallied to our support in this crisis and led by Viscount Shibusawa and Baron Sakatani, adequate provision was made by the proffer of the Imperial Theatre with a seating capacity of 2,300 by Baron Okura in the name of its Board of Directors.

Messages of Sympathy

Cablegrams, telegrams and letters of sympathy came from all parts of the world and offers of financial support in the crisis were freely made but respectfully declined by the Japanese leaders.

The magnificent spirit of the Japanese people was voiced by Baron Sakatani who after the destruction of the building in an address said, "Let us go forward with courage."

Cablegrams, telegrams and letters of good will and sympathy were received from President Woodrow Wilson, the Honorable Lloyd George, the Imperial Greek Government through Charge d'Affaires S. X. Constantinidi who was an accredited delegate, the Honorable Arthur Meighan, Premier of Canada, Viscount Kentaro Kaneko for the Japan-American Society, the Most Rev. Randall, Archbishop of Canterbury, Honorable Edward Bell, Charge d'Affaires for the United States at Tokyo, Honorable John Wanamaker, Dr. J. H. Jowett, Governor Cox, Senator Harding and others.

Many Distinguished Men Present

The Convention delegation included many distinguished missionaries, ministers, educators, business men and leaders in the field of religious education from all parts of the world.

Presentation of Gavel

Justice J. J. Maclaren the presiding officer of the Convention was presented with a gavel made of oak by Prince Tokugawa who suggested that "the wood was the symbol of the strength of truth."

The Convention Program

The Convention program was built around the General Theme—"The Sunday School and World Progress" and a daily theme which expressed the special emphasis of each day. The program was a masterly production which evidenced the large vision and statesmanship of Dr. Frank L. Brown, Mr. James W. Kinnear and the Program Committee. A rare balance was preserved giving to the delegates instruction and inspiration. The morning and evening sessions were given over to general sessions, while on each afternoon specialization conferences were held.

Pageantry, Music and Art

Under the direction of Prof. and Mrs. H. Augustine Smith assisted by Japanese leaders a rare program of Pageantry, Music and Art was provided which was closely related to the theme.

This program included four great pageants, stereopticon lectures, instruction in Sunday school music as well as inspirational song esrvices. This work carried us to greater heights than could have been reached by addresses alone and deepened the impressions made by the speakers.

In paying tribute to the pageantry Viscount Shibusawa said "The pageants were beautiful, grand and still delicate. In Japan and other countries they attempt such things, but the efforts are partial, small in scale and lack delicateness presentation."

Unveiling of Portraits

Portraits in oil of Their Majesties the Emperor and Empress of Japan, gifts from the delegates, were unveiled at the Imperial Theatre with appropriate ceremony. They were later presented by a special committee to Their Majesties at the Imperial Household.

These portraits were the work of the distinguished Canadian artist, Mr. J. W. L. Forster, a delegate from Toronto and are the first ever made of the Japanese Imperial Family by a western artist.

Portraits of our fallen leaders were also unveiled, including Mr. Edward K. Warren, Dr. George W. Bailey, and Sir Robert Laidlaw. An oil portrait of Rev. Hiromichi

Kozaki, the present President of the National Sunday School Association of Japan, was presented to the Association.

Special Courtesies

With rare grace and elaborate preparation in perfect keeping with this great World enterprise the Japanese people entertained the officers and delegates of the Convention at special functions.

Two complimentary excursions with chartered trains were given all delegates to Kamakura the ancient capital of Japan and to Yokohama, one of her great seaport cities, where the visitors were royally entertained by the Governor, Mayors and the leading citizens of these great municipalities.

The Patrons Association entertained 1,500 people at the Imperial Theatre on Thursday night with an elaborate box dinner, music and pageantry, at which Baron Sakatani presided making the opening address. Viscount Shibusawa's address was read by his secretary and responses were made by Count Y. Uchida, Minister of Foreign Affairs, Chief Justice MacLaren and Dr. Frank L. Brown.

On Friday morning the officers and speakers were entertained royally at the Nobles' club.

On the last night the Emperor sent a message by a personal representative expressing the interest of the Imperial Household in the success of the Convention. This is without precedent in the history of Japan.

Tokyo Municipality Entertains

A reception was given by the City of Tokyo at Hibiya Park by a large company of her municipal officials. A large number greatly appreciated the cordial welcome and the elaborate supper. An address was made by His Honor the Mayor, Viscount Tajira, who said "We appreciate your coming to Tokyo, for you come here for the sake of Christianity and humanity. In the name of Christ and in the spirit of Christianity we are brothers, we are sisters."

Dr. Frank L. Brown responded and led the delegates in three banzais in response to those given by the Japanese led by the Mayor for the delegates.

Grand Sunday School Parade and Rally

On Sunday afternoon a grand parade of the delegates and Sunday schools was followed by a rally at Hibiya Park. Each delegation and Sunday school marched under its own banner. Fully 20,000 people assembled to hear the Sunday school addresses. It was an inspiring sight to witness a sea of pennants, carried by all, waving in the air and to hear the great multitude of Sunday school children sing the songs of the Kingdom that gave evidence that the childhood of Japan was fast catching the Sunday school spirit.

The splendid Exhibit which attracted 40,000 people, and the 51 extension meetings throughout Tokyo attended by 33,000 were under the supervision of our Educational Secretary for Japan, Horace E. Coleman. Fifty cities over Japan were visited, and meetings addressed by delegates from abroad; and an around-the-world party of forty, including specialists, is carrying the Convention message to Korea, China, India, Egypt and other lands.

The Convention Enrollment

The accredited foreign delegates from the various islands, countries and continents were as follows:

Siam 1; India 5; Holland 4; Formosa 1; Africa 1; Netherland Indies 1; Scotland 5; England 9; Australia 7; South America 6; Hawaii 8; Philippine Islands 29; China 17; Korea 44; Canada 75; United States 513; Japan (Foreigners) 275; Japanese delegates 813. Grand Total 1814.

Our Tomorrow

The future is very bright with promise and what we saw and heard at Tokyo and in other lands through which we traveled is but the earnest of a greater program of religious education which is to follow, through which was the blessing of our Heavenly Father our living Christ is to become the Savior of the world.

One of the great climaxes of the gathering was the Investment Service when $40,000 per year for four years was contributed by the delegates to World's work.

World's Sunday School Association Officers

Another assurance of success is the magnificent leadership which was elected to guide the ministry of this great organization for the next quadrenium.

The officers for the next quadrenium are as follows:

President—Hon. John Wanamaker, Philadelphia.

Treasurer—Mr. Paul Sturdevant, New York.

The Executive was organized by the election of James W. Kinnear, Pittsburgh Chairman and Mr. Arthur M. Harris, New York, Vice Chairman. Frank L. Brown, LL.D., was reelected General Secretary. By request of the British Section all the work of the World's Association will hereafter be centered in the office in New York City, 216 Metropolitan Tower.

| J. A. Garber PRESIDENT | Our Young People at Work | E. A. Rowsey SECRETARY |

Advertising Christian Endeavor

By Earl Huette, Publicity Department

‡-‡-‡

Pastors: DO NOT READ THROUGH THIS BUT READ IT THOROUGHLY.

Are you having trouble in keeping your young people on the job?

Do you know where they are on Sunday evening when they are not at the church services?

Is their under-shepherd on the job when it comes to directing their Christian lives and activities?

Can they always look to you for advice and comfort such as only a pastor is able to give, through the guidance of the Holy Spirit?

Do they come to you and offer their services?

Are You able to give them all the training which they need and which the church should give?

Do you have young people who are trained to do the work necessary when you are away or upon special occasions?

Do you know that there is an organization which (when its principles are carried out) will train your young people for service in the Master's work?

Do you boost that organization?

Do you help and advice its leaders in their efforts to direct its influence?

Come on, Pastors,

Get interested in Christian Endeavor.

A good, live and working Endeavor society will help you in your work and also will make your church an influence in the community.

SEND ALL MONEY FOR
General Home, Kentucky and
Foreign Missions to

MISSIONS

WILLIAM A. GEARHART
General Missionary Secretary
906 American Bldg., Dayton, O.

KENTUCKY MISSIONS

At the General Conference at Winona Lake, last September no special effort was made to take Kentucky pledges as had been done in the years past but pursuant to an action by the Home Mission Board Kentucky Missions were placed on the regular budget to be raised at Thanksgiving time. Our budget has thus been increased to over $5,000.00 and the goal fixed at $1.00 per member.

Riverside

The school at Riverside has never had a brighter outlook than it has at the present time. The rooms are filled with pupils and the dormitories are crowded. The grade school this year as for several years in the past, is supported by the State under the supervision of our superintendent, G. E. Drushal. This relieves the Home Mission Board of entirely supporting the grade work, which is distinctly the duty of the State. But yet, having the grade work as we do in our buildings and under our supervision it brings the grade pupils under the influence of a Christian school where the Bible is taught so efficiently by Brother and Sister Drushal and the other members of the faculty.

The Faculty

The Home Mission Board this year is supporting entirely the following workers at Riverside: Brother G. E. Drushal, Superintendent; Brother C. N. Aikens, Financial Secretary-Treasurer and teacher; Miss Anna Bethke as Matron and Miss Hulda Ewert as teaching also. The teachers of the grade work are Miss Byrd, who teaches the first, second, third and fourth grades and Miss Bessie Hooks, who teaches the fifth, sixth, seventh and eighth grades. The two latter teachers are supported by the state.

The Local Committee

The local committee of five prominent citizens of Lost Creek and vicinity have been selected to co-operate with the Home Mission Board in planning and executing the work at Riverside. Splendid suggestions have been offered by these men as to the conduct of the school and the farm and we trust that this new feature will bring about a better co-operation between the citizens of this community and the Home Mission Board and that the work will go forward with greater zeal and more efficiently than ever before.

The Light Plant

One of the great needs of Riverside was met last year by the installation of a modern light plant. This eliminates some of the dangers of the oil lamp and at the same time gives the students better light in their rooms for studying and provides efficient light for the chapel and church services. The last word from Brother Drushal is that the plant is working fine.

The Lost Creek Church

The Brethren church of Lost Creek has its services at the chapel in Riverside each Sunday. Brother Drushal has been its pastor ever since its organization and under his leader-

ship is making commendable progress. Sunday school services and regular preaching services are held. The noticeable feature of the work here is the increase of the gifts for pastors, etc.

Krypton

The work at Krypton for the past year has been under the supervision of Brother and Sister Rempel. Many very perplexing problems have come to our Brother and Sister in the work here. Yet the Lord is blessing the efforts put forth. The coal mining industry in the vicinity of Krypton has made it possible for the local membership to contribute more than ever before and we trust that the work at this place will soon progress to a point where it will be self-supporting.

The Needs

Riverside needs a new building to be used as a dining room for the students. It should be built with basement equipped for a laundry. The present basement of the girls' dormitory, which is used as a dining room is entirely too small, and besides this room is needed for other purposes. The Board will gladly receive any special gifts to start this building fund.

A nurse should also be found who will go to Riverside at once and stay at least until April 1st, 1921. More school desks could be used to replace the old ones, which are worn out.

The Budget

The Kentucky Budget this year calls for an expenditure of over $5,000.00, which is more than one-third of the entire Home Mission budget. There is no disposition on the part of the Mission Board to hinder the work in Kentucky by cutting the budget, but we want to do all we can to help the needy fields everywhere. Our goal is $1.00 per member which if reached will give the Home Board sufficient funds to take care of the Kentucky work in an adequate way, as well as other needy fields. May the Lord give us the greatest Thanksgiving we have yet received.

Orion E. BOWMAN, Chairman,
Kentucky Committee of Home Mission Board.

Sad News From One of Our Home Mission Points

In a letter from Elder and Mrs. George E. Cone, they gave us the sad news of the death of their darling child on Sunday, November 14th from the effects of burns received while Brother Cone was rescuing it from a burning building, Saturday evening. Brother Cone also was seriously burned on his face and hands and will be unable to work for several weeks. The doctor says that he will recover.

Brother Cone is the pastor of the Fort Scott, Kansas, Mission church, which was shown on the front cover of the Evangelist No. 43, dated November 10th, and which is one of the many mission points which our Thanksgiving offering will help to support.

Now, my dear brethren and sisters, all over

our brotherhood, will you not please join with me in prayer to our heavenly Father in behalf of Brother and Sister Cone, that they may be comforted in their great bereavement, and that our dear brother may speedily recover from his painful wounds? We are among those who believe that the faithful, fervent prayer of God's righteous people availeth much. Please pray for them as soon as you have finished reading this sad news.

WILLIAM A. GEARHART,

A UNIQUE METHOD OF EVANGELISM

In these days when secular publications such as the Wall Street Journal, the Manufacturers Record, Leslie's Weekly and others keep telling their readers from time to time that the country's chief need is a revival of old-fashioned religion, it is of interest to know that a unique method of evangelism has recently been inaugurated by Mr. Charles M. Alexander, the famous gospel song conductor and soloist.

Recently Mr. Alexander reported remarkable success with his first church campaign attempt along the new line, made in the North Woodward Avenue Methodist Episcopal church of Detroit, Michigan. He went to stay for four weeks, but remained for seven. He had decided to make it a "Bible revival" and began by enrolling the two pastors and their wives, the sexton and his wife, and all the official board and their wives in the Pocket Testament League, personally presenting a Testament to each and securing their signatures to the following statement, which is printed on the fly-leaf of the League Testament:

"I hereby accept membership in the Pocket League by making it the rule of my life to read at least one chapter in the Bible each day, and to carry a Bible or Testament with me wherever I go."

This was followed by similarly enrolling a large percentage of both church and Sunday school membership, and night by night the enthusiasm grew as the idea of winning people through handing them a Testament and securing their promise to read the Bible daily took hold. Presently the fire spread to other churches until more than sixty Detroit churches were enrolled by the revival. 31,400 persons received a Testament and signed the pledge, including a number of the City's leading business men, and partial reports recorded over 1800 conversions.

Mr. Alexander was accompanied by his associate, Mr. George T. B. Davis, who is authority for the statement that Mr. Alexander has personally given away testaments in recent years to the amount of $30,000.

In the last twenty-seven years Mr. Alexander has participated in a thousand or more evangelistic campaigns in cities and towns of the United States, Canada, Great Britain, Australia and many other countries. He has circled the world three times, crossed the Atlantic twenty-seven times, and seven million hymn books have been issued through his instrumentality.

NEWS FROM THE FIELD

AT CONFERENCE—WHAT I NOTICED

After days and nights and weeks and months of painful sufferings, I once again enjoyed the pleasure of being for a few hours at a Brethren conference.

While the recent Indiana district conference was in session at Flora, two brethren, Pearson and Allbaugh, came to our humble home one morning and said, "They want you and wife at conference and we have come after you." Wife just recovering from a severe spell of sickness and yet weak, we could not see how we could take that trip of twenty miles, but said if it were a day later I might arrange to have some one stay with the woman and I think I could go. They said, "Do that, and we'll be after you in the morning and bring you home in the evening." The time was set for them to be here and in the meantime my arrangements were completed and they were here next morning at the appointed hour. This time it was Pearson and Catson.

What I Noticed

On arrival I noticed the jam of autos about that grand structure called the church, but I did not see much of a crowd of people outside; they apparently had just convened for the forenoon service and were inside the church.

Directly Brother Humbert came with his smiling countenance and said, "I want to show you through the basement." While there looking with admiration at some up-to-date improvements, Brother Johnson came to me and said, "They want you up there on the pulpit, and we want you to give us a little talk." Directly after being seated there, the Moderator, Brother McInturff, introduced me to the conference. Having been so suddenly nabbed and taken by surprise I hardly knew on the spur of the moment what I should talk about. Nevertheless I expressed my thankfulness for being once again able to be at a Brethren conference and also made mention of one of the various incidents of my experience at Flora in the early days of the church. That was the first effort for the Brethren cause at Flora, at which time, (evening of November 26, 1883) three persons took a resolute stand for the Brethren faith—the Gospel alone as a rule of faith and a guide for practice.

Having made a little bungling speech along the aforesaid lines and being seated again, here comes Brother Johnson bearing something that looked like a contribution box which he said contained just one hundred dollars and presented it to me as a gift by the conference, and it was then so announced by the Moderator. With mingled feelings of surprise and gratitude I was compelled to restrain my emotions for a moment before thanking that benevolent people for their act of kindness, charity and benevolence. I then committed the bulk of bills and coin to the care of Brother Johnson for the time being, which after a little, was returned transformed into a check calling for one hundred and ten dollars.

Now while we feel heartily thankful to the donors for that handsome present we cannot feel ourselves worthy of the gift.

Enjoyed Much

While at that noble conference I enjoyed much. I heard the speech by Brother Willis Ronk on Pastoral Evangelism which was grand, and the address by Brother Rench on District Evangelism. We who know Brother Rench know that when he opens his mouth to talk he always says something. We enjoyed his address greatly. Then, too, we heard and saw the song service led by Brother Grisso, who when he sings sings all over. At the noon hour was enjoyed the social chat, the renewing of acquaintance sand the forming of new ones. And all in all, it was a grand time while there. I was returned home by Brethren Allbaugh and Rinehart. Many thanks to all and God bless the brethren.

Another Shower

A few days after our return from the Flora meeting we received a letter from Brother John Parr of the Bethel congregation containing thirty-two dollars, which was sent by the church (Bethel) at Berne, Indiana, also as a gift. Such favors are highly appreciated, not alone for what they are worth in themselves, but also the kindly spirit in which they re made.

J. H. AND LUCINDA SWIHART.

EVANGELISTIC LEAGUE SERVICES AT BUCKEYE CITY, OHIO

After closing my week's prophetic lectures at Berne, Indiana, on Sunday night, I took the midnight train for Lansing, Michigan. I stopped a few hours to see my daughter, Mrs. Deitrick and my son and left Monday night for Buckeye City, Ohio. By traveling both Sunday and Monday nights I made the same connections I would have made to Buckeye if I had stayed at Berne till Monday morning.

We held a three weeks' meeting here, closing on Monday night, October 4 with Communion.

They have had no regular pastor here for a long time and the members seemed somewhat discouraged. The interest kept increasing to the very last. We had about 22 confessions. Twenty united with the church. One went to the Methodists and one was baptized but did not join the church.

If they will get a good pastor there now and push the work I believe that a strong Brethren church can be built up there.

I felt some misgivings about this meeting because of the condition of the church. But the Lord did above our expectations. I will never forget the kindness of the people. They loaned us a Ford machine for most of the time for two weeks and we traveled over the hills of Ohio visiting the people. They bore all the expenses of the meeting, thus enabling the League to use its funds upon poorer churches. They also signed a number of the League cards providing funds for the needy churches.

I had expected to go from Buckeye to Buena Vista, Virginia, but I received a telegram that they wanted me to hold a three weeks' meeting at the Third Brethren church of Philadelphia. The last conference year I was only home two weeks in twelve months. I was very glad to accept the call as I could be home every night for three weeks. After closing the Buckeye City meeting with a splendid communion, I was taken 18 miles by auto and took a back track to Columbus, Ohio, and by taking an extra fare train I reached A. and Tioga church in Philadelphia just in time for preaching, after being on the train all night.

Will report the Philadelphia meeting in my next article.

ISAAC D. BOWMAN,
1942 South 17th Street, Philadelphia, Pa.

PLEASANT HILL, OHIO

Dear Evangelist Family:

Just a few words from the Pleasant Hill Brethren church. We have been working all summer and our work here grew all summer. For six weeks before October 31st, we had on the Lincoln Highway contest, and to say we succeeded is putting it very mildly. For this church has been here for more than 45 years, they tell me, and we finished the auto contest with a Rally Day service and had 211 present in Sunday school and over $17.00 in offering. This is by far the largest Sunday school ever assembled in the church. We are not dead yet, have just been napping.

Our Christian Endeavor is still alive too, for we have from 30 to 40 present every Sunday night at 6:00 P. M. And the church in general is moving along. We have had 23 additions to the church since the 10th of last April since I became pastor and our Wednesday night Bible Study is well attended—from 35 to 55 being present every week and increasing all the time. We are studying the Book of Revelation now. Everybody is busy and we expect to build an addition to the church in the spring to house our prospering Sunday school. Brethren, pray for us. Our creed is the Bible, the whole Bible, and nothing but the Bible.

S. LOWMAN, Pastor.

WINONA TABERNACLE AGAIN

It is well along toward three months since the annual gathering of the Brethren clans at Winona, where we agreed to accept the pledge we had made to the management of the Winona Assembly at the conference of 1919. Right nobly did some respond to the call of the conference's committee on the matter, making it possible to secure a loan from the Foreign Missionary Society for the balance due from the congregations. But the limit of the promise given by the committee to the Foreign Missionary Society has been reached, and still we are far from having the amount necessary to make good with our brethren.

Now I have been wanting to "say some things" for some time, and so if you want to leave before I begin, now is your chance. I have, for several years noticed a tendency among our folks to seemingly all get an idea at the same time, and then each put forth their claims at about the same time that some one else is asking for notice. Witness, if you will this situation: The National Conference authorized the loan from the Foreign Missionary Society of $1,000.00, for a term of 60 days, with the understanding that the pastors and delegates were to go home and make immediate canvass in their congregations to raise their quota of this fund and forward it to the proper parties. Some did as the conference requested. Some districts waited until the meeting of the district conference (losing a month of valuable time) and then took action again authorizing the congregations to raise the money. NOW WHY THE DELAY? Our church is ULTRA congregational anyway and if the churches don't want to take this offering they will not do it if forty conferences ask or insist upon them doing so. AND AGAIN, nine out of every ten churches WILL take such offerings if the pastors present the matter as a duty and earnestly request them to do so. WHY the dilly-dallying around for two or three months?

Now as the result of such "whipping the devil about the stump" we are faced with this situation, viz., Before we get the Winona offering out of the way, along comes the Publishing House with a request for an offering (and with a perfectly good permit for their action), but we haven't the other one out of the way yet. AND WHICH SHALL WAIT? And the College needs a HEN—one with feathers—to help knock the stilts from under old H. C. L., and who shall say them nay to present their appeal when they feel like it? And the "General Mission Board" is expecting every church to raise the equivalent of ONE DOLLAR per member at Thanksgiving time as an offering for Home Mission Work. And we have given them right of way at Thanksgiving time for these many years. And besides all this most churches that are to be counted on for all the above has a pastor to support and a few local expenses to meet, besides the Red Cross Roll Call which is ON about now, and the Girl Scout Week, and the Christmas Seals, etc., etc., etc., etc.

Allow me to say that I am NOT afraid of my salary. I have always gotten it—and that on time. I am NOT jealous of any of these calls, for I support them all, and they get their money about on time. But I AM in favor of a bit more prompt action on the part of some one in attending to these calls. AND I DO BELIEVE WE NEED A BIT MORE SYSTEM IN THE MANNER OF PRESENTING THE FINANCIAL CLAIMS OF THE VARIOUS AUXILIARIES OF THE GENERAL CHURCH TO THE INDIVIDUAL CONGREGATIONS. As it is we have a "feast or a famine." We have offerings galore at one time, and then we wait a while and get our breath, and then we "go some more." The rights of the regular established dates should be respected by all the rest of the interests having claims to present, and thus prevent the piling up of calls as we have had for the last two months.

And to those who are responsible for the gathering of these offerings in the various congregations it comes to be a matter of prompt and persistent presentation of the calls as they come, and get them out of the way for the others are on the way. It seems to me that it were better to present the claim and get something than to wait until another call overtakes the first one and then have them both on hand and have the members get "scared" at having so many calls, and possibly turn them all down. "A half a loaf is better than none" to these various organizations, and prompt action will go far toward getting a pretty fair-sized loaf from most congregations. OF COURSE SOME CONGREGATIONS ARE SO SELFISH THAT NO PREACHER WILL BE ABLE TO GET MUCH OUT OF THEM FOR ANY CALL BUT FOR THEIR OWN NEEDS. SUCH SHOULD BE LEFT WITHOUT A PREACHER FOR A WHILE UNTIL THEY EXPERIENCE A CHANGE OF HEART.

But some one has by this time about made up his mind to write a reply to this and say that "most any one can find fault, but it takes some one with brains to suggest a remedy." Well, I am willing to be counted in both classes this time, so here's my suggestion as to a remedy. FIRST, if the churches would be in a position to heed the calls whenthey come, let them take God's method of financing the kingdom, and practice it and they will have enough and to spare. TITHE, and do it HONESTLY, and we shall be able to do more than the most visionary of us have ever dreamed of. SECONDLY, let there be a committee chosen by National Conference whose duty it shall be to pass upon the claims of the various auxiliaries and NOT DENY THEM PLACE in the churches' programme, BUT DETERMINE WHEN THEY MAY PRESENT THEIR PLEA BEFORE THE BROTHERHOOD. Not otherwise, as far as I can see, will we ever escape this nerve-racking task of most pastors to keep one call moving fast enough to keep out of the way of the next, and sandwich in the regular financial plans of the congregation between times.

FOR FEAR I FORGET IT, WHEN CAN WE LOOK FOR THAT OFFERING FROM YOUR CONGREGATION FOR THE WINONA TABERNACLE FUND? You can send it to Herman Roscoe, Goshen, Indiana, Care Salem Bank, or to me. BUT PLEASE SEND IT SOON. And some Pennsylvania churches need to hurry a bit with their contribution to the Tabernacle Fund as time is passing and other calls are rapidly approaching.

Yours for Business,
DYOLL BELOTE,
61 Highland Ave., Uniontown, Pa.

HOLLIDAYSBURG, PENNSYLVANIA

I held one week's meeting at Yellow Creek, and closed with communion which was well attended. I baptized eleven as an immediate result of the week's meeting. This church I organized a number of years ago. Brother Edward Byers was pastor at the time of his death. We expect one young man from these to go to Ashland College in the near future. This field will produce if worked.

E. H. SMITH.

FREDONIA, KANSAS

I have been preaching in a neighborhood called Row Valley, where there had been no preaching for a number of years. As a result of my labors in the Lord twenty came out on the Lord's side and made a good confession.

I am to return tomorrow and continue the meetings over Sunday and baptize quite a number, and possibly continue a week or so olnger. All have agreed to unite in organizing a Brethren church. Pray for me.
W. B. SELL,
Box 804,   Fredonia, Kansas.
(Row Valley is 18 miles north of Fredonia).

GOSHEN, INDIANA

Mr. Editor, can you remember when I wrote you a news letter? Well, no matter about that, I have something to write now. We closed the Four Year Program with every goal gained but one. This was one of the most successful efforts of our congregation. We hope that the coming program will be bigger and better in results, but one thing is sure and that is it must be more definite than it is now if we are to get hold of it.

During the past year we have spent over one thousand dollars for repairs and improvements on the church. Last spring we increased our budget thirty-three and one-third percent. This with the expenditures for repairs makes a very large increase in local expenses, but we went over with a bang. Some time ago the men of the Men's Bible Class built us a "home for Henry" in the rear of the parsonage lot. This was a very nice gift and we appreciated it and "so did Henry." If our memory is good the budget has increased from a little over $1,900.00 three years ago to $5,500.00 for this year.

Church Services

The attendance at the services is still increasing. From actual count we have gained in attendance. We count all adults leaving Sunday school and at the end of the month publish the number and designate the number of our members who "have the habit." This helped to "cure us." Then we try to make the services interesting as well as worshipful. In regard to mid-week service, we have here broken our record. The best we did was two hundred and eight. The average is very good. For more than a year we lectured on the "Life of Christ using the text book, "In the Days of His Flesh," by David Smith. This is the best Life of Christ written according to Dr. Miller. This we believe was the beginning of increased interest. Following this we used, "The Great Doctrines of the Bible" by Evans, and now are entering into "The Life and Letters of Saint Paul," by David Smith. We state this because many ministers have asked about the program of our meetings.

The W. M. S. and S. M. M. have also the largest membership in their history with the largest meetings. These two organizations are becoming very important factors in the life of our church here.

The Sunday school is progressing very well. The Children's Division is making exceptionally good under Mr. Roscoe and has increased about 1 percent with a much more efficient teaching force. But the one difficulty is room. This will be cared for in the future. The Adult school is doing well but has not increased so much, but is more efficient and more regular. All considered the school is growing.

Our Six Week Program

More than three years ago, before we became pastor the church bought the present parsonage but made no effort to complete the payment at that time. Some had been paid by the W. M. S. but the remainder of more than twenty-two hundred remained. This with other indebtedness made the total twenty-five hundred. The reason this debt was carried so long was the war conditions. We planned to take an offering through the church organizations and pay it off AND WE DID. But as the program will show you, we also made it practical and a means of growth. We are clear of debt, and are looking into the future, and we see something, but WHAT? One goal in the program was very interesting, and we believe educational. It was the two week's tithing. The offering was $500.00. Just 408 persons tithed according to the names written on the envelopes. To be sure these represented the wage earners. About one-half responded. Their tithe was $250.00, per week. If all had tithed it would have been about $500.00 per week. This was an experiment and was very valuable as an educational effort.

Revival with Dr. Bell

We began with a full house and the week has been a success. We are hoping for a great meeting and we will have it. This will be reported later.

J. A. McINTURFF.

THE PROGRAM AND RESULTS

(With the thought that the Goshen church's program may be suggestive to others and to show how it enlisted every department of the church and made provision for spiritual as well as financial attainment, we are publishing the following program taken from one of Brother McInturff's calendars. The result of the several goals is indicated in black type.—Editor.

CHURCH GOALS:

1. Deepening the Spiritual life of the church. Progress.
   (a) Pastor and Deacons visiting.
   (b) Pastor, Moderator and Secretary sending letters to the families relative to the church work.
2. 25 percent increase in church attendance. Gained.
3. Organized choir. (Goal Directors, Mr. Roscoe and Mr. Wysong). Gained.
4. 10 percent increase at the Prayer Meetings. Lost.
5. Two weeks of tithing—Oct. 17th to Oct. 31. Gained $500.00.
   Note. This offering will be made in an envelope with name or names written on the envelope plainly and dropped in the tithing chest which will be placed in the church.

SUNDAY SCHOOL GOALS:

1. 25 percent increase in attendance. Gained.
2. 25 percent increase in membership of all classes. Progress.

(a) Note. These two goals will be attained by soliciting of new members. This will be carried out through the Sunday School Cabinet and classes.
3. 90 percent Sunday school adults at the church services. Gained.
4. $1,000.00 (one thousand) free-will offering Oct 31. Gained, $1,355.15.
   (a) Note. See program as applied by S. S. Cabinet to the different classes.

WOMAN'S MISSIONARY SOCIETY:

1. 25 new members. Progress.
2. 8) percent membership at September meeting. Lost.
3. $100.00 free-will offering Oct 31. Gained, $100.00.

SISTERHOOD OF MARTHA AND MARY:

1. 12 new members. Gained.
3. $150.00 free-will offering Oct 31. Gained.
   Note. The Sisterhood has accepted the goals and has 9 new members and has made all plans to cover goal 3. Good.

CHRISTIAN ENDEAVORERS, Senior, Intermediate and Junior:

1. 20 percent increase in membership. Progress.
2. 75 percent membership in the October meetings. Gained.
3. Offering by each society in October for charity. Gained.
4. $50.00 free-will offering Oct. 31. Gained, $61.00.

HAGERSTOWN, MARYLAND

This report indicates that we are still striving steadily onward for the Master. Nothing but results of routine activities mark progress with us. We, as well as others, find the work exceedingly difficult in these post-war times. The abnormal interest manifested during days of anxiety and fear, has faded like a will-o-the-wisp and pleasure-seeking is the order of the day. Since last reporting the usual fall events have taken place. Coming home from our General Conference, we are filled with enthusiasm to do greater and better things than before, and thus it should be. But alas, how soon our ardor becomes chilled when you find a cold indifference and only a half-hearted response from those who are in covenant relations to encourage you. We held our Rally Day and Promotion exercises the last Sunday in September. The attendance was not up to former years; this caused the pastor some anxiety and upon investigation found that such was the situation of the other churches of the city. The promotion exercises were most gratifying, for a large number of the Elementary Division received promotion certificates and passed on to higher grades in the church's school. We have labored strenuously to make the work of the school as efficient as possible because we believe there is the future church. Efficiency is the goal in officers, teachers and work done. May God direct and we be willing to be directed that his work of saving grace shall be accomplished.

Our fall communion services were held the first Sunday of October. A larger number than usually gather in the fall, surrounded the Lord's tables. The general spiritual atmosphere was one of brotherly love and sweet

fellowship which strengthens the soul. The auxiliaries are doing their part of the work and are making steady progress. We are now preparing for the Home Mission offering and for a series of meetings under the tried veteran of the cross, Brother I. D. Bowman. Pray that the Lord will be blessed with precious fruit.

A. B. COVER.

ACCIDENT, MARYLAND

It was my privilege to spend eight days with the Pleasant Valley church near Accident, Maryland, after closing my meeting at Terra Alta. This church is also under the pastoral care of V. U. Flora and he is doing a splendid work here too. We regret to know that he is soon leaving this church as the work was forging ahead nicely under his leadership. I am sure that whoever shall be his successor will find splendid people with whom to labor and abundant opportunity to build up the kingdom. Had it not been necessary to return home and move, having sold my farm, I believe another week would have brought many into the kingdom here. In the eight days I received seven confessions. Splendid audiences greeted us at each service and we moved on thanking the Lord for the score of souls he gave us for our labors among the Brethren in the hills. After a meeting in Indiana we will return to Pennsylvania for a meeting or two.

We have yet a few open dates for the New Year. Yours under the Precious Blood,

C. C. GRISSO.

Communion Notice

The First Brethren church of Louisville, Ohio, will hold their lovefeast and communion services, Sunday evening, November 28, at 6:30.

Neighboring brethren are invited to share the blessings of this service.

E. M. RIDDLE, Pastor.

THE TIE THAT BINDS

WALLACE-PETERSEN—On Saturday evening, February 7, 1920, at the home of the pastor in Cerro Gordo, Illinois, Homer C. Wallace and Miss Edith Dell Petersen, were united in marriage. The bride is a member of the Cerro Gordo Brethren church.

D. A. C. TRETER.

SCHAFFER-FLOWERS—On October 5th, 1920, in the First Brethren church of Pittsburgh, Pa., Miss Helen Schaffer, daughter of Mr. and Mrs. Wm. H. Schaffer of Allentown, Pa., and Mr. Flowers of North Carolina, were united in holy wedlock by the writer. The bride is a member of the First Brethren church of Allentown. For the present they will reside in Pittsburgh. They have the best wishes of a host of friends.

E. M. FEHNEL.

IN THE SHADOW

HUSTEAD—Guy J. Hustead closed the forty years and thirteen days of his earthly pilgrimage and passed to be with the Master on November 7, 1920. He was an ultimate victim of pneumonia, superinduced by the Flu, and had been suffering for several months, death coming as release from constant weakness and fatigue.

He was married to Nannie J. Griffith on June 21, 1904, and leaves the wife and two sons, two sisters and four brothers as the near relatives who mourn his leaVetaking.

On August 15, 1920, the undersigned received the confession of sin and of faith in the SaVior, and on subsequent visits he found joy in listening to the Word and prayer.

Funeral services were held at the old Griffith homestead, in Georges township, Fayette county, Pennsylvania, on November 11, and the body was laid to rest in the cemetery at Uniontown. Services by the undersigned. DYOLL BELOTE.

SHOWALTER — Curtis Leedy Showalter was born February 28, 1907 and was called to his heavenly home November 8, 1920. He was a promising lad and liked by eVerybody. His life was cut short by diabetis. Besides his parents, sisters and grandfather and other relatives, he is mourned by a host of friend. Elder Irvin V. Enos of the Church of the Brethren conducted the funeral and the body was laid to rest in the family lot in the Adrian, Missouri, cemetery.

SIMMONS—Mary A. Simmons of Allegheny county, Virginia, passed to her eternal reward November 5, 1920, at the age of 85 years and 28 days. She lived a beautifully Christian life and was a member of the Brethren church for fifty years. She leaves two sons and four daughters, two brothers, one sister and thirty-seven grandchildren, besides a hostof friends to mourn their loss. Her husband preceded her in death nearly thirteen years. Two sons, John Simmons of Cabin Creek and H. E. Simmons of Oak Hill, live in West Virginia, while the four daughters reside in Allegheny county, Virginia. The funeral was held in the Union church at Arritts, Virginia, with Rev. J. W. Jamison officiating. The body was laid to rest in the family burying grounds, accompanied by many and Very beautiful floral tributes, which reveal the high esteem in which she was held by her friends.

D. O. BOWYER.

TRENT—Charles Trent, son of Mr. and Mrs. Albert Trent, of Rich Valley, passed out of this life into the life beyond, August 17, 1920, aged 14 years, 11 months, 23 days. He united with the Brethren church at College Corner at the age of nine, remembering his Creator in the days of his youth. He leaves father, mother, sister, and a number of other relatives and a host of friends. Services conducted from the College Corner church by the writer and assisted by Rev. Homer Anderson of the Pleasant Grove church, Iowa.

D. A. C. TEETER.

GASSETT—Mahala Jane Gassett, was born in Rockingham county, Virginia, July 9 1847, and died July 25, 1920, at the age of 73 years and 16 days. Funeral services were conducted from the home in Cerro Gordo, Illinois by the writer D. A. C. TEETER.

WALKER—Following a long illness Charley Walker, aged 72 years, departed out of this life into the life everlasting on February 3, 1920. He was a member of the Cisco M. E. church. Services were conducted from Cerro Gordo Brethren church by D. A. C. TEETER.

CONE—Frank Augustus Cone, only child of Rev. and Mrs. Geo. E. Cone, pastor of the Brethren church in Fort Scott, Kansas, was born December 23rd, 1918 at Hamlin, Kansas. He passed away Sunday, November 14th, 1920, at 12:30 P. M., aged 1 years, 10 months and 21 days.

His death resulted from the effects of burns receiVed in a fire Saturday eVening.

The funeral serVices were held from the home of Geo. W. Mayberry, at 2:30 P. M., Tuesday and were conducted by Dr. L. S. Buckner, pastor of the First M. E. church of the city, assisted by the pastors of the other churches. The remains were taken to Leon, Iowa for interment.

REYNOLDS — Ann Fahrney Reynolds passed from this earthly life June 17th, 1920. She was a patient sufferer of some months but the end came peacefully, passing away while a brother minister was praying at her bedside. She was a member of the church here. Services by her pastor, the writer.

A. B COVER.

REYNOLDS—William Reynolds, husband of the aforesaid Ann Reynolds died just a few months after his companion. He dropped dead on his way home from work. He was Very lonely after the death of his wife and expressed a desire to follow soon. He also was a member of the church here. A daughter and a son remain to mourn the loss of parents. The writer was assisted at both serVices by Dr. Clever, pastor of Christ's Reformed church of the city.

A. B. COVER.

DORSEY—John W. Dorsey passed to his reward July 23, 1920. He was a retired farmer living at Heuyetts Cross Roads. He was a member of the St. James congregation and was formerly active in church work. His wife preceded him to the spirit world. Services by the writer, assisted by Rev. Roy S. Long at the Broadfording (Dunkard) church.

A. B. COVER.

STEWART—Benjamin F. Stewart, an aged county resident, died at the home of Mrs. Howard Lehmen, November 5th, having reached nearly the 83rd milestone. "Uncle Ben," as he was known, mended shoes and was widely known. Services were held from the home amidst a large gathering of sympathizing friends. Services by the writer.

A. B. COVER.

MURRAY—George Murray, a young man of 35 summers, died very suddenly at Washington, D. C., November 5th. He was stricken on his way to work from the dinner hour. He passed away shortly after reaching the hospital. He is survived by his wife, and three small children. May God comfort the bereft. A. B. COVER.

BECHTEL—Mary Catherine Bechtel, wife of David Bechtel, departed this life at her home near La Paz, Indiana, NoVember 6th, 1920, at the age of 66 years, 8 months and 10 days. She united with the Brethren church about eight years ago, under the ministry of Elder P. M. Fisher, and died in the triumphs of the faith. Funeral serVices held in the La Paz Brethren church on November 8, in charge of the writer. C. C. GRISSO.

FETTERS—Grace P. Hostetler Fetters, wife of Elder Enoch Fetters, passed to her long eternal home from their home in La Paz, Indiana, on NoVember 8, 1920, at the age of 39 years, 4 months and 4 days. She was united in marriage to Enoch Fetters on Easter Sunday, April 16, 1911. This union was blessed with two sons, Enoch Platon, and John Samuel, aged 8 and 5 years. These two boys, with her companion and two brothers are the immediate relatives left to sustain their great loss. At the early age of nine years, she took Christ as her Savior, and from that time until her departure, it was the joy of her life to giVe herself in his serVice. Her work in the churches at North Liberty, Columbus and Fort Scott, is spoken of in the most commendable terms by those with whom she labored. At the latter place she was ordained to the eldership of the church. The Lord was pleased to use her greatly in building up his kingdom, and blest her ministry by giving her scores of souls. She labored earnestly wth her husband until three years ago when they were compelled to giVe up the ministry on account of her failing health. Her last days were days of intense suffering, but her faith never waned. Her sick room was a Veritable mount of transfiguration where we who were present beheld the glory of the Lord reflected in the face of his serVant. She was perfectly resigned to his will whatever that will might be. If further service awaited her, well. If promotion to higher serVice, it was far better. She died in the faith of our fathers. Truly, her life liVes on in others that haVe felt the transforming touch of this life. Her work, her words, the character she built, and the influences she set in motion will outliVe the stars. The last sad rites were held in La Paz, Indiana, on Thursday, November 6, in the presence of a Very large congregation, in charge of her pastor, the writer, who spoke from the text, "For me to live in Christ, and to die is gain." We were assisted in the serVices by Elders Strang, Wade and Whetstone.

C. C. GRISSO.

LICHTY—Allen W. Lichty was born near Somerset, Pennsylvania, on April 3, 1850, and departed this life at Omaha, Nebraska, on November 1st, 1920, aged 70 years, 6 months and 28 days. At the age of seVenteen he moVed from Pennsylvnia to Waterloo, Iowa, at which place he remained until in 1870, when he moved to Illinois, where he was united in marriage to Miss Evaline Saylor at Dutchtown, Illinois, on November 27, 1870. To this union ten children were born; Anna M., Jennie S., John CalVin, Joseph C., Corda M., Edward M., Lulu L., Lela D. Homer L., and Nona L., all of whom surViVe except Lela, who died in infancy. There are seventeen grandchildren and three great-grandchildren, two brohers, Samuel J., and Wm. H., both of Waterloo, Iowa, and one sister, Mrs. Mary Miller of Somerset, Pennsylvania, who surViVe him. Following his marriage he resided at a number of places, but finally settled at his late home in Morrill, Kansas.

Mr. Lichty went through the pioneering days and had the nerVe and ambition to hold fast with many others of his early friends and thereby reaped the benefits of the ultimate deVelopment of the then prairie country. He was always interested in the affairs of county and state and contributed his share to the public service and uplift. He served his county as commissioner three successive terms, besides giVing much time to his township and its developments. Greater, howeVer, was his interest in his church. At the age of seVenteen he hnited with the Church of the Brethren, and was loyal thereto until the time when the church suffered a diVision, he casting his lot with the Brethren, which organization has receiVed his conscientious support eVer since. His church duties and obliiations neVer came too thick and fast for him to regard them as a pleasure. He was conscientious, loyal, sympathetic and kind in his Christian ministration. For twenty-five years he serVed as Sunday school superintendent, besides serVing in the office of deacon and other respnsible positions. The place he leaves vacant will be hard to fill.

Until a few months ago he had always enjoyed exceptionally good health, but during the late months he began to fail. It was found that he was afflicted with a stomach disorder which finally necessitated an operation, which was performed in St. Joseph's Hospital in Omaha, Nebraska, Saturday morning, October 30th. All that medical attention and kind hands could do was done, but early morning, November 1st, he laid down the work of this world and went to be with him whom he had serVed throughout his adult life.

Funeral serVices were conducted on Wednesday, November 3, by the undersigned, his pastor, assisted by H. F. Stuckman and John Burnworth. A. E. WHITTED.

Business Manager's Corner

THE GOOD WORK GOES ON

While there has been an appreciable slacking up in the offerings received to help the Publishing Company meet its heaVy paper bills, yet a number of substantial gifts haVe been receiVed since our last week's report. We are glad to be able to report that with the assistance of our friends we were able to meet the $1,000.00 note that fell due last week, and we trust what help may yet come in will, with the receipts from our regular business, enable us to meet the $2,000.00 note that falls due the middle of December.

This week we have the following contributions to report: Morrill Brethren church, $15.00; Mrs. Chas. Martin, $5.00; Elkhart Brethren church, $25.00; Samuel Houenshell, $3.00; Ardmore Brethren church, $5.00; Yellow Creek Brethren church, $3.70; Uniontown Brethern church, $21.10; Mrs. E. G. Goode, $3.00; College Corner Brethren church, $10.00; Zion Hill Brethren church, $12.50; Isaiah Kreider, $1.00; Lordsburg Brethren church, $18.00.

There are still other churches that are making up their apportionment for this fund that have not yet sent in their offering. Perhaps some have thought it too close to the Thanksgiving offering to respond at this time. We would not lay a straw in the way of the Thanksgiving offering. We want that to be the largest offering the church has ever made; but there is plenty for all the needs of the church, and we trust no church will fail in making a contribution to this fund for which we have been making our appeals for the last month or more. Any time will suit us, but of course the sooner the better.

One of our pastors who has already made a personal contribution to the Evangelist fund for the amount of $10.00 tells us he will be one of ONE HUNDRED men to give another FIVE to the fund. Are there ninety nine men in the brotherhood that will accept this challenge and make this brother pay up? The Business Manager has already made his contribution through the regular channel of the church he serves, but he will be the ninety ninth man to make up the balance. Now, who will be the ninety-eighth?

R. R. TEETER,
Business Manager.

I FILL UP
That which is Behind
OF THE
Afflictions of Christ
(COLOSSIANS 1:24)

The gospel of a broken heart demands the ministry of bleeding hearts. If that succession is broken we lose fellowship with the King. As soon as we cease to bleed, we cease to bless. When our sympathy loses its pang we can no longer be the servants of the passion.

—Dr. J. H. Jowett.

Published every W^nesday at Ashland, Ohio. All matter for publication must reach the Editor not later than Friday noon of the preceding week.

George S. Baer, Editor

The Brethren Evangelist

When ordering your paper changed give old as well as new address. Subscriptions discontinued at expiration. To avoid missing any numbers renew two weeks in advance.

R. R. Teeter, Business Manager

ASSOCIATE EDITORS: J. Fremont Watson, Louis S. Bauman, A. B. Cover, Alva J. McClain, B. T. Burnworth.

OFFICIAL ORGAN OF THE BRETHREN CHURCH

Subscription price, $2.00 per year, payable in advance.
Entered at the Post Office at Ashland, Ohio, as second-class matter.
Acceptance for mailing at special rate of postage provided for in section 1103, Act of October 3, 1917, authorized September 9, 1918.
Address all matter for publication to **Geo. S. Baer, Editor of the Brethren Evangelist,** and all business communications to **R. R. Teeter, Business Manager, Brethren Publishing Company, Ashland, Ohio.** Make all checks payable to the Brethren Publishing Company.

TABLE OF CONTENTS

EDITORIAL

The Pre-Eminence of Jesus Christ

The greatest of the great, the mightiest of the mighty, the most glorious of the glorious, the most faithful of the faithful, the kindest of the kind, the most merciful of the merciful, the tenderest of the tender, the truest of the true, the purest of the pure, the sweetest of the sweet,—that is Jesus Christ! "That in all things he might have the pre-eminence," was the unspeakable longing in the heart of the most pre-eminent of men outside himself.

Nothing so stirs the Satanic anger as to have pre-eminence given to Jesus Christ. Unquestionably this is the reason why the doctrine of the Deity of Jesus Christ is so bitterly denied and so universally hated among the unregenerate. It is that Satan himself has ever sought the pre-eminence, as the prophet Isaiah so clearly sets forth (14:12-15). The tremendous price Satan laid at the feet of the Christ when together they stood on that wilderness mountain-top, was a price for the pre-eminence. "All these things (the kingdoms of the world and the glory of them!) will I give thee if thou wilt fall down and worship me!" And the dethroned prince of the powers of darkness worries not for one moment over any man who refuses to give pre-eminence to the Son of God!

Jesus Christ claims pre-eminence as to his Person. The first and most fundamental test of all true theology is right here. Errors at other points may be admissible. Error here is fatal! The eighth chapter of John records a memorable battle between Jesus Christ and the rulers of the Jewish nation. The battle was as to his Person. "Except ye believe that I am he, ye shall die in your sins," was the fiat of the One Pre-eminent over all, he will continue to command forever the spirits of men. If he is not, he must step aside and cease to be the spiritual Leader among men. The whole fabric of the church he came to build, will stand or fall with the pre-eminence of his Person.

He claims pre-eminence as to his word. The first involves the second. If he is pre-eminent as to his Person, then he is also pre-eminent as to his word. There is a perfect Babylon of voices in the world today, claiming pre-eminence. Such a Babylon was in the days of his first coming, when the city of Rome and the cities of Greece were filled with every sort of soothsayer pretending to possess Oriental wisdom. No wonder the pagan Pilate sneeringly cried: "What is truth?" Above that confusion, the heavens opened one day and gave answer: "This is my beloved Son! Hear ye him!" HE is truth! Since that moment, the least word that ever fell from his lips outweighs in its abundance of eternal truth all the accumulated wealth of man's wisdom since the earth rolled out of star-dust into her present orbit. And, when some would-be-wiser-than-God scientist, philosopher, or

professor and possessor of man's wisdom, steps forth to question even the least word of the Christ, we can only remark: "Mr. Professor Wise-Man, when the mighty heavens above your head rend asunder, and the voice of the Eternal thunders forth from his everlasting throne, 'HEAR YE HIM!' then will we consider as to whether we shall surrender the least of the words of Jesus Christ for yours!" "GOD HATH SPOKEN UNTO US IN HIS SON!" (Heb. 1:2).

He claims pre-eminence in temporal authority. In the choice of your life's work, are you compelled to admit, O man, O woman, that you would not be where you are if you were yielding him the pre-eminence in temporal matters? As you stand at the marriage altar, precious young life, are you there yielding pre-eminence to the Christ? In matters of business and of state, have you given Jesus Christ and his kingdom first place? After all, is it possible to yield unto Jesus Christ pre-eminence in spiritual matters, and then withhold from him pre-eminence in temporal matters?

He claims pre-eminence in spiritual authority. The church plunged into her night and the world was hurled into the "Dark Ages" when she (the church) declared: "At the command of the Virgin, all things obey, even God!" In that sentence she robbed the Pre-eminent of his eternal pre-eminence, and was spewed out. And whenever the church shall so far forget her glorious Head as to give the pre-eminence to one far less than the Virgin,—to such an infinitely lesser one as Mary Baker Eddy as do "Christian Scientists" so-called; or, to the ghosts of some fallen race as do "Spiritualists" so-called; or, to the exceedingly uncertain grey-matter of men of science as do "the Higher Critics" so-called; then will come the last deeper and darker night with its fury of Divine wrath!

And here, many well-meaning children of God need a most solemn warning. For, the anathema of God must likewise rest upon the man or set of men who shall rob Jesus Christ of his pre-eminence and bestow it upon a sect or creed. It is agreed that the short-sightedness of men has compelled the existence of so unbiblical a thing as denominationalim. But woe betide the man who is more loyal to his "denomination" than he is to the Head of the church, and will be unfaithful to Jesus Christ rather than be accused of unfaithfulness to his denimination! Christendom teems with her hundreds of thousands that unhesitatingly bow to the mandate of a creed even though it means disobedience to the Lord of glory! In the battle of the creeds, how often is the Lord himself forgotten!

Members of The Brethren church! We are members of the Brethren church because (or should be because) before our God we believe that in no other denomination on the face of this earth can we preach and practise a fuller Gospel and worship God and his Son whom he set, so acceptably. We challenge proof that there is a better place to this end. But, if ever The Brethren church should so forsake her glorious Head as to "worship and serve the creature more than the Creator" (Rom. 1:25), then we must cast her aside as we would a polluted and outworn garment,—a castaway! Verily, there are doctrines upon which, because of short-sightedness, the children of God may disagree, and yet be neighborly, to say the least. But, when it comes to the PERSON of Jesus Christ; or, to the WORD of Jesus Christ; or, to the AUTHORITY of Jesus Christ in the whole realm of life,—at these points disloyalty is simply treason, and every limit of toleration has been reached so far as the Faithful are concerned. At these points in these apostate times, there is no place for mincing words. Verily, let every man among us stand in his place to say, that, please God, The Brethren church shall not fail here; "that, in all things he might have the pre-eminence!"

LOUIS S. BAUMAN.

EDITORIAL REVIEW

Are you planning a White Gift Christmas service? There are two reasons why you should. (1) It is the most appropriate way of celebrating the birthday of our Savior and King. (2) The needs of the Lord's work require it. Read what Brethren Watson and Gearhart have to say in this connection on other pages in this issue.

Brother A. T. Ronk states, in a communication to our office, that the evangelistic campaign which he and Brother Coleman are conducting at the Flora, Indiana, church in conjunction with the pastor, Brother W. E. Thomas, is about to be brought to a close and that more than a score of souls have already accepted Christ as their Savior. A report is promised in the near future.

We met Brother A. L. Lynn on the streets of Ashland the other day and he told us of having conducted a Thanksgiving service at his Ankenytown charge and of his people making him a thank offering of eats of all kinds. He said the donation was so large it was a real problem to know how to get it all home. We judged it was a rather pleasant problem. And he remarked that the good sisters helped him solve it by expressing the goods to his home. It is evident that Brother Lynn has a warm place in the hearts of these loyal people.

Brother I. D. Bowman had a very successful meeting for the saving of souls in the Third church of Philadelphia, a report of which he encloses in this issue. He gives much credit to Brother Braker, the pastor, and Brother H. C. Cassel for the high state of spirituality which he found there. The fact that most of the converts came from the Sunday school is a demonstration of the value of that organization when it functions rightly.

Brother Dyoll Belote, pastor at Uniontown, Pennsylvania, reports the good meeting he and Brother Bell recently had in that church. They were up against handicaps of time and conditions, but the thoroughness of the pastor and the stirring enthusiasm of the evangelist and the consecration of the two brought success nevertheless.

Brother Martin Shively, the Bursar of Ashland College, is now engaged in an evangelistic campaign with Brother Lyman B. Wilkins, pastor of the church near Washington Court House, Ohio. Brother Wilkins assures us that no interest of the church will suffer; that all special days will be observed and that the Bicentenary Movement is already being pushed in his congregation. He recently sent for a hundred Bicentenary programs to be used to acquaint his people with the Movement.

A report from Brother Herman E. Roscoe, of Goshen, Indiana, concerning the Winona Tabernacle Fund, he states that a number of churches in "Indiana and Pennsylvania need to be reminded that they have not paid their apportionment. The report came too late for publication in this issue, but we mention it here that you may get the word sooner and begin to make arrangements to meet your obligation. We are wondering if the few in Ohio who have not come

across on this proposition will soon remit their apportionment of 16 cents per member to Brother Roscoe, and thus enable Ohio to have a clear slate.

Waynesboro, under the leadership of Brother M. A. Witter, deserves great credit for the most thorough manner in which they won their way on the Evangelist Honor Roll. We congratulate them. See the Business Manager's Corner for the evidences of Brethren loyalty all over the brotherhood, and we are sure the returns are not all in yet.

Brother C. Forney, one of the fathers in Israel, writes concerning a revival recently held at Maple Grove, Kansas, by the pastor, Brother Dodds. When he speaks regretfully of the lack of union and co-operation between the branches of the Brethren fraternity, he strikes a very sympathetic cord in many hearts.

Brother W. T. Lytle, pastor of the Burlington and Darwin churches in Indiana informs us of the fact that both these congregations have had a season of refreshing. Brother L. A. Myers assisted him in the meeting at Darwin and Brother B. T. Burnworth was the evangelist for Burlington. At the latter place some regrettable difficulties were encountered, but the campaign was a success in spite of these.

Nappanee, Indiana, is still going in the right direction, following the efficient leadership of Brother E. L. Miller. They have put on two campaigns for the saving of souls since General Conference. Where the spirit of evangelism abounds there is life, and no one will doubt that the Nappanee church is alive.

Brother B. T. Burnworth, one of our associate editors, recently called at our office, while passing through here on his way home from a revival meeting at Louisville, Ohio. He expressed himself as greatly pleased with our new plant which he saw for the first time. We were glad for his visit as we shall be for the visits of other brethren who may find it convenient to stop at Ashland.

EDITORIAL SQUIBS

He who would extend a helping hand to lift the fallen must keep his other hand in Christ's or he himself shall be pulled down instead of lifting his brother up.

"Give and it shall be given unto you," and of like kind; if a smile you give, a smile you shall receive or if a frown, a frown shall be returned unto you.

No Christian can be all he ought to be, or do all he ought to do, or give all he ought to give until he has learned to say "No," to appetite, to deny himself of many of the innocent pleasures and pastimes and even to sacrifice some of the apparently needful things of life.

According to the United States Bureau of Standards, 93 cents out of every dollar of Uncle Sam's money this year goes for war, past, present or future. Only one cent out of every dollar goes for education and the improvement of public health. Whereas the cities spend an average of six dollars per capita for education per year, and the states and private agencies about three dollars per capita for education, Uncle Sam with his huge billions only spends six cents per capita for education,—and some of that goes to the "land grant" colleges for military drill. According to this analysis, the national government is levying a tax of $50 this year for every man, woman and child in the United States, and of this amount $46.50 goes for war and militarism. And to top it all, Congressman Julius Kahn of California is proposing a system of universal military training that will cost the country in the neighborhood of a billion dollars a year.

With grasping hand and heart of strife
He seeks the fame that briefly lingers,
And all the while the gold prize, Life,
Is slipping through his heedless fingers.—Selected.

THE BRETHREN BICENTENARY MOVEMENT PAGE

1723 - - - - - - 1923

Dr. Charles A. Bame, Editor

Expectation

I am at Expectation Corner, enroute home. I have come down from the Fayette Mountain—a very dangerous trip by auto, to catch the C. & O. No. 3. Arriving with but a few moments to get my ticket, the agent says, No. 3 is two hours late! Two hours late and all my hopes of well-figured connections smashed to smithereens! For about three weeks at off times I had been trying to figure out how I might get home in the day's run. I had been unable to do it, but now, all the second best hopes have fled and it will be a good many hours later than I had any idea, that I shall return to my loved ones. A few minutes later I was at Expectation Corner full of hope; now, I am at Patience station trying to say something that will be worth the space it will occupy on our Bicentenary Page.

But I am at another expectation corner. I am waiting with bated breath to see what shall be the news from the churches as to Stewardship Day. I know by the word from my good private secretary, Mrs. Bame, that reports have been coming in but what they contain, I have not the slightest hint. What have the churches done with the message as to Stewardship? I had thought that this epistle to the churches should have reported something along the line of progress; but here I am and shall not be able to get the page full if I do not write without knowing. So, here is my second expectation corner. It will be a fine day for the denomination when we shall find that we have 10,000 tithers. We shall have some recruits. Shall we get the dollars to man the army? Brother Gearhart, I presume is getting reports from the churches as to the second day of the Movement. We are most assured that if we have a lot of new tithers, we shall have no trouble to get that Day's work further along in the tens of thousands than ever before. So, we are anxious to hear from both.

Our Lord's Expectation

If thus we wait for the reports, how must the good Master in heaven wait? How anxious he has been for twenty centuries that the church awake to her opportunity and privilege. During the past weeks it has been my good fortune to be connected with a number of people of other faiths. The proprietor of the hotel where I had lived for more than three weeks told me that he was a liberal giver and though he does not profess to be over religious, he said, "I never gave that I did not get more back." How universal is this idea. If the good Lord had not promised more than twenty centuries ago that he would give it back if we gave, then we might be hunting around for this evidence, but he did. It is just "up to us" to prove it. He has even asked us to prove it and we are going to do so, are we not? Well, I'll tell you in the next what has been done among the churches. Sorry that I can not do so today.

"The Signs of the Times"

This is a frequent topic among the pre-millennialists. But this is not to be a discussion of that prolific topic. The signs of the times are that the churches are passing through a severe testing. We need not turn to prophecy to find out that there is today, a falling away—an apostasy. Every leech of a sect that is drawing members away from the true churches is a sign of the apostasy. Sects that do not try particularly to convert sinners but to proselyte members from the orthodox churches, are only serving to reveal the superficiality of the Christianity that some thought was the real article. Well, as to the signs. The signs are that the real Christians will have to make up for the apostates if the work of the church is to go on with just the usual vigor. They will have to work more; pay more; pray more. And they will. They are, right in the Brethren Bicentenary Movement. I share no feeling of pessimism as to the heart of the Brethren character. It is strong, true, steady. We have the Bible; we have the Christ; we have the Holy Spirit. The God of heaven is with us; we shall not be moved. Indeed, I feel sure that we are being kept for a wonderful day. If it please God that his return shall be long delayed, for whom we look, then, I am sure that if we "occupy" there shall be a good and great place for us in his great plan. To be ready for that time and to be doing his will, let the admonitions of this page and the leadings of the good spirit keep us true.

Ready for the Time

I dare not say here all I wish. But as other divisions of the church have served their day and lapsed into coma in the Lord's task, and another always came to take up its place, so may it not be that we are being prepared for a time like that? So, I verily believe. When some of the now, great organizations go a bit further in neglecting the "thus saith the Lord" of his word, who shall say there it is; God says it in his word. That is what Brethren preachers are now saying and bless God may it never be otherwise.

Heralding with Renewed Zeal

Let me refer the preachers again to the late Evangelist, to this page and to the topics of Brother Rench. Remember that a few churches are to be tested as to whether their preacher is doing the task. Inside of three months, some preacher will be "on the grill" and if the reporter says that he has not preached on the topics or some of them, what can we say of him? No one doubts the standing or loyalty or ability of Brother Rench properly to direct the preachers along the line of doctrine. What we need then is a lot of good followers and I am trying in this way to recall to you that now is the time to get busy. During the winter is the time to preach doctrine. Before and during and after the revival. Let us not think there is little need of it. Not only the new members, but the older ones are constantly up against the shallow and superficial slights of the Word and the commandments, in a way that makes it important that they have them offset at the only place they can expect it have it rightly done—in the Brethren pulpit. Brother minister, I am aware of the difficulty; I realize how hard it is to get to it. But no man will deny that the heralding of these topics is what made the Brethren church and is about all the excuse she has for existence. Preach the word, then. Be instant in season and out of season; reprove, rebuke with all long-suffering and doctrine. For in so doing, you are "in the steps" of the great preachers of all time. May the good Lord give you grace to accept and fulfill the place he has commissioned you to fill. Believe that you are in a very special way his ambassador and one of his most faithful friends and to betray him is to crucify him afresh before the world. God save you and all from that appalling crime.

A Secret

Let me tell you a secret. You know that Brother Bell occupied the seat of Brother Rench in the former program. Well, the secret is that Bell got the "blues." He came to my house one time in the last year of the other program and said, "If they do not want to preach on the topics as outlined, what is the use of doing it?" Now, Dr. Rench never thought that many preachers would not try to keep the pace he sets in this Movement. So loyal to the faith, he thinks of course that we all are as diligent in the preaching of these topics as he is. Well, if we have not been and if we do not try to be, who can say that he too may not become discouraged? The only way to keep the Movement, is to keep moving. If we keep moving, we shall arrive. "Keep Moving," then.

BAME.

GENERAL ARTICLES

Character-Making Factors of the Young Men's Christian Association
BY H. F. E. O'NEILL
(An address given before the Students and Alumni of Ashland College, October 19, 1920)

The Young Men's Christian Association is an organization of laymen of the Protestant Evangelical churches established in the name of those churches and co-operating with them in the extension of Christ's kingdom among men and boys. In all its activities it seeks to supplement the work of the church which it recognizes as the fundamental and primary agency for the promotion of the religious life.

In fulfilling its mission the Association seeks to promote the spiritual, social, educational and physical welfare of men and boys within and without its membership, offering its service without regard to faith or creed.

The Association's supreme aim is accomplished only as it leads men and boys into the Christian life and into active membership with the church of their choice. It is "the Protestant church at work seven days a week."

The question is often raised, Is the Community "Y" the Railroad "Y," the Industrial "Y," or the College "Y," a part of the regular "Y" work? The answer is "Yes, all are parts of the same work, only each is specializing for the group of men within their reach. And in each division there is the same supreme aim,—the building of Christian character.

What is character? Consider a definition. Here is the Catholic theological definition: "The ineffaceable mark received through the rites of the church." R. G. White says, "Character is like an inward and spiritual grace of which reputation is, or should be the outward visible sign." Character is what one really is; reputation is what he is thought to be. Thus defined my subject is a very simple one, namely, The Church at Work (or in action) Seven Days a Week on One's Best Self. Now consider again the definition we gave of the Association, "An association of laymen of the Protestant Evangelical churches established in the name of those churches and co-operating with them in the extension of Christ's kingdom among men and boys. In all of its activities it seeks to supplement the work of the church which it recognizes as the fundamental and primary agency for the promotion of the spiritual life." The Young Men's Christian Association seeks to deepen the spiritual life of its members by presenting the Gospel of Christ in evangelistic meetings, Bible classes and by personal work. The Association never has, and I hope never will try to supplant the the church, but to supplement it by aiding it and co-operating with it in every way possible.

Consider a few illustrations from personal experiences of Y. M. C. A. men that will show how the Association has been a factor in helping young men to build worth-while character and in leading them into the Christian life.

(1) A young man in high school fought the idea of the Men's United Fellowship Week efforts. He was a genuine "rough neck," and one day he met the Y. M. C. A. secretary in the outskirts of the town. The young fellow was large and overgrown, much larger in physique than the secretary. He began to slander the secretary, and with the most insulting language challenged him to a fight. The secretary pulled off his coat and made a lurch for the rough neck, who when he saw the Y. M. C. A. man meant business dropped back and said, "I didn't think you were made of that kind of stuff and I don't want to fight now." The secretary replied, "Well, I do, and there is going to be a fight staged right here and now with you as one of the participants unless you consent to an interview in the M. U. F. effort." The results were that the young fellow not only signed up for an interview, but was instrumental in getting about fifteen other boys in the high school to sign up, and this same young fellow is now a leader in Christian work.

(2) A Sophomore in high school and a quarterback on a football team became interested in the Y. M. C. A. secretary. He urged his parents to invite the secretary to their home, but he parents were un-Christian, drinking people and not interested in any form of religious work. After persistent efforts the boy finally succeeded in getting the secretary to his home, and after a number of visits the father, mother and two sons were led to accept Jesus Christ as their Savior. This same father became the instigator of and is now the president of the Young Men's Christian Association in one of our Pennsylvania cities.

(3) At the State Sunday School Convention held in Pittsburgh last year there was a young man, who while a mere boy working in a coal mine in Eastern Pennsylvania, was influenced by the Y. M. C. A. secretary to take up educational work and to attend the Bible classes. He is now the leader of the older boys' group in the State Sunday School Association work.

(4) On entering the elevator at 347 Madison avenue not long since, one of our Y. M. C. A. secretaries was stopped by a young man who was just stepping off the elevator. He took the secretary by the arm, looked him in the eyes and said to him, "You are Mr. Blank, aren't you? You don't know me but I know you. You interested me when a mere boy in getting into one of your night school classes and the Bible classes at the Y. M. C. A. You kept encouraging me to go to school, which I did . I completed my college course and am now private secretary to Dr. John R. Mott."

(5) A man intoxicated walked into a Y. M. C. A. building. The secretary met him and discovered that he had a wife and two children and was spending his time and money drinking, gambling and fighting. It was also discovered that he was no novice with his fists. After several friendly conversations this man, together with his family was led into the Christian life, and is now secretary in the Y. M. C. A. These are only a few of the many illustrations as to how the Y. M. C. A. is and may be used for the building of Christian character.

These, you say, are very good, but they occurred in a Y. M. C. A. where they had a paid force and a building with privileges, etc., but is there any use in a Christian college, especially in a church school where there is the seminary with its theological courses and religious education in the college? After fifteen years' experience in Y. M. C. A. work, I am convinced that there is need and a large field of usefulness in any college, not excepting Ashland. And I wish to set forth my reasons why the Association has a rightful place in our own church school.

(1) It is a connecting medium between the students and the great Student Volunteer Movement with which the Y. M. C. A. is so closely connected.

(2) It is also a connecting link between the students and one of the strongest forces for righteousness and with some of the brightest minds of the world, through attendance at its international and state conventions and Summer Schools. Examples of the men they come in touch with are Dr. John R. Mott, Dr. Robert E. Speer, Dr. W. S. Hall, Judge S. Spencer, Judge Joseph A. Bluffington, and John D. Rockefeller, Jr. At these conferences and conventions you get the benefit of training in leadership in various forms of religious work and are brought in contact with men of note in all callings.

(3) It is the one correlating force to harmonize and spiritualize the feelings of the different fraternities, and it is often the one place where faculty and students can meet

together on an equal basis and both feel comfortable. This is also true of the Industrial, Railroad and Army Y. M. C. A.

(4) It is a training school in unselfish service. It encourages both consideration of and service for others.

(5) It serves to keep the students in touch with the great movements that are promoted by the Y. M. C. A., such as the M. U. F., Find Yourself Campaign, Thrift Week (and some of the students who are here or who have been here need to learn the lesson of thrift) and Christian Callings Campaign.

(6) And best of all it affords a splendid opportunity for evangelism by the evangelistic meetings, Bible classes and, more important, by personal work. I believe the greatest and most far-reaching results are obtained by personal interviews. I am sorry to say, but nevertheless it is true, that many of our young men and women who enter our colleges and far to many who come out of them are not filled with the spirit of Christ, and there is need of this evangelistic emphasis to intensify their spiritual lives. And may I say by way of parenthesis. Then, too, not all the men and women who come to college are professing Christians, and some are mere professors and have never experienced conversion. Here is our greatest field of service.

Let me illustrate what I am saying; and since my audience is composed of the girls of the Y. W. C. A., as well as of the boys of the Y. M. C. A., I will take my illustration from the ladies' side of the house. The daughter of wealthy parents was in the freshman class in college. She was generous in spirit and shared all the "goodies" which her parents sent her with her fellow students. She became very popular, and the girls all loved her, at first. But gradually an ugly disposition showed itself which caused her friends to drop off one by one. She ceased to be the popular girl and more and more the girls began to shun her. She was left almost alone and she became greatly discouraged and homesick, but nobody seemed to pity her. Finally one of

the older girls, a Senior, took it upon herself to tactfully take the Freshman into her confidence and to point out her faults. She became voluntarily the advisor, counsellor and friend of this deserted girl, whose whole life was changed into a really lovely girl who both deserved and won the friendship of all her fellow students. This change had a great influence upon the entire freshman class, and all because one girl did not fail to influence by personal interview another girl for Christ.

The Y. M. C. A. seeks not only to lead men to Christ, but into the church where they can be trained for further service. And what I say about the Y. M. C. A. could be said also about the Y. W. C. A. Many of our young men and women in college are not only led to accept Christ as their Lord and Savior, but also to hear and heed the call of God to dedicate their lives to some form of Christian service. Mr. McLachin of China, a very dear friend of mine, said that when he first went to the foreign field his great object was to lead men into the Christian life and was quite satisfied with that, but he says he has since learned that his greatest privilege is not merely to lead men to Christ, but to teach and train them to lead others to Christ. A class in personal work for Christ will repay a college Y. M. or Y. W. for all the time, effort and expense they put upon it.

I have found that many of our clergymen, while they can preach effective sermons are as ill at ease in dealing with an individual with a view to leading him to Christ as most people are in their first attempt to operate an automobile.

In closing let me say that our best and most consecrated leaders in the Y. M. C. A. work were led into it because of the personal touch of some consecrated Y. M. C. A. worker. And many of these men have entered this calling, influenced by the opportunities afforded for personal contact with men and boys.

Pittsburgh, Pennsylvania.

Christian Baptism. By E. E. Roberts
II. The How? of Baptism

We have shown that baptism is immersion, but people practice different things which they call baptism. If important at all, it is most important to know how Christ commanded, and how the Apostles practiced baptism.

Our contentions are

(1) That no man claiming to be a grammarian would dare to parse the Commission, as given in Matthew 28:19, as meaning anything else than a three-fold immersion.

(2) That the symbol of the act require a triune immersion, which, briefly stated is—

(a) That we have repented of our sins against God, for all sin is against him (Ps. 51:4).

(b) That we believe that Christ is the Son of God, and that he is our Savior.

(c) That we yield ourselves to the guidance and infilling of the Holy Spirit.

Secondly, Paul says in Romans 6:3-5, that it is typical of three other things:

(a) That "we are baptized in the likeness of his death." Therefore it typifies the death of the old man of sin; and "if in the likeness of his death," which we find in John 19:30 was by the bowing of his head, we must be baptized by a forward bowing of the head under the water. All acts of worship are forward—the backward action is only typical of sin and misfortunes (1 Sam. 4:18; John 18:6).

(b) It is a symbol of burial, hence it must be a covering of the body of the old man of sin in the watery grave. Anything but a covering would be meaningless, and be no symbol.

(c) It is also a symbol of the resurrection, or birth of the new creation, (Rom. 6:4-5; John 3:5) by the coming forth from a hidden state in the water, to "walk in a new-

ness of life." This cannot be typified in the least by sprinkling, or in any other way.

(2) Early Christian writers testify to Triune Immersion, beginning with the "Didache," or Teaching of the Apostles, possibly written as early as A. D. 65. Section 7 expressly commands triune immersion, in the name of the Father, and of the Son, and of the Holy Spirit. Cyprian, A. D. 220, Augustine A. D. 345, and in fact all the church fathers contend for it and it only.

(3) Modern writers admit it, though many do not practice it. Alexander Campbell, (founder of the Disciple church,) in his "Debate with Rice," p. 258, says, "Not only Mosheim and Neander, but all historians, trace triune immersion to the times of the Apostles." Martin Luther says: "Let the baptist dip her head three times under the water" (Walscheas Life of Luther, part 10, p. 2637). Luther also says: "Without a doubt it was instituted by Christ." John Calvin (Vol. 4. 15-19) says, "The very word signifies to immerse, and it is certain that immersion was the practice of the early church." John Wesley (More's Life, Vol. 1, p. 425): "When Mr. Wesley baptized adults professing conversion, he did so by immersion."

Rev. Wm. Cathcart, D.D. (Baptist) in his "Baptism of the Ages and Nations," says, "Triune immersion was the practice of the early Christian church, the proof is overwhelming."

Conebeare and Howson (Episcopalians) say: Romans 6:4, cannot be understood unless it be borne in mind that the primitive mode of baptism was by immersion.

Dean Stanley (Church of England) says in "History of Eastern Church," p. 117, "There can be no question that the original mode of baptism was by complete immersion." These few must suffice: hundreds more could be quoted.

(4) Triune immersion not only began with Christ and the Apostles, but has continued all the time to the present, and now has a larger body of people practicing it than any other form. The Greek church, in whose language the Gospel was written, always has and still practices triune immersion. They ought to know what Greek means.

Again, we can tell when and how sprinkling and pouring began. Single immersion is first heard of in connection with the Eunomain Heresy, A. D. 350, and called forth the condemnation of the Church fathers. Then later because of the Arian heresy, the Pope claiming authority to change the. Lord's command in A. D. 633, advised the single forward immersion; but the first backward single immersion was that of a fanatic, named Thomas Munzer, on the first day of March, 1522. The first case of pouring was that of Novatian A. D. 250, who, being supposedly dying was three times poured upon, but recovering, his baptism was not

counted valid by the church fathers. The Council of Neo-Caesarea, in the fourth century, declared, "If a man is baptized in time of sickness, he shall not be ordained as a Presbyter, because his faith was not voluntary, but of constraint." The first record of sprinkling was A. D. 255. Cyprian replying to an inquiry, says: "You have asked me regarding those who have received the grace of God in time of sickness. . . . Let them run no further risk, if they recover, let them be baptized." It has never been considered valid by over 160 million of Greeks, Hebrews, and others of all nations. Reader, such are the facts briefly told. It seems to me—does it not to you, that it is the rankest folly to accept anything but triune immersion? which every church in Christendom admits is valid, and which will give us membership in any church on earth, and, may I add, in heaven, too. Let us reject these young substitutes for the good old way.

Recruiting the Ministry.

The above subject is trite, uninteresting, and uninviting to many, but I have come to regard it with the years as representing one of the most urgent needs of our church. This is also true of most other churches.

The ministry needs recruiting, for by many young persons, it is misunderstood. The delight of service in this field are not, in most cases, evident to the young people of our church. Hence, the opportunities, obligations, and rewards of the ministry must be repeatedly presented to those who are casting about for a life of service. I am writing this article on my own initiative in the light of our proposed period of expansion and also that of the present enrollment in our Seminary. I am not speaking for any organization or committee within the church but wholly from the standpoint of the college.

The enrollment in the Seminary this year is not up to that of last year. This is not wholly alarming, for enrollments are certain to fluctuate within limits. Moreover, figures do not always represent the situation, for sometimes the total enrollment will include the wives of students, others who are preparing for Christian work but not for the ministry within our church, and still sometimes young women who are preparing for calls as nurses, etc., to the foreign field. While these are necessary, I am not having these so much in mind as those young men who are preparing to go out and man places in our congregations. There is now a dearth in this direction.

What is the solution? There is but one and that is the local minister and the local church. The College can not extend its arms across the continent and bring young people to see the advisability of entering the ministry, but the local pastor and the local church can. I may be wholly mistaken. but to my mind the ministry will be recruited no faster than the pastors make it possible. The college stands to serve. It is equipped to serve but it can not serve those who will not come. I suppose it is a waste of time, but I want to appeal again to the pastors to remind their young people of this field of service. Last summer I sent a letter with advertising matter to every pastor in the church and I had two replies.

As I have suggested elsewhere, we talk missions, expansion, enlargement, and yet we are not preparing workers in as great numbers as we ought. Last spring, the College brought Brethren Shively, Wolford, and DeLozier here, taking three men out of the active ministry and sent from the graduating class back into the church, two from the long course and one from the short course. Fine chance for enlargement thus! If even three men of the right sort should drop out of our ministry, even so small a number as that would seriously handicap us. The passing of Brethren Trout and Edward Byers very noticeably increased the shortage of available men.

Some churches have men here in the Seminary practi-

cally all the time. Others have never had any and never will. I have every sympathy with the pastors in their duties, but I want to lay this burden upon their hearts once more.

Ashland, Ohio.

By President Edwin E. Jacobs

An Open Letter to Martin Luther

My Dear Brother Luther:—I am indeed surprised and deeply humiliated to have the early reports of your conduct at Wittenberg so fully confirmed. It is not that I doubt some corrupt—or, at least, unwise—practices have crept into our holy Catholic Church, or that I doubt your ability to point them out and to secure a considerable following among the dissatisfied and those who by nature are ever ready to take up with any who attack the established order.

As to John Tetzel, you are probably right in criticizing his actions somewhat. He has certainly gone a bit beyond bounds in allowing men to purchase the privilege of sinning. But, even so, remember he is a Bachelor of Theology, and prior of the Dominican Order, commissioner of our most holy Father at Rome—and, above all, he is your brother.

Now, Brother Martin, your nailing up those ninety-five theses and proposing to debate upon them is probably within your rights, but is it not a bit too common, does it not savor of play to the galleries, and is it not apt to lead to ill-feeling and a lack of respect for the constituted authorities?

Martin, Martin, trust your brethren. It is well enough to be interested in the truth, but the great thing is love. Trust your brethren.

I do so hate controversy, and I fear your actions are leading us into it, especially as they seem to have aroused so many of the commoner type of people against the established order in our holy church.

Try to trust your brethren,

With deep love,

AMICUS.

Oh you, the rising race of America . . . you in whom, for better or for worse, is vested the empire of the world; make it the empire of your King Jesus! The science of the ages has come with its gifts and poured them at your feet. Literature, art, medicine, the philosophy of mind and nature, have enriched your souls and multiplied your powers and thoughts. The prizes of wealth and power are in your grasp. But what are these compared with wealth of souls and power over nations being born into new life? Use these treasures right. Knowledge has often led men astray from God; let yours be brought a willing slave to the feet of him in whom is all knowledge. Wealth has often deadened the soul; let yours be a joyous offering at his feet, who, though rich, became poor.—W. T. A. Barber, M. A.

THE BRETHREN PULPIT

AN ADVENTURE OF FAITH

A Pilgrim Tercentenary Sermon by Miles J. Snyder

TEXT: "By faith he went out, not knowing whither he went." "By faith he endured, as seeing Him who is invisible."
(HEBREWS 11:8; 11:27)

The Pilgrims were a God-fearing people who were persecuted in England and for that reason migrated to Holland; and, after fourteen years spent there, they made the great adventure of faith across the Atlantic to the American shores. They sailed from Holland in July, 1620, to Southampton, England, there to join the "Mayflower" which was awaiting them. On September 6, 1620, one hundred and two Pilgrims sailed from Plymouth, England, on what was to be a most memorable voyage across the Atlantic. They experienced great hardships aboard ship on an uncertain voyage which required sixty-four days. And then they spent five more weary weeks in search of a site suitable for founding their new settlement. At last, on December 21, 1620, they disembarked from the good ship Mayflower and landed at a spot which they named Plymouth, after the English port from which they had sailed sixteen weeks before.

As Longfellow said:

"They came to the Plymouth Rock, which was to their feet
as a doorstep
Into a world unknown,—the corner-stone of a nation!"

My purpose is to consider the spirit of the Pilgrims rather than the Pilgrims themselves. Much has been said out of prejudice and ignorance and sin against the Pilgrim, and the Puritan from whom he came. He has been pictured as a narrow, morbid soul; as a religious fanatic; as one enshrouded in gloom and sadness, without laughter and love and song. But this is far from the truth. Granted, the Pilgrims had peculiarities and faults and frailties. What people does not have? They were human beings, not translated saints. Some of them even became criminals in after years. But let us not lose sight of the fact (which it is safe to assume will never be said of their critics and caricaturists in three hundred years from now) that over and beyond all their littlenesses and limitations and shortcomings, they had a spirit which has lived; and, after three hundred years have passed by and the things of earth have dropped away, there shines forth from their life and achievement the spirit of liberty and the firm-set faith of strong endeavor. Looking back across the centuries, the world today beholds in wonder the sublime heights of spiritual vision and truth they occupied and from which they wrought, with the unbroken strength of souls unimpaired by sin and self-indulgence and frivolity, the deeds that made men free and nations great.

The spirit of the Pilgrim was a spirit not his own. It was in the world long before the Pilgrims went to Holland and across the sea and landed on these barren shores. Animated by this same spirit, Abraham, in obedience to God's call, "went out, not knowing whither he went." Likewise, Moses was impelled by the same spirit when he forsook the splendors of the kingly court of Egypt and championed the cause of an oppressed people that they might be free, and through long years of suffering and hardship and trial "endured as seeing him who is invisible." Daniel also had the spirit of the Pilgrim when he faced the wild beast's fury in a lion's den rather than refuse to worship the true and living God after the manner of his people. John the Baptist, crying in the wilderness and calling the people to repentance, was moved by the same spirit of freedom and faithfulness to God. And St. Paul, lifting his hands in chains, fettered as a prisoner, and indicting the king on his throne, was also sustained by the spirit of the Pilgrim. The form in which this spirit appears changes from age to age, but the spirit abides the same and is a force for righteousness wherever it is found.

In thinking of this "Adventure of Faith" we should consider the priceless inheritance which has come to us out of the past because of the sacrifice and the blood and the deeds and the ideals of the Pilgrim forefathers. This inheritance brings with it a grave responsibility; it is something not to be lived upon, but to be lived up to. We can best honor the heritage they afforded us by giving the spirit which dominated them, form and expression in the needy world in which we find ourselves. The blessings which have come down to us through the achievements of the Pilgrims do not constitute a legacy for selfish enjoyment, but rather a trophy to be continually re-won by those who fight the good fight of faith. As heirs of those who have gone before, the great task that confronts us in our day is not so much to preserve that which has been provided for us, but to create a living social and moral order, rich in freedom and friendship, fruitful to the arts of peace and the service of mankind, faithful to the highest ideals and the Word of God.

In this twentieth century there are certain great lessons that we may profitably learn from the Pilgrims. While they did not know life throbbing with industry and power as we know it, nor did they find themselves in a society as complex and intricate as our own, yet fundamental problems are essentially the same; and in studying the Pilgrims we have illustrious exemplification of vital principles and eternal truths applied to the common problems and tasks of human life.

Notable in the life of the Pilgrims was a supreme and unfaltering faith in God. They went out not knowing whither, but they were confident that God was in that unseen place and in that unknown future. From them God was not far removed at any time. They passed through sore trials and hard sufferings and great discouragements, but through all these they kept their faith in God, and believed that he was in the world and that their life had both meaning and high destiny.

The practical value of such a faith is that this sense of God makes for holiness in character and heroism in conduct. The Pilgrim put the emphasis on goodness, and nothing else satisfied him. Wickedness and sin were things to be hated and gotten rid of. And this is just the type of manhood and womanhood that our age pre-eminently needs, but it is wholly impossible without an individual consciousness of God. The Pilgrim's belief in God meant to him that he should strive to live a godly life. In his thought, to be saved was not merely for security, but for holiness. His daily conduct was but the natural outcome, the blossoming forth, of his living faith in God.

Another thing worthy of consideration, growing out of his faith in God, was his deep desire for fellowship with God. The Pilgrim sought to live as though the eye of God were constantly upon him, as though the ear of God heard all the words he spoke, as though the mind of God knew every secret thought, as though the presence of God was ever at his side. That meant being conscious of the spiritual fellowship of God, and it was this deep personal concern which developed that peculiar entity sometimes called the "New England conscience."

We need to consider anew the Pilgrim's fear of displeasing God as he sought to have fellowship with him. The tendency today is to think of God as an amiable, good-natured being, not to be taken too seriously. But the Pilgrim was right. Every individual is personally accountable to God for his conduct, and the sooner we have the conviction dominating our lives that friendship and fellowship with God is the most important thing we can strive after the better it will be for us. What a blessing it would be today if a lot of criminal profiteers, if the giddy throngs that delight in every excess of gayety, if the thousands dishonoring the marriage vow and crowding the divorce courts,—if all these and others equally blameworthy had a wholesome fear of God and a feeling of personal accountability to him.

Another lesson that comes to us from the Pilgrims is the supreme importance of religion. As men and women, religion was their first concern; and their meeting houses had more men in them than women, showing that their's was a masculine religion. Their temporal life was dominated by their spiritual life. It seems hard for the modern man to understand how one can submerge a longing for pleasure and a passion for material gain, into a consuming desire to be God's friend and to do his sovereign will. But that was the Pilgrim's conception of the purpose of life. The tendency today is to look upon the profession of religion as a cloak of respectability, a comfort in tottering old age, a help in times of storm when the threatening waves beat hard against us.

But the constant concern of the Pilgrim was the type of his daily life. Religion was a real, dominating thing to him. It was at once vital and vitalizing, a religion of a positive, earnest, and enduring type. He preferred the sweet content and peace and power which "the life of God in the soul of man through faith in Christ" assures, rather than the acclaim of men and the gains of earth and the pleasures of the world. To know God, to serve him, to enjoy him, to receive his commendation, that was the aim and end of the Pilgrim's life. He was not concerned about having his name carved on tables of stone, but he did want it recorded in the Lamb's Book of Life.

Again, a lesson for us is seen in the way the Pilgrims used the Bible. The Bible was their chart as they went out not knowing whither they went; and it was the anchor that held them true in every time of storm. We are told that every family that sailed in the Mayflower had a copy of the Bible, and, what is more, they diligently studied it that they might "receive further light." The Bible was the foundation of their religion, the keynote of their worship, and the guide of their daily conduct. It truly was "a lamp unto their feet and a light unto their path."

The historian further tells us that every question that arose among them was "discussed, disputed, and cleared up by the Word of God," and it was not considered settled until it was found "agreeable to the Holy Scriptures." Furthermore, we are told that public officials were selected according to the directions given in the Bible, and that the qualifications there demanded were set up as the standard for all office-holders! All their hopes of civil and religious well-being hung upon the Word of God. They diligently studied the Book so that they might know themselves, so that they might know each other, but principally that they might know God. Before deciding upon any course of action, they sought to ascertain his will. And as they studied the Bible it did for them what it will do for every people; it quickened their thoughts, purified the springs of conduct, cleared their vision, became a system of practical ethics, and transformed their lives.

Again, we find in the Pilgrims worthy examples of heroic courage. Few in number, they undertook one of the greatest enterprises the world has ever known. Speaking of them a few weeks ago, Lloyd George said, "By the alchemy of faith the Pilgrim fathers transformed their experiences and sufferings into a great adventure." Think what courage it took to turn from friends and break home ties and journey to Holland, and there establish a residence among people of strange language and stranger manners. Then think again of the undaunted courage in leaving there and sailing in a little boat across untried and dangerous seas, to a land unknown and bleak and inhospitable and wild, beset with savages. But they did not quail before the prospect of a great adventure of faith; instead they grew stronger as the shadow of danger deepened.

And, their sublime courage marks them as great idealists. Like Abraham, they went out not knowing whither they went; but they were in quest of high ideals and neither the hardships they encountered nor the engrossments of this life stopped them. And like them, we too, in spite of our entanglements here, our interests, our cares, our pleasures, should be seeking a heavenly home, and should permit nothing to divert us from our course or prevent us from realizing the ideals of our pilgrimage.

Looking back across the centuries, then, we conclude that the spirit of the Pilgrims is the richest legacy that the generations have bequeathed to us; and it is our responsibility, our opportunity, to give this spirit expression in our day and hand it on unimpaired and enriched to our children's children. The call of the present hour is a call to a stern moral awakening. What would it profit us if our country is the richest nation in the world if character should be bankrupt? Incalculable physical resources are valueless if there is no moral strength and stability. Intellectual and aesthetic achievements are but vapors that pass away if men are without pure and animating spiritual hopes.

On this three hundredth anniversary of the landing of the Pilgrims their challenge comes to us with renewed power. It is a call to unfaltering faith in God, to cultivate a spiritual fellowship with him, to vitalize personal religion, to exalt the Bible as the Book of Life and Light, to moral courage, and to high idealism. To heed this call and to meet the challenge will be to honor our forefathers more than to build monuments of marble and fashion tablets of bronze.

"The Pilgrim of the olden time,
How calm and firm and true!
Unspotted by its wrong and crime,
He walked the dark earth through.
The lust of power, the love of gain,
The thousand lures of sin
Around him, had no power to stain
The purity within.

"With that deep insight which detects
All great things in the small,
And knows how each man's life affects
The spiritual life of all,
He walked by faith and not by sight,
By love and not by law;
The presence of the wrong or right
He rather felt than saw.

"O Spirit of that early day,
So pure and strong and true,
Be with us in the narrow way
Our faithful fathers knew.
Give strength the evil to forsake,
The cross of Truth to bear,
And love and reverent fear to make
Our daily lives a prayer."

Milledgeville, Illinois.

The Lord does not light up the entire road leading from the calling to the goal. He just lights up the bit of road we have got to travel today, and the rest is still in darkness. He takes us partly into his counsel. "Now I know in part." The lamp is lit of which we have present need. "Abraham went out not knowing whither he went." "We walk by faith and not by sight."—Dr. J. H. Jowett.

THE SUNDAY SCHOOL

H. H. WOLFORD
General Secretary-Treasurer.
Ashland, Ohio

White Gifts for the King. By J. Fremont Watson

I am glad that the modern Sunday school is turning the Christmas entertainment from a "Santa Claus" revel into one of real worship. We are ceasing to celebrate the birthday of our Lord by the aid of a make-believe "Santa Claus," fur clad and pillow stuffed, with nine parts hilarity and one part worship. Were the Wise Men so unwise as to take with them a "Santa Claus" to add amusement to the first Christmas entertainment? Try to suppose that they had done so; think you that the choicest musicians from heaven's choir would have played the opening prelude on their harps of gold and sung the opening hymn?

A better way to celebrate Christmas has been given to the church by Mrs. Phoebe A. Curtiss in her beautiful little story book entitled, "White Gifts for the King." This story is introduced by an old legend entitled, "The Legend of Cathay." It is not a fairy tale, nor yet a fancy tale, but is more like one of the parables of our Lord. The story is given thus:

"There was once a strange country called Cathay, the ruler whereof was one King Kubla Kahn. Though a mighty warrior, the king was a wise and beneficient ruler, greatly revered by all his subjects, who were bound to him by strong ties of love and loyalty. Now the king's birthday was always observed by all his people in what was known as the "White Feast," at which time the king and his court assembled in the Royal Palace, all dressed in white apparel. The floors were laid in the whitest marble, the walls and windows were draped in costly white silk.

"Every subject brought the king a birthday gift and every gift was a white gift to show that the love and loyalty of the giver was pure and without stain. The rich brought gifts of pearls, carvings in ivory, costly white embroidered garments and spans of white horses for their king, while the poor brought white doves or pigeons, or perchance a mere handful of rice. Nor did the king regard one gift above another so long as all were white! And so they kept the king's birthday, year by year."

The new form of service, when properly carried out, makes an irresistible appeal to every member of the Sunday school to bring some sort of white gift to the king on his birthday. There is such a spirit of loving unselfishness and benevolence in it all that the service ought to arouse the church to a new interest and sweeten the world with its fragrance.

There are three kinds of gifts proposed but they include all the gifts which the King of kings desires: a birthday gift of self—to the King; a gift or pledge of service—to the church; a gift or pledge—of substance to the poor and needy.

For the Sunday school to prefer another form of Christmas service, knowing the gracious and abiding results of this, would seem like preferring noise to music, silver to gold, and amusement to spiritual blessing.

We appeal to our Sunday school forces to loyally stand by the work of the National Sunday School Association. Our budget this year is approximately $3,500. Judging from what our schools have done other years, this will not be difficult to reach. The former record of our schools is commendable but we can do better. We trust that every school will begin plans for a service which will honor the King with our substance and result in great blessings to the givers. Every year you have exceeded that of the former in your gifts, which, to say the least, speaks well for your zeal in the work. Make it a "White Gift Service" and a "White Gift Offering" worthy of the name to our King.

Johnstown, Pennsylvania.

That College Hen, Again

The little blue pullet has a lot of company now, but there is room for more, as you furnish it. And I know you are going to do it, for the interest in the project is growing as you will see from the following report:

Previously reported,	$51.25
Turlock, California, Sunday school,	5.00
Mrs. Melvin Woodruff, Williamstown, Ohio,	1.00
Henry V. Wall, Long Beach, California,	5.00
Mrs. George Griffin, Uniontown, Pennsylvania,	2.00
Catherine Madelene Wolf, North Liberty, Indiana,	1.00
Paul Lowell Wolf, North Liberty, Indiana,	1.00
Margaret Jeanette Wolf, North Liberty, Indiana,	1.00
Beginners' Class, Fairview, by Mrs. Himiller,	5.50
Elizabeth Junk,	.50
Pearl Baer, Meyersdale, Pennsylvania,	2.00
Primary Department, North Liberty, Indiana,	2.06
Mrs. Oliver Winters, Fremont, Ohio,	1.00
Total to date,	$78.51

The fund is reaching quite respectable proportions, and will be much larger, I am sure. Two more of our largest Sunday schools presented the cause last Sunday, but their reports are not in. Watch for them, and get in with them.

Faithfully, your servant,
MARTIN SHIVELY, Ashland College. Ashland, Ohio.

J. A. Garber
PRESIDENT

Our Young People at Work

E. A. Rowsey
SECRETARY

Young People Cultivating the Spiritual Life. By E. M. Riddle

(An address prepared for the Christian Endeavor session of General Conference)

As I ponder this subject I think of a stream with for its source a spring. In close connection I recall the words of our Lord to the woman at Samaria about a well of living water springing up into eternal life. At the very beginning one desires to know what are the contributing factors to the spiritual life and how to cultivate them.

Such verses as these will be helpful and inspiring for this consideration: "If any man thirst, let him come unto me and drink;" "He that believeth on me, from within him shall flow rivers of living water;" "As the hart panteth after the water brooks, so my soul panteth after thee, O God;" and another Psalm says, "Glorious things are spoken of thee, O city of God," and ends with, "They that shall

sing shall say, "All my fountains are in thee." From these beautiful words, we can readily discern the source of the true fountain or stream of life.

As I try to discover the things that help to cultivate the spiritual life, I repeat the words of a noted servant, First, appropriate study of available, reliable knowledge of God; and 2nd., persistent fellowship with God. In brief, I should say, Bible Study and Prayer. Prayer is the interchange of thought, the interplay of feeling, which takes place between the heavenly Father and his human child. You may ask, How does Bible study contribute to effective praying? First, Bible study is an incentive to prayer, because the Bible reports the experience of the great religious pioneers of humanity who have found God in prayer and who urge others to seek the same experience. The Bible is one long call to prayer, sounding through the centuries and issuing from the experience of great praying souls. Secondly, the Bible presents a God who is personal, and with whom personal intercourse in prayer is possible. It is hard for the modern man, who sees the vastness of the universe, to conceive that it is filled by a personal Being. Moreover, the Bible presents Jesus as a living personality, ready, through personal association with his disciples, to train them in prayer. The praying soul of Christ rises up in the soul of the disciples and communicates to them his own spirit of prayer.

"If ye abide in me and my words abide in you, ye shall ask what ye will and it shall be done unto you." The Bible clearly and insistently cultivates in us an unselfish regard for the man. The prayer in which Jesus can be expected to join must be one which has due regard for the interests of other men, for Jesus is as vitally interested in them as he is in the man who is praying. In other words, we should cultivate an interest in the Kingdom for it was the chief interest of Jesus.

The spiritual life is a problem of, first a clearer understanding and a heartier acceptance of the ideals of Jesus, and a closer adjustment to his person. The first comes through Bible study and the second through prayer.

Young people may cultivate their gifts by activity. The athlete develops himself for his game by constant persistent training. The marksman gains a steady hand and a sure eye by practice. Nor should it be vastly different with the finer inner nature of man.

Christian Endeavorers should be spiritually minded. There is no better way to cultivate this fine characteristic than by being active in the thing we wish to become. For instance, if one desires to be a soul-winner, then I maintain that the best preparation for this joyful service is to begin now the task of winning men. There is no more convincing way to feel that one's spiritual life is being cultivated than by having it tested in activity for God.

You may be asking, Why it is that so many people in this life seem almost void of spirituality? It is, I believe, because of indifference, which to my mind is a sin second to that of unbelief. So many if they ever had a spark of spirituality, smothered it under a bushel. When people are so covered by the world that the inner life is never allowed to cast a shadow, then growing conditions are not favorable for the

soul. We are often Samsons shorn of power, slaves who should be free, because of hidden sin. In the late war we saw many instances when in the hour of need men could not go to the front, who were pronounced "unfit for service," because of dishonorable lives. Then we think how many are unfit for service in the great conflict of the Kingdom today. Would God dare trust you with his power? "If a man therefore purge himself from these, he shall be a vessel unto honor, sanctified, and meet for the Master's use."

The young person who has the consciousness of God in his or her life has gone a long way in cultivating a beautiful character. It is the greatest and most precious possession of life. With this possesion young people can go out fearlessly to meet every life problem. The late Ex-president Roosevelt once said to a body of students, that character was made up chiefly of three elements; plain honesty, courage and common sense. I am wondering if the young people of the Brethren church can face the arduous tasks of our beloved church with these great elements. You may have read John Foster's book, "Decision of Character." Three great suggestions come to us from this work: First, think a thing through; second, make the decision; third, act on the decision.

If this is a common sense way to consider the facts of the world and I believe there is, then let us be determined, and not lacking in these things that are vital for a young life in the making.

Do you dread to know the will of God? The Apostle Paul says, "We may know what is that good and acceptable and perfect will of God." What kind of a child would you be if every moment you were afraid to know the will of God? Some are fearful that God may call them to be a missionary for foreign service or a minister of the Gospel. How inconsistent! Did you not when you surrendered your sinful life to him, also surrender your best self? You should have allowed him to become Lord of all your life. Because of this timidity, this fearfulness of God's will, it is necessary to make great appeals for recruits, and comrades and servants for the work of the Kingdom.

This should not be so. In the words of Henry Drummond, "There is no grander possession for any Christian life than the transparently simple mechanism of a sincere obeying heart. And if we could keep the machinery clear, there would be lives in thousands doing Gods' will on earth even as it is done in heaven."

Louisville, Ohio.

SEND ALL MONEY FOR
General Home, Kentucky and
Foreign Missions to

MISSIONS

WILLIAM A. GEARHART
General Missionary Secretary
906 American Bldg., Dayton, O.

Importance of the "White Gift" to the Kentucky Mission Field

Retrospective

About seven years ago a church building was contemplated at Krypton, Kentucky, and one of our dear brethren suggested that funds might be raised at Christmas time through "White Gift" offerings for this proposition, and surely a building was needed badly. The idea was promptly carried out. Money was raised and the building was erected in due time where regular services have been conducted these years. Ever since that time the National Sunday School Association has been assisting in support of the Kentucky work. One Thousand Dollars of the White Gift money has been turned over to the Home Mission Board yearly for the Kentucky fund. Had it not been for this generous contribution our Kentucky Missions would never have been extended as much as they have been.

It would be unwise no doubt to use much space in our church paper to call our attention to things that have transpired in our Kentucky mission field during the sixteen years that our people have so generously supported the work at Lost Creek and Krypton. We wish however, to state that about the best way to learn what has been accomplished, is to visit with some of these mountaineers and talk to them personally as a number of us have been privileged to do. Expressions such as the following can be heard from their lips: "We would not think of remaining here if it were not for the benefits we derive from our mission station." "We would not feel safe without the mission." "The people are so different since Christianity has been brought to us, etc. We may not feel satisfied with the accomplishments of the past, but

surely we must admit that the work and sacrifice of the workers was not in vain and that the Lord has wonderfuly blessed the people of that field under the leadership of Elder and Mrs. Geo. E. Drushal, Elder and Mrs. Jas. S. Cook, Elder and Mrs. Jas. A. Rempel and their helpers White Gifts have helped to make this great work possible. May we assume the attitude of the apostle Paul when he said, "Forgetting the things which are behind, etc." and let us for a moment see what is being done at the present time.

Introspective

Brother Orion E. Bowman, chairman of our Kentucky Committee, has given recently through this paper some of the things that are being accomplished at the present time, therefore we shall be brief. The financial support from the mountaineers is much better than it has been in the past, and we hope the grace of freely giving of their substance (though it may be small as it surely must be in many homes) will continue to grow. It is an indication that people are more deeply interested if they are more willing to contribute to the support of any work.

Elder L. D. Bowman, who recently conducted evangelistic campaigns at both places, gave us encouraging reports through our church papers. Many souls were regenerated and added to the Lord's army.

This is, after all, to my mind, the most important part of the missionary's duty, to teach and preach the Gospel of Jesus Christ first, and social work, reform work, secular education, etc., should be secondary, and will naturally follow where the true Gospel seed is first sown. Jesus said, "Seek ye first the Kingdom of God and his righteousness and all these things shall be added unto you." Oh, that all of us might be more willing to obey our Master's injunction. We trust that our missionaries everywhere, will not neglect to teach the Bible even though they may be handicapped in their other educational work. At Lost Creek we are fortunate in having the grades taught in our own building under the supervision of Brother Drushal. This gives our missionaries the wonderful opportunity of inculcating the Bible truths into the minds and hearts of the students under instruction.

Prospective

Since the people of Lost Creek and Krypton are growing in the grace of giving more liberally for the support of the mission work which is of such vital concern to them; we are looking forward to the time when our Kentucky stations at Lost Creek and Krypton will be more nearly self-supporting, which condition, if obtained, will open the way for the use of more of our mission funds for other worthy points in the mountains of Kentucky, the great Northwest and many other localities where the Gospel seed has not been sown and where the people are calling for help. The budget for our mission field in Kentucky is slightly larger this year than it ever has been due to the increase in salary paid to our missionaries. If the Thanksgiving offering reaches the goal of "One Dollar per member," and if the National Sunday School Association contributes one thousand dollars again this year from the White Gift offerings, we shall be able to meet the budget for

Home Missions and have a little surplus for extension work.

We hope arrangements can be made at Krypton to hold three months subscription school at the close of the regular school term which is abolt the holidays. This has been done in past years and according to statements from Brethren Cook and Bempel, it is very fruitful way to train the young lives under Christian influences. We are wondering if there is a consecrated teacher in our brotherhood who would be willing to make the sacrifice to go to Krypton for the months of January, February and March, 1921, and teach these rugged and earnest mountaineers, if a sufficient number of pupils can be enrolled to provide for the support of the teacher.

About the first thing the Krypton folks would want to know before pledging support, would be, Will the teacher be efficient and aggressive? If there is a desire for the three months 'tuition school, and the proper arrangements can be made, announcement will be made through the Evangelist. In the meantime let us pray and boost for a splendid White Gift Offering.

WILLIAM A. GEARHART,
General Missionary Secretary.

NEWS FROM THE FIELD

NAPPANEE, INDIANA

Present! Our quarterly report being due, I will endeavor to relate some of our doings with a prayer and hope that they might help in the general good. National and district conferences have both come and gone since last we wrote and they were both enjoyed to the full by pastor and as many of the people as could attend both of them. The national conference found quite one hundred Nappanee folks on the job, and the district conference, although at the southern end of the district, was attended by an even dozen Nappaneeites, the largest delegation from any one church. The reason I mention this is because I feel such attendance is what conduces to the better development of a church, and gives one a church well informed as I can assure you the Nappanee church is. One week after general conference, Miss Aboud came with us for a two weeks' meeting. The weather was ideal and the largest crowd that ever attended meetings in this church were on hand to greet the sister. We simply could not accommodate all who tried to get in the church. On several evenings scores were turned away, or they sat in the autos lined around the church in effort to hear the messages. Miss Aboud delivered the goods and regaled the people with her expositions of the Word. Her work on themes with a strictly oriental setting and flavor was most excellent. We had made no special preparation Miss Aboud came here to fill time that had been cancelled elsewhere. And two weeks is only enough time to get started, so we cannot report any additions to the work as a result of the meeting, but we do know that there was seed sown that will produce fruit in season. Miss Aboud has a place to fill among

us and our prayer is that she might be used to the glory of God and the salvation of souls as well as the instruction of others.

Following the close of the meetings we held our annual business meeting. According to the reports of the officers we went through one of the most prosperous years in the history of the church. If money is any index in church work, and I feel that it is, then we surely made good the past year. With the largest budget in the history of the church we cleaned it up and went several hundreds of dollars to the good. We have a large band of tithers here and that helps wonderfully. Then our feeling is that the church has prospered spiritually, without which all would be failure. The services of the church and auxiliaries are well attended and keen interest is shown in the work all through. The pastor is kept quite busy preaching twice each Sabbath, teaching the Men's Bible class, leading the Teacher Training class, acting as Scoutmaster for a troop of wiry youngsters, looking after the prayer meeting and choir rehearsals besides other odds and ends of church and community work that demand time and effort. But so long as people appreciate one's efforts and try to see some good in you and what you are trying to do, a fellow feels like keeping the tugs stretched tight even to the breaking point. I must say that we have a goodly body of regular stand-bys who are the very salt of the work. I wish that some others who have united with the church might sense the duty they owe to God and themselves, what a church this church would be if they too were loyal in all things!

At this writing we are engaged in our revival meetings. The first week of the meet-

ings is being conducted by Mr. and Mrs. J. M. Harris of Chicago. They are conducting a prophetic and victorious life conference after which the pastor will continue with the meetings for two or three weeks. The first day of the meetings large crowds greeted the speakers and we feel that we are in for a real revival of religion among our folks and the community. Pray for us.

Our church has made all the goals set and is already well paid up on the obligations of the present church year. The people seem to have a mind to work as did those who assisted Nehemiah of old, and so we work together, my Lord, my people and I. The Sunday school recently lifted an offering toward the installation of an inverted lighting system in the church. They made their goal and ere this is published we will very likely be using the new system. With all our other obligations we have given the Muncie church about five hundred dollars toward its new building. We do not enumerate these things boastfully, but it is with a sense of pride that the people of the Nappanee church can go over their last year's attainments, knowing that the records tell of victories won and progress made.

We are praying for a successful year in evangelism throughout the brotherhood this year, and we again solicit an interest in your prayers that our humble efforts may be honored of God to the salvation of some. Let us tell the old, old story with renewed zeal. As Brother Harris puts it, "If it's new it isn't true, and if it's true it isnt' new." So let us concern ourselves with the truth which is as old as the hills. Our man-made systems of thought have collapsed, so back to God and his Word for the world's redemption.

E. L. MILLER.

FROM MAPLE GROVE, KANSAS

In accordance with the announcement of J. G. Dodds, pastor of the Maple Grove church, Norton county, Kansas, that he would hold a revival in the church, commencing October 17th to continue a couple weeks, I availed myself of the pleasure of attending those meetings most of the time and listening to the sermons which were well prepared and suited for the occasion. Yet owing to certain conditions in the community the results were not all we could wish for. Here we have two churches within less than two miles of each other, doctrinaly the same, that ought to be one. It seems to me they might be, if it were not for a decision of the Annual Meeting of the Church of the Brethren now on record, to the effect that they do not want any fraternal relations with the Brethren church. Christ says, "He that doeth the will of my Father which is in heaven the same is my brother and sister". (See Matthew 12:49, 50). It seems a little hard to reconcile or harmonize such a decision with the Gospel as sighted.

The meetings were good in general and a number worked in harmony from both churches. But it could easily be noted that the divided condition in the community and the neighborhood was not conducive to the best interests of the meeting and made it impossible to do the best for the people in the church and the neighborhood. It is not strange that Jesus so earnestly prayed that his people might be one as he and the Father are one. It is bad to be doctrinally divided, but worse to protest against union when we are doctrinally united. God help us to be united and be one.

C. FORNEY.

BURLINGTON AND DARWIN BRETHREN CHURCHES

We are very glad to again let the brotherhood know of some of the victories and some of the defeats that have befallen us in our work at Burlington and Darwin.

Darwin

We began a meeting at this church following the National Conference and then Brother L. A. Myers of Sidney came and for two weeks preached some very fine sermons which showed much study and earnest effort had been put forth to make them both convincing and plain. Many good things were accomplished in this meeting. While no visible results by way of immediate accessions were accomplished yet in the future we are sure some men and women are going to decide because of the fine spirit and presentation of the truth by Brother Meyers. We held our communion service on the evening of November 4th, a fair representation of the church being present. A fine spirit of fellowship was experienced, yet no visiting brethren were with us.

Burlington

We have just closed our campaign here under the leadership of Brother B. T. Burnworth who was with us for three weeks. We were made to feel that this was one of the very best meetings Burlington has had for a number of years. The position of our church was set forth positively and distinctly and evidence was presented which caused people to

say like men of old, "We have never seen it on this wise."

Of course one thing happened where ever a "Campbellite Church" is operating; they yell "Christian" like a "Wapoo Indian" and act like a bunch of heathen. Well, Brother Burnworth gave them evidence of the Trinity and they were stirred to be contemptible and spoiled our arrangement with the school, by interfering with the "High School night" by putting on a special program of outside talent, advertising that they would have on exhibition a full-fledged converted anarchist right from Russia, and urged the school to attend in a body the same. Thus, Brother Burnworth's plan to speak to the high school was greatly interfered with and no one is to blame except the poor "Old Devil."

Our meeting progressed nevertheless and a number of splendid people accepted Christ and others are deciding. Of course the nearer we came to election time, the more folks had their attention divided. Yet those things did not interfere as much as the fact that some of our forces were in the hospital at Indianapolis and others were there in attendance at their bedsides. Our Brother W. Polk, who is always very faithful with his family was at the hospital, and Brother and Sister Bock's daughter (Sister Milburn was at the hospital undergoing a very serious operation and those were days of anxious waiting for both these splendid families and their friends.) This of course caused a division of interest. Thank God, he blessed them all and the very latest news is that all are getting along splendidly.

Both Brethren Myers and Burnworth made many friends and many took these men into their confidence because they proved such splendid Christian gentlemen and these two brethren seemed to enjoy the hospitality of our open-hearted folks.

When you brethren read this, we will be with our Brother Myers at College Corner in a short campaign. Pray for us and our work that we may be faithful.

W. T. LYTLE,

Burlington, Indiana.

REVIVAL MEETING UNDER THE AUSPICES OF THE EVANGELISTIC AND BIBLE STUDY LEAGUE

Third Brethren church of Philadelphia, Pa.

I received a telegram from Brother Cassel while at Buckeye City, Ohio, to hold this meeting. In order to comply with this request I had to shift the Buena Vista, Virginia meeting three weeks ahead. As I am away from home all the time this was a great treat for me to hold a meeting in the city where I could be home every night.

Several good members of the church said that they pitied me as the field had been so well worked that little reaping could be done. Brother Bell held them a splendid meeting under the Evangelistic League about six months before.

The Lord blessed us beyond our expectation but it was because of the live Sunday school.

The first Sunday I was there they had in the Sunday school 178 which packed in the little church beyond measure.

This wonderful aggressive work is run

wholly along spiritual lines. They do nothing questionable in the Sunday school, or in any of the church work. The high spiritual standard that Brother Braker and Brother Cassel have held up there from the inception of that work is the secret of their success.

I have seen in many churches the Holy Ghost unseated and by worldliness they would build up a mushroom work that would go all to pieces as quickly as built or become such an iceburg that you could skate in it.

What we need today is the old time Gospel preached in the demonstration and power of the Holy Ghost, backed by a pure Godly life. If this is done, the Brethren church will double in influence, power and numbers in a few years.

I am daily praying for a deeper work of grace in my own heart, for our pastors, churches, mission boards, college and publishing house, that we may let the Holy Ghost have the right of way, that he may melt us together that the whole world may hear and learn of a "Whole Gospel."

May the Lord awaken such a spirit of evangelism that may not only stir the church to save our dying churches but reach out and plant a whole gospel in every large city in the land, and then reach out to the country, until we will complete the "Bride" and bring back the coming King.

We had thirty-one confessions at the Third church, most of them from the Sunday school. They should have at once a new church building, as their little building is inadequate for their needs. I surely have a warm heart for the Third church and if they keep along the present lines of work I believe they will become a great and strong body. I am praying that the Lord will send them the money to build, this coming summer, as it is a prospective work.

I am now in the midst of the greatest revival I have had for years, but will report after I am through here.

I am looking for wife to come tomorrow. She will be with me here a few days till I close at Buena Vista, and then she will go to Rockingham and visit her old home and I will go to Hagerstown, Maryland, for a two weeks' campaign. She may come by there a day or two on her return trip.

Pray earnestly that the Lord may greatly bless me in the evangelistic field.

ISAAC D. BOWMAN,

1942 S. 17th St. Philadelphia, Pennsylvania.

P. S.—Sister Vianna Detwiler's mother died very suddenly. She has been a mother to me.

—I. D. B.

WASHINGTON C. H., OHIO

Evangelist Readers, Greetings:

Brother Martin Shively of the College will begin a meeting here at Fairview, Washington C. H., Ohio, Sunday, November the 28th. We would be pleased to have our near neighbors visit with us.

Your brethren at Dayton and Columbus could give us considerable help by coming over for a service or two. If you come, let us know.

The church here is moving along in the usual way and while we are not doing wonderful things, nevertheless we are going forward. We are well organized on the Bicentenary Movement with seven local secretaries. We recently submitted a letter to the head of this movement setting forth our position, etc., but I suppose he was too busy to give us the usual recognition.

We are going to observe all special days as we have in the past and we are planning to go over the top for Thanksgiving. We are going to see each member and acquaint him with the responsibility of his share of this offering. We are mailing fifty letters today to those who are "afar off" and hope to have a large ingathering. God pity the man or woman who tries to get through this world and into the great heaven beyond without meeting these urgent calls. We need more men and women whose first consideration is the church (Matthew 10:37) and whose chiefest desire is to see the various interests of the church move forward.

We need a return to the good old faith of our fathers. We need to have a new vision, a vision that will lift us out of this 20th century rut and replant our feet on the soil of the great Master builder. I pray God for a religion—or Christian experience—which will manifest itself in acts rather than words. I believe the new Bicentenary Movement is the most forward step the church has taken since Holsinger proclaimed the blessing of a united effort upon the parts of those who believed in freedom. And the church should not fail to assume her full share of responsibility in this movement. If we do no more than get the church on her knees we will have done a great service.

If you will permit I would like to say a word regarding Brother Shively's "chicken plea." I was over the ground with Brother Shively at conference time and was very much impressed with his arrangements for his chicken farm. We tried to approach this impression in a material way and if the brethren in Ohio, as well as other churches—for Ashland belongs to all the churches—will get a vision and send along ten or twenty dollars, Shively's chicken farm will become a reality. Come on folks, let us put one thousand hens in the college farm.

LYMAN B. WILKINS, Pastor.

UNIONTOWN, PENNSYLVANIA, REVIVAL

On October 10th, Brother W. S. Bell came to conduct the revival services for the church at this place. It was no new combination when he and the writer yoked up for this campaign, for we had worked together for a like purpose upon four previous occasions.

Brother Bell came to us with the same gospel which he always preaches, and which the devil doesn't like one bit better now than he ever did. And of course the devil got busy, and Hallowe'en was celebrated for two weeks of the three through which the meeting continued. And of course we had to elect a president this fall and men were not sure just which candidate it were better to support, so they had to hear the League of Nations discussed—and the Republicans "cuss" the Democrats and vice versa. And then just the

sinful desires and inclinations of the human heart prompted the unconverted to stay away, "lest they should hear with their ears, and understand with their hearts, and be converted." At no time were the crowds large, but despite that fact the interest was good and God was not left without witness to the power of the Gospel. Eleven made the good confession, of which ten were baptized and received into membership—one being hindered by parental influence. Two others were received by relation, making the total of accessions twelve. This may seem small for a meeting of that duration, but personally I consider it a real success without specifying reasons.

Brother Bell made his home with the pastor and we renewed old friendships and talked over the work and needs and future of our beloved fraternity, as we sensed them. Not always did we agree, but we are still brethren and willing to work and sacrifice for the church of our choice. Brother Bell left Uniontown for a short visit among old friends at Johnstown, and to present the claims of the Evangelistic and Bible Study League, and then on to Goshen, Indiana, for a campaign for souls. With him goes the good will and prayers of the Uniontown brethren that he may be used of God for his glory among the brethren there.

The semi-annual communion services of the congregation were held on Monday evening, December 1, with the pastor conducting the service and seventy souls around the tables. The service was most enjoyable, a number assuring the pastor of their personal enjoyment of the occasion.

We are now planning for the Christmas services of the Sunday school, expecting to put on a Cantata or stated programme. The interest in the work of the church is good and the attendance at the services is all that we expect at present. But we are hoping for better things and ask an interest in the prayers of the brotherhood. On November 11, Miss Mae Smith was with us for an evening gathering of the women, and spoke to a goodly assemblage of the sisters of the church. The women learned some things about the work of the W. M. S. and received some inspiration to continued and larger efforts.

Uniontown faces the same problems that the brethren everywhere are "up against," and has but one solution for any and all of the ills to which humanity is heir, and that is the glorious Gospel of the Son of God. In that we believe, that we preach, by that men can be saved, and without that this old world is lost. God help us to be true to "the faith once delivered to the saints."

DYOLL BELOTE.

MINUTES OF PENNSYLVANIA CONFERENCE

(Continued from issue of November 17).

A motion carried that the chair appoint a committee of three to confer with members of the Mission Board present and to report back to this conference a policy concerning the work of the board for the coming year. The chair appointed on this committee, Brethren Henry Wise, J. F. Watson, A. J. McClain, H. C. Cassel, and W. C. Benshoff.

Brother H. F. E. O'Neill presented the fol-

lowing report of the Board of Benevolences. The report was accepted and is as follows:

Report of Board of Benevolence
Number of churches—43.
Churches contributing—in 1919, 24; 1920, 20.
Percentage of churches contributing,—1919, 55 5-6; 1920, 46½.
Percentage of churches not contributing,— 1919, 44⅙; 1920, 53½.
Churches increase this year, 11. Progressing.
Churches decrease this year, 3.
Same as last year, 1. Lukewarm.
Gave last year and not this year 8 Backsliders.
Loss of 4 churches.
Gave this year and not last, 4 Grown in grace and liberality.
This shows a loss of four churches this year.
Total amount given by churches and Sunday schools in 1919, $538.66.
Number of individuals giving in 1919, 1; amount, $25.00.
District total, 1919—$563.66.
Churches, Sunday schools and Christian Endeavor giving in 1920—$751.47.
Individuals giving in 1920, 5; amount—$17.50.
District total, 1920—$768.97.
Total increase over 1919, $205.31 or 36%+.
Total members in Pennsylvania Districts, 4,214.
Raised per capita to 50c.
Raised beneficiaries' salaries to $20.00 per month.

H. F. E. O'NEILL.

Wednesday Afternoon

Christian Endeavor Session

At this session President Eleanor Wilcox of the District Christian Endeavor Society presided, and conducted the devotions. After prayer by Miss Wilcox, two hymns were sung and five earnest short prayers were offered. John 15 was read by the president.

A solo was sung by Miss Herb.

Mrs. Carl Gross, C. E. Field Secretary reported her work for the year. She plead for a more hearty response to correspondence sent out to the societies and emphasized the importance of training, organization and prayer.

Rev. E. A. Rowsey addressed the conference on "Christian Endeavor Handicaps." Three handicaps were pointed out—uninteresting meetings, only a few present, and only a few taking part. We hope to see the address in full in the Evangelist.

Rev. H. H. Wolford spoke on the "Program of the Year—Bicentenary Program." We hope to see this clear outline of the goals under seven heads in the columns of the Evangelist.

Rev. A. J. McClain spoke on C. E. work.

Miss Margaret Rau, Superintendent of Pittsburgh Juniors, presented the Juniors of the Pittsburgh church and spoke briefly of their work.

Immediately following the C. E. session, the work of the W. M. S. was ably presented in an earnest address by Miss Mae Smith, Field Secretary of the W. M. S.

At the close of this session one item of conference business was acted upon. The conference accepted the following report of the committee appointed to confer with members of the District Mission Board.

1. That Conference recommend to the Mission Board the policy of concentration.

2. That Conference recommend the immediate application of this policy on the following mission points—Armstrong county, Third church, Philadelphia, and Third church, Johnstown.

3. That conference recommend that the Mission Board secure the active co-operation of the Evangelistic and Bible Study League for evangelistic meetings in other points, as authorized by the board.

4. That conference recommend that the Mission Board continues its present policy in other points as nearly as possible.

W. C. BENSHOFF,
ALVA J. McCLAIN,
HENRY WISE,
H. C. CASSEL,
J. FREMONT WATSON,
Committee.

The afternoon session was closed with the benediction.

Wednesday Evening
Bicentenary Movement Session

After spirited song service the devotions were conducted by Brother H. C. Cassel, who read portions of Romans 11 and 12 and led in prayer. A solo by Mrs. Wm. Smith was enjoyed by all.

The entire evening was given to the consideration of the seven goals of the Bicentenary Movement.

Elder M. A. Witter addressed conference on "The Spiritual Life."

Elder H. H. Wolford spoke of "Education—College and Seminary, and Religious Education."

Elder W. C. Benshoff spoke on "Stewardship of Life and of Possessions."

Elder L. G. Wood spoke on "Evangelism."

Elder A. J. McClain spoke on "Missions and Extension."

Elder J. F. Watson spoke on "Publication Interests."

Brother H. F. E. O'Neill spoke on "Benevolences."

This was a session of real inspiration and was fruitful in creating an earnest purpose to make the Brethren Bicentenary Movement a success in this district and in setting clearly before the conference to goals to be attained.

Brother S. R. Smouse sang, "How Lovely Are Thy Dwellings."

An offering of $13.43 was taken and the session closed with hymn and benediction.

Thursday Morning
Business Session

The devotional period was conducted by Elder Jos. L. Gingrich. After spirited congregational singing voluntary prayer was offered by many of the delegates. Brother Gingrich read Matthew 7:1-12 and gave a helpful message, inspiring to helpfulness and recognition of others.

The minutes of former sessions were read and approved.

The Credential Committee made its final report of 53 lay credentials and 33 ministerial credentials, a total of 86 credentials presented and approved. The report was accepted and the committee dismissed with thanks.

The responsibility of the Pennsylvania District touching the Winona Tabernacle fund was clearly explained by Elder Dyoll Belote. Churches of the district should send their contributions to this fund to Elder Dyoll Belote, 61 Highland Ave., Uniontown, Pa.

The Statistical Report of the District was made by Elder M. A. Witter. The report follows:

Report of Pennsylvania District Statistician Of the Brethren Churches for 1919, 1920

	1919	1920
Number of churches listed,	43	41
Number of churches reporting,	27	33
Number of churches failing to report	16	8
Churches owned in fee simple,	24	34
Union houses owned,	1	1-4
Halls and school houses used,	0	1
Parsonages owned,	7	12
Churches owning other property,	3	7
Preaching services:		
Twice weekly,	13	13
Once weekly,	1	3
Twice bi-weekly,	2	2
Once bi-weekly,	10	11
Six times each month,		2

Membership

Total membership of churches reporting	2875	4214
Male members,	1193	1748
Female members,	1680	2466
Revivals held,	16	22
Accessions in revivals,	145	184
Accessions at regular services,	60	84
Accessions by letter,	34	38
Accessions by relation,	5	21
Accessions by baptism,	167	228
Total accessions 1920,	200	308
Lost by death, letter, etc.,	142	103
Net gain in churches reporting,	34	217

Prayer Meetings

Churches having prayer meetings,	15	19
Total attendance,	351	426
Average attendance, prayer meetings,	23	23+

Financial Values

Received from the Value of church houses, lots and fixtures $170,815.75 $238,378.74

Interest in Union Houses,	500.00	150.00
Value of parsonages,	21,800.00	46,800.00
Value other property,	31,200.00	27,275.00

Total valuations, $233,815.74 $323,103.74

Financial Receipts

Amount raised by the churches,	$ 36,951.69	$ 57,471.90
Received by church from Sunday school	1,677.25	13685.62
W. M. S.,	504.06	2,951.67
Received from the C. E. Societies,	663.34	55.27

Total receipts from all sources, ... $ 39,796.34 $ 63,347.49

Financial Disbursements

Paid for Pastor's Salaries,	$ 17,610.60	$ 24,258.52
Paid for Evangelistic Services,	2,596.76	2,453.43
For Current Expenses,	13,713.59	34,330.48
For District Missions,	1,342.12	1,373.15
For National Home Missions,	1,251.39	1,676.78
For Foreign Missions,	1,233.74	2,495.70
For Miscellaneous Benevolences,	4,788.63	3,244.98

Total paid by church, $ 35,631.40 $ 67,644.20

Miscellaneous

Number of Deacons,	67	98
Number of Deaconesses,	27	33
Number of Elders,	44	49
Number of Evangelist Subscribers,	490	700

Note.—There are eight churches, Aleppo, Highland, McAllisterville, Quiet Dell, Ridgely, Md., Sugar Grove, Vandergrift and Windber, from which no report was received but in those cases such information as was available from other sources has been included in the report making the totals as nearly accurate as is possible without the missing reports. It is believed that the report of membership and of financial values are fairly accurate for the district. The receipts and expenditures are too low as given in the report as no information is available from a number of the churches not reporting.

Respectfully submitted,
M. A. WITTER, Statistician.

The following District Christian Endeavor Society officers were elected:

Miss Eleanor Wilcox, President.

Carl Gross, Vice-President.

Miss Agnes Simpson, Secretary-Treasurer.

Mrs. Carl Gross, Field Secretary (West).

Elder E. E. Fehnel, Field Secretary (East).

Elder W. C. Benshoff was elected District Director of the Brethren Bicentenary Movement.

Brethren Ira S. Wilcox and B. F. Bole were elected delegates at large from the Pennsylvania District to General Conference.

By motion the Conference officers were empowered to issue eight additional credentials to General Conference to members of this District present at the General Conference but not representing any congregation as delegates.

The Womans Missionary Society reported the election of the following District officers:

Miss E. Mae Minnich, President.

Mrs. Jos. L. Gingrich, Vice President.

Mrs. H. M. Harley, Secretary-Treasurer.

A motion was passed that the District Mission Board be constituted a committee to cooperate with the Evangelistic and Bible Study League in its work in this district.

The following Conference Officers were elected:

Elder W. C. Benshoff, Moderator.

Brother H. F. E. O'Neill, Vice-Moderator.

Elder Jos. L. Gingrich, Secretary.

Elder E. E. Fehnel, Treasurer.

Elder M. A. Witter, Statistician.

Elder J. Fremont Watson was nominated for Trustee of Ashland College and Elder L. G. Smith was named as alternate.

Elders W. S. Baker and Dyoll Belote were elected members of the District Conference Executive Committee.

A motion was carried that a Conference Membership Committee for next conference be appointed. The Moderator named George H. Jones, L. G. Wood, and H. C. Cassel.

A motion prevailed that a committee be appointed to arrange a satisfactory basis of representation of churches and auxiliaries at District Conference and of conference fees and that they be asked to report at next District Conference. The moderator appointed J. Fremont Watson, Dyoll Belote, and Jos. L. Gingrich.

This session was closed by benediction by Elder Henry Wise.

Thursday Afternoon, 1:30 P. M.

A short devotional session with but one item of business filled the half hour of this session. "Jesus Included Me" was sung. Brother H. C. Cassel brought a helpful message which we hope to see in the Evangelist and offered fervent prayer.

Conference received an invitation by telegram to meet for the 1921 Conference in the First church, Philadelphia. The invitation was accepted by unanimous vote of conference.

Conference then adjourned and the afternoon was spent by the delegates in an automobile trip of about 24 miles seeing the notable points of interest in the city, a delightful evidence of the hospitality of the Pittsburgh congregation.

Thursday Evening Session, 7:30 P. M.

This session was opened by singing "O My Soul Bless Thou Jehovah." Elder J. I. Hall led the devotions, three short prayers were made by Brethren Cassel, Watson and Witter. Scripture was read by Brother Hall with comment appropriate to last session of conference. "Be a Hero" was sung.

The Moderator introduced the representative of Ashland College, Elder H. H. Wolford, who spoke with optimism of the work and the future of Ashland College. A strong plea for the loyal support of the seminary was made No institution can do effective work without proper equipment. A new Library building is now assured. This will mean much to the work of the seminary. There is great need for deep spiritual and sacrificial service in the support of this essential work.

"Just When I Need Him Most" was sung. An offering of $16.93 was taken.

The Committee on Resolutions made the following report which was accepted:

Resolutions

Realizing that the membership of the Brethren churches of the Pennsylvania District have since we last met in conference session enjoyed the blessings of the Heavenly Father and that our work has been fruitful and has resulted in much good to the glory and praise of the great Leader, the Lord Jesus Christ,

Be it resolved: That we feel deeply indebted to God, the Father, for his riches in grace through Jesus Christ, and that we render him most profound and heartfelt thanks and that we recognize the necessity of the leadership of the Holy Spirit in all the activities of the church,

Be it resolved: That most hearty thanks be extended to the pastor, membership and friends of the Pittsburgh church for their part in making this conference a source of blessing to all of us by considering so well our comfort and giving gracious reception into their homes.

That we tender to the officers of this conference our sincere thanks for the faithful and impartial manner in which they have discharged their duties.

That we recognize the great loss to this conference and the church at large in the death of Brethren Trout and Byers and that we express our appreciation of their splendid eladership and our Christian sympathy and love to their families and that the secretary of this conference be instructed to convey the same to their families.

That we call upon our churches, pastors and various auxiliaries to co-operate with the Bicentenary Committee (in every way possible) looking toward the accomplishment of all the goals of the Bicentenary Movement.

That we call the attention of Christian womanhood to the opportunity which is now theirs in the exercise of suffrage for the protection of the home and nation.

That we extend our appreciation to those who filled their regular places on the program, to those who rendered service in song, to our delight and worship, and to Brethren Teeter, Wolford, Rowsey, and Miss Mae Smith who were present and lent help and enthusiasm to the conference.

That we urge upon all of the men of the church the giving of the tithe in the exercise of Christian stewardship and a revival of the Bible study and the family altar as the best way to increase the spiritual life and usefulness of the church.

W. C. BENSHOFF,
J. F. WATSON,
E. E. ROBERTS,
Committee.

The Minutes of the sessions of this day were read and approved.

The Treasurer, E. E. Fehnel, made his final report which was accepted. The report follows:

Conference Treasurer's Report

Balance on hand from last year,	.....$ 64.92
Interest,	.... 1.95
	$ 66.87

Receipts

Income from credentials,	...........$ 57.00
Offering, October 4,	.... 15.59
Offering October 5,	.... 18.43
Offering October 6,	.... 29.44
Offering October 7,	.... 16.93
Total received at conference,	...$137.39
Total receipts,	............$204.26

Expenditures

1. Publishing Co.,	............$ 3.50
R. R. Teeter's carfare,	.... 8.00
	$ 11.50
2. Moderators expenses,	............$ 2.18
3. M. A. Witter, Sec., Salary,	.....$ 5.00
Statistician,	.... 5.00
Postage and Stationery,	.... 3.55
Total,	.........................$ 13.55
4. Printing credentials and cards,	...$ 4.75
5. H. H. Wolford's Expenses,	.... 9.50
6. Stationery and Printing for S. S.,	.. 4.75
7. L. G. Smith expense to meeting of	

Ashland College Trustees, ... 34.45

Total expenses ....$ 80.64

Balance in Treasury, Oct. 7, 1920, ...$123.58
E. E. FEHNEL, Treasurer.

At this time a selection was sung by the quartet. The congregation sang, ''Leaning on the Everlasting Arm.''

The closing message of the conference was brought in the stirring sermon of Elder Dyoll Belote on ''The Control of Religion.'' He took for his text, Nehemiah 5:15—''But so did not I, because of the fear of God.'' This sermon will be published in the Evangelist.

The last hymn of the session was ''I Would Be Like Jesus.'' Moderator H. M. Harley offered the closing prayer and benediction.

M. A. WITTER, Secretary.

Business Manager's Corner

THE HONOR ROLL AGAIN

After an absence of several weeks we are glad that the Evangelist Honor Roll has an opportunity to appear once more in the columns of the Evangelist.

This time it is Waynesboro, Pennsylvania, that wins out and is honored by a place among the other Honor Roll churches of the brotherhood. We know the pastor, Marcus A. Witter, has worked strenuously for several months to get this feat accomplished, but it was a worthy achievement. It has been but a short time since the Waynesboro church ceased to be a mission point and became a self-supporting church. But it is going at the work in a systematic way, and realizes the importance of keeping the entire congregation informed along all Brethren lines, and with the budget system of finance it· has placed the Evangelist in ONE · HUNDRED percent of the families of the church, making in all eighty-six subscriptions. This is a larger list than many of the older churches with a larger total membership have included in their budgets.

We are also glad to report that the only Brethren church in the state of Wisconsin has again asked to be counted among the Honor Roll churches. This is the little band at Eau Claire, Wisconsin, under the leadership of Brother J. A. Baker. This is the second year for Eau Claire.

The Special Fund

It is with pleasure that we report the constant growth of the fund to meet the excessive cost paper stock. Since our report last week the following offerings have been received:

Brethren church, Ankenytown, Ohio, $10.00; Anna A. Ruble, $2.75; Sarah Droltke, $5.00; Brethren church, Campbell, Michigan, $10.00; W. O. Benshop, $1.00; Brethren church, Sergeantsville, New Jersey, $7.75; Nancy Haines, $2.00; Third Brethren church, Johnstown, Pennsylvania, $17.76; Brethren church, Mexico, Indiana, $17.00; Brethren church, Roann, Indiana, $3.40; Brethren church, Oakville, Indiana, $12.00; Brethren church, Roanoke, Virginia, $54.58.·

For all these we are thankful, and we trust the good work may continue until every church in the brotherhood has had a part in it.

R. R. TEETER,
Business Manager.·

Volume XLII
Number 47

December 8
1920

The BRETHREN EVANGELIST

-ONE·IS·YOUR·MASTER·AND·ALL·YE·ARE·BRETHREN-

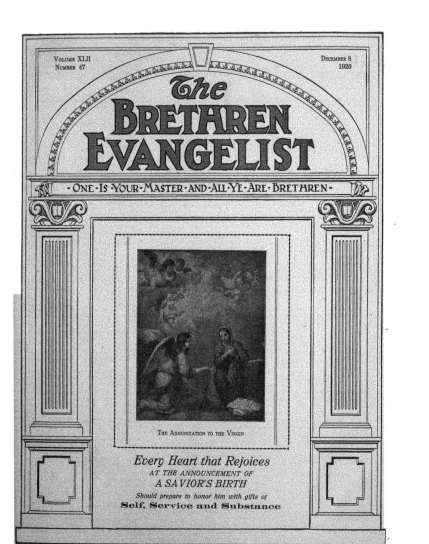

The Annunciation to the Virgin

Every Heart that Rejoices
AT THE ANNOUNCEMENT OF
A SAVIOR'S BIRTH
Should prepare to honor him with gifts of
Self, Service and Substance

Published every Wednesday at Ashland, Ohio. All matter for publication must reach the Editor not later than Friday noon of the preceding week.

George S. Baer, Editor

The
Brethren
Evangelist

When ordering your paper changed give old as well as new address. Subscriptions discontinued at expiration. To avoid missing any numbers renew two weeks in advance.

R. R. Teeter, Business Manager

ASSOCIATE EDITORS: J. Fremont Watson, Louis S. Bauman, A. B. Cover, Alva J. McClain, B. T. Burnworth.

OFFICIAL ORGAN OF THE BRETHREN CHURCH

Subscription price, $2.00 per year, payable in advance.
Entered at the Post Office at Ashland, Ohio, as second-class matter.
Acceptance for mailing at special rate of postage provided for in section 1103, Act of October 3, 1917, authorized September 9, 1918.
Address all matter for publication to Geo. S. Baer, Editor of the Brethren Evangelist, and all business communications to R. R. Teeter, Business Manager, Brethren Publishing Company, Ashland, Ohio. Make all checks payable to the Brethren Publishing Company.

TABLE OF CONTENTS

EDITORIAL

Permanent Church Literature and The Bicentenary Movement

By this time the brotherhood should be quite generally informed concerning the program and aims of our Bicentenary Movement. The program itself has been published in the columns of The Evangelist, and in almost every issue the Executive Secretary, Brother Bame, and his co-workers have a page dealing with some phase of the Movement's proposed activities. The widest publicity is being given to this the greatest task the Brethren church has yet set before herself. And it shall continue to be our policy to co-operate to the fullest extent in the effort to carry the program and its aims down to the last member of the last church of the brotherhood. And if in any way not yet understood by the editor and his associates, the official organ of our beloved fraternity can be made to serve more efficiently these ends, suggestions of such a nature will be warmly received.

But the thing that is being borne home to us more strongly every day is the fact that this program cannot be carried out satisfactorily until we put ourselves seriously to the task of making more than a temporary literature. This program involves an extensive educational policy, to meet the demands of which a periodical devoted mainly to general church and hortatory material is not sufficient. This paper deals with all the various phases of church interests included in this Movement from time to time, but it cannot deal with them in the thorough and detailed manner that might be desired; nor can it bring all the various suggestions, instructions and points of interest connected with the different divisions of the Movement into one convenient and compact volume or number of volumes. To do this we must resort to the making of permanent literature. We must have hosts of pamphlets and inexpensive booklets to put into every home of the brotherhood. These pamphlets should deal with all the essential phases of the program. And only as we have this permanent literature and give it the widest distribution can we hope to realize the extensive program of education which the culmination of this Movement anticipates.

This need of a pamphlet literature dealing with the Movement interests has been sensed by the Bicentenary directors and there are little beginnings toward meeting this need already on foot. The program as outlined is published in a neat little folder and other helps are soon to be forthcoming, so we understand. But the demands are big and urgent. We need pamphlets and booklets dealing with our denominational principles and practices, with the cultivation of the spiritual life, religious education, stewardship of life and substance, personal evangelism and missions at home and abroad. And these needs should be met in the immediate future. Every moment we delay is so much time wasted. The three years scheduled by our Bicentenary Movement should be one solid period of intensive education along the lines essential to church growth and Kingdom building. The first year has already begun its speedy flight, and the incentives and material for such education should be supplied promptly.

The pulpit is a wonderfully educative force and it is being counted upon to wield the full weight of its influence, not merely to enthuse and move to action but to educate and to lay the foundation for greater things. No amount of printed page can take the place of the consecrated and intelligent preacher-teacher. But the printed page will find its way into many homes that are comparatively little influenced by the pulpit, and it will remain in homes and with individuals to give repeated emphasis to the message it carries. Every preacher recognizes the limitations of the spoken word and the great benefit to be derived from having it supplemented with the printed page. Every evangelist recognizes the opportunity of more widely extending his ministry, particularly the instructional type, by carrying along with him for distribution some choice pamphlets and booklets. Every lay worker even of brief experience understands how important it is to have at his command literature of this nature which will give him in small compass the best thought of the brotherhood on the great Bible doctrines and practices of the church together with the scriptures and references setting forth such doctrines. There is scarcely anyone of understanding but will acknowledge the great practical benefit and the possibilities of a far-reaching influence and an abiding ministry of a permanent church literature of an inexpensive character.

But as a church we are greatly impoverished from this standpoint. We were not always so much so as we are now. But for a number of years the ministry of the pamphlet has been neglected until today scarcely any one ever thinks of ordering either denominational or general tracts, and scarcely one good order could be filled if it were received. We have overlooked the importance of this type of the printed page, and with it we have overlooked the importance of teaching our distinctive denominational tenets. Great numbers of our people are losing the consciousness which once was prevalent in all hearts, that we as a church have a definite, positive and distinctive mission to fill and their minds are no longer filled with intelligence concerning the doctrines and practices which are peculiar to us as a denomination, so that they are able to give a reason for the faith that is within them. As a result it matters little in many quarters whether one is a member of the Brethren church or some other church. They have little appreciation of the peculiar function and faith of the Brethren church because they have been taught very little about it. While there are the traditional "seven thousand" who have not bowed the knee to indifference in this matter, yet that there is a notable weakness here is being recognized by members of the ministry both old and young. There is a need of reviving doctrinal instruction of the kind that gives the Brethren church an important and distinctive place in the divine economy. We do not plead for that type of denominational instruction that will make for a bigoted, selfish, combative and unco-operative denomination, but for that kind that exalts the mission of our church and makes for denominational loyalty. This is one of the laudable aims of the Bicentenary Movement.

Aside from the need of a revival of this kind of instruction in the pulpit, it must be revived by means of the tract as well. Oral instruction can never be so thorough as when supplemented by the printed page. It may be that we have not appreciated the ministry of the printed page in permanent form in these later years as we ought, and so have not made sufficient demand for its publication. Perhaps we need a revival of appreciation and demand along this line. It may be that we have not sensed the demand and responded to it as we ought, and so need more aggressiveness in this matter. It may be that those to whom we might have looked for the writing of the needed pamphlets have been so busy preaching or writing for immediate consumption that they have neglected this important service. Whatever be the cause or causes we may assign for our present poverty in this kind of literature, it is certainly evident that something must be done to improve the situation. Perhaps the demands of our Bicentenary will be the immediate incentive for the creation of a more adequate, serviceable permanent literature. Surely our program cannot be carried out in any thorough manner without it. If we had a preacher for every pulpit this would still be true. But in view of the great scarcity of preachers, the demand is all the greater that concisely written and inexpensively printed tracts be made and given the widest and most careful distribution possible. If our Bicentenary Movement should not accomplish all its aims, yet if it succeeds in creating an adequate, usable pamphlet literature, it will have been abundantly worth while.

EDITORIAL REVIEW

Each year should be better than the last. Make this the banner White Gift offering.

Mrs. G. W. Dowell, secretary of the Middle West Conference gives a very compact but interesting report of the proceedings of that district conference; they are found in this issue.

Brother M. E. Horner, the Goshen correspondent, informs us by post card that Brother Bell's meeting was "fine" and that during the last three nights the "house was crowded to the entrance." A report is promised soon.

Brother S. P. Fogle continues his work of preaching the gospel to the scattered and neglected groups of Brethren among the mountains of Virginia. He finds some very appreciative hearts among these people as is evidenced by their gifts from time to time.

Brother W. R. Deeter and his helpmeet are doing a splendid work at Oakville, Indiana. They are enjoying a new parsonage in the construction of which Brother Deeter himself had a hand. The Sunday school and church are growing and they are soon to enjoy an evangelistic effort with Brother A. L. Lynn as evangelist.

From Los Angeles, First church comes another good letter from Brother A. P. Reed, the correspondent of that church. A successful evangelistic meeting has recently been held there with Brother Bauman doing the preaching. With two able preachers possessing the evangelistic zeal that these two brethren, L. S. Bauman and N. W. Jennings, have, yoked together in a single campaign, it would have to be a very difficult field that would not yield results. This church is steadily going forward from victory to victory.

Brother C. W. Yoder writes an encouraging letter concerning the progress of the work at Morrill, Kansas, where Brother A. E. Whitted is pastor. He commends Sister Whitted as a very efficient assistant to her husband in the pastorate.

Miss Charlotte Hillegas requests us to announce "that the African party would appreciate having the Sisterhood girls make bandages which they may take with them. The party expects to sail January 18. Address Sister Hillegas at Berlin, Pennsylvania.

From Brother H. C. Marlin's report in this issue we judge that the Pleasant Hill, Ohio, church is rallying loyally about Brother Lowman, and we feel sure that if such hearty co-operation is continued, God will use Brother Lowman to lead them into a great future as a church.

A new method of saving printing bills comes to our notice. Brother H. M. Harley of Pittsburgh is putting out his four-page weekly bulletin by means of the typewriter and the mimeograph or Rotospeed. It is done very neatly and doubtless serves the purpose just as well as the printed form.

Brother and Sister J. E. Ham who now live in Fort Wayne, Indiana, are calling for the names of Brethren people or those of Brethren leaning, who may live in that city. That is the way the early church in the days of the Apostles grew, and likewise in the early days of Brethrenism, by every member being a missionary wherever they went.

Have you paid anything to the Winona Tabernacle Fund? Has your church? If not, don't fail to read Brother Roscoe's notice in this issue. You may have had ever so good intentions and have simply forgotten it, but if so you are nevertheless causing great embarrassment to those whom we delegated to look after this matter for us. Do it now.

The meeting at Goshen where Brother Bell and Brother McInturff were laboring together resulted in great victory, but Brother Bell, as usual, modestly leaves the particulars to be reported by some local representative of the church. Brother Bell is now "at home" at Sunnyside, Washington, where he will supply the pulpit during Brother Ashman's absence.

Brother H. E. Eppley reports the work at Eaton, Indiana, where he is pastor, in good condition, and also mentions the fact that a "truly great meeting" was held at Clay City. With such a variety of talent as Henderson, Thomas and Eppley would afford brought together into one evangelistic team and consecrated to the one task of lifting up Christ in the community, we do not doubt that the hearts of the people would be stirred greatly.

One of the enthusiastic members of the Manteca, California, congregation writes concerning the progress of that promising little work. It is evident that the spirit of faith and triumph possess these noble people and under the consecrated leadership of Brother Platt they are certain by the grace of God to realize a splendid future. They are appealing for financial aid.

There are always "Doings at Dayton" and Brother W. C. Teeter is a careful reporter of them. They are doing some intensive Bible study under the direction of Brother E. M. Cobb. Their recent communion was unusual in attendance and spirit. We will all look forward with interest to the results of the proposed evangelistic campaign. One could hardly plan a stronger team than will be hitched up together here, in the persons of Brethren Bame, Cobb and Lynn.

A card from Sister Vianna Detwiler, who has been making her home recently with her brother at Los Angeles, and was instructed by her physician to take a long rest, states, "I shall have to make a change. I began Bible teaching too soon and am down again. As soon as arrangements can be made I will leave for Ridgely,—I can't say home any more, my mother having gone." Sister Detwiler's many friends will regret that she has not been able to regain her health and will pray that when she comes back east she may be able to withdraw from all responsibilities until her strength is restored. In behalf of our Evangelist family we extend sincerest sympathy to her and her brothers and sisters in the loss of their mother.

THE BRETHREN BICENTENARY MOVEMENT PAGE

1723 - - - - - - 1923

Dr. Charles A. Bame, Editor

Hundreds Are Being Won For Christ

When this year is over it will mark the greatest effort ever made by our denomination for winning men to Christ. The report of great victories are continually coming to us. The ministry of the church are taking things serious in this campaign and are being backed by a faithful laity. Yes, hundreds have already been won for Christ in this evangelistic drive and we hope to see thousands before next Annual Conference. Just a word to the churches that have

pastors who have evangelistic ability—Give your pastor time off for one, or more meetings this year. We must have the help of some pastors to reach the calls coming for revivals, we do not have evangelists enough to reach all the demands. We are glad that some churches are already doing this. HOW ABOUT YOUR CHURCH? Have you made arrangements for a revival yet? Do not fail Christ and the Program of the church.

Here Is An Additional List of Churches Who Have Had Successful Meetings

CHURCH	PASTOR	EVANGELIST
Limestone	Miss Pence	Miss Aboud
Peru	Carpenter	Miss Aboud
Terra Alta	Flora	Grisso
Flora	Thomas	Coleman & Ronk
Goshen	McInturff	Bell
McLouth	Howell	Coleman & Ronk
Masontown	Gingrich	Gingrich
Zion Hill	Lynn	Lynn
Pleasant Grove	Anderson	Anderson
Fillmore	Beal	Oliver (Union)
La Paz	Grisso	Grisso

Will your church be on this honor Roll? WHY NOT? ? ?

W. S. BELL, Director of Evangelism.

One of the finest things about all the evangelism of the Brethren churches, is that we have so many pastors that are evangelistic. That is also according to the "Bible, the whole Bible and nothing but the Bible." The church was born in a revival, and it was a genuine revival. What a time the Holy Spirit had on his hands when he started that meeting in the upper room on Pentecost. Less than forty days before, one of the chosen ones had turned traitor, one had denied him, and the last one had "forsaken him and fled." Preachers and evangelists, sometimes we refer to the church to which we come as ice-cold or frigid; but I do not think I ever came to such a church as that one. Nothing is too hard for the Lord. No place has people all so completely given over to Satan that nothing could or can be lone. The word can not return to the Lord void. Good must come of it. Numbers may not always be great, but good must come from a faithful presentation of the Word of the Lord. "It is quick and powerful and sharp" and must do its work, All the Power of God is in his word. Therefore, "Preach the word" and you shall have that power behind you. Let me tell you of one of the finest evidences I have ever had of the truthfulness of this. It was only last year. It was in one of the Indiana cities. A sisterhood of girls, most of whom were not Christian had come to a three weeks' meeting and the preacher had set his heart on their salvation and preached and prayed for the victory in their lives. Sometimes they would make a night, but very seldom; a few times, I think they went from the meeting to a dance—their besetting sin. The end of the meeting came and the last invitation was given and the girls had not come. The next night was to be the communion and baptism of all who were ready. The evangelist and the singer, without much concern, singing some duets and solos while the crowd was leisurely gathering amid a downpour of rain. Presently the pastor came ready for baptism and several applicants came forward for the rite. The invitation was further extended and the "bevy" of girls began to come forward, and lo, hallelujah! the last one of them all were there ready for

baptism and communion! Once more, in my last meeting the going had been hard. At the first call 38 came; then we were disappointed many times and they had not come save a few at a time. The victory was not continual as we love to see after the break has come. But in the last meeting, there was a windfall and they came. Boys made the first grand rush; then the girls started and the older folks, foreigners, boozers, cigarette fiends and who not! Once more, hallelujah! So, my fellow-workers, believe the word; preach the word; attempt great things for God; attain great victories with God and for God. You are the greatest salesmen in the world. You have the best article; you have more talking points. Decided gain is guaranteed with your product. Follow the leadership of your Director and leader in his great attempts to gain for the Lord this year, more than we have ever gained and give God the glory.

BAME.

Besieged in Aintab

The Near East Relief is carrying on its beneficient work as the representative of the American people in spite of very great hindrances in various sections of Asia Minor. Aintab, one of the principal points of attack by the Turk Nationalist army, has been under siege since early in March of this year. The French relieved the besieged city twice, but the Turks regained it. They have had Urfa under siege since February 9th, but the Nationalist leaders have permitted the Near East Relief to continue its work there. Marash has also been cut off from the world for nearly all of this year, but the Near East Relief manages to keep its work going there as well. There are about 10,000 Armenian refugees shut up in this city, from which the French departed in February, and these are in peril of extermination by the Turks. It is the generosity of benevolent America, and the ingenuity and devotion of the representatives of the Near East Relief at work in this section that makes their preservation possible.

CONCERNING THAT
WHITE GIFT OFFERING

An Urgent Call

BY PROF. H. H. WOLFORD

Secretary-Treasurer, National Sunday School Association

We may rightly call the request for a large "White Gift Offering" an urgent call. This is true because the bulk of the offering goes to the support of two vital tasks of the church, namely, home missions and religious education. Unless the Brethren church honestly and sincerely faces these two tasks it can not be effective in the great work unto which its Lord has called it. The foreign program of the church will suffer unless there is a strong home base. The home base can never be strengthened and built up without trained men. Men are not trained for Christian service without religious education.

The call of the National Sunday School Association is primarily for these two causes. One thousand dollars is budgeted for the work in Kentucky. This is home missions. The United States presents many waiting fields to the church. Some of these fields are white unto the harvest. West of the Mississippi are many opportunities. These new fields can not be manned and taken care of without money to support the work. Our church is already in the field of Kentucky. This work must be maintained and enlarged. There are many new fields near Lost Creek and Krypton which ought to be opened. As we put these points upon a self-supporting basis we will be able to go out into other fields. The Sunday school workers will be glad for the opportunity of making a liberal contribution to this work. You will thus be doing a definite work for the needed and neglected fields of Kentucky. More than this you will be rendering unto the Lord that which belongs to him. Out of our abundance we want to give unto those who have not.

The other cause which our White Gift offering is to help is that of religious education in our college. If there are many fields to be occupied it will take many men and women to occupy them. These men and women must be trained. The only college which the church has is not being supported to the extent that it ought to be. The church has not yet come to recognize how necessary it is to maintain a college and maintain it rightly. Money, men and equipment are needed. The Sunday school composed for the most part of young men and women and children who appreciate the value of education will gladly give to the support of the college. Within the college religious instruction must be given if our young men and women are to be fully equipped for a life of service. To help support the work of religious instruction and especially that which is definitely along the line of preparing the student for active and practical service in religious education, we will give largely. Twelve hundred dollars is set aside this year for this purpose!

The other two items in our budget are the necessary expense account in the Association work and the partial support of a field worker. This last item is vital for we need to send trained workers into the field to help the local worker sin planning for larger and more definite Sunday school work. Part of your White Gift offering will go for this purpose.

The Largest Offering Yet is our slogan.
Ashland, Ohio.

The White Gift And Religious Education

PRESIDENT EDWIN E. JACOBS

A distinguished college president recently made the statement that the pressing need now in education was a larger degree of religious motivation. This statement was made after he had been in communication with six presidents of state controlled schools, for they confided to him that they were anxiously trying to introduce a more positive form of religious spirit into their student bodies.

Now this religious education, so-called, may take two forms. First, it may mean only to hold up the spirit of Jesus in all learning. His spirit may be made to permeate the study of sociology, ethics, philosophy, and it is not even adverse to the spirit of modern biology. This is possible only where the teacher is both able and consecrated. This spirit on the part of the teacher might not be shown in any sort of an examination, even if he were to be tried before some church board, and certainly would not appear in examination for certification.

If I am not in error, this spirit is noticeably lacking in our high schools. We are so utterly afraid that we might have the so-called union of church and state, a thing that has never happened in America, that we recoil from even mentioning religion in the public schools. Perhaps this point of view could be defended but at the same time, there is a danger here. A well known divine, one, too, who is not given to hasty statements, recently said that the danger now in America is that she ceases to be plainly religious.

But a second form of religious education, and the one with which the White Gift has most to do, is that which offers courses in religious education. These courses include Bible study, religious pedagogy, Sunday school pedagogy, and allied courses. Ashland College by the good graces of the Sunday schools and Christian Endeavor societies of the brotherhood, is enabled to sustain such a department.

This department is under the direction of the Seminary and has become one of the regularly established lines of work. If the church at large does not feel in time the effect of this department, then I shall be sadly disappointed for we are turning back to the church, in all too small numbers to be sure, young people from year to year who ought to be able to do a large service in the Sunday school and the Christian Endeavor. If young people who do not expect to enter the ministry but who do expect to live in Brethren congregations, would come here, for at least two years and get the spirit of modern education as well as some positive knowledge about the Sunday school and the Christian Endeavor, and then go back and be effective in their home congregations, the church would be well repaid for the gift made us at the White Gift season of the year. I can not be too insistent upon this point. The department is here and along with it the other departments of the school are open. Brethren young people ought to take advantage of this opportunity.

The College is grateful for the gifts made it from this offering. The money is husbanded carefully and under God the department has been blessed and is a blessing.
Ashland, Ohio.

GENERAL ARTICLES

Stewardship. BY H. W. ANDERSON

And the Lord said, Who then is that faithful and wise steward, whom his lord will make ruler over his household to give them their portion of meat in due season (Luke 12: 42)? Let a man so account of us, as the ministers of Christ, and stewards of the mysteries of God (1 Cor. 4:1). From these two references we find a class of stewards that are set over the household of their lord. And the lesser steward is the servant of the higher steward. The lesser stewards are the flock and the higher steward is the shepherd over the flock. So then I shall direct my thought to the ministry, and give the laity a chance to see what the duty of the higher steward is.

Too many pastors are blaming the laity and not willing to take any of the blame unto themselves for the church losing its grip. Jesus left the church in the hands of the laity never; he left it in the hands of the Apostles, who were his stewards. To them he said, Who then is the faithful and wise steward whom his lord shall make ruler over his household. Now who are the faithful and wise stewards?

Then Jesus said, "Go ye therefore, and teach all nations, baptizing them into the name of the Father, and of the Son, and of the Holy Spirit: teaching them to observe all things whatsoever I have commanded you: and, lo, I am with you alway, even unto the end of the world. Here is the test. Sometime ago, I saw an article in The Evangelist on Christian Stewardship. The writer referred to feet washing, saying that we ought to be as much concerned about stewardship as we are about feet washing, and I firmly believe that we ought. But I believe also that we ought to be concerned about whether we as stewards are really concerned about feet washing, and whether we are teaching it or not. The same article made a reference to baptism and said We ought to be as much concerned about our stewardship as we are about baptism. That is true, but we ought to know whether we as stewards are faithful in teaching baptism. These are some of the ordinances that Jesus said for us to teach all nations to observe. And we are treading on holy ground when we observe them, but

that is where Jesus wants us to walk. We cannot be faithful stewards and lay any of them aside, for if we do, we lay aside some things that Jesus told us to do.

I am thinking very seriously that if the Brethren church is to have a future, we shall have to find more real Brethren stewards, who will be willing to fill Brethren pulpits and do this teaching of all things which we are commanded to teach. There is not much use to try to make the goals of our Bicentenary Movement by 1923, if our Brethren stewards keep on leaving the Brethren pulpits vacant. There is not much use to build new churches until the churches we have are supplied with preachers. And if we do not have college students to fill the pulpits, we will have to go back to the old way of filling them from the farm and the shop. What is the matter with the stewards of the household of God? Where are they?

We must have more stewards, and stewards of the kind that are willing to teach all that Jesus taught and commanded. This is necessary. Some years ago we listened to a steward preach against the "isms," and now he is working among the "isms." We must not throw down the bars and let every "ism" and creed walk into our church. We have creed enough, which is the whole gospel. Why do we stand for the whole gospel and not preach it? At our General Conference we have never heard a doctrinal sermon. Are we ashamed to preach in General Conference what we teach in our local churches? Why should we have the Virgin birth so plainly taught us and not have taught the commandments of him who was born of the Virgin Mary?

I am convinced that if the Brethren church is to have a future we must have some real Brethren stewards. And Brethren stewardship will be Christian stewardship, for Brethren, if true to their creed will be true to Christ. Let us make the Brethren church what she ought to be by being true ministers of Christ and faithful stewards of the mysteries of God.

North English, Iowa.

Christ Our Example In Love and Service. BY N. J. PAUL

By invitation we will try by the help of the Holy Spirit to discuss this great topic. In the discussion of this subject, it will be of great value for us first, to notice the SINLESSNESS OF CHRIST, the perfect freedom of Christ, not only from all outward acts of sin, but also from all inward inclination to sin. The Old Testament prophecies relating to Christ, whether symbolically expressed or uttered in words, point to his perfect purity (see Matt. 29:30; John 4:34; 6:38; 8:29, 46; 15:10;17:4! Acts 3;14; Rom. 8:3; 2 Corinthians 5:21; Heb. 4:15; 1 Peter 1:10; 2:22; 1 John 2:2; 3:5). It is distinctly stated that Christ was tempted, and if so we must admit the abstract possibility of his sinning. Yet his temptations were in no case such as spring from a sinful nature, and the fact remains that he was absolutely without sin. We want to hold up Christ as the example, this is why we want to show the sinlessness of Christ. He taught men to confess their sins, but he made no such confession; he taught men to pray for forgiveness, but uttered no such prayer for himself; he declared the necessity of the new birth by the work of the Holy Spirit, but it was for others. He recognized in himself no such necessity. And thus it follows that in Christ we find a reversal of the law which prevails with respect to all limited measure of human excellence, or, he was supremely excellent, absolutely without sin. Christ, because he was sinless, is one of the highest, may we not say, the highest of the

credentials of Christianity. He is a mortal miracle, and is himself greater than all his miracles; Christ in his sinlessness exhibits to us the highest good. He was not free from poverty, and persecution, and hatred, and loneliness, and death, but he was free from sin. Neither can we be free from poverty or persecutions, or hatred, or loneliness or temptations or death, but we can by the assistance of the Holy Spirit keep free from sin. His offering of himself was of unspeakable value because he was spotless (see 1 Peter 1:19; comp. John 1:29). Likewise the efficacy of his intercession is based upon the same fact (John 2:1; Heb. 4:14-16). This fact also throws light upon his offer of new life to men. He is at the same time our perfect example, and the one through whom we receive power to follow in his steps (John 10:10; 1 Peter 2:21).

Christ, Our Example in Love

Go with me through the three and a half years of our Lord's ministry, and notice how his sympathy and love, was manifested upon all with whom he came in contact. He always had a kind look, a good word, and a loving act for men and women in all walks of life. There were none too high, or too low, but what the Lord would let his sympathy go out, and assist them in whatever condition he found them. If only the church of the First Born could lift up her eyes, and see the need of ruling out, and extending her love, and sympathy for falling humanity, as the

Christ extended his, and actually meet that need, then would she be able to claim to be holding up the Christ as her example. Notice how his love went out for the harlot, as well as for the rich young ruler. There were none preferred above the other with the Christ; they all looked precious to him.

Let a man be possessed of wealth, fame and everything that constitutes prosperity, and see the friends flock around about him: Oh, how they love him! Love him, did I say? Ah! there is the mistake. They appear to love him, but wait awhile. Wait until adversity comes and he loses his wealth, or he has committed some great sin, thus exposing the weakness of his character, and causing him to be stripped of his good reputation, then take another look and you will see that the number of his friends has been divided and subtracted, until you will find it necessary to take another, a searching look, in order to tell whether he now has any friends at all. Yes, we love when everything is lovely and all goes well. But when one is struggling against misfortune, or is bending low beneath a burden of guilt—a crushing burden—just the time when he needs friends, real friends, it is then that as a rule he finds he is all alone. Brethren, do you not find this to be the case with ninety-seven out of every hundred of those whom you have seen fall through some weakness? Oh, the bitterness of it all! No one knows but those who have had experience along that line. Despair, yet, black despair, is pictured on the face, and the heart is heavy as lead. Who is to extend the helping hand? This can be borne awhile, but the time comes when it can be borne no longer, and in great distress of soul, man cries out to his God for help, and lo, he finds to his surprise that God loves not as men love, for God hears his despairing cry, and in a tone full of love and compassion he says, "Come unto me!" No sinner is so vile, so wretched, so weighted down beneath the load of guilt that he will be hindered from accepting the loving invitation. Ah, no, for God hath said, "Though your sins be as scarlet, they shall be as white as snow; though they be red like crimson, they shall be as wool." My prayer, and heart's desire is, that the church may possess this kind of love, a love to reach out, take hold, and rescue fallen humanity. Is Christ our example? "By their fruits ye shall know them."

Christ Our Example for Peace

What is a home, without peace? What is a family without peace? Even though all the children be married and separated, when they meet together at the home of their parents, what enjoyment will they have if peace does not reign? What is a church, if peace hath no place in it? Oh, that we could call to mind the prayers that were offered up in our behalf, that we might be one, "even as Christ and his Father were One." This prayer fell from the lips of our Lord, time after time, that his disciples might be one and that they might have peace. In homes, in families, in churches, where love abounds, you may rest assured peace also abounds.

Our Example in Service

We want to note first, that when we are in reality serving Christ, we are his servants. We are either in the service of Christ, or we are in the service of Satan. Therefore, we are the servants of Christ, or we are the servants of the Devil. "No servant can serve two masters: for either he will hate the one, and love the other; or else he will hold to the one, and despise the other. Ye can not serve God and mammon." I firmly believe in the great day of the judgment, there will be thousands, yea millions of professed Christians who will be compelled to got to the left, for the simple reason, that they took the preacher for their example, in place of the Christ.

Christ as a Missionary

Consider Christ for one moment, and think how he left the courts of glory, to come to earth to suffer, and to die on the shameful cross that you and I might have life. See the sacrifice he made; gave up all, even his life. Should he not be our example? In mission work among the different creeds of the United States, there is more than $60,000,000 spent each year to push the cause of Christianity, and to establish peace. And yet, a number of these creeds fail to hold up the word of God, as they should, and show the Savior as the true example. Would to God that the Brethren church could "lay aside every weight, and the sin which doth so easily beset us, looking unto Jesus the author and finisher of our faith.

When we are in the true service of the Master, taking him as our guide, we are not thinking of this world, or the things that are of the world. Our thoughts, our lips, our minds and our hearts are striving to get closer to him, who is our great and true example, and pattern for us all. Can we do too much for him? Can we live too close to him? Can we be too thankful? Or, on the other hand, is there not a danger of our following him afar off. The Climax of it all is simply this, If we have love for one another, we will serve one another. If we have love for the church, we will serve the church. If we have love for the Christ, we will be his servants, and be always found in his service. If we love the world, we will be serving the world, even though we have our names on some class book. "Love not the world, neither the things that are in the world. If any man love the world, the love of the Father is not in him.

Losantville, Indiana.

The Universal Man.   BY T. DARLEY ALLEN

"Jesus never advocated patriotism," says Frank Crane, the essayist, "but desired his followers to regard all mankind as their brethren."

The Jewish people were very exclusive and believed themselves to be much better than any other race. Yet Christ, one of this race, so proved of its nationality, taught the doctrine of the brotherhood of man and so taught it as to bring men and women from all the races of mankind into one great brotherhood, a body that gives promise in time of becoming universal.

How different are other religions from Christianity as regards adaptability to those whom they reach. However well a few of them may be able to meet the conditions of the people among whom they originated they are not successful as missionary religions or capable of welding races in different parts of the globe into one faith with a common hope and similar aspirations.

Efforts have been made to introduce Buddhism into America, but without success further than the conversion of a few men and women who seem blind to the beauty of Christianity and to the fact that in this religion alone is

there hope for a bright future in India and other lands of Asia where Buddhism has flourished for ages and where the people are degraded and all forms of immorality are practiced even in the temples. Can anyone conceive of worse conditions than have existed in India for ages with the "Light of Asia" "shining" all the time?

The religion of Christ goes to the South Sea cannibals and to the most degraded races of people in all parts of the world and fits them as members of a happy brotherhood that embraces the most enlightened people of the globe.

How thankful we should be for such a religion and for such a wonderful Savior as we have and how zealous we should be to carry the blessings that have come to us through Christ to those who sit in darkness who are our brethren and are as dear to our Heavenly Father as those of us who already know him!

Cleveland, Ohio.

Prayer is either a tremendous force, or else it's a disgraceful farce. If a farce, you may pray much and get little; if a force, you may pray little and get much.

FROM OUR CONFERENCE PLATFORMS

Pastoral Evangelism.   By Willis E. Ronk

A paper read at the Indiana state conference

The subject of this address, "Pastoral Evangelism," covers far too much territory for the speaker to do more than to talk on some one part of the subject; therefore, it is important that first of all, we should define and clarify the issue. What is Pastoral Evangelism? Evangelism is the carrying forth of the "Good Message" to others. Pastoral Evangelism is the carrying forth of the message by pastors. Very well—, but in what respect does evangelism by the pastor differ from that of the regular evangelist? To say that the difference is not in purpose is merely stating the self-evident. The difference, if there is any, is not in purpose but in method.

On the one hand the evangelist may come into a community and church, both being, in the vernacular, "as dead as a door nail." He is clearly at a disadvantage. He is given two or three weeks in which "to deliver the goods" in the form of a successful meeting. Woe be unto him if he does not, for certainly his good name will suffer. What he does he must do quickly and above all he must get plenty of "joiners." His chief aim is to bring people to an immediate decision for the Master. He then leaves the converts in the hands of the pastor to instruct in the way of righteousness. And sometimes the task left to the pastor is all but an impossible one. Many are led to a decision who have not fully counted the cost. To train them in the "Christian Way" is a gigantic task. If the evangelist is a man of real tact, he may lighten the task of the pastor. Too often converts are converted to the preacher and not to Christ and when the preacher goes along goes their Christianity. Not infrequently has the evangelist, by one method or another brought discord between pastor and people, which has ultimately caused the severing of their relations. We do not propose to lay the blame all at the evangelist's door,—the trouble often lies with the church and what she expects of the man.

On the other hand, the pastor-evangelist, if he is in his own church, has a whole year in which to accomplish his task and there is always the possibility of another year's labor. If he is called to a neighboring church for a meeting, likely he knows something of the field or is possibly on more or less intimate terms with the pastor. As great results are not expected as there are of the evangelist he enters the field and step by step, he reinforces what the pastor has already said many times and with a quiet persuasion urges to a decision. If the results are not all that he thinks they should be, he may go home, feeling that the seed has been sown and that the local pastor may reap the fruit during the coming months. In other words, he is free.

It is not my intention to give a lengthy discussion on the contrast of the two types of evangelism, nor yet to criticize so called professional evangelism, but rather to sum up as briefly as possible, and yet retain clearness, the requirements for successful Pastoral Evangelism.

First, successful Pastoral Evangelism depends on proper teachings. He who fails to recognize the importance of careful, day by day teaching, cannot hope to reap an adequate harvest. How great is the loss of effort, of money and the most sad of all the loss of human souls! We are permitting our boys and girls to grow to manhood and womanhood without the proper religious training. When they are grown we put forth a stupendous effort to bring them within the fold and alas! too often we are failing together. Then too the ignorance of many church people of today is amazing. Not long ago a certain Christian was seen trying to find the Gospel of John in the Old Testament. There are those who think that little is required of him that knows little and they proceed to remain in their ignorance. We are fast drifting away from a recognition of the necessity of teaching. Turn back over the pages of history and study the life of the peoples of primitive civilization or better still go into the heart of Africa or into the far East and you will find that as the youth approaches manhood he is not only taught the traditions of of his fathers, but he is introduced to his father's Gods. It seems that only modern civilized man has failed to see the importance of the proper teaching of the young. How can we expect our children to grow up and be Christians when the Bible is a forgotten book in many a home? I visited in the home of one of my members where there was sickness—out in Ohio—and as it came time to leave, the head of the house said, "We would like to have a sample of your prayers before you go." Then was started a hunt for the family Bible. Although I insisted that we could get along very well without it, relying on memory, the hunt continued until every room was searched and so far as I know it has not been found yet. Back to the Bible and religious teaching we must go. We must teach TEACH, for precept must be upon precept, precept upon precept; line upon line, line upon line; here a little and there a little.

As to Evangelism, people must be taught the need. A great many of our church people are provincial in thought. They have been born, have grown up and lived all of their lives in their local communities and the world to them is just like that which they have seen. They know nothing of the great need of the world. And many do not see the great need of their own communities. Crying needs—needs of the great moment—are often not seen by the church people. Having been brought up under Christian influences, they do not know of any other kind of a life. Many who are crying out, "We have plenty to do at home," and "We have enough heathen here," are failing either to see the real need or to do anything to meet the need. The greatest sins exist under their very eyes and "having eyes they see not." Too often a new church building which fails to materialize, or a petty church quarrel, the origin of which no one knows, keeps otherwise very fine people from seeing that great numbers are being lost—eternally lost—while they are doing nothing.

And above everything else, people must be taught not only the fact of sin, but the awfulness of sin. We are passing lightly over the fact of sin today. Things are done today and merely passed over with a laugh or a joke—things that should bring a blush of shame to our cheeks,—yes, things that a few years ago would have put one beyond the pale of good society, to say nothing of meeting the condemnation of the church. The church dares not be silent on the great moral issues. One who has committed nearly every sin in the category, dies and the last words we hear are, "he was a good neighbor, a good friend and we leave him in the hands of a just and merciful God," as if to say, it does not matter just so one is a good neighbor and a good friend, God will be merciful. People must be made to realize that sin is not just error, but sin is sin,—damnable sin. There must be positive teachings on the fact and presence of sin in the life, if we would succeed. Then can we follow the consolation of a God who can and will forgive to the uttermost all who will believe.

Successful evangelism depends upon prevailing prayer. The pastor or evangelist who trusts to the great message presented, to the work of his assistants or the congregation or even to the Holy Spirit and forgets the place of prayer, is certain to be disappointed in the results. These things are aids to move man, while prayer is to move God. Not that God will change his mind, but the asking produces the change in us and fulfills such conditions as render it consistent for God to do the thing asked. However strong the message and the appeal, however strong the effort put forth, all will be in vain, unless men will lay hold of God in prevailing prayer. If one would prevail in prayer, he must be definite in the asking. A long prayer for the heathen, however great their need, or even a prayer for sinners in general, will do little to save John Brown who comes to church every night but who cannot get victory. John Brown must be prayed for specifically. Then here is Mr. Jones in whose path is an obstacle. We must pray that the obstacle will be removed. If our people will learn to pray definitely for their friends and enemies, then we may look for success. You are a father and your little boy comes to you and says, "Daddy, I want money," or "I want to go to the fair," or "I want some marbles," or "I want new tops, like Jimmie Jones," that would be definite. On the other hand suppose he should say, "Daddy, I am quite sure I want something very badly. I don't know just what I want, but I think I should have it. That is, if you want me to have it." If he should come to you in this way, you would take the boy's temperature, put him to bed and call the doctor. And yet we are often just as rambling and as indefinite in our prayers to God. Let us be definite and specific in the things we ask.

Then too, we should pray as though we expected to be heard and answered. There is a danger that we may be so willing to submit to God's will that we really become indifferent. Indifference should not be confused with submitting to his will. We should study God's word and try to discern his will, then act accordingly. One thing is clear, the great invitations of the Bible are universal; they are to all who will believe. Thus the only barrier is man's will. Certainly we may here be sure that we can continue to agonize for our unsaved friends. Though rarely put in words, there is a general feeling that there are a few individuals in every community who cannot be reached. I have often heard, while making a survey previous to a meeting, "Yes, there is Mr. Brown, Mr. Jones, and a few others but there is no use wasting your time on them. Why, we have some of the best preachers in the Brethren church here, and they have failed to reach them and there is not much use in you trying it. There is the case of Mr. R—, John, as every one calls him. Ha! ha! Say, that man can 'cuss' and swear. There is not much use in talking to him, but you might put his name down." I lived next door to him for a year and never heard him swear or utter an ugly word. Today he is a saved man, because someone would not give up. He is also superintendent of a Sunday school. This is not the question of a big preacher; but can God save the man? If he can't he saves none. Never did man sink so low in the mire that God could not save him,—but you could never convince some people that this is so. If God cannot and does not save to the uttermost, then is our preaching in vain. Definite, understanding, expectant prayer will prevail.

Now we have a new building and a big preacher, now wont things just go fine. "Now we can just recline on flowery beds of ease" is often the first step in the decline of a church or in the failure of an evangelistic effort. It seems that it should not be necessary to mention such an essential as a labor of love, yet there are many who do not recognize the great importance of labor, at least; so we judge from their lives. Some people are perpetually tired and must be ever singing:

I heard the voice of Jesus say,
Come unto me and rest,
Lay down thou weary one, lay down
Thy head upon my breast. Or

Just lean upon the arms of Jesus,
Then leave all to him,
Leave all to him, Leave all to him.

That a large percent of the church people are doing scarcely anything to reach their fellowmen, is a statement that will scarcely be challenged, and yet the very existence of the church depends upon individual service. This is taught in the New Testament and has been proven by the history of the church. I would let no man outdo me in demanding faith—by all means, let us have more faith, but faith and prayer are not sufficient. James says, (Jas. 2:17) "Even so faith if it hath not works is dead," also "faith without works is dead." James further says, "I will show thee my faith, by my works." I will not spend my time trying to point out the necessity of work; but certainly if we are to succeed as a pastor-evangelist, we must teach the people the importance of work. We cannot hope to be able to reach others unless individuals shall be willing to carry the message.

In the church there is work for all,
There are dying souls to rescue—hear the call-

All through our teachings there must run the note of love. Men may see and men may know, but it takes an all consuming love to impel men to lives of service. There is the service of duty, but the service of love is higher.

Many apparently well laid plans for a revival fail because we stress the importance of well laid plans and insist on strenuous effort and then go forth trying to attain success. Any effort put forth for the savation of souls is certain to fail, IF the person and office of the Holy Spirit are overlooked. We must preach, pray, work and have faith; but the Spirit convicts men of sin and leads them out into all truth. Far too often the Spirit is left out of our calculations and out of our message. Many think of the Holy Spirit as an influence working in the lives of men. This takes the heart out of Christianity. The teaching of the New Testament is that the Holy Spirit is a person.—HE convicts. HE leads out into all truth. HE is the personal leader. We need a lot more preaching of the old time Holy Ghost power. If we would succeed, we must rely on the Holy Spirit.

This then is all there is to successful Pastoral Evangelism? Not by any means. I have often heard people say, "Just preach the plain gospel as it is written and you will succeed," yet there are some fine, consecrated men who have done this very thing and then their efforts have not been crowned with success. Wherein is the trouble? Successful evangelism depends upon not only the message, but upon the MAN AND THE MESSAGE.

First, the man must live his message. Now may I say right in the beginning that I am not looking for perfection in the person of the preacher, far from it. The preacher is human and since he is, depend upon it, he will make his mistakes. When he does let us then withhold our condemnation and try to lift him up. I know at least three young ministers who have been lost to the ministry of our church, because at the time of their first little mistakes they found no sympathy or help, but only abuse and condemnation and because of discouragement and lack of faith in applied Christianity, they have gone to still more grievous mistakes and sins and are lost to the ministry if not worse. Some churches by their counsel and help, make successful men while others are men-killers. The minister needs help and sympathy. Now to the other side, we say that the preacher is human and makes his mistakes, so he does. Too often a man's humanity is made the excuse for any and all sins. There are sins or mistakes that we might dispute about, but there are sins that meet specific condemnation in the Word. Our humanity does not excuse us when we commit them. The man behind the message must live a clean moral life, or else success will not be his. He must be Spirit-filled and Spirit-led.

Then the man must use his own personality. Many a preacher fails because he tries to preach like another. Wm. A. Sunday is a strong and successful man, but there is only one Wm. A. Sunday. The man who imitates him will not meet success in fullest measure. The man will make his greatest mark by being natural. His own personality will win for him when otherwise he would fail.

Then, too, the message should be sensational; that is,

Send
WHITE GIFT
OFFERINGS to

THE SUNDAY SCHOOL

H. H. WOLFORD
General Secretary-Treasurer
Ashland, Ohio

Announcement of Editorial Changes. BY A. D. GNAGEY

In accordance with certain recommendations made by the editor of the Sunday school literature, the Brethren Publication Board, representing the church at large, at its recent sessions, Winona Lake, Indiana, authorized the following enlargement of the editorial staff:

Prof. J. A. Garber, Department of Religious Education, Ashland College, becomes associate editor **The Teacher and Educator.** The Review Section of this publication will be under the editorial supervision of Prof. Garber. In this department he hopes to develop and carry forward a program of Religious Education—a field in which he has specialized, and a service for which he is eminently qualified. The editors have already under way well defined plans looking toward the enlargement and usefulness of this publication.

Dr. J. Allen Miller, Dean of the Seminary, Ashland College, will write the notes for the **Brethren Advanced Quarterly,** in the department now bearing the title, "A Study of the Scripture Passage." Dr. Miller is too well known as a Bible scholar in the Brethren church to need any introduction to the brotherhood. This arrangement with Dr. Miller will mean a valuable acquisition to the editorial staff and give added influence to the publication to which he will contribute editorially.

Rev. A. V. Kimmell, pastor of the Brethren church, Whittier, California, one of the most successful and growing young men in the brotherhood, will prepare the lesson helps for the **Youths' (Intermediate) Quarterly.** Rev. Kimmell has given both time and thought to the study of the needs of teen age pupils, and his contributions to this publication will be welcomed by the church.

The special editorial work in the **Home Department Quarterly** will be under the supervision of Mrs. J. Allen Miller, who will bring to these pages not only the fruit of a well trained mind and cultivated heart, but also the experience of a mother and a teacher, having been for many years and being at present a member of the Ashland College Faculty. The lesson helps in the Home Department Quarterly are adapted from those in the Brethren Advanced Quarterly.

This enlargement of the editorial staff of our Sunday school publications will mean a corresponding enlargement of the value and usefulness of these publications, more nearly in accordance with the forward look of the church's program adopted at its late General Conference. It will mean also a more representative literature, interpretive of the thought of the church.

Rev. George H. Jones, pastor of the Brethren church at Conemaugh, Pennsylvania, will prepare the editorial section (six front pages and cover pages) of the **Intermediate Quarterly.** He will also prepare the Lesson Helps for the **Boys and Girls Quarterly** (Junior). Rev. Jones has given both time and thought to the study of Junior and teen age pupils, and is eminently qualified for the task which the Brethren Publishing Company has committed to him.

The editorial section (six front pages and cover pages) of the **Boys and Girls Quarterly** (Junior) is conducted by Miss Lois Frazier, Nappanee, Indiana, a graduate of Ashland College and teacher in High School. She is a person of rare qualities and ability and her service in this connection will add much to the attractiveness and helpfulness of this publication.

What Leonard Wood Says

Major-General Wood, in writing for the Metropolitan Magazine for November, has the following to say about the Eighteenth Amendment:

"There has been a great decrease in crime and in the ment of our people today is in favor of prohibition, and that those who are looking for political assets in which to trade will gain rather than lose by standing squarely for the Eighteenth Amendment. The Amendment has come to stay.

"There is, it is true, less activity at present by those who are in favor of prohibition than there was prior to the action by the states on the Amendment. This simply means that patriotic and law abiding citizens and organizations support the enforcement of the laws of the nation and that they have confidence that the Government is going to see that the Amendment is enforced. If there is any ultimate laxity in so doing, this same element will, eventually, take the necessary steps to secure the enforcement of the law.

"There has been a great recrease in crime and in the number of accidents. More money is spent for necessities, such as food, clothing, etc., and as a result there has been marked diminution in the demands for charity. Women and children are better taken care of. There is much less dissipation, and there has been no corresponding increase in the use of drugs, although this has been held as sure to occur.

"From our knowledge of the effect of the steady use of alcoholic liquors we can expect, with confidence, great eventual improvement in the physical and mental quality of the children to be born, now that these drinks are no longer available. We can look for greater economic efficiency, a continued decrease in crime, decrease in vice diseases and a better race physically and morally: These are results worth while."

Pastoral Evangelism
Continued from page 9

it should appeal to the senses. Do not misunderstand me. I am not favoring ultra-sensational or spectacular preaching, far from it. But if preaching is to keep people awake, say nothing about reaching their hearts, it must be done in such a way as to appeal to the senses. All successful preachers, while they would likely not admit it, are in their way sensational. But let them be sensational; they are in good company. There stands Noah preaching repentance and predicting the flood; there is Jonah preaching, "yet forty days and Nineveh shall be destroyed; there are Isaiah, Jeremiah, Hosea and a host of others to say nothing of Christ himself. It is not sufficient that we should present the Message in such a way that men will say, "What a beautiful Gospel or what a beautiful Christ," but rather in such a way that men will cry out, "men and brethren, what shall we do to be saved?"

May we then realize the importance of teaching constantly the fundamentals of the gospel. The large task of "Pastoral Evangelism" is teaching with a constant appeal. This is the chief task. An understanding, praying, working, loving spirit filled church and the man with the message will bring an abundant harvest. Let us believe as our forefathers did, that the message WILL reach and touch hearts. Let us not once or twice, but time and again impress upon the minds of Christians the crying need of the hour—saving the men all around us, who are drifting to a Christless grave.

O ye saints, arouse, be earnest,
Up and work while yet 'tis day;
Ere the night of death o'ertake thee,
Strive for souls while yet you may.

Roann, Indiana.

Our Young People at Work

Christian Endeavor Inspiring Missions.   BY JAMES S. COOK

(Address prepared for the Ohio Conference, which Brother Cook was unavoidably hindered from attending and which hindrance occurred too late to enable the sending of the manuscript to be read at conference).

I have looked forward to this conference at Ashland with exceedingly great interest. Seven long years have passed since I left these sacred walls, but fond memories have ever been a source of strength and uplift to me, and I have longed to see these halls once more, and to imagine, if I can, that I hear once more those once familiar voices. I fancy now, I can hear the voice and see that pleasant and familiar smile playing over the face of our beloved Edward Byers. Likewise I can sense the presence of many others whom we learned to know and to love.

Somehow I felt that I must say, what I have said before coming directly to the subject assigned me.

When I received my Evangelist a couple or three weeks ago, which contained the program of this conference, I opened it, and was scanning the contents when my eyes fell upon the subject assigned me," Christian Endeavor Inspiring Missions." I at once thought of several persons who were better acquainted with Christian Endeavor work and whom I knew could discuss the question much better than myself.

However I began to turn the subject over and over in my mind and then to dissect it as we used to do flowers in our botany class, or as a boy might pick a watch to pieces to see how and from what it was made. There are only four words, as you see, and we want to know the true and full meaning that each of them conveys. I took the first word CHRISTIAN and held it up before me as I had done many times before my people, and asked the question, What is a Christian? I do not doubt that we all know what a Christian is, and what a Christian ought to do. I am not saying that all who bear the name, Christian are worthy of the name. But God has been kind enough to give us a few of them, and we know when we meet one and we also know when we see a Christian.

Then I took up the word ENDEAVOR in like manner, and after I had turned it over several times, I said to myself, Well, MR. ENDEAVORER, it seems we have met a few times before; we are not such strangers as I had first thought. You are one of those determined fellows who is going to reach your goal or die trying. Yes, we have worked together many times. And now if you want to see things hum, just hitch Mr. Christian, that Holy man of God, together with Mr. Endeavorer, that fellow who is ever putting forth a determined effort to do something, and you are going to see something move. Such a combination always has moved things and it always will.

Now we have Mr. Christian Endeavorer, but even yet I wandered back in my imagination, and asked myself the question, does this just include those who have signed the pledge of some society, and for myself I answered that question in the negative. To me in the broad and fullest sense of the term, it means every truly converted CHRISTIAN. When you offer your life, your all, to serve Christ, is not that just as binding as any vow that man could write. And when we come to the place where we are not willing to serve the Lord, and endeavor to do what he wants us to do, it is time we were ceasing to be a hypocrite, and disrobe ourselves of the name. For really every true Christian is an ENDEAVORER.

Now, if what I have just said is true, Francis E. Clark is not the originator of CHRISTIAN ENDEAVOR. It must have existed since the days of Christ and the apostles, and what Francis E. Clark did in the midst of the great receding tide of youthful energies was to rediscover it. Like electricity it existed long before it was ever discovered, and harnessed for work. Neither did Clark create Christian Endeavor; it was created and he discovered it. What he really did in my judgment was to bring together a few of these determined, enthused, inspired Christians, though weak they may have been and conferred upon them no new title, no new name, but simply called them by the name with which he found them. He further submitted to them on that evening of February 2nd, 1881, plans, outlines and helps by which they could the better go forth conquering and to conquer.

Now since we have seen who Christian Endeavorers really are, and what they really do, it is not a large stretch of the imagination to see how CHRISTIAN ENDEAVOR INSPIRES MISSIONS. How could missions be inspired were they not inspired by Christian endeavorers. It is certainly true that Satan lends no inspiration. That he is on the job we all know, and just as cunning as in the garden of Eden. Much of the inspiration comes from those devoted, consecrated Christian endeavorers who are ever mindful of the Lord's work and his workers.

I want to very briefly stress two ways in which, "Christian Endeavor Inspires Missions."

First I shall say through prayer. If there are those who know how to pray and do pray, it is those who know God. It is the ones who have fully dedicated their lives to the Lord to be used of him. Their prayers not only give strength to themselves, but are a source of strength and uplift to those already in the service. Our missionaries in Africa, in South America and in our own land not only need our money, but ever more than all that, our constant upholding of them before the throne of grace. And I pray tell me, whom do we find doing this thing more than Christian Endeavorers,

How does "Christian Endeavor Inspire Missions?" By furnishing the missionaries to deliver the goods. If I have been rightly informed, there are now already over five thousand of these recruits actively engaged in some mission work. Were it not for the work that Christian Endeavor is doing—gathering up recruits, preparing them, inspiring them, and sending them out, this great army of men and women,—how small would our work be? And how could we look Matthew 28:18-20 in the face? And too, he who gave us that great commission was himself a missionary, and he too was the first true Endeavorer.

I question however if there are many missionaries who cannot trace their inspiration and perhaps their call to the field to some Christian Endeavorer or some work in which they were engaged through the Christian Endeavor. How many of us can trace our first public prayers back to the Christian Endeavor? Likewise our own little feeble public speech? It was here we learned to do these things, and here that we developed our various talents and perhaps caught the spark of enthusiasm that has led us to find our place in the Lord's work.

Therefore we are very grateful to Mr. Francis E. Clark for the finding of Christian Endeavor, for the idea of searching out and grouping together those Christian Endeavorers who already were the bulwark for the inspiration and evangelization of the world.

Clayton, Ohio.

ALL

You can give without loving. You can't love without giving. When you love as God did, you will give as God did—all.—J. Campbell White.

SEND ALL MONEY FOR
General Home, Kentucky and
Foreign Missions to

MISSIONS

WILLIAM A. GEARHART
General Missionary Secretary
906 American Bldg., Dayton, O.

A Valuable Contribution To Missionary Literature

"The Missionary Outlook in the Light of the War" One of the Most Important Books of the Year.. A Review by Howard B. Grose.

It is long since a volume of the quality and worth of "The Missionary Outlook in the Light of the War," issued by the Committee on the War and the Religious Outlook has come to the editorial desk. The report is a model of missionary apologetics. It is as convincing as it is clear and comprehensive. Its vision sweeps the whole range of foreign missions in the light of the results consequent upon the World War. We wish that every intelligent man who regards missions with a question mark or with indifference could be led to read this setting forth of great facts and vital truths. Once begun, the reading is not likely to be discontinued by those who take thought of the essential values in life and civilization.

See the range of topics: Introduction by Robert E. Speer, full of meat for missionary sermons; Foreign Missions as a Preparation for the New Internationalism; What Foreign Missions Can Contribute to an Effective League of Nations; Foreign Missions and Democracy in Non-Christian Lands; Enlarged Outlook of Foreign Missions; Effect of the War on the Vitality of Non-Christian Religions; the War and New Influences Among Oriental Women; the War and the Missionary Outlook in India, China, Japan, Korea, Africa, Moslem Lands, and Latin America; the Effect of War on Missionary Activity; Lessons from the War as to Propaganda for Missions; New Demands Regarding the Character and Training of Missionaries; Reconsideration of Missionary Methods; the War and Literary Aspects of Missions; Missions and American Business and Professional Men Abroad; Bearing of Economics and Business on Foreign Missions; Missionary Agencies in Relation to Students from Other Lands.; Foreign Policies of the United States and the Success of Foreign Missions; Relation of Foreign Missions to International Policies; with synopsis of contents and bibliography. The

names of the contributors to this list of subjects show that outstanding missionaries and special students of missions have been called upon for first-hand knowledge, while at the same time the whole has been skillfully edited into unity.

Few men can say as much in as small space or as pungently as Dr. Speer says in the brief introduction. Instantly he links the missionary enterprise with the moral aims of the nation in its recent conflict, and then shows how the missionary movement has been in the world as an instrumentality of peace and international good will, a great agency of righteousness, of human service, of human unity and concord. Never was this agency so needed as now, strong, living, aggressive. The great negative energies of destruction such as war releases can never achieve the things that have to be done in the world. In Christ alone today is the power of saving men and of redeeming society. This is the keynote of the volume.

In a day when we all recognize the need of a new spirit of internationalism if world peace is to be secured and preserved, the analysis which this report presents of the contributions made by foreign missions to the new internationalism is highly significant:

1. The Christian missionary movement has been the basis for the best there is in the confidence which the nations of the East and the West have in each other as moral, righteous, and dependable institutions.

2. Foreign missions has been the greatest agency in the past century in breaking down racial barriers and interpreting the East and West to each other.

3. Foreign missions is the one agency that has not only proclaimed, but incarnated the spirit of human brotherhood and service.

4. Foreign missions has for more than a hundred years been developing in non-Christian lands a high class of native leadership sympathetic to democracy and internationalism.

Significant indeed on this last point is the fact that at the Peace Conference at Versailles two of the three representatives of the Chinese Republic were Christians, one of them, C. T. Wang, for many years secretary of the Chinese Y. M. C. A. Equally convincing are the points as to what foreign missions can contribute to the success of a League of Nations, including the spirit of brotherhood and service, the attitude of faith, and the mutual understanding that is developed by the boon of a common religious faith, without which a full and permanent brotherhood is impossible.

So we might go on through the chapters, if space permitted. Each chapter possesses some special interest, some suggestive impulse. One of the most informing sections is that on the war's effect on the Vitality of the non-Christian religions. Evidences of revival in Hinduism, Buddhism, Shintoism, Confucianism, and Mohammedanism are first given, and then evidences of weakening. The whole is illuminating and a fresh contribution of moment. In some way this Volume should be gotten into the hands of pastors throughout the country. Its reading could not fail to stir them with the immediacy of the gospel need and opportunity in all lands at this vital moment in human history. Light is thrown at every point, but there are no hysterics, simply the array of facts. Whether one accepts all the conclusions or not, they all call for serious consideration.

In its five reports, two of which have already appeared, the Committee on the War and the Religious Outlook, is rendering a service of distinct and permanent Value. This Committee is an outcome of the General War-Time Commission of the churches appointed by the Federal Council. Professor William Adams Brown is the chairman of the Committee; President King, of Oberlin, and Rev. Charles W. Gilkey, vice-chairmen; and Rev. Samuel McCrea Cavert, Secretary. The volumes are published in attractive form by Association Press, 347 Madison Avenue, New York.

NEWS FROM THE FIELD

EVANGELISTIC NEWS

We are now at Reliance, Virginia (Mt. Zion church) for a few days. We cannot hope for many additions to the church, as the young people of our Brethren families have gone for the big wages, just as in many other places. But I come into this district not for the money I get for my work, but for the love and pity for the old folks at home. I have been in this work now for the ninth year, so I have come to love the people.

I baptized one dear old brother and wife there this week, and there are still a few to

be gathered into the Shepherd's fold. We added five last year.

Last week I was at Piney Hill, Nethers, Virginia, where we have no church building, but a place by the wayside where we go and conduct worship. We have been going there three or four years. We had nice weather this time, was there four days and had good congregations and interest. They sent me cans of fruit, all from Brother Seth Jenkins and family. We are thankful for such useful tokens of appreciation. Our collection was

about enough to pay car fare. Such places as these where there are only a few of Brethren folks are the places that are usually neglected, though they are hungry for the Word.

We were hoping for Brother I. D. Bowman's help at the Hammer mission, Franklin, West Virginia, in November, but a card from Brother Cover yesterday says he cannot reach there before some time in December. As that section often gets snow- and ice-bound in the winter, we had better defer the meeting till early spring, when we hope to have Brother Bowman at the Hammer church. I shall go there one trip yet, over this fifth Sunday (of October). May we all keep singing and praying God's belssing on these out-of-the-way places, until we can do more for them in the future than we have in the past.

S. P. FOGLE.

OAKVILLE, INDIANA

No news having been sent in from here for some time, I will endeavor to do so now. The work in general is doing nicely, and some vital things have come to pass. After graduating from Ashland College last June we packed our goods and bid farewell to Ashland as our home and shipped goods to Hoosierdom. During the month of July the church granted us our vacation. We spent nine days in the Kansas harvest fields with our home people near Norcatur. I preached one Sunday at the Federated Church in the town. One Sunday at our home church in the country eight miles from town. It was indeed a joy to see a packed house of our old neighbors and friends who had come out to "see how we fared." We gave them a large dose of the good old Gospel. Some came 15 miles to see how it tasted, but none were moved to accept it in full. We spent one day in central Missouri. This was the warmest day we ever experienced, as Missouri is known as a "hot state." We spent five happy days in our old parish, Udell, Iowa, where we tried to preach the Gospel for thirty months in the first five years of our ministry. Here full houses greeted us over one Sunday. It was a great pleasure to have old friends before us again. These were some of the most happy days we had during the summer. This is the home of our dear Brother Staley, now in Ashland College, of Brother Atkinson who graduated last June and now lives at Delta, Colorado.

We landed back in Oakville for the first Sunday in August, but was assigned to preach in the city park at a union service with the Muncie Mission, Maple Grove and Oakville. This was a beautiful service together and our association was uplifting.

We jumped into work with the Brethren on the parsonage, and stayed with it from the ground up, acting as "apprentice" under the boss carpenter.

We put the last shingle, the last lath on, cement floor in basement, and anything our hands found to do. The last of September we called the Board together and decided we would have to borrow $500, after dedication to finish our bills. On October 3rd we called Brother Shively of Ashland to be with us. And a great day we had, one that marks a VICTORY in the history of the church. After a brief sermonette in the morning, we proceeded to raise funds, and in thirty minutes we had gone over the top,—beyond our expectations. The people responded well, and a fine lot of people we have too.

We now have a seven room house, basement under the entire main part, furnace, electric lights, gas to cook with, veranda 8x30, pastor's study nicely equipped. At the least figure it is worth $3,500.00. The total cost outside of donation work was nearly $2,800.

After living in one room of the school house for ten weeks you may believe that we were glad when moving day came. We now feel more at home than since leaving Ashland last June.

We have a Ford and are trying to make good use of it in the Lord's work whenever we can.

The Sunday school is keeping up well. Our average attendance so far this year has been 70 plus. Average offerings about $10.00. One new feature now is the superintendent's sending out of four people from four different classes for several Sundays to other schools to observe work and report back anything that may be commendable. So far nothing has been found that is ahead of our own school. We are planning on having a Christmas program. We are crowded for room with our 8 classes, and Mrs. Deeter who now has charge of the Juniors meets them in the parsonage for the full hour. She is having them outline the Book of Mark along with their study.

We will have an all-day Thanksgiving service at the church. This is something this church has never had before. We are looking forward to a blessed service.

We are preparing the field for our coming revival, beginning Sunday, December the 19th, with Brother A. L. Lynn as evangelist. Brother Lynn and I were college chums and it will be a joy to have him work among us and bring some of his powerful messages.

Four of our members are moving to West Virginia, one of which has been our efficient Sunday school secretary for some time. The Sunday school gave her a vote of thanks for her faithfulness, and wished her well in her new home. We have added 45 names to the church roll since we have been among this people,—less than two years.

We will appreciate the prayers of God's people elsewhere, in our behalf and for continued success in our work. Our interest and prayers are for the glory of God's Kingdom everywhere. May the Lord bless you all.

W. R. DEETER

MANTECA, CALIFORNIA
November 12, 1920

Since our last report we have many more things to be thankful for in Manteca. Activity in all departments of our work makes this possible.

Our Rally Day exercises on September 26 were enjoyable as well as profitable. There were over one hundred present to listen to the program, which was as follows:

Greeting, ... Ruby Larson
Piano Solo, ... Mae Elliott
Recitation—"If We Try,"
          Enid Platt and Donald Bigham
Violin Duet,
          J. Wesley Platt and Frank Larson
Male Quartet:
   C. Johnson, L. Powell, W. Platt, W. Reyner
Recitation, ... Josie Mayberry
Piano Duet, ... Eleanor and Adeline Wolfe
Exercise—"Take Care,"
   By three boys and three girls from Intermediate Class.
Piano Duet,
          J. Wesley Platt and Darrel Reyner

Flower Exercise, ... Beginners' Class
Song—"Beautiful City,"
   By Mrs. Frank Larson and daughter, Laura, accompanied by Mr. Larson on the violin.
Bible Exercise and Drill by 24 boys and girls of the Intermediate Class.

After the Sunday school exercises were brought to a close, Brother Platt took charge of the services and preached a powerful sermon. When the invitation was given Mrs. Thorson went forward and gave her heart to Jesus and accepted him as her personal Savior. It was indeed a privilege to be there and see the joy in her face after she had made the confession. She said, "I am so happy now. Such a big burden has gone from my heart." She was raised a Catholic, married a Protestant and her life was made miserable by the priests. She certainly is a new creature in Christ. Her young daughter (about 12 years old) went forward also.

On the evening of October 8th, we enjoyed communion services and there were 26 present. These were all members of our local organization, excepting one dear old brother who had been baptized only a few weeks previously, and who took part in the communion and foot washing for the first time in his life, though he had been a Christian for years. He is a member of the Swedish church but he attends our evening services quite regularly. He told Brother Platt there was one thing he desired and that was to be buried with Christ in baptism. So Brother Platt baptized him and he has a satisfaction now that he had never experienced before. There have been four other baptisms since our last report, and we are expecting more to take the stand for Jesus at most any service as the interest is good, likewise, the sermons. Our membership now totals 34 and we feel the need of a church house more and more each week.

We have our regular cottage prayer meetings every Wednesday evening; also a teacher training class; Sunday school twice monthly, and Christian Endeavor every Sunday evening at 7 o'clock. Last night we had for our Christian Endeavor prayer meeting service the reading of a long and interesting letter from Brother Gribble, the letter having been reprinted and divided into paragraphs so that each one present should have a portion to read, with any additional comments they had to offer. Only one-half of the letter was gone over but we expect to take the remaining five pages for next Sunday evening. It makes us feel much more keenly the experience of our dear brethren in the distant fields. To those of us who have missed our opportunity I would say, "Give and pray." To the young folks who have their lives before them, I would say, "Go; obey the command of Jesus to teach all nations."

Brother Platt took up the services immediately following Christian Endeavor and chose for the lesson the 12th chapter of Romans. The first verse, "I beseech you therefore, brethren, by the mercies of God, that ye present your bodies a living sacrifice, holy acceptable unto God, which is your reasonable service," was the foundation for his impressive talk.

God grant that from our little band at Manteca may go forth laborers into the harvest, is our earnest prayer.

To those who are interested in the work of the Brethren in Manteca, I would say in regard to our church building, that we are ready to start, but we need some help financially. We have a fine corner lot 100x130 feet in the best portion of the city, facing the state highway and the lot is all paid for. We also have a monthly subscription list sufficient to meet the Building & Loan installments, but we are in need of more cash to be able to get out the loan. Our progress is blocked until we can get the cash to start with. Our Finance committee is working hard to get the required amount, but as none of our members possess much of this world's goods we are going to give everyone a chance to help us. Mrs. Bertha Elliott of Manteca is the secretary of the Finance committee and she will be more than glad to receive any amount the Lord may lay upon the hearts of the Brethren to give. This money will be put into the building fund and will positively be used for that purpose only.

We ask you to pray for the work at Manteca.

SUSIE G. REYNER,
Chairman Finance Committee.

FIRST BRETHREN CHURCH

Los Angeles, California

A few more things that may be of interest have come to us since our last letter. A three weeks' evangelistic campaign closed November 7th, conducted by our pastor, assisted by Brother L. S. Bauman of Long Beach. Brother Jennings did quite a good deal of visiting in the homes of the people and otherwise advertized and planned from day to day. Brother Bauman did all the preaching except on Sunday mornings when each pastor conducted his own service in his own church. The evangelist seemed to be at his best and preached with a good deal of vigor and power. A fine spirit prevailed all through the meeting and a very large percent of the membership stood faithfully by the work.

The choir did exceedingly well under the leadership of Brother Brilhart who is an artist in the use of the trombone as well as a fine soloist and leader of song.

The results that we can tabulate are as follows: Total confessions, 18. Baptized, 13. By letter, 1. By relation, 1. Not yet baptized and received into the church, 3.

Just after the close of the meeting, Tuesday, November 9th, a communion service was held at which 125 participated. We had a few visitors from Long Beach and from the Compton Avenue church, including the pastor, Brother Leatherman. It was one of the largest and best communion services we have ever enjoyed here. We were also pleased to have with us Sister Vianna Detwiler, so well known throughout the brotherhood, and who will spend the winter in our beautiful Southern California.

Our people take charge of the services one evening a month at the Union Rescue Mission,

145 North Main street, at which our pastor preaches the sermon. He has also preached there on a number of other occasions by invitation of the superintendent, Brother Price. Brother Jennings is always ready to assist in any good work where the people need to be encouraged and helped to a better life. He and some of our members have also visited the Old Folks' Home and talked and sung for the aged inmates. This too is a blessed work.

We recall now that three of our people who have been sick have called for the anointing service, and these services have resulted in great spiritual blessing.

Our people are greatly encouraged, we believe, and are being built up in the Christian life, and as conversions have been occurring right along from time to time during the past year, we anticipate a continued, steady and healthy growth in the year to come.

Yours in Christian love,
A. P. REED.

4910 Wadsworth Street.

PLEASANT HILL, OHIO

It is seldom that the Pleasant Hill church breaks into print through the columns of the Evangelist, but nevertheless this congregation is still moving forward in the work.

Since Brother S. Lowman has come to us the work here has taken on new life. Interest in things Brethren is being manifested throughout the community. Attendance is increasing and several more additions to the church have been made.

At the Rally Day services which were held a few weeks ago, all attendance records for the Sunday school have been broken, which means something when you realize that the church has been organized for above thirty years.

We feel fortunate indeed to have secured the services of Brother S. Lowman, and would be inclined to boast if it were not that we realize the serious need of more men like him in the brotherhood.

That Brother Lowman had a big job on his hands when he took up the work here is well known to all of the men who have had previous experience in this field, and that the work is progressing under his supervision is certainly encouraging.

We are made to feel that the rapid progress made in the past few months is only the beginning of bigger and greater things.

It would not be fair to our pastor if we conveyed the impression that he is merely a good organizer—he is more than that; he is a consecrated Bible teacher as well, and we feel that his sermons are well worth serious consideration. We trust that the work at this place will have a place in your prayers.

H. C. MARLIN.

EATON, INDIANA

This is a rural church and one naturally expects the attendance to slow up just a little through the busy season when the farmers are hard at work. But this has not happened this summer. Our attendance has been right at

normal with the exception of a very few Sundays.

Holy communion was observed on the evening of November seventh. The attendance was good but not record-breaking. The interest and impressiveness of the service were more than ordinary. Each participant seemed to and I believe did receive a special blessing. These are truly seasons of refreshing and strengthening.

Clay City

In response to a telegram from Henderson and Thomas I made haste to get down to Clay City that we might have a complete team—avoirdupois, pep, and noise. This was truly a great meeting—not in numbers but in other respects. It is one meeting which cannot rightly be put on paper. One had to begin it to realize its greatness. There is a fine leadership here and next year they should come to Oakville and say to the Mission Board, "We are full grown now and can walk alone."

Huntington

This is another of Indiana's mission points and on the 28th of November I expect to begin a series of meetings for them. It has never been my privilege to work in a meeting with Brother Brower but I am anticipating a great time. I covet the prayers of God's people that I and the Huntington workers may do our best in this meeting and we will leave the results with the Lord. (Come on, Clay City, help Huntington with your prayers.)

H. E. EPPLEY.

MORRILL, KANSAS

Rev. A. E. Whitted has begun his third year as pastor of the church at this place. Mrs. Whitted is a very efficient assistant in the work. She has charge of the Junior Endeavorers and is assistant superintendent of the Sunday school. All departments of the work are in running order.

The Sunday school has had a slightly increased attendance this year, despite the fact that it suffered an unusually heavy loss by removals last spring. Mrs. Whitted had charge of the Temperance Day programme. After paying her respects to John Barleycorn, she said some things for the benefit of the tobacco users. And the boys who have not yet begun the habit. If more people felt as Mrs. Whitted does on this subject, and voted as they felt, there would not be many inveterate tobacco users placed in responsible positions in the church. The Sunday school provides the teachers of the boys' classes and the superintendent of the Temperance department, with copies of the No Tobacco Educator, published at Pittsburgh, Pa.

At the fall business meeting two men who had been re-elected to the official board, declined to serve in order to give some new men a chance. And why not? If official positions in the church are rightly to be regarded as opportunities to serve the church, Why should one man be given several of them year after year while others, just as competent are never given an opportunity to render such service or to develop the latent talent they may possess!

A. W. Lichty who had served the church for many years as deacon and superintendent of the Sunday school, died in an Omaha hospital recently.

Rev. and Mrs. J. H. Burnworth visited here recently. Brother Burnworth settled in this community forty-six years ago before the prairie was fenced, and was a charter member of the old Pony Creek church, which later became the Morrill church.

Rev. Ashman has been engaged to hold our revival meeting, beginning the last week in December.

C. W. YODER, Correspondent.

DOINGS AT DAYTON

Among the many things that have been doing at Dayton, we will mention a few to let the readers of the Evangelist know we are not inactive, but pushing the Master's work at the First Brethren church. The pastor, Dr. E. M. Cobb, is just as enthusiastic and interested in forwarding and promoting a greater zeal in the hearts of its membership for the systematic study of God's Word, as he was when entering his pastorate over two years ago. Special Bible study classes began active work October First, Tuesday and Wednesday evenings, and recently he has organized the "Bible Class," an extension class of the Los Angeles Bible Institute, which meets every Friday evening and has a fine membership. Surely the membership of our church is not wanting in specific Bible instruction, and while the classes are well attended, many more should take advantage of the opportunity at hand which will not always last. Elder Arthur Lynn, assistant to the pastor, has just returned from his vacation, during which he filled two evangelistic engagements, as music director at Fremont and Ohio City, Ohio, respectively, and reports very favorable results in conversions at both points, and a great interest in the meetings with large attendance. He started in another two weeks' engagement last night, at the St. Paul's M. E. church, Dayton, Ohio. He is kept very busy, and unable to fill all his calls, especially during his time demanded at the First Brethren, but has been given a furlough of two months from February First to meet some of his most urgent calls, after which he will return to his regular work here.

We are anticipating a great revival campaign to begin Sunday, January second, and count ourselves very fortunate in securing the services of Dr. Charles A. Bame, as evangelist to assist us in the meetings, and with Brother Arthur Lynn as music director, and our pastor, Dr. Cobb, the trio, with the help of the active personal workers in the church, we have good reason to believe that under the directing hand, and Spirit of the Great Shepherd, many souls should be won for him, in the campaign, and to this end we pray and seek an interest in the prayers of the membership in our great brotherhood!

Our Thanksgiving offering of Sunday, November 21st, was very satisfactory, and funds are still being received from absentees. Final report may be made later. Our communion service was held on the evening of the same date. I will quote from our church calendar of November 28th: "Now honest, wasn't

that about the finest love feast you ever attended? It was the largest ever held in the church, if not in the denomination. Every seat downstairs in the main auditorium was taken; the rear section of the balcony only was reserved for visitors and the rest was occupied by communicants, and half of the choir loft was taken. What a glorious sight! What beautiful solemnity! The Spirit of God reigneth supreme. And such order. The brethren and sisters were surely mindful that they were in the presence of the Lord. Then too, the management was superb (under the direction of Brother W. A. Gearhart, chairman of our Deacon Board). The large concourse of people were served in exactly two hours, 6:15 to 8:15. That is a record."

On Thanksgiving day at 5:30 the church was literally packed to witness an exquisitely beautiful church wedding, at which the pastor was "Past master" to a nicety in performing a double ring ceremony, when one of our choir girls, Miss Helen Coy, was united in wedlock with Mr. John Siebenthaler. There were about 300 invited guests, but an invitation was extended to the church membership, and many took the invitation seriously, see! The floral decorations, the solos, marches, and ceremony were all very aesthetic indeed! May a beautiful Christian life exemplify the wedded ones.

The pastor, Dr. Cobb, has again been called to deliver a course of lectures on Fundamentals at Rochester, New York, Gospel Center; and also to speak at Buffalo, on several occasions, and will leave about December 1st to fill the engagements. Elders Lynn, Minderman and others will occupy the home base during his stay in the east. Last Sunday morning at the close of the church service, a baptismal service was held at which seven were immersed and one was received into church fellowship by relation, and the interest in the congregation shows that a fine harvest should be gathered in our anticipated January campaign. Other things of interest must wait for later report, lest we weary you.

WILLIAM C. TEETER,
Corresponding Secretary.

FIELD REPORT OF EVANGELISTIC AND BIBLE STUDY LEAGUE

Goshen Meetings

Four years ago I had the pleasure of holding a meeting here with these good people when Brother J. L. Kimmel was pastor and God gave us a great victory. When I returned to hold another meeting this year I was a little fearful that coming back so soon we might not have the same response, but that fear vanished before the first week was over. From the very first, we had good audiences, the church being filled to overflowing several evenings.

Brother McInturff had everything ready and the church lined up for the campaign, and beginning with the second week we had confessions nearly all the remaining nights. The Lord gave us another great victory and we were glad to see several husbands and their wives walk down the aisles and give themselves to Christ.

This is one of our largest and most active

churches in the denomination and Brother McInturff is to be congratulated for his leadership and victories won here during his pastorate. Since I was here before they have secured and purchased a fine parsonage and only a few weeks ago had a rally day and raised $2,500.00. The work here is moving along nicely. The building that they now have is not big enough for the large Sunday school, which is crowding Dayton for first place in the brotherhood. The attendance a few Sundays ago at one service was 562. In the days to come they will have to push their walls out farther and make room for more. Goshen, we wish you prosperity and increase with God's blessing.

Back Home

I have not seen my family since the middle of August and have been going day and night and feel the need of a rest. I am returning to my home in Sunnyside, Washington, where I will spend the winter and supply for the church there, while Brother Ashman takes my place in the field. He will hold meetings in Falls City, Nebraska, Morrill, Kansas, Johnstown and Pittsburgh, Pennsylvania.

W. S. BELL.

MINUTES OF THE MIDDLE WEST DISTRICT CONFERENCE HELD AT FORT SCOTT, OCTOBER 12-14, 1920

The first session of the conference was held Tuesday evening at 7:30, opened with devotionals led by Moderator A. E. Whitted. Conference sermon was delivered by E. S. Flora, who preached a very able sermon using for his theme, "Faith of Our Fathers," and reading for a Scripture lesson Genesis 28.

The Moderator appointed as a credential committee, J. B. Enslow, E. S. Flora and Mrs. G. W. Dowell.

This session closed with benediction by J. B. Enslow.

Wednesday morning session opened at 9 o'clock. Devotions were conducted by Vice Moderator Roy Brumbaugh.

E. E. Otto gave an address of welcome to the visiting delegates.

Responses were made by a number of delegates.

The report of the credential committee showed 8 ministerial and 12 lay delegates present.

The Moderator's message was given by A. E. Whitted. He spoke of the great loss to this district in the death of John Lichty of Falls City and Sadie Gibbons Eggleston, of St. Joseph.

He showed that the work had progressed during the past year, that 9 out of ten churches had regular pastors, the majority of the churches had adopted the budget system and each church had held a series of meetings. This district is represented among the banner churches.

The majority of the Sunday schools are front line, and the W. M. S. societies are second to none.

The election of conference officers took place at this time. The following officers were elected: Moderator, Roy Brumbaugh;

Vice Moderator, E. S. Flora; Secretary-Treasurer, Mrs. G. W. Dowell.

Report of the Home Mission Board was given by Elias Lichty who made excellent suggestions regarding this work for the coming year. After thorough discussion of the plans, a motion was made to elect two members on the board, S. C. Flickinger of Morrill, N. P. Eglin of Hamlin being elected. A song and benediction brought this session to a close.

The first of the excellent meals prepared by the ladies of Fort Scott was served to the delegates in the upper story of the church.

Wednesday afternoon session opened at two. Devotions were conducted by E. S. Flora. The first address of the afternoon was on the subject, "Stewardship of Life," by Roy Brumbaugh, who very ably discussed this theme and showed the great importance of each one doing their part to hold high our Bible and to extend our Christian faith. He spoke of the many excuses offered for not doing our duty.

Prof. J. A. Garber of Ashland, Ohio, was introduced by the Moderator and gave a splendid talk on The Curriculum of the Sunday School. He made his statements so clear that even the smallest child could understand them. He gave the definition of curriculum—as a series of stepping stones by which the child mounts from its present position to that place we would have it reach. He emphasized the importance of instilling into the immature mind the things we would have developed in the mature mind.

Wednesday evening session opened with a song service and devotions conducted by H. F. Stuckman and a solo by Mr. Scott of the M. E. church. The address of the evening was given by J. A. Garber on the subject, "Religious Education." He told of the interest being manifested in the college by the people of Ashland, the improvements that are being made and the appreciation shown of the good work that is being accomplished at Ashland. Closing song, "Count your Blessings;" benediction by E. S. Flora.

Thursday morning the last session, was opened by a special prayer service in behalf of Mrs. Fetler (the wife of a former Fort Scott minister) who was very ill at Columbus, Ohio.

The first period of this session was devoted to the transaction of the conference business. By motion, A. E. Whitted of Morrill was elected Director of the Bicentenary Movement in this district.

By motion, E. S. Flora of Beaver City, was elected District Director of the Spiritual Lief in the Bicentenary Movement.

By motion Marie Lichty of Falls City, Lillie B. Johnson of Beaver City, Hazel B. Gaston of Hamlin were elected to serve as a Religious Education Committee from this district.

By motion, the conference accepted the invitation of the Morrill church to hold the next session at Morrill.

By motion, H. F. Stuckman was elected Evangelistic Director of this district.

By motion, S. C. Flickinger, Morrill, H. S.

Brumbaugh, of Portis, were named as Middle West nominees for Ashland College Trustees.

A vote of thanks was tendered the Fort Scott people for their hospitality and kindness to the visiting delegates.

The next hour was given to the W. M. S. society. Vice President, Mrs. Lewis, presided. She explained the goals for the coming year and gave helpful suggestions along the line of reaching them. Mrs. Whitted's report from W. M. S. session of National Conference was full of inspiration and help for all who heard it. She also gave encouragement and help to the Sisterhood Girls.

By motion, Mrs. H. F. Stuckman was elected president of the W. M. S.; Mrs. Jennie Lewis, Vice President; Mrs. A. E. Whitted, Secretary-Treasurer.

The closing number on the program was the Bicentenary Movement which was a very able discussion by H. F. Stuckman. He emphasized the deep importance of starting at once to make the goals. "God be with you till we meet again," was sung and J. B. Ensworth offered the closing prayer.

MRS. G. W. DOWELL,
Secretary.

APPEAL TO DELINQUENT CHURCHES

There is yet a large number of our churches in the Indiana and Pennsylvania districts as well as a few scattered churches in other sections who have not responded to the various appeals published. This is an obligation that must be paid and is just as sacred to us as the giving of money for missions and the many other good things which the Brethren are doing.

The money will have to be raised in some manner and it is not fair to the entire brotherhood who have done their share for a few to neglect their duty in this important matter. Pastors, take it upon yourself to look into this matter and see if your church has paid; if not make arrangements at once to do so. The apportionment is fifteen cents per member and the amount yet to be collected and paid is $700.00.

We are hoping that this will be the last appeal that will be necessary to close this matter. Send all checks to H. E. Roscoe, Treasurer Tabernacle Fund, Goshen, Indiana.

NOTICE

Will those having friends in Fort Wayne, Indiana, who are members of, or in sympathy with, the Brethren church, please send name and full address of same to,

MR. and MRS. J. E. HAM,
815 Clay St., Ft. Wayne, Indiana.

THE TIE THAT BINDS

SMITH-MORT: IRVINE-CLOA — At the home of Brother and Sister Samuel Smith near Sidney, Indiana, on Thanksgiving Day occurred the wedding of their son, Dorsey, to Vernice Mort, and also the wedding of their daughter, Cloa, to Edwin Irvine. These are all fine Christian young folks and we pray God's richest blessing and benediction on them. The ceremony was said by the writer. A. T. RONK.

RUFF-HALL—At the home of the bride's aunt occurred the wedding of Mr. Melvin Ruff and Miss Wilma Hall, Wednesday evening, October 6. The bride is a daughter of

Brother and Sister Ralph Hall, and the groom is a farmer in the neighborhood. The wedding was before a large number of friends and relatives. These young people are members of the Carlton church and are very popular in the community. May the choicest blessings be theirs through life. Ceremony by FREEMAN ANKRUM.

IN THE SHADOW

FOLTZ—William W. Foltz, a son of Mr. and Mrs. Elijah Foltz, was born in St. Joseph county, Indiana, on October 12, 1865 and departed from this life on November 8th, 1926, aged 55 years. His marriage to Miss Anna Elizabeth Wise took place on October 17th, 1886. His wife, two children, two grandchildren, a brother and four sisters survive him.

Brother Foltz has been a faithful and loyal member of the Brethren church for 13 years. His family and many friends will miss his presence. Funeral services were conducted by the writer, assisted by Brother Kimmel, of Muncie.   B. S. STOFFER.

SNYDER—Emanuel Snyder, son of Albert and Annie (Varner) Snyder, parted from this life on November first, in his fortieth year. Death was due to injuries received while at work in the Cambria Steel Co., on the last day of October. He is survived by his wife, Grace (Page) Snyder, and eight children. May the God of ease comfort their hearts. Funeral services conducted in the Wesley (M. E.) Chapel, by the undersigned.
E. F. BYERS.

BURKHART—Roscoe L. Burkhart, son of David F. and Ellen (Shaffer) Burkhart, passed from death unto life, Saturday morning, November 6th, in his 39th year. Death was due to Bright's disease and heart trouble. Brother Burkhart was a member of the Brethren church for 27 years, having united with the church when but 12 years of age. He was a good man, a Christian, one whose life corresponded with the profession of his lips. He is survived by his parents, and the following brothers and sisters: Hulda, wife of Hite Rorabaugh, of Conemaugh; Lettia, wife of Irvin Wissinger, of Milwood; Harry L., of Milwood; and Ruby and Olin at home. May the God that raised up Jesus from the dead comfort the hearts of those who mourn the loss of a splendid son and a good brother. Services conducted in the Pike Brethren church, by the undersigned, assisted by Rev. G. H. Jones of Conemaugh, Pa.
E. F. BYERS.

EAST, WEST, HOME'S BEST

It has been said that The Youth's Companion has had more readers per copy than any other publication in America. There is a good reason to believe this to be true. But the important thing is that the influence of the paper upon its millions of readers has always been directed to building character. "East, west, home's best," has been its unuttered slogan. In its articles, editorial and otherwise, it has dwelt upon the importance of good citizenship. In all its contents it has aimed to give not only entertainment, but "stepping-stones to higher things."

A year of The Youth's Companion brings a tremendous tide of delightful and diversified reading that cannot be found elsewhere.

The 52 issues of 1921 will be crowded with serial stories, short stories, editorials, poetry, facts and fun. Subscribe now and receive:
1. The Youth's Companion—52 issues in 1921.
2. All the remaining issues of 1920.
3. The Companion Home Calendar for 1921. All the above for $2.50.
4. McCall's Magazine for 1921. The monthly authority on fashions, $1.50 a year. Both publications, only $3.50.

THE YOUTH'S COMPANION
Commonwealth Ave. & St. Paul St. Boston, Mass.

New Subscriptions Received at this Office.

CHRISTMAS MORN -

*"Glory to God in the Highest
And on Earth, Peace
And Good Will among Men."*

Published every Wednesday at
Ashland, Ohio. All matter for publication must reach the Editor not
later than Friday noon of the preceding week.

George S. Baer, Editor

The

Brethren

Evangelist

When ordering your paper changed
give old as well as new address.
Subscriptions discontinued at expiration. To avoid missing any numbers renew two weeks in advance.

R. R. Teeter, Business Manage

ASSOCIATE EDITORS: J. Fremont Watson, Louis S. Bauman, A. B. Cover, Alva J. McClain, B. T. Burnworth.

OFFICIAL ORGAN OF THE BRETHREN CHURCH

Subscription price, $2.00 per year, payable in advance.
Entered at the Post Office at Ashland, Ohio, as second-class matter.
Acceptance for mailing at special rate of postage provided for in section 1103, Act of October 3, 1917, authorized September 9, 1918.
Address all matter for publication to Geo. S. Baer, Editor of the Brethren Evangelist, and all business communications to R. R. Teeter,
Business Manager, Brethren Publishing Company, Ashland, Ohio. Make all checks payable to the Brethren Publishing Company.

TABLE OF CONTENTS

EDITORIAL

What Does Christmas Mean to You?

To some Christmas means merely a holiday and a time of jollity and receiving and giving of gifts. It is merely one of the most joy-bringing of the many holidays in the year's calendar. They scarcely know how the day originated or why it is maintained. There is a vague impression among them that one Jesus was born many years ago and that he is somehow associated with this day. But as to the real significance of the day, they have no consciousness of it. Of such we expect no White Gift to aid in the great work that the National Sunday School Association is carrying on in the Lord's name.

There are others to whom Christmas means more than a mere holiday; it is the day on which was born the greatest Man who ever lived,—a man whose influence has spread over the world and transformed the nations thereof. It is a day that celebrates the birth of a life as does Washington's birthday or Lincoln's, though much more wonderful and inexplicable. They honor the Christ because he was a great reformer. The strength of his character, the courage of his convictions, his friendship for the poor and the unparalleled beauty and perfection of his teaching, they appreciate, and so they celebrate Christmas. They will give gifts more noble than the former class, and may give more generously, but we cannot expect them to be White Gifts of self, service and substance like the wise men brought, —gifts that are inspired by love, devotion and adoration such as cause the heart to rejoice in sacrifice.

To others Christmas means the celebration of the birth of the Son of God among men. They look upon Jesus to be truly the promised Messiah; his credentials are accepted as genuine. They marvel at his mighty works of healing and teaching, and every manifestation of divine power. He was all that he claimed to be; he was the Christ of God; he was the Lord of heaven and earth. And as such they honor him and stand in awe before his majesty and goodness. They reverence him and keep sacred the day of his birth. They even give many and costly gifts to alleviate the suffering and distress of their fellow-humans, because the giving spirit is that which dominated the life of him whom they would honor. But they give not the White Gifts which are so much part and parcel of the giver that they throb with his life, glow with the warmth of his love and reflect the sincerity of his interest.

But there are hosts of noble souls who look upon Christmas as commemorating not only the birth of the Son of God in human form, but the coming of him who was to be the Savior of the world and who is their own personal Savior. They have grasped the meaning of that heavenly declaration of Christ when he said, "For God so loved the world that he gave his only begotten Son that whosoever believeth in him might not perish but have everlasting life." In their own hearts they have felt the constraint of that love, and in self-confessed weakness and humility they have turned the eye of faith to the all-sufficient Savior and have experienced the thrills of his quickening and transforming power. To them Jesus is not a vague historical personage; he is not merely a great reformer; not merely the Son of God; he is their blessed Redeemer. It was to this end that the angel of the Lord declared the Christ should be born,—"Thou shalt call his name Jesus for he shall save his people from their sins." It is in the performance of this mission that he wins the disciples of the purest and deepest love, the truest and most persevering loyalty and the most sincere and self-sacrificing service. And it is from such as these—men and women who have personally experienced the saving grace of the Son of God in their hearts and who rejoice in the full realization of the purpose of his coming—that we can expect gifts pure and white and worthy to do honor to the King on his birthday. From such as these will come gifts of self, service and substance such as will constitute a worthy token and sincere acknowledgment of the Lordship of Christ and the stewardship of their own life.

He who thus appreciates the significance of Christmas and possesses an abiding and deep love for him who was born on Christmas day cannot be silent or selfish about the joy that blesses his life. The spirit of Christ cannot be confined and restrained in the soul of man. He who attempts it will soon find that the good spirit has left him and an evil spirit has taken its place. The Christian is by the very fact of his new birth unselfish and concerned about the welfare of others. The peace he knows he wants others to possess. The joy that fills his heart he wants to pass on to others. The Christ he loves he wants to tell others about. The gratitude that fills his heart because "God so loved the world that he gave his only begotten

Son'' must find expression in word and life and gifts. It is just as natural and inevitable that the Christian should communicate his joy to others as that the bird should sing its songs in the springtime. He whose heart is throbbing with the life of Christ cannot be silent concerning the news of a Savior's birth, nor belfish with the "unspeakable gift" which God has given in the person of his Son.

Now, would we dare repeat the question with which we started out, making it very personal? "What does Christmas mean to you?" Does it seem too personal? That is Christ's way. He always puts things very personally. In fact, what Christmas means to you depends entirely upon your personal attitude toward Christ.

In the first place Christmas cannot mean to you what it may and ought to mean until you have taken Christ to be your personal Savior and have experienced his regenerating power in your life. You may believe him to be the Son of God and may speak words and give gifts in his honor, but there is no other gift that will be acceptable to him until you have given him yourself. That is the first White Gift that you can give.

When you have given yourself to Christ and he has become the center of your life, the meaning of Christmas in its larger sense is still dependent upon your personal attitude toward Christ. He would be your Lord as well as your Savior. He wants your service as well as your life. Your time, your talents, your opportunities,—what will you do with them? This Christmas can never mean what it ought to mean to you until you are willing to give to the Christ of Christmas every service of which you are capable.

Yet again is the meaning of Christmas dependent upon your personal attitude towards Christ. He would be not only your Savior and Lord, but the recognized owner of all that you possess. Christ is never satisfied so long as his ownership and man's stewardship is not recognized and acknowledged—he is not satisfied because man thereby denies himself of an experience which would otherwise greatly enrich his life. And if you desire that Christmas shall be full of meaning for you, bring to him as did the wise men of old gifts of your substance, in loving acknowledgment of his ownership of all.

Thus may we honor the King on his birthday, and Christmas will come to be in reality what it is in name,—a Christ-mas, or sacred service.

EDITORIAL REVIEW

Buy Christmas seals and fight tuberculosis.

Remember the suffering of Armenia and the starving of China at the Christmas season.

You will notice some Home Mission reports from Brother Gearheart in this issue. Has your name been reported. Or have you paid up yet?

A really great victory has been won at Brighton, Indiana, and the Brethren there are greatly encouraged and going forward under the enthusiastic leadership of Brother J. W. Clark.

The "Paper Fund" is still growing and all connected with the Publishing Company are grateful for the splendid support that is being given the publishing interests. The Evangelist Honor Roll is being maintained in a splendid manner.

A brother who is a careful reader of The Evangelist writes appreciatingly of Brother E. E. Robert's articles on "Christian Baptism," and requests the sending of a copy on a missionary journey to a friend.

The good people of Gratis, Ohio, are endeavoring to keep their house in order until the arrival of their new pastor, Brother Roy Brumbaugh. Workers from a number of the Miami Valley churches are giving them noble assistance.

"Expect great things from God; attempt great things for God," quotes our correspondent from the Long Beach church, Sister N. H. Nielsen. And in their expecting and attempting, God is working through them for the accomplishing of great things.

Brother A. P. Reed reports further ingatherings at the First church of Los Angeles where the Lord's work is going steadily forward under the leadership of Brother N. W. Jennings. The Sunday school is also giving evidences of this gowth.

Send your White Gift offerings to Prof. H. H. Wolford, Ashland, Ohio.

Brother Claude Studebaker who was formerly at home among the little group of Brethren at Mulberry Grove, Illinois, has decided to give himself to full-time service for the Lord and has accepted the pastorate of the Hamlin, Kansas, church. May the Lord prosper him.

Christians should live in the world, but not be filled with it. A ship lives in the water; but if the water gets into the ship, she goes to the bottom. So Christians may live in the world; but if the world gets into them, they sink.

A new voice in a Brethren pulpit is now heard at the Sergeantsville-Calvary charge where Brother Orville Jobson is acting as pastor until a resident pastor can be secured. Brother Jobson is doing school work in Philadelphia in the Bible school where Brother McClain is teaching.

An even hundred confessions of Christ is a great victory. That was the numerical report of the evangelistic meeting held by Brother I. D. Bowman at Buena Vista, Virginia. The presence of the Holy Spirit in great power was very evident. That is always an essential to successful evangelism, or any other work for the Lord.

The West Alexandria church has no thought of hanging "a crepe on the door," according to the enthusiastic correspondent who is known to us only as "M. S." Brother C. E. Beekley has taken charge of the work at this place and things seem to be moving forward with much prospect.

Brother Bame reports a successful evangelistic campaign conducted at Mount Hope, Virginia. It is at the Mount of Hope where such success usually occurs. Not only hope but faith and prayer must have been strong at this point because of the remarkable meeting they had.

The "Christmas Message" which appears on page 10 of this issue, comes from The United American Press, the common imprint over which more than 35 Evangelical Christian churches of the United States and Canada are planning to publish literature for adults who do not read the English language. This literature will seek to set forth the ideals and principles of Jesus as the Savior and Lord of all.

If all our people could have just a little experience in our mission fields and understand conditions as they really are, the work would be more adequately supported and the needs more quickly met. Brother and Sister Teall of Elkhart, Indiana, who were in Kentucky helping in the work for a time give their testimony as to the need of a nurse at Lost Creek.

Silence does not spell slump for Masontown. says Brother Joseph Gingrich, the hustling pastor. He had the courage to launch into a revival meeting without any outside help and it proved to be a real revival, though no additions to the church were realized. The church is giving him loyal co-operation, as it knows how to do, and we dare say that they will under God be able to realize their aim and need—an enlarged church building.

The greatest ingathering yet reported this year from a single campaign is the one about which Brother C. H. Ashman writes in this issue. A hundred additions to a church should mean great things for the future of that church and will undoubtedly mean great work for the pastor. It is remarkable the success was attained in spite of the sad and fatal accident to one member of the evangelistic party. This great victory should be a splendid preparation for Brother Ashman as he enters upon his evangelistic tour.

We are in receipt of the "Industrial Bulletin" of The Colorado Fuel and Iron Company, located at Denver, and in it we find the notice of the election of Brother A. H. Lichty to the vice presidency of that company. In that capacity, the "Bulletin" states, "He will devote his attention exclusively to matters bearing on employees' representation and conditions affecting employment." The Evangelist family among whom he is so widely known will be pleased to learn of this new advancement and the opportunity of Christian welfare work which the position offers. Those who knew "Bert" Lichty in his school days believed that he was a man of extraordinary ability and his steady climb has proven that he was not wrongly estimated.

CONCERNING THAT WHITE GIFT OFFERING

White Gifts For The King

By Prof. H. H. Wolford
Secretary Treasurer National Sunday School Association

Our gifts to Christ at Christmas time have rightly been called "White Gifts." White is the emblem of purity. We are promised white robes in his kingdom, emblems of our purity as we shall ever be before him.

Let us ask ourselves the question as to how our gifts should be given and what kind of gifts are really "White Gifts" to him.

If our gifts are to be pure and while they must be given in love. Great love for him ought to be our characteristic Christian virtue. "We love him because he first loved us." God's great love was and is manifested unto us through Jesus Christ our Savior. How much we ought to love him when we continually realize that through him we have the forgiveness of our sins. Christ's love to us has been bountiful and forgiving. Our gifts to him should be great. Unto him whom we love we will give our best. But we will also give white gifts because we love others. Indeed our gift of money to him will be used for others. Those who do not have the great opportunities that we have, should be recipients of our gifts. We love them and wish to give to them the same Christian joy that we possess. They have not heard of him. How shall they hear except some one be sent? How can any one be sent without the money necessary to send and keep them? Therefore because we love those who know not Christ we will give "White Gifts" to them.

Again our gifts will be white if they are given cheerfully. God loveth a cheerful giver. Indeed our gifts can not be truly gifts of love unless they are given cheerfully. God has given to us in abundance; we will give to him cheerfully. As we cheerfully give, we will pray that God may use that gift to its fullest extent in helping some one into the blessed light of the Gospel.

Our gifts will be White if given in proportion to what God has given us. As the Lord has prospered us, so will we give unto him. We can not withhold because, while men may not know how much we have received, God knows. We can not deceive him. Not according to our measure should we give but according to his measure as he has prospered us. When we give to him let us remember his supreme gift to us, and then also the gift of material things which have come from him. All we are, all we have and all we hope to be is through him. That which is his, we will give him.

For the most part our Sunday schools make but one gift to others. The time for that gift has now come. You are familiar with the budget as given elsewhere in this paper. Let our gifts be "White" because of our great love for Christ and others. Let it also be cheerfully given and in proportion to his gift to us in material things.

Ashland, Ohio.

ADORATION OF THE SHEPHERDS. (MURILLO)

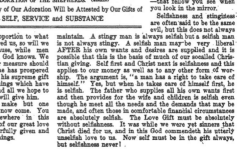

The Sincerity of Our Adoration Will be Attested by Our Gifts of SELF, SERVICE and SUBSTANCE

Christmas Love Gifts

By A. V. Kimmell
Vice President National Sunday School Association

FOR GOD SO LOVED THAT HE GAVE

No other words so adequately express the reason every Christmas gift should be a love gift. That the gift was the human birth of his Son, the Word so emphatically attests. That the day called Christmas is appointed for the celebration of his birth is recognized by all civilized nations. Thus fundamentally a Christmas gift is a love gift.

Are we straying from the fundamental in the keeping of this day? An oft repeated caption would so indicate. Many songs are being written to the "spirit of Christmas;" many recitations are being spoken headed "the spirit of Christmas;" many addresses are being given upon "the spirit of Christmas." The world is strong on "the spirit of Christmas;" the infidel is blatant in lauding the "spirit of Christmas;" the Christ denying preachers are masters in using the expression, and in so doing they have taken THE CHRIST out of Christmas and in his place are offering for worship in a popular way THE SPIRIT OF A HOLIDAY. Now hear the shout of the angels before the city of Bethlehem on that glad morning, "For unto you is born this day in the city of David a Savior, which is Christ the Lord." These words kept ringing in our ears will keep Christ in Christmas and will keep us recognizing that he is the greatest Love Gift ever given.

The Love Gift Must Be Unselfish

Even in the lives of recognized liberal people self plays an important part. Self is largely responsible for habits, likes and dislikes, temperament, etc. Of course this works for good as well as evil, but the point is that self must be reckoned with, —that fellow you see when you look in the mirror.

Selfishness and stinginess are often said to be the same evil, but this does not always maintain. A stingy man is always selfish but a selfish man is not always stingy. A selfish man may be very liberal AFTER his own wants and desires are supplied and it is possible that this is the basis of much of our socalled Christian giving. Self first and Christ next is selfishness and this applies to our money as well as to any other form of worship. The argument is, "a man has a right to take care of himself." Yes, but when he takes care of himself first, he is selfish. The father who supplies all his own wants first and then provides for the wife and children is selfish even though he meet all the needs and the demands that may be made, and often those in comfortable financial circumstances are absolutely selfish. The Love Gift must be absolutely without selfishness. It was while we were yet sinners that Christ died for us, and in this God commendeth his utterly unselfish love to us. Now self must be in the gift always, but selfishness never!

The White Gift as a Love Gift

At no time in the year should we give so unstintingly and without measure as at the Christmas time, especially this Christmas time. 1. Our Substance: This is the hardest place for many to be liberal. When a man's pocket-book,—his possessions—his substance, is wholly given to the Lord the rest is usually upon the altar. The various uses of the White Gift offerings call out that we make this truly an unselfish love gift.

2. Our Service: Hear this, people, your all belongs to the Lord. Not merely your money but your time, energy, ability, works, words, acts, it all belongs to him. You are a steward entrusted with these precious God-given avenues for service. The Book says, "It is required of a steward that he be found faithful." Some day you must give an accounting. What will you say as to the service you have so long withheld from him?

3. Self: All the above without YOU is worthless. Your service, your money amounts to nothing without YOU. There was a time when men were called to die for Christ. At this time in our own land, at least, there is a call to live for him. "I beseech you therefore, brethren, by the mercies of God, that ye present your bodies a LIVING SACRIFICE, holy, acceptable unto God, which is your reasonable service.

May this Christmas time find the peace of him, to whom the angels sang, filling your heart to overflowing because you have offered as your love gift SELF AND SERVICE AND SUBSTANCE.

Whittier, California.

GENERAL ARTICLES

Natural Men, and Spiritual Men   By Samuel Kiehl

Christ hath redeemed us from the curse of the law, being made a curse for us, that we (men, women and children) might receive the promise of the Spirit through faith (Gal. 4:13). Our theme includes all, but treats of men only.

There are in the world, according to the "Word," two classes; natural men and spiritual men (1 Cor. 2:14, 15, Gal. 6:1). Natural men are born once (Job 14:1); spiritual men, twice (John 3:7). The natural man is begotten of his father, born of his mother, and from them inherits human nature. The spiritual man is begotten of God (with the word of truth, Jas. 1:18), born of the spirit (John 3:6), and is a partaker of the divine nature (2 Pet. 1:4). The natural birth is an egress, the spiritual birth is an ingress (John 7:39; 1 Cor. 2:12). He who has the Spirit of God dwelling in him, is in the Spirit (Rom. 8:9); is born again; is a spiritual man. The natural man is a free moral agent, he can accept, or reject Jesus Christ as his Savior and Lord. The spiritual man, (standing fast in the liberty wherewith Christ hath made him free. Gal. 5:1), is Christ's voluntary servant and devoted follower. The initial steps to be taken by the natural man to become a spiritual man are, "Repentance toward God, and faith toward our Lord Jesus Christ" (Jesus, —Mark 1:15; 16:16. Paul,—Acts 20:21; Rom. 10:9).

The natural man receiveth not the things of the Spirit of God, for they (salvation, regeneration, eternal life, etc., received by faith in Christ the only begotten Son of God) are foolishness unto him; neither can he know them because they are spiritually discerned (1 Cor. 2:14). The things of God knoweth no man, but the Spirit of God (1 Cor. 2:11), and the natural man (before receiving Christ as his personal Savior and Lord), not having the spirit of God dwelling in him, has no spiritual vision, saving faith, or Christian experience. He cannot say concerning spiritual things, "One thing I know, that, whereas I was blind, now I see."

The carnal mind (the natural man's mind) is enmity against God; for it is not subject to the law of God, neither indeed can be. So then they that are in the flesh cannot please (obey) God (Rom. 8:7, 8). Paul says, I keep under my body, and bring it into subjection (1 Cor. 9:27). The natural man cannot do that according to Romans 8:7, 8 Jesus says, If ye love me keep my commandments (John 14:15). Who can love Christ and keep his commandments? The "word" (Rom. 8: 7, 8; 1 Cor. 2:14) teaches that the natural man cannot do so. Why? Because the God-given power, the Holy Ghost (1 Cor. 6:19), received by faith in Christ (John 7:39), is not dwelling in him. Those to whom God hath given the Holy Ghost obey him (Acts 5:32) He who obeys God is subject to his law. Romans 9:7 says, the carnal mind cannot be subject to the law of God. That is final.

Is there no hope for such? Yes, there is, praise the Lord! Christ Jesus came into the world to save natural men and women (1 Tim. 1:15). He gave himself a ransom for all (1 Tim. 2:6). And the Holy Scriptures are able to make them wise unto salvation through faith which is in Christ Jesus (2 Tim. 3:15). When Peter, on the day of Pentecost, preached Christ to natural men (Christ rejecting Jews), as many as gladly received his word, repented, believed, and were baptized (Acts 2:41). Such baptized believers,—saved, consecrated, spiritual men (not natural men, or baptized hypocrites, lovers of pleasures more than lovers of God, 2 Tim. 3:4),—the Lord is adding to his church daily (Mat. 16:18; Acts 2:47). That is the scriptural way the church receives substantial, numerical strength and spiritual power. If the pure gospel is preached, and the godly life is daily lived by those in the church, the Lord will do the adding. Let us not set a "goal" for him. He knoweth those that are his (2 Tim. 2:19), and will take care of them (John 10:28). Bless his holy name.

Natural men are men of the world (their environment is on a horizontal, worldly plane), therefore speak they of the world, and the world heareth them (1 John 4:5). The spiritual man is not a man of the world. His life is hid with Christ in God (Col. v:3). His physical environment is on a horizontal, earthly plane, but his spiritual environment is in a vertical, heavenly plane. He is seeking those things which are above, where Christ sitteth on the right hand of God. His affection is set on things above, not on things on the earth (Col. 3:1, 2). He knows that Christ hath gone to prepare a place for him, and some day will come again, and receive him unto himself; that where Christ is, there he may be also (John 14:2, 3). Such a bright, heavenly prospect fills his soul "with joy unspeakable and full of glory (1 Pet. 1:8).

Dear reader, (if you have not yet received Christ as your personal Savior and Lord), please listen, Christ dwells in the heart by faith (Eph. 3:17). Receive him now into your heart, and give him full possession and control of your spirit, soul, and body, having his will done in you, not your own, thus receiving the Holy Ghost by faith in Christ (John 7:39), born of the Spirit (John 3:6), Regenerated (Titus 3: 5), you too will be spiritual, a child of God (Gal. 3:26); always rejoicing in the Lord (Phil. 4:4) who is able to keep you from falling, and to present you faultless before the presence of his glory with exceeding joy (Jude 24). Receive him now. The joy will be yours. Be it so, we ask in his name.

1940 Watervleit Ave., Dayton, Ohio.

The New Testament Our Sufficient Creed   By C. Forney

Our subject heading this article is of great importance and should be the accepted creed of every true follower and servant of God. As our creed, so will be our service. The creed assigned us is the New Testament which is our all sufficient creed, and forever settles the kind of creed I am to write upon. This suits me exactly as it is the only safe ground upon which to build, as all othher ground is but sinking sand. The New Testament is the record that God gave us of his Son who is the author of eternal salvation to all them that believe, whether Jew or Gentile, bond or free (Romans 1:16, 17) Read also John 12:44, and to the end of the chapter for important information). Remember that the Father dictates to the Son and the Son obeys the Father, and as the Son obeys, so we should follow his example. This is our New Testament creed, of which Christ is the author, making Christ our example. He sealed our creed with his own blood.

Christ proved his mission by his life. By living our lives in Christ we thereby glorify God and show our love to him. We must show our faith by what we do as exemplified by the Author of our faith and creed.

A few references from our New Testament creed as to what a penitent believer must do to be saved. See Acts 2:37-39 for an answer; "Repent and be baptized in the name of Jesus Christ for the remission of sins and ye shall receive the gift of the Holy Ghost." Note that when we obey from the heart the form of doctrine delivered us we are made free from sin and have our "fruit unto holiness and everlasting life" (Romans 6:17, 18). God gives the Holy Ghost to all who believe and obey him (Acts 5:22). All who do the will of our Father in heaven are our brethren and are entitled to a seat with us at the Lord's table (See Matthew 12:49, 50). According to our New Testament creed we have no right to reject any from fraternal relation with us who obey the gospel as we do. They are our brethren according to Christ's plain statement. Any creed which differs from the New Testament is wrong, and any creed just like it is not necessary. My observation and experience is that the Brethren church has been amply blest because of her acceptance and strict observance of the New Testament in its fullness as her creed. No people or class of people doubt that we do too little in the acceptance and observance of its teachings. No true servant of Jesus Christ is brought to doubt the need of doing so much, but on the contrary, because of the joy and blessings which come to him because of his obedience he is brought to testify with God's servant of old who said, "There failed not aught of any good thing which theh Lord had spoken... All came to pass." "If ye know these things, happy are ye if ye do them."

The Gospel Creed is all we need
To lead us home on heavens' street;
For as we would to God be true,
The Father's will we all may do.

As in the steps of Christ we walk,
And of his goodness always talk,
We all shall him the better know
As we together always go.

The Savior's prayer for us will be
That we his glory all may see.
And seeing it may know and share
In that Homeland over there.

There we will be at God's right hand,
And with the bloodwashed we will stand.
There'll be no sorrow over there,
If we for heaven here prepare.

With loved ones gone before we'll meet,
And lovingly each other greet;
And there we'll never say good-bye,
For in that land none ever die.

Beaver City, Nebraska.

Christian Baptism.   By E. E. Roberts

III. The Who of Baptism

(Continued from issue of December 7)

Having discovered the nature and manner of baptism, we will proceed to consider the Who? of baptism. Who are fit subjects for baptism? This we can discover only by searching the Word. Placing side by side Matthew 28:19, Mark 16:16, Acts 2:38 and 8:37, we can omit the rest, for in these we have all the requirements stated; viz., Matthew tells us that we are "to go and teach all nations." Mark says, "Go ye. . . . preach the gospel." The Greek is, announce or proclaim, to do which is preaching. Peter and Philip in Acts had both taught and proclaimed the gospel to their hearers; hence their hearers must have been of sufficient age and mental ability to comprehend the meaning and to appreciate the importance of the matter preached; hence, they could not have been children.

The next step, Mark tells us, "he that believeth." Peter's hearers showed by their cry—"What must we do?" that they believed. Philip tells the Eunuch, "If thou believeth." Belief comes only to those whose brain is sufficiently developed to weigh the evidence and decide the validity of the claims of the gospel. This a baby cannot do, therefore they are not fit subjects for the rite of immersion.

Peter tells his hearers, who doubtless were a part of the crowd which had cried, "Crucify him, crucify him!" that though they were sorry that they had killed Christ, and thereby missed the blessings he had come to give them, yet their sorrow was not "godly sorrow that needeth not to be repented of," but was like the sorrow of a disobedient boy who has gotten into his mother's preserves, and seeing a good whipping in sight, he is not sorry that he has grieved his mother by disobedience, but sorry that he is going to get a whipping. So Peter emphasizes the necessity of repentance of the right kind, the kind that always goes with true faith which realizes what great sins we have committed against "our Father in heaven." Then comes that deep heart sorrow that fits us for immersion. As a child is utterly unable to realize this, it is not a fit subject for the rite.

But the Master in Matthew tells the Apostles that after they have baptized those who have been fit subjects, they must "teach them to observe all things whatsoever I have commanded you." Not having been able to receive the first instruction, they surely cannot receive the second class of instruction: hence a baby is not a fit subject for the rite of immersion.

We cannot enter into the subject further. The above Scripture is enough to show any fair-minded man the error of baby sprinkling. The early church did not practice it, but forbade it. But to show the utter folly of it, we feel to quote from an article in the "Christian Advocate," the official organ of a church that practices baby sprinkling. It points out what would be the results if every baby were sprinkled, and taken into the church:

(1) It would set aside believer's baptism, because there would be no believers to baptize.

(2) It would destroy the promise "He that believeth and is baptized shall be saved."

(3) There would be no need of preaching, all would be in the church.

(4) All would be in the church without exercising their faith.

(5) There would not be, could not be, a converted member in all the church, for all would be there before they could be converted.

(6) If all were baptized into the church in infancy, every wicked person would be in the church, because all would be in it.

(7) There would be no line between the world and the church, for there would be no world, because all would be in the church.

(8) There being no regenerated persons in the church, there could be no Christians in the church; hence, such a practice would wipe out the Christian church.

We have in no sense of the word, exhausted the arguments against such an unscriptural practice, but believe these are abundantly sufficient to convince any thinking person of its folly. We will proceed to consider next the WHY of baptism.

Philadelphia, Pa.

Financial Righteousness By H. M. Harley

(A plain statement of facts).

We all know, either from experience or from heresay, that it takes gasoline to run an automobile, that it takes electricity to run a street car, and that it takes brains and finance to conduct a successful business. But so many folks seem to forget that it takes money, as well as work and spirituality, to carry on the work of the church.

Never have the demands upon the church been so many and so great for aid of one kind or another, and never have there been so many opportunities for real Christian service that counts for something as right now. But so often the church is handicapped because of a lack of funds. And it isn't because her members are without the means, either. The reason is found in the fact that Christians fail to manifest the real spirit of Christianity, which is, "'Freely ye have received, freely give."

We need so much of what we have for our own wants, that there is generally little, and ofttimes nothing, left for the work of Christ and his church. And all the while that we are withholding our gifts from the church we are not only robbing God of that which really belongs to him, according to Malachi 3:8 (read it), but we are robbing ourselves of that which God promises to the liberal soul. Read Luke 6: 38). And at the same time we are retarding the progress of the church and of his Kingdom.

And why are we asked to give liberally to the work of God? Surely not that God really needs it, in order to carry on his work in the world. He could have ordained otherwise. But he says, and surely he knows, that it is to our advantage both materially and spiritually, both for this and for the future world, that we give liberally and cheerfully

to the furtherance of his work among men. Paul tells us in 2 Corinthians 8, that the measure of our giving is really the measure of our sincerity and of our love for the work of the Lord, and that all we give redounds to our own welfare, even more than to the one receiving the direct benefit of our gifts.

Remember, we are asked, "Not to forsake the assembling of ourselves together for worship," and we are also asked to worship, not only with the singing of hymns and the praying of prayers, but with our gifts and our lives. We are to give, not as unto men but as unto God," "even as the Lord has prospered us," yea, even as he has directed all through his Word. And if people would heed this, and try the tithe for a while, they would never give otherwise, for it would not only bring great blessing to them, but it would solve every financial problem of the church, as well as many other problems.

The Treasurers' reports of many churches are continually showing a shortage of funds. This ought not so to be. Surely we do not want the work of the Lord to go begging. Let us make this a subject of prayers, and then let every one of us give even as we pray, and thus prove the sincerity of our prayers, and the measure of our love for Christ and his church. As this Christmas time approaches, let us remember our church with a gift, as well as our friends, especially let us remember our White Gift Sunday school offering in a generous way. And we will be able to do a larger and a better work in the year before us than in any year past. Why not give God's plan of tithing a fair trial, and see whether he will not do as he says. I believe,—yea, I know that he will.

Pittsburgh, Pennsylvania.

A Brief Christmas Message Mrs. Geo. Stanley Baer

"Thanks be unto God for his unspeakable gift."—"For unto you is born this day a Savior, which is Christ the Lord." The "gift," an expression of love, was the gift of a life. That first Christmas gift was not a gift to a child; it was the gift of a Child. As the coming of a child often transforms a family much more the coming of the Christ-Child transformed a world of families. In that far-off day no one suspected that the Child in the manger was to revolutionize all thoughts of childhood. The wise men brought their gifts and laid them at the feet of him who was to become the Savior of the world, and lo! the leaders of modern society are bringing the best treasures the nation possesses to offer at the feet of little children. If once society was unconcerned about the child now it exists for the child's sake. Every law and institution revolves around the cradle out from which goes cheer and sunshine to brighten the home, even as the light of Christ brightens the whole world.

But what does Christmas mean to us directly? What did it mean to the principal characters in the Christmas story? It meant first of all joy; "They rejoiced with exceeding great joy," and "Behold, I bring you good tidings of great joy." Christmas means that to us, of course. The The spirit of Christmas as we celebrate it is just that—joy. But has the second great meaning of Christmas come to us? The angel choir on the first Christmas sang: "Glory to God in the highest." What are we going to do this Christmas to bring glory to God? God will give us Christmas joy; will we deny him his Christmas glory? A heart given to Christ,

a life dedicated to his service, a child consecrated to him, the poor made happy, the sick cared for or a lonely neighbor cheered, all mean glory to God. And a heartfelt, sincere prayer, thanking God for his goodness to any one of us, this too, means glory to God. To us is given exceeding great joy;" to God, "Glory in the highest." Shall we do our part?

Ashland, Ohio.

POSSIBILITY OF MORE ARMENIAN DEPORTATIONS

There are probabilities of further deportations of Armenians by the Turks according to statements received at the New York headquarters of the Near East Relief. One of their workers who has just come home from a term of service in the medical work of that organization says that the Turks in Marash are threatening to deport the Armenians that remain in that center, which has suffered many times from the cruelty and hatred of the Turks, and was the scene of one of the worst massacres of the entire war period last year. Only Mustapha Kemal's orders are preventing it, and it is a question if even the Nationalist leader can continue to ward it off for long. The Christians are subjected to all sorts of persecution. They are not allowed to work or trade in the markets, consequently they have no money and can buy no food. The Near East Relief is feeding and caring for five thousand people daily in Marash, and is also helping the suffering people in many other ways.

THE BRETHREN PULPIT

Quench Not The Spirit. By C. R. Koontz

TEXT: Quench not the Spirit. I Thessalonians 5: 19

These words are found in the concluding exhortation of Paul to the Thessalonian converts. Undoubtedly Paul had just reason to feel proud of these people for they had remained faithful in spite of terrible persecutions; and their infuence had been felt throughout Greece and Macedonia. In the light of these facts the question may be raised why such an exhortation, for these people seem to·be the least in need of it. Their work of faith and their labor of love and patience of hope in the Lord Jesus Christ were continually remembered by St. Paul.

It seems to be a case of whom the Lord loveth he chasteneth. Paul's great love for this people, and his realization of the great ministry of the Holy Spirit made him feel the importance of dropping this helpful suggestion as a note of warning, which to us carries a two fold implication. (1) The Ministry of the Spirit; (2) The Possibility of Quenching the Spirit.

The Ministry of the Spirit

This phase of the subject at once raises two questions: Who is the Spirit and What does he do for man?

In answer to the first, without going into any theological technicalities, he is more than an influence or emanation. He is a divine person, having the distinctive characteristics or marks of personality. Paul in his various writings attributes to him the following: Knowledge, feeling, and will. In a word, the Holy Spirit is God himself, in vital contact and communion and communication with the spirits of men. One who wishes to know what the Holy Spirit was to the Apostolic church should sit down and carefully yet rapidly read the Epistles, noting the many operations of power and grace of the living Spirt of God as they are represented. These letters were written in the atmosphere of power by inspired men, as much so as holy men of old who stood in the presence of Jehovah or the disciples in the days of Jesus.

In answer to the second, may I suggest the following line of thought from the lips of our blessed Savior. While Jesus was yet in the upper room after that Judas had gone out, he told his disciples that he was soon to leave them, but that they should not let their hearts be troubled, for he would not leave them as orphans, but would pray the Father and the father would send them another Comforter to take his place. ·

The Greek word translated Comforter means a comforter plus a great deal more. It means "one who pleads another's cause before a judge; an advocate, an intercessor; in the widest sense, a helper, a suceorer, aider, assistant, so of the Holy Spirit destined to take the place of Christ with the apostles, to lead them to a deeper knowledge of gospel truth, and to give them the divine strength needed to enable them to undergo the trials and persecutions on behalf of the divine kingdom." In addition to this Christ said that "when the Spirit is come he will convict the world of sin and of righteousness and of judgment." Hence we see that the work of the Spirit in the world is to convince or implant among the convictions of men the abiding.convictions of the soul,—what sin really is in the sight of God, what righteousness as a goal really amounts to, and, that there cometh a day when the world shall be judged. The doctrine may be hard to explain and interpret but the fact and reality of it remain just the same. It is here that we find the answer to the awakenings of public conscience concerning moral issues. These changes do not come about by chance but are the workings of the Holy Spirit in the lives of men.

While it may be said that this is the broadest work of the Spirit done in the world, the deeper work is done in the church or in the hearts of the individuals that make , up the visible body of Christ here on earth. ·His work differs in much the same way as did the work and teaching of Jesus differ between the world and his followers. Jesus promised the disciples that when the Spirit should come then he, the Spirit, would guide them into all truth; and again, "He shall teach you all things, and bring all things to your remembrance, whatsoever I have said unto you." This may be a long process in progress because of our weaknesses and limitations, but the fact remains that it is the privilege of the humblest believer to have a divine person as his daily instructor of the truth of God. He that willeth to do shall know the truth, and the truth shall make him free, and he shall be free indeed. Here is to be found one of the significant lessons for us who live this side of the days of Jesus. It is not our privilege to walk and talk with Jesus as it was the privilege of the disciples; nor are we accorded the opportunity of sitting at his feet as a student as was Mary, but thanks be unto God for the unspeakable gift of his Holy Spirit. It is ours to share in the baptism of the Spirit and to share in revival of the Pentecostal experience. Where God's Spirit is there will be no coldness but warm affections, fiery impulses, hearts aglow with a living, conquering energy and enthusiasm for the Kingdom of God. It is the indwelling of the Holy Spirit that accounts for the tireless activity of St. Paul as well as the rest of the apostolic workers. And as fire is the best visible symbol of the Holy Spirit, Paul exhorts the brethren at Thessalonica that they quench not the Spirit.

Possibility of Quenching the Spirit

With every added opportunity there comes also an , added responsibility. The more a question is involved the greater the care exercised in its solution. The finer the mechanism of our machinery the greater care we. should take of it lest we get it out of adjustment, or proper working order. So it is in this case. God in his wise providential way has made great provision for us. Man has journeyed a long way across the years of civilization. Many days have been spent in the university of experience. We today should be able to stand and build on the foundations laid by others; in a word, God expects us to profit by the past. All these years he has been interested in us and trying to do all for us that we will let him. In the last days he revealed his will in the Person of his Son, who was to be the perfect and complete revelation. Now we have the Spirit to bring to our remembrance all that Jesus taught us ⏌ and to lead us in to all truth. By this we can see that we hold a very responsible place in the sight of God, and if such be the case we should be very careful lest we do not measure up to our position. Herein I believe to be the reason why Paul exhorts them to be very careful of their conduct lest they quench the power of the Spirit.

How may we quench the Spirit? Following the suggestion of the symbol that the Spirit is like unto fire, implied in the text, there are at least three ways by which fire can be put out.

The easiest way to quench a little fire is simply to neglect it. Start a little fire ever so carefully but neglect to provide it with fuel and it will soon burn itself out. How true is this in the life of every individual and the church as well. Take for instance the condition that prevails at revival time. Enthusiasm and attendance increases, earnestness upon the part of the members is manifest, souls are born into the kingdom, and we say surely this is the outpouring of the Holy Spirit, and justly so. But my point is how long does this condition last after the meeting closes? Only so long as we keep adding the right kind of fuel. The sin of neglect is one that needs to be guarded against for it is one of the easiest ways to quench the work of the Spirit. How many are the opportunities that we allow to pass by, not intentionally but simply because of neglect?

But there are some fires that we dare not neglect, for there is plenty of fuel at hand to do a great deal of damage. When fire is mentioned the first thing we think of is water. As water quenches fire, so there is no surer way to quench the spirit than to apply the water of scorn and criticism. In fact, this is the natural outcome of the first. After neglect comes rejection and scorn. What better way is there to quench the promptings and revelations of the Spirit than to reject them. How long do we present a beneficent proposition to the man who rejects or scorns it. How natural because of the hardness of some hearts is it to think of the Spirit being quenched. Esau despised his birthright for a mess of cabbage, and forfeited his right to a future of high privilege. May it not be said of us that when we sell our interest in things spiritual for material possessions of whatsoever kind they may be, and the pleasures of the most trivial sort we despise and quench the Spirit?

But there are some fires that we not only dare not let alone, but we dare not pour water on them for it only tends to spread them. I refer to the oil fire. In the fighting of them the smothering method has been found to be very successful. Many automobile owners carry a fire extinguisher of this sort with their equipment, so that in case of fire about the motor or garage, it can be smothered out at once. How truly this represents the life experience of many members of the church. The Spirit kindles the spark of life and lights up their soul. The devil knows that this bids fair to a full surrender of that life to the cause of Jesus Christ. To neglect it will not do; to pour the water of persecution upon it will only tend to spread it and cause a greater loss to his kingdom of darkness. Therefore he tries to smother it out by bringing before the Christian, or would-be-follower of Christ, all the trials, vexations, hindrances, and weaknesses that human flesh is heir to and suggests that they be put on the fire. And the sad thing of it all is his voice is heeded rather than that of the Spirit. It is no wonder that the Spirit is grieved and quenched when he comes as our great Comforter, Teacher and Guide, and we try to pile upon him all the rubbish of our complaints, failings, and weaknesses.

So then in conclusion, may I suggest that the Holy Spirit is to us what Jehovah was to the Israelites, and what Jesus was to the disciples, and it is my prayer that we may not quench the Spirit of God by our neglect, or our rejecting or despising his illuminating revelations and divine promptings, or by shunting his power because of our weakness. But may we rather be led of the Spirit to do his full and complete will. Amen.

Woodstock, Virginia.

OUR DEVOTIONAL

The Daily Guidance of the Spirit

By Albert G. Hartman

OUR SCRIPTURE

God is a Spirit: and they that worship him must worship him in spirit and in truth (John 4:24). Except a man be born of water and of the Spirit, he cannot enter the kingdom of God. That which is born of the flesh is flesh; and that which is born of the Spirit is spirit (John 3:5-6). If we live in the Spirit, let us also walk in the Spirit (Gal. 5:25). For he that soweth to his flesh shall of the flesh reap corruption; but he that soweth to the Spirit shall of the Spirit reap life everlasting (Gal. 6:8). There is therefore now no condemnation to them which are in Christ Jesus, who walk not after the flesh, but after the Spirit (Romans 8:1). For as many as are led by the Spirit of God, they are all the sons of God (Romans 8:14).

OUR MEDITATION

What a blessed hope is within us who seek daily to be guided in all things by the Spirit of God. God is a Spirit, we are told in the Scriptures, and yet how many of us in times past have failed to put our trust in him as such. God's omniscience, his omnipotence, and his omnipresence are all evidences of his being a spirit. Can we doubt his ability to be ever present with us, if we will but give him a chance? A lack of faith on our part can never lessen his power to do mighty works, but it may cause us the loss of an opportunity to receive a blessing from him.

Complying with such verses as Galatians 5:25, we must strive always to walk in the Spirit if we are to live in the Spirit. This will not be difficult if we will but take God at his word. We must simply bring our own desires in subjection to his divine will, and be willing to follow every step of the way. For instruction in this regard it is necessary not only to search the Scriptures, but to go to God in prayer, and ask his guidance in all things that we do.

From personal experience we learn that the strict observance of the "Quiet Hour" is the best way to bring ourselves in closest contact with God. The few minutes thus spent in prayer and Bible reading are the sweetest moments of the whole day. If we neglect to bring ourselves in touch with the Spirit; if we fail to commune regularly with him, then we cannot hope to be led continually by his loving kindness. True regularity is one of the best features of the "Quiet Hour."

Let us not be unmindful of the fact, also, that the indirect results of the "Quiet Hour" are very far-reaching. The spiritual blessings we receive are not confined to the short period of time spent in communion, but is extended throughout the whole day; for we are always left in a different mood after a heart to heart talk with the Master. The man or woman who is wiling to let Christ come into the heart, and is willing to be dominated entirely by his spirit, enjoys the pleasure of Christian service not occasionally, but all the time. Influenced by the desire to do effective Christian work, we will be impelled to perform deeds of kindness from day to day. Every act which we commit will be actuated by a love of righteousness and we can move forward, making great strides, knowing that we are moving in the right channel.

In the light of such knowledge as we have already gained in our Christian living, let us then strive to follow even more closely the leading of the Spirit. May we be more fully consecrated to the Master's work. May we be willing to forget self and remember only Jesus Christ and him crucified. We need not worry about our own temporal welfare; our needs will be provided for according to God's divine wisdom. Then guided daily by the Spirit, as was the Apostle Paul, we can "press toward the mark for the prize of high calling of God in Christ Jesus."

OUR PRAYER

Blessed Father, we thank thee for the guidance thou hast given us in the past, and for the promise which we hold for the future. We pray that we may be filled with thy Spirit to the extent that all our acts will be in conformity with thy will. Wilt thou instill in our lives a desire to be helpful to those about us. May we dedicate our time and our talents to thy service. Be with us as we seek to do thy bidding form day to day. We pray not for greatness, but for faithfulness. Use us in whatever way seemeth best in thy sight. Guide us continually in spiritual growth until our earthly career is ended; and at last save us to live eternally with Jesus our Redeemer. Amen.

Warsaw, Indiana.

He loves not Christ sincerely, who loves him not supremely.

THE SUNDAY SCHOOL

"Importance of A White Gift From Every Member of Every School."

I By C. E. Johnson

Superintendent of the Brethren Sunday School at Turlock, California

What a blessed thing it is for us to realize that we belong to the great Sunday school Army. What a blessed thing to also realize that we have something definite to perform; that we have given our promise to do some definite work for our King. Just in so far as we, members of this great army, respond will that work progress. Surely the Lord is depending on us. The workers are also depending on us. Therefore let every member of every school give a White Gift this Christmas that the name of our King may be glorified and our promise redeemed. It is but our simple duty yet in the doing of it we will surely receive a blessing from him who knows how to give the best.

Turlock, California.

II By C. D. Whitmer

Superintendent First Brethren Sunday School, South Bend, Indiana

"For God so loved the world that he gave his only begotten Son."

If God so loved, likewise must a Christian so love. But God so loved that he gave. So if a Christian so loves he must give. The dominating thought in this gem verse is to love so much that we will give.

If God so loved us as to give his greatest gift, his only Son, how much more should we love all humanity to the extent that we give our greatest gift possible, in order that all people may know of this gift that Christianity has received, and that all people, whosoever will, may have.

Therefore, let us realize the importance of every member of every school, having a part in bestowing this gift to the lost world. To me there is no better time to show my appreciation for God's gift than at Christmas time, when all eyes are turned toward that Star of Bethlehem, and when the note of joy is vibrating in the hearts of Christian people, by remembering our White Gift service.

Let every member of every school make this Christmas time the greatest in our history, to the end that we may have the largest White Gift offering ever.

South Bend, Indiana.

III By Frank J. Weaver

Superintendent of the Brethren Sunday School at New Lebanon, Ohio

The Yuletide season is, in my estimation, the most opportune time for every member of every Bible school to be interested in making a White Gift offering. Everyone whether in the Bible school or out of it has been reading and hearing much about the sufferings and distress of millions in southern and eastern Europe as well as in China, and Christian hearts will be going out in sympathy and material relief as they are able. But our hearts are not only made sympathetic for the foreign sufferers but for those who need both physical and spiritual relief in the mountains of Kentucky. There is no time when we are more deeply moved to give to meet the needs of such needy people, as well as to help in the spiritual preparation of those who are to go in person to minister to such as these. And so in this time of stress every one should do his part by making a generous White Gift offering.

Another reason why every one should participate in this offering is that the general financial conditions make it necessary that all shall help in order that the work of Kentucky missions and religious education may be carried forward unhindered. These fields stand in great need just now. What effect will the slump in business in the various parts of our land have upon this offering? Thirty-four thousand people in Dayton are idle, and if this condition obtains all over our land, as I believe it does, it surely will be the duty of every member of every Bible school to do what he can to-

ward holding up the work of our Sunday School Association that it may not suffer because of this condition.

And then, too, for a far higher reason, we should give liberally to this glorious cause because the Master has said, "Freely ye have received, freely give." And we know that those who give in the Master's name shall not lose their reward.

Our White Gift Offering Budget

By H. H. Wolford

Let us remind you again of the budget for the Christmas offering for the work of the National Sunday School Association. This work under the direction of the Association is the work of all the Sunday schools of the Brethren church and as such every Sunday school will be glad to do their part. The offering this year will provide the funds for the following budget:

Kentucky Missions	$1,000.00
Religious Education	1,200.00
Field Worker	500.00
Expenses of National Association	200.00
Total	$2,900.00

As an Association we must depend upon our superintendents and officers to keep it before the school. More than this it will be necessary for each school in the way which seems best to make a definite presentation of this work and ask for an offering for it. Many schools will render a program at Christmas time and ask for an offering. This method has proven very effective in the past. The "White Gift Service" is very appropriate and can be made very impressive.

Send your offering to the Secretary-Treasurer of the National Sunday School Association, H. H. Wolford, 311 College Avenue, Ashland, Ohio.

The Christmas Message

(as the Bible states it)

God will judge between the nations . . . and they shall beat their swords into plowshares, and their spears into pruning hooks; nation shall not lift up sword against nation, neither shall they learn war any more (Isaiah 2:4). They shall not hurt nor destroy in all my holy mountain: for the earth shall be full of the knowledge of the Lord, as the waters cover the sea (Isaiah 11:9). Be not afraid; for behold I bring you good tidings of great joy which shall be to all people: for there is born to you this day in the city of David a Savior, who is Christ the Lord.

Glory to God in the highest,

And on earth peace among men in whom he is well pleased (Luke 2:10, 11, 14).

He became flesh, and dwelt among us (and we beheld his glory, glory as of the only begotten from the Father), full of grace and truth (John 1:14).

He hath showed strength with his arm;

He hath scattered the proud in the imagination of their heart.

He hath put down princes from their thrones

And hath exalted them of low degree (Luke 1:51.52).

Come unto me, all ye that labor and are heavy laden, and I will give you rest. Take my yoke upon you, and learn of me; for I am meek and lowly in heart: and ye shall find rest unto your souls (Matthew 11:28, 29).

Now abideth faith, hope, love, these three; and the greatest of these is love (1 Corinthians 13:13).

J. A. Garber
PRESIDENT

Our Young People at Work

E. A. Rowsey
SECRETARY

December: Quiet Hour Month   By Prof. J. A. Garber

The Quiet Hour department has the right of way during December. The purpose of the special emphasis is to bring to the attention of young people the great importance of daily Bible study and prayer.

Now is the time to line our folks up with section three of our Bicentenary program. It is designated thus

III Devotion

1. The value of private Bible study and prayer faithfully stressed.
2. The enrollment of Comrades of the Quiet Hour.
3. Individual participation in society and church prayer meetings urged.

All enrollments should be reported to our Quiet Hour superintendent, Brother E. M. Riddle, Louisville, Ohio, who recently had an article in these columns on "Cultivating the Devotional Life of Young People." As additional stimulus we reprint below an article from The Ohio Endeavorer, of which our General Secretary, Brother E. A. Rowsey, is Associate Editor.

"Draw Nigh to God'

"Draw nigh to God and he will draw nigh to you," is a telling admonition from the Apostle James. James doubtless knew what he was talking about. He with other apostles, knew all the hardships and struggles of those first days of vital Christianity. Christian endeavor was not popular. To be engaged in the service of Christ meant persecution, sufering and ofttimes death. The carnal nature in the hearts of men that dogged the steps of the sinless Son of God to the cross, was still "breathing out threatenings" against his followers. James had doubtless found the words of Jesus to be reality—"Lo I am with you alway" and from that intimate knowledge gave the exhortation, "Draw nigh to God."

"Draw nigh to God, and he will draw nigh to you." That means that God places a special premium upon the cultivation of the spiritual. There are some folks who are closer to God than others. They have deliberately chosen the better part. And God has rewarded that choice with his presence. These are days when we ought as young people to draw nigh. Only thus can we stem the tide of worldliness, resist the siren voices of sin, escape the seductive snare of false teaching, and "perfect holiness in the fear of God."

Three reasons for drawing nigh are: 1st. That you may be a real Christian. If you would be a real Christian, Christ must be a reality. Christ can never be real to the heart that has no time to draw nigh to him. You are unwilling to unburden your heart to a stranger or the heart. No more will Christ reveal the wonders of his love and grace to the chance and hurried visitor. Draw nigh. Tarry. Wait upon his Word. He will then show himself as Reality to your heart.

2nd. That you may be a joyous Christian. Draw nigh to God for joy. A real Christian is a joyous Christian. Many have just enough religion to make them miserable. They have neither found nor tasted the "joy of the Lord." They are bad "examples." They have not learned the secret of "Drawing nigh to God." From that sacred audience one draws "Joy unspeakable and full of glory" and is enabled to meet all the vicissitudes of life with the conqueror's tread, because the "joy of the Lord" is his strength.

3rd. That you may be a successful Christian. One of the most disheartening things is failure. Peter met failure when he "followed afar off." Sorrow filled the young man's heart when he "went away" from Jesus. Judas met his tragic end after he "went out" from the presence of Jesus into the night. It is safe to say that these and all others who

have met defeat could have won, had they "drawn nigh." It is in the "secret of his presence" that strength is given. Look back over your own experience, is it not so that lack of prayer preceded every failure?

We have been thinking of the negative side. Turn to the positive. "Draw nigh to God and he will draw nigh to you." That is the secret of success. "Wait upon the Lord," that you may renew your strength." "Wait I say, on the Lord."

Activities at Altoona

Greetings to the C. E. Societies throughout the brotherhood: Not having seen a report from Altoona for some time and thinking we might be accorded a little space in the Christian Endeavor doings of the Evangelist, we are taking the liberty to drop a few lines at this time. November 28th was a time of Thanksgiving. Very much in season, and with the help of our blessed Savior we arranged for special services in the Christian Endeavor meeeting in the form of a rally, with the three societies of our church taking an active part. Our societies' work in harmony one with the other for the glory of Jesus Christ from whom we receive our strength. We are proud of our Christian Endeavor work and what has evolved from it for God's glory. Three of our good working members having entered Ashland College to prepare for a higher school of endeavor. Now a little explanation of our services on the 28th, if I may be allowed the space. First: It pays to advertise; it pays big. The attendance almost reached the two hundred mark. We have the hearty co-operation of both of our daily papers without charge, for which we are very thankful.

Our society is a member of the city union of Christian Endeavor and our leader for the rally was the president of the city union whom we are pleased to say was our former president, Brother Carl Grosse. And the least we can say of Brother Carl is that he is a "Live wire". C. E. worker. On our program we were fortunate to have Rec. Lockard of the Grace Reformed church who is another live wire in C. E. work. He delivered the address of the evening on the subject, "The Relation of Christian Endeavor to the Church." He talked for twenty minutes in a powerful and instructive way. This was followed by a recitation by Miss Gertrude Mills, whose subject was "Unaware." This was delivered in a masterful and touching manner. Miss Mills is from the First Lutheran society. Special music was interspersed throughout the service; this added much indeed to it. Brother Francis Weidel, one of our promising Intermediates read "The Parson's Vacation," in his usual inimitable style. The Junior department followed with several recitations and we heartily thank Sister Davis who is the Junior superintendent and really a mother to these little ones.

We were indeed glad to have with us at this service Brother Barnard of Ashland who delivered the message to us during the day, and we can truthfully say, he has had the vision.

Brother Arthur Cashman and sister Irene, were very much present, both being enthusiastic C. E. workers. We are very sorry that Brother Hubert Hammond could not be present. He was one of the pillars of our society, but now is in Ashland College.

We thank our blessed Savior for his many blessings in keeping the interest up. We are without a pastor, but the good work goes on and we pray for his help in all things. And may the Lord keep watch between me and thee while we are absent one from the other. Amen.

W. W. WERTMAN, Secretary Senior Society.
2726 Maple Avenue, Altoona, Pa.

NEWS FROM THE FIELD

MASONTOWN, PENNSYLVANIA

Silence, by no means spells slump or defeat, surely not at Masontown. Some time has elapsed since the readers heard anything from this district. It affords me, as pastor, much pleasure to report at this time.

Through Brother Bell's report in the Evangelist you noticed we were preparing for a revival. The meetings began November 3 and concluded November 20. Although there were no visible results by way of conversions, we have every reason to believe that the seed was sown. Many have expressed their desire to unite with the church but did not during the meetings. Attendance and spirit were all that the pastor could hope for and grew as the meetings progressed. Every one considers the revival a success for the church is stronger and the spirit deeper. Just a word concerning the last Sunday of the revival. The Sunday morning services were fitly given to the observance of Thanksgiving, at which time the special Thanksgiving sermon was preached and the offering which amounted to $123.50 was laid upon the altar. In the evening we observed our semi-annual communion. Every table was filled and a splendid spirit prevailed through the entire service. We closed by singing, "Praise God from whom all blessings flow." These services were conducted by the local pastor due to the fact that they were held on Sunday and could not secure the assistance of neighboring pastors.

November 20 three classes in our Sunday school held a bazaar in the school auditorium. They realized over $400.00. Thus it will be seen that with a heart for the task and the spirit to urge us forward we have realized our purpose and materialized our goal.

The church of Masontown realizes that to do much effective work it will be necessary to enlarge the church building. All are co-operating to increase the building fund. Plans are soon to be effected for the extension work.

"Where there is no vision the people perish." JOSEPH. L. GINGRICH, Pastor.

MOUNT HOPE

This was the scene of my last battle for the Lord. If it were true to name, perhaps they would not have needed an evangelist to tell the old gospel story but how often, indeed, are places as well as people untrue to the name they bear. If anyone needs wealth and if they think money is a blessing, let them go to Mt. Hope where the good Lord pressed into splendid shape veins of the hottest coal in the U. S. A. Plenty of wealth but alas! wealth does not guarantee wealth of grace. Of course it ought to. Money ought to bring blessings to its possessor but too many times the possessor is like the poor rich man of Hades fame. What a wail he has made all these 2,000 years since the good Lord told the story. Still crying, "Send Lazarus, oh, send Lazarus to dip his finger in water that he may cool this tongue for I am tormented." Money must be separated from selfishness or it is a curse.

Disappointments

Never so many came at me in all my experience. Cold rooms for services; for we chased around to find a place suitable to hold the meeting and then wound up in the church and movie theater. It was a notable meeting in many ways. The first call for penitents listed 33 and the last more than 50. It was a hallelujah meeting when we saw a millionaire give himself to the Master- a man who already has been noted for his goodness and his gifts to the church of his father. Notable again on the last night when an Italian business man and his family surrendered to the Man of Galilee. Notable again when after the first service one of the pretty girls of the town who has been a notable dancer said, "I'm done with it all," and who was useful in leading other girls into the kingdom. And again when more than 100 boys in a single meeting promised to give up cigarettes. Notable once more because Miss Marie Duncan, school teacher and musician, granddaughter of the patriarch, Elder A. B. Duncan, definitely offered herself for the African Brethren mission. Praise the Lord! So, our disappointments were not all for the devil's good. I do like to work among these needy and appreciative people. Slow? Yes, slow to tell you that you have preached a good sermon or to fall in line with a radical presentation of the plain gospel, but nevertheless, appreciative. I covet more of the hard work and am sure the Lord has more for me to do there.

Near Home

Now, I am but a few miles away from home. After a wait of more than an hour, I'll be started to see the ones I love most and who spend my money. But what a joy it is to give it to the ones you love. What a happy meeting one gets when, after being away a long time, they welcome you back with open arms. Home! How wonderfully sweet is the word. "I'll soon be at home over there," in North Manchester and Indiana God, when all these trips are over, it will be "over there" where partings never come. My next is Sidney, Indiana, only ten miles away from home and a new Ford! Ha! Ha! Hurrah for the Lord's work in evangelism in the next few months. Say Amen! Everybody! CHARLES A. BAME.

FIRST BRETHREN CHURCH
Los Angeles, California

The ingathering to the church here continues. Sunday morning, November 21st, there were four confessions, a mother and daughter and two young ladies. A sister baptized the previous week was received into our number by the ceremony of the laying on of hands and the right hand of fellowship. At the evening service two more came forward, a husband and wife, Brother and Sister Noll, coming to us from the Presbyterian church. They live near our church and have been co-operating with us for several months.

A reception has been planned for the new converts, to be held Friday evening, November 26th. There will be supper in the basement dining room at 6:30, followed by a program in the main auditorium at 7:30. We are very happy to receive these new members into our number. Several of them have been members of our Sunday school, and it is an evidence of the good work being done by our teachers.

Here is an item previously overlooked. The day after returning from National Conference, Brother Jennings was called to Whittier to conduct the funeral of Clifford Kimmell, little son of Brother A. V. Kimmell, pastor of the Whittier Brethren church. Clifford passed from this life September 8th, having lived in this world a little more than a year, and most of that time spent in great suffering. We are told that he was much loved and that he is greatly missed by those who are left to mourn his loss.

With the exception of Rally Day, we reached the highest record of attendance in the Sunday school on November 14th, 170. An interesting and successful business session of the Sunday School Cabinet was held Friday evening, November 19th, after having a basket lunch together in the basement. We have a fine staff of teachers who are on time and conscientious in their work. A. P. REED. 4910 Wadsworth St.

BRIGHTON, INDIANA

The church at this place is one of the oldest in the Indiana district and has been served by some of our best men. But the last three years have been a time of God's testing and we have hesitated to report. We are glad the tide has turned and things look bright for the future of this work. It seemed at first a losing fight, but with the help of the faithful few and our trust in him who is able to give the victory, we stayed by it. We closed a revival on November 21, having held two and one-half weeks, with the visible results of 19 confessions. Six have been baptized and received into the church and others are to follow. But the good that has been done cannot be measured at the present time. The church as a whole has been helped. The confidence of the community has been won back, at least in a measure. Nobody will know what that means to the good brethren hereabouts who are acquainted with the local conditions.

So what seemed like defeat God has turned into a blessing for us, and this he is willing to do everywhere his people are willing to trust him.

We have a banner Woman's Missionary Society which deserves much credit for the work that has been done here. When things looked the darkest they stood faithful and steadfast. The Sunday school is not as good as it might be, but it is making progress.

The pastor, who is the writer, did his own preaching in the meeting, but he was ably assisted by Brother Harley Zumbaugh, who had charge of the singing. Brother Zumbaugh will be long remembered by the good folks here for the way he sang the Gospel into their hearts. We can highly recommend Brother Zumbaugh to any one desiring a singer. He is Brethren through and through. We ask the brotherhood to remember these good people at the throne of grace that the Lord of glory may save this work through us.

Yours in his service,

J. W. CLARK.

P. S.—The writer and Mrs. Clark wishes to thank these good people for the shower of good things to eat that were given us. All these were very much appreciated.—J. W. C.

NEWS FROM GRATIS, OHIO

As we have not had any news in the Evangelist for some time we must tell the brethren what we are doing. Since October 1st we have been without a pastor. But we are having services every two weeks. Brother A. A. Maysellis of the U. B. church gave a splendid temperance talk the Sunday preceding election day. Brother Hugh Marlin of Pleasant Hill came next, preaching both morning and evening.

November 14th our Sunday school had Rally Day with Brother Orion Bowman of Dayton for our speaker. Last Sunday Brother Bowman came again and preached for us. Brother Lynn will be with us December 19th. We have heard some splendid sermons and surely appreciate the kindness of our Brethren in preaching for us. Our W. M. S. is planning a Christmas sale and free will offering December 18th. Three new members were added to our roll at our last business meeting. Our Sunday school is doing fine. Sister Florence Focht's class of girls gave a parcel post social a few weeks ago, which was enjoyed by every one present. We are glad to see our young people working so earnestly and our prayers are with them.

Our Sunday school will give a Christmas entertainment and all are asked to help.

We have given Brother Roy Brumbaugh of Portis, Kansas, a call to our church as a pastor. He has accepted and will be with us just as soon as the Portis Brethren can secure another pastor. Until that time Gratis Brethren mean, by God's help, to "Keep the church Fires Burning."   A SISTER.

WEST ALEXANDRIA, OHIO

It has been some time since a report from this church has appeared in the Evangelist, and in fact I suppose some people think we are dead. We have been told to hang crape on the door and have our funeral preached, and many other discouraging remarks have gone out, but there are always two sides to the question.

I will let the readers of the Evangelist decide from the brief report that follows.

A called business meeting was held Wednesday, October 20th. The attendance was above the average and a keen interest was manifested.

At this time we gave Rev. C. E. Beekley a call for half time—a man whom we have known for three years and surely no man can say aught against him. On the following Sunday we had very good attendance, both morning and evening. Then we were handicapped for several weeks on account of furnace trouble, but since the repair we have had excellent crowds.

The Sunday school is growing and nearing the 100 mark and are now preparing their Christmas program.

The W. M. S. has been doing splendid work and we have learned to depend on them in time of need. Just recently the interior of the church has been redecorated and varnished for which we give the W. M. S. the credit.

On Sunday, November 28th, we observed our communion service with about 70 surrounding the Lord's tables and indeed it was a good meeting, the best we have had for years. And under the efficient leadership of Rev. Beekley we hope to move forward, for Brother Beekley is surely a man called of God with great ability to proclaim the Gospel.

Sunday, December 5th we had a very good attendance at Sunday school and an excellent church service. In the afternoon about 15 drove to Farmersville for the anointing service of our dear Brother David Lowman, one of the charter members of the church. And it surely was a blessed service, one long to be remembered. Then in the evening we listened again to the Gospel as it fell from the lips of one of God's anointed.

We also want to report that we have one fine young lady in Ashland College this year.

The church needs the prayers of the brotherhood for the continued blessing of God that his name may be glorified and his kingdom advanced in all the earth.

Per M. S., Corresponding Secretary.

EVANGELISM IN SUNNYSIDE WASHINGTON

During the month of October, we joined with the other churches of Sunnyside in a Tabernacle Campaign. A tabernacle seating 1800 was built. A choir of 250 voices was organized and other means of evangelism were set in motion. The evangelistic party was composed of Dr. E. J. Bulgin, evangelist, Bob Lewis manager and Chorus director, Mrs. Lewis, pianist, and Arthur Bulgin, soloist and chairman of personal work. A most pathetic tragedy occurred during the second week of the campaign when, while hunting pheasants in the immediate vicinity, Arthur was accidentally shot and killed. The writer stood within 20 feet of him when the fatal shot was fired. On the very night after the accident, Dr. Bulgin, the father, in spite of his broken heart, gave a powerful message and many made confession of Christ. The details of how the meeting continued regardless of this tragedy will be omitted. It is sufficient to say that the campaign was a great success. This party did the most effective and reliable work of evangelism of any we have ever known. It meant something to make a confession under their direction. They were loyal to the church and made no "Come Outers." The benefits of the campaign to our church are as follows. There were 25 members of the church who publicly reconsecrated and became more rooted and grounded in grace. Up to this writing, we have baptized and received 87 new members. Five have been received by relation, making a total received of 92. We have, in addition to these, baptized 10, who will be received by Brother Bell when he arrives. Then there are some yet to be baptized, so the final total can not be given. Part of these were our natural

constituency, but many new families have been added to our family. The attendance of the Sunday school has been increased by 75.

The communion, held two weeks after the campaign, was the largest for some years. There has been only once before when as many surrounded the tables to partake of the Lord's Supper. Many for the first time enjoyed the blessed happiness of the three fold communion.

Yes, the instructing of these new members in the doctrines of the church has been cared for. In sermon and in private, they have been given an intelligent, scriptural reason for these things. In fact these doctrines were what led many of them to seek fellowship with us. And, of course, these things prevented some from doing this. But God has wonderfully blessed his Word.

This is written as we are about to take our leave for a tour of evangelism including Falls City, Morrill, Johnstown, and Pittsburgh. Brother Bell will arrive within ten days to serve as pastor until our return in the spring. It will be like getting back home for him for he served here most faithfully and effectively in the beginning of the work.

CHARLES H. ASHMAN.

THE BRETHREN CHURCHES OF SERGEANTSVILLE AND CALVARY, NEW JERSEY

Elder M. L. Sands, a very efficient pastor, who for five years served these two churches, began new relations with the First Brethren church of Fremont, Ohio, on the first of September, leaving Sergeantsville and Calvary without a pastor.

Brother J. D. Wilson, member of the Sergeantsville church corresponded with Brother Alva J. McClain, with the view of obtaining some one to supply the pulpit. Brother McClain, my pastor, after consulting me, suggested to Brother Wilson, that I serve them while attending the "Philadelphia School of the Bible." This suggestion was accepted by the church and I began work on September 19, 1920.

September 5th and 12th, during which time neither Brother Sands nor myself were there, the pulpits were filled by Brother J. W. Porte, Elder of the Sergeantsville church.

The Sergeantsville church has a membership of (63) sixty-three, willing working people, and an empty parsonage, waiting for a pastor. Who will come?

The Calvary church (dependent on the pastor of Sergeantsville for services) has a membership of thirty. The country surrounding Calvary church is unworked, a splendid chance for Home Mission Work, and the building of Calvary Mission to a self-supporting church. Act Brethren!

During my short stay with them I have learned to love them. They have indeed made me welcome. I appreciate the courtesy to me as I grow in grace among them. But Brethren, I can do no pastoral work among them. The sole need for fuller development is a pastor.

Correspond with Brother W. C. Myers, Sergeantsville, New Jersey.

ORVILLE D. JOBSON, Jr.,
Acting Pastor.

LONG BEACH, CALIFORNIA

"Expect great things from God; attempt great things for God." The Long Beach church is now in the midst of a great evangelistic campaign for Christ, in this city. These are days, indeed, when the Christian needs to be on the alert; the unsaved need anchorage upon the Rock of Ages. Every member possible has been lined up for definite work during these meetings. Three prayer meetings, the one for men, another for women, and the third composed of the young people are in session for a half hour preceding the service. Brother Bauman, standing for the Whole Gospel, is assisted in the singing by Mr. Brillhart of Los Angeles. Already there is reason to rejoice over the fruit which is being gathered as a result of the Word sown.

Brother Bauman has been kept very busy since his return this fall. During his absence he circled the States, attending and speaking at various Bible conferences.

Previous to our own meetings, the pastor held revival services in the First church of Los Angeles. Brother Jennings has been greatly blessed in his work at that place. One Monday evening over one hundred members of the Long Beach congregation were in attendance. Before returning homeward, over that twenty mile stretch of California highway, the kind hospitality of those brethren was expressed by refreshments served in the basement of their new building. Such pleasant associations only remind us, that the churches of Southern California are just one large family. The most remote is reached by only a few hours' ride.

Our assistant pastor, Percy Yett, has recently left us, to attend the Zenia Seminary at St. Louis, Missouri. His duties were most worthily and cheerfully performed, and we have already felt his absence in the church and Sunday school work. The results of Rally Day were largely due to his efforts. There were four hundred and fifty in attendance with an offering over fifty dollars. However, we are glad to see Brother Yett go forward in training for the Lord's work. This was expressed by a large number of the members who gathered at Brother Bauman's home, and presented Brother Yett with a large pocketbook. The contents therein, express in one way appreciation for his earnest efforts along with us.

Only about two weeks following his return from National Conference, our Brother Srack was suddenly called to his eternal reward. Brother and Sister Srack had presented themselves as applicants for the African field, along with Brother and Sister Bush, also from the Long Beach church. Though rejected by the Board upon the physical examination, it was no easy matter to refuse those, who are willing to lay down their lives for him when past the prime of life. Sister Srack, who was continuing her work with the views from Africa, reached home the day after her husband departed from this world. Brother Srack was a deacon and a trustee in the Long Beach church. His Christian life and loyalty to his Savior will ever live among us.

During the past weeks the Dorcas committee of the Missionary Society has been meeting to sew for our missionaries, Sister Foulke

in China, the Rollier children in Africa, and Sister Bush, who is preparing her outfit for the African field.

During the past months we have enjoyed hearing several prominent speakers, and Christian workers. Dr. Pink, the noted Bible teacher and author held a week of meetings in our church. He is one who stands for the fundamentals of the Old Book, in these days.

One Sunday, Brother and Sister Waldron were guests of Brother Bauman. Mrs. Waldron is a daughter of Brother Harry Cassell of Philadelphia. She brought a message in song, and her husband occupied the pulpit in the evening.

Most inspiring was the morning service held recently by Mr. and Mrs. Morton, the well known missionaries of Belgium. The eagerness of the people for the Word of God in that land of Catholicism compels the Christian to respond to the call. Over five hundred dollars was subscribed to this cause. Though only a week later, and our Thanksgiving offering of $2,200 was to be taken in connection with the work here. Our Home Missionary Offering is always included in the church budget. We are told to lay up treasure in heaven where neither moth nor rust does destroy. Behold, the night cometh when no man can work; we must needs be about "Our Father's Business."

MRS. N. H. NIELSEN.

EVANGELISTIC SERVICES HELD FOR THE EVANGELISTIC AND BIBLE STUDY LEAGUE, BUENA, VISTA, VIRGINIA

I left home Friday, October 29, to hold a four weeks' meeting at Buena Vista, Virginia. On Saturday night I had about fifteen people present. Sunday morning we had a half a house and Sunday night about full. From that date on we had great crowds. We borrowed fifty chairs from the Church of the Brethren and then could not begin to seat the crowds.

On account of some injudicious management of the officers, the church was run down and the people very much discouraged. There were only about twelve active members. They were holding on, but were tempted to write me that it was no use to come as a revival in the present state of the church was impossible. The Holy Spirit fell upon the people until before it closed many said they never had such a meeting in Buena Vista before.

It was about a week before we had any confessions and then they came flocking home to God. The third Sunday we had sixteen confessions, and the fourth Sunday 18. The last Tuesday night there were nine confessions; on Wednesday night eight and the last night at the close of the communion I gave an invitation and came forward.

One good brother said before the meeting closed—a week before—we will have a hundred confessions. On Tuesday before it closed we lacked 13; on Wednesday night we still lacked five. We expected to close with 95 confessions. I was impressed to give an invitation at the close of the communion and the five came, making exactly 100 confessions. Some were reclaimed, some were baptized and a few will go to other churches. Most

of them united with the church, but I do not know the exact number.

The interest was intense when I closed. I should have remained over the coming Sunday but I could not well push my next meeting forward. I feel more and more impressed that the addition was not the best part of the meeting, but I did all in my power to put the work upon a permanent and solid basis. I will be greatly disappointed if you do not hear of better work done at Buena Vista than ever before.

We closed the services with the largest communion service they have had for a long time. Some fifteen or more could not be seated at the tables, so we served them with sandwiches.

I was royally treated by these big hearted Virginians. I shall never forget it. I had a royal home at Brother and Sister Jennings'. They did all they possibly could for me. I also took many meals out among the dear people there. Sister Jennings is pastor of the church. She seems to be universally loved by the people there. This was the first meeting I ever held where she preached. I had no idea she was such a tireless and faithful worker. They have lived there for seven years and both of them are actively working for the church. She is pastor and Brother Jennings superintendent of the Sunday school.

How she gets her house work done, canvasses the town to make payments on their house and preaches every Sunday and visits everybody who is a prospective member for the church I cannot see. If they would pay her better and let her rest some and get some of the good men from Roanoke to do some of the preaching it would rest her and also help the church. Mrs. Jennings seems to be unselfish and void of jealousy and is willing to do anything to make the work go.

My wife came from Philadelphia five days before the meeting closed. She went with my youngest brother, J. S. Bowman, to Roanoke to visit his children one day.

On Friday afternoon we left for Port Republic, the most precious spot on earth to both my wife and myself as we were both raised there.

My older brother met us with his Ford. We spent the night there and the next day I took his Ford and we went to see my only sister at Bridgewater, Virginia. Her husband, Rev. Samuel A. Sanger, one of the best men I ever knew, insisted that I come to see him before he dies as he has cancer of the kidneys. He takes it heroically. He says he would love to live if it is the Lords will, if not, he will be glad to go home.

We stopped a few minutes at Brother J. M. Bowmans, but he was not at home. We also stopped to see his mother, Aunt Sarah Bowman, who is in her eighty-first year. We also stopped to see an aunt of my wife, who is eighty-four. She cannot walk a step but is happy. So after riding about 40 miles, we went home in the rain, ate supper, gave wife and all good-bye and brother took me to the train where I waited in the rain for three hours. The depot was locked but a neighbor took me in. I boarded the train for Hagerstown, where I am pleasantly situated for a short meeting of two weeks. Weather is bad. Christmas is near and the field well worked, so that we cannot expect a large ingathering here, but we leave that matter entirely with the Lord.

Wife will visit a couple of weeks and then come by here and stop off a day or two on her way to Philadelphia, and I will go an opposite direction to West Virginia. So is life. I get homesick for the Lord's return when meeting and parting will be known no more.

I will write an article concerning this good Hagerstown church and congregation later, the Lord willing.

I want to say to my beloved brethren that I have received many calls by letter and telegrams that I have been compelled to turn down because of undue haste for your meetings. Please write and give me time to fix dates. I have turned possibly a dozen calls down this fall so far.

I neglected to say one thing that I meant to say about the Buena Vista work. They need teaching concerning giving. They gave more during this meeting than they ever gave before but not more than half of what they should have given. We would have gotten much more money if it had not been that many of the shops were partly or wholly shut down. Many of the women and men were laid off and they were much discouraged financially.

I recommended a better organization along this line and I believe from this on they will do much better.

ISAAC D. BOWMAN,
1942 S. 17th St., Philadelphia, Pa.

REPORT OF RECEIPTS FOR MISSIONS
(Explanatory)

N. B.—In making Financial Reports on Missions it has been advised that in order to conserve space in the EVANGELIST, that detail receipts of less than $5.00 could be omitted and reported as miscellaneous. However, we will be pleased to list smaller amounts for children or others if specially requested.

Home Missions for July and August
General Fund:

Mrs. W. A. Price, Nappanee, Ind., H. G.,	$ 5.00
Martin Shively, Ashland, O., H. G.,	5.00
W. G. M., Philadelphia, Pa., Interest,	72.07
Mary C. Wenger, Treas. W. M. S., Nat.	25.00
J. C. Bentz, Treas., Hagerstown, Md.,	10.00
1st Brethren,	10.00
Mrs. Alta Wright, Tiosa, Ind., H. E.,	5.00
Br. Ch., Tiosa, Ind.,	15.00
W. Homer Br. Ch., Homerville, O.,	5.00
Sarah A. Bock, Burlington, Ind., H. G.,	5.00
Mrs. C. N. Johns, Sidney, Ind., H. G.,	5.00
Br. Ch., Waterloo, Iowa, Landis, Tr.,	40.00
Mary C. Wenger, Treas, Nat. W. M. S.,	25.00
G. L. Maus, Bryan, Ohio, H. G.,	5.00
Horace Kolb, Philadelphia, Pa., H. G.,	5.00
Mrs. Emma Kolb, Philadelphia, Pa., H. G.,	5.00
William Kolb, Jr., Phila., Pa., H. G.,	5.00
Sisterhood Girls, 1st Br., H. G.,	5.00
First Br. Ch., Philadelphia, Pa.,	50.00
Cora Culp, Nappanee, Ind., H. G.,	5.00
Mary C. Wenger, Treas., Nat. W.M.S.,	25.00
Mr. & Mrs. Peter Pontius,	5.00
Mr. & Mrs. Claude Studebaker, Mulberry Grove, Ill.,	10.00
Reimbursement from other funds,	285.84
Miscellaneous receipts,	17.35
	$650.26

Kentucky Support Fund:

S. Ind. S.S. & C. E. Bal. Denver, Ind. (Maus),	$ 6.80
Mr. & Mrs. L. L. Kilmer, N. Liberty	

Indiana,	12.50
Mrs. T. M. McKinley, Eaton, Ind.,	5.00
Br. C. E., Louisville, O., I. E. Hang,	5.00
J. C. Bentz, Treas., Hagerstown, Md.,	10.00
Dyoll Belote, Uniontown, Pa.,	5.00
Brethren Church, Krypton, Ky.,	8.00
Miss Mary Stacy, Uniontown, Pa.,	10.00
O. E. First Br. Ch., Flora, Ind.,	5.00
C. E. First B. ch., Sarah Phillips,	15.00
Hudson, Br. C. E. (Boardman),	25.00
Roann, Ind. (M. M. Sisterhood (Bloom),	
Sarah E. Phillips, Mid. Branch, O.,	15.00
Sidney, Ind. W. M. S., Br Church, Hickman,	25.00
W. W. S. S. Class, New Lebanon, O., (Eck),	5.00
Oakville, Ind., Br. Ch., (Kern),	12.97
Mr. & Mrs. Henry V. Wall, Long Beach, California,	200.00
Mrs. Ella Fudge, Gratis, Ohio,	5.00
Mrs. Nell Wycoff Wentz, Portland, Indiana,	10.00
Br. Ch., Gratis, O. (Kimmel),	25.00
Union S. S., New Lebanon, Ohio (Weaver),	20.00
Dorothy Whitted, Morrill, Kans.,	10.00
J. L. Young, Geneva, Ind.,	5.00
W. M. S., Ankenytown, Ohio, Br. Ch. (Garber),	10.00
Eld. A. T. Wirick, S. Bend., Ind.,	50.00
Y. W. C. A. Ashland College (Lichty),	10.00
Eld. A. R. CoVer, Hagerstown, Md.,	5.00
Pleasant Hill, O. C. E. (Stout),	7.40
Eld. A. T. Ronk, Warsaw, Ind.,	10.00
A. C. Hendrickson, Ashland, O.,	5.00
C. E. Society, Roanoke, Va. (Rowsey),	5.00
W. M. S., Ankenytown, O. (Leedy),	10.00
C. E. Jones Mills, Pa., (Miller),	15.00
W. M. S., Dayton, O., 1st Br. (Kem),	20.00
Albert Trent, Johnstown, Pa.,	10.00
Eld. G. E. Cone, Ft. Scott, Kans.,	15.00
W. M. S., Zion Hill, O, (Crider),	5.00
Dr. E. M. Cobb, Dayton, O.,	5.00
W. M. S., Warsaw, Ind. (Shaffer),	10.00
Mrs. J. E. Ham, Ft. Wayne, Ind.,	5.00
Archie Lytle, Burlington, Ind.,	5.00
Mrs. E. M. Biddle, Louisville, O.,	10.00
C. E. Stewart — J. M. Fox, Loree, Indiana,	5.00
Eld. & Mrs. G. S. Baer, Ashland, O.,	5.00
Leroy N. Haney, Dayton, Ohio,	5.00
C. E., Peru, Ind., (Carpenter),	5.00
Mrs. C. G. Wolfe, N. Liberty, Ind.,	5.00
W. R. Deeter, Oakville, Ind.,	5.00
J. E. Braker, Phila, Pa., (Struth),	5.00
Third Br. Ch. S.S., Phila., Pa.,	10.00
Sisterhood Girls, Phila., Pa., (Eaton),	5.00
Br. S. S., Roann, Ind. (Needham),	25.00
R. A. Hazen, Ashland, Ohio,	5.00
C. E., 1st Br. Ch. Phila, Pa. (Kolb),	50.00
Mr. & Mrs. H. S. Rutt, Smithville, O.,	25.00
Annie D. Bunch, Leon, Iowa,	5.00
Br. S. S., Altoona, Pa. (Benshoff,	10.00
Campbell Br. .Ch., Clarksville, Mich.,	5.00
Loyal Helpers S. S. Class, Waterloo, Iowa,	10.00
C. E. Fremont, O. (Oberholtzer),	5.00
Br. Ch., Lost Creek, Ky.,	54.32
Mrs. J. DaVis, Philadelphia, Pa.,	5.00
Eld. S. E. Christiansen, Columbus, O.,	5.00
Eld. Henry Wise, Parkersburg, W. Virginia,	5.00
C. E. Society, Dayton, O., (Askin),	110.00
Mr. & Mrs. Peter Pontius, Elkhart, Indiana,	5.00
W. M. Derr, Cerro Gordo, Ill.,	10.00
Luella Miller, Urbana, Ill.,	5.00
D. L. Minderman, Dayton, O.,	5.00
Miscellaneous receipts,	5.00
Total,	$1,096.99

Miscellaneous Funds:

Ky. Kitchen Shower, Mrs. L. L. Kilmer,	$ 5.00
Campbell B. Ch., Mich (Price),	5.00
Total,	$ 10.00

Ky. Light Plant:

Mrs. Nell Wentz, Portland, Ind.,	5.00
Dr. E. W. Longenecker, Dayton, O.,	35.00

Lathrop Br. Ch., Calif(Coykendall),	6.12
Ruth Bixler, Marion, Ind.,	5.00
R. I. Humberd, Chicago, Ill.,	5.00
Waterloo, Ia., Br. Ch. (Puterbaugh),	53.00
Long Beach, Calif., 1st Br. Ch.,	79.85
Whittier, Calif. Br. Ch., (Flory),	12.00
Miscellaneous receipts,	2.00
Total,	$ 202.97
W. M. S., New Paris, Ind., Spokane Missions,	10.00
W. W. Bible Class, Dayton, Educational Fund,	9.75
Ky. Extension Fund (Krypton Land Sale),	400.00
Total Miscellaneous,	$ 632.72

WILLIAM A. GEARHART,
General Missionary Secretary.

BETHANY CHURCH, HAMLIN KANSAS

After deciding to give up all our material interests for the ministration of the Gospel of our Lord, we soon came in touch with Brother N. P. Eglin of the Hamlin church, who was looking for a pastor. Soon after conference we arranged to visit them on September 19th. The church giving us a unanimous call to the pastorate. We arrived in Hamlin, November 10th. Hamlin is a small town of about 200, with an extremely high class of folks. This church is an old organization but has not the power it should have as a Brethren church, with the whole Gospel to proclaim to lost men. Brother Bell held a successful meeting here last January, but they have been without a pastor for a year and are feeling a little discouraged, but we shall give our best endeavors to help them move out and possess the land for Christ and the church. Hope we may be able to give you some real interesting church news later on. We crave an interest in the prayers of the saints.

CLAUDE STUDEBAKER.

THE TIE THAT BINDS

MULL—McEWAN—On Thanksgiving Day the marriage of Noble Mull to Miss Ruth McEwan took place at the home of Mr. and Mrs. E. F. Owen at Ashland, Ohio. Mrs. Mull, who is a sister to Mrs. Owen, was formerly from Montreal, Canada, but has been living in Ashland since May, 1918. In that time she has held a position at the Brethren Publishing Company, and has rendered splendid service. Mr. Mull came to Ashland from Roann, Indiana. He is a splendid young man, very industrious and energetic. They are both loyal members of the Brethren church. The wishes of their many friends are that success and prosperity may follow them in all their endeavors and that they may enjoy a long and happy married life.

BENJ. F. OWEN.

IN THE SHADOW

CUBITT—Mrs. Mary Cubitt was born at Whitehaven, England, fifty-three years ago and died at her home at Listie, Pa., November 19, 1920. She united with the Listie church about seven years ago, and since that time has been one of its faithful and devoted members. She leaves to mourn her departure a husband, one daughter and five grandchildren, besides a host of friends. Funeral services on Sunday, November 21, 1920, by the Rev. H. S. Myers and her pastor.

W. S. BAKER.

TAYLOR—George W. Taylor was born in Scioto county, 1876 and departed this life November 20, 1920, aged 44 years 4 months and 16 days. He was united in marriage to Miss A. C. Curtiss, who died five years ago.

He was later married again. He united with the Brethren church in 1912 and remained a faithful member until his death, which came suddenly, he being sick only four hours. We sorrow with his bereaved wife and his four children by his first marriage and pray that God may greatly sustain them. The services were held at the Glenford church by the writer. BENJ. F. OWEN.

DETWILER—Mrs. Mary (Culp) Detwiler, after a two days' illness, passed peacefully away November 17, 1920. She was born November 26, 1837, near Columbiana, Ohio. She was married December 4, 1859 to Abram Detwiler, who died eight years after the celebration of their golden wedding. Fourteen children were born to this union; of this number thirteen, four sons and nine daughters, survive. During Mrs. Detwiler's 83rd year she never complained of illness until the last two days. Her old age was full of interest and energy. She loved good books and especially did she delight in studying the Bible, much of which she had memorized and could recite in two languages. She and her husband were charter members of the Ridgely Brethren church. Her face in death was lit up with a smile as she crossed to be with her Master. Her daughter, Vianna, who was ill in Los Angeles, and not able to return, had sent some beautiful flowers as a Thanksgiving remembrance to her mother. They arrived the day after the funeral. One son lives in Montreal, three daughters in Ohio, a son and a daughter in Los Angeles and the rest in or near Ridgely, Maryland. The funeral was conducted in the home church, Rev. A. J. McClain, assisted by Rev. H. L. Hoisinger and Rev. J. Frank White, officiating.

EDNA M. DETWILER.

CARTHEW—Bertha S., infant daughter of James and Agnes Carthew of Fairfield Ave., Johnstown, Pa., was called into the arms of the Good Shepherd at the age of seven weeks. Funeral service from the home, Novembr 25, 1920, by the writer. The mother is a member of the Third Brethren church of Johnstown, and little Bertha was a member of the Cradle Roll. The parents have the deep sympathy of a large circle of friends.

L. G. WOOD.

RHOADS—After a long illness due to heart trouble and goiter David Bennett Rhoads, aged 66 years, 11 months, 27 days, passed beyond earth's shadows to greet the dawning of eternity on the morning of November 18, 1920. The deceased is survived by his companion, Mrs. Etta B. Rhoads, two daughters and one son, two brothers, A. B. and R. P. Rhoads. The departed brother, earlier in life, made a private confession in a little devotional meeting with Rev. Martin Shively. May the Father of grace comfort and sustain the bereaved in this time of sorrow. Service by the undersigned.

REV. JOSEPH L. GINGRICH.

WILSON—After a very brief sickness of membranous croup, terminating in bronchial pneumonia, Harry Wilson, 3 year old stepson of Mr. and Mrs. Rose of Jefferson, peaceably answered the summons to come home, Thursday, Thanksgiving Day. Interment was held in Church Hill cemetery, Saturday at 1:30 P. M. Funeral services by the writer.

REV. JOSEPH L. GINGRICH.

STADDEN—Paul A. Stadden, son of Mrs. J. Stadden, was drowned several months ago near Dayton in the Miami River. He was working with the Conservancy deepening the river channel when he and another young man met their death. He had spent three years in the navy, but had returned home and was helping to support his widowed mother. Services conducted by the writer and assisted by Miss Emma Aboud.

J. S. COOK.

LEATHERMAN—Christian A. Leatherman was born March 23rd, 1861 and departed this life, October 23, 1920. He had not been well for almost a year but was confined to his bed but a few days. He recently came into the church but had read the New Testament through and had begun on the Old Testament a few days before he passed away. Two days before his death he bore a beautiful testimony to God's saving grace, in the presence of his pastor. Services were held in the New Lebanon church by the writer.

J. S. COOK.

SAYLOR—Joseph M. Saylor was born in Somerset county, Pennsylvania, near Meyersdale, November 25th, 1837, and passed away at the home of his daughter, Mrs. Eliza Schrock on October 30th, 1920, at the ripe age of almost 83 years. In 1860 he was united in marriage to Mary Buechly of Meyersdale; and in 1863 they moved to Iowa, settling in Orange township south of Waterloo. Brother locality,, and he followed his occupation until Saylor was one of the pioneer farmers in this he removed to Waterloo, 26 years ago. He was a member of the Church of the Brethren up to the time of the division, when he came over to the Progressive wing of the church. He was a charter member of the Enon church, and after cominf to town he was closely allied with the church in the city until his death. Brother Saylor was a loyal, faithful Brethren. Because of his faithfulness he will be missed. A son and daughter survive him. His wife preceded him in death in 1918. He felt that his course had been run and he was patiently awaiting his summons to go. The funeral was in charge of the church. WM. H. BEACHLER.

KLINGAMAN—Silas L. Klingaman was born in Somerset county, Pennsylvania, September 13th, 1842 and departed this life at his home in Waterloo, November 17th, 1920, at the age of 78 years. Brother Klingaman served the last year in the Civil War, and shortly after the close of the war he came to Iowa. He followed farming up until 19 years ago at which time he removed to Waterloo. In January of 1865 he was united in marriage to Martha Cain. To this union were born four sons and a daughter. All of the children, the wife and mother, and sixteen grandchildren survive. Brother Klingaman's death was the first break in this family circle. He was originally a member of the Church of the Brethren, but at the time of the division he identified himself with the Brethren movement. He was closely associated with the church at Enon until he moved to Waterloo. And from then until his death he was loyal to the work in the city. His death marks the removal of another of the pioneers in the church and in the community. The funeral was in charge of the pastor, assisted by Brother Edward Boardman at the church. A very large concourse of people was present, including the local G. A. R. and the Women's Relief Corps.

WM. H. BEACHLER.

BICKLEY—Samuel B. Blickley was born in West Moreland county, Pennsylvania, August 21st, 1848, and died November 22nd, 1920, at the age of 72 years, 3 months, and 1 day. Although Brother Bickley had been in failing health for some time, his death came very suddenly as a result of heart failure. When but a child, Brother Bickley's parents moved to Ohio, settling in Wayne county. From that place he came to Waterloo, Iowa as a young man in his later 'teens. He had been a farmer up until 20 years ago when he came to Waterloo. He became a Christian at 12 years of age, having given to his Master 60 years of service. His wife and a daughter preceded him to that better world. A son and four grandchildren survive him. His first religious activities were in the Church of the Brethren, but in its very beginning he became a member of the Brethren fraternty. He was active in the Enon church, and upon moving to the city he was just as active and faithful in the Waterloo work. In his death a heavy loss comes to the community, the local congregation, and to the general brotherhood. Brother Bickley was a man of splendid missionary vision, and of broad, benevolent tendencies. He has been for many years a substantial supporter of our own missionary interests both home and foreign. In addition to this, he has during the years educated one Chinese native who is now a Christian worker. And at the time of his death he was supporting two native Chinese students in a Mission school. In his will Brother Bickley made substantial provision for our Foreign Mission work, the College, and an orphanage in Iowa. He stood for the best things in the city and community, and he coveted growth and progress for the Kingdom of God. Faithful to every service of the church, for many years a Sunday school teacher, his life will be long remembered and his place will not be easily filled. Funeral in the church in charge of the pastor. WM. H. BEACHLER.

ABRAHAM—Andrew Charles Abraham was born in South Union township, Fayette county, Pennsylvania, April 17, 1874, the son of T. B. and Margaret J. Abraham. For the last eighteen years the family has resided in Uniontown. Deceased was married to Miss Gertrude Kellis, of Lynchburg, Ohio, on Nov. 25, 1903. To this union one child, Elizabeth was born. She, together with the wife and mother, and two half brothers are left to mourn his sudden leave-taking. Brother Abraham was a member of the Uniontown Brethren church, having united under the ministry of Brother E. L. Miller, and on November 17, at his own request received the ordinance of anointing for healing, at the time expressing his desire for a continued lease on life, but a willingness to abide God's dealings in his life. He passed away suddenly while resting on the couch in his home on December 7, 1920. Death came at the age of 46 years, 6 months and 20 days. Funeral services conducted by his pastor, assisted by Rev. Paige of the Free Methodist church. Services and burial at the Tent church, in Georges township, on Dec. 9. Peace to the departed and grace for the mourning friends be granted by our God.

DYOLL BELOTE.

Business Manager's Corner

CONTRIBUTIONS STILL COMING IN

We are indeed glad to be able to report that offerings for the "Paper Fund" are still coming in, and some churches that have taken up an offering for this purpose have not yet made the remittance of the offering, while others have reported that an offering would be made at a later and more convenient season. But still others have made no report at all. However, we feel no church will want to be left out of this proposition and we will expect to hear from a number of good churches that have not yet made any report.

Since our last report we have received the following offerings for this fund: Brethren church, Portis, Kansas, $10.62; Brethren church, Limestone, Tennessee, $8.00; 1st Brethren church, Los Angeles, $17.00; Brethren church, Berlin, Pennsylvania, $27.00; 1st Brethren church, Johnstown, $50.00; Brethren church, Roanoke,, Virginia, (additional) $1.75; Mrs. Wm. Williams, $1.00; F. C. Schaper, $3.00; Mr. and Mrs. A. L. DeLozier, $5.00; Mrs. Ella Ovelman, $1.00; Mrs. Edward S. Reynolds, $1.00—total to date, $1,172.35.

We repeat for all this we are thankful. On Wednesday we have a two thousand dollar note to meet, given in settlement for the paper bill, and at the close of business last Saturday we did not have sufficient funds in the bank to meet the obligation, but we will receive enough in our business before Wednesday to make up what is lacking. This will then leave a balance of about $1,900.00 still to be provided for in the near future. So the churches that have not yet made up their portion for this fund can easily see they are still needed in this good work.

We rejoice further that three of our churches that are already on the Evangelist Honor Roll have renewed their subscription lists and retain their places. Lanark has renewed for the fourth year and we are sure so long as Brother Burnworth remains as their pastor they will always keep their place among the Honor Roll churches. Elkhart, Indiana has renewed its list with a goodly increase in the number of subscribers. This is the third year for Elkhart, and the pastor at this time is Bryan S. Stoffer. The third church we have to report this week is the "Little Brown Church of Peru." This is the second year for this mission church and we are sure the pastor, G. C. Carpenter has realized the helpfulness of the Evangelist in the homes of his congregation.

A goodly number of churches should renew their lists within the next thirty days; and whenever possible the cash should accompany the order for the renewal. That would help us greatly in the matter of meeting our obligations that are coming due with the regularity of the months of the calendar.

We began mailing the Adult Bible Class quarterlies more than a week ago and we will mail the others just as rapidly as we can get them completed so as to cause no delays in our Sunday schools.

R. R. TEETER,
Business Manager.

VOLUME XLII
NUMBER 49

DECEMBER 22
1920

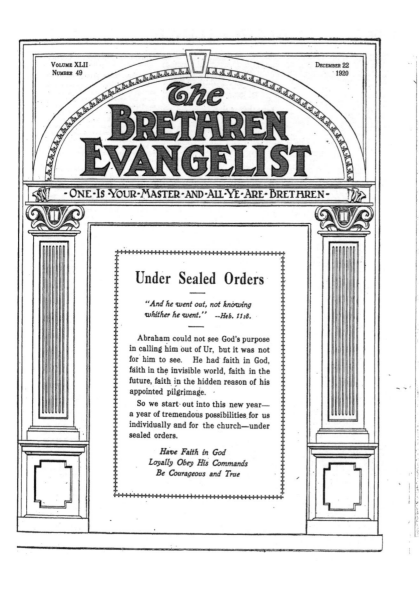

The BRETHREN EVANGELIST

- ONE · IS · YOUR · MASTER · AND · ALL · YE · ARE · BRETHREN -

Under Sealed Orders

*"And he went out, not knowing
whither he went."* --Heb. 11:8.

Abraham could not see God's purpose
in calling him out of Ur, but it was not
for him to see. He had faith in God,
faith in the invisible world, faith in the
future, faith in the hidden reason of his
appointed pilgrimage.

So we start out into this new year—
a year of tremendous possibilities for us
individually and for the church—under
sealed orders.

*Have Faith in God
Loyally Obey His Commands
Be Courageous and True*

Published every Wednesday at Ashland, Ohio. All matter for publication must reach the Editor not later than Friday noon of the preceding week.

George S. Baer, Editor

The Brethren Evangelist

When ordering your paper changed give old as well as new address. Subscriptions discontinued at expiration. To avoid missing any numbers renew two weeks in advance.

R. R. Teeter, Business Manager

ASSOCIATE EDITORS: J. Fremont Watson, Louis S. Bauman, A. B. Cover, Alva J. McClain, B. T. Burnworth.

OFFICIAL ORGAN OF THE BRETHREN CHURCH

Subscription price, $2.00 per year, payable in advance.
Entered at the Post Office at Ashland, Ohio, as second-class matter.
Acceptance for mailing at special rate of postage provided for in section 1103, Act of October 3, 1917, authorized September 9, 1918.
Address all matter for publication to Geo. S. Baer, Editor of the Brethren Evangelist, and all business communications to R. R. Teeter, Business Manager, Brethren Publishing Company, Ashland, Ohio. Make all checks payable to the Brethren Publishing Company.

TABLE OF CONTENTS

EDITORIAL

GOD'S REDEMPTIVE PURPOSE

In every great movement—intellectual, moral, or spiritual—there must be a central fact or principle. So in God's vast scheme for the world's betterment, there must be a central fact. Nor is it necessary to lose any time speculating as to where such a central fact may be found.

The incarnation of God in the person of his Son, Jesus Christ, for the salvation of the human race forms the central point in the history and development of mankind. How finely it is put in that noble passage in the Epistle to the Galatians! "But when the fullness of time was come, God sent forth his Son, made of woman, made under the law, to redeem them that were under the law, that we might receive the adoption of sons"—the fullness of the time, the harvest of the centuries, the point upon which their forces and influences had from the beginning been focalized. All former history served only as a preparation for this event. All the time preceding it was used by Providence for the working toward it. And, as all the time prior to this event was but a preparation for it, so is it equally true that all time subsequent thereto is but the development of its divine significance. In order to realize the millennial dream of all its prophets and poets, the world needs only to accept in its fullness and apply in its life the great fact that "God was in Christ, reconciling the world unto himself."

The recognition of this as the central fact of history is absolutely essential to a correct interpretation of history. There is a great difference in the way men regard the past.

Faithless interpreters have always proved false interpreters. To them the events of the world's life seem a hopeless jumble of confused and disorderly occurrences. Thus Gibbon and Voltaire each declared that history is only the register of the crimes and misfortunes of mankind; while our Christian President, Garfield, wrote: "The world's history is a divine poem. Its strains have been pealing along down the centuries; and though there have been mingled the discords of warring cannon and dying men, yet to the Christian philosopher and historian—the humble listener—there has been a divine melody running through the song." Tennyson had the faith to discern that "through the ages one increasing purpose runs," and to see the goal of all in that

"One far-off divine event
To which the whole creation moves."

In this great fact the incarnation of God is the key to a proper understanding of his movements in time and his purpose for the race.

Now, if this truth be central in God's purpose, then it must be vitally related to the cause of human progress. The statement, "God was in Christ reconciling the world unto himself," really contains the principle of the secret of its growth towards better things. The world progresses toward an ideal civilization in proportion as it accepts the mind of the Master as its standard and applies his mind in every department of life. The Spirit of God is the organizer of civilization. It is easy for the modern man to boast of what he has done. But what has he done? He has been a discoverer, a learner. The foundations upon which he has builded were provided by divine forethought. It was Kepler who said, "In reading the secrets of nature I am thinking the thought of God after him." The man of the twentieth century is superior intellectually to the man of the tenth century in that he has learned to do this more effectively. God and man have wrought together for the achievement of this end. The very first breath of inspired utterance presents the Spirit of God as moving upon the face of the waters, bringing order out of chaos. The Eternal Spirit has ever been true to this mighty mission. He has been moving through the centuries upon the face of human life, bringing order out of chaos, light out of darkness, systems out of confusion, moral beauty out of moral desolation and ugliness. This has primarily, for man, secondarily be the honor of the better day and the larger life to which the world in its progress has come.

It is interesting to note the material upon which the Spirit of God works. He directs his redemptive energies upon the raw material of human life. With all its limitations, its natural ugliness and inherent degradation, human nature is yet capable of redemption under the touch of the divine hand. Left to itself, it would be utterly hopeless; but considered with respect to its capacity for the divine, it contains the sure promise of high and worthy achievement. The essential factor in the development of man is not as to whether he has been evolved from a lower order of the world's life. "Here is a manlike ape. He is, as far as history is concerned, an older being than man; he can boast a more venerable ancestry; he is a more ancient habitant of our planet, and has had, therefore, the greater opportunities, a longer course of time has supplied in which to develop the resources that are in him and achieve his manlike apehood. But how stands the case? He stands today precisely where his most ancient ancestry stood; he cracks his nuts and feeds himself in the ancestral manner; he lives in the old home in the old way, swings himself from tree to tree by the same organ and with the same dexterity; he emits sounds of alarm or ferocity or affection, cries of defiance or of solicitation; which men may try to imitate, but can understand only by ceasing as much as possible to be men and becoming apes. In a word, he began as a brute and a brute he remains.

"BUT WHAT OF MAN?" He may have begun by dwelling in caves and holes of the earth, but he has not continued to dwell there. His first efforts in art may have been rude pictures on the walls of his cave, but he has not stayed at the stage where he first used tools. Man's social life may have begun in a state of savage war, where the weak man went to the wall. But out of that stage he slowly and painfully emerged into a social and political order, where law reigns and restrains. In fact, no day dawns that does not see some new wonder added to the race.

The principle of differentiation from every other form of life is not found in his bodily structure but in the quality of his soul. His capacity to think God's thoughts after him, to receive God's life into him, and to live God's life with God—these are the things which differentiate him from other forms of life. All that is necessary to secure to man his highest and divinest possibility is that the Spirit of God should have a fair, free, and full chance at him.

This is preeminently the case of the truths which group themselves about the revelation of God in Jesus Christ. For a man to admit these truths into his being and to make them the law of his life is for him to escape the low plane of the human and to mount upward to the plane of the divine.

In Christ he has shown us that the world was never far adrift in supposing that human life was in some sense an expression of this divine mode of being. Men were not wrong in fancying certain resemblances between God and themselves, but in failing to invest him with proper attributes, and to apprehend him as holiness and love. Christ will convince those who accept him as the ultimate revelation of God that the Infinite does relate himself personally to all the experiences of men. No logic will prove this declaration, but a spiritual fellowship with Christ will evidence it.

On a famous bridge spanning the river which flows through an Austrian city there are twelve statues of Jesus, representing him in various characteristic vocations of life. There is Christ as physician, teacher, carpenter—Christ in twelve separate callings. The weary men who cross the bridge at morning, noon, and night may turn their eyes towards the Christ who, touching human experience at every point, has brought God within the compass of every devout heart willing to receive him. It is this universality of Christ's adaptation to the needs of men which constrains them to see in him the perfect manifestation of God. When once this conviction has seized the soul, he will ignore the difficulties which pure reason may suggest, and, out of his consciousness that Christ fulfills the deepest requirements of his nature, he will exclaim with the hesitant but loyal disciple of old, "My Lord and my God."

J. FREMONT WATSON.

ARMENIA'S NEED A CHALLENGE TO YOUR CHRISTMAS SPIRIT

When one talks profusely of the Christmas spirit in the presence of dire need and offers no hand of relief and provision his profession may well be challenged. Among no people is there so much said of the spirit of love and giving that flowed so freely on the first Christmas as among the Christian people of America. And consequently of no people is so much expected in the way of a practical demonstration of the true Christmas spirit as of American Christians. And possibly by our unequaled generosity we have given occasion for the world to expect much of us. But however much we have excelled other peoples in our giving, we have never reached the measure of our ability and of the need. Much more is this true in this very year and at this very season.

Just now as we are approaching the sacred Christmas season with its attendant cheer and gifts of love, and when the horn of plenty pours forth its viands in such profusion, over across the sea in the afflicted country of Armenia are thousands of helpless, starving children. Due to Turkish cruelty and oppression they are without homes or parents. Crusts are their only food and rags their only clothing. There are 54,600 homeless children being cared for in orphanages instituted by the Near East Relief, while 55,039 receive partial support outside of orphanages. Every Armenian orphan looks to America for food and clothing. By constant and difficult labor on the part of those who are giving their lives to the relief of these sufferers, backed

by American contributions of money, many pitiable waifs have been saved. But the great unanswered need comes as a direct challenge to the genuineness of our Christmas spirit. Poverty such as we can hardly imagine is the common lot there. To banish this poverty and to alleviate their abject condition requires an outlay of money. Winter is on and they are without the common necessities of life. Whatever measure of warmth and cheer they will be granted depends on the thousands of American Christians who have enough and to spare. All gifts are wisely applied by the Near East Relief, One Madison Avenue, New York.

EDITORIAL REVIEW

Welcome, La Paz, to the Evangelist Honor Roll. We are glad to count you as a member of the "family."

Sister Mary C. Wenger gives an interesting sketch of her recent trip to Kentucky in company with Miss Huldah Ewert, who is the new cook for the Riverside Institute.

Brother A. T. Wirick reports the Bryan revival meeting from the evangelist's standpoint and displays a splendid spirit and attitude on the part of an evangelist toward a pastor.

In addition to the fine report which Brother Ora Paul supplies for the Evangelist readers, we learn that every officer of the Sunday school, from the pastor down is a tither. That is a great record.

Brother Shively's "College Hen" is getting quite a large brood and apparently is insured of being well housed and well fed, judging from the way the contributions are coming in.

Brother Huette's advertisement of Christian Endeavor should stimulate some societies to New Year resolves for better work and on the same page Prof. Garber mentions a matter that ought to receive the hearty response of every Endeavorer. Do it Now.

Brother Shively, the Bursar of Ashland College, writes an interesting letter regarding his leaving of the pastorate and entrance upon his new work. Brother Shively's service in the pastorate has been among the longest and most successful of our ministry.

If you have ever waited for an important piece of news that never came when the very success of a work delegated to you depended on its coming, you will understand how Brother Bame feels at the failure of some pastors to report on the Stewardship campaign of the Bicentenary Movement.

It was indeed a great victory that the Lord's forces realized at Bryan, Ohio, when Brother A. T. Wirick as evangelist was yoked up with Brother G. L. Maus, the pastor, in an evangelistic campaign. The Bryan people are wide-awake and aggressive in every phase of the Lord's work.

The letter from Brother C. F. Yoder, of Rio Cuarto, Argentina, is very encouraging. It shows that the work there is going steadily forward and is being built up carefully and substantially. The brotherhood will rejoice to know that Sister Yoder's recovery is going forward so splendidly that she is now able to do much in the work of the mission.

Brother E. M. Riddle reviews the splendid work of the Louisville church and states among other things that the church has decided to have full time service, beginning the first of the year. This is a step that promises much for this splendid people and a thing they have contemplated for some time.

President Jacobs' "College News" mentions a number of items of interest, among them is the good financial condition of the Purple and Gold, the college paper. In addition to this encouraging feature we wish to commend the excellent editorial work that gives quality and beauty to this student publication.

Help your General Missionary Secretary by sending your Thanksgiving offerings to him promptly, if you have not already done so. Remember this offering goes to Wm. A. Gearhart, 906 American Building, Dayton, Ohio. Do not send White Gift offerings to him; send them to H. H. Wolford, Ashland, Ohio. The White Gift offering goes to the National Sunday School Association which uses it both to help Kentucky missions and Ashland College department of Religious Education and a smaller portion for the great work of the Sunday School Association itself.

THE BRETHREN BICENTENARY MOVEMENT PAGE

1723 - - - - - - 1923

Dr. Charles A. Bame, Editor

Don't Hold Your Breath

In my last letter, you remember that I was listening with bated breath for the replies from the pastors as to the reports from STEWARDSHIP DAY. Well, I hope that you have not held your breath for them. If you have you will suffocate. For, you would be ashamed to be a member of the denomination, I fear, if I were to tell you how few have reported. Some doubtless have their reasons for not reporting, but too many have none. I thought that I would surely, by this time, be ready to give a good report. But I am not. If no more churches report and if no more have tithers than did report, I am sure that there will be a lot of disappointed people when the entire report is made.

Ashamed

I just wrote a paragraph and cut it out, of which I am ashamed. But it was all the truth. The truth hurts and it would have hurt too much in this case. I'd like to tell the whole truth all the time but sometimes we find ourselves in the "strait" of the Master, "Ye can not bear them now." But if you had made several trips of hundreds of miles and if you sent out 150 self-addressed letters and if you were hired to get a thing done that ought to be done and must be done and then,—if you only got about one-tenth as many replies after waiting two months as you thought you ought to have and then, if you had gotten several slams on top of that, some in the church paper, what do you think you would write?

Spending the Money

I am spending the money the conference gave me, just as if the churches were going to put the Movement across. It takes a lot of money to get done what needs to be done for a Movement like this and I am carrying out the commands of the Conference as best I can, and if we do not get results, it will not be my fault.

What They Say

Now, of course, some of the preachers and congregations have not tried to do what the Conference asked of them and so, they do not know how it feels to get into line with the purposes of God on Stewardship. But that they may know what some of the real leaders of the church are saying of this work, I'll pass on to them, what many have said. Here is one: "We like the new Movement and bespeak for it success." Another says, "We had a very stormy day. . . I'm glad for the nine, however." "Will take it up later," says another. A pastor of one of our large churches says, "We made a special plea for both above and find that as yet we have but three or four tithers. . . I have been emphasizing Stewardship during the past year." Good for them all but it is too bad that a pastor emphasizes what the Lord wants among his people and gets but three or four to respond. Too bad!

See Here!

If you think the Movement strikes all alike, listen to this discordant note: "We will determine the number of tithers when we secure the scroll,—this from Pennsylvania, and this from Indiana: "You are NOT; to send me a scroll on which to enroll the names of tithers; our people do not want the publicity that the scroll would give them." Now why? Why would any one object to have it known that they have money for the Lord if he gives it to them? Why WHY? One pastor writes, "We have now thirty six tithers among our church members, this being one of our regular efforts."

But This

Of all the answers this one, I think, caps the climax: "Number of recruits, 0. Tithers SOME. Number will be determined later." This from a prominent member of the organization of the officers of the Movement. If all answered like that, what would be the good of the effort, my dear pastor? Now, answer right and do it quick!

A Hero

This pastor is made of the stuff that makes the kingdom come. I imagine that there are a good many like him but—and that "but" is enough to make one miss heaven. "Did my best. Preached on Stewardship and urged decisions both for money and life; no response." He tried and was courageous enough to return the self-addressed card, even though he could not put on it what he would like to see. But he served the Movement according to its plan, nevertheless.

Best of All

From one of our newer churches and pastors comes this finest of all messages: "Brother Bame, I pray God will bless you in this work you are doing for the greatest of all institutions, the church. Your greater reward is in heaven." Heaven's blessing be upon you, dear pastor, for this encouragement. It compensates, in a small way for some of the things one has to suffer for a cause such as this. I am sure that you are as happy as some who knock and I am a lot happier. It does no one harm to give good encouragement and it will not take much time to do it and if we can thus assist each other in the Lord's work, why not do it?

Why Not, Preachers?

Why not return the cards, brethren? If you have nothing to put on—if you did not and if you will not, we shall all be better off if you will say that much. Why not make your kick if you have one and let us all know where we are leading against the Spirit, if you see it thus? We shall be glad for your opinion, even though we do not agree with you. Maybe you can tell us what we ought to do and maybe we can tell you where you are wrong, but at any rate, let us understand each other.

Fine! Fine!

That's what I have to say to those who tried to do their duty. Angels could do no more. We have a good many Life Recruits but not enough for the tomorrow of the church. If your program has been just too full to get the thing across, remember that any day is a good day to do things like this for the church. Do not put it off too long for there are many days yet on this year's program and you will need to get them out of the way on schedule if we get where we ought in this campaign—and we shall get where we ought if we all intend to be in the mind of Christ, whom we are trying to serve in it all.   BAME.

GENERAL ARTICLES

Through the New Year With Christ. By R. Paul Miller

"Brethren, I count not myself to have apprehended: but this one thing I do, forgetting those things which are behind and reaching forth unto those things which are before, I press toward the mark for the prize of the high calling of God in Christ Jesus" (Phil. 3:13, 14).

First, just a word on another year for the world without Christ. We have passed through many of them and the world has passed through about 6,000 Christless years and each one increasing in turmoil, bloodshed and calamity by leaps and bounds. The year just past is still fresh in memory, and the anticipation of another year of Bolshevism, anarchy and rebellion against God even worse than before is surely not pleasant to the soul of most of us. Especially since there is nothing in sight in the world's plans to stop it but the arm of flesh which has failed for 6,000 years. Surely the future of this world in its heedless plunging on in Christian rejection is not a peaceful and comforting thought. Now what will it mean to go through this year with Christ?

First of all it will mean waiting on him. The besetting sin of Christians today is substituting the energies of the flesh for the leading and working of the Holy Spirit. We take counsel of ourselves, decide what to do, lay our plans, roll up our sleeves and then try to bring it all to pass by the working of the human hand and head. Not that we should lay down and do nothing and cover up laziness with prayer, but that we should make sure that God is leading in the way we are going and in the work we are doing. Just because a work is a good work is no indication that the Holy Spirit sponsors it. There are many so-called good works that the devil is trying to substitute for the real work of God. The only way to do real lasting work and pleasing in the sight of God is to be sure that God is leading. If we would spend more breath in praying, we would waste less in crying over our failures. This is an age of rush and hurry but you cannot rush God and his work. If we would wait on God at all times we might not do so many things this year, but we would accomplish more and do better and more successful things. We plunge ahead and ask God to bless when it would be a lot better to ask God to lead and then follow. It will save much disappointment and misspent energy and embarrassment. To go through WITH Christ MEANS WITH him, not AHEAD of him. Hours with God mean days of power and victory.

In the second place, to go through the year with Christ means hard, diligent labor. "My Father worketh hitherto, and I work." None ever worked as Jesus worked—early and late,—for none others saw the awful need and suffering and sin and eternal loss as he saw it. And if we go through this year with Christ we will get such a vision of humanity as we never had before. We will see this world, not so much a place to live in and enjoy yourself in, as a world full of lost souls going down and down to a Christless eternity without a hand raised to help or stay the tide. When we get this vision we cannot take things so easy. Surprisingly few are they who overwork in the Master's vineyard. "Lift up your eyes unto the whitened harvest," says the Master. "Get the vision of the awful procession of death and see if you can remain unconcerned." Finney got that vision; Jonathan Edwards got it; Moody got it; and they burned up in their passion to save the lost. Many you could save today will be gone tomorrow. "Work for the night is coming." There will be no ease in Zion if we go through this year with Christ.

In the third place, to go through this year with Christ will mean warfare of the bitterest kind. "For many false prophets are gone out into the world." Paul fought them in his day with all his power. We owe many of his glorious epistles to the battles he fought for the truth. Among them are Galatians, Colossians and 1 Thessalonions. It would have been easier for Paul to have kept still and not opposed the false teachers. He might have waited for his sweet and pliant influence to shame them into silence, but he did not. He couldn't stand it to see the flock of God decimated by them. He knew also that we would have them to face today and warned us against them. He also knew the power of the enemy; he had felt their blows only too often. "We fight not against flesh and blood, but against principalities, powers and world rulers of this darkness, spiritual hosts of wickedness." If we go through this year with Jesus we will have to measure swords with the same implacable enemy Paul faced. We may also have more enemies and bitter ones, but likewise more friends and truer ones. We will know Jesus better after fighting through the battle with him. We will have less fear of man and more of that spirit of dear old Thomas who, when he thought that to follow Jesus back to Judea meant death to them all, said, "Let us also go with him that we may die with him." Oh, let us hold his glorious banner high and unsullied and lunge into the fray and if we fall in the thick of the fight, let us fall with our face to the enemy, true to the last. So may we also, as we lay down our mantle, cry, 'I have fought a good fight, I have finished my course, I have kept the faith.'

In the fourth place it will mean a determined purpose and program. Old Sanballat and his gang are on the job every minute seeking to turn the church away from her high and pilgrim calling of preparing men to meet their God, to trying to make a heaven on earth for a God-hating generation. Education, social service, legislation and reform are all right in their places, but the church is called to preach the Gospel. Some seem to think that God's plan is not quick enough, but the quickest way under heaven to make this world a fit place to live in is to preach the pure gospel to them—if men reject the gospel, there is nothing else for them. After all, God's way is the best and quickest way, in fact the only way. It is when the church has departed from this program that she lost her power. Turn a deaf ear to all the specious arguments and attacks and like Nehemiah, "Refuse to come down."

In the fifth place it will mean true loyalty, no matter what the cost. The days are fearful and ominous; the test of faith is getting more severe every day. The days of the martyrs may be repeated. Some folks have fairweather loyalty that fades at the first test, others stand quite a bit, but who will stand true to the end? Tradition tells of Peter running from Rome when persecution against the faith got severe. In the darkness he suddenly saw a white figure and looking closely he recognized the Lord going towards Rome bearing his cross. In his surprise he cried, "Where goest thou, Lord?" Jesus answered, "I go to Rome to be crucified again." Peter, feeling the sting of his own cowardice and shame, turned back to Rome and death. "Faith of our fathers living still, we will be true to thee till death."

In the last place, to go through the year with Christ will mean peace of soul and victory. The path of duty is the only place of security. No matter where it leads, all is well if he has laid out the course. While the world restlessly turns from one thing to another, if we walk with Christ, our path never swerves. It may be through fire or deep waters but if he goes through with us all is well and perfect peace and tranquility is ours. So it was with Daniel and the three Hebrew children. There is no safety or protection for the Christian who is flying from the path of duty. What peace to know that your path is the one he has chosen for you! And the joy of it is in the victory all the way from January to Christmas. What achievements, what success, what blessing if we go through the year with Christ! Not a long record of failures and disappointments, but one fair record, fit for his pages, of souls won, goals gained, and Christ glorified! "Thanks be to God who giveth us the victory through our Lord Jesus Christ." Spokane, Washington.

What are We Educating for?   By President Edwin E Jacobs

A survey of the present enrollment of students in Ashland College reveals some very suggestive facts and while this is only for the current year, yet doubtless the figures would not vary much for any recent year.

As nearly as I could determine, out of a total of 105 students in the regular college work, about 16 are preparing for some profession, 24 are doing college work with no definite aim as yet, 35 are preparing for teaching and some 30 are enrolled in the Seminary. To be added to this number are some 60 in music. Out of the total enrollment in the College of Arts and Sciences of 105 about 60 are from Brethren homes and some 45 are from other homes. Practically every student is a member of some church. Out of the 105, 63 are men.

These figures raise two questions in my mind. First, does it pay the church to sustain a college to prepare young men and women for other than Christian work? My answer is quick and certain. It does, if, as it trains for secular occupations, it also seeks to develop a sterling, unique, and outstanding quality of Christian character. Think what it might mean to have 35 young people preparing for teaching. Now there is no greater calling than this, if done in the right way. The opportunity here is surpassingly great. Our mission fields are not all abroad. Certainly our own American culture needs the leaven of Christian influence and I am so bold as to say that it is very much in need of quite a bit of Brethrenism. If any man doubts this, let him look

today at the utter folly of over dressing, extreme amusements, cheap and silly reading matter, and so on. I have an ambition, shared by all these, I am confident, who have a part in the affairs of Ashland, that she shall stand four square against these and other forms of nonsense. At a small town I visited recently, one store was displaying what they said to be $80,000 worth of ladies' furs. In China, babies are starving for bread. And in America men and women are dying for that bread which cometh down from above. This is but a passing remark and is not particularly related to my theme, but it is worth making and I am very earnest in my desire that students at Ashland may be able to answer rightly the Master's question, "What doth it profit a man if he gain the whole world and lose his own soul?"

Secondly, should not there be started a league within the church, say by the National Ministerial Association, to encourage young men to enter the ministry? The seminary is on my mind day and night. I do not believe we have ever had a more promising body of young people in this department than we have now, but it is too small. So far as I know, there is not a young person enrolled there this year that does not have the work of the church at heart. If so, the exception is slight. Discipline in this department is nil this year, but I could wish to see the number of enrollments doubled. Pray ye therefore that laborers be thrust into the harvest.

Ashland, Ohio.

The Great Jewish Lawgiver.   By T. Darley Allen

In answer to a question who desired to know the name of the first republic, The Cleveland Press said recently that "The first republic of which there is authentic record was the commonwealth which was organized by the Jews after they were led out of Egypt," and gave other information showing that under the Jewish form of government the people had advantages greater than were enjoyed by the people of any other nation of their time.

Moses was the world's greatest lawgiver. Milman the historian said that this great leader "has exercised a more extensive and permanent influence over the destinies of man than any other individual in the history of the world."

Hollis Read says in "God in History:" "The Mosaic code was the first in the world to recognize the equal rights of the citizen; reverence for law, constitutional government, the principle of trial by jury, general education, freedom of opinion, social order and individual enterprise and industry as sources of national prosperity and happiness. . . Plato's ideal republic is perhaps a fairer specimen of the real conception which the intelligent Greeks had of civil liberty than any realization of liberty which they could furnish. This ideal republic bears evident marks of being borrowed from the Hebrew commonwealth, and Plato's ideal laws and institutions from the code of Moses. And this Grecian liberty—this Hebrew element—became incorporated into the Roman republic, where it found even a more congenial soil till choked and smothered by the avarice and ambition of selfish men. The famous Twelve Tables were confessedly borrowed from the Greeks and betray a Mosaic origin. Through these channels, as well as from the Bible itself, the principles of the Mosaic code have found their way into the jurisprudence of all civilized nations."

Professor E. C. Wines in "'The Laws of the Ancient Hebrew'' says, "Sir Matthew Hale has traced the influence of the Bible, generally, on the laws of England. Sismondi testified that Alfred the Great, in causing a republication of the Saxon laws, inserted several statutes from the code of Moses to give strength and cogency to the principles of morality. The same historian also states that one of the first acts of the clergy under Pepin and Charlemagne was to improve the legislation of the Franks by the introduction of several of the Mosaic laws."

Hollis Read tells us that the laws of Sweden were permeated with the same leaven. "And no laws and institutions are more thoroughly pervaded by the spirit and wisdom of the Hebrew legislator than those of the United States."

We have heard a great deal in late years about the "mistakes" of Moses, but perhaps not so much during the lifetime of a famous infidel lawyer and orator who made those mistakes "the subject of a lecture." Another man who was not a believer in Christianity was Huxley, who said, "There is no code of legislation, ancient or modern, at once so just and so merciful, so tender to the weak and poor, as the Jewish law."

And it is worthy of note that political economists find much in the Mosaic laws to commend.

Many of the Single Taxers are not believers in the inspiration of the Scriptures, yet Henry George found a great ideal in the laws of Moses that he believed must be commended by every wise student of economics.

The teachings of Moses concerning hygiene and dietetics have been highly praised by competent authorities, and modern scientists have written much to prove that those laws are the most wonderful the world has known.

It is a fact abundantly supported by evidence that the Jews live longer on an average than any other race, and there are life insurance companies in Great Britain that have cheaper rates for them than for Gentiles. For whether the lower death rate and greater longevity of the Jews are the result of many centuries of observance of those health laws of Moses by the Jewish people, thus bequeathing to present-day members of that race sounder bodies than other peoples have, or whether there is some other cause, the fact remains that the Jew is undeniably superior to his Gentile neighborhood in this respect and is characterized by unparalleled vitality and vigor.

The very fact that the Jew exists after the persecutions of long ages has been referred to as a striking illustration of the law of "the survival of the fittest." He has outlived his ancient enemies in spite of disasters that are greater than have come to any other people without destroying them. Persecution has been unable to cause his destruction or merge him with the cause his nations and he exists after over eighteen centuries without a country of his own and therefore without the means one would naturally suppose necessary to enable a people to preserve their national characteristics and racial integrity. It is claimed that pride in his religion and a belief in his superiority to all other races have been the means of keeping him apart and making him exclusive, who was it but Moses who gave him laws and instilled in him ideas that showed he was favored of God? What other man before Christ ever had an influence upon the world approaching that of Moses?

Cleveland, Ohio.

Christian Baptism. By E. E. Roberts

IV. The Why? of Baptism.

Personally we do not believe that the simple act of baptism will save anyone, although there are some who believe that it will, basing their belief on Peter's words in Acts 2: 38, "Repent and be baptized every one of you . . . for the remission of sins," and Acts 22:16, where Paul said that Ananias should "Arise and be baptized, and wash away your sins." We hold that it is the Blood that saves, and the Blood alone, not the washing away of the filth of the flesh; and that it is the heart-sorrow for sins committed against God, and a belief in Christ the Son of God as our Savior, which puts us under the Blood and brings us into a condition for salvation, or in which we may be saved. Such condition existing in us, we will not rest until we have confessed that such conditions do exist in our hearts by being publicly "buried with him in baptism." And it follows logically, that where there is no willingness to obey in baptism, the condition that saves does not exist in one's heart.

But if baptism does not save, some may ask, of what use is it for us to be baptized? We reply, that we baptize for the following reasons:

(1) Salvation is only promised to those who are baptized (Mark 16:16).

(2) Salvation is nowhere spoken of as being possessed by any one, except those who have been baptized (1 Cor. 6: 11; Heb. 10:22; Eph. 5:26; Titus 3:5).

(3) Because Christ commanded it as a part of my duty (Matt. 28:19).

(4) Because the disciples obeyed that command and observed it (Acts 2:38; 8:38; 1 Cor. 13:14-16).

(5) Because there is no record of the descent of the Holy Spirit upon any one except those who had been baptized, save those in acts 10:44; and it took the descending of the Spirit, as well as a vision, to overcome Peter's prejudice against the Gentiles.

As I cannot live a successful Christian life nor have necessary power without the baptism of the Holy Spirit, therefore by baptism I place myself in a position to receive the Spirit with all his power.

Let us hear the conclusion of the matter:

We have briefly stated a few of the main facts without arguments, so that this might be quickly read and thoroughly digested in a brief space of time. Reader, if you were far from home, the night starless and dark, and two roads lay before you; the one you knew had been trodden for many years by the feet of the wise and good in their homeward journey; the other was a new way, little trodden, not above suspicion, one that you only hoped would bring you safely home,—we appeal to you—which one would you take? Reader, such a journey lays before us, not to an earthly, but to an eternal home. Let us be as wise in spiritual things as in temporal ones. Let us take no foolish risks. Let us be sure our feet are treading where the saints of old have trodden. So that like them we may enter in through the gates into the city of our God.

(This series of articles is published in pamphlet form and may be secured of E. E. Roberts, 2335 Frankford Avenue, Philadelphia, Pa.—Ed).

THE BRETHREN PULPIT

Reaching Forth In 1921. By Miss Mary Pence

Text: Forgetting those things which are behind, and reaching forth unto those things which are before, I press toward the mark for the prize of the high calling of God in Christ Jesus" (Phil. 3:13, 14).

This text readily calls to mind Hebrews 12:1 which reads in part, "Let us lay aside every weight, and the sin which doth so easily beset us, and let us run with patience the race that is set before us, looking unto Jesus the author and finisher of our faith."

However much inspiration there may be in one's past, to continually live in the past is to fail to get from the present hour what one should. But we must at some time reckon with the past of our lives. Every honest man will confess there is much in his past he wishes might have been different because he sees his past failures—instances in which Satan gained decided victories. The mature Christian cannot be found who does not say, O, if I had only begun to serve Christ earlier in life, if I had only done thus and so, or left that undone. But to the Christian who has the faith of our Lord Jesus Christ and cherishes the hope of God in his heart the future holds out the joy of successes yet to come. Praise God for hope; praise him for putting the desire into our hearts to want to have a better future than the past has been and to be and to do what he wills. Blessed be the name of the Lord for the strong right arm to lead us out of the lust of the flesh, the lust of the eye, and the pride of life into the glorious liberty of the sons of God. Thank God for a future in which he moves.

Paul did not forget his past in that he was indifferent to it. He remembered with sorrow how he held the coats of those who stoned Stephen; how he persecuted the Christians generally. Indifference to the past is no remedy for its evils. What we need is to do as Paul did,—rid ourselves of past sins or successes either of which may be a weight to progress. We can do two thing with the past. We can get the forgiveness for all past sin which follows confession. "If we confess our sins he is faithful and just to forgive our sins and to cleanse us from all unrighteousness." Then we can give the past to him, let him bless its good while hiding its failures and sins under the blood.

The Brethren church now has a past year behind it. As individuals and as a church there has without doubt been much said and done that has pleased God and we know he has blessed us. But there have been many things said and done that have pleased God and we know he has blessed us. But there have been many things said and done by the church and in the name of the church that have reflected neither the Spirit nor teaching of Jesus. But to run in the race before us and reach forth we must be rid of anything that is a weight to progress. We can bury all in Jesus, forget them in him. To rest by the wayside with the fact that we have done some good work for God is a weight to progress. He that has wrought in an evil way, who has shunned to declare the whole counsel of God, who has shirked the burden of the church, or he who carries in his bosom deadly sins, secret or otherwise, has weight to progress. God can use only cleansed vessels, and that the church and individuals might be clean he opened up a fountain for cleansing in the blood of Jesus. We praise God we can confess our sins and lay our weights on Jesus. What the church needs is more tears of deep repentance that will bring the joy of forgiveness and the joy of fruitful service.

Bad habits we must lay aside,
They'll surely hinder in the race.
All hatred that will blind our eyes
And tend our spirits to debase.

"Pride goes before a fall" they say,
With stumbling feet we cannot win,
While envy clouds the busy brain
And helps mean thoughts to enter in.

"Doubt fills the heart with foolish fears
And clouds the past with shadows grim.
Then unbelief, its comrade dread,
Waits but the word our faith to dim.

"The secret sins we cherish so,
Are hindering weights that fall and fret,
No compromise with evil things,
Lest in the shining gold forget.

"Lay them aside, lay them aside,
Cast in a heap at Jesus' feet."

Then can we say with Paul, "Forgetting those things which are behind, and reaching forth unto those things which are before, I press toward the mark for the prize of the high calling of God in Christ Jesus." A sham Christian does not get far with God. God walks only with the upright in heart. I plead for clean Christians and therefore a clean church; a clean college supported and run by clean people so that its product may be cleansed vessels to be filled, to be used, to be carried, and led, and driven by the Spirit here and there for God; clean mission Boards who by their prayers and labors send out cleansed missionaries; cleansed preachers and teachers; clean church literature. In Jesus is a fountain of daily cleansing. Let us bathe in it. We are by nature unclean creatures but we can be cleansed. His are the promises to claim and in desiring them and reaching out for them we put off the filth of the flesh and are washed by the blood and the Word.

God help us by his Spirit, Brethren, to clean up our lives and cast aside the weights and sins that hinder for before the church right now is a mighty task and we need the unobstructed use of all our faculties if we are to be used of God in our allotted part of this great task. The forces of good and evil are in great conflict. It is as though Satan were gathering together his mighty army for a last great assault against the church of Jesus Christ. You may not or you may see this locally. But if conditions are what conditions should be in and around your church it is an exception to the general condition of churches. O, the cold indifference! And hundreds of ministers, so called, are not using subjects for sermons that are calculated to command Christians, so called, to take up the bed on which they are sleeping and walk. Christ alone can quicken but Christ is not being preached by even hundreds. "Was Charlie Chaplin born a fool or did he cultivate it;" or "God's duty to man," are subjects used by some California ministers. Thus they shun to declare the counsel of God. Recently one Lord's day morning I sat through an hour's service held in a very large city church. Save in songs or prayer, I noticed the name of Christ or God mentioned twice in the expression, "Christ's disciples." Nevertheless a certain man of the town was held up as a fit example for us to follow. Satan uses anything to hide the blood of Christ without which there is no remission. And so the flock scatters about

seeking its own pasture, each sheep becoming a law unto himself, disregarding the laws of God.

We experienced the fact that it took millions of men and billions of dollars to overthrow militarism but we are also experiencing the fact that the godless philosophy that fostered militarism is leavening the whole of human society. These conditions and others give sufficient reason for the declaration that has gone forth, that "the supreme need of the hour is a revival in the church," and we would send forth to our own body of believers that we give ourselves answer to prayer, that witnessing must take its true place in the life of believers, and, that we must exercise faith with deeper conviction in the person and work of God, the Holy Spirit.

If we as a church want to do greater things during 1921, we must pray. There is no power that can prevail against the praying church—a church on its knees. Much depends on the ministry of the church and praying members make a good ministry. A poor prayer life of the pew is no doubt cause of some of the smallness of the pulpit. A church cannot expect to rise higher than its prayers. The whole trend of scripture is that God knows every need and desire of the human heart yet he ordained the means of prayer by which to get these things from him. Back of all our great church leaders of this and ages past, such men as Moody, Whitefield, Wesley, were men and women in the closest of intercession. The prayer of one righteous man availeth much; what would not the effectual fervent prayer of many avail? "Prayer changes things," yes and people— the prayer, the home, the church, souls are saved, and the world is changed because of prayer. Why not the Brethren church dedicate herself to prayer during 1921? May God help us to spend more time at the place of prayer until the place is shaken and God's presence and power manifested because we are praying. It can be so.

Again if the Brethren church would be a power for God among this world's evil, it must open its mouth boldly and speak the things it should speak. The church is to preach the gospel, to proclaim salvation. The church has no time nor business in any other realm. Science, art, learning and a lot of other things are good things and have their appointed place but the Gospel is a thing apart and has its appointed mission and I declare unto you it alone will God bless to the salvation of souls. If any man preach any other gospel let him be accursed, and God will see to it. Most of us need the dumb spirits cast out of us. I mean in reality we are possessed with dumb spirits. In the days of Peter and John the Sanhedrin tried to stop their testimony and on the peril of their lives they were to speak no more in the name of Jesus of Nazareth. But no dumb spirit took hold of those faithful apostles.

My brother, hast thou a dumb spirit so thou dost not testify of God's saving grace and blessing in your home, to friends, and in the church and out of the church? When the church through prayer rises up as one man from its seat of silence to give testimony to the power of God and his Gospel high heaven will rejoice, God will be glorified, souls will be saved. Lord Jesus, during 1921 free pen, pulpit, and pew from the power that is shutting up their testimony while the devil speaks contrary to the name of Jesus. Grant that utterance may be given unto us that we may open our mouths to speak boldly for thee and thy Gospel as we ought to speak.

And, again, if the Brethren church is to press forward against the host of wickedness it must have faith. "But let him ask in faith nothing wavering. For he that wavereth is like a wave of the sea driven with the wind and tossed. For let not that man think that he shall receive anything of the Lord."

God's power and wisdom is at the disposal of any who will pay the price of faith. We pay money for food and raiment, but to obtain that which is impossible to man we must pay the price of faith. "Nothing shall be impossible unto you" if you ask in faith. In the olden days "faith subdued kingdoms, wrought righteousness, obtained promises, stopped the mouths of lions, quenched the violence of fire, escaped the edge of the sword, out of weakness were made strong, waxed valiant in fight, turned to flight the enemies of the aliens.'' That is just the quality of faith we need now, a faith shown by mighty works. The Holy Spirit is here to bestow great faith upon the church; God is waiting to pour out his blessing. Then will lives be lifted up, souls saved, God glorified in our lives, and the way paved for the coming of the Lord.

Lord, pour out upon the church the old time faith that overcomes evil and barriers, and obtains promises. Inspire for Jesus; inspire her with a faith that advances thy Kingdom, a faith that forgets the things that are behind and reaches forth unto the things that are before, presses toward the mark for the prize of the high calling of God in Christ Jesus.

Limestone, Tennessee.

OUR DEVOTIONAL

New Consecration for the New Year
By Miss E. Mae Minnich

OUR SCRIPTURE

Oh the depth of the riches both of the wisdom and knowledge of God! How unsearchable are his judgments, and his ways past finding out! For who hath known the mind of the Lord? Or who hath been his counsellor? Or who hath first given to him, and it shall be recompensed unto him again? For of him, and through him, and to him, are all things: to whom be glory forever. Amen. I beseech you therefore, brethren, by the mercies of God, that ye present your bodies a living sacrifice, holy, acceptable unto God, which is your reasonable service. And be not conformed to this world; but be ye transformed by the renewing of your mind, that ye may prove what is that good, and acceptable, and perfect, will of God (Rom. 11:33—12:2). Neither yield ye your members as instruments of unrighteousness unto sin; but yield yourselves unto God, as those that are alive from the dead, and your members as instruments of righteousness unto God. Know ye not, that to whom ye yield yourselves servants to obey, his servants ye are to whom ye obey; whether of sin unto death, or of obedience unto righteousness (Rom. 6:13, 16; 19)? By him therefore let us offer the sacrifice of praise to God continually, that is, the fruit of our lips giving thanks to his name. But to do good and to communicate forget not: for with such sacrifices God is well pleased (Heb. 13:15, 15). And this they did, not as we hoped, but first gave their own selves to the Lord, and unto us by the will of God (2 Cor. 8:5). Brethren, I count not myself to have apprehended; but this one thing I do, forgetting those things which are behind, and reaching forth unto those things which are before, I press toward the mark for the prize of the high calling of God in Christ Jesus (Phil. 3:13, 14).

OUR MEDITATION

We have come once more to the threshold of a new year. Bearing in our spirit the scars of battle, sobered by the sins and griefs of yesterday, many will face the future with uncertainty and fear. But since a Divine hand guides the helm, we can begin the new year with courage and confidence, resting assured that to those who trust in God and do his will, all good things will come to pass.

Consecration is a dedication or setting apart of self for the service of God. It means that the one consecrated be wholly given over to his using, and be entirely devoted to sacred purposes. ''Present your bodies a living sacrifice which is your reasonable service.'' No part must be withheld. Then we will not yield our members to unrighteousness but will be holy individuals, maintaining a pure, clean and holy life. If we will take stock of the past twelve months, we will find that the rust of selfishness and worldliness have corroded our wicket gate of consecration through which the abundant life would flow and fill our souls.

Let every reader make a real consecration of self at the beginning of this new year. Let every talent be set aside as sacred to our Lord. If every professing Christian would do this what a wonderful change would be wrought in this troubled and sinful world. O, how we do need just this type of men and women who are steadfast, always abounding in the work of the Lord. Jesus Christ fully exemplified our ideal of consecration. He said, ''My meat is to do the will of him that sent me, and to finish his work'' (John 4:34). ''O my Father, if it be possible let this cup pass from me; nevertheless not as I will, but as thou wilt'' (Matt. 26:39). Here should be our life motto: ''I delight to do thy will, O my God'' (Ps. 40:8). That is true consecration. All ambition should start and end there. Duty is simple obedience. The highest thing possible in this world for any life is what God would make out of it. Since Christ himself filled his life with such loving devotion to his Father's will it should be our highest joy to do the same. ''A soul cannot be regarded as truly subdued and consecrated in its will, and as having passed into union with the divine will, until it has a disposition to do promptly and faithfully all that God requires, as well as to endure patiently and thankfully all that he imposes.''

Paul says, ''I press toward the mark for the prize of the high calling of God is Christ Jesus.'' How may we know the mark of our high calling? God will reveal it to us if we earnestly pray for guidance. After we possess that compelling conviction of our course of duty, may we never say, ''No, Lord, our way is too hard.'' Indeed it will mean sacrifice, temptations to be resisted, habits to be overcome, ideals to be attained, but with his help we shall prevail. We are leaving the old year behind but we are not leaving Christ in the dead year. We need not fear to go forward if we go with him. May God help us to be true to all that is highest and noblest in our heart, mind and soul, then will the new year be a constant achievement in spiritual things. Let us appropriate a part of the beautiful hymn of Frances Havergal as our individual consecration vow:

> ''Take my life and let it be
> Consecrated Lord to thee;
> Take my hands and let them move
> At the impulse of thy love.
>
> Take my love, my God, I pour
> At thy feet its treasure store;
> Take myself and I will be
> Ever, only, all for thee.''

OUR PRAYER

Father of all wisdom and knowledge, grant us guidance for this new and untried year. We confess that we have been too much engrossed with the things of this world, but create in us a deeper craving for spiritual things. Help us to crucify self and to enthrone thee as the absolute ruler of our whole being. Take our lives as we lay them in glad consecration on the altar for Jesus, to be used when and where he pleases. Give us thy protecting grace and strength to meet every vicissitude of this life. Keep our feet ever in the pathway of duty, our hands ready to serve thee, and our hearts always willing to hear and heed thy call. May al thy children and ''first give their own selves to the Lord.'' Then help us to faithfully remember to give thee and thy work first place during the whole year. Grant that day by day we may grow in wisdom, in faith, in self denial and to be heavenly minded. Help us to adore all thy purposes without knowing them and to have no other desire than to accomplish thy will, Hear us, for Jesus' sake. Amen.

Greencastle, Pennsylvania.

Send
WHITE GIFT
OFFERINGS to

THE SUNDAY SCHOOL

H. H. WOLFORD
General Secretary-Treasurer
Ashland, Ohio

Brethren Sunday School at Muncie, Indiana. By Ora C. Paul

The Sunday school here was organized in the home of N. J. Paul, 1309 South Macedonia Avenue, March 28, 1915. Mrs. Rosalie Garrett was chosen for superintendent, for a term of three months, and the writer as assistant. The first two sessions were held (April 4 and 11), in an old wagon shop on Ohio Avenue, near the Big Four Railroad tracks, but this building was sold and we were ordered out. We then rented a building a short distance from there at 505 Wolf Street, which had been built and used for a barn for a number of years, but for some time had been converted into a dwelling.

Mrs. Garrett proved her ability as a superintendent for two months, at the end of which she was quarantined for several weeks, because scarlet fever had invaded her home. The assistant superintendent assumed the duties of superintending the school on the 6th day of June, was elected to that office on the 27th day of the same month, and has been favored with the honor ever since.

On the 28th of April, 1918, the little Sunday school bid farewell forever to the shabby old building which had been its home for just three years and two weeks. On the next Sunday, May 5th, the session was held in the Brethren tent on Ohio Avenue, on the lots which the church had bought the autumn before, and which are to be decorated with a beautiful church next year.

Here we tented it through for five months. October 6th we held our first session in the "Little White Chapel," where we are still trying to honor the Great Teacher.

Our first training class was graduated and received diplomas September 23, 1917, during a campaign which was being conducted by Brother Sylvester Lowman who delivered the class address. Six were enrolled in the class at the beginning, but because of a lingering illness which lasted many months, Mrs. Susie Garrett was unable to complete the course. Brother M. M. Hoover, who was our pastor and also our class instructor, moved away, leaving four to finish the study. Those completing the course were, T. A. Hartley, Mrs. Rosalie Garrett, Mrs. Bessie Paul, and her husband. All of these are at present engaged in official duty in the Sunday school.

Our school received its "Front Line Diploma," at the General Conference of 1916, and has attained an additional seal each year since. In the beginning of 1919 when the Waterloo Sunday school heralded the four month challenge, we entered the contest. As a result we gained third place with seventy-eight points to our credit. Ashland was second with seventy-nine points and Milledgeville first with eighty. At present we are not only Front Line in denominational requirements, but also 100 percent in the International.

On the 18th day of last month our township convention was held. The township officers gave, as an inducement for attendance, a beautiful silk American flag, about 26x40 inches. When the winner was announced, it was with no little pleasure that our worthy pastor, Brother J. L. Kimmel and your humble servant walked side and side down the aisle amidst the ringing cheers of the overflowing audience that taxed the seating capacity of the large church, and bore Old Glory away. Possibly by the time you read these lines our "Prize" flag will be framed and decorating the walls of the little chapel.

The county president pronounced ours the best little school in Delaware county. Other county and township workers say similar things. To all that is, or may be said to the credit of the school here, we only say "Praise the Lord." He is the doer of it all. We are but his stewards.

One of our members is county superintendent of Ad-

ministration for a second term, and another is county superintendent of Publicity. Nearly all our young people and several children have made the good choice.

Once More, That College Hen

The "College Hen" is delighted, and so is her sponsor, at the response which has been made to his appeal. No, I am not surprised, for I felt that I knew what kind of folks our Sunday school people are, and now I am convinced more than ever, that I do. I knew you would want to help, and here is what you have already done, which augurs well for what will yet come. When you are all done, I will tell you in detail what you have made possible. So hurry up, and get the story.

Previously reported,	$ 78.31
Alice Cunningham, Masontown, Pa.,	2.00
Class No. 12, Masontown Sunday School,	9.00
Eva Walek and mother, Masontown,	5.00
Morrill, Kansas, Sunday School,	4.85
North Liberty, Ind., Sunday School,	5.00
Oakville, Ind.,—Primary Dept.,	1.00
Mrs. Laura Hegler, Washington C. H., O.,	2.00
Compton Ave. Sunday School, Los Angeles, Cal.,	
What So Ever Bible Class,	7.10
B: Y. P. S., Young People's Class,	4.55
Willing Workers—Boys;	2.55
Sunbeams — Girls,	1.01
Guiding Stars—Girls,	1.00
Gideon Band—Boys,	.88
Shepherd Boys,	.45
R. B. Rittenhouse, Santa Cruz, Cal.,	2.00
Peru, Ind., Sunday School,	12.22
Hudson, Iowa, Sunday School,	5.00
O. E. Bowman, Dayton, Ohio,	10.00
H. W. Sutton, Canton, Ohio,	2.00
Gratis, Ohio, Primary Dept.,	2.57
Waterloo, Iowa, Sunday School,	21.57
Ruth and Vada Weimer, Bealeton, Va.,	2.00

Total cash contributions to date, ... $179.52

In addition to this, Ronald and Raymond Drushal of Ankenytown, Ohio, sent us two splendid white Leghorn hens, and Mr. J. I. Hereter, of Gettysburgh, Pa., sent a pen of full-blooded Barred Rocks, consisting of three hens and a rooster. But the biggest bunch of live chickens, came from the Lanark, Illinois, Sunday school, for Brother B. T. Burnworth shipped us a coop with 23 hens in it, all of which had been contributed by members of the Sunday school. There are enough fowls in the pen now to give us a real chorus, of their kind of music, whenever Brother Petit feeds them.

There is still room for any help which you may care to end and I know the rest of our Sunday schools will be heard from.   MARTIN SHIVELY,
Ashland College, Ashland, Ohio.

A Home-Coming Service

Just a line to let you know that the Brethren Sunday school at Elkhart, is not dead but is going forward with God's hand guiding us.

November 21 we held our second annual Home-Coming Day and broke all records of attendance. Our faithful worker, Miss Mamie Leonard, had charge of the program and any one who knows Miss Leonard knows this program was 100 percent perfect. We are not the largest school in the brotherhood but I think I am safe in saying it is one of the most faithful and loyal and we invite you one and all to pay us a visit at any time.

The following program was given to an attendance of 284, with an offering of $30.89:

Piano Selection, ... Miss Fern Baugher
Song—"All Hail the Power of Jesus' Name," .. Congregation
Prayer, ... W. G. Hall
Scripture Reading—Psalm 100, ... Ward Duel
Greetings, ... Miss Mamie Leonard
Vocal Solo .... Miss Nellie Benson
                    Accompanied by Mrs. O. B. Fields
Roll Call of Classes,
Address of Welcome, ... A. J. Wineland

Song—"Blest Be the Tie That Binds," ..... Congregation
Offering.
Vocal Solo, ... Mr. H. E. Weigner
                    Accompanied by Miss Ruth Harden
History of Our School, ... Miss Naomi Wilson
A Message from our First Superintendent, Samuel Maintjoy
A Message from our Former Pastor, .. Prof. H. H. Wolford
Saxophone Solo, ... Mr. Lee Willis
                    Accompanied by Mrs. Lee Willis
Address by Our Pastor, ... Rev. B. S. Stoffer
Song—"Keep the Heart Singing," .... Congregation
Benediction.
                    A. J. WINELAND, Superintendent,
                    617 McDonald St. Elkhart, Indiana.

| J. A. Garber | Our Young People at Work | E. A. Rowsey |
| PRESIDENT | | SECRETARY |

Advertising Christian Endeavor. By Earl Huette

Publicity Department of Christian Endeavor

Do Not Read This

Unless you are an officer in your Christian Endeavor Society.

Did you hear what Harriet James said about your society? Well, she said, "That C. E. society is as dead as can be. I was down there last Sunday evening and all they had was the same old program, two songs, two sentence prayers, some newspaper clippings or something like that and Mart Wabash gave the same "spiel" which he has given for the last ten years; then the benediction, and when it was out, I did not see a single person shake hands with his neighbor. It was so cold, I almost shivered."

Is this the kind of talk that is going the rounds about your society?

Are you allowing it to be said that the Christian Endeavor organization is DEAD?

If you are, then here is where we come to the "Battle of Words."

How about it?
Where do you stand?
Do these suggestions suit your case?
Would you like to have some information concerning the greater activities of Christian Endeavor?

Do you want to have your society listed among those of the Front Line rank?

Watch these columns weekly.

Or if you desire personal helps, write to your President, Prof. J. A. Garber, Ashland, Ohio, or Publicity Superintendent, Earl Huette, 11 Marion St., Dayton, Ohio.

CHRISTIAN ENDEAVOR IS NOT DEAD.

Some Endeavorers are dead, but that does not mean that the organization is dead.

If your society is not active in your church let us analyze the situation with the following remarks:

1. The officers are DEAD to Christian Endeavor activities and have been for some time.
2. Your membership has not given the officers the proper support.
3. The parents of the young people in the church have not been solicited for their support.
4. You have not sought the support and cooperation of the pastor.
5. You have not kept in touch with the C. E. work in county, state and national and international circles.
6. You have not been present at the regular county C. E. meetings.
7. You have not had a variation of prayer meeting programmes.

8. You are not alive to the possibilities that lie in having a good live C. E. society.

An Urgent, Important Request

Could your Christian Endeavor society use a handy reference guide? Would you accept the same if it were sent to you free of cost?

Through the generosity of its new General Secretary, Rev. E. A. Rowsey, 612 White Haines Building, Columbus, Ohio, our National Union is able and ready to send you a complimentary copy of a comprehensive "Handbook." It will inform you fully concerning every phase of Christian Endeavor. It will be sent you on this condition: that you send the undersigned the name and address of your president or corresponding secretary. The book is too valuable to be lost in the mail.

To make it easy for you to supply the desired information and to secure statistical data that will enable us to check up on our attainments at the first of the calendar year we are providing a blank below. All you need to do is to fill in the blank spaces and mail the same to the writer. Act while the impulse is strong. Delay means loss.

Christian Endeavor Week is rapidly approaching. With this recurring celebration this year we celebrate our fortieth anniversary. Excellent suggestive helps will appear in the Christian Endeavor World, the Brethren Evangelist and the Angelus. This great week presents a splendid opportunity to set forward our Bicentenary program. The little book mentioned above will show you how to do it.

Extending in behalf of all our national officers heartiest Christmas greetings and best wishes for a victorious New Year, I am,
                    Your servant,
                    J. A. GARBER, Ashland, Ohio.

Christian Endeavor Report from ....
President .... Address ....
Cor. Sec. .... Address ....
Active Members ..... Associate...... C. E. Experts ......
Tithers............. Life Work Recruits ....
Special Items:
Intermediates .... Superintendent ....
       Address ....
Juniors .... Superintendent ....
       Address ....

Note: The foregoing communication was sent recently to a former correspondent in each society. Officers will do well to inquire if it has had the attention it deserves. If for any reason no copy was received by your society use this printed one.—Editor.

SEND ALL MONEY FOR
General Home, Kentucky and
Foreign Missions to

MISSIONS

WILLIAM A. GEARHART
General Missionary Secretary
906 American Bldg., Dayton, O.

RIO CUARTO, ARGENTINA

I must beg pardon of the readers of . the readers of the Evangelist for not reporting our work oftener. I realize that those who contribute for the support of the work have a right to expect frequent reports of its progress and it would be better to neglect something else rather than to neglect these reports. But if you will forgive me this time I will try to write more frequently hereafter.

When I wrote the last time Brother Edwards and family had moved to Huinca Renanco where he had gone before to explore the land and found an opening so good that the Field Council was unanimous in believing it our duty to occupy the field at once. Brother Edwards will report the work there more in detail but I may say in passing that it is beginning with more interest than we have been able to arouse in other places after years of labor, and if nothing happens to prevent it we should soon be able to reach out from this center to the numerous growing towns round about.

Last week I made my monthly visit to Carlota and Los Cisnes. In Carlota we had twenty-five children this time in the Sunday school although a number were absent on account of sickness. We need a school teacher in this place to conduct a private primary school and care for the Sunday school. Or, a pastor here could at the same time preach in Canals on one side and Los Cisnes on the other. In both these towns there are a number of believers and a desire for the Gospel. After Sunday school in Carlota I went to Los Cisnes and preached in the open air and then again in the evening in a vacant room formerly used as a bakery. There was good interest in both meetings.

Here in Rio Cuarto we have just closed a revival effort which continued through the month of October. We are thankful for seventeen who publicly accepted Christ, two of whom have been baptized and the rest will be prepared as rapidly as possible. However, the indifference of the public in general is most distressing. Although we are respected and many sympathize with our work, yet there is a sort of a hoodoo about the mission which makes people afraid to come lest they be laughed at by some relative or friend. In our regular work here I preach and teach in nine or ten meetings a week.

When I have opportunities to speak in other places, the people attend better than in the church. One night during the meeting after preaching in the church I gave a lecture on "The Origin and Destiny of Man" for the workingmen's organization and the large hall which they use was entirely filled with men.

Sunday afternoons we have meetings in the square in front of the church and also in the central plaza in connection with the Salvation Army which now has meetings there every Sunday. In these plaza meetings we sometimes have three hundred or four hundred people. On the second of November everybody goes to the cemetery to decorate the graves. This year besides distributing thousands of tracts we held a meeting there to explain to the people the Gospel teaching

about the dead. The priests and monks all go to the cemetery on this day to say responses for the dead for which they receive pay according to the length of the jargon they go through. But they are not doing so thriving a business as formerly. When we first came here a Protestant could not be buried in the cemetery except in the corner reserved for criminals. Even last year one of our young men was arrested for selling tracts and another was ordered out by a priest at the point of a revolver. This year they tried to prevent our meetings but were not able to do so.

November first corresponds to May at home, and is the month of flowers. The first Sunday in November we celebrated Mother's Day. We had a beautiful day and the church was filled. The mothers and babies who live at a distance we brought in with the Bible auto and all enjoyed the program very much. The church was filled again at the evening service and there is a good spirit prevailing among the members. We hope to have another love feast soon and prepare a Christmas program. In two weeks more one of our young men will graduate from the college and will then accompany Brother Sickel for a time with the auto, but later he must report for military service.

We have received safely the communion set that was so kindly donated to the work by Sister Holmes and also a box of post cards from the Christian Endeavor Society of Los Angeles. These have been useful with the baloptieon and we thank the donors very much. We have learned that small packages (about 4x4x6 inches) sent by registered mail come through all right but larger packages, or those not registered are sure to get into the customs house and cost dearly.

We are glad to hear that several new workers have been selected for the field but we wish that they could come at once. It is better to learn the language and study the problems right on the field. I would say to any who contemplated coming that it no longer pays to bring new furniture along. We will be glad to correspond with anyone who is interested in coming.

The best dentist in Rio Cuarto wishes to have a North American dentist for a partner. He has a diploma and a very large practice. A dentist coming in cannot practice where there is a dentist with a diploma until he also has one and it is almost impossible to get one without taking the course in this country.

The best doctor here also wishes to employ a woman capable of directing his hospital, directing the work in his absence, etc. He prefers a North American lady.

I am glad to say that Mrs. Yoder is gradually recovering her sight and her strength and is able to help again in nearly all the work of the mission. Our two daughters have been away to school but one of them has now returned. We hope to be able to send them to Ashland by another year.

Our church library has been approved by the National Library Association and they have sent us a box of books free and will duplicate any sum that we raise for books. Quite a number of our people, especially the

young men, make good use of the library and we loan out large numbers of books.

By the time this reaches the readers it will be almost Christmas and we send best wishes to all for a merry Christmas and a happy New Year.

C. F. YODER,
Rio Cuarto, Argentina, Nov. 8, 1920.

THE NEED OF A NURSE FOR LOST CREEK

Brother Editor, we see in The Evangelist that they are calling for a nurse at Lost Creek. We want to say as two who have had some experience there that we feel that the church ought not try to run a school at that place and ask people to go there and work without providing them with a nurse and a good one at that. As it is almost out of the question to get a doctor during the winter months, owing to the bad roads and being eight miles to the nearest one, and as they must either walk, ride a mule or a wagon, during the months when they are most apt to need medical attention they ought to have a nurse on the grounds all the time. We were there several weeks last winter and we did not see a buggy in the entire neighborhood, nor did we see an auto for twenty-five miles either way from Lost Creek. It is almost impossible to use either one in the summer and less possible in the winter.

I presume that Brother Gearhart and his good wife are a thousand times grateful to that ladies' auxiliary that sent a nurse there last winter in the person of Miss Hade of Pennylvania, to administer unto him so faithfully during his sickness at that place. She will be long remembered by us as well as by him. How she would wade the deep mud in her rubber boots and ride the mules while going to see her patients in the vicinity. We are in a position to appreciate the sacrifice that the workers are making while they are at Lost Creek. And we hope that much good may be done in the name of the Lord.

MR. AND MRS. CHAS. TEALL.

REPORT OF RECEIPTS FOR MISSIONS

(Explanatory)

N. B.—In making Financial Reports on Missions it has been advised that in order to conserve space in the EVANGELIST, that detail receipts of less than $5.00 could be omitted and reported as miscellaneous. However, we will be pleased to list smaller amounts for children or others if specially requested.

Home Missions—September and October, 1920
General Fund:

Church offering, Sunday at National Conference,	$149.71
S. S. at National Conf.,	825.13
Mrs. Rowena DonaVan, Modesta, Cal., H G.,	5.00
Eld. & Mrs. J. W. Brower, Huntington, Indiana, H. G.,	5.00
Albert H. Postle, Phila., Pa., H. G.,	5.00
John M. Freeland, Terra Alta, W. Virginia, H. G.,	5.00
Mary C. Wenger, Treas. Nat. W. M. S.,	150.00
Mrs. Sylvia Nickerson, Lake Odessa, Mich., H. G.,	5.00

Mrs. C. G. Wolfe, North Liberty, Indiana, H. G., ... 5.00
Br. S. S., Conemaugh, Pa. (Stutzman), 33.00
Mrs. Wm. Garwood, South Bend, Indiana, H. G., ... 5.00
Emma Olinger, Meyersdale, Pa. H. G., 5.00
Sarah J. Olinger, Meyersdale, Pa., H. G., ... 5.00
Miscellaneous receipts, Sept & Oct., 9.01

Total receipts, ... $1,211.85

Kentucky Fund:
Cash on pledges and loose offering at Conference .... $ 303.11
C. E., Nappanee, Ind. 1919-1920 pledges, ... 35.00
C. E., N. Liberty, Ind. (Whitmer Tr.), 10.00
S. S. Carleton, Neb. (Kemper), ... 5.00
W. W. Bible Class, Huntington, Indiana, (Brower), ... 10.00
C. E., Warsaw, Ind. (Bennett), ... 10.00
Br. Ch., Berlin, Pa. (Cober), ... 10.00
Br. Ch., Lanark Ill. (Burnworth),.. 9.03
S. M. M., Huntington, Ind. (Brower), 15.00
Clara Zollers, Huntington, Ind., ... 5.00
C. E. Martinsburg Pa. (Treech), ... 10.00
Br. Ch., Berlin, Pa. (Hay), ... 10.00
S. M. M. LouisVille, O. (Oyster), .. 5.00
Jr. C. E., Center Chapel Ch., Ind., (Sampson), ... 15.00
C. E., Ashland O. (Kilhefner), ... 50.00

Mr. & Mrs. B. H. Lehman, Glendale, Arizona, ... 25.00
Br. Ch., LaVerne, Cal. (Good), ... 7.50
C. E., LouisVille, O. (Hang), ... 10.00
Br. Ch., Lost Creek, Ky., ... 16.20
Mrs. Anna Clays, Sandusky, Ohio, (Fremont Ch.) 5.00
John Eck, New Lebanon, Ohio, Br. Ch. Pldg., ... 15.00
Loose offering at Nat. Con. for Ky,, 25.00
S. A. Lowman, Pleasant Hill, Ohio, H. G., ... 5.00
Jr. C. E. Society, LouisVille, Ohio, (Painter) H. G., ... 5.00
Loyal Helpers Class, Waterloo, Ia., H. G., ... 10.00
Excelsior Bible Class, Allentown, Pa., H. G., ... 10.00
Arthur Carey, Troy, Ohio, Pleasant Hill Ch., H. G., ... 5.00
A. G. Brandenberg, Harry, Kentucky Mission, ... 10.00
W. M. S. 1st Br. Ch., Phila., Pa., H. G., ... 25.00
Hazel Keiser, Bryan, O, H. G., ... 25.00
Mr, & Mrs. Wm. Garwood, S. Bend, Ind., H. G., ... 10.00
Mrs. R. D. Martin, Pioneer, Ohio, H. G., ... 10.00
Young Ladies Class, Berne, Indiana, Bethel, H. G., ... 13.00

Miscellaneous receipts, ... 1.00

Total receipts, ... $ 734.84

Miscellaneous Funds:
Missionary Education Fund:
Rev. Miss Emma Aboud, Dayton, O., H. G., ... $ 125.75
W. W. Bible Class, Dayton, O., ... 6.25
W. W. Bible Class, Dayton, O,, ... 27.25
W. W. Bible Class, Dayton, O., ... 4.75

Total receipts, ... $ 164.00

PLEASE NOTE: Our attention has been called to the Pittstown, New Jersey, Brethren Mission about last Easter offering. The same had been included in Unclassified Receipts, but should have been listed as follows:
Pittstown, N. J. Breth. Mission, unclassified receipts, ... $18.50
H. K. Wright, ... 10.00
Mr. & Mrs. S. F. Weber, ... 12.00
Mrs. Edith Schubiger, ... 10.00
Mr. & Mrs. E. C. Hackett, ... 22.00

Individual Totals, ... $54.00

Total offering last Easter, ... $72.50
WILLIAM A. GEARHART,
General Missionary Secretary.

NEWS FROM THE FIELD

THE LORD'S VICTORY AT BRYAN, OHIO

The work at Bryan is going forward with renewed zeal and vigor. We have not said anything through the columns of the Evangelist for some time. But because we have not written anything by no means indicates we have not been at work.

We are now on our fifth year at this place and are beginning to realize some of the fruits of our labors with these people. Bryan has her problems to solve just like any other church, but she has some mighty good people to work with that are ever ready and willing to help a pastor and his wife to solve them. God forbid that we should say this boastfully, but we feel the work here is up to the standard of the average congregation.

In the Four Year Program we set out to reach every goal and when the program closed and the goals were tabulated we found we were short four. We are indeed proud of our effort, though we did not reach them all. Now that we are entering on the Bicentenary Movement we are lining up with the work and we hope to reach every goal by 1923. Stewardship Day was observed with good results in many ways while not so good as hoped for in other ways. Our Thanksgiving offering was what we expected it would be and we met the goal of one dollar per member.

The Sunday school has been doing splendid work. It is usually the case that during the summer months there is a slump, but it was not with us. We gained in attendance almost each Sunday all summer. On the second Sunday in October we observed rally day, and it was a rally day for Bryan. We set our goal for 150 in attendance, and decided to make a public recognition of the class having the largest attendance, the largest offering and the largest offering per capita. Everybody was right there on time and when the

final count was made, it revealed there were 235 present with an offering of $115.35. At the close of the service the young people's class issued a challenge to the younger married peoples' class for a contest for three months, ending with the last Sunday in December. The points for the contest were to be worked out by the officers of the two classes. At the close, the losers were to give a banquet to the winners and the winners to furnish a program. A fine spirit prevails between these two classes and some good work is being done.

The W. M. S. is one of the live adjuncts of this church. They are keeping pace with the National work and are anxiously awaiting for Miss Smith to come that they may share in the raising of the $10,000 bequest fund. Their attendance and interest are increasing at each meeting.

Then, lest we forget, there are those faithful S. M. M. girls. Always something new in the way of a program at each meeting. A live bunch of Christian girls, always ready to help the church in whatever way they can.

Last July the church began to plan for a campaign for the saving of souls to begin about the first of November. By a unanimous vote Brother A. T. Wirick of South Bend, Indiana, was chosen to be the evangelist. We began at once to plan for this meeting. Every sermon that was preached and the prayers of the church were directed to this special meeting.

On November 2, (election night) Brother Wirick came. Of course when an evangelist comes on the field to help the people of God to save souls the devil gets extra busy. But we gave him the chase of his life. For four full weeks Brother Wirick preached against sin, ever holding up before the people the old time Gospel and contending for the faith of the Brethren church. The people of the

brotherhood who know him know he does not put the soft pedal on when he goes after the devil. When people sin in English he rebukes them in English. He preached, and we visited and prayed and plead with people to give their lives to Christ. As a result of our efforts 56 souls made that good confession. Fifty of them have been baptized, 3 came from our sister church, the Church of the Brethren, and 3 remain to receive Christian baptism. This meeting was brought to a close Sunday evening, November 28, at which service gave their hearts to Christ. We have felt condemned for closing this meeting at this time, believing if we had continued another week we would have had at least 25 or 50 more who would have made that good confession. However, we feel this meeting is not over, as last Sunday evening after we had preached our sermon and given the usual invitation, we discovered there were two husbands and their wives who were under conviction, but for some cause or other they would not cut loose from the world and take their stand for Christ. In all the meetings we have never seen so many confessions of adults. Three-fourths of those who came were heads of families. On Monday night, November 29, we held our communion with the largest attendance in the history of this church.

Brother Wirick certainly won his way into the hearts of the people while here. The last night of the meeting with the house packed from pulpit to door every person in the house by raising his or her hand, expressed their desire for him to return again to hold another meeting.

I am sure we feel the added responsibility that now rests upon our shoulders to doctrinate and shepherd these precious souls who have been added to our ranks. By the help of God we will do our best, and we feel the need of the prayers of the entire brotherhood in this work. It is our prayer that every one of our churches may have the Lord to pour out his blessing upon them as he did for Bryan.

G. L. MAUS.

COLLEGE NEWS

School has closed for the Holidays, most of the students having returned to their homes. The fall term was on the whole very good. The athletic interests were well taken care of, the College winning its share and more of the games played. The Purple and Gold came out regularly and at this writing there is almost enough money in the Business Manager's hands to pay for the rest of the numbers up to the end of the school year. Already enough of subscriptions to the annual, Pine Whispers, have been secured to make that publication secure. The Debating League has already taken up the matter of the intercollegiate debates and prospects are good for the usual number of these contests. While it is a bit early to safely forecast the finances, yet indications are that we will be able to meet all our obligations as they come due. The enrollment in the regular work is well over one hundred with more to come in. This is an increase of some ten percent over former years. The music departments are up to and over the normal enrollment.

Professors Wolford, Haun, Garber, Miller, and others have done their share of publicity work in the way of making addresses and Dr. Shively has been enabled to spend two weeks with an Ohio church in the interests both of the College and of that congregation. This was made possible by others taking care of his work here. The College in conjunction with the local church held a weeks meeting in November, the preaching being done by members of the College faculty and the Publishing House staff.

Moreover, my appeal for some sort of a league within the church and among the ministers has already brought good results. Some have decided to take up this matter and try to not only help worthy young men through school, but what is vastly more important, try to SEEK OUT AND SELECT WORTHY YOUNG MEN for the ministry. If we could put but two through a year, in addition to those who would come any way, it would be a big help. There are denominations that will take any likely young man graduating from a high school and fit him for, and put him into, a pulpit without a dollar of expense to the young person. We have young men here in school now, who, if the church would allow them to stop for the need of funds, would represent untold loss in after years. I earnestly hope that this movement may result in large returns.

Taken all in all, the work of the school up to this point has been very encouraging.

I am open to calls to nearby churches for services over Sunday at no more expense than the church chooses to assume.

EDWIN E. JACOBS.

THANKSGIVING OFFERING

We are pleased to report that our churches are responding very generously to the call for the greatest Thanksgiving offering for Home Missions that was ever made by the Brethren people. Some churches are not content to merely reach the goal of $1.00 per member, but are giving considerably more, while others are falling below the mark. Some have sent in their offering with the statement that more would be sent later. If your church did not reach the goal and you desire to do so before the final report is made for the year, please remember that you can send it in any time before June 1, 1921 and receive credit.

Report of receipts during November and December will be sent to the Evangelist early in January, and we are anxious to have as complete a report of the Thanksgiving offerings as possible. If you expect your of-

fering to be in that report, it must reach my office prior to January 1st.

Quite a number of churches have sent me their offerings, but failed to give the list of names and addresses of those who gave $5.00 or more. This information must be furnished if Home Guard Souvenir cards are desired and the names are to appear in the Evangelist. Gifts amounting to less than $5.00 will not be published unless special request is made to do so. Some have reported the names with the statement that they gave $5.00 or more, which is not sufficient information to make the proper report. State the exact amount given, and if there is a request from the donor that the amount should not be published, we will gladly withhold it.

White Gift offerings from the Sunday schools should not be sent to this office, unless you are paying your pledge or making a special offering for some missionary purpose. Please read carefully instructions in this Evangelist as to the purpose of the WHITE GIFT offering.

WILLIAM A. GEARHART,
General Missionary Secretary,
906 American Building, Dayton, Ohio.

BRYAN, OHIO

On November second we began a meeting at Bryan. This was our fifth meeting with this church and our third time to be yoked up with Brother Maus. When I was with him in two meetings in Iowa, we were then after money for a new church, and the beautiful church at Dallas Center was the result of those two meetings; as well as many additions to the church.

In our meeting at Bryan we gave our whole time and strength to winning souls and the Lord was with us in a wonderful meeting which I will leave Brother Maus report.

We found Brother Maus hard at work pushing the work through the Sunday school and other organizations of the church. At present Mrs. Maus is not able to put her time and energy into the work was she usually does, and the girls and women feel the loss of their leader very keenly.

With Mrs. Maus unable to be up part of the time it was easy to keep the pastor busy. He fits in nicely as nurse, cook, washwoman, preacher, song leader, Sunday school teacher, assistant janitor as well as chauffeur for the evangelist.

This is Brother Maus' fifth year at this place and we hope it may be his best.

Many of our old friends at Bryan have gone to their rest. Others were too sick to attend the meetings, but many of the old wheel horses are still there and they seem to like the Old Gospel story better than ever.

Almost all the religious frills and freaks on the map are represented in Bryan, but none seem to grip the heart like the Godsent, Blood-bought, Spirit-sealed, salvation from sin, as plainly revealed in the good old Book.

The Bryan brethren will get a larger vision home day and rise up and build a church that will send out a light, such as has never been seen around there, and the poor deluded crowds now disgusted with much that goes under the name of religion will flock to the doors and find the old, old story sweeter to their souls than any modern delusion of the devil has ever been.

I am hoping this will be the year the Whole Gospel story will win as never before.

ARTHUR T. WIRICK.

KENTUCKY NEWS

It was my privilege quite recently to accompany one of our own dear Dayton girls to Riverside,—Miss Huldah Ewert, a consecrated Christian girl who feels that she should give at least a part of her young life in some needy mission work. Huldah is the new cook at Riverside Institute.

Leaving Dayton early in the morning, we arrived at Haddix near 7 P. M. This depot has a waiting room in one end of a box car. After meeting Brother Aikens, we were trying to penetrate through the darkness, and wondering what kind of a wagon we would be expected to ride in when we were very much surprised to hear Brother Aikens say he had brought a couple of animals for us. Then and there we began having some new experiences, some that we shall never forget. Through the kindness and patience of Brother Aiken, and the help of a barrel, I finally found myself on the back of a mule, equipped with a man's saddle. I have often thanked the Lord for the light of a new day, and for sunshine, but never before did I thank him for darkness, but that night I certainly did. As we followed the trail or track along those mountains, I thought I never saw such a headstrong mule; he would not walk in a straight path one minute. I thought Y was going straight up the mountain; the next minute I went just as far in the other direction. I held tight to the saddle, to keep from taking a header. The saddle seemed the only reliable thing within reach.

We were received very kindly by all the workers, and indeed glad were they to welcome a cook.

I lived in the "Dorm." for a few days; there I met the girls and learned to love them. As I went into the school room again and again, and saw and heard these earnest, consecrated, Christian teachers, and looked into the faces of the boys and girls, and saw their keen interest, and the advancement they have made in education, it was all a pleasant surprise to me. I think we as a church should appreciate the fact that the state of Kentucky provides and pays two teachers to teach the grades from July to December. Six months, and that this teaching is done under the supervision of Brother Drushal. The grades are very well taken care of in this way. This leaves Brother Drushal and Brother Aikens to care for the high school department, which they are doing in a very splendid way.

The Bible is regularly taught, and it is most interesting to hear the Primary people name perfectly the divisions and books of the Bible, recite the Beatitudes, numerous Psalms, etc. The regular systematic Bible study is proving a safeguard to the other pupils against the perverted teachings of ignorant leaders, and is building them up in truth and doctrine.

It does not take tact to get into a mountain home, but it sometimes takes genuine tact to get out. They greet you with a ready smile, and a "Howdy," and forthwith invite you to stay all day.

The needs at Riverside are numerous, but the greatest need in my judgment is a laundry room, or rather a dining room and then use the present dining room for a laundry. The present dining room is in the basement, and would make a much better laundry than it does a dining room. I hope at this Christmastide, at our White Gift service, we may remember this great need. Let us start a "Fund" for this much needed room. If you will stipulate where you want your money to go, there it will go without fail. Let us boost for this building at once.

On my return trip to Haddix on my way to Krypton, I walked over the same road I had traveled, on that never to be forgotten trip. My estimate of "Kentucky Jim" was raised very high. I yet wonder how a mule could pick his way as well as this mule did that dark night. A wheeled vehicle seems to me to be almost useless; nothing but a low wooden sledge will keep right side up.

In leaving Haddix I waited two hours in that box car waiting room after dark. My train was late again. Soon a typical mountaineer came to the door, apologizing for the lateness of the train, and said, "Don't be afraid, I'll see that nothing will hurt you." He then handed me a large red apple which

I took, thanking him. I felt perfectly safe under the protection of this rough mountaineer.

Commercialized Vice has no foothold here in this land of sunshine and "Moonshine." Thieves and tramps are unheard of. It is said a girl can go alone anywhere in the mountains safely.

I arrived at Krypton after dark. Here I was very much disappointed in finding that Brother Rempel and his wife were in Lexington. Sister Eversole the mother of several girls at Riverside, knowing that the Rempels were not home, met me at the depot with a large lamp in her hand, and took me to her house. I felt very grateful for this act of kindness. Here we find conditions changed somewhat. Seventeen new houses have been built on the ground next to the church. Here we find no idle men; with the coming of the railroads, and the opening of the mines, this place has taken on a new activity. Financially they are doing well. I would not be surprised if before many years this church will be self supporting.

These people are proud, sensitive pioneers. These mountaineers inherit brains. You may occasionally find Volumes of Horace and Virgil, with the names of remote ancestors inscribed therein. Education has lapsed; mental attitude has not.

Here I want to speak of Sister Tiery whom I met for the first time,—a consecrated Christian woman who showed me every kindness. I thank my Lord for women like Mrs. Tiery. She is an earnest worker in our church and Sunday school. She, with her husband, who is superintendent of the mine at this place, remained with me till my train left Krypton, late in the evening. I shall always remember their kindness.

The greatest need here it seems to me is for some consecrated teacher to go into this field. They have been unfortunate in not having good teachers for their public schools for several years. I believe a subscription school with a good, teacher would be a wonderful uplift at this place.

With opportunity will come responsibility, with responsibility will come wonderful development, I believe.

MISS MARY C. WENGER,
230 North Western Ave., Dayton, Ohio.

BUENA VISTA, VIRGINIA

We think probably it would be of interest to the readers of the Evangelist to have a report from Buena Vista at this time. In the first place probably the greatest meeting in the history of the First Brethren church at this place came to a close Thanksgiving night, Rev. I. D. Bowman, D.D., the evangelist, opened fire at this place, Saturday, October 30. Brother Bowman preached the old-time Gospel with unusual force and power. The church had been getting ready for some time. And consequently there were conversions almost from the very beginning of these services. The visible results of this meeting were an even hundred conversions. The gratifying feature was the large number of grown people reached. Brother Bowman administered the ordinance of baptism to 28 candidates before leaving. We have a number to be baptized Sunday, December 12. There was a large number of reconsecrations to God in these services. We regret very much that we could not get all of this number in our church. Some few went to the other churches of the city. We observed Holy Communion on Thanksgiving night, when 90 surrounded the Lord's tables and participated in the service. It was a most beautiful scene. In the last few weeks we have indeed experienced a wonderful time in the Lord.

It is useless for me to say that the preaching of Dr. Bowman is of the highest order. The people of this section of the city are deeply appreciative of the great message. All of them fell in love with him and regretted very much that his stay was so short. I feel

sure that if Brother Bowman could have stayed with us two weeks longer there would have been a hundred more to confess Christ. The writer never witnessed such a manifestation of divine power as on this occasion. There were men convicted to such an extent that they actually left the house of God and never came back. And their testimony to men on the streets was that they would never be saved because they had turned God down at the opportune moment. I speak for the church as a whole, that we are confident that the Lord sent Dr. Bowman to this place.

Since the close of the meeting the Sunday school and church attendance have increased at least fifty percent. For all we give God the praise. Amen. We solicit the prayers of the brotherhood in behalf of the work at this place.

Fraternally,
M. M. TEAGUE.

LOUISVILLE, OHIO

The calendar reveals that the time has arrived again for a report of our work.

As we approach the last lap of our second year of labor together, we feel grateful to our God for precious leading and for a degree of satisfaction at seeing some things well done. Every organization as an auxiliary to the church is well organized and the work being done is of fine order because of the consecrated spirit-filled lives who lead and direct as officers.

Our Sunday school, both primary and adult departments are preparing special and separate Christmas services. New recruits are coming into our Sunday school ranks almost weekly. At present a contest is being arranged with Canton Brethren Sunday school. The two schools on the average are quite the same, so we are looking for some keen interest in this friendly contest.

Christian Endeavor is flourishing. New members have recently been received. The new officers are proving themselves. It has been said by others, that Louisville has the strongest Endeavor work in the church. The Senior work is being fed by a strong Junior department under the direction of Sister Painter. Her worthy husband is president of the Senior society.

The woman's work, including Missionary Society and Sisterhood girls is of inestimable worth to the church. Special attention is given to their programs. A fine missionary spirit is prevalent. Much practical work has been done among the sick, aged and among the newcomers to the town.

Revival

On election day we began a revival meeting. Brother B. T. Burnworth of Lanark, Illinois, came to do the preaching. He had been in a battle for three weeks at Burlington, Indiana, but came here in good trim. His stay was all too short, only ten days. His sermons were strong, well prepared and forcifully and convincingly delivered. Our initial plan was to have had the meeting started by at least a week before the evangelist arrived, but owing to the date of the Ohio Conference it was not possible to carry out the plan. To do the next best thing the meeting was continued until the close of the second week. As to results we are glad to say that much more good was done than can be tabulated. Seven were added to the church. Two others were received just before the meeting, thus nine have recently been added to our number.

Full Time Service

October 1 it was decided that this church should have the entire service of the pastor beginning January 1. Heretofore we shared half our Sundays with the North Georgetown congregation. Therefore our services at North Georgetown will soon end and a report will be given in these columns. We are hoping that by being in this pulpit every Sunday to be able to have more power and prestige in the community and among our own people.

A Merry Christmas and a Happy New Year

from Louisville First Brethren church to all our friends. E. M. RIDDLE, Pastor.

FROM THE PASTORATE TO THE COLLEGE

For months I have wanted to give this message to my many friends in the church in which I have served so many years, but want of time has held it back. I feel that I owe to them an explanation for the step which has been taken, and most of all, I owe it to the hundreds of loyal friends whom I left at Masontown; when I gave up the pulpit there. During the 33 years which have been devoted entirely to the preaching of the precious Gospel, it has been my privilege to serve in many localities, and I like to think that in every place where I have served, there are those who follow my effort with a prayerful interest, and of whom I am justified in believing that I have in them friends, and friends in that deeper sense in which our Lord applied the term to his disciples. Later if the editor consents I want to tell my readers about some of these and some of the things which forged the tie which will bind until death shall bring its consumation, where partings do not come. But now, I want to speak more especially about my last pastorate, and the one of which I shall always think as among the most precious, if indeed not at the very head of the list. During the winter of 1914, I accepted an invitation to come to Masontown to hold some evangelistic meetings. For a year the church had been without a regular pastor, and except for such care as Brother Goughnour gave them from Meyersdale, they shifted for themselves and kept alive. The co-operation which they gave me in that special effort was both immediate and complete, and the results were in every way most encouraging. A few months thereafter, at their earnest request, I became their pastor, and for six years we worked together with never a hitch to mar the pleasure of the relationship. The more than 200 additions to the church during this period were by no means the results of pulpit effort alone, but as in every other instance, were, from a human standpoint, due to the ready response which was given to every suggestion or appeal of the pastor. Many are deserving of personal mention in this connection, but I shall ever give much of the credit for results achieved, on the human side, to the unfailing helpfulness of Sallie Griffith, now Mrs. Dugan. She never once failed me, and I can wish nothing better for any pastor, than that he may have a helper at the piano as efficient and loyal as she. And then, there were "my men," who never balked at any appeal for financial help which was made to them, and who were a constant source of inspiration to me. Indeed the whole Sunday school was of such caliber, and when I looked at the board which told of the offerings, my heart was always warmed by the story which it proclaimed, of loving response in acknowledgement of our fullest dependence upon the Father. While I could not but be deeply appreciative of the many expressions of loving sympathy which both school and church gave me, I can hardly be blamed if the class seems a bit nearer my heart than any of the rest. I became its teacher at once, and found an enrollment of 12 men, with an average attendance of 8. We grew until at one time we had an enrollment of 71, with an average attendance of near 50, and for the entire six years, we had an average attendance of above 50 with an average attendance of above 25, and offerings which shall always stand out in my memory as being the best I have ever known. I could not forget then if I tried the many pressed so many tokens of their love upon me, that their marks are ineffacable. While I live, that bunch of men will remain inexpressibly dear to my heart.

But it is not alone the living, who bind my heart to this my last pastorate, for the precious dust of many whom I learned to love as if they had been my very own. For death came often to a community so densely populated, and more than a hundred times was I called to comfort the living, as we laid away their dead. In a pastorate as long as mine has been, such duties come often, and not infrequently the task is made doubly hard, because the shaft has taken one who was exceptionally dear to the pastor. One such experience which came to me at Masontown, and I can scarcely think coherently about it even now, though a year has passed since the blow fell. A young man of foreign birth, Adam Walek by name, the cleanest, and most practically Christian young man of all my experience, was killed in a mine accident and from the pastor, through all the list of the men of the church, we wept as little children as we heard of it, and later tried to look upon the multilated face which we scarce could see through our tears. Some time I want to tell the readers of the Evangelist about him, for I know the story will be helpful to all, and especially young men, but tears so blind me yet as I try to write, that the story must wait.

One thing goes far toward reconciling me to the change from even such a pastorate, to the work in which I am now engaged, as Bursar of the college. In this institution; the denomination has its largest investment, and rightly so. If I can be of such service here, as will conserve that investment, and preserve it too, and help to make it fruitful to the ends for which it stands, I feel that I shall be making a contribution to the church at large, more essential to its success, than I could make in the pastorate. For the denomination must look to Ashland College for its future ministers, missionaries, editors and in fact its leadership in every department of its activities. In a paper which I hope to find time to write soon, I want to tell my readers what I have found here, but in the meantime, let me assure you that our college is Brethren, even to the very core. For the pastorate at Masontown, and for every other with which I have been associated, yes, and for that aggregation of pastorates which constitute the Brethren church, I shall ever have the warmest sympathy, for the pastorate is the firing line, on which the battle is waged. As for Masontown, I am comforted in the thought that under the leadership of Brother Gingrich, who has both training and consecration, splendid days await both it and him, and as for me,— still "press toward the mark for the prize of the high calling in Christ Jesus," though in another field of Christian endeavor. May God bless both the work and the workers.

MARTIN SHIVELY,
Ashland College, Ashland, Ohio.

IN THE SHADOW

BROWN—Mrs. Amanda Brown was born in Seneca county, Ohio, January 9, 1842, and departed this life November 23, 1920, aged 78 years, 10 months and 14 days. She received her education in the district school and at Williams Center Academy, Ohio, and taught school at South Bend, Indiana, and in Williams county, Ohio. On January 1, 1862, she was united in marriage to Abner K. Brown, to which union were born eight boys and two girls, one of the latter passing away in early childhood. Father and Mother Brown were reared in Christian homes and in the winter of 1877-1878, they united with the German Baptist Brethren church, and when the split came they cast their lot with the Progressive branch, being charter members in Williams county. Mother Brown was zealous in her love of patriotism, and many were the hours she spent in reading history and patriotics stories to her children. Her abhorrence of the saloon was great and she rejoiced to live to see the Eighteenth Amendment passed. On February 7, 1897, her husband passed on before, and during her widowhood, Mother Brown was called upon to give up her youngest son, Lemine, September 9, 1906, and her next older son, Ira L., December 5, 1910. Those who remain to mourn her departure are Ora L., of Conneaut, Ohio; Reuben G., Parsons, Kansas; Mrs. Blanche Deemer, Rocky Ford, Colorado; Jacob A., Edmond, Kansas; Orton K., Montpelier, Ohio; Harry O., Burlington, Colorado; and Melvin C, Everett, Michigan.

O. L. BROWN.

MILLER—Brother A. J. Miller of Jones' Mills, Pa., was born November 19th, 1862, died December 5th, 1920. His death was a great shock to the church and to the community at large as it was wholly unexpected. Brother Miller was a man who touched life at many points. In his earlier life he was a teacher in the public schools of the township in which he lived. Later he engaged in the mercantile business and was known far and wide for his honesty and integrity. As a citizen he was always interested in the betterment of the social and economic conditions of the community.

He was for many years a faithful member of the Brethren church, and at the time of his death was superintendent of the Jones' Mills Brethren Sunday School. He was also a deacon in the church, and president of the Christian Endeavor society. He was faithful and regular in his attendance on the means of grace, and believed most sincerely in the distinctive doctrines of the church. His place in the church will be very hard to fill.

On the evening of December 5th, he retired about 9 o'clock in about his usual health and shortly after breathed his last. Truly in the midst of life we are in death. He leaves to mourn their loss a wife, a sister and two brothers. Funeral services in his late home to a great throng of people conducted by the writer. Interment in the Miller cemetery.

J. L. BOWMAN.

KLINGMAN—Sally Bickley Klingman, youngest daughter of Elias K. Bickley, was born in Meyersdale, Somerset Co., Pa., February 21st, 1847. She came to Waterloo, Iowa with her parents in March, 1860. On April 1st,, 1866, she was married to J. F. Klingaman, of Waterloo. To this union was born seven children, of whom five are living: Walter E., of Vinton, Iowa; Mrs. P. L. A. Ferguson and Mrs. Jennie Haffa, of Waterloo, Iowa; Mrs. F. C. Blanchard, of Long Beach, Cal.; and Miss Minnie Klingaman, of Los Angeles, Cal. She was a charter member of the First Brethren church of Waterloo, Iowa, and was a faithful, consistent Christian in fellowship with the same until her death. Sister Klingaman, with her husband, came to Long Beach less than two weeks before her sudden departure from this life on Sunday morning,, December 5th, 1920. She was sick only one night, and the end came very suddenly and unexpectedly. Brother and Sister Klingaman have together spent the last five winters here in Long Beach. The precious dust of our sister will be kept here in California until March, when it will be taken back to Waterloo. The funeral services were conducted by the undersigned, basing our remarks on the blessed hope set forth for our comfort in 1 Thess. 4: 13-18. May God "comfort with these words" all that mourn.

LOUIS S. BAUMAN.

Business Manager's Corner

THE SECOND MILE

A great many people have wondered just what interpretation they should put upon the words of Jesus: "If a man compel thee to go with him a mile go twain." Brother C. C. Grisso who has recently taken up the work of the church at La Paz, Indiana, has given a very good interpretation of this saying in a practical manner. This week we received a list of Evangelist subscriptions from him from the La Paz church and he said, "This list represents ONE HUNDRED AND TEN PERCENT of the families belonging to the La Paz church." Do you get the point? This places the La Paz church on the Evangelist Honor Roll, **cum laude**, if you real Latin scholars will allow the use of that expression in this connection. We can say further of Brother Grisso's achievement that it increased the subscription list of the La Paz church more than FIVE HUNDRED percent. So you see there is still room for the Evangelist subscription list to grow. There must be nearly fifty Brethren churches, or pastors, that have not yet caught the vision.

It may be of interest to our churches to know that the success of our Budget and Honor Roll system has attracted the attention of other church publications. We have been in recent correspondence with the editor and publisher of a church paper in the south that is considering the feasibility of adopting the plan with his publication.

There are a number of our churches that should renew their lists within the next four weeks. It will be of great financial assistance to the Company, if they will do so promptly.

Not much has been received in the way of contributions to our "paper bill" since our last report, but we have received ten dollars from B. L. Gordon and two dollars from A Friend.

We hope to get the Conference Minutes and the Brethren Annual completed early in January. We did not receive any of the copy until it was too late to do anything with it until after the Sunday school quarterlies are out of the way. In fact we do not have all the copy for the Conference Report yet. But we hope to get it soon.

R. R. TEETER,
Business Manager.

EVANGELIST HONOR ROLL

The following churches having met the requirements laid down by the Brethren Publishing Company regarding the placing of the Evangelist in the homes of the congregations are entitled to a place on the Evangelist Honor Roll:

Church	Pastor
Akron, Ind., (New Highland), ...	(Vacant)
Allentown, Pa., 3rd Year, ...	C. E. Kolb
Ankenytown, Ohio, 3rd Yr., ...	A. L. Lynn
Ardmore Indiana, ...	A. T. Wirick
Ashland, Ohio, 4th Yr., ...	J. A. Garber
Beaver City, Nebr., (3rd Yr.), ..	E. S. Flora
Berlin, Pa., (2nd Yr.), ...	W. C. Benshoff
Berne, Indiana, 3rd Yr., ...	W. F. Johnson
Bryan, Ohio, 3rd Yr.	G. L. Maus
Buckeye City, O., ...	Glen Peterson
Burlington, Ind., (3rd Yr.)	W. T. Lytle
Center Chapel, Ind., ...	K. R. Ronk
Clay City, Indiana, 3rd Yr., ..	S C Henderson
College Corner, Ind., 3rd Yr., ..	L. A. Myers
Conemaugh, Pa., 3rd Yr.	G. H. Jones
Columbus, Ohio, ...	S. E. Christiansen
Darwin, Indiana, 2nd Yr.	W. T. Lytle
Dallas Center, Iowa, 2nd Yr. ...	R. F. Porte
Dayton, Ohio, ...	E. M. Cobb
Elkhart, Ind., 3rd Yr., ...	B. S. Stoffer
Eaton, Indiana, 2nd Yr., ...	H. E. Eppley
Eau Claire,, ,Wis., 2nd Yr., ...	J. A. Baker
Fair Haven,, Ohio,, ,3rd Yr., ...	B. F. Owen
Falls City, Nebr., 3rd Yr., ..	H. F. Stuckman
Fillmore, Calif.,, 2nd Yr., ...	J. C. Beal
Flora, Ind, 2nd Yr., ...	W. E. Thomas
Fostoria, Ohio, 2nd Yr., ...	M. S. White
Goshen, Indiana, 2nd Yr. ..	J. A. McInturff
Fremont,, O., 3rd Yr., ...	M. L. Sands
Gretna,, Ohio, 4th Yr., ...	R. R. Teeter
Gratis Ohio, ...	C. E. Beekley
Hagerstown, Maryland, ...	A. B. Cover
Harrisonburg, Va. (Bethlehem)	
Huntington, Ind., 2nd Yr., ...	J. W. Brower
Hudson, Ia., ...	Edwin Boardman
Johnstown, Pa., 1st Ch., 2nd Yr.	J. F. Watson
Johnstown, Pa., 3rd Ch., ...	L. G. Wood
Lanark, Ill., 4th Yr., ...	B. T. Burnworth
La Paz, Indiana, ...	C. C. Grisso
La Verne, Calif., 2nd Yr., ...	T. H. Broad
Limestone, Tenn., 2nd Yr., ...	Mary Pence
Long Beach, Calif., 3rd Yr., ...	L. S. Bauman
Loree, Indiana,, 3rd Yr., ...	C. A. Stewart
Los Angeles,, Cal, 1st Ch.,, ...	N. W. Jennigs
Los Angeles, Cal., Comp. Av. 2d Yr.	J. C. Beal
Louisville, O, 3rd Yr., ...	E. M. Riddle
Mansfield, Ohio, ...	A. L. DeLozier
Martinsburg, Pa., 2nd Yr., ...	J. I. Hall
Masontown, Pennsylvania, ..	J. L. Gingrich
Mexico, Ind., 3rd Yr., ...	J. W. Clark
Milford, Indiana, ...	E. H. Detsch
Milledgeville, Ill., 3rd Yr.,..	Miles J. Snyder
Morrill, Kans., 3rd Yr.	A. E. Whitted
Mt,. View, Va., 3rd Yr.	J. E. Patterson
Munice, Indiana, 2nd Yr.	J. L. Kimmel
Nappanee, Ind., 3rd Yr.	E. L. Miller
New Enterprise, Pa.	Edward Byers
New Lebanon., O., 2nd Yr.	G. W. Kinzie
New Paris, Ind., 3rd Yr.	W. I. Duker
North Manchester, Ind., ..	Charles A. Bame
N. Liberty, Ind., 2nd Yr.	C. C. Grisso
Norcatur, Kansas, ...	J. G. Dodds
Oakville, Ind., 2nd Yr.	W. R. Deeter
Peru, Indiana, 2nd Yr. ..	Geo. C. Carpenter
Philadelphia, Pa. (1st Br.) ..	Alva J. McClain
Philadelphia, Pa., 3rd church, ..	J. E. Baker
Portis, Kans., 3rd Yr.	Roy Brumbaugh
Rittman, Ohio, 2nd Yr.	J. Allen Miller
Roann, ,Indiana, 3rd Yr.	W. E. Ronk
Roanoke,, Indiana	W. F. Johnson
Roanoke, Va., ...	H. M. Oberholtzer
South Bend, Indiana	G. W. Rench
Sidney, Indiana, 3rd Yr.	L. A. Myers
Tiosa, Ind., 3rd Yr. ...	Sylvester Whetstone
Turlock, California, ...	J. Francis Reagan
Washington, C. H., O., 4th Yr.	L. B. Wilkins
Waynesboro, Penna.	M. A. Witter
Waterloo, Iowa, 3rd Yr.	W. H. Beachler
Whittier, Cal., 2nd Yr.	A. V. Kimmel
Windber, Pennsylvania	E. F. Byers
Yellow Creek, Pa., ...	Edward Byers
Zion Hill, Ohio, 2nd Yr.	A. L. Lynn

VOLUME XLII
NUMBER 50

DECEMBER 29
1920

The BRETHREN EVANGELIST

- ONE · IS · YOUR · MASTER · AND · ALL · YE · ARE · BRETHREN -

Keeping on Year After Year

Laborers in bronze factories, as they labor upon the massive doors, clean the surfaces, trim the edges, fill the cavities, touch and retouch the outlines, shape and smooth and polish one part after another, and then go back and do the same thing over again. A visitor once said to one of them, "I shouldn't think you would know when you were through." "We are never through," was the workman's reply, "so long as they will let us keep at it. We stop when they take the panels away. That's all the finishing there is to it." One of the hardest lessons to learn is that we must go over our character year after year, cleaning, trimming, shaping, smoothing, polishing, touching and retouching. But what a holy joy it will be, if when the Lord comes to take these characters away, they are "Complete in him!"—I. Q. M.

"He that endureth to the end shall be saved." (MATTHEW 10:22.)

"Be thou faithful unto death and I will give you a crown of life." (REVELATION 2:10.)

Published every Wednesday at Ashland, Ohio. All matter for publication must reach the Editor not later than Friday noon of the preceding week.

George S. Baer, Editor

The Brethren Evangelist

When ordering your paper changed give old as well as new address. Subscriptions discontinued at expiration. To avoid missing any numbers renew two weeks in advance.

R. R. Teeter, Business Manage

ASSOCIATE EDITORS: J. Fremont Watson, Louis S. Baumann, A. B. Cover, Alva J. McClain, B. T. Burnworth.

OFFICIAL ORGAN OF THE BRETHREN CHURCH

Subscription price, $2.00 per year, payable in advance.
Entered at the Post Office at Ashland, Ohio, as second-class matter.
Acceptance for mailing at special rate of postage provided for in section 1103, Act of October 3, 1917, authorized September 9, 1918.
Address all matter for publication to Geo. S. Baer, Editor of the Brethren Evangelist, and all business communications to R. R. Teeter, Business Manager, Brethren Publishing Company, Ashland, Ohio. Make all checks payable to the Brethren Publishing Company.

TABLE OF CONTENTS

EDITORIAL

Experimental Religion Versus Second-Hand Religion

The Apostle Paul was fond of paradoxical expressions, a noted one in his writings being, "I am crucified with Christ, nevertheless I live, yet not I, but Christ liveth in me" (Gal. 2:20). Gilbert Chesterton, our modern master of paradox, says, "It is truth standing on its head to attract attention." If that be true then our failure to see or accept the truth reflects upon our blindness or else our perverseness. Truth should be recognized standing upright as we come face to face with it. Truth looks us steadily in the eye and a perfectly sincere youth meets it four square, but when he becomes a man, if it be a distasteful fact he meets, he gets down and plays or turns away.

To reverse the figure then, it is not truth standing on its head but standing the man on his head. Since the world began this has been true, "We see as it were through a glass darkly," and what we need besides ordinary sight is extraordinary insight. It is said, "Man lives at first in a fancy world in which his senses trick him at every turn." It is not strange then that he might mistake the artificial for the genuine in religion.

First, then Paul is saying that he is dead but Christ is alive. Foolish, says the world; Jesus is crucified and Paul is alive. There may be some people living who think they are dead but that is not as prevalent as those that are dead and do not know it. Forget the paradox and see the truth for it is a challenge to both our faith and reason. See the truth then that the religion of Jesus Christ is a first hand experience of the soul. Not as a mere form of worship, for the form is the shell that may preserve the kernel; it does not make it. Not as a system of doctrine or creedal statement, but the distinctive and divine power of direct revelation in the human soul.

You read about the melody in music or song, hear others speak about it until you feel that you really know what melody is, but one day its sound falls upon your ear and you then for the first have experienced what true melody is. So with religion, you hear others testify, and you may even profess it, but to have the peace and power of God communicated to your soul is quite another thing. It is the difference between saint and sinner, nominal follower and fervent disciple, the difference between first hand experimental religion and second hand intellectual assent.

Secondly, then I note the apostle's use of the terms "life" and "death." How vast, how solemn and how unfathomable are they, yet life and death explain all of this sojourn—all our experiences in the final analysis. Touch life or death and you touch self. In the religious realm, "He that hath the Son hath life and he that hath not the son hath not life." It is one thing to come trembling in desperation and touch the hem of his garment and another thing to lean upon his bosom in the fulness of perfect love that casteth out all fear. Too much of our religion is like the missionary barrel whose contents are garments that have been well tried and worn by others. We clothe our soul in the second hand garments of salvation and we are speechless for a reason when a new wedding garment is provided. Paul said it is the difference between life and death, a figure that meant you are alive when you have a real experience of the soul and are dead without. Saul the sinner is dead, Paul the Christian is alive. He had not simply turned over a new leaf, made a few praiseworthy resolutions, Christened, catechised and vaccinated and none of it took, but Saul was crucified, dead and buried. He had witnessed the funeral, one in which there were few mourners—just Satan and the companions of the old life, but it was a death that caused rejoicing. We have three things here, a first-hand faith, a wonderful experience and a remarkable witness. There was nothing second hand about it. He had not inherited it as some inherit both their religion and politics, and are utterly unable to give a reason for either.

Now note the result. He had a powerful message and he was a living witness. He had not been fed like a robin, as some preachers feed their flocks without labeling it, but his hungering soul had found the manna and he had that peace the world knoweth not of, but that passeth all understanding except to those that have first instead of second hand religion. So here is Paul's statement of what it means to be a Christian. We either crucify Christ anew or else we as lesser christs re-incarnate him in our lives. The world is looking for a panacea. We are saying there is something wrong with our social and economic systems, but the cure is to bring Christ back to the world and let him live in and through you and me. This is the only hope for sinful men. To let him once more be the wellspring of truth, revivifying, life-giving, life-saving in you is the means whereby the gladdening, sanctifying power of Christ may find expression in a sinning, sighing, sorrowing world. This is what genuine, experimental, first-hand religion means, versus the shelf-worn second-hand impotency about us.

What is yours then? Have you had a great experience and was your soul born anew or was it handed to you worn, faded and lifeless? In the Gifford lectures of the late Professor James on the "Varieties of Christian Experiences," occurs this fine passage quoted in essence, "I speak not of your ordinary believer who follows the conventional observances of his country; his religion has been made for him by another; communicated to him by tradition; determined in fixed forms by imitation and retained by habit.

Is it not then dear friends who may read this, a matter of gratitude that the humblest believer may have an original experience of God's grace. There is too much second hand religion in the world. It may be the best second hand goods you can get but they are not the garments of salvation. Buy a second hand automobile if you will, furnish your home at the second hand store if you must, but don't look for a bargain counter when seeking religion. The dinner of your neighbor won't satisfy you when you are hungry by a rehearsal of the menu; another's testimony may inspire you but it will never satisfy you.

I am pleading for first hand religion, the old fashioned kind that gives you a flaming message, a burning loyalty and makes you a living witness. Move up closer to the original fount and drink deeply for yourself and don't be deceived. What this world needs is not a change of environment but a change of heart.

B. T. BURNWORTH.

To Writers for the Evangelist

We are very grateful for the very loyal co-operation that has been given to the editor by so many different people from every part of the brotherhood. Never was the co-operation more generous and cordial than now. We wish to express, at the beginning of this new year, our sincere thanks to all who are giving of time and thought to add to the worth of our beloved paper and to acknowledge that it is this hearty co-operation of the brotherhood that makes The Evangelist the valued paper that our readers tell us it is. More and more we are coming in touch with new talents in various parts and we are finding that even the leaders of our church have never begun to realize how much latent talent there is in our brotherhood. And we rejoice to say that we have found a very ready and willing spirit to be manifested on the part of most of our talented Brethren—both men and women. With this ever increasing number of writers, we believe the future of periodical literature is unusually bright. We wish to commend the pastors for their readiness to use their pens and for bringing us in touch with the gifted members of their congregations. We shall be pleased to receive from any pastor names of Brethren people who are able to use the pen for the glory of Christ. And on the other hand, we shall appreciate the co-operation of the laity in urging their pastors to send in some especially helpful and uplifting sermons as they are preached from time to time. More and more we are seeking to make our paper representative and we covet your continued co-operation.

Just this word about manuscripts. Write on only one side of paper. Write double space if you use the typewriter. If you write with pen leave space enough between lines so that descending letters of line above do not interlink with ascending letters of line below. Write legibly so that every word is easily discernible. Prose is always more acceptable to our readers than poetry. Poetry is difficult to read and hard to write. Remember The Evangelist brings you in touch with approximately 20,000 readers. No pastor enjoys the privilege of preaching to so large a concourse of people. Such a great number of earnest readers deserve the very best efforts of every one who attempts to use the pen for the glory of Christ. And let him to whom God has given a talent not hide it away in a napkin. It is your paper as much as mine. We are laborers together with God. Continued co-operation with one another and dependence on God will make "The Evangelist" an increasingly useful organ in the Kingdom of God.

EDITORIAL REVIEW

The local church's view of the successful meeting recently held at Buena Vista, Virginia, by Brother I. D. Bowman and reported by the evangelist, is given in this issue by Brother M. M. Teague.

Brother A. B. Cover reports a successful though brief meeting recently conducted in his church at Hagerstown by Brother I. D. Bowman.

You will notice a report of the meeting of the wide-awake ministers of Indiana held at the time of their state conference. Brother C. A. Stewart the secretary, makes the report.

Every pastor and Sunday school worker should study the Sunday School page this week.

From Nappanee comes a "Postscript" informing our readers of the splendid results of their prophetic and victorious life conference and evangelistic campaign. Brother E. L. Miller was his own evangelist.

Send your White Gift offering as promptly as possible to Prof. H. H. Wolford, Ashland, Ohio. All General Home or Foreign Mission offerings should be sent to Wm. A. Gearhart, 906 American Building, Dayton, Ohio.

"The News from Milford" speaks encouragingly concerning the work at that place. They have secured as pastor Brother Earl H. Detsch, an Ashland College student, and are already placing confidence in his leadership.

The Ohio conference minutes are in type and will appear in next week's paper, if at all possible. They are the last district conference minutes to be published this year, but Ohio folks will say, by no means the least in importance.

The Christian Endeavorers will find some things of interest on the Christian Endeavor page, especially will they be interested in the announcement concerning the new Intermediate and Junior Superintendent, who is Miss Frieda Price, of Nappanee, Indiana.

Brother I. D. Bowman speaks of his pleasant visit and campaign with the Hagerstown people, where a number of souls were saved. Brother Cover's report, concerning which we have made mention elsewhere in these items, reached us last week, but was crowded out for lack of space, as were some other letters also.

Brother H. E. Eppley, pastor of the Eaton, Indiana, church gave assistance to Brother Brower and the Huntington church in an evangelistic campaign which resulted successfully and is reported by Brother Eppley. He speaks a good word for Brother Brower's work in this field which he is now leaving.

The Falls City, Nebraska, church of which Brother H. F. Stuckman is the faithful shepherd has recently experienced another season of refreshing and soul saving under the evangelistic leadership of Brother Charles Ashman, pastor of the Sunnyside, Washington, church. Brother Ashman commends the membership for their loyal co-operation.

Brother C. C. Grisso has had a successful revival meeting in the La Paz, Indiana, congregation of which he is pastor; and it seems that a real awakening has taken place here. The good people of the pastorate he just closed, North Liberty, showed their appreciation of his services by a farewell reception to himself and Mrs. Grisso.

Progress has characterized the faithful people and pastor of the Pittsburgh Brethren church. Willingly and earnestly they co-operate in every general interest of the church and energetically they are prosecuting their local work. Brother Harley in a personal note to us expressed his appreciation of the Evangelist and mentioned certain things in particular. We rejoice for Christ's sake that our beloved paper is doing a worthy service.

We have a good letter from Brother W. C. Benshoff, in which he tells of his leave-taking at Altoona and his arrival at the Berlin pastorate. That Brother Benshoff was greatly appreciated at Altoona is evident and the splendid leadership which he exercised while there gave reason for the affection that grew up between pastor and people.

"And the Lord added unto the church daily such as were being saved" seems to be true of the First Brethren church of Los Angeles as well as of the "First" church of Jerusalem. Brother Reed, our correspondent tells of the steady growth. He also mentions the fact that Sister Vianna Detwiler is in the hospital, threatened with pneumonia and asks the brotherhood to pray for her recovery. May there be a general response to this request.

It is surprising how much being "dead in earnest" counts in the Lord's work as well as in other activities of life. Often in the most successful, earnestness makes up for a lack of native ability which others, less successful, possess in greater abundance. And the happy thing about it is that while all may not possess talents of equal magnitude, any one who will may possess the spirit of earnestness in unlimited abundance.

THE BRETHREN BICENTENARY MOVEMENT PAGE

1723 - - - - - - 1923

Dr. Charles A. Bame, Editor

Some New Instructions

Doubtless there will may· questions arise as to the procedure of the new movement among our churches, as we go along. I hope there will. If questions are asked, then I shall know that I am not the only one that is thinking. I get a "slam" once in a while that hurts a bit, but after a time, I let it slide and go ahead. I'd rather have questions than slams. It is not so easy to promote a Movement like this with seven directors scattered all over the country and with every man so busy with the things he must do that he has but small spare time for other things. I have been very busy this fall as all know who have followed me in my work. The privilege of filling my engagements for six months was granted me at the start or I would not be Director-in-Chief of the Movement. I simply needed the experience that would come from it and, when that time has passed and I am really working at this job as I hope to be at the end of the six months, you can expect more of me than now. Until that time, do not expect me to do the impossible—to answer all the demands of this Movement. I'll try to answer all the necessary questions possible and do all I can for any church that is ready to run ahead of the Movement, but I do not care to go ahead of my own clear ideas on any part of it.

Enthusiastic.

A very few of our pastors seem very enthusiastic about the progress of the Program. Thank· God for a few! Two pastors of Ohio are doing all they can and awaiting orders that can not yet be given. They are ahead of the Directors on some things. That is, they are asking for directions that I can not yet give because we have not yet planned it ourselves. On my desk is the letter head· of a church that is fully organized with all the seven departmental heads and in a letter to the State Secretary, on a least two points he says, "We lack instructions." Well, on those two points, so do I. So does the Director, for the special day for both of those divisions is some time in the future and so far, no definite plan is worked out among the members of the committee or directors. But on every other point, there is a plenty to be done and this is the time of the year as planned by the directors, for the pushing of them. Say, Spiritual Life, Stewardship, Evangelism, Missions and Publications. How very wide is the latitude for activity at this· time of the year on all of them!

Further Bible Study!

On religious education, you remember, there is a big place for your church to go ahead. Have a Week's Bible lectures at your church. Or, get the churches of other denominations to join you and get a big man from some of the good schools and have a School of Missions as is directed under Education, Sec. 2, Art. 3. Turn to your leaflet and see what it asks of you there. NOW.

About Finances.

One question that has come to me is "Will the general directors furnish the necessary funds for the work of the district secretaries?" Well, I wish we had the money to do that, but it is not in sight. Indeed, we shall need every cent we have doubtless, and then some for the work we have set for ourselves. And, by the way, the secretary informs me that not all of the Money subscribed at the Conference at Winona for this fund has been sent in. If your pledge remains unpaid, will you not look up at once your responsibility and remit?

A New Director.

Many of the brethren will be sorry that we have been called to accept the resignation of Dr. Rench from the directorate of this Movement. The burning of his church at South Bend has thrown upon him, too many new responsibilities, and asking for his release, the other directors have acquiesed. Brother Rench had some good plans started and we know that he would have done faithful service for the church and our misfortune is only compensated by the fact that we have secured Dr. J. Allen Miller to accept the place and he has been duly elected by the other directors to fill the place made vacant by Dr. Rench. This is his commission and your information that the Spiritual Life work of the Movement will be directed by Dr. Miller. And by the way, I hope that many family altars are being erected this year and· that each pastor and evangelist is preaching more and more on the value of the home spiritual life which must grow if our country is to maintain its place of leadership among the nations.

What Shall State Secretaries Do?

There's a plenty. So far as I know they have absolute authority to go ahead and do everything they can to get every church ready for the progress of the Movement. They ought to see that every church is trying to function along the lines of the Movement and· that, ON TIME. One bar to progress in this and every other program is that so many pastors and churches allow other things to crowd off the program on the day set for it and then, before they know another has come and they have no place for the former. This Movement must as far as possible, function ON TIME. But it is not, or else there are not many pastors reporting about Stewardship Day. To date I have not enough replies to forward to the secretary. It would be a mighty fine thing for the state officers to find out why this neglect. The general secretary will furnish the stamps for this work, twice a year.

It Came Suddenly.

Yes, unfortunately it did. But enough has been said since to have it made mighty clear that that was not the only day, for the stewardship plea. This day is a good day to align your membership up for this most important proof of our discipleship. The Lord will come suddenly too, and pray that we be found faithful stewards when· he does come.

The Charts.

The·scroll for the churches will come to them sometime early in the new year. When you see it, you will know why it is a long time coming. You will be proud of it and give it a fine place in your church. You will see the whole ideal and much good information right there each time you look. It is a masterpiece of beauty, I think and the artist is a member of the church.

Stationery.

We·are planning to supply each pastor and worker in the brotherhood with stationery with the symbol of the movement. It will be forwarded a little later than the scroll. Some information and instruction will come with it and it will be supplied for the work of correspondence in the work of the Movement and wherever it will advance the Cause. The Fairview Brethren Church, Lyman B. Wilkins, pastor, is ahead of us on this. Already they have a very neat letter-head representing the organization of their church in full. Congratulations! But we expect to give them some of ours, too, with the emblem of the Movement, when it is ready. It all waits on the emblem.

Hats Off To Ohio.

Ohio directors, or secretaries as I'd rather call them, Dr. Shively and Editor Baer have already gotten out a circular letter one of which has come to me, asking the churches to get in line on the seven-fold organization. It is a good letter and closes with this fine appeal: ''Realizing that delay means handicap, we are ambitious that every church in Ohio shall get into this Movement whole-hearted-ly, at the very outset. And if in any way either or both of us can serve you, do not hesitate to command us. We stand ready to co-operate in any way possible.'' Good advice for every church in the brotherhood! Get busy!

Bame.

GENERAL ARTICLES

Problems of the Pioneer Church   By J. G. Dodds

The above subject is trite and uninteresting to many, but it is of vital importance to the pioneer church and should have the ACTIVE attention of every member of the Brethren church. The Four Year Program circulated propaganda for the rebuilding of weak churches and the establishing of Brethren churches where heretofore none had been. Such widespread activity to build on the ''True and Solid Foundation'' by preaching the Whole Gospel shall not remain barren. Four years of united prayer and Gospel teaching for this work, which shall have been seven years by 1923 will be not void of abundant fruit. Pioneer Brethren churches will be more abundant ten years hence. May parents open their lives unto the Holy Spirit to train their OWN children for the great task before us.

A dearth in the supply and adequacy of workers is and will continue to be, a grave problem of the pioneer Sunday school. The pioneer church may flourish so long as an efficient leader remains on the field but such leaders seldom remain a ''Pioneer.'' Some flourishing (?) church having more congenial (worldly) surroundings calls—the pioneer Sunday school has no pastor. No doubt this problem is more often true of the rural and small village church and in regions of uncertain crops. This is the more evident that the Brethren church should solve the problem. The church ought to go in and possess the large unchurched rural districts of the Middle West. Think of the souls that should be saved when at least one from every Brethren home allows God to dedicate him or her for definite Christian work.

The second problem is an effect of the first. Idleness produces disinterest, inactivity, indifference. Lack of cooks to administer proper food allows starvation. For lack of shepherds the wolves howl and devour. Allowed to continue, the end of these things is death: The solution of this problem requires patient years of praying, teaching, and work. Pray God that your Sunday school and church may never experience the tribulation of this destructive problem.

Then, too, a great majority of the present day isms crowd and jostle at the outskirts and into many homes of the ''Middle West'' pioneer Sunday school. Millennial Dawnism, Spiritualism, Christian Scienceism, Mormonism, Another-chanceism, Atheism, Just-so-you-do-what-you-think ism, and many others. Such insidious vipers are found mostly in homes irregular and unfaithful in church attendance. Propagators of these isms are not neglectful to get their venomous literature into every home possible at the first convenient opportunity. The present generation of children are absorbing this poison. What will the harvest be twenty-five years hence? To keep the homes supplied with Gospel and church literature, tracts, papers, tactful stories, etc., might, many times, prove the proper antidote when accompanied by prayer and diligent teaching. ''Give diligence to present thyself approved unto God, a workman that needeth not to be ashamed, handling aright the word of truth.''

Of course, as with many other churches, the pioneer Sunday school has many of the more common problems. May it suffice to name a few. There is the problem of irregular attendance on the part of many, some of whom might become giants for God if once they were brought to realize that God has a purpose in their lives which can only be worked out through Christ. There is the problem of carelessness and indifference on the part of many and will continue until the finger of the Almighty Father touches their lives awakening them to the need of valiant soldiers of the Cross. Finance is a troublesome problem that is always solved when the great love of God fills the heart so full that service to God becomes the supreme purpose of life. Also, the want of a complete corps of ever present workers, is probably one of the great worrying problems. No manmade remedy for this problem has yet proven efficacious.

Because of the progress made during the Four Year Program and the advancement that shall have been made by the close of the Bicentenary Movement is it not high time the Brethren church be solving the hindering problems of pioneer work by preparing to combat them before they arise? A church literature to be used to help spread the Whole Gospel to the whole world is greatly needed. A vast army of adequately equipped and thoroughly trained Christian workers is needed. ''Pray ye therefore the Lord of the harvest, that he send forth laborers into his harvest.'' Then when God calls you, reveal your sincerity by doing as did Isaiah. The need is at hand. May every Brethren home hear the call.

Norcatur, Kansas.

''Nothing of Importance.''   By George M. Warner

''Nothing of Importance'' is the title of a little book by John Bernard Adams published in 1917 by Methue & Co., Ltd., London. The author was a young Englishman of true culture and high ideals; he won a classical scholarship at St. John's College, Cambridge, served as Warden at the Hostel for Indian Students in South Kensington, joined a Welsh regiment, as lieutenant, in 1914, went to the front in 1915, was wounded and returned to England in 1916, went out again and in 1917 was again wounded and died in the field hospital.

The following are his conclusions as thought out in an Autumn afternoon (1916) during his convalescence at the residence of his aunt, in one of the most beautiful parts of Kent.

''First of all, War is evil—utterly evil. Let us be sure of that first. It is an evil instrument, even if it be used for motives that are good. I, who have been through war and know it, say that it is evil. I knew it before the war; instinct, reason, religion told me that war was evil; now experience has told me also.

''For I have seen the real face of war; I have seen men killed, mutilated, blown to little pieces; I have seen men crippled for life; I have looked in the face of madness, and I know that many have gone mad under its grip. I have seen fine natures break and crumble under the strain. I have seen men grow brutalized, and coarsened in this war. (God will judge justly in the end; meanwhile, there are thousands among us yet—yes, and among our enemy, too—brutalized through no fault of theirs.) I have lost friends killed (and shall lose more yet), friends with whom I have lived and suffered so long.

''War is evil. Justice is stronger than Force. Yet, was

there need of all this bloodshed to prove this? For this war is not as past wars; this is every man's war; a war of civilians, a war of men who hate war, of men who fight for a cause, who are compelled to kill and hate it. That is another thing that people will not face. Men whisper that Tommy does not hate Fritz. Again I say, away with this whispering. Let us speak it out plain and bold. Private Davies, my orderly, formerly a shepherd of Blaenau Festiniog, has no quarrel with one Fritz Schneider of Hamburg who is sitting in the trench opposite the Matterhorn sap; yet he will bayonet him certainly if he comes over the top, or if we go over into the German trenches; ay, he will perform this action with a certain amount of brutality too, for I have watched him jabbing at rats with a bayonet through the wires of a rat trap, and I know that he has in him a savage vein of cruelty. But when peace is declared, he and Fritz will light a bonfire of trench stores in No Man's Land, and there will be the end of their quarrel. I say boldly, I know. For indeed I know Davies very well indeed.

"Again I say, was there need of all this bloodshed? Who is responsible? Who is responsible for Lance-Corporal Allen lying in the trench in Maple Redoubt? Again I see yon glittering eyes looking down upon me in the arena. And, Davies, too, in his slow simple way, is beginning to take you in, and to ask you why he is put there to fight? Is it for your pleasure? Is it for your expediency? Is it a necessary part of your great game? Necessary? Necessary for whom? Davies and Fritz alike are awaiting your answer.

"It is hard to trace ultimate causes. It is hard to fix absolute responsibility. There were many seeds sown, scattered, and secretly fostered before they produced this harvest of blood. The seeds of cruelty, selfishness, ambition, avarice, and indifference, are always liable to swell, grow, and bud, and blossom suddenly into the red flower of war. Let every man look into his heart, and if the seeds are there let him make quick to root them out while there is time; unless he wishes to join those glittering eyes that look down upon the arena.

"These are the seeds of war. And it is because they know that we, too, are not free from them, that certain men have stood out from the arena as a protest against war. These men are real heroes, who for their conscience' sake are enduring taunts, ignominy, misunderstanding and worse. Most men and women in the arena are cursing them, and as they struggle in agony and anguish, they beat their hands at them and cry, 'You do not care.' I, too, have cursed them, when I was mad with pain. But I know them,

and I know that they are true men. I would not have one less. They are witnesses against war, and, I too am fighting war. Men do not understand them now, but one day they will.''

"But what of the future? How are we to save future generations from going down into the arena? We will rearrange the map of Europe; we will secure the independence of small states; we will give the power to the people; there shall be an end of tyrannies. So men speak easily of an international spirit, of a world conference for peace. There is so great a will-power against war, they say, that we will secure the world for the future. Millions of men know the vileness of war; they will devise ways and means to prevent its recurrence. I agree. Let us try all ways. Yet I see no guarantee in all this against the glittering eyes; I see no power in all this knowledge against a new generation fostering and harvesting the seeds of war. Men have long shown that war is evil. Did that knowledge prevent this war? Will that knowledge secure India or China from the power of the glittering eyes?

"There is only one sure way, I said at first. And again a clear conviction filled me. There is only one way to put an end to the arena. Pledges and treaties have failed; and force will fail. These things may bring peace for a time,. but they cannot crush those glittering eyes. There is only one Man whose eyes have never glittered. Look at the palms of your hands, you, who have had a bullet through the middle of it! Did they not give you morphia to ease the pain? And did you not often cry out in the darkness in the terrible agony that you did not care who won the war if only the pain would cease? Yet one Man there was who held out His hand upon the wood, while they knocked, knocked, knocked in the nail, every knock bringing a jarring, excruciating pain,.every hit as bad as yours. And any moment His will-power could have weakened and He could have saved Himself that awful pain. And they nailed through the other hand; and then the feet. And as they lifted the Cross all the weight came upon the pierced hands. And when He had tasted the vinegar He would not drink. And any moment He could have come down from the Cross; and yet He so cared that love should win in the war against evil, that He never wavered, His eyes never glittered. Do you want to put an end to the arena? Here is a Man to follow."

War cannot kill War, nor Militarism cure Prussian autocracy. For what shall America stand in the coming years, the Mailed Fist or the Pierced Hand? Caesar or Christ?　　　　Germantown, Pennsylvania.

Lessons from the Great Teacher and Winner of Souls　　By Mrs. C. E. Nicholas

Christ has justly been called, "The Great Teacher" and the greatest of all soul-winners. By his doctrines and his deeds Christ is the educator of humanity.

Rich and poor, learned and unlearned, the ignorant and depraved have listened to his simple words of truth. Through the influence of our Great Teacher, faith has been awakened, hope inspired, love quickened and man redeemed from sin by his power. Millions of lives have been influenced by the sweetness and purity of his character.

Every Christian must be a student of this great Teacher,—then we must study the how, or his method in teaching, and the what, or the truths and doctrines he taught.

Christ always suited himself to his hearers. He did not appear above his people but rather humbled himself. The secret of his power lay in his diction—he always put his teachings in a simple form that they might be understood by all classes of people. So simple and direct were his teachings that a child could understand them.

When Nicodemus appeared to him, he at once plunged into the profound doctrines, but when he met the poor ignorant woman, he lead her by the simplest method to the truth. He is the most remarkable example of the teacher suiting

himself to his pupils. So he did much of his teaching in parables—teaching the spiritual through the natural, or going from the known to the unknown.

When he wished to teach the evil of covetousness he told them of a certain rich man. He encouraged faithfulness by the parables of the talents. He taught mercy by the account of the good Samaritan. So always by suitable illustrations he taught the greatest truths.

Christ was a lover of nature and many lessons he taught from the plants, the fowls of the air, the sowing of the grain and the reaping of the harvest. "Consider the lillies," "Behold the fowls of the air," "A sower went forth to sow," "Lift up your eyes and behold the fields,"—these and scores of others show he was familiar with nature and knew just how to apply her vital truths.

Christ sacrificed everything for truth. His life, his words, his acts went to establish eternal truth. When we listen to his words, we feel we are listening to the voice of this truth? The closer you follow your divine Teacher, the greater will be your power in winning souls for him.

The secret of our failure lies in not teaching the truth.

Our teaching has lost its power. So many popular teachers have tried to explain the truth till scarcely the fragments remain—nothing tangible remains—it has lost its power. Our slogan must be "Get back to the simplicity of Christ; teach the truth as he taught and the problem of winning souls will be solved."

Nothing is more convincing in his teaching than the zeal and earnestness with which he went about his Father's business. It always aroused the people, even his enemies. Much of our trouble today is no doubt due to the lack of zeal and earnestness we put into our Christian work.

You cannot make people feel something you do not feel yourself. You must feel, live and act what you teach. To convince people, you must first be convinced. There must be no doubt expressed if you hope to influence lives for good. Christ always believed, lived and acted the truth he taught; so must you and I.

Christ's sympathy went out to all classes of humanity—we found him wherever there were sinners. He became the companion of the outcasts; he labored among the guilty, he spoke tenderly and lovingly to those whom society considered unclean. Christ went out in the storm and cold to seek the lost sheep. Christ was not afraid his garments would be soiled by sin. His work was to seek and save the lost. We must go out after them. It is a lamentable fact that our churches have allowed so much of the "going out after them" to the Salvation Army workers. We have fallen here. We have grown satisfied by inviting them to come to our churches, but when they do not come we must go where they are. Follow your Teacher if you win souls for him.

Christ loved to bind up the broken-hearted; he breathed life into the dying; he lifted the fallen and was ever ready to relieve suffering.

The sight of the depraved and ignorant never repelled him as it does so many of us. It never chilled his ardor for saving souls. His ear was open to every sigh of distress and his hand extended to the fallen. This great sympathy for human suffering and sin was a great factor in winning souls to a better life. The world needs it today. Are we extending that hand as Christ did?

Christ's object was not to compel but to persuade—to gain willing consent. He never compelled people to accept his teaching but sought to lead them to the truth by reason-

ing. The good and wise shepherd will lead his flock—he never compels them to enter the bold but uses the power of persuasion.

Today there are teachers who try to compel people to enter the church with "fire and brimstone." Never was a greater injustice done to Christ's teachings. He never drove people into the Kingdom, neither did he frighten them into it.

Such methods are false methods and give rise to evil results. Your power of persuasion will be measured by the kind of doctrine you teach and how you teach it.

Christ lived his teaching. If he preached forgiveness, he prayed for his enemies. If he taught self denial, he subjected himself to persecution. If he taught piety, he spent hours in prayer and in the last hour drank from the cup his Father gave him.

As Christ went about doing good and suffering evil, he became our example fit for our imitation. Do you regard him as your example, or is he only your model?

Here lies our failure in soul winning (personal)— too many regard him as a model and not an example. You copy the outline of a model; you imitate the spirit of an example. Christ is our example and not our model. You may copy a picture, but you are not Christ-like. On the other hand you imitate Christ and you get his spirit; you live his words and the very essence of his life penetrates your whole being. Thus to you Christ is an example. When Christ is our example in reality we are then examples of him before men. When we live the spirit of his life, surely souls will be influenced by the truth.

Every professor of religion should become a student of the Great Teacher, learn his doctrines and his principles of presenting his truths, that his teachings may be faithfully lived and acted and taught.

Every truth our Savior taught must become a personal lesson to you. The more we study the life and work of Jesus the more we learn to consider others, to see their needs and wants, to suffer with them in their trouble, to care for them to the extent of forgetfulness of self and in the effort renounce every thought of personal ease and comfort and live that we may spend and be spent for others. Then we will have learned the great lesson Christ taught, "It is more blessed to give than to receive."

Dowagiac, Michigan.

"Pep" or Enthusiasm--Which? By Dyoll Belote

For some time I have had it in mind to relieve myself of an opinion or two that have been bothering me considerably and seeking for an outlet, but which I have feared to release lest they should bring down a storm of applause (?) upon my unlucky head. But I can endure their tormenting me no longer—and whether other folks will be able to do so remains to be seen.

At a Christian Endeavor Rally, recently, the minister who was conducting the devotions read the Christian Endeavor chapter, Romans 12, and in the course of the reading he called attention to the fact that the teaching of Paul is that we are to be enthused about the work of the kingdom. "En Theos"—God in us, is the meaning of our English "enthuse." Now it has been from the very start a senseless mixture of terms for Christian preachers and leaders to be using a mongrel word "Pep," which sprang from no one knows where, to express an evident thought which could be so much more sensibly and expressively set forth in language which has the sanction of good usage, and in addition fits in with Biblical suggestion and meaning.

Brethren, God knows we need all of the article which some would have us comprehend when they make use of the term "pep," but I for one am in favor of using a term which sounds more like a Biblical term and which in its very make-up conveys a Scriptural significance. Why need the workers of the kingdom stoop to pick up some slang expression,

which is on the lips of every street corner barrister and pool room frequenter, to set forth the facts and verities of the Kingdom of Almighty God?

To the discard with such, and let us have life, spirit enthusiasm, both in our labors and in our speech. WHAT SAY YOU?

Uniontown, Pennsylvania.

THE BIBLE

The London Times, a secular paper, not long ago published the following significant announcement—such an announcement shows that there are still many believers in the Bible as a supernatural revelation:

"The Bible! What is it? To this stupendous question, there is but one equally stupendous answer. It is the written Word of God. It is God speaking to men individually and collectively, through the instrumentality of other men, specially inspired for the purpose. It is the authoritative Revelation from God of supernatural things, and things of God and of eternity. It is the one fountain of truth. It is far above the word of any man or men. It is free to all, and addressed to all. It is the greatest treasure the world possesses. It is folly to neglect it, and a crime to despise it. Eternal life is the reward for accepting it, and eternal death the penalty for rejecting it."

THE BRETHREN PULPIT

"Drifting."   By A. E. Whitted

"That we henceforth be no more children, tossed to and fro, and carried about with every wind of doctrine, by the sleight of men and cunning craftiness, whereby they lie in wait to deceive; but speaking the truth in love, may grow up into him in all things which is the head, even Christ." (Eph. 4:14-15.)

I think we all understand the meaning of the term drifting. We know that it takes but little or no effort to drift. When we talk of drifting our minds naturally turn to water. Once upon a time a party of young men and women were boating on a large river. In the course of their careless pleasure and giddy conversation the ones at the oars ceased their efforts and were absorbed in the merry-making of the party. Soon one of the party chanced to look toward the shore and was very much startled to find the boat a half mile or more down the stream. They had been drifting rapidly under the power of the current of which they had not been conscious. It took a very hard pull on the part of the oarsmen to regain the lost space. I am sure that the word drifting carried an entirely different meaning to those young people after this experience.

It is the spiritual "drifting" however, that I am interested in just now. We may many of us be drifting spiritually. Perhaps as unconscious of it as were these young folks on the river. It behooves every one to "lookout," to be careful, to mind the oars.

First of all, let us notice that drifting is an unconscious process. As we have already said, it requires but little effort. Because of this very fact it becomes very fascinating and in the end perilous. While the process of drifting is unconscious it is very liable to be ceaseless in drawing the wrong way. If you are a Christian and are resting on your oars, to listen for a season to the whirl and hum of the world, or have laid them aside for a while to investigate for yourself some new theology or tainted ISM, mark you, you will be losing ground. O, I know you fancy that nothing harmful is taking place in your life, but when you awaken and become conscious of your loss, you will be startled to find how very far you are from God.

This drifting in a spiritual and moral sense is very liable to be more rapid than we think. The movement may be as vehement, as impetuous, as the mighty rushing of the swollen river. We must remember also that the peaceful quiet surface of a stream gives little hint of the real rapidity of the under current which unnoticeably draws downward. How true is our moral and spiritual life. It is hard to determine sometimes whether a certain thing that enters our life will cause us to be builded up or torn down. Let us not take it for granted that because we are making some effort in the right direction that we must be going forward. These efforts may not be enough to counteract the forces of the current; we may really be drifting backward. O, how we must watch and be careful, as the apostle Peter puts it, "Be sober, be vigilant; because your adversary the devil, as a roaring lion, walketh about seeking whom he may devour; whom resist steadfast in the faith knowing that the same afflictions are accomplished in your brethren that are in the world."

This moral and spiritual drifting is very likely to become fatal. "Therefore we ought to give the more earnest heed to the things which we have heard, lest we drift away from them." And in this connection remember also this, "How shall we escape if we neglect so great salvation?" Negligence so often spells ruin. By simple neglect men have been hurled over the mighty Niagara to death. We cannot expect to save ourselves by good intention or good resolutions. Sam Jones has said, the way to hell is paved with good intentions. By simple neglect many souls have let themselves drift out past redemption point on the perilous river of life. Procrastination is not only a thief of time, but a thief of souls as well.

Secondly, let us consider the direction of the tide. How did Peter put it? Like this, was it not? "Lest haply we drift away from—." O, yes, this tide sets us in the direction away from God and all that is godly. We all know that. This tide flows out toward laxity of belief, leading on to unbelief and to laxity of conduct as well. The mind that is adrift is not anchored to any truth. Distrust yourself, therefore and trust only and always in the Lord. Anchor fast to Christ. This is the only preventative of drifting away. Be not blown about by every wind of doctrine. If we are not staid in these perilous times, how terrible the disturbances from the many gales of false doctrines! What a wonder if the ship of our soul reach the peaceful harbor under such conditions!

An unanchored ship may be lying on waters as smooth as glass, and yet before the master is aware his keel is on the rocks. The tide which he could not see had born him away softly, silently to his regret. So are thousands of people, and not a few of them, so-called Christians, too, carried to their undoing onto the rocks not so many times by the outward sins, not by gales of adversity, but by the sugar coated vices, the under-current of strong temptation. One man is slowly seduced into slavery by his appetite. One cup with friends, just a taste here and another there, until he wakens to find himself in chains. Another feels the grip of sensual temptation, yes he has been slipping for some time, but is not in the least alarmed until he strikes the rock of shame with a hideous rent in his character, which will forever leave an ugly scar and perchance one that will never heal. And here is a church member, sad there are so many, who insensibly drifts into neglect of his Bible. Oh, yes, he has one and his intentions are good, but he excuses himself by saying that he is busy. It is true, in his hurry and bustle, so many other things come between him and his Bible. For the same or similar reasons, puny as they are, he forgets to pray—really forgets to pray.

When the day is dark and dreary,
  Don't forget to pray;
Prayer will make your pathway brighter,
  Drive the clouds away.
For your loving heavenly Father
  Listens when you call,
And in mercy he will answer,
  Trust Him for it all.
When the sun is brightly shining,
  Don't forget to pray;
Let the Savior share your gladness,
  On your pilgrim way,
For He longs to walk beside you,
  Your most trusted friend,
And abide through storm and sunshine,
  To your journey's end.

Another gets into an under-current of utter worldliness; it swings him along slowly but surely until he has lost sight of his lighthouse. He goes sleepily along and when we look for him where he used to be, and where he ought still to be, he is not there. O, can we not learn that the direction of the tide is away from Christ! Yet men will still drift on.

"Drifting away from the Savior,
  Drifting to lands unknown,
Drifting away by night and by day
  Drifting, yes, drifting alone.
Drifting away from the Savior,
  He who would bear your load,

Drifting away by night and by day,
Drifting, yes, drifting from God.
    Drifting away from the Savior,
    Fearlessly on you go; .
    Drifting away by night and by day,
    Drifting to regions of woe.
Drifting away from the Savior,
Even the angels weep;
Still you drift on with mirth and song,
Out on the fathomless deep.

But in closing I would have you notice, that there is a
remedy for drifting. First of all, the remedy is steady rowing. The idle oarsmen had to turn up stream and bend to
the oars to regain their safe retreat. So with those who
have been idle spiritually. Those who have drifted away
from the Savior must turn and pull as a good yoke-fellow,
if they would make their way to a safe retreat. This does
not mean that salvation is won by self-effort, but by a willingness to use the means afforded. Thus men should avail
themselves of the opportunity to keep off the rocks while
there is yet time and means.

The remedy is not only found in steady rowing but also in stout or secure anchoring. This means more than
mere idleness; it means a "binding of the soul to God under
the stress of wind and rain which make personal effort
futile. To every one these days come. Times of bereavement
and fiery trial, when nothing short of being securely anchored to the rock of Christ Jesus can avail us or hold us
firm.

O, friend, drift no longer with the tide, bend every effort to the oar. "Watch ye, stand fast in the faith, quit
you like men, be strong." Anchor in Jesus, who is the refuge for the storm tossed soul. "Lay hold on eternal life."
Morrill, Kansas.

OUR DEVOTIONAL

In Touch With Christ
Jessie D. Whitehair

. "Behold, I stand at the door and knock, if any man
hear my voice and open the door, I will come in to him,
and will sup with him, and he with me" (Rev. 8:20).
"Come unto me, all ye that labor and are heavy laden, and
I will give you rest" (Matt. 11:28). "If a man love me he
will keep my words and my Father will love him, and we
will come unto him, and make our abode with him" (John
14:25). "Thou wilt keep him in perfect peace, whose mind
is stayed on thee" (Isa. 26:3). "Great stumbling block"
Ps. 119:165). .

To be in touch with Christ means that we are really
living with him, obeying, and doing his will. But how is a
person to do this? First, we must let Christ into our lives.
As soon as we are conscious of our own unworthiness, our
sinfulness and weakness; when we are willing to give up
all for him, and believe, simply believe that he saves us,
then Christ can come into our lives. That is the first that
we can truly say we are in touch with Christ. The moment
the Lord sees that one trusts him, he will then be able to
trust that soul with peace and joy. We must even take
peace and joy by faith, simply believing

. There are three steps to take to enter into a victorious
life of union with Christ.

First, yield your heart, will and thought to be controlled by Jesus each moment in just the same way you
yielded your life the first time to Jesus to be saved. Let
him have the right to think through you, act through you
and to move and live through you every day. It is not
enough just to trust in the Lord, but do his will, work for
. him. It is one thing to give your heart to Jesus, and it is

another thing to have Jesus in all his power in your heart
and life. "I will come into him and will sup with him"
(Rev. 3:20).

Second, trust him as you open your heart to him in
this new relationship to come in and fill you with himself.
Trust him to keep you peaceful in storms of doubt and
fear, to keep you rejoicing in sorrow. He said to his disciples, "If a man love me, he will keep my words; and my
father will love him, and we will come unto him and make
our abode with him." .

Third, obey the still small voice within you. Jesus is
the One now who is working in you and to do right is not
hard. "If we make a mistake and confess our sin, he is
faithful and just to forgive us our sin."

There is always some blessing to receive from God, but
there must be a need. When there is a need tell God about
it in prayer. No matter about the eloquence of the prayer,
if it is filled with earnestness. Prayer is a little talk with
Jesus about a definite thing. Then there comes praise.
Prayer is asking and praise is taking. Holding up the need
to him, asking him and then let it be answered through the
gates of praise, and, then, you will know what it is to receive anything from Jesus.

Living in touch with Christ implies more than yielding, doing, asking, and receiving. Yes much more, it signifies peace in our souls. We never would know the real
peace of God unless we were in the midst of disturbing elements, for it is a peace which the world cannot give. There
is one little word that compromises the whole question,
"Where are you centered?" No matter how fast the wheel
goes around, the center of the hub is perfectly still. The
only place where there is no vibration is in the heart of
Christ. You must get in the centre of himself. Center your
thoughts in him. "Thou wilt keep him in perfect peace,
whose mind is stayed on thee" (Isa. 26:3). The reason that
doubts and fears beset us is because we allow them to be
entertained in our thoughts, if even just for a moment. Reject them not by will effort, but by bringing in the thought
of Jesus. Center your trust in him. When circumstances are
pressing, if work is above your strength, remember not only
the name of Jesus but with it the power of that name. In an
unconverted person's life peace is kept by outward tranquility. In the life of a Christian peace is kept by the inward abiding of Christ.

Center your love in him. People, ways, and plans disturb us when they cross our plans and the way we like to
have things. This disturbance shows that we are centered in
ourselves rather than in him. "Great peace have they which
love thy law; and they shall have no stumbling block" (Ps.
119:16).

How can we centre and keep centered our thought, our
trust, and our love on him alone? "Lord, thou wilt ordain
peace for us; for thou also hast wrought all our works in
us" (Isa. 26:12). Then indeed it is that peace, real peace,
abides and it "passeth all understanding."

. Thus it is to be in touch with Christ.

Our Prayer

Our Father, we pray that our lives may be so lived and
be so used that we can bring others in touch with Christ.
May thy holy name be honored and praised in us, and may
the peace and love of thine only begotten Son be within
us and then be manifested to the world so that all may come
to see with spiritual eyes.

In Christ's name we pray. Amen.
Terra Alta, West Virginia.

Building Own Cells

A few years ago, the convicts at Dartmoor prison were
employed to build cells of stone to replace those of cor-
rugated iron in which they were temporarily put. When
completed they were transferred to the new and more secure cells. So many are found building their own prison
chambers.

Send
WHITE GIFT
OFFERINGS to

THE SUNDAY SCHOOL

H. H. WOLFORD
General Secretary-Treasurer
Ashland, Ohio

From Superintendent of Religious Education

(A circular letter sent out to Sunday School workers and published by permission as an open letter.—Editor.)

ATTENTION OF PASTORS AND DIRECTORS OF RELIGIOUS EDUCATION.

Your attention is hereby directed to the "Religious Education" section of our Bicentenary Movement. It consists of three parts, relating to the home, community and church.

To reach the desired objective in each instance a completely unified and closely articulated organization becomes an urgent necessity. This Association took cognizance of that pressing need and recommended the creation of a church board of Religious Education. After adopting the recommendation General Conference elected these members: Wm. H. Beachler, Waterloo, Iowa; W. I. Duker, Goshen, Indiana; E. G. Mason, West Salem, Ohio; H. H. Wolford, Ashland, Ohio; J. A. Garber, Ashland, Ohio.

The recommendation asked for a similar board in each district to direct the Sunday school and young people's work. And provision was made for the same in each of the fall conferences, as you doubtless observed through participation in your own conferences.

Next in order is the election of a board of the local church. It may consist of three or five members with a tenure of office that will cause the term of one member to expire annually. In addition to Christian character and church loyalty these persons should believe in religious education, have capacity for a study of its problems and possess executive ability. With the help received from the general and district boards they will see to correlate and direct the various educational agencies and activities of the church. That they may be circularized with literature you should send the name and address of each member to the undersigned.

We recommend the following helpful publications: "Religious Education in the Family," Cope; "Religious Education in the Church," Cope; "Church School," Athearn; "How to Teach Religion," Betts; and these magazines "The Church School," "Religious Education." It is assumed that you have access to our "Teacher and Educator."

Awaiting the report on your board and assuring you of our willingness to render any assistance within our power, we are,

Your servants,
The Church Board,
By J. A. Garber.

Standard of Excellence for Brethren Church Schools

(The Standard of Excellence has been revised since last we published it in The Evangelist and for the benefit of our schools we give it place at this time.—Editor.)

I. HOME. (10 Points.)
An active Cradle Roll. 5 Points.
A working Home Department. 5 Points.

II. ORGANIZED CLASSES. (10 Points.)
One or more organized classes in Adult Division. 5 Points.
One or more organized classes in Young People's Division. 5 Points.

III. TEACHER TRAINING. (10 Points.)
Teacher training classes. 5 Points.
Fifty percent of teachers graduates. 5 Points.

IV. GRADATION. (10 Points.)
Graded School with annual promotion. 5 Points.
Graded instruction in at least one department. 5 Points.

V. MISSIONS. (10 Points.)
Co-operation in annual school of missions. 5 Points.
Annual White Gift offering. 5 Points.

VI. TEMPERANCE
Temperance instruction quarterly. 5 Points.
Participation in some form of benovelence. 5 Points.

VII. DECISIONS
Decision day observed annually. 5 Points.
Life work decisions emphasized. 5 Points.

VIII. CONFERENCES. (10 Points.)
Workers' conferences regularly held. 5 Points.
Delegates to some convention. 5 Points.

IX. DENOMINATIONAL. (10 Points.)
Records accurately kept and statistics furnished to secretary-treasurer. 5 Points.
Use of Brethren Publications. 5 Points.

X. LIBRARY. (10 Points.)
At least one book chosen from each division of suggested list.

Has the Church Really Collapsed?

A New York minister, who has broken from all denominational ties and turned his former church into a "Community Church," says that it has. "All attempts to disguise the utter collapse of the churches," said he, "have now become futile and ridiculous. The churches all are alike, mere survivals of the past." One who knows the churches of the country will not be unduly alarmed by such a statement. At no time in the past had the churches so varied and helpful social activities as today. But the charge of empty pews can not be so easily met. Ask the average man why he doesn't go to church and he will tell you the average preacher doesn't give him anything. For the preacher it should be said he has a harder task than in the days of our fathers when the pulpit was the sole or principal source of instruction. The pulpit now must compete with the printed page, the moving picture theater and a Sunday given over to recreation. All preachers are not eloquent and interesting, yet it is a good deal to ask that one who speaks twice a Sunday to the same congregation, should equal in eloquence and interest the occasional lecturer. On the other hand the average man has a right to expect from the average preacher something in the way of warm spiritual insight and suggestion not always found in lectures or books, or walks in the woods, or golf. Let us suggest to the preachers that they live up to this expectation. And let everyone who has been "knocking" the church quit for awhile, and for a solid month go to church. The increased congregations will put new life into discouraged preachers and help give their messages an inspiration now lacking.—Leslie's Weekly.

J. A. Garber
PRESIDENT

Our Young People at Work

E. A. Rowsey
SECRETARY

Advertising Christian Endeavor

BY EARL HUETTE

Publicity Department of Christian Endeavor

INFIDEL OR CHRISTIAN. WHICH?

This is the question that every mother and father faces as a future for their child.

It Is Not Enough For You To

Put a New Testament in their hands and expect them to read and study it.

Teach them to say, "Now I lay me down to sleep, etc."

Repeat the Twenty-Third Psalm.

Send them to Sunday School when they feel like going.

But It IS Necessary That You—

Urge them to identify themselves with an organization which will give them the opportunity of learning in a systematic way, about Jesus and his saving grace. .

Endorse some approved method of Bible study in order that they may become better acquainted with the Book.

Give them the opportunity which you possibly did not enjoy—that of learning to speak in public.

CHRISTIAN ENDEAVOR WILL GIVE THEM THESE OPPORTUNITIES.

It may be that you have never known just what Christian Endeavor would really do for your child and incidentally your home.

Perhaps you have taken it for granted that Christian Endeavor is just a social organization.

If that is what you think, YOU ARE MISTAKEN.

Christian Endeavor is intended to

Train your child for

Christian living and

Christian Service.

Before Another Day Passes,

See your pastor and ask him about Christian Endeavor.

Get in touch with the president of your Christian Endeavor society or some other member. He or she will explain Christian Endeavor to you.

REMEMBER: The FUTURE of YOUR CHILD is at stake and it lies within the scope of Christian Endeavor activities to help you in making the life of your child, that of a CHRISTIAN instead of an INFIDEL.

The Purpose of Christian Endeavor

From the Brethren Bulletin, Pittsburg, Pennsylvania.

I don't believe we have to emphasize the NEED of Christian Endeavor to our people. The first Society was formed to answer a definite need in the church. That need still exists—and just so long as the need does exist, just that long must we have an answer to it, or lose our young people.

Rev. Francis E. Clark, the founder and president of all Christian Endeavor, has an article in the Christian Endeavor World, containing these statements: "The first Christian Endeavor Societies succeeded because they were adapted as training schools, to the needs of Christian young people. They have flourished so long because these needs are the same now as forty years ago—the same in every generation and every land."

The purpose of the Christian Endeavor Society is shown in the beginning of our Covenant. The pledge starts out with the words—"Trusting in the Lord Jesus Christ for strength, I promise him that I will strive to do whatever he would

like to have me do." Can you think of a better foundation for people of any age than that?

Our Society is a place for service, for fellowship, and for endeavor, for consecrated service for God, for happy fellowship, socials and good times, so long as the social does not detract from our service, for endeavoring to pray, to sing, to witness for Christ and to help others. It is not an exhibition of those who can do these things well, but it's a chance for us to try, knowing that we are not alone.

"Come thou with us, and we will do thee good,

"Come thou with us, and we will let thee do good for others."

Yours for a flourishing Christian Endeavor Society,

Miss Eleanor Wilcox, President.

A New Superintendent

When the National Sunday School Association selected Miss Nora Bracken to superintend the Children's Division it became necessary to choose a new Junior-Intermediate superintendent.

The nominating committee recommended the election of Miss Freida E. Price of Nappanee, Indiana. She is a talented daughter of Doctor and Mrs. W. A. Price. After graduating from high school she spent several years in Ashland College. Later she taught in the public schools, and then withdrew to specialize in kindergarten work at Indianapolis. Now she is engaged in teaching the children of Nappanee.

In addition Miss Price finds time to help with the work of her church. She teaches in the Sunday school and superintends the Junior Endeavor. It is her sincere desire to assist other superintendents. To this end correspondence is solicited. Additional help in the form of stories, methods and plans will be given through the Evangelist and Angelus.   J. A. GARBER.

Junior-- Intermediate Endeavor

New Year Greetings to all Christian Endeavor Societies of the Brotherhood. We are ready to start on another New Year. Have we decided to make it the best? Yes—so let us look about and find places that can be made better in our C. E. work. I should like to suggest that each C. E. Society ask themselves this question, "What are we doing for the children who are too young to belong to our C. E. Society?" or perhaps, "What can we do for the children?" Help them to organize a Junior C. E. and an Intermediate C. E. Give them food they can digest, start them right and they will put so much enthusiasm in it that the Senior Society will feel its effects.

We would like to know what the Junior and Intermediate Societies already organized are doing. Send your reports to me that others may read and be inspired to greater service. In this way we can help each other, so let us hear from you.   Frieda E. Price Nappanee, Indiana.

"The true mourners will not crowd each other at the funeral of the man who lives chiefly to himself."

"The size of a person's gift to a good cause is often determined by the number of people who are looking on."

"Go break to the needy, sweet charity's bread,
For giving is living," the angel said.
"And must I be giving again and again,"
My peevish and pitiless answer ran?
"Oh no," said the angel, piercing me through,
"Just give till the Master stops giving to you."

THE BRETHREN EVANGELIST

SEND ALL MONEY FOR
General Home, Kentucky and
Foreign Missions to

MISSIONS

WILLIAM A. GEARHART
General Missionary Secretary
906 American Bldg., Dayton, O.

Excerpts from a Letter from Tokyo, Japan

(Written by Miss Edith Newlin, a missionary of the Friend's church to Japan, to her sister, Mrs. Mary Bradfield, who with her husband, Landis Bradfield, is attending school at Ashland College. By the courtesy of Sister Bradfield, we are permitted to publish this portion of the letter).

World's Sunday School Convention

The Convention was considered a great success. They had crowds of people and there was no adequate room for them so the whole thing was rather unwieldy. It was a wonderful sight to see the Japanese so interested in Christian teaching. After the building, which was a temporary affair built for the convention, burned on the opening day, the managers of the Imperial Theater offered that large building so we were well taken care of. In fact it was touching to see the efforts the influential Japanese put forth to make the guests comfortable. It was true from the first, and after the burning of the building they did much more. Some who openly said they were not Christians made addresses of welcome in which they said they realized that if Japan was to be developed into a strong country the spiritual side must not be neglected. They said they believed the Christian Sunday school was one of the best agencies for doing that and they heartily welcomed the movement. The Emperor sent three messages, I believe it was, to the convention or its leading men, and welcomed the convention and the spirit back of it. This warm spirit was a surprise to us all. And the way the Japanese turned out to the meeting was also a surprise. Of course only the regular delegates' tickets would let any one into the main meetings, but overflow meetings were held in three or four places and they were well attended. The room in the theatre was at a premium and it brought tears to our eyes to see the sea of faces eagerly listening to the strong messages and joining in the hymns. Surely some good will come of it all. Christianity has never been made so prominent before and now it is over we want to follow it up by getting all we can into the Sunday schools and Bible classes.

"They had a big Sunday school rally on the last First-day (Sunday) of the convention when 1,500 children of the Sunday schools of Tokyo only, marched to one of the central parks of the city and united in singing of Christian hymns. This was only a part of the regular Sunday school children, for all could not get there.

"Prof. Augustine Smith of Boston University had charge of the pictures used on the screen, and of the music and the pageants. These were used very effectively in telling the truths of the Bible. The most impressive pageant was the one entitled, "From Bethlehem to Tokyo." We saw the star first, then the wise men came in. Then there was the Babe in the manger and the mother hovering over it. Around it gathered the wise men and the shepherds. Then a girl dressed in white representing the spirit of Christ's teaching lighted a torch at the cradle and called others to come to this same light and go out to win others. First a Kindergarten teacher came and lighted her torch and went out to teach the little children; then a Bible teacher came and lighted her torch and went then a teacher of teachers; then a business man; then a man in civic life; then a worker for the world. These all went after others. The kindergarten teacher brought back a number of little children, both foreign and Japanese, and they gathered round the cradle and sang, "Jesus loves me" in Japanese. The Bible teacher brought a number of young men students; the preacher brought people of all ages; the teacher brought a number of girls; the business man brought men; the man in civic life brought people of all classes in Japan and the man who went out after the world brought those of 'Every nation, every tongue." This was very impressive and the truth of it was brought home to the hundreds who saw it both times it was given.

"The other pageants were also good, but I liked this one best of all. There were many good speakers here also. Dr. Poole of London and Margaret Slattery, the author of the books for boys and girls were two whom the Japanese liked.

The Japanese-California Question

"The last three days have been national holidays here. The thirty-first (of October) is observed each year as the Emperor's official holiday. Then this year they have completed a very beautiful shrine for the former Emperor Meji, the father of the present Emperor, thousands of people have come to Tokyo for this festive time. . .

"There is a great deal in the papers here about the Japanese-California question. The stir that has been made in the United States on this subject by the presidential candidates has been reflected here. The people here seem to be of different opinions, just as they are at home. Some of the newspapers as well as the people are inclined to work for peace, and some for trouble. Despite it all, to the average Japanese the United States is a land of bliss and they all cherish the hope that some fine day they may visit there. The unprecedented influx of tourists of all kinds to Japan since the war, has brought much that is undesirable as well as much that is good. If we could bring only the good and leave behind what is bad how much easier our Christian work would be!

Tobacco and Whiskey

"Tobacco and whiskey have come here, and these words and the use of the vile things are known to all the people. When I see these words written in the kind of characters they always use for foreign words, and know that every one who can read must know they are most likely English, I am too ashamed to look a little innocent child in the face, for sooner or later his life will be tainted by them. Many women smoke and nearly all the men. Then the man is the exception who does not use intoxicants in some form. The women are not free from its use as a beverage and some kinds they use at funerals, weddings, New Years, and in their common cooking. To make Japanese strictly temperate will be a difficult task. There is a growing interest in the temperance cause on the part of thinking people, and some effort is being made to begin temperance teaching. Our plan this year is to begin a campaign in the country where we have groups of Christian Japanese. Some of the posters made by the girls in the Girls' school, for which prizes were offered by Alice Lewis, were very good. The poster which took first was a unique idea.

"A man was falling from his airplane and sake ("Sake" is a fermented liquor made from rice.—Ed.) bottles and all were smashed. Over him a big bird was flying majestically. The bird's mouth was open as it laughed at the man who had no more sense than to fill up on sake before he tried to fly. A bird has more sense than that. This was especially good for the aviators here always take a drink for good luck before they fly. And the accidents of aviators are worse than in almost any other country.

"We are having beautiful fall weather. As yet we have not needed fire for heat. The sun is a great warmer here. When it is cloudy we feel the chill. Just now we are having the fall fruits. Apples come from the northern island. We have also been having figs, grapes and plums. The persimmon is in the market now and there is nothing better, I think. There are a number of varieties. I like the ones best which are a deep red in color and are so soft that they must be eaten with a spoon. The others are good. Their color is more of an orange. The largest ones are the size of big apples, but there are also smaller ones the size of crab apples.

Japan's First Census

"The first census was taken in Japan this fall. There was great excitement over it. First they sent out trial papers like trial ballots to teach the people. Then the real ones came later. These had to be made on a certain day and taken up as near simultaneously as possible so that they would not miss any one or count any one twice. Some people who did not understand refused to fill out the blanks and had to be threatened. The general opinion is that Tokyo will not have as great a population as she has been credited with. However there are plenty here I should think and no cause for worry on that score. Everywhere we go are little children by the scores. They seem to come out of the ground like the lice in Pharaoh's day, only that is not a very happy figure, for they are as dear as they can be when they have the proper care.

"Just now there have been a number of salutes fired. We have heard these all day and every day of the festival. The drum at the temple near here has been pounded all day. This afternoon we saw an airplane twice. This is a strange mixture of the modern and the ancient."

(Sub-heads inserted are the editor's.)

NEWS FROM THE FIELD

NAPPANEE, INDIANA, POSTSCRIPT

When we wrote a few weeks ago we were just on the verge of entering our revival meeting. Now since the meetings are over it may be of interest to the brotherhood to report our success. It is aimed at by the Bicentenary committee to make this a year of evangelism and Brother Bell's report urge that we let folks know how we are doing. Our meeting commenced with one week of prophetic and Victorious life conference conducted by Mr. J. M. Harris and wife of Chicago. Brother Harris is a converted Jew and his wife a Gentile. They did us a good work and laid the foundation for much teaching and work throughout the coming year. Then on the Saturday evening of the week which they opened the pastor commenced his part of the work. For three weeks and two nights we held forth the Word as best we could with the prayers of the Lord's people supporting us. At times the weather seemed to be against us, but we forgot about the fact that we were having weather and went at it with a hearty good will. The attendance was good from the beginning especially considering that the pastor was holding his own meeting. Then some evenings the house was filled completely and made us feel that somebody prayed for success. One Sunday morning during the meetings we had Decision Day in the Sunday school and six came at that time. The summarized results are as follows: Total received were thirty. Of these twenty-four were received by confession of faith and baptism. Three were reconsecrations of those who in years gone by had been members of the Brethren church. One was a reconsecration of a former Methodist who was baptized by triune-immersion. And there were two received by letter. The general feeling among the church is that we had a fine spiritual time together and that the church was revived greatly as a result of the efforts put forth. In closing we would like to say that our revival is not over if we are any judge of such things. Others are counting the cost and our prayers are that God will have his way with them. Let us praise his holy name for souls born into the kingdom.

E. L. MILLER.

PASTORAL AND EVANGELISTIC SKETCHES

It is always a pleasure to bring to the Evangelist family our budget of news. I am sure that we are all rejoicing together in these days for the wonderful victories throughout the brotherhood.

According to our plans we opened fire in the evening at the old County Line church near LaPaz, Indiana, on November 21 and continued for nearly three weeks. There was as usual those things that detracted very materially from the general interest and attendance, but in the face of these hindrances the folks were generally faithful and responsive to our efforts and gave us splendid audiences from night to night. The revival started at once with two confessions at the first service, and when we came to the close we found that eighteen persons had taken their stand with the people of God. Twelve of this number were baptized in the church at North Liberty on last Lord's Day. Two came by relation, two by letter, and two await the rite. In this number were four whole families and were such as will mean much to the future of the work here.

When we recall that this church was pronounced dead for several years and that there was little hopes for a resurrection even among the most faithful, it will help you to appreciate with us the victory. Our Sunday school is near the 100 mark and things seem to be forging ahead in every way. I expect to soon conduct another meeting in the town

of La Paz, where there are prospects for a splendid harvest for the Brethren. We have succeeded in placing the Evangelist in every home. This alone would mean a great victory. My! how our homes need a revival in the reading of the right sort of literature.

I am now at home for a five days' resting up for our next trip to the east where we have several meetings scheduled. Have yet an open date or two for the new year. If there is any rundown pastorless church somewhere wanting an old-time, genuine revival, we will give you the preference. I somehow enjoy this kind of work and the Lord has been pleased to bless us abundantly as we have gone to these fields that nobody else seemed to want. Who is next?

While tarrying at home a few days recently about 60 of the good-brethren here at North Liberty gave us an old-fashioned surprise, and just to show their appreciation of our efforts and labors while pastor here gave us this farewell reception and presented the pastor with a very beautiful leather chair, and Mrs. Grisso with a satin shopping bag and a purse of $15. Well, any preacher can have a reception when he arrives on the field, but isn't it great to know that they are equally glad to have him go? We shall always cherish their good will I am sure and take this way of publicly expressing our gratitude for all these gifts.

With love to all the brethren, I am yours Under the Blood.

C. CLARENCE GRISSO.

HAGERSTOWN, MARYLAND

We have recently closed a splendid short meeting under the leadership of Brother I. D. Bowman. This was our first meeting with this tried veteran but we yoked very well and we much enjoyed the fellowship. He appeared to be in excellent form and brought us messages that made old Satan squirm and exalted the Christ. He made it evident that the way of the transgressor is hard and ends in condemnation, and while the Christian does not find the pathway of life strewn with endless flowers it is far easier than the way of sin, and that it ends in eternal blessedness. Brother Bowman's years of Biblical study and long experience as pastor and evangelist has made him a clear Bible teacher and a practical preacher.

When we report this meeting as a successful one, we do not only measure it in terms of visible results, although there are encouraging. There were seven confessions, six united with the church. Among these were two husbands a wife and three splendid young people of the Sunday school. In these additions we enter three new homes, which is always encouraging for it is the open door of future growth. We feel that these visible results are but a part of the good feast. We feel that the membership has been greatly strengthened spiritually. In these days we need the truth to make us free, and preaching the Word will not be in vain it will either quicken or condemn. We believe that there will be further reaping as a result of this splendid sowing. The attendance at the meetings on Sundays were very commendable; large audiences greeting the speaker, but during the week the number attending was somewhat smaller due to the time being near the holidays. In our city as elsewhere the celebration of Christmas does not always exalt the Christ. So considering everything: The short meeting, (only two weeks), and close to the holiday season, we rejoice in the Lord for giving us victory and pray God to mightily use Brother Bowman in saving souls for the coming Kingdom.

On the closing night of the meeting Brother Bowman presented the work and aims of

the Evangelistic and Bible Study League, which resulted in securing a number of memberships from the church.

A. B. COVER.

LOS ANGELES, CALIFORNIA

Our heavenly Father is still richly blessing us here in his work. The attendance and interest in the Sunday school is better than ever before. Our hearts were filled with joy last Sunday at the close of the morning preaching service to see another of our intermediate boys walk to the front and give himself to Christ.

Sunday evening, November 28th, Brother Jennings had the great satisfaction and privilege of leading six adults into the baptismal waters and baptizing them into the name of the Father and of the Son and of the Holy Spirit; three men and three women, all heads of families. Sunday evening, December 5th, two were baptized, a father and his little daughter. The wife and mother had been baptized the week previous. It was a beautiful sight to see both father and child go into the baptistry together, and while the little girl was being baptized she had her father right there in front of her standing reverently looking on. Then while kind hands cared for her, he knelt and was himself baptized, and any one could tell by the look on his face that he was a new man in Christ Jesus which fact he also confirmed by his own words. A week later, Sunday, December 12th, these three were received into the church by the laying on of hands and prayer, the mother in the morning service and the father and little daughter at the close of the evening service, both bowing at once and receiving the laying on of hands and prayer at the altar. It made a beautiful picture.

This same evening another sin-sick soul came forward at the close of the service and made a public confession of the Savior, a middle aged woman who has been attending our services for some time and no doubt has been counting the cost. Truly we have been having some refreshing seasons as we have met together for worship from time to time during the last few weeks,

One man seventy-five years old who has been sick lately, father of our Sister Snavely, gave his heart to God last week and the pastor baptized him at his home. Several of us visited him last Sunday afternoon and received him into the church in the usual way. It was fine to see his face light up and bear him tell of his new-found interest in life which is so near the end.

Sister Vianna Detwiler has been quite ill lately and has been for several days in the hospital threatened with pneumonia and some other complications, but we are glad to report that when the pastor visited her yesterday there was a marked improvement. Kindly remember her in your devotions and ask that she may soon be restored to health again that she may continue her work she so much loves to do.

An interesting Christmas program is being planned for in which the children will receive a treat, and at the same time a White Gift service will be held in which our people will be asked to give as usual with us here for the National Home Mission work with particular reference to the Kentucky field.

The regular Annual business meeting will be held on New Year's Day in the afternoon and evening with a social meal together in the basement dining room at about five thirty or six o'clock. We are planning for and expecting the largest possible attendance at this meeting in view of the new members we have received during the recent months.

Every day seems a little better than the

day before. We might go on and tell several other interesting things but our letter
will grow too long.

A. P. REED,
4910 Wadsworth Street.

ALTOONA TO BERLIN, PENNSYLVANIA

It has been some time since the writer has
been heard from through the columns of the
Evangelist, but feel that it is due three congregations that I send in a report. It is a
pleasure to write of the work. On the last
Sunday in September we closed a five year
pastorate with the Brethren at Altoona. It
was a day that we will ever remember. During the time spent together, associations
were formed which were hard to sever. The
real strength of the ties binding us was only
fully realized on the closing day of our relation as pastor and people.

In Altoona, we found a people loyal to all
of the interests of the denomination; we
found them ready to follow their leader and
to co-operate in the doing of the Lord's work.
This fine spirit made possible the results
which were realized. This congregation has
sustained, during the last five years, some
real losses. "Some went back and walked
no more with him;" others moved from the
city; while a number of the pillars of the
church were called by death. Serious enough,
but sadder had there been no gains. More
than a hundred were added to the church by
baptism, a number of whom have proven
faithful and efficient workers. Stress was
laid upon the importance of the individual
finding his place to work in the organization.
The doctrine of stewardship was taught, and
this congregation succeeded in making all but
one of the goals of the Four Year Program.
From time to time, improvements were made
to the church property, such as the re-decor-
ating of the walls and re-carpeting the floor.
The last and most needy thing done, was the
purchasing of a parsonage, thereby providing
an immediate home for the coming pastor.

From time to time, these people gave genuine expression of their appreciation of our
weak endeavor through words of encouragement and many substantial and material tokens of their love. On Monday evening before
our last Sunday, members and friends of the
congregation crowded into the parsonage,
bringing a farewell shower of gifts for each
member of the family. A nice sum of money
was also given. All we could do, was to
thank these good people and to pray that the
Lord would richly bless and reward them.

September 29th was moving day. The
goods were sent the seventy-five miles across
the country in auto trucks. Through the
kindness of Brother and Sister L. Z. Replogle of Altoona, we were privileged to motor
to Berlin. The time spent among these good
people was indeed pleasant, and, we trust,
profitable. We continue to pray for them and
to trust that the Lord will lead this congregation to still greater things.

Berlin

We began our work with the Berlin people
the first Sunday in October. Here we succeeded our dear Brother Trout, who departed
this life last March. Brother Trout was held
in high esteem by the people of the church
and the community. One of the good things
accomplished by our predecessor was the
work of consolidation. The country churches
were abandoned and the members encouraged
to place their memberships in the town
church, most of whom either have or will do
so. We have here now but one preaching
point instead of four. We have been privileged to enjoy with this people in addition to
the regular services, Rally Day in the Sunday
school and holy communion. Services were
held a few evenings prior to communion and
as a result, three were added to the church
by confession of faith and baptism. This
field is large and some needs are apparent.
The first and most pressing need is that of
a new house of worship. If this congregation

is to do its appointed work, to nourish and
develop its present membership, it must have
a new church building. We are now in the
midst of our revival meeting with Miss Emma
Aboud leading us. Large crowds attend and
already a number of converts. A report of
this will appear later.

Linwood, Maryland

Beginning Monday evening, November 1st,
I held a two weeks' meeting with the Brethren at this place. This congregation has been
without a pastor for some time but the work
is being cared for by Brethren Tombaugh and
Long out of Hagerstown. It took the first
week to get started, the second week came
the results. The members of the church and
the people of the community responded to the
preaching of the Gospel. Through prayer a
conviction of sin was brought upon many
hearts. Eight responded to the invitation
and were added to the church. The membership is small but mighty loyal. We shall ever
remember their kindness and hospitality. The
evangelist was well paid for his services.
This meeting closed with communion. Sixty-
eight gathered around the Lord's tables. We
were assisted in this, as in some of the former services, by Brother Roy Long. We were
glad to know that this congregation is soon
to have a pastor for full time. May the
Lord richly bless them.

WM. C. BENSHOFF.

Editor's Note: We are in receipt of a clipping from the Altoona Times Tribune under
date of September 27, 1920, which, together
with a picture of Brother Benshoff, gives the
following report concerning the pastorate and
the farewell services.

"Rev. W. C. Benshoff, for five years pastor
of the First Brethren church, Maple avenue
and Thirtieth street, closed his pastorate with
the local congregation last evening at a farewell service which was so largely attended
that large numbers of people were unable to
crowd into the church. All the services of
the day were attended by capacity audiences.
Rev. Benshoff reviewed the quarters' lessons
before the Sunday school at 9:30, and at
10:30, after an impressive opening service,
he delivered an address in which he set forth
the relation existing between the pastor and
the laity.

"The final service in the evening was unusually impressive and was very perceptibly
tinged with evidence of the strong emotions
engendered by the thought of the impending
separation. A special program of music was
rendered, featured by vocal solos by Rev.
Benshoff and Prof. S. R. Smouse. The subject of the sermon was "Love of Christ."
After the service many of the members of the
congregation and friends remained to tender
expressions of regret at the pastor's leaving.

"Rev. Benshoff came here to serve the
Maple avenue church from California and on
Wednesday morning will remove his family
to Berlin, Somerset county, in answer to the
call from that congregation. The family will
make the trip by motor in the company of
Mr. and Mrs. L. Z. Replogle, 1331 Seventh
avenue, who will help to establish them in
their new home.

"During the five years of Rev. Benshoff's
pastorate in the local church he conducted
41 funerals, officiated at 28 marriages, and
received 122 members into the church fellowship. The average attendance at the mid-
week prayer service for the duration of the
pastorate was 34."

HUNTINGTON, INDIANA

Huntington is one of our mission points. I
had heard much about the place and work
and had been through the town twice and
when an agreement was reached whereby I
should conduct an evangelistic campaign for

them I was eager to see and know more about
the work.

We began the effort on November 28 and
closed December 19, a period of three weeks.
The numerical result of the meeting was ten,
nine baptized and one to be baptized who
came the last evening. The interest was good
and many expressed themselves as much benefitted. The hospitality shown was of the
highest character. I wish here to express my
appreciation of the same.

A Change

The pastor, J. W. Brower, has tendered his
resignation and will leave the work April
first. A successor has not yet been selected.
Brother Brower is a business man who was
called to the ministry and later selected by
the Mission Board to shepherd the work at
Huntington. His spiritual qualities and conscientious efforts together with his sound
business methods have made his work at
Huntington a success. With the proper support this work should be self-supporting in a
few years.

H. E. EPPLEY, Eaton, Indiana.

THE NEWS FROM MILFORD

Thinking that a short message from the
Milford church might be acceptable, it is
with pleasure that we report the following
notes.

Rev. C. E. Kolb closed his pastorate about
the first of October, and Brother Earl H.
Detsch, applying for the pastorate, was called
to preach a trial sermon. He made a favorable impression, and is now our pastor for the
coming year. Despite the fact that he is limited by the time he must needs spend during
the week at college, Brother Detsch is progressing splendidly. There is no friction
whatsoever in the church machinery. Consequently it is operating smoothly.

Rally Day was one of the "red letter"
days during the month of October. An extensive and interesting program was arranger
for the occasion. The church was decorated a
la Autumn,—i. e., crimsoned leaves, hanging
clusters of grapes, etc. Rare talent, and uplifting addresses figured in the program. At
the noon hour the entire congregation sat
down to the tables in the basement of the
church, embellished with food prepared by
many of the "wives and mothers."

On Sunday evening, November 17th, Holy
communion was served, conducted by Rev.
Detsch. The communion was intensely uplifting, and all present felt the Spirit's presence.

The services are well attended. Especially
are the Sunday evening services "witnessed
by many" for the church is usually quite
full. The choir under the direction of Mrs.
Young is doing effective work, and with the
host of young voices, is a great asset to the
work.

We have a large Christmas pageant under
way now, which will be given Christmas eve.
All have entered the work of the pageant
whole-heartedly, The Music Director, the
play-director, the electrician, scenery-makers,
etc., have all taken their work almost invol-
untarily. There is quite an extensive cast:

Herod is impersonated by Dr. Young; the prophet, Ceon Scott; Joseph, Wm. Bushong; Mary, Mrs. Charlene Fuller; the Angel, Jeannette Lentz; the Inn keeper, Egbert Gawthrop; 1st Wise man, Ed. Lentz; 2nd Wise man, Earl H. Detsch; 3rd Wise man, Emanuel Dubbs; Shepherds, Bert McCloughen, Amos Gawthrop, and Earl Tom; Scribes, O.ville Neff, N. F. McDonald. Hosts of boys and girls, attendants and messengers. Pianist during the pageant, Mrs. F. J. Young.

Such Christmas exercises as these are always attended, or have been in past years, by many, many people outside as well as inside of town. We hope that the pageant will be an impressive "sermon," and that the Christ will be glorified, and that young minds as well as old, will see and hear things that memory will hold fast.

May God bless the church as we start out the new year with a new leader!

MRS HATTIE V. GROVES,
Corresponding Secretary.
Milford, Indiana, December 20, 1920.

HAGERSTOWN, MARYLAND REVIVAL
Held Under the Auspices of the Evangelistic and Bible Study League

I was indeed made happy to work with our dear Brother Cover in a meeting. I found that he had the church in a good working condition and the field well worked when I arrived. They wanted the meeting earlier but it was impossible for me to hold it sooner hence we only had a two weeks' meeting and the holiday rush interfered considerably with it. We should have had a three weeks' meeting by all means but it was too near Christmas, so we closed on December the 10th with an excellent interest and with a large congregation.

Five came forward the last night. One for re-consecration and four confessions. One excellent man that we had hoped would come, I am glad to have learned, came and was baptized right after I closed. We did not have very many additions but considering all the circumstances I think we had an excellent meeting. Brother Cover promised to write up the meeting hence will say very little about it.

I spent some happy hours with our dear Brother Tombaugh who lives here. His health is now good and he is doing considerable preaching. Brother Roy Long also attended nearly every night and he also preaches some but has a good position here where he works through the week but often runs out over Sunday.

I was agreeably surprised one night to find the pastor of the Meyersdale church present. He went with me to my room and we had a very pleasant visit for three hours. He is one of those modest lawyers and preachers who preaches every Sunday but says nothing about it through the Evangelist. "Ed." with his keen intellect should use it for the benefit of the whole church by writing for our paper.

I had royal treatment, rested each Saturday, and feasted off of the fat of the land among those good people.

I met many dear friends while there from St. James, Mapleville and Downsville, three places where I preached when I had my first pastorate, 32 years ago. These Hagerstown people then drove two miles to Funkstown to preaching as they had no building in Hagerstown. Now they have a splendid congregation and the prettiest church in the brotherhood with a fine Mollar pipe organ in it. Their singing was excellent. They treated me so well I loathed to leave. Surely they know how to treat an evangelist there. I am happy to say that this meeting did not cost the Evangelistic and Bible Study League anything.

In closing this article I want to say I found the pastor thoroughly orthodox and holding up a high spiritual standard.

I will not mention many of the dear friends for want of time but I would like to state briefly that I was pleased especially to meet our dear Brother Tilman Fahrney, who did more for me in my deep poverty than any other man ever did when I was a boy preacher and as poor as a church mouse. God bless him, I shall never forget his kindness and unselfishness to me. He advertised a time sale when I moved from St. James, took the whole matter in his own hands, and had me to hold a revival up to the time of leaving, then took all the sale notes and paid me cash for them. How many he collected or never collected I do not know to this day and it was over 30 years ago. I think the bill has run out of date and I will never be asked to pay it. In my travels I sometimes find churches killing their preachers and robbing them, but not so with Tilman.

I was also glad to find Dr. Mary Laughlin, whom I baptized in Philadelphia more than 20 years ago. She is an excellent and popular physician and loyal member of the Hagerstown church.

I am now at Gatewood, West Virginia, having large crowds and a good interest but the roads are almost impassable. Will report this meeting later.

I preached over Sunday at Mt. Olive, Virginia, before coming to Gatewood. Attended a splendid communion service there on Saturday night, then preached Sunday and Sunday night. Wife and I were here together. I left for West Virginia and she for Philadelphia the same day. Brother Chambers is the pastor here and is well liked.

ISAAC D. BOWMAN,
Gatewood, West Virginia.

EVANGELISTIC CAMPAIGN AT FALLS CITY, UNDER THE DIRECTION OF THE EVANGELISTIC AND BIBLE STUDY LEAGUE

On the day before Thanksgiving, we bid farewell to our loved ones and our church at Sunnyside, Washington, to be absent until the middle of March. There is only one Person and only one organization in existence for whom and for which we would absent ourselves from our family for both Thanksgiving and Christmas. That Person is Jesus Christ! That organization is The Evangelistic and Bible Study League! Brother W. S. Bell will be our supply pastor until our return.

The campaign here was of three weeks' duration. The rank and file of the church was faithful from the very opening service. Of course, there are always a few worldly minded, careless, indifferent members in whom you can put no dependence and this church was no exception. But the vast majority of the members were loyal. They attended faithfully. In fact, according to the local verdict, the attendance was the largest in years. They prayed faithfully. They enlisted in personal visitation of the unsaved. They cared for the evangelist in a way that few churches have learned the secret of doing. The interest throughout was excellent and sustained, although we were approaching the distracting Christmas season. The Holy Spirit's presence was in evidence. Seldom have we had greater liberty and power in proclaiming the Gospel.

Early in the campaign, deep conviction settled upon hardened sinners. But several inevitable facts of condition made it impossible at this time to secure a large ingathering. Just a little over six months had elapsed since the campaign conducted by Brother Bell. At this time, practically all the available recruits were gathered from the Sunday school. The months intervening were not the ones during which usually new ones are brought in. Consequently, our task was to secure the decisions of the hardened ones or go out after entirely new material. This is a most difficult task in Falls City where the attendance of the unsaved public is almost impossible to secure at a campaign of this nature. But victory crowned our efforts in 14 confessions. All of these are adults, except one and over half are heads of families. There were about a dozen who came to the point of deep conviction, but rather than yield stopped coming entirely.

The Prophetic Studies, given in the afternoons, were well attended and most appreciatively received. Several were given in the evening by request of the men, so they could attend. Prophetic study has received an impetus here, we believe.

The offering was an excellent one. It was raised in exactly ten minutes, freely and willingly. It will more than pay for the exact expenses of this individual campaign. 28 new members were received into the League. Falls City certainly knows how and is wiling to give. Thank you, Brethren!

Being too far away to return home and it being unwise to open the campaign at Morrill until Sunday, December 26, we will sojourn among the brethren here for this week of rest.

We rejoice to read of the successful meetings being held in the different churches. Let us pray for each other, brethren! I am praying for the success of the Lord's work under your direction. Do the same for me.

CHARLES H. ASHMAN.

SPARKS FROM BUSY PITTSBURGH

The first day of December just past, marks the end of the sixth, and the beginning of the seventh year of our pastorate in The Steel City. (You will note that we didn't say, "The Smoky City," for we who live in Pittsburgh know that the smoke is only an incident to the making of our city as the greatest steel center of the world. And at that,—smoke conditions are not nearly so bad as they used to be.) In our six years' work among these good people, we have been able to do some good, we believe, with their cooperation and by God's help. But oh, there is so much yet to be done. But we thank God for the victories won and take courage for the stupendous tasks that are facing the church everywhere today.

We are like "Mac" of Goshen,—we hardly remember when we last reported the work, so don't recall where we left off in naming our activities. But we know that we have not reported anything since the summer vacation,—so here goes.

During the summer months, we experimented with a combined service,—The Sunday evening service being taken care of jointly by the Christian Endeavor and the church. The services were held in the basement of the church, which room is always cool, even in the very warmest weather. The time consumed was generally about an hour and a quarter,—the Christian Endeavor taking the fore part of the same with an interesting and snappy program and then the pastor following it with a sermon on the topic for that evening. And it worked sufficiently well for us to commend it to others for a trial.

The church here then granted their pastor a whole month's vacation with pay, and it was very much appreciated, as well as put to good use. In the pastor's absence, Brethren Oass, Myers and O'Neill very kindly filled the pulpit for the morning services. The extended vacation granted the pastor permitted him to spend three weeks with his home people at Allentown, where he gave the people a lift, since that church was pastorless at the time. And let me say right here, that the Allentown people missed very much the able services of both Brother and Sister DeLozier. They all spoke in the very highest terms of their noble efforts and splendid work while in their service. And we believe that Brother Clarence Kolb will find the same co-operation and loyal support, as he takes up the work among this people. (Success to you "Dick," among the Pennsylvania Dutch, which are among the best in the land).

While in the East, the pastor enjoyed a most wonderful privilege, and that was of preaching in what is known as "Kline's Meeting House," near Schwenksville, Montgomery county, Pennsylvania, one of the first Dunkard churches built on American soil, and alongside of which church lies the remains of Peter Becker, one of the founders of Brethrenism in this country. The Harley reunion was held in this church on a Saturday afternoon, and on the following Lord's Day morning, the writer was asked to fill the pulpit and preach the English sermon. We considered this a wonderful privilege, which he hopes the congregation enjoyed as much as he himself did. We also at this time learned a very interesting bit of family history. About the time that Peter Becker came to this country from Germany, one Rudolf Harley came over from England. And in time, Rudolf's son married Peters' daughter, thus very closely linking "The Harley Freundschaft" with the Founders of Brethrenism. May we as a family be as true to the teachings of the Word, and as zealous to disseminate the truths of the same, as were our forbears. The pastor never enjoyed and appreciated a vacation as much as this one, and takes this privilege of again saying so, even to those of his own people who shall read these lines.

Immediately on returning to our work at the close of National Conference, we began preparations for the entertaining of our District Conference. And here again the people all rallied most loyally, and left nothing undone that might help to make this Conference one of the best ever. And we hope that all who attended the same, enjoyed themselves as much as did we who considered it a real privilege to act as their hosts.

Soon after conference, came our communion, which was well attended, 116 being at the tables, all of whom seemed to enter into the full spirit of the same, and enjoyed it to the full. And here again the pastor, as he always does, enjoyed the co-operation of the two elders and the six deacons who are real co-workers with him, in the work of this congregation.

Early in November, the Sunday school and church unitedly observed Father and Son's Day,—the pastor talking to fathers on the Lord's day morning, and to sons especially in the evening. And then on the following Monday evening, the Sunday school staged a Father and Son's Banquet, the expenses of which were met by two good brethren, and which gathering was both enjoyed and appreciated by all present.

The next new or special feature, was the organization of a Woman's Missionary Society, with 20 charter members, with a number of others ready to enter at the next monthly meeting. Mrs. H. F. E. O'Neill and Mrs. M. C. Myers were elected as the leaders of this new organization, which was an outgrowth of the visit made sometime ago by Miss Mae Smith, which visit was well worth while. We are glad that her efforts were not in vain.

Another thing worthy of note is that the Ladies' and Men's Bible classes were engaged in a contest during the summer months, with the hope that it would help to keep up interest during the time when ordinarily we would expect a slump, especially in the city. And it proved a success, even though the ladies lost out. They were game losers, and entertained the men to a splendid repast and a fine evening's program.

The Sunday school and Christian Endeavor are both in the best of working condition, and are rendering good service. The first-named organization has been thoroughly reorganized, and is now fully graded, and using the regular graded work through the Primary and in part of the Junior Department. Brother H. B. Landis is doing his utmost to make ours a First Rank school in every particular, and is doing a splendid work, with commendable results. The Sunday school is right now planning a White Gift program, with all that is included in the same.

Our Christian Endeavor under the able leadership of Miss Eleanor Wilcox, is also coming to the forefront. The Christian Endeavor services are very well attended, and the interest runs high. Just this last week, a number of our Endeavorers had charge of the service in the famous Trotter Mission, with the pastor bringing the message of the evening. And when the invitation was given, nineteen men came forward, and knelt for prayer, they themselves asking for forgiveness and for salvation. It was certainly a most touching and inspiring sight. Our Endeavorers are hoping to do more of this kind of work. Our Junior Christian Endeavor, under the leadership of Miss Marguerite Rau, is also in a most flourishing condition, and is doing a most splendid work, not only among our own, but among the children of the community. The fact of the matter is that we are reaching more outsiders than we are of our own families, which gives us promise for good work in time to come. You will hear more of our Juniors some of these times.

This evening the Men's Bible Class is entertaining all the members and friends of the Bible school and church. And on New Year's eve, we will have open house at the church, with the Ladies' Bible Class in charge.

And so the good work goes on. We are planning for several new and big features, with the beginning of the New Year, off which you will hear more later on. But the biggest thing we are looking forward to at this time, is the evangelistic campaign sometime in February, under the leadership of Brother C. H. Ashman. We are hoping and planning, and praying for big things, and trust that we shall not be disappointed. We wish for all of the Brethren churches all and even more of good than we desire for ourselves, and we want to assure both our readers, and the leaders of our beloved church that the Pittsburgh Brethren will not lag in any good work, whether for the church at home, or for the needy conditions in the regions beyond. We hope that we may be found occupied, even until he comes again.

H. M. HARLEY, Pastor.

INDIANA MINISTERIUM

The following is a report of the Indiana Ministerium, that assembled at Flora, Indiana at the time of the state conference, October 5, 1920. The Ministerial Association was called to order by the Moderator, J. A. McInturff, with thirteen members present. Brother Wirick was elected chairman, and Brother Deeter secretary, in the absence of Brother Stewart, who was elected to serve another year.

A discussion then followed in regard to credentials. The final result was that we accept credentials of non-active ministers in good standing if they were not present at conference. The committee was instructed to report credentials received of those that were not present.

A proposition was then submitted by G. W. Rench from a Mrs. Ash at Shipshewana Lake offering to make a gift of four lots to the Brethren church providing they place material on the ground for the erection of a tabernacle next spring. No action was taken.

On October 6th, Brother Wirick called the meeting to order. After prayer the erection of a tabernacle at Shipshewana Lake was taken up and discussed. The final result was that Brethren McInturff, Wirick and Rench submit to the conference a resolution concerning the proposition.

Brother Grisso then brought before the assembly the matter of a benevolent fund to be presented to Brother Swihart. Brother Johnson was chosen as the man to make the presentation.

Brother Bell then made an appeal to all ministers that were open for a meeting to report to him that arrangements could be made.

Brother Wirick then brought us a message on the subject of "The Place of Theology in the Brethren Conferences and Pulpits," in which he brought out the fact that criticism was not so destructive after all as it brought man to a closer study of God's Word. A discussion then followed concerning credal statements. Brother Bell then made a plea that the ministers of Indiana stay by the Word and the fundamental teaching of the Scripture, such as the Virgin Birth and the Deity of Christ. He then said there was no real cause for alarm and nervousness that exists among the ministers of the Brethren church and that there was more of a unity today than three years ago.

On October 7th Brother Wirick called the meeting to order after prayer. Brother McInturff presented the matter of a Bible Conference to be held in the spring. It was suggested that those who should make addresses put them in writing so that tracts on the distinctive doctrines of the church may be printed. Subjects were then submitted to be discussed at that conference, such as the following: "Why Am I a Member of the Brethren Church?" "The Teaching of the Basin and Towel" was given to Brother Rench. Brother Rench was then asked to bring a message on Baptism. The subject of evangelism was given to Brother Wirick and Brother Grisso the subject of anointing. It was then suggested that part of the conference be given to Bible reading.

A motion was made and carried that the Indiana Ministerial Association endorse the Executive Committee of National Conference in its action in regard to the placing of Dr. Evans on the conference platform. The secretary was instructed to communicate such intelligence to the secretary of the National Conference Executive Committee.

Brother Lytle then brought us a forceful message on "How to Get More Successful Evangelism in our Churches," in which he said we should have messages instead of sentiment. We should have messengers who should speak the truth, and prove all things —prove the field and the need and supply it. The meeting was brought to a close by prayer.

A. T. WIRICK, Moderator,
C. A. STEWART, Secretary.

Lightning Source UK Ltd.
Milton Keynes UK
UKHW020405070219
336748UK00007BC/445/P